Comparison

Explication

In-Depth Study of an Author

Paper Incorporating Critical Approaches

Paper-in-Progress

Research Paper

LaunchPad Solo for Literature

The Online, Interactive
Guide to Close Reading

**macmillanhighered.com
/launchpadsolo/literature**

Inside *LaunchPad Solo for Literature*:

- Interactive modules
- Quizzes (nearly 500 to choose from)
- Author videos
- Additional selections (over 200 to choose
  from)

If your book did not come packaged with
an access code, you can purchase access to
LaunchPad Solo for Literature at
**macmillanhighered.com/launchpadsolo
/literature**.

ELEVENTH EDITION

THE BEDFORD INTRODUCTION TO LITERATURE

Reading · Thinking · Writing

Michael Meyer

University of Connecticut

Bedford/St. Martin's

A Macmillan Education Imprint

Boston • New York

For Bedford/St. Martin's

Vice President, Editorial, Macmillan Higher Education Humanities: Edwin Hill
Editorial Director, English and Music: Karen S. Henry
Executive Editor: Vivian Garcia
Developmental Editor: Christina Gerogiannis
Production Editor: Deborah Baker
Media Producer: Allison Hart
Production Supervisor: Robert Cherry
Marketing Manager: Joy Fisher Williams
Copyeditor: Jennifer Greenstein
Indexer: Steve Csipke
Director of Rights and Permissions: Hilary Newman
Senior Art Director: Anna Palchik
Cover Design: John Callahan
Cover Art/Cover Photo: Patti Mollica/Superstock
Composition: Cenveo Publisher Services
Printing and Binding: RR Donnelley and Sons

Manufactured in the United States of America.

0 9 8 7 6 5
f e d c b a

For information, write: Bedford/St. Martin's, 75 Arlington Street, Boston, MA 02116
(617-399-4000)

ISBN   978-1-319-00218-3 (College Edition)
ISBN   978-1-319-03465-8 (High School Edition)

Acknowledgments

FICTION

Toni Cade Bambara. "Sweet Town" from *Gorilla, My Love* by Toni Cade Bambara. Copyright © 1959, 1960, 1963, 1964, 1965, 1968, 1970, 1971, 1972 by Toni Cade Bambara. Used by permission of Random House, an imprint and division of Penguin Random House LLC. All rights reserved. Any third party use of this material, outside of this publication, is prohibited. Interested parties must apply directly to Penguin Random House LLC for permission.

John Barth. "On Minimalist Fiction" from "A Few Words about Minimalism" by John Barth, originally published in the *New York Times*. Copyright © 1995 by John Barth. Used by permission of the Wylie Agency LLC.

Text acknowledgments and copyrights appear at the back of the book on pages 1740–49, which constitute an extension of the copyright page. Art acknowledgments and copyrights appear on the same page as the art selections they cover. It is a violation of the law to reproduce these selections by any means whatsoever without the written permission of the copyright holder.

For My Wife
Regina Barreca

About Michael Meyer

Michael Meyer, Emeritus Professor of English, taught writing and literature courses for more than thirty years — since 1981 at the University of Connecticut and before that at the University of North Carolina at Charlotte and the College of William and Mary. In addition to being an experienced teacher, Meyer is a highly regarded literary scholar. His scholarly articles have appeared in distinguished journals such as *American Literature, Studies in the American Renaissance,* and *Virginia Quarterly Review.* An internationally recognized authority on Henry David Thoreau, Meyer is a former president of the Thoreau Society and coauthor (with Walter Harding) of *The New Thoreau Handbook,* a standard reference source. His first book, *Several More Lives to Live: Thoreau's Political Reputation in America,* was awarded the Ralph Henry Gabriel Prize by the American Studies Association. He is also the editor of *Frederick Douglass: The Narrative and Selected Writings.* He has lectured on a variety of American literary topics from Cambridge University to Peking University. His other books for Bedford/St. Martin's include *The Compact Bedford Introduction to Literature,* Tenth Edition; *Literature to Go,* Second Edition; *Thinking and Writing about Poetry;* and *Thinking and Writing about Literature,* Second Edition.

Preface for Instructors

Like its predecessors, the eleventh edition of *The Bedford Introduction to Literature* assumes that reading and understanding literature offers a valuable means of apprehending life in its richness and diversity. This book also reflects the hope that its selections will inspire students to become lifelong readers of imaginative literature, as well as more thoughtful and skillful writers.

As before, the text is flexibly organized into four parts focusing on fiction, poetry, drama, and critical thinking and writing. The first three parts explain the literary elements of each genre and how to write about them. These three parts also explore several additional approaches to reading literature and conclude with an anthology of literary works. The fourth part provides detailed instruction on thinking, reading, and writing about literature that can be assigned selectively throughout the course. Sample student papers and more than 2,000 assignments appear in the text, offering students the support they need to read and write about literature.

Class-tested in thousands of literature courses, *The Bedford Introduction to Literature* accommodates many different teaching styles. New to the eleventh edition are a thematic case study in the fiction section on war, a cultural case study on John Patrick Shanley's play *Doubt*, and eighty-eight carefully chosen stories, poems, and plays — as well as new art throughout the book.

FEATURES OF *THE BEDFORD INTRODUCTION TO LITERATURE,* ELEVENTH EDITION

A description of the features and content that have long made *The Bedford Introduction to Literature* a favorite of students and teachers follows. What is new to this edition is described starting on page ix.

A wide and well-balanced selection of literature

66 stories, 375 poems, and 18 plays represent a variety of periods, nationalities, cultures, styles, and voices — from the serious to the humorous, and from the traditional to the contemporary. Each selection has been chosen for its appeal to students and for its effectiveness in demonstrating the elements, significance, and pleasures of literature. As in previous editions, canonical works by Ernest Hemingway, John Keats, Susan Glaspell, and many others are generously represented. In addition, there are many contemporary selections from well-regarded writers including Kay Ryan, Kevin Young, Alice Munro, and David Ives.

Many options for teaching and learning about literature

Over eleven editions, in its continuing effort to make literature come to life for students and the course a pleasure to teach for instructors, *The Bedford Introduction to Literature* has developed and refined these innovative features:

PERSPECTIVES ON LITERATURE   More than one hundred intriguing documents—including personal journals, letters, critical essays, interviews, and contextual images—appear throughout the book to stimulate class discussion and writing.

CONNECTIONS BETWEEN "POPULAR" AND "LITERARY" CULTURE   The fiction, poetry, and drama introductions incorporate examples from popular culture,

From "Encountering Poetry."

Roz Chast The New Yorker Collection/The Cartoon Bank.

effectively introducing students to the literary elements of a given genre through what they already know. For example, students are introduced to the elements of fiction through excerpts from a romance novel and from *Tarzan of the Apes;* to the elements of poetry through greeting card verse; and to elements of drama through a television script from *Seinfeld.* Unique visual portfolios, Encountering Fiction, Encountering Poetry, and Encountering Drama, present images that demonstrate how literature is woven into the fabric of popular culture and art. Students encounter **fiction** through comics and graphic novels; **poetry** through the visual arts, advertisements, posters, and cartoons; and **drama** through popular

images of *Hamlet* in art and performance. These images help students recognize the imprint of literature on their everyday lives.

ENHANCED TREATMENT OF AUTHORS IN DEPTH Each genre section includes chapters that focus closely on two major figures. There are three stories each by Nathaniel Hawthorne and Flannery O'Connor; an extensive selection of poems by Emily Dickinson and Robert Frost; and one play by Sophocles and two by Shakespeare. Complementing the literature in these chapters are biographical introductions (with author photographs); chronologies; critical perspectives; cultural documents (such as letters and draft manuscript pages); and

Library of Congress, Prints and Photographs Division.

From Chapter 13: A Critical Case Study: William Faulkner's "Barn Burning."

Cofield Collection, Archives and Special Collections, University of Mississippi Libraries.

a generous collection of images that serve to contextualize the works. A variety of critical thinking and writing questions follow the selections to stimulate student responses. All these supplementary materials engage students more fully with the writers and their works.

From Chapter 36, a Cultural Case Study on four Harlem Renaissance poets.
The Granger Collection.

CULTURAL, CRITICAL, AND THEMATIC CASE STUDIES
Each *Cultural Case Study* presents a literary work together with documents and images to help students understand the work in its cultural context. For example, James Joyce's "Eveline" is accompanied by a facsimile of its first appearance in an Irish periodical, photographs, a poster, a letter, and an excerpt from a temperance almanac. Each *Critical Case Study* gathers four or more critical analyses of a single work — for example, Henrik Ibsen's *A Doll's House* — to illustrate a variety of contemporary critical approaches. Each *Thematic Case Study* invites students to explore literature through a particular topic, such as "War" in fiction, and "The Natural World" in poetry.

ACCESSIBLE COVERAGE OF LITERARY THEORY   For instructors who wish to incorporate literary theory into their courses, Chapter 51, "Critical Strategies for Reading," introduces students to a variety of critical strategies, ranging from formalism to cultural criticism. In brief examples the approaches are applied in analyzing Kate Chopin's "The Story of an Hour" as well as other works, so that students will develop a sense of how to use these strategies in their own reading and writing.

Plenty of help with reading, writing, and research

CRITICAL READING*   Advice on how to read literature appears at the beginning of each genre section. Sample Close Readings of selections including William Faulkner's "A Rose for Emily" (Fiction), William Hathaway's "Oh, Oh" (Poetry), and Susan Glaspell's *Trifles* (Drama) provide analyses of the language, images, and other literary elements at work in these selections. Interpretive annotations clearly show students the process of close reading and provide examples of the kind of critical thinking that leads to strong academic writing.

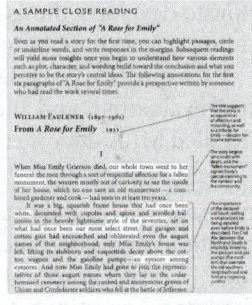

---

*A reference chart on the book's inside front cover outlines all of the book's help for reading and writing about literature.

Later in the book, Chapter 52, "Reading and the Writing Process," provides more instruction on how to read a work closely, annotate a text, take notes, keep a reading journal, and develop a topic into a thesis, with a section on arguing persuasively about literature. An Index of Terms appears at the back of the book, and a glossary provides thorough explanations of more than two hundred terms central to the study of literature.

THE WRITING AND RESEARCH PROCESS Seven chapters (2, 10, 21, 30, 43, 52, 53) cover every step of the writing process — from generating topics to documenting sources — while sample student papers model the results.

Of these chapters, three — "Writing about Fiction" (2), "Writing about Poetry" (21), and "Writing about Drama" (43) — focus on genre-specific writing assignments. Another, "Reading and the Writing Process" (52), offers models of the types of papers most frequently assigned in the introductory course.

Twenty-four sample student papers — all with MLA-style documentation — model how to analyze and argue about literature and how to support ideas by citing examples. The papers are integrated throughout the book, as are nine "Questions for Writing" units that guide students through particular writing tasks: reading and writing responsively; developing a topic into a revised thesis; incorporating secondary sources; applying a critical approach to a work; and writing about multiple works by an author.

A sample student paper on Ralph Ellison's "Battle Royal" makes an argument about the story and includes parenthetical citations and a Works Cited page.

Two unique chapters, "Combining the Elements of Fiction: A Writing Process" (10) and "Combining the Elements of Poetry: A Writing Process" (30), help students understand how literary elements work together, and how to write papers on the interplay of elements. For fiction, the emphasis is on how to develop a thesis and write an analysis paper, and for poetry, the focus is on writing an explication of a poem.

Chapter 53, "The Literary Research Paper," offers detailed advice for finding, evaluating, and incorporating sources in a paper and includes current, detailed MLA documentation guidelines.

QUESTIONS FOR CRITICAL READING AND WRITING More than two thousand questions and assignments — "Considerations for Critical Thinking and Writing," "Connections to Other Selections," "First Response" prompts, "Critical Strategies" questions, and "Creative Response" assignments — spark students' interest, sharpen their thinking, and improve their reading, discussion, and writing skills.

NEW TO THIS EDITION

88 classic and contemporary selections

12 STORIES, 73 POEMS, AND 3 PLAYS representing canonical, multicultural, contemporary, and popular literature are new to this edition. Complementing the addition of several classic literary works are numerous stories, poems, and plays not frequently anthologized. These include stories by Alice Walker, Geoff Wyss, and Lydia Davis; poems by Willa Cather, Seamus Heaney, and Martín Espada; and plays by John Patrick Shanley and Wendy Wasserstein. The stories, poems, and plays new to this edition are a rich collection of traditional, contemporary, and multicultural literature — works that will make classroom discussion come alive.

A thematic case study on war fiction

This timely chapter includes vivid stories in a range of styles and points of view so that every student will find something they will remember. The stories included explore perennial concerns as well as contemporary responses to war, and confront its profound impact on both soldiers and civilians.

Muriel Spark, author of "The First Year of My Life."
© Hulton-Deutsch Collection/CORBIS.

Phil Klay, author of "Redeployment."
© Beowulf Sheehan/Corbis.

A cultural case study on John Patrick Shanley's play Doubt

Returning to the anthology by popular request, the play is now accompanied by nonfiction critical and contextual works — giving students a new, deeper appreciation of a modern classic and its place in our culture.

ACKNOWLEDGMENTS

This book has benefited from the ideas, suggestions, and corrections of scores of careful readers who helped transform various stages of an evolving manuscript into a finished book and into subsequent editions. I remain grateful to those I have thanked in previous prefaces, particularly the late Robert Wallace of Case Western Reserve University. In addition, many instructors who used the tenth edition of *The Bedford Introduction to Literature* responded to a questionnaire for the book. For their valuable comments and advice, I am grateful to James Aubrey, Metropolitan State University of Denver; Eileen Baland, Mountain

View College; Anita Baxter, Rowlett High School; Keri Bell, Harmony Public Schools; Miriam Bellis, University of Alabama at Birmingham; Mary Bradley, Eastern Florida State College; Janice Brantley, University of Arkansas at Pine Bluff; Akilah Brown, Santa Fe College; David Calonne, Eastern Michigan University; Denise Coulter, Atlantic Cape Community College; Julie Gibson, Greenville Technical College; Dianna Hyde, Jefferson State Community College; Jennifer Jordan-Henley, Roane State Community College; Tamara Kuzmenkov, Tacoma Community College; Debbie Lelekis, Florida Institute of Technology; James Machor, Kansas State University; Debra Magai, Stuarts Draft High School; Diann Mason, Paris Junior College; James Minor, South Piedmont Community College; Paul Nagy, Clovis Community College; Troy Nordman, Butler Community College; Joe Payne, Centennial High School; David Pulling, Louisiana State University Eunice; Nancy Risch, Caldwell Community College and Technical Institute; Cathy Rusco, Muskegon Community College; Zahir Small, Santa Fe College; Joel Sperber, Seton Hall University; Susan Topping, Three Rivers Community College; John Valliere, Eastern Florida State College; Joette Waddle, Roane State Community College; Fontaine Wallace, Florida Institute of Technology; Rita Weeks, Spartanburg Community College; Jenny Williams, Spartanburg Community College; and Joyce Williams, University of Alabama at Birmingham.

I would also like to give special thanks to the following instructors who contributed teaching tips to *Resources for Teaching the Bedford Introduction to Literature*: Sandra Adickes, Helen J. Aling, Sr. Anne Denise Brenann, Robin Calitri, James H. Clemmer, Robert Croft, Thomas Edwards, Elizabeth Kleinfeld, Olga Lyles, Timothy Peters, Catherine Rusco, Robert M. St. John, Richard Stoner, Nancy Veiga, Karla Walters, and Joseph Zeppetello.

I am also indebted to those who cheerfully answered questions and generously provided miscellaneous bits of information. What might have seemed to them like inconsequential conversations turned out to be important leads. Among these friends and colleagues are Raymond Anselment, Barbara Campbell, Ann Charters, Karen Chow, John Christie, Eleni Coundouriotis, Irving Cummings, William Curtin, Patrick Hogan, Lee Jacobus, Thomas Jambeck, Bonnie Januszewski-Ytuarte, Greta Little, George Monteiro, Brenda Murphy, Joel Myerson, Rose Quiello, Thomas Recchio, William Sheidley, Stephanie Smith, Milton Stern, Kenneth Wilson, and the dedicated reference librarians at the Homer Babbidge Library, University of Connecticut. I am particularly happy to acknowledge the tactful help of Roxanne Cody, owner of R. J. Julia Booksellers in Madison, Connecticut, whose passion for books authorizes her as the consummate matchmaker for writers, readers, and titles. It's a wonder that somebody doesn't call the cops.

I continue to be grateful for what I have learned from teaching my students and for the many student papers I have received over the years that I have used in various forms to serve as good and accessible models of student writing. I am also indebted to Valerie Duff-Strautmann for her extensive work on the eleventh edition of *Resources for Teaching the Bedford Introduction to Literature*.

At Bedford/St. Martin's, my debts once again require more time to acknowledge than the deadline allows. Charles H. Christensen and Joan E. Feinberg initiated this project and launched it with their intelligence, energy, and sound advice. This book has also benefited from the savvy insights of Denise Wydra, Edwin Hill, Vivian Garcia, Maura Shea, and Steve Scipione. Earlier editions of the book were shaped by editors Karen Henry, Kathy Retan, Alanya Harter, Aron Keesbury, and Ellen Thibault; their work was as first rate as it was essential. As my development editor, Christina Gerogiannis expertly kept the book on track and made the journey a pleasure to the end; her valuable contributions richly remind me of how fortunate I am to be a Bedford/St. Martin's author. Cara Kaufman, editorial assistant, gracefully handled a variety of editorial tasks. Permissions were deftly arranged by Kalina Ingham, Arthur Johnson, Martha Friedman, and Susan Doheny. The difficult tasks of production were skillfully managed by Deborah Baker, whose attention to details and deadlines was essential to the completion of this project. Jennifer Greenstein provided careful copyediting, and Anne True and Angela Morrison did meticulous proofreading. I thank all of the people at Bedford/St. Martin's — including John Callahan, who designed the cover, and Joy Fisher Williams, the marketing manager — who helped to make this formidable project a manageable one.

Finally, I am grateful to my sons Timothy and Matthew for all kinds of help, but mostly I'm just grateful they're my sons. And for making all the difference, I thank my wife, Regina Barreca.

— Michael Meyer

GET THE MOST OUT OF YOUR COURSE WITH *THE BEDFORD INTRODUCTION TO LITERATURE*

The Bedford Introduction to Literature doesn't stop with a book. Bedford/St. Martin's offers resources that help you and your students get even more out of your book and course. You'll also find convenient instructor resources, and even a nationwide community of teachers. To learn more about or to order any of the following products, contact your Bedford/St. Martin's sales representative, visit **macmillanhighered.com/myrep**, or visit **macmillanhighered.com/meyerlit/catalog**.

Assign LaunchPad Solo for Literature — *the online, interactive, guide to close reading*

macmillanhighered.com/meyerlit/catalog

To get the most out of *The Bedford Introduction to Literature*, assign it with *LaunchPad Solo for Literature*, which can be packaged at **a significant discount**. With easy-to-use and easy-to-assign modules, reading comprehension quizzes, and engaging author videos, *LaunchPad Solo for Literature* guides students through three common assignment types: responding to a reading, drawing connections between two or more texts, and instructor-led collaborative close reading. Get all of our great resources and activities in one fully customizable space online; then use our tools with your own content.

Package one of our best-selling brief handbooks at a discount

Do you need a pocket-sized handbook for your course? Package *Easy Writer* by Andrea Lunsford or *A Pocket Style Manual* by Diana Hacker and Nancy Sommers with this text at a 20% discount. For more information, go to **macmillanhighered.com/easywriter/catalog** or **macmillanhighered.com /pocket/catalog**.

Teach longer works at a nice price

Volumes from our Literary Reprint series—the Case Studies in Contemporary Criticism series, Bedford Cultural Edition series, the Bedford Shakespeare series, and the Bedford College Editions—can be shrinkwrapped with *The Bedford Introduction to Literature* at a discount. For a complete list of available titles, visit **macmillanhighered.com/literaryreprints/catalog**.

Trade Up and save 50%

Add more value and choice to your students' learning experiences by packaging their Bedford/St. Martin's textbook with one of a thousand titles from our sister publishers, including Farrar, Straus and Giroux and St. Martin's Press—at a discount of 50% off the regular price. Visit **macmillanhighered .com/tradeup** for details.

Access your instructor resources and get teaching ideas you can use today

Are you looking for professional resources for teaching literature and writing? How about some help with planning classroom activities?

REQUEST OR DOWNLOAD YOUR INSTRUCTOR'S MANUAL This comprehensive manual offers teaching support for every selection, useful for new and experienced instructors alike. Resources include commentaries, biographical information, and writing assignments, as well as teaching tips from instructors who have taught with the book, additional suggestions for connections among the selections, and thematic groupings with questions for discussion and writing. The manual is available in print and online at **macmillanhighered .com/meyerlit/catalog**.

JOIN OUR COMMUNITY The Macmillan English Community is home to Bedford/St. Martin's professional resources, featuring content to support the teaching of literature—including our popular blog, *LitBits*, as well as articles, research studies, and testimonials on the importance of literature in our classrooms and in our lives. Community members may also review projects and ideas in the pipeline. Join at **community.macmillan.com**.

ORDER CONTENT FOR YOUR COURSE MANAGEMENT SYSTEM Content cartridges for the most common course management systems — Blackboard, Canvas, Angel, Moodle, Sakai, and Desire2Learn — allow you to easily download Bedford/St. Martin's digital materials for your course. For more information, visit **macmillanhighered.com/coursepacks**.

Brief Contents

DRAMA

Contents

KATE CHOPIN
Missouri Historical
Society, St. Louis.

2. Writing about Fiction   *46*

3. Plot   *66*

WILLIAM FAULKNER
Cofield Collection, Archives and Special Collections, University of Mississippi Libraries.

FAY WELDON
© Steve Ellison/
Corbis.

Approaches to Fiction 313

NATHANIEL HAWTHORNE
© Peabody Essex Museum, Salem, Massachusetts.

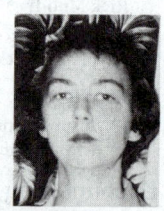

FLANNERY O'CONNOR
© Corbis.

14. A Cultural Case Study: James Joyce's "Eveline" 430

A Brief Biography and Introduction 431

Documents 440

15. A Study of Dagoberto Gilb: The Author Reflects on Three Stories 448

Introduction 448

A Brief Biography 449

DAGOBERTO GILB
Courtesy of Dagoberto Gilb.

ZORA NEALE HURSTON
Library of Congress, Print and Photographs Division.

POETRY   585

The Elements of Poetry   587

JOHN UPDIKE
Boston Globe/Getty Images.

22. Word Choice, Word Order, and Tone 635

JOANNE DIAZ
Jason Reblando.

STEPHEN CRANE
© Bettmann/CORBIS.

JEAN TOOMER
© Bettmann/Corbis.

27. Patterns of Rhythm   *754*

28. Poetic Forms 775

EDNA ST. VINCENT MILLAY
© Corbis.

Approaches to Poetry   827

EMILY DICKINSON
Todd-Bingham
Picture Collection,
1837–1966 (inclusive). Manuscripts
& Archives, Yale
University.

ROBERT FROST
The Estate of Robert Frost.

JULIA ALVAREZ
© Jeffrey Allan Salter/
Corbis Outline.

36. A Cultural Case Study: Harlem Renaissance Poets Claude McKay, Georgia Douglas Johnson, Langston Hughes, and Countee Cullen 959

LANGSTON HUGHES
© Corbis.

37. A Thematic Case Study: Love and Longing 996

38. A Thematic Case Study: Humor and Satire 1008

KAY RYAN
© Christopher Felver/
Corbis.

An Anthology of Poems 1041

WILLIAM BUTLER
YEATS
© Hulton-Deutsch
Collection/Corbis.

DRAMA   1073

The Study of Drama   1075

LARRY DAVID
© Dan Winters.

ETHAN HAWKE AS HAMLET
The Kobal Collection at Art Resource, NY.

SCENE FROM *DOUBT*
Sara Krulwich/*The New York
Times*/Redux.

Plays in Performance

Photos of scenes from:

SCENE FROM *DEATH OF A SALESMAN*
Photo by W. Eugene Smith, The LIFE Picture Collection/Getty Images.

49. A Thematic Case Study: An Album of Contemporary Humor and Satire 1465

A Collection of Plays   1487

50. Plays for Further Reading 1489

WENDY WASSERSTEIN
Jack Mitchell/Getty Images.

CRITICAL THINKING AND WRITING 1639

MARGARET ATWOOD
Kathy deWitt/Alamy.

DOROTHY PARKER
© Bettmann/Corbis.

INTRODUCTION

Reading
Imaginative Literature

To seek the source, the impulse of a story is like tearing a flower to pieces for wantonness.
— KATE CHOPIN

Missouri Historical Society, St. Louis.

THE NATURE OF LITERATURE

Literature does not lend itself to a single tidy definition because the making of it over the centuries has been as complex, unwieldy, and natural as life itself. Is literature everything that has been written, from ancient prayers to graffiti? Does it include songs and stories that were not written down until many years after they were recited? Does literature include the television scripts from *Modern Family* as well as Shakespeare's *King Lear*? Is literature only writing that has permanent value and continues to move people? Must literature be true or beautiful or moral? Should it be socially useful?

Although these kinds of questions are not conclusively answered in this book, they are implicitly raised by the stories, poems, and plays included here. No definition of literature, particularly a brief one, is likely to satisfy everyone because definitions tend to weaken and require qualification when confronted by the uniqueness of individual works. In this context it is worth recalling Herman Melville's humorous use of a definition of a whale in *Moby-Dick* (1851). In the course of the novel Melville presents his imaginative and symbolic whale as inscrutable, but he begins with a quotation from Georges Cuvier, a French naturalist who defines a whale in his nineteenth-century study *The Animal Kingdom* this way: "The whale is a mammiferous animal without hind feet." Cuvier's description is technically correct, of course, but there is little wisdom in it. Melville understood that the reality of the whale (which he describes as the "ungraspable phantom of life") cannot be caught by isolated facts. If the full meaning of the whale is to be understood, it must be sought on the open sea of experience, where the whale itself is, rather than in exclusionary definitions. Facts and definitions are helpful; however, they do not always reveal the whole truth.

Despite Melville's reminder that a definition can be too limiting and even comical, it is useful for our purposes to describe literature as a fiction consisting of carefully arranged words designed to stir the imagination. Stories, poems, and plays are fictional. They are made up — imagined — even when based on actual historic events. Such imaginative writing differs from other kinds of writing because its purpose is not primarily to transmit facts or ideas. Imaginative literature is a source more of pleasure than of information, and we read it for basically the same reasons we listen to music or view a dance: enjoyment, delight, and satisfaction. Like other art forms, imaginative literature offers pleasure and usually attempts to convey a perspective, mood, feeling, or experience. Writers transform the facts the world provides — people, places, and objects — into experiences that suggest meanings.

Consider, for example, the difference between the following factual description of a snake and a poem on the same subject. Here is *Webster's Eleventh New Collegiate Dictionary*'s definition:

> any of numerous limbless scaled reptiles (suborder Serpentes syn. Ophidia) with a long tapering body and with salivary glands often modified to produce venom which is injected through grooved or tubular fangs.

Contrast this matter-of-fact definition with Emily Dickinson's poetic evocation of a snake in "A narrow Fellow in the Grass":

A narrow Fellow in the Grass
Occasionally rides —
You may have met Him — did you not
His notice sudden is —

The Grass divides as with a Comb —   5
A spotted shaft is seen —
And then it closes at your feet
And opens further on —

He likes a Boggy Acre
A floor too cool for Corn —   10
Yet when a Boy, and Barefoot —
I more than once at Noon

Have passed, I thought, a Whip lash
Unbraiding in the Sun
When stooping to secure it   15
It wrinkled, and was gone —

Several of Nature's People
I know, and they know me —
I feel for them a transport
Of cordiality —   20

But never met this Fellow
Attended, or alone
Without a tighter breathing
And Zero at the Bone —

The dictionary provides a succinct, anatomical description of what a snake is, while Dickinson's poem suggests what a snake can mean. The definition offers facts; the poem offers an experience. The dictionary would probably allow someone who had never seen a snake to sketch one with reasonable accuracy. The poem also provides some vivid subjective descriptions — for example, the snake dividing the grass "as with a Comb" — yet it offers more than a picture of serpentine movements. The poem conveys the ambivalence many people have about snakes — the kind of feeling, for example, so evident on the faces of visitors viewing the snakes at a zoo. In the poem there is both a fascination with and a horror of what might be called snakehood; this combination of feelings has been coiled in most of us since Adam and Eve.

That "narrow Fellow" so cordially introduced by way of a riddle (the word *snake* is never used in the poem) is, by the final stanza, revealed as a snake in the grass. In between, Dickinson uses language expressively to convey her meaning. For instance, in the line "His notice sudden is," listen to the *s* sound in each word and note how the verb *is* unexpectedly appears at the end, making the snake's hissing presence all the more "sudden." And anyone who has ever been surprised by a snake knows the "tighter breathing / And Zero at the Bone" that Dickinson evokes so successfully by the rhythm of her word choices and line breaks. Perhaps even more significant, Dickinson's poem allows those who have never encountered a snake to imagine such an experience.

A good deal more could be said about the numbing fear that undercuts the affection for nature at the beginning of this poem, but the point here is that imaginative literature gives us not so much the full, factual proportions of the world as some of its experiences and meanings. Instead of defining the world, literature encourages us to try it out in our imaginations.

THE VALUE OF LITERATURE

Mark Twain once shrewdly observed that a person who chooses not to read has no advantage over a person who is unable to read. In industrialized societies today, however, the question is not who reads, because nearly everyone can and does, but what is read. Why should anyone spend precious time with literature when there is so much reading material available that provides useful information about everything from the daily news to personal computers? Why should a literary artist's imagination compete for attention that could be spent on the firm realities that constitute everyday life? In fact, national best-seller lists much less often include collections of stories, poems, or plays than they do cookbooks and, not surprisingly, diet books. Although such fare may be filling, it doesn't stay with you. Most people have other appetites too.

Certainly one of the most important values of literature is that it nourishes our emotional lives. An effective literary work may seem to speak directly to us, especially if we are ripe for it. The inner life that good writers reveal in their characters often gives us glimpses of some portion of ourselves. We can be moved to laugh, cry, tremble, dream, ponder, shriek, or rage with a character by simply turning a page instead of turning our lives upside down. Although the experience itself is imagined, the emotion is real. That's why the final chapters of a good adventure novel can make a reader's heart race as much as a 100-yard dash or why the repressed love of Hester Prynne in *The Scarlet Letter* by Nathaniel Hawthorne is painful to a sympathetic reader. Human emotions speak a universal language regardless of when or where a work was written.

In addition to appealing to our emotions, literature broadens our perspectives on the world. Most of the people we meet are pretty much like ourselves, and what we can see of the world even in a lifetime is astonishingly limited. Literature allows us to move beyond the inevitable boundaries of our own lives and culture because it introduces us to people different from ourselves, places remote from our neighborhoods, and times other than our own. Reading makes us more aware of life's possibilities as well as its subtleties and ambiguities. Put simply, people who read literature experience more life and have a keener sense of a common human identity than those who do not. It is true, of course, that many people go through life without reading imaginative literature, but that is a loss rather than a gain. They may find themselves troubled by the same kinds of questions that reveal Daisy Buchanan's restless, vague discontentment in F. Scott Fitzgerald's *The Great Gatsby:* "What'll we do with ourselves this afternoon?" cried Daisy, "and the day after that, and the next thirty years?"

Sometimes students mistakenly associate literature more with school than with life. Accustomed to reading it in order to write a paper or pass an examination, students may perceive such reading as a chore instead of a pleasurable opportunity, something considerably less important than studying for the "practical" courses that prepare them for a career. The study of literature, however, is also practical because it engages you in the kinds of problem solving important in a variety of fields, from philosophy to science and technology. The interpretation of literary texts requires you to deal with uncertainties, value judgments, and emotions; these are unavoidable aspects of life.

People who make the most significant contributions to their professions — whether in business, engineering, teaching, or some other area — tend to be challenged rather than threatened by multiple possibilities. Instead of retreating to the way things have always been done, they bring freshness and creativity to their work. F. Scott Fitzgerald once astutely described the "test of a first-rate intelligence" as "the ability to hold two opposed ideas in the mind at the same time, and still retain the ability to function." People with such intelligence know how to read situations, shape questions, interpret details, and evaluate competing points of view. Equipped with a healthy respect for facts, they also understand the value of pursuing hunches and exercising their imaginations. Reading literature encourages a suppleness of mind that is helpful in any discipline or work.

Once the requirements for your degree are completed, what ultimately matters are not the courses listed on your transcript but the sensibilities and habits of mind that you bring to your work, friends, family, and, indeed, the rest of your life. A healthy economy changes and grows with the times; people do too if they are prepared for more than simply filling a job description. The range and variety of life that literature affords can help you to interpret your own experiences and the world in which you live.

To discover the insights that literature reveals requires careful reading and sensitivity. One of the purposes of a college introduction to literature class is to cultivate the analytic skills necessary for reading well. Class discussions often help establish a dialogue with a work that perhaps otherwise would not speak to you. Analytic skills can also be developed by writing about what you read. Writing is an effective means of clarifying your responses and ideas because it requires you to account for the author's use of language as well as your own. This book is based on two premises: that reading literature is pleasurable and that reading and understanding a work sensitively by thinking, talking, or writing about it increases the pleasure of the experience of it.

Understanding its basic elements — such as point of view, symbol, theme, tone, irony, and so on — is a prerequisite to an informed appreciation of literature. This kind of understanding allows you to perceive more in a literary work in much the same way that a spectator at a tennis match sees more if he or she understands the rules and conventions of the game. But literature is not simply a spectator sport. The analytic skills that open up literature also have their uses when you watch a television program or film and, more important, when you attempt to sort out the significance of the people, places, and events that constitute your own life. Literature enhances and sharpens your perceptions. What could be more lastingly practical as well as satisfying?

THE CHANGING LITERARY CANON

Perhaps the best reading creates some kind of change in us: we see more clearly; we're alert to nuances; we ask questions that previously didn't occur to us. Henry David Thoreau had that sort of reading in mind when he remarked in *Walden* that the books he valued most were those that caused him to date "a new era in his life from the reading." Readers are sometimes changed by literature, but it is also worth noting that the life of a literary work can also be affected by its readers. Melville's *Moby-Dick,* for example, was not valued as a classic until the 1920s, when critics rescued the novel from the obscurity of being cataloged in many libraries (including Yale's) not under fiction but under cetology, the study of whales. Indeed, many writers contemporary to Melville who were important and popular in the nineteenth century — William Cullen Bryant, Henry Wadsworth Longfellow, and James Russell Lowell, to name a few — are now mostly unread; their names appear more often on elementary schools built early in the twentieth century than in anthologies. Clearly, literary reputations and what is valued as great literature change over time and in the eyes of readers.

Such changes have steadily accelerated as the literary *canon* — those works considered by scholars, critics, and teachers to be the most important to read and study — has undergone a significant series of shifts. Writers who previously were overlooked, undervalued, neglected, or studiously ignored have been brought into focus in an effort to create a more diverse literary canon, one that recognizes the contributions of the many cultures that make up American society. Since the 1960s, for example, some critics have reassessed writings by women who had been left out of the standard literary traditions dominated by male writers. Many more female writers are now read alongside the male writers who traditionally populated literary history. Hence, a reader of Mark Twain and Stephen Crane is now just as likely to encounter Kate Chopin in a literary anthology. Until fairly recently Chopin was mostly regarded as a minor local colorist of Louisiana life. In the 1960s, however, the feminist movement helped to establish her present reputation as a significant voice in American literature owing to the feminist concerns so compellingly articulated by her female characters. This kind of enlargement of the canon also resulted from another reform movement of the 1960s. The civil rights movement sensitized literary critics to the political, moral, and esthetic necessity of rediscovering African American literature, and more recently Asian and Hispanic writers have been making their way into the canon. Moreover, on a broader scale the canon is being revised and enlarged to include the works of writers from parts of the world other than the West, a development that reflects the changing values, concerns, and complexities of recent decades, when literary landscapes have shifted as dramatically as the political boundaries of much of the world.

No semester's reading list — or anthology — can adequately or accurately echo all the new voices competing to be heard as part of the mainstream literary canon, but recent efforts to open up the canon attempt to sensitize readers to the voices of women, minorities, and writers from all over the world. This development has not occurred without its urgent advocates or passionate dissenters. It's no surprise that issues about race, gender, and class often get people off the fence and on their feet. (These controversies are discussed further in Chapter 51, "Critical Strategies for Reading.") Although what we regard as literature — whether it's called great, classic, or canonical — continues to generate debate, there is no question that such controversy will continue to reflect readers' values as well as the writers they admire.

FICTION

The Elements
of Fiction

1

Reading Fiction

You don't find out you're an artist because you do something really well. You find out you're an artist because when you fail you have something within you — strength or belief or just craziness — that picks you back up again.

— JUNOT DÍAZ

READING FICTION RESPONSIVELY

Reading a literary work responsively can be an intensely demanding activity. Henry David Thoreau — about as intense and demanding a reader and writer as they come — insists that "books must be read as deliberately and reservedly as they were written." Thoreau is right about the necessity for a conscious, sustained involvement with a literary work. Imaginative literature does demand more from us than, say, browsing through *People* magazine in a dentist's waiting room, but Thoreau makes the process sound a little more daunting than it really is. For when we respond to the demands of responsive reading, our efforts are usually rewarded with pleasure as well as understanding. Careful, deliberate reading — the kind that engages a reader's imagination as it calls forth the writer's — is a means of exploration that can take a reader outside whatever circumstance or experience previously defined his or her world. Just as we respond moment by moment to people and situations in our lives, we also respond to literary works as we read them, though we may not be fully aware of how we are affected at each point along the way. The more conscious we are of how and why we respond to works in particular ways, the more likely we are to be imaginatively engaged in our reading.

In a very real sense both the reader and the author create the literary work. How a reader responds to a story, poem, or play will help to determine its meaning. The author arranges the various elements that constitute his or her craft — elements such as plot, character, setting, point of view, symbolism, theme, and style, which you will be examining in subsequent chapters and which are defined in the Glossary of Literary Terms (p. 1716) — but the author cannot completely control the reader's response any more than a person can absolutely predict how a remark or action will be received by a stranger, a friend, or even a family member. Few authors *tell* readers how to respond. Our sympathy, anger, confusion, laughter, sadness, or whatever the feeling might be is left up to us to experience. Writers may have the talent to evoke such feelings, but they don't have the power and authority to enforce them. Because of the range of possible responses produced by imaginative literature, there is no single, correct, definitive response or interpretation. There can be readings that are wrongheaded or foolish, and some readings are better than others — that is, more responsive to a work's details and more persuasive — but that doesn't mean there is only one possible reading of a work (see Chapter 2, "Writing about Fiction").

Experience tells us that different people respond differently to the same work. Consider, for example, how often you've heard Melville's *Moby-Dick* described as one of the greatest American novels. This, however, is how a reviewer in *New Monthly Magazine* described the book when it was published in 1851: it is "a huge dose of hyperbolical slang, maudlin sentimentalism and tragic-comic bubble and squeak." Melville surely did not intend or desire this response; but there it is, and it was not a singular, isolated reaction. This reading — like any reading — was influenced by the values, assumptions, and expectations that the readers brought to the novel from both previous readings and life experiences. The reviewer's refusal to take the book seriously may have caused him to miss the boat from the perspective of many other readers of *Moby-Dick*, but it indicates that even "classics" (perhaps especially those kinds of works) can generate disparate readings.

Consider the following brief story by Kate Chopin, a writer whose fiction (like Melville's) sometimes met with indifference or hostility in her own time. As you read, keep track of your responses to the central character, Mrs. Mallard. Write down your feelings about her in a substantial paragraph when you finish the story. Think, for example, about how you respond to the emotions she expresses concerning news of her husband's death. What do you think of her feelings about marriage? Do you think you would react the way she does under similar circumstances?

Kate Chopin (1851–1904)

The Story of an Hour   1894

Missouri Historical Society, St. Louis.

Knowing that Mrs. Mallard was afflicted with a heart trouble, great care was taken to break to her as gently as possible the news of her husband's death.

It was her sister Josephine who told her, in broken sentences; veiled hints that revealed in half concealing. Her husband's friend Richards was there, too, near her. It was he who had been in the newspaper office when intelligence of the railroad disaster was received, with Brently Mallard's name leading the list of "killed." He had only taken the time to assure himself of its truth by a second telegram, and had hastened to forestall any less careful, less tender friend in bearing the sad message.

She did not hear the story as many women have heard the same, with a paralyzed inability to accept its significance. She wept at once, with sudden, wild abandonment, in her sister's arms. When the storm of grief had spent itself she went away to her room alone. She would have no one follow her.

There stood, facing the open window, a comfortable, roomy armchair. Into this she sank, pressed down by a physical exhaustion that haunted her body and seemed to reach into her soul.

She could see in the open square before her house the tops of trees that were all 5 aquiver with the new spring life. The delicious breath of rain was in the air. In the street below a peddler was crying his wares. The notes of a distant song which some one was singing reached her faintly, and countless sparrows were twittering in the eaves.

There were patches of blue sky showing here and there through the clouds that had met and piled one above the other in the west facing her window.

She sat with her head thrown back upon the cushion of the chair, quite motionless, except when a sob came up into her throat and shook her, as a child who has cried itself to sleep continues to sob in its dreams.

She was young, with a fair, calm face, whose lines bespoke repression and even a certain strength. But now there was a dull stare in her eyes, whose gaze was fixed away off yonder on one of those patches of blue sky. It was not a glance of reflection, but rather indicated a suspension of intelligent thought.

There was something coming to her and she was waiting for it, fearfully. What was it? She did not know; it was too subtle and elusive to name. But she felt it, creeping out of the sky, reaching toward her through the sounds, the scents, the color that filled the air.

Now her bosom rose and fell tumultuously. She was beginning to recognize this 10 thing that was approaching to possess her, and she was striving to beat it back with her will—as powerless as her two white slender hands would have been.

When she abandoned herself a little whispered word escaped her slightly parted lips. She said it over and over under her breath: "free, free, free!" The vacant stare and the look of terror that had followed it went from her eyes. They stayed keen and bright. Her pulses beat fast, and the coursing blood warmed and relaxed every inch of her body.

She did not stop to ask if it were or were not a monstrous joy that held her. A clear and exalted perception enabled her to dismiss the suggestion as trivial.

She knew that she would weep again when she saw the kind, tender hands folded in death; the face that had never looked save with love upon her, fixed and gray and dead. But she saw beyond that bitter moment a long procession of years to come that would belong to her absolutely. And she opened and spread her arms out to them in welcome.

There would be no one to live for her during those coming years; she would live for herself. There would be no powerful will bending hers in that blind persistence with which men and women believe they have a right to impose a private will upon a fellow-creature. A kind intention or a cruel intention made the act seem no less a crime as she looked upon it in that brief moment of illumination.

And yet she had loved him — sometimes. Often she had not. What did it mat- 15 ter! What could love, the unsolved mystery, count for in face of this possession of self-assertion which she suddenly recognized as the strongest impulse of her being!

"Free! Body and soul free!" she kept whispering.

Josephine was kneeling before the closed door with her lips to the keyhole, imploring for admission. "Louise, open the door! I beg; open the door — you will make yourself ill. What are you doing, Louise? For heaven's sake open the door."

"Go away. I am not making myself ill." No; she was drinking in a very elixir of life through that open window.

Her fancy was running riot along those days ahead of her. Spring days, and summer days, and all sorts of days that would be her own. She breathed a quick prayer that life might be long. It was only yesterday she had thought with a shudder that life might be long.

She arose at length and opened the door to her sister's importunities. There was 20 a feverish triumph in her eyes, and she carried herself unwittingly like a goddess of Victory. She clasped her sister's waist, and together they descended the stairs. Richards stood waiting for them at the bottom.

Some one was opening the front door with a latchkey. It was Brently Mallard who entered, a little travel-stained, composedly carrying his gripsack and umbrella. He had been far from the scene of accident, and did not even know there had been one. He stood amazed at Josephine's piercing cry; at Richards' quick motion to screen him from the view of his wife.

But Richards was too late.

When the doctors came they said she had died of heart disease — of joy that kills.

A SAMPLE CLOSE READING

An Annotated Section of "The Story of an Hour"

Even as you read a story for the first time, you can highlight passages, circle or underline words, and write responses in the margins. Subsequent readings will yield more insights once you begin to understand how various elements such as plot, characterization, and wording build toward the conclusion and what you perceive to be the story's central ideas. The following annotations for the first eleven paragraphs of "The Story of an Hour" provide a perspective written by someone who had read the work several times. Your own approach might, of course, be quite different — as the sample paper that follows the annotated passage amply demonstrates.

KATE CHOPIN (1851–1904)

The Story of an Hour   1894

Knowing that Mrs. Mallard was afflicted with a heart trouble, great care was taken to break to her as gently as possible the news of her husband's death.

It was her sister Josephine who told her, in broken sentences; veiled hints that revealed in half concealing. Her husband's friend Richards was there, too, near her. It was he who had been in the newspaper office when intelligence of the railroad disaster was received, with Brently Mallard's name leading the list of "killed." He had only taken the time to assure himself of its truth by a second telegram, and had hastened to forestall any less careful, less tender friend in bearing the sad message.

She did not hear the story as many women have heard the same, with a paralyzed inability to accept its significance. She wept at once, with sudden, wild abandonment, in her sister's arms. When the storm of grief had spent itself she went away to her room alone. She would have no one follow her.

There stood, facing the open window, a comfortable, roomy armchair. Into this she sank, pressed down by a physical exhaustion that haunted her body and seemed to reach into her soul.

She could see in the open square before her house the tops 5 of trees that were all aquiver with the new spring life. The delicious breath of rain was in the air. In the street below a peddler was crying his wares. The notes of a distant song which some one was singing reached her faintly, and countless sparrows were twittering in the eaves.

There were patches of blue sky showing here and there through the clouds that had met and piled one above the other in the west facing her window.

She sat with her head thrown back upon the cushion of the chair, quite motionless, except when a sob came up into her throat and shook her, as a child who has cried itself to sleep continues to sob in its dreams.

She was young, with a fair, calm face, whose lines bespoke repression and even a certain strength. But now there was a dull stare in her eyes, whose gaze was fixed away off yonder on one of those patches of blue sky. It was not a glance of reflection, but rather indicated a suspension of intelligent thought.

There was something coming to her and she was waiting for it, fearfully. What was it? She did not know; it was too subtle

---

Marginal annotations:

The title could point to the brevity of the story — only 23 short paragraphs — or to the decisive nature of what happens in a very short period of time. Or both.

Mrs. Mallard's first name (Louise) is not given until paragraph 17, yet her sister Josephine is named immediately. This emphasizes Mrs. Mallard's married identity.

Given the nature of the cause of Mrs. Mallard's death at the story's end, it's worth noting the ambiguous description that she "was afflicted with a heart trouble." Is this one of Chopin's (rather than Josephine's) "veiled hints"?

When Mrs. Mallard weeps with "wild abandonment," the reader is again confronted with an ambiguous phrase: she grieves in an overwhelming manner yet seems to express relief at being abandoned by Brently's death.

These 3 paragraphs create an increasingly "open" atmosphere that leads to the "delicious" outside where there are inviting sounds and "patches of blue sky." There's a definite tension between the inside and outside worlds.

Though still stunned by grief, Mrs. Mallard begins to feel a change come over her owing to her growing awareness of a world outside her room. What that change is remains "too subtle and elusive to name."

Mrs. Mallard's conflicted struggle is described in passionate, physical terms as if she is "possess[ed]" by a lover she is "powerless" to resist.

Once she has "abandoned" herself (see the "abandonment" in paragraph 3), the reader realizes that her love is to be "free, free, free." Her recognition is evident in the "coursing blood [that] warmed and relaxed every inch of her body."

and elusive to name. But she felt it, creeping out of the sky, reaching toward her through the sounds, the scents, the color that filled the air.

Now her bosom rose and fell tumultuously. She was 10 beginning to recognize this thing that was approaching to possess her, and she was striving to beat it back with her will — as powerless as her two white slender hands would have been.

When she abandoned herself a little whispered word escaped her slightly parted lips. She said it over and over under her breath: "free, free, free!" The vacant stare and the look of terror that had followed it went from her eyes. They stayed keen and bright. Her pulses beat fast, and the coursing blood warmed and relaxed every inch of her body. . . .

Do you find Mrs. Mallard a sympathetic character? Some readers think that she is callous, selfish, and unnatural — even monstrous — because she ecstatically revels in her newly discovered sense of freedom so soon after learning of her husband's presumed death. Others read her as a victim of her inability to control her own life in a repressive, male-dominated society. Is it possible to hold both views simultaneously, or are they mutually exclusive? Are your views in any way influenced by your being male or female? Does your age affect your perception? What about your social and economic background? Does your nationality, race, or religion in any way shape your attitudes? Do you have particular views about the institution of marriage that inform your assessment of Mrs. Mallard's character? Have other reading experiences — perhaps a familiarity with some of Chopin's other stories — predisposed you one way or another to Mrs. Mallard?

Understanding potential influences might be useful in determining whether a particular response to Mrs. Mallard is based primarily on the story's details and their arrangement or on an overt or a subtle bias that is brought to the story. If you unconsciously project your beliefs and assumptions onto a literary work, you run the risk of distorting it to accommodate your prejudice. Your feelings can be a reliable guide to interpretation, but you should be aware of what those feelings are based on.

Often specific questions about literary works cannot be answered definitively. For example, Chopin does not explain why Mrs. Mallard suffers a heart attack at the end of this story. Is the shock of seeing her "dead" husband simply too much for this woman "afflicted with a heart trouble"? Does she die of what the doctors call a "joy that kills" because she is so glad to see her husband? Is she so profoundly guilty about feeling "free" at her husband's expense that she has a heart attack? Is her death a kind of willed suicide in reaction to her loss of freedom? Your answers to these questions will depend on which details you emphasize in your interpretation of the story and the kinds of perspectives and values you bring to it. If, for example, you read the story from a feminist perspective, you would be likely to pay close attention to Chopin's comments about marriage in paragraph 14. Or if you read the story as an oblique attack on the insensitivity of physicians of the period, you might want to find out whether Chopin wrote elsewhere about doctors (she did) and compare her comments with historic sources. (A number of critical strategies for reading, including feminist and historical approaches, appear in Chapter 51.)

Reading responsively makes you an active participant in the process of creating meaning in a literary work. The experience that you and the author create will most likely not be identical to another reader's encounter with the same work, but then that's true of nearly any experience you'll have, and it is part of the pleasure of reading. Indeed, talking and writing about literature is a way of sharing responses so that they can be enriched and deepened.

A SAMPLE PAPER

Differences in Responses to Kate Chopin's "The Story of an Hour"

The following paper was written in response to an assignment that called for a three- to four-page discussion of how different readers might interpret Mrs. Mallard's character. The paper is based on the story as well as on the discussion of reader-response criticism (pp. 1659–61) in Chapter 51, "Critical Strategies for Reading." As that discussion indicates, reader-response criticism is a critical approach that focuses on the reader rather than on the work itself in order to describe how the reader creates meaning from the text.

Wally Villa

Professor Brian

English 210

12 January 2015

Differences in Responses to

Kate Chopin's "The Story of an Hour"

Kate Chopin's "The Story of an Hour" appears merely to explore a woman's unpredictable reaction to her husband's assumed death and reappearance, but actually Chopin offers Mrs. Mallard's bizarre story to reveal problems that are inherent in the institution of marriage. By offering this depiction of a marriage that stifles the woman to the point that she celebrates the death of her kind and loving husband, Chopin challenges her readers to examine their own views of marriage and relationships between men and women. Each reader's judgment of Mrs. Mallard and her behavior inevitably stems from his or her own personal feelings about marriage and the influences of societal expectations. Readers of differing genders, ages, and marital experiences are, therefore, likely to react differently to Chopin's startling portrayal of the Mallards' marriage, and that certainly is true of my response to the story compared to my father's and grandmother's responses.

Marriage often establishes boundaries between people that make them unable to communicate with each other. The Mallards' marriage was evidently crippled by both their inability to talk to one another and Mrs. Mallard's conviction that her marriage was defined by a "powerful will bending hers in that blind persistence with which men and women believe they have a right to impose a private will upon a fellow-creature" (16). Yet she does not recognize that it is not just men who impose their will upon women and that the problems inherent in marriage affect men and women equally. To me, Mrs. Mallard is a somewhat sympathetic character, and I appreciate her longing to live out the "years to come that would belong to her absolutely" (16). However, I also believe that she could have tried to improve her own situation somehow, either by reaching out to her husband or by abandoning the marriage altogether. Chopin uses Mrs. Mallard's tragedy to illuminate aspects of marriage that are harmful and, in this case, even deadly. Perhaps the Mallards' relationship should be taken as a warning to others: sacrificing

---

Thesis providing writer's interpretation of story's purpose

Introduction setting up other reader responses discussed later in paper

Analysis of story's portrayal of marriage, with textual evidence

Analysis of character and plot, connecting with story's purpose

one's own happiness in order to satisfy societal expectations can poison one's life and even destroy entire families.

When my father read "The Story of an Hour," his reaction to Mrs. Mallard was more antagonistic than my own. He sees Chopin's story as a timeless "battle of the sexes," serving as further proof that men will never really be able to understand what it is that women want. Mrs. Mallard endures an obviously unsatisfying marriage without ever explaining to her husband that she feels trapped and unfulfilled. Mrs. Mallard dismisses the question of whether or not she is experiencing a "monstrous joy" (15) as trivial, but my father does not think that this is a trivial question. He believes Mrs. Mallard is guilty of a monstrous joy because she selfishly celebrates the death of her husband without ever having allowed him the opportunity to understand her feelings. He believes that, above all, Brently Mallard should be seen as the most victimized character in the story. Mr. Mallard is a good, kind man, with friends who care about him and a marriage that he thinks he can depend on. He "never looked save with love" (16) upon his wife, his only "crime" (16) was his presence in the house, and yet he is the one who is bereaved at the end of the story, for reasons he will never understand. Mrs. Mallard's passion for her newly discovered freedom is perhaps understandable, but according to my father, Mr. Mallard is the character most deserving of sympathy.

Maybe not surprisingly, my grandmother's interpretation of "The Story of an Hour" was radically different from both mine and my father's. My grandmother was married in 1936 and widowed in 1959 and therefore can identify with Chopin's characters, who live at the turn of the twentieth century. Her first reaction, aside from her unwavering support for Mrs. Mallard and her predicament, was that this story demonstrates the differences between the ways men and women related to each other a century ago and the way they relate today. Unlike my father, who thinks Mrs. Mallard is too passive, my grandmother believes that Mrs. Mallard doesn't even know that she is feeling repressed until after she is told that Brently is dead. In 1894, divorce was so scandalous and stigmatized that it simply wouldn't have been an option for Mrs. Mallard, and so her only way out of the marriage would have been one

Marginal notes:

Contrasting summary and analysis of another reader's response

Contrasting summary and analysis of another reader's response

Cultural and historical background providing context for response and story itself of their deaths. Being relatively young, Mrs. Mallard probably considered herself doomed to a long life in an unhappy marriage. My grandmother also feels that, in spite of all we know of Mrs. Mallard's feelings about her husband and her marriage, she still manages to live up to everyone's expectations of her as a woman both in life and in death. She is a dutiful wife to Brently, as she is expected to be. She weeps "with sudden, wild abandonment" when she hears the news of his death; she locks herself in her room to cope with her new situation, and she has a fatal heart attack upon seeing her husband arrive home. Naturally the male doctors would think that she died of the "joy that kills" (16)—nobody could have guessed that she was unhappy with her life, and she would never have wanted them to know.

Interpretations of "The Story of an Hour" seem to vary according to the gender, age, and experience of the reader. While both male and female readers can certainly sympathize with Mrs. Mallard's plight, female readers—as was evident in our class discussions—seem to relate more easily to her predicament and more quickly exonerate her of any responsibility for her unhappy situation. Conversely, male readers are more likely to feel compassion for Mr. Mallard, who loses his wife for reasons that will always remain entirely unknown to him. Older readers probably understand more readily the strength of social forces and the difficulty of trying to deny societal expectations concerning gender roles in general and marriage in particular. Younger readers seem to feel that Mrs. Mallard is too passive and that she could have improved her domestic life immeasurably if she had taken the initiative to either improve or end her relationship with her husband. Ultimately, how each individual reader responds to Mrs. Mallard's story reveals his or her own ideas about marriage, society, and how men and women communicate with each other.

Analysis supported with textual evidence

Conclusion summarizing reader responses explored in the paper

Work Cited

Chopin, Kate. "The Story of an Hour." *The Bedford Introduction to Literature*. Ed. Michael Meyer. 11th ed. Boston: Bedford/St. Martin's, 2016. 15–16. Print.

Before beginning your own writing assignment on fiction, you should review Chapter 2, "Writing about Fiction," as well as Chapter 52, "Reading and the Writing Process," which provides a step-by-step explanation of how to choose a topic, develop a thesis, and organize various types of writing assignments. If you use outside sources, you should also be familiar with the conventional documentation procedures described in Chapter 53, "The Literary Research Paper."

EXPLORATIONS AND FORMULAS

Each time we pick up a work of fiction, go to the theater, or turn on the television, we have a trace of the same magical expectation that can be heard in the voice of a child who begs, "Tell me a story." Human beings have enjoyed stories ever since they learned to speak. Whatever the motive for creating stories — even if simply to delight or instruct — the basic human impulse to tell and hear stories existed long before the development of written language. Myths about the origins of the world and legends about the heroic exploits of demigods were among the earliest forms of storytelling to develop into oral traditions, which were eventually written down. These narratives are the ancestors of the stories we read on the printed page today. Unlike the early listeners to ancient myths and legends, we read our stories silently, but the pleasure derived from the mysterious power of someone else's artfully arranged words remains largely the same. Every one of us likes a good story.

The stories that appear in anthologies for college students are generally chosen for their high literary quality. Such stories can affect us at the deepest emotional level, reveal new insights into ourselves or the world, and stretch us by exercising our imaginations. They warrant careful reading and close study to appreciate the art that has gone into creating them. The following chapters on plot, character, setting, and the other elements of literature are designed to provide the terms and concepts that can help you understand how a work of fiction achieves its effects and meanings. It is worth acknowledging, however, that many people buy and read fiction that is quite different from the stories usually anthologized in college texts. What about all those paperbacks with exciting, colorful covers near the cash registers in shopping malls and corner drugstores?

These books, known as *formula fiction*, are the adventure, western, detective, science fiction, and romance novels that entertain millions of readers annually. What makes them so popular? What do their characters, plots, and themes offer readers that accounts for the tremendous sales of stories with titles like *Caves of Doom, Silent Scream, Colt .45,* and *Forbidden Ecstasy?* Many of the writers included in this book have enjoyed wide popularity and written best-sellers, but there are more readers of formula fiction than there are readers of Ernest Hemingway, William Faulkner, or Joyce Carol Oates, to name only a few. Formula novels do provide entertainment, of course, but that makes them no different from serious stories, if entertainment means pleasure. Any of the stories in this or any other anthology can be read for pleasure.

Formula fiction, though, is usually characterized as escape literature. There are sensible reasons for this description. Adventure stories about soldiers of fortune are eagerly read by men who live pretty average lives doing ordinary jobs. Romance novels about attractive young women falling in love with tall, dark, handsome men are read mostly by women who dream themselves out of their familiar existences. The excitement, violence, and passion that such stories provide are a kind of reprieve from everyday experience.

And yet readers of serious fiction may also use it as a refuge, a liberation from monotony and boredom. Mark Twain's humorous stories have, for example, given countless hours of pleasurable relief to readers who would rather spend time in Twain's light and funny world than in their own. Others might prefer the terror of Edgar Allan Poe's fiction or the painful predicament of two lovers in a Joyce Carol Oates story.

Thus, to get at some of the differences between formula fiction and serious literature, it is necessary to go beyond the motives of the reader to the motives of the writer and the qualities of the work itself.

Unlike serious fiction, the books displayed next to the cash registers (and their short story equivalents on the magazine racks) are written with essentially one goal: to be sold. They are aimed at specific consumer markets that can be counted on to buy them. This does not mean that all serious writers must live in cold garrets writing for audiences who have not yet discovered their work. No one writes to make a career of poverty. It does mean, however, that if a writer's primary purpose is to anticipate readers' generic expectations about when the next torrid love scene, bloody gunfight, or thrilling chase is due, there is little room to be original or to have something significant to say. There is little if any chance to explore seriously a character, idea, or incident if the major focus is not on the integrity of the work itself.

Although the specific elements of formula fiction differ depending on the type of story, some basic ingredients go into all westerns, mysteries, adventures, science fiction, and romances. From the very start, a reader can anticipate a happy ending for the central character, with whom he or she will identify. There may be suspense, but no matter what or how many the obstacles, complications, or near defeats, the hero or heroine succeeds and reaffirms the values and attitudes the reader brings to the story. Virtue triumphs, love conquers all, honesty is the best policy, and hard work guarantees success. Hence, the villains are corralled, the wedding vows are exchanged, the butler confesses, and gold is discovered at the last moment. The visual equivalents of such formula stories are readily available at movie theaters and in television series. Some are better than others, but all are relatively limited by the writer's goal of giving an audience what will sell.

Although formula fiction may not offer many surprises, it provides pleasure to a wide variety of readers. College professors, for example, are just as likely to be charmed by formula stories as anyone else. Readers of serious fiction who revel in exploring more challenging imaginative worlds can also enjoy formulaic stories, which offer little more than an image of the world as a simple place in which our assumptions and desires are confirmed. The familiarity of a given formula is emotionally satisfying because we are secure in our expectations of it. We know at the start of a Sherlock Holmes story that the mystery will be solved by that famous detective's relentless scientific analysis of the clues, but we take pleasure in seeing how Holmes unravels the mystery before us. Similarly, we know that James Bond's wit, grace, charm, courage, and skill will ultimately prevail over the diabolic schemes of eccentric villains, but we volunteer for the mission anyway.

Perhaps that happens for the same reason that we climb aboard a roller coaster: no matter how steep and sharp the curves, we stay on a track that is both exciting and safe. Although excitement, adventure, mystery, and romance are major routes to escape in formula fiction, most of us make that trip only temporarily, for a little relaxation and fun. Momentary relief from our everyday concerns is as healthy and desirable as an occasional daydream or fantasy. Such reading is a form of play because we — like spectators of or participants in a game — experience a formula of excitement, tension, and then release that can fascinate us regardless of how many times the game is played.

There are many kinds of formulaic romance novels; some include psychological terrors, some use historical settings, and some even incorporate time travel so that the hero or heroine can travel back in time and fall in love, and still others create mystery and suspense. A number of publishers routinely release romances that reflect contemporary social concerns and issues. In addition to vampires and werewolves, Harlequin Enterprises, an enormously popular publisher that releases more than one hundred titles per month, offered two series of military novels titled *Uniformly Hot!* and *Heroes Come Home*, both reflecting America's involvement in longstanding conflicts in the Middle East; hence, the all-important cover art on bookstore shelves includes Navy Seals as well as werewolves. Multicultural couples and gay and lesbian relationships as well as more explicit descriptions of sexual activities are now sometimes featured in romance books. In general, however, the majority of romance novels are written to appeal to a readership that embraces more traditional societal expectations and values.

Many publishers of formula fiction — such as romance, adventure, or detective stories — issue a set number of new novels each month. Readers can buy them in stores or subscribe to them through the mail. These same publishers send "tip sheets" on request to authors who want to write for a particular series. The details of the formula differ from one series to another, but each tip sheet covers the basic elements that go into a story.

The following composite tip sheet summarizes the typical advice offered by publishers of romance novels. These are among the most popular titles published in the United States; it has been estimated that four out of every ten paperbacks sold are romance novels. The categories and the tone of the language in this composite tip sheet are derived from a number of publishers and provide a glimpse of how formula fiction is written and what the readers of romance novels are looking for in their escape literature.

A Composite of a Romance Tip Sheet

PLOT

The story focuses on the growing relationship between the heroine and hero. After a number of complications, they discover lasting love and make a permanent commitment to each other in marriage. The plot should move quickly. Background information about the heroine should be kept to a minimum. The hero should appear as early as possible (preferably in the first chapter and no later than the second), so that the hero's and heroine's feelings about each other are in the foreground as they cope with misperceptions that keep them apart until the final pages of the story. The more tension created by their uncertainty about each other's love, the greater the excitement and anticipation for the reader.

Love is the major interest. Do not inject murder, extortion, international intrigue, hijacking, horror, or supernatural elements into the plot. Controversial social issues and politics, if mentioned at all, should never be allowed a significant role. Once the heroine and hero meet, they should clearly be interested in each other, but that interest should be complicated by some kind of misunderstanding. He, for example, might find her too ambitious, an opportunist, cold, or flirtatious; or he might assume that she is attached to someone else. She might think he is haughty, snobbish, power hungry, indifferent, or contemptuous of her. The reader knows what they do not: that eventually these obstacles will be overcome. Interest is sustained by keeping the lovers apart until very near the end so that the reader will stay with the plot to see how they get together.

HEROINE

The heroine is a modern American woman between the ages of nineteen and twenty-eight who reflects today's concerns. The story is told in the third person from her point of view. She is attractive and nicely dressed but not glamorous; glitter and sophistication should be reserved for the other woman (the heroine's rival for the hero), whose flashiness will compare unfavorably with the heroine's modesty. When the heroine does dress up, however, her beauty should be stunningly apparent. Her trim figure is appealing but not abundant; a petite healthy appearance is desirable. Both her looks and her clothes should be generously detailed.

Her personality is spirited and independent without being pushy or stubborn because she knows when to give in. Although sensitive, she doesn't cry every time she is confronted with a problem (though she might cry in private moments). A sense of humor is helpful. Because she is on her own, away from parents (usually deceased) or other protective relationships, she is self-reliant as well as vulnerable.

The story may begin with her on the verge of an important decision about her life. She is clearly competent but not entirely certain of her own qualities. She does not take her attractiveness for granted or realize how much the hero is drawn to her.

Common careers for the heroine include assistant, nurse, teacher, interior 5 designer, assistant manager, department store buyer, travel expert, or struggling photographer (no menial work). She can also be a doctor, lawyer, or other professional. Her job can be described in some detail and made exciting, but it must not dominate her life. Although she is smart, she is not extremely intellectual or defined by her work. Often she meets the hero through work, but her major concerns center on love, marriage, home, and family. White wine is okay, but she never drinks alone — or uses drugs. She may be troubled, frustrated, threatened, and momentarily thwarted in the course of the story, but she never totally gives in to despair or desperation. She has strengths that the hero recognizes and admires.

Hero

The hero should be about ten years older than the heroine and can be foreign or American. He needn't be handsome in a traditional sense, but he must be strongly masculine. Always tall and well built (not brawny or thick) and usually dark, he looks as terrific in a three-piece suit as he does in sports clothes. His clothes reflect good taste and an affluent life-style. Very successful professionally and financially, he is a man in charge of whatever work he's engaged in (financier, doctor, publisher, architect, business executive, airline pilot, artist, etc.). His wealth is manifested in his sophistication and experience.

His past may be slightly mysterious or shrouded by some painful moment (perhaps with a woman) that he doesn't want to discuss. Whatever the circumstance — his wife's death or divorce are common — it was not his fault. Avoid chronic problems such as alcoholism, drug addiction, or sexual dysfunctions. To others he may appear moody, angry, unpredictable, and explosively passionate, but the heroine eventually comes to realize his warm, tender side. He should be attractive not only as a lover but also as a potential husband and father.

Secondary Characters

Because the major interest is in how the heroine will eventually get together with the hero, the other characters are used to advance the action. There are three major types:

(1) *The Other Woman:* Her vices serve to accent the virtues of the heroine; immediately beneath her glamorous sophistication is a deceptive, selfish, mean-spirited, rapacious predator. She may seem to have the hero in her clutches, but she never wins him in the end.

(2) *The Other Man:* He usually falls into two types: (a) the decent sort who 10 is there when the hero isn't around and (b) the selfish sort who schemes rather than loves. Neither is a match for the hero.

(3) *Other Characters:* Like furniture, they fill in the background and are useful for positioning the hero and heroine. These characters are familiar types

such as the hero's snobbish aunt, the heroine's troubled younger siblings, the loyal friend, or the office gossip. They should be realistic, but they must not be allowed to obscure the emphasis on the lovers. The hero may have children from a previous marriage, but they should rarely be seen or heard. It's usually simpler and better not to include them.

SETTING

The setting is usually contemporary. Romantic, exciting places are best: New York City, London, Paris, Rio, the mountains, the ocean — wherever it is exotic and love's possibilities are the greatest. Marriage may take the heroine and hero to a pretty suburb or small town.

LOVE SCENES

The hero and heroine may make love before marriage. The choice will depend largely on the heroine's sensibilities and circumstances. She should reflect modern attitudes. If the lovers do engage in premarital sex, it should be made clear that neither is promiscuous, especially the heroine. Even if their relationship is consummated before marriage, their lovemaking should not occur until late in the story. There should be at least several passionate scenes, but complications, misunderstandings, and interruptions should keep the couple from actually making love until they have made a firm commitment to each other. Descriptions should appeal to the senses; however, detailed, graphic close-ups are unacceptable. Passion can be presented sensually but not clinically; the lovemaking should be seen through a soft romantic lens. Violence and any out-of-the-way sexual acts should not even be hinted at. No coarse language.

WRITING

Avoid extremely complex sentences, very long paragraphs, and lengthy descriptions. Use concise, vivid details to create the heroine's world. Be sure to include full descriptions of the hero's and heroine's physical features and clothes. Allow the reader to experience the romantic mood surrounding the lovers. Show how the heroine feels; do not simply report her feelings. Dialogue should sound like ordinary conversation, and the overall writing should be contemporary English without slang, difficult foreign expressions, strange dialects, racial epithets, or obscenities (*hell, damn,* and a few other mild swears are all right).

LENGTH

55,000 to 65,000 words in ten to twelve chapters.

15

CONSIDERATIONS FOR CRITICAL THINKING AND WRITING

1. FIRST RESPONSE. Given the expectations implied by the tip sheet, what generalizations can you make about those likely to write formula fiction? Does the tip sheet change the way you think about romantic fiction or other kinds of formula fiction?

Romance novel. The cover for *The Vampire Affair* (Silhouette, 2009) illustrates another convention of romance formula fiction: its packaging demands an image of a man clasping a passionate beauty to his manly chest. This novel is a vampire romance — a subcategory of the romance formula — and so a few of the guidelines on the tip sheet are modified (the prohibition against violence, for example). But most of the guidelines apply: Michael is strong and so is Jessie's powerful love.

2. Who is the intended audience for this type of romance? Try to describe the audience in detail: How does a romance novel provide escape for these readers?

3. Why is it best that the heroine be "attractive and nicely dressed but not glamorous"? Why do you think publishers advise writers to include detailed descriptions of her clothes? Do you find the heroine appealing? Why or why not?

4. Why should the hero be "about ten years older than the heroine"? If he is divorced, why is it significant that "it was not his fault"?

5. Why do you think the hero and heroine are kept apart by complications until the end of the story? Does the outline of the plot sound familiar to you or remind you of any other stories?

6. Why do you think restrictions are placed on the love scenes?

7. Why are "extremely complex sentences, very long paragraphs, and lengthy descriptions" discouraged?

8. To what extent does the tip sheet describe the strategies used in popular television soap operas? How do you account for the appeal of these shows?

9. Explain how the tip sheet confirms traditional views of male and female roles in society. Does it accommodate any broken traditions?

10. Carefully examine the romance book cover (p. 29). How do the cover's images and copy reinforce what readers can expect from a romance novel?

11. Write a tip sheet for another kind of popular formula story, such as a western or a detective story, that you have observed in a novel, television show, or film. How is the plot patterned? How are the characters made familiar? How is the setting related to the story? What are the obligatory scenes? How is the overall style consistent? To get started, you might consider an Agatha Christie novel, an episode from a police series on television, or a James Bond film.

12. Try writing a scene for a formula romance, or read the excerpt from Edgar Rice Burroughs's *Tarzan of the Apes* (p. 69) and try an adventure scene.

A COMPARISON OF TWO STORIES

Each of the following contemporary pieces of fiction is about a woman who experiences deep sorrow. The first, from *A Secret Sorrow* by Karen van der Zee, is an excerpt from a romance by Harlequin Books, a major publisher of formula fiction that has sold well over a billion copies of its romance titles — enough for about 20 percent of the world's population. The second piece, Gail Godwin's "A Sorrowful Woman," is a complete short story that originally appeared in *Esquire;* it is not a formula story. Unlike *A Secret Sorrow*, Godwin's story does not have a standard plot pattern employing familiar character types that appear in a series of separate but similar works.

Read each selection carefully and look for evidence of formulaic writing in the chapters from *A Secret Sorrow*. Pay particular attention to the advice on plotting and characterization offered in the composite tip sheet. As you read Godwin's short story, think about how it is different from van der Zee's excerpt; note also any similarities. The questions that follow the stories should help you consider how the experiences of reading the two are different.

Karen van der Zee (b. 1947)

Born and raised in Holland, Karen van der Zee lives in the United States, where she has become a successful romance writer, contributing more than thirty novels to the popular Harlequin series. This excerpt consists of the final two chapters of *A Secret Sorrow*. This is what has happened so far: the central character, Faye, is recuperating from the psychological effects of a serious car accident in which she received a permanent internal injury. After the accident, she quits her job and breaks her engagement to Greg. She moves into her brother Chuck's house and falls in love with Kai, a visiting Texan and good friend of her brother. At the end of Chapter 10, Kai insists on knowing why she will not marry him and asks, "Who is Doctor Jaworski?"

By permission of the author.

From A Secret Sorrow   1981

Chapter Eleven

Faye could feel the blood drain from her face and for one horrifying moment she thought she was going to faint right in Kai's arms. The room tilted and everything swirled around in a wild madman's dance. She clutched at him for support, fighting for control, trying to focus at some point beyond his shoulder. Slowly, everything steadied.

"I . . . I don't know him," she murmured at last. "I. . . ."

He reached in the breast pocket of his shirt, took out a slip of paper, and held it out for her to see. One glance and Faye recognized it as the note from Doctor Martin with Doctor Jaworski's name scrawled on it, thickly underlined.

"How did you get that?" Her voice was a terrified whisper. She was still holding on, afraid she would fall if she let go.

"I found it on the floor in my bedroom. It must have fallen out of your wallet along with everything else on Saturday morning." 5

Yes — oh God! Her legs were shaking so badly, she knew it was only his arms that kept her from falling.

"Who is Doctor Jaworski, Faye?" His voice was patiently persistent.

"I . . . he. . . ." Her voice broke. "Let me go, please let me go." She felt as if she were suffocating in his embrace and she struggled against him, feebly, but it was no use.

"He's a psychiatrist, isn't he?" His voice was gentle, very gentle, and she looked up at him in stunned surprise.

He knew, oh God, he knew. She closed her eyes, a helpless sense of inevitability 10 engulfing her.

"You know," she whispered. "How do you know?"

"Simple. Two minutes on the phone to Chicago." He paused. "Doctor Martin — was he one of the doctors who treated you at the hospital?"

"Yes."

"Why did he give you Doctor Jaworski's name? Did he want you to make an appointment with him?"

"Yes." Despondency overtook her. There was no going back now. No escape 15 from the truth. No escape from his arms. Resistance faded and she felt numbed and lifeless. It didn't matter any more. Nothing mattered.

"Did you?" Kai repeated.

"Did I what?"

"See him — Doctor Jaworski."

"No."

"Why did Doctor Martin want you to see a psychiatrist?" 20

"I...." Faye swallowed miserably. "It's...it's therapy for grieving... mourning." She made a helpless gesture with her hand. "When people lose a...a wife, or husband for instance, they go through a more or less predictable pattern of emotions...." She gave him a quick glance, then looked away. "Like denial, anger...."

"...depression, mourning, acceptance," Kai finished for her, and she looked back at him in surprise.

"Yes."

His mouth twisted in a little smile. "I'm not totally ignorant about subjects other than agronomy." There was a momentary pause as he scrutinized her face. "Why did you need that kind of therapy, Faye?"

And then it was back again, the resistance, the revolt against his probing ques- 25 tions. She stiffened in defense — her whole body growing rigid with instinctive rebellion.

"It's none of your business!"

"Oh, yes, it is. We're talking about our life together. Your life and mine."

She strained against him, hands pushing against his chest. "Let me go! Please let me go!" Panic changed into tears. She couldn't take his nearness any more, the feel of his hard body touching hers, the strength of him.

"No, Faye, no. You're going to tell me. Now. I'm not letting you go until you've told me everything. Everything, you hear?"

"I can't!" she sobbed. "I can't!" 30

"Faye," he said slowly, "you'll *have* to. You told me you love me, but you don't want to marry me. You have given me no satisfactory reasons, and I'll be damned if I'm going to accept your lack of explanations."

"You have no right to demand an explanation!"

"Oh, yes, I have. You're part of me, Faye. Part of my life."

"You talk as if you own me!" She was trembling, struggling to get away from him. She couldn't stand there, so close to him with all the pent-up despair inside her, the anger, the fear of what she knew not how to tell him.

His hands were warm and strong on her back, holding her steady. Then, with 35 one hand, he tilted back her head and made her look at him. "You gave me your love — I own that," he said softly. "True loving involves commitment, vulnerability, trust. Don't you trust me, Faye?"

New tears ran silently down her cheeks. "If I told you," she blurted out, "you wouldn't . . . you wouldn't. . . ."

"I wouldn't *what?*"

"You wouldn't want me any more!" The words were wrenched from her in blind, agonizing grief. "You wouldn't *want* me any more!"

He shook his head incredulously. "What makes you think you can make that decision for me? Do you have so little trust in my love for you?"

Faye didn't answer, couldn't answer. Through a mist of tears he was nothing but 40 a blur in front of her eyes.

"What is so terrible that you can't tell me?"

She shrank inwardly, as if shriveling away in pain. "Let me go," she whispered. "Please let me go and I'll tell you."

After a moment's hesitation Kai released her. Faye backed away from him, feeling like a terrified animal. She stood with her back against the wall, glad for the support, her whole body shaking. She took a deep breath and wiped her face dry with her hand.

"I'm afraid . . . afraid to marry you."

"Afraid?" He looked perplexed. "Afraid of what? Of me? Of marriage?" 45

Faye closed her eyes, taking another deep breath. "I can't be what you want me to be. We can't have the kind of life you want." She looked at him, standing only a few feet away, anguish tearing through her. "I'm so afraid . . . you'll be disappointed," she whispered.

"Oh God, Faye," he groaned, "I love you." He came toward her and panic surged through her as he held her against the wall, his hands reaching up to catch her face between them.

"Don't," she whispered. "Please, don't touch me." But it was no use. His mouth came down on hers and he kissed her with a hard, desperate passion.

"I love you," he said huskily. "I love you."

Faye wrenched her face free from his hands. "Don't touch me! Please don't 50 touch me!" She was sobbing now, her words barely audible. Her knees gave way and her back slid down along the wall until she crumpled on to the floor, face in her hands.

Kai took a step backward and pulled her up. "Stand up, Faye. For God's sake stand up!" He held her against the wall and she looked at him, seeing every line in his dark face, the intense blue of his eyes, and knew that this was the moment, that there was no more waiting.

And Kai knew it too. His eyes held hers locked in unrelenting demand. "Why should I be disappointed, Faye? *Why?*"

Her heart was thundering in her ears and it seemed as if she couldn't breathe, as if she were going to drown.

"Because . . . because I can't give you children! Because I can't get pregnant! I can't have babies! That's why!" Her voice was an agonized cry, torn from the depths of her misery. She yanked down his arms that held her locked against the wall and moved away from him. And then she saw his face.

It was ashen, gray under his tan. He stared at her as if he had never seen her 55 before.

"Oh my God, Faye. . . ." His voice was low and hoarse. "Why didn't you tell me, why. . . ."

Faye heard no more. She ran out the door, snatching her bag off the chair as she went by. The only thought in her mind was to get away — away from Kai and what was in his eyes.

She reached for Kai's spare set of car keys in her bag, doing it instinctively, knowing she couldn't walk home alone in the dark. How she managed to get the keys in the door lock and in the ignition she never knew. Somehow, she made it home.

The phone rang as Faye opened the front door and she heard Chuck answer it in the kitchen.

"She's just got in," he said into the mouthpiece, smiling at Faye as she came into 60
view. He listened for a moment, nodded. "Okay, fine with me."

Faye turned and walked up the stairs, taking deep breaths to calm her shattered nerves. Kai hadn't wasted any time checking up on her. She didn't care what he was telling Chuck, but she wasn't going to stand there listening to a one-sided conversation. But only a second later Chuck was behind her on the stairs.

"Kai wanted to know whether you'd arrived safely."

"I did, thank you," she said levelly, her voice surprisingly steady.

"I take it you ran out and took off with his car?"

"Did he say that?" 65

"No. He was *worried* about you. He wanted to make sure you went home." He sounded impatient, and she couldn't blame him. She was making life unbearable for everyone around her. Everybody worried about her. Everybody loved her. Everything should be right. Only it wasn't.

"Well, I'm home now, and I'm going to bed. Good night."

"Good night, Faye."

Faye lay in bed without any hope of sleep. Mechanically she started to sort through her thoughts and emotions, preparing mentally for the next confrontation. There would be one, she didn't doubt it for a moment. But she needed time — time to clear her head, time to look at everything in a reasonable, unemotional way.

It was a temptation to run — get in the car and keep driving, but it would be a 70
stupid thing to do. There was no place for her to go, and Kai would find her, no matter what. If there was one thing she knew about Kai it was his stubbornness and his persistence. She had to stick it out, right here, get it over with, deal with it. Only she didn't know how.

She lay listening to the stillness, just a few sounds here and there — the house creaking, a car somewhere in the distance, a dog barking. She had to think, but her mind refused to cooperate. She *had* to think, decide what to say to Kai the next time she saw him, but she couldn't think, she *couldn't think*.

And then, as she heard the door open in the silence, the quiet footsteps coming up the stairs, she knew it was too late, that time had run out.

Without even knocking he came into her room and walked over to the bed. She could feel the mattress sag as his weight came down on it. Her heart was pounding like a sledgehammer, and then his arms came around her and he drew her against him.

"Faye," he said quietly, "please marry me."

"No," she said thickly. "No." She could feel him stiffen against her and she 75
released herself from his arms and slid off the bed. She switched on the light and stood near the window, far from the bed, far from Kai. "I don't expect you to play the gentleman, I don't expect you to throw out a life of dreams just for the sake of chivalry. You don't have to marry me, Kai." She barely recognized

her own voice. It was like the cool calm sound of a stranger, unemotional, cold. "You don't have to marry me," she repeated levelly, giving him a steady look.

Her words were underlined by the silence that followed, a silence loaded with a strange, vibrating energy, a force in itself, filling the room.

Kai rose to his feet, slowly, and the face that looked at her was like that of a stranger, a dangerous, angry stranger. Never before had she seen him so angry, so full of hot, fuming fury.

"Shut up," he said in a low, tight voice. "Shut up and stop playing the martyr!"

The sound of his voice and the words he said shocked Faye into silence. She stared at him open-mouthed, and then a slow, burning anger arose inside her.

"How dare you! How. . . ." 80

He strode toward her and took her upper arms and shook her. "Shut up and listen to me! What the hell are you thinking? What the hell did you expect me to do when you told me? You throw me a bomb and then walk out on me! What did you expect my reaction to be? Was I supposed to stay cool and calm and tell you it didn't matter? Would you have married me then? Well, let me tell you something! It matters! It matters to me! I am not apologizing for my reaction!" He paused, breathing hard. "You know I always wanted children, but what in God's name makes you think you're the only one who has the right to feel bad about it? I have that right too, you hear! I love you, dammit, and I want to marry you, and if we can't have children I have all the right in the world to feel bad about it!"

He stopped talking. He was still breathing hard and he looked at her with stormy blue eyes. Faye felt paralyzed by his tirade and she stared at him, incapable of speech. She couldn't move, she couldn't think.

"Why do you think I want you for my wife?" he continued on a calmer note. "Because you're some kind of baby factory? What kind of man do you think I am? I love *you*, not your procreating ability. So we have a problem. Well, we'll learn to deal with it, one way or another."

There was another silence, and still Faye didn't speak, and she realized she was crying, soundlessly, tears slowly dripping down her cheeks. She was staring at his chest, blindly, not knowing what to think, not thinking at all.

He lifted her chin, gently. "Look at me, Faye." 85

She did, but his face was only a blur.

"Faye, we're in this together — you and I. Don't you see that? It's not just *your* problem, it's *ours*."

"No," she whispered. "No!" She shook her head wildly. "You have a choice, don't you see that? You don't have to marry me. You could marry someone else and have children of your own."

"Oh, God, Faye," he groaned, "you're wrong. Don't you know? Don't you see? I *don't* have a choice. I never did have a choice, or a chance. Not since I met you and fell in love with you. I don't *want* anybody else, don't you understand that? I want you, only you."

She wanted to believe it, give in to him. Never before had she wanted any- 90 thing more desperately than she wanted to give in to him now. But she couldn't, she couldn't. . . . She closed her eyes, briefly, fighting for reason, common sense.

"Kai, I . . . I can't live all my life with your regret and your disappointment. Every time we see some pregnant woman, every time we're with somebody else's children I'll feel I've failed you! I. . . ." Her voice broke and new sobs came unchecked.

He held her very tightly until she calmed down and then he put her from him a little and gave her a dark, compelling look.

"It's not *my* regret, or *my* disappointment," he said with quiet emphasis. "It's *ours*. We're not talking about *you* or *me*. We're talking about *us*. I love you, and you love me, and that's the starting point, that comes first. From then on we're in it together."

Faye moved out of his arms, away from him, but her legs wouldn't carry her and she sank into a chair. She covered her face with her hands and tried desperately to stop the crying, to stop the tears from coming and coming as if they would never end.

"How . . . how can I ever believe it?"   95

"Because I'm asking you to," he said quietly. He knelt in front of her, took her hands away from her wet face. "Look at me, Faye. No other woman can give me what you can — yourself, your love, your warmth, your sense of humor. All the facets of your personality that make up the final you. I've known other women, Faye, but none of them have ever stirred in me any feelings that come close to what I feel for you. You're an original, remember? There's no replacement for an original. There are only copies, and I don't want a copy. To me you're special, and you'll have to believe it, take it on faith. That's what love is all about."

He was holding her hands in his, strong brown hands, and she was looking down on them, fighting with herself, fighting with everything inside her to believe what he was saying, to accept it, to give in to it.

Leaning forward, Kai kissed her gently on the mouth and smiled. "It's all been too much too soon for you, hasn't it? You never really got a chance to get over the shock, and when I fell in love with you it only made things worse." He smiled ruefully and Faye was surprised at his insight.

"Yes," she said. "It all happened too fast."

"Bad timing. If only we could have met later, after you'd sorted it all out in your   100 mind, then it would never have been such a crisis."

She looked at him doubtfully. "It wouldn't have changed the facts."

"No, but it might have changed your perspective."

Would it have? she wondered. Could she ever feel confident and secure in her worth as a woman? Or was she at this moment too emotionally bruised to accept that possibility?

"I don't understand," he said, "why I never guessed what was wrong. Now that I know, it all seems so obvious." He looked at her thoughtfully. "Faye," he said gently, "I want you to tell me exactly what happened to you, what Doctor Martin told you."

She stared at him, surprised a little. A thought stirred in the back of her mind.   105 Greg. He had never even asked. The why and the what had not interested him. But Kai, he wanted to know. She swallowed nervously and began the story, slowly, word for word, everything Doctor Martin had said. And he listened, quietly, not interrupting. "So you see," she said at last, "we don't have to hope for any miracles either."

"We'll make our own miracles," he said, and smiled. "Come here," he said then, "kiss me."

She did, shyly almost, until he took over and lifted her up and carried her to the bed. He looked down on her, eyes thoughtful. "I won't pretend I understand your feelings about this, the feelings you have about yourself as a woman, but I'll try." He paused for a moment. "Faye," he said then, speaking with slow emphasis, "don't *ever*, not for a single moment, think that you're not good enough for me. You're the best there is, Faye, the very best."

His mouth sought hers and he kissed her with gentle reassurance at first, then with rising ardor. His hands moved over her body, touching her with sensual, intimate caresses.

"You're my woman, Faye, you're mine. . . ."

Her senses reeled. She could never love anyone like she loved him. No one had ever evoked in her this depth of emotion. This was real, this was forever. Kai wanted her as much as ever. No chivalry, this, no game of pretense, she was very sure of that. And when he lifted his face and looked at her, it was all there in his eyes and the wonder of it filled her with joy. 110

"Do you believe me now?" he whispered huskily. "Do you believe I love you and want you and need you?"

She nodded wordlessly, incapable of uttering a sound.

"And do you love me?"

Again she nodded, her eyes in his.

"Okay, then." In one smooth flowing movement he got to his feet. He crossed to the closet, opened it, and took out her suitcases. He put one on the end of the bed and began to pile her clothes in it, taking armfuls out of the closet. 115

Faye watched incredulously. "What are you doing?" she managed at last.

Kai kept on moving around, opening drawers, taking out her things, filling the suitcase until it could hold no more. "Get dressed. We're going home."

"Home . . . ?"

For a moment he stopped and he looked at her with a deep blue glitter in his eyes. "Yes, *home* — where you belong. With me, in my house, in my bed, in my arms."

"Oh, Kai," she said tremulously, smiling suddenly. "It's midnight!" 120

His eyes were very dark. "I've waited long enough, I'm not waiting any more. You're coming with me, now. And I'm not letting you out of my sight until we're safely married. I don't want you getting any crazy ideas about running off to save me from myself, or some such notion."

Her throat was dry. "Please, let's not rush into it! Let's think about it first!"

Calmly he zipped up the full suitcase, swung it off the bed, and put it near the door. "I'm not rushing into anything," he said levelly. "I've wanted to marry you for quite a while, remember?"

He crossed to the bed, sat down next to her, and put his arm around her. "Faye, I wish you wouldn't worry so. I'm not going to change my mind. And I haven't shelved my hopes for a family, either." There was a brief silence. "When we're ready to have kids, we'll have them. We'll adopt them. There are orphanages the world over, full of children in need of love and care. We'll do whatever it takes. We'll get them, one way or another."

Faye searched his face, faint hope flickering deep inside her. 125

"Would you want that?"

"Why not?"

"I don't know, really. I thought you . . . it isn't the same."

"No," he said levelly, "it isn't. Adoption is a different process from pregnancy and birth, but the kids will be ours just the same and we'll love them no less."

"Yes," she said, "yes." And suddenly it seemed as if a light had been turned on inside her, as if suddenly she could see again, a future with Kai, a future with children. 130

A bronzed hand lifted her face. "Look, Faye, I'll always be sorry. I'll always be sorry not to see you pregnant, not to see you with a big stomach knowing you're carrying my child, but I'll live."

Faye lowered her eyes and tears threatened again. With both his hands he cupped her face.

"Look at me, Faye. I want you to stop thinking of yourself as a machine with a defect. You're not a damaged piece of merchandise, you hear? You're a living, breathing human being, a warm-blooded female, and I love you."

Through a haze of tears she looked at him, giving a weak smile. "I love you too." She put her arms around him and he heaved an unsteady breath.

"Faye," he said huskily, "you're my first and only choice."   135

Chapter Twelve

Kai and Faye had their family, two girls and a boy. They came to them one at a time, from faraway places, with small faces and large dark eyes full of fear. In their faces Faye could read the tragedies of war and death and poverty. They were hungry for love, hungry for nourishment and care. At night they woke in terror, screaming, their memories alive in sleep.

Time passed, and in the low white ranch house under the blue skies of Texas they flourished like the crops in the fields. They grew tall and straight and healthy and the fear in their dark eyes faded. Like their father they wore jeans and boots and large-brimmed hats, and they rode horses and played the guitar. They learned to speak English with a Southern twang.

One day Kai and Faye watched them as they played in the garden, and joy and gratitude overflowed in Faye's heart. Life was good and filled with love.

"They're all ours," she said. Even now after all these years she sometimes still couldn't believe it was really so.

Kai smiled at her. His eyes, still very blue, crinkled at the corners. "Yes, and   140 you're all mine."

"They don't even look like us," she said. "Not even a tiny little bit." No blondes, no redheads.

Taking her in his arms, Kai kissed her. "They're true originals, like their mother. I wouldn't want it any other way."

There was love in his embrace and love in his words and in her heart there was no room now for doubt, no room for sorrow.

Sometimes in the night he would reach for her and she would wake to his touch, his hands on her breast, her stomach, searching. In the warm darkness of their bed she would come to him and they would hold each other close and she knew he had been dreaming.

She knew the dream. She was walking away from him, calling out that she   145 couldn't marry him, the words echoing all around. *"I can't marry you! I can't marry you!"* And Kai was standing there watching her go, terrified, unable to move, his legs frozen to the ground. He wanted to follow her, keep her from leaving, but his legs wouldn't move.

Kai had told her of the dream, of the panic that clutched at him as he watched her walk out of his life. And always he would wake and search for her in the big bed, and she knew of only one way to reassure him. And in the warm afterglow of lovemaking, their bodies close together, she knew that to him she was everything, to him she was the only woman, beautiful, complete, whole.

GAIL GODWIN (B. 1937)

Born in Birmingham, Alabama, Gail Godwin was educated at the University of North
Carolina and the University of Iowa, where
she earned a Ph.D. in English in 1971. She is
a full-time writer who has won grants from
the National Endowment for the Arts, the Guggenheim Foundation, and the American Institute for the Arts and Letters. Among her novels
are *Glass People* (1971), *A Mother and Two
Daughters* (1981), *The Finishing School* (1985),
Evensong (1999), *Queen of the Underworld*

Alan Carey / The Image Works.

(2006), and *Flora* (2015). Her short stories have been collected in several volumes including *Dream Children* (1976) and *Mr. Bedford and the Muses* (1983).

A Sorrowful Woman   1971

Once upon a time there was a wife and mother one too many times

One winter evening she looked at them: the husband durable, receptive, gentle; the
child a tender golden three. The sight of them made her so sad and sick she did not
want to see them ever again.

She told the husband these thoughts. He was attuned to her; he understood
such things. He said he understood. What would she like him to do? "If you could
put the boy to bed and read him the story about the monkey who ate too many
bananas, I would be grateful." "Of course," he said. "Why, that's a pleasure." And he
sent her off to bed.

The next night it happened again. Putting the warm dishes away in the cupboard, she turned and saw the child's gray eyes approving her movements. In the
next room was the man, his chin sunk in the open collar of his favorite wool shirt.
He was dozing after her good supper. The shirt was the gray of the child's trusting
gaze. She began yelping without tears, retching in between. The man woke in alarm
and carried her in his arms to bed. The boy followed them up the stairs, saying, "It's
all right, Mommy," but this made her scream. "Mommy is sick," the father said, "go
wait for me in your room."

The husband undressed her, abandoning her only long enough to root beneath
the eiderdown for her flannel gown. She stood naked except for her bra, which hung
by one strap down the side of her body; she had not the impetus to shrug it off. She
looked down at the right nipple, shriveled with chill, and thought, How absurd, a
vertical bra. "If only there were instant sleep," she said, hiccuping, and the husband
bundled her into the gown and went out and came back with a sleeping draught
guaranteed swift. She was to drink a little glass of cognac followed by a big glass of
dark liquid and afterwards there was just time to say Thank you and could you get
him a clean pair of pajamas out of the laundry, it came back today.

The next day was Sunday and the husband brought her breakfast in bed and 5
let her sleep until it grew dark again. He took the child for a walk, and when they
returned, red-cheeked and boisterous, the father made supper. She heard them
laughing in the kitchen. He brought her up a tray of buttered toast, celery sticks,
and black bean soup. "I am the luckiest woman," she said, crying real tears. "Nonsense," he said. "You need a rest from us," and went to prepare the sleeping draught,
find the child's pajamas, select the story for the night.

She got up on Monday and moved about the house till noon. The boy, delighted
to have her back, pretended he was a vicious tiger and followed her from room
to room, growling and scratching. Whenever she came close, he would growl and
scratch at her. One of his sharp little claws ripped her flesh, just above the wrist, and
together they paused to watch a thin red line materialize on the inside of her pale
arm and spill over in little beads. "Go away," she said. She got herself upstairs and
locked the door. She called the husband's office and said, "I've locked myself away
from him. I'm afraid." The husband told her in his richest voice to lie down, take
it easy, and he was already on the phone to call one of the baby-sitters they often
employed. Shortly after, she heard the girl let herself in, heard the girl coaxing the
frightened child to come and play.

After supper several nights later, she hit the child. She had known she was
going to do it when the father would see. "I'm sorry," she said, collapsing on the
floor. The weeping child had run to hide. "What has happened to me, I'm not myself
anymore." The man picked her tenderly from the floor and looked at her with much
concern. "Would it help if we got, you know, a girl in? We could fix the room downstairs. I want you to feel freer," he said, understanding these things. "We have the
money for a girl. I want you to think about it."

And now the sleeping draught was a nightly thing, she did not have to ask. He
went down to the kitchen to mix it, he set it nightly beside her bed. The little glass and
the big one, amber and deep rich brown, the flannel gown and the eiderdown.

The man put out the word and found the perfect girl. She was young, dynamic,
and not pretty. "Don't bother with the room, I'll fix it up myself." Laughing, she
employed her thousand energies. She painted the room white, fed the child lunch,
read edifying books, raced the boy to the mailbox, hung her own watercolors on
the fresh-painted walls, made spinach soufflé, cleaned a spot from the mother's
coat, made them all laugh, danced in stocking feet to music in the white room
after reading the child to sleep. She knitted dresses for herself and played chess
with the husband. She washed and set the mother's soft ash-blonde hair and gave
her neck rubs, offered to.

The woman now spent her winter afternoons in the big bedroom. She made a 10
fire in the hearth and put on slacks and an old sweater she had loved at school, and
sat in the big chair and stared out the window at snow-ridden branches, or went
away into long novels about other people moving through other winters.

The girl brought the child in twice a day, once in the later afternoon when he
would tell of his day, all of it tumbling out quickly because there was not much time,
and before he went to bed. Often now, the man took his wife to dinner. He made a
courtship ceremony of it, inviting her beforehand so she could get used to the idea.
They dressed and were beautiful together again and went out into the frosty night.
Over candlelight he would say, "I think you are better, you know." "Perhaps I am,"
she would murmur. "You look . . . like a cloistered queen," he said once, his voice
breaking curiously.

One afternoon the girl brought the child into the bedroom. "We've been out playing in the park. He found something he wants to give you, a surprise." The little boy approached her, smiling mysteriously. He placed his cupped hands in hers and left a live dry thing that spat brown juice in her palm and leapt away. She screamed and wrung her hands to be rid of the brown juice. "Oh, it was only a grasshopper," said the girl. Nimbly she crept to the edge of the curtain, did a quick knee bend, and reclaimed the creature, led the boy competently from the room.

"The girl upsets me," said the woman to her husband. He sat frowning on the side of the bed he had not entered for so long. "I'm sorry, but there it is." The husband stroked his creased brow and said he was sorry too. He really did not know what they would do without that treasure of a girl. "Why don't you stay here with me in bed," the woman said.

Next morning she fired the girl who cried and said, "I loved the little boy, what will become of him now?" But the mother turned away her face and the girl took down the watercolors from the walls, sheathed the records she had danced to, and went away.

"I don't know what we'll do. It's all my fault, I know. I'm such a burden, I know that." 15

"Let me think. I'll think of something." (Still understanding these things.)

"I know you will. You always do," she said.

With great care he rearranged his life. He got up hours early, did the shopping, cooked the breakfast, took the boy to nursery school. "We will manage," he said, "until you're better, however long that is." He did his work, collected the boy from the school, came home and made the supper, washed the dishes, got the child to bed. He managed everything. One evening, just as she was on the verge of swallowing her draught, there was a timid knock on her door. The little boy came in wearing his pajamas. "Daddy has fallen asleep on my bed and I can't get in. There's not room."

Very sedately she left her bed and went to the child's room. Things were much changed. Books were rearranged, toys. He'd done some new drawings. She came as a visitor to her son's room, wakened the father and helped him to bed. "Ah, he shouldn't have bothered you," said the man, leaning on his wife. "I've told him not to." He dropped into his own bed and fell asleep with a moan. Meticulously she undressed him. She folded and hung his clothes. She covered his body with the bedclothes. She flicked off the light that shone in his face.

The next day she moved her things into the girl's white room. She put her hair- 20 brush on the dresser; she put a note pad and pen beside the bed. She stocked the little room with cigarettes, books, bread, and cheese. She didn't need much.

At first the husband was dismayed. But he was receptive to her needs. He understood these things. "Perhaps the best thing is for you to follow it through," he said. "I want to be big enough to contain whatever you must do."

All day long she stayed in the white room. She was a young queen, a virgin in a tower; she was the previous inhabitant, the girl with all the energies. She tried these personalities on like costumes, then discarded them. The room had a new view of streets she'd never seen that way before. The sun hit the room in late afternoon and she took to brushing her hair in the sun. One day she decided to write a poem. "Perhaps a sonnet." She took up her pen and pad and began working from words that had lately lain in her mind. She had choices for the sonnet, ABAB or ABBA for a start. She pondered these possibilities until she tottered into a larger choice: she did not have to write a sonnet. Her poem could be six, eight, ten, thirteen lines, it could be any number of lines, and it did not even have to rhyme.

She put down the pen on top of the pad.

In the evenings, very briefly, she saw the two of them. They knocked on her door, a big knock and a little, and she would call Come in, and the husband would smile though he looked a bit tired, yet somehow this tiredness suited him. He would put her sleeping draught on the bedside table and say, "The boy and I have done all right today," and the child would kiss her. One night she tasted for the first time the power of his baby spit.

"I don't think I can see him anymore," she whispered sadly to the man. And 25 the husband turned away, but recovered admirably and said, "Of course, I see."

So the husband came alone. "I have explained to the boy," he said. "And we are doing fine. We are managing." He squeezed his wife's pale arm and put the two glasses on her table. After he had gone, she sat looking at the arm.

"I'm afraid it's come to that," she said. "Just push the notes under the door; I'll read them. And don't forget to leave the draught outside."

The man sat for a long time with his head in his hands. Then he rose and went away from her. She heard him in the kitchen where he mixed the draught in batches now to last a week at a time, storing it in a corner of the cupboard. She heard him come back, leave the big glass and the little one outside on the floor.

Outside her window the snow was melting from the branches, there were more people on the streets. She brushed her hair a lot and seldom read anymore. She sat in her window and brushed her hair for hours, and saw a boy fall off his new bicycle again and again, a dog chasing a squirrel, an old woman peek slyly over her shoulder and then extract a parcel from a garbage can.

In the evening she read the notes they slipped under her door. The child could 30 not write, so he drew and sometimes painted his. The notes were painstaking at first; the man and boy offering the final strength of their day to her. But sometimes, when they seemed to have had a bad day, there were only hurried scrawls.

One night, when the husband's note had been extremely short, loving but short, and there had been nothing from the boy, she stole out of her room as she often did to get more supplies, but crept upstairs instead and stood outside their doors, listening to the regular breathing of the man and boy asleep. She hurried back to her room and drank the draught.

She woke earlier now. It was spring, there were birds. She listened for sounds of the man and the boy eating breakfast; she listened for the roar of the motor when they drove away. One beautiful noon, she went out to look at her kitchen in the daylight. Things were changed. He had bought some new dish towels. Had the old ones worn out? The canisters seemed closer to the sink. She got out flour, baking powder, salt, milk (he bought a different brand of butter), and baked a loaf of bread and left it cooling on the table.

The force of the two joyful notes slipped under her door that evening pressed her into the corner of the little room; she had hardly space to breathe. As soon as possible, she drank the draught.

Now the days were too short. She was always busy. She woke with the first bird. Worked till the sun set. No time for hair brushing. Her fingers raced the hours.

Finally, in the nick of time, it was finished one late afternoon. Her veins 35 pumped and her forehead sparkled. She went to the cupboard, took what was hers, closed herself into the little white room and brushed her hair for a while.

The man and boy came home and found: five loaves of warm bread, a roast stuffed turkey, a glazed ham, three pies of different fillings, eight molds of the boy's favorite custard, two weeks' supply of fresh-laundered sheets and shirts and towels, two hand-knitted sweaters (both of the same gray color), a sheath of marvelous watercolor beasts accompanied by mad and fanciful stories nobody could ever make up again, and a tablet full of love sonnets addressed to the man. The house smelled redolently of renewal and spring. The man ran to the little room, could not contain himself to knock, flung back the door.

"Look, Mommy is sleeping," said the boy. "She's tired from doing all our things again." He dawdled in a stream of the last sun for that day and watched his father roll tenderly back her eyelids, lay his ear softly to her breast, test the delicate bones of her wrist. The father put down his face into her fresh-washed hair.

"Can we eat the turkey for supper?" the boy asked.

CONSIDERATIONS FOR CRITICAL THINKING AND WRITING

1. FIRST RESPONSE. How did you respond to the excerpt from *A Secret Sorrow* and to "A Sorrowful Woman"? Do you like one more than the other? Is one of the women — Faye or Godwin's unnamed wife — more likable than the other? Why do you think you respond the way you do to the characters and the stories — is your response intellectual, emotional, a result of authorial intent, a mix of these, or something else entirely?

2. Describe what you found appealing in each story. Can you point to passages in both that strike you as especially well written or interesting? Was there anything in either story that did not appeal to you? Why?

3. How do the two women's attitudes toward family life differ? How does that difference constitute the problem in each story?

4. How is the woman's problem in "A Sorrowful Woman" made more complex than Faye's in *A Secret Sorrow*? What is the purpose of the husband and child in Godwin's story?

5. How would you describe the theme — the central point and meaning — in each story?

6. To what extent might "A Sorrowful Woman" be regarded as an unromantic sequel to *A Secret Sorrow*?

7. Can both stories be read a second or third time and still be interesting? Why or why not?

8. Explain how you think a romance formula writer would end "A Sorrowful Woman," or write the ending yourself.

9. Contrast what marriage means in the two stories.

10. Discuss your feelings about the woman in "A Sorrowful Woman." How does she remain a sympathetic character in spite of her refusal to be a traditional wife and mother? (It may take more than one reading of the story to see that Godwin does sympathize with her.)

11. The happy ending of *A Secret Sorrow* may seem like that of a fairy tale, but it is realistically presented because there is nothing strange, mysterious, or fabulous that strains our ability to believe it could happen. In contrast, "A Sorrowful Woman" begins with an epigraph (*"Once upon a time . . ."*) that causes us to expect a fairy-tale ending, but that story is clearly a fairy tale gone wrong. Consider the two stories as fairy tales. How might "A Sorrowful Woman" be read as a dark version of "Sleeping Beauty"?

12. CRITICAL STRATEGIES. Read the section on feminist criticism in Chapter 54, "Critical Strategies for Reading." Based on that discussion, what do you think a feminist critic might have to say about these two stories?

Perspectives

KAY MUSSELL (B. 1943)

Are Feminism and Romance Novels
Mutually Exclusive?   1997

If feminism and romance are mutually exclusive, a lot of romance writers and readers haven't heard the news yet. In my experience, the only people who think they are mutually exclusive are people who don't know much about romances — or about women, or dare I add about feminism? That last point may be provocative and subject to real debate.

Twenty years ago, when romance novels were getting a lot of attention in the media, I thought that their increased popularity and changing content had something to do with the challenge mounted by feminism to more traditional women. I saw romances back then as a kind of backlash against the more aggressive and controversial aspects of feminism — something that reaffirmed traditional values and made women who hadn't bought into the feminist critique feel validated about their own choices. I also expected romances to fade away as more and more women entered the labor force and became practical feminists if not theoretical or political feminists.

Was I ever wrong! Instead of quietly going the way of the Western (which is much less popular now than it was a few decades ago), romances have become one of the hottest areas of publishing. One reason, of course, is that romances have changed with the times. The newer romances incorporate feminist themes while still reaffirming more traditional notions about love and family. Moreover, many romance writers have openly claimed feminist values and, in the process, rejected easy stereotypes about themselves and their work. For example, see the essays by romance writers collected in Jayne Ann Krentz's *Dangerous Men & Adventurous Women*.

More difficult to illustrate, but I think equally important, is change in feminist thinking itself. Twenty or so years ago, when academic feminists first became interested in the romance genre, there was wider agreement among feminists themselves on what the feminist agenda should be — and conventional romantic relationships, widely assumed to be discriminatory toward women, were not part of it. Thus romances were seen as threatening to female autonomy. But as feminism has matured — and as feminist scholars have come to recognize a broader range of female experience — some scholars have challenged those earlier notions in productive ways.

I don't know how you can read many romances today as anything but feminist. To take just one issue: Heroes and heroines meet each other on a much more equal playing field. Heroes don't always dominate and heroines are frequently right. Heroines have expertise and aren't afraid to show it. Heroes aren't the fount of all wisdom and they actually have things to learn from heroines. This is true of both contemporary and historical romances. I'm not trying to argue that all romances before the 1990s featured unequal relationships or that all romances today are based on equality. That's clearly not the case. But in general heroines today have a lot more independence and authority than their counterparts did in earlier romances. I think that's clear evidence of the influence of feminism on romances and of the ability of romance novels to address contemporary concerns that women share.

From *All About Romance: The Back Fence for Lovers of Romance Novels,*
accessed at likesbooks.com/mussell.html

Considerations for Critical Thinking and Writing

1. How might the excerpt from *A Secret Sorrow* be read "as a kind of backlash against the more aggressive and controversial aspects of feminism"?

2. Examine some recent romance novel covers and back-cover copy in a bookstore. What evidence is there to support or refute Mussell's claim that "newer romances incorporate feminist themes while still reaffirming more traditional notions about love and family"?

3. Write an essay in which you consider a book, film, or television program that seems to appeal to male fantasies, and explore some of the similarities and differences between male and female tastes in popular fiction.

Thomas Jefferson (1743–1826)
On the Dangers of Reading Fiction   1818

A great obstacle to good education is the inordinate passion prevalent for novels, and the time lost in that reading which should be instructively employed. When this poison infects the mind, it destroys its tone and revolts it against wholesome reading. Reason and fact, plain and unadorned, are rejected. Nothing can engage attention unless dressed in all the figments of fancy, and nothing so bedecked comes amiss. The result is a bloated imagination, sickly judgment, and disgust towards all the real businesses of life. This mass of trash, however, is not without some distinction; some few modeling their narratives, although fictitious, on the incidents of real life, have been able to make them interesting and useful vehicles of a sound morality. . . . For a like reason, too, much poetry should not be indulged. Some is useful for forming style and taste. Pope, Dryden, Thompson, Shakespeare, and of the French, Molière, Racine, the Corneilles, may be read with pleasure and improvement.

Letter to Nathaniel Burwell, March 14, 1818,
in *The Writings of Thomas Jefferson*

Considerations for Critical Thinking and Writing

1. Jefferson voices several common objections to fiction. What, according to him, are the changes associated with reading fiction? Are these concerns still expressed today? Why or why not? To what extent are Jefferson's arguments similar to twentieth-century objections to watching television?

2. Explain why you agree or disagree that works of fiction should serve as "useful vehicles of a sound morality."

3. How do you think Jefferson would regard Harlequin romances?

2

Writing about Fiction

Writing permits me to experience life as any number of strange creations.

— ALICE WALKER

Courtesy of Jean Weisinger/© Jean Weisinger, 1991.

FROM READING TO WRITING

There's no question about it: writing about fiction is a different experience than reading it. The novelist William Styron amply concedes that writing to him is not so much about pleasure as it is about work: "Let's face it, writing is hell." Although Styron's lament concerns his own feelings about writing prose fiction, he no doubt speaks for many other writers, including essayists. Writing is, of course, work, but it is also a pleasure when it goes well — when ideas feel solid and the writing is fluid. You can experience that pleasure as well, if you approach writing as an intellectual and emotional opportunity rather than merely a sentence.

Just as reading fiction requires an imaginative, conscious response, so does writing about fiction. Composing an essay is not just recording your interpretive response to a work because the act of writing can change your response as you explore, clarify, and discover relationships you hadn't previously considered or recognized. Most writers discover new ideas and connections as they move through the process of rereading and annotating the text, taking notes, generating ideas, developing a thesis, and organizing an argumentative essay. (These matters are detailed in Chapter 52, "Reading and the Writing Process.") To become more conscious of the writing process, first study the following questions specifically aimed at sharpening your response to reading and writing about fiction. Then examine the case study of a student's paper in progress that takes you through writing a first response to reading, brainstorming for a paper topic, writing a first draft, revising, and writing the final paper.

Questions for Responsive Reading and Writing

The following questions can help you consider important elements of fiction that reveal your responses to a story's effects and meanings. The questions are general, so they will not always be relevant to a particular story. Many of them, however, should prove useful for thinking, talking, and writing about a work of fiction. If you are uncertain about the meaning of a term used in a question, consult the Glossary of Literary Terms beginning on page 1716 of this book. You should also find useful the discussion of various critical approaches to literature in Chapter 51, "Critical Strategies for Reading."

PLOT

1. Does the plot conform to a formula? Is it like those of any other stories you have read? Did you find it predictable?

2. What is the source and nature of the conflict for the protagonist? Was your major interest in the story based on what happens next or on some other concern? What does the title reveal now that you've finished the story?

3. Is the story told chronologically? If not, in what order are its events told, and what is the effect of that order on your response to the action?

4. What does the exposition reveal? Are flashbacks used? Did you see any foreshadowings? Where is the climax?

5. Is the conflict resolved at the end? Would you characterize the ending as happy, unhappy, or somewhere in between?

6. Is the plot unified? Is each incident somehow related to some other element in the story?

CHARACTER

7. Do you identify with the protagonist? Who (or what) is the antagonist?

(continued)

8. Did your response to any characters change as you read? What do you think caused the change? Do any characters change and develop in the course of the story? How?

9. Are round, flat, or stock characters used? Is their behavior motivated and plausible?

10. How does the author reveal characters? Are they directly described or indirectly presented? Are the characters' names used to convey something about them?

11. What is the purpose of the minor characters? Are they individualized, or do they primarily represent ideas or attitudes?

SETTING

12. Is the setting important in shaping your response? If it were changed, would your response to the story's action and meaning be significantly different?

13. Is the setting used symbolically? Are the time, place, and atmosphere related to the theme?

14. Is the setting used as an antagonist?

POINT OF VIEW

15. Who tells the story? Is it a first-person or third-person narrator? Is it a major or minor character or one who does not participate in the action at all? How much does the narrator know? Does the point of view change at all in the course of the story?

16. Is the narrator reliable and objective? Does the narrator appear too innocent, emotional, or self-deluded to be trusted?

17. Does the author directly comment on the action?

18. If it were told from a different point of view, how would your response to the story change? Would anything be lost?

SYMBOLISM

19. Did you notice any symbols in the story? Are they actions, characters, settings, objects, or words?

20. How do the symbols contribute to your understanding of the story?

THEME

21. Did you find a theme? If so, what is it?

22. Is the theme stated directly, or is it developed implicitly through the plot, characters, or some other element?

23. Is the theme a confirmation of your values, or does it challenge them?

STYLE, TONE, AND IRONY

24. Do you think the style is consistent and appropriate throughout the story? Do all the characters use the same kind of language, or did you hear different voices?

25. Would you describe the level of diction as formal or informal? Are the sentences short and simple, long and complex, or some combination?

26. How does the author's use of language contribute to the tone of the story? Did it seem, for example, intense, relaxed, sentimental, nostalgic, humorous, angry, sad, or remote?

27. Do you think the story is worth reading more than once? Does the author's use of language bear close scrutiny so that you feel and experience more with each reading?

CRITICAL STRATEGIES

28. Is there a particular critical approach that seems especially appropriate for this story? (See the discussion of critical strategies for reading beginning on p. 1641.)

29. How might biographical information about the author help you to determine the central concerns of the story?

30. How might historical information about the story provide a useful context for interpretation?

31. What kinds of evidence from the story are you focusing on to support your interpretation? Does your interpretation leave out any important elements that might undercut or qualify your interpretation?

32. To what extent do your own experiences, values, beliefs, and assumptions inform your interpretation?

33. Given that there are a variety of ways to interpret the story, which one seems the most useful to you?

A SAMPLE PAPER IN PROGRESS

The following student paper was written in response to an assignment that asked for a comparison and contrast of the treatment of marriage in the excerpt from Karen van der Zee's novel *A Secret Sorrow* (p. 31) and in Gail Godwin's short story "A Sorrowful Woman" (p. 39). The final draft of the paper is preceded by four distinct phases of composition: (1) an initial response, (2) a brainstorming exercise, (3) a preliminary draft of the paper, and (4) an annotated version of the preliminary draft that shows how the student thought about revising the paper. Maya Leigh's First Response is an informal paper based on questions supplied by the instructor: "How did you respond to each story? Do you like one more than the other? Is one of the women more likable than the other? Why do you think you respond the way you do? Is your response to the characters and the stories primarily intellectual, emotional, a result of authorial intention, a mix of these, or something else entirely?" (Spelling and grammatical errors in Maya's preliminary drafts have been silently corrected so as not to distract from her developing argument.)

A First Response to A Secret Sorrow and "A Sorrowful Woman"

Reading the excerpt from the Harlequin I was irritated by the seeming helplessness of Faye; in the first chapter she is constantly on the edge of hysteria and can hardly stand up. I could do without all of the fainting, gasping, and general theatrics. I've read Harlequins before, and I usually skim through that stuff to get to the good romantic parts and the happy ending. What I like about these kinds of romance novels is the happy ending. Even though the ending is kind of clichéd with the white fence and blue skies, there is still something satisfying about having everything work out okay.

The Godwin story, of course, does not have a happy ending. It is a much more powerful story, and it is one that I could read several times, unlike the Harlequin. The Godwin woman bothers me too, because I can't really see what she has to complain about. Her husband is perfectly accommodating and understanding. It seems that if she were unhappy with her life as a wife and mother and wanted to work or do something else, he wouldn't have a problem with it. She seems to throw away her life and hurt her family for nothing.

I enjoyed reading the Godwin story more just because it is well written and more complex, but I liked the ending of the Harlequin more. I think on an emotional level I liked the Harlequin better, and on an intellectual level I liked the Godwin story more. It is more satisfying emotionally to see a romance develop and end happily than it is to see the deterioration of a marriage and the suicide of a depressed woman. I don't really find either character particularly likable; toward the end when the Godwin woman comes out of her room and starts doing things again I begin to feel sympathy for her—I can understand her having a period of depression, but I want her to pull herself out of it, and when she doesn't, I am disappointed. Even though Faye is annoying in the beginning, because everything ends happily I am almost willing to forgive and forget my previous annoyance with her. If the Godwin woman hadn't killed herself and had returned to her family life, I would have liked her better, but because she doesn't I leave the story feeling discouraged.

Brainstorming

By listing these parallel but alternate treatments of marriage in each story, Maya begins to assemble an inventory of relevant topics related to the assignment. What becomes clear to her is that her approach will emphasize the differences in each story's portrayal of marriage.

A Sample Brainstorming List

<table>
<tr><td colspan="2" align="center">Marriage</td></tr>
<tr><td align="center">Godwin</td><td align="center">Harlequin</td></tr>
<tr><td>marriage as end of life — confining, weighty</td><td>marriage as end, goal — dreamlike, idyllic</td></tr>
<tr><td>husband — durable, receptive, understanding</td><td>husband — understanding, manly</td></tr>
<tr><td>p. 39 sight of family makes her sad and sick</td><td>p. 38 watching kids she feels that life is good + filled with love</td></tr>
<tr><td>house in winter — girl paints room white</td><td>white house in Texas under blue skies</td></tr>
<tr><td>the power of his baby spit and looking at arm p. 42</td><td>in husband's embrace no room for doubt or sorrow p. 38</td></tr>
<tr><td>family makes her sad</td><td>family makes her happy</td></tr>
<tr><td>weight pressing on her</td><td>weight lifted off her</td></tr>
<tr><td>impersonal — the husband, the child</td><td>Kai, Faye, our children</td></tr>
<tr><td>emphasis on roles</td><td></td></tr>
<tr><td>dead in the end</td><td>beautiful, whole, complete in the end</td></tr>
<tr><td>crisis due to fear of always having husband and kid</td><td>crisis due to fear of never having husband and kids</td></tr>
<tr><td>feels incomplete and depressed as only wife and mother</td><td>feels incomplete and depressed not being wife and mother</td></tr>
</table>

Revising: First and Second Drafts

Maya's first draft of the paper pursues and develops many of the topics she noted while brainstorming. She explores the differences between each story's treatment of marriage in detail by examining each protagonist's role as wife and mother, her husband's response, the role played by her children, and the ending of each story. The second draft's annotations indicate that Maya has been able to distance herself enough from her first draft to critique its weak moments. In the annotations she recognizes, for example, that she needs a clearer thesis, some stronger transitions between paragraphs, some crisper and more detailed sentences to clarify points, and a more convincing conclusion as well as a more pointed title.

A Sample First Draft: Separate Sorrows

Separate Sorrows

In both the excerpt from *A Secret Sorrow* and "A Sorrowful Woman,"
by Gail Godwin, the story is centered around ideas of marriage and family.
However, marriage and family are presented in very different lights in the
two stories. Karen van der Zee presents marriage with children as perfect and
somewhat dreamlike; it is what Faye, the heroine of *A Secret Sorrow*, wants,
and what is necessary for her happiness. For Godwin's heroine, marriage
and family are almost the antithesis of happiness; her home life seems to
suffocate her and eventually leads her to commit suicide.

Both of the female protagonists in the two stories experience a crisis
of sorts. In *A Secret Sorrow,* Faye's crisis comes before marriage. She is
distraught because she cannot have children and fears that this will prevent
her from marrying the man she loves. Both she and her beloved, Kai, have
always wanted a marriage with children, and it is assumed that only under
these circumstances will they truly be happy. Faye feels that her inability
to have children is a fatal flaw. "Every time we see some pregnant woman,
every time we're with somebody else's children I'll feel I've failed you!"
(35). In "A Sorrowful Woman," however, the crisis comes after the marriage,
when the woman has already procured her husband and child. Faye would
be ecstatic in this woman's situation. The protagonist of the Godwin story,
however, is not. Her husband and son bring her such sorrow that eventually
she is unable to see them at all, and communicates only through notes stuck
under her bedroom door. Faye's anxiety and fear is based on the thought of
losing her man and never having children. In contrast, Godwin's character
has a loving husband and child and is still filled with grief. In a Harlequin
such as *A Secret Sorrow*, this is unimaginable; it goes against every formula
of romance writing, where books always end with a wedding, and happiness
after that is just assumed.

In *A Secret Sorrow*, marriage is portrayed as the end, as the goal of
the story. It is what the heroine wants. The author works to let the reader
know that only in this way will Faye be fulfilled and happy; it is what the
entire story, with all the plot twists and romantic interludes, has been
working toward. In "A Sorrowful Woman," marriage is the end, but is not the

goal—it is quite literally the end of the woman's life. Though we don't see what her life was like before her emotional crisis, there are hints of it. When she moves into the new room she mentions seeing the streets from a whole new perspective, suggesting the previous monotony of her daily life. In addition, in the final paragraphs of the story when the character bakes pies and bread and washes and folds the laundry, her son says, "she's tired from doing all our things again" (43), giving us an idea of what "our things" were, and what the woman did with her time before becoming ill.

In *A Secret Sorrow,* Faye's inability to have children does not end Kai's love for her, and the two go on to get married and adopt children. Faye's married life is described in a very idyllic way—she raises her son and two daughters in a "white ranch house under the blue skies of Texas" (38). In other words, once she is married and has children there is no more anxiety, nothing more to fear. The author leads us to the conclusion that marriage solves all problems and is a source of unending happiness for all. This is a great difference from the Godwin tale, which takes place in the winter and maintains a sense of cold throughout the whole thing. Whenever Godwin describes the family it is not in the light, glowing terms of van der Zee, but always with a sense of weight or guilt or failure about it. The child's trusting gaze makes the protagonist begin "yelping without tears" (39). Any sign of life or love increases her sorrow and makes her want to be rid of it. For example, when the hired girl brings her son to visit her with a grasshopper he's found—something both alive and from the outside world—she gets very upset and forces her husband to fire her. The girl is too much of an infringement on her space, and too much of a reminder of what she can no longer be.

Never is the difference between the two authors' portrayals of marriage more apparent than when both the women are viewing their families. Faye, sitting with her husband and watching her children play, felt that "life was good and filled with love" (38). Godwin's protagonist, on the other hand, reacts this way: "The sight of them made her so sad and sick she did not want to see them ever again" (39). When Kai, now her husband, embraces Faye, she feels that "there was love in his embrace and love in his words and in her heart there was no room now for doubt, no room for sorrow" (38). When Godwin's heroine feels the loving touch of her husband's arm and the kiss of her child she cannot bear it and cuts off all direct contact with them. The situation of her marriage pushes her into a self-imposed imprisonment and lethargy. She feels unbearably sad because she can no longer be who they want and need her to be. She avoids them not because she does not love them, but rather because she loves them so much that it is too painful to see them and feel her failure.

When Faye's fears of losing Kai are assuaged, and she is happily married, it is as though a great weight has been lifted off of her. Godwin's character, on the other hand, feels her marriage as a great weight pressing in on her. The love of her husband and child weighs on her and immobilizes her. When she leaves her room for a day and leaves out freshly baked bread for her husband and son, they express their happiness in the notes they write to her that night, and "the force of the two joyful notes . . . pressed her into the corner of the little room; she hardly had space to breathe" (42). Faye can be a traditional wife and mother, so her family is a source of joy. Godwin's character can no longer do this, and so her family is a representation of her failure, and the guilt presses her further and further into herself, until she can retreat no further and ends her life.

The endings of the two stories are powerful illustrations of the differences between them. In the end of *A Secret Sorrow,* the author shows us Faye feeling "beautiful, complete, whole" (38) in her role as wife and mother. Godwin, on the other hand, shows us her heroine dead on her bed. Godwin first gives the reader hope, by showing all that the woman has done, and saying that "the house smelled redolently of renewal and spring" (43). This makes the blow even harder when we then discover, along with the husband and child, the woman's suicide.

Karen van der Zee creates a story full of emotional highs and lows, but one that leads up to—and ends with—marriage. After the marriage all plot twists and traumas come to a halt. Faye is brought to new life by her marriage and children; in it she finds completion of herself and total happiness. Godwin's tale, on the other hand, is full of anguish and emotion, but it all takes place after the marriage. The character she creates is stifled and killed by her marriage. There is no portrayal of unending happiness in her tale, but rather unending woe.

A Sample Second Draft: Separate Sorrows

Maya Leigh   Leigh 1
Professor Herlin
English 104
February 11, 2015

title works for Godwin— but does it for van der Zee? →

Separate Sorrows)

Karen van der Zee's novel   *Gail Godwin's short story*

In both the excerpt from *A Secret Sorrow* and "A Sorrowful Woman," ~~by~~

plot   *s*

~~Gail Godwin,~~ the ~~story is~~ centered around ideas of marriage and family.

need a clear thesis here — is it that SS endorses marriage while SW problematizes it?

However, marriage and family are presented in very different lights in the

two stories. Karen van der Zee presents marriage with children as perfect and

totally fulfilling   *protagonist*

~~somewhat dream-like~~; it is what Faye, the ~~heroine~~ of *A Secret Sorrow*, wants/

unnamed protagonist,

and what is necessary for her happiness. For Godwin's ~~heroine,~~ marriage and

does she? or is she consumed by her role?

family are almost the antithesis of happiness; her home life seems to suffo-

cate her and eventually leads her to commit suicide.

Both of the female protagonists in the two stories experience a crisis

~~of sorts~~. In *A Secret Sorrow,* Faye's crisis comes before marriage. She is

distraught because she cannot have children and fears that this will

prevent her from marrying the man she loves. Both she and her beloved, Kai,

unclear *referent*

have always wanted a marriage with children, and (it) is assumed that only

under these circumstances will they truly be happy. Faye feels that her inabil-

that cuts her off from Kai's love

ity to have children is a fatal flaw. "Every time we see some pregnant woman,

every time we're with somebody else's children I'll feel I've failed you!" (35).

In "A Sorrowful Woman," however, the crisis comes after the marriage, when

secured   *[Unlike who]*

the woman has already ~~procured~~ her husband and child. Faye would be

s

ecstatic in this woman's situation, ~~The protagonist of the~~ Godwin story/~~how-~~

Inexplicably,

~~ever,~~ is not. Her husband and son bring her such sorrow that eventually she is

ing

unable to see them at all, ~~and~~ communicates only through notes stuck under

her bedroom door. Faye's anxiety and fear are based on the thought of losing

her man and never having children. ~~In contrast,~~ Godwin's character has a

Leigh 2

yet she ⟨in a Harlequin romance because⟩

loving husband and child ~~and~~ is still\filled with grief. ~~In a Harlequin such as~~
sense of defeat would be   *one of the most popular*
~~*A Secret Sorrow*,~~ this ~~is~~ unimaginable⸝it goes against ~~every~~ formula of
                     the plot
romance writing; ~~where books~~ always end⸝with a wedding, ~~and happiness~~
with the assumption that the rest is happily ever after.
~~after that is just assumed.~~

In *A Secret Sorrow*, marriage is portrayed as ~~the end, as~~ the goal of the
                                                      Van der Zee
story. ~~It is what the heroine wants. The author~~ works to let the reader know that

only in this way will Faye be fulfilled and happy; it is what the entire story,

with all the plot twists and romantic interludes, ~~has been~~ working toward. ~~In~~
                                                                              ^
                                    also   *is*
"A Sorrowful Woman," ⟨marriage is the end⟩ but not ~~as~~ the goal—it is quite | *I like*
                                                                                  | *this!*
literally the end of the woman's life. Though we don't see what her life was

like before her emotional crisis, there are hints of it. When she moves into
                                                            need p. ref
the new room she mentions seeing the streets from a whole new perspective,

suggesting the previous monotony of her daily life. In addition, in the final

paragraphs of the story when the character bakes pies and bread and washes

and folds the laundry, her son says, "she's tired from doing all our things | *is she really*
                                                                                | *ill? or just*
again" (43), giving us an idea of what "our things" were, and what the | *withdrawing*
                                                                                | *from her life?*
woman did with her time before becoming ill.

In *A Secret Sorrow*, Faye's inability to have children does not end Kai's | *need*
                                                                              | *transition*
love for her, and the two go on to get married and adopt children. Faye's

married life is described in a very idyllic way—she raises her son and two

daughters in a "white ranch house under the blue skies of Texas" (38). ~~In~~

~~other words,~~ once she is married and has children there is no more anxiety,
because the plot
~~nothing more to fear. The author~~ leads us to the conclusion that marriage

solves all problems and is a source of unending happiness ~~for all.~~ This ~~is a~~
  ly   *s*   *s*
great difference from ~~the~~ Godwin tale, which takes place in the winter and

maintains a sense of cold ~~throughout the whole thing.~~ Whenever Godwin
                                                    that suggest
describes the family it is ~~not~~ in ~~the light, glowing~~ terms of van der Zee, ~~but~~

Leigh 3

~~always with a sense of~~ weight, ~~or~~ guilt, or failure ~~about it~~. The child's trusting

gaze makes the protagonist begin "yelping without tears" (39). ^and ^Any sign
unclear referent

of life or love increases her sorrow and makes her want to be rid of (it.) For

example, when the hired girl brings her son to visit her with a grasshopper

he's found ; something both alive and from the outside world ; she gets very

the girl *Apparently,*

upset and forces her husband to fire ~~her~~. ~~T~~he girl is too much of an infringe-

ment on her space, and too much of a reminder of what she can no longer be.

Never is the difference between the two authors' portrayals of marriage

more apparent than when both the women are viewing their families. Faye,

sitting with her husband and watching her children play, felt that "life was

good and filled with love" (38). Godwin's protagonist, on the other hand,

reacts this way: "The sight of them made her so sad and sick she did not want

to see them ever again" (39). When Kai, now her husband, embraces Faye,

she feels that "there was love in his embrace and love in his words and in

her heart there was no room now for doubt, no room for sorrow" (38). When

Godwin's heroine feels the loving touch of her husband's arm and the kiss of

her child, she cannot bear it and cuts off all direct contact with them. The

situation of her marriage pushes her into a self-imposed imprisonment and

lethargy. She feels unbearably sad because she can no longer be who they

*should I use
epigram
here? or
work into the
thesis?*

want and need her to be. She avoids them not because she does not love

them, but rather because she loves them so much that it is too painful to see

them and feel her failure.

*need→
transition* When Faye's fears of losing Kai are assuaged, and she is happily mar-

ried, it is as though a great weight has been lifted off of her. Godwin's char-

acter, on the other hand, feels her marriage as a great weight pressing in on

and *,ing*

her, ~~The love of her husband and child weighs on her and~~ immobilizes her.

puts

When she leaves her room for a day and ~~leaves~~ out freshly baked bread for

Leigh 4

her husband and son, they express their happiness in the notes they write to

her that night, and "the force of the two joyful notes . . . pressed her into

the corner of the little room; she hardly had space to breathe" (42). Faye can

be a [*the*] traditional wife and mother, so her family is a source of joy. Godwin's

character can no longer do this, and so her family is a representation of her [*'s own*]

failure, and the guilt presses her further and further into herself until she

can retreat no further and ends her life.

   The endings of the two stories are powerful illustrations of the

differences between them. In the end of *A Secret Sorrow,* the author shows us

Faye feeling "beautiful, complete, whole" (38) in her role as wife and mother.

Godwin, on the other hand, shows us her heroine [*protagonist*] dead on her bed. Godwin

first [*seems to*] gives the reader hope by showing all that the woman has done and

saying that "the house smelled redolently of renewal and spring" (43). This

[*margin: same idyllic surroundings as VDZ's blue skies?*]

makes the blow even harder when we then discover, along with the husband

and child, the woman's suicide [*death*].

   Karen van der Zee creates a story full of emotional highs and lows but

one that leads up to—and ends with—marriage. After the marriage all plot

twists and traumas come to a halt. Faye is brought to new life by her mar-

riage and children, in it she finds completion of herself [*fulfillment*] and total happiness.

Godwin's tale, on the other hand, [*story, however,*] is full of anguish and emotion, but it [*confusion (?) that*] all

[*margin: need some very brief quotes to make conclusion stronger?*]

takes place after the marriage. The character she creates is stifled and killed

by her marriage. There is no portrayal of unending happiness in her tale, but

rather unending woe. [*is this the right word, since she dies?*]

Need to add Works Cited!

Final Paper

The changes noted in Maya's annotations on her second draft are put to good use in the following final draft. By not insisting that Godwin's protagonist actually commits suicide, Maya shifts her attention away from this indeterminable death to the causes and effects of it. This shift leads her to a stronger thesis — that Godwin raises questions about the efficacy of marriage rather than endorsing it as a certain recipe for happiness the way van der Zee does. Maya also incorporates additional revisions, such as transitions (see, for example, the revision between paragraphs 3 and 4), sentence clarity, and a fuller and more persuasive concluding paragraph.

Final Paper: *Fulfillment or Failure?*
***Marriage in* A Secret Sorrow *and* "A Sorrowful Woman"**

Maya Leigh

Professor Herlin

English 104

13 February 2015

Fulfillment or Failure?

Marriage in *A Secret Sorrow* and "A Sorrowful Woman"

  In both the excerpt from Karen van der Zee's novel *A Secret Sorrow* and in Gail Godwin's short story "A Sorrowful Woman," the plots center around ideas of marriage and family. However, marriage and family are presented in very different lights in the two stories. Karen van der Zee presents marriage with children as perfect and totally fulfilling; it is what Faye, the protagonist of *A Secret Sorrow,* wants and what is necessary for her happiness. For Godwin's unnamed protagonist, marriage and family are almost the antithesis of happiness; her home life seems to suffocate her and eventually leads to her death. *A Secret Sorrow* directly endorses and encourages marriage, whereas "A Sorrowful Woman" indirectly questions and discourages it.

  Both of the female protagonists in the two stories experience a crisis. In *A Secret Sorrow,* Faye's crisis comes before the marriage. She is distraught because she cannot have children and fears that this will prevent her from marrying the man she loves. Both she and her beloved, Kai, desire marriage with children, and van der Zee suggests that only with these things will they truly be happy. Faye feels that her inability to have children is a fatal flaw that cuts her off from Kai's love. "Every time we see some pregnant woman, every time we're with somebody else's children I'll feel I've failed you!" (35). Faye's anxiety and fear are based on the thought of losing her man and never having children. In "A Sorrowful Woman," however, the crisis comes after the marriage, when the woman has already secured her husband and child. Unlike Faye, who would be ecstatic in this woman's situation, the protagonist of Godwin's story is not. Inexplicably, her husband and son bring her such sorrow that eventually she is unable to see them at all, communicating only through notes stuck under her bedroom door. Godwin's character has a

Introduction comparing plots of both stories

Thesis contrasting treatment of marriage in both stories

Discussion of crisis in A Secret Sorrow with textual evidence

Discussion of crisis in "A Sorrowful Woman"

loving husband and child, yet she is still filled with grief. This sense of defeat would be unimaginable in a Harlequin romance because it goes against one of the most popular formulas of romance writing: the plot always ends with a wedding, with the assumption that the rest is happily ever after.

In *A Secret Sorrow*, marriage is portrayed as the goal. Van der Zee works to let the reader know that only in this way will Faye be fulfilled and happy; it is what the entire story, with all the plot twists and romantic interludes, works toward. Marriage is also the end in "A Sorrowful Woman" but not as in the goal: it is quite literally the end of the woman's life. Though we don't see what her life was like before her emotional crisis, there are hints of it. When she moves into a new bedroom—away from her husband—she mentions seeing the streets from a whole new perspective (41), suggesting the previous monotony of her daily life. In addition, in the final paragraphs of the story—when the character bakes pies and bread and washes and folds the laundry—her son says, "She's tired from doing all our things again" (43), giving us an idea of what "our things" were and what the woman did with her time before her crisis.

This monotony of marriage is absent in *A Secret Sorrow*. Faye's inability to have children does not end Kai's love for her, and the two go on to marry and adopt children. Faye's married life is described in a very idyllic way: she raises her son and two daughters in a "white ranch house under the blue skies of Texas" (38). Once she is married and has children, there is no more anxiety because the plot leads us to the conclusion that marriage solves all problems and is a source of unending happiness. This greatly differs from Godwin's tale, which takes place in winter and maintains a sense of cold. Whenever Godwin describes the family, it is in terms that suggest weight, guilt, or failure. The child's trusting gaze makes the protagonist begin "yelping without tears" (39), and any sign of life or love increases her sorrow and makes her want to be alone. For example, when the hired girl brings her son to visit her with a grasshopper he's found (41)—something both alive and from the outside world—she gets very upset and forces her husband to fire the girl. Apparently, the girl is too much of an infringement on her space, too much of a reminder of what she can no longer be.

Statements contrasting crises in the plots of the two stories

Discussion contrasting function of marriage in both stories

Textual evidence supporting analysis of "A Sorrowful Woman"

Discussion contrasting married life and family in both stories, with textual evidence

Leigh 3

Never is the difference between the two authors' portrayals of marriage more apparent than when both women are viewing their families. Faye, sitting with her husband and watching her children play, feels that "life was good and filled with love" (38). Godwin's protagonist, on the other hand, reacts this way: "The sight of them made her so sad and sick she did not want to see them ever again" (39). When Kai, now her husband, embraces Faye, she feels, "There was love in his embrace and love in his words and in her heart there was no room now for doubt, no room for sorrow" (38). When Godwin's heroine feels the loving touch of her husband's arm and the kiss of her child, she cannot bear it and cuts off all direct contact with them. The situation of her marriage pushes her into a self-imposed imprisonment and lethargy. She feels unbearably sad because she can no longer be who they want and need her to be. She avoids them not because she does not love them but rather because she loves them so much that it is too painful to see them and feel her failure. The epigram to Godwin's story tells us that "once upon a time there was a wife and mother one too many times" (39). The addition of "one too many times" to this traditional story opening forces the idea of repetition and monotony: it suggests that it is not that state of being a wife and mother that is inherently bad but rather the fact that that is all Godwin's character is. Day in and day out, too many times over, the woman is just a wife and a mother, and it isn't enough for her.

In van der Zee's story, there could be no such thing as too much motherhood or too much of being a wife. When Faye's fears of losing Kai are assuaged, and she is happily married, it is as though a great weight has been lifted off her. Godwin's character, on the other hand, feels her marriage as a great weight pressing on her and immobilizing her. When she leaves her room for a day and puts out freshly baked bread for her husband and son, they express their happiness in the notes they write to her that night, and "the force of the two joyful notes . . . pressed her into the corner of the little room; she had hardly space to breathe" (42). Faye can be a traditional wife and mother, so her family is a source of joy. Godwin's character can no longer be the traditional wife and mother, and so her family represents her own

Analysis contrasting emotions of protagonists in both stories, with textual evidence

Analysis contrasting protagonists' experience of traditional roles, with textual evidence failure, and the guilt presses her further and further into herself until she can retreat no further and ends her life.

The endings of the two stories are powerful illustrations of the differences between them. In the end of *A Secret Sorrow,* the author shows us Faye feeling "beautiful, complete, whole" (38) in her role as wife and mother. Godwin, on the other hand, shows us her protagonist dead on her bed. Godwin seems to give the reader hope by showing all that the woman has done and saying that "the house smelled redolently of renewal and spring" (43). This makes the blow even harder when we then discover, along with the husband and child, the woman's death. The ambiguous way the death of Godwin's unnamed protagonist is dealt with reinforces the author's negative portrayal of marriage. It isn't explicitly written as a suicide, and Godwin seems to encourage her readers to see it as the inevitable consequence of her marriage.

Van der Zee creates a story full of emotional highs and lows, but one that leads up to and ends with marriage. After the marriage all of the plot twists and traumas come to a halt, replaced with peace and happiness. Faye is brought to new life by her marriage and children; she finds fulfillment of all of her desires in them. Godwin's story, however, is full of postmarital anguish and confusion. The character she creates is stifled and most definitely unfulfilled by her marriage. A burst of creative energy right before her death produces, among other things, "a sheath of marvelous watercolor beasts accompanied by mad and fanciful stories nobody could ever make up again, and a tablet full of love sonnets addressed to the man" (43). It is clear that the woman had talents and desires not met by the routine duties of her marital life. For Faye, the protagonist of *A Secret Sorrow,* marriage is the happily-ever-after ending she has wanted all of her life; for Godwin's protagonist, on the other hand, marriage is just a monotonous and interminable ever after.

Analysis contrasting conclusions of the two stories

Conclusion summarizing paper's analyses

Works Cited

Godwin, Gail. "A Sorrowful Woman." Meyer 39–43.

Meyer, Michael, ed. *The Bedford Introduction to Literature*. 11th ed. Boston: Bedford/St. Martin's, 2016. Print.

Van der Zee, Karen. "From *A Secret Sorrow*." Meyer 31–38.

3

Plot

Never mistake motion for action.
— ERNEST HEMINGWAY

Created by a writer's imagination, a work of fiction need not be factual or historically accurate. Although actual people, places, and events may be included in fiction, facts are not as important as is the writer's use of them. We can learn much about Russian life in the early part of the nineteenth century from Leo Tolstoy's *War and Peace,* but that historical information is incidental to Tolstoy's exploration of human nature. Tolstoy, like most successful writers, makes us accept as real the world in his novel no matter how foreign it may be to our own reality. One of the ways a writer achieves this acceptance and engagement — and one of a writer's few obligations — is to interest us in what is happening in the story. We are carried into the writer's fictional world by the plot.

Plot is the author's arrangement of incidents in a story. It is the organizing principle that controls the order of events. This structure is, in a sense, what remains after a writer edits out what is irrelevant to the story being told. We don't need to know, for example, what happens to Rip Van Winkle's faithful dog, Wolf, during his amiable master's twenty-year nap in the Catskill Mountains in order to be enchanted by Washington Irving's story of a henpecked husband. Instead, what is told takes on meaning as it is brought into focus by a skillful writer who selects and orders the events that constitute the story's plot.

Events can be presented in a variety of orders. A chronological arrangement begins with what happens first, then second, and so on, until the last incident is related. That is how "Rip Van Winkle" is told. The events in William Faulkner's "A Rose for Emily," however, are not arranged in chronological order because that would give away the story's surprise ending; instead, Faulkner moves back and forth between the past and present to provide information that leads up to the final startling moment (which won't be given away here either; the story begins on p. 78).

Some stories begin at the end and then lead up to why or how events worked out as they did. If you read the first paragraph of Ralph Ellison's "Battle Royal" (p. 227), you'll find an example of this arrangement that will make it difficult for you to stop reading. Stories can also begin in the middle of things (the Latin term for this common plot strategy is *in medias res*). In this kind of plot we enter the story on the verge of some important moment. John Updike's "A & P" (p. 200) begins with the narrator, a teenager working at a checkout counter in a supermarket, telling us: "In walks these three girls in nothing but bathing suits." Right away we are brought into the middle of a situation that will ultimately create the conflict in the story.

Another common strategy is the *flashback*, a device that informs us about events that happened before the opening scene of a work. Nearly all of Ellison's "Battle Royal" takes the form of a flashback as the narrator recounts how his identity as a black man was shaped by the circumstances that attended a high-school graduation speech he delivered twenty years earlier in a hotel ballroom before a gathering of the town's leading white citizens, most of whom were "quite tipsy." Whatever the plot arrangement, you should be aware of how the writer's conscious ordering of events affects your responses to the action.

EDGAR RICE BURROUGHS (1875–1950)

A great many stories share a standard plot pattern. The following excerpt from Edgar Rice Burroughs's novel *Tarzan of the Apes* provides a conventional plot pattern in which the *character*, an imagined person in the story, is confronted with a problem leading to a climactic struggle that is followed by a resolution of the problem. The elements of a conventional plot are easily recognizable to readers familiar with fast-paced, action-packed mysteries, spy thrillers, westerns, or adventure stories. These page-turners are carefully plotted so that the reader is swept up by the action. More serious writers sometimes use similar strategies, but they do so with greater subtlety and for some purpose that goes beyond providing a thrill a minute. The writer of serious fiction is usually less concerned with what happens next to the central character than with why it happens. In Burroughs's adventure story, however, the emphasis is clearly on action. *Tarzan of the Apes* may add little or nothing to our understanding of life, but it is useful for delineating some important elements of plot. Moreover, it is great fun.

Burroughs Memorial Collection, Rare Books, Archives & Special Collections, University of Louisville.

Although Burroughs wrote *Tarzan of the Apes* some one hundred years ago, the novel and its subsequent films, television shows, comic books, and numerous other spin-offs continue to thrive in the undergrowth of American popular culture.

Tarzan first appeared in the October 1912 issue of *The All-Story* magazine, a pulp serial that sold for 15 cents a copy. Instead of publishing the lengthy novel in serial segments, *All-Story* published *Tarzan of the Apes: A Romance of the Jungle* in a single issue that featured a provocative cover and exotic illustrations. The enormous popularity of the *Tarzan* issue led to the publication of the 1914 novel that spawned two dozen books, more than forty movies, hundreds of comic books and radio and television programs, and countless products, from toys to running shoes. Edgar Rice Burroughs became one of the most popular authors of the twentieth century, and Tarzan remains one of the world's best-known characters.

Burroughs Memorial Collection, Rare Books, Archives & Special Collections, University of Louisville.

Curiously, one such by-product even includes a pseudo-autobiography titled *Me Cheeta: My Life in Hollywood* (2009), a memoir allegedly written by the chimpanzee that appeared in the Tarzan movies but never in the novels, an oddity that suggests the action continues in the Tarzan trade.

Burroughs's novel, published in 1914 and the first in the series, charts the growth to manhood of a child raised in the African jungle by great apes. Tarzan struggles to survive his primitive beginnings and to reconcile what he has learned in the jungle with his equally powerful instincts to be a civilized human being. One of the more exciting moments in Tarzan's development is his final confrontation with his old enemy, Terkoz, a huge tyrannical ape that has kidnapped Jane, a pretty nineteen-year-old from Baltimore, Maryland, who has accompanied her father on an expedition to the jungle.

In the chapter preceding this excerpt, Tarzan falls in love with Jane and writes this pointed, if not eloquent, note to her: "I am Tarzan of the Apes. I want you. I am yours. You are mine." Just as he finishes the note, he hears "the agonized screams of a woman" and rushes to their source to find Esmeralda, Jane's maid, hysterical with fear and grief. She reports that Jane, the fair and gentle embodiment of civilization in the story, has been carried off by a gorilla. Here is the first half of the next chapter, which illustrates how Burroughs plots the sequence of events so that the emphasis is on physical action.

From Tarzan of the Apes 1914

From the time Tarzan left the tribe of great anthropoids in which he had been raised, it was torn by continual strife and discord. Terkoz proved a cruel and capricious king, so that, one by one, many of the older and weaker apes, upon whom he was particularly prone to vent his brutish nature, took their families and sought the quiet and safety of the far interior.

But at last those who remained were driven to desperation by the continued truculence of Terkoz, and it so happened that one of them recalled the parting admonition of Tarzan:

"If you have a chief who is cruel, do not do as the other apes do, and attempt, any one of you, to pit yourself against him alone. But, instead, let two or three or four of you attack him together. Then, if you will do this, no chief will dare to be other than he should be, for four of you can kill any chief who may ever be over you."

And the ape who recalled this wise counsel repeated it to several of his fellows, so that when Terkoz returned to the tribe that day he found a warm reception awaiting him.

There were no formalities. As Terkoz reached the group, five huge, hairy beasts 5 sprang upon him.

At heart he was an arrant coward, which is the way with bullies among apes as well as among men; so he did not remain to fight and die, but tore himself away from them as quickly as he could and fled into the sheltering boughs of the forest.

Two more attempts he made to rejoin the tribe, but on each occasion he was set upon and driven away. At last he gave it up, and turned, foaming with rage and hatred, into the jungle.

For several days he wandered aimlessly, nursing his spite and looking for some weak thing on which to vent his pent anger.

It was in this state of mind that the horrible, manlike beast, swinging from tree to tree, came suddenly upon two women in the jungle.

He was right above them when he discovered them. The first intimation Jane 10 Porter had of his presence was when the great hairy body dropped to the earth beside her, and she saw the awful face and the snarling, hideous mouth thrust within a foot of her.

One piercing scream escaped her lips as the brute hand clutched her arm. Then she was dragged toward those awful fangs which yawned at her throat. But ere they touched that fair skin another mood claimed the anthropoid.

The tribe had kept his women. He must find others to replace them. This hairless white ape would be the first of his new household, and so he threw her roughly across his broad, hairy shoulders and leaped back into the trees, bearing Jane away.

Esmeralda's scream of terror had mingled once with that of Jane, and then, as was Esmeralda's manner under stress of emergency which required presence of mind, she swooned.

But Jane did not once lose consciousness. It is true that that awful face, pressing close to hers, and the stench of the foul breath beating upon her nostrils, paralyzed her with terror; but her brain was clear, and she comprehended all that transpired.

With what seemed to her marvelous rapidity the brute bore her through the 15 forest, but still she did not cry out or struggle. The sudden advent of the ape had confused her to such an extent that she thought now that he was bearing her toward the beach.

For this reason she conserved her energies and her voice until she could see that they had approached near enough to the camp to attract the succor she craved.

She could not have known it, but she was being borne farther and farther into the impenetrable jungle.

The scream that had brought Clayton and the two older men stumbling through the undergrowth had led Tarzan of the Apes straight to where Esmeralda lay, but it was not Esmeralda in whom his interest centered, though pausing over her he saw that she was unhurt.

For a moment he scrutinized the ground below and the trees above, until the ape that was in him by virtue of training and environment, combined with the intelligence that was his by right of birth, told his wondrous woodcraft the whole story as plainly as though he had seen the thing happen with his own eyes.

And then he was gone again into the swaying trees, following the high-flung 20 spoor which no other human eye could have detected, much less translated.

At boughs' ends, where the anthropoid swings from one tree to another, there is most to mark the trail, but least to point the direction of the quarry; for there the pressure is downward always, toward the small end of the branch, whether the ape be leaving or entering a tree. Nearer the center of the tree, where the signs of passage are fainter, the direction is plainly marked.

Here, on this branch, a caterpillar has been crushed by the fugitive's great foot, and Tarzan knows instinctively where that same foot would touch in the next stride. Here he looks to find a tiny particle of the demolished larva, ofttimes not more than a speck of moisture.

Again, a minute bit of bark has been upturned by the scraping hand, and the direction of the break indicates the direction of the passage. Or some great limb, or the stem of the tree itself has been brushed by the hairy body, and a tiny shred of hair tells him by the direction from which it is wedged beneath the bark that he is on the right trail.

Nor does he need to check his speed to catch these seemingly faint records of the fleeing beast.

To Tarzan they stand out boldly against all the myriad other scars and bruises 25 and signs upon the leafy way. But strongest of all is the scent, for Tarzan is pursuing up the wind, and his trained nostrils are as sensitive as a hound's.

There are those who believe that the lower orders are specially endowed by nature with better olfactory nerves than man, but it is merely a matter of development.

Man's survival does not hinge so greatly upon the perfection of his senses. His power to reason has relieved them of many of their duties, and so they have, to some extent, atrophied, as have the muscles which move the ears and scalp, merely from disuse.

The muscles are there, about the ears and beneath the scalp, and so are the nerves which transmit sensations to the brain, but they are underdeveloped because they are not needed.

Not so with Tarzan of the Apes. From early infancy his survival had depended upon acuteness of eyesight, hearing, smell, touch, and taste far more than upon the more slowly developed organ of reason.

The least developed of all in Tarzan was the sense of taste, for he could eat lus- 30 cious fruits, or raw flesh, long buried, with almost equal appreciation; but in that he differed but slightly from more civilized epicures.

Almost silently the ape-man sped on in the track of Terkoz and his prey, but the sound of his approach reached the ears of the fleeing beast and spurred it on to greater speed.

Three miles were covered before Tarzan overtook them, and then Terkoz, see-ing that further flight was futile, dropped to the ground in a small open glade, that he might turn and fight for his prize or be free to escape unhampered if he saw that the pursuer was more than a match for him.

He still grasped Jane in one great arm as Tarzan bounded like a leopard into the arena which nature had provided for this primeval-like battle.

When Terkoz saw that it was Tarzan who pursued him, he jumped to the con-clusion that this was Tarzan's woman, since they were of the same kind — white and hairless — and so he rejoiced at this opportunity for double revenge upon his hated enemy.

To Jane the strange apparition of this godlike man was as wine to sick nerves. 35

From the description which Clayton and her father and Mr. Philander had given her, she knew that it must be the same wonderful creature who had saved them, and she saw in him only a protector and a friend.

But as Terkoz pushed her roughly aside to meet Tarzan's charge, and she saw the great proportions of the ape and the mighty muscles and the fierce fangs, her heart quailed. How could any vanquish such a mighty antagonist?

Like two charging bulls they came together, and like two wolves sought each other's throat. Against the long canines of the ape was pitted the thin blade of the man's knife.

Jane — her lithe, young form flattened against the trunk of a great tree, her hands tight pressed against her rising and falling bosom, and her eyes wide with mingled horror, fascination, fear, and admiration — watched the primordial ape battle with the primeval man for possession of a woman — for her.

As the great muscles of the man's back and shoulders knotted beneath the 40 tension of his efforts, and the huge biceps and forearm held at bay those mighty tusks, the veil of centuries of civilization and culture were swept from the blurred vision of the Baltimore girl.

When the long knife drank deep a dozen times of Terkoz's heart's blood, and the great carcass rolled lifeless upon the ground, it was a primeval woman who sprang forward with outstretched arms toward the primeval man who had fought for her and won.

And Tarzan?

He did what no red-blooded man needs lessons in doing. He took his woman in his arms and smothered her upturned, panting lips with kisses.

For a moment Jane lay there with half-closed eyes. For a moment — the first in her young life — she knew the meaning of love.

But as suddenly as the veil had been withdrawn it dropped again, and an out- 45 raged conscience suffused her face with its scarlet mantle, and a mortified woman thrust Tarzan of the Apes from her and buried her face in her hands.

Tarzan had been surprised when he had found the girl he had learned to love after a vague and abstract manner a willing prisoner in his arms. Now he was surprised that she repulsed him.

He came close to her once more and took hold of her arm. She turned upon him like a tigress, striking his great breast with her tiny hands.

Tarzan could not understand it.

A moment ago, and it had been his intention to hasten Jane back to her people, but that little moment was lost now in the dim and distant past of things which were but can never be again, and with it the good intention had gone to join the impossible.

Since then Tarzan of the Apes had felt a warm, lithe form close pressed to his. 50 Hot, sweet breath against his cheek and mouth had fanned a new flame to life within his breast, and perfect lips had clung to his in burning kisses that had seared a deep brand into his soul — a brand which marked a new Tarzan.

Again he laid his hand upon her arm. Again she repulsed him. And then Tarzan of the Apes did just what his first ancestor would have done.

He took his woman in his arms and carried her into the jungle.

This episode begins with **exposition**, the background information the reader needs to make sense of the situation in which the characters are placed. The first eight paragraphs let us know that Terkoz has been overthrown as leader of the ape tribe and that he is roaming the jungle "looking for some weak thing on which to vent his pent anger." This exposition is in the form of a flashback. (Recall that the previous chapter ended with Esmeralda's report of the kidnapping; now we will see what happened.)

Once this information supplies a context for the characters, the plot gains momentum with the **rising action**, a complication that intensifies the situation: Terkoz, looking for a victim, discovers the vulnerable Esmeralda and Jane. His first impulse is to kill Jane, but his "mood" changes when he remembers that he has no woman of his own after having been forced to leave the tribe (more exposition). Hence, there is a further complication in the rising action when he decides to carry her off. Just when it seems that the situation could not get any worse, it does. The reader is invited to shudder even more than if Terkoz had made a meal of Jane because she may have to endure the "awful face," "foul breath," and lust of this beast.

At this point we are brought up to the action that ended the preceding chapter. Tarzan races to the rescue by unerringly following the trail from the place where Jane was kidnapped. He relentlessly tracks Terkoz. Unfortunately, Burroughs slows down the pursuit here by including several paragraphs that abstractly consider the evolutionary development of human reliance on reason more than on their senses for survival. This discussion offers a rationale for Tarzan's remarkable ability to track Jane, but it is an interruption in the chase.

When Tarzan finally catches up to Terkoz, the **conflict** of this episode fully emerges. Tarzan must save the woman he loves by defeating his long-standing enemy. For Terkoz seeks to achieve a "double revenge" by killing Tarzan and taking his woman. Terkoz's assumption that Jane is Tarzan's woman is a **foreshadowing**, a suggestion of what is yet to come. In this conflict Tarzan is the **protagonist** or **hero**, the central character who engages our interest and empathy. *Protagonist* is often a more useful term than *hero* or **heroine**, however, because the central character of a story can be despicable as well as heroic. In Edgar Allan Poe's "The Tell-Tale Heart," for example, the central character is a madman and murderer. Terkoz is the **antagonist**, the force that opposes the protagonist.

The battle between Tarzan and Terkoz creates **suspense** because the reader is made anxious about what is going to happen. Burroughs makes certain that the reader will worry about the outcome by having Jane wonder, "How could any vanquish such a mighty antagonist?" If we are caught up in the moment, we watch the battle, as Jane does, with "mingled horror, fascination, fear, and admiration" to see what will happen next. The moment of greatest emotional tension, the **climax**, occurs when Tarzan kills Terkoz. Tarzan's victory is the **resolution** of the conflict, also known as the **dénouement** (a French word meaning the "untying of the knot"). This could have been the conclusion to the episode except that Jane and Tarzan simultaneously discover their "primeval" selves sexually drawn to each other. Burroughs resolves one conflict — the battle with Terkoz — but then immediately creates another — by raising the question of what a respectable professor's daughter from Baltimore is doing in the sweaty arms of a panting, half-naked man.

For a brief moment the cycle of conflict, suspense, and resolution begins again as Jane passionately kisses Tarzan; then her "outraged conscience" causes her to regain her sense of propriety and she pushes him away. Although Tarzan succeeds in the encounter with Terkoz, he is not successful with Jane. However, Burroughs creates suspense for a third time at the very end of the episode, when the "new Tarzan," having been transformed by this sexual awakening, "took his woman in his arms and carried her into the jungle." What will he do next? Despite the novel's implausibility (beginning with the premise that apes could raise a human child) and its heavy use of coincidences (not the least of which is Tarzan's donning a loincloth for the first time only four pages before he meets Jane), the story is difficult to put down. The plot swings us swiftly and smoothly from incident to incident, even if there is an occasional interruption, such as Burroughs's discussion of evolution, in the flow of the action.

Although this pattern of exposition, rising action, conflict, suspense, climax, and resolution provides a useful outline of many plots that emphasize physical action, a greater value of this pattern is that it helps us to see how innovative artists move beyond formula fiction by manipulating and changing the pattern for their own purposes. At the furthest extreme are those modern storytellers who reject traditional plotting techniques in favor of experimental approaches. Instead of including characters who wrestle with conflicts, experimental fiction frequently may concern the writer's own efforts to create a story. Rather than ordering experience, such writers disrupt it by insisting that meanings in fiction are as elusive — or nonexistent — as meanings in life; they are likely to reject both traditional values and traditional forms of writing. Most writers, however, use conflicts in their plots to reveal characters and convey meanings. The nature of those conflicts can help determine how important physical action is to the plot.

The primary conflict that Tarzan experiences in his battle with Terkoz is external. External conflict is popular in adventure stories because the protagonist's physical struggles with a formidable foe or the ever-present dangers of a dense jungle echoing wild screams provide plenty of excitement. External conflicts may place the protagonist in opposition to another individual, nature, or society. Tarzan's battle with societal values begins the moment he instinctively takes Jane in his arms to carry her off into the jungle. He will learn that an individual's conflict with society can be as frustrating as it is complex, which is why so many plots in serious fiction focus on this conflict. It can be seen, to cite only two examples, in a mysterious stranger's alienation from a materialistic culture in Herman Melville's "Bartleby, the Scrivener" (p. 130) and in a young black man's struggle with racism in Ellison's "Battle Royal" (p. 227).

Conflict may also be internal; in such a case some moral or psychological issue must be resolved within the protagonist. Inner conflicts frequently accompany external ones, as in Godwin's "A Sorrowful Woman" (p. 39). Godwin's story is quiet and almost uneventful compared with *Tarzan of the Apes*. The conflict, though puzzling, is more significant in "A Sorrowful Woman" because that story subtly explores some troubling issues that cannot be resolved simply by "huge biceps" or a "lithe, young form." The protagonist struggles with both internal and external forces. We are not told why she withdraws from her considerate husband and beautiful son. There is no exposition to explain why she is hopelessly "sad and sick" of them. There is no readily identifiable antagonist in her way, but there are several possibilities. Her antagonist is some part of herself that cannot find satisfaction in playing the roles of wife and mother, yet her husband and child also seem to bear some of the responsibility, as does the domestic environment that defines her.

Godwin creates questions for the reader rather than suspense. We are compelled to keep asking why the protagonist in her story is so unhappy instead of what is going to happen next. The story ends with her flurry of domestic activity and her death, but we do not feel as if we have come to a resolution. "A Sorrowful Woman" will not let us go because we keep coming back to what causes the protagonist's rejection of her role. Has she gone mad? Are the husband and child not what they seem to be? Is her domestic life stifling rather than nourishing? Does her family destroy rather than support her? Who or what is to blame? No one is able to rescue the sorrowful woman from her conflict, nor does the design of Godwin's plot relieve the reader of the questions the story raises. The meaning of the action is not self-evident as it is in *Tarzan of the Apes*. It must be drawn from a careful reading of the interrelated details and dialogues that constitute this story's action.

Although Burroughs makes enormous demands on Tarzan to survive the perils of the jungle, the author makes few demands on the reader. In part, that's why *Tarzan of the Apes* is so much fun: we sit back while Tarzan does all the work, struggling heroically through all the conflicts Burroughs has planted along his jungle paths. Godwin's story, in contrast, illustrates that there are other kinds of plots, less dependent on action but equally full of conflict. This kind of reading is more demanding, but ultimately more satisfying, because as we confront conflicts in serious fiction we read not only absorbing stories but also ourselves. We are invited not to escape life but to look long and hard at it. Although serious fiction can be as diverting and pleasurable as most standard action-packed plots, serious fiction offers an additional important element: a perspective on experience that reflects rather than deflects life.

The following three stories — Alice Walker's "The Flowers" William Faulkner's "A Rose for Emily," and Andre Dubus's "Killings" — are remarkable for the different kinds of tension produced in each by a subtle use of plot.

ALICE WALKER (B. 1944)

Novelist, poet, and political activist, Alice Walker was born in 1944 to Minnie Tallulah Grant Walker and Willie Lee Walker, sharecroppers in Eatonton, Georgia. A promising student from the beginning, Walker started her collegiate career at Spelman College in Atlanta, but graduated from Sarah Lawrence College in New York in 1965. After teaching history in Mississippi, she won a fellowship from the Radcliffe Institute and went on to teach at Wellesley College, where she pioneered one of the first women's studies courses in the country. Walker has published several volumes of poetry, including *Once* (1968), *Revolutionary Petunias and Other Poems* (1973), *Horses Make a Landscape Look More Beautiful* (1984), *Collected Poems* (2005), *Hard Times Require Furious Dancing* (2000), and a book of essays, *Living by the Word* (1988). Her numerous works of fiction include *In Love and Trouble: Stories of Black Women* (1973), *The Temple of My Familiar* (1989), *Possessing the Secret of Joy* (1992), *The Complete Stories* (1994), *By the Light of My Father's*

Courtesy of Jean Weisinger/© Jean Weisinger, 1991.

Smile (1998), *Now Is the Time to Open Your Heart* (2004), and *The Color Purple* (1982), which was made into a major motion picture. The acclaim for her novel *Meridian* (1976) won her a Guggenheim Fellowship and led her to San Francisco, where she still lives. Walker's writing career has been defined largely by political interests that have not waned since the sixties, and she has contributed substantially to the antinuclear and environmental movements, women's rights, and the movement for the protection of indigenous peoples.

The Flowers 1973

It seemed to Myop as she skipped lightly from hen house to pigpen to smokehouse that the days had never been as beautiful as these. The air held a keenness that made her nose twitch. The harvesting of the corn and cotton, peanuts and squash, made each day a golden surprise that caused excited little tremors to run up her jaws.

Myop carried a short, knobby stick. She struck out at random at chickens she liked, and worked out the beat of a song on the fence around the pigpen. She felt light and good in the warm sun. She was ten, and nothing existed for her but her song, the stick clutched in her dark brown hand, and the tat-de-ta-ta-ta of accompaniment.

Turning her back on the rusty boards of her family's sharecropper cabin, Myop walked along the fence till it ran into the stream made by the spring. Around the spring, where the family got drinking water, silver ferns and wild-flowers grew. Along the shallow banks pigs rooted. Myop watched the tiny white bubbles disrupt the thin black scale of soil and the water that silently rose and slid away down the stream.

She had explored the woods behind the house many times. Often, in late autumn, her mother took her to gather nuts among the fallen leaves. Today she made her own path, bouncing this way and that way, vaguely keeping an eye out for snakes. She found, in addition to various common but pretty ferns and leaves, an armful of strange blue flowers with velvety ridges and a sweet-suds bush full of the brown, fragrant buds.

By twelve o'clock, her arms laden with sprigs of her findings, she was a 5 mile or more from home. She had often been as far before, but the strangeness of the land made it not as pleasant as her usual haunts. It seemed gloomy in the little cove in which she found herself. The air was damp, the silence close and deep.

Myop began to circle back to the house, back to the peacefulness of the morning. It was then she stepped smack into his eyes. Her heel became lodged in the broken ridge between brow and nose, and she reached down quickly, unafraid, to free herself. It was only when she saw his naked grin that she gave a little yelp of surprise.

He had been a tall man. From feet to neck covered a long space. His head lay beside him. When she pushed back the leaves and layers of earth and debris Myop saw that he'd had large white teeth, all of them cracked or broken, long fingers, and very big bones. All his clothes had rotted away except some threads of blue denim from his overalls. The buckles of the overalls had turned green.

Myop gazed around the spot with interest. Very near where she'd stepped into the head was a wild pink rose. As she picked it to add to her bundle she noticed a raised mound, a ring, around the rose's root. It was the rotted remains of a noose, a bit of shredding plowline, now blending benignly into the soil. Around an overhanging limb of a great spreading oak clung another piece. Frayed, rotted, bleached, and frazzled—barely there—but spinning restlessly in the breeze. Myop laid down her flowers.

And the summer was over.

CONSIDERATIONS FOR CRITICAL THINKING AND WRITING

1. FIRST RESPONSE. How do you interpret the final line of the story? What is the effect of the brevity of that sentence?

2. Describe the atmosphere and tone of the first three paragraphs. What emotions do they produce concerning Myop's childhood?

3. How might paragraph 5 be described as an example of foreshadowing?

4. What is the conflict in the story? What is its climax? Is there a resolution to the conflict? Explain.

5. What do you think is the central point of this story?

CONNECTIONS TO OTHER SELECTIONS

1. Discuss the significance of Myop's experience and that of the narrator in Ralph Ellison's "Battle Royal" (p. 227).

2. Write an essay comparing the ending of Walker's story with that of William Faulkner's "A Rose for Emily" (p. 78). What is the effect of the ending on your reading of each story?

WILLIAM FAULKNER (1897–1962)

Born into an old Mississippi family that had lost its influence and wealth during the Civil War, William Faulkner lived nearly all his life in the South writing about Yoknapatawpha County, an imagined Mississippi county similar to his home in Oxford. Among his novels based on this fictional location are *The Sound and the Fury* (1929), *As I Lay Dying* (1930), *Light in August* (1932), and *Absalom, Absalom!* (1936). Although his writings are regional in their emphasis on local social history, his concerns are broader. In his 1950 acceptance speech for the Nobel Prize for Literature, he insisted that

Cofield Collection, Archives and Special Collections, University of Mississippi Libraries.

the "problems of the human heart in conflict with itself . . . alone can make good writing because only that is worth writing about, worth the agony and the sweat." This commitment is evident in his novels and in *The Collected Stories of William Faulkner* (1950). "A Rose for Emily," about the mysterious life of Emily Grierson, presents a personal conflict rooted in her southern identity. It also contains a grim surprise.

A Rose for Emily   1931

I

When Miss Emily Grierson died, our whole town went to her funeral: the men through a sort of respectful affection for a fallen monument, the women mostly out of curiosity to see the inside of her house, which no one save an old manservant — a combined gardener and cook — had seen in at least ten years.

It was a big, squarish frame house that had once been white, decorated with cupolas and spires and scrolled balconies in the heavily lightsome style of the seventies, set on what had once been our most select street. But garages and cotton gins had encroached and obliterated even the august names of that neighborhood; only Miss Emily's house was left, lifting its stubborn and coquettish decay above the cotton wagons and the gasoline pumps — an eyesore among eyesores. And now Miss Emily had gone to join the representatives of those august names where they lay in the cedar-bemused cemetery among the ranked and anonymous graves of Union and Confederate soldiers who fell at the battle of Jefferson.

Alive, Miss Emily had been a tradition, a duty, and a care; a sort of hereditary obligation upon the town, dating from that day in 1894 when Colonel Sartoris, the mayor — he who fathered the edict that no Negro woman should appear on the streets without an apron — remitted her taxes, the dispensation dating from the death of her father on into perpetuity. Not that Miss Emily would have accepted charity. Colonel Sartoris invented an involved tale to the effect that Miss Emily's father had loaned money to the town, which the town, as a matter of business, preferred this way of repaying. Only a man of Colonel Sartoris' generation and thought could have invented it, and only a woman could have believed it.

When the next generation, with its more modern ideas, became mayors and aldermen, this arrangement created some little dissatisfaction. On the first of the year they mailed her a tax notice. February came, and there was no reply. They wrote her a formal letter, asking her to call at the sheriff's office at her convenience. A week later the mayor wrote her himself, offering to call or to send his car for her, and received in reply a note on paper of an archaic shape, in a thin, flowing calligraphy in faded ink, to the effect that she no longer went out at all. The tax notice was also enclosed, without comment.

They called a special meeting of the Board of Aldermen. A deputation waited 5 upon her, knocked at the door through which no visitor had passed since she ceased giving china-painting lessons eight or ten years earlier. They were admitted by the old Negro into a dim hall from which a stairway mounted into still more shadow. It smelled of dust and disuse — a close, dank smell. The Negro led them into the parlor. It was furnished in heavy, leather-covered furniture. When the Negro opened the blinds of one window, they could see that the leather was cracked; and when they sat down, a faint dust rose sluggishly about their thighs, spinning with slow motes in the single sun-ray. On a tarnished gilt easel before the fireplace stood a crayon portrait of Miss Emily's father.

They rose when she entered — a small, fat woman in black, with a thin gold chain descending to her waist and vanishing into her belt, leaning on an ebony cane with a tarnished gold head. Her skeleton was small and spare; perhaps that was why what would have been merely plumpness in another was obesity in her. She looked bloated, like a body long submerged in motionless water, and of that pallid hue. Her eyes, lost in the fatty ridges of her face, looked like two small pieces of coal pressed into a lump of dough as they moved from one face to another while the visitors stated their errand.

She did not ask them to sit. She just stood in the door and listened quietly until the spokesman came to a stumbling halt. Then they could hear the invisible watch ticking at the end of the gold chain.

Her voice was dry and cold. "I have no taxes in Jefferson. Colonel Sartoris explained it to me. Perhaps one of you can gain access to the city records and satisfy yourselves."

"But we have. We are the city authorities, Miss Emily. Didn't you get a notice from the sheriff, signed by him?"

"I received a paper, yes," Miss Emily said. "Perhaps he considers himself the 10 sheriff . . . I have no taxes in Jefferson."

"But there is nothing on the books to show that, you see. We must go by the —"

"See Colonel Sartoris. I have no taxes in Jefferson."

"But, Miss Emily —"

"See Colonel Sartoris." (Colonel Sartoris had been dead almost ten years.) "I have no taxes in Jefferson. Tobe!" The Negro appeared. "Show these gentlemen out."

II

So she vanquished them, horse and foot, just as she had vanquished their fathers 15 thirty years before about the smell. That was two years after her father's death and a short time after her sweetheart — the one we believed would marry her — had deserted her. After her father's death she went out very little; after her sweetheart went away, people hardly saw her at all. A few of the ladies had the temerity to call, but were not received, and the only sign of life about the place was the Negro man — a young man then — going in and out with a market basket.

"Just as if a man — any man — could keep a kitchen properly," the ladies said; so they were not surprised when the smell developed. It was another link between the gross, teeming world and the high and mighty Griersons.

A neighbor, a woman, complained to the mayor, Judge Stevens, eighty years old.

"But what will you have me do about it, madam?" he said.

"Why, send her word to stop it," the woman said. "Isn't there a law?"

"I'm sure that won't be necessary," Judge Stevens said. "It's probably just a snake 20 or a rat that nigger of hers killed in the yard. I'll speak to him about it."

The next day he received two more complaints, one from a man who came in diffident deprecation. "We really must do something about it, Judge. I'd be the last one in the world to bother Miss Emily, but we've got to do something." That night the Board of Aldermen met — three graybeards and one younger man, a member of the rising generation.

"It's simple enough," he said. "Send her word to have her place cleaned up. Give her a certain time to do it in, and if she don't . . ."

"Dammit, sir," Judge Stevens said, "will you accuse a lady to her face of smelling bad?"

So the next night, after midnight, four men crossed Miss Emily's lawn and slunk about the house like burglars, sniffing along the base of the brickwork and at the cellar openings while one of them performed a regular sowing motion with his hand out of a sack slung from his shoulder. They broke open the cellar door and sprinkled lime there, and in all the outbuildings. As they recrossed the lawn, a window that had been dark was lighted and Miss Emily sat in it, the light behind her, and her upright torso motionless as that of an idol. They crept quietly across the lawn and into the shadow of the locusts that lined the street. After a week or two the smell went away.

That was when people had begun to feel really sorry for her. People in our town, remembering how old lady Wyatt, her great-aunt, had gone completely crazy at last, believed that the Griersons held themselves a little too high for what they really were. None of the young men were quite good enough for Miss Emily and such. We had long thought of them as a tableau, Miss Emily a slender figure in white in the background, her father a spraddled silhouette in the foreground, his back to her and clutching a horsewhip, the two of them framed by the back-flung front door. So when she got to be thirty and was still single, we were not pleased exactly, but vindicated; even with insanity in the family she wouldn't have turned down all of her chances if they had really materialized.

When her father died, it got about that the house was all that was left to her; and in a way, people were glad. At last they could pity Miss Emily. Being left alone, and a pauper, she had become humanized. Now she too would know the old thrill and the old despair of a penny more or less.

The day after his death all the ladies prepared to call at the house and offer condolence and aid, as is our custom. Miss Emily met them at the door, dressed as usual and with no trace of grief on her face. She told them that her father was not dead. She did that for three days, with the ministers calling on her, and the doctors, trying to persuade her to let them dispose of the body. Just as they were about to resort to law and force, she broke down, and they buried her father quickly.

We did not say she was crazy then. We believed she had to do that. We remembered all the young men her father had driven away, and we knew that with nothing left, she would have to cling to that which had robbed her, as people will.

III

She was sick for a long time. When we saw her again, her hair was cut short, making her look like a girl, with a vague resemblance to those angels in colored church windows — sort of tragic and serene.

The town had just let the contracts for paving the sidewalks, and in the summer after her father's death they began the work. The construction company came with niggers and mules and machinery, and a foreman named Homer Barron, a Yankee — a big, dark, ready man, with a big voice and eyes lighter than his face. The little boys would follow in groups to hear him cuss the niggers, and the niggers singing in time to the rise and fall of picks. Pretty soon he knew everybody in town. Whenever you heard a lot of laughing anywhere about the square, Homer Barron would be in the center of the group. Presently we began to see him and Miss Emily on Sunday afternoons driving in the yellow-wheeled buggy and the matched team of bays from the livery stable.

At first we were glad that Miss Emily would have an interest, because the ladies all said, "Of course a Grierson would not think seriously of a Northerner, a day laborer." But there were still others, older people, who said that even grief could not cause a real lady to forget *noblesse oblige*° — without calling it *noblesse oblige*. They just said, "Poor Emily. Her kinsfolk should come to her." She had some kin in Alabama; but years ago her father had fallen out with them over the estate of old

noblesse oblige: The obligation of people of high social position.

lady Wyatt, the crazy woman, and there was no communication between the two families. They had not even been represented at the funeral.

And as soon as the old people said, "Poor Emily," the whispering began. "Do you suppose it's really so?" they said to one another. "Of course it is. What else could . . ." This behind their hands; rustling of craned silk and satin behind jalousies closed upon the sun of Sunday afternoon as the thin, swift clop-clop-clop of the matched team passed: "Poor Emily."

She carried her head high enough — even when we believed that she was fallen. It was as if she demanded more than ever the recognition of her dignity as the last Grierson; as if it had wanted that touch of earthiness to reaffirm her imperviousness. Like when she bought the rat poison, the arsenic. That was over a year after they had begun to say "Poor Emily," and while the two female cousins were visiting her.

"I want some poison," she said to the druggist. She was over thirty then, still a slight woman, though thinner than usual, with cold, haughty black eyes in a face the flesh of which was strained across the temples and about the eye-sockets as you imagine a lighthouse-keeper's face ought to look. "I want some poison," she said.

"Yes, Miss Emily. What kind? For rats and such? I'd recom —"   35

"I want the best you have. I don't care what kind."

The druggist named several. "They'll kill anything up to an elephant. But what you want is —"

"Arsenic," Miss Emily said. "Is that a good one?"

"Is . . . arsenic? Yes, ma'am. But what you want —"

"I want arsenic."   40

The druggist looked down at her. She looked back at him, erect, her face like a strained flag. "Why, of course," the druggist said. "If that's what you want. But the law requires you to tell what you are going to use it for."

Miss Emily just stared at him, her head tilted back in order to look him eye for eye, until he looked away and went and got the arsenic and wrapped it up. The Negro delivery boy brought her the package; the druggist didn't come back. When she opened the package at home there was written on the box, under the skull and bones: "For rats."

IV

So the next day we all said, "She will kill herself"; and we said it would be the best thing. When she had first begun to be seen with Homer Barron, we had said, "She will marry him." Then we said, "She will persuade him yet," because Homer himself had remarked — he liked men, and it was known that he drank with the younger men in the Elks' Club — that he was not a marrying man. Later we said, "Poor Emily" behind the jalousies as they passed on Sunday afternoon in the glittering buggy, Miss Emily with her head high and Homer Barron with his hat cocked and a cigar in his teeth, reins and whip in a yellow glove.

Then some of the ladies began to say that it was a disgrace to the town and a bad example to the young people. The men did not want to interfere, but at last the ladies forced the Baptist minister — Miss Emily's people were Episcopal — to call upon her. He would never divulge what happened during that interview, but he refused to go back again. The next Sunday they again drove about the streets, and the following day the minister's wife wrote to Miss Emily's relations in Alabama.

So she had blood-kin under her roof again and we sat back to watch develop-   45
ments. At first nothing happened. Then we were sure that they were to be married. We learned that Miss Emily had been to the jeweler's and ordered a man's toilet set

in silver, with the letters H. B. on each piece. Two days later we learned that she had bought a complete outfit of men's clothing, including a nightshirt, and we said, "They are married." We were really glad. We were glad because the two female cousins were even more Grierson than Miss Emily had ever been.

So we were not surprised when Homer Barron — the streets had been finished some time since — was gone. We were a little disappointed that there was not a public blowing-off, but we believed that he had gone on to prepare for Miss Emily's coming, or to give her a chance to get rid of the cousins. (By that time it was a cabal, and we were all Miss Emily's allies to help circumvent the cousins.) Sure enough, after another week they departed. And, as we had expected all along, within three days Homer Barron was back in town. A neighbor saw the Negro man admit him at the kitchen door at dusk one evening.

And that was the last we saw of Homer Barron. And of Miss Emily for some time. The Negro man went in and out with the market basket, but the front door remained closed. Now and then we would see her at a window for a moment, as the men did that night when they sprinkled the lime, but for almost six months she did not appear on the streets. Then we knew that this was to be expected too; as if that quality of her father which had thwarted her woman's life so many times had been too virulent and too furious to die.

When we next saw Miss Emily, she had grown fat and her hair was turning gray. During the next few years it grew grayer and grayer until it attained an even pepper-and-salt iron-gray, when it ceased turning. Up to the day of her death at seventy-four it was still that vigorous iron-gray, like the hair of an active man.

From that time on her front door remained closed, save for a period of six or seven years, when she was about forty, during which she gave lessons in china-painting. She fitted up a studio in one of the downstairs rooms, where the daughters and granddaughters of Colonel Sartoris' contemporaries were sent to her with the same regularity and in the same spirit that they were sent to church on Sundays with a twenty-five-cent piece for the collection plate. Meanwhile her taxes had been remitted.

Then the newer generation became the backbone and the spirit of the town, 50 and the painting pupils grew up and fell away and did not send their children to her with boxes of color and tedious brushes and pictures cut from the ladies' magazines. The front door closed upon the last one and remained closed for good. When the town got free postal delivery, Miss Emily alone refused to let them fasten the metal numbers above her door and attach a mailbox to it. She would not listen to them.

Daily, monthly, yearly we watched the Negro grow grayer and more stooped, going in and out with the market basket. Each December we sent her a tax notice, which would be returned by the post office a week later, unclaimed. Now and then we would see her in one of the downstairs windows — she had evidently shut up the top floor of the house — like the carven torso of an idol in a niche, looking or not looking at us, we could never tell which. Thus she passed from generation to generation — dear, inescapable, impervious, tranquil, and perverse.

And so she died. Fell ill in the house filled with dust and shadows, with only a doddering Negro man to wait on her. We did not even know she was sick; we had long since given up trying to get information from the Negro. He talked to no one, probably not even to her, for his voice had grown harsh and rusty, as if from disuse.

She died in one of the downstairs rooms, in a heavy walnut bed with a curtain, her gray head propped on a pillow yellow and moldy with age and lack of sunlight.

V

The Negro met the first of the ladies at the front door and let them in, with their hushed, sibilant voices and their quick, curious glances, and then he disappeared. He walked right through the house and out the back and was not seen again.

The two female cousins came at once. They held the funeral on the 55 second day, with the town coming to look at Miss Emily beneath a mass of bought flowers, with the crayon face of her father musing profoundly above the bier and the ladies sibilant and macabre; and the very old men — some in their brushed Confederate uniforms — on the porch and the lawn, talking of Miss Emily as if she had been a contemporary of theirs, believing that they had danced with her and courted her perhaps, confusing time with its mathematical progression, as the old do, to whom all the past is not a diminishing road but, instead, a huge meadow which no winter ever quite touches, divided from them now by the narrow bottle-neck of the most recent decade of years.

Already we knew that there was one room in that region above stairs which no one had seen in forty years, and which would have to be forced. They waited until Miss Emily was decently in the ground before they opened it.

The violence of breaking down the door seemed to fill this room with pervading dust. A thin, acrid pall as of the tomb seemed to lie everywhere upon this room decked and furnished as for a bridal: upon the valance curtains of faded rose color, upon the rose-shaded lights, upon the dressing table, upon the delicate array of crystal and the man's toilet things backed with tarnished silver, silver so tarnished that the monogram was obscured. Among them lay a collar and tie, as if they had just been removed, which, lifted, left upon the surface a pale crescent in the dust. Upon a chair hung the suit, carefully folded; beneath it the two mute shoes and the discarded socks.

The man himself lay in the bed.

For a long while we just stood there, looking down at the profound and fleshless grin. The body had apparently once lain in the attitude of an embrace, but now the long sleep that outlasts love, that conquers even the grimace of love, had cuckolded him. What was left of him, rotted beneath what was left of the nightshirt, had become inextricable from the bed in which he lay; and upon him and upon the pillow beside him lay that even coating of the patient and biding dust.

Then we noticed that in the second pillow was the indentation of a head. One 60 of us lifted something from it, and leaning forward, that faint and invisible dust dry and acrid in the nostrils, we saw a long strand of iron-gray hair.

CONSIDERATIONS FOR CRITICAL THINKING AND WRITING

1. FIRST RESPONSE. How might this story be rewritten as a piece of formula fiction? You could write it as a romance, detective, or horror story — whatever strikes your fancy. Does Faulkner's version have elements of formulaic fiction?

2. What is the effect of the final paragraph of the story? How does it contribute to your understanding of Emily? Why is it important that we get this information last rather than at the beginning of the story?

3. What details foreshadow the conclusion of the story? Did you anticipate the ending?

4. Contrast the order of events as they happen in the story with the order in which they are told. How does this plotting create interest and suspense?

5. Faulkner uses a number of gothic elements in this plot: the imposing decrepit house, the decayed corpse, and the mysterious secret horrors connected with Emily's life. How do these elements forward the plot and establish the atmosphere?

6. How does the information provided by the exposition indicate the nature of the conflict in the story? What does Emily's southern heritage contribute to the story?

7. Who or what is the antagonist of the story? Why is it significant that Homer Barron is a construction foreman and a northerner?

8. In what sense does the narrator's telling of the story serve as "A Rose for Emily"? Why do you think the narrator uses *we* rather than *I*?

9. Explain how Emily's reasons for murdering Homer are related to her personal history and to the ways she handled previous conflicts.

10. Discuss how Faulkner's treatment of the North and South contributes to the meaning of the story.

11. Provide an alternative title and explain how the emphasis in your title is reflected in the story.

CONNECTIONS TO OTHER SELECTIONS

1. Contrast Faulkner's ordering of events with Tim O'Brien's "How to Tell a True War Story" (p. 488). How does each author's arrangement of incidents create different effects on the reader?

2. To what extent do concepts of honor and tradition influence the action in "A Rose for Emily" and "How to Tell a True War Story"?

Perspective

WILLIAM FAULKNER (1897–1962)
On "A Rose for Emily"   1959

Q. What is the meaning of the title "A Rose for Emily"?

A. Oh, it's simply the poor woman had had no life at all. Her father had kept her more or less locked up and then she had a lover who was about to quit her, she had to murder him. It was just "A Rose for Emily" — that's all.

Q. . . . What ever inspired you to write this story?

A. That to me was another sad and tragic manifestation of man's condition in which he dreams and hopes, in which he is in conflict with himself or with his environment or with others. In this case there was the young girl with a young girl's normal aspirations to find love and then a husband and a family, who was browbeaten and kept down by her father, a selfish man who didn't want her to leave home because he wanted a housekeeper, and it was a natural instinct of — repressed which — you can't repress it — you can mash it down but it comes up somewhere else and very likely in a tragic form, and that was simply another manifestation of man's injustice to man, of the poor tragic human being struggling with its own heart, with others, with its environment, for the simple things which all human beings want. In that case it was a young girl that just wanted to be loved and to love and to have a husband and a family.

Q. And that purely came from your imagination?

A. Well, the story did but the condition is there. It exists. I didn't invent that condition, I didn't invent the fact that young girls dream of someone to love and children and a home, but the story of what her own particular tragedy was was invented, yes. . . .

Q. Sir, it has been argued that "A Rose for Emily" is a criticism of the North, and others have argued saying that it is a criticism of the South. Now, could this story, shall we say, be more properly classified as a criticism of the times?

A. Now that I don't know, because I was simply trying to write about people. The writer uses environment — what he knows — and if there's a symbolism in which the lover represented the North and the woman who murdered him represents the South, I don't say that's not valid and not there, but it was no intention of the writer to say, Now let's see, I'm going to write a piece in which I will use a symbolism for the North and another symbol for the South, that he was simply writing about people, a story which he thought was tragic and true, because it came out of the human heart, the human aspiration, the human — the conflict of conscience with glands, with the Old Adam. It was a conflict not between North and the South so much as between, well you might say, God and Satan.

Q. Sir, just a little more on that thing. You say it's a conflict between God and Satan. Well, I don't quite understand what you mean. Who is — did one represent the —

A. The conflict was in Miss Emily, that she knew that you do not murder people. She had been trained that you do not take a lover. You marry, you don't take a lover. She had broken all the laws of her tradition, her background, and she had finally broken the law of God too, which says you do not take human life. And she knew she was doing wrong, and that's why her own life was wrecked. Instead of murdering one lover, and then to go and take another and when she used him up to murder him, she was expiating her crime.

Q. Was the "Rose for Emily" an idea or a character? Just how did you go about it?

A. That came from a picture of the strand of hair on the pillow. It was a ghost story. Simply a picture of a strand of hair on the pillow in the abandoned house.

From *Faulkner in the University*, edited by
Frederick Gwynn and Joseph Blotner

CONSIDERATIONS FOR CRITICAL THINKING AND WRITING

1. Discuss whether you think Faulkner's explanation of the conflict between "God and Satan" limits or expands the meaning of the story for you.

2. In what sense is "A Rose for Emily" a ghost story?

A SAMPLE CLOSE READING

An Annotated Section of "A Rose for Emily"

Even as you read a story for the first time, you can highlight passages, circle or underline words, and write responses in the margins. Subsequent readings will yield more insights once you begin to understand how various elements such as plot, character, and wording build toward the conclusion and what you perceive to be the story's central ideas. The following annotations for the first five paragraphs of "A Rose for Emily" provide a perspective written by someone who had read the work several times.

WILLIAM FAULKNER (1897–1962)

From *A Rose for Emily* 1931

> The title suggests that the story is an expression of affection and mourning, as well as a tribute, for Emily — despite her bizarre behavior.

I

When Miss Emily Grierson died, our whole town went to her funeral: the men through a sort of respectful affection for a fallen monument, the women mostly out of curiosity to see the inside of her house, which no one save an old manservant — a combined gardener and cook — had seen in at least ten years.

> The story begins (and ends) with death, and the "fallen monument" signals Emily's special meaning to the narrator and the community.

It was a big, squarish frame house that had once been white, decorated with cupolas and spires and scrolled balconies in the heavily lightsome style of the seventies, set on what had once been our most select street. But garages and cotton gins had encroached and obliterated even the august names of that neighborhood; only Miss Emily's house was left, lifting its stubborn and coquettish decay above the cotton wagons and the gasoline pumps — an eyesore among eyesores. And now Miss Emily had gone to join the representatives of those august names where they lay in the cedar-bemused cemetery among the ranked and anonymous graves of Union and Confederate soldiers who fell at the battle of Jefferson.

> The importance of the decayed old South setting is emphasized by being detailed even before Emily is described. The Civil War between the North and South is implicitly linked to the garages and gas pumps (the modern) that overtake the old southern neighborhood and hint at a lingering conflict.

Alive, Miss Emily had been a tradition, a duty, and a care; a sort of hereditary obligation upon the town, dating from that day in 1894 when Colonel Sartoris, the mayor — he who fathered the edict that no Negro woman should appear on the streets without an apron — remitted her taxes, the dispensation dating from the death of her father on into perpetuity. Not that Miss Emily would have accepted charity. Colonel Sartoris invented an involved tale to the effect that Miss Emily's father had loaned money to the town, which the town, as a matter of business, preferred this way of repaying. Only a man of Colonel Sartoris' generation and thought could have invented it, and only a woman could have believed it.

> Emily is associated with southern tradition, duty, and privilege that require protection. This helps explain why the townspeople attend her funeral.

Like Emily, her "archaic," "thin," and "faded" note resists change and "modern ideas." She dismisses any attempts by the town to assess her for taxes or for anything else. She won't even leave the house.

When the next generation, with its more modern ideas, became mayors and aldermen, this arrangement created some little dissatisfaction. On the first of the year they mailed her a tax notice. February came, and there was no reply. They wrote her a formal letter, asking her to call at the sheriff's office at her convenience. A week later the mayor wrote her himself, offering to call or to send his car for her, and received in reply a note on paper of an archaic shape, in a thin, flowing calligraphy in faded ink, to the effect that she no longer went out at all. The tax notice was also enclosed, without comment.

The description of the "dank" house smelling of "dust and disuse" reinforces Emily's connection with the past and her refusal to let go of it. As the men sat down, "a faint dust rose" around them. The passage of time is alluded to in each of these paragraphs and ultimately emerges as a kind of antagonist.

They called a special meeting of the Board of Aldermen. 5 A deputation waited upon her, knocked at the door through which no visitor had passed since she ceased giving china-painting lessons eight or ten years earlier. They were admitted by the old Negro into a dim hall from which a stairway mounted into still more shadow. It smelled of dust and disuse — a close, dank smell. The Negro led them into the parlor. It was furnished in heavy, leather-covered furniture. When the Negro opened the blinds of one window, they could see that the leather was cracked; and when they sat down, a faint dust rose sluggishly about their thighs, spinning with slow motes in the single sunray. On a tarnished gilt easel before the fireplace stood a crayon portrait of Miss Emily's father.

A SAMPLE STUDENT RESPONSE

Josiah Parker

Professor Altschuler

English 200-A

14 December 2015

Conflict in the Plot of William Faulkner's "A Rose for Emily"

The conflict of William Faulkner's "A Rose for Emily" is the driving force of the story's plot. However, the conflict is not the act of murder, nor is it Miss Emily's bizarre, reclusive lifestyle. The conflict is located instead in Miss Emily's background, her history. She is portrayed as a hardened, bitter old woman, but we soon realize she herself is a victim. She has been oppressed her entire life by her domineering father, unable to take a suitor and marry, which is what she desires most. This lifelong oppression becomes the central conflict, and is what drives Miss Emily, causing her "to cling to that which had robbed her" (Faulkner, "Rose" 80).

After her father's death, Miss Emily immediately takes a lover, then poisons him when he tries to leave her. Both actions are what Faulkner himself claims "had broken all the laws of her tradition" (Faulkner, "On 'A Rose'" 85). She has been taught her whole life not to take a lover, certainly not to take a life. Her willingness to go against what she has always known to be moral and right creates dramatic tension and advances the story. In this way, the act of murder is nothing more than a portion of the plot, "the author's arrangement of incidents in a story," rather than the conflict itself (Meyer 66). . . .

Parker 5

Works Cited

Faulkner, William. "A Rose for Emily." Meyer 78–83.

---. "On 'A Rose for Emily.'" Meyer 84–85.

Meyer, Michael, ed. *The Bedford Introduction to Literature*. 11th ed. Boston: Bedford/St. Martin's, 2016. Print.

ANDRE DUBUS (1936–1999)

Though a native of Louisiana, where he attended the Christian Brothers School and McNeese State College, Andre Dubus lived much of his life in Massachusetts; many of his stories are set in the Merrimack Valley north of Boston. After college Dubus served as an officer for five years in the Marine Corps. He then took an M.F.A. at the University of Iowa in 1966 and began teaching at Bradford College in Massachusetts. His fiction earned him numerous awards, and he was both a Guggenheim

© Marion Ettlinger.

and a MacArthur Fellow. Among his collections of fiction are *Separate Flights* (1975); *Adultery and Other Choices* (1977); *Finding a Girl in America* (1980), from which "Killings" is taken; *The Last Worthless Evening* (1986); *Collected Stories* (1988); and *Dancing after Hours* (1996). In 1991 he published *Broken Vessels,* a collection of autobiographical essays. His stories are often tense with violence, anger, tenderness, and guilt; they are populated by characters who struggle to understand and survive their experiences, painful with failure and the weight of imperfect relationships. In "Killings," the basis for a 2001 film titled *In the Bedroom,* Dubus offers a powerful blend of intimate domestic life and shocking violence.

Killings   1979

On the August morning when Matt Fowler buried his youngest son, Frank, who had lived for twenty-one years, eight months, and four days, Matt's older son, Steve, turned to him as the family left the grave and walked between their friends, and said: "I should kill him." He was twenty-eight, his brown hair starting to thin in front where he used to have a cowlick. He bit his lower lip, wiped his eyes, then said it again. Ruth's arm, linked with Matt's, tightened; he looked at her. Beneath her eyes there was swelling from the three days she had suffered. At the limousine Matt stopped and looked back at the grave, the casket, and the Congregationalist minister who he thought had probably had a difficult job with the eulogy though he hadn't seemed to, and the old funeral director who was saying something to the six young pallbearers. The grave was on a hill and overlooked the Merrimack, which he could not see from where he stood; he looked at the opposite bank, at the apple orchard with its symmetrically planted trees going up a hill.

Next day Steve drove with his wife back to Baltimore where he managed the branch office of a bank, and Cathleen, the middle child, drove with her husband back to Syracuse. They had left the grandchildren with friends. A month after the funeral Matt played poker at Willis Trottier's because Ruth, who knew this was the second time he had been invited, told him to go, he couldn't sit home with her for the rest of her life, she was all right. After the game Willis went outside to tell everyone good night and, when the others had driven away, he walked with Matt to his car. Willis was a short, silver-haired man who had opened a diner after World War II, his trade then mostly very early breakfast, which he cooked, and then lunch for the men who worked at the leather and shoe factories. He now owned a large restaurant.

"He walks the Goddamn streets," Matt said.

"I know. He was in my place last night, at the bar. With a girl."

"I don't see him. I'm in the store all the time. Ruth sees him. She sees him too 5 much. She was at Sunnyhurst today getting cigarettes and aspirin, and there he was. She can't even go out for cigarettes and aspirin. It's killing her."

"Come back in for a drink."

Matt looked at his watch. Ruth would be asleep. He walked with Willis back into the house, pausing at the steps to look at the starlit sky. It was a cool summer night; he thought vaguely of the Red Sox, did not even know if they were at home tonight; since it happened he had not been able to think about any of the small pleasures he believed he had earned, as he had earned also what was shattered now forever: the quietly harried and quietly pleasurable days of fatherhood. They went inside. Willis's wife, Martha, had gone to bed hours ago, in the rear of the large house which was rigged with burglar and fire alarms. They went downstairs to the game room: the television set suspended from the ceiling, the pool table, the poker table with beer cans, cards, chips, filled ashtrays, and the six chairs where Matt and his friends had sat, the friends picking up the old banter as though he had only been away on vacation; but he could see the affection and courtesy in their eyes. Willis went behind the bar and mixed them each a Scotch and soda; he stayed behind the bar and looked at Matt sitting on the stool.

"How often have you thought about it?" Willis said.

"Every day since he got out. I didn't think about bail. I thought I wouldn't have to worry about him for years. She sees him all the time. It makes her cry."

"He was in my place a long time last night. He'll be back."   10

"Maybe he won't."

"The band. He likes the band."

"What's he doing now?"

"He's tending bar up to Hampton Beach. For a friend. Ever notice even the worst bastard always has friends? He couldn't get work in town. It's just tourists and kids up to Hampton. Nobody knows him. If they do, they don't care. They drink what he mixes."

"Nobody tells me about him."   15

"I hate him, Matt. My boys went to school with him. He was the same then. Know what he'll do? Five at the most. Remember that woman about seven years ago? Shot her husband and dropped him off the bridge in the Merrimack with a hundred-pound sack of cement and said all the way through it that nobody helped her. Know where she is now? She's in Lawrence now, a secretary. And whoever helped her, where the hell is he?"

"I've got a .38 I've had for years, I take it to the store now. I tell Ruth it's for the night deposits. I tell her things have changed: we got junkies here now too. Lots of people without jobs. She knows though."

"What does she know?"

"She knows I started carrying it after the first time she saw him in town. She knows it's in case I see him, and there's some kind of a situation —"

He stopped, looked at Willis, and finished his drink. Willis mixed him another.   20

"What kind of situation?"

"Where he did something to me. Where I could get away with it."

"How does Ruth feel about that?"

"She doesn't know."

"You said she does, she's got it figured out."   25

He thought of her that afternoon: when she went into Sunnyhurst, Strout was waiting at the counter while the clerk bagged the things he had bought; she turned down an aisle and looked at soup cans until he left.

"Ruth would shoot him herself, if she thought she could hit him."

"You got a permit?"

"No."

"I do. You could get a year for that."   30

"Maybe I'll get one. Or maybe I won't. Maybe I'll just stop bringing it to the store."

Richard Strout was twenty-six years old, a high school athlete, football scholarship to the University of Massachusetts where he lasted for almost two semesters before quitting in advance of the final grades that would have forced him not to return. People then said: Dickie can do the work; he just doesn't want to. He came home and did construction work for his father but refused his father's offer to learn the business; his two older brothers had learned it, so that Strout and Sons trucks going about town, and signs on construction sites, now slashed wounds into Matt Fowler's life. Then Richard married a young girl and became a bartender, his salary and tips augmented and perhaps sometimes matched by his father, who also posted his bond. So his friends, his enemies (he had those: fist fights or, more often, boys and then young men who had not fought him when they thought they should have), and those who simply knew him by face and name, had a series of images of him which they recalled when they heard of the killing: the high school running back, the young drunk in bars, the oblivious hard-hatted young man eating lunch at a counter, the bartender who could perhaps be called courteous but not more than that: as he tended bar, his dark eyes and dark, wide-jawed face appeared less sullen, near blank.

One night he beat Frank. Frank was living at home and waiting for September, for graduate school in economics, and working as a lifeguard at Salisbury Beach, where he met Mary Ann Strout, in her first month of separation. She spent most days at the beach with her two sons. Before ten o'clock one night Frank came home; he had driven to the hospital first, and he walked into the living room with stitches over his right eye and both lips bright and swollen.

"I'm all right," he said, when Matt and Ruth stood up, and Matt turned off the television, letting Ruth get to him first: the tall, muscled but slender suntanned boy. Frank tried to smile at them but couldn't because of his lips.

"It was her husband, wasn't it?" Ruth said.   35

"Ex," Frank said. "He dropped in."

Matt gently held Frank's jaw and turned his face to the light, looked at the stitches, the blood under the white of the eye, the bruised flesh.

"Press charges," Matt said.

"No."

"What's to stop him from doing it again? Did you hit him at all? Enough so he   40
won't want to next time?"

"I don't think I touched him."

"So what are you going to do?"

"Take karate," Frank said, and tried again to smile.

"That's not the problem," Ruth said.

"You know you like her," Frank said.   45

"I like a lot of people. What about the boys? Did they see it?"

"They were asleep."

"Did you leave her alone with him?"

"He left first. She was yelling at him. I believe she had a skillet in her hand."

"Oh for God's sake," Ruth said.   50

Matt had been dealing with that too: at the dinner table on evenings when Frank wasn't home, was eating with Mary Ann; or, on the other nights — and Frank was with her every night — he talked with Ruth while they watched television, or lay in bed with the windows open and he smelled the night air and imagined, with both pride and muted sorrow, Frank in Mary Ann's arms. Ruth didn't like it because Mary Ann was in the process of divorce, because she had two children, because she was four years older than Frank, and finally — she told this in bed, where she had during all of their marriage told him of her deepest feelings: of love, of passion, of fears about one of the children, of pain Matt had caused her or she had caused him — she was against it because of what she had heard: that the marriage had gone bad early, and for most of it Richard and Mary Ann had both played around.

"That can't be true," Matt said. "Strout wouldn't have stood for it."

"Maybe he loves her."

"He's too hot-tempered. He couldn't have taken that."

But Matt knew Strout had taken it, for he had heard the stories too. He won- 55
dered who had told them to Ruth; and he felt vaguely annoyed and isolated: living with her for thirty-one years and still not knowing what she talked about with
her friends. On these summer nights he did not so much argue with her as try to
comfort her, but finally there was no difference between the two: she had concrete
objections, which he tried to overcome. And in his attempt to do this, he neglected
his own objections, which were the same as hers, so that as he spoke to her he felt
as disembodied as he sometimes did in the store when he helped a man choose a
blouse or dress or piece of costume jewelry for his wife.

"The divorce doesn't mean anything," he said. "She was young and maybe she
liked his looks and then after a while she realized she was living with a bastard. I see
it as a positive thing."

"She's not divorced yet."

"It's the same thing. Massachusetts has crazy laws, that's all. Her age is no problem. What's it matter when she was born? And that other business: even if it's true,
which it probably isn't, it's got nothing to do with Frank, and it's in the past. And
the kids are no problem. She's been married six years; she ought to have kids. Frank
likes them. He plays with them. And he's not going to marry her anyway, so it's not
a problem of money."

"Then what's he doing with her?"

"She probably loves him, Ruth. Girls always have. Why can't we just leave it at 60
that?"

"He got home at six o'clock Tuesday morning."

"I didn't know you knew. I've already talked to him about it."

Which he had: since he believed almost nothing he told Ruth, he went to Frank
with what he believed. The night before, he had followed Frank to the car after
dinner.

"You wouldn't make much of a burglar," he said.

"How's that?" 65

Matt was looking up at him; Frank was six feet tall, an inch and a half taller
than Matt, who had been proud when Frank at seventeen outgrew him; he had only
felt uncomfortable when he had to reprimand or caution him. He touched Frank's
bicep, thought of the young taut passionate body, believed he could sense the desire,
and again he felt the pride and sorrow and envy too, not knowing whether he was
envious of Frank or Mary Ann.

"When you came in yesterday morning, I woke up. One of these mornings
your mother will. And I'm the one who'll have to talk to her. She won't interfere with
you. Okay? I know it means —" But he stopped, thinking: I know it means getting
up and leaving that suntanned girl and going sleepy to the car, I know —

"Okay," Frank said, and touched Matt's shoulder and got into the car.

There had been other talks, but the only long one was their first one: a night
driving to Fenway Park, Matt having ordered the tickets so they could talk, and

knowing when Frank said yes, he would go, that he knew the talk was coming too. It took them forty minutes to get to Boston, and they talked about Mary Ann until they joined the city traffic along the Charles River, blue in the late sun. Frank told him all the things that Matt would later pretend to believe when he told them to Ruth.

"It seems like a lot for a young guy to take on," Matt finally said.   70

"Sometimes it is. But she's worth it."

"Are you thinking about getting married?"

"We haven't talked about it. She can't for over a year. I've got school."

"I *do* like her," Matt said.

He did. Some evenings, when the long summer sun was still low in the sky,   75 Frank brought her home; they came into the house smelling of suntan lotion and the sea, and Matt gave them gin and tonics and started the charcoal in the back-yard, and looked at Mary Ann in the lawn chair: long and very light brown hair (Matt thinking that twenty years ago she would have dyed it blonde), and the long brown legs he loved to look at; her face was pretty; she had probably never in her adult life gone unnoticed into a public place. It was in her wide brown eyes that she looked older than Frank; after a few drinks Matt thought what he saw in her eyes was something erotic, testament to the rumors about her; but he knew it wasn't that, or all that: she had, very young, been through a sort of pain that his children, and he and Ruth, had been spared. In the moments of his recognizing that pain, he wanted to tenderly touch her hair, wanted with some gesture to give her solace and hope. And he would glance at Frank, and hope they would love each other, hope Frank would soothe that pain in her heart, take it from her eyes; and her divorce, her age, and her children did not matter at all. On the first two evenings she did not bring her boys, and then Ruth asked her to bring them the next time. In bed that night Ruth said, "She hasn't brought them because she's embarrassed. She shouldn't feel embarrassed."

Richard Strout shot Frank in front of the boys. They were sitting on the living room floor watching television, Frank sitting on the couch, and Mary Ann just return-ing from the kitchen with a tray of sandwiches. Strout came in the front door and shot Frank twice in the chest and once in the face with a 9 mm automatic. Then he looked at the boys and Mary Ann, and went home to wait for the police.

It seemed to Matt that from the time Mary Ann called weeping to tell him until now, a Saturday night in September, sitting in the car with Willis, parked beside Strout's car, waiting for the bar to close, that he had not so much moved through his life as wandered through it, his spirit like a dazed body bumping into furniture and corners. He had always been a fearful father: when his children were young, at the start of each summer he thought of them drowning in a pond or the sea, and he was relieved when he came home in the evenings and they were there; usually that relief was his only acknowledgment of his fear, which he never spoke of, and which he controlled within his heart. As he had when they were very young and all of them in turn, Cathleen too, were drawn to the high oak in the backyard, and had to climb it. Smiling, he watched them, imagining the fall: and he was poised to catch the small body before it hit the earth. Or his legs were poised; his hands were in his pockets or his arms were folded and, for the child looking down, he appeared relaxed and confident while his heart beat with the two words he wanted to call out but did not: *Don't fall.* In winter he was less afraid: he made sure the ice would hold him before they skated, and he brought or sent them to places where they could sled without ending in the street. So he and his children had survived their childhood, and he only worried about them when he knew they were driving a long distance, and then he lost Frank in a way no father expected to lose his son, and he felt that all the fears he had borne while they were growing up, and all the grief he had been afraid of, had backed up like a huge wave and struck him on the beach and swept him out to sea. Each day he felt the same and when he was able to forget how he felt, when he was able to force himself not to feel that way, the eyes of his clerks and customers defeated him. He wished those eyes were oblivious, even cold; he felt he was withering in their tenderness. And beneath his listless wandering, every day in his soul he shot Richard Strout in the face; while Ruth, going about town on errands, kept seeing him. And at nights in bed she would hold Matt and cry, or sometimes she was silent and Matt would touch her tightening arm, her clenched fist.

As his own right fist was now, squeezing the butt of the revolver, the last of the drinkers having left the bar, talking to each other, going to their separate cars which were in the lot in front of the bar, out of Matt's vision. He heard their voices, their cars, and then the ocean again, across the street. The tide was in and sometimes it smacked the sea wall. Through the windshield he looked at the dark red side wall of the bar, and then to his left, past Willis, at Strout's car, and through its windows he could see the now-emptied parking lot, the road, the sea wall. He could smell the sea.

The front door of the bar opened and closed again and Willis looked at Matt then at the corner of the building; when Strout came around it alone Matt got out of the car, giving up the hope he had kept all night (and for the past week) that Strout would come out with friends, and Willis would simply drive away; thinking: *All right then. All right;* and he went around the front of Willis's car, and at Strout's he stopped and aimed over the hood at Strout's blue shirt ten feet away. Willis was aiming too, crouched on Matt's left, his elbow resting on the hood.

"Mr. Fowler," Strout said. He looked at each of them, and at the guns. 80
"Mr. Trottier."

Then Matt, watching the parking lot and the road, walked quickly between the car and the building and stood behind Strout. He took one leather glove from his pocket and put it on his left hand.

"Don't talk. Unlock the front and back and get in."

Strout unlocked the front door, reached in and unlocked the back, then got in, and Matt slid into the back seat, closed the door with his gloved hand, and touched Strout's head once with the muzzle.

"It's cocked. Drive to your house."

When Strout looked over his shoulder to back the car, Matt aimed at his temple 85
and did not look at his eyes.

"Drive slowly," he said. "Don't try to get stopped."

They drove across the empty front lot and onto the road, Willis's headlights shining into the car; then back through town, the sea wall on the left hiding the beach, though far out Matt could see the ocean; he uncocked the revolver; on the right were the places, most with their neon signs off, that did so much business in summer: the lounges and cafés and pizza houses, the street itself empty of traffic, the way he and Willis had known it would be when they decided to take Strout at the bar rather than knock on his door at two o'clock one morning and risk that one insomniac neighbor. Matt had not told Willis he was afraid he could not be alone with Strout for very long, smell his smells, feel the presence of his flesh, hear his voice, and then shoot him. They left the beach town and then were on the high bridge over the channel: to the left the smacking curling white at the breakwater and beyond that the dark sea and the full moon, and down to his right the small fishing boats bobbing at anchor in the cove. When they left the bridge, the sea was blocked by abandoned beach cottages, and Matt's left hand was sweating in the glove. Out here in the dark in the car he believed Ruth knew. Willis had come to his house at eleven and asked if he wanted a nightcap; Matt went to the bedroom for his wallet, put the gloves in one trouser pocket and the .38 in the other and went back to the living room, his hand in his pocket covering the bulge of the cool cylinder pressed against his fingers, the butt against his palm. When Ruth said good night she looked at his face, and he felt she could see in his eyes the gun, and the night he was going to. But he knew he couldn't trust what he saw. Willis's wife had taken her sleeping pill, which gave her eight hours — the reason, Willis had told Matt, he had the alarms installed, for nights when he was late at the restaurant — and when it was all done and Willis got home he would leave ice and a trace of Scotch and soda in two glasses in the game room and tell Martha in the morning that he had left the restaurant early and brought Matt home for a drink.

"He was making it with my wife." Strout's voice was careful, not pleading.

Matt pressed the muzzle against Strout's head, pressed it harder than he wanted to, feeling through the gun Strout's head flinching and moving forward; then he lowered the gun to his lap.

"Don't talk," he said.

Strout did not speak again. They turned west, drove past the Dairy Queen closed until spring, and the two lobster restaurants that faced each other and were crowded all summer and were now also closed, onto the short bridge crossing the tidal stream, and over the engine Matt could hear through his open window the water rushing inland under the bridge; looking to his left he saw its swift moon-lit current going back into the marsh which, leaving the bridge, they entered: the salt marsh stretching out on both sides, the grass tall in patches but mostly low and leaning earthward as though windblown, a large dark rock sitting as though rested on nothing but itself, and shallow pools reflecting the bright moon.

Beyond the marsh they drove through woods, Matt thinking now of the hole he and Willis had dug last Sunday afternoon after telling their wives they were going to Fenway Park. They listened to the game on a transistor radio, but heard none of it as they dug into the soft earth on the knoll they had chosen because elms and maples sheltered it. Already some leaves had fallen. When the hole was deep enough they covered it and the piled earth with dead branches, then cleaned their shoes and pants and went to a restaurant farther up in New Hampshire where they ate sandwiches and drank beer and watched the rest of the game on television. Looking at the back of Strout's head he thought of Frank's grave; he had not been back to it; but he would go before winter, and its second burial of snow.

He thought of Frank sitting on the couch and perhaps talking to the children as they watched television, imagined him feeling young and strong, still warmed from the sun at the beach, and feeling loved, hearing Mary Ann moving about in the kitchen, hearing her walking into the living room; maybe he looked up at her and maybe she said something, looking at him over the tray of sandwiches, smiling at him, saying something the way women do when they offer food as a gift, then the front door opening and this son of a bitch coming in and Frank seeing that he meant the gun in his hand, this son of a bitch and his gun the last person and thing Frank saw on earth.

90

When they drove into town the streets were nearly empty: a few slow cars, a policeman walking his beat past the darkened fronts of stores. Strout and Matt both glanced at him as they drove by. They were on the main street, and all the stoplights were blinking yellow. Willis and Matt had talked about that too: the lights changed at midnight, so there would be no place Strout had to stop and where he might try to run. Strout turned down the block where he lived and Willis's headlights were no longer with Matt in the back seat. They had planned that too, had decided it was best for just the one car to go to the house, and again Matt had said nothing about his fear of being alone with Strout, especially in his house: a duplex, dark as all the houses on the street were, the street itself lit at the corner of each block. As Strout turned into the driveway Matt thought of the one insomniac neighbor, thought of some man or woman sitting alone in the dark living room, watching the all-night channel from Boston. When Strout stopped the car near the front of the house, Matt said: "Drive it to the back."

He touched Strout's head with the muzzle.   95

"You wouldn't have it cocked, would you? For when I put on the brakes."

Matt cocked it, and said: "It is now."

Strout waited a moment; then he eased the car forward, the engine doing little more than idling, and as they approached the garage he gently braked. Matt opened the door, then took off the glove and put it in his pocket. He stepped out and shut the door with his hip and said: "All right."

Strout looked at the gun, then got out, and Matt followed him across the grass, and as Strout unlocked the door Matt looked quickly at the row of small backyards on either side, and scattered tall trees, some evergreens, others not, and he thought of the red and yellow leaves on the trees over the hole, saw them falling soon, probably in two weeks, dropping slowly, covering. Strout stepped into the kitchen.

"Turn on the light."   100

Strout reached to the wall switch, and in the light Matt looked at his wide back, the dark blue shirt, the white belt, the red plaid pants.

"Where's your suitcase?"

"My suitcase?"

"Where is it?"

"In the bedroom closet."   105

"That's where we're going then. When we get to a door you stop and turn on the light."

They crossed the kitchen, Matt glancing at the sink and stove and refrigerator: no dishes in the sink or even the dish rack beside it, no grease splashings on the stove, the refrigerator door clean and white. He did not want to look at any more but he looked quickly at all he could see: in the living room magazines and newspapers in a wicker basket, clean ashtrays, a record player, the records shelved next to it, then down the hall where, near the bedroom door, hung a color photograph of Mary Ann and the two boys sitting on a lawn — there was no house in the picture — Mary Ann smiling at the camera or Strout or whoever held the camera, smiling as she had on Matt's lawn this summer while he waited for the charcoal and they all talked and he looked at her brown legs and at Frank touching her arm, her shoulder, her hair; he moved down the hall with her smile in his mind, wondering: was that when they were both playing around and she was smiling like that at him and they were happy, even sometimes, making it worth it? He recalled her eyes, the pain in them, and he was conscious of the circles of love he was touching with the hand that held the revolver so tightly now as Strout stopped at the door at the end of the hall.

"There's no wall switch."

"Where's the light?"

"By the bed." 110

"Let's go."

Matt stayed a pace behind, then Strout leaned over and the room was lighted: the bed, a double one, was neatly made; the ashtray on the bedside table clean, the bureau top dustless, and no photographs; probably so the girl—who *was* she?—would not have to see Mary Ann in the bedroom she believed was theirs. But because Matt was a father and a husband, though never an ex-husband, he knew (and did not want to know) that this bedroom had never been theirs alone. Strout turned around; Matt looked at his lips, his wide jaw, and thought of Frank's doomed and fearful eyes looking up from the couch.

"Where's Mr. Trottier?"

"He's waiting. Pack clothes for warm weather."

"What's going on?" 115

"You're jumping bail."

"Mr. Fowler—"

He pointed the cocked revolver at Strout's face. The barrel trembled but not much, not as much as he had expected. Strout went to the closet and got the suitcase from the floor and opened it on the bed. As he went to the bureau, he said: "He was making it with my wife. I'd go pick up my kids and he'd be there. Sometimes he spent the night. My boys told me."

He did not look at Matt as he spoke. He opened the top drawer and Matt stepped closer so he could see Strout's hands: underwear and socks, the socks rolled, the underwear folded and stacked. He took them back to the bed, arranged them neatly in the suitcase, then from the closet he was taking shirts and trousers and a jacket; he laid them on the bed and Matt followed him to the bathroom and watched from the door while he packed those things a person accumulated and that became part of him so that at times in the store Matt felt he was selling more than clothes.

"I wanted to try to get together with her again." He was bent over the suitcase. 120 "I couldn't even talk to her. He was always with her. I'm going to jail for it; if I ever get out I'll be an old man. Isn't that enough?"

"You're not going to jail."

Strout closed the suitcase and faced Matt, looking at the gun. Matt went to his rear, so Strout was between him and the lighted hall; then using his handkerchief he turned off the lamp and said: "Let's go."

They went down the hall, Matt looking again at the photograph, and through the living room and kitchen, Matt turning off the lights and talking, frightened that he was talking, that he was telling this lie he had not planned: "It's the trial. We can't go through that, my wife and me. So you're leaving. We've got you a ticket, and a job. A friend of Mr. Trottier's. Out west. My wife keeps seeing you. We can't have that anymore."

Matt turned out the kitchen light and put the handkerchief in his pocket, and they went down the two brick steps and across the lawn. Strout put the suitcase on the floor of the back seat, then got into the front seat and Matt got in the back and put on his glove and shut the door.

"They'll catch me. They'll check passenger lists." 125

"We didn't use your name."

"They'll figure that out too. You think I wouldn't have done it myself if it was that easy?"

He backed into the street, Matt looking down the gun barrel but not at the profiled face beyond it.

"You were alone," Matt said. "We've got it worked out."

"There's no planes this time of night, Mr. Fowler."   130

"Go back through town. Then north on 125."

They came to the corner and turned, and now Willis's headlights were in the car with Matt.

"Why north, Mr. Fowler?"

"Somebody's going to keep you for a while. They'll take you to the airport." He uncocked the hammer and lowered the revolver to his lap and said wearily: "No more talking."

As they drove back through town, Matt's body sagged, going limp with his 135 spirit and its new and false bond with Strout, the hope his lie had given Strout. He had grown up in this town whose streets had become places of apprehension and pain for Ruth as she drove and walked, doing what she had to do; and for him too, if only in his mind as he worked and chatted six days a week in his store; he wondered now if his lie would have worked, if sending Strout away would have been enough; but then he knew that just thinking of Strout in Montana or whatever place lay at the end of the lie he had told, thinking of him walking the streets there, loving a girl there (who *was* she?) would be enough to slowly rot the rest of his days. And Ruth's. Again he was certain that she knew, that she was waiting for him.

They were in New Hampshire now, on the narrow highway, passing the shopping center at the state line, and then houses and small stores and sandwich shops. There were few cars on the road. After ten minutes he raised his trembling hand, touched Strout's neck with the gun, and said: "Turn in up here. At the dirt road."

Strout flicked on the indicator and slowed.

"Mr. Fowler?"

"They're waiting here."

Strout turned very slowly, easing his neck away from the gun. In the moonlight 140 the road was light brown, lighter and yellowed where the headlights shone; weeds and a few trees grew on either side of it, and ahead of them were the woods.

"There's nothing back here, Mr. Fowler."

"It's for your car. You don't think we'd leave it at the airport, do you?"

He watched Strout's large, big-knuckled hands tighten on the wheel, saw Frank's face that night: not the stitches and bruised eye and swollen lips, but his own hand gently touching Frank's jaw, turning his wounds to the light. They rounded a bend in the road and were out of sight of the highway: tall trees all around them now, hiding the moon. When they reached the abandoned gravel pit on the left, the bare flat earth and steep pale embankment behind it, and the black crowns of trees at its top, Matt said: "Stop here."

Strout stopped but did not turn off the engine. Matt pressed the gun hard against his neck, and he straightened in the seat and looked in the rearview mirror, Matt's eyes meeting his in the glass for an instant before looking at the hair at the end of the gun barrel.

"Turn it off."   145

Strout did, then held the wheel with two hands, and looked in the mirror.

"I'll do twenty years, Mr. Fowler; at least. I'll be forty-six years old."

"That's nine years younger than I am," Matt said, and got out and took off the glove and kicked the door shut. He aimed at Strout's ear and pulled back the hammer. Willis's headlights were off and Matt heard him walking on the soft thin layer of dust, the hard earth beneath it. Strout opened the door, sat for a moment in the interior light, then stepped out onto the road. Now his face was pleading. Matt did not look at his eyes, but he could see it in the lips.

"Just get the suitcase. They're right up the road."

Willis was beside him now, to his left. Strout looked at both guns. Then he opened the back door, leaned in, and with a jerk brought the suitcase out. He was turning to face them when Matt said: "Just walk up the road. Just ahead."

Strout turned to walk, the suitcase in his right hand, and Matt and Willis followed; as Strout cleared the front of his car he dropped the suitcase and, ducking, took one step that was the beginning of a sprint to his right. The gun kicked in Matt's hand, and the explosion of the shot surrounded him, isolated him in a nimbus of sound that cut him off from all his time, all his history, isolated him standing absolutely still on the dirt road with the gun in his hand, looking down at Richard Strout squirming on his belly, kicking one leg behind him, pushing himself forward, toward the woods. Then Matt went to him and shot him once in the back of the head.

Driving south to Boston, wearing both gloves now, staying in the middle lane and looking often in the rearview mirror at Willis's headlights, he relived the suitcase dropping, the quick dip and turn of Strout's back, and the kick of the gun, the sound of the shot. When he walked to Strout, he still existed within the first shot, still trembled and breathed with it. The second shot and the burial seemed to be happening to someone else, someone he was watching. He and Willis each held an arm and pulled Strout face-down off the road and into the woods, his bouncing sliding belt white under the trees where it was so dark that when they stopped at the top of the knoll, panting and sweating, Matt could not see where Strout's blue shirt ended and the earth began. They pulled off the branches then dragged Strout to the edge of the hole and went behind him and lifted his legs and pushed him in. They stood still for a moment. The woods were quiet save for their breathing, and Matt remembered hearing the movements of birds and small animals after the first shot. Or maybe he had not heard them. Willis went down to the road. Matt could see him clearly out on the tan dirt, could see the glint of Strout's car and, beyond the road, the gravel pit. Willis came back up the knoll with the suitcase. He dropped it in the hole and took off his gloves and they went down to his car for the spades. They worked quietly. Sometimes they paused to listen to the woods. When they were finished Willis turned on his flashlight and they covered the earth with leaves and branches and then went down to the spot in front of the car, and while Matt held the light Willis crouched and sprinkled dust on the blood, backing up till he reached the grass and leaves, then he used leaves until they had worked up to the grave again. They did not stop. They walked around the grave and through the woods, using the light on the ground, looking up through the trees to where they ended at the lake. Neither of them spoke above the sounds of their heavy and clumsy strides through low brush and over fallen branches. Then they reached it: wide and dark, lapping softly at the bank, pine needles smooth under Matt's feet, moonlight on the lake, a small island near its middle, with black, tall evergreens. He took out the gun and threw for the island: taking two steps back on the pine needles, striding with the throw and going to one knee as he followed through, looking up to see the dark shapeless object arcing downward, splashing.

They left Strout's car in Boston, in front of an apartment building on Commonwealth Avenue. When they got back to town Willis drove slowly over the bridge and Matt threw the keys into the Merrimack. The sky was turning light. Willis let him out a block from his house, and walking home he listened for sounds from the houses he passed. They were quiet. A light was on in his living room. He turned it off and undressed in there, and went softly toward the bedroom; in the hall he smelled the smoke, and he stood in the bedroom doorway and looked at the orange of her cigarette in the dark. The curtains were closed. He went to the closet and put his shoes on the floor and felt for a hanger.

"Did you do it?" she said.

He went down the hall to the bathroom and in the dark he washed his hands 155 and face. Then he went to her, lay on his back, and pulled the sheet up to his throat.

"Are you all right?" she said.

"I think so."

Now she touched him, lying on her side, her hand on his belly, his thigh.

"Tell me," she said.

He started from the beginning, in the parking lot at the bar; but soon with his 160 eyes closed and Ruth petting him, he spoke of Strout's house: the order, the woman presence, the picture on the wall.

"The way she was smiling," he said.

"What about it?"

"I don't know. Did you ever see Strout's girl? When you saw him in town?"

"No."

"I wonder who she was." 165

Then he thought: *not was: is. Sleeping now she is his girl.* He opened his eyes, then closed them again. There was more light beyond the curtains. With Ruth now he left Strout's house and told again his lie to Strout, gave him again that hope that Strout must have for a while believed, else he would have to believe only the gun pointed at him for the last two hours of his life. And with Ruth he saw again the dropping suitcase, the darting move to the right: and he told of the first shot, feeling her hand on him but his heart isolated still, beating on the road still in that explosion like thunder. He told her the rest, but the words had no images for him, he did not see himself doing what the words said he had done; he only saw himself on that road.

"We can't tell the other kids," she said. "It'll hurt them, thinking he got away. But we mustn't."

"No."

She was holding him, wanting him, and he wished he could make love with her but he could not. He saw Frank and Mary Ann making love in her bed, their eyes closed, their bodies brown and smelling of the sea; the other girl was faceless, bodiless, but he felt her sleeping now; and he saw Frank and Strout, their faces alive; he saw red and yellow leaves falling on the earth, then snow: falling and freezing and falling; and holding Ruth, his cheek touching her breast, he shuddered with a sob that he kept silent in his heart.

CONSIDERATIONS FOR CRITICAL THINKING AND WRITING

1. FIRST RESPONSE. How do you feel about Matt's act of revenge? Trace the emotions his character produces in you as the plot unfolds.

2. Discuss the significance of the title. Why is "Killings" a more appropriate title than "Killers"?

3. What are the effects of Dubus's ordering of events in the story? How would the effects be different if the story were told in a chronological order?

4. Describe the Fowler family before Frank's murder. How does the murder affect Matt?

5. What is learned about Richard from the flashback in paragraphs 32 through 75? How does this information affect your attitude toward him?

6. What is the effect of the description of Richard shooting Frank in paragraph 76?

7. How well planned is Matt's revenge? Why does he lie to Richard about sending him out west?

8. Describe Matt at the end of the story when he tells his wife about the killing. How do you think this revenge killing will affect the Fowler family?

9. How might "Killings" be considered a love story as well as a murder story?

10. CRITICAL STRATEGIES. Read the section on psychological criticism (pp. 1649–51) in Chapter 51, "Critical Strategies for Reading." How do the details of the killing and the disposal of Richard's body reveal Matt's emotions? What is he thinking and feeling as he performs these actions? How did you feel as you read about them?

CONNECTIONS TO OTHER SELECTIONS

1. Compare and contrast Matt's motivation for murder with Emily's in "A Rose for Emily" (p. 78). Which character made you feel more empathy and sympathy for his or her actions? Why?

2. Explore the father-son relationships in "Killings" and William Faulkner's "Barn Burning" (p. 406). Read the section on psychological criticism in Chapter 50, "Critical Strategies for Reading." How do you think a psychological critic would interpret these relationships in each story?

Perspective

A. L. BADER

Nothing Happens in Modern Short Stories 1945

Any teacher who has ever confronted a class with representative modern short stories will remember the disappointment, the puzzled "so-what" attitude, of certain members of the group. "Nothing happens in some of these stories," "They just end," or "They're not real stories" are frequent criticisms. . . . Sometimes the phrase "Nothing happens" seems to mean that nothing significant happens, but in a great many cases it means that the modern short story is charged with a lack of narrative structure. Readers and critics accustomed to an older type of story are baffled by a newer type. They sense the underlying and unifying design of the one, but they find nothing equivalent to it in the other. Hence they maintain that the modern short story is plotless, static, fragmentary, amorphous — frequently a mere character sketch or vignette, or a mere reporting of a transient moment, or the capturing of a mood or nuance — everything, in fact, except a story.

From "The Structure of the Modern Story" in *College English*

CONSIDERATIONS FOR CRITICAL THINKING AND WRITING

1. What is the basic objection to the "newer type" of short story? How does it differ from the "older type"?

2. Read a recent story published in the *New Yorker* or *Harper's* and compare its narrative structure with that of Faulkner's "A Rose for Emily" (p. 78).

ENCOUNTERING FICTION: COMICS AND GRAPHIC STORIES

In the beginning of storytelling was the drawn picture, not the written word. The cave paintings produced thousands of years ago told stories without words, but the development of written language and the invention of printing cast visual storytelling into the shadows until the late nineteenth century when the first comic strips brought words and pictures together in what has become an enormously popular art. From the quirky humor of *Peanuts* characters to the sexy action adventures of Japanese graphic novels, comic strips and graphic stories have become a significant part of the growth of the visual culture that we daily encounter.

Comic strips and graphic stories — told by a series of related drawings containing words that advance the plot — are certainly not to everyone's taste, but their increasing popularity is undeniable. A perusal of the shelf space devoted to comic books and graphic novels in your local bookstore will confirm the growing demand for this kind of storytelling. Like the conventional books that surround them, comic strips and graphic stories vary in quality. The best create seamless relationships between words and images that can be humorous, satirical, disturbing, or provocative. The strips that follow below and throughout the fiction section of *The Bedford Introduction to Literature* by Edward Gorey, Lynda Barry, Marjane Satrapi, and Matt Groening manage to take on important subjects with seriousness but also with humor. There can be no question that reading a graphic story is not identical to reading a short story, but it is nevertheless a form of reading — and the strips a form of storytelling. What similarities and differences do you find between the narrative elements in the strips and in the short stories you have read?

EDWARD GOREY (1925–2000), From *The Hapless Child*

Born in Chicago, Edward Gorey read *Dracula, Alice in Wonderland, Frankenstein*, and the works of Victor Hugo by the time he was eight. After one semester at the Art Institute of Chicago (his only formal art training), Gorey was drafted for a three-year stint in the army as a wartime clerk. He went on to study French literature at Harvard, where he roomed with the poet Frank O'Hara, and then worked as illustrator and designer for Doubleday Anchor Books. Since his first book in 1953 (*The Unstrung Harp*), Gorey published nearly one hundred illustrated books and designed sets for theatrical productions. He is best known for *The Gashlycrumb Tinies* (1963), a cautionary alphabet of twenty-six doomed children ("A is for Amy who fell down the stairs"). Gorey's works have been described as "macabre, yet delicate; grim but amusing; ghoulish without a drop of blood." Following are excerpts from *The Hapless Child* (1961), a satire of the nineteenth-century gothic novel. In the story, an innocent orphan is unjustly tormented before meeting her tragic demise, ironically under the wheels of a carriage driven by her supposedly dead father. Gorey, who disliked "exhaustive writers" who left nothing for the reader's imagination, preferred to leave his own readers with unanswered questions. He once commented: "Since I leave out most of the connections and very little is pinned down, I feel that I'm doing the minimum damage to other possibilities that might arise in a reader's mind."

THE HAPLESS CHILD

There was once a little girl named Charlotte Sophia.

One day her father, a colonel in the army, was ordered to Africa.

Several months later he was reported killed in a native uprising.

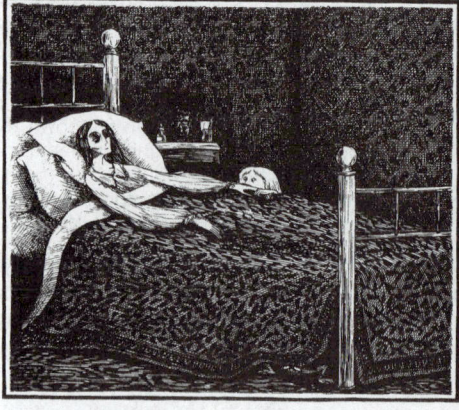

Her mother fell into a decline that proved fatal.

Charlotte Sophia was left in the hands of the family lawyer.

He at once put her into a boarding-school.

There she was punished by the teachers for things she hadn't done.

During the day Charlotte Sophia hid as much as possible.

At night she lay awake weeping and weeping.

When she could bear it no longer she fled from the school at dawn.

CONSIDERATIONS AND CONNECTION TO ANOTHER SELECTION

1. Discuss the use of light and dark in the drawings. How are these shadings related to the plot?

2. Compare the style of the printed letters in Gorey's drawings and in Lynda Barry's "Spelling" (p. 157). How is the lettering related to the style and tone of each story?

3. Does this story have a happy ending? Why or why not?

4. Compare the themes in "The Hapless Child" and in "The Story of the Good Little Boy" by Mark Twain (p. 525).

4

Character

When I find a well-drawn character
in fiction or biography, I generally
take a warm personal interest in him,
for the reason that I have known him
before — met him on the river.
— MARK TWAIN

Character is essential to plot. Without characters Burroughs's *Tarzan of the Apes* would be a travelogue through the jungle and Faulkner's "A Rose for Emily" little more than a faded history of a sleepy town in the South. If stories were depopulated, the plots would disappear because characters and plots are interrelated. A dangerous jungle is important only because we care what effect it has on a character. Characters are influenced by events just as events are shaped by characters. Tarzan's physical strength is the result of his growing up in the jungle, and his strength, along with his inherited intelligence, allows him to be master there.

The methods by which a writer creates people in a story so that they seem actually to exist are called ***characterization***. Huck Finn never lived yet those who have read Mark Twain's novel about his adventures along the Mississippi River feel as if they know him. A good writer gives us the illusion that a character is real, but we should also remember that a character is not an actual person but instead has been created by the author. Though we might walk out of a room in which Huck Finn's Pap talks racist nonsense, we would not throw away the book in a similar fit of anger. This illusion of reality is the magic that allows us to move beyond the circumstances of our own lives into a writer's fictional world, where we can encounter everyone from royalty to paupers, murderers, lovers, cheaters, martyrs, artists, destroyers, and, nearly always, some part of ourselves. The life that a writer breathes into a character adds to our own experiences and enlarges our view of the world.

A character is usually but not always a person. In Jack London's *Call of the Wild,* the protagonist is a devoted sled dog; in Herman Melville's *Moby-Dick,* the antagonist is an unfathomable whale. Perhaps the only possible qualification to be placed on character is that whatever it is — whether an animal or even an inanimate object, such as a robot — it must have some recognizable human qualities. The action of the plot interests us primarily because we care about what happens to people and what they do. We may identify with a character's desires and aspirations, or we may be disgusted by his or her viciousness and selfishness. To understand our response to a story, we should be able to recognize the methods of characterization the author uses.

CHARLES DICKENS (1812–1870)

Charles Dickens is well known for creating characters who have stepped off the pages of his fictions into the imaginations and memories of his readers. His characters are successful not because readers might have encountered such people in their own lives, but because his characterizations are vivid and convincing. He manages to make strange and eccentric people appear familiar. The following excerpt from *Hard Times* is the novel's entire first chapter. In it Dickens introduces and characterizes a school principal addressing a classroom full of children.

© Bettmann/CORBIS.

From Hard Times 1854

"Now, what I want is, Facts. Teach these boys and girls nothing but Facts. Facts alone are wanted in life. Plant nothing else, and root out everything else. You can only form the minds of reasoning animals upon Facts: nothing else will ever be of any service to them. This is the principle on which I bring up my own children, and this is the principle on which I bring up these children. Stick to Facts, sir!"

The scene was a plain, bare, monotonous vault of a schoolroom, and the speaker's square forefinger emphasized his observations by underscoring every sentence with a line on the schoolmaster's sleeve. The emphasis was helped by the speaker's square wall of a forehead, which had his eyebrows for its base, while his eyes found commodious cellarage in two dark caves, overshadowed by the wall. The emphasis was helped by the speaker's mouth, which was wide, thin, and hard set. The emphasis was helped by the speaker's voice, which was inflexible, dry, and dictatorial. The emphasis was helped by the speaker's hair, which bristled on the skirts of his bald head, a plantation of firs to keep the wind from its shining surface, all covered with knobs, like the crust of a plum pie, as if the head had scarcely warehouse-room for the hard facts stored inside. The speaker's obstinate carriage, square coat, square legs, square shoulders — nay, his very neckcloth, trained to take him by the throat with an unaccommodating grasp, like a stubborn fact, as it was — all helped the emphasis.

"In this life, we want nothing but Facts, sir; nothing but Facts!"

The speaker, and the schoolmaster, and the third grown person present, all backed a little, and swept with their eyes the inclined plane of little vessels then and there arranged in order, ready to have imperial gallons of facts poured into them until they were full to the brim.

Dickens withholds his character's name until the beginning of the second chapter; he calls this fact-bound educator Mr. Gradgrind. Authors sometimes put as much time and effort into naming their characters as parents invest in naming their children. Names can be used to indicate qualities that the writer associates with the characters. Mr. Gradgrind is precisely what his name suggests. The "schoolmaster" employed by Gradgrind is Mr. M'Choakumchild. Pronounce this name aloud and you have the essence of this teacher's educational philosophy. In Nathaniel Hawthorne's *The Scarlet Letter,* Chillingworth is cold and relentless in his single-minded quest for revenge. The innocent and youthful protagonist in Herman Melville's *Billy Budd* is nipped in the bud by the evil Claggart, whose name simply sounds unpleasant.

Names are also used in films to suggest a character's nature. One example that is destined to be a classic is the infamous villain Darth Vader, whose name identifies his role as an invader allied with the dark and death. On the heroic side, it makes sense that Marion Morrison decided to change his box-office name to John Wayne in order to play tough, masculine roles because both the first and last of his chosen names are unambiguously male and to the point, while his given name is androgynous. There may also be some significance to the lack of a specific identity. In Godwin's "A Sorrowful Woman" (p. 39) the woman, man, boy, and girl are reduced to a set of domestic functions, and their not being named emphasizes their roles as opposed to their individual identities. Of course, not every name is suggestive of the qualities a character may embody, but it is frequently worth determining what is in a name.

The only way to tell whether a name reveals character is to look at the other information the author supplies about the character. We evaluate fictional characters in much the same way we understand people in our own lives. By piecing together bits of information, we create a context that allows us to interpret their behavior. We can predict, for instance, that an acquaintance who is a chronic complainer is not likely to have anything good to say about a roommate. We interpret words and actions in the light of what we already know about someone, and that is why keeping track of what characters say (and how they say it) along with what they do (and don't do) is important.

Authors reveal characters by other means too. Physical descriptions can indicate important inner qualities; disheveled clothing, a crafty smile, or a blush might communicate as much as or more than what a character says. Characters can also be revealed by the words and actions of others who respond to them. In literature, moreover, we have one great advantage that life cannot offer; a work of fiction can give us access to a person's thoughts. Although in Herman Melville's "Bartleby, the Scrivener" (p. 130) we learn about Bartleby primarily through descriptive details, words, actions, and his relationships with the other characters, Melville allows us to enter the lawyer's consciousness.

Authors have two major methods of presenting characters: **showing** and **telling**. Characters shown in dramatic situations reveal themselves indirectly by what they say and do. In the first paragraph of the excerpt from *Hard Times*, Dickens shows us some of Gradgrind's utilitarian educational principles by having him speak. We can infer the kind of person he is from his reference to boys and girls as "reasoning animals," but we are not told what to think of him until the second paragraph. It would be impossible to admire Gradgrind after reading the physical description of him and the school that he oversees. The adjectives in the second paragraph make the author's evaluation of Gradgrind's values and personality clear: everything about him is rigidly "square"; his mouth is "thin, and hard set"; his voice is "inflexible, dry, and dictatorial"; and he presides over a "plain, bare, monotonous vault of a schoolroom." Dickens directly lets us know how to feel about Gradgrind, but he does so artistically. Instead of simply being presented with a statement that Gradgrind is destructively practical, we get a detailed and amusing description.

We can contrast Dickens's direct presentation in this paragraph with the indirect showing that Gail Godwin uses in "A Sorrowful Woman." Godwin avoids telling us how we should think about the characters. Their story includes little description and no evaluations or interpretations by the author. To determine the significance of the events, the reader must pay close attention to what the characters say and do. Like Godwin, many twentieth-century authors favor showing over telling because showing allows readers to discover the meanings, which modern authors are often reluctant to impose on an audience for whom fixed meanings and values are not as strong as they once were. However, most writers continue to reveal characters by telling as well as showing when the technique suits their purposes — when, for example, a minor character must be sketched economically or when a long time has elapsed, causing changes in a major character. Telling and showing complement each other.

Characters can be convincing whether they are presented by telling or showing, provided their actions are **motivated**. There must be reasons for how they behave and what they say. If adequate motivation is offered, we can understand and find **plausible** their actions no matter how bizarre. In "A Rose for Emily" (p. 78), Faulkner makes Emily Grierson's intimacy with a corpse credible by preparing us with information about her father's death along with her inability to leave the past and live in the present. Emily turns out to be *consistent*. Although we are surprised by the ending of the story, the behavior it reveals is compatible with her temperament.

Some kinds of fiction consciously break away from our expectations of traditional realistic stories. Consistency, plausibility, and motivation are not very useful concepts for understanding and evaluating characterizations in modern **absurdist literature**, for instance, in which characters are often alienated from themselves and their environment in an irrational world. In this world there is no possibility for traditional heroic action; instead we find an **antihero** who has little control over events. Yossarian from Joseph Heller's *Catch-22* is an example of a protagonist who is thwarted by the absurd terms on which life offers itself to many twentieth-century characters.

In most stories we expect characters to act plausibly and in ways consistent with their personalities, but that does not mean that characters cannot develop and change. A **dynamic** character undergoes some kind of change because of the action of the plot. Huck Finn's view of Jim, the runaway slave in Mark Twain's novel, develops during their experiences on the raft. Huck discovers Jim's humanity and, therefore, cannot betray him because Huck no longer sees his companion as merely the property of a white owner. On the other hand, Huck's friend, Tom Sawyer, is a **static** character because he does not change. He remains interested only in high adventure, even at the risk of Jim's life. As static characters often do, Tom serves as a foil to Huck; his frivolous concerns are contrasted with Huck's serious development. A **foil** helps to reveal by contrast the distinctive qualities of another character.

The protagonist in a story is usually a dynamic character who experiences some conflict that makes an impact on his or her life. Less commonly, static characters can also be protagonists. Rip Van Winkle wakes up from his twenty-year sleep in Washington Irving's story to discover his family dramatically changed and his country no longer a British colony, but none of these important events has an impact on his character; he continues to be the same shiftless and idle man that he was before he fell asleep. The protagonist in Faulkner's "A Rose for Emily" is also a static character; indeed, she rejects all change. Our understanding of her changes, but she does not. Ordinarily, however, a plot contains one or two dynamic characters with any number of static characters in supporting roles. This is especially true of short stories, in which brevity limits the possibilities of character development.

The extent to which a character is developed is another means by which character can be analyzed. The novelist E. M. Forster coined the terms *flat* and *round* to distinguish degrees of character development. A **flat character** embodies one or two qualities, ideas, or traits that can be readily described in a brief summary. For instance, Mr. M'Choakumchild in Dickens's *Hard Times* stifles students instead of encouraging them to grow. Flat characters tend to be one-dimensional. They are readily accessible because their characteristics are few and simple; they are not created to be psychologically complex.

Some flat characters are immediately recognizable as **stock characters**. These stereotypes are particularly popular in formula fiction, television programs, and action movies. Stock characters are types rather than individuals.

The poor but dedicated writer falls in love with a hard-working understudy, who gets nowhere because the corrupt producer favors his boozy, pampered mistress for the leading role. Characters such as these — the loyal servant, the mean stepfather, the henpecked husband, the dumb blonde, the sadistic army officer, the dotty grandmother — are prepackaged; they lack individuality because their authors have, in a sense, not imaginatively created them but simply summoned them from a warehouse of clichés and social prejudices. Stock characters can become fresh if a good writer makes them vivid, interesting, or memorable, but too often a writer's use of these stereotypes is simply weak characterization.

Round characters are more complex than flat or stock characters. Round characters have more depth and require more attention. They may surprise us or puzzle us. Although they are more fully developed, round characters are also more difficult to summarize because we are aware of competing ideas, values, and possibilities in their lives. As a flat character, Huck Finn's alcoholic, bigoted father is clear to us; we know that Pap is the embodiment of racism and irrationality. But Huck is considerably less predictable because he struggles with what Twain calls a "sound heart and a deformed conscience."

In making distinctions between flat and round characters, you must understand that an author's use of a flat character — even as a protagonist — does not necessarily represent an artistic flaw. Moreover, both flat and round characters can be either dynamic or static. Each plot can be made most effective by its own special kind of characterization. Terms such as *round* and *flat* are helpful tools to use to determine what we know about a character, but they are not an infallible measurement of the quality of a story.

The next three stories — Jamaica Kincaid's "Girl," May-lee Chai's "Saving Sourdi," and Herman Melville's "Bartleby, the Scrivener" — offer character studies worthy of close analysis. As you read them, notice the methods of characterization used to bring each to life.

A SAMPLE STUDENT RESPONSE

Crispin Shea

Professor Atwood

English 102

20 January 2015

Character Development in Charles Dickens's *Hard Times*

In the first chapter of *Hard Times*, by Charles Dickens, the speaker, or focal character, develops slowly and is brought to life through dialogue and description. We understand him as a character not only through what he says, but through how he says it. Learning, to him, means nothing more than absorbing facts; there is no discussion, no debate. Facts are given to the students, "poured into them until they were full to the brim," and the children must take every word as truth (109). Understanding the speaker's view on learning helps us to understand the man himself, and he quickly becomes a fully developed character: a person hard-nosed and unyielding, with little interest in middle ground.

After the character speaks, Dickens gives us a physical description to reinforce our initial opinion of the speaker. He is described as having a "square wall of a forehead," and eyes that find "commodious cellarage in two dark caves" (109). His mouth is "thin, and hard set" (109). Dickens's description emphasizes the character's rigidity. He portrays the speaker as someone who is callous and difficult. This does not mean, however, that all characters with harsh physical features are unpleasant or villainous (just as attractive characters are not always pleasant). Certainly Dickens could have focused on the speaker's best traits, physical or otherwise, and created a more endearing character. Instead, he focuses on what he wants us to read as the true essence of this particular person, using physical details to "indicate [the character's] important inner qualities" (Meyer 110). . . .

Shea 6

Works Cited

Dickens, Charles. "From *Hard Times*." Meyer 108–09.

Meyer, Michael, ed. *The Bedford Introduction to Literature*. 11th ed. Boston: Bedford/St. Martin's, 2016. Print.

Jamaica Kincaid (b. 1949)

Jamaica Kincaid was born Elaine Potter Richardson on the Caribbean island of Antigua. She moved to New York in 1965 to work as an au pair, studied photography at both the New School for Social Research and Franconia College, and changed her name to Jamaica Kincaid in 1973 with her first publication, "When I Was 17," a series of interviews. Over the next few years, she wrote for the *New Yorker* magazine, first as a freelancer and then as a staff writer. In 1978, Kincaid wrote her first piece of fiction, "Girl," published in the *New Yorker* and included in her debut short story collection, *At the Bottom of the River* (1983), which won an award from the Academy and Institute of Arts and Letters and was nominated for the PEN/Faulkner Award. Her other work includes *Annie John* (1985), *Lucy* (1990), *Autobiography of My Mother* (1994), *See Now Then* (2013), and three nonfiction books, *A Small Place* (1988), *My Brother* (1997), and *Mr. Potter* (2002). Whether autobiographical fiction or nonfiction, her work usually focuses on the perils of postcolonial society, paralleled by an examination of rifts in mother-daughter relationships.

Trix Rosen.

Girl 1978

Wash the white clothes on Monday and put them on the stone heap; wash the color clothes on Tuesday and put them on the clothesline to dry; don't walk barehead in the hot sun; cook pumpkin fritters in very hot sweet oil; soak your little cloths right after you take them off; when buying cotton to make yourself a nice blouse, be sure that it doesn't have gum on it, because that way it won't hold up well after

a wash; soak salt fish overnight before you cook it; is it true that you sing benna°
in Sunday school?; always eat your food in such a way that it won't turn someone
else's stomach; on Sundays try to walk like a lady and not like the slut you are so
bent on becoming; don't sing benna in Sunday school; you mustn't speak to wharf-
rat boys, not even to give directions; don't eat fruits on the street — flies will follow
you; *but I don't sing benna on Sundays at all and never in Sunday school;* this is how
to sew on a button; this is how to make a buttonhole for the button you have just
sewed on; this is how to hem a dress when you see the hem coming down and so
to prevent yourself from looking like the slut I know you are so bent on becoming;
this is how you iron your father's khaki shirt so that it doesn't have a crease; this is
how you iron your father's khaki pants so that they don't have a crease; this is how
you grow okra — far from the house, because okra tree harbors red ants; when you
are growing dasheen,° make sure it gets plenty of water or else it makes your throat
itch when you are eating it; this is how you sweep a corner; this is how you sweep
a whole house; this is how you sweep a yard; this is how you smile to someone you
don't like too much; this is how you smile to someone you don't like at all; this is
how you smile to someone you like completely; this is how you set a table for tea;
this is how you set a table for dinner; this is how you set a table for dinner with an
important guest; this is how you set a table for lunch; this is how you set a table for
breakfast; this is how to behave in the presence of men who don't know you very
well, and this way they won't recognize immediately the slut I have warned you
against becoming; be sure to wash every day, even if it is with your own spit; don't
squat down to play marbles — you are not a boy, you know; don't pick people's
flowers — you might catch something; don't throw stones at blackbirds, because it
might not be a blackbird at all; this is how to make a bread pudding; this is how to
make doukona;° this is how to make pepper pot;° this is how to make a good medicine for a cold; this is how to make a good medicine to throw away a child before
it even becomes a child; this is how to catch a fish; this is how to throw back a fish
you don't like, and that way something bad won't fall on you; this is how to bully
a man; this is how a man bullies you; this is how to love a man, and if this doesn't
work there are other ways, and if they don't work don't feel too bad about giving
up; this is how to spit up in the air if you feel like it, and this is how to move quick
so that it doesn't fall on you; this is how to make ends meet; always squeeze bread
to make sure it's fresh; *but what if the baker won't let me feel the bread?;* you mean to
say that after all you are really going to be the kind of woman who the baker won't
let near the bread?

Considerations for Critical Thinking and Writing

1. **FIRST RESPONSE.** Explain whether or not the "Girl" is the protagonist or antagonist in this story.

2. Consider whether the mother is a stock or round character.

3. What details indicate the nature of the mother's advice? How would you
   describe her perceptions of her daughter?

---

benna: Calypso music.
dasheen: The edible rootstock of taro, a tropical plant.
doukona: A spicy plantain pudding.
pepper pot: A stew.

4. How does the mother inadvertently reveal and characterize herself?

5. Describe the daughter's responses to the mother's admonitions.

6. **CREATIVE RESPONSE.** Write a one-paragraph response to the mother from the daughter's perspective.

CONNECTIONS TO OTHER SELECTIONS

1. Compare the teenager's relationship to authority in Kincaid's story and in John Updike's "A & P" (p. 200).

2. Discuss the mother-daughter relationship in "Girl" and in Julia Alvarez's poem "Dusting" (p. 931).

MAY-LEE CHAI

Jason Doiy.

May-lee Chai, the first of her family to be born in the United States, is a San Francisco author and graduate of Yale University. Chai has worked as a reporter for the Associated Press and taught creative writing at San Francisco State University, the University of Wyoming, and Amherst College. She is the author of *My Lucky Face* (1997), a novel about a woman's marriage in contemporary China; *Glamorous Asians: Short Stories and Essays* (2004); and coauthor, with her father, Winberg Chai, of *The Girl from Purple Mountain* (2001), a family memoir about her grandparents' journey from China to America. *Hapa Girl: A Memoir* (2007) describes the bigotry her family encounters in rural South Dakota.

> **WHEN I WRITE** "When I was a teenager, I lived on a farm. I'd get up early in the morning while it was still dark and write bad sci-fi stories for 20 minutes before I had to go out for chores. That was my escape. The stories were terrible, but the act of writing was my salvation." — MAY-LEE CHAI

Saving Sourdi 2001

Once, when my older sister, Sourdi, and I were working alone in our family's restaurant, just the two of us and the elderly cook, some men got drunk and I stabbed one of them. I was eleven.

I don't remember where Ma had gone that night. But I remember we were tired and it was late. We were one of the only restaurants that stayed open past nine in those days. The men had been growing louder, until they were our only customers, and, finally, one of them staggered up and put his arm across Sourdi's shoulders. He called her his "China doll," and his friends hooted at this.

Sourdi looked distressed and tried to remove his arm, but he held her tighter. She said, "Please," in her incense-sweet voice, and he smiled and said, "Say it again nice and I might just have to give you a kiss."

That summer we'd just moved to South Dakota. After all the crummy jobs Ma had had to take in Texas, where we'd first come to the U.S., where our sponsors lived, we were so proud to be working in our own restaurant. When we moved to South Dakota, I thought we'd find the real America, the one where we were supposed to be, not the hot sweaty America where we lived packed together in an apartment with bars on the windows on a street where angry boys in cars played loud music and shot guns at each other in the night. The summer we moved to join my uncle's family to run the Silver Palace, I was certain we would at last find the life we deserved.

Now I was panicked. I wanted Ma to be there. Ma would know what to do. She 5 always did. I stood there, chewing my nails, wishing I could make them go away. The men's voices were so loud in my ears, I was drowning in the sound.

I ran into the kitchen. I had this idea to get the cook and the cleaver, but the first thing that caught my eye was this little paring knife on the counter next to a bowl of oranges. I grabbed the knife and ran back out to Sourdi.

"Get away from my sister!" I shouted, waving the paring knife.

The men were silent for about three seconds, then they burst into laughter.

I charged and stabbed the man in the sleeve.

In a movie or a television show this kind of scene always unfolds in slow 10 motion, but everything happened so fast. I stabbed the man, Sourdi jumped free, Ma came rushing in the front door waving her arms. "Omigod! What happen?"

"Jesus Christ!" The man shook his arm as though it were on fire, but the paring knife was stuck in the fabric of his jeans jacket.

I thought Ma would take care of everything now. And I was right, she did, but not the way I had imagined. She started apologizing to the man, and she helped him take off his jacket. She made Sourdi get the first-aid kit from the bathroom, "Quick! Quick!" Ma even tried to put some ointment on his cut, but he just shrugged her off.

I couldn't believe it. I wanted to take the knife back and stab myself. That's how I felt when I heard her say, "No charge, on the house," for their dinner, despite the $50-worth of pitchers they'd had.

Ma grabbed me by the shoulders. "Say you sorry. Say it." I pressed my lips firmly together and hung my head. Then she slapped me.

I didn't start crying until after the men had left. "But, Ma," I said, "he was hurt- 15 ing Sourdi!"

"Then why Sourdi not do something?" Ma twisted my ear. "You not thinking. That your problem. You always not think!"

Afterwards, Sourdi said I was lucky. The knife had only grazed the man's skin. They could have sued us. They could have pressed charges.

"I don't care!" I hissed then. "I shoulda killed him! I shoulda killed that sucker!"

Sourdi's face changed. I'd never seen my sister look like that. Not ever. Especially not at me. I was her favorite. But she looked then the way I felt inside. Like a big bomb was ticking behind her eyes.

We were sitting together in the bathroom. It was late at night, and everyone 20 else was asleep. Sometimes we locked ourselves in the bathroom then, just the two of us, so we could talk about things like boys at school or who was the cutest actor on television shows we liked or how we felt when our family fought, when Uncle and Auntie yelled at each other, or when Ma grew depressed and smoked too much and looked at us as though she wished we'd never been born.

This night, however, Sourdi looked at me grimly. "Oh, no, Nea. Don't ever say that. Don't ever talk like that."

I was going to smile and shrug and say something like "I was just kidding," but something inside me couldn't lie tonight. I crossed my arms over my flat chest, and I stuck out my lower lip, like I'd seen the tough girls at school do. "Anyone mess like that with me, I'm gonna kill him!"

Sourdi took me by the shoulders then and shook me so hard I thought she was going to shake my head right off my body. She wouldn't stop even after I started to cry.

"Stop, stop!" I begged. "I'll be good! I promise, I'll be good!"

Finally, she pushed me away from her and sat on the toilet, with her head in her 25 hands. Although she'd been the one hurting me, she looked as though she'd been beaten up, the way she sat like that, her shoulders hunched over her lap, as though she were trying to make herself disappear.

"I was trying to protect you," I said through my tears. "I was trying to save you. You're so stupid! I should just let that man diss you!"

Sourdi's head shot up and I could see that she had no patience left. Her eyes were red and her nostrils flared. She stood up and I took a step back quickly. I thought she was going to grab me and shake me again, but this time she just put her hand on my arm. "They could take you away. The police, they could put you in a foster home. All of us."

A chill ran through my whole body, like a live current. We all knew about foster homes. Rudy Gutierrez in third grade was taken away from his parents after the teacher noticed some bruises on his back. He'd tried to shoplift some PayDays from the 7-Eleven and got caught. When his dad got home that weekend, he let him have it. But after the school nurse took a look at him, Rudy was taken away from his parents and sent to live in a foster home. His parents couldn't speak English so good and didn't know what was happening until too late. Anyway, what kind of lawyer could they afford? We heard later from his cousin in Mrs. Chang's homeroom that Rudy's foster-dad had molested him. The cousin said Rudy ran away from that home, but he got caught. At any rate, none of us ever saw him again.

"You want to go to a foster home?" Sourdi asked me.

"No," I whispered. 30

"Then don't be so stupid!"

I started crying again, because I realized Sourdi was right. She kissed me on the top of my head and hugged me to her. I leaned my head against her soft breasts that had only recently emerged from her chest and pretended that I was a good girl and that I would always obey her. What I didn't tell Sourdi was that I was still a wicked girl. I was glad I'd stabbed that man. I was crying only because life was so unfair.

We used to say that we'd run away, Sourdi and me. When we were older. After she graduated. She'd be my legal guardian. We'd go to California to see the stars. Paris. London. Cambodia even, to light incense for the bones of our father. We'd earn money working in Chinese restaurants in every country we visited. We had enough experience; it had to be worth something.

We'd lie awake all night whispering back and forth. I'd climb into Sourdi's bed, claiming that I couldn't sleep, curling into a ball beside my older sister, the smell of her like salt and garlic and a sweet scent that emanated directly from her skin. Sometimes I'd stroke Sourdi's slick hair, which she plaited into a thick wet braid so that it would be wavy in the morning. I would stay awake all night, pinching the inside of Sourdi's arm, the soft flesh of her thigh, to keep my sister from falling asleep and leaving me alone.

When she first started seeing Duke, I used to think of him as something like a 35 bookmark, just holding a certain space in her life until it was time for her to move on. I never thought of him as a fork in the road, dividing my life with Sourdi from Sourdi's life with men.

In those days, I didn't understand anything.

Ma had hired Duke to wash dishes at the Palace that first summer. At first, we paid him no mind. He was just this funny-looking white kid, hair that stuck up straight from his head when he wasn't wearing his silly baseball cap backwards, skinny as a stalk of bamboo, long legs and long arms that seemed to move in opposition to each other. Chopstick-boy I called him, just to be mean. He took it as a compliment.

I could see why he fell in love with Sourdi. My sister was beautiful. Really beautiful, not like the girls in magazines with their pale, pinched faces, pink and powdery, brittle girls. Sourdi looked like a statue that had been rescued from the sea. She was smooth where I had angles and soft where I was bone. Sourdi's face was round, her nose low and wide, her eyes crescent-shaped like the quarter moon, her hair sleek as seaweed. Her skin was a burnished cinnamon color. Looking at Sourdi, I could pretend I was beautiful, too. She had so much to spare.

At first, Duke and Sourdi only talked behind the Palace, pretending to take a break from the heat of the kitchen. I caught them looking at the stars together.

The first time they kissed, I was there, too. Duke was giving us a ride after 40 school in his pickup. He had the music on loud and the windows were open. It was a hot day for October, and the wind felt like a warm ocean that we could swim in forever. He was going to drop us off at the Palace, but then Duke said he had something to show us, and we circled around the outskirts of town, taking the gravel road that led to the open fields, beyond the highway where the cattle ranches lay. Finally, he pulled off the gravel road and parked.

"You want us to look at cows?" I asked impatiently, crossing my arms.

He laughed at me then and took Sourdi by the hand. We hiked through a ditch to the edge of an empty cornfield long since harvested, the stubble of cornstalks poking up from the black soil, pale and bonelike. The field was laced with a barbed-wire fence to keep the cattle in, though I couldn't see any cows at all. The whole place gave me the creeps.

Duke held the strands of barbed wire apart for Sourdi and me and told us to crawl under the fence.

"Just trust me," he said.

We followed him to a spot in the middle of the field. "It's the center of the 45 world," Duke said. "Look." And he pointed back to where we'd come from, and suddenly I realized the rest of the world had disappeared. The ground had appeared level, but we must have walked into a tiny hollow in the plains, because from where we stood there was only sky and field for as far as our eyes could see. We could no longer see the road or Duke's pickup, our town, or even the green smudge of cottonwoods that grew along the Yankton River or the distant hills of Nebraska. There was nothing overhead, either; the sky was unbroken by clouds, smooth as an empty rice bowl. "It's just us here," Duke said. "We're alone in the whole universe."

All at once, Sourdi began to breathe funny. Her face grew pinched, and she wiped at her eyes with the back of her hand.

"What's wrong?" Duke asked stupidly.

Then Sourdi was running wildly. She took off like an animal startled by a gunshot. She was trying to head back to the road, but she tripped over the cornstalks and fell onto her knees. She started crying for real.

I caught up to her first — I've always been a fast runner. As Duke approached, I put my arms around Sourdi.

"I thought you'd like it," Duke said. 50

"We're city girls," I said, glaring at him. "Why would we like this hick stuff?"

"I'm sorry," Sourdi whispered. "I'm so sorry."

"What are you sorry for? It's his fault!" I pointed out.

Now Duke was kneeling next to Sourdi. He tried to put his arm over her shoulder, too. I was going to push him away, when Sourdi did something very surprising. She put both her arms around his neck and leaned against him, while Duke said soft, dumb-sounding things that I couldn't quite hear. Then they were kissing.

I was so surprised, I stared at them before I forced myself to look away. Then I 55 was the one who felt like running, screaming, for the road.

On the way back to the Palace, Duke and Sourdi didn't talk, but they held hands. The worst part was I was sitting between them.

Ma didn't seem to notice anything for a while, but then with Ma it was always hard to know what she was thinking, what she knew and what she didn't. Sometimes she seemed to go through her days like she was made of stone. Sometimes she erupted like a volcano.

Uncle fired Duke a few weeks later. He said it was because Duke had dropped a tray of dishes. It was during the Saturday lunch rush when Sourdi and I weren't working and couldn't witness what had happened.

"He's a clumsy boy," Ma agreed after work that night, when we all sat around in the back booths and ate our dinner.

Sourdi didn't say anything. She knew Ma knew. 60

She kept seeing Duke, of course. They were both juniors, and there was only one high school in town. Now when I crept into Sourdi's bed at night, when she talked about running away, she meant Duke and her. I was the one who had to pipe up that I was coming with them, too. What we didn't know was that Ma was making plans as well.

Uncle first introduced his friend Mr. Chhay in the winter. I'd had a strange dream the night before. I hadn't remembered it at all until Mr. Chhay walked into the Palace, with his hangdog face and his suit like a salesman's. He sat in a corner booth with Uncle and, while they talked, he shredded a napkin, then took the scraps of paper and rolled them between his thumb and index finger into a hundred tiny red balls. He left them in the ashtray, like a mountain of fish eggs. Seeing them, I remembered my dream.

I was swimming in the ocean. I was just a small child, but I wasn't afraid at all. The sea was liquid turquoise, the sunlight yellow as gold against my skin. Fish were swimming alongside me. I could see through the clear water to the bottom of the sea. The fish were schooling around me and below me, and they brushed against my feet when I kicked the water. Their scales felt like bones scraping my toes. I tried to push them away, but the schools grew more dense, until I was swimming amongst them under the waves.

The fish began to spawn around me and soon the water was cloudy with eggs. I tried to break through the film, but the eggs clung to my skin. The water darkened as we entered a sea of kelp. I pushed against the dark slippery strands like Sourdi's hair. I realized I was pushing against my sister, wrapped in the kelp, suspended just below the surface of the water. Then I woke up.

I thought about that dream seeing that old guy Mr. Chhay with Uncle and I 65 knew they were up to no good. I wanted to warn Sourdi, but she seemed to understand without my having to tell her anything.

Uncle called over to her and introduced her to his friend. But Sourdi wouldn't even look at Mr. Chhay. She kept her eyes lowered, though he tried to smile and talk to her. She whispered so low in reply that no one could understand a word she said. I could tell the man was disappointed when he left. His shoulders seemed barely able to support the weight of his jacket.

Mr. Chhay wrote letters to Uncle, to Ma. He thanked them for their hospitality and enclosed pictures of his business and his house, plus a formal portrait of himself looking ridiculous in another suit, standing in front of some potted plants, his hair combed over the bald spot in the middle of his head.

The next time he came to visit the Palace, he brought gifts. A giant Chinese vase for Ma, Barbie dolls for my younger sisters and cousin, a Christian music cassette tape for me, and a bright red leather purse for Sourdi.

Ma made Sourdi tell him thank you.

And that was all she said to him.   70

But this old guy was persistent. He took us all out to eat at a steakhouse once. He said he wanted to pay back Uncle for some good deed he'd done a long time ago when they both first came to America. I could have told him, Sourdi hated this kind of food. She preferred Mexican, tacos, not this Midwest cowboy stuff. But Ma made us all thank him.

"Thank you, Mr. Chhay," we said dutifully. He'd smiled so all his yellow teeth showed at once. "Oh, please, call me Older Brother," he said.

It was the beginning of the end. I should have fought harder then. I should have stabbed this man, too.

I saw Duke at Sourdi's wedding. She invited him for the ceremony proper, the reception, too, but he didn't show up until the end. I almost didn't see him at all. He was slouching through the parking lot of St. Agnes, wearing his best hightops and the navy-blue suit that his mother had insisted upon buying for graduation. I wasn't used to him looking like a teenage undertaker, but I recognized his loping gait immediately. That afternoon of Sourdi's wedding, he was holding a brown bag awkwardly behind his back, as if trying to conceal the fact that he was drinking as conspicuously as possible.

I was standing inside the bingo hall, before the row of squat windows, my back 75 turned to the festivities, the exploding flash capturing the tipsy toasts, the in-laws singing off-key to the rented karaoke machine.

Then it really became too much to bear, and I had to escape the terrible heat, the flickering fluorescent lights. I slipped from the church into the ferocious March wind and gave it my best shot, running across the hard lawn, but the too-tight heels pinched my toes and the stiff taffeta bodice of the cotton-candy-pink bridesmaid's dress might as well have been a vise around my rib cage. I had intended to make it off church property, run to the empty field that stretched low and dark all the way to the horizon, but I only made it to the end of the walk near the rectory before vomiting into Sister Kevin's over-tended tulip patch.

Duke came over and sat on his haunches beside me, while I puked. I let him hold back my hair, while the wedding cake and wine cooler that I'd tried poured from my mouth.

Finally, I spat a few times to clear my mouth, then sat back on my rear end.

After a few minutes, I could take a sip from Duke's beer.

We didn't talk. 80

I took out the pack of cigarettes I'd stolen from Ma's purse and lit one. It took five puffs before I could mask the taste of bile and sugar.

The wind was blowing fiercely from the northwest, whipping my hair about my face like a widow's veil, throwing dust from the parking lot around us like wedding rice.

After a long while, Duke stood up and walked back down the sidewalk lined with yellow daffodils. He walked bow-legged, like all the boys in our town, farmers' sons, no matter how cool Duke tried to be. I buried my head in my arms and watched him from under one polyester-covered armpit as he climbed back into his pickup and pulled away with a screech. As he left the parking lot, he tossed the brown bag with the empty bottle of Bud out the window. It fell into the street, where it rolled and rolled until it disappeared into a ditch.

Ma liked Sourdi's husband. He had a steady job, a house. She didn't mind he was so old and Sourdi just eighteen when they married. In her eyes, eighteen was a good age to start a family. "I was younger than Sourdi when I get married," Ma liked to say.

When Sourdi sent pictures home for the holidays, Ma ooohed and aaahed as 85 though they were winning lottery tickets. My sister and her old husband in front of a listing Christmas tree, a pile of presents at their feet. Then, the red-faced baby sprawled on a pink blanket on the living room carpet, drooling in its shiny high chair, slumped in its Snugli like a rock around Sourdi's neck.

"Look. Sony," Ma pointed at the big-screen television in the background of the New Year's pictures. "Sourdi say they got all new washer/dryer, too. Maytag."

When I looked at my sister's pictures, I could see that she looked tired.

Sourdi always said that Ma used to be a very brave woman. She also said that Ma used to be a beautiful woman who liked to have her hair fixed in salons, who wore pretty dresses and knew how to dance in all the fashionable styles. I don't remember this mother. I remember the mother who worked two jobs for us.

I might never have seen Duke again if it were not for Sourdi's strange phone call one Saturday evening nearly two years after her wedding. I was fourteen and a half.

At first, I hadn't recognized my older sister's voice. 90

"Who is this?" I demanded, thinking: heavy breathing, prank caller.

"Who d'you think?" Sourdi was crying, a tiny crimped sound that barely crept out of the receiver. Then her voice steadied with anger and grew familiar. "Is Ma there?"

"What's the matter? What happened?"

"Just let me speak to Ma, O.K.?" There was a pause, as Sourdi blew her nose. "Tell her it's important."

I lured Ma from the TV room without alerting my younger sisters. Ma paced back and forth in the kitchen between the refrigerator and the stove, nodding and muttering, "Mmm, mmm, uh-hmm." I could just hear the tinny squeak of Sourdi's panicked voice.

I sat on the floor, hugging my knees, in the doorway to the hall, just out of Ma's line of sight.

Finally, Ma said, in the tone normally reserved for refusing service to the unruly or arguing with a customer who had a complaint, "It's always like this. Every marriage is hard. Sometimes there is nothing you can do —"

Then Ma stopped pacing. "Just minute," she said and she took the phone with her into the bathroom, shutting the door firmly behind her.

When she came out again, twenty-two minutes later, she ignored me completely. She set the phone back on the counter without saying a word.

"So?" I prompted.

"I'm tired." Ma rubbed her neck with one hand. "Just let me rest. You girls, it's always something. Don't let your old mother rest."

She yawned extravagantly. She claimed she was too tired to watch any more TV. She had to go to bed, her eyes just wouldn't stay open.

I tried calling Sourdi, but the phone only rang and rang.

The next morning, Sunday, I called first thing, but then *he* picked up, my sister's husband.

"Oh, is this Nea?" he said, so cheerfully it was obvious he was hiding something.

"Yes, I'd like to speak to my sister."

"I'm sorry, Little Sister." I just hated when he called me that. "My wife is out right now. But I'll tell her you called. She'll be sorry she missed you."

It was eight o'clock in the morning, for Chrissake.

"Oh, thank you," I said, sweet as pie. "How's the baby?"

"So well!" Then he launched into a long explanation about his daughter's eating habits, her rather average attempts to crawl, the simple words she was trying to say. For all I knew, Sourdi could have been right there, fixing his breakfast, washing his clothes, cleaning up his messes. I thought of my sister's voice in my ear, the tiny sound like something breaking.

It was all I could do to disguise the disdain in my voice. "Be sure to tell Sourdi to call back. Ma found that recipe she wanted. That special delicious recipe she was looking for. I can't tell you what it is, Ma's secret recipe, but you'll really be surprised."

"Oh, boy," the jerk said. "I didn't know about any secret recipe."

"That's why it's a secret." I hung up. I couldn't breathe. My chest hurt. I could feel my swollen heart pressing against my ribs.

The next afternoon, I tried calling back three more times, but no one answered.

At work that evening, Ma was irritable. She wouldn't look me in the eyes when I tried to get her attention. Some little kid spilled his Coke into a perfectly good plate of House Special Prawns and his parents insisted they be given a new order — and a new Coke — on the house. There was a minor grease fire around quarter to nine — the smoke alarms all went off at the same time — and then the customers started complaining about the cold, too, once we had opened all the doors and windows to clear the air. Fairly average as far as disasters went, but they put Ma in a sour mood.

Ma was taking a cigarette break out back by the dumpsters, smoke curling from her nostrils, before I could corner her. She wasn't in the mood to talk, but after the nicotine fix took hold, she didn't tell me to get back to work, either.

I asked Ma if I could have a smoke. She didn't get angry. She smiled in her tired way, the edges of her mouth twitching upwards just a little, and said, "Smoking will kill you." Then she handed me her pack.

"Maybe Sourdi should come back home for a while," I suggested.

"She's a married woman. She has her own family now."

"She's still part of our family." 120

Ma didn't say anything, just tilted her head back and blew smoke at the stars, so I continued, "Well, don't you think she might be in trouble? She was crying, you know. It's not like Sourdi." My voice must have slipped a tad, just enough to sound disrespectful, because Ma jerked upright, took the cigarette out of her mouth and glared at me.

"What you think? You so smart? You gonna tell me what's what?" Ma threw her cigarette onto the asphalt. "You not like your sister. Your sister know how to bear things!"

She stormed back into the kitchen, and Ma ignored me for the rest of the evening.

I called Sourdi one more time, after Ma and my sisters had gone to bed and I finally had the kitchen to myself, the moon spilling from the window onto the floor in a big, blue puddle. I didn't dare turn on the lights.

This time, my sister answered. "Mmm . . . Hello?" 125

"Sourdi?"

"What time is it?"

"Sssh." My heart beat so loudly, I couldn't hear my own voice. "How are you doing?"

"Oh, we're fine. The baby, she's doing real good. She's starting to talk —"

"No, no, no. I mean, what happened the other night?" 130

"What?"

Another voice now, low, a man's voice, just beneath the snow on the line. Then suddenly a shriek.

"Uh-oh. I just woke her up." Sourdi's voice grew fainter as she spoke to him: "Honey, can you check the baby's diaper?" Then she said to me, "I have to go. The baby, she's hungry, you know."

"Let him handle it. I have to talk to you a minute, O.K.? Just don't go, Sourdi. What's going on? What did you say to Ma?"

Sourdi sighed, like a balloon losing its air. "Oh . . . nothing. Look, I really have 135 to go. Talk to you later, Nea." She hung up.

I called back in twenty minutes, surely long enough to change a diaper, but the phone only rang forlornly, ignored.

I considered taking Ma's car, but then Ma wouldn't be able to get to work and I wasn't sure how long I needed to be gone. Then I thought of Duke.

Even though it was far too late in the night, I called Duke. He was still in town, two years after graduation. I'd heard he was working as a mechanic at the Standard station. I found his number in the phone book.

"It's Nea. Pick up your phone, Duke," I hissed into his machine. "It's an emergency!"

"Nea?!" He was yawning. "My God. What time is it?"   140

"Duke! It's important! It's Sourdi, she's in trouble."

There was a pause while I let him absorb all this.

"You have to drive me to Des Moines. We have to get her."

"What happened?"

"Look, I don't have time to explain. We have to go tonight. It's an emergency.   145
A matter of life and death."

"Did you call the police?"

"Don't be stupid. Sourdi would never call the cops. She loves that jerk."

"What?" Duke whispered, "Her husband, he beat her up?"

"Duke, I told you, I can't say anything right now. But you have to help me."

He agreed to meet me at the corner, where there'd be no chance Ma could hear   150
his truck. I'd be waiting.

It was freezing. The wind stung my cheeks, which wasn't a good sign. Could be rain coming, or worse, snow. Even when the roads were clear, it was a good six-hour drive. I didn't want to think how long it would take if we ran into a late-season blizzard.

There was the roar of a souped-up engine and then a spray of gravel. Snoop Doggy Dogg growled over the wind.

"Duke! What took you?"

He put his hand over the door, barring me from climbing up. "You want me to help or not?"

"Don't joke."   155

I pulled myself inside and then made Duke back up rather than run in front of the house. Just in case Ma woke up.

"How come your Ma didn't want to come?"

"She doesn't know."

"Sourdi didn't want to worry her?"

"Mmm." There was no point trying to shout above Snoop Dogg.   160

He was obviously tired. When Duke was tired, he turned his music up even louder than normal. I'd forgotten that. Now the bass underneath the rap was vibrating in my bones. But at least he did as I asked and took off toward the highway.

Soon the squat buildings of town, the used-car lots on the route in from the interstate with their flapping colored flags, and the metal storage units of the Sav-U-Lot passed from view, and there was nothing before us but the black sky and the highway and the patches of snow on the shoulders glowing briefly in the wake of the headlights.

I must have fallen asleep, though I don't remember feeling tired. I was standing on the deck of a boat in an inky ocean, trying to read the stars, but every time I found one constellation, the stars began to blink and fade. I squinted at them, but the stars would not stay in place. Then my head snapped forward as the pickup careened off the shoulder.

The pickup landed in a ditch. Metal glittered in the headlights; the fields on this side of the highway were strung with barbed wire.

We got out by sacrificing our jackets, stuffing them under the back tires until   165
we had enough traction to slide back onto the pavement.

I insisted upon driving. "I got my license," I lied. "And I'm not tired at all."

Duke settled into the passenger seat, his arms folded across his chest, his head tilted back, preparing to go to sleep again.

"D'ya think she'll be happy to see me?" he said out of the blue. "Sourdi sent me a Christmas card with a picture of the baby. Looks just like . . . But I didn't write back or nothing. She probably thought I was angry. She mad at me, you think?"

"Sourdi's never mad at anybody."

"She must be mad at her husband if she wants you to come get her."   170

"She doesn't know we're coming."

"What!"

"I didn't have time to explain to her."

"You're not running away from home, are you?" Duke's eyes narrowed and his voice grew slow as if he thought he was suddenly being clever.

"Yeah, I'm running away to Des Moines."   175

Once upon a time, in another world, a place almost unimaginable to me sitting in the pickup with Madonna singing "Lucky Star" on the radio, Sourdi had walked across a minefield, carrying me on her back. She was nine and I was four. Because she'd told me, I could see it all clearly, better than if I actually remembered: the startled faces of people who'd tripped a mine, their limbs in new arrangements, the bones peeking through the earth. Sourdi had said it was safest to step on the bodies; that way you knew a mine was no longer there.

This was nothing I would ever tell Duke. It was our own personal story, just for Sourdi and me to share. Nobody's business but ours.

I would walk on bones for my sister, I vowed. I would put my bare feet on rotting flesh. I would save Sourdi.

We found the house in West Des Moines after circling for nearly an hour through the identical streets with their neat lawns and boxy houses and chain link fences. I refused to allow Duke to ask for directions from any of the joggers or the van that sputtered by, delivering the *Register*. He figured people in the neighborhood would know, just ask where the Oriental family lived. I told him to go to hell. Then we didn't talk for a while.

But as soon as we found Locust Street, I recognized the house. I knew it was   180
Sourdi's even though it had been painted a different color since the last set of pictures. The lace undercurtains before the cheerful flowered draperies, the flourishing plants in the windows, next to little trinkets, figurines in glass that caught the light. Every space crammed with something sweet.

The heater in Duke's truck began to make a high-pitched, sick-cat whine as we waited, parked across the street, staring at Sourdi's house.

"So, are we going to just sit here?"

"Shh," I said irritably. "Just wait a minute." Somehow I had imagined that Sourdi would sense our presence, the curtains would stir, and I'd only have to wait a moment for my sister to come running out the front door. But we sat patiently, shivering, staring at Sourdi's house. Nothing moved.

"Her husband's home," I said stupidly. "He hasn't gone to work yet."

"He wouldn't dare try anything. Not with the both of us here. We should just 185 go and knock."

"They're probably still asleep."

"Nea, what's the matter with you? What are you afraid of all of a sudden?"

I'd had it with Duke. He just didn't understand anything. I hopped out of the truck and ran through the icy air, my arms wrapped around my body. The sidewalk was slick beneath my sneakers, still damp from the ditch, and I slid onto my knees on the driveway. My right hand broke the fall. A sharp jagged pain shot up to my elbow and stayed there, throbbing. I picked myself up and ran limping to the door and rang.

No one answered for a minute, and then it was him.

"What on earth? Nea!" Sourdi's husband was dressed for work, but he hadn't 190 shaved yet. He looked even older than I remembered, his thinning hair flat across his skull, his bloodshot eyes and swollen lids still heavy from sleep. He might have been handsome once, decades ago, but I saw no evidence of it now. He held the door open and I slipped into the warmth without even removing my shoes first. "How did you get here? Is your mother coming, too?"

My eyes started to water, the transition from cold to heat. Slowly the room came into focus. It was a mess. Baby toys on the carpet, shoes in a pile by the door, old newspapers scattered on an end table anchored by a bowl of peanut shells. The TV was blaring somewhere, and a baby was crying.

Sourdi emerged from the kitchen, dressed in a bright pink sweatsuit emblazoned with the head of Minnie Mouse, pink slippers over her feet, the baby on her hip. She had a bruise across her cheekbone and the purple remains of a black eye. Sourdi didn't say anything for a few seconds as she stared at me, blinking, her mouth falling open. "Where's Ma?"

"Home."

"Oh, no." Sourdi's face crumpled. "Is everything all right?"

I couldn't believe how dense my sister had become. We used to be able to com- 195 municate without words. "Everything's fine . . . at home. Of course." I tried to give her a look so that she'd understand that I had come to rescue her, but Sourdi stood rigidly in place in the doorway to the kitchen, her mouth twitching, puzzled.

"Please, Little Sister, sit down," her husband said. "Let me make you some tea."

Someone banged on the front door, three times. Before I could begin to feel annoyed that Duke couldn't even wait five minutes, that he just had to ruin everything, my sister's husband opened the door again. I didn't bother to turn, instead I watched Sourdi's eyes widen and her wide mouth pucker into an O as she gasped, "Duke!"

"What's goin' on?" Duke said.

Then everyone stared at me with such identical expressions of noncomprehension that I had to laugh. Then I couldn't stop, because I hadn't slept and it was so cold and my nose was running and I didn't have any Kleenex.

"I said, what the hell is going on?" Duke repeated. 200

Sourdi's husband approached Duke. He smiled. "You must be Nea's —"

But by now, Duke had seen Sourdi's bruises. His mouth twisted into a sneer. "You bastard! I oughtta —" He punched Sourdi's husband in the nose. Sourdi screamed, her husband bent over double. Duke drew back his fist again, but Sourdi ran forward and grabbed him. She was punching him on the chest, "Out! Out! You!

I'll call the police!" She tried to claw him with her nails, but Duke threw his arms up around his head.

Sourdi's husband stood up. Blood gushed from his nose all over his white shirt and tie.

"Come on!" I said stupidly. "Come on, Sourdi, let's go!"

But it was pretty obvious that she didn't want to leave. 205

The baby began shrieking.

I started crying, too.

After everyone had calmed down, Duke went down the street to the 7-Eleven to get a bag of ice for Mr. Chhay, who kept saying "I'm fine, don't worry," even though his nose had turned a deep scarlet and was starting to swell.

It turned out Sourdi's husband hadn't beaten her up. An economy-size box of baby wipes had fallen off the closet shelf and struck her full in the eye.

While Mr. Chhay went into the bedroom to change his clothes, I sat with 210 Sourdi in the kitchen as she tried to get the squawling baby to eat its breakfast.

"Nea, what's wrong with you?"

"What's wrong with me? Don't you get it? I was trying to help you!"

Sourdi sighed as the baby spat a spoonful of the glop onto the table. "I'm a married woman. I'm not just some girl anymore. I have my own family. You understand that?"

"You were crying." I squinted at my sister. "I heard you."

"I'm gonna have another baby, you know. That's a big step. That's a big thing." 215 She said this as though it explained everything.

"You sound like an old lady. You're only twenty, for Chrissake. You don't have to live like this. Ma is wrong. You can be anything, Sourdi."

Sourdi pinched her nose between two fingers. "Everything's gonna be fine. We just had a little argument, but it's O.K. We had a good talk. He understands now. I'm still gonna go to school. I haven't changed my mind. After the baby gets a little bigger, I mean, both babies. Maybe when they start pre-school."

Just then her husband came back into the kitchen. He had to use the phone to call work. His face looked like a gargoyle's.

Sourdi looked at me then, so disappointed. I knew what she was thinking. She had grown up, and I had merely grown unworthy of her love.

After Duke got back with the ice, he and Sourdi's husband shook hands. Duke kept 220 saying, "Gosh, I'm so sorry," and Mr. Chhay kept repeating, "No problem, don't worry."

Then Sourdi's husband had to go. We followed him to the driveway. My sister kissed him before he climbed into his Buick. He rolled down the window, and she leaned in and kissed him again.

I turned away. I watched Duke standing in the doorway, holding the baby in his arms, cooing at its face. In his tough wannabe clothes, the super-wide jeans and his fancy sneakers and the chain from his wallet to his belt loops, he looked surprisingly young.

Sourdi lent us some blankets and matching his-and-hers Donald and Daisy Duck sweatshirts for the trip back, since our coats were still wet and worthless.

"Don't tell Ma I was here, O.K.?" I begged Sourdi. "We'll be home by afternoon. She'll just think I'm with friends or something. She doesn't have to know, O.K.?"

Sourdi pressed her full lips together into a thin line and nodded in a way 225 that seemed as though she were answering a different question. And I knew that I couldn't trust my sister to take my side anymore.

As we pulled away from Sourdi's house, the first icy snowflakes began to fall across the windshield.

Sourdi stood in the driveway with the baby on her hip. She waved to us as the snow swirled around her like ashes.

She had made her choice, and she hadn't chosen me.

Sourdi told me a story once about a magic serpent, the Naga, with a mouth so large, it could swallow people whole. Our ancestors carved Naga into the stones of Angkor Wat to scare away demons. Sourdi said people used to believe they could come alive in times of great evil and protect the temples. They could eat armies.

I wished I was a Naga. I would have swallowed the whole world in one gulp.   230
But I have no magic powers. None whatsoever.

CONSIDERATIONS FOR CRITICAL THINKING AND WRITING

1. FIRST RESPONSE. How does your response to Nea develop over the course of the story? Is she a dynamic or a static character?

2. Explain how Nea and Sourdi serve as character foils to one another.

3. Discuss whether you think Duke is a flat or a round character.

4. What is the effect of the story's being told from Nea's perspective? How might the story be different if it were told from the mother's point of view?

5. Do you think Mr. Chhay is a good or bad husband?

6. How does the information about Nea and Sourdi's trip through the minefield affect your understanding of Nea's relationship with her sister?

7. Comment on the title. Why wouldn't an alternative like "Nea the Troublemaker" be appropriate?

CONNECTIONS TO OTHER SELECTIONS

1. Discuss the process of immigrants becoming Americanized in this story and in Julia Alvarez's poem "Queens, 1963" (p. 924).

2. Compare the characterization of Nea in "Saving Sourdi" and of Sammy in John Updike's "A & P" (p. 200). In what sense do both characters see themselves as rescuers?

HERMAN MELVILLE (1819–1891)

Hoping to improve his distressed financial situation, Herman Melville left New York and went to sea as a young common sailor. He returned to become an uncommon writer. His experiences at sea became the basis for his early novels: *Typee* (1846), *Omoo* (1847), *Mardi* (1849), *Redburn* (1849), and *White-Jacket* (1850). Ironically, with the publication of his masterpiece, *Moby-Dick* (1851), Melville lost the popular success he had enjoyed with his earlier books because his readers were not ready for its philosophical complexity.

Library of Congress, Prints and Photographs Division.

Although he wrote more, Melville's works were read less and slipped into obscurity. His final short novel, *Billy Budd,* was not published until the 1920s, when critics rediscovered him. In "Bartleby, the Scrivener," Melville presents a quiet clerk in a law office whose baffling "passive resistance" disrupts the life of his employer, a man who attempts to make sense of Bartleby's refusal to behave reasonably.

Bartleby, the Scrivener 1853

A Story of Wall Street

I am a rather elderly man. The nature of my avocations, for the last thirty years, has brought me into more than ordinary contact with what would seem an interesting and somewhat singular set of men, of whom, as yet, nothing, that I know of, has ever been written — I mean, the law-copyists, or scriveners. I have known very many of them, professionally and privately, and, if I pleased, could relate diverse histories, at which good-natured gentlemen might smile, and sentimental souls might weep. But I waive the biographies of all other scriveners, for a few passages in the life of Bartleby, who was a scrivener, the strangest I ever saw, or heard of. While, of other law-copyists, I might write the complete life, of Bartleby nothing of that sort can be done. I believe that no materials exist, for a full and satisfactory biography of this man. It is an irreparable loss to literature. Bartleby was one of those beings of whom nothing is ascertainable, except from the original sources, and, in his case, those are very small. What my own astonished eyes saw of Bartleby, *that* is all I know of him, except, indeed, one vague report, which will appear in the sequel.

Ere introducing the scrivener, as he first appeared to me, it is fit I make some mention of myself, my *employés,* my business, my chambers, and general surroundings, because some such description is indispensable to an adequate understanding of the chief character about to be presented. Imprimis:° I am a man who, from his youth upwards, has been filled with a profound conviction that the easiest way of life is the best. Hence, though I belong to a profession proverbially energetic and nervous, even to turbulence, at times, yet nothing of that sort have I ever suffered to invade my peace. I am one of those unambitious lawyers who never address a jury, or in any way draw down public applause; but, in the cool tranquillity of a snug retreat, do a snug business among rich men's bonds, and mortgages, and title-deeds. All who know me, consider me an eminently *safe* man. The late John Jacob Astor,° a personage little given to poetic enthusiasm, had no hesitation in pronouncing my first grand point to be prudence; my next, method. I do not speak it in vanity, but simply record the fact, that I was not unemployed in my profession by the late John Jacob Astor; a name which, I admit, I love to repeat; for it hath a rounded and orbicular sound to it, and rings like unto bullion. I will freely add, that I was not insensible to the late John Jacob Astor's good opinion.

Some time prior to the period at which this little history begins, my avocations had been largely increased. The good old office, now extinct in the State of

Imprimis: In the first place.
John Jacob Astor (1763–1848): An enormously wealthy American capitalist.

New York, of a Master in Chancery, had been conferred upon me. It was not a very arduous office, but very pleasantly remunerative. I seldom lose my temper; much more seldom indulge in dangerous indignation at wrongs and outrages; but I must be permitted to be rash here and declare, that I consider the sudden and violent abrogation of the office of Master in Chancery, by the new Constitution, as a —— premature act; inasmuch as I had counted upon a life-lease of the profits, whereas I only received those of a few short years. But this is by the way.

My chambers were up stairs, at No. — Wall Street. At one end, they looked upon the white wall of the interior of a spacious skylight shaft, penetrating the building from top to bottom.

This view might have been considered rather tame than otherwise, deficient 5 in what landscape painters call "life." But, if so, the view from the other end of my chambers offered, at least, a contrast, if nothing more. In that direction, my windows commanded an unobstructed view of a lofty brick wall, black by age and everlasting shade; which wall required no spyglass to bring out its lurking beauties, but, for the benefit of all near-sighted spectators, was pushed up to within ten feet of my window-panes. Owing to the great height of the surrounding buildings, and my chambers being on the second floor, the interval between this wall and mine not a little resembled a huge square cistern.

At the period just preceding the advent of Bartleby, I had two persons as copyists in my employment, and a promising lad as an office-boy. First, Turkey; second, Nippers; third, Ginger Nut. These may seem names, the like of which are not usually found in the Directory. In truth, they were nicknames, mutually conferred upon each other by my three clerks, and were deemed expressive of their respective persons or characters. Turkey was a short, pursy Englishman, of about my own age — that is, somewhere not far from sixty. In the morning, one might say, his face was of a fine florid hue, but after twelve o'clock, meridian — his dinner hour — it blazed like a grate full of Christmas coals; and continued blazing — but, as it were, with a gradual wane — till six o'clock, P.M., or thereabouts; after which, I saw no more of the proprietor of the face, which, gaining its meridian with the sun, seemed to set with it, to rise, culminate, and decline the following day, with the like regularity and undiminished glory. There are many singular coincidences I have known in the course of my life, not the least among which was the fact, that, exactly when Turkey displayed his fullest beams from his red and radiant countenance, just then, too, at that critical moment, began the daily period when I considered his business capacities as seriously disturbed for the remainder of the twenty-four hours. Not that he was absolutely idle, or averse to business then; far from it. The difficulty was, he was apt to be altogether too energetic. There was a strange, inflamed, flurried, flighty recklessness of activity about him. He would be incautious in dipping his pen into his inkstand. All his blots upon my documents were dropped there after twelve o'clock, meridian. Indeed, not only would he be reckless, and sadly given to making blots in the afternoon, but, some days, he went further, and was rather noisy. At such times, too, his face flamed with augmented blazonry, as if cannel coal had been heaped on anthracite. He made an unpleasant racket with his chair; spilled his sand-box; in mending his pens, impatiently split them all to pieces, and threw them on the floor in a sudden passion; stood up, and leaned over his table, boxing his papers about in a most indecorous manner, very sad to behold in an elderly man like him. Nevertheless, as he was in many ways a most valuable person to me, and all the time before twelve o'clock, meridian, was the quickest, steadiest creature, too, accomplishing a great deal of work in a style not easily to be matched — for these reasons, I was willing to overlook his eccentricities, though, indeed, occasionally, I remonstrated with him. I did this very gently, however, because, though the civilest, nay, the blandest and most reverential of men in the morning, yet, in the afternoon, he was disposed, upon provocation, to be slightly rash with his tongue — in fact, insolent. Now, valuing his morning services as I did, and resolved not to lose them — yet, at the same time, made uncomfortable by his inflamed ways after twelve o'clock — and being a man of peace, unwilling by my admonitions to call forth unseemly retorts from him, I took upon me, one Saturday noon (he was always worse on Saturdays) to hint to him, very kindly, that, perhaps, now that he was growing old, it might be well to abridge his labors; in short, he need not come to my chambers after twelve o'clock, but, dinner over, had best go home to his lodgings, and rest himself till tea-time. But no; he insisted upon his afternoon devotions. His countenance became intolerably fervid, as he oratorically assured me — gesticulating with a long ruler at the other end of the room — that if his services in the morning were useful, how indispensable, then, in the afternoon?

"With submission, sir," said Turkey, on this occasion, "I consider myself your right-hand man. In the morning I but marshal and deploy my columns; but in the afternoon I put myself at their head, and gallantly charge the foe, thus" — and he made a violent thrust with the ruler.

"But the blots, Turkey," intimated I.

"True; but, with submission, sir, behold these hairs! I am getting old. Surely, sir, a blot or two of a warm afternoon is not to be severely urged against gray hairs. Old age — even if it blot the page — is honorable. With submission, sir, we *both* are getting old."

This appeal to my fellow-feeling was hardly to be resisted. At all events, 10 I saw that go he would not. So, I made up my mind to let him stay, resolving, nevertheless, to see to it that, during the afternoon, he had to do with my less important papers.

Nippers, the second on my list, was a whiskered, sallow, and, upon the whole, rather piratical-looking young man, of about five-and-twenty. I always deemed him the victim of two evil powers — ambition and indigestion. The ambition was evinced by a certain impatience of the duties of a mere copyist, an unwarrantable usurpation of strictly professional affairs such as the original drawing up of legal documents. The indigestion seemed betokened in an occasional nervous testiness and grinning irritability, causing the teeth to audibly grind together over mistakes committed in copying; unnecessary maledictions, hissed, rather than spoken, in the heat of business; and especially by a continual discontent with the height of the table where he worked. Though of a very ingenious mechanical turn, Nippers could never get this table to suit him. He put chips under it, blocks of various sorts, bits of pasteboard, and at last went so far as to attempt an exquisite adjustment, by final pieces of folded blotting-paper. But no invention would answer. If, for the sake of easing his back, he brought the table-lid at a sharp angle well up towards his chin, and wrote there like a man using the steep roof of a Dutch house for his desk, then he declared that it stopped the circulation in his arms. If now he lowered the table to his waistbands, and stooped over it in writing, then there was a sore aching in his back. In short, the truth of the matter was, Nippers knew not what he wanted. Or, if he wanted anything, it was to be rid of a scrivener's table altogether. Among the manifestations of his diseased ambition was a fondness he had for receiving visits from certain ambiguous-looking fellows in seedy coats, whom he called his clients. Indeed, I was aware that not only was he, at times, considerable of a ward-politician, but he occasionally did a little business at the justices' courts, and was not unknown on the steps of the Tombs.° I have good reason to believe, however, that one individual who called upon him at my chambers, and who, with a grand air, he insisted was his client, was no other than a dun, and the alleged title-deed, a bill. But, with all his failings, and the annoyances he caused me, Nippers, like his compatriot Turkey, was a very useful man to me; wrote a neat, swift hand; and, when he chose, was not deficient in a gentlemanly sort of deportment. Added to this, he always dressed in a gentlemanly sort of way; and so, incidentally, reflected credit upon my chambers. Whereas, with respect to Turkey, I had much ado to keep him from being a reproach to me. His clothes were apt to look oily, and smell of eating-houses. He wore his pantaloons very loose and baggy in summer. His coats were execrable, his hat not to be handled. But while the hat was a thing of indifference to me, inasmuch as his natural civility and deference, as a dependent Englishman, always led him to doff it the moment he entered the room, yet his coat was another matter. Concerning his coats, I reasoned with him; but with no effect. The truth was, I suppose, that a man with so small an income could not afford to sport such a lustrous face and a lustrous coat at one and the same time. As Nippers once observed, Turkey's money went chiefly for red ink. One winter day, I presented Turkey with a highly respectable-looking coat of my own — a padded gray coat, of a most comfortable warmth, and which buttoned straight up from the knee to the neck. I thought Turkey would appreciate the favor, and abate his rashness and obstreperousness of afternoons. But no; I verily believe that buttoning himself up in so downy and blanket-like a coat had a pernicious effect upon him — upon the same principle that too much oats are bad for horses. In fact, precisely as a rash, restive horse is said to feel his oats, so Turkey felt his coat. It made him insolent. He was a man whom prosperity harmed.

Though, concerning the self-indulgent habits of Turkey, I had my own private surmises, yet, touching Nippers, I was well persuaded that, whatever might be his faults in other respects, he was, at least, a temperate young man. But indeed, nature herself seemed to have been his vintner, and, at his birth, charged him so thoroughly with an irritable, brandy-like disposition, that all subsequent potations were needless. When I consider how, amid the stillness of my chambers, Nippers would sometimes impatiently rise from his seat, and stooping over his table, spread his arms wide apart, seize the whole desk, and move it, and jerk it, with a grim, grinding motion on the floor, as if the table were a perverse voluntary agent, intent on thwarting and vexing him, I plainly perceive that, for Nippers, brandy-and-water were altogether superfluous.

It was fortunate for me that, owing to its peculiar cause — indigestion — the irritability and consequent nervousness of Nippers were mainly observable in the morning, while in the afternoon he was comparatively mild. So that, Turkey's paroxysms only coming on about twelve o'clock, I never had to do with their eccentricities at one time. Their fits relieved each other, like guards. When Nippers' was on, Turkey's was off; and *vice versa*. This was a good natural arrangement, under the circumstances.

the Tombs: A jail in New York City.

Ginger Nut, the third on my list, was a lad, some twelve years old. His father was a carman, ambitious of seeing his son on the bench instead of a cart, before he died. So he sent him to my office, as student at law, errand-boy, cleaner, and sweeper, at the rate of one dollar a week. He had a little desk to himself, but he did not use it much. Upon inspection, the drawer exhibited a great array of the shells of various sorts of nuts. Indeed, to this quick-witted youth, the whole noble science of the law was contained in a nutshell. Not the least among the employments of Ginger Nut, as well as one which he discharged with the most alacrity, was his duty as cake and apple purveyor for Turkey and Nippers. Copying lawpapers being proverbially a dry, husky sort of business, my two scriveners were fain to moisten their mouths very often with Spitzenbergs, to be had at the numerous stalls nigh the Custom House and Post Office. Also, they sent Ginger Nut very frequently for that peculiar cake — small, flat, round, and very spicy — after which he had been named by them. Of a cold morning, when business was but dull, Turkey would gobble up scores of these cakes, as if they were mere wafers — indeed, they sell them at the rate of six or eight for a penny — the scrape of his pen blending with the crunching of the crisp particles in his mouth. Of all the fiery afternoon blunders and flurried rashness of Turkey, was his once moistening a ginger-cake between his lips, and clapping it on to a mortgage, for a seal. I came within an ace of dismissing him then. But he mollified me by making an oriental bow, and saying —

"With submission, sir, it was generous of me to find you in stationery on my 15 own account."

Now my original business — that of a conveyancer and title hunter, and drawer-up of recondite documents of all sorts — was considerably increased by receiving the Master's office. There was now great work for scriveners. Not only must I push the clerks already with me, but I must have additional help.

In answer to my advertisement, a motionless young man one morning stood upon my office threshold, the door being open, for it was summer. I can see that figure now — pallidly neat, pitiably respectable, incurably forlorn! It was Bartleby.

After a few words touching his qualifications, I engaged him, glad to have among my corps of copyists a man of so singularly sedate an aspect, which I thought might operate beneficially upon the flighty temper of Turkey, and the fiery one of Nippers.

I should have stated before that ground-glass folding-doors divided my premises into two parts, one of which was occupied by my scriveners, the other by myself. According to my humor, I threw open these doors, or closed them. I resolved to assign Bartleby a corner by the folding-doors, but on my side of them, so as to have this quiet man within easy call, in case any trifling thing was to be done. I placed his desk close up to a small side-window in that part of the room, a window which originally had afforded a lateral view of certain grimy brickyards and bricks, but which, owing to subsequent erections, commanded at present no view at all, though it gave some light. Within three feet of the panes was a wall, and the light came down from far above, between two lofty buildings, as from a very small opening in a dome. Still further to a satisfactory arrangement, I procured a high green folding screen, which might entirely isolate Bartleby from my sight, though not remove him from my voice. And thus, in a manner, privacy and society were conjoined.

At first, Bartleby did an extraordinary quantity of writing. As if long famish- 20 ing for something to copy, he seemed to gorge himself on my documents. There was no pause for digestion. He ran a day and night line, copying by sunlight and by candle-light. I should have been quite delighted with his application, had he been cheerfully industrious. But he wrote on silently, palely, mechanically.

It is, of course, an indispensable part of a scrivener's business to verify the accuracy of his copy, word by word. Where there are two or more scriveners in an office, they assist each other in this examination, one reading from the copy, the other holding the original. It is a very dull, wearisome, and lethargic affair. I can readily imagine that, to some sanguine temperaments, it would be altogether intolerable. For example, I cannot credit that the mettlesome poet, Byron, would have contentedly sat down with Bartleby to examine a law document of, say five hundred pages, closely written in a crimpy hand.

Now and then, in the haste of business, it had been my habit to assist in comparing some brief document myself, calling Turkey or Nippers for this purpose. One object I had, in placing Bartleby so handy to me behind the screen, was, to avail myself of his services on such trivial occasions. It was on the third day, I think, of his being with me, and before any necessity had arisen for having his own writing examined, that, being much hurried to complete a small affair I had in hand, I abruptly called to Bartleby. In my haste and natural expectancy of instant compliance, I sat with my head bent over the original on my desk, and my right hand sideways, and somewhat nervously extended with the copy, so that, immediately upon emerging from his retreat, Bartleby might snatch it and proceed to business without the least delay.

In this very attitude did I sit when I called to him, rapidly stating what it was I wanted him to do — namely, to examine a small paper with me. Imagine my surprise, nay, my consternation, when, without moving from his privacy, Bartleby, in a singularly mild, firm voice, replied, "I would prefer not to."

I sat awhile in perfect silence, rallying my stunned faculties. Immediately it occurred to me that my ears had deceived me, or Bartleby had entirely misunderstood my meaning. I repeated my request in the clearest tone I could assume; but in quite as clear a one came the previous reply, "I would prefer not to."

"Prefer not to," echoed I, rising in high excitement, and crossing the room with 25 a stride. "What do you mean? Are you moonstruck? I want you to help me compare this sheet here — take it," and I thrust it towards him.

"I would prefer not to," said he.

I looked at him steadfastly. His face was leanly composed; his gray eye dimly calm. Not a wrinkle of agitation rippled him. Had there been the least uneasiness, anger, impatience, or impertinence in his manner; in other words, had there been anything ordinarily human about him, doubtless I should have violently dismissed him from the premises. But as it was, I should have as soon thought of turning my pale plaster-of-paris bust of Cicero out of doors. I stood gazing at him awhile, as he went on with his own writing, and then reseated myself at my desk. This is very strange, thought I. What had one best do? But my business hurried me. I concluded to forget the matter for the present, reserving it for my future leisure. So, calling Nippers from the other room, the paper was speedily examined.

A few days after this, Bartleby concluded four lengthy documents, being quadruplicates of a week's testimony taken before me in my High Court of Chancery. It became necessary to examine them. It was an important suit, and great accuracy was imperative. Having all things arranged, I called Turkey, Nippers, and Ginger Nut, from the next room, meaning to place the four copies in the hands of my four clerks, while I should read from the original. Accordingly, Turkey, Nippers, and

Ginger Nut had taken their seats in a row, each with his document in his hand, when I called to Bartleby to join this interesting group.

"Bartleby! quick, I am waiting."

I heard a slow scrape of his chair legs on the uncarpeted floor, and soon he 30 appeared standing at the entrance of his hermitage.

"What is wanted?" said he, mildly.

"The copies, the copies," said I, hurriedly. "We are going to examine them. There" — and I held towards him the fourth quadruplicate.

"I would prefer not to," he said, and gently disappeared behind the screen.

For a few moments I was turned into a pillar of salt, standing at the head of my seated column of clerks. Recovering myself, I advanced towards the screen, and demanded the reason for such extraordinary conduct.

"*Why* do you refuse?"   35

"I would prefer not to."

With any other man I should have flown outright into a dreadful passion, scorned all further words, and thrust him ignominiously from my presence. But there was something about Bartleby that not only strangely disarmed me, but, in a wonderful manner, touched and disconcerted me. I began to reason with him.

"These are your own copies we are about to examine. It is labor saving to you, because one examination will answer for your four papers. It is common usage. Every copyist is bound to help examine his copy. Is it not so? Will you not speak? Answer!"

"I prefer not to," he replied in a flute-like tone. It seemed to me that, while I had been addressing him, he carefully revolved every statement that I made; fully comprehended the meaning; could not gainsay the irresistible conclusion; but, at the same time, some paramount consideration prevailed with him to reply as he did.

"You are decided, then, not to comply with my request — a request made 40 according to common usage and common sense?"

He briefly gave me to understand, that on that point my judgment was sound. Yes: his decision was irreversible.

It is not seldom the case that, when a man is browbeaten in some unprecedented and violently unreasonable way, he begins to stagger in his own plainest faith. He begins, as it were, vaguely to surmise that, wonderful as it may be, all the justice and all the reason is on the other side. Accordingly, if any disinterested persons are present, he turns to them for some reinforcement for his own faltering mind.

"Turkey," said I, "what do you think of this? Am I not right?"

"With submission, sir," said Turkey, in his blandest tone, "I think that you are."

"Nippers," said I, "what do *you* think of it?"   45

"I think I should kick him out of the office."

(The reader of nice perceptions will have perceived that, it being morning, Turkey's answer is couched in polite and tranquil terms, but Nippers replies in ill-tempered ones. Or, to repeat a previous sentence, Nippers' ugly mood was on duty, and Turkey's off.)

"Ginger Nut," said I, willing to enlist the smallest suffrage in my behalf, "what do *you* think of it?"

"I think, sir, he's a little *luny*," replied Ginger Nut, with a grin.

"You hear what they say," said I, turning towards the screen, "come forth and 50 do your duty."

But he vouchsafed no reply. I pondered a moment in sore perplexity. But once more business hurried me. I determined again to postpone the consideration of this dilemma to my future leisure. With a little trouble we made out to examine the papers without Bartleby, though at every page or two Turkey deferentially dropped his opinion, that this proceeding was quite out of the common; while Nippers, twitching in his chair with a dyspeptic nervousness, ground out, between his set teeth, occasional hissing maledictions against the stubborn oaf behind the screen. And for his (Nippers') part, this was the first and the last time he would do another man's business without pay.

Meanwhile Bartleby sat in his hermitage, oblivious to everything but his own peculiar business there.

Some days passed, the scrivener being employed upon another lengthy work. His late remarkable conduct led me to regard his ways narrowly. I observed that he never went to dinner; indeed, that he never went anywhere. As yet I had never, of my personal knowledge, known him to be outside of my office. He was a perpetual sentry in the corner. At about eleven o'clock though, in the morning, I noticed that Ginger Nut would advance toward the opening in Bartleby's screen, as if silently beckoned thither by a gesture invisible to me where I sat. The boy would then leave the office, jingling a few pence, and reappear with a handful of ginger-nuts, which he delivered in the hermitage, receiving two of the cakes for his trouble.

He lives, then, on ginger-nuts, thought I; never eats a dinner, properly speaking; he must be a vegetarian, then, but no; he never eats even vegetables, he eats nothing but ginger-nuts. My mind then ran on in reveries concerning the probable effects upon the human constitution of living entirely on ginger-nuts. Ginger-nuts are so called, because they contain ginger as one of their peculiar constituents, and the final flavoring one. Now, what was ginger? A hot, spicy thing. Was Bartleby hot and spicy? Not at all. Ginger, then, had no effect upon Bartleby. Probably he preferred it should have none.

Nothing so aggravates an earnest person as a passive resistance. If the individual so resisted be of a not inhumane temper, and the resisting one perfectly harmless in his passivity, then, in the better moods of the former, he will endeavor charitably to construe to his imagination what proves impossible to be solved by his judgment. Even so, for the most part, I regarded Bartleby and his ways. Poor fellow! thought I, he means no mischief; it is plain he intends no insolence; his aspect sufficiently evinces that his eccentricities are involuntary. He is useful to me. I can get along with him. If I turn him away, the chances are he will fall in with some less indulgent employer, and then he will be rudely treated, and perhaps driven forth miserably to starve. Yes. Here I can cheaply purchase a delicious self-approval. To befriend Bartleby; to humor him in his strange wilfulness, will cost me little or nothing, while I lay up in my soul what will eventually prove a sweet morsel for my conscience. But this mood was not invariable with me. The passiveness of Bartleby sometimes irritated me. I felt strangely goaded on to encounter him in new opposition — to elicit some angry spark from him answerable to my own. But, indeed, I might as well have essayed to strike fire with my knuckles against a bit of Windsor soap. But one afternoon the evil impulse in me mastered me, and the following little scene ensued:

"Bartleby," said I, "when those papers are all copied, I will compare them with you."

"I would prefer not to."

"How? Surely you do not mean to persist in that mulish vagary?"

No answer.

I threw open the folding-doors nearby, and turning upon Turkey and Nippers, 60 exclaimed:

"Bartleby a second time says, he won't examine his papers. What do you think of it, Turkey?"

It was afternoon, be it remembered. Turkey sat glowing like a brass boiler; his bald head steaming; his hands reeling among his blotted papers.

"Think of it?" roared Turkey. "I think I'll just step behind his screen, and black his eyes for him!"

So saying, Turkey rose to his feet and threw his arms into a pugilistic position. He was hurrying away to make good his promise, when I detained him, alarmed at the effect of incautiously rousing Turkey's combativeness after dinner.

"Sit down, Turkey," said I, "and hear what Nippers has to say. What do you think 65 of it, Nippers? Would I not be justified in immediately dismissing Bartleby?"

"Excuse me, that is for you to decide, sir. I think his conduct quite unusual, and, indeed, unjust, as regards Turkey and myself. But it may only be a passing whim."

"Ah," exclaimed I, "you have strangely changed your mind, then — you speak very gently of him now."

"All beer," cried Turkey; "gentleness is effects of beer — Nippers and I dined together to-day. You see how gentle *I* am, sir. Shall I go and black his eyes?"

"You refer to Bartleby, I suppose. No, not to-day, Turkey," I replied; "pray, put up your fists."

I closed the doors, and again advanced towards Bartleby. I felt additional 70 incentives tempting me to my fate. I burned to be rebelled against again. I remembered that Bartleby never left the office.

"Bartleby," said I, "Ginger Nut is away; just step around to the Post Office, won't you?" (it was but a three minutes' walk) "and see if there is anything for me."

"I would prefer not to."

"You *will* not?"

"I *prefer* not."

I staggered to my desk, and sat there in a deep study. My blind inveteracy 75 returned. Was there any other thing in which I could procure myself to be ignominiously repulsed by this lean, penniless wight? — my hired clerk? What added thing is there, perfectly reasonable, that he will be sure to refuse to do?

"Bartleby!"

No answer.

"Bartleby," in a louder tone.

No answer.

"Bartleby," I roared. 80

Like a very ghost, agreeably to the laws of magical invocation, at the third summons, he appeared at the entrance of his hermitage.

"Go to the next room, and tell Nippers to come to me."

"I prefer not to," he respectfully and slowly said, and mildly disappeared.

"Very good, Bartleby," said I, in a quiet sort of serenely-severe self-possessed tone, intimating the unalterable purpose of some terrible retribution very close at hand. At the moment I half intended something of the kind. But upon the whole, as it was drawing towards my dinner-hour, I thought it best to put on my hat and walk home for the day, suffering much from perplexity and distress of mind.

Shall I acknowledge it? The conclusion of this whole business was, that it soon 85 became a fixed fact of my chambers, that a pale young scrivener, by the name of Bartleby, had a desk there; that he copied for me at the usual rate of four cents a folio (one hundred words); but he was permanently exempt from examining the work done by him, that duty being transferred to Turkey and Nippers, out of compliment, doubtless, to their superior acuteness; moreover, said Bartleby was never, on any account, to be dispatched on the most trivial errand of any sort; and that even if entreated to take upon him such a matter, it was generally understood that he would "prefer not to" — in other words, that he would refuse point-blank.

As days passed on, I became considerably reconciled to Bartleby. His steadiness, his freedom from all dissipation, his incessant industry (except when he chose to throw himself into a standing revery behind his screen), his great stillness, his unalterableness of demeanor under all circumstances, made him a valuable acquisition. One prime thing was this — *he was always there* — first in the morning, continually through the day, and the last at night. I had a singular confidence in his honesty. I felt my most precious papers perfectly safe in his hands. Sometimes, to be sure, I could not, for the very soul of me, avoid falling into sudden spasmodic passions with him. For it was exceeding difficult to bear in mind all the time those strange peculiarities, privileges, and unheard-of exemptions, forming the tacit stipulations on Bartleby's part under which he remained in my office. Now and then, in the eagerness of dispatching pressing business, I would inadvertently summon Bartleby, in a short, rapid tone, to put his finger, say, on the incipient tie of a bit of red tape with which I was about compressing some papers. Of course, from behind the screen the usual answer, "I prefer not to," was sure to come; and then, how could a human creature, with the common infirmities of our nature, refrain from bitterly exclaiming upon such perverseness — such unreasonableness? However, every added repulse of this sort which I received only tended to lessen the probability of my repeating the inadvertence.

Here it must be said, that, according to the custom of most legal gentlemen occupying chambers in densely populated law buildings, there were several keys to my door. One was kept by a woman residing in the attic, which person weekly scrubbed and daily swept and dusted my apartments. Another was kept by Turkey for convenience sake. The third I sometimes carried in my own pocket. The fourth I knew not who had.

Now, one Sunday morning I happened to go to Trinity Church, to hear a celebrated preacher, and finding myself rather early on the ground I thought I would walk round to my chambers for a while. Luckily I had my key with me; but upon applying it to the lock, I found it resisted by something inserted from the inside. Quite surprised, I called out; when to my consternation a key was turned from within; and thrusting his lean visage at me, and holding the door ajar, the apparition of Bartleby appeared, in his shirt-sleeves, and otherwise in a strangely tattered *deshabille,* saying quietly that he was sorry, but he was deeply engaged just then, and — preferred not admitting me at present. In a brief word or two, he moreover added, that perhaps I had better walk round the block two or three times, and by that time he would probably have concluded his affairs.

Now, the utterly unsurmised appearance of Bartleby, tenanting my law-chambers of a Sunday morning, with his cadaverously gentlemanly *nonchalance,* yet withal firm and self-possessed, had such a strange effect upon me, that incontinently I slunk away from my own door, and did as desired. But not without sundry twinges of impotent rebellion against the mild effrontery of this unaccountable scrivener. Indeed, it was his wonderful mildness chiefly, which not only disarmed me, but unmanned me, as it were. For I consider that one, for the time, is sort of unmanned when he tranquilly permits his hired clerk to dictate to him, and order him away from his own premises. Furthermore, I was full of uneasiness as to what Bartleby could possibly be doing in my office in his shirt-sleeves, and in an otherwise dismantled condition of a Sunday morning. Was anything amiss going on? Nay, that was out of the question. It was not to be thought of for a moment that Bartleby was an immoral person. But what could he be doing there? — copying? Nay again, whatever might be his eccentricities, Bartleby was an eminently decorous person. He would be the last man to sit down to his desk in any state approaching to nudity. Besides, it was Sunday; and there was something about Bartleby that forbade the supposition that he would by any secular occupation violate the proprieties of the day.

Nevertheless, my mind was not pacified; and full of a restless curiosity, at last I 90 returned to the door. Without hindrance I inserted my key, opened it, and entered. Bartleby was not to be seen. I looked round anxiously, peeped behind his screen; but it was very plain that he was gone. Upon more closely examining the place, I surmised that for an indefinite period Bartleby must have ate, dressed, and slept in my office, and that too without plate, mirror, or bed. The cushioned seat of a rickety old sofa in one corner bore the faint impress of a lean, reclining form. Rolled away under his desk, I found a blanket; under the empty grate, a blacking box and brush; on a chair, a tin basin, with soap and a ragged towel; in a newspaper a few crumbs of ginger-nuts and a morsel of cheese. Yes, thought I, it is evident enough that Bartleby has been making his home here, keeping bachelor's hall all by himself. Immediately then the thought came sweeping across me, what miserable friendlessness and loneliness are here revealed! His poverty is great; but his solitude, how horrible! Think of it. Of a Sunday, Wall Street is deserted as Petra;° and every night of every day it is an emptiness. This building, too, which of week-days hums with industry and life, at nightfall echoes with sheer vacancy, and all through Sunday is forlorn. And here Bartleby makes his home; sole spectator of a solitude which he has seen all populous — a sort of innocent and transformed Marius brooding among the ruins of Carthage?°

For the first time in my life a feeling of overpowering stinging melancholy seized me. Before, I had never experienced aught but a not unpleasing sadness. The bond of a common humanity now drew me irresistibly to gloom. A fraternal melancholy! For both I and Bartleby were sons of Adam. I remembered the bright silks and sparkling faces I had seen that day, in gala trim, swan-like sailing down the Mississippi of Broadway; and I contrasted them with the pallid copyist, and thought to myself, Ah, happiness courts the light, so we deem the world is gay; but misery hides aloof, so we deem that misery there is none. These sad fancyings — chimeras, doubtless, of a sick and silly brain — led on to other and more special thoughts, concerning the eccentricities of Bartleby. Presentiments of strange discoveries hovered round me. The scrivener's pale form appeared to me laid out, among uncaring strangers, in its shivering winding-sheet.

Suddenly I was attracted by Bartleby's closed desk, the key in open sight left in the lock.

I mean no mischief, seek the gratification of no heartless curiosity, thought I; besides, the desk is mine, and its contents, too, so I will make bold to look within.

Petra: An ancient Arabian city whose ruins were discovered in 1812.
Marius . . . of Carthage: Gaius Marius (157–86 B.C.), an exiled Roman general, sought refuge in the African city-state of Carthage, which had been destroyed by the Romans in the Third Punic War. Later writers, describing his arrival, compared the ruins of Marius's political career to the devastated city.

Everything was methodically arranged, the papers smoothly placed. The pigeon-holes were deep, and removing the files of documents, I groped into their recesses. Presently I felt something there, and dragged it out. It was an old bandanna hand-kerchief, heavy and knotted. I opened it, and saw it was a saving's bank.

I now recalled all the quiet mysteries which I had noted in the man. I remembered that he never spoke but to answer; that, though at intervals he had considerable time to himself, yet I had never seen him reading — no, not even a newspaper; that for long periods he would stand looking out, at his pale window behind the screen, upon the dead brick wall; I was quite sure he never visited any refectory or eating-house; while his pale face clearly indicated that he never drank beer like Turkey; or tea and coffee even, like other men; that he never went anywhere in particular that I could learn; never went out for a walk, unless, indeed, that was the case at present; that he had declined telling who he was, or whence he came, or whether he had any relatives in the world; that though so thin and pale, he never complained of ill-health. And more than all, I remembered a certain unconscious air of pallid — how shall I call it? — of pallid haughtiness, say, or rather an austere reserve about him, which had positively awed me into my tame compliance with his eccentricities, when I had feared to ask him to do the slightest incidental thing for me, even though I might know, from his long-continued motionlessness, that behind his screen he must be standing in one of those dead-wall reveries of his.

Revolving all these things, and coupling them with the recently discovered 95 fact, that he made my office his constant abiding place and home, and not forgetful of his morbid moodiness; revolving all these things, a prudential feeling began to steal over me. My first emotions had been those of pure melancholy and sincerest pity; but just in proportion as the forlornness of Bartleby grew and grew to my imagination, did that same melancholy merge into fear, that pity into repulsion. So true it is, and so terrible, too, that up to a certain point the thought or sight of misery enlists our best affections; but, in certain special cases, beyond that point it does not. They err who would assert that invariably this is owing to the inherent selfishness of the human heart. It rather proceeds from a certain hopelessness of remedying excessive and organic ill. To a sensitive being, pity is not seldom pain. And when at last it is perceived that such pity cannot lead to effectual succor, common sense bids the soul be rid of it. What I saw that morning persuaded me that the scrivener was the victim of innate and incurable disorder. I might give alms to his body; but his body did not pain him; it was his soul that suffered, and his soul I could not reach.

I did not accomplish the purpose of going to Trinity Church that morning. Somehow, the things I had seen disqualified me for the time from church-going. I walked homeward, thinking what I would do with Bartleby. Finally, I resolved upon this — I would put certain calm questions to him the next morning, touching his history, etc., and if he declined to answer them openly and unreservedly (and I supposed he would prefer not), then to give him a twenty dollar bill over and above whatever I might owe him, and tell him his services were no longer required; but that if in any other way I could assist him, I would be happy to do so, especially if he desired to return to his native place, wherever that might be, I would willingly help to defray the expenses. Moreover, if, after reaching home, he found himself at any time in want of aid, a letter from him would be sure of a reply.

The next morning came.

"Bartleby," said I, gently calling to him behind his screen.

No reply.

"Bartleby," said I, in a still gentler tone, "come here; I am not going to ask you to do anything you would prefer not to do — I simply wish to speak to you." 100

Upon this he noiselessly slid into view.

"Will you tell me, Bartleby, where you were born?"

"I would prefer not to."

"Will you tell me *anything* about yourself?"

"I would prefer not to." 105

"But what reasonable objection can you have to speak to me? I feel friendly towards you."

He did not look at me while I spoke, but kept his glance fixed upon my bust of Cicero, which, as I then sat, was directly behind me, some six inches above my head.

"What is your answer, Bartleby?" said I, after waiting a considerable time for a reply, during which his countenance remained immovable, only there was the faintest conceivable tremor of the white attenuated mouth.

"At present I prefer to give no answer," he said, and retired into his hermitage.

It was rather weak in me I confess, but his manner, on this occasion, nettled 110 me. Not only did there seem to lurk in it a certain calm disdain, but his perverseness seemed ungrateful, considering the undeniable good usage and indulgence he had received from me.

Again I sat ruminating what I should do. Mortified as I was at his behavior, and resolved as I had been to dismiss him when I entered my office, nevertheless I strangely felt something superstitious knocking at my heart, and forbidding me to carry out my purpose, and denouncing me for a villain if I dared to breathe one bitter word against this forlornest of mankind. At last, familiarly drawing my chair behind his screen, I sat down and said: "Bartleby, never mind, then, about revealing your history; but let me entreat you, as a friend, to comply as far as may be with the usages of this office. Say now, you will help to examine papers tomorrow or next day: in short, say now, that in a day or two you will begin to be a little reasonable: — say so, Bartleby."

"At present I would prefer not to be a little reasonable," was his mildly cadaverous reply.

Just then the folding-doors opened, and Nippers approached. He seemed suffering from an unusually bad night's rest, induced by severer indigestion than common. He overheard those final words of Bartleby.

"*Prefer not*, eh?" gritted Nippers — "I'd *prefer* him, if I were you, sir," addressing me — "I'd *prefer* him; I'd give him preferences, the stubborn mule! What is it, sir, pray, that he *prefers* not to do now?"

Bartleby moved not a limb. 115

"Mr. Nippers," said I, "I'd prefer that you would withdraw for the present."

Somehow, of late, I had got into the way of involuntarily using this word "prefer" upon all sorts of not exactly suitable occasions. And I trembled to think that my contact with the scrivener had already and seriously affected me in a mental way. And what further and deeper aberration might it not yet produce? This apprehension had not been without efficacy in determining me to summary measures.

As Nippers, looking very sour and sulky, was departing, Turkey blandly and deferentially approached.

"With submission, sir," said he, "yesterday I was thinking about Bartleby here, and I think that if he would but prefer to take a quart of good ale every day, it would do much towards mending him, and enabling him to assist in examining his papers."

"So you have got the word, too," said I, slightly excited. 120

"With submission, what word, sir?" asked Turkey, respectfully crowding himself into the contracted space behind the screen, and by so doing, making me jostle the scrivener. "What word, sir?"

"I would prefer to be left alone here," said Bartleby, as if offended at being mobbed in his privacy.

"*That's* the word, Turkey," said I — "*that's* it."

"Oh, *prefer?* oh yes — queer word. I never use it myself. But, sir, as I was saying, if he would but prefer —"

"Turkey," interrupted I, "you will please withdraw." 125

"Oh certainly, sir, if you prefer that I should."

As he opened the folding-door to retire, Nippers at his desk caught a glimpse of me, and asked whether I would prefer to have a certain paper copied on blue paper or white. He did not in the least roguishly accent the word "prefer." It was plain that it involuntarily rolled from his tongue. I thought to myself, surely I must get rid of a demented man, who already has in some degree turned the tongues, if not the heads of myself and clerks. But I thought it prudent not to break the dismission at once.

The next day I noticed that Bartleby did nothing but stand at his window in his dead-wall revery. Upon asking him why he did not write, he said that he had decided upon doing no more writing.

"Why, how now? what next?" exclaimed I, "do no more writing?"

"No more." 130

"And what is the reason?"

"Do you not see the reason for yourself?" he indifferently replied.

I looked steadfastly at him, and perceived that his eyes looked dull and glazed. Instantly it occurred to me, that his unexampled diligence in copying by his dim window for the first few weeks of his stay with me might have temporarily impaired his vision.

I was touched. I said something in condolence with him. I hinted that of course he did wisely in abstaining from writing for a while; and urged him to embrace that opportunity of taking wholesome exercise in the open air. This, however, he did not do. A few days after this, my other clerks being absent, and being in a great hurry to dispatch certain letters by the mail, I thought that, having nothing else earthly to do, Bartleby would surely be less inflexible than usual, and carry these letters to the Post Office. But he blankly declined. So, much to my inconvenience, I went myself.

Still added days went by. Whether Bartleby's eyes improved or not, I could not 135 say. To all appearance, I thought they did. But when I asked him if they did, he vouchsafed no answer. At all events, he would do no copying. At last, in replying to my urgings, he informed me that he had permanently given up copying.

"What!" exclaimed I; "suppose your eyes should get entirely well — better than ever before — would you not copy then?"

"I have given up copying," he answered, and slid aside.

He remained as ever, a fixture in my chamber. Nay — if that were possible — he became still more of a fixture than before. What was to be done? He would do nothing in the office; why should he stay there? In plain fact, he had now become a millstone to me, not only useless as a necklace, but afflictive to bear. Yet I was sorry for him. I speak less than truth when I say that, on his own account, he occasioned me uneasiness. If he would but have named a single relative or friend, I would instantly have written, and urged their taking the poor fellow away to some convenient retreat. But he seemed alone, absolutely alone in the universe. A bit of wreck in the mid-Atlantic. At length, necessities connected with my business tyrannized over all other considerations. Decently as I could, I told Bartleby that in six days' time he must unconditionally leave the office. I warned him to take measures, in the interval, for procuring some other abode. I offered to assist him in this endeavor, if he himself would but take the first step towards a removal. "And when you finally quit me, Bartleby," added I, "I shall see that you go not away entirely unprovided. Six days from this hour, remember."

At the expiration of that period, I peeped behind the screen, and lo! Bartleby was there.

I buttoned up my coat, balanced myself; advanced slowly towards him, touched his shoulder, and said, "The time has come; you must quit this place; I am sorry for you; here is money; but you must go." 140

"I would prefer not," he replied, with his back still towards me.

"You *must*."

He remained silent.

Now I had an unbounded confidence in this man's common honesty. He had frequently restored to me sixpences and shillings carelessly dropped upon the floor, for I am apt to be very reckless in such shirt-button affairs. The proceeding, then, which followed will not be deemed extraordinary.

"Bartleby," said I, "I owe you twelve dollars on account; here are thirty-two, the odd twenty are yours — Will you take it?" and I handed the bills towards him. 145

But he made no motion.

"I will leave them here, then," putting them under a weight on the table. Then taking my hat and cane and going to the door, I tranquilly turned and added — "After you have removed your things from these offices, Bartleby, you will of course lock the door — since every one is now gone for the day but you — and if you please, slip your key underneath the mat, so that I may have it in the morning. I shall not see you again; so good-bye to you. If, hereafter, in your new place of abode, I can be of any service to you, do not fail to advise me by letter. Good-bye, Bartleby, and fare you well."

But he answered not a word; like the last column of some ruined temple, he remained standing mute and solitary in the middle of the otherwise deserted room.

As I walked home in a pensive mood, my vanity got the better of my pity. I could not but highly plume myself on my masterly management in getting rid of Bartleby. Masterly I call it, and such it must appear to any dispassionate thinker. The beauty of my procedure seemed to consist in its perfect quietness. There was no vulgar bullying, no bravado of any sort, no choleric hectoring, and striding to and fro across the apartment, jerking out vehement commands for Bartleby to bundle himself off with his beggarly traps. Nothing of the kind. Without loudly bidding Bartleby depart — as an inferior genius might have done — I *assumed* the ground that depart he must; and upon that assumption built all I had to say. The more I thought over my procedure, the more I was charmed with it. Nevertheless, next morning, upon awakening, I had my doubts — I had somehow slept off the fumes of vanity. One of the coolest and wisest hours a man has, is just after he awakes in the morning. My procedure seemed as sagacious as ever — but only in theory. How it would prove in practice — there was the rub. It was truly a beautiful thought to have assumed Bartleby's departure; but, after all, that assumption was simply my own, and none of Bartleby's. The great point was, not whether I had assumed that he would quit me, but whether he would prefer to do so. He was more a man of preferences than assumptions.

After breakfast, I walked down town, arguing the probabilities *pro* and *con.*   150 One moment I thought it would prove a miserable failure, and Bartleby would be found all alive at my office as usual; the next moment it seemed certain that I should find his chair empty. And so I kept veering about. At the corner of Broadway and Canal Street, I saw quite an excited group of people standing in earnest conversation.

"I'll take odds he doesn't," said a voice as I passed.

"Doesn't go? — done!" said I, "put up your money."

I was instinctively putting my hand in my pocket to produce my own, when I remembered that this was an election day. The words I had overheard bore no reference to Bartleby, but to the success or non-success of some candidate for the mayoralty. In my intent frame of mind, I had, as it were, imagined that all Broadway shared in my excitement, and were debating the same question with me. I passed on, very thankful that the uproar of the street screened my momentary absent-mindedness.

As I had intended, I was earlier than usual at my office door. I stood listening for a moment. All was still. He must be gone. I tried the knob. The door was locked. Yes, my procedure had worked to a charm; he indeed must be vanished. Yet a certain melancholy mixed with this: I was almost sorry for my brilliant success. I was fumbling under the door mat for the key, which Bartleby was to have left there for me, when accidentally my knee knocked against a panel, producing a summoning sound, and in response a voice came to me from within — "Not yet; I am occupied."

It was Bartleby.   155

I was thunderstruck. For an instant I stood like the man who, pipe in mouth, was killed one cloudless afternoon long ago in Virginia, by summer lightning; at his own warm open window he was killed, and remained leaning out there upon the dreamy afternoon, till some one touched him, when he fell.

"Not gone!" I murmured at last. But again obeying that wondrous ascendancy which the inscrutable scrivener had over me, and from which ascendancy, for all my chafing, I could not completely escape, I slowly went down stairs and out into the street, and while walking round the block, considered what I should next do in this unheard-of perplexity. Turn the man out by an actual thrusting I could not; to drive him away by calling him hard names would not do; calling in the police was an unpleasant idea; and yet, permit him to enjoy his cadaverous triumph over me — this, too, I could not think of. What was to be done? or, if nothing could be done, was there anything further that I could *assume* in the matter? Yes, as before I had prospectively assumed that Bartleby would depart, so now I might retrospectively assume that departed he was. In the legitimate carrying out of this assumption, I might enter my office in a great hurry, and pretending not to see Bartleby at all, walk straight against him as if he were air. Such a proceeding would in a singular degree have the appearance of a home-thrust. It was hardly possible that Bartleby could withstand such an application of the doctrine of assumption. But upon second thoughts the success of the plan seemed rather dubious. I resolved to argue the matter over with him again.

"Bartleby," said I, entering the office, with a quietly severe expression, "I am seriously displeased. I am pained, Bartleby. I had thought better of you. I had imagined you of such a gentlemanly organization, that in any delicate dilemma a slight hint would suffice — in short, an assumption. But it appears I am deceived. Why," I added, unaffectedly starting, "you have not even touched that money yet," pointing to it, just where I had left it the evening previous.

He answered nothing.

"Will you, or will you not, quit me?" I now demanded in a sudden passion, 160 advancing close to him.

"I would prefer *not* to quit you," he replied, gently emphasizing the *not.*

"What earthly right have you to stay here? Do you pay any rent? Do you pay my taxes? Or is this property yours?"

He answered nothing.

"Are you ready to go on and write now? Are your eyes recovered? Could you copy a small paper for me this morning? or help examine a few lines? or step round to the Post Office? In a word, will you do anything at all, to give a coloring to your refusal to depart the premises?"

He silently retired into his hermitage. 165

I was now in such a state of nervous resentment that I thought it but prudent to check myself at present from further demonstrations. Bartleby and I were alone. I remembered the tragedy of the unfortunate Adams and the still more unfortunate Colt° in the solitary office of the latter; and how poor Colt, being dreadfully incensed by Adams, and imprudently permitting himself to get wildly excited, was at unawares hurried into his fatal act — an act which certainly no man could possibly deplore more than the actor himself. Often it had occurred to me in my ponderings upon the subject that had that altercation taken place in the public street, or at a private residence, it would not have terminated as it did. It was the circumstance of being alone in a solitary office, up stairs, of a building entirely unhallowed by humanizing domestic associations — an uncarpeted office, doubtless, of a dusty, haggard sort of appearance — this it must have been, which greatly helped to enhance the irritable desperation of the hapless Colt.

But when this old Adam of resentment rose in me and tempted me concerning Bartleby, I grappled him and threw him. How? Why, simply by recalling the divine injunction: "A new commandment give I unto you, that ye love one another." Yes, this it was that saved me. Aside from higher considerations, charity often operates as a vastly wise and prudent principle — a great safeguard to its possessor. Men have committed murder for jealousy's sake, and anger's sake, and hatred's sake, and selfishness' sake, and spiritual pride's sake; but no man, that ever I heard of, ever committed a diabolical murder for sweet charity's sake. Mere self-interest, then, if no better motive can be enlisted, should, especially with high-tempered men, prompt all beings to charity and philanthropy. At any rate, upon the occasion in question, I strove to drown my exasperated feelings towards the scrivener by benevolently construing his conduct. Poor fellow, poor fellow! thought I, he don't mean anything; and besides, he has seen hard times, and ought to be indulged.

I endeavored, also, immediately to occupy myself, and at the same time to comfort my despondency. I tried to fancy, that in the course of the morning, at such time as might prove agreeable to him, Bartleby, of his own free accord, would emerge from his hermitage and take up some decided line of march in the direction of the door. But no. Half-past twelve o'clock came; Turkey began to glow in the face,

---

Adams . . . Colt: Samuel Adams was killed by John C. Colt, brother of the gun maker, during a quarrel in 1842. After a sensational court case, Colt committed suicide just before he was to be hanged.

overturn his inkstand, and become generally obstreperous; Nippers abated down into quietude and courtesy; Ginger Nut munched his noon apple; and Bartleby remained standing at his window in one of his profoundest dead-wall reveries. Will it be credited? Ought I to acknowledge it? That afternoon I left the office without saying one further word to him.

Some days now passed, during which, at leisure intervals I looked a little into "Edwards on the Will," and "Priestley on Necessity."° Under the circumstances, those books induced a salutary feeling. Gradually I slid into the persuasion that these troubles of mine, touching the scrivener, had been all predestined from eternity, and Bartleby was billeted upon me for some mysterious purpose of an all-wise Providence, which it was not for a mere mortal like me to fathom. Yes, Bartleby, stay there behind your screen, thought I; I shall persecute you no more; you are harmless and noiseless as any of these old chairs; in short, I never feel so private as when I know you are here. At last I see it, I feel it; I penetrate to the predestined purpose of my life. I am content. Others may have loftier parts to enact; but my mission in this world, Bartleby, is to furnish you with office-room for such period as you may see fit to remain.

I believe that this wise and blessed frame of mind would have continued with 170 me, had it not been for the unsolicited and uncharitable remarks obtruded upon me by my professional friends who visited the rooms. But thus it often is, that the constant friction of illiberal minds wears out at last the best resolves of the more generous. Though to be sure, when I reflected upon it, it was not strange that people entering my office should be struck by the peculiar aspect of the unaccountable Bartleby, and so be tempted to throw out some sinister observations concerning him. Sometimes an attorney, having business with me, and calling at my office, and finding no one but the scrivener there, would undertake to obtain some sort of precise information from him touching my whereabouts; but without heeding his idle talk, Bartleby would remain standing immovable in the middle of the room. So after contemplating him in that position for a time, the attorney would depart, no wiser than he came.

Also, when a reference was going on, and the room full of lawyers and witnesses, and business driving fast, some deeply-occupied legal gentleman present, seeing Bartleby wholly unemployed, would request him to run round to his (the legal gentleman's) office and fetch some papers for him. Thereupon, Bartleby would tranquilly decline, and yet remain idle as before. Then the lawyer would give a great stare, and turn to me. And what could I say? At last I was made aware that all through the circle of my professional acquaintance, a whisper of wonder was running round, having reference to the strange creature I kept at my office. This worried me very much. And as the idea came upon me of his possibly turning out a long-lived man, and keeping occupying my chambers, and denying my authority; and perplexing my visitors; and scandalizing my professional reputation; and casting a general gloom over the premises; keeping soul and body together to the last upon his savings (for doubtless he spent but half a dime a day), and in the end perhaps outlive me, and claim possession of my office by right of his perpetual occupancy: as all these dark anticipations crowded upon me more and more, and my friends continually intruded their relentless remarks upon the apparition in my room; a great change was wrought in me. I resolved to gather all my faculties together, and forever rid me of this intolerable incubus.

"*Edwards . . . Necessity*": Jonathan Edwards, in *Freedom of the Will* (1754), and Joseph Priestley, in *Doctrine of Philosophical Necessity* (1777), both argued that human beings do not have free will.

Ere revolving any complicated project, however, adapted to this end, I first simply suggested to Bartleby the propriety of his permanent departure. In a calm and serious tone, I commended the idea to his careful and mature consideration. But, having taken three days to meditate upon it, he apprised me, that his original determination remained the same; in short, that he still preferred to abide with me.

What shall I do? I now said to myself, buttoning up my coat to the last button. What shall I do? what ought I to do? what does conscience say I *should* do with this man, or, rather, ghost. Rid myself of him, I must; go, he shall. But how? You will not thrust him, the poor, pale, passive mortal — you will not thrust such a helpless creature out of your door? you will not dishonor yourself by such cruelty? No, I will not, I cannot do that. Rather would I let him live and die here, and then mason up his remains in the wall. What, then, will you do? For all your coaxing, he will not budge. Bribes he leaves under your own paper-weight on your table; in short, it is quite plain that he prefers to cling to you.

Then something severe, something unusual must be done. What! surely you will not have him collared by a constable, and commit his innocent pallor to the common jail? And upon what ground could you procure such a thing to be done? — a vagrant, is he? What! he a vagrant, a wanderer, who refuses to budge? It is because he will *not* be a vagrant, then, that you seek to count him *as* a vagrant. That is too absurd. No visible means of support: there I have him. Wrong again: for indubitably he *does* support himself, and that is the only unanswerable proof that any man can show of his possessing the means so to do. No more, then. Since he will not quit me, I must quit him. I will change my offices; I will move elsewhere, and give him fair notice, that if I find him on my new premises I will then proceed against him as a common trespasser.

Acting accordingly, next day I thus addressed him: "I find these chambers too far from the City Hall; the air is unwholesome. In a word, I propose to remove my offices next week, and shall no longer require your services. I tell you this now, in order that you may seek another place."

He made no reply, and nothing more was said.

On the appointed day I engaged carts and men, proceeded to my chambers, and having but little furniture, everything was removed in a few hours. Throughout, the scrivener remained standing behind the screen, which I directed to be removed the last thing. It was withdrawn; and, being folded up like a huge folio, left him the motionless occupant of a naked room. I stood in the entry watching him a moment, while something from within me upbraided me.

I re-entered, with my hand in my pocket — and — and my heart in my mouth.

"Good-bye, Bartleby; I am going — good-bye, and God some way bless you; and take that," slipping something in his hand. But it dropped upon the floor, and then — strange to say — I tore myself from him whom I had so longed to be rid of.

Established in my new quarters, for a day or two I kept the door locked, and started at every footfall in the passages. When I returned to my rooms, after any little absence, I would pause at the threshold for an instant, and attentively listen, ere applying my key. But these fears were needless. Bartleby never came nigh me.

I thought all was going well, when a perturbed-looking stranger visited me, inquiring whether I was the person who had recently occupied rooms at No. — Wall Street.

Full of forebodings, I replied that I was.

"Then, sir," said the stranger, who proved a lawyer, "you are responsible for the man you left there. He refuses to do any copying; he refuses to do anything; he says he prefers not to; and he refuses to quit the premises."

"I am very sorry, sir," said I, with assumed tranquillity, but an inward tremor, "but, really, the man you allude to is nothing to me — he is no relation or apprentice of mine, that you should hold me responsible for him."

"In mercy's name, who is he?" 185

"I certainly cannot inform you. I know nothing about him. Formerly I employed him as a copyist; but he has done nothing for me now for some time past."

"I shall settle him, then — good morning, sir."

Several days passed, and I heard nothing more; and, though I often felt a charitable prompting to call at the place and see poor Bartleby, yet a certain squeamishness, of I know not what, withheld me.

All is over with him, by this time, thought I, at last, when, through another week, no further intelligence reached me. But, coming to my room the day after, I found several persons waiting at my door in a high state of nervous excitement.

"That's the man — here he comes," cried the foremost one, whom I recognized 190 as the lawyer who had previously called upon me alone.

"You must take him away, sir, at once," cried a portly person among them, advancing upon me, and whom I knew to be the landlord of No. — Wall Street. "These gentlemen, my tenants, cannot stand it any longer; Mr. B —— ," pointing to the lawyer, "has turned him out of his room, and he now persists in haunting the building generally, sitting upon the banisters of the stairs by day, and sleeping in the entry by night. Everybody is concerned; clients are leaving the offices; some fears are entertained of a mob; something you must do, and that without delay."

Aghast at this torrent, I fell back before it, and would fain have locked myself in my new quarters. In vain I persisted that Bartleby was nothing to me — no more than to any one else. In vain — I was the last person known to have anything to do with him, and they held me to the terrible account. Fearful, then, of being exposed in the papers (as one person present obscurely threatened), I considered the matter, and, at length, said, that if the lawyer would give me a confidential interview with the scrivener, in his (the lawyer's) own room, I would, that afternoon, strive my best to rid them of the nuisance they complained of.

Going up stairs to my old haunt, there was Bartleby silently sitting upon the banister at the landing.

"What are you doing here, Bartleby?" said I.

"Sitting upon the banister," he mildly replied. 195

I motioned him into the lawyer's room, who then left us.

"Bartleby," said I, "are you aware that you are the cause of great tribulation to me, by persisting in occupying the entry after being dismissed from the office?"

No answer.

"Now one of two things must take place. Either you must do something, or something must be done to you. Now what sort of business would you like to engage in? Would you like to re-engage in copying for some one?"

"No; I would prefer not to make any change." 200

"Would you like a clerkship in a dry-goods store?"

"There is too much confinement about that. No, I would not like a clerkship; but I am not particular."

"Too much confinement," I cried, "why, you keep yourself confined all the time!"

"I would prefer not to take a clerkship," he rejoined, as if to settle that little item at once.

"How would a bar-tender's business suit you? There is no trying of the eye- 205 sight in that."

"I would not like it at all; though, as I said before, I am not particular."

His unwonted wordiness inspirited me. I returned to the charge.

"Well, then, would you like to travel through the country collecting bills for the merchants? That would improve your health."

"No, I would prefer to be doing something else."

"How, then, would going as a companion to Europe, to entertain some young 210
gentleman with your conversation — how would that suit you?"

"Not at all. It does not strike me that there is anything definite about that. I like to be stationary. But I am not particular."

"Stationary you shall be, then," I cried, now losing all patience, and, for the first time in all my exasperating connection with him, fairly flying into a passion. "If you do not go away from these premises before night, I shall feel bound — indeed, I *am* bound — to — to quit the premises myself!" I rather absurdly concluded, knowing not with what possible threat to try to frighten his immobility into compliance. Despairing of all further efforts, I was precipitately leaving him, when a final thought occurred to me — one which had not been wholly unindulged before.

"Bartleby," said I, in the kindest tone I could assume under such exciting circumstances, "will you go home with me now — not to my office, but my dwelling — and remain there till we can conclude upon some convenient arrangement for you at our leisure? Come, let us start now, right away."

"No: at present I would prefer not to make any change at all."

I answered nothing; but, effectually dodging every one by the suddenness and 215
rapidity of my flight, rushed from the building, ran up Wall Street towards Broadway, and, jumping into the first omnibus, was soon removed from pursuit. As soon as tranquillity returned, I distinctly perceived that I had now done all that I possibly could, both in respect to the demands of the landlord and his tenants, and with regard to my own desire and sense of duty, to benefit Bartleby, and shield him from rude persecution. I now strove to be entirely care-free and quiescent; and my conscience justified me in the attempt; though, indeed, it was not so successful as I could have wished. So fearful was I of being again hunted out by the incensed landlord and his exasperated tenants, that, surrendering my business to Nippers, for a few days, I drove about the upper part of the town and through the suburbs, in my rockaway; crossed over to Jersey City and Hoboken, and paid fugitive visits to Manhattanville and Astoria. In fact, I almost lived in my rockaway for the time.

When again I entered my office, lo, a note from the landlord lay upon the desk. I opened it with trembling hands. It informed me that the writer had sent to the police, and had Bartleby removed to the Tombs as a vagrant. Moreover, since I knew more about him than any one else, he wished me to appear at that place, and make a suitable statement of the facts. These tidings had a conflicting effect upon me. At first I was indignant; but, at last, almost approved. The landlord's energetic, summary disposition, had led him to adopt a procedure which I do not think I would have decided upon myself; and yet, as a last resort, under such peculiar circumstances, it seemed the only plan.

As I afterwards learned, the poor scrivener, when told that he must be conducted to the Tombs, offered not the slightest obstacle, but, in his pale, unmoving way, silently acquiesced.

Some of the compassionate and curious by-standers joined the party; and headed by one of the constables arm-in-arm with Bartleby, the silent procession filed its way through all the noise, and heat, and joy of the roaring thoroughfares at noon.

The same day I received the note, I went to the Tombs, or, to speak more properly, the Halls of Justice. Seeking the right officer, I stated the purpose of my call, and was informed that the individual I described was, indeed, within. I then assured the functionary that Bartleby was a perfectly honest man, and greatly to be compassionated, however unaccountably eccentric. I narrated all I knew, and closed by suggesting the idea of letting him remain in as indulgent confinement as possible, till something less harsh might be done — though, indeed, I hardly knew what. At all events, if nothing else could be decided upon, the almshouse must receive him. I then begged to have an interview.

Being under no disgraceful charge, and quite serene and harmless in all his ways, they had permitted him freely to wander about the prison, and, especially, in the inclosed grass-platted yards thereof. And so I found him there, standing all alone in the quietest of the yards, his face towards a high wall, while all around, from the narrow slits of the jail windows, I thought I saw peering out upon him the eyes of murderers and thieves. 220

"Bartleby!"

"I know you," he said, without looking round — "and I want nothing to say to you."

"It was not I that brought you here, Bartleby," said I, keenly pained at his implied suspicion. "And to you, this should not be so vile a place. Nothing reproachful attaches to you by being here. And see, it is not so sad a place as one might think. Look, there is the sky, and here is the grass."

"I know where I am," he replied, but would say nothing more, and so I left him.

As I entered the corridor again, a broad meat-like man, in an apron, accosted me, and, jerking his thumb over his shoulder, said — "Is that your friend?" 225

"Yes."

"Does he want to starve? If he does, let him live on the prison fare, that's all."

"Who are you?" asked I, not knowing what to make of such an unofficially speaking person in such a place.

"I am the grub-man. Such gentlemen as have friends here, hire me to provide them with something good to eat."

"Is this so?" said I, turning the turnkey. 230

He said it was.

"Well, then," said I, slipping some silver into the grub-man's hands (for so they called him), "I want you to give particular attention to my friend there; let him have the best dinner you can get. And you must be as polite to him as possible."

"Introduce me, will you?" said the grub-man, looking at me with an expression which seemed to say he was all impatience for an opportunity to give a specimen of his breeding.

Thinking it would prove of benefit to the scrivener, I acquiesced; and, asking the grub-man his name, went up with him to Bartleby.

"Bartleby, this is a friend; you will find him very useful to you." 235

"Your sarvant, sir, your sarvant," said the grub-man, making a low salutation behind his apron. "Hope you find it pleasant here, sir; nice grounds — cool apartments — hope you'll stay with us some time — try to make it agreeable. What will you have for dinner to-day?"

"I prefer not to dine to-day," said Bartleby, turning away. "It would disagree with me; I am unused to dinners." So saying, he slowly moved to the other side of the inclosure, and took up a position fronting the deadwall.

"How's this?" said the grub-man, addressing me with a stare of astonishment. "He's odd, ain't he?"

"I think he is a little deranged," said I, sadly.

"Deranged? deranged is it? Well, now, upon my word, I thought that friend of 240 yourn was a gentleman forger; they are always pale and genteel-like, them forgers. I can't help pity 'em — can't help it, sir. Did you know Monroe Edwards?" he added, touchingly, and paused. Then, laying his hand piteously on my shoulder, sighed, "he died of consumption at Sing-Sing. So you weren't acquainted with Monroe?"

"No, I was never socially acquainted with any forgers. But I cannot stop longer. Look to my friend yonder. You will not lose by it. I will see you again."

Some few days after this, I again obtained admission to the Tombs, and went through the corridors in quest of Bartleby; but without finding him.

"I saw him coming from his cell not long ago," said a turnkey, "may be he's gone to loiter in the yards."

So I went in that direction.

"Are you looking for the silent man?" said another turnkey, passing me. "Yonder 245 he lies — sleeping in the yard there. 'Tis not twenty minutes since I saw him lie down."

The yard was entirely quiet. It was not accessible to the common prisoners. The surrounding walls, of amazing thickness, kept off all sounds behind them. The Egyptian character of the masonry weighed upon me with its gloom. But a soft imprisoned turf grew under foot. The heart of the eternal pyramids, it seemed, wherein, by some strange magic, through the clefts, grass-seed, dropped by birds, had sprung.

Strangely huddled at the base of the wall, his knees drawn up, and lying on his side, his head touching the cold stones, I saw the wasted Bartleby. But nothing stirred. I paused; then went close up to him; stooped over, and saw that his dim eyes were open; otherwise he seemed profoundly sleeping. Something prompted me to touch him. I felt his hand, when a tingling shiver ran up my arm and down my spine to my feet.

The round face of the grub-man peered upon me now. "His dinner is ready. Won't he dine to-day, either? Or does he live without dining?"

"Lives without dining," said I, and closed the eyes.

"Eh! — He's asleep, ain't he?" 250

"With kings and counselors,"° murmured I.

There would seem little need for proceeding further in this history. Imagination will readily supply the meagre recital of poor Bartleby's interment. But, ere parting with the reader, let me say, that if this little narrative has sufficiently interested him, to awaken curiosity as to who Bartleby was, and what manner of life he led prior to the present narrator's making his acquaintance, I can only reply, that in such curiosity I fully share, but am wholly unable to gratify it. Yet here I hardly know whether I should divulge one little item of rumor, which came to my ear a few months after the scrivener's decease. Upon what basis it rested, I could never ascertain; and hence, how true it is I cannot now tell. But, inasmuch as this vague report has not been without a certain suggestive interest to me, however sad, it may prove the same with some others; and so I will briefly mention it. The report was this: that Bartleby had been a subordinate clerk in the Dead Letter Office at Washington, from which he had been suddenly removed by a change in the administration. When I think over this rumor, hardly can I express the emotions which seize me. Dead letters! does it not sound like dead men? Conceive a man by nature and misfortune prone to a pallid hopelessness,

---

"With kings and counselors": From Job 3:13–14: "then had I been at rest, / With kings and counselors of the earth, / which built desolate places for themselves."

can any business seem more fitted to heighten it than that of continually handling these dead letters, and assorting them for the flames? For by the cart-load
they are annually burned. Sometimes from out the folded paper the pale clerk
takes a ring — the finger it was meant for, perhaps, moulders in the grave; a bank-
note sent in swiftest charity — he whom it would relieve, nor eats nor hungers any
more; pardon for those who died despairing; hope for those who died unhoping;
good tidings for those who died stifled by unrelieved calamities. On errands of
life, these letters speed to death.

Ah, Bartleby! Ah, humanity!

CONSIDERATIONS FOR CRITICAL THINKING AND WRITING

1. FIRST RESPONSE. How does the lawyer's description of himself serve to characterize him? Why is it significant that he is a lawyer? Are his understandings
   and judgments about Bartleby and himself always sound?

2. Why do you think Turkey, Nippers, and Ginger Nut are introduced to the
   reader before Bartleby?

3. Describe Bartleby's physical characteristics. How is his physical description a
   foreshadowing of what happens to him?

4. How does Bartleby's "I would prefer not to" affect the routine of the lawyer
   and his employees?

5. What is the significance of the subtitle: "A Story of Wall Street"?

6. Who is the protagonist? Whose story is it?

7. Does the lawyer change during the story? Does Bartleby? Who is the
   antagonist?

8. What motivates Bartleby's behavior? Why do you think Melville withholds
   the information about the Dead Letter Office until the end of the story? Does
   this background adequately explain Bartleby?

9. Does Bartleby have any lasting impact on the lawyer?

10. Do you think Melville sympathizes more with Bartleby or with the lawyer?

11. Describe the lawyer's changing attitudes toward Bartleby.

12. Consider how this story could be regarded as a kind of protest with nonnego-
    tiable demands.

13. Discuss the story's humor and how it affects your response to Bartleby.

14. Trace your emotional reaction to Bartleby as he is revealed in the story.

15. CRITICAL STRATEGIES. Read the section on biographical criticism (pp. 1647–49)
    in Chapter 51, "Critical Strategies for Reading," and use the library or go
    online to learn about Melville's reputation as a writer at the time of his writing
    "Bartleby." How might this information produce a provocative biographical
    approach to the story?

CONNECTIONS TO OTHER SELECTIONS

1. Compare Bartleby's withdrawal from life with that of the protagonist in Gail
   Godwin's "A Sorrowful Woman" (p. 39). Why does each character choose
   death?

2. How is Melville's use of Bartleby's experience in the Dead Letter Office similar to
   Nathaniel Hawthorne's use of Brown's forest encounter with the devil in "Young
   Goodman Brown" (p. 321)? Why is each experience crucial to an understanding
   of what informs the behavior of these characters?

Perspectives

NATHANIEL HAWTHORNE (1804–1864)

On Herman Melville's Philosophic Stance 1856

[Melville] stayed with us from Tuesday till Thursday; and, on the intervening day, we took a pretty long walk together, and sat down in a hollow among the sand hills (sheltering ourselves from the high, cool wind) and smoked a cigar. Melville, as he always does, began to reason of Providence and futurity, and of everything that lies beyond human ken, and informed me that he had "pretty much made up his mind to be annihilated"; but still he does not seem to rest in that anticipation; and, I think, will never rest until he gets hold of a definite belief. It is strange how he persists — and has persisted ever since I knew him, and probably long before — in wandering to-and-fro over these deserts, as dismal and monotonous as the sand hills amid which we were sitting. He can neither believe, nor be comfortable in his unbelief; and he is too honest and courageous not to try to do one or the other. If he were a religious man, he would be one of the most truly religious and reverential; he has a very high and noble nature, and better worth immortality than most of us.

From The American Notebooks

CONSIDERATIONS FOR CRITICAL THINKING AND WRITING

1. How does this description of Melville shed light on the central concerns of "Bartleby, the Scrivener"?
2. Which side does Hawthorne seem to be on — "belief" or "unbelief"? Why?
3. Compare Hawthorne's description with Melville's view of Hawthorne (p. 354). What attitudes about life do they share?
4. Write an essay about the issue of "belief" and "unbelief" in "Bartleby, the Scrivener" and Ernest Hemingway's "Soldier's Home" (p. 162).

DAN McCALL (1940–2012)

On the Lawyer's Character in "Bartleby, the Scrivener" 1989

The overwhelming majority of the Bartleby Industry reads the narrator of the story in a way that is not only different from mine but quite incompatible with mine. Every virtue I see in the man, they see as a vice; where I see his strength, they see his weakness; what I see as his genuine responsiveness, they see as his cold self-absorption. Some critics read the story as I do, but we are in a distinct minority. There are several reasons this should be so, and I think I understand at least some of them, but first I should like to present as fairly as I can the majority opinion.

Robert Weisbuch, who has said the Lawyer is Charles Dickens, refers to the Lawyer as "unnatural," "anti-natural," "lifeless," "self-satisfied," "pompous," and "rationalizing." The Lawyer "investigates Bartleby but refuses authentic emotional commitment in so doing," and "Bartleby rightly refuses to credit the Lawyer's false commitment." The Lawyer is guilty of "toadyism" and his final heartbroken outburst, "Ah, Bartleby! Ah, humanity!" is no more than "a someways hollow and unfeeling exclamation."[1] Another critic calls the Lawyer a "smug fool" who is "terribly unkind to a very sick man."[2] I had always thought of the Lawyer as a kind of stand-in for us, a figure we could identify with as we struggled to understand Bartleby. On the contrary, the narrator is "deficient in humanity and quite obtuse towards human beings." I must have had it backwards, for "surely this was Melville's intention: to have his reader *not* sympathize with the Lawyer, *not* to identify with him, *not* to put himself in the Lawyer's place" (*his* italics, not mine).[3] Another critic says, "The narrator attains new heights of vague sentimentality rather than a peak of awareness in his climactic and highly revealing sigh: 'Ah, Bartleby! Ah, humanity!'" This reader provides dismissive certainty in answering the question

> Who then is Melville's narrator? He is the sort of man one tends to find in high places: the snug man whose worldly success has convinced him that this is the "best of all possible worlds," and whose virtues cluster around a "prudential" concern for maintaining his own situation. The narrator can never fully understand or truly befriend Bartleby because the narrator is simply too complacent, both philosophically and morally, to sympathize with human dissatisfaction and despair.[4]

Still another reader tells us the Lawyer's commentary "rings with blasphemy" and demonstrates "grotesque manifestations of diseased conscience."[5]

Authority is the enemy here. In the extended quotation just above it is taken for granted that the "sort of man one tends to find in high places" is superficial and selfish. Worldly success is bad for the character. The Lawyer has to be bad, or he wouldn't be in an office on Wall Street. Hershel Parker tells us that "our ultimate opinion" of the Lawyer "is not contempt so much as bleak astonishment at his secure blindness. With a bitterer irony than the narrator is capable of, we murmur something like 'Ah, narrator! Ah, humanity!' In his self-consciously eloquent sequel, after all, the lawyer has merely made his last cheap purchase of a 'delicious self-approval.'" Parker maintains that when "this easy-conscienced" man speaks of kings and counselors, "he is experiencing a comfortable, self-indulgent variety of melancholy"; when he quotes words from the Book of Job he does so "with prideful aptness," and "characteristically perverts them from profound lament to sonorous urbanity."[6]

This last feature of Parker's argument is interesting to me because it reminds me of the first time I read the story, at eighteen. I was overwhelmed by the discovery that Bartleby had died, and I didn't know that "With kings and counselors" was a quotation from the Book of Job. The phrase "With kings and counselors" seemed to me majestic and solemn and final. That "murmured I" put a deep hush around

---

[1] Robert Weisbuch, "Melville's 'Bartleby' and the Dead Letter of Charles Dickens," *Atlantic Double-Cross: American Literature and British Influence in the Age of Emerson* (Chicago: University of Chicago Press, 1986), pp. 44, 45–47.

[2] David Shusterman, "The 'Reader Fallacy' and 'Bartleby, the Scrivener,'" *New England Quarterly* 45 (March 1972): 122–23.

[3] Ibid., p. 121.

[4] Allan Emery, "The Alternatives of Melville's 'Bartleby,'" *Nineteenth-Century Fiction* 31 (1976): 186–87.

[5] William Bysshe Stein, "Bartleby: The Christian Conscience," in *Melville Annual 1965, A Symposium: "Bartleby, the Scrivener,"* ed. Howard P. Vincent (Kent, Ohio: Kent State University Press, 1966), p. 107.

[6] Hershel Parker, "The Sequel in 'Bartleby,'" in *Bartleby the Inscrutable: A Collection of Commentary on Herman Melville's Tale "Bartleby, the Scrivener,"* ed. M. Thomas Inge (Hamden, Conn.: Archon Books, 1979), pp. 159–65, 163–64.

it. But it never occurred to me that the man who said those words was "easy-conscienced" or "self-indulgent" or the sort of man who "characteristically perverts" a "profound lament to sonorous urbanity." The figure of Bartleby seemed so weird and funny and painful, his death at once inevitable and shocking, that I did not see it as an occasion for the man who was telling me about it to make a "last cheap purchase" of "delicious self-approval." I trusted that Lawyer.

Thirty years later, I still do. He seems to me extremely intelligent, whimsical and ironic, generous, self-aware, passionate, and thoroughly competent.

From *The Silence of Bartleby*

Considerations for Critical Thinking and Writing

1. How does McCall characterize the "majority opinion" on the lawyer's character? What is his opinion of the lawyer?

2. How does McCall's opinion of the lawyer compare with Hawthorne's opinion of Herman Melville in the preceding Perspective?

3. Write an essay explaining whether you find the "majority opinion" or McCall's view of the lawyer more convincing.

ENCOUNTERING FICTION: COMICS AND GRAPHIC STORIES

LYNDA BARRY (B. 1956), *Spelling*

Lynda Barry is the creator of the syndicated comic strip *Ernie Pook's Comeek* and author of more than a dozen illustrated books that she classifies as "autobifictionalography," or part fiction, part autobiography. Barry's characters range from the "life-grooving" Marlys (featured in the following strip, from *Down the Street* [1986]), to herself in *One Hundred Demons* (2002). Her work focuses on childhood and adolescent experience, and among her influences are Dr. Seuss, R. Crumb, Grimm's fairy tales, *Ripley's Believe It or Not!*, cave paintings, and religious art of India. "When I write," said Barry in a 2003 interview, "I don't plan the story first, I don't pencil anything in. . . . I try really hard not to plan anything beyond the movement of the brush and the next word." Barry's first comic strip was published in 1977 in the Evergreen State College student newspaper, where friend and classmate Matt Groening served as coeditor. She lives in Wisconsin.

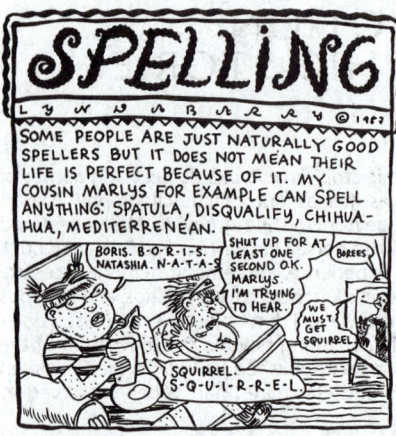

"Spelling" by Lynda Barry from *The! Greatest! Of Marlys!* (Sasquatch Books 2000.) Copyright © 2000 by Lynda Barry. Used courtesy of Darhansoff and Verrill Literary Agents.

CONSIDERATIONS AND CONNECTION TO ANOTHER SELECTION

1. How does Barry's drawing serve to characterize Marlys? Write a paragraph that articulates what the drawing shows about Marlys's character.

2. Why is spelling an especially appropriate and symbolic endeavor in this narrative?

3. Try drawing and writing a fifth frame for "Spelling" that depicts Marlys after her job interview.

4. CREATIVE RESPONSE. Reread the brief excerpt from *Hard Times* by Charles Dickens (p. 108) and use it as an inspiration to write a vivid, detailed one-paragraph description of Marlys that captures her character for you.

5

Setting

My role is to look at the world, get a true,
not an idealized vision of it and hand it over
to you in fictional form.
— FAY WELDON

© Steve Ellison/Corbis.

Setting is the context in which the action of a story occurs. The major elements
of setting are time, place, and the social environment that frames the characters. These elements establish the world in which the characters act. In most
stories they also serve as more than backgrounds and furnishings. If we are
sensitive to the contexts provided by setting, we are better able to understand
the behavior of the characters and the significance of their actions. It may be
tempting to read quickly through a writer's descriptions and ignore the details
of the setting once a geographic location and a historic period are established.
But if you read a story so impatiently, the significance of the setting may slip by
you. That kind of reading is similar to traveling on interstate highways: a lot of
ground gets covered, but very little is seen along the way.

Settings can be used to evoke a mood or atmosphere that will prepare the reader for what is to come. In "Young Goodman Brown" (p. 321),
Nathaniel Hawthorne has his pious protagonist leave his wife and village one
night to keep an appointment in a New England forest near the site of the

seventeenth-century witch trials. This is Hawthorne's description of Brown entering the forest:

> He had taken a dreary road, darkened by all the gloomiest trees of the forest, which barely stood aside to let the narrow path creep through, and closed immediately behind. It was all as lonely as could be; and there is this peculiarity in such a solitude, that the traveler knows not who may be concealed by the innumerable trunks and the thick boughs overhead; so that with lonely footsteps he may yet be passing through an unseen multitude.

The atmosphere established in this descriptive setting is somber and threatening. Careful reading reveals that the forest is not simply the woods; it is a moral wilderness, where anything can happen.

If we ask why a writer chooses to include certain details in a work, then we are likely to make connections that relate the details to some larger purpose, such as the story's meaning. The final scene in Godwin's "A Sorrowful Woman" (p. 39) occurs in the spring, an ironic time for the action to be set because instead of rebirth for the protagonist there is only death. There is usually a reason for placing a story in a particular time or location. Katherine Mansfield has the protagonist in "Miss Brill" (p. 259) discover her loneliness and old age in a French vacation town, a lively atmosphere that serves as a cruel contrast to an elderly (and foreign) lady's painful realization.

Melville's "Bartleby, the Scrivener" (p. 130) takes on meaning as Bartleby's "dead-wall reveries" begin to reflect his shattered vision of life. He is surrounded by walls. A folding screen separates him from others in the office; he is isolated. The office window faces walls; there is no view to relieve the deadening work. Bartleby faces a wall at the prison where he dies; the final wall is death. As the subtitle indicates, this is "A Story of Wall Street." Unless the geographic location or the physical details of a story are used merely as necessary props, they frequently shed light on character and action. All offices have walls, but Melville transforms the walls into an antagonist that represents the limitations Bartleby sees and feels all around him but does not speak of.

Time, location, and the physical features of a setting can all be relevant to the overall purpose of a story. So too is the social environment in which the characters are developed. In Faulkner's "A Rose for Emily" (p. 78) the changes in her southern town serve as a foil for Emily's tenacious hold on a lost past. She is regarded as a "fallen monument," as old-fashioned and peculiar as the "stubborn and coquettish decay" of her house. Neither she nor her house fits into the modern changes that are paving and transforming the town. Without the social context, this story would be mostly an account of a bizarre murder rather than an exploration of the conflicts Faulkner associated with the changing South. Setting enlarges the meaning of Emily's actions.

Some settings have traditional associations that are closely related to the action of a story. Adventure and romance, for example, flourish in the fertile soil of most exotic settings: the film version of Isak Dinesen's novel *Out of Africa* is a lush visual demonstration of how setting can play a significant role in generating the audience's expectations of love and excitement.

Sometimes, writers reverse traditional expectations. When a tranquil garden is the scene for a horrendously bloody murder, we are as much taken by surprise as the victim is. In John Updike's "A & P" (p. 200) there seems to be little possibility for heroic action in so mundane a place as a supermarket, but the setting turns out to be appropriate for the important, unexpected decision the protagonist makes about life. Traditional associations are also disrupted in "A Sorrowful Woman," in which Godwin disassociates home from the safety, security, and comfort usually connected with it by presenting the protagonist's home as a deadly trap. By drawing on traditional associations, a writer can fulfill or disrupt a reader's expectations about a setting in order to complement the elements of the story.

Not every story uses setting as a means of revealing mood, idea, meaning, or characters' actions. Some stories have no particularly significant setting. It is entirely possible to envision a story in which two characters speak to each other about a conflict between them and little or no mention is made of the time or place they inhabit. If, however, a shift in setting would make a serious difference to our understanding of a story, then the setting is probably an important element in the work. Consider how different "Bartleby, the Scrivener" would be if it were set in a relaxed, pleasant, sunny town in the South rather than in the grinding, limiting materialism of Wall Street. Bartleby's withdrawal from life would be less comprehensible and meaningful in such a setting. The setting is integral to that story.

The following three stories — Ernest Hemingway's "Soldier's Home," F. Scott Fitzgerald's "The Ice Palace," and Fay Weldon's "IND AFF, or Out of Love in Sarajevo" — include settings that serve to shape their meanings.

ERNEST HEMINGWAY (1899–1961)

In 1918, a year after graduating from high school in Oak Park, Illinois, Ernest Hemingway volunteered as an ambulance driver in World War I. At the Italian front, he was seriously wounded. This experience haunted him and many of the characters in his short stories and novels. *In Our Time* (1925) is a collection of short stories, including "Soldier's Home," that reflect some of Hemingway's own attempts to readjust to life back home after the war. *The Sun Also Rises* (1926), *A Farewell to Arms* (1929), and *For Whom the Bell Tolls* (1940) are also about war and its impact on people's lives. Hemingway courted violence all his life in war, the bullring, the boxing ring, and big game hunting. When he was sixty-two years old and terminally ill with cancer,

Ermeni Studio, Milan. Courtesy of the Ernest Hemingway Photographic Collection, John Fitzgerald Kennedy Library, Boston.

he committed suicide by shooting himself with a shotgun. "Soldier's Home" takes place in a small town in Oklahoma; the war, however, is never distant from the protagonist's mind as he struggles to come home again.

Soldier's Home 1925

Krebs went to the war from a Methodist college in Kansas. There is a picture which shows him among his fraternity brothers, all of them wearing exactly the same height and style collar. He enlisted in the Marines in 1917 and did not return to the United States until the second division returned from the Rhine in the summer of 1919.

There is a picture which shows him on the Rhine with two German girls and another corporal. Krebs and the corporal look too big for their uniforms. The German girls are not beautiful. The Rhine does not show in the picture.

By the time Krebs returned to his home town in Oklahoma the greeting of heroes was over. He came back much too late. The men from the town who had been drafted had all been welcomed elaborately on their return. There had been a great deal of hysteria. Now the reaction had set in. People seemed to think it was rather ridiculous for Krebs to be getting back so late, years after the war was over.

At first Krebs, who had been at Belleau Wood, Soissons, the Champagne, St. Mihiel, and in the Argonne° did not want to talk about the war at all. Later he felt the need to talk but no one wanted to hear about it. His town had heard too many atrocity stories to be thrilled by actualities. Krebs found that to be listened to at all he had to lie, and after he had done this twice he, too, had a reaction against the war and against talking about it. A distaste for everything that had happened to him in the war set in because of the lies he had told. All of the times that had been able to make him feel cool and clear inside himself when he thought of them; the times so long back when he had done the one thing, the only thing for a man to do, easily and naturally, when he might have done something else, now lost their cool, valuable quality and then were lost themselves.

His lies were quite unimportant lies and consisted in attributing to himself 5 things other men had seen, done, or heard of, and stating as facts certain apocryphal incidents familiar to all soldiers. Even his lies were not sensational at the pool room. His acquaintances, who had heard detailed accounts of German women found chained to machine guns in the Argonne forest and who could not comprehend, or were barred by their patriotism from interest in, any German machine gunners who were not chained, were not thrilled by his stories.

Krebs acquired the nausea in regard to experience that is the result of untruth or exaggeration, and when he occasionally met another man who had really been a soldier and they talked a few minutes in the dressing room at a dance he fell into the easy pose of the old soldier among other soldiers: that he had been badly, sickeningly frightened all the time. In this way he lost everything.

During this time, it was late summer, he was sleeping late in bed, getting up to walk down town to the library to get a book, eating lunch at home, reading on the front porch until he became bored, and then walking down through the town to spend the hottest hours of the day in the cool dark of the pool room. He loved to play pool.

Belleau Wood . . . Argonne: Sites of battles in World War I in which American troops were instrumental in pushing back the Germans.

In the evening he practiced on his clarinet, strolled down town, read, and went to bed. He was still a hero to his two young sisters. His mother would have given him breakfast in bed if he had wanted it. She often came in when he was in bed and asked him to tell her about the war, but her attention always wandered. His father was noncommittal.

Before Krebs went away to the war he had never been allowed to drive the family motor car. His father was in the real estate business and always wanted the car to be at his command when he required it to take clients out into the country to show them a piece of farm property. The car always stood outside the First National Bank building where his father had an office on the second floor. Now, after the war, it was still the same car.

Nothing was changed in the town except that the young girls had grown up.   10 But they lived in such a complicated world of already defined alliances and shifting feuds that Krebs did not feel the energy or the courage to break into it. He liked to look at them, though. There were so many good-looking young girls. Most of them had their hair cut short. When he went away only little girls wore their hair like that or girls that were fast. They all wore sweaters and shirt waists with round Dutch collars. It was a pattern. He liked to look at them from the front porch as they walked on the other side of the street. He liked to watch them walking under the shade of the trees. He liked the round Dutch collars above their sweaters. He liked their silk stockings and flat shoes. He liked their bobbed hair and the way they walked.

When he was in town their appeal to him was not very strong. He did not like them when he saw them in the Greek's ice cream parlor. He did not want them themselves really. They were too complicated. There was something else. Vaguely he wanted a girl but he did not want to have to work to get her. He would have liked to have a girl but he did not want to have to spend a long time getting her. He did not want to get into the intrigue and the politics. He did not want to have to do any courting. He did not want to tell any more lies. It wasn't worth it.

He did not want any consequences. He did not want any consequences ever again. He wanted to live alone without consequences. Besides he did not really need a girl. The army had taught him that. It was all right to pose as though you had to have a girl. Nearly everybody did that. But it wasn't true. You did not need a girl. That was the funny thing. First a fellow boasted how girls mean nothing to him, that he never thought of them, that they could not touch him. Then a fellow boasted that he could not get along without girls, that he had to have them all the time, that he could not go to sleep without them.

That was all a lie. It was all a lie both ways. You did not need a girl unless you thought about them. He learned that in the army. Then sooner or later you always got one. When you were really ripe for a girl you always got one. You did not have to think about it. Sooner or later it would come. He had learned that in the army.

Now he would have liked a girl if she had come to him and not wanted to talk. But here at home it was all too complicated. He knew he could never get through it all again. It was not worth the trouble. That was the thing about French girls and German girls. There was not all this talking. You couldn't talk much and you did not need to talk. It was simple and you were friends. He thought about France and then he began to think about Germany. On the whole he had liked Germany better. He did not want to leave Germany. He did not want to come home. Still, he had come home. He sat on the front porch.

He liked the girls that were walking along the other side of the street. He liked   15 the look of them much better than the French girls or the German girls. But the world they were in was not the world he was in. He would like to have one of them. But it was not worth it. They were such a nice pattern. He liked the pattern. It was exciting. But he would not go through all the talking. He did not want one badly enough. He liked to look at them all, though. It was not worth it. Not now when things were getting good again.

He sat there on the porch reading a book on the war. It was a history and he was reading about all the engagements he had been in. It was the most interesting reading he had ever done. He wished there were more maps. He looked forward with a good feeling to reading all the really good histories when they would come out with good detail maps. Now he was really learning about the war. He had been a good soldier. That made a difference.

One morning after he had been home about a month his mother came into his bedroom and sat on the bed. She smoothed her apron.

"I had a talk with your father last night, Harold," she said, "and he is willing for you to take the car out in the evenings."

"Yeah?" said Krebs, who was not fully awake. "Take the car out? Yeah?"

"Yes. Your father has felt for some time that you should be able to take the car 20 out in the evenings whenever you wished but we only talked it over last night."

"I'll bet you made him," Krebs said.

"No. It was your father's suggestion that we talk the matter over."

"Yeah. I'll bet you made him," Krebs sat up in bed.

"Will you come down to breakfast, Harold?" his mother said.

"As soon as I get my clothes on," Krebs said. 25

His mother went out of the room and he could hear her frying something downstairs while he washed, shaved, and dressed to go down into the dining-room for breakfast. While he was eating breakfast his sister brought in the mail.

"Well, Hare," she said. "You old sleepyhead. What do you ever get up for?"

Krebs looked at her. He liked her. She was his best sister.

"Have you got the paper?" he asked.

She handed him the Kansas City *Star* and he shucked off its brown wrapper 30 and opened it to the sporting page. He folded the *Star* open and propped it against the water pitcher with his cereal dish to steady it, so he could read while he ate.

"Harold," his mother stood in the kitchen doorway, "Harold, please don't muss up the paper. Your father can't read his *Star* if it's been mussed."

"I won't muss it," Krebs said.

His sister sat down at the table and watched him while he read.

"We're playing indoor over at school this afternoon," she said. "I'm going to pitch."

"Good," said Krebs. "How's the old wing?" 35

"I can pitch better than lots of the boys. I tell them all you taught me. The other girls aren't much good."

"Yeah?" said Krebs.

"I tell them all you're my beau. Aren't you my beau, Hare?"

"You bet."

"Couldn't your brother really be your beau just because he's your brother?" 40

"I don't know."

"Sure you know. Couldn't you be my beau, Hare, if I was old enough and if you wanted to?"

"Sure. You're my girl now."

"Am I really your girl?"

"Sure." 45

"Do you love me?"

"Uh, huh."

"Will you love me always?"

"Sure."

"Will you come over and watch me play indoor?" 50

"Maybe."

"Aw, Hare, you don't love me. If you loved me, you'd want to come over and watch me play indoor."

Krebs's mother came into the dining-room from the kitchen. She carried a plate with two fried eggs and some crisp bacon on it and a plate of buckwheat cakes.

"You run along, Helen," she said. "I want to talk to Harold."

She put the eggs and bacon down in front of him and brought in a jug of maple 55 syrup for the buckwheat cakes. Then she sat down across the table from Krebs.

"I wish you'd put down the paper a minute, Harold," she said.

Krebs took down the paper and folded it.

"Have you decided what you are going to do yet, Harold?" his mother said, taking off her glasses.

"No," said Krebs.

"Don't you think it's about time?" His mother did not say this in a mean way. 60 She seemed worried.

"I hadn't thought about it," Krebs said.

"God has some work for everyone to do," his mother said. "There can be no idle hands in His Kingdom."

"I'm not in His Kingdom," Krebs said.

"We are all of us in His Kingdom."

Krebs felt embarrassed and resentful as always. 65

"I've worried about you so much, Harold," his mother went on. "I know the temptations you must have been exposed to. I know how weak men are. I know what your own dear grandfather, my own father, told us about the Civil War and I have prayed for you. I pray for you all day long, Harold."

Krebs looked at the bacon fat hardening on his plate.

"Your father is worried, too," his mother went on. "He thinks you have lost your ambition, that you haven't got a definite aim in life. Charley Simmons, who is just your age, has a good job and is going to be married. The boys are all settling down; they're all determined to get somewhere; you can see that boys like Charley Simmons are on their way to being really a credit to the community."

Krebs said nothing.

"Don't look that way, Harold," his mother said. "You know we love you and I 70 want to tell you for your own good how matters stand. Your father does not want to hamper your freedom. He thinks you should be allowed to drive the car. If you want to take some of the nice girls out riding with you, we are only too pleased. We want you to enjoy yourself. But you are going to have to settle down to work, Harold. Your father doesn't care what you start in at. All work is honorable as he says. But you've got to make a start at something. He asked me to speak to you this morning and then you can stop in and see him at his office."

"Is that all?" Krebs said.

"Yes. Don't you love your mother, dear boy?"

"No," Krebs said.

His mother looked at him across the table. Her eyes were shiny. She started crying.

"I don't love anybody," Krebs said.   75

It wasn't any good. He couldn't tell her, he couldn't make her see it. It was silly to have said it. He had only hurt her. He went over and took hold of her arm. She was crying with her head in her hands.

"I didn't mean it," he said. "I was just angry at something. I didn't mean I didn't love you."

His mother went on crying. Krebs put his arm on her shoulder.

"Can't you believe me, mother?"

His mother shook her head.   80

"Please, please, mother. Please believe me."

"All right," his mother said chokily. She looked up at him. "I believe you, Harold."

Krebs kissed her hair. She put her face up to him.

"I'm your mother," she said. "I held you next to my heart when you were a tiny baby."

Krebs felt sick and vaguely nauseated.   85

"I know, Mummy," he said. "I'll try and be a good boy for you."

"Would you kneel and pray with me, Harold?" his mother asked.

They knelt down beside the dining-room table and Krebs's mother prayed.

"Now, you pray, Harold," she said.

"I can't," Krebs said.   90

"Try, Harold."

"I can't."

"Do you want me to pray for you?"

"Yes."

So his mother prayed for him and then they stood up and Krebs kissed his 95 mother and went out of the house. He had tried so to keep his life from being complicated. Still, none of it had touched him. He had felt sorry for his mother and she had made him lie. He would go to Kansas City and get a job and she would feel all right about it. There would be one more scene maybe before he got away. He would not go down to his father's office. He would miss that one. He wanted his life to go smoothly. It had just gotten going that way. Well, that was all over now, anyway. He would go over to the schoolyard and watch Helen play indoor baseball.

CONSIDERATIONS FOR CRITICAL THINKING AND WRITING

1. FIRST RESPONSE. The title, "Soldier's Home," focuses on the setting. Do you have a clear picture of Krebs's home? Describe it, filling in missing details from your associations of home, Krebs's routine, or anything else you can use.

2. What does the photograph of Krebs, the corporal, and the German girls reveal?

3. Belleau Wood, Soissons, the Champagne, St. Mihiel, and the Argonne were the sites of fierce and bloody fighting. What effect have these battles had on Krebs? Why do you think he won't talk about them to the people at home?

4. Why does Krebs avoid complications and consequences? How has the war changed his attitudes toward work and women? How is his hometown different from Germany and France? What is the conflict in the story?

5. Why do you think Hemingway refers to the protagonist as Krebs rather than Harold? What is the significance of his sister calling him "Hare"?

6. How does Krebs's mother embody the community's values? What does Krebs think of those values?

7. Why can't Krebs pray with his mother?

8. What is the resolution to Krebs's conflict?

9. Comment on the appropriateness of the story's title.

10. Explain how Krebs's war experiences are present throughout the story even though we get no details about them.

11. CRITICAL STRATEGIES. Read the section on reader-response criticism (pp. 1659–61) in Chapter 51, "Critical Strategies for Reading," and consider the following: Perhaps, after having been away from home for a time, you have returned to find yourself alienated from your family or friends. Describe your experience. What caused the change? How does this experience affect your understanding of Krebs? Alternately, if alienation hasn't been your experience, how does that difference affect your reading of Krebs?

CONNECTIONS TO OTHER SELECTIONS

1. Contrast the attitudes toward patriotism implicit in this story with those in Tim O'Brien's "How to Tell a True War Story" (p. 488). How do the stories' settings help to account for the differences between them?

2. How might Krebs's rejection of his community's values be related to Sammy's relationship to his supermarket job in John Updike's "A & P" (p. 200)? What details does Updike use to make the setting in "A & P" a comic, though nonetheless serious, version of Krebs's hometown?

3. Explain how the violent details that O'Brien uses to establish the setting in "How to Tell a True War Story" can be considered representative of the kinds of horrors that haunt Krebs after he returns home.

Perspective

ERNEST HEMINGWAY (1899–1961)

On What Every Writer Needs 1954

The most essential gift for a good writer is a built-in, shock-proof, shit detector. This is the writer's radar and all great writers have had it.

From *Writers at Work: The Paris Review Interviews* (Second Series)

CONSIDERATIONS FOR CRITICAL THINKING AND WRITING

1. Hemingway is typically forthright here, but it is tempting to dismiss his point as simply humorous. Take him seriously. What does he insist a good writer must be able to do?

2. How might Krebs in Hemingway's "Soldier's Home" (p. 162) be seen as having a similar kind of "shit detector" and "radar"?

3. Try writing a pithy, quotable statement that makes an observation about reading or writing.

F. Scott Fitzgerald (1896–1940)

F. Scott Fitzgerald grew up in St. Paul, Minnesota. He attended Princeton University but left before graduating to join the army as a second lieutenant during World War I. While at a training camp in the South he met Zelda Sayre, who was later to become his wife. Fitzgerald's rise to fame was rapid during the 1920s, when in his fiction he became the voice of the Jazz Age. After the success of his first novel, *This Side of Paradise* (1920), two collections of his short stories appeared in quick succession: *Flappers and Philosophers* (1921) and *Tales of the Jazz Age* (1922). Among his other writings, *The Great Gatsby* (1925) and *Tender Is the Night* (1934) are the most effective representations of his nostalgic disillusionment with success in America. However, by the time of his death, his personal life had unraveled because of his alcoholism and his wife's insanity. The depression years of the 1930s were inhospitable to the stories Fitzgerald wrote depicting the high and reckless living of the previous decade. In "The Ice Palace" a young woman is confronted with a choice between making a new life in the North or staying at home in the South. The settings reveal the nature of the conflict that develops.

© Minnesota Historical Society/CORBIS.

The Ice Palace 1920

I

The sunlight dripped over the house like golden paint over an art jar, and the freckling shadows here and there only intensified the rigor of the bath of light. The Butterworth and Larkin houses flanking were entrenched behind great stodgy trees; only the Happer house took the full sun, and all day long faced the dusty road-street with a tolerant kindly patience. This was the city of Tarleton in southernmost Georgia, September afternoon.

Up in her bedroom window Sally Carrol Happer rested her nineteen-year-old chin on a fifty-two-year-old sill and watched Clark Darrow's ancient Ford turn the corner. The car was hot—being partly metallic it retained all the heat it absorbed or evolved—and Clark Darrow sitting bolt upright at the wheel wore a pained, strained expression as though he considered himself a spare part, and rather likely to break. He laboriously crossed two dust ruts, the wheels squeaking indignantly at the encounter, and then with a terrifying expression he gave the steering-gear a final wrench and deposited self and car approximately in front of the Happer steps. There was a plaintive heaving sound, a death-rattle, followed by a short silence; and then the air was rent by a startling whistle.

Sally Carrol gazed down sleepily. She started to yawn, but finding this quite impossible unless she raised her chin from the windowsill, changed her mind and continued silently to regard the car, whose owner sat brilliantly if perfunctorily at attention as he waited for an answer to his signal. After a moment the whistle once more split the dusty air.

"Good mawnin'."

With difficulty Clark twisted his tall body round and bent a distorted glance on 5 the window.

" 'Tain't mawnin', Sally Carrol."

"Isn't it, sure enough?"

"What you doin'?"

"Eatin' 'n apple."

"Come on go swimmin' — want to?" 10

"Reckon so."

"How 'bout hurryin' up?"

"Sure enough."

Sally Carrol sighed voluminously and raised herself with profound inertia from the floor, where she had been occupied in alternately destroying parts of a green apple and painting paper dolls for her younger sister. She approached a mirror, regarded her expression with a pleased and pleasant languor, dabbed two spots of rouge on her lips and a grain of powder on her nose, and covered her bobbed corn-colored hair with a rose-littered sunbonnet. Then she kicked over the painting water, said, "Oh, damn!" — but let it lay — and left the room.

"How you, Clark?" she inquired a minute later as she slipped nimbly over the 15 side of the car.

"Mighty fine, Sally Carrol."

"Where we go swimmin'?"

"Out to Walley's Pool. Told Marylyn we'd call by an' get her an' Joe Ewing."

Clark was dark and lean, and when on foot was rather inclined to stoop. His eyes were ominous and his expression somewhat petulant except when startlingly illuminated by one of his frequent smiles. Clark had "a income" — just enough to keep himself in ease and his car in gasoline — and he had spent the two years since he graduated from Georgia Tech in dozing round the lazy streets of his home town, discussing how he could best invest his capital for an immediate fortune.

Hanging round he found not at all difficult; a crowd of little girls had grown 20 up beautifully, the amazing Sally Carrol foremost among them; and they enjoyed being swum with and danced with and made love to in the flower-filled summery evenings — and they all liked Clark immensely; When feminine company palled there were half a dozen other youths who were always just about to do something, and meanwhile were quite willing to join him in a few holes of golf, or a game of billiards, or the consumption of a quart of "hard yella licker." Every once in a while one of these contemporaries made a farewell round of calls before going up to New York or Philadelphia or Pittsburgh to go into business, but mostly they just stayed round in this languid paradise of dreamy skies and firefly evenings and noisy niggery street fairs—and especially of gracious, soft-voiced girls, who were brought up on memories instead of money.

The Ford having been excited into a sort of restless resentful life Clark and Sally Carrol rolled and rattled down Valley Avenue into Jefferson Street, where the dust road became a pavement; along opiate Millicent Place, where there were half a dozen prosperous, substantial mansions; and on into the downtown section. Driving was perilous here, for it was shopping time; the population idled casually across the streets and a drove of low-moaning oxen were being urged along in front of a placid streetcar; even the shops seemed only yawning their doors and blinking their windows in the sunshine before retiring into a state of utter and finite coma.

"Sally Carrol," said Clark suddenly, "it a fact that you're engaged?"

She looked at him quickly.

"Where'd you hear that?"

"Sure enough, you engaged?"   25

" 'At's a nice question!"

"Girl told me you were engaged to a Yankee you met up in Asheville last summer."

Sally Carrol sighed.

"Never saw such an old town for rumors."

"Don't marry a Yankee, Sally Carrol. We need you round here." Sally Carrol   30
was silent a moment.

"Clark," she demanded suddenly, "who on earth shall I marry?"

"I offer my services."

"Honey, you couldn't support a wife," she answered cheerfully. "Anyway, I know you too well to fall in love with you."

" 'At doesn't mean you ought to marry a Yankee," he persisted.

"S'pose I love him?"   35

He shook his head.

"You couldn't. He'd be a lot different from us, every way."

He broke off as he halted the car in front of a rambling, dilapidated house. Marylyn Wade and Joe Ewing appeared in the doorway.

" 'Lo, Sally Carrol."

"Hi!"   40

"How you-all?"

"Sally Carrol," demanded Marylyn as they started off again, "you engaged?"

"Lawdy, where'd all this start? Can't I look at a man 'thout everybody in town engagin' me to him?"

Clark stared straight in front of him at a bolt on the clattering windshield.

"Sally Carrol," he said with a curious intensity, "don't you like us?"   45

"What?"

"Us down here?"

"Why, Clark, you know I do. I adore all you boys."

"Then why you gettin' engaged to a Yankee?"

"Clark, I don't know. I'm not sure what I'll do, but—well, I want to go places and   50
see people. I want my mind to grow. I want to live where things happen on a big scale."

"What you mean?"

"Oh, Clark, I love you, and I love Joe here, and Ben Arrot, and you-all, but you'll—you'll—"

"We'll all be failures?"

"Yes. I don't mean only money failures, but just sort of—of ineffectual and sad, and—oh, how can I tell you?"

"You mean because we stay here in Tarleton?"   55

"Yes, Clark; and because you like it and never want to change things or think or go ahead."

He nodded and she reached over and pressed his hand.

"Clark," she said softly, "I wouldn't change you for the world. You're sweet the way you are. The things that'll make you fail I'll love always — the living in the past, the lazy days and nights you have, and all your carelessness and generosity."

"But you're goin' away?"

"Yes — because I couldn't ever marry you. You've a place in my heart no one else could have, but tied down here I'd get restless. I'd feel I was — wastin' myself. There's two sides to me, you see. There's the sleepy old side you love; an' there's a sort of energy — the feelin' that makes me do wild things. That's the part of me that may be useful somewhere, that'll last when I'm not beautiful any more." 60

She broke off with characteristic suddenness and sighed, "Oh, sweet cooky!" as her mood changed.

Half closing her eyes and tipping back her head till it rested, on the seat-back she let the savory breeze fan her eyes and ripple the fluffy curls of her bobbed hair. They were in the country now, hurrying between tangled growths of bright-green coppice and grass and tall trees that sent sprays of foliage to hang a cool welcome over the road. Here and there they passed a battered Negro cabin, its oldest white-haired inhabitant smoking a corncob pipe beside the door, and half a dozen scantily clothed pickaninnies parading tattered dolls on the wild-grown grass in front. Farther out were lazy cotton-fields, where even the workers seemed intangible shadows lent by the sun to the earth, not for toil but to while away some age-old tradition in the golden September fields. And round the drowsy picturesqueness, over the trees and shacks and muddy rivers, flowed the heat, never hostile, only comforting, like a great warm nourishing bosom for the infant earth.

"Sally Carrol, we're here!"

"Poor chile's soun' asleep."

"Honey, you dead at last outa sheer laziness?" 65

"Water, Sally Carrol! Cool water waitin' for you!"

Her eyes opened sleepily.

"Hi!" she murmured, smiling.

II

In November Harry Bellamy, tall, broad, and brisk, came down from his Northern city to spend four days. His intention was to settle a matter that had been hanging fire since he and Sally Carrol had met in Asheville, North Carolina, in mid-summer. The settlement took only a quiet afternoon and an evening in front of a glowing open fire, for Harry Bellamy had everything she wanted; and, besides, she loved him — loved him with that side of her she kept especially for loving. Sally Carrol had several rather clearly defined sides.

On his last afternoon they walked, and she found their steps tending half-unconsciously toward one of her favorite haunts, the cemetery. When it came in sight, gray-white and golden-green under the cheerful late sun, she paused, irresolute, by the iron gate. 70

"Are you mournful by nature, Harry?" she asked with a faint smile.

"Mournful? Not I."

"Then let's go in here. It depresses some folks, but I like it."

They passed through the gateway and followed a path that led through a wavy valley of graves — dusty-gray and moldy for the fifties; quaintly carved with flowers and jars for the seventies; ornate and hideous for the nineties, with fat marble cherubs lying in sodden sleep on stone pillows, and great impossible growths of nameless granite flowers. Occasionally they saw a kneeling figure with tributary flowers, but over most of the graves lay silence and withered leaves with only the fragrance that their own shadowy memories could waken in living minds.

They reached the top of a hill where they were fronted by a tall, round head- 75
stone, freckled with dark spots of damp and half grown over with vines.

"Margery Lee," she read; "1844–1873. Wasn't she nice? She died when she was
twenty-nine. Dear Margery Lee," she added softly. "Can't you see her, Harry?"

"Yes, Sally Carrol."

He felt a little hand insert itself into his.

"She was dark, I think; and she always wore her hair with a ribbon in it, and
gorgeous hoopskirts of alice blue and old rose."

"Yes." 80

"Oh, she was sweet, Harry! And she was the sort of girl born to stand on a wide,
pillared porch and welcome folks in. I think perhaps a lot of men went away to war
meanin' to come back to her; but maybe none of 'em ever did."

He stooped down close to the stone, hunting for any record of marriage.

"There's nothing here to show."

"Of course not. How could there be anything there better than just 'Margery
Lee,' and that eloquent date?"

She drew close to him and an unexpected lump came into his throat as her yel- 85
low hair brushed his cheek.

"You see how she was, don't you, Harry?"

"I see," he agreed gently. "I see through your precious eyes. You're beautiful
now, so I know she must have been."

Silent and close they stood, and he could feel her shoulders trembling a
little. An ambling breeze swept up the hill and stirred the brim of her floppidy
hat.

"Let's go down there!"

She was pointing to a flat stretch on the other side of the hill where along the 90
green turf were a thousand grayish-white crosses stretching in endless, ordered
rows like the stacked arms of a battalion.

"Those are the Confederate dead," said Sally Carrol simply.

They walked along and read the inscriptions, always only a name and a date,
sometimes quite indecipherable.

"The last row is the saddest — see, 'way over there. Every cross has just a date
on it, and the word 'Unknown.' "

She looked at him and her eyes brimmed with tears.

"I can't tell you how real it is to me, darling — if you don't know." 95

"How you feel about it is beautiful to me."

"No, no, it's not me, it's them — that old time that I've tried to have live in me.
These were just men, unimportant evidently or they wouldn't have been 'unknown';
but they died for the most beautiful thing in the world — the dead South. You see,"
she continued, her voice still husky, her eyes glistening with tears, "people have
these dreams they fasten onto things, and I've always grown up with that dream. It
was so easy because it was all dead and there weren't any disillusions comin' to me.
I've tried in a way to live up to those past standards of noblesse oblige — there's just
the last remnants of it, you know, like the roses of an old garden dying all round
us — streaks of strange courtliness and chivalry in some of these boys an' stories I
used to hear from a Confederate soldier who lived next door, and a few old darkies.
Oh, Harry, there was something, there was something! I couldn't ever make you
understand, but it was there."

"I understand," he assured her again quietly.

Sally Carrol smiled and dried her eyes on the tip of a handkerchief protruding
from his breast pocket.

"You don't feel depressed, do you, lover? Even when I cry I'm happy here, and I   100
get a sort of strength from it."

Hand in hand they turned and walked slowly away. Finding soft grass she
drew him down to a seat beside her with their backs against the remnants of a low
broken wall.

"Wish those three old women would clear out," he complained. "I want to kiss
you, Sally Carrol."

"Me, too."

They waited impatiently for the three bent figures to move off, and then she
kissed him until the sky seemed to fade out and all her smiles and tears to vanish in
an ecstasy of eternal seconds.

Afterward they walked slowly back together, while on the corners twilight   105
played at somnolent black-and-white checkers with the end of day.

"You'll be up about mid-January," he said, "and you've got to stay a month at
least. It'll be slick. There's a winter carnival on, and if you've never really seen snow
it'll be like fairyland to you. There'll be skating and skiing and tobogganing and
sleigh-riding, and all sorts of torchlight parades on snowshoes. They haven't had
one for years, so they're going to make it a knockout."

"Will I be cold, Harry?" she asked suddenly.

"You certainly won't. You may freeze your nose, but you won't be shivery cold.
It's hard and dry, you know."

"I guess I'm a summer child. I don't like any cold I've ever seen."

She broke off and they were both silent for a minute.   110

"Sally Carrol," he said very slowly, "what do you say to — March?"

"I say I love you."

"March?"

"March, Harry."

III

All night in the Pullman it was very cold. She rang for the porter to ask for another   115
blanket, and when he couldn't give her one she tried vainly, by squeezing down
into the bottom of her berth and doubling back the bedclothes, to snatch a few
hours' sleep. She wanted to look her best in the morning.

She rose at six and sliding uncomfortably into her clothes stumbled up to the
diner for a cup of coffee. The snow had filtered into the vestibules and covered the
floor with a slippery coating. It was intriguing, this cold, it crept in everywhere. Her
breath was quite visible and she blew into the air with a naive enjoyment. Seated in the
diner she stared out the window at white hills and valleys and scattered pines whose
every branch was a green platter for a cold feast of snow. Sometimes a solitary farmhouse would fly by, ugly and bleak and lone on the white waste; and with each one she
had an instant of chill compassion for the souls shut in there waiting for spring.

As she left the diner and swayed back into the Pullman she experienced a surging rush of energy and wondered if she was feeling the bracing air of which Harry
had spoken. This was the North, the North — her land now!

"Then blow, ye winds, heigho!
A-roving I will go,"

she chanted exultantly to herself.

"What's 'at?" inquired the porter politely.

"I said: 'Brush me off.'"

The long wires of the telegraph-poles doubled; two tracks ran up beside the 120
train — three — four; came a succession of white-roofed houses, a glimpse of a
trolley-car with frosted windows, streets — more streets — the city.

She stood for a dazed moment in the frosty station before she saw three fur-
bundled figures descending upon her.

"There she is!"

"Oh, Sally Carrol!"

Sally Carrol dropped her bag.

"Hi!" 125

A faintly familiar icy-cold face kissed her, and then she was in a group of faces
all apparently emitting great clouds of heavy smoke; she was shaking hands. There
were Gordon, a short, eager man of thirty who looked like an amateur knocked-
about model for Harry, and his wife, Myra, a listless lady with flaxen hair under
a fur automobile cap. Almost immediately Sally Carrol thought of her as vaguely
Scandinavian. A cheerful chauffeur adopted her bag, and amid ricochets of half-
phrases, exclamations, and perfunctory listless "my dears" from Myra, they swept
each other from the station.

Then they were in a sedan bound through a crooked succession of snowy
streets where dozens of little boys were hitching sleds behind grocery wagons and
automobiles.

"Oh," cried Sally Carrol, "I want to do that! Can we, Harry?"

"That's for kids. But we might ——"

"It looks like such a circus!" she said regretfully. 130

Home was a rambling frame house set on a white lap of snow, and there she met
a big, gray-haired man of whom she approved, and a lady who was like an egg, and
who kissed her — these were Harry's parents. There was a breathless indescribable
hour crammed full of half-sentences, hot water, bacon and eggs and confusion; and
after that she was alone with Harry in the library, asking him if she dared smoke.

It was a large room with a Madonna over the fireplace and rows upon rows of
books in covers of light gold and dark gold and shiny red. All the chairs had little
lace squares where one's head should rest, the couch was just comfortable, the books
looked as if they had been read — some — and Sally Carrol had an instantaneous
vision of the battered old library at home, with her father's huge medical books, and
the oil-paintings of her three great-uncles, and the old couch that had been mended
up for forty-five years and was still luxurious to dream in. This room struck her as
being neither attractive nor particularly otherwise. It was simply a room with a lot
of fairly expensive things in it that all looked about fifteen years old.

"What do you think of it up here?" demanded Harry eagerly. "Does it surprise
you? Is it what you expected, I mean?"

"You are, Harry," she said quietly, and reached out her arms to him.

But after a brief kiss he seemed anxious to extort enthusiasm from her. 135

"The town, I mean. Do you like it? Can you feel the pep in the air?"

"Oh, Harry," she laughed, "you'll have to give me time. You can't just fling questions at me."

She puffed at her cigarette with a sigh of contentment.

"One thing I want to ask you," he began rather apologetically; "you Southerners put quite an emphasis on family, and all that — not that it isn't quite all right, but
you'll find it a little different here. I mean — you'll notice a lot of things that'll seem
to you sort of vulgar display at first, Sally Carrol; but just remember that this is a

three-generation town. Everybody has a father, and about half of us have grandfa-thers. Back of that we don't go."

"Of course," she murmured.   140

"Our grandfathers you see, founded the place, and a lot of them had to take some pretty queer jobs while they were doing the founding. For instance, there's one woman who at present is about the social model for the town; well, her father was the first public ash man — things like that."

"Why," said Sally Carrol, puzzled; "did you s'pose I was goin' to make remarks about people?"

"Not at all," interrupted Harry; "and I'm not apologizing for any one either. It's just that — well, a Southern girl came up here last summer and said some unfortu-nate things, and — oh, I just thought I'd tell you."

Sally Carrol felt suddenly indignant — as though she had been unjustly spanked — but Harry evidently considered the subject closed, for he went on with a great surge of enthusiasm.

"It's carnival time, you know. First in ten years. And there's an ice palace they're   145 building now that's the first they've had since eighty-five. Built out of blocks of the clearest ice they could find — on a tremendous scale."

She rose and walking to the window pushed aside the heavy Turkish portières and looked out.

"Oh!" she cried suddenly. "There's two little boys makin' a snow man! Harry, do you reckon I can go out an' help 'em?"

"You dream! Come here and kiss me."

She left the window rather reluctantly.

"I don't guess this is a very kissable climate, is it? I mean, it makes you so you   150 don't want to sit round, doesn't it?"

"We're not going to. I've got a vacation for the first week you're here, and there's a dinner-dance tonight."

"Oh, Harry," she confessed, subsiding in a heap, half in his lap, half in the pil-lows, "I sure do feel confused. I haven't got an idea whether I'll like it or not, an' I don't know what people expect, or anythin'. You'll have to tell me, honey."

"I'll tell you," he said softly, "if you'll just tell me you're glad to be here."

"Glad — just awful glad!" she whispered, insinuating herself into his arms in her own peculiar way. "Where you are is home for me, Harry."

And as she said this she had the feeling for almost the first time in her life that   155 she was acting a part.

That night, amid the gleaming candles of a dinner-party, where the men seemed to do most of the talking while the girls sat in a haughty and expensive aloofness, even Harry's presence on her left failed to make her feel at home.

"They're a good-looking crowd, don't you think?" he demanded. "Just look round. There's Spud Hubbard, tackle at Princeton last year, and Junie Morton — he and the red-haired fellow next to him were both Yale hockey captains; Junie was in my class. Why, the best athletes in the world come from these States round here. This is a man's country, I tell you. Look at John J. Fishburn!"

"Who's he?" asked Sally Carrol innocently.

"Don't you know?"

"I've heard the name."   160

"Greatest wheat man in the Northwest, and one of the greatest financiers in the country."

She turned suddenly to a voice on her right.

"I guess they forgot to introduce us. My name's Roger Patton."

"My name is Sally Carrol Happer," she said graciously.

"Yes, I know. Harry told me you were coming." 165

"You a relative?"

"No, I'm a professor."

"Oh," she laughed.

"At the university. You're from the South, aren't you?"

"Yes; Tarleton, Georgia." 170

She liked him immediately — a reddish-brown mustache under watery blue eyes that had something in them that these other eyes lacked, some quality of appreciation. They exchanged stray sentences through dinner, and she made up her mind to see him again.

After coffee she was introduced to numerous good-looking young men who danced with conscious precision and seemed to take it for granted that she wanted to talk about nothing except Harry.

"Heavens," she thought, "they talk as if my being engaged made me older than they are — as if I'd tell their mothers on them!"

In the South an engaged girl, even a young married woman, expected the same amount of half-affectionate badinage and flattery that would be accorded a débutante, but here all that seemed banned. One young man, after getting well started on the subject of Sally Carrol's eyes, and how they had allured him ever since she entered the room, went into a violent confusion when he found she was visiting the Bellamys — was Harry's fiancée. He seemed to feel as though he had made some risqué and inexcusable blunder, became immediately formal and left her at the first opportunity.

She was rather glad when Roger Patton cut in on her and suggested that they 175 sit out a while.

"Well," he inquired, blinking cheerily, "how's Carmen from the South?"

"Mighty fine. How's — how's Dangerous Dan McGrew? Sorry, but he's the only Northerner I know much about."

He seemed to enjoy that.

"Of course," he confessed, "as a professor of literature I'm not supposed to have read Dangerous Dan McGrew."

"Are you a native?" 180

"No, I'm a Philadelphian. Imported from Harvard to teach French. But I've been here ten years."

"Nine years, three hundred an' sixty-four days longer than me."

"Like it here?"

"Uh-huh. Sure do!"

"Really?" 185

"Well, why not? Don't I look as if I were havin' a good time?"

"I saw you look out the window a minute ago — and shiver."

"Just my imagination," laughed Sally Carrol. "I'm used to havin' everythin' quiet outside, an' sometimes I look out an' see a flurry of snow, an' it's just as if somethin' dead was movin'."

He nodded appreciatively.

"Ever been North before?"

"Spent two Julys in Asheville, North Carolina." 190

"Nice-looking crowd, aren't they?" suggested Patton, indicating the swirling floor.

Sally Carrol started. This had been Harry's remark.

"Sure, are! They're — canine."

"What?"   195

She flushed.

"I'm sorry; that sounded worse than I meant it. You see I always think of people
as feline or canine, irrespective of sex."

"Which are you?"

"I'm feline. So are you. So are most Southern men an' most of these girls here."

"What's Harry?"   200

"Harry's canine distinctly. All the men I've met tonight seem to be canine."

"What does 'canine' imply? A certain conscious masculinity as opposed to
subtlety?"

"Reckon so. I never analyzed it — only I just look at people an' say 'canine' or
'feline' right off. It's right absurd, I guess."

"Not at all. I'm interested. I used to have a theory about these people. I think
they're freezing up."

"What?"   205

"I think they're growing like Swedes — Ibsenesque, you know. Very gradually
getting gloomy and melancholy. It's these long winters. Ever read any Ibsen?"

She shook her head.

"Well, you find in his characters a certain brooding rigidity. They're righteous,
narrow, and cheerless, without infinite possibilities for great sorrow or joy."

"Without smiles or tears?"

"Exactly. That's my theory. You see there are thousands of Swedes up here. They   210
come, I imagine, because the climate is very much like their own, and there's been a
gradual mingling. There're probably not half a dozen here tonight, but — we've had
four Swedish governors. Am I boring you?"

"I'm mighty interested."

"Your future sister-in-law is half Swedish. Personally I like her, but my theory is
that Swedes react rather badly on us as a whole. Scandinavians, you know, have the
largest suicide rate in the world."

"Why do you live here if it's so depressing?"

"Oh, it doesn't get me. I'm pretty well cloistered, and I suppose books mean
more than people to me anyway."

"But writers all speak about the South being tragic. You know — Spanish   215
señoritas, black hair and daggers an' haunting music."

He shook his head.

"No, the Northern races are the tragic races — they don't indulge in the cheering luxury of tears."

Sally Carrol thought of her graveyard. She supposed that that was vaguely what
she had meant when she said it didn't depress her.

"The Italians are about the gayest people in the world — but it's a dull subject,"
he broke off. "Anyway, I want to tell you you're marrying a pretty fine man."

Sally Carrol was moved by an impulse of confidence.   220

"I know. I'm the sort of person who wants to be taken care of after a certain
point, and I feel sure I will be."

"Shall we dance? You know," he continued as they rose, "it's encouraging to find
a girl who knows what she's marrying for. Nine-tenths of them think of it as a sort of
walking into a moving-picture sunset."

She laughed, and liked him immensely.

Two hours later on the way home she nestled near Harry in the back seat.

"Oh, Harry," she whispered, "it's so co-old!"   225
"But it's warm in here, darling girl."
"But outside it's cold; and oh, that howling wind!"
      She buried her face deep in his fur coat and trembled involuntarily as his cold
lips kissed the tip of her ear.

IV

The first week of her visit passed in a whirl. She had her promised toboggan-ride
at the back of an automobile through a chill January twilight. Swathed in furs she
put in a morning tobogganing on the country-club hill; even tried skiing, to sail
through the air for a glorious moment and then land in a tangled laughing bundle on a soft snowdrift. She liked all the winter sports, except an afternoon spent
snowshoeing over a glaring plain under pale yellow sunshine, but she soon realized that these things were for children — that she was being humored and that the
enjoyment round her was only a reflection of her own.
      At first the Bellamy family puzzled her. The men were reliable and she liked   230
them; to Mr. Bellamy especially, with his iron-gray hair and energetic dignity she
took an immediate fancy, once she found that he was born in Kentucky; this made
of him a link between the old life and the new. But toward the women she felt a definite hostility. Myra, her future sister-in-law, seemed the essence of spiritless conventionality. Her conversation was so utterly devoid of personality that Sally Carrol,
who came from a country where a certain amount of charm and assurance could be
taken for granted in the women, was inclined to despise her.
      "If those women aren't beautiful," she thought, "they're nothing. They just fade
out when you look at them. They're glorified domestics. Men are the center of every
mixed group."
      Lastly there was Mrs. Bellamy, whom Sally Carrol detested. The first day's
impression of an egg had been confirmed — an egg with a cracked, veiny voice and
such an ungracious dumpiness of carriage that Sally Carrol felt that if she once fell
she would surely scramble. In addition, Mrs. Bellamy seemed to typify the town in
being innately hostile to strangers. She called Sally Carrol "Sally," and could not be
persuaded that the double name was anything more than a tedious ridiculous nick-
name. To Sally Carrol this shortening of her name was like presenting her to the
public half clothed. She loved "Sally Carrol"; she loathed "Sally." She knew also that
Harry's mother disapproved of her bobbed hair; and she had never dared smoke
downstairs after that first day when Mrs. Bellamy had come into the library sniffing
violently.
      Of all the men she met she preferred Roger Patton, who was a frequent visitor
at the house. He never again alluded to the Ibsenesque tendency of the populace,
but when he came in one day and found her curled upon the sofa bent over "Peer
Gynt" he laughed, and told her to forget what he'd said — that it was all rot.
      And then one afternoon in her second week she and Harry hovered on the edge
of a dangerously steep quarrel. She considered that he precipitated it entirely, though
the Serbia in the case was an unknown man who had not had his trousers pressed.
      They had been walking homeward between mounds of high-piled snow and   235
under a sun which Sally Carrol scarcely recognized. They passed a little girl done
up in gray wool until she resembled a small Teddy bear and Sally Carrol could not
resist a gasp of maternal appreciation.

"Look! Harry!"

"What?"

"That little girl — did you see her face?"

"Yes, why?"

"It was red as a little strawberry. Oh, she was cute!"   240

"Why, your own face is almost as red as that already! Everybody's healthy here. We're out in the cold as soon as we're old enough to walk. Wonderful climate!"

She looked at him and had to agree. He was mighty healthy-looking; so was his brother. And she had noticed the new red in her own cheeks that very morning.

Suddenly their glances were caught and held, and they stared for a moment at the street-corner ahead of them. A man was standing there, his knees bent, his eyes gazing upward with a tense expression as though he were about to make a leap toward the chilly sky. And then they both exploded into a shout of laughter, for coming closer they discovered it had been a ludicrous momentary illusion produced by the extreme bagginess of the man's trousers.

"Reckon that's one on us," she laughed.

"He must be a Southerner, judging by those trousers," suggested Harry   245 mischievously.

"Why, Harry!"

Her surprised look must have irritated him.

"Those damn Southerners!"

Sally Carrol's eyes flashed.

"Don't call 'em that!"   250

"I'm sorry, dear," said Harry, malignantly apologetic, "but you know what I think of them. They're sort of — sort of degenerates — not at all like the old Southerners. They've lived so long down there with all the colored people that they've gotten lazy and shiftless."

"Hush your mouth, Harry!" she cried angrily. "They're not! They may be lazy — anybody would be in that climate — but they're my best friends, an' I don't want to hear 'em criticized in any such sweepin' way. Some of 'em are the finest men in the world."

"Oh, I know. They're all right when they come North to college, but of all the hangdog, ill-dressed, slovenly lot I ever saw, a bunch of small-town Southerners are the worst!"

Sally Carrol was clinching her gloved hands and biting her lip furiously.

"Why," continued Harry, "there was one in my class at New Haven, and we all   255 thought that at last we'd found the true type of Southern aristocrat, but it turned out that he wasn't an aristocrat at all — just the son of a Northern carpetbagger, who owned about all the cotton round Mobile."

"A Southerner wouldn't talk the way you're talking now," she said evenly.

"They haven't the energy!"

"Or the somethin' else."

"I'm sorry, Sally Carrol, but I've heard you say yourself that you'd never marry——"

"That's quite different. I told you I wouldn't want to tie my life to any of the boys   260 that are round Tarleton now, but I never made any sweepin' generalities."

They walked along in silence.

"I probably spread it on a bit thick, Sally Carrol. I'm sorry."

She nodded but made no answer. Five minutes later as they stood in the hallway she suddenly threw her arms round him.

"Oh, Harry," she cried, her eyes brimming with tears, "let's get married next week. I'm afraid of having fusses like that. I'm afraid, Harry. It wouldn't be that way if we were married."

But Harry, being in the wrong, was still irritated.   265

"That'd be idiotic. We decided on March."

The tears in Sally Carrol's eyes faded; her expression hardened slightly.

"Very well — I suppose I shouldn't have said that."

Harry melted.

"Dear little nut!" he cried. "Come and kiss me and let's forget."   270

That very night at the end of a vaudeville performance the orchestra played "Dixie" and Sally Carrol felt something stronger and more enduring than her tears and smiles of the day brim up inside her; She leaned forward gripping the arms of her chair until her face grew crimson.

"Sort of get you, dear?" whispered Harry.

But she did not hear him. To the spirited throb of the violins and the inspiring beat of the kettledrums her own old ghosts were marching by and on into the darkness, and as fifes whistled and sighed in the low encore they seemed so nearly out of sight that she could have waved good-by.

"Away, away,
    Away down South in Dixie!
Away, away,
    Away down South in Dixie!"

V

It was a particularly cold night. A sudden thaw had nearly cleared the streets the day before, but now they were traversed again with a powdery wraith of loose snow that traveled in wavy lines before the feet of the wind, and filled the lower air with a fine-particled mist. There was no sky — only a dark, ominous tent that draped in the tops of the streets and was in reality a vast approaching army of snowflakes — while over it all, chilling away the comfort from the brown-and-green glow of lighted windows and muffling the steady trot of the horse pulling their sleigh, interminably washed the north wind. It was a dismal town after all, she thought — dismal.

Sometimes at night it had seemed to her as though no one lived here — they   275
had all gone long ago — leaving lighted houses to be covered in time by tombing heaps of sleet. Oh, if there should be snow on her grave! To be beneath great piles of it all winter long, where even her headstone would be a light shadow against light shadows. Her grave — a grave that should be flower-strewn and washed with sun and rain.

She thought again of those isolated country houses that her train had passed, and of the life there the long winter through — the ceaseless glare through the windows, the crust forming on the soft drifts of snow, finally the slow, cheerless melting, and the harsh spring of which Roger Patton had told her. Her spring — to lose it forever — with its lilacs and the lazy sweetness it stirred in her heart. She was laying away that spring — afterward she would lay away that sweetness.

With a gradual insistence the storm broke. Sally Carrol felt a film of flakes melt quickly on her eyelashes, and Harry reached over a furry arm and drew down her complicated flannel cap. Then the small flakes came in skirmish-line, and the horse bent his neck patiently as a transparency of white appeared momentarily on his coat.

"Oh, he's cold, Harry," she said quickly.

"Who? The horse? Oh, no, he isn't. He likes it!"

After another ten minutes they turned a corner and came in sight of their desti-   280
nation. On a tall hill outlined in vivid glaring green against the wintry sky stood the
ice palace. It was three stories in the air, with battlements and embrasures and narrow icicled windows, and the innumerable electric lights inside made a gorgeous
transparency of the great central hall. Sally Carrol clutched Harry's hand under the
fur robe.

"It's beautiful!" he cried excitedly. "My golly, it's beautiful, isn't it! They haven't
had one here since eighty-five!"

Somehow the notion of there not having been one since eighty-five oppressed
her. Ice was a ghost, and this mansion of it was surely peopled by those shades of the
eighties, with pale faces and blurred snow-filled hair.

"Come on, dear," said Harry.

She followed him out of the sleigh and waited while he hitched the horse. A
party of four — Gordon, Myra, Roger Patton, and another girl — drew up beside
them with a mighty jingle of bells. There were quite a crowd already, bundled in fur
or sheepskin, shouting and calling to each other as they moved through the snow,
which was now so thick that people could scarcely be distinguished a few yards
away.

"It's a hundred and seventy feet tall," Harry was saying to a muffled figure   285
beside him as they trudged toward the entrance; "covers six thousand square yards."

She caught snatches of conversation: "One main hall" — "walls twenty to forty
inches thick" — "and the ice cave has almost a mile of — " — "this Canuck who built
it — "

They found their way inside, and dazed by the magic of the great crystal walls
Sally Carrol found herself repeating over and over two lines from "Kubla Khan":

"It was a miracle of rare device,
A sunny pleasure-dome with caves of ice!"

In the great glittering cavern with the dark shut out she took a seat on a wooden
bench, and the evening's oppression lifted. Harry was right — it was beautiful; and
her gaze traveled the smooth surface of the walls, the blocks for which had been
selected for their purity and clearness to obtain this opalescent, translucent effect.

"Look! Here we go — oh, boy!" cried Harry.

A band in a far corner struck up "Hail, Hail, the Gang's All Here!" which   290
echoed over to them in wild muddled acoustics, and then the lights suddenly went
out; silence seemed to flow down the icy sides and sweep over them. Sally Carrol
could still see her white breath in the darkness, and a dim row of pale faces over on
the other side.

The music eased to a sighing complaint, and from outside drifted in the full-
throated resonant chant of the marching clubs. It grew louder like some pæan of a
viking tribe traversing an ancient wild; it swelled — they were coming nearer; then
a row of torches appeared, and another and another, and keeping time with their
moccasined feet a long column of gray-mackinawed figures swept in, snowshoes
slung at their shoulders, torches soaring and flickering as their voices rose along the
great walls.

The gray column ended and another followed, the light streaming luridly this
time over red toboggan caps and flaming crimson mackinaws, and as they entered
they took up the refrain; then came a long platoon of blue and white, of green, of
white, of brown and yellow.

"Those white ones are the Wacouta Club," whispered Harry eagerly. "Those are the men you've met round at dances."

The volume of the voices grew; the great cavern was a phantasmagoria of torches waving in great banks of fire, of colors and the rhythm of soft-leather steps. The leading column turned and halted, platoon deployed in front of platoon until the whole procession made a solid flag of flame, and then from thousands of voices burst a mighty shout that filled the air like a crash of thunder, and sent the torches wavering. It was magnificent, it was tremendous! To Sally Carrol it was the North offering sacrifice on some mighty altar to the gray pagan God of Snow. As the shout died the band struck up again and there came more singing, and then long reverberating cheers by each club. She sat very quiet listening while the staccato cries rent the stillness; and then she started, for there was a volley of explosion, and great clouds of smoke went up here and there through the cavern — the flash-light photographers at work — and the council was over. With the band at their head the clubs formed in column once more, took up their chant, and began to march out.

"Come on!" shouted Harry. "We want to see the labyrinths downstairs before 295 they turn the lights off!"

They all rose and started toward the chute — Harry and Sally Carrol in the lead, her little mitten buried in his big fur gantlet. At the bottom of the chute was a long empty room of ice, with the ceiling so low that they had to stoop — and their hands were parted. Before she realized what he intended Harry had darted down one of the half-dozen glittering passages that opened into the room and was only a vague receding blot against the green shimmer.

"Harry!" she called.

"Come on!" he cried back.

She looked round the empty chamber; the rest of the party had evidently decided to go home, were already outside somewhere in the blundering snow. She hesitated and then darted in after Harry.

"Harry!" she shouted. 300

She had reached a turning-point thirty feet down; she heard a faint muffled answer far to the left, and with a touch of panic fled toward it. She passed another turning, two more yawning alleys.

"Harry!"

No answer. She started to run straight forward, and then turned like lightning and sped back the way she had come, enveloped in a sudden icy terror.

She reached a turn — was it here? — took the left and came to what should have been the outlet into the long, low room, but it was only another glittering passage with darkness at the end. She called again but the walls gave back a flat, lifeless echo with no reverberations. Retracing her steps she turned another corner, this time following a wide passage. It was like the green lane between the parted waters of the Red Sea, like a damp vault connecting empty tombs.

She slipped a little now as she walked, for ice had formed on the bottom of 305 her overshoes; she had to run her gloves along the half-slippery, half-sticky walls to keep her balance.

"Harry!"

Still no answer. The sound she made bounced mockingly down to the end of the passage.

Then on an instant the lights went out, and she was in complete darkness. She gave a small, frightened cry, and sank down into a cold little heap on the ice. She felt her left knee do something as she fell, but she scarcely noticed it as some deep terror far greater than any fear of being lost settled upon her. She was alone with this presence that came out of the North, the dreary loneliness that rose from ice-bound whalers, in the Arctic seas, from smokeless, trackless wastes where were strewn the whitened bones of adventure. It was an icy breath of death; it was rolling down low across the land to clutch at her.

With a furious despairing energy she rose again and started blindly down the darkness. She must get out. She might be lost in here for days, freeze to death and lie embedded in the ice like corpses she had read of, kept perfectly preserved until the melting of a glacier. Harry probably thought she had left with the others — he had gone by now; no one would know until late next day. She reached pitifully for the wall. Forty inches thick, they had said — forty inches thick!

"Oh!"   310

On both sides of her along the walls she felt things creeping, damp souls that haunted this palace, this town, this North.

"Oh, send somebody — send somebody!" she cried aloud.

Clark Darrow — he would understand; or Joe Ewing; she couldn't be left here to wander forever — to be frozen, heart, body, and soul. This her — this Sally Carrol! Why, she was a happy thing. She was a happy little girl. She liked warmth and summer and Dixie. These things were foreign — foreign.

"You're not crying," something said aloud. "You'll never cry any more. Your tears would just freeze; all tears freeze up here!"   315

She sprawled full length on the ice.

"Oh, God!" she faltered.

A long single file of minutes went by, and with a great weariness she felt her eyes closing. Then some one seemed to sit down near her and take her face in warm, soft hands. She looked up gratefully.

"Why, it's Margery Lee," she crooned softly to herself. "I knew you'd come." It really was Margery Lee, and she was just as Sally Carrol had known she would be, with a young, white brow, and wide, welcoming eyes, and a hoopskirt of some soft material that was quite comforting to rest on.

"Margery Lee."

It was getting darker now and darker — all those tombstones ought to be 320 repainted, sure enough, only that would spoil 'em, of course. Still, you ought to be able to see 'em.

Then after a succession of moments that went fast and then slow, but seemed to be ultimately resolving themselves into a multitude of blurred rays converging toward a pale-yellow sun, she heard a great cracking noise break her newfound stillness.

It was the sun, it was a light; a torch, and a torch beyond that, and another one, and voices; a face took flesh below the torch, heavy arms raised her, and she felt something on her cheek — it felt wet. Some one had seized her and was rubbing her face with snow. How ridiculous — with snow!

"Sally Carrol! Sally Carrol!"

It was Dangerous Dan McGrew; and two other faces she didn't know.

"Child, child! We've been looking for you two hours! Harry's half-crazy!"   325

Things came rushing back into place — the singing, the torches, the great shout of the marching clubs. She squirmed in Patton's arms and gave a long low cry.

"Oh, I want to get out of here! I'm going back home. Take me home" — her voice rose to a scream that sent a chill to Harry's heart as he came racing down the next passage — "tomorrow!" she cried with delirious, unrestrained passion — "Tomorrow! Tomorrow! Tomorrow!"

VI

The wealth of golden sunlight poured a quite enervating yet oddly comforting heat over the house where day long it faced the dusty stretch of road. Two birds were making a great to-do in a cool spot found among the branches of a tree next door, and down the street a colored woman was announcing herself melodiously as a purveyor of strawberries. It was April afternoon.

Sally Carrol Happer, resting her chin on her arm, and her arm on an old window-seat gazed sleepily down over the spangled dust whence the heat waves were rising for the first time this spring. She was watching a very ancient Ford turn a perilous corner and rattle and groan to a jolting stop at the end of the walk. She made no sound, and in a minute a strident familiar whistle rent the air. Sally Carrol smiled and blinked.

"Good mawnin.'"   330

A head appeared tortuously from under the car-top below.

" 'Tain't mawnin', Sally Carrol."

"Sure enough!" she said in affected surprise. "I guess maybe not."

"What you doin'?"

"Eatin' green peach. 'Spect to die any minute."   335

Clark twisted himself a last impossible notch to get a view of her face.

"Water's warm as a kettla steam, Sally Carrol. Wanta go swimmin'?"

"Hate to move," sighed Sally Carrol lazily, "but I reckon so."

Considerations for Critical Thinking and Writing

1. **FIRST RESPONSE.** How is the South presented in Part I? How is the atmosphere of the setting established? What seems to be Fitzgerald's attitude toward the South?

2. Why does Sally Carrol want to leave the South? What does she associate with the North?

3. What do we learn about Sally Carrol's feelings about the South at Margery Lee's grave?

4. What is the difference between the gold colors in Part I and those Sally Carrol sees in the library at Harry's home in Part III? What other differences between North and South are established in Part III?

5. What is Roger Patton's function in the story? Why does Sally Carrol classify him as "feline" rather than "canine"? Why is it appropriate that he later rescues Sally Carrol?

6. Why do you think Mrs. Bellamy insists upon calling Sally Carrol "Sally"? What does this reveal about her attitude toward her future daughter-in-law?

7. Examine the descriptive language in the first three paragraphs of Part V. How does this description foreshadow the subsequent events of this part?

8. Explain how Sally Carrol's experience in the ice palace encapsulates her trip North.

9. Does the description of the setting in Part VI resolve the conflict in the story? Do you find the resolution convincing?

10. Discuss Fitzgerald's view of the South and North. Is his treatment of each region a stereotype?

11. Consider how valid Sally Carrol's categories of "feline" and "canine" are in describing types of people. Are there other kinds of animals that you would use to classify people?

CONNECTIONS TO OTHER SELECTIONS

1. Compare Fitzgerald's treatment of the differences between the South and North with Faulkner's in "A Rose for Emily" (p. 78).

2. Discuss the significance attached to the hometown values of the respective protagonists in "The Ice Palace" and "Soldier's Home" (p. 162).

FAY WELDON (B. 1933)

Born in England and raised in New Zealand, Fay Weldon graduated from St. Andrew's University in Scotland. She wrote advertising copy for various companies and was a propaganda writer for the British Foreign Office before turning to fiction. She has written novels, short stories, plays, and radio scripts. In 1971 her script for an episode of *Upstairs, Downstairs* won an award from the Society of Film and Television Arts. She has written more than thirty novels, including *The Fat Woman's Joke* (1967), *Down Among the Women* (1971), *Praxis* (1978), *The Life and Loves of a She-Devil* (1983), *Life Force* (1991), *The Bulgari Connection* (2001), *She May Not Leave* (2005), *The Stepmother's Diary* (2008),

© Steve Ellison/Corbis.

Chalcot Crescent (2010), *Kehua!* (2011), and *Habits of the House* (2012), and an equal number of plays and scripts. Her collections of short stories include *Moon over Minneapolis* (1992), *Wicked Women* (American edition, 1997), *A Hard Time to Be a Father* (1998), and *Nothing to Wear and Nowhere to Hide* (2002). Weldon often uses ironic humor to portray carefully drawn female characters coming to terms with the facts of their lives. Awarded a CBE (Commander of the Order of the British Empire) in 2001, Weldon currently teaches creative writing at Bath Spa University in Bath, England.

IND AFF 1988

or Out of Love in Sarajevo

This is a sad story. It has to be. It rained in Sarajevo, and we had expected fine weather.

The rain filled up Sarajevo's pride, two footprints set into a pavement which mark the spot where the young assassin Princip stood to shoot the Archduke Franz Ferdinand and his wife. (Don't forget his wife: everyone forgets his wife, the archduchess.) That was in the summer of 1914. Sarajevo is a pretty town, Balkan style, mountain-rimmed. A broad, swift, shallow river runs through its center, carrying the mountain snow away, arched by many bridges. The one nearest the two footprints has been named the Princip Bridge. The young man is a hero in these parts. Not only does he bring in the tourists — look, look, the spot, the very spot! — but by his action, as everyone knows, he lit a spark which fired the timber which caused World War I which crumbled the Austro-Hungarian Empire, the crumbling of which made modern Yugoslavia possible. Forty million dead (or was it thirty?) but who cares? So long as he loved his country.

The river, they say, can run so shallow in the summer it's known derisively as "the wet road." Today, from what I could see through the sheets of falling rain, it seemed full enough. Yugoslavian streets are always busy — no one stays home if they can help it (thus can an indecent shortage of housing space create a sociable nation) and it seemed as if by common consent a shield of bobbing umbrellas had been erected two meters high to keep the rain off the streets. It just hadn't worked around Princip's corner.

"Come all this way," said Peter, who was a professor of classical history, "and you can't even see the footprints properly, just two undistinguished puddles." Ah, but I loved him. I shivered for his disappointment. He was supervising my thesis on varying concepts of morality and duty in the early Greek States as evidenced in their poetry and drama. I was dependent upon him for my academic future. He said I had a good mind but not a first-class mind and somehow I didn't take it as an insult. I had a feeling first-class minds weren't all that good in bed.

Sarajevo is in Bosnia, in the center of Yugoslavia, that grouping of unlikely 5 states, that distillation of languages into the phonetic reasonableness of Serbo-Croatian. We'd sheltered from the rain in an ancient mosque in Serbian Belgrade; done the same in a monastery in Croatia; now we spent a wet couple of days in Sarajevo beneath other people's umbrellas. We planned to go on to Montenegro, on the coast, where the fish and the artists come from, to swim and lie in the sun, and recover from the exhaustion caused by the sexual and moral torments of the last year. It couldn't possibly go on raining forever. Could it? Satellite pictures showed black clouds swishing gently all over Europe, over the Balkans, into Asia — practically all the way from Moscow to London, in fact. It wasn't that Peter and myself were being singled out. No. It was raining on his wife, too, back in Cambridge.

Peter was trying to decide, as he had been for the past year, between his wife and myself as his permanent life partner. To this end we had gone away, off the beaten track, for a holiday; if not with his wife's blessing, at least with her knowledge. Were we really, truly suited? We had to be sure, you see, that this was more than just any old professor-student romance; that it was the Real Thing, because the longer the indecision went on the longer Mrs. Piper would be left dangling in uncertainty and distress. They had been married for twenty-four years; they had stopped loving each other a long time ago, of course — but there would be a fearful personal and practical upheaval entailed if he decided to leave permanently and shack up, as he put it, with me. Which I certainly wanted him to do. I loved him. And so far I was winning hands down. It didn't seem much of a contest at all, in fact. I'd been cool and thin and informed on the seat next to him in a Zagreb theater (Mrs. Piper was sweaty and only liked telly); was now eager and anxious for social and political instruction in Sarajevo (Mrs. Piper spat in the face of knowledge, he'd once told me); and planned to be lissome (and I thought topless but I hadn't quite decided: this might be the area where the age difference showed) while I splashed and shrieked like a bathing belle in the shallows of the Montenegrin coast. (Mrs. Piper was a swimming coach: I imagined she smelt permanently of chlorine.)

In fact so far as I could see, it was no contest at all between his wife and myself. But Peter liked to luxuriate in guilt and indecision. And I loved him with an inordinate affection.

Princip's prints are a meter apart, placed as a modern cop on a training shoot-out would place his feet — the left in front at a slight outward angle, the right behind, facing forward. There seemed great energy focused here. Both hands on the gun, run, stop, plant the feet, aim, fire! I could see the footprints well enough, in spite of Peter's complaint. They were clear enough to me.

We went to a restaurant for lunch, since it was too wet to do what we loved to do: that is, buy bread, cheese, sausage, wine, and go off somewhere in our hired car, into the woods or the hills, and picnic and make love. It was a private restaurant — Yugoslavia went over to a mixed capitalist-communist economy years back, so you get either the best or worst of both systems, depending on your mood — that is to say, we knew we would pay more but be given a choice. We chose the wild boar.

"Probably ordinary pork soaked in red cabbage water to darken it," said Peter. 10 He was not in a good mood.

Cucumber salad was served first.

"Everything in this country comes with cucumber salad," complained Peter. I noticed I had become used to his complaining. I supposed that when you had been married a little you simply wouldn't hear it. He was forty-six and I was twenty-five.

"They grow a lot of cucumber," I said.

"If they can grow cucumbers," Peter then asked, "why can't they grow *mange-tout*°?" It seemed a why-can't-they-eat-cake sort of argument to me, but not knowing enough about horticulture not to be outflanked if I debated the point, I moved the subject on to safer ground.

"I suppose Princip's action couldn't really have started World War I," I 15 remarked. "Otherwise, what a thing to have on your conscience! One little shot and the deaths of thirty million."

"Forty," he corrected me. Though how they reckon these things and get them right I can't imagine. "Of course he didn't start the war. That's just a simple tale to keep the children quiet. It takes more than an assassination to start a war. What happened was that the buildup of political and economic tensions in the Balkans was such that it had to find some release."

"So it was merely the shot that lit the spark that fired the timber that started the war, et cetera?"

"Quite," he said. "World War I would have had to have started sooner or later."

---

mange-tout: A sugar pea or bean (French).

"A bit later or a bit sooner," I said, "might have made the difference of a million or so; if it was you on the battlefield in the mud and the rain you'd notice; exactly when they fired the starting-pistol; exactly when they blew the final whistle. Is that what they do when a war ends; blow a whistle? So that everyone just comes in from the trenches."

But he wasn't listening. He was parting the flesh of the soft collapsed orangey- 20
red pepper which sat in the middle of his cucumber salad; he was carefully extract-ing the pips. His nan had once told him they could never be digested, would stick inside and do terrible damage. I loved him for his dexterity and patience with his knife and fork. I'd finished my salad yonks ago, pips and all. I was hungry. I wanted my wild boar.

Peter might be forty-six, but he was six foot two and grizzled and muscled with it, in a dark-eyed, intelligent, broad-jawed kind of way. I adored him. I loved to be seen with him. "Muscular academic, not weedy academic" as my younger sister Clare once said. "Muscular academic is just a generally superior human being: everything works well from the brain to the toes. Weedy academic is when there isn't enough vital energy in the person, and the brain drains all the strength from the other parts." Well, Clare should know. Clare is only twenty-three, but of the superior human vari-ety kind herself, vividly pretty, bright and competent — somewhere behind a heavy curtain of vibrant red hair, which she only parts for effect. She had her first degree at twenty. Now she's married to a Harvard professor of economics seconded to the United Nations. She can even cook. I gave up competing yonks ago. Though she too is capable of self-deception. I would say her husband was definitely of the weedy academic rather than the muscular academic type. And they have to live in Brussels.

The archduke's chauffeur had lost his way, and was parked on the corner try-ing to recover his nerve when Princip came running out of a café, planted his feet, aimed, and fired. Princip was nineteen — too young to hang. But they sent him to prison for life and, since he had TB to begin with, he only lasted three years. He died in 1918, in an Austrian prison. Or perhaps it was more than TB: perhaps they gave him a hard time, not learning till later, when the Austro-Hungarian Empire collapsed, that he was a hero. Poor Princip, too young to die — like so many other millions. Dying for love of a country.

"I love you," I said to Peter, my living man, progenitor already of three children by his chlorinated, swimming-coach wife.

"How much do you love me?"

"Inordinately! I love you with inordinate affection." It was a joke between us. 25
Ind Aff!

"Inordinate affection is a sin," he'd told me. "According to the Wesleyans. John Wesley° himself worried about it to such a degree he ended up abbreviating it in his diaries, Ind Aff. He maintained that what he felt for young Sophy, the eighteen-year-old in his congregation, was not Ind Aff, which bears the spirit away from God towards the flesh: he insisted that what he felt was a pure and spiritual, if passionate, concern for her soul."

Peter said now, as we waited for our wild boar, and he picked over his pepper, "Your Ind Aff is my wife's sorrow, that's the trouble." He wanted, I knew, one of the long half-wrangles, half soul-sharings that we could keep going for hours, and led to piercing pains in the heart which could only be made better in bed. But our bedroom at the Hotel Europa was small and dark and looked out into the well of

---

John Wesley (1703–1791): English religious leader and founder of Methodism.

the building — a punishment room if ever there was one. (Reception staff did sometimes take against us.) When Peter had tried to change it in his quasi-Serbo-Croa-
tian, they'd shrugged their Bosnian shoulders and pretended not to understand, so
we'd decided to put up with it. I did not fancy pushing hard single beds together — it
seemed easier not to have the pain in the heart in the first place. "Look," I said, "this
holiday is supposed to be just the two of us, not Mrs. Piper as well. Shall we talk
about something else?"

Do not think that the archduke's chauffeur was merely careless, an inefficient
chauffeur, when he took the wrong turning. He was, I imagine, in a state of shock,
fright, and confusion. There had been two previous attempts on the archduke's life
since the cavalcade had entered town. The first was a bomb which got the car in
front and killed its driver. The second was a shot fired by none other than young
Princip, which had missed. Princip had vanished into the crowd and gone to sit
down in a corner café and ordered coffee to calm his nerves. I expect his hand
trembled at the best of times — he did have TB. (Not the best choice of assassin,
but no doubt those who arrange these things have to make do with what they can
get.) The archduke's chauffeur panicked, took the wrong road, realized what he'd
done, and stopped to await rescue and instructions just outside the café where
Princip sat drinking his coffee.
   "What shall we talk about?" asked Peter, in even less of a good mood.
   "The collapse of the Austro-Hungarian Empire?" I suggested. "How does an   30
empire collapse? Is there no money to pay the military or the police, so everyone
goes home? Or what?" He liked to be asked questions.
   "The Hungro-Austrarian Empire," said Peter to me, "didn't so much collapse
as fail to exist any more. War destroys social organizations. The same thing happened after World War II. There being no organized bodies left between Moscow
and London — and for London read Washington, then as now — it was left to
these two to put in their own puppet governments. Yalta, 1944. It's taken the best
part of forty-five years for nations of West and East Europe to remember who
they are."
   "Austro-Hungarian," I said, "not Hungro-Austrarian."
   "I didn't say Hungro-Austrarian," he said.
   "You did," I said.
   "Didn't," he said. "What the hell are they doing about our wild boar? Are they   35
out in the hills shooting it?"
   My sister Clare had been surprisingly understanding about Peter. When I worried about him being older, she pooh-poohed it; when I worried about him being
married, she said, "Just go for it, sister. If you can unhinge a marriage, it's ripe for
unhinging, it would happen sooner or later, it might as well be you. See a catch, go
ahead and catch! Go for it!"
   Princip saw the archduke's car parked outside, and went for it. Second
chances are rare in life: they must be responded to. Except perhaps his second
chance was missing in the first place? Should he have taken his cue from fate,
and just sat and finished his coffee, and gone home to his mother? But what's
a man to do when he loves his country? Fate delivered the archduke into his
hands: how could he resist it? A parked car, a uniformed and medaled chest,
the persecutor of his country — how could Princip not, believing God to be
on his side, but see this as His intervention, push his coffee aside and leap to
his feet?

Two waiters stood idly by and watched us waiting for our wild boar. One was young and handsome in a mountainous Bosnian way—flashing eyes, hooked nose, luxuriant black hair, sensuous mouth. He was about my age. He smiled. His teeth were even and white. I smiled back, and instead of the pain in the heart I'd become accustomed to as an erotic sensation, now felt, quite violently, an associated yet different pang which got my lower stomach. The true, the real pain of Ind Aff!

"Fancy him?" asked Peter.

"No," I said. "I just thought if I smiled the wild boar might come quicker." 40

The other waiter was older and gentler: his eyes were soft and kind. I thought he looked at me reproachfully. I could see why. In a world which for once, after centuries of savagery, was finally full of young men, unslaughtered, what was I doing with this man with thinning hair?

"What are you thinking of?" Professor Piper asked me. He liked to be in my head.

"How much I love you," I said automatically, and was finally aware how much I lied. "And about the archduke's assassination," I went on, to cover the kind of tremble in my head as I came to my senses, "and let's not forget his wife, she died too—how can you say World War I would have happened anyway. If Princip hadn't shot the archduke, something else, some undisclosed, unsuspected variable, might have come along and defused the whole political/ military situation, and neither World War I nor II ever happened. We'll just never know, will we?"

I had my passport and my travelers' checks with me. (Peter felt it was less confusing if we each paid our own way.) I stood up, and took my raincoat from the peg.

"Where are you going?" he asked, startled. 45

"Home," I said. I kissed the top of his head, where it was balding. It smelt gently of chlorine, which may have come from thinking about his wife so much, but might merely have been that he'd taken a shower that morning. ("The water all over Yugoslavia, though safe to drink, is unusually chlorinated": Guide Book.) As I left to catch a taxi to the airport the younger of the two waiters emerged from the kitchen with two piled plates of roasted wild boar, potatoes duchesse, and stewed peppers. ("Yugoslavian diet is unusually rich in proteins and fats": Guide Book.) I could tell from the glisten of oil that the food was no longer hot, and I was not tempted to stay, hungry though I was. Thus fate—or was it Bosnian willfulness?—confirmed the wisdom of my intent.

And that was how I fell out of love with my professor, in Sarajevo, a city to which I am grateful to this day, though I never got to see very much of it, because of the rain.

It was a silly sad thing to do, in the first place, to confuse mere passing academic ambition with love: to try and outdo my sister Clare. (Professor Piper was spiteful, as it happened, and did his best to have my thesis refused, but I went to appeal, which he never thought I'd dare, and won. I had a first-class mind after all.) A silly sad episode, which I regret. As silly and sad as Princip, poor young man, with his feverish mind, his bright tubercular cheeks, and his inordinate affection for his country, pushing aside his cup of coffee, leaping to his feet, taking his gun in both hands, planting his feet, aiming, and firing—one, two, three shots—and starting World War I. The first one missed, the second got the wife (never forget the wife), and the third got the archduke and a whole generation, and their children, and their children's children, and on and on forever. If he'd just hung on a bit, there in Sarajevo, that June day, he might have come to his senses. People do, sometimes quite quickly.

Considerations for Critical Thinking and Writing

1. FIRST RESPONSE. Do you agree with Weldon's first line, "This is a sad story"? Explain why or why not.

2. How does the rain establish the mood for the story in the first five paragraphs?

3. Characterize Peter. What details concerning him reveal his personality?

4. Describe the narrator's relationship with Peter. How do you think he regards her? Why is she attracted to him?

5. Why is Sarajevo important for the story's setting? What is the effect of having the story of Princip's assassination of the Archduke Franz Ferdinand and his wife woven through the plot?

6. Describe Mrs. Piper. Though she doesn't appear in the story, she does have an important role. What do you think her role is?

7. What is "Ind Aff"? Why is it an important element of this story?

8. What is the significance of the two waiters (paras. 38–41)? How do they affect the narrator?

9. Why does the narrator decide to go home (para. 46)? Do you think she makes a reasoned or an impulsive decision? Explain why you think so.

10. Discuss the relationship between the personal history and the public history recounted in the story. How are the two interconnected? Explain whether you think it is necessary to be familiar with the assassinations in Sarajevo before reading the story.

11. CRITICAL STRATEGIES. Read the section on cultural criticism (pp. 1654–55) in Chapter 51, "Critical Strategies for Reading." How do you think a cultural critic might describe the nature of the narrator's relationship with her professor given the current attitudes on college campuses concerning teacher-student affairs?

Connections to Other Selections

1. Explain how Weldon's concept of "Ind Aff" — "inordinate affection" — can be used to make sense of the relationship between Georgiana and Aylmer in Nathaniel Hawthorne's "The Birthmark" (p. 339).

2. Compare and contrast "IND AFF" and David Updike's "Summer" (p. 301) as love stories. Do you think that the stories end happily or the way you would want them to? Are the endings problematic?

Perspective

FAY WELDON (B. 1933)

On the Importance of Place in "IND AFF" 1997

I'm the kind of writer who lives mostly in her head, looking inwards not outwards, more sensitive to people than places, unless the place turns out to be some useful metaphor. In Sarajevo, on a book tour, brooding about Ind. Aff., inordinate affection, these days more unkindly known as neurotic dependency, I was taken to see Princip's footsteps in the sidewalk. Fancy fell away. Here was the metaphor taken in physical form — chance and death, so like chance and love. Then later we went up into the hills to eat wild boar and the intellectual Englishmen I was with seemed so pallid and absurd compared to the here-and-now mountain men: people came into perspective inside a landscape. I have a kind of rule of thumb: three preoccupations make a story. I interweaved them, delivered them into paper, and fell back into jet-lagged torpor.

From an interview with Michael Meyer, November 15, 1997

CONSIDERATIONS FOR CRITICAL THINKING AND WRITING

1. Weldon's description of how she began "IND AFF" draws on her personal experience in Sarajevo. How does that experience make its way into the story?

2. Consider Weldon's observation that "here was the metaphor taken in physical form — chance and death, so like chance and love." Do you think her observation works as a summary of the story?

3. Choose any other story in this anthology that can serve as an example of how "people [come] into perspective inside a landscape," and write an essay about it.

A SAMPLE STUDENT RESPONSE

Karita Perez

Professor Hoffs

English 202

30 November 2015

The Significance of Setting in Fay Weldon's "IND AFF"

In the first line of Fay Weldon's "IND AFF," we are told "This is a sad story" (Weldon 186), and the setting immediately reflects that. The story takes place in Sarajevo, where the skies are dark and the rain never stops. A young woman and her lover (twenty years her senior, and also her university professor) are on holiday visiting the landmark where Archduke Ferdinand was assassinated. The trip is meant to be pleasant, a break from their lives to determine if they are "truly suited" for each other. But just as the rains spoil their trip, their relationship is spoiled by a reality they cannot control. The main character feels guilt and sympathizes with her lover's wife: "It was raining on his wife, too" (186). She begins to see her lover in a new light, and her hopes for something beautiful give way to disappointment.

The setting also creates a mood that shapes the story, what Michael Meyer calls an "atmosphere that will prepare the reader for what is to come" (159). Along with the dismal weather, the descriptions of the landscape represent what the characters are going through. Despite the rains, there is beauty here; the town is "mountain-rimmed," and a "shallow river runs through its center, carrying the mountain snow away, arched by many bridges" (Weldon 186). This majestic scenery can be read as connected to the physical stature of Peter. The main character, despite her doubts, has strong feelings for Peter and is drawn to his height and attractiveness: "he was six foot two and grizzled and muscled with it, in a dark-eyed, intelligent, broad-jawed kind of way. I adored him" (188). . . .

Works Cited

Meyer, Michael, ed. *The Bedford Introduction to Literature*. 11th ed. Boston: Bedford/St. Martin's, 2016. Print.

Weldon, Fay. "IND AFF, or Out of Love in Sarajevo." Meyer 186–91.

6

Point of View

It is not necessary to portray many characters. The center of gravity should be in two persons: him and her.
— ANTON CHEKHOV

© Austrian Archives/CORBIS.

Because one of the pleasures of reading fiction consists of seeing the world through someone else's eyes, it is easy to overlook the eyes that control our view of the plot, characters, and setting. *Point of view* refers to who tells us the story and how it is told. What we know and how we feel about the events in a story are shaped by the author's choice of a point of view. The teller of a story, the *narrator*, inevitably affects our understanding of the characters' actions by filtering what is told through his or her own perspective. The narrator should not be confused with the author who has created the narrative voice because the two are usually distinct (more on this point later).

If the narrative voice is changed, the story will change. Consider, for example, how different "Bartleby, the Scrivener" (p. 130) would be if Melville had chosen to tell the story from Bartleby's point of view instead of the lawyer's. With Bartleby as narrator, much of the mystery concerning his behavior would be lost. The peculiar force of his saying "I would prefer not to" would be lessened amid all the other things he would have to say as narrator. Moreover, the lawyer's reaction — puzzled, upset, outraged, and finally sympathetic to Bartleby — would be lost too. It would be entirely possible, of course, to write a story from Bartleby's point of view, but it would not be the story Melville wrote.

The possible ways of telling a story are many, and more than one point of view can be worked into a single story. However, the various points of view that storytellers draw on can be conveniently grouped into two broad categories: (1) the third-person narrator and (2) the first-person narrator. The third-person narrator uses *he, she,* or *they* to tell the story and does not participate in the action. The first-person narrator uses *I* and is a major or minor participant in the action. A second-person narrator, *you*, is possible but is rarely used because of the awkwardness in thrusting the reader into the story, as in "You are minding your own business on a park bench when a drunk steps out of the bushes and demands your lunch bag."

Let's look now at the most important and most often used variations within first- and third-person narrations.

THIRD-PERSON NARRATOR (Nonparticipant)

1. Omniscient (the narrator takes us inside the character[s])
2. Limited omniscient (the narrator takes us inside one or two characters)
3. Objective (the narrator is outside the character[s])

No type of third-person narrator appears as a character in a story. The *omniscient narrator* is all-knowing. From this point of view, the narrator can move from place to place and pass back and forth through time, slipping into and out of characters as no human being possibly could in real life. This narrator can report the characters' thoughts and feelings as well as what they say and do. In the excerpt from *Tarzan of the Apes* (p. 69), Burroughs's narrator tells us about events concerning Terkoz in another part of the jungle that long preceded the battle between Terkoz and Tarzan. We also learn Tarzan's and Jane's inner thoughts and emotions during the episode. And Burroughs's narrator describes Terkoz as "an arrant coward" and a bully, thereby evaluating the character for the reader. This kind of intrusion is called *editorial omniscience*. In contrast, narration that allows characters' actions and thoughts to speak for themselves is known as *neutral omniscience*. Most modern writers use neutral omniscience so that readers can reach their own conclusions.

The *limited omniscient narrator* is much more confined than the omniscient narrator. With limited omniscience the author very often restricts the narrator to the single perspective of either a major or a minor character. Sometimes a narrator can see into more than one character, particularly in a longer work that focuses, for example, on two characters alternately from one chapter to the next. Short stories, however, frequently are restricted by length to a single character's point of view. The way people, places, and events appear to that character is the way they appear to the reader. The reader has access to the thoughts and feelings of the characters revealed by the narrator, but neither the reader nor the character has access to the inner lives of any of the other characters in the story. The events in Katherine Mansfield's "Miss Brill" (p. 259) are viewed entirely through the protagonist's eyes; we see a French vacation town as an elderly woman does. Miss Brill represents the central consciousness of the story. She unifies the story by being present through all the action. We are not told of anything that happens away from the character because the narration is based on her perception of things.

The most intense use of a central consciousness in narration can be seen in the **stream-of-consciousness technique** developed by modern writers such as James Joyce, Virginia Woolf, and William Faulkner. This technique takes a reader inside a character's mind to reveal perceptions, thoughts, and feelings on a conscious or unconscious level. A stream of consciousness suggests the flow of thought as well as its content; hence, complete sentences may give way to fragments as the character's mind makes rapid associations free of conventional logic or transitions.

The following passage is from Joyce's *Ulysses,* a novel famous for its extended use of this technique. In this paragraph Joyce takes us inside the mind of a character who is describing a funeral:

> Coffin now. Got here before us, dead as he is. Horse looking round at it with his plume skeowways [askew]. Dull eye: collar tight on his neck, pressing on a bloodvessel or something. Do they know what they cart out of here every day? Must be twenty or thirty funerals every day. Then Mount Jerome for the protestants. Funerals all over the world everywhere every minute. Shovelling them under by the cartload doublequick. Thousands every hour. Too many in the world.

The character's thoughts range from specific observations to speculations about death. Joyce creates the illusion that we are reading the character's thoughts as they occur. The stream-of-consciousness technique provides an intimate perspective on a character's thoughts.

In contrast, the **objective point of view** employs a narrator who does not see into the mind of any character. From this detached and impersonal perspective, the narrator reports action and dialogue without telling us directly what the character feels and thinks. We observe the characters in much the same way we would perceive events in a film or play: we supply the meanings; no analysis or interpretation is provided by the narrator. This point of view places a heavy premium on dialogue, actions, and details to reveal character.

In Hemingway's "Soldier's Home" (p. 162), a limited omniscient narration is the predominant point of view. Krebs's thoughts and reaction to being home from the war are made available to the reader by the narrator, who tells us that Krebs "felt embarrassed and resentful" or "sick and vaguely nauseated" by the small-town life he has reentered. Occasionally, however, Hemingway uses an objective point of view when he dramatizes particularly tense moments between Krebs and his mother. In the following excerpt, Hemingway's narrator shows us Krebs's feelings instead of telling us what they are. Krebs's response to his mother's concerns is presented without comment. The external details of the scene reveal his inner feelings.

> "I've worried about you so much, Harold," his mother went on. "I know the temptations you must have been exposed to. I know how weak men are. I know what your own dear grandfather, my own father, told us about the Civil War and I have prayed for you. I pray for you all day long, Harold."
>
> Krebs looked at the bacon fat hardening on his plate.
>
> "Your father is worried, too," his mother went on. "He thinks you have lost your ambition, that you haven't got a definite aim in life. Charley Simmons, who is just your age, has a good job and is going to be married. The boys are all settling down; they're all determined to get somewhere; you can see that boys like Charley Simmons are on their way to being really a credit to the community."
>
> Krebs said nothing.
>
> "Don't look that way, Harold. . . ."

When Krebs looks at the bacon fat, we can see him cooling and hardening too. Hemingway does not describe the expression on Krebs's face, yet we know it is a look that disturbs his mother as she goes on about what she thinks she knows. Krebs and his mother are clearly tense and upset; the details, action, and dialogue reveal that without the narrator telling the reader how each character feels.

FIRST-PERSON NARRATOR (Participant)

1. Major character
2. Minor character

With a *first-person narrator*, the *I* presents the point of view of only one character's consciousness. The reader is restricted to the perceptions, thoughts, and feelings of that single character. This is Melville's technique with the lawyer in "Bartleby, the Scrivener" (p. 130). Everything learned about the characters, action, and plot comes from the unnamed lawyer. Bartleby remains a mystery because we are limited to what the lawyer knows and reports. The lawyer cannot explain what Bartleby means because he does not entirely know himself. Melville's use of the first person encourages us to identify with the lawyer's confused reaction to Bartleby so that we pay attention not only to the scrivener but to the lawyer's response to him. We are as perplexed as the lawyer and share his effort to make sense of Bartleby.

The lawyer is a major character in Melville's story; indeed, many readers take him to be the protagonist. A first-person narrator can, however, also be a minor character (imagine how different the story would be if it were told by, say, Ginger Nut or by an observer who had little or nothing to do with the action). Faulkner uses an observer in "A Rose for Emily" (p. 78). His *we*, though plural and representative of the town's view of Emily, is nonetheless a first-person narrator.

One of the primary reasons for identifying the point of view in a story is to determine where the author stands in relation to the story. Behind the narrative voice of any story is the author, manipulating events and providing or withholding information. It is a mistake to assume that the narrative voice of a story is the author. The narrator, whether a first-person participant or a third-person nonparticipant, is a creation of the writer. A narrator's perceptions may be accepted, rejected, or modified by an author, depending on how the narrative voice is articulated.

Faulkner seems to have shared the fascination, sympathy, and horror of the narrator in "A Rose for Emily," but Melville must not be so readily identified with the lawyer in "Bartleby, the Scrivener." The lawyer's description of himself as "an eminently *safe* man," convinced "that the easiest way of life is the best," raises the question of how well equipped he is to fathom Bartleby's protest. To make sense of Bartleby, it is also necessary to understand the lawyer's point of view. Until the conclusion of the story, this "*safe* man" is too self-serving, defensive, and obtuse to comprehend the despair embodied in Bartleby and the deadening meaninglessness of Wall Street life.

The lawyer is an **unreliable narrator**, whose interpretation of events is different from the author's. We cannot entirely accept the lawyer's assessment of Bartleby because we see that the lawyer's perceptions are not totally to be trusted. Melville does not expect us, for example, to agree with the lawyer's suggestion that the solution to Bartleby's situation might be to "entertain some young gentleman with your conversation" on a trip to Europe. Given Bartleby's awful silences, this absurd suggestion reveals the lawyer's superficial understanding. The lawyer's perceptions frequently do not coincide with those Melville expects his readers to share. Hence, the lawyer's unreliability preserves Bartleby's mysterious nature while revealing the lawyer's sensibilities. The point of view is artistically appropriate for Melville's purposes because the eyes through which we perceive the plot, characters, and setting are also the subject of the story.

Narrators can be unreliable for a variety of reasons: they might lack self-knowledge, like Melville's lawyer, or they might be innocent and inexperienced, like Ralph Ellison's young narrator in "Battle Royal" (p. 227). Youthful innocence frequently characterizes a **naive narrator** such as Mark Twain's Huck Finn or Holden Caulfield, J. D. Salinger's twentieth-century version of Huck in *The Catcher in the Rye*. These narrators lack the sophistication to interpret accurately what they see; they are unreliable because the reader must go beyond their understanding of events to comprehend the situations described. Huck and Holden describe their respective social environments, but the reader, with more experience, supplies the critical perspective that each boy lacks. In "Battle Royal" that perspective is supplemented by Ellison's dividing the narration between the young man who experiences events and the mature man who reflects back on those events.

Few generalizations can be made about the advantages or disadvantages of using a specific point of view. What can be said with confidence, however, is that writers choose a point of view to achieve particular effects because point of view determines what we know about the characters and events in a story.

We should, therefore, be aware of who is telling the story and whether the narrator sees things clearly and reliably.

The next three works warrant a careful examination of their points of view. In John Updike's "A & P," the youthful narrator makes a crucial decision that will change his sensibilities. In Alice Munro's "Wild Swans," an eager, inexperienced young woman has a tense encounter with a stranger on a train. And in Maggie Mitchell's "It Would Be Different If," a woman reflects upon an early rejection in her life.

JOHN UPDIKE (1932–2009)

John Updike grew up in the small town of Shillington, Pennsylvania, and on a family farm nearby. Academic success in school earned him a scholarship to Harvard, where he studied English and graduated in 1954. He soon sold his first story and poem to the *New Yorker*. Also an artist, Updike studied drawing in Oxford, England, and returned to take a position on the staff at the *New Yorker*. His first book, a collection of poems titled *The Carpentered Hen and Other Tame Creatures*, appeared in 1958, and the following year he published a book of stories and a novel, *The Poorhouse Fair*, which received the Rosenthal Foundation Award in 1960.

Boston Globe / Getty Images.

Updike produced his second novel, *Rabbit, Run,* in the same year. The prolific Updike lived in Massachusetts the rest of his life and continued to publish essays, poems, a novel, or a book of stories nearly every year, including *The Centaur* (1963), winner of the National Book Award; *Rabbit Is Rich* (1981) and *Rabbit at Rest* (1990), both Pulitzer Prize winners; and *The Witches of Eastwick* (1984), which was made into a major motion picture (Warner Bros., 1987). His last novel was *Terrorist* (2006), and his last short story collection was *My Father's Tears and Other Stories* (2009). Updike's fiction is noted for its exemplary use of storytelling conventions, its unique prose style, and its engaging picture of middle-class American life.

A & P 1961

In walks these three girls in nothing but bathing suits. I'm in the third checkout slot, with my back to the door, so I don't see them until they're over by the bread. The one that caught my eye first was the one in the plaid green two-piece. She was a chunky kid, with a good tan and a sweet broad soft-looking can with those two crescents of white just under it, where the sun never seems to hit, at the top of the backs of her legs. I stood there with my hand on a box of HiHo crackers trying to remember if I rang it up or not. I ring it up again and the customer starts giving me hell. She's one of these cash-register-watchers, a witch about fifty with rouge on her cheekbones and no eyebrows, and I know it made her day to trip me up. She'd been watching cash registers for fifty years and probably never seen a mistake before.

By the time I got her feathers smoothed and her goodies into a bag — she gives me a little snort in passing, if she'd been born at the right time they would have burned her over in Salem — by the time I get her on her way the girls had circled around the bread and were coming back, without a pushcart, back my way along the counters, in the aisle between the checkouts and the Special bins. They didn't even have shoes on. There was this chunky one, with the two-piece — it was bright green and the seams on the bra were still sharp and her belly was still pretty pale so I guessed she just got it (the suit) — there was this one, with one of those chubby berry-faces, the lips all bunched together under her nose, this one, and a tall one, with black hair that hadn't quite frizzed right, and one of these sunburns right across under the eyes, and a chin that was too long — you know, the kind of girl other girls think is very "striking" and "attractive" but never quite makes it, as they very well know, which is why they like her so much — and then the third one, that wasn't quite so tall. She was the queen. She kind of led them, the other two peeking around and making their shoulders round. She didn't look around, not this queen, she just walked straight on slowly, on these long white prima-donna legs. She came down a little hard on her heels, as if she didn't walk in her bare feet that much, putting down her heels and then letting the weight move along to her toes as if she was testing the floor with every step, putting a little deliberate extra action into it. You never know for sure how girls' minds work (do you really think it's a mind in there or just a little buzz like a bee in a glass jar?) but you got the idea she had talked the other two into coming in here with her, and now she was showing them how to do it, walk slow and hold yourself straight.

She had on a kind of dirty-pink — beige maybe, I don't know — bathing suit with a little nubble all over it and, what got me, the straps were down. They were off her shoulders looped loose around the cool tops of her arms, and I guess as a result the suit had slipped a little on her, so all around the top of the cloth there was this shining rim. If it hadn't been there you wouldn't have known there could have been anything whiter than those shoulders. With the straps pushed off, there was nothing between the top of the suit and the top of her head except just *her,* this clean bare plane of the top of her chest down from the shoulder bones like a dented sheet of metal tilted in the light. I mean, it was more than pretty.

She had sort of oaky hair that the sun and salt had bleached, done up in a bun that was unraveling, and a kind of prim face. Walking into the A & P with your straps down, I suppose it's the only kind of face you *can* have. She held her head so high her neck, coming up out of those white shoulders, looked kind of stretched, but I didn't mind. The longer her neck was, the more of her there was.

She must have felt in the corner of her eye me and over my shoulder Stokesie 5 in the second slot watching, but she didn't tip. Not this queen. She kept her eyes moving across the racks, and stopped, and turned so slow it made my stomach rub the inside of my apron, and buzzed to the other two, who kind of huddled against her for relief, and then they all three of them went up the cat-and-dogfood-breakfast-cereal-macaroni-rice-raisins-seasonings-spreads-spaghetti-soft-drinks-crackers-and-cookies aisle. From the third slot I look straight up this aisle to the meat counter, and I watched them all the way. The fat one with the tan sort of fumbled with the cookies, but on second thought she put the package back. The sheep pushing their carts down the aisle — the girls were walking against the usual traffic (not that we have one-way signs or anything) — were pretty hilarious. You could see them, when Queenie's white shoulders dawned on them, kind of jerk, or hop, or hiccup, but their eyes snapped back to their own baskets and on they pushed. I bet you could set off dynamite in an A & P and the people would by and large keep reaching and checking oatmeal off their lists and muttering "Let me see, there was a third thing, began with A, asparagus, no, ah, yes, applesauce!" or whatever it is they do mutter. But there was no doubt, this jiggled them. A few houseslaves in pin curlers even looked around after pushing their carts past to make sure what they had seen was correct.

You know, it's one thing to have a girl in a bathing suit down on the beach, where what with the glare nobody can look at each other much anyway, and another thing in the cool of the A & P, under the fluorescent lights, against all those stacked packages, with her feet paddling along naked over our checker-board green-and-cream rubber-tile floor.

"Oh Daddy," Stokesie said beside me. "I feel so faint."

"Darling," I said. "Hold me tight." Stokesie's married, with two babies chalked up on his fuselage already, but as far as I can tell that's the only difference. He's twenty-two, and I was nineteen this April.

"Is it done?" he asks, the responsible married man finding his voice. I forgot to say he thinks he's going to be manager some sunny day, maybe in 1990 when it's called the Great Alexandrov and Petrooshki Tea Company or something.

What he meant was, our town is five miles from a beach, with a big summer colony out on the Point, but we're right in the middle of town, and the women generally put on a shirt or shorts or something before they get out of the car into the street. And anyway these are usually women with six children and varicose veins mapping their legs and nobody, including them, could care less. As I say, we're right in the middle of town, and if you stand at our front doors you can see two banks and the Congregational church and the newspaper store and three real-estate offices and about twenty-seven old freeloaders tearing up Central Street because the sewer broke again. It's not as if we're on the Cape, we're north of Boston and there's people in this town haven't seen the ocean for twenty years.

The girls had reached the meat counter and were asking McMahon something. He pointed, they pointed, and they shuffled out of sight behind a pyramid of Diet Delight peaches. All that was left for us to see was old McMahon patting his mouth and looking after them sizing up their joints. Poor kids, I began to feel sorry for them, they couldn't help it.

Now here comes the sad part of the story, at least my family says it's sad, but I don't think it's so sad myself. The store's pretty empty, it being Thursday afternoon, so there was nothing much to do except lean on the register and wait for the girls to show up again. The whole store was like a pinball machine and I didn't know which tunnel they'd come out of. After a while they come around out of the far aisle, around the light bulbs, records at discount of the Caribbean Six or Tony Martin Sings or some such gunk you wonder they waste the wax on, sixpacks of candy bars, and plastic toys done up in cellophane that fall apart when a kid looks at them anyway. Around they come, Queenie still leading the way, and holding a little gray jar in her hands. Slots Three through Seven are unmanned and I could see her wondering between Stokes and me, but Stokesie with his usual luck draws an old party in baggy gray pants who stumbles up with four giant cans of pineapple juice (what do these bums *do* with all that pineapple juice? I've often asked myself). So the girls come to me.

10

Queenie puts down the jar and I take it into my fingers icy cold. Kingfish Fancy Herring Snacks in Pure Sour Cream: 49¢. Now her hands are empty, not a ring or a bracelet, bare as God made them, and I wonder where the money's coming from. Still with that prim look she lifts a folded dollar bill out of the hollow at the center of her nubbled pink top. The jar went heavy in my hand. Really, I thought that was so cute.

Then everybody's luck begins to run out. Lengel comes in from haggling with a truck full of cabbages on the lot and is about to scuttle into that door marked MANAGER behind which he hides all day when the girls touch his eye. Lengel's pretty dreary, teaches Sunday school and the rest, but he doesn't miss that much. He comes over and says, "Girls, this isn't the beach."

Queenie blushes, though maybe it's just a brush of sunburn I was noticing for the first time, now that she was so close. "My mother asked me to pick up a jar of herring snacks." Her voice kind of startled me, the way voices do when you see the people first, coming out so flat and dumb yet kind of tony, too, the way it ticked over "pick up" and "snacks." All of a sudden I slid right down her voice into the living room. Her father and the other men were standing around in ice-cream coats and bow ties and the women were in sandals picking up herring snacks on toothpicks off a big glass plate and they were all holding drinks the color of water with olives and sprigs of mint in them. When my parents have somebody over they get lemonade and if it's a real racy affair Schlitz in tall glasses with "They'll Do It Every Time" cartoons stenciled on.

"That's all right," Lengel said. "But this isn't the beach." His repeating this 15 struck me as funny, as if it had just occurred to him, and he had been thinking all these years the A & P was a great big dune and he was the head lifeguard. He didn't like my smiling — as I say he doesn't miss much — but he concentrates on giving the girls that sad Sunday-school-superintendent stare.

Queenie's blush is no sunburn now, and the plump one in plaid, that I liked better from the back — a really sweet can — pipes up, "We weren't doing any shopping. We just came in for the one thing."

"That makes no difference," Lengel tells her, and I could see from the way his eyes went that he hadn't noticed she was wearing a two-piece before. "We want you decently dressed when you come in here."

"We *are* decent," Queenie says suddenly, her lower lip pushing, getting sore now that she remembers her place, a place from which the crowd that runs the A & P must look pretty crummy. Fancy Herring Snacks flashed in her very blue eyes.

"Girls, I don't want to argue with you. After this come in here with your shoulders covered. It's our policy." He turns his back. That's policy for you. Policy is what the kingpins want. What the others want is juvenile delinquency.

All this while, the customers had been showing up with their carts but, you 20 know, sheep, seeing a scene, they had all bunched up on Stokesie, who shook open a paper bag as gently as peeling a peach, not wanting to miss a word. I could feel in the silence everybody getting nervous, most of all Lengel, who asks me, "Sammy, have you rung up their purchase?"

I thought and said "No" but it wasn't about that I was thinking. I go through the punches, 4, 9, GROC. TOT — it's more complicated than you think, and after you do it often enough, it begins to make a little song, that you hear words to, in my case "Hello *(bing)* there, you *(gung)* hap-py pee-pul *(splat)!*" — the *splat* being the drawer flying out. I uncrease the bill, tenderly as you may imagine, it just having come from between the two smoothest scoops of vanilla I had ever known were there, and pass a half and a penny into her narrow pink palm, and nestle the herrings in a bag and twist its neck and hand it over, all the time thinking.

The girls, and who'd blame them, are in a hurry to get out, so I say "I quit" to Lengel quick enough for them to hear, hoping they'll stop and watch me, their unsuspected hero. They keep right on going, into the electric eye; the door flies open and they flicker across the lot to their car, Queenie and Plaid and Big Tall Goony-Goony (not that as raw material she was so bad), leaving me with Lengel and a kink in his eyebrow.

"Did you say something, Sammy?"

"I said I quit."

"I thought you did."   25

"You didn't have to embarrass them."

"It was they who were embarrassing us."

I started to say something that came out "Fiddle-de-doo." It's a saying of my grandmother's, and I know she would have been pleased.

"I don't think you know what you're saying," Lengel said.

"I know you don't," I said. "But I do." I pull the bow at the back of my apron and   30 start shrugging it off my shoulders. A couple customers that had been heading for my slot begin to knock against each other, like scared pigs in a chute.

Lengel sighs and begins to look very patient and old and gray. He's been a friend of my parents for years. "Sammy, you don't want to do this to your Mom and Dad," he tells me. It's true, I don't. But it seems to me that once you begin a gesture it's fatal not to go through with it. I fold the apron, "Sammy" stitched in red on the pocket, and put it on the counter, and drop the bow tie on top of it. The bow tie is theirs, if you've ever wondered. "You'll feel this for the rest of your life," Lengel says, and I know that's true, too, but remembering how he made the pretty girl blush makes me so scrunchy inside I punch the No Sale tab and the machine whirs "pee-pul" and the drawer splats out. One advantage to this scene taking place in summer, I can follow this up with a clean exit, there's no fumbling around getting your coat and galoshes, I just saunter into the electric eye in my white shirt that my mother ironed the night before, and the door heaves itself open, and outside the sunshine is skating around on the asphalt.

I look around for my girls, but they're gone, of course. There wasn't anybody but some young married screaming with her children about some candy they didn't get by the door of a powder-blue Falcon station wagon. Looking back in the big windows, over the bags of peat moss and aluminum lawn furniture stacked on the pavement, I could see Lengel in my place in the slot, checking the sheep through. His face was dark gray and his back stiff, as if he'd just had an injection of iron, and my stomach kind of fell as I felt how hard the world was going to be to me hereafter.

Considerations for Critical Thinking and Writing

1. FIRST RESPONSE. Describe the setting. How accurate do you think Updike's treatment of the A & P is?

2. What kind of person is Sammy? How do his actions and speech constitute his own individual style?

3. Analyze the style of the first paragraph. How does it set the tone for the rest of the story?

4. What is the story's central conflict? Does it seem to be a serious or trivial conflict to you?

5. With what kind of values is Lengel associated? Do you feel any sympathy for him?

6. What do you think is Stokesie's function in the story?

7. Consider Sammy's treatment of the three girls. Do you think his account of them is sexist? Explain why or why not.

8. Locate the climax of the story. How does the climax affect your attitude toward Sammy?

9. How do you think the story would be different if it were told from another character's point of view instead of Sammy's?

10. Discuss the thematic significance of the story's final paragraph. Would you read the story differently if this last paragraph were eliminated?

CONNECTION TO ANOTHER SELECTION

1. Compare the tone established by the point of view in this story and in Maggie Mitchell's "It Would Be Different If" (p. 213).

ALICE MUNRO (B. 1931)

Alice Munro began writing in her teens in the small rural town of Wingham, Ontario. She published her first story in 1950 when she was a student at Western Ontario University. Munro's first book, *Dance of the Happy Shades,* was published in 1968, and she went on to publish a number of acclaimed short story collections including *Lives of Girls and Women* (1971), *Something I've Been Meaning to Tell You* (1974), *The Beggar Maid* (1978), *The Moons of Jupiter* (1982), *The Progress of Love* (1986), *Friend of My Youth* (1990), *Open Secrets* (1994), *The Love of a Good Woman* (1998), *Vintage Munro* (2004), *The View from Castle Rock* (2006), *Too Much Happiness* (2009), and *Dear Life* (2012). Among her many awards have been the Governor General's Award (Canada's highest literary prize), the Marian Engel Award, the Man Booker International Prize, and the Nobel Prize for Literature. Often dealing with the "emotional reality" of her characters, Munro's stories have appeared in the *New Yorker,* the *Atlantic, Grand Street, Mademoiselle,* and the *Paris Review.*

Maclean's Magazine/Rich Chard/Canadian Press Images.

Wild Swans 1978

Flo said to watch for White Slavers. She said this was how they operated: an old woman, a motherly or grandmotherly sort, made friends while riding beside you on a bus or train. She offered you candy, which was drugged. Pretty soon you began to droop and mumble, were in no condition to speak for yourself. Oh, help, the woman said, my daughter (granddaughter) is sick, please somebody help me get her off so that she can recover in the fresh air. Up stepped a polite gentleman, pretending to be a stranger, offering assistance. Together, at the next stop, they hustled you off the train or bus, and that was the last the ordinary world ever saw of you. They kept you a prisoner in the White Slave place (to which you had been transported drugged and bound so you wouldn't even know where you were), until such time as you were thoroughly degraded and in despair, your insides torn up by drunken men and invested with vile disease, your mind destroyed by drugs, your hair and teeth fallen out. It took about three years for you to get to this state. You wouldn't want to go home then; maybe couldn't remember home, or find your way if you did. So they let you out on the streets.

Flo took ten dollars and put it in a little cloth bag, which she sewed to the strap of Rose's slip. Another thing likely to happen was that Rose would get her purse stolen.

Watch out, Flo said as well, for people dressed up as ministers. They were the worst. That disguise was commonly adopted by White Slavers, as well as those after your money.

Rose said she didn't see how she could tell which ones were disguised.

Flo had worked in Toronto once. She had worked as a waitress in a coffee shop 5 in Union Station. That was how she knew all she knew. She never saw sunlight, in those days, except on her days off. But she saw plenty else. She saw a man cut another man's stomach with a knife, just pull out his shirt and do a tidy cut, as if it was a watermelon not a stomach. The stomach's owner just sat looking down surprised, with no time to protest. Flo implied that that was nothing, in Toronto. She saw two bad women (that was what Flo called whores, running the two words together, like badminton) get into a fight, and a man laughed at them, other men stopped and laughed and egged them on, and they had their fists full of each other's hair. At last the police came and took them away, still howling and yelping.

She saw a child die of a fit too. Its face was black as ink.

"Well, I'm not scared," said Rose provokingly. "There's the police, anyway."

"Oh, them! They'd be the first ones to diddle you!"

She did not believe anything Flo said on the subject of sex. Consider the undertaker.

A little bald man, very neatly dressed, would come into the store sometimes 10 and speak to Flo with a placating expression.

"I only wanted a bag of candy. And maybe a few packages of gum. And one or two chocolate bars. Could you go to the trouble of wrapping them?"

Flo in her mock-deferential tone would assure him that she could. She wrapped them in heavy-duty white paper, so they were something like presents. He took his time with the selection, humming and chatting, then dawdled for a while. He might ask how Flo was feeling. And how Rose was, if she was there.

"You look pale. Young girls need fresh air." To Flo he would say, "You work too hard. You've worked hard all your life."

"No rest for the wicked," Flo would say agreeably.

When he went out she hurried to the window. There it was — the old black 15 hearse with its purple curtains.

"He'll be after them today!" Flo would say as the hearse rolled away at a gentle pace, almost a funeral pace. The little man had been an undertaker, but he was retired now. The hearse was retired too. His sons had taken over the undertaking and bought a new one. He drove the old hearse all over the country, looking for women. So Flo said. Rose could not believe it. Flo said he gave them the gum and the candy. Rose said he probably ate them himself. Flo said he had been seen, he had been heard. In mild weather he drove with the windows down, singing, to himself or to somebody out of sight in the back.

"Her brow is like the snowdrift
Her throat is like the swan . . ."

Flo imitated him singing. Gently overtaking some woman walking on a back road, or resting at a country crossroads. All compliments and courtesy and chocolate bars, offering a ride. Of course every woman who reported being asked said she had turned him down. He never pestered anybody, drove politely on. He called in at houses, and if the husband was home he seemed to like just as well as anything to sit and chat. Wives said that was all he ever did anyway but Flo did not believe it.

"Some women are taken in," she said. "A number." She liked to speculate on what the hearse was like inside. Plush. Plush on the walls and the roof and the floor. Soft purple, the color of the curtains, the color of dark lilacs.

All nonsense, Rose thought. Who could believe it, of a man that age?

Rose was going to Toronto on the train for the first time by herself. She had been once before, but that was with Flo, long before her father died. They took along their own sandwiches and bought milk from the vendor on the train. It was sour. Sour chocolate milk. Rose kept taking tiny sips, unwilling to admit that something so much desired could fail her. Flo sniffed it, then hunted up and down the train until she found the old man in his red jacket, with no teeth and the tray hanging around his neck. She invited him to sample the chocolate milk. She invited people nearby to smell it. He let her have some ginger ale for nothing. It was slightly warm.

"I let him know," Flo said, looking around after he had left. "You have to let 20 them know."

A woman agreed with her but most people looked out the window. Rose drank the warm ginger ale. Either that, or the scene with the vendor, or the conversation Flo and the agreeing woman now got into about where they came from, why they were going to Toronto, and Rose's morning constipation which was why she was lacking color, or the small amount of chocolate milk she had got inside her, caused her to throw up in the train toilet. All day long she was afraid people in Toronto could smell vomit on her coat.

This time Flo started the trip off by saying, "Keep an eye on her, she's never been away from home before!" to the conductor, then looking around and laughing, to show that was jokingly meant. Then she had to get off. It seemed the conductor had no more need for jokes than Rose had, and no intention of keeping an eye on anybody. He never spoke to Rose except to ask for her ticket. She had a window seat, and was soon extraordinarily happy. She felt Flo receding, West Hanratty flying away from her, her own wearying self discarded as easily as everything else. She loved the towns less and less known. A woman was standing at her back door in her nightgown, not caring if everybody on the train saw her. They were travelling south, out of the snowbelt, into an earlier spring, a tenderer sort of landscape. People could grow peach trees in their back yards.

Rose collected in her mind the things she had to look for in Toronto. First, things for Flo. Special stockings for her varicose veins. A special kind of cement for sticking handles on pots. And a full set of dominoes.

For herself Rose wanted to buy hair-remover to put on her arms and legs, and if possible an arrangement of inflatable cushions, supposed to reduce your hips and thighs. She thought they probably had hair-remover in the drugstore in Hanratty, but the woman in there was a friend of Flo's and told everything. She told Flo who bought hair dye and slimming medicine and French safes. As for the cushion business, you could send away for it but there was sure to be a comment at the Post Office, and Flo knew people there as well. She also planned to buy some bangles, and an angora sweater. She had great hopes of silver bangles and powder-blue angora. She thought they could transform her, make her calm and slender and take the frizz out of her hair, dry her underarms and turn her complexion to pearl.

The money for these things, as well as the money for the trip, came from a 25 prize Rose had won, for writing an essay called "Art and Science in the World of Tomorrow." To her surprise, Flo asked if she could read it, and while she was reading it, she remarked that they must have thought they had to give Rose the prize for swallowing the dictionary. Then she said shyly, "It's very interesting."

She would have to spend the night at Cela McKinney's. Cela McKinney was her father's cousin. She had married a hotel manager and thought she had gone up in the world. But the hotel manager came home one day and sat down on the dining-room floor between two chairs and said, "I am never going to leave this house again." Nothing unusual had happened, he had just decided not to go out of the house again, and he didn't, until he died. That had made Cela McKinney odd and nervous. She locked her doors at eight o'clock. She was also very stingy. Supper was usually oatmeal porridge, with raisins. Her house was dark and narrow and smelled like a bank.

The train was filling up. At Brantford a man asked if she would mind if he sat down beside her.

"It's cooler out than you'd think," he said. He offered her part of his newspaper. She said no thanks.

Then, lest he think her rude, she said it really was cooler. She went on looking out the window at the spring morning. There was no snow left, down here. The trees and bushes seemed to have a paler bark than they did at home. Even the sunlight looked different. It was as different from home, here, as the coast of the Mediterranean would be, or the valleys of California.

"Filthy windows, you'd think they'd take more care," the man said. "Do you 30 travel much by train?"

She said no.

Water was lying in the fields. He nodded at it and said there was a lot this year.

"Heavy snows."

She noticed his saying "snows," a poetic-sounding word. Anyone at home would have said "snows."

"I had an unusual experience the other day. I was driving out in the country. In 35 fact, I was on my way to see one of my parishioners, a lady with a heart condition —"

She looked quickly at his collar. He was wearing an ordinary shirt and tie and a dark-blue suit.

"Oh, yes," he said. "I'm a United Church minister. But I don't always wear my uniform. I wear it for preaching in. I'm off duty today.

"Well, as I said, I was driving through the country and I saw some Canada geese down on a pond, and I took another look, and there were some swans down with them. A whole great flock of swans. What a lovely sight they were. They would be on their spring migration, I expect, heading up North. What spectacle. I never saw anything like it."

Rose was unable to think appreciatively of the wild swans because she was afraid he was going to lead the conversation from them to Nature in general and then to God, the way a minister would feel obliged to do. But he did not, he stopped with the swans.

"A very fine sight. You would have enjoyed them."   40

He was between fifty and sixty years old, Rose thought. He was short, and energetic-looking, with a square ruddy face and bright waves of gray hair combed straight up from his forehead. When she realized he was not going to mention God she felt she ought to show her gratitude.

She said they must have been lovely.

"It wasn't even a regular pond, it was only some water lying in a field. It was just luck the water was lying there and they came down and I came driving by at the right time. Just luck. They come in at the east end of Lake Erie, I think. But I never was lucky enough to see them before."

She turned by degrees to the window, and he returned to his paper. She remained slightly smiling, so as not to seem rude, not to seem to be rejecting conversation altogether. The morning really was cool, and she had taken down her coat off the hook where she put it when she first got on the train; she had spread it over herself, like a lap robe. She had set her purse on the floor when the minister sat down, to give him room. He took the sections of the paper apart, shaking and rustling them in a leisurely, rather showy way. He seemed to her the sort of person who does everything in a showy way. A ministerial way. He brushed aside the sections he didn't want at the moment. A corner of newspaper touched her leg, just at the edge of her coat.

She thought for some time that it was the paper. Then she said to herself, What   45
if it is a hand? That was the kind of thing she could imagine. She would sometimes look at men's hands, at the fuzz on their forearms, their concentrating profiles. She would think about everything they could do. Even the stupid ones. For instance, the driver-salesman who brought the bread to Flo's store. The ripeness and confidence of manner, the settled mixture of ease and alertness with which he handled the bread truck. A fold of mature belly over the belt did not displease her. Another time she had her eye on the French teacher at school. Not a Frenchman at all, really, his name was McLaren, but Rose thought teaching French had rubbed off on him, made him look like one. Quick and sallow; sharp shoulders; hooked nose and sad eyes. She saw him lapping and coiling his way through slow pleasures, a perfect autocrat of indulgences. She had a considerable longing to be somebody's object. Pounded, pleasured, reduced, exhausted.

But what if it was a hand? What if it really was a hand? She shifted slightly, moved as much as she could toward the window. Her imagination seemed to have created this reality, a reality she was not prepared for at all. She found it alarming. She was concentrating on that leg, that bit of skin with the stocking over it. She could not bring herself to look. Was there a pressure, or was there not? She shifted again. Her legs had been, and remained, tightly closed. It was. It was a hand. It was a hand's pressure.

Please don't. That was what she tried to say. She shaped the words in her mind, tried them out, then couldn't get them past her lips. Why was that? The embarrassment, was it, the fear that people might hear? People were all around them, the seats were full.

It was not only that.

She did manage to look at him, not raising her head but turning it cautiously. He had tilted his seat back and closed his eyes. There was his dark-blue suit sleeve, disappearing under the newspaper. He had arranged the paper so that it overlapped Rose's coat. His hand was underneath, simply resting, as if flung out in sleep.

Now, Rose could have shifted the newspaper and removed her coat. If he was 50 not asleep, he would have been obliged to draw back his hand. If he was asleep, if he did not draw it back, she could have whispered *Excuse me* and set his hand firmly on his own knee. This solution, so obvious and foolproof, did not occur to her. And she would have to wonder, Why not? The minister's hand was not, or not yet, at all welcome to her. It made her feel uncomfortable, resentful, slightly disgusted, trapped, and wary. But she could not take charge of it, to reject it. She could not insist that it was there, when he seemed to be insisting that it was not. How could she declare him responsible, when he lay there so harmless and trusting, resting himself before his busy day, with such a pleased and healthy face? A man older than her father would be, if he were living, a man used to deference, an appreciator of Nature, delighter in wild swans. If she did say *Please don't* she was sure he would ignore her, as if overlooking some silliness or impoliteness on her part. She knew that as soon as she said it she would hope he had not heard.

But there was more to it than that. Curiosity. More constant, more imperious, than any lust. A lust in itself, that will make you draw back and wait, wait too long, risk almost anything, just to see what will happen. *To see what will happen.*

The hand began, over the next several miles, the most delicate, the most timid, pressures and investigations. Not asleep. Or if he was, his hand wasn't. She did feel disgust. She felt a faint, wandering nausea. She thought of flesh: lumps of flesh pink snouts, fat tongues, blunt fingers, all on their way trotting and creeping and lolling and rubbing, looking for their comfort. She thought of cats in heat rubbing themselves along the top of board fences, yowling with their miserable complaint. It was pitiful, infantile, this itching and shoving and squeezing. Spongy tissues, inflamed membranes, tormented nerve-ends, shameful smells; humiliation.

All that was starting. His hand, that she wouldn't ever have wanted to hold, that she wouldn't have squeezed back, his stubborn patient hand was able, after all, to get the ferns to rustle and the streams to flow, to waken a sly luxuriance.

Nevertheless, she would rather not. She would still rather not. Please remove this, she said out the window. Stop it, please, she said to the stumps and barns. The hand moved up her leg past the top of her stocking to her bare skin, had moved higher, under her suspender, reached her underpants and the lower part of her belly. Her legs were still crossed, pinched together. While her legs stayed crossed she could lay claim to innocence, she had not admitted anything. She could still believe that she would stop this in a minute. Nothing was going to happen, nothing more. Her legs were never going to open.

But they were. They were. As the train crossed the Niagara Escarpment above 55 Dundas, as they looked down at the preglacial valley, the silver-wooded rubble of little hills, as they came sliding down to the shores of Lake Ontario, she would make this slow, and silent, and definite declaration, perhaps disappointing as much as satisfying the hand's owner. He would not lift his eyelids, his face would not alter, his fingers would not hesitate, but would go powerfully and discreetly to work. Invasion, and welcome, and sunlight flashing far and wide on the lake water; miles of bare orchards stirring round Burlington.

This was disgrace, this was beggary. But what harm in that, we say to ourselves at such moments, what harm in anything, the worse the better, as we ride the cold wave of greed, of greedy assent. A stranger's hand, or root vegetables or humble kitchen tools that people tell jokes about; the world is tumbling with innocent-seeming objects ready to declare themselves, slippery and obliging. She was careful of her breathing. She could not believe this. Victim and accomplice she was borne past

Glassco's Jams and Marmalades, past the big pulsating pipes of oil refineries. They glided into suburbs where bedsheets, and towels used to wipe up intimate stains, flapped leeringly on the clotheslines, where even the children seemed to be frolicking lewdly in the schoolyards, and the very truck drivers stopped at the railway crossings must be thrusting their thumbs gleefully into curled hands. Such cunning antics now, such popular visions. The gates and towers of the Exhibition Grounds came into view, the painted domes and pillars floated marvellously against her eyelids' rosy sky. Then flew apart in celebration. You could have had such a flock of birds, wild swans, even, wakened under one big dome together, exploding from it, taking to the sky.

She bit the edge of her tongue. Very soon the conductor passed through the train, to stir the travellers, warn them back to life.

In the darkness under the station the United Church minister, refreshed, opened his eyes and got his paper folded together, then asked if she would like some help with her coat. His gallantry was self-satisfied, dismissive. No, said Rose, with a sore tongue. He hurried out of the train ahead of her. She did not see him in the station. She never saw him again in her life. But he remained on call, so to speak, for years and years, ready to slip into place at a critical moment, without even any regard, later on, for husband or lovers. What recommended him? She could never understand it. His simplicity, his arrogance, his perversely appealing lack of handsomeness, even of ordinary grown-up masculinity? When he stood up she saw that he was shorter even than she had thought, that his face was pink and shiny, that there was something crude and pushy and childish about him.

Was he a minister, really, or was that only what he said? Flo had mentioned people who were not ministers, dressed up as if they were. Not real ministers dressed as if they were not. Or, stranger still, men who were not real ministers pretending to be real but dressed as if they were not. But that she had come as close as she had, to what could happen, was an unwelcome thing. Rose walked through Union Station feeling the little bag with the ten dollars rubbing at her, knew she would feel it all day long, rubbing its reminder against her skin.

She couldn't stop getting Flo's messages, even with that. She remembered, 60 because she was in Union Station, that there was a girl named Mavis working here, in the gift shop, when Flo was working in the coffee shop. Mavis had warts on her eyelids that looked like they were going to turn into sties but they didn't, they went away. Maybe she had them removed, Flo didn't ask. She was very good-looking, without them. There was a movie star in those days she looked a lot like. The movie star's name was Frances Farmer.°

Frances Farmer. Rose had never heard of her.

That was the name. And Mavis went and bought herself a big hat that dipped over one eye and a dress entirely made of lace. She went off for the weekend to Georgian Bay, to a resort up there. She booked herself in under the name of Florence Farmer. To give everybody the idea she was really the other one, Frances Farmer, but calling herself Florence because she was on holiday and didn't want to be recognized. She had a little cigarette holder that was black and mother-of-pearl. She could have been arrested, Flo said. For the *nerve*.

Rose almost went over to the gift shop to see if Mavis was still there and if she could recognize her. She thought it would be an especially fine thing to manage a transformation like that. To dare it; to get away with it, to enter on preposterous adventures in your own, but newly named, skin.

Frances Farmer (1904–1970): A Hollywood film star of the late 1930s and early 1940s.

CONSIDERATIONS FOR CRITICAL THINKING AND WRITING

1. **FIRST RESPONSE.** Did you find Rose to be a sympathetic character? Does the narrator? Were you surprised by her behavior? Was it credible? Explain why or why not.

2. Describe Flo's view of the world. How does Rose respond to her warnings about life?

3. How is Rose's experience on her trip to Toronto with Flo (paragraphs 19–22) relevant to her subsequent trip by herself?

4. How is West Hanratty implicitly contrasted with Toronto? What is the significance of these two settings?

5. Choose a passage that you think especially reveals Rose's character and explain what it indicates about her.

6. Why do you think Rose does not ask the minister to withdraw his hand? What explanation does the narrator offer?

7. The narrator describes Rose as both a "victim" and an "accomplice" (para. 56). Discuss this assessment and indicate whether you agree.

8. What do you think is the story's theme?

9. How is the story about Mavis related to Rose's story?

10. Comment on the story's title. Why do you suppose Munro chose "Wild Swans" rather than, say, "Victim and Accomplice"?

11. **CRITICAL STRATEGIES.** Read the section on psychological criticism (pp. 1649–51) in Chapter 51, "Critical Strategies for Reading." How would a psychological critic discuss Rose's behavior?

CONNECTIONS TO OTHER SELECTIONS

1. Discuss the treatment of desire and passion in this story and in Susan Minot's "Lust" (p. 282). What important similarities and differences do you see?

2. Consider the endings of "Wild Swans" and Updike's "A & P" (p. 200), paying attention to the tone of each ending. In what ways do the endings resemble each other? How do they differ?

MAGGIE MITCHELL (B. 1970)

Josh Masters.

Maggie Mitchell grew up in a small town in the northernmost part of New York State, on the Canadian border. She received an undergraduate degree in English from Cornell University and a Ph.D. from the University of Connecticut, and she now teaches English at the University of West Georgia. Her first novel, *Pretty Is* (2015), has been widely translated. Mitchell's short fiction has appeared in a number of literary magazines, including *New Ohio Review*, *American Literary Review,* and *Green Mountains Review*. The stark landscape of her childhood often finds its way into her short stories, as it does in "It Would Be Different If," which originally appeared in *New South*.

It Would Be Different If   2011

Here's what I remember. If I could hate you, this is what I would hate you for. It's a summer night, humid, starry. It's already pretty late but we're all heading over to Canada, to a bar called the Shipyard. She is there, which surprises me, because the Shipyard is the kind of place where people crack beer bottles over each other's heads, and I wouldn't have thought it was her scene. But she's been hanging out with your sister Megan all summer, working down at the restaurant, back when it was still the Riverside. She's always around. She annoys me, but I don't suspect anything yet. There are two boats; we're splitting into groups. I'm standing on the dock, a beer in my hand. I've had a little too much to drink already, probably, because everything seems very dark, slightly confused. I'm trying to figure out which boat you're in so I don't get stuck in the other one. Just then a car happens to go by on Water Street and its headlights flicker across us. You're already in the first boat, and you're reaching your hand up toward the dock, smiling. I move blindly in your direction, thinking you're reaching for me, when another flash of light shows me that she is grabbing for your hand, you're swinging her down, the smile is for her, it's not a mistake. I stand on the dock in a miniskirt and a very skimpy cropped top, my hair sprayed into a sort of stiff gold cloud because it is the 80s. I feel, for the first time in my life, completely ridiculous. There's no turning back, though. I can't just announce, like a little kid, that I'm going home, I don't want to play anymore, though that's exactly what I feel.

The first boat is full. The headlights veer away: everything is dark again. I tumble somehow into the second boat, wishing I had something to cover myself with: I feel naked, although back then I always dressed like that, we all did. At the Shipyard I mostly stay in the bathroom, drinking and crying. I don't remember the boat ride home. But that's it, that's the end of it. That much I remember.

I've heard variations on this story from everyone, over the years. I'm always the victim, the one people feel sorry for. Maybe there are other versions where I get what's coming to me, where I've always needed to be put in my place, something like that, but I doubt it. People have never liked Amber much; they tend to be on my side. Or at least they did: as the years go by, I notice, that's less true. It's so long ago that people can't get too worked up about it anymore. Now they talk as if it was somehow inevitable, and we just didn't know it yet — you know, isn't life funny, but look how it all works out in the end. Except when it doesn't.

It would be different if we lived in the kind of place where people can disappear, never see each other again. It would be different if I could pretend you didn't exist. But there you are: you are at the post office, peering into your mailbox, pulling out a stack of envelopes and catalogues while I drop my electric bill in the mail slot; I wait till you turn around, to make sure you see me. You would rather not see me. You're at the table on the other side of the restaurant, bending forward to speak to her, or wiping food off your kid's face. You're getting gas, staring off into the distance, forgetting what you are doing. You don't notice that I'm driving by. What are you thinking of? You're everywhere. I think you have ruined my life.

And now she's the one they feel sorry for. Yes, of course I know what you've been   5 up to. Everyone knows. I see your truck in the parking lot at Jude's every night, and they say you don't tend to leave alone. I see her sometimes: Amber. She looks smaller, paler, less pretty. I could almost feel sorry for her myself, to tell you the truth. I don't blame you, of course. It's just because it's all wrong. I could have told you it would happen.

I wasn't supposed to be one of those people, the unmarryable ones. I never expected to be. I had you, and we had plans, ever since our junior year: Nikki and Jeff. Nikki Gilbert. It sounded right. We joked about getting old, how you would go bald and I'd go pure white, and we'd go fishing in the summer, cross-country skiing in the winter, with our dog. It was a beagle. I had a bit of a stoop; you had put on some weight. You can't cancel that out.

It wasn't fair. She had gone away — to college, the city, whatever. She was the kind of person who goes away, doesn't come back: that's what everyone expected. But she did come back and she chose you, of all people. Why you? You're not like her. You are like us.

Well. Here's what I imagine. It's the best I can do. I am working, finishing up someone's hair. It's late afternoon — that quiet time when the sun starts to come in sideways. Whose hair? Someone like Deb White, not much of a talker, but lots of hair, complicated hair, ever since Don got his job back and they gave up on that hippie phase. I'm finished with the cut and now I'm styling it, taking my time because I don't have any more appointments that day, blowing it out section by section, working through the layers. Her eyes are half closed, I hum a little. It's nice.

Then I hear the door clang as it swings shut behind someone. I glance over and it's you. I am calm; we say nothing. I just nod, and you pick up a magazine and sit down on the couch to wait. Like anyone else. I don't rush Deb. If anything I slow down, taking extra time with each wave, making it perfect. You're just sitting there but somehow you fill the air, you're everywhere and invisible. I breathe you, I walk on you, I curl you into Deb's frosted waves. But I don't shake, or sweat. I'm not nervous. You're like a birthday, a red X on the calendar. Sooner or later you'll happen, one way or the other: it doesn't matter what I do. Eventually Deb rises to her feet, admires herself in the mirror. She writes a check; I don't take credit cards. It seems to take her forever, like one of those women in line at the grocery store. In the meantime I sweep up the heap of doll-like hair around the chair, straighten up the station. She makes an appointment for the next month. Finally she drifts toward the door and I follow her, because she is chatting about something, telling me a story about one of her daughters; she always does this. I wave as she maneuvers herself into her car, careful not to disturb her hair.

When I return to the shop you have seated yourself in the chair that is probably 10 still warm from its contact with Deb White's bony behind. I think of this, for some reason. I see myself smile in the mirror and our eyes, for the first time, meet each other's reflections. I drape a hunter green smock across you, attach it behind your neck with velcro straps.

I cut your hair. I use four different kinds of scissors, a razor, two combs, a touch of mousse. I used to cut your hair in high school, for practice. Now I do it better. Mostly I keep my eyes focused on your head, like an artist putting the final touches on some life-sized sculpture, but every now and then I look up, and there you are in the mirror. We always look at the same moment. We know exactly how long to wait between looks; we know not to overdo it. Your eyes are still the same blue as always but there are crinkles, now, at the corners. I think you are better looking than ever. My work does you justice: this is the best haircut you will ever, ever get.

I remove the smock when it's over. You do not pay. You don't speak. You look at me one more time, and you touch my hand — so far, given the circumstances, I have been the one to do all the touching — and then you leave. I wait until your truck has pulled away to sweep up the short brown hairs. I can't throw them away, so I tilt the contents of the dustpan into one of the nice creamy envelopes I use for gift certificates.

I don't know what happens after that. Probably you don't leave her right away. But sooner or later I know you'll come. I'll be waiting. For now I'll settle for the trimmings, glossy and shampoo-scented, and for the traces of your reflection that you seem to have left in the mirror. You flicker endlessly between the stiff curls of middle-aged ladies in pastel pantsuits, the long doomed locks of small terrified boys, the towering, glittery updos of girls on their way to the prom. You remind me to wait, promise that things will be different. I believe you.

Considerations for Critical Thinking and Writing

1. **FIRST RESPONSE.** What actually happens in this story? What is the status of the present in relation to memory and imagination?

2. How does the narrator invite the reader's sympathy? Is it important that we sympathize with her?

3. How trustworthy is the narrator's version of events? What specific lines or passages reinforce or undermine her perspective?

4. What kind of resolution does this story offer? Would you say that the conflict has been resolved, in any sense?

5. What does the narrator's way of relating this story — not *what* she says, but the way she says it — reveal about her world or about her character?

6. What sense do you get of the town in which this story is set? How important is the setting to your understanding of the story and the characters?

7. What is the significance of the final line of the story?

8. **CREATIVE RESPONSE.** Use what you think you can infer about the narrator from this story to craft a paragraph from a third-person point of view in which Nikki is portrayed unsympathetically.

Connection to Another Selection

1. In a short essay, compare this narrator's representation of her past to that of the narrator in Muriel Spark's "The First Year of My Life" (p. 483). What is the relationship between the narrative present and the remembered past in each story? How does it shape the ending in each case?

ENCOUNTERING FICTION: COMICS AND GRAPHIC STORIES

Marjane Satrapi (b. 1969), "The Trip," From *Persepolis*

Marjane Satrapi was born in Rasht, Iran, and grew up in Tehran. The daughter of politically liberal parents but also a princess (her great-grandfather was the last Qadjar emperor of Iran), Satrapi attended Tehran's Lycée Français, and left at age fourteen to study illustration in Vienna and Strasbourg. Her graphic memoir, *Persepolis,* excerpted in the following pages, is an account of her experiences as a young girl during the 1979 Iranian Revolution, from the ages of six to fourteen. In her preface she writes: "This old and great civilization has been discussed mostly in connection with fundamentalism, fanaticism, and terrorism. As an Iranian who has lived more than half of my life in Iran, I know that this image is far from the truth. This is why writing *Persepolis* was so important to me." Satrapi's work has been compared to Art Spiegelman's *Maus,* a graphic novel about the Holocaust, a work that greatly influenced her. "When I read him, I thought . . . it's possible to tell a story and make a point this way. It was amazing."

THE TRIP

OH SHIT!

THEY'VE OCCUPIED THE U.S. EMBASSY!!

WHO'S "THEY"?

WHO DO YOU THINK? THE FUNDA- MENTALIST STUDENTS HAVE TAKEN THE AMERICANS HOSTAGE!!

REALLY?

THEY CALL IT "A NEST OF SPIES." HA HA! YOU'D THINK IT WAS A JAMES BOND MOVIE.

YOU'RE NOT INTERESTED?

I COULDN'T CARE LESS.

ANYWAY, THE AMERICANS ARE DUMMIES.

MAYBE, BUT NOW NO ONE CAN GO TO THE UNITED STATES.

WHY'S THAT ??

THINK ABOUT IT. NO EMBASSY, NO VISA!

SO, MY GREAT DREAM WENT UP IN SMOKE. I WOULDN'T BE ABLE TO GO TO THE UNITED STATES.

KAVEH, THEY CLOSED THE U.S. EMBASSY TODAY. I WON'T BE ABLE TO COME AND SEE YOU...

THE DREAM WASN'T THE USA. IT WAS SEEING MY FRIEND KAVEH, WHO HAD LEFT TO GO LIVE IN THE STATES A YEAR EARLIER.

CONSIDERATIONS FOR CRITICAL THINKING AND WRITING

1. How does point of view in "The Trip" affect your understanding of the impact of the Islamic Revolution in Iran?

2. What specific cultural and political issues are raised by Satrapi's narrative? How does the strip comment on those issues?

3. How are Islamic fundamentalists portrayed in the strip? Explain whether you think this is a fair depiction.

7

Symbolism

Everett Collection/Newscom.

Now mind, I recognize no dichotomy
between art and protest.
—RALPH ELLISON

A *symbol* is a person, object, or event that suggests more than its literal meaning. This basic definition is simple enough, but the use of symbol in literature makes some students slightly nervous because they tend to regard it as a booby trap, a hidden device that can go off during a seemingly harmless class discussion. "I didn't see that when I was reading the story" is a frequently heard comment. This sort of surprise and recognition is both natural and common. Most readers go through a story for the first time getting their bearings, figuring out what is happening to whom and so on. Patterns and significant details often require a second or third reading before they become evident—before a symbol sheds light on a story. Then the details of a work may suddenly fit together, and its meaning may be reinforced, clarified, or enlarged by the symbol. Symbolic meanings are usually embedded in the texture of a story, but they are not "hidden"; instead, they are carefully placed. Reading between the lines (where there is only space) is unnecessary. What is needed is a careful consideration of the elements of the story, a sensitivity to its language, and some common sense.

Common sense is a good place to begin. Symbols appear all around us; anything can be given symbolic significance. Without symbols our lives would be stark and vacant. Awareness of a writer's use of symbols is not all that different from the kinds of perceptions and interpretations that allow us to make sense of our daily lives. We know, for example, that a ring used in a wedding is more than just a piece of jewelry because it suggests the unity and intimacy of a closed circle. The bride's gown may be white because we tend to associate innocence and purity with that color. Or consider the meaning of a small polo pony sewn on a shirt or some other article of clothing. What started as a company trademark has gathered around it a range of meanings suggesting everything from quality and money to preppiness and silliness. The ring, the white gown, and the polo pony trademark are symbolic because each has meanings that go beyond its specific qualities and functions.

Symbols such as these that are widely recognized by a society or culture are called **conventional symbols**. The Christian cross, the Star of David, a swastika, or a nation's flag all have meanings understood by large groups of people. Certain kinds of experiences also have traditional meanings in Western cultures. Winter, the setting sun, and the color black suggest death, while spring, the rising sun, and the color green evoke images of youth and new beginnings. (It is worth noting, however, that individual cultures sometimes have their own conventions; some Eastern cultures associate white rather than black with death and mourning. And obviously the polo pony trademark would mean nothing to anyone totally unfamiliar with American culture.) These broadly shared symbolic meanings are second nature to us.

Writers use conventional symbols to reinforce meanings. Kate Chopin, for example, emphasizes the spring setting in "The Story of an Hour" (p. 15) as a way of suggesting the renewed sense of life that Mrs. Mallard feels when she thinks herself free from her husband.

A **literary symbol** can include traditional, conventional, or public meanings, but it may also be established internally by the total context of the work in which it appears. In "Soldier's Home" (p. 162), Hemingway does not use Krebs's family home as a conventional symbol of safety, comfort, and refuge from the war. Instead, Krebs's home becomes symbolic of provincial, erroneous presuppositions compounded by blind innocence, sentimentality, and smug middle-class respectability. The symbolic meaning of his home reveals that Krebs no longer shares his family's and town's view of the world. Their notions of love, the value of a respectable job, and a belief in God seem to him petty, complicated, and meaningless. The significance of Krebs's home is determined by the events within the story, which reverse and subvert the traditional associations readers might bring to it. Krebs's interactions with his family and the people in town reveal what home has come to mean to him.

A literary symbol can be a setting, character, action, object, name, or anything else in a work that maintains its literal significance while suggesting other meanings. Symbols cannot be restricted to a single meaning; they are suggestive rather than definitive. Their evocation of multiple meanings allows a writer to say more with less. Symbols are economical devices for evoking complex ideas without having to resort to painstaking explanations that would make a story more like an essay than an experience. The many walls in Melville's "Bartleby, the Scrivener" (p. 130) cannot be reduced to one idea. They have multiple meanings that unify the story. The walls are symbols of the deadening, dehumanizing, restrictive repetitiveness of the office routine, as well as of the confining, materialistic sensibilities of Wall Street. They suggest whatever limits and thwarts human aspirations, including death itself. We don't know precisely what shatters Bartleby's will to live, but the walls in the story, through their symbolic suggestiveness, indicate the nature of the limitations that cause the scrivener to slip into hopelessness and his "dead-wall reveries."

When a character, object, or incident indicates a single, fixed meaning, the writer is using **allegory** rather than symbol. Whereas symbols have literal functions as well as multiple meanings, the primary focus in allegory is on the abstract idea called forth by the concrete object. John Bunyan's *Pilgrim's Progress*, published during the seventeenth century, is a classic example of allegory because the characters, action, and setting have no existence beyond their abstract meanings. Bunyan's purpose is to teach his readers the exemplary way to salvation and heaven. The protagonist, named Christian, flees the City of Destruction in search of the Celestial City. Along the way he encounters characters who either help or hinder his spiritual journey. Among them are Mr. Worldly Wiseman, Faithful, Prudence, Piety, and a host of others named after the virtues or vices they display. These characters, places, and actions exist solely to illustrate religious doctrine. Allegory tends to be definitive rather than suggestive. It drives meaning into a corner and keeps it there. Most modern writers prefer the exploratory nature of symbol to the reductive nature of pure allegory.

Stories often include symbols that you may or may not perceive on a first reading. Their subtle use is a sign of a writer's skill in weaving symbols into the fabric of the characters' lives. Symbols may sometimes escape you, but that is probably better than finding symbols where only literal meanings are intended. Allow the text to help you determine whether a symbolic reading is appropriate. Once you are clear about what literally happens, read carefully and notice the placement of details that are emphasized. The pervasive references to time in Faulkner's "A Rose for Emily" (p. 78) and the many kinds of walls that appear throughout "Bartleby, the Scrivener" call attention to themselves and warrant symbolic readings. A symbol, however, need not be repeated to have an important purpose in a story. We don't learn until the very end of "Bartleby, the Scrivener" that Bartleby once worked as a clerk in the Dead Letter Office in Washington, D.C. This information is offered as merely an offhand rumor by the narrator, but its symbolic value is essential for understanding what motivates Bartleby's behavior. Indeed, Bartleby's experiences in the Dead Letter Office suggest enough about the nature of his thwarted hopes and desires to account for Bartleby's rejection of life.

By keeping track of the total context of the story, you should be able to decide whether your reading is reasonable and consistent with the other facts; plenty of lemons in literature yield no symbolic meaning even if they are squeezed. Be sensitive to the meanings that the author associates with people, places, objects, and actions. You may not associate home with provincial innocence as Hemingway does in "Soldier's Home," but a close reading of the story will permit you to see how and why he constructs that symbolic meaning. If you treat stories like people — with tact and care — they ordinarily are accessible and enjoyable.

The next four stories — Tobias Wolff's "That Room," Ralph Ellison's "Battle Royal," Michael Oppenheimer's "The Paring Knife," and Dagoberto Gilb's "Romero's Shirt" — rely on symbols to convey meanings that go far beyond the specific incidents described in their plots.

TOBIAS WOLFF (B. 1945)

Born in Birmingham, Alabama, Tobias Wolff grew up in the state of Washington. After quitting high school, he worked on a ship and for a carnival. In the army he served four years as a paratrooper, after which he studied to pass the entrance exams for Oxford University, from which he graduated with high honors. He has published two memoirs — *This Boy's Life* (1989) and *In Pharaoh's Army: Memories of the Lost War* (1994). In addition to his two novels, *The Barracks Thief* (1984) and *Old School* (2003), he has published four short story collections: *In the Garden of North American Martyrs* (1981), *Back in the World* (1985), *The Night in Question* (1996), and *Our Story Begins* (2008). Wolff has taught literature and creative writing courses at Stanford University since 1997.

> **WHEN I WRITE** "I revise until I can't see a way to make a story better. Only then do I show it to a few trusted readers. If they spot a real weakness, I'll go back to work. Knowing when it's finished is a matter of instinct — an instinct that grows sharper with time and experience." — TOBIAS WOLFF

That Room 2008

The summer after my first year of high school, I got a case of independence and started hitchhiking to farms up and down the valley for daywork picking berries and mucking out stalls. Then I found a place where the farmer paid me ten cents an hour over minimum wage, and his plump, childless wife fed me lunch and fussed over me while I ate, so I stayed on there until school started.

While shoveling shit or hacking weeds out of a drainage ditch, I'd sometimes stop to gaze out toward the far fields, where the hands, as the farmer called them, were bucking bales of hay into a wagon, stacking them to teetering heights. Now and then a bark of laughter reached me, a tag end of conversation. The farmer hadn't let me work in the hay because I was too small, but I beefed up over the winter, and the following summer he let me join the crew.

So I was a hand. A hand! I went a little crazy with that word, with the pleasure of applying it to myself. Having a job like this changed everything. It delivered you from the reach of your parents, from the caustic scrutiny of your friends. It set you free among strangers in the eventful world, where you could practice being someone else until you *were* someone else. It put money in your pocket and allowed you to believe that your other life — your inessential, parenthetical life at home and school — was just a sop to those deluded enough to imagine you still needed them.

There were three others working the fields with me: the farmer's shy, muscle-bound nephew, Clemson, who was in my class at school but to whom I condescended because he was just an inexperienced kid, and two Mexican brothers, Miguel and Eduardo. Miguel, short and stolid and solitary, spoke very little English, but rakish Eduardo did the talking for both of them. While the rest of us did the heavy work, Eduardo provided advice about girls and told stories in which he featured as a trickster and deft, indefatigable swordsman. He played it for laughs, but in the very materials of his storytelling — the dance halls and bars, the bumbling border guards, the clod-brained farmers and their insatiable wives, the larcenous cops, the whores who loved him — I felt the actuality of a life I knew nothing about yet somehow contrived to want for myself: a real life in a real world.

While Eduardo talked, Miguel labored silently beside us, now and then grunt- 5 ing with the weight of a bale, his acne-scarred face flushed with heat, narrow eyes narrowed even tighter against the sun. Clemson and I sprinted and flagged, sprinted and flagged, laughing at Eduardo's stories, goading him with questions. Miguel never flagged, and never laughed. He sometimes watched his brother with what appeared to be mild curiosity; that was all.

The farmer, who owned a big spread with a lot of hay to bring in, should have hired more hands. He had only the four of us, and there was always the danger of rain. He was a relaxed, amiable man, but as the season wore on he grew anxious and began to push us harder and keep us longer. During the last week or so I spent the nights with Clemson's family, just down the road, so I could get to the farm with the others at sunup and work until dusk. The bales were heavy with dew when we started bringing them in. The air in the loft turned steamy from fermentation, and Eduardo warned the farmer that the hay might combust, but he held us to his schedule. Limping, sunburned, covered with scratches, I could hardly get out of bed in the morning. But although I griped with Clemson and Eduardo, I was secretly glad to take my place beside them, to work as if I had no choice.

Eduardo's car broke down toward the end of the week, and Clemson started driving him and Miguel to and from the decrepit motel where they lived with other seasonal workers. Sometimes, pulling up to their door, we'd all just sit there, saying nothing. We were that tired. Then one night Eduardo asked us in for a drink. Clemson, being a good boy, tried to beg off, but I got out with Miguel and Eduardo, knowing he wouldn't leave me. "Come on, Clem," I said, "don't be a homo." He looked at me, then turned the engine off.

That room. Jesus. The brothers had done their best, making their beds, keeping their clothes neatly folded in open suitcases, but you got swamped by the smell of mildew the moment you stepped inside. The floor was mushy underfoot and shedding squares of drab linoleum, the ceiling bowed and stained. The overhead light didn't quite reach the corners. Behind the mildew was another, unsettling smell.

Clemson was a fastidious guy and writhed in distress as I made a show of being right at home.

We poured rye into our empty stomachs and listened to Eduardo, and before long we were all drunk. Someone came to the door and spoke to him in Spanish, and Eduardo went outside and didn't come back. Miguel and I kept drinking. Clemson was half asleep, his chin declining slowly toward his chest and snapping up again. Then Miguel looked at me. He slitted his eyes and looked at me hard, without blinking, and began to protest an injustice done him by our boss, or maybe another boss. I could barely understand his English, and he kept breaking into Spanish, which I didn't understand at all. But he was angry—I understood that much.

At some point he went across the room and came back and put a pistol on the table, right in front of him. A revolver, long barrel, most of the bluing worn off. Miguel stared at me over the pistol and resumed his complaint, entirely in Spanish. He was looking at me, but I knew he was seeing someone else. I had rarely heard him speak before. Now the words poured out in an aggrieved singsong, and I saw that his own voice was lashing him on somehow, the very sound of his indignation proving that he had been wronged, feeding his rage, making him hate whoever he thought I was. I was too afraid to speak. All I could do was smile.

That room — once you enter it, you never really leave. You can forget you're there, you can go on as if you hold the reins, that the course of your life, yea even its *length,* will reflect the force of your character and the wisdom of your judgments. And then you hit an icy patch on a turn one sunny March day and the wheel in your hands becomes a joke and you no more than a spectator to your own dreamy slide toward the verge, and then you remember where you are.

Or you board a bus with thirty other young men. It's early, just before dawn. That's when the buses always leave, their lights dimmed, to avoid the attention of the Quakers outside the gate, but it doesn't work and they're waiting, silently holding up their signs, looking at you not with reproach but with sadness and sympathy as the bus drives past them and on toward the airport and the plane that will take you where you would not go — and at this moment you know exactly what your desires count for, and your plans, and all your strength of body and will. Then you know where you are, as you will know where you are when those you love die before their time — the time you had planned for them, for yourself with them — and when your daily allowance of words and dreams is withheld from you, and when your daughter drives the car straight into a tree. And if she walks away without a scratch you still feel that dark ceiling close overhead, and know where you are. And what can you do but what you did back in this awful room, with Miguel hating you for nothing and a pistol ready to hand? Smile and hope for a change of subject.

It came, this time. Clemson bolted up from his chair, bent forward, and puked all over the table. Miguel stopped talking. He stared at Clemson as if he'd never seen him before, and when Clemson began retching again Miguel jumped up and grabbed him by the shirt and pushed him toward the door. I took over and helped Clemson outside while Miguel looked on, shrieking his disgust. Disgust! Now *he* was the fastidious one. Revulsion had trumped rage, had trumped even hatred. Oh, how sweetly I tended Clemson that night! I thought he'd saved my life. And maybe he had.

The farmer's barn burned to the ground that winter. When I heard about it, I said, "Didn't I tell him? I did, I told that stupid sumbitch not to put up wet hay."

CONSIDERATIONS FOR CRITICAL THINKING AND WRITING

1. FIRST RESPONSE. Why does the narrator describe his "life at home and school" as "inessential, parenthetical" (para. 3) in comparison to "a real life in a real world" (para. 4)?

2. Why is the work the narrator does on the farm important to him?

3. How are Eduardo and Miguel foils to one another?

4. Why is Miguel so angry?

5. How does the motel room and what happens in it take on symbolic meaning in this plot?

6. Discuss the significance of paragraphs 11 through 12. Why do you think they appear where they do and are set off from the rest of the story?

7. How is the bus trip described in paragraph 12 relevant to the narrator's experience? What kind of perspective on life is expressed in this paragraph?

8. Discuss your reading of the story's final paragraph and how it relates to the rest of the narration.

CONNECTION TO ANOTHER SELECTION

1. Discuss the similarities and differences related to the nature of what the protagonist learns about life in "That Room" and in either John Updike's "A & P" (p. 200) or Ralph Ellison's "Battle Royal" (p. 227).

RALPH ELLISON (1914–1994)

Everett Collection/Newscom.

Born in Oklahoma and educated at the Tuskegee Institute in Alabama, where he studied music, Ralph Ellison gained his reputation as a writer on the strength of his only published novel, *Invisible Man* (1952). He also published some scattered short stories and two collections of essays, *Shadow and Act* (1964) and *Going to the Territory* (1986). Although his writing was not extensive, it is important because Ellison wrote about race relations in the context of universal human concerns. *Invisible Man* is the story of a young black man who moves from the South to the North and discovers what it means to be black in America. "Battle Royal," published in 1947 as a short story, became the first chapter of *Invisible Man*. It concerns the beginning of the protagonist's long struggle for an adult identity in a world made corrupt by racial prejudice.

Battle Royal   1947

It goes a long way back, some twenty years. All my life I had been looking for something, and everywhere I turned someone tried to tell me what it was. I accepted their answers too, though they were often in contradiction and even self-contradictory. I was naive. I was looking for myself and asking everyone except myself questions which I, and only I, could answer. It took me a long time and much painful boomeranging of my expectations to achieve a realization everyone else appears to have been born with: That I am nobody but myself. But first I had to discover that I am an invisible man!

And yet I am no freak of nature, nor of history. I was in the cards, other things having been equal (or unequal) eighty-five years ago. I am not ashamed of my grandparents for having been slaves. I am only ashamed of myself for having at one time been ashamed. About eighty-five years ago they were told that they were free, united with others of our country in everything pertaining to the common good, and, in everything social, separate like the fingers of the hand. And they believed it. They exulted in it. They stayed in their place, worked hard, and brought up my father to do the same. But my grandfather is the one. He was an odd old guy, my grandfather, and I am told I take after him. It was he who caused the trouble. On his deathbed he called my father to him and said, "Son, after I'm gone I want you to keep up the good fight. I never told you, but our life is a war and I have been a traitor all my born days, a spy in the enemy's country ever since I gave up my gun back in the Reconstruction. Live with your head in the lion's mouth. I want you to overcome 'em with yeses, undermine 'em with grins, agree 'em to death and destruction, let 'em swoller you till they vomit or bust wide open." They thought the old man had gone out of his mind. He had been the meekest of men. The younger children were rushed from the room, the shades drawn and the flame of the lamp turned so low that it sputtered on the wick like the old man's breathing. "Learn it to the young-uns," he whispered fiercely; then he died.

But my folks were more alarmed over his last words than over his dying. It was as though he had not died at all, his words caused so much anxiety. I was warned emphatically to forget what he had said and, indeed, this is the first time it has been mentioned outside the family circle. It had a tremendous effect upon me, however. I could never be sure of what he meant. Grandfather had been a quiet old man who never made any trouble, yet on his deathbed he had called himself a traitor and a spy, and he had spoken of his meekness as a dangerous activity. It became a constant puzzle which lay unanswered in the back of my mind. And whenever things went well for me I remembered my grandfather and felt guilty and uncomfortable. It was as though I was carrying out his advice in spite of myself. And to make it worse, everyone loved me for it. I was praised by the most lily-white men of the town. I was considered an example of desirable conduct — just as my grandfather had been. And what puzzled me was that the old man had defined it as *treachery*. When I was praised for my conduct I felt a guilt that in some way I was doing something that was really against the wishes of the white folks, that if they had understood they would have desired me to act just the opposite, that I should have been sulky and mean, and that that really would have been what they wanted, even though they were fooled and thought they wanted me to act as I did. It made me afraid that some day they would look upon me as a traitor and I would be lost. Still I was more afraid to act any other way because they didn't like that at all. The old man's words were like a curse. On my graduation day I delivered an oration in which I showed that humility was the secret, indeed, the very essence of progress. (Not that I believed this — how could I, remembering my grandfather? — I only believed that it worked.) It was a great success. Everyone praised me and I was invited to give the speech at a gathering of the town's leading white citizens. It was a triumph for our whole community.

It was in the main ballroom of the leading hotel. When I got there I discovered that it was on the occasion of a smoker, and I was told that since I was to be there anyway I might as well take part in the battle royal to be fought by some of my schoolmates as part of the entertainment. The battle royal came first.

All of the town's big shots were there in their tuxedoes, wolfing down the buf- 5 fet foods, drinking beer and whiskey and smoking black cigars. It was a large room with a high ceiling. Chairs were arranged in neat rows around three sides of a portable boxing ring. The fourth side was clear, revealing a gleaming space of polished floor. I had some misgivings over the battle royal, by the way. Not from a distaste for fighting, but because I didn't care too much for the other fellows who were to take part. They were tough guys who seemed to have no grandfather's curse worrying their minds. No one could mistake their toughness. And besides, I suspected that fighting a battle royal might detract from the dignity of my speech. In those pre-invisible days I visualized myself as a potential Booker T. Washington. But the other fellows didn't care too much for me either, and there were nine of them. I felt superior to them in my way, and I didn't like the manner in which we were all crowded together into the servants' elevator. Nor did they like my being there. In fact, as the warmly lighted floors flashed past the elevator we had words over the fact that I, by taking part in the fight, had knocked one of their friends out of a night's work.

We were led out of the elevator through a rococo hall into an anteroom and told to get into our fighting togs. Each of us was issued a pair of boxing gloves and ushered out into the big mirrored hall, which we entered looking cautiously about us and whispering, lest we might accidentally be heard above the noise of the room. It was foggy with cigar smoke. And already the whiskey was taking effect. I was shocked to see some of the most important men of the town quite tipsy. They were all there — bankers, lawyers, judges, doctors, fire chiefs, teachers, merchants. Even one of the more fashionable pastors. Something we could not see was going on up front. A clarinet was vibrating sensuously and the men were standing up and moving eagerly forward. We were a small tight group, clustered together, our bare upper bodies touching and shining with anticipatory sweat; while up front the big shots were becoming increasingly excited over something we still could not see. Suddenly I heard the school superintendent, who had told me to come, yell, "Bring up the shines, gentlemen! Bring up the little shines!"

We were rushed up to the front of the ballroom, where it smelled even more strongly of tobacco and whiskey. Then we were pushed into place. I almost wet my pants. A sea of faces, some hostile, some amused, ringed around us, and in the center, facing us, stood a magnificent blonde — stark naked. There was dead silence. I felt a blast of cold air chill me. I tried to back away, but they were behind me and around me. Some of the boys stood with lowered heads, trembling. I felt a wave of irrational guilt and fear. My teeth chattered, my skin turned to goose flesh, my knees knocked. Yet I was strongly attracted and looked in spite of myself. Had the price of looking been blindness, I would have looked. The hair was yellow like that of a circus kewpie doll, the face heavily powdered and rouged, as though to form an abstract mask, the eyes hollow and smeared a cool blue, the color of a baboon's butt.

I felt a desire to spit upon her as my eyes brushed slowly over her body. Her breasts were firm and round as the domes of East Indian temples, and I stood so close as to see the fine skin texture and beads of pearly perspiration glistening like dew around the pink and erected buds of her nipples. I wanted at one and the same time to run from the room, to sink through the floor, or go to her and cover her from my eyes and the eyes of the others with my body; to feel the soft thighs, to caress her and destroy her, to love her and murder her, to hide from her, and yet to stroke where below the small American flag tattooed upon her belly her thighs formed a capital V. I had a notion that of all in the room she saw only me with her impersonal eyes.

And then she began to dance, a slow sensuous movement; the smoke of a hundred cigars clinging to her like the thinnest of veils. She seemed like a fair bird-girl girdled in veils calling to me from the angry surface of some gray and threatening sea. I was transported. Then I became aware of the clarinet playing and the big shots yelling at us. Some threatened us if we looked and others if we did not. On my right I saw one boy faint. And now a man grabbed a silver pitcher from a table and stepped close as he dashed ice water upon him and stood him up and forced two of us to support him as his head hung and moans issued from his thick bluish lips. Another boy began to plead to go home. He was the largest of the group, wearing dark red fighting trunks much too small to conceal the erection which projected from him as though in answer to the insinuating low-registered moaning of the clarinet. He tried to hide himself with his boxing gloves.

And all the while the blonde continued dancing, smiling faintly at the big shots who watched her with fascination, and faintly smiling at our fear. I noticed a certain merchant who followed her hungrily, his lips loose and drooling. He was a large man who wore diamond studs in a shirtfront which swelled with the ample paunch underneath, and each time the blonde swayed her undulating hips he ran his hand through the thin hair of his bald head and, with his arms upheld, his posture clumsy like that of an intoxicated panda, wound his belly in a slow and obscene grind. This creature was completely hypnotized. The music had quickened. As the dancer flung herself about with a detached expression on her face, the men began reaching out to touch her. I could see their beefy fingers sink into the soft flesh. Some of the others tried to stop them as she began to move around the floor in graceful circles, as they gave chase, slipping and sliding over the polished floor. It was mad. Chairs went crashing, drinks were spilt, as they ran laughing and howling after her. They caught her just as she reached a door, raised her from the floor, and tossed her as college boys are tossed at a hazing, and above her red, fixed-smiling lips I saw the terror and disgust in her eyes, almost like my own terror and that which I saw in some of the other boys. As I watched, they tossed her twice and her soft breasts seemed to flatten against the air and her legs flung wildly as she spun. Some of the more sober ones helped her to escape. And I started off the floor, heading for the anteroom with the rest of the boys.

Some were still crying in hysteria. But as we tried to leave we were stopped and 10 ordered to get into the ring. There was nothing to do but what we were told. All ten of us climbed under the ropes and allowed ourselves to be blindfolded with broad bands of white cloth. One of the men seemed to feel a bit sympathetic and tried to cheer us up as we stood with our backs against the ropes. Some of us tried to grin. "See that boy over there?" one of the men said. "I want you to run across at the bell and give it to him right in the belly. If you don't get him, I'm going to get you. I don't like his looks." Each of us was told the same. The blindfolds were put on. Yet even then I had been going over my speech. In my mind each word was as bright as flame. I felt the cloth pressed into place, and frowned so that it would be loosened when I relaxed.

But now I felt a sudden fit of blind terror. I was unused to darkness. It was as though I had suddenly found myself in a dark room filled with poisonous cottonmouths. I could hear the bleary voices yelling insistently for the battle royal to begin.

"Get going in there!"

"Let me at that big nigger!"

I strained to pick up the school superintendent's voice, as though to squeeze some security out of that slightly more familiar sound.

"Let me at those black sonsabitches!" someone yelled.   15

"No, Jackson, no!" another voice yelled. "Here, somebody, help me hold Jack."

"I want to get at that ginger-colored nigger. Tear him limb from limb," the first voice yelled.

I stood against the ropes trembling. For in those days I was what they called ginger-colored, and he sounded as though he might crunch me between his teeth like a crisp ginger cookie.

Quite a struggle was going on. Chairs were being kicked about and I could hear voices grunting as with a terrific effort. I wanted to see, to see more desperately than ever before. But the blindfold was tight as a thick skin-puckering scab and when I raised my gloved hands to push the layers of white aside a voice yelled, "Oh, no you don't, black bastard! Leave that alone!"

"Ring the bell before Jackson kills him a coon!" someone boomed in the sud-   20
den silence. And I heard the bell clang and the sound of the feet scuffling forward.

A glove smacked against my head. I pivoted, striking out stiffly as someone went past, and felt the jar ripple along the length of my arm to my shoulder. Then it seemed as though all nine of the boys had turned upon me at once. Blows pounded me from all sides while I struck out as best I could. So many blows landed upon me that I wondered if I were not the only blindfolded fighter in the ring, or if the man called Jackson hadn't succeeded in getting me after all.

Blindfolded, I could no longer control my motions. I had no dignity. I stumbled about like a baby or a drunken man. The smoke had become thicker and with each new blow it seemed to sear and further restrict my lungs. My saliva became like hot bitter glue. A glove connected with my head, filling my mouth with warm blood. It was everywhere. I could not tell if the moisture I felt upon my body was sweat or blood. A blow landed hard against the nape of my neck. I felt myself going over, my head hitting the floor. Streaks of blue light filled the black world behind the blindfold. I lay prone, pretending that I was knocked out, but felt myself seized by hands and yanked to my feet. "Get going, black boy! Mix it up!" My arms were like lead, my head smarting from blows. I managed to feel my way to the ropes and held on, trying to catch my breath. A glove landed in my mid-section and I went over again, feeling as though the smoke had become a knife jabbed into my guts. Pushed this way and that by the legs milling around me, I finally pulled erect and discovered that I could see the black, sweat-washed forms weaving in the smoky-blue atmosphere like drunken dancers weaving to the rapid drumlike thuds of blows.

Everyone fought hysterically. It was complete anarchy. Everybody fought everybody else. No group fought together for long. Two, three, four, fought one, then turned to fight each other, were themselves attacked. Blows landed below the belt and in the kidney, with the gloves open as well as closed, and with my eye partly opened now there was not so much terror. I moved carefully, avoiding blows, although not too many to attract attention, fighting from group to group. The boys groped about like blind, cautious crabs crouching to protect their mid-sections, their heads pulled in short against their shoulders, their arms stretched nervously before them, with their fists testing the smoke-filled air like the knobbed feelers of hypersensitive snails. In one corner I glimpsed a boy violently punching the air and heard him scream in pain as he smashed his hand against a ring post. For a second I saw him bent over holding his hand, then going down as a blow caught his unprotected head. I played one group against the other, slipping in and throwing a punch then stepping out of range while pushing the others into the melee to take the blows blindly aimed at me. The smoke was agonizing and there were no rounds, no bells at three minute intervals to relieve our exhaustion. The room spun round me, a swirl of lights, smoke, sweating bodies surrounded by tense white faces. I bled from both nose and mouth, the blood spattering upon my chest.

The men kept yelling, "Slug him, black boy! Knock his guts out!"

"Uppercut him! Kill him! Kill that big boy!"   25

Taking a fake fall, I saw a boy going down heavily beside me as though we were felled by a single blow, saw a sneaker-clad foot shoot into his groin as the two who had knocked him down stumbled upon him. I rolled out of range, feeling a twinge of nausea.

The harder we fought the more threatening the men became. And yet, I had begun to worry about my speech again. How would it go? Would they recognize my ability? What would they give me?

I was fighting automatically when suddenly I noticed that one after another of the boys was leaving the ring. I was surprised, filled with panic, as though I had been left alone with an unknown danger. Then I understood. The boys had arranged it among themselves. It was the custom for the two men left in the ring to slug it out for the winner's prize. I discovered this too late. When the bell sounded two men in tuxedoes leaped into the ring and removed the blindfold. I found myself facing Tatlock, the biggest of the gang. I felt sick at my stomach. Hardly had the bell stopped ringing in my ears than it clanged again and I saw him moving swiftly toward me. Thinking of nothing else to do I hit him smash on the nose. He kept coming, bringing the rank sharp violence of stale sweat. His face was a black blank of a face, only his eyes alive — with hate of me and aglow with a feverish terror from what had happened to us all. I became anxious. I wanted to deliver my speech and he came at me as though he meant to beat it out of me. I smashed him again and again, taking his blows as they came. Then on a sudden impulse I struck him lightly and as we clinched, I whispered, "Fake like I knocked you out, you can have the prize."

"I'll break your behind," he whispered hoarsely.

"For *them?*"   30

"For *me*, sonofabitch!"

They were yelling for us to break it up and Tatlock spun me half around with a blow, and as a joggled camera sweeps in a reeling scene, I saw the howling red faces crouching tense beneath the cloud of blue-gray smoke. For a moment the world wavered, unraveled, flowed, then my head cleared and Tatlock bounced before me. That fluttering shadow before my eyes was his jabbing left hand. Then falling forward, my head against his damp shoulder, I whispered,

"I'll make it five dollars more."

"Go to hell!"

But his muscles relaxed a trifle beneath my pressure and I breathed, "Seven?"   35
"Give it to your ma," he said, ripping me beneath the heart.

And while I still held him I butted him and moved away. I felt myself bombarded with punches. I fought back with hopeless desperation. I wanted to deliver my speech more than anything else in the world, because I felt that only these men could judge truly my ability, and now this stupid clown was ruining my chances. I began fighting carefully now, moving in to punch him and out again with my greater speed. A lucky blow to his chin and I had him going too — until I heard a loud voice yell, "I got my money on the big boy."

Hearing this, I almost dropped my guard. I was confused: Should I try to win against the voice out there? Would not this go against my speech, and was not this a moment for humility, for nonresistance? A blow to my head as I danced about sent my right eye popping like a jack-in-the-box and settled my dilemma. The room went red as I fell. It was a dream fall, my body languid and fastidious as to where to land, until the floor became impatient and smashed up to meet me. A moment later I came to. An hypnotic voice said FIVE emphatically. And I lay there, hazily watching a dark red spot of my own blood shaping itself into a butterfly, glistening and soaking into the soiled gray world of the canvas.

When the voice drawled TEN I was lifted up and dragged to a chair. I sat dazed. My eye pained and swelled with each throb of my pounding heart and I wondered if now I would be allowed to speak. I was wringing wet, my mouth still bleeding. We were grouped along the wall now. The other boys ignored me as they congratulated Tatlock and speculated as to how much they would be paid. One boy whimpered over his smashed hand. Looking up front, I saw attendants in white jackets rolling the portable ring away and placing a small square rug in the vacant space surrounded by chairs. Perhaps, I thought, I will stand on the rug to deliver my speech.

Then the M.C. called to us, "Come on up here boys and get your money." We   40
ran forward to where the men laughed and talked in their chairs, waiting. Everyone seemed friendly now.

"There it is on the rug," the man said. I saw the rug covered with coins of all dimensions and a few crumpled bills. But what excited me, scattered here and there, were the gold pieces.

"Boys, it's all yours," the man said. "You get all you grab."

"That's right, Sambo," a blond man said, winking at me confidentially.

I trembled with excitement, forgetting my pain. I would get the gold and the bills, I thought. I would use both hands. I would throw my body against the boys nearest me to block them from the gold.

"Get down around the rug now," the man commanded, "and don't anyone   45
touch it until I give the signal."

"This ought to be good," I heard.

As told, we got around the square rug on our knees. Slowly the man raised his freckled hand as we followed it upward with our eyes.

I heard, "These niggers look like they're about to pray!"

Then, "Ready," the man said. "Go!"

I lunged for a yellow coin lying on the blue design of the carpet, touching it   50
and sending a surprised shriek to join those rising around me. I tried frantically to remove my hand but could not let go. A hot, violent force tore through my body, shaking me like a wet rat. The rug was electrified. The hair bristled up on my head as I shook myself free. My muscles jumped, my nerves jangled, writhed. But I saw that this was not stopping the other boys. Laughing in fear and embarrassment, some

were holding back and scooping up the coins knocked off by the painful contortions of the others. The men roared above us as we struggled.

"Pick it up, goddamnit, pick it up!" someone called like a bass-voiced parrot. "Go on, get it!"

I crawled rapidly around the floor, picking up the coins, trying to avoid the coppers and to get greenbacks and the gold. Ignoring the shock by laughing, as I brushed the coins off quickly, I discovered that I could contain the electricity — a contradiction, but it works. Then the men began to push us onto the rug. Laughing embarrassedly, we struggled out of their hands and kept after the coins. We were all wet and slippery and hard to hold. Suddenly I saw a boy lifted into the air, glistening with sweat like a circus seal, and dropped, his wet back landing flush upon the charged rug, heard him yell and saw him literally dance upon his back, his elbows beating a frenzied tattoo upon the floor, his muscles twitching like the flesh of a horse stung by many flies. When he finally rolled off, his face was gray and no one stopped him when he ran from the floor amid booming laughter.

"Get the money," the M.C. called. "That's good hard American cash!"

And we snatched and grabbed, snatched and grabbed. I was careful not to come too close to the rug now, and when I felt the hot whiskey breath descend upon me like a cloud of foul air I reached out and grabbed the leg of a chair. It was occupied and I held on desperately.

"Leggo, nigger! Leggo!"   55

The huge face wavered down to mine as he tried to push me free. But my body was slippery and he was too drunk. It was Mr. Colcord, who owned a chain of movie houses and "entertainment palaces." Each time he grabbed me I slipped out of his hands. It became a real struggle. I feared the rug more than I did the drunk, so I held on, surprising myself for a moment by trying to topple *him* upon the rug. It was such an enormous idea that I found myself actually carrying it out. I tried not to be obvious, yet when I grabbed his leg, trying to tumble him out of the chair, he raised up roaring with laughter, and, looking at me with soberness dead in the eye, kicked me viciously in the chest. The chair leg flew out of my hand and I felt myself going and rolled. It was as though I had rolled through a bed of hot coals. It seemed a whole century would pass before I would roll free, a century in which I was seared through the deepest levels of my body to the fearful breath within me and the breath seared and heated to the point of explosion. It'll all be over in a flash, I thought as I rolled clear. It'll all be over in a flash.

But not yet, the men on the other side were waiting, red faces swollen as though from apoplexy as they bent forward in their chairs. Seeing their fingers coming toward me I rolled away as a fumbled football rolls off the receiver's fingertips, back into the coals. That time I luckily sent the rug sliding out of place and heard the coins ringing against the floor and the boys scuffling to pick them up and the M.C. calling, "All right, boys, that's all. Go get dressed and get your money."

I was limp as a dish rag. My back felt as though it had been beaten with wires.

When we had dressed the M.C. came in and gave us each five dollars, except Tatlock, who got ten for being last in the ring. Then he told us to leave. I was not to get a chance to deliver my speech, I thought. I was going out into the dim alley in despair when I was stopped and told to go back. I returned to the ballroom, where the men were pushing back their chairs and gathering in groups to talk.

The M.C. knocked on a table for quiet. "Gentlemen," he said, "we almost forgot   60 an important part of the program. A most serious part, gentlemen. This boy was brought here to deliver a speech which he made at his graduation yesterday . . ."

"Bravo!"

"I'm told that he is the smartest boy we've got out there in Greenwood. I'm told that he knows more big words than a pocket-sized dictionary."

Much applause and laughter.

"So now, gentlemen, I want you to give him your attention."

There was still laughter as I faced them, my mouth dry, my eye throbbing. 65 I began slowly, but evidently my throat was tense, because they began shouting, "Louder! Louder!"

"We of the younger generation extol the wisdom of that great leader and educator," I shouted, "who first spoke these flaming words of wisdom: 'A ship lost at sea for many days suddenly sighted a friendly vessel. From the mast of the unfortunate vessel was seen a signal: "Water, water; we die of thirst!" The answer from the friendly vessel came back: "Cast down your bucket where you are." The captain of the distressed vessel, at last heeding the injunction, cast down his bucket, and it came up full of fresh sparkling water from the mouth of the Amazon River.' And like him I say, and in his words, 'To those of my race who depend upon bettering their condition in a foreign land, or who underestimate the importance of cultivating friendly relations with the Southern white man, who is his next-door neighbor, I would say: "Cast down your bucket where you are" — cast it down in making friends in every manly way of the people of all races by whom we are surrounded . . .'"

I spoke automatically and with such fervor that I did not realize that the men were still talking and laughing until my dry mouth, filling up with blood from the cut, almost strangled me. I coughed, wanting to stop and go to one of the tall brass, sand-filled spittoons to relieve myself, but a few of the men, especially the superintendent, were listening and I was afraid. So I gulped it down, blood, saliva, and all, and continued. (What powers of endurance I had during those days! What enthusiasm! What a belief in the rightness of things!) I spoke even louder in spite of the pain. But still they talked and still they laughed, as though deaf with cotton in dirty ears. So I spoke with greater emotional emphasis. I closed my ears and swallowed blood until I was nauseated. The speech seemed a hundred times as long as before, but I could not leave out a single word. All had to be said, each memorized nuance considered, rendered. Nor was that all. Whenever I uttered a word of three or more syllables a group of voices would yell for me to repeat it. I used the phrase "social responsibility" and they yelled:

"What's that word you say, boy?"

"Social responsibility," I said.

"What?" 70

"Social . . ."

"Louder."

". . . responsibility."

"More!"

"Respon —" 75

"Repeat!"

"— sibility."

The room filled with the uproar of laughter until, no doubt, distracted by having to gulp down my blood, I made a mistake and yelled a phrase I had often seen denounced in newspaper editorials, heard debated in private.

"Social . . ."

"What?" they yelled. 80

". . . equality —"

The laughter hung smokelike in the sudden stillness. I opened my eyes, puzzled. Sounds of displeasure filled the room. The M.C. rushed forward. They shouted hostile phrases at me. But I did not understand.

A small dry mustached man in the front row blared out, "Say that slowly, son!"

"What, sir?"

"What you just said!"   85

"Social responsibility, sir," I said.

"You weren't being smart, were you, boy?" he said, not unkindly.

"No, sir!"

"You sure that about 'equality' was a mistake?"

"Oh, yes, sir," I said. "I was swallowing blood."   90

"Well, you had better speak more slowly so we can understand. We mean to do right by you, but you've got to know your place at all times. All right, now, go on with your speech."

I was afraid. I wanted to leave but I wanted also to speak and I was afraid they'd snatch me down.

"Thank you, sir," I said, beginning where I had left off, and having them ignore me as before.

Yet when I finished there was a thunderous applause. I was surprised to see the superintendent come forth with a package wrapped in white tissue paper, and, gesturing for quiet, address the men.

"Gentlemen, you see that I did not overpraise this boy. He makes a good speech 95 and some day he'll lead his people in the proper paths. And I don't have to tell you that that is important in these days and times. This is a good, smart boy, and so to encourage him in the right direction, in the name of the Board of Education I wish to present him a prize in the form of this . . ."

He paused, removing the tissue paper and revealing a gleaming calfskin brief case.

". . . in the form of this first-class article from Shad Whitmore's shop."

"Boy," he said, addressing me, "take this prize and keep it well. Consider it a badge of office. Prize it. Keep developing as you are and some day it will be filled with important papers that will help shape the destiny of your people."

I was so moved that I could hardly express my thanks. A rope of bloody saliva forming a shape like an undiscovered continent drooled upon the leather and I wiped it quickly away. I felt an importance that I had never dreamed.

"Open it and see what's inside," I was told.   100

My fingers a-tremble, I complied, smelling the fresh leather and finding an official-looking document inside. It was a scholarship to the state college for Negroes. My eyes filled with tears and I ran awkwardly off the floor.

I was overjoyed; I did not even mind when I discovered that the gold pieces I had scrambled for were brass pocket tokens advertising a certain make of automobile.

When I reached home everyone was excited. Next day the neighbors came to congratulate me. I even felt safe from grandfather, whose deathbed curse usually spoiled my triumphs. I stood beneath his photograph with my brief case in hand and smiled triumphantly into his stolid black peasant's face. It was a face that fascinated me. The eyes seemed to follow everywhere I went.

That night I dreamed I was at a circus with him and that he refused to laugh at the clowns no matter what they did. Then later he told me to open my brief case and read what was inside and I did, finding an official envelope stamped with the state seal; and inside the envelope I found another and another, endlessly, and I thought I would fall of weariness. "Them's years," he said. "Now open that one." And I did and in it I found an engraved document containing a short message in letters of gold. "Read it," my grandfather said. "Out loud!"

"To Whom It May Concern," I intoned. "Keep This Nigger-Boy Running." 105 I awoke with the old man's laughter ringing in my ears.

(It was a dream I was to remember and dream again for many years after. But at that time I had no insight into its meaning. First I had to attend college.)

CONSIDERATIONS FOR CRITICAL THINKING AND WRITING

1. FIRST RESPONSE. Discuss how the protagonist's expectations are similar to what has come to be known as the American dream — the assumption that ambition, hard work, perseverance, intelligence, and virtue always lead to success. Do you believe in the American dream?

2. How does the first paragraph of the story sum up the conflict that the narrator confronts? In what sense is he "invisible"?

3. Why do his grandfather's last words cause so much anxiety in the family? What does his grandfather mean when he says, "I want you to overcome 'em with yeses, undermine 'em with grins, agree 'em to death" (para. 2)?

4. What is the symbolic significance of the naked blonde? What details reveal that she represents more than a sexual tease in the story?

5. How does the battle in the boxing ring and the scramble for money afterward suggest the kind of control whites have over blacks in the story?

6. Why is it significant that the town is named Greenwood and that the briefcase award comes from Shad Whitmore's shop? Can you find any other details that serve to reinforce the meaning of the story?

7. What is the narrator's perspective as an educated adult telling the story, in contrast to his assumptions and beliefs as a recent high school graduate? How is this contrast especially evident in the speech before the "leading white citizens" of the town?

8. How can the dream at the end of the story be related to the major incidents that precede it?

9. Given the grandfather's advice, explain how "meekness" can be a "dangerous activity" and a weapon against oppression.

10. Imagine the story as told from a third-person point of view. How would this change the story? Do you think the story would be more or less effective told from a third-person point of view? Explain your answer.

11. CRITICAL STRATEGIES. Read the section on mythological criticism (pp. 1657–59) in Chapter 51, "Critical Strategies for Reading," and "What Is an Initiation Story?" by Mordecai Marcus (following). Discuss "Battle Royal" as an archetypal initiation story.

CONNECTION TO ANOTHER SELECTION

1. Compare and contrast Ellison's view of the South with William Faulkner's in "A Rose for Emily" (p. 78).

Perspective

MORDECAI MARCUS (1925–2014)
What Is an Initiation Story?   1960

An initiation story may be said to show its young protagonist experiencing a significant change of knowledge about the world or himself, or a change of character, or of both, and this change must point or lead him toward an adult world. It may or may not contain some form of ritual, but it should give some evidence that the change is at least likely to have permanent effects.

Initiation stories obviously center on a variety of experiences and the initiations vary in effect. It will be useful, therefore, to divide initiations into types according to their power and effect. First, some initiations lead only to the threshold of maturity and understanding but do not definitely cross it. Such stories emphasize the shocking effect of experience, and their protagonists tend to be distinctly young. Second, some initiations take their protagonists across a threshold of maturity and understanding but leave them enmeshed in a struggle for certainty. These initiations sometimes involve self-discovery. Third, the most decisive initiations carry their protagonists firmly into maturity and understanding, or at least show them decisively embarked toward maturity. These initiations usually center on self-discovery. For convenience, I will call these types tentative, uncompleted, and decisive initiations.

> From "What Is an Initiation Story?" in *The Journal*
> *of Aesthetics and Art Criticism*

CONSIDERATIONS FOR CRITICAL THINKING AND WRITING

1. For a work to be classified as an initiation story, why should it "give some evidence that the change [in the protagonist] is at least likely to have permanent effects"?

2. Marcus divides initiations into three broad types: tentative, uncompleted, and decisive. Explain how you would categorize the initiation in Ellison's "Battle Royal."

A SAMPLE CLOSE READING

An Annotated Section of "Battle Royal"

Even as you read a story for the first time, you can highlight passages, circle or underline words, and write responses in the margins. Subsequent readings will yield more insights once you begin to understand how various elements such as plot, character, and wording build toward the conclusion and what you perceive to be the story's central ideas. The following annotations for paragraphs 3–6 of "Battle Royal" provide a perspective written by someone who had read the work several times.

On his "graduation day," the narrator is about to be initiated into a world of racial degradations that will make him an "invisible man."

The narrator's "humility" is a pragmatic strategy to achieve success in a white world and connects him to his grandfather's subversive advice "to overcome 'em with yeses."

The "leading" whites in the "leading" hotel represent the respectable pillars of the community, but they are only leading the blacks to a battle with each other rather than to some kind of recognition and "triumph."

The town's leaders are described as "wolfing" down their food, an appropriate image for their predatory relationship to the boys.

The narrator's "dignity" exists in his own mind but not in the minds of the whites or his fellow fighters.

The advice that the narrator quotes from Washington, a symbol of racial accommodation, in his speech (para. 66) is undercut by the battle royal to come.

RALPH ELLISON (1914–1994)

Battle Royal   1947

[. . . On my graduation day I delivered an oration in which I showed that humility was the secret, indeed, the very essence of progress. (Not that I believed this — how could I, remembering my grandfather? — I only believed that it worked.) It was a great success. Everyone praised me and I was invited to give the speech at a gathering of the town's leading white citizens. It was a triumph for our whole community.

It was in the main ballroom of the leading hotel. When I got there I discovered that it was on the occasion of a smoker, and I was told that since I was to be there anyway I might as well take part in the battle royal to be fought by some of my schoolmates as part of the entertainment. The battle royal came first.

All of the town's big shots were there in their tuxedoes, wolfing down the buffet foods, drinking beer and whiskey and smoking black cigars. It was a large room with a high ceiling. Chairs were arranged in neat rows around three sides of a portable boxing ring. The fourth side was clear, revealing a gleaming space of polished floor. I had some misgivings over the battle royal, by the way. Not from a distaste for fighting, but because I didn't care too much for the other fellows who were to take part. They were tough guys who seemed to have no grandfather's curse worrying their minds. No one could mistake their toughness. And besides, I suspected that fighting a battle royal might detract from the dignity of my speech. In those pre-invisible days I visualized myself as a potential Booker T. Washington. But the other fellows didn't care too much for me either, and there were nine of them. I felt superior to them in my way, and I didn't like the manner in which we were all crowded together into the servants' elevator. Nor did they like my being there. In fact, as the warmly lighted floors flashed past the elevator we had words over the fact that I, by taking part in the fight, had knocked one of their friends out of a night's work.

We were led out of the elevator through a rococo hall into an anteroom and told to get into our fighting togs. Each of us was issued a pair of boxing gloves and ushered out into the big mirrored hall, which we entered looking cautiously about us and whispering, lest we might accidentally be heard above the noise of the room. It was foggy with cigar smoke. And already the whiskey was taking effect. I was shocked to see some of the most important men of the town quite tipsy. They were all there — bankers, lawyers, judges, doctors, fire chiefs, teachers, merchants. Even one of the more fashionable pastors. Something we could not see was going on up front. A clarinet was vibrating sensuously and the men were standing up and moving eagerly forward. We were a small tight group, clustered together, our bare upper bodies touching and shining with anticipatory sweat; while up front the big shots were becoming increasingly excited over something we still could not see. Suddenly I heard the school superintendent, who had told me to come, yell, "Bring up the shines, gentlemen! Bring up the little shines!"

> The narrator's innocence is demonstrated by his shocked response to seeing "the most important men of the town," including a pastor, at the smoker.

> The school superintendent not only participates but appears to be in charge of the smoker. His yelling "Bring up the shines" is filled with unintended irony.

A SAMPLE STUDENT RESPONSE

Katz 1

Lila Katz

Professor West

English 200

2 February 2015

Symbolism in Ralph Ellison's "Battle Royal"

In Ralph Ellison's story "Battle Royal," a young African American man, proud of his achievements, is asked to read his high school graduation speech to the "town's big shots" (228). The event, which the narrator initially looks forward to as "a triumph for our whole community" (228), turns out to be a spectacle of ridicule and abuse. He and other young black men are degraded and forced to fight gladiator-style—all for the amusement of drunken white men. This experience, as horrible as it is, allows the main character to better understand the world and the place he is expected to occupy in it. The story can be considered a coming-of-age or initiation story, in which the main character experiences change. Ellison's character is taken "across a threshold of maturity and understanding" yet is still "enmeshed in a struggle for certainty" (Marcus 237). And through the story's powerful symbolism, the reader can better understand that struggle.

The battle itself can be read as a representation of the society in which the narrator lives—in which nothing makes sense, in which whites hold the power, and in which blacks must struggle against racism and violence. In this battle, part of the narrator's initiation into society, the young black men are stripped of power, blindfolded, and turned against each other. The lead-up to the battle, the dance of the naked white woman branded with an American flag tattoo, is symbolic, too. Read as a representation of America, she is what the young black men cannot have. In the aftermath of the battle, when it is time for the men to finally be paid, they are forced to crawl on the floor and grapple not for money but for worthless tokens. Ellison offers these symbols to define the inequalities of race and class that the African Americans endure in the story. . . .

Works Cited

Ellison, Ralph. "Battle Royal." Meyer 227–36.

Marcus, Mordecai. "What Is an Initiation Story?" Meyer 237.

Meyer, Michael, ed. *The Bedford Introduction to Literature*. 11th ed. Boston: Bedford/St. Martin's, 2016. Print.

MICHAEL OPPENHEIMER (B. 1943)

Born in Berkeley, California, Michael Oppenheimer grew up on a cattle ranch in the Rocky Mountains of southwest Colorado. He graduated from Antioch College and earned a master of arts in English and art at Lone Mountain College / University of San Francisco. Oppenheimer has published short stories and worked as a reporter, teacher, and publisher of a press; he currently lives in Bellingham, Washington, where he creates kinetic environmental art.

The Paring Knife   1982

I found a knife under the refrigerator while the woman I love and I were cleaning our house. It was a small paring knife that we lost many years before and had since forgotten about. I showed the knife to the woman I love and she said, "Oh. Where did you find it?" After I told her, she put the knife on the table and then went into the next room and continued to clean. While I cleaned the kitchen floor, I remembered something that happened four years before that explained how the knife had gotten under the refrigerator.

We had eaten a large dinner and had drunk many glasses of wine. We turned all the lights out, took our clothing off, and went to bed. We thought we would make love, but something happened and we had an argument while making love. We had never experienced such a thing. We both became extremely angry. I said some very hurtful things to the woman I love. She kicked at me in bed and I got out and went into the kitchen. I fumbled for a chair and sat down. I wanted to rest my arms on the table and then rest my head in my arms, but I felt the dirty dishes on the table and they were in the way. I became incensed. I swept everything that was on the table onto the floor. The noise was tremendous, but then the room was very quiet and I suddenly felt sad. I thought I had destroyed everything. I began to cry. The woman I love came into the kitchen and asked if I was all right. I said, "Yes." She turned the light on and we looked at the kitchen floor. Nothing much was broken, but the floor was very messy. We both laughed and then went back to bed and made love. The next morning we cleaned up the mess, but obviously overlooked the knife.

I was about to ask the woman I love if she remembered that incident when she came in from the next room and without saying a word, picked up the knife from the table and slid it back under the refrigerator.

CONSIDERATIONS FOR CRITICAL THINKING AND WRITING

1. FIRST RESPONSE. Why do you think the woman slides the knife back under the refrigerator at the end of the story?
2. Consider whether the knife is used as a conventional symbol or as a literary symbol in the story.
3. Discuss the significance of the title.
4. How does the flashback in the second paragraph provide the necessary exposition to create the elements of a complex plot?
5. CREATIVE RESPONSE. Rewrite the second paragraph without revising the first and third paragraphs so that the woman's motivation for sliding the knife under the refrigerator must be read in a very different way than you read it now.

CONNECTIONS TO OTHER SELECTIONS

1. Compare the narrator's emotions at the end of this story and in Maggie Mitchell's "It Would Be Different If" (p. 213).

2. Explain how symbolism is central to understanding the resolution of the conflicts in "The Paring Knife" and in Raymond Carver's "Popular Mechanics" (p. 277).

DAGOBERTO GILB (B. 1950)

A brief biography and introduction to Dagoberto Gilb's work appear in Chapter 15, "A Study of Dagoberto Gilb: The Author Reflects on Three Stories" (p. 448). Chapter 15 features Gilb's commentaries on three additional stories, as well as nonfiction excerpts from his writing, photographs, manuscript drafts, and an interview.

Romero's Shirt   1993

Juan Romero, a man not unlike many in this country, has had jobs in factories, shops, and stores. He has painted houses, dug ditches, planted trees, hammered, sawed, bolted, snaked pipes, picked cotton and chile and pecans, each and all for wages. Along the way he has married and raised his children and several years ago he finally arranged it so that his money might pay for the house he and his family live in. He is still more than twenty years away from being the owner. It is a modest house even by El Paso standards. The building, in an adobe style, is made of stone which is painted white, though the paint is gradually chipping off or being absorbed by the rock. It has two bedrooms, a den which is used as another, a small dining area, a living room, a kitchen, one bathroom, and a garage which, someday, he plans to turn into another place to live. Although in a development facing a paved street and in a neighborhood, it has the appearance of being on almost half an acre. At the front is a garden of cactus — nopal, ocotillo, and agave — and there are weeds that grow tall with yellow flowers which seed into thorn-hard burrs. The rest is dirt and rocks of various sizes, some of which have been lined up to form a narrow path out of the graded dirt, a walkway to the front porch — where, under a tile and one-by tongue and groove overhang, are a wooden chair and a love seat, covered by an old bedspread, its legless frame on the red cement slab. Once the porch looked onto oak trees. Two of them are dried-out stumps; the remaining one has a limb or two which still can produce leaves, but with so many amputations, its future is irreversible. Romero seldom runs water through a garden hose, though in the back yard some patchy grass can almost seem suburban, at least to him, when he does. Near the corner of his land, in the front, next to the sidewalk, is a juniper shrub, his only bright green plant, and Romero does not want it to yellow and die, so he makes special efforts on its behalf, washing off dust, keeping its leaves neatly pruned and shaped.

These days Romero calls himself a handyman. He does odd jobs, which is exactly how he advertises — "no job too small" — in the throwaway paper. He hangs wallpaper and doors, he paints, lays carpet, does just about anything someone will call and ask him to do. It doesn't earn him much, and sometimes it's barely enough, but he's his own boss, and he's had so many bad jobs over those other years, ones no more dependable, he's learned that this suits him. At one time Romero did want more, and he'd believed that he could have it simply through work, but no matter what he did his children still had to be born at the county hospital. Even years later it was there that his oldest son went for serious medical treatment because Romero couldn't afford the private hospitals. He tried not to worry about how he earned his money. In Mexico, where his parents were born and he spent much of his youth, so many things weren't available, and any work which allowed for food, clothes, and housing was to be honored — by the standards there, Romero lived well. Except this wasn't Mexico, and even though there were those who did worse even here, there were many who did better and had more, and a young Romero too often felt ashamed by what he saw as his failure. But time passed, and he got older. As he saw it, he didn't live in poverty, and *here,* he finally came to realize, was where he was, where he and his family were going to stay. Life in El Paso was much like the land — hard, but one could make do with what was offered. Just as his parents had, Romero always thought it was a beautiful place for a home.

Yet people he knew left — to Houston, Dallas, Los Angeles, San Diego, Denver, Chicago — and came back for holidays with stories of high wages and acquisition. And more and more people crossed the river, in rags, taking work, his work, at any price. Romero constantly had to discipline himself by remembering the past, how his parents lived; he had to teach himself to appreciate what he did have. His car, for example, he'd kept up since his early twenties. He'd had it painted three times in that period and he worked on it so devotedly that even now it was in as good a condition as almost any car could be. For his children he tried to offer more — an assortment of clothes for his daughter, lots of toys for his sons. He denied his wife nothing, but she was a woman who asked for little. For himself, it was much less. He owned some work clothes and T-shirts necessary for his jobs as well as a set of good enough, he thought, shirts he'd had since before the car. He kept up a nice pair of custom boots, and in a closet hung a pair of slacks for a wedding or baptism or important mass. He owned two jackets, a leather one from Mexico and a warm nylon one for cold work days. And he owned a wool plaid Pendleton shirt, his favorite piece of clothing, which he'd bought right after the car and before his marriage because it really was good-looking besides being functional. He wore it anywhere and everywhere with confidence that its quality would always be both in style and appropriate.

The border was less than two miles below Romero's home, and he could see, down the dirt street which ran alongside his property, the desert and mountains of Mexico. The street was one of the few in the city which hadn't yet been paved. Romero liked it that way, despite the run-off problems when heavy rains passed by, as they had the day before this day. A night wind had blown hard behind the rains, and the air was so clean he could easily see buildings in Juárez. It was sunny, but a breeze told him to put on his favorite shirt before he pulled the car up alongside the house and dragged over the garden hose to wash it, which was something he still enjoyed doing as much as anything else. He was organized, had a special bucket, a special sponge, and he used warm water from the kitchen sink. When he started soaping the car he worried about getting his shirt sleeves wet, and once he was moving around he decided a T-shirt would keep him warm enough. So he took off the wool shirt and draped it, conspicuously, over the juniper near him, at the corner of his property. He thought that if he couldn't help but see it, he couldn't forget it, and forgetting something outside was losing it. He lived near a school, and teenagers passed by all the time, and also there was regular foot-traffic — many people walked the sidewalk in front of his house, many who had no work.

After the car was washed, Romero went inside and brought out the car wax. 5 Waxing his car was another thing he still liked to do, especially on a weekday like this one when he was by himself, when no one in his family was home. He could work faster, but he took his time, spreading with a damp cloth, waiting, then wiping off the crust with a dry cloth. The exterior done, he went inside the car and waxed the dash, picked up some trash on the floorboard, cleaned out the glove compartment. Then he went for some pliers he kept in a toolbox in the garage, returned and began to wire up the rear license plate which had lost a nut and bolt and was hanging awkwardly. As he did this, he thought of other things he might do when he finished, like prune the juniper. Except his old shears had broken, and he hadn't found another used pair, because he wouldn't buy them new.

An old man walked up to him carrying a garden rake, a hoe, and some shears. He asked Romero if there was some yard work needing to be done. After spring, tall weeds grew in many yards, but it seemed a dumb question this time of year, particularly since there was obviously so little ever to be done in Romero's yard. But Romero listened to the old man. There were still a few weeds over there, and he could rake the dirt so it'd be even and level, he could clip that shrub, and probably there was something in the back if he were to look. Romero was usually brusque with requests such as these, but he found the old man unique and likeable and he listened and finally asked how much he would want for all those tasks. The old man thought as quickly as he spoke and threw out a number. Ten. Romero repeated the number, questioningly, and the old man backed up, saying well, eight, seven. Romero asked if that was for everything. Yes sir, the old man said, excited that he'd seemed to catch a customer. Romero asked if he would cut the juniper for three dollars. The old man kept his eyes on the evergreen, disappointed for a second, then thought better of it. Okay, okay, he said, but, I've been walking all day, you'll give me lunch? The old man rubbed his striped cotton shirt at his stomach.

Romero liked the old man and agreed to it. He told him how he should follow the shape which was already there, to cut it evenly, to take a few inches off all of it just like a haircut. Then Romero went inside, scrambled enough eggs and chile and cheese for both of them and rolled it all in some tortillas. He brought out a beer.

The old man was clearly grateful, but since his gratitude was keeping the work from getting done — he might talk an hour about his little ranch in Mexico, about his little turkeys and his pig — Romero excused himself and went inside. The old man thanked Romero for the food, and, as soon as he was finished with the beer, went after the work sincerely. With dull shears — he sharpened them, so to speak, against a rock wall — the old man snipped garishly, hopping and jumping around the bush, around and around. It gave Romero such great pleasure to watch that this was all he did from his front window.

The work didn't take long, so, as the old man was raking up the clippings, Romero brought out a five-dollar bill. He felt that the old man's dancing around that bush, in those baggy old checkered pants, was more inspiring than religion, and a couple of extra dollars was a cheap price to see old eyes whiten like a boy's.

The old man was so pleased that he invited Romero to that little ranch of his in 10 Mexico where he was sure they could share some aguardiente, or maybe Romero could buy a turkey from him — they were skinny but they could be fattened — but in any case they could enjoy a bottle of tequila together, with some sweet lemons. The happy old man swore he would come back no matter what, for he could do many things for Romero at his beautiful home. He swore he would return, maybe in a week or two, for surely there was work that needed to be done in the back yard.

Romero wasn't used to feeling so virtuous. He so often was disappointed, so often dwelled on the difficulties of life, that he had become hard, guarding against compassion and generosity. So much so that he'd even become spare with his words, even with his family. His wife whispered to the children that this was because he was tired, and, since it wasn't untrue, he accepted it as the explanation too. It spared him that worry, and from having to discuss why he liked working weekends and taking a day off during the week, like this one. But now an old man had made Romero wish his family were there with him so he could give as much, *more,* to them too, so he could watch their spin around dances — he'd missed so many — and Romero swore he would take them all into Juárez that night for dinner. He might even convince them to take a day, maybe two, for a drive to his uncle's house in Chihuahua instead, because he'd promised that so many years ago — so long ago they probably thought about somewhere else by now, like San Diego, or Los Angeles. Then he'd take them there! They'd go for a week, spend whatever it took. No expense could be so great, and if happiness was as easy as some tacos and a five-dollar bill, then how stupid it had been of him not to have offered it all this time.

Romero felt so good, felt such relief, he napped on the couch. When he woke up he immediately remembered his shirt, that it was already gone before the old man had even arrived — he remembered they'd walked around the juniper before it was cut. Nevertheless, the possibility that the old man took it wouldn't leave Romero's mind. Since he'd never believed in letting down, giving into someone like that old man, the whole experience became suspect. Maybe it was part of some ruse which ended with the old man taking his shirt, some food, money. This was how Romero thought. Though he held a hope that he'd left it somewhere else, that it was a lapse of memory on his part — he went outside, inside, looked everywhere twice, then one more time after that — his cynicism had flowered, colorful and bitter.

Understand that it was his favorite shirt, that he'd never thought of replacing it and that its loss was all Romero could keep his mind on, though he knew very well it wasn't a son, or a daughter, or a wife, or a mother or father, not a disaster of any kind. It was a simple shirt, in the true value of things not very much to lose. But understand also that Romero was a good man who tried to do what was right and who would harm no one willfully. Understand that Romero was a man who had taught himself to not care, to not want, to not desire for so long that he'd lost many words, avoided many people, kept to himself, alone, almost always, even when his wife gave him his meals. Understand that it was his favorite shirt and though no more than that, for him it was no less. Then understand how he felt like a fool paying that old man who, he considered, might even have taken it, like a fool for feeling so friendly and generous, happy, when the shirt was already gone, like a fool for having all those and these thoughts for the love of a wool shirt, like a fool for not being able to stop thinking them all, but especially the one reminding him that this was what he had always believed in, that loss was what he was most prepared for. And so then you might understand why he began to stare out the window of his home, waiting for someone to walk by absently with it on, for the thief to pass by, careless. He kept a watch out the window as each of his children came in, then his wife. He told them only what had happened and, as always, they left him alone. He stared out that window onto the dirt street, past the ocotillos and nopales and agaves, the junipers and oaks and mulberries in front of other homes of brick or stone, painted or not, past them to the buildings in Juárez, and he watched the horizon darken and the sky light up with the moon and stars, and the land spread with shimmering lights, so bright in the dark blot of night. He heard dogs barking until another might bark farther away, and then another, back and forth like that, the small rectangles and squares of their fences plotted out distinctly in his mind's eye as his lids closed. Then he heard a gust of wind bend around his house, and then came the train, the metal rhythm getting closer until it was as close as it could be, the steel pounding the earth like a beating heart, until it diminished and then faded away and then left the air to silence, to its quiet and dark, so still it was like death, or rest, sleep, until he could hear a grackle, and then another gust of wind, and then finally a car.

He looked in on his daughter still so young, so beautiful, becoming a woman who would leave that bed for another, his sons still boys when they were asleep, who dreamed like men when they were awake, and his wife, still young in his eyes in the morning shadows of their bed.

Romero went outside. The juniper had been cut just as he'd wanted it. He got   15
cold and came back in and went to the bed and blankets his wife kept so clean, so neatly arranged as she slept under them without him, and he lay down beside her.

CONSIDERATIONS FOR CRITICAL THINKING AND WRITING

1. FIRST RESPONSE. How do Romero's attitudes toward work reveal his character and values?

2. Which details about El Paso seem important to you as a means of establishing the setting and the context of Romero's life?

3. What do you think is the function of the old man in the story? How does he affect Romero?

4. Write a sentence that captures what you think is the story's theme. Explain whether the theme is explicitly stated or is implicitly embedded in, for example, character, action, plot, or some other element in the story.

5. How might the use of a first-person point of view, instead of the third person, affect your understanding of and response to Romero?

6. Choose a substantial paragraph from the story and analyze its style, considering such elements as diction, sentence structure, and tone. How is the style related to its content?

7. Why do you think the story is titled "Romero's Shirt"? What symbolic values are associated with it in the story?

CONNECTIONS TO OTHER SELECTIONS

1. Discuss the treatment of domestic life, and in particular the image of the fathers, in "Romero's Shirt" and in Gilb's "Shout" (p. 462).

2. Consider the ending and tone of "Romero's Shirt," keeping in mind two poems about work: Jan Beatty's "My Father Teaches Me to Dream" (p. 1033) and Michael Chitwood's "Men Throwing Bricks" (p. 1034). Which of the two poems do you think seems to describe Romero's sensibilities more completely?

8

Theme

To produce a mighty book, you must choose a mighty theme.
— HERMAN MELVILLE,
from *Moby-Dick*, 1851

Theme is the central idea or meaning of a story. It provides a unifying point around which the plot, characters, setting, point of view, symbols, and other elements of a story are organized. In some works the theme is explicitly stated. Nathaniel Hawthorne's "Wakefield," for example, begins with the author telling the reader that the point of his story is "done up neatly, and condensed into the final sentence." Most modern writers, however, present their themes implicitly (as Hawthorne does in the majority of his stories), so determining the underlying meaning of a work often requires more effort than it does from the reader of "Wakefield." One reason for the difficulty is that the theme is fused into the elements of the story, and these must be carefully examined in relation to one another as well as to the work as a whole. But then that's the value of determining the theme, for it requires a close analysis of all the elements of a work. Such a close reading often results in sharper insights into this overlooked character or that seemingly unrelated incident. Accounting for the details and seeing how they fit together result in greater understanding of the story. Such familiarity creates pleasure in much the same way that a musical piece heard more than once becomes a rich experience rather than simply a repetitive one.

Themes are not always easy to express, but some principles can aid you in articulating the central meaning of a work. First distinguish between the theme of a story and its subject. They are not equivalents. Many stories share identical subjects, such as fate, death, innocence, youth, loneliness, racial prejudice, and disillusionment. Yet each story usually makes its own statement about the subject and expresses some view of life. Hemingway's "Soldier's Home" (p. 162) and Faulkner's "Barn Burning" (p. 406) both describe young men who are unhappy at home and decide that they must leave, but the meaning of each story is quite different. A thematic generalization about "Soldier's Home" could be something like this: "The brutal experience of war can alienate a person from those — even family and friends — who are innocent of war's reality." The theme of Faulkner's story could be stated this way: "No matter how much one might love one's father, there comes a time when family loyalties must be left behind in order to be true to one's self."

These two statements of theme do not definitively sum up each story — there is no single, absolute way of expressing a work's theme — but they do describe a central idea in each. Furthermore, the emphasis in each of these themes could be modified or expanded because interpretations of interesting, complex works are always subject to revision. People have different responses to life, and so it is hardly surprising that responses to literature are not identical. When theme is considered, the possibilities for meaning are usually expanded and not reduced to categories such as "right" or "wrong."

Although readers may differ in their interpretations of a story, that does not mean that *any* interpretation is valid. If we were to assert that the soldier's dissatisfactions in Hemingway's story could be readily eliminated by his settling down to marriage and a decent job (his mother's solution), we would have missed Hemingway's purposes in writing the story; we would have failed to see how Krebs's war experiences have caused him to reexamine the assumptions and beliefs that previously nurtured him but now seem unreal to him. We would have to ignore much in the story in order to arrive at such a reading. To be valid, the statement of the theme should be responsive to the details of the story. It must be based on evidence within the story rather than solely on experiences, attitudes, or values the reader brings to the work — such as personally knowing a war veteran who successfully adjusted to civilian life after getting a good job and marrying. Familiarity with the subject matter of a story can certainly be an aid to interpretation, but it should not get in the way of seeing the author's perspective.

Sometimes readers too hastily conclude that a story's theme always consists of a moral, some kind of lesson that is dramatized by the various elements of the work. There are stories that do this — Hawthorne's "Wakefield," for example. Here are the final sentences in his story about a middle-aged man who drops out of life for twenty years:

> He has left us much food for thought, a portion of which shall lend its wisdom to a moral, and be shaped into a figure. Amid the seeming confusion of our mysterious world, individuals are so nicely adjusted to a system, and systems to one another and to a whole, that, by stepping aside for a moment, a man exposes himself

to a fearful risk of losing his place forever. Like Wakefield, he may become, as it were, the Outcast of the Universe.

Most stories, however, do not include such direct caveats about the conduct of life. A tendency to look for a lesson in a story can produce a reductive and inaccurate formulation of its theme. Consider the damage done to Godwin's "A Sorrowful Woman" (p. 39) if its theme is described as this: "The woman in the story is too selfish to cope with the responsibilities of marriage." Godwin's focus in this story is on the woman's desperate response to domestic identity rather than on her inability to be a good wife. In fact, a good many stories go beyond traditional social values to explore human behavior instead of condemning or endorsing it.

Determining the theme of a story can be a difficult task because all the story's elements may contribute to its central idea. Indeed, you may discover that finding the theme is more challenging than coming to grips with the author's values as they are revealed in the story. There is no precise formula that can take you to the center of a story's meaning and help you to articulate it. However, several strategies are practical and useful once you have read the story. Apply these pointers during a second or third reading:

1. Pay attention to the title of the story. It often provides a lead to a major symbol (Faulkner's "Barn Burning," p. 406) or to the subject around which the theme develops (Godwin's "A Sorrowful Woman," p. 39).

2. Look for details in the story that have potential for symbolic meanings. Careful consideration of names, places, objects, minor characters, and incidents can lead you to the central meaning — for example, think of the stripper in Ellison's "Battle Royal" (p. 227). Be especially attentive to elements you did not understand on the first reading.

3. Decide whether the protagonist changes or develops some important insight as a result of the action. Carefully examine any generalizations the protagonist or narrator makes about the events in the story.

4. When you formulate the theme of the story in your own words, write it down in one or two complete sentences that make some point about the subject matter. Revenge may be the subject of a story, but its theme should make a statement about revenge: "Instead of providing satisfaction, revenge defeats the best in one's self" is one possibility.

5. Be certain that your expression of the theme is a generalized statement rather than a specific description of particular people, places, and incidents in the story. Contrast the preceding statement of a theme on revenge with this too-specific one: "In Nathaniel Hawthorne's *The Scarlet Letter,* Roger Chillingworth loses his humanity owing to his single-minded attempts to punish Arthur Dimmesdale for fathering a child with Chillingworth's wife, Hester." Hawthorne's theme is not restricted to a single fictional character named Chillingworth but to anyone whose life is ruined by revenge. Be certain that your statement of theme does not focus on only part of the story. The theme just cited for *The Scarlet Letter,* for example, relegates Hester to the status of a minor character. What it says about Chillingworth is true, but the statement is incomplete as a generalization about the novel.

6. Be wary of using clichés as a way of stating theme. They tend to short-circuit ideas instead of generating them. It may be tempting to resort to something like "an eye for an eye" as a statement of the theme of *The Scarlet Letter*; however, even the slightest second thought reveals how much more ambiguous the ending of that story is.

7. Be aware that some stories emphasize theme less than others. Stories that have as their major purpose adventure, humor, mystery, or terror may have little or no theme. In Edgar Allan Poe's "The Pit and the Pendulum," for example, the protagonist is not used to condemn torture; instead, he becomes a sensitive gauge to measure the pain and horror he endures at the hands of his captors.

What is most valuable about articulating the theme of a work is the process by which the theme is determined. Ultimately, the theme is expressed by the story itself and is inseparable from the experience of reading the story. Tim O'Brien's explanation of "How to Tell a True War Story" (p. 488) is probably true of most kinds of stories: "In a true war story, if there's a moral [or theme] at all, it's like the thread that makes the cloth. You can't tease it out. You can't extract the meaning without unraveling the deeper meaning." Describing the theme should not be a way to consume a story, to be done with it. It is a means of clarifying our thinking about what we've read and probably felt intuitively.

Stephen Crane's "The Bride Comes to Yellow Sky," Katherine Mansfield's "Miss Brill," and Xu Xi's "Famine" are three stories whose respective themes emerge from the authors' skillful use of plot, character, setting, and symbol.

STEPHEN CRANE (1871–1900)

Born in Newark, New Jersey, Stephen Crane attended Lafayette College and Syracuse University and then worked as a freelance journalist in New York City. He wrote newspaper pieces, short stories, poems, and novels for his entire, brief adult life. His first book, *Maggie: A Girl of the Streets* (1893), is a story about New York slum life and prostitution. His most famous novel, *The Red Badge of Courage* (1895), gives readers a vivid, convincing re-creation of Civil War battles, even though Crane had never been to war. However, Crane was personally familiar with the American West, where he traveled as a reporter. "The Bride Comes to Yellow Sky" includes some of the ingredients of a typi-

© Bettmann/CORBIS.

cal popular western — a confrontation between a marshal and a drunk who shoots up the town — but the story's theme is less predictable and more serious than the plot seems to suggest.

The Bride Comes to Yellow Sky 1898

I

The great Pullman was whirling onward with such dignity of motion that a glance from the window seemed simply to prove that the plains of Texas were pouring eastward. Vast flats of green grass, dull-hued spaces of mesquit and cactus, little groups of frame houses, woods of light and tender trees, all were sweeping into the east, sweeping over the horizon, a precipice.

A newly married pair had boarded this coach at San Antonio. The man's face was reddened from many days in the wind and sun, and a direct result of his new black clothes was that his brick-colored hands were constantly performing in a most conscious fashion. From time to time he looked down respectfully at his attire. He sat with a hand on each knee, like a man waiting in a barber's shop. The glances he devoted to other passengers were furtive and shy.

The bride was not pretty, nor was she very young. She wore a dress of blue cashmere, with small reservations of velvet here and there, and with steel buttons abounding. She continually twisted her head to regard her puff sleeves, very stiff, straight, and high. They embarrassed her. It was quite apparent that she had cooked, and that she expected to cook, dutifully. The blushes caused by the careless scrutiny of some passengers as she had entered the car were strange to see upon this plain, under-class countenance, which was drawn in placid, almost emotionless lines.

They were evidently very happy. "Ever been in a parlor-car before?" he asked, smiling with delight.

"No," she answered; "I never was. It's fine, ain't it?" 5

"Great! And then after a while we'll go forward to the diner, and get a big lay-out. Finest meal in the world. Charge a dollar."

"Oh, do they?" cried the bride. "Charge a dollar? Why, that's too much — for us — ain't it, Jack?"

"Not this trip, anyhow," he answered bravely. "We're going to go the whole thing."

Later he explained to her about the trains. "You see, it's a thousand miles from one end of Texas to the other; and this train runs right across it, and never stops but four times." He had the pride of an owner. He pointed out to her the dazzling fittings of the coach; and in truth her eyes opened wider as she contemplated the sea-green figured velvet, the shining brass, silver, and glass, the wood that gleamed as darkly brilliant as the surface of a pool of oil. At one end a bronze figure sturdily held a support for a separated chamber, and at convenient places on the ceiling were frescoes in olive and silver.

To the minds of the pair, their surroundings reflected the glory of their marriage 10 that morning in San Antonio; this was the environment of their new estate; and the man's face in particular beamed with an elation that made him appear ridiculous to the negro porter. This individual at times surveyed them from afar with an amused and superior grin. On other occasions he bullied them with skill in ways that did not make it exactly plain to them that they were being bullied. He subtly used all the manners of the most unconquerable kind of snobbery. He oppressed them; but of this oppression they had small knowledge, and they speedily forgot that infrequently a number of travelers covered them with stares of derisive enjoyment. Historically there was supposed to be something infinitely humorous in their situation.

"We are due in Yellow Sky at 3:42," he said, looking tenderly into her eyes.

"Oh, are we?" she said, as if she had not been aware of it. To evince surprise at her husband's statement was part of her wifely amiability. She took from a pocket a little silver watch; and as she held it before her, and stared at it with a frown of attention, the new husband's face shone.

"I bought it in San Anton' from a friend of mine," he told her gleefully.

"It's seventeen minutes past twelve," she said, looking up at him with a kind of shy and clumsy coquetry. A passenger, noting this play, grew excessively sardonic, and winked at himself in one of the numerous mirrors.

At last they went to the dining-car. Two rows of negro waiters, in glowing white 15 suits, surveyed their entrance with the interest, and also the equanimity, of men who had been forewarned. The pair fell to the lot of a waiter who happened to feel pleasure in steering them through their meal. He viewed them with the manner of a fatherly pilot, his countenance radiant with benevolence. The patronage, entwined with the ordinary deference, was not plain to them. And yet, as they returned to their coach, they showed in their faces a sense of escape.

To the left, miles down a long purple slope, was a little ribbon of mist where moved the keening Rio Grande. The train was approaching it at an angle, and the apex was Yellow Sky. Presently it was apparent that, as the distance from Yellow Sky grew shorter, the husband became commensurately restless. His brick-red hands were more insistent in their prominence. Occasionally he was even rather absent-minded and far-away when the bride leaned forward and addressed him.

As a matter of truth, Jack Potter was beginning to find the shadow of a deed weigh upon him like a leaden slab. He, the town marshal of Yellow Sky, a man known, liked, and feared in his corner, a prominent person, had gone to San Antonio to meet a girl he believed he loved, and there, after the usual prayers, had actually induced her to marry him, without consulting Yellow Sky for any part of the transaction. He was now bringing his bride before an innocent and unsuspecting community.

Of course people in Yellow Sky married as it pleased them in accordance with a general custom; but such was Potter's thought of his duty to his friends, or of their idea of his duty, or of an unspoken form which does not control men in these matters, that he felt he was heinous. He had committed an extraordinary crime. Face to face with this girl in San Antonio, and spurred by his sharp impulse, he had gone headlong over all the social hedges. At San Antonio he was like a man hidden in the dark. A knife to sever any friendly duty, any form, was easy to his hand in that remote city. But the hour of Yellow Sky — the hour of daylight — was approaching.

He knew full well that his marriage was an important thing to his town. It could only be exceeded by the burning of the new hotel. His friends could not forgive him. Frequently he had reflected on the advisability of telling them by telegraph, but a new cowardice had been upon him. He feared to do it. And now the train was hurrying him toward a scene of amazement, glee, and reproach. He glanced out of the window at the line of haze swinging slowly in toward the train.

Yellow Sky had a kind of brass band, which played painfully, to the delight of the 20 populace. He laughed without heart as he thought of it. If the citizens could dream of his prospective arrival with his bride, they would parade the band at the station and escort them, amid cheers and laughing congratulations, to his adobe home.

He resolved that he would use all the devices of speed and plainscraft in making the journey from the station to his house. Once within that safe citadel, he could issue some sort of vocal bulletin, and then not go among the citizens until they had time to wear off a little of their enthusiasm.

The bride looked anxiously at him. "What's worrying you, Jack?"

He laughed again. "I'm not worrying, girl; I'm only thinking of Yellow Sky."

She flushed in comprehension.

A sense of mutual guilt invaded their minds and developed a finer tenderness. 25
They looked at each other with eyes softly aglow. But Potter often laughed the same nervous laugh; the flush upon the bride's face seemed quite permanent.

The traitor to the feelings of Yellow Sky narrowly watched the speeding landscape. "We're nearly there," he said.

Presently the porter came and announced the proximity of Potter's home. He held a brush in his hand, and, with all his airy superiority gone, he brushed Potter's new clothes as the latter slowly turned this way and that way. Potter fumbled out a coin and gave it to the porter, as he had seen others do. It was a heavy and muscle-bound business, as that of a man shoeing his first horse.

The porter took their bag, and as the train began to slow they moved forward to the hooded platform of the car. Presently the two engines and their long string of coaches rushed into the station of Yellow Sky.

"They have to take water here," said Potter, from a constricted throat and in mournful cadence, as one announcing death. Before the train stopped his eye had swept the length of the platform, and he was glad and astonished to see there was none upon it but the station-agent, who, with a slightly hurried and anxious air, was walking toward the water-tanks. When the train had halted, the porter alighted first, and placed in position a little temporary step.

"Come on, girl," said Potter, hoarsely. As he helped her down they each laughed 30
on a false note. He took the bag from the negro, and bade his wife cling to his arm. As they slunk rapidly away, his hang-dog glance perceived that they were unloading the two trunks, and also that the station-agent, far ahead near the baggage-car, had turned and was running toward him, making gestures. He laughed, and groaned as he laughed, when he noted the first effect of his marital bliss upon Yellow Sky. He gripped his wife's arm firmly to his side, and they fled. Behind them the porter stood, chuckling fatuously.

II

The California express on the Southern Railway was due at Yellow Sky in twenty-one minutes. There were six men at the bar of the Weary Gentleman saloon. One was a drummer° who talked a great deal and rapidly; three were Texans who did not care to talk at that time; and two were Mexican sheep-herders, who did not talk as a general practice in the Weary Gentleman saloon. The barkeeper's dog lay on the board walk that crossed in front of the door. His head was on his paws, and he glanced drowsily here and there with the constant vigilance of a dog that is kicked on occasion. Across the sandy street were some vivid green grass-plots, so wonderful in appearance, amid the sands that burned near them in a blazing sun, that they caused a doubt in the mind. They exactly resembled the grass mats used to represent lawns on the stage. At the cooler end of the railway station, a man without a coat sat in a tilted chair and smoked his pipe. The fresh-cut bank of the Rio Grande circled near the town, and there could be seen beyond it a great plum-colored plain of mesquit.

drummer: Traveling salesman.

Save for the busy drummer and his companions in the saloon, Yellow Sky was dozing. The new-comer leaned gracefully upon the bar, and recited many tales with the confidence of a bard who has come upon a new field.

" — and at the moment that the old man fell downstairs with the bureau in his arms, the old woman was coming up with two scuttles of coal, and of course — "

The drummer's tale was interrupted by a young man who suddenly appeared in the open door. He cried: "Scratchy Wilson's drunk, and has turned loose with both hands." The two Mexicans at once set down their glasses and faded out of the rear entrance of the saloon.

The drummer, innocent and jocular, answered: "All right, old man. S'pose he   35
has? Come in and have a drink, anyhow."

But the information had made such an obvious cleft in every skull in the room that the drummer was obliged to see its importance. All had become instantly solemn. "Say," said he, mystified, "what is this?" His three companions made the introductory gesture of eloquent speech; but the young man at the door forestalled them.

"It means, my friend," he answered, as he came into the saloon, "that for the next two hours this town won't be a health resort."

The barkeeper went to the door, and locked and barred it; reaching out of the window, he pulled in heavy wooden shutters, and barred them. Immediately a solemn, chapel-like gloom was upon the place. The drummer was looking from one to another.

"But, say," he cried, "what is this, anyhow? You don't mean there is going to be a gun-fight?"

"Don't know whether there'll be a fight or not," answered one man, grimly; "but   40
there'll be some shootin' — some good shootin'."

The young man who had warned them waved his hand. "Oh, there'll be a fight fast enough, if any one wants it. Anybody can get a fight out there in the street. There's a fight just waiting."

The drummer seemed to be swayed between the interest of a foreigner and a perception of personal danger.

"What did you say his name was?" he asked.

"Scratchy Wilson," they answered in chorus.

"And will he kill anybody? What are you going to do? Does this happen often?   45
Does he rampage around like this once a week or so? Can he break in that door?"

"No; he can't break down that door," replied the barkeeper. "He's tried it three times. But when he comes you'd better lay down on the floor, stranger. He's dead sure to shoot at it, and a bullet may come through."

Thereafter the drummer kept a strict eye upon the door. The time had not yet called for him to hug the floor, but, as a minor precaution, he sidled near the wall. "Will he kill anybody?" he said again.

The men laughed low and scornfully at the question.

"He's out to shoot, and he's out for trouble. Don't see any good in experimentin' with him."

"But what do you do in a case like this? What do you do?"   50

A man responded: "Why, he and Jack Potter — "

"But," in chorus the other men interrupted, "Jack Potter's in San Anton'."

"Well, who is he? What's he got to do with it?"

"Oh, he's the town marshal. He goes out and fights Scratchy when he gets on one of these tears."

"Wow!" said the drummer, mopping his brow. "Nice job he's got."   55

The voices had toned away to mere whisperings. The drummer wished to ask further questions, which were born of an increasing anxiety and bewilderment; but when he attempted them, the men merely looked at him in irritation and motioned him to remain silent. A tense waiting hush was upon them. In the deep shadows of the room their eyes shone as they listened for sounds from the street. One man made three gestures at the barkeeper; and the latter, moving like a ghost, handed him a glass and a bottle. The man poured a full glass of whisky, and set down the bottle noiselessly. He gulped the whisky in a swallow, and turned again toward the door in immovable silence. The drummer saw that the barkeeper, without a sound, had taken a Winchester from beneath the bar. Later he saw this individual beckoning to him, so he tiptoed across the room.

"You better come with me back of the bar."

"No thanks," said the drummer, perspiring; "I'd rather be where I can make a break for the back door."

Whereupon the man of bottles made a kindly but peremptory gesture. The drummer obeyed it, and, finding himself seated on a box with his head below the level of the bar, balm was laid upon his soul at sight of various zinc and copper fittings that bore a resemblance to armor-plate. The barkeeper took a seat comfortably upon an adjacent box.

"You see," he whispered, "this here Scratchy Wilson is a wonder with a gun — a 60 perfect wonder; and when he goes on the war-trail, we hunt our holes — naturally. He's about the last one of the old gang that used to hang out along the river here. He's a terror when he's drunk. When he's sober he's all right — kind of simple — wouldn't hurt a fly — nicest fellow in town. But when he's drunk — whoo!"

There were periods of stillness. "I wish Jack Potter was back from San Anton'," said the barkeeper. "He shot Wilson up once — in the leg — and he would sail in and pull out the kinks in this thing."

Presently they heard from a distance the sound of a shot, followed by three wild yowls. It instantly removed a bond from the men in the darkened saloon. There was a shuffling of feet. They looked at each other. "Here he comes," they said.

III

A man in a maroon-colored flannel shirt, which had been purchased for purposes of decoration, and made principally by some Jewish women on the East Side of New York, rounded a corner and walked into the middle of the main street of Yellow Sky. In either hand the man held a long, heavy, blue-black revolver. Often he yelled, and these cries rang through a semblance of a deserted village, shrilly flying over the roofs in a volume that seemed to have no relation to the ordinary vocal strength of a man. It was as if the surrounding stillness formed the arch of a tomb over him. These cries of ferocious challenge rang against walls of silence. And his boots had red tops with gilded imprints, of the kind beloved in winter by little sledding boys on the hillsides of New England.

The man's face flamed in a rage begot of whisky. His eyes, rolling, and yet keen for ambush, hunted the still doorways and windows. He walked with the creeping movement of the midnight cat. As it occurred to him, he roared menacing information. The long revolvers in his hands were as easy as straws; they were removed with an electric swiftness. The little fingers of each hand played sometimes in a musician's way. Plain from the low collar of the shirt, the cords of his neck straightened and sank, straightened and sank, as passion moved him. The only sounds were his terrible invitations. The calm adobes preserved their demeanor at the passing of this small thing in the middle of the street.

There was no offer of fight — no offer of fight. The man called to the sky. There 65 were no attractions. He bellowed and fumed and swayed his revolvers here and everywhere.

The dog of the barkeeper of the Weary Gentleman saloon had not appreciated the advance of events. He yet lay dozing in front of his master's door. At sight of the dog, the man paused and raised his revolver humorously. At sight of the man, the dog sprang up and walked diagonally away, with a sullen head, and growling. The man yelled, and the dog broke into a gallop. As it was about to enter the alley, there was a loud noise, a whistling, and something spat the ground directly before it. The dog screamed, and, wheeling in terror, galloped headlong in a new direction. Again there was a noise, a whistling, and sand was kicked viciously before it. Fear-stricken, the dog turned and flurried like an animal in a pen. The man stood laughing, his weapons at his hips.

Ultimately the man was attracted by the closed door of the Weary Gentleman saloon. He went to it and, hammering with a revolver, demanded drink.

The door remaining imperturbable, he picked a bit of paper from the walk, and nailed it to the framework with a knife. He then turned his back contemptuously upon this popular resort and, walking to the opposite side of the street and spinning there on his heel quickly and lithely, fired at the bit of paper. He missed it by a half inch. He swore at himself, and went away. Later he comfortably fusilladed the windows of his most intimate friend. The man was playing with this town; it was a toy for him.

But still there was no offer of fight. The name of Jack Potter, his ancient antagonist, entered his mind, and he concluded that it would be a glad thing if he should go to Potter's house, and by bombardment induce him to come out and fight. He moved in the direction of his desire, chanting Apache scalp-music.

When he arrived at it, Potter's house presented the same still front as had the 70 other adobes. Taking up a strategic position, the man howled a challenge. But this house regarded him as might a great stone god. It gave no sign. After a decent wait, the man howled further challenges, mingling with them wonderful epithets.

Presently there came the spectacle of a man churning himself into deepest rage over the immobility of a house. He fumed at it as the winter wind attacks a prairie cabin in the North. To the distance there should have gone the sound of a tumult like the fighting of two hundred Mexicans. As necessity bade him, he paused for breath or to reload his revolvers.

IV

Potter and his bride walked sheepishly and with speed. Sometimes they laughed together shamefacedly and low.

"Next corner, dear," he said finally.

They put forth the efforts of a pair walking bowed against a strong wind. Potter was about to raise a finger to point the first appearance of the new home when, as they circled the corner, they came face to face with a man in a maroon-colored shirt, who was feverishly pushing cartridges into a large revolver. Upon the instant the man dropped his revolver to the ground and, like lightning, whipped another from its holster. The second weapon was aimed at the bridegroom's chest.

There was a silence. Potter's mouth seemed to be merely a grave for his tongue. 75 He exhibited an instinct to at once loosen his arm from the woman's grip, and he dropped the bag to the sand. As for the bride, her face had gone as yellow as old cloth. She was a slave to hideous rites, gazing at the apparitional snake.

The two men faced each other at a distance of three paces. He of the revolver smiled with a new and quiet ferocity.

"Tried to sneak up on me," he said. "Tried to sneak up on me!" His eyes grew more baleful. As Potter made a slight movement, the man thrust his revolver venomously forward. "No, don't you do it, Jack Potter. Don't you move a finger toward a gun just yet. Don't you move an eyelash. The time has come for me to settle with you and I'm goin' to do it my own way, and loaf along with no interferin'. So if you don't want a gun bent on you, just mind what I tell you."

Potter looked at his enemy. "I ain't got a gun on me, Scratchy," he said. "Honest, I ain't." He was stiffening and steadying, but yet somewhere at the back of his mind a vision of the Pullman floated: the sea-green figured velvet, the shining brass, silver, and glass, the wood that gleamed as darkly brilliant as the surface of a pool of oil — all the glory of marriage, the environment of the new estate. "You know I fight when it comes to fighting, Scratchy Wilson; but I ain't got a gun on me. You'll have to do all the shootin' yourself."

His enemy's face went livid. He stepped forward, and lashed his weapon to and fro before Potter's chest. "Don't you tell me you ain't got no gun on you, you whelp. Don't tell me no lie like that. There ain't a man in Texas ever seen you without no gun. Don't take me for no kid." His eyes blazed with light, and his throat worked like a pump.

"I ain't takin' you for no kid," answered Potter. His heels had not moved an inch 80 backward. "I'm takin' you for a damn fool. I tell you I ain't got a gun, and I ain't. If you're goin' to shoot me up, you better begin now; you'll never get a chance like this again."

So much enforced reasoning had told on Wilson's rage; he was calmer. "If you ain't got a gun, why ain't you got a gun?" he sneered. "Been to Sunday-school?"

"I ain't got a gun because I've just come from San Anton' with my wife. I'm married," said Potter. "And if I'd thought there was going to be any galoots like you prowling around when I brought my wife home, I'd had a gun, and don't you forget it."

"Married!" said Scratchy, not at all comprehending.

"Yes, married. I'm married," said Potter, distinctly.

"Married?" said Scratchy. Seemingly for the first time, he saw the drooping, 85 drowning woman at the other man's side. "No!" he said. He was like a creature allowed a glimpse of another world. He moved a pace backward, and his arm, with the revolver, dropped to his side. "Is this the lady?" he asked.

"Yes; this is the lady," answered Potter.

There was another period of silence.

"Well," said Wilson at last, slowly, "I s'pose it's all off now."

"It's all off if you say so, Scratchy. You know I didn't make the trouble." Potter lifted his valise.

"Well, I 'low it's off, Jack," said Wilson. He was looking at the ground. "Mar- 90 ried!" He was not a student of chivalry; it was merely that in the presence of this foreign condition he was a simple child of the earlier plains. He picked up his starboard revolver, and, placing both weapons in their holsters, he went away. His feet made funnel-shaped tracks in the heavy sand.

Considerations for Critical Thinking and Writing

1. **first response.** Think of a western you've read or seen: any of Larry McMurtry's books would work, such as *Lonesome Dove* or *Evening Star*. You might also try Charles Portis's novel *True Grit* or one of its two film versions.

Compare and contrast the setting, characters, action, and theme in Crane's story with your western.

2. What is the nature of the conflict Marshal Potter feels on the train in Part I? Why does he feel that he committed a "crime" in bringing home a bride to Yellow Sky?

3. What is the function of the "drummer," the traveling salesman, in Part II?

4. How do Mrs. Potter and Scratchy Wilson serve as foils for each other? What does each represent in the story?

5. What is the significance of the setting?

6. How does Crane create suspense about what will happen when Marshal Potter meets Scratchy Wilson? Is suspense the major point of the story?

7. Is Scratchy Wilson too drunk, comical, and ineffective to be a sympathetic character? What is the meaning of his conceding that "I s'pose it's all off now" at the end of Part IV? Is he a dynamic or a static character?

8. What details seem to support the story's theme? Consider, for example, the descriptions of the bride's clothes and Scratchy Wilson's shirt and boots.

9. Explain why the heroes in western stories are rarely married and why Crane's use of marriage is central to his theme.

10. CRITICAL STRATEGIES. Read the section on gender strategies (pp. 1655–57) in Chapter 51, "Critical Strategies for Reading." Explore the heterosexual and potentially homosexual issues that a gender critic might discover in the story.

CONNECTIONS TO OTHER SELECTIONS

1. Although Scratchy Wilson and the title character in Katherine Mansfield's "Miss Brill" (below) are radically different kinds of people, they share a painful recognition at the end of their stories. What does each of them learn? Discuss whether you think what each of them learns is of equal importance in changing his or her life.

2. Write an essay comparing Crane's use of suspense with William Faulkner's in "A Rose for Emily" (p. 78).

KATHERINE MANSFIELD (1888–1923)

Born in New Zealand, Katherine Mansfield moved to London when she was a young woman and began writing short stories. Her first collection, *In a German Pension,* appeared in 1911. Subsequent publications, which include *Bliss and Other Stories* (1920) and *The Garden Party* (1922), secured her reputation as an important writer. The full range of her short stories is available in *The Collected Short Stories of Katherine Mansfield* (1945). Mansfield tends to focus her stories on intelligent, sensitive protagonists who undergo subtle but important changes in their lives. In "Miss Brill," an aging Englishwoman

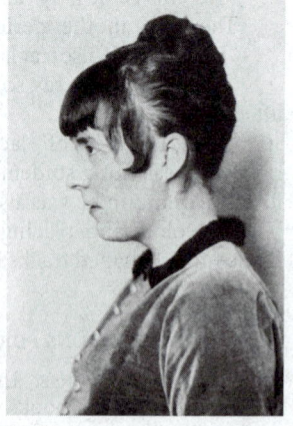

© Corbis.

spends the afternoon in a park located in an unnamed French vacation town watching the activities of the people around her. Through those observations, Mansfield characterizes Miss Brill and permits us to see her experience a moment that changes her view of the world as well as of herself.

Miss Brill   1922

Although it was so brilliantly fine—the blue sky powdered with gold and great spots of light like white wine splashed over the Jardins Publiques—Miss Brill was glad that she had decided on her fur. The air was motionless, but when you opened your mouth there was just a faint chill, like a chill from a glass of iced water before you sip, and now and again a leaf came drifting—from nowhere, from the sky. Miss Brill put up her hand and touched her fur. Dear little thing! It was nice to feel it again. She had taken it out of its box that afternoon, shaken out the moth-powder, given it a good brush, and rubbed the life back into the dim little eyes. "What has been happening to me?" said the sad little eyes. Oh, how sweet it was to see them snap at her again from the red eiderdown! . . . But the nose, which was of some black composition, wasn't at all firm. It must have had a knock, somehow. Never mind—a little dab of black sealing-wax when the time came—when it was absolutely necessary. . . . Little rogue! Yes, she really felt like that about it. Little rogue biting its tail just by her left ear. She could have taken it off and laid it on her lap and stroked it. She felt a tingling in her hands and arms, but that came from walking, she supposed. And when she breathed, something light and sad—no, not sad, exactly—something gentle seemed to move in her bosom.

There were a number of people out this afternoon, far more than last Sunday. And the band sounded louder and gayer. That was because the Season had begun. For although the band played all the year round on Sundays, out of season it was never the same. It was like someone playing with only the family to listen; it didn't care how it played if there weren't any strangers present. Wasn't the conductor wearing a new coat, too? She was sure it was new. He scraped with his foot and flapped his arms like a rooster about to crow, and the bandsmen sitting in the green rotunda blew out their cheeks and glared at the music. Now there came a little "flutey" bit—very pretty!—a little chain of bright drops. She was sure it would be repeated. It was; she lifted her head and smiled.

Only two people shared her "special" seat: a fine old man in a velvet coat, his hands clasped over a huge carved walking-stick, and a big old woman, sitting upright, with a roll of knitting on her embroidered apron. They did not speak. This was disappointing, for Miss Brill always looked forward to the conversation. She had become really quite expert, she thought, at listening as though she didn't listen, at sitting in other people's lives just for a minute while they talked around her.

She glanced, sideways, at the old couple. Perhaps they would go soon. Last Sunday, too, hadn't been as interesting as usual. An Englishman and his wife, he wearing a dreadful Panama hat and she button boots. And she'd gone on the whole time about how she ought to wear spectacles; she knew she needed them; but that it was no good getting any; they'd be sure to break and they'd never keep on. And he'd been so patient. He'd suggested everything—gold rims, the kind that curved round your ears, little pads inside the bridge. No, nothing would please her. "They'll always be sliding down my nose!" Miss Brill had wanted to shake her.

The old people sat on the bench, still as statues. Never mind, there was always   5
the crowd to watch. To and fro, in front of the flower-beds and the band rotunda,
the couples and groups paraded, stopped to talk, to greet, to buy a handful of
flowers from the old beggar who had his tray fixed to the railings. Little children
ran among them, swooping and laughing; little boys with big white silk bows
under their chins, little girls, little French dolls, dressed up in velvet and lace. And
sometimes a tiny staggerer came suddenly rocking into the open from under the
trees, stopped, stared, as suddenly sat down "flop," until its small high-stepping
mother, like a young hen, rushed scolding to its rescue. Other people sat on the
benches and green chairs, but they were nearly always the same, Sunday after Sunday, and — Miss Brill had often noticed — there was something funny about nearly
all of them. They were odd, silent, nearly all old, and from the way they stared
they looked as though they'd just come from dark little rooms or even — even
cupboards!

Behind the rotunda the slender trees with yellow leaves down drooping, and
through them just a line of sea, and beyond the blue sky with gold-veined clouds.

Tum-tum-tum tiddle-um! tiddle-um! tum tiddley-um tum ta! blew the band.

Two young girls in red came by and two young soldiers in blue met them, and
they laughed and paired and went off arm-in-arm. Two peasant women with funny
straw hats passed, gravely, leading beautiful smoke-colored donkeys. A cold, pale
nun hurried by. A beautiful woman came along and dropped her bunch of violets,
and a little boy ran after to hand them to her, and she took them and threw them
away as if they'd been poisoned. Dear me! Miss Brill didn't know whether to admire
that or not! And now an ermine toque and a gentleman in grey met just in front of
her. He was tall, stiff, dignified, and she was wearing the ermine toque she'd bought
when her hair was yellow. Now everything, her hair, her face, even her eyes, was the
same color as the shabby ermine, and her hand, in its cleaned glove, lifted to dab her
lips, was a tiny yellowish paw. Oh, she was so pleased to see him — delighted! She
rather thought they were going to meet that afternoon. She described where she'd
been — everywhere, here, there, along by the sea. The day was so charming — didn't
he agree? And wouldn't he, perhaps? . . . But he shook his head, lighted a cigarette,
slowly breathed a great deep puff into her face, and, even while she was still talking
and laughing, flicked the match away and walked on. The ermine toque was alone;
she smiled more brightly than ever. But even the band seemed to know what she
was feeling and played more softly, played tenderly, and the drum beat, "The Brute!
The Brute!" over and over. What would she do? What was going to happen now?
But as Miss Brill wondered, the ermine toque turned, raised her hand as though
she'd seen some one else, much nicer, just over there, and pattered away. And the
band changed again and played more quickly, more gaily than ever, and the old
couple on Miss Brill's seat got up and marched away, and such a funny old man with
long whiskers hobbled along in time to the music and was nearly knocked over by
four girls walking abreast.

Oh, how fascinating it was! How she enjoyed it! How she loved sitting here,
watching it all! It was like a play. It was exactly like a play. Who could believe the sky
at the back wasn't painted? But it wasn't till a little brown dog trotted on solemn and
then slowly trotted off, like a little "theatre" dog, a little dog that had been drugged,
that Miss Brill discovered what it was that made it so exciting. They were all on the
stage. They weren't only the audience, not only looking on; they were acting. Even
she had a part and came every Sunday. No doubt somebody would have noticed if
she hadn't been there; she was part of the performance after all. How strange she'd

never thought of it like that before! And yet it explained why she made such a point of starting from home at just the same time each week—so as not to be late for the performance—and it also explained why she had quite a queer, shy feeling at telling her English pupils how she spent her Sunday afternoons. No wonder! Miss Brill nearly laughed out loud. She was on the stage. She thought of the old invalid gentleman to whom she read the newspaper four afternoons a week while he slept in the garden. She had got quite used to the frail head on the cotton pillow, the hollowed eyes, the open mouth, and the high pinched nose. If he'd been dead she mightn't have noticed for weeks; she wouldn't have minded. But suddenly he knew he was having the paper read to him by an actress! "An actress!" The old head lifted; two points of light quivered in the old eyes. "An actress—are ye?" And Miss Brill smoothed the newspaper as though it were the manuscript of her part and said gently: "Yes, I have been an actress for a long time."

The band had been having a rest. Now they started again. And what they played 10 was warm, sunny, yet there was just a faint chill—a something, what was it?—not sadness—no, not sadness—a something that made you want to sing. The tune lifted, lifted, the light shone; and it seemed to Miss Brill that in another moment all of them, all the whole company, would begin singing. The young ones, the laughing ones who were moving together, they would begin, and the men's voices, very resolute and brave, would join them. And then she too, she too, and the others on the benches—they would come in with a kind of accompaniment—something low, that scarcely rose or fell, something so beautiful—moving. . . . And Miss Brill's eyes filled with tears and she looked smiling at all the other members of the company. Yes, we understand, we understand, she thought—though what they understood she didn't know.

Just at that moment a boy and a girl came and sat down where the old couple had been. They were beautifully dressed; they were in love. The hero and heroine, of course, just arrived from his father's yacht. And still soundlessly singing, still with that trembling smile, Miss Brill prepared to listen.

"No, not now," said the girl. "Not here, I can't."

"But why? Because of that stupid old thing at the end there?" asked the boy. "Why does she come here at all—who wants her? Why doesn't she keep her silly old mug at home?"

"It's her fu-fur which is so funny," giggled the girl. "It's exactly like a fried whiting."

"Ah, be off with you!" said the boy in an angry whisper. Then: "Tell me, ma 15 petite chère ——"

"No, not here," said the girl. "Not *yet.*"

On her way home she usually bought a slice of honey-cake at the baker's. It was her Sunday treat. Sometimes there was an almond in her slice, sometimes not. It made a great difference. If there was an almond it was like carrying home a tiny present—a surprise—something that might very well not have been there. She hurried on the almond Sundays and struck the match for the kettle in quite a dashing way.

But today she passed the baker's by, climbed the stairs, went into the little dark room—her room like a cupboard—and sat down on the red eiderdown. She sat there for a long time. The box that the fur came out of was on the bed. She unclasped the necklet quickly; quickly, without looking, laid it inside. But when she put the lid on she thought she heard something crying.

CONSIDERATIONS FOR CRITICAL THINKING AND WRITING

1. FIRST RESPONSE. There is almost no physical description of Miss Brill in the story. What do you think she looks like? Develop a detailed description that would be consistent with her behavior.

2. How does the calculated omission of Miss Brill's first name contribute to her characterization?

3. What details make Miss Brill more than a stock characterization of a frail old lady?

4. What do Miss Brill's observations about the people she encounters reveal about her?

5. What is the conflict in the story? Who or what is the antagonist?

6. Locate the climax of the story. How is it resolved?

7. What is the purpose of the fur piece? What is the source of the crying in the final sentence of the story?

8. Is Miss Brill a static or a dynamic character?

9. Describe Miss Brill's sense of herself at the end of the story.

10. Discuss the function of the minor characters mentioned in the story. Analyze how Mansfield used them to reveal Miss Brill's character.

CONNECTIONS TO OTHER SELECTIONS

1. Compare Miss Brill's recognition with that of the narrator in Fay Weldon's "IND AFF, or Out of Love in Sarajevo" (p. 186).

2. Write an essay comparing the themes in "Miss Brill" and James Joyce's "Eveline" (p. 436).

XU XI (B. 1954)

Raised in Hong Kong and a resident there until her mid-twenties, Xu Xi graduated from the M.F.A. Program for Poets and Writers at the University of Massachusetts and has taught at the City University of Hong Kong. Among her published fictions are *Chinese Walls* (1994), *Hong Kong Rose* (1997), *The Unwalled City* (2001), and *Habit of a Foreign Sky* (2010) — and four collections of stories and essays — *Daughters of Hui* (1996), *History's Fiction* (2001), *Overleaf Hong Kong* (2004), and *Access: Thirteen Tales* (2011). "Famine" was chosen for the *O. Henry Prize Stories 2006*.

AFP/Getty Images.

Famine   2004

I escape. I board Northwest 18 to New York, via Tokyo. The engine starts, there is no going back. Yesterday, I taught the last English class and left my job of thirty-two years. Five weeks earlier, A-Ma died of heartbreak, within days of my father's sudden death. He was ninety-five, she ninety. Unlike A-Ba, who saw the world by crewing on tankers, neither my mother nor I ever left Hong Kong.

Their deaths rid me of responsibility at last, and I could forfeit my pension and that dreary existence. I am fifty-one and an only child, unmarried.

I never expected my parents to take so long to die.

This meal is *luxurious,* better than anything I imagined.

My colleagues who fly every summer complain of the indignities of travel. 5 Cardboard food, cramped seats, long lines, and these days, too much security nonsense, they say. They fly Cathay, our "national" carrier. This makes me laugh. We have never been a nation; "national" isn't our adjective. *Semantics,* they say, dismissive, just as they dismiss what I say of debt, that it is not an inevitable state, or that children exist to be taught, not spoilt. My colleagues live in overpriced, new, mortgaged flats and indulge 1 to 2.5 children. Most of my students are uneducable.

Back, though, to this in-flight meal. Smoked salmon and cold shrimp, endive salad, strawberries and melon to clean the palate. Then, steak with mushrooms, potatoes *au gratin,* a choice between a shiraz or cabernet sauvignon. Three cheeses, white chocolate mousse, coffee, and port or a liqueur or brandy. Foods from the pages of a novel, perhaps.

My parents ate sparingly, long after we were no longer impoverished, and disdained "unhealthy" Western diets. A-Ba often said that the only thing he really discovered from travel was that the world was hungry, and that there would never be enough food for everyone. It was why, he said, he did not miss the travel when he retired.

I have no complaints of my travels so far.

My complaining colleagues do not fly business. This seat is an *island* of a bed, surrounded by air. I did not mean to fly in dignity, but having never traveled in summer, or at all, I didn't plan months ahead, long before flights filled up. I simply rang the airlines and booked Northwest, the first one that had a seat, only in business class.

Friends and former students, who do fly business when their companies foot 10 the bill, were horrified. *You paid full fare? No one does!* I have money, I replied, why shouldn't I? *But you've given up your "rice bowl." Think of the future.*

I hate rice, always have, even though I never left a single grain, because under my father's watchful glare, A-Ma inspected my bowl. Every meal, even after her eyes dimmed.

The Plaza Suite is nine hundred square feet, over three times the size of home. I had wanted the Vanderbilt or Ambassador and would have settled for the Louis XV, but they were all booked, by those more important than I, no doubt. Anyway, this will have to do. "Nothing unimportant" happens here at the Plaza is what their website literature claims.

The porter arrives, and wheels my bags in on a trolley.

My father bought our tiny flat in a village in Shatin with his disability settlement. When he was forty-five and I one, a falling crane crushed his left leg and groin, thus ending his sailing and procreating career. Shatin isn't very rural anymore, but our home has denied progress its due. We didn't get a phone till I was in my thirties.

I tip the porter five dollars and begin unpacking the leather luggage set. There   15
is too much space for my things.

Right about now, you're probably wondering, along with my colleagues, former students, and friends, *What on earth does she think she's doing?* It was what my parents shouted when I was twelve and went on my first hunger strike.

My parents were illiterate, both refugees from China's rural poverty. A-Ma fried tofu at Shatin market. Once A-Ba recovered from his accident, he worked there also as a cleaner, cursing his fate. They expected me to support them as soon as possible, which should have been after six years of primary school, the only compulsory education required by law in the sixties.

As you see, I clearly had no choice but to strike, since my exam results proved I was smart enough for secondary school. My father beat me, threatened to starve me. *How dare I,* when others were genuinely hungry, unlike me, the only child of a tofu seller who always ate. *Did I want him and A-Ma to die of hunger just to send me to school? How dare I risk their longevity and old age?*

But I was unpacking a Spanish leather suitcase when the past, that country bumpkin's territory, so rudely interrupted.

Veronica, whom I met years ago at university while taking a literature course,   20
foisted this luggage on me. She runs her family's garment enterprise, and is married to a banker. Between them and their three children, they own four flats, three cars, and at least a dozen sets of luggage. Veronica invites me out to dinner (she always pays) whenever she wants to complain about her family. Lately, we've dined often.

"Kids," she groaned over our rice porridge, two days before my trip. "My daughter won't use her brand-new Loewe set because, she says, that's *passé.* All her friends at Stanford sling these canvas bags with one fat strap. Canvas, imagine. Not even leather."

"Ergonomics," I told her, annoyed at this bland and inexpensive meal. "It's all about weight and balance." And cost, I knew, because the young overspend to conform, just as Veronica eats rice porridge because she's overweight and no longer complains that I'm thin.

She continued. "You're welcome to take the set if you like."

"Don't worry yourself. I can use an old school bag."

"But that's barely a cabin bag! Surely not enough to travel with."   25

In the end, I let her nag me into taking this set, which is more bag than clothing.

Veronica sounded worried when I left her that evening. "Are you *sure* you'll be okay?"

And would she worry, I wonder, if she could see me now, here, in this suite, this enormous space where one night's bill would have taken my parents years, no, *decades,* to earn and even for me, four years' pay, at least when I first started teaching in my rural enclave (though you're thinking, of course, quite correctly, *Well, what about inflation,* the thing economists cite to dismiss these longings of an English teacher who has spent her life instructing those who care not a whit for our "official language," the one they never speak, at least not if they can choose, especially not now when there is, increasingly, a choice).

My unpacking is done; the past need not intrude. I draw a bath, as one does in English literature, to wash away the heat and grime of both cities in summer. *Why New York?* Veronica asked, at the end of our last evening together. Because, I told her, it will be like nothing I've ever known. For the first time since we've known each other, Veronica actually seemed to envy *me*, although perhaps it was my imagination.

The phone rings, and it's "Guest Relations" wishing to welcome me and offer hos- 30
pitality. The hotel must wonder, since I grace no social register. I ask for a table at Lutèce tonight. Afterwards, I tip the concierge ten dollars for successfully making the reservation. As you can see, I am no longer an ignorant bumpkin, even though I never left the schools in the New Territories, our urban countryside now that no one farms anymore. Besides, Hong Kong magazines detail lives of the rich and richer so I've read of the famous restaurant and know about the greasy palms of New Yorkers.

I order tea and scones from Room Service. It will hold me till dinner at eight.

The first time I ever tasted tea and scones was at the home of my private student. To supplement income when I enrolled in Teacher Training, I tutored Form V students who needed to pass the School Certificate English exam. This was the compromise I agreed to with my parents before they would allow me to qualify as a teacher. Oh yes, there was a second hunger strike two years prior, before they would let me continue into Form IV. That time, I promised to keep working in the markets after school with A-Ma, which I did.

Actually, my learning English at all was a stroke of luck, since I was *hardly* at a "name school" of the elite. An American priest taught at my secondary school, so I heard a native speaker. He wasn't a very good teacher, but he paid attention to me because I was the only student who liked the subject. A little attention goes a long way.

Tea and scones! I am *supposed* to be eating, not dwelling on the ancient past. The opulence of the tray Room Service brings far surpasses what that pretentious woman served, mother of the hopeless boy, my first private student of many, who only passed his English exam because he cheated (he paid a friend to sit the exam for him), not that I'd ever tell since he's now a wealthy international businessman of some repute who can hire staff to communicate in English with the rest of the world, since he still cannot, at least not with any credibility. That scone ("from Cherikoff," she bragged) was cold and dry, hard as a rock.

Hot scones, oozing with butter. To ooze. I like the lasciviousness of that word, 35
with its excess of vowels, the way an excess of wealth allows people to waste kindness on me, as my former student still does, every lunar new year, by sending me a *laisee* packet with a generous check which I deposit in my parents' bank account, the way I surrender all my earnings, as any filial and responsible unmarried child should, or so they said.

I eat two scones oozing with butter and savor tea enriched by cream and sugar, here at this "greatest hotel in the world," to vanquish, once and for all, my parents' fear of death and opulence.

Eight does not come soon enough. In the taxi on the way to Lutèce, I ponder the question of pork.

When we were poor but not impoverished, A-Ma once dared to make pork for dinner. It was meant to be a treat, to give me a taste of meat, because I complained that tofu was bland. A-Ba became a vegetarian after his accident and prohibited meat at home; eunuchs are angry people. She dared because he was not eating with us that night, a rare event in our family (I think some sailors he used to know invited him out).

I shat a tapeworm the next morning — almost ten inches long — and she never cooked pork again.

I have since tasted properly cooked pork, naturally, since it's unavoidable in Chi- 40 nese cuisine. In my twenties, I dined out with friends, despite my parents' objections. But friends marry and scatter; the truth is that there is no one but family in the end, so over time, I submitted to their way of being and seldom took meals away from home, meals my mother cooked virtually till the day she died.

I am distracted. The real question, of course, is whether or not I should order pork tonight.

I did not expect this trip to be fraught with pork!

At Lutèce, I have the distinct impression that the two couples at the next table are talking about me. Perhaps they pity me. People often pitied me my life. *Starved of affection,* they whispered, although why they felt the need to whisper what every-one could hear I failed to understand. All I desired was greater gastronomic variety, but my parents couldn't bear the idea of my eating without them. I ate our plain diet and endured their perpetual skimping because they did eventually learn to leave me alone. That much filial propriety was reasonable payment. I just didn't expect them to *stop* complaining, to fear for what little fortune they had, because somewhere someone was less fortunate than they. That fear made them cling hard to life, forc-ing me to suffer their fortitude, their good health, and their longevity.

I should walk over to those overdressed people and tell them how things are, about famine, I mean, the way I tried to tell my students, the way my parents dinned it into me as long as they were alive.

Famine has no menu! The waiter waits as I take too long to study the menu. 45 He does not seem patient, making him an oxymoron in his profession. My students would no more learn the oxymoron than they would learn about famine. *Daughter, did you lecture your charges today about famine?* A-Ba would ask every night before dinner. *Yes,* I learned to lie, giving him the answer he needed. This waiter could take a lesson in patience from me.

Finally, I look up at this man who twitches, and do not order pork. *Very good,* he says, as if I should be graded for my literacy in menus. He returns shortly with a bottle of the most expensive red available, and now I *know* the people at the next table are staring. The minute he leaves, the taller of the two men from that table comes over.

"Excuse me, but I believe we met in March? At the U.S. Consulate cocktail in Hong Kong? You're Kwai-sin Ho, aren't you?" He extends his hand. "Peter Martin."

Insulted, it's my turn to stare at this total stranger. I look *nothing* like that sim-pering socialite who designs wildly fashionable hats that are all the rage in Asia. Hats! We don't have the weather for hats, especially not those things, which are good for neither warmth nor shelter from the sun.

Besides, what use are hats for the hungry?

I do not accept his hand. "I'm her twin sister," I lie. "Kwai-sin and I are 50 estranged."

He looks like he's about to protest, but retreats. After that, they don't stare, although I am sure they discuss me now that I've contributed new gossip for those who are nurtured by the crumbs of the rich and famous. But at least I can eat in peace.

It's my outfit, probably. Kwai-sin Ho is famous for her *cheongsams*, which is all she ever wears, the way I do. It was my idea. When we were girls together in school, I said the only thing I'd ever wear when I grew up was the *cheongsam*, the shapely dress with side slits and a neck-strangling collar. She grimaced and said they weren't fashionable, that only spinster schoolteachers and prostitutes wore them, which, back in the sixties, wasn't exactly true, but Kwai-sin was never too bright or imaginative.

That was long ago, before she became Kwai-sin in the *cheongsam* once these turned fashionable again, long before her father died and her mother became the mistress of a prominent businessman who whisked them into the stratosphere high above mine. For a little while, she remained my friend, but then we grew up, she married one of the shipping Hos, and became the socialite who refused, albeit politely, to recognize me the one time we bumped into each other at some function in Hong Kong.

So now, vengeance is mine. I will not entertain the people who fawn over her and possess no powers of recognition.

Food is getting sidelined by memory. This is unacceptable. I cannot allow all these 55
intrusions. I must get back to the food, which is, after all, the point of famine.

This is due to a lack of diligence, as A-Ma would say, this lazy meandering from what's important, this succumbing to sloth. My mother was terrified of sloth, almost as much as she was terrified of my father.

She used to tell me an old legend about sloth.

There once was a man so lazy he wouldn't even lift food to his mouth. When he was young, his mother fed him, but as his mother aged, she couldn't. So he marries a woman who will feed him as his mother did. For a time, life is bliss.

Then one day, his wife must return to her village to visit her dying mother. "How will I eat?" he exclaims in fright. The wife conjures this plan. She bakes a gigantic cookie and hangs it on a string around his neck. All the lazy man must do is bend forward and eat. "Wonderful!" he says, and off she goes, promising to return.

On the first day, the man nibbles the edge of the cookie. Each day, he nibbles 60
further. By the fourth day, he's eaten so far down there's no more cookie unless he turns it, which his wife expected he would since he could do this with his mouth.

However, the man's so lazy he lies down instead and waits for his wife's return. As the days pass, his stomach growls and begins to eat itself. Yet the man still won't turn the cookie. By the time his wife comes home, the lazy man has starved to death.

Memory causes such unaccountable digressions! There I was in Lutèce, noticing that people pitied me. Pity made my father livid, which he took out on A-Ma and me. Anger was his one escape from timidity. He wanted no sympathy for either his dead limb or useless genitals.

Perhaps people find me odd rather than pitiful. I will describe my appearance and let you judge. I am thin but not emaciated and have strong teeth. This latter feature is most unusual for a Hong Kong person of my generation. Many years ago, a dentist courted me. He taught me well about oral hygiene, trained as he had been at an American university. Unfortunately, he was slightly rotund, which offended A-Ba. I think A-Ma wouldn't have minded the marriage, but she always sided with my father, who believed it wise to marry one's own physical type (illiteracy did not prevent him from developing philosophies, as you've already witnessed). I was then in my mid-thirties. After the dentist, there were no other men and as a result, I never left home, which is our custom for unmarried women and men, a loathsome custom but difficult to overthrow. We all must pick our battles, and my acquiring English, which my parents naturally knew not a word, was a sufficiently drastic defiance to last a lifetime, or at least till they expired.

This dinner at Lutèce has come and gone, and you haven't tasted a thing. It's what happens when we converse overmuch and do not concentrate on the food. At home, we ate in the silence of A-Ba's rage.

What a shame, but never mind, I promise to share the bounty next time. This 65 meal must have been good because the bill is in the thousands. I pay by traveler's checks because, not believing in debt, I own no credit cards.

Last night's dinner weighs badly, despite my excellent digestion, so I take a long walk late in the afternoon and end up in Chelsea. New York streets are dirtier than I imagined. Although I did not really expect pavements of gold, in my deepest fantasies, there did reign a glitter and sheen.

No one talks to me here.

The air is fetid with the day's leftover heat and odors. Under a humid, darkening sky, I almost trip over a body on the corner of Twenty-fourth and Seventh. It cannot be a corpse! Surely cadavers aren't left to rot in the streets.

A-Ma used to tell of a childhood occurrence in her village. An itinerant had stolen food from the local pig trough. The villagers caught him, beat him senseless, cut off his tongue and arms, and left him to bleed to death behind the rubbish heap. In the morning, my mother was at play, and while running, tripped over the body. She fell into a blood pool beside him. The corpse's eyes were open.

He surely didn't mean to steal, she always said in the telling, her eyes burning 70 from the memory. *Try to forget,* my father would say. My parents specialized in memory. They both remained lucid and clearheaded till they died.

But this body moves. It's a man awakening from sleep. He mumbles something. Startled, I move away. He is still speaking. I think he's saying he's hungry.

I escape. A taxi whisks me back to my hotel, where my table is reserved at the restaurant.

The ceiling at the Oak Room is roughly four times the height of an average basketball player. The ambience is not as seductive as promised by the Plaza's literature. The problem with reading the wrong kind of literature is that you are bound to be disappointed.

This is a man's restaurant, with a menu of many steaks. Hemingway and Fitzgerald used to eat here. Few of my students have heard of these two, and none of them will have read a single book by either author.

As an English teacher, especially one who was not employed at a "name school" 75 of the elite, I became increasingly marginal. Colleagues and friends converse in Cantonese, the only official language out of our three that people live as well as speak. The last time any student read an entire novel was well over twenty years ago. English literature is not on anyone's exam roster anymore; to desire it in a Chinese colony is as irresponsible as it was of me to master it in our former British one.

Teaching English is little else than a linguistic requirement. Once, it was my passion and flight away from home. Now it is merely my entrée to this former men's club.

But I must order dinner and stop thinking about literature.

The entrées make my head spin, so I turn to the desserts. There is no gooseberry tart! Ever since *David Copperfield,* I have wanted to taste a gooseberry tart (or perhaps it was another book, I don't remember). I tell the boy with the water jug this.

He says. "The magician, madam?"

"The orphan," I reply.   80

He stands, openmouthed, without pouring water. What is this imbecility of the young? They neither serve nor wait.

The waiter appears. "Can I help with the menu?"

"Why?" I snap. "It isn't heavy."

But what upsets me is the memory of my mother's story, which I'd long forgotten until this afternoon, just as I hoped to forget about the teaching of English literature, about the uselessness of the life I prepared so hard for.

The waiter hovers. "Are you feeling okay?"   85

I look up at the sound of his voice and realize my hands are shaking. Calming myself, I say, "*Au jus.* The prime rib, please, and escargots to start," and on and on I go, ordering in the manner of a man who retreats to a segregated club, who indulges in oblivion because he can, who shuts out the stirrings of the groin and the heart.

I wake to a ringing phone. Housekeeping wants to know if they may clean. It's already past noon. This must be jet lag. I tell Housekeeping, Later.

It's so *comfortable* here that I believe it is possible to forget.

I order brunch from Room Service. Five-star hotels in Hong Kong serve brunch buffets on weekends. The first time I went to one, Veronica paid. We were both students at university. She wasn't wealthy, but her parents gave her spending money, whereas my entire salary (I was already a working teacher by then) belonged to my parents. The array of food made my mouth water. *Pace yourself,* Veronica said. *It's all you can eat.* I wanted to try everything, but gluttony frightened me.

Meanwhile, A-Ba's voice. *After four or more days without food, your stomach*   90
begins to eat itself, and his laugh, dry and caustic.

But I was choosing brunch.

Mimosa. Smoked salmon. Omelet with Swiss cheese and chives. And salad, the expensive kind that's imported back home, crisp Romaine in a Caesar. Room Service asks what I'd like for dessert, so I say chocolate ice-cream sundae. Perhaps I'm more of a bumpkin than I care to admit. My colleagues, former students, and friends would consider my choices boring, unsophisticated, lacking in culinary imagination. They're right, I suppose, since everything I've eaten since coming to New York I could just as easily have obtained back home. They can't understand, though. It's not *what* but *how much.* How opulent. The opulence is what counts to stop the cannibalism of internal organs.

Will that be all?

I am tempted to say, Bring me an endless buffet, whatever your chef concocts, whatever your tongues desire.

How long till my money runs out, my finite account, ending this sweet exile?   95

Guest Relations knocks, insistent. I have not let anyone in for three days. I open the door wide to show the manager that everything is fine, that their room is not wrecked, that I am not crazy even if I'm not on the social register. If you read the news, as I do, you know it's necessary to allay fears. So I do, because I do not wish to give the wrong impression. I am not a diva or an excessively famous person who trashes hotel rooms because she can.

I say, politely, that I've been a little unwell, nothing serious, and to please have Housekeeping stop in now. The "please" is significant; it shows I am not odd, that I am, in fact, cognizant of civilized language in English. The manager withdraws, relieved.

For dinner tonight, I decide on two dozen oysters, lobster, and filet mignon. I select a champagne and the wines, one white and one red. Then, it occurs to me that since this is a suite, I can order enough food for a party, so I tell Room Service that there will be a dozen guests for dinner, possibly more. *Very good,* he says, and asks how many extra bottles of champagne and wine, to which I reply, As many as needed.

My students will be my guests. They more or less were visitors during those years I tried to teach. You mustn't think I was always disillusioned, though I seem so now. To prove it to you I'll invite all my colleagues, the few friends I have, like Veronica, the dentist who courted me and his wife and two children, even Kwai-sin and my parents. I bear no grudges; I am not bitter towards them. What I'm uncertain of is whether or not they will come to my supper.

This room, this endless meal, can save me. I feel it. I am vanquishing my fear of 100 death and opulence.

There was a time we did not care about opulence and we dared to speak of death. You spoke of famine because everyone knew the stories from China were true. Now, even in this country, people more or less know. You could educate students about starvation in China or Africa or India because they knew it to be true, because they saw the hunger around them, among the beggars in our streets, and for some, even in their own homes. There was a time it was better *not* to have space, or things to put in that space, and to dream of having instead, because no one had much, except royalty and movie stars and they were *meant* to be fantasy — untouchable, unreal — somewhere in a dream of manna and celluloid.

But you can't speak of famine anymore. Anorexia's fashionable and desirably profitable on runways, so students simply *can't see the hunger.* My colleagues and friends also can't, and refuse to speak of it, changing the subject to what they prefer to see. Even our journalists can't seem to see, preferring the reality they fashion rather than the reality that is. I get angry, but then, when I'm calm, I am simply baffled. Perhaps my parents, and friends and colleagues and memory, are right, that I *am* too stubborn, perhaps even too slothful because instead of *seeing* reality, I've hidden in my parents' home, in my life as a teacher, even though the years were dreary and long, when what I truly wanted, what I desired, was to embrace the opulence, forsake the hunger, but was too lazy to turn the cookie instead.

I mustn't be angry at them, by which I mean all the "thems" I know and don't know, the big impersonal "they." Like a good English teacher I tell my students, you *must* define the "they." Students are students and continue to make the same mistakes, and all I can do is remind them that "they" are you and to please, please, try to remember because language is a root of life.

Most of the people can't be wrong all the time. Besides, whose fault is it if the dream came true? Postdream is like postmodern; no one understands it, but everyone condones its existence.

Furthermore, what you can't, or won't see, *doesn't* exist. 105

Comfort, like food, exists, *surrounds* me here.

Not wishing to let anger get the better of me, I eat. Like the Romans, I disgorge and continue. It takes hours to eat three lobsters and three steaks, plus consume five glasses of champagne and six of wine, yet still the food is not enough.

The guests arrive and more keep coming. Who would have thought all these people would show up, all these people I thought I left behind. Where do they come from? My students, colleagues, the dentist and his family, a horde of strangers. Even

Kwai-sin and her silly hats, and do you know something, we *do* look a little alike, so Peter Martin wasn't completely wrong. I changed my language to change my life, but still the past throngs, bringing all these people and their Cantonese chatter. The food is not enough, the food is never enough.

Room Service obliges round the clock.

Veronica arrives and I feel a great relief, because the truth is, I no longer   110
cared for her anymore when all we ate was rice porridge. It was mean-spirited, I was ungrateful, forgetting that once she fed me my first buffet, teasing my appetite. *Come out, travel,* she urged over the years. It's not her fault I stayed at home, afraid to abandon my responsibility, traveling only in my mind.

Finally, my parents arrive. My father sits down first to the feast. His leg is whole, and sperm gushes out from between his legs. *It's not so bad here,* he says, and gestures for my mother to join him. This is good. A-Ma will eat if A-Ba does, they're like that, those two. My friends don't understand, not even Veronica. She repeats now what she often has said, that my parents are "controlling." Perhaps, I say, but that's unimportant. I'm only interested in not being responsible anymore.

The noise in the room is deafening. We can barely hear each other above the din. Cantonese is a noisy language, unlike Mandarin or English, but it is alive. This suite that was too empty is stuffed with people, all needing to be fed.

I gaze at the platters of food, piled in this space with largesse. What does it matter if there *are* too many mouths to feed? A phone call is all it takes to get more food, and more. I am fifty-one and have waited too long to eat. They're right, they're all right. If I give in, if I let go, I will vanquish my fears. *This* is bliss, truly.

A-Ma smiles at the vast quantities of food. This pleases me because she so rarely smiles. She says, *Not like lazy cookie man, hah?*

Feeling benevolent, I smile at my parents. *No, not like him,* I say. *Now, eat.*   115

CONSIDERATIONS FOR CRITICAL THINKING AND WRITING

1. FIRST RESPONSE. How does Xu Xi engage the reader in the first three paragraphs of the story?

2. Explain how the narrator's parents' values and sensibilities are revealed through exposition.

3. How do Veronica and Kwai-sin function as foils to the narrator?

4. What is the relevance of the narrator's having been an English teacher for her entire career?

5. Do you find any humor in "Famine"? Describe the story's tone. Is it consistent?

6. Choose a paragraph in which Xu Xi uses details particularly well to create a mood, set a scene, or unify the plot, and discuss how that effect is achieved through her carefully chosen language.

7. Can you find the story's theme (or themes) stated directly in a specific paragraph, or is it developed implicitly through the plot, characters, symbols, or some other literary element?

CONNECTIONS TO OTHER SELECTIONS

1. Compare the cultural ambitions of the narrator in "Famine" with those of the man in Mark Halliday's "Young Man on Sixth Avenue" (p. 533).

2. Discuss the narrator's symbolic relationship to food in "Famine" and in Sally Croft's poem "Home-Baked Bread" (p. 684).

9

Style, Tone, and Irony

I like it when there is some feeling of threat or sense of menace in short stories. I think a little menace is fine to have in a story.
—RAYMOND CARVER

© Marion Ettlinger.

STYLE

Style is a concept that everyone understands on some level because in its broadest sense it refers to the particular way in which anything is made or done. Style is everywhere around us. The world is saturated with styles in cars, clothing, buildings, teaching, dancing, music, politics — in anything that reflects a distinctive manner of expression or design. Consider, for example, how a tune sung by the Beatles differs from the same tune performed by a string orchestra. There's no mistaking the two styles.

Authors also have different characteristic styles. *Style* refers to the distinctive manner in which a writer arranges words to achieve particular effects. That arrangement includes individual word choices and matters such as the length of sentences, their structure and tone, and the use of irony.

Diction refers to a writer's choice of words. Because different words evoke different associations in a reader's mind, the writer's choice of words is crucial in controlling a reader's response. The diction must be appropriate for the characters and the situations in which the author places them. Consider how

272

inappropriate it would have been if Melville had had Bartleby respond to the lawyer's requests with "Hell no!" instead of "I would prefer not to." The word *prefer* and the tentativeness of *would* help reinforce the scrivener's mildness, his dignity, and even his seeming reasonableness — all of which frustrate the lawyer's efforts to get rid of him. Bartleby, despite his passivity, seems to be in control of the situation. If he were to shout "Hell no!" he would appear angry, aggressive, desperate, and too informal, none of which would fit with his solemn, conscious decision to die. Melville makes the lawyer the desperate party by carefully choosing Bartleby's words.

Sentence structure is another element of a writer's style. Hemingway's terse, economical sentences are frequently noted and readily perceived. Here are the concluding sentences of Hemingway's "Soldier's Home" (p. 162), in which Krebs decides to leave home:

> He had tried so to keep his life from being complicated. Still, none of it had touched him. He had felt sorry for his mother and she had made him lie. He would go to Kansas City and get a job and she would feel all right about it. There would be one more scene maybe before he got away. He would not go down to his father's office. He would miss that one. He wanted his life to go smoothly. It had just gotten going that way. Well, that was all over now, anyway. He would go over to the schoolyard and watch Helen play indoor baseball.

Hemingway expresses Krebs's thought the way Krebs thinks. The style avoids any "complicated" sentence structures. Seven of the eleven sentences begin with the word *He*. There are no abstractions or qualifications. We feel as if we are listening not only to *what* Krebs thinks but to *how* he thinks. The style reflects his firm determination to make, one step at a time, a clean, unobstructed break from his family and the entangling complications they would impose on him.

Contrast this straightforward style with Vladimir Nabokov's description of a woman in his short story "The Vane Sisters." The sophisticated narrator teaches French literature at a women's college and is as observant as he is icily critical of the woman he describes in this passage:

> Her fingernails were gaudily painted, but badly bitten and not clean. Her lovers were a silent young photographer with a sudden laugh and two older men, brothers, who owned a small printing establishment across the street. I wondered at their tastes whenever I glimpsed, with a secret shudder, the higgledy-piggledy striation of black hairs that showed all along her pale shins through the nylon of her stockings with the scientific distinctness of a preparation flattened under glass; or when I felt, at her every movement, the dullish, stalish, not particularly conspicuous but all-pervading and depressing emanation that her seldom bathed flesh spread from under weary perfumes and creams.

This portrait — etched with a razor blade — is restrained but devastating. The woman's fingernails are "gaudily painted." She has no taste in men either. One of her lovers is "silent" except for a "sudden laugh," a telling detail that suggests a strikingly odd personality. Her other lovers, the two brothers (!), run a "small" business. We are invited to "shudder" along with the narrator as he vividly describes the "striation of black hairs" on her legs; we see the woman as if she were displayed under a microscope, an appropriate perspective given the narrator's close inspection. His scrutiny is relentless, and its object smells as awful as it looks (notice the difference in the language between this blunt description and the narrator's elegant distaste). He finds the woman "depressing" because the weight of her unpleasantness oppresses him.

The narrator reveals nearly as much about himself as about the woman, but Nabokov leaves the reader with the task of assessing the narrator's fastidious reactions. The formal style of this description is appropriately that of an educated, highly critical, close observer of life who knows how to convey the "dullish, stalish" essence of this woman. But, you might ask, what about the curious informality of "higgledy-piggledy"? Does that fit the formal professorial voice? Given Nabokov's well-known fascination with wit and, more important, the narrator's obvious relish for verbally slicing this woman into a slide specimen, the term is revealed as appropriately chosen once the reader sees the subtle, if brutal, pun on *piggledy*.

Hemingway's and Nabokov's uses of language are very different, yet each style successfully fuses what is said with how it is said. We could write summaries of both passages, but our summaries, owing to their styles, would not have the same effect as the originals. And that makes all the difference.

TONE

Style reveals ***tone***, the author's implicit attitude toward the people, places, and events in a story. When we speak, tone is conveyed by our voice inflections, our wink of an eye, or some other gesture. A professor who says "You're going to fail the next exam" may be indicating concern, frustration, sympathy, alarm, humor, or indifference, depending on the tone of voice. In a literary work that spoken voice is unavailable; instead we must rely on the context in which a statement appears to interpret it correctly.

In Chopin's "The Story of an Hour" (p. 15), for example, we can determine that the author sympathizes with Mrs. Mallard despite the fact that her grief over her husband's assumed death is mixed with joy. Though Mrs. Mallard thinks she's lost her husband, she experiences relief because she feels liberated from an oppressive male-dominated life. That's why she collapses when she sees her husband alive at the end of the story. Chopin makes clear by the tone of the final line ("When the doctors came they said she had died of heart disease — of joy that kills") that the men misinterpret both her grief and joy, for in the larger context of Mrs. Mallard's emotions we see, unlike the doctors, that her death may well have been caused not by a shock of joy but by an overwhelming recognition of her lost freedom.

If we are sensitive to tone, we can get behind a character and see him or her from the author's perspective. In Melville's "Bartleby, the Scrivener" (p. 130) everything is told from the lawyer's point of view, but the tone of his remarks often separates him from the author's values and attitudes. When the lawyer characterizes himself at the beginning of the story, his use of language effectively allows us to see Melville disapproving of what the lawyer takes pride in:

> The late John Jacob Astor, a personage little given to poetic enthusiasm, had no hesitation in pronouncing my first grand point to be prudence; my next, method. I do not speak it in vanity.

But, of course, he is vain and a name-dropper as well. He likes the "rounded and orbicular sound" of Astor's name because it "rings like unto bullion." Tone, here, helps to characterize the lawyer. Melville doesn't tell us that the lawyer is status conscious and materialistic; instead, we discover that through the tone. This stylistic technique is frequently an important element for interpreting a story. An insensitivity to tone can lead a reader astray in determining the theme of a work. Regardless of who is speaking in a story, it is wise to listen for the author's voice too.

IRONY

One of the enduring themes in literature is that things are not always what they seem to be. What we see — or think we see — is not always what we get. The unexpected complexity that often surprises us in life — what Herman Melville in *Moby-Dick* called the "universal thump" — is fertile ground for writers of imaginative literature. They cultivate that ground through the use of *irony*, a device that reveals a reality different from what appears to be true.

Verbal irony consists of a person saying one thing but meaning the opposite. If a student driver smashes into a parked car and the angry instructor turns to say "You sure did well today," the statement is an example of verbal irony. What is meant is not what is said. Verbal irony that is calculated to hurt someone by false praise is commonly known as *sarcasm*. In literature, however, verbal irony is usually not openly aggressive; instead, it is more subtle and restrained though no less intense.

In Godwin's "A Sorrowful Woman" (p. 39), a woman retreats from her family because she cannot live in the traditional role that her husband and son expect of her. When the husband tries to be sympathetic about her withdrawal from family life, the narrator tells us three times that "he understood such things" and that in "understanding these things" he tried to be patient by "still understanding these things." The narrator's repetition of these phrases constitutes verbal irony because they call attention to the fact that the husband doesn't understand his wife at all. His "understanding" is really only a form of condescension that represents part of her problem rather than a solution.

Situational irony exists when there is an incongruity between what is expected to happen and what actually happens. For instance, at the climactic showdown between Marshal Potter and Scratchy Wilson in Crane's "The Bride Comes to Yellow Sky" (p. 251), there are no gunshots, only talk — and what subdues Wilson is not Potter's strength and heroism but the fact that the marshal is now married. To take one more example, the protagonist in Godwin's "A Sorrowful Woman" seems, by traditional societal standards, to have all that a wife and mother could desire in a family, but, given her needs, that turns out not to be enough to sustain even her life, let alone her happiness. In each of these instances the ironic situation creates a distinction between appearances and realities and brings the reader closer to the central meaning of the story.

Another form of irony occurs when an author allows the reader to know more about a situation than a character knows. *Dramatic irony* creates a discrepancy between what a character believes or says and what the reader understands to be true. In Flannery O'Connor's "Revelation" (p. 385) the insecure Mrs. Turpin, as a member of "the home-and-land owner" class, believes herself to be superior to "niggers," "white-trash," and mere "home owners." She takes pride in her position in the community and in what she perceives to be her privileged position in relation to God. The reader, however, knows that her remarks underscore her failings rather than any superiority. Dramatic irony can be an effective way for an author to have a character unwittingly reveal himself or herself.

As you read Raymond Carver's "Popular Mechanics," Susan Minot's "Lust," Rick Moody's "Boys," and Geoff Wyss's "How to Be a Winner," pay attention to the authors' artful use of style, tone, and irony to convey meanings.

RAYMOND CARVER (1938–1988)

Born in 1938 in Clatskanie, Oregon, to working-class parents, Carver grew up in Yakima, Washington, was educated at Humboldt State College in California, and did graduate work at the University of Iowa. He married at age nineteen and during his college years worked at a series of low-paying jobs to help support his family. These difficult years eventually ended in divorce. He taught at a number of universities, among them the University of California, Berkeley; the University of Iowa; the University of Texas, El Paso; and Syracuse University. Carver's collections of stories include *Will You Please Be Quiet, Please?* (1976); *What We Talk*

© Marion Ettlinger.

about When We Talk about Love (1981), from which "Popular Mechanics" is taken; *Cathedral* (1984); and *Where I'm Calling From: New and Selected Stories* (1988). Though extremely brief, "Popular Mechanics" describes a stark domestic situation with a startling conclusion.

Popular Mechanics 1981

Early that day the weather turned and the snow was melting into dirty water. Streaks of it ran down from the little shoulder-high window that faced the back-yard. Cars slushed by on the street outside, where it was getting dark. But it was getting dark on the inside too.

He was in the bedroom pushing clothes into a suitcase when she came to the door.

I'm glad you're leaving! I'm glad you're leaving! she said. Do you hear?

He kept on putting his things into the suitcase.

Son of a bitch! I'm so glad you're leaving! She began to cry. You can't even look 5 me in the face, can you?

Then she noticed the baby's picture on the bed and picked it up.

He looked at her and she wiped her eyes and stared at him before turning and going back to the living room.

Bring that back, he said.

Just get your things and get out, she said.

He did not answer. He fastened the suitcase, put on his coat, looked around 10 the bedroom before turning off the light. Then he went out to the living room.

She stood in the doorway of the little kitchen, holding the baby.

I want the baby, he said.

Are you crazy?

No, but I want the baby. I'll get someone to come by for his things.

You're not touching this baby, she said. 15

The baby had begun to cry and she uncovered the blanket from around his head.

Oh, oh, she said, looking at the baby.

He moved toward her.

For God's sake! she said. She took a step back into the kitchen.

I want the baby. 20

Get out of here!

She turned and tried to hold the baby over in a corner behind the stove.

But he came up. He reached across the stove and tightened his hands on the baby.

Let go of him, he said.

Get away, get away! she cried. 25

The baby was red-faced and screaming. In the scuffle they knocked down a flowerpot that hung behind the stove.

He crowded her into the wall then, trying to break her grip. He held on to the baby and pushed with all his weight.

Let go of him, he said.

Don't, she said. You're hurting the baby, she said.

I'm not hurting the baby, he said. 30

The kitchen window gave no light. In the near-dark he worked on her fisted fingers with one hand and with the other hand he gripped the screaming baby up under an arm near the shoulder.

She felt her fingers being forced open. She felt the baby going from her.

No! she screamed just as her hands came loose.

She would have it, this baby. She grabbed for the baby's other arm. She caught the baby around the wrist and leaned back.

But he would not let go. He felt the baby slipping out of his hands and he pulled 35
back very hard.

In this manner, the issue was decided.

CONSIDERATIONS FOR CRITICAL THINKING AND WRITING

1. FIRST RESPONSE. Discuss the story's final lines. What is the "issue" that is "decided"?

2. Though there is little description of the setting in this story, how do the few details that are provided help to establish the tone?

3. How do small actions take on larger significance in the story? Consider the woman picking up the baby's picture and the knocked-down flowerpot.

4. Why is this couple splitting up? Do we know? Does it matter? Explain your response.

5. Discuss the title of the story. The original title was "Mine." Which do you think is more effective?

6. What is the conflict? How is it resolved?

7. Read 1 Kings 3 in the Bible for the story of Solomon. How might "Popular Mechanics" be read as a retelling of this story? What significant differences do you find in the endings of each?

8. Explain how Carver uses irony to convey theme.

CONNECTIONS TO OTHER SELECTIONS

1. Compare Carver's style with Ernest Hemingway's in "Soldier's Home" (p. 162).

2. How is the ending of "Popular Mechanics" similar to the ending of Nathaniel Hawthorne's "The Birthmark" (p. 339)?

Perspective

JOHN BARTH (B. 1930)

On Minimalist Fiction   1987

Minimalism (of one sort or another) is the principle (one of the principles, anyhow) underlying (what I and many another interested observer consider to be perhaps) the most impressive phenomenon on the current (North American, especially the United States) literary scene (the gringo equivalent of *el boom* in the Latin American novel): I mean the new flowering of the (North) American short story (in particular the kind of terse, oblique, realistic or hyperrealistic, slightly plotted, extrospective, cool-surfaced fiction associated in the last five or ten years with such excellent writers as Frederick Barthelme, Ann Beattie, Raymond Carver, Bobbie Ann Mason, James Robison, Mary Robison, and Tobias Wolff, and both praised and damned under such labels as "K-Mart realism," "hick chic," "Diet-Pepsi minimalism," and "post-Vietnam, post-literary, postmodernist blue-collar neo-early-Hemingwayism"). . . .

The genre of the short story, as Poe distinguished it from the traditional tale in his 1842 review of Hawthorne's first collection of stories, is an early manifesto of modern narrative minimalism: "In the whole composition there should be no word written, of which the tendency... is not to the pre-established design.... Undue length is ... to be avoided." Poe's codification informs such later nineteenth-century masters of terseness, selectivity, and implicitness (as opposed to leisurely once-upon-a-timelessness, luxuriant abundance, explicit and extended analysis) as Guy de Maupassant and Anton Chekhov. Show, don't tell, said Henry James in effect and at length in his prefaces to the 1908 New York edition of his novels. And don't tell a word more than you absolutely need to, added young Ernest Hemingway, who thus described his "new theory" in the early 1920's: "You could omit anything if you knew that you omitted, and the omitted part would strengthen the story and make people feel something more than they understood...."

Old or new, fiction can be minimalist in any or all of several ways. There are minimalisms of unit, form, and scale: short words, short sentences and paragraphs, [and] super-short stories.... There are minimalisms of style: a stripped-down vocabulary; a stripped-down syntax that avoids periodic sentences, serial predications, and complex subordinating constructions; a stripped-down rhetoric that may eschew figurative language altogether; a stripped-down, non-emotive tone. And there are minimalisms of material: minimal characters, minimal exposition ("all that David Copperfield kind of crap," says J. D. Salinger's *Catcher in the Rye*), minimal *mises en scène,* minimal action, minimal plot.

From Weber Studies

CONSIDERATIONS FOR CRITICAL THINKING AND WRITING

1. To what extent do Ernest Hemingway's "Soldier's Home" (p. 162) and Raymond Carver's "Popular Mechanics" fulfill Barth's description of minimalist fiction? How does each story suggest that less is more?

2. Write an essay explaining why one of the short stories by Nathaniel Hawthorne, William Faulkner, or Flannery O'Connor in this anthology is not a minimalist story.

A SAMPLE STUDENT RESPONSE

Skyler Hansen

Professor Ríos

English 200

6 November 2015

The Minimalist Style of Raymond Carver's "Popular Mechanics"

Raymond Carver provides little information in the story "Popular Mechanics." We are not given a complete background of the characters or vivid descriptions of setting. Even the dialogue is limited, and we are thrown into a scene already in progress. However, even though Carver does not tell us "a word more than [he] absolutely need[s] to" (Barth 279), all the necessary elements of a story are right there in front of us. Despite the minimalist style, we understand the characters and their motives by reading closely.

The plot of the story is simple: in the wake of a bitter fight, a man packs his suitcase and is about to leave the mother of his child. Many seemingly important details are missing. We're not certain whether the couple is married or what they are arguing about. We don't even know their names. However, all the story's complexities are there. The main conflict emerges when the man decides that he wants the baby. And while we might initially assume this has always been his intention, we realize that's not the case. He first plans to take a picture of the baby, and when the woman won't let him, he suddenly decides to raise the stakes:

> He did not answer. He fastened the suitcase, put on his
> coat, looked around the bedroom before turning off the light.
> Then he went out to the living room.
>
> She stood in the doorway of the little kitchen, holding
> the baby.
>
> I want the baby, he said. (277)

Here, we are practically able to watch the man's thought process. He feels so much anger toward the woman that he wants to hurt her before he leaves. As he packs, he searches for something he can take from her, and finally decides on the baby. His motive has little (perhaps nothing) to do with the child.

He seeks only to devastate the child's mother.

Though the story appears to be open-ended, the resolution is clear. The two struggle for the baby, forcefully, violently, unwilling to give in to the other:

> She caught the baby around the wrist and leaned back.
>
> But he would not let go. He felt the baby slipping out of his hands and he pulled back very hard.
>
> In this manner, the issue was decided. (277–78)

While we do not know the extent of the damage, or what will become of these people, we do know that the baby suffers most as a result of the altercation, a theme Carver makes clear. . . .

Works Cited

Barth, John. "On Minimalist Fiction." Meyer 278.

Carver, Raymond. "Popular Mechanics." Meyer 277–78.

Meyer, Michael, ed. *The Bedford Introduction to Literature*. 11th ed. Boston: Bedford/St. Martin's, 2016. Print.

SUSAN MINOT (B. 1956)

Born and raised in Massachusetts, Susan Minot earned a B.A. at Brown University and an M.F.A. at Columbia University. Before devoting herself full-time to writing, Minot worked as an assistant editor at *Grand Street* magazine. Her stories have appeared in the *Atlantic*, *Harper's*, the *New Yorker*, *Mademoiselle*, and *Paris Review*. Her short stories have been collected in *Lust and Other Stories* (1989), and she has published five novels — *Monkeys* (1986), *Folly* (1992), *Evening* (1998), *Rapture* (2002), and *Thirty Girls* (2014), as well as one volume of poetry, *Poems 4 A.M.* (2002).

Ulf Andersen/Getty Images.

Lust 1984

Leo was from a long time ago, the first one I ever saw nude. In the spring before the Hellmans filled their pool, we'd go down there in the deep end, with baby oil, and like that. I met him the first month away at boarding school. He had a halo from the campus light behind him. I flipped.

Roger was fast. In his illegal car, we drove to the reservoir, the radio blaring, talking fast, fast, fast. He was always going for my zipper. He got kicked out sophomore year.

By the time the band got around to playing "Wild Horses," I had tasted Bruce's tongue. We were clicking in the shadows on the other side of the amplifier, out of Mrs. Donovan's line of vision. It tasted like salt, with my neck bent back, because we had been dancing so hard before.

Tim's line: "I'd like to see you in a bathing suit." I knew it was his line when he said the exact same thing to Annie Hines.

You'd go on walks to get off campus. It was raining like hell, my sweater as   5
sopped as a wet sheep. Tim pinned me to a tree, the woods light brown and dark brown, a white house half hidden with the lights already on. The water was as loud as a crowd hissing. He made certain comments about my forehead, about my cheeks.

We started off sitting at one end of the couch and then our feet were squished against the armrest and then he went over to turn off the TV and came back after he had taken off his shirt and then we slid onto the floor and he got up again to close the door, then came back to me, a body waiting on the rug.
    You'd try to wipe off the table or to do the dishes and Willie would untuck your shirt and get his hands up under in front, standing behind you, making puffy noises in your ear.

He likes it when I wash my hair. He covers his face with it and if I start to say something, he goes, "Shush."

For a long time, I had Philip on the brain. The less they noticed you, the more you got them on the brain.

My parents had no idea. Parents never really know what's going on, especially   10
when you're away at school most of the time. If she met them, my mother might say, "Oliver seems nice" or "I like that one" without much of an opinion. If she didn't like them, "He's a funny fellow, isn't he?" or "Johnny's perfectly nice but a drink of water." My father was too shy to talk to them at all unless they played sports and he'd ask them about that.

The sand was almost cold underneath because the sun was long gone. Eben piled a mound over my feet, patting around my ankles, the ghostly surf rumbling behind him in the dark. He was the first person I ever knew who died, later that summer, in a car crash. I thought about it for a long time.

"Come here," he says on the porch.

I go over to the hammock and he takes my wrist with two fingers.

"What?"

He kisses my palm then directs my hand to his fly.   15

Songs went with whichever boy it was. "Sugar Magnolia" was Tim, with the line "Rolling in the rushes / down by the riverside." With "Darkness Darkness," I'd picture Philip with his long hair. Hearing "Under My Thumb" there'd be the smell of Jamie's suede jacket.

We hid in the listening rooms during study hall. With a record cover over the door's window, the teacher on duty couldn't look in. I came out flushed and heady and back at the dorm was surprised how red my lips were in the mirror.

One weekend at Simon's brother's, we stayed inside all day with the shades down, in bed, then went out to Store 24 to get some ice cream. He stood at the magazine rack and read through *MAD* while I got butterscotch sauce, craving something sweet.

I could do some things well. Some things I was good at, like math or painting or even sports, but the second a boy put his arm around me, I forgot about wanting to do anything else, which felt like a relief at first until it became like sinking into a muck.

It was different for a girl.   20

When we were little, the brothers next door tied up our ankles. They held the door of the goat house and wouldn't let us out till we showed them our underpants. Then they'd forget about being after us and when we played whiffle ball, I'd be just as good as they were.

Then it got to be different. Just because you have on a short skirt, they yell from the cars, slowing down for a while, and if you don't look, they screech off and call you a bitch.

"What's the matter with me?" they say, point-blank.

Or else, "Why won't you go out with me? I'm not asking you to get married," about to get mad.

Or it'd be, trying to be reasonable, in a regular voice, "Listen, I just want to have   25 a good time."

So I'd go because I couldn't think of something to say back that wouldn't be obvious, and if you go out with them, you sort of have to do something.

I sat between Mack and Eddie in the front seat of the pickup. They were having a fight about something. I've a feeling about me.

Certain nights you'd feel a certain surrender, maybe if you'd had wine. The surrender would be forgetting yourself and you'd put your nose to his neck and feel like a squirrel, safe, at rest, in a restful dream. But then you'd start to slip from that and the dark would come in and there'd be a cave. You make out the dim shape of the windows and feel yourself become a cave, filled absolutely with air, or with a sadness that wouldn't stop.

Teenage years. You know just what you're doing and don't see the things that start to get in the way.

Lots of boys, but never two at the same time. One was plenty to keep you in a 30 state. You'd start to see a boy and something would rush over you like a fast storm cloud and you couldn't possibly think of anyone else. Boys took it differently. Their eyes perked up at any little number that walked by. You'd act like you weren't noticing.

The joke was that the school doctor gave out the pill like aspirin. He didn't ask you anything. I was fifteen. We had a picture of him in assembly, holding up an IUD shaped like a T. Most girls were on the pill, if anything, because they couldn't handle a diaphragm. I kept the dial in my top drawer like my mother and thought of her each time I tipped out the yellow tablets in the morning before chapel.

If they were too shy, I'd be more so. Andrew was nervous. We stayed up with his family album, sharing a pack of Old Golds. Before it got light, we turned on the TV. A man was explaining how to plant seedlings. His mouth jerked to the side in a tic. Andrew thought it was a riot and kept imitating him. I laughed to be polite. When we finally dozed off, he dared to put his arm around me, but that was it.

You wait till they come to you. With half fright, half swagger, they stand one step down. They dare to touch the button on your coat then lose their nerve and quickly drop their hand so you — you'd do anything for them. You touch their cheek.

The girls sit around in the common room and talk about boys, smoking their heads off.

"What are you complaining about?" says Jill to me when we talk about 35 problems.

"Yeah," says Giddy. "You always have a boyfriend."

I look at them and think, As if.

I thought the worst thing anyone could call you was a cock-teaser. So, if you flirted, you had to be prepared to go through with it. Sleeping with someone was perfectly normal once you had done it. You didn't really worry about it. But there were other problems. The problems had to do with something else entirely.

Mack was during the hottest summer ever recorded. We were renting a house on an island with all sorts of other people. No one slept during the heat wave, walking around the house with nothing on which we were used to because of the nude beach. In the living room, Eddie lay on top of a coffee table to cool off. Mack and I, with the bedroom door open for air, sweated and sweated all night.

"I can't take this," he said at three a.m. "I'm going for a swim." He and some 40 guys down the hall went to the beach. The heat put me on edge. I sat on a cracked chest by the open window and smoked and smoked till I felt even worse, waiting for something — I guess for him to get back.

One was on a camping trip in Colorado. We zipped our sleeping bags together, the coyotes' hysterical chatter far away. Other couples murmured in other tents. Paul was up before sunrise, starting a fire for breakfast. He wasn't much of a talker in the daytime. At night, his hand leafed about in the hair at my neck.

There'd be times when you overdid it. You'd get carried away. All the next day, you'd be in a total fog, delirious, absent-minded, crossing the street and nearly getting run over.

The more girls a boy has, the better. He has a bright look, having reaped fruits, blooming. He stalks around, sure-shouldered, and you have the feeling he's got more in him, a fatter heart, more stories to tell. For a girl, with each boy it's as though a petal gets plucked each time.

Then you start to get tired. You begin to feel diluted, like watered-down stew.

Oliver came skiing with us. We lolled by the fire after everyone had gone to bed. 45
Each creak you'd think was someone coming downstairs. The silver loop bracelet he gave me had been a present from his girlfriend before.

On vacations, we went skiing, or you'd go south if someone invited you. Some people had apartments in New York that their families hardly ever used. Or summer houses, or older sisters. We always managed to find someplace to go.

We made the plan at coffee hour. Simon snuck out and met me at Main Gate after lights-out. We crept to the chapel and spent the night in the balcony. He tasted like onions from a submarine sandwich.

The boys are one of two ways: either they can't sit still or they don't move. In front of the TV, they won't budge. On weekends they play touch football while we sit on the sidelines, picking blades of grass to chew on, and watch. We're always watching them run around. We shiver in the stands, knocking our boots together to keep our toes warm, and they whizz across the ice, chopping their sticks around the puck. When they're in the rink, they refuse to look at you, only eyeing each other beneath low helmets. You cheer for them but they don't look up, even if it's a face-off when nothing's happening, even if they're doing drills before any game has started at all.

Dancing under the pink tent, he bent down and whispered in my ear. We slipped away to the lawn on the other side of the hedge. Much later, as he was leaving the buffet with two plates of eggs and sausage, I saw the grass stains on the knees of his white pants.

Tim's was shaped like a banana, with a graceful curve to it. They're all differ- 50
ent. Willie's like a bunch of walnuts when nothing was happening, another's as thin as a thin hot dog. But it's like faces; you're never really surprised.

Still, you're not sure what to expect.

I look into his face and he looks back. I look into his eyes and they look back at mine. Then they look down at my mouth so I look at his mouth, then back to his eyes then, backing up, at his whole face. I think, Who? Who are you? His head tilts to one side.

I say, "Who are you?"

"What do you mean?"

"Nothing." 55

I look at his eyes again, deeper. Can't tell who he is, what he thinks.

"What?" he says. I look at his mouth.

"I'm just wondering," I say and go wandering across his face. Study the chin line. It's shaped like a persimmon.

"Who are you? What are you thinking?"

He says, "What the hell are you talking about?" 60

Then they get mad after, when you say enough is enough. After, when it's easier to explain that you don't want to. You wouldn't dream of saying that maybe you weren't really ready to in the first place.

Gentle Eddie. We waded into the sea, the waves round and plowing in, buffalo-headed, slapping our thighs. I put my arms around his freckled shoulders and he held me up, buoyed by the water, and rocked me like a sea shell.

I had no idea whose party it was, the apartment jam-packed, stepping over people in the hallway. The room with the music was practically empty, the bare floor, me in red shoes. This fellow slides onto one knee and takes me around the waist and we rock to jazzy tunes, with my toes pointing heavenward, and waltz and spin and dip to "Smoke Gets in Your Eyes" or "I'll Love You Just for Now." He puts his head to my chest, runs a sweeping hand down my inside thigh and we go loose-limbed and sultry and as smooth as silk and I stamp my red heels and he takes me into a swoon. I never saw him again after that but I thought, I could have loved that one.

You wonder how long you can keep it up. You begin to feel as if you're showing through, like a bathroom window that only lets in grey light, the kind you can't see out of.

They keep coming around. Johnny drives up at Easter vacation from Balti- 65
more and I let him in the kitchen with everyone sound asleep. He has friends waiting in the car.

"What are you, crazy? It's pouring out there," I say.

"It's okay," he says. "They understand."

So he gets some long kisses from me, against the refrigerator, before he goes because I hate those girls who push away a boy's face as if she were made out of Ivory soap, as if she's that much greater than he is.

The note on my cubby told me to see the headmaster. I had no idea for what. He had received complaints about my amorous displays on the town green. It was Willie that spring. The headmaster told me he didn't care what I did but that Casey Academy had a reputation to uphold in the town. He lowered his glasses on his nose. "We've got twenty acres of woods on this campus," he said. "If you want to smooch with your boyfriend, there are twenty acres for you to do it out of the public eye. You read me?"

Everybody'd get weekend permissions for different places, then we'd all go to   70
someone's house whose parents were away. Usually there'd be more boys than girls.
We raided the liquor closet and smoked pot at the kitchen table and you'd never
know who would end up where, or with whom. There were always disasters. Ceci
got bombed and cracked her head open on the banister and needed stitches. Then
there was the time Wendel Blair walked through the picture window at the Lowes'
and got slashed to ribbons.

He scared me. In bed, I didn't dare look at him. I lay back with my eyes closed,
luxuriating because he knew all sorts of expert angles, his hands never fumbling,
going over my whole body, pressing the hair up and off the back of my head, giving
an extra hip shove, as if to say *There.* I parted my eyes slightly, keeping the screen of
my lashes low because it was too much to look at him, his mouth loose and pink and
parted, his eyes looking through my forehead, or kneeling up, looking through my
throat. I was ashamed but couldn't look him in the eye.

You wonder about things feeling a little off-kilter. You begin to feel like a piece
of pounded veal.

At boarding school, everyone gets depressed. We go in and see the house-
mother, Mrs. Gunther. She got married when she was eighteen. Mr. Gunther was
her high school sweetheart, the only boyfriend she ever had.
"And you knew you wanted to marry him right off?" we ask her.
She smiles and says, "Yes."   75
"They always want something from you," says Jill, complaining about her
boyfriend.
"Yeah," says Giddy. "You always feel like you have to deliver something."
"You do," says Mrs. Gunther. "Babies."

After sex, you curl up like a shrimp, something deep inside you ruined,
slammed in a place that sickens at slamming, and slowly you fill up with an overwhelming sadness, an elusive gaping worry. You don't try to explain it, filled with
the knowledge that it's nothing after all, everything filling up finally and absolutely
with death. After the briskness of loving, loving stops. And you roll over with death
stretched out alongside you like a feather boa, or a snake, light as air, and you . . .
you don't even ask for anything or try to say something to him because it's obviously
your own damn fault. You haven't been able to — to what? To open your heart. You
open your legs but can't, or don't dare anymore, to open your heart.

It starts this way: 80
You stare into their eyes. They flash like all the stars are out. They look at you
seriously, their eyes at a low burn and their hands no matter what starting off shy
and with such a gentle touch that the only thing you can do is take that tenderness
and let yourself be swept away. When, with one attentive finger they tuck the hair
behind your ear, you —
You do everything they want.
Then comes after. After when they don't look at you. They scratch their balls,
stare at the ceiling. Or if they do turn, their gaze is altogether changed. They are
surprised. They turn casually to look at you, distracted, and get a mild distracted
surprise. You're gone. Their blank look tells you that the girl they were fucking is not
there anymore. You seem to have disappeared.

CONSIDERATIONS FOR CRITICAL THINKING AND WRITING

1. **FIRST RESPONSE.** What do you think of the narrator? Why? Do you agree with the definition the story offers for *lust*?

2. Do you think that the narrator's depiction of male and female responses to sex are accurate? Explain why or why not.

3. How effective is the narrator's description of teenage sex? What do you think she means when she says "You know just what you're doing and don't see the things that start to get in the way" (para. 29)?

4. What is the story's conflict? Explain whether you think the conflict is resolved.

5. Discuss the story's tone. Is it what you expected from the title?

6. What do you think is the theme of "Lust"? Does its style carry its theme?

7. What is the primary setting for the story? What does it reveal about the nature of the narrator's economic and social class?

8. In a *Publishers Weekly* interview (November 6, 1992), Minot observed, "There's more fictional material in unhappiness and disappointment and frustration than there is in happiness. Who was it that said, 'Happiness is like a blank page'?" What do you think of this observation?

CONNECTIONS TO OTHER SELECTIONS

1. Compare the treatments of youthful sexuality in "Lust" and David Updike's "Summer" (p. 301). Do you prefer one story to the other? Why?

2. Write an essay explaining the sort of advice the narrator of Fay Weldon's "IND AFF, or Out of Love in Sarajevo" (p. 186) might give to the narrator of "Lust." You might try writing this in the form of a letter.

RICK MOODY (B. 1961)

Born in New York City, Rick Moody grew up in Connecticut and earned his undergraduate degree at Brown University and his M.F.A. at Columbia University. His first of five novels, *Garden State* (1992), won the Pushcart Editor's Choice Award. *The Ice Storm* (1994) was made into a popular film directed by Ang Lee in 1997 and was followed by three more novels: *Purple America* (1996), *The Diviners* (2005), and *The Four Fingers of Death* (2010). Moody has also published three collections of short stories and novellas: *The Ring of Brightest Angels Along Heaven* (1995); *Demonology* (2001), which collects "Boys"; and *Right Livelihoods* (2007). "Boys" was included in *The Best American Short Stories 2001*, in which Moody

© Colin McPherson/Corbis.

describes how this experimental story began. He had heard a fellow writer, Max Steele, use the phrase "Then the boys entered the house" at a reading and found himself "preoccupied" with what is "perhaps the most essential gesture in a boy's life." He then "started playing around with the sentence."

Boys 2000

Boys enter the house, boys enter the house. Boys, and with them the ideas of boys (ideas leaden, reductive, inflexible), enter the house. Boys, two of them, wound into hospital packaging, boys with infant-pattern baldness, slung in the arms of parents, boys dreaming of breasts, enter the house. Twin boys, kettles on the boil, boys in hideous vinyl knapsacks that young couples from Edison, N.J., wear on their shirt fronts, knapsacks coated with baby saliva and staphylococcus and milk vomit, enter the house. Two boys, one striking the other with a rubberized hot dog, enter the house. Two boys, one of them striking the other with a willow switch about the head and shoulders, the other crying, enter the house. Boys enter the house speaking nonsense. Boys enter the house calling for mother. On a Sunday, in May, a day one might nearly describe as perfect, an ice cream truck comes slowly down the lane, chimes inducing salivation, and children run after it, not long after which boys dig a hole in the back yard and bury their younger sister's dolls two feet down, so that she will never find these dolls and these dolls will rot in hell, after which boys enter the house. Boys, trailing after their father like he is the Second Goddamned Coming of Christ Goddamned Almighty, enter the house, repair to the basement to watch baseball. Boys enter the house, site of devastation, and repair immediately to the kitchen, where they mix lighter fluid, vanilla pudding, drain-opening lye, balsamic vinegar, blue food coloring, calamine lotion, cottage cheese, ants, a plastic lizard one of them received in his Christmas stocking, tacks, leftover mashed potatoes, Spam, frozen lima beans, and chocolate syrup in a medium-sized saucepan and heat over a low flame until thick, afterward transferring the contents of this saucepan into a Pyrex lasagna dish, baking the Pyrex lasagna dish in the oven for nineteen minutes before attempting to persuade their sister that she should eat the mixture; later they smash three family heirlooms (the last, a glass egg, intentionally) in a two-and-a-half-hour stretch, whereupon they are sent to their bedroom until freed, in each case thirteen minutes after. Boys enter the house, starchy in pressed shirts and flannel pants that itch so bad, fresh from Sunday school instruction, blond and brown locks (respectively) plastered down but even so with a number of cowlicks protruding at odd angles, disconsolate and humbled, uncertain if boyish things — such as shooting at the neighbor's dog with a pump-action BB gun and gagging the fat boy up the street with a bandanna and showing their shriveled boy-penises to their younger sister — are exempted from the commandment to *Love the Lord thy God with all thy heart and with all thy soul and with all thy mind, and thy neighbor as thyself.* Boys enter the house in baseball gear (only one of the boys can hit): in their spikes, in mismatched tube socks that smell like Stilton cheese. Boys enter the house in soccer gear. Boys enter the house carrying skates. Boys enter the house with lacrosse sticks, and soon after, tossing a lacrosse ball lightly in the living room, they destroy a lamp. One boy enters the house sporting basketball clothes, the other wearing jeans and a sweatshirt. One boy enters the house bleeding profusely and is taken out to get stitches, the other watches. Boys enter the house at the end of term carrying report cards, sneak around the house like spies of foreign nationality, looking for a place to hide the report cards for the time being (under a toaster? in a medicine cabinet?). One boy with a black eye enters the house, one boy without. Boys with acne enter the house and squeeze and prod large skin blemishes in front of their sister. Boys with acne-treatment products hidden about their persons enter the house. Boys, standing just up the street, sneak cigarettes behind a willow in the Elys' yard, wave smoke away from their natural fibers, hack terribly, experience nausea, then enter the house. Boys call each other *Retard, Homo, Geek,* and, later, *Neckless Thug, Theater Fag,* and enter the house exchanging further epithets. Boys enter house with nose-hair clippers, chase sister around house threatening to depilate her eyebrows. She cries. Boys attempt to induce girls to whom they would not have spoken only six or eight months prior to enter the house with them. Boys enter the house with girls efflorescent and homely and attempt to induce girls to sneak into their bedroom, as they still share a single bedroom; girls refuse. Boys enter the house, go to separate bedrooms. Boys, with their father (an arm around each of them), enter the house, but of the monologue preceding and succeeding this entrance, not a syllable is preserved. Boys enter the house having masturbated in a variety of locales. Boys enter the house having masturbated in train-station bathrooms, in forests, in beach houses, in football bleachers at night under the stars, in cars (under a blanket), in the shower, backstage, on a plane, the boys masturbate constantly, identically, three times a day in some cases, desire like a madness upon them, at the mere sound of certain words, words that sound like other words, *interrogative* reminding them of *intercourse, beast* reminding them of *breast, sects* reminding them of *sex,* and so forth, the boys are not very smart yet, and as they enter the house they feel, as always, immense shame at the scale of this self-abusive cogitation, seeing a classmate, seeing a billboard, seeing a fire hydrant, seeing things that should not induce thoughts of masturbation (their sister, e.g.) and then thinking of masturbation anyway. Boys enter the house, go to their rooms, remove sexually explicit magazines from hidden stashes, put on loud music, feel despair. Boys enter the house worried; they argue. The boys are ugly, they are failures, they will never be loved, they enter the house. Boys enter the house and kiss their mother, who feels differently now they have outgrown her. Boys enter the house, kiss their mother, she explains the seriousness of their sister's difficulty, her diagnosis. Boys enter the house, having attempted to locate the spot in their yard where the dolls were buried, eight or nine years prior, without success; they go to their sister's room, sit by her bed. Boys enter the house and tell their completely bald sister jokes about baldness. Boys hold either hand of their sister, laying aside differences, having trudged grimly into the house. Boys skip school, enter house, hold vigil. Boys enter the house after their parents have both gone off to work, sit with their sister and with their sister's nurse. Boys enter the house carrying cases of beer. Boys enter the house, very worried now, didn't know more worry was possible. Boys enter the house carrying controlled substances, neither having told the other that he is carrying a controlled substance, though an intoxicated posture seems appropriate under the circumstances. Boys enter the house weeping and hear weeping around them. Boys enter the house embarrassed, silent, anguished, keening, afflicted, angry, woeful, grief-stricken. Boys enter the house on vacation, each clasps the hand of the other with genuine warmth, the one wearing dark colors and having shaved a portion of his head, the other having grown his hair out longish and wearing, uncharacteristically, a tie-dyed shirt. Boys enter the house on vacation and argue bitterly about politics (other subjects are no longer discussed), one boy supporting the Maoist insurgency in a certain Southeast Asian country, one believing that to change the system you need to work inside it; one boy threatens to beat the living shit out of the other, refuses crème brûlée, though it is created by his mother in order to keep the peace. One boy writes home and thereby enters the house only through a mail slot: he argues that the other boy is crypto-fascist, believing that the market can seek its own level on questions of ethics and morals; boys enter the house on vacation and announce future professions; boys enter the house on vacation and change their minds about professions; boys enter the house on vacation, and one boy brings home a sweetheart but throws a tantrum when it is suggested that the sweetheart will have to retire on the folding bed in the basement; the other boy, having no sweetheart, is distant and withdrawn, preferring to talk late into the night about family members gone from this world. Boys enter the house several weeks apart. Boys enter the house on days of heavy rain. Boys enter the house, in different calendar years, and upon entering, the boys seem to do nothing but compose manifestos, for the benefit of parents; they follow their mother around the place, having fashioned these manifestos in celebration of brand-new independence: *Mom, I like to lie in bed late into the morning watching game shows*, or, *I'm never going to date anyone but artists from now on, mad girls, dreamers, practicers of black magic*, or, *A man should eat bologna, sliced meats are important*, or, *An American should bowl at least once a year*, but these manifestos apply only for brief spells, after which they are reversed or discarded. Boys don't enter the house at all, except as ghostly afterimages of younger selves, fleeting images of sneakers dashing up a staircase; soggy towels on the floor of the bathroom; blue jeans coiled like asps in the basin of the washing machine; boys as an absence of boys, blissful at first, you put a thing down on a spot, put this book down, come back later, it's still there; you buy a box of cookies, eat three, later three are missing. Nevertheless, when boys next enter the house, which they ultimately must do, it's a relief, even if it's only in preparation for weddings of acquaintances from boyhood, one boy has a beard, neatly trimmed, the other has rakish sideburns, one boy wears a hat, the other boy thinks hats are ridiculous, one boy wears khakis pleated at the waist, the other wears denim, but each changes into his suit (one suit fits well, one is a little tight), as though suits are the liminary marker of adulthood. Boys enter the house after the wedding and they are slapping each other on the back and yelling at anyone who will listen, *It's a party!* One boy enters the house, carried by friends, having been arrested (after the wedding) for driving while intoxicated, complexion ashen; the other boy tries to keep his mouth shut: the car is on its side in a ditch, the car has the top half of a tree broken over its bonnet, the car has struck another car, which has in turn struck a third, *Everyone will have seen*. One boy misses his brother horribly, misses the past, misses a time worth being nostalgic over, a time that never existed, back when they set their sister's playhouse on fire; the other boy avoids all mention of that time; each of them is once the boy who enters the house alone, missing the other, each is devoted and each callous, and each plays his part on the telephone, over the course of months. Boys enter the house with fishing gear, according to prearranged date and time, arguing about whether to use lures or live bait, in order to meet their father for the fishing adventure, after which boys enter the house again, almost immediately, with live bait, having settled the question; boys boast of having caught fish in the past, though no fish has ever been caught: *Remember when the blues were biting?* Boys enter the house carrying their father, slumped. Happens so fast. Boys rush into the house leading EMTs to the couch in the living room where the body lies, boys enter the house, boys enter the house, boys enter the house. Boys hold open the threshold, awesome threshold that has welcomed them when they haven't even been able to welcome themselves, that threshold which welcomed them when they had to be taken in, here is its tarnished knocker, here is its euphonious bell, here's where the boys had to sand the door down because it never would hang right in the frame, here are the scuff marks from when boys were on the wrong side of the door demanding, here's where there were once milk bottles for the milkman, here's where the newspaper always landed, here's the mail slot, here's the light on the front step, illuminated, here's where the boys are standing, as that beloved man is carried out. Boys, no longer boys, exit.

CONSIDERATIONS FOR CRITICAL THINKING AND WRITING

1. FIRST RESPONSE. Write a paragraph that describes in detail the style of this story. In what ways is it conventional as well as unconventional?

2. What is the story's basic plot? What actually happens? Does it have any kind of pattern to it?

3. Who are the major characters? Is there an antagonist who produces a conflict? Explain why or why not.

4. How well do you think Moody captures boys' lives?

5. How is the plot related to the story's style?

6. What do you think is the significance of the final sentence?

CONNECTIONS TO OTHER SELECTIONS

1. Discuss how time is conveyed stylistically in this narrative and in Mark Halliday's "Young Man on Sixth Avenue" (p. 533).

2. Compare the literary styles and their effects in this story and in David Foster Wallace's "Incarnations of Burned Children" (p. 535).

GEOFF WYSS (B. 1968)

Raised in Peoria, Illinois, Geoff Wyss moved to teach high school English in New Orleans, where many of his stories are set. He has a degree in creative writing from Kansas State University. The author of a novel, *Tiny Clubs* (2007), and *How* (2012), a collection of short stories and winner of the Ohio State University Fiction Prize, he has also published short stories in *Image, Painted Bride Quarterly, Northwest Review, Tin House,* and *Glimmer Train.* In "How to Be a Winner," Wyss combines humor and satire in an ironically detailed style.

© 2011, Samantha Scheel.

How to Be a Winner 2012

The first thing is, it takes guts. Let me hear you say it! Guts!

Men, when you have gotten to know me better, you will understand I am an individual who I am prepared to repeatedly demand or ask a question until I get my desired response. I am an individual who in my mind and heart there is constant focus on a goal. When you boys have locked up your pads and you're on your way home to Mommy or maybe you're quote kicking it with friends, I am a person who odds are almost a hundred percent I am still in my office devising a punishing, foolproof offense. I have in my office there's a coffee maker for late nights and film of you name the coverage or blocking scheme and I've got film of it, and this is me choosing to excel. Or sometimes, for health reasons and what have you, I drink green tea.

So my prerequisite question I'm asking is, are you able to look in the mirror and say this is a person with guts? Not am I a cruel person. Not am I unsportsmanlike in terms of hits to the knee or do I fall into the trap of performance-enhancing drugs, that whole spectrum. But am I a person who could fashion my own tourniquet in a war setting and return to battle? Am I a person who the Ten Commandments is my guiding code, which things like the Internet make it harder for you as young people than it was for me? Am I man enough to befriend a homosexual or a retarded individual despite I am a looked-up-to athlete, because everyone is deserving of respect? If you can say yes to these integrity benchmarks, my vow here today is that maybe you are five-foot-one like this gentleman in the front row, and maybe you have a, what is that, son, an eye patch? over your eye, but I will teach you how to be a winner.

So you are 0-5, 0-2 in district play. OK. Your coach has contacted me for the purpose of we're going to rectify that. My name is Cleveland Miller, and I am what is known as a sports behavior consultant, or simply a consultant. As a coach, my players referred to me as *Coach Killer* for the style of play I harped. I had a trademark of everyone in the state knew I was going to run the football and I ran the football anyway. In my last three years at Meequeepanassatommee High School, Storrs, Connecticut, my teams compiled a record of 36-1 and brought home two state titles. For the last four years, I have been an individual brought into various programs and et cetera, work environments and even governments, for mental toughness and success orientation. You may recall in your memory a period when Jay Cutler of the NFL Denver Broncos lost confidence in his mid-range game, specifically over the middle. This was widely reported. The person called in on that matter to restore Jay's way of thinking vis-à-vis throw with your eyes, not with your arm was me, and I induced him with anecdotes of let's look at how the greats did it and a visualization mini-retreat, which the next week he threw three touchdown passes. My moniker or what have you is I mix modern technology with old-fashioned I know what makes people tick. But I want to let you know that in your case today, I have waived my fee because I have watched the tapes your coach sent me and heard his cry from the wilderness. Men, be not afraid. Follow me. I have come to lead you forth.

Specifics of you're doing this wrong and you're doing that wrong we'll save for 5 the field. But what the tapes are showing as a general sphere are missed tackles and confusion about where do I line up for the play in question, which these are mental or will-power mistakes. My notes indicate a recurring facet of it basically looks like you're handing the ball to the opposing team, which this is like giving candy to a girl who's already trying to kick you in the nuts. I saw individuals in this room trip and fall purposely to avoid physical contact. Then there are what you would call the football stupidity or a nicer word would be lack of knowledge issues. The offensive unit lined up on the wrong side of the ball not once this season but twice. That's five yards right there. I had to make a new category in Excel for plays you ran with only ten men on the field. Then, number three, there are the issues of lack of self-caring about yourself and your teammates. One particular individual whose number I won't state but whose position involves predominantly running the ball with stamina was captured for posterity lighting a cigarette under the bleachers and slowly enjoying the rich tobacco flavor. Let me guess that the reason I hear giggling in the back of the room is listen now and see if I've got it is because you have told yourself if we are going to lose anyway, then losing will not hurt as much if I put myself in a passive or female position, go ahead, other team, eff me and get it over with. See, here's the thing is, I have coached losers before. I know and sympathize the mentality. I have coached many losers successfully, and this is what qualifies me to aggress and incent you. At Meequeepanassatommee High School, Storrs, Connecticut, I took young men whose major yearn was huffing chemicals and self-touching themselves in the lavatory, and I turned them into *yes-ma'am, yes-sir* type of people who would have eaten my enemy's heart off a spear. Did I have my critics, so to say? Yes, I did. But a rule of life you can say Cleveland Miller taught you is your critics are people who secretly wish they could be you. They are frequently English teachers and Math teachers, and they sit on school boards and whisper-campaign about what they call abusive and coercive treatment. They are people who according to a tape measure may be the size of a full-size person, but they preside in your memory as approximately a midget. They never played the game, and they will never know the inner joy and feeling of hit or be hit. They notify their decisions to you on the letterhead of a law firm instead of we're going to speak to you face to face and fire you as a man. Son, look at me. Spit out that gum, look at me, and listen as I tell you the story of Michael Wiltonberry.

There are many types of loser. Michael Wiltonberry was the kind where the word I use for it is smug. This is a word that means clever combined with a sort of facial look that is begging authority figures to punch you in the mouth. I knew Michael as a student in my health class with leather wrist bracelets on his wrists and hair over his eyes, which that was his message he wanted to send and I got the message. His main hobby in class was writing offensive material on small pieces of paper, this would be female vaginas and jokes about my teaching approach, and passing them to other students. But all that changed the day I entered the student lavatory on what they call a whim and intercessed Michael handing a plastic bag of narcotics to a fellow student. If there is a national or international drug of people everywhere who have no goals, it is marijuana or weed, which was the contents of this bag, which I plucked into my keeping. But: did I see this incident as this is a bad or negative moment in life, no good can come of it? Something to get downhearted? No: because winners are never downhearted, this is a hallmark. Because fate may have given Michael Wiltonberry a father who only saw the sun when the law dragged him out into it, but it also gave him a six-foot-three frame with high physical I.Q. and surprising foot speed. I took the plastic bag like this, and I placed it in the toilet like so, and I applied the flushing mechanism. And I looked at Michael the same way I am looking at you, young man, as an individual of infinite potential. And I expressed my hope that he would show up for spring football practice the next morning with cleats and a hairstyle suitable to a young man of the male gender.

This seventeen-year-old boy had the lungs of a coal miner, but I addressed that situation by making him throw up his old lungs every day until he developed new ones. Experience had taught Michael he could remedy a cure for everything by crying, and I provided him a new experience where crying gave him more things to cry about. I saw Michael's car entering a McDonald's one night after practice, a cry-for-help mobile with heavy metal or maybe the lingo is goth markings, and I took him home so my wife could make him a proper supper. A sit-down meal is one of my messages to you, men. Plates you can't fold and forks made out of metal, you report to your parents regarding I learned this or that about the world today, what wisdom do you have for me, your loving son. My wife served I'll always remember it was pot roast that night, and Michael took seconds. His favorite dish in the long run was this baked chicken with my wife puts bread crumbs on it, which Michael came to my residence for every Monday night, Monday being the night his mother was pre-engaged committing adultery in various taverns. How anyone could become so wasteful with what God has given them, which you would think loving and caring for your child would be universal, this is the question I ask myself. My wife was unable to have children personally. There was a medical term we were given. But — but my point I'm trying to express to you young men here today is how I ran Michael at practice and fed him at home and dragged him out of parties by the neck to reverse-motivate his bad habits and, yes, a couple times at the beginning I let my players teach him lessons of respect in the locker room. And eventually the outside loser was washed away to reveal the inside winner of Michael James Wiltonberry. This was remarked by everyone who crossed his path, including his grades went up in his core subjects. And next fall he led my team to the state finals, where he played the last nine minutes of the fourth quarter with a torn ACL. So when I tell you this is a winner and that is a winner, and when I use a word like son in the context of that's how I saw Michael, you will understand certain things the school board did not, such as maybe there is a good reason a player would spend the night at a coach's house. Such as maybe human life doesn't always fit your rule book. So I had to leave that job. But I still speak to Michael by phone, and I want you to know that he excelled in Division II college football until he was reinjured and today is a grocery store manager or is on that track is what they call it, and he has two healthy children.

I sometimes consider that today's world possibly makes young people afraid to win. Whether there is something to that. That there is a sense of everything is dirty, everyone is lying. That there is a so-called hedonism of I have to always be enjoying myself. But, men, please understand, and there is no doubt in my mind or should be in yours about this: the world is broken down into half the world is winners and half the world is losers. We have what is known as a locked struggle. The losers are trying to make losers of us all. This is their armageddon goal, and they are constantly attaining toward this goal with persuasive this and attractive that, mostly things of the body. But if we winners surrender, the world can say good-bye to the following. The precision excellence of football. American military superiority. Inventions to improve the daily lives of people from caveman times to now. Trust among humans based on here is my word and handshake. And hello to the following. Constant sex jokes in films, suck you, suck me. Everyone is obese. Cities are you can't even go into them without a machine gun. And one day when we're all watching TV, Ayatollah Busybody gets elected President of the World. It's a locked struggle. The championship of the world is at stake. You can take the first step toward winning that championship when we go out onto the field today.

So grab your helmets, men. I am going to teach you speed concepts, and I am going to teach you pre-game. I have studied Buddhist meditation, and tomorrow I will insert that component. I asked you to spit out that gum, son. Only losers have to always be doing something with their mouths. That's the main organ of losers, their mouths. Ours is our guts, men. Say it with me! Guts!

CONSIDERATIONS FOR CRITICAL THINKING AND WRITING

1. FIRST RESPONSE. To what extent is Cleveland Miller similar or dissimilar to coaches you have known? Is his characterization credible to you?

2. Cite specific examples of how diction, grammar, sentence structure, and logic reveal the coach's character.

3. How is Cleveland Miller's coaching style similar to his style of teaching?

4. What was the coach's experience in his previous job?

5. Why does the coach tell the story about Michael Wiltonberry? Why do you think the author includes it?

6. How does the penultimate paragraph suggest the coach's politics and world view?

7. Discuss the nature of the satire in this story. Explain why you found it humorous — or why you did not.

CONNECTIONS TO OTHER SELECTIONS

1. Compare the treatment of the boys' lives in Wyss's story and in Rick Moody's "Boys" (p. 289).

2. Write an essay that compares how style reveals character in "How to Be a Winner" and in the excerpt from Charles Dickens's *Hard Times* (p. 108).

ENCOUNTERING FICTION: COMICS AND GRAPHIC STORIES

Matt Groening (b. 1954), *Life in Hell*

A native of Portland, Oregon, cartoon artist Matt Groening moved to Los Angeles in 1977 to become a writer for television. There he began recording his observations of life in the comic strip *Life in Hell,* a strip that he began as "an ongoing series of self-help cartoons." First published in 1980 in the *Los Angeles Reader, Life in Hell* was quickly syndicated and has been collected in many volumes beginning with *Love Is Hell* (1984). In his preface to *The Big Book of Hell,* from which the following cartoon is reprinted, Groening writes: "All my life I've been torn between frivolity and despair, between the desire to amuse and the desire to annoy, between dread-filled insomnia and a sense of my own goofiness. Just like you, I worry about love and sex and work and suffering and injustice and death, but I also dig drawing bulgy-eyed rabbits with tragic overbites." Groening is best known as the creator of *The Simpsons,* an animated sitcom satirizing family, life, and culture in America. He describes its central character, Bart Simpson, as "a more entertaining version of myself."

Reprinted from *The Big Book of Hell: A Cartoon Book* by Matt Groening © 1990 Matt Groening Productions, Inc. Published by Pantheon Books, a division of Random House, Inc. New York.

CONSIDERATIONS AND CONNECTION TO ANOTHER SELECTION

1. What do you think of the father's explanation of death? What does he think about his own ideas?

2. What is the story's tone? How do the images and the words set the tone?

3. Does this strip rely more heavily on the drawings or on the words for its meanings? Explain your answer.

4. Discuss the perspective on death in Groening's strip and in Tim O'Brien's "How to Tell a True War Story" (p. 488).

10

Combining the Elements of Fiction: A Writing Process

Library of Congress, Prints and Photographs Division.

A skillful artist has constructed a tale. He has not fashioned his thoughts to accommodate his incidents, but having deliberately conceived a certain single *effect* to be wrought, he then invents such incidents . . . as may best serve him in establishing the preconceived effect. There should be no word written of which the tendency, direct or indirect, is not to the one pre-established design.

— EDGAR ALLAN POE, Review of
Hawthorne's *Twice-Told Tales*

THE ELEMENTS TOGETHER

The elements of fiction that you have examined in Chapters 1–9 provide terms and concepts that enable you to think, talk, and write about fiction in a variety of ways. As those chapters have indicated, there are many means available to you for determining a story's effects and meanings. By considering elements of fiction such as characterization, conflict, setting, point of view, symbolism, style, and theme, you can better articulate your understanding of a particular work. A careful reading of the work's elements allows you to see how the parts contribute to the whole.

The parts or elements of a story work together rather than in isolation to create a particular kind of experience, emotion, or insight for a reader. The symbolic significance of the free and easy Mississippi River setting of *The Adventures of Huckleberry Finn*, for example, cannot be excavated from Huck's first-person point of view. Nor can the "smothery" ways of the corrupt towns along the river be understood without the pious frauds, hypocrites, cowards, and other sordid characters that populate them. Add the plot that has Jim on the run from slavery and the unconscious ironic tone that Mark Twain invests in Huck—all constitute interrelated elements that add up to serious themes commenting on nineteenth-century society. Understanding the ways in which these elements work together produces a richer and more satisfying reading of a plot that might otherwise be read simply as a children's story.

MAPPING THE STORY

Writing about a story requires your creation of a clear path that a reader can take in order to follow your experience and understanding of the work. The path offers perspectives and directions that are informed by what caught your attention along the way. Your paper points out what you thought worth revisiting and taking the reader to see. Whatever the thesis of the paper, your role as a guide remains the same as you move from one element of the story to the next, offering an overall impression about the story. And as you already know, the best tours are always guided by informed and interesting voices.

This chapter presents an example of how one student, Janice Reardon, arrived at a thesis, combining her understanding of several elements of fiction for an assigned topic on David Updike's short story "Summer." After reviewing the elements of fiction covered in Chapters 1–9, Janice read the story several times, paying careful attention to plot, character, setting, point of view, symbolism, and so on. She then developed her ideas by brainstorming, drafting, and using the Questions for Writing (p. 305) to develop her thesis into a statement that makes a definite claim about a specific idea and provides a clear sense of direction for the paper to come. As you read "Summer," think about what you might want to say about the relationship—or lack thereof—between Homer and Sandra. Pay attention to how the various elements of fiction work together to establish or reinforce that relationship.

DAVID UPDIKE (B. 1957)

Born in Ipswich, Massachusetts, David Updike is the son of author John Updike. David received his B.A. in art history at Harvard and his M.A. from Teachers College, Columbia University. His acclaimed children's books include *An Autumn Tale* (1988), *A Spring Story* (1989), *Seven Times Eight* (1990), *The Sounds of Summer* (1993), and *A Helpful Alphabet of Friendly Objects* (1998), which he coauthored with his father. "Summer," a poignant tale for adults, is part of *Out on the Marsh: Stories* (1988), a collection of his short fiction. A second collection, *Old Girlfriends,* appeared in 2009.

Jan Brown.

Summer 1985

It was the first week in August, the time when summer briefly pauses, shifting between its beginning and its end: the light had not yet begun to change, the leaves were still full and green on the trees, the nights were still warm. From the woods and fields came the hiss of crickets; the line of distant mountains was still dulled by the edge of summer haze, the echo of fireworks was replaced by the rumble of thunder and the hollow premonition of school, too far off to imagine though dimly, dully felt. His senses were consumed by the joy of their own fulfillment: the satisfying swat of a tennis ball, the dappled damp and light of the dirt road after rain, the alternating sensations of sand, mossy stone, and pine needles under bare feet. His days were spent in the adolescent pursuit of childhood pleasures: tennis, a haphazard round of golf, a variant of baseball adapted to the local geography: two pine trees as foul poles, a broomstick as the bat, the apex of the small, secluded house the dividing line between home runs and outs. On rainy days they swatted bottle tops across the living room floor, and at night vented budding cerebral energy with games of chess thoughtfully played over glasses of iced tea. After dinner they would paddle the canoe to the middle of the lake, and drift beneath the vast, blue-black dome of sky, looking at the stars and speaking softly in tones which, with the waning summer, became increasingly philosophical: the sky's blue vastness, the distance and magnitude of stars, an endless succession of numbers, gave way to a rising sensation of infinity, eternity, an imagined universe with no bounds. But the sound of the paddle hitting against the side of the canoe, the faint shadow of surrounding mountains, the cry of a nocturnal bird brought them back to the happy, cloistered finity of their world, and they paddled slowly home and went to bed.

Homer woke to the slant and shadow of a summer morning, dressed in their shared cabin, and went into the house where Mrs. Thyme sat alone, looking out across the flat blue stillness of the lake. She poured him a cup of coffee and they quietly talked, and it was then that his happiness seemed most tangible. In this summer month with the Thymes, freed from the complications of his own family, he had released himself to them and, as interim member — friend, brother, surrogate son — he lived in a blessed realm between two worlds.

From the cool darkness of the porch, smelling faintly of moldy books and kerosene and the tobacco of burning pipes, he sat looking through the screen to the lake, shimmering beneath the heat of a summer afternoon: a dog lay sleeping in the sun, a bird hopped along a swaying branch, sunlight came in through the trees and collapsed on the sandy soil beside a patch of moss, or mimicked the shade and cadence of stones as they stepped to the edge of a lake where small waves lapped a damp rock and washed onto a sandy shore. An inverted boat lay decaying under a tree, a drooping American flag hung from its gnarled pole, a haphazard dock started out across the cove toward distant islands through which the white triangle of a sail silently moved.

The yellowed pages of the book from which he occasionally read swam before him: "... Holmes clapped the hat upon his head. It came right over the forehead and settled on the bridge of his nose. 'It is a question of cubic capacity' said he ..." Homer looked up. The texture of the smooth, unbroken air was cleanly divided by the sound of a slamming door, echoing up into the woods around him. Through the screen he watched Fred's sister Sandra as she came ambling down the path, stepping lightly between the stones in her bare feet. She held a towel in one hand, a book in the other, and wore a pair of pale blue shorts — faded relics of another era. At the end of the dock she stopped, raised her hands above her head, stretching, and then sat down. She rolled over onto her stomach and, using the book as a pillow, fell asleep.

Homer was amused by the fact, that although she did this every day, she didn't 5 get any tanner. When she first came in her face was faintly flushed, and there was a pinkish line around the snowy band where her bathing suit strap had been, but the back of her legs remained an endearing, pale white, the color of eggshells, and her back acquired only the softest, brownish blur. Sometimes she kept her shoes on, other times a shirt, or sweater, or just collapsed onto the seat of the boat, her pale eyelids turned upward toward the pale sun; and as silently as she arrived, she would leave, walking back through the stones with the same, casual sway of indifference. He would watch her, hear the distant door slam, the shower running in the far corner of the house. Other times he would just look up and she would be gone.

On the tennis court she was strangely indifferent to his heroics. When the crucial moment arrived — Homer serving in the final game of the final set — the match would pause while she left, walking across the court, stopping to call the dog, swaying out through the gate. Homer watched her as she went down the path, and, impetus suddenly lost, he double faulted, stroked a routine backhand over the back fence, and the match was over.

When he arrived back at the house she asked him who won, but didn't seem to hear his answer. "I wish I could go sailing," she said, looking distractedly out over the lake.

At night, when he went out to the cottage where he and Fred slept, he could see her through the window as she lay on her bed, reading, her arm folded beneath her head like a leaf. Her nightgown, pulled and buttoned to her chin, pierced him with a regret that had no source or resolution, and its imagined texture floated in the air above him as he lay in bed at night, suspended in the surrounding darkness, the scent of pine, the hypnotic cadence of his best friend's breathing.

Was it that he had known her all his life, and as such had grown up in the shadow of her subtle beauty? Was it the condensed world of the lake, the silent reverence of surrounding woods, mountains, which heightened his sense of her and brought the warm glow of her presence into soft, amorous focus? She had the hair of a baby, the freckles of a child, and the sway of motherhood. Like his love, her beauty rose up in the world which spawned and nurtured it, and found in the family the medium in which it thrived, and in Homer distilled to a pure distant longing for something he had never had.

One day they climbed a mountain, and as the components of family and 10 friends strung out along the path on their laborious upward hike, he found himself tromping along through the woods with her with nobody else in sight. Now and then they would stop by a stream, or sit on a stump, or stone, and he would speak to her, and then they would set off again, he following her. But in the end this day exhausted him, following her pale legs and tripping sneakers over the ruts and stones and a thousand roots, all the while trying to suppress a wordless, inarticulate passion, and the last mile or so he left her, sprinting down the path in a reckless, solitary release, howling into the woods around him. He was lying on the grass, staring up into the patterns of drifting clouds when she came ambling down. "Wher'd you go? I thought I'd lost you," she said, and sat heavily down in the seat of the car. On the ride home, his elbow hopelessly held in the warm crook of her arm, he resolved to release his love, give it up, on the grounds that it was too disruptive to his otherwise placid life. But in the days to follow he discovered that his resolution had done little to change her, and her life went on its oblivious, happy course without him.

His friendship with Fred, meanwhile, continued on its course of athletic and boyhood fulfillment. Alcohol seeped into their diet, and an occasional cigarette, and at night they would drive into town, buy two enormous cans of Australian beer and sit at a small cove by the lake, talking. One night on the ride home Fred accelerated over a small bridge, and as the family station wagon left the ground their heads floated up to the ceiling, touched, and then came crashing down as the car landed and Fred wrestled the car back onto course. Other times they would take the motorboat out onto the lake and make sudden racing turns around buoys, sending a plume of water into the air and everything in the boat crashing to one side. But always with these adventures Homer felt a pang of absence, and was always relieved when they headed back toward the familiar cove, and home.

As August ran its merciless succession of beautiful days, Sandra drifted in and out of his presence in rising oscillations of sorrow and desire. She worked at a bowling alley on the other side of the lake, and in the evening Homer and Fred would drive the boat over, bowl a couple of strings, and wait for her to get off work. Homer sat at the counter and watched her serve up sloshing cups of coffee, secretly loathing the leering gazes of whiskered truck drivers, and loving her oblivious, vacant stare in answer, hip cocked, hand on counter, gazing up into the neon air above their heads. When she was finished, they would pile into the boat and skim through darkness the four or five miles home, and it was then, bundled beneath sweaters and blankets, the white hem of her waitressing dress showing through the darkness, their hair swept in the wind and their voices swallowed by the engine's slow, steady growl, that he felt most powerless to her attraction. As the boat rounded corners he would close his eyes and release himself to gravity, his body's warmth swaying into hers, guising his attraction in the thin veil of centrifugal force. Now and then he would lean into the floating strands of her hair and speak into her fragrance, watching her smile swell in the pale half-light of the moon, the umber glow of the boat's rear light, her laughter spilling backward over the swirling "V" of wake.

Into the humid days of August a sudden rain fell, leaving the sky a hard, unbroken blue and the nights clear and cool. In the morning when he woke, leaving Fred a heap of sighing covers in his bed, he stepped out into the first rays of sunlight that came through the branches of the trees and sensed, in the cool vapor that rose from damp pine needles, the piercing cry of a blue jay, that something had changed. That night as they ate dinner — hamburgers and squash and corn-on-the-cob — everyone wore sweaters, and as the sun set behind the undulating line of distant mountains — burnt, like a filament of summer into his blinking eyes — it was with an autumnal tint, a reddish glow. Several days later the tree at the end of the point bloomed with a sprig of russet leaves, one or two of which occasionally fell, and their lives became filled with an unspoken urgency. Life of summer went on in the silent knowledge that, with the slow, inexorable seepage of an hourglass, it was turning into fall. Another mountain was climbed, annual tennis matches were arranged and played. Homer and Fred became unofficial champions of the lake by trouncing the elder Dewitt boys, unbeaten in several years. "Youth, youth," glum Billy Dewitt kept saying over iced tea afterward, in jest, though Homer could tell he was hiding some greater sense of loss.

And the moment, the conjunction of circumstance that, through the steady exertion of will, minor adjustments of time and place, he had often tried to induce, never happened. She received his veiled attentions with a kind of amused curiosity, as if smiling back on innocence. One night they had been the last ones up, and there was a fleeting, shuddering moment before he stepped through the woods to his cabin and she went to her bed that he recognized, in a distant sort of way, as the moment of truth. But to touch her, or kiss her, seemed suddenly incongruous, absurd, contrary to something he could not put his finger on. He looked down at the floor and softly said goodnight. The screen door shut quietly behind him and he went out into the darkness and made his way through the unseen sticks and stones, and it was only then, tripping drunkenly on a fallen branch, that he realized he had never been able to imagine the moment he distantly longed for.

The Preacher gave a familiar sermon about another summer having run 15 its course, the harvest of friendship reaped, and a concluding prayer that, "God willing, we will all meet again in June." That afternoon Homer and Fred went sailing, and as they swept past a neighboring cove Homer saw in its sullen shadows a girl sitting alone in a canoe, and in an eternal, melancholy signal of parting, she waved to them as they passed. And there was something in the way that she raised her arm which, when added to the distant impression of her fullness, beauty, youth, filled him with longing as their boat moved inexorably past, slapping the waves, and she disappeared behind a crop of trees.

The night before they were to leave they were all sitting in the living room after dinner — Mrs. Thyme sewing, Fred folded up with the morning paper, Homer reading on the other end of the couch where Sandra was lying — when the dog leapt up and things shifted in such a way that Sandra's bare foot was lightly touching Homer's back. Mrs. Thyme came over with a roll of newspaper, hit the dog on the head and he leapt off. But to Homer's surprise Sandra's foot remained, and he felt, in the faint sensation of exerted pressure, the passive emanation of its warmth, a distant signal of acquiescence. And as the family scene continued as before it was with the accompanying drama of Homer's hand, shielded from the family by a haphazard wall of pillows, migrating over the couch to where, in a moment of breathless abandon, settled softly on the cool hollow of her arch. She laughed at something her mother had said, her toe twitched, but her foot remained. It was only then, in the presence of the family, that he realized she was his accomplice, and that, though this was as far as it would ever go, his love had been returned.

CONSIDERATIONS FOR CRITICAL THINKING AND WRITING

1. **FIRST RESPONSE.** How do you respond to this love story? Would the story be more satisfying if Homer and Sandra openly acknowledged their feelings for each other and kissed at the end? Why or why not?

2. What details in the first paragraph evoke particular feelings about August? What sort of mood is created by these details?

3. How is Homer's attraction to Sandra made evident in paragraphs 5 through 9?

4. Why do you think August is described as a "merciless succession of beautiful days" (para. 12)?

5. Analyze the images in paragraph 13 that evoke the impending autumn. What does Billy Dewitt's lament about "youth, youth" add to this description?

6. Discuss the transition between paragraphs 14 and 15. How is the mood effectively changed between the night and the next day?

7. What effect does Homer's friendship with Fred and his relationship with the Thyme family have on your understanding of his reticent attraction to Sandra?

8. What, if any, significance can you attach to the names of Homer, Sandra, Thyme, and the Dewitt boys?

9. How successful do you think Updike is in evoking youthful feeling about summer in this story? Explain why you responded positively or negatively to this evocation of summer.

CONNECTIONS TO OTHER SELECTIONS

1. Compare David Updike's treatment of summer as the setting of his story with John Updike's use of summer as the setting in "A & P" (p. 200).

2. Discuss "Summer" and Dagoberto Gilb's "Love in L.A." (p. 458) as love stories. Explain why you might prefer one over the other.

As you read "Summer," what potential paper topics occurred to you? Annotating the text and brainstorming are both good ways to identify moments in a text that you will feel moved to write about if your instructor does not assign a paper topic to you. Even after you come up with a topic — say, the relationship between Homer and Sandra — you still need to turn it into a thesis. The following questions should prove useful in choosing a topic that you can develop into a thesis, the central idea of your paper. As you become increasingly engaged in your topic, you're likely to discover new ideas and perhaps change your ideas, so at the beginning stages it's best to regard your thesis as tentative. This will allow you to remain open to unexpected insights along the way.

Questions for Writing

DEVELOPING A TOPIC INTO A REVISED THESIS

1. If the topic is assigned, have you specifically addressed the prescribed subject matter?

2. If you choose your own topic, have you used your annotations, notes, and first response writing to help you find a suitable topic?

3. Is the topic too broad or too narrow? Is the topic focused enough to be feasible and manageable for the assigned length of the paper?

4. Is the topic too difficult or specialized for you to write about successfully? If you need information and expertise that goes well beyond the scope of the assignment, would it be better to choose another topic?

5. Is the topic too simple or obvious to allow you to develop a strong thesis?

6. Once you have focused your topic, what do you think you want to say about it? What is the central idea — the tentative thesis — of the paper?

7. Have you asked questions about the topic to help generate a thesis?

8. Have you tried brainstorming or freewriting as a means of producing ideas that would lead to a thesis?

9. Have you tried writing a rough outline or simply jotting down ideas to see if your tentative thesis can be supported or qualified and made firmer?

10. Is your thesis statement precise or vague? What is the central argument that your thesis makes?

11. Does the thesis help provide an organizing principle—a sense of direction—for the paper?

12. Does the thesis statement consist of one or more complete declarative sentences (not framed as a question) written in clear language that express a complete idea?

13. Is the thesis supported by specific references to the text you are discussing? Have you used brief quotations to illustrate important points and provide evidence for the argument?

14. Is everything included in the paper in some way related to the thesis? Should any sentences or paragraphs be deleted because they are irrelevant to the central point?

15. Does the thesis appear in the introductory paragraph? If not, is there a particular reason for including it later in the paper?

16. If during the course of writing the paper you shifted direction or changed your mind about its central point, have you revised (or completely revamped) your thesis to reflect that change?

17. Have you developed a thesis that genuinely interests you? Are you interested enough in the thesis to write a paper that will also engage your reader?

A SAMPLE BRAINSTORMING LIST

After Janice has read the story twice carefully, she is ready to start working on turning the assigned topic into a defined thesis. Her instructor asked the class to answer the first question in the Considerations for Critical Thinking and Writing: *Would the story be more satisfying if Homer and Sandra openly acknowledged their feelings for each other and kissed at the end?* Janice uses the technique of brainstorming to come up with a more specific approach to the topic, thinking carefully about elements of the story like plot, setting, action, character, symbolism, tone, and theme.

— *plot with subtle drama* — why?

— "blessed realm between two worlds" — adolescence, the school years, real home life (Homer with another family), state of desire before culmination

— *action*: regular, familiar, relatively uneventful, savoring state of vague desire

— *setting*: tranquil, idyllic, familiar, warm, unabrasive "happy, cloistered finity of their world" — unthreatening, known; things happen as they're expected to; navigable, happy, image of summer

> — *character*: Homer is shy but sensitive; Sandra seems a little more in control; both are on the threshold of adulthood
>
> — *symbolism*: "blessed realm between two worlds" — adolescent summer life on the lake vs. school and the adult world, summer month with Thymes vs. real home life
>
> — *tone*: easy, light tone, vague but pleasant romantic longing
>
> — *theme*: love acknowledged but kept as part of summer life

A SAMPLE FIRST THESIS

Reviewing her brainstorming list, Janice sees a connection between the plot and the setting that helps her to address the question and to draft a thesis.

> David Updike's short story "Summer" is a love story with little drama or complication. This lack of action in the plot is mirrored by Updike's rendering of the setting and general atmosphere, which are evoked by the description of the picturesque cabin on a lake, the season of summer, and the symbolic "season" of adolescence. The fact that there is no great culmination to Homer's attraction to Sandra is not a failure of the characters or of the fiction's drama. Instead, this nearly actionless plot captures and reflects the sense of adolescence and summer as a state of protected happiness.

A SAMPLE REVISED THESIS

After this initial attempt at a thesis, Janice asks herself several of the Questions for Writing on pages 305–06 and writes out her responses, realizing along the way how she needs to revise her thesis.

> *Is the topic (that the action reflects the setting to create a sense of "happy, cloistered finity") too simple? I could discuss whether the story succeeds in creating this sense. It does — through description of setting and of Homer's thoughts.*
>
> *Is the thesis statement precise? Not quite; I think I need to say in the thesis what would be appealing about "between two worlds." Updike describes it in*

(continued)

*positive tones, but suggests with the word "cloistered" that there's some-
thing they're closing themselves away from, implies there's a world outside.
Why is the cloistered state happy and blessed? (I should also comment on
the religious terminology, but maybe not in the thesis statement, since it's
not the most important descriptive technique in the story.)*

*Does my thesis offer a direction for the paper, an organizing principle? I think
that if I add onto the last sentence something about why the "realm between
two worlds" is blessed, I'd be able to organize the paper as a discussion moving between action and setting to argue that the lack of action isn't a failure
but a kind of fulfillment or contentment.*

*Is the thesis supported by specific references to the text you are discuss-
ing? Instead of saying "protected happiness" I should use one of the quotes
I've been mentioning: "the happy, cloistered finity of their world" (para. 1) and
"a blessed realm between two worlds" (para. 2).*

*David Updike's short story "Summer" involves little action or complication,
but this lack of action in the plot is made meaningful by the rendering of the
idyllic setting. Combined, these create a particular sense of summer, the
symbolic "season" of adolescence, and of adolescent love. The fact that there
is no great culmination to Homer's attraction to Sandra is not a failure of the
characters or of the plot. Instead, the light tone of this nearly actionless
plot captures and reflects the theme — a sense of adolescence and summer
as "a blessed realm between two worlds" (para. 2), in which the characters
are relatively free of the constraints of more complex adult relationships but
may enjoy something of adult consciousness of feeling.*

Compare the two thesis statements. Does the revised version seem more
effective to you? Why or why not? Can you think of ways to further improve
the revised version? Do you think the thesis would be more effective if more or
fewer elements were included in it?

Before you begin writing your own paper, review the Questions for Responsive Reading and Writing (pp. 47–49) in Chapter 2, "Writing about Fiction."
These questions will help you to focus and sharpen your critical thinking and
writing. You'll also find help in Chapter 52, "Reading and the Writing Process,"
which offers a systematic overview of choosing a topic, developing a thesis,
and organizing various types of assignments. If you use outside sources for the
paper, be sure to acknowledge them adequately by using the conventional documentation procedures detailed in Chapter 53, "The Literary Research Paper."

A SAMPLE STUDENT RESPONSE

Janice Reardon

Professor Halovanic

English 102

21 January 2015

Plot and Setting in David Updike's "Summer"

David Updike's short story "Summer" is a love story with little drama
or complication, but the lack of action in the plot is made meaningful by
the rendering of the idyllic setting, as well as through metaphor and subtle
detail. Combined, these elements create a particular sense of summer, the
symbolic "season" of adolescence, and of adolescent love. The fact that
there is no great culmination to Homer's attraction to Sandra is not a
failure of Updike's characters or plot. Instead, the light tone of this nearly
actionless plot reflects a specific period of adolescence, a moment between
one stage of life and the next. During this time, the characters experience—
perhaps for the first time—adult emotions, yet they are still free of the
constraints of more complex adult relationships.

From the start, the story establishes a theme of transition through
setting. The story takes place in early August "when summer briefly pauses,
shifting between its beginning and its end" (301). The days are still long
and warm, yet change looms. The sound of fireworks is replaced by distant
thunder. Thoughts of the approaching school year become stronger. This
setting (both the physical setting as well as the time of year) is a metaphor
for the characters, who are also dealing with change. The characters are
caught in this same "pause" of summer, experiencing changes in their lives,
anticipating other changes to come.

Also like the setting, the characters are at a midpoint, poised
between where they have been and where they are going. Both Homer and
Sandra are maturing. Homer suddenly has an interest in Sandra, though he
has known her all his life. He sees her as having "the hair of a baby, the
freckles of a child, and the sway of motherhood" (302). This description
suggests the dichotomy of adolescence, a time when a person is caught
"between two worlds" (301), between youth and adulthood. Though they

recognize the changes they are going through, the characters still cling to their childhood. Homer spends his days playing games: tennis, golf, baseball. Sandra wears shorts faded by time—"faded relics of another era" (302)—a token of her past, perhaps one she is unwilling to give up just yet. These characters are pulled between what they have been all their lives and what lies ahead. They are no longer children and not quite adults, but the emotions they experience are no less real or significant.

The story has few active scenes, and Updike focuses on internal monologue and detail; it is this inaction that drives the plot. Homer does little to express his love for Sandra. He spends his days watching her intently as she lies in the sun, but he loathes the truck drivers' "leering gazes" (303) in the bowling alley diner where Sandra works. He deals with his newfound love for Sandra by focusing on and analyzing detail, much like the reader of the story. He cannot tell Sandra how he feels, even when the moment warrants it. When they are the last two awake and share a subtle, intimate moment, the thought of kissing her seems "absurd," and Homer can only look at the floor and say goodnight (304). At times, Homer even tries to use his inaction to get what he wants. When the pain of Sandra's seeming indifference becomes too much, he decides to give up his love for her, only to find that she continues on her "oblivious, happy course without him" (303). But it is Homer's inaction that helps us to understand what he is going through; in many ways his inaction creates more drama than action would.

While Homer does little to act on his love for Sandra, he does *react*. His desire for Sandra causes him to go to extremes. During their hike, when Homer is overcome by his "inarticulate passion" for Sandra, he runs from her at full speed, "howling into the woods" (302). At other times, he and Fred behave recklessly, speeding their car over bridges, racing their motorboat between buoys. They get in the habit of having a beer and a cigarette each night. These impulsive actions are a "solitary release" for Homer, a way for him to expend some of the anguish he's experiencing (302). This is not uncommon in life or in fiction. Sammy in John Updike's "A & P" reacts similarly to a difficult situation. After seeing two teenage girls humiliated by his boss, Sammy decides to take a stand. He quits his job, despite the possibility of upsetting his parents:

> "Sammy, you don't want to do this to your Mom and Dad,"
> he tells me. It's true, I don't. But it seems to me that
> once you begin a gesture it's fatal not to go through
> with it. (204)

Here, Sammy, like Homer, acts without considering the consequences, a behavior common to adolescents.

Keeping with the themes of time and transition, the story ends when the summer ends. The nights grow cold; the preacher speaks of "another summer having run its course" (D. Updike 304). It is only then that Homer and Sandra share a simple, tender moment, a touch, and Homer's love for Sandra is finally—albeit subtly—requited. And with this small dramatic peak, the characters enter a new phase of adulthood. The two will no longer live "between two worlds." They will move on to the next stage of their lives, taking with them memories: memories of this period of their lives, of summer, and of each other.

Works Cited

Meyer, Michael, ed. *The Bedford Introduction to Literature*. 11th ed. Boston: Bedford/St. Martin's, 2016. Print.

Updike, David. "Summer." Meyer 301–04.

Updike, John. "A & P." Meyer 200–04.

Approaches
to Fiction

11

A Study of
Nathaniel Hawthorne

© Peabody Essex Museum, Salem,
Massachusetts.

[My] book, if you would see anything
in it, requires to be read in the clear,
brown, twilight atmosphere in which it
was written; if opened in the sunshine,
it is apt to look exceedingly like a
volume of blank pages.

—HAWTHORNE, *Preface to
Twice-Told Tales* (1851)

The three short stories by Nathaniel Hawthorne included in this chapter provide an opportunity to study a major fiction writer in depth. Getting to know an author's work is similar to developing a friendship with someone: the more encounters, the more intimate the relationship becomes. Familiarity with a writer's concerns and methods in one story can help to illuminate another story. As we become accustomed to someone's voice — a friend's or a writer's — we become attuned to nuances in tone and meaning. The nuances in Hawthorne's fiction warrant close analysis. Although the stories included are not wholly representative of his work, they suggest some of the techniques and concerns that characterize it. The three stories provide a useful context

© Peabody Essex Museum, Salem, Massachusetts.

"The Old Manse." The Hawthornes spent some of their happiest years (from the summer of 1842 to 1845) at the Old Manse, a house built by the family of Ralph Waldo Emerson (c. 1770). The garden held a special attraction for Hawthorne, as he describes in *Mosses from an Old Manse:* "I used to visit and revisit it a dozen times a day, and stand in deep contemplation over my vegetable progeny with a love that nobody could share or conceive of who had never taken part in the process of creation. It was one of the most bewitching sights in the world, to observe a hill of beans thrusting aside the soil, or a row of early peas just peeping forth sufficiently to trace a line of delicate green. . . ." © Lee Snider.

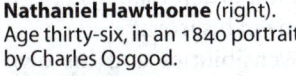

"The Witch of the Woodlands"
(above). Because Hawthorne's
family tree included a judge who
participated in the Salem witchcraft trials (1692–93), witchcraft
was an important theme in Hawthorne's writing. This illustration
from an eighteenth-century book
on witchcraft features "a grave
and dark-clad company" such
as Goodman Brown describes
(see "Young Goodman Brown,"
p. 321). Witches were thought to
commune in the forest and associate with evil creatures or strange
animals known as "familiars."

© Peabody Essex Museum, Salem,
Massachusetts.

Nathaniel Hawthorne (right).
Age thirty-six, in an 1840 portrait
by Charles Osgood.

© Peabody Essex Museum, Salem,
Massachusetts.

for reading individual stories. Moreover, the works invite comparisons and contrasts in their styles and themes. Following the three stories are some brief commentaries by and about Hawthorne that establish additional contexts for understanding his fiction.

A BRIEF BIOGRAPHY AND INTRODUCTION

Nathaniel Hawthorne (1804–1864) once described himself as "the obscurest man of letters in America." During the early years of his career, this self-assessment was mostly accurate, but the publication of *The Scarlet Letter* in 1850 marked the beginning of Hawthorne's reputation as a major American writer. His novels and short stories have entertained and challenged generations of readers; they have wide appeal because they can be read on many levels. Hawthorne skillfully creates an atmosphere of complexity and ambiguity that makes it difficult to reduce his stories to a simple view of life. The moral and psychological issues that he examines through the conflicts his characters experience are often intricate and mysterious. Readers are frequently made to feel that in exploring Hawthorne's characters they are also encountering some part of themselves.

Hawthorne achieved success as a writer only after a steady and intense struggle. His personal history was hardly conducive to producing a professional writer. Born in Salem, Massachusetts, Hawthorne came from a Puritan family of declining fortunes that prided itself on an energetic pursuit of practical matters such as law and commerce. He never knew his father, a sea captain who died in Dutch Guiana when Hawthorne was only four years old, but he did have a strong imaginative sense of an early ancestor, who as a Puritan judge persecuted Quakers, and of a later ancestor, who was a judge during the Salem witchcraft trials. His forebears seemed to haunt Hawthorne, so that in some ways he felt more involved in the past than in the present.

In "The Custom-House," the introduction to *The Scarlet Letter,* Hawthorne considers himself in relation to his severe Puritan ancestors:

> No aim, that I have ever cherished, would they recognize as laudable; no success of mine . . . would they deem otherwise than worthless, if not positively disgraceful. "What is he?" murmurs one gray shadow of my forefathers to the other. "A writer of story-books! What kind of a business in life, — what mode of glorifying God, or being serviceable to mankind in his day and generation, — may that be? Why, the degenerate fellow might as well have been a fiddler!" Such are the compliments bandied between my great-grandsires and myself, across the gulf of time! And yet, let them scorn me as they will, strong traits of their nature have intertwined with mine.

Hawthorne's sense of what his forebears might think of his work caused him to worry that the utilitarian world was more real and important than his imaginative creations. This issue became a recurring theme in his work.

Despite the Puritan strain in Hawthorne's sensibilities and his own deep suspicion that a literary vocation was not serious or productive work,

Hawthorne was determined to become a writer. He found encouragement at Bowdoin College in Maine and graduated in 1825 with a class that included the poet Henry Wadsworth Longfellow and Franklin Pierce, who would be elected president of the United States in the early 1850s. After graduation Hawthorne returned to his mother's house in Salem, where for the next twelve years he read New England history as well as writers such as John Milton, William Shakespeare, and John Bunyan. During this time he lived a relatively withdrawn life devoted to developing his literary art. Hawthorne wrote and revised stories as he sought a style that would express his creative energies. Many of these early efforts were destroyed when they did not meet his high standards. His first novel, *Fanshawe*, was published anonymously in 1828; it concerns a solitary young man who fails to realize his potential and dies young. Hawthorne very nearly succeeded in reclaiming and destroying all the published copies of this work. It was not attributed to the author until after his death; not even his wife was aware that he had written it. The stories eventually published as *Twice-Told Tales* (1837) represent work that was carefully revised and survived Hawthorne's critical judgments.

Writing did not provide an adequate income, so like nearly all nineteenth-century American writers, Hawthorne had to take on other employment. He worked in the Boston Custom House from 1839 through 1840 to save money to marry Sophia Peabody, but he lost that politically appointed job when administrations changed. In 1841 he lived at Brook Farm, a utopian community founded by idealists who hoped to combine manual labor with art and philosophy. Finding that monotonous physical labor left little time for thinking and writing, Hawthorne departed after seven months. The experience failed to improve his financial situation, but it did eventually serve as the basis for a novel, *The Blithedale Romance* (1852).

Married in the summer of 1842, Hawthorne and his wife moved to the Old Manse in Concord, Massachusetts, where their neighbors included Ralph Waldo Emerson, Henry David Thoreau, Amos Bronson Alcott, and other writers and thinkers who contributed to the lively literary environment of that small town. Although Hawthorne was on friendly terms with these men, his skepticism concerning human nature prevented him from sharing either their optimism or their faith in radical reform of individuals or society. Hawthorne's view of life was chastened by a sense of what he called in "Wakefield" the "iron tissue of necessity." His sensibilities were more akin to Herman Melville's. When Melville and Hawthorne met while Hawthorne was living in the Berkshires of western Massachusetts, they responded to each other intensely. Melville admired the "power of blackness" he discovered in Hawthorne's writings and dedicated *Moby-Dick* to him.

During the several years he lived in the Old Manse, Hawthorne published a second collection of *Twice-Told Tales* (1842) and additional stories in *Mosses from an Old Manse* (1846). To keep afloat financially, he worked in the Salem Custom House from 1846 until 1849, when he again lost his job through a change in administrations. This time, however, he discovered that by leaving the oppressive materialism of the Custom House he found more energy to write: "So little adapted is the atmosphere of a Custom House to the delicate harvest of fancy and sensibility, that, had I remained there through ten Presidencies yet to come, I doubt whether the tale of 'The Scarlet Letter' would ever have been brought before the public. My imagination was a tarnished mirror [there.]" Free of the Custom House, Hawthorne was at the height of his creativity and productivity during the early 1850s. In addition to *The Scarlet Letter* and *The Blithedale Romance*, he wrote *The House of the Seven Gables* (1851); *The Snow-Image, and Other Twice-Told Tales* (1851); a campaign biography of his Bowdoin classmate, *The Life of Franklin Pierce* (1852); and two collections of stories for children, *A Wonder Book* (1852) and *Tanglewood Tales* (1853).

Hawthorne's financial situation improved during the final decade of his life. In 1853 his friend President Pierce appointed him to the U.S. consulship in Liverpool, where he remained for the next four years. Following a tour of Europe from 1858 to 1860, Hawthorne and his family returned to Concord, and he published *The Marble Faun* (1860), his final completed work of fiction. He died while traveling through New Hampshire with former president Pierce.

Hawthorne's stories are much more complex than the melodramatic but usually optimistic fiction published in many magazines contemporary to him. Instead of cheerfully confirming public values and attitudes, his work tends to be dark and brooding. Modern readers remain responsive to Hawthorne's work — despite the fact that his nineteenth-century style takes some getting used to — because his psychological themes are as fascinating as they are disturbing. The range of his themes is not broad, but their treatment is remarkable for its insights.

Hawthorne wrote about individuals who suffer from inner conflicts caused by sin, pride, untested innocence, hidden guilt, perverse secrecy, cold intellectuality, and isolation. His characters are often consumed by their own passions, whether those passions are motivated by an obsession with goodness or evil. He looks inside his characters and reveals to us that portion of their hearts, minds, and souls that they keep from the world and even from themselves. This emphasis accounts for the private, interior, and sometimes gloomy atmosphere in Hawthorne's works. His stories rarely end on a happy note because the questions his characters raise are almost never completely answered. Rather than positing solutions to the problems and issues his characters encounter, Hawthorne leaves us with ambiguities suggesting that experience cannot always be fully understood and controlled. Beneath the surface appearances in his stories lurk ironies and shifting meanings that point to many complex truths instead of a single simple moral.

The following three Hawthorne stories provide an opportunity to study this writer in some depth. These stories are not intended to be entirely representative of the 120 or so that Hawthorne wrote, but they do offer some sense of the range of his techniques and themes. Hawthorne's fictional world of mysterious incidents and sometimes bizarre characters increases in meaning the more his stories are read in the context of one another.

Chronology

1804	Born on July 4 in Salem, Massachusetts.
1808	Hawthorne's father, a sea captain, dies in Surinam, Dutch Guiana, leaving the family dependent on relatives.
1821–25	Attends Bowdoin College in Maine. Franklin Pierce (later to become president) and Henry Wadsworth Longfellow are classmates. Graduates eighteenth in a class of thirty-eight.
1828	Publishes *Fanshawe: A Tale* anonymously at his own expense.
1830–37	Publishes numerous stories in periodicals anonymously or pseudonymously, collected in *Twice-Told Tales*.
1838	Becomes engaged to Sophia Peabody.
1839–40	Works in Boston Custom House.
1841	From April to November, lives at the utopian Brook Farm Community.
1842–45	Marries (eventually has three children) and lives at the Old Manse in Concord, Massachusetts, where he meets Ralph Waldo Emerson and Henry David Thoreau.
1846	Publishes his second collection of stories, *Mosses from an Old Manse*.
1846–49	Works as a surveyor in the Salem Custom House.
1850	Publishes *The Scarlet Letter*; becomes a friend of Herman Melville.
1851	Publishes *The House of the Seven Gables*; *The Snow-Image, and Other Twice-Told Tales*; and *True Stories from History and Biography*.
1852	Publishes *The Blithedale Romance*; *A Wonder Book for Girls and Boys*; and *The Life of Franklin Pierce*, a campaign biography.
1853–57	Serves as United States Consul at Liverpool on appointment by President Pierce.
1858–59	Lives in Rome and Florence.
1860	Publishes *The Marble Faun*; returns to Concord.
1863	Publishes *Our Old Home: A Series of English Sketches*.
1864	Dies on May 19 at Plymouth, New Hampshire.

Young Goodman Brown   1835

Young Goodman Brown came forth at sunset into the street at Salem village; but put his head back, after crossing the threshold, to exchange a parting kiss with his young wife. And Faith, as the wife was aptly named, thrust her own pretty head into the street, letting the wind play with the pink ribbons of her cap while she called to Goodman Brown.

"Dearest heart," whispered she, softly and rather sadly, when her lips were close to his ear, "prithee put off your journey until sunrise and sleep in your own bed tonight. A lone woman is troubled with such dreams and such thoughts that she's afeared of herself sometimes. Pray tarry with me this night, dear husband, of all nights in the year."

"My love and my Faith," replied young Goodman Brown, "of all nights in the year, this one night must I tarry away from thee. My journey, as thou callest it, forth and back again, must needs be done 'twixt now and sunrise. What, my sweet, pretty wife, dost thou doubt me already, and we but three months married?"

"Then God bless you!" said Faith, with the pink ribbons; "and may you find all well when you come back."

"Amen!" cried Goodman Brown. "Say thy prayers, dear Faith, and go to bed at 5
dusk, and no harm will come to thee."

So they parted; and the young man pursued his way until, being about to turn the corner by the meeting-house, he looked back and saw the head of Faith still peeping after him with a melancholy air, in spite of her pink ribbons.

"Poor little Faith!" thought he, for his heart smote him. "What a wretch am I to leave her on such an errand! She talks of dreams, too. Methought as she spoke there was trouble in her face, as if a dream had warned her what work is to be done tonight. But no, no; 't would kill her to think it. Well, she's a blessed angel on earth; and after this one night I'll cling to her skirts and follow her to heaven."

With this excellent resolve for the future, Goodman Brown felt himself justified in making more haste on his present evil purpose. He had taken a dreary road, darkened by all the gloomiest trees of the forest, which barely stood aside to let the narrow path creep through, and closed immediately behind. It was all as lonely as could be; and there is this peculiarity in such a solitude, that the traveler knows not who may be concealed by the innumerable trunks and the thick boughs overhead; so that with lonely footsteps he may yet be passing through an unseen multitude.

"There may be a devilish Indian behind every tree," said Goodman Brown to himself; and he glanced fearfully behind him as he added, "What if the devil himself should be at my very elbow!"

His head being turned back, he passed a crook of the road, and, looking for- 10
ward again, beheld the figure of a man, in grave and decent attire, seated at the foot of an old tree. He arose at Goodman Brown's approach and walked onward side by side with him.

"You are late, Goodman Brown," said he. "The clock of the Old South was strik-ing as I came through Boston, and that is full fifteen minutes agone."

"Faith kept me back a while," replied the young man, with a tremor in his voice, caused by the sudden appearance of his companion, though not wholly unexpected.

It was now deep dusk in the forest, and deepest in that part of it where these two were journeying. As nearly as could be discerned, the second traveler was about fifty years old, apparently in the same rank of life as Goodman Brown, and bearing a considerable resemblance to him, though perhaps more in expression than features. Still they might have been taken for father and son. And yet, though the elder person was as simply clad as the younger, and as simple in manner too, he had an indescribable air of one who knew the world, and who would not have felt abashed at the governor's dinner table or in King William's court, were it pos-sible that his affairs should call him thither. But the only thing about him that could be fixed upon as remarkable was his staff, which bore the likeness of a great black snake, so curiously wrought that it might almost be seen to twist and wriggle itself like a living serpent. This, of course, must have been an ocular deception, assisted by the uncertain light.

"Come, Goodman Brown," cried his fellow-traveler, "this is a dull pace for the beginning of a journey. Take my staff, if you are so soon weary."

"Friend," said the other, exchanging his slow pace for a full stop, "having kept 15 covenant by meeting thee here, it is my purpose now to return whence I came. I have scruples touching the matter thou wot'st° of."

"Sayest thou so?" replied he of the serpent, smiling apart. "Let us walk on, nevertheless, reasoning as we go; and if I convince thee not thou shalt turn back. We are but a little way in the forest yet."

"Too far! too far!" exclaimed the goodman, unconsciously resuming his walk. "My father never went into the woods on such an errand, nor his father before him. We have been a race of honest men and good Christians since the days of the martyrs; and shall I be the first of the name of Brown that ever took this path and kept" —

"Such company, thou wouldst say," observed the elder person, interpreting his pause. "Well said, Goodman Brown! I have been as well acquainted with your family as with ever a one among the Puritans; and that's no trifle to say. I helped your grandfather, the constable, when he lashed the Quaker woman so smartly through the streets of Salem; and it was I that brought your father a pitch-pine knot, kindled at my own hearth, to set fire to an Indian village, in King Philip's war.° They were my good friends, both; and many a pleasant walk have we had along this path, and returned merrily after midnight. I would fain be friends with you for their sake."

"If it be as thou sayest," replied Goodman Brown, "I marvel they never spoke of these matters; or, verily, I marvel not, seeing that the least rumor of the sort would have driven them from New England. We are a people of prayer, and good works to boot, and abide no such wickedness."

"Wickedness or not," said the traveler with the twisted staff, "I have a very 20 general acquaintance here in New England. The deacons of many a church have drunk the communion wine with me; the selectmen of divers towns make me their chairman; and a majority of the Great and General Court are firm supporters of my interest. The governor and I, too — But these are state secrets."

"Can this be so?" cried Goodman Brown, with a stare of amazement at his undisturbed companion. "Howbeit, I have nothing to do with the governor and council; they have their own ways, and are no rule for a simple husbandman like me. But, were I to go on with thee, how should I meet the eye of that good old man, our minister, at Salem village? Oh, his voice would make me tremble both Sabbath day and lecture day."

Thus far the elder traveler had listened with due gravity; but now burst into a fit of irrepressible mirth, shaking himself so violently that his snakelike staff actually seemed to wriggle in sympathy.

"Ha! ha! ha!" shouted he again and again; then composing himself, "Well, go on, Goodman Brown, go on; but, prithee, don't kill me with laughing."

---

wot'st: Know.
King Philip's war (1675–76): War between the colonists and an alliance of Indian tribes led by Metacan (also known as Metacomet), leader of the Wampanoags, who was called King Philip by the colonists.

"Well, then, to end the matter at once," said Goodman Brown, considerably nettled, "there is my wife, Faith. It would break her dear little heart; and I'd rather break my own."

"Nay, if that be the case," answered the other, "e'en go thy ways, Goodman 25 Brown. I would not for twenty old women like the one hobbling before us that Faith should come to any harm."

As he spoke he pointed his staff at a female figure on the path, in whom Goodman Brown recognized a very pious and exemplary dame, who had taught him his catechism in youth, and was still his moral and spiritual adviser, jointly with the minister and Deacon Gookin.

"A marvel, truly that Goody Cloyse should be so far in the wilderness at nightfall," said he. "But with your leave, friend, I shall take a cut through the woods until we have left this Christian woman behind. Being a stranger to you, she might ask whom I was consorting with and whither I was going."

"Be it so," said his fellow-traveler. "Betake you to the woods, and let me keep the path."

Accordingly the young man turned aside, but took care to watch his companion, who advanced softly along the road until he had come within a staff's length of the old dame. She, meanwhile, was making the best of her way, with singular speed for so aged a woman, and mumbling some indistinct words — a prayer, doubtless — as she went. The traveler put forth his staff and touched her withered neck with what seemed the serpent's tail.

"The devil!" screamed the pious old lady. 30

"Then Goody Cloyse knows her old friend?" observed the traveler, confronting her and leaning on his writhing stick.

"Ah, forsooth, and is it your worship indeed?" cried the good dame. "Yea, truly is it, and in the very image of my old gossip, Goodman Brown, the grandfather of the silly fellow that now is. But — would your worship believe it? — my broomstick hath strangely disappeared, stolen, as I suspect, by that unhanged witch, Goody Cory, and that, too, when I was all anointed with the juice of smallage, and cinquefoil, and wolfsbane" —

"Mingled with fine wheat and the fat of a newborn babe," said the shape of old Goodman Brown.

"Ah, your worship knows the recipe," cried the old lady, cackling aloud. "So, as I was saying, being all ready for the meeting, and no horse to ride on, I made up my mind to foot it; for they tell me there is a nice young man to be taken into communion tonight. But now your good worship will lend me your arm, and we shall be there in a twinkling."

"That can hardly be," answered her friend. "I may not spare you my arm, 35 Goody Cloyse; but here is my staff, if you will."

So saying, he threw it down at her feet, where, perhaps, it assumed life, being one of the rods which its owner had formerly lent to the Egyptian magi. Of this fact, however, Goodman Brown could not take cognizance. He had cast up his eyes in astonishment, and, looking down again, beheld neither Goody Cloyse nor the serpentine staff, but his fellow-traveler alone, who waited for him as calmly as if nothing had happened.

"That old woman taught me my catechism," said the young man; and there was a world of meaning in this simple comment.

They continued to walk onward, while the elder traveler exhorted his companion to make good speed and persevere in the path, discoursing so aptly that his arguments seemed rather to spring up in the bosom of his auditor than to be suggested by himself. As they went, he plucked a branch of maple to serve for a walking stick, and began to strip it of the twigs and little boughs, which were wet with evening dew. The moment his fingers touched them they became strangely withered and dried up as with a week's sunshine. Thus the pair proceeded, at a good free pace, until suddenly, in a gloomy hollow of the road, Goodman Brown sat himself down on the stump of a tree and refused to go any farther.

"Friend," he said, stubbornly, "my mind is made up. Not another step will I budge on this errand. What if a wretched old woman do choose to go to the devil when I thought she was going to heaven: is that any reason why I should quit my dear Faith and go after her?"

"You will think better of this by and by," said his acquaintance, composedly. "Sit   40 here and rest yourself a while; and when you feel like moving again, there is my staff to help you along."

Without more words, he threw his companion the maple stick, and was as speedily out of sight as if he had vanished into the deepening gloom. The young man sat a few moments by the roadside, applauding himself greatly, and thinking with how clear a conscience he should meet the minister in his morning walk, nor shrink from the eye of good old Deacon Gookin. And what calm sleep would be his that very night, which was to have been spent so wickedly, but so purely and sweetly now, in the arms of Faith! Amidst these pleasant and praiseworthy meditations, Goodman Brown heard the tramp of horses along the road, and deemed it advisable to conceal himself within the verge of the forest, conscious of the guilty purpose that had brought him thither, though now so happily turned from it.

On came the hoof tramps and the voices of the riders, two grave old voices, conversing soberly as they drew near. These mingled sounds appeared to pass along the road, within a few yards of the young man's hiding-place; but, owing doubtless to the depth of the gloom at that particular spot, neither the travelers nor their steeds were visible. Though their figures brushed the small boughs by the wayside, it could not be seen that they intercepted, even for a moment, the faint gleam from the strip of bright sky athwart which they must have passed. Goodman Brown alternately crouched and stood on tiptoe, pulling aside the branches and thrusting forth his head as far as he durst without discerning so much as a shadow. It vexed him the more, because he could have sworn, were such a thing possible, that he recognized the voices of the minister and Deacon Gookin, jogging along quietly, as they were wont to do, when bound to some ordination or ecclesiastical council. While yet within hearing, one of the riders stopped to pluck a switch.

"Of the two, reverend sir," said the voice like the deacon's, "I had rather miss an ordination dinner than tonight's meeting. They tell me that some of our community are to be here from Falmouth and beyond, and others from Connecticut and Rhode Island, besides several of the Indian powwows, who, after their fashion, know almost as much deviltry as the best of us. Moreover, there is a goodly young woman to be taken into communion."

"Mighty well, Deacon Gookin!" replied the solemn old tones of the minister. "Spur up, or we shall be late. Nothing can be done, you know, until I get on the ground."

The hoofs clattered again; and the voices, talking so strangely in the empty air,   45 passed on through the forest, where no church had ever been gathered or solitary Christian prayed. Whither, then, could these holy men be journeying so deep into the heathen wilderness? Young Goodman Brown caught hold of a tree for support, being ready to sink down on the ground, faint and overburdened with the heavy sickness of his heart. He looked up to the sky, doubting whether there really was a heaven above him. Yet there was the blue arch, and the stars brightening in it.

"With heaven above and Faith below, I will yet stand firm against the devil!" cried Goodman Brown.

While he still gazed upward into the deep arch of the firmament and had lifted his hands to pray, a cloud, though no wind was stirring, hurried across the zenith and hid the brightening stars. The blue sky was still visible, except directly overhead, where this black mass of cloud was sweeping swiftly northward. Aloft in the air, as if from the depths of the cloud, came a confused and doubtful sound of voices. Once the listener fancied that he could distinguish the accents of townspeople of his own, men and women, both pious and ungodly, many of whom he had met at the communion table, and had seen others rioting at the tavern. The next moment, so indistinct were the sounds, he doubted whether he had heard aught but the murmur of the old forest, whispering without a wind. Then came a stronger swell of those familiar tones, heard daily in the sunshine at Salem village, but never until now from a cloud of night. There was one voice, of a young woman, uttering lamentations, yet with an uncertain sorrow, and entreating for some favor, which, perhaps, it would grieve her to obtain; and all the unseen multitude, both saints and sinners, seemed to encourage her onward.

"Faith!" shouted Goodman Brown, in a voice of agony and desperation; and the echoes of the forest mocked him, crying, "Faith! Faith!" as if bewildered wretches were seeking her all through the wilderness.

The cry of grief, rage, and terror was yet piercing the night, when the unhappy husband held his breath for a response. There was a scream, drowned immediately in a louder murmur of voices, fading into far-off laughter, as the dark cloud swept away, leaving the clear and silent sky above Goodman Brown. But something fluttered lightly down through the air and caught on the branch of a tree. The young man seized it, and beheld a pink ribbon.

"My Faith is gone!" cried he after one stupefied moment. "There is no good on 50 earth; and sin is but a name. Come, devil; for to thee is this world given."

And, maddened with despair, so that he laughed loud and long, did Goodman Brown grasp his staff and set forth again, at such a rate that he seemed to fly along the forest path rather than to walk or run. The road grew wilder and drearier and more faintly traced, and vanished at length, leaving him in the heart of the dark wilderness, still rushing onward with the instinct that guides mortal man to evil. The whole forest was peopled with frightful sounds — the creaking of the trees, the howling of wild beasts, and the yell of Indians; while sometimes the wind tolled like a distant church bell, and sometimes gave a broad roar around the traveler, as if all Nature were laughing him to scorn. But he was himself the chief horror of the scene, and shrank not from its other horrors.

"Ha! ha! ha!" roared Goodman Brown when the wind laughed at him. "Let us hear which will laugh loudest. Think not to frighten me with your deviltry. Come witch, come wizard, come Indian powwow, come devil himself, and here comes Goodman Brown. You may as well fear him as he fear you."

In truth, all through the haunted forest there could be nothing more frightful than the figure of Goodman Brown. On he flew among the black pines, brandishing his staff with frenzied gestures, now giving vent to an inspiration of horrid blasphemy, and now shouting forth such laughter as set all the echoes of the forest laughing like demons around him. The fiend in his own shape is less hideous than when he rages in the breast of man. Thus sped the demoniac on his course, until, quivering among the trees, he saw a red light before him, as when the felled trunks and branches of a clearing have been set on fire, and throw up their lurid blaze against the sky, at the hour of midnight. He paused, in a lull of the tempest that had driven him onward, and heard the swell of what seemed a hymn, rolling solemnly from a distance with the weight of many voices. He knew the tune; it was a familiar one in the choir of the village meeting-house. The verse died heavily away, and was lengthened by a chorus, not of human voices, but of all the sounds of the benighted wilderness pealing in awful harmony together. Goodman Brown cried out, and his cry was lost to his own ear by its unison with the cry of the desert.

In the interval of silence he stole forward until the light glared full upon his eyes. At one extremity of an open space, hemmed in by the dark wall of the forest, arose a rock, bearing some rude, natural resemblance either to an altar or a pulpit, and surrounded by four blazing pines, their tops aflame, their stems untouched, like candles at an evening meeting. The mass of foliage that had overgrown the summit of the rock was all on fire, blazing high into the night and fitfully illuminating the whole field. Each pendent twig and leafy festoon was in a blaze. As the red light arose and fell, a numerous congregation alternately shone forth, then disappeared in shadow, and again grew, as it were, out of the darkness, peopling the heart of the solitary woods at once.

"A grave and dark-clad company," quoth Goodman Brown.   55

In truth they were such. Among them, quivering to and fro between gloom and splendor, appeared faces that would be seen next day at the council board of the province, and others which, Sabbath after Sabbath, looked devoutly heavenward, and benignantly over the crowded pews, from the holiest pulpits in the land. Some affirm that the lady of the governor was there. At least there were high dames well known to her, and wives of honored husbands, and widows, a great multitude, and ancient maidens, all of excellent repute, and fair young girls, who trembled lest their mothers should espy them. Either the sudden gleams of light flashing over the obscure field bedazzled Goodman Brown, or he recognized a score of the church members of Salem village famous for their especial sanctity. Good old Deacon Gookin had arrived, and waited at the skirts of that venerable saint, his revered pastor. But, irreverently consorting with these grave, reputable, and pious people, these elders of the church, these chaste dames and dewy virgins, there were men of dissolute lives and women of spotted fame, wretches given over to all mean and filthy vice, and suspected even of horrid crimes. It was strange to see that the good shrank not from the wicked, nor were the sinners abashed by the saints. Scattered also among their pale-faced enemies were the Indian priests, or powwows, who had often scared their native forest with more hideous incantations than any known to English witchcraft.

"But where is Faith?" thought Goodman Brown; and, as hope came into his heart, he trembled.

Another verse of the hymn arose, a slow and mournful strain, such as the pious love, but joined to words which expressed all that our nature can conceive of sin, and darkly hinted at far more. Unfathomable to mere mortals is the lore of fiends. Verse after verse was sung; and still the chorus of the desert swelled between like the deepest tone of a mighty organ; and with the final peal of that dreadful anthem there came a sound, as if the roaring wind, the rushing streams, the howling beasts, and every other voice of the unconcerted wilderness were mingling and according with the voice of guilty man in homage to the prince of all. The four blazing pines threw up a loftier flame, and obscurely discovered shapes and visages of horror on the smoke wreaths above the impious assembly. At the same moment the fire on the rock shot redly forth and formed a glowing arch above its base, where now appeared a figure. With reverence be it spoken, the figure bore no slight similitude, both in garb and manner, to some grave divine of the New England churches.

"Bring forth the converts!" cried a voice that echoed through the field and rolled into the forest.

At the word, Goodman Brown stepped forth from the shadow of the trees 60 and approached the congregation, with whom he felt a loathful brotherhood by the sympathy of all that was wicked in his heart. He could have well-nigh sworn that the shape of his own dead father beckoned him to advance, looking downward from a smoke wreath, while a woman, with dim features of despair, threw out her hand to warn him back. Was it his mother? But he had no power to retreat one step, nor to resist, even in thought, when the minister and good old Deacon Gookin seized his arms and led him to the blazing rock. Thither came also the slender form of a veiled female, led between Goody Cloyse, that pious teacher of the catechism, and Martha Carrier, who had received the devil's promise to be queen of hell. A rampant hag was she. And there stood the proselytes beneath the canopy of fire.

"Welcome, my children," said the dark figure, "to the communion of your race. Ye have found thus young your nature and your destiny. My children, look behind you!"

They turned; and flashing forth, as it were, in a sheet of flame, the fiend worshipers were seen; the smile of welcome gleamed darkly on every visage.

"There," resumed the sable form, "are all whom ye have reverenced from youth. Ye deemed them holier than yourselves and shrank from your own sin, contrasting it with their lives of righteousness and prayerful aspirations heavenward. Yet here are they all in my worshiping assembly. This night it shall be granted you to know their secret deeds: how hoary-bearded elders of the church have whispered wanton words to the young maids of their households; how many a woman, eager for widows' weeds, has given her husband a drink at bedtime and let him sleep his last sleep in her bosom; how beardless youths have made haste to inherit their fathers' wealth; and how fair damsels — blush not, sweet ones — have dug little graves in the garden, and bidden me, the sole guest, to an infant's funeral. By the sympathy of your human hearts for sin ye shall scent out all the places — whether in church, bedchamber, street, field, or forest — where crime has been committed, and shall exult to behold the whole earth one stain of guilt, one mighty blood spot. Far more than this. It shall be yours to penetrate, in every bosom, the deep mystery of sin, the fountain of all wicked arts, and which inexhaustibly supplies more evil impulses than human power — than my power at its utmost — can make manifest in deeds. And now, my children, look upon each other."

They did so; and, by the blaze of the hell-kindled torches, the wretched man beheld his Faith, and the wife her husband, trembling before that unhallowed altar.

"Lo, there ye stand, my children," said the figure, in a deep and solemn tone, 65 almost sad with its despairing awfulness, as if his once angelic nature could yet mourn for our miserable race. "Depending upon one another's hearts, ye had still hoped that virtue were not all a dream. Now are ye undeceived. Evil is the nature of mankind. Evil must be your only happiness. Welcome again, my children, to the communion of your race."

"Welcome," repeated the fiend worshipers; in one cry of despair and triumph.

And there they stood, the only pair, as it seemed, who were yet hesitating on the verge of wickedness in this dark world. A basin was hollowed, naturally, in the rock. Did it contain water, reddened by the lurid light? or was it blood? or, perchance, a liquid flame? Herein did the shape of evil dip his hand and prepare to lay the mark of baptism upon their foreheads, that they might be partakers of the mystery of sin, more conscious of the secret guilt of others, both in deed and thought, than they could now be of their own. The husband cast one look at his pale wife, and Faith at him. What polluted wretches would the next glance show them to each other, shuddering alike at what they disclosed and what they saw!

"Faith! Faith!" cried the husband, "look up to heaven, and resist the wicked one."

Whether Faith obeyed he knew not. Hardly had he spoken when he found himself amid calm night and solitude, listening to a roar of the wind which died heavily away through the forest. He staggered against the rock, and felt it chill and damp; while a hanging twig, that had been all on fire, besprinkled his cheek with the coldest dew.

The next morning young Goodman Brown came slowly into the street of ⁊₀ Salem village, staring around him like a bewildered man. The good old minister was taking a walk along the graveyard to get an appetite for breakfast and meditate his sermon, and bestowed a blessing, as he passed, on Goodman Brown. He shrank from the venerable saint as if to avoid an anathema. Old Deacon Gookin was at domestic worship, and the holy words of his prayer were heard through the open window. "What God doth the wizard pray to?" quoth Goodman Brown. Goody Cloyse, that excellent old Christian, stood in the early sunshine at her own lattice, catechizing a little girl who had brought her a pint of morning's milk. Goodman Brown snatched away the child as from the grasp of the fiend himself. Turning the corner by the meeting-house, he spied the head of Faith, with the pink ribbons, gazing anxiously forth, and bursting into such joy at sight of him that she skipped along the street and almost kissed her husband before the whole village. But Goodman Brown looked sternly and sadly into her face, and passed on without a greeting.

Had Goodman Brown fallen asleep in the forest and only dreamed a wild dream of a witch-meeting?

Be it so if you will; but, alas! it was a dream of evil omen for young Goodman Brown. A stern, a sad, a darkly meditative, a distrustful, if not a desperate man did he become from the night of that fearful dream. On the Sabbath day, when the congregation were singing a holy psalm, he could not listen because an anthem of sin rushed loudly upon his ear and drowned all the blessed strain. When the minister spoke from the pulpit with power and fervid eloquence, and, with his hand on the open Bible, of the sacred truths of our religion, and of saintlike lives and triumphant deaths, and of future bliss or misery unutterable, then did Goodman Brown turn pale, dreading lest the roof should thunder down upon the gray blasphemer and his hearers. Often, awaking suddenly at midnight, he shrank from the bosom of Faith; and at morning or eventide, when the family knelt down at prayer, he scowled and muttered to himself, and gazed sternly at his wife, and turned away. And when he had lived long, and was borne to his grave a hoary corpse, followed by Faith, an aged woman, and children and grandchildren, a goodly procession, besides neighbors not a few, they carved no hopeful verse upon his tombstone, for his dying hour was gloom.

CONSIDERATIONS FOR CRITICAL THINKING AND WRITING

1. FIRST RESPONSE. Try to summarize "Young Goodman Brown" with a tidy moral. Is it possible? What makes this story complex?

2. What is the significance of Goodman Brown's name?

3. What is the symbolic value of the forest in this story? How are the descriptions of the forest contrasted with those of Salem village?

4. Characterize Goodman Brown at the beginning of the story. Why does he go into the forest? What does he mean when he says "Faith kept me back a while" (para. 12)?

5. What function do Faith's ribbons have in the story?

6. What foreshadows Goodman Brown's meeting with his "fellow-traveler" (para. 14)? Who is he? How do we know that Brown is keeping an appointment with a supernatural being?

7. The narrator describes the fellow-traveler's staff wriggling like a snake but then says, "This, of course, must have been an ocular deception, assisted by the uncertain light" (para. 13). What is the effect of this and other instances of ambiguity in the story?

8. What does Goodman Brown discover in the forest? What does he come to think of his ancestors, the church and state, Goody Cloyse, and even his wife?

9. Is Salem populated by hypocrites who cover hideous crimes with a veneer of piety and respectability? Do Faith and the other characters Brown sees when he returns from the forest appear corrupt to you?

10. Near the end of the story the narrator asks, "Had Goodman Brown fallen asleep in the forest and only dreamed a wild dream of a witch-meeting?" (para. 71). Was it a dream, or did the meeting actually happen? How does the answer to this question affect your reading of the story? Write an essay giving an answer to the narrator's question.

11. How is Goodman Brown changed by his experience in the forest? Does the narrator endorse Brown's unwillingness to trust anyone?

12. Consider the story as a criticism of the village's hypocrisy.

13. CRITICAL STRATEGIES. Read the section on psychological criticism (pp. 1649–51) in Chapter 51, "Critical Strategies for Reading," and discuss this story as an inward, psychological journey in which Goodman Brown discovers the power of blackness in himself but refuses to acknowledge that dimension of his personality.

CONNECTIONS TO OTHER SELECTIONS

1. Compare and contrast Goodman Brown's reasons for withdrawal with those of Melville's Bartleby (p. 130). Do you find yourself more sympathetic with one character than the other? Explain.

2. To what extent is Hawthorne's use of dreams crucial in this story and in "The Birthmark" (p. 339)? Explain how Hawthorne uses dreams as a means to complicate our view of his characters.

3. What does Goodman Brown's pursuit of sin have in common with Aylmer's quest for perfection in "The Birthmark"? How do these pursuits reveal the characters' personalities and shed light on the theme of each story?

The Minister's Black Veil   1836

A Parable°

The sexton stood in the porch of Milford meeting-house, pulling lustily at the bell-rope. The old people of the village came stooping along the street. Children, with bright faces, tript merrily beside their parents, or mimicked a graver gait, in the conscious dignity of their Sunday clothes. Spruce bachelors looked sidelong at the pretty maidens, and fancied that the Sabbath sunshine made them prettier than on weekdays. When the throng had mostly streamed into the porch, the sexton began to toll the bell, keeping his eye on the Reverend Mr. Hooper's door. The first glimpse of the clergyman's figure was the signal for the bell to cease its summons.

"But what has good Parson Hooper got upon his face?" cried the sexton in astonishment.

All within hearing immediately turned about, and beheld the semblance of Mr. Hooper, pacing slowly his meditative way towards the meeting-house. With one accord they started, expressing more wonder than if some strange minister were coming to dust the cushions of Mr. Hooper's pulpit.

"Are you sure it is our parson?" inquired Goodman Gray of the sexton.

"Of a certainty it is good Mr. Hooper," replied the sexton. "He was to have   5 exchanged pulpits with Parson Shute of Westbury; but Parson Shute sent to excuse himself yesterday, being to preach a funeral sermon."

The cause of so much amazement may appear sufficiently slight. Mr. Hooper, a gentlemanly person of about thirty, though still a bachelor, was dressed with due clerical neatness, as if a careful wife had starched his band, and brushed the weekly dust from his Sunday's garb. There was but one thing remarkable in his appearance. Swathed about his forehead, and hanging down over his face, so low as to be shaken by his breath, Mr. Hooper had on a black veil. On a nearer view, it seemed to consist of two folds of crape, which entirely concealed his features, except the mouth and chin, but probably did not intercept his sight, farther than to give a darkened aspect to all living and inanimate things. With this gloomy shade before him, good Mr. Hooper walked onward, at a slow and quiet pace, stooping somewhat and looking on the ground, as is customary with abstracted men, yet nodding kindly to those of his parishioners who still waited on the meeting-house steps. But so wonder-struck were they, that his greeting hardly met with a return.

"I can't really feel as if good Mr. Hooper's face was behind that piece of crape," said the sexton.

"I don't like it," muttered an old woman, as she hobbled into the meeting-house. "He has changed himself into something awful, only by hiding his face."

"Our parson has gone mad!" cried Goodman Gray, following him across the threshold.

Another clergyman in New England, Mr. Joseph Moody, of York, Maine, who died about eighty years since, made himself remarkable by the same eccentricity that is here related of the Reverend Mr. Hooper. In his case, however, the symbol had a different import. In early life he had accidentally killed a beloved friend; and from that day till the hour of his own death, he hid his face from men. [Hawthorne's note.]

A rumor of some unaccountable phenomenon had preceded Mr. Hooper 10 into the meeting-house, and set all the congregation astir. Few could refrain from twisting their heads towards the door; many stood upright, and turned directly about; while several little boys clambered upon the seats, and came down again with a terrible racket. There was a general bustle, a rustling of the women's gowns and shuffling of the men's feet, greatly at variance with that hushed repose which should attend the entrance of the minister. But Mr. Hooper appeared not to notice the perturbation of his people. He entered with an almost noiseless step, bent his head mildly to the pews on each side, and bowed as he passed his oldest parishioner, a white-haired great-grandsire, who occupied an arm-chair in the center of the aisle. It was strange to observe, how slowly this venerable man became conscious of something singular in the appearance of his pastor. He seemed not fully to partake of the prevailing wonder, till Mr. Hooper had ascended the stairs, and showed himself in the pulpit, face to face with his congregation, except for the black veil. That mysterious emblem was never once withdrawn. It shook with his measured breath as he gave out the psalm; it threw its obscurity between him and the holy page, as he read the Scriptures; and while he prayed, the veil lay heavily on his uplifted countenance. Did he seek to hide it from the dread Being whom he was addressing?

Such was the effect of this simple piece of crape, that more than one woman of delicate nerves was forced to leave the meeting-house. Yet perhaps the pale-faced congregation was almost as fearful a sight to the minister, as his black veil to them.

Mr. Hooper had the reputation of a good preacher, but not an energetic one: he strove to win his people heavenward, by mild persuasive influences, rather than to drive them thither, by the thunders of the Word. The sermon which he now delivered, was marked by the same characteristics of style and manner, as the general series of his pulpit oratory. But there was something, either in the sentiment of the discourse itself, or in the imagination of the auditors, which made it greatly the most powerful effort that they had ever heard from their pastor's lips. It was tinged, rather more darkly than usual, with the gentle gloom of Mr. Hooper's temperament. The subject had reference to secret sin, and those sad mysteries which we hide from our nearest and dearest, and would fain conceal from our own consciousness, even forgetting that the Omniscient can detect them. A subtle power was breathed into his words. Each member of the congregation, the most innocent girl, and the man of hardened breast, felt as if the preacher had crept upon them, behind his awful veil, and discovered their hoarded iniquity of deed or thought. Many spread their clasped hands on their bosoms. There was nothing terrible in what Mr. Hooper said; at least, no violence; and yet, with every tremor of his melancholy voice, the hearers quaked. An unsought pathos came hand in hand with awe. So sensible were the audience of some unwonted attribute in their minister, that they longed for a breath of wind to blow aside the veil, almost believing that a stranger's visage would be discovered, though the form, gesture, and voice were those of Mr. Hooper.

At the close of the services, the people hurried out with indecorous confusion, eager to communicate their pent-up amazement, and conscious of lighter spirits, the moment they lost sight of the black veil. Some gathered in little circles, huddled closely together, with their mouths all whispering in the center; some went homeward alone, wrapt in silent meditation; some talked loudly, and profaned the Sabbath-day with ostentatious laughter. A few shook their sagacious heads, intimating that they could penetrate the mystery; while one or two affirmed that there was no mystery at all, but only that Mr. Hooper's eyes were so weakened by the midnight lamp, as to require a shade. After a brief interval, forth came good Mr. Hooper also, in the rear of his flock. Turning his veiled face from one group to another, he paid due reverence to the hoary heads, saluted the middle-aged with kind dignity, as their friend and spiritual guide, greeted the young with mingled authority and love, and laid his hands on the little children's heads to bless them. Such was always his custom on the Sabbath-day. Strange and bewildered looks repaid him for his courtesy. None, as on former occasions, aspired to the honor of walking by their pastor's side. Old Squire Saunders, doubtless by an accidental lapse of memory, neglected to invite Mr. Hooper to his table, where the good clergyman had been wont to bless the food, almost every Sunday since his settlement. He returned, therefore, to the parsonage, and, at the moment of closing the door, was observed to look back upon the people, all of whom had their eyes fixed upon the minister. A sad smile gleamed faintly from beneath the black veil, and flickered about his mouth, glimmering as he disappeared.

"How strange," said a lady, "that a simple black veil, such as any woman might wear on her bonnet, should become such a terrible thing on Mr. Hooper's face!"

"Something must surely be amiss with Mr. Hooper's intellects," observed 15 her husband, the physician of the village. "But the strangest part of the affair is the effect of this vagary, even on a sober-minded man like myself. The black veil, though it covers only our pastor's face, throws its influence over his whole person, and makes him ghost-like from head to foot. Do you not feel it so?"

"Truly do I," replied the lady; "and I would not be alone with him for the world. I wonder he is not afraid to be alone with himself!"

"Men sometimes are so," said her husband.

That afternoon service was attended with similar circumstances. At its conclusion, the bell tolled for the funeral of a young lady. The relatives and friends were assembled in the house, and the more distant acquaintances stood about the door, speaking of the good qualities of the deceased, when their talk was interrupted by the appearance of Mr. Hooper, still covered with his black veil. It was now an appropriate emblem. The clergyman stepped into the room where the corpse was laid, and bent over the coffin, to take a last farewell of his deceased parishioner. As he stooped, the veil hung straight down from his forehead, so that, if her eye-lids had not been closed for ever, the dead maiden might have seen his face. Could Mr. Hooper be fearful of her glance, that he so hastily caught back the black veil? A person, who watched the interview between the dead and living, scrupled not to affirm, that, at the instant when the clergyman's features were disclosed, the corpse had slightly shuddered, rustling the shroud and muslin cap, though the countenance retained the composure of death. A superstitious old woman was the only witness of this prodigy. From the coffin, Mr. Hooper passed into the chamber of the mourners, and thence to the head of the staircase, to make the funeral prayer. It was a tender and heart-dissolving prayer, full of sorrow, yet so imbued with celestial hopes, that the music of a heavenly harp, swept by the fingers of the dead, seemed faintly to be heard among the saddest accents of the minister. The people trembled, though they but darkly understood him, when he prayed that they, and himself, and all of mortal race, might be ready, as he trusted this young maiden had been, for the dreadful hour that should snatch the veil from their faces. The bearers went heavily forth, and the mourners followed, saddening all the street, with the dead before them, and Mr. Hooper in his black veil behind.

"Why do you look back?" said one in the procession to his partner.

"I had a fancy," replied she, "that the minister and the maiden's spirit were 20 walking hand in hand."

"And so had I, at the same moment," said the other.

That night, the handsomest couple in Milford village were to be joined in wedlock. Though reckoned a melancholy man, Mr. Hooper had a placid cheerfulness for such occasions, which often excited a sympathetic smile, where livelier merriment would have been thrown away. There was no quality of his disposition which made him more beloved than this. The company at the wedding awaited his arrival with impatience, trusting that the strange awe, which had gathered over him throughout the day, would now be dispelled. But such was not the result. When Mr. Hooper came, the first thing that their eyes rested on was the same horrible black veil, which had added deeper gloom to the funeral, and could portend nothing but evil to the wedding. Such was its immediate effect on the guests, that a cloud seemed to have rolled duskily from beneath the black crape, and dimmed the light of the candles. The bridal pair stood up before the minister. But the bride's cold fingers quivered in the tremulous hand of the bridegroom, and her deathlike paleness caused a whisper, that the maiden who had been buried a few hours before, was come from her grave to be married. If ever another wedding were so dismal, it was that famous one, where they tolled the wedding-knell. After performing the ceremony, Mr. Hooper raised a glass of wine to his lips, wishing happiness to the new-married couple, in a strain of mild pleasantry that ought to have brightened the features of the guests, like a cheerful gleam from the hearth. At that instant, catching a glimpse of his figure in the looking-glass, the black veil involved his own spirit in the horror with which it overwhelmed all others. His frame shuddered — his lips grew white — he spilt the untasted wine upon the carpet — and rushed forth into the darkness. For the Earth, too, had on her Black Veil.

The next day, the whole village of Milford talked of little else than Parson Hooper's black veil. That, and the mystery concealed behind it, supplied a topic for discussion between acquaintances meeting in the street, and good women gossiping at their open windows. It was the first item of news that the tavernkeeper told to his guests. The children babbled of it on their way to school. One imitative little imp covered his face with an old black handkerchief, thereby so affrighting his playmates, that the panic seized himself, and he well nigh lost his wits by his own waggery.

It was remarkable, that, of all the busy-bodies and impertinent people in the parish, not one ventured to put the plain question to Mr. Hooper, wherefore he did this thing. Hitherto, whenever there appeared the slightest call for such interference, he had never lacked advisers, nor shown himself averse to be guided by their judgment. If he erred at all, it was by so painful a degree of self-distrust, that even the mildest censure would lead him to consider an indifferent action as a crime. Yet, though so well acquainted with this amiable weakness, no individual among his parishioners chose to make the black veil a subject of friendly remonstrance. There was a feeling of dread, neither plainly confessed nor carefully concealed, which caused each to shift the responsibility upon another, till at length it was found expedient to send a deputation of the church, in order to deal with Mr. Hooper about the mystery, before it should grow into a scandal. Never did an embassy so ill discharge its duties. The minister received them with friendly courtesy, but became silent, after they were seated, leaving to his visitors the whole burthen of introducing their important business. The topic, it might be supposed, was obvious enough. There was the black veil, swathed round Mr. Hooper's forehead, and concealing every feature above his placid mouth, on which, at times, they could perceive the glimmering of a melancholy smile. But that piece of crape, to their imagination, seemed to hang down before his heart, the symbol of a fearful secret between him and them. Were the veil but cast aside, they might speak freely of it, but not till then. Thus they sat a considerable time, speechless, confused, and shrinking uneasily from Mr. Hooper's eye, which they felt to be fixed upon them with an invisible glance. Finally, the deputies returned abashed to their constituents, pronouncing the matter too weighty to be handled, except by a council of the churches, if, indeed, it might not require a general synod.

But there was one person in the village, unappalled by the awe with which the black veil had impressed all beside herself. When the deputies returned without an explanation, or even venturing to demand one, she, with the calm energy of her character, determined to chase away the strange cloud that appeared to be settling round Mr. Hooper, every moment more darkly than before. As his plighted wife, it should be her privilege to know what the black veil concealed. At the minister's first visit, therefore, she entered upon the subject, with a direct simplicity, which made the task easier both for him and her. After he had seated himself, she fixed her eyes steadfastly upon the veil, but could discern nothing of the dreadful gloom that had so overawed the multitude: it was but a double fold of crape, hanging down from his forehead to his mouth, and slightly stirring with his breath.

"No," said she aloud, and smiling, "there is nothing terrible in this piece of crape, except that it hides a face which I am always glad to look upon. Come, good sir, let the sun shine from behind the cloud. First lay aside your black veil: then tell me why you put it on."

Mr. Hooper's smile glimmered faintly.

"There is an hour to come," said he, "when all of us shall cast aside our veils. Take it not amiss, beloved friend, if I wear this piece of crape till then."

"Your words are a mystery too," returned the young lady. "Take away the veil for them, at least."

"Elizabeth, I will," said he, "so far as my vow may suffer me. Know, then, this veil is a type and a symbol, and I am bound to wear it ever, both in light and darkness, in solitude and before the gaze of multitudes, and as with strangers, so with my familiar friends. No mortal eye will see it withdrawn. This dismal shade must separate me from the world: even you, Elizabeth, can never come behind it!"

"What grievous affliction hath befallen you," she earnestly inquired, "that you should thus darken your eyes for ever?"

"If it be a sign of mourning," replied Mr. Hooper, "I, perhaps, like most other mortals, have sorrows dark enough to be typified by a black veil."

"But what if the world will not believe that it is the type of an innocent sorrow?" urged Elizabeth. "Beloved and respected as you are, there may be whispers, that you hide your face under the consciousness of secret sin. For the sake of your holy office, do away this scandal!"

The color rose into her cheeks, as she intimated the nature of the rumors that were already abroad in the village. But Mr. Hooper's mildness did not forsake him. He even smiled again — that same sad smile, which always appeared like a faint glimmering of light, proceeding from the obscurity beneath the veil.

"If I hide my face for sorrow, there is cause enough," he merely replied; "and if I cover it for secret sin, what mortal might not do the same?"

And with this gentle, but unconquerable obstinacy, did he resist all her entreaties. At length Elizabeth sat silent. For a few moments she appeared lost in thought, considering, probably, what new methods might be tried, to withdraw her lover from so dark a fantasy, which, if it had no other meaning, was perhaps a symptom of mental disease. Though of a firmer character than his own, the tears rolled down her cheeks. But, in an instant, as it were, a new feeling took the place of sorrow: her eyes were fixed insensibly on the black veil, when, like a sudden twilight in the air, its terrors fell around her. She arose, and stood trembling before him.

"And do you feel it then at last?" said he mournfully.

She made no reply, but covered her eyes with her hand, and turned to leave the room. He rushed forward and caught her arm.

"Have patience with me, Elizabeth!" cried he passionately. "Do not desert me, though this veil must be between us here on earth. Be mine, and hereafter there shall be no veil over my face, no darkness between our souls! It is but a mortal veil — it is not for eternity! Oh! you know not how lonely I am, and how frightened to be alone behind my black veil. Do not leave me in this miserable obscurity for ever!"

"Lift the veil but once, and look me in the face," said she.   40

"Never! It cannot be!" replied Mr. Hooper.

"Then, farewell!" said Elizabeth.

She withdrew her arm from his grasp, and slowly departed, pausing at the door, to give one long, shuddering gaze, that seemed almost to penetrate the mystery of the black veil. But, even amid his grief, Mr. Hooper smiled to think that only a material emblem had separated him from happiness, though the horrors which it shadowed forth, must be drawn darkly between the fondest of lovers.

From that time no attempts were made to remove Mr. Hooper's black veil, or, by a direct appeal, to discover the secret which it was supposed to hide. By persons who claimed a superiority to popular prejudice, it was reckoned merely an eccentric whim, such as often mingles with the sober actions of men otherwise rational, and tinges them all with its own semblance of insanity. But with the multitude, good Mr. Hooper was irreparably a bugbear. He could not walk the streets with any peace of mind, so conscious was he that the gentle and timid would turn aside to avoid him, and that others would make it a point of hardihood to throw themselves in his way. The impertinence of the latter class compelled him to give up his customary walk, at sunset, to the burial ground, for when he leaned pensively over the gate, there would always be faces behind the grave-stones, peeping at his black veil. A fable went the rounds that the stare of the dead people drove him thence. It grieved him, to the very depth of his kind heart, to observe how the children fled from his approach, breaking up their merriest sports, while his melancholy figure was yet afar off. Their instinctive dread caused him to feel, more strongly than aught else, that a preternatural horror was interwoven with the threads of the black crape. In truth, his own antipathy to the veil was known to be so great, that he never willingly passed before a mirror, nor stooped to drink at a still fountain, lest, in its peaceful bosom, he should be affrighted by himself. This was what gave plausibility to the whispers, that Mr. Hooper's conscience tortured him for some great crime, too horrible to be entirely concealed, or otherwise than so obscurely intimated. Thus, from beneath the black veil, there rolled a cloud into the sunshine, an ambiguity of sin or sorrow, which enveloped the poor minister, so that love or sympathy could never reach him. It was said, that ghost and fiend consorted with him there. With self-shudderings and outward terrors, he walked continually in its shadow, groping darkly within his own soul, or gazing through a medium that saddened the whole world. Even the lawless wind, it was believed, respected his dreadful secret, and never blew aside the veil. But still good Mr. Hooper sadly smiled, at the pale visages of the worldly throng as he passed by.

Among all its bad influences, the black veil had the one desirable effect, 45 of making its wearer a very efficient clergyman. By the aid of his mysterious emblem — for there was no other apparent cause — he became a man of awful power, over souls that were in agony for sin. His converts always regarded him with a dread peculiar to themselves, affirming, though but figuratively, that, before he brought them to celestial light, they had been with him behind the black veil. Its gloom, indeed, enabled him to sympathize with all dark affections. Dying sinners cried aloud for Mr. Hooper, and would not yield their breath till he appeared; though ever, as he stooped to whisper consolation, they shuddered at the veiled face so near their own. Such were the terrors of the black veil, even when Death had bared his visage! Strangers came long distances to attend service at his church, with the mere idle purpose of gazing at his figure, because it was forbidden them to behold his face. But many were made to quake ere they departed! Once, during Governor Belcher's administration, Mr. Hooper was appointed to preach the election sermon. Covered with his black veil, he stood before the chief magistrate, the council, and the representatives, and wrought so deep an impression, that the legislative measures of that year were characterized by all the gloom and piety of our earliest ancestral sway.

In this manner Mr. Hooper spent a long life, irreproachable in outward act, yet shrouded in dismal suspicions; kind and loving, though unloved, and dimly feared; a man apart from men, shunned in their health and joy, but ever summoned to their aid in mortal anguish. As years wore on, shedding their snows above his sable veil, he acquired a name throughout the New-England churches, and they called him Father Hooper. Nearly all his parishioners, who were of mature age when he was settled, had been borne away by many a funeral: he had one congregation in the church, and a more crowded one in the churchyard; and having wrought so late into the evening, and done his work so well, it was now good Father Hooper's turn to rest.

Several persons were visible by the shaded candlelight, in the death-chamber of the old clergyman. Natural connections he had none. But there was the decorously grave, though unmoved physician, seeking only to mitigate the last pangs of the patient whom he could not save. There were the deacons, and other eminently pious members of his church. There, also, was the Reverend Mr. Clark, of Westbury, a young and zealous divine, who had ridden in haste to pray by the bedside of the expiring minister. There was the nurse, no hired handmaiden of death, but one whose calm affection had endured thus long, in secrecy, in solitude, amid the chill of age, and would not perish, even at the dying hour. Who, but Elizabeth! And there lay the hoary head of good Father Hooper upon the death-pillow, with the black veil still swathed about his brow and reaching down over his face, so that each more difficult gasp of his faint breath caused it to stir. All through life that piece of crape had hung between him and the world: it had separated him from cheerful brotherhood and woman's love, and kept him in that saddest of all prisons, his own heart; and still it lay upon his face, as if to deepen the gloom of his darksome chamber, and shade him from the sunshine of eternity.

For some time previous, his mind had been confused, wavering doubtfully between the past and the present, and hovering forward, as it were, at intervals, into the indistinctness of the world to come. There had been feverish turns, which tossed him from side to side, and wore away what little strength he had. But in his most convulsive struggles, and in the wildest vagaries of his intellect, when no other thought retained its sober influence, he still showed an awful solicitude lest the black veil should slip aside. Even if his bewildered soul could have forgotten, there was a faithful woman at his pillow, who, with averted eyes, would have covered that aged face, which she had last beheld in the comeliness of manhood. At length the death-stricken old man lay quietly in the torpor of mental and bodily exhaustion, with an imperceptible pulse, and breath that grew fainter and fainter, except when a long, deep, and irregular inspiration seemed to prelude the flight of his spirit.

The minister of Westbury approached the bedside.

"Venerable Father Hooper," said he, "the moment of your release is at hand.   50 Are you ready for the lifting of the veil, that shuts in time from eternity?"

Father Hooper at first replied merely by a feeble motion of his head; then, apprehensive, perhaps, that his meaning might be doubtful, he exerted himself to speak.

"Yea," said he, in faint accents, "my soul hath a patient weariness until that veil be lifted."

"And is it fitting," resumed the Reverend Mr. Clark, "that a man so given to prayer, of such a blameless example, holy in deed and thought, so far as mortal judgment may pronounce; is it fitting that a father in the church should leave a shadow on his memory, that may seem to blacken a life so pure? I pray you, my venerable brother, let not this thing be! Suffer us to be gladdened by your triumphant aspect, as you go to your reward. Before the veil of eternity be lifted, let me cast aside this black veil from your face!"

And thus speaking, the Reverend Mr. Clark bent forward to reveal the mystery of so many years. But, exerting a sudden energy, that made all the beholders stand aghast, Father Hooper snatched both his hands from beneath the bedclothes, and pressed them strongly on the black veil, resolute to struggle, if the minister of Westbury would contend with a dying man.

"Never!" cried the veiled clergyman. "On earth, never!"   55

"Dark old man!" exclaimed the affrighted minister, "with what horrible crime upon your soul are you now passing to the judgment?"

Father Hooper's breath heaved; it rattled in his throat; but, with a mighty effort, grasping forward with his hands, he caught hold of life, and held it back till he should speak. He even raised himself in bed; and there he sat, shivering with the arms of death around him, while the black veil hung down, awful, at that last moment, in the gathered terrors of a life-time. And yet the faint, sad smile, so often there, now seemed to glimmer from its obscurity, and linger on Father Hooper's lips.

"Why do you tremble at me alone?" cried he, turning his veiled face round the circle of pale spectators. "Tremble also at each other! Have men avoided me, and women shown no pity, and children screamed and fled, only for my black veil? What, but the mystery which it obscurely typifies, has made this piece of crape so awful? When the friend shows his inmost heart to his friend; the lover to his best-beloved; when man does not vainly shrink from the eye of his Creator, loathsomely treasuring up the secret of his sin; then deem me a monster, for the symbol beneath which I have lived, and die! I look around me, and, lo! on every visage a Black Veil!"

While his auditors shrank from one another, in mutual affright, Father Hooper fell back upon his pillow, a veiled corpse, with a faint smile lingering on the lips. Still veiled, they laid him in his coffin, and a veiled corpse they bore him to the grave. The grass of many years has sprung up and withered on that grave, the burial-stone is moss-grown, and good Mr. Hooper's face is dust; but awful is still the thought, that it moldered beneath the Black Veil!

CONSIDERATIONS FOR CRITICAL THINKING AND WRITING

1. FIRST RESPONSE. Why do you think Hooper wears the veil? Explain whether you think Hooper is right or wrong to wear it.
2. Describe the veil Hooper wears. How does it affect his vision?
3. Characterize the townspeople. How does the community react to the veil?
4. What is Hooper's explanation for why he wears the veil? Is he more or less effective as a minister because he wears it?
5. What is the one feature of Hooper's face that we see? What does that feature reveal about him?
6. Describe what happens at the funeral and wedding ceremonies at which Hooper officiates. How are the incidents at these events organized around the veil?
7. Why does Elizabeth think "it should be her privilege to know what the black veil concealed" (para. 25)? Why doesn't Hooper remove it at her request?
8. How does Elizabeth react to Hooper's refusal to take off the veil? Why is her response especially significant?
9. How do others in town explain why Hooper wears the veil? Do these explanations seem adequate to you? Why or why not?
10. Why is Hooper buried with the veil? Of what significance is it that grass "withered" on his grave (para. 59)?
11. Describe the story's point of view. How would a first-person narrative change the story dramatically?

CONNECTIONS TO OTHER SELECTIONS

1. How might this story be regarded as a sequel to "Young Goodman Brown"? How are the themes similar?
2. Explain how Faith in "Young Goodman Brown," Georgiana in "The Birthmark" (below), and Elizabeth in "The Minister's Black Veil" are used to reveal some truth about the central male characters in each story. Describe the similarities that you see among these women characters.
3. Compare Hawthorne's use of symbol in "The Minister's Black Veil" and "The Birthmark." Write an essay explaining which symbol you think works more effectively to evoke the theme of its story.

The Birthmark   1843

In the latter part of the last century there lived a man of science, an eminent proficient in every branch of natural philosophy, who not long before our story opens had made experience of a spiritual affinity more attractive than any chemical one. He had left his laboratory to the care of an assistant, cleared his fine countenance from the furnace smoke, washed the stain of acids from his fingers, and persuaded a beautiful woman to become his wife. In those days when the comparatively recent discovery of electricity and other kindred mysteries of Nature seemed to open paths into the region of miracle, it was not unusual for the love of science to rival the love of woman in its depth and absorbing energy. The higher intellect, the imagination, the spirit, and even the heart might all find their congenial aliment in pursuits which, as some of their ardent votaries believed, would ascend from one step of powerful intelligence to another, until the philosopher should lay his hand on the secret of creative force and perhaps make new worlds for himself. We know not whether Aylmer possessed this degree of faith in man's ultimate control over Nature. He had devoted himself, however, too unreservedly to scientific studies ever to be weaned from them by any second passion. His love for his young wife might prove the stronger of the two; but it could only be by intertwining itself with his love of science, and uniting the strength of the latter to his own.

Such a union accordingly took place, and was attended with truly remarkable consequences and a deeply impressive moral. One day, very soon after their marriage, Aylmer sat gazing at his wife with a trouble in his countenance that grew stronger until he spoke.

"Georgiana," said he, "has it never occurred to you that the mark upon your cheek might be removed?"

"No, indeed," said she, smiling; but perceiving the seriousness of his manner, she blushed deeply. "To tell you the truth it has been so often called a charm that I was simple enough to imagine it might be so."

"Ah, upon another face perhaps it might," replied her husband; "but never on 5 yours. No, dearest Georgiana, you came so nearly perfect from the hand of Nature that this slightest possible defect, which we hesitate whether to term a defect or a beauty, shocks me, as being the visible mark of earthly imperfection."

"Shocks you, my husband!" cried Georgiana, deeply hurt; at first reddening with momentary anger, but then bursting into tears. "Then why did you take me from my mother's side? You cannot love what shocks you!"

To explain this conversation it must be mentioned that in the center of Georgiana's left cheek there was a singular mark, deeply interwoven, as it were, with the texture and substance of her face. In the usual state of her complexion — a healthy though delicate bloom — the mark wore a tint of deeper crimson, which imperfectly defined its shape amid the surrounding rosiness. When she blushed it gradually became more indistinct, and finally vanished amid the triumphant rush of blood that bathed the whole cheek with its brilliant glow. But if any shifting motion caused her to turn pale, there was the mark again, a crimson stain upon the snow, in what Aylmer sometimes deemed an almost fearful distinctness. Its shape bore not a little similarity to the human hand, though of the smallest pygmy size. Georgiana's lovers were wont to say that some fairy at her birth hour had laid her tiny hand upon the infant's cheek, and left this impress there in token of the magic endowments that were to give her such sway over all hearts. Many a desperate swain would have risked life for the privilege of pressing his lips to the mysterious hand. It must not be concealed, however, that the impression wrought by this fairy sign manual varied exceedingly, according to the difference of temperament in the beholders. Some fastidious persons — but they were exclusively of her own sex — affirmed that the bloody hand, as they chose to call it, quite destroyed the effect of Georgiana's beauty, and rendered her countenance even hideous. But it would be as reasonable to say that one of those small blue stains which sometimes occur in the purest statuary marble would convert the Eve of Powers to a monster. Masculine observers, if the birthmark did not heighten their admiration, contented themselves with wishing it away, that the world might possess one living specimen of ideal loveliness without the semblance of a flaw. After his marriage, — for he thought little or nothing of the matter before, — Aylmer discovered that this was the case with himself.

Had she been less beautiful, — if Envy's self could have found aught else to sneer at, — he might have felt his affection heightened by the prettiness of this mimic hand, now vaguely portrayed, now lost, now stealing forth again and glimmering to and fro with every pulse of emotion that throbbed within her heart; but seeing her otherwise so perfect, he found this one defect grow more and more intolerable with every moment of their united lives. It was the fatal flaw of humanity which Nature, in one shape or another, stamps ineffaceably on all her productions, either to imply that they are temporary and finite, or that their perfection must be wrought by toil and pain. The crimson hand expressed the ineludible gripe° in which mortality clutches the highest and purest of earthly mold, degrading them into kindred with the lowest, and even with the very brutes, like whom their visible frames return to dust. In this manner, selecting it as the symbol of his wife's liability to sin, sorrow, decay, and death, Aylmer's somber imagination was not long in rendering the birthmark a frightful object, causing him more trouble and horror than ever Georgiana's beauty, whether of soul or sense, had given him delight.

At all the seasons which should have been their happiest, he invariably and without intending it, nay, in spite of a purpose to the contrary, reverted to this one disastrous topic. Trifling as it at first appeared, it so connected itself with innumerable trains of thought and modes of feeling that it became the central point of all. With the morning twilight Aylmer opened his eyes upon his wife's face and recognized the symbol of imperfection; and when they sat together at the evening hearth his eyes wandered stealthily to her cheek, and beheld, flickering with the blaze of the wood fire, the spectral hand that wrote mortality where he would fain have worshiped. Georgiana soon learned to shudder at his gaze. It needed but a glance with the peculiar expression that his face often wore to change the roses of her cheek into a deathlike paleness, amid which the crimson hand was brought strongly out, like a bas-relief of ruby on the whitest marble.

Late one night when the lights were growing dim, so as hardly to betray the stain on the poor wife's cheek, she herself, for the first time, voluntarily took up the subject. 10

"Do you remember, my dear Aylmer," said she, with a feeble attempt at a smile, "have you any recollection of a dream last night about this odious hand?"

"None! none whatever!" replied Aylmer, starting; but then he added, in a dry, cold tone, affected for the sake of concealing the real depth of his emotion, "I might well dream of it; for before I fell asleep it had taken a pretty firm hold of my fancy."

"And you did dream of it?" continued Georgiana hastily, for she dreaded lest a gush of tears should interrupt what she had to say. "A terrible dream! I wonder that you can forget it. Is it possible to forget this one expression? — 'It is in her heart now; we must have it out!' Reflect, my husband; for by all means I would have you recall that dream."

The mind is in a sad state when Sleep, the all-involving, cannot confine her specters within the dim region of her sway, but suffers them to break forth,

gripe: Grip.

affrighting this actual life with secrets that perchance belong to a deeper one. Aylmer now remembered his dream. He had fancied himself with his servant Aminadab, attempting an operation for the removal of the birthmark; but the deeper went the knife, the deeper sank the hand, until at length its tiny grasp appeared to have caught hold of Georgiana's heart; whence, however, her husband was inexorably resolved to cut or wrench it away.

When the dream had shaped itself perfectly in his memory, Aylmer sat in his 15 wife's presence with a guilty feeling. Truth often finds its way to the mind close muffled in robes of sleep, and then speaks with uncompromising directness of matters in regard to which we practice an unconscious self-deception during our waking moments. Until now he had not been aware of the tyrannizing influence acquired by one idea over his mind, and of the lengths which he might find in his heart to go for the sake of giving himself peace.

"Aylmer," resumed Georgiana solemnly, "I know not what may be the cost to both of us to rid me of this fatal birthmark. Perhaps its removal may cause cureless deformity; or it may be the stain goes as deep as life itself. Again: do we know that there is a possibility, on any terms, of unclasping the firm grip of this little hand which was laid upon me before I came into the world?"

"Dearest Georgiana, I have spent much thought upon the subject," hastily interrupted Aylmer. "I am convinced of the perfect practicability of its removal."

"If there be the remotest possibility of it," continued Georgiana, "let the attempt be made at whatever risk. Danger is nothing to me; for life, while this hateful mark makes me the object of your horror and disgust, — life is a burden which I would fling down with joy. Either remove this dreadful hand, or take my wretched life! You have deep science. All the world bears witness of it. You have achieved great wonders. Cannot you remove this little, little mark, which I cover with the tips of two small fingers? Is this beyond your power, for the sake of your own peace, and to save your poor wife from madness?"

"Noblest, dearest, tenderest wife," cried Aylmer rapturously, "doubt not my power. I have already given this matter the deepest thought — thought which might almost have enlightened me to create a being less perfect than yourself. Georgiana, you have led me deeper than ever into the heart of science. I feel myself fully competent to render this dear cheek as faultless as its fellow; and then, most beloved, what will be my triumph when I shall have corrected what Nature left imperfect in her fairest work! Even Pygmalion, when his sculptured woman assumed life, felt not greater ecstasy than mine will be."

"It is resolved, then," said Georgiana, faintly smiling. "And, Aylmer, spare me 20 not, though you should find the birthmark take refuge in my heart at last."

Her husband tenderly kissed her cheek — her right cheek — not that which bore the impress of the crimson hand.

The next day Aylmer apprised his wife of a plan that he had formed whereby he might have opportunity for the intense thought and constant watchfulness which the proposed operation would require; while Georgiana, likewise, would enjoy the perfect repose essential to its success. They were to seclude themselves in the extensive apartments occupied by Aylmer as a laboratory, and where, during his toilsome youth, he had made discoveries in the elemental powers of Nature that had roused the admiration of all the learned societies in Europe. Seated calmly in this laboratory, the pale philosopher had investigated the secrets of the highest cloud region and of the profoundest mines; he had satisfied himself of the causes that kindled and kept alive the fires of the volcano; and had explained the mystery of fountains, and how it is that they gush forth, some so bright and pure, and others with such rich medicinal virtues, from the dark bosom of the earth. Here, too, at an earlier period, he had studied the wonders of the human frame, and attempted to fathom the very process by which Nature assimilates all her precious influences from earth and air, and from the spiritual world, to create and foster man, her masterpiece. The latter pursuit, however, Aylmer had long laid aside in unwilling recognition of the truth — against which all seekers sooner or later stumble — that our great creative Mother, while she amuses us with apparently working in the broadest sunshine, is yet severely careful to keep her own secrets, and, in spite of her pretended openness, shows us nothing but results. She permits us, indeed, to mar, but seldom to mend, and, like a jealous patentee, on no account to make. Now, however, Aylmer resumed these half-forgotten investigations, — not, of course, with such hopes or wishes as first suggested them, but because they involved much physiological truth and lay in the path of his proposed scheme for the treatment of Georgiana.

As he led her over the threshold of the laboratory, Georgiana was cold and tremulous. Aylmer looked cheerfully into her face, with intent to reassure her, but was so startled with the intense glow of the birthmark upon the whiteness of her cheek that he could not restrain a strong convulsive shudder. His wife fainted.

"Aminadab! Aminadab!" shouted Aylmer, stamping violently on the floor.

Forthwith there issued from an inner apartment a man of low stature, but 25 bulky frame, with shaggy hair hanging about his visage, which was grimed with the vapors of the furnace. This personage had been Aylmer's underworker during his whole scientific career, and was admirably fitted for that office by his great mechanical readiness, and the skill with which, while incapable of comprehending a single principle, he executed all the details of his master's experiments. With his vast strength, his shaggy hair, his smoky aspect, and the indescribable earthiness that encrusted him, he seemed to represent man's physical nature; while Aylmer's slender figure, and pale, intellectual face, were no less apt a type of the spiritual element.

"Throw open the door of the boudoir, Aminadab," said Aylmer, "and burn a pastille."

"Yes, master," answered Aminadab, looking intently at the lifeless form of Georgiana; and then he muttered to himself, "If she were my wife, I'd never part with that birthmark."

When Georgiana recovered consciousness she found herself breathing an atmosphere of penetrating fragrance, the gentle potency of which had recalled her from her deathlike faintness. The scene around her looked like enchantment. Aylmer had converted those smoky, dingy, somber rooms, where he had spent his brightest years in recondite pursuits, into a series of beautiful apartments not unfit to be the secluded abode of a lovely woman. The walls were hung with gorgeous curtains, which imparted the combination of grandeur and grace that no other species of adornment can achieve; and as they fell from the ceiling to the floor, their rich and ponderous folds, concealing all angles and straight lines, appeared to shut in the scene from infinite space. For aught Georgiana knew, it might be a pavilion among the clouds. And Aylmer, excluding the sunshine, which would have interfered with his chemical processes, had supplied its place with perfumed lamps, emitting flames of various hue, but all uniting in a soft, empurpled radiance. He now knelt by his wife's side, watching her earnestly, but without alarm; for he was confident in his science, and felt that he could draw a magic circle round her within which no evil might intrude.

"Where am I? Ah, I remember," said Georgiana faintly; and she placed her hand over her cheek to hide the terrible mark from her husband's eyes.

"Fear not, dearest!" exclaimed he. "Do not shrink from me! Believe me, Georgiana, I even rejoice in this single imperfection, since it will be such a rapture to remove it." 30

"Oh, spare me!" sadly replied his wife. "Pray do not look at it again. I never can forget that convulsive shudder."

In order to soothe Georgiana, and, as it were, to release her mind from the burden of actual things, Aylmer now put in practice some of the light and playful secrets which science had taught him among its profounder lore. Airy figures, absolutely bodiless ideas, and forms of unsubstantial beauty came and danced before her, imprinting their momentary footsteps on beams of light. Though she had some indistinct idea of the method of these optical phenomena, still the illusion was almost perfect enough to warrant the belief that her husband possessed sway over the spiritual world. Then again, when she felt a wish to look forth from her seclusion, immediately, as if her thoughts were answered, the procession of external existence flitted across a screen. The scenery and the figures of actual life were perfectly represented, but with that bewitching, yet indescribable difference which always makes a picture, an image, or a shadow so much more attractive than the original. When wearied of this, Aylmer bade her cast her eyes upon a vessel containing a quantity of earth. She did so, with little interest at first; but was soon startled to perceive the germ of a plant shooting upward from the soil. Then came the slender stalk; the leaves gradually unfolded themselves; and amid them was a perfect and lovely flower.

"It is magical!" cried Georgiana. "I dare not touch it."

"Nay, pluck it," answered Aylmer: "pluck it, and inhale its brief perfume while you may. The flower will wither in a few moments and leave nothing save its brown seed vessels; but thence may be perpetuated a race as ephemeral as itself."

But Georgiana had no sooner touched the flower than the whole plant suffered 35 a blight, its leaves turning coal-black as if by the agency of fire.

"There was too powerful a stimulus," said Aylmer thoughtfully.

To make up for this abortive experiment, he proposed to take her portrait by a scientific process of his own invention. It was to be effected by rays of light striking upon a polished plate of metal. Georgiana assented; but, on looking at the result, was affrighted to find the features of the portrait blurred and indefinable; while the minute figure of a hand appeared where the cheek should have been. Aylmer snatched the metallic plate and threw it into a jar of corrosive acid.

Soon, however, he forgot these mortifying failures. In the intervals of study and chemical experiment he came to her flushed and exhausted, but seemed invigorated by her presence, and spoke in glowing language of the resources of his art. He gave a history of the long dynasty of the alchemists, who spent so many ages in quest of the universal solvent by which the golden principle might be elicited from all things vile and base. Aylmer appeared to believe that, by the plainest scientific logic, it was altogether within the limits of possibility to discover this long-sought medium; "but," he added, "a philosopher who should go deep enough to acquire the power would attain too lofty a wisdom to stoop to the exercise of it." Not less singular were his opinions in regard to the elixir vitae. He more than intimated that it was at his option to concoct a liquid that should prolong life for years, perhaps interminably; but that it would produce a discord in Nature which all the world, and chiefly the quaffer of the immortal nostrum, would find cause to curse.

"Aylmer, are you in earnest?" asked Georgiana, looking at him with amazement and fear. "It is terrible to possess such power, or even to dream of possessing it."

"Oh, do not tremble, my love," said her husband. "I would not wrong either you 40 or myself by working such inharmonious effects upon our lives; but I would have you consider how trifling, in comparison, is the skill requisite to remove this little hand."

At the mention of the birthmark, Georgiana, as usual, shrank as if a red-hot iron had touched her cheek.

Again Aylmer applied himself to his labors. She could hear his voice in the distant furnace-room giving directions to Aminadab, whose harsh, uncouth, misshapen tones were audible in response, more like the grunt or growl of a brute than human speech. After hours of absence, Aylmer reappeared and proposed that she should now examine his cabinet of chemical products and natural treasures of the earth. Among the former he showed her a small vial, in which, he remarked, was contained a gentle yet most powerful fragrance, capable of impregnating all the breezes that blow across a kingdom. They were of inestimable value, the contents of that little vial; and, as he said so, he threw some of the perfume into the air and filled the room with piercing and invigorating delight.

"And what is this?" asked Georgiana, pointing to a small crystal globe containing a gold-colored liquid. "It is so beautiful to the eye that I could imagine it the elixir of life."

"In one sense it is," replied Aylmer; "or rather, the elixir of immortality. It is the most precious poison that ever was concocted in this world. By its aid I could apportion the lifetime of any mortal at whom you might point your finger. The strength of the dose would determine whether he were to linger out years, or drop dead in the midst of a breath. No king on his guarded throne could keep his life if I, in my private station, should deem that the welfare of millions justified me in depriving him of it."

"Why do you keep such a terrific drug?" inquired Georgiana in horror. 45

"Do not mistrust me, dearest," said her husband, smiling; "its virtuous potency is yet greater than its harmful one. But see! here is a powerful cosmetic. With a few drops of this in a vase of water, freckles may be washed away as easily as the hands are cleansed. A stronger infusion would take the blood out of the cheek, and leave the rosiest beauty a pale ghost."

"Is it with this lotion that you intend to bathe my cheek?" asked Georgiana, anxiously.

"Oh, no," hastily replied her husband; "this is merely superficial. Your case demands a remedy that shall go deeper."

In his interviews with Georgiana, Aylmer generally made minute inquiries as to her sensations and whether the confinement of the rooms and the temperature of the atmosphere agreed with her. These questions had such a particular drift that Georgiana began to conjecture that she was already subjected to certain physical influences, either breathed in with the fragrant air or taken with her food. She fancied likewise, but it might be altogether fancy, that there was a stirring up of her system — a strange, indefinite sensation creeping through her veins, and tingling, half painfully, half pleasurably, at her heart. Still, whenever she dared to look into the mirror, there she beheld herself pale as a white rose and with the crimson birthmark stamped upon her cheek. Not even Aylmer now hated it so much as she.

To dispel the tedium of the hours which her husband found it necessary to 50 devote to the processes of combination and analysis, Georgiana turned over the volumes of his scientific library. In many dark old tomes she met with chapters full of romance and poetry. They were the works of the philosophers of the middle ages, such as Albertus Magnus, Cornelius Agrippa, Paracelsus, and the famous friar who created the prophetic Brazen Head. All these antique naturalists stood in advance of their centuries, yet were imbued with some of their credulity, and therefore were believed, and perhaps imagined themselves to have acquired from the investigation of Nature a power above Nature, and from physics a sway over the spiritual world. Hardly less curious and imaginative were the early volumes of the Transactions of the Royal Society, in which the members, knowing little of the limits of natural possibility, were continually recording wonders or proposing methods whereby wonders might be wrought.

But to Georgiana the most engrossing volume was a large folio from her husband's own hand, in which he had recorded every experiment of his scientific career, its original aim, the methods adopted for its development, and its final success or failure, with the circumstances to which either event was attributable. The book, in truth, was both the history and emblem of his ardent, ambitious, imaginative, yet practical and laborious life. He handled physical details as if there were nothing beyond them; yet spiritualized them all, and redeemed himself from materialism by his strong and eager aspiration towards the infinite. In his grasp the veriest clod of earth assumed a soul. Georgiana, as she read, reverenced Aylmer and loved him more profoundly than ever, but with a less entire dependence on his judgment than heretofore. Much as he had accomplished, she could not but observe that his most splendid successes were almost invariably failures, if compared with the ideal at which he aimed. His brightest diamonds were the merest pebbles, and felt to be so by himself, in comparison with the inestimable gems which lay hidden beyond his reach. The volume, rich with achievements that had won renown for its author, was yet as melancholy a record as ever mortal hand had penned. It was the sad confession and continual exemplification of the shortcomings of the composite man, the spirit burdened with clay and working in matter, and of the despair that assails the higher nature at finding itself so miserably thwarted by the earthly part. Perhaps every man of genius in whatever sphere might recognize the image of his own experience in Aylmer's journal.

So deeply did these reflections affect Georgiana that she laid her face upon the open volume and burst into tears. In this situation she was found by her husband.

"It is dangerous to read in a sorcerer's books," said he with a smile, though his countenance was uneasy and displeased. "Georgiana, there are pages in that volume which I can scarcely glance over and keep my senses. Take heed lest it prove as detrimental to you."

"It has made me worship you more than ever," said she.

"Ah, wait for this one success," rejoined he, "then worship me if you will. I shall deem myself hardly unworthy of it. But come, I have sought you for the luxury of your voice. Sing to me, dearest."

So she poured out the liquid music of her voice to quench the thirst of his spirit. He then took his leave with a boyish exuberance of gaiety, assuring her that her seclusion would endure but a little longer, and that the result was already certain. Scarcely had he departed when Georgiana felt irresistibly impelled to follow him. She had forgotten to inform Aylmer of a symptom which for two or three hours past had begun to excite her attention. It was a sensation in the fatal birthmark, not painful, but which induced a restlessness throughout her system. Hastening after her husband, she intruded for the first time into the laboratory.

The first thing that struck her eye was the furnace, that hot and feverish worker, with the intense glow of its fire, which by the quantities of soot clustered above it seemed to have been burning for ages. There was a distilling apparatus in full operation. Around the room were retorts, tubes, cylinders, crucibles, and other apparatus of chemical research. An electrical machine stood ready for immediate use. The atmosphere felt oppressively close, and was tainted with gaseous odors which had been tormented forth by the processes of science. The severe and homely simplicity of the apartment, with its naked walls and brick pavement, looked strange, accustomed as Georgiana had become to the fantastic elegance of her boudoir. But what chiefly, indeed almost solely, drew her attention, was the aspect of Aylmer himself.

He was pale as death, anxious and absorbed, and hung over the furnace as if it depended upon his utmost watchfulness whether the liquid which it was distilling should be the draught of immortal happiness or misery. How different from the sanguine and joyous mien that he had assumed for Georgiana's encouragement!

"Carefully now, Aminadab; carefully, thou human machine; carefully, thou man of clay!" muttered Aylmer, more to himself than his assistant. "Now, if there be a thought too much or too little, it is all over."

"Ho! ho!" mumbled Aminadab. "Look, master! look!"   60

Aylmer raised his eyes hastily, and at first reddened, then grew paler than ever, on beholding Georgiana. He rushed towards her and seized her arm with a gripe that left the print of his fingers upon it.

"Why do you come hither? Have you no trust in your husband?" cried he impetuously. "Would you throw the blight of that fatal birthmark over my labors? It is not well done. Go, prying woman, go!"

"Nay, Aylmer," said Georgiana with the firmness of which she possessed no stinted endowment, "it is not you that have a right to complain. You mistrust your wife; you have concealed the anxiety with which you watch the development of this experiment. Think not so unworthily of me, my husband. Tell me all the risk we run, and fear not that I shall shrink; for my share in it is far less than your own."

"No, no, Georgiana!" said Aylmer impatiently; "it must not be."

"I submit," replied she calmly. "And, Aylmer, I shall quaff whatever draught you   65
bring me; but it will be on the same principle that would induce me to take a dose of poison if offered by your hand."

"My noble wife," said Aylmer, deeply moved, "I knew not the height and depth of your nature until now. Nothing shall be concealed. Know, then, that this crimson hand, superficial as it seems, has clutched its grasp into your being with a strength of which I had no previous conception. I have already administered agents powerful enough to do aught except to change your entire physical system. Only one thing remains to be tried. If that fails us we are ruined."

"Why did you hesitate to tell me this?" asked she.

"Because, Georgiana," said Aylmer in a low voice, "there is danger."

"Danger? There is but one danger — that this horrible stigma shall be left upon my cheek!" cried Georgiana. "Remove it, remove it, whatever be the cost, or we shall both go mad!"

"Heaven knows your words are too true," said Aylmer sadly. "And now, dearest, 70
return to your boudoir. In a little while all will be tested."

He conducted her back and took leave of her with a solemn tenderness which spoke far more than his words how much was now at stake. After his departure Georgiana became rapt in musings. She considered the character of Aylmer, and did it completer justice than at any previous moment. Her heart exulted, while it trembled, at his honorable love — so pure and lofty that it would accept nothing less than perfection nor miserably make itself contented with an earthlier nature than he had dreamed of. She felt how much more precious was such a sentiment than that meaner kind which would have borne with the imperfection for her sake, and have been guilty of treason to holy love by degrading its perfect idea to the level of the actual; and with her whole spirit she prayed that, for a single moment, she might satisfy his highest and deepest conception. Longer than one moment she well knew it could not be; for his spirit was ever on the march, ever ascending, and each instant required something that was beyond the scope of the instant before.

The sound of her husband's footsteps aroused her. He bore a crystal goblet containing a liquor colorless as water, but bright enough to be the draught of immortality. Aylmer was pale; but it seemed rather the consequence of a highly wrought state of mind and tension of spirit than of fear or doubt.

"The concoction of the draught has been perfect," said he, in answer to Georgiana's look. "Unless all my science have deceived me, it cannot fail."

"Save on your account, my dearest Aylmer," observed his wife, "I might wish to put off this birthmark of mortality by relinquishing mortality itself in preference to any other mode. Life is but a sad possession to those who have attained precisely the degree of moral advancement at which I stand. Were I weaker and blinder it might be happiness. Were I stronger, it might be endured hopefully. But, being what I find myself, methinks I am of all mortals the most fit to die."

"You are fit for heaven without tasting death!" replied her husband. "But why 75 do we speak of dying? The draught cannot fail. Behold its effect upon this plant."

On the window seat there stood a geranium diseased with yellow blotches, which had overspread all its leaves. Aylmer poured a small quantity of the liquid upon the soil in which it grew. In a little time, when the roots of the plant had taken up the moisture, the unsightly blotches began to be extinguished in a living verdure.

"There needed no proof," said Georgiana quietly. "Give me the goblet. I joyfully stake all upon your word."

"Drink, then, thou lofty creature!" exclaimed Aylmer, with fervid admiration. "There is no taint of imperfection on thy spirit. Thy sensible frame, too, shall soon be all perfect."

She quaffed the liquid and returned the goblet to his hand.

"It is grateful," said she, with a placid smile. "Methinks it is like water from a 80 heavenly fountain; for it contains I know not what of unobtrusive fragrance and deliciousness. It allays a feverish thirst that had parched me for many days. Now, dearest, let me sleep. My earthly senses are closing over my spirit like the leaves around the heart of a rose at sunset."

She spoke the last words with a gentle reluctance, as if it required almost more energy than she could command to pronounce the faint and lingering syllables. Scarcely had they loitered through her lips ere she was lost in slumber. Aylmer sat by her side, watching her aspect with the emotions proper to a man the whole value of whose existence was involved in the process now to be tested. Mingled with this mood, however, was the philosophic investigation characteristic of the man of science. Not the minutest symptom escaped him. A heightened flush of the cheek, a slight irregularity of breath, a quiver of the eyelid, a hardly perceptible tremor through the frame, — such were the details which, as the moments passed, he wrote down in his folio volume. Intense thought had set its stamp upon every previous page of that volume, but the thoughts of years were all concentrated upon the last.

While thus employed, he failed not to gaze often at the fatal hand, and not without a shudder. Yet once, by a strange and unaccountable impulse, he pressed it with his lips. His spirit recoiled, however, in the very act; and Georgiana, out of the midst of her deep sleep, moved uneasily and murmured as if in remonstrance. Again Aylmer resumed his watch. Nor was it without avail. The crimson hand, which at first had been strongly visible upon the marble paleness of Georgiana's cheek, now grew more faintly outlined. She remained not less pale than ever; but the birthmark, with every breath that came and went, lost somewhat of its former distinctness. Its presence had been awful; its departure was more awful still. Watch the stain of the rainbow fading out of the sky, and you will know how that mysterious symbol passed away.

"By Heaven! it is well-nigh gone!" said Aylmer to himself, in almost irrepressible ecstasy. "I can scarcely trace it now. Success! success! And now it is like the faintest rose color. The lightest flush of blood across her cheek would overcome it. But she is so pale!"

He drew aside the window curtain and suffered the light of natural day to fall into the room and rest upon her cheek. At the same time he heard a gross, hoarse chuckle, which he had long known as his servant Aminadab's expression of delight.

"Ah, clod! ah, earthly mass!" cried Aylmer, laughing in a sort of frenzy, "you 85 have served me well! Matter and spirit — earth and heaven — have both done their part in this! Laugh, thing of the senses! You have earned the right to laugh."

These exclamations broke Georgiana's sleep. She slowly unclosed her eyes and gazed into the mirror which her husband had arranged for that purpose. A faint smile flitted over her lips when she recognized how barely perceptible was now that crimson hand which had once blazed forth with such disastrous brilliancy as to scare away all their happiness. But then her eyes sought Aylmer's face with a trouble and anxiety that he could by no means account for.

"My poor Aylmer!" murmured she.

"Poor? Nay, richest, happiest, most favored!" exclaimed he. "My peerless bride, it is successful! You are perfect!"

"My poor Aylmer," she repeated, with a more than human tenderness, "you have aimed loftily; you have done nobly. Do not repent that with so high and pure a feeling, you have rejected the best the earth could offer. Aylmer, dearest Aylmer, I am dying!"

Alas! it was too true! The fatal hand had grappled with the mystery of life, and 90 was the bond by which an angelic spirit kept itself in union with a mortal frame. As the last crimson tint of the birthmark — that sole token of human imperfection — faded from her cheek, the parting breath of the now perfect woman passed into the atmosphere, and her soul, lingering a moment near her husband, took its heavenward flight. Then a hoarse, chuckling laugh was heard again! Thus ever does the gross fatality of earth exult in its invariable triumph over the immortal essence which, in this dim sphere of half development, demands the completeness of a higher state. Yet, had Aylmer reached a profounder wisdom, he need not thus have flung away the happiness which would have woven his mortal life of the selfsame texture with the celestial. The momentary circumstance was too strong for him; he failed to look beyond the shadowy scope of time, and, living once for all in eternity, to find the perfect future in the present.

CONSIDERATIONS FOR CRITICAL THINKING AND WRITING

1. FIRST RESPONSE. Consider this story as an early version of our contemporary obsession with physical perfection. What significant similarities — and differences — do you find?

2. Is Aylmer evil? Is he simply a stock version of a mad scientist? In what sense might he be regarded as an idealist?

3. What does the birthmark symbolize? How does Aylmer's view of it differ from the other perspectives provided in the story? What is the significance of its handlike shape?

4. Does Aylmer love Georgiana? Why does she allow him to risk her life to remove the birthmark?

5. In what sense can Aylmer be characterized as guilty of the sin of pride?

6. How is Aminadab a foil for Aylmer?

7. What is the significance of the descriptions of Aylmer's laboratory?

8. What do Aylmer's other experiments reveal about the nature of his work? How do they constitute foreshadowings of what will happen to Georgiana?

9. What is the theme of the story? What point is made about what it means to be a human being?

10. Despite the risks to Georgiana, Aylmer conducts his experiments in the hope and expectation of achieving a higher good. He devotes his life to science, and yet he is an egotist. Explain.

11. Discuss the extent to which Georgiana is responsible for her own death.

CONNECTION TO ANOTHER SELECTION

1. Compare Aylmer's unwillingness to accept things as they are with Goodman Brown's refusal to be a part of a community he regards as fallen.

Perspectives on Hawthorne

NATHANIEL HAWTHORNE

On Solitude   1837

Dear Sir,

Not to burthen you with my correspondence, I have delayed a rejoinder to your very kind and cordial letter, until now. It gratifies me to find that you have occasionally felt an interest in my situation. . . . You would have been nearer the truth if you had pictured me as dwelling in an owl's nest; for mine is about as dismal; and, like the owl I seldom venture abroad till after dark. By some witchcraft or other — for I really cannot assign any reasonable why and wherefore — I have been carried apart from the main current of life, and find it impossible to get back again. Since we last met . . . I have secluded myself from society; and yet I never meant any such thing, nor dreamed what sort of life I was going to lead. I have made a captive of myself and put me into a dungeon, and now I cannot find the key to let myself out — and if the door were open, I should be almost afraid to come out. You tell me that you have met with troubles and changes. I know not what they may have been; but I can assure you that trouble is the next best thing to enjoyment, and that there is no fate in this world so horrible as to have no share in either its joys or sorrows. For the last ten years, I have not lived, but only dreamed about living. It may be true that there have been some unsubstantial pleasures here in the shade, which I should have missed in the sunshine, but you cannot conceive how utterly devoid of satisfaction all my retrospects are. I have laid up no treasure of pleasant remembrances, against old age; but there is some comfort in thinking that my future years can hardly fail to be more varied, and therefore more tolerable, than the past.

You give me more credit than I deserve, in supposing that I have led a studious life. I have, indeed, turned over a good many books, but in so desultory a way that it cannot be called study, nor has it left me the fruits of study. As to my literary efforts, I do not think much of them — neither is it worthwhile to be ashamed of them. They would have been better, I trust, if written under more favorable circumstances. I have had no external excitement — no consciousness that the public would like what I wrote, nor much hope nor a very passionate desire that they should do so. Nevertheless, having nothing else to be ambitious of, I have felt considerably interested in literature; and if my writings had made any decided impression, I should probably have been stimulated to greater exertions; but there has been no warmth of approbation, so that I have always written with benumbed fingers. I have another great difficulty, in the lack of materials; for I have seen so little of the world, that I have nothing but thin air to concoct my stories of, and it is not easy to give a lifelike semblance to such shadowy stuff. Sometimes, through a peep-hole, I have caught a glimpse of the real world; and the two or three articles, in which I have portrayed such glimpses, please me better than the others. I have now, or shall soon have, one sharp spur to exertion, which I lacked at an earlier period; for I see little prospect but that I must scribble for a living. But this troubles me much less than you would suppose. I can turn my pen to all sorts of drudgery, such as children's books, etc., and by and by, I shall get some editorship that will answer my purpose. Frank Pierce, who was with us at college, offered me his influence to obtain an office in the Exploring Expedition; but I believe that he was mistaken in supposing that a vacancy existed. If such a post were attainable, I should certainly accept it; for, though fixed so long to one spot, I have always had a desire to run around the world.

The copy of my Tales was sent to Mr. Owen's, the bookseller's in Cambridge. I am glad to find that you had read and liked some of the stories. To be sure, you could not well help flattering me a little; but I value your praise too highly not to have faith in its sincerity. When I last heard from the publisher — which was not very recently — the book was doing pretty well. Six or seven hundred copies had been sold. I suppose, however, these awful times have now stopped the sale.

I intend in a week or two to come out of my owl's nest, and not return to it till late in the summer — employing the interval in making a tour somewhere in New England. You, who have the dust of distant countries on your "sandalshoon," cannot imagine how much enjoyment I shall have in this little excursion. Whenever I get abroad, I feel just as young as I did, ten years ago. What a letter I am inflicting on you! I trust you will answer it.

Yours sincerely,
Nath. Hawthorne.

From a letter to Henry Wadsworth Longfellow, June 4, 1837

CONSIDERATIONS FOR CRITICAL THINKING AND WRITING

1. How does Hawthorne regard his solitude? How does he feel it has affected his life and writing?

2. Hawthorne explains to Longfellow, one of his Bowdoin classmates, that "there is no fate in this world so horrible as to have no share in either its joys or sorrows" (para. 1). Explain how this idea is worked into "Young Goodman Brown" (p. 321).

3. Does Hawthorne indicate any positive results for having lived in his "owl's nest" (para. 1)? Consider how "The Minister's Black Veil" (p. 331) and this letter shed light on each other.

NATHANIEL HAWTHORNE

On the Power of the Writer's Imagination   1850

... Moonlight, in a familiar room, falling so white upon the carpet, and showing all its figures so distinctly — making every object so minutely visible, yet so unlike a morning or noontide visibility — is a medium the most suitable for a romance-writer° to get acquainted with his illusive guests. There is the little domestic scenery of the well-known apartment; the chairs, with each its separate individuality; the center-table, sustaining a work-basket, a volume or two, and an extinguished lamp; the sofa; the book-case; the picture on the wall — all these details, so completely seen, are so spiritualized by the unusual light, that they seem to lose their actual substance, and become things of intellect. Nothing is too small or too trifling to undergo this change, and acquire dignity thereby. A child's shoe; the doll, seated in her little wicker carriage; the hobbyhorse — whatever, in a word, has been used or played with, during the day, is now invested with a quality of strangeness and remoteness, though still almost as vividly present as by daylight. Thus, therefore, the floor of our familiar room has become a neutral territory, somewhere between the real world and fairyland, where the Actual and the Imaginary may meet, and each imbue itself with the nature of the other. Ghosts might enter here, without affrighting us. It would be too much in keeping with the scene to excite surprise, were we to look about us and discover a form, beloved, but gone hence, now sitting quietly in a streak of this magic moonshine, with an aspect that would make us doubt whether it had returned from afar, or had never once stirred from our fireside.

The somewhat dim coal-fire has an essential influence in producing the effect which I would describe. It throws its unobtrusive tinge throughout the room, with a faint ruddiness upon the walls and ceiling, and a reflected gleam from the polish of the furniture. This warmer light mingles itself with the cold spirituality of the moonbeams, and communicates, as it were, a heart and sensibilities of

---

romance-writer: Hawthorne distinguished romance writing from novel writing. In the preface to *The House of the Seven Gables* he writes:

> The latter form of composition is presumed to aim at a very minute fidelity, not merely to the possible, but to the probable and ordinary course of man's experience. The former — while, as a work of art, it must rigidly subject itself to laws, and while it sins unpardonably so far as it may swerve aside from the truth of the human heart — has fairly a right to present that truth under circumstances, to a great extent, of the writer's own choosing or creation.

human tenderness to the forms which fancy summons up. It converts them from snow-images into men and women. Glancing at the looking-glass, we behold — deep within its haunted verge — the smouldering glow of the half-extinguished anthracite, the white moonbeams on the floor, and a repetition of all the gleam and shadow of the picture, with one remove farther from the actual, and nearer to the imaginative. Then, at such an hour, and with this scene before him, if a man, sitting all alone, cannot dream strange things, and make them look like truth, he need never try to write romances.

From The Scarlet Letter

Considerations for Critical Thinking and Writing

1. Explain how Hawthorne uses light as a means of invoking the transforming powers of the imagination.
2. How do Hawthorne's stories fulfill his definition of romance writing? Why can't they be regarded as realistic?
3. Choose one story and discuss it as an attempt to evoke "the truth of the human heart."

Nathaniel Hawthorne

On His Short Stories 1851

[These stories] have the pale tint of flowers that blossomed in too retired a shade — the coolness of a meditative habit, which diffuses itself through the feeling and observation of every sketch. Instead of passion there is sentiment; and, even in what purport to be pictures of actual life, we have allegory, not always warmly dressed in its habiliments of flesh and blood as to be taken into the reader's mind without a shiver. Whether from lack of power, or an unconquerable reserve, the Author's touches have often an effect of tameness; the merriest man can hardly contrive to laugh at his broadest humor; the tenderest woman, one would suppose, will hardly shed warm tears at his deepest pathos. The book, if you would see anything in it, requires to be read in the clear brown, twilight atmosphere in which it was written; if opened in the sunshine, it is apt to look exceedingly like a volume of blank pages.

From the preface to the 1851 edition of Twice-Told Tales

Considerations for Critical Thinking and Writing

1. How does Hawthorne characterize his stories? Does his assessment accurately describe the stories you've read?
2. Why is a "twilight atmosphere" more conducive to an appreciation of Hawthorne's art than "sunshine"?
3. Write a one-page description of Hawthorne's stories in which you generalize about his characteristic approach to one of these elements: plot, character, setting, symbol, theme, tone.

HERMAN MELVILLE (1819–1891)

On Nathaniel Hawthorne's Tragic Vision   1851

There is a certain tragic phase of humanity which, in our opinion, was never more powerfully embodied than by Hawthorne. We mean the tragicalness of human thought in its own unbiased, native, and profounder workings. We think that in no recorded mind has the intense feeling of the visable truth ever entered more deeply than into this man's. By visable truth, we mean the apprehension of the absolute condition of present things as they strike the eye of the man who fears them not, though they do their worst to him — the man who, like Russia or the British Empire, declares himself a sovereign nature (in himself) amid the powers of heaven, hell, and earth. He may perish; but so long as he exists he insists upon treating with all Powers upon an equal basis. If any of those other Powers choose to withhold certain secrets, let them; that does not impair my sovereignty in myself; that does not make me tributary. And perhaps, after all, there is *no* secret. We incline to think that the Problem of the Universe is like the Freemason's° mighty secret, so terrible to all children. It turns out, at last, to consist in a tri-angle, a mallet, and an apron — nothing more! . . . There is the grand truth about Nathaniel Hawthorne. He says NO! in thunder; but the Devil himself cannot make him say *yes.* For all men who say *yes,* lie; and all men who say *no* — why, they are in the happy condition of judicious, unincumbered travelers in Europe; they cross the frontiers into Eternity with nothing but a carpetbag — that is to say, the Ego. Whereas those *yes*-gentry, they travel with heaps of baggage, and, damn them! they will never get through the Custom House. What's the reason, Mr. Hawthorne, that in the last stages of metaphysics a fellow always falls to *swearing* so? I could rip an hour.

From a letter to Hawthorne, April 16(?), 1851

Freemason: A member of the secret fraternity of Freemasonry.

CONSIDERATIONS FOR CRITICAL THINKING AND WRITING

1. What qualities in Hawthorne does Melville admire?
2. Explain how these qualities are embodied in one of the Hawthorne stories.
3. How might Melville's lawyer in "Bartleby, the Scrivener" (p. 130) be character-ized as one of "those *yes*-gentry"?

GAYLORD BREWER (B. 1965)

The Joys of Secret Sin   2006

— *after Hawthorne*

"For the Earth, too, had on her Black Veil"?
Can you blame her? The better to avoid
the humbug of these two soldiers of melancholy —
that young, good man who soils the world

with his dark dream; a sweat-lipped preacher   5
smugly trembling behind twin folds of crape.

The Earth doesn't appreciate her name
sullied — always, winds howling and bestial
cries. Wife and fiancée fare no better —
poor plump Faith, her pink ribbons disavowed;   10
long-suffering Elizabeth, left old by cryptic
evasions. Who in the village doesn't
recognize the human face or needs reminding?
Black veil on every visage? Dying hour of gloom?
That's the rectitude that compels them all —   15
deacon, farmer, child, maiden, hag —
toward your welcoming smile, avuncular wink,
kindly dip of black staff, so curiously
entwined it seems almost to writhe. There,
just ahead: the forest's mossy, crooked path,   20
a canopy of flames, a guiltless hearth of stone.

Considerations for Critical Thinking and Writing

1. Write a paraphrase of this poem. How does it provide a reading of "Young Goodman Brown" (p. 321) and "The Minister's Black Veil" (p. 331)?

2. CREATIVE RESPONSE. Using Brewer's poem as a source of inspiration (but not necessarily its style and form), try writing a poem based on your reading of "The Birthmark" (p. 339).

12

A Study of Flannery O'Connor

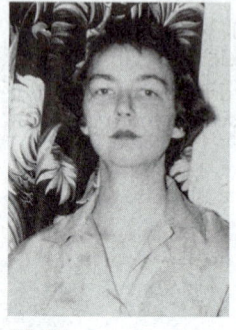

© Corbis.

In most English classes the short story has become a kind of literary specimen to be dissected. Every time a story of mine appears in a Freshman anthology, I have a vision of it, with its little organs laid open, like a frog in a bottle.

— FLANNERY O'CONNOR

I am always having it pointed out to me that life in Georgia is not at all the way I picture it, that escaped criminals do not roam the roads exterminating families, nor Bible salesmen prowl about looking for girls with wooden legs.

— FLANNERY O'CONNOR

When Flannery O'Connor (1925–1964) died of lupus before her fortieth birthday, her work was cruelly cut short. Nevertheless, she had completed two novels, *Wise Blood* (1952) and *The Violent Bear It Away* (1960), as well as thirty-one short stories. Despite her brief life and relatively modest output, her work is regarded as among the most distinguished American fiction of the mid-twentieth century. Her two collections of short stories, *A Good Man Is Hard to Find* (1955) and *Everything That Rises Must Converge* (1965), were included in *The Complete Stories of Flannery O'Connor* (1971), which won the National Book Award. The stories included in this chapter offer a glimpse into the work of this important twentieth-century writer.

Cheers,
Flannery

A BRIEF BIOGRAPHY AND INTRODUCTION

O'Connor's fiction grapples with living a spiritual life in a secular world. Although this major concern is worked into each of her stories, she takes a broad approach to spiritual issues by providing moral, social, and psychological contexts that offer a wealth of insights and passion that her readers have found both startling and absorbing. Her stories are challenging because her characters, who initially seem radically different from people we know, turn out to be, by the end of each story, somehow familiar — somehow connected to us.

O'Connor inhabited simultaneously two radically different worlds. The world she created in her stories is populated with bratty children, malcontents, incompetents, pious frauds, bewildered intellectuals, deformed cynics, rednecks, hucksters, racists, perverts, and murderers who experience dramatically intense moments that surprise and shock readers. Her personal life, however, was largely uneventful. She humorously acknowledged its quiet nature in 1958 when she claimed that "there won't be any biographies of me because, for only one reason, lives spent between the house and the chicken yard do not make exciting copy."

A broad outline of O'Connor's life may not offer very much "exciting copy," but it does provide clues about why she wrote such powerful fiction. The only child of Catholic parents, O'Connor was born in Savannah, Georgia, where she attended a parochial grammar school and high school. When she was thirteen, her father became ill with disseminated lupus, a rare, incurable blood disease, and had to abandon his real-estate business. The family moved to Milledgeville in central Georgia, where her mother's family had lived for generations. Because there were no Catholic schools in Milledgeville, O'Connor attended a public high school. In 1942, the year after her father died of lupus, O'Connor graduated from high school and enrolled in Georgia State College for Women. There she wrote for the literary magazine until receiving her diploma in 1945. Her stories earned her a fellowship to the Writers' Workshop at the University of Iowa, and for two years she learned to write steadily and seriously. She sold her first story to *Accent* in 1946 and earned her master of fine arts degree in 1947. She wrote stories about life in the rural South, and this subject matter, along with her devout Catholic perspective, became central to her fiction.

With her formal education behind her, O'Connor was ready to begin her professional career at the age of twenty-two. Equipped with determination ("No one can convince me that I shouldn't rewrite as much as I do") and offered the opportunity to be around other practicing writers, she moved to New York, where she worked on her first novel, *Wise Blood*. In 1950, however, she was diagnosed as having lupus, and, returning to Georgia for treatment, she took up permanent residence on her mother's farm in Milledgeville. There she lived a severely restricted but productive life, writing stories and raising peacocks.

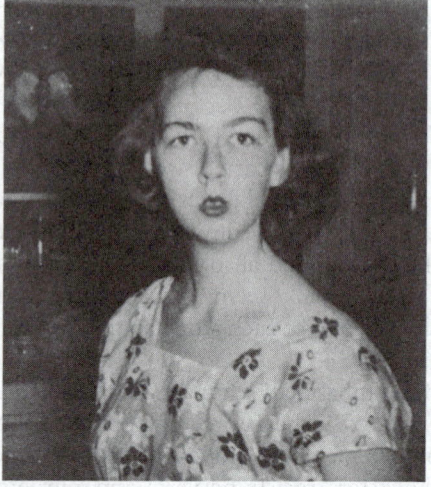

Flannery O'Connor (above left) at age twelve and (above right) in her teens (age sixteen or seventeen). O'Connor, whose youth was marked by the declining health and death of her father, once wrote, "[A]nybody who has survived childhood has enough information about life to last him the rest of the days."

Flannery O'Connor and a Self-Portrait. The author poses in front of an accurate, if rather fierce self-portrait with one of her beloved ring-necked pheasants. As a child, O'Connor enjoyed raising birds, a passion that was sparked when one of her chickens, "a buff Cochin Bantam [that] had the distinction of being able to walk either forward or backward," was reported on in the press. "I had to have more and more chickens. . . . I wanted one with three legs or three wings but nothing in that line turned up. . . . My quest, whatever it was for, ended with peacocks," she wrote.

The *Corinthian* Staff (above). Flannery O'Connor (seated, center) as editor of the *Corinthian*, the literary magazine at Georgia State College for Women (now Georgia College and State University). O'Connor attended the college from 1942 through 1945 and earned a B.A. in social science.

Courtesy of Ina Dillard Russell Library Special Collections, Georgia College and State University.

With the exception of O'Connor's early years in Iowa and New York and some short lecture trips to other states, she traveled little. Although she made a pilgrimage to Lourdes (apparently more for her mother's sake than for her own) and then to Rome for an audience with the pope, her life was centered in the South. Like those of William Faulkner and many other southern writers, O'Connor's stories evoke the rhythms of rural southern speech and manners in insulated settings where widely diverse characters mingle. Also like Faulkner, she created works whose meanings go beyond their settings. She did not want her fiction to be seen in the context of narrowly defined regionalism: she complained that "in almost every hamlet you'll find at least one old lady writing epics in Negro dialect and probably two or three old gentlemen who have impossible historical novels on the way." Refusing to be caricatured, she knew that "the woods are full of regional writers, and it is the great horror of every serious Southern writer that he will become one of them." O'Connor's stories are rooted in rural southern culture, but in a larger sense they are set within the psychological and spiritual landscapes of the human soul. This interior setting universalizes local materials in much the same way that Nathaniel Hawthorne's New England stories do. Indeed, O'Connor once described herself as "one of his descendants": "I feel more of a kinship with him than any other American."

O'Connor's deep spiritual convictions coincide with the traditional emphasis on religion in the South, where, she said, there is still the belief "that man has fallen and that he is only perfectible by God's grace, not by his own unaided efforts." Although O'Connor's Catholicism differs from the prevailing Protestant fundamentalism of the South, the religious ethos so pervasive even in rural southern areas provided fertile ground for the spiritual crises her characters experience. In a posthumous collection of her articles, essays, and reviews aptly titled *Mystery and Manners* (1969), she summarized her basic religious convictions:

> I am no disbeliever in spiritual purpose and no vague believer. I see from the standpoint of Christian orthodoxy. This means that for me the meaning of life is centered in our Redemption by Christ and what I see in the world I see in its relation to that. I don't think that this is a position that can be taken halfway or one that is particularly easy in these times to make transparent in fiction.

O'Connor realized that she was writing against the grain of the readers who discovered her stories in the *Partisan Review, Sewanee Review, Mademoiselle,* or *Harper's Bazaar.* Many readers thought that Christian dogma would make her writing doctrinaire, but she insisted that the perspective of Christianity allowed her to interpret the details of life and guaranteed her "respect for [life's] mystery." O'Connor's stories contain no prepackaged prescriptions for living, no catechisms that lay out all the answers. Instead, her characters struggle with spiritual questions in bizarre, incongruous situations. Their lives are grotesque — even comic — precisely because they do not understand their own spiritual natures. Their actions are extreme and abnormal. O'Connor explains the reasons for this in *Mystery and Manners;* she says she sought to expose the "distortions" of "modern life" that appear "normal" to her audience. Hence, she used "violent means" to convey her vision to a "hostile audience." "When you can assume that your audience holds the same beliefs you do, you can relax a little and use more normal means of talking to it." But when the audience holds different values, "you have to make your vision apparent by shock — to the hard of hearing you shout, and for the almost-blind you draw large and startling figures." O'Connor's characters lose or find their soul-saving grace in painful, chaotic circumstances that bear little or no resemblance to the slow but sure progress to the Celestial City of repentant pilgrims in traditional religious stories.

Because her characters are powerful creations who live convincing, even if ugly, lives, O'Connor's religious beliefs never supersede her storytelling. One need not be either Christian or Catholic to appreciate her concerns about human failure and degradation and her artistic ability to render fictional lives that are alternately absurdly comic and tragic. The ironies that abound in her work leave plenty of room for readers of all persuasions. O'Connor's work is narrow in the sense that her concerns are emphatically spiritual, but her compassion and her belief in human possibilities — even among the most unlikely characters — afford her fictions a capacity for wonder that is exhilarating. Her precise, deft use of language always reveals more than it seems to tell.

Like Hawthorne's fiction, O'Connor's stories present complex experiences that cannot be tidily summarized; it takes the entire story to suggest the meanings. Read the following three stories for the pleasure of entering the remarkable world O'Connor creates. You're in for some surprises.

Chronology

1925	Born on March 25 in Savannah, Georgia.
1938	Moves with family to Milledgeville, Georgia; enters the public Peabody High School.
1941	Father dies of lupus.
1942	Graduates from Peabody High School; enters Georgia State College for Women (now Georgia College and State University).
1943–45	Writes stories and poems for college literary magazine; graduates from Georgia State with an undergraduate degree in English.
1945–47	Enters writing program at the University of Iowa and earns a master of fine arts degree in creative writing.
1948–49	Attends Yaddo artists' colony near Saratoga Springs, New York, for several months; lives in New York and Connecticut.
1950	After an illness, returns to Milledgeville and is diagnosed as suffering from lupus, an incurable disease. Lives on her family's dairy farm the rest of her life.
1952	*Wise Blood* receives mixed reviews and upsets some Milledgeville residents.
1955	*A Good Man Is Hard to Find and Other Stories* receives critical praise; the Guggenheim Foundation rejects her fellowship application for a second time.
1956	A degenerating hip forces her to use crutches; the first telephone is installed on the farm.
1957	Lectures at several universities; dislikes a television version of the short story "The Life You Save May Be Your Own"; receives a grant from the National Institute of Arts and Letters.
1958	Visits Lourdes and Rome.
1960	Publishes *The Violent Bear It Away.*
1962–63	Receives honorary doctorate from Saint Mary's women's college of the University of Notre Dame; speaks at a number of colleges in the South about her writing.
1964	Dies on August 3, 1964.
1965	*Everything That Rises Must Converge* published posthumously.

A Good Man Is Hard to Find   1953

The grandmother didn't want to go to Florida. She wanted to visit some of her connections in east Tennessee and she was seizing at every chance to change Bailey's mind. Bailey was the son she lived with, her only boy. He was sitting on the edge of his chair at the table, bent over the orange sports section of the *Journal*. "Now look here, Bailey," she said, "see here, read this," and she stood with one hand on her thin hip and the other rattling the newspaper at his bald head. "Here this fellow that calls himself The Misfit is aloose from the Federal Pen and headed toward Florida and you read here what it says he did to these people. Just you read it. I wouldn't take my children in any direction with a criminal like that aloose in it. I couldn't answer to my conscience if I did."

Bailey didn't look up from his reading so she wheeled around then and faced the children's mother, a young woman in slacks, whose face was as broad and innocent as a cabbage and was tied around with a green headkerchief that had two points on the top like a rabbit's ears. She was sitting on the sofa, feeding the baby his apricots out of a jar. "The children have been to Florida before," the old lady said. "You all ought to take them somewhere else for a change so they would see different parts of the world and be broad. They never have been to east Tennessee."

The children's mother didn't seem to hear her but the eight-year-old boy, John Wesley, a stocky child with glasses, said, "If you don't want to go to Florida, why dontcha stay at home?" He and the little girl, June Star, were reading the funny papers on the floor.

"She wouldn't stay at home to be queen for a day," June Star said without raising her yellow head.

"Yes and what would you do if this fellow, The Misfit, caught you?" the grand-   5
mother asked.

"I'd smack his face," John Wesley said.

"She wouldn't stay at home for a million bucks," June Star said. "Afraid she'd miss something. She has to go everywhere we go."

"All right, Miss," the grandmother said. "Just remember that the next time you want me to curl your hair."

June Star said her hair was naturally curly.

The next morning the grandmother was the first one in the car, ready to go. She   10
had her big black valise that looked like the head of a hippopotamus in one corner, and underneath it she was hiding a basket with Pitty Sing, the cat, in it. She didn't intend for the cat to be left alone in the house for three days because he would miss her too much and she was afraid he might brush against one of the gas burners and accidentally asphyxiate himself. Her son, Bailey, didn't like to arrive at a motel with a cat.

She sat in the middle of the back seat with John Wesley and June Star on either side of her. Bailey and the children's mother and the baby sat in front and they left Atlanta at eight forty-five with the mileage on the car at 55890. The grandmother wrote this down because she thought it would be interesting to say how many miles they had been when they got back. It took them twenty minutes to reach the outskirts of the city.

The old lady settled herself comfortably, removing her white cotton gloves and putting them up with her purse on the shelf in front of the back window. The children's mother still had on slacks and still had her head tied up in a green kerchief, but the grandmother had on a navy blue straw sailor hat with a bunch of white violets on the brim and a navy blue dress with a small white dot in the print. Her collars and cuffs were white organdy trimmed with lace and at her neckline she had pinned a purple spray of cloth violets containing a sachet. In case of an accident, anyone seeing her dead on the highway would know at once that she was a lady.

She said she thought it was going to be a good day for driving, neither too hot nor too cold, and she cautioned Bailey that the speed limit was fifty-five miles an hour and that the patrolmen hid themselves behind billboards and small clumps of trees and sped out after you before you had a chance to slow down. She pointed out interesting details of the scenery: Stone Mountain; the blue granite that in some places came up to both sides of the highway; the brilliant red clay banks slightly streaked with purple; and the various crops that made rows of green lace-work on the ground. The trees were full of silver-white sunlight and the meanest of them sparkled. The children were reading comic magazines and their mother had gone back to sleep.

"Let's go through Georgia fast so we won't have to look at it much," John Wesley said.

"If I were a little boy," said the grandmother, "I wouldn't talk about my native 15 state that way. Tennessee has the mountains and Georgia has the hills."

"Tennessee is just a hillbilly dumping ground," John Wesley said, "and Georgia is a lousy state too."

"You said it," June Star said.

"In my time," said the grandmother, folding her thin veined fingers, "children were more respectful of their native states and their parents and everything else. People did right then. Oh look at the cute little pickaninny!" she said and pointed to a Negro child standing in the door of a shack. "Wouldn't that make a picture, now?" she asked and they all turned and looked at the little Negro out of the back window. He waved.

"He didn't have any britches on," June Star said.

"He probably didn't have any," the grandmother explained. "Little niggers in 20 the country don't have things like we do. If I could paint, I'd paint that picture," she said.

The children exchanged comic books.

The grandmother offered to hold the baby and the children's mother passed him over the front seat to her. She set him on her knee and bounced him and told him about the things they were passing. She rolled her eyes and screwed up her mouth and stuck her leathery thin face into his smooth bland one. Occasionally he gave her a faraway smile. They passed a large cotton field with five or six graves fenced in the middle of it, like a small island. "Look at the graveyard!" the grandmother said, pointing it out. "That was the old family burying ground. That belonged to the plantation."

"Where's the plantation?" John Wesley asked.

"Gone With the Wind," said the grandmother. "Ha. Ha."

When the children finished all the comic books they had brought, they opened 25 the lunch and ate it. The grandmother ate a peanut butter sandwich and an olive and would not let the children throw the box and the paper napkins out the window. When there was nothing else to do they played a game by choosing a cloud and making the other two guess what shape it suggested. John Wesley took one the shape of a cow and June Star guessed a cow and John Wesley said, no, an automobile, and June Star said he didn't play fair, and they began to slap each other over the grandmother.

The grandmother said she would tell them a story if they would keep quiet. When she told a story, she rolled her eyes and waved her head and was very dramatic. She said once when she was a maiden lady she had been courted by a Mr. Edgar Atkins Teagarden from Jasper, Georgia. She said he was a very good-looking man and a gentleman and that he brought her a watermelon every Saturday afternoon with his initials cut in it, E.A.T. Well, one Saturday, she said, Mr. Teagarden brought the watermelon and there was nobody at home and he left it on the front porch and returned in his buggy to Jasper, but she never got the watermelon, she said, because a nigger boy ate it when he saw the initials, E.A.T.! This story tickled

John Wesley's funny bone and he giggled and giggled but June Star didn't think it was any good. She said she wouldn't marry a man that just brought her a watermelon on Saturday. The grandmother said she would have done well to marry Mr. Teagarden because he was a gentleman and had bought Coca-Cola stock when it first came out and that he had died only a few years ago, a very wealthy man.

They stopped at The Tower for barbecued sandwiches. The Tower was a part stucco and part wood filling station and dance hall set in a clearing outside of Timothy. A fat man named Red Sammy Butts ran it and there were signs stuck here and there on the building and for miles up and down the highway saying, TRY RED SAMMY'S FAMOUS BARBECUE. NONE LIKE FAMOUS RED SAMMY'S! RED SAM! THE FAT BOY WITH THE HAPPY LAUGH. A VETERAN! RED SAMMY'S YOUR MAN!

Red Sammy was lying on the bare ground outside The Tower with his head under a truck while a gray monkey about a foot high, chained to a small chinaberry tree, chattered nearby. The monkey sprang back into the tree and got on the highest limb as soon as he saw the children jump out of the car and run toward him.

Inside, The Tower was a long dark room with a counter at one end and tables at the other and dancing space in the middle. They all sat down at a board table next to the nickelodeon and Red Sam's wife, a tall burnt-brown woman with hair and eyes lighter than her skin, came and took their order. The children's mother put a dime in the machine and played "The Tennessee Waltz," and the grandmother said that tune always made her want to dance. She asked Bailey if he would like to dance but he only glared at her. He didn't have a naturally sunny disposition like she did and trips made him nervous. The grandmother's brown eyes were very bright. She swayed her head from side to side and pretended she was dancing in her chair. June Star said play something she could tap to so the children's mother put in another dime and played a fast number and June Star stepped out onto the dance floor and did her tap routine.

"Ain't she cute?" Red Sam's wife said, leaning over the counter. "Would you like 30 to come be my little girl?"

"No I certainly wouldn't," June Star said. "I wouldn't live in a broken-down place like this for a million bucks!" and she ran back to the table.

"Ain't she cute?" the woman repeated, stretching her mouth politely.

"Aren't you ashamed?" hissed the grandmother.

Red Sam came in and told his wife to quit lounging on the counter and hurry up with these people's order. His khaki trousers reached just to his hip bones and his stomach hung over them like a sack of meal swaying under his shirt. He came over and sat down at a table nearby and let out a combination sigh and yodel. "You can't win," he said. "You can't win," and he wiped his sweating red face off with a gray handkerchief. "These days you don't know who to trust," he said. "Ain't that the truth?"

"People are certainly not nice like they used to be," said the grandmother. 35

"Two fellers come in here last week," Red Sammy said, "driving a Chrysler. It was a old beat-up car but it was a good one and these boys looked all right to me. Said they worked at the mill and you know I let them fellers charge the gas they bought? Now why did I do that?"

"Because you're a good man!" the grandmother said at once.

"Yes'm, I suppose so," Red Sam said as if he were struck with this answer.

His wife brought the orders, carrying the five plates all at once without a tray, two in each hand and one balanced on her arm. "It isn't a soul in this green world of God's that you can trust," she said. "And I don't count nobody out of that, not nobody," she repeated, looking at Red Sammy.

"Did you read about that criminal, The Misfit, that's escaped?" asked the 40 grandmother.

"I wouldn't be a bit surprised if he didn't attack this place right here," said the woman. "If he hears about it being here, I wouldn't be none surprised to see him. If he hears it's two cent in the cash register, I wouldn't be a tall surprised if he. . . ."

"That'll do," Red Sam said. "Go bring these people their Co'-Colas," and the woman went off to get the rest of the order.

"A good man is hard to find," Red Sammy said. "Everything is getting terrible. I remember the day you could go off and leave your screen door unlatched. Not no more."

He and the grandmother discussed better times. The old lady said that in her opinion Europe was entirely to blame for the way things were now. She said the way Europe acted you would think we were made of money and Red Sam said it was no use talking about it, she was exactly right. The children ran outside into the white sunlight and looked at the monkey in the lacy chinaberry tree. He was busy catching fleas on himself and biting each one carefully between his teeth as if it were a delicacy.

They drove off again into the hot afternoon. The grandmother took cat naps 45 and woke up every few minutes with her own snoring. Outside of Toombsboro she woke up and recalled an old plantation that she had visited in this neighborhood once when she was a young lady. She said the house had six white columns across the front and that there was an avenue of oaks leading up to it and two little wooden trellis arbors on either side in front where you sat down with your suitor after a stroll in the garden. She recalled exactly which road to turn off to get to it. She knew that Bailey would not be willing to lose any time looking at an old house, but the more she talked about it, the more she wanted to see it once again and find out if the little twin arbors were still standing. "There was a secret panel in this house," she said craftily, not telling the truth but wishing that she were, "and the story went that all the family silver was hidden in it when Sherman° came through but it was never found. . . ."

"Hey!" John Wesley said. "Let's go see it! We'll find it! We'll poke all the woodwork and find it! Who lives there? Where do you turn off at? Hey Pop, can't we turn off there?"

"We never have seen a house with a secret panel!" June Star shrieked. "Let's go to the house with the secret panel! Hey Pop, can't we go see the house with the secret panel!"

"It's not far from here, I know," the grandmother said. "It won't take over twenty minutes."

Bailey was looking straight ahead. His jaw was as rigid as a horseshoe. "No," he said.

The children began to yell and scream that they wanted to see the house with 50 the secret panel. John Wesley kicked the back of the front seat and June Star hung over her mother's shoulder and whined desperately into her ear that they never had any fun even on their vacation, that they could never do what THEY wanted to do. The baby began to scream and John Wesley kicked the back of the seat so hard that his father could feel the blows in his kidney.

"All right!" he shouted and drew the car to a stop at the side of the road. "Will you all shut up? Will you all just shut up for one second? If you don't shut up, we won't go anywhere."

Sherman: William Tecumseh Sherman (1820–1891), Union Army commander who led infamous marches through the South during the Civil War.

"It would be very educational for them," the grandmother murmured.

"All right," Bailey said, "but get this: this is the only time we're going to stop for anything like this. This is the one and only time."

"The dirt road that you have to turn down is about a mile back," the grandmother directed. "I marked it when we passed."

"A dirt road," Bailey groaned.   55

After they had turned around and were headed toward the dirt road, the grandmother recalled other points about the house, the beautiful glass over the front doorway and the candle-lamp in the hall. John Wesley said that the secret panel was probably in the fireplace.

"You can't go inside this house," Bailey said. "You don't know who lives there."

"While you all talk to the people in front, I'll run around behind and get in a window," John Wesley suggested.

"We'll all stay in the car," his mother said.

They turned onto the dirt road and the car raced roughly along in a swirl of   60
pink dust. The grandmother recalled the times when there were no paved roads and thirty miles was a day's journey. The dirt road was hilly and there were sudden washes in it and sharp curves on dangerous embankments. All at once they would be on a hill, looking down over the blue tops of trees for miles around, then the next minute, they would be in a red depression with the dust-coated trees looking down on them.

"This place had better turn up in a minute," Bailey said, "or I'm going to turn around."

The road looked as if no one had traveled on it for months.

"It's not much farther," the grandmother said and just as she said it, a horrible thought came to her. The thought was so embarrassing that she turned red in the face and her eyes dilated and her feet jumped up, upsetting her valise in the corner. The instant the valise moved, the newspaper top she had over the basket under it rose with a snarl and Pitty Sing, the cat, sprang onto Bailey's shoulder.

The children were thrown to the floor and their mother, clutching the baby, was thrown out the door onto the ground; the old lady was thrown into the front seat. The car turned over once and landed right-side-up in a gulch off the side of the road. Bailey remained in the driver's seat with the cat — gray-striped with a broad white face and an orange nose — clinging to his neck like a caterpillar.

As soon as the children saw they could move their arms and legs, they scram-   65
bled out of the car, shouting, "We've had an ACCIDENT!" The grandmother was curled up under the dashboard, hoping she was injured so that Bailey's wrath would not come down on her all at once. The horrible thought she had before the accident was that the house she had remembered so vividly was not in Georgia but in Tennessee.

Bailey removed the cat from his neck with both hands and flung it out the window against the side of a pine tree. Then he got out of the car and started looking for the children's mother. She was sitting against the side of the red gutted ditch, holding the screaming baby, but she only had a cut down her face and a broken shoulder. "We've had an ACCIDENT!" the children screamed in a frenzy of delight.

"But nobody's killed," June Star said with disappointment as the grandmother limped out of the car, her hat still pinned to her head but the broken front brim standing up at a jaunty angle and the violet spray hanging off the side. They all sat down in the ditch, except the children, to recover from the shock. They were all shaking.

"Maybe a car will come along," said the children's mother hoarsely.

"I believe I have injured an organ," said the grandmother, pressing her side, but no one answered her. Bailey's teeth were clattering. He had on a yellow sport shirt with bright blue parrots designed in it and his face was as yellow as the shirt. The grandmother decided that she would not mention that the house was in Tennessee.

The road was about ten feet above and they could see only the tops of the trees   70 on the other side of it. Behind the ditch they were sitting in there were more woods, tall and dark and deep. In a few minutes they saw a car some distance away on top of a hill, coming slowly as if the occupants were watching them. The grandmother stood up and waved both arms dramatically to attract their attention. The car continued to come on slowly, disappeared around a bend and appeared again, moving even slower, on top of the hill they had gone over. It was a big black battered hearse-like automobile. There were three men in it.

It came to a stop just over them and for some minutes, the driver looked down with a steady expressionless gaze to where they were sitting, and didn't speak. Then he turned his head and muttered something to the other two and they got out. One was a fat boy in black trousers and a red sweat shirt with a silver stallion embossed on the front of it. He moved around on the right side of them and stood staring, his mouth partly open in a kind of loose grin. The other had on khaki pants and a blue striped coat and a gray hat pulled down very low, hiding most of his face. He came around slowly on the left side. Neither spoke.

The driver got out of the car and stood by the side of it, looking down at them. He was an older man than the other two. His hair was just beginning to gray and he wore silver-rimmed spectacles that gave him a scholarly look. He had a long creased face and didn't have on any shirt or undershirt. He had on blue jeans that were too tight for him and was holding a black hat and a gun. The two boys also had guns.

"We've had an ACCIDENT!" the children screamed.

The grandmother had the peculiar feeling that the bespectacled man was someone she knew. His face was as familiar to her as if she had known him all her life but she could not recall who he was. He moved away from the car and began to come down the embankment, placing his feet carefully so that he wouldn't slip. He had on tan and white shoes and no socks, and his ankles were red and thin. "Good afternoon," he said. "I see you all had you a little spill."

"We turned over twice!" said the grandmother.   75

"Oncet," he corrected. "We seen it happen. Try their car and see will it run, Hiram," he said quietly to the boy with the gray hat.

"What you got that gun for?" John Wesley asked. "Whatcha gonna do with that gun?"

"Lady," the man said to the children's mother, "would you mind calling them children to sit down by you? Children make me nervous. I want all you all to sit down right together there where you're at."

"What are you telling US what to do for?" June Star asked.

Behind them the line of woods gaped like a dark open mouth. "Come here,"   80 said their mother.

"Look here now," Bailey said suddenly, "we're in a predicament! We're in. . . ."

The grandmother shrieked. She scrambled to her feet and stood staring. "You're The Misfit!" she said. "I recognized you at once!"

"Yes'm," the man said, smiling slightly as if he were pleased in spite of himself to be known, "but it would have been better for all of you, lady, if you hadn't of reckernized me."

Bailey turned his head sharply and said something to his mother that shocked even the children. The old lady began to cry and The Misfit reddened.

"Lady," he said, "don't you get upset. Sometimes a man says things he don't 85
mean. I don't reckon he meant to talk to you thataway."

"You wouldn't shoot a lady, would you?" the grandmother said and removed a
clean handkerchief from her cuff and began to slap at her eyes with it.

The Misfit pointed the toe of his shoe into the ground and made a little hole
and then covered it up again. "I would hate to have to," he said.

"Listen," the grandmother almost screamed, "I know you're a good man. You
don't look a bit like you have common blood. I know you must come from nice
people!"

"Yes mam," he said, "finest people in the world." When he smiled he showed
a row of strong white teeth. "God never made a finer woman than my mother and
my daddy's heart was pure gold," he said. The boy with the red sweat shirt had come
around behind them and was standing with his gun at his hip. The Misfit squatted
down on the ground. "Watch them children, Bobby Lee," he said. "You know they
make me nervous." He looked at the six of them huddled together in front of him
and he seemed to be embarrassed as if he couldn't think of anything to say. "Ain't a
cloud in the sky," he remarked, looking up at it. "Don't see no sun but don't see no
cloud neither."

"Yes, it's a beautiful day," said the grandmother. "Listen," she said, "you 90
shouldn't call yourself The Misfit because I know you're a good man at heart. I can
just look at you and tell."

"Hush!" Bailey yelled. "Hush! Everybody shut up and let me handle this!" He
was squatting in the position of a runner about to sprint forward but he didn't move.

"I pre-chate that, lady," The Misfit said and drew a little circle in the ground
with the butt of his gun.

"It'll take a half a hour to fix this here car," Hiram called, looking over the raised
hood of it.

"Well, first you and Bobby Lee get him and that little boy to step over yonder
with you," The Misfit said, pointing to Bailey and John Wesley. "The boys want to ast
you something," he said to Bailey. "Would you mind stepping back in them woods
there with them?"

"Listen," Bailey began, "we're in a terrible predicament! Nobody realizes what 95
this is," and his voice cracked. His eyes were as blue and intense as the parrots in his
shirt and he remained perfectly still.

The grandmother reached up to adjust her hat brim as if she were going to
the woods with him but it came off in her hand. She stood staring at it and after
a second she let it fall to the ground. Hiram pulled Bailey up by the arm as if
he were assisting an old man. John Wesley caught hold of his father's hand and
Bobby Lee followed. They went off toward the woods and just as they reached
the dark edge, Bailey turned and supporting himself against a gray naked pine
trunk, he shouted, "I'll be back in a minute, Mamma, wait on me!"

"Come back this instant!" his mother shrilled but they all disappeared into the
woods.

"Bailey Boy!" the grandmother called in a tragic voice but she found she was
looking at The Misfit squatting on the ground in front of her. "I just know you're a
good man," she said desperately. "You're not a bit common!"

"Nome, I ain't a good man," The Misfit said after a second as if he had considered her statement carefully, "but I ain't the worst in the world neither. My daddy
said I was a different breed of dog from my brothers and sisters. 'You know,' Daddy
said, 'it's some that can live their whole life out without asking about it and it's others

has to know why it is, and this boy is one of the latters. He's going to be into every-thing!'" He put on his black hat and looked up suddenly and then away deep into the woods as if he were embarrassed again. "I'm sorry I don't have on a shirt before you ladies," he said, hunching his shoulders slightly. "We buried our clothes that we had on when we escaped and we're just making do until we can get better. We bor-rowed these from some folks we met," he explained.

"That's perfectly all right," the grandmother said. "Maybe Bailey has an extra   100 shirt in his suitcase."

"I'll look and see terrectly," The Misfit said.

"Where are they taking him?" the children's mother screamed.

"Daddy was a card himself," The Misfit said. "You couldn't put anything over on him. He never got in trouble with the Authorities though. Just had the knack of handling them."

"You could be honest too if you'd only try," said the grandmother. "Think how wonderful it would be to settle down and live a comfortable life and not have to think about somebody chasing you all the time."

The Misfit kept scratching in the ground with the butt of his gun as if he were   105 thinking about it. "Yes'm, somebody is always after you," he murmured.

The grandmother noticed how thin his shoulder blades were just behind his hat because she was standing up looking down on him. "Do you ever pray?" she asked.

He shook his head. All she saw was the black hat wiggle between his shoulder blades. "Nome," he said.

There was a pistol shot from the woods, followed closely by another. Then silence. The old lady's head jerked around. She could hear the wind move through the tree tops like a long satisfied insuck of breath. "Bailey Boy!" she called.

"I was a gospel singer for a while," The Misfit said. "I been most everything. Been in the arm service, both land and sea, at home and abroad, been twict mar-ried, been an undertaker, been with the railroads, plowed Mother Earth, been in a tornado, seen a man burnt alive oncet," and he looked up at the children's mother and the little girl who were sitting close together, their faces white and their eyes glassy; "I even seen a woman flogged," he said.

"Pray, pray," the grandmother began, "pray, pray. . . ."   110

"I never was a bad boy that I remember of," The Misfit said in an almost dreamy voice, "but somewheres along the line I done something wrong and got sent to the penitentiary. I was buried alive," and he looked up and held her attention to him by a steady stare.

"That's when you should have started to pray," she said. "What did you do to get sent to the penitentiary that first time?"

"Turn to the right, it was a wall," The Misfit said, looking up again at the cloud-less sky. "Turn to the left, it was a wall. Look up it was a ceiling, look down it was a floor. I forget what I done, lady. I set there and set there, trying to remember what it was I done and I ain't recalled it to this day. Oncet in a while, I would think it was coming to me, but it never come."

"Maybe they put you in by mistake," the old lady said vaguely.

"Nome," he said. "It wasn't no mistake. They had the papers on me."   115

"You must have stolen something," she said.

The Misfit sneered slightly. "Nobody had nothing I wanted," he said. "It was a head-doctor at the penitentiary said what I had done was kill my daddy but I known that for a lie. My daddy died in nineteen ought nineteen of the epidemic flu and I never had a thing to do with it. He was buried in the Mount Hopewell Baptist churchyard and you can see for yourself."

"If you would pray," the old lady said, "Jesus would help you."

"That's right," The Misfit said.

"Well then, why don't you pray?" she asked trembling with delight suddenly.   120

"I don't want no hep," he said. "I'm doing all right by myself."

Bobby Lee and Hiram came ambling back from the woods. Bobby Lee was dragging a yellow shirt with bright blue parrots in it.

"Throw me that shirt, Bobby Lee," The Misfit said. The shirt came flying at him and landed on his shoulder and he put it on. The grandmother couldn't name what the shirt reminded her of. "No, lady," The Misfit said while he was buttoning it up, "I found out the crime don't matter. You can do one thing or you can do another, kill a man or take a tire off his car, because sooner or later you're going to forget what it was you done and just be punished for it."

The children's mother had begun to make heaving noises as if she couldn't get her breath. "Lady," he asked, "would you and that little girl like to step off yonder with Bobby Lee and Hiram and join your husband?"

"Yes, thank you," the mother said faintly. Her left arm dangled helplessly and   125 she was holding the baby, who had gone to sleep, in the other. "Hep that lady up, Hiram," The Misfit said as she struggled to climb out of the ditch, "and Bobby Lee, you hold onto that little girl's hand."

"I don't want to hold hands with him," June Star said. "He reminds me of a pig."

The fat boy blushed and laughed and caught her by the arm and pulled her off into the woods after Hiram and her mother.

Alone with The Misfit, the grandmother found that she had lost her voice. There was not a cloud in the sky nor any sun. There was nothing around her but woods. She wanted to tell him that he must pray. She opened and closed her mouth several times before anything came out. Finally she found herself saying, "Jesus, Jesus," meaning Jesus will help you, but the way she was saying it, it sounded as if she might be cursing.

"Yes'm," The Misfit said as if he agreed. "Jesus thrown everything off balance. It was the same case with Him as with me except He hadn't committed any crime and they could prove I had committed one because they had the papers on me. Of course," he said, "they never shown me my papers. That's why I sign myself now. I said long ago, you get your signature and sign everything you do and keep a copy of it. Then you'll know what you done and you can hold up the crime to the punishment and see do they match and in the end you'll have something to prove you ain't been treated right. I call myself The Misfit," he said, "because I can't make what all I done wrong fit what all I gone through in punishment."

There was a piercing scream from the woods, followed closely by a pistol   130 report. "Does it seem right to you, lady, that one is punished a heap and another ain't punished at all?"

"Jesus!" the old lady cried. "You've got good blood! I know you wouldn't shoot a lady! I know you come from nice people! Pray! Jesus, you ought not to shoot a lady. I'll give you all the money I've got!"

"Lady," The Misfit said, looking beyond her far into the woods, "there never was a body that give the undertaker a tip."

There were two more pistol reports and the grandmother raised her head like a parched old turkey hen crying for water and called, "Bailey Boy, Bailey Boy!" as if her heart would break.

"Jesus was the only One that ever raised the dead," The Misfit continued, "and He shouldn't have done it. He thown everything off balance. If He did what He said, then it's nothing for you to do but thow away everything and follow Him, and if He didn't, then it's nothing for you to do but enjoy the few minutes you got left the best way you can — by killing somebody or burning down his house or doing some other meanness to him. No pleasure but meanness," he said and his voice had become almost a snarl.

"Maybe He didn't raise the dead," the old lady mumbled, not knowing what she 135 was saying and feeling so dizzy that she sank down in the ditch with her legs twisted under her.

"I wasn't there so I can't say He didn't," The Misfit said. "I wisht I had of been there," he said, hitting the ground with his fist. "It ain't right I wasn't there because if I had of been there I would of known. Listen lady," he said in a high voice, "if I had of been there I would of known and I wouldn't be like I am now." His voice seemed about to crack and the grandmother's head cleared for an instant. She saw the man's face twisted close to her own as if he were going to cry and she murmured, "Why you're one of my babies. You're one of my own children!" She reached out and touched him on the shoulder. The Misfit sprang back as if a snake had bitten him and shot her three times through the chest. Then he put his gun down on the ground and took off his glasses and began to clean them.

Hiram and Bobby Lee returned from the woods and stood over the ditch, looking down at the grandmother who half sat and half lay in a puddle of blood with her legs crossed under her like a child's and her face smiling up at the cloudless sky.

Without his glasses, The Misfit's eyes were red-rimmed and pale and defenseless-looking. "Take her off and thow her where you thown the others," he said, picking up the cat that was rubbing itself against his leg.

"She was a talker, wasn't she?" Bobby Lee said, sliding down the ditch with a yodel.

"She would of been a good woman," The Misfit said, "if it had been somebody 140 there to shoot her every minute of her life."

"Some fun!" Bobby Lee said.

"Shut up, Bobby Lee," The Misfit said. "It's no real pleasure in life."

CONSIDERATIONS FOR CRITICAL THINKING AND WRITING

1. **FIRST RESPONSE.** How does O'Connor portray the family? What is comic about them? What qualities about them are we meant to take seriously? Are you shocked by what happens to them? Does your attitude toward them remain constant during the course of the story?

2. How do the grandmother's concerns about the trip to Florida foreshadow events in the story?

3. Describe the grandmother. How does O'Connor make her the central character?

4. What is Red Sammy's purpose in the story? Relate his view of life to the story's conflicts.

5. Characterize The Misfit. What makes him so? Can he be written off as simply insane? How does the grandmother respond to him?

6. Why does The Misfit say that "Jesus thown everything off balance" (para. 129)? What does religion have to do with the brutal action of this story?

7. What does The Misfit mean at the end when he says about the grandmother, "She would of been a good woman . . . if it had been somebody there to shoot her every minute of her life"?

8. Describe the story's tone. Is it consistent? What is the effect of O'Connor's use of tone?

9. How is coincidence used to advance the plot? How do coincidences lead to ironies in the story?

10. Explain how the title points to the story's theme.

CONNECTIONS TO OTHER SELECTIONS

1. What makes "A Good Man Is Hard to Find" so difficult to interpret in contrast, say, to Nathaniel Hawthorne's "The Birthmark" (p. 339)?

2. How does this family compare with the Snopeses in Faulkner's "Barn Burning" (p. 406)? Which family are you more sympathetic to?

3. Consider the criminal behavior of The Misfit and Abner Snopes. What motivates each character? Explain the significant similarities and differences between them.

Good Country People 1955

Besides the neutral expression that she wore when she was alone, Mrs. Freeman had two others, forward and reverse, that she used for all her human dealings. Her forward expression was steady and driving like the advance of a heavy truck. Her eyes never swerved to left or right but turned as the story turned as if they followed a yellow line down the center of it. She seldom used the other expression because it was not often necessary for her to retract a statement, but when she did, her face came to a complete stop, there was an almost imperceptible movement of her black eyes, during which they seemed to be receding, and then the observer would see that Mrs. Freeman, though she might stand there as real as several grain sacks thrown on top of each other, was no longer there in spirit. As for getting anything across to her when this was the case, Mrs. Hopewell had given it up. She might talk her head off. Mrs. Freeman could never be brought to admit herself wrong on any point. She would stand there and if she could be brought to say anything, it was something like, "Well, I wouldn't of said it was and I wouldn't of said it wasn't," or letting her gaze range over the top kitchen shelf where there was an assortment of dusty bottles, she might remark, "I see you ain't ate many of them figs you put up last summer."

They carried on their most important business in the kitchen at breakfast. Every morning Mrs. Hopewell got up at seven o'clock and lit her gas heater and Joy's. Joy was her daughter, a large blonde girl who had an artificial leg. Mrs. Hopewell thought of her as a child though she was thirty-two years old and highly educated. Joy would get up while her mother was eating and lumber into the bathroom and slam the door, and before long, Mrs. Freeman would arrive at the back door. Joy would hear her mother call, "Come on in," and then they would talk for a while in low voices that were indistinguishable in the bathroom. By the time Joy came in, they had usually finished the weather report and were on one or the other of Mrs. Freeman's daughters, Glynese or Carramae, Joy called them Glycerin and Caramel. Glynese, a redhead, was eighteen and had many admirers; Carramae, a blonde, was only fifteen but already married and pregnant. She could not keep anything in her stomach. Every morning Mrs. Freeman told Mrs. Hopewell how many times she had vomited since the last report.

Mrs. Hopewell liked to tell people that Glynese and Carramae were two of the finest girls she knew and that Mrs. Freeman was a *lady* and that she was never ashamed to take her anywhere or introduce her to anybody they might meet. Then she would tell how she had happened to hire the Freemans in the first place and how they were a godsend to her and how she had had them four years. The reason for her keeping them so long was that they were not trash. They were good country people. She had telephoned the man whose name they had given as a reference and he had told her that Mr. Freeman was a good farmer but that his wife was the nosiest woman ever to walk the earth. "She's got to be into everything," the man said. "If she don't get there before the dust settles, you can bet she's dead, that's all. She'll want to know all your business. I can stand him real good," he had said, "but me nor my wife neither could have stood that woman one more minute on this place." That had put Mrs. Hopewell off for a few days.

She had hired them in the end because there were no other applicants but she had made up her mind beforehand exactly how she would handle the woman. Since she was the type who had to be into everything, then, Mrs. Hopewell decided, she would not only let her be into everything, she would *see to it* that she was into everything — she would give her the responsibility of everything, she would put her in charge. Mrs. Hopewell had no bad qualities of her own but she was able to use other people's in such a constructive way that she never felt the lack. She had hired the Freemans and she had kept them four years.

Nothing is perfect. This was one of Mrs. Hopewell's favorite sayings. Another 5 was: that is life! And still another, the most important, was: well, other people have their opinions too. She would make these statements, usually at the table, in a tone of gentle insistence as if no one held them but her, and the large hulking Joy, whose constant outrage had obliterated every expression from her face, would stare just a little to the side of her, her eyes icy blue, with the look of someone who has achieved blindness by an act of will and means to keep it.

When Mrs. Hopewell said to Mrs. Freeman that life was like that, Mrs. Freeman would say, "I always said so myself." Nothing had been arrived at by anyone that had not first been arrived at by her. She was quicker than Mr. Freeman. When Mrs. Hopewell said to her after they had been on the place a while, "You know, you're the wheel behind the wheel," and winked, Mrs. Freeman had said, "I know it. I've always been quick. It's some that are quicker than others."

"Everybody is different," Mrs. Hopewell said.

"Yes, most people is," Mrs. Freeman said.

"It takes all kinds to make the world."

"I always said it did myself." 10

The girl was used to this kind of dialogue for breakfast and more of it for dinner; sometimes they had it for supper too. When they had no guest they ate in the kitchen because that was easier. Mrs. Freeman always managed to arrive at some point during the meal and to watch them finish it. She would stand in the doorway if it were summer but in the winter she would stand with one elbow on top of the refrigerator and look down on them, or she would stand by the gas heater, lifting the back of her skirt slightly. Occasionally she would stand against the wall and roll her head from side to side. At no time was she in any hurry to leave. All this was very trying on Mrs. Hopewell but she was a woman of great patience. She realized that nothing is perfect and that in the Freemans she had good country people and that if, in this day and age, you get good country people, you had better hang onto them.

She had had plenty of experience with trash. Before the Freemans she had averaged one tenant family a year. The wives of these farmers were not the kind you would want to be around you for very long. Mrs. Hopewell, who had divorced her husband long ago, needed someone to walk over the fields with her; and when Joy had to be impressed for these services, her remarks were usually so ugly and her face so glum that Mrs. Hopewell would say, "If you can't come pleasantly, I don't want you at all," to which the girl, standing square and rigid-shouldered with her neck thrust slightly forward, would reply, "If you want me, here I am — LIKE I AM."

Mrs. Hopewell excused this attitude because of the leg (which had been shot off in a hunting accident when Joy was ten). It was hard for Mrs. Hopewell to realize that her child was thirty-two now and that for more than twenty years she had had only one leg. She thought of her still as a child because it tore her heart to think instead of the poor stout girl in her thirties who had never danced a step or had any *normal* good times. Her name was really Joy but as soon as she was twenty-one and away from home, she had had it legally changed. Mrs. Hopewell was certain that she had thought and thought until she had hit upon the ugliest name in any language. Then she had gone and had the beautiful name, Joy, changed without telling her mother until after she had done it. Her legal name was Hulga.

When Mrs. Hopewell thought the name, Hulga, she thought of the broad blank hull of a battleship. She would not use it. She continued to call her Joy to which the girl responded but in a purely mechanical way.

Hulga had learned to tolerate Mrs. Freeman who saved her from taking walks 15 with her mother. Even Glynese and Carramae were useful when they occupied attention that might otherwise have been directed at her. At first she had thought she could not stand Mrs. Freeman for she had found that it was not possible to be rude to her. Mrs. Freeman would take on strange resentments and for days together she would be sullen but the source of her displeasure was always obscure; a direct attack, a positive leer, blatant ugliness to her face — these never touched her. And without warning one day, she began calling her Hulga.

She did not call her that in front of Mrs. Hopewell who would have been incensed but when she and the girl happened to be out of the house together, she would say something and add the name Hulga to the end of it, and the big spectacled Joy-Hulga would scowl and redden as if her privacy had been intruded upon. She considered the name her personal affair. She had arrived at it first purely on the basis of its ugly sound and then the full genius of its fitness had struck her. She had a vision of the name working like the ugly sweating Vulcan° who stayed in the furnace and to whom, presumably, the goddess had to come when called. She saw it as the name of her highest creative act. One of her major triumphs was that her mother had not been able to turn her dust into Joy, but the greater one was that she had been able to turn it herself into Hulga. However, Mrs. Freeman's relish for using the name only irritated her. It was as if Mrs. Freeman's beady steel-pointed eyes had penetrated far enough behind her face to reach some secret fact. Something about her seemed to fascinate Mrs. Freeman and then one day Hulga realized that it was the artificial leg. Mrs. Freeman had a special fondness for the details of secret infections, hidden deformities, assaults upon children. Of diseases, she preferred the lingering or incurable. Hulga had heard Mrs. Hopewell give her the details of the hunting accident, how the leg had been literally blasted off, how she had never lost consciousness. Mrs. Freeman could listen to it any time as if it had happened an hour ago.

Vulcan: Roman god of fire.

When Hulga stumped into the kitchen in the morning (she could walk without making the awful noise but she made it — Mrs. Hopewell was certain — because it was ugly-sounding), she glanced at them and did not speak. Mrs. Hopewell would be in her red kimono with her hair tied around her head in rags. She would be sitting at the table, finishing her breakfast and Mrs. Freeman would be hanging by her elbow outward from the refrigerator, looking down at the table. Hulga always put her eggs on the stove to boil and then stood over them with her arms folded, and Mrs. Hopewell would look at her — a kind of indirect gaze divided between her and Mrs. Freeman — and would think that if she would only keep herself up a little, she wouldn't be so bad looking. There was nothing wrong with her face that a pleasant expression wouldn't help. Mrs. Hopewell said that people who looked on the bright side of things would be beautiful even if they were not.

Whenever she looked at Joy this way, she could not help but feel that it would have been better if the child had not taken the Ph.D. It had certainly not brought her out any and now that she had it, there was no more excuse for her to go to school again. Mrs. Hopewell thought it was nice for girls to go to school to have a good time but Joy had "gone through." Anyhow, she would not have been strong enough to go again. The doctors had told Mrs. Hopewell that with the best of care, Joy might see forty-five. She had a weak heart. Joy had made it plain that if it had not been for this condition, she would be far from these red hills and good country people. She would be in a university lecturing to people who knew what she was talking about. And Mrs. Hopewell could very well picture her there, looking like a scarecrow and lecturing to more of the same. Here she went about all day in a six-year-old skirt and a yellow sweat shirt with a faded cowboy on a horse embossed on it. She thought this was funny; Mrs. Hopewell thought it was idiotic and showed simply that she was still a child. She was brilliant but she didn't have a grain of sense. It seemed to Mrs. Hopewell that every year she grew less like other people and more like herself — bloated, rude, and squint-eyed. And she said such strange things! To her own mother she had said — without warning, without excuse, standing up in the middle of a meal with her face purple and her mouth half full — "Woman! do you ever look inside? Do you ever look inside and see what you are *not*? God!" she had cried sinking down again and staring at her plate, "Malebranche° was right: we are not our own light. We are not our own light!" Mrs. Hopewell had no idea to this day what brought that on. She had only made the remark, hoping Joy would take it in, that a smile never hurt anyone.

The girl had taken the Ph.D. in philosophy and this left Mrs. Hopewell at a complete loss. You could say, "My daughter is a nurse," or "My daughter is a schoolteacher," or even, "My daughter is a chemical engineer." You could not say, "My daughter is a philosopher." That was something that had ended with the Greeks and Romans. All day Joy sat on her neck in a deep chair, reading. Sometimes she went for walks but she didn't like dogs or cats or birds or flowers or nature or nice young men. She looked at nice young men as if she could smell their stupidity.

One day Mrs. Hopewell had picked up one of the books the girl had just put down and opening it at random, she read, "Science, on the other hand, has to assert its soberness and seriousness afresh and declare that it is concerned solely with what-is. Nothing — how can it be for science anything but a horror and a phantasm? If science is right, then one thing stands firm: science wishes to know nothing of nothing. Such is after all the strictly scientific approach to Nothing.

Malebranche: Nicolas Malebranche (1638–1715), a French philosopher.

We know it by wishing to know nothing of Nothing." These words had been underlined with a blue pencil and they worked on Mrs. Hopewell like some evil incantation in gibberish. She shut the book quickly and went out of the room as if she were having a chill.

This morning when the girl came in, Mrs. Freeman was on Carramae. "She thrown up four times after supper," she said, "and was up twict in the night after three o'clock. Yesterday she didn't do nothing but ramble in the bureau drawer. All she did. Stand up there and see what she could run up on."

"She's got to eat," Mrs. Hopewell muttered, sipping her coffee, while she watched Joy's back at the stove. She was wondering what the child had said to the Bible salesman. She could not imagine what kind of a conversation she could possibly have had with him.

He was a tall gaunt hatless youth who had called yesterday to sell them a Bible. He had appeared at the door, carrying a large black suitcase that weighted him so heavily on one side that he had to brace himself against the door facing. He seemed on the point of collapse but he said in a cheerful voice, "Good morning, Mrs. Cedars!" and set the suitcase down on the mat. He was not a bad-looking young man though he had on a bright blue suit and yellow socks that were not pulled up far enough. He had prominent face bones and a streak of sticky-looking brown hair falling across his forehead.

"I'm Mrs. Hopewell," she said.

"Oh!" he said, pretending to look puzzled but with his eyes sparkling, "I saw it 25 said 'The Cedars' on the mailbox so I thought you was Mrs. Cedars!" and he burst out in a pleasant laugh. He picked up the satchel and under cover of a pant, he fell forward into her hall. It was rather as if the suitcase had moved first, jerking him after it. "Mrs. Hopewell!" he said and grabbed her hand. "I hope you are well!" and he laughed again and then all at once his face sobered completely. He paused and gave her a straight earnest look and said, "Lady, I've come to speak of serious things."

"Well, come in," she muttered, none too pleased because her dinner was almost ready. He came into the parlor and sat down on the edge of a straight chair and put the suitcase between his feet and glanced around the room as if he were sizing her up by it. Her silver gleamed on the two sideboards; she decided he had never been in a room as elegant as this.

"Mrs. Hopewell," he began, using her name in a way that sounded almost intimate, "I know you believe in Chrustian service."

"Well yes," she murmured.

"I know," he said and paused, looking very wise with his head cocked on one side, "that you're a good woman. Friends have told me."

Mrs. Hopewell never liked to be taken for a fool. "What are you selling?" she 30 asked.

"Bibles," the young man said and his eye raced around the room before he added, "I see you have no family Bible in your parlor, I see that is the one lack you got!"

Mrs. Hopewell could not say, "My daughter is an atheist and won't let me keep the Bible in the parlor." She said, stiffening slightly, "I keep my Bible by my bedside." This was not the truth. It was in the attic somewhere.

"Lady," he said, "the word of God ought to be in the parlor."

"Well, I think that's a matter of taste," she began. "I think . . ."

"Lady," he said, "for a Chrustian, the word of God ought to be in every room 35 in the house besides in his heart. I know you're a Chrustian because I can see it in every line of your face."

She stood up and said, "Well, young man, I don't want to buy a Bible and I smell my dinner burning."

He didn't get up. He began to twist his hands and looking down at them, he said softly, "Well lady, I'll tell you the truth—not many people want to buy one nowadays and besides, I know I'm real simple. I don't know how to say a thing but to say it. I'm just a country boy." He glanced up into her unfriendly face. "People like you don't like to fool with country people like me!"

"Why!" she cried, "good country people are the salt of the earth! Besides, we all have different ways of doing, it takes all kinds to make the world go 'round. That's life!"

"You said a mouthful," he said.

"Why, I think there aren't enough good people in the world!" she said, stirred.   40
"I think that's what's wrong with it!"

His face had brightened. "I didn't introduce myself," he said. "I'm Manley Pointer from out in the country around Willohobie, not even from a place, just from near a place."

"You wait a minute," she said. "I have to see about my dinner." She went out to the kitchen and found Joy standing near the door where she had been listening.

"Get rid of the salt of the earth," she said, "and let's eat."

Mrs. Hopewell gave her a pained look and turned the heat down under the vegetables. "I can't be rude to anybody," she murmured and went back into the parlor.

He had opened the suitcase and was sitting with a Bible on each knee.   45

"You might as well put those up," she told him. "I don't want one."

"I appreciate your honesty," he said. "You don't see any more real honest people unless you go way out in the country."

"I know," she said, "real genuine folks!" Through the crack in the door she heard a groan.

"I guess a lot of boys come telling you they're working their way through college," he said, "but I'm not going to tell you that. Somehow," he said, "I don't want to go to college. I want to devote my life to Chrustian service. See," he said, lowering his voice, "I got this heart condition. I may not live long. When you know it's something wrong with you and you may not live long, well then, lady . . ." He paused, with his mouth open, and stared at her.

He and Joy had the same condition! She knew that her eyes were filling with   50
tears but she collected herself quickly and murmured, "Won't you stay for dinner? We'd love to have you!" and was sorry the instant she heard herself say it.

"Yes mam," he said in an abashed voice, "I would sher love to do that!"

Joy had given him one look on being introduced to him and then throughout the meal had not glanced at him again. He had addressed several remarks to her, which she had pretended not to hear. Mrs. Hopewell could not understand deliberate rudeness, although she lived with it, and she felt she had always to overflow with hospitality to make up for Joy's lack of courtesy. She urged him to talk about himself and he did. He said he was the seventh child of twelve and that his father had been crushed under a tree when he himself was eight years old. He had been crushed very badly, in fact, almost cut in two and was practically not recognizable. His mother had got along the best she could by hard working and she had always seen that her children went to Sunday School and that they read the Bible every evening. He was now nineteen years old and he had been selling Bibles for four months. In that time he had sold seventy-seven Bibles and had the promise of two more sales. He wanted to become a missionary because he thought that was the way you could do most for people. "He who losest his life shall find it," he said simply and he was so sincere, so genuine and earnest that Mrs. Hopewell would not for the world have smiled. He prevented his peas from sliding onto the table by blocking them with a piece of bread which he later cleaned his plate with. She could see Joy observing sidewise how he handled his knife and fork and she saw too that every few minutes, the boy would dart a keen appraising glance at the girl as if he were trying to attract her attention.

After dinner Joy cleared the dishes off the table and disappeared and Mrs. Hopewell was left to talk with him. He told her again about his childhood and his father's accident and about various things that had happened to him. Every five minutes or so she would stifle a yawn. He sat for two hours until finally she told him she must go because she had an appointment in town. He packed his Bibles and thanked her and prepared to leave, but in the doorway he stopped and wrung her hand and said that not on any of his trips had he met a lady as nice as her and he asked if he could come again. She had said she would always be happy to see him.

Joy had been standing in the road, apparently looking at something in the distance, when he came down the steps toward her, bent to the side with his heavy valise. He stopped where she was standing and confronted her directly. Mrs. Hopewell could not hear what he said but she trembled to think what Joy would say to him. She could see that after a minute Joy said something and that then the boy began to speak again, making an excited gesture with his free hand. After a minute Joy said something else at which the boy began to speak once more. Then to her amazement, Mrs. Hopewell saw the two of them walk off together, toward the gate. Joy had walked all the way to the gate with him and Mrs. Hopewell could not imagine what they had said to each other, and she had not yet dared to ask.

Mrs. Freeman was insisting upon her attention. She had moved from the 55 refrigerator to the heater so that Mrs. Hopewell had to turn and face her in order to seem to be listening. "Glynese gone out with Harvey Hill again last night," she said. "She had this sty."

"Hill," Mrs. Hopewell said absently, "is the one who works in the garage?"

"Nome, he's the one that goes to chiropractor school," Mrs. Freeman said. "She had this sty. Been had it two days. So she says when he brought her in the other night he says, 'Lemme get rid of that sty for you,' and she says, 'How?' and he says, 'You just lay yourself down acrost the seat of that car and I'll show you.' So she done it and he popped her neck. Kept on a-popping it several times until she made him quit. This morning," Mrs. Freeman said, "she ain't got no sty. She ain't got no traces of a sty."

"I never heard of that before," Mrs. Hopewell said.

"He ast her to marry him before the Ordinary,"° Mrs. Freeman went on, "and she told him she wasn't going to be married in no *office*."

"Well, Glynese is a fine girl," Mrs. Hopewell said. "Glynese and Carramae are 60 both fine girls."

"Carramae said when her and Lyman was married Lyman said it sure felt sacred to him. She said he said he wouldn't take five hundred dollars for being married by a preacher."

"How much would he take?" the girl asked from the stove.

"He said he wouldn't take five hundred dollars," Mrs. Freeman repeated.

"Well we all have work to do," Mrs. Hopewell said.

"Lyman said it just felt more sacred to him," Mrs. Freeman said. "The doctor 65 wants Carramae to eat prunes. Says instead of medicine. Says them cramps is coming from pressure. You know where I think it is?"

Ordinary: Justice of the peace.

"She'll be better in a few weeks," Mrs. Hopewell said.

"In the tube," Mrs. Freeman said. "Else she wouldn't be as sick as she is."

Hulga had cracked her two eggs into a saucer and was bringing them to the table along with a cup of coffee that she had filled too full. She sat down carefully and began to eat, meaning to keep Mrs. Freeman there by questions if for any reason she showed an inclination to leave. She could perceive her mother's eye on her. The first round-about question would be about the Bible salesman and she did not wish to bring it on. "How did he pop her neck?" she asked.

Mrs. Freeman went into a description of how he had popped her neck. She said he owned a '55 Mercury but that Glynese said she would rather marry a man with only a '36 Plymouth who would be married by a preacher. The girl asked what if he had a '32 Plymouth and Mrs. Freeman said what Glynese had said was a '36 Plymouth.

Mrs. Hopewell said there were not many girls with Glynese's common sense.   70 She said what she admired in those girls was their common sense. She said that reminded her that they had had a nice visitor yesterday, a young man selling Bibles. "Lord," she said, "he bored me to death but he was so sincere and genuine I couldn't be rude to him. He was just good country people, you know," she said, "— just the salt of the earth."

"I seen him walk up," Mrs. Freeman said, "and then later — I seen him walk off," and Hulga could feel the slight shift in her voice, the slight insinuation, that he had not walked off alone, had he? Her face remained expressionless but the color rose into her neck and she seemed to swallow it down with the next spoonful of egg. Mrs. Freeman was looking at her as if they had a secret together.

"Well, it takes all kinds of people to make the world go 'round," Mrs. Hopewell said. "It's very good we aren't all alike."

"Some people are more alike than others," Mrs. Freeman said.

Hulga got up and stumped, with about twice the noise that was necessary, into her room and locked the door. She was to meet the Bible salesman at ten o'clock at the gate. She had thought about it half the night. She had started thinking of it as a great joke and then she had begun to see profound implications in it. She had lain in bed imagining dialogues for them that were insane on the surface but that reached below to depths that no Bible salesman would be aware of. Their conversation yesterday had been of this kind.

He had stopped in front of her and had simply stood there. His face was bony   75 and sweaty and bright, with a little pointed nose in the center of it, and his look was different from what it had been at the dinner table. He was gazing at her with open curiosity, with fascination, like a child watching a new fantastic animal at the zoo, and he was breathing as if he had run a great distance to reach her. His gaze seemed somehow familiar but she could not think where she had been regarded with it before. For almost a minute he didn't say anything. Then on what seemed an insuck of breath, he whispered, "You ever ate a chicken that was two days old?"

The girl looked at him stonily. He might have just put this question up for consideration at the meeting of a philosophical association. "Yes," she presently replied as if she had considered it from all angles.

"It must have been mighty small!" he said triumphantly and shook all over with little nervous giggles, getting very red in the face, and subsiding finally into his gaze of complete admiration, while the girl's expression remained exactly the same.

"How old are you?" he asked softly.

She waited some time before she answered. Then in a flat voice she said, "Seventeen."

His smiles came in succession like waves breaking on the surface of a little lake. 80 "I see you got a wooden leg," he said. "I think you're brave. I think you're real sweet."

The girl stood blank and solid and silent.

"Walk to the gate with me," he said. "You're a brave sweet little thing and I liked you the minute I seen you walk in the door."

Hulga began to move forward.

"What's your name?" he asked, smiling down on the top of her head.

"Hulga," she said. 85

"Hulga," he murmured, "Hulga. Hulga. I never heard of anybody name Hulga before. You're shy, aren't you, Hulga?" he asked.

She nodded, watching his large red hand on the handle of the giant valise.

"I like girls that wear glasses," he said. "I think a lot. I'm not like these people that a serious thought don't ever enter their heads. It's because I may die."

"I may die too," she said suddenly and looked up at him. His eyes were very small and brown, glittering feverishly.

"Listen," he said, "don't you think some people was meant to meet on account 90 of what all they got in common and all? Like they both think serious thoughts and all?" He shifted the valise to his other hand so that the hand nearest her was free. He caught hold of her elbow and shook it a little. "I don't work on Saturday," he said. "I like to walk in the woods and see what Mother Nature is wearing. O'er the hills and far away. Pic-nics and things. Couldn't we go on a pic-nic tomorrow? Say yes, Hulga," he said and gave her a dying look as if he felt his insides about to drop out of him. He had even seemed to sway slightly toward her.

During the night she had imagined that she seduced him. She imagined that the two of them walked on the place until they came to the storage barn beyond the two back fields and there, she imagined, that things came to such a pass that she very easily seduced him and that then, of course, she had to reckon with his remorse. True genius can get an idea across even to an inferior mind. She imagined that she took his remorse in hand and changed it into a deeper understanding of life. She took all his shame away and turned it into something useful.

She set off for the gate at exactly ten o'clock, escaping without drawing Mrs. Hopewell's attention. She didn't take anything to eat, forgetting that food is usually taken on a picnic. She wore a pair of slacks and a dirty white shirt, and as an afterthought, she had put some Vapex° on the collar of it since she did not own any perfume. When she reached the gate no one was there.

She looked up and down the empty highway and had the furious feeling that she had been tricked, that he had only meant to make her walk to the gate after the idea of him. Then suddenly he stood up, very tall, from behind a bush on the opposite embankment. Smiling, he lifted his hat which was new and wide-brimmed. He had not worn it yesterday and she wondered if he had bought it for the occasion. It was toast-colored with a red and white band around it and was slightly too large for him. He stepped from behind the bush still carrying the black valise. He had on the same suit and the same yellow socks sucked down in his shoes from walking. He crossed the highway and said, "I knew you'd come!"

The girl wondered acidly how he had known this. She pointed to the valise and asked, "Why did you bring your Bibles?"

He took her elbow, smiling down on her as if he could not stop. "You can never 95 tell when you'll need the word of God, Hulga," he said. She had a moment in which

---

Vapex: Trade name for a nasal spray.

she doubted that this was actually happening and then they began to climb the embankment. They went down into the pasture toward the woods. The boy walked lightly by her side, bouncing on his toes. The valise did not seem to be heavy today; he even swung it. They crossed half the pasture without saying anything and then, putting his hand easily on the small of her back, he asked softly, "Where does your wooden leg join on?"

She turned an ugly red and glared at him and for an instant the boy looked abashed. "I didn't mean you no harm," he said. "I only meant you're so brave and all. I guess God takes care of you."

"No," she said, looking forward and walking fast, "I don't even believe in God."

At this he stopped and whistled. "No!" he exclaimed as if he were too astonished to say anything else.

She walked on and in a second he was bouncing at her side, fanning with his hat. "That's very unusual for a girl," he remarked, watching her out of the corner of his eye. When they reached the edge of the wood, he put his hand on her back again and drew her against him without a word and kissed her heavily.

The kiss, which had more pressure than feeling behind it, produced that extra   100
surge of adrenaline in the girl that enables one to carry a packed trunk out of a burning house, but in her, the power went at once to the brain. Even before he released her, her mind, clear and detached and ironic anyway, was regarding him from a great distance, with amusement but with pity. She had never been kissed before and she was pleased to discover that it was an unexceptional experience and all a matter of the mind's control. Some people might enjoy drain water if they were told it was vodka. When the boy, looking expectant but uncertain, pushed her gently away, she turned and walked on, saying nothing as if such business, for her, were common enough.

He came along panting at her side, trying to help her when he saw a root that she might trip over. He caught and held back the long swaying blades of thorn vine until she had passed beyond them. She led the way and he came breathing heavily behind her. Then they came out on a sunlit hillside, sloping softly into another one a little smaller. Beyond, they could see the rusted top of the old barn where the extra hay was stored.

The hill was sprinkled with small pink weeds. "Then you ain't saved?" he asked suddenly, stopping.

The girl smiled. It was the first time she had smiled at him at all. "In my economy," she said, "I'm saved and you are damned but I told you I didn't believe in God."

Nothing seemed to destroy the boy's look of admiration. He gazed at her now as if the fantastic animal at the zoo had put its paw through the bars and given him a loving poke. She thought he looked as if he wanted to kiss her again and she walked on before he had the chance.

"Ain't there somewheres we can sit down sometime?" he murmured, his voice   105
softening toward the end of the sentence.

"In that barn," she said.

They made for it rapidly as if it might slide away like a train. It was a large two-story barn, cool and dark inside. The boy pointed up the ladder that led into the loft and said, "It's too bad we can't go up there."

"Why can't we?" she asked.

"Yer leg," he said reverently.

The girl gave him a contemptuous look and putting both hands on the ladder,   110
she climbed it while he stood below, apparently awestruck. She pulled herself

expertly through the opening and then looked down at him and said, "Well, come on if you're coming," and he began to climb the ladder, awkwardly bringing the suitcase with him.

"We won't need the Bible," she observed.

"You never can tell," he said, panting. After he had got into the loft, he was a few seconds catching his breath. She had sat down in a pile of straw. A wide sheath of sunlight, filled with dust particles, slanted over her. She lay back against a bale, her face turned away, looking out the front opening of the barn where hay was thrown from a wagon into the loft. The two pink-speckled hillsides lay back against a dark ridge of woods. The sky was cloudless and cold blue. The boy dropped down by her side and put one arm under her and the other over her and began methodically kissing her face, making little noises like a fish. He did not remove his hat but it was pushed far enough back not to interfere. When her glasses got in his way, he took them off of her and slipped them into his pocket.

The girl at first did not return any of the kisses but presently she began to and after she had put several on his cheek, she reached his lips and remained there, kissing him again and again as if she were trying to draw all the breath out of him. His breath was clear and sweet like a child's and the kisses were sticky like a child's. He mumbled about loving her and about knowing when he first seen her that he loved her, but the mumbling was like the sleepy fretting of a child being put to sleep by his mother. Her mind, throughout this, never stopped or lost itself for a second to her feelings. "You ain't said you loved me none," he whispered finally, pulling back from her. "You got to say that."

She looked away from him off into the hollow sky and then down at a black ridge and then down farther into what appeared to be two green swelling lakes. She didn't realize he had taken her glasses but this landscape could not seem exceptional to her for she seldom paid any close attention to her surroundings.

"You got to say it," he repeated. "You got to say you love me."   115

She was always careful how she committed herself. "In a sense," she began, "if you use the word loosely, you might say that. But it's not a word I use. I don't have illusions. I'm one of those people who see *through* to nothing."

The boy was frowning. "You got to say it. I said it and you got to say it," he said.

The girl looked at him almost tenderly. "You poor baby," she murmured. "It's just as well you don't understand," and she pulled him by the neck, face-down, against her. "We are all damned," she said, "but some of us have taken off our blindfolds and see that there's nothing to see. It's a kind of salvation."

The boy's astonished eyes looked blankly through the ends of her hair. "Okay," he almost whined, "but do you love me or don'tcher?"

"Yes," she said and added, "in a sense. But I must tell you something. There   120
mustn't be anything dishonest between us." She lifted his head and looked him in the eye. "I am thirty years old," she said. "I have a number of degrees."

The boy's look was irritated but dogged. "I don't care," he said. "I don't care a thing about what all you done. I just want to know if you love me or don'tcher?" and he caught her to him and wildly planted her face with kisses until she said, "Yes, yes."

"Okay then," he said, letting her go. "Prove it."

She smiled, looking dreamily out on the shifty landscape. She had seduced him without even making up her mind to try. "How?" she asked, feeling that he should be delayed a little.

He leaned over and put his lips to her ear. "Show me where your wooden leg joins on," he whispered.

The girl uttered a sharp little cry and her face instantly drained of color. The obscenity of the suggestion was not what shocked her. As a child she had sometimes been subject to feelings of shame but education had removed the last traces of that as a good surgeon scrapes for cancer; she would no more have felt it over what he was asking than she would have believed in his Bible. But she was as sensitive about the artificial leg as a peacock about his tail. No one ever touched it but her. She took care of it as someone else would his soul, in private and almost with her own eyes turned away. "No," she said.

"I known it," he muttered, sitting up. "You're just playing me for a sucker."

"Oh no no!" she cried. "It joins on at the knee. Only at the knee. Why do you want to see it?"

The boy gave her a long penetrating look. "Because," he said, "it's what makes you different. You ain't like anybody else."

She sat staring at him. There was nothing about her face or her round freezing-blue eyes to indicate that this had moved her; but she felt as if her heart had stopped and left her mind to pump her blood. She decided that for the first time in her life she was face to face with real innocence. This boy, with an instinct that came from beyond wisdom, had touched the truth about her. When after a minute, she said in a hoarse high voice, "All right," it was like surrendering to him completely. It was like losing her own life and finding it again, miraculously, in his.

Very gently he began to roll the slack leg up. The artificial limb, in a white sock and brown flat shoe, was bound in a heavy material like canvas and ended in an ugly jointure where it was attached to the stump. The boy's face and his voice were entirely reverent as he uncovered it and said, "Now show me how to take it off and on."

She took it off for him and put it back on again and then he took it off himself, handling it as tenderly as if it were a real one. "See!" he said with a delighted child's face. "Now I can do it myself!"

"Put it back on," she said. She was thinking that she would run away with him and that every night he would take the leg off and every morning put it back on again. "Put it back on," she said.

"Not yet," he murmured, setting it on its foot out of her reach. "Leave it off for a while. You got me instead."

She gave a little cry of alarm but he pushed her down and began to kiss her again. Without the leg she felt entirely dependent on him. Her brain seemed to have stopped thinking altogether and to be about some other function that it was not very good at. Different expressions raced back and forth over her face. Every now and then the boy, his eyes like two steel spikes, would glance behind him where the leg stood. Finally she pushed him off and said, "Put it back on me now."

"Wait," he said. He leaned the other way and pulled the valise toward him and opened it. It had a pale blue spotted lining and there were only two Bibles in it. He took one of these out and opened the cover of it. It was hollow and contained a pocket flask of whiskey, a pack of cards, and a small blue box with printing on it. He laid these out in front of her one at a time in an evenly-spaced row, like one presenting offerings at the shrine of a goddess. He put the blue box in her hand. THIS PRODUCT TO BE USED ONLY FOR THE PREVENTION OF DISEASE, she read, and dropped it. The boy was unscrewing the top of the flask. He stopped and pointed, with a smile, to the deck of cards. It was not an ordinary deck but one with an obscene picture on the back of each card. "Take a swig," he said, offering her the bottle first. He held it in front of her, but like one mesmerized, she did not move.

Her voice when she spoke had an almost pleading sound. "Aren't you," she murmured, "aren't you just good country people?"

The boy cocked his head. He looked as if he were just beginning to understand that she might be trying to insult him. "Yeah," he said, curling his lip slightly, "but it ain't held me back none. I'm as good as you any day in the week."

"Give me my leg," she said.

He pushed it farther away with his foot. "Come on now, let's begin to have us a good time," he said coaxingly. "We ain't got to know one another good yet."

"Give me my leg!" she screamed and tried to lunge for it but he pushed her 140 down easily.

"What's the matter with you all of a sudden?" he asked, frowning as he screwed the top on the flask and put it quickly back inside the Bible. "You just a while ago said you didn't believe in nothing. I thought you was some girl!"

Her face was almost purple. "You're a Christian!" she hissed. "You're a fine Christian! You're just like them all — say one thing and do another. You're a perfect Christian, you're . . ."

The boy's mouth was set angrily. "I hope you don't think," he said in a lofty indignant tone, "that I believe in that crap! I may sell Bibles but I know which end is up and I wasn't born yesterday and I know where I'm going!"

"Give me my leg!" she screeched. He jumped up so quickly that she barely saw him sweep the cards and the blue box into the Bible and throw the Bible into his valise. She saw him grab the leg and then she saw it for an instant slanted forlornly across the inside of the suitcase with a Bible at either side of its opposite ends. He slammed the lid shut and snatched up the valise and swung it down the hole and then stepped through himself.

When all of him had passed but his head, he turned and regarded her with a 145 look that no longer had any admiration in it. "I've gotten a lot of interesting things," he said. "One time I got a woman's glass eye this way. And you needn't to think you'll catch me because Pointer ain't really my name. I use a different name at every house I call at and don't stay nowhere long. And I'll tell you another thing, Hulga," he said, using the name as if he didn't think much of it, "you ain't so smart. I been believing in nothing ever since I was born!" and then the toast-colored hat disappeared down the hole and the girl was left, sitting on the straw in the dusty sunlight. When she turned her churning face toward the opening, she saw his blue figure struggling successfully over the green speckled lake.

Mrs. Hopewell and Mrs. Freeman, who were in the back pasture, digging up onions, saw him emerge a little later from the woods and head across the meadow toward the highway. "Why, that looks like that nice dull young man that tried to sell me a Bible yesterday," Mrs. Hopewell said, squinting. "He must have been selling them to the Negroes back in there. He was so simple," she said, "but I guess the world would be better off if we were all that simple."

Mrs. Freeman's gaze drove forward and just touched him before he disappeared under the hill. Then she returned her attention to the evil-smelling onion shoot she was lifting from the ground. "Some can't be that simple," she said. "I know I never could."

CONSIDERATIONS FOR CRITICAL THINKING AND WRITING

1. FIRST RESPONSE. What do you think of Hulga's conviction that intelligence and education are incompatible with religious faith?

2. Why is it significant that Mrs. Hopewell's daughter has two names? How do the other characters' names serve to characterize them?

3. Why do you think Mrs. Freeman and Mrs. Hopewell are introduced before Hulga? What do they contribute to Hulga's story?

4. Identify the conflict in this story. How is it resolved?

5. Hulga and the Bible salesman play a series of jokes on each other. How are these deceptions related to the theme?

6. What is the effect of O'Connor's use of the phrase "good country people" throughout the story? Why is it an appropriate title?

7. The Bible salesman's final words to Hulga are "You ain't so smart. I been believing in nothing ever since I was born!" What religious values are expressed in the story?

8. After the Bible salesman leaves Hulga at the end of the story, O'Connor adds two more paragraphs concerning Mrs. Hopewell and Mrs. Freeman. What is the purpose of these final paragraphs?

9. Hulga's perspective on life is ironic, but she is also the subject of O'Connor's irony. Explain how O'Connor uses irony to reveal Hulga's character.

10. This story would be different if told from Hulga's point of view. Describe how the use of a limited omniscient narrator contributes to the story's effects.

CONNECTIONS TO OTHER SELECTIONS

1. How do Mrs. Hopewell's assumptions about life compare with those of Krebs's mother in Hemingway's "Soldier's Home" (p. 162)? Explain how the conflict in each story is related to what the mothers come to represent in the eyes of the central characters.

2. Discuss the treatment of faith in this story and in Hawthorne's "Young Goodman Brown" (p. 321).

Revelation   1964

The doctor's waiting room, which was very small, was almost full when the Turpins entered and Mrs. Turpin, who was very large, made it look even smaller by her presence. She stood looming at the head of the magazine table set in the center of it, a living demonstration that the room was inadequate and ridiculous. Her little bright black eyes took in all the patients as she sized up the seating situation. There was one vacant chair and a place on the sofa occupied by a blond child in a dirty blue romper who should have been told to move over and make room for the lady. He was five or six, but Mrs. Turpin saw at once that no one was going to tell him to move over. He was slumped down in the seat, his arms idle at his sides and his eyes idle in his head; his nose ran unchecked.

Mrs. Turpin put a firm hand on Claud's shoulder and said in a voice that included anyone who wanted to listen, "Claud, you sit in that chair there," and gave

him a push down into the vacant one. Claud was florid and bald and sturdy, somewhat shorter than Mrs. Turpin, but he sat down as if he were accustomed to doing
what she told him to.

Mrs. Turpin remained standing. The only man in the room besides Claud was
a lean stringy old fellow with a rusty hand spread out on each knee, whose eyes
were closed as if he were asleep or dead or pretending to be so as not to get up
and offer her his seat. Her gaze settled agreeably on a well-dressed gray-haired lady
whose eyes met hers and whose expression said: if that child belonged to me, he
would have some manners and move over — there's plenty of room there for you
and him too.

Claud looked up with a sigh and made as if to rise.

"Sit down," Mrs. Turpin said. "You know you're not supposed to stand on that   5
leg. He has an ulcer on his leg," she explained.

Claud lifted his foot onto the magazine table and rolled his trouser leg up to
reveal a purple swelling on a plump marble-white calf.

"My!" the pleasant lady said. "How did you do that?"

"A cow kicked him," Mrs. Turpin said.

"Goodness!" said the lady.

Claud rolled his trouser leg down.   10

"Maybe the little boy would move over," the lady suggested, but the child did
not stir.

"Somebody will be leaving in a minute," Mrs. Turpin said. She could not
understand why a doctor — with as much money as they made charging five dollars a day to just stick their head in the hospital door and look at you — couldn't
afford a decent-sized waiting room. This one was hardly bigger than a garage. The
table was cluttered with limp-looking magazines and at one end of it there was a big
green glass ash tray full of cigarette butts and cotton wads with little blood spots on
them. If she had had anything to do with the running of the place, that would have
been emptied every so often. There were no chairs against the wall at the head of
the room. It had a rectangular-shaped panel in it that permitted a view of the office
where the nurse came and went and the secretary listened to the radio. A plastic
fern in a gold pot sat in the opening and trailed its fronds down almost to the floor.
The radio was softly playing gospel music.

Just then the inner door opened and a nurse with the highest stack of yellow
hair Mrs. Turpin had ever seen put her face in the crack and called for the next
patient. The woman sitting beside Claud grasped the two arms of her chair and
hoisted herself up; she pulled her dress free from her legs and lumbered through the
door where the nurse had disappeared.

Mrs. Turpin eased into the vacant chair, which held her tight as a corset. "I wish
I could reduce," she said, and rolled her eyes and gave a comic sigh.

"Oh, *you* aren't fat," the stylish lady said.   15

"Ooooo I am too," Mrs. Turpin said. "Claud he eats all he wants to and never
weighs over one hundred and seventy-five pounds, but me I just look at something
good to eat and I gain some weight," and her stomach and shoulders shook with
laughter. "You can eat all you want to, can't you, Claud?" she asked, turning to him.

Claud only grinned.

"Well, as long as you have such a good disposition," the stylish lady said, "I
don't think it makes a bit of difference what size you are. You just can't beat a good
disposition."

Next to her was a fat girl of eighteen or nineteen, scowling into a thick blue book which Mrs. Turpin saw was entitled *Human Development.* The girl raised her head and directed her scowl at Mrs. Turpin as if she did not like her looks. She appeared annoyed that anyone should speak while she tried to read. The poor girl's face was blue with acne and Mrs. Turpin thought how pitiful it was to have a face like that at that age. She gave the girl a friendly smile but the girl only scowled the harder. Mrs. Turpin herself was fat but she had always had good skin, and though she was forty-seven years old, there was not a wrinkle in her face except around her eyes from laughing too much.

Next to the ugly girl was the child, still in exactly the same position, and next to him was a thin leathery old woman in a cotton print dress. She and Claud had three sacks of chicken feed in their pump house that was in the same print. She had seen from the first that the child belonged with the old woman. She could tell by the way they sat — kind of vacant and white-trashy, as if they would sit there until Doomsday if nobody called and told them to get up. And at right angles but next to the well-dressed pleasant lady was a lank-faced woman who was certainly the child's mother. She had on a yellow sweat shirt and wine-colored slacks, both gritty-looking, and the rims of her lips were stained with snuff. Her dirty yellow hair was tied behind with a little piece of red paper ribbon. Worse than niggers any day, Mrs. Turpin thought.

The gospel hymn playing was, "When I looked up and He looked down," and Mrs. Turpin, who knew it, supplied the last line mentally, "And wona these days I know I'll we-eara crown."

Without appearing to, Mrs. Turpin always noticed people's feet. The well-dressed lady had on red and gray suede shoes to match her dress. Mrs. Turpin had on her good black patent leather pumps. The ugly girl had on Girl Scout shoes and heavy socks. The old woman had on tennis shoes and the white-trashy mother had on what appeared to be bedroom slippers, black straw with gold braid threaded through them — exactly what you would have expected her to have on.

Sometimes at night when she couldn't go to sleep, Mrs. Turpin would occupy herself with the question of who she would have chosen to be if she couldn't have been herself. If Jesus had said to her before he made her, "There's only two places available for you. You can either be a nigger or white-trash," what would she have said? "Please, Jesus, please," she would have said, "just let me wait until there's another place available," and he would have said, "No, you have to go right now and I have only those two places so make up your mind." She would have wiggled and squirmed and begged and pleaded but it would have been no use and finally she would have said, "All right, make me a nigger then — but that don't mean a trashy one." And he would have made her a neat clean respectable Negro woman, herself but black.

Next to the child's mother was a red-headed youngish woman, reading one of the magazines and working a piece of chewing gum, hell for leather, as Claud would say. Mrs. Turpin could not see the woman's feet. She was not white-trash, just common. Sometimes Mrs. Turpin occupied herself at night naming the classes of people. On the bottom of the heap were most colored people, not the kind she would have been if she had been one, but most of them; then next to them — not above, just away from — were the white-trash; then above them were the homeowners, and above them the home-and-land owners, to which she and Claud belonged. Above she and Claud were people with a lot of money and much bigger houses and much more land. But here the complexity of it would begin to bear in on her, for some of the people with a lot of money were common and ought to be below she and Claud and some of the people who had good blood had lost their money and had to rent and then there were colored people who owned their homes and land as well. There was a colored dentist in town who had two red Lincolns and a swimming pool and a farm with registered white-face cattle on it. Usually by the time she had fallen asleep all the classes of people were moiling and roiling around in her head, and she would dream they were all crammed in together in a box car, being ridden off to be put in a gas oven.

"That's a beautiful clock," she said and nodded to her right. It was a big wall 25 clock, the face encased in a brass sunburst.

"Yes, it's very pretty," the stylish lady said agreeably. "And right on the dot too," she added, glancing at her watch.

The ugly girl beside her cast an eye upward at the clock, smirked, then looked directly at Mrs. Turpin and smirked again. Then she returned her eyes to her book. She was obviously the lady's daughter because, although they didn't look anything alike as to disposition, they both had the same shape of face and the same blue eyes. On the lady they sparkled pleasantly but in the girl's seared face they appeared alternately to smolder and to blaze.

What if Jesus had said, "All right, you can be white-trash or a nigger or ugly"!

Mrs. Turpin felt an awful pity for the girl, though she thought it was one thing to be ugly and another to act ugly.

The woman with the snuff-stained lips turned around in her chair and looked 30 up at the clock. Then she turned back and appeared to look a little to the side of Mrs. Turpin. There was a cast in one of her eyes. "You want to know wher you can get you one of themther clocks?" she asked in a loud voice.

"No, I already have a nice clock," Mrs. Turpin said. Once somebody like her got a leg in the conversation, she would be all over it.

"You can get you one with green stamps," the woman said. "That's most likely wher he got hisn. Save you up enough, you can get you most anythang. I got me some joo'ry."

Ought to have got you a wash rag and some soap, Mrs. Turpin thought.

"I get contour sheets with mine," the pleasant lady said.

The daughter slammed her book shut. She looked straight in front of her, 35 directly through Mrs. Turpin and on through the yellow curtain and the plate glass window which made the wall behind her. The girl's eyes seemed lit all of a sudden with a peculiar light, an unnatural light like night road signs give. Mrs. Turpin turned her head to see if there was anything going on outside that she should see, but she could not see anything. Figures passing cast only a pale shadow through the curtain. There was no reason the girl should single her out for her ugly looks.

"Miss Finley," the nurse said, cracking the door. The gum-chewing woman got up and passed in front of her and Claud and went into the office. She had on red high-heeled shoes.

Directly across the table, the ugly girl's eyes were fixed on Mrs. Turpin as if she had some very special reason for disliking her.

"This is wonderful weather, isn't it?" the girl's mother said.

"It's good weather for cotton if you can get the niggers to pick it," Mrs. Turpin said, "but niggers don't want to pick cotton any more. You can't get the white folks to pick it and now you can't get the niggers — because they got to be right up there with the white folks."

"They gonna *try* anyways," the white-trash woman said, leaning forward. 40
"Do you have one of the cotton-picking machines?" the pleasant lady asked.

"No," Mrs. Turpin said, "they leave half the cotton in the field. We don't have much cotton anyway. If you want to make it farming now, you have to have a little of everything. We got a couple of acres of cotton and a few hogs and chickens and just enough white-face that Claud can look after them himself."

"One thang I don't want," the white-trash woman said, wiping her mouth with the back of her hand. "Hogs. Nasty stinking things, a-gruntin and a-rootin all over the place."

Mrs. Turpin gave her the merest edge of her attention. "Our hogs are not dirty and they don't stink," she said. "They're cleaner than some children I've seen. Their feet never touch the ground. We have a pig parlor — that's where you raise them on concrete," she explained to the pleasant lady, "and Claud scoots them down with the hose every afternoon and washes off the floor." Cleaner by far than that child right there, she thought. Poor nasty little thing. He had not moved except to put the thumb of his dirty hand into his mouth.

The woman turned her face away from Mrs. Turpin. "I know I wouldn't scoot 45 down no hog with no hose," she said to the wall.

You wouldn't have no hog to scoot down, Mrs. Turpin said to herself.

"A-gruntin and a-rootin and a-groanin," the woman muttered.

"We got a little of everything," Mrs. Turpin said to the pleasant lady. "It's no use in having more than you can handle yourself with help like it is. We found enough niggers to pick our cotton this year but Claud he has to go after them and take them home again in the evening. They can't walk that half a mile. No they can't. I tell you," she said and laughed merrily, "I sure am tired of buttering up niggers, but you got to love em if you want em to work for you. When they come in the morning, I run out and I say, 'Hi yawl this morning?' and when Claud drives them off to the field I just wave to beat the band and they just wave back." And she waved her hand rapidly to illustrate.

"Like you read out of the same book," the lady said, showing she understood perfectly.

"Child, yes," Mrs. Turpin said. "And when they come in from the field, I run 50 out with a bucket of icewater. That's the way it's going to be from now on," she said. "You may as well face it."

"One thang I know," the white-trash woman said. "Two thangs I ain't going to do: love no niggers or scoot down no hog with no hose." And she let out a bark of contempt.

The look that Mrs. Turpin and the pleasant lady exchanged indicated they both understood that you had to *have* certain things before you could *know* certain things. But every time Mrs. Turpin exchanged a look with the lady, she was aware that the ugly girl's peculiar eyes were still on her, and she had trouble bringing her attention back to the conversation.

"When you got something," she said, "you got to look after it." And when you ain't got a thing but breath and britches, she added to herself, you can afford to come to town every morning and just sit on the Court House coping and spit.

A grotesque revolving shadow passed across the curtain behind her and was thrown palely on the opposite wall. Then a bicycle clattered down against the outside of the building. The door opened and a colored boy glided in with a tray from the drugstore. It had two large red and white paper cups on it with tops on them. He was a tall, very black boy in discolored white pants and a green nylon shirt. He was chewing gum slowly, as if to music. He set the tray down in the office opening next to the fern and stuck his head through to look for the secretary. She was not in there. He rested his arms on the ledge and waited, his narrow bottom stuck out, swaying to the left and right. He raised a hand over his head and scratched the base of his skull.

"You see that button there, boy?" Mrs. Turpin said. "You can punch that and 55 she'll come. She's probably in the back somewhere."

"Is that right?" the boy said agreeably, as if he had never seen the button before. He leaned to the right and put his finger on it. "She sometime out," he said and twisted around to face his audience, his elbows behind him on the counter. The nurse appeared and he twisted back again. She handed him a dollar and he rooted in his pocket and made the change and counted it out to her. She gave him fifteen cents for a tip and he went out with the empty tray. The heavy door swung to slowly and closed at length with the sound of suction. For a moment no one spoke.

"They ought to send all them niggers back to Africa," the white-trash woman said. "That's wher they come from in the first place."

"Oh, I couldn't do without my good colored friends," the pleasant lady said.

"There's a heap of things worse than a nigger," Mrs. Turpin agreed. "It's all kinds of them just like it's all kinds of us."

"Yes, and it takes all kinds to make the world go round," the lady said in her 60 musical voice.

As she said it, the raw-complexioned girl snapped her teeth together. Her lower lip turned downwards and inside out, revealing the pale pink inside of her mouth. After a second it rolled back up. It was the ugliest face Mrs. Turpin had ever seen anyone make and for a moment she was certain that the girl had made it at her. She was looking at her as if she had known and disliked her all her life — all of Mrs. Turpin's life, it seemed too, not just all the girl's life. Why, girl, I don't even know you, Mrs. Turpin said silently.

She forced her attention back to the discussion. "It wouldn't be practical to send them back to Africa," she said. "They wouldn't want to go. They got it too good here."

"Wouldn't be what they wanted — if I had anythang to do with it," the woman said.

"It wouldn't be a way in the world you could get all the niggers back over there," Mrs. Turpin said. "They'd be hiding out and lying down and turning sick on you and wailing and hollering and raring and pitching. It wouldn't be a way in the world to get them over there."

"They got over here," the trashy woman said. "Get back like they got over." 65

"It wasn't so many of them then," Mrs. Turpin explained.

The woman looked at Mrs. Turpin as if here was an idiot indeed but Mrs. Turpin was not bothered by the look, considering where it came from.

"Nooo," she said, "they're going to stay here where they can go to New York and marry white folks and improve their color. That's what they all want to do, every one of them, improve their color."

"You know what comes of that, don't you?" Claud asked.

"No, Claud, what?" Mrs. Turpin said. 70

Claud's eyes twinkled. "White-faced niggers," he said with never a smile.

Everybody in the office laughed except the white-trash and the ugly girl. The girl gripped the book in her lap with white fingers. The trashy woman looked around her from face to face as if she thought they were all idiots. The old woman in the feed sack dress continued to gaze expressionless across the floor at the high-top shoes of the man opposite her, the one who had been pretending to be asleep when the Turpins came in. He was laughing heartily, his hands still spread out on his knees. The child had fallen to the side and was lying now almost face down in the old woman's lap.

While they recovered from their laughter, the nasal chorus on the radio kept the room from silence.

"You go to blank blank
And I'll go to mine
But we'll all blank along
To-geth-ther,
And all along the blank
We'll hep each other out
Smile-ling in any kind of
Weath-ther!"

Mrs. Turpin didn't catch every word but she caught enough to agree with the spirit of the song and it turned her thoughts sober. To help anybody out that needed it was her philosophy of life. She never spared herself when she found somebody in need, whether they were white or black, trash or decent. And of all she had to be thankful for, she was most thankful that this was so. If Jesus had said, "You can be high society and have all the money you want and be thin and svelte-like, but you can't be a good woman with it," she would have had to say, "Well don't make me that then. Make me a good woman and it don't matter what else, how fat or how ugly or how poor!" Her heart rose. He had not made her a nigger or white-trash or ugly! He had made her herself and given her a little of everything. Jesus, thank you! she said. Thank you thank you thank you! Whenever she counted her blessings she felt as buoyant as if she weighed one hundred and twenty-five pounds instead of one hundred and eighty.

"What's wrong with your little boy?" the pleasant lady asked the white-trashy 75 woman.

"He has a ulcer," the woman said proudly. "He ain't give me a minute's peace since he was born. Him and her are just alike," she said, nodding at the old woman, who was running her leathery fingers through the child's pale hair. "Look like I can't get nothing down them two but Co' Cola and candy."

That's all you try to get down em, Mrs. Turpin said to herself. Too lazy to light the fire. There was nothing you could tell her about people like them that she didn't know already. And it was not just that they didn't have anything. Because if you gave them everything, in two weeks it would all be broken or filthy or they would have chopped it up for lightwood. She knew all this from her own experience. Help them you must, but help them you couldn't.

All at once the ugly girl turned her lips inside out again. Her eyes fixed like two drills on Mrs. Turpin. This time there was no mistaking that there was something urgent behind them.

Girl, Mrs. Turpin exclaimed silently, I haven't done a thing to you! The girl might be confusing her with somebody else. There was no need to sit by and let herself be intimidated. "You must be in college," she said boldly, looking directly at the girl. "I see you reading a book there."

The girl continued to stare and pointedly did not answer.   80

Her mother blushed at this rudeness. "The lady asked you a question, Mary Grace," she said under her breath.

"I have ears," Mary Grace said.

The poor mother blushed again. "Mary Grace goes to Wellesley College," she explained. She twisted one of the buttons on her dress. "In Massachusetts," she added with a grimace. "And in the summer she just keeps right on studying. Just reads all the time, a real book worm. She's done real well at Wellesley; she's taking English and Math and History and Psychology and Social Studies," she rattled on, "and I think it's too much. I think she ought to get out and have fun."

The girl looked as if she would like to hurl them all through the plate glass window.

"Way up north," Mrs. Turpin murmured and thought, well, it hasn't done much   85 for her manners.

"I'd almost rather to have him sick," the white-trash woman said, wrenching the attention back to herself. "He's so mean when he ain't. Look like some children just take natural to meanness. It's some gets bad when they get sick but he was the opposite. Took sick and turned good. He don't give me no trouble now. It's me waitin to see the doctor," she said.

If I was going to send anybody back to Africa, Mrs. Turpin thought, it would be your kind, woman. "Yes, indeed," she said aloud, but looking up at the ceiling, "it's a heap of things worse than a nigger." And dirtier than a hog, she added to herself.

"I think people with bad dispositions are more to be pitied than anyone on earth," the pleasant lady said in a voice that was decidedly thin.

"I thank the Lord he has blessed me with a good one," Mrs. Turpin said. "The day has never dawned that I couldn't find something to laugh at."

"Not since she married me anyways," Claud said with a comical straight face.   90

Everybody laughed except the girl and the white-trash.

Mrs. Turpin's stomach shook. "He's such a caution," she said, "that I can't help but laugh at him."

The girl made a loud ugly noise through her teeth.

Her mother's mouth grew thin and tight. "I think the worst thing in the world," she said, "is an ungrateful person. To have everything and not appreciate it. I know a girl," she said, "who has parents who would give her anything, a little brother who loves her dearly, who is getting a good education, who wears the best clothes, but who can never say a kind word to anyone, who never smiles, who just criticizes and complains all day long."

"Is she too old to paddle?" Claud asked.   95

The girl's face was almost purple.

"Yes," the lady said, "I'm afraid there's nothing to do but leave her to her folly. Some day she'll wake up and it'll be too late."

"It never hurt anyone to smile," Mrs. Turpin said. "It just makes you feel better all over."

"Of course," the lady said sadly, "but there are just some people you can't tell anything to. They can't take criticism."

"If it's one thing I am," Mrs. Turpin said with feeling, "it's grateful. When I think 100 who all I could have been besides myself and what all I got, a little of everything, and a good disposition besides, I just feel like shouting, 'Thank you, Jesus, for making everything the way it is!' It could have been different!" For one thing, somebody else could have got Claud. At the thought of this, she was flooded with gratitude and a terrible pang of joy ran through her. "Oh thank you, Jesus, Jesus, thank you!" she cried aloud.

The book struck her directly over her left eye. It struck almost at the same instant that she realized the girl was about to hurl it. Before she could utter a sound, the raw face came crashing across the table toward her, howling. The girl's fingers sank like clamps into the soft flesh of her neck. She heard the mother cry out and Claud shout, "Whoa!" There was an instant when she was certain that she was about to be in an earthquake.

All at once her vision narrowed and she saw everything as if it were happening in a small room far away, or as if she were looking at it through the wrong end of a telescope. Claud's face crumpled and fell out of sight. The nurse ran in, then out, then in again. Then the gangling figure of the doctor rushed out of the inner door. Magazines flew this way and that as the table turned over. The girl fell with a thud and Mrs. Turpin's vision suddenly reversed itself and she saw everything large instead of small. The eyes of the white-trashy woman were staring hugely at the floor. There the girl, held down on one side by the nurse and on the other by her mother, was wrenching and turning in their grasp. The doctor was kneeling astride her, trying to hold her arm down. He managed after a second to sink a long needle into it.

Mrs. Turpin felt entirely hollow except for her heart which swung from side to side as if it were agitated in a great empty drum of flesh.

"Somebody that's not busy call for the ambulance," the doctor said in the off-hand voice young doctors adopt for terrible occasions.

Mrs. Turpin could not have moved a finger. The old man who had been sitting 105 next to her skipped nimbly into the office and made the call, for the secretary still seemed to be gone.

"Claud!" Mrs. Turpin called.

He was not in his chair. She knew she must jump up and find him but she felt like some one trying to catch a train in a dream, when everything moves in slow motion and the faster you try to run the slower you go.

"Here I am," a suffocated voice, very unlike Claud's, said.

He was doubled up in the corner on the floor, pale as paper, holding his leg. She wanted to get up and go to him but she could not move. Instead, her gaze was drawn slowly downward to the churning face on the floor, which she could see over the doctor's shoulder.

The girl's eyes stopped rolling and focused on her. They seemed a much lighter 110 blue than before, as if a door that had been tightly closed behind them was now open to admit light and air.

Mrs. Turpin's head cleared and her power of motion returned. She leaned forward until she was looking directly into the fierce brilliant eyes. There was no doubt in her mind that the girl did know her, knew her in some intense and personal way, beyond time and place and condition. "What you got to say to me?" she asked hoarsely and held her breath, waiting, as for a revelation.

The girl raised her head. Her gaze locked with Mrs. Turpin's. "Go back to hell where you came from, you old wart hog," she whispered. Her voice was low but clear. Her eyes burned for a moment as if she saw with pleasure that her message had struck its target.

Mrs. Turpin sank back in her chair.

After a moment the girl's eyes closed and she turned her head wearily to the side.

The doctor rose and handed the nurse the empty syringe. He leaned over and 115 put both hands for a moment on the mother's shoulders, which were shaking. She was sitting on the floor, her lips pressed together, holding Mary Grace's hand in her lap. The girl's fingers were gripped like a baby's around her thumb. "Go on to the hospital," he said. "I'll call and make the arrangements."

"Now let's see that neck," he said in a jovial voice to Mrs. Turpin. He began to inspect her neck with his first two fingers. Two little moon-shaped lines like pink fish bones were indented over her windpipe. There was the beginning of an angry red swelling above her eye. His fingers passed over this also.

"Lea' me be," she said thickly and shook him off. "See about Claud. She kicked him."

"I'll see about him in a minute," he said and felt her pulse. He was a thin gray-haired man, given to pleasantries. "Go home and have yourself a vacation the rest of the day," he said and patted her on the shoulder.

Quit your pattin me, Mrs. Turpin growled to herself.

"And put an ice pack over that eye," he said. Then he went and squatted down 120
beside Claud and looked at his leg. After a moment he pulled him up and Claud limped after him into the office.

Until the ambulance came, the only sounds in the room were the tremulous moans of the girl's mother, who continued to sit on the floor. The white-trash woman did not take her eyes off the girl. Mrs. Turpin looked straight ahead at nothing. Presently the ambulance drew up, a long dark shadow, behind the curtain. The attendants came in and set the stretcher down beside the girl and lifted her expertly onto it and carried her out. The nurse helped the mother gather up her things. The shadow of the ambulance moved silently away and the nurse came back in the office.

"That ther girl is going to be a lunatic, ain't she?" the white-trash woman asked the nurse, but the nurse kept on to the back and never answered her.

"Yes, she's going to be a lunatic," the white-trash woman said to the rest of them.

"Po' critter," the old woman murmured. The child's face was still in her lap. His eyes looked idly out over her knees. He had not moved during the disturbance except to draw one leg up under him.

"I thank Gawd," the white-trash woman said fervently, "I ain't a lunatic." 125
Claud came limping out and the Turpins went home.

As their pick-up truck turned into their own dirt road and made the crest of the hill, Mrs. Turpin gripped the window ledge and looked out suspiciously. The land sloped gracefully down through a field dotted with lavender weeds and at the start of the rise their small yellow frame house, with its little flower beds spread out around it like a fancy apron, sat primly in its accustomed place between two giant hickory trees. She would not have been startled to see a burnt wound between two blackened chimneys.

Neither of them felt like eating so they put on their house clothes and lowered the shade in the bedroom and lay down, Claud with his leg on a pillow and herself with a damp washcloth over her eye. The instant she was flat on her back, the image of a razor-backed hog with warts on its face and horns coming out behind its ears snorted into her head. She moaned, a low quiet moan.

"I am not," she said tearfully, "a wart hog. From hell." But the denial had no force. The girl's eyes and her words, even the tone of her voice, low but clear, directed only to her, brooked no repudiation. She had been singled out for the message, though there was trash in the room to whom it might justly have been applied. The full force of this fact struck her only now. There was a woman there who was neglecting her own child but she had been overlooked. The message had been given to Ruby Turpin, a respectable, hard-working, church-going woman. The tears dried. Her eyes began to burn instead with wrath.

She rose on her elbow and the washcloth fell into her hand. Claud was lying on   130
his back, snoring. She wanted to tell him what the girl had said. At the same time, she did not wish to put the image of herself as a wart hog from hell into his mind.

"Hey, Claud," she muttered and pushed his shoulder.

Claud opened one pale baby blue eye.

She looked into it warily. He did not think about anything. He just went his way.

"Wha, whasit?" he said and closed the eye again.

"Nothing," she said. "Does your leg pain you?"   135

"Hurts like hell," Claud said.

"It'll quit terreckly," she said and lay back down. In a moment Claud was snoring again. For the rest of the afternoon they lay there. Claud slept. She scowled at the ceiling. Occasionally she raised her fist and made a small stabbing motion over her chest as if she was defending her innocence to invisible guests who were like the comforters of Job, reasonable-seeming but wrong.

About five-thirty Claud stirred. "Got to go after those niggers," he sighed, not moving.

She was looking straight up as if there were unintelligible handwriting on the ceiling. The protuberance over her eye had turned a greenish-blue. "Listen here," she said.

"What?"   140

"Kiss me."

Claud leaned over and kissed her loudly on the mouth. He pinched her side and their hands interlocked. Her expression of ferocious concentration did not change. Claud got up, groaning and growling, and limped off. She continued to study the ceiling.

She did not get up until she heard the pick-up truck coming back with the Negroes. Then she rose and thrust her feet in her brown oxfords, which she did not bother to lace, and stumped out onto the back porch and got her red plastic bucket. She emptied a tray of ice cubes into it and filled it half full of water and went out into the back yard. Every afternoon after Claud brought the hands in, one of the boys helped him put out hay and the rest waited in the back of the truck until he was ready to take them home. The truck was parked in the shade under one of the hickory trees.

"Hi yawl this evening?" Mrs. Turpin asked grimly, appearing with the bucket and the dipper. There were three women and a boy in the truck.

"Us doin nicely," the oldest woman said. "Hi you doin?" and her gaze struck   145
immediately on the dark lump on Mrs. Turpin's forehead. "You done fell down, ain't you?" she asked in a solicitous voice. The old woman was dark and almost toothless. She had on an old felt hat of Claud's set back on her head. The other two women were younger and lighter and they both had new bright green sunhats. One of them had hers on her head; the other had taken hers off and the boy was grinning beneath it.

Mrs. Turpin set the bucket down on the floor of the truck. "Yawl hep yourselves," she said. She looked around to make sure Claud had gone. "No, I didn't fall down," she said, folding her arms. "It was something worse than that."

"Ain't nothing bad happen to you!" the old woman said. She said it as if they all knew that Mrs. Turpin was protected in some special way by Divine Providence. "You just had you a little fall."

"We were in town at the doctor's office for where the cow kicked Mr. Turpin," Mrs. Turpin said in a flat tone that indicated they could leave off their foolishness. "And there was this girl there. A big fat girl with her face all broke out. I could look at that girl and tell she was peculiar but I couldn't tell how. And me and her mama was just talking and going along and all of a sudden WHAM! She throws this big book she was reading at me and . . ."

"Naw!" the old woman cried out.

"And then she jumps over the table and commences to choke me."   150

"Naw!" they all exclaimed, "naw!"

"Hi come she do that?" the old woman asked. "What ail her?"

Mrs. Turpin only glared in front of her.

"Somethin ail her," the old woman said.

"They carried her off in an ambulance," Mrs. Turpin continued, "but before she   155
went she was rolling on the floor and they were trying to hold her down to give her a shot and she said something to me." She paused. "You know what she said to me?"

"What she say?" they asked.

"She said," Mrs. Turpin began, and stopped, her face very dark and heavy. The sun was getting whiter and whiter, blanching the sky overhead so that the leaves of the hickory tree were black in the face of it. She could not bring forth the words. "Something real ugly," she muttered.

"She sho shouldn't said nothin ugly to you," the old woman said. "You so sweet. You the sweetest lady I know."

"She pretty too," the one with the hat on said.

"And stout," the other one said. "I never knowed no sweeter white lady."   160

"That's the truth befo' Jesus," the old woman said. "Amen! You des as sweet and pretty as you can be."

Mrs. Turpin knew exactly how much Negro flattery was worth and it added to her rage. "She said," she began again and finished this time with a fierce rush of breath, "that I was an old wart hog from hell."

There was an astounded silence.

"Where she at?" the youngest woman cried in a piercing voice.

"Lemme see her. I'll kill her!"   165

"I'll kill her with you!" the other one cried.

"She b'long in the sylum," the old woman said emphatically. "You the sweetest white lady I know."

"She pretty too," the other two said. "Stout as she can be and sweet. Jesus satisfied with her!"

"Deed he is," the woman declared.

Idiots! Mrs. Turpin growled to herself. You could never say anything intelli-   170
gent to a nigger. You could talk at them but not with them. "Yawl ain't drunk your water," she said shortly. "Leave the bucket in the truck when you're finished with it. I got more to do than just stand around and pass the time of day," and she moved off and into the house.

She stood for a moment in the middle of the kitchen. The dark protuberance over her eye looked like a miniature tornado cloud which might any moment sweep across the horizon of her brow. Her lower lip protruded dangerously. She squared her massive shoulders. Then she marched into the front of the house and out the side door and started down the road to the pig parlor. She had the look of a woman going single-handed, weaponless, into battle.

The sun was deep yellow now like a harvest moon and was riding westward very fast over the far tree line as if it meant to reach the hogs before she did. The road was rutted and she kicked several good-sized stones out of her path as she strode along. The pig parlor was on a little knoll at the end of a lane that ran off from the side of the barn. It was a square of concrete as large as a small room, with a board fence about four feet high around it. The concrete floor sloped slightly so that the hog wash could drain off into a trench where it was carried to the field for fertilizer. Claud was standing on the outside, on the edge of the concrete, hanging onto the top board, hosing down the floor inside. The hose was connected to the faucet of a water trough nearby.

Mrs. Turpin climbed up beside him and glowered down at the hogs inside. There were seven long-snouted bristly shoats in it — tan with liver-colored spots — and an old sow a few weeks off from farrowing. She was lying on her side grunting. The shoats were running about shaking themselves like idiot children, their little slit pig eyes searching the floor for anything left. She had read that pigs were the most intelligent animal. She doubted it. They were supposed to be smarter than dogs. There had even been a pig astronaut. He had performed his assignment perfectly but died of a heart attack afterwards because they left him in his electric suit, sitting upright throughout his examination when naturally a hog should be on all fours.

A-gruntin and a-rootin and a-groanin.

"Gimme that hose," she said, yanking it away from Claud. "Go on and carry   175 them niggers home and then get off that leg."

"You look like you might have swallowed a mad dog," Claud observed, but he got down and limped off. He paid no attention to her humors.

Until he was out of earshot, Mrs. Turpin stood on the side of the pen, holding the hose and pointing the stream of water at the hind quarters of any shoat that looked as if it might try to lie down. When he had had time to get over the hill, she turned her head slightly and her wrathful eyes scanned the path. He was nowhere in sight. She turned back again and seemed to gather herself up. Her shoulders rose and she drew in her breath.

"What do you send me a message like that for?" she said in a low fierce voice, barely above a whisper but with the force of a shout in its concentrated fury. "How am I a hog and me both? How am I saved and from hell too?" Her free fist was knotted and with the other she gripped the hose, blindly pointing the stream of water in and out of the eye of the old sow whose outraged squeal she did not hear.

The pig parlor commanded a view of the back pasture where their twenty beef cows were gathered around the hay-bales Claud and the boy had put out. The freshly cut pasture sloped down to the highway. Across it was their cotton field and beyond that a dark green dusty wood which they owned as well. The sun was behind the wood, very red, looking over the paling of the trees like a farmer inspecting his own hogs.

"Why me?" she rumbled. "It's no trash around here, black or white, that I   180 haven't given to. And break my back to the bone every day working. And do for the church."

She appeared to be the right size woman to command the arena before her. "How am I a hog?" she demanded. "Exactly how am I like them?" and she jabbed the stream of water at the shoats. "There was plenty of trash there. It didn't have to be me.

"If you like trash better, go get yourself some trash then," she railed. "You could have made me trash. Or a nigger. If trash is what you wanted why didn't you make me trash?" She shook her fist with the hose in it and a watery snake appeared momentarily in the air. "I could quit working and take it easy and be filthy," she growled. "Lounge about the sidewalks all day drinking root beer. Dip snuff and spit in every puddle and have it all over my face. I could be nasty.

"Or you could have made me a nigger. It's too late for me to be a nigger," she said with deep sarcasm, "but I could act like one. Lay down in the middle of the road and stop traffic. Roll on the ground."

In the deepening light everything was taking on a mysterious hue. The pasture was growing a peculiar glassy green and the streak of highway had turned lavender. She braced herself for a final assault and this time her voice rolled out over the pasture. "Go on," she yelled, "call me a hog! Call me a hog again. From hell. Call me a wart hog from hell. Put that bottom rail on top. There'll still be a top and bottom!"

A garbled echo returned to her.   185

A final surge of fury shook her and she roared, "Who do you think you are?"

The color of everything, field and crimson sky, burned for a moment with a transparent intensity. The question carried over the pasture and across the highway and the cotton field and returned to her clearly like an answer from beyond the wood.

She opened her mouth but no sound came out of it.

A tiny truck, Claud's, appeared on the highway, heading rapidly out of sight. Its gears scraped thinly. It looked like a child's toy. At any moment a bigger truck might smash into it and scatter Claud's and the niggers' brains all over the road.

Mrs. Turpin stood there, her gaze fixed on the highway, all her muscles rigid,   190
until in five or six minutes the truck reappeared, returning. She waited until it had had time to turn into their own road. Then like a monumental statue coming to life, she bent her head slowly and gazed, as if through the very heart of mystery, down into the pig parlor at the hogs. They had settled all in one corner around the old sow who was grunting softly. A red glow suffused them. They appeared to pant with a secret life.

Until the sun slipped finally behind the tree line, Mrs. Turpin remained there with her gaze bent to them as if she were absorbing some abysmal life-giving knowledge. At last she lifted her head. There was only a purple streak in the sky, cutting through a field of crimson and leading, like an extension of the highway, into the descending dusk. She raised her hands from the side of the pen in a gesture hieratic and profound. A visionary light settled in her eyes. She saw the streak as a vast swinging bridge extending upward from the earth through a field of living fire. Upon it a vast horde of souls were rumbling toward heaven. There were whole companies of white-trash, clean for the first time in their lives, and bands of black niggers in white robes, and battalions of freaks and lunatics shouting and clapping and leaping like frogs. And bringing up the end of the procession was a tribe of people whom she recognized at once as those who, like herself and Claud, had always had a little of everything and the God-given wit to use it right. She leaned forward to observe them closer. They were marching behind the others with great dignity, accountable as they had always been for good order and common sense and respectable behavior. They alone were on key. Yet she could see by their shocked and altered faces that even their virtues were being burned away. She lowered her hands and gripped the rail of the hog pen, her eyes small but fixed unblinkingly on what lay ahead. In a moment the vision faded but she remained where she was, immobile.

At length she got down and turned off the faucet and made her slow way on the darkening path to the house. In the woods around her the invisible cricket choruses had struck up, but what she heard were the voices of the souls climbing upward into the starry field and shouting hallelujah.

CONSIDERATIONS FOR CRITICAL THINKING AND WRITING

1. FIRST RESPONSE. Does your attitude toward Mrs. Turpin change or remain the same during the story? Do you *like* her more at some points than at others? Explain why.

2. Why is it appropriate that the two major settings for the action in this story are a doctor's waiting room and a "pig parlor"?

3. How does Mrs. Turpin's treatment of her husband help to characterize her?

4. Mrs. Turpin notices people's shoes. What does this and her thoughts about "classes of people" (para. 24) reveal about her? How does she see herself in relation to other people?

5. Why does Mary Grace attack Mrs. Turpin?

6. Why is it significant that the book Mary Grace reads is *Human Development*? What is the significance of her name?

7. What does the background music played on the radio contribute to the story?

8. To whom does Mrs. Turpin address this anguished question: "What do you send me a message [Mary Grace's whispered words telling her "Go back to hell where you came from, you old wart hog"] like that for?" (para. 178). Why is Mrs. Turpin so angry and bewildered?

9. What is the "abysmal life-giving knowledge" that Mrs. Turpin discovers in the next to the last paragraph? Why is it "abysmal"? How is it "life-giving"?

10. Given the serious theme, consider whether the story's humor is appropriate.

11. When Mrs. Turpin returns home bruised, a hired African American woman tells her that nothing really "bad" happened: "You just had you a little fall" (para. 147). Pay particular attention to the suggestive language of this sentence, and discuss its significance in relation to the rest of the story.

12. CRITICAL STRATEGIES. Choose a critical approach from Chapter 51, "Critical Strategies for Reading," that you think is particularly useful for explaining the themes of this story.

CONNECTIONS TO OTHER SELECTIONS

1. Compare and contrast Mary Grace with Hulga of "Good Country People."

2. Explain how "Revelation" could be used as a title for any of the O'Connor stories you have read.

3. Discuss Mrs. Turpin's prideful hypocrisy in connection with the racial attitudes expressed by the white men at the "smoker" in Ralph Ellison's "Battle Royal" (p. 227). How do pride and personal illusions inform these characters' racial attitudes?

4. Explore the nature of the "revelation" in O'Connor's story and in John Updike's "A & P" (p. 200).

Perspectives on O'Connor

FLANNERY O'CONNOR
On the Use of Exaggeration and Distortion 1969

When I write a novel in which the central action is a baptism, I am very well aware that for a majority of my readers, baptism is a meaningless rite, and so in my novel I have to see that this baptism carries enough awe and mystery to jar the reader into some kind of emotional recognition of its significance. To this end I have to bend the whole novel — its language, its structure, its action. I have to make the reader feel, in his bones if nowhere else, that something is going on here that counts. Distortion in this case is an instrument; exaggeration has a purpose, and the whole structure of the story or novel has been made what it is because of belief. This is not the kind of distortion that destroys; it is the kind that reveals, or should reveal.

From "Novelist and Believer" in *Mystery and Manners*

CONSIDERATIONS FOR CRITICAL THINKING AND WRITING

1. It has been observed that in many of O'Connor's works the central action takes the form of some kind of "baptism" that initiates, tests, or purifies a character. Select a story that illustrates this generalization, and explain how the conflict results in a kind of baptism.

2. O'Connor says that exaggeration and distortion reveal something in her stories. What is the effect of such exaggeration and distortion? Typically, what is revealed by it? Focus your comments on a single story to illustrate your points.

3. Do you think that O'Connor's stories have anything to offer a reader who has no religious faith? Explain why or why not.

JOSEPHINE HENDIN (B. 1946)
On O'Connor's Refusal to "Do Pretty" 1970

There is, in the memory of one Milledgeville matron, the image of O'Connor at nineteen or twenty who, when invited to a wedding shower for an old family friend, remained standing, her back pressed against the wall, scowling at the group of women who had sat down to lunch. Neither the devil nor her mother could make her say yes to this fiercely gracious female society, but Flannery O'Connor could not say no even in a whisper. She could not refuse the invitation but she would not accept it either. She did not exactly "fuss" but neither did she "do pretty."

From *The World of Flannery O'Connor*

CONSIDERATIONS FOR CRITICAL THINKING AND WRITING

1. How is O'Connor's personality revealed in this anecdote about her ambivalent response to society? Allow the description to be suggestive for you, and flesh out a brief portrait of her.

2. Consider how this personality makes itself apparent in any one of O'Connor's stories you have read. How does the anecdote help to characterize the narrator's voice in the story?

3. To what extent do you think biographical details such as this — assuming the Milledgeville matron's memory to be accurate — can shed light on a writer's works?

CLAIRE KATZ (B. 1935)
The Function of Violence in O'Connor's Fiction 1974

From the moment the reader enters O'Connor's backwoods, he is poised on the edge of a pervasive violence. Characters barely contain their rage; images reflect a hostile nature; and even the Christ to whom the characters are ultimately driven is a threatening figure . . . full of the apocalyptic wrath of the Old Testament.

O'Connor's conscious purpose is evident enough . . . : to reveal the need for grace in a world grotesque without a transcendent context. "I have found that my subject in fiction is the action of grace in territory largely held by the devil," she wrote [in *Mystery and Manners*], and she was not vague about what the devil is: "an evil intelligence determined on its own supremacy." It would seem that for O'Connor, given the fact of original Sin, any intelligence determined on its own supremacy was intrinsically evil. For in each work, it is the impulse toward secular autonomy, the smug confidence that human nature is perfectible by its own efforts, that she sets out to destroy, through an act of violence so intense that the character is rendered helpless, a passive victim of a superior power. Again and again she creates a fiction in which a character attempts to live autonomously, to define himself and his values, only to be jarred back to what she calls "reality" — the recognition of helplessness in the face of contingency, and the need for absolute submission to the power of Christ.

From "Flannery O'Connor's Rage of Vision"
in *American Literature*

CONSIDERATIONS FOR CRITICAL THINKING AND WRITING

1. Choose an O'Connor story, and explain how grace — the divine influence from God that redeems a person — is used in it to transform a character.

2. Which O'Connor characters can be accurately described as having an "evil intelligence determined on its own supremacy" (para. 2)? Choose one character, and write an essay explaining how this description is central to the conflict of the story.

3. Compare an O'Connor story with one of Hawthorne's "in which a character attempts to live autonomously, to define himself and his values, only to be jarred back to . . . 'reality' — the recognition of helplessness in the face of contingency . . ." (para. 2).

EDWARD KESSLER (B. 1927)
On O'Connor's Use of History 1986

In company with other Southern writers . . . who aspire to embrace a lost tradition and look on history as a repository of value, Flannery O'Connor seems a curious anomaly. She wrote of herself: "I am a Catholic peculiarly possessed of the modern consciousness . . . unhistorical, solitary, and guilty." Likewise her characters comprise a gallery of misfits isolated in a present and sentenced to a lifetime of exile from the human community. In O'Connor's fiction, the past neither justifies nor even explains what is happening. If she believed, for example, in the importance of the past accident that maimed Joy in "Good Country People," she could have demonstrated how the event predetermined her present rejection of both human and external nature; but Joy's past is parenthetical: "Mrs. Hopewell excused this attitude because of the leg (which had been shot off in a hunting accident when Joy was ten)." Believing that humankind is fundamentally flawed, O'Connor spends very little time constructing a past for her characters. The cure is neither behind us nor before us but within us; therefore, the past — even historical time itself — supplies only a limited base for self-discovery.

From *Flannery O'Connor and the Language of Apocalypse*

CONSIDERATIONS FOR CRITICAL THINKING AND WRITING

1. Consider how O'Connor uses history in any one of her stories in this anthology and compare that "unhistorical" vision with Hawthorne's in "Young Goodman Brown" (p. 321) or "The Minister's Black Veil" (p. 331).

2. Write an essay in which you discuss Kessler's assertion that for O'Connor the "past is parenthetical," in contrast to most southern writers, who "embrace a lost tradition and look on history as a repository of value." For your point of comparison choose either William Faulkner's "A Rose for Emily" (p. 78) or "Barn Burning" (p. 406).

Time *Magazine, on* A Good Man Is Hard to Find and Other Stories 1962

Highly unladylike . . . a brutal irony, a slam-bang humor, and a style of writing as balefully direct as a death sentence.

From a *Time* magazine blurb quoted on the cover of the second American edition of *A Good Man Is Hard to Find and Other Stories*

CONSIDERATIONS FOR CRITICAL THINKING AND WRITING

1. How accurate do you think this blurb is in characterizing the three O'Connor stories in this chapter?

2. CREATIVE RESPONSE. Write your own blurb for the three stories and be prepared to justify your pithy description.

13

A CRITICAL CASE STUDY

William Faulkner's "Barn Burning"

> The writer's only responsibility is to his art. . . . He has a dream. It anguishes him so much he must get rid of it. He has no peace until then.
> —WILLIAM FAULKNER

> It is the writer's privilege to help man endure by lifting his heart.
> —WILLIAM FAULKNER

This chapter offers several critical approaches to a well-known short story by William Faulkner. Though there are many possible critical approaches to any given work (see Chapter 51, "Critical Strategies for Reading," for a discussion of a variety of methods), and there are numerous studies of Faulkner from formalist, biographical, historical, mythological, psychological, sociological, and other perspectives, it is worth noting that each reading of a work or writer is predicated on accepting certain assumptions about literature and life. Those assumptions or premises may be complementary or mutually exclusive, and they may appeal to you or appall you. What is interesting, however, is how various approaches reveal the text (as well as its readers and critics) by calling attention to certain elements or leaving others out. The critical excerpts following the story suggest only a portion of the range of possibilities, but even a small representation of approaches can help you to raise new questions, develop insights, recognize problems, and suggest additional ways of reading the text.

WILLIAM FAULKNER (1897–1962)

A biographical note for William Faulkner appears on page 77, before his story "A Rose for Emily." In "Barn Burning" Faulkner portrays a young boy's love and revulsion for his father, a frightening man who lives by a "ferocious conviction in the rightness of his own actions."

William Faulkner, Author Photo for *Sanctuary*, 1931. William Faulkner was born in New Albany, Mississippi, the first of four sons born to Murry and Maud Butler Falkner (as their name was then spelled). He was named after his deceased great-grandfather, William Clark Falkner — family patriarch, lawyer, politician, planter, businessman, railroad financier, and best-selling writer (*The White Rose of Memphis*) — who was known as the "Old Colonel." When Faulkner was five, his family moved forty miles west to the town of Oxford in Lafayette County. Following the move, Murry's father abruptly sold the railroad founded by the "Old Colonel," and Murry was forced to take a series of jobs in Oxford to support his family. Oxford and its surrounding county — its landscape, history, and inhabitants — became a rich source for William Faulkner's writing and the inspiration for his fictional Yoknapatawpha County. "Beginning with *Sartoris* [1929, his third novel]," Faulkner wrote, "I discovered that my own little postage stamp of native soil was worth writing about, and that I would never live long enough to exhaust it."

Rowan Oak. In 1930, Faulkner purchased a large, dilapidated plantation house in Oxford known as "The Bailey Place." The house predated the Civil War and was set on thirty-two acres (known as "Bailey's Woods") where Faulkner had played as a boy. He renamed the house "Rowan Oak," and from 1930 on, he did most of his writing here. Despite the financial strain that Rowan Oak presented, the house and land also represented for Faulkner the reclaiming of the genteel life of "The Colonel": Faulkner would never inherit a plantation, so he bought one.

Library of Congress, Prints and Photographs Division.

William Faulkner (May 6, 1955). The author in the spot where he did most of his writing — his living room at Rowan Oak — bent over a glass-topped table with a pen.
© Bettmann/CORBIS.

Barn Burning 1939

The store in which the Justice of the Peace's court was sitting smelled of cheese. The boy, crouched on his nail keg at the back of the crowded room, knew he smelled cheese, and more: from where he sat he could see the ranked shelves close-packed with the solid, squat, dynamic shapes of tin cans whose labels his stomach read, not from the lettering which meant nothing to his mind but from the scarlet devils and the silver curve of fish—this, the cheese which he knew he smelled and the hermetic meat which his intestines believed he smelled coming in intermittent gusts momentary and brief between the other constant one, the smell and sense just a little of fear because mostly of despair and grief, the old fierce pull of blood. He could not see the table where the Justice sat and before which his father and his father's enemy (*our enemy* he thought in that despair; *ourn! mine and hisn both! He's my father!*) stood, but he could hear them, the two of them that is, because his father had said no word yet:

"But what proof have you, Mr. Harris?"

"I told you. The hog got into my corn. I caught it up and sent it back to him. He had no fence that would hold it. I told him so, warned him. The next time I put the hog in my pen. When he came to get it I gave him enough wire to patch up his pen. The next time I put the hog up and kept it. I rode down to his house and saw the wire I gave him still rolled on to the spool in his yard. I told him he could have the hog when he paid me a dollar pound fee. That evening a nigger came with the dollar and got the hog. He was a strange nigger. He said, 'He say to tell you wood and hay kin burn.' I said, 'What?' 'That whut he say to tell you,' the nigger said. 'Wood and hay kin burn.' That night my barn burned. I got the stock out but I lost the barn."

"Where is the nigger? Have you got him?"

"He was a strange nigger, I tell you. I don't know what became of him."

"But that's not proof. Don't you see that's not proof?"

"Get that boy up here. He knows." For a moment the boy thought too that the man meant his older brother until Harris said, "Not him. The little one. The boy," and, crouching, small for his age, small and wiry like his father, in patched and faded jeans even too small for him, with straight, uncombed, brown hair and eyes gray and wild as storm scud, he saw the men between himself and the table part and become a lane of grim faces, at the end of which he saw the Justice, a shabby, collarless, graying man in spectacles, beckoning him. He felt no floor under his bare feet; he seemed to walk beneath the palpable weight of the grim turning faces. His father, stiff in his black Sunday coat donned not for the trial but for the moving, did not even look at him. *He aims for me to lie,* he thought, again with that frantic grief and despair. *And I will have to do hit.*

"What's your name, boy?" the Justice said.

"Colonel Sartoris Snopes," the boy whispered.

"Hey?" the Justice said. "Talk louder. Colonel Sartoris? I reckon anybody named for Colonel Sartoris in this country can't help but tell the truth, can they?" The boy said nothing. *Enemy! Enemy!* he thought; for a moment he could not even see, could not see that the Justice's face was kindly nor discern that his voice was troubled when he spoke to the man named Harris: "Do you want me to question this boy?" But he could hear, and during those subsequent long seconds while there was absolutely no sound in the crowded little room save that of quiet and intent breathing it was as if he had swung outward at the end of a grape vine, over a ravine, and at the top of the swing had been caught in a prolonged instant of mesmerized gravity, weightless in time.

5

10

"No!" Harris said violently, explosively. "Damnation! Send him out of here!" Now time, the fluid world, rushed beneath him again, the voices coming to him again through the smell of cheese and sealed meat, the fear and despair and the old grief of blood:

"This case is closed. I can't find against you, Snopes, but I can give you advice. Leave this country and don't come back to it."

His father spoke for the first time, his voice cold and harsh, level, without emphasis: "I aim to. I don't figure to stay in a country among people who . . ." he said something unprintable and vile, addressed to no one.

"That'll do," the Justice said. "Take your wagon and get out of this country before dark. Case dismissed."

His father turned, and he followed the stiff black coat, the wiry figure walking   15 a little stiffly from where a Confederate provost's man's musket ball had taken him in the heel on a stolen horse thirty years ago, followed the two backs now, since his older brother had appeared from somewhere in the crowd, no taller than the father but thicker, chewing tobacco steadily, between the two lines of grim-faced men and out of the store and across the worn gallery and down the sagging steps and among the dogs and half-grown boys in the mild May dust, where as he passed a voice hissed:

"Barn burner!"

Again he could not see, whirling; there was a face in a red haze, moonlike, bigger than the full moon, the owner of it half again his size, he leaping in the red haze toward the face, feeling no blow, feeling no shock when his head struck the earth, scrabbling up and leaping again, feeling no blow this time either and tasting no blood, scrabbling up to see the other boy in full flight and himself already leaping into pursuit as his father's hand jerked him back, the harsh, cold voice speaking above him: "Go get in the wagon."

It stood in a grove of locusts and mulberries across the road. His two hulking sisters in their Sunday dresses and his mother and her sister in calico and sunbonnets were already in it, sitting on or among the sorry residue of the dozen and more movings which even the boy could remember — the battered stove, the broken beds and chairs, the clock inlaid with mother-of-pearl, which would not run, stopped at some fourteen minutes past two o'clock of a dead and forgotten day and time, which had been his mother's dowry. She was crying, though when she saw him she drew her sleeve across her face and began to descend from the wagon. "Get back," the father said.

"He's hurt. I got to get some water and wash his . . ."

"Get back in the wagon," his father said. He got in too, over the tail-gate. His   20 father mounted to the seat where the older brother already sat and struck the gaunt mules two savage blows with the peeled willow, but without heat. It was not even sadistic; it was exactly that same quality which in later years would cause his descendants to over-run the engine before putting a motor car in motion, striking and reining back in the same movement. The wagon went on, the store with its quiet crowd of grimly watching men dropped behind; a curve in the road hid it. *Forever* he thought. *Maybe he's done satisfied now, now that he has . . .* stopping himself, not to say it aloud even to himself. His mother's hand touched his shoulder.

"Does hit hurt?" she said.

"Naw," he said. "Hit don't hurt. Lemme be."

"Can't you wipe some of the blood off before hit dries?"

"I'll wash to-night," he said. "Lemme be, I tell you."

The wagon went on. He did not know where they were going. None of them 25 ever did or ever asked, because it was always somewhere, always a house of sorts waiting for them a day or two days or even three days away. Likely his father had already arranged to make a crop on another farm before he . . . Again he had to stop himself. He (the father) always did. There was something about his wolflike independence and even courage when the advantage was at least neutral which impressed strangers, as if they got from his latent ravening ferocity not so much a sense of dependability as a feeling that his ferocious conviction in the rightness of his own actions would be of advantage to all whose interest lay with his.

That night they camped, in a grove of oaks and beeches where a spring ran. The nights were still cool and they had a fire against it, of a rail lifted from a nearby fence and cut into lengths—a small fire, neat, niggard almost, a shrewd fire; such fires were his father's habit and custom always, even in freezing weather. Older, the boy might have remarked this and wondered why not a big one; why should not a man who had not only seen the waste and extravagance of war, but who had in his blood an inherent voracious prodigality with material not his own, have burned everything in sight? Then he might have gone a step farther and thought that that was the reason: that niggard blaze was the living fruit of nights passed during those four years in the woods hiding from all men, blue or gray, with his strings of horses (captured horses, he called them). And older still, he might have divined the true reason: that the element of fire spoke to some deep mainspring of his father's being, as the element of steel or of powder spoke to other men, as the one weapon for the preservation of integrity, else breath were not worth the breathing, and hence to be regarded with respect and used with discretion.

But he did not think this now and he had seen those same niggard blazes all his life. He merely ate his supper beside it and was already half asleep over his iron plate when his father called him, and once more he followed the stiff back, the stiff and ruthless limp, up the slope and on to the starlit road where, turning, he could see his father against the stars but without face or depth—a shape black, flat, and bloodless as though cut from tin in the iron folds of the frockcoat which had not been made for him, the voice harsh like tin and without heat like tin:

"You were fixing to tell them. You would have told him."

He didn't answer. His father struck him with the flat of his hand on the side of the head, hard but without heat, exactly as he had struck the two mules at the store, exactly as he would strike either of them with any stick in order to kill a horse fly, his voice still without heat or anger. "You're getting to be a man. You got to learn. You got to learn to stick to your own blood or you ain't going to have any blood to stick to you. Do you think either of them, any man there this morning, would? Don't you know all they wanted was a chance to get at me because they knew I had them beat? Eh?" Later, twenty years later, he was to tell himself, "If I had said they wanted only truth, justice, he would have hit me again." But now he said nothing. He was not crying. He just stood there. "Answer me," his father said.

"Yes," he whispered. His father turned.   30

"Get on to bed. We'll be there tomorrow."

Tomorrow they were there. In the early afternoon the wagon stopped before a paintless two-room house identical almost with the dozen others it had stopped before even in the boy's ten years, and again, as on the other dozen occasions, his mother and aunt got down and began to unload the wagon, although his two sisters and his father and brother had not moved.

"Likely hit ain't fitten for hawgs," one of the sisters said.

"Nevertheless, fit it will and you'll hog it and like it," his father said. "Get out of them chairs and help your Ma unload."

The two sisters got down, big, bovine, in a flutter of cheap ribbons; one of them 35 drew from the jumbled wagon bed a battered lantern, the other a worn broom. His father handed the reins to the older son and began to climb stiffly over the wheel. "When they get unloaded, take the team to the barn and feed them." Then he said, and at first the boy thought he was still speaking to his brother: "Come with me."

"Me?" he said.

"Yes," his father said. "You."

"Abner," his mother said. His father paused and looked back — the harsh level stare beneath the shaggy, graying, irascible brows.

"I reckon I'll have a word with the man that aims to begin tomorrow owning me body and soul for the next eight months."

They went back up the road. A week ago — or before last night, that is — he 40 would have asked where they were going, but not now. His father had struck him before last night but never before had he paused afterward to explain why; it was as if the blow and the following calm, outrageous voice still rang, repercussed, divulging nothing to him save the terrible handicap of being young, the light weight of his few years, just heavy enough to prevent his soaring free of the world as it seemed to be ordered but not heavy enough to keep him footed solid in it, to resist it and try to change the course of events.

Presently he could see the grove of oaks and cedars and the other flowering trees and shrubs where the house would be, though not the house yet. They walked beside a fence massed with honeysuckle and Cherokee roses and came to a gate swinging open between two brick pillars, and now, beyond a sweep of drive, he saw the house for the first time and at that instant he forgot his father and the terror and despair both, and even when he remembered his father again (who had not stopped) the terror and despair did not return. Because, for all the twelve movings, they had sojourned until now in a poor country, a land of small farms and fields and houses, and he had never seen a house like this before. *Hit's big as a courthouse* he thought quietly, with a surge of peace and joy whose reason he could not have thought into words, being too young for that: *They are safe from him. People whose lives are a part of this peace and dignity are beyond his touch, he no more to them than a buzzing wasp: capable of stinging for a little moment but that's all; the spell of this peace and dignity rendering even the barns and stable and cribs which belong to it impervious to the puny flames he might contrive . . .* this, the peace and joy, ebbing for an instant as he looked again at the stiff black back, the stiff and implacable limp of the figure which was not dwarfed by the house, for the reason that it had never looked big anywhere and which now, against the serene columned backdrop, had more than ever that impervious quality of something cut ruthlessly from tin, depthless, as though, sidewise to the sun, it would cast no shadow. Watching him, the boy remarked the absolutely undeviating course which his father held and saw the stiff foot come squarely down in a pile of fresh droppings where a horse had stood in the drive and which his father could have avoided by a simple change of stride. But it ebbed only for a moment, though he could not have thought this into words either, walking on in the spell of the house, which he could even want but without envy, without sorrow, certainly never with that ravening and jealous rage which unknown to him walked in the ironlike black coat before him: *Maybe he will feel it too. Maybe it will even change him now from what maybe he couldn't help but be.*

They crossed the portico. Now he could hear his father's stiff foot as it came down on the boards with clocklike finality, a sound out of all proportion to the displacement of the body it bore and which was not dwarfed either by the white door before it, as though it had attained to a sort of vicious and ravening minimum not to be dwarfed by anything — the flat, wide, black hat, the formal coat of broadcloth which had once been black but which had now that friction-glazed greenish cast of the bodies of old house flies, the lifted sleeve which was too large, the lifted hand like a curled claw. The door opened so promptly that the boy knew the Negro must have been watching them all the time, an old man with neat grizzled hair, in a linen jacket, who stood barring the door with his body, saying, "Wipe yo foots, white man, fo you come in here. Major ain't home nohow."

"Get out of my way, nigger," his father said, without heat too, flinging the door back and the Negro also and entering, his hat still on his head. And now the boy saw the prints of the stiff foot on the doorjamb and saw them appear on the pale rug behind the machinelike deliberation of the foot which seemed to bear (or transmit) twice the weight which the body compassed. The Negro was shouting "Miss Lula! Miss Lula!" somewhere behind them, then the boy, deluged as though by a warm wave by a suave turn of the carpeted stair and a pendant glitter of chandeliers and a mute gleam of gold frames, heard the swift feet and saw her too, a lady — perhaps he had never seen her like before either — in a gray, smooth gown with lace at the throat and an apron tied at the waist and the sleeves turned back, wiping cake or biscuit dough from her hands with a towel as she came up the hall, looking not at his father at all but at the tracks on the blond rug with an expression of incredulous amazement.

"I tried," the Negro cried. "I tole him to . . ."

"Will you please go away?" she said in a shaking voice. "Major de Spain is not at 45 home. Will you please go away?"

His father had not spoken again. He did not speak again. He did not even look at her. He just stood stiff in the center of the rug, in his hat, the shaggy iron-gray brows twitching slightly above the pebble-colored eyes as he appeared to examine the house with brief deliberation. Then with the same deliberation he turned; the boy watched him pivot on the good leg and saw the stiff foot drag round the arc of the turning, leaving a final long and fading smear. His father never looked at it, he never once looked down at the rug. The Negro held the door. It closed behind them, upon the hysteric and indistinguishable woman-wail. His father stopped at the top of the steps and scraped his boot clean on the edge of it. At the gate he stopped again. He stood for a moment, planted stiffly on the stiff foot, looking back at the house. "Pretty and white, ain't it?" he said. "That's sweat. Nigger sweat. Maybe it ain't white enough yet to suit him. Maybe he wants to mix some white sweat with it."

Two hours later the boy was chopping wood behind the house within which his mother and aunt and the two sisters (the mother and aunt, not the two girls, he knew that; even at this distance and muffled by walls the flat loud voices of the two girls emanated an incorrigible idle inertia) were setting up the stove to prepare a meal; when he heard the hooves and saw the linen-clad man on a fine sorrel mare, whom he recognized even before he saw the rolled rug in front of the Negro youth following on a fat bay carriage horse — a suffused, angry face vanishing, still at full gallop, beyond the corner of the house where his father and brother were sitting in the two tilted chairs; and a moment later, almost before he could have put the axe down, he heard the hooves again and watched the sorrel mare go back out of the yard, already galloping again. Then his father began to shout one of the sisters' names, who presently emerged backward from the kitchen door dragging the rolled rug along the ground by one end while the other sister walked behind it.

"If you ain't going to tote, go on and set up the wash pot," the first said.

"You, Sarty!" the second shouted. "Set up the wash pot!" His father appeared at the door, framed against that shabbiness, as he had been against that other bland perfection, impervious to either, the mother's anxious face at his shoulder.

"Go on," the father said. "Pick it up." The two sisters stopped, broad, lethargic; 50 stooping, they presented an incredible expanse of pale cloth and a flutter of tawdry ribbons.

"If I thought enough of a rug to have to git hit all the way from France I wouldn't keep hit where folks coming in would have to tromp on hit," the first said. They raised the rug.

"Abner," the mother said. "Let me do it."

"You go back and git dinner," his father said. "I'll tend to this."

From the woodpile through the rest of the afternoon the boy watched them, the rug spread flat in the dust beside the bubbling wash pot, the two sisters stooping over it with that profound and lethargic reluctance, while the father stood over them in turn, implacable and grim, driving them though never raising his voice again. He could smell the harsh homemade lye they were using; he saw his mother come to the door once and look toward them with an expression not anxious now but very like despair; he saw his father turn, and he fell to with the axe and saw from the corner of his eye his father raise from the ground a flattish fragment of field stone and examine it and return to the pot, and this time his mother actually spoke: "Abner. Abner. Please don't. Please, Abner."

Then he was done too. It was dusk; the whippoorwills had already begun. 55 He could smell coffee from the room where they would presently eat the cold food remaining from the midafternoon meal, though when he entered the house he realized they were having coffee again probably because there was a fire on the hearth, before which the rug now lay spread over the backs of the two chairs. The tracks of his father's foot were gone. Where they had been were now long, water-cloudy scoriations resembling the sporadic course of a lilliputian mowing machine.

It still hung there while they ate the cold food and then went to bed, scattered without order or claim up and down the two rooms, his mother in one bed, where his father would later lie, the older brother in the other, himself, the aunt, and the two sisters on pallets on the floor. But his father was not in bed yet. The last thing the boy remembered was the depthless, harsh silhouette of the hat and coat bending over the rug and it seemed to him that he had not even closed his eyes when the silhouette was standing over him, the fire almost dead behind it, the stiff foot prodding him awake. "Catch up the mule," his father said.

When he returned with the mule his father was standing in the black door, the rolled rug over his shoulder. "Ain't you going to ride?" he said.

"No. Give me your foot."

He bent his knee into his father's hand, the wiry, surprising power flowed smoothly, rising, he rising with it, on to the mule's bare back (they had owned a saddle once; the boy could remember it though not when or where) and with the same effortlessness his father swung the rug up in front of him. Now in the starlight they retraced the afternoon's path, up the dusty road rife with honeysuckle, through the gate and up the black tunnel of the drive to the lightless house, where he sat on the mule and felt the rough warp of the rug drag across his thighs and vanish.

"Don't you want me to help?" he whispered. His father did not answer and   60
now he heard again that stiff foot striking the hollow portico with that wooden
and clocklike deliberation, that outrageous overstatement of the weight it carried.
The rug, hunched, not flung (the boy could tell that even in the darkness) from his
father's shoulder struck the angle of wall and floor with a sound unbelievably loud,
thunderous, then the foot again, unhurried and enormous; a light came on in the
house and the boy sat, tense, breathing steadily and quietly and just a little fast,
though the foot itself did not increase its beat at all, descending the steps now; now
the boy could see him.

"Don't you want to ride now?" he whispered. "We kin both ride now," the light
within the house altering now, flaring up and sinking. *He's coming down the stairs
now,* he thought. He had already ridden the mule up beside the horse block; presently his father was up behind him and he doubled the reins over and slashed the
mule across the neck, but before the animal could begin to trot the hard, thin arm
came around him, the hard, knotted hand jerking the mule back to a walk.

In the first red rays of the sun they were in the lot, putting plow gear on the
mules. This time the sorrel mare was in the lot before he heard it at all, the rider collarless and even bareheaded, trembling, speaking in a shaking voice as the woman
in the house had done, his father merely looking up once before stooping again to
the hame he was buckling, so that the man on the mare spoke to his stooping back:

"You must realize you have ruined that rug. Wasn't there anybody here, any of
your women . . ." he ceased, shaking, the boy watching him, the older brother leaning now in the stable door, chewing, blinking slowly and steadily at nothing apparently. "It cost a hundred dollars. But you never had a hundred dollars. You never
will. So I'm going to charge you twenty bushels of corn against your crop. I'll add it
in your contract and when you come to the commissary you can sign it. That won't
keep Mrs. de Spain quiet but maybe it will teach you to wipe your feet before you
enter her house again."

Then he was gone. The boy looked at his father, who still had not spoken or
even looked up again, who was now adjusting the logger-head in the hame.

"Pap," he said. His father looked at him — the inscrutable face, the shaggy brows   65
beneath which the gray eyes glinted coldly. Suddenly the boy went toward him, fast,
stopping as suddenly. "You done the best you could!" he cried. "If he wanted hit done
different why didn't he wait and tell you how? He won't git no twenty bushels! He
won't git none! We'll gether hit and hide hit! I kin watch . . ."

"Did you put the cutter back in that straight stock like I told you?"

"No, sir," he said.

"Then go do it."

That was Wednesday. During the rest of that week he worked steadily, at what
was within his scope and some which was beyond it, with an industry that did
not need to be driven nor even commanded twice; he had this from his mother,
with the difference that some at least of what he did he liked to do, such as splitting
wood with the half-size axe which his mother and aunt had earned, or saved money
somehow, to present him with at Christmas. In company with the two older women
(and on one afternoon, even one of the sisters), he built pens for the shoat and the
cow which were part of his father's contract with the landlord, and one afternoon,
his father being absent, gone somewhere on one of the mules, he went to the field.

They were running a middle buster now, his brother holding the plow straight   70
while he handled the reins, and walking beside the straining mule, the rich black
soil shearing cool and damp against his bare ankles, he thought *Maybe this is the*

end of it. Maybe even that twenty bushels that seems hard to have to pay for just a rug will be a cheap price for him to stop forever and always from being what he used to be; thinking, dreaming now, so that his brother had to speak sharply to him to mind the mule: *Maybe he even won't collect the twenty bushels. Maybe it will all add up and balance and vanish — corn, rug, fire; the terror and grief; the being pulled two ways like between two teams of horses — gone, done with for ever and ever.*

Then it was Saturday; he looked up from beneath the mule he was harnessing and saw his father in the black coat and hat. "Not that," his father said. "The wagon gear." And then, two hours later, sitting in the wagon bed behind his father and brother on the seat, the wagon accomplished a final curve, and he saw the weathered paintless store with its tattered tobacco- and patent-medicine posters and the tethered wagons and saddle animals below the gallery. He mounted the gnawed steps behind his father and brother, and there again was the lane of quiet, watching faces for the three of them to walk through. He saw the man in spectacles sitting at the plank table and he did not need to be told this was a Justice of the Peace; he sent one glare of fierce, exultant, partisan defiance at the man in collar and cravat now, whom he had seen but twice before in his life, and that on a galloping horse, who now wore on his face an expression not of rage but of amazed unbelief which the boy could not have known was at the incredible circumstance of being sued by one of his own tenants, and came and stood against his father and cried at the Justice: "He ain't done it! He ain't burnt . . ."

"Go back to the wagon," his father said.

"Burnt?" the Justice said. "Do I understand this rug was burned too?"

"Does anybody here claim it was?" his father said. "Go back to the wagon." But he did not, he merely retreated to the rear of the room, crowded as that other had been, but not to sit down this time, instead, to stand pressing among the motionless bodies, listening to the voices:

"And you claim twenty bushels of corn is too high for the damage you did to   75 the rug?"

"He brought the rug to me and said he wanted the tracks washed out of it. I washed the tracks out and took the rug back to him."

"But you didn't carry the rug back to him in the same condition it was in before you made the tracks on it."

His father did not answer, and now for perhaps half a minute there was no sound at all save that of breathing, the faint, steady suspiration of complete and intent listening.

"You decline to answer that, Mr. Snopes?" Again his father did not answer. "I'm going to find against you, Mr. Snopes. I'm going to find that you were responsible for the injury to Major de Spain's rug and hold you liable for it. But twenty bushels of corn seems a little high for a man in your circumstances to have to pay. Major de Spain claims it cost a hundred dollars. October corn will be worth about fifty cents. I figure that if Major de Spain can stand a ninety-five dollar loss on something he paid cash for, you can stand a five-dollar loss you haven't earned yet. I hold you in damages to Major de Spain to the amount of ten bushels of corn over and above your contract with him, to be paid to him out of your crop at gathering time. Court adjourned."

It had taken no time hardly, the morning was but half begun. He thought they   80 would return home and perhaps back to the field, since they were late, far behind all other farmers. But instead his father passed on behind the wagon, merely indicating with his hand for the older brother to follow with it, and crossed the road toward the blacksmith shop opposite, pressing on after his father, overtaking him, speaking, whispering up at the harsh, calm face beneath the weathered hat: "He won't git no ten bushels neither. He won't git one. We'll . . ." until his father glanced for an instant down at him, the face absolutely calm, the grizzled eyebrows tangled above the cold eyes, the voice almost pleasant, almost gentle:

"You think so? Well, we'll wait till October anyway."

The matter of the wagon — the setting of a spoke or two and the tightening of the tires — did not take long either, the business of the tires accomplished by driving the wagon into the spring branch behind the shop and letting it stand there, the mules nuzzling into the water from time to time, and the boy on the seat with the idle reins, looking up the slope and through the sooty tunnel of the shed where the slow hammer rang and where his father sat on an upended cypress bolt, easily, either talking or listening, still sitting there when the boy brought the dripping wagon up out of the branch and halted it before the door.

"Take them on to the shade and hitch," his father said. He did so and returned. His father and the smith and a third man squatting on his heels inside the door were talking, about crops and animals; the boy, squatting too in the ammoniac dust and hoof-parings and scales of rust, heard his father tell a long and unhurried story out of the time before the birth of the older brother even when he had been a professional horsetrader. And then his father came up beside him where he stood before a tattered last year's circus poster on the other side of the store, gazing rapt and quiet at the scarlet horses, the incredible poisings and convolutions of tulle and tights and the painted leers of comedians, and said, "It's time to eat."

But not at home. Squatting beside his brother against the front wall, he watched his father emerge from the store and produce from a paper sack a segment of cheese and divide it carefully and deliberately into three with his pocket knife and produce crackers from the same sack. They all three squatted on the gallery and ate, slowly, without talking; then in the store again, they drank from a tin dipper tepid water smelling of the cedar bucket and of living beech trees. And still they did not go home. It was a horse lot this time, a tall rail fence upon and along which men stood and sat and out of which one by one horses were led, to be walked and trotted and then cantered back and forth along the road while the slow swapping and buying went on and the sun began to slant westward, they — the three of them — watching and listening, the older brother with his muddy eyes and his steady, inevitable tobacco, the father commenting now and then on certain of the animals, to no one in particular.

It was after sundown when they reached home. They ate supper by lamplight, then, sitting on the doorstep, the boy watched the night fully accomplish, listening to the whippoorwills and the frogs, when he heard his mother's voice: "Abner! No! No! Oh, God. Oh, God. Abner!" and he rose, whirled, and saw the altered light through the door where a candle stub now burned in a bottle neck on the table and his father, still in the hat and coat, at once formal and burlesque as though dressed carefully for some shabby and ceremonial violence, emptying the reservoir of the lamp back into the five-gallon kerosene can from which it had been filled, while the mother tugged at his arm until he shifted the lamp to the other hand and flung her back, not savagely or viciously, just hard, into the wall, her hands flung out against the wall for balance, her mouth open and in her face the same quality of hopeless despair as had been in her voice. Then his father saw him standing in the door.

"Go to the barn and get that can of oil we were oiling the wagon with," he said. The boy did not move. Then he could speak.

"What . . ." he cried. "What are you . . ."

"Go get that oil," his father said. "Go."

Then he was moving, running, outside the house, toward the stable: this the old habit, the old blood which he had not been permitted to choose for himself, which had been bequeathed him willy nilly and which had run for so long (and who knew where, battening on what of outrage and savagery and lust) before it came to him. *I could keep on,* he thought. *I could run on and on and never look back, never need to see his face again. Only I can't. I can't,* the rusted can in his hand now, the liquid sploshing in it as he ran back to the house and into it, into the sound of his mother's weeping in the next room, and handed the can to his father.

"Ain't you going to even send a nigger?" he cried. "At least you sent a nigger 90 before!"

This time his father didn't strike him. The hand came even faster than the blow had, the same hand which had set the can on the table with almost excruciating care flashing from the can toward him too quick for him to follow it, gripping him by the back of his shirt and on to tiptoe before he had seen it quit the can, the face stooping at him in breathless and frozen ferocity, the cold, dead voice speaking over him to the older brother who leaned against the table, chewing with that steady, curious, sidewise motion of cows:

"Empty the can into the big one and go on. I'll catch up with you."

"Better tie him up to the bedpost," the brother said.

"Do like I told you," the father said. Then the boy was moving, his bunched shirt and the hard, bony hand between his shoulder-blades, his toes just touching the floor, across the room and into the other one, past the sisters sitting with spread heavy thighs in the two chairs over the cold hearth, and to where his mother and aunt sat side by side on the bed, the aunt's arms about his mother's shoulders.

"Hold him," the father said. The aunt made a startled movement. "Not you," 95 the father said. "Lennie. Take hold of him. I want to see you do it." His mother took him by the wrist. "You'll hold him better than that. If he gets loose don't you know what he is going to do? He will go up yonder." He jerked his head toward the road. "Maybe I'd better tie him."

"I'll hold him," his mother whispered.

"See you do then." Then his father was gone, the stiff foot heavy and measured upon the boards, ceasing at last.

Then he began to struggle. His mother caught him in both arms, he jerking and wrenching at them. He would be stronger in the end, he knew that. But he had no time to wait for it. "Lemme go!" he cried. "I don't want to have to hit you!"

"Let him go!" the aunt said. "If he don't go, before God, I am going up there myself!"

"Don't you see I can't?" his mother cried. "Sarty! Sarty! No! No! Help me, 100 Lizzie!"

Then he was free. His aunt grasped at him but it was too late. He whirled, running, his mother stumbled forward on to her knees behind him, crying to the nearer sister. "Catch him, Net! Catch him!" But that was too late too, the sister (the sisters were twins, born at the same time, yet either of them now gave the impression of being, encompassing as much living meat and volume and weight as any other two of the family) not yet having begun to rise from the chair, her head, face, alone merely turned, presenting to him in the flying instant an astonishing expanse of young female features untroubled by any surprise even, wearing only an expression of bovine interest. Then he was out of the room, out of the house, in the mild dust of the starlit road and the heavy rifeness of honeysuckle, the pale ribbon unspooling with terrific slowness under his running feet, reaching the gate at last and turning in, running, his heart and lungs drumming, on up the drive toward the lighted house, the lighted door. He did not knock, he burst in, sobbing for breath, incapable for the moment of speech; he saw the astonished face of the Negro in the linen jacket without knowing when the Negro had appeared.

"De Spain!" he cried, panted. "Where's . . ." then he saw the white man too emerging from a white door down the hall. "Barn!" he cried. "Barn!"

"What?" the white man said. "Barn?"

"Yes!" the boy cried. "Barn!"

"Catch him!" the white man shouted. 105

But it was too late this time too. The Negro grasped his shirt, but the entire sleeve, rotten with washing, carried away, and he was out that door too and in the drive again, and had actually never ceased to run even while he was screaming into the white man's face.

Behind him the white man was shouting, "My horse! Fetch my horse!" and he thought for an instant of cutting across the park and climbing the fence into the road, but he did not know the park nor how high the vine-massed fence might be and he dared not risk it. So he ran on down the drive, blood and breath roaring; presently he was in the road again though he could not see it. He could not hear either: the galloping mare was almost upon him before he heard her, and even then he held his course, as if the very urgency of his wild grief and need must in a moment more find him wings, waiting until the ultimate instant to hurl himself aside and into the weed-choked roadside ditch as the horse thundered past and on, for an instant in furious silhouette against the stars, the tranquil early summer night sky which, even before the shape of the horse and rider vanished, strained abruptly and violently upward: a long, swirling roar incredible and soundless, blotting the stars, and he springing up and into the road again, running again, knowing it was too late yet still running even after he heard the shot and, an instant later, two shots, pausing now without knowing he had ceased to run, crying "Pap! Pap!," running again before he knew he had begun to run, stumbling, tripping over something and scrabbling up again without ceasing to run, looking backward over his shoulder at the glare as he got up, running on among the invisible trees, panting, sobbing, "Father! Father!"

At midnight he was sitting on the crest of a hill. He did not know it was midnight and he did not know how far he had come. But there was no glare behind him now and he sat now, his back toward what he had called home for four days anyhow, his face toward the dark woods which he would enter when breath was strong again, small, shaking steadily in the chill darkness, hugging himself into the remainder of his thin, rotten shirt, the grief and despair now no longer terror and fear but just grief and despair. *Father. My father,* he thought. "He was brave!" he cried suddenly, aloud but not loud, no more than a whisper: "He was! He was in the war! He was in Colonel Sartoris' cav'ry!" not knowing that his father had gone to that war a private in the fine old European sense, wearing no uniform, admitting the authority of and giving fidelity to no man or army or flag, going to war as Malbrouck° himself did: for booty — it meant nothing and less than nothing to him if it were enemy booty or his own.

The slow constellations wheeled on. It would be dawn and then sun-up after a while and he would be hungry. But that would be tomorrow and now he was only

---

Malbrouck: John Churchill, duke of Marlborough (1650–1722), English military commander who led the armies of England and Holland in the War of Spanish Succession.

cold, and walking would cure that. His breathing was easier now and he decided to get up and go on, and then he found that he had been asleep because he knew it was almost dawn, the night almost over. He could tell that from the whippoor-wills. They were everywhere now among the dark trees below him, constant and inflectioned and ceaseless, so that, as the instant for giving over to the day birds drew nearer and nearer, there was no interval at all between them. He got up. He was a little stiff, but walking would cure that too as it would the cold, and soon there would be the sun. He went on down the hill, toward the dark woods within which the liquid silver voices of the birds called unceasing — the rapid and urgent beating of the urgent and quiring heart of the late spring night. He did not look back.

CONSIDERATIONS FOR CRITICAL THINKING AND WRITING

1. FIRST RESPONSE. Who is "Barn Burning" about? Explain your choice.

2. Is Sarty a dynamic or a static character? Why? Which term best describes his father? Why?

3. Who is the central character in this story? Explain your choice.

4. How are Sarty's emotions revealed in the story's opening paragraphs? What seems to be the function of the italicized passages there and elsewhere?

5. What do we learn from the story's exposition that helps us understand Abner's character? How does his behavior reveal his character? What do other people say about him?

6. How does Faulkner's physical description of Abner further our understanding of his personality?

7. Explain how the justice of the peace, Mr. Harris, and Major de Spain serve as foils to Abner. Discuss whether you think they are round or flat characters.

8. Who are the story's stock characters? What is their purpose?

9. Explain how the description of Major de Spain's house helps to frame the main conflicts that Sarty experiences in his efforts to remain loyal to his father.

10. Write an essay describing Sarty's attitudes toward his father as they develop and change throughout the story.

11. What do you think happens to Sarty's father and brother at the end of the story? How does your response to this question affect your reading of the last paragraph?

12. How does the language of the final paragraph suggest a kind of resolution to the conflicts Sarty has experienced?

CONNECTIONS TO OTHER SELECTIONS

1. Compare and contrast Faulkner's characterizations of Abner Snopes in this story and Miss Emily in "A Rose for Emily" (p. 78). How does the author generate sympathy for each character even though both are guilty of terrible crimes? Which character do you find more sympathetic? Explain why.

2. How does Abner Snopes's motivation for revenge compare with Matt Fowler's in Andre Dubus's "Killings" (p. 89)? How do the victims of each character's revenge differ and thereby help to shape the meanings of each story?

3. Read the section on mythological criticism in Chapter 51, "Critical Strategies for Reading." How do you think a mythological critic would make sense of Sarty Snopes and Matt Fowler?

Perspectives on Faulkner

JANE HILES (B. 1951)

Hiles uses a biographical approach (see pp. 1647–49 in Chapter 51, "Critical Strategies for Reading") to determine Faulkner's intentions in his characterization of how Sarty responds to the conflicts he feels about his father.

Blood Ties in "Barn Burning"   1985

"'You're getting to be a man. . . . You got to learn to stick to your own blood or you ain't going to have any blood to stick to you'": Abner Snopes's admonition to his son, Colonel Sartoris (or "Sarty"), introduces a central issue in Faulkner's "Barn Burning" — the kinship bond, which the story's narrator calls the "old fierce pull of blood." The interpretive crux of the work is a conflict between determinism, represented by the blood tie that binds Sarty to his clan, and free will, dramatized by the boy's ultimate repudiation of family ties and his decampment. Dissonances between the structure and the imagery of the work develop and amplify Sarty's conflict: viewed in the light of the narrator's deterministic assumptions, the story's denouement is a red herring which only appears to resolve the complexities created by evocative language. Sarty's seeming interruption of the antisocial pattern established by his father is actually a continuation of it, and the ostensible resolution of his moral dilemma actually no resolution at all. . . .

In an interview in Japan sixteen years after the publication of "Barn Burning," Faulkner delivered an appraisal of the phenomenon of clannishness that bears considerable relevance to Abner Snopes's defensive posture in "Barn Burning":

> Yes, we are country people and we have never had too much in material possessions because 60 or 70 years ago we were invaded and we were conquered. So we have been thrown back on our selves not only for entertainment but certain [sic] amount of defense. We have to be clannish just like the people in the Scottish highlands, each springing to defend his own blood whether it be right or wrong. Just a matter of custom and habit, we have to do it; interrelated that way, and usually there is hereditary head [sic] of the whole lot, as usually, the oldest son of the oldest son and each looked upon as chief of his own particular clan. That is the tone they live by. But I am sure it is because only a comparatively short time ago we were invaded by our own people — speaking in our own language which is always a pretty savage sort of warfare.

In Faulkner's estimation, the old pull of blood transcends considerations of caste, class, and occupation:

> . . . [I]t is regional. It is through what we call the "South." It doesn't matter what the people do. They can be land people, farmers, and industrialists, but there still exists the feeling of blood, of clan, blood for blood. It is pretty general through all the classes.[1]

---

[1] James B. Meriwether and Michael Millgate, eds., *Lion in the Garden* (New York: Random House, 1968), p. 191.

Faulkner's explanation of the phenomenon of Southern clannishness touches upon a number of the issues that arise in "Barn Burning." In each case, alienation from the politically and economically dominant group leads to dependence upon an alternative source of security. Just as beleaguered Southerners, Faulkner suggests, have had to look to themselves for "defense" since the South was defeated, so Ab Snopes must turn to his kin for defense not only from Union troops but also from the landed Southern aristocrat who, in what Ab perceives as a failure of paternalism, "aims to begin . . . owning [him] body and soul." The clan's identifying characteristic, then, is its orientation to survival. Perhaps most interestingly, the comments made in the interview impinge upon the central issue of the morality of Sarty's choice. Faulkner's recognition here of a private code of honor suggests that Sarty's conduct is somewhat more questionable than is generally recognized, and his articulation in the interview of a necessity for clannishness suggests at least a modicum of sympathy for the "custom and habit" of "each springing to defend his own blood whether it be right or wrong."

From *Mississippi Quarterly: The Journal of Southern Culture*

CONSIDERATIONS FOR CRITICAL THINKING AND WRITING

1. To what extent does Faulkner's description of clannishness in the South affect your understanding of whether Sarty resolves his dilemma at the end of the story?

2. Do you agree with Hiles that "Sarty's conduct is somewhat more questionable than is generally recognized" (para. 4)?

BENJAMIN DeMOTT (1924–2005)

DeMott pays close attention to matters of culture, race, class, and power that affect Abner Snopes, and from those perspectives Abner is seen as more than simply malevolent.

Abner Snopes as a Victim of Class 1988

We know that Ab Snopes is harsh to his wife, his sons, and his daughters, and that he is particularly cruel to his stock. We know that his hatred of the planters with whom he enters into sharecropping agreements repeatedly issues in acts of wanton destruction. We know that he's ridden with suspicion of his own closest kin, expecting them to betray him. And we know that — worse than any of this — he often behaves with fearful coldness to those who try desperately to communicate the loving respect they feel for him.

Given such a combination of racism, destructiveness, and blank insensitivity, it's tempting to imagine Ab as a figure in whom ignorance and brutality obliterate every sympathetic impulse, every normative response to peace, dignity, or beauty. Major de Spain seems to reach something close to that conclusion after the rug-laundering episode ("Wasn't there anybody here, any of your women . . ."). And although Ab's son is intensely loyal to his father and indignant at the injustice of the Major's twenty-bushel "charge" for the destruction of the rug, Sarty clearly has a conviction that "peace and dignity" are somehow "*beyond his [father's] touch, he no more to them than a buzzing wasp.*" Is there anything to be made of Ab Snopes except a person whose raging malevolence has badly stunted if not crippled his humanity?

Denying the force of the malevolence is impossible — but tracing it solely to ignorance and insensitivity falsifies Ab's nature. Uneducated, probably illiterate, schooled in none of the revolutionary traditions which, in urban settings, were shaping popular protests against "economic injustice" when this story was written in the late 1930s, Ab nevertheless has managed, through the exercise of his own primitive intelligence, to make sense of his world, to arrive at a vision of the relations between labor, money, and the beautiful. It's a vision that's miles away from transforming itself into a broadly historical account of capital accumulation. Ab Snopes can't frame a theory to himself about, say, proletarian enslavement; he has no language in which to imagine a class solidarity leading to political action aimed at securing justice and truth. Indeed, he would explode at the notion that considerations of truth and justice have any pertinence either to the interests of the authorities opposing him or to his own interests in defying them. ("Later, twenty years later, [Sarty] was to tell himself, 'If I had said they wanted only truth, justice, he would have hit me again.'") For Ab Snopes the only principle lending significance to his war with the de Spains of this world is that of blood loyalty — determination to beat your personal enemy if you can and keep faith, at all costs, with your clan.

Yet despite all this, Ab does see that part of the power of the beautiful and the orderly to command our respect depends upon our refusal to remind ourselves that they have been brought into existence by other people's labor — by effort that often in history has been slave labor and has seldom been fairly recompensed. Sarty Snopes, grown up, presumably arrives finally at an understanding both that his father's situation was one of economic oppression and that the oppressors, when sitting in a court of law, are capable of attempting to reach beyond selfishness to a decent distribution of justice. But his father had, at the time, no grip on any of this.

Yet Ab is not a fool, and brutality and insensitivity are not the only features of character that we can make out in him. What we need also to summon is the terrible frustration of an undeveloped mind — aware of the weight of an immense unfairness, aware of the habit of the weak perpetually to behave as though the elegance, grace, beauty, and order found often in the neighborhoods of the rich somehow were traceable exclusively to the superior nature of the rich — and yet unable to move forward from either awareness to anything approaching rational protest. His rage cannot become a force leading toward any positive principle; it has no way to express itself except in viciousness to those closest at hand. It can't begin to make a serious bid for admiration, because whatever inclination we might have to admire it is instantly crossed by repugnance at the cruelty inherent in it.

But it remains true that, together with the ignorance and brutality in Ab Snopes, there is a ferocious, primitive undeceivedness in his reading of the terms of the relationship between rich and poor, lucky and unlucky, advantaged and disadvantaged. Ab Snopes has seen a portion of the truth of the world that many on his level, and most who are luckier, never see. We can damn him for allowing that truth to wreck his humanity, but when we fully bring him to life as a character, it's impossible not to include with our indictment a sense of pity.

From *Close Imagining: An Introduction to Literature*

CONSIDERATIONS FOR CRITICAL THINKING AND WRITING

1. DeMott acknowledges Abner's ignorance and brutality, but he also presents him as a man who suffers injustices. What are those injustices? Discuss whether you think they warrant a more balanced assessment of Abner's character.

2. Why doesn't Abner protest his "oppression" (para. 4)? Given DeMott's perspective on him, how might Abner — in another story — have been the hero rather than a terrible source of conflict?

3. To what extent can DeMott's approach to Abner's circumstances be described as a Marxist perspective? (For a discussion of Marxist criticism, see p. 1653.)

GAYLE EDWARD WILSON (B. 1931)

The following analysis combines psychology and myth as a means of understanding the conflicts in "Barn Burning." The "Apollonian man" alluded to in the discussion (para. 1) refers to the myth of Apollo and implies a person who values order, community, balance, and self-knowledge to establish true relations between the individual and his world.

Conflict in "Barn Burning" 1990

Ruth Benedict's descriptions of two major patterns of culture provide an advantageous starting point for a discussion of the way in which Faulkner develops the content of "Barn Burning." The Paranoid way of life, she comments, has "no political organization. In a strict sense it has no legality."[1] As a consequence of the Paranoid man's adherence to this life-style, he is "lawless," and is feared as a warrior who will hesitate "at no treachery" (p. 121). In such a culture, "every man's hand is against every other man," and as a result each man relies upon blood ties to form social alliances and to sanction his actions (pp. 122–23). The Apollonian man, on the other hand, "keeps to the middle of the road, stays within the known map," and strives to fulfill his civic role in terms of the expectations of the community at large (p. 70). Men in such a society, although the blood tie is relatively important as a bond, turn to the community and its collected wisdom, as it is embodied in the law, for the approval of their actions and for their security. Thus the sanction for a man's "acts comes from the formal structure, not the individual" (p. 99) — from the community, not the blood kin. In "Barn Burning" Faulkner develops the ideas contained in these descriptions of dissimilar life-styles in a way which creates the central tension in the story and keeps it constantly before the reader. The reader is thus made aware of the pervasiveness of Sarty's *"terror and the grief, the being pulled two ways like between two teams of horses."*

The tension is made evident by the presence of effects which follow from actions taken in accord with the dominant characteristic of each life-style. Abner's "wolflike independence . . . his latent ravening ferocity . . . [and] conviction in the rightness of his own actions," which have frequently manifested themselves in acts of destruction against the property of an established community, clearly mark him as a follower of

[1] *Patterns of Culture* (New York, 1959), p. 122.

the Paranoid way. As such, his actions inevitably, and repeatedly, alienate him from each settled society into which he moves. His disregard for a "formal structure" of any kind is indicated by such a minor detail as that which occurs when Abner fuels his fire with "a rail lifted from a nearby fence and cut into lengths," an act which is symbolic of his rejection of any societally imposed limits. It is by burning barns, however, that Abner's Paranoid life-style and its consequences are most forcefully dramatized. At Abner's trial for barn burning, Sarty sees the men "between himself and the table part and become a lane of grim faces." Abner and Sarty then walk between the "two lines of grim-faced men" and they leave a "quiet crowd of grimly watching men." This separation of the Snopes family from the larger society as a consequence of acts motivated by Abner's "ravening ferocity" is underscored by the Justice's command to Abner: "Take your wagon and get out of this country before dark." The Snopes's wagon, containing "the sorry residue of the dozen and more movings," becomes, therefore, a symbol of the transient and nomadic way of life which the Snopes family is forced to adopt because of Abner's adherence to the Paranoid way. The de Spain tenant house and the manner in which the Snopes family lives in it are also effects of a life-style which is not concerned with permanence or order or boundaries or limits. The house is a "paintless two-room" structure "identical almost with the dozen others" in which the family has lived as a result of its nomadic existence, and the members of the family are found "scattered without order or claim up and down the two rooms."

On the other hand, the Harris and de Spain barns represent productivity and fertility, permanence and continuity, because they house the equipment, stock, and seed by which a society produces the goods to sustain and perpetuate itself. A barn and its contents are the effects of a society which is built upon the willingness of men to subordinate their unfettered desires to a communal consensus in order to develop a permanent community. The importance of a barn to the Apollonian way is illustrated by Sarty's thoughts when he sees the effect brought about by what a barn symbolizes. When he comes upon the de Spain house for the first time, he feels that "*the spell*" of "*peace and dignity*" cast by the magnificent house will render "*even the barns and stable and cribs which belong to it impervious to the puny flames he* [Abner] *might contrive.*" The sight of this apotheosis of the Apollonian way has a profound effect on Sarty: he "at that instant . . . forgot his father. . . ." It is most revealing that Sartoris should compare this house which symbolizes the "*peace and dignity*" of the Apollonian way with another kind of building which, because of what it represents, embodies the very essence of an ordered society: "*Hit's big as a courthouse* he thought quietly, with a surge of peace and joy."

Essentially, it is the concept of law, as symbolized by the de Spain house, that gives Sarty his sense of "peace and joy," for it is the law that provides man with the peace necessary to develop the "formal structure" of a communal, stable society. Without law, as Hobbes tells us, "there is no place for Industry; because the fruit thereof is uncertain: and consequently no Culture of the Earth; . . . no commodius Building; . . . no Society; and which is worst of all, continuall feare, and danger of violent death; And the life of man, solitary, poore, nasty, brutish, and short."[2] At its best, the law is moderate, even, and impartial. It protects as well as punishes; it is

---

[2] Chapter XIII, "*Of the NATURAL CONDITION of Mankind, as concerning their Felicity, and Misery,*" *Leviathan* . . . (1651) in *Seventeenth-Century Verse and Prose*, ed. Helen White, Ruth Wallerstein, and Ricardo Quintana (New York, 1967), I, 223.

an elaborately worked out system designed to join men together in a common purpose, to insure the presumption of innocence until guilt is proved, and to make the
punishment commensurate with the crime. In "Barn Burning" the primacy of the
law in an Apollonian society is made quite evident. It is represented in a minor way
by the contract in which Snopes engages with de Spain to work for eight months
in return for a share of the crop. It is developed in a major way in the two trials
which take place. In the first trial, the law protects Abner from unwarranted conclusions. Concerning the charge that Abner burned Harris's barn, the Justice asks Harris, "But what proof have you, Mr. Harris?" Harris tells of the Negro who appeared
and gave him the cryptic message, "'wood and hay kin burn,'" to which the Justice
replies, "But that's not proof. Don't you see that's not proof?" In the second trial, de
Spain's unreasonable assessment of twenty bushels of corn in payment for the rug
Abner ruined is not allowed. Abner is fined ten bushels, not twenty, as de Spain had
wanted. For the men in "Barn Burning," . . . then, the law and its equitable application to all men is the *sine qua non* of the Apollonian way. . . . It is this belief in the
law and its extensions of "justice" and "civilization" which guides and controls the
behavior of the Apollonian man. This is the same realization that young Sarty is
only able to articulate "twenty years" after Abner strikes him for not being willing to
lie in his defense at the trial. "'If I had said they only wanted truth, justice, he would
have hit me again.'"

From *Mississippi Quarterly*

CONSIDERATIONS FOR CRITICAL THINKING AND WRITING

1. What distinctions are drawn between the "Paranoid man" and the "Apollonian
   man" (para. 1)? How do these two different types serve to frame the conflicts in
   "Barn Burning"?
2. How is Snopes's wagon an appropriate symbol of the "Paranoid way" (para. 1),
   and how are the Harris and de Spain barns fitting symbols of the "Apollonian
   way" (para. 3)?
3. In an essay explain why you think Sarty chooses one way of life over the other
   at the end of the story.
4. Compare Wilson's description of the story's conflicts with Hiles's and DeMott's.

JAMES FERGUSON (B. 1928)

Ferguson's formalist approach (see pp. 1645–47 in Chapter 51, "Critical Strategies
for Reading") relates Faulkner's use of point of view to his thematic concerns in the
story.

Narrative Strategy in "Barn Burning" 1991

The point of view is largely limited to the consciousness of Sarty Snopes, but in
spite of his sensitivity and his intuitive sense of right and wrong, the little boy is
far too young to understand his father and the complexities of the moral choice he

must make. To enhance the pathos of his situation and the drama of Sarty's initiation into life, Faulkner felt the need for the occasional intrusion of an authorial voice giving the reader insights far beyond the capabilities of the youthful protagonist. A passage, for example, about the fires Abner Snopes builds affords us a sense of the rationale for the man's actions, of his strangely perverse integrity, which could not be supplied to us by the consciousness of his son:

> The nights were still cool and they had a fire against it, of a rail lifted from a nearby fence and cut into lengths — a small fire, neat, niggard almost, a shrewd fire; such fires were his father's habit and custom always, even in freezing weather. Older, the boy might have remarked this and wondered why not a big one; why should not a man who had not only seen the waste and extravagance of war, but who had in his blood an inherent voracious prodigality with material not his own, have burned everything in sight? Then he might have gone a step farther and thought that that was the reason: that niggard blaze was the living fruit of nights passed during those four years in the woods hiding from all men, blue or gray, with his strings of horses (captured horses, he called them). And older still, he might have divined the true reason: that the element of fire spoke to some deep mainspring of his father's being, as the element of steel or of powder spoke to other men, as the one weapon for the preservation of integrity, else breath were not worth the breathing, and hence to be regarded with respect and used with discretion.

Again, near the end of the story, after Sarty has betrayed his father, there is another brief shift away from the consciousness of the protagonist:

> "He was brave!" he cried suddenly, aloud but not loud, no more than a whisper: "He was! He was in the war! He was in Colonel Sartoris' cav'ry!" not knowing that his father had gone to that war a private in the fine old European sense, wearing no uniform, admitting the authority of and giving fidelity to no man or army or flag, going to war as Malbrouck himself did: for booty — it meant nothing and less than nothing to him if it were enemy booty or his own.

"Barn Burning" is incomparably richer than it would have been without such additions not only because they supply us with ironies otherwise unavailable to us but also because these manipulations of point of view dramatize *on the level of technique* the thematic matter of the story. The tensions between the awareness of the boy and the information supplied us by the authorial voice undergird and emphasize the conflicts between youth and age, innocence and sophistication, intuition and abstraction, decency and corruption, all of which lie at the core of the work.

From *Faulkner's Short Fiction*

CONSIDERATIONS FOR CRITICAL THINKING AND WRITING

1. In the first passage quoted by Ferguson, how does the narrator's analysis of Abner Snopes become progressively sophisticated in explaining his reasons for building a small fire?

2. What other examples of shifts away from the consciousness of Sarty to a more informed point of view can you find in the story? Choose what you judge to be a significant example and write an essay about how Faulkner's use of point of view contributes to the story's themes.

INCORPORATING THE CRITICS

The following questions can help you to incorporate materials from critical essays into your own writing about a literary work. You may initially feel intimidated by the prospect of responding to the arguments of professional critics in your own paper. However, the process will not defeat you if you have clearly formulated your own response to the literary work and are able to distinguish it from the critics' perspectives. Reading the critics can help you to develop your own thesis — perhaps, to cite just two examples, by using them as supporting evidence or by arguing with them in order to clarify or qualify their points about the literary work. As you write and discover how to advance your thesis, you'll find yourself participating in a dialogue with the critics. This sort of conversation will help you to improve your thinking and hone your argument.

Keep in mind that the work of professional critics is a means of enriching your understanding of a literary work rather than a substitution for your own analysis and interpretation of that work. Quoting, paraphrasing, or summarizing a critic's perspective does not relieve you of the obligation of choosing a topic, organizing information, developing a thesis, and arguing your point of view by citing sufficient evidence from the text you are examining. These matters are discussed in further detail in Chapter 52, "Reading and the Writing Process." You should also be familiar with the methods for documenting sources that are explained in Chapter 53, "The Literary Research Paper"; this chapter also contains important information about how to avoid plagiarism.

No doubt you won't find all literary criticism equally useful: some critics' arguments won't address your own areas of concern; some will be too difficult for you to get a handle on; and some will seem wrongheaded. However, much of the criticism you read will serve to make a literary work more accessible and interesting to you, and disagreeing with others' arguments will often help you to develop your own ideas about a work. When you use the work of critics in your own writing, you should consider the following questions. Responding to these questions will help you to ensure that you have a clear understanding of what a critic is arguing about a work, to what extent you agree with that argument, and how you plan to incorporate and respond to the critic's reading in your own paper. The more questions you can ask yourself in response to this list or as a result of your own reading, the more you'll be able to think critically about how you are approaching both the critics and the literary work under consideration.

1. Have you read the literary work carefully and taken notes of your own impressions before reading any critical perspectives so that your initial insights are not lost to the arguments made by the critics? Have you articulated your own responses to the work in a journal entry prior to reading the critics?

(continued)

2. Are you sufficiently familiar with the literary work that you can determine the accuracy, fairness, and thoroughness of the critic's use of evidence from the work?

3. Have you read the critic's piece carefully? Try summarizing the critic's argument in a brief paragraph. Do you understand the nature and purpose of the critic's argument? Which passages are especially helpful to you? Which seem unclear? Why?

4. Is the critic's reading of the literary work similar to or different from your own reading? Why do you agree or disagree? What generational, historical, cultural, or biographical considerations might help to account for any differences between the critic's responses and your own?

5. How has your reading of the critic influenced your understanding of the literary work? Do issues that previously seemed unimportant now seem significant? What are these issues, and how does a consideration of them affect your reading of the work?

6. Are you too quickly revising or even discarding your own reading because the critic's perspective seems so polished and persuasive? Are you making use of your reading notes and the responses in your journal entries?

7. How would you classify the critic's approach? Through what kind of lens does the critic view the literary work? Is the critical approach formalist, biographical, psychological, historical, mythological, reader-response, deconstructionist, or some combination of these or possibly other strategies? (For a discussion of these approaches, see Chapter 51, "Critical Strategies for Reading.")

8. What biases, if any, can you detect in the critic's approach? How might, for example, a southern critic's reading of "Barn Burning" differ from a northern critic's?

9. Can you determine how other critics have responded to the critic's work? Is the critic's work cited and taken seriously in other critics' books and articles? Is the work dated by having been superseded by subsequent studies?

10. Are any passages or topics that you deem important left out by the critic? Do these omissions qualify or refute the critic's argument?

11. What judgments does the critic seem to make about the work? Is the work regarded, for example, as significant, unified, representative, trivial, inept, or irresponsible? Do you agree with these judgments? If not, can you develop and support a thesis about your difference of opinion?

12. What important disagreements do critics reveal in their approaches to the work? Do you find one perspective more convincing than another? Why? Is there a way of resolving their conflicting views that could serve as a thesis for your paper?

13. Can you extend or qualify the critic's argument to matters in the literary text that are not covered by the critic's perspective? Will this allow you to develop your own topic while acknowledging the critic's useful insights?

14. Have you quoted, paraphrased, or summarized the critic accurately and fairly? Have you avoided misrepresenting the critic's arguments in any way?

15. Are the critic's words, ideas, opinions, and insights adequately acknowledged and documented in the correct format? Do you understand the difference between common knowledge and plagiarism? Have you avoided quoting excessively? Are the quotations smoothly integrated into your own text?

16. Are you certain that your incorporation of the critic's work is for the purpose of developing your paper's thesis rather than for name-dropping or padding your paper? How can you explain to yourself why the critic's work is useful for your argument?

A SAMPLE STUDENT PAPER

The Fires of Class Conflict in William Faulkner's "Barn Burning" (excerpt)

The following excerpt consists of the first few paragraphs of a paper in which the student develops a thesis based on her reading of critical perspectives by Benjamin DeMott (p. 419) and Gayle Edward Wilson (p. 421). Sonia Metzger uses the two critics' different approaches to "Barn Burning" to develop a thesis that goes beyond either critic's perspective. The rest of her paper (not included) argues her thesis that a recognition of the class conflicts suppressed by Faulkner in the story makes Abner Snopes's violent response to the economic power inherent in Major de Spain's Apollonian values appear to be justifiable, rather than merely the desperate activity of a Paranoid man. Abner has good reason to fear Apollonian values because de Spain's world is carefully constructed to exclude him while simultaneously exploiting him.

Sonia Metzger

Professor Wolf

English 109

15 April 2015

The Fires of Class Conflict in William Faulkner's "Barn Burning"

The central conflict in William Faulkner's "Barn Burning" concerns a young boy named Sarty Snopes who must choose between loyalty to his father and his family and loyalty to society and humanity. A first reading of the story probably leaves most readers with the sense that the boy must turn away from his father's vicious sensibilities if he is to grow into a responsible adult. Sarty faces tremendous pressure from his father to lie in court so that his father will not be convicted of barn burning. He knows his father wants him "to stick to your own blood or you ain't going to have any blood to stick to you" (408).

Unlike the selfish, mean, vengeful father who despises the wealth and gentility of the southern aristocracy and is relentless in his contempt for the upper-class world of Major de Spain, Sarty is a gentle, vulnerable character who engages our sympathy. He is divided between wanting his father's love and loving the "peace and dignity" (409) that de Spain's house evokes within him. Gayle Edward Wilson, one of the critics I've read, mostly agrees with this view of the story's conflict, but Benjamin DeMott goes beyond the focus on Sarty's conflicted conscience to examine another, more subtle dimension of the story—the reasons for Abner Snopes's ferocious rejection of the world he wants to burn down.

Our understanding of Abner and his son is, according to Wilson, deepened by employing two concepts from Ruth Benedict's *Patterns of Culture* that she calls the "Paranoid man" and the "Apollonian man" (421). Abner is a version of the Paranoid man. His culture consists of a lawless, clannish, fierce world in which his nomadic, lonely existence is characterized by violence, hatred, force, and destruction. Except for blood ties, he rejects forms of any kind: the stability created by the Apollonian man (Major de Spain) through law and order in a community is his enemy. He will not be bound by any societal regulations; instead, he destroys any sense of community through his barn burning and his erratic antisocial behavior. For Wilson,

---

Margin annotations:

Thesis identifying conflict of story, supported with textual evidence

Writer's analysis of central character and conflict

Identification of two critics' views of conflict

Analysis of critics' views, set in contrast to each other

Sarty must turn away from the Paranoid man to the Apollonian man if he is to pledge his loyalty to justice and civilization (421). This conflict is also recognized by Benjamin DeMott, who acknowledges Abner's harshness, cruelty, destructiveness, paranoia, and coldness but who also raises an important question that shifts some of our focus from Sarty onto Abner: "Is there anything to be made of Ab Snopes except a person whose raging malevolence has badly stunted if not crippled his humanity?" (420).

By considering when "Barn Burning" was written—during the depression of the late 1930s—DeMott suggests a kind of defense for understanding and even sympathizing with Abner by pointing to issues of class and power embedded in the capitalistic culture and the nearly slave-labor conditions endured by Abner. This version of Abner is not merely brutish but also suffering from "the terrible frustration of an undeveloped mind—aware of the weight of an immense unfairness . . . and yet unable to move forward . . . to anything approaching rational protest" (420). DeMott suggests that Abner warrants our pity rather than total repudiation and that he, however imperfectly, does feel (even if he doesn't comprehend) the pain produced by the miserable gap between the rich and the poor. With this gap in mind, I want to go further than DeMott goes and argue, using Wilson's categories, that Faulkner's portrayal of Apollonian values avoids confronting the economic oppression that Abner experiences but that neither he nor Sarty can articulate. Abner may fit much of the description associated with the Paranoid man, but there are important social reasons for his rightfully fearing the economic power of the Apollonian man.

> Writer's response to critics' views

Works Cited

DeMott, Benjamin. "Abner Snopes as a Victim of Class." Meyer 419–20.

Faulkner, William. "Barn Burning." Meyer 406–17.

Meyer, Michael, ed. *The Bedford Introduction to Literature.* 11th ed. Boston: Bedford/St. Martin's, 2016. Print.

Wilson, Gayle Edward. "Conflict in 'Barn Burning.'" Meyer 421–23.

14

A CULTURAL CASE STUDY
James Joyce's "Eveline"

Ireland is the old sow that eats her farrow.
— JAMES JOYCE

I've put in [my writing] so many enigmas and puzzles that it will keep the professors busy for centuries arguing over what I meant.
— JAMES JOYCE

Close reading is an essential and important means of appreciating the literary art of a text. This formalist approach to literature explores the subtle, complex relationships between how a work is constructed using elements such as plot, characterization, point of view, diction, metaphor, symbol, irony, and other literary techniques to create a coherent structure that contributes to a work's meaning. (For a more detailed discussion of formalistic approaches to literary works, see Chapter 51, "Critical Strategies for Reading.") The formalist focuses on the text itself rather than the historical, political, economic, and other contexts of a text. A formalist reading of *The Scarlet Letter,* for example, is more likely to examine how the book is structured around a series of scenes in which the main characters appear on or near the town scaffold than to analyze how the text portrays the social and religious values of Nathaniel Hawthorne or of seventeenth-century Puritan New Englanders. Although recent literary criticism has continued to demonstrate the importance of close readings to discover how a text creates its effects on a reader, scholars also have made a sustained effort to place literary texts in their historical and cultural contexts.

Cultural critics, like literary historians, place literary works in the contexts of their times, but they do not restrict themselves to major historical moments or figures. Instead of focusing on, perhaps, Hawthorne's friendship with Herman Melville, a cultural critic might examine the relationship between Hawthorne's writing and popular contemporary domestic novels that are now obscure. Cultural critics might even examine the classic comic book version of *The Scarlet Letter* or one of its many film versions to gain insight into how our culture has reinterpreted Hawthorne's writing. The materials used by cultural critics are taken from both "high culture" and popular culture. A cultural critic's approach to James Joyce's work might include discussions of Dublin's saloons, political pamphlets, and Catholic sexual mores as well as connections to Ezra Pound or T. S. Eliot.

The documents that follow Joyce's "Eveline" in this chapter offer a glimpse of how cultural criticism can be used to provide a rich and revealing historical context for a literary work. They include an early twentieth-century photograph of Dublin, a portion of a temperance tract, a letter from an Irish woman who emigrated to Australia, and a plot synopsis of the opera *The Bohemian Girl*: all these documents figure in one way or another in "Eveline." These documents are suggestive rather than exhaustive, but they do evoke some of the culture contemporary to Joyce that informs the world he creates in "Eveline" and thereby allow readers to gain a broader and deeper understanding of the story itself.

A BRIEF BIOGRAPHY AND INTRODUCTION

James Joyce (1882–1941) was born in Dublin, Ireland, during a time of political upheaval. The country had endured nearly a century of economic depression and terrible famine and continued to suffer under what many Irish regarded as British oppression. Irish nationalism and independence movements attempted to counter British economic exploitation and cultural arrogance. Joyce, influenced by a climate in which ecclesiastical privilege and governmental authority were at once powerful and suspect, believed the Irish were also unable to free themselves from the Catholic church's compromises and their own political ineptitude. Change was in the air, but Ireland was slow to be moved by the reform currents already rippling through the Continent.

Modernism, as it was developing on the Continent, challenged traditional attitudes about God, humanity, and society. Scientific and industrial advances created not only material progress but also tremendous social upheaval, which sometimes produced a sense of discontinuity, fragmentation, alienation, and despair. Firm certainties gave way to anxious doubts, and the past was considered more as something to be overcome than as something to revere. Heroic action seemed remote and theatrical to a writer like Joyce, who rejected the use of remarkable historic events in his fiction and instead focused on the everyday lives of ordinary people trying to make sense of themselves.

Joyce himself came from a declining middle-class family of more than a dozen children, eventually reduced to poverty by his father's drinking.

Nevertheless, Joyce received a fine classical education at Jesuit schools, including University College, Dublin. His strict early education was strongly traditional in its Catholicism, but when he entered University College, he rejected both his religion and his national heritage. By the time he took his undergraduate degree in 1902, he was more comfortable casting himself as an alienated writer than as a typical citizen of Dublin, who he thought lived a life of mediocrity, sentimentality, and self-deception. While at college he studied modern languages and taught himself Norwegian so he could read the plays of Henrik Ibsen in their original language (see p. 1357 for Ibsen's *A Doll's House*). Joyce responded deeply to Ibsen's dramatizations of troubled individuals who repudiate public morality and social values in their efforts to create lives of integrity amid stifling families, institutions, and cultures.

After graduation Joyce left Dublin for Paris to study medicine, but that career soon ended when he dropped out of the single course for which he had registered. Instead, he wrote poetry, which was eventually published in 1907 as *Chamber Music*. In 1903 he returned to Dublin to be with his mother, then dying of cancer. The next summer he met Nora Barnacle, while she was working in a Dublin boardinghouse. After leaving Dublin with Nora in 1905 to return to the Continent, he visited his native city only a few times (the final visit was in 1912), and he lived the rest of his life in Europe. From 1920 until shortly before his death, Joyce settled in Paris, where he enjoyed the stimulation of living amid writers and artists. He lived with Nora his entire life, having two children and eventually marrying her in 1931.

Joyce earned a living by teaching at a Berlitz language school, tutoring, and working in a bank, but mostly he gathered impressions of the world around him — whether in Trieste, Zurich, Rome, or Paris — that he would incorporate into his literary work. His writings, however, were always about life in Ireland rather than the European cities in which he lived. Fortunately, Joyce's talents attracted several patrons who subsidized his income and helped him to publish.

Dubliners, Joyce's first major publication in fiction, was a collection of stories that he published in 1914 and that included "Eveline." Two years later Joyce published *A Portrait of the Artist as a Young Man*, a novel. Joyce strongly identified with the protagonist, who, like Joyce, rejected custom and tradition. If the price of independence from deadening sensibilities, crass materialism, and a circumscribed life was alienation, then so be it. Joyce believed that if the artist was to see clearly and report what he saw freshly, it was necessary to stand outside the commonplace responses to experience derived from family, church, or country. His next novel, *Ulysses* (1922), is regarded by many readers as Joyce's masterpiece. This remarkably innovative novel is an account of one day in the life of an Irish Jew named Leopold Bloom, who, despite his rather ordinary life in Dublin, represents a microcosm of all human experience. Joyce's stream-of-consciousness technique revealed the characters' thoughts as they experienced them (see p. 197 for a discussion of this technique). These uninhibited thoughts were censored in the United States until 1933, when a judge ruled in a celebrated court case that the book was not obscene. Though *Ulysses* is Joyce's most famous book, *Finnegans Wake* (1939) is his most

THE
IRISH HOMESTEAD
The Organ of Irish Agricultural and Industrial Development

By Post 1½d.

SEPTEMBER 10, 1904.   THE IRISH HOMESTEAD.   761

OUR WEEKLY STORY.

EVELINE.
BY STEPHEN DAEDALUS.

First Publication of "Eveline." In 1904, the editor of the farmer's magazine *The Irish Homestead* asked James Joyce to write some "simple" stories about Irish life. The magazine published "The Sisters," "Eveline," and "After the Race," before deciding that Joyce's work was not suitable for *Homestead* readers. After some initial trouble with his publisher over the risk of libel, Joyce in 1914 published the stories in *Dubliners,* a book that he called "a moral history" of his country. "I call the series *Dubliners,*" he writes, "to betray the soul of that hemiplegia or paralysis which many consider a city." Though Joyce never lived in Dublin again after he eloped with Nora Barnacle in 1905, Dublin is the setting of almost all of his work. Shown here is a facsimile of the first publication of "Eveline," on September 10, 1904. Joyce signed the story "Stephen Daedalus," his early pen name and the name of the protagonist in *A Portrait of the Artist as a Young Man* (1916) who later reappears in *Ulysses* (1922). **Joyce is shown here at age twenty-two**, the year his stories appeared in *The Irish Homestead.*

All images: Courtesy of the Poetry/Rare Books Collection, UB Libraries, State University of New York at Buffalo.

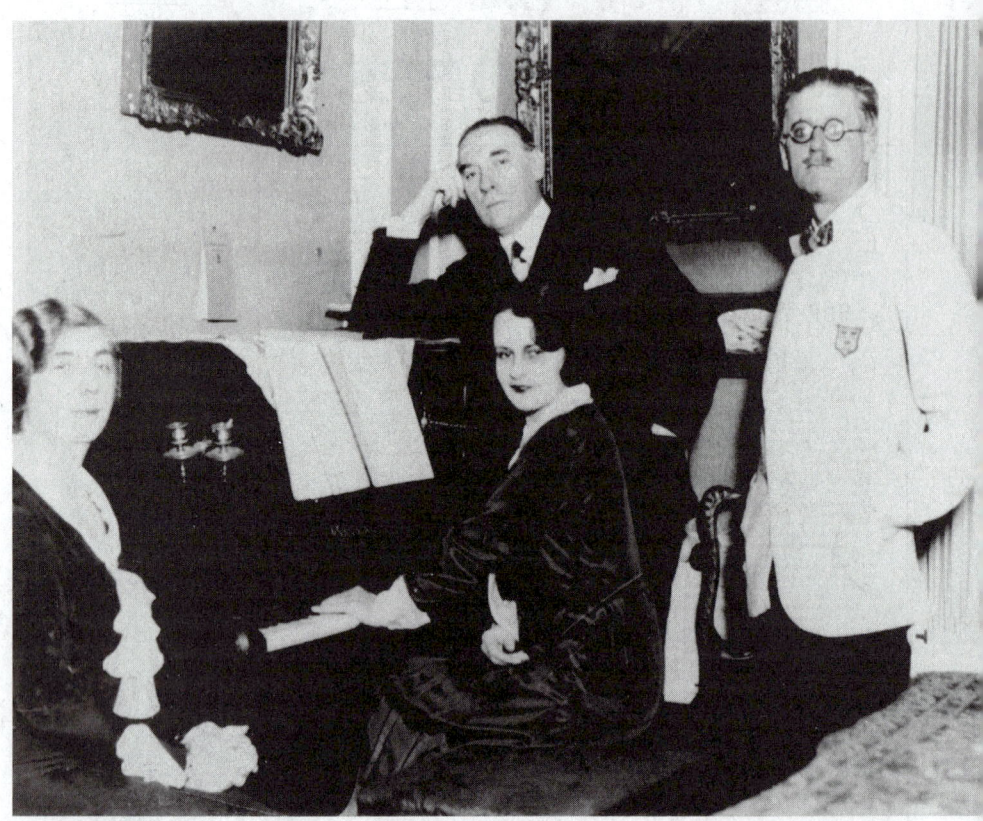

James Joyce with Nora and Friends (top). James Joyce, Nora Barnacle (left), and their friends the Sullivans, at a piano in Paris. Joyce grew up in a musical family and was said to have a beautiful tenor voice. He loved music and frequently incorporated it in his writing — his works contain thousands of musical references and allusions.

Courtesy of the Poetry/Rare Books Collection, UB Libraries, State University of New York at Buffalo.

James Joyce in Paris (right). James Joyce and Sylvia Beach, proprietor of the Parisian bookstore Shakespeare & Company, during the "roaring twenties." In 1920 Joyce and his family relocated to Paris, and in 1922 Beach published the first edition of *Ulysses*.

© Bettmann/CORBIS.

challenging. Even more unconventional and experimental than *Ulysses,* it endlessly plays with language within a fluid dream world in which the characters' experiences evolve into continuously expanding meanings produced through complex allusions and elaborate puns in multiple languages. The novel's plot defies summation, but its language warrants exploration, which is perhaps best begun by hearing a recording of Joyce reading aloud from the book. His stylistic innovations in *Ulysses* and *Finnegans Wake* had as great an influence on literature as the automobile and the radio did on people's daily lives, when people started covering more ground and hearing more voices than ever before.

Dubliners is Joyce's quarrel with his native city, and his homage to it. Written between 1904 and 1907, it is the most accessible of Joyce's works. It consists of a series of fifteen stories about characters who struggle with oppressive morality, plodding routines, somber shadows, self-conscious decency, restless desires, and frail gestures toward freedom. These stories contain no conventional high drama or action-filled episodes; instead, they are made up of small, quiet moments that turn out to be important in their characters' lives. Most of the characters are on the brink of discovering something, such as loss, shame, failure, or death. Typically, the protagonist suddenly experiences a deep realization about himself or herself, a truth that is grasped in an ordinary rather than melodramatic moment. Joyce called such a moment — when a character is overcome by a flash of recognition — an **epiphany** and defined it as a "sudden spiritual manifestation, whether in the vulgarity of speech or gesture or in a memorable phase of the mind itself." Even the most commonplace experience might yield a spontaneous insight into the essential nature of a person or situation. Joyce's characters may live ordinary lives cluttered with mundane details, but their lives have significance. Indeed, they seem to stumble onto significance when they least expect it.

Joyce weaves his characters' dreams and longings into the texture of Dublin life, a social fabric that appears to limit his characters' options. He once explained to his publisher that his intention in *Dubliners* "was to write a chapter of the moral history of my country," and he focused on Dublin because that city seemed to him "the center of paralysis." The major causes of his characters' paralysis are transmitted by their family life, Catholicism, economic situations, and vulnerability to political forces. His characters have lives consisting largely of self-denial and drab duties, but they also have an irrepressible desire for something more — as in "Eveline," which focuses on a dutiful daughter's efforts to run away with her lover.

Chronology

1882   Born on February 2 in Dublin, Ireland.

1888–98   Studies at Jesuit schools in preparation for university.

1898–1902   Attends University College, Dublin, another Jesuit school, and graduates with a degree in modern languages.

1902	Studies medicine in Paris but soon abandons it for writing.
1903	Returns to be at his mother's deathbed in Dublin.
1904	Meets Nora Barnacle, with whom he will have two children and live his entire life.
1905	Moves to the Continent to teach at the Berlitz school in Trieste and write.
1907	After working in a bank for a year in Rome, he returns to Trieste; publishes *Chamber Music*, a volume of poems.
1912	Makes his final visit to Ireland.
1914	Publishes *Dubliners* after eight years of censorship battles.
1916	Publishes *A Portrait of the Artist as a Young Man*.
1917	Has the first of a series of debilitating eye operations.
1918	Publishes *Exiles*, a play.
1920	Settles in Paris with his family.
1922	Publishes *Ulysses* amid controversy concerning its alleged obscenity.
1927	Publishes *Pomes Penyeach*.
1931	Marries Nora Barnacle.
1934	Publishes *Collected Poems*.
1939	Publishes *Finnegans Wake*.
1940	After the German occupation of Paris, the Joyces move to Zurich.
1941	Dies of a perforated ulcer on January 13 at Zurich.

Eveline 1914

She sat at the window watching the evening invade the avenue. Her head was leaned against the window curtains and in her nostrils was the odor of dusty cretonne. She was tired.

Few people passed. The man out of the last house passed on his way home; she heard his footsteps clacking along the concrete pavement and afterwards crunching on the cinder path before the new red houses. One time there used to be a field there in which they used to play every evening with other people's children. Then a man from Belfast bought the field and built houses in it — not like their little brown houses but bright brick houses with shining roofs. The children of the avenue used to play together in that field — the Devines, the Waters, the Dunns, little Keogh the cripple, she and her brothers and sisters. Ernest, however, never played: he was too grown up. Her father used often to hunt them in out of the field with his blackthorn stick; but usually little Keogh used to keep *nix* and call out when he saw her father coming. Still they seemed to have been rather happy then. Her father was not so bad then; and besides, her mother was alive. That was a long time ago; she and her brothers and sisters were all grown up; her mother was dead. Tizzie Dunn was dead, too, and the Waters had gone back to England. Everything changes. Now she was going to go away like the others, to leave her home.

Home! She looked round the room, reviewing all its familiar objects which she had dusted once a week for so many years, wondering where on earth all the dust came from. Perhaps she would never see again those familiar objects from which she had never dreamed of being divided. And yet during all those years she had never found out the name of the priest whose yellowing photograph hung on the wall above the broken harmonium beside the colored print of the promises made to Blessed Margaret Mary Alacoque. He had been a school friend of her father. Whenever he showed the photograph to a visitor her father used to pass it with a casual word:

— He is in Melbourne now.

She had consented to go away, to leave her home. Was that wise? She tried to 5 weigh each side of the question. In her home anyway she had shelter and food; she had those whom she had known all her life about her. Of course she had to work hard both in the house and at business. What would they say of her in the Stores when they found out that she had run away with a fellow? Say she was a fool, perhaps; and her place would be filled up by advertisement. Miss Gavan would be glad. She had always had an edge on her, especially whenever there were people listening.

— Miss Hill, don't you see these ladies are waiting?

— Look lively, Miss Hill, please.

She would not cry many tears at leaving the Stores.

But in her new home, in a distant unknown country, it would not be like that. Then she would be married — she, Eveline. People would treat her with respect then. She would not be treated as her mother had been. Even now, though she was over nineteen, she sometimes felt herself in danger of her father's violence. She knew it was that that had given her the palpitations. When they were growing up he had never gone for her, like he used to go for Harry and Ernest, because she was a girl; but latterly he had begun to threaten her and say what he would do to her only for her dead mother's sake. And now she had nobody to protect her. Ernest was dead and Harry, who was in the church decorating business, was nearly always down somewhere in the country. Besides, the invariable squabble for money on Saturday nights had begun to weary her unspeakably. She always gave her entire wages — seven shillings — and Harry always sent up what he could but the trouble was to get any money from her father. He said she used to squander the money, that she had no head, that he wasn't going to give her his hard-earned money to throw about the streets, and much more, for he was usually fairly bad of a Saturday night. In the end he would give her the money and ask her had she any intention of buying Sunday's dinner. Then she had to rush out as quickly as she could and do her marketing, holding her black leather purse tightly in her hand as she elbowed her way through the crowds and returning home late under her load of provisions. She had hard work to keep the house together and to see that the two young children who had been left to her charge went to school regularly and got their meals regularly. It was hard work — a hard life — but now that she was about to leave it she did not find it a wholly undesirable life.

She was about to explore another life with Frank. Frank was very kind, manly, 10 open-hearted. She was to go away with him by the night-boat to be his wife and to live with him in Buenos Aires where he had a home waiting for her. How well she remembered the first time she had seen him; he was lodging in a house on the main road where she used to visit. It seemed a few weeks ago. He was standing at the gate, his peaked cap pushed back on his head and his hair tumbled forward over a face of bronze. Then they had come to know each other. He used to meet her outside the Stores every evening and see her home. He took her to see *The Bohemian Girl* and she felt elated as she sat in an unaccustomed part of the theater with him. He was awfully fond of music and sang a little. People knew that they were courting and, when he sang about the lass that loves a sailor, she always felt pleasantly confused. He used to call her Poppens out of fun. First of all it had been an excitement for her to have a fellow and then she had begun to like him. He had tales of distant countries. He had started as a deck boy at a pound a month on a ship of the Allan Line going out to Canada. He told her the names of the ships he had been on and the names of the different services. He had sailed through the Straits of Magellan and he told her stories of the terrible Patagonians. He had fallen on his feet in Buenos Aires, he said, and had come over to the old country just for a holiday. Of course, her father had found out the affair and had forbidden her to have anything to say to him.

— I know these sailor chaps, he said.

One day he had quarreled with Frank and after that she had to meet her lover secretly.

The evening deepened in the avenue. The white of two letters in her lap grew indistinct. One was to Harry; the other was to her father. Ernest had been her favorite but she liked Harry too. Her father was becoming old lately, she noticed; he would miss her. Sometimes he could be very nice. Not long before, when she had been laid up for a day, he had read her out a ghost story and made toast for her at the fire. Another day, when their mother was alive, they had all gone for a picnic to the Hill of Howth. She remembered her father putting on her mother's bonnet to make the children laugh.

Her time was running out but she continued to sit by the window, leaning her head against the window curtain, inhaling the odor of dusty cretonne. Down far in the avenue she could hear a street organ playing. She knew the air. Strange that it should come that very night to remind her of the promise to her mother, her promise to keep the home together as long as she could. She remembered the last night of her mother's illness; she was again in the close dark room at the other side of the hall and outside she heard a melancholy air of Italy. The organ-player had been ordered to go away and given sixpence. She remembered her father strutting back into the sickroom saying:

— Damned Italians! coming over here!   15

As she mused the pitiful vision of her mother's life laid its spell on the very quick of her being — that life of commonplace sacrifices closing in final craziness. She trembled as she heard again her mother's voice saying constantly with foolish insistence:

— Derevaun Seraun! Derevaun Seraun!°

She stood up in a sudden impulse of terror. Escape! She must escape! Frank would save her. He would give her life, perhaps love, too. But she wanted to live. Why should she be unhappy? She had a right to happiness. Frank would take her in his arms, fold her in his arms. He would save her.

She stood among the swaying crowd in the station at the North Wall. He held her hand and she knew that he was speaking to her, saying something about the passage over and over again. The station was full of soldiers with brown baggages.

Derevaun Seraun!: "The end of pleasure is pain!" (Gaelic).

Through the wide doors of the sheds she caught a glimpse of the black mass of the boat, lying in beside the quay wall, with illumined portholes. She answered nothing. She felt her cheek pale and cold and, out of a maze of distress, she prayed to God to direct her, to show her what was her duty. The boat blew a long mournful whistle into the mist. If she went, tomorrow she would be on the sea with Frank, steaming toward Buenos Aires. Their passage had been booked. Could she still draw back after all he had done for her? Her distress awoke a nausea in her body and she kept moving her lips in silent fervent prayer.

A bell clanged upon her heart. She felt him seize her hand: 20

—Come!

All the seas of the world tumbled about her heart. He was drawing her into them: he would drown her. She gripped with both hands at the iron railing.

—Come!

No! No! No! It was impossible. Her hands clutched the iron in frenzy. Amid the seas she sent a cry of anguish!

—Eveline! Evvy!   25

He rushed beyond the barrier and called to her to follow. He was shouted at to go on but he still called to her. She set her white face to him, passive, like a helpless animal. Her eyes gave him no sign of love or farewell or recognition.

CONSIDERATIONS FOR CRITICAL THINKING AND WRITING

1. FIRST RESPONSE. Explain why you agree or disagree with Eveline's decision.
2. Describe the character of Eveline. What do you think she looks like? Though there are no physical details about her in the story, write a one-page description of her as you think she would appear at the beginning of the story looking out the window.
3. Describe the physical setting of Eveline's home. How does she feel about living at home?
4. What sort of relationship does Eveline have with her father? Describe the range of her feelings toward him.
5. How is Frank characterized? Why does Eveline's father forbid them to see each other?
6. Why does thinking of her mother make Eveline want to "escape"?
7. Before she meets him at the dock, how does Eveline expect Frank to change her life?
8. Why doesn't she go with Frank to Buenos Aires?
9. What associations do you have about Buenos Aires? What symbolic value does this Argentine city have in the story?
10. Read carefully the water imagery in the final paragraphs of the story. How does this imagery help to suggest Eveline's reasons for not leaving with Frank?

CONNECTIONS TO OTHER SELECTIONS

1. How does Eveline's response to her life at home compare with that of the narrator in D. H. Lawrence's "The Horse Dealer's Daughter" (p. 558)? Write an essay that explores the similarities and differences in their efforts to escape to something better.
2. Write an essay about the meaning of "home" to the protagonists in "Eveline" and Ernest Hemingway's "Soldier's Home" (p. 162).

DOCUMENTS

CONSIDERATIONS FOR CRITICAL THINKING AND WRITING

1. Describe what this photograph tells you. What does it tell you about life in Dublin? Explain whether you think this photograph confirms or challenges the view of Dublin presented by Joyce in "Eveline."

2. Write an essay describing the mood evoked by this photograph, and compare it with the tone associated with urban life in "Eveline."

Poole Street in Dublin. The street in this photograph, taken during the period 1880–1914, gives a sense of the "little brown house" that Eveline calls home.

Image Courtesy of the National Library of Ireland.

THE ALLIANCE TEMPERANCE ALMANACK
On the Resources of Ireland   1910

The Alliance Temperance Almanack was published in London. The following excerpt describes the cost of Ireland's drinking habits in economic terms.

Much of the public attention is at this time drawn to the wants of the labouring poor of Ireland, and the great decay of her trade and manufactures. It may therefore be worth while to lay before our countrymen some calculations of the quantity of produce and employment which might arise from the whole population of that country agreeing to apply the vast sum, which, as stated below, is spent annually on whiskey in Ireland, to the encouragement of home manufactures, and the employment of the people. These advantages would follow in the most simple and natural course from the purchase of those articles of prime necessity, or of substantial comfort, the desire for which arises in the mind of every poor man whose habits do not lead him to prefer whiskey to domestic happiness. The Linen Manufacture, which *was* the staple trade of that island, the woollen trade, and the other more useful and indispensable occupations in a civilized community, are chiefly referred to; and the observer will be struck with the immense loss which that country sustains from the propensity to the use of Distilled Spirits.

"It appears from parliamentary returns, that the average quantity of Whiskey which paid excise duty in Ireland for each of the years 1826, 1827, 1828, and 1829, was Ten millions of Gallons. To this, if there be added one-sixth for reduction of strength by retailers, and also about Two Millions, Five Hundred Thousand Gallons made, but which did not pay duty, we shall have a total of upwards of *Fourteen Millions of Gallons, costing, at nine shillings per gallon, by retail, Six Millions Three Hundred Thousand Pounds sterling;* and being equal to a yearly consumption of more than Two Gallons for every man, woman, and child of our population."

•   •   •

The above remarks, though intended exclusively for Ireland, apply with great force to the United Kingdom generally. The ardent spirits, at full proof, on which duty was paid for home consumption in the year ending January 6, 1830, amounted to *twenty-seven millions five hundred and thirteen thousand two hundred and sixty gallons,* imperial measure. To this if we add, at a very low estimate as above, one-sixth, for the reduction of strength by retailers, without computing either the adulterations notoriously made, the spirits smuggled from the continent, or the still greater quantity produced by illicit distillation in Scotland and Ireland, we find that we have expended in one year for ardent spirits, *eighteen millions nine hundred and eleven thousand six hundred and fifty-eight pounds, ten shillings.*

Table I.   Shewing that the sum of Six Millions Three Hundred Thousand Pounds, which the People of Ireland pay annually for Whiskey, if expended as follows, would provide

1. The population of Ireland, (computed at eight millions) with 2½ yards of linen each, amounting to 20,000,000 yards, at 1s. 3d. per yard	£1,250,000
2. Ten thousand men in each county in Ireland with 3½ yards of Corduroy each, amounting to 1,120,000 yards, at 1s. per yard	56,000
3. Four thousand men in each county with 3 yards of Kersey each, amounting to 384,000 yards, at 2s. 4d. per yard	44,800
4. Ten thousand men in each county with 2½ yards of Broad Cloth, amounting to 720,000 yards, at 4s. per yard	144,000
5. Four thousand men in each county with one hat each, amounting to 128,000 hats, at 5s. per hat	32,000
6. Three millions of women and children with 1¼ yard of Check, amounting to 3,750,000 yards, at 10d. per yard.	156,250
7. One million of women and children with 6 yards of stuff each, amounting to 6,000,000 yards, at 8d. per yard	200,000
8. Three millions of women and children with 6 yards of printed calico, each, amounting to 18,000,000 yards, at 8d. per yard	600,000
9. Three hundred and twenty thousand women with 2¼ yards of grey cloaking, amounting to 720,000 yards, at 2s. 8d. per yard	96,000
10. Four millions of men, women, and children, with 2½ yards of Flannel each, amounting to 10,000,000 yards, at 1s. per yard	500,000
11. Four millions of men, women, and children, with one pair of shoes each, at 5s. per pair	1,000,000
12. Four millions of men, women and children, with one pair of stockings each, at 1s. 3d. per pair	250,000
13. Ten thousand families in each county with one pair of blankets each, amounting to 320,000 pair, at 10s. per pair	160,000
14. Four hundred tons of oatmeal for each county, amounting to 12,800 tons, at £15 per ton	192,000
15. Three hundred tons of wheat meal for each county, amounting to 9,600 tons, at £18 per ton	172,800
16. Two thousand pigs for each county, amounting to 64,000 pigs at £2 per pig	128,000
17. Two thousand sheep for each county, amounting to 64,000 sheep, at £1 5s. per sheep	80,000
18. Five hundred cows for each county, amounting to 16,000 cows, at £10 per cow	160,000
19. And pay one thousand labourers in each county, (reclaiming land, &c.) amounting to 32,000 labourers, at 6s. per week each, or £15 12s. per year	499,200
20. And support 1,000 aged and infirm in each county, amounting to 32,000 at 6d. per day, or £9 per year each	288,000
21. And build fifty school-houses in each county, amounting to 1,600 at £100 each	160,000
22. And pay fifty school-masters at £50, and fifty school-mistresses at £30 per year, in each county, amounting to 3,200 teachers, at an average salary of £40 each	128,000
23. Leaving for other charitable purposes	2,950
Total £6,300,000	

Let us now see what might be done by a proper application of the money, which the most moderate habitual tippler spends on whiskey in the course of a year.

One glass of whiskey per day, commonly called by drinking men "*their morning,*" costs (at three half-pence per glass) Two pounds Five Shillings and Sevenpence Half-penny, yearly! which sum, if laid by, would provide the following clothing, viz.: —

	£	s	d
Three yards of Kersey for great coat, at 2s. 4d. per yard	£0	7	0
Two yards and a quarter of Broad Cloth for coat and waistcoat, at 5s. 4d. per yard	0	12	0
Three yards and a half of Corduroy for Trowsers, at 1s. per yard	0	3	6
Two Neck Handkerchiefs	0	1	7½
One Hat	0	5	0
One Pair of Shoes	0	7	0
Two Pair of Stockings	0	8	0
Two Shirts	0	8	6
	£2	5	7½

Six million three hundred thousand sovereigns in gold would extend in a line from the town of Roscommon to the Circular Road of Dublin, being a distance of 66¾ Irish miles, or 85 English miles, and would require 49 horses and carts to draw them, at one ton weight each draft.

The same sum, if laid down in shillings, would extend in a line of 1442 Irish miles, or 1835 English miles, and would require 669 horses and carts to draw them, at one ton weight each draft.

The same sum, if laid down in penny pieces, would extend in a line of 25,000 miles, equal to the computed distance round the globe!

The three last year's expenditure on whiskey, say £18,900,000, would afford nine guineas for each family (four persons), in Ireland, allowing the population as already stated, at eight millions of souls!

Note. — The cost of ardent spirits in the United Kingdom which exceeds *eighteen millions nine hundred and eleven thousand pounds sterling, yearly,* would, on the calculations given, afford employment to *four hundred and twenty-eight thousand seven hundred and fifty men;* circulating among them nearly *six million pounds sterling* in wages only.

Our magistrates have already publicly declared that this enormous expenditure of £18,911,658 10s. is not to be regarded as merely useless, but horribly injurious; and their testimony is amply supported by the voice of *ninety five thousand offenders* committed within the past year to the prisons of England and Wales only. On high authority it is asserted that four-fifths of the crimes, three-fourths of the beggary, and one-half of all the madness of our countrymen arise from drinking. Have we nothing to learn from America, where, by the associated efforts of the sober and intelligent for the purpose of discouraging the use of ardent spirits, their consumption is already diminished one-third throughout the whole Union?

From *The Alliance Temperance Almanack* for 1910

CONSIDERATIONS FOR CRITICAL THINKING AND WRITING

1. Describe the tone of this analysis of Ireland's consumption of alcohol. Why is it significant that this temperance publication originates from England?

2. What sort of economic argument is made here? Explain why you do or do not find it convincing.

3. How does this document speak to the conditions of Eveline Hill's life? Pay particular attention to paragraph 9 of the story.

BRIDGET BURKE

A Letter Home from an Irish Emigrant 1882

The excerpt below comes from a letter written by Bridget Burke, who, at the age of twenty-one, emigrated from Galway, Ireland, to Brisbane, Australia. Though her spelling is rough, her affection for her brother John is clear.

Dear John

I am 40 Miles from My uncle. I feal Quare without a Home to goe to when on My sunday out. I often wish to Have you out Heare. I ame verry strange out Here. I cannot make free with any body. I often Have a Walk with Patt [her brother] & Has a long yarn of Home. He is verry Kind became a steady fellow since He Left Home & also I could not expect My father to be a bit better than My Uncle. His wife & children is all right it is a nice place to go but it is to [too] far away but My brother is near me & comes to see me 2 or 3 times a week. We often Have some fun talking of the Old times at Home.

Dear John you wanted to know How do I Like the Country or what sort of people are heare. John that Queston I cannot answer. There is all sortes black & white misted & married together & Living in pretty Cotages Just the same as the white people. Thire is English Irish French German Italian black Chineease and not forgetin the Juse [Jews]. There are verry rich fancy John white girls marrid to a black man & Irish girls to [too] & to Yellow Chinaman with their Hair platted down there[?] black back. Sow [so] you see that girls dont care what the do in this Country. The would do anny think [anything] before the worke & a great Lot of them does worse[?] than that same. & this is a fine Country for a Young person that can take care of himselfe.

Now John I must ask you for all my Aunts & Uncles Cousins friends & Neighbours sweet Harts & all also did Cannopy die yet. Now John I must Conclude Hoping that You will send me as Long a Letter as I have send you & Lett me know all about Home. Dirrect Your Letter as[?] Patt told you for me, I Have more[?] to say but remaning yours fond sister for ever

BDB

From David Fitzpatrick, *Oceans of Consolation: Personal Accounts of Irish Migration to Australia*, Cornell University Press (1994)

CONSIDERATIONS FOR CRITICAL THINKING AND WRITING

1. How does Bridget feel about living in Australia? How does she feel about Ireland?

2. How is Australia's social structure different from Ireland's?

3. How does this letter help to fill in Eveline's feelings about leaving Ireland for Buenos Aires?

4. Research life in Buenos Aires during the first fifteen years of the twentieth century. What would it have been like to live there then? How would it be different from Ireland?

A Plot Synopsis of The Bohemian Girl   1843

The following synopsis recounts the story of The Bohemian Girl, *a well-loved opera by Michael William Balfe that played in the principal capitals of Europe, North America, and South America. It gives a sense of the romantic narrative Eveline and Frank would have seen at the opera.*

The action of this drama commences at the chateau of Count Arnheim, in Austria. The peasantry and retainers of the Count are making preparations for the chase, when Thaddeus, a Polish exile and fugitive from the Austrian troops, arrives in search of shelter and concealment. Here he encounters a band of Gipsies, headed by one Devilshoof, who, learning from Thaddeus that he is pursued by soldiers, gives him a disguise, conceals him, and puts the pursuing troops on the wrong track. Just at this time, shouts of distress are heard, and Florestein appears surrounded by huntsmen. The Count's child and her attendant have been attacked by an infuriated stag in the forest, and are probably destroyed. Hearing this, Thaddeus seizes a rifle, and hastens to their relief, and by a well-aimed shot kills the animal, and saves them from destruction. The Count now returns in time to hear of the peril of his darling child, and to see Thaddeus bearing her wounded form in his arms. Overjoyed to find her still alive, the Count overwhelms Thaddeus with grateful thanks, and invites him to join in the festivities about to take place. Thaddeus at first declines, but being warmly entreated to remain, at length consents to do so. They seat themselves at table, and the Count proposes as a toast, "Health and long life to the Emperor!" All except Thaddeus do honor to the toast, and his silence being observed, the Count challenges him to empty his goblet as the rest have done. Thaddeus, to the surprise of all, dashes the wine to the earth; this, of course, produces a burst of indignation. The assembled guests are infuriated by such an indignity to their monarch, and threaten the life of Thaddeus. At this moment Devilshoof returns, and at once takes sides with Thaddeus. The Count orders Devilshoof to be secured. The attendants seize and carry him into the castle. Thaddeus departs, and festivities are resumed. During the *fête*, Devilshoof escapes, taking with him the Count's infant daughter, Arline; and his flight being almost immediately discovered, the greatest excitement prevails. Peasants, huntsmen, and attendants hasten in search of the daring fugitive, and he is seen bearing the child across a dangerous precipice; he escapes, and the unhappy father sinks in despair as the First Act ends.

Twelve years are supposed to elapse, and we are transported to the city of Presburg, in the suburbs of which the Gipsies are encamped with the Queen of their tribe in whose tent dwells the Count's daughter, Arline, now a fine young

The **Bohemian Girl** (1843). Carefully chosen fragments of opera and popular music are woven into stories in *Dubliners,* providing texture and advancing the dramatic action. In "Eveline" Frank takes Eveline to a performance of an operetta by Michael William Balfe: "He took her to see *The Bohemian Girl* and she felt elated as she sat in an unaccustomed part of the theater with him. . . . He had tales of distant countries." Shown here is a program for a performance of the operetta. The white castle in the upper left corner of the image reflects Eveline's yearning for "another life."

Bohemian Sun Dreamer (oil on canvas), Mucha, Alphonse Marie (1860–1939)/Private Collection/Photo © Christie's Images/Bridgeman Images.

woman. Florestein, a foppish *attaché* to the Court, is met by Devilshoof and his companions, who relieve him of his jewelry, among which is a medallion, which Devilshoof carries off. Thaddeus, who has joined the tribe, is now enamored of Arline, and he tells her that it was he who saved her life in infancy, but he still carefully conceals from her the secret of her birth. Arline confesses her love for Thaddeus, and they are betrothed according to the custom of the Gipsy tribe.

A grand fair is in progress in the plaza of the city, and hither, of course, come all the Gipsies, who add to the gayety and life of the scene by their peculiar dances, songs, etc. Florestein appears, and is quite fascinated by the beauty of Arline. While trying to engage her attention, he perceives his medallion hanging on her neck and claims it, charging her with having stolen it. This leads to great excitement: the guard is called, Arline is arrested, and the crowd dispersed by the soldiery. The supposed culprit is brought before Count Arnheim; Florestein presses the charge, and circumstances strengthen the appearance of guilt against Arline, when the Count perceives the mark left by the wound inflicted by the deer on Arline's arm. He asks its origin. She repeats the story as related to her by Thaddeus. The Count recognizes his long-lost child, and the Act ends with an effective *tableau*.

In the Third Act we find Arline restored to her rank and the home of her father; but the change in her prospects does not diminish her love for Thaddeus. He, daring all dangers for an interview, seeks and finds her here. He comes to bid her farewell, and prays that she will, even when surrounded by other admirers, give a thought to him who saved her life, and who loves her. She promises fidelity, and declares herself his and his only. Here we find that the Gipsy Queen, who also loves Thaddeus, has been plotting to take him from Arline. By her device the medallion was discovered in the possession of Arline. Even now she is conspiring to separate the lovers, but her plots fail. Thaddeus relates his history to Count Arnheim, who, in gratitude to the preserver of his child, bestows her upon him. Desire for vengeance now fills the heart of the Gipsy Queen; she induces one of her tribe to fire at Thaddeus as he is embracing Arline, but by a timely movement of Devilshoof the bullet reaches her own heart.

From *The Bohemian Girl,* edited by Richard Aldrich (1902)

CONSIDERATIONS FOR CRITICAL THINKING AND WRITING

1. Describe the action of this opera. How does its plot compare with Eveline's life?
2. Why do you suppose Joyce has Frank take Eveline to this particular opera?
3. One of the songs of *The Bohemian Girl* is titled "Tis Sad to Leave Our Fatherland" and contains these verses: "Without / friends, and without a home, my country too! yes, I'm exiled from thee; what / fate, what fate awaits me here, now! Pity, Heav'n! oh calm my despair!" How do these lines shed light on Eveline's situation?

15

A Study of Dagoberto Gilb: The Author Reflects on Three Stories

Courtesy of Dagoberto Gilb.

For me, fiction is life transformed and fueled by imagination.
— DAGOBERTO GILB

INTRODUCTION

Dagoberto Gilb chose the three short stories in this chapter (as well as a fourth story, "Romero's Shirt," in Chapter 7, p. 242) and provides commentary on each of them. Along with his personal observations on the stories are relevant images and documents that offer perspectives for interpreting and appreciating his fiction. Gilb's candid comments on the stories are written specifically for readers who are interested in why and how the stories were composed. He reveals some of the biographical contexts and circumstances that led him to become an avid reader and then a successful writer (despite the dismal grade

Courtesy of Dagoberto Gilb.

he received for his first college English paper) and how he managed to build a fictional world while working full time on construction sites.

In addition to the stories and commentaries, this chapter also offers contexts for the stories, including photographs of his family and his life as a construction carpenter in Los Angeles, California, and El Paso, Texas. Also included are a draft manuscript page from an essay collection, an edited galley from the short story "Uncle Rock" originally published in *The New Yorker*, Gilb's comments on physical labor and popular perceptions of Mexican American culture, and an interview with Michael Meyer that ranges from issues of political correctness to how "advocacy" is embedded in Gilb's literary art. You'll find this ex-carpenter to be a straightforward storyteller who makes a point of being on the level.

A BRIEF BIOGRAPHY

Born in Los Angeles in 1950, Dagoberto Gilb worked as a construction worker and a journeyman high-rise carpenter with the United Brotherhood of Carpenters for some sixteen years as he began hammering out his fiction. Though born and raised in California, he considered both Los Angeles and El Paso to be home. His Anglo father was a laconic, hardened World War II Marine Corps veteran who worked for nearly fifty years in a Los Angeles industrial laundry, his mother was an undocumented Mexican immigrant, and their marriage ended early. Gilb's life, like his fiction, is grounded by working-class circumstances in which laborers sweat to pay bills and put food on the table. He does not list any unpaid internships on his résumé.

As Gilb acknowledges in *Gritos*, a collection of essays, he was not in his youth "precocious in matters of literature, even to the end of my teenage years when I still thought of 'book' more as a verb." He did, however, read on the job and make his way to junior college and then to the University of California, Santa Barbara, where he earned a B.A. and an M.A. studying philosophy and religious studies. In college, he devoured canonical American and European writers and then discovered Chicano literature, works that ultimately inspired him to write about his own experiences. After graduate school, he followed construction jobs between Los Angeles and El Paso, making a living and finding the material for framing much of his writing.

Following some success in publishing a number of short stories in literary journals, a chapbook-size collection of stories, *Winners on the Pass Line*, appeared in 1985. His first full collection, the critically acclaimed book *The Magic of Blood* (1993), won the PEN/Ernest Hemingway Award as well as the Jesse Jones Award from the Texas Institute of Letters and was a finalist for the PEN/Faulkner Award. On the heels of a National Endowment for the Arts Fellowship, he published a novel, *The Last Known Residence of Mickey Acuna* (1994), which was followed by a Guggenheim Foundation Fellowship. *Gritos* (2003), consisting of previously published essays in such venues as *The New Yorker*, the *New York Times*, the *Los Angeles Times*, and *The Nation*, along with commentaries written for National Public Radio's "Fresh Air," offers a perspective on how a Mexican American working man became a nationally

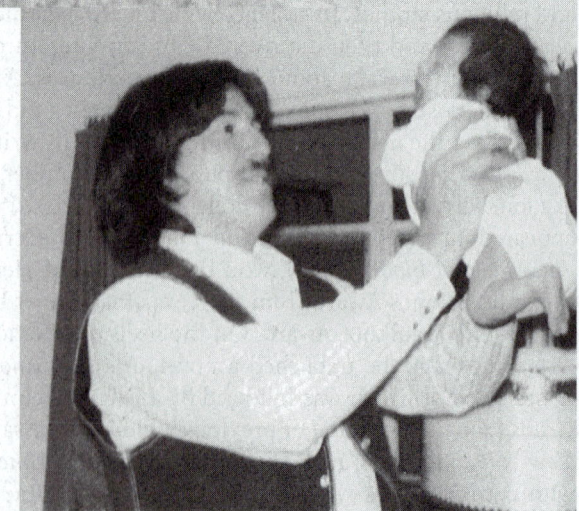

(*Top*) Dagoberto Gilb's mother. Los Angeles, California, late 1940s.
Courtesy of Dagoberto Gilb.

(*Right*) Dagoberto Gilb with his older son, Antonio. El Paso, Texas, 1978.
Courtesy of Dagoberto Gilb.

The author with his son, Antonio. Los Angeles, California, 1981. The
'62 Chevy pictured here is the very one mentioned on page 461.
Courtesy of Dagoberto Gilb.

recognized working writer. Another novel, *The Flowers* (2008), and two more
collections of stories, *Woodcuts of Women* (2001) and *Before the End, After the
Beginning* (2011), have solidified his reputation as a highly regarded fiction
writer. His works have been translated into Spanish, French, German, Italian,
Japanese, Chinese, and Turkish, and he has been invited to be a visiting writer
at a number of schools, including the University of Texas at Austin, the University of Wyoming, the University of Arizona, and Vassar College.

Previously a tenured professor in the Creative Writing Program at Texas State
University in San Marcos, Gilb is currently writer-in-residence and executive
director of Centro Victoria, a center for Mexican American literature and culture
at the University of Houston in Victoria, Texas, where the undergraduate student
body is primarily Latino, a school he describes as "the smallest, most just barely at
its beginning university in the country." Located equidistant from Houston, Austin,
San Antonio, and Corpus Christi, in a state that in several years will be 50 percent
Latino, Centro Victoria was founded, in part, to educate Texans of all ethnicities
and educational levels — and others outside the state — about the history and culture of Mexican Americans, who make up two-thirds of the Latino population

Dagoberto Gilb at work. Los Angeles, California, 1986.
Courtesy of Dagoberto Gilb.

in the United States. The purpose of the center is to foster an understanding and appreciation of Mexican American literature and art in Texas and beyond.

One of Centro Victoria's major projects is to provide Texas students and teachers with lesson plans based on *Hecho en Tejas: An Anthology of Texas Mexican Literature* (2006), edited by Gilb, which ranges from sixteenth-century exploration narratives to twenty-first-century poetry and prose. By integrating Mexican American arts into the curriculum, the program elevates the vicissitudes of Latinos' lives — satisfactions as well as challenges — to an art and helps to validate the very existence and presence of Latinos in the United States who never before had the opportunity to read about their own unique experiences. Gilb makes clear in his introduction to *Hecho en Tejas* that the predominant popular attitude toward people of Mexican descent in the United States, whether toward legitimate citizens or the undocumented, what some in the media call "illegals," is shaped by cultural distortions:

> The kindest attitude portrays the culture as an homage in a children's museum, or as in a folklorico dance show, and the prevailing images, framed and shelved in the state's unconscious, are of men in sombreros and serapes walking burros, women patting tortillas or stuffing tamales in color-frilled white housedresses, while the stories of Mexican adventures are of border whorehouses and tequila drunks — not meant as harmful, only fascinating, and wild.

Gilb insists on moving beyond such patronizing images and passionately announces as the anthology's major theme: "We have been here, we are still here." (For a brief provocative comparison of Mexican American and African American cultural experiences in the West and South, see Gilb's "On Distortions of Mexican American Culture," p. 473.)

(*Left*) The author in 2002, on the Brownsville, Texas–Matamoros, Mexico, borderline.
Courtesy of Dagoberto Gilb.

(*Below*) Dagoberto Gilb with his younger son, Ricardo. Uruapan, Mexico, 2005.
Courtesy of Dagoberto Gilb.

(*Top*) The author at the Pirámedes del Sol y Luna, Mexico, 2008.
Courtesy of Dagoberto Gilb.

(*Right*) Dagoberto Gilb at the PEN/ Faulkner Reading at the Folger Shakespeare Library. Washington, D.C., 2012.
Courtesy of Dagoberto Gilb.

Furthering his goal of making Mexican Americans apparent in American culture, in 2011 Gilb founded *Huizache: The Magazine of Latino Literature,* published by Centro Victoria at the University of Houston–Victoria. Featuring literary works from mostly Latino writers who are largely neglected or ignored, the magazine also opens its pages to all fiction, poetry, and essays that challenge ethnic, gender, or social stereotyping. "A huizache," as explained on the title page, "is an acacia tree that is native to Mexico but also grows wild in South and East Texas. It irritates the regional farmers because, no matter what they do, it keeps growing and populating." The editor, Diana López, asks readers to "think of this journal as the nursery that fosters this tree and any species considered 'invasive.'" *Huizache* is founded on the energy, ambition, and neglected talent of Latino and Latina writers in Texas and the Southwest.

Gilb's own writing offers a broad landscape of Mexican American experience in a direct, straightforward style that is energized by his unapologetically hearty and robust take on ordinary life. His characters work pretty hard in the face of ugly inequities, make money but not enough of it, get fired, find work, fall in love, desire marriage, settle on divorce, suffer loss, maintain dignity, strive to succeed, frequently fail, raise kids, embody fear, and stubbornly persevere—all of them serially engaged in the disorderly conduct of being human.

Chronology

1950	Born in Los Angeles, California.
1950–70	Raised in Los Angeles.
1973	Graduates from University of California, Santa Barbara, with a B.A.
1976	Graduates from University of California, Santa Barbara, with an M.A.
1976–92	Moves to El Paso and begins to write fiction while employed as a construction worker.
1980	Joins the United Brotherhood of Carpenters and becomes a journeyman, high-rise carpenter.
1985	Publishes *Winners on the Pass Line*, short stories.
1988	Visiting writer, University of Texas at Austin.
1992	Awarded a National Endowment for the Arts Fellowship.
1992	Visiting writer, University of Arizona.

The story "Love in L.A." (p. 458) is from *The Magic of Blood*, published in 1993 by Grove Press.

1993	Publishes *The Magic of Blood*, short stories; winner of the PEN/Hemingway Award.
1994	Visiting Writer, University of Wyoming.
1994	Publishes *The Last Known Residence of Mickey Acuna*, a novel.
1995	Awarded a Guggenheim Foundation Fellowship.
1997–2009	Professor of English, Creative Writing Program at Southwest Texas State University (now Texas State University).
2001	Publishes *Woodcuts of Women*, short stories.
2003	Publishes *Gritos*, essays.
2005	Visiting writer, Vassar College.
2006	Publishes *Hecho en Tejas: An Anthology of Texas Mexican Literature*, winner of the PEN Southwest Award for nonfiction.
2008	Publishes *The Flowers*, a novel.
2009–Present	Writer-in-residence, University of Houston–Victoria; executive director of Centro Victoria, Center for Mexican American Literature and Culture.
2011	Publishes *Before the End, After the Beginning*, short stories; founds *Huizache: The Magazine of Latino Literature*.

The story "Shout" (p. 462) is from *Woodcuts of Women*, published in 2001 by Grove Press.

Cover of *Woodcuts of Women* by Dagoberto Gilb used by permission of Grove/Atlantic, Inc. Any third party use of this material, outside of this publication, is prohibited.

The story "Uncle Rock" (p. 466) is from *Before the End, After the Beginning*, published in 2011 by Grove Press.

Cover of *Before the End, After the Beginning* by Dagoberto Gilb used by permission of Grove/Atlantic, Inc. Any third party use of this material, outside of this publication, is prohibited.

Huizache: The Magazine of Latino Literature was founded in 2011 and is published by Centro Victoria: Center for Mexican American Literature and Culture, where Gilb serves as executive director.

Courtesy of Dagoberto Gilb.

Dagoberto Gilb

How Books Bounce   2012

Many have asked me, how did you become a writer? This is one of those ordinary questions that comes at Q&A's, but at mine I sometimes catch a snarky or world-weary, all-caps emphasis on the *you*. I could snap off a couple of words in defense, but the truth is that I, too, find me a curious representative of literature. Real writers are bred like champion racehorses, the offspring of Seabiscuit and Secretariat. When real writers discuss their careers, they refer back (modestly, of course) to what they published before their double-digit birthdays. They had books at home (that's all I need to say there). The very classiest universities begged them to be undergrads, and while there they briefly thought they might become a molecular chemist or an avant-garde sculptor. Now, modestly, these real writers will say they were probably better at one of those. Whereas, in contrast, I read my first book when I was seventeen because, in a less than advanced English class for we special few (I worked a full-time, graveyard shift job as a janitor), one day the teacher mentioned a novel hippies were reading. I wanted to know what hippies read because they seemed to have all kinds of easy goings-on that weren't like mine. And nothing in mine included any books. My pre-janitor years I can't say were busy with any poetic forms other than chrome spokes on wheels and girls who didn't read poetry either. Where I came up, balls were as close to books as I got. I bounced them, hit them, threw them, caught them, guarded them, blocked them, kicked them, jump-shot them. They weren't books. Nobody expected me to read them. I didn't. Neither was it suggested that maybe I try an actual volume with unrounded corners, though if anyone had, I would have made it bounce too.

I was not, in other words, born a writer. And then I went to a junior college. Much of that incentive was not so much improving my brains as not losing them, or my legs, walking point in Vietnam (older friends, drafted, came back not doing great). My first freshman comp paper I got a D. The teacher told me she was being generous. When I failed the class, I was smart enough to know who took night classes — on the curve with the most tired day job students (mine was full-time too, a department store stock boy), this time, at a lesser community college, I got a B. I did not consider a major in chemistry. The only sculpture I knew of came from Mexico, which, cool-looking and deep, I couldn't say I understood any better than what was taught in art history (nothing Mexican, indigenous, colonial, or modern). I tried a business law class. I liked math but too much homework. Sociology, political science, geography, history, philosophy — each offered original news to me. I was learning. Excited, I began eating it all up. Though I still feared English. That second semester requirement, when you study literature, I remember having to look up a word in virtually every sentence of Melville's *Billy Budd*. Supposedly American, I thought it had to be from a foreign language, and I wasn't sure if I understood what exactly happened to Mr. Budd. I took the teacher at his word for the explanation of it. Great story!

Oh, how I then fell in love. In the beginning it was any books I called on or which called on me. Books stacked and piled and neatly lined up in rows, new or used or checked out (I even stole them, yes, I here confess!). There were the small ones forgotten in quirky, cramped bottom corners, and ones that took tall ladders to touch, and ones that saw so little light their covers seemed to have recast inward — I loved them the most, these difficult ones, hard to get to know, to understand, odd, too quiet and bashful, secret. When suddenly I became furtive: though I would never take a lit class again, I was reading novels and poetry.

How did I become a writer? Something happened, that's pretty clear. Did lightning strike and skip the ears hearing, override the memory but alter the brain? Am I the product of some secret government experiment that maybe went wrong? How did a boy who cared only about sports — what little reading I would do young was from a newspaper sports page — become a man who would idealize books like classic teams and then become one of its professional "athletes"?

I've always been obsessed with story. Whether it's nature or nurture, or what I like to call my family mess, I cannot recall a time when I wasn't listening to a story being told. Maybe because I have only a single blurry memory of my father leaving my childhood home, it opens with ones about him and my mother. Of German descent, he was born in Kentucky but came to Los Angeles young. She was baptized in Mexico City at the Basilica de Guadalupe. He joined the Marines to fight the Japanese at Pearl Harbor. She kept the rising sun flag he'd captured as an advanced scout. Older, he watched her growing up next door to the industrial laundry where he started working when he was thirteen, where she eventually did too as a teenager (not for long). She grew up in that house next door with her mother, who was my grandmother, who was the mistress of the owner of the laundry who owned the house (what in Spanish is known as *la casa chica*). My grandmother came to the United States after her husband, my grandfather, was killed. By knife, went the story, and in the back. My grandmother came to the United States following her sister, my great-aunt, whose mother — this story! — had been married at fourteen to a man in his sixties and she had . . . not sure how many but a number of children by him. When my great-aunt turned eighteen, her mother traveled from Xalapa and in the capital rented the finest limousine for a visit to the presidential palace. And thus, my great-aunt represented Mexico on a tour to Europe and the United States as an opera singer. She wound up in Hollywood, married to a minor French director. My grandmother died young, making my mother closer to my great-aunt. By the time I am old enough to first see her — old, a widow for years, hard for a young person to imagine any glamorous youth attaching to her — she is nothing but a seamstress who needed money, a job, one of fifty at the industrial laundry where my father had become the floor supervisor. She repaired the elastic on bras, my father, bitter by divorce and who knows, enjoyed pointing out. He gave me a job there when I too turned thirteen. And this was when I begin to have stories.

When I think about being a writer now, I can't help but think of the improbable travel that my genes have made to get here. This journey. And to think we *each* have one, no matter to what breeding or privilege we were born. Why we perk up to listen, why we are driven to, I have no idea. It's so fun to bounce books on your ride — it's a necessary skill. But go, get out there, and what I know is you'll meet people, you'll see places, you'll hear stories that only you will be able to tell.

—D.G.

Dagoberto Gilb

Love in L.A. 1993

Jake slouched in a clot of near motionless traffic, in the peculiar gray of concrete, smog, and early morning beneath the overpass of the Hollywood Freeway on Alvarado Street. He didn't really mind because he knew how much worse it could be trying to make a left onto the onramp. He certainly didn't do that every day of his life, and he'd assure anyone who'd ask that he never would either. A steady occupation had its advantages and he couldn't deny thinking about that too. He needed an FM radio in something better than this '58 Buick he drove. It would have crushed velvet interior with electric controls for the L.A. summer, a nice warm heater and defroster for the winter drives at the beach, a cruise control for those longer trips, mellow speakers front and rear of course, windows that hum closed, snuffing out that nasty exterior noise of freeways. The fact was that he'd probably have to change his whole style. Exotic colognes, plush, dark nightclubs, maitais and daiquiris, necklaced ladies in satin gowns, misty and sexy like in a tequila ad. Jake could imagine lots of possibilities when he let himself, but none that ended up with him pressed onto a stalled freeway.

Jake was thinking about this freedom of his so much that when he glimpsed its green light he just went ahead and stared bye bye to the steadily employed. When he turned his head the same direction his windshield faced, it was maybe one second too late. He pounced the brake pedal and steered the front wheels away from the tiny brakelights but the smack was unavoidable. Just one second sooner and it would only have been close. One second more and he'd be crawling up the Toyota's trunk. As it was, it seemed like only a harmless smack, much less solid than the one against his back bumper.

Jake considered driving past the Toyota but was afraid the traffic ahead would make it too difficult. As he pulled up against the curb a few carlengths ahead, it occurred to him that the traffic might have helped him get away too. He slammed the car door twice to make sure it was closed fully and to give himself another second more, then toured front and rear of his Buick for damage on or near the bumpers. Not an impressionable scratch even in the chrome. He perked up. Though the car's beauty was secondary to its ability to start and move, the body and paint were clean except for a few minor dings. This stood out as one of his few clearcut accomplishments over the years.

Before he spoke to the driver of the Toyota, whose looks he could see might present him with an added complication, he signaled to the driver of the car that hit him, still in his car and stopped behind the Toyota, and waved his hands and shook his head to let the man know there was no problem as far as he was concerned. The driver waved back and started his engine.

"It didn't even scratch my paint," Jake told her in that way of his. "So how you 5 doin? Any damage to the car? I'm kinda hoping so, just so it takes a little more time and we can talk some. Or else you can give me your phone number now and I won't have to lay my regular b.s. on you to get it later."

He took her smile as a good sign and relaxed. He inhaled her scent like it was clean air and straightened out his less than new but not unhip clothes.

"You've got Florida plates. You look like you must be Cuban."

"My parents are from Venezuela."

"My name's Jake." He held out his hand.

"Mariana." 10

They shook hands like she'd never done it before in her life.

"I really am sorry about hitting you like that." He sounded genuine. He fondled the wide dimple near the cracked taillight. "It's amazing how easy it is to put a dent in these new cars. They're so soft they might replace waterbeds soon." Jake was confused about how to proceed with this. So much seemed so unlikely, but there was always possibility. "So maybe we should go out to breakfast somewhere and talk it over."

"I don't eat breakfast."

"Some coffee then."

"Thanks, but I really can't." 15

"You're not married, are you? Not that that would matter that much to me. I'm an openminded kinda guy."

She was smiling. "I have to get to work."

"That sounds boring."

"I better get your driver's license," she said.

Jake nodded, disappointed. "One little problem," he said. "I didn't bring it. I just 20 forgot it this morning. I'm a musician," he exaggerated greatly, "and, well, I dunno, I left my wallet in the pants I was wearing last night. If you have some paper and a pen I'll give you my address and all that."

He followed her to the glove compartment side of her car.

"What if we don't report it to the insurance companies? I'll just get it fixed for you."

"I don't think my dad would let me do that."

"Your dad? It's not your car?"

"He bought it for me. And I live at home." 25

"Right." She was slipping away from him. He went back around to the back of her new Toyota and looked over the damage again. There was the trunk lid, the bumper, a rear panel, a taillight.

"You do have insurance?" she asked, suspicious, as she came around the back of the car.

"Oh yeah," he lied.

"I guess you better write the name of that down too."

He made up a last name and address and wrote down the name of an insurance 30 company an old girlfriend once belonged to. He considered giving a real phone number but went against that idea and made one up.

"I act too," he lied to enhance the effect more. "Been in a couple of movies."

She smiled like a fan.

"So how about your phone number?" He was rebounding maturely.

She gave it to him.

"Mariana, you are beautiful," he said in his most sincere voice. 35

"Call me," she said timidly.

Jake beamed. "We'll see you, Mariana," he said holding out his hand. Her hand felt so warm and soft he felt like he'd been kissed.

Back in his car he took a moment or two to feel both proud and sad about his performance. Then he watched the rear view mirror as Mariana pulled up behind him. She was writing down the license plate numbers on his Buick, ones that he'd taken off a junk because the ones that belonged to his had expired so long ago. He turned the ignition key and revved the big engine and clicked into drive. His sense of freedom swelled as he drove into the now moving street traffic, though he couldn't stop the thought about that FM stereo radio and crushed velvet interior and the new car smell that would even make it better.

DAGOBERTO GILB

On Writing "Love in L.A." 2012

I was unemployed when I wrote "Love in L.A." I wasn't happy about that. I had two young sons and a wife and a landlord and utility companies I supported and I drove an older car that needed, at the very least, springs and shocks and often gas. When

I'd come back to L.A. in the early '80s after many years here and there but mostly El Paso, I did so with dreams of good money as a construction worker with high-rise skills. I'd joined the carpenter's union, and I was a journeyman, and there were cranes in the skyline everywhere. I was good at it. And work was great when I was working, but a job ended, and it always ended too fast. . . . As I was saying, I drove an old car, a 1962 Chevy II wagon. I used to joke around that it was a vintage classic. It came with a red vinyl interior its previous owner had done pretty in Juárez, and I kept the rest up. It roared with a rebuilt six-cylinder, and I did the tune-ups myself. I'd gotten it super cheap and the best you could say about it, years later, was that it still ran. I had no money for anything else. And I was, again, unemployed, close to broke.

I'd been going like this for years by then, surviving. Only surviving. Should I be trying to find some better line of work? Not to say that I hadn't tried before. Physically able, I could do this if there were regular paychecks. The last time there were no checks for too long, we lost our apartment. Could be this is nothing but the way life is. Lots of my friends didn't do much better. But with me there was also this: was it really that I was trying to be a writer? If I stopped wanting that, maybe even construction work would get easier for me to find because I would give in to it only. They were parallel dream worlds, one where I made a good living as a carpenter, another where I made a living as a writer. Most thought the writer one was fantasy. I didn't, but then I didn't know any better. I did know that I was having a hard time.

Were mine dreams that you have to push forward to reach, or were they fantasies that you get over?

Writing is like having a fever: your brain can't shy away, won't stop. It's a few lines of a lyric or melody that you can't shut down, a word or lover's name that follows you, whether you're talking to who you know or overhearing strangers, an image that has superimposed itself so equally on the familiar and not, that it can't be "out there," only in you. It won't quit you until you write it.

Her: I do not remember where I was driving from one day when I was inching 5 along in some ridiculous street traffic caused by a minor accident. Except nothing in this part of Los Angeles, on Melrose Avenue, is minor, right? And it wasn't really so minor, as car-only damage goes. It was an elderly man, nondescript, whose little car had been rear-ended. He was standing there. A tall, leggy, too curvy woman in the bigger car (her hood wouldn't shut) was pacing and going on, upset as though it weren't her fault. She wore the highest heels and the slinkiest dress. It wasn't three in the morning, it was three in the afternoon. Like everyone else crawling by, it didn't seem like the man knew how to respond other than to stare at her.

Him: many years earlier, I knew a creepy guy who pretended his occupation was connected to Hollywood movies and that he had money. Since he was dark, he saw himself in an ethnic category of an Anthony Quinn or even a Charles Bronson, though more leading man — he would say that people thought he looked like Omar Sharif. Really only he saw Dr. Zhivago in his mirror. He combed his hair with a quality mousse once he began to share an apartment with an older dude who had done some TV show westerns, who knows what else, and drove a red Corvette convertible. Only slightly dangerous (low-level Tony Montana), he scored his women with props — he might lay out a black book to a certain page, incidentally, where no one could miss the famous names he had fake numbers for.

I worried I was as messed up as him, worse in a way, because I had a family. No I wasn't. Yes I was. No. Yes. Was I a construction worker pretending to be a writer? Writing was this full of it dude who was getting me. Or was I this man looking in a mirror, not seeing the screws tightening or falling out under my hardhat? Was I doing the right thing? Did I know what the right thing was? I worried that writing was that woman in the accident — excessive, spoiled, flashy, gaudy, not responsible for the wreck. Writing was beautiful, and sexy, and dramatic. Writing was fun even when there was a minor accident. Writing was L.A., cruising Melrose, a neighborhood where rich people lived lives unlike mine, drove Mercedes.

Then I wrote this story. I'd lived alone for a bit over by 3rd and Alvarado, an older *mexicano* part of town. I made her Venezuelan because I wanted her to be the fairy tale Latina beauty. I wanted her to be driving an economical Toyota. I wanted her to smile. I wanted her to have a family and be getting an education. I didn't want her to be a fool. Him, surviving, I wanted in an old luxury car with dreams, or fantasies, of a better one without dings, a little lost, a little scared, not in the system. I wanted them both in a brief moment together. The writer, I didn't know which of the two characters I was. The carpenter, I got another job out of the union hall soon after.

DAGOBERTO GILB

Shout   2001

He beat on the screen door. "Will somebody open this?!" Unlike most men, he didn't leave his hard hat in his truck, he took it inside his home, and he had it in his hand. His body was dry now, at least wasn't like it was two hours ago at work, when he wrung his T-shirt of sweat, made it drool between the fingers of his fist, he and his partner making as much of a joke out of it as they could. That's how hot it was, how humid, and it'd been like this, in the nineties and hundreds, for two weeks, and it'd been hot enough before that. All he could think about was unlacing his dirty boots, then peeling off those stinky socks, then the rest. He'd take a cold one into the shower. The second one. He'd down the first one right at the refrigerator. "Come on!" Three and four were to be appreciated, five was mellow, and six let him nap before bed.

"I didn't hear you," his wife said.

"Didn't *hear* me? How *couldn't* you hear me? And why's it locked anyways? When I get here I don't feel like waiting to come in. Why can't you leave the thing unlocked?"

"Why do you think?"

"Well don't let the baby open it. I want this door open when I get home." He ⁵ carried on in Spanish, *hijos* de and *putas* and *madres* and *chingadas*. This was the only Spanish he used at home. He tossed the hard hat near the door, relieved to be inside, even though it was probably hotter than outside, even though she was acting mad. He took it that she'd been that way all day already.

Their children, three boys, were seven, four, and almost two, and they were, as should be expected, battling over something.

"Everybody shut up and be quiet!" he yelled. Of course that worsened the situation, because when he got mad he scared the baby, who immediately started crying.

"I'm so tired," he muttered.

She glared at him, the baby in her arms.

"You know sometimes I wish you were a man cuz I wouldn't let you get away ¹⁰ with looks like that. I wouldn't take half the shit I take from you." He fell back into the wooden chair nobody sat in except him when he laced the high-top boots on, or off, as he already had. "You know how hot it was today? A hundred and five. It's unbelievable." He looked at her closely, deeply, which he didn't often do, especially this month. She was trying to settle down the baby and turned the TV on to distract the other two.

"It's too hard to breathe," he said to her. He walked bare-footed for the beer and took out two. They were in the door tray of the freezer and almost frozen.

"So nothing happened today?" she asked. Already she wasn't mad at him. It was how she was, why they could get along.

"Nothing else was said. Maybe nothing's gonna happen. God knows this heat's making everybody act unnatural. But tomorrow's check day. If he's gonna get me most likely it'll be tomorrow." He finished a beer leaning against the tile near the kitchen sink, enjoying a peace that had settled into the apartment. The baby was content, the TV was on, the Armenians living an arm's reach away were chattering steadily, there was a radio on from an apartment in a building across from them, Mexican TV upstairs, pigeons, a dog, traffic noise, the huge city out there groaning its sound — all this silence in the apartment.

"There's other jobs," he said. "All of 'em end no matter what anyways."

It was a job neither of them wanted to end too soon. This year he'd been   15 laid up for months after he fell and messed up his shoulder and back. He'd been drunk — a happy one that started after work — but he did it right there at his own front door, playing around. At the same time the duplex apartment they'd been living in for years had been sold and they had to move here. It was all they could get, all they were offered, since so few landlords wanted three children, boys no less, at a monthly rent they could afford. They were lucky to find it and it wasn't bad as places went, but they didn't like it much. They felt like they were starting out again, and that did not seem right. They'd talked this over since they'd moved in until it degenerated into talk about separation. And otherwise, in other details, it also wasn't the best year of their lives.

He showered in warm water, gradually turning the hot water down until it came out as cold as the summer allowed, letting the iced beer do the rest.

She was struggling getting dinner together, the boys were loud and complaining about being hungry, and well into the fifth beer, as he sat near the bright color and ever-happy tingle of the TV set, his back stiffening up, he snapped.

"Everybody has to shut up! I can't stand this today! I gotta relax some!"

She came back at him screaming too. "I can't stand *you!*"

He leaped. "You don't talk to me like that!"   20

She came right up to him. "You gonna hit me?!" she dared him.

The seven-year-old ran to his bed but the other two froze up, waiting for the tension to ease enough before their tears squeezed out.

"Get away from me," he said trying to contain himself. "You better get away from me right now. You know, just go home, go to your mother's, just go."

"*You* go! *You* get out! We're gonna stay!"

He looked through her, then slapped a wall, rocking what seemed like the   25 whole building. "You don't know how close you are."

He wouldn't leave. He walked into the bedroom, then walked out, sweating. He went into the empty kitchen — they were all in the children's room, where there was much crying — and he took a plate and filled it with what she'd made and went in front of the tube and he clicked on a ball game, told himself to calm himself and let it all pass at least tonight, at least while the weather was like it was and while these other things were still bothering both of them, and then he popped the sixth beer. He wasn't going to fall asleep on the couch tonight.

Eventually his family came out, one by one peeking around a corner to see what he looked like. Then they ate in a whisper, even cutting loose here and there with a little giggle or gripe. Eventually the sun did set, though that did nothing to wash off the glue of heat.

And eventually the older boys felt comfortable enough to complain about bedtime. Only the baby cried—he was tired and wanted to sleep but couldn't because a cold had clogged his nose. Still, they were all trying to maintain the truce when from outside, a new voice came in: SHUT THAT FUCKING KID UP YOU FUCK-ING PEOPLE! HEY! SHUT THAT FUCKING KID UP OVER THERE!

It was like an explosion except that he flew toward it. He shook the window screen with his voice. "You fuck yourself, asshole! You stupid asshole, you shut your mouth!" He ran out the other way, out the screen door and around and under the heated stars. "Come on out here, mouth! Come out and say that to my face!" He squinted at all the windows around him, no idea where it came from. "So come on! Say it right now!" There was no taker, and he turned away, his blood still bright red.

When he came back inside, the children had gone to bed and she was lying down   30 with the baby, who'd fallen asleep. He went back to the chair. The game ended, she came out, half-closing the door behind her, and went straight to their bed. He followed.

"I dunno," he said after some time. He'd been wearing shorts and nothing else since his shower, and it shouldn't have taken him so long, yet he just sat there on the bed. Finally he turned on the fan and it whirred, ticking as it pivoted left and right. "It doesn't do any good, but it's worse without it." He looked at her like he did earlier. "I'm kinda glad nobody came out. Afterwards I imagined some nut just shooting me, or a few guys coming. I'm getting too old for that shit."

She wasn't talking.

"So what did they say?" he asked her. "At the clinic?"

"Yes."

"Yes what?"   35

"That I am."

They both listened to the fan and to the mix of music from the Armenians and that TV upstairs.

"I would've never thought it could happen," he said. "That one time, and it wasn't even good."

"Maybe for you. I knew it then."

"You did?"   40

She rolled on her side.

"I'm sorry about all the yelling," he said.

"I was happy you went after that man. I always wanna do stuff like that."

He rolled to her.

"I'm too sticky. It's too hot."   45

"I have to. We do. It's been too long, and now it doesn't matter."

"It does matter," she said. "I love you."

"I'm sorry," he said, reaching over to touch her breast. "You know I'm sorry."

He took another shower afterward. A cold shower. His breath sputtered and noises hopped from his throat. He crawled into the bed naked, onto the sheet that seemed as hot as ever, and listened to outside, to that mournful Armenian music mixing with Spanish, and to the fan, and it had stilled him. It was joy, and it was so strange. She'd fallen asleep and so he resisted kissing her, telling her. He thought he should hold on to this as long as he could, until he heard the pitch of the freeway climb, telling him that dawn was near and it was almost time to go back to work.

DAGOBERTO GILB

On Writing "Shout" 2012

I suspect that younger readers — though older ones too — believe that a writer would enjoy going back and reading his earlier work. Probably a few do. I do not. It's like going back and looking at old photographs. I see a younger me, and I think of all the decisions I made, or didn't, because I didn't know what I didn't know. Worse, I read these stories and see what I would cut over there and add right here. And who am I to do that now to these full-grown stories? I think about where I was in my head when I wrote them . . . but let me give you this easier where: when I wrote "Shout," we were living in an East Hollywood apartment building beneath an elderly Armenian couple who grew parsley in the cracks of the cement pathways, who were miserable whenever my two baby boys rode their noisy Big Wheels. If the horrible thing about construction work was those times I didn't have a job, one of the great things was those times when I didn't have a job — not banging nails meant, instead, me getting to stay home at my wooden desk. (I still had the one I bought used in college. Beside me then was a Mexican calavera who oversaw whatever was on it, which it does to this day, on a newer wood desk.) That was when I allowed myself to write "officially" these pages I wanted published, the ones crafted, the ones you read. Not to say I was not always writing. Even working eleven hours, six days a week for as many months as a job would hold me, I wrote every day, but it would be in a notebook, recording conversations, incidents, descriptions, deep philosophical insights, and dear diary type boo-hoos or longings. Thousands of pages accumulated. My best writing hours were when my sons were asleep, and there was quiet, though once I got onto something, I could work anytime, in any noise.

It's surely obvious that much of my fiction comes from my own life and experiences. "Shout," for instance, could be said to have come out of the same period of my life as "Love in L.A." Hard to avoid what lasted over a decade. It used to be that most writers wrote out of their lived experience. Herman Melville, of *Moby Dick* (and *Billy Budd*), was a whaler. Nowadays people expect fiction to be nothing but mental creation and research, drawn on the page. Art is the imagination, goes this view, is the writer's desk alone, and the discipline there. That's not untrue, and it alone works well for very many. Gustave Flaubert, imagining a life as a woman, is said to have written one of the greatest novels of a woman, *Madame Bovary*. For me, fiction is life transformed and fueled by imagination. Experience often teaches by surprise — what cannot be predicted by the best reader in the library. My own favorite writers are out there, feeling the wind, on an adventure. Fiction I admire the most captures what, like life, smacks you when and where you're not looking, and the blow can seem so small, and it's so big.

Which brings up the subject of the small and the big, the short story and the novel. In many respects, a novel is simply a short story that is made larger, fuller, with more characters, more involved situations, a longer and more casual read. Thus, many short stories can be expanded into novels, or become segments of one. But I want to say that the best short fiction has more kinship with poetry: the goal is to reduce words and condense, and it is driven more by image than plot, both contrary to the novel. War can be described in a hundred pages of a battle scene, but might be more lastingly understood in an image of a tear falling, red itself or what is seen through it. There are never enough pages for love, but isn't it only the neighbor's *gallo* waking you up angry until you see, sound asleep next to you. . . .

The small. If novels are often about epic sweeps of history and issues, the big ideas of big egos, characters who are larger than whole nations and journeys that are bold, short fiction goes for what's left off-screen, following characters who would be minor against the headliners in those novels, but whose conclusions, The Ends, if less grandiose and more subtle, are anything shy of large.

And so, my own stories are about the small things and the people who aren't seen much in literature. There was a time when characters like those who populate my fiction were written about more, just not very much in recent decades. By that I mean common Americans, what many call working people, be they employed or looking to be. There are not a lot of stories about men like the main character in "Shout." I have found over the years that many know them as fathers and uncles, brothers and husbands, but they are not in the books they read. What you see in "Shout" as well is this man in a Mexican American family, yet another huge segment of American culture seldom read about. What I hoped to offer was not a simple portrayal of a construction worker coming home from work exhausted from a long day in the heat, not just a domestic squabble he causes with a patient wife, the mother of their three children. Left there, it would be a working-class cliché, the macho stereotype not only of that kind of man but also of a Mexican male. What I wanted seen was the same bullish rage he had in his home being used to defend his family when a stranger screams at them. And then the intimacy, what is hidden in the broad, usual expectation, what is forgotten when you don't know characters as living people, that the man and woman are lovers.

DAGOBERTO GILB

Uncle Rock 2011

In the morning, at his favorite restaurant, Erick got to order his favorite American food, sausage and eggs and hash-brown *papitas*° fried crunchy on top. He'd be sitting there, eating with his mother, not bothering anybody, and life was good, when a man started changing it all. Lots of times it was just a man staring too much — but then one would come over. Friendly, he'd put his thick hands on the table as if he were touching water, and squat low, so that he was at sitting level, as though he were so polite, and he'd smile, with coffee-and-tobacco-stained teeth. He might wear a bolo tie and speak in a drawl. Or he might have on a tan uniform, a company logo on the back, an oval name patch on the front. Or he'd be in a nothing-special work shirt, white or striped, with a couple of pens clipped onto the left side pocket, tucked into a pair of jeans or chinos that were morning-clean still, with a pair of scuffed work boots that laced up higher than regular shoes. He'd say something about her earrings, or her bracelet, or her hair, or her eyes, and if she had on her white uniform how nice it looked on her. Or he'd come right out with it and tell her how pretty she was, how he couldn't keep himself from walking up, speaking to her directly, and could they talk again? Then he'd wink at Erick. Such a fine-looking boy! How old is he, eight or nine? Erick wasn't even small for an eleven-year-old. He tightened his jaw then, slanted his eyes up from his plate at his mom and not the man, definitely not this man he did not care for. Erick drove a fork into a goopy

---

papitas: Potatoes.

American egg yolk and bled it into his American potatoes. She wouldn't offer the man Erick's correct age either, saying only that he was growing too fast.

She almost always gave the man her number if he was wearing a suit. Not a sports coat but a buttoned suit with a starched white shirt and a pinned tie meant something to her. Once in a while, Erick saw one of these men again at the front door of the apartment in Silverlake. The man winked at Erick as if they were buddies. Grabbed his shoulder or arm, squeezed the muscle against the bone. What did Erick want to be when he grew up? A cop, a jet-airplane mechanic, a travel agent, a court reporter? A dog groomer? Erick stood there, because his mom said that he shouldn't be impolite. His mom's date said he wanted to take Erick along with them sometime. The three of them. What kind of places did Erick think were fun? Erick said nothing. He never said anything when the men were around, and not because of his English, even if that was what his mother implied to explain his silence. He didn't talk to any of the men and he didn't talk much to his mom either. Finally they took off, and Erick's night was his alone. He raced to the grocery store and bought half a gallon of chocolate ice cream. When he got back, he turned on the TV, scooted up real close, as close as he could, and ate his dinner with a soup spoon. He was away from all the men. Even though a man had given the TV to them. He was a salesman in an appliance store who'd bragged that a rich customer had given it to him and so why shouldn't he give it to Erick's mom, who couldn't afford such a good TV otherwise?

When his mom was working as a restaurant hostess, and was going to marry the owner, Erick ate hot-fudge sundaes and drank chocolate shakes. When she worked at a trucking company, the owner of all the trucks told her he was getting a divorce. Erick climbed into the rigs, with their rooms full of dials and levers in the sky. Then she started working in an engineer's office. There was no food or fun there, but even he could see the money. He was not supposed to touch anything, but what was there to touch — the tubes full of paper? He and his mom were invited to the engineer's house, where he had two horses and a stable, a swimming pool, and two convertible sports cars. The engineer's family was there: his grown children, his gray-haired parents. They all sat down for dinner in a dining room that seemed bigger than Erick's apartment, with three candelabras on the table, and a tablecloth and cloth napkins. Erick's mom took him aside to tell him to be well mannered at the table and polite to everyone. Erick hadn't said anything. He never spoke anyway, so how could he have said anything wrong? She leaned into his ear and said that she wanted them to know that he spoke English. That whole dinner he was silent, chewing quietly, taking the smallest bites, because he didn't want them to think he liked their food.

When she got upset about days like that, she told Erick that she wished they could just go back home. She was tired of worrying. "Back," for Erick, meant mostly the stories he'd heard from her, which never sounded so good to him: she'd had to share a room with her brothers and sisters. They didn't have toilets. They didn't have electricity. Sometimes they didn't have enough food. He saw this Mexico as if it were the backdrop of a movie on afternoon TV, where children walked around barefoot in the dirt or on broken sidewalks and small men wore wide-brimmed straw hats and baggy white shirts and pants. The women went to church all the time and prayed to alcoved saints and, heads down, fearful, counted rosary beads. There were rocks everywhere, and scorpions and tarantulas and rattlesnakes, and vultures and no trees and not much water, and skinny dogs and donkeys, and ugly bad guys with guns and bullet vests who rode laughing into town to drink and shoot off their pistols and rifles, driving their horses all over like dirt bikes on desert dunes. When they spoke English, they had stupid accents — his mom didn't have an accent like theirs. It didn't make sense to him that Mexico would only be like that, but what if it was close? He lived on paved, lighted city streets, and a bicycle ride away were the Asian drugstore and the Armenian grocery store and the corner where black Cubans drank coffee and talked Dodgers baseball.

When he was in bed, where he sometimes prayed, he thanked God for his 5 mom, who he loved, and he apologized for not talking to her, or to anyone, really, except his friend Albert, and he apologized for her never going to church and for his never taking Holy Communion, as Albert did — though only to God would he admit that he wanted to only because Albert did. He prayed for good to come, for his mom and for him, since God was like magic, and happiness might come the way of early morning, in the trees and bushes full of sparrows next to his open window, louder and louder when he listened hard, eyes closed.

The engineer wouldn't have mattered if Erick hadn't told Albert that he was his dad. Albert had just moved into the apartment next door and lived with both his mother and his father, and since Albert's mother already didn't like Erick's mom, Erick told him that his new dad was an engineer. Erick actually believed it, too, and thought that he might even get his own horse. When that didn't happen, and his mom was lying on her bed in the middle of the day, blowing her nose, because she didn't have the job anymore, that was when Roque came around again. Roque was nobody — or he was anybody. He wasn't special, he wasn't not. He tried to speak English to Erick, thinking that was the reason Erick didn't say anything when he was there. And Erick had to tell Albert that Roque was his uncle, because the engineer was supposed to be his new dad any minute. Uncle Rock, Erick said. His mom's brother, he told Albert. Roque worked at night and was around during the day, and one day he offered Erick and Albert a ride. When his mom got in the car, she scooted all the way over to Roque on the bench seat. Who was supposed to be her brother, Erick's Uncle Rock. Albert didn't say anything, but he saw what had happened, and that was it for Erick. Albert had parents, grandparents, and a brother and a sister, and he'd hang out only when one of his cousins wasn't coming by. Erick didn't need a friend like him.

What if she married Roque, his mom asked him one day soon afterward. She told Erick that they would move away from the apartment in Silverlake to a better neighborhood. He did want to move, but he wished that it weren't because of Uncle Rock. It wasn't just because Roque didn't have a swimming pool or horses or a big ranch house. There wasn't much to criticize except that he was always too willing and nice, too considerate, too generous. He wore nothing flashy or expensive, just ordinary clothes that were clean and ironed, and shoes he kept shined. He combed and parted his hair neatly. He didn't have a buzzcut like the men who didn't like kids. He moved slow, he talked slow, as quiet as night. He only ever said yes to Erick's mom. How could she not like him for that? He loved her so much — anybody could see his pride when he was with her. He signed checks and gave her cash. He knocked on their door carrying cans and fruit and meat. He was there when she asked, gone when she asked, back whenever, grateful. He took her out to restaurants on Sunset, to the movies in Hollywood, or on drives to the beach in rich Santa Monica.

Roque knew that Erick loved baseball. Did Roque like baseball? It was doubtful that he cared even a little bit — he didn't listen to games on the radio or TV, and he never looked at a newspaper. He loved boxing though. He knew the names of all the Mexican fighters as if they lived here, as if they were Dodgers players like Steve Yeager, Dusty Baker, Kenny Landreaux or Mike Marshall, or Pedro Guerrero. Roque did know about Fernando Valenzuela, everyone did, even his mom, which is why she agreed to let Roque take them to a game. What Mexican didn't love Fernando? Dodger Stadium was close to their apartment. He'd been there once with Albert and his family — well, outside it, on a nearby hill, to see the fireworks for Fourth of July. His mom decided that all three of them would go on a Saturday afternoon, since Saturday night, Erick thought, she might want to go somewhere else, even with somebody else.

Roque, of course, didn't know who the Phillies were. He knew nothing about the strikeouts by Steve Carlton or the homeruns by Mike Schmidt. He'd never heard of Pete Rose. It wasn't that Erick knew very much either, but there was nothing that Roque could talk to him about, if they were to talk.

If Erick showed his excitement when they drove up to Dodger Stadium and   10 parked, his mom and Roque didn't really notice it. They sat in the bleachers, and for him the green of the field was a magic light; the stadium decks surrounding them seemed as far away as Rome. His body was somewhere it had never been before. The fifth inning? That's how late they were. Or were they right on time, because they weren't even sure they were sitting in the right seats yet when he heard the crack of the bat, saw the crowd around them rising as it came at them. Erick saw the ball. He had to stand and move and stretch his arms and want that ball until it hit his bare hands and stayed there. Everybody saw him catch it with no bobble. He felt all the eyes and voices around him as if they were every set of eyes and every voice in the stadium. His mom was saying something, and Roque, too, and then, finally, it was just him and that ball and his stinging hands. He wasn't even sure if it had been hit by Pete Guerrero. He thought for sure it had been, but he didn't ask. He didn't watch the game then — he couldn't. He didn't care who won. He stared at his official National League ball, reimagining what had happened. He ate a hot dog and drank a soda and he sucked the salted peanuts and the wooden spoon from his chocolate-malt ice cream. He rubbed the bumpy seams of his homerun ball.

Game over, they were the last to leave. People were hanging around, not going straight to their cars. Roque didn't want to leave. He didn't want to end it so quickly, Erick thought, while he still had her with him. Then one of the Phillies came out of the stadium door and people swarmed — boys mostly, but also men and some women and girls — and they got autographs before the player climbed onto the team's bus. Joe Morgan, they said. Then Garry Maddox appeared. Erick clutched the ball but he didn't have a pen. He just watched, his back to the gray bus the Phillies were getting into.

Then a window slid open. *Hey, big man,* a voice said. Erick really wasn't sure. *Gimme the ball, la pelota,°* the face in the bus said. *I'll have it signed, comprendes?°* *Échalo,°* *just toss it to me.* Erick obeyed. He tossed it up to the hand that was reaching out. The window closed. The ball was gone a while, so long that his mom came up to him, worried that he'd lost it. The window slid open again and the voice spoke to her. *We got the ball, Mom. It's not lost, just a few more.* When the window opened once more, this time the ball was there. *Catch.* There were all

la pelota: The ball.
comprendes?: Understand?
Échalo: Throw it.

kinds of signatures on it, though none that he could really recognize except for Joe Morgan and Pete Rose.

Then the voice offered more, and the hand threw something at him. *For your mom, okay? Comprendes?* Erick stared at the asphalt lot where the object lay, as if he'd never seen a folded-up piece of paper before. *Para tu mamá, bueno?* He picked it up, and he started to walk over to his mom and Roque, who were so busy talking they hadn't noticed anything. Then he stopped. He opened the note himself. No one had said he couldn't read it. It said, *I'd like to get to know you. You are muy linda. Very beautiful and sexy. I don't speak Spanish very good, may be you speak better English, pero No Importa.°* Would you come by tonite and let me buy you a drink? There was a phone number and a hotel room number. A name, too. A name that came at him the way that the homerun had.

Erick couldn't hear. He could see only his mom ahead of him. She was talking to Roque, Roque was talking to her. Roque was the proudest man, full of joy because he was with her. It wasn't his fault he wasn't an engineer. Now Erick could hear again. Like sparrows hunting seed, boys gathered round the bus, calling out, while the voice in the bus was yelling at him, *Hey, big guy! Give it to her!* Erick had the ball in one hand and the note in the other. By the time he reached his mom and Roque, the note was already somewhere on the asphalt parking lot. *Look*, he said in a full voice. *They all signed my ball.*

pero No Importa: It doesn't matter.

Dagoberto Gilb

On Writing "Uncle Rock" 2012

Mostly I don't like talking about my work. What can I say without implying a boast that it is fine writing you will want to know at least as well as me, if not better? (Of course it is!) Not only tasteless, it's a little questionable. Because, of course, this is somebody else's occupation, not my mirror's. Do you go to a restaurant telling you that it has "The Best Mexican Food in Texas!" (Of course it does, right?) All this aside, "Uncle Rock" might be one of my easiest stories to disassemble to see how it was put together.

As a craft, what I do isn't that much different than what a tile setter does. My fictional tiles, however, are broken, chipped, cracked, and come in different sizes and proportions and colors, and what I do is make a mosaic. There are sentences based on experience of my own years ago, and there are graphs which are what I remember doing with my sons when they were children; there are objects much like I owned, and a character who is memories of two people on the body of a third I worked with. Even within a single sentence, the imaginary is beside the Googled. The drama is invention. "Uncle Rock" appears to be a story of an eleven-year-old boy's life in the '80s, when really it is a set of disconnected images from several decades flipped through so quickly that it gives the illusion of movement (yes, like a "movie"), a story of a single experience. People read this story and assume it must be autobiographical. A compliment to my craft. You now know it was written willfully, by design.

Where the shards of tiles come from is what distinguishes what's mine from another writer's. And no doubt there are all sorts of piles to go through. I studied religion in college. That wasn't because I made a mistake and picked a degree plan that I thought I would cash in on. It's that I learned we live on a circling planet and noticed that I am alive and conscious. My curiosity about this has driven me to where I am. What I write is called literary fiction. The purpose of commercial fiction is, besides making money, to pass the time pleasantly, to get some relief from the grind — to entertain. Though this used to be more the function of reading in the past, now that is primarily handled by television and film. Literary fiction intends to entertain as well (and I say it does, more and especially so when it's great), and wishes to make money, but its goal — as is mine — is to reach out from the ordinary to realize the extraordinary. To point to the mystery that is being alive, in a strange place, in a time — a reader's, a writer's — that is not only in time. Is Erick's story about the '60s, '80s, these teens? Is his mom or Roque only a product of a class or culture? Is this story about males and single women, about the boundaries of love between a fatherless boy and a mother?

Don't think I'm denying that my fiction has autobiography in it. But this is true of most works of art, no more mine than many. Still, "Uncle Rock" could be used to do a clinical, psychological take on me through my work, digging out the root troubles haunting me. Most likely not wrong. It could be pointed out that, for instance, how the too wild single mother theme and character comes up here as it does in other pieces by me. That I have a *mami* issue. Probably true. But in my defense, my mom really did create some stories. Say you were the littlest broke, or even felt like splurging, treating yourself, or just felt like making life easy for yourself, and you knew where there was a chest of gold coins. Wouldn't you go there and grab one? It's only one here, and another couple in the past, not like I got greedy and grabbed the whole suitcase.

It's easiest for me to talk about my work when it has to do with advocacy. I would argue that all art advocates, like it or not, and that a writer represents a group of people and their interests. My fiction is very much about the common people in America, those who work and support families with their hands and bodies for hourly wages, who go about their lives hidden from media and celebrity links. Characters with "careers" like Erick's mother or Roque are not read about. Which brings up the American West — it is still unusual to read literary work set in and written by those who live west of the Mississippi. But it is more than rare to read stories set in the American Southwest, and more so still when they are about Mexican American people in their historical homeland — why the mountains and rivers and cities have names in Spanish. And I do that. My stories represent the Chicano story. It could be said that this is unavoidable for me, and that's not wrong, but my advocacy began only vaguely when I was young. In college I was lucky enough to see Luis Valdez's plays performed by his Teatro Campesino. I went to events supporting, and featuring, Cesar Chavez. Both were synonymous with the farm workers' movement. Broccoli, to me, only came from a Safeway grocery store, and other people ate that kind of food. But the urban Mexican American was, obviously, always there too. There was simply little to no publicly documented evidence of it. Many call this an "invisibility" of the culture and history in the United States. I don't see it that way, not when what's loved about the Mexican American West, from cowboys to adobes, from margaritas to enchiladas, tacos, and burritos, are now as American as an iPod and a hamburger. I say Mexican

Americans are being ignored willfully, an ignorance that has gotten worse in the past decade as a seismic demographic shift is altering the region's, and nation's, political landscape.

Which finally brings me back to "Uncle Rock." Take it apart, and you find a description of the Mexican American situation: Roque, a working man who struggles with English, an anybody, nobody special, who only works hard and is steady, is the only one who treats Erick's mother well. He adores her. But, despite the humiliation she endures, she wants more than what he is able to offer. She is beautiful and attracts all kinds of attention, so how can she not want more than what everyone else accepts? Her American dream. Erick is as embarrassed by his mom as he is attached to her. He is bothered so much that he has gone mute — he does not want to talk to anyone but God and his friend Albert. From the outside, it would appear that his is a struggle with the English language. One day he realizes a dream. In the days of Fernandomania, Roque takes him and his mom to a Dodgers game. Not only does he get to go to his first professional baseball game, not only does he catch a homerun ball, but a famous baseball player wants to meet his mother. At first thrilled, as young as he is Erick knows the offer is disrespectful and crude. And when he walks back to the two of them, who are unaware of what happened, he speaks to them. I want Erick's voice to get louder, smarter, and more confident.

Perspectives

DAGOBERTO GILB

On Physical Labor   2003

From "Work Union," *Gritos*

Not everybody wants to sit at a desk for a living. So many of us come from cultures where it is expected that we will move our bodies in the wind and sun, at dawn and into dusk. Many of us have been taught by family that physical work feels good and is good — when the day is over, we know what we did because we see it, we feel the efforts in our feet and hands and bones, and when we go home, when the wife puts food on the table and the family sits down and eats, there is unmistakable pride that all of it is because we have done our job.

It is human to work, to bend and grip, to lift and pull. It's never about getting tired or dirty. There is nothing wrong with sweat and toil. It is only about conditions and decent wages that there can come complaint. This is what so many people don't understand, especially those who sit in chairs in offices. They see us tired, they see us worried. They say, Well, if you don't like your situation, why don't you get a better job? Because it isn't the job, the kind of work. The job is good. Being a carpenter, an electrician, a plumber, an ironworker, a laborer, those are all good. What isn't good is to be earning a living that can't bring in enough money to raise a healthy family, buy a home, go to a dentist and doctor, and be around comfortably for grandchildren.

A writer from Detroit who worked years for the Fisher Body Plant in Flint, Michigan, has recently been profiled in the newspapers because he won a prize for his writing. In the exultation of winning, he has been quoted often about those years he worked on the assembly line, saying, "I can't stress to you enough how much I hated it." This writer, he is certainly a good man, but like so many, he simply forgot what a joy employment is, what a job means to people and their families. There is only good in work, and the very best people are those who work hard.

DAGOBERTO GILB

On Distortions of Mexican American Culture 2011

From "La Próxima Parada Is Next," *American Book Review*

When Americans think of the South, some might think of its white society, Antebellum and post, its white literature, its wealth, yet the black culture is undeniably ever there, present. Others might discuss the history of the South in terms of black people, their history of slavery, their struggle with poverty, as the homeland of African Americans. This binary is a permanent overlay on the topography of the Southeast region, that quadrangle of the U.S. It is a black-white that has come to define much of America's internal history. Now consider a comparable Southwest quadrangle, one whose historical binary could be called — should be called — brown and white. We are all taught passionately about the American expansion into the West, cattle drives, cowboys and Indians, John Wayne movies, but if someone were to say it is the homeland of Mexican Americans, would anyone associate that with populations in Los Angeles, the state of New Mexico, El Paso, San Antonio, the Rio Grande Valley? Visitors thrill at oversized enchilada plates and the bountiful bowls of tortilla chips (Americanisms, both), visits to seventeenth- and early eighteenth-century missions, and they see and hear the vast numbers of "Mexican" people who speak to them in homegrown English at shops, stores, and stations — and yet somehow, relaxing in adobe-themed motels or new Spanish Villa homes, the binary here is not brown and white but *blank* and white, the dominant Mexican culture as if from an uninhabited ghost town. Meanwhile, what brown people they encounter — what articles appear in the media — are recent immigrants, invaders from the border. Part of American history? Curiously, if we were to assert that we are part of Mexico's history — which nobody here or there ever has or does — that would be far more of an outrage than lament that, unless photographed in folklorico costume, we have no images in our nation's history other than as foreigners.

Michael Meyer Interviews Dagoberto Gilb 2012

Meyer: Here is a potentially annoying but sincere usage question concerning a simple matter of terms that has caused me and my students to sometimes stumble: Do we (do you) use Chicano or Latino, Hispanic or Mexican American or Tex Mex to describe your writings? Should I even bring up feminine endings and hyphens as well? Do the terms define important distinctions? Is there a single umbrella term? Can you help sort this out for us?

Gilb: Aww, the rage of the nomenclature. All these words are better than the ones when I was young — "beaner" and "wetback" are the hit oldies, but just the word "Mexican," with but a soft decibel of racist tone, could clear the bench. The Chicano period was the beginning of the alternative. The problem with that became the masculine "o" at the end. Since the linguistic rules of Spanish reflected a macho boys' club mentality that did rule beyond usage, Chicanas rightfully fought for the equal status of the feminine "a," which has since created the slash usage, Chicana/o. It was the Nixon administration which came in with the word "Hispanic" as a "non-political" term (Chicanos and Chicanas, college-educated, did not vote Republican). It is a word now predominantly used in Republican circles. Latino, Latina, and Latina/o are the alternative to that. For me the problem with this is its application in the West. While Mexican Americans are close to 70 percent of the national demographic, Latinas and Latinos in the West are 95 percent Mexican American. One may note that neither do I love the hyphen that can be used in "Mexican American" (as in, the diminutive, hyphenated American). Me being me, I don't love the exhausting bureaucracy of slash world, and me being as American as the rest of us, I want nicknames of one or at most two syllables, so I've been going with the gender-neutral "MexAm" when it fits in easily. Sorry for the extra cap. And so it goes.

Meyer: It's not likely that any of your characters subscribe to the *American Book Review,* because they are mostly working-class, hard-working individuals struggling to earn a living. Do you think your work reaches an audience that includes the kind of characters that you write about? Do you worry about making the connection?

Gilb: Sadly, yes, improbable that an under-educated community would read or receive suggestions to read any of my writing, fiction or nonfiction. Is that because reading has become a luxury item? Is education a luxury item? Historically this has been true in most countries, in Europe, in Mexico, in Latin America. It was just less true in ours. At least as ideals went. Today, it would seem that's our direction. But putting that aside, my writing does reach a segment of the population that does care. And it touches enough even in my own community of people who recognize family members in the stories, who recognize their own voices through hearing mine. And I was invited into a literary world that has rewarded me. Not only have my books been published by Grove Press (the house whose books I was most infatuated with as a young reader), but my work has been in the most honored pages of the literary establishment — the *New Yorker* and *Harper's* magazines — and has been granted their finer awards. That doesn't mean that the mainstream public cares about what I do enough to make me a rich author, but it does mean that there is a respect in our country's literary marketplace for the ideas that pass through me and the people those ideas intend to honor. I am proud that this is true.

Meyer: In your comments about "Uncle Rock" you write that "It's easiest for me to talk about my work when it has to do with advocacy." Which of the four stories that you've chosen to include in this anthology do you think most fully seems to be an "advocacy story"?

Gilb: All art advocates. The one who says his doesn't, he's someone who's advocating for the way things are, someone who's comfortable. I'm not saying that's right or wrong (though I'm sure I would pick a better or worse), only that

Hecho en Tejas: An Anthology of Texas Mexican Literature was edited by Gilb and published in 2006 by the University of New Mexico Press.

From *Hecho en Tejas* by Dagoberto Gilb
© 2006, University of New Mexico Press.

An event celebrating the anthology at the historic Cine El Rey Theatre. McAllen, Texas, 2007.
Courtesy of Dagoberto Gilb.

it is a stance. For those who are less than comfortable, that status of ghosts, in situations that are less romantic or sitcom popular. I myself have gone through stages of understanding about the role of advocacy. I used to think that, like Dostoevsky, it — the politics, the spirituality — was contained in the art of the fiction alone, not in tracts or marches. A writer writes quietly alone, no option. It's in the finished work, and readers who are ready to find it, will. But I have changed. Maybe because I became a parent. Maybe because, as a journeyman, I worked with an apprentice often. Maybe because I was a coach for nine years and both yelled at and encouraged boys and girls who needed the coaching and got better. Once I became a teacher, a professor even, I found that, being in front of a class, students knowing that it was real and could be earned and I'd come from where they did, their learning altered their views, broke down their clichés and stereotypes. How

Dagoberto Gilb's desk — and the Mexican *calavera* that oversees it, mentioned in his essay "On Writing 'Shout'" (p. 465).
Courtesy of Dagoberto Gilb.

many Chicano professors of English have you had? Why should it be surprising, even, that Mexican Americans have as many professional and personal complexities as others? As to the stories in this anthology, I don't really think of any one of them having more or less advocacy than another. Choose any of mine anywhere. A different emphasis in that one as opposed to this one, that's it. As to me, I am simply more aware of saying aloud, maybe saying louder, HEY! LOOK! Not sure if that's me, or survival in noisy times.

Meyer: In interviews and essays you have described the disadvantages of not being a northeastern writer snugly situated in the New York literary scene. Are there any encouraging advantages to being a southwestern writer in today's literary market?

Gilb: If you're from San Francisco, you're a Bay Area writer. From Oregon or Washington, a writer from the Pacific Northwest. Colorado, Utah, Wyoming, Montana, a western writer. If you're from the Southeast, a southern writer. If you live in New York, even Boston, you're a national writer. Hard to argue with the economic demographics and the number of readers who live in those cities and the history of colleges and universities there, as well as magazines and publishers. Traditions groove permanent paths. Hard for anyone to not follow the money, and that's where the money is, too. Also hard not to be born where you're born. The Southwest has always had an exoticized legacy. D. H. Lawrence and Georgia O'Keeffe are New Mexico. Meanwhile, the MexAm Southwest has barely registered on an art stat, but no doubt that too has to change. The Apaches came to learn the force of America's westward expansion onto their land. Mexican Americans — though probably less, are no more immigrant than those from European descent, despite the demagoguery — will be 50 percent of the American Southwest soon, and its beautiful culture and epic history is unavoidably blending into the American mainstream.

Meyer: You suffered a debilitating stroke in 2009 from which you have since remarkably recovered, but if you were to write a short story about that experience, the fact that it is your writing hand that remains impaired seems to conjure all kinds of symbolic meanings. What has that stroke meant to you as a writer?

Gilb: A story titled "please, thank you," first published in *Harper's* and then collected in *Before the End, After the Beginning*, does deal with a character, Mr. Sanchez, who suffered a stroke similar to the one I did. He and I have had to learn how to type only, first one-handed, then slowly with one finger on the other hand, instead of using a pen to write. I can't say I like it a lot, so I do not recommend anyone use the technique to gain insights or to seek material. Yes, it's hard not to consider the metaphor: a writer losing the use of his writing hand. Add to that it happening the night he is celebrating the beginning of a new future as a full-time writer. But that metaphor is only one. Another is the obstacle it is for many of us to be writers. To be artists. To do what we dream, not what is expected, not what we accept. What we have to work hard for. That has always been me, and so adding this new element is not really new. When I wrote the stories for my last collection (mentioned above), for me it was an act of calm defiance — no, I am not done yet — but also gratitude for the generous gifts still given. I'm lucky I can do what I always wanted to do, that I am a writer, and I only need a keyboard. That's not so bad.

gilb / story
8

~~I don't want that, but then again, yes, that'd probaby be better, because, then again, I don't believe~~ [au: not quite clear what "that" refers to]

~~that's the explanation.~~ a third Mexican American This is a campus where my work can be taught in a Chicano lit course only. I [and I don't grasp this wholly either; it's me alone, I think, but run your danger] will
wonder when, if ever, we ~~would~~ be considered gourmet enough, talented enough, important enough.

I am guilty too because I don't think I'm smart enough. Flawed in a couple of personal areas,

I wish I could claim to be better here, I wish instead of wanting to collapse and watch HBO (even, I

admit, those cheap ~~TV~~ judge shows), I read another book. I know those kind of writers. My God, [ok] [and overu...]

they are so brilliant and articulate. I ~~even~~ know a couple who are genuises. But what I ~~can~~ only hope

might be seen is what gets undervalued: Not only has writing saved my life, projected it into New
and Washington, D.C.,
York and European fantasylands I'd never know otherwise, ~~but~~ it has offered me joy and fun. ~~In this,~~

there are limits to how much that might be seen in these essays. I assure you, everyone of them has

given me such pleasure and satisfaction, the same kind I ~~have~~ had when I used to cut wood with my
huge
skilsaw and drive nails and build, watch a building rise high, a fun of the kind that trowels the back
a
of a tile with adhesive and sets it in, the pattern mounting. Each word is rock I've placed personally [yes] [it's right]
then
into a wall—five go in and I pick through a pile and find another, shift them around until I like it,

I've chipped and knicked at most so ~~that~~ they look to me like good sentences, good paragraphs. If I
of
don't think of myself as the smartest, I do feel a strength in my working the craft, so that everytime I [e!]
maybe too
finish something I'm impressed proud of myself, can hardly believe I did it, that I could. ~~Because it's~~ [or?]
the words The words are
~~almost as though it came from another consciousness,~~ beyond my own physical self or nature,
not
because I don't think I was born to be a writer, I've just done it anyway. Often this work is outright

fun, almost as fun as ~~it would be at~~ a good construction job where we were all muscles sweating and

laughing and building shit and getting paid ~~all~~ at the same time—living and working—except writing

work is alone, only an imaginary crew. Sometimes you see that laughter in these essays, but even

4G

A draft manuscript page for the introduction to Gilb's essay collection, *Gritos*, published in 2003 by Grove Press.
Courtesy of Dagoberto Gilb.

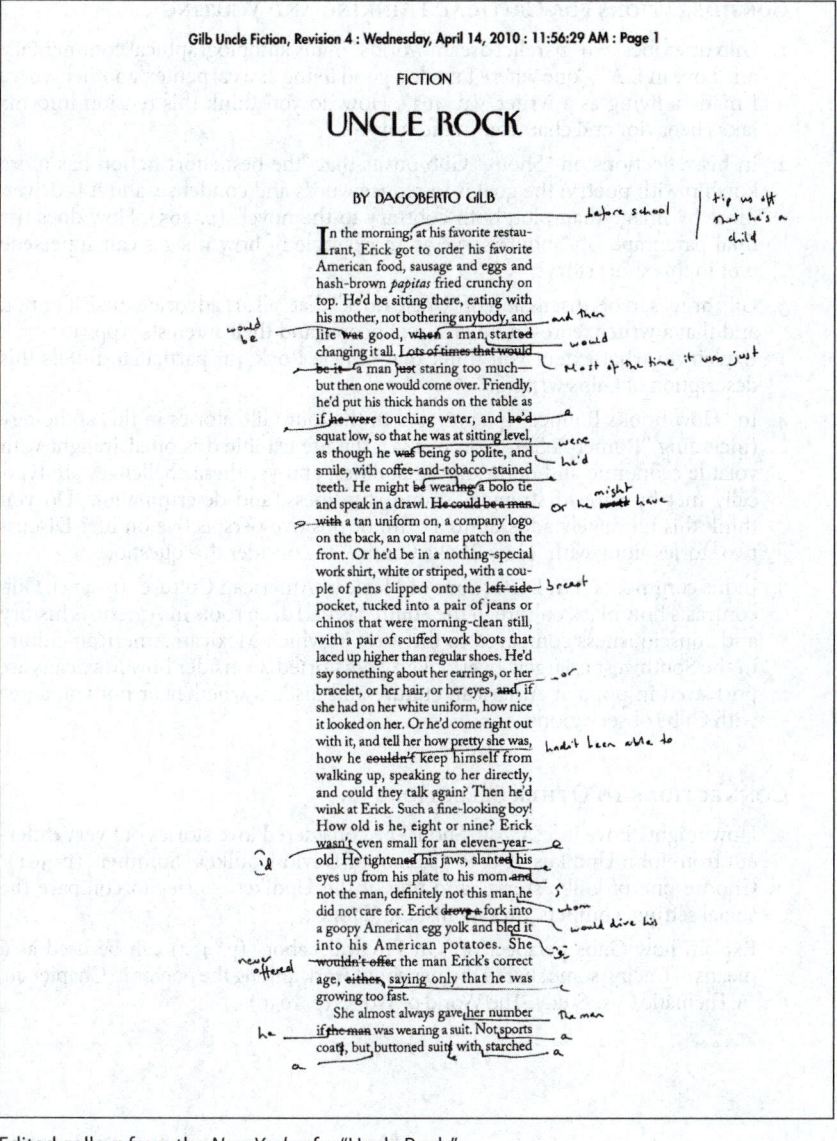

FICTION

UNCLE ROCK

BY DAGOBERTO GILB

In the morning, at his favorite restaurant, Erick got to order his favorite American food, sausage and eggs and hash-brown *papitas* fried crunchy on top. He'd be sitting there, eating with his mother, not bothering anybody, and life was good, when a man started changing it all. Lots of times that would be it—a man just staring too much— but then one would come over. Friendly, he'd put his thick hands on the table as if he were touching water, and he'd squat low, so that he was at sitting level, as though he was being so polite, and smile, with coffee-and-tobacco-stained teeth. He might be wearing a bolo tie and speak in a drawl. He could be a man with a tan uniform on, a company logo on the back, an oval name patch on the front. Or he'd be in a nothing-special work shirt, white or striped, with a couple of pens clipped onto the left side pocket, tucked into a pair of jeans or chinos that were morning-clean still, with a pair of scuffed work boots that laced up higher than regular shoes. He'd say something about her earrings, or her bracelet, or her hair, or her eyes, and, if she had on her white uniform, how nice it looked on her. Or he'd come right out with it, and tell her how pretty she was, how he couldn't keep himself from walking up, speaking to her directly, and could they talk again? Then he'd wink at Erick. Such a fine-looking boy! How old is he, eight or nine? Erick wasn't even small for an eleven-year-old. He tightened his jaws, slanted his eyes up from his plate to his mom and not the man, definitely not this man he did not care for. Erick drove a fork into a goopy American egg yolk and bled it into his American potatoes. She wouldn't offer the man Erick's correct age, either, saying only that he was growing too fast.

She almost always gave her number if the man was wearing a suit. Not sports coats, but buttoned suits with starched

Edited galleys from the *New Yorker* for "Uncle Rock."
Courtesy of Dagoberto Gilb.

CONSIDERATIONS FOR CRITICAL THINKING AND WRITING

1. Gilb describes two "parallel dream worlds" in his autobiographical commentary on "Love in L.A.": "one where I made a good living as a carpenter, another where I made a living as a writer" (p. 461). How do you think this tension informs Jake's behavior and character in the story?

2. In his reflections on "Shout," Gilb posits that "the best short fiction has more kinship with poetry: the goal is to reduce words and condense, and it is driven more by image than plot, both contrary to the novel" (p. 465). How does the final paragraph of "Shout" serve as an example of how images can supersede plot in this short story?

3. Gilb argues in his discussion of "Uncle Rock" that "all art advocates, like it or not, and that a writer represents a group of people and their interests" (pp. 471–72). Explain to what extent you think that "Uncle Rock," in particular, fulfills this description of Gilb's writing.

4. In "How Books Bounce" (p. 456) and in the four Gilb stories in this anthology (including "Romero's Shirt" on p. 242), the life exhibited is often fraught with volatile economic and domestic instabilities, and yet these challenges are typically met by shrewd strength, sound sturdiness, and determination. Do you think this ultimately adds up to a grim or positive perspective on life? Discuss two stories along with "How Books Bounce" to consider this question.

5. In his comments "On Distortions of Mexican American Culture" (p. 473), Gilb contrasts how black culture in the South has had deep roots in America's history and consciousness compared to the ways in which Mexican American culture in the Southwest is largely overlooked or distorted. Consider how Mexicans are portrayed in popular American culture and discuss whether or not you agree with Gilb's observations.

CONNECTIONS TO OTHER SELECTIONS

1. How might "Love in L.A." or "Shout" be considered love stories but very different from John Updike's "A & P" (p. 200) or David Updike's "Summer" (p. 301)? Choose one of Gilb's stories and one of the Updikes' stories to compare the social setting, conflicts, protagonists, and tone.

2. Explain how Gilb's perspective "On Physical Labor" (p. 472) can be used as a means of tracing some shared themes about work among the poems in Chapter 40, "A Thematic Case Study: The World of Work" (p. 1030).

16

A THEMATIC CASE STUDY
War

© Hulton-Deutsch Collection / CORBIS.

I've often wondered that — am I just
left with my past? But no . . .
— MURIEL SPARK

The literature of war is, lamentably, a major and persistent topic for writers and readers because human history has marched to a steady drumbeat of violent conflict. Wars are legion. In *What Every Person Should Know about War* (2003), Chris Hedges, a best-selling author and a former foreign correspondent for the *New York Times,* reports that for the past 3,400 years complete peace has been established in only 268 years. This means that in 92 percent of recorded history, some portion of the world has been at war. Since the beginning of the twenty-first century, when this estimate was made, the percentage of peacetime has not increased. Peace may briefly break out, but almost any daily newspaper imprints upon us the dominating fact of life that war is a permanent course of human action. It is not surprising, then, that writers are simultaneously attracted to war and appalled by it.

This chapter offers four short stories about war written within the last half century. Such a limited selection cannot be representative of the thematic and stylistic range of such narratives, but these stories do suggest some perennial concerns as well as contemporary responses to war. They maneuver around the profound impact of war on people, both combatants and civilians, who confront its meaning and its meaninglessness. What emerges from the fog is a series of complicated contradictions that map its confusion, brutality, horror, boredom, and futility, along with the courage, sacrifice, love, and even the beauty that the landscape of war presents. What Tim O'Brien describes in "How to Tell a True War Story" (p. 488) as "the awful majesty of combat" is the discovery of the intensity of life amid the possibility, indeed the likelihood, of death. This extraordinary tension italicizes immediate experience even though the broader context of political abstractions and historical justifications might raise fatal questions about the efficacy of war. Ernest Hemingway suggests as much in a little-read introduction he wrote for *Men at War*, an anthology he put together in 1942, one year into World War II: "The editor of this anthology, who took part and was wounded in the last war to end war [World War I], hates war and hates all the politicians whose mismanagement, gullibility, cupidity, selfishness and ambition brought this present war and made it inevitable. But once we have a war there is only one thing to do." The stories that follow explore some of the things one might do.

In addition to O'Brien's work about Vietnam, the chapter includes Muriel Spark's evocation of World War I in "The First Year of My Life" (p. 483), and two recent stories concerning war in the Middle East, Gavin Ford Kovite's "When Engaging Targets, Remember" (p. 497) and Phil Klay's "Redeployment" (p. 506). Two other classic war stories elsewhere in this anthology are Stephen Crane's "An Episode of War" (p. 546), about the Civil War, and Hemingway's "Soldier's Home" (p. 162), about returning from World War I. Each of these six stories offers a fresh and original approach to understanding war that goes beyond the sort of reductive assumptions produced by sentimental bombast or platitudinous declarations that war is hell.

MURIEL SPARK (1918–2006)

© Hulton-Deutsch Collection / CORBIS.

Born in Edinburgh, Scotland, Muriel Spark was a highly regarded novelist, short story writer, poet, and essayist honored as a Dame Commander of the British Empire (DBE). Although she didn't begin writing novels until she was nearly forty and a struggling single mother, she had a prolific career. Among her more than twenty-five novels are *The Comforters* (1957), *Memento Mori* (1959), *The Prime of Miss Jean Brodie* (1961), *The Mandelbaum Gate* (1965), *The Driver's Seat* (1970), *Loitering with Intent* (1981), *Symposium* (1990), and *The Finishing School* (2004). Her *Complete Short Stories* appeared in 2001 and *All the Poems* in 2004. Death and violence as well as eccentric behavior are often present in her fiction, but so are humor and irony. Spark characterized her own writing as having "a comic strain" that is also "serious." "The First Year of My Life" serves as a fine example of that self-description of her work.

The First Year of My Life   1975

I was born on the first day of the second month of the last year of the First World War, a Friday. Testimony abounds that during the first year of my life I never smiled. I was known as the baby whom nothing and no one could make smile. Everyone who knew me then has told me so. They tried very hard, singing and bouncing me up and down, jumping around, pulling faces. Many times I was told this later by my family and their friends; but, anyway, I knew it at the time.

You will shortly be hearing of that new school of psychology, or maybe you have heard of it already, which after long and far-adventuring research and experiment has established that all of the young of the human species are born omniscient. Babies, in their waking hours, know everything that is going on everywhere in the world; they can tune in to any conversation they choose, switch on to any scene. We have all experienced this power. It is only after the first year that it was brainwashed out of us; for it is demanded of us by our immediate environment that we grow to be of use to it in a practical way. Gradually, our know-all brain-cells are blacked out, although traces remain in some individuals in the form of E.S.P., and in the adults of some primitive tribes.

It is not a new theory. Poets and philosophers, as usual, have been there first. But scientific proof is now ready and to hand. Perhaps the final touches are being put to the new manifesto in some cell at Harvard University. Any day now it will be given to the world, and the world will be convinced.

Let me therefore get my word in first, because I feel pretty sure, now, about the authenticity of my remembrance of things past. My autobiography, as I very well perceived at the time, started in the very worst year that the world had ever seen so far. Apart from being born bedridden and toothless, unable to raise myself on the pillow or utter anything but farmyard squawks or police-siren wails, my bladder and my bowels totally out of control, I was further depressed by the curious behavior of the two-legged mammals around me. There were those black-dressed people, females of the species to which I appeared to belong, saying they had lost their sons. I slept a great deal. Let them go and find their sons. It was like the special pin for my nappies which my mother or some other hoverer dedicated to my care was always losing. These careless women in black lost their husbands and their brothers. Then they came to visit my mother and clucked and crowed over my cradle. I was not amused.

"Babies never really smile till they're three months old," said my mother. 5 "They're not *supposed* to smile till they're three months old."

My brother, aged six, marched up and down with a toy rifle over his shoulder:

The grand old Duke of York
He had ten thousand men;
He marched them up to the top of the hill
And he marched them down again.

And when they were up, they were up.
And when they were down, they were down.

And when they were neither down nor up
They were neither up nor down.

"Just listen to him!"
"Look at him with his rifle!"
I was about ten days old when Russia stopped fighting. I tuned in to the Czar, a prisoner, with the rest of his family, since evidently the country had put him off his throne and there had been a revolution not long before I was born. Everyone was talking about it. I tuned in to the Czar. "Nothing would ever induce me to sign the treaty of Brest-Litovsk," he said to his wife. Anyway, nobody had asked him to.

At this point I was sleeping twenty hours a day to get my strength up. And   10 from what I discerned in the other four hours of the day I knew I was going to need it. The Western Front on my frequency was sheer blood, mud, dismembered bodies, blistered crashes, hectic flashes of light in the night skies, explosions, total terror. Since it was plain I had been born into a bad moment in the history of the world, the future bothered me, unable as I was to raise my head from the pillow and as yet only twenty inches long. "I truly wish I were a fox or a bird," D. H. Lawrence was writing to somebody. Dreary old creeping Jesus. I fell asleep.

Red sheets of flame shot across the sky. It was 21st March, the fiftieth day of my life, and the German Spring Offensive had started before my morning feed. Infinite slaughter. I scowled at the scene, and made an effort to kick out. But the attempt was feeble. Furious, and impatient for some strength, I wailed for my feed. After which I stopped wailing but continued to scowl.

The grand old Duke of York
He had ten thousand men . . .

They rocked the cradle. I never heard a sillier song. Over in Berlin and Vienna the people were starving, freezing, striking, rioting and yelling in the streets. In London everyone was bustling to work and muttering that it was time the whole damn business was over.

The big people around me bared their teeth; that meant a smile, it meant they were pleased or amused. They spoke of ration cards for meat and sugar and butter.

"Where will it all end?"

I went to sleep. I woke and tuned in to Bernard Shaw who was telling someone to shut up. I switched over to Joseph Conrad who, strangely enough, was saying precisely the same thing. I still didn't think it worth a smile, although it was expected of me any day now. I got on to Turkey. Women draped in black huddled and chattered in their harems; yak-yak-yak. This was boring, so I came back to home base.

In and out came and went the women in British black. My mother's brother,   15 dressed in his uniform, came coughing. He had been poison-gassed in the trenches. "*Tout le monde à la bataille!*"° declared Marshal Foch the old swine. He was now Commander-in-Chief of the Allied Forces. My uncle coughed from deep within his lungs, never to recover but destined to return to the Front. His brass buttons gleamed in the firelight. I weighed twelve pounds by now; I stretched and kicked for exercise, seeing that I had a lifetime before me, coping with this crowd. I took six feeds a day and kept most of them down by the time the *Vindictive* was sunk in Ostend harbor, on which day I kicked with special vigor in my bath.

Tout le monde à la bataille!: Everyone to the battle!

In France the conscripted soldiers leapfrogged over the dead on the advance and littered the fields with limbs and hands, or drowned in the mud. The strongest men on all fronts were dead before I was born. Now the sentries used bodies for barricades and the fighting men were unhealthy from the start. I checked my toes and fingers, knowing I was going to need them. *The Playboy of the Western World* was playing at the Court Theatre in London, but occasionally I beamed over to the House of Commons which made me drop off gently to sleep. Generally, I preferred the Western Front where one got the true state of affairs. It was essential to know the worst, blood and explosions and all, for one had to be prepared, as the boy scouts said. Virginia Woolf yawned and reached for her diary. Really, I preferred the Western Front.

In the fifth month of my life I could raise my head from my pillow and hold it up. I could grasp the objects that were held out to me. Some of these things rattled and squawked. I gnawed on them to get my teeth started. "She hasn't smiled yet?" said the dreary old aunties. My mother, on the defensive, said I was probably one of those late smilers. On my wavelength Pablo Picasso was getting married and early in that month of July the Silver Wedding of King George V and Queen Mary was celebrated in joyous pomp at St. Paul's Cathedral. They drove through the streets of London with their children. Twenty-five years of domestic happiness. A lot of fuss and ceremonial handing over of swords went on at the Guildhall where the King and Queen received a cheque for £53,000 to dispose of for charity as they thought fit. *Tout le monde à la bataille!* Income tax in England had reached six shillings in the pound. Everyone was talking about the Silver Wedding; yak-yak-yak, and ten days later the Czar and his family, now in Siberia, were invited to descend to a little room in the basement. Crack, crack, went the guns; screams and blood all over the place, and that was the end of the Romanoffs. I flexed my muscles. "A fine healthy baby," said the doctor; which gave me much satisfaction.

Tout le monde à la bataille! That included my gassed uncle. My health had improved to the point where I was able to crawl in my playpen. Bertrand Russell was still cheerily in prison for writing something seditious about pacifism. Tuning in as usual to the Front Lines it looked as if the Germans were winning all the battles yet losing the war. And so it was. The upper-income people were upset about the income tax at six shillings to the pound. But all women over thirty got the vote. "It seems a long time to wait," said one of my drab old aunts, aged twenty-two. The speeches in the House of Commons always sent me to sleep which was why I missed, at the actual time, a certain oration by Mr. Asquith following the armistice on 11th November. Mr. Asquith was a greatly esteemed former prime minister later to be an Earl, and had been ousted by Mr. Lloyd George. I clearly heard Asquith, in private, refer to Lloyd George as "that damned Welsh goat."

The armistice was signed and I was awake for that. I pulled myself on to my feet with the aid of the bars of my cot. My teeth were coming through very nicely in my opinion, and well worth all the trouble I was put to in bringing them forth. I weighed twenty pounds. On all the world's fighting fronts the men killed in action or dead of wounds numbered 8,538,315 and the warriors wounded and maimed were 21,219,452. With these figures in mind I sat up in my high chair and banged my spoon on the table. One of my mother's black-draped friends recited:

I have a rendezvous with Death
At some disputed barricade,
When spring comes back with rustling shade
And apple blossoms fill the air —
I have a rendezvous with Death.

Most of the poets, they said, had been killed. The poetry made them dab their 20
eyes with clean white handkerchiefs.

Next February on my first birthday, there was a birthday-cake with one candle.
Lots of children and their elders. The war had been over two months and twenty-
one days. "Why doesn't she smile?" My brother was to blow out the candle. The
elders were talking about the war and the political situation. Lloyd George and
Asquith, Asquith and Lloyd George. I remembered recently having switched on to
Mr. Asquith at a private party where he had been drinking a lot. He was playing
cards and when he came to cut the cards he tried to cut a large box of matches by
mistake. On another occasion I had seen him putting his arm around a lady's shoulder in a Daimler motor car, and generally behaving towards her in a very friendly
fashion. Strangely enough she said, "If you don't stop this nonsense immediately I'll
order the chauffeur to stop and I'll get out." Mr. Asquith replied, "And pray, what
reason will you give?" Well anyway it was my feeding time.

The guests arrived for my birthday. It was so sad, said one of the black widows,
so sad about Wilfred Owen who was killed so late in the war, and she quoted from
a poem of his:

> What passing-bells for these who die as cattle?
> Only the monstrous anger of the guns.

The children were squealing and toddling around. One was sick and another
wet the floor and stood with his legs apart gaping at the puddle. All was mopped up.
I banged my spoon on the table of my high chair.

> But I've a rendezvous with Death
> At midnight in some flaming town;
> When spring trips north again this year,
> And I to my pledged word am true,
> I shall not fail that rendezvous.

More parents and children arrived. One stout man who was warming his
behind at the fire, said, "I always think those words of Asquith's after the armistice
were so apt . . . "

They brought the cake close to my high chair for me to see, with the candle 25
shining and flickering above the pink icing. "A pity she never smiles."

"She'll smile in time," my mother said, obviously upset.

"What Asquith told the House of Commons just after the war," said that stout
gentleman with his backside to the fire, " — so apt, what Asquith said. He said that
the war has cleansed and purged the world, by God! I recall his actual words: 'All
things have become new. In this great cleansing and purging it has been the privilege of our country to play her part . . .'"

That did it. I broke into a decided smile and everyone noticed it, convinced that
it was provoked by the fact that my brother had blown out the candle on the cake.
"She smiled!" my mother exclaimed. And everyone was clucking away about how
I was smiling. For good measure I crowed like a demented raven. "My baby's smiling!" said my mother.

"It was the candle on her cake," they said.

The cake be damned. Since that time I have grown to smile quite naturally, 30
like any other healthy and house-trained person, but when I really mean a smile,

deeply felt from the core, then to all intents and purposes it comes in response to the words uttered in the House of Commons after the First World War by the distinguished, the immaculately dressed and the late Mr. Asquith.

CONSIDERATIONS FOR CRITICAL THINKING AND WRITING

1. FIRST RESPONSE. Discuss the story's point of view and its effect on you.
2. What is the significance of the settings? Why are they crucial to the plot?
3. What finally causes the baby to smile?
4. How does the use of language serve to characterize the narrator? Choose a paragraph in which the style seems to represent the narrator's sensibilities, and analyze the way in which diction and phrasing reveal tone.
5. Research one of the historical allusions to actual events, writers, and politicians that you are unfamiliar with in the story and discuss how it contributes to your understanding of the themes.
6. Stories about the horrors of war are not infrequent in literature. How does Spark avoid being predictable, clichéd, or sentimental?
7. Characterize the humor in the story. What adjectives would you employ to describe it?

CONNECTIONS TO OTHER SELECTIONS

1. Use the historical context as a means of explaining Krebs's behavior in Ernest Hemingway's "Soldier's Home" (p. 162).
2. Write an essay comparing the themes of Spark's story with those in E. E. Cummings's "next to of course god america i" (p. 718) and Wilfred Owen's "Dulce et Decorum Est" (p. 681).

TIM O'BRIEN (B. 1946)

Born in Austin, Minnesota, Tim O'Brien was educated at Macalester College and Harvard University. He was drafted to serve in the Vietnam War and received a Purple Heart. His work is heavily influenced by his service in the war. His first book, *If I Die in a Combat Zone, Box Me Up and Ship Me Home* (1973), is a blend of fiction and actual experiences during his tour of duty. *Going after Cacciato,* judged by many critics to be the best work of American fiction about the Vietnam War, won the National Book Award in 1978. He has also published five other novels, *Northern Lights* (1974), *The Nuclear*

© Marion Ettlinger.

Age (1985), *In the Lake of the Woods* (1994), *Tomcat in Love* (1998), and *July, July* (2002). "How to Tell a True War Story" is from a collection of interrelated stories titled *The Things They Carried* (1990). Originally published in *Esquire,* this story is at once grotesque and beautiful in its attempt to be true to experience.

How to Tell a True War Story 1987

This is true.

I had a buddy in Vietnam. His name was Bob Kiley, but everybody called him Rat.

A friend of his gets killed, so about a week later Rat sits down and writes a letter to the guy's sister. Rat tells her what a great brother she had, how strack° the guy was, a number one pal and comrade. A real soldier's soldier, Rat says. Then he tells a few stories to make the point, how her brother would always volunteer for stuff nobody else would volunteer for in a million years, danger-ous stuff, like doing recon° or going out on these really badass night patrols. Stainless steel balls, Rat tells her. The guy was a little crazy, for sure, but crazy in a good way, a real daredevil, because he liked the challenge of it, he liked testing himself, just man against gook. A great, great guy, Rat says.

Anyway, it's a terrific letter, very personal and touching. Rat almost bawls writ-ing it. He gets all teary telling about the good times they had together, how her brother made the war seem almost fun, always raising hell and lighting up villes° and bringing smoke to bear every which way. A great sense of humor, too. Like the time at this river when he went fishing with a whole damn crate of hand grenades. Probably the funniest thing in world history, Rat says, all that gore, about twenty zillion dead gook fish. Her brother, he had the right attitude. He knew how to have a good time. On Halloween, this real hot spooky night, the dude paints up his body all different colors and puts on this weird mask and goes out on ambush almost stark naked, just boots and balls and an M-16. A tremendous human being, Rat says. Pretty nutso sometimes, but you could trust him with your life.

And then the letter gets very sad and serious. Rat pours his heart out. He says 5 he loved the guy. He says the guy was his best friend in the world. They were like soul mates, he says, like twins or something, they had a whole lot in common. He tells the guy's sister he'll look her up when the war's over.

So what happens?

Rat mails the letter. He waits two months. The dumb cooze never writes back.

A true war story is never moral. It does not instruct, nor encourage virtue, nor sug-gest models of proper human behavior, nor restrain men from doing the things they have always done. If a story seems moral, do not believe it. If at the end of a war story you feel uplifted, or if you feel that some small bit of rectitude has been salvaged from the larger waste, then you have been made the victim of a very old and terrible lie. There is no rectitude whatsoever. There is no virtue. As a first rule of thumb, therefore, you can tell a true war story by its absolute and uncompromis-ing allegiance to obscenity and evil. Listen to Rat Kiley. *Cooze,* he says. He does not say *bitch.* He certainly does not say *woman,* or *girl.* He says *cooze.* Then he spits and stares. He's nineteen years old—it's too much for him—so he looks at you with those big gentle killer eyes and says *cooze,* because his friend is dead, and because it's so incredibly sad and true: she never wrote back.

You can tell a true war story if it embarrasses you. If you don't care for obscenity, you don't care for the truth; if you don't care for the truth, watch how you vote. Send guys to war, they come home talking dirty.

strack: A strict military appearance.
doing recon: Reconnaissance, or exploratory survey of enemy territory.
villes: Villages.

Listen to Rat: "Jesus Christ, man, I write this beautiful fucking letter, I slave 10 over it, and what happens? The dumb cooze never writes back."

The dead guy's name was Curt Lemon. What happened was, we crossed a muddy river and marched west into the mountains, and on the third day we took a break along a trail junction in deep jungle. Right away, Lemon and Rat Kiley started goofing off. They didn't understand about the spookiness. They were kids; they just didn't know. A nature hike, they thought, not even a war, so they went off into the shade of some giant trees — quadruple canopy, no sunlight at all — and they were giggling and calling each other motherfucker and playing a silly game they'd invented. The game involved smoke grenades, which were harmless unless you did stupid things, and what they did was pull out the pin and stand a few feet apart and play catch under the shade of those huge trees. Whoever chickened out was a motherfucker. And if nobody chickened out, the grenade would make a light popping sound and they'd be covered with smoke and they'd laugh and dance around and then do it again.

It's all exactly true.

It happened nearly twenty years ago, but I still remember that trail junction and the giant trees and a soft dripping sound somewhere beyond the trees. I remember the smell of moss. Up in the canopy there were tiny white blossoms, but no sunlight at all, and I remember the shadows spreading out under the trees where Lemon and Rat Kiley were playing catch with smoke grenades. Mitchell Sanders sat flipping his yo-yo. Norman Bowker and Kiowa and Dave Jensen were dozing, or half-dozing, and all around us were those ragged green mountains.

Except for the laughter things were quiet.

At one point, I remember, Mitchell Sanders turned and looked at me, not quite 15 nodding, then after a while he rolled up his yo-yo and moved away.

It's hard to tell what happened next.

They were just goofing. There was a noise, I suppose, which must've been the detonator, so I glanced behind me and watched Lemon step from the shade into bright sunlight. His face was suddenly brown and shining. A handsome kid, really. Sharp gray eyes, lean and narrow-waisted, and when he died it was almost beautiful, the way the sunlight came around him and lifted him up and sucked him high into a tree full of moss and vines and white blossoms.

In any war story, but especially a true one, it's difficult to separate what happened from what seemed to happen. What seems to happen becomes its own happening and has to be told that way. The angles of vision are skewed. When a booby trap explodes, you close your eyes and duck and float outside yourself. When a guy dies, like Lemon, you look away and then look back for a moment and then look away again. The pictures get jumbled; you tend to miss a lot. And then afterward, when you go to tell about it, there is always that surreal seemingness, which makes the story seem untrue, but which in fact represents the hard and exact truth as it seemed.

In many cases a true war story cannot be believed. If you believe it, be skeptical. It's a question of credibility. Often the crazy stuff is true and the normal stuff isn't because the normal stuff is necessary to make you believe the truly incredible craziness.

In other cases you can't even tell a true war story. Sometimes it's just 20 beyond telling.

I heard this one, for example, from Mitchell Sanders. It was near dusk and we were sitting at my foxhole along a wide, muddy river north of Quang Ngai. I remember how peaceful the twilight was. A deep pinkish red spilled out on the river, which moved without sound, and in the morning we would cross the river and march west into the mountains. The occasion was right for a good story.

"God's truth," Mitchell Sanders said. "A six-man patrol goes up into the mountains on a basic listening-post operation. The idea's to spend a week up there, just lie low and listen for enemy movement. They've got a radio along, so if they hear anything suspicious — anything — they're supposed to call in artillery or gunships, whatever it takes. Otherwise they keep strict field discipline. Absolute silence. They just listen."

He glanced at me to make sure I had the scenario. He was playing with his yo-yo, making it dance with short, tight little strokes of the wrist.

His face was blank in the dusk.

"We're talking hardass LP.° These six guys, they don't say boo for a solid week. 25 They don't got tongues. *All* ears."

"Right," I said.

"Understand me?"

"Invisible."

Sanders nodded.

"Affirm," he said. "Invisible. So what happens is, these guys get themselves 30 deep in the bush, all camouflaged up, and they lie down and wait and that's all they do, nothing else, they lie there for seven straight days and just listen. And man, I'll tell you — it's spooky. This is mountains. You don't *know* spooky till you been there. Jungle, sort of, except it's way up in the clouds and there's always this fog — like rain, except it's not raining — everything's all wet and swirly and tangled up and you can't see jack, you can't find your own pecker to piss with. Like you don't even have a body. Serious spooky. You just go with the vapors — the fog sort of takes you in. . . . And the sounds, man. The sounds carry forever. You hear shit nobody should *ever* hear."

Sanders was quiet for a second, just working the yo-yo, then he smiled at me. "So, after a couple days the guys start hearing this real soft, kind of wacked-out music. Weird echoes and stuff. Like a radio or something, but it's not a radio, it's this strange gook music that comes right out of the rocks. Faraway, sort of, but right up close, too. They try to ignore it. But it's a listening post, right? So they listen. And every night they keep hearing this crazyass gook concert. All kinds of chimes and xylophones. I mean, this is wilderness — no way, it can't be real — but there it *is*, like the mountains are tuned in to Radio Fucking Hanoi. Naturally they get nervous. One guy sticks Juicy Fruit in his ears. Another guy almost flips. Thing is, though, they can't report music. They can't get on the horn and call back to base and say, 'Hey, listen, we need some firepower, we got to blow away this weirdo gook rock band.' They can't do that. It wouldn't go down. So they lie there in the fog and keep their mouths shut. And what makes it extra bad, see, is the poor dudes can't horse around like normal. Can't joke it away. Can't even talk to each other except maybe in whispers, all hush-hush, and that just revs up the willies. All they do is listen."

Again there was some silence as Mitchell Sanders looked out on the river. The dark was coming on hard now, and off to the west I could see the mountains rising in silhouette, all the mysteries and unknowns.

LP: Listening post.

"This next part," Sanders said quietly, "you won't believe."

"Probably not," I said.

"You won't. And you know why?"

"Why?"

35

He gave me a tired smile. "Because it happened. Because every word is absolutely dead-on true."

Sanders made a little sound in his throat, like a sigh, as if to say he didn't care if I believed it or not. But he did care. He wanted me to believe, I could tell. He seemed sad, in a way.

"These six guys, they're pretty fried out by now, and one night they start hearing voices. Like at a cocktail party. That's what it sounds like, this big swank gook cocktail party somewhere out there in the fog. Music and chitchat and stuff. It's crazy, I know, but they hear the champagne corks. They hear the actual martini glasses. Real hoity-toity, all very civilized, except this isn't civilization. This is Nam.

"Anyway, the guys try to be cool. They just lie there and groove, but after 40 a while they start hearing—you won't believe this—they hear chamber music. They hear violins and shit. They hear this terrific mama-san soprano. Then after a while they hear gook opera and a glee club and the Haiphong Boys Choir and a barbershop quartet and all kinds of weird chanting and Buddha-Buddha stuff. The whole time, in the background, there's still that cocktail party going on. All these different voices. Not human voices, though. Because it's the mountains. Follow me? The rock—it's *talking*. And the fog, too, and the grass and the goddamn mongooses. Everything talks. The trees talk politics, the monkeys talk religion. The whole country. Vietnam, the place talks.

"The guys can't cope. They lose it. They get on the radio and report enemy movement—a whole army, they say—and they order up the firepower. They get arty° and gunships. They call in air strikes. And I'll tell you, they fuckin' crash that cocktail party. All night long, they just smoke those mountains. They make jungle juice. They blow away trees and glee clubs and whatever else there is to blow away. Scorch time. They walk napalm up and down the ridges. They bring in the Cobras and F-4s, they use Willie Peter and HE° and incendiaries. It's all fire. They make those mountains burn.

"Around dawn things finally get quiet. Like you never even *heard* quiet before. One of those real thick, real misty days—just clouds and fog, they're off in this special zone—and the mountains are absolutely dead-flat silent. Like Brigadoon°—pure vapor, you know? Everything's all sucked up inside the fog. Not a single sound, except they still *hear* it.

"So they pack up and start humping. They head down the mountain, back to base camp, and when they get there they don't say diddly. They don't talk. Not a word, like they're deaf and dumb. Later on this fat bird colonel comes up and asks what the hell happened out there. What'd they hear? Why all the ordnance? The man's ragged out, he gets down tight on their case. I mean, they spent six trillion dollars on firepower, and this fatass colonel wants answers, he wants to know what the fuckin' story is.

"But the guys don't say zip. They just look at him for a while, sort of funny-like, sort of amazed, and the whole war is right there in that stare. It says everything you

---

arty: Artillery.

Willie Peter and HE: White phosphorus, an incendiary substance, and high explosives.

Brigadoon: A fictional village in Scotland that appears only once every one hundred years; subject of a popular American musical (1947).

can't ever say. It says, man, you got *wax* in your ears. It says, poor bastard, you'll never know—wrong frequency—you don't *even* want to hear this. Then they salute the fucker and walk away, because certain stories you don't ever tell."

You can tell a true war story by the way it never seems to end. Not then, not ever. 45 Not when Mitchell Sanders stood up and moved off into the dark.

It all happened.

Even now I remember that yo-yo. In a way, I suppose, you had to be there, you had to hear it, but I could tell how desperately Sanders wanted me to believe him, his frustration at not quite getting the details right, not quite pinning down the final and definitive truth.

And I remember sitting at my foxhole that night, watching the shadows of Quang Ngai, thinking about the coming day and how we would cross the river and march west into the mountains, all the ways I might die, all the things I did not understand.

Late in the night Mitchell Sanders touched my shoulder.

"Just came to me," he whispered. "The moral, I mean. Nobody listens. Nobody 50 hears nothing. Like that fatass colonel. The politicians, all the civilian types, what they need is to go out on LP. The vapors, man. Trees and rocks—you got to *listen* to your enemy."

And then again, in the morning, Sanders came up to me. The platoon was preparing to move out, checking weapons, going through all the little rituals that preceded a day's march. Already the lead squad had crossed the river and was filing off toward the west.

"I got a confession to make," Sanders said. "Last night, man, I had to make up a few things."

"I know that."

"The glee club. There wasn't any glee club."

"Right." 55

"No opera."

"Forget it, I understand."

"Yeah, but listen, it's still true. Those six guys, they heard wicked sound out there. They heard sound you just plain won't believe."

Sanders pulled on his rucksack, closed his eyes for a moment, then almost smiled at me.

I knew what was coming but I beat him to it. 60

"All right," I said, "what's the moral?"

"Forget it."

"No, go ahead."

For a long while he was quiet, looking away, and the silence kept stretching out until it was almost embarrassing. Then he shrugged and gave me a stare that lasted all day.

"Hear that quiet, man?" he said. "There's your moral." 65

In a true war story, if there's a moral at all, it's like the thread that makes the cloth. You can't tease it out. You can't extract the meaning without unraveling the deeper meaning. And in the end, really, there's nothing much to say about a true war story, except maybe "Oh."

True war stories do not generalize. They do not indulge in abstraction or analysis.

For example: War is hell. As a moral declaration the old truism seems perfectly true, and yet because it abstracts, because it generalizes, I can't believe it with my stomach. Nothing turns inside.

It comes down to gut instinct. A true war story, if truly told, makes the stomach believe.

This one does it for me. I've told it before — many times, many versions — but 70
here's what actually happened.

We crossed the river and marched west into the mountains. On the third day, Curt Lemon stepped on a booby-trapped 105 round. He was playing catch with Rat Kiley, laughing, and then he was dead. The trees were thick; it took nearly an hour to cut an LZ for the dustoff.°

Later, higher in the mountains, we came across a baby VC° water buffalo. What it was doing there I don't know — no farms or paddies — but we chased it down and got a rope around it and led it along to a deserted village where we set for the night. After supper Rat Kiley went over and stroked its nose.

He opened up a can of C rations, pork and beans, but the baby buffalo wasn't interested.

Rat shrugged.

He stepped back and shot it through the right front knee. The animal did not make 75
a sound. It went down hard, then got up again, and Rat took careful aim and shot off an ear. He shot it in the hindquarters and in the little hump at its back. He shot it twice in the flanks. It wasn't to kill; it was just to hurt. He put the rifle muzzle up against the mouth and shot the mouth away. Nobody said much. The whole platoon stood there watching, feeling all kinds of things, but there wasn't a great deal of pity for the baby water buffalo. Lemon was dead. Rat Kiley had lost his best friend in the world. Later in the week he would write a long personal letter to the guy's sister, who would not write back, but for now it was a question of pain. He shot off the tail. He shot away chunks of meat below the ribs. All around us there was the smell of smoke and filth, and deep greenery, and the evening was humid and very hot. Rat went to automatic. He shot randomly, almost casually, quick little spurts in the belly and butt. Then he reloaded, squatted down, and shot it in the left front knee. Again the animal fell hard and tried to get up, but this time it couldn't quite make it. It wobbled and went down sideways. Rat shot it in the nose. He bent forward and whispered something, as if talking to a pet, then he shot it in the throat. All the while the baby buffalo was silent, or almost silent, just a light bubbling sound where the nose had been. It lay very still. Nothing moved except the eyes, which were enormous, the pupils shiny black and dumb.

Rat Kiley was crying. He tried to say something, but then cradled his rifle and went off by himself.

The rest of us stood in a ragged circle around the baby buffalo. For a time no one spoke. We had witnessed something essential, something brand-new and profound, a piece of the world so startling there was not yet a name for it.

Somebody kicked the baby buffalo.

It was still alive, though just barely, just in the eyes.

"Amazing," Dave Jensen said. "My whole life, I never seen anything like it." 80
"Never?"

LZ for the dustoff: Landing zone for a helicopter evacuation of a casualty.
VC: Vietcong (North Vietnamese).

"Not hardly. Not once."

Kiowa and Mitchell Sanders picked up the baby buffalo. They hauled it across the open square, hoisted it up, and dumped it in the village well.

Afterward, we sat waiting for Rat to get himself together.

"Amazing," Dave Jensen kept saying.　　　　　　　　　　　　　　　　　　　　85

"For sure."

"A new wrinkle. I never seen it before."

Mitchell Sanders took out his yo-yo.

"Well, that's Nam," he said. "Garden of Evil. Over here, man, every sin's real fresh and original."

How do you generalize?　　　　　　　　　　　　　　　　　　　　　　　　　90

War is hell, but that's not the half of it, because war is also mystery and terror and adventure and courage and discovery and holiness and pity and despair and longing and love. War is nasty; war is fun. War is thrilling; war is drudgery. War makes you a man; war makes you dead.

The truths are contradictory. It can be argued, for instance, that war is grotesque. But in truth war is also beauty. For all its horror, you can't help but gape at the awful majesty of combat. You stare out at tracer rounds unwinding through the dark like brilliant red ribbons. You crouch in ambush as a cool, impassive moon rises over the nighttime paddies. You admire the fluid symmetries of troops on the move, the harmonies of sound and shape and proportion, the great sheets of metal-fire streaming down from a gunship, the illumination rounds, the white phosphorous, the purply black glow of napalm, the rocket's red glare. It's not pretty, exactly. It's astonishing. It fills the eye. It commands you. You hate it, yes, but your eyes do not. Like a killer forest fire, like cancer under a microscope, any battle or bombing raid or artillery barrage has the aesthetic purity of absolute moral indifference — a powerful, implacable beauty — and a true war story will tell the truth about this, though the truth is ugly.

To generalize about war is like generalizing about peace. Almost everything is true. Almost nothing is true. At its core, perhaps, war is just another name for death, and yet any soldier will tell you, if he tells the truth, that proximity to death brings with it a corresponding proximity to life. After a fire fight, there is always the immense pleasure of aliveness. The trees are alive. The grass, the soil — everything. All around you things are purely living, and you among them, and the aliveness makes you tremble. You feel an intense, out-of-the-skin awareness of your living self — your truest self, the human being you want to be and then become by the force of wanting it. In the midst of evil you want to be a good man. You want decency. You want justice and courtesy and human concord, things you never knew you wanted. There is a kind of largeness to it; a kind of godliness. Though it's odd, you're never more alive than when you're almost dead. You recognize what's valuable. Freshly, as if for the first time, you love what's best in yourself and in the world, all that might be lost. At the hour of dusk you sit at your foxhole and look out on a wide river turning pinkish red, and at the mountains beyond, and although in the morning you must cross the river and go into the mountains and do terrible things and maybe die, even so, you find yourself studying the fine colors on the river, you feel wonder and awe at the setting of the sun, and you are filled with a hard, aching love for how the world could be and always should be, but now is not.

Mitchell Sanders was right. For the common soldier, at least, war has the feel — the spiritual texture — of a great ghostly fog, thick and permanent. There is no clarity. Everything swirls. The old rules are no longer binding, the old truths no longer true. Right spills over into wrong. Order blends into chaos, love into hate, ugliness into beauty, law into anarchy, civility into savagery. The vapors suck you in. You can't tell where you are, or why you're there, and the only certainty is absolute ambiguity.

In war you lose your sense of the definite, hence your sense of truth itself, and 95 therefore it's safe to say that in a true war story nothing much is ever very true.

Often in a true war story there is not even a point, or else the point doesn't hit you until twenty years later, in your sleep, and you wake up and shake your wife and start telling the story to her, except when you get to the end you've forgotten the point again. And then for a long time you lie there watching the story happen in your head. You listen to your wife's breathing. The war's over. You close your eyes. You smile and think, Christ, what's the *point?*

This one wakes me up.

In the mountains that day, I watched Lemon turn sideways. He laughed and said something to Rat Kiley. Then he took a peculiar half step, moving from shade into bright sunlight, and the booby-trapped 105 round blew him into a tree. The parts were just hanging there, so Norman Bowker and I were ordered to shinny up and peel him off. I remember the white bone of an arm. I remember pieces of skin and something wet and yellow that must've been the intestines. The gore was horrible, and stays with me, but what wakes me up twenty years later is Norman Bowker singing "Lemon Tree" as we threw down the parts.

You can tell a true war story by the questions you ask. Somebody tells a story, let's say, and afterward you ask, "Is it true?" and if the answer matters, you've got your answer.

For example, we've all heard this one. Four guys go down a trail. A grenade 100 sails out. One guy jumps on it and takes the blast and saves his three buddies.

Is it true?

The answer matters.

You'd feel cheated if it never happened. Without the grounding reality, it's just a trite bit of puffery, pure Hollywood, untrue in the way all such stories are untrue. Yet even if it did happen — and maybe it did, anything's possible — even then you know it can't be true, because a true war story does not depend upon that kind of truth. Happeningness is irrelevant. A thing may happen and be a total lie; another thing may not happen and be truer than the truth. For example: four guys go down a trail. A grenade sails out. One guy jumps on it and takes the blast, but it's a killer grenade and everybody dies anyway. Before they die, though, one of the dead guys says, "The fuck you do *that* for?" and the jumper says, "Story of my life, man," and the other guy starts to smile but he's dead.

That's a true story that never happened.

Twenty years later, I can still see the sunlight on Lemon's face. I can see him turn- 105 ing, looking back at Rat Kiley, then he laughed and took that curious half step from shade into sunlight, his face suddenly brown and shining, and when his foot touched down, in that instant, he must've thought it was the sunlight that was killing him. It was not the sunlight. It was a rigged 105 round. But if I could ever get the story right, how the sun seemed to gather around him and pick him up and lift him into a tree, if I could somehow recreate the fatal whiteness of that light, the quick glare, the obvious cause and effect, then you would believe the last thing Lemon believed, which for him must've been the final truth.

Now and then, when I tell this story, someone will come up to me afterward and say she liked it. It's always a woman. Usually it's an older woman of kindly temperament and humane politics. She'll explain that as a rule she hates war stories, she can't understand why people want to wallow in blood and gore. But this one she liked. Sometimes, even, there are little tears. What I should do, she'll say, is put it all behind me. Find new stories to tell.

I won't say it but I'll think it.

I'll picture Rat Kiley's face, his grief, and I'll think, *You dumb cooze.*

Because she wasn't listening.

It wasn't a war story. It was a love story. It was a ghost story. 110

But you can't say that. All you can do is tell it one more time, patiently, adding and subtracting, making up a few things to get at the real truth. No Mitchell Sanders, you tell her. No Lemon, no Rat Kiley. And it didn't happen in the mountains, it happened in this little village on the Batangan Peninsula, and it was raining like crazy, and one night a guy named Stink Harris woke up screaming with a leech on his tongue. You can tell a true war story if you just keep on telling it.

In the end, of course, a true war story is never about war. It's about the special way that dawn spreads out on a river when you know you must cross the river and march into the mountains and do things you are afraid to do. It's about love and memory. It's about sorrow. It's about sisters who never write back and people who never listen.

CONSIDERATIONS FOR CRITICAL THINKING AND WRITING

1. FIRST RESPONSE. What implicit problem is created about the story by its first line, "This is true"? How is the notion of "truth" problematized throughout the story and subjected to irony?

2. Why is Rat Kiley so upset over Curt Lemon's sister's not writing back?

3. How are you affected by the descriptions of Curt Lemon being blown up in paragraphs 17, 98, and 105?

4. Analyze the story told about the six-man patrol in paragraphs 19–65. How is this story relevant to the rest of the plot?

5. What emotions did you feel as you read about the shooting of the water buffalo? How does paragraph 75 achieve these effects?

6. Explain what you think O'Brien means when he writes "After a fire fight, there is always the immense pleasure of aliveness" (para. 93).

7. Trace the narrator's comments about what constitutes a true war story. What do you think these competing and contradictory ideas finally add up to?

8. Characterize the narrator. Why must he repeatedly "keep on telling" his war story?

9. Consider O'Brien's use of profanity and violence in this story. Do you think they are essential or merely sensational?

10. CRITICAL STRATEGIES. Read the discussion concerning historical criticism (pp. 1651–55) in Chapter 51, "Critical Strategies for Reading," and

research American protests and reactions to the war in Vietnam. How are these responses relevant to O'Brien's story, particularly paragraphs 1–10 and 106–11?

CONNECTIONS TO OTHER SELECTIONS

1. Imagine Krebs from Ernest Hemingway's "Soldier's Home" (p. 162) writing a letter home recommending "How to Tell a True War Story" to his parents. Write that letter from Krebs's point of view.

2. How does the treatment of violence in O'Brien's story compare with that in Andre Dubus's "Killings" (p. 89)? Write an essay that points to specific descriptions and explains the function of the violence in each story.

3. "In the end, of course," O'Brien writes, "a true war story is never about war" (para. 112). How might this idea be applied to Stephen Crane's short story "An Episode of War" (p. 546)?

GAVIN FORD KOVITE (B. 1981)

Gavin Ford Kovite led an infantry platoon in Iraq from 2004 to 2005. He attended New York University Law School and has served as an army lawyer. His writing career began with the NYU Veterans Writing Workshop, where his work was published in its journal *Nine Lives*. With Christopher Robinson, he has cowritten a novel, *War of the Encyclopaedists* (2015), that focuses on two friends whose lives go in different directions after college, one fighting in Iraq, the other studying at a Boston graduate school. "When Engaging Targets, Remember" appeared in *Fire and Forget* (2013), an anthology of war fiction written by veterans. In the story Kovite employs a choose-your-own-adventure narrative point of view to achieve powerful effects.

When Engaging Targets, Remember   2013

(1) On the Road

You are a United States infantryman. An Imperial Grunt. The emblem of American militarism. Your rank is: Specialist. It is late 2004, and you are behind a machine gun in al-Anbar, Iraq, swathed in bulky armor and expensive gear and sitting — almost reclining — in a wide nylon sling slung across the roof of a Humvee that's as cartoonishly bulky as you. Your job as a Humvee gunner is to provide rear security for a convoy of fuel tankers that's currently wending its way from the Baghdad airport to a Forward Operating Base one hundred miles east.

You're no fool; you're a college kid. You were just about to declare a poli-sci major at UC Riverside when you got the letter ordering you to active duty for Iraq, along with the rest of your California National Guard brigade. You're smart, and you get the joke. The fuel will be used to fill the vehicles and generators of the combat and combat support units at the base, whose main task is to secure the area around Kut, the security of which presumably increases the security of the country and then the region, which helps to secure the world in general and the United

States in particular. It's tough to make a direct connection between what you're doing right now and the peace and prosperity of your hometown of Riverside, but that's no surprise because global security is all about action that's collective as well as synergistic, as far as you understand it.

As you think this, you reach into one of the nylon pouches of your vest. You pull out a Met-RX Big 100 protein bar and unwrap it with your teeth while your left hand rests on the handle of the Browning .50 caliber machine gun mounted to a swivel in front of you. The air smells of dust and burning garbage. The sky is eggshell white with brown and black highlights. You're about to see some action, although you don't know it quite yet.

At the front of your field of vision is the enormous black barrel of an M2 .50 caliber machine gun, a weapon that's longer than you are tall and that shoots rounds the size of small dildos. In the middle range of your vision, fifty meters away, is a pack of cars following your convoy. Any one of them could be a suicide car bomb, but they're probably just average Joes, day-to-day Iraqis trying to get somewhere. The reason they're all fifty meters away is that there's a large, white, bilingual sign affixed to your Humvee's rear that reads "US CONVOY DO NOT APPROACH WITHIN 50 METERS OR YOU WILL BE FIRED UPON," the Operation Iraqi Freedom version of the good old "IF YOU CAN READ THIS YOU'RE DRIVING TOO CLOSE." And of course, there's you, crouched in the gunner's hatch menacing everyone with the .50 cal.

It doesn't always work. Some hajjis are weirdly — almost nihilistically, you think — unresponsive to menacing. You wonder if nihilistic is the right word to use. Your PHIL 101 Intro to Western Philosophy course went over nihilism last semester, but thanks to the letter you got sending you here, you never finished it. Your PHIL 101 professor was nice about you leaving midway through, although he kept on saying he was, "So, so sorry," as if someone you loved had contracted a terminal illness. 5

Your thoughts drift. You know the importance of vigilance and constant scanning, but you are perhaps too imaginative for sentry work or rolling down Baghdad highways day in and day out. Consider: there is a large crater in the intersection outside your unit's walled-off living area on the edge of the Green Zone where a silver BMW exploded, beheading rush-hour commuters and landing a guy from 1st Cavalry Division in the ICU with "polytrauma," which is the new buzzword for injuries sustained in the kind of blast that would kill anyone lacking 100 pounds of Kevlar and ceramic armor and twenty-first-century surgical care. Thanks to a recent mop-up operation, you can now mentally produce a photorealistic image of what your own body would look like after such an explosion, and this image comes unbidden to your mind during long stretches of highway.

The protein bar is incredibly dry and needs to be washed down frequently with rubbery-tasting water from the hose of your CamelBak. You think about going back to UC Riverside and enrolling in ENGL 302 with no lower jaw or tongue, having to write out your conversation or type through some text-to-speech thing like a twenty-year-old Stephen Hawking, your old roommates looking at you with kindness and awkwardness and pity, no one really wanting to talk to you in that condition, and you not wanting to talk to anyone either. Sex with the Riverside coeds would be out of the question, with you looking like either the Phantom of the Opera or that Marine in the *New York Times Magazine* with his face and scalp totally burned off and scarred over, a too-scary-for-PG version of the guy in *Goonies*. And that's just what could happen to your head. A bomb could leave you dickless and castrated too, which would probably take at least one leg off pretty close, which would lead the few girls you have gotten with to suspect that it's worse than it looks and to have nightmares of what's become of you "down there." Your buddies wouldn't be able to take you out for drinks without acknowledging it and thinking about it, the worst thing that could happen to a guy, your catheter filling your bag with fluid after a few Heinekens and one of your friends, most of whom front like they're assholes but are actually really nice guys, changing it out for you, trying to decide whether wisecracking about it or refraining from wisecracking would make you feel worse.

You're not a worrywart, though. You cut that train of thought off and start mouthing Jay-Z lyrics while swiveling the Fifty around and aiming at cars and windows and the rooftops of the drab apartment buildings that line the highways. One interesting tidbit you heard from the 3rd Infantry Division troops, whom you relieved, is that some gunners have been ordered to crouch way down in the hatch, like too far down to really be able to see anything, since the main danger is IEDs, which you won't see anyway, but which will take your head off in a close blast or in a rollover if you're standing up tall and trying to scan this way and that.

In your (albeit limited) army experience, this is the kind of decision that sergeants or officers make for you, but you haven't been instructed either way, probably because your sergeants and officers, being new here themselves, either haven't thought of it or aren't sure whether it's wise. You figure you're probably justified in going either way, even though you're the rear security and are supposed to be keeping an eye out for threats coming from the rear of the convoy. You can crouch down low, popping up for a quick scan every fifteen or twenty seconds. You might miss the telltale lumps of a roadside IED that didn't detonate, but this also means you'd avoid taking the blast in your face if it does. All in all it seems prudent. On the other hand, there are things you know you don't know and things you don't know you don't know. And as long as you're crouched down, you're not watching the convoy's six.

DO YOU: 10
Crouch down in the turret and pop up to scan every twenty seconds? TURN TO SECTION (2).
Remain standing and scanning as before? TURN TO SECTION (3).

(2) Turtle Down

Here's the worst situation: after having mulled over keeping your head down, you decide to keep it up, and then you get hit with an IED, which burns your face off or gives you the kind of brain trauma that disables you for the rest of your life but doesn't erase the memory of mulling over and then failing to take a simple precaution that could have saved you. You feel around for a comfortable sitting position and then settle into it, figuring out by trial and error the best method for hauling your heavily armored self up at twenty-second intervals for a quick scan. Your armor and equipment increase your body weight by about seventy pounds, and human nature and muscle fatigue being what they are, the twenty-second intervals become more like thirty seconds as the hours wear on. The convoy is keeping speed and making good time. The traffic is staying fifty meters away from you. You pass a billboard advertising Mr. Brown Canned Iced Coffee, which has actually become a personal favorite and is sold by the case by Ali at a kiosk he set up at the outskirts of your Forward Operating Base. Body armor is uncomfortable to move around in, but the immobility (along with the drone of the engine) can be somewhat sleep inducing in the heat, hence the regular drinking of Mr. Browns. The cartoon Mr. Brown himself looks jolly and avuncular. Popping back down into a sitting position on the turret's swinging foot-sling, you dig a strawberry-yogurt-flavored protein bar (that you've added for snack purposes) out of the extra ammo pouch on your flak vest and take a bite. Guardo, the medic, is sitting in the right rear seat looking troglodytic and pudgy-faced in his helmet and armor. Your boots have been resting on his trauma bag since you've assumed your new, protected position. Guardo does not seem to object to this. He holds a fist up, and you give it a bump.

The explosion sounds like a huge beam of hardwood snapping in half. The driver and your squad leader, Staff Sergeant Boyle, call out, "IED." Your gun truck runs over a large pothole almost immediately, smacking your neck painfully against the edge of the turret and pushing your Kevlar down over your eyes. Your platoon leader is yelling something indecipherable on the radio, and Guardo is yanking at the bag under your feet. You hear some of the gunners farther up in the column open fire. You untangle your feet and yank yourself back up behind the Fifty.

You are surprised to see a black BMW sedan passing you on the left at a high 15 rate of speed and headed straight for the fuel trucks about fifty meters up in the middle of the convoy. Your Rules of Engagement (ROE) card, which you are required to keep in your left chest pocket at all times, reads:

THESE RULES APPLY AT ALL TIMES AND ON ALL OPERATIONS

1. **Positive Identification (PID) is required prior to engagement.** PID is a reasonable certainty that the target you are engaging is exhibiting hostile intent or committing a hostile act. Once you have PID, you may use escalated force up to and including deadly force, to eliminate the threat.

2. **When engaging targets, remember:**
   a. Escalation of force. Always use the minimum amount of force necessary to eliminate the threat. If time and circumstances permit, use the following degrees of force when responding to hostile act or hostile intent:

   - Shout verbal warnings to halt.
   - Show your weapon and demonstrate intent to use it.
   - Shoot a warning shot (vehicles only).
   - Shoot a disabling shot (vehicles only).
   - Shoot to eliminate target.

In bold is the caveat:

NOTHING ON THIS CARD PREVENTS YOU FROM USING ALL FORCE NECESSARY TO DEFEND YOURSELF.

By the time you get the barrel swung around, the BMW has passed you. The time for warning or disabling shots is over, given that a shot going into the engine block at this angle would also go through the driver's head. You either engage the BMW or let it drive right into the middle of the convoy.

DO YOU:

Fire on the BMW? TURN TO (5).

Let the BMW pass into the convoy? TURN TO (6).   20

(3) Look Out

You'll try and find a way to broach the subject with your squad leader tomorrow in a way that doesn't sound like you're just being a pussy. For now, your job is rear security and you have to be scanning at all times. You stay standing and facing the rear like a good trooper, only every once in a while allowing half of your mind to slip into a daydream about mom's kitchen or the Riverside coeds, and you wonder if thinking about whether you're a wartime cliché prevents you from being a wartime cliché.

About an hour after you made your decision to stand, an IED goes off at the front of the column. You can feel it as well as hear it: a pocket of stiffened air busting by with a sound like an enormous firecracker.* As soon as the IED goes off, your truck swerves slightly and hits a pothole, jolting you against the rear of the turret and pushing your Kevlar forward over your eyes. You push it back up and see that a black BMW about fifty meters away has floored it in the left lane and looks like it's going to try to pass you. After about a second's worth of deer-in-the-headlights hesitation, you remember your Rules of Engagement, which are printed on a small, yellow folding card that you keep in your left chest pocket. The card reads:

THESE RULES APPLY AT ALL TIMES
AND ON ALL OPERATIONS

1. **Positive Identification (PID) is required prior to engagement:** PID is a reasonable certainty that the target you are engaging is exhibiting hostile intent or committing a hostile act. Once you have PID, you may use escalated force up to and including deadly force, to eliminate the threat.

---

*Most people have only seen large explosions in movies and so understandably assume that a large bomb makes a sort of loud but sort of wet and rumbly sound, because this is the sound it makes in theaters. But theater explosions are made by the vibrations of speaker cones, whereas an actual explosion is the sound of air expanding at like twenty thousand feet per second, which for obvious legal as well as technical reasons even the fanciest Dolby-surround-sound systems cannot reproduce. If you've never heard a large explosion go off nearby, just think of one of those little Black Cat firecrackers that tween boys like to light and throw on the street around the Fourth of July, then multiply it by a thousand or ten thousand until it's a loud, sharp, and pretty scary sound that you can feel as well as hear, and (because you can feel it) always seems surprisingly close.

2. **When engaging targets, remember:**

    a. Escalation of force. Always use the minimum amount of force necessary to eliminate the threat. If time and circumstances permit, use the following degrees of force when responding to hostile act or hostile intent:

- Shout verbal warnings to halt.
- Show your weapon and demonstrate intent to use it.
- Shoot a warning shot (vehicles only).
- Shoot a disabling shot (vehicles only).
- Shoot to eliminate target.

In bold is the caveat:

NOTHING ON THIS CARD PREVENTS YOU FROM USING ALL FORCE NECESSARY TO DEFEND YOURSELF.

    Many would have seized up in a situation like this, but you remember the ROE and go by the numbers as per your training, first yelling Hey and Stay Back. The meaning of this should be obvious by the context, even to non-English speakers, but the BMW keeps coming and is now within thirty meters. The next step in the ROE — Show (show your presence and weapon) — is a constant, given the huge DO NOT APPROACH sign, not to mention the enormous and unmistakable Fifty. Next is Shoot (a warning shot), which you now do, fully aware that gunfire at the rear of the column is going to freak out the rest of the group, but whatever, he's at twenty-five meters now, and you lower the Fifty and fire into the concrete behind your truck, not trusting yourself to be able to put it close to but not in the car, given that your truck's starting to hit potholes and swerve around, and a single round could take ten people's heads off if they were lined up right.

    The car seems to hesitate for a moment, then continues ahead. It'll be past your bumper in a few seconds. You're probably within blast radius right now, and the thought that you should just duck pops into your head. You push it away. The ROE is all about your personal subjective threat assessment, an assessment that, given al-Qaeda's well-known tactic of impersonating civilians, is very hard to make. The ROE card makes clear however, that NOTHING ON THIS CARD PREVENTS YOU FROM USING ALL FORCE NECESSARY TO DEFEND YOURSELF, which is either a smart reminder of priorities or an end-run around the rules themselves. Your NCOs have made it clear to you that you are absolutely permitted and expected to light up a hajji that's intent on plowing into the convoy and won't respond to shouts, warning shots, and so on. The step now is to walk fire up into the engine block and then into the driver. You've just about committed to blow the BMW away when you remember the two-liter water bottle next to you and wonder if you can just fling it onto their windshield, like maybe the driver is too dense to realize that you're going to shoot him unless he stops, or is spooked and needs to be snapped out of it. You're out of time. 25

DO YOU:
Try and fling the water bottle onto the BMW's windshield? TURN TO (4).
Engage the BMW with the .50 caliber? TURN TO (5).

(4) Water

You grab the water bottle in one of your green, fuzzy gloves and chuck it. Your aim is true. The bottle caroms off the windshield right in front of the driver. This would get a reaction out of you for sure. But instead of stopping, the BMW driver steps on it and speeds past you in the next lane while you're trying to get the Fifty around. There's no longer a question of warning shots, but you could still stop the vehicle before it reaches the tankers. If you blow it away, you run the risk of Swiss-cheesing a family. If you don't stop it and it's a VBIED and it gets to one of the JP-4 Tankers, it could wipe out half the convoy.

DO YOU:
Fire on the BMW? TURN TO (5).
Let the BMW pass into the convoy? TURN TO (6). 30

(5) Fire

The M2 Browning .50 caliber machine gun was designed near the end of the First World War, and its design reflects its heritage. It is black and 100 percent steel and more than five feet long, weighing well over one hundred pounds loaded. Each round is almost half a foot long, and they are clipped together in long steel belts that disintegrate into shell casing and projectile with a sound that is described as "barking" but of course doesn't sound like anything else except for the repeated detonations of about 250 grains of propellant reverberating through a four-foot-long steel barrel. There is a widespread misconception among American combat soldiers that its use against human targets is banned by a number of treaties, and recruits have been told by generations of drill sergeants to aim a Fifty at enemy soldiers' "equipment" rather than their bodies. The persistence of this myth can probably be explained by the fact that while smaller bullets punch holes in humans, the Fifty takes them apart.

You draw a bead at the piece of concrete just in front of the BMW and depress the butterfly trigger. It is terrifically loud. You struggle to keep the muzzle from moving up and right as it spits out five huge slugs per second — the BMW is right next to the trucks and heaven forfend you put a round into one of your buddies or a tanker. Your grandmother used to say "heaven forfend," and the phrase is repeated in your panic brain in a queer voice that is somewhere between your grandmother's and your own. You quit firing after three bursts, unwilling to continue to shoot alongside (heaven forfend) your own column. You watch gratefully as another gunner a few trucks down opens up as well.

The riddled BMW swerves to the left and slows. Your ribcage expands, as it 35 seems like a physical weight has been lifted. You have not killed your friends, either with a bullet or through inaction. No one will suffer polytrauma because of you, you think, and to know that after a few seconds of not knowing it gives you a euphoria almost palpably chemical, the dopamine hitting your brain and a wave of pleasure moving from your scalp to your balls.

The column is moving slowly forward and your truck follows. The BMW slows and lists to port. It has no remaining windows. There is no blood visible, though of course there must be a sea of blood. A Browning .50 caliber round puts a hole in a human body the size of a grapefruit. The hole is much larger than the slug itself because of the kinetic force of the slug hitting flesh at approximately 2,910 feet per second.

It is afternoon and the sun is at about a forty-five-degree angle from the ground and very bright. Through the lattice of complex shadows you can see what is probably a human body in the back seat. One of the silhouette's hands is up by its shoulder, as though it is calling a waiter. You can see into the car more easily because all of the bullets make the shadow cast by the car's roof and sides somewhat translucent. You are convinced for a second that the person sitting up in the backseat is alive and unharmed. There are now a few thin streams of blood running from a bullet hole low in the passenger door and onto the concrete. The smell of burned-up ammunition propellant is acrid and strong. You briefly remember that the BMW could still be a bomb and duck back into your hatch after making a quick 360-degree scan. You then pass the location of the IED explosion and are out on the open road again, picking up speed, the radio buzzing furiously.

TURN TO (7).

(6) Denouement (I)

You have about two seconds to make this decision. Your heart tightens up, and your thumbs clench a bit, but you do not press the trigger. Maybe you decided at the time that the statistical probability of any black BMW sprinting into a US convoy in al-Anbar being an actual suicide bomber was low enough that the risk of death should be borne by your comrades rather than the BMW's occupants. More probably you just froze up in the moment and couldn't bring yourself to fire on a human being — a normal enough problem for troops throughout history. You're a smart person, and you'll have years to rationalize the decision.

The BMW floors it up through the convoy until it gets to the fourth truck, where Boyce sees it and is faster on the trigger than you. He yells at the BMW and puts a few rounds into the concrete in front of it. The BMW keeps going. As per SOP, Boyce then puts down a steady stream of fire in front of the vehicle, and the car drives right through it like a pole of fresh timber though a mill saw. The car swings to the left and smashes up against the median. The convoy's radios are all going furiously. Drivers don't know whether to drive in the right lane closest to the IED and the dirt berm that was drawing the convoy's fire, or in the left lane closest to the now-smoking BMW that everyone assumes is a possible VBIED.

You have gone back to scanning the rear, but allow yourself a long glance at the BMW as it passes by your right shoulder. Aside from the scattered dents in the roof, it looks from the rear like the driver just parked it up against the median for some inscrutable reason. You think you see at least one other person in the vehicle besides the driver. Soon the convoy clears the IED, and the spread-out broken glass and parked-looking, corpse-filled vehicle recede into the distance as you pick up speed.

You'll be chewed out but good for letting some random car come right into the convoy like that. You'll get a lot of meaningful glances from the other members of your platoon, too, who also spend time thinking about getting their jaws or dicks blown off, and who depend on you to fend off bombers. The next morning, your squad leader informs you that he's swapping you out with the driver. You'll be behind the wheel for the rest of the rotation.

THE END

(7) Denouement (II)

They do not ask how you knew that BMW was a VBIED; the whole crux of the terrorist tactic is to take what looks like an innocent civilian family sedan or produce truck and rig it to blow. The idea is to use your own humanity against you — if you are fast on the trigger, you will end up stopping car bombers but killing civilians, doing al-Qaeda's work for it. If you hold your fire past the point of no return, you will start to get hit more often as al-Qaeda realizes that convoys are soft targets. It is the other asymmetry of this type of asymmetric warfare: heads they win, tails you lose.

It was a good shoot — the vehicle was speeding into the convoy. The LT 45 arranges for you to see the chaplain anyway, because he suspects (with what you imagine is near certainty) that the BMW was full of civilians, the driver maybe having been spooked by the IED and thinking the thing to do was just step on it. Possibly he was drunk, unusual at midafternoon, but who knows? You shot them, regardless. You accept this, at first, as an unfortunate happenstance that is sort of the by-product of a landscape in which every enemy appears by design to be a civilian, which means that every civilian appears as a possible enemy. It will become a small hard nut of guilt and self-pity that you carry around, and that will, in subtle ways, color your opinions about yourself and the government and the people around you. You will find it hard to concentrate and your mind will frequently wander. You will stew in anger over insults that you imagine in daydreams. You will want to kill again, for a time. You will never quite be the same, although of course, no one can be certain whether or not this is a bad thing.

THE END

CONSIDERATIONS FOR CRITICAL THINKING AND WRITING

1. FIRST RESPONSE. Describe the point of view. If the story were told from a different point of view, how do you think your response might change?

2. Select a substantial paragraph that reveals the narrator's character and analyze how the details, tone, and action contribute to his characterization.

3. To what extend is the setting used as an antagonist in the story?

4. What do you think is the effect and the purpose of the narrator's detailed description of the Browning .50 caliber machine gun?

5. How does Kovite create suspense in the plot?

6. What kind of choices did you make at the end of each numbered section? Did you read straight through or choose to turn to subsequent sections? What difference in your ordering of the plot did those choices make?

7. What function do the Rules of Engagement serve in the story? How are they related to the conflict?

8. Compare the alternative endings in sections 6 and 7. Consider how the theme(s) of the story differ depending upon which one you choose. What themes emerge when you combine both?

CONNECTIONS TO OTHER SELECTIONS

1. Write an essay exploring the similarities and differences of the protagonists' responses to war in Kovite's story and in Phil Klay's "Redeployment" (below).

2. "The idea is to use your own humanity against you" (para. 44). Explain how this dilemma plays out in this story and in one of the three war stories listed in this chapter.

PHIL KLAY (B. 1984)

Born in White Plains, New York, Phil Klay graduated from Dartmouth College and earned an M.F.A. from Hunter College. In between degrees, he enlisted in the Marine Corps and served in Iraq as a public affairs officer in Anbar Province from 2007 to 2008 during the surge. His work has appeared in *Tin House, The Best American Nonrequired Reading,* the *Daily Beast,* and elsewhere. In *Redeployment,* winner of the 2014 National Book Award for Fiction, he uses a variety of character's voices to examine the radical differences between military and civilian life. Klay describes this dis-

© Beowulf Sheehan/Corbis.

juncture and locates it midway through his tour of duty, when he was on leave: "I literally went straight to New York City from Iraq, which was bizarre, and complicated. I was walking down Madison Avenue and it was spring, and people were smartly dressed, and it was so strange because there was no sense that we were at war. It was something to grapple with." In the title story, "Redeployment," Klay's protagonist tries to make sense of his life back home after experiencing the chaos and death of Fallujah.

Redeployment   2014

We shot dogs. Not by accident. We did it on purpose, and we called it Operation Scooby. I'm a dog person, so I thought about that a lot.

First time was instinct. I hear O'Leary go, "Jesus," and there's a skinny brown dog lapping up blood the same way he'd lap up water from a bowl. It wasn't American blood, but still, there's that dog, lapping it up. And that's the last straw, I guess, and then it's open season on dogs.

At the time, you don't think about it. You're thinking about who's in that house, what's he armed with, how's he gonna kill you, your buddies. You're going block by block, fighting with rifles good to 550 meters, and you're killing people at five in a concrete box.

The thinking comes later, when they give you the time. See, it's not a straight shot back, from war to the Jacksonville mall. When our deployment was up, they put us on TQ, this logistics base out in the desert, let us decompress a bit. I'm not sure what they meant by that. Decompress. We took it to mean jerk off a lot in the showers. Smoke a lot of cigarettes and play a lot of cards. And then they took us to Kuwait and put us on a commercial airliner to go home.

So there you are. You've been in a no-shit war zone and then you're sitting 5 in a plush chair, looking up at a little nozzle shooting air-conditioning, thinking, What the fuck? You've got a rifle between your knees, and so does everyone else. Some Marines got M9 pistols, but they take away your bayonets because you aren't allowed to have knives on an airplane. Even though you've showered, you all look grimy and lean. Everybody's hollow-eyed, and their cammies are beat to shit. And you sit there, and close your eyes, and think.

The problem is, your thoughts don't come out in any kind of straight order. You don't think, Oh, I did A, then B, then C, then D. You try to think about home, then you're in the torture house. You see the body parts in the locker and the retarded guy in the cage. He squawked like a chicken. His head was shrunk down to a coconut. It takes you a while to remember Doc saying they'd shot mercury into his skull, and then it still doesn't make any sense.

You see the things you saw the times you nearly died. The broken television and the hajji corpse. Eicholtz covered in blood. The lieutenant on the radio.

You see the little girl, the photographs Curtis found in a desk. First had a beautiful Iraqi kid, maybe seven or eight years old, in bare feet and a pretty white dress like it's First Communion. Next she's in a red dress, high heels, heavy makeup. Next photo, same dress, but her face is smudged and she's holding a gun to her head.

I tried to think of other things, like my wife, Cheryl. She's got pale skin and fine dark hairs on her arms. She's ashamed of them, but they're soft. Delicate.

But thinking of Cheryl made me feel guilty, and I'd think about Lance Corporal 10 Hernandez, Corporal Smith, and Eicholtz. We were like brothers, Eicholtz and me. The two of us saved this Marine's life one time. A few weeks later, Eicholtz is climbing over a wall. Insurgent pops out a window, shoots him in the back when he's halfway over.

So I'm thinking about that. And I'm seeing the retard, and the girl, and the wall Eicholtz died on. But here's the thing. I'm thinking a lot, and I mean a lot, about those fucking dogs.

And I'm thinking about my dog. Vicar. About the shelter we'd got him from, where Cheryl said we had to get an older dog because nobody takes older dogs. How we could never teach him anything. How he'd throw up shit he shouldn't have eaten in the first place. How he'd slink away all guilty, tail down and head low and back legs crouched. How his fur started turning gray two years after we got him and he had so many white hairs on his face that it looked like a mustache.

So there it was. Vicar and Operation Scooby, all the way home.

Maybe, I don't know, you're prepared to kill people. You practice on man-shaped targets so you're ready. Of course, we got targets they call "dog targets." Target shape Delta. But they don't look like fucking dogs.

And it's not easy to kill people, either. Out of boot camp, Marines act like they're 15 gonna play Rambo, but it's fucking serious, it's professional. Usually. We found this one insurgent doing the death rattle, foaming and shaking, fucked up, you know? He's hit with a 7.62 in the chest and pelvic girdle; he'll be gone in a second, but the company XO walks up, pulls out his KA-BAR, and slits his throat. Says, "It's good to kill a man with a knife." All the Marines look at each other like, "What the fuck?" Didn't expect that from the XO. That's some PFC bullshit.

On the flight, I thought about that, too.

It's so funny. You're sitting there with your rifle in your hands but no ammo in sight. And then you touch down in Ireland to refuel. And it's so foggy you can't see shit, but, you know, this is Ireland, there's got to be beer. And the plane's captain, a fucking civilian, reads off some message about how general orders stay in effect until you reach the States, and you're still considered on duty. So no alcohol.

Well, our CO jumped up and said, "That makes about as much sense as a god-damn football bat. All right, Marines, you've got three hours. I hear they serve Guinness." Oo-fucking-rah.

Corporal Weissert ordered five beers at once and had them laid out in front of him. He didn't even drink for a while, just sat there looking at 'em all, happy. O'Leary said, "Look at you, smiling like a faggot in a dick tree," which is a DI expression Curtis loves.

So Curtis laughs and says, "What a horrible fucking tree," and we all start 20 cracking up, happy just knowing we can get fucked up, let our guard down.

We got crazy quick. Most of us had lost about twenty pounds and it'd been seven months since we'd had a drop of alcohol. MacManigan, second award PFC, was rolling around the bar with his nuts hanging out of his cammies, telling Marines, "Stop looking at my balls, faggot." Lance Corporal Slaughter was there all of a half hour before he puked in the bathroom, with Corporal Craig, the sober Mormon, helping him out, and Lance Corporal Greeley, the drunk Mormon, puking in the stall next to him. Even the Company Guns got wrecked.

It was good. We got back on the plane and passed the fuck out. Woke up in America.

Except when we touched down in Cherry Point, there was nobody there. It was zero dark and cold, and half of us were rocking the first hangover we'd had in months, which at that point was a kind of shitty that felt pretty fucking good. And we got off the plane and there's a big empty landing strip, maybe a half dozen red patchers and a bunch of seven tons lined up. No families.

The Company Guns said that they were waiting for us at Lejeune. The sooner we get the gear loaded on the trucks, the sooner we see 'em.

Roger that. We set up working parties, tossed our rucks and seabags into the 25 seven tons. Heavy work, and it got the blood flowing in the cold. Sweat a little of the alcohol out, too.

Then they pulled up a bunch of buses and we all got on, packed in, M16s sticking everywhere, muzzle awareness gone to shit, but it didn't matter.

Cherry Point to Lejeune's an hour. First bit's through trees. You don't see much in the dark. Not much when you get on 24, either. Stores that haven't opened yet. Neon lights off at the gas stations and bars. Looking out, I sort of knew where I was, but I didn't feel home. I figured I'd be home when I kissed my wife and pet my dog.

We went in through Lejeune's side gate, which is about ten minutes away from our battalion area. Fifteen, I told myself, way this fucker is driving. When we got to McHugh, everybody got a little excited. And then the driver turned on A Street. Battalion area's on A, and I saw the barracks and I thought, There it is. And then they stopped about four hundred meters short. Right in front of the armory. I could've jogged down to where the families were. I could see there was an area behind one of the barracks where they'd set up lights. And there were cars parked everywhere. I could hear the crowd down the way. The families were there. But we all got in line, thinking about them just down the way. Me thinking about Cheryl and Vicar. And we waited.

When I got to the window and handed in my rifle, though, it brought me up short. That was the first time I'd been separated from it in months. I didn't know where to rest my hands. First I put them in my pockets, then I took them out and crossed my arms, and then I just let them hang, useless, at my sides.

After all the rifles were turned in, First Sergeant had us get into a no-shit 30 parade formation. We had a fucking guidon waving out front, and we marched down A Street. When we got to the edge of the first barracks, people started cheering. I couldn't see them until we turned the corner, and then there they were, a big wall of people holding signs under a bunch of outdoor lights, and the lights were bright and pointed straight at us, so it was hard to look into the crowd and tell who was who. Off to the side there were picnic tables and a Marine in woodlands grilling hot dogs. And there was a bouncy castle. A fucking bouncy castle.

We kept marching. A couple more Marines in woodlands were holding the crowd back in a line, and we marched until we were straight alongside the crowd, and then First Sergeant called us to a halt.

I saw some TV cameras. There were a lot of U.S. flags. The whole MacManigan clan was up front, right in the middle, holding a banner that read: OO RAH PRIVATE FIRST CLASS BRADLEY MACMANIGAN. WE ARE SO PROUD.

I scanned the crowd back and forth. I'd talked to Cheryl on the phone in Kuwait, not for very long, just, "Hey, I'm good," and, "Yeah, within forty-eight hours. Talk to the FRO, he'll tell you when to be there." And she said she'd be there, but it was strange, on the phone. I hadn't heard her voice in a while.

Then I saw Eicholtz's dad. He had a sign, too. It said: WELCOME BACK HEROES OF BRAVO COMPANY. I looked right at him and remembered him from when we left, and I thought, That's Eicholtz's dad. And that's when they released us. And they released the crowd, too.

I was standing still, and the Marines around me, Curtis and O'Leary and 35 MacManigan and Craig and Weissert, they were rushing out to the crowd. And the crowd was coming forward. Eicholtz's dad was coming forward.

He was shaking the hand of every Marine he passed. I don't think a lot of guys recognized him, and I knew I should say something, but I didn't. I backed off. I looked around for my wife. And I saw my name on a sign: SGT PRICE, it said. But the rest was blocked by the crowd, and I couldn't see who was holding it. And then I was moving toward it, away from Eicholtz's dad, who was hugging Curtis, and I saw the rest of the sign. It said: SGT PRICE, NOW THAT YOU'RE HOME YOU CAN DO SOME CHORES. HERE'S YOUR TO-DO LIST. 1) ME. 2) REPEAT NUMBER 1.

And there, holding the sign, was Cheryl.

She was wearing cammie shorts and a tank top, even though it was cold. She must have worn them for me. She was skinnier than I remembered. More makeup, too. I was nervous and tired and she looked a bit different. But it was her.

All around us were families and big smiles and worn-out Marines. I walked up to her and she saw me and her face lit. No woman had smiled at me like that in a long time. I moved in and kissed her. I figured that was what I was supposed to do. But it'd been too long and we were both too nervous and it felt like just lip on lip pushed together, I don't know. She pulled back and looked at me and put her hands on my shoulders and started to cry. She reached up and rubbed her eyes, and then she put her arms around me and pulled me into her.

Her body was soft and it fit into mine. All deployment, I'd slept on the ground 40 or on canvas cots. I'd worn body armor and kept a rifle slung across my body. I hadn't felt anything like her in seven months. It was almost like I'd forgotten how she felt, or never really known it, and now here was this new feeling that made everything else black and white fading before color. Then she let me go and I took her by the hand and we got my gear and got out of there.

She asked me if I wanted to drive and hell yeah I did, so I got behind the wheel. A long time since I'd done that, too. I put the car in reverse, pulled out, and started driving home. I was thinking I wanted to park somewhere dark and curl up with her in the backseat like high school. But I got the car out of the lot and down McHugh. And driving down McHugh it felt different from the bus. Like, This is Lejeune. This is the way I used to get to work. And it was so dark. And quiet.

Cheryl said, "How are you?" which meant, How was it? Are you crazy now?

I said, "Good. I'm fine."

And then it was quiet again and we turned down Holcomb. I was glad I was driving. It gave me something to focus on. Go down this street, turn the wheel, go down another. One step at a time. You can get through anything one step at a time.

She said, "I'm so happy you're home."   45

Then she said, "I love you so much."

Then she said, "I'm proud of you."

I said, "I love you, too."

When we got home, she opened the door for me. I didn't even know where my house keys were. Vicar wasn't at the door to greet me. I stepped in and scanned around, and there he was on the couch. When he saw me, he got up slow.

His fur was grayer than before, and there were weird clumps of fat on his legs, 50 these little tumors that Labs get but that Vicar's got a lot of now. He wagged his tail. He stepped down off the couch real careful, like he was hurting. And Cheryl said, "He remembers you."

"Why's he so skinny?" I said, and I bent down and scratched him behind the ears.

"The vet said we had to keep him on weight control. And he doesn't keep a lot of food down these days."

Cheryl was pulling on my arm. Pulling me away from Vicar. And I let her.

She said, "Isn't it good to be home?"

Her voice was shaky, like she wasn't sure of the answer. And I said, "Yeah, yeah, 55 it is." And she kissed me hard. I grabbed her in my arms and lifted her up and carried her to the bedroom. I put a big grin on my face, but it didn't help. She looked a bit scared of me, then. I guess all the wives were probably a little bit scared.

And that was my homecoming. It was fine, I guess. Getting back feels like your first breath after nearly drowning. Even if it hurts, it's good.

I can't complain. Cheryl handled it well. I saw Lance Corporal Curtis's wife back in Jacksonville. She spent all his combat pay before he got back and she was five months pregnant, which, for a Marine coming back from a seven-month deployment, is not pregnant enough.

Corporal Weissert's wife wasn't there at all when we got back. He laughed, said she probably got the time wrong, and O'Leary gave him a ride to his house. They get there and it's empty. Not just of people, of everything: furniture, wall hangings, everything. Weissert looks at this shit and shakes his head, starts laughing. They went out, bought some whiskey, and got fucked up right there in his empty house.

Weissert drank himself to sleep, and when he woke up, MacManigan was right next to him, sitting on the floor. And MacManigan, of all people, was the one who cleaned him up and got him into base on time for the classes they make you take about, Don't kill yourself. Don't beat your wife. And Weissert was like, "I can't beat my wife. I don't know where the fuck she is."

That weekend they gave us a ninety-six, and I took on Weissert duty for Friday. 60 He was in the middle of a three-day drunk, and hanging with him was a carnival freak show filled with whiskey and lap dances. Didn't get home until four, after I dropped him off at Slaughter's barracks room, and I woke Cheryl coming in. She didn't say a word. I figured she'd be mad, and she looked it, but when I got in bed she rolled over to me and gave me a little hug, even though I was stinking of booze.

Slaughter passed Weissert to Addis, Addis passed him to Greeley, and so on. We had somebody with him the whole weekend until we were sure he was good.

When I wasn't with Weissert and the rest of the squad, I sat on the couch with Vicar, watching the baseball games Cheryl'd taped for me. Sometimes Cheryl and I talked about her seven months, about the wives left behind, about her family, her job, her boss. Sometimes she'd ask little questions. Sometimes I'd answer. And glad as I was to be in the States, and even though I hated the past seven months and the only thing that kept me going was the Marines I served with and the thought of coming home, I started feeling like I wanted to go back. Because fuck all this.

The next week at work was all half days and bullshit. Medical appointments to deal with injuries guys had been hiding or sucking up. Dental appointments. Admin. And every evening, me and Vicar watching TV on the couch, waiting for Cheryl to get back from her shift at Texas Roadhouse.

Vicar'd sleep with his head in my lap, waking up whenever I'd reach down to feed him bits of salami. The vet told Cheryl that's bad for him, but he deserved something good. Half the time when I pet him, I'd rub up against one of his tumors, and that had to hurt. It looked like it hurt him to do everything, wag his tail, eat his chow. Walk. Sit. And when he'd vomit, which was every other day, he'd hack like he was choking, revving up for a good twenty seconds before anything came out. It was the noise that bothered me. I didn't mind cleaning the carpet.

And then Cheryl'd come home and look at us and shake her head and smile 65 and say, "Well, you're a sorry bunch."

I wanted Vicar around, but I couldn't bear to look at him. I guess that's why I let Cheryl drag me out of the house that weekend. We took my combat pay and did a lot of shopping. Which is how America fights back against the terrorists.

So here's an experience. Your wife takes you shopping in Wilmington. Last time you walked down a city street, your Marine on point went down the side of the road, checking ahead and scanning the roofs across from him. The Marine behind him checks the windows on the top levels of the buildings, the Marine behind him gets the windows a little lower, and so on down until your guys have the street level covered, and the Marine in back has the rear. In a city there's a million places they can kill you from. It freaks you out at first. But you go through like you were trained, and it works.

In Wilmington, you don't have a squad, you don't have a battle buddy, you don't even have a weapon. You startle ten times checking for it and it's not there. You're safe, so your alertness should be at white, but it's not.

Instead, you're stuck in an American Eagle Outfitters. Your wife gives you some clothes to try on and you walk into the tiny dressing room. You close the door, and you don't want to open it again.

Outside, there're people walking around by the windows like it's no big deal. 70 People who have no idea where Fallujah is, where three members of your platoon died. People who've spent their whole lives at white.

They'll never get even close to orange. You can't, until the first time you're in a firefight, or the first time an IED goes off that you missed, and you realize that everybody's life, everybody's, depends on you not fucking up. And you depend on them.

Some guys go straight to red. They stay like that for a while and then they crash, go down past white, down to whatever is lower than "I don't fucking care if I die." Most everybody else stays orange, all the time.

Here's what orange is. You don't see or hear like you used to. Your brain chemistry changes. You take in every piece of the environment, everything. I could spot a dime in the street twenty yards away. I had antennae out that stretched down the block. It's hard to even remember exactly what that felt like. I think you take in too much information to store so you just forget, free up brain space to take in everything about the next moment that might keep you alive. And then you forget that moment, too, and focus on the next. And the next. And the next. For seven months.

So that's orange. And then you go shopping in Wilmington, unarmed, and you think you can get back down to white? It'll be a long fucking time before you get down to white.

By the end of it I was amped up. Cheryl didn't let me drive home. I would have 75 gone a hundred miles per hour. And when we got back, we saw Vicar had thrown up again, right by the door. I looked for him and he was there on the couch, trying to stand on shaky legs. And I said, "Goddamn it, Cheryl. It's fucking time."

She said, "You think I don't know?"

I looked at Vicar.

She said, "I'll take him to the vet tomorrow."

I said, "No."

She shook her head. She said, "I'll take care of it."   80

I said, "You mean you'll pay some asshole a hundred bucks to kill my dog."

She didn't say anything.

I said, "That's not how you do it. It's on me."

She was looking at me in this way I couldn't deal with. Soft. I looked out the window at nothing.

She said, "You want me to go with you?"   85

I said, "No. No."

"Okay," she said. "But it'd be better."

She walked over to Vicar, leaned down, and hugged him. Her hair fell over her face and I couldn't see if she was crying. Then she stood up, walked to the bedroom, and gently closed the door.

I sat down on the couch and scratched Vicar behind the ears, and I came up with a plan. Not a good plan, but a plan. Sometimes that's enough.

There's a dirt road near where I live and a stream off the road where the light 90 filters in around sunset. It's pretty. I used to go running there sometimes. I figured it'd be a good spot for it.

It's not a far drive. We got there right at sunset. I parked just off the road, got out, pulled my rifle out of the trunk, slung it over my shoulders, and moved to the passenger side. I opened the door and lifted Vicar up in my arms and carried him down to the stream. He was heavy and warm, and he licked my face as I carried him, slow, lazy licks from a dog that's been happy all his life. When I put him down and stepped back, he looked up at me. He wagged his tail. And I froze.

Only one other time I hesitated like that. Midway through Fallujah, an insurgent snuck through our perimeter. When we raised the alarm, he disappeared. We freaked, scanning everywhere, until Curtis looked down in this water cistern that'd been used as a cesspit, basically a big round container filled a quarter way with liquid shit.

The insurgent was floating in it, hiding beneath the liquid and only coming up for air. It was like a fish rising up to grab a fly sitting on the top of the water. His mouth would break the surface, open for a breath, and then snap shut, and he'd submerge. I couldn't imagine it. Just smelling it was bad enough. About four or five Marines aimed straight down, fired into the shit. Except me.

Staring at Vicar, it was the same thing. This feeling, like, something in me is going to break if I do this. And I thought of Cheryl bringing Vicar to the vet, of some stranger putting his hands on my dog, and I thought, I have to do this.

I didn't have a shotgun, I had an AR-15. Same, basically, as an M16, what I'd 95
been trained on, and I'd been trained to do it right. Sight alignment, trigger control,
breath control. Focus on the iron sights, not the target. The target should be blurry.

I focused on Vicar, then on the sights. Vicar disappeared into a gray blur. I
switched off the safety. There had to be three shots. It's not just pull the trigger and
you're done. Got to do it right. Hammer pair to the body. A final well-aimed shot to
the head.

The first two have to be fired quick, that's important. Your body is mostly water,
so a bullet striking through is like a stone thrown in a pond. It creates ripples. Throw
in a second stone soon after the first, and in between where they hit, the water gets
choppy. That happens in your body, especially when it's two 5.56 rounds traveling at
supersonic speeds. Those ripples can tear organs apart.

If I were to shoot you on either side of your heart, one shot . . . and then another,
you'd have two punctured lungs, two sucking chest wounds. Now, you're good and
fucked. But you'll still be alive long enough to feel your lungs fill up with blood.

If I shoot you there with the shots coming fast, it's no problem. The ripples
tear up your heart and lungs and you don't do the death rattle, you just die. There's
shock, but no pain.

I pulled the trigger, felt the recoil, and focused on the sights, not on Vicar, three 100
times. Two bullets tore through his chest, one through his skull, and the bullets
came fast, too fast to feel. That's how it should be done, each shot coming quick after
the last so you can't even try to recover, which is when it hurts.

I stayed there staring at the sights for a while. Vicar was a blur of gray and
black. The light was dimming. I couldn't remember what I was going to do with the
body.

Considerations for Critical Thinking and Writing

1. **FIRST RESPONSE.** Consider the ambiguity of the title "Redeployment," a term
   that refers to troops returning home from assignments as well as those starting
   another tour of duty. Why is this term especially appropriate for evoking the
   conflicts in this story?

2. "We shot dogs. Not by accident." How does Klay manage to make the narrator
   a sympathetic character despite this startling and chilling opening sentence?

3. Discuss the significance of how the protagonist feels when he hands in his rifle
   (para. 29). Explain how this scene contributes to the story's themes.

4. Describe the ways in which the protagonist's fellow marines experience their
   return home from the war. To what extent does this information affect your
   response to the protagonist?

5. Discuss Vicar's function in the plot. Why do you think he is named Vicar?
   Consult a dictionary for the word's meaning and origin.

6. Why do you suppose Klay chose American Eagle Outfitters as the store the
   protagonist visits in Wilmington?

7. Consider the detailed account of Vicar being shot. How does it affect your view
   of the protagonist? What purpose do you think it serves thematically?

8. Based on your experience reading and/or viewing war stories, describe what
   you think constitutes a typical plot. How does "Redeployment" seem similar to
   and/or different from what you are familiar with?

CONNECTIONS TO OTHER SELECTIONS

1. Consider how "Redeployment" could be read as a kind of sequel to Kovite's "When Engaging Targets, Remember" (p. 497).

2. In one of his stories in *Redeployment*, "Psychological Operations," Klay quotes a joke: "How many Vietnam vets does it take to change a light bulb?" Answer: "You wouldn't know. You weren't there." How does the significance underlying this joke manifest itself in "Redeployment" and in O'Brien's "How to Tell a True War Story" (p. 488) or Hemingway's "Soldier's Home" (p. 162)?

17

A THEMATIC CASE STUDY

Humor and Satire

It is the writer's privilege to help man endure by lifting his heart.
—WILLIAM FAULKNER

Cofield Collection, Archives and Special Collections, University of Mississippi Libraries.

Let's get serious: although some austere readers may assume that humor and satire require a rationale or apology, a reading life without laughter would be grimly monochromed and dull. We laugh in color, not just in black and white, because humor is often used as a play of light that allows us to perceive shades of meaning that might otherwise be invisible. Wit, irony, exaggeration, understatement, caricature, parody, and any number of other methods through which a writer opens our eyes to the complexities of human experience illuminate what high seriousness sometimes demands is no laughing matter. Flannery O'Connor's fiction, for example, is heavily freighted with pain, perversity, and tragic attempts at religious salvation, but a responsive reader will also find that her stories include startling humor, despite the presence of murder, a stolen artificial leg, and some lunatic characters (see her three stories in Chapter 12, "A Study of Flannery O'Connor"). Even Herman Melville's weird protagonist in "Bartleby, the Scrivener" (p. 130), who engages in a suicidal withdrawal from life, is invested with a comic dimension. To test this idea, try reading the very brief story that begins this chapter, Annie Proulx's "55 Miles to the Gas Pump."

Of course people don't always agree about what's amusing, owing to their personal sensibilities and experiences. "That's not funny" is a sentiment that commonly measures the difference in varying responses. Humor can open people's eyes, but it can also cause people to shut them if they feel offended by it. A passionate animal rights advocate might argue that the topic of a family pet's death wholly removes any possibilities for humor in Ron Hansen's "My Kid's Dog" (p. 521). As Mark Twain makes surprisingly clear in "The Story of the Good Little Boy" (p. 525), even Sunday school can be unexpectedly funny, because humor often asserts that nothing is sacred. It wears social restraints lightly and refuses to sit still, preferring that others grapple with discomfort. Effective humor — like the jogger's in "Hi Howya Doin" by Joyce Carol Oates (p. 518) — isn't afraid to take your breath away with a startling ending that some readers might find "inappropriate" (a term demanding compliance that has always crippled humor), but most readers of Oates's story are more likely to feel that they've experienced an invigorating run as well as a plot that's perfectly worked out. The humor in the stories composing this chapter will keep you on your toes and will also help you to keep your balance.

ANNIE PROULX (B. 1935)

Annie Proulx was born in 1935 and did not finish her first book until 1988. She received a B.A. from the University of Vermont in 1969 and a master's degree from Sir George Williams University, both in history, and later became a freelance writer of articles for magazines in the United States. She published short stories occasionally until she had enough to make her first collection, *Heart Songs and Other Stories* (1988), which she followed with the novel *Post-cards* in 1992. Her breakthrough novel was *The*

John Harding/The Life Images Collection/ Getty Images.

Shipping News (1993), which won both the Pulitzer Prize and the National Book Award, and she has since produced two novels, *Accordion Crimes* (1996) and *The Old Ace in the Hole* (2003), and three books of short stories, *Close Range: Wyoming Stories* (1999), *Bad Dirt: Wyoming Stories 2* (2004), and *Fine Just the Way It Is: Wyoming Stories 3* (2008). Setting her works in places as distant as Newfoundland and Wyoming, Proulx conveys her dark, comic stories by creating a strong sense of place, using her talent for keen detail and for reproducing the peculiarities of local speech. *The Shipping News* and the short story "Brokeback Mountain" from *Close Range* were made into popular films. In 2011, Proulx published *Bird Cloud: A Memoir,* about her life in Wyoming.

55 Miles to the Gas Pump   1999

Rancher Croom in handmade boots and filthy hat, that walleyed cattleman, stray hairs like curling fiddle string ends, that warm-handed, quick-foot dancer on splintery boards or down the cellar stairs to a rack of bottles of his own strange beer, yeasty, cloudy, bursting out in garlands of foam, Rancher Croom at night galloping drunk over the dark plain, turning off at a place he knows to arrive at a canyon brink where he dismounts and looks down on tumbled rock, waits, then steps out, parting the air with his last roar, sleeves surging up windmill arms, jeans riding over boot tops, but before he hits he rises again to the top of the cliff like a cork in a bucket of milk.

Mrs. Croom on the roof with a saw cutting a hole into the attic where she has not been for twelve years thanks to old Croom's padlocks and warnings, whets to her desire, and the sweat flies as she exchanges the saw for a chisel and hammer until a ragged slab of peak is free and she can see inside: just as she thought: the corpses of Mr. Croom's paramours — she recognizes them from their photographs in the paper: MISSING WOMAN — some desiccated as jerky and much the same color, some moldy from lying beneath roof leaks, and all of them used hard, covered with tarry handprints, the marks of boot heels, some bright blue with the remnants of paint used on the shutters years ago, one wrapped in newspaper nipple to knee.

When you live a long way out you make your own fun.

CONSIDERATIONS FOR CRITICAL THINKING AND WRITING

1. FIRST RESPONSE. Do you think this story is humorous? Why or why not?

2. What kinds of assumptions about rural and urban life are made in the story? To what extent does Proulx challenge or endorse conventional views of rural and urban values?

3. Consider whether Mr. and Mrs. Croom are round, flat, or stock characters.

4. Is there a resolution to the conflict(s) in the plot?

5. How important is the setting?

6. Write a sentence that expresses your reading of the theme.

7. Describe the style and tone of each paragraph. How do they contribute to the theme?

8. CREATIVE RESPONSE. Substitute Proulx's title and final paragraph with your own. How do these changes affect your interpretation of the entire work?

CONNECTIONS TO OTHER SELECTIONS

1. Despite their brevity, how do "55 Miles to the Gas Pump" and Raymond Carver's "Popular Mechanics" (p. 277) manage to create compelling fictional worlds?

2. Compare Proulx's humorous treatment of the West to Stephen Crane's in "The Bride Comes to Yellow Sky" (p. 251).

3. Consider the use of irony in Proulx's story and in Mark Twain's "The Story of the Good Little Boy" (p. 525). Explain why you find the endings of the stories similar or different in tone.

JOYCE CAROL OATES (B. 1938)

Raised in upstate New York, Joyce Carol Oates earned degrees at Syracuse University and the University of Wisconsin. Both the range and volume of her writing are extraordinarily extensive. A writer of novels, plays, short stories, poetry, and literary criticism, she has published over eighty books. Oates has described the subject matter of her fiction as "real people in a real society," but her method of expression ranges from the realistic to the experimental. Her novels include *them* (1969), *Do with Me What You Will* (1973), *Childwold* (1976), *Bellefleur* (1980), *A Bloodsmoor Romance*

© Beth Gwinn.

(1982), *Marya: A Life* (1986), *You Must Remember This* (1987), *Black Water* (1992), *I'll Take You There* (2003), *Missing Mom* (2005), *Mudwoman* (2012), *Carthage* (2014), and *Sacrifice* (2015). Among her collections of short stories are *Marriages and Infidelities* (1972), *Raven's Wing* (1986), *The Assignation* (1988), *Heat* (1991), *Haunted: Tales of the Grotesque* (1994), *Will You Always Love Me? and Other Stories* (1996), *The Collector of Hearts* (1998), *Small Avalanches and Other Stories* (2004), *High Lonesome: New and Selected Stories 1966–2006* (2006), *Dear Husband* (2009), *The Corn Maiden and Other Stories* (2011), and *Lovely, Dark, Deep: Stories* (2014). Oates teaches at Princeton University.

Hi Howya Doin   2007

Good-looking husky guy six-foot-four in late twenties or early thirties, Caucasian male, as the initial police report will note, he's solid-built as a fire hydrant, carries himself like an athlete, or an ex-athlete just perceptibly thickening at the waist, otherwise in terrific condition like a bronze figure in motion, sinewy arms pumping as he runs, long muscled legs, chiseled-muscled calves, he's hurtling along the moist woodchip path at the western edge of the university arboretum at approximately six P.M., Thursday evening, and there comes, from the other direction, a woman jogger on the path, female in her late thirties, flushed face, downturned eyes, dark hair threaded with gray like cobwebs, an awkward runner, fleshy lips parted, holds her arms stiff at her sides, in a shrunken pullover shirt with a faded tiger cat on its front, not-large but sizable breasts shaking as she runs, mimicked in the slight shaking of her cheeks, and her hips in carrot-colored sweatpants, this is Madeline Hersey frowning at the woodchip path before her, Madeline's exasperating habit of staring at the ground when she runs, oblivious of the arboretum, though at this time in May it's dazzling with white dogwood, pink dogwood, vivid yellow forsythia, Madeline is a lab technician at Squibb, lost in a labyrinth of her own tangled thoughts (career, lover, lover's "learning disabled" child), startled out of her reverie by the loud aggressive-friendly greeting *Hi! Howya doin!* flung out at her like a playful slap on the buttocks as the tall husky jogger passes Madeline with the most fleeting of glances, big-toothed bemused smile, and Madeline loses her stride, in a faltering voice *Fine — thank you —* but the other jogger is past, unhearing and now on the gravel path behind the university hospital, now on the grassy towpath beside the old canal, in the greenly lushness of University Dells Park where, in the late afternoon, into dusk joggers are running singly and in couples, in groups of three or more, track-team runners from the local high school, college students, white-haired older runners both male and female, to these the husky jogger in skin-tight mustard-yellow T-shirt, short navy-blue shorts showing his chiseled thigh muscles, size-twelve Nikes calls out *Hi Howya doin* in a big bland booming voice, *Hi Howya doin* and a flash of big horsy teeth, long pumping legs, pumping arms, it's his practice to come up close behind a solitary jogger, a woman maybe, a girl, or an older man, so many "older" men (forties, fifties, sixties, and beyond) in the university community, sometimes a younger guy who's sweated through his clothes, beginning to breathe through his mouth, size-twelve Nikes striking the earth like mallets, *Hi! Howya doin!* jolting Kyle Lindeman out of dreamy-sexy thoughts, jolting Michelle Rossley out of snarled anxious thoughts, there's Diane Hendricks who'd been an athlete in high school now twenty pounds overweight, divorced, no kid, replaying in her head a quarrel she'd had with a woman friend, goddamn she's angry! goddamn she's not going to call Ginny back, this time! trying to calm her rush of thoughts like churning roiling water, trying to measure her breaths Zen-fashion, inhale, exhale, inhale and out of nowhere into this reverie a tall husky hurtling figure bears down upon her, toward her, veering into her line of vision, instinctively Diane bears to the right to give him plenty of room to pass her, hopes this is no one she knows from work, no one who knows her, trying not to look up at him, tall guy, husky, must weigh two-twenty, works out, has got to be an athlete, or ex-athlete, a pang of sexual excitement courses through her, or is it sexual dread even as *Hi! Howya doin!* rings out loud and bemused like an elbow in Diane's left breast as the stranger pounds past her, in his wake an odor of male sweat, acrid-briny male sweat and an impression of big glistening teeth bared in a brainless grin or is it a mock-grin, death's-head grin? — thrown off stride, self-conscious and stumbling, Diane manages to stammer *Fine — I'm fine* as if the stranger brushing past her is interested in her, or in her well-being, in the slightest, what a fool Diane is! — yet another day, moist-bright morning in the university dells along the path beside the seed-stippled lagoon where amorous-combative male mallard ducks are pursuing female ducks with much squawking, flapping of wings, and splashing water, there comes the tall husky jogger, Caucasian male six-foot-four, two-twenty pounds, no ID as the initial police report will note, on this occasion the jogger is wearing a skin-tight black Judas Priest T-shirt, very short white-nylon shorts revealing every surge, ripple, sheen of chiseled thigh muscles, emerging out of a shadowy pathway at the edge of the birch woods to approach Dr. Rausch of the university's geology department, older man, just slightly vain of being "fit," dark-tinted aviator glasses riding the bridge of his perspiring nose, Dr. Rausch panting as he runs, not running so fast as he'd like, rivulets of sweat like melting grease down his back, sides, sweating through his shirt, in baggy khaki shorts to the knee, Dr. Rausch grinding his jaws in thought (departmental budget cuts! his youngest daughter's wrecked marriage! his wife's biopsy next morning at seven A.M., he will drive her to the medical center and wait for her, return her home and yet somehow get to the tenure committee meeting he's chairing at eleven A.M.) when *Hi! Howya doin!* jolts Dr. Rausch as if the husky jogger in the black Judas Priest T-shirt has extended a playful size-twelve foot into Dr. Rausch's path to trip him, suddenly he's thrown off-stride, poor old guy, hasn't always been sixty-four years old, sunken-chested, skinny white legs sprouting individual hairs like wires, hard little pot belly straining at the unbelted waistline of the khaki shorts, Dr. Rausch looks up squinting, is this someone he knows? should know? who knows *him*? across the vertiginous span of thirty years in the geology department Dr. Rausch has had so many students, but before he can see who this is, or make a panting effort to reply in the quick-casual way of youthful joggers, the husky jogger has passed by Dr. Rausch without a second glance, legs like pistons of muscle, shimmering sweat-film like a halo about his body, fair-brown, russet-brown hair in curls like wood shavings lifting halo-like from his large uplifted head, big toothy smile, large broad nose made for deep breathing, enormous dark nostrils that look as if thumbs have been shoved into them, soon again this shimmering male figure appears on the far side of the dells, another afternoon on the Institute grounds, hard-pounding feet, muscled arms pumping, on this day a navy blue T-shirt faded from numerous launderings, another time the very short navy-blue shorts, as he runs he exudes a yeasty body odor, sighting a solitary male jogger ahead he quickens his pace to overtake him, guy in his early twenties, university student, no athlete, about five-eight, skinny guy, running with some effort, breathing through his mouth, and in his head a swirl of numerals, symbols, equations, quantum optics, quantum noise, into this reverie *Hi! Howya doin* is like a firecracker tossed by a prankish kid, snappishly the younger jogger replies *I'm okay* as his face flushes, how like high school, junior high kids pushing him around, in that instant he's remembering, almost now limping, lost the stride, now life seems pointless, you know it's pointless, you live, you die, look how his grandfather died, what's the point, there is none, as next day, next week, late Friday afternoon of the final week in May along the canal towpath past Linden Road where there are fewer joggers looming up suddenly in your line of vision, approaching you, a tall husky male jogger running in the center of the path, instinctively you bear to the right, instinctively you turn your gaze downward, no eye contact on the towpath, you've been lost in thought, coils of thought like electric currents burning-hot, scalding-hot, the very pain, anguish, futility of your thoughts, for what is your soul but your thoughts, upright flame cupped between your hands silently pleading *Don't speak to me, respect my privacy please* even as the oncoming jogger continues to approach, in the center of the path, inexorably, unstoppably, curly hairs on his arms shimmering with a bronze-roseate glow, big teeth bared in a smile *Hi! Howya doing!* loud and bland and booming mock-friendly, and out of the pocket of your nylon jacket you fumble to remove the snub-nosed, twenty-two-caliber Smith & Wesson revolver you'd stolen from your stepfather's lodge in Jackson Hole, Wyoming, three years before, hateful of the old drunk asshole you'd waited for him to ask if you'd taken it, were you the one to take his gun that's unlicensed, and your stepfather never asked, and you never told, and you lift the toy-like gun in a hand trembling with excitement, with trepidation, with anticipation, aim at the face looming at you like a balloon-face up close and fire and the bullet leaps like magic from the toy-weapon with unexpected force and short-range accuracy and enters the face at the forehead directly above the big-nostriled nose, in an instant the husky jogger in the mustard-yellow T-shirt drops to his knees on the path, already the mustard-yellow T-shirt is splashed with blood, on his belly now and brawny arms outspread, face flattened against the path fallen silent and limp as a cloth puppet when the puppeteer has lost interest and dropped the puppet, he's dead, *That's how I'm doin.*

CONSIDERATIONS FOR CRITICAL THINKING AND WRITING

1. **FIRST RESPONSE.** How is the style of this story particularly suited to jogging?
2. What is the effect of the narrator's mentioning the "initial police report" in the second line?

3. Explain how the male jogger is a character foil to Madeline Hersey. How do the other joggers' responses to him further define his character?

4. How might this story be regarded as a kind of sociology of jogging? Consider whether or not it seems like an accurate rendition of it to you.

5. How does Oates subtly convey the passage of time in the narrative?

6. The inevitable question: Is this story funny? Why or why not?

Connections to Other Selections

1. Compare the tone of the humor in this story with that in Ron Hansen's "My Kid's Dog" (p. 521).

2. Comment on the ways in which style is related to content in "Hi Howya Doin" and in Rick Moody's "Boys" (p. 289).

Ron Hansen (b. 1947)

Born in Omaha, Nebraska, Ron Hansen holds a B.A. from Creighton University, an M.F.A. from the University of Iowa, and an M.A. in spirituality from Santa Clara University. He has received numerous fellowships and awards, including the Award in Literature from the American Academy and Institute of Arts and Letters. Hansen has

Ulf Andersen/Getty Images.

taught writing and literature at Stanford, the University of Michigan, Cornell, and the University of Iowa, and is currently the Gerard Manley Hopkins, S.J., Professor in the Arts and Humanities at Santa Clara University. He is the author of a number of novels — *Desperadoes: A Novel* (1979), *The Assassination of Jesse James by the Coward Robert Ford* (1983), *Mariette in Ecstasy* (1992), *Atticus* (1996), *Hitler's Niece* (1999), *Isn't It Romantic?* (2003), *Exiles* (2008), and *A Wild Surge of Guilty Passion* (2011) — two collections of short fiction — *Nebraska: Stories* (1989) and *She Loves Me Not: New and Selected Stories* (2012) — and a children's book, *The Shadowmaker* (1987). Hansen's works tend to smudge generic lines, partaking freely of popular modes such as the murder mystery and the western, and to emphasize spiritual conflicts within his characters.

My Kid's Dog   2003

My kid's dog died.
    Sparky.
    I hated that dog.
    The feeling was mutual.
    We got off on the wrong foot. Whining in his pen those first nights. My squirt   5
gun in his face and him blinking from the water. And then the holes in the yard.

The so-called accidents in the house. His nose snuffling into my Brooks Brothers trousers. Him slurping my fine Pilsner beer or sneaking bites of my Dagwood sandwich when I fell asleep on the sofa. Also his inability to fetch, to take a joke, to find the humor in sudden air horns. To be dandled, roughhoused, or teased. And then the growling, the skulking, the snapping at my ankles, the hiding from me under the house, and literally thousands of abject refusals to obey. Like, *Who the hell are you?*

You'd have thought he was a cat. When pushed to the brink I shouted, "I'll cut your face off and show it to you," and the small-brained mammal just stared at me.

But with the kids or my wife little Foo-Foo was a changeling, conning them with the tail, the prance, the peppiness, the soft chocolate eyes, the sloppy expressions of love, the easy tricks that if I performed I'd get no credit for.

Oh, we understood each other all right. I was on to him.

And then, at age ten, and none too soon, he kicked the bucket. You'd think that would be it. End of story. But no, he had to get even.

Those who have tears, prepare to shed them. 10

I was futzing with the hinges on the front-yard gate on a Saturday afternoon, my tattersall shirtsleeves rolled up and mind off in Oklahoma, when I noticed Fido in the California shade, snoozing, but for once a little wistful too, and far more serene than he usually was in my offensive presence. I tried to surprise him with my standard patriarchal shout, but it was no go, so I walked over and prodded the little guy with my wingtip. Nothing doing. And not so much as a flutter in his oddly abstracted face. Surely this was the big sleep, I thought.

She who must be obeyed was at the mall, provisioning, so I was safe from objection or inquiry on that account. I then made an inventory of my progeny: Buzz in the collegiate East, in the realm of heart-attack tuitions, Zack in the netherworld of the surf shop, Suzy, my last kid, on her bike and somewhere with her cousin. Were I to bury Rover with due haste and dispatch I could forestall the waterworks, even convince them that he'd signed up with the circus, run afoul of Cruella De Vil° — anything but died.

I got a green tarpaulin from the garage and laid it out on the front lawn where I hesitated before using my shoe to roll Spot into his funeral shroud, then dragged him back into the victory garden where summer's dying zucchini plants were in riot. With trusty spade I dug his burial place, heaped earth atop him, tamped it down with satisfying *whumps.*

I was feeling good about myself, heroic, as if, miraculously, compassion and charity had invaded not only my bones but my sinewy muscle tissues. I fixed myself a tall glass of gin and tonic and watched the first quarter of the USC football game.

And then pangs of conscience assailed me. Hadn't my investigation of 15 said demise of Precious been rather cursory? Wouldn't I, myself, closely cross-examine a suspect whose emotions were clouded, whose nefarious wishes were well established, whose veterinary skills were without credential? The innocence of my childhood had been spoiled with the tales of Edgar Allan Poe, so it was not difficult to conjure images of Scruffy clawing through tarpaulin and earth as he fought for one last gasp of air, air that others could more profitably use.

I marched out to the garden with aforementioned spade and with great lumbar strain exhumed our darling lapdog. Considering the circumstances, he seemed none the worse for wear, but I did detect a marked disinclination to respirate, which I took as a sign either of his inveterate stubbornness or of his having reached the Stygian shore. The latter seemed more likely. I heard in my fuddled head a line from

---

Cruella De Vil: A fictional character popularized in Disney films who kidnapped puppies.

The Wild Bunch when a critically injured gunman begs his outlaw gang to "finish it." And in the healing spirit of Hippocrates I lifted high the shovel and whanged it down on Harvey's head.

To my relief, not a whimper issued from him. I was confident he was defunct.

With care I shrouded and buried him again, committing earth to earth and dust to dust and so on, and with spritelike step conveyed myself to the kitchen where I made another gin and tonic and, in semiprone position, settled into the game's third quarter, the fabled Trojan running attack grinding out, it would seem, another win.

I was shocked awake by the impertinence of a ringing telephone, which I, with due caution, answered. It was my wife's friend Vicki inquiring about the pooch, for it was her assertion that Snip had fancied a taste of her son's upper calf and without invitation or permission to do so had partaken of same within the last twenty-four hours. Even while I was wondering what toxicity lurked in the child's leg and to what extent the poison was culpably responsible for our adored pet's actionable extinction, a loss we would feel for our lifetimes, Vicki insisted that I have the dog checked out by a vet to ascertain if he had rabies.

Cause of death: rabies? It seemed unlikely. Notwithstanding his surliness, 20 there'd been no Cujoesque frothing or lunging at car windows; but my familiarity with torts has made me both careful and rather unctuous in confrontation with a plaintiff, and so I assured the complainant that I would accede to her request.

Off to the back yard again, my pace that of a woebegone trudge, and with my implement of agriculture I displaced the slack and loosened earth. This was getting old. With an accusatory tone I said, "You're doing this on purpose, aren't you," and I took his silence as a plea of nolo contendere.°

My plan, of course, was to employ the Oldsmobile 88 to transport my burden to the canine's autopsy at Dr. Romo's office just a half mile away. However, upon settling into its plush front seat, it came to my attention that Zack — he who is but a sojourner on this earth — had not thought to replenish the fuel he'd used up on his trip to the Hollywood Bowl last night. The vehicle was not in a condition of plenitude. Would not ferry us farther than a block.

With Buster lying in the altogether on the driveway, not yet unsightly but no calendar page, I went into the house and found an old leather suitcase in the attic, then stuffed the mutt into the larger flapped compartment before hefting him on his final journey to those veterinary rooms he always shivered in.

I am, as I may have implied, a man of depth, perspicacity, and nearly Olympian strength, but I found myself hauling my heavy and lifeless cargo to Dr. Romo's with a pronounced lack of vigor and resolve. The September afternoon was hot, the Pasadena streets were vacant, the entire world seemed to have found entertainment and surcease in ways that I had not. I was, in a word, in a sweaty snit, and after many panting and pain-filled stops, my spine in Quasimodo configuration and my right arm gradually inching longer than my left, it was all I could do not to heave the suitcase containing Wonderdog into a haulaway behind the Chinese restaurant.

But during our joint ordeal I had developed a grudging affection for our pet; he 25 who'd been so quick to defend my kith and kin against the noise of passing trucks, who took loud notice of the squirrels outside, who held fast in the foyer, hackles

---

nolo contendere: Latin for "I do not wish to contend."

raised, fearlessly barking, whenever company arrived at the front door. With him I seemed calm, masterful, and uneccentric, the Superior Man that the *I Ching* talks so much about. Without him, I thought, I would be otherwise.

I put down the suitcase to shake the ache from my fingers and subtract affliction from my back, and it was then that my final indignity came. An angel of mercy spied my plight, braked his ancient Cadillac, and got out, his facial piercings and tattoos and shoot-the-marbles eyes belying the kindness and decency of his heart as he asked, "Can I help you with that suitcase?"

"I can handle it."

"Are you sure?"

"I'm just two blocks away."

"What the heck's in it?" he asked.   30

And for some reason I said, "A family heirloom."

"Wow!" he said. "Why don't you put it in my trunk and I'll help you with it? I got nothin' better to do."

Well, I did not just fall off the turnip truck. I would have been, in other circumstances, suspicious. But I was all too aware of the weight and worthlessness of my cumbrance, and so I granted his specified offer, hoisting the deceased into the Seville and slamming down the trunk lid. And, in evidence of our fallen state, my Samaritan immediately took off without me, jeering and peeling rubber and speeding west toward Los Angeles.

I could only lift my hand in a languid wave. *So long, old sport.*

Our world being the location of penance and recrimination, it was only right   35
that my last kid should pedal up to me on her bike just then and ask, "Daddy, what are you doing here?"

Waving to a guy, I thought, *who's about to become an undertaker.*

And then I confessed. Sparky's sudden death, the burial, not the exhumation and execution attempt, but the imputation of rabies and my arduous efforts to acquit his reputation with a pilgrimage to the vet's.

Suzy took it in with sangfroid for a little while, but then the lip quivered and tears spilled from her gorgeous eyes, and as I held her close she begged me to get her another dog just like Sparky. And that was Sparky's final revenge, for I said, "Okay, honey. Another dog, just like him."

Considerations for Critical Thinking and Writing

1. **FIRST RESPONSE.** What's so funny about a family's dog dying? How does Hansen transform this unpromising subject matter into humorous material?

2. Is there anything likable about the narrator despite the way he treats Sparky and his wife and children? Explain why or why not.

3. How does the narrator's use of language help to characterize him? Choose a paragraph in which his language seems representative of his personality, and analyze the way in which his diction and phrasing reveal his character.

4. Point to specific moments in the story when Hansen further complicates the plot and delays resolving the story's conflicts.

5. Trace the names that the narrator calls the dog throughout the story. Do they suggest anything about how he really feels about him?

6. In what sense is this story a revenge plot?

7. Discuss the tone of the final paragraph. Is it consistent with the rest of the story? Why or why not?

Connections to Other Selections

1. Compare the opening lines of this story with the openings of several others in this anthology. Discuss how their respective writers immediately engage their readers' interest.

2. Compare the tone of this revenge story with that of Edgar Allan Poe's "The Cask of Amontillado" (p. 579).

Mark Twain (1835–1910)

© Bettmann/CORBIS.

Mark Twain is the pen name of Samuel Clemens, born in Missouri in 1835. Twain spent most of his childhood in Hannibal, Missouri, on the Mississippi River, and after the death of his father when he was eleven, he worked at a series of jobs to help support his family. A newspaper job prepared him to wander east working for papers and exploring St. Louis, New York, and Philadelphia. Later he trained as a steamboat pilot on the Mississippi and piloted boats professionally until the onset of the Civil War. Clemens had used a couple of different pseudonyms for minor publications before this point, but in 1863 he signed a travel narrative "Mark Twain," from a boating term that means "two fathoms deep," and the name for the great American humorist was created. Twain gained fame in 1865 with his story "The Celebrated Jumping Frog of Calaveras County," which appeared in the New York–based *Saturday Press*. He then became a traveling correspondent, writing pieces on his travels to Europe and the Middle East, and returned to the United States in 1870, when he married and moved to Connecticut. Twain produced *Roughing It* (1872) and *The Gilded Age* (1873) while he toured the country lecturing, and in 1876 published *The Adventures of Tom Sawyer*, an instant hit. His subsequent publications include *A Tramp Abroad* (1880), *The Prince and the Pauper* (1881), and the masterpiece *The Adventures of Huckleberry Finn* (1884). Often traveling and lecturing, Twain wrote several more books, including story collections, *The Tragedy of Pudd'nhead Wilson* (1894), and *Tom Sawyer, Detective* (1896), before he died in Italy in 1910. His work is noted for the combination of rough humor and vernacular language it often uses to convey keen social insights. In "The Story of the Good Little Boy" Twain offers his version of a Sunday-school lesson.

The Story of the Good Little Boy   1870

Once there was a good little boy by the name of Jacob Blivens. He always obeyed his parents, no matter how absurd and unreasonable their demands were; and he always learned his book, and never was late at Sabbath-school. He would not play hookey, even when his sober judgment told him it was the most profitable thing he could do. None of the other boys could ever make that boy out, he acted so strangely. He wouldn't lie, no matter how convenient it was. He just said it was wrong to lie, and that was sufficient for him. And he was so honest that he was simply ridiculous. The curious ways that that Jacob had, surpassed everything. He wouldn't play marbles on Sunday, he wouldn't rob birds' nests, he wouldn't give hot pennies to organ-grinders' monkeys; he didn't seem to take any interest in any kind of rational amusement. So the other boys used to try to reason it out and come to an understanding of him, but they couldn't arrive at any satisfactory conclusion. As I said before, they could only figure out a sort of vague idea that he was "afflicted," and so they took him under their protection, and never allowed any harm to come to him.

This good little boy read all the Sunday-school books; they were his greatest delight. This was the whole secret of it. He believed in the good little boys they put in the Sunday-school books; he had every confidence in them. He longed to come across one of them alive once; but he never did. They all died before his time, maybe. Whenever he read about a particularly good one he turned over quickly to the end to see what became of him, because he wanted to travel thousands of miles and gaze on him; but it wasn't any use; that good little boy always died in the last chapter, and there was a picture of the funeral, with all his relations and the Sunday-school children standing around the grave in pantaloons that were too short, and bonnets that were too large, and everybody crying into handkerchiefs that had as much as a yard and a half of stuff in them. He was always headed off in this way. He never could see one of those good little boys on account of his always dying in the last chapter.

Jacob had a noble ambition to be put in a Sunday-school book. He wanted to be put in, with pictures representing him gloriously declining to lie to his mother, and her weeping for joy about it; and pictures representing him standing on the doorstep giving a penny to a poor beggar-woman with six children, and telling her to spend it freely, but not to be extravagant, because extravagance is a sin; and pictures of him magnanimously refusing to tell on the bad boy who always lay in wait for him around the corner as he came from school, and welted him over the head with a lath, and then chased him home, saying, "Hi! hi!" as he proceeded. That was the ambition of young Jacob Blivens. He wished to be put in a Sunday-school book. It made him feel a little uncomfortable sometimes when he reflected that the good little boys always died. He loved to live, you know, and this was the most unpleasant feature about being a Sunday-school-book boy. He knew it was not healthy to be good. He knew it was more fatal than consumption to be so supernaturally good as the boys in the books were; he knew that none of them had ever been able to stand it long, and it pained him to think that if they put him in a book he wouldn't ever see it, or even if they did get the book out before he died it wouldn't be popular without any picture of his funeral in the back part of it. It couldn't be much of a Sunday-school book that couldn't tell about the advice he gave to the community when he was dying. So at last, of course, he had to make up his mind to do the best he could under the circumstances — to live right, and, hang on as long as he could, and have his dying speech all ready when his time came.

But somehow nothing ever went right with this good little boy; nothing ever turned out with him the way it turned out with the good little boys in the books. They always had a good time, and the bad boys had the broken legs; but in his case there was a screw loose somewhere, and it all happened just the other way. When he found Jim Blake stealing apples, and went under the tree to read to him about the bad little boy who fell out of a neighbor's apple tree and broke his arm, Jim fell out of the tree, too, but he fell on *him* and broke *his* arm, and Jim wasn't hurt at all. Jacob couldn't understand that. There wasn't anything in the books like it.

And once, when some bad boys pushed a blind man over in the mud, and   5
Jacob ran to help him up and receive his blessing, the blind man did not give him any blessing at all, but whacked him over the head with his stick and said he would like to catch him shoving *him* again, and then pretending to help him up. This was not in accordance with any of the books. Jacob looked them all over to see.

One thing that Jacob wanted to do was to find a lame dog that hadn't any place to stay, and was hungry and persecuted, and bring him home and pet him and have that dog's imperishable gratitude. And at last he found one and was happy; and he brought him home and fed him, but when he was going to pet him the dog flew at him and tore all the clothes off him except those that were in front, and made a spectacle of him that was astonishing. He examined authorities, but he could not understand the matter. It was of the same breed of dogs that was in the books, but it acted very differently. Whatever this boy did he got into trouble. The very things the boys in the books got rewarded for turned out to be about the most unprofitable things he could invest in.

Once, when he was on his way to Sunday-school, he saw some bad boys starting off pleasuring in a sailboat. He was filled with consternation, because he knew from his reading that boys who went sailing on Sunday invariably got drowned. So he ran out on a raft to warn them, but a log turned with him and slid him into the river. A man got him out pretty soon, and the doctor pumped the water out of him, and gave him a fresh start with his bellows, but he caught cold and lay sick abed nine weeks. But the most unaccountable thing about it was that the bad boys in the boat had a good time all day, and then reached home alive and well in the most surprising manner. Jacob Blivens said there was nothing like these things in the books. He was perfectly dumbfounded.

When he got well he was a little discouraged, but he resolved to keep on trying anyhow. He knew that so far his experiences wouldn't do to go in a book, but he hadn't yet reached the allotted term of life for good little boys, and he hoped to be able to make a record yet if he could hold on till his time was fully up. If everything else failed he had his dying speech to fall back on.

He examined his authorities, and found that it was now time for him to go to sea as a cabin-boy. He called on a ship-captain and made his application, and when the captain asked for his recommendations he proudly drew out a tract and pointed to the word, "To Jacob Blivens, from his affectionate teacher." But the captain was a coarse, vulgar man, and he said, "Oh, that be blowed! *that* wasn't any proof that he knew how to wash dishes or handle a slush-bucket, and he guessed he didn't want him." This was altogether the most extraordinary thing that ever happened to Jacob in all his life. A compliment from a teacher, on a tract, had never failed to move the tenderest emotions of ship-captains, and open the way to all offices of honor and profit in their gift — it never had in any book that ever *he* had read. He could hardly believe his senses.

This boy always had a hard time of it. Nothing ever came out according to the   10
authorities with him. At last, one day, when he was around hunting up bad little boys to admonish, he found a lot of them in the old iron-foundry fixing up a little joke on fourteen or fifteen dogs, which they had tied together in long procession, and were going to ornament with empty nitroglycerin cans made fast to their

tails. Jacob's heart was touched. He sat down on one of those cans (for he never minded grease when duty was before him), and he took hold of the foremost dog by the collar, and turned his reproving eye upon wicked Tom Jones. But just at that moment Alderman McWelter, full of wrath, stepped in. All the bad boys ran away, but Jacob Blivens rose in conscious innocence and began one of those stately little Sunday-school-book speeches which always commence with "Oh, sir!" in dead opposition to the fact that no boy, good or bad, ever starts a remark with "Oh, sir." But the alderman never waited to hear the rest. He took Jacob Blivens by the ear and turned him around, and hit him a whack in the rear with the flat of his hand; and in an instant that good little boy shot out through the roof and soared away toward the sun, with the fragments of those fifteen dogs stringing after him like the tail of a kite. And there wasn't a sign of that alderman or that old iron-foundry left on the face of the earth; and, as for young Jacob Blivens, he never got a chance to make his last dying speech after all his trouble fixing it up, unless he made it to the birds; because, although the bulk of him came down all right in a tree-top in an adjoining county, the rest of him was apportioned around among four townships, and so they had to hold five inquests on him to find out whether he was dead or not, and how it occurred. You never saw a boy scattered so.[1]

Thus perished the good little boy who did the best he could, but didn't come out according to the books. Every boy who ever did as he did prospered except him. His case is truly remarkable. It will probably never be accounted for.

[1] This glycerin catastrophe is borrowed from a floating newspaper item, whose author's name I would give if I knew it. M.T.

CONSIDERATIONS FOR CRITICAL THINKING AND WRITING

1. FIRST RESPONSE. This story is about the death of a child. What's so funny about that?

2. What is the story's central irony?

3. Which sentences are particularly effective in imitating the style of Sunday-school books? Which sentences are clearly Twain's style? What is the effect of having both styles side by side?

4. How does the story's irony reveal Twain's attitude toward Jacob? Find specific passages to support your points.

5. What sort of lesson does Twain's version of Sunday-school instruction teach?

6. Is there a serious point to the humor here? What is the theme of the story?

7. It might be tempting to sum up this story with something like "Nice guys finish last." Discuss the adequacy of this as a statement of theme.

8. Characterize the tone of voice that tells the story. Is it indignant, amused, cynical, bitter, disinterested, or what?

CONNECTIONS TO OTHER SELECTIONS

1. Compare Jacob's fate with that of the central character in Ralph Ellison's "Battle Royal" (p. 227).

2. Write an essay explaining the extent to which this story and Stephen Crane's "The Bride Comes to Yellow Sky" (p. 251) are dependent on a reader's familiarity with the formulaic qualities of Sunday-school stories or traditional westerns.

18

A THEMATIC CASE STUDY
Remarkably Short Short Stories

A ratio of failures is built into the process of writing. The wastebasket has evolved for a reason.
— MARGARET ATWOOD

© Kathy deWitt/Alamy.

All of the seven very short stories in this chapter are fewer than three pages in length and can be read in less than five minutes. These numbers do not measure what the stories achieve as works of literature, however. Their remarkably focused form gives you an intense opportunity to read fiction carefully and deliberately in order to enhance your understanding and pleasure.

Short-short stories have developed into a genre of their own in recent years; they are known variously as *sudden, flash, fast, quick, micro,* or *mini fiction.* A number of anthologies have now compiled stories that are only a few pages long. Authors enjoy the challenge of writing in such an intense and disciplined form, while readers appreciate the express journeys into writers' imaginations that are skillfully mapped and allow readers to travel at their own pace. These brief works do not sacrifice complexity, depth, seriousness, or subtlety. You'll find in these stories some characters who will make you laugh, wince, feel wistful, and experience the full weight of human loss and tragedy. Moreover, while the plots are not long, they are intriguing because they engage the characters in conflicts that are crucial to them and will likely matter to you. Give it five minutes. You'll see.

LYDIA DAVIS (B. 1947)

Born in Northampton, Massachusetts, Lydia Davis graduated from Barnard College in 1970, after which she began work as a translator of French literature. Her success as a translator can be measured in part by the French government's awarding her the Chevalier of the Order of Arts. She has won high praise particularly for her translations of Marcel Proust. As a fiction writer, Davis has appeared in numerous literary periodicals while publishing one novel, *The End of the Story* (1995), and a number of collections of short stories, including *Break It Down* (1986); *Almost No*

© Colin McPherson/Corbis.

Memory (1997); *Samuel Johnson Is Indignant* (2001), *Varieties of Disturbances: Stories* (2007); *The Collected Stories of Lydia Davis* (2009); and *Can't and Won't* (2014), the collection from which "Negative Emotions" is reprinted. Among the prestigious literary prizes that Davis has been awarded are fellowships from the MacArthur and Guggenheim foundations, a Lannan Literary Award, and a Whiting Writer's Award. She has taught at several schools, including Bard College and the University at Albany. Davis is well known for her brief, compact, sharp, and often humorous fictions that survey contemporary life. "In such a form," she observes, "each word has to be right."

Negative Emotions 2014

A well-meaning teacher, inspired by a text he had been reading, once sent all the other teachers in his school a message about negative emotions. The message consisted entirely of advice quoted from a Vietnamese Buddhist monk.

Emotion, said the monk, is like a storm: it stays for a while and then it goes. Upon perceiving the emotion (like a coming storm), one should put oneself in a stable position. One should sit or lie down. One should focus on one's abdomen. One should focus, specifically, on the area just below one's navel, and practice mindful breathing. If one can identify the emotion as an emotion, it may then be easier to handle.

The other teachers were puzzled. They did not understand why their colleague had sent them a message about negative emotions. They resented the message, and they resented their colleague. They thought he was accusing them of having negative emotions and needing advice about how to handle them. Some of them were, in fact, angry.

The teachers did not choose to regard their anger as a coming storm. They did not focus on their abdomens. They did not focus on the area just below their navels.

Instead, they wrote back immediately, declaring that because they did not understand why he had sent it, his message had filled them with negative emotions. They told him that it would take a lot of practice for them to get over the negative emotions caused by his message. But, they went on, they did not intend to do this practice. Far from being troubled by their negative emotions, they said, they in fact liked having negative emotions, particularly about him and his message.

CONSIDERATIONS FOR CRITICAL THINKING AND WRITING

1. FIRST RESPONSE. Why does it make sense that the author of this story is also a professional translator? What does that fact suggest about her sensitivity to diction and tone?
2. Describe the movement of the story's plot. What elements of a typical plot (see the glossary entry for *plot*) can you find in the story?
3. Which paragraphs seem particularly humorous to you? Explain why the story does or doesn't make a serious point.
4. To what extent do you think these paragraphs constitute a short story?

CONNECTION TO ANOTHER SELECTION

1. Compare the style, tone, and irony of Davis's story with those of Annie Proulx's "55 Miles to the Gas Pump" (p. 517).

RON CARLSON (B. 1947)

Born in Logan, Utah, Ron Carlson is emeritus professor of English at Arizona State University. He has published his fiction widely in magazines such as the *New Yorker, Esquire,* and *Harper's*. To date he has published four novels, the most recent being *The Signal* (2010), and five collections of short stories, the last *The Blue Box* (2014). On his own work Carlson has commented: "I think all stories, long and short, require astonishing attention.... Attention is the ruler of craft." And for a discussion of his own short story writing, see *Ron Carlson Writes a Story* (2007).

> WHEN I WRITE "After I finish a story, I wait a few days and make sure I've got every beat, every moment that I wanted. I look for the thing I've omitted or hurried past. I also read everything I write aloud." —RON CARLSON

Max   1986

Max is a crotch dog. He has powerful instinct and insistent snout, and he can ruin a cocktail party faster than running out of ice. This urge of his runs deeper than any training can reach. He can sit, heel, fetch; he'll even fetch a thrown snowball from a snowfield, bringing a fragment of it back to you delicately in his mouth. And then he'll poke your crotch, and be warned: it is no gentle nuzzling.

So when our friend Maxwell came by for a drink to introduce us to his new girlfriend, our dog Max paddled up to him and jabbed him a sharp one, a stroke so clean and fast it could have been a boxing glove on a spring. Maxwell, our friend, lost his breath and sat on the couch suddenly and heavily, unable to say anything beyond a hoarse whisper of "*Scotch.* Just *scotch.* No ice."

Cody put Max out on the back porch, of course, where he has spent a good measure of this long winter, and Maxwell took a long nourishing sip on his scotch and began recovering. He's not athletic at all, but I admired the way he had folded, crumpling just like a ballplayer taking an inside pitch in the nuts. It wasn't enough to change my whole opinion of him, but it helped me talk to him civilly for five minutes while Cody calmed the dog. I think I had seen a sly crocodile smile on Max's face after he'd struck, pride in a job well done, possibly, and then again, possibly a deeper satisfaction. He had heard Cody and me talk about Maxwell before, and Max is a smart dog.

Maxwell, his color returning, was now explaining that his new girlfriend, Laurie, would be along in a minute; she had been detained at aerobics class. Life at the museum was hectic and lovely, he was explaining. It was frustrating for him to be working with folk so ignorant of what made a good show, of counterpoint, of even the crudest elements of art. Let alone business, the business of curating, the business of public responsibility, the business in general. I was hoping to get him on his arch tirade about how the average intelligence in his department couldn't make a picture by connecting the dots, a routine which Cody could dial up like a phone number. But I wasn't going to get it tonight; he was already on business, his favorite topic.

The truth is that Maxwell is a simple crook. He uses his office to travel like a 5 pasha; he damages borrowed work, sees to the insurance, and then buys some of it for himself; he only mounts three shows a year; and he only goes in four days a week.

Cody came in for one of her favorite parts, Maxwell's catalogue (including stores and prices) of the clothing and jewelry he was wearing tonight. Cody always asked about the clerks, and so his glorious monologue was sprinkled with diatribes about the help. Old Maxwell.

When his girlfriend, Laurie, finally did arrive, breathless and airy at the same time, Maxwell had all three rings on the coffee table and he was showing Cody his new watch. Laurie tossed her head three times taking off her coat; we were in for a record evening.

Maxwell would show her off for a while, making disparaging remarks about exercise *of any kind,* and she would admire his rings, ranking them like tokens on the table, going into complex and aesthetic reasons for her choices. I would fill her full of the white wine that all of Maxwell's girlfriends drink, and then when she asked where the powder room was, I would rise with her and go into the kitchen, wait, count to twenty-five while selecting another Buckhorn out of the fridge, and let Max in.

CONSIDERATIONS FOR CRITICAL THINKING AND WRITING

1. FIRST RESPONSE. Why do you think the story is titled "Max" rather than "Maxwell"?

2. What details are especially effective in characterizing Maxwell and his girlfriend?

3. How does the narrator serve as an implicit foil to Maxwell?

4. CREATIVE RESPONSE. Write an additional final paragraph that describes what happens when Max is let back into the house, a paragraph that is worthy of the humor in the rest of the story.

5. Why do you think Carlson didn't write that paragraph?

CONNECTION TO ANOTHER SELECTION

1. Compare the narrator's relationship to his dog in "Max" and in Howard Nemerov's "Walking the Dog" (p. 1012).

MARK HALLIDAY (B. 1949)

Born in Ann Arbor, Michigan, Mark Halliday earned a B.A. and an M.A. from Brown University and a Ph.D. from Brandeis University. A teacher at Ohio University, his short stories and poems have appeared in a variety of periodicals, including the *Massachusetts Review, Michigan Quarterly Review, Chicago Review,* and the *New Republic.* Among his six collections of poetry, *Little Star* was selected by the National Poetry Series for publication in 1987. He has also written a critical study on poet Wallace Stevens titled *Stevens and the Interpersonal* (1991).

WHEN I WRITE "After fifty, a year can seem strangely brief, and even a decade can vanish like a dream. I wrote this story when I was around forty, thinking about my father and how mysterious to him the racing away of his youth must seem. Now that I'm over sixty, the story's feeling has come closer to home." — MARK HALLIDAY

Young Man on Sixth Avenue   1995

He was a young man in the big city. He was a young man in the biggest, the most overwhelming city — and he was not overwhelmed. For see, he strode across Fifth Avenue just before the light changed, and his head was up in the sharp New York wind and he was thriving upon the rock of Manhattan, in 1938. His legs were long and his legs were strong; there was no question about his legs; they were unmistakable in their length and strength; they were as bold and dependable as any American machine, moving him across Fifth just in time, his brown shoes attaining the sidewalk without any faltering, his gait unaware of the notion that legs might ever want to rest. Forty-ninth Street! He walked swiftly through the haste and blare, through the chilly exclamation points of taxis and trucks and people. He was a man! In America, '38, New York, two o'clock in the afternoon, sunlight chopping down between buildings, Forty-ninth Street. And his hair was so dark, almost black, and it had a natural wave in it recognized as a handsome feature by everyone, recognized universally, along with his dark blue eyes and strong jaw. Women saw him, they all had to see him, all the young women had to perceive him reaching the corner of Forty-ninth and Sixth, and they had to know he was a candidate. He knew they knew. He knew they knew he would *get* some of them, and he moved visibly tall with the tall potential of the not-finite twentieth-century getting that would be his inheritance; and young women who glanced at him on Sixth Avenue knew that he knew. They felt that they or their sisters would have to take him into account, and they touched their scarves a little nervously.

He was twenty-five years old, and this day in 1938 was the present. It was so obviously and totally the present, so unabashed and even garish with its present-ness, beamingly right there right now like Rita Hayworth,° all Sixth Avenue was in fact at two o'clock a thumping bright Rita Hayworth and the young man strode south irresistibly. If there was only one thing he knew, crossing Forty-eighth, it was that this day was the present, out of which uncounted glories could and must blossom — when? — in 1938, or in 1939, soon, or in the big brazen decade ahead, in 1940, soon; so he walked with fistfuls of futures that could happen in all his pockets.

And his wavy hair was so dark, almost black. And he knew the right restaurant for red roast beef, not too expensive. And in his head were some sharp ideas about Dreiser, and Thomas Wolfe, and John O'Hara.

On Forty-seventh between two buildings (buildings taller even than him) there was an unexpected zone of deep shade. He paused for half a second, and he shivered for some reason. Briskly then, briskly he moved ahead.

In the restaurant on Seventh Avenue he met his friend John for a witty late   5
lunch. Everything was — the whole lunch was good. It was right. And what they said was both hilarious and notably well informed. And then soon he was taking the stairs two at a time up to an office on Sixth for his interview. The powerful lady seemed to like his sincerity and the clarity of his eyes — a hard combination to beat — and the even more powerful man in charge sized him up and saw the same things, and he got the job.

That job lasted three years, then came the War, then another job, then Judy, and the two kids, and a better job in Baltimore, and those years — those years. And those years. "Those years" — and the kids went to college with new typewriters. In the blue chair, with his work on his lapboard, after a pleasant dinner of macaroni and sausage and salad, he dozed off. Then he was sixty. Sixty? Then he rode back and forth on trains, Judy became ill, doctors offered opinions, comas were decep-tive, Judy died. But the traffic on Coleytown Road next morning still moved casu-ally too fast. And in a minute he was seventy-five and the phone rang with news that witty John of the great late lunches was dead. The house pulsed with silence.

Something undone? What? The thing that would have saved — what? Wak-ing in the dark — maybe something unwritten, that would have made people say "*Yes* that's why you matter so much." Ideas about Wolfe. Dreiser. Or some lost point about John O'Hara.

Women see past him on the street in this pseudo-present and he feels they are so stupid and walks fierce for a minute but then his shoulders settle closer to his skeleton with the truth about these women: not especially stupid; only young. In this pseudo-present he blinks at a glimpse of that young man on Sixth Avenue, young man as if still out there in the exclamation of Sixth Avenue — that young man ready to stride across — but a taxi makes him step back to the curb, he'll have to wait a few more seconds, he can wait.

Rita Hayworth (1918–1987): A Hollywood movie star.

CONSIDERATIONS FOR CRITICAL THINKING AND WRITING

1. FIRST RESPONSE. Do you identify with the young man as he is described in the first paragraph? Is he appealing to you? Why or why not?
2. Why do you think this story opens in 1938? Why is the Manhattan setting important?
3. The American novelists Theodore Dreiser, Thomas Wolfe, and John O'Hara are mentioned in paragraphs 3 and 7. Of what significance are these novelists in this story? You may have to research these writers to answer this question.
4. What is the conflict in the story?
5. Locate the climax in the story. Is there a resolution to the conflict? Explain.

CONNECTIONS TO OTHER SELECTIONS

1. Discuss the significance of the Manhattan setting in "Young Man on Sixth Avenue" and in Xu Xi's "Famine" (p. 263).
2. Write an essay comparing the ending of Halliday's story with that of Raymond Carver's "Popular Mechanics" (p. 277). What is the effect of the ending on your reading of each story?

DAVID FOSTER WALLACE (1962–2008)

© Gary Hannabarger/CORBIS.

Born in Ithaca, New York, David Foster Wallace grew up in Illinois and graduated with a B.A. from Amherst College and an M.F.A. from the University of Arizona. He taught in the English department at Illinois State University and then became a professor of English at Pomona College. His essays and fiction appeared in magazines ranging from the *New Yorker* to the *Paris Review.* These, along with his three novels — *The Broom of the System* (1987), *Infinite Jest* (1996), and *The Pale King* (2011) — and three short story collections — *Girl with Curious Hair* (1989), *Brief Interviews with Hideous Men* (1999), and *Oblivion* (2004) — earned him a meteoric literary reputation as an innovative writer. "Incarnations of Burned Children" was originally published in *Esquire.*

Incarnations of Burned Children   2000

The Daddy was around the side of the house hanging a door for the tenant when he heard the child's screams and the Mommy's voice gone high between them. He could move fast, and the back porch gave onto the kitchen, and before the screen door had banged shut behind him the Daddy had taken the scene in whole, the overturned pot on the floortile before the stove and the burner's blue jet and the floor's pool of water still steaming as its many arms extended, the toddler in his baggy diaper standing rigid with steam coming off his hair and his chest and shoulders scarlet and his eyes rolled up and mouth open very wide and seeming somehow separate from the sounds that issued, the Mommy down on one knee with the dishrag dabbing pointlessly at him and matching the screams with cries of her own, hysterical so she was almost frozen. Her one knee and the bare little soft feet were still in the steaming pool and the Daddy's first act was to take the child under the arms and lift him away from it and take him to the sink, where he threw out plates and struck the tap to let cold well water run over the boy's feet while with his cupped hand he gathered and poured or flung cold water over his head and shoulders and chest, wanting first to see the steam stop coming off him, the Mommy over his shoulder invoking God until he sent her for towels and gauze if they had it, the Daddy moving quickly and well and his man's mind empty of everything but purpose, not yet aware of how smoothly he moved or that he'd ceased to hear the high screams because to hear them would freeze him and make impossible what had to be done to help his child, whose screams were regular as breath and went on so long they'd become already a thing in the kitchen, something else to move quickly around. The tenant side's door outside hung half off its top hinge and moved slightly in the wind, and a bird in the oak across the driveway appeared to observe the door with a cocked head as the cries still came from inside. The worst scalds seemed to be the right arm and shoulder, the chest and stomach's red was fading to pink under the cold water and his feet's soft soles weren't blistered that the Daddy could see, but the toddler still made little fists and screamed except now merely on reflex from fear, the Daddy would know he thought possible later, small face distended and thready veins standing out at the temples and the Daddy kept saying he was here he was here, adrenaline ebbing and an anger at the Mommy for allowing this thing to happen just starting to gather in wisps at his mind's extreme rear still hours from expression. When the Mommy returned he wasn't sure whether to wrap the child in a towel or not but he wet the towel down and did, swaddled him tight and lifted his baby out of the sink and set him on the kitchen table's edge to soothe him while the Mommy tried to check the feet's soles with one hand waving around in the area of her mouth and uttering objectless words while the Daddy bent in and was face to face with the child on the table's checked edge repeating the fact that he was here and trying to calm the toddler's cries but still the child breathlessly screamed, a high pure shining sound that could stop his heart and his bitty lips and gums now tinged with the light blue of a low flame the Daddy thought, screaming as if almost still under the tilted pot in pain. A minute, two like this that seemed much longer, with the Mommy at the Daddy's side talking sing-song at the child's face and the lark on the limb with its head to the side and the hinge going white in a line from the weight of the canted door until the first wisp of steam came lazy from under the wrapped towel's hem and the parents' eyes met and widened — the diaper, which when they opened the towel and leaned their little boy back on the checkered cloth and unfastened the softened tabs and tried to remove it resisted slightly with new high cries and was hot, their baby's diaper burned their hand and they saw where the real water'd fallen and pooled and been burning their baby all this time while he screamed for them to help him and they hadn't, hadn't thought and when they got it off and saw the state of what was there the Mommy said their God's first name and grabbed the table to keep her feet while the father turned away and threw a haymaker at the air of the kitchen and cursed both himself and the world for not the last time while his child might now have been sleeping if not for the rate of his breathing and the tiny stricken motions of his hands in the air above where he lay, hands the size of a grown man's thumb that had clutched the Daddy's thumb in the crib while he'd watched the Daddy's mouth move in song, his head cocked and seeming to see way past him into something his eyes made the Daddy lonesome for in a sideways way. If you've never wept and want to, have a child. Break your heart inside and something will a child is the twangy song the Daddy hears again as if the radio's lady was almost there with him looking down at what they've done, though hours later what the Daddy won't most forgive is how badly he wanted a cigarette right then as they diapered the child as best they could in gauze and two crossed hand-towels and the Daddy lifted him like a newborn with his skull in one palm and ran him out to the hot truck and burned custom rubber all the way to town and the clinic's ER with the tenant's door hanging open like that all day until the hinge gave but by then it was too late, when it wouldn't stop and they couldn't make it the child had learned to leave himself and watch the whole rest unfold from a point overhead, and whatever was lost never thenceforth mattered, and the child's body expanded and walked about and drew pay and lived its life untenanted, a thing among things, its self's soul so much vapor aloft, falling as rain and then rising, the sun up and down like a yoyo.

CONSIDERATIONS FOR CRITICAL THINKING AND WRITING

1. FIRST RESPONSE. Describe the emotions this narration produces in you. What elements in the story are most effective in creating them for you?

2. How do you interpret the ending of this story? What do you think happens at the very end?

3. At one point the narrator steps in front of the action and addresses the reader: "If you've never wept and want to, have a child." Explain whether that sentence adequately sums up the theme of the story for you.

4. What do you make of the title?

CONNECTIONS TO OTHER SELECTIONS

1. Describe the unconventional style of Wallace's story and Joyce Carol Oates's "Hi Howya Doin" (p. 518). How is the style related to content in each story?

2. Compare the relationship between the husband and wife in "Incarnations of Burned Children" and in "Popular Mechanics" by Raymond Carver (p. 277).

MARK BUDMAN (B. 1950)

Born and raised in the former Soviet Union, Mark Budman came to the United States in the 1980s. After working at IBM and creating some of his own patents, he turned to short stories, focusing on flash fiction. In 2000 he cofounded with Sue O'Neil *Vestal Review,* a magazine devoted to flash fiction. He has published a semiautobiographical novel, *My Life at First Try,* that is told in very brief chapters and a collection titled *Lady Gaga's Dress and Other Absurd Stories* (2012). Budman has also coedited with Tom Hazuka *You Have*

Time for This: Contemporary Short-Short Stories (2007), and they have, along with Christine Perkins-Hazuka, edited *Sudden Flash Youth: 65 Short-Short Stories* (2011).

The Diary of a Salaryman 2007

Today I was promoted to a junior coordinator of coordinating activities. This means I'll get a 3% salary raise spread over five years. This also means I get to stay at work longer.

Wife bore quintuplets. Was allowed to take three days off from work. Brought home the laptop and had a telecon during the delivery.

My cubicle mate was laid off. Had to pick up his workload. When I bent over the crib today, one of the quintuplets peed in my face, from a foot away. I think it was a boy.

Wife e-mailed me a picture of the kids on their first day in school.

Was promoted to an associate coordinator of coordinating activities. This   5
means I'll get a 4% salary raise spread over five years. This also means I get to stay at work longer.

Today I saw a car with five teenagers leaving my garage. They waved at me. Is wife renting the garage out?

The new cubicle mate had a heart attack. While they were getting him on the stretcher, had a conversation with a guy from across the aisle. His name was Pete, and he's been with the company for twenty-four years. Twenty years in the same cubicle. Same as me.

Was promoted to a senior coordinator of coordinating activities. This means I'll get a 5% salary raise spread over five years. This also means I get to stay at work longer.

They laid me off today. Counted the remaining Valiums. Only three. Not enough for suicide.

Took my five grandchildren to a ball game today. Had ice cream in the park.   10
My chest was heaving and a strange sound came from my throat. I guess they call it laughter.

Wife retired. Ran out of Viagra, but had sex with her anyway. She screamed and raked my back with her nails. Wow. The last time she'd done that was nine months before the quintuplets were born.

Got a call from work today. They want to re-hire me. E-mailed them a pic of myself flipping the bird.

Today is my last diary entry for a while. Too busy planting strawberries in my garden. Wife takes a bubble bath. Means it's going to be a busy night, too.

CONSIDERATIONS FOR CRITICAL THINKING AND WRITING

1. **FIRST RESPONSE.** How is the world of work comically portrayed in the story? What other responses does the character evoke besides laughter?

2. Explain how the passage of time is deftly conveyed.

3. Discuss the effects of the repeated lines.

4. **CREATIVE RESPONSE.** Write a one-paragraph job description, preserving the narrator's tone, that explains what you imagine "a senior coordinator of coordinating activities" is actually doing at work.

CONNECTION TO ANOTHER SELECTION

1. Write an essay that discusses the plot and style of Budman's story and of Mark Halliday's "Young Man on Sixth Avenue" (p. 533).

PETER MEINKE (B. 1932)

Born in Brooklyn, New York, Peter Meinke was educated at Hamilton College (B.A., 1955), the University of Michigan (M.A., 1961), and the University of Minnesota (Ph.D., 1965). He has taught literature and creative writing at a number of schools, including Hamline University, Eckerd College, and Old Dominion University. Among his many poetry books are *Nightwatch on the Chesapeake* (1987), *Scars* (1996), *The Contracted World* (2006), and *Lucky Bones* (2014), which are notable for their powerful use of detail from everyday life as well as simple — and serious — humor. They have earned him two National Endowment for the Arts fellowships. Though Meinke is primarily a poet, he has also published two collections of short stories: *Piano Tuner* (1986), which won the Flannery O'Connor Award, and *Unheard Music* (2007). In a 1990 interview in *Clockwatch Review,* Meinke discussed the similarities he sees between short stories and poetry: "I think that certainly poetry and short stories are more alike than short stories and novels, because that's the main decision — leaving out the boffo endings, leaving out conversations that are extraneous. There's a big empty spot around poems and short stories, certainly. That's the thing they have very strongly in common." "The Cranes" is a fine example of the kind of literary economy that Meinke believes poetry and short stories often share.

WHEN I READ "It's important for poets to read fiction, and fiction writers to read poetry — this could add depth to the fiction and clarity to the poetry." — PETER MEINKE

The Cranes 1987

"Oh!" she said, "what are those, the huge white ones?" Along the marshy shore two tall and stately birds, staring motionless toward the Gulf, towered above the bobbing egrets and scurrying plovers.

"Well, I can't believe it," he said. "I've been coming here for years and never saw one."

"But what are they? Don't make me guess or anything; it makes me feel dumb." They leaned forward in the car, and the shower curtain spread over the front seat crackled and hissed.

"They've got to be whooping cranes, nothing else so big." One of the birds turned gracefully, as if to acknowledge the old Dodge parked alone in the tall grasses. "See the black legs and black wingtips? Big! Why don't I have my binoculars?" He looked at his wife and smiled.

"Well," he continued after a while, "I've seen enough birds. But whooping 5 cranes, they're rare. Not many left."

"They're lovely. They make the little birds look like clowns."

"I could use a few clowns," he said. "A few laughs never hurt anybody."

"Are you all right?" She put a hand on his thin arm. "I feel I'm responsible. Maybe this is the wrong thing."

"God, no!" His voice changed. "No way. I can't smoke, can't drink martinis, no coffee, no candy. I not only can't leap buildings in a single bound, I can hardly get up the goddamn stairs."

She was smiling. "Do you remember the time you drank nine martinis and 10 asked that young priest to step outside and see whose side God was on?"

"What a jerk I was! How have you put up with me all this time?"

"Oh no! I was proud of you. You were so funny, and that priest was a snot."

"Now you tell me." The cranes were moving slowly over a small hillock, wings opening and closing like bellows. "It's all right. It's enough," he said again. "How old am I anyway, 130?"

"Really," she said, "it's me. Ever since the accident it's been one thing after another. I'm just a lot of trouble to everybody."

"Let's talk about something else," he said. "Do you want to listen to the radio? 15 How about turning on that preacher station so we can throw up?"

"No," she said, "I just want to watch the birds. And listen to you."

"You must be pretty tired of that."

She turned her head from the window and looked into his eyes. "I never got tired of listening to you. Never."

"Well, that's good," he said. "It's just that when my mouth opens, your eyes tend to close."

"They do not!" she said, and began to laugh, but the laugh turned into a cough 20 and he had to pat her on the back until she stopped. They leaned back in silence and looked toward the Gulf stretching out beyond the horizon. In the distance, the water looked like metal, still and hard.

"I wish they'd court," he said. "I wish we could see them court, the cranes. They put on a show. He bows like Nijinsky and jumps straight up in the air."

"What does she do?"

"She lies down and he lands on top of her."

"No," she said, "I'm serious."

"Well, I forget. I've never seen it. But I do remember that they mate for life and 25 live a long time. They're probably older than we are. Their feathers are falling out and their kids never write."

She was quiet again. He turned in his seat, picked up an object wrapped in a plaid towel, and placed it between them in the front. "Here's looking at *you*, kid," he said.

"Do they really mate for life? I'm glad — they're so beautiful."

"Yep. Audubon said that's why they're almost extinct: a failure of imagination."

"I don't believe that," she said. "I think there'll always be whooping cranes."

"Why not?" he said.

"I wish the children were more settled. I keep thinking it's my fault."

"You think everything's your fault. Nicaragua. Ozone depletion. Nothing is your fault. They'll be fine, and anyway, they're not children anymore. Kids are different today, that's all. You were terrific." He paused. "You were terrific in ways I couldn't tell the kids about."

"I should hope not." She laughed and began coughing again, but held his hand when he reached over. When the cough subsided they sat quietly, looking down at their hands as if they were objects in a museum. "I used to have pretty hands," she said.

"I remember."

"Do you? Really?"

"I remember everything," he said.

"You always forgot everything."

"Well, now I remember."

"Did you bring something for your ears?"

"No, I can hardly hear anything, anyway." But he turned his head at a sudden squabble among the smaller birds. The cranes were stepping delicately away from the commotion.

"I'm tired," she said.

"Yes." He leaned over and kissed her, barely touching her lips. "Tell me," he said, "did I really drink nine martinis?"

But she had already closed her eyes and only smiled. Outside, the wind ruffled the bleached-out grasses, and the birds in the white glare seemed almost transparent. The hull of the car gleamed beetle-like — dull and somehow sinister in its metallic isolation.

Suddenly, the two cranes plunged upward, their great wings beating the air and their long slender necks pointed like arrows toward the sun.

Considerations for Critical Thinking and Writing

1. FIRST RESPONSE. What happens at the end of "The Cranes"? What do you think this story is about?

2. Does the couple's behavior seem motivated and plausible to you? Explain why or why not.

3. Point to incidences of suspenseful foreshadowing and discuss how they affect your understanding of the plot. Were you aware of the foreshadowing elements on a first reading or only after subsequent readings?

4. How might the cranes be read as both conventional and literary symbols in this story?

Connection to Another Selection

1. Consider how symbols convey the central meanings of "The Cranes" and of either Kate Chopin's "The Story of an Hour" (p. 15) or Gail Godwin's "A Sorrowful Woman" (p. 39).

TERRY L. TILTON

The following story by Terry L. Tilton appeared as a contest winner in *The World's Shortest Stories,* edited by Steve Moss. The book is described on the cover as follows: "Murder. Love. Horror. Suspense. All this and much more in the most amazing short stories ever written — each one just fifty-five words long!" And indeed they are all limited to fifty-five words — every one drawn from stories submitted in a contest with the winners selected for publication. If Terry L. Tilton has published more than these fifty-five words, they are not readily available, but here's a story that provided a positive answer to a question that the editor raised in his introduction: "Does such a stingy word count allow for a really satisfying read?" That's a good question. See what you think.

That Settles That 1998

Tom was a handsome, fun-loving young man, albeit a bit drunk when he got into the argument with Sam, his roommate of just two months.

"You can't. You can *not* write a short story in just 55 words, you idiot!"

Sam shot him dead on the spot.

"Oh, yes you can," Sam said, smiling.

CONSIDERATIONS FOR CRITICAL THINKING AND WRITING

1. FIRST RESPONSE. How satisfying a read is this as a short story?
2. Specifically, what elements of fiction can you identify in these fifty-five words?
3. CREATIVE RESPONSE. Write your own short story using precisely fifty-five words.

19

Stories for Further Reading

I mean to live and die by my own mind.

— ZORA NEALE HURSTON

Library of Congress, Prints and Photographs Division.

TONI CADE BAMBARA (1939–1995)

Raised in New York City's Harlem and Bedford-Stuyvesant communities, Toni Cade Bambara graduated from Queens College in 1959, studied in Florence and Paris, and earned her M.A. at City College of New York in 1964. She also studied dance, linguistics, and filmmaking and worked a variety of jobs in welfare, recreation, and community housing, in addition to teaching at various schools, including Rutgers University and Spelman College. She described her writing as "straight-up fiction . . . 'cause I value my family and friends, and mostly 'cause I lie a lot anyway." Her fiction has been collected in *Gorilla, My Love* (1972) and *The Sea Birds Are Still Alive* (1977), and in 1980 she published her first novel, *The Salt Eaters,* followed by *If Blessing Comes* (1987). Her most recent books, *Deep Sightings and Rescue Missions* (1996) and *These Bones Are Not My Child* (1999), were published posthumously. A number of her screenplays have been produced, including *Epitaph for Willie* and *Tar Baby.* In the following story an adolescent reflects on a memorable summer.

Sweet Town 1959

It is hard to believe that there was only one spring and one summer apiece that year, my fifteenth year. It is hard to believe that I so quickly squandered my youth in the sweet town playground of the sunny city, that wild monkeybardom of my fourth-grade youthhood. However, it was so.

"Dear Mother" — I wrote one day on her bathroom mirror with a candle sliver — "please forgive my absence and my decay and overlook the freckled dignity and pockmarked integrity plaguing me this season."

I used to come on even wilder sometimes and write her mad cryptic notes on the kitchen sink with charred matches. Anything for a bit, we so seldom saw each other. I even sometimes wrote her a note on paper. And then one day, having romped my soul through the spectrum of sunny colors, I dashed up to her apartment to escape the heat and found a letter from her which eternally elated my heart to the point of bursture and generally endeared her to me forever. Written on the kitchen table in cake frosting was the message, "My dear, mad, perverse young girl kindly take care and paint the fire escape in your leisure . . ." All the *i*'s were dotted with marmalade, the *t*'s were crossed with orange rind. Here was a sight to carry with one forever in the back of the screaming eyeballs somewhere. I howled for at least five minutes out of sheer madity and vowed to love her completely. Leisure. As if bare-armed spring ever let up from its invitation to perpetuate the race. And as if we ever owned a fire escape. "Zweep," I yelled, not giving a damn for intelligibility and decided that if ever I was to run away from home, I'd take her with me. And with that in mind, and with Penelope splintering through the landscape and the pores secreting animal champagne, I bent my youth to the season's tempo and proceeded to lose my mind.

There is a certain glandular disturbance all beautiful, wizardy, great people have second sight to, that trumpets through the clothes, sets the nerves up for the kill, and torments the senses to orange explosure. It has something to do with the cosmic interrelationship between the cellular atunement of certain designated organs and the firmental correlation with the axis shifts of the globe. My mother calls it sex and my brother says it's groin-fever time. But then, they were always ones for brevity. Anyway, that's the way it was. And in this spring race, the glands always win and the muses and the brain core must step aside to ride in the trunk with the spare tire. It was during this sweet and drugged madness time that I met B. J., wearing his handsomeness like an article of clothing, for an effect, and wearing his friend Eddie like a necessary pimple of adolescence. It was on the beach that we met, me looking great in a pair of cut-off dungarees and them with beards. Never mind the snows of yesteryear, I told myself, I'll take the sand and sun blizzard any day.

"Listen, Kit," said B. J. to me one night after we had experienced such we-   5
encounters with the phenomenal world at large as a two-strawed mocha, duo-jaywalking summons, twosome whistling scenes, and other such like we-experiences, "the thing for us to do is hitch to the Coast and get into films."

"Righto," said Ed. "And soon."

"Sure thing, honeychile," I said, and jumped over an unknown garbage can. "We were made for celluloid — beautifully chiseld are we, not to mention well-buffed." I ran up and down somebody's stoop, whistling "Columbia the Gem of the Ocean" through my nose. And Eddie made siren sounds and walked a fence. B. J. grasped a parking-sign pole and extended himself parallel to the ground. I

applauded, not only the gymnastics but also the offer. We liked to make bold direc-
tionless overtures to action like those crazy teenagers you're always running into
on the printed page or MGM movies.

"We could buy a sleeping bag," said B. J., and challenged a store cat to duel.

"We could buy a sleeping bag," echoed Eddie, who never had any real contribution to make in the say of statements.

"Three in a bag," I said while B. J. grasped me by the belt and we went flying down 10
a side street. "Hrumph," I coughed, and perched on a fire hydrant. "Only one bag?"

"Of course," said B. J.

"Of course," said Ed. "And hrumph."

We came on like this the whole summer, even crazier. All of our friends
abandoned us, they couldn't keep the pace. My mother threatened me with dis-
inheritance. And my old roommate from camp actually turned the hose on me
one afternoon in a fit of Florence Nightingale therapy. But hand in hand, me and
Pan, and Eddie too, whizzed through the cement kaleidoscope making our own
crazy patterns, singing our own song. And then one night a crazy thing happened.
I dreamt that B. J. was running down the street howling, tearing his hair out and
making love to the garbage cans on the boulevard. I was there laughing my head
off and Eddie was spinning a beer bottle with a faceless person I didn't even know.
I woke up and screamed for no reason I know of and my roommate, who was living with us, threw a Saltine cracker at me in way of saying something about silence,
peace, consideration, and sleepdom. And then on top of that another crazy thing
happened. Pebbles were flying into my opened window. The whole thing struck
me funny. It wasn't a casement window and there was no garden underneath.
I naturally laughed my head off and my roommate got really angry and cursed me
out viciously. I explained to her that pebbles were coming in, but she wasn't one for
imagination and turned over into sleepdom. I went to the window to see who I was
going to share my balcony scene with, and there below, standing on the milkbox,
was B. J. I climbed out and joined him on the stoop.

"What's up?" I asked, ready to take the world by storm in my mixed-match
baby-doll pajamas. B. J. motioned me into the foyer and I could see by the distraught mask that he was wearing that serious discussion was afoot.

"Listen, Kit," he began, looking both ways with, unnecessary caution. "We're 15
leaving, tonight, now. Me and Eddie. He stole some money from his grandmother,
so we're cutting out."

"Where're ya going?" I asked. He shrugged. And just then I saw Eddie dash
across the stoop and into the shadows. B. J. shrugged and he made some kind of
desperate sound with his voice like a stifled cry. "It's been real great. The summer
and you ... but ... "

"Look here," I said with anger. "I don't know why the hell you want to hang
around with that nothing." I was really angry but sorry too. It wasn't at all what I
wanted to say. I would have liked to have said, "Apollo, we are the only beautiful
people in the world. And because our genes are so great, our kid can't help but burst
through the human skin into cosmic significance." I wanted to say, "You will bear in
mind that I am great, brilliant, talented, good-looking, and am going to college at
fifteen. I have the most interesting complexes ever, and despite Freud and Darwin I
have made a healthy adjustment as an earthworm." But didn't tell him this. Instead,
I revealed that petty, small, mean side of me by saying "Eddie is a shithead."

B. J. scratched his head, swung his foot in an arc, groaned and took off. "Maybe
next summer ... " he started to say but his voice cracked and he and Eddie went

dashing down the night street, arm in arm. I stood there with my thighs bare and my soul shook. Maybe we will meet next summer, I told the mailboxes. Or maybe I'll quit school and bum around the country. And in every town I'll ask for them as the hotel keeper feeds the dusty, weary traveler that I'll be. "Have you seen two guys one great, the other acned? If you see 'em, tell 'em Kit's looking for them." And I'd bandage up my cactus-torn feet and sling the knapsack into place and be off. And in the next town, having endured dust storms, tornadoes, earthquakes, and coyotes, I'll stop at the saloon and inquire. "Yeh, they travel together," I'd say in a voice somewhere between W. C. Fields and Gladys Cooper. "Great buddies. Inseparable. Tell 'em for me that Kit's still a great kid."

And legends'll pop up about me and my quest. Great long twelve-bar blues ballads with eighty-nine stanzas. And a strolling minstrel will happen into the feedstore where B. J.'ll be and hear and shove the farmer's daughter off his lap and mount up to find me. Or maybe we won't meet ever, or we will but I won't recognize him cause he'll be an enchanted frog or a bald-headed, fat man and I'll be God knows what. No matter. Days other than the here and now, I told myself, will be dry and sane and sticky with the rotten apricots oozing slowly in the sweet time of my betrayed youth.

STEPHEN CRANE (1871–1900)

A biographical note and a photograph of Stephen Crane appear on page 250, before his story "The Bride Comes to Yellow Sky."

An Episode of War 1899

The lieutenant's rubber blanket lay on the ground, and upon it he had poured the company's supply of coffee. Corporals and other representatives of the grimy and hot-throated men who lined the breast-work had come for each squad's portion.

The lieutenant was frowning and serious at this task of division. His lips pursed as he drew with his sword various crevices in the heap, until brown squares of coffee, astoundingly equal in size, appeared on the blanket. He was on the verge of a great triumph in mathematics, and the corporals were thronging forward, each to reap a little square, when suddenly the lieutenant cried out and looked quickly at a man near him as if he suspected it was a case of personal assault. The others cried out also when they saw blood upon the lieutenant's sleeve.

He had winced like a man stung, swayed dangerously, and then straightened. The sound of his hoarse breathing was plainly audible. He looked sadly, mystically, over the breast-work at the green face of a wood, where now were many little puffs of white smoke. During this moment the men about him gazed statue-like and silent, astonished and awed by this catastrophe which happened when catastrophes were not expected — when they had leisure to observe it.

As the lieutenant stared at the wood, they too swung their heads, so that for another instant all hands, still silent, contemplated the distant forest as if their minds were fixed upon the mystery of a bullet's journey.

The officer had, of course, been compelled to take his sword into his left hand. 5 He did not hold it by the hilt. He gripped it at the middle of the blade, awkwardly. Turning his eyes from the hostile wood, he looked at the sword as he held it there, and seemed puzzled as to what to do with it, where to put it. In short, this weapon had of a sudden become a strange thing to him. He looked at it in a kind of stupefaction, as if he had been endowed with a trident, a sceptre, or a spade.

Finally he tried to sheathe it. To sheathe a sword held by the left hand, at the middle of the blade, in a scabbard hung at the left hip, is a feat worthy of a sawdust ring. This wounded officer engaged in a desperate struggle with the sword and the wobbling scabbard, and during the time of it he breathed like a wrestler.

But at this instant the men, the spectators, awoke from their stone-like poses and crowded forward sympathetically. The orderly-sergeant took the sword and tenderly placed it in the scabbard. At the time, he leaned nervously backward, and did not allow even his finger to brush the body of the lieutenant. A wound gives strange dignity to him who bears it. Well men shy from his new and terrible majesty. It is as if the wounded man's hand is upon the curtain which hangs before the revelations of all existence — the meaning of ants, potentates, wars, cities, sunshine, snow, a feather dropped from a bird's wing; and the power of it sheds radiance upon a bloody form, and makes the other men understand sometimes that they are little. His comrades look at him with large eyes thoughtfully. Moreover, they fear vaguely that the weight of a finger upon him might send him headlong, precipitate the tragedy, hurl him at once into the dim, gray unknown. And so the orderly-sergeant, while sheathing the sword, leaned nervously backward.

There were others who proffered assistance. One timidly presented his shoulder and asked the lieutenant if he cared to lean upon it, but the latter waved him away mournfully. He wore the look of one who knows he is the victim of a terrible disease and understands his helplessness. He again stared over the breast-work at the forest, and then, turning, went slowly rearward. He held his right wrist tenderly in his left hand as if the wounded arm was made of very brittle glass.

And the men in silence stared at the wood, then at the departing lieutenant; then at the wood, then at the lieutenant.

As the wounded officer passed from the line of battle, he was enabled to see 10 many things which as a participant in the fight were unknown to him. He saw a general on a black horse gazing over the lines of blue infantry at the green woods which veiled his problems. An aide galloped furiously, dragged his horse suddenly to a halt, saluted, and presented paper. It was, for a wonder, precisely like a historical painting.

To the rear of the general and his staff a group, composed of a bugler, two or three orderlies, and the bearer of the corps standard, all upon maniacal horses, were working like slaves to hold their ground, preserve their respectful interval, while the shells boomed in the air about them, and caused their chargers to make furious quivering leaps.

A battery, a tumultuous and shining mass, was swirling toward the right. The wild thud of hoofs, the cries of the riders shouting blame and praise, menace and encouragement, and, last, the roar of the wheels, the slant of the glistening guns, brought the lieutenant to an intent pause. The battery swept in curves that stirred the heart; it made halts as dramatic as the crash of a wave on the rocks, and when it fled onward this aggregation of wheels, levers, motors had a beautiful unity, as if it were a missile. The sound of it was a war-chorus that reached into the depths of man's emotion.

The lieutenant, still holding his arm as if it were of glass, stood watching this battery until all detail of it was lost, save the figures of the riders, which rose and fell and waved lashes over the black mass.

Later, he turned his eyes toward the battle, where the shooting sometimes crackled like bush fires, sometimes sputtered with exasperating irregularity, and sometimes reverberated like the thunder. He saw the smoke rolling upward and saw crowds of men who ran and cheered, or stood and blazed away at the inscrutable distance.

He came upon some stragglers, and they told him how to find the field hos- 15 pital. They described its exact location. In fact, these men, no longer having part in the battle, knew more of it than others. They told the performance of every corps, every division, the opinion of every general. The lieutenant, carrying his wounded arm rearward, looked upon them with wonder.

At the roadside a brigade was making coffee and buzzing with talk like a girls' boarding school. Several officers came out to him and inquired concerning things of which he knew nothing. One, seeing his arm, began to scold. "Why, man, that's no way to do. You want to fix that thing." He appropriated the lieutenant and the lieutenant's wound. He cut the sleeve and laid bare the arm, every nerve of which softly fluttered under his touch. He bound his handkerchief over the wound, scolding away in the meantime. His tone allowed one to think that he was in the habit of being wounded every day. The lieutenant hung his head, feeling, in this presence, that he did not know how to be correctly wounded.

The low white tents of the hospital were grouped around an old schoolhouse. There was here a singular commotion. In the foreground two ambulances interlocked wheels in the deep mud. The drivers were tossing the blame of it back and forth, gesticulating and berating, while from the ambulances, both crammed with wounded, there came an occasional groan. An interminable crowd of bandaged men were coming and going. Great numbers sat under the trees nursing heads or arms or legs. There was a dispute of some kind raging on the steps of the schoolhouse. Sitting with his back against a tree a man with a face as gray as a new army blanket was serenely smoking a corncob pipe. The lieutenant wished to rush forward and inform him that he was dying.

A busy surgeon was passing near the lieutenant. "Good morning," he said, with a friendly smile. Then he caught sight of the lieutenant's arm, and his face at once changed. "Well, let's have a look at it." He seemed possessed suddenly of a great contempt for the lieutenant. This wound evidently placed the latter on a very low social plane. The doctor cried out impatiently: "What mutton-head tied it up that way anyhow?" The lieutenant answered, "Oh, a man."

When the wound was disclosed the doctor fingered it disdainfully. "Humph," he said, "You come along with me and I'll tend to you." His voice contained the same scorn as if he were saying, "You will have to go to jail."

The lieutenant had been very meek, but now his face flushed, and he looked 20 into the doctor's eyes. "I guess I won't have it amputated," he said.

"Nonsense, man! Nonsense! Nonsense!" cried the doctor. "Come along, now. I won't amputate it. Come along. Don't be a baby."

"Let go of me," said the lieutenant, holding back wrathfully, his glance fixed upon the door of the old schoolhouse, as sinister to him as the portals of death.

And this is the story of how the lieutenant lost his arm. When he reached home, his sisters, his mother, his wife, sobbed for a long time at the sight of the flat sleeve. "Oh, well," he said, standing shamefaced amid these tears, "I don't suppose it matters so much as all that."

CHARLOTTE PERKINS GILMAN (1860–1935)

Born in Hartford, Connecticut, Charlotte Perkins Gilman was raised by her mother in strained economic circumstances because her father deserted the family soon after her birth. She briefly attended the Rhode Island School of Design and subsequently worked as an artist and teacher to support herself before her first marriage, which ended in divorce after she had a nervous breakdown following her daughter's birth. In California she remarried and became an influential writer, lecturer, and activist, focusing on feminist issues concerning labor, economics, ethics, and social reform. Among her books urging women to achieve financial autonomy in order to further social justice are *Women and Economics* (1898) and *The Man-Made World* (1900). Her best-known fiction is "The Yellow Wallpaper," a short story based on her mental breakdown and the problematic treatment she received. Her other works include a volume of poetry, *In This Our World* (1893); a utopian novel *Herland* (1915); and numerous short stories, novels, and essays on social reform. The female protagonist in "If I Were a Man" explores gender issues from a provocative point of view.

If I Were a Man   1914

"If I were a man, . . ." that was what pretty little Mollie Mathewson always said when Gerald would not do what she wanted him to — which was seldom.

That was what she said this bright morning with a stamp of her little high-heeled slipper, just because he had made a fuss about that bill, the long one with the "account rendered," which she had forgotten to give him the first time and been afraid to the second — and now he had taken it from the postman himself.

Mollie was "true to type." She was a beautiful instance of what is reverentially called "a true woman." Little, of course — no true woman may be big. Pretty, of course — no true woman could possibly be plain. Whimsical, capricious, charming, changeable, devoted to pretty clothes and always "wearing them well," as the esoteric phrase has it. (This does not refer to the clothes — they do not wear well in the least — but to some special grace of putting them on and carrying them about, granted to but few, it appears.)

She was also a loving wife and a devoted mother possessed of "the social gift" and the love of "society" that goes with it, and, with all these was fond and proud of her home and managed it as capably as — well, as most women do.

If ever there was a true woman it was Mollie Mathewson, yet she was wishing heart and soul she was a man. 5

And all of a sudden she was!

She was Gerald, walking down the path so erect and square-shouldered, in a hurry for his morning train, as usual, and, it must be confessed, in something of a temper.

Her own words were ringing in her ears — not only the "last word," but several that had gone before, and she was holding her lips tight shut, not to say something she would be sorry for. But instead of acquiescence in the position taken by that angry little figure on the veranda, what she felt was a sort of superior pride, a sympathy as with weakness, a feeling that "I must be gentle with her," in spite of the temper.

A man! Really a man — with only enough subconscious memory of herself remaining to make her recognize the differences.

At first there was a funny sense of size and weight and extra thickness, the feet 10 and hands seemed strangely large, and her long, straight, free legs swung forward at a gait that made her feel as if on stilts.

This presently passed, and in its place, growing all day, wherever she went, came a new and delightful feeling of being *the right size.*

Everything fitted now. Her back snugly against the seat-back, her feet comfortably on the floor. Her feet? . . . His feet! She studied them carefully. Never before, since her early school days, had she felt such freedom and comfort as to feet — they were firm and solid on the ground when she walked; quick, springy, safe — as when, moved by an unrecognizable impulse, she had run after, caught, and swung aboard the car.

Another impulse fished in a convenient pocket for change — instantly, automatically, bringing forth a nickel for the conductor and a penny for the newsboy.

These pockets came as a revelation. Of course she had known they were there, had counted them, made fun of them, mended them, even envied them; but she never had dreamed of how it *felt* to have pockets.

Behind her newspaper she let her consciousness, that odd mingled conscious- 15 ness, rove from pocket to pocket, realizing the armored assurance of having all those things at hand, instantly get-at-able, ready to meet emergencies. The cigar case gave her a warm feeling of comfort — it was full; the firmly held fountain pen, safe unless she stood on her head; the keys, pencils, letters, documents, notebook, checkbook, bill folder — all at once, with a deep rushing sense of power and pride, she felt what she had never felt before in all her life — the possession of money, of her own earned money — hers to give or to withhold, not to beg for, tease for, wheedle for — hers.

That bill — why, if it had come to her — to him, that is — he would have paid it as a matter of course, and never mentioned it — to her.

Then, being he, sitting there so easily and firmly with his money in his pockets, she wakened to his life-long consciousness about money. Boyhood — its desires and dreams, ambitions. Young manhood — working tremendously for the wherewithal to make a home — for her. The present years with all their net of cares and hopes and dangers; the present moment, when he needed every cent for special plans of great importance, and this bill, long overdue and demanding payment, meant an amount of inconvenience wholly unnecessary if it had been given him when it first came; also, the man's keen dislike of that "account rendered."

"Women have no business sense!" she found herself saying. "And all that money just for hats — idiotic, useless, ugly things!"

With that she began to see the hats of the women in the car as she had never seen hats before. The men's seemed normal, dignified, becoming, with enough variety for personal taste, and with distinction in style and in age, such as she had never noticed before. But the women's —

With the eyes of a man and the brain of a man; with the memory of a whole 20 lifetime of free action wherein the hat, close-fitting on cropped hair, had been no handicap; she now perceived the hats of women.

The massed fluffed hair was at once attractive and foolish, and on that hair, at every angle, in all colors, tipped, twisted, tortured into every crooked shape, made of any substance chance might offer, perched these formless objects. Then, on their formlessness the trimmings — these squirts of stiff feathers, these violent outstanding bows of glistening ribbon, these swaying, projecting masses of plumage which tormented the faces of bystanders.

Never in all her life had she imagined that this idolized millinery could look, to those who paid for it, like the decorations of an insane monkey.

And yet, when there came into the car a little woman, as foolish as any, but pretty and sweet-looking, up rose Gerald Mathewson and gave her his seat. And, later, when there came in a handsome red-cheeked girl, whose hat was wilder, more violent in color and eccentric in shape than any other — when she stood nearby and her soft curling plumes swept his cheek once and again — he felt a sense of sudden pleasure at the intimate tickling touch — and she, deep down within, felt such a wave of shame as might well drown a thousand hats forever.

When he took his train, his seat in the smoking car, she had a new surprise. All about him were the other men, commuters too, and many of them friends of his.

To her, they would have been distinguished as "Mary Wade's husband," "the 25 man Belle Grant is engaged to," "that rich Mr. Shopworth," or "that pleasant Mr. Beale." And they would all have lifted their hats to her, bowed, made polite conversation if near enough — especially Mr. Beale.

Now came the feeling of open-eyed acquaintance, of knowing men — as they were. The mere amount of this knowledge was a surprise to her — the whole background of talk from boyhood up, the gossip of barber-shop and club, the conversation of morning and evening hours on trains, the knowledge of political affiliation, of business standing and prospects, of character — in a light she had never known before.

They came and talked to Gerald, one and another. He seemed quite popular. And as they talked, with this new memory and new understanding, an understanding which seemed to include all these men's minds, there poured in on the submerged consciousness beneath a new, a startling knowledge — what men really think of women.

Good, average, American men were there; married men for the most part, and happy — as happiness goes in general. In the minds of each and all there seemed to be a two-story department, quite apart from the rest of their ideas, a separate place where they kept their thoughts and feelings about women.

In the upper half were the tenderest emotions, the most exquisite ideals, the sweetest memories, all lovely sentiments as to "home" and "mother," all delicate admiring adjectives, a sort of sanctuary, where a veiled statue, blindly adored, shared place with beloved yet commonplace experiences.

In the lower half — here that buried consciousness woke to keen dis- 30 tress — they kept quite another assortment of ideas. Here, even in this clean-minded husband of hers, was the memory of stories told at men's dinners, of worse ones overheard in street or car, of base traditions, coarse epithets, gross experiences — known, though not shared.

And all these in the department "woman," while in the rest of the mind — here was new knowledge indeed.

The world opened before her. Not the world she had been reared in — where Home had covered all the map, almost, and the rest had been "foreign," or "unexplored country," but the world as it was — man's world, as made, lived in, and seen, by men.

It was dizzying. To see the houses that fled so fast across the car window, in terms of builders' bills, or of some technical insight into materials and methods;

to see a passing village with lamentable knowledge of who "owned it" and of how its Boss was rapidly aspiring in state power, or of how that kind of paving was a failure; to see shops, not as mere exhibitions of desirable objects, but as business ventures, many were sinking ships, some promising a profitable voyage — this new world bewildered her.

She — as Gerald — had already forgotten about that bill, over which she — as Mollie — was still crying at home. Gerald was "talking business" with this man, "talking politics" with that, and now sympathizing with the carefully withheld troubles of a neighbor.

Mollie had always sympathized with the neighbor's wife before.   35

She began to struggle violently with this large dominant masculine consciousness. She remembered with sudden clearness things she had read, lectures she had heard, and resented with increasing intensity this serene masculine preoccupation with the male point of view.

Mr. Miles, the little fussy man who lived on the other side of the street, was talking now. He had a large complacent wife; Mollie had never liked her much, but had always thought him rather nice — he was so punctilious in small courtesies.

And here he was talking to Gerald — such talk!

"Had to come in here," he said. "Gave my seat to a dame who was bound to have it. There's nothing they won't get when they make up their minds to it — eh?"

"No fear!" said the big man in the next seat. "They haven't much mind to make   40
up, you know — and if they do, they'll change it."

"The real danger," began the Rev. Alfred Smythe, the new Episcopal clergyman, a thin, nervous, tall man with a face several centuries behind the times, "is that they will overstep the limits of their God-appointed sphere."

"Their natural limits ought to hold 'em, I think," said cheerful Dr. Jones. "You can't get around physiology, I tell you."

"I've never seen any limits, myself, not to what they want, anyhow," said Mr. Miles. "Merely a rich husband and a fine house and no end of bonnets and dresses, and the latest thing in motors, and a few diamonds — and so on. Keeps us pretty busy."

There was a tired gray man across the aisle. He had a very nice wife, always beautifully dressed, and three unmarried daughters, also beautifully dressed — Mollie knew them. She knew he worked hard, too, and she looked at him now a little anxiously.

But he smiled cheerfully.   45

"Do you good, Miles," he said. "What else would a man work for? A good woman is about the best thing on earth."

"And a bad one's the worst, that's sure," responded Miles.

"She's a pretty weak sister, viewed professionally," Dr. Jones averred with solemnity, and the Rev. Alfred Smythe added, "She brought evil into the world."

Gerald Mathewson sat up straight. Something was stirring in him which he did not recognize — yet could not resist.

"Seems to me we all talk like Noah," he suggested drily. "Or the ancient Hindu   50
scriptures. Women have their limitations, but so do we, God knows. Haven't we known girls in school and college just as smart as we were?"

"They cannot play our games," coldly replied the clergyman.

Gerald measured his meager proportions with a practiced eye.

"I never was particularly good at football myself," he modestly admitted, "but I've known women who could outlast a man in all-round endurance. Besides — life isn't spent in athletics!"

This was sadly true. They all looked down the aisle where a heavy ill-dressed man with a bad complexion sat alone. He had held the top of the columns once, with headlines and photographs. Now he earned less than any of them.

"It's time we woke up," pursued Gerald, still inwardly urged to unfamiliar 55 speech. "Women are pretty much *people*, seems to me. I know they dress like fools — but who's to blame for that? We invent all those idiotic hats of theirs, and design their crazy fashions, and, what's more, if a woman is courageous enough to wear common-sense clothes — and shoes — which of us wants to dance with her?

"Yes, we blame them for grafting on us, but are we willing to let our wives work? We are not. It hurts our pride, that's all. We are always criticizing them for making mercenary marriages, but what do we call a girl who marries a chump with no money? Just a poor fool, that's all. And they know it.

"As for Mother Eve — I wasn't there and can't deny the story, but I will say this. If she brought evil into the world, we men have had the lion's share of keeping it going ever since — how about that?"

They drew into the city, and all day long in his business, Gerald was vaguely conscious of new views, strange feelings, and the submerged Mollie learned and learned.

ZORA NEALE HURSTON (1901–1960)

Raised in Eatonville, Florida, the first black incorporated township established in the United States, Zora Neale Hurston attended Howard University and graduated from Barnard College with an emphasis on anthropology. This abiding interest is reflected in her use of African American folklore in her fiction. An important figure writing stories and plays during the Harlem Renaissance in the 1920s and 1930s, she insisted on making known the humanity of black people and depicted their cultural heritage with respect and affection in an effort to overcome the crude stereotyping of the period. Hurston is the author of four novels, *Jonah's Gourd Vine* (1934), *Their Eyes Were Watching God* (1937), *Moses, Man of the Mountain* (1939), and *Seraph of the Sewanee* (1948), and her short stories are collected in *The Complete Stories* (1948). Her work, though largely neglected late in her life, was rediscovered in the 1970s through the conscientious inclusiveness of the women's movement.

Library of Congress, Prints and Photographs Division.

Spunk   1925

A giant of a brown-skinned man sauntered up the one street of the village and out into the palmetto thickets with a small pretty woman clinging lovingly to his arm.

"Looka theah, folkses!" cried Elijah Mosley, slapping his leg gleefully. "Theah they go, big as life an' brassy, as tacks."

All the loungers in the store tried to walk to the door with an air of nonchalance but with small success.

"Now pee-eople!" Walter Thomas gasped. "Will you look at 'em!"

"But that's one thing Ah likes about Spunk Banks — he ain't skeered of nothin' on God's green footstool — *nothin'!* He rides that log down at sawmill jus' like he struts 'round wid another man's wife — jus' don't give a kitty. When Tes' Miller got cut to giblets on that circle-saw, Spunk steps right up and starts ridin'. The rest of us was skeered to go near it."

A round-shouldered figure in overalls much too large came nervously in the door and the talking ceased. The men looked at each other and winked.

"Gimme some soda-water. Sass'prilla Ah reckon," the newcomer ordered, and stood far down the counter near the open pickled pig-feet tub to drink it.

Elijah nudged Walter and turned with mock gravity to the newcomer.

"Say, Joe, how's everything up yo' way? How's yo' wife?"

Joe started and all but dropped the bottle he was holding. He swallowed several times painfully and his lips trembled.

"Aw 'Lige, you oughtn't to do nothin' like that," Walter grumbled. Elijah ignored him.

"She jus' passed heah a few minutes ago goin' thata way," with a wave of his hand in the direction of the woods.

Now Joe knew his wife had passed that way. He knew that the men lounging in the general store had seen her, moreover, he knew that the men knew *he* knew. He stood there silent for a long moment staring blankly, with his Adam's apple twitching nervously up and down his throat. One could actually *see* the pain he was suffering, his eyes, his face, his hands, and even the dejected slump of his shoulders. He set the bottle down upon the counter. He didn't bang it, just eased it out of his hand silently and fiddled with his suspender buckle.

"Well, Ah'm goin' after her to-day. Ah'm goin' an' fetch her back. Spunk's done gone too fur."

He reached deep down into his trouser pocket and drew out a hollow ground razor, large and shiny, and passed his moistened thumb back and forth over the edge.

"Talkin' like a man, Joe. 'Course that's *yo'* fambly affairs, but Ah like to see grit in anybody."

Joe Kanty laid down a nickel and stumbled out into the street.

Dusk crept in from the woods. Ike Clarke lit the swinging oil lamp that was almost immediately surrounded by candle-flies. The men laughed boisterously behind Joe's back as they watched him shamble woodward.

"You oughtn't to said whut you said to him, 'Lige — look how it worked him up," Walter chided.

"And Ah hope it did work him up. Tain't even decent for a man to take and take like he do."

"Spunk will sho' kill him."

"Aw, Ah doan know. You never kin tell. He might turn him up an' spank him fur gettin' in the way, but Spunk wouldn't shoot no unarmed man. Dat razor he carried outa heah ain't gonna run Spunk down an' cut him, an' Joe ain't got the nerve to go to Spunk with it knowing he totes that Army .45. He makes that break outa heah to bluff us. He's gonna hide that razor behind the first palmetto root an' sneak back home to bed. Don't tell me nothin' 'bout that rabbit-foot colored man. Didn't he meet Spunk an' Lena face to face one day las' week an' mumble sumthin' to Spunk 'bout lettin' his wife alone?"

"What did Spunk say?" Walter broke in. "Ah like him fine but tain't right the way he carries on wid Lena Kanty, jus' 'cause Joe's timid 'bout fightin'."

"You wrong theah, Walter. Tain't 'cause Joe's timid at all, it's 'cause Spunk wants Lena. If Joe was a passle of wile cats Spunk would tackle the job just the same. He'd go after *anything* he wanted the same way. As Ah wuz sayin' a minute ago, he tole Joe right to his face that Lena was his. 'Call her and see if she'll come. A woman knows her boss an' she answers when he calls.' 'Lena, ain't I yo' husband?' Joe sorter whines out. Lena looked at him real disgusted but she don't answer and she don't move outa her tracks. Then Spunk reaches out an' takes hold of her arm an' says: 'Lena, youse mine. From now on Ah works for you an' fights for you an' Ah never wants you to look to nobody for a crumb of bread, a stitch of close or a shingle to go over yo' head, but *me* long as Ah live. Ah'll git the lumber foh owah house tomorrow. Go home an' git yo' things together!'

"'Thass mah house,' Lena speaks up. 'Papa gimme that.'   25

"'Well,' says Spunk, 'doan give up what's yours, but when youse inside doan forgit youse mine, an' let no other man git outa his place wid you!'

"Lena looked up at him with her eyes so full of love that they wuz runnin' over, an' Spunk seen it an' Joe seen it too, and his lip started to tremblin' and his Adam's apple was galloping up and down his neck like a race horse. Ah bet he's wore out half a dozen Adam's apples since Spunk's been on the job with Lena. That's all he'll do. He'll be back heah after while swallowin' an' workin' his lips like he wants to say somethin' an' can't."

"But didn't he do *nothin'* to stop 'em?"

"Nope, not a frazzlin' thing—jus' stood there. Spunk took Lena's arm and walked off jus' like nothin' ain't happened and he stood there gazin' after them till they was outa sight. Now you know a woman don't want no man like that. I'm jus' waitin' to see whut he's goin' to say when he gits back."

But Joe Kanty never came back, never. The men in the store heard the sharp report   30
of a pistol somewhere distant in the palmetto thicket and soon Spunk came walking leisurely, with his big black Stetson set at the same rakish angle and Lena clinging to his arm, came walking right into the general store. Lena wept in a frightened manner.

"Well," Spunk announced calmly, "Joe came out there wid a meat axe an' made me kill him."

He sent Lena home and led the men back to Joe—crumpled and limp with his right hand still clutching his razor.

"See mah back? Mah close cut clear through. He sneaked up an' tried to kill me from the back, but Ah got him, an' got him good, first shot," Spunk said.

The men glared at Elijah, accusingly.

"Take him up an' plant him in Stony Lonesome," Spunk said in a careless voice. "Ah   35
didn't wanna shoot him but he made me do it. He's a dirty coward, jumpin' on a man from behind."

Spunk turned on his heel and sauntered away to where he knew his love wept in fear for him and no man stopped him. At the general store later on, they all talked of locking him up until the sheriff should come from Orlando, but no one did anything but talk.

A clear case of self-defense, the trial was a short one, and Spunk walked out of the court house to freedom again. He could work again, ride the dangerous log-carriage that fed the singing, snarling, biting circle-saw; he could stroll the soft dark lanes with his guitar. He was free to roam the woods again; he was free to return to Lena. He did all these things.

"Whut you reckon, Walt?" Elijah asked one night later. "Spunk's gittin' ready to marry Lena!"

"Naw! Why, Joe ain't had time to git cold yit. Nohow Ah didn't figger Spunk was the marryin' kind."

"Well, he is," rejoined Elijah. "He done moved most of Lena's things—and her 40 along wid 'em—over to the Bradley house. He's buying it. Jus' like Ah told yo' all right in heah the night Joe was kilt. Spunk's crazy 'bout Lena. He don't want folks to keep on talkin' 'bout her—thass reason he's rushin' so. Funny thing 'bout that bob-cat, wan't it?"

"What bob-cat, 'Lige? Ah ain't heered 'bout none."

"Ain't cher? Well, night befo' las' as they was goin' to bed, a big black bob-cat, black all over, you hear me, *black,* walked round and round that house and howled like forty, an' when Spunk got his gun an' went to the winder to shoot it, he says it stood right still an' looked him in the eye, an' howled right at him. The thing got Spunk so nervoused up he couldn't shoot. But Spunk says twan't no bob-cat nohow. He says it was Joe done sneaked back from Hell!"

"Humph!" sniffed Walter, "he oughter be nervous after what he done. Ah reckon Joe come back to dare him to marry Lena, or to come out an' fight. Ah bet he'll be back time and again, too. Know what Ah think? Joe wuz a braver man than Spunk."

There was a general shout of derision from the group.

"Thass a fact," went on Walter. "Lookit whut he done; took a razor an' went out 45 to fight a man he knowed toted a gun an' wuz a crack shot, too; 'nother thing Joe wuz skeered of Spunk, skeered plumb stiff! But he went jes' the same. It took him a long time to get his nerve up. Tain't nothin' for Spunk to fight when he ain't skeered of nothin'. Now, Joe's done come back to have it out wid the man that's got all he ever had. Y'all know Joe ain't never had nothin' nor wanted nothin' besides Lena. It musta been a h'ant cause ain't nobody never seen no black bob-cat."

"'Nother thing," cut in one of the men, "Spunk was cussin' a blue streak to-day 'cause he 'lowed dat saw wuz wobblin'—almos' got 'im once. The machinist come, looked it over an' said it wuz alright. Spunk musta been leanin' t'wards it some. Den he claimed somebody pushed 'im but twan't nobody close to 'im. Ah wuz glad when knockin' off time came. I'm skeered of dat man when he gits hot. He'd beat you full of button holes as quick as he'd look atcher."

The men gathered the next evening in a different mood, no laughter. No badinage this time.

"Look, 'Lige, you goin' to set up wid Spunk?"

"Naw, Ah reckon not, Walter. Tell yuh the truth, Ah'm a li'l bit skittish. Spunk died too wicket—died cussin' he did. You know he thought he was done outa life."

"Good Lawd, who'd he think done it?" 50

"Joe."

"Joe Kanty? How come?"

"Walter, Ah b'leeve Ah will walk up thata way an' set. Lena would like it Ah reckon."

"But whut did he say, 'Lige?"

Elijah did not answer until they had left the lighted store and were strolling 55 down the dark street.

"Ah wuz loadin' a wagon wid scantlin' right near the saw when Spunk fell on the carriage but 'fore Ah could git to him the saw got him in the body — awful sight. Me an' Skint Miller got him off but it was too late. Anybody could see that. The fust thing he said wuz: 'He pushed me, 'Lige — the dirty hound pushed me in the back!' — he was spittin' blood at ev'ry breath. We laid him on the sawdust pile with his face to the East so's he could die easy. He helt mah han' till the last, Walter, and said: 'It was Joe, 'Lige . . . the dirty sneak shoved me . . . he didn't dare come to mah face . . . but Ah'll git the son-of-a-wood louse soon's Ah get there an' make hell too hot for him . . . Ah felt him shove me . . . !' Thass how he died."

"If spirits kin fight, there's a powerful tussle goin' on somewhere ovah Jordan 'cause Ah b'leeve Joe's ready for Spunk an' ain't skeered any more — yas, Ah b'leeve Joe pushed 'im mahself."

They had arrived at the house. Lena's lamentations were deep and loud. She had filled the room with magnolia blossoms that gave off a heavy sweet odor. The keepers of the wake tipped about whispering in frightened tones. Everyone in the village was there, even old Jeff Kanty, Joe's father, who a few hours before would have been afraid to come within ten feet of him, stood leering triumphantly down upon the fallen giant as if his fingers had been the teeth of steel that laid him low.

The cooling board consisted of three sixteen-inch boards on saw horses, a dingy sheet was his shroud.

The women ate heartily of the funeral baked meats and wondered who would 60 be Lena's next. The men whispered coarse conjectures between guzzles of whiskey.

D. H. LAWRENCE (1885–1930)

David Herbert Lawrence was born near Nottingham, England, in 1885. As a teenager, he worked as a factory clerk but became ill and, during his recuperation, became drawn to writing and teaching. He received a teaching certificate from University College, Nottingham, in 1908, having already published his first story. Lawrence achieved literary success early, publishing poems in the prestigious *English Review,* whose editor helped him to publish his first novel, *The White Peacock* (1911), which he followed with *The Trespasser* (1912) and *Sons and Lovers* (1913). In the meantime, he eloped

© Hulton-Deutsch Collection/Corbis.

with Freida Weekly, the German wife of a professor in Nottingham, and they were married in 1914. After World War I, Lawrence and his wife left England and never again resided there. The couple lived in Italy and traveled and lived in Ceylon, Australia, the United States, and Mexico. Lawrence published several novels and books of nonfiction along the way, including *The Rainbow* (1915), *Women in Love* (1920), *Lost Girl* (1920), *Aaron's Rod* (1922), *The Plumed Serpent* (1926), *Movements in European History* (1921), *Studies in Classic American Literature* (1923), and two books on psychoanalysis. Lawrence had already transgressed norms of decency with *The Rainbow,* considered obscene in England, and his next work, *Lady Chatterley's Lover,* was published privately in 1928 because of its explicit sexual descriptions. Also the author of plays, poems, and such famous short stories as "The Odour of Chrysanthemums" and "Daughters of the Vicar," Lawrence innovated in ways that go far beyond his challenge to standards of obscenity. His works characteristically probe the nature of unconscious experience and promote a new receptiveness to sexuality, intuition, and emotion. In 1930, Lawrence died of tuberculosis in the south of France.

The Horse Dealer's Daughter 1922

"Well, Mabel, and what are you going to do with yourself?" asked Joe, with foolish flippancy. He felt quite safe himself. Without listening for an answer, he turned aside, worked a grain of tobacco to the tip of his tongue, and spat it out. He did not care about anything, since he felt safe himself.

The three brothers and the sister sat round the desolate breakfast-table, attempting some sort of desultory consultation. The morning's post had given the final tap to the family fortunes, and all was over. The dreary dining-room itself, with its heavy mahogany furniture, looked as if it were waiting to be done away with.

But the consultation amounted to nothing. There was a strange air of ineffectuality about the three men, as they sprawled at table, smoking and reflecting vaguely on their own condition. The girl was alone, a rather short, sullen-looking young woman of twenty-seven. She did not share the same life as her brothers. She would have been good-looking, save for the impressive fixity of her face, "bull-dog," as her brothers called it.

There was a confused tramping of horses' feet outside. The three men all sprawled round in their chairs to watch. Beyond the dark holly bushes that separated the strip of lawn from the high-road, they could see a cavalcade of shire horses swinging out of their own yard, being taken for exercise. This was the last time. These were the last horses that would go through their hands. The young men watched with critical, callous looks. They were all frightened at the collapse of their lives, and the sense of disaster in which they were involved left them no inner freedom.

Yet they were three fine, well-set fellows enough. Joe, the eldest, was a man 5 of thirty-three, broad and handsome in a hot, flushed way. His face was red, he twisted his black mustache over a thick finger, his eyes were shallow and restless. He had a sensual way of uncovering his teeth when he laughed, and his bearing was stupid. Now he watched the horses with a glazed look of helplessness in his eyes, a certain stupor of downfall.

The great draft-horses swung past. They were tied head to tail, four of them, and they heaved along to where a lane branched off from the high-road, planting their great hoofs floutingly in the fine black mud, swinging their great rounded haunches sumptuously, and trotting a few sudden steps as they were led into the lane, round the corner. Every movement showed a massive, slumbrous strength, and a stupidity which held them in subjection. The groom at the head looked back, jerking the leading rope. And the cavalcade moved out of sight up the lane, the tail of the last horse, bobbed up tight and stiff, held out taut from the swinging great haunches as they rocked behind the hedges in a motionlike sleep.

Joe watched with glazed hopeless eyes. The horses were almost like his own body to him. He felt he was done for now. Luckily he was engaged to a woman as old as himself, and therefore her father, who was steward of a neighboring estate, would provide him with a job. He would marry and go into harness. His life was over, he would be a subject animal now.

He turned uneasily aside, the retreating steps of the horses echoing in his ears. Then, with foolish restlessness, he reached for the scraps of bacon-rind from the plates, and making a faint whistling sound, flung them to the terrier that lay against the fender. He watched the dog swallow them, and waited till the creature looked into his eyes. Then a faint grin came on his face, and in a high, foolish voice he said:

"You won't get much more bacon, shall you, you little b———?"

The dog faintly and dismally wagged its tail, then lowered its haunches, cir- 10
cled round, and lay down again.

There was another helpless silence at the table. Joe sprawled uneasily in his seat, not willing to go till the family conclave was dissolved. Fred Henry, the second brother, was erect, clean-limbed, alert. He had watched the passing of the horses with more *sang-froid.*° If he was an animal, like Joe, he was an animal which controls, not one which is controlled. He was master of any horse, and he carried himself with a well-tempered air of mastery. But he was not master of the situations of life. He pushed his coarse brown mustache upwards, off his lip, and glanced irritably at his sister, who sat impassive and inscrutable.

"You'll go and stop with Lucy for a bit, shan't you?" he asked. The girl did not answer.

"I don't see what else you can do," persisted Fred Henry.

"Go as a skivvy,"° Joe interpolated laconically.

The girl did not move a muscle. 15

"If I was her, I should go in for training for a nurse," said Malcolm, the youngest of them all. He was the baby of the family, a young man of twenty-two, with a fresh, jaunty *museau.*°

But Mabel did not take any notice of him. They had talked at her and round her for so many years, that she hardly heard them at all.

The marble clock on the mantelpiece softly chimed the half-hour, the dog rose uneasily from the hearth-rug and looked at the party at the breakfast-table. But still they sat on in ineffectual conclave.

"Oh, all right," said Joe suddenly, apropos of nothing. "I'll get a move on."

He pushed back his chair, straddled his knees with a downward jerk, to get 20
them free, in horsey fashion, and went to the fire. Still he did not go out of the room; he was curious to know what the others would do or say. He began to charge his pipe, looking down at the dog and saying in a high, affected voice:

"Going wi' me? Going wi' me are ter? Tha'rt goin' further than tha counts on just now, dost hear?"

---

sang-froid: Coolness, composure.
skivvy: Domestic worker.
museau: Slang for "face."

The dog faintly wagged its tail, the man stuck out his jaw and covered his pipe with his hands, and puffed intently, losing himself in the tobacco, looking down all the while at the dog with an absent brown eye. The dog looked up at him in mournful distrust. Joe stood with his knees stuck out, in real horsey fashion.

"Have you had a letter from Lucy?" Fred Henry asked of his sister.

"Last week," came the neutral reply.

"And what does she say?"   25

There was no answer.

"Does she *ask* you to go and stop there?" persisted Fred Henry.

"She says I can if I like."

"Well, then, you'd better. Tell her you'll come on Monday."

This was received in silence.   30

"That's what you'll do then, is it?" said Fred Henry, in some exasperation.

But she made no answer. There was a silence of futility and irritation in the room. Malcolm grinned fatuously.

"You'll have to make up your mind between now and next Wednesday," said Joe loudly, "or else find yourself lodgings on the curbstone."

The face of the young woman darkened, but she sat on immutable.

"Here's Jack Fergusson!" exclaimed Malcolm, who was looking aimlessly out   35
of the window.

"Where?" exclaimed Joe loudly.

"Just gone past."

"Coming in?"

Malcolm craned his neck to see the gate.

"Yes," he said.   40

There was a silence. Mabel sat on like one condemned, at the head of the table. Then a whistle was heard from the kitchen. The dog got up and barked sharply. Joe opened the door and shouted:

"Come on."

After a moment a young man entered. He was muffled up in overcoat and a purple woolen scarf, and his tweed cap, which he did not remove, was pulled down on his head. He was of medium height, his face was rather long and pale, his eyes looked tired.

"Hello, Jack! Well, Jack!" exclaimed Malcolm and Joe. Fred Henry merely said: "Jack."

"What's doing?" asked the newcomer, evidently addressing Fred Henry.   45

"Same. We've got to be out by Wednesday. Got a cold?"

"I have — got it bad, too."

"Why don't you stop in?"

"*Me* stop in? When I can't stand on my legs, perhaps I shall have a chance," the young man spoke huskily. He had a slight Scotch accent.

"It's a knock-out, isn't it," said Joe, boisterously, "if a doctor goes round croak-   50
ing with a cold. Looks bad for the patients, doesn't it?"

The young doctor looked at him slowly.

"Anything the matter with *you*, then?" he asked sarcastically.

"Not as I know of. Damn your eyes, hope not. Why?"

"I thought you were very concerned about the patients, wondered if you might be one yourself."

"Damn it, no, I've never been patient to no flaming doctor, and hope I never   55
shall be," returned Joe.

At this point Mabel rose from the table, and they all seemed to become aware of her existence. She began putting the dishes together. The young doctor looked at her, but did not address her. He had not greeted her. She went out of the room with the tray, her face impassive and unchanged.

"When are you off then, all of you?" asked the doctor.

"I'm catching the eleven-forty," replied Malcolm. "Are you goin' down wi' th' trap,° Joe?"

"Yes, I've told you I'm going down wi' th' trap, haven't I?"

"We'd better be getting her in then. So long, Jack, if I don't see you before I go," said Malcolm, shaking hands. 60

He went out, followed by Joe, who seemed to have his tail between his legs.

"Well, this is the devil's own," exclaimed the doctor, when he was left alone with Fred Henry. "Going before Wednesday, are you?"

"That's the orders," replied the other.

"Where, to Northampton?"

"That's it." 65

"The devil!" exclaimed Fergusson, with quiet chagrin.

And there was silence between the two.

"All settled up, are you?" asked Fergusson.

"About."

There was another pause. 70

"Well, I shall miss yer, Freddy, boy," said the young doctor.

"And I shall miss thee, Jack," returned the other.

"Miss you like hell," mused the doctor.

Fred Henry turned aside. There was nothing to say. Mabel came in again, to finish clearing the table.

"What are *you* going to do, then, Miss Pervin?" asked Fergusson. "Going to 75 your sister's, are you?"

Mabel looked at him with her steady, dangerous eyes, that always made him uncomfortable, unsettling his superficial ease.

"No," she said.

"Well, what in the name of fortune *are* you going to do? Say what you mean to do," cried Fred Henry, with futile intensity.

But she only averted her head, and continued her work. She folded the white table-cloth, and put on the chenille cloth.

"The sulkiest bitch that ever trod!" muttered her brother. 80

But she finished her task with perfectly impassive face, the young doctor watching her interestedly all the while. Then she went out.

Fred Henry stared after her, clenching his lips, his blue eyes fixing in sharp antagonism, as he made a grimace of sour exasperation.

"You could bray her into bits, and that's all you'd get out of her," he said, in a small, narrowed tone.

The doctor smiled faintly.

"What's she *going* to do, then?" he asked. 85

"Strike me if *I* know!" returned the other.

There was a pause. Then the doctor stirred.

"I'll be seeing you tonight, shall I?" he said to his friend.

"Ay — where's it to be? Are we going over to Jessdale?"

---

trap: A light two-wheeled carriage.

"I don't know. I've got such a cold on me. I'll come round to the 'Moon and 90
Stars,' anyway."

"Let Lizzie and May miss their night for once, eh?"

"That's it — if I feel as I do now."

"All's one ——"

The two young men went through the passage and down to the back door together. The house was large, but it was servantless now, and desolate. At the back was a small bricked houseyard and beyond that a big square, graveled fine and red, and having stables on two sides. Sloping, dank, winter-dark fields stretched away on the open sides.

But the stables were empty. Joseph Pervin, the father of the family, had been a 95
man of no education, who had become a fairly large horse dealer. The stables had been full of horses, there was a great turmoil and come-and-go of horses and of dealers and grooms. Then the kitchen was full of servants. But of late things had declined. The old man had married a second time, to retrieve his fortunes. Now he was dead and everything was gone to the dogs, there was nothing but debt and threatening.

For months, Mabel had been servantless in the big house, keeping the home together in penury for her ineffectual brothers. She had kept house for ten years. But previously it was with unstinted means. Then, however brutal and coarse everything was, the sense of money had kept her proud, confident. The men might be foul-mouthed, the women in the kitchen might have bad reputations, her brothers might have illegitimate children. But so long as there was money, the girl felt herself established, and brutally proud, reserved.

No company came to the house, save dealers and coarse men. Mabel had no associates of her own sex, after her sister went away. But she did not mind. She went regularly to church, she attended to her father. And she lived in the memory of her mother, who had died when she was fourteen, and whom she had loved. She had loved her father, too, in a different way, depending upon him, and feeling secure in him, until at the age of fifty-four he married again. And then she had set hard against him. Now he had died and left them all hopelessly in debt.

She had suffered badly during the period of poverty. Nothing, however, could shake the curious, sullen, animal pride that dominated each member of the family. Now, for Mabel, the end had come. Still she would not cast about her. She would follow her own way just the same. She would always hold the keys of her own situation. Mindless and persistent, she endured from day to day. Why should she think? Why should she answer anybody? It was enough that this was the end, and there was no way out. She need not pass any more darkly along the main street of the small town, avoiding every eye. She need not demean herself any more, going into the shops and buying the cheapest food. This was at an end. She thought of nobody, not even of herself. Mindless and persistent, she seemed in a sort of ecstasy to be coming nearer to her fulfillment, her own glorification, approaching her dead mother, who was glorified.

In the afternoon she took a little bag, with shears and sponge and a small scrubbing-brush, and went out. It was a gray, wintry day, with saddened, dark green fields and an atmosphere blackened by the smoke of foundries not far off. She went quickly, darkly along the causeway, heeding nobody, through the town to the churchyard.

There she always felt secure, as if no one could see her, although as a mat- 100
ter of fact she was exposed to the stare of everyone who passed along under the churchyard wall. Nevertheless, once under the shadow of the great looming

church, among the graves, she felt immune from the world, reserved within the thick churchyard wall as in another country.

Carefully she clipped the grass from the grave, and arranged the pinky white, small chrysanthemums in the tin cross. When this was done, she took an empty jar from a neighboring grave, brought water, and carefully, most scrupulously sponged the marble headstone and the coping-stone.

It gave her sincere satisfaction to do this. She felt in immediate contact with the world of her mother. She took minute pains, went through the park in a state bordering on pure happiness, as if in performing this task she came into a subtle, intimate connection with her mother. For the life she followed here in the world was far less real than the world of death she inherited from her mother.

The doctor's house was just by the church. Fergusson, being a mere hired assistant, was slave to the countryside. As he hurried now to attend to the outpatients in the surgery, glancing across the graveyard with his quick eye, he saw the girl at her task at the grave. She seemed so intent and remote, it was like looking into another world. Some mystical element was touched in him. He slowed down as he walked, watching her as if spellbound.

She lifted her eyes, feeling him looking. Their eyes met. And each looked again at once, each feeling, in some way, found out by the other. He lifted his cap and passed on down the road. There remained distinct in his consciousness, like a vision, the memory of her face, lifted from the tombstone in the churchyard, and looking at him with slow, large, portentous eyes. It *was* portentous, her face. It seemed to mesmerize him. There was a heavy power in her eyes which laid hold of his whole being, as if he had drunk some powerful drug. He had been feeling weak and done before. Now the life came back into him, he felt delivered from his own fretted, daily self.

He finished his duties at the surgery as quickly as might be, hastily filling up 105 the bottles of the waiting people with cheap drugs. Then, in perpetual haste, he set off again to visit several cases in another part of his round, before teatime. At all times he preferred to walk if he could, but particularly when he was not well. He fancied the motion restored him.

The afternoon was falling. It was gray, deadened, and wintry, with a slow, moist, heavy coldness sinking in and deadening all the faculties. But why should he think or notice? He hastily climbed the hill and turned across the dark green fields, following the black cinder-track. In the distance, across a shallow dip in the country, the small town was clustered like smoldering ash, a tower, a spire, a heap of low, raw, extinct houses. And on the nearest fringe of the town, sloping into the dip, was Oldmeadow, the Pervins' house. He could see the stables and the outbuildings distinctly, as they lay towards him on the slope. Well, he would not go there many more times! Another resource would be lost to him, another place gone: the only company he cared for in the alien, ugly little town he was losing. Nothing but work, drudgery, constant hastening from dwelling to dwelling among the colliers and the iron-workers. It wore him out, but at the same time he had a craving for it. It was a stimulant to him to be in the homes of the working people, moving, as it were, through the innermost body of their life. His nerves were excited and gratified. He could come so near, into the very lives of the rough, inarticulate, powerful emotional men and women: He grumbled, he said he hated the hellish hole. But as a matter of fact it excited him, the contact with the rough, strongly-feeling people was a stimulant applied direct to his nerves.

Below Oldmeadow, in the green, shallow, soddened hollow of fields, lay a square, deep pond. Roving across the landscape, the doctor's quick eye detected a figure in black passing through the gate of the field, down towards the pond. He looked again. It would be Mabel Pervin. His mind suddenly became alive and attentive.

Why was she going down there? He pulled up on the path on the slope above, and stood staring. He could just make sure of the small black figure moving in the hollow of the failing day. He seemed to see her in the midst of such obscurity, that he was like a clairvoyant, seeing rather with the mind's eye than with ordinary sight. Yet he could see her positively enough, whilst he kept his eye attentive. He felt, if he looked away from her, in the thick, ugly falling dusk, he would lose her altogether.

He followed her minutely as she moved, direct and intent, like something transmitted rather than stirring in voluntary activity, straight down from the field towards the pond. There she stood on the bank for a moment. She never raised her head. Then she waded slowly into the water.

He stood motionless as the small black figure walked slowly and deliberately 110 towards the center of the pond, very slowly, gradually moving deeper into the motionless water, and still moving forward as the water got up to her breast. Then he could see her no more in the dusk of the dead afternoon.

"There!" he exclaimed. "Would you believe it?"

And he hastened straight down, running over the wet, soddened fields, pushing through the hedges, down into the depression of callous wintry obscurity. It took him several minutes to come to the pond. He stood on the bank, breathing heavily. He could see nothing. His eyes seemed to penetrate the dead water. Yes, perhaps that was the dark shadow of her black clothing beneath the surface of the water.

He slowly ventured into the pond. The bottom was deep, soft clay, he sank in, and the water clasped dead cold round his legs. As he stirred he could smell the cold, rotten clay that fouled up into the water. It was objectionable in his lungs. Still, repelled and yet not heeding, he moved deeper into the pond. The cold water rose over his thighs, over his loins, upon his abdomen. The lower part of his body was all sunk in the hideous cold element. And the bottom was so deeply soft and uncertain, he was afraid of pitching with his mouth underneath. He could not swim, and was afraid.

He crouched a little, spreading his hands under the water and moving them round, trying to feel for her. The dead cold pond swayed upon his chest. He moved again, a little deeper, and again, with his hands underneath, he felt all around under the water. And he touched her clothing. But it evaded his fingers. He made a desperate effort to grasp it.

And so doing he lost his balance and went under, horribly, suffocating in the 115 foul earthy water, struggling madly for a few moments. At last, after what seemed an eternity, he got his footing, rose again into the air, and looked around. He gasped, and knew he was in the world. Then he looked at the water. She had risen near him. He grasped her clothing, and drawing her nearer, turned to make his way to land again.

He went very slowly, carefully, absorbed in the slow progress. He rose higher, climbing out of the pond. The water was now only about his legs; he was thankful, full of relief to be out of the clutches of the pond. He lifted her and staggered on to the bank, out of the horror of wet, gray clay.

He laid her down on the bank. She was quite unconscious and running with water. He made the water come from her mouth, he worked to restore her. He did not have to work very long before he could feel the breathing begin again in her; she was breathing naturally. He worked a little longer. He could feel her live beneath his hands; she was coming back. He wiped her face, wrapped her in his overcoat, looked round into the dim, dark gray world, then lifted her and staggered down the bank and across the fields.

It seemed an unthinkably long way, and his burden so heavy he felt he would never get to the house. But at last he was in the stable-yard, and then in the house-yard. He opened the door and went into the house. In the kitchen he laid her down on the hearth-rug and called. The house was empty. But the fire was burning in the grate.

Then again he kneeled to attend to her. She was breathing regularly, her eyes were wide open and as if conscious, but there seemed something missing in her look. She was conscious in herself, but unconscious of her surroundings.

He ran upstairs, took blankets from a bed, and put them before the fire to 120 warm. Then he removed her saturated, earthy-smelling clothing, rubbed her dry with a towel, and wrapped her naked in the blankets. Then he went into the dining-room, to look for spirits. There was a little whiskey. He drank a gulp himself, and put some into her mouth.

The effect was instantaneous. She looked full into his face, as if she had been seeing him for some time, and yet had only just become conscious of him.

"Dr. Fergusson?" she said.

"What?" he answered.

He was divesting himself of his coat, intending to find some dry clothing upstairs. He could not bear the smell of the dead, clayey water, and he was mortally afraid for his own health.

"What did I do?" she asked. 125

"Walked into the pond," he replied. He had begun to shudder like one sick, and could hardly attend to her. Her eyes remained full on him, he seemed to be going dark in his mind, looking back at her helplessly. The shuddering became quieter in him, his life came back to him, dark and unknowing, but strong again.

"Was I out of my mind?" she asked, while her eyes were fixed on him all the time.

"Maybe, for the moment," he replied. He felt quiet, because his strength had come back. The strange fretful strain had left him.

"Am I out of my mind now?" she asked.

"Are you?" he reflected a moment. "No," he answered truthfully, "I don't see 130 that you are." He turned his face aside. He was afraid now, because he felt dazed, and felt dimly that her power was stronger than his, in this issue. And she continued to look at him fixedly all the time. "Can you tell me where I shall find some dry things to put on?" he asked.

"Did you dive into the pond for me?" she asked.

"No," he answered. "I walked in. But I went in overhead as well."

There was silence for a moment. He hesitated. He very much wanted to go upstairs to get into dry clothing. But there was another desire in him. And she seemed to hold him. His will seemed to have gone to sleep, and left him, standing there slack before her. But he felt warm inside himself. He did not shudder at all, though his clothes were sodden on him.

"Why did you?" she asked.

"Because I didn't want you to do such a foolish thing," he said. 135

"It wasn't foolish," she said, still gazing at him as she lay on the floor, with a sofa cushion under her head. "It was the right thing to do. *I* knew best, then."

"I'll go and shift these wet things," he said. But still he had not the power to move out of her presence, until she sent him. It was as if she had the life of his body in her hands, and he could not extricate himself. Or perhaps he did not want to.

Suddenly she sat up. Then she became aware of her own immediate condition. She felt the blankets about her, she knew her own limbs. For a moment it seemed as if her reason were going. She looked round, with wild eyes, as if seeking something. He stood still with fear. She saw her clothing lying scattered.

"Who undressed me?" she asked, her eyes resting full and inevitable on his face.

"I did," he replied, "to bring you round." 140

For some moments she sat and gazed at him, awfully, her lips parted.

"Do you love me, then?" she asked.

He only stood and stared at her, fascinated. His soul seemed to melt.

She shuffled forward on her knees, and put her arms round him, round his legs, as he stood there, pressing her breasts against his knees and thighs, clutching him with strange, convulsive certainty, pressing his thighs against her, drawing him to her face, her throat, as she looked up at him with flaring, humble eyes of transfiguration, triumphant in first possession.

"You love me," she murmured, in strange transport, yearning and triumphant 145 and confident. "You love me. I know you love me, I know."

And she was passionately kissing his knees, through the wet clothing, passionately and indiscriminately kissing his knees, his legs, as if unaware of everything.

He looked down at the tangled wet hair, the wild, bare, animal shoulders. He was amazed, bewildered, and afraid. He had never thought of loving her. He had never wanted to love her. When he rescued her and restored her, he was a doctor, and she was a patient. He had had no single personal thought of her. Nay, this introduction of the personal element was very distasteful to him, a violation of his professional honor. It was horrible to have her there embracing his knees. It was horrible. He revolted from it, violently. And yet — and yet — he had not the power to break away.

She looked at him again, with the same supplication of powerful love, and that same transcendent, frightening light of triumph. In view of the delicate flame which seemed to come from her face like a light, he was powerless. And yet he had never intended to love her. He had never intended. And something stubborn in him could not give way.

"You love me," she repeated, in a murmur of deep, rhapsodic assurance. "You love me."

Her hands were drawing him, drawing him down to her. He was afraid, even 150 a little horrified. For he had, really, no intention of loving her. Yet her hands were drawing him towards her. He put out his hand quickly to steady himself, and grasped her bare shoulder. A flame seemed to burn the hand that grasped her soft shoulder. He had no intention of loving her: his whole will was against his yielding. It was horrible. And yet wonderful was the touch of her shoulders, beautiful the shining of her face. Was she perhaps mad? He had a horror of yielding to her. Yet something in him ached also.

He had been staring away at the door, away from her. But his hand remained on her shoulder. She had gone suddenly very still. He looked down at her. Her eyes were now wide with fear, with doubt, the light was dying from her face, a shadow of terrible grayness was returning. He could not bear the touch of her eyes' question upon him, and the look of death behind the question.

With an inward groan he gave way, and let his heart yield towards her. A sudden gentle smile came on his face. And her eyes, which never left his face, slowly, slowly filled with tears. He watched the strange water rise in her eyes, like some slow fountain coming up. And his heart seemed to burn and melt away in his breast.

He could not bear to look at her any more. He dropped on his knees and caught her head with his arms and pressed her face against his throat. She was very still. His heart, which seemed to have broken, was burning with a kind of agony in his breast. And he felt her slow, hot tears wetting his throat. But he could not move.

He felt the hot tears wet his neck and the hollows of his neck, and he remained motionless, suspended through one of man's eternities. Only now it had become indispensable to him to have her face pressed close to him; he could never let her go again. He could never let her head go away from the close clutch of his arm. He wanted to remain like that for ever, with his heart hurting him in a pain that was also life to him. Without knowing, he was looking down on her damp, soft brown hair.

Then, as it were suddenly, he smelt the horrid stagnant smell of that water. And at the same moment she drew away from him and looked at him. Her eyes were wistful and unfathomable. He was afraid of them, and he fell to kissing her, not knowing what he was doing. He wanted her eyes not to have that terrible, wistful, unfathomable look. 155

When she turned her face to him again, a faint delicate flush was glowing, and there was again dawning that terrible shining of joy in her eyes, which really terrified him, and yet which he now wanted to see, because he feared the look of doubt still more.

"You love me?" she said, rather faltering.

"Yes." The word cost him a painful effort. Not because it wasn't true. But because it was too newly true, the *saying* seemed to tear open again his newly-torn heart. And he hardly wanted it to be true, even now.

She lifted her face to him, and he bent forward and kissed her on the mouth, gently, with the one kiss that is an eternal pledge. And as he kissed her his heart strained again in his breast. He never intended to love her. But now it was over. He had crossed over the gulf to her, and all that he had left behind had shriveled and become void.

After the kiss, her eyes again slowly filled with tears. She sat still, away from him, with her face drooped aside, and her hands folded in her lap. The tears fell very slowly. There was complete silence. He too sat there motionless and silent on the hearth-rug. The strange pain of his heart that was broken seemed to consume him. That he should love her? That this was love! That he should be ripped open in this way! Him, a doctor! How they would all jeer if they knew! It was agony to him to think they might know. 160

In the curious naked pain of the thought he looked again to her. She was still sitting there drooped into a muse. He saw a tear fall, and his heart flared hot. He saw for the first time that one of her shoulders was quite uncovered, one arm bare, he could see one of her small breasts; dimly, because it had become almost dark in the room.

"Why are you crying?" he asked, in an altered voice.

She looked up at him, and behind her tears the consciousness of her situation for the first time brought a dark look of shame to her eyes.

"I'm not crying, really," she said, watching him, half frightened.

He reached his hand, and softly closed it on her bare arm. 165

"I love you! I love you!" he said in a soft, low vibrating voice, unlike himself.

She shrank, and dropped her head. The soft, penetrating grip of his hand on her arm distressed her. She looked up at him.

"I want to go," she said. "I want to go and get you some dry things."

"Why?" he said. "I'm all right."

"But I want to go," she said. "And I want you to change your things."   170

He released her arm, and she wrapped herself in the blanket, looking at him rather frightened. And still she did not rise.

"Kiss me," she said wistfully.

He kissed her, but briefly, half in anger.

Then, after a second, she rose nervously, all mixed up in the blanket. He watched her in her confusion as she tried to extricate herself and wrap herself up so that she could walk. He watched her relentlessly, as she knew. And as she went, the blanket trailing, and as he saw a glimpse of her feet and her white leg, he tried to remember her as she was when he had wrapped her in the blanket. But then he didn't want to remember, because she had been nothing to him then, and his nature revolted from remembering her as she was when she was nothing to him.

A tumbling, muffled noise from within the dark house startled him. Then he   175 heard her voice: "There are clothes." He rose and went to the foot of the stairs, and gathered up the garments she had thrown down. Then he came back to the fire, to rub himself down and dress. He grinned at his own appearance when he had finished.

The fire was sinking, so he put on coal. The house was now quite dark, save for the light of a street-lamp that shone in faintly from beyond the holly trees. He lit the gas with matches he found on the mantelpiece. Then he emptied the pockets of his own clothes, and threw all his wet things in a heap into the scullery. After which he gathered up her sodden clothes, gently, and put them in a separate heap on the copper-top in the scullery.

It was six o'clock on the clock. His own watch had stopped. He ought to go back to the surgery. He waited, and still she did not come down. So he went to the foot of the stairs and called:

"I shall have to go."

Almost immediately he heard her coming down. She had on her best dress of black voile, and her hair was tidy, but still damp. She looked at him — and in spite of herself, smiled.

"I don't like you in those clothes," she said.   180

"Do I look a sight?" he answered.

They were shy of one another.

"I'll make you some tea," she said.

"No, I must go."

"Must you?" And she looked at him again with the wide, strained, doubtful   185 eyes. And again, from the pain of his breast, he knew how he loved her. He went and bent to kiss her, gently, passionately, with his heart's painful kiss.

"And my hair smells so horrible," she murmured in distraction. "And I'm so awful, I'm so awful! Oh, no, I'm too awful." And she broke into bitter, heart-broken sobbing. "You can't want to love me, I'm horrible."

"Don't be silly, don't be silly," he said, trying to comfort her, kissing her, holding her in his arms. "I want you, I want to marry you, we're going to be married, quickly, quickly — tomorrow if I can."

But she only sobbed terribly, and cried:

"I feel awful. I feel awful. I feel I'm horrible to you."

"No, I want you, I want you," was all he answered, blindly, with that terrible   190 intonation which frightened her almost more than her horror lest he should *not* want her.

JACK LONDON (1876–1916)

Born in San Francisco, Jack London was raised in Oakland, California. Though he never completed a degree at the University of California, Berkeley, his informal education ranged widely throughout the world from oyster pirating in San Francisco Bay to seal hunting in Japan and Siberia. By the

Hulton Archive/Getty Images.

time he was twenty-one, he was in Alaska attempting to strike it rich in the Klondike Gold Rush. These early experiences provided rich materials for the start of his writing career so that within six years he did, indeed, find gold in *The Call of the Wild* (1903), which became an international best-seller. Among his later works were *The Sea-Wolf* (1904), *White Fang* (1906), and *The Iron Heel* (1908). During his lifetime, London was enormously prolific and arguably the most popular American writer in the world. He demonstrated in both his career and his plots how to survive.

To Build a Fire 1908

Day had broken cold and grey, exceedingly cold and grey, when the man turned aside from the main Yukon trail and climbed the high earth-bank, where a dim and little-travelled trail led eastward through the fat spruce timberland. It was a steep bank, and he paused for breath at the top, excusing the act to himself by looking at his watch. It was nine o'clock. There was no sun nor hint of sun, though there was not a cloud in the sky. It was a clear day, and yet there seemed an intangible pall over the face of things, a subtle gloom that made the day dark, and that was due to the absence of sun. This fact did not worry the man. He was used to the lack of sun. It had been days since he had seen the sun, and he knew that a few more days must pass before that cheerful orb, due south, would just peep above the skyline and dip immediately from view.

The man flung a look back along the way he had come. The Yukon lay a mile wide and hidden under three feet of ice. On top of this ice were as many feet of snow. It was all pure white, rolling in gentle undulations where the ice jams of the freeze-up had formed. North and south, as far as his eye could see, it was unbroken white, save for a dark hairline that curved and twisted from around the spruce-covered island to the south, and that curved and twisted away into the north, where it disappeared behind another spruce-covered island. This dark hairline was the trail — the main trail — that led south five hundred miles to the Chilcoot Pass, Dyea, and salt water; and that led north seventy miles to Dawson, and still on to the north a thousand miles to Nulato, and finally to St. Michael, on Bering Sea, a thousand miles and half a thousand more.

But all this — the mysterious, far-reaching hairline trail, the absence of sun from the sky, the tremendous cold, and the strangeness and weirdness of it all — made no impression on the man. It was not because he was long used to it.

He was a newcomer in the land, a *chechaquo,* and this was his first winter. The trouble with him was that he was without imagination. He was quick and alert in the things of life, but only in the things, and not in the significances. Fifty degrees below zero meant eighty-odd degrees of frost. Such fact impressed him as being cold and uncomfortable, and that was all. It did not lead him to meditate upon his frailty as a creature of temperature, and upon man's frailty in general, able only to live within certain narrow limits of heat and cold; and from there on it did not lead him to the conjectural field of immortality and man's place in the universe. Fifty degrees below zero stood for a bite of frost that hurt and that must be guarded against by the use of mittens, ear flaps, warm moccasins, and thick socks. Fifty degrees below zero. That there should be anything more to it than that was a thought that never entered his head.

As he turned to go on, he spat speculatively. There was a sharp explosive crackle that startled him. He spat again. And again, in the air, before it could fall to the snow, the spittle crackled. He knew that at fifty below spittle crackled on the snow, but this spittle had crackled in the air. Undoubtedly it was colder than fifty below — how much colder he did not know. But the temperature did not matter. He was bound for the old claim on the left fork of Henderson Creek, where the boys were already. They had come over across the divide from the Indian Creek country, while he had come the roundabout way to take a look at the possibilities of getting out logs in the spring from the islands in the Yukon. He would be in to camp by six o'clock; a bit after dark, it was true, but the boys would be there, a fire would be going, and a hot supper would be ready. As for lunch, he pressed his hand against the protruding bundle under his jacket. It was also under his shirt, wrapped up in a handkerchief and lying against the naked skin. It was the only way to keep the biscuits from freezing. He smiled agreeably to himself as he thought of those biscuits, each cut open and sopped in bacon grease, and each enclosing a generous slice of fried bacon.

He plunged in among the big spruce trees. The trail was faint. A foot of snow 5 had fallen since the last sled had passed over, and he was glad he was without a sled, travelling light. In fact, he carried nothing but the lunch wrapped in the handkerchief. He was surprised, however, at the cold. It certainly was cold, he concluded, as he rubbed his numb nose and cheekbones with his mittened hand. He was a warm-whiskered man, but the hair on his face did not protect the high cheekbones and the eager nose that thrust itself aggressively into the frosty air.

At the man's heels trotted a dog, a big native husky, the proper wolf-dog, grey-coated and without any visible or temperamental difference from its brother, the wild wolf. The animal was depressed by the tremendous cold. It knew that it was no time for travelling. Its instinct told it a truer tale than was told to the man by the man's judgment. In reality, it was not merely colder than fifty below zero; it was colder than sixty below, than seventy below. It was seventy-five below zero. Since the freezing point is thirty-two above zero, it meant that one hundred and seven degrees of frost obtained. The dog did not know anything about thermometers. Possibly in its brain there was no sharp consciousness of a condition of very cold such as was in the man's brain. But the brute had its instinct. It experienced a vague but menacing apprehension that subdued it and made it slink along at the man's heels, and that made it question eagerly every unwonted movement of the man as if expecting him to go into camp or to seek shelter somewhere and build a fire. The dog had learned fire, and it wanted fire, or else to burrow under the snow and cuddle its warmth away from the air.

The frozen moisture of its breathing had settled on its fur in a fine powder of frost, and especially were its jowls, muzzle, and eyelashes whitened by its crystalled breath. The man's red beard and moustache were likewise frosted, but more solidly, the deposit taking the form of ice and increasing with every warm, moist breath he exhaled. Also, the man was chewing tobacco, and the muzzle of ice held his lips so rigidly that he was unable to clear his chin when he expelled the juice. The result was that a crystal beard of the colour and solidity of amber was increasing its length on his chin. If he fell down it would shatter itself, like glass, into brittle fragments. But he did not mind the appendage. It was the penalty all tobacco chewers paid in that country, and he had been out before in two cold snaps. They had not been so cold as this, he knew, but by the spirit thermometer at Sixty Mile he knew they had been registered at fifty below and at fifty-five.

He held on through the level stretch of woods for several miles, crossed a wide flat of nigger heads, and dropped down a bank to the frozen bed of a small stream. This was Henderson Creek, and he knew he was ten miles from the forks. He looked at his watch. It was ten o'clock. He was making four miles an hour, and he calculated that he would arrive at the forks at half-past twelve. He decided to celebrate that event by eating his lunch there.

The dog dropped in again at his heels, with a tail drooping discouragement, as the man swung along the creek bed. The furrow of the old sled trail was plainly visible, but a dozen inches of snow covered up the marks of the last runners. In a month no man had come up or down that silent creek. The man held steadily on. He was not much given to thinking, and just then particularly he had nothing to think about save that he would eat lunch at the forks and that at six o'clock he would be in camp with the boys. There was nobody to talk to; and, had there been, speech would have been impossible because of the ice muzzle on his mouth. So he continued monotonously to chew tobacco and to increase the length of his amber beard.

Once in a while the thought reiterated itself that it was very cold and that he had never experienced such cold. As he walked along he rubbed his cheekbones and nose with the back of his mittened hand. He did this automatically, now and again changing hands. But, rub as he would, the instant he stopped his cheek-bones went numb, and the following instant the end of his nose went numb. He was sure to frost his cheeks; he knew that, and experienced a pang of regret that he had not devised a nose strap of the sort Bud wore in cold snaps. Such a strap passed across the cheeks, as well, and saved them. But it didn't matter much, after all. What were frosted cheeks? A bit painful, that was all; they were never serious.

Empty as the man's mind was of thoughts, he was keenly observant, and he noticed the changes in the creeks, the curves and bends and timber jams, and always he sharply noted where he placed his feet. Once, coming round a bend, he shied abruptly, like a startled horse, curved away from the place where he had been walking, and retreated several paces back along the trail. The creek he knew was frozen clear to the bottom — no creek could contain water in that arctic winter — but he knew also that there were springs that bubbled out from the hillsides and ran along under the snow and on top of the ice of the creek. He knew that the coldest snaps never froze these springs, and he knew likewise their danger. They were traps. They hid pools of water under the snow that might be three inches deep, or three feet. Sometimes a skin of ice half an inch thick covered them, and in turn was covered by snow. Sometimes there were alternate layers of water and ice skin, so that when one broke through he kept on breaking through for a while, sometimes wetting himself to the waist.

That was why he had shied in such a panic. He had felt the give under his feet and heard the crackle of a snow-hidden ice skin. And to get his feet wet in such a temperature meant trouble and danger. At the very least it meant delay, for he would be forced to stop and build a fire, and under its protection to bare his feet while he dried his socks and moccasins. He stood and studied the creek bed and its banks, and decided that the flow of water came from the right. He reflected awhile, rubbing his nose and cheeks, then skirted to the left, stepping gingerly and testing the footing for each step. Once clear of the danger, he took a fresh chew of tobacco and swung along at his four-mile gait.

In the course of the next two hours he came upon several similar traps. Usually the snow above the hidden pools had a sunken, candied appearance that advertised the danger. Once again, however, he had a close call; and once, suspecting danger, he compelled the dog to go on in front. The dog did not want to go. It hung back until the man shoved it forward, and then it went quickly across the white, unbroken surface. Suddenly it broke through, floundered to one side, and got away to firmer footing. It had wet its forefeet and legs, and almost immediately the water that clung to it turned to ice. It made quick efforts to lick the ice off its legs, then dropped down in the snow and began to bite out the ice that had formed between the toes. This was a matter of instinct. To permit the ice to remain would mean sore feet. It did not know this. It merely obeyed the mysterious prompting that arose from the deep crypts of its being. But the man knew, having achieved a judgment on the subject, and he removed the mitten from his right hand and helped to tear out the ice particles. He did not expose his fingers more than a minute, and was astonished at the swift numbness that smote them. It certainly was cold. He pulled on the mitten hastily, and beat the hand savagely across his chest.

At twelve o'clock the day was at its brightest. Yet the sun was too far south on its winter journey to clear the horizon. The bulge of the earth intervened between it and Henderson Creek, where the man walked under a clear sky at noon and cast no shadow. At half-past twelve, to the minute, he arrived at the forks of the creek. He was pleased at the speed he had made. If he kept it up, he would certainly be with the boys by six. He unbuttoned his jacket and shirt and drew forth his lunch. The action consumed no more than a quarter of a minute, yet in that brief moment the numbness laid hold of the exposed fingers. He did not put the mitten on, but, instead, struck the fingers a dozen sharp smashes against his leg. Then he sat down on a snow-covered log to eat. The sting that followed upon the striking of his fingers against his leg ceased so quickly that he was startled. He had had no chance to take a bite of biscuit. He struck the fingers repeatedly and returned them to the mitten, baring the other hand for the purpose of eating. He tried to take a mouthful, but the ice muzzle prevented. He had forgotten to build a fire and thaw out. He chuckled at his foolishness, and as he chuckled he noted the numbness creeping into the exposed fingers. Also, he noted that the stinging which had first come to his toes when he sat down was already passing away. He wondered whether the toes were warm or numb. He moved them inside the moccasins and decided that they were numb.

He pulled the mitten on hurriedly and stood up. He was a bit frightened. He 15 stamped up and down until the stinging returned into the feet. It certainly was cold, was his thought. That man from Sulphur Creek had spoken the truth when telling how cold it sometimes got in the country. And he had laughed at him at the time! That showed one must not be too sure of things. There was no mistake about it, it *was* cold. He strode up and down, stamping his feet and threshing his arms, until reassured by the returning warmth. Then he got out matches and proceeded to make a fire. From the undergrowth, where high water of the previous spring had lodged a supply of seasoned twigs, he got his firewood. Working carefully from a small beginning, he soon had a roaring fire, over which he thawed the ice from his face and in the protection of which he ate his biscuits. For the moment the cold of space was outwitted. The dog took satisfaction in the fire, stretching out close enough for warmth and far enough away to escape being singed.

When the man had finished, he filled his pipe and took his comfortable time over a smoke. Then he pulled on his mittens, settled the ear-flaps of his cap firmly about his ears, and took the creek trail up the left fork. The dog was disappointed and yearned back towards the fire. This man did not know cold. Possibly all the generations of his ancestry had been ignorant of cold, of real cold, of cold one hundred and seven degrees below freezing point. But the dog knew; all its ancestry knew, and it had inherited the knowledge. And it knew that it was not good to walk abroad in such fearful cold. It was the time to lie snug in a hole in the snow and wait for a curtain of cloud to be drawn across the face of outer space whence this cold came. On the other hand, there was no keen intimacy between the dog and the man. The one was the toil slave of the other, and the only caresses it had ever received were the caresses of the whip lash and of harsh and menacing throat sounds that threatened the whip lash. So the dog made no effort to communicate its apprehension to the man. It was not concerned in the welfare of the man; it was for its own sake that it yearned back towards the fire. But the man whistled, and spoke to it with the sound of whip lashes, and the dog swung in at the man's heels and followed after.

The man took a chew of tobacco and proceeded to start a new amber beard. Also, his moist breath quickly powdered with white his moustache, eyebrows, and lashes. There did not seem to be so many springs on the left fork of the Henderson, and for half an hour the man saw no signs of any. And then it happened. At a place where there were no signs, where the soft, unbroken snow seemed to advertise solidity beneath, the man broke through. It was not deep. He wet himself half-way to the knees before he floundered out to the firm crust.

He was angry, and cursed his luck aloud. He had hoped to get into camp with the boys at six o'clock, and this would delay him an hour, for he would have to build a fire and dry out his footgear. This was imperative at that low temperature — he knew that much; and he turned aside to the bank, which he climbed. On top, tangled in the underbrush about the trunks of several small spruce trees, was a high-water deposit of dry firewood — sticks and twigs, principally, but also larger portions of seasoned branches and fine, dry, last year's grasses. He threw down several large pieces on top of the snow. This served for a foundation and prevented the young flame from drowning itself in the snow it otherwise would melt. The flame he got by touching a match to a small shred of birch bark that he took from his pocket. This burned even more readily than paper. Placing it on the foundation, he fed the young flame with wisps of dry grass and with the tiniest dry twigs.

He worked slowly and carefully, keenly aware of his danger. Gradually, as the flame grew stronger, he increased the size of the twigs with which he fed it. He squatted in the snow pulling the twigs out from their entanglement in the brush and feeding directly to the flame. He knew there must be no failure. When it is seventy-five below zero, a man must not fail in his first attempt to build a fire — that is, if his feet are wet. If his feet are dry, and he fails, he can run along the trail for half a mile and restore his circulation. But the circulation of wet and freezing feet cannot be restored by running when it is seventy-five below. No matter how fast he runs, the wet feet will freeze the harder.

All this the man knew. The old-timer on Sulphur Creek had told him about 20 it the previous fall, and now he was appreciating the advice. Already all sensation had gone out of his feet. To build the fire he had been forced to remove his mittens, and the fingers had quickly gone numb. His pace of four miles an hour had kept his heart pumping blood to the surface of his body and to all the extremities. But the instant he stopped, the action of the pump eased down. The cold of space smote the unprotected tip of the planet, and he, being on that unprotected tip, received the full force of the blow. The blood of his body recoiled before it. The blood was alive, like the dog, and like the dog it wanted to hide away and cover itself up from the fearful cold. So long as he walked four miles an hour, he pumped that blood, willy-nilly, to the surface; but now it ebbed away and sank down into the recesses of his body. The extremities were the first to feel its absence. His wet feet froze the faster, and his exposed fingers numbed the faster, though they had not yet begun to freeze. Nose and cheeks were already freezing, while the skin of all his body chilled as it lost its blood.

But he was safe. Toes and nose and cheeks would be only touched by the frost, for the fire was beginning to burn with strength. He was feeding it with twigs the size of his finger. In another minute he would be able to feed it with branches the size of his wrist, and then he could remove his wet footgear, and, while it dried, he could keep his naked feet warm by the fire, rubbing them at first, of course, with snow. The fire was a success. He was safe. He remembered the advice of the old-timer on Sulphur Creek, and smiled. The old-timer had been very serious in laying down the law that no man must travel alone in the Klondike after fifty below. Well, here he was; he had had the accident; he was alone; and he had saved himself. Those old-timers were rather womanish, some of them, he thought. All a man had to do was to keep his head, and he was all right. Any man who was a man could travel alone. But it was surprising, the rapidity with which his cheeks and nose were freezing. And he had not thought his fingers could go lifeless in so short a time. Lifeless they were, for he could scarcely make them move together to grip a twig, and they seemed remote from his body and from him. When he touched a twig, he had to look and see whether or not he had hold of it. The wires were pretty well down between him and his finger ends.

All of which counted for little. There was the fire, snapping and crackling and promising life with every dancing flame. He started to untie his moccasins. They were coated with ice; the thick German socks were like sheaths of iron halfway to the knees; and the moccasin strings were like rods of steel all twisted and knotted as by some conflagration. For a moment he tugged with his numb fingers, then, realizing the folly of it, he drew his sheath knife.

But before he could cut the strings, it happened. It was his own fault, or, rather, his mistake. He should not have built the fire under the spruce tree. He should have built it in the open. But it had been easier to pull the twigs from the brush and drop them directly on the fire. Now the tree under which he had done this carried a weight of snow on its boughs. No wind had blown for weeks, and each bough was fully freighted. Each time he had pulled a twig he had communicated a slight agitation to the tree — an imperceptible agitation, so far as he was concerned, but an agitation sufficient to bring about the disaster. High up in the tree one bough capsized its load of snow. This fell on the boughs beneath, capsizing them. This process continued, spreading out and involving the whole tree. It grew like an avalanche, and it descended without warning upon the man and the fire, and the fire was blotted out! Where it had burned was a mantle of fresh and disordered snow.

The man was shocked. It was as though he had just heard his own sentence of death. For a moment he sat and stared at the spot where the fire had been. Then he grew very calm. Perhaps the old-timer on Sulphur Creek was right. If he had only had a trail mate he would have been in no danger now. The trail mate could have built the fire. Well, it was up to him to build the fire over again, and this second time there must be no failure. Even if he succeeded, he would most likely lose some toes. His feet must be badly frozen by now, and there would be some time before the second fire was ready.

Such were his thoughts, but he did not sit and think them. He was busy all the 25 time they were passing through his mind. He had made a new foundation for a fire, this time in the open, where no treacherous tree could blot it out. Next he gathered dry grasses and tiny twigs from the high-water flotsam. He could not bring his fingers together to pull them out, but he was able to gather them by the handful. In this way he got many rotten twigs and bits of green moss that were undesirable, but it was the best he could do. He worked methodically, even collecting an armful of the larger branches to be used later when the fire gathered strength. And all the while the dog sat and watched him, a certain yearning wistfulness in its eyes, it looked upon him as the fire provider, and the fire was slow in coming.

When all was ready, the man reached in his pocket for a second piece of birch bark. He knew the bark was there, and, though he could not feel it with his fingers, he could hear its crisp rustling as he fumbled for it. Try as he would, he could not clutch hold of it. And all the time, in his consciousness, was the knowledge that each instant his feet were freezing. This thought tended to put him in a panic, but he fought against it and kept calm. He pulled on his mittens with his teeth, and threshed his arms back and forth, beating his hands with all his might against his sides. He did this sitting down, and he stood up to do it; and all the while the dog sat in the snow, its wolf brush of a tail curled around warmly over its forefeet, its sharp wolf ears pricked forward intently as it watched the man. And the man, as he beat and threshed with his arms and hands, felt a great surge of envy as he regarded the creature that was warm and secure in its natural covering.

After a time he was aware of the first faraway signals of sensation in his beaten fingers. The faint tingling grew stronger till it evolved into a stinging ache that was excruciating, but which the man hailed with satisfaction. He stripped the mitten from his right hand and fetched forth the birch bark. The exposed fingers were quickly going numb again. Next he brought out his bunch of sulphur matches. But the tremendous cold had already driven the life out of his fingers. In his effort to separate one match from the others, the whole bunch fell in the snow. He tried to pick it out of the snow, but failed. The dead fingers could neither touch nor clutch. He was very careful. He drove the thought of his freezing feet, and nose, and cheeks, out of his mind, devoting his whole soul to the matches. He watched, using the sense of vision in place of that of touch, and when he saw his fingers on each side the bunch, he closed them — that is, he willed to close them, for the wires were down, and the fingers did not obey. He pulled the mitten on the right hand, and beat it fiercely against the knee. Then with both mittened hands, he scooped the bunch of matches, along with much snow, into his lap. Yet he was no better off.

After some manipulation he managed to get the bunch between the heels of his mittened hands. In this fashion he carried it to his mouth. The ice crackled and snapped when by a violent effort he opened his mouth. He drew the lower jaw in, curled the upper lip out of the way, and scraped the bunch with his upper teeth in order to separate a match. He succeeded in getting one, which he dropped on his lap. He was no better off. He could not pick it up. Then he devised a way. He picked it up in his teeth and scratched it on his leg. Twenty times he scratched before he succeeded in lighting it. As it flamed he held it with his teeth to the birch bark. But the burning brimstone went up his nostrils and into his lungs, causing him to cough spasmodically. The match fell into the snow and went out.

The old-timer on Sulphur Creek was right, he thought in the moment of controlled despair that ensued: after fifty below, a man should travel with a partner. He beat his hands, but failed in exciting any sensation. Suddenly he bared both hands, removing the mittens with his teeth. He caught the whole bunch between the heels of his hands. His arm muscles not being frozen enabled him to press the hand heels tightly against the matches. Then he scratched the bunch along his leg. It flared into flame, seventy sulphur matches at once! There was no wind to blow them out. He kept his head to one side to escape the strangling fumes, and held the blazing bunch to the birch bark. As he so held it, he became aware of sensation in his hand. His flesh was burning. He could smell it. Deep down below the surface he could feel it. The sensation developed into pain that grew acute. And still he endured it, holding the flame of the matches clumsily to the bark that would not light readily because his own burning hands were in the way, absorbing most of the flame.

At last, when he could endure no more, he jerked his hands apart. The blazing   30 matches fell sizzling into the snow, but the birch bark was alight. He began laying dry grasses and the tiniest twigs on the flame. He could not pick and choose, for he had to lift the fuel between the heels of his hands. Small pieces of rotten wood and green moss clung to the twigs, and he bit them off as well as he could with his teeth. He cherished the flame carefully and awkwardly. It meant life, and it must not perish. The withdrawal of blood from the surface of his body now made him begin to shiver, and he grew more awkward. A large piece of green moss fell squarely on the little fire. He tried to poke it out with his fingers, but his shivering frame made him poke too far, and he disrupted the nucleus of the little fire, the burning grasses and tiny twigs separating and scattering. He tried to poke them together again, but in spite of the tenseness of the effort, his shivering got away with him, and the twigs were hopelessly scattered. Each twig gushed a puff of smoke and went out. The fire provider had failed. As he looked apathetically about him, his eyes chanced on the dog, sitting across the ruins of the fire from him, in the snow, making restless, hunching movements, slightly lifting one forefoot and then the other, shifting its weight back and forth on them with wistful eagerness.

The sight of the dog put a wild idea into his head. He remembered the tale of the man, caught in a blizzard, who killed a steer and crawled inside the carcass, and so was saved. He would kill the dog and bury his hands in the warm body until the numbness went out of them. Then he could build another fire. He spoke to the dog, calling it to him; but in his voice was a strange note of fear that frightened the animal, who had never known the man to speak in such a way before. Something was the matter, and its suspicious nature sensed danger — it knew not what danger but somewhere, somehow, in its brain arose an apprehension of the man. It flattened its ears down at the sound of the man's voice, and its restless, hunching movements and the liftings and shiftings of its forefeet became more pronounced; but it would not come to the man. He got on his hands and knees and crawled towards the dog. This unusual posture again excited suspicion, and the animal sidled mincingly away.

The man sat up in the snow for a moment and struggled for calmness. Then he pulled on his mittens, by means of his teeth, and got upon his feet. He glanced down at first in order to assure himself that he was really standing up, for the absence of sensation in his feet left him unrelated to the earth. His erect position in itself started to drive the webs of suspicion from the dog's mind; and when he spoke peremptorily, with the sound of whip lashes in his voice, the dog rendered its customary allegiance and came to him. As it came within reaching distance, the man lost his control. His arms flashed out to the dog, and he experienced genuine surprise when he discovered that his hands could not clutch, that there was neither bend nor feeling in the fingers. He had forgotten for the moment that they were frozen and that they were freezing more and more. All this happened quickly, and before the animal could get away, he encircled its body with his arms. He sat down in the snow, and in this fashion held the dog, while it snarled and whined and struggled.

But it was all he could do, hold its body encircled in his arms and sit there. He realized he could not kill the dog. There was no way to do it. With his helpless hands he could neither draw nor hold his sheath knife nor throttle the animal. He released it, and it plunged wildly away, with tail between its legs, and still snarling. It halted forty feet away and surveyed him curiously, with ears pricked forward.

The man looked down at his hands in order to locate them, and found them hanging on the ends of his arms. It struck him as curious that one should have to use his eyes in order to find out where his hands were. He began threshing his arms back and forth, beating the mittened hands against his sides. He did this for five minutes, violently, and his heart pumped enough blood up to the surface to put a stop to his shivering. But no sensation was aroused in the hands. He had an impression that they hung like weights on the ends of his arms, but when he tried to run the impression down, he could not find it.

A certain fear of death, dull and oppressive, came to him. This fear quickly 35 became poignant as he realized that it was no longer a mere matter of freezing his fingers and toes, or of losing his hands and feet, but that it was a matter of life and death with the chances against him. This threw him into a panic, and he turned and ran up the creek bed along the old, dim trail. The dog joined in behind him and kept up with him. He ran blindly, without intention, in fear such as he had never known in his life. Slowly, as he ploughed and floundered through the snow, he began to see things again — the banks of the creek, the old timber jams, the leafless aspens, and the sky. The running made him feel better. He did not shiver. Maybe, if he ran on, his feet would thaw out; and, anyway, if he ran far enough, he would reach camp and the boys. Without doubt he would lose some fingers and toes and some of his face; but the boys would take care of him, and save the rest of him when he got there. And at the same time there was another thought in his mind that said he would never get to the camp and the boys; that it was too many miles away, that the freezing had too great a start on him, and that he would soon be stiff and dead. This thought he kept in the background and refused to consider. Sometimes it pushed itself forward and demanded to be heard, but he thrust it back and strove to think of other things.

It struck him as curious that he could run at all on feet so frozen that he could not feel them when they struck the earth and took the weight of his body. He seemed to himself to skim along above the surface, and to have no connection with the earth. Somewhere he had once seen a winged Mercury, and he wondered if Mercury felt as he felt when skimming over the earth.

His theory of running until he reached camp and the boys had one flaw in it: he lacked the endurance. Several times he stumbled, and finally he tottered, crumpled up, and fell. When he tried to rise, he failed. He must sit and rest, he decided, and next time he would merely walk and keep on going. As he sat and regained his breath, he noted that he was feeling quite warm and comfortable. He was not shivering, and it even seemed that a warm glow had come to his chest and trunk. And yet, when he touched his nose or cheeks, there was no sensation. Running would not thaw them out. Nor would it thaw out his hands and feet. Then the thought came to him that the frozen portions of his body must be extending. He tried to keep this thought down, to forget it, to think of something else; he was aware of the panicky feeling that it caused, and he was afraid of the panic. But the thought asserted itself, and persisted, until it produced a vision of his body totally frozen. This was too much, and he made another wild run along the trail. Once he slowed down to a walk, but the thought of the freezing extending itself made him run again.

And all the time the dog ran with him, at his heels. When he fell down a second time, it curled its tail over its forefeet and sat in front of him, facing him, curiously eager and intent. The warmth and security of the animal angered him, and he cursed it till it flattened down its ears appeasingly. This time the shivering came more quickly upon the man. He was losing in his battle with the frost. It was creeping into his body from all sides. The thought of it drove him on, but he ran no more than a hundred feet, when he staggered and pitched headlong. It was his last panic. When he had recovered his breath and control, he sat up and entertained in his mind the conception of meeting death with dignity. However, the conception did not come to him in such terms. His idea of it was that he had been making a fool of himself, running around like a chicken with its head cut off — such was the simile that occurred to him. Well, he was bound to freeze anyway, and he might as well take it decently. With this new-found peace of mind came the first glimmerings of drowsiness. A good idea, he thought, to sleep off to death. It was like taking an anaesthetic. Freezing was not so bad as people thought. There were lots worse ways to die.

He pictured the boys finding his body next day. Suddenly he found himself with them, coming along the trail looking for himself. And, still with them, he came around a turn in the trail and found himself lying in the snow. He did not belong with himself any more, for even then he was out of himself, standing with the boys and looking at himself in the snow. It certainly was cold, was his thought. When he got back to the States he could tell the folks what real cold was. He drifted on from this to a vision of the old-timer on Sulphur Creek. He could see him quite clearly, warm and comfortable, and smoking a pipe.

"You were right, old hoss; you were right," the man mumbled to the old-timer 40 of Sulphur Creek.

Then the man drowsed off into what seemed to him the most comfortable and satisfying sleep he had ever known. The dog sat facing him and waiting. The brief day drew to a close in a long, slow twilight. There were no signs of a fire to be made, and, besides, never in the dog's experience had it known a man to sit like that in the snow and make no fire. As the twilight drew on, its eager yearning for the fire mastered it, and with a great lifting and shifting of forefeet, it whined softly, then flattened its ears down in anticipation of being chidden by the man. But the man remained silent. Later the dog whined loudly. And still later it crept close to the man and caught the scent of death. This made the animal bristle and back away. A little longer it delayed, howling under the stars that leaped and danced and shone brightly in the cold sky. Then it turned and trotted up the trail in the direction of the camp it knew, where were the other food providers and fire providers.

EDGAR ALLAN POE (1809–1849)

Edgar Allan Poe grew up in the home of John Allan, in Richmond, Virginia, after his mother died in 1811, and he was educated in Scotland and England for five years before completing his classical education in Richmond. After a short stint at the University of Virginia, Poe went to Boston, where he began publishing his poetry. His foster father sent him to West Point Military Academy, but Poe was expelled and moved on to New York, where he published a book of poems inspired by the Romantic movement. Moving among editorial jobs in Baltimore,

Library of Congress, Prints and Photographs Division.

Richmond, and New York, Poe married his thirteen-year-old cousin Virginia Clemm. Early in his story-writing career, Poe published his only novel-length piece, *The Narrative of Arthur Gordon Pym* (1838), and the following year, he began to work in the genre of the supernatural and horrible, with the stories "William Wilson" and "The Fall of the House of Usher." He gained publicity with the detective story "The Murders in the Rue Morgue," became nationally famous with the publication of his poem "The Raven" in 1845, and died four years later in Baltimore after a drinking binge. Poe theorized that the short story writer should plan every word toward the achievement of a certain effect, and that stories should be read in a single sitting. Morbidity and dreamlike flights of fancy, for which Poe is often recognized, do not detract from his lucid crafting of suspense and his erudite control of language and symbol.

The Cask of Amontillado 1846

The thousand injuries of Fortunato I had borne as I best could; but when he ventured upon insult, I vowed revenge. You, who so well know the nature of my soul, will not suppose, however, that I gave utterance to a threat. *At length* I would be avenged; this was a point definitely settled — but the very definitiveness with which it was resolved precluded the idea of risk. I must not only punish, but punish with impunity. A wrong is unredressed when retribution overtakes its redresser. It is equally unredressed when the avenger fails to make himself felt as such to him who has done the wrong.

It must be understood, that neither by word nor deed had I given Fortunato cause to doubt my good-will. I continued, as was my wont, to smile in his face, and he did not perceive that my smile *now* was at the thought of his immolation.

He had a weak point — this Fortunato — although in other regards he was a man to be respected and even feared. He prided himself on his connoisseurship in wine. Few Italians have the true virtuoso spirit. For the most part their enthusiasm is adopted to suit the time and opportunity — to practise imposture upon the British and Austrian *millionnaires*. In painting and gemmary Fortunato, like his countrymen, was a quack — but in the matter of old wines he was sincere. In this respect I did not differ from him materially: I was skilful in the Italian vintages myself, and bought largely whenever I could.

It was about dusk, one evening during the supreme madness of the carnival season, that I encountered my friend. He accosted me with excessive warmth, for he had been drinking much. The man wore motley. He had on a tight-fitting parti-striped dress, and his head was surmounted by the conical cap and bells. I was so pleased to see him, that I thought I should never have done wringing his hand.

I said to him: "My dear Fortunato, you are luckily met. How remarkably well 5 you are looking to-day! But I have received a pipe° of what passes for Amontillado, and I have my doubts."

"How?" said he. "Amontillado? A pipe? Impossible! And in the middle of the carnival!"

"I have my doubts," I replied; "and I was silly enough to pay the full Amontillado price without consulting you in the matter. You were not to be found, and I was fearful of losing a bargain."

"Amontillado!"

"I have my doubts."

"Amontillado!"   10

"And I must satisfy them."

"Amontillado!"

"As you are engaged, I am on my way to Luchesi. If any one has a critical turn, it is he. He will tell me ——"

"Luchesi cannot tell Amontillado from Sherry."

"And yet some fools will have it that his taste is a match for your own."   15

"Come, let us go."

"Whither?"

"To your vaults."

"My friend, no; I will not impose upon your good nature. I perceive you have an engagement. Luchesi ——"

"I have no engagement; — come."   20

"My friend, no. It is not the engagement, but the severe cold with which I perceive you are afflicted. The vaults are insufferably damp. They are encrusted with nitre."

"Let us go, nevertheless. The cold is merely nothing. Amontillado! You have been imposed upon. And as for Luchesi, he cannot distinguish Sherry from Amontillado."

Thus speaking, Fortunato possessed himself of my arm. Putting on a mask of black silk, and drawing a *roquelaire*° closely about my person, I suffered him to hurry me to my palazzo.

There were no attendants at home; they had absconded to make merry in honor of the time. I had told them that I should not return until the morning,

pipe: A large keg.
roquelaire: A short cloak.

and had given them explicit orders not to stir from the house. These orders were sufficient, I well knew, to insure their immediate disappearance, one and all, as soon as my back was turned.

I took from their sconces two flambeaux, and giving one to Fortunato, bowed 25 him through several suites of rooms to the archway that led into the vaults. I passed down a long and winding staircase, requesting him to be cautious as he followed. We came at length to the foot of the descent, and stood together on the damp ground of the catacombs of the Montresors.

The gait of my friend was unsteady, and the bells upon his cap jingled as he strode.

"The pipe?" said he.

"It is farther on," said I; "but observe the white web-work which gleams from these cavern walls."

He turned toward me, and looked into my eyes with two filmy orbs that distilled the rheum of intoxication.

"Nitre?" he asked, at length. 30

"Nitre," I replied. "How long have you had that cough?"

"Ugh! ugh! ugh! — ugh! ugh! ugh! — ugh! ugh! ugh! — ugh! ugh! ugh! — ugh! ugh! ugh!"

My poor friend found it impossible to reply for many minutes.

"It is nothing," he said, at last.

"Come," I said, with decision, "we will go back; your health is precious. You 35 are rich, respected, admired, beloved; you are happy, as once I was. You are a man to be missed. For me it is no matter. We will go back; you will be ill, and I cannot be responsible. Besides, there is Luchesi ——"

"Enough," he said; "the cough is a mere nothing; it will not kill me. I shall not die of a cough."

"True — true," I replied; "and, indeed, I had no intention of alarming you unnecessarily; but you should use all proper caution. A draught of this Medoc will defend us from the damps."

Here I knocked off the neck of a bottle which I drew from a long row of its fellows that lay upon the mould.

"Drink," I said, presenting him the wine.

He raised it to his lips with a leer. He paused and nodded to me familiarly, 40 while his bells jingled.

"I drink," he said, "to the buried that repose around us."

"And I to your long life."

He again took my arm, and we proceeded.

"These vaults," he said, "are extensive."

"The Montresors," I replied, "were a great and numerous family." 45

"I forget your arms."

"A huge human foot d'or,° in a field azure; the foot crushes a serpent rampant whose fangs are imbedded in the heel."

"And the motto?"

"*Nemo me impune lacessit.*"°

"Good!" he said. 50

---

d'or: Of gold.
Nemo . . . lacessit (Latin): No one wounds me with impunity.

The wine sparkled in his eyes and the bells jingled. My own fancy grew warm with the Medoc. We had passed through walls of piled bones, with casks and puncheons intermingling into the inmost recesses of the catacombs. I paused again, and this time I made bold to seize Fortunato by an arm above the elbow.

"The nitre!" I said; "see, it increases. It hangs like moss upon the vaults. We are below the river's bed. The drops of moisture trickle among the bones. Come, we will go back ere it is too late. Your cough ——"

"It is nothing," he said; "let us go on. But first, another draught of the Medoc."

I broke and reached him a flagon of De Grâve. He emptied it at a breath. His eyes flashed with a fierce light. He laughed and threw the bottle upward with a gesticulation I did not understand.

I looked at him in surprise. He repeated the movement — a grotesque one.   55

"You do not comprehend?" he said.

"Not I," I replied.

"Then you are not of the brotherhood."

"How?"

"You are not of the masons."   60

"Yes, yes," I said; "yes, yes."

"You? Impossible! A mason?"

"A mason," I replied.

"A sign," he said.

"It is this," I answered, producing a trowel from beneath the folds of my   65
roquelaire.

"You jest," he exclaimed, recoiling a few paces. "But let us proceed to the Amontillado."

"Be it so," I said, replacing the tool beneath the cloak, and again offering him my arm. He leaned upon it heavily. We continued our route in search of the Amontillado. We passed through a range of low arches, descended, passed on, and descending again, arrived at a deep crypt, in which the foulness of the air caused our flambeaux rather to glow than flame.

At the most remote end of the crypt there appeared another less spacious. Its walls had been lined with human remains, piled to the vault overhead, in the fashion of the great catacombs of Paris. Three sides of this interior crypt were still ornamented in this manner. From the fourth the bones had been thrown down, and lay promiscuously upon the earth, forming at one point a mound of some size. Within the wall thus exposed by the displacing of the bones, we perceived a still interior recess, in depth about four feet, in width three, in height six or seven. It seemed to have been constructed for no especial use within itself, but formed merely the interval between two of the colossal supports of the roof of the catacombs, and was backed by one of their circumscribing walls of solid granite.

It was in vain that Fortunato, uplifting his dull torch, endeavored to pry into the depth of the recess. Its termination the feeble light did not enable us to see.

"Proceed," I said; "herein is the Amontillado. As for Luchesi ——"   70

"He is an ignoramus," interrupted my friend, as he stepped unsteadily forward, while I followed immediately at his heels. In an instant he had reached the extremity of the niche, and finding his progress arrested by the rock, stood stupidly bewildered. A moment more and I had fettered him to the granite. In its surface were two iron staples, distant from each other about two feet, horizontally. From one of these depended a short chain, from the other a padlock. Throwing the links about his waist, it was but the work of a few seconds to secure it. He was too much astounded to resist. Withdrawing the key I stepped back from the recess.

"Pass your hand," I said, "over the wall; you cannot help feeling the nitre. Indeed it is *very* damp. Once more let me *implore* you to return. No? Then I must positively leave you. But I must first render you all the little attentions in my power."

"The Amontillado!" ejaculated my friend, not yet recovered from his astonishment.

"True," I replied; "the Amontillado."

As I said these words I busied myself among the pile of bones of which I have 75 before spoken. Throwing them aside, I soon uncovered a quantity of building stone and mortar. With these materials and with the aid of my trowel, I began vigorously to wall up the entrance of the niche.

I had scarcely laid the first tier of the masonry when I discovered that the intoxication of Fortunato had in a great measure worn off. The earliest indication I had of this was a low moaning cry from the depth of the recess. It was *not* the cry of a drunken man. There was then a long and obstinate silence. I laid the second tier, and the third, and the fourth; and then I heard the furious vibrations of the chain. The noise lasted for several minutes, during which, that I might hearken to it with the more satisfaction, I ceased my labors and sat down upon the bones. When at last the clanking subsided, I resumed the trowel, and finished without interruption the fifth, the sixth, and the seventh tier. The wall was now nearly upon a level with my breast. I again paused, and holding the flambeaux over the masonwork, threw a few feeble rays upon the figure within.

A succession of loud and shrill screams, bursting suddenly from the throat of the chained form, seemed to thrust me violently back. For a brief moment I hesitated — I trembled. Unsheathing my rapier, I began to grope with it about the recess; but the thought of an instant reassured me. I placed my hand upon the solid fabric of the catacombs, and felt satisfied. I reapproached the wall. I replied to the yells of him who clamored. I reechoed — I aided — I surpassed them in volume and in strength. I did this, and the clamorer grew still.

It was now midnight, and my task was drawing to a close. I had completed the eighth, the ninth, and the tenth tier. I had finished a portion of the last and the eleventh; there remained but a single stone to be fitted and plastered in. I struggled with its weight; I placed it partially in its destined position. But now there came from out the niche a low laugh that erected the hairs upon my head. It was succeeded by a sad voice, which I had difficulty in recognizing as that of the noble Fortunato. The voice said —

"Ha! ha! ha! — he! he! — a very good joke indeed — an excellent jest. We will have many a rich laugh about it at the palazzo — he! he! he! — over our wine — he! he! he!"

"The Amontillado!" I said. 80

"He! he! he! — he! he! he! — yes, the Amontillado. But is it not getting late? Will not they be awaiting us at the palazzo, the Lady Fortunato and the rest? Let us be gone."

"Yes," I said, "let us be gone."

"For the love of God, Montresor!"

"Yes," I said, "for the love of God!"

But to these words I hearkened in vain for a reply. I grew impatient. I called 85 aloud:

"Fortunato!"

No answer. I called again:

"Fortunato!"

No answer still, I thrust a torch through the remaining aperture and let it fall within. There came forth in return only a jingling of the bells. My heart grew sick — on account of the dampness of the catacombs. I hastened to make an end of my labor. I forced the last stone into its position; I plastered it up. Against the new masonry I re-erected the old rampart of bones. For the half of a century no mortal has disturbed them. *In pace requiescat!°*

In pace requiescat! (Latin): In peace may he rest!

POETRY

The Elements
of Poetry

20

Reading Poetry

Ink runs from the corners of my mouth.
There is no happiness like mine.
I have been eating poetry.
— MARK STRAND

READING POETRY RESPONSIVELY

Perhaps the best way to begin reading poetry responsively is not to allow yourself to be intimidated by it. Come to it, initially at least, the way you might listen to a song on the radio. You probably listen to a song several times before you hear it all, before you have a sense of how it works, where it's going, and how it gets there. You don't worry about analyzing a song when you listen to it, even though after repeated experiences with it you know and anticipate a favorite part and know, on some level, why it works for you. Give yourself a chance to respond to poetry. The hardest work has already been done by the poet, so all you need to do at the start is listen for the pleasure produced by the poet's arrangement of words.

Try reading the following poem aloud. Read it aloud before you read it silently. You may stumble once or twice, but you'll make sense of it if you pay attention to its punctuation and don't stop at the end of every line where there is no punctuation. The title gives you an initial sense of what the poem is about.

LISA PARKER (B. 1972)

Snapping Beans   1998

For Fay Whitt

I snapped beans into the silver bowl
that sat on the splintering slats
of the porchswing between my grandma and me.
I was home for the weekend,
from school, from the North,   5
Grandma hummed "What A Friend We Have In Jesus"
as the sun rose, pushing its pink spikes
through the slant of cornstalks,
through the fly-eyed mesh of the screen.
We didn't speak until the sun overcame   10
the feathered tips of the cornfield
and Grandma stopped humming. I could feel
the soft gray of her stare
against the side of my face
when she asked, *How's school a-goin'?*   15
I wanted to tell her about my classes,
the revelations by book and lecture,
as real as any shout of faith
and potent as a swig of strychnine.
She reached the leather of her hand   20
over the bowl and cupped
my quivering chin; the slick smooth of her palm
held my face the way she held tomatoes
under the spigot, careful not to drop them,
and I wanted to tell her   25
about the nights I cried into the familiar
heartsick panels of the quilt she made me,
wishing myself home on the evening star.
I wanted to tell her
the evening star was a planet,   30
that my friends wore noserings and wrote poetry
about sex, about alcoholism, about Buddha.
I wanted to tell her how my stomach burned
acidic holes at the thought of speaking in class,
speaking in an accent, speaking out of turn,   35
how I was tearing, splitting myself apart
with the slow-simmering guilt of being happy
despite it all.
I said, *School's fine.*
We snapped beans into the silver bowl between us   40
and when a hickory leaf, still summer green,
skidded onto the porchfront,
Grandma said,
It's funny how things blow loose like that.

CONSIDERATIONS FOR CRITICAL THINKING AND WRITING

1. FIRST RESPONSE. Describe the speaker's feelings about starting a life at college. How do those feelings compare with your own experiences?

2. How does the grandmother's world differ from the speaker's at school? What details especially reveal those differences?

3. Discuss the significance of the grandmother's response to the hickory leaf in line 44. How do you read the last line?

The next poem creates a different kind of mood. Think about the title, "Those Winter Sundays," before you begin reading the poem. What associations do you have with winter Sundays? What emotions does the phrase evoke in you?

ROBERT HAYDEN (1913–1980)

Those Winter Sundays 1962

Sundays too my father got up early
and put his clothes on in the blueblack cold,
then with cracked hands that ached
from labor in the weekday weather made
banked fires blaze. No one ever thanked him.   5

I'd wake and hear the cold splintering, breaking.
When the rooms were warm, he'd call,
and slowly I would rise and dress,
fearing the chronic angers of that house,

Speaking indifferently to him,   10
who had driven out the cold
and polished my good shoes as well.
What did I know, what did I know
of love's austere and lonely offices?

Does the poem match the feelings you have about winter Sundays? Either way, your response can be useful in reading the poem. For most of us, Sundays are days at home; they might be cozy and pleasant experiences or they might be dull and depressing. Whatever they are, Sundays are more evocative than, say, Tuesdays. Hayden uses that response to call forth a sense of missed opportunity in the poem. The person who reflects on those winter Sundays didn't know until much later how much he had to thank his father for "love's austere and lonely offices." This is a poem about a cold past and a present reverence for his father — elements brought together by the phrase "Winter Sundays." *His* father? You may have noticed that the poem doesn't use a masculine pronoun; hence the voice could be a woman's. Does the gender of the voice make any difference to your reading? Would it make any difference about which details are included or what language is used?

What is most important about your initial readings of a poem is that you ask questions. If you read responsively, you'll find yourself asking all kinds of questions about the words, descriptions, sounds, and structure of a poem. The specifics of those questions will be generated by the particular poem. We don't, for example, ask how humor is achieved in "Those Winter Sundays" because there is none, but it is worth asking what kind of tone is established by the description of "the chronic angers of that house." The remaining chapters in this part of the book will help you formulate and answer questions about a variety of specific elements in poetry, such as speaker, image, metaphor, symbol, rhyme, and rhythm. For the moment, however, read the following poem several times and note your response at different points in the poem. Then write down a half-dozen or so questions about what produces your response to the poem. To answer questions, it's best to know first what the questions are, and that's what the rest of this chapter is about.

John Updike (1932–2009)

Dog's Death 1969

She must have been kicked unseen or brushed by a car.
Too young to know much, she was beginning to learn
To use the newspapers spread on the kitchen floor
And to win, wetting there, the words, "Good dog! Good dog!"

We thought her shy malaise was a shot reaction. 5
The autopsy disclosed a rupture in her liver.
As we teased her with play, blood was filling her skin
And her heart was learning to lie down forever.

Monday morning, as the children were noisily fed
And sent to school, she crawled beneath the youngest's bed. 10
We found her twisted and limp but still alive.
In the car to the vet's, on my lap, she tried

To bite my hand and died. I stroked her warm fur
And my wife called in a voice imperious with tears.
Though surrounded by love that would have upheld her, 15
Nevertheless she sank and, stiffening, disappeared.

Back home, we found that in the night her frame,
Drawing near to dissolution, had endured the shame
Of diarrhoea and had dragged across the floor
To a newspaper carelessly left there. *Good dog.* 20

Here's a simple question to get started with your own questions: What would the poem's effect have been if Updike had titled it "Good Dog" instead of "Dog's Death"?

THE PLEASURE OF WORDS

The impulse to create and appreciate poetry is as basic to human experience as language itself. Although no one can point to the precise origins of poetry, it is one of the most ancient of the arts, because it has existed ever since human beings discovered pleasure in language. The tribal ceremonies of peoples without written languages suggest that the earliest primitive cultures incorporated rhythmic patterns of words into their rituals. These chants, very likely accompanied by the music of a simple beat and the dance of a measured step, expressed what people regarded as significant and memorable in their lives. They echoed the concerns of the chanters and the listeners by chronicling acts of bravery, fearsome foes, natural disasters, mysterious events, births, deaths, and whatever else brought people pain or pleasure, bewilderment or revelation. Later cultures, such as the ancient Greeks, made poetry an integral part of religion.

Thus, from its very beginnings, poetry has been associated with what has mattered most to people. These concerns — whether natural or supernatural — can, of course, be expressed without vivid images, rhythmic patterns, and pleasing sounds, but human beings have always sensed a magic in words that goes beyond rational, logical understanding. Poetry is not simply a method of communication; it is a unique experience in itself.

What is special about poetry? What makes it valuable? Why should we read it? How is reading it different from reading prose? To begin with, poetry pervades our world in a variety of forms, ranging from advertising jingles to song lyrics. These may seem to be a long way from the chants heard around a primitive campfire, but they serve some of the same purposes. Like poems printed in a magazine or book, primitive chants, catchy jingles, and popular songs attempt to stir the imagination through the carefully measured use of words.

Although reading poetry usually makes more demands than does the kind of reading we use to skim a magazine or newspaper, the appreciation of poetry comes naturally enough to anyone who enjoys playing with words. Play is an important element of poetry. Consider, for example, how the following words appeal to the children who gleefully chant them in playgrounds:

I scream, you scream
We all scream
For ice cream.

These lines are an exuberant evocation of the joy of ice cream. Indeed, chanting the words turns out to be as pleasurable as eating ice cream. In poetry, the expression of the idea is as important as the idea expressed.

But is "I scream . . ." poetry? Some poets and literary critics would say that it certainly is one kind of poem because the children who chant it experience some of the pleasures of poetry in its measured beat and repeated sounds. However, other poets and critics would define poetry more narrowly and insist, for a variety of reasons, that this isn't true poetry but merely **doggerel**, a term used for lines whose subject matter is trite and whose rhythm and sounds are monotonously heavy-handed.

Although probably no one would argue that "I scream . . ." is a great poem, it does contain some poetic elements that appeal, at the very least, to children. Does that make it poetry? The answer depends on one's definition, but poetry has a way of breaking loose from definitions. Because there are nearly as many definitions of poetry as there are poets, Edwin Arlington Robinson's succinct observations are useful: "[P]oetry has two outstanding characteristics. One is that it is undefinable. The other is that it is eventually unmistakable."

This comment places more emphasis on how a poem affects a reader than on how a poem is defined. By characterizing poetry as "undefinable," Robinson acknowledges that it can include many different purposes, subjects, emotions, styles, and forms. What effect does the following poem have on you?

WILLIAM HATHAWAY (B. 1944)

Oh, Oh 1982

William Hathaway.

My girl and I amble a country lane,
moo cows chomping daisies, our own
sweet saliva green with grass stems.
"Look, look," she says at the crossing,
"the choo-choo's light is on." And sure
enough, right smack dab in the middle
of maple dappled summer sunlight
is the lit headlight — so funny.
An arm waves to us from the black window.
We wave gaily to the arm. "When I hear
trains at night I dream of being president,"
I say dreamily. "And me first lady," she
says loyally. So when the last boxcars,
named after wonderful, faraway places,
and the caboose chuckle by we look   15
eagerly to the road ahead. And there,
poised and growling, are fifty Hell's Angels.

A SAMPLE CLOSE READING

An Annotated Version of "Oh, Oh"

After you've read a poem two or three times, a deeper, closer reading — line by line, word by word, syllable by syllable — will help you discover even more about the poem. Ask yourself: What happens (or does not happen) in the poem? What are the poem's central ideas? How do the poem's words, images, and sounds, for example, contribute to its meaning? What is the poem's overall tone? How is the poem put together?

You can flesh out your close reading by writing your responses in the margins of the page. The following interpretive notes offer but one way to read Hathaway's poem.

WILLIAM HATHAWAY (B. 1944)

Oh, Oh   1982

My girl and I amble a country lane,

moo cows chomping daisies, our own

sweet saliva green with grass stems.

"Look, look," she says at the crossing,

"the choo-choo's light is on." And sure   5

enough, right smack dab in the middle

of maple dappled summer sunlight

is the lit headlight — so funny.

An arm waves to us from the black window.

We wave gaily to the arm. "When I hear   10

trains at night I dream of being president,"

I say dreamily. "And me first lady," she

says loyally. So when the last boxcars,

named after wonderful, faraway places,

and the caboose chuckle by we look   15

eagerly to the road ahead. And there,

poised and growling, are fifty Hell's Angels.

Margin annotations:

The title offers an interjection expressing strong emotion and foreboding.

The informal language conjures up an idyllic picture of a walk in the country, where the sights, sounds, and tastes are full of pleasure.

The carefully orchestrated d's, m's, p's, and s's of lines 6–8 create sounds that are meant to be savored.

Filled with confidence and hope, the couple imagines a successful future together in exotic locations. Even the train is happy for them as it "chuckle[s]" in approval of their dreams.

The visual effect of the many o's in lines 1–5 (and 15) suggests an innocent, wide-eyed openness to experience while the repetitive oo sounds echo a kind of reassuring, satisfied cooing.

"Right smack dab in the middle" of the poem, the "black window" hints that all is not well.

Not until the very last line does "the road ahead" yield a terrifying surprise. The strategically "poised" final line derails the leisurely movement of the couple and brings their happy story to a dead stop. The emotional reversal parked in the last few words awaits the reader as much as it does the couple. The sight and sound of the motorcycle gang signal that what seemed like heaven is, in reality, hell: Oh, oh.

Hathaway's poem serves as a convenient reminder that poetry can be full of surprises. Full of confidence, this couple, like the reader, is unprepared for the shock to come. When we see those "fifty Hell's Angels," we are confronted with something like a bucket of cold water in the face.

But even though our expectations are abruptly and powerfully reversed, we are finally invited to view the entire episode from a safe distance — the distance provided by the delightful humor in this poem. After all, how seriously can we take a poem that is titled "Oh, Oh"? The poet has his way with us, but we are brought in on the joke, too. The terror takes on comic proportions as the innocent couple is confronted by no fewer than *fifty* Hell's Angels. This is the kind of raucous overkill that informs a short animated film produced some years ago titled *Bambi Meets Godzilla*: you might not have seen it, but you know how it ends. The poem's good humor comes through when we realize how pathetically inadequate the response of "Oh, Oh" is to the circumstances.

As you can see, reading a description of what happens in a poem is not the same as experiencing a poem. The exuberance of "I scream . . ." and the surprise of Hathaway's "Oh, Oh" are in the hearing or reading rather than in the retelling. A *paraphrase* is a prose restatement of the central ideas of a poem in your own language. Consider the difference between the following poem and the paraphrase that follows it. What is missing from the paraphrase?

ROBERT FRANCIS (1901–1987)

Catch   1950

Two boys uncoached are tossing a poem together,
Overhand, underhand, backhand, sleight of hand, every hand,
Teasing with attitudes, latitudes, interludes, altitudes,
High, make him fly off the ground for it, low, make him stoop,
Make him scoop it up, make him as-almost-as-possible miss it,   5
Fast, let him sting from it, now, now fool him slowly,
Anything, everything tricky, risky, nonchalant,
Anything under the sun to outwit the prosy,
Over the tree and the long sweet cadence down,
Over his head, make him scramble to pick up the meaning,   10
And now, like a posy, a pretty one plump in his hands.

Paraphrase: A poet's relationship to a reader is similar to a game of catch. The poem, like a ball, should be pitched in a variety of ways to challenge and create interest. Boredom and predictability must be avoided if the game is to be engaging and satisfying.

A paraphrase can help us achieve a clearer understanding of a poem, but, unlike a poem, it misses all the sport and fun. It is the poem that "outwit[s] the prosy" because the poem serves as an example of what it suggests poetry should be. Moreover, the two players — the poet and the reader — are "uncoached."

They know how the game is played, but their expectations do not preclude spontaneity and creativity or their ability to surprise and be surprised. The solid pleasure of the workout — of reading poetry — is the satisfaction derived from exercising your imagination and intellect.

That pleasure is worth emphasizing. Poetry uses language to move and delight even when it includes a cast of fifty Hell's Angels. The pleasure is in having the poem work its spell on us. For that to happen, it is best to relax and enjoy poetry rather than worry about definitions of it. Pay attention to what the poet throws you. We read poems for emotional and intellectual discovery — to feel and to experience something about the world and ourselves. The ideas in poetry — what can be paraphrased in prose — are important, but the real value of a poem consists in the words that work their magic by allowing us to feel, see, and be more than we were before. Perhaps the best way to approach a poem is similar to what Francis's "Catch" implies: expect to be surprised, stay on your toes, and concentrate on the delivery.

A SAMPLE STUDENT ANALYSIS

Tossing Metaphors Together in Robert Francis's "Catch"

The following sample paper on Robert Francis's "Catch" was written in response to an assignment that asked students to discuss the use of metaphor in the poem. Notice that Chris Leggett's paper is clearly focused and well organized. His discussion of the use of metaphor in the poem stays on track from beginning to end without any detours concerning unrelated topics (for a definition of **metaphor**, see p. 690). His title draws on the central metaphor of the poem, and he organizes the paper around four key words used in the poem: "attitudes, latitudes, interludes, altitudes." These constitute the heart of the paper's four substantive paragraphs, and they are effectively framed by introductory and concluding paragraphs. Moreover, the transitions between paragraphs clearly indicate that the author was not merely tossing a paper together.

Chris Leggett

Professor Lyles

English 203-1

9 November 2015

Tossing Metaphors Together in Robert Francis's "Catch"

> **Exploration of the meaning of the word *catch*.**

The word *catch* is an attention getter. It usually means something is about to be hurled at someone and that he or she is expected to catch it. *Catch* can also signal a challenge to another player if the toss is purposefully difficult. Robert Francis, in his poem "Catch," uses the

> **Thesis statement identifying purpose of poem's metaphors.**

extended metaphor of two boys playing catch to explore the considerations a poet makes when "tossing a poem together" (line 1). Line 3 of "Catch" enumerates these considerations metaphorically as "attitudes, latitudes, interludes, [and] altitudes." While regular prose is typically straightforward and easily understood, poetry usually takes great effort to understand

> **Reference to specific language in poem, around which the paper is organized.**

and appreciate. To exemplify this, Francis presents the reader not with a normal game of catch with the ball flying back and forth in a repetitive and predictable fashion, but with a physically challenging game in which one must concentrate, scramble, and exert oneself to catch the ball, as one must stretch the intellect to truly grasp a poem.

> **Introductory analysis of the poem's purpose.**

The first consideration mentioned by Francis is attitude. Attitude, when applied to the game of catch, indicates the ball's pitch in flight—upward, downward, or straight. It could also describe the players' attitudes toward each other or toward the game in general. Below this literal level lies

> **Analysis of the meaning of *attitude* in the poem.**

attitude's meaning in relation to poetry. Attitude in this case represents a poem's tone. A poet may "Teas[e] with attitudes" (3) by experimenting with different tones to achieve the desired mood. The underlying tone of "Catch"

> **Discussion of how the attitude metaphor contributes to poem's tone.**

is a playful one, set and reinforced by the use of a game. This playfulness is further reinforced by such words and phrases as "[t]easing" (3), "outwit" (8), and "fool him" (6).

Considered also in the metaphorical game of catch is latitude, which, when applied to the game, suggests the range the object may be thrown—how high, how low, or how far. Poetic latitude, along similar lines, concerns

> **Analysis of the meaning of *latitude* in the poem.**

a poem's breadth, or the scope of topic. Taken one level further, latitude suggests freedom from normal restraints or limitations, indicating the ability to

Leggett 2

go outside the norm to find originality of expression. The entire game of catch described in Francis's poem reaches outside the normal expectations of something being merely tossed back and forth in a predictable manner. The ball is thrown in almost every conceivable fashion, "Overhand, underhand . . . every hand" (2). Other terms describing the throws—such as "tricky," "risky," "Fast," "slowly," and "Anything under the sun" (6-8)—express endless latitude for avoiding predictability in Francis's game of catch and metaphorically in writing poetry.

> Discussion of how the latitude metaphor contributes to the poem's scope and message.

During a game of catch the ball may be thrown at different intervals, establishing a steady rhythm or a broken, irregular one. Other intervening features, such as the field being played on or the weather, could also affect the game. These features of the game are alluded to in the poem by the use of the word *interludes*. *Interlude* in the poetic sense represents the poem's form, which can similarly establish or diminish rhythm or enhance meaning. Lines 6 and 9, respectively, show a broken and a flowing rhythm. Line 6 begins rapidly as a hard toss that stings the catcher's hand is described. The rhythm of the line is immediately slowed, however, by the word "now" followed by a comma, followed by the rest of the line. In contrast, line 9 flows smoothly as the reader visualizes the ball flying over the tree and sailing downward. The words chosen for this line function perfectly. The phrase "the long sweet cadence down" establishes a sweet rhythm that reads smoothly and rolls off the tongue easily. The choice of diction not only affects the poem's rhythmic flow but also establishes through connotative language the various levels at which the poem can be understood, represented in "Catch" as altitude.

> Analysis of the meaning of *interlude* in the poem.

> Discussion of how the interlude metaphor contributes to the poem's form and rhythm.

While *altitudes* when referring to the game of catch means how high an object is thrown, in poetry it could refer to the level of diction, lofty or down-to-earth, formal or informal. It suggests also the levels at which a poem can be comprehended, the literal as well as the interpretive. In Francis's game of catch, the ball is thrown high to make the player reach, low to "make him stoop" (4), or "Over his head [to] make him scramble" (10), implying that the player should have to exert himself to catch it. So too, then, should the reader of poetry put great effort into understanding the full meaning of a poem. Francis exemplifies this consideration in writing poetry by giving "Catch" not only an enjoyable literal meaning concerning the

> Analysis of the meaning of *altitudes* in the poem.

game of catch, but also a rich metaphorical meaning—reflecting the process of writing poetry. Francis uses several phrases and words with multiple meanings. The phrase "tossing a poem together" (1) can be understood as tossing something back and forth or the process of constructing a poem. While "prosy" (8) suggests prose itself, it also means the mundane or the ordinary. In the poem's final line the word *posy* of course represents a flower, while it is also a variant of the word *poesy*, meaning poetry, or the practice of composing poetry.

> **Discussion of how the altitude metaphor contributes to the poem's literal and symbolic meanings, with references to specific language.**

Francis effectively describes several considerations to be taken in writing poetry in order to "outwit the prosy" (8). His use of the extended metaphor in "Catch" shows that a poem must be unique, able to be comprehended on multiple levels, and a challenge to the reader. The various rhythms in the lines of "Catch" exemplify the ideas they express. While achieving an enjoyable poem on the literal level, Francis has also achieved a rich metaphorical meaning. The poem offers a good workout both physically and intellectually.

> **Conclusion summarizing ideas explored in paper.**

Work Cited

Francis, Robert. "Catch." *The Bedford Introduction to Literature.* Ed. Michael Meyer. 11th ed. Boston: Bedford/St. Martin's, 2016. 596. Print.

Before beginning your own writing assignment on poetry, you should review Chapter 21, "Writing about Poetry," and Chapter 52, "Reading and the Writing Process," which provides a step-by-step overview of how to choose a topic, develop a thesis, and organize various types of writing assignments. If you are using outside sources in your paper, you should make sure that you are familiar with the conventional documentation procedures described in Chapter 53, "The Literary Research Paper."

How does the speaker's description in Francis's "Catch" of what readers might expect from reading poetry compare with the speaker's expectations concerning fiction in the next poem by Philip Larkin?

PHILIP LARKIN (1922–1985)

A Study of Reading Habits   1964

When getting my nose in a book
Cured most things short of school,
It was worth ruining my eyes
To know I could still keep cool,
And deal out the old right hook   5
To dirty dogs twice my size.

Later, with inch-thick specs,
Evil was just my lark:
Me and my cloak and fangs
Had ripping times in the dark.   10
The women I clubbed with sex!
I broke them up like meringues.

Don't read much now: the dude
Who lets the girl down before
The hero arrives, the chap   15
Who's yellow and keeps the store,
Seem far too familiar. Get stewed:
Books are a load of crap.

In "A Study of Reading Habits," Larkin distances himself from a speaker whose sensibilities he does not wholly share. The poet — and many readers — might identify with the reading habits described by the speaker in the first twelve lines, but Larkin uses the last six lines to criticize the speaker's attitude toward life as well as reading. The speaker recalls in lines 1–6 how as a schoolboy he identified with the hero, whose virtuous strength always triumphed over "dirty dogs," and in lines 7–12 he recounts how his schoolboy fantasies were transformed by adolescence into a fascination with violence and sex. This description of early reading habits is pleasantly amusing, because many readers of popular fiction will probably recall having moved through similar stages, but at the end of the poem the speaker provides more information about himself than he intends to.

As an adult the speaker has lost interest in reading because it is no longer an escape from his own disappointed life. Instead of identifying with heroes or villains, he finds himself identifying with minor characters who are irresponsible and cowardly. Reading is now a reminder of his failures, so he turns to alcohol. His solution, to "Get stewed" because "Books are a load of crap," is obviously self-destructive. The speaker is ultimately exposed by Larkin as someone who never grew beyond fantasies. Getting drunk is consistent with the speaker's immature reading habits. Unlike the speaker, the poet understands that life is often distorted by escapist fantasies, whether through a steady diet of popular fiction or through alcohol. The speaker in this poem, then, is not Larkin but a created identity whose voice is filled with disillusionment and delusion.

The problem with Larkin's speaker is that he misreads books as well as his own life. Reading means nothing to him unless it serves as an escape from himself. It is not surprising that Larkin has him read fiction rather than poetry because poetry places an especially heavy emphasis on language. Fiction, indeed any kind of writing, including essays and drama, relies on carefully chosen and arranged words, but poetry does so to an even greater extent. Notice, for example, how Larkin's deft use of trite expressions and slang characterizes the speaker so that his language reveals nearly as much about his dreary life as what he says. Larkin's speaker would have no use for poetry.

What is "unmistakable" in poetry (to use Robinson's term again) is its intense, concentrated use of language — its emphasis on individual words to convey meanings, experiences, emotions, and effects. Poets never simply process words; they savor them. Words in poems frequently create their own tastes, textures, scents, sounds, and shapes. They often seem more sensuous than ordinary language, and readers usually sense that a word has been hefted before making its way into a poem. Although poems are crafted differently from the ways a painting, sculpture, or musical composition is created, in each form of art the creator delights in the medium. Poetry is carefully orchestrated so that the words work together as elements in a structure to sustain close, repeated readings. The words are chosen to interact with one another to create the maximum desired effect, whether the purpose is to capture a mood or feeling, create a vivid experience, express a point of view, narrate a story, or portray a character.

Here is a poem that looks quite different from most *verse*, a term used for lines composed in a measured rhythmical pattern, which are often, but not necessarily, rhymed.

ROBERT MORGAN (B. 1944)

Mountain Graveyard   1979

for the author of "Slow Owls"

Spore Prose

stone	notes
slate	tales
sacred	cedars
heart	earth
asleep	please
hated	death

Though unconventional in its appearance, this is unmistakably poetry because of its concentrated use of language. The poem demonstrates how serious play with words can lead to some remarkable discoveries. At first glance "Mountain Graveyard" may seem intimidating. What, after all, does this list of words add up to? How is it in any sense a poetic use of language? But if the words are examined closely, it is not difficult to see how they work. The wordplay here is literally in the form of a game. Morgan uses a series of **anagrams** (words made from the letters of other words, such as *read* and *dare*) to evoke feelings about death. "Mountain Graveyard" is one of several poems that Morgan has called "Spore Prose" (another anagram) because he finds in individual words the seeds of poetry. He wrote the poem in honor of the fiftieth birthday of another poet, Jonathan Williams, the author of "Slow Owls," whose title is also an anagram.

The title, "Mountain Graveyard," indicates the poem's setting, which is also the context in which the individual words in the poem interact to provide a larger meaning. Morgan's discovery of the words on the stones of a graveyard is more than just clever. The observations he makes among the silent graves go beyond the curious pleasure a reader experiences in finding that the words *sacred cedars,* referring to evergreens common in cemeteries, consist of the same letters. The surprise and delight of realizing the connection between *heart* and *earth* are tempered by the more sober recognition that everyone's story ultimately ends in the ground. The hope that the dead are merely asleep is expressed with a plea that is answered grimly by a hatred of death's finality.

Little is told in this poem. There is no way of knowing who is buried or who is looking at the graves, but the emotions of sadness, hope, and pain are unmistakable — and are conveyed in fewer than half the words of this sentence. Morgan takes words that initially appear to be a dead, prosaic list and energizes their meanings through imaginative juxtapositions.

The following poem also involves a startling discovery about words. With the peculiar title "l(a," the poem cannot be read aloud, so there is no sound, but is there sense, a **theme** — a central idea or meaning — in the poem?

E. E. CUMMINGS (1894–1962)

l(a 1958

l(a

le
af
fa

ll
s)
one
l

iness

© Bettmann/Corbis.

CONSIDERATIONS FOR CRITICAL THINKING AND WRITING

1. **FIRST RESPONSE.** Discuss the connection between what appears inside and outside the parentheses in this poem.

2. What does Cummings draw attention to by breaking up the words? How do this strategy and the poem's overall shape contribute to its theme?

3. Which seems more important in this poem — what is expressed or the way it is expressed?

Although "Mountain Graveyard" and "l(a" do not resemble the kind of verse that readers might recognize immediately as poetry on a page, both are actually a very common type of poem, called the *lyric*, usually a brief poem that expresses the personal emotions and thoughts of a single speaker. Lyrics are often written in the first person, but sometimes — as in "Mountain Graveyard" and "l(a" — no speaker is specified. Lyrics present a subjective mood, emotion, or idea. Very often they are about love or death, but almost any subject or experience that evokes some intense emotional response can be found in lyrics. In addition to brevity and emotional intensity, lyrics are also frequently characterized by their musical qualities. The word *lyric* derives from the Greek word *lyre,* meaning a musical instrument that originally accompanied the singing of a lyric. Lyric poems can be organized in a variety of ways, such as the sonnet, elegy, and ode (see Chapter 28), but it is enough to point out here that lyrics are an extremely popular kind of poetry with writers and readers.

The following anonymous lyric was found in a sixteenth-century manuscript.

Anonymous

Western Wind   ca. 1500

Western wind, when wilt thou blow,
The small rain down can rain?
Christ, if my love were in my arms,
And I in my bed again!

This speaker's intense longing for his lover is characteristic of lyric poetry. He impatiently addresses the western wind that brings spring to England and could make it possible for him to be reunited with the woman he loves. We do not know the details of these lovers' lives because this poem focuses on the speaker's emotion. We do not learn why the lovers are apart or if they will be together again. We don't even know if the speaker is a man. But those issues are not really important. The poem gives us a feeling rather than a story.

A poem that tells a story is called a *narrative poem*. Narrative poetry may be short or very long. An *epic,* for example, is a long narrative poem on a serious subject chronicling heroic deeds and important events. Among the most famous epics are Homer's *Iliad* and *Odyssey,* the Old English *Beowulf,* Dante's *Divine Comedy,* and John Milton's *Paradise Lost.* More typically, however, narrative poems are considerably shorter, as is the case with the following poem, which tells the story of a child's memory of her father.

WHEN I WRITE "There are lots of things that are going on in the world, in your room, or in that book you didn't read for class that could set you on fire if you gave them a chance. Poetry isn't only about what you feel, it's about what you think, and about capturing the way the world exists in one particular moment." — REGINA BARRECA

Regina Barreca (b. 1957)

Nighttime Fires   1986

When I was five in Louisville
we drove to see nighttime fires. Piled seven of us,
all pajamas and running noses, into the Olds,
drove fast toward smoke. It was after my father
lost his job, so not getting up in the morning
gave him time: awake past midnight, he read old
    newspapers
with no news, tried crosswords until he split the pencil
between his teeth, mad. When he heard
the wolf whine of the siren, he woke my mother,

© Nicolette Theriault.

and she pushed and shoved   10
us all into waking. Once roused we longed for burnt wood
and a smell of flames high into the pines. My old man liked
driving to rich neighborhoods best, swearing in a good mood
as he followed fire engines that snaked like dragons
and split the silent streets. It was festival, carnival.   15

If there were a Cadillac or any car
in a curved driveway, my father smiled a smile
from a secret, brittle heart.
His face lit up in the heat given off by destruction
like something was being made, or was being set right.   20
I bent my head back to see where sparks
ate up the sky. My father who never held us
would take my hand and point to falling cinders that
covered the ground like snow, or, excited, show us
the swollen collapse of a staircase. My mother   25
watched my father, not the house. She was happy
only when we were ready to go, when it was finally over
and nothing else could burn.
Driving home, she would sleep in the front seat
as we huddled behind. I could see his quiet face in the   30
rearview mirror, eyes like hallways filled with smoke.

    This narrative poem could have been a short story if the poet had wanted to say more about the "brittle heart" of this unemployed man whose daughter so vividly remembers the desperate pleasure he took in watching fire consume other people's property. Indeed, a reading of William Faulkner's famous short story "Barn Burning" (p. 406) suggests how such a character can be further developed and how his child responds to him. The similarities between Faulkner's angry character and the poem's father, whose "eyes [are] like hallways filled with smoke," are coincidental, but the characters' sense of "something . . . being set right" by flames is worth comparing. Although we do not know everything about this man and his family, we have a much firmer sense of their story than we do of the story of the couple in "Western Wind."

Although narrative poetry is still written, short stories and novels have largely replaced the long narrative poem. Lyric poems tend to be the predominant type of poetry today. Regardless of whether a poem is a narrative or a lyric, however, the strategies for reading it are somewhat different from those for reading prose. Try these suggestions for approaching poetry.

Suggestions for Approaching Poetry

1. Assume that it will be necessary to read a poem more than once. Give yourself a chance to become familiar with what the poem has to offer. Like a piece of music, a poem becomes more pleasurable with each encounter.

2. Pay attention to the title; it will often provide a helpful context for the poem and serve as an introduction to it. Larkin's "A Study of Reading Habits" is precisely what its title describes.

3. As you read the poem for the first time, avoid becoming entangled in words or lines that you don't understand. Instead, give yourself a chance to take in the entire poem before attempting to resolve problems encountered along the way.

4. On a second reading, identify any words or passages that you don't understand. Look up words you don't know; these might include names, places, historical and mythical references, or anything else that is unfamiliar to you.

5. Read the poem aloud (or perhaps have a friend read it to you). You'll probably discover that some puzzling passages suddenly fall into place when you hear them. You'll find that nothing helps, though, if the poem is read in an artificial, exaggerated manner. Read in as natural a voice as possible, with slight pauses at line breaks. Silent reading is preferable to imposing a te-tumpty-te-tum reading on a good poem.

6. Read the punctuation. Poems use punctuation marks — in addition to the space on the page — as signals for readers. Be especially careful not to assume that the end of a line marks the end of a sentence, unless it is concluded by punctuation. Consider, for example, the opening lines of Hathaway's "Oh, Oh":

   > My girl and I amble a country lane,
   > moo cows chomping daisies, our own
   > sweet saliva green with grass stems.

   Line 2 makes little or no sense if a reader stops after "own." Keeping track of the subjects and verbs will help you find your way among the sentences.

7. Paraphrase the poem to determine whether you understand what happens in it. As you work through each line of the poem, a paraphrase will help you to see which words or passages need further attention.

8. Try to get a sense of who is speaking and what the setting or situation is. Don't assume that the speaker is the author; often it is a created character.

9. Assume that each element in the poem has a purpose. Try to explain how the elements of the poem work together.

10. Be generous. Be willing to entertain perspectives, values, experiences, and subjects that you might not agree with or approve of. Even if baseball bores you, you should be able to comprehend its imaginative use in Francis's "Catch."

11. Try developing a coherent approach to the poem that helps you to shape a discussion of the text. See Chapter 51, "Critical Strategies for Reading," to review formalist, biographical, historical, psychological, feminist, and other possible critical approaches.

12. Don't expect to produce a definitive reading. Many poems do not resolve all the ideas, issues, or tensions in them, and so it is not always possible to drive their meaning into an absolute corner. Your reading will explore rather than define the poem. Poems are not trophies to be stuffed and mounted. They're usually more elusive. And don't be afraid that a close reading will damage the poem. Poems aren't hurt when we analyze them; instead, they come alive as we experience them and put into words what we discover through them.

A list of more specific questions using the literary terms and concepts discussed in the following chapters begins on page 628. That list, like the suggestions just made, raises issues and questions that can help you read just about any poem closely. These strategies should be a useful means for getting inside poems to understand how they work. Furthermore, because reading poetry inevitably increases sensitivity to language, you're likely to find yourself a better reader of words in any form — whether in a novel, a newspaper editorial, an advertisement, a political speech, or a conversation — after having studied poetry. In short, many of the reading skills that make poetry accessible also open up the world you inhabit.

You'll probably find some poems amusing or sad, some fierce or tender, and some fascinating or dull. You may find, too, some poems that will get inside you. Their kinds of insights — the poet's and yours — are what Emily Dickinson had in mind when she defined poetry this way: "If I read a book and it makes my whole body so cold no fire can ever warm me, I know that it is poetry. If I feel physically as if the top of my head were taken off, I know that it is poetry." Dickinson's response may be more intense than most — poetry was, after all, at the center of her life — but you, too, might find yourself moved by poems in unexpected ways. In any case, as Edwin Arlington Robinson knew, poetry is, to an alert and sensitive reader, "eventually unmistakable."

BILLY COLLINS (B. 1941)

Introduction to Poetry   1988

I ask them to take a poem
and hold it up to the light
like a color slide

or press an ear against its hive.

I say drop a mouse into a poem 5
and watch him probe his way out,

or walk inside the poem's room
and feel the walls for a light switch.

I want them to water-ski
across the surface of a poem 10
waving at the author's name on the shore.

But all they want to do
is tie the poem to a chair with rope
and torture a confession out of it.

They begin beating it with a hose 15
to find out what it really means.

CONSIDERATIONS FOR CRITICAL THINKING AND WRITING

1. FIRST RESPONSE. In what sense does this poem offer suggestions for approaching poetry? What advice does the speaker provide in lines 1–11?

2. How does the mood of the poem change beginning in line 12? What do you make of the shift from "them" to "they"?

3. Paraphrase the poem. How is your paraphrase different from what is included in the poem?

POETRY IN POPULAR FORMS

Before you try out these strategies for reading on a few more poems, it is worth acknowledging that the verse that enjoys the widest readership appears not in collections, magazines, or even anthologies for students, but in greeting cards. A significant amount of the personal daily mail delivered in the United States consists of greeting cards. That represents millions of lines of verse going by us on the street and in planes over our heads. These verses share some similarities with the poetry included in this anthology, but there are also important differences that indicate the need for reading serious poetry closely rather than casually.

The popularity of greeting cards is easy to explain: just as many of us have neither the time nor the talent to make gifts for birthdays, weddings, anniversaries, graduations, Valentine's Day, Mother's Day, and other holidays, we are unlikely to write personal messages when cards conveniently say them for us. Although impersonal, cards are efficient and convey an important message no matter what the occasion for them: I care. These greetings are rarely serious poetry; they are not written to be. Nevertheless, they demonstrate the impulse in our culture to generate and receive poetry.

In a handbook for greeting-card freelancers, a writer and past editor of such verse began with this advice:

Once you determine what you want to say — and in this regard it is best to stick to one basic idea — you must choose your words to do several things at the same time:

1. Your idea must be expressed as a complete idea; it must have a beginning, a middle, and an end.

2. There must be coherence in your verse. Every line must be linked logically and smoothly with its neighbors.

3. Your expressions . . . must be conversational. High-flown language rarely comes off successfully in greeting-card writing.

4. You must write with emphasis — and something else: enthusiasm. It's necessary to create interest in that all-important first line. From that point on, writing your verse is a matter of developing your idea and bringing it to a peak of emphasis in the last line. Occasionally you will find that you have shot your wad too early in the verse, and whatever you say after that point sounds like an afterthought.

5. You must do all of the above and at the same time make everything come out right in the meter-and-rhyme department.[1]

This advice is followed by a list of approximately fifty of the most frequently used rhyme sounds accompanied by rhyming words, such as *love, of, above* for the sound *uv.* The point of these prescriptions is that the verse must be written so that it is immediately accessible — consumable — by both the buyer and the recipient. Writers of these cards are expected to avoid any complexity.

Compare the following greeting-card verse with the poem that comes after it. "Magic of Love," by Helen Farries, has been a longtime favorite in a major greeting-card company's "wedding line"; with different endings it has been used also in valentines and friendship cards.

If you're college age, you might not send very many greeting cards at this point in your life, though the card industry figures that you will once you get married or start a household. You might also prefer mailing — or e-mailing — cards that include more humor and sarcasm than you'll find in the example that follows, but the vast majority of older consumers enjoy sending the sort of traditional card written by Helen Farries.

HELEN FARRIES (1918–2008)

Magic of Love   date unknown

There's a wonderful gift that can give you a lift,
It's a blessing from heaven above!
It can comfort and bless, it can bring happiness —
It's the wonderful MAGIC OF LOVE!

Like a star in the night, it can keep your faith bright,   5
Like the sun, it can warm your hearts, too —
It's a gift you can give every day that you live,
And when given, it comes back to you!

When love lights the way, there is joy in the day
And all troubles are lighter to bear,   10

[1] Chris Fitzgerald, "Conventional Verse: The Sentimental Favorite," *The Greeting Card Writer's Handbook,* ed. H. Joseph Chadwick (Cincinnati: Writer's Digest, 1975), 13, 17.

Love is gentle and kind, and through love you will find
There's an answer to your every prayer!

May it never depart from your two loving hearts,
May you treasure this gift from above —
You will find if you do, all your dreams will come true,   15
In the wonderful MAGIC OF LOVE!

JOHN FREDERICK NIMS (1913–1999)

Love Poem   1947

My clumsiest dear, whose hands shipwreck vases,
At whose quick touch all glasses chip and ring,
Whose palms are bulls in china, burs in linen,
And have no cunning with any soft thing

Except all ill-at-ease fidgeting people: 5
The refugee uncertain at the door
You make at home; deftly you steady
The drunk clambering on his undulant floor.

Unpredictable dear, the taxi drivers' terror,
Shrinking from far headlights pale as a dime   10
Yet leaping before red apoplectic streetcars —
Misfit in any space. And never on time.

A wrench in clocks and the solar system. Only
With words and people and love you move at ease.
In traffic of wit expertly maneuver   15
And keep us, all devotion, at your knees.

Forgetting your coffee spreading on our flannel,
Your lipstick grinning on our coat,
So gaily in love's unbreakable heaven
Our souls on glory of spilt bourbon float.   20

Be with me, darling, early and late. Smash glasses —
I will study wry music for your sake.
For should your hands drop white and empty
All the toys of the world would break.

CONSIDERATIONS FOR CRITICAL THINKING AND WRITING

1. FIRST RESPONSE. Read these two works aloud. How are they different? How the same?

2. To what extent does the advice to would-be greeting-card writers apply to each work?

3. Compare the two speakers. Which do you find more appealing? Why?

4. How does Nims's description of love differ from Farries's?

In contrast to poetry, which transfigures and expresses an emotion or experience through an original use of language, the verse in "Magic of Love" relies on ***clichés*** — ideas or expressions that have become tired and trite from overuse, such as describing love as "a blessing from heaven above." Clichés anesthetize readers instead of alerting them to the possibility of fresh perceptions. They are used to draw out ***stock responses*** — predictable, conventional reactions to language, characters, symbols, or situations; God, heaven, the flag, motherhood, hearts, puppies, and peace are some often-used objects of stock responses. Advertisers manufacture careers from this sort of business.

Clichés and stock responses are two of the major ingredients of sentimentality in literature. ***Sentimentality*** exploits the reader by inducing responses that exceed what the situation warrants. This pejorative term should not be confused with *sentiment,* which is synonymous with *emotion* or *feeling.* Sentimentality cons readers into falling for the mass murderer who is devoted to stray cats, and it requires that we not think twice about what we're feeling because those tears shed for the little old lady, the rage aimed at the vicious enemy soldier, and the longing for the simple virtues of poverty might disappear under the slightest scrutiny. The experience of sentimentality is not unlike biting into a swirl of cotton candy; it's momentarily sweet but wholly insubstantial.

Clichés, stock responses, and sentimentality are generally the hallmarks of weak writing. Poetry — the kind that is unmistakable — achieves freshness, vitality, and genuine emotion that sharpen our perceptions of life.

POEMS FOR FURTHER STUDY

MARY OLIVER (B. 1935)

The Poet with His Face in His Hands 2005

You want to cry aloud for your
mistakes. But to tell the truth the world
doesn't need any more of that sound.

So if you're going to do it and can't
stop yourself, if your pretty mouth can't   5
hold it in, at least go by yourself across

the forty fields and the forty dark inclines
of rocks and water to the place where
the falls are flinging out their white sheets

like crazy, and there is a cave behind all that   10
jubilation and water fun and you can
stand there, under it, and roar all you

want and nothing will be disturbed; you can
drip with despair all afternoon and still,
on a green branch, its wings just lightly touched   15

by the passing foil of the water, the thrush,
puffing out its spotted breast, will sing
of the perfect, stone-hard beauty of everything.

CONSIDERATIONS FOR CRITICAL THINKING AND WRITING

1. FIRST RESPONSE. Describe the kind of poet the speaker characterizes. What is the speaker's attitude toward that sort of poet?

2. Explain which single phrase used by the speaker to describe the poet most reveals for you the speaker's attitude toward the poet.

3. How is nature contrasted with the poet?

CONNECTION TO ANOTHER SELECTION

1. Compare the thematic use of nature in Oliver's poem and in Robert Frost's "Design" (p. 885).

WHEN I WRITE "When I'm creating a story, I try to keep writing until I finish a draft — same for a poem, but I don't set aside a specific block of time. When the inkling of a poem is there, I write. When it's not, I go for a walk until it arrives." — JIM TILLEY

JIM TILLEY (B. 1950)

The Big Questions   2011

The big questions are big only
because they have never been answered.
Some questions, big as they seem,
are big only in the moment,
like when you're hiking a trail alone   5

and you encounter a mammoth
grizzly who hasn't had lunch
in a fortnight, and he eyes you
as the answer to his only big question.
Life turns existential, and you can't   10

help questioning why you are here —
in this place on this planet
within this universe —
at this precise time,
or why he is, and you know he's not,   15

even for a moment, wondering
the same thing, because he's already
figured it out. And you, too,
know exactly what to do.
So, this can be a defining moment,   20

but not a big question,
because no one ever figures those out.
Still, one day when someone does,
might it not be a person like you
staring down a bear looking for lunch?   25

Considerations for Critical Thinking and Writing

1. **FIRST RESPONSE.** What are the "big questions" raised in this poem?
2. Explain whether or not you think the bear and his "lunch" have much in common.
3. How does Tilley's use of language create a poem that is philosophically serious as well as genuinely funny?

Connection to Another Selection

1. To what extent does Mary Oliver's "The Poet with His Face in His Hands" (p. 611) also raise the existential question of "why you are here"?

Alberto Ríos (b. 1952)

Seniors 1985

Alberto Ríos.

William cut a hole in his Levi's pocket
so he could flop himself out in class
behind the girls so the other guys
could see and shit what guts we all said.
All Konga wanted to do over and over   5
was the rubber band trick, but he showed
everyone how, so nobody wanted to see
anymore and one day he cried, just cried
until his parents took him away forever.
Maya had a Hotpoint refrigerator standing   10
in his living room, just for his family to show
anybody who came that they could afford it.

Me, I got a French kiss, finally, in the catholic
darkness, my tongue's farthest half vacationing
loudly in another mouth like a man in Bermudas,   15
and my body jumped against a flagstone wall,
I could feel it through her thin, almost
nonexistent body: I had, at that moment, that moment,
a hot girl on a summer night, the best of all
the things we tried to do. Well, she   20
let me kiss her, anyway, all over.

Or it was just a flagstone wall
with a flaw in the stone, an understanding cavity
for burning young men with smooth dreams —
the true circumstance is gone, the true   25
circumstances about us all then
are gone. But when I kissed her, all water,
she would close her eyes, and they into somewhere
would disappear. Whether she was there
or not, I remember her, clearly, and she moves   30
around the room, sometimes, until I sleep.

I have lain on the desert in watch
low in the back of a pick-up truck
for nothing in particular, for stars, for
the things behind stars, and nothing comes   35
more than the moment: always now, here in a truck,
the moment again to dream of making love and sweat,
this time to a woman, or even to all of them
in some allowable way, to those boys, then,
who couldn't cry, to the girls before they were   40
women, to friends, me on my back, the sky over me
pressing its simple weight into her body
on me, into the bodies of them all, on me.

CONSIDERATIONS FOR CRITICAL THINKING AND WRITING

1. FIRST RESPONSE. Comment on the use of slang in the poem. Does it surprise you? How does it characterize the speaker?

2. How does the language of the final stanza differ from that of the first stanza? To what purpose?

3. Write an essay that discusses the speaker's attitudes toward sex and life. How are they related?

CONNECTION TO ANOTHER SELECTION

1. Think about "Seniors" as a kind of love poem and compare the speaker's voice here with the one in T. S. Eliot's "The Love Song of J. Alfred Prufrock" (p. 948). How are these two voices used to evoke different cultures? Of what value is love in these cultures?

ALFRED, LORD TENNYSON (1809–1892)

The Eagle 1851

Fragment

He clasps the crag with crooked hands;
Close to the sun in lonely lands,
Ringed with the azure world, he stands.

The wrinkled sea beneath him crawls:
He watches from his mountain walls,
And like a thunderbolt he falls.

CONSIDERATIONS FOR CRITICAL THINKING AND WRITING

1. FIRST RESPONSE. How does the speaker distinguish between the eagle's movements in the second stanza and those in the first stanza?

2. Although this poem is considered to be a fragment by Tennyson, how might it also be considered as a kind of complete portrait of an eagle?

CONNECTION TO ANOTHER SELECTION

1. Why can "The Eagle" and the anonymously written "Western Wind" (p. 604) be accurately described as lyric poems?

EDGAR ALLAN POE (1809–1849)

Sonnet — To Science 1845

Science! true daughter of Old Time thou art!
  Who alterest all things with thy peering eyes.
Why preyest thou thus upon the poet's heart,
  Vulture, whose wings are dull realities?
How should he love thee? or how deem thee wise,   5
  Who wouldst not leave him in his wandering
To seek for treasure in the jewelled skies,
  Albeit he soared with an undaunted wing?
Hast thou not dragged Diana° from her car?   *goddess of hunting and the moon*
  And driven the Hamadryad° from the wood   *tree nymph*   10
To seek a shelter in some happier star?
  Hast thou not torn the Naiad° from her flood,   *water nymph*
The Elfin from the green grass, and from me
The summer dream beneath the tamarind tree?°   *exotic Asian tree*

CONSIDERATIONS FOR CRITICAL THINKING AND WRITING

1. FIRST RESPONSE. How is science characterized in lines 1–4? Which words are particularly revealing?

2. Given the references to Diana, the Hamadryad, the Naiad, the Elfin, and the tamarind tree, how would you describe the poet's world compared to the scientist's?

3. How do you think a scientist might respond to this poem?

CONNECTION TO ANOTHER SELECTION

1. Compare the speaker's attitudes toward what Poe calls in this poem "peering eyes" with the speaker's attitude toward the readers in Billy Collins's "Introduction to Poetry" (p. 607).

WILLA CATHER (1873–1947)

Prairie Spring 1913

Evening and the flat land,
Rich and sombre and always silent;
The miles of fresh-plowed soil,
Heavy and black, full of strength and harshness;
The growing wheat, the growing weeds,   5

The toiling horses, the tired men;
The long empty roads,
Sullen fires of sunset, fading,
The eternal, unresponsive sky.
Against all this, Youth,   10
Flaming like the wild roses,
Singing like the larks over the plowed fields,
Flashing like a star out of the twilight;
Youth with its insupportable sweetness,
Its fierce necessity,   15
Its sharp desire,
Singing and singing,
Out of the lips of silence,
Out of the earthy dusk.

CONSIDERATIONS FOR CRITICAL THINKING AND WRITING

1. FIRST RESPONSE. To what extent do lines 1–9 present competing perspectives on the prairie?

2. Compare the poet's description of youth with that of the prairie.

3. Discuss the appropriateness of the title.

CONNECTION TO ANOTHER SELECTION

1. How might the themes in Mary Oliver's "The Poet with His Face in His Hands" (p. 611) indicate what she might have to say about "Prairie Spring"?

CORNELIUS EADY (B. 1954)

The Supremes 1991

We were born to be gray. We went to school,
Sat in rows, ate white bread,
Looked at the floor a lot. In the back
Of our small heads

A long scream. We did what we could,   5
And all we could do was
Turn on each other. How the fat kids suffered!
Not even being jolly could save them.

And then there were the anal retentives,
The terrified brown-noses, the desperately   10
Athletic or popular. This, of course,
Was training. At home

Our parents shook their heads and waited.
We learned of the industrial revolution,
The sectioning of the clock into pie slices.   15

We drank cokes and twiddled our thumbs. In the
Back of our minds

A long scream. We snapped butts in the showers,
Froze out shy girls on the dance floor,
Pin-pointed flaws like radar.   20
Slowly we understood: this was to be the world.

We were born insurance salesmen and secretaries,
Housewives and short order cooks,
Stock room boys and repairmen,
And it wouldn't be a bad life, they promised,   25
In a tone of voice that would force some of us
To reach in self-defense for wigs,
Lipstick,

Sequins.

CONSIDERATIONS FOR CRITICAL THINKING AND WRITING

1. FIRST RESPONSE. Who were the Supremes? Why is the title so crucial for this poem?

2. Explain how the meanings and mood of this poem would change if it ended with line 25.

3. How does the speaker's recollection of school experiences compare with your own?

CONNECTION TO ANOTHER SELECTION

1. Discuss the speakers' memories of school in "The Supremes" and in Judy Page Heitzman's "The Schoolroom on the Second Floor of the Knitting Mill" (p. 701).

TED KOOSER (B. 1939)

Selecting a Reader   1974

First, I would have her be beautiful,
and walking carefully up on my poetry
at the loneliest moment of an afternoon,
her hair still damp at the neck
from washing it. She should be wearing   5
a raincoat, an old one, dirty
from not having money enough for the cleaners.
She will take out her glasses, and there
in the bookstore, she will thumb
over my poems, then put the book back   10
up on its shelf. She will say to herself,
"For that kind of money, I can get
my raincoat cleaned." And she will.

CONSIDERATIONS FOR CRITICAL THINKING AND WRITING

1. FIRST RESPONSE. What do the descriptive details in this poem reveal about the kind of reader the poet desires?

2. Based on this description of the poet's desired reader, write a one-paragraph description of the poem's speaker. Try to include some imaginative details that suggest his personality.

ENCOUNTERING POETRY: IMAGES OF POETRY IN POPULAR CULTURE

© Kevin Fleming/Corbis.

Although poets may find it painful to acknowledge, poetry is not nearly as popular as prose among contemporary readers. A quick prowl through almost any bookstore reveals many more shelves devoted to novels or biographies, for example, than the meager space allotted to poetry. Moreover, very few poems are made into films, and few collections of poetry have earned their authors extraordinary wealth or celebrity status.

Despite these facts, however, there is plenty of poetry being produced that saturates our culture and suggests just how essential it is to our lives. When in 2001 Billy Collins was named the poet laureate of the United States, he shrewdly observed that "we should notice that there is no *prose* laureate." What Collins implicitly acknowledges here is the importance of poetry. He acknowledges the idea that poetry is central to any literature because it is the art closest to language itself; its emphasis on getting each word just right speaks to us and for us. The audience for poetry may be relatively modest in comparison to the readership of prose, but there is nothing shy about poetry's presence in contemporary life. Indeed, a particularly observant person might find it difficult to reach the end of a day without encountering poetry in some shape or form.

You may, for instance, read yet again that magnetic poem composed on your refrigerator door as you reach for your breakfast juice, or perhaps you'll be surprised by some poetic lines while riding the bus or subway, where you might encounter a Poetry in Motion poster, featuring the work of a local poet or well-known author such as Dorothy Parker. What the poems have in common is the celebration of language as a means of surprising, delighting, provoking, or inspiring their readers. There's no obligation and no quiz. The poems are for the taking: all for pleasure.

The following portfolio of images—including provocative posters, a humorous cartoon, poetry-related art in public spaces, and vibrant photographs from the poetry slam scene—illustrate the significance of poetry in our culture. These images recognize the importance not only of such canonical authors as Carl Sandburg and T. S. Eliot but also of aspiring poets—spoken word performers or Magnetic Poetry authors, for example—whose works reflect the growth of poetry as a popular form of expression.

Perhaps the largest, most recent explosion of poetry can be found on the Internet. The number of poetry sites is staggering; these include sites that provide poems, audio readings, e-zines, reviews, criticism, festivals, slams, conferences, workshops, and even collaborative poetry writing in real time. This growth in poetry on the Internet is significant because it reflects an energy and a vitality about the poetic activity in our daily lives. Poetry may not be rich and famous, but it is certainly alive and well. Consider, for example, the following images of poetry that can be found in contemporary life. What do they suggest to you about the nature of poetry and its audience?

DOROTHY PARKER, *Unfortunate Coincidence*

Begun in New York City in 1992, the Poetry in Motion program has spread from coast to coast on buses and subways. Offering works ranging from ancient Chinese poetry to contemporary poetry, Poetry in Motion posters give riders more to look at than their own reflections in the window. In this example, Dorothy Parker, a poet known for her sharp wit, becomes a presence on a New York subway car.
Viking Penguin.

POETRY IN MOTION

UNFORTUNATE COINCIDENCE

By the time you swear you're his,
     Shivering and sighing,
And he vows his passion is
     Infinite, undying —
Lady, make a note of this:
     One of you is lying.

—Dorothy Parker (1893–1967)

CONSIDERATIONS FOR CRITICAL THINKING AND WRITING

1. How does the unromantic nature of this poem seem especially appropriate for New York City subway riders?

2. What kinds of poetry do you find on billboards or public transportation in your own environment? If there is none, what poem would you choose to post on a bus or train in your area?

Carl Sandburg, *Window*

This mural, painted on a station wall of the Chicago El, features the poem "Window," from a collection of poems by Carl Sandburg titled *Chicago*. This work transforms the evening commute into an encounter with a vivid image.
Jason Reblando.

Considerations for Critical Thinking and Writing

1. Discuss the effectiveness of the images in these two lines.

2. **CREATIVE RESPONSE.** Try writing two lines of vivid imagery that capture the movement seen from a quickly moving automobile during daylight.

ROZ CHAST, *The Love Song of J. Alfred Crew*

This *New Yorker* cartoon by Roz Chast (b. 1954) updates lines from T. S. Eliot's "The Love Song of J. Alfred Prufrock" (pp. 948–52, lines 120–24) with the kind of language used in the popular J. Crew clothing catalog. Though published in 1917, Eliot's poem clearly remains fashionable.

Roz Chast The New Yorker Collection/The Cartoon Bank.

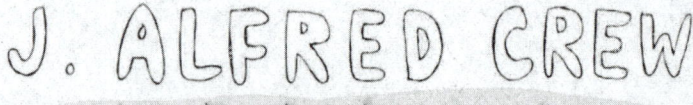

CONSIDERATIONS FOR CRITICAL THINKING AND WRITING

1. Read "The Love Song of J. Alfred Prufrock" (p. 948) and compare the speaker's personality to the kind of image associated with the typical J. Crew customer. How does this comparison serve to explain the humor in the cartoon?

2. Explain why you think the J. Crew company would be flattered or annoyed to have its image treated this way in a cartoon.

TIM TAYLOR, *I shake the delicate apparatus*

Magnetic Poetry kits are available in a number of languages, including Yiddish, Norwegian, and sign language, along with a variety of thematic versions such as those dedicated to cats, love, art, rock and roll, college, and Shakespeare. This poem by Tim Taylor (b. 1957) graces his Manhattan apartment refrigerator and is but one example of the creative expression that poetry magnets inspire in kitchens around the world.

Reprinted by permission of Tim Taylor (poem) and Pelle Cass (image).

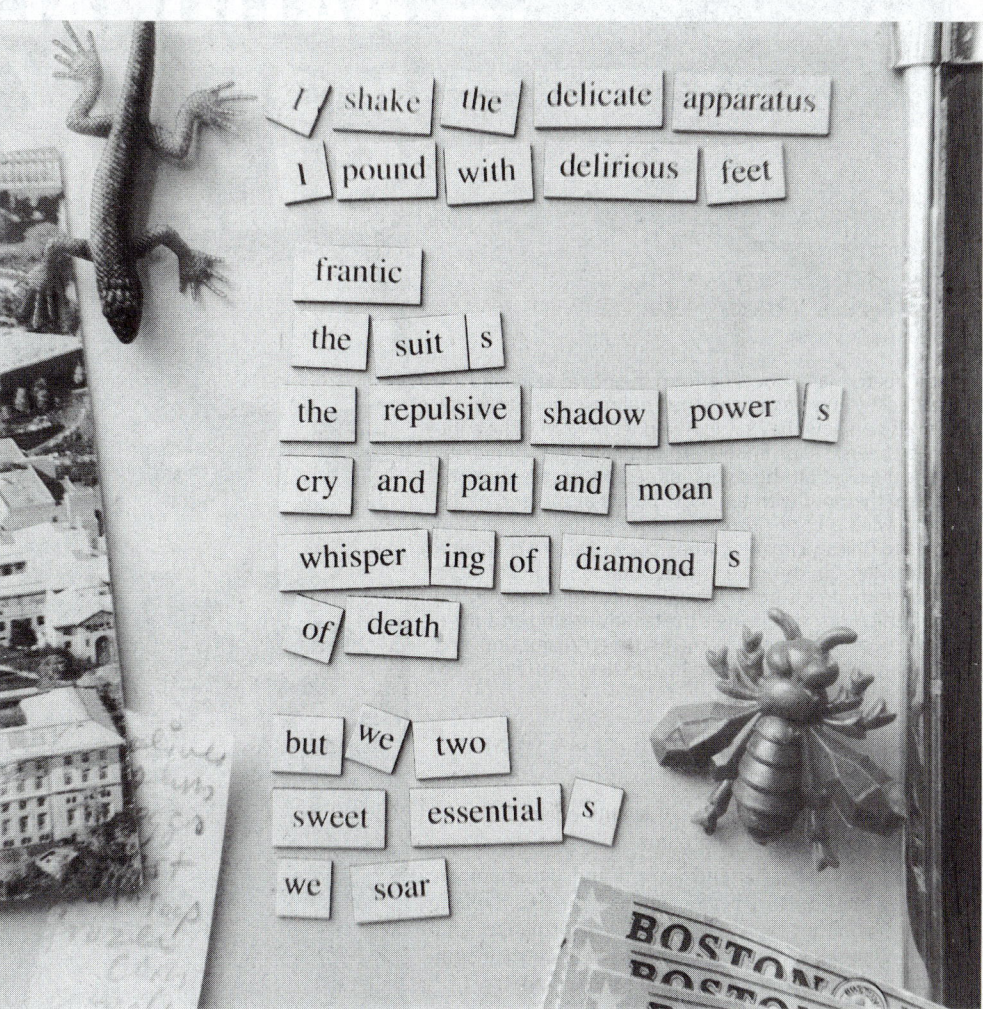

CONSIDERATIONS FOR CRITICAL THINKING AND WRITING

1. Write a paragraph that describes what you think is the essential meaning of this poem.

2. How do you explain the enormous popularity of Magnetic Poetry?

Eric Dunn, Mike Wigton, and Kevin Fleming, *National Poetry Slam*

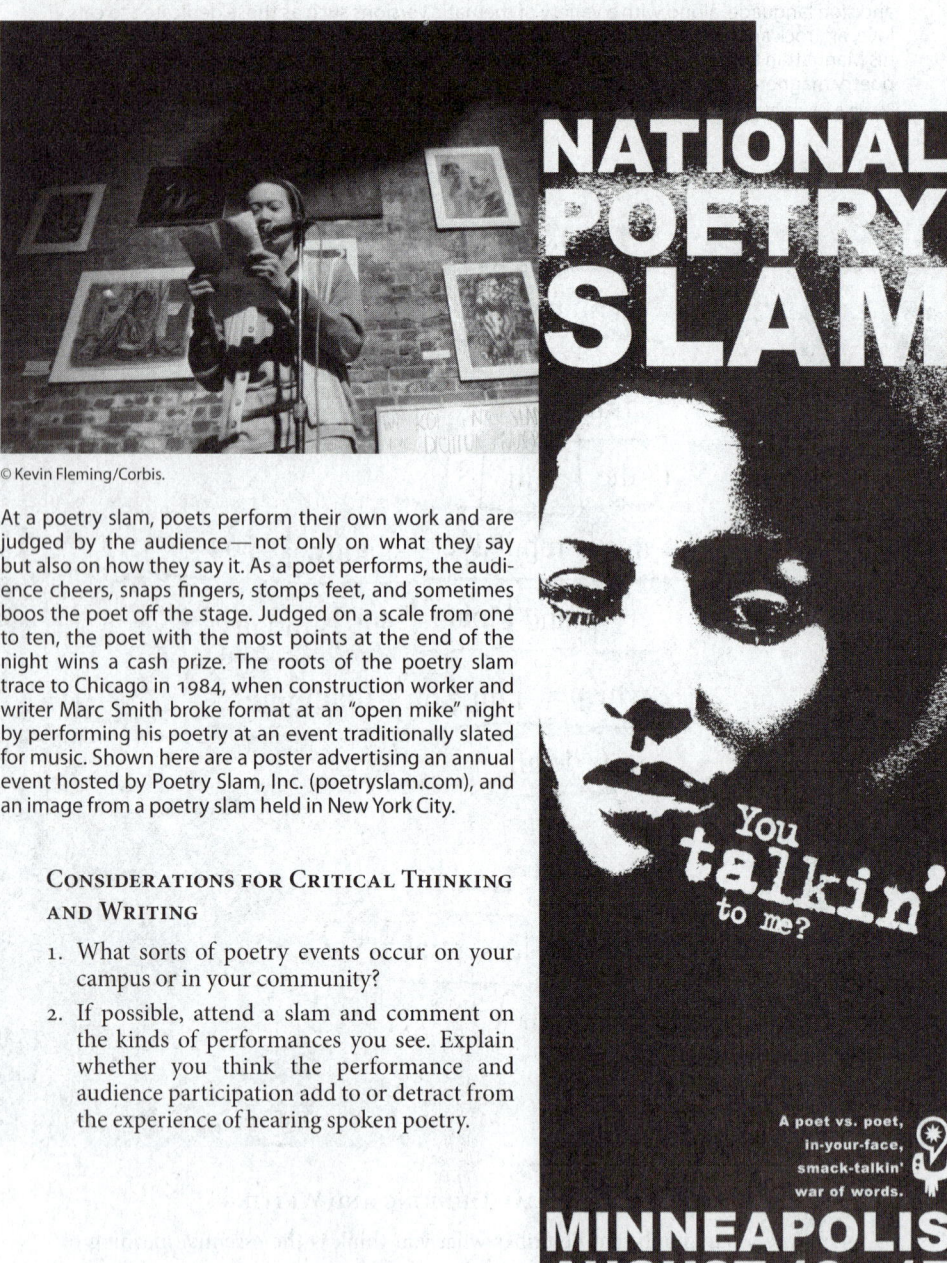

© Kevin Fleming/Corbis.

At a poetry slam, poets perform their own work and are judged by the audience—not only on what they say but also on how they say it. As a poet performs, the audience cheers, snaps fingers, stomps feet, and sometimes boos the poet off the stage. Judged on a scale from one to ten, the poet with the most points at the end of the night wins a cash prize. The roots of the poetry slam trace to Chicago in 1984, when construction worker and writer Marc Smith broke format at an "open mike" night by performing his poetry at an event traditionally slated for music. Shown here are a poster advertising an annual event hosted by Poetry Slam, Inc. (poetryslam.com), and an image from a poetry slam held in New York City.

Considerations for Critical Thinking and Writing

1. What sorts of poetry events occur on your campus or in your community?

2. If possible, attend a slam and comment on the kinds of performances you see. Explain whether you think the performance and audience participation add to or detract from the experience of hearing spoken poetry.

NATIONAL POETRY SLAM

You talkin' to me?

A poet vs. poet, in-your-face, smack-talkin' war of words.

MINNEAPOLIS AUGUST 13 - 17

Visit www.nps2002.com for event locations and times.

Reprinted by permission of Eric Dunn and Mike Wigton (designer/copywriter), and by permission of Poetry Slam, Inc.

Ted Kooser, *American Life in Poetry*

AMERICAN LIFE IN POETRY

A PROJECT FOR NEWSPAPERS BY TED KOOSER, POET LAUREATE OF THE UNITED STATES 2004-2006

Ted Kooser, U.S. Poet Laureate 2004-2006   Photo © Sarah Greene

American Life in Poetry provides newspapers and online publications with a free weekly column featuring contemporary American poems. The sole mission of this project is to promote poetry: American Life in Poetry seeks to create a vigorous presence for poetry in our culture. There are no costs for reprinting the columns; we do require that you register your publication here and that the text of the column be reproduced without alteration.

The poem in each column is brief and will be enjoyable and enlightening to readers of newspapers and online publications. Each week, a new column will be posted. Registered publications will receive new columns by email. Our archive of previous columns is also available for publication.

American Life in Poetry: Column 357

The title of this beautiful poem by Edward Hirsch contradicts the poem, which is indeed a prayer. Hirsch lives in New York and is president of the John Simon Guggenheim Memorial Foundation, one of our country's most distinguished cultural endowments.

Read the column >>

American Life in Poetry (americanlifeinpoetry.org) is a weekly newspaper column featuring a contemporary poem and brief introduction. Initiated by Ted Kooser, a poet laureate of the United States, and supported by the Poetry Foundation in partnership with the Library of Congress, this popular source is distributed free to newspapers and online publications. The site provides countless readers with a wide variety of high-quality, accessible poems.

The next page reprints one of Kooser's columns as it appeared online.

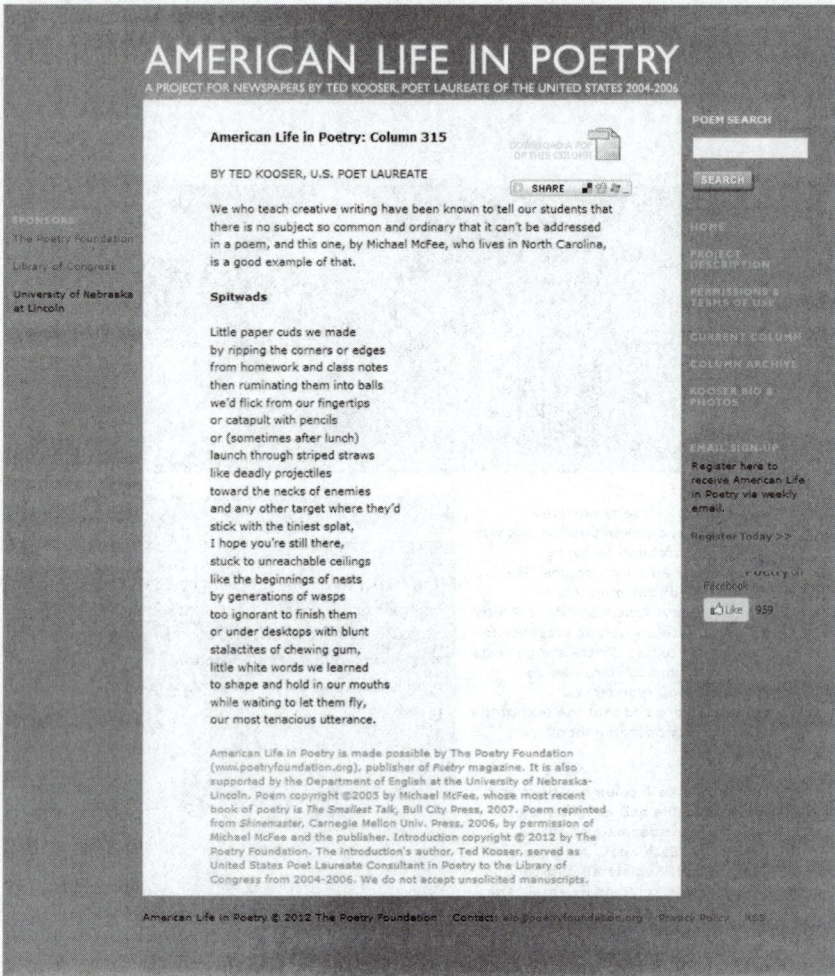

AMERICAN LIFE IN POETRY
A PROJECT FOR NEWSPAPERS BY TED KOOSER, POET LAUREATE OF THE UNITED STATES 2004-2006

American Life in Poetry: Column 315

BY TED KOOSER, U.S. POET LAUREATE

We who teach creative writing have been known to tell our students that there is no subject so common and ordinary that it can't be addressed in a poem, and this one, by Michael McFee, who lives in North Carolina, is a good example of that.

Spitwads

Little paper cuds we made
by ripping the corners or edges
from homework and class notes
then ruminating them into balls
we'd flick from our fingertips
or catapult with pencils
or (sometimes after lunch)
launch through striped straws
like deadly projectiles
toward the necks of enemies
and any other target where they'd
stick with the tiniest splat,
I hope you're still there,
stuck to unreachable ceilings
like the beginnings of nests
by generations of wasps
too ignorant to finish them
or under desktops with blunt
stalactites of chewing gum,
little white words we learned
to shape and hold in our mouths
while waiting to let them fly,
our most tenacious utterance.

American Life in Poetry is made possible by The Poetry Foundation (www.poetryfoundation.org), publisher of *Poetry* magazine. It is also supported by the Department of English at the University of Nebraska-Lincoln. Poem copyright ©2005 by Michael McFee, whose most recent book of poetry is *The Smallest Talk*, Bull City Press, 2007. Poem reprinted from *Shinemaster*, Carnegie Mellon Univ. Press, 2006, by permission of Michael McFee and the publisher. Introduction copyright © 2012 by The Poetry Foundation. The introduction's author, Ted Kooser, served as United States Poet Laureate Consultant in Poetry to the Library of Congress from 2004-2006. We do not accept unsolicited manuscripts.

American Life in Poetry © 2012 The Poetry Foundation   Contact: alp@poetryfoundation.org   Privacy Policy   RSS

POEM SEARCH

SEARCH

SPONSORS
The Poetry Foundation
Library of Congress
University of Nebraska at Lincoln

HOME
PROJECT DESCRIPTION
PERMISSIONS & TERMS OF USE
CURRENT COLUMN
COLUMN ARCHIVE
KOOSER BIO & PHOTOS

EMAIL SIGN-UP
Register here to receive American Life in Poetry via weekly email.
Register Today >>

Facebook
Like 959

Considerations for Critical Thinking and Writing

1. Put together a cluster of images that reflect your encounters with poetry. Where do you find poetry? How is it used? What do these images suggest to you about the state of poetry in contemporary culture?

2. Surely not all manifestations of poetry in popular culture represent good poetry. Does bad poetry undercut good poetry? Does it cheapen its value? At this point in your study of poetry — the beginning — how do you define a good poem or a bad poem?

3. What is your favorite poem? Where did you first encounter it? Why is it important to you? Alternatively, if you can't come up with a favorite poem, why can't you?

21

Writing about Poetry: From Inquiry to Final Paper

Many people, especially beginning writers, think that writing is mostly inspiration. The muse tosses down a lightning bolt and you write something good. I think writing is mostly perspiration. You go to your chair or desk, and you stay there.

— MICHAEL CHITWOOD

Derek Anderson.

FROM READING TO WRITING

Writing about poetry can be a rigorous means of testing the validity of your own reading of a poem. Anyone who has been asked to write several pages about a fourteen-line poem knows how intellectually challenging this exercise is, because it means paying close attention to language. Such scrutiny of words, however, sensitizes you not only to the poet's use of language but also to your own use of language. At first you may feel intimidated by having to compose a paper that is longer than the poem you're writing about, but a careful reading will reveal that there's plenty to write about what the poem says and how it says it. Keep in mind that your job is not to produce a definitive reading of the poem — even Carl Sandburg once confessed that "I've written some poetry I don't understand myself." It is enough to develop an interesting thesis and to present it clearly and persuasively.

An interesting thesis will come to you if you read and reread, take notes, annotate the text, and generate ideas (for a discussion of this process, see Chapter 52, "Reading and the Writing Process"). Although it requires energy to read closely and to write convincingly about the charged language found in poetry, there is nothing mysterious about such reading and writing. This chapter provides a set of questions designed to sharpen your reading and writing about poetry. Following these questions is a sample paper that offers a clear and well-developed thesis concerning Elizabeth Bishop's "Manners."

Questions for Responsive Reading and Writing

The following questions can help you respond to important elements that reveal a poem's effects and meanings. The questions are general, so not all of them will necessarily be relevant to a particular poem. Many, however, should prove useful for thinking, talking, and writing about each poem in this collection. If you are uncertain about the meaning of a term used in a question, consult the Glossary of Literary Terms beginning on page 1716.

Before addressing these questions, read the poem you are studying in its entirety. Don't worry about interpretation on a first reading; allow yourself the pleasure of enjoying whatever makes itself apparent to you. Then on subsequent readings, use the questions to understand and appreciate how the poem works.

1. Who is the speaker? Is it possible to determine the speaker's age, sex, sensibilities, level of awareness, and values?
2. Is the speaker addressing anyone in particular?
3. How do you respond to the speaker? Favorably? Negatively? What is the situation? Are there any special circumstances that inform what the speaker says?
4. Is there a specific setting of time and place?
5. Does reading the poem aloud help you understand it?
6. Does a paraphrase reveal the basic purpose of the poem?
7. What does the title emphasize?
8. Is the theme presented directly or indirectly?
9. Do any allusions enrich the poem's meaning?
10. How does the diction reveal meaning? Are any words repeated? Do any carry evocative connotative meanings? Are there any puns or other forms of verbal wit?
11. Are figures of speech used? How does the figurative language contribute to the poem's vividness and meaning?
12. Do any objects, persons, places, events, or actions have allegorical or symbolic meanings? What other details in the poem support your interpretation?

13. Is irony used? Are there any examples of situational irony, verbal irony, or dramatic irony? Is understatement or paradox used?

14. What is the tone of the poem? Is the tone consistent?

15. Does the poem use onomatopoeia, assonance, consonance, or alliteration? How do these sounds affect you?

16. What sounds are repeated? If there are rhymes, what is their effect? Do they seem forced or natural? Is there a rhyme scheme? Do the rhymes contribute to the poem's meaning?

17. Do the lines have a regular meter? What is the predominant meter? Are there significant variations? Does the rhythm seem appropriate for the poem's tone?

18. Does the poem's form — its overall structure — follow an established pattern? Do you think the form is a suitable vehicle for the poem's meaning and effects?

19. Is the language of the poem intense and concentrated? Do you think it warrants more than one or two close readings?

20. Did you enjoy the poem? What, specifically, pleased or displeased you about what was expressed and how it was expressed?

21. Is there a particular critical approach that seems especially appropriate for this poem? (See Chapter 51, "Critical Strategies for Reading.")

22. How might biographical information about the author help to determine the poem's central concerns?

23. How might historical information about the poem provide a useful context for interpretation?

24. To what extent do your own experiences, values, beliefs, and assumptions inform your interpretation?

25. What kinds of evidence from the poem are you focusing on to support your interpretation? Does your interpretation leave out any important elements that might undercut or qualify your interpretation?

26. Given that there are a variety of ways to interpret the poem, which one seems the most useful to you?

ELIZABETH BISHOP (1911–1979)

Manners   1965

for a Child of 1918

My grandfather said to me
as we sat on the wagon seat,
"Be sure to remember to always
speak to everyone you meet."

© Bettmann/Corbis.

We met a stranger on foot   5
My grandfather's whip tapped his hat.
"Good day, sir. Good day. A fine day."
And I said it and bowed where I sat.

Then we overtook a boy we knew
with his big pet crow on his shoulder.   10
"Always offer everyone a ride;
don't forget that when you get older,"

my grandfather said. So Willy
climbed up with us, but the crow
gave a "Caw!" and flew off. I was worried.   15
How would he know where to go?

But he flew a little way at a time
from fence post to fence post, ahead;
and when Willy whistled he answered.
"A fine bird," my grandfather said,   20

"and he's well brought up. See, he answers
nicely when he's spoken to.
Man or beast, that's good manners.
Be sure that you both always do."

When automobiles went by,   25
the dust hid the people's faces,
but we shouted "Good day! Good day!
Fine day!" at the top of our voices.

When we came to Hustler Hill,
he said that the mare was tired,   30
so we all got down and walked,
as our good manners required.

A SAMPLE CLOSE READING

An Annotated Version of "Manners"

The following annotations represent insights about the relationship of various elements at work in the poem gleaned only after several close readings. Don't expect to be able to produce these kinds of interpretive notes on a first reading because such perceptions will not be apparent until you've read the poem and then gone back to the beginning to discover how each word, line, and stanza contributes to the overall effect. Writing your responses in the margins of the page can be a useful means of recording your impressions as well as discovering new insights as you read the text closely.

ELIZABETH BISHOP (1911–1979)

Manners 1965

for a Child of 1918

My grandfather said to me
as we sat on the wagon seat,
"Be sure to remember to always
speak to everyone you meet."

We met a stranger on foot.   5
My grandfather's whip tapped his hat.
"Good day, sir. Good day. A fine day."
And I said it and bowed where I sat.

Then we overtook a boy we knew
with his big pet crow on his shoulder.   10
"Always offer everyone a ride;
don't forget that when you get older,"

my grandfather said. So Willy
climbed up with us, but the crow
gave a "Caw!" and flew off. I was worried.   15
How would he know where to go?

But he flew a little way at a time
from fence post to fence post, ahead;
and when Willy whistled he answered.
"A fine bird," my grandfather said,   20

"and he's well brought up. See, he answers
nicely when he's spoken to.
Man or beast, that's good manners.
Be sure that you both always do."

When automobiles went by,   25
the dust hid the people's faces,

Marginal annotations:

Title refers to what is socially correct, polite, and/or decent behavior.

WWI ended in 1918 and denotes a shift in values and manners that often follows rapid social changes brought about by war.

Wagon seat suggests a simpler past—as does simple language and informal diction of the child speaker.

Grandfather seems kind, but he also carries a whip that reinforces his authoritative voice.

Idea that values "always" transcend time is emphasized by the grandfather's urging: "don't forget."

"My grandfather," repeated four times in first five stanzas, reflects the child's affection and a sense of belonging in his world. The crow, however, worries the child and indicates an uncertain future.

Predictable quatrains and *abcb* rhyme scheme throughout the poem take the worry out of where they—and the crow—are headed.

The modern symbolic automobile races by, raising dust that obscures everyone's vision and forces them to shout. Rhymes in lines 26 and 28 are off (unlike all the other rhymes) just enough to suggest the dissonant future that will supersede the calm wagon ride.

Third time the grandfather says "always." This and the inverted syntax of line 24 call attention, again, to idea that good manners are forever important.

but we shouted "Good day! Good day!
Fine day!" at the top of our voices.

When we came to Hustler Hill,

The horse, like ——— he said that the mare was tired,   30
the simple past
it symbolizes, is   so we all got down and walked,
weakened by the
hustle of modern   as our good manners required.
life, but even
so, "our" good
manners prevail,
internalized from
the grandfather's
values.

A SAMPLE STUDENT ANALYSIS

Memory in Elizabeth Bishop's "Manners"

The following sample paper on Elizabeth Bishop's "Manners" was written in response to an assignment that called for a 750-word discussion of the ways in which at least five of the following elements work to develop and reinforce the poem's themes:

diction and tone	irony	form
images	sound and rhyme	speaker
figures of speech	rhythm and meter	setting and situation
symbols		

In her paper, Debra Epstein discusses the ways in which a number of these elements contribute to what she sees as a central theme of "Manners": the loss of a way of life that Bishop associates with the end of World War I. Not all of the elements of poetry are covered equally in Epstein's paper because some, such as the speaker and setting, are more important to her argument than others. Notice how rather than merely listing each of the elements, Epstein mentions them in her discussion as she needs to in order to develop the thesis that she clearly and succinctly expresses in her opening paragraph.

Epstein 1

Debra Epstein

Professor Brown

English 210

1 May 2015

Memory in Elizabeth Bishop's "Manners"

The subject of Elizabeth Bishop's "Manners" has to do with behaving

well, but the theme of the poem has more to do with a way of life than with

etiquette. The poem suggests that modern society has lost something

important—a friendly openness, a generosity of spirit, a sense of decency

and consideration—in its race toward progress. Although the narrative is

simply told, Bishop enriches this poem about manners by developing an

implicit theme through her subtle use of such elements of poetry as speaker,

setting, rhyme, meter, symbol, and images.

The dedication suggests that the speaker is "a Child of 1918" who

accompanies his or her grandfather on a wagon ride and who is urged to

practice good manners by greeting people, offering everyone a ride, and

speaking when spoken to by anyone. During the ride they say hello to a

stranger, give a ride to a boy with a pet crow, shout greetings to a passing

automobile, and get down from the wagon when they reach a hill because

the horse is tired. They walk because "good manners required" (line 32) such

consideration, even for a horse. This summary indicates what goes on in the

poem but not its significance. That requires a closer look at some of the

poem's elements.

Given the speaker's simple language (there are no metaphors or

similes and only a few words out of thirty-two lines are longer than two

syllables), it seems likely that he or she is a fairly young child rather than

an adult reminiscing. (It is interesting to note that Bishop herself, though

not identical with the speaker, would have been seven in 1918.) Because the

speaker is a young child who uses simple diction, Bishop has to show us the

ride's significance indirectly rather than having the speaker explicitly state it.

The setting for the speaker's narrative is important because 1918

was the year World War I ended, and it marked the beginning of a new era

of technology that was the result of rapid industrialization during the war.

Horses and wagons would soon be put out to pasture. The grandfather's

---

Marginal notes:

Thesis providing interpretation of poem.

Statement of elements in poem to be discussed in paper.

Summary of poem's narrative and introduction to discussion of elements.

Analysis of speaker in poem.

Analysis of poem's setting.

manners emphasize a time gone by; the child must be told to "remember" what the grandfather says because he or she will take that advice into a new and very different world.

The grandfather's world of the horse and wagon is uncomplicated, and this is reflected in both the simple quatrains that move predictably along in an *abcb* rhyme scheme and the frequent anapestic meter (ǎs wě sát ǒn thě wágǒn [2]) that pulls the lines rapidly and lightly. The one moment Bishop breaks the set rhyme scheme is in the seventh stanza when the automobile (the single four-syllable word in the poem) rushes by in a cloud of dust so that people cannot see or hear each other. The only off rhymes in the poem—"faces" (26) and "voices" (28)—are also in this stanza, which suggests that the automobile and the people in it are somehow off or out of sync with what goes on in the other stanzas. The automobile is a symbol of a way of life in which people—their faces hidden—and manners take a backseat to speed and noise. The people in the car don't wave, don't offer a ride, and don't speak when spoken to.

Maybe the image of the crow's noisy cawing and flying from post to post is a foreshadowing that should prepare readers for the automobile. The speaker feels "worried" about the crow's apparent directionlessness: "How would he know where to go?" (16). However, neither the child nor the grandfather (nor the reader on a first reading) clearly sees the two worlds that Bishop contrasts in the final stanza.

"Hustler Hill" is the perfect name for what finally tires out the mare. There is no hurry for the grandfather and child, but there is for those people in the car and the postwar hustle and bustle they represent. The fast-paced future overtakes the tired symbol of the past in the poem. The pace slows as the wagon passengers get down to walk, but the reader recognizes that the grandfather's way has been lost to a world in which good manners are not required.

Marginal notes:
Analysis of rhyme scheme and meter.

Analysis of symbols.

Analysis of images.

Conclusion supporting thesis on poem's theme.

Work Cited

Bishop, Elizabeth. "Manners." *The Bedford Introduction to Literature.* Ed. Michael Meyer. 11th ed. Boston: Bedford/St. Martin's, 2016. 629–30. Print.

22

Word Choice, Word Order, and Tone

The Granger Collection.

I still feel that a poet has a duty to words, and that words can do wonderful things. And it's too bad to just let them lie there without doing anything with and for them.
— GWENDOLYN BROOKS

WORD CHOICE

Diction

Like all good writers, poets are keenly aware of **diction**, their choice of words. Poets, however, choose words especially carefully because the words in poems call attention to themselves. Characters, actions, settings, and symbols may appear in a poem, but in the foreground, before all else, is the poem's language. Also, poems are usually briefer than other forms of writing. A few inappropriate words in a 200-page novel (which would have about 100,000 words) create fewer problems than they would in a 100-word poem. Functioning in a compressed atmosphere, the words in a poem must convey meanings gracefully and economically. Readers therefore have to be alert to the ways in which those meanings are released.

Although poetic language is often more intensely charged than ordinary speech, the words used in poetry are not necessarily different from everyday speech. Inexperienced readers may sometimes assume that language must be high-flown and out-of-date to be included in a poem: instead of reading about a boy "enjoying a swim," they expect to read about a boy "disporting with pliant arm o'er a glassy wave." During the eighteenth century this kind of *poetic diction* — the use of elevated language rather than ordinary language — was highly valued in English poetry, but since the nineteenth century poets have generally overridden the distinctions that were once made between words used in everyday speech and those used in poetry. Today all levels of diction can be found in poetry.

A poet, like any writer, has several levels of diction from which to choose; they range from formal to middle to informal. *Formal diction* consists of a dignified, impersonal, and elevated use of language. Notice, for example, the formality of Thomas Hardy's description of the sunken luxury liner *Titanic* in this stanza from "The Convergence of the Twain" (the entire poem appears on p. 652):

> In a solitude of the sea
> Deep from human vanity,
> And the Pride of Life that planned her, stilly couches she.

There is nothing casual or relaxed about these lines. Hardy's use of "stilly," meaning "quietly" or "calmly," is purely literary; the word rarely, if ever, turns up in everyday English.

The language used in Sharon Olds's "Last Night" (p. 650) represents a less formal level of diction; the speaker uses a *middle diction* spoken by most educated people. Consider how Olds's speaker struggles the next day to comprehend her passion:

> Love? It was more like dragonflies
> in the sun, 100 degrees at noon,
> the ends of their abdomens stuck together, I
> close my eyes when I remember.

The words used to describe this encounter are common enough, yet it is precisely Olds's use of language that evokes the extraordinary nature of this couple's connection.

Informal diction is evident in Philip Larkin's "A Study of Reading Habits" (p. 601). The speaker's account of his early reading is presented *colloquially*, in a conversational manner that in this instance includes slang expressions not used by the culture at large:

> When getting my nose in a book
> Cured most things short of school,
> It was worth ruining my eyes
> To know I could still keep cool,
> And deal out the old right hook
> To dirty dogs twice my size.

This level of diction is clearly not that of Hardy's or Olds's speakers.

Poets may also draw on another form of informal diction, called *dialect*. Dialects are spoken by definable groups of people from a particular geographic region, economic group, or social class. New England dialects are often heard in Robert Frost's poems, for example. Gwendolyn Brooks uses a black dialect in "We Real Cool" (p. 662) to characterize a group of pool players. Another form of diction related to particular groups is *jargon*, a category of language defined by a trade or profession. Sociologists, photographers, carpenters, baseball players, and dentists, for example, all use words that are specific to their fields. Sally Croft offers an appetizing dish of cookbook jargon in "Home-Baked Bread" (p. 684).

Many levels of diction are available to poets. The variety of diction to be found in poetry is enormous, and that is how it should be. No language is foreign to poetry because it is possible to imagine any human voice as the speaker of a poem. When we say a poem is formal, informal, or somewhere in between, we are making a descriptive statement rather than an evaluative one. What matters in a poem is not only which words are used but how they are used.

Denotations and Connotations

One important way that the meaning of a word is communicated in a poem is through sound: snakes *hiss,* saws *buzz.* This and other matters related to sound are discussed in Chapter 26. Individual words also convey meanings through denotations and connotations. *Denotations* are the literal, dictionary meanings of a word. For example, *bird* denotes a feathered animal with wings (other denotations for the same word include a shuttlecock, an airplane, or an odd person), but in addition to its denotative meanings, *bird* also carries *connotations* — associations and implications that go beyond a word's literal meanings. Connotations derive from how the word has been used and the associations people make with it. Therefore, the connotations of *bird* might include fragility, vulnerability, altitude, the sky, or freedom, depending on the context in which the word is used. Consider also how different the connotations are for the following types of birds: hawk, dove, penguin, pigeon, chicken, peacock, duck, crow, turkey, gull, owl, goose, coot, and vulture. These words have long been used to refer to types of people as well as birds. They are rich in connotative meanings.

Connotations derive their resonance from a person's experiences with a word. Those experiences may not always be the same, especially when the people having them are in different times and places. *Theater,* for instance, was once associated with depravity, disease, and sin, whereas today the word usually evokes some sense of high culture and perhaps visions of elegant opulence. In several ethnic communities in the United States many people would find *squid* appetizing, but elsewhere the word is likely to produce negative connotations. Readers must recognize, then, that words written in other times and places may have unexpected connotations. Annotations usually help in these matters, which is why it makes sense to pay attention to them when they are available.

Ordinarily, though, the language of poetry is accessible, even when the circumstances of the reader and the poet are different. Although connotative language may be used subtly, it mostly draws on associations experienced by many people. Poets rely on widely shared associations rather than on the idiosyncratic response that an individual might have to a word. Someone who has received a severe burn from a fireplace accident may associate the word *hearth* with intense pain instead of home and family life, but that reader must not allow a personal experience to undermine the response the poet intends to evoke. Connotative meanings are usually public meanings.

Perhaps this can be seen most clearly in advertising, where language is also used primarily to convey moods and feelings rather than information. For instance, three decades of increasing interest in nutrition and general fitness have created a collective consciousness that advertisers have capitalized on successfully. Knowing that we want to be slender or lean or slim (not *spare* or *scrawny* and certainly not *gaunt*), advertisers have created a new word to describe beers, wines, sodas, cheeses, canned fruits, and other products that tend to overload what used to be called sweatclothes and sneakers. The word is *lite*. The assumed denotative meaning of *lite* is "low in calories," but as close readers of ingredient labels know, some *lites* are heavier than regularly prepared products. There can be no doubt about the connotative meaning of *lite*, however. Whatever is *lite* cannot hurt you; less is more. Even the word is lighter than *light;* there is no unnecessary droopy *g* or plump *h*. *Lite* is a brilliantly manufactured use of connotation.

Connotative meanings are valuable because they allow poets to be economical and suggestive simultaneously. In this way emotions and attitudes are carefully woven into the texture of the poem's language. Read the following poem and pay close attention to the connotative meanings of its words.

RANDALL JARRELL (1914–1965)

The Death of the Ball Turret Gunner 1945

From my mother's sleep I fell into the State
And I hunched in its belly till my wet fur froze.
Six miles from earth, loosed from its dream of life,
I woke to black flak and the nightmare fighters.
When I died they washed me out of the turret with a hose.

The title of this poem establishes the setting and the speaker's situation. Like the setting of a short story, the setting of a poem is important when the time and place influence what happens. "The Death of the Ball Turret Gunner" is set in the midst of a war and, more specifically, in a ball turret — a Plexiglas sphere housing machine guns on the underside of a bomber. The speaker's situation obviously places him in extreme danger; indeed, his fate is announced in the title.

Although the poem is written in the first-person singular, its speaker is clearly not the poet. Jarrell uses a **persona**, a speaker created by the poet. In this poem the persona is a disembodied voice that makes the gunner's story all the more powerful. What is his story? A paraphrase might read something like this:

> After I was born, I grew up to find myself at war, cramped into the turret of a bomber's belly some 31,000 feet above the ground. Below me were exploding shells from antiaircraft guns and attacking fighter planes. I was killed, but the bomber returned to base, where my remains were cleaned out of the turret so the next man could take my place.

This paraphrase is accurate, but its language is much less suggestive than the poem's. The first line of the poem has the speaker emerge from his "mother's sleep," the anesthetized sleep of her giving birth. The phrase also suggests the comfort, warmth, and security he knew as a child. This safety was left behind when he "fell," a verb that evokes the danger and involuntary movement associated with his subsequent "State" (*fell* also echoes, perhaps, the fall from innocence to experience related in the Bible).

Several dictionary definitions appear for the noun *state*; it can denote a territorial unit, the power and authority of a government, a person's social status, or a person's emotional or physical condition. The context provided by the rest of the poem makes clear that "State" has several denotative meanings here: because it is capitalized, it certainly refers to the violent world of a government at war, but it also refers to the gunner's vulnerable status as well as his physical and emotional condition. By having "State" carry more than one meaning, Jarrell has created an intentional ambiguity. **Ambiguity** allows for two or more simultaneous interpretations of a word, a phrase, an action, or a situation, all of which can be supported by the context of a work. Through his ambiguous use of "State," Jarrell connects the horrors of war not just to bombers and gunners but to the governments that control them.

Related to this ambiguity is the connotative meaning of "State" in the poem. The context demands that the word be read with a negative charge. The word is used not to indicate patriotic pride but to suggest an anonymous, impersonal "State" that kills rather than nurtures the life in its "belly." The state's "belly" is a bomber, and the gunner is "hunched" like a fetus in the cramped turret, where, in contrast to the warmth of his mother's womb, everything is frozen, even the "wet fur" of his flight jacket (newborn infants have wet fur too). The gunner is not just 31,000 feet from the ground but "Six miles from earth." *Six miles* has roughly the same denotative meaning as 31,000 feet, but Jarrell knew that the connotative meaning of *six miles* makes the speaker's position seem even more remote and frightening.

When the gunner is born into the violent world of war, he finds himself waking up to a "nightmare" that is all too real. The poem's final line is grimly understated, but it hits the reader with the force of an exploding shell: what the State-bomber-turret gives birth to is a gruesome death that is merely one of an endless series. It may be tempting to reduce the theme of this poem to the idea that "war is hell," but Jarrell's target is more specific. He implicates the "State," which routinely executes such violence, and he does so without preaching or hysterical denunciations. Instead, his use of language conveys his theme subtly and powerfully.

WORD ORDER

Meanings in poems are conveyed not only by denotations and connotations but also by the poet's arrangement of words into phrases, clauses, and sentences to achieve particular effects. The ordering of words into meaningful verbal patterns is called **syntax**. A poet can manipulate the syntax of a line to place emphasis on a word; this is especially apparent when a poet varies normal word order. In Emily Dickinson's "A narrow Fellow in the Grass" (p. 2), for example, the speaker says about the snake that "His notice sudden is." Ordinarily, that would be expressed as "his notice is sudden." By placing the verb *is* unexpectedly at the end of the line, Dickinson creates the sense of surprise we feel when we suddenly come upon a snake. Dickinson's inversion of the standard word order also makes the final sound of the line a hissing *is*.

TONE

Tone is the writer's attitude toward the subject, the mood created by all the elements in the poem. Writing, like speech, can be characterized as serious or light, sad or happy, private or public, angry or affectionate, bitter or nostalgic, or by any other attitudes and feelings that human beings experience. In Jarrell's "The Death of the Ball Turret Gunner," the tone is clearly serious; the voice in the poem even sounds dead. Listen again to the persona's final words: "When I died they washed me out of the turret with a hose." The brutal, restrained matter-of-factness of this line is effective because the reader is called on to supply the appropriate anger and despair — a strategy that makes those emotions all the more convincing.

Consider how tone is used to convey meaning in the next poem, inspired by the poet's contemplation of mortality.

MARILYN NELSON (B. 1946)

How I Discovered Poetry   1997

It was like soul-kissing, the way the words
filled my mouth as Mrs. Purdy read from her desk.
All the other kids zoned an hour ahead to 3:15,
but Mrs. Purdy and I wandered lonely as clouds borne
by a breeze off Mount Parnassus. She must have seen
the darkest eyes in the room brim: The next day
she gave me a poem she'd chosen especially for me
to read to the all except for me white class.
She smiled when she told me to read it, smiled harder,
said oh yes I could. She smiled harder and harder   10
until I stood and opened my mouth to banjo playing
darkies, pickaninnies, disses and dats. When I finished
my classmates stared at the floor. We walked silent
to the buses, awed by the power of words.

> **WHEN I WRITE** "Although I usually wind up showing my poems to my best friend, sometimes I ask other people to be first-readers because I don't want to ask too much of my friend! I recently joined a poetry group. Their suggestions are useful, mostly in helping me see what I'm really trying to get at." —MARILYN NELSON

CONSIDERATIONS FOR CRITICAL THINKING AND WRITING

1. **FIRST RESPONSE.** Trace your response to Mrs. Purdy from the beginning to the end of the poem.
2. What do the references to William Wordsworth's poem "I Wandered Lonely as a Cloud" (see p. 1069) and Mount Parnassus (look it up) in lines 4 and 5 suggest to you about the speaker?
3. How do you interpret the tone of the final two lines?

The next work is a ***dramatic monologue***, a type of poem in which a character — the speaker — addresses a silent audience in such a way as to reveal unintentionally some aspect of his or her temperament or personality. What tone is created by Machan's use of a persona?

KATHARYN HOWD MACHAN (B. 1952)

Hazel Tells LaVerne   1976

last night
im cleanin out my
howard johnsons ladies room
when all of a sudden
up pops this frog
musta come from the sewer
swimmin aroun an tryin ta
climb up the sida the bowl
so i goes ta flushm down

> **WHEN I WRITE** "When a poem begins to find its shape and form and voice inside you, let your heart and your head join to give it the best life you can: passion! imagery! music! And if it will let you, humor: ah, the world needs all it can get."
> —KATHARYN HOWD MACHAN

but sohelpmegod he starts talkin 10
bout a golden ball
an how i can be a princess
me a princess
well my mouth drops
all the way to the floor 15
an he says
kiss me just kiss me
once on the nose
well i screams
ya little green pervert 20
an i hitsm with my mop
an has ta flush
the toilet down three times
me
a princess 25

CONSIDERATIONS FOR CRITICAL THINKING AND WRITING

1. FIRST RESPONSE. What do you imagine the situation and setting are for this poem? Do you like this revision of the fairy tale "The Frog Prince"?

2. What creates the poem's humor? How does Hazel's use of language reveal her personality? Is her treatment of the frog consistent with her character?

3. Although it has no punctuation, this poem is easy to follow. How does the arrangement of the lines organize Hazel's speech for clarity and emphasis?

4. What is the theme? Is it conveyed through denotative or connotative language?

5. CREATIVE RESPONSE. Write what you think might be LaVerne's reply to Hazel. First, write LaVerne's response as a series of ordinary sentences, and then try editing and organizing them into poetic lines.

CONNECTION TO ANOTHER SELECTION

1. Although Robert Browning's "My Last Duchess" (p. 726) is a more complex poem than Machan's, both use dramatic monologues to reveal character. How are the strategies in each poem similar?

A SAMPLE STUDENT RESPONSE

Alex Georges

Professor Myerov

English 200

2 October 2015

Tone in Katharyn Howd Machan's "Hazel Tells LaVerne"

"Tone," Michael Meyer writes, "is the writer's attitude toward the subject, the mood created by all the elements in the poem" (640) and is used to convey meaning and character. In her dramatic monologue, "Hazel Tells LaVerne," the poet Katharyn Howd Machan reveals through the persona of Hazel—a funny, tough-talking, no-nonsense cleaning lady—a satirical revision of "The Frog Prince" fairy tale. Hazel's attitude toward the possibility of a fairy-tale romance is evident in her response to the frog prince. She has no use for him or his offers "bout a golden ball / an how i can be a princess" (lines 11-12). If Hazel is viewed by the reader as a princess, it is clear from her words and tone that she is far from a traditional one.

Machan's word choice and humorous tone also reveal much about Hazel's personality and circumstances. Through the use of slang, alternate spellings, and the omission of punctuation, we learn a great deal about the character:

> well i screams
>
> ya little green pervert
>
> an i hitsm with my mop
>
> an has ta flush
>
> the toilet down three times
>
> me
>
> a princess (19-25)

Listening to her speak, the reader understands that Hazel, a cleaner at Howard Johnson's, does not have an extensive education. She speaks in the colloquial, running words into one another and using phrases like "ya little green pervert" (20) and "i screams" (19). The lack of complete sentences, capital letters, and punctuation adds to her informal tone. Hazel's speech defines her social status, brings out details of her personality, and gives the reader her view of herself. She is accustomed to the thankless daily grind of work and will not allow herself even a moment's fantasy of becoming a princess. It is a notion that she has to flush away—literally, has "ta flush . . . down three times." She tells LaVerne that the very idea of such fantasy is absurd to her, as she states in the final lines: "me / a princess" (24-25).

Works Cited

Machan, Katharyn Howd. "Hazel Tells LaVerne." Meyer 641–42.

Meyer, Michael, ed. *The Bedford Introduction to Literature*. 11th ed. Boston: Bedford/St. Martin's, 2016. Print.

Martín Espada (b. 1957)
Latin Night at the Pawnshop 1987

> **When I Write** "As a poet and a reader, I am most interested in the theme of justice. I am interested in poems that address justice vividly, concretely, specifically. Poets are, as Shelley put it, the 'unacknowledged legislators of the world.' We shouldn't leave justice to the lawyers and the politicians." — Martín Espada

Chelsea, Massachusetts
Christmas, 1987

The apparition of a salsa band
gleaming in the Liberty Loan
pawnshop window:

Golden trumpet,
silver trombone,
congas, maracas, tambourine,

all with price tags dangling
like the city morgue ticket
on a dead man's toe.

CONSIDERATIONS FOR CRITICAL THINKING AND WRITING

1. FIRST RESPONSE. What is "Latin" about this night at the pawnshop?
2. What kind of tone is created by the poet's word choice and by the poem's rhythm?
3. Does it matter that this apparition occurs on Christmas night? Why or why not?
4. What do you think is the central point of this poem? How do the speaker's attitude and tone change during the course of this next poem?

PAUL LAURENCE DUNBAR (1872–1906)

To a Captious Critic   1903

Dear critic, who my lightness so deplores,
Would I might study to be prince of bores,
Right wisely would I rule that dull estate —
But, sir, I may not; till you abdicate.

CONSIDERATIONS FOR CRITICAL THINKING AND WRITING

1. FIRST RESPONSE. How do Dunbar's vocabulary and syntax signal the level of diction used in the poem?
2. Describe the speaker's tone. How does it characterize the speaker as well as the critic?
3. CREATIVE RESPONSE. Using "To a Captious Critic" as a model, try writing a four-line witty reply to someone in your own life — perhaps a roommate, coach, teacher, waiter, dentist, or anyone else who provokes a strong response in you.

DICTION AND TONE IN FOUR LOVE POEMS

The first three of these love poems share the same basic situation and theme: a male speaker addresses a female (in the first poem it is a type of female) urging that love should not be delayed because time is short. This theme is as familiar in poetry as it is in life. In Latin this tradition is known as *carpe diem*, "seize the day." Notice how the poets' diction helps create a distinctive tone in each poem, even though the subject matter and central ideas are similar (although not identical) in all three.

ROBERT HERRICK (1591–1674)

To the Virgins, to Make Much of Time   1648

Gather ye rose-buds while ye may,
   Old Time is still a-flying;
And this same flower that smiles today,
   Tomorrow will be dying.

The glorious lamp of heaven, the sun,
   The higher he's a-getting,
The sooner will his race be run,
   And nearer he's to setting.

That age is best which is the first,
   When youth and blood are warmer;
But being spent, the worse, and worst
   Times still succeed the former.

Then be not coy, but use your time,
   And while ye may, go marry;
For having lost but once your prime,
   You may for ever tarry.

© Hulton-Deutsch Collection/Corbis.

CONSIDERATIONS FOR CRITICAL THINKING AND WRITING

1. FIRST RESPONSE. Would there be any change in meaning if the title of this poem were "To Young Women, to Make Much of Time"? Do you think the poem can apply to young men, too?

2. What do the virgins have in common with the flowers (lines 1–4) and the course of the day (5–8)?

3. How does the speaker develop his argument? What will happen to the virgins if they don't "marry"? Paraphrase the poem.

4. What is the tone of the speaker's advice?

The next poem was also written in the seventeenth century, but it includes some words that have changed in usage and meaning over the past three hundred years. The title of Andrew Marvell's "To His Coy Mistress" requires some explanation. "Mistress" does not refer to a married man's illicit lover but to a woman who is loved and courted—a sweetheart. Marvell uses "coy" to describe a woman who is reserved and shy rather than coquettish or flirtatious. Often such shifts in meanings over time are explained in the notes that accompany reprintings of poems. You should keep in mind, however, that it is helpful to have a reasonably thick dictionary available when you are reading poetry. The most thorough is the *Oxford English Dictionary* (*OED*), which provides histories of words. The *OED* is a multivolume leviathan, but there are other useful unabridged dictionaries and desk dictionaries and many are available online.

Knowing a word's original meaning can also enrich your understanding of why a contemporary poet chooses a particular word. In "Design" (p. 885), Robert Frost raises provocative questions about the nature of evil and the existence of God in his dark examination of a moth's death, all presented in unexpected images of whiteness. He ends the poem with a series of questions concerning what causes "death and blight," wondering if it is a "design of darkness to appall" or no design at all, a universe informed only by random meaninglessness. Frost's precise contemporary use of "appall" captures the sense of consternation and dismay that such a frightening contemplation of death might evoke, but a dictionary reveals some further relevant insights. The dictionary's additional information about the history of *appall* shows us why it is the perfect word to establish the overwhelming effect of the poem. The word comes from the Middle English *appallen*, meaning "to grow faint," and in Old French *apalir* means "to grow pale" or white. These meanings reinforce the powerful sense of death buried in the images of whiteness throughout the poem. Moreover, Frost's "appall" also echoes a funereal pall, or coffin, allowing the word to bear even more connotative weight. Knowing the origin of *appall* gives us the full heft of the poet's word choice.

Although some of the language in "To His Coy Mistress" requires annotations for the modern reader, this poem continues to serve as a powerful reminder that time is a formidable foe, even for lovers.

© Michael Nicholson/CORBIS.

ANDREW MARVELL (1621–1678)

To His Coy Mistress   1681

Had we but world enough, and time,
This coyness, lady, were no crime.
We would sit down, and think which way
To walk, and pass our long love's day.
Thou by the Indian Ganges'° side   5
Shouldst rubies find; I by the tide
Of Humber° would complain.° I would   *write love songs*
Love you ten years before the Flood,
And you should, if you please, refuse
Till the conversion of the Jews.   10
My vegetable love should grow°
Vaster than empires, and more slow;
An hundred years should go to praise
Thine eyes and on thy forehead gaze,
Two hundred to adore each breast,   15
But thirty thousand to the rest:
An age at least to every part,
And the last age should show your heart.
For, lady, you deserve this state,
Nor would I love at lower rate.   20
     But at my back I always hear
Time's wingèd chariot hurrying near;
And yonder all before us lie
Deserts of vast eternity.
Thy beauty shall no more be found,   25
Nor in thy marble vault shall sound
My echoing song; then worms shall try

---

5 *Ganges:* A river in India sacred to the Hindus.   7 *Humber:* A river that flows through Marvell's native town, Hull.   11 *My vegetable love . . . grow:* A slow, unconscious growth.

That long preserved virginity,
And your quaint honor turn to dust,
And into ashes all my lust.
The grave's a fine and private place,   30
But none, I think, do there embrace.
    Now, therefore, while the youthful hue
Sits on thy skin like morning dew,
And while thy willing soul transpires°   *breathes forth*   35
At every pore with instant fires,
Now let us sport us while we may,
And now, like amorous birds of prey,
Rather at once our time devour
Than languish in his slow-chapped° power.   *slow-jawed*   40
Let us roll all our strength and all
Our sweetness up into one ball,
And tear our pleasures with rough strife
Thorough° the iron gates of life.   *through*
Thus, though we cannot make our sun
Stand still, yet we will make him run.   45

Considerations for Critical Thinking and Writing

1. **FIRST RESPONSE.** Do you think this *carpe diem* poem is hopelessly dated, or does it speak to our contemporary concerns?

2. This poem is divided into a three-part argument. Briefly summarize each section: if (lines 1–20), but (21–32), therefore (33–46).

3. What is the speaker's tone in lines 1–20? How much time would he spend adoring his mistress? Is he sincere? How does he expect his mistress to respond to these lines?

4. How does the speaker's tone change beginning with line 21? What is his view of time in lines 21–32? What does this description do to the lush and leisurely sense of time in lines 1–20? How do you think his mistress would react to lines 21–32?

5. In the final lines of Herrick's "To the Virgins, to Make Much of Time" (p. 645), the speaker urges the virgins to "go marry." What does Marvell's speaker urge in lines 33–46? How is the pace of these lines (notice the verbs) different from that of the first twenty lines of the poem?

6. This poem is sometimes read as a vigorous but simple celebration of flesh. Is there more to the theme than that?

The third in this series of *carpe diem* poems is a twenty-first-century work. The language of Ann Lauinger's "Marvell Noir" is more immediately accessible than that of Marvell's "To His Coy Mistress"; an ordinary dictionary will quickly identify any words unfamiliar to a reader. But the title might require an online search or a dictionary of biography for the reference to Marvell, as well as a dictionary of allusions to provide a succinct description that explains the reference to film noir. An ***allusion*** is a brief cultural reference to a person, a place, a thing, an event, or an idea in history or literature. Allusive words, like connotative words, are both suggestive and economical; poets use allusions to conjure up biblical authority, scenes from Shakespeare's plays, historic figures, wars, great love stories, and anything else that might serve to deepen and enrich their own work. The title of "Marvell Noir" makes two allusions that an ordinary dictionary may not explain, because it alludes to Marvell's most famous poem, "To His Coy Mistress," and to dark crime films (*noir* is "black" in French) of the 1940s that were often filmed in black and white featuring tough-talking, cynical heroes — such as those portrayed by Humphrey Bogart — and hardened, cold women — like the characters played by Joan Crawford. Lauinger assumes that her reader will understand the allusions.

Allusions imply reading and cultural experiences shared by the poet and the reader. Literate audiences once had more in common than they do today because more people had similar economic, social, and educational backgrounds. But a judicious use of specialized dictionaries, encyclopedias, and online reference tools such as Google Search can help you decipher allusions that grow out of this body of experience. As you read more, you'll be able to make connections based on your own experiences with literature. In a sense, allusions make available what other human beings have deemed worth remembering, and that is certainly an economical way of supplementing and enhancing your own experience.

Lauinger's version of the *carpe diem* theme follows. What strikes you as particularly modern about it?

ANN LAUINGER (B. 1948)

Marvell Noir   2005

> **WHEN I READ** "As a writer, my best friends are some very dead poets. Reading them is what made me want to write, and re-reading them keeps me writing." — ANN LAUINGER

Sweetheart, if we had the time,
A week in bed would be no crime.
I'd light your Camels, pour your Jack;
You'd do shiatsu on my back.
When you got up to scramble eggs,   5
I'd write a sonnet to your legs,
And you could watch my stubble grow.
Yes, gorgeous, we'd take it slow.
I'd hear the whole sad tale again:
A roadhouse band; you can't trust men;   10
He set you up; you had to eat,
And bitter with the bittersweet
Was what they dished you; Ginger lied;
You weren't there when Sanchez died;
You didn't know the pearls were fake . . .   15
Aw, can it, sport! Make no mistake,
You're in it, doll, up to your eyeballs!
Tears? Please! You'll dilute our highballs,
And make that angel face a mess
For the nice Lieutenant. I confess   20
I'm nuts for you — but take the rap?
You must think I'm some other sap!
And, precious, I kind of wish I was.
Well, when they spring you, give a buzz;
Guess I'll get back to Archie's wife,   25
And you'll get twenty-five to life.
You'll have time then, more than enough,

To reminisce about the stuff
That dreams are made of, and the men
You suckered. Sadly, in the pen   30
Your kind of talent goes to waste.
But Irish bars are more my taste
Than iron ones: stripes ain't my style.
You're going down; I promise I'll
Come visit every other year.   35
Now kiss me, sweet — the squad car's here.

CONSIDERATIONS FOR CRITICAL THINKING AND WRITING

1. FIRST RESPONSE. How does Lauinger's poem evoke Marvell's *carpe diem* poem
   (p. 645) and the tough-guy tone of a "noir" narrative, a crime story or thriller
   that is especially dark?

2. Discuss the ways in which time is a central presence in the poem.

3. Explain the allusion to dreams in lines 28–29.

CONNECTION TO ANOTHER SELECTION

1. Compare the speaker's voice in this poem with that of the speaker in "To His
   Coy Mistress" (p. 647). What significant similarities and differences do you
   find?

This fourth love poem is a twentieth-century work in which the speaker's
voice is a woman's. How does it sound different from the way the men speak in
the previous three poems?

SHARON OLDS (B. 1942)

Last Night   1996

The next day, I am almost afraid.
Love? It was more like dragonflies
in the sun, 100 degrees at noon,
the ends of their abdomens stuck together, I
close my eyes when I remember. I hardly   5
knew myself, like something twisting and
twisting out of a chrysalis,
enormous, without language, all
head, all shut eyes, and the humming
like madness, the way they writhe away,   10
and do not leave, back, back,
away, back. Did I know you? No kiss,
no tenderness — more like killing, death-grip
holding to life, genitals
like violent hands clasped tight   15
barely moving, more like being closed
in a great jaw and eaten, and the screaming
I groan to remember it, and when we started

to die, then I refuse to remember,
the way a drunkard forgets. After,   20
you held my hands extremely hard as my
body moved in shudders like the ferry when its
axle is loosed past engagement, you kept me
sealed exactly against you, our hairlines
wet as the arc of a gateway after   25
a cloudburst, you secured me in your arms till I slept —
that was love, and we woke in the morning
clasped, fragrant, buoyant, that was
the morning after love.

CONSIDERATIONS FOR CRITICAL THINKING AND WRITING

1. FIRST RESPONSE. How is your response to this poem affected by the fact that the speaker is female? Explain why this is or isn't a *carpe diem* poem.

2. Comment on the descriptive passages of "Last Night." Which images seem especially vivid to you? How do they contribute to the poem's meaning?

3. Explain how the poem's tone changes from beginning to end.

CONNECTIONS TO OTHER SELECTIONS

1. How does the speaker's description of intimacy compare with Herrick's and Marvell's?

2. Compare the speaker's voice in Olds's poem with the voice you imagine for the coy mistress in Marvell's poem.

3. CRITICAL STRATEGIES. Read the section on formalist criticism (pp. 1645–47) in Chapter 51, "Critical Strategies for Reading," and compare the themes in Olds's poem and Philip Larkin's "A Study of Reading Habits" (p. 601) the way you think a feminist critic might analyze them.

Perspective

GENE WEINGARTEN (B. 1951), DAN WEINGARTEN (B. 1984), AND DAVID CLARK (B. 1960)

Barney & Clyde 2012

cartoonistgroup.com.

CONSIDERATIONS FOR CRITICAL THINKING AND WRITING

1. Did you get the joke? Probably not, but how does a Google search help you?

2. Additional strips of *Barney & Clyde* can be found on the Internet, which provides information about the comic's characters as well as its writers and illustrator. How does that information serve to characterize the type of humor in the strip?

3. Choose a poem from Chapter 41, "A Collection of Poems," that is rich in allusions and use the Internet to explain their function in the poem.

POEMS FOR FURTHER STUDY

WALT WHITMAN (1819–1892)

The Dalliance of the Eagles   1880

Skirting the river road, (my forenoon walk, my rest,)
Skyward in air a sudden muffled sound, the dalliance of the eagles,
The rushing amorous contact high in space together,
The clinching interlocking claws, a living, fierce, gyrating wheel,
Four beating wings, two beaks, a swirling mass tight grappling,   5
In tumbling turning clustering loops, straight downward falling,
Till o'er the river pois'd, the twain yet one, a moment's lull,
A motionless still balance in the air, then parting, talons loosing,
Upward again on slow-firm pinions slanting, their separate diverse flight,
She hers, he his, pursuing.   10

CONSIDERATIONS FOR CRITICAL THINKING AND WRITING

1. FIRST RESPONSE. Why do you think Whitman chose the word *dalliance* rather than, perhaps, *mating*?

2. List the verbs in the poem and comment on their effects in evoking the scene.

CONNECTION TO ANOTHER SELECTION

1. Compare Whitman's treatment of the eagles with Tennyson's description of "The Eagle" (p. 614). Which do you find more powerful? Why?

THOMAS HARDY (1840–1928)

The Convergence of the Twain   1912

Lines on the Loss of the "Titanic"°

I

In a solitude of the sea
Deep from human vanity,
And the Pride of Life that planned her, stilly couches she.

"*Titanic*": A luxurious ocean liner, reputed to be unsinkable, which sank after hitting an iceberg on its maiden voyage in 1912. Only a third of the 2,200 passengers survived.

II

Steel chambers, late the pyres
    Of her salamandrine fires,°   5
Cold currents thrid,° and turn to rhythmic tidal lyres.   *thread*

III

Over the mirrors meant
    To glass the opulent
The sea-worm crawls — grotesque, slimed, dumb, indifferent.

IV

Jewels in joy designed   10
    To ravish the sensuous mind
Lie lightless, all their sparkles bleared and black and blind.

V

Dim moon-eyed fishes near
    Gaze at the gilded gear
And query: "What does this vaingloriousness down here?"   15

VI

Well: while was fashioning
    This creature of cleaving wing,
The Immanent Will that stirs and urges everything

VII

Prepared a sinister mate
    For her — so gaily great —   20
A Shape of Ice, for the time far and dissociate.

VIII

And as the smart ship grew
    In stature, grace, and hue,
In shadowy silent distance grew the Iceberg too.

IX

Alien they seemed to be: 25
    No mortal eye could see
The intimate welding of their later history,

---

5 *salamandrine fires:* Salamanders were, according to legend, able to survive fire; hence the
ship's fires burned even though under water.

X

    Or sign that they were bent
    By paths coincident
On being anon twin halves of one august event,   30

XI

    Till the Spinner of the Years
    Said "Now!" And each one hears,
And consummation comes, and jars two hemispheres.

CONSIDERATIONS FOR CRITICAL THINKING AND WRITING

1. FIRST RESPONSE. Describe a contemporary disaster comparable to the sinking of the *Titanic*. How was your response to it similar to or different from the speaker's response to the fate of the *Titanic*?

2. How do the words used to describe the ship in this poem reveal the speaker's attitude toward the *Titanic*?

3. The diction of the poem suggests that the *Titanic* and the iceberg participate in something like an arranged marriage. What specific words imply this?

4. Who or what causes the disaster? Does the speaker assign responsibility?

DAVID R. SLAVITT (B. 1935)

Titanic   1983

Who does not love the *Titanic*?
If they sold passage tomorrow for that same crossing,
who would not buy?

To go down . . . We all go down, mostly
alone. But with crowds of people, friends, servants,   5
well fed, with music, with lights! Ah!

And the world, shocked, mourns, as it ought to do
and almost never does. There will be the books and movies
to remind our grandchildren who we were
and how we died, and give them a good cry.   10

Not so bad, after all. The cold
water is anesthetic and very quick.
The cries on all sides must be a comfort.

We all go: only a few, first-class.

CONSIDERATIONS FOR CRITICAL THINKING AND WRITING

1. FIRST RESPONSE. What, according to the speaker in this poem, is so compelling about the *Titanic*? Do you agree?

2. Discuss the speaker's tone. Is "Titanic" merely a sarcastic poem?

3. What is the effect of the poem's final line? What emotions does it elicit?

CONNECTIONS TO OTHER SELECTIONS

1. How does "Titanic" differ in its attitude toward opulence from "The Convergence of the Twain" (p. 652)?

2. Which poem, "Titanic" or "The Convergence of the Twain," is more emotionally satisfying to you? Explain why.

3. Compare the speakers' tones in "Titanic" and "The Convergence of the Twain."

4. **CRITICAL STRATEGIES.** Read the section on Marxist criticism (p. 1653) in Chapter 51, "Critical Strategies for Reading," and analyze the attitudes toward opulence that are manifested in the two poems.

JOANNE DIAZ (B. 1972)

On My Father's Loss of Hearing 2006

*I'd like to see more poems treat the deaf as being abled
differently, not lost or missing something, weakened,
deficient.   —from a listserv for the deaf*

Abled differently — so vague compared
with *deaf*, obtuse but true to history,
from *deave*: to deafen, stun, amaze with noise.

Perhaps that's what we've done — amazed him
with our sorrows and complaints, the stupid jabs,
the loneliness of boredom in the house,

Jason Reblando.

our wants so foreign to his own. What else
is there but loss? He's lost the sarcasm
in subtle jokes, the snarky dialogue

of British films eludes him, and phone calls   10
cast him adrift in that cochlear maze
that thrums and bristles even now, when

it doesn't have to: an unnecessary kind
of elegance, the vestige of a sense
no longer obligated to transmit   15

the crack of thawing ice that fills the yard's
wide dip in winter, or the silver scrape
of his dull rake in spring, its prongs' vibration

thrilled by grass. Imagine his desires
released like saffron pistils in the wind;   20
observe their trace against the cords of wood

he spent the summer splitting. See his quiet
flicker like a film, a Super-8
projected on the wall, and all of us

there, laughing on the porch without a sound.   25
No noisy cruelty, no baffled rage,
no aging children sullen in their lack.

CONSIDERATIONS FOR CRITICAL THINKING AND WRITING

1. FIRST RESPONSE. Why does the speaker prefer the word *deaf* to the phrase "abled differently" as a means of describing her father? Which description do you prefer? Why?

2. Explain how sound and silence move through the poem from beginning to end.

3. Choose a single word from each stanza that strikes you as particularly effective, and explain why you think Diaz chose it over other possibilities.

4. What do you make of the poem's final line? How does it relate to the tone of the rest of the poem?

CONNECTION TO ANOTHER SELECTION

1. Discuss the relationship between love and pain in "On My Father's Loss of Hearing" and in Theodore Roethke's "My Papa's Waltz" (p. 772).

DANUSHA LAMÉRIS (B. 1971)

Names 2014

What happens to the ones that fall out of favor:
the Dorises and Archibalds,
the Theodores and Eunices?
They all had their day,
once roamed the earth in multitudes   5
alongside Gerties and Wyatts —
at least one in every classroom.
Names written in neat block print,
scratched into tree bark,
engraved on heart-shaped lockets,   10
filling the morning paper
with weddings and engagements.
How could they have known
that one-by-one the Constances
and Clydes would disappear,   15
replaced by Jennifers, Jacobs,
Ashleys and Aidens.
That few would ever dance again,
corsages pinned to their breasts
or hear their names on the radio   20
whispered in dedication,
or uttered in darkness
by a breathless voice,
or even shouted out in anger —
"Seymour!"—   25
as they grabbed the keys and stormed out the door.
Each name fading quietly from daily life
as though it had never existed,

except for the letters etched into stone,
warmed by the sun   30
and at night, lit by a crescent moon.

Considerations for Critical Thinking and Writing

1. FIRST RESPONSE. What connotations do you think are associated with your own given name?
2. What names do you think are currently in and out of "favor"?
3. Why is the poem about more than just what its title indicates?

Connection to Another Selection

1. How do you think the speaker of "Names" would categorize the names in Katharyn Howd Machan's "Hazel Tells LaVerne" (p. 641).

Mary Oliver (b. 1935)

Oxygen   2005

Everything needs it: bone, muscles, and even,
while it calls the earth its home, the soul.
So the merciful, noisy machine

stands in our house working away in its
lung-like voice. I hear it as I kneel   5
before the fire, stirring with a

stick of iron, letting the logs
lie more loosely. You, in the upstairs room,
are in your usual position, leaning on your

right shoulder which aches   10
all day. You are breathing
patiently; it is a

beautiful sound. It is
your life, which is so close
to my own that I would not know   15

where to drop the knife of
separation. And what does this have to do
with love, except

everything? Now the fire rises
and offers a dozen, singing, deep-red   20
roses of flame. Then it settles

to quietude, or maybe gratitude, as it feeds
as we all do, as we must, upon the invisible gift:
our purest, sweet necessity: the air.

CONSIDERATIONS FOR CRITICAL THINKING AND WRITING

1. FIRST RESPONSE. Though this is a poem about someone who is seriously ill, its tone isn't sad. Why not?
2. What is the connection between the loved one's breathing and the fire? How does the speaker's choice of words to describe each connect them?
3. In what sense might this celebration of oxygen be considered a love poem?

CATHY SONG (B. 1955)

The Youngest Daughter 1983

The sky has been dark
for many years.
My skin has become as damp
and pale as rice paper
and feels the way   5
mother's used to before the drying sun
parched it out there in the fields.

    Lately, when I touch myself,
my hands react as if
I had just touched something   10
hot enough to burn.
My skin, aspirin-colored,
tingles with migraine. Mother
has been massaging the left side of my face
especially in the evenings   15
when it flares up.

This morning
her breathing was graveled,
her voice gruff with affection
when I took her into the bath.   20
She was in good humor,
making jokes about her great breasts,
floating in the milky water
like two walruses,
flaccid and whiskered around the nipples.   25
I scrubbed them with a sour taste
in my mouth, thinking:
six children and an old man
have sucked from these brown nipples.

I was almost tender   30
when I came to the blue bruises
that freckle her body,
places where she has been injecting insulin
for thirty years, ever since
I can remember. I soaped her slowly,   35
she sighed deeply, her eyes closed.

In the afternoons
when she has rested,
she prepares our ritual of tea and rice,
garnished with a shred of gingered fish,   40
a slice of pickled turnip
a token for my white body.
We eat in the familiar silence.
She knows I am not to be trusted,
even now planning my escape.   45
As I toast to her health
with the tea she has poured,
a thousand cranes curtain the window,
fly up in a sudden breeze.

Considerations for Critical Thinking and Writing

1. **FIRST RESPONSE.** Though the speaker is the youngest daughter in the family, how old do you think she is based on the description of her in the poem? What, specifically, makes you think so?

2. How would you characterize the relationship between mother and daughter? How are lines 44–45 ("She knows I am not to be trusted, / even now planning my escape") particularly revealing of the nature of the relationship?

3. Interpret the final four lines of the poem. Why do you think it ends with this image?

Angela Alaimo O'Donnell (b. 1960)

Messenger   2013

5PM
& again

you're calling
me to supper.

Across the red fence   5
you sing my name —

An-ge-la —
three notes

that rise and fall,
each a bright bell   10

knelling *now.*
Though I know

you are dead
as those days,

as that small girl   15
I used to be,

I'm still
running,

And you're still
calling me.   20

CONSIDERATIONS FOR CRITICAL THINKING AND WRITING

1. FIRST RESPONSE. Describe the speaker's relationship to her mother in the past and now.

2. Is the tone of the poem consistent throughout? Why or why not?

3. How does the diction transform the ordinary experience of a child being called for supper into something more significant?

CONNECTION TO ANOTHER SELECTION

1. Compare the themes of "Messenger" with the themes in Cathy Song's "The Youngest Daughter" (p. 658).

JOHN KEATS (1795–1821)
Ode on a Grecian Urn   1819

I

Thou still unravished bride of quietness,
    Thou foster-child of silence and slow time,
Sylvan° historian, who canst thus express
    A flowery tale more sweetly than our rhyme:
What leaf-fringed legend haunts about thy shape   5
    Of deities or mortals, or of both,
        In Tempe or the dales of Arcady?°
What men or gods are these? What maidens loath?
    What mad pursuit? What struggle to escape?
        What pipes and timbrels? What wild ecstasy?   10

II

Heard melodies are sweet, but those unheard
    Are sweeter; therefore, ye soft pipes, play on;
Not to the sensual ear, but, more endeared,
    Pipe to the spirit ditties of no tone:
Fair youth, beneath the trees, thou canst not leave   15
    Thy song, nor ever can those trees be bare;
        Bold Lover, never, never canst thou kiss,
Though winning near the goal — yet, do not grieve;
    She cannot fade, though thou hast not thy bliss,
        For ever wilt thou love, and she be fair!   20

3 *Sylvan:* Rustic. The urn is decorated with a forest scene.   7 *Tempe, Arcady:* Beautiful rural valleys in Greece.

III

Ah, happy, happy boughs! that cannot shed
  Your leaves, nor ever bid the Spring adieu;
And, happy melodist, unwearièd,
  For ever piping songs for ever new;
More happy love! more happy, happy love!   25
  For ever warm and still to be enjoyed,
    For ever panting, and for ever young;
All breathing human passion far above,
  That leaves a heart high-sorrowful and cloyed,
    A burning forehead, and a parching tongue.   30

IV

Who are these coming to the sacrifice?
  To what green altar, O mysterious priest,
Lead'st thou that heifer lowing at the skies,
  And all her silken flanks with garlands drest?
What little town by river or sea shore,   35
  Or mountain-built with peaceful citadel,
    Is emptied of this folk, this pious morn?
And, little town, thy streets for evermore
  Will silent be; and not a soul to tell
    Why thou art desolate, can e'er return.   40

V

O Attic° shape! Fair attitude! with brede°
  Of marble men and maidens overwrought,
With forest branches and the trodden weed;
  Thou, silent form, dost tease us out of thought
As doth eternity: Cold Pastoral!   45
  When old age shall this generation waste,
    Thou shalt remain, in midst of other woe
Than ours, a friend to man, to whom thou say'st,
  Beauty is truth, truth beauty — that is all
    Ye know on earth, and all ye need to know.   50

41 *Attic:* Possessing classic Athenian simplicity; *brede:* Design.

CONSIDERATIONS FOR CRITICAL THINKING AND WRITING

1. **FIRST RESPONSE.** What does the speaker's diction reveal about his attitude toward the urn in this ode? Does his view develop or change?
2. How is the happiness in stanza 3 related to the assertion in lines 11–12 that "Heard melodies are sweet, but those unheard / Are sweeter"?
3. What is the difference between the world depicted on the urn and the speaker's world?
4. What do lines 49 and 50 suggest about the relation of art to life? Why is the urn described as a "Cold Pastoral" (line 45)?

5. Which world does the speaker seem to prefer, the urn's or his own?

6. Describe the overall tone of the poem.

CONNECTIONS TO OTHER SELECTIONS

1. Write an essay comparing the view of time in this ode with that in Marvell's "To His Coy Mistress" (p. 647). Pay particular attention to the connotative language in each poem.

2. Compare the tone and attitude toward life in this ode with those in John Keats's "To Autumn" (p. 685).

GWENDOLYN BROOKS (1917–2000)

We Real Cool 1960

The Pool Players.
Seven at the Golden Shovel.

We real cool. We
Left school. We

Lurk late. We
Strike straight. We

Sing sin. We
Thin gin. We

Jazz June. We
Die soon.

CONSIDERATIONS FOR CRITICAL THINKING AND WRITING

1. FIRST RESPONSE. How does the speech of the pool players in this poem help to characterize them? What is the effect of the pronouns coming at the ends of the lines? How would the poem sound if the pronouns came at the beginnings of lines?

2. What is the author's attitude toward the players? Is there a change in tone in the last line?

3. How is the pool hall's name related to the rest of the poem and its theme?

JOAN MURRAY (B. 1945)

We Old Dudes 2006

We old dudes. We
White shoes. We

Golf ball. We
Eat mall. We

> **WHEN I READ** "Reading stretches your mind and imagination. It lets you discover what you like and admire. Sometimes after I read a poem, I want to write one. It's as if someone's speaking my language, and I want to converse." — JOAN MURRAY

Soak teeth. We
Palm Beach; We

Vote red. We
Soon dead.

CONSIDERATIONS FOR CRITICAL THINKING AND WRITING

1. FIRST RESPONSE. Consider the poem's humor. To what extent does it make a serious point?

2. What does the reference to Palm Beach tell you about these "old dudes"?

3. CREATIVE RESPONSE. Write a poem similar in style that characterizes your life as a student.

CONNECTION TO ANOTHER SELECTION

1. Compare the themes of "We Old Dudes" and Brooks's "We Real Cool." How do the two poems speak to each other?

ALICE JONES (B. 1949)

The Lungs   1997

WHEN I WRITE "The process of becoming a writer involves recognizing the desire to write, allowing ourselves to take the desire seriously, and then learning to recognize the obstacles we put in our own way." — ALICE JONES

In the tidal flux, the lobed pair avidly
    grasp the invisible.

Along oblique fissures, gnarled vascular roots
    anchor the puffed cushions,

soot-mottled froth, the pink segmented sponges
    that soak up the atmosphere,

then squeezed by the rising dome of the diaphragm's
    muscular bellows, exhale.

Braids of vessels and cartilage descend
    in vanishing smallness,   5

to grape clusters of alveoli, the sheerest
    of membranes, where oxygen

crosses the infinite cellular web, where air turns
    to blood, spirit to flesh,

in a molecular transubstantiation, to bring rich
    food to that red engine,

the heart, which like an equitable mother, pumps
    to each organ and appendage

according to need, so even the cells in the darkest
    corners can breathe.   10

CONSIDERATIONS FOR CRITICAL THINKING AND WRITING

1. FIRST RESPONSE. Why do you think the lines in this poem are arranged in pairs? How does the length of the sentences contribute to the poem's meaning?

2. Make a list of words and phrases from the poem that strike you as scientific, and compare those with a list of words that seem poetic. How do they compete or complement each other in terms of how they affect your reading?

3. Comment on the use of personification (see the glossary, p. 1716) in the poem.

CONNECTION TO ANOTHER SELECTION

1. Compare the diction and the ending in "The Lungs" with those of "The Foot" (p. 764), another poem by Jones.

LOUIS SIMPSON (1923–2012)

In the Suburbs 1963

There's no way out.
You were born to waste your life.
You were born to this middleclass life

As others before you
Were born to walk in procession
To the temple, singing.

CONSIDERATIONS FOR CRITICAL THINKING AND WRITING

1. FIRST RESPONSE. Is the title of this poem especially significant? What images does it conjure up for you?

2. What does the repetition in lines 2–3 suggest?

3. Discuss the possible connotative meanings of lines 5 and 6. Who are the "others before you"?

CONNECTION TO ANOTHER SELECTION

1. Write an essay on suburban life based on this poem and John Ciardi's "Suburban" (p. 1009).

GARRISON KEILLOR (B. 1942)

The Anthem 2006

If famous poets had written "The Star-Spangled Banner"

Whose flag this is I think I know
His house is being bombed now though
He will not see that I have come
To watch the twilight's ebbing glow.

My little horse must think it dumb,   5
The cannons' pandemonium,
The rockets bursting in the air,
The sound of bugle, fife, and drum.

He turns and shakes his derrière
To show me that he doesn't care   10
Who takes this battle flag or why,
When in the redness of the glare

I see the banner flying high
Through the tumult in the sky
And, knowing all is now okay,   15
We walk away, my horse and I.

The flag is lovely, hip hooray,
But I have things to do today,
Some here and others far away,
Before I stop to hit the hay.   20
—Robert Frost

CONSIDERATIONS FOR CRITICAL THINKING AND WRITING

1. FIRST RESPONSE. Explain why a familiarity with both "The Star-Spangled Banner" and Robert Frost's "Stopping by Woods on a Snowy Evening" (p. 881) is vital to an informed reading of Keillor's "Anthem."

2. Discuss the lines from each poem that Keillor appropriates for his own purposes.

3. What makes this poem humorous?

4. CREATIVE RESPONSE. "Anthem" is reprinted from an issue of the *Atlantic* (Jan.–Feb. 2006) in which Keillor also includes versions of "The Star-Spangled Banner" as if written by Emily Dickinson and by Billy Collins. (You might want to look those poems up.) Choose a poet whose style you find interesting and write a version of the anthem as if written by that poet.

A NOTE ON READING TRANSLATIONS

Sometimes translation can inadvertently be a comic business. Consider, for example, the discovery made by John Steinbeck's wife, Elaine, when in a Yokohama bookstore she asked for a copy of her husband's famous novel *The Grapes of Wrath* and learned that it had been translated into Japanese as *Angry Raisins*. Close but no cigar (perhaps translated as: Nearby, yet no smoke). As amusing as that *Angry Raisins* title is, it teaches an important lesson about the significance of a poet's or a translator's choices when crafting a poem: a powerful piece moves us through diction and tone, both built word by careful word. Translations are frequently regarded as merely vehicular, a way to arrive at the original work. It is, of course, the original work — its spirit, style, and meaning — that most readers expect to find in a translation. Even so, it is important to understand that a translation is *by nature* different from the original — and that despite that difference, a fine translation can be an important part of the journey and become part of the literary landscape itself. Reading a translation of a poem is not the same as reading the original, but neither is watching two different performances of *Hamlet*. The translator provides a reading of the poem in much the same way that a director shapes the play. Each interprets the text from a unique perspective.

Basically, there are two distinct approaches to translation: literal translations and adaptations. A literal translation sets out to create a word-for-word equivalent that is absolutely faithful to the original. As simple and direct as this method may sound, literal translations are nearly impossible over extended passages because of the structural differences between languages. Moreover, the meaning of a single word in one language may not exist in another language, or it may require a phrase, clause, or entire sentence to capture its implications. Adaptations of works offer broader, more open-ended approaches to translation. Unlike a literal translation, an adaptation moves beyond denotative meanings in an attempt to capture the spirit of a work so that its idioms, dialects, slang, and other conventions are re-created in the language of the translation.

The question we ask of an adaptation should not be "Is this exactly how the original reads?" Instead, we ask, "Is this an insightful, graceful rendering worth reading?" To translate poetry it is not enough to know the language of the original; it is also necessary that the translator be a poet. A translated poem is more than a collation of decisions based on dictionaries and grammars; it must also be poetry. However undefinable poetry may be, it is unmistakable in its intense use of language. Poems are not merely translated; they are savored.

Three Translations of a Poem by Sappho

Sappho, born about 630 B.C. and a native of the Greek island of Lesbos, is the author of a hymn to Aphrodite, the goddess of love and beauty in Greek myth. The three translations that follow suggest how widely translations can differ from one another. The first, by Henry T. Wharton, is intended to be a literal prose translation of the original Greek.

© Bettmann/Corbis.

SAPPHO (CA. 630 B.C.–CA. 570 B.C.)
Immortal Aphrodite of the broidered throne   date unknown

TRANSLATED BY HENRY T. WHARTON (1885)

Immortal Aphrodite of the broidered throne,
daughter of Zeus, weaver of wiles, I pray thee break
not my spirit with anguish and distress, O Queen.
But come hither, if ever before thou didst hear my

voice afar, and listen, and leaving thy father's golden house camest with chariot yoked, and fair fleet sparrows drew thee, flapping fast their wings around the dark earth, from heaven through mid sky. Quickly arrived they; and thou, blessed one, smiling with immortal countenance, didst ask What now is befallen me, and Why now I call, and What I in my mad heart most desire to see. "What Beauty now wouldst thou draw to love thee? Who wrongs thee, Sappho? For even if she flies she shall soon follow, and if she rejects gifts shall yet give, and if she loves not shall soon love, however loth." Come, I pray thee, now too, and release me from cruel cares; and all that my heart desires to accomplish, accomplish thou, and be thyself my ally.

Beautiful-throned, immortal Aphrodite

TRANSLATED BY THOMAS WENTWORTH HIGGINSON (1871)

Beautiful-throned, immortal Aphrodite,
Daughter of Zeus, beguiler, I implore thee,
Weigh me not down with weariness and anguish
    O Thou most holy!

Come to me now, if ever thou in kindness   5
Hearkenedst my words, — and often hast thou hearkened —
Heeding, and coming from the mansions golden
    Of thy great Father,

Yoking thy chariot, borne by the most lovely
Consecrated birds, with dusky-tinted pinions,   10
Waving swift wings from utmost heights of heaven
    Through the mid-ether;

Swiftly they vanished, leaving thee, O goddess,
Smiling, with face immortal in its beauty,
Asking why I grieved, and why in utter longing   15
    I had dared call thee;

Asking what I sought, thus hopeless in desiring,
Wildered in brain, and spreading nets of passion —
Alas, for whom? and saidst thou, "Who has harmed thee?
    "O my poor Sappho!   20

"Though now he flies, ere long he shall pursue thee;
"Fearing thy gifts, he too in turn shall bring them;
"Loveless to-day, to-morrow he shall woo thee,
    "Though thou shouldst spurn him."

Thus seek me now, O holy Aphrodite!   25
Save me from anguish; give me all I ask for,
Gifts at thy hand; and thine shall be the glory,
    Sacred protector!

Prayer to my lady of Paphos

TRANSLATED BY MARY BARNARD (1958)

Dapple-throned Aphrodite,
eternal daughter of God,
snare-knitter! Don't, I beg you,

cow my heart with grief! Come,
as once when you heard my far-   5
off cry and, listening, stepped

from your father's house to your
gold car, to yoke the pair whose
beautiful thick-feathered wings

oaring down mid-air from heaven   10
carried you to light swiftly
on dark earth; then, blissful one,

smiling your immortal smile
you asked, What ailed me now that
made me call you again? What   15

was it that my distracted
heart most wanted? "Whom has
Persuasion to bring round now

"to your love? Who, Sappho, is
unfair to you? For, let her   20
run, she will soon run after;

"if she won't accept gifts, she
will one day give them; and if
she won't love you — she soon will

"love, although unwillingly . . . "   25
If ever — come now! Relieve
this intolerable pain!

What my heart most hopes will
happen, make happen; you your-
self join forces on my side!   30

CONSIDERATIONS FOR CRITICAL THINKING AND WRITING

1. FIRST RESPONSE. Try rewriting Wharton's prose version in contemporary language. How does your prose version differ in tone from Wharton's?
2. Which of the two verse translations seems closer to Wharton's prose version? Explain your answer.
3. Discuss the images and metaphors in Higginson's and Barnard's versions. Which version is more appealing to you? Explain why.
4. Which version seems to you to be the most contemporary in its use of language? Explain your choice.

23

Images

I think poetry is always a kind of faith. It is the kind that I have.
—NATASHA TRETHEWEY

AP Photo/Rogelio V. Solis.

POETRY'S APPEAL TO THE SENSES

A poet, to borrow a phrase from Henry James, is one on whom nothing is lost. Poets take in the world and give us impressions of what they experience through images. An *image* is language that addresses the senses. The most common images in poetry are visual; they provide verbal pictures of the poets' encounters — real or imagined — with the world. But poets also create images that appeal to our other senses. Li Ho arouses several senses in this excerpt from "A Beautiful Girl Combs Her Hair":

Awake at dawn
she's dreaming
by cool silk curtains

fragrance of spilling hair
half sandalwood, half aloes

windlass creaking at the well
singing jade

These vivid images deftly blend textures, fragrances, and sounds that tease out the sensuousness of the moment. Images give us the physical world to experience in our imaginations. Some poems, like the following one, are written to do just that; they make no comment about what they describe.

WILLIAM CARLOS WILLIAMS (1883–1963)

Poem 1934

As the cat
climbed over
the top of

the jamcloset
first the right   5
forefoot

carefully
then the hind
stepped down

into the pit of   10
the empty
flowerpot

This poem defies paraphrase because it is all an image of agile movement. No statement is made about the movement; the title, "Poem"—really no title—signals Williams's refusal to comment on the movements. To impose a meaning on the poem, we'd probably have to knock over the flowerpot.

We experience the image in Williams's "Poem" more clearly because of how the sentence is organized into lines and groups of lines, or stanzas. Consider how differently the sentence is read if it is arranged as prose:

> As the cat climbed over the top of the jamcloset, first the right forefoot carefully then the hind stepped down into the pit of the empty flowerpot.

The poem's line and stanza division transforms what is essentially an awkward prose sentence into a rhythmic verbal picture. Especially when the poem is read aloud, this line and stanza division allows us to feel the image we see. Even the lack of a period at the end suggests that the cat is only pausing.

Images frequently do more than offer only sensory impressions, however. They also convey emotions and moods, as in the following poem's view of Civil War troops moving across a river.

WALT WHITMAN (1819–1892)

Cavalry Crossing a Ford 1865

A line in long array where they wind betwixt green islands,
They take a serpentine course, their arms flash in the sun — hark to the
    musical clank,
Behold the silvery river, in it the splashing horses loitering stop to drink,
Behold the brown-faced men, each group, each person, a picture, the
    negligent rest on the saddles,
Some emerge on the opposite bank, others are just entering the ford — while,
Scarlet and blue and snowy white,
The guidon flags flutter gaily in the wind.

CONSIDERATIONS FOR CRITICAL THINKING AND WRITING

1. **FIRST RESPONSE.** Do the colors and sounds establish the mood of this poem? What is the mood?
2. How would the poem's mood have been changed if Whitman had used "look" or "see" instead of "behold" (lines 3–4)?
3. Where is the speaker as he observes this troop movement?
4. Does "serpentine" in line 2 have an evil connotation in this poem? Explain your answer.

Whitman seems to capture momentarily all of the troop's actions, and through carefully chosen, suggestive details — really very few — he succeeds in making "each group, each person, a picture." Specific details, even when few are provided, give us the impression that we see the entire picture; it is as if those are the details we would remember if we had viewed the scene ourselves. Notice, too, that the movement of the "line in long array" is emphasized by the continuous winding syntax of the poem's lengthy lines.

Movement is also central to the next poem, in which action and motion are created through carefully chosen verbs.

DAVID SOLWAY (B. 1941)

Windsurfing 1993

It rides upon the wrinkled hide
of water, like the upturned hull
of a small canoe or kayak
waiting to be righted — yet its law
is opposite to that of boats,
it floats upon its breastbone and
brings whatever spine there is to light.

> **WHEN I READ** "The good poet always generates a sense of lexical surprise, an openness toward the unexpected, a feeling of novelty and delight."
> — DAVID SOLWAY

5

A thin shaft is slotted into place.
Then a puffed right-angle of wind
pushes it forward, out into the bay,   10
where suddenly it glitters into speed,
tilts, knifes up, and for the moment's
nothing but a slim projectile
of cambered fiberglass,
peeling the crests.   15

           The man's
clamped to the mast, taut as a guywire.
Part of the sleek apparatus
he controls, immaculate nerve
of balance, plunge and curvet,   20
he clinches all component movements
into single motion.
It bucks, stalls, shudders, yaws, and dips
its hissing sides beneath the surface
that sustains it, tensing   25
into muscle that nude ellipse
of lunging appetite and power.

And now the mechanism's wholly
dolphin, springing toward its prey
of spume and beaded sunlight,   30
tossing spray, and hits the vertex
of the wide, salt glare of distance,
and reverses.

           Back it comes through
a screen of particles,   35
scalloped out of water, shimmer
and reflection, the wind snapping
and lashing it homeward,
shearing the curve of the wave,
breaking the spell of the caught breath   40
and articulate play of sinew, to enter
the haven of the breakwater
and settle in a rush of silence.

Now the crossing drifts
in the husk of its wake   45
and nothing's the same again
as, gliding elegantly on a film of water,
the man guides
his brash, obedient legend
into shore.   50

CONSIDERATIONS FOR CRITICAL THINKING AND WRITING

1. **FIRST RESPONSE.** Draw a circle around the verbs that seem especially effective in conveying a strong sense of motion, and explain why they are effective.
2. How is the man made to seem to be one with his board and sail?
3. How does the rhythm of the poem change beginning with line 45?

CONNECTION TO ANOTHER SELECTION

1. Consider the effects of the images in "Windsurfing" and Robert Frost's "Birches" (p. 877). In an essay, explain how these images elicit the emotional responses they do.

"Windsurfing" is awash with images of speed, fluidity, and power. Even the calming aftermath of the breakwater is described as a "rush of silence," adding to the sense of motion that is detailed and expanded throughout the poem.

Poets choose details the way they choose the words to present those details: only telling ones will do. Consider the images Theodore Roethke uses in "Root Cellar."

THEODORE ROETHKE (1908–1963)

Root Cellar 1948

Nothing would sleep in that cellar, dank as a ditch,
Bulbs broke out of boxes hunting for chinks in the dark,
Shoots dangled and drooped,
Lolling obscenely from mildewed crates,
Hung down long yellow evil necks, like tropical snakes.   5
And what a congress of stinks!
Roots ripe as old bait,
Pulpy stems, rank, silo-rich,
Leaf-mold, manure, lime, piled against slippery planks.
Nothing would give up life: 10
Even the dirt kept breathing a small breath.

CONSIDERATIONS FOR CRITICAL THINKING AND WRITING

1. **FIRST RESPONSE.** Explain why you think this is a positive or negative rendition of a root cellar.
2. What senses are engaged by the images in this poem? Is the poem simply a series of sensations, or do the detailed images make some kind of point about the root cellar?
3. What controls the choice of details in the poem? Why isn't there, for example, a rusty shovel leaning against a dirt wall or a worn gardener's glove atop one of the crates?

4. Look up *congress* in a dictionary for its denotative meanings. Explain why "congress of stinks" (line 6) is especially appropriate given the nature of the rest of the poem's imagery.

5. What single line in the poem suggests a theme?

6. CREATIVE RESPONSE. Try writing a poem of ten lines or so that consists of a series of evocative images that creates a strong impression about something you know well.

The tone of the images and mood of the speaker are consistent in Roethke's "Root Cellar." In Matthew Arnold's "Dover Beach," however, they shift as the theme is developed.

MATTHEW ARNOLD (1822–1888)

Dover Beach 1867

The sea is calm tonight.
The tide is full, the moon lies fair
Upon the straits; — on the French coast the light
Gleams and is gone; the cliffs of England stand,
Glimmering and vast, out in the tranquil bay.   5
Come to the window, sweet is the night-air!
Only, from the long line of spray
Where the sea meets the moon-blanched land,
Listen! you hear the grating roar
Of pebbles which the waves draw back, and fling,   10
At their return, up the high strand,
Begin, and cease, and then again begin,
With tremulous cadence slow, and bring
The eternal note of sadness in.

Sophocles long ago   15
Heard it on the Aegean, and it brought
Into his mind the turbid ebb and flow
Of human misery;° we
Find also in the sound a thought,
Hearing it by this distant northern sea.   20

The Sea of Faith
Was once, too, at the full, and round earth's shore
Lay like the folds of a bright girdle furled.
But now I only hear
Its melancholy, long, withdrawing roar,   25
Retreating, to the breath
Of the night-wind, down the vast edges drear
And naked shingles° of the world.   *pebble beaches*

Ah, love, let us be true
To one another! for the world, which seems   30

15–18 *Sophocles ... misery:* In *Antigone* (lines 656–77), Sophocles likens the disasters that beset the house of Oedipus to a "mounting tide."

To lie before us like a land of dreams,
So various, so beautiful, so new,
Hath really neither joy, nor love, nor light,
Nor certitude, nor peace, nor help for pain;
And we are here as on a darkling plain   35
Swept with confused alarms of struggle and flight,
Where ignorant armies clash by night.

CONSIDERATIONS FOR CRITICAL THINKING AND WRITING

1. FIRST RESPONSE. Discuss what you consider to be this poem's central point. How do the speaker's descriptions of the ocean work toward making that point?

2. Contrast the images in lines 4–8 and 9–13. How do they reveal the speaker's mood? To whom is he speaking?

3. What is the cause of the "sadness" in line 14? What is the speaker's response to the ebbing "Sea of Faith"? Is there anything to replace his sense of loss?

4. What details of the beach seem related to the ideas in the poem? How is the sea used differently in lines 1–14 and 21–28?

5. Describe the differences in tone between lines 1–8 and 35–37. What has caused the change?

6. CRITICAL STRATEGIES. Read the section on mythological strategies (pp. 1657–59) in Chapter 51, "Critical Strategies for Reading," and discuss how you think a mythological critic might make use of the allusion to Sophocles in this poem.

CONNECTION TO ANOTHER SELECTION

1. Explain how the images in Wilfred Owen's "Dulce et Decorum Est" (p. 681) develop further the ideas and sentiments suggested by Arnold's final line concerning "ignorant armies clash[ing] by night."

Consider the appetite for images displayed in the celebration of poetry in the following poem.

RUTH FORMAN (B. 1968)

Poetry Should Ride the Bus   1993

poetry should hopscotch in a polka dot dress
wheel cartwheels
n hold your hand
when you walk past the yellow crackhouse

poetry should wear bright red lipstick
n practice kisses in the mirror
for all the fine young men with fades
shootin craps around the corner
poetry should dress in fine plum linen suits
n not be so educated that it don't stop in

Photograph by Christine Bennett, www
.cbimages.org.

every now n then to sit on the porch
and talk about the comins and goins of the world

poetry should ride the bus
in a fat woman's Safeway bag
between the greens n chicken wings   15
to be served with tuesday's dinner

poetry should drop by a sweet potato pie
ask about the grandchildren
n sit through a whole photo album
on a orange plastic covered lazy boy with no place to go   20

poetry should sing red revolution love songs
that massage your scalp
and bring hope to your blood
when you think you're too old to fight

yeah   25
poetry should whisper electric blue magic
all the years of your life
never forgettin to look you in the soul
every once in a while
n smile   30

CONSIDERATIONS FOR CRITICAL THINKING AND WRITING

1. FIRST RESPONSE. How do the images in each stanza reveal the speaker's attitude toward poetry? Do you agree with the poem's ideas about what poetry should do and be?

2. What does the poem's diction tell you about the speaker?

3. Discuss the tone of this poem and why you think it does or does not work.

CONNECTION TO ANOTHER SELECTION

1. How does Forman's speaker's view of poetry compare with that of the speaker in Billy Collins's "Introduction to Poetry" (p. 607)?

POEMS FOR FURTHER STUDY

AMY LOWELL (1874–1925)

The Pond 1919

Cold, wet leaves
Floating on moss-colored water,
And the croaking of frogs —
Cracked bell-notes in the twilight.

CONSIDERATIONS FOR CRITICAL THINKING AND WRITING

1. FIRST RESPONSE. This poem is not a complete sentence. What is missing? Does it matter in terms of understanding what is described by the images?

2. What senses are stimulated by the images? Which sense seems to be the most dominant in the poem? Why?

3. CREATIVE RESPONSE. Is the title of the poem necessary to convey its meaning? Choose an appropriate alternate title and explain how it subtly suggests something different from "The Pond."

ADELAIDE CRAPSEY (1878–1914)

November Night   1913

Listen . . .

With faint dry sound,
Like steps of passing ghosts,
The leaves, frost-crisp'd, break from the trees
And fall.

CONSIDERATIONS FOR CRITICAL THINKING AND WRITING

1. FIRST RESPONSE. Which senses are evoked in the poem? What sort of tone do the words produce?

2. Explain whether or not you think "November Night" has a theme.

CONNECTION TO ANOTHER SELECTION

1. Compare the use of images and their effects in this poem and in E. E. Cummings's "l(a" (p. 603).

RUTH FAINLIGHT (B. 1931)

Crocuses   2006

Pale, bare, tender stems rising
from the muddy winter-faded grass,

shivering petals the almost luminous
blue and mauve of bruises on the naked

bodies of men, women, children
herded into a forest clearing

before the shouted order, crack of gunfire,
final screams and prayers and moans.

CONSIDERATIONS FOR CRITICAL THINKING AND WRITING

1. FIRST RESPONSE. Comment on Fainlight's choice of title. What effect does it have on your reading of the poem?

2. Trace your response to each image in the poem and describe the poem's tone as it moves from line to line.

3. CREATIVE RESPONSE. Try writing an eight-line poem in the style of Fainlight's based on images that gradually but radically shift in tone.

MARY ROBINSON (1758–1800)

London's Summer Morning   1806

Who has not wak'd to list° the busy sounds	*listen to*
Of summer's morning, in the sultry smoke	
Of noisy London? On the pavement hot	
The sooty chimney-boy, with dingy face	
And tatter'd covering, shrilly bawls his trade,	5
Rousing the sleepy housemaid. At the door	
The milk-pail rattles, and the tinkling bell	
Proclaims the dustman's office; while the street	
Is lost in clouds impervious. Now begins	
The din of hackney-coaches, waggons, carts;	10
While tinmen's shops, and noisy trunk-makers,	
Knife-grinders, coopers, squeaking cork-cutters,	
Fruit-barrows, and the hunger-giving cries	
Of vegetable venders, fill the air.	
Now ev'ry shop displays its varied trade,	15
And the fresh-sprinkled pavement cools the feet	
Of early walkers. At the private door	
The ruddy housemaid twirls the busy mop,	
Annoying the smart 'prentice, or neat girl,	
Tripping with band-box° lightly. Now the sun	*hatbox* 20
Darts burning splendour on the glitt'ring pane,	
Save where the canvas awning throws a shade	
On the gay merchandize. Now, spruce and trim,	
In shops (where beauty smiles with industry),	
Sits the smart damsel; while the passenger	25
Peeps thro' the window, watching ev'ry charm.	
Now pastry dainties catch the eye minute	
Of humming insects, while the limy snare	
Waits to enthral them. Now the lamp-lighter	
Mounts the tall ladder, nimbly vent'rous,	30
To trim the half-fill'd lamp; while at his feet	
The pot-boy° yells discordant! All along	*drink server*
The sultry pavement, the old-clothes-man cries	
In tones monotonous, and side-long views	
The area for his traffic: now the bag	35
Is slily open'd, and the half-worn suit	
(Sometimes the pilfer'd treasure of the base	
Domestic spoiler), for one half its worth,	
Sinks in the green abyss. The porter now	
Bears his huge load along the burning way;	40
And the poor poet wakes from busy dreams,	
To paint the summer morning.	

Considerations for Critical Thinking and Writing

1. **FIRST RESPONSE.** How effective is this picture of a London summer morning in 1806? Which images do you find particularly effective?
2. How does the end of the poem bring us full circle to its beginning? What effect does this structure have on your understanding of the poem?
3. **CREATIVE RESPONSE.** Try writing about the start of your own day — in the dormitory, at home, at the start of a class — using a series of images that provide a vivid sense of what happens and how you experience it.

Connection to Another Selection

1. How does Robinson's description of London differ from William Blake's "London," the next poem? What would you say is the essential difference in purpose between the two poems?

WILLIAM BLAKE (1757–1827)

London 1794

I wander through each chartered° street,   *defined by law*
Near where the chartered Thames does flow,
And mark in every face I meet
Marks of weakness, marks of woe.

In every cry of every man,   5
In every Infant's cry of fear,
In every voice, in every ban,
The mind-forged manacles I hear.

How the Chimney-sweeper's cry
Every black'ning Church appalls;   10
And the hapless Soldier's sigh
Runs in blood down Palace walls.

But most through midnight streets I hear
How the youthful Harlot's curse
Blasts the new-born Infant's tear,   15
And blights with plagues the Marriage hearse.

Considerations for Critical Thinking and Writing

1. **FIRST RESPONSE.** What feelings do the visual images in this poem suggest to you?
2. What is the predominant sound heard in the poem?
3. What is the meaning of line 8? What is the cause of the problems that the speaker sees and hears in London? Does the speaker suggest additional causes?
4. The image in lines 11 and 12 cannot be read literally. Comment on its effectiveness.
5. How does Blake's use of denotative and connotative language enrich this poem's meaning?
6. An earlier version of Blake's last stanza appeared this way:

> But most the midnight harlot's curse
> From every dismal street I hear,

Weaves around the marriage hearse
And blasts the new-born infant's tear.

Examine carefully the differences between the two versions. How do Blake's revisions affect his picture of London life? Which version do you think is more effective? Why?

A SAMPLE STUDENT RESPONSE

Anna Tamara

Professor Burton

English 211

30 September 2015

Imagery in William Blake's "London" and Mary Robinson's

"London's Summer Morning"

Both William Blake and Mary Robinson use strong imagery to examine and bring to life the city of London, yet each writer paints a very different picture. The images in both poems "[address] the senses," as Meyer writes (669). But while Blake's images depict a city weighed down by oppression and poverty, Robinson's images are lighter, happier, and, arguably, idealized. Both poems use powerful imagery in very different ways to establish theme.

In Blake's poem, oppression and social discontent are defined by the speaker, who sees "weakness" and "woe" (line 4) in the faces he meets; he hears cries of men and children and "mind-forged manacles" (8). And, through imagery, the poem makes a political statement:

> How the Chimney-sweeper's cry
>
> Every black'ning Church appalls;
>
> And the hapless Soldier's sigh
>
> Runs in blood down Palace walls. (9-12)

These images indicate the speaker's dark view of the religious and governmental institutions that he believes cause the city's suffering. The "black'ning Church" and bloody "Palace walls" can be seen to represent misused power and corruption, while the "manacles" are the rules and physical and psychological burdens that lead to societal ills. In Blake's view of London, children are sold into servitude (as chimney sweeps) and soldiers pay in blood.

Tamara 2

Robinson's poem, on the other hand, offers the reader a pleasant view of a sunny London morning through a different series of images. The reader hears "the tinkling bell" (7) and sees a bright moment in which "the sun / Darts burning splendour on the glitt'ring pane" (20-21). Even the chimney-boy is shown in a rosy glow. Though he is described as having a "dingy face / And tatter'd covering," he wakes the "sleepy" house servant when he "shrilly bawls his trade" (4-6). In contrast to the chimney-sweep of Blake's "London," Robinson's boy is painted as a charming character who announces the morning amid a backdrop of happy workers. Also unlike Blake's London, Robinson's is a city of contentment in which a "ruddy housemaid twirls the busy mop" (18) . . .

Tamara 4

Works Cited

Blake, William. "London." Meyer 679.

Meyer, Michael, ed. *The Bedford Introduction to Literature*. 11th ed. Boston: Bedford/St. Martin's, 2016. Print.

Robinson, Mary. "London's Summer Morning." Meyer 678.

WILFRED OWEN (1893–1918)

Dulce et Decorum Est   1920

Bent double, like old beggars under sacks,
Knock-kneed, coughing like hags, we cursed through sludge,
Till on the haunting flares we turned our backs,
And towards our distant rest began to trudge.
Men marched asleep. Many had lost their boots,   5
But limped on, blood-shod. All went lame, all blind;
Drunk with fatigue; deaf even to the hoots
Of gas-shells dropping softly behind.

Gas! GAS! Quick, boys! — An ecstasy of fumbling,
Fitting the clumsy helmets just in time,   10

But someone still was yelling out and stumbling
And flound'ring like a man in fire or lime. —
Dim through the misty panes and thick green light,
As under a green sea, I saw him drowning.

In all my dreams before my helpless sight   15
He plunges at me, guttering, choking, drowning.
If in some smothering dreams, you too could pace
Behind the wagon that we flung him in,
And watch the white eyes writhing in his face,
His hanging face, like a devil's sick of sin,   20
If you could hear, at every jolt, the blood
Come gargling from the froth-corrupted lungs
Obscene as cancer, bitter as the cud
Of vile, incurable sores on innocent tongues, —
My friend, you would not tell with such high zest   25
To children ardent for some desperate glory,
The old lie: *Dulce et decorum est*
Pro patria mori.

CONSIDERATIONS FOR CRITICAL THINKING AND WRITING

1. FIRST RESPONSE. The Latin quotation in lines 27 and 28 is from Horace: "It is sweet and fitting to die for one's country." Owen served as a British soldier during World War I and was killed. Is this poem unpatriotic? What is its purpose?

2. Which images in the poem are most vivid? To which senses do they speak?

3. Describe the speaker's tone. What is his relationship to his audience?

4. How are the images of the soldiers in this poem different from the images that typically appear in recruiting posters?

PATRICIA SMITH (B. 1955)

What It's Like to Be a Black Girl (for Those of You Who Aren't) 1991

First of all, it's being 9 years old and
feeling like you're not finished, like your
edges are wild, like there's something,
everything, wrong. it's dropping food coloring
in your eyes to make them blue and suffering   5
their burn in silence. it's popping a bleached
white mophead over the kinks of your hair and
primping in front of the mirrors that deny your
reflection. it's finding a space between your
legs, a disturbance at your chest, and not knowing 10
what to do with the whistles. it's jumping
double dutch until your legs pop, it's sweat
and vaseline and bullets, it's growing tall and
wearing a lot of white, it's smelling blood in
your breakfast, it's learning to say fuck with   15

grace but learning to fuck without it, it's
flame and fists and life according to motown,
it's finally having a man reach out for you
then caving in
around his fingers.   20

CONSIDERATIONS FOR CRITICAL THINKING AND WRITING

1. **FIRST RESPONSE.** Describe the speaker's tone. What images in particular contribute to it? How do you account for the selected tone?

2. How does the speaker characterize her life? On which elements of it does she focus?

3. Discuss the poem's final image. What sort of emotions does it elicit in you?

CHARLES SIMIC (B. 1938)

Fork   1969

This strange thing must have crept
Right out of hell.
It resembles a bird's foot.
Worn around the cannibal's neck.

As you hold it in your hand,
As you stab with it into a piece of meat,
It is possible to imagine the rest of the bird:
Its head which like your fist
Is large, bald, beakless, and blind.

CONSIDERATIONS FOR CRITICAL THINKING AND WRITING

1. **FIRST RESPONSE.** How is the speaker's tone revealed by the images that describe the fork?

2. Explain how the final two lines broaden the poem's themes.

SEAMUS HEANEY (1939–2013)

The Pitchfork   1991

Of all implements, the pitchfork was the one
That came near to an imagined perfection:
When he tightened his raised hand and aimed with it,
It felt like a javelin, accurate and light.

So whether he played the warrior or the athlete   5
Or worked in earnest in the chaff and sweat,
He loved its grain of tapering, dark-flecked ash
Grown satiny from its own natural polish.

Riveted steel, turned timber, burnish, grain,
Smoothness, straightness, roundness, length and sheen.   10

Sweat-cured, sharpened, balanced, tested, fitted.
The springiness, the clip and dart of it.

And then when he thought of probes that reached the
        farthest,
He would see the shaft of a pitchfork sailing past
Evenly, imperturbably through space,   15
Its prongs starlit and absolutely soundless —

But has learned at last to follow that simple lead
Past its own aim, out to an other side
Where perfection — or nearness to it — is imagined
Not in the aiming but the opening hand.   20

CONSIDERATIONS FOR CRITICAL THINKING AND WRITING

1. FIRST RESPONSE. Provide an alternate title that you think captures the poem's meaning.

2. How do the images make this pitchfork more than merely one of many "implements"?

3. What does the thrower of the pitchfork learn in lines 13-16?

CONNECTION TO ANOTHER SELECTION

1. The images used to describe the pitchfork in this poem and the fork in Charles Simic's "Fork" (p. 683) invest significance in these otherwise ordinary objects. Write an essay that discusses how the images in these two poems give these objects qualities that are not inherent in either pitchforks or forks.

SALLY CROFT (B. 1935)
Home-Baked Bread   1981

Nothing gives a household a greater sense of stability and common comfort than the aroma of cooling bread. Begin, if you like, with a loaf of whole wheat, which requires neither sifting nor kneading, and go on from there to more cunning triumphs.
                                                    — *The Joy of Cooking*

What is it she is not saying?
Cunning triumphs. It rings
of insinuation. Step into my kitchen,
I have prepared a cunning triumph
for you. Spices and herbs   5
sealed in this porcelain jar,

a treasure of my great-aunt
who sat up past midnight
in her Massachusetts bedroom
when the moon was dark. Come,   10
rest your feet. I'll make
you tea with honey and slices

of warm bread spread with peach butter.
I picked the fruit this morning
still fresh with dew. The fragrance   15
is seductive? I hoped you would say that.
See how the heat rises
when the bread opens. Come,

we'll eat together, the small flakes
have scarcely any flavor. What cunning   20
triumphs we can discover in my upstairs room
where peach trees breathe their sweetness
beside the open window and
sun lies like honey on the floor.

CONSIDERATIONS FOR CRITICAL THINKING AND WRITING

1. FIRST RESPONSE. Why does the speaker in this poem seize on the phrase "cunning triumphs" from the *Joy of Cooking* excerpt?

2. Distinguish between the voice we hear in lines 1–3 and the second voice in lines 3–24. Who is the "you" in the poem?

3. Why is the word "insinuation" an especially appropriate choice in line 3?

4. How do the images in lines 20–24 bring together all the senses evoked in the preceding lines?

5. CREATIVE RESPONSE. Write a paragraph — or stanza — that describes the sensuous (and perhaps sensual) qualities of a food you enjoy.

JOHN KEATS (1795–1821)

To Autumn   1819

I

Season of mists and mellow fruitfulness,
    Close bosom-friend of the maturing sun;
Conspiring with him how to load and bless
    With fruit the vines that round the thatch-eves run;
To bend with apples the mossed cottage-trees,   5
    And fill all fruit with ripeness to the core;
        To swell the gourd, and plump the hazel shells
    With a sweet kernel; to set budding more,
And still more, later flowers for the bees,
Until they think warm days will never cease,   10
        For summer has o'er-brimmed their clammy cells.

II

Who hath not seen thee oft amid thy store?
    Sometimes whoever seeks abroad may find
Thee sitting careless on a granary floor,
    Thy hair soft-lifted by the winnowing wind;   15
Or on a half-reaped furrow sound asleep,

Drowsed with the fume of poppies, while thy hook°   *scythe*
   Spares the next swath and all its twinèd flowers:
And sometimes like a gleaner thou dost keep
   Steady thy laden head across a brook;   20
   Or by a cider-press, with patient look,
     Thou watchest the last oozings hours by hours.

III

Where are the songs of spring? Ay, where are they?
   Think not of them, thou hast thy music too —
While barred clouds bloom the soft-dying day,   25
   And touch the stubble-plains with rosy hue;
Then in a wailful choir the small gnats mourn
   Among the river swallows,° borne aloft   *willows*
     Or sinking as the light wind lives or dies;
And full-grown lambs loud bleat from hilly bourn;°   *territory* 30
   Hedge-crickets sing; and now with treble soft
   The redbreast whistles from a garden-croft,
     And gathering swallows twitter in the skies.

CONSIDERATIONS FOR CRITICAL THINKING AND WRITING

1. **FIRST RESPONSE.** How is autumn made to seem like a person in each stanza of this ode?

2. Which senses are most emphasized in each stanza?

3. How is the progression of time expressed in the ode?

4. How does the imagery convey tone? Which words have especially strong connotative values?

5. What is the speaker's view of death?

CONNECTIONS TO OTHER SELECTIONS

1. Compare this poem's tone and perspective on death with those of Robert Frost's "After Apple-Picking" (p. 876).

2. Write an essay comparing the significance of this poem's images of "mellow fruitfulness" (line 1) with that of the images of ripeness in Theodore Roethke's "Root Cellar" (p. 673). Explain how the images in each poem lead to very different feelings about the same phenomenon.

Perspective

T. E. HULME (1883–1917)

On the Differences between Poetry and Prose 1924

In prose as in algebra concrete things are embodied in signs or counters which are moved about according to rules, without being visualized at all in the process. There are in prose certain type situations and arrangements of words, which move as automatically into certain other arrangements as do functions in algebra. One only changes the *X*'s and the *Y*'s back into physical things at the end of the process. Poetry, in one aspect at any rate, may be considered as an effort to avoid this characteristic of prose. It is not a counter language, but a visual concrete one. It is a compromise for a language of intuition which would hand over sensations bodily. It always endeavors to arrest you, and to make you continuously see a physical thing, to prevent you gliding through an abstract process. It chooses fresh epithets and fresh metaphors, not so much because they are new, and we are tired of the old, but because the old cease to convey a physical thing and become abstract counters. A poet says a ship "coursed the seas" to get a physical image, instead of the counter word "sailed." Visual meanings can only be transferred by the new bowl of metaphor; prose is an old pot that lets them leak out. Images in verse are not mere decoration, but the very essence of an intuitive language. Verse is a pedestrian taking you over the ground, prose — a train which delivers you at a destination.

From "Romanticism and Classicism," in *Speculations,*
edited by Herbert Read

CONSIDERATIONS FOR CRITICAL THINKING AND WRITING

1. What distinctions does Hulme make between poetry and prose? Which seems to be the most important difference?

2. Write an essay that discusses Hulme's claim that poetry "is a compromise for a language of intuition which would hand over sensations bodily."

24

Figures of Speech

© Bettmann/Corbis.

Like a piece of ice on a hot stove the
poem must ride on its own melting.
— ROBERT FROST

Figures of speech are broadly defined as a way of saying one thing in terms of
something else. An overeager funeral director might, for example, be described
as a vulture. Although figures of speech are indirect, they are designed to clarify, not obscure, our understanding of what they describe. Poets frequently use
them because, as Emily Dickinson said, the poet's work is to "tell all the Truth
but tell it slant" to capture the reader's interest and imagination. But figures of
speech are not limited to poetry. Hearing them, reading them, or using them is
as natural as using language itself.

Suppose that in the middle of a class discussion concerning the economic
causes of World War II your history instructor introduces a series of statistics
by saying, "Let's get down to brass tacks." Would anyone be likely to expect
a display of brass tacks for students to examine? Of course not. To interpret
the statement literally would be to wholly misunderstand the instructor's point
that the time has come for a close look at the economic circumstances leading
to the war. A literal response transforms the statement into the sort of hilari-
ously bizarre material often found in a sketch by Woody Allen.

The class does not look for brass tacks because, in a nutshell, they understand that the instructor is speaking figuratively. They would understand, too, that in the preceding sentence "in a nutshell" refers to brevity and conciseness rather than to the covering of a kernel of a nut. Figurative language makes its way into our everyday speech and writing as well as into literature because it is a means of achieving color, vividness, and intensity.

Consider the difference, for example, between these two statements:

Literal: The diner strongly expressed anger at the waiter.
Figurative: The diner leaped from his table and roared at the waiter.

The second statement is more vivid because it creates a picture of ferocious anger by likening the diner to some kind of wild animal, such as a lion or tiger. By comparison, "strongly expressed anger" is neither especially strong nor especially expressive; it is flat. Not all figurative language avoids this kind of flatness, however. Figures of speech such as "getting down to brass tacks" and "in a nutshell" are clichés because they lack originality and freshness. Still, they suggest how these devices are commonly used to give language some color, even if that color is sometimes a bit faded.

There is nothing weak about William Shakespeare's use of figurative language in the following passage from *Macbeth*. Macbeth has just learned that his wife is dead, and he laments her loss as well as the course of his own life.

WILLIAM SHAKESPEARE (1564–1616)

From Macbeth *(Act V, Scene v)*   1605–1606

Tomorrow, and tomorrow, and tomorrow
Creeps in this petty pace from day to day
To the last syllable of recorded time;
And all our yesterdays have lighted fools
The way to dusty death. Out, out, brief candle!   5
Life's but a walking shadow, a poor player,
That struts and frets his hour upon the stage,
And then is heard no more. It is a tale
Told by an idiot, full of sound and fury,
Signifying nothing.   10

This passage might be summarized as "life has no meaning," but such a brief paraphrase does not take into account the figurative language that reveals the depth of Macbeth's despair and his view of the absolute meaninglessness of life. By comparing life to a "brief candle," Macbeth emphasizes the darkness and death that surround human beings. The light of life is too brief and unpredictable to be of any comfort. Indeed, life for Macbeth is a "walking shadow," futilely playing a role that is more farcical than dramatic, because life is, ultimately, a desperate story filled with pain and devoid of significance. What the figurative language provides, then, is the emotional force of Macbeth's assertion; his comparisons are disturbing because they are so apt.

The remainder of this chapter discusses some of the most important figures of speech used in poetry. A familiarity with them will help you to understand how poetry achieves its effects.

SIMILE AND METAPHOR

The two most common figures of speech are simile and metaphor. Both compare things that are ordinarily considered unlike each other. A *simile* makes an explicit comparison between two things by using words such as *like, as, than, appears,* or *seems*: "A sip of Mrs. Cook's coffee is like a punch in the stomach." The force of the simile is created by the differences between the two things compared. There would be no simile if the comparison were stated this way: "Mrs. Cook's coffee is as strong as the cafeteria's coffee." This is a literal comparison because Mrs. Cook's coffee is compared with something like it, another kind of coffee. Consider how simile is used in this poem.

MARGARET ATWOOD (B. 1939)

you fit into me   1971

you fit into me
like a hook into an eye

a fish hook
an open eye

© Sophie Bassouls/Sygma/Corbis.

If you blinked on a second reading, you got the point of this poem because you recognized that the simile "like a hook into an eye" gives way to a play on words in the final two lines. There the hook and eye, no longer a pleasant domestic image of a clothing fastener or door latch that fits closely together, become a literal, sharp fishhook and a human eye. The wordplay qualifies the simile and drastically alters the tone of this poem by creating a strong and unpleasant surprise.

A *metaphor*, like a simile, makes a comparison between two unlike things, but it does so implicitly, without words such as *like* or *as*: "Mrs. Cook's coffee is a punch in the stomach." Metaphor asserts the identity of dissimilar things. Macbeth tells us that life *is* a "brief candle," life *is* "a walking shadow," life *is* "a poor player," life *is* "a tale / Told by an idiot." Metaphor transforms people, places, objects, and ideas into whatever the poet imagines them to be, and if metaphors are effective, the reader's experience, understanding, and appreciation of what is described are enhanced. Metaphors are frequently more demanding than similes because they are not signaled by particular words. They are both subtle and powerful.

Here is a poem about presentiment, a foreboding that something terrible is about to happen.

EMILY DICKINSON (1830–1886)

Presentiment — is that long Shadow — on the lawn —　ca. 1863

Presentiment — is that long Shadow — on the lawn —
Indicative that Suns go down —

The notice to the startled Grass
That Darkness — is about to pass —

The metaphors in this poem define the abstraction "Presentiment." The sense of foreboding that Dickinson expresses is identified with a particular moment — the moment when darkness is just about to envelop an otherwise tranquil, ordinary scene. The speaker projects that fear onto the "startled Grass" so that it seems any life must be frightened by the approaching "Shadow" and "Darkness" — two richly connotative words associated with death. The metaphors obliquely tell us ("tell it slant" was Dickinson's motto, remember) that presentiment is related to a fear of death, and, more important, the metaphors convey the feelings that attend that idea.

Some metaphors are more subtle than others because their comparison of terms is less explicit. Notice the difference between the following two metaphors, both of which describe a shaggy derelict refusing to leave the warmth of a hotel lobby: "He was a mule standing his ground" is a quite explicit comparison. The man is a mule; X is Y. But this metaphor is much more covert: "He brayed his refusal to leave." This second version is an *implied metaphor* because it does not explicitly identify the man with a mule. Instead it hints at or alludes to the mule. Braying is associated with mules and is especially appropriate in this context because of the mule's reputation for stubbornness. Implied metaphors can slip by readers, but they offer the alert reader the energy and resonance of carefully chosen, highly concentrated language.

Some poets write extended comparisons in which part or all of the poem consists of a series of related metaphors or similes. Extended metaphors are more common than extended similes. In "Catch" (p. 596), Robert Francis creates an *extended metaphor* that compares poetry to a game of catch. The entire poem is organized around this comparison. Because these comparisons are at work throughout the entire poem, they are called *controlling metaphors*. Extended comparisons can serve as a poem's organizing principle; they are also a reminder that in good poems metaphor and simile are not merely decorative but inseparable from what is expressed.

Notice the controlling metaphor in this poem, published posthumously by a woman whose contemporaries identified her more as a wife and mother than as a poet. Bradstreet's first volume of poetry, *The Tenth Muse*, was published by her brother-in-law in 1650 without her prior knowledge.

ANNE BRADSTREET (CA. 1612–1672)

The Author to Her Book 1678

Thou ill-formed offspring of my feeble brain,
Who after birth did'st by my side remain,
Till snatched from thence by friends, less wise than true,
Who thee abroad exposed to public view;
Made thee in rags, halting, to the press to trudge,   5
Where errors were not lessened, all may judge.
At thy return my blushing was not small,
My rambling brat (in print) should mother call;
I cast thee by as one unfit for light,
Thy visage was so irksome in my sight;   10
Yet being mine own, at length affection would
Thy blemishes amend, if so I could:
I washed thy face, but more defects I saw,
And rubbing off a spot, still made a flaw.
I stretched thy joints to make thee even feet,   15
Yet still thou run'st more hobbling than is meet;
In better dress to trim thee was my mind,
But nought save homespun cloth in the house I find.
In this array, 'mongst vulgars may'st thou roam;
In critics' hands beware thou dost not come;   20
And take thy way where yet thou are not known.
If for thy Father asked, say thou had'st none;
And for thy Mother, she alas is poor,
Which caused her thus to send thee out of door.

The extended metaphor likening her book to a child came naturally
to Bradstreet and allowed her to regard her work both critically and affectionately. Her conception of the book as her child creates just the right tone of
amusement, self-deprecation, and concern.

The controlling metaphor in the following poem is identified by the title.

RICHARD WILBUR (B. 1921)

The Writer 1976

In her room at the prow of the house
Where light breaks, and the windows are tossed with linden,
My daughter is writing a story.

I pause in the stairwell, hearing
From her shut door a commotion of typewriter-keys   5
Like a chain hauled over a gunwale.

Young as she is, the stuff
Of her life is a great cargo, and some of it heavy:
I wish her a lucky passage.

But now it is she who pauses,   10
As if to reject my thought and its easy figure.
A stillness greatens, in which

The whole house seems to be thinking,
And then she is at it again with a bunched clamor
Of strokes, and again is silent.   15

I remember the dazed starling
Which was trapped in that very room, two years ago;
How we stole in, lifted a sash

And retreated, not to affright it;
And how for a helpless hour, through the crack of the door,   20
We watched the sleek, wild, dark

And iridescent creature
Batter against the brilliance, drop like a glove
To the hard floor, or the desk-top,

And wait then, humped and bloody,   25
For the wits to try it again; and how our spirits
Rose when, suddenly sure,

It lifted off from a chair-back,
Beating a smooth course for the right window
And clearing the sill of the world.   30

It is always a matter, my darling,
Of life or death, as I had forgotten. I wish
What I wished you before, but harder.

CONSIDERATIONS FOR CRITICAL THINKING AND WRITING

1. **FIRST RESPONSE.** How does the speaker reveal affection for the daughter? What makes it authentic rather than sentimental?

2. In what sense do you think lines 1–11 represent an "easy figure" to the speaker?

3. Describe the effect of Wilbur's second extended metaphor concerning the "dazed starling" (line 16). How does it convey the poem's major ideas?

CONNECTION TO ANOTHER SELECTION

1. Compare the speaker's use of metaphor in "The Writer" with the father's method of offering advice in Jan Beatty's "My Father Teaches Me to Dream" (p. 1033). What's the essential difference between how the two parents express themselves?

OTHER FIGURES

Perhaps the humblest figure of speech — if not one of the most familiar — is the pun. A *pun* is a play on words that relies on a word having more than one meaning or sounding like another word. For example, "A fad is in one era and out the other" is the sort of pun that produces obligatory groans. But most of us find pleasant and interesting surprises in puns. Here's one that has a slight edge to its humor.

EDMUND CONTI (B. 1929)

Pragmatist 1985

Apocalypse soon
Coming our way
Ground zero at noon
Halve a nice day.

Grimly practical under the circumstances, the pragmatist divides the familiar cheerful cliché by half. As simple as this poem is, its tone is mixed because it makes us laugh and wince at the same time.

Puns can be used to achieve serious effects as well as humorous ones. Although we may have learned to underrate puns as figures of speech, it is a mistake to underestimate their power and the frequency with which they appear in poetry. A close examination, for example, of Henry Reed's "Naming of Parts" (p. 725), Robert Frost's "Design" (p. 885), or almost any lengthy passage from a Shakespeare play will confirm the value of puns.

Synecdoche is a figure of speech in which part of something is used to signify the whole: a neighbor is a "wagging tongue" (a gossip); a criminal is placed "behind bars" (in prison). Less typically, synecdoche refers to the whole used to signify the part: "Germany invaded Poland"; "Princeton won the fencing match." Clearly, certain individuals participated in these activities, not all of Germany or Princeton. Another related figure of speech is **metonymy**, in which something closely associated with a subject is substituted for it: "She preferred the silver screen [motion pictures] to reading." "At precisely ten o'clock the paper shufflers [office workers] stopped for coffee."

Synecdoche and metonymy may overlap and are therefore sometimes difficult to distinguish. Consider this description of a disapproving minister entering a noisy tavern: "As those pursed lips came through the swinging door, the atmosphere was suddenly soured." The pursed lips signal the presence of the minister and are therefore a synecdoche, but they additionally suggest an inhibiting sense of sin and guilt that makes the bar patrons feel uncomfortable. Hence the pursed lips are also a metonymy, as they are in this context so closely connected with religion. Although the distinction between synecdoche and metonymy can be useful, a figure of speech is usually labeled a metonymy when it overlaps categories.

Knowing the precise term for a figure of speech is, finally, less important than responding to its use in a poem. Consider how metonymy and synecdoche convey the tone and meaning of the following poem.

DYLAN THOMAS (1914–1953)

The Hand That Signed the Paper   1936

© Hulton-Deutsch Collection/Corbis.

The hand that signed the paper felled a city;
Five sovereign fingers taxed the breath,
Doubled the globe of dead and halved a
    country;
These five kings did a king to death.

The mighty hand leads to a sloping shoulder,
The finger joints are cramped with chalk;
A goose's quill has put an end to murder
That put an end to talk.

The hand that signed the treaty bred a fever,
And famine grew, and locusts came;   10
Great is the hand that holds dominion over
Man by a scribbled name.

The five kings count the dead but do not soften
The crusted wound nor stroke the brow;
A hand rules pity as a hand rules heaven;   15
Hands have no tears to flow.

The "hand" in this poem is a synecdoche for a powerful ruler because it is a part of someone used to signify the entire person. The "goose's quill" is a metonymy that also refers to the power associated with the ruler's hand. By using these figures of speech, Thomas depersonalizes and ultimately dehumanizes the ruler. The final synecdoche tells us that "Hands have no tears to flow." It makes us see the political power behind the hand as remote and inhuman. How is the meaning of the poem enlarged when the speaker says, "A hand rules pity as a hand rules heaven"?

One of the ways writers energize the abstractions, ideas, objects, and animals that constitute their created worlds is through *personification*, the attribution of human characteristics to nonhuman things: temptation pursues the innocent; trees scream in the raging wind; mice conspire in the cupboard. We are not explicitly told that these things are people; instead, we are invited to see that they behave like people. Perhaps it is human vanity that makes personification a frequently used figure of speech. Whatever the reason, personification, a form of metaphor that connects the nonhuman with the human, makes the world understandable in human terms. Consider this concise example from William Blake's *The Marriage of Heaven and Hell*, a long poem that takes delight in attacking conventional morality: "Prudence is a rich ugly old maid courted by Incapacity." By personifying prudence, Blake transforms what is usually considered a virtue into a comic figure hardly worth emulating.

Often related to personification is another rhetorical figure called **apostrophe**, an address either to someone who is absent and therefore cannot hear the speaker or to something nonhuman that cannot comprehend. Apostrophe provides an opportunity for the speaker of a poem to think aloud, and often the thoughts expressed are in a formal tone. John Keats, for example, begins "Ode on a Grecian Urn" (p. 660) this way: "Thou still unravished bride of quietness." Apostrophe is frequently accompanied by intense emotion that is signaled by phrasing such as "O Life." In the right hands — such as Keats's — apostrophe can provide an intense and immediate voice in a poem, but when it is overdone or extravagant it can be ludicrous. Modern poets are more wary of apostrophe than their predecessors because apostrophizing strikes many self-conscious twenty-first-century sensibilities as too theatrical. Thus modern poets tend to avoid exaggerated situations in favor of less charged though equally meditative moments, as in this next poem, with its amusing, half-serious cosmic twist.

JANICE TOWNLEY MOORE (B. 1939)

To a Wasp   1984

You must have chortled
finding that tiny hole
in the kitchen screen. Right
into my cheese cake batter
you dived,   5
no chance to swim ashore,
no saving spoon,
the mixer whirring
your legs, wings, stinger,
churning you into such   10
delicious death.
Never mind the bright April day.
Did you not see
rising out of cumulus clouds
That fist aimed at both of us?   15

> **WHEN I WRITE** "I began writing poetry as a freshman in college. I wrote using poetic diction and sometimes rhyme. Then I discovered 'modern poetry.' Seeing what was published in literary magazines quickly changed my style."
> — JANICE TOWNLEY MOORE

Moore's apostrophe "To a Wasp" is based on the simplest of domestic circumstances; there is almost nothing theatrical or exaggerated in the poem's tone until "That fist" in the last line, when exaggeration takes center stage. As a figure of speech, exaggeration is known as **overstatement** or **hyperbole** and adds emphasis without intending to be literally true: "The teenage boy ate everything in the house." Notice how the speaker of Andrew Marvell's "To His Coy Mistress" (p. 647) exaggerates his devotion in the following overstatement:

> An hundred years should go to praise
> Thine eyes and on thy forehead gaze,
> Two hundred to adore each breast,
> But thirty thousand to the rest:

That comes to 30,500 years. What is expressed here is heightened emotion, not deception.

The speaker also uses the opposite figure of speech, **understatement**, which says less than is intended. In the next section he sums up why he cannot take 30,500 years to express his love:

> The grave's a fine and private place,
> But none, I think, do there embrace.

The speaker is correct, of course, but by deliberately understating — saying "I think" when he is actually certain — he makes his point, that death will overtake their love, all the more emphatic. Another powerful example of understatement appears in the final line of Randall Jarrell's "The Death of the Ball Turret Gunner" (p. 638), when the disembodied voice of the machine-gunner describes his death in a bomber: "When I died they washed me out of the turret with a hose."

Paradox is a statement that initially appears to be self-contradictory but that, on closer inspection, turns out to make sense: "The pen is mightier than the sword." In a fencing match, anyone would prefer the sword, but if the goal is to win the hearts and minds of people, the art of persuasion can be more compelling than swordplay. To resolve the paradox, it is necessary to discover the sense that underlies the statement. If we see that "pen" and "sword" are used as metonymies for writing and violence, then the paradox rings true. **Oxymoron** is a condensed form of paradox in which two contradictory words are used together. Combinations such as "sweet sorrow," "silent scream," "sad joy," and "cold fire" indicate the kinds of startling effects that oxymorons can produce. Paradox is useful in poetry because it arrests a reader's attention by its seemingly stubborn refusal to make sense, and once a reader has penetrated the paradox, it is difficult to resist a perception so well earned. Good paradoxes are knotty pleasures. Here is a simple but effective one.

TAJANA KOVICS (B. 1985)

Text Message   2011

> Because I think you're nearly perfect,
> I want to love you best:
> And since absence makes the heart grow fonder,
> We should see each other less.

As the title suggests, the medium is part of the implicit subtext in this quatrain. Consider how the very idea of romantic love is conveyed and built on separation rather than intimacy in this witty paradox.

The following poems are rich in figurative language. As you read and study them, notice how their figures of speech vivify situations, clarify ideas, intensify emotions, and engage your imagination. Although the terms for the various figures discussed in this chapter are useful for labeling the particular devices used in poetry, they should not be allowed to get in the way of your response to a poem. Don't worry about rounding up examples of figurative language. First relax and let the figures work their effects on you. Use the terms as a means of taking you further into poetry, and they will serve your reading well.

POEMS FOR FURTHER STUDY

GARY SNYDER (B. 1930)

How Poetry Comes to Me 1992

It comes blundering over the
Boulders at night, it stays
Frightened outside the
Range of my campfire
I go to meet it at the
Edge of the light

CONSIDERATIONS FOR CRITICAL THINKING AND WRITING

1. FIRST RESPONSE. How does personification in this poem depict the creative process?

2. Why do you suppose Snyder makes each successive line shorter?

3. CREATIVE RESPONSE. How would eliminating the title change your understanding of the poem? Substitute another title that causes you to reinterpret it.

A SAMPLE STUDENT RESPONSE

Jennifer Jackson

Professor Kahane

English 215

16 October 2015

Metaphor in Gary Snyder's "How Poetry Comes to Me"

"A metaphor," Michael Meyer writes, "makes a comparison between two unlike things . . . implicitly, without words such as *like* or *as*" (690). In his poem "How Poetry Comes to Me," Gary Snyder uses metaphor to compare poetic inspiration and creativity with a kind of wild creature.

In this work, poetry itself is both an ungraceful beast and a timid animal. It is something big and unwieldy, that "comes blundering over the / Boulders at night" (lines 1-2). The word "blunder" suggests that poetic inspiration moves clumsily, blindly—not knowing where it will go next—and somewhat dangerously. Yet it is hesitant and "stays / Frightened outside the / Range of [the] campfire" (2-4). According to Snyder's poem, the creature poetry comes only partway to meet the poet; the poet has to go to meet it on its terms, "at the / Edge of the light" (5-6). The metaphor of the poem as wild animal tells the reader that poetic inspiration is elusive and unpredictable. It must be sought out carefully or it will run back over the boulders, by the way it came. . . .

Works Cited

Meyer, Michael, ed. *The Bedford Introduction to Literature*. 11th ed. Boston: Bedford/St. Martin's, 2016. Print.

Snyder, Gary. "How Poetry Comes to Me." Meyer 698.

Martín Espada (b. 1957)

The Mexican Cabdriver's Poem for His Wife, Who Has Left Him   2000

We were sitting in traffic
on the Brooklyn Bridge,
so I asked the poets
in the backseat of my cab
to write a poem for you.   5

They asked
if you are like the moon
or the trees.

I said no,
she is like the bridge   10
when there is so much traffic
I have time
to watch the boats
on the river.

Considerations for Critical Thinking and Writing

1. **First response.** What do you think is the speaker's attitude toward the cabdriver?

2. Explore the potential meanings of the similes concerning the moon, trees, and the bridge. How does the bridge differ from the other two?

Connection to Another Selection

1. Compare the source of poetry in this poem and in Gary Snyder's "How Poetry Comes to Me" (p. 698).

William Carlos Williams (1883–1963)

To Waken an Old Lady   1921

Old age is
a flight of small
cheeping birds
skimming
bare trees   5
above a snow glaze.
Gaining and failing
they are buffeted
by a dark wind —
But what?   10
On harsh weedstalks

the flock has rested,
the snow
is covered with broken
seedhusks   15
and the wind tempered
by a shrill
piping of plenty.

CONSIDERATIONS FOR CRITICAL THINKING AND WRITING

1. FIRST RESPONSE. Consider the images and figures of speech in this poem
   and explain why you think it is a positive or negative assessment of
   old age.
2. How does the title relate to the rest of the poem?

ERNEST SLYMAN (B. 1946)

Lightning Bugs   1988

In my backyard,
They burn peepholes in the night
And take snapshots of my house.

CONSIDERATIONS FOR CRITICAL THINKING AND WRITING

1. FIRST RESPONSE. Explain why the title is essential to this poem.
2. What makes the description of the lightning bugs effective? How do the second and third lines complement each other?
3. CREATIVE RESPONSE. As Slyman has done, take a simple, common fact of nature
   and make it vivid by using a figure of speech to describe it.

> WHEN I WRITE "Only on very rare occasions is a poem complete in a first draft. The first draft of a
> poem can sit for a long time waiting for its other half, or its meaning. Save everything you write,
> no matter how unhappy you are with it. You often won't see the beauty until later."
> — JUDY PAGE HEITZMAN

JUDY PAGE HEITZMAN (B. 1952)

The Schoolroom on the Second Floor of the Knitting Mill   1991

While most of us copied letters out of books,
Mrs. Lawrence carved and cleaned her nails.
Now the red and buff cardinals at my back-room window
make me miss her, her room, her hallway,
even the chimney outside   5
that broke up the sky.

In my memory it is afternoon.
Sun streams in through the door
next to the fire escape where we are lined up
getting our coats on to go out to the playground,   10
the tether ball, its towering height, the swings.
She tells me to make sure the line
does not move up over the threshold.
That would be dangerous.
So I stand guard at the door.   15
Somehow it happens
the way things seem to happen when we're not really looking,
or we are looking, just not the right way.
Kids crush up like cattle, pushing me over the line.

Judy is not a good leader is all Mrs. Lawrence says.   20
She says it quietly. Still, everybody hears.
Her arms hang down like sausages.
I hear her every time I fail.

CONSIDERATIONS FOR CRITICAL THINKING AND WRITING

1. FIRST RESPONSE. Does your impression of Mrs. Lawrence change from the beginning to the end of the poem? How so?

2. How can line 2 be read as an implied metaphor?

3. Discuss the use of similes in the poem. How do they contribute to the poem's meaning?

STEPHEN CRANE (1871–1900)

The Wayfarer   1899

The wayfarer
Perceiving the pathway to truth
Was struck with astonishment.
It was thickly grown with weeds.
"Ha," he said,   5
"I see that none has passed here
"In a long time."
Later he saw that each weed
Was a singular knife.
"Well," he mumbled at last,   10
"Doubtless there are other roads."

CONSIDERATIONS FOR CRITICAL THINKING AND WRITING

1. FIRST RESPONSE. How does the metaphor in this poem produce its theme?

2. Why do you think the person is described as a "wayfarer" rather than simply as a "traveler"?

1. Discuss how metaphors create meaning in "The Wayfarer" and in Robert Frost's "The Road Not Taken" (p. 871).

WILLIAM WORDSWORTH (1770–1850)

London, 1802   1802

Milton!° thou should'st be living at this hour:
England hath need of thee: she is a fen
Of stagnant waters: altar, sword, and pen,
Fireside, the heroic wealth of hall and bower,
Have forfeited their ancient English dower   5
Of inward happiness. We are selfish men;
Oh! raise us up, return to us again;
And give us manners, virtue, freedom, power.
Thy soul was like a star, and dwelt apart:
Thou hadst a voice whose sound was like the sea: 10
Pure as the naked heavens, majestic, free,
So didst thou travel on life's common way,
In cheerful godliness; and yet thy heart
The lowliest duties on herself did lay.

1 *Milton:* John Milton (1608–1674), poet, famous especially for his religious epic *Paradise Lost* and his defense of political freedom.

CONSIDERATIONS FOR CRITICAL THINKING AND WRITING

1. FIRST RESPONSE. Describe the poem's tone. Is it nostalgic, angry, or something else?

2. Explain the metonymies in lines 3–6 of this poem. What is the speaker's assessment of England?

3. How would the effect of the poem be different if it were in the form of an address to Wordsworth's contemporaries rather than an apostrophe to Milton? What qualities does Wordsworth attribute to Milton by the use of figurative language?

4. CRITICAL STRATEGIES. Read the section on literary history criticism (pp. 1651–55) in Chapter 51, "Critical Strategies for Reading," and use the Internet to find out about the state of London in 1802. How does the poem reflect or refute the social values of its time?

JIM STEVENS (B. 1922)

Schizophrenia   1992

It was the house that suffered most.

It had begun with slamming doors, angry feet scuffing the carpets,
dishes slammed onto the table,
greasy stains spreading on the cloth.

Certain doors were locked at night,   5
feet stood for hours outside them,
dishes were left unwashed, the cloth
disappeared under a hardened crust.

The house came to miss the shouting voices,
the threats, the half-apologies, noisy   10
reconciliations, the sobbing that followed.

Then lines were drawn, borders established,
some rooms declared their loyalties,
keeping to themselves, keeping out the other.
The house divided against itself.   15

Seeing cracking paint, broken windows,
the front door banging in the wind,
the roof tiles flying off, one by one,
the neighbors said it was a madhouse.

It was the house that suffered most.   20

CONSIDERATIONS FOR CRITICAL THINKING AND WRITING

1. FIRST RESPONSE. What is the effect of personifying the house in this poem?

2. How are the people who live in the house characterized? What does their behavior reveal about them? How does the house respond to them?

3. Comment on the title. If the title were missing, what, if anything, would be missing from the poem? Explain your answer.

JOHN DONNE (1572–1631)

A Valediction: Forbidding Mourning   1611

As virtuous men pass mildly away,
   And whisper to their souls to go,
While some of their sad friends do say,
   The breath goes now, and some say, no:

So let us melt, and make no noise,   5
   No tear-floods, nor sigh-tempests move;
'Twere profanation of our joys
   To tell the laity our love.

Moving of th' earth° brings harms and fears,   *earthquakes*
   Men reckon what it did and meant,   10
But trepidation of the spheres,°
   Though greater far, is innocent.

---

11 *trepidation of the spheres:* According to Ptolemaic astronomy, the planets sometimes moved violently, as in earthquakes, but these movements were not felt by people on Earth.

Dull sublunary° lovers' love
    (Whose soul is sense) cannot admit
Absence, because it doth remove   15
    Those things which elemented° it.   *composed*

But we by a love so much refined,
    That ourselves know not what it is,
Inter-assured of the mind,
    Care less, eyes, lips, and hands to miss.   20

Our two souls therefore, which are one,
    Though I must go, endure not yet
A breach, but an expansion,
    Like gold to airy thinness beat.

If they be two, they are two so   25
    As stiff twin compasses are two;
Thy soul the fixed foot, makes no show
    To move, but doth, if th' other do.

And though it in the center sit,
    Yet when the other far doth roam,   30
It leans, and hearkens after it,
    And grows erect, as that comes home.

Such wilt thou be to me, who must
    Like th' other foot, obliquely run;
Thy firmness makes my circle just,°   35
    And makes me end, where I begun.

13 *sublunary:* Under the moon; hence, mortal and subject to change.   35 *circle just:* The circle is a traditional symbol of perfection.

CONSIDERATIONS FOR CRITICAL THINKING AND WRITING

1. **FIRST RESPONSE.** A valediction is a farewell. Donne wrote this poem for his wife before leaving on a trip to France. What kind of "mourning" is the speaker forbidding?

2. Explain how the simile in lines 1–4 is related to the couple in lines 5–8. Who is described as dying?

3. How does the speaker contrast the couple's love to "sublunary lovers' love" (line 13)?

4. Explain the similes in lines 24 and 25–36.

LINDA PASTAN (B. 1932)

Marks   1978

My husband gives me an A
for last night's supper,
an incomplete for my ironing,

a B plus in bed.
My son says I am average,   5
an average mother, but if
I put my mind to it
I could improve.
My daughter believes
in Pass/Fail and tells me   10
I pass. Wait 'til they learn
I'm dropping out.

CONSIDERATIONS FOR CRITICAL THINKING AND WRITING

1. FIRST RESPONSE. Explain the appropriateness of the controlling metaphor in this poem. How does it reveal the woman's relationship to her family?

2. Discuss the meaning of the title.

3. How does the last line serve as the climax of both the woman's story and the poem's controlling metaphor?

KAY RYAN (B. 1945)

Learning   1996

Whatever must be learned
is always on the bottom,
as with the law of drawers
and the necessary item.
It isn't pleasant,
whatever they tell children,
to turn out on the floor
the folded things in them.

CONSIDERATIONS FOR CRITICAL THINKING AND WRITING

1. FIRST RESPONSE. Why does the speaker consider learning to be unpleasant and difficult?

2. Why is unfolding what must be learned an especially apt metaphor?

LUCILLE CLIFTON (1936–2010)

come home from the movies   1974

come home from the movies,
black girls and boys,
the picture be over and the screen
be cold as our neighborhood.
come home from the show,
don't be the show.
take off some flowers and plant them,
pick us some papers and read them,
stop making some babies and raise them.

© Christopher Felver.

come home from the movies
black girls and boys,
show our fathers how to walk like men,
they already know how to dance.

CONSIDERATIONS FOR CRITICAL THINKING AND WRITING

1. FIRST RESPONSE. What are the "movies" a metaphor for?
2. What advice does the speaker urge upon "black girls and boys"?
3. Explain the final two lines. Why do they come last?

RONALD WALLACE (B. 1945)

Building an Outhouse　1991

> WHEN I WRITE "I've always admired people who can make beautiful things — out of wood, or paint, or the movement of the human body, or the strings of a musical instrument. I have spent my life trying to make beautiful things out of words."
> — RONALD WALLACE

Is not unlike building a poem: the pure
mathematics of shape; the music of hammer
and tenpenny nail, of floor joist, stud wall,
and sill; the cut wood's sweet smell.

If the Skil saw rear up in your unpracticed hand,　5
cussing, hawking its chaw of dust,
and you're lost in the pounding particulars
of fly rafters, siding, hypotenuse, and load,
until nothing seems level or true
but the scorn of the tape's clucked tongue,　10

let the nub of your plainspoken pencil prevail
and it's up! Functional. Tight as a sonnet.
It will last forever (or at least for awhile)
though the critics come sit on it, and sit on it.

CONSIDERATIONS FOR CRITICAL THINKING AND WRITING

1. FIRST RESPONSE. Explain how the poem's diction contributes to the extended simile. Why is the language of building especially appropriate here?
2. What is the effect of the repetition and sounds in the final line? How does that affect the poem's tone?
3. Consult the Glossary of Literary Terms (p. 1716) for the definition of *sonnet*. To what extent does "Building an Outhouse" conform to a sonnet's structure?

ELAINE MAGARRELL (1928–2014)

The Joy of Cooking　1988

I have prepared my sister's tongue,
scrubbed and skinned it,
trimmed the roots, small bones, and gristle.

Carved through the hump it slices thin and neat.
Best with horseradish   5
and economical — it probably will grow back.
Next time perhaps a creole sauce
or mold of aspic?

I will have my brother's heart,
which is firm and rather dry,   10
slow cooked. It resembles muscle
more than organ meat
and needs an apple-onion stuffing
to make it interesting at all.
Although beef heart serves six   15
my brother's heart barely feeds two.
I could also have it braised
and served in sour sauce.

Considerations for Critical Thinking and Writing

1. **first response.** Describe the poem's tone. Do you find it amusing, bitter, or something else?

2. How are the tongue and heart used to characterize the sister and brother in this poem?

3. How is the speaker's personality revealed in the poem's language?

Connection to Another Selection

1. Write an essay that explains how cooking becomes a way of talking about something else in this poem and in Sally Croft's "Home-Baked Bread" (p. 684).

Perspective

John R. Searle (b. 1932)

Figuring Out Metaphors   1979

If you hear somebody say, "Sally is a block of ice," or, "Sam is a pig," you are likely to assume that the speaker does not mean what he says literally, but that he is speaking metaphorically. Furthermore, you are not likely to have very much trouble figuring out what he means. If he says, "Sally is a prime number between 17 and 23," or "Bill is a barn door," you might still assume he is speaking metaphorically, but it is much harder to figure out what he means. The existence of such utterances — utterances in which the speaker means metaphorically something different from what the sentence means literally — poses a series of questions for any theory of language and communication: What is metaphor, and how does it differ from both literal and other forms of figurative utterances? Why do we use expressions metaphorically instead of saying exactly and literally what we mean? How do metaphorical utterances work, that is, how is it possible for speakers to communicate to hearers when speaking metaphorically inasmuch as they do not say what they mean? And why do some metaphors work and others do not?

From *Expression and Meaning*

CONSIDERATIONS FOR CRITICAL THINKING AND WRITING

1. Searle poses a series of important questions. Write an essay that explores one of these questions, basing your discussion on the poems in this chapter.

2. CREATIVE RESPONSE. Try writing a brief poem that provides a context for the line "Sally is a prime number between 17 and 23" or the line "Bill is a barn door." Your task is to create a context so that either one of these metaphoric statements is as readily understandable as "Sally is a block of ice" or "Sam is a pig." Share your poem with your classmates and explain how the line generated the poem you built around it.

25

Symbol, Allegory, and Irony

Barbara Savage Cheresh.

Poetry is serious business; literature is the apparatus through which the world tries to keep intact its important ideas and feelings.
— MARY OLIVER

SYMBOL

A **symbol** is something that represents something else. An object, a person, a place, an event, or an action can suggest more than its literal meaning. A handshake between two world leaders might be simply a greeting, but if it is done ceremoniously before cameras, it could be a symbolic gesture signifying unity, issues resolved, and joint policies that will be followed. We live surrounded by symbols. When a $100,000 Mercedes-Benz comes roaring by in the fast lane, we get a quick glimpse of not only an expensive car but also an entire lifestyle that suggests opulence, broad lawns, executive offices, and power. One of the reasons some buyers are willing to spend roughly the cost of five Chevrolets for a single Mercedes-Benz is that they are aware of the car's symbolic value. A symbol is a vehicle for two things at once: it functions as itself, and it implies meanings beyond itself.

The meanings suggested by a symbol are determined by the context in which it appears. The Mercedes could symbolize very different things depending on where it was parked. Would an American political candidate be likely to appear in a Detroit blue-collar neighborhood with such a car? Probably not. Although a candidate might be able to afford the car, it would be an inappropriate symbol for someone seeking votes from all of the people. As a symbol, the German-built Mercedes would backfire if voters perceived it as representing an entity partially responsible for layoffs of automobile workers or, worse, as a sign of decadence and corruption. Similarly, a huge portrait of Mao Tse-tung conveys different meanings to residents of Beijing than it would to farmers in Prairie Center, Illinois. Because symbols depend on contexts for their meaning, literary artists provide those contexts so that the reader has enough information to determine the probable range of meanings suggested by a symbol.

In the following poem, the speaker describes walking at night. How is the night used symbolically?

ROBERT FROST (1874–1963)

Acquainted with the Night   1928

I have been one acquainted with the night.
I have walked out in rain — and back in rain.
I have outwalked the furthest city light.

I have looked down the saddest city lane.
I have passed by the watchman on his beat   5
And dropped my eyes, unwilling to explain.

I have stood still and stopped the sound of feet
When far away an interrupted cry
Came over houses from another street,

But not to call me back or say good-by;   10
And further still at an unearthly height
One luminary clock against the sky

Proclaimed the time was neither wrong nor right.
I have been one acquainted with the night.

In approaching this or any poem, you should read for literal meanings first and then allow the elements of the poem to invite you to symbolic readings, if they are appropriate. Here the somber tone suggests that the lines have symbolic meaning, too. The flat matter-of-factness created by the repetition of "I have" (lines 1–5, 7, 14) understates the symbolic subject matter of the poem, which is, finally, more about the "night" located in the speaker's mind or soul than it is about walking away from a city and back again. The speaker is "acquainted with the night." The importance of this phrase is emphasized by Frost's title and by the fact that he begins and ends the poem with it. Poets frequently use this kind of repetition to alert readers to details that carry more than literal meanings.

The speaker in this poem has personal knowledge of the night but does not indicate specifically what the night means. To arrive at the potential meanings of the night in this context, it is necessary to look closely at its connotations, along with the images provided in the poem. The connotative meanings of night suggest, for example, darkness, death, and grief. By drawing on these connotations, Frost uses a ***conventional symbol*** — something that is recognized by many people to represent certain ideas. Roses conventionally symbolize love or beauty; laurels, fame; spring, growth; the moon, romance. Poets often use conventional symbols to convey tone and meaning.

Frost uses the night as a conventional symbol, but he also develops it into a ***literary*** or ***contextual symbol*** that goes beyond traditional, public meanings. A literary symbol cannot be summarized in a word or two. It tends to be as elusive as experience itself. The night cannot be reduced to or equated with darkness or death or grief, but it evokes those associations and more. Frost took what perhaps initially appears to be an overworked, conventional symbol and prevented it from becoming a cliché by deepening and extending its meaning.

The images in "Acquainted with the Night" lead to the poem's symbolic meaning. Unwilling, and perhaps unable, to explain explicitly to the watchman (and to the reader) what the night means, the speaker nevertheless conveys feelings about it. The brief images of darkness, rain, sad city lanes, the necessity for guards, the eerie sound of a distressing cry coming over rooftops, and the "luminary clock against the sky" proclaiming "the time was neither wrong nor right" all help to create a sense of anxiety in this tight-lipped speaker. Although we cannot know what unnamed personal experiences have acquainted the speaker with the night, the images suggest that whatever the night means, it is somehow associated with insomnia, loneliness, isolation, coldness, darkness, death, fear, and a sense of alienation from humanity and even time. Daylight — ordinary daytime thoughts and life itself — seems remote and unavailable in this poem. The night is literally the period from sunset to sunrise, but, more important, it is an internal state of being felt by the speaker and revealed through the images.

Frost used symbols rather than an expository essay that would explain the conditions that cause these feelings because most readers can provide their own list of sorrows and terrors that evoke similar emotions. Through symbol, the speaker's experience is compressed and simultaneously expanded by the personal darkness that each reader brings to the poem. The suggestive nature of symbols makes them valuable for poets and evocative for readers.

ALLEGORY

Unlike expansive, suggestive symbols, ***allegory*** is a narration or description usually restricted to a single meaning because its events, actions, characters, settings, and objects represent specific abstractions or ideas. Although the elements in an allegory may be interesting in themselves, the emphasis tends to be on what they ultimately mean. Characters may be given names such as Hope, Pride, Youth, and Charity; they have few, if any, personal qualities beyond their abstract meanings. These personifications are a form of extended metaphor, but their meanings are severely restricted. They are not symbols because, for instance, the meaning of a character named Charity is precisely that virtue.

There is little or no room for broad speculation and exploration in allegories. If Frost had written "Acquainted with the Night" as an allegory, he might have named his speaker Loneliness and had him leave the City of Despair to walk the Streets of Emptiness, where Crime, Poverty, Fear, and other characters would define the nature of city life. The literal elements in an allegory tend to be deemphasized in favor of the message. Symbols, however, function both literally and symbolically, so that "Acquainted with the Night" is about both a walk and a sense that something is terribly wrong.

Allegory especially lends itself to **didactic poetry**, which is designed to teach an ethical, moral, or religious lesson. Many stories, poems, and plays are concerned with values, but didactic literature is specifically created to convey a message. "Acquainted with the Night" does not impart advice or offer guidance. If the poem argued that city life is self-destructive or sinful, it would be didactic; instead, it is a lyric poem that expresses the emotions and thoughts of a single speaker.

Although allegory is often enlisted in didactic causes because it can so readily communicate abstract ideas through physical representations, not all allegories teach a lesson. Here is a poem describing a haunted palace while also establishing a consistent pattern that reveals another meaning.

EDGAR ALLAN POE (1809–1849)

The Haunted Palace   1839

I

In the greenest of our valleys,
  By good angels tenanted,
Once a fair and stately palace —
  Radiant palace — reared its head.
In the monarch Thought's dominion —   5
  It stood there!
Never seraph spread a pinion
  Over fabric half so fair.

II

Banners yellow, glorious, golden,
  On its roof did float and flow;
(This — all this — was in the olden   10
  Time long ago)
And every gentle air that dallied,
  In that sweet day,
Along the ramparts plumed and pallid,   15
  A wingèd odor went away.

III

Wanderers in that happy valley
   Through two luminous windows saw
Spirits moving musically
   To a lute's well-tunèd law,   20
Round about a throne, where sitting
   (Porphyrogene!)°   *born to purple, royal*
In state his glory well befitting,
   The ruler of the realm was seen.

IV

And all with pearl and ruby glowing   25
   Was the fair palace door,
Through which came flowing, flowing, flowing
   And sparkling evermore,
A troop of Echoes whose sweet duty
   Was but to sing,   30
In voices of surpassing beauty,
   The wit and wisdom of their king.

V

But evil things, in robes of sorrow,
   Assailed the monarch's high estate;
(Ah, let us mourn, for never morrow
   Shall dawn upon him, desolate!)   35
And, round about his home, the glory
   That blushed and bloomed
Is but a dim-remembered story
   Of the old time entombed.   40

VI

And travelers now within that valley,
   Through the red-litten windows see
Vast forms that move fantastically
   To a discordant melody;
While, like a rapid ghastly river,   45
   Through the pale door,
A hideous throng rush out forever,
   And laugh — but smile no more.

     On one level this poem describes how a once happy palace is desolated by "evil things" (line 33). If the reader pays close attention to the diction, however, an allegorical meaning becomes apparent on a second reading. A systematic pattern develops in the choice of words used to describe the palace, so that it comes to stand for a human mind. The palace, banners, windows, door, echoes, and throng are equated with a person's head, hair, eyes, mouth, voice, and laughter. That mind, once harmoniously ordered, is overthrown by evil, haunting thoughts that lead to the mad laughter in the poem's final lines. Once the general pattern is seen, the rest of the details fall neatly into place to strengthen the parallels between the surface description of a palace and the allegorical representation of a disordered mind.

Modern writers generally prefer symbol over allegory because they tend to be more interested in opening up the potential meanings of an experience instead of transforming it into a closed pattern of meaning. Perhaps the major difference is that while allegory may delight a reader's imagination, symbol challenges and enriches it.

IRONY

Another important resource writers use to take readers beyond literal meanings is *irony*, a technique that reveals a discrepancy between what appears to be and what is actually true. Here is a classic example in which appearances give way to the underlying reality.

EDWIN ARLINGTON ROBINSON (1869–1935)

Richard Cory   1897

Whenever Richard Cory went down town,
We people on the pavement looked at him:
He was a gentleman from sole to crown,
Clean favored, and imperially slim.

And he was always quietly arrayed,   5
And he was always human when he talked;
But still he fluttered pulses when he said,
"Good-morning," and he glittered when he walked.

And he was rich — yes, richer than a king —
And admirably schooled in every grace: 10
In fine, we thought that he was everything
To make us wish that we were in his place.

So on we worked, and waited for the light,
And went without the meat, and cursed the bread;
And Richard Cory, one calm summer night,   15
Went home and put a bullet through his head.

Richard Cory seems to have it all. Those less fortunate, the "people on the pavement," regard him as well-bred, handsome, tasteful, and richly endowed with both money and grace. Until the final line of the poem, the reader, like the speaker, is charmed by Cory's good fortune, so quietly expressed in his decent, easy manner. That final, shocking line, however, shatters the appearances of

Cory's life and reveals him to have been a desperately unhappy man. While everyone else assumes that Cory represented "everything" to which they aspire, the reality is that he could escape his miserable life only as a suicide. This discrepancy between what appears to be true and what actually exists is known as **situational irony**: what happens is entirely different from what is expected. We are not told why Cory shoots himself; instead, the irony in the poem shocks us into the recognition that appearances do not always reflect realities.

Words are also sometimes intended to be taken at other than face value. **Verbal irony** is saying something different from what is meant. If after reading "Richard Cory," you said, "That rich gentleman sure was happy," your statement would be ironic. Your tone of voice would indicate that just the opposite was meant; hence verbal irony is usually easy to detect in spoken language. In literature, however, a reader can sometimes take literally what a writer intends ironically. The remedy for this kind of misreading is to pay close attention to the poem's context. There is no formula that can detect verbal irony, but contradictory actions and statements as well as the use of understatement and overstatement can often be signals that verbal irony is present.

A SAMPLE STUDENT RESPONSE

Diaz 1

Cipriano Diaz

Professor Young

English 200

16 September 2015

Irony in Edwin Arlington Robinson's "Richard Cory"

In Edwin Arlington Robinson's poem "Richard Cory," appearances are not reality. The character Richard Cory, viewed by the townspeople as "richer than a king" (line 9) and "a gentleman from sole to crown" (3), is someone who inspires envy. The poem's speaker says, "we thought that he was every-thing / To make us wish that we were in his place" (11-12). However, the final shocking line of the poem creates a situational irony that emphasizes the difference between what seems—and what really is.

In lines 1 through 14, the speaker sets up a shining, princely image of Cory, associating him with such regal words as "imperially" (4), "crown" (3), and "king" (9). Cory is viewed by the townspeople from the "pavement" (2) as if he is on a pedestal; far below him, those who must work and "[go] without the meat" (14) stand in stark contrast. Further, not only is Cory a gentleman, he is so good-looking that he "flutter[s] pulses" (7) of those around him when he speaks. He's a rich man who "glitter[s] when he walk[s]" (8). He is also a decent man who is "always human when he talk[s]" (6). However, this noble image of Cory is unexpectedly shattered "one calm summer night" (15) in the final couplet. What the speaker and townspeople believed Cory to be and aspired to imitate was merely an illusion. The irony is that what Cory seemed to be—a happy, satisfied man—is exactly what he was not. . . .

Work Cited

Robinson, Edwin Arlington. "Richard Cory." *The Bedford Introduction to Literature*. Ed. Michael Meyer. 11th ed. Boston: Bedford/St. Martin's, 2016. 715. Print.

Consider how verbal irony is used in this poem.

KENNETH FEARING (1902–1961)

AD   1938

Wanted: Men;
Millions of men are *wanted at once* in a big new field;
New, tremendous, thrilling, great.
If you've ever been a figure in the chamber of horrors,
If you've ever escaped from a psychiatric ward,   5
If you thrill at the thought of throwing poison into wells, have heavenly
     visions of people, by the thousands, dying in flames —

You are the very man we want
We mean business and our business is *you*
Wanted: A race of brand-new men.

Apply: Middle Europe;   10
No skill needed;
No ambition required; no brains wanted and no character allowed;

Take a permanent job in the coming profession
Wages: *Death.*

This poem was written as Nazi troops stormed across Europe at the start of World War II. The advertisement suggests on the surface that killing is just an ordinary job, but the speaker indicates through understatement that there is nothing ordinary about the "business" of this "*coming profession.*" Fearing uses verbal irony to indicate how casually and mindlessly people are prepared to accept the horrors of war.

"AD" is a *satire*, an example of the literary art of ridiculing a folly or vice in an effort to expose or correct it. The object of satire is usually some human frailty; people, institutions, ideas, and things are all fair game for satirists. Fearing satirizes the insanity of a world mobilizing itself for war: his irony reveals the speaker's knowledge that there is nothing "*New, tremendous, thrilling,* [or] *great*" about going off to kill and be killed. The implication of the poem is that no one should respond to advertisements for war. The poem serves as a satiric corrective to those who would troop off armed with unrealistic expectations: wage war, and the wages consist of death.

Dramatic irony is used when a writer allows a reader to know more about a situation than a character does. This creates a discrepancy between what a character says or thinks and what the reader knows to be true. Dramatic irony is often used to reveal character. In the following poem the speaker delivers a public address that ironically tells us more about him than it does about the patriotic holiday he is commemorating.

E. E. Cummings (1894–1962)

next to of course god america i 1926

"next to of course god america i
love you land of the pilgrims' and so forth oh
say can you see by the dawn's early my
country 'tis of centuries come and go
and are no more what of it we should worry   5
in every language even deafanddumb
thy sons acclaim your glorious name by gorry
by jingo by gee by gosh by gum
why talk of beauty what could be more beautiful than these heroic happy dead   10
who rushed like lions to the roaring slaughter
they did not stop to think they died instead
then shall the voice of liberty be mute?"

He spoke. And drank rapidly a glass of water

This verbal debauch of chauvinistic clichés (notice the run-on phrases and lines) reveals that the speaker's relationship to God and country is not, as he claims, one of love. His public address suggests a hearty mindlessness that leads to "roaring slaughter" rather than to reverence or patriotism. Cummings allows the reader to see through the speaker's words to their dangerous emptiness. What the speaker means and what Cummings means are entirely different. Like Fearing's "AD," this poem is a satire that invites the reader's laughter and contempt in order to deflate the benighted attitudes expressed in it.

When a writer uses God, destiny, or fate to dash the hopes and expectations of a character or humankind in general, it is called **cosmic irony**. In "The Convergence of the Twain" (p. 652), for example, Thomas Hardy describes how "The Immanent Will" brought together the *Titanic* and a deadly iceberg. Technology and pride are no match for "the Spinner of the Years." Here's a painfully terse version of cosmic irony.

STEPHEN CRANE (1871–1900)

A Man Said to the Universe   1899

A man said to the universe:
"Sir, I exist!"
"However," replied the universe,
"The fact has not created in me
A sense of obligation."

Unlike in "The Convergence of the Twain," there is the slightest bit of humor in Crane's poem, but the joke is on us.

Irony is an important technique that allows a writer to distinguish between appearances and realities. In situational irony a discrepancy exists between what we expect to happen and what actually happens; in verbal irony a discrepancy exists between what is said and what is meant; in dramatic irony a discrepancy exists between what a character believes and what the reader knows to be true; and in cosmic irony a discrepancy exists between what a character aspires to and what universal forces provide. With each form of irony, we are invited to move beyond surface appearances and sentimental assumptions to see the complexity of experience. Irony is often used in literature to reveal a writer's perspective on matters that previously seemed settled.

POEMS FOR FURTHER STUDY

BOB HICOK (B. 1960)

Making it in poetry   2004

The young teller
at the credit union
asked why so many

small checks
from universities?
Because I write   5
poems I said. Why
haven't I heard
of you? Because
I write poems   10
I said.

CONSIDERATIONS FOR CRITICAL THINKING AND WRITING

1. FIRST RESPONSE. Explain how the speaker's verbal irony is central to the poem's humor.

2. What sort of portrait of the poet-speaker emerges from this very brief poem?

JANE KENYON (1947–1995)

Not Writing   1993

A wasp rises to its papery
nest under the eaves
where it daubs

at the gray shape,
but seems unable
to enter its own house.

Donald Hall.

CONSIDERATIONS FOR CRITICAL THINKING AND WRITING

1. FIRST RESPONSE. Why is the title crucial to an understanding of this poem?

2. Which words serve to reinforce the symbolic meaning that concerns writing?

CONNECTION TO ANOTHER SELECTION

1. Discuss the treatment of what it is to be a writer in this poem and in Richard Wilbur's "The Writer" (p. 692).

KEVIN PIERCE (B. 1958)

Proof of Origin   2005

NEWSWIRE — A U.S. judge ordered a Georgia school district to remove from text-
books stickers challenging the theory of evolution.

Though close to their hearts is the version that starts
With Adam and Eve and no clothes,
What enables their grip as the stickers they strip
Is Darwinian thumbs that oppose.

CONSIDERATIONS FOR CRITICAL THINKING AND WRITING

1. FIRST RESPONSE. How do the rhymes contribute to the humorous tone?
2. Discuss the levels of irony in the poem.
3. How do you read the title? Can it be explained in more than one way?

CARL SANDBURG (1878–1967)

A Fence 1916

Now the stone house on the lake front is finished and the workmen
    are beginning the fence.
The palings are made of iron bars with steel points that can stab the
    life out of any man who falls on them.
As a fence, it is a masterpiece, and will shut off the rabble and all
    vagabonds and hungry men and all wandering children looking
    for a place to play.
Passing through the bars and over the steel points will go nothing
    except Death and the Rain and Tomorrow.

CONSIDERATIONS FOR CRITICAL THINKING AND WRITING

1. FIRST RESPONSE. What is the effect of the capital letters in the final line?
2. Discuss the symbolic meaning of the fence and whether you think the symbolism is too spelled out or not.

CONNECTION TO ANOTHER SELECTION

1. Consider the themes in "A Fence" and Robert Frost's "Mending Wall" (p. 874). Which poem do you prefer? Why?

WALLACE STEVENS (1879–1955)

Anecdote of the Jar 1923

I placed a jar in Tennessee,
And round it was, upon a hill.
It made the slovenly wilderness
Surround that hill.

The wilderness rose up to it,   5
And sprawled around, no longer wild.
The jar was round upon the ground
And tall and of a port in air.

It took dominion everywhere.
The jar was gray and bare.   10
It did not give of bird or bush,
Like nothing else in Tennessee.

CONSIDERATIONS FOR CRITICAL THINKING AND WRITING

1. FIRST RESPONSE. How is the jar different from its surroundings? What effect does the jar's placement have upon the "slovenly wilderness" (line 3)?

2. What do you make of all the "round" sounds in lines 2, 4, 6, and 7? How do they echo the relationship between the jar and the wilderness?

3. In what sense might this poem be regarded as an anecdote about the power and limitations of art and nature?

CONNECTION TO ANOTHER SELECTION

1. Compare the thematic function of the jar in Stevens's poem with that of the urn in John Keats's "Ode on a Grecian Urn" (p. 660). What important similarities and differences do you see in the meanings of each? Discuss why you think Stevens and Keats have similar or different ideas about art.

JULIO MARZÁN (B. 1946)
Ethnic Poetry   1994

> WHEN I WRITE "Words you are sure convey your truest feelings or thoughts may record only sentiment, not a line of poetry, while another arrangement, different words in another tone or rhythm, unlock and reveal what you really wanted to say." — JULIO MARZÁN

The ethnic poet said: "The earth is maybe
a huge maraca / and the sun a trombone /
and life / is to move your ass / to slow beats."
The ethnic audience roasted a suckling pig.

The ethnic poet said: "Oh thank Goddy, Goddy /   5
I be me, my toenails curled downward /
deep, deep, deep into Mama earth."
The ethnic audience shook strands of sea shells.

The ethnic poet said: "The sun was created black /
so we should imagine light / and also dream /   10
a walrus emerging from the broken ice."
The ethnic audience beat on sealskin drums.

The ethnic poet said: "Reproductive organs /
Eagles nesting California redwoods /
Shut up and listen to my ancestors."   15
The ethnic audience ate fried bread and honey.

The ethnic poet said: "Something there is that
doesn't love a wall / That sends
the frozen-ground-swell under it."
The ethnic audience deeply understood humanity.   20

CONSIDERATIONS FOR CRITICAL THINKING AND WRITING

1. FIRST RESPONSE. What is the implicit definition of *ethnic poetry* in this poem?

2. The final stanza quotes lines from Robert Frost's "Mending Wall" (p. 874). Read the entire poem. Why do you think Marzán chooses these lines and this particular poem as one kind of ethnic poetry?

3. What is the poem's central irony? Pay particular attention to the final line. What is being satirized here?

4. CRITICAL STRATEGIES. Read the section on the literary canon (pp. 1644–45) in Chapter 51, "Critical Strategies for Reading," and discuss how the formation of the literary canon is related to the theme of "Ethnic Poetry."

CONNECTION TO ANOTHER SELECTION

1. Write an essay that discusses the speakers' ideas about what poetry should be in "Ethnic Poetry" and in Ruth Forman's "Poetry Should Ride the Bus" (p. 675).

MARK HALLIDAY (B. 1949)

Graded Paper   1991

On the whole this is quite successful work:
your main argument about the poet's ambivalence —
how he loves the very things he attacks —
is mostly persuasive and always engaging.

At the same time,   5
                          there are spots
where your thinking becomes, for me,
alarmingly opaque, and your syntax seems to jump
backwards through unnecessary hoops,
as on p. 2 where you speak of "precognitive awareness   10
not yet disestablished by the shell that encrusts
each thing that a person actually says"
or at the top of p. 5 where your discussion of
"subverbal undertow miming the subversion of self-belief
woven counter to desire's outreach"   15
leaves me groping for firmer footholds.
(I'd have said it differently,
or rather, said something else.)
And when you say that women "could not fulfill themselves" (p. 6)
"in that era" (only forty years ago, after all!)   20
are you so sure that the situation is so different today?
Also, how does Whitman bluff his way into
your penultimate paragraph? He is the *last* poet
I would have quoted in this context!
What plausible way of behaving   25
does the passage you quote represent? Don't you think
literature should ultimately reveal possibilities for *action*?

Please notice how I've repaired your use of semicolons.

And yet, despite what may seem my cranky response,
I do admire the freshness of   30
your thinking and your style; there is
a vitality here; your sentences thrust themselves forward

with a confidence as impressive as it is cheeky. . . .
You are not
            me, finally,
and though this is an awkward problem, involving
the inescapable fact that you are so young, so young
it is also a delightful provocation.

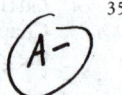

35

CONSIDERATIONS FOR CRITICAL THINKING AND WRITING

1. FIRST RESPONSE. How do you characterize the grader of this paper based on the comments about the paper?

2. Is the speaker a man or a woman? What makes you think so? Does the gender of the speaker affect your reading of the poem? How?

3. Explain whether or not you think the teacher's comments on the paper are consistent with the grade awarded it. How do you account for the grade?

CONNECTION TO ANOTHER SELECTION

1. Compare the ways in which Halliday reveals the speaker's character in this poem with the strategies used by Robert Browning in "My Last Duchess" (p. 726).

JAMES MERRILL (1926–1995)

Casual Wear   1984

Your average tourist: Fifty. 2.3
Times married. Dressed, this year, in Ferdi Plinthbower
Originals. Odds 1 to 9
Against her strolling past the Embassy

Today at noon. Your average terrorist: 5
Twenty-five. Celibate. No use for trends,
At least in clothing. Mark, though, where it ends.
People have come forth made of colored mist

Unsmiling on one hundred million screens
To tell of his prompt phone call to the station,   10
"Claiming responsibility" — devastation
Signed with a flourish, like the dead wife's jeans.

CONSIDERATIONS FOR CRITICAL THINKING AND WRITING

1. FIRST RESPONSE. What is the effect of the statistics in this poem?

2. Describe the speaker's tone. Is it appropriate for the subject matter? Explain why or why not.

3. Comment on the ironies that emerge from the final two lines. How are the tourist and terrorist linked by the speaker's description? Explain why you think the speaker sympathizes more with the tourist or the terrorist — or with neither.

CONNECTION TO ANOTHER SELECTION

1. Compare the satire in this poem with that in Kenneth Fearing's "AD" (p. 717). What is satirized in each poem? Which satire do you think is more pointed?

HENRY REED (1914–1986)

Naming of Parts   1946

Today we have naming of parts. Yesterday,
We had daily cleaning. And tomorrow morning,
We shall have what to do after firing. But today,
Today we have naming of parts. Japonica
Glistens like coral in all of the neighboring gardens,   5
        And today we have naming of parts.

This is the lower sling swivel. And this
Is the upper sling swivel, whose use you will see,
When you are given your slings. And this is the piling swivel,
Which in your case you have not got. The branches   10
Hold in the gardens their silent, eloquent gestures,
        Which in our case we have not got.

This is the safety-catch, which is always released
With an easy flick of the thumb. And please do not let me
See anyone using his finger. You can do it quite easy   15
If you have any strength in your thumb. The blossoms
Are fragile and motionless, never letting anyone see
        Any of them using their finger.

And this you can see is the bolt. The purpose of this
Is to open the breech, as you see. We can slide it   20
Rapidly backwards and forwards: we call this
Easing the spring. And rapidly backwards and forwards
The early bees are assaulting and fumbling the flowers:
        They call it easing the Spring.

They call it easing the Spring: it is perfectly easy   25
If you have any strength in your thumb: like the bolt,
And the breech, and the cocking-piece, and the point of balance,
Which in our case we have not got; and the almond-blossom
Silent in all of the gardens and the bees going backwards and forwards,
        For today we have naming of parts.   30

CONSIDERATIONS FOR CRITICAL THINKING AND WRITING

1. **FIRST RESPONSE.** Characterize the two speakers in this poem. Identify the lines spoken by each. How do their respective lines differ in tone?
2. What is the effect of the last line of each stanza?

3. How do ambiguities and puns contribute to the poem's meaning?
4. What symbolic contrast is made between the rifle instruction and the gardens? How is this contrast ironic?

ROBERT BROWNING (1812–1889)

My Last Duchess 1842

© Corbis.

Ferrara°

That's my last Duchess painted on the wall,
Looking as if she were alive. I call
That piece a wonder, now: Frà Pandolf's°
        hands
Worked busily a day, and there she stands.
Will't please you sit and look at her? I said
"Frà Pandolf" by design, for never read
Strangers like you that pictured countenance,
The depth and passion of its earnest glance,
But to myself they turned (since none puts by
The curtain I have drawn for you, but I)   10
And seemed as they would ask me, if they durst,
How such a glance came there; so, not the first
Are you to turn and ask thus. Sir, 'twas not
Her husband's presence only, called that spot
Of joy into the Duchess' cheek: perhaps   15
Frà Pandolf chanced to say "Her mantle laps
Over my lady's wrist too much," or "Paint
Must never hope to reproduce the faint
Half-flush that dies along her throat": such stuff
Was courtesy, she thought, and cause enough   20
For calling up that spot of joy. She had
A heart — how shall I say? — too soon made glad,
Too easily impressed; she liked whate'er
She looked on, and her looks went everywhere.
Sir, 'twas all one! My favor at her breast,   25
The dropping of the daylight in the West,
The bough of cherries some officious fool
Broke in the orchard for her, the white mule
She rode with round the terrace — all and each
Would draw from her alike the approving speech,   30
Or blush, at least. She thanked men, — good! but thanked
Somehow — I know not how — as if she ranked
My gift of a nine-hundred-years-old name
With anybody's gift. Who'd stoop to blame
This sort of trifling? Even had you skill   35
In speech — which I have not — to make your will

Ferrara: In the sixteenth century, the duke of this Italian city arranged to marry a second time after the mysterious death of his very young first wife.   3 *Frà Pandolf:* A fictitious artist.

Quite clear to such an one, and say, "Just this
Or that in you disgusts me; here you miss,
Or there exceed the mark" — and if she let
Herself be lessoned so, nor plainly set   40
Her wits to yours, forsooth, and made excuse,
— E'en then would be some stooping; and I choose
Never to stoop. Oh sir, she smiled, no doubt,
Whene'er I passed her; but who passed without
Much the same smile? This grew; I gave commands;   45
Then all smiles stopped together. There she stands
As if alive. Will't please you rise? We'll meet
The company below, then. I repeat,
The Count your master's known munificence
Is ample warrant that no just pretense   50
Of mine for dowry will be disallowed;
Though his fair daughter's self, as I avowed
At starting, is my object. Nay, we'll go
Together down, sir. Notice Neptune, though,
Taming a sea-horse, thought a rarity,   55
Which Claus of Innsbruck° cast in bronze for me!

56 *Claus of Innsbruck:* Also a fictitious artist.

Considerations for Critical Thinking and Writing

1. FIRST RESPONSE. What do you think happened to the duchess?

2. To whom is the duke addressing his remarks about the duchess in this poem? What is ironic about the situation?

3. Why was the duke unhappy with his first wife? What does this reveal about him? What does the poem's title suggest about his attitude toward women in general?

4. What seems to be the visitor's response (lines 53–54) to the duke's account of his first wife?

Connection to Another Selection

1. Write an essay describing the ways in which the speakers of "My Last Duchess" and Katharyn Howd Machan's "Hazel Tells LaVerne" (p. 641) inadvertently reveal themselves.

William Blake (1757–1827)

A Poison Tree   1794

I was angry with my friend:
I told my wrath, my wrath did end.
I was angry with my foe:
I told it not, my wrath did grow.

And I water'd it in fears,
Night & morning with my tears;   5

And I sunned it with smiles,
And with soft deceitful wiles.

And it grew both day and night,
Till it bore an apple bright. 10
And my foe beheld it shine,
And he knew that it was mine,

And into my garden stole,
When the night had veild the pole;
In the morning glad I see 15
My foe outstretched beneath the tree.

CONSIDERATIONS FOR CRITICAL THINKING AND WRITING

1. FIRST RESPONSE. Considering the "apple bright" allusion in the third stanza, how can "A Poison Tree" be read as more than a meditation on a personal relationship gone bad?

2. What is the speaker's attitude toward anger and revenge? What do you think the speaker wants the reader's attitude to be?

PAUL MULDOON (B. 1951)

Symposium 1998

You can lead a horse to water but you can't make it hold
its nose to the grindstone and hunt with the hounds.
Every dog has a stitch in time. Two heads? You've been sold
one good turn. One good turn deserves a bird in the hand.

A bird in the hand is better than no bread. 5
To have your cake is to pay Paul.
Make hay while you can still hit the nail on the head.
For want of a nail the sky might fall.

People in glass houses can't see the wood
for the new broom. Rome wasn't built between two stools. 10
Empty vessels wait for no man.

A hair of the dog is a friend indeed.
There's no fool like the fool
who's shot his bolt. There's no smoke after the horse is gone.

CONSIDERATIONS FOR CRITICAL THINKING AND WRITING

1. FIRST RESPONSE. What meanings can you draw from the poem on a first reading? Do the lines mean more to you after subsequent readings? Why or why not?

2. To what extent are these bits of clichés and aphorisms connected to each other? Explain why you find the poem coherent or not.

3. Look up the meaning and origin of *symposium* in a dictionary. Why is this an apt title for this poem?

CONNECTION TO ANOTHER SELECTION

1. Discuss the use of irony in this poem and in E. E. Cummings's "next to of course god america i" (p. 718).

Perspective

EZRA POUND (1885–1972)

On Symbols 1912

I believe that the proper and perfect symbol is the natural object, that if a man uses "symbols" he must so use them that their symbolic function does not obtrude; so that *a* sense, and the poetic quality of the passage, is not lost to those who do not understand the symbol as such, to whom, for instance, a hawk is a hawk.

From "Prolegomena," *Poetry Review*, February 1912

CONSIDERATIONS FOR CRITICAL THINKING AND WRITING

1. Discuss whether you agree with Pound that the "perfect symbol" is a "natural object" that does not insist on being read as a symbol.
2. Write an essay in which you discuss Carl Sandburg's "A Fence" (p. 721) as an example of the "perfect symbol" Pound proposes.

26

Sounds

© Bettmann/Corbis.

In a poem the words should be as
pleasing to the ear as the meaning is
to the mind.
—MARIANNE MOORE

LISTENING TO POETRY

Poems yearn to be read aloud. Much of their energy, charm, and beauty come
to life only when they are heard. Poets choose and arrange words for their
sounds as well as for their meanings. Most poetry is best read with your lips,
teeth, and tongue because they serve to articulate the effects that sound may
have in a poem. When a voice is breathed into a good poem, there is pleasure
in the reading, the saying, and the hearing.

The earliest poetry — before writing and painting — was chanted or sung.
The rhythmic quality of such oral performances served two purposes: it helped
the chanting bard remember the lines and it entertained audiences with patterned sounds of language, which were sometimes accompanied by musical
instruments. Poetry has always been closely related to music. Indeed, as the
word suggests, lyric poetry evolved from songs. "Western Wind" (p. 604), an
anonymous Middle English lyric, survived as song long before it was written
down. Had Robert Frost lived in a nonliterate society, he probably would have
sung some version — a very different version to be sure — of "Acquainted with

the Night" (p. 711) instead of writing it down. Even though Frost creates a speaking rather than a singing voice, the speaker's anxious tone is distinctly heard in any careful reading of the poem.

Like lyrics, early narrative poems were originally part of an anonymous oral folk tradition. A **ballad** such as "Bonny Barbara Allan" (p. 1043) told a story that was sung from one generation to the next until it was finally transcribed. Since the eighteenth century, this narrative form has sometimes been imitated by poets who write *literary ballads*. John Keats's "La Belle Dame sans Merci" (p. 1057) is, for example, a more complex and sophisticated nineteenth-century reflection of the original ballad traditions that developed in the fifteenth century and earlier. In considering poetry as sound, we should not forget that poetry traces its beginnings to song.

These next lines exemplify poetry's continuing relation to song. What poetic elements can you find in this ballad, which was adapted by Paul Simon and Art Garfunkel and became a popular antiwar song in the 1960s?

ANONYMOUS

Scarborough Fair   date unknown

Where are you going? To Scarborough Fair?
Parsley, sage, rosemary, and thyme,
Remember me to a bonny lass there,
For once she was a true lover of mine.

Tell her to make me a cambric shirt,   5
Parsley, sage, rosemary, and thyme,
Without any needle or thread work'd in it,
And she shall be a true lover of mine.

Tell her to wash it in yonder well,
Parsley, sage, rosemary, and thyme,   10
Where water ne'er sprung nor a drop of rain fell,
And she shall be a true lover of mine.

Tell her to plough me an acre of land,
Parsley, sage, rosemary, and thyme,
Between the sea and the salt sea strand,   15
And she shall be a true lover of mine.

Tell her to plough it with one ram's horn,
Parsley, sage, rosemary, and thyme,
And sow it all over with one peppercorn,
And she shall be a true lover of mine.   20

Tell her to reap it with a sickle of leather,
Parsley, sage, rosemary, and thyme,
And tie it all up with a tom tit's feather,
And she shall be a true lover of mine.

Tell her to gather it all in a sack, 25
Parsley, sage, rosemary, and thyme,
And carry it home on a butterfly's back,
And then she shall be a true lover of mine.

CONSIDERATIONS FOR CRITICAL THINKING AND WRITING

1. FIRST RESPONSE. What do you associate with "Parsley, sage, rosemary, and thyme"? What images does this poem evoke? How so?
2. What kinds of demands does the speaker make on his former lover? What do these demands have in common?
3. What is the tone of this ballad?
4. Choose a contemporary song that you especially like and examine the lyrics. Write an essay explaining whether or not you consider the lyrics poetic.

Of course, reading "Scarborough Fair" is not the same as hearing it. Like the lyrics of a song, many poems must be heard — or at least read with listening eyes — before they can be fully understood and enjoyed. The sounds of words are a universal source of music for human beings. This has been so from ancient tribes to bards to the two-year-old child in a bakery gleefully chanting "Cuppitycake, cuppitycake!"

Listen to the sound of this poem as you read it aloud. How do the words provide, in a sense, their own musical accompaniment?

JOHN UPDIKE (1932–2009)

Player Piano 1958

My stick fingers click with a snicker
And, chuckling, they knuckle the keys;
Light-footed, my steel feelers flicker
And pluck from these keys melodies.

My paper can caper; abandon 5
Is broadcast by dint of my din,
And no man or band has a hand in
The tones I turn on from within.

At times I'm a jumble of rumbles,
At others I'm light like the moon, 10
But never my numb plunker fumbles,
Misstrums me, or tries a new tune.

The speaker in this poem is a piano that can play automatically by means of a mechanism that depresses keys in response to signals on a perforated roll. Notice how the speaker's voice approximates the sounds of a piano. In each stanza a predominant sound emerges from the carefully chosen words. How is the sound of each stanza tuned to its sense?

Like Updike's "Player Piano," this next poem also employs sounds to reinforce meanings.

EMILY DICKINSON (1830–1886)
A Bird came down the Walk —   ca. 1862

A Bird came down the Walk —
He did not know I saw —
He bit an Angleworm in halves
And ate the fellow, raw,

And then he drank a Dew   5
From a convenient Grass —
And then hopped sidewise to the Wall
To let a Beetle pass —

He glanced with rapid eyes
That hurried all around —   10
They looked like frightened Beads, I thought —
He stirred his Velvet Head

Like one in danger, Cautious,
I offered him a Crumb
And he unrolled his feathers   15
And rowed him softer home —

Than Oars divide the Ocean,
Too silver for a seam —
Or Butterflies, off Banks of Noon
Leap, plashless as they swim.   20

This description of a bird offers a close look at how differently a bird moves when it hops on the ground than when it flies in the air. On the ground the bird moves quickly, awkwardly, and irregularly as it plucks up a worm, washes it down with dew, and then hops aside to avoid a passing beetle. The speaker recounts the bird's rapid, abrupt actions from a somewhat superior, amused perspective. By describing the bird in human terms (as if, for example, it chose to eat the worm "raw"), the speaker is almost condescending. But when the attempt to offer a crumb fails and the frightened bird flies off, the speaker is left looking up instead of down at the bird.

With that shift in perspective the tone shifts from amusement to awe in response to the bird's graceful flight. The jerky movements of lines 1 to 13 give way to the smooth motion of lines 15 to 20. The pace of the first three stanzas is fast and discontinuous. We tend to pause at the end of each line, and this reinforces a sense of disconnected movements. In contrast, the final six lines are to be read as a single sentence in one flowing movement, lubricated by various sounds.

Read again the description of the bird flying away. Several *o*-sounds contribute to the image of the serene, expansive, confident flight, just as the *s*-sounds serve as smooth transitions from one line to the next. Notice how these sounds are grouped in the following vertical columns:

unrolled	softer	Too	his	Ocean	Banks
rowed	Oars	Noon	feathers	silver	plashless
home	Or		softer	seam	as
Ocean	off		Oars	Butterflies	swim

This blending of sounds (notice how "Leap, plashless" brings together the *p*- and *l*-sounds without a ripple) helps convey the bird's smooth grace in the air. Like a feathered oar, the bird moves seamlessly in its element.

The repetition of sounds in poetry is similar to the function of the tones and melodies that are repeated, with variations, in music. Just as the patterned sounds in music unify a work, so do the words in poems, which have been carefully chosen for the combinations of sounds they create. These sounds are produced in a number of ways.

The most direct way in which the sound of a word suggests its meaning is through **onomatopoeia,** which is the use of a word that resembles the sound it denotes: *quack, buzz, rattle, bang, squeak, bowwow, burp, choo-choo, ding-a-ling, sizzle.* The sound and sense of these words are closely related, but such words represent a very small percentage of the words available to us. Poets usually employ more subtle means for echoing meanings.

Onomatopoeia can consist of more than just single words. In its broadest meaning the term refers to lines or passages in which sounds help to convey meanings, as in these lines from Updike's "Player Piano":

> My stick fingers click with a snicker
> And, chuckling, they knuckle the keys.

The sharp, crisp sounds of these two lines approximate the sounds of a piano; the syllables seem to "click" against one another. Contrast Updike's rendition with the following lines:

> My long fingers play with abandon
> And, laughing, they cover the keys.

The original version is more interesting and alive because the sounds of the words are pleasurable and reinforce the meaning through a careful blending of consonants and vowels.

Alliteration is the repetition of the same consonant sounds at the beginnings of nearby words: "*d*escending *d*ewdrops," "*l*uscious *l*emons." Sometimes the term is also used to describe the consonant sounds within words: "trespass-er's reproach," "we*dd*ed la*d*y." Alliteration is based on sound rather than spelling. "Keen" and "car" alliterate, but "car" does not alliterate with "cite." Rarely is heavy-handed alliteration effective. Used too self-consciously, it can be distracting instead of strengthening meaning or emphasizing a relation between words. Consider the relentless *h*'s in this line: "Horrendous horrors haunted

Helen's happiness." Those *h*'s certainly suggest that Helen is being pursued, but they have a more comic than serious effect because they are overdone.

   Assonance is the repetition of the same vowel sound in nearby words: "asl*ee*p under a tr*ee*," "t*i*me and t*i*de," "h*au*nt" and "*aw*esome," "*ea*ch *e*vening." Both alliteration and assonance help to establish relations among words in a line or a series of lines. Whether the effect is *euphony* (lines that are musically pleasant to the ear and smooth, like the final lines of Dickinson's "A Bird came down the Walk—") or *cacophony* (lines that are discordant and difficult to pronounce, like the claim that "never my numb plunker fumbles" in Updike's "Player Piano"), the sounds of words in poetry can be as significant as the words' denotative or connotative meanings.

A SAMPLE STUDENT RESPONSE

Ryan Lee

Professor McDonough

English 211

1 December 2015

Sound in Emily Dickinson's "A Bird came down the Walk—"

In her poem "A Bird came down the Walk—" Emily Dickinson uses the sound and rhythm of each line to reflect the motion of a bird walking awkwardly—and then flying gracefully. Particularly when read aloud, the staccato phrases and stilted breaks in lines 1 through 14 create a sense of the bird's movement on land, quick and off-balanced, which helps bring the scene to life.

The first three stanzas are structured to make the bird's movement consistent. The bird hops around, eating worms while keeping guard for any threats. Vulnerable on the ground, the bird is intensely aware of danger:

> He glanced with rapid eyes
>
> That hurried all around—
>
> They looked like frightened Beads, I thought—
>
> He stirred his Velvet Head (9-12)

In addition to choosing words that portray the bird as cautious—it "glanced with rapid eyes" (9) that resemble "frightened Beads" (11)—Dickinson chooses to end each line abruptly. This abrupt halting of sound allows the reader to experience the bird's fear more immediately, and the effect is similar to the missing of a beat or a breath.

These halting lines stand in contrast to the smoothness of the last six lines, during which the bird takes flight. The sounds in these lines are pleasingly soft, and rich in the "s" sound. The bird

> unrolled his feathers
> And rowed him softer home—
>
> Than Oars divide the Ocean,
> Too silver for a seam— (15-18). . . .

Work Cited

Dickinson, Emily. "A Bird came down the Walk—." *The Bedford Introduction to Literature.* Ed. Michael Meyer. 11th ed. Boston: Bedford/St. Martin's, 2016. 733. Print.

RHYME

Like alliteration and assonance, **rhyme** is a way of creating sound patterns. Rhyme, broadly defined, consists of two or more words or phrases that repeat the same sounds: *happy* and *snappy*. Rhyme words often have similar spellings, but that is not a requirement of rhyme; what matters is that the words sound alike: *vain* rhymes with *reign* as well as *rain*. Moreover, words may look alike but not rhyme at all. In **eye rhyme** the spellings are similar, but the pronunciations are not, as with *bough* and *cough,* or *brow* and *blow*.

Not all poems use rhyme. Many great poems have no rhymes, and many weak verses use rhyme as a substitute for poetry. These are especially apparent in commercial messages and greeting-card lines. At its worst, rhyme is merely a distracting decoration that can lead to dullness and predictability. But used skillfully, rhyme creates lines that are memorable and musical.

Here is a poem using rhyme that you might remember the next time you are in a restaurant.

RICHARD ARMOUR (1906–1989)
Going to Extremes   1954

Shake and shake
  The catsup bottle
None'll come —
  And then a lot'll.

The experience recounted in Armour's poem is common enough, but the rhyme's humor is special. The final line clicks the poem shut — an effect that is often achieved by the use of rhyme. That click provides a sense of a satisfying and fulfilled form. Rhymes have a number of uses: they can emphasize words, direct a reader's attention to relations between words, and provide an overall structure for a poem.

Rhyme is used in the following poem to imitate the sound of cascading water.

ROBERT SOUTHEY (1774–1843)
From "The Cataract of Lodore"   1820

    "How does the water
    Come down at Lodore?"

· ·

From its sources which well
  In the tarn on the fell;
    From its fountains   5
      In the mountains,
    Its rills and its gills;
Through moss and through brake,
  It runs and it creeps
  For awhile, till it sleeps   10
    In its own little lake.
  And thence at departing,
  Awakening and starting,
  It runs through the reeds
  And away it proceeds,   15
Through meadow and glade,
  In sun and in shade,

And through the wood-shelter,
  Among crags in its flurry,
    Helter-skelter,
    Hurry-scurry.   20
  Here it comes sparkling,
And there it lies darkling;
Now smoking and frothing
  Its tumult and wrath in,   25
    Till in this rapid race
      On which it is bent,
    It reaches the place
    Of its steep descent.

. . . .

Dividing and gliding and sliding,   30
And falling and brawling and sprawling,
And driving and riving and striving,
And sprinkling and twinkling and wrinkling,
And sounding and bounding and rounding,
And bubbling and troubling and doubling,   35
And grumbling and rumbling and tumbling,
And clattering and battering and shattering;
Retreating and beating and meeting and sheeting,
Delaying and straying and playing and spraying,
Advancing and prancing and glancing and dancing,   40
Recoiling, turmoiling and toiling and boiling,
And gleaming and streaming and steaming and beaming,
And rushing and flushing and brushing and gushing,
And flapping and rapping and clapping and slapping,
And curling and whirling and purling and twirling,   45
And thumping and plumping and bumping and jumping,
And dashing and flashing and splashing and clashing;
And so never ending, but always descending,
Sounds and motions forever and ever are blending,
All at once and all o'er, with a mighty uproar;   50
And this way the water comes down at Lodore.

    This deluge of rhymes consists of "Sounds and motions forever and ever . . . blending" (line 49). The pace quickens as the water creeps from its mountain source and then descends in rushing cataracts. As the speed of the water increases, so do the number of rhymes, until they run in fours: "dashing and flashing and splashing and clashing" (line 47). Most rhymes meander through poems instead of flooding them; nevertheless, Southey's use of rhyme suggests how sounds can flow with meanings. "The Cataract of Lodore" has been criticized, however, for overusing onomatopoeia. Some readers find the poem silly; others regard it as a brilliant example of sound effects. What do you think?

    A variety of types of rhyme is available to poets. The most common form, **end rhyme**, comes at the ends of lines (lines 14–17).

> It runs through the reeds
>> And away it proceeds,
> Through meadow and glade,
>> In sun and in shade.

Internal rhyme places at least one of the rhymed words within the line, as in "Dividing and gliding and sliding" (line 30) or, more subtly, in the fourth and final words of "In mist or cloud, on mast or shroud."

The rhyming of single-syllable words such as *glade* and *shade* is known as *masculine rhyme*, as we see in these lines from A. E. Housman:

> Loveliest of trees, the cherry now
> Is hung with bloom along the bough.

Rhymes using words of more than one syllable are also called masculine when the same sound occurs in a final stressed syllable, as in *defend, contend; betray, away*. A *feminine rhyme* consists of a rhymed stressed syllable followed by one or more rhymed unstressed syllables, as in *butter, clutter; gratitude, attitude; quivering, shivering*. This rhyme is evident in John Millington Synge's verse:

> Lord confound this surly sister,
> Blight her brow and blotch and blister.

All of the examples so far have been *exact rhymes* because they share the same stressed vowel sounds as well as any sounds that follow the vowel. In *near rhyme* (also called *off rhyme*, *slant rhyme*, and *approximate rhyme*), the sounds are almost but not exactly alike. There are several kinds of near rhyme. One of the most common is *consonance*, an identical consonant sound preceded by a different vowel sound: *home, same; worth, breath; trophy, daffy*. Near rhyme can also be achieved by using different vowel sounds with identical consonant sounds: *sound, sand; kind, conned; fellow, fallow*. The dissonance of *blade* and *blood* in the following lines from Wilfred Owen helps to reinforce their grim tone:

> Let the boy try along this bayonet-blade
> How cold steel is, and keen with hunger of blood.

Near rhymes greatly broaden the possibility for musical effects in English, a language that, compared with Spanish or Italian, contains few exact rhymes. Do not assume, however, that a near rhyme represents a failed attempt at exact rhyme. Near rhymes allow a musical subtlety and variety and can avoid the sometimes overpowering jingling effects that exact rhymes may create.

These basic terms hardly exhaust the ways in which the sounds in poems can be labeled and discussed, but the terms can help you to describe how poets manipulate sounds for effect. Read Gerard Manley Hopkins's "God's Grandeur" (p. 740) aloud and try to determine how the sounds of the lines contribute to their sense.

Perspective

DAVID LENSON (B. 1945)
On the Contemporary Use of Rhyme 1988

One impediment to a respectable return to rhyme is the popular survival of "functional" verse: greeting cards, pedagogical and mnemonic devices ("Thirty days hath September"), nursery rhymes, advertising jingles, and of course song lyrics. Pentameters, irregular rhymes, and free verse aren't much use in songwriting, where the meter has to be governed by the time signature of the music.

Far from universities, there has been a revival of rhymed couplets in rap music, in which, to the accompaniment of synthesizers, vocalists deliver lengthy first-person narratives in tetrameter. While most writing teachers would dismiss such lyrics as doggerel, the aim of the songs is really not so far from that of Alexander Pope: to use rhyme to sharpen social insight, in the hope that the world may be reordered.

From The Chronicle of Higher Education, February 24, 1988

CONSIDERATIONS FOR CRITICAL THINKING AND WRITING

1. Read some contemporary song lyrics from a wide range of groups or vocalists. Is Lenson correct in his assessment that irregular rhyme is not much use in songwriting?

2. Examine the rhymed couplets of some rap music. Discuss whether they are used "to sharpen social insight." What is the effect of using rhymes in rap music?

3. What is your own response to rhymed poetry? Do you like yours with or without? What do you think informs your preference?

SOUND AND MEANING

GERARD MANLEY HOPKINS (1844–1889)
God's Grandeur 1877

The world is charged with the grandeur of God.
 It will flame out, like shining from shook foil;°   *shaken gold foil*
 It gathers to a greatness, like the ooze of oil
Crushed.° Why do men then now not reck his rod?°
Generations have trod, have trod, have trod;   5
 And all is seared with trade; bleared, smeared with toil;
 And wears man's smudge and shares man's smell: the soil
Is bare now, nor can foot feel, being shod.

---

4 *Crushed:* Olives crushed in their oil; *reck his rod:* Obey God.

And for all this, nature is never spent;
  There lives the dearest freshness deep down things;   10
And though the last lights off the black West went
  Oh, morning, at the brown brink eastward, springs —
Because the Holy Ghost over the bent
  World broods with warm breast and with ah! bright wings.

The subject of this poem is announced in the title and the first line: "The world is charged with the grandeur of God." The poem is a celebration of the power and greatness of God's presence in the world, but the speaker is also perplexed and dismayed by people who refuse to recognize God's authority and grandeur as they are manifested in the creation. Instead of glorifying God, "men" have degraded the earth through meaningless toil and cut themselves off from the spiritual renewal inherent in the beauty of nature. The relentless demands of commerce and industry have blinded people to the earth's natural and spiritual resources. Despite this abuse and insensitivity to God's grandeur, however, "nature is never spent"; the morning light that "springs" in the east redeems the "black West" of the night and is a sign that the spirit of the Holy Ghost is ever present in the world. This summary of the poem sketches some of the thematic significance of the lines, but it does not do justice to how they are organized around the use of sound. Hopkins's poem, unlike Southey's "The Cataract of Lodore," uses sounds in a subtle and complex way.

In the opening line Hopkins uses alliteration — a device apparent in almost every line of the poem — to connect "Go*d*" to the "worl*d*," which is "charge*d*" with his "gran*d*eur." These consonants unify the line as well. The alliteration in lines 2 and 3 suggests a harmony in the creation: the *f*'s in "*f*lame" and "*f*oil," the *sh*'s in "*sh*ining" and "*sh*ook," the *g*'s in "*g*athers" and "*g*reatness," and the visual (not alliterative) similarities of "*ooze of oil*" emphasize a world that is held together by God's will.

That harmony is abruptly interrupted by the speaker's angry question in line 4: "Why do men then now not reck his rod?" The question is as painful to the speaker as it is difficult to pronounce. The arrangement of the alliteration ("*n*ow," "*n*ot"; "*r*eck," "*r*od"), the assonance ("n*o*t," "r*o*d"; "m*e*n," "th*e*n," "r*e*ck"), and the internal rhyme ("m*en*," "th*en*") contribute to the difficulty in saying the line — a difficulty associated with human behavior. That behavior is introduced in line 5 by the repetition of "have trod" to emphasize the repeated mistakes — sins — committed by human beings. The tone is dirgelike because humanity persists in its mistaken path rather than progressing. The speaker's horror at humanity is evident in the cacophonous sounds of lines 6 to 8. Here the alliteration of "*sm*eared," "*sm*udge," and "*sm*ell" along with the internal rhymes of "s*eared*," "bl*eared*," and "sm*eared*" echo the disgust with which the speaker views humanity's "toil" with the "soil," an end rhyme that calls attention to our mistaken equation of nature with production rather than with spirituality.

In contrast to this cacophony, the final six lines build toward the joyful recognition of the new possibilities that accompany the rising sun. This recognition leads to the euphonic description of the "Holy Ghost *over*" (notice the reassuring consistency of the assonance) the world. Traditionally represented as a dove, the Holy Ghost brings love and peace to the "*world*," and "*broods* with *warm breast* and *with* ah! *bright wings*." The effect of this alliteration is mellifluous: the sound bespeaks the harmony that prevails at the end of the poem resulting from the speaker's recognition that "nature is never spent" because God loves and protects the world.

The sounds of "God's Grandeur" enhance the poem's theme; more can be said about its sounds, but it is enough to point out here that for this poem the sound strongly echoes the theme in nearly every line. Here are some more poems in which sound plays a significant role.

POEMS FOR FURTHER STUDY

Diane Lockward (b. 1953)

Linguini 2006

> When I Read "Consider each poem you like or that intrigues you. Learn from the poem. Notice its moves. Ask yourself how they are achieved. Then imitate. Yes, imitate. This will teach you craft and help you develop your personal style." —Diane Lockward

It was always linguini between us.
Linguini with white sauce, or
red sauce, sauce with basil snatched from
the garden, oregano rubbed between
our palms, a single bay leaf adrift amidst   5
plum tomatoes. Linguini with meatballs,
sausage, a side of brascioli. Like lovers
trying positions, we enjoyed it every way
we could — artichokes, mushrooms, little
neck clams, mussels, and calamari — linguini   10
twining and braiding us each to each.
Linguini knew of the kisses, the smooches,
the *molti baci.*° It was never spaghetti   *many kisses*
between us, not cappellini, nor farfalle,
vermicelli, pappardelle, fettucini, perciatelli,   15
or even tagliarini. Linguini we stabbed, pitched,
and twirled on forks, spun round and round
on silver spoons. Long, smooth, and always
al dente. In dark trattorias, we broke crusty panera,
toasted each other — *La dolce vita!*° — and sipped   *The Sweet Life* 20
Amarone,° wrapped ourselves in linguini,   *Italian wine*
briskly boiled, lightly oiled, salted, and lavished
with sauce. *Bellissimo, paradisio, belle gente!*°   *Beautiful, paradise, beautiful people*
Linguini witnessed our slurping, pulling, and
sucking, our unraveling and raveling, chins   25
glistening, napkins tucked like bibs in collars,
linguini stuck to lips, hips, and bellies, cheeks

flecked with *formaggio*° — parmesan, romano,   *cheese*
and shaved pecorino — strands of linguini flung
around our necks like two fine silk scarves.   30

CONSIDERATIONS FOR CRITICAL THINKING AND WRITING

1. **FIRST RESPONSE.** Read this poem aloud. Which words and sounds do you think
   make this such an exuberant celebration of linguini?
2. Comment on the effect of the repetitions of sound in the poem.
3. Consider the poem's final image. What would be missing if the "two fine silk
   scarves" were omitted?

LEWIS CARROLL (CHARLES LUTWIDGE DODGSON/1832–1898)

Jabberwocky   1871

'Twas brillig, and the slithy toves
   Did gyre and gimble in the wabe:
All mimsy were the borogoves,
   And the mome raths outgrabe.

"Beware the Jabberwock, my son!   5
   The jaws that bite, the claws that catch!
Beware the Jubjub bird, and shun
   The frumious Bandersnatch!"

He took his vorpal sword in hand;
   Long time the manxome foe he sought —   10
So rested he by the Tumtum tree,
   And stood awhile in thought.

And, as in uffish thought he stood,
   The Jabberwock, with eyes of flame,
Came whiffling through the tulgey wood,   15
   And burbled as it came!

One, two! One, two! And through and through
   The vorpal blade went snicker-snack!
He left it dead, and with its head
   He went galumphing back.   20

"And hast thou slain the Jabberwock?
   Come to my arms, my beamish boy!
O frabjous day! Callooh, Callay!"
   He chortled in his joy.

'Twas brillig, and the slithy toves   25
   Did gyre and gimble in the wabe:
All mimsy were the borogoves,
   And the mome raths outgrabe.

CONSIDERATIONS FOR CRITICAL THINKING AND WRITING

1. FIRST RESPONSE. What happens in this poem? Does it have any meaning?

2. Not all of the words used in this poem appear in dictionaries. In *Through the Looking Glass*, Humpty Dumpty explains to Alice that "'slithy' means 'lithe and slimy.' 'Lithe' is the same as 'active.' You see it's like a portmanteau — there are two meanings packed up into one word." Are there any other port-manteau words in the poem?

3. Which words in the poem sound especially meaningful, even if they are devoid of any denotative meanings?

CONNECTION TO ANOTHER SELECTION

1. Compare Carroll's strategies for creating sound and meaning with those used by Updike in "Player Piano" (p. 732).

WILLIAM HEYEN (B. 1940)

The Trains 1984

Signed by Franz Paul Stangl, Commandant,
there is in Berlin a document,
an order of transmittal from Treblinka:

248 freight cars of clothing,
400,000 gold watches,
25 freight cars of women's hair.   5

Some clothing was kept, some pulped for paper.
The finest watches were never melted down.
All the women's hair was used for mattresses, or dolls.

Would these words like to use some of that same paper?   10
One of those watches may pulse in your own wrist.
Does someone you know collect dolls, or sleep on human hair?

He is dead at last, Commandant Stangl of Treblinka,
but the camp's three syllables still sound like freight cars
straining around a curve, Treblinka,   15

Treblinka. Clothing, time in gold watches,
women's hair for mattresses and dolls' heads.
Treblinka. The trains from Treblinka.

CONSIDERATIONS FOR CRITICAL THINKING AND WRITING

1. FIRST RESPONSE. How does the sound of the word *Treblinka* inform your under-standing of the poem?

2. Why does the place name of Treblinka continue to resonate over time? To learn more about Treblinka, search the Web, perhaps starting at ushmm.org, the site of the United States Holocaust Memorial Museum.

3. Why do you suppose Heyen uses the word *in* instead of *on* in line 11?

4. Why is sound so important for establishing the tone of this poem? In what sense do "the camp's three syllables still sound like freight cars" (line 14)?

5. CRITICAL STRATEGIES. Read the section on reader-response strategies (pp. 1659–61) in Chapter 51, "Critical Strategies for Reading." How does this poem make you feel? Why?

JOHN DONNE (1572–1631)

Song 1633

Go and catch a falling star,
 Get with child a mandrake root,°
Tell me where all past years are,
 Or who cleft the Devil's foot,
Teach me to hear mermaids singing,   5
 Or to keep off envy's stinging,
   And find
   What wind
Serves to advance an honest mind.

If thou be'st borne to strange sights,   10
 Things invisible to see,
Ride ten thousand days and nights,
 Till age snow white hairs on thee,
Thou, when thou return'st, wilt tell me
 All strange wonders that befell thee,   15
   And swear
   Nowhere
Lives a woman true, and fair.

If thou findst one, let me know,
 Such a pilgrimage were sweet —   20
Yet do not, I would not go,
 Though at next door we might meet;
Though she were true, when you met her,
 And last, till you write your letter,
   Yet she   25
   Will be
False, ere I come, to two or three.

2 *mandrake root*: This V-shaped root resembles the lower half of the human body.

CONSIDERATIONS FOR CRITICAL THINKING AND WRITING

1. FIRST RESPONSE. What is the speaker's tone in this poem? What is his view of a woman's love? What does the speaker's use of hyperbole reveal about his emotional state?

2. Do you think Donne wants the speaker's argument to be taken seriously? Is there any humor in the poem?

3. Most of these lines end with masculine rhymes. What other kinds of rhymes are used for end rhymes?

WILFRED OWEN (1893–1918)

Futility 1918

Move him into the sun —
Gently its touch awoke him once,
At home, whispering of fields half-sown.
Always it woke him, even in France,
Until this morning and this snow.   5
If anything might rouse him now
The kind old sun will know.

Think how it wakes the seeds —
Woke once the clays of a cold star.
Are limbs, so dear achieved, are sides   10
Full-nerved, still warm, too hard to stir?
Was it for this the clay grew tall?
— O what made fatuous sunbeams toil
To break earth's sleep at all?

CONSIDERATIONS FOR CRITICAL THINKING AND WRITING

1. FIRST RESPONSE. Why is the date of this poem relevant to an appreciation of it?

2. Discuss the effects of Owen's use of rhyme.

3. How do the images and tone shift in lines 10–14 compared to lines 1–9?

CONNECTION TO ANOTHER SELECTION

1. Compare the themes of this poem and Kenneth Fearing's "AD" (p. 717).

ANDREW HUDGINS (B. 1951)

The Ice-Cream Truck 2009

From blocks away the music floats
to my enchanted ears.
It builds. It's here! And then it fades —
and I explode in tears.

I kick the TV set, and scream,   5
sobbing to extort her,
while Mom stares at *One Life to Live,*
and won't give me a quarter.

I pause, change tactics, snatch a coin
from the bottom of her purse,   10

then race to catch the ice-cream truck,
ignoring Mama's curse.

I stop the truck, I start to choose —
then see I won't be eating.
I stare down at a goddamn dime,   15
and trudge home to my beating.

CONSIDERATIONS FOR CRITICAL THINKING AND WRITING

1. FIRST RESPONSE. Describe the tone of each stanza. How do the rhymes serve to establish the tone?
2. Characterize the speaker. How do you reconcile what is said in the first stanza with the description in the final stanza?
3. This poem appeared in a collection by Hudgins titled *Shut Up, You're Fine: Poems for Very, Very Bad Children*. How does that context affect your reading of it?
4. CREATIVE RESPONSE. Add a four-line stanza in Hudgins's style that rhymes and concludes back at home.

PAUL HUMPHREY (1915–2001)

Blow   1983

Her skirt was lofted by the gale;
When I, with gesture deft,
Essayed to stay her frisky sail
She luffed, and laughed, and left.

CONSIDERATIONS FOR CRITICAL THINKING AND WRITING

1. FIRST RESPONSE. How do alliteration and assonance contribute to the euphonic effects in this poem?
2. What is the poem's controlling metaphor? Why is it especially appropriate?
3. Explain the ambiguity of the title.

ROBERT FRANCIS (1901–1987)

The Pitcher   1953

His art is eccentricity, his aim
How not to hit the mark he seems to aim at,

His passion how to avoid the obvious,
His technique how to vary the avoidance.

The others throw to be comprehended. He   5
Throws to be a moment misunderstood.

Yet not too much. Not errant, arrant, wild,
But every seeming aberration willed.

Not to, yet still, still to communicate
Making the batter understand too late.   10

CONSIDERATIONS FOR CRITICAL THINKING AND WRITING

1. FIRST RESPONSE. Explain how each pair of lines in this poem works together to describe the pitcher's art.

2. Consider how the poem itself works the way a good pitcher does. Which lines illustrate what they describe?

3. Comment on the effects of the poem's rhymes. How are the final two lines different in their rhyme from the previous lines? How does sound echo sense in lines 9–10?

4. Write an essay that examines "The Pitcher" as an extended metaphor for talking about poetry. How well does the poem characterize strategies for writing poetry as well as pitching?

5. Write an essay that develops an extended comparison between writing or reading poetry and playing or watching another sport.

CONNECTION TO ANOTHER SELECTION

1. Write an essay comparing "The Pitcher" with another work by Francis, "Catch" (p. 596). One poem defines poetry implicitly; the other defines it explicitly. Which poem do you prefer? Why?

HELEN CHASIN (B. 1938)

The Word Plum   1968

The word *plum* is delicious

pout and push, luxury of
self-love, and savoring murmur
full in the mouth and falling
like fruit   5

taut skin
pierced, bitten, provoked into
juice, and tart flesh

question
and reply, lip and tongue   10
of pleasure.

CONSIDERATIONS FOR CRITICAL THINKING AND WRITING

1. FIRST RESPONSE. What is the effect of the repetitions of the alliteration and assonance throughout the poem? How does it contribute to the poem's meaning?

2. Which sounds in the poem are like the sounds one makes while eating a plum?

3. Discuss the title. Explain whether you think this poem is more about the word *plum* or about the plum itself. Can the two be separated in the poem?

RICHARD WAKEFIELD (B. 1952)

The Bell Rope   2005

In Sunday school the boy who learned a psalm
by heart would get to sound the steeple bell
and send its tolling through the sabbath calm
to call the saved and not-so-saved as well.
For lack of practice all the lines are lost —
something about how angels' hands would bear
me up to God — but on one Pentecost
they won me passage up the steeple stair.
I leapt and grabbed the rope up high to ride
it down, I touched the floor, the rope went slack,   10
the bell was silent. Then, beatified,
I rose, uplifted as the rope pulled back.
I leapt and fell again; again it took
me up, but still the bell withheld its word —
until at last the church foundation shook   15
in bass approval, felt as much as heard,
and after I let go the bell tolled long
and loud as if repaying me for each
unanswered pull with heaven-rending song
a year of Sunday school could never teach   20
and that these forty years can not obscure.
Some nights when sleep won't come I think of how
just once there came an answer, clear and sure.
If I could find that rope I'd grasp it now.

WHEN I READ "I like poems that don't tell me how the writer feels; they tell me how the world looks to someone who feels that way. They make sense by engaging the senses, and so they become an experience. The reader is not merely an audience but a participant."

— RICHARD WAKEFIELD

CONSIDERATIONS FOR CRITICAL THINKING AND WRITING

1. FIRST RESPONSE. Describe the rhyme scheme and then read the poem aloud. How does Wakefield manage to avoid making this heavily rhymed poem sound clichéd or sing-songy?

2. Comment on the appropriateness of Wakefield's choice of diction and how it relates to the poem's images.

3. Explain how sound becomes, in a sense, the theme of the poem.

CONNECTION TO ANOTHER SELECTION

1. Compare the images and themes of "The Bell Rope" with those in Robert Frost's "Birches" (p. 877).

JEAN TOOMER (1894–1967)

Unsuspecting   ca. 1929

There is a natty kind of mind
That slicks its thoughts,
Culls its oughts,

Trims its views,
Prunes its trues,
And never suspects it is a rind.

CONSIDERATIONS FOR CRITICAL THINKING AND WRITING

1. FIRST RESPONSE. What sort of person do you think is described by the speaker?

2. Comment on the poem's diction and use of rhyme. Which word (or words) do you think are the most crucial for determining the poem's central idea?

CONNECTION TO ANOTHER SELECTION

© Bettmann/Corbis.

1. Discuss the tone and themes in "Unsuspecting" and in Stephen Crane's "The Wayfarer" (p. 702).

JOHN KEATS (1795–1821)

Ode to a Nightingale   1819

I

My heart aches, and a drowsy numbness pains
  My sense, as though of hemlock° I had drunk,   *a poison*
Or emptied some dull opiate to the drains
  One minute past, and Lethe-wards° had sunk:
'Tis not through envy of thy happy lot,   5
  But being too happy in thine happiness —
    That thou, light-wingèd Dryad° of the trees,   *wood nymph*
      In some melodious plot
Of beechen green, and shadows numberless,
    Singest of summer in full-throated ease.   10

II

O, for a draught of vintage! that hath been
  Cooled a long age in the deep-delved earth,
Tasting of Flora° and the country green,   *goddess of flowers*
  Dance, and Provençal song,° and sunburnt mirth!
O for a beaker full of the warm South,   15
  Full of the true, the blushful Hippocrene,°
    With beaded bubbles winking at the brim,
      And purple-stainèd mouth;
That I might drink, and leave the world unseen,
  And with thee fade away into the forest dim.   20

---

4 *Lethe-wards:* Toward Lethe, the river of forgetfulness in the Hades of Greek mythology.
14 *Provençal song:* The medieval troubadours of Provence, France, were known for their singing.
16 *Hippocrene:* The fountain of the Muses in Greek mythology.

III

Fade far away, dissolve, and quite forget
   What thou among the leaves hast never known,
The weariness, the fever, and the fret
   Here, where men sit and hear each other groan;
Where palsy shakes a few, sad, last gray hairs,   25
     Where youth grows pale, and specter-thin, and dies,
        Where but to think is to be full of sorrow
          And leaden-eyed despairs,
     Where Beauty cannot keep her lustrous eyes;
        Or new Love pine at them beyond tomorrow.   30

IV

Away! away! for I will fly to thee,
   Not charioted by Bacchus and his pards,°
But on the viewless wings of Poesy,
   Though the dull brain perplexes and retards:
Already with thee! tender is the night,   35
     And haply the Queen-Moon is on her throne,
        Clustered around by all her starry Fays;
         But here there is no light,
     Save what from heaven is with the breezes blown
        Through verdurous glooms and winding mossy ways.   40

V

I cannot see what flowers are at my feet,
   Nor what soft incense hangs upon the boughs,
But, in embalmèd° darkness, guess each sweet   *perfumed*
   Wherewith the seasonable month endows
The grass, the thicket, and the fruit-tree wild;   45
     What hawthorn, and the pastoral eglantine;
        Fast fading violets covered up in leaves;
         And mid-May's eldest child,
     The coming musk-rose, full of dewy wine,
        The murmurous haunt of flies on summer eves.   50

VI

Darkling° I listen; and for many a time   *in the dark*
   I have been half in love with easeful Death,
Called him soft names in many a musèd rhyme,
   To take into the air my quiet breath;
Now more than ever seems it rich to die,   55
     To cease upon the midnight with no pain,
        While thou art pouring forth thy soul abroad
         In such an ecstasy!

---

32 *Bacchus and his pards:* The Greek god of wine traveled in a chariot drawn by leopards.

Still wouldst thou sing, and I have ears in vain —
　To thy high requiem become a sod.　　　　　　　　　　60

VII

Thou wast not born for death, immortal Bird!
　No hungry generations tread thee down;
The voice I hear this passing night was heard
　In ancient days by emperor and clown:
Perhaps the selfsame song that found a path　　　　　　65
　Through the sad heart of Ruth,° when, sick for home,
　　She stood in tears amid the alien corn:
　　　The same that oft-times hath
　Charmed magic casements, opening on the foam
　Of perilous seas, in faery lands forlorn.　　　　　　70

VIII

Forlorn! the very word is like a bell
　To toll me back from thee to my sole self!
Adieu! the fancy cannot cheat so well
　As she is famed to do, deceiving elf.
Adieu! adieu! thy plaintive anthem fades　　　　　　75
　Past the near meadows, over the still stream,
　　Up the hill side; and now 'tis buried deep
　　　In the next valley-glades:
　Was it a vision, or a waking dream?
　　Fled is that music: — Do I wake or sleep?　　　　80

66 *Ruth:* A young widow in the Bible (see the book of Ruth).

CONSIDERATIONS FOR CRITICAL THINKING AND WRITING

1. FIRST RESPONSE. Why does the speaker in this ode want to leave his world for the nightingale's? What might the nightingale symbolize?

2. How does the speaker attempt to escape his world? Is he successful?

3. What changes the speaker's view of death at the end of stanza VI?

4. What does the allusion to Ruth (line 66) contribute to the ode's meaning?

5. In which lines is the imagery especially sensuous? How does this effect add to the conflict presented?

6. What calls the speaker back to himself at the end of stanza VII and the beginning of stanza VIII?

7. Choose a stanza and explain how sound is related to its meaning.

8. How regular is the stanza form of this ode?

KAY RYAN (B. 1945)

Dew   1996

As neatly as peas
in their green canoe,
as discretely as beads
strung in a row,
sit drops of dew
along a blade of grass.
But unattached and
subject to their weight,
they slip if they accumulate.
Down the green tongue
out of the morning sun
into the general damp,
they're gone.

© Christopher Felver/Corbis.

CONSIDERATIONS FOR CRITICAL THINKING AND WRITING

1. FIRST RESPONSE. How does reading the poem aloud affect your understanding of Ryan's use of rhyme to create a particular tone?

2. Explain whether the images in the poem are simply descriptive or are presented as a means of producing a theme. What is the role of the title?

HOWARD NEMEROV (1920–1991)

Because You Asked about the Line between Prose and Poetry   1980

Sparrows were feeding in a freezing drizzle
That while you watched turned into pieces of snow
Riding a gradient invisible
From silver aslant to random, white, and slow.

There came a moment that you couldn't tell.
And then they clearly flew instead of fell.

CONSIDERATIONS FOR CRITICAL THINKING AND WRITING

1. FIRST RESPONSE. Describe the distinction that this poem makes between prose and poetry. How does the poem itself become an example of that distinction?

2. Identify the kinds of rhymes Nemerov employs. How do the rhymes in the first and second stanzas differ from each other?

3. Comment on the poem's punctuation. How is it related to theme?

27

Patterns of Rhythm

I would define, in brief, the Poetry of words as the Rhythmical Creation of Beauty. Its sole arbiter is Taste.

—EDGAR ALLAN POE

The rhythms of everyday life surround us in regularly recurring movements and sounds. As you read these words, your heart pulsates while somewhere else a clock ticks, a cradle rocks, a drum beats, a dancer sways, a foghorn blasts, a wave recedes, or a child skips. We may tend to overlook rhythm because it is so tightly woven into the fabric of our experience, but it is there nonetheless, one of the conditions of life. Rhythm is also one of the conditions of speech because the voice alternately rises and falls as words are stressed or unstressed and as the pace quickens or slackens. In poetry *rhythm* refers to the recurrence of stressed and unstressed sounds. Depending on how the sounds are arranged, this can result in a pace that is fast or slow, choppy or smooth.

SOME PRINCIPLES OF METER

Poets use rhythm to create pleasurable sound patterns and to reinforce meanings. "Rhythm," Edith Sitwell once observed, "might be described as, to the world of sound, what light is to the world of sight. It shapes and gives new meaning." Prose can use rhythm effectively too, but prose that does so tends to be an exception. The following exceptional lines are from a speech by Winston Churchill to the House of Commons after Allied forces lost a great battle to German forces at Dunkirk during World War II:

> We shall not flag or fail. We shall go on to the end. We shall fight in France, we shall fight on the seas and oceans, we shall fight with growing confidence and growing strength in the air, we shall defend our island, whatever the cost may be, we shall fight on the beaches, we shall fight on the landing grounds, we shall fight in the fields and in the streets, we shall fight in the hills; we shall never surrender.

The stressed repetition of "we shall" bespeaks the resolute singleness of purpose that Churchill had to convey to the British people if they were to win the war. Repetition is also one of the devices used in poetry to create rhythmic effects. In the following excerpt from "Song of the Open Road," Walt Whitman urges the pleasures of limitless freedom on his reader:

> Allons!° the road is before us!   *Let's go!*
> It is safe — I have tried it — my own feet have tried it well — be not detain'd!
> Let the paper remain on the desk unwritten, and the book on the
>   shelf unopen'd!
> Let the tools remain in the workshop! Let the money remain unearn'd!
> Let the school stand! mind not the cry of the teacher!   5
> Let the preacher preach in his pulpit! Let the lawyer plead in the
>   court, and the judge expound the law.
>
> Camerado,° I give you my hand!   *friend*
> I give you my love more precious than money,
> I give you myself before preaching or law;
> Will you give me yourself? will you come travel with me?   10
> Shall we stick by each other as long as we live?

These rhythmic lines quickly move away from conventional values to the open road of shared experiences. Their recurring sounds are created not by rhyme or alliteration and assonance (see Chapter 26) but by the repetition of words and phrases.

Although the repetition of words and phrases can be an effective means of creating rhythm in poetry, the more typical method consists of patterns of accented or unaccented syllables. Words contain syllables that are either stressed or unstressed. A **stress** (or **accent**) places more emphasis on one syllable than on another. We say "*syl*lable" not "syl*lable*," "*em*phasis" not "em*pha*sis." We routinely stress syllables when we speak: "*Is* she con*tent* with the *con*tents of the *yel*low *pack*age?" To distinguish between two people we might say "Is *she* content . . . ?" In this way stress can be used to emphasize a particular word in a sentence. Poets often arrange words so that the desired meaning is suggested by the rhythm; hence emphasis is controlled by the poet rather than left entirely to the reader.

When a rhythmic pattern of stresses recurs in a poem, the result is **meter**. Taken together, all the metrical elements in a poem make up what is called the poem's **prosody**. **Scansion** consists of measuring the stresses in a line to determine its metrical pattern. Several methods can be used to mark lines. One widely used system uses ´ for a stressed syllable and ˘ for an unstressed syllable. In a sense, the stress mark represents the equivalent of tapping one's foot to a beat:

> Híckŏrў, díckŏrў, dóck,
> Tħe móuse răn úp tħe clóck.
> Tħe clóck strŭck ońe,
> Ańd dowń hĕ ruń,
> Híckŏrў, díckŏrў, dóck.

In the first two lines and the final line of this familiar nursery rhyme we hear three stressed syllables. In lines 3 and 4, where the meter changes for variety, we hear just two stressed syllables. The combination of stresses provides the pleasure of the rhythm we hear.

To hear the rhythms of "Hickory, dickory, dock" does not require a formal study of meter. Nevertheless, an awareness of the basic kinds of meter that appear in English poetry can enhance your understanding of how a poem achieves its effects. Understanding the sound effects of a poem and having a vocabulary with which to discuss those effects can intensify your pleasure in poetry. Although the study of meter can be extremely technical, the terms used to describe the basic meters of English poetry are relatively easy to comprehend.

The *foot* is the metrical unit by which a line of poetry is measured. A foot usually consists of one stressed and one or two unstressed syllables. A vertical line is used to separate the feet: "Tħe clóck | strŭck ońe" consists of two feet. A foot of poetry can be arranged in a variety of patterns; here are five of the chief ones:

Foot	Pattern	Example
iamb	˘ ´	ăwáy
trochee	´ ˘	Lóveľy
anapest	˘ ˘ ´	uňdĕrstánd
dactyl	´ ˘ ˘	déspĕraťe
spondee	´ ´	déad sét

The most common lines in English poetry contain meters based on iambic feet. However, even lines that are predominantly iambic will often include variations to create particular effects. Other important patterns include trochaic, anapestic, and dactylic feet. The spondee is not a sustained meter but occurs for variety or emphasis.

Iambic
> Whăt képt | hĭs eyés | frŏm gív | iňg báck | tħe gáze

Trochaic
> Hé wăs | loúdĕr | thán tħe | préachĕr

Anapestic
> Ĭ ăm caľled | tŏ tħe frónt | ŏf tħe roóm

Dactylic
> Sińg ĭt aľl | mérrĭlў

These meters have different rhythms and can create different effects. Iambic and anapestic are known as **rising meters** because they move from unstressed to stressed sounds, while trochaic and dactylic are known as **falling meters**. Anapests and dactyls tend to move more lightly and rapidly than iambs or trochees. Although no single kind of meter can be considered always better than another for a given subject, it is possible to determine whether the meter of a specific poem is appropriate for its subject. A serious poem about a tragic death would most likely not be well served by lilting rhythms. Keep in mind, too, that though one or another of these four basic meters might constitute the predominant rhythm of a poem, variations can occur within lines to change the pace or call attention to a particular word.

A **line** is measured by the number of feet it contains. Here, for example, is an iambic line with three feet: "If she | shŏuld wrîte | ă nóte." These are the names for line lengths:

monometer: one foot   pentameter: five feet

dimeter: two feet   hexameter: six feet

trimeter: three feet   heptameter: seven feet

tetrameter: four feet   octameter: eight feet

By combining the name of a line length with the name of a foot, we can describe the metrical qualities of a line concisely. Consider, for example, the pattern of feet and length of this line:

I didn't want the boy to hit the dog.

The iambic rhythm of this line falls into five feet; hence it is called **iambic pentameter**. Iambic is the most common pattern in English poetry because its rhythm appears so naturally in English speech and writing. Unrhymed iambic pentameter is called **blank verse**; Shakespeare's plays are built on such lines.

Less common than the iamb, trochee, anapest, or dactyl is the **spondee**, a two-syllable foot in which both syllables are stressed (´´). Note the effect of the spondaic foot at the beginning of this line:

Déad sét | ăgaińst | the plan | hĕ wént | ăwáy.

Spondees can slow a rhythm and provide variety and emphasis, particularly in iambic and trochaic lines. Also less common is a **pyrrhic** foot, which consists of two unstressed syllables, as in Shakespeare's "A horse! A horse! My kingdom for a horse!" Pyrrhic feet are typically variants for iambic verse rather than predominant patterns in lines. A line that ends with a stressed syllable is said to have a **masculine ending**, whereas a line that ends with an extra unstressed syllable is said to have a **feminine ending**. Consider, for example, these two lines from Timothy Steele's "Waiting for the Storm" (the entire poem appears on p. 760):

feminine: The sánd | ăt my feet | grŏw cóld | er,
masculine: The damp | aír chíll | and spréad.

The effects of English meters are easily seen in the following lines by Samuel Taylor Coleridge, in which the rhythm of each line illustrates the meter described in it:

SAMUEL TAYLOR COLERIDGE (1772–1834)

Mnemonic 1803

Trochee trips from long to short;
From long to long in solemn sort
Slow Spondee stalks; strong foot yet ill able
Ever to come up with Dactylic trisyllable.
Iambics march from short to long —
With a leap and a bound the swift Anapests throng.

CONSIDERATIONS FOR CRITICAL THINKING AND WRITING

1. FIRST RESPONSE. Scan each of the lines and see how this little handbook of a poem works.
2. Memorize this poem (Coleridge wrote it for his son). By doing so, you will have learned from a master.

The speed of a line is also affected by the number of pauses in it. A pause within a line is called a *caesura* and is indicated by a double vertical line (‖). A caesura can occur anywhere within a line and need not be indicated by punctuation:

Camerado, ‖ I give you my hand!
I give you my love ‖ more precious than money.

A slight pause occurs within each of these lines and at its end. Both kinds of pauses contribute to the lines' rhythm.

When a line has a pause at its end, it is called an ***end-stopped line***. Such pauses reflect normal speech patterns and are often marked by punctuation. A line that ends without a pause and continues into the next line for its meaning is called a ***run-on line***. Running over from one line to another is also called ***enjambment***. The first and eighth lines of the following poem are run-on lines; the rest are end-stopped.

WILLIAM WORDSWORTH (1770–1850)

My Heart Leaps Up 1807

My heart leaps up when I behold
   A rainbow in the sky:
So was it when my life began;
So is it now I am a man;
So be it when I shall grow old,
   Or let me die!

The child is father of the Man;
And I could wish my days to be
Bound each to each by natural piety.

Run-on lines have a different rhythm from end-stopped lines. Lines 3 and 4 and lines 8 and 9 are iambic, but the effect of their two rhythms is very different when we read these lines aloud. The enjambment of lines 8 and 9 reinforces their meaning; just as the "days" are bound together, so are the lines.

The rhythm of a poem can be affected by several devices: the kind and number of stresses within lines, the length of lines, and the kinds of pauses that appear within lines or at their ends. In addition, as we saw in Chapter 26, the sound of a poem is affected by alliteration, assonance, rhyme, and consonance. These sounds help to create rhythms by controlling our pronunciations, as in the following lines excerpted from "An Essay on Criticism," a poem by Alexander Pope:

Soft is the strain when Zephyr gently blows,
And the smooth stream in smoother numbers flows;
But when loud surges lash the sounding shore,
The hoarse, rough verse should like the torrent roar.

These lines are effective because their rhythm and sound work with their meaning.

Suggestions for Scanning a Poem

These suggestions should help you in talking about a poem's meter.

1. After reading the poem through, read it aloud and mark the stressed syllables in each line. Then mark the unstressed syllables.

2. From your markings, identify what kind of foot is dominant (iambic, trochaic, dactylic, or anapestic) and divide the lines into feet, keeping in mind that the vertical line marking a foot may come in the middle of a word as well as at its beginning or end.

3. Determine the number of feet in each line. Remember that there may be variations; some lines may be shorter or longer than the predominant meter. What is important is the overall pattern. Do not assume that variations represent the poet's inability to fulfill the overall pattern. Notice the effects of variations and whether they emphasize words and phrases or disrupt your expectation for some other purpose.

4. Listen for pauses within lines and mark the caesuras; many times there will be no punctuation to indicate them.

5. Recognize that scansion does not always yield a definitive measurement of a line. Even experienced readers may differ over the scansion of a given line. What is important is not a precise description of the line but an awareness of how a poem's rhythms contribute to its effects.

The following poem demonstrates how you can use an understanding of meter and rhythm to gain a greater appreciation for what a poem is saying.

Timothy Steele (b. 1948)

Waiting for the Storm 1986

Bréeze sént | ă wrink | lǐng dárk | něss
Ácróss | thĕ bay. || Ĭ knélt
Bĕneáth | ăn úp | turnĕd bóat,
Aňd, mo | mĕnt by mo | mĕnt, félt

Thĕ sánd | ăt my féet | grŏw cóld | ĕr,
Thĕ damp | áir chíll | ăňd spréad.
Thĕn thĕ | first ráin | dróps sóund | ĕd
Oň thĕ húll | abóve | mў héad.

The predominant meter of this poem is iambic trimeter, but there is plenty of variation as the storm rapidly approaches and finally begins to pelt the sheltered speaker. The emphatic spondee ("Breeze sent") pushes the darkness quickly across the bay while the caesura at the end of the sentence in line 2 creates a pause that sets up a feeling of suspense and expectation that is measured in the ticking rhythm of line 4, a run-on line that brings us into the chilly sand and air of the second stanza. Perhaps the most impressive sound effect used in the poem appears in the second syllable of "sounded" in line 7. That "ed" precedes the sound of the poem's final word, "head," just as if it were the first drop of rain hitting the hull above the speaker. The visual, tactile, and auditory images make "Waiting for the Storm" an intense sensory experience.

A SAMPLE STUDENT RESPONSE

Marco Pacini

Professor Fierstein

English 201

2 November 2015

The Rhythm of Anticipation in Timothy Steele's "Waiting for the Storm"

In his poem "Waiting for the Storm," Timothy Steele uses run-on lines, or enjambment, to create a feeling of anticipation. Every line ends unfinished or is a continuation of the previous line, so we must read on to gain completion. This open-ended rhythm mirrors the waiting experienced by the speaker of the poem.

Nearly every line of the poem leaves the reader in suspense:

> I knelt
> Beneath an upturned boat,
> And, moment by moment, felt
>
> The sand at my feet grow colder,
> The damp air chill and spread. (2-6)

Action is interrupted at every line break. We have to wait to find out where the speaker knelt and what was felt, since information is given in small increments. So, like the speaker, we must take in the details of the storm little by little, "moment by moment" (4). Even when the first drops of rain hit the hull, the poem ends before we can see or feel the storm's full force, and we are left waiting, in a continuous state of anticipation. . . .

Work Cited

Steele, Timothy. "Waiting for the Storm." *The Bedford Introduction to Literature*. Ed. Michael Meyer. 11th ed. Boston: Bedford/St. Martin's, 2016. 760. Print.

This next poem also reinforces meanings through its use of meter and rhythm.

WILLIAM BUTLER YEATS (1865–1939)
That the Night Come   1912

She lived | in storm | and strife,
Her soul | had such | desire
For what | proud death | may bring
That it | could not | endure
The com | mon good | of life,   5
But lived | as 'twere | a king
That packed | his mar | riage day
With ban | neret | and pen | non,
Trumpet | and ket | tledrum,
And the | outrag | eous can | non,   10
To bun | dle time | away
That the | night come.

Scansion reveals that the predominant meter here is iambic trimeter: each line contains three stressed and unstressed syllables that form a regular, predictable rhythm through line 7. That rhythm is disrupted, however, when the speaker compares the woman's longing for what death brings to a king's eager anticipation of his wedding night. The king packs the day with noisy fanfares and celebrations to fill up time and distract himself. Unable to accept "The common good of life," the woman fills her days with "storm and strife." In a determined effort "To bundle time away," she, like the king, impatiently awaits the night.

Lines 8–10 break the regular pattern established in the first seven lines. The extra unstressed syllable in lines 8 and 10 along with the trochaic feet in lines 9 ("Trúmpĕt") and 10 ("Ănd thĕ") interrupt the basic iambic trimeter and parallel the woman's and the king's frenetic activity. These lines thus echo the inability of the woman and king to "endure" regular or normal time. The last line is the most irregular in the poem. The final two accented syllables sound like the deep resonant beats of a kettledrum or a cannon firing. The words "night come" dramatically remind us that what the woman anticipates is not a lover but the mysterious finality of death. The meter serves, then, in both its regularity and variations to reinforce the poem's meaning and tone.

The following poems are especially rich in their rhythms and sounds. As you read and study them, notice how patterns of rhythm and the sounds of words reinforce meanings and contribute to the poems' effects. And, perhaps most important, read the poems aloud so that you can hear them.

POEMS FOR FURTHER STUDY

WILLIAM TROWBRIDGE (B. 1941)

Drumming behind You in the High School Band   1989

Rehearsing in street clothes after school,
we measured off the football field
in the spice and chill of early fall.
Through roll-off, counterpoint, and turn,
by the grunt and pop of blocking drill,   5
I marked the cadence of switching hips
no martial air could ever hold.
How left was left, how right was right!
We had a rhythm all our own
and made them march to it, slowing "The Stars   10
and Stripes Forever" as the sun stretched
our shadows toward the rising moon
and my heart kept stepping on my heels.

CONSIDERATIONS FOR CRITICAL THINKING AND WRITING

1. FIRST RESPONSE. Describe the various "cadences" of this poem.

2. How are the rhythms of the lines related to their meaning?

3. Using the images from the poem to make your point, discuss whether the
   speaker is simply an ogling cad or something else.

ALFRED, LORD TENNYSON (1809–1892)

Break, Break, Break   1842

Break, break, break,
    On thy cold gray stones, O Sea!
And I would that my tongue could utter
    The thoughts that arise in me.

O, well for the fisherman's boy,   5
    That he shouts with his sister at play!
O, well for the sailor lad,
    That he sings in his boat on the bay!

And the stately ships go on
    To their haven under the hill;   10
But O for the touch of a vanished hand,
    And the sound of a voice that is still!

Break, break, break
    At the foot of thy crags, O Sea!
But the tender grace of a day that is dead   15
    Will never come back to me.

1. FIRST RESPONSE. Paraphrase the poem and describe its tone.

2. How do lines 1 and 13 differ from the predominant meter of the rest of the lines? How do these lines control the poem's tone?

3. What is the effect of the repetition? What does "break" refer to in addition to the waves?

ALICE JONES (B. 1949)

The Foot 1993

Our improbable support, erected
on the osseous architecture
of the calcaneus, talus, cuboid,
navicular, cuneiforms, metatarsals,
phalanges, a plethora of hinges,   5

all strung together by gliding
tendons, covered by the pearly
plantar fascia, then fat-padded
to form the sole, humble surface
of our contact with earth.   10

Here the body's broadest tendon
anchors the heel's fleshy base,
the finely wrinkled skin stretches
forward across the capillaried arch,
to the ball, a balance point.   15

A wide web of flexor tendons
and branched veins maps the dorsum,
fades into the stub-laden bone
splay, the stuffed sausage sacks
of toes, each with a tuft   20

of proximal hairs to introduce
the distal nail, whose useless
curve remembers an ancestor,
the vanished creature's wild
and necessary claw.   25

CONSIDERATIONS FOR CRITICAL THINKING AND WRITING

1. FIRST RESPONSE. What is the effect of the diction? What sort of tone is established by the use of anatomical terms? How do the terms affect the rhythm?

2. Jones has described the form of "The Foot" as "five stubby stanzas." Explain why the lines of this poem may or may not warrant this description of the stanzas.

3. CRITICAL STRATEGIES. Read the section on formalist strategies (pp. 1645–47) in Chapter 51, "Critical Strategies for Reading." Describe the effect of the final stanza. How would your reading be affected if the poem ended after the comma in the middle of line 22?

A. E. Housman (1859–1936)

When I was one-and-twenty   1896

When I was one-and-twenty
  I heard a wise man say,
"Give crowns and pounds and guineas
  But not your heart away;
Give pearls away and rubies   5
  But keep your fancy free."
But I was one-and-twenty,
  No use to talk to me.

When I was one-and-twenty
  I heard him say again,   10
"The heart out of the bosom
  Was never given in vain;
'Tis paid with sighs a plenty
  And sold for endless rue."
And I am two-and-twenty,   15
  And oh, 'tis true, 'tis true.

Considerations for Critical Thinking and Writing

1. **First response.** How does the basic metrical pattern affect your understanding of the speaker?

2. How do lines 1–8 parallel lines 9–16 in their use of rhyme and metaphor? Are there any significant differences between the stanzas?

3. What do you think has happened to change the speaker's attitude toward love?

4. Explain why you agree or disagree with the advice given by the "wise man."

5. What is the effect of the repetition in line 16?

Virginia Hamilton Adair (1913–2004)

Pro Snake   1998

Some say the Bible teaches fear of women, snakes,
and God, who killed his manchild for our sakes
and puts a mark beside our least mistakes,
and beats us all until our spirit breaks.

Must we believe his godly finger shakes
at Eve for every apple pie she bakes?
I'd rather take my chances with the snakes.

Considerations for Critical Thinking and Writing

1. **First response.** Scan the poem, marking the stressed and unstressed syllables. Which words are particularly stressed? Why?

2. Every line ends with the same rhyme. Why do you suppose Adair chose that scheme? How does it affect the tone of the peom?

3. Is there a serious theme coiled in the humor of "Pro Snake"?

RACHEL HADAS (B. 1948)

The Red Hat   1995

It started before Christmas. Now our son
officially walks to school alone.
Semi-alone, it's accurate to say:
I or his father track him on the way.
He walks up on the east side of West End,   5
we on the west side. Glances can extend
(and do) across the street; not eye contact.
Already ties are feeling and not fact.
Straus Park is where these parallel paths part;
he goes alone from there. The watcher's heart   10
stretches, elastic in its love and fear,
toward him as we see him disappear,
striding briskly. Where two weeks ago,
holding a hand, he'd dawdle, dreamy, slow,
he now is hustled forward by the pull   15
of something far more powerful than school.

The mornings we turn back to are no more
than forty minutes longer than before,
but they feel vastly different — flimsy, strange,
wavering in the eddies of this change,   20
empty, unanchored, perilously light
since the red hat vanished from our sight.

CONSIDERATIONS FOR CRITICAL THINKING AND WRITING

1. **FIRST RESPONSE.** What emotions do the parents experience throughout the poem? How do you think the boy feels? Does the metrical pattern affect your understanding of the parents or the boy?

2. What prevents the rhymed couplets in this poem from sounding sing-songy? What is the predominant meter?

3. What is it that "pull[s]" the boy along in lines 15–16?

4. Why do you think Hadas titled the poem "The Red Hat" rather than, for example, "Paths Part" (line 9)?

5. **CRITICAL STRATEGIES.** Read the section on psychological strategies (pp. 1649–51) in Chapter 51, "Critical Strategies for Reading." How does the speaker reveal her personal psychology in this poem?

ROBERT HERRICK (1591–1674)

Delight in Disorder   1648

A sweet disorder in the dress
Kindles in clothes a wantonness.
A lawn° about the shoulders thrown   *linen scarf*
Into a fine distraction;

An erring lace, which here and there   5
Enthralls the crimson stomacher,
A cuff neglectful, and thereby
Ribbons to flow confusedly;
A winning wave, deserving note,
In the tempestuous petticoat;   10
A careless shoestring, in whose tie
I see a wild civility;
Do more bewitch me than when art
Is too precise in every part.

Considerations for Critical Thinking and Writing

1. FIRST RESPONSE. Why does the speaker in this poem value "disorder" so highly? How do the poem's organization and rhythmic order relate to its theme? Are they "precise in every part" (line 14)?

2. Which words in the poem indicate disorder? Which words indicate the speaker's response to that disorder? What are the connotative meanings of each set of words? Why are they appropriate? What do they suggest about the woman and the speaker?

3. Write a short essay in which you agree or disagree with the speaker's views on dress.

BEN JONSON (1573–1637)

Still to Be Neat   1609

Still° to be neat, still to be dressed,   *continually*
As you were going to a feast;
Still to be powdered, still perfumed;
Lady, it is to be presumed,
Though art's hid causes are not found,   5
All is not sweet, all is not sound.

Give me a look, give me a face
That makes simplicity a grace;
Robes loosely flowing, hair as free;
Such sweet neglect more taketh me   10
Then all th' adulteries of art.
They strike mine eyes, but not my heart.

Considerations for Critical Thinking and Writing

1. FIRST RESPONSE. What are the speaker's reservations about the lady in the first stanza? What do you think "sweet" means in line 6?

2. What does the speaker want from the lady in the second stanza? How has the meaning of "sweet" shifted from line 6 to line 10? What other words in the poem are especially charged with connotative meanings?

3. How do the rhythms of Jonson's lines help to reinforce meanings? Pay particular attention to lines 6 and 12.

CONNECTIONS TO OTHER SELECTIONS

1. Write an essay comparing the themes of "Still to Be Neat" and Herrick's preceding poem, "Delight in Disorder." How do the speakers make similar points but from different perspectives?

2. How does the rhythm of "Still to Be Neat" compare with that of "Delight in Disorder"? Which do you find more effective? Explain why.

WILLIAM BLAKE (1757–1827)

The Lamb   1789

© Corbis.

> Little Lamb, who made thee?
> Dost thou know who made thee?
> Gave thee life, and bid thee feed
> By the stream and o'er the mead;
> Gave thee clothing of delight,
> Softest clothing, wooly, bright;
> Gave thee such a tender voice,
> Making all the vales rejoice?
> Little Lamb, who made thee?
> Dost thou know who made thee?   10
>
> Little Lamb, I'll tell thee,
> Little Lamb, I'll tell thee:
> He is callèd by thy name,
> For he calls himself a Lamb.
> He is meek, and he is mild;   15
> He became a little child.
> I a child, and thou a lamb,
> We are callèd by his name.
> Little Lamb, God bless thee!
> Little Lamb, God bless thee!   20

CONSIDERATIONS FOR CRITICAL THINKING AND WRITING

1. FIRST RESPONSE. This poem is from Blake's *Songs of Innocence*. Describe its tone. How do the meter, rhyme, and repetition help to characterize the speaker's voice?

2. Why is it significant that the animal addressed by the speaker is a lamb? What symbolic value would be lost if the animal were, for example, a doe?

3. How does the second stanza answer the question raised in the first? What is the speaker's view of the creation?

WILLIAM BLAKE (1757–1827)

The Tyger   1794

> Tyger! Tyger! burning bright
> In the forests of the night,
> What immortal hand or eye
> Could frame thy fearful symmetry?

In what distant deeps or skies   5
Burnt the fire of thine eyes?
On what wings dare he aspire?
What the hand dare seize the fire?

And what shoulder, and what art,
Could twist the sinews of thy heart?   10
And when thy heart began to beat,
What dread hand? and what dread feet?

What the hammer? what the chain?
In what furnace was thy brain?
What the anvil? what dread grasp   15
Dare its deadly terrors clasp?

When the stars threw down their spears,
And watered heaven with their tears,
Did he smile his work to see?
Did he who made the Lamb make thee?   20

Tyger! Tyger! burning bright
In the forests of the night,
What immortal hand or eye
Dare frame thy fearful symmetry?

CONSIDERATIONS FOR CRITICAL THINKING AND WRITING

1. FIRST RESPONSE. This poem from Blake's *Songs of Experience* is often paired with
   "The Lamb." Describe the poem's tone. Is the speaker's voice the same here as
   in "The Lamb"? Which words are repeated, and how do they contribute to the
   tone?

2. What is revealed about the nature of the tiger by the words used to describe its
   creation? What do you think the tiger symbolizes?

3. Unlike in "The Lamb," more than one question is raised in "The Tyger." What
   are these questions? Are they answered?

4. Compare the rhythms in "The Lamb" and "The Tyger." Each basically uses a
   seven-syllable line, but the effects are very different. Why?

5. Using these two poems as the basis of your discussion, describe what distinguishes innocence from experience.

CARL SANDBURG (1878–1967)

Chicago 1916

Hog Butcher for the World,
Tool Maker, Stacker of Wheat,
Player with Railroads and the Nation's Freight Handler;
Stormy, husky, brawling,
City of the Big Shoulders: 5

They tell me you are wicked and I believe them, for I have seen your painted
        women under the gas lamps luring the farm boys.

And they tell me you are crooked and I answer: Yes, it is true I have seen the
    gunman kill and go free to kill again.
And they tell me you are brutal and my reply is: On the faces of women and
    children I have seen the marks of wanton hunger.
And having answered so I turn once more to those who sneer at this my city, and I
    give them back the sneer and say to them:
Come and show me another city with lifted head singing so proud to be alive and
    coarse and strong and cunning.   10
Flinging magnetic curses amid the toil of piling job on job, here is a tall bold
    slugger set vivid against the little soft cities;
Fierce as a dog with tongue lapping for action, cunning as a savage pitted against
    the wilderness,
    Bareheaded,
    Shoveling,
    Wrecking,   15
    Planning,
    Building, breaking, rebuilding,
Under the smoke, dust all over his mouth, laughing with white teeth,
Under the terrible burden of destiny laughing as a young man laughs,
Laughing even as an ignorant fighter laughs who has never lost a battle,   20
Bragging and laughing that under his wrist is the pulse, and under his ribs the
      heart of the people,
    Laughing!
Laughing the stormy, husky, brawling laughter of Youth, half-naked, sweating,
    proud to be Hog Butcher, Tool Maker, Stacker of Wheat, Player with
    Railroads and Freight Handler to the Nation.

CONSIDERATIONS FOR CRITICAL THINKING AND WRITING

1. FIRST RESPONSE. Sandburg's personification of Chicago creates a strong identity
for the city. Explain why you find the city attractive or not.

2. How do the length and rhythm of lines 1–5 compare with those of the final lines?

3. CREATIVE RESPONSE. Using "Chicago" as a model for style, try writing a tribute
to or a condemnation of a place that you know well. Make an effort to use vivid
images and stylistic techniques that capture its rhythms.

CONNECTION TO ANOTHER SELECTION

1. Compare "Chicago" with William Blake's "London" (p. 679) in style and theme.

E. E. CUMMINGS (1894–1962)

O sweet spontaneous   1920

O sweet spontaneous
earth how often have
the
doting

    fingers of   5
prurient philosophers pinched

and
poked

thee
, has the naughty thumb   10
of science prodded
thy

  beauty   .how
often have religions taken
thee upon their scraggy knees   15
squeezing and

buffeting thee that thou mightest conceive
gods
   (but
true   20

to the incomparable
couch of death thy
rhythmic
lover

  thou answerest   25

them only with

  spring)

CONSIDERATIONS FOR CRITICAL THINKING AND WRITING

1. FIRST RESPONSE. What is the controlling metaphor that Cummings uses to characterize philosophers, scientists, and theologians? How is the earth portrayed?

2. In what sense is spring the answer to the issues raised in the poem?

3. To what extent does the arrangement of lines on the page serve to establish rhythm?

CONNECTION TO ANOTHER SELECTION

1. Discuss the treatment of science in "O sweet spontaneous" and in Edgar Allan Poe's "Sonnet — To Science" (p. 615).

JOHN MALONEY (B. 1947)

Good! 1999

The ball goes up off glass and rebounded
down the court, outlet flung to the quick guard
like clicking seconds: he dribbles, hounded
by hands, calls the play, stops short, looking hard
for a slant opening, fakes it twice, passes   5
into the center — he lobs to the small
forward, top of the key, a pick: asses

crash (the pick-and-roll), he cuts, bumps, the ball
reaches him as he turns, dribbles, sends it
back to the baseline, forward back to him,   10
jump — and in midair, twisting, he bends it
over a tangle of arms — SHOOTS, the rim
rattles as it jerks against the back joints,
and into the net, trippingly drop two points.

CONSIDERATIONS FOR CRITICAL THINKING AND WRITING

1. FIRST RESPONSE. Comment on the effects of the lines' rhythms.
2. Notice the precise pattern of rhyme. How is that related to the action in the poem?

THEODORE ROETHKE (1908–1963)

My Papa's Waltz   1948

The whiskey on your breath
Could make a small boy dizzy;
But I hung on like death:
Such waltzing was not easy.

We romped until the pans   5
Slid from the kitchen shelf;
My mother's countenance
Could not unfrown itself.

The hand that held my wrist
Was battered on one knuckle;   10
At every step you missed
My right ear scraped a buckle.

You beat time on my head
With a palm caked hard by dirt,
Then waltzed me off to bed   15
Still clinging to your shirt.

CONSIDERATIONS FOR CRITICAL THINKING AND WRITING

1. FIRST RESPONSE. What details characterize the father in this poem? How does the speaker's choice of words reveal his feeling about his father? Is the remembering speaker still a boy?
2. Characterize the rhythm of the poem. Does it move "like death" (line 3) or is it more like a waltz? Is the rhythm regular throughout the poem? What is its effect?
3. Comment on the appropriateness of the title. Why do you suppose Roethke didn't use "My Father's Waltz"?

RONALD WALLACE (B. 1945)

Dogs 1997

When I was six years old I hit one with
a baseball bat. An accident, of course,
and broke his jaw. They put that dog to sleep,
a euphemism even then I knew
could not excuse me from the lasting wrath   5
of memory's flagellation. My remorse
could dog me as it would, it wouldn't keep
me from the life sentence that I drew:

For I've been barked at, bitten, nipped, knocked flat,
slobbered over, humped, sprayed, beshat,   10
by spaniel, terrier, retriever, bull, and Dane.
But through the years what's given me most pain
of all the dogs I've been the victim of
are those whose slow eyes gazed at me, in love.

CONSIDERATIONS FOR CRITICAL THINKING AND WRITING

1. FIRST RESPONSE. Discuss the relationship between the poem's first sentence and
   its last. What's happened to the speaker in between?
2. Comment on the rhyme scheme. Would you characterize it as obvious or
   subtle? Explain why.
3. How does Wallace's use of caesura and enjambement affect the poem's rhythm?

CONNECTION TO OTHER SELECTIONS

1. Compare this poem's theme with that of John Updike's "Dog's Death" (p. 592).
2. In an essay, discuss the strategies used in this sonnet and in Shakespeare's "My
   mistress' eyes are nothing like the sun" (p. 781) to create emotion in the reader.

Perspective

LOUISE BOGAN (1897–1970)

On Formal Poetry 1953

What is formal poetry? It is poetry written in form. And what is *form*? The elements of form, so far as poetry is concerned, are meter and rhyme. Are these elements merely mold and ornaments that have been impressed upon poetry from
without? Are they indeed restrictions which bind and fetter language and the
thought and emotion behind, under, within language in a repressive way? Are they
arbitrary rules which have lost all validity since they have been broken to good
purpose by "experimental poets," ancient and modern? Does the breaking up of

form, or its total elimination, always result in an increase of power and of effect; and is any return to form a sort of relinquishment of freedom, or retreat to old fogeyism?

From *A Poet's Alphabet*

CONSIDERATIONS FOR CRITICAL THINKING AND WRITING

1. Choose one of the questions Bogan raises and write an essay in response to it using two or three poems from this chapter to illustrate your answer.

2. CREATIVE RESPONSE. Try writing a poem in meter and rhyme. Does the experience make your writing feel limited or not?

28

Poetic Forms

Writing a poem is like repacking a small suitcase for a long trip over and over. The balance of want and need.
—WILLIAM HATHAWAY

William Hathaway.

Poems come in a variety of shapes. Although the best poems always have their own unique qualities, many of them also conform to traditional patterns. Frequently the *form* of a poem — its overall structure or shape — follows an already established design. A poem that can be categorized by the patterns of its lines, meter, rhymes, and stanzas is considered a *fixed form* because it follows a prescribed model such as a sonnet. However, poems written in a fixed form do not always fit models precisely; writers sometimes work variations on traditional forms to create innovative effects.

Not all poets are content with variations on traditional forms. Some prefer to create their own structures and shapes. Poems that do not conform to established patterns of meter, rhyme, and stanza are called *free verse* or *open form* poetry. (See Chapter 29 for further discussion of open forms.) This kind of poetry creates its own ordering principles through the careful arrangement of words and phrases in line lengths that embody rhythms appropriate to the meaning. Modern and contemporary poets in particular have learned to use the blank space on the page as a significant functional element (for a vivid example, see E. E. Cumming's "l(a," p. 603). Good poetry of this kind is structured in ways that can be as demanding, interesting, and satisfying as fixed forms. Open and fixed forms represent different poetic styles, but they are identical in the sense that both use language in concentrated ways to convey meanings, experiences, emotions, and effects.

SOME COMMON POETIC FORMS

A familiarity with some of the most frequently used fixed forms of poetry is useful because it allows for a better understanding of how a poem works. Classifying patterns allows us to talk about the effects of established rhythm and rhyme and to recognize how significant variations from them affect the pace and meaning of the lines. An awareness of form also allows us to anticipate how a poem is likely to proceed. As we shall see, a sonnet creates a different set of expectations in a reader from those of, say, a limerick. A reader isn't likely to find in limericks the kind of serious themes that often make their way into sonnets. The discussion that follows identifies some of the important poetic forms frequently encountered in English poetry.

The shape of a fixed-form poem is often determined by the way in which the lines are organized into stanzas. A *stanza* consists of a grouping of lines, set off by a space, that usually has a set pattern of meter and rhyme. This pattern is ordinarily repeated in other stanzas throughout the poem. What is usual is not obligatory, however; some poems may use a different pattern for each stanza, somewhat like paragraphs in prose.

Traditionally, though, stanzas do share a common *rhyme scheme*, the pattern of end rhymes. We can map out rhyme schemes by noting patterns of rhyme with lowercase letters: the first rhyme sound is designated *a,* the second becomes *b,* the third *c,* and so on. Using this system, we can describe the rhyme scheme in the following poem this way: *aabb, ccdd, eeff.*

A. E. HOUSMAN (1859–1936)
Loveliest of trees, the cherry now 1896

Loveliest of trees, the cherry now	*a*
Is hung with bloom along the bough,	*a*
And stands about the woodland ride	*b*
Wearing white for Eastertide.	*b*
Now, of my threescore years and ten,	*c*
Twenty will not come again,	*c*
And take from seventy springs a score,	*d*
It only leaves me fifty more.	*d*
And since to look at things in bloom	*e*
Fifty springs are little room,	*e*

5

10

About the woodlands I will go   *f*
To see the cherry hung with snow.   *f*

CONSIDERATIONS FOR CRITICAL THINKING AND WRITING

1. FIRST RESPONSE. What is the speaker's attitude in this poem toward time and life?
2. Why is spring an appropriate season for the setting rather than, say, winter?
3. Paraphrase each stanza. How do the images in each reinforce the poem's themes?
4. Lines 1 and 12 are not intended to rhyme, but they are close. What is the effect of the near rhyme of "now" and "snow"? How does the rhyme enhance the theme?

Poets often create their own stanzaic patterns; hence there is an infinite number of kinds of stanzas. One way of talking about stanzaic forms is to describe a given stanza by how many lines it contains.

A *couplet* consists of two lines that usually rhyme and have the same meter; couplets are frequently not separated from each other by space on the page. A *heroic couplet* consists of rhymed iambic pentameter. Here is an example from Alexander Pope's "Essay on Criticism":

One science only will one genius fit;   *a*
So vast is art, so narrow human wit: *a*
Not only bounded to peculiar arts,   *b*
But oft in those confined to single parts. *b*

A *tercet* is a three-line stanza. When all three lines rhyme, they are called a *triplet*. Two triplets make up this captivating poem.

ROBERT HERRICK (1591–1674)

Upon Julia's Clothes   1648

Whenas in silks my Julia goes,   *a*
Then, then, methinks, how sweetly flows   *a*
That liquefaction of her clothes.   *a*

Next, when I cast mine eyes, and see   *b*
That brave vibration, each way free,   *b*
O, how that glittering taketh me!   *b*

CONSIDERATIONS FOR CRITICAL THINKING AND WRITING

1. FIRST RESPONSE. What purpose does alliteration serve in this poem?
2. Comment on the effect of the meter. How is it related to the speaker's description of Julia's clothes?

3. Look up the word *brave* in the *Oxford English Dictionary.* Which of its meanings is appropriate to describe Julia's movement? Some readers interpret lines 4–6 to mean that Julia has no clothes on. What do you think?

CONNECTION TO ANOTHER SELECTION

1. Compare the tone of this poem with that of Paul Humphrey's "Blow" (p. 747). Are the situations and speakers similar? Is there any difference in tone between these two poems?

Terza rima consists of an interlocking three-line rhyme scheme: *aba, bcb, cdc, ded,* and so on. Dante's *Divine Comedy* uses this pattern, as does Robert Frost's "Acquainted with the Night" (p. 711) and Percy Bysshe Shelley's "Ode to the West Wind" (p. 795).

A *quatrain*, or four-line stanza, is the most common stanzaic form in the English language and can have various meters and rhyme schemes (if any). The most common rhyme schemes are *aabb, abba, aaba,* and *abcb.* This last pattern is especially characteristic of the popular *ballad stanza*, which consists of alternating eight- and six-syllable lines. Samuel Taylor Coleridge adopted this pattern in "The Rime of the Ancient Mariner"; here is one representative stanza:

> All in a hot and copper sky
> The bloody Sun, at noon,
> Right up above the mast did stand,
> No bigger than the Moon.

There are a number of longer stanzaic forms, and the list of types of stanzas could be extended considerably, but knowing these three most basic patterns should prove helpful to you in talking about the form of a great many poems. In addition to stanzaic forms, there are fixed forms that characterize entire poems. Lyric poems can be, for example, sonnets, villanelles, sestinas, or epigrams.

Sonnet

The *sonnet* has been a popular literary form in English since the sixteenth century, when it was adopted from the Italian *sonnetto,* meaning "little song." A sonnet consists of fourteen lines, usually written in iambic pentameter. Because the sonnet has been such a favorite form, writers have experimented with many variations on its essential structure. Nevertheless, there are two basic types of sonnets: the Italian and the English.

The *Italian sonnet* (also known as the *Petrarchan sonnet*, from the fourteenth-century Italian poet Petrarch) divides into two parts. The first eight lines (the *octave*) typically rhyme *abbaabba.* The final six lines (the *sestet*) may vary; common patterns are *cdecde, cdcdcd,* and *cdccdc.* Very often the octave presents a situation, an attitude, or a problem that the sestet comments upon or resolves, as in John Keats's "On First Looking into Chapman's Homer."

JOHN KEATS (1795–1821)

On First Looking into Chapman's Homer° 1816

© Corbis.

Much have I traveled in the realms of gold,
    And many goodly states and kingdoms
        seen;
    Round many western islands have I been
Which bards in fealty to Apollo° hold.
Oft of one wide expanse had I been told
    That deep-browed Homer ruled as his
        demesne;
    Yet did I never breathe its pure serene°   *atmosphere*
Till I heard Chapman speak out loud and bold:
Then felt I like some watcher of the skies
    When a new planet swims into his ken;   10
Or like stout Cortez° when with eagle eyes
    He stared at the Pacific — and all his men
Looked at each other with a wild surmise —
    Silent, upon a peak in Darien.

Chapman's Homer: Before reading George Chapman's (ca. 1560–1634) poetic Elizabethan translations of Homer's *Iliad* and *Odyssey*, Keats had known only stilted and pedestrian eighteenth-century translations.   4 *Apollo:* Greek god of poetry.   11 *Cortez:* Vasco Núñez de Balboa, not Hernando Cortés, was the first European to sight the Pacific from Darien, a peak in Panama.

CONSIDERATIONS FOR CRITICAL THINKING AND WRITING

1. FIRST RESPONSE. How do the images shift from the octave to the sestet? How does the tone change? Does the meaning change as well?

2. What is the controlling metaphor of this poem?

3. What is it that the speaker discovers?

4. How does the rhythm of the lines change between the octave and the sestet? How does that change reflect the tones of both the octave and the sestet?

5. Does Keats's mistake concerning Cortés and Balboa affect your reading of the poem? Explain why or why not.

The Italian sonnet pattern is also used in the next sonnet, but notice that the thematic break between octave and sestet comes within line 9 rather than between lines 8 and 9. This unconventional break helps to reinforce the speaker's impatience with the conventional attitudes he describes.

WILLIAM WORDSWORTH (1770–1850)

The World Is Too Much with Us   1807

The world is too much with us; late and soon,
Getting and spending, we lay waste our powers;
Little we see in Nature that is ours;
We have given our hearts away, a sordid boon!
This Sea that bares her bosom to the moon;   5
The winds that will be howling at all hours,
And are up-gathered now like sleeping flowers;
For this, for everything, we are out of tune;
It moves us not. — Great God! I'd rather be
A Pagan suckled in a creed outworn;   10
So might I, standing on this pleasant lea,
Have glimpses that would make me less forlorn;
Have sight of Proteus rising from the sea;
Or hear old Triton blow his wreathèd horn.

CONSIDERATIONS FOR CRITICAL THINKING AND WRITING

1. FIRST RESPONSE. What is the speaker's complaint in this sonnet? How do the
   conditions described affect him?
2. Look up "Proteus" and "Triton." What do these mythological allusions contribute to the sonnet's tone?
3. What is the effect of the personification of the sea and wind in the octave?

CONNECTION TO ANOTHER SELECTION

1. Compare the theme of this sonnet with that of Gerard Manley Hopkins's
   "God's Grandeur" (p. 740).

The **English sonnet**, more commonly known as the **Shakespearean sonnet**, is organized into three quatrains and a couplet, which typically rhyme
abab cdcd efef gg. This rhyme scheme is more suited to English poetry because
English has fewer rhyming words than Italian. English sonnets, because of
their four-part organization, also have more flexibility about where thematic
breaks can occur. Frequently, however, the most pronounced break or turn
comes with the concluding couplet.

In the following Shakespearean sonnet, the three quatrains compare the
speaker's loved one to a summer's day and explain why the loved one is even
more lovely. The couplet bestows eternal beauty and love upon both the loved
one and the sonnet.

WILLIAM SHAKESPEARE (1564–1616)

Shall I compare thee to a summer's day?   1609

Shall I compare thee to a summer's day?
Thou art more lovely and more temperate:

Rough winds do shake the darling buds of May,
And summer's lease hath all too short a date.
Sometime too hot the eye of heaven shines,   5
And often is his gold complexion dimmed;
And every fair from fair sometime declines,
By chance, or nature's changing course, untrimmed.
But thy eternal summer shall not fade,
Nor lose possession of that fair thou ow'st°   *possess* 10
Nor shall death brag thou wand'rest in his shade,
When in eternal lines to time thou grow'st.
    So long as men can breathe or eyes can see,
    So long lives this, and this gives life to thee.

CONSIDERATIONS FOR CRITICAL THINKING AND WRITING

1. FIRST RESPONSE. Describe the shift in tone and subject matter that begins in line 9.
2. Why is the speaker's loved one more lovely than a summer's day? What qualities does he admire in the loved one?
3. What does the couplet say about the relation between art and love?
4. Which syllables are stressed in the final line? How do these syllables relate to the line's meaning?

Sonnets have been the vehicles for all kinds of subjects, including love, death, politics, and cosmic questions. Although most sonnets tend to treat their subjects seriously, this fixed form does not mean a fixed expression; humor is also possible in it. Compare this next Shakespearean sonnet with "Shall I compare thee to a summer's day?" They are, finally, both love poems, but their tones are markedly different.

WILLIAM SHAKESPEARE (1564–1616)

My mistress' eyes are nothing like the sun   1609

My mistress' eyes are nothing like the sun;
Coral is far more red than her lips' red;
If snow be white, why then her breasts are dun;
If hairs be wires, black wires grow on her head.
I have seen roses damasked red and white,   5
But no such roses see I in her cheeks;
And in some perfumes is there more delight
Than in the breath that from my mistress reeks.
I love to hear her speak, yet well I know
That music hath a far more pleasing sound;   10
I grant I never saw a goddess go:
My mistress, when she walks, treads on the ground.
    And yet, by heaven, I think my love as rare
    As any she,° belied with false compare.   *lady*

CONSIDERATIONS FOR CRITICAL THINKING AND WRITING

1. FIRST RESPONSE. What does "mistress" mean in this sonnet? Write a description of this particular mistress based on the images used in the sonnet.

2. What sort of person is the speaker? Does he truly love the woman he describes?

3. In what sense are this sonnet and "Shall I compare thee to a summer's day?" about poetry as well as love?

EDNA ST. VINCENT MILLAY (1892–1950)

I will put Chaos into fourteen lines 1954

© Corbis.

I will put Chaos into fourteen lines
And keep him there; and let him thence escape
If he be lucky; let him twist, and ape
Flood, fire, and demon — his adroit designs
Will strain to nothing in the strict confines
Of this sweet Order, where, in pious rape,
I hold his essence and amorphous shape,
Till he with Order mingles and combines.
Past are the hours, the years, of our duress,
His arrogance, our awful servitude: 10
I have him. He is nothing more nor less
Than something simple not yet understood;
I shall not even force him to confess;
Or answer. I will only make him good.

CONSIDERATIONS FOR CRITICAL THINKING AND WRITING

1. FIRST RESPONSE. Does the poem contain "Chaos"? If so, how? If not, why not?

2. What properties of a sonnet does this poem possess?

3. What do you think is meant by the phrase "pious rape" in line 6?

4. What is the effect of the personification in the poem?

CONNECTION TO ANOTHER SELECTION

1. Compare the theme of this poem with that of Robert Frost's "Design" (p. 885).

A SAMPLE STUDENT RESPONSE

Alexia Sykes

Professor Jones

English 211

1 December 2015

The Fixed Form in Edna St. Vincent Millay's

"I will put Chaos into fourteen lines"

In her poem "I will put Chaos into fourteen lines," Edna St. Vincent Millay does exactly what her title promises. Though the poem is of a fixed form, using patterns in meter, rhyme, line, and stanza, a sense of chaos is created through a complex structure, only to be calmed in the last six lines by a simpler rhyme scheme.

The first octave of the poem is structured *abbaabba,* a structure commonly found in sonnets. Although this is a fixed structure, the rhyme scheme is so complex that a chaotic tone is established:

> Flood, fire, and demon—his adroit designs
>
> Will strain to nothing in the strict confines
>
> Of this sweet Order, where, in pious rape,
>
> I hold his essence and amorphous shape,
>
> Till he with Order mingles and combines. (lines 4-8)

Rhyming couplets are fired at the reader and the seemingly haphazard pattern gives the impression that there is little or no structure at all, particularly on a first reading. It is difficult to determine the framework of the poem, and the absence of a decipherable structure creates in the reader a feeling of randomness, the same disorder mentioned by the speaker. It is not until the end of the poem that relief is provided. The final six lines contain a much simpler, more repetitive structure: *cdcdcd*. This rhyme scheme provides stability and consistency. The pattern is simple and predictable; order is restored. Chaos has been tamed and made "good" (14) by the poem's form. . . .

Sykes 3

Work Cited

Millay, Edna St. Vincent. "I will put Chaos into fourteen lines." *The Bedford Introduction to Literature*. Ed. Michael Meyer. 11th ed. Boston: Bedford/St. Martin's, 2016. 782. Print.

SHERMAN ALEXIE (B. 1966)

The Facebook Sonnet   2011

Welcome to the endless high-school
Reunion. Welcome to past friends
And lovers, however kind or cruel.
Let's undervalue and unmend

The present. Why can't we pretend   5
Every stage of life is the same?
Let's exhume, resume, and extend
Childhood. Let's all play the games

That occupy the young. Let fame
And shame intertwine. Let one's search   10
For God become public domain.
Let church.com become our church.

Let's sign up, sign in, and confess
Here at the altar of loneliness.

CONSIDERATIONS FOR CRITICAL THINKING AND WRITING

1. FIRST RESPONSE. Why does a fixed form rather than an open form seem especially appropriate for the themes of this poem?
2. What type of sonnet is this?
3. How might Facebook be regarded as the "altar of loneliness" (line 14)? Explain why you agree or disagree with the speaker's assessment.

CONNECTION TO ANOTHER SELECTION

1. Write an essay comparing the themes of "The Facebook Sonnet" and Thomas A. Moore's "At the Berkeley Free Speech Café" (p. 1019).

THOMAS HARDY (1840–1928)

At the Altar-Rail   1914

"My bride is not coming, alas!" says the groom,
And the telegram shakes in his hand. "I own

It was hurried! We met at a dancing-room
When I went to the Cattle-Show alone,
And then, next night, where the Fountain leaps,   5
And the Street of the Quarter-Circle sweeps.

"Ay, she won me to ask her to be my wife —
'Twas foolish perhaps! — to forsake the ways
Of the flaring town for a farmer's life.
She agreed. And we fixed it. Now she says: 10
It's sweet of you, dear, to prepare me a nest,
But a swift, short, gay life suits me best.
What I really am you have never gleaned;
I had eaten the apple ere you were weaned."

CONSIDERATIONS FOR CRITICAL THINKING AND WRITING

1. FIRST RESPONSE. To what extent are the reader's expectations disrupted by the
   content of the poem in relation to its title?

2. Describe the type of sonnet Hardy has written here.

3. What is the speaker's tone? Consider whether or not that is also the tone Hardy
   creates for the reader.

R. S. GWYNN (B. 1948)

Shakespearean Sonnet   2010

With a first line taken from the tv listings

A man is haunted by his father's ghost.
Boy meets girl while feuding families fight.
A Scottish king is murdered by his host.
Two couples get lost on a summer night.
A hunchback murders all who block his way.   5
A ruler's rivals plot against his life.
A fat man and a prince make rebels pay.
A noble Moor has doubts about his wife.
An English king decides to conquer France.
A duke learns that his best friend is a she.   10
A forest sets the scene for this romance.
An old man and his daughters disagree.
A Roman leader makes a big mistake.
A sexy queen is bitten by a snake.

CONSIDERATIONS FOR CRITICAL THINKING AND WRITING

1. FIRST RESPONSE. How many Shakespearean plays can you identify from the
   fourteen encapsulated plots that make up this poem?

2. Discuss the significance of the title.

3. CREATIVE RESPONSE. Try your hand at creating a poem — a sonnet or another
   from — in whole or in part from TV listings.

Villanelle

The **villanelle** is a fixed form consisting of nineteen lines of any length divided
into six stanzas: five tercets and a concluding quatrain. The first and third lines
of the initial tercet rhyme; these rhymes are repeated in each subsequent tercet
(*aba*) and in the final two lines of the quatrain (*abaa*). Moreover, line 1 appears
in its entirety as lines 6, 12, and 18, while line 3 appears as lines 9, 15, and 19.
This form may seem to risk monotony, but in competent hands a villanelle can
create haunting echoes, as in Dylan Thomas's "Do Not Go Gentle into That
Good Night."

DYLAN THOMAS (1914–1953)

Do Not Go Gentle into That Good Night   1952

Do not go gentle into that good night,
Old age should burn and rave at close of day;
Rage, rage against the dying of the light.

Though wise men at their end know dark is right,
Because their words had forked no lightning they   5
Do not go gentle into that good night.

Good men, the last wave by, crying how bright
Their frail deeds might have danced in a green bay,
Rage, rage against the dying of the light.

Wild men who caught and sang the sun in flight,   10
And learn, too late, they grieved it on its way,
Do not go gentle into that good night.

Grave men, near death, who see with blinding sight
Blind eyes could blaze like meteors and be gay,
Rage, rage against the dying of the light.   15

And you, my father, there on the sad height,
Curse, bless, me now with your fierce tears, I pray.
Do not go gentle into that good night.
Rage, rage against the dying of the light.

CONSIDERATIONS FOR CRITICAL THINKING AND WRITING

1. FIRST RESPONSE. How does Thomas vary the meanings of the poem's two
   refrains: "Do not go gentle into that good night" and "Rage, rage against the
   dying of the light"?
2. Thomas's father was close to death when this poem was written. How does the
   tone contribute to the poem's theme?
3. How is "good" used in line 1?

4. Characterize the men who are "wise" (line 4), "Good" (7), "Wild" (10), and "Grave" (13).
5. What do figures of speech contribute to this poem?
6. Discuss this villanelle's sound effects.

EDWIN ARLINGTON ROBINSON (1869–1935)

The House on the Hill   1894

They are all gone away,
   The House is shut and still,
There is nothing more to say.

Through broken walls and gray
   The winds blow bleak and shrill:
They are all gone away.   5

Nor is there one to-day
   To speak them good or ill:
There is nothing more to say.

Why is it then we stray
   Around the sunken sill?   10
They are all gone away,

And our poor fancy-play
   For them is wasted skill:
There is nothing more to say.   15

There is ruin and decay
   In the House on the Hill:
They are all gone away,
There is nothing more to say.

CONSIDERATIONS FOR CRITICAL THINKING AND WRITING

1. FIRST RESPONSE. What connotations does "on the hill" suggest to you?
2. Is this poem about a house or something else?

CONNECTION TO ANOTHER SELECTION

1. Compare the images and themes of "The House on the Hill" with those of Edgar Allan Poe's "The Haunted Palace" (p. 713).

Sestina

Although the **sestina** usually does not rhyme, it is perhaps an even more demanding fixed form than the villanelle. A sestina consists of thirty-nine lines of any length divided into six six-line stanzas and a three-line concluding stanza called an **envoy**. The difficulty lies in repeating the six words at the ends of the first stanza's lines at the ends of the lines in the other five six-line stanzas as well. Those words must also appear in the final three lines, where they often resonate important themes. The sestina originated in the Middle Ages, but contemporary poets continue to find it a fascinating and challenging form.

ALGERNON CHARLES SWINBURNE (1837–1909)

Sestina 1872

I saw my soul at rest upon a day
As a bird sleeping in the nest of night,
Among soft leaves that give the starlight way
To touch its wings but not its eyes with light;
So that it knew as one in visions may,   5
And knew not as men waking, of delight.

This was the measure of my soul's delight;
It had no power of joy to fly by day,
Nor part in the large lordship of the light;
But in a secret moon-beholden way   10
Had all its will of dreams and pleasant night,
And all the love and life that sleepers may.

But such life's triumph as men waking may
It might not have to feed its faint delight
Between the stars by night and sun by day,   15
Shut up with green leaves and a little light;
Because its way was as a lost star's way,
A world's not wholly known of day or night.

All loves and dreams and sounds and gleams of night
Made it all music that such minstrels may,   20
And all they had they gave it of delight;
But in the full face of the fire of day
What place shall be for any starry light,
What part of heaven in all the wide sun's way?

Yet the soul woke not, sleeping by the way,   25
Watched as a nursling of the large-eyed night,
And sought no strength nor knowledge of the day,
Nor closer touch conclusive of delight,
Nor mightier joy nor truer than dreamers may,
Nor more of song than they, nor more of light.   30

For who sleeps once and sees the secret light
Whereby sleep shows the soul a fairer way
Between the rise and rest of day and night,
Shall care no more to fare as all men may,
But be his place of pain or of delight,   35
There shall he dwell, beholding night as day.

Song, have thy day and take thy fill of light
Before the night be fallen across thy way;
Sing while he may, man hath no long delight.

CONSIDERATIONS FOR CRITICAL THINKING AND WRITING

1. FIRST RESPONSE. How are the six end words — "day," "night," "way," "light," "may," and "delight" — central to the sestina's meaning?

2. Number the end words of the first stanza 1, 2, 3, 4, 5, and 6, and then use those numbers for the corresponding end words in the remaining five stanzas to see how the pattern of the line-end words is worked out in this sestina. Also locate the six end words in the envoy.

3. Underline the images that seem especially vivid to you. What effects do they create? What is the tone of the sestina?

4. CRITICAL STRATEGIES. Read the section on psychological strategies (pp. 1649– 51) in Chapter 51, "Critical Strategies for Reading." Write a brief essay explaining why you think a poet might derive pleasure from writing in a fixed form such as a villanelle or sestina. Can you think of similar activities outside the field of writing in which discipline and restraint give pleasure? How might this reflect an author's personal psychology?

FLORENCE CASSEN MAYERS (B. 1940)

All-American Sestina   1996

One nation, indivisible
two-car garage
three strikes you're out
four-minute mile
five-cent cigar   5
six-string guitar

six-pack Bud
one-day sale
five-year warranty
two-way street   10
fourscore and seven years ago
three cheers

three-star restaurant
sixty-
four-dollar question   15
one-night stand
two-pound lobster
five-star general

five-course meal
three sheets to the wind   20
two bits
six-shooter

one-armed bandit
four-poster

four-wheel drive 25
five-and-dime
hole in one
three-alarm fire
sweet sixteen
two-wheeler 30

two-tone Chevy
four rms, hi flr, w/vu
six-footer
high five
three-ring circus 35
one-room schoolhouse

two thumbs up, five-karat diamond
Fourth of July, three-piece suit
six feet under, one-horse town

CONSIDERATIONS FOR CRITICAL THINKING AND WRITING

1. FIRST RESPONSE. Discuss the significance of the title; what is "All-American" about this sestina?

2. How is the structure of this poem different from that of a conventional sestina? (What structural requirement does Mayers add for this sestina?)

3. Do you think important themes are raised by this poem, as is traditional for a sestina? If so, what are they? If not, what is being played with by using this convention?

CONNECTION TO ANOTHER SELECTION

1. Describe and compare the strategy used to create meaning in "All-American Sestina" with that used by E. E. Cummings in "next to of course god america i" (p. 718).

Epigram

An *epigram* is a brief, pointed, and witty poem. Although most rhyme and they are often written in couplets, epigrams take no prescribed form. Instead, they are typically polished bits of compressed irony, satire, or paradox. Here is an epigram that defines itself.

SAMUEL TAYLOR COLERIDGE (1772–1834)

What Is an Epigram? 1802

What is an epigram? A dwarfish whole;
Its body brevity, and wit its soul.

These additional examples by David McCord and Paul Laurence Dunbar satisfy Coleridge's definition.

David McCord (1897–1997)

Epitaph on a Waiter   1954

By and by
God caught his eye.

Paul Laurence Dunbar (1872–1906)

Theology   1896

There is a heaven, for ever, day by day,
The upward longing of my soul doth tell
    me so.
There is a hell, I'm quite as sure; for pray,
If there were not, where would my
     neighbors go?

© Corbis.

Considerations for Critical Thinking and Writing

1. **First response.** In what sense is each of these two epigrams, as Coleridge puts it, a "dwarfish whole"?
2. Explain how all three epigrams, in addition to being witty, make a serious point.
3. **Creative response.** Try writing a few epigrams that say something memorable about whatever you choose to focus on.

Limerick

The **limerick** is always light and humorous. Its usual form consists of five predominantly anapestic lines rhyming *aabba;* lines 1, 2, and 5 contain three feet, while lines 3 and 4 contain two. Limericks have delighted everyone from schoolchildren to sophisticated adults, and they range in subject matter from the simply innocent and silly to the satiric or obscene. The sexual humor helps to explain why so many limericks are written anonymously. Here is one that is more concerned with physics than physiology.

Arthur Henry Reginald Butler (1874–1944)

There was a young lady named Bright   1923

There was a young lady named Bright,
Whose speed was far faster than light,
   She set out one day,
   In a relative way,
And returned home the previous night.

This next one is a particularly clever definition of a limerick.

LAURENCE PERRINE (1915–1995)

The limerick's never averse 1982

The limerick's never averse
To expressing itself in a terse
    Economical style,
    And yet, all the while,
The limerick's *always* a verse.

CONSIDERATIONS FOR CRITICAL THINKING AND WRITING

1. **FIRST RESPONSE.** How does this limerick differ from others you know? How is it similar?

2. Scan Perrine's limerick. How do the lines measure up to the traditional fixed metrical pattern?

3. **CREATIVE RESPONSE.** Try writing a limerick. Use the following basic pattern.

    ⌣ ⌣ ´   ⌣ ⌣ ´   ⌣ ⌣ ´
    ⌣ ⌣ ´   ⌣ ⌣ ´   ⌣ ⌣ ´
           ⌣ ⌣ ´   ⌣ ⌣ ´
           ⌣ ⌣ ´   ⌣ ⌣ ´
    ⌣ ⌣ ´   ⌣ ⌣ ´   ⌣ ⌣ ´

You might begin with a friend's name or the name of your school or town. Your instructor is, of course, fair game, too, provided your tact matches your wit.

Haiku

Another brief fixed poetic form, borrowed from the Japanese, is the **haiku**. A haiku is usually described as consisting of seventeen syllables organized into three unrhymed lines of five, seven, and five syllables. Owing to language difference, however, English translations of haiku are often only approximated, because a Japanese haiku exists in time (Japanese syllables have duration). The number of syllables in our sense is not as significant as the duration in Japanese. These poems typically present an intense emotion or vivid image of nature, which, in the Japanese, is also designed to lead to a spiritual insight.

MATSUO BASHŌ (1644–1694)

Under cherry trees date unknown

Under cherry trees
Soup, the salad, fish and all . . .
Seasoned with petals.

CAROLYN KIZER (B. 1925)

After Bashō 1984

Tentatively, you
slip onstage this evening,
pallid, famous moon.

AMY LOWELL (1874–1925)

Last night it rained 1921

Last night it rained.
Now, in the desolate dawn,
Crying of blue jays.

GARY SNYDER (B. 1930)

A Dent in a Bucket 2004

Hammering a dent out of a bucket
   a woodpecker
      answers from the woods

CONSIDERATIONS FOR CRITICAL THINKING AND WRITING

1. FIRST RESPONSE. What different emotions do these four haiku evoke?
2. What differences and similarities are there between the effects of a haiku and those of an epigram?
3. CREATIVE RESPONSE. Compose a haiku. Try to make it as allusive and suggestive as possible.

Elegy

An elegy in classical Greek and Roman literature was written in alternating hexameter and pentameter lines. Since the seventeenth century, however, the term *elegy* has been used to describe a lyric poem written to commemorate someone who is dead. The word is also used to refer to a serious meditative poem produced to express the speaker's melancholy thoughts. Elegies no longer conform to a fixed pattern of lines and stanzas, but their characteristic subject is related to death and their tone is mournfully contemplative.

BEN JONSON (1573–1637)

On My First Son 1603

Farewell, thou child of my right hand,° and joy.
My sin was too much hope of thee, loved boy;

---

1 *child of my right hand:* This phrase translates the Hebrew name "Benjamin," Jonson's son.

Seven years thou wert lent to me, and I thee pay,
Exacted by thy fate, on the just day.°   *his birthday*
Oh, could I lose all father° now. For why   *fatherhood*   5
Will man lament the state he should envy? —
To have so soon 'scaped world's and flesh's rage,
And, if no other misery, yet age.
Rest in soft peace, and asked, say, "Here doth lie
Ben Jonson his best piece of poetry,"   10
For whose sake henceforth all his vows be such
As what he loves may never like too much.

CONSIDERATIONS FOR CRITICAL THINKING AND WRITING

1. FIRST RESPONSE. Describe the tone of this elegy. What makes it so emotionally convincing?

2. In what sense is Jonson's son "his best piece of poetry" (line 10)?

3. Interpret the final two lines. Do they seem consistent with the rest of the poem? Why or why not?

ANDREW HUDGINS (B. 1951)

Elegy for My Father, Who Is Not Dead   1991

One day I'll lift the telephone
and be told my father's dead. He's ready.
In the sureness of his faith, he talks
about the world beyond this world
as though his reservations have   5
been made. I think he wants to go,
a little bit — a new desire
to travel building up, an itch
to see fresh worlds. Or older ones.
He thinks that when I follow him   10
he'll wrap me in his arms and laugh,
the way he did when I arrived
on earth. I do not think he's right.
He's ready. I am not. I can't
just say good-bye as cheerfully   15
as if he were embarking on a trip
to make my later trip go well.
I see myself on deck, convinced
his ship's gone down, while he's convinced
I'll see him standing on the dock   20
and waving, shouting, Welcome back.

CONSIDERATIONS FOR CRITICAL THINKING AND WRITING

1. FIRST RESPONSE. Why does this speaker elegize his father if the father "is not dead"?

2. How does the speaker's view of immortality differ from his father's?

3. Explain why you think this is an optimistic or a pessimistic poem — or explain why these two categories fail to describe the poem.

4. In what sense can this poem be regarded as an elegy?

CONNECTION TO ANOTHER SELECTION

1. Write an essay comparing attitudes toward death in this poem and in Dylan Thomas's "Do Not Go Gentle into That Good Night" (p. 786). Both speakers invoke their fathers, nearer to death than they are; what impact does this invocation have?

Ode

An *ode* is characterized by a serious topic and formal tone, but no prescribed formal pattern describes all odes. In some odes the pattern of each stanza is repeated throughout, while in others each stanza introduces a new pattern. Odes are lengthy lyrics that often include lofty emotions conveyed by a dignified style. Typical topics include truth, art, freedom, justice, and the meaning of life. Frequently such lyrics tend to be more public than private, and their speakers often use apostrophe.

PERCY BYSSHE SHELLEY (1792–1822)

Ode to the West Wind 1820

I

O wild West Wind, thou breath of Autumn's being,
Thou, from whose unseen presence the leaves dead
Are driven, like ghosts from an enchanter fleeing,

Yellow, and black, and pale, and hectic red,
Pestilence-stricken multitudes: O thou,   5
Who chariotest to their dark wintry bed

The wingèd seeds, where they lie cold and low,
Each like a corpse within its grave, until
Thine azure sister of the Spring shall blow

Her clarion o'er the dreaming earth, and fill   10
(Driving sweet buds like flocks to feed in air)
With living hues and odors plain and hill:

Wild Spirit, which art moving everywhere;
Destroyer and preserver; hear, oh, hear!

II

Thou on whose stream, mid the steep sky's commotion,   15
Loose clouds like earth's decaying leaves are shed,
Shook from the tangled boughs of Heaven and Ocean,

Angels° of rain and lightning: there are spread   *messengers*
On the blue surface of thine airy surge,
Like the bright hair uplifted from the head   20

Of some fierce Maenad,° even from the dim verge
Of the horizon to the zenith's height,
The locks of the approaching storm. Thou dirge

Of the dying year, to which this closing night
Will be the dome of a vast sepulcher,   25
Vaulted with all thy congregated might

Of vapors, from whose solid atmosphere
Black rain, and fire, and hail will burst: oh, hear!

III

Thou who didst waken from his summer dreams
The blue Mediterranean, where he lay,   30
Lulled by the coil of his crystálline streams,

Beside a pumice isle in Baiae's bay,°
And saw in sleep old palaces and towers
Quivering within the wave's intenser day,

All overgrown with azure moss and flowers   35
So sweet, the sense faints picturing them! Thou
For whose path the Atlantic's level powers

Cleave themselves into chasms, while far below
The sea-blooms and the oozy woods which wear
The sapless foliage of the ocean, know   40

Thy voice, and suddenly grow gray with fear,
And tremble and despoil themselves: oh, hear!

IV

If I were a dead leaf thou mightest bear;
If I were a swift cloud to fly with thee;
A wave to pant beneath thy power, and share   45

The impulse of thy strength, only less free
Than thou, O uncontrollable! If even
I were as in my boyhood, and could be

The comrade by thy wanderings over Heaven,
As then, when to outstrip thy skyey speed   50
Scarce seemed a vision; I would ne'er have striven

As thus with thee in prayer in my sore need.
Oh, lift me as a wave, a leaf, a cloud!
I fall upon the thorns of life! I bleed!

A heavy weight of hours has chained and bowed   55
One too like thee: tameless, and swift, and proud.

---

21 *Maenad:* In Greek mythology, a frenzied worshipper of Dionysus, god of wine and fertility.   32 *Baiae's bay:* A bay in the Mediterranean Sea.

V

Make me thy lyre,° even as the forest is:
What if my leaves are falling like its own!
The tumult of thy mighty harmonies

Will take from both a deep, autumnal tone,   60
Sweet though in sadness. Be thou, Spirit fierce,
My spirit! Be thou me, impetuous one!

Drive my dead thoughts over the universe
Like withered leaves to quicken a new birth!
And, by the incantation of this verse,   65

Scatter, as from an unextinguished hearth
Ashes and sparks, my words among mankind!
Be through my lips to unawakened earth

The trumpet of a prophecy! O Wind,
If Winter comes, can Spring be far behind?   70

57 *Make me thy lyre:* Sound is produced on an Aeolian lyre, or wind harp, by wind blowing
across its strings.

Considerations for Critical Thinking and Writing

1. FIRST RESPONSE. Write a summary of each of this ode's five sections.
2. What is the speaker's situation? What is his "sore need" (line 52)? What does
   the speaker ask of the wind in lines 57–70?
3. What does the wind signify in this ode? How is it used symbolically?
4. Determine the meter and rhyme of the first five stanzas. How do these elements contribute to the ode's movement? Is this pattern continued in the other
   four sections?

Parody

A *parody* is a humorous imitation of another, usually serious, work. It can
take any fixed or open form because parodists imitate the tone, language, and
shape of the original. While a parody may be teasingly close to a work's style, it
typically deflates the subject matter to make the original seem absurd. Parody
can be used as a kind of literary criticism to expose the defects in a work, but it
is also very often an affectionate acknowledgment that a well-known work has
become both institutionalized in our culture and fair game for some fun. Read
Robert Frost's "The Road Not Taken" (p. 871) and then study this parody.

Blanche Farley (b. 1937)

The Lover Not Taken   1984

Committed to one, she wanted both
And, mulling it over, long she stood,
Alone on the road, loath

To leave, wanting to hide in the undergrowth.
This new guy, smooth as a yellow wood 5

Really turned her on. She liked his hair,
His smile. But the other, Jack, had a claim
On her already and she had to admit, he did wear
Well. In fact, to be perfectly fair,
He understood her. His long, lithe frame 10

Beside hers in the evening tenderly lay.
Still, if this blond guy dropped by someday,
Couldn't way just lead on to way?
No. For if way led on and Jack
Found out, she doubted if he would ever come back. 15

Oh, she turned with a sigh.
Somewhere ages and ages hence,
She might be telling this. "And I —"
She would say, "stood faithfully by."
But by then who would know the difference? 20

With that in mind, she took the fast way home,
The road by the pond, and phoned the blond.

WHEN I WRITE "Keep your work, even if it is unfinished or not to your liking. It can be revised or even rewritten in another form. Maybe the original idea is what will prove valuable. Most importantly, despite all else going on in your life, despite rejection or feelings of discouragement, keep writing." —BLANCHE FARLEY

CONSIDERATIONS FOR CRITICAL THINKING AND WRITING

1. **FIRST RESPONSE.** To what degree does this poem duplicate Frost's style? How does it differ?

2. Does this parody seem successful to you? Explain what you think makes a successful parody.

3. **CREATIVE RESPONSE.** Choose a poet whose work you know reasonably well or would like to know better and determine what is characteristic about his or her style. Then choose a poem to parody. It's probably best to attempt a short poem or a section of a long work. If you have difficulty selecting an author, you might consider Herrick, Blake, Keats, Dickinson, Whitman, Hughes, or Frost, as a number of their works are included in this book.

Picture Poem

By arranging lines into particular shapes, poets can sometimes organize typography into *picture poems* of what they describe. Words have been arranged into all kinds of shapes, from apples to light bulbs. Notice how the shape of this next poem embodies its meaning.

WHEN I WRITE "I've shared my poems with a friend, who's also a poet, for decades now. He marks them up and gives them back; I do the same for him. You need a sympathetic critic who is not you, to help make your poetry as strong and clear as possible to readers who are not you." —MICHAEL MCFEE

MICHAEL McFEE (B. 1954)

In Medias Res° 1985

His waist
like the plot
thickens, wedding
pants now breathtaking,
belt no longer the cinch   5
it once was, belly's cambium
expanding to match each birthday,
his body a wad of anonymous tissue
swung in the same centrifuge of years
that separates a house from its foundation,   10
undermining sidewalks grim with joggers
and loose-filled graves and families
and stars collapsing on themselves,
no preservation society capable
of plugging entropy's dike,   15
under his zipper's sneer
a belly hibernation-
soft, ready for
the kill.

In Medias Res: A Latin term for a story that begins "in the middle of things."

CONSIDERATIONS FOR CRITICAL THINKING AND WRITING

1. FIRST RESPONSE. Explain how the title is related to this poem's shape and meaning.
2. Identify the puns. How do they work in the poem?
3. What is "cambium" (line 6)? Why is the phrase "belly's cambium" especially appropriate?
4. What is the tone of this poem? Is it consistent throughout?

Perspective

ELAINE MITCHELL (1924–2012)

Form 1994

Is it a corset
or primal wave?
Don't try to force it.

Even endorse it
to shape and deceive.   5
Ouch, too tight a corset.

Take it off. No remorse. It
's an ace up your sleeve.
No need to force it.

Can you make a horse knit?   10
Who would believe?
Consider. Of course, it

might be a resource. Wit,
your grateful slave.
Form. Sometimes you force it,   15

sometimes divorce it
to make it behave.
So don't try to force it.
Respect a good corset.

Considerations for Critical Thinking and Writing

1. FIRST RESPONSE. What is the speaker's attitude toward form?
2. Explain why you think the form of this poem does or does not conform to the speaker's advice.
3. Why is the metaphor of a corset an especially apt image for this poem?

29

Open Form

I'm not very good at communicating verbally. I'm somebody who listens more than talks. I like to listen and absorb. But when I need to connect with people and I need to reach out, I write.

— RUTH FORMAN

Photograph by Christine Bennett, www.cbimages.org.

Many poems, especially those written in the past century, are composed of lines that cannot be scanned for a fixed or predominant meter. Moreover, very often these poems do not rhyme. Known as *free verse* (from the French, *vers libre*), such lines can derive their rhythmic qualities from the repetition of words, phrases, or grammatical structures; the arrangement of words on the printed page; or some other means. In recent years the term **open form** has been used in place of *free verse* to avoid the erroneous suggestion that this kind of poetry lacks all discipline and shape.

Although the following poem does not use measurable meters, it does have rhythm.

WALT WHITMAN (1819–1892)

From "I Sing the Body Electric" 1855

Library of Congress, Prints and Photographs Division.

O my body! I dare not desert the likes of you in
    other men and women, nor the likes of the
    parts of you,
I believe the likes of you are to stand or fall with
    the likes of the soul, (and that they are the
    soul,)
I believe the likes of you shall stand or fall with
    my poems, and that they are my poems.
Man's, woman's, child's, youth's, wife's, husband's,
    mother's, father's, young man's, young
    woman's poems.
Head, neck, hair, ears, drop and tympan of the
    ears.   5
Eyes, eye-fringes, iris of the eye, eyebrows, and
    the waking or sleeping of the lids,
Mouth, tongue, lips, teeth, roof of the mouth, jaws, and the jaw-hinges,
Nose, nostrils of the nose, and the partition,
Cheeks, temples, forehead, chin, throat, back of the neck, neck-slue,
Strong shoulders, manly beard, scapula, hind-shoulders, and the ample
    side-round of the chest,   10
Upper-arm, armpit, elbow-socket, lower-arm, arm-sinews, arm-bones,
Wrist and wrist-joints, hand, palm, knuckles, thumb, forefinger, finger-joints,
    finger-nails,
Broad breast-front, curling hair of the breast, breast-bone, breast-side,
Ribs, belly, backbone, joints of the backbone,
Hips, hip-sockets, hip-strength, inward and outward round, man-balls,
    man-root,   15
Strong set of thighs, well carrying the trunk above,
Leg-fibers, knee, knee-pan, upper-leg, under-leg,
Ankles, instep, foot-ball, toes, toe-joints, the heel;
All attitudes, all the shapeliness, all the belongings of my or your body or of
    any one's body, male or female,
The lung-sponges, the stomach-sac, the bowels sweet and clean,   20
The brain in its folds inside the skull-frame,
Sympathies, heart-valves, palate-valves, sexuality, maternity,
Womanhood, and all that is a woman, and the man that comes from woman,
The womb, the teats, nipples, breast-milk, tears, laughter, weeping, love-looks,
    love-perturbations and risings,
The voice, articulation, language, whispering, shouting aloud,   25
Food, drink, pulse, digestion, sweat, sleep, walking, swimming,
Poise on the hips, leaping, reclining, embracing, arm-curving and tightening,
The continual changes of the flex of the mouth, and around the eyes,
The skin, the sunburnt shade, freckles, hair,

The curious sympathy one feels when feeling with the hand the naked
    meat of the body,   30
The circling rivers the breath, and breathing it in and out,
The beauty of the waist, and thence of the hips, and thence downward toward
    the knees,
The thin red jellies within you or within me, the bones and the marrow in the
    bones,
The exquisite realization of health;
O I say these are not the parts and poems of the body only, but of the soul,   35
O I say now these are the soul!

Considerations for Critical Thinking and Writing

1. FIRST RESPONSE. What informs this speaker's attitude toward the human body?
2. Read the poem aloud. Is it simply a tedious enumeration of body parts, or do the lines achieve some kind of rhythmic cadence?

Perspective

WALT WHITMAN (1819–1892)

On Rhyme and Meter   1855

The poetic quality is not marshaled in rhyme or uniformity or abstract addresses to things nor in melancholy complaints or good precepts, but is the life of these and much else and is in the soul. The profit of rhyme is that it drops seeds of a sweeter and more luxuriant rhyme, and of uniformity that it conveys itself into its own roots in the ground out of sight. The rhyme and uniformity of perfect poems show the free growth of metrical laws and bud from them as unerringly and loosely as lilacs or roses on a bush, and take shapes as compact as the shapes of chestnuts and oranges and melons and pears, and shed the perfume impalpable to form. The fluency and ornaments of the finest poems or music or orations or recitations are not independent but dependent. All beauty comes from beautiful blood and a beautiful brain. If the greatnesses are in conjunction in a man or woman it is enough . . . the fact will prevail through the universe . . . but the gaggery and gilt of a million years will not prevail. Who troubles himself about his ornaments or fluency is lost.

From the preface to the 1855 edition of Leaves of Grass

Considerations for Critical Thinking and Writing

1. According to Whitman, what determines the shape of a poem?
2. Why does Whitman prefer open forms over fixed forms such as the sonnet?
3. Is Whitman's poetry devoid of any structure or shape? Choose one of his poems (listed in the index) to illustrate your answer.

A SAMPLE STUDENT RESPONSE

Avery Bloom

Professor Rios

English 212

7 October 2015

The Power of Walt Whitman's Open Form Poem

"I Sing the Body Electric"

Walt Whitman's "I Sing the Body Electric" is an ode to the human body. The poem is open form, without rhymes or consistent meter, and instead relies almost entirely on the use of language and the structure of lists to affect the reader. The result is a thorough inventory of parts of the body that illustrates the beauty of the human form and its intimate connection to the soul.

At times, Whitman lists the parts of the body with almost complete objectivity, making it difficult to understand the poem's purpose. The poem initially appears to do little more than recite the names of body parts: "Head, neck, hair, ears, drop and tympan of the ears" (line 5); "Mouth, tongue, lips, teeth, roof of the mouth, jaws, and the jaw-hinges" (7). There are no end rhymes, but the exhaustive and detailed list of body parts— from the brain to the "thin red jellies . . . , the bones and the marrow in the bones" (33)—offers language that has a certain rhythm. The language and rhythm of the list create a visual image full of energy and momentum that builds, emphasizing the body's functions and movements. As Michael Meyer writes, open form poems "rely on an intense use of language to establish rhythms and relations between meaning and form. [They] use the arrangement of words and phrases . . . to create unique forms" (page 805). No doubt Whitman chose the open form for this work—relying on his "intense use of language" and the rhythm of the list—because it allowed a basic structure that held together but did not restrain, and a full freedom and range of motion to create a poem that is alive with movement and electricity. . . .

Bloom 4

Works Cited

Meyer, Michael, ed. *The Bedford Introduction to Literature*. 11th ed. Boston:
    Bedford/St. Martin's, 2016. Print.
Whitman, Walt. "From 'I Sing the Body Electric.'" Meyer 802–03.

Open form poetry is sometimes regarded as formless because it is unlike the strict fixed forms of a sonnet, villanelle, or sestina. But even though open form poems may not employ traditional meters and rhymes, they still rely on an intense use of language to establish rhythms and relations between meaning and form. Open form poems use the arrangement of words and phrases on the printed page, pauses, line lengths, and other means to create unique forms that express their particular meaning and tone.

The excerpt from Whitman's "I Sing the Body Electric" demonstrates how rhythmic cadences can be aligned with meaning, but there is one kind of open form poetry that doesn't even look like poetry on a page. A ***prose poem*** is printed as prose and represents, perhaps, the most clear opposite of fixed forms. Here are two brief examples.

DAVID SHUMATE (B. 1950)

Shooting the Horse   2004

I unlatch the stall door, step inside, and stroke the silky neck of the old mare like a lover about to leave. I take an ear in hand, fold it over, and run my fingers across her muzzle. I coax her head up so I can blow into those nostrils. All part of the routine we taught each other long ago. I turn a half turn, pull a pistol from my coat, raise it to that long brow with the white blaze and place it between her sleepy eyes. I clear my throat. A sound much louder than it should be. I squeeze the trigger and the horse's feet fly out from under her as gravity gives way to a force even more austere, which we have named mercy.

CONSIDERATIONS FOR CRITICAL THINKING AND WRITING

1. FIRST RESPONSE. Describe the range of emotions that this poem produces for you.
2. Think of other words that could be substituted for *mercy* in the final line. How does your choice change the tone and theme of the poem?

3. Rearrange the poem so that its words, phrases, and sentences are set up to use the white space on the page to convey tone and meaning. Which version do you prefer? Why?

RICHARD HAGUE (B. 1947)

Directions for Resisting the SAT   1996

Do not believe in October or May
or in any Saturday morning with pencils.
Do not observe the rules of gravity,
commas, history.
Lie about numbers.   5
Blame your successes,
every one of them,
on rotten luck.
Resign all clubs and committees.
Go down with the ship — any ship.   10
Speak nothing like English.
Desire to live whole,
like an oyster or snail,
and follow no directions.
Listen to no one.   15

Make your marks on everything.

> WHEN I READ "In an increasingly distracting and distracted world, poems are countercultural. They can pay attention — to public and private life, to the world of nature and rituals and things, in ways akin to prayer, or to precise and pointed cursing — like magic spells. They name what ails us." — RICHARD HAGUE

CONSIDERATIONS FOR CRITICAL THINKING AND WRITING

1. FIRST RESPONSE. What is the speaker's subversive message? What do you think of the advice offered?

2. What kinds of assumptions do you suppose Hague makes about readers' attitudes toward the SAT? To what extent do you share those attitudes?

3. Discuss Hague's use of spacing and line breaks. What is the effect of the space between lines 15 and 16?

Much of the poetry published today is written in open form; however, many poets continue to take pleasure in the requirements imposed by fixed forms. Some write both fixed form and open form poetry. Each kind offers rewards to careful readers as well. Here are several more open form poems that establish their own unique patterns.

MICHAEL RYAN (B. 1946)

I   2013

When did I learn the word "I"?
What a mistake. For some,
    it may be a placeholder,
    for me it's a contagion.

For some, it's a thin line, a bare wisp,   5
    just enough to be somewhere
    among the gorgeous troublesome you's.
For me, it's a thorn, a spike, its slimness
    a deceit, camouflaged like a stick insect:
    touch it and it becomes what it is: 10
ravenous slit, vertical cut, little boy
    standing upright in his white
    communion suit and black secret.

CONSIDERATIONS FOR CRITICAL THINKING AND WRITING

1. FIRST RESPONSE. What do you think the speaker is suggesting by regarding his identity as a "contagion"?
2. Explain how the poem's images evoke its subject matter.
3. What emotion do you think lines 11–13 produce in the speaker?

CONNECTION TO ANOTHER SELECTION

1. Compare the sense of one's self in "I" and in the excerpt from Walt Whitman's "I Sing the Body Electric" (p. 802).

E. E. CUMMINGS (1894–1962)

old age sticks 1958

old age sticks
up Keep
Off
signs)&

youth yanks them   5
down(old
age
cries No

Tres)&(pas)
youth laughs   10
(sing
old age

scolds Forbid
den Stop
Must   15
n't Don't

&)youth goes
right on
gr
owing old   20

CONSIDERATIONS FOR CRITICAL THINKING AND WRITING

1. FIRST RESPONSE. What distinctions does the speaker make between age and youth?

2. Paraphrase each stanza. What gets lost in the process if you write out these lines as you would write an ordinary prose sentence?

3. How does the final stanza complicate the poem's central idea?

WILLIAM CARLOS WILLIAMS (1883–1963)

The Red Wheelbarrow   1923

so much depends
upon

a red wheel
barrow

glazed with rain
water

beside the white
chickens.

CONSIDERATIONS FOR CRITICAL THINKING AND WRITING

1. FIRST RESPONSE. What "depends upon" the things mentioned in the poem? What is the effect of these images? Do they have a particular meaning?

2. Do these lines have any kind of rhythm?

3. How does this poem resemble a haiku? How is it different?

NATASHA TRETHEWEY (B. 1966)

On Captivity   2007

Being all Stripped as Naked as We were Born, and endeavoring to hide our Naked-
ness, these Cannaballs took [our] Books, and tearing out the Leaves would give each
of us a Leaf to cover us . . .

— *Jonathan Dickinson, 1699*

At the hands now
          of their captors, those
                    they've named *savages,*
          do they say the word itself
savagely — hissing   5

that first letter,
      the serpent's image,
        releasing
    thought into speech?
For them now,

everything is flesh
    as if their thoughts, made
        suddenly corporeal,
    reveal even more
their nakedness —

AP Photo/Rogelio V. Solis.

the shame of it:
    their bodies rendered
        plain as the natives' —
    homely and pale,
their ordinary sex,   20

the secret illicit hairs
    that do not (cannot)
        cover enough.
    This is how they are brought,
naked as newborns,   25

to knowledge. Adam and Eve
    in the New World,
        they have only the Bible
    to cover them. Think of it:
a woman holding before her   30

the torn leaves of *Genesis,*
    and a man covering himself
        with the Good Book's
    frontispiece — his own name
inscribed on the page.   35

Considerations for Critical Thinking and Writing

1. **FIRST RESPONSE.** Trethewey has written about the sources of her epigraph: "Because the conquerors made use of the written word to claim land [in North America] inhabited by native people, I found the detail of settlers forced to cover themselves with torn pages from books a compelling irony" (*The Best American Poetry 2008,* p. 182). How does this comment contribute to the central irony in the poem?

2. Discuss Trethewey's use of alliteration in lines 1–9.

3. In what sense are the captors "brought, / naked as newborns, / to knowledge" (lines 24–26)?

Julio Marzán (b. 1946)

The Translator at the Reception for Latin American Writers 1997

Air-conditioned introductions,
then breezy Spanish conversation
fan his curiosity to know
what country I come from.
"Puerto Rico and the Bronx."   5

Spectacled downward eyes
translate disappointment
like a poison mushroom
puffed in his thoughts as if,
after investing a sizable   10
intellectual budget, transporting
a huge cast and camera crew
to film on location
Mayan pyramid grandeur,
indigenes whose ancient gods   15
and comet-tail plumage
inspire a glorious epic
of revolution across a continent,
he received a lurid script
for a social documentary   20
rife with dreary streets
and pathetic human interest,
meager in the profits of high culture.

Understandably he turns,
catches up with the hostess,   25
praising the uncommon quality
of her offerings of cheese.

Considerations for Critical Thinking and Writing

1. **FIRST RESPONSE.** What is the speaker's attitude toward the person he meets at the reception? What lines in particular lead you to that conclusion?

2. Why is that person so disappointed about the answer, "Puerto Rico and the Bronx" (line 5)?

3. Explain lines 6–23. How do they reveal both the speaker and the person encountered at the reception?

4. Why is the setting of this poem significant?

CHARLES HARPER WEBB (B. 1952)

Descent   1998

For my son

Let
there be
amino acids,
and there were: a slop
of molecules in ancient seas,
building cell walls to keep their
distance, dividing, replicating, starting
to diversify, one growing oars, one rotors, one
a wiry tail, lumping into clusters — cyanobacteria, sea-
worms, medusae, trilobites, lobe-finned fish dragging onto
land, becoming thrinaxodon, protoceratops, growing larger —
diplodocus, gorgosaurus — dying out — apatosaurus, tyrannosaurus —
mammals evolving from shrew-like deltatheridium into hyenadon, eohippus,
mammoth, saber-tooth, dire wolf, australopithecus rising on two feet, homo erectus
tramping from Africa into Europe and Asia, thriving like a weed that will grow anywhere —
jungle, desert, snow-pack — the genetic rivers flowing downhill now: a husband's skull crushed
in the Alps, a Tartar raping a green-eyed girl who dies in childbirth, whose daughter falls in
love with a Viking who takes her to Istanbul, a Celt who marries a Saxon, a weaver
who abducts the daughter of a witch, a son who steals his father's gold, a girl
who loses one eye leaping from a tree, dozens who die of smallpox,
cholera, black plague, a knight, a prostitute, thieves, carpenters,
farmers, poachers, blacksmiths, seamstresses, peddlers of
odds and ends, an Irishman who sells his family into
servitude, a Limey who jumps ship in New York,
Jews who flee Hungary, a midwife, an X-ray
machine repairman, a psychologist,
a writer, all flowing down,
converging on the great
delta, the point
of all this:
you.

CONSIDERATIONS FOR CRITICAL THINKING AND WRITING

1. **FIRST RESPONSE.** What do you make of the shape of this poem? Given its content, why is the shape appropriate?

2. Describe the significance of the change in diction from the first half of the poem to the second half.

3. Why do you think Webb titled the poem "Descent" rather than "Ascent"?

CONNECTION TO ANOTHER SELECTION

1. Compare the themes in "Descent" with those in Robert Frost's "Design" (p. 885).

KEVIN YOUNG (B. 1970)

Eddie Priest's Barbershop & Notary 1995

Tod Martens.

Closed Mondays

is music is   *men*
off early from work   is waiting
for the chance at the chair
while the eagle claws holes
in your pockets   keeping
time   by the turning
of rusty fans   steel flowers with
cold breezes   is having nothing
better to do   than guess at the years
of hair   matted beneath the soiled caps   10
of drunks   the pain of running
a fisted comb through stubborn
knots   is the dark dirty low
down blues   the tender heads
of sons fresh from cornrows   all   15
wonder at losing   half their height
is a mother gathering hair   for good
luck   for a soft wig   is the round
difficulty of ears   the peach
faced boys asking Eddie   20
to cut in parts and arrows
wanting to have their names read
for just a few days   and among thin
jazz   is the quick brush of a done
head   the black flood around   25
your feet   grandfathers
stopping their games of ivory
dominoes   just before they read the bone
yard   is winking widowers announcing
cut it clean off   I'm through courting   30
and hair only gets in the way   is the final
spin of the chair   a reflection of
a reflection   that sting of wintergreen
tonic   on the neck of a sleeping snow
haired man   when you realize it is   35
your turn   you are next

CONSIDERATIONS FOR CRITICAL THINKING AND WRITING

1. FIRST RESPONSE. What does the speaker think and feel about the barbershop?
2. What is the effect of using extra word space as a substitute for conventional punctuation?
3. What do you think comes "next" in the last line?

ANONYMOUS

The Frog   date unknown

What a wonderful bird the frog are!
When he stand he sit almost;
When he hop he fly almost.
He ain't got no sense hardly;
He ain't got no tail hardly either.
When he sit, he sit on what he ain't got almost.

CONSIDERATIONS FOR CRITICAL THINKING AND WRITING

1. FIRST RESPONSE. How is the poem a description of the speaker as well as of a frog?
2. Though this poem is ungrammatical, it does have a patterned structure. How does the pattern of sentences create a formal structure?

DAVID HERNANDEZ   (B. 1971)

All-American   2012

I'm this tiny, this statuesque, and everywhere
in between, and everywhere in between
bony and overweight, my shadow cannot hold
one shape in Omaha, in Tuscaloosa, in Aberdeen.
My skin is mocha brown, two shades darker   5
than taupe, your question is racist, nutmeg, beige,
I'm not offended by your question at all.
Penis or vagina? Yes and yes. Gay or straight?
Both boxes. Bi, not bi, who cares, stop
fixating on my sex life, Jesus never leveled   10
his eye to a bedroom's keyhole. I go to church
in Tempe, in Waco, the one with the exquisite
stained glass, the one with a white spire
like the tip of a Klansman's hood. Churches
creep me out, I never step inside one,   15
never utter hymns, Sundays I hide my flesh
with camouflage and hunt. I don't hunt
but wish every deer wore a bulletproof vest
and fired back. It's cinnamon, my skin,
it's more sandstone than any color I know.   20
I voted for Obama, McCain, Nader, I was too
apathetic to vote, too lazy to walk one block,
two blocks to the voting booth. For or against
a woman's right to choose? Yes, for and against.
For waterboarding, for strapping detainees   25
with snorkels and diving masks. Against burning
fossil fuels, let's punish all those smokestacks
for eating the ozone, bring the wrecking balls,

but build more smokestacks, we need jobs
here in Harrisburg, here in Kalamazoo. Against   30
gun control, for cotton bullets, for constructing
a better fence along the border, let's raise
concrete toward the sky, why does it need
all that space to begin with? For creating
holes in the fence, adding ladders, they're not   35
here to steal work from us, no one dreams
of crab walking for hours across a lettuce field
so someone could order the Caesar salad.
No one dreams of sliding a squeegee down
the cloud-mirrored windows of a high-rise,   40
but some of us do it. Some of us sell flowers.
Some of us cut hair. Some of us carefully
steer a mower around the cemetery grounds.
Some of us paint houses. Some of us monitor
the power grid. Some of us ring you up   45
while some of us crisscross a parking lot
to gather the shopping carts into one long,
rolling, clamorous and glittering backbone.

CONSIDERATIONS FOR CRITICAL THINKING AND WRITING

1. FIRST RESPONSE. How does the arrangement of lines communicate a sense of
   energy and vitality?

2. How does the speaker characterize the United States?

3. Discuss the tone and thematic significance of the final image in lines 46–48.

CONNECTION TO ANOTHER SELECTION

1. How does Hernandez's description of what is "All-American" compare with Julio
   Marzán's in "The Translator at the Reception for Latin American Writers" (p. 810)?

CHRISTINA GEROGIANNIS (B. 1981)

Headland   2007

1

There is no sadness
but held in the bedroom of the
rented house from two years ago.

I should say no
definite sadness.   5

2

On the dresser:
a small sample of jasper.
Late summer, the house smelled of bleach.

In every corner we tried
to clean it of the day.   10

3

The telephone rang in the living day.
After that, the prepared slideshow, the
walking in and walking out.

The photos on corkboard.
The ordeal over.   15

4

The quilt stained white in places
from mopping bleach onto the ceiling
and not moving the quilt.

I could smell bleach underneath and
thought of the acres around the house.   20

5

Here, in the driveway,
is Celeste in her workout clothes.
This is ending everything.

Quarries, unfamiliar, not
just unfamiliar —   25

6

Home is over for us.
Here, in the kitchen,
we learn of a new death.

Celeste is polite and leaves. Acres surround
the house, protection from nothing, really.   30

7

In the living world I collected rocks
and minerals, and was interested in
telescopes, meridians. Hills, quarries —

the land at home, whatever it was.
At this hour, clean. Later, start again.   35

QUESTIONS FOR CRITICAL THINKING AND WRITING

1. FIRST RESPONSE. What is lost in "Headland"? How does "no definite sadness" characterize feelings about a place that has been lost?

2. What does Gerogiannis achieve by describing emotions, places, and objects in ambiguous terms? Are there parallel details to "no definite sadness" that characterize the absences referred to in the poem?

3. Is "Headland" a place, a geological formation, or a mental territory? How does this affect your sense of the title?

CONNECTION TO ANOTHER SELECTION

1. Why are the speaker's sensory perceptions jumbled in this poem? Discuss "Headland" in terms Emily Dickinson identifies in "The Bustle in a House" (p. 848).

Found Poem

This next selection is a *found poem*, unintentional verse discovered in a non-poetic context, such as a conversation, news story, or an advertisement. Found poems are playful reminders that the words in poems are very often the language we use every day. Whether such found language should be regarded as a poem is an issue left for you to consider.

DONALD JUSTICE (1925–2004)

Order in the Streets   1969

(*From instructions printed on a child's toy, Christmas 1968, as reported in the* New York Times)

1. 2. 3.
Switch on.

Jeep rushes
to the scene
of riot   5

Jeep goes
in all directions
by mystery action.

Jeep stops periodically
to turn hood over   10

machine gun appears
with realistic
shooting noise.

After putting down riot,
jeep goes   15
back to the headquarters.

CONSIDERATIONS FOR CRITICAL THINKING AND WRITING

1. FIRST RESPONSE. What is the effect of arranging these instructions in discrete lines? How are the language and meaning enhanced by this arrangement?

2. How does this poem connect upon the many riots that occurred throughout the United States during the late sixties?

3. CREATIVE RESPONSE. Look for phrases or sentences in ads, textbooks, labels, or directions — in anything that might inadvertently contain provocative material that would be revealed by arranging the words in verse lines. You may even discover some patterns of rhyme and rhythm. After arranging the lines, explain why you organized them as you did.

30

Combining the Elements of Poetry: A Writing Process

In poetry you have a form looking for a subject and a subject looking for a form. When they come together successfully you have a poem.
— W. H. AUDEN

© Corbis.

THE ELEMENTS TOGETHER

The elements of poetry that you have studied in the preceding ten chapters of this book offer a vocabulary and a series of perspectives that open up avenues of inquiry into a poem. As you have learned, there are many potential routes that you can take. By asking questions about the speaker, diction, figurative language, sounds, rhythm, tone, or theme, you clarify your understanding while simultaneously sensitizing yourself to elements and issues especially relevant to the poem under consideration. This process of careful, informed reading allows you to see how the various elements of the poem reinforce its meanings.

A poem's elements do not exist in isolation, however. They work together to create a complete experience for the reader. Knowing how the elements combine helps you understand the poem's structure and appreciate it as a whole. Robert Herrick's "Delight in Disorder" (p. 766), for example, is more easily understood (and the humor of the poem is better appreciated) when meter and rhyme are considered together with the poem's meaning. Musing about how he is more charmed by a naturally disheveled appearance than by those that seem contrived, the speaker lists several attributes of dishevelment and concludes that they

> Do more bewitch me than when art
> Is too precise in every part.

Noticing how the couplet's precise and sing-songy rhythm combines with the solid, obvious, and final rhyme of *art / part* helps in understanding what the speaker means by "too precise," as the lines are a little too precise themselves. Noticing this, you may even want to chart how rhythm and rhyme work together throughout the early (more disheveled) lines of the poem. Finding a pattern in the ways the elements work together throughout the poem will help you understand how the poem works.

MAPPING THE POEM

When you write about a poem, you are, in some ways, providing a guide for a place that might otherwise seem unfamiliar and remote. Put simply, writing enables you to chart a work so that you can comfortably move around in it to discuss or write about what interests you. Your paper represents a record and a map of your intellectual journey through the poem, pointing out the things worth noting and your impressions about them. Your role as writer is to offer insights into the challenges, pleasures, and discoveries that the poem harbors. These insights are a kind of sightseeing, as you navigate the various elements of the poem to make some overall point about it.

This chapter shows you how one student, Rose Bostwick, moves through the stages of writing about how a poem's elements combine for a final effect. Included here are Rose's annotated version of the poem, her first response, her informal outline, and the final draft of an explication of John Donne's "Death Be Not Proud." A detailed explanation of what is implicit in a poem, an *explication* requires a line-by-line examination of the poem. (For more on explication, see page 1679 in Chapter 52, "Reading and the Writing Process.") After reviewing the elements of poetry covered in the preceding chapters, Rose read the poem (which follows) several times, paying careful attention to diction, figurative language, irony, symbol, rhythm, sound, and so on. Her final paper is more concerned with the overall effect of the combination of elements than with a line-by-line breakdown, and her annotated version of the poem details her attention to that task. As you read and reread "Death Be Not Proud," keep notes on how *you* think the elements of this poem work together and to what overall effect.

John Donne (1572–1631)

John Donne, now regarded as a major poet of the early seventeenth century, wrote love poems at the beginning of his career but shifted to religious themes after converting from Catholicism to Anglicanism in the early 1590s. Although trained in law, he was also ordained a priest and became dean of St. Paul's Cathedral in London in 1621. The following poem, from "Holy Sonnets," reflects both his religious faith and his ability to create elegant arguments in verse.

© Michael Nicholson/CORBIS.

Death Be Not Proud   1611

Death be not proud, though some have callèd thee
Mighty and dreadful, for thou art not so;
For those whom thou think'st thou dost overthrow
Die not, poor Death, nor yet canst thou kill me.
From rest and sleep, which but thy pictures° be,   *images*   5
Much pleasure; then from thee much more must flow,
And soonest our best men with thee do go,
Rest of their bones, and soul's delivery.°   *deliverance*
Thou art slave to Fate, Chance, kings, and desperate men,
And dost with Poison, War, and Sickness dwell;   10
And poppy or charms can make us sleep as well,
And better than thy stroke; why swell'st° thou then?   *swell with pride*
One short sleep past, we wake eternally
And death shall be no more; Death, thou shalt die.

Considerations for Critical Thinking and Writing

1. **First response.** Why doesn't the speaker fear death? Explain why you find the argument convincing or not.

2. How does the speaker compare death with rest and sleep in lines 5–8? What is the point of this comparison?

3. Discuss the poem's rhythm by examining the breaks and end-stopped lines. How does the poem's rhythm contribute to its meaning?

4. What are the signs that this poem is structured as a sonnet?

ASKING QUESTIONS ABOUT THE ELEMENTS

After reading a poem, use the Questions for Responsive Reading and Writing (pp. 628–29) to help you think, talk, and write about any poem. Before you do, though, be sure that you have read the poem several times without worrying actively about interpretation. With poetry, as with all literature, it's important to allow yourself the pleasure of enjoying whatever makes itself apparent to you. On subsequent readings, use the questions to understand and appreciate how the poem works; remember to keep in mind that not all questions will necessarily be relevant to a particular poem. A good starting point is to ask yourself what elements are exemplified in the parts of the poem that especially interest you. Then ask the Questions for Responsive Reading and Writing that relate to those elements. Finally, as you begin to get a sense of what elements are important to the poem and how those elements fit together, it often helps to put your impressions on paper.

A SAMPLE CLOSE READING

An Annotated Version of "Death Be Not Proud"

As she read the poem closely several times, Rose annotated it with impressions and ideas that would lead to insights on which her analysis would be built. Her close examination of the poem's elements allowed her to understand how its parts contribute to its overall effect; her annotations provide a useful map of her thinking.

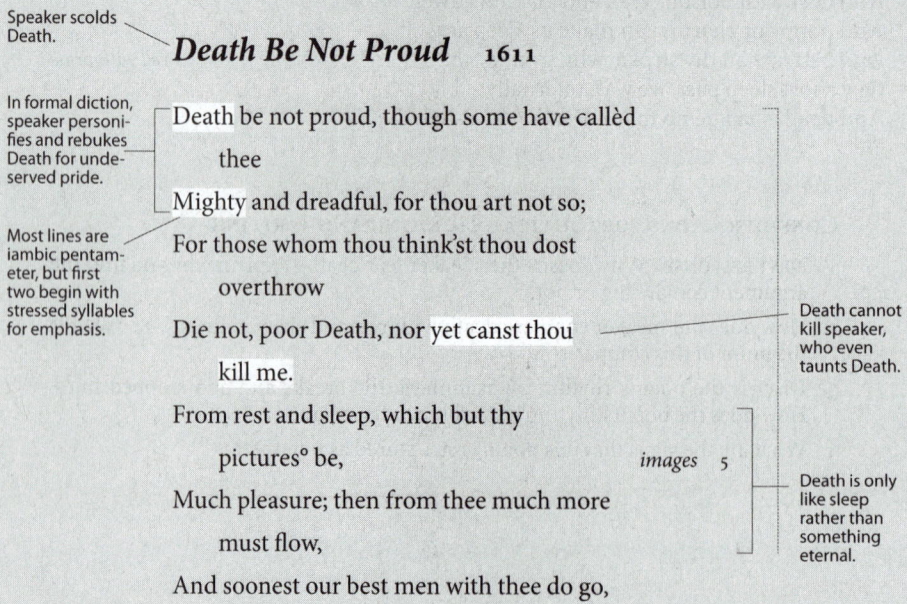

Speaker scolds Death.

Death Be Not Proud   1611

In formal diction, speaker personifies and rebukes Death for undeserved pride.

Most lines are iambic pentameter, but first two begin with stressed syllables for emphasis.

Death be not proud, though some have callèd
    thee
Mighty and dreadful, for thou art not so;
For those whom thou think'st thou dost
    overthrow
Die not, poor Death, nor yet canst thou
    kill me.
From rest and sleep, which but thy
    pictures° be,   *images* 5
Much pleasure; then from thee much more
    must flow,
And soonest our best men with thee do go,

Death cannot kill speaker, who even taunts Death.

Death is only like sleep rather than something eternal.

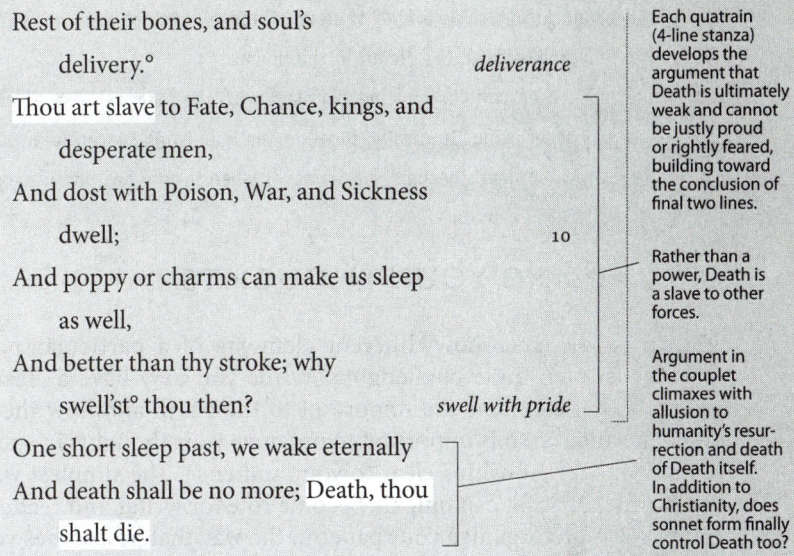

Rest of their bones, and soul's delivery.°   *deliverance*

Thou art slave to Fate, Chance, kings, and desperate men,

And dost with Poison, War, and Sickness dwell;   10

And poppy or charms can make us sleep as well,

And better than thy stroke; why swell'st° thou then?   *swell with pride*

One short sleep past, we wake eternally

And death shall be no more; Death, thou shalt die.

Marginal annotations:

Each quatrain (4-line stanza) develops the argument that Death is ultimately weak and cannot be justly proud or rightly feared, building toward the conclusion of final two lines.

Rather than a power, Death is a slave to other forces.

Argument in the couplet climaxes with allusion to humanity's resurrection and death of Death itself. In addition to Christianity, does sonnet form finally control Death too?

A SAMPLE FIRST RESPONSE

After Rose carefully read "Death Be Not Proud" and had a sense of how the elements work, she took the first step toward a formal explication by writing informally about the relevant elements and addressing the question *Why doesn't the speaker fear death? Explain why you find the argument convincing or not.* Note that at this point, she was not as concerned with textual evidence and detail as she would need to be in her final paper.

> I've read the poem "Death Be Not Proud" by John Donne a few times now, and I have a sense of how it works. The poem is a sonnet, and each of the three quatrains presents a piece of the argument that Death should not be proud, because it is not really all-powerful, and may even be a source of pleasure. As a reader, I resist this seeming paradox at first, but I know it must be a trick, a riddle of some sort that the poem will proceed to untangle. I think one of the reasons the poem comes off as such a powerful statement is that Donne at first seems to be playful and paradoxical in his characterizations of Death. He's almost teasing Death. But beneath the teasing tone you feel the strong foundation of the real reason Death should not be proud—Donne's faith in the immortality of the soul. The poem begins to feel more solemn as it progresses, as the hints at the idea of immortality become more clearly articulated.
>
> Donne utilizes two literary conventions to increase the effect of this poem: he uses the convention of personifying death, so that he can address it directly, and he

uses the metaphor of death as a kind of sleep. These two things determine the tone and the progression from playful to solemn in the poem.

The last clause of the poem (line 14) plays with the paradoxical-seeming character of what he's been declaring. Ironically, it seems the only thing susceptible to death is death itself. Or, when death becomes powerless is when it only has power over itself.

ORGANIZING YOUR THOUGHTS

Showing in a paper how different elements of a particular poem work together is often quite challenging. While you may have a clear intuitive sense of what elements are important to the poem and how they complement one another, it is important to organize your thoughts in such a way as to make the relationships clear to your audience. The simplest way is to go line by line, but that can quickly become rote for writer and reader. Because you will want to organize your paper in the way that best serves your thesis, it may help to write an informal outline that charts how you think the argument moves. You may find, for example, that the argument is not persuasive if you start with the final lines and go back to the beginning of the poem or passage. However you decide to organize your argument, keep in mind that a single idea, or thesis, will have to run throughout the entire paper.

A SAMPLE INFORMAL OUTLINE

In her informal outline (following), Rose discovers that her argument works best if she begins at the beginning. Note that, though her later paper concerns itself with how several elements of poetry contribute to the poem's theme and message, her informal outline concerns itself much more with what that message is and how it develops as the poem progresses. She will fill in the details later.

Thesis: From the very first word, addressing "Death" directly, Donne uses the literary conventions of personifying death and comparing it to sleep to begin an argument that Death should not be proud of its might or dreadfulness. But these two elements of his argument come to be seen as the superficial points when the true reason for death's powerlessness becomes clear. The Christian belief in the immortality of the soul is the reason for death's powerlessness and likeness to sleep.

Body of essay: Show how argument proceeds by quatrains from playful address to Death, and statement that Death is much like sleep, its "picture," to statement that Death is "slave" to other forces (and so should not be proud of being the mightiest), to the couplet, which articulates clearly the idea of immortality and gives the final paradox, "Death, thou shalt die."

Conclusion: Donne's faith in the immortality of the soul enables him to "prove" in this argument that Death is truly like its metaphorical representation, sleep. Faith allows him to derive a source for this conventional trope, and it allows him to state his truth in paradoxes. He relies on the conventional idea that death is an end, and a conqueror, and the only all-powerful force, to make the paradoxes that lend his argument the force of mystery — the mystery of faith.

THE ELEMENTS AND THEME

As you create an informal outline, your understanding of the poem will grow, change, and finally, solidify. You will develop a much clearer sense of what the poem's elements combine to create, and you will have chosen a scheme for organizing your argument. The next step before drafting is to determine the paper's thesis, which will not only keep your paper focused but will also help you center your thoughts. For papers that discuss how the elements of poetry come together, the thesis is a single and concise statement of what the elements combine to create — the idea around which all the elements revolve. In the earlier discussion of Robert Herrick's "Delight in Disorder," for example, the two elements, rhythm and rhyme, work together to create the speaker's self-directed irony. To state this as a thesis, we might say that by making his own rhythm and rhyme "too precise," Herrick's speaker is making fun of himself while complimenting a certain type of woman. (You may ask yourself if he's doing a little flirting.)

Once you understand how all of the elements of the poem fit together and have articulated your understanding in the thesis statement, the next step is to flesh out your argument. By including quotations from the poem to illustrate the points you will be making, you will better explain exactly how each element relates to the others and, more specifically, to your thesis, and you will have created a finished paper that helps readers navigate the poem's geography.

A SAMPLE EXPLICATION

The Use of Conventional Metaphors for Death in John Donne's "Death Be Not Proud"

In Rose's final draft, she focuses on the use of metaphor in "Death Be Not Proud." Her essay provides a coherent reading that relates each line of the poem to the speaker's intense awareness of death. Although the essay discusses each stanza in order, the introductory paragraph provides a brief overview explaining how the poem's metaphor and arguments contribute to its total meaning. In addition, Rose does not hesitate to discuss a line out of sequence when it can be usefully connected to another phrase. She also works quotations into her sentences to support her points. When she adds something to a quotation to clarify it, she encloses her words in brackets so that they will not be mistaken for the poet's, and she uses a slash to indicate line divisions: "soonest . . . with thee do go, / [for] Rest of their bones, and soul's delivery." Finally, Rose is sure to cite the line numbers for any direct quotations from the poem. As you read through her final draft, remember that the word *explication* comes from the Latin *explicare*, "to unfold." How successful do you think Rose is at unfolding this poem to reveal how its elements — here ranging from metaphor, structure, meter, personification, paradox, and irony to theme — contribute to its meaning?

Rose Bostwick

English 101

Professor Hart

24 February 2015

The Use of Conventional Metaphors for Death
in John Donne's "Death Be Not Proud"

Thesis providing interpretation of the poem's use of metaphor and how it contributes to the poem's central argument

In the sonnet that begins "Death be not proud . . ." John Donne argues that death is not "mighty and dreadful" but is more like its metaphorical representation, sleep. Death, Donne puts forth, is even a source of pleasure and rest. The poet builds this argument on two foundations. One is made up of the metaphors and literary conventions for death: death is compared with sleep and is often personified so that it can be addressed directly. The poem is an address to death that at first seems paradoxical and somewhat playful, but which then rises in all the emotion of faith as it reveals the second foundation of the argument—the Christian belief in the immortality of the soul. Seen against the backdrop of this belief, death loses its powerful threat and is seen as only a metaphorical sleep, or rest.

Discussion of how form and meter contribute to the poem's central argument

The poem is an ironic argument that proceeds according to the structure of the sonnet form. Each quatrain contains a new development or aspect of the argument, and the final couplet serves as a conclusion. The metrical scheme is mainly iambic pentameter, but in several places in the poem, the stress pattern is altered for emphasis. For example, the first foot of the poem is inverted, so that "Death," the first word, receives the stress. This announces to us right away that Death is being personified and addressed. This inversion also serves to begin the poem energetically and forcefully. The second line behaves in the same way. The first syllable of "Mighty" receives the stress, emphasizing the meaning of the word and its assumed relation to Death.

Discussion of how personification contributes to the poem's central argument

This first quatrain offers the first paradox and sets up the argument that death has been conventionally personified with the wrong attributes, might and dreadfulness. The poet tells death not to be proud, "though some have callèd thee / Mighty and dreadful," because, he says, death is "not so" (lines 1-2). Donne will turn this conventional characterization of death on its head with the paradox of the third and fourth lines: he says the people overthrown by death (as if by a conqueror) "Die not, poor death, nor yet canst thou kill me." These lines establish the paradox of death not being able to cause death.

The next quatrain will not begin to answer the question of why this paradox is so, but will posit another slight paradox—the idea of death as pleasurable. In lines 5-8, Donne uses the literary convention of describing death as a metaphorical sleep, or rest, to construct the argument that death must give pleasure: "From rest and sleep, which but thy pictures be, / Much pleasure; then from thee much more must flow" (5-6). At this point, the argument seems almost playful, but is carefully hinting at the solemnity of the deeper foundation of the belief in immortality. The metaphor of sleep for death includes the idea of waking; one doesn't sleep forever. The next two lines put forth the idea that death is pleasurable enough to be desired by "our best men" who "soonest . . . with thee do go, / [for] Rest of their bones, and soul's delivery" (7-8). This last line comes closer to announcing the true reason for death's powerlessness and pleasure: it is the way to the "soul's delivery" from the body and life on earth, and implicitly, into another, better realm.

> Discussion of how metaphor of sleep and idea of immortality support the poem's central argument

A new reason for death's powerlessness arises in the next four lines. The poet says to death:

> Thou art slave to Fate, Chance, kings, and desperate men,
>
> And dost with Poison, War, and Sickness dwell;
>
> And poppy or charms can make us sleep as well,
>
> And better than thy stroke; why swell'st thou then? (9-12)

Donne argues here that there are forces more powerful than death that actually control it. Fate and chance determine when death occurs, and to whom it comes. Kings, with the powers of law and war, can summon death and throw it on whom they wish. And desperate men, murderers or suicides, can also summon death with the strength of their emotions. In lines 11 and 12, Donne again uses the metaphor of death as a kind of sleep, but says that drugs or "charms" give one a better sleep than death. And he asks playfully why death should be so proud, after all these illustrations of its weakness have been given: "why swell'st thou then?" (12).

> Discussion of how language and tone contribute to the poem's central argument

Discussion of function of religious faith in the poem and how word order and meter create emphasis

Finally, with the last couplet, Donne reveals the true, deeper reason behind his argument that death should not be proud of its power. These lines also offer an explanation of the metaphor for death of sleep, or rest: "One short sleep past, we wake eternally / And death shall be no more; Death, thou shalt die" (13-14). After death, the soul lives on, according to Christian theology and belief. In the Christian heaven, where the soul is immortal, death will no longer exist, and so this last paradox, "Death, thou shalt die," becomes true. Again in this line, a significant inversion of metrical stress occurs. "Death," in the second clause, receives the stress, recalling the first line, emphasizing that it is an address and giving the clause a forceful sense of finality. His belief in the immortality of the soul

Conclusion supporting thesis in context of poet's beliefs

enables Donne to "prove" in this argument that death is in actuality like its metaphorical representation, sleep. His faith allows him to derive a source for this conventional metaphor and to "disprove" the metaphor of death as an all-powerful conqueror. His Christian beliefs also allow him to state his truth in paradoxes, the mysteries that are justified by the mystery of faith.

Work Cited

Donne, John. "Death Be Not Proud." *The Bedford Introduction to Literature*. Ed. Michael Meyer. 11th ed. Boston: Bedford/St. Martin's, 2016. 819. Print.

Before you begin writing your own paper on poetry, review the Suggestions for Approaching Poetry (pp. 606–07) and Chapter 21, "Writing about Poetry: From Inquiry to Final Paper," particularly the Questions for Responsive Reading and Writing (pp. 628–29). These suggestions and questions will help you focus and sharpen your critical thinking and writing. You'll also find help in Chapter 52, "Reading and the Writing Process," which offers a systematic overview of choosing a topic, developing a thesis, and organizing various types of assignments. If you use outside sources for the paper, be sure to acknowledge them adequately by using the conventional documentation procedures detailed in Chapter 53, "The Literary Research Paper."

Approaches
to Poetry

31

A Study of Emily Dickinson

My business is circumference.

— EMILY DICKINSON

In this chapter you'll find a variety of poems by Emily Dickinson so that you can study her work in some depth. While this collection is not wholly representative of her work, it does offer enough poems to suggest some of the techniques and concerns that characterize her writings. The poems speak not only to readers but also to one another. That's natural enough: the more familiar you are with a writer's work, the easier it is to perceive and enjoy the strategies and themes the poet uses. If you are asked to write about a number of poems by the same author, you may find useful the Questions for Writing about an Author in Depth (p. 858) and the sample paper on Dickinson's attitudes toward religious faith in four of her poems (pp. 861–63).

Emily E. Dickinson.

This daguerreotype of Emily Dickinson, taken shortly after her sixteenth birthday, and the silhouette (*opposite page*), created when she was fourteen years old, are the only authenticated mechanically produced images of the poet.

Todd-Bingham Picture Collection, 1837-1966 (inclusive). Manuscripts and Archives, Yale University.

A BRIEF BIOGRAPHY

Emily Dickinson (1830–1886) grew up in a prominent and prosperous household in Amherst, Massachusetts. Along with her younger sister, Lavinia, and older brother, Austin, she experienced a quiet and reserved family life headed by her father, Edward Dickinson. In a letter to Austin at law school, she once described the atmosphere in her father's house as "pretty much all sobriety."

(*Below*) This recently discovered print of a mid-1850s daguerreotype, acquired by the scholar Philip F. Gura in 2000, may represent the poet in her twenties.

Philip and Leslie Gura.

(*Right*) This silhouette shows Dickinson at age fourteen.

Todd-Bingham Picture Collection, 1837-1966 (inclusive). Manuscripts and Archives, Yale University.

Her mother, Emily Norcross Dickinson, was not as powerful a presence in her life; she seems not to have been as emotionally accessible as Dickinson would have liked. Her daughter is said to have characterized her as not the sort of mother "to whom you hurry when you are troubled." Both parents raised Dickinson to be a cultured Christian woman who would one day be responsible for a family of her own. Her father attempted to protect her from reading books that might "joggle" her mind, particularly her religious faith, but Dickinson's individualistic instincts and irreverent sensibilities created conflicts that did not allow her to fall into step with the conventional piety, domesticity, and social duty prescribed by her father and the orthodox Congregationalism of Amherst.

The Dickinsons were well known in Massachusetts. Her father was a lawyer and served as the treasurer of Amherst College (a position Austin eventually took up as well), and her grandfather was one of the college's founders. Although nineteenth-century politics, economics, and social issues do not appear in the foreground of her poetry, Dickinson lived in a family environment that was steeped in them: her father was an active town official and served in the General Court of Massachusetts, the state senate, and the U.S. House of Representatives.

Dickinson, however, withdrew not only from her father's public world but also from almost all social life in Amherst. She refused to see most people, and aside from a single year at South Hadley Female Seminary (now Mount Holyoke College), one excursion to Philadelphia and Washington, and several brief trips to Boston to see a doctor about eye problems, she lived all her life in her father's house. She dressed only in white and developed a reputation as a reclusive eccentric. Dickinson selected her own society carefully and frugally. Like her poetry, her relationship to the world was intensely reticent. Indeed, during the last twenty years of her life she rarely left the house.

Though Dickinson never married, she had significant relationships with several men who were friends, confidants, and mentors. She also enjoyed an intimate relationship with her friend Susan Huntington Gilbert, who became her sister-in-law by marrying Austin. Susan and her husband lived next door and were extremely close with Dickinson. Biographers have attempted to find in a number of her relationships the source for the passion of some of her love poems and letters. Several possibilities have been put forward as the person she addressed in three letters as "Dear Master": Benjamin Newton, a clerk in her father's office who talked about books with her; Samuel Bowles, editor of the *Springfield Republican* and friend of the family; the Reverend Charles Wadsworth, a Presbyterian preacher with a reputation for powerful sermons; and an old friend and widower, Judge Otis P. Lord. Despite these speculations, no biographer has been able to identify definitively the object of Dickinson's love. What matters, of course, is not with whom she was in love — if, in fact, there was any single person — but that she wrote about such passions so intensely and convincingly in her poetry.

Choosing to live life internally within the confines of her home, Dickinson brought her life into sharp focus, for she also chose to live within the limitless expanses of her imagination — a choice she was keenly aware of and which she described in one of her poems this way: "I dwell in Possibility —" (p. 845). Her small circle of domestic life did not impinge on her creative sensibilities. Like Henry David Thoreau, she simplified her life so that doing without was a means of being within. In a sense, she redefined the meaning of deprivation because being denied something — whether faith, love, literary recognition, or some other desire — provided a sharper, more intense understanding than she would have experienced had she achieved what she wanted: " 'Heaven,' " she wrote, "is what I cannot reach!" This poem (p. 842) — along with many others, such as "Water, is taught by thirst" (p. 838) and "Success is counted sweetest / By those who ne'er succeed" (p. 837) — suggests just how persistently she saw deprivation as a way of sensitizing herself to the value of what she was missing. For Dickinson, hopeful expectation was always more satisfying than achieving a golden moment. Perhaps that's one reason she was so attracted to John Keats's poetry (see, for example, his "Ode on a Grecian Urn," p. 660).

Dickinson enjoyed reading Keats as well as Emily and Charlotte Brontë; Robert and Elizabeth Barrett Browning; Alfred, Lord Tennyson; and George Eliot. Even so, these writers had little or no effect on the style of her writing. In her own work she was original and innovative, but she did draw on her knowledge of the Bible, classical myths, and Shakespeare for allusions and references in her poetry. She also used contemporary popular church hymns, transforming their standard rhythms into free-form hymn meters. Among American writers she appreciated Ralph Waldo Emerson and Thoreau, but she apparently felt Walt Whitman was better left unread. She once mentioned to Thomas Wentworth Higginson, a leading critic with whom she corresponded about her poetry, that as for Whitman "I never read his Book — but was told that he was disgraceful" (for the kind of Whitman poetry she had been warned against, see his "I Sing the Body Electric," p. 802). Nathaniel Hawthorne, however, intrigued her with his faith in the imagination and his dark themes: "Hawthorne appals — entices," a remark that might be used to describe her own themes and techniques.

AN INTRODUCTION TO HER WORK

Today, Dickinson is regarded as one of America's greatest poets, but when she died at the age of fifty-six after devoting most of her life to writing poetry, her nearly two thousand poems — only a dozen of which were published, anonymously, during her lifetime — were unknown except to a small number of friends and relatives. Dickinson was not recognized as a major poet until the twentieth century, when modern readers ranked her as a major new voice whose literary innovations were unmatched by any other nineteenth-century poet in the United States.

Dickinson neither completed many poems nor prepared them for publication. She wrote her drafts on scraps of paper, grocery lists, and the backs of recipes and used envelopes. Early editors of her poems took the liberty of making them more accessible to nineteenth-century readers when several volumes of selected poems were published in the 1890s. The poems were made to appear like traditional nineteenth-century verse by assigning them titles, rearranging their syntax, normalizing their grammar, and regularizing their capitalizations. Instead of dashes, editors used standard punctuation; instead of the highly elliptical telegraphic lines so characteristic of her poems, editors added articles, conjunctions, and prepositions to make them more readable and in line with conventional expectations. In addition, the poems were made more predictable by organizing them into categories such as friendship, nature, love, and death. Not until 1955, when Thomas Johnson published Dickinson's complete works in a form that attempted to be true to her manuscript versions, did readers have the opportunity to see the full range of her style and themes.

Like that of Robert Frost, Dickinson's popular reputation has sometimes relegated her to the role of a New England regionalist who writes quaint uplifting verses that touch the heart. In 1971 that image was mailed first class all over the country by the U.S. Postal Service. In addition to issuing a commemorative stamp featuring a portrait of Dickinson, the postal service affixed the stamp to a first-day-of-issue envelope that included an engraved rose and one of her poems. Here's the poem chosen from among the nearly two thousand she wrote:

If I can stop one Heart from breaking   ca. 1864

If I can stop one Heart from breaking
I shall not live in vain
If I can ease one Life the Aching
or cool one Pain

Or help one fainting Robin
Unto his Nest again
I shall not live in Vain.

This is typical not only of many nineteenth-century popular poems but also of the kind of verse that can be found in contemporary greeting cards. The speaker tells us what we imagine we should think about and makes the point simply with a sentimental image of a "fainting Robin." To point out that robins don't faint or that altruism isn't necessarily the only rule of conduct by which one should live one's life is to make trouble for this poem. Moreover, its use of language is unexceptional; the metaphors used, like that robin, are a bit weary. If this poem were characteristic of Dickinson's poetry, the U.S. Postal Service probably would not have been urged to issue a stamp in her honor, nor would you be reading her poems in this anthology or many others. Here's a poem by Dickinson that is more typical of her writing:

If I shouldn't be alive   ca. 1860

If I shouldn't be alive
When the Robins come,
Give the one in Red Cravat,
A Memorial crumb.

If I couldn't thank you,
Being fast asleep,
You will know I'm trying
With my Granite lip!

    This poem is more representative of Dickinson's sensibilities and techniques. Although the first stanza sets up a rather mild concern that the speaker might not survive the winter (a not uncommon fear for those who fell prey to pneumonia, for example, during Dickinson's time), the concern can't be taken too seriously—a gentle humor lightens the poem when we realize that all robins have red cravats and are therefore the speaker's favorite. Furthermore, the euphemism that describes the speaker "Being fast asleep" in line 6 makes death seem not so threatening after all. But the sentimental expectations of the first six lines—lines that could have been written by any number of popular nineteenth-century writers—are dashed by the penultimate word of the last line. *Granite* is the perfect word here because it forces us to reread the poem and to recognize that it's not about feeding robins or offering a cosmetic treatment of death; rather, it's a bone-chilling description of a corpse's lip that evokes the cold, hard texture and grayish color of tombstones. These lips will never say "thank you" or anything else.

    Instead of the predictable rhymes and sentiments of "If I can stop one Heart from breaking," this poem is unnervingly precise in its use of language and tidily points out how much emphasis Dickinson places on an individual word. Her use of near rhyme with "asleep" and "lip" brilliantly mocks a euphemistic approach to death by its jarring dissonance. This is a better poem, not because it's grim or about death, but because it demonstrates Dickinson's skillful use of language to produce a shocking irony.

    Dickinson found irony, ambiguity, and paradox lurking in the simplest and commonest experiences. The materials and subject matter of her poetry are quite conventional. Her poems are filled with robins, bees, winter light, household items, and domestic duties. These materials represent the range of what she experienced in and around her father's house. She used them because they constituted so much of her life and, more important, because she found meanings latent in them. Though her world was simple, it was also complex in its beauties and its terrors. Her lyric poems capture impressions of particular moments, scenes, or moods, and she characteristically focuses on topics such as nature, love, immortality, death, faith, doubt, pain, and the self.

    Though her materials were conventional, her treatment of them was innovative because she was willing to break whatever poetic conventions stood in the way of the intensity of her thought and images. Her conciseness, brevity, and wit are tightly packed. Typically she offers her observations via one or two images that reveal her thought in a powerful manner. She once characterized her literary art by writing, "My business is circumference." Her method is to reveal the inadequacy of declarative statements by evoking qualifications and questions with images that complicate firm assertions and affirmations. In one of her poems she describes her strategies this way: "Tell all the Truth but tell it slant — / Success in Circuit lies" (p. 849). This might well stand as a working definition of Dickinson's aesthetics and is embodied in the following poem:

The Thought beneath so slight a film —   ca. 1860

The Thought beneath so slight a film —
Is more distinctly seen —
As laces just reveal the surge —
Or Mists — the Apennine°   *Italian mountain range*

Paradoxically, "Thought" is more clearly understood precisely because a slight "film" — in this case language — covers it. Language, like lace, enhances what it covers and reveals it all the more — just as a mountain range is more engaging to the imagination if it is covered in mists rather than starkly presenting itself. Poetry for Dickinson intensifies, clarifies, and organizes experience.

Dickinson's poetry is challenging because it is radical and original in its rejection of most traditional nineteenth-century themes and techniques. Her poems require active engagement from the reader because she seems to leave out so much with her elliptical style and remarkable contracting metaphors. But these apparent gaps are filled with meaning if we are sensitive to her use of devices such as personification, allusion, symbolism, and startling syntax and grammar. Because her use of dashes is sometimes puzzling, it helps to read her poems aloud to hear how carefully the words are arranged. What might initially seem intimidating on a silent page can surprise the reader with meaning when heard. It's also worth keeping in mind that Dickinson was not always consistent in her views and that they can change from poem to poem, depending on how she felt at a given moment. For example, her definition of religious belief in "'Faith' is a fine invention" (p. 859) reflects an ironically detached wariness in contrast to the faith embraced in "I never saw a Moor —" (p. 860). Dickinson was less interested in absolute answers to questions than she was in examining and exploring their "circumference."

Because Dickinson's poems are all relatively brief (none is longer than fifty lines), they invite browsing and sampling, but perhaps a useful way into their highly metaphoric and witty world is this "how to" poem that reads almost like a recipe:

To make a prairie it takes a clover and one bee   date unknown

To make a prairie it takes a clover and one bee,
One clover, and a bee,
And revery.
The revery alone will do,
If bees are few.

This quiet but infinite claim for a writer's imagination brings together the range of ingredients in Dickinson's world of domestic and ordinary natural details. Not surprisingly, she deletes rather than adds to the recipe, because the one essential ingredient is the writer's creative imagination. *Bon appétit.*

Success is counted sweetest   ca. 1859

Success is counted sweetest
By those who ne'er succeed.
To comprehend a nectar
Requires sorest need.

Not one of all the purple Host   5
Who took the Flag today
Can tell the definition
So clear of Victory

As he defeated — dying —
On whose forbidden ear   10
The distant strains of triumph
Burst agonized and clear!

CONSIDERATIONS FOR CRITICAL THINKING AND WRITING

1. FIRST RESPONSE. How is "success" defined in this poem? To what extent does that definition agree with your own understanding of the word?
2. What do you think is meant by the use of "comprehend" in line 3? How can a nectar be comprehended?
3. Why do the defeated understand victory better than the victorious?
4. Discuss the effect of the poem's final line.

CONNECTION TO ANOTHER SELECTION

1. In an essay compare the themes of this poem with those of John Keats's "Ode on a Grecian Urn" (p. 660).

Water, is taught by thirst   ca. 1859

Water, is taught by thirst.
Land — by the Oceans passed.
Transport — by throe —
Peace — by its battles told —
Love, by Memorial Mold —
Birds, by the Snow.

CONSIDERATIONS FOR CRITICAL THINKING AND WRITING

1. FIRST RESPONSE. Which image in the poem do you find most powerful? Explain why.

2. How is the paradox of each line of the poem resolved? How is the first word of each line "taught" by the phrase that follows it?

3. CREATIVE RESPONSE. Try your hand at writing similar lines in which something is "taught."

CONNECTIONS TO OTHER SELECTIONS

1. What does this poem have in common with "Success is counted sweetest" (p. 837)? Which poem do you think is more effective? Explain why.

2. How is the crucial point of this poem related to "I like a look of Agony" (p. 842)?

Papa above!   ca. 1859

Papa above!
Regard a Mouse
O'erpowered by the Cat!
Reserve within thy kingdom
A "Mansion" for the Rat!

Snug in seraphic Cupboards
To nibble all the day,
While unsuspecting Cycles°   *time periods*
Wheel solemnly away!

CONSIDERATIONS FOR CRITICAL THINKING AND WRITING

1. FIRST RESPONSE. What do you think about the speaker's familiar way of addressing God? Describe the speaker's tone.

2. Comment on the levels of diction in this poem: formal, middle, and informal. Explain why you think they are appropriate or not.

3. Describe the view of God and heaven presented in this poem.

CONNECTION TO ANOTHER SELECTION

1. Discuss attitudes toward traditional views of God in "Papa above!" and "I know that He exists" (p. 859).

Safe in their Alabaster Chambers — 1859 version

Safe in their Alabaster Chambers —
Untouched by Morning
And untouched by Noon —
Sleep the meek members of the Resurrection —
Rafter of satin,   5
And Roof of stone.

Light laughs the breeze
In her Castle above them —
Babbles the Bee in a stolid Ear,
Pipe the Sweet Birds in ignorant cadence —   10
Ah, what sagacity perished here!

Safe in their Alabaster Chambers — 1861 version

Safe in their Alabaster Chambers —
Untouched by Morning —
And untouched by Noon —
Lie the meek members of the Resurrection —
Rafter of Satin — and Roof of Stone!   5

Grand go the Years — in the Crescent — above them —
Worlds scoop their arcs —
And Firmaments — row —
Diadems — drop — and Doges° — surrender —
Soundless as dots — on a Disc of Snow —   10

9 *Doges:* Chief magistrates of Venice from the twelfth to the sixteenth centuries.

CONSIDERATIONS FOR CRITICAL THINKING AND WRITING

1. FIRST RESPONSE. Dickinson permitted the 1859 version of this poem, titled "The Sleeping," to be printed in the *Springfield Republican.* The second version she sent privately to Thomas Wentworth Higginson. Why do you suppose she would agree to publish the first but not the second version?

2. Are there any significant changes in the first stanzas of the two versions? If you answered yes, explain the significance of the changes.

3. Describe the different kinds of images used in the two second stanzas. How do those images affect the tones and meanings of those stanzas?

4. Discuss why you prefer one version of the poem to the other.

CONNECTIONS TO OTHER SELECTIONS

1. Compare the theme in the 1861 version with the theme of Robert Frost's "Design" (p. 885).

2. In an essay discuss the attitude toward death in the 1859 version and in "Apparently with no surprise" (p. 860).

Portraits are to daily faces   ca. 1860

Portraits are to daily faces
As an Evening West,
To a fine, pedantic sunshine —
In a satin Vest!

CONSIDERATIONS FOR CRITICAL THINKING AND WRITING

1. FIRST RESPONSE. Dickinson once described her literary art this way: "My business is circumference." Does this poem fit her characterization of her poetry?

2. How is the basic strategy of this poem similar to the following statement: "Doorknob is to door as button is to sweater"?

3. Identify the four metonymies in the poem. Pay close attention to their connotative meanings.

4. If you don't know the meaning of "pedantic" (line 3), look it up in a dictionary. How does its meaning affect your reading of "fine" (line 3)?

CONNECTIONS TO OTHER SELECTIONS

1. Compare Dickinson's view of poetry in this poem with Robert Francis's perspective in "Catch" (p. 596). What important similarities and differences do you find?

2. Write an essay describing Robert Frost's strategy in "Mending Wall" (p. 874) or "Birches" (p. 877) as the "business of circumference."

3. How is the theme of this poem related to the central idea in "The Thought beneath so slight a film —" (p. 836)?

4. Compare the use of the word "fine" here with its use in "'Faith' is a fine invention" (p. 859).

Some keep the Sabbath going to Church —   ca. 1860

Some keep the Sabbath going to Church —
I keep it, staying at Home —
With a Bobolink for a Chorister —
And an Orchard, for a Dome —

Some keep the Sabbath in Surplice°   *holy robes*   5
I just wear my Wings —
And instead of tolling the Bell, for Church,
Our little Sexton — sings.

God preaches, a noted Clergyman —
And the sermon is never long,   10
So instead of getting to Heaven, at last —
I'm going, all along.

CONSIDERATIONS FOR CRITICAL THINKING AND WRITING

1. FIRST RESPONSE. What is the effect of referring to "Some" people (line 1)?
2. Characterize the speaker's tone.
3. How does the speaker distinguish himself or herself from those who go to church?
4. How might "Surplice" (line 5) be read as a pun?
5. According to the speaker, how should the Sabbath be observed?

CONNECTION TO ANOTHER SELECTION

1. Write an essay that discusses nature in this poem and in Walt Whitman's "When I Heard the Learn'd Astronomer" (p. 1069).

I taste a liquor never brewed —   1861

I taste a liquor never brewed —
From Tankards scooped in Pearl —
Not all the Vats upon the Rhine
Yield such an Alcohol!

Inebriate of Air — am I —   5
And Debauchee of Dew —
Reeling — thro endless summer days —
From inns of Molten Blue —

When "Landlords" turn the drunken Bee
Out of the Foxglove's door —   10
When Butterflies — renounce their "drams" —
I shall but drink the more!

Till Seraphs° swing their snowy Hats —   *angels*
And Saints — to windows run —
To see the little Tippler   15
Leaning against the — Sun —

CONSIDERATIONS FOR CRITICAL THINKING AND WRITING

1. FIRST RESPONSE. What is the poem's central metaphor? How is it developed in each stanza?

2. Which images suggest the causes of the speaker's intoxication?

3. Characterize the speaker's relationship to nature.

CONNECTION TO ANOTHER SELECTION

1. In an essay compare this speaker's relationship with nature to that of "A narrow Fellow in the Grass" (p. 2).

"Heaven" — is what I cannot reach! ca. 1861

"Heaven" — is what I cannot reach!
The Apple on the Tree —
Provided it do hopeless — hang —
That — "Heaven" is — to Me!

The Color, on the Cruising Cloud —   5
The interdicted Land —
Behind the Hill — the House behind —
There — Paradise — is found!

Her teasing Purples — Afternoons —
The credulous — decoy —   10
Enamored — of the Conjuror —
That spurned us — Yesterday!

CONSIDERATIONS FOR CRITICAL THINKING AND WRITING

1. FIRST RESPONSE. How does the speaker define *heaven*? How does that definition compare with conventional views of heaven?

2. Look up the myth of Tantalus and explain the allusion in line 3.

3. Given the speaker's definition of *heaven*, how do you think he or she would describe hell?

CONNECTIONS TO OTHER SELECTIONS

1. Write an essay that discusses desire in this poem and in "Water, is taught by thirst" (p. 838).

2. Discuss the speakers' attitudes toward pleasure in this poem and in Sharon Olds's "Last Night" (p. 650).

I like a look of Agony ca. 1861

I like a look of Agony,
Because I know it's true —
Men do not sham Convulsion,
Nor simulate, a Throe —

The Eyes glaze once — and that is Death —
Impossible to feign
The Beads upon the Forehead
By homely Anguish strung.

CONSIDERATIONS FOR CRITICAL THINKING AND WRITING

1. FIRST RESPONSE. Why does the speaker "like a look of Agony"? How do you respond to her appreciation of "Convulsion" (line 3)?

2. Discuss the image of "The Eyes glaze once —" (line 5). Why is that a particularly effective metaphor for death?

3. Characterize the speaker. One critic described the voice in this poem as "almost a hysterical shriek." Explain why you agree or disagree.

CONNECTION TO ANOTHER SELECTION

1. Write an essay on Dickinson's attitudes toward pain and deprivation, using this poem and "'Heaven' — is what I cannot reach!" (p. 842).

Wild Nights — Wild Nights! ca. 1861

Wild Nights — Wild Nights!
Were I with thee
Wild Nights should be
Our luxury!

Futile — the Winds —   5
To a Heart in port —
Done with the Compass —
Done with the Chart!

Rowing in Eden —
Ah, the Sea!   10
Might I but moor — Tonight —
In Thee!

CONSIDERATIONS FOR CRITICAL THINKING AND WRITING

1. FIRST RESPONSE. Thomas Wentworth Higginson, Dickinson's mentor, once said he was afraid that some "malignant" readers might "read into [a poem like this] more than that virgin recluse ever dreamed of putting there." What do you think?

2. Look up the meaning of *luxury* in a dictionary. Why does this word work especially well here?

3. Given the imagery of the final stanza, do you think the speaker is a man or a woman? Explain why.

4. CRITICAL STRATEGIES. Read the section on psychological strategies (pp. 1649–51) in Chapter 51, "Critical Strategies for Reading." What do you think this poem reveals about the author's personal psychology?

CONNECTION TO ANOTHER SELECTION

1. Write an essay that compares the voice, figures of speech, and theme of this poem with those of Margaret Atwood's "you fit into me" (p. 690).

The Soul selects her own Society —   ca. 1862

The Soul selects her own Society —
Then — shuts the Door —
To her divine Majority —
Present no more —

Unmoved — she notes the Chariots — pausing —   5
At her low Gate —
Unmoved — an Emperor be kneeling
Upon her Mat —

I've known her — from an ample nation —
Choose One —   10
Then — close the Valves of her attention —
Like Stone —

CONSIDERATIONS FOR CRITICAL THINKING AND WRITING

1. FIRST RESPONSE. Characterize the speaker. Is she self-reliant and self-sufficient? Cold? Angry?

2. Why do you suppose the "Soul" in this poem is female? Would it make any difference if it were male?

3. Discuss the effect of the images in the final two lines. Pay particular attention to the meanings of "Valves" in line 11.

Much Madness is divinest Sense —   ca. 1862

Much Madness is divinest Sense —
To a discerning Eye —
Much Sense — the starkest Madness —
'Tis the Majority
In this, as All, prevail —
Assent — and you are sane —
Demur — you're straightway dangerous —
And handled with a Chain —

CONSIDERATIONS FOR CRITICAL THINKING AND WRITING

1. FIRST RESPONSE. Thomas Wentworth Higginson's wife once referred to Dickinson as the "partially cracked poetess of Amherst." Assuming that Dickinson had some idea of how she was regarded by "the Majority" (line 4), how might this poem be seen as an insight into her life?

2. Discuss the conflict between the individual and society in this poem. Which images are used to describe each? How do these images affect your attitudes about them?

3. Comment on the effectiveness of the poem's final line.

CONNECTION TO ANOTHER SELECTION

1. Discuss the theme of self-reliance in this poem and in "The Soul selects her own Society —" (p. 844).

I dwell in Possibility —   ca. 1862

I dwell in Possibility —
A fairer House than Prose —
More numerous of Windows —
Superior — for Doors —

Of Chambers as the Cedars —   5
Impregnable of Eye —
And for an Everlasting Roof
The Gambrels° of the Sky —   *angled roofs*

Of Visitors — the fairest —
For Occupation — This —   10
The spreading wide my narrow Hands
To gather Paradise —

CONSIDERATIONS FOR CRITICAL THINKING AND WRITING

1. FIRST RESPONSE. What distinction is made between poetry and prose in this poem? Explain why you agree or disagree with the speaker's distinctions.

2. What is the poem's central metaphor in the second and third stanzas?

3. How does the use of metaphor in this poem become a means for the speaker to envision and create a world beyond the circumstances of his or her actual life?

CONNECTIONS TO OTHER SELECTIONS

1. Compare what this poem says about poetry and prose with T. E. Hulme's comments in "On the Differences between Poetry and Prose" (p. 686).

2. How can the speaker's sense of expansiveness in this poem be reconciled with the speaker's insistence on contraction in "The Soul selects her own Society —" (p. 844)? Are these poems contradictory? Explain why or why not.

After great pain, a formal feeling comes — ca. 1862

After great pain, a formal feeling comes —
The Nerves sit ceremonious, like Tombs —
The stiff Heart questions was it He, that bore,
And Yesterday, or Centuries before?

The Feet, mechanical, go round — 5
Of Ground, or Air, or Ought —
A Wooden way
Regardless grown,
A Quartz contentment, like a stone —

This is the Hour of Lead — 10
Remembered, if outlived,
As Freezing persons, recollect the Snow —
First — Chill — then Stupor — then the letting go —

CONSIDERATIONS FOR CRITICAL THINKING AND WRITING

1. FIRST RESPONSE. What do you think has caused the speaker's pain?
2. How does the rhythm of the lines create a slow, somber pace?
3. Discuss why "the Hour of Lead" (line 10) could serve as a useful title for this poem.

CONNECTION TO ANOTHER SELECTION

1. How might this poem be read as a kind of sequel to "The Bustle in a House" (p. 848)?

I heard a Fly buzz — when I died — ca. 1862

I heard a Fly buzz — when I died —
The Stillness in the Room
Was like the Stillness in the Air —
Between the Heaves of Storm —

The Eyes around — had wrung them dry — 5
And Breaths were gathering firm
For that last Onset — when the King
Be witnessed — in the Room —

I willed my Keepsakes — Signed away
What portion of me be 10
Assignable — and then it was
There interposed a Fly —

With Blue — uncertain stumbling Buzz —
Between the light — and me —
And then the Windows failed — and then 15
I could not see to see —

CONSIDERATIONS FOR CRITICAL THINKING AND WRITING

1. FIRST RESPONSE. What was expected to happen "when the King" was "witnessed" (lines 7–8)? What happened instead?
2. Why do you think Dickinson chooses a fly rather than perhaps a bee or gnat?
3. What is the effect of the last line? Why not end the poem with "I could not see" instead of the additional "to see"?
4. Discuss the sounds in the poem. Are there any instances of onomatopoeia?

CONNECTION TO ANOTHER SELECTION

1. Consider the meaning of "light" (line 14) in this poem and in "There's a certain Slant of light" (p. 1680).

Because I could not stop for Death —   ca. 1863

Because I could not stop for Death —
He kindly stopped for me —
The Carriage held but just Ourselves —
And Immortality.

We slowly drove — He knew no haste   5
And I had put away
My labor and my leisure too,
For His Civility —

We passed the School, where Children strove
At Recess — in the Ring —   10
We passed the Fields of Gazing Grain —
We passed the Setting Sun —

Or rather — He passed Us —
The Dews drew quivering and chill —
For only Gossamer, my Gown —   15
My Tippet° — only Tulle —   *shawl*

We paused before a House that seemed
A Swelling of the Ground —
The Roof was scarcely visible —
The Cornice — in the Ground —   20

Since then — 'tis Centuries — and yet
Feels shorter than the Day
I first surmised the Horses' Heads
Were toward Eternity —

CONSIDERATIONS FOR CRITICAL THINKING AND WRITING

1. FIRST RESPONSE. Why couldn't the speaker "stop for Death"?
2. How is death personified in this poem? How does the speaker respond to him? Why are they accompanied by Immortality?

3. What is the significance of the things they "passed" in the third stanza?

4. What is the "House" in lines 17–20?

5. Discuss the rhythm of the lines. How, for example, is the rhythm of line 14 related to its meaning?

CONNECTIONS TO OTHER SELECTIONS

1. Compare the tone of this poem with that of Dickinson's "Apparently with no surprise" (p. 860).

2. Write an essay comparing Dickinson's view of death in this poem and in "If I shouldn't be alive" (p. 835). Which poem is more powerful for you? Explain why.

I felt a Cleaving in my Mind —   ca. 1864

I felt a Cleaving in my Mind —
As if my Brain had split —
I tried to match it — Seam by Seam —
But could not make them fit.

The thought behind, I strove to join
Unto the thought before —
But Sequence ravelled out of Sound
Like Balls — upon a Floor.

CONSIDERATIONS FOR CRITICAL THINKING AND WRITING

1. FIRST RESPONSE. What is going on in the speaker's mind?

2. What is the poem's controlling metaphor? Describe the simile in lines 7 and 8. How does it clarify the first stanza?

3. Discuss the rhymes. How do they reinforce meaning?

CONNECTION TO ANOTHER SELECTION

1. Compare the power of the speaker's mind described here with the power of imagination described in "To make a prairie it takes a clover and one bee" (p. 837).

The Bustle in a House   ca. 1866

The Bustle in a House
The Morning after Death
Is solemnest of industries
Enacted upon Earth —

The Sweeping up the Heart
And putting Love away
We shall not want to use again
Until Eternity.

CONSIDERATIONS FOR CRITICAL THINKING AND WRITING

1. FIRST RESPONSE. What is the relationship between love and death in this poem?

2. Why do you think mourning (notice the pun in line 2) is described as industry?

3. Discuss the tone of the poem's ending. Consider whether you think it is hopeful, sad, resigned, or some other mood.

CONNECTIONS TO OTHER SELECTIONS

1. Compare this poem with "After great pain, a formal feeling comes —" (p. 846). Which poem is, for you, a more powerful treatment of mourning?

2. How does this poem qualify "I like a look of Agony" (p. 842)? Does it contradict the latter poem? Explain why or why not.

Tell all the Truth but tell it slant —   ca. 1868

Tell all the Truth but tell it slant —
Success in Circuit lies
Too bright for our infirm Delight
The Truth's superb surprise

As Lightning to the Children eased
With explanation kind
The Truth must dazzle gradually
Or every man be blind —

CONSIDERATIONS FOR CRITICAL THINKING AND WRITING

1. FIRST RESPONSE. What do you think the first line means? Why should truth be told "slant" and circuitously?

2. How does the second stanza explain the first?

3. How is this poem an example of its own theme?

CONNECTIONS TO OTHER SELECTIONS

1. How does the first stanza of "I know that He exists" (p. 859) suggest an idea similar to this poem's? Why do you think the last eight lines of the former aren't similar in theme to this poem?

2. Write an essay on Dickinson's attitudes about the purpose and strategies of poetry by considering this poem as well as "The Thought beneath so slight a film —" (p. 836) and "Portraits are to daily faces" (p. 840).

Oh Sumptuous moment   ca. 1868

Oh Sumptuous moment
Slower go
That I may gloat on thee —
'Twill never be the same to starve
Now I abundance see —

Which was to famish, then or now —
The difference of Day
Ask him unto the Gallows led —
With morning in the sky

CONSIDERATIONS FOR CRITICAL THINKING AND WRITING

1. FIRST RESPONSE. How do the sounds of the first stanza contribute to its meaning?
2. What kind of moment do you imagine the speaker is describing?
3. How do the final three lines shed light on the meaning of lines 1–6?

CONNECTIONS TO OTHER SELECTIONS

1. Compare and contrast the themes of this poem, "Water, is taught by thirst" (p. 838), and "Heaven' — is what I cannot reach!" (p. 842).

A Route of Evanescence   ca. 1879

A Route of Evanescence
With a revolving Wheel —
A Resonance of Emerald —
A Rush of Cochineal —
And every Blossom on the Bush
Adjusts its tumbled Head —
The mail from Tunis, probably,
An easy Morning's Ride —

CONSIDERATIONS FOR CRITICAL THINKING AND WRITING

1. FIRST RESPONSE. What does this poem describe?
2. Discuss the effectiveness of the poem's images in capturing what is described.
3. Consider how the poem's sounds contribute to its meanings.
4. How do the last two lines affect the poem's tone?

CONNECTION TO ANOTHER SELECTION

1. Discuss the style and theme of this poem and Dickinson's "A Bird came down the Walk —" (p. 733).

From all the Jails the Boys and Girls   ca. 1881

From all the Jails the Boys and Girls
Ecstatically leap —
Beloved only Afternoon
That Prison doesn't keep

They storm the Earth and stun the Air,
A Mob of solid Bliss —
Alas — that Frowns should lie in wait
For such a Foe as this —

CONSIDERATIONS FOR CRITICAL THINKING AND WRITING

1. FIRST RESPONSE. What are the "Jails"?
2. Comment on the effectiveness of the description in lines 5 and 6.
3. How might "Frowns" be read symbolically?

CONNECTION TO ANOTHER SELECTION

1. In an essay discuss the treament of childhood in this poem and in Robert Frost's "'Out, Out —'" (p. 879).

Perspectives on Emily Dickinson

EMILY DICKINSON

A Description of Herself   1862

Mr Higginson,
    Your kindness claimed earlier gratitude — but I was ill — and write today, from my pillow.
    Thank you for the surgery — it was not so painful as I supposed. I bring you others° — as you ask — though they might not differ —
    While my thought is undressed — I can make the distinction, but when I put them in the Gown — they look alike, and numb.
    You asked how old I was? I made no verse — but one or two° — until this winter — Sir —
    I had a terror — since September — I could tell to none — and so I sing, as the Boy does by the Burying Ground — because I am afraid — You inquire my Books — For Poets — I have Keats — and Mr and Mrs Browning. For Prose — Mr Ruskin — Sir Thomas Browne — and the Revelations. I went to school — but in your manner of the phrase — had no education. When a little Girl, I had a friend, who taught me Immortality — but venturing too near,

---

others: Dickinson had sent poems to Higginson for his opinions and enclosed more with this letter.   *one or two:* Actually she had written almost 300 poems.

himself — he never returned — Soon after, my Tutor, died — and for several years, my Lexicon — was my only companion — Then I found one more — but he was not contented I be his scholar — so he left the Land.

You ask of my Companions Hills — Sir — and the Sundown — and a Dog — large as myself, that my Father bought me — They are better than Beings — because they know — but do not tell — and the noise in the Pool, at Noon — excels my Piano. I have a Brother and Sister — My Mother does not care for thought — and Father, too busy with his Briefs — to notice what we do — He buys me many Books — but begs me not to read them — because he fears they joggle the Mind. They are religious — except me — and address an Eclipse, every morning — whom they call their "Father." But I fear my story fatigues you — I would like to learn — Could you tell me how to grow — or is it unconveyed — like Melody — or Witchcraft?

From a letter to Thomas Wentworth Higginson,
April 25, 1862

CONSIDERATIONS FOR CRITICAL THINKING AND WRITING

1. What impression does this letter give you of Dickinson?
2. What kinds of thoughts are there in the foreground of her thinking?
3. To what extent is the style of her letter writing like that of her poetry?

THOMAS WENTWORTH HIGGINSON (1823–1911)

On Meeting Dickinson for the First Time 1870

A large county lawyer's house, brown brick, with great trees & a garden — I sent up my card. A parlor dark & cool & stiffish, a few books & engravings & an open piano....

A step like a pattering child's in entry & in glided a little plain woman with two smooth bands of reddish hair & a face a little like Belle Dove's; not plainer — with no good feature — in a very plain & exquisitely clean white pique & a blue net worsted shawl. She came to me with two day lilies which she put in a sort of childlike way into my hand & said "These are my introduction" in a soft frightened breathless childlike voice — & added under her breath Forgive me if I am frightened; I never see strangers & hardly know what I say — but she talked soon & thenceforward continuously — & deferentially — sometimes stopping to ask me to talk instead of her — but readily recommencing ... thoroughly ingenuous & simple ... & saying many things which you would have thought foolish & I wise — & some things you wd. hv. liked. I add a few over the page....

"Women talk; men are silent; that is why I dread women."

"My father only reads on Sunday — he reads *lonely* & *rigorous* books."

"If I read a book [and] it makes my whole body so cold no fire ever can warm me I know *that* is poetry. If I feel physically as if the top of my head were taken off, I know *that* is poetry. These are the only ways I know it. Is there any other way."

"How do most people live without any thoughts. There are many people in the world (you must have noticed them in the street) How do they live. How do they get strength to put on their clothes in the morning"

"When I lost the use of my Eyes it was a comfort to think there were so few real *books* that I could easily find some one to read me all of them"

"Truth is such a *rare* thing it is delightful to tell it."

"I find ecstasy in living — the mere sense of living is joy enough"

I asked if she never felt want of employment, never going off the place & never seeing any visitor "I never thought of conceiving that I could ever have the slightest approach to such a want in all future time" (& added) "I feel that I have not expressed myself strongly enough."

From a letter to his wife, August 16, 1870

CONSIDERATIONS FOR CRITICAL THINKING AND WRITING

1. How old is Dickinson when Higginson meets her? Does this description seem commensurate with her age? Explain why or why not.

2. Choose one of the quotations from Dickinson that Higginson includes and write an essay about what it reveals about her.

MABEL LOOMIS TODD (1856–1932)

The Character *of Amherst*   1881

I must tell you about the *character* of Amherst. It is a lady whom the people call the *Myth.* She is a sister of Mr. Dickinson, & seems to be the climax of all the family oddity. She has not been outside of her own house in fifteen years, except once to see a new church, when she crept out at night, & viewed it by moonlight. No one who calls upon her mother & sister ever see her, but she allows little children once in a great while, & one at a time, to come in, when she gives them cake or candy, or some nicety, for she is very fond of little ones. But more often she lets down the sweetmeat by a string, out of a window, to them. She dresses wholly in white, & her mind is said to be perfectly wonderful. She writes finely, but no one *ever* sees her. Her sister, who was at Mrs. Dickinson's party, invited me to come & sing to her mother sometime. . . . People tell me the *myth* will hear every note — she will be near, but unseen. . . . Isn't that like a book? So interesting.

From a letter to her parents, November 6, 1881

CONSIDERATIONS FOR CRITICAL THINKING AND WRITING

1. Todd, who in the 1890s would edit Dickinson's poems and letters, had known her for only two months when she wrote this letter. How does Todd characterize Dickinson?

2. Does this description seem positive or negative to you? Explain your answer.

3. A few of Dickinson's poems, such as "Much Madness is divinest Sense —" (p. 844), suggest that she was aware of this perception of her. Refer to her poems in discussing Dickinson's response to this perception.

RICHARD WILBUR (B. 1921)

On Dickinson's Sense of Privation   1960

What did Emily Dickinson do, as a poet, with her sense of privation? One thing she quite often did was to pose as the laureate and attorney of the empty-handed, and question God about the economy of His creation. Why, she asked, is a fatherly God so sparing of His presence? Why is there never a sign that prayers are heard? Why does Nature tell us no comforting news of its Maker? Why do some receive a whole loaf, while others must starve on a crumb? Where is the benevolence in shipwreck and earthquake? By asking such questions as these, she turned complaint into critique, and used her own sufferings as experiential evidence about the nature of the deity. The God who emerges from these poems is a God who does not answer, an unrevealed God whom one cannot confidently approach through Nature or through doctrine.

But there was another way in which Emily Dickinson dealt with her sentiment of lack — another emotional strategy which was both more frequent and more fruitful. I refer to her repeated assertion of the paradox that privation is more plentiful than plenty; that to renounce is to possess the more; that "The Banquet of abstemiousness / Defaces that of wine." We all know how the poet illustrated this ascetic paradox in her behavior — how in her latter years she chose to live in relative retirement, keeping the world, even in its dearest aspects, at a physical remove. She would write her friends, telling them how she missed them, then flee upstairs when they came to see her; afterward, she might send a note of apology, offering the odd explanation that "We shun because we prize." Any reader of Dickinson biographies can furnish other examples, dramatic or homely, of this prizing and shunning, this yearning and renouncing: in my own mind's eye is a picture of Emily Dickinson watching a gay circus caravan from the distance of her chamber window.

> From "Sumptuous Destitution" in *Emily Dickinson: Three Views*,
> by Richard Wilbur, Louise Bogan, and Archibald MacLeish

CONSIDERATIONS FOR CRITICAL THINKING AND WRITING

1. Which poems by Dickinson reprinted in this anthology suggest that she was "the laureate and attorney of the empty-handed"?
2. Which poems suggest that "privation is more plentiful than plenty"?
3. Of these two types of poems, which do you prefer? Write an essay that explains your preference.

SANDRA M. GILBERT (B. 1936) AND
SUSAN GUBAR (B. 1944)

On Dickinson's White Dress   1979

Today a dress that the Amherst Historical Society assures us is *the* white dress Dickinson wore — or at least one of her "Uniforms of Snow" — hangs in a dry-cleaner's plastic bag in the closet of the Dickinson homestead. Perfectly preserved, beautifully flounced and tucked, it is larger than most readers would have expected this self-consciously small poet's dress to be, and thus reminds visiting scholars of the enduring enigma of Dickinson's central metaphor, even while it draws gasps from more practical visitors, who reflect with awe upon the difficulties of maintaining such a costume. But what exactly did the literal and figurative whiteness of this costume represent? What rewards did it offer that would cause an intelligent woman to overlook those practical difficulties? Comparing Dickinson's obsession with whiteness to [Herman] Melville's, William R. Sherwood suggests that "it reflected in her case the Christian mystery and not a Christian enigma . . . a decision to announce . . . the assumption of a worldly death that paradoxically involved regeneration." This, he adds, her gown — "a typically slant demonstration of truth" — should have revealed "to anyone with the wit to catch on."[1]

We might reasonably wonder, however, if Dickinson herself consciously intended her wardrobe to convey any one message. The range of associations her white poems imply suggests, on the contrary, that for her, as for Melville, white is the ultimate symbol of enigma, paradox, and irony, "not so much a color as the visible absence of color, and at the same time the concrete of all colors." Melville's question [in *Moby-Dick*] might, therefore, also be hers: "is it for these reasons that there is such a dumb blankness, full of meaning, in a wide landscape of snows — a colorless, all-color of atheism from which we shrink?" And his concluding speculation might be hers too, his remark "that the mystical cosmetic which produces every one of [Nature's] hues, the great principle of light, for ever remains white or colorless in itself, and if operating without medium upon matter, would touch all objects . . . with its own blank tinge." For white, in Dickinson's poetry, frequently represents both the energy (the white heat) of Romantic creativity, and the loneliness (the polar cold) of the renunciation or tribulation Romantic creativity may demand, both the white radiance of eternity — or Revelation — and the white terror of a shroud.

> From *The Madwoman in the Attic: The Woman Writer and the Nineteenth-Century Literary Imagination*

[1] *Circumference and Circumstance: Stages in the Mind and Art of Emily Dickinson* (New York: Columbia UP, 1968), 152, 231.

CONSIDERATIONS FOR CRITICAL THINKING AND WRITING

1. What meanings do Gilbert and Gubar attribute to Dickinson's white dress?

2. Discuss the meaning of the implicit whiteness in "Safe in their Alabaster Chambers —" (p. 839) and "After great pain, a formal feeling comes —" (p. 846). To what extent do these poems incorporate the meanings of whiteness that Gilbert and Gubar suggest?

3. What other reasons can you think of that might account for Dickinson's wearing only white?

PAULA BENNETT (B. 1936)

On "I heard a Fly buzz — when I died —" 1990

Dickinson's rage against death, a rage that led her at times to hate both life and death, might have been alleviated, had she been able to gather hard evidence about an afterlife. But, of course, she could not. "The *Bareheaded life* — under the grass — ," she wrote to Samuel Bowles in c. 1860, "worries one like a Wasp." If death was the gate to a better life in "the childhood of the kingdom of Heaven," as the sentimentalists — and Christ — claimed, then, perhaps, there was compensation and healing for life's woes. . . . But how do we know? What can we know? In "I heard a Fly buzz — when I died," Dickinson concludes that we do not know much. . . .

Like many people in her period, Dickinson was fascinated by death-bed scenes. How, she asked various correspondents, did this or that person die? In particular, she wanted to know if their deaths revealed any information about the nature of the afterlife. In this poem, however, she imagines her own death-bed scene, and the answer she provides is grim, as grim (and, at the same time, as ironically mocking) as anything she ever wrote.

In the narrowing focus of death, the fly's insignificant buzz, magnified tenfold by the stillness in the room, is all that the speaker hears. This kind of distortion in scale is common. It is one of the "illusions" of perception. But here it is horrifying because it defeats every expectation we have. Death is supposed to be an experience of awe. It is the moment when the soul, departing the body, is taken up by God. Hence the watchers at the bedside wait for the moment when the "King" (whether God or death) "be witnessed" in the room. And hence the speaker assigns away everything but that which she expects God (her soul) or death (her body) to take.

What arrives instead, however, is neither God nor death but a fly, "[w]ith Blue — uncertain — stumbling Buzz," a fly, that is, no more secure, no more sure, than we are. Dickinson had associated flies with death once before in the exquisite lament, "How many times these low feet / staggered." In this poem, they buzz "on the / chamber window," and speckle it with dirt, reminding us that the housewife, who once protected us from such intrusions, will protect us no longer. Their presence is threatening but only in a minor way, "dull" like themselves. They are a background noise we do not have to deal with yet.

In "I heard a Fly buzz," on the other hand, there is only one fly and its buzz is not only foregrounded. Before the poem is over, the buzz takes up the entire field of perception, coming between the speaker and the "light" (of day, of life, of knowledge). It is then that the "Windows" (the eyes that are the windows of the soul as well as, metonymically, the light that passes through the panes of glass) "fail" and the speaker is left in darkness — in death, in ignorance. She cannot "see" to "see" (understand).

Given that the only sure thing we know about "life after death" is that flies — in their adult form and more particularly, as maggots — devour us, the poem is at the very least a grim joke. In projecting her death-bed scene, Dickinson confronts her ignorance and gives back the only answer human knowledge can with any certainty give. While we may hope for an afterlife, no one, not even the dying, can prove it exists.

From *Emily Dickinson: Woman Poet*

CONSIDERATIONS FOR CRITICAL THINKING AND WRITING

1. According to Bennett, what is the symbolic value of the fly?

2. Does Bennett leave out any significant elements of the poem in her analysis? Explain why you think she did or did not.

3. Choose a Dickinson poem and write a detailed analysis that attempts to account for all of its major elements.

Martha Nell Smith (b. 1953)

On "Because I could not stop for Death —" 1993

That this poem begins and ends with humanity's ultimate dream of self-importance — Immortality and Eternity — could well be the joke central to its meaning, for Dickinson carefully surrounds the fantasy of living ever after with the dirty facts of life — dusty carriage rides, schoolyards, and farmers' fields. Many may contend that, like the Puritans and metaphysicals before her, Dickinson pulls the sublime down to the ridiculous but unavoidable facts of existence, thus imbues life on earth with its real import. On the other hand, Dickinson may have argued otherwise. Very late in her life, she wrote, "When Jesus tells us about his Father, we distrust him. When he shows us his Home, we turn away, but when he confides to us that he is 'acquainted with Grief,' we listen, for that is also an Acquaintance of our own." Instead of sharing their faith, Dickinson may be showing the community around her, most of whom were singing "When we all get to Heaven what a day of rejoicing that will be," how selfishly selective is their belief in a system that bolsters egocentrism by assuring believers not only that their individual identities will survive death, but also that they are one of the exclusive club of the saved. Waiting for the return of Eden or Paradise, which "is always eligible" and which she "never believed . . . to be a superhuman site," those believers may simply find themselves gathering dust. Surrounded by the faithful, Dickinson struggled with trust and doubt in Christian promises herself, but whether she believed in salvation or even in immortality is endlessly debatable. Readers can select poems and letters and construct compelling arguments to prove that she did or did not. But for every declaration evincing belief, there is one like that to Elizabeth Holland:

> The Fiction of "Santa Claus" always reminds me of the reply to my early question of "Who made the Bible" — "Holy Men moved by the Holy Ghost," and though I have now ceased my investigations, the Solution is insufficient —

What "Because I could not stop for Death —" will not allow is any hard and fast conclusion to be drawn about the matter. Once again . . . by mixing tropes and tones Dickinson underscores the importance of refusing any single-minded response to a subject and implicitly attests to the power in continually opening possibilities by repeatedly posing questions.

From *Comic Power in Emily Dickinson*, by Suzanne Juhasz,
Cristanne Miller, and Martha Nell Smith

Considerations for Critical Thinking and Writing

1. In what sense, according to Smith, could a joke be central to the meaning of "Because I could not stop for Death — "(p. 847)?

2. Compare the potential joke in this poem and in "I know that He exists" (p. 859). How is your reading of each poem influenced by considering them together?

3. Read the sample paper on "Religious Faith in Four Poems by Emily Dickinson" (pp. 861–63) and write an analysis of "Because I could not stop for Death —" that supports or refutes the paper's thesis.

Questions for Writing about an Author in Depth

As you read multiple works by the same author, you're likely to be struck by the similarities and differences in those selections. You'll begin to recognize situations, events, characters, issues, perspectives, styles, and strategies — even recurring words or phrases — that provide a kind of signature, making the poems in some way identifiable with that particular writer.

The following questions can help you respond to multiple works by the same author. They should help you listen to how a writer's works can speak to one another and to you. Additional useful questions can be found in other chapters of this book. See Chapter 21, "Writing about Poetry: From Inquiry to Final Paper" and Arguing about Literature (p. 1670) in Chapter 52, "Reading and the Writing Process."

1. What topics reappear in the writer's work? What seem to be the major concerns of the author?

2. Does the author have a definable worldview that can be discerned from work to work? Is, for example, the writer liberal, conservative, apolitical, or religious?

3. What social values come through in the author's work? Does he or she seem to identify with a particular group or social class?

4. Is there a consistent voice or point of view from work to work? Is it a persona or the author's actual self?

5. How much of the author's own life experiences and historical moment make their way into the works?

6. Does the author experiment with style from work to work, or are the works mostly consistent with one another?

7. Can the author's work be identified with a literary tradition, such as *carpe diem* poetry, that aligns his or her work with that of other writers?

8. What is distinctive about the author's writing? Is the language innovative? Are the themes challenging? Are the voices conventional? Is the tone characteristic?

9. Could you identify another work by the same author without a name being attached to it? What are the distinctive features that allow you to do so?

10. Do any of the writer's works seem *not* to be by that writer? Why?

11. What other writers are most like this author in style and content? Why?

12. Has the writer's work evolved over time? Are there significant changes or developments? Are there new ideas and styles, or do the works remain largely the same?

13. How would you characterize the author's writing habits? Is it possible to anticipate what goes on in different works, or are you surprised by their content or style?

14. Can difficult or ambiguous passages in a work be resolved by referring to a similar passage in another work?

15. What does the writer say about his or her own work? Do you trust the teller or the tale? Which do you think is more reliable?

A SAMPLE IN-DEPTH STUDY

The following paper was written for an assignment that called for an analysis (about 750 words) on any topic that could be traced in three or four poems by Dickinson. The student, Michael Weitz, chose "'Faith' is a fine invention," "I know that He exists," "I never saw a Moor —," and "Apparently with no surprise."

Previous knowledge of a writer's work can set up useful expectations in a reader. In the case of the four Dickinson poems included in this section, religion emerges as a central topic linked to a number of issues, including faith, immortality, skepticism, and the nature of God. The student selected these poems because he noticed Dickinson's intense interest in religious faith owing to the many poems that explore a variety of religious attitudes in her work. He chose these four because they were closely related, but he might have found equally useful clusters of poems about love, nature, domestic life, or writing. What especially intrigued him was some of the information he read about Dickinson's sternly religious father and the orthodox nature of the religious values of her hometown of Amherst, Massachusetts. Because this paper was not a research paper, he did not pursue these issues beyond the level of the general remarks provided in an introduction to her poetry (though he might have). He did, however, use this biographical and historical information as a means of framing his search for poems that were related to one another. In doing so he discovered consistent concerns along with contradictory themes that became the basis of his paper.

"Faith" is a fine invention   ca. 1860

"Faith" is a fine invention
When Gentlemen can *see* —
But *Microscopes* are prudent
In an Emergency.

I know that He exists   ca. 1862

I know that He exists.
Somewhere — in Silence —
He has hid his rare life
From our gross eyes.

'Tis an instant's play.   5
'Tis a fond Ambush —
Just to make Bliss
Earn her own surprise!

But — should the play
Prove piercing earnest —
Should the glee-glaze —
In Death's — stiff — stare — 10

Would not the fun
Look too expensive!
Would not the jest —
Have crawled too far! 15

I never saw a Moor — ca. 1865

I never saw a Moor —
I never saw the Sea —
Yet know I how the Heather looks
And what a Billow be.

I never spoke with God
Nor visited in Heaven —
Yet certain am I of the spot
As if the Checks were given —

Apparently with no surprise ca. 1884

Apparently with no surprise
To any happy Flower
The Frost beheads it at its play —
In accidental power —
The blond Assassin passes on —
The Sun proceeds unmoved
To measure off another Day
For an Approving God.

A SAMPLE STUDENT PAPER

Religious Faith in Four Poems by Emily Dickinson

Michael Weitz

Professor Pearl

English 270

5 May 2015

Religious Faith in Four Poems by Emily Dickinson

Throughout much of her poetry, Emily Dickinson wrestles with complex notions of God, faith, and religious devotion. She adheres to no consistent view of religion; rather, her poetry reveals a vision of God and faith that is constantly evolving. Dickinson's gods range from the strict and powerful Old Testament father to a loving spiritual guide to an irrational and ridiculous imaginary figure. Through these varying images of God, Dickinson portrays contrasting images of the meaning and validity of religious faith. Her work reveals competing attitudes toward religious devotion as conventional religious piety struggles with a more cynical perception of God and religious worship.

> Introduction providing overview of faith in Dickinson's work

> Thesis analyzing poet's attitudes toward God and religion

Dickinson's "I never saw a Moor—" reveals a vision of traditional religious sensibilities. Although the speaker readily admits that "I never spoke with God / Nor visited in Heaven—" (lines 5-6), her devout faith in a supreme being does not waver. The poem appears to be a straightforward profession of true faith stemming from the argument that the proof of God's existence is the universe's existence. Dickinson's imagery therefore evolves from the natural to the supernatural, first establishing her convictions that moors and seas exist, in spite of her lack of personal contact with either. This leads to the foundation of her religious faith, again based not on physical experience but on intellectual convictions. The speaker professes that she believes in the existence of Heaven even without conclusive evidence: "Yet certain am I of the spot / As if the Checks were given—" (7-8). But the appearance of such idealistic views of God and faith in "I never saw a Moor—" are transformed in Dickinson's other poems into a much more skeptical vision of the validity of religious piety.

> Analysis of religious piety in "I never saw a Moor —" supported with textual evidence

> Contrast between attitudes in "Moor" and other poems

While faith is portrayed as an authentic and deeply important quality in "I never saw a Moor—," Dickinson's "'Faith' is a fine invention" portrays faith as much less essential. Faith is defined in the poem as "a fine invention" (1), suggesting that it is created by man for man and therefore is not a crucial aspect of the natural universe. Thus the strong idealistic faith of "I never saw a Moor—" becomes discredited in the face of scientific rationalism. The speaker compares religious faith with actual microscopes, both of which are meant to enhance one's vision in some way. But "Faith" is useful only "When Gentlemen can *see*—" already (2); "In an Emergency," when one ostensibly cannot see, "*Microscopes* are prudent" (4, 3). Dickinson pits religion against science, suggesting that science, with its tangible evidence and rational attitude, is a more reliable lens through which to view the world. Faith is irreverently reduced to a mere "invention" and one that is ultimately less useful than microscopes or other scientific instruments.

Analysis of scientific rationalism in "'Faith' is a fine invention" supported with textual evidence

Rational, scientific observations are not the only contributing factor to the portrayal of religious skepticism in Dickinson's poems; nature itself is seen to be incompatible in some ways with conventional religious ideology. In "Apparently with no surprise," the speaker recognizes the inexorable cycle of natural life and death as a morning frost kills a flower. But the tension in this poem stems not from the "happy Flower" (2) struck down by the frost's "accidental power" (4) but from the apparent indifference of the "Approving God" (8) who condones this seemingly cruel and unnecessary death. God is seen as remote and uncompromising, and it is this perceived distance between the speaker and God that reveals the increasing absurdity of traditional religious faith. The speaker understands that praying to God or believing in religion cannot change the course of nature, and as a result feels so helplessly distanced from God that religious faith becomes virtually meaningless.

Analysis of God and nature in "Apparently with no surprise" supported with textual evidence

Dickinson's religious skepticism becomes even more explicit in "I know that He exists," in which the speaker attempts to understand the connection between seeing God and facing death. In this poem Dickinson characterizes God as a remote and mysterious figure; the speaker mockingly asserts, "I know that He exists" (1), even though "He has hid his rare life / From our gross eyes" (3-4). The skepticism toward religious faith revealed in this poem stems from the speaker's recognition of the paradoxical quest that

Analysis of characterization of God in "I know that He exists" supported with textual evidence

Weitz 3

people undertake to know and to see God. A successful attempt to see God, to win the game of hide-and-seek that He apparently is orchestrating, results inevitably in death. With this recognition the speaker comes to view religion as an absurd and reckless game in which the prize may be "Bliss" (7) but more likely is "Death's—stiff—stare—" (12). For, to see God and to meet one's death as a result certainly suggests that the game of trying to see God (the so-called "fun" of line 13) is much "too expensive" and that religion itself is a "jest" that, like the serpent in Genesis, has "crawled too far" (14-16).

Ultimately, the vision of religious faith that Dickinson describes in her poems is one of suspicion and cynicism. She cannot reconcile the physical world to the spiritual existence that Christian doctrine teaches, and as a result the traditional perception of God becomes ludicrous. "I never saw a Moor—" does attempt to sustain a conventional vision of religious devotion, but Dickinson's poems overall are far more likely to suggest that God is elusive, indifferent, and often cruel, thus undermining the traditional vision of God as a loving father worthy of devout worship. Thus, not only religious faith but also those who are religiously faithful become targets for Dickinson's irreverent criticism of conventional belief.

> Conclusion providing well-supported final analysis of poet's views on God and faith

Weitz 5

Works Cited

Dickinson, Emily. "Apparently with no surprise." Meyer 860.

---. "'Faith' is a fine invention." Meyer 859.

---. "I know that He exists." Meyer 859–60.

---. "I never saw a Moor—." Meyer 860.

Meyer, Michael, ed. *The Bedford Introduction to Literature*. 11th ed. Boston: Bedford/St. Martin's, 2016. Print.

SUGGESTED TOPICS FOR LONGER PAPERS

1. Irony is abundant in Dickinson's poetry. Choose five poems from this chapter that strike you as especially ironic and discuss her use of irony in each. Taken individually and collectively, what do these poems suggest to you about the poet's sensibilities and her ways of looking at the world?

2. Readers have sometimes noted that Dickinson's poetry does not reflect very much of the social, political, economic, religious, and historical events of her lifetime. Using the poems in this chapter as the basis of your discussion, what can you say about the contexts in which Dickinson wrote? What kind of world do you think she inhabited, and how did she respond to it?

Poetry and the Visual Arts

In the "Reading" chapter of *Walden* (1854), Henry David Thoreau confidently asserts: "A written word is the choicest of relics. It is something at once more intimate with us and more universal than any other work of art. It is the work of art nearest to life itself." This proclivity was true for Thoreau, but it may not be true for you and may register simply as the bias of a committed writer. No doubt a good many writers and avid readers would readily agree with Thoreau's preference for literature, but his contention would likely be qualified or even refuted by painters, musicians, sculptors, architects, filmmakers, and anyone else who creates or deeply connects to an art medium that relies on materials other than the written word. Our own experiences and preferences — whether we are producers or audiences or both — determine what kinds of works of art are "nearest to life itself." Moreover, these various media aren't mutually exclusive, as is demonstrated by eclectic audiences who enjoy the arts without making sweeping claims about the intimate and universal. Literature needn't compete with the visual arts; indeed, over time it has allied itself with other arts, as the six poems in this section will demonstrate.

The poems included here are examples of ekphrasis, from the Greek term *ekphrasis* (*ek,* "out of," and *phrasis,* "expression" or "speech"), which is often translated simply as "description." Ekphrastic literature consists of works that attempt to capture some quality or essential feature of another work of art. Such attempts are common in other types of art as well: a sculpture, for example, might evoke a heroic figure from a painting depicting a famous battle while a musical score might capture the explosive violence of the same painting. In literature, to cite an example from this anthology that you might have already read, John Keats's "Ode to a Grecian Urn" (p. 660) explores the possible meanings to be discovered concerning the lovers portrayed on a now-celebrated piece of pottery. One of the intriguing features of ekphrasis is the opportunity to contemplate an inspired artist in one medium prompted by another artist's work in a different medium.

This section offers six ekphrastic poems that reflect on the visual arts represented by a range of styles in four paintings, a woodblock print, and a memorial sculpture.

Questions for Responding to the Visual Arts

The following questions can help you respond to important elements in the visual arts. The questions may not apply to every work nor are they exhaustive, but they should help you organize your thoughts, discussions, and writing about each piece in this section. These questions will encourage you to see what's going on in a painting or some other media rather than to merely look at it. An analysis of particular elements will allow you to understand how various parts of a work contribute to its entire effect (to review Questions for Responsive Reading and Writing about poetry, see pp. 628–29).

1. What does the title reveal? How does it lead you into the work?

2. What is the subject matter? Is there a definable setting of time and place that makes the historical context important?

3. What details seem particularly significant? How does the artist relate them to one another and achieve a mood or tone in terms of proportion, lights and darks, colors, lines, and perspective?

4. How do the foreground, middleground, and background create a focus in the work?

5. Is it possible to describe the overall style as realistic, impressionistic, or abstract?

6. Do any of the details have symbolic significance or make allusions to other works, historical moments, contemporary events, people, or myths?

7. Does the artist offer a particular point of view or set of values associated with the subject matter?

8. Is there any humor, satire, or irony in the work?

9. How do the artist's choices of what is included in the work also suggest what has been purposely omitted from it?

10. After examining the work closely, have you confirmed, expanded, or qualified your first impression? Would you want to have a copy of this art in your room? Why or why not?

AMERICAN GOTHIC

Grant Wood (1891–1942) was born in Anamosa, Iowa. After studying at the School of the Art Institute of Chicago, he continued his studies for a number of years in Europe, but unlike a number of Americans traveling abroad in the 1920s, he returned home declaring that "all the really good ideas I'd ever had came to me while I was milking a cow. So I went back to Iowa." One of his early self-portraits has him in overalls similar to those worn by the farmer in *American Gothic* (1930), a work that made him an extraordinarily popular painter during the Depression of the 1930s when midwestern security and solidity offered simple American perseverance as an antidote to economic chaos. Curiously, many commentators regarded the painting as a satire of small-town parochialism and provincialism. Some viewers interpreted the painting as a negative critique of rural life rather than a celebration of it. John Stone's treatment of *American Gothic* doesn't resolve that issue, but it clearly appreciates the humanity of the couple depicted in the painting. Stone, born in Jackson, Mississippi, was both a poet and a cardiologist. After earning a medical degree at Washington University School of Medicine in St. Louis, he served on the medical faculty at Emory University School of Medicine, where he had a strong reputation for dealing with patients, students, and ultimately readers with directness and humor. Among his collections are *Where Water Begins* (1998) and *Music from Apartment 8: New and Selected Poems* (2004). In his "American Gothic," he makes a cordial and good-natured house call.

American Gothic Painted with oil on beaver board in 1930, *American Gothic* was created in a precise, realistic style reminiscent of fifteenth-century northern European artists. It earned a bronze medal at the Art Institute of Chicago's annual painting competition. The museum purchased it soon after, and it has been housed there ever since. Grant Wood, American, 1891–1942, *American Gothic,* 1930, Oil on Beaver Board, 78 × 65.3 cm (30¾ × 25¾ in.), Friends of American Art Collection, 1930.934, The Art Institute of Chicago. Photography © The Art Institute of Chicago. Art © Figge Art Museum successors to the Estate of Nan Wood Graham/Licensed by VAGA, New York, NY.

JOHN STONE (1936–2008)
American Gothic   1998

after the painting by Grant Wood, 1930

Just outside the frame
there has to be a dog
chickens, cows and hay

and a smokehouse
where a ham in hickory   5
is also being preserved

Here for all time
the borders of the Gothic window
anticipate the ribs

of the house   10
the tines of the pitchfork
repeat the triumph

of his overalls
and front and center
the long faces, the sober lips   15

above the upright spines
of this couple
arrested in the name of art

These two
by now   20
the sun this high

ought to be
in mortal time
about their businesses

Instead they linger here   25
within the patient fabric
of the lives they wove

he asking the artist silently
how much longer
and worrying about the crops   30

she no less concerned about the crops
but more to the point just now
whether she remembered

to turn off the stove.

CONSIDERATIONS FOR CRITICAL THINKING AND WRITING

1. FIRST RESPONSE. In what sense can Stone's poem be regarded as an analysis of the painting? Explain whether you think he sees Grant's depiction of the two figures more as a satire or a celebration. How do you read them?

2. What symbolic elements can you describe in the painting?

3. Discuss the humor in the poem. Explain whether you find any humor in the painting.

CONNECTION TO ANOTHER SELECTION

1. Choose a poem from among those collected in Chapter 40, "A Thematic Case Study: The World of Work," and compare its treatment of work with that of Stone's in "American Gothic."

GIRL POWDERING HER NECK

Little is known about the actual details of Kitagawa Utamaro's life (1753–1806). An eighteenth-century Japanese painter and printmaker especially appreciated for his woodblock prints called *ukiyo-e,* Utamaro focuses on the

Girl Powdering Her Neck This woodblock print is one of many of Utamaro's masterfully composed studies of women, a genre known as *bijin-ga.* © RMN-Grand Palais/Art Resource, NY.

intimate world of cultivated courtesans and geishas who entertained male clients. His work includes nature scenes and martial themes, but he is best known for his mysterious delicate portraits of beautiful sensuous women whose inner lives are subtly revealed, as in *Girl Powdering Her Neck* (ca. 1795). Cathy Song, of Chinese and Korean descent, was born in Honolulu, Hawaii, and was educated at Wellesley College and Boston University. Her poetry frequently explores the world of family and ancestry. Among her collections of poetry are *Frameless Windows, Squares of Light* (1988) and *Cloud Moving Hands* (2007). In "Girl Powdering Her Neck," Song responds to Utamaro's print with a series of vivid images that add imaginative details to the woodblock while simultaneously scrutinizing the female's life depicted in Utamaro's image.

Cathy Song (b. 1955)
Girl Powdering Her Neck   1983

from a ukiyo-e print by Utamaro

The light is the inside
sheen of an oyster shell,
sponged with talc and vapor,
moisture from a bath.

A pair of slippers   5
are placed outside
the rice-paper doors.
She kneels at a low table
in the room,
her legs folded beneath her   10
as she sits on a buckwheat pillow.

Her hair is black
with hints of red,
the color of seaweed
spread over rocks.   15

Morning begins the ritual
wheel of the body,
the application of translucent skins.
She practices pleasure:
the pressure of three fingertips   20
applying powder.
Fingerprints of pollen
some other hand will trace.

The peach-dyed kimono
patterned with maple leaves   25
drifting across the silk,
falls from right to left
in a diagonal, revealing
the nape of her neck
and the curve of a shoulder   30
like the slope of a hill
set deep in snow in a country
of huge white solemn birds.
Her face appears in the mirror,
a reflection in a winter pond,   35
rising to meet itself.

She dips a corner of her sleeve
like a brush into water
to wipe the mirror;
she is about to paint herself.   40
The eyes narrow
in a moment of self-scrutiny.
The mouth parts
as if desiring to disturb
the placid plum face;   45
break the symmetry of silence.
But the berry-stained lips,
stenciled into the mask of beauty,
do not speak.

Two chrysanthemums   50
touch in the middle of the lake
and drift apart.

Considerations for Critical Thinking and Writing

1. **first response.** What does Song's poem add to the visual information provided in Utamaro's woodcut?

2. Explain whether you think Song's treatment of the girl is sympathetic or something else.

3. Discuss the relationship of the final three lines to the rest of the poem. What effect do they have on you?

Connection to Another Selection

1. Discuss how the respective points of view in this poem and in Song's "The Youngest Daughter" (p. 658) affect your understanding of the poems.

THE VIETNAM VETERANS MEMORIAL WALL

The Vietnam Veterans Memorial Wall was designed by Maya Lin to honor U.S. troops who fought and died in the Vietnam War. Installed on the National Mall in Washington D.C., the memorial wall is made up of two intersecting pieces set into the ground, ranging in depth from 8 inches at their outside edges, to 10 feet in the center, where the two sections of the wall meet. More than 58,000 names of the dead and missing are etched into the polished black granite in the chronological order in which they died or disappeared. At first, the wall generated controversy because, though it made no statement about the divisive war, its stark design was created by a twenty-one-year-old Asian student at Yale University and was perceived by some as an insensitive memorial to those who had died. Yusef Komunyakaa's "Facing It" is based on his service as a correspondent in the war for which he was awarded a Bronze Star. His reflections on the wall offer a different take from the way it was initially received. Among his dozen poetry collections is *Dien Cai* (1988), often cited as one of the best poetry collections about the war.

YUSEF KOMUNYAKAA (B. 1947)

Facing It   1988

My black face fades,
hiding inside the black granite.
I said I wouldn't,
dammit: No tears.
I'm stone. I'm flesh.   5
My clouded reflection eyes me
like a bird of prey, the profile of night
slanted against morning. I turn
this way — the stone lets me go.
I turn that way — I'm inside   10
the Vietnam Veterans Memorial
again, depending on the light
to make a difference.
I go down the 58,022 names,
half-expecting to find   15
my own in letters like smoke.
I touch the name Andrew Johnson;
I see the booby trap's white flash.
Names shimmer on a woman's blouse
but when she walks away   20
the names stay on the wall.
Brushstrokes flash, a red bird's

Vietnam Veterans Memorial Wall   The wall is the best-known part of the larger Vietnam Veterans Memorial. Here, one can see the haunting effect the black granite creates with a visitor's reflection. Millions of people visit the wall each year. Library of Congress, Prints and Photographs Division.

wings cutting across my stare.
The sky. A plane in the sky.
A white vet's image floats   25
closer to me, then his pale eyes
look through mine. I'm a window.
He's lost his right arm
inside the stone. In the black mirror
a woman's trying to erase names: 30
No, she's brushing a boy's hair.

CONSIDERATIONS FOR CRITICAL THINKING AND WRITING

1. FIRST RESPONSE. Explain the significance of the title. How are the speaker's war experiences reflected in the war memorial?

2. Discuss the possible meanings of the poem's final lines: "In the black mirror / a woman's trying to erase names: / No, she's brushing a boy's hair."

3. Explain why you think the speaker's response to the memorial indicates that its conception and composition are successful or unsuccessful as a public memorial.

CONNECTION TO ANOTHER SELECTION

1. Discuss the speaker's tone and attitudes toward war in "Facing It" and in E. E. Cummings's "next to of course god america i" (p. 718).

TWO MONKEYS

Though it is not clear when or where Pieter Bruegel the Elder (ca. 1525–1569) was born, he eventually settled in Brussels and is considered to be a major northern European painter of the mid-sixteenth century, particularly of peasant life (Bruegel dropped the *h* in his name, originally Brueghel, but his sons later restored it). In *Two Monkeys,* Bruegel moves away from depicting peasant life directly, but he seems to imply that the two primates nonetheless evoke a common human condition since they are in chains. Beyond them, in contrast, a sky is populated with soaring birds and a waterfront bay filled with sailboats. This subject matter appealed to Wisława Szymborska, who was born in Kraków, Poland, where she studied literature and sociology and where her education and sensibilities were shaped by living under Nazi occupation during World War II (1939–1945). The year before she published "Bruegel's Two Monkeys," Poland was threatened by Soviet Russian armies under the orders of Joseph Stalin. Szymborska was no stranger to her country's history of violence, oppression, and death. Among her translated volumes are *Poems: New and Collected, 1957–1997* (1998) and *Here: New Poems* (2010). In 1996, she was awarded the Nobel Prize for Literature.

WISŁAWA SZYMBORSKA (1923–2012)
Bruegel's Two Monkeys   1957

Translated from the Polish by Stanislaw Barańczak and Clare Cavanagh

This is what I see in my dreams about final exams:
two monkeys, chained to the floor, sit on the windowsill,
the sky behind them flutters,
the sea is taking its bath.

Two Monkeys   This oil on wood painting is housed in Germany's Gemaldegalerie in Berlin. Bruegel is believed to have completed the work in 1562.   © Francis G. Mayer/Corbis.

The exam is History of Mankind.   5
I stammer and hedge.

One monkey stares and listens with mocking disdain,
the other seems to be dreaming away —
but when it's clear I don't know what to say
he prompts me with a gentle   10
clinking of his chain.

Considerations for Critical Thinking and Writing

1. **FIRST RESPONSE.** Why do you suppose Bruegel chooses monkeys as his subject? What does that have to do with taking an exam on the "History of Mankind"?

2. What kind of answer do you think the "gentle / clinking of his chain" prompts in the speaker? What does it mean to you?

3. Consider the shape of the space created by the arch and the monkey's tails. What does that suggest about their situation?

Connection to Another Selection

1. Discuss the theme in this poem and in Kay Ryan's "Turtle" (p. 1027).

HOUSE BY THE RAILROAD

Edward Hopper (1882–1967) became an influential realist painter during his long painting career in the twentieth century. His seemingly simple rural and urban scenes sparsely populated with figures that appear vaguely anxious and uncomfortable produce a complexity that is often mysterious in its capacity to evoke a pervading sense of loneliness and alienation. In *House by the Railroad* (1925), Hopper brings together a solitary old Victorian house looming beside a railroad track that slices across the bottom of the painting. The house is clearly the dominant image, but the angle of vision creates a problematic perspective that makes the train tracks a powerful presence. Edward Hirsch explores the effects of that presence in "Edward Hopper and the House by the Railroad (1925)." Born in Chicago and educated at the University of Pennsylvania, where he earned a Ph.D. in folklore, Hirsch has published poetry collections that include *Wild Gratitude* (1986), *Earthly Measures* (1989), *Special Orders* (2003), and *The Living Fire* (2010). Hirsch's poem ruminates on the relationship between what the culture of the house represents and what the culture of the railroad implies about the pending nature of American life.

EDWARD HIRSCH (B. 1950)

Edward Hopper and the House by the Railroad (1925)   1982

Out here in the exact middle of the day,
This strange, gawky house has the expression
Of someone being stared at, someone holding
His breath underwater, hushed and expectant;

This house is ashamed of itself, ashamed   5
Of its fantastic mansard rooftop
And its pseudo-Gothic porch, ashamed
of its shoulders and large, awkward hands.

But the man behind the easel is relentless.
He is as brutal as sunlight, and believes   10
The house must have done something horrible
To the people who once lived here

Because now it is so desperately empty,
It must have done something to the sky
Because the sky, too, is utterly vacant   15
And devoid of meaning. There are no

Trees or shrubs anywhere — the house
Must have done something against the earth.
All that is present is a single pair of tracks
Straightening into the distance. No trains pass.   20

Now the stranger returns to this place daily
Until the house begins to suspect
That the man, too, is desolate, desolate
And even ashamed. Soon the house starts

To stare frankly at the man. And somehow   25
The empty white canvas slowly takes on
The expression of someone who is unnerved,
Someone holding his breath underwater.

And then one day the man simply disappears.
He is a last afternoon shadow moving   30
Across the tracks, making its way
Through the vast, darkening fields.

This man will paint other abandoned mansions,
And faded cafeteria windows, and poorly lettered
Storefronts on the edges of small towns.   35
Always they will have this same expression,

The utterly naked look of someone
Being stared at, someone American and gawky.
Someone who is about to be left alone
Again, and can no longer stand it.   40

House by the Railroad   Art patron Stephen Clark donated this oil on canvas painting to the Museum of Modern Art in New York City in 1930. It was the first oil painting the museum acquired for its collection.   Digital Image © The Museum of Modern Art/Licensed by SCALA/Art Resource, NY.

CONSIDERATIONS FOR CRITICAL THINKING AND WRITING

1. FIRST RESPONSE. Why do you think Hopper places railroad tracks rather than a paved road directly in front of the house?

2. The title of this poem and the poem itself include both the painting and the painter. What do you think is the effect of incorporating Hopper into the poem?

3. Try to match particular images in the poem with the physical details in the painting. How do both create the tone and potential themes?

CONNECTION TO ANOTHER SELECTION

1. Discuss the images and themes associated with the house in this poem and in Edgar Allan Poe's "The Haunted Palace" (p. 713) or Jim Stevens's "Schizophrenia" (p. 703).

THE MILKMAID

Johannes Vermeer (1632–1675), born in Delft, the Netherlands, had no formal training as a painter. Although he enjoyed only a modest reputation in his lifetime based upon some thirty paintings, he was rediscovered in the nineteenth century and is now widely regarded as a major artist of the golden age of Dutch painting. *The Milkmaid* (ca. 1660), housed in Amsterdam's Rijksmuseum, is considered a national treasure. Vermeer is celebrated for his detailed, almost photographic, representations of middle-class life, particularly his depictions of women performing simple domestic tasks that reveal the subjects' quiet strength and ordinary beauty. During the mid-seventeenth century, however, the world outside his paintings was daubed with the tumult produced by war, plague, and economic crisis. In "Vermeer," Wisława Szymborska reflects upon the significance of the painting's serenity in contrast to her own historical moment more than 350 years later. Born in Poland, Szymborska lived in Kraków most of her life. Although she steadfastly refused to reveal autobiographical details, insisting that her poems, essays, and translations should speak for themselves, the fact that she survived the genocidal Nazi occupation of Poland during World War II clearly affected her response to twentieth-century history, as well as her calm appreciation of everyday human concerns. In an interview, she once said, "[M]y poems are strictly not political. They are more about people and life." Among the collections of her poems that have been translated into English are *Poems, New and Collected, 1957–1997* (1998) and *Here: New Poems* (2010). Her reading of *The Milkmaid* in "Vermeer" helps explain the painting's enduring appeal, and, fittingly, her international reputation was made secure in 1996 when she was awarded the Nobel Prize for Literature.

Wisława Szymborska (1923–2012)

Vermeer   2010

Translated by Clare Cavanagh and Stanisław Barańczak

So long as that woman from the Rijksmuseum
in painted quiet and concentration
keeps pouring milk day after day
from the pitcher to the bowl
the World hasn't earned
the world's end.

The Milkmaid   This small, oil-on-canvas painting is housed in the Netherlands' Rijksmuseum in Amsterdam. Vermeer is believed to have completed the work around 1660.   Erich Lessing/Art Resource, NY.

CONSIDERATIONS FOR CRITICAL THINKING AND WRITING

1. **FIRST RESPONSE.** Why do you suppose Szymborska capitalizes "World" in line 5 but not in line 6?

2. Describe the ways in which the line length and shape of the poem relate to its content.

3. How does the poem's treatment of time and motion invest significance in the simple act of pouring milk into a bowl?

CONNECTION TO ANOTHER SELECTION

1. Compare the tone and theme of "Vermeer" with those of John Stone's "American Gothic" (Poetry and the Visual Arts insert, p. D).

32

A Study of Robert Frost

A poem . . . begins as a lump in
the throat, a sense of wrong, a
homesickness, a love-sickness. . . . It
finds the thought and the thought finds
the words.
— ROBERT FROST

Dartmouth College.

Every poem is doubtlessly affected by the personal history of its composer, but
Robert Frost's poems are especially known for their reflection of New England
life. Although the poems included in this chapter evoke the landscapes of Frost's
life and work, the depth and range of those landscapes are far more complicated
than his popular reputation typically acknowledges. He was an enormously private man and a much more subtle poet than many of his readers have expected
him to be. His poems warrant careful, close readings. As you explore his poetry,

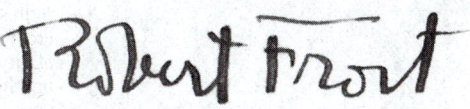

The Estate of Robert Frost.

you may find useful the Questions for Writing about an Author in Depth (p. 858) as a means of stimulating your thinking about his life and work.

A BRIEF BIOGRAPHY

Few poets have enjoyed the popular success that Robert Frost (1874–1963) achieved during his lifetime, and no twentieth-century American poet has had his or her work as widely read and honored. Frost is as much associated with New England as the stone walls that help define its landscape; his reputation, however, transcends regional boundaries. Although he was named poet laureate of Vermont only two years before his death, he was for many years the nation's unofficial poet laureate. Frost collected honors the way some people pick up burrs on country walks. Among his awards were four Pulitzer Prizes, the Bollingen Prize, a Congressional Medal, and dozens of honorary degrees. Perhaps his most moving appearance was his recitation of

Robert Frost at age eighteen (1892), the year he graduated from high school. "Education," Frost once said, "is the ability to listen to almost anything without losing your temper or your self-confidence."
Dartmouth College.

Robert Frost at age forty-seven (1921) at Stone Cottage in Shaftsbury, Vermont. Frost wrote, "I would have written of me on my stone: / I had a lover's quarrel with the world." Dartmouth College.

Robert Frost at his writing desk in Franconia, New Hampshire, 1915. "I have never started a poem whose end I knew," Frost said, "writing a poem is discovering."
The Estate of Robert Frost.

"The Gift Outright" for millions of Americans at the inauguration of John F. Kennedy in 1961.

Frost's recognition as a poet is especially remarkable because his career as a writer did not attract any significant attention until he was nearly forty years old. He taught himself to write while he labored at odd jobs, taught school, or farmed.

Frost's early identity seems very remote from the New England soil. Although his parents were descended from generations of New Englanders, he was born in San Francisco and was named Robert Lee Frost after the Confederate general. After his father died in 1885, his mother moved the family back to Massachusetts to live with relatives. Frost graduated from high school sharing valedictorian honors with the classmate who would become his wife three years later. Between high school and marriage, he attended Dartmouth College for a few months and then taught. His teaching prompted him to enroll at Harvard in 1897, but after less than two years he withdrew without a degree (though Harvard would eventually award him an honorary doctorate in 1937, four years after Dartmouth conferred its honorary degree on him). For the next decade, Frost read and wrote poems when he was not chicken farming or teaching. In 1912, he sold his farm and moved his family to England, where he hoped to find the audience that his poetry did not have in America.

Three years in England made it possible for Frost to return home as a poet. His first two volumes of poetry, *A Boy's Will* (1913) and *North of Boston* (1914), were published in England. During the next twenty years, honors and awards were conferred on collections such as *Mountain Interval* (1916), *New Hampshire* (1923), *West-Running Brook* (1928), and *A Further Range* (1936). These are the volumes on which most of Frost's popular and critical reputation rests. Later collections include *A Witness Tree* (1942), *A Masque of Reason* (1945), *Steeple Bush* (1947), *A Masque of Mercy* (1947), *Complete Poems* (1949), and *In the Clearing* (1962). In addition to publishing his works, Frost endeared himself to audiences throughout the country by presenting his poetry almost as conversations. He also taught at a number of schools, including Amherst College, the University of Michigan, Harvard University, Dartmouth College, and Middlebury College.

Frost's countless poetry readings generated wide audiences eager to claim him as their poet. The image he cultivated resembled closely what the public likes to think a poet should be. Frost was seen as a lovable, wise old man; his simple wisdom and cracker-barrel sayings appeared comforting and homey. From this Yankee rustic, audiences learned that "There's a lot yet that isn't understood" or "We love the things we love for what they are" or "Good fences make good neighbors."

In a sense, Frost packaged himself for public consumption. "I am . . . my own salesman," he said. When asked direct questions about the meanings of his poems, he often winked or scratched his head to give the impression that the customer was always right. To be sure, there is a simplicity in Frost's language, but that simplicity does not fully reflect the depth of the man, the complexity of his themes, or the richness of his art.

The folksy optimist behind the public lectern did not reveal his private troubles to his audiences, although he did address those problems at his writing desk. Frost suffered from professional jealousies, anger, and depression. His family life was especially painful. Three of his four children died: a son at the age of four, a daughter in her late twenties from tuberculosis, and another son by suicide. His marriage was filled with tension. Although Frost's work is landscaped with sunlight, snow, birches, birds, blueberries, and squirrels, it is important to recognize that he was also intimately "acquainted with the night," a phrase that serves as the haunting title of one of his poems (see p. 711).

As a corrective to Frost's popular reputation, one critic, Lionel Trilling, described the world Frost creates in his poems as a "terrifying universe," characterized by loneliness, anguish, frustration, doubts, disappointment, and despair. To point this out is not to annihilate the pleasantness and even good-natured cheerfulness that can be enjoyed in Frost's poetry, but to say that Frost is not so one-dimensional as he is sometimes assumed to be. Frost's poetry requires readers who are alert and willing to penetrate the simplicity of its language to see the elusive and ambiguous meanings that lie below the surface.

AN INTRODUCTION TO HIS WORK

Frost's treatment of nature helps explain the various levels of meaning in his poetry. The familiar natural world his poems evoke is sharply detailed. We hear icy branches clicking against themselves, we see the snow-white trunks of birches, we feel the smarting pain of a twig lashing across a face. The aspects of the natural world Frost describes are designated to give pleasure, but they are also frequently calculated to provoke thought. His use of nature tends to be symbolic. Complex meanings are derived from simple facts, such as a spider killing a moth or the difference between fire and ice (see "Design," p. 885, and "Fire and Ice," p. 880). Although Frost's strategy is to talk about particular events and individual experiences, his poems evoke universal issues.

Frost's poetry has strong regional roots and is "versed in country things," but it flourishes in any receptive imagination because, in the final analysis, it is concerned with human beings. Frost's New England landscapes are the occasion rather than the ultimate focus of his poems. Like the rural voices he creates in his poems, Frost typically approaches his themes indirectly. He explained the reason for this in a talk titled "Education by Poetry":

> Poetry provides the one permissible way of saying one thing and meaning another. People say, "Why don't you say what you mean?" We never do that, do we, being all of us too much poets. We like to talk in parables and in hints and in indirections — whether from diffidence or some other instinct.

The result is that the settings, characters, and situations that make up the subject matter of Frost's poems are vehicles for his perceptions about life.

In "Stopping by Woods on a Snowy Evening" (p. 881), for example, Frost uses the kind of familiar New England details that constitute his poetry for more than descriptive purposes. He shapes them into a meditation on the tension we sometimes feel between life's responsibilities and the "lovely, dark and deep" attraction that death offers. When the speaker's horse "gives his harness bells a shake," we are reminded that we are confronting a universal theme as well as a quiet moment of natural beauty.

Among the major concerns that appear in Frost's poetry are the fragility of life, the consequences of rejecting or accepting the conditions of one's life, the passion of inconsolable grief, the difficulty of sustaining intimacy, the fear of loneliness and isolation, the inevitability of change, the tensions between the individual and society, and the place of tradition and custom.

Whatever theme is encountered in a poem by Frost, a reader is likely to agree with him that "the initial delight is in the surprise of remembering something I didn't know." To achieve that fresh sense of discovery, Frost allowed himself to follow his instincts; his poetry

> inclines to the impulse, it assumes direction with the first line laid down, it runs a course of lucky events, and ends in a clarification of life — not necessarily a great clarification, such as sects and cults are founded on, but in a momentary stay against confusion.

This description from "On the Figure a Poem Makes," Frost's brief introduction to *Complete Poems,* may sound as if his poetry is formless and merely "lucky," but his poems tend to be more conventional than experimental: "The artist in me," as he put the matter in one of his poems, "cries out for design."

From Frost's perspective, "free verse is like playing tennis with the net down." He exercised his own freedom in meeting the challenges of rhyme and meter. His use of fixed forms such as couplets, tercets, quatrains, blank verse, and sonnets was not slavish because he enjoyed working them into the natural English speech patterns — especially the rhythms, idioms, and tones of speakers living north of Boston — that give voice to his themes. Frost often liked to use "Stopping by Woods on a Snowy Evening" as an example of his graceful way of making conventions appear natural and inevitable. He explored "the old ways to be new."

Frost's eye for strong, telling details was matched by his ear for natural speech rhythms. His flexible use of what he called "iambic and loose iambic" enabled him to create moving lyric poems that reveal the personal thoughts of a speaker and dramatic poems that convincingly characterize people caught in intense emotional situations. The language in his poems appears to be little more than a transcription of casual and even rambling speech, but it is in actuality Frost's poetic creation, carefully crafted to reveal the joys and sorrows that are woven into people's daily lives. What is missing from Frost's poems is artificiality, not art. Consider this poem.

The Road Not Taken   1916

Two roads diverged in a yellow wood,
And sorry I could not travel both
And be one traveler, long I stood
And looked down one as far as I could
To where it bent in the undergrowth;   5

Then took the other, as just as fair,
And having perhaps the better claim,
Because it was grassy and wanted wear;
Though as for that the passing there
Had worn them really about the same,   10

And both that morning equally lay
In leaves no step had trodden black.
Oh, I kept the first for another day!
Yet knowing how way leads on to way,
I doubted if I should ever come back.   15

I shall be telling this with a sigh
Somewhere ages and ages hence:
Two roads diverged in a wood, and I —
I took the one less traveled by,
And that has made all the difference.   20

This poem intrigues readers because it is at once so simple and so deeply resonant. Recalling a walk in the woods, the speaker describes how he came to a fork in the road, which forced him to choose one path over another. Though "sorry" that he "could not travel both," he made a choice after carefully weighing his two options. This, essentially, is what happens in the poem; there is no other action. However, the incident is charged with symbolic significance by the speaker's reflections on the necessity and consequences of his decision.

The final stanza indicates that the choice concerns more than simply walking down a road, for the speaker says that choosing the "less traveled" path has affected his entire life — that "that has made all the difference." Frost draws on a familiar enough metaphor when he compares life to a journey, but he is also calling attention to a less commonly noted problem: despite our expectations, aspirations, appetites, hopes, and desires, we can't have it all. Making one choice precludes another. It is impossible to determine what particular decision the speaker refers to: perhaps he had to choose a college, a career, a spouse; perhaps he was confronted with mutually exclusive ideas, beliefs, or values. There is no way to know because Frost wisely creates a symbolic choice and implicitly invites us to supply our own circumstances.

The speaker's reflections about his choice are as central to an understanding of the poem as the choice itself; indeed, they may be more central. He describes the road taken as "having perhaps the better claim, / Because it was grassy and wanted wear"; he prefers the "less traveled" path. This seems to be an expression of individualism, which would account for "the difference" his choice made in his life. But Frost complicates matters by having the speaker also acknowledge that there was no significant difference between the two roads; one was "just as fair" as the other; each was "worn . . . really about the same"; and "both that morning equally lay / In leaves no step had trodden black."

The speaker imagines that in the future, "ages and ages hence," he will recount his choice with "a sigh" that will satisfactorily explain the course of his life, but Frost seems to be having a little fun here by showing us how the speaker will embellish his past decision to make it appear more dramatic. What we hear is someone trying to convince himself that the choice he made significantly changed his life. When he recalls what happened in the "yellow wood," a color that gives a glow to that irretrievable moment when his life seemed to be on the verge of a momentous change, he appears more concerned with the path he did not choose than with the one he took. Frost shrewdly titles the poem to suggest the speaker's sense of loss at not being able to "travel both" roads. When the speaker's reflections about his choice are examined, the poem reveals his nostalgia instead of affirming his decision to travel a self-reliant path in life.

The rhymed stanzas of "The Road Not Taken" follow a pattern established in the first five lines (*abaab*). This rhyme scheme reflects, perhaps, the speaker's efforts to shape his life into a pleasing and coherent form. The natural speech rhythms Frost uses allow him to integrate the rhymes unobtrusively, but there is a slight shift in lines 19 and 20, when the speaker asserts self-consciously that the "less traveled" road — which we already know to be basically the same as the other road — "made all the difference." Unlike all of the other rhymes in the poem, "difference" does not rhyme precisely with "hence." The emphasis that must be placed on "differ*ence*" to make it rhyme perfectly with "hence" may suggest that the speaker is trying just a little too hard to pattern his life on his earlier choice in the woods.

Perhaps the best way to begin reading Frost's poetry is to accept the invitation he placed at the beginning of many volumes of his poems. "The Pasture" means what it says, of course; it is about taking care of some farm chores, but it is also a means of "saying one thing in terms of another."

The Pasture 1913

I'm going out to clean the pasture spring;
I'll only stop to rake the leaves away
(And wait to watch the water clear, I may):
I shan't be gone long. — You come too.

I'm going out to fetch the little calf
That's standing by the mother. It's so young
It totters when she licks it with her tongue.
I sha'n't be gone long. — You come too.

"The Pasture" is a simple but irresistible songlike invitation to the pleasure of looking at the world through the eyes of a poet.

Mowing 1913

There was never a sound beside the wood but one,
And that was my long scythe whispering to the ground.
What was it it whispered? I knew not well myself;
Perhaps it was something about the heat of the sun,
Something, perhaps, about the lack of sound —   5
And that was why it whispered and did not speak.
It was no dream of the gift of idle hours,
Or easy gold at the hand of fay or elf:
Anything more than the truth would have seemed too weak
To the earnest love that laid the swale in rows,   10
Not without feeble-pointed spikes of flowers
(Pale orchises), and scared a bright green snake.
The fact is the sweetest dream that labour knows.
My long scythe whispered and left the hay to make.

Considerations for Critical Thinking and Writing

1. First response. Describe the tone of "Mowing." How does reading the poem aloud affect your understanding of it?
2. Discuss the image of the scythe. Do you think it has any symbolic value? Explain why or why not.
3. Paraphrase the poem. What do you think its theme is?
4. Describe the type of sonnet Frost uses in "Mowing."

My November Guest   1913

My Sorrow, when she's here with me,
   Thinks these dark days of autumn rain
Are beautiful as days can be;
She loves the bare, the withered tree;
   She walks the sodden pasture lane.   5

Her pleasure will not let me stay.
   She talks and I am fain to list:
She's glad the birds are gone away,
She's glad her simple worsted grey
   Is silver now with clinging mist.   10

The desolate, deserted trees,
   The faded earth, the heavy sky,
The beauties she so truly sees,
She thinks I have no eye for these,
   And vexes me for reason why.   15

Not yesterday I learned to know
   The love of bare November days
Before the coming of the snow,
But it were vain to tell her so,
   And they are better for her praise.   20

CONSIDERATIONS FOR CRITICAL THINKING AND WRITING

1. FIRST RESPONSE. How is "Sorrow" personified? What sort of relationship does
   the speaker have with her?

2. What kind of tone do the poem's images create?

3. What do you think is this poem's theme?

CONNECTION TO ANOTHER SELECTION

1. Compare Frost's treatment of November with Dave Lucas's evocation of
   "November" (p. 1024). Explain why you prefer one poem over the other.

Mending Wall   1914

Something there is that doesn't love a wall,
That sends the frozen-ground-swell under it,
And spills the upper boulders in the sun;
And makes gaps even two can pass abreast.
The work of hunters is another thing: 5
I have come after them and made repair
Where they have left not one stone on a stone,
But they would have the rabbit out of hiding,
To please the yelping dogs. The gaps I mean,

No one has seen them made or heard them made,   10
But at spring mending-time we find them there.
I let my neighbor know beyond the hill;
And on a day we meet to walk the line
And set the wall between us once again.
We keep the wall between us as we go.   15
To each the boulders that have fallen to each.
And some are loaves and some so nearly balls
We have to use a spell to make them balance:
"Stay where you are until our backs are turned!"
We wear our fingers rough with handling them.   20
Oh, just another kind of outdoor game,
One on a side. It comes to little more:
There where it is we do not need the wall:
He is all pine and I am apple orchard.
My apple trees will never get across   25
And eat the cones under his pines, I tell him.
He only says, "Good fences make good neighbors."
Spring is the mischief in me, and I wonder
If I could put a notion in his head:
"*Why* do they make good neighbors? Isn't it   30
Where there are cows? But here there are no cows.
Before I built a wall I'd ask to know
What I was walling in or walling out,
And to whom I was like to give offense.
Something there is that doesn't love a wall,   35
That wants it down." I could say "Elves" to him,
But it's not elves exactly, and I'd rather
He said it for himself. I see him there
Bringing a stone grasped firmly by the top
In each hand, like an old-stone savage armed.   40
He moves in darkness as it seems to me,
Not of woods only and the shade of trees.
He will not go behind his father's saying,
And he likes having thought of it so well
He says again, "Good fences make good neighbors."   45

CONSIDERATIONS FOR CRITICAL THINKING AND WRITING

1. FIRST RESPONSE. What might the "Something" be that "doesn't love a wall" (line 1)? Why does the speaker remind his neighbor each spring that the wall needs to be repaired? Is it ironic that the *speaker* initiates the mending? Is there anything good about the wall?

2. How do the speaker and his neighbor differ in sensibilities? What is suggested about the neighbor in lines 41 and 42?

3. The neighbor likes the saying "Good fences make good neighbors" so well that he repeats it (lines 27, 45). Does the speaker also say something twice? What else suggests that the speaker's attitude toward the wall is not necessarily Frost's?

4. Although the speaker's language is colloquial, what is poetic about the sounds and rhythms he uses?

5. This poem was first published in 1914; Frost read it to an audience when he visited Russia in 1962. What do these facts suggest about the symbolic value of "Mending Wall"?

CONNECTIONS TO OTHER SELECTIONS

1. How do you think the neighbor in this poem would respond to Emily Dickinson's idea of imagination in "To make a prairie it takes a clover and one bee" (p. 837)?

2. What similarities and differences does the neighbor have with the people Frost describes in "Neither Out Far nor In Deep" (p. 884)?

After Apple-Picking   1914

My long two-pointed ladder's sticking through a tree
Toward heaven still,
And there's a barrel that I didn't fill
Beside it, and there may be two or three
Apples I didn't pick upon some bough.   5
But I am done with apple-picking now.
Essence of winter sleep is on the night,
The scent of apples: I am drowsing off.
I cannot rub the strangeness from my sight
I got from looking through a pane of glass   10
I skimmed this morning from the drinking trough
And held against the world of hoary grass.
It melted, and I let it fall and break.
But I was well
Upon my way to sleep before it fell,   15
And I could tell
What form my dreaming was about to take.
Magnified apples appear and disappear,
Stem end and blossom end,
And every fleck of russet showing clear.   20
My instep arch not only keeps the ache,
It keeps the pressure of a ladder-round.
I feel the ladder sway as the boughs bend.
And I keep hearing from the cellar bin
The rumbling sound   25
Of load on load of apples coming in.
For I have had too much
Of apple-picking: I am overtired
Of the great harvest I myself desired.
There were ten thousand thousand fruit to touch,   30
Cherish in hand, lift down, and not let fall.
For all
That struck the earth,
No matter if not bruised or spiked with stubble,
Went surely to the cider-apple heap   35

As of no worth.
One can see what will trouble
This sleep of mine, whatever sleep it is.
Were he not gone,
The woodchuck could say whether it's like his   40
Long sleep, as I describe its coming on,
Or just some human sleep.

CONSIDERATIONS FOR CRITICAL THINKING AND WRITING

1. FIRST RESPONSE. How does this poem illustrate Frost's view that "poetry provides the one permissible way of saying one thing and meaning another"? When do you first sense that the detailed description of apple picking is being used that way?

2. What comes after apple picking? What does the speaker worry about in the dream beginning in line 18?

3. Why do you suppose Frost uses apples rather than, say, pears or squash?

Birches 1916

When I see birches bend to left and right
Across the lines of straighter darker trees,
I like to think some boy's been swinging them.
But swinging doesn't bend them down to stay
As ice-storms do. Often you must have seen them   5
Loaded with ice a sunny winter morning
After a rain. They click upon themselves
As the breeze rises, and turn many-colored
As the stir cracks and crazes their enamel.
Soon the sun's warmth makes them shed crystal shells   10
Shattering and avalanching on the snow-crust —
Such heaps of broken glass to sweep away
You'd think the inner dome of heaven had fallen.
They are dragged to the withered bracken by the load,
And they seem not to break; though once they are bowed   15
So low for long, they never right themselves:
You may see their trunks arching in the woods
Years afterwards, trailing their leaves on the ground
Like girls on hands and knees that throw their hair
Before them over their heads to dry in the sun.   20
But I was going to say when Truth broke in
With all her matter-of-fact about the ice-storm,
I should prefer to have some boy bend them
As he went out and in to fetch the cows —
Some boy too far from town to learn baseball,   25
Whose only play was what he found himself,
Summer or winter, and could play alone.
One by one he subdued his father's trees

By riding them down over and over again
Until he took the stiffness out of them,   30
And not one but hung limp, not one was left
For him to conquer. He learned all there was
To learn about not launching out too soon
And so not carrying the tree away
Clear to the ground. He always kept his poise   35
To the top branches, climbing carefully
With the same pains you use to fill a cup
Up to the brim, and even above the brim.
Then he flung outward, feet first, with a swish,
Kicking his way down through the air to the ground.   40
So was I once myself a swinger of birches.
And so I dream of going back to be.
It's when I'm weary of considerations,
And life is too much like a pathless wood
Where your face burns and tickles with the cobwebs   45
Broken across it, and one eye is weeping
From a twig's having lashed across it open.
I'd like to get away from earth awhile
And then come back to it and begin over.
May no fate willfully misunderstand me   50
And half grant what I wish and snatch me away
Not to return. Earth's the right place for love:
I don't know where it's likely to go better.
I'd like to go by climbing a birch tree,
And climb black branches up a snow-white trunk,   55
Toward heaven, till the tree could bear no more,
But dipped its top and set me down again.
That would be good both going and coming back.
One could do worse than be a swinger of birches.

CONSIDERATIONS FOR CRITICAL THINKING AND WRITING

1. **FIRST RESPONSE.** What do you think the swinging of birches symbolizes?

2. Why does the speaker in this poem prefer the birches to have been bent by boys instead of ice storms?

3. How is "Earth" (line 52) described in the poem? Why does the speaker choose it over "heaven" (line 56)?

4. How might the effect of this poem be changed if it were written in heroic couplets instead of blank verse?

5. **CRITICAL STRATEGIES.** Read the section on reader-response strategies (pp. 1659–61) in Chapter 51, "Critical Strategies for Reading." Trace your response to this poem over three successive careful readings. How does your understanding of the poem change or develop?

"Out, Out —"° 1916

The buzz-saw snarled and rattled in the yard
And made dust and dropped stove-length sticks of wood,
Sweet-scented stuff when the breeze drew across it.
And from there those that lifted eyes could count
Five mountain ranges one behind the other 5
Under the sunset far into Vermont.
And the saw snarled and rattled, snarled and rattled,
As it ran light, or had to bear a load.
And nothing happened: day was all but done.
Call it a day, I wish they might have said 10
To please the boy by giving him the half hour
That a boy counts so much when saved from work.
His sister stood beside them in her apron
To tell them "Supper." At the word, the saw,
As if to prove saws knew what supper meant, 15
Leaped out at the boy's hand, or seemed to leap —
He must have given the hand. However it was,
Neither refused the meeting. But the hand!
The boy's first outcry was a rueful laugh,
As he swung toward them holding up the hand 20
Half in appeal, but half as if to keep
The life from spilling. Then the boy saw all —
Since he was old enough to know, big boy
Doing a man's work, though a child at heart —
He saw all spoiled. "Don't let him cut my hand off — 25
The doctor, when he comes. Don't let him, sister!"
So. But the hand was gone already.
The doctor put him in the dark of ether.
He lay and puffed his lips out with his breath.
And then — the watcher at his pulse took fright. 30
No one believed. They listened at his heart.
Little — less — nothing! — and that ended it.
No more to build on there. And they, since they
Were not the one dead, turned to their affairs.

"Out, Out —": From Act V, Scene v, of Shakespeare's *Macbeth*.

CONSIDERATIONS FOR CRITICAL THINKING AND WRITING

1. FIRST RESPONSE. This narrative poem is about the accidental death of a Vermont boy. What is the purpose of the story? Some readers have argued that the final lines reveal the speaker's callousness and indifference. What do you think?

2. How does Frost's allusion to *Macbeth* contribute to the meaning of this poem? Does the speaker seem to agree with the view of life expressed in Macbeth's lines?

3. CRITICAL STRATEGIES. Read the section on Marxist criticism (p. 1651) in Chapter 51, "Critical Strategies for Reading." How do you think a Marxist critic would interpret the family and events described in this poem?

Connections to Other Selections

1. What are the similarities and differences in theme between this poem and Frost's "Dust of Snow" (p. 881)?
2. Compare the tone and theme of "'Out, Out —'" with those of Stephen Crane's "A Man Said to the Universe" (p. 719).

The Oven Bird   1916

There is a singer everyone has heard,
Loud, a mid-summer and a mid-wood bird,
Who makes the solid tree trunks sound again.
He says that leaves are old and that for flowers
Mid-summer is to spring as one to ten.   5
He says the early petal-fall is past
When pear and cherry bloom went down in showers
On sunny days a moment overcast;
And comes that other fall we name the fall.
He says the highway dust is over all.   10
The bird would cease and be as other birds
But that he knows in singing not to sing.
The question that he frames in all but words
Is what to make of a diminished thing.

Considerations for Critical Thinking and Writing

1. FIRST RESPONSE. What kind of sonnet is this poem? What is the relationship between the octave and the sestet?
2. The ovenbird is a warbler that makes its domed nest on the ground. What kinds of observations does the speaker have it make about spring, summer, and fall?
3. The final two lines invite symbolic readings. What do you make of them?
4. CRITICAL STRATEGIES. Read the section on critical thinking (pp. 1641–44) in Chapter 51, "Critical Strategies for Reading," and then research critical commentary on this poem. Write an essay describing the range of interpretations that you find. Which interpretation do you think is the most convincing? Why?

Fire and Ice   1923

Some say the world will end in fire,
Some say in ice.
From what I've tasted of desire
I hold with those who favor fire.
But if it had to perish twice,
I think I know enough of hate
To say that for destruction ice
Is also great
And would suffice.

CONSIDERATIONS FOR CRITICAL THINKING AND WRITING

1. FIRST RESPONSE. What characteristics of human behavior does the speaker associate with fire and with ice?

2. What theories about the end of the world are alluded to in lines 1 and 2?

3. How does the speaker's use of understatement and rhyme affect the tone of this poem?

Dust of Snow   1923

The way a crow
Shook down on me
The dust of snow
From a hemlock tree

Has given my heart
A change of mood
And saved some part
Of a day I had rued.

CONSIDERATIONS FOR CRITICAL THINKING AND WRITING

1. FIRST RESPONSE. Explain why you are inclined to read this poem literally or symbolically.

2. What connotations are evoked by Frost's diction?

3. How would you describe the speaker's relation to nature?

CONNECTION TO ANOTHER SELECTION

1. Compare the themes in "Dust of Snow" and in Mary Oliver's "The Poet with His Face in His Hands" (p. 619).

Stopping by Woods on a Snowy Evening   1923

Whose woods these are I think I know.
His house is in the village, though;
He will not see me stopping here
To watch his woods fill up with snow.

My little horse must think it queer   5
To stop without a farmhouse near
Between the woods and frozen lake
The darkest evening of the year.

He gives his harness bells a shake
To ask if there is some mistake.   10
The only other sound's the sweep
Of easy wind and downy flake.

The woods are lovely, dark and deep,
But I have promises to keep,
And miles to go before I sleep,   15
And miles to go before I sleep.

CONSIDERATIONS FOR CRITICAL THINKING AND WRITING

1. FIRST RESPONSE. What is the significance of the setting in this poem? How is tone conveyed by the images?

2. What does the speaker find appealing about the woods? What is the purpose of the horse in the poem?

3. Although the last two lines are identical, they are not read at the same speed. Why the difference? What is achieved by the repetition?

4. What is the poem's rhyme scheme? What is the effect of the rhyme in the final stanza?

CONNECTION TO ANOTHER SELECTION

1. What do you think Frost might have to say about "A Parodic Interpretation of 'Stopping by Woods on a Snowy Evening'" by Herbert R. Coursen Jr. (p. 889)?

The Need of Being Versed in Country Things 1923

The house had gone to bring again
To the midnight sky a sunset glow.
Now the chimney was all of the house that stood,
Like a pistil after the petals go.

The barn opposed across the way,   5
That would have joined the house in flame
Had it been the will of the wind, was left
To bear forsaken the place's name.

No more it opened with all one end
For teams that came by the stony road   10
To drum on the floor with scurrying hoofs
And brush the mow with the summer load.

The birds that came to it through the air
At broken windows flew out and in,
Their murmur more like the sigh we sigh   15
From too much dwelling on what has been.

Yet for them the lilac renewed its leaf,
And the aged elm, though touched with fire;
And the dry pump flung up an awkward arm;
And the fence post carried a strand of wire.   20

For them there was really nothing sad.
But though they rejoiced in the nest they kept,
One had to be versed in country things
Not to believe the phoebes wept.

CONSIDERATIONS FOR CRITICAL THINKING AND WRITING

1. FIRST RESPONSE. What kinds of moods are produced in the speaker by the house and the birds?
2. How is Frost's use of personification of thematic significance?
3. Why is it necessary for the speaker to be "versed in country things"?
4. Do you think this poem is sentimental? Why or why not?

CONNECTION TO ANOTHER SELECTION

1. Compare what the speaker learns in this poem with the speaker's response to nature in "Design" (p. 885).

Nothing Gold Can Stay   1923

Nature's first green is gold,
Her hardest hue to hold.
Her early leaf's a flower;
But only so an hour.
Then leaf subsides to leaf.
So Eden sank to grief.
So dawn goes down to day.
Nothing gold can stay.

CONSIDERATIONS FOR CRITICAL THINKING AND WRITING

1. FIRST RESPONSE. What is meant by "gold" in the poem? Why can't it "stay"?
2. What do the leaf, humanity, and a day have in common?

CONNECTION TO ANOTHER SELECTION

1. Write an essay comparing the tone and theme of "Nothing Gold Can Stay" with those of Robert Herrick's "To the Virgins, to Make Much of Time" (p. 645).

Once by the Pacific   1928

The shattered water made a misty din.
Great waves looked over others coming in,
And thought of doing something to the shore
That water never did to land before.
The clouds were low and hairy in the skies,   5
Like locks blown forward in the gleam of eyes.
You could not tell, and yet it looked as if
The shore was lucky in being backed by cliff,
The cliff in being backed by continent;
It looked as if a night of dark intent   10
Was coming, and not only a night, an age.
Someone had better be prepared for rage.
There would be more than ocean-water broken
Before God's last *Put out the Light* was spoken.

CONSIDERATIONS FOR CRITICAL THINKING AND WRITING

1. FIRST RESPONSE. How is nature presented in the poem? How do you know this is about more than just an approaching storm?

2. What kind of sonnet is this poem? Does its form seem suited to the subject matter? Why or why not?

3. Comment on the title. What purpose does it serve?

4. Write an alternative line for line 14 and explain how your line changes the poem's effect and meaning.

CONNECTION TO ANOTHER SELECTION

1. Write an essay that discusses Frost's use of the ocean in "Once by the Pacific" and in "Neither Out Far nor In Deep" (p. 884).

Neither Out Far nor In Deep 1936

The people along the sand
All turn and look one way.
They turn their back on the land.
They look at the sea all day.

As long as it takes to pass   5
A ship keeps raising its hull;
The wetter ground like glass
Reflects a standing gull.

The land may vary more;
But wherever the truth may be —   10
The water comes ashore,
And the people look at the sea.

They cannot look out far.
They cannot look in deep.
But when was that ever a bar   15
To any watch they keep?

CONSIDERATIONS FOR CRITICAL THINKING AND WRITING

1. FIRST RESPONSE. Frost built this poem around a simple observation that raises some questions. Why do people at the beach almost always face the ocean? What feelings and thoughts are evoked by looking at the ocean?

2. Notice how the verb *look* takes on added meaning as the poem progresses. What are the people looking for?

3. How does the final stanza extend the poem's significance?

4. Does the speaker identify with the people described, or does he ironically distance himself from them?

Neither Out Far nor In Deep
The people along the sand
All turn and look one way.
They turn their backs on the land;
They look at the sea all day.

As long as it takes to pass
A ship keeps raising its hull.
The wetter ground like glass
Reflects a standing gull.

The land may vary more,
But wherever the truth may be —
The water comes ashore
And the people look at the sea.

They cannot look out far;
They cannot look in deep;
But when was that ever a bar
To any watch they keep.

Robert Frost

With the permission of The Yale Review.

Manuscript page for Robert Frost's "Neither Out Far nor In Deep" (*opposite*), which was first published in the *Yale Review* in 1934 and again in 1936, with a few punctuation changes, in *A Further Range.*
The Estate of Robert Frost

Design   1936

I found a dimpled spider, fat and white,
On a white heal-all,° holding up a moth
Like a white piece of rigid satin cloth —

2 *heal-all:* A common flower, usually blue, once used for medicinal purposes.

Assorted characters of death and blight
Mixed ready to begin the morning right,   5
Like the ingredients of a witches' broth —
A snow-drop spider, a flower like a froth,
And dead wings carried like a paper kite.

What had the flower to do with being white,
The wayside blue and innocent heal-all?   10
What brought the kindred spider to that height,
Then steered the white moth thither in the night?
What but design of darkness to appall? —
If design govern in a thing so small.

CONSIDERATIONS FOR CRITICAL THINKING AND WRITING

1. **FIRST RESPONSE.** What kinds of speculations are raised in the poem's final two lines? Consider the meaning of the title. Is there more than one way to read it?

2. How does the division of the octave and sestet in this sonnet serve to organize the speaker's thoughts and feelings? What is the predominant rhyme? How does that rhyme relate to the poem's meaning?

3. Which words seem especially rich in connotative meanings? Explain how they function in the sonnet.

CONNECTIONS TO OTHER SELECTIONS

1. Compare the ironic tone of "Design" with the tone of William Hathaway's "Oh, Oh" (p. 594). What would you have to change in Hathaway's poem to make it more like Frost's?

2. In an essay discuss Frost's view of God in this poem and Emily Dickinson's perspective in "I know that He exists" (p. 859).

3. Compare "Design" with "In White," Frost's early version of it (p. 887).

The Gift Outright 1942

The land was ours before we were the land's.
She was our land more than a hundred years
Before we were her people. She was ours
In Massachusetts, in Virginia,
But we were England's, still colonials,   5
Possessing what we still were unpossessed by,
Possessed by what we now no more possessed.
Something we were withholding made us weak
Until we found out that it was ourselves
We were withholding from our land of living,   10
And forthwith found salvation in surrender.
Such as we were we gave ourselves outright

(The deed of gift was many deeds of war)
To the land vaguely realizing westward,
But still unstoried, artless, unenhanced, 15
Such as she was, such as she would become.

CONSIDERATIONS FOR CRITICAL THINKING AND WRITING

1. FIRST RESPONSE. Frost once described this poem as "a history of the United States in sixteen lines." Is it? What events in American history does the poem focus on? What does it leave out?

2. This poem is built on several paradoxes. How are the paradoxes in lines 1, 6, 7, and 11 resolved?

CONNECTION TO ANOTHER SELECTION

1. Compare and contrast the theme and tone of this poem with those of E. E. Cummings's "next to of course god america i" (p. 718).

Perspectives on Robert Frost

ROBERT FROST

"In White": An Early Version of "Design" 1912

A dented spider like a snow drop white
On a white Heal-all, holding up a moth
Like a white piece of lifeless satin cloth —
Saw ever curious eye so strange a sight? —
Portent in little, assorted death and blight 5
Like the ingredients of a witches' broth? —
The beady spider, the flower like a froth,
And the moth carried like a paper kite.

What had that flower to do with being white,
The blue prunella every child's delight. 10
What brought the kindred spider to that height?
(Make we no thesis of the miller's° plight.) °*miller moth*
What but design of darkness and of night?
Design, design! Do I use the word aright?

CONSIDERATIONS FOR CRITICAL THINKING AND WRITING

1. Read "In White" and "Design" (p. 885) aloud. Which version sounds better to you? Why?

2. Compare these versions line for line, paying particular attention to word choice. List the differences and try to explain why you think Frost revised the lines.

3. How does the change in titles reflect a shift in emphasis in the poem?

ROBERT FROST

On the Living Part of a Poem   1914

The living part of a poem is the intonation entangled somehow in the syntax, idiom, and meaning of a sentence. It is only there for those who have heard it previously in conversation. . . . It is the most volatile and at the same time important part of poetry. It goes and the language becomes dead language, the poetry dead poetry. With it go the accents, the stresses, the delays that are not the property of vowels and syllables but that are shifted at will with the sense. Vowels have length there is no denying. But the accent of sense supersedes all other accent, overrides it and sweeps it away. I will find you the word *come* variously used in various passages, a whole, half, third, fourth, fifth, and sixth note. It is as long as the sense makes it. When men no longer know the intonations on which we string our words they will fall back on what I may call the absolute length of our syllables, which is the length we would give them in passages that meant nothing. . . . I say you can't read a single good sentence with the salt in it unless you have previously heard it spoken. Neither can you with the help of all the characters and diacritical marks pronounce a single word unless you have previously heard it actually pronounced. Words exist in the mouth not books.

From a letter to Sidney Cox in *A Swinger of Birches: A Portrait of Robert Frost*

CONSIDERATIONS FOR CRITICAL THINKING AND WRITING

1. FIRST RESPONSE. Why does Frost place so much emphasis on hearing poetry spoken?

2. Choose a passage from "After Apple-Picking" (p. 876) or "Birches" (p. 877) and read it aloud. How does Frost's description of his emphasis on intonation help explain the effects he achieves in the passage you have selected?

3. Do you think it is true that all poetry must be heard? Do "[w]ords exist in the mouth not books"?

AMY LOWELL (1874–1925)

On Frost's Realistic Technique   1915

I have said that Mr. Frost's work is almost photographic. The qualification was unnecessary, it is photographic. The pictures, the characters, are reproduced directly from life, they are burnt into his mind as though it were a sensitive plate. He gives out what has been put in unchanged by any personal mental process. His imagination is bounded by what he has seen, he is confined within the limits of his experience (or at least what might have been his experience) and bent all one way like the windblown trees of New England hillsides.

From a review of *North of Boston, The New Republic*, February 20, 1915

CONSIDERATIONS FOR CRITICAL THINKING AND WRITING

1. Consider the "photographic" qualities of Frost's poetry by discussing particular passages that strike you as having been "reproduced directly from life."

2. Write an essay that supports or refutes Lowell's assertion that "[Frost] gives out what has been put in unchanged by any personal mental process."

HERBERT R. COURSEN JR. (1932–2011)

A Parodic Interpretation of "Stopping by Woods on a Snowy Evening" 1962

Much ink has spilled on many pages in exegesis of this little poem. Actually, critical jottings have only obscured what has lain beneath critical noses all these years. To say that the poem means merely that a man stops one night to observe a snowfall, or that the poem contrasts the mundane desire for creature comfort with the sweep of aesthetic appreciation, or that it renders worldly responsibilities paramount, or that it reveals the speaker's latent death-wish is to miss the point rather badly. Lacking has been that mind simple enough to see what is *really* there. . . .

The "darkest evening of the year" in New England is December 21st, a date near that on which the western world celebrates Christmas. It may be that December 21st *is* the date of the poem, or (and with poets this seems more likely) that this is the closest the poet can come to Christmas without giving it all away. Who has "promises to keep" at or near this date, and who must traverse much territory to fulfill these promises? Yes, and who but St. Nick would know the location of *each* home? Only he would know who had "just settled down for a long winter's nap" (the poem's third line — "He will not see me stopping here" — is clearly a veiled allusion) and would not be out inspecting his acreage this night. The unusual phrase "fill up with snow," in the poem's fourth line, is a transfer of Santa's occupational preoccupation to the countryside; he is mulling the filling of countless stockings hung above countless fireplaces by countless careful children. "Harness bells," of course, allude to "Sleighing Song," a popular Christmas tune of the time the poem was written in which the refrain "Jingle Bells! Jingle Bells!" appears; thus again are we put on the Christmas track. The "little horse," like the date, is another attempt at poetic obfuscation. Although the "rein-reindeer" ambiguity has been eliminated from the poem's final version,[1] probably because too obvious, we may speculate that the animal is really a reindeer disguised as a horse by the poet's desire for obscurity, a desire which we must concede has been fulfilled up to now.

The animal is clearly concerned, like the faithful Rudolph — another possible allusion (post facto, hence unconscious) — lest his master fail to complete his mission. Seeing no farmhouse in the second quatrain, but pulling a load of presents, no wonder the little beast wonders! It takes him a full two quatrains to rouse his driver

---

[1] The original draft contained the following line: "That bid me give the reins a shake" (Stageberg-Anderson, *Poetry as Experience* [New York, 1952], p. 457). [Coursen's note.]

to remember all the empty stockings which hang ahead. And Santa does so reluctantly at that, poor soul, as he ponders the myriad farmhouses and villages which spread between him and his own "winter's nap." The modern St. Nick, lonely and overworked, tosses no "Happy Christmas to all and to all a good night!" into the precipitation. He merely shrugs his shoulders and resignedly plods away.

> From "The Ghost of Christmas Past: 'Stopping by Woods
> on a Snowy Evening,'" *College English,* December 1962

Considerations for Critical Thinking and Writing

1. Is this critical spoof at all credible? Does the interpretation hold any water? Is the evidence reasonable? Why or why not? Which of the poem's details are accounted for, and which are ignored?

2. Choose a Frost poem and try writing a parodic interpretation of it.

3. What criteria do you use to distinguish between a sensible interpretation of a poem and an absurd one?

Peter D. Poland

On "Neither Out Far nor In Deep"   1994

Robert Frost's cryptic little lyric "Neither Out Far nor In Deep" remains as elusive as "the truth" that is so relentlessly pursued in the poem itself. The poem is very much "about" this search for truth, and scholars, for the most part, persistently maintain that such effort is both necessary and noble, adding slowly but inexorably to the storehouse of human knowledge. Suggestive though such an interpretation might be, it distorts Frost's intentions — as a close examination of the curious image of "a standing gull," located strategically at the very heart of this enigmatic work (lines 7–8, its literal and thematic center), will reveal.

As "the people" stare vacantly seaward in search of "the truth," mesmerized by the mysterious, limitless sea, they closely resemble standing (as opposed to flying) gulls. Never directly stated, this comparison, so crucial to the poem's meaning, is clearly implied, and it works very much to the people's disadvantage. For the gull is doing what comes naturally, staring into the teeming sea that is its source of life (that is, of food), and it is merely resting from its life-sustaining labors. "The people," implies Frost, in literally and symbolically turning their backs on their domain, the land, to stare incessantly seaward, are unnatural. Their efforts are life-denying in the extreme.

Frost underscores the life-denying nature of their mindless staring by introducing not a flock of standing gulls, but a single gull only — surprising in that standing gulls (or, more accurately, terns, which typically station themselves en masse by the water's edge) are rarely found alone. The solitary gull points up just what "the people" are doing and how isolating and dehumanizing such activity is. So absorbed are they in their quest for "truth" that they have become oblivious of all else but their own solipsistic pursuit. They have cut themselves off from the land world and all that it represents (struggles and suffering, commitments, obligations, responsibilities) and from one another as well. They have become isolates, like the solitary gull that they resemble. Furthermore, Frost emphasizes not the bird itself but only its reflected image in the glassy surface of the shore; it is the reflected image that is the object of our concern, for it bears significantly on "the people" themselves. In an ironic version of Plato's Parable of the Cave, these relentless pursuers of truth have willfully turned their backs on the only "reality" they can ever know — the land world and all that it represents — and in so doing have been reduced to insubstantial images, shadowy reflections of true human beings engaged in genuinely fruitful human endeavor. Nameless, faceless, mindless, they have become pale copies of the real thing.

All of this adds up to one inescapable conclusion: "The people" are indeed "gulls" — that is, "dupes." In their search for ultimate reality they have been tricked, cheated, conned. It is all a fraud, insists Frost (for all that they do see is the occasional passing ship mentioned in lines 5 and 6), and he clearly holds their vain efforts in contempt. As the final stanzas make dramatically clear, they are wasting away their lives in a meaningless quest, for whatever it is and wherever it might be, "the truth" is surely not here. In short, they can look "Neither Out Far nor In Deep." So why bother?

The poem cries out for comparison with Frost's most famous work, his personal favorite, "Stopping by Woods on a Snowy Evening," wherein the seductive woods — "lovely, dark and deep" — recall the mysterious sea of "Neither Out Far nor In Deep." But the narrator of "Stopping by Woods" realizes how dangerously alluring the woods are. He realizes that he has "promises to keep," that he cannot "sleep" in the face of his societal obligations, and so he shortly turns homeward. "The people" of the present poem, however, continue to "look at the sea all day," seduced by its deep, dark, mysterious depths. Turning their backs on the land world, their world, they have violated their promises; they are asleep to their human responsibilities, as their comparison to the reflected image of a solitary gull suggests. For "gulls" they surely are.

From *The Explicator* 52.2 (Winter 1994)

CONSIDERATIONS FOR CRITICAL THINKING AND WRITING

1. Do you agree with Poland's interpretation of this poem or do you agree with the other readers he mentions who argue that the people on the shore are engaged in a "necessary and noble" pursuit of the truth?

2. How does Poland use "Stopping by Woods on a Snowy Evening" (p. 881) to further his argument?

3. Explain whether or not you think Poland's reading of "Neither Out Far nor In Deep" is consistent with your understanding of Frost's attitudes toward human aspiration in "Birches" (p. 877).

SUGGESTED TOPICS FOR LONGER PAPERS

1. Research Frost's popular reputation and compare that with recent biographical accounts of his personal life. How does knowledge of his personal life affect your reading of his poetry?

2. Frost has been described as a cheerful poet of New England who creates pleasant images of the region as well as a poet who creates a troubling, frightening world bordered by anxiety, anguish, doubts, and darkness. How do the poems in this chapter support both of these readings of Frost's poetry?

33

A Study of Billy Collins:
The Author Reflects on Five Poems

More interesting to me than what a poem means is how it travels. In the classroom, I like to substitute for the question, "What is the meaning of the poem?" other questions: "How does this poem go?" or "How does this poem travel through itself in search of its own ending?"
— BILLY COLLINS

© Lynn Goldsmith/Corbis.

Billy Collins selected the five poems presented in this chapter and provided commentaries for each so that readers of this anthology might gain a sense of how he, a former poet laureate and teacher, writes and thinks about poetry. In his perspectives on the poems, Collins explores a variety of literary elements ranging from the poems' origins, allusions, images, metaphors, symbols, and tone to his strategies for maintaining his integrity and sensitivity to both language and the reader. Be advised, however, that these discussions do not constitute CliffsNotes to the poems; Collins does not interpret a single one of them for us. Instead of "beating it with a hose / to find out what it really means," as he writes in his poem "Introduction to Poetry" (p. 607), he "hold[s] it up to the light" so that we can see more clearly how each poem works. He explains that the purpose of his discussions is to have students "see how a poem gets written from the opening lines, through the shifts and maneuvers of the body to whatever closure the poem manages to achieve . . . to make the process of writing a poem less mysterious without taking away the mystery that is at the heart of every good poem."

Along with Collins's illuminating and friendly tutorial, the chapter also provides some additional contexts, such as photos from the poet's personal collection; screen shots that offer a look at his unique — and dynamic — Web presence, including a collection of short animated films set to his work; a collection of draft manuscript pages; and an interview with Michael Meyer.

A BRIEF BIOGRAPHY AND AN INTRODUCTION TO HIS WORK

Born in New York City in 1941, Billy Collins grew up in Queens, the only child of a nurse and an electrician. His father had hoped that he might go to the Harvard Business School, but following his own lights, after graduating from Holy Cross College, he earned a Ph.D. at the University of California,

> **"I climbed into the building where all the letters of the alphabet and all the numbers were waiting for me."**

Billy Collins on his first day as a student at St. Joan of Arc School, Jackson Heights, New York, 1948.

Riverside, in Romantic poetry, and then began a career in the English department at Lehman College, City University of New York, where he taught writing and literature for more than thirty years. He has also tutored writers at the National University of Ireland at Galway, Sarah Lawrence University, Arizona State University, Columbia University, and Rollins College. Along the way, he wrote poems that eventually earned him a reputation among many people as the most popular living poet in America.

Billy Collins on his first day at Holy Cross College, 1959.
Reprinted with permission by Chris Calhoun Agency, © Billy Collins.

(*Left*) Billy Collins, senior photo, Holy Cross College, 1963.
Reprinted with permission by Chris Calhoun Agency, © Billy Collins.

(*Below*) Of this photo, Collins remarks, "The striped pants must be blamed on the '70s. I might add that quitting smoking was about the coolest thing I have ever done."
Reprinted with permission by Chris Calhoun Agency, © Billy Collins.

Among his numerous collections of poetry are *Aimless Love* (2013), *Horoscopes for the Dead* (2011), *Ballistics* (2008), *The Trouble with Poetry* (2005), *Nine Horses* (2002), *Sailing Alone Around the Room* (2001), *Picnic, Lightning* (1998), *The Art of Drowning* (1995), *Questions About Angels* (1991), and *The Apple That Astonished Paris* (1988). Collins also edited two anthologies of contemporary poetry designed to entice high school students: *Poetry 180: A Turning Back to Poetry* (2003) and *180 More: Extraordinary Poems for Every Day* (2005). His many honors include fellowships from the New York Foundation for the Arts, the National Endowment for the Arts, and the Guggenheim Foundation. *Poetry* magazine has awarded him the Oscar Blumenthal Prize, the Bess Hokin Prize, the Frederick Bock Prize, and the Levinson Prize.

Collins characterizes himself as someone who was once a professor who wrote poems but who is now a poet who occasionally teaches. This transformation was hard earned because he didn't publish his first complete book of poems until he was in his early forties, with no expectation that twenty years later he would be named United States poet laureate (a gift of hope to writers everywhere). Just as writing poetry has been good for Billy Collins, he has been good for poetry. Both their reputations have risen simultaneously owing to his appeal to audiences that pack high school auditoriums, college halls, and public theaters all over the country. His many popular readings — including broadcasts on National Public Radio — have helped to make him a best-selling poet, a phrase that is ordinarily an oxymoron in America.

Unlike many poetry readings, Collins's are attended by readers and fans who come to whoop, holler, and cheer after nearly every poem, as well as to laugh out loud. His audiences are clearly relieved to be in the presence of a poet who speaks to (not down to) them without a trace of pretension, superiority, or presumption. His work is welcoming and readable because he weaves observations about the commonplace materials of our lives — the notes we write in the margins of our books, the food we eat, the way we speak, even the way we think of death — into startling, evocative insights that open our eyes wider than they were before.

To understand Collins's attraction to audiences is to better understand his appeal on the page. He wins the affection of audiences with his warmth and genial charm, an affability that makes him appear unreserved and approachable but never intrusive or over-the-top. He is a quieter, suburban version of Walt Whitman — with a dash of Emily Dickinson's reserve. He gives just enough and lets the poems do the talking so that he remains as mysteriously appealing as his poems. His persona is well crafted and serves to engage readers in the world of his art rather than in his personal life. In a parallel manner, he has often described the openings of his poems as "hospitable" — an invitation to the reader to move further into the poem without having to worry about getting lost in the kind of self-referential obscurity and opacity that sometimes characterize modern poetry.

(*Above*) The poet with his dog, Luke. Scarsdale, New York, 1970s.

Reprinted with permission by Chris Calhoun Agency, © Billy Collins.

(*Left*) Billy Collins, in his office at Lehman College, 1984.

Reprinted with permission by Chris Calhoun Agency, © Billy Collins.

Perhaps not surprisingly, some critics and fellow poets have objected that Collins's poems may sometimes bear up to little more than the pleasures of one reading. Collins, however, believes immediate pleasure can be a primary motivation for reading poetry, and he argues that a poem using simple language should not be considered simpleminded. In his work the ordinary, the everyday, and the familiar often become curious, unusual, and surprising the more closely the poems are read. In interviews, he has compared a first reading of his poems to a reading of the large *E* at the top of an eye chart in an optometrist's office. What starts out clear and unambiguous gradually becomes more complicated and demanding as we squint to make our way to the end. That big *E*—it might be read as "enter"—welcomes us in and gives us the confidence to enjoy the experience, but it doesn't mean that there aren't challenges ahead. The casual, "easy" read frequently becomes a thought-provoking compound of humor, irony, and unconventional wisdom. Humor is such an essential part of Collins's work that in 2004 he was the first recipient of the Poetry Foundation's Mark Twain Award for Humor in Poetry. Given this remarkable trifecta of humor, popularity, and book sales, it is hardly to be unexpected that Collins gives some of his colleagues—as Mark Twain might have put it—the "fantods," but his audiences and readers eagerly anticipate whatever poetic pleasures he will offer them next. In any case, Whitman made the point more than 150 years ago in his preface to *Leaves of Grass:* "The proof of a poet is that his country absorbs him as affectionately as he has absorbed it."

BILLY COLLINS

"How Do Poems Travel?"   2008

Asking a poet to examine his or her own work is a bit like trying to get a puppy interested in looking in a mirror. Parakeets take an interest in their own reflections but not puppies, who are too busy smelling everything and tumbling over themselves to have time for self-regard. Maybe the difficulty is that most imaginative poems issue largely from the intuitive right side of the brain, whereas literary criticism draws on the brain's more rational, analytic left side. So, writing about your own writing involves getting up, moving from one room of the brain to another, and taking all the furniture with you. When asked about the source of his work, one contemporary poet remarked that if he knew where his poems came from, he would go there and never come back. What he was implying is that much of what goes on in the creative moment takes place on a stealthy level beneath the writer's conscious awareness. If creative work did not offer access to this somewhat mysterious, less than rational region, we would all be writing annual reports or law briefs, not stories, plays, and poems.

Just because you don't know what you are doing doesn't mean you are not doing it; so let me say what I do know about the writing process. While writing a poem, I am also listening to it. As the poem gets underway, I am pushing it forward—after all, I am the one holding the pencil—but I am also ready to be pulled in the direction that the poem seems to want to go. I am willfully writing the poem, but I am also submitting to the poem's will. Emerson once compared writing poetry to ice-skating. I think he meant that both the skater on a frozen pond and the poet on the page might end up going places they didn't intend to go. And Mario Andretti, the Grand Prix driver, once remarked that "If you think everything is under control, you're just not driving fast enough."

Total control over any artistic material eliminates the possibility of surprise. I would not bother to start a poem if I already knew how it was going to end. I try to "maintain the benefits of my ignorance," as another poet put it, letting the poem work toward an understanding of itself (and of me) as I go along. In a student essay, the idea is to stick to the topic. In much imaginative poetry, the pleasure lies in finding a way to escape the initial topic, to transcend the subject and ride the poem into strange, unforeseen areas. As poet John Ashbery put it: "In the process of writing, all sorts of unexpected things happen that shift the poet away from his plan; these accidents are really what we mean whenever we talk about Poetry." Readers of poetry see only the finished product set confidently on the page; but the process of writing a poem involves uncertainty, ambiguity, improvisation, and surprise.

I think of poetry as the original travel literature in that a poem can take me to an imaginative place where I have never been. A good poem often progresses by a series of associative leaps, including sudden shifts in time and space, all of which results in a kind of mental journey. I never know the ending of the poem when I set out, but I am aware that I am moving the poem toward some destination, and when I find the ending, I recognize it right away. More interesting to me than what a poem means is how it travels. In the classroom, I like to substitute for the question, "What is the meaning of the poem?" other questions: "How does this poem go?" or "How does this poem travel through itself in search of its own ending?" Maybe a few of my poems that follow will serve as illustrations, and I hope what I have said so far will help you articulate how poems go and how they find their endings.

BILLY COLLINS

Osso Buco° 1995

I love the sound of the bone against the plate
and the fortress-like look of it
lying before me in a moat of risotto,
the meat soft as the leg of an angel
who has lived a purely airborne existence.   5
And best of all, the secret marrow,
the invaded privacy of the animal
prized out with a knife and swallowed down
with cold, exhilarating wine.

I am swaying now in the hour after dinner,   10
a citizen tilted back on his chair,
a creature with a full stomach —
something you don't hear much about in poetry,
that sanctuary of hunger and deprivation.
You know: the driving rain, the boots by the door,   15
small birds searching for berries in winter.

Osso Buco: An Italian veal dish; translated as "hole [*buco*] bone [*osso*]."

But tonight, the lion of contentment
has placed a warm, heavy paw on my chest,
and I can only close my eyes and listen
to the drums of woe throbbing in the distance   20
and the sound of my wife's laughter
on the telephone in the next room,
the woman who cooked the savory osso buco,
who pointed to show the butcher the ones she wanted.
She who talks to her faraway friend   25
while I linger here at the table
with a hot, companionable cup of tea,
feeling like one of the friendly natives,
a reliable guide, maybe even the chief's favorite son.

Somewhere, a man is crawling up a rocky hillside   30
on bleeding knees and palms, an Irish penitent
carrying the stone of the world in his stomach;
and elsewhere people of all nations stare
at one another across a long, empty table.
But here, the candles give off their warm glow,   35
the same light that Shakespeare and Izaak Walton wrote by,
the light that lit and shadowed the faces of history.
Only now it plays on the blue plates,
the crumpled napkins, the crossed knife and fork.

In a while, one of us will go up to bed   40
and the other one will follow.
Then we will slip below the surface of the night
into miles of water, drifting down and down
to the dark, soundless bottom
until the weight of dreams pulls us lower still,   45
below the shale and layered rock,
beneath the strata of hunger and pleasure,
into the broken bones of the earth itself,
into the marrow of the only place we know.

Billy Collins

On Writing "Osso Buco"   2008

The critic Terry Eagleton pointed out that "writing is just language which can function perfectly well in the physical absence of its author." In other words, the author does not have to accompany his or her writing into the world to act as its interpreter or chaperone. One way for a poem to achieve that kind of independence is to exhibit a certain degree of clarity, at least in the opening lines. The ideal progression of a poem is from the clear to the mysterious. A poem that begins simply can engage the reader by establishing a common ground and then lead the reader into more challenging, less familiar territory. Robert Frost's poems are admirable models of this process of deepening. Of course, if the initial engagement is not made early, it's hard to see how the participation of a reader can be counted on.

"Osso Buco" opens with a gourmand's appreciation of a favorite dish, one commonly served up in Italian restaurants. The one thing I knew at the outset was that the poem was going to be a meditation on the subject of contentment. Misery, despondency, melancholy, and just plain human wretchedness are more likely to be the moods of poetry. Indeed, happiness in serious literature is often mistaken for a kind of cowlike stupidity. I thought I would address that imbalance by taking on the challenge of writing about the pleasures of a full stomach. Even the gloomiest of philosophers admits that there are occasional interruptions in the despondency that is the human lot; so why not pay those moments some poetic attention?

To me, the image of "the lion of contentment" suggested a larger set of metaphors connected to African exploration that might add glue to the poem. A metaphor can be deployed in one line of a poem and then dropped, but other times the poem develops an interest in its own language and a metaphor can be extended and explored. The result can bind together a number of disparate thoughts by giving them a common vocabulary. Thus, in this extended metaphor that begins with "the lion of contentment," "drums of woe" are heard "throbbing in the distance," and later the speaker feels like "one of the friendly natives" or "even the chief's favorite son."

In the fourth stanza, the camera pulls back from the domestic scene of the poem and its mood of contentment to survey examples of human suffering taking place elsewhere. The man with bleeding knees is a reference to the religious pilgrims who annually climb Croagh Patrick, a rocky mountain in the west of Ireland. The image of the "long, empty table" is meant to express the condition of world hunger and famine. But the poem offers those images only in contrast to its insistent theme: satisfaction. Back in the kitchen, there is the candle-lit scene of pleasures recently taken. The mention of Shakespeare and Izaak Walton, who wrote *The Compleat Angler,* a whimsical book on the pleasures of fly-fishing, adds some historic perspective and shows the speaker to be a person of some refinement, an appreciator of literature, history, and, of course, food.

The poem so far has made two noticeable maneuvers, shifting to a global then a historical perspective, but in the final stanza the poem takes its biggest turn when it hits upon the resolving metaphor of geology. The couple retires to bed — another pleasure — descends into sleep, then deeper into dreams, then deeper still through the layers of the earth and into its very center, a "marrow" which harkens back to the bone marrow of the eaten calf. Thus the poem travels from the domestic setting of a kitchen to the plains of Africa, a mountain in Ireland, then back to the kitchen before boring into the core of the earth itself — a fairly extensive journey for a poem of only fifty lines, but not untypical of the kind of ground a lyric poem can quickly cover.

BILLY COLLINS

Nostalgia 1991

Remember the 1340s? We were doing a dance called
    the Catapult.
You always wore brown, the color craze of the decade,
and I was draped in one of those capes that were popular,
the ones with unicorns and pomegranates in needlework.
Everyone would pause for beer and onions in the afternoon,   5
and at night we would play a game called "Find the Cow."
Everything was hand-lettered then, not like today.

Where has the summer of 1572 gone? Brocade and sonnet
marathons were the rage. We used to dress up in the flags
of rival baronies and conquer one another in cold rooms
    of stone.   10
Out on the dance floor we were all doing the Struggle
while your sister practiced the Daphne all alone in her room.
We borrowed the jargon of farriers for our slang.
These days language seems transparent, a badly broken code.

The 1790s will never come again. Childhood was big.   15
People would take walks to the very tops of hills
and write down what they saw in their journals without
    speaking.
Our collars were high and our hats were extremely soft.
We would surprise each other with alphabets made of twigs.
It was a wonderful time to be alive, or even dead.   20

I am very fond of the period between 1815 and 1821.
Europe trembled while we sat still for our portraits.
And I would love to return to 1901 if only for a moment,
time enough to wind up a music box and do a
    few dance steps,
or shoot me back to 1922 or 1941, or at least let me   25
recapture the serenity of last month when we picked
berries and glided through afternoons in a canoe.

Even this morning would be an improvement over
    the present.
I was in the garden then, surrounded by the hum of bees
and the Latin names of flowers, watching the early light   30
flash off the slanted windows of the greenhouse
and silver the limbs on the rows of dark hemlocks.

As usual, I was thinking about the moments of the past,
letting my memory rush over them like water
rushing over the stones on the bottom of a stream.   35
I was even thinking a little about the future, that place
where people are doing a dance we cannot imagine,
a dance whose name we can only guess.

BILLY COLLINS

On Writing "Nostalgia"   2008

"Nostalgia" offers me the opportunity to say something about poetic form. Broadly speaking, *form* can mean any feature of a poem that keeps it together and gives it unity. Form is the nails and glue that hold the emotions and thoughts of a poem in place. Naturally, poets are in the business of self-expression, but paradoxically they are always looking for limits. Form can be inherited — the sonnet is an enduring example — or the poet may make up his own rules as he goes along. He might even decide at some point to break the very rules he just imposed upon himself. In either case, formal rules give the poet an enclosed space in which to work, and they keep the poem from descending into chaos or tantrum. As poet Stephen Dunn put it, "form is the pressure that an artist puts on his material in order to see what it will bear."

The Irish poet W. B. Yeats felt that "all that is personal will rot unless it is packed in ice and salt." For a formalist poet like Yeats, "ice and salt," which were common food preservatives of his day, probably meant rhyme and meter. After Walt Whitman showed in *Leaves of Grass* (1855) that poems could be written without those two traditional supporting pillars, poets still had many other formal devices at their disposal. Just because poets could now write poems without a design of rhyme words at the ends of lines or a regular meter such as iambic pentameter did not mean they had abandoned form. Some of these alternative formal strategies would include line length, stanza choice, repetition, rhetorical development (beginning–middle–end), and thematic recurrence as well as patterns of sound and imagery. Focusing on form allows us to see that poetry can combine a high level of imaginative freedom with the imposition of boundaries and rules of procedure. For the reader, the coexistence of these two contrary elements — liberty and restriction — may be said to create a pleasurable tension found to a higher degree in poetry than in any other literary genre.

An apparent formal element in "Nostalgia," besides its use of stanza breaks, is the chronological sequence it obediently follows. After the absurd opening question (to which the only answer is no), the poem moves forward from the Middle Ages (the 1340s would place us smack in the middle of the Black Death) to the Renaissance, to the beginnings of English Romanticism, that being 1798, when the first edition of *Lyrical Ballads,* a poetic collaboration between Wordsworth and Coleridge, was published. The poem then continues to travel forward in time, but now more whimsically with dates that seem plucked out of the air — 1901, 1922, 1941 — before arriving rather abruptly at "last month" and then "this morning." If nothing else, the poem demonstrates poetry's freedom from normal time constraints as it manages to travel more than 600 years from the Middle Ages to the present in only twenty-eight lines.

When the poem does arrive at the present, the speaker morphs from a kind of thousand-year-old man into an actual person, a sympathetic fellow who likes to garden and who appreciates the sounds and sights of the natural world. The imaginary historical journey of the poem ends amid the bees and flowers of the speaker's garden, where he continues to dwell nostalgically on the past until his attention turns to the future, really the only place left for him to go. Having relinquished his power as an eyewitness to centuries of human civilization, the speaker trails off in a dreamy speculation about the unknowable dance crazes of the future.

The poem takes a lot of imaginative liberties in the oddness of its premise and its free-ranging images, yet, formally speaking, it is held together by a strict chronological line drawn from the distant historical past right through the present moment and into the future.

I don't recall how a lot of my poems got started, but I do remember that this poem arose out of a kind of annoyance. Just as a grain of sand can irritate an oyster into producing a pearl by coating it with a smooth surface, so a poem may be irked into being. What was bugging me in this case was the popular twentieth-century habit of breaking the past into decades ("the fifties," "the sixties," and so forth), constructs which amounted to little more than a collage of stereotypes. What a gross simplification of this mysterious, invisible thing we call the past, I thought. Even worse, each decade was so sentimentalized as to make one feel that its passing was cause for feelings of melancholy and regret. "Nostalgia," then, is a poem with a motive, that is, to satirize that kind of enforced nostalgia.

BILLY COLLINS

Questions About Angels   1991

Of all the questions you might want to ask
about angels, the only one you ever hear
is how many can dance on the head of a pin.

No curiosity about how they pass the eternal time
besides circling the Throne chanting in Latin   5
or delivering a crust of bread to a hermit on earth
or guiding a boy and girl across a rickety wooden bridge.

Do they fly through God's body and come out singing?
Do they swing like children from the hinges
of the spirit world saying their names backwards and
              forwards?   10
Do they sit alone in little gardens changing colors?

What about their sleeping habits, the fabric of their robes,
their diet of unfiltered divine light?
What goes on inside their luminous heads? Is there a wall
these tall presences can look over and see hell?   15

If an angel fell off a cloud, would he leave a hole
in a river and would the hole float along endlessly
filled with the silent letters of every angelic word?

If an angel delivered the mail, would he arrive
in a blinding rush of wings or would he just assume   20
the appearance of the regular mailman and
whistle up the driveway reading the postcards?

No, the medieval theologians control the court.
The only question you ever hear is about
the little dance floor on the head of a pin   25
where halos are meant to converge and drift invisibly.

It is designed to make us think in millions,
billions, to make us run out of numbers and collapse
into infinity, but perhaps the answer is simply one:
one female angel dancing alone in her stocking feet,   30
a small jazz combo working in the background.

She sways like a branch in the wind, her beautiful
eyes closed, and the tall thin bassist leans over
to glance at his watch because she has been dancing
forever, and now it is very late, even for musicians.   35

BILLY COLLINS
On Writing "Questions About Angels" 2008

I find that it doesn't take much to get a poem going. A poem can start casually
with something trivial and then develop significance along the way. The first
inkling may act as a keyhole that allows the poet to look into an imaginary room.
When I started to write "Questions About Angels," I really had nothing on my
mind except that odd, speculative question: How many angels can dance on the
head of a pin? Seemingly unanswerable, the question originated as an attempt
to mock certain medieval philosophers (notably Thomas Aquinas) who sought
to solve arcane theological mysteries through the sheer application of reason. I
had first heard the question when I was studying theology at a Jesuit college, but
well before that, the phrase had made its way into the mainstream of modern
parlance. It was typical of me to want to begin a poem with something everyone
knows and then proceed from there. The poem found a direction to go in when
it occurred to me to open up the discussion to include other questions. At that
point, it was "Game on."

My investigation really begins in the second stanza, which draws on traditional
images of angels in religious art, either worshipping God or paying helpful visits to
earth, assisting the poor and protecting the innocent. Then the questions become
more fanciful — off-the-wall, really: "Do they fly through God's body and come out
singing?" No doubt you could come up with questions of your own about angel
behavior; clearly, that has become the poem's game — an open inquiry into the
spirit life of these creatures.

After the poem's most bizarre question, which involves a hole that a fallen
angel has left in a river, the interrogation descends into the everyday with the
image of an angel delivering mail, not gloriously "in a blinding rush of wings" but
just like "the regular mailman." After a reminder of the monopoly "the medieval
theologians" seem to have on questions about angels, the poem makes a sudden
turn (one I did not see coming) by offering a simple, irreducible answer to that
unanswerable question. On the little word "but" (line 29), the poem drops down
abruptly from "billions" to "one," and the scene shrinks from heaven to a jazz club
located in eternity.

In the process of composing a poem, the poet is mentally juggling many concerns, one of the most dominant and persistent being how the poem is going to find
a place to end, a point where the journey of the poem was meant to stop, a point
where the poet does not want to say any more, and the reader has heard just enough.

In this case, the moment she appeared—rather miraculously, as I remember—
I knew that this beautiful angel "dancing alone in her stocking feet" was how the
poem would close. She was the hidden destination the poem was moving toward all
along without my knowing it. I had only to add the detail of the bored bassist and
the odd observation that even musicians playing in eternity cannot be expected to
stay awake forever.

BILLY COLLINS

Litany 2002

You are the bread and the knife,
The crystal goblet and the wine.
            —Jacques Crickillon

You are the bread and the knife,
the crystal goblet and the wine.
You are the dew on the morning grass,
and the burning wheel of the sun.
You are the white apron of the baker,   5
and the marsh birds suddenly in flight.

However, you are not the wind in the orchard,
the plums on the counter,
or the house of cards.
And you are certainly not the pine-scented air.   10
There is no way you are the pine-scented air.

It is possible that you are the fish under the bridge,
maybe even the pigeon on the general's head,
but you are not even close
to being the field of cornflowers at dusk.   15

And a quick look in the mirror will show
that you are neither the boots in the corner
nor the boat asleep in its boathouse.

It might interest you to know,
speaking of the plentiful imagery of the world,   20
that I am the sound of rain on the roof.

I also happen to be the shooting star,
the evening paper blowing down an alley,
and the basket of chestnuts on the kitchen table.

I am also the moon in the trees   25
and the blind woman's teacup.
But don't worry, I am not the bread and the knife.
You are still the bread and the knife.
You will always be the bread and the knife,
not to mention the crystal goblet and—somehow—   30
        the wine.

BILLY COLLINS

On Writing "Litany" 2008

As the epigraph to this poem indicates, "Litany" was written in reaction to another poem, a love poem I came across in a literary magazine by a poet I had not heard of. What struck me about his poem was its reliance on a strategy that had its heyday in the love sonnets of the Elizabethan age, namely, the convention of flattering the beloved by comparing her to various aspects of nature. Typically, her eyes were like twin suns, her lips red as coral or rubies, her skin pure as milk, and her breath as sweet as flowers or perfume. Such exaggerations were part of the overall tendency to idealize women who were featured in the courtly love poetry of the time, each of whom was as unattainable as she was beautiful and as cruel as she was fair. It took Shakespeare to point out the ridiculousness of these hyperboles, questioning in one of his sonnets the very legitimacy of comparisons ("Shall I compare thee to a summer's day?" [p. 780]), then drenching the whole process with the cold water of realism ("My mistress' eyes are nothing like the sun" [p. 781]). You might think that would have put an end to the practice, but the habit of appealing to women's vanity through comparisons persists even in the poetry of today. That poem in the magazine prompted me to respond.

Starting with the same first two lines, "Litany" seeks to rewrite the earlier poem by offering a corrective. It aims to point out the latent silliness in such comparisons and perhaps the potential absurdity at the heart of metaphor itself. The poem even wants us to think about the kind of romantic relationships that would permit such discourse.

The poem opens by adding some new metaphors (morning dew, baker's apron, marsh birds) to the pile, but in the second stanza, the poem reverses direction by trading in flattery for a mock-serious investigation of what this woman might be and what she is not. Instead of appealing to her sense of her own beauty, the speaker is perfectly willing to insult her by bringing up her metaphoric short-comings. By the time he informs her that "There is no way you are the pine-scented air" and "you are not even close / to being the field of cornflowers at dusk," we know that this is a different kind of love poem altogether.

The second big turn comes in the fifth stanza when the speaker unexpectedly begins comparing himself to such things as "the sound of rain on the roof." Notice that the earlier comparisons were not all positive. The "pigeon on the general's head" should remind us of an equestrian statue in a park, and we all know what pigeons like to do to statues. But the speaker is not the least bit ashamed to flatter himself with a string of appealing images including a "shooting star," a "basket of chestnuts," and "the moon in the trees." Turning attention away from the "you" of the poem to the speaker is part of the poem's impertinence — the attentive lover turns into an egomaniac — but it echoes a strategy used by Shakespeare himself. Several of his sonnets begin by being about the beloved but end by being about the poet, specifically about his power to bestow immortality on the beloved through his art. Thus, what begins as a love poem ends as a self-love poem.

The last thing to notice is that "Litany" has a circular structure: It ends by swinging back to its beginning, to the imagery of the epigraph. True to the cheekiness of the speaker, his last words are devoted to tossing the woman a bit of false reassurance that she is still and will always be "the bread and the knife." For whatever that's worth.

BILLY COLLINS

Building with Its Face Blown Off   2005

How suddenly the private
is revealed in a bombed-out city,
how the blue and white striped wallpaper

of a second story bedroom is now
exposed to the lightly falling snow   5
as if the room had answered the explosion

wearing only its striped pajamas.
Some neighbors and soldiers
poke around in the rubble below

and stare up at the hanging staircase,   10
the portrait of a grandfather,
a door dangling from a single hinge.

And the bathroom looks almost embarrassed
by its uncovered ochre walls,
the twisted mess of its plumbing,   15

the sink sinking to its knees,
the ripped shower curtain,
the torn goldfish trailing bubbles.

It's like a dollhouse view
as if a child on its knees could reach in   20
and pick up the bureau, straighten a picture.

Or it might be a room on a stage
in a play with no characters,
no dialogue or audience,

no beginning, middle and end —   25
just the broken furniture in the street,
a shoe among the cinder blocks,

a light snow still falling
on a distant steeple, and people
crossing a bridge that still stands.   30

And beyond that — crows in a tree,
the statue of a leader on a horse,
and clouds that look like smoke,

and even farther on, in another country
on a blanket under a shade tree,   35
a man pouring wine into two glasses

and a woman sliding out
the wooden pegs of a wicker hamper
filled with bread, cheese, and several kinds of olives.

Perspective

On "Building with Its Face Blown Off": Michael Meyer Interviews Billy Collins 2009

Meyer: The subject matter of your poetry is well known for being typically about the patterns and rhythms of everyday life, along with its delights, humor, ironies, and inevitable pain. "Building with Its Face Blown Off," however, explicitly concerns war and is implicitly political. What prompted this minority report in your writing?

Collins: It's true that I usually steer away from big historical subjects in my poems. I don't want to assume a level of authority beyond what a reader might trust, nor do I want to appear ridiculous by taking a firm stand against some moral horror that any other humane person would naturally oppose. A few years back, I consciously avoided joining the movement called "Poets against the War" because I thought it was as self-obviating as "Generals for the War." A direct approach to subjects as enormous as war or slavery or genocide carries the risk that the poet will be smothered under the weight of the topic. Plus, readers are already morally wired to respond in a certain way to such things. As a writer, you want to *create* an emotion, not merely activate one that already exists in the reader. And who wants to preach to the choir? I have come across few readers of poetry who are all for war; and, besides, poets have enough work to do without trying to convert the lost. William Butler Yeats put it best in his "On Being Asked for a War Poem":

> I think it better that in times like these
> A poet's mouth be silent, for in truth
> We have no gift to set a statesman right;
> He has had enough of meddling who can please
> A young girl in the indolence of her youth,
> Or an old man upon a winter's night.

Before poetry can be political, it must be personal.

That's my dim view of poems that do little more than declare that the poet, walking the moral high road, is opposed to ethically reprehensible acts. But the world does press in on us, and I was stopped in my tracks one morning when I saw in a newspaper still another photograph of a bombed-out building, which echoed all the similar images I had seen for too many decades in too many conflicts around the world in Dresden, Sarajevo, or Baghdad, wherever shells happen to fall. That photograph revealed one personal aspect of the war: the apartment of a family blown wide open for all to see. "Building with Its Face Blown Off" was my response.

Meyer: The images in the poem have a photojournalistic quality, but they are snapped through the lens of personification rather than a camera. Isn't a picture better than a thousand words?

Collins: I wanted to avoid the moralistic antiwar rhetoric that the underlying subject invites, so I stuck to the visual. A photojournalist once observed that to capture the horrors of war, you don't have to go to the front lines and photograph actual armed conflict: just take a picture of a child's shoe lying on a road. That picture would be worth many words, but as a poet I must add, maybe not quite a thousand. In this poem, I wanted to downplay the horrible violence of the destruction by treating the event as a mere social embarrassment, an invasion of domestic privacy. As Chekhov put it, if you want to get the reader emotionally involved, write cold. For the same reason, I deployed nonviolent metaphors such as the dollhouse and the theater, where the fourth wall is absent. The poem finds a way to end by withdrawing from the scene like a camera pulling back to reveal a larger world. Finally, we are looking down as from a blimp on another country, one where the absence of war provides the tranquility that allows a man and a woman to have a picnic.

A reader once complimented me for ending this poem with olives, the olive branch being a traditional symbol of peace. Another reader heard an echo of Ernest Hemingway's short story "In Another Country," which concerns World War I. Just between you and me, neither of these references had ever occurred to me; but I am always glad to take credit for such happy accidents even if it is similar to drawing a target around a bullet hole. No writer can — or should want to — have absolute control over the reactions of his readers.

Meyer: In your essay on writing "Nostalgia," you point out that "formal rules give the poet an enclosed space in which to work, and they keep the poem from descending into chaos or tantrum" (p. 903). How does form in "Building with Its Face Blown Off" prevent its emotions and thoughts from being reduced to a prose bumper sticker such as "War is hell"?

Collins: I hope what keeps this poem from getting carried away with its traumatic subject is its concentration on the photograph so that the poem maintains a visual, even cinematic, focus throughout. You could think of the poem as a one-minute movie — a short subject about a big topic. Another sign of apparent form here is the division of the poem into three-line stanzas, or tercets, which slow down the reader's progress through the poem. Just as readers should pause slightly at the end of every poetic line (even an unpunctuated one — the equivalent of half a comma), they should also observe a little pause between stanzas. Poetry is famous for condensing large amounts of mental and emotional material into small packages, and it also encourages us to slow down from the speed at which we usually absorb information. The stanzas give the poem a look of regularity, and some of them make visible the grammatical structure of the poem's sentences. Regular stanzas suggest that the poem comes in sections, and they remind us that poetry is a spatial arrangement of words on the page. Think of such stanzas as stones in a stream; the reader steps from one to the next to get to the other side.

Meyer: In a classroom discussion of the final two stanzas, one of my students read the couple's picnic scene as "offering an image of hope and peace in contrast to the reckless destruction that precedes it," while another student countered that the scene appeared to be a depiction of "smug indifference and apathy to suffering." Care to comment?

Collins: I find it fascinating that such contrary views of the poem's ending could exist. Probably the most vexing question in poetry studies concerns interpretation. One thing to keep in mind is that readers of poetry, students especially, are much more preoccupied with "meaning" than poets are. While I am writing, I am not thinking about the poem's meaning; I am only trying to write a good poem, which involves securing the form of the poem and getting the poem to hold together so as to stay true to itself. Thinking about what my poem means would only distract me from the real work of poetry. Neurologically speaking, I am trying to inhabit the intuitive side of the brain, not the analytical side where critical thought and "study questions" come from. "Meaning," if I think of it at all, usually comes as an afterthought.

But the question remains: How do poets react to interpretations of their work? Generally speaking, once a poem is completed and then published, it is out of the writer's hands. I'm disposed to welcome interpretations that I did not consciously intend — that doesn't mean my unconscious didn't play a role — as long as those readings do not twist the poem out of shape. In "Building with Its Face Blown Off," I added the picnicking couple simply as a sharp contrast to the scene of destruction in the war-torn city. The man and woman are free to enjoy the luxury of each other's company, the countryside, wine, cheese, and even a choice of olives. Are they a sign of hope? Well, yes, insofar as they show us that the whole world is not at war. Smugness? Not so much to my mind, even though that strikes me as a sensible reaction. But if a reader claimed that the couple represented Adam and Eve, or more absurdly, Antony and Cleopatra, or Donny and Marie Osmond, then I would question the person's common sense or sanity. I might even ring for Security. Mainly, the couple is there simply to show us what is no longer available to the inhabitants of the beleaguered city and to give me a place to end the poem.

The Library of Congress — Poem # ▢ **GO**

Poetry 180
a poem a day for american high schools

list of all 180 poems

poetry and literature center

RSS Feeds

Welcome to Poetry 180. Poetry can and should be an important part of our daily lives. Poems can inspire and make us think about what it means to be a member of the human race. By just spending a few minutes reading a poem each day, new worlds can be revealed.

Poetry 180 is designed to make it easy for students to hear or read a poem on each of the 180 days of the school year. I have selected the poems you will find here with high school students in mind. They are intended to be listened to, and I suggest that all members of the school community be included as readers. A great time for the readings would be following the end of daily announcements over the public address system.

Listening to poetry can encourage students and other learners to become members of the circle of readers for whom poetry is a vital source of pleasure. I hope Poetry 180 becomes an important and enriching part of the school day.

New Poems!

Billy Collins
Former Poet Laureate of the United States

more about this program | how to read a poem out loud | read our legal notices

Billy Collins writes: "Poetry can and should be an important part of our daily lives. Poems can inspire and make us think about what it means to be a member of the human race. By just spending a few minutes reading a poem each day, new worlds can be revealed." As United States poet laureate, Collins instituted an ongoing student program through the Library of Congress called "Poetry 180: A Poem a Day for American High Schools." He chose 180 poems for the project — one for each day of the public school year — and offered some advice on reading poems aloud. (See loc.gov/poetry/180, where the poems can be read online.)
Library of Congress.

1st

Splash ?   Dec 14   faucets
                08

The Bath

Nothing much to ~~really~~ tell really —

the soap resting in its soap dish,

hot water blasting from the spigot

¶ hills of bubbles rising,

~~my ankles co~~

only ankles crossed

and the mirror going blind ~~into~~ with steam

¶ ~~and~~ But there is
      ~~A~~the wish to apologize

to R W B Lewis for letting his
                    American Adam

slip from my wet hands into the water

¶ the book I propped up to dry

tub-side, like a diving bird

drying ~~its~~ its wings on the shore of
              a ~~volcanic~~ lake.

              prehistoric, //

A draft of the unpublished poem "The Bath" from an entry in one of Collins's notebooks, dated December 14, 2008.

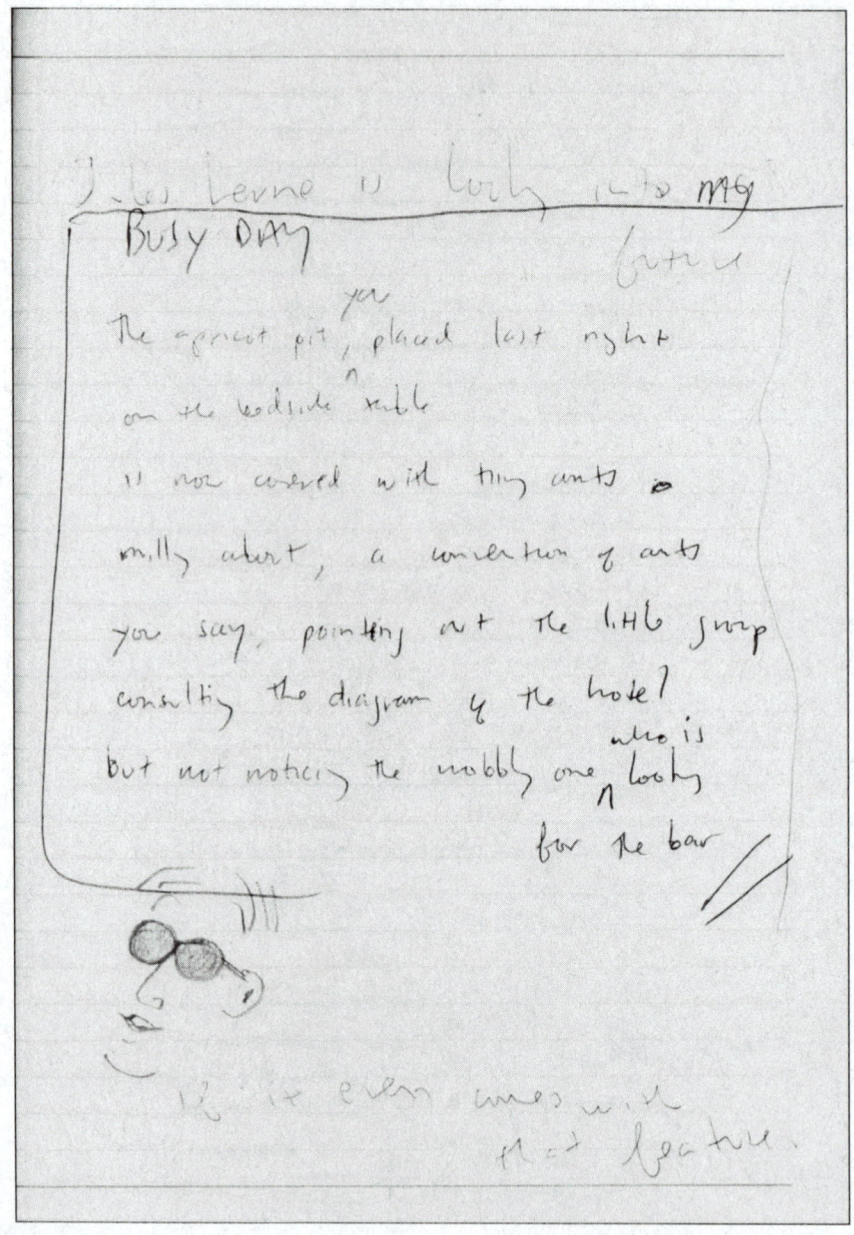

A draft of the unpublished poem "Busy Day" from an undated page of Collins's notebooks.
Reprinted by permission by Chris Calhoun Agency © Billy Collins.

The Gathering

Outside, the scene was ~~mostly~~
the low, gray clouds looked heavy
and there was just enough wind
so blow down the last of the
yellow leaves.

2 But the house was different that
day,
so distant
~~twisted away~~ from the other houses,
like a planet inhabited by a
dozen people
revolving slowly on its invisible
axis.

A draft page of "The Gathering" (working title) from an undated page in Collins's notebooks. Published in 2006 in the *New York Times* as "For Your Digestion; The Gathering."

Reprinted by permission by Chris Calhoun Agency © Billy Collins.

Billy Collins Action Poetry Web Site.
In a 2003 interview with the American Booksellers Association, Billy Collins explained that his goal as United States poet laureate was for poetry "to pop up in unexpected places, like the daily announcement in high schools and on airplanes." At the Web site for the Billy Collins Action Poetry film project (www.bcactionpoet.org), you can view artful new interpretations of the poet's work and hear them read aloud by Collins himself, in what makes for an imaginative and elegant combination of poetry and technology.
Library of Congress (Produced by the J. Walter Thompson ad agency and the Sundance Channel).

CONSIDERATIONS FOR CRITICAL THINKING AND WRITING

1. In his commentary on "Osso Buco," Collins observes that "happiness in serious literature is often mistaken for a kind of cowlike stupidity" (p. 901). How does the language of the poem maneuver around that kind of sentimental quicksand?

2. What other "formal strategies" can you find in "Nostalgia" (p. 902) in addition to the use of stanza breaks and the chronological sequence that Collins discusses? What other poetic elements serve to unify this satiric poem?

3. CREATIVE RESPONSE. Collins explains that he began "Questions About Angels" by setting out to mock the medieval speculative question of how many angels can dance on the head of a pin. He also describes his discovery of how to end the poem in line 29 after the word "but" (p. 905) with the image of the female angel dancing by herself in a jazz club. That was his solution. Try writing your own final six lines as you discover them from the preceding twenty-nine.

4. As Collins indicates, the speaker in "Litany" writes a parodic love poem that "ends as a self-love poem" (p. 907). Is the "cheekiness" in his language appealing to you? Explain why or why not.

5. In his final paragraph in "On 'Building with Its Face Blown Off'" (p. 911), Collins offers some commonsense observations about literary interpretation and how to read a poem sensitively and sensibly. He also acknowledges that wild misreadings might cause him to "ring for Security." Write an essay on "How Not to Interpret a Poem" that articulates what you think are some of the most important problems to avoid.

CONNECTION TO ANOTHER SELECTION

1. Compare one of the commentaries by Collins on a poem of your choice with a commentary by Julia Alvarez on one of her poems in Chapter 34, "A Study of Julia Alvarez: The Author Reflects on Five Poems." How do the commentaries compare in their subject, tone, and emphasis on the art of composition? Describe how each poet's distinct voice emerges from the commentary.

SUGGESTED TOPICS FOR LONGER PAPERS

1. Analyze the humor in four of Collins's poems included in this anthology (see also "Introduction to Poetry," p. 607). What purpose does the humor serve? Does the humor appeal to you? Explain why or why not, giving examples.

2. View the poems available on the Billy Collins Action Poetry Web site (see p. 916 and www.bcactionpoet.org), where you can find visual interpretations of individual poems and hear Collins read the poems aloud. Choose three of the poems and write an analysis of how the visual and auditory representations affect your response to the poems' language. Explain why you think this approach enhances or diminishes — or is simply different from — reading the poem on a page.

34

A Study of Julia Alvarez:
The Author Reflects
on Five Poems

When I'm asked what made me into
a writer, I point to the watershed
experience of coming to this country.
Not understanding the language, I
had to pay close attention to each
word — great training for a writer.
— JULIA ALVAREZ

This chapter offers five poems, chosen by Julia Alvarez for this anthology, with commentaries written by the poet herself. Alvarez's insights on each work, in addition to accompanying images and documents, provide a variety of contexts — personal, cultural, and historical — for understanding and appreciating her poems.

In her introductions to each of the poems, Alvarez shares her reasons for writing, what was on her mind when she wrote each work, and what she thinks now looking back at them, as well as providing a bird's-eye view into her writing process (see especially the drafts of the poem in progress on pp. 936–38). She also evokes the voices of those who have inspired her — muses that range from women talking and cooking in a kitchen to a character in *The Arabian Nights* to the poets Walt Whitman, Langston Hughes, and others. Alvarez writes, "A poem can be a resting place for the soul . . . a world teeming with discoveries and luminous little *ah-ha!* moments, a 'place for the genuine,' as Marianne Moore calls it." Read on and find out, for example, who her real "First Muse" was, and what, according to Alvarez, a famous American poet and the Chiquita Banana have in common.

In addition to Alvarez's inviting and richly detailed introductions, the chapter also presents a number of visual contexts, such as a photo of a 1963 civil rights demonstration in Queens, New York; the poet's passport photo taken at age ten, just before she moved back to the United States; a collection of draft manuscript pages; and an image of one of Alvarez's poems set in a bronze plaque in a sidewalk — part of "Library Way" in New York City. Further, a critical essay — which complements Alvarez's own perspectives throughout the chapter — by Kelli Lyon Johnson (p. 943) allows readers to consider Alvarez's work in a critical framework. (For a discussion on reading a work alongside critical theory, see Chapter 51, "Critical Strategies for Reading," p. 1641.)

A BRIEF BIOGRAPHY

Although Julia Alvarez was born (1950) in New York City, she lived in the Dominican Republic until she was ten years old. She returned to New York after her father, a physician, was connected to a plot to overthrow the dictatorship of Rafael Trujillo, and the family had to flee. Growing up in Queens was radically different from the Latino Caribbean world she experienced during her early childhood. A new culture and new language sensitized Alvarez to her surroundings and her use of language so that emigration from the Dominican Republic to Queens was the beginning of her movement toward becoming a writer. Alvarez quotes the Polish poet Czeslaw Milosz's assertion that "language is the only homeland" to explain her own sense that what she really settled into was not so much the United States as the English language.

Her fascination with English continued into high school and took shape in college as she became a serious writer — first at Connecticut College from 1967 to 1969 and then at Middlebury College, where she earned her B.A. in 1971. At Syracuse University she was awarded the American Academy of Poetry Prize and, in 1975, earned an M.A. in creative writing.

Since then Alvarez has served as a writer-in-residence for the Kentucky Arts Commission, the Delaware Arts Council, and the Arts Council of Fayetteville, North Carolina. She has taught at California State College (Fresno), College of Sequoias, Phillips Andover Academy, the University of Vermont,

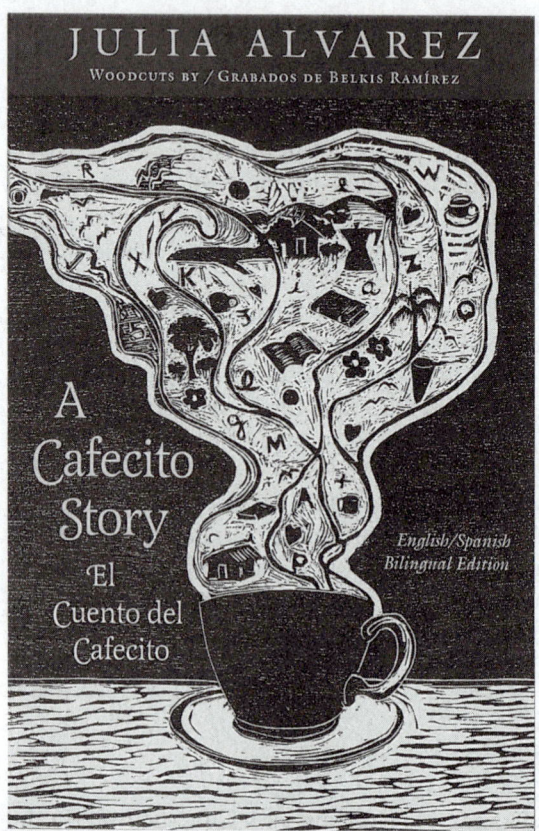

(*Left*) *A Cafecito Story* (2001), which Alvarez describes as a modern "eco-parable" or "green fable" and love story, was inspired by the author's work with local coffee growers in the Dominican Republic.

Reprinted from *A Cafecito Story* © 2002 used with permission from Chelsea Green Publishing (www.chelseagreen.com).

(*Below*) Julia Alvarez with students from Middlebury College at her coffee farm, Alta Gracia, in the Dominican Republic.

George Washington University, the University of Illinois, and, since 1988, at Middlebury College, where she has been a professor of literature and creative writing and is currently a part-time writer-in-residence. Alvarez divides her time between Vermont and the Dominican Republic, where she and her husband have set up an organic coffee farm, Alta Gracia, that supports a literacy school for children and adults. *A Cafecito Story* (2001), which Alvarez considers a "green fable" or "eco-parable," grew out of their experiences promoting fair trade and sustainability for coffee farmers in the Dominican Republic.

AN INTRODUCTION TO HER WORK

Alvarez's poetry has been widely published in journals and magazines ranging from the *New Yorker* to *Mirabella* to the *Kenyon Review*. Her first book of poems, *Homecoming* (1984; a new expanded verison, *Homecoming: New and Collected Poems,* was published in 1996 by Plume/Penguin), uses simple — yet incisive — language to explore issues related to love, domestic life, and work. Her second book of poetry, *The Other Side/El Otro Lado* (1995), is a collection of meditations on her childhood memories of immigrant life that shaped her adult identity and sensibilities. Some of these concerns are also manifested in her book of essays, titled *Something to Declare* (1998), a collection that describes her abiding concerns about how to respond to competing cultures. In her third poetry collection, *The Woman I Kept to Myself* (2004), Alvarez reflects on her personal life and development as a writer from the vantage point of her mid-fifties in seventy-five poems, each consisting of three ten-line stanzas.

In addition to writing a number of books for children and young adults, Alvarez has also published six novels. The first, *How the García Girls Lost Their Accents* (1991), is a collection of fifteen separate but interrelated stories that cover thirty years of the lives of the García sisters from the late 1950s to the late 1980s. Drawing on her own experiences, Alvarez describes the sisters fleeing the Dominican Republic and growing up Latina in the United States. *In the Time of the Butterflies* (1994) is a fictional account of a true story concerning four sisters who opposed Trujillo's dictatorship. Three of the sisters were murdered in 1960 by the government, and the surviving fourth sister recounts the events of their personal and political lives that led to her sisters' deaths. Shaped by the history of Dominican freedom and tyranny, the novel also explores the sisters' relationships to each other and their country.

In ¡*Yo!* (1997), Alvarez focuses on Yolanda, one of the García sisters from her first novel, who is now a writer. Written in the different voices of Yo's friends and family members, this fractured narrative constructs a complete picture of a woman who uses her relationships as fodder for fiction, a woman who is self-centered, aggravating, and finally lovable — who is deeply embedded in American culture while remaining aware of her Dominican roots. ¡*Yo!,* which means "I" in English, is a meditation on points of view and narrative.

In the Name of Salomé (2000) is a fictional account of Salomé Ureña, who was born in the 1850s and considered to be "the Emily Dickinson of the Dominican Republic," and her daughter's efforts late in life to reconcile her relationship to her mother's reputation and her own response to Castro's revolution in Cuba. Alvarez published her sixth and most recent novel, *Saving the World,* in 2006, a story that also links two women's lives, one from the past and one from the present, around personal and political issues concerning humanitarian efforts to end smallpox in the nineteenth century and the global AIDS epidemic in the twenty-first century.

In "Queens, 1963," Alvarez remembers the neighborhood she lived in when she was a thirteen-year-old and how "Everyone seemed more American / than we, newly arrived." The tensions that arose when new immigrants and ethnic groups moved onto the block were mirrored in many American neighborhoods in 1963. Indeed, the entire nation was made keenly aware of such issues as integration when demonstrations were organized across the South and a massive march on Washington in support of civil rights for African Americans drew hundreds of thousands of demonstrators who listened to Martin Luther King Jr. deliver his electrifying "I have a dream" speech. But the issues were hardly resolved, as evidenced by 1963's two best-selling books: *Happiness Is a Warm Puppy* and *Security Is a Thumb and a Blanket,* by Charles M. Schulz of *Peanuts* cartoon fame. The popularity of these books is, perhaps, understandable given the tensions that moved across the country and which seemed to culminate on November 22, 1963, when President Kennedy was assassinated in Dallas, Texas. These events are not mentioned in "Queens, 1963," but they are certainly part of the context that helps us understand Alvarez's particular neighborhood. In the following introductory essay, Alvarez reflects on the cultural moment of 1963 and her reasons for writing the poem.

Julia Alvarez
On Writing "Queens, 1963" 2006

I remember when we finally bought our very own house after three years of living in rentals. Back then, Queens, New York, was not the multicultural, multilingual place it is today. But the process was beginning. Our neighborhood was sprinkled with ethnicities, some who had been here longer than others. The Germans down the block — now we would call them German Americans — had been Americans for a couple of generations as had our Jewish neighbors, and most definitely, the Midwesterners across the street. Meanwhile, the Greek family next door were newcomers as were we, our accents still heavy, our cooking smells commingling across our backyard fences during mealtimes: their Greek lamb with rosemary, our Dominican habichuelas with sofrito.°

It seemed a peaceable enough kingdom until a black family moved in across the street. What a ruckus got started! Of course, it was the early 1960s: the civil rights movement was just getting under way in this country. Suddenly,

---

habichuelas with sofrito: Kidney beans prepared with a sautéed mixture of spices, herbs, garlic, onion, pepper, and tomato.

Julia Alvarez, age ten, in her 1960 passport photo.

our neighborhood was faced with discrimination, but coming from the very same people who themselves had felt discrimination from other, more mainstream Americans. It was my first lesson in hypocrisy and in realizing that America was still an experiment in process. The words on the Statue of Liberty (see "Sometimes the Words Are So Close," p. 935) were only a promise, not yet a practice in the deep South or in Queens, New York.

In writing this poem I wanted to suggest the many ethnic families in the neighborhood. Of course, I couldn't use their real names and risk being sued. (Though, come to think of it, I've never heard of a poem being sued, have you?) Plus, there is the matter of failing memory. (This was forty-two years ago!) So I chose names that suggested other languages, other places, and also — always the poet's ear at work — names that fit in with the rhythm and cadence of the lines.

Julia Alvarez

Queens, 1963   1992

Everyone seemed more American
than we, newly arrived,
foreign dirt still on our soles.
By year's end, a sprinkler waving
like a flag on our mowed lawn,   5
we were blended into the block,
owned our own mock Tudor house.
Then the house across the street
sold to a black family.
Cop cars patrolled our block   10
from the Castellucci's at one end
to the Balakian's on the other.
We heard rumors of bomb threats,
a burning cross on their lawn.
(It turned out to be a sprinkler.)   15
Still the neighborhood buzzed.
The barber's family, Haralambides,
our left-side neighbors, didn't want trouble.
They'd come a long way to be free!
Mr. Scott, the retired plumber,   20
and his plump midwestern wife,
considered moving back home
where white and black got along
by staying where they belonged.
They had cultivated our street   25
like the garden she'd given up
on account of her ailing back,
bad knees, poor eyes, arthritic hands.
She went through her litany daily.
Politely, my mother listened —   30
¡Ay, Mrs. Scott, qué pena!°
—her Dominican good manners
still running on automatic.
The Jewish counselor next door,
had a practice in her house;   35
clients hurried up her walk
ashamed to be seen needing.
(I watched from my upstairs window,
gloomy with adolescence,
and guessed how they too must have   40
hypocritical old-world parents.)
Mrs. Bernstein said it was time
the neighborhood opened up.
As the first Jew on the block,

---

31 *qué pena:* What a shame!

she remembered the snubbing she got   45
a few years back from Mrs. Scott.
But real estate worried her,
our houses' plummeting value.
She shook her head as she might
at a client's grim disclosures.   50
Too bad the world works this way.
The German girl playing the piano
down the street abruptly stopped
in the middle of a note.
I completed the tune in my head   55
as I watched *their* front door open.
A dark man in a suit
with a girl about my age
walked quickly into a car.
My hand lifted but fell   60
before I made a welcoming gesture.
On her face I had seen a look
from the days before we had melted
into the United States of America.
It was hardness mixed with hurt.   65
It was knowing she never could be
the right kind of American.
A police car followed their car.
Down the street, curtains fell back.
Mrs. Scott swept her walk   70
as if it had just been dirtied.
Then the German piano commenced
downward scales as if tracking
the plummeting real estate.
One by one I imagined the houses   75
sinking into their lawns,
the grass grown wild and tall
in the past tense of this continent
before the first foreigners owned
any of this free country.   80

CONSIDERATIONS FOR CRITICAL THINKING AND WRITING

1. FIRST RESPONSE. What nationalities are the people in this neighborhood in the New York City borough of Queens? Are they neighborly to each other?

2. In line 3, why do you suppose Alvarez writes "foreign dirt still on our soles" rather than "foreign soil still on our shoes"? What does Alvarez's word choice suggest about her feelings for her native country?

3. Characterize the speaker. How old is she? How does she feel about having come from the Dominican Republic? About living in the United States?

4. Do you think this poem is optimistic or pessimistic about racial relations in the United States? Explain your answer by referring to specific details in the poem.

CONNECTIONS TO OTHER SELECTIONS

1. Compare the use of irony in "Queens, 1963" with that in John Ciardi's "Suburban" (p. 1009). How does irony contribute to each poem?

2. Write an essay comparing and contrasting the tone and theme in "Queens, 1963" and in David Hernandez's "All-American" (p. 813).

Queens Civil Rights Demonstration   1963

In this photograph police remove a Congress of Racial Equality (CORE) demonstrator from a Queens construction site. Demonstrators blocked the delivery entrance to the site because they wanted more African Americans and Puerto Ricans hired in the building-trade industry.
Associated Press.

CONSIDERATIONS FOR CRITICAL THINKING AND WRITING

1. Discuss the role played by the police in this photograph and in "Queens, 1963." What attitudes toward the police do the photograph and the poem display?

2. How do you think the Scotts and Mrs. Bernstein would have responded to this photograph in 1963?

3. Compare the tensions in "Queens, 1963" to those depicted in this photo. How do the speaker's private reflections relate to this public protest?

Perspective

MARNY REQUA (B. 1971)

From an Interview with Julia Alvarez 1997

M.R. What was it like when you came to the United States?

J.A. When we got to Queens, it was really a shock to go from a totally Latino, *familia* Caribbean world into this very cold and kind of forbidding one in which we didn't speak the language. I didn't grow up with a tradition of writing or reading books at all. People were always telling stories but it wasn't a tradition of literary . . . reading a book or doing something solitary like that. Coming to this country I discovered books, I discovered that it was a way to enter into a portable homeland that you could carry around in your head. You didn't have to suffer what was going on around you. I found in books a place to go. I became interested in language because I was learning a language intentionally at the age of ten. I was wondering, "Why is it that word and not another?" which any writer has to do with their language. I always say I came to English late but to the profession early. By high school I was pretty set: That's what I want to do, be a writer.

M.R. Did you have culture shock returning to the Dominican Republic as you were growing up?

J.A. The culture here had an effect on me—at the time this country was coming undone with protests and flower children and drugs. Here I was back in the Dominican Republic and I wouldn't keep my mouth shut. I had my own ideas and I had my own politics, and it, I just didn't gel anymore with the family. I didn't quite feel I ever belonged in this North American culture and I always had this nostalgia that when I went back I'd belong, and then I found out I didn't belong there either.

M.R. Was it a source of inspiration to have a foot in both cultures?

J.A. I only came to that later. [Then], it was a burden because I felt torn. I wanted to be part of one culture and then part of the other. It was a time when the model for the immigrant was that you came and you became an American and you cut off your ties and that was that. My parents had that frame of mind, because they were so afraid, and they were "Learn your English" and "Become one of them," and that left out so much. Now I see the richness. Part of what I want to do with my work is that complexity, that richness. I don't want it to be simplistic and either/or.

From "The Politics of Fiction," *Frontera* magazine 5 (1997)

CONSIDERATIONS FOR CRITICAL THINKING AND WRITING

1. What do you think Alvarez means when she describes books as "a portable homeland that you could carry around in your head"?

2. Why is it difficult for Alvarez to feel that she belongs in either the Dominican or the North American culture?

3. Alvarez says that in the 1960s "the model for the immigrant was that you came and you became an American and you cut off your ties and that was that." Do you think this model has changed in the United States since then? Explain your response.

4. How might this interview alter your understanding of "Queens, 1963"? What light is shed, for example, on the speaker's feeling that her family "blended into the block" in line 6?

JULIA ALVAREZ

On Writing "Housekeeping Cages" and Her Housekeeping Poems   1998

I can still remember the first time I heard my own voice on paper. It happened a few years after I graduated from a creative writing master's program. I had earned a short-term residency at Yaddo, the writer's colony, where I was assigned a studio in the big mansion — the tower room at the top of the stairs. The rules were clear: we artists and writers were to stick to our studios during the day and come out at night for supper and socializing. Nothing was to come between us and our work.

I sat up in my tower room, waiting for inspiration. All around me I could hear the typewriters going. Before me lay a blank sheet of paper, ready for the important work I had come there to write. That was the problem, you see. I was trying to do IMPORTANT work and so I couldn't hear myself think. I was trying to pitch my voice to "Turning and turning in the widening gyre," or, "Of man's first disobedience, and the fruit of that forbidden tree," or, "Sing in me, Muse, and through me tell the story." I was tuning my voice to these men's voices because I thought that was the way I had to sound if I wanted to be a writer. After all, the writers I read and admired sounded like that.

But the voice I heard when I listened to myself think was the voice of a woman, sitting in her kitchen, gossiping with a friend over a cup of coffee. It was the voice of Gladys singing her sad boleros, Belkis putting color on my face with tales of her escapades, Tití naming the orchids, Ada telling me love stories as we made the beds. I had, however, never seen voices like these in print. So, I didn't know poems could be written in those voices, *my* voice.

So there I was at Yaddo, trying to write something important and coming up with nothing. And then, hallelujah — I heard the vacuum going up and down the hall. I opened the door and introduced myself to the friendly, sweating woman, wielding her vacuum cleaner. She invited me down to the kitchen so we wouldn't disturb the other guests. There I met the cook, and as we all sat, drinking coffee, I paged through her old cookbook, *knead, poach, stew, whip, score, julienne, whisk, sauté, sift.* Hmm. I began hearing a music in these words. I jotted down the names of implements:

> Cup, spoon, ladle, pot, kettle,
> grater and peeler,
> colander, corer,
> waffle iron, small funnel.

"You working on a poem there?" the cook asked me.
I shook my head.

A little later, I went upstairs and wrote down in my journal this beautiful vocabulary of my girlhood. As I wrote, I tapped my foot on the floor to the rhythm of the words. I could see Mami and the aunts with the cook in the kitchen bending their heads over a pot of habichuelas, arguing about what flavor was missing — what could it be they had missed putting in it? And then, the thought of Mami recalled Gladys, the maid who loved to sing, and that thought led me through the house, the mahogany furniture that needed dusting, the beds that needed making, the big bin of laundry that needed washing.

That day, I began working on a poem about dusting. Then another followed on sewing; then came a sweeping poem, an ironing poem. Later, I would collect these into a series I called "the housekeeping poems," poems using the metaphors, details, language of my first apprenticeship as a young girl. Even later, having found my woman's voice, I would gain confidence to explore my voice as a Latina and to write stories and poems using the metaphors, details, rhythms of that first world I had left behind in Spanish.

But it began, first, by discovering my woman's voice at Yaddo where I had found it as a child. Twenty years after learning to sing with Gladys, I was reminded of the lessons I had learned in childhood: that my voice would not be found up in a tower, in those upper reaches or important places, but down in the kitchen among the women who first taught me about service, about passion, about singing as if my life depended on it.

From Something to Declare

Julia Alvarez

Housekeeping Cages   1994

Sometimes people ask me why I wrote a series of poems about housekeeping if I'm a feminist. Don't I want women to be liberated from the oppressive roles they were condemned to live? I don't see housekeeping that way. They were the crafts we women had, sewing, embroidering, cooking, spinning, sweeping, even the lowly dusting. And like Dylan Thomas said, we sang in our chains like the sea. Isn't it already thinking from the point of view of the oppressor to say to ourselves, what we did was nothing?

You use what you have, you learn to work the structure to create what you need. I don't feel that writing in traditional forms is giving up power, going over to the enemy. The word belongs to no one, the houses built of words belong to no one. We have to take them back from those who think they own them.

Sometimes I get in a mood. I tell myself I am taken over. I am writing under somebody else's thumb and tongue. See, English was not my first language. It was, in fact, a colonizing language to my Spanish Caribbean. But then Spanish was also a colonizer's language; after all, Spain colonized Quisqueya. There's no getting free. We are always writing in a form imposed on us. But then, I'm Scheherazade in the Sultan's room. I use structures to survive and triumph! To say what's important to me as a woman and as a Latina.

I think of form as territory that has been colonized, but that you can free. See, I feel subversive in formal verse. A voice is going to inhabit that form that was barred from entering it before! That's what I tried in the "33" poems, to use my woman's voice in a sonnet as I would use it sitting in the kitchen with a close friend, talking womanstuff. In school, I was always trying to inhabit those forms as the male writers had. To pitch my voice to "Of man's first disobedience, and the fruit. . . ." If it didn't hit the key of "Sing in me, Muse, and through me tell the story," how could it be important poetry? The only kind.

While I was in graduate school some of the women in the program started a Women's Writing Collective in Syracuse. We were musing each other into unknown writing territory. One woman advised me to listen to my own voice, deep inside, and put that down on paper. But what I heard when I listened were voices that said things like "Don't put so much salt on the lettuce, you'll wilt the salad!" I'd never heard that in a poem. So how could it be poetry? Then, with the "33" sonnet sequence, I said, I'm going to go in there and I'm going to sound like myself. I took on the whole kaboodle. I was going into form, sonnets no less. Wow.

What I wanted from the sonnet was the tradition that it offered as well as the structure. The sonnet tradition was one in which women were caged in golden cages of beloved, in perfumed gas chambers of stereotype. I wanted to go in that heavily mined and male labyrinth with the string of my own voice. I wanted to explore it and explode it too. I call my sonnets free verse sonnets. They have ten syllables per line, and the lines are in a loose iambic pentameter. But they are heavily enjambed and the rhymes are often slant-rhymes, and the rhyme scheme is peculiar to each sonnet. One friend read them and said, "I didn't know they were sonnets. They sounded like you talking!"

By learning to work the sonnet structure and yet remaining true to my own voice, I made myself at home in that form. When I was done with it, it was a totally different form from the one I learned in school. I have used other traditional forms. In my poem about sweeping, since you sweep with the broom and you dance — it's a coupling — I used rhyming couplets. I wrote a poem of advice mothers give to their daughters in a villanelle, because it's such a nagging form. But mostly the sonnet is the form I've worked with. It's the classic form in which we women were trapped, love objects, and I was trapped inside that voice and paradigm, and I wanted to work my way out of it.

My idea of traditional forms is that as women much of our heritage is trapped in them. But the cage can turn into a house if you housekeep it the right way. You housekeep it by working the words just so.

> From *A Formal Feeling Comes: Poems in Form by Contemporary Women*,
> edited by Annie Finch

CONSIDERATIONS FOR CRITICAL THINKING AND WRITING

1. **FIRST RESPONSE.** How does Alvarez connect housekeeping to "writing in traditional forms"?

2. Compare "Sometimes the Words Are So Close" (p. 935) to Alvarez's description in her essay of how she writes sonnets. How closely does the poem's form follow her description?

3. Why does Alvarez consider "Dusting" (p. 931) and "Ironing Their Clothes" (p. 933) to be feminist poems? How can the poems be read as feminist in their sensibility?

JULIA ALVAREZ

On Writing "Dusting" 2006

Finally, I took the leap and began to write poems in my own voice and the voices of the women in my past, who inevitably were talking about their work, housekeeping. I had to trust that those voices, while not conventionally important, still had something to say. At school, I had been taught the formal canon of literature: epic poems with catalogues of ships, poems about wars and the rumors of wars. Why not write a poem in the voice of a mother cataloguing the fabrics, with names as beautiful as those of ships ("gabardine, organdy, wool, madras" from "Naming the Fabrics") or a poem about sweeping while watching a news report about the Vietnam War on TV ("How I Learned to Sweep")? Each time I delved into one of the housekeeping "arts," I discovered deeper, richer materials and metaphors than I had anticipated. This is wonderful news for a writer. As Robert Frost once said about rhymes in a poem, "No surprise for the writer, no surprise for the reader." The things we discover while writing what we write tingle with that special energy and delight of not just writing a poem, but enlarging our understanding.

Dusting is the lowliest of the housekeeping arts. Any little girl with a rag can dust. But rather than dust, the little girl in my poem is writing her name on the furniture, something her mother keeps correcting. What a perfect metaphor for the changing roles of women which I've experienced in my own life: the mother believing that a woman's place is in the home, not in the public sphere; the girl from a younger generation wanting to make a name for herself.

And in writing "Dusting," I also discovered a metaphor about writing. A complicated balancing act: like the mother, the artist has to disappear in her work; it's the poem that counts, not the name or celebrity of the writer. But the artist also needs the little girl's pluck and ambition to even imagine a public voice for herself. Otherwise, she'd be swallowed up in self-doubt, silenced by her mother's old-world way of viewing a woman's role.

JULIA ALVAREZ

Dusting 1981

Each morning I wrote my name
on the dusty cabinet, then crossed
the dining table in script, scrawled
in capitals on the backs of chairs,
practicing signatures like scales   5
while Mother followed, squirting

linseed from a burping can
into a crumpled-up flannel.

She erased my fingerprints
from the bookshelf and rocker,   10
polished mirrors on the desk
scribbled with my alphabets.
My name was swallowed in the towel
with which she jeweled the table tops.
The grain surfaced in the oak   15
and the pine grew luminous.
But I refused with every mark
to be like her, anonymous.

Considerations for Critical Thinking and Writing

1. **first response.** Describe the central conflict between the speaker and the mother.
2. Explain why the image of dusting is a particularly appropriate metaphor for evoking the central conflict.
3. Discuss the effect of the rhymes in lines 15–18.
4. Consider the tone of each stanza. Explain why you see the tones as identical or not.

Connection to Another Selection

1. Discuss the mother-daughter relationships in "Dusting" and in Cathy Song's "The Youngest Daughter" (p. 658).

Julia Alvarez

On Writing "Ironing Their Clothes"   2006

Maybe because ironing is my favorite of all the housekeeping chores, this is my favorite of the housekeeping poems. In the apprenticeship of household arts, ironing is for the advanced apprentice. After all, think about it, you're wielding an instrument that could cause some damage: You could burn yourself, you could burn the clothes. I was not allowed to iron clothes until I was older and could be trusted to iron all different kinds of fabrics ("gabardine, organdy, wool, madras") just right.

Again, think of how ironing someone's clothes can be a metaphor for all kinds of things. You have this power to take out the wrinkles and worries from someone's outer skin! You can touch and caress and love someone and not be told that you are making a nuisance of yourself!

In writing this poem I wanted the language to mirror the process. I wanted the lines to suggest all the fussy complications of trying to get your iron into hard corners and places ("I stroked the yoke, / the breast pocket, collar and cuffs, / until the rumpled heap relaxed . . .") and then the smooth sailing of a line that sails over the line break into the next line ("into the shape / of my father's broad chest . . ."). I wanted to get the hiss of the iron in those last four lines. I revised and revised this poem, especially the verbs, most especially the verbs that have to do the actual work of the iron. When I finally got that last line with its double rhymes ("express / excess"; "love / cloth"), I felt as if I'd done a whole laundry basket worth of ironing just right.

JULIA ALVAREZ

Ironing Their Clothes　1981

With a hot glide up, then down, his shirts,
I ironed out my father's back, cramped
and worried with work. I stroked the yoke,
the breast pocket, collar and cuffs,
until the rumpled heap relaxed into the shape　　　　5
of my father's broad chest, the shoulders shrugged off
the world, the collapsed arms spread for a hug.
And if there'd been a face above the buttondown neck,
I would have pressed the forehead out, I would
have made a boy again out of that tired man!　　　　10

If I clung to her skirt as she sorted the wash
or put out a line, my mother frowned,
a crease down each side of her mouth.
This is no time for love! But here
I could linger over her wrinkled bedjacket,　　　　15
kiss at the damp puckers of her wrists
with the hot tip. Here I caressed
collars, scallops, ties, pleats which made
her outfits test of the patience of my passion.
Here I could lay my dreaming iron on her lap.　　　　20

The smell of baked cotton rose from the board
and blew with a breeze out the window
to the family wardrobe drying on the clothesline,
all needing a touch of my iron. Here I could tickle
the underarms of my big sister's petticoat　　　　25
or secretly pat the backside of her pajamas.
For she too would have warned me not to muss
her fresh blouses, starched jumpers, and smocks,
all that my careful hand had ironed out,
forced to express my excess love on cloth.　　　　30

CONSIDERATIONS FOR CRITICAL THINKING AND WRITING

1. FIRST RESPONSE. Explain how the speaker expresses her love for her family in the extended metaphor of ironing.

2. How are ironing and the poem itself expressions of the speaker's "excess love" (line 30)? In what sense is her love excessive?

3. Explain how the speaker's relationship to her father differs from her relationship to her mother.

CONNECTION TO ANOTHER SELECTION

1. CREATIVE RESPONSE. Compare the descriptions of mothers in this poem and in Alvarez's "Dusting" (p. 931). Write a one-paragraph character sketch that uses vivid details and metaphoric language to describe them.

JULIA ALVAREZ

On Writing "Sometimes the Words Are So Close" 2006
From the "33" Sonnet Sequence

I really believe that being a reader turns you into a writer. You connect with the voice in a poem at a deeper and more intimate level than you do with practically anyone in your everyday life. Seems like the years fall away, differences fall away, and when George Herbert asks in his poem, "The Flower,"

> Who would have thought my shrivel'd heart
> Could have recover'd greennesse?

You want to stroke the page and answer him, "I did, George." Instead you write a poem that responds to the feelings in his poem; you recover greenness for him and for yourself.

With the "33" sonnet sequence, I wanted the voice of the speaker to sound like a real woman speaking. A voice at once intimate and also somehow universal, essential. This sonnet #42 ["Sometimes the Words Are So Close"] is the last one in the sequence, a kind of final "testimony" about what writing is all about.

I mentioned that when you love something you read, you want to respond to it. You want to say it again, in fresh new language. Robert Frost speaks to this impulse in the poet when he says, "Don't borrow, steal!" Well, I borrowed / stole two favorite passages. One of them is from the poem on the Statue of Liberty, which was written by Emma Lazarus (1849–1887), titled "The New Colossus" [p. 1059]. These lines will sound familiar to you, I'm sure:

> "Give me your tired, your poor,
> Your huddled masses yearning to breathe free,
> The wretched refuse of your teeming shore.
> Send these, the homeless, tempest-tost to me,
> I lift my lamp beside the golden door!"

I think of these lines, not just as an invitation to the land of the brave and home of the free, but an invitation to poetry! A poem can be a resting place for the soul yearning to breathe free, a form that won't tolerate the misuses and abuses of language, a world teeming with discoveries and luminous little *ah-ha!* moments, a "place for the genuine," as Marianne Moore calls it in her poem, "On Poetry." William Carlos Williams said that we can't get the news from poems, practical information, hard facts, but "men die daily for lack of what is found there."

I not only agreed with this idea, but I wanted to say so in my own words, and so I echoed those lines from the Statue of Liberty in my sonnet:

> Those of you lost and yearning to be free,
> who hear these words, take heart from me.

Another favorite line comes from Walt Whitman's book-length "Leaves of Grass": "Who touches this [book] touches a man." As a young, lonely immigrant girl reading Whitman, those words made me feel so accompanied, so connected. And so I borrowed / stole that line and made it my own at the end of this poem.

JULIA ALVAREZ

Sometimes the Words Are So Close 1982
From the "33" Sonnet Sequence

Sometimes the words are so close I am
more who I am when I'm down on paper
than anywhere else as if my life were
practicing for the real me I become
unbuttoned from the anecdotal and   5
unnecessary and undressed down
to the figure of the poem, line by line,
the real text a child could understand.
Why do I get confused living it through?
Those of you lost and yearning to be free,   10
who hear these words, take heart from me.
I once was in as many drafts as you.
But briefly, essentially, here I am.
Who touches this poem touches a woman.

Drafts of "Sometimes the Words Are So Close": A Poet's Writing Process

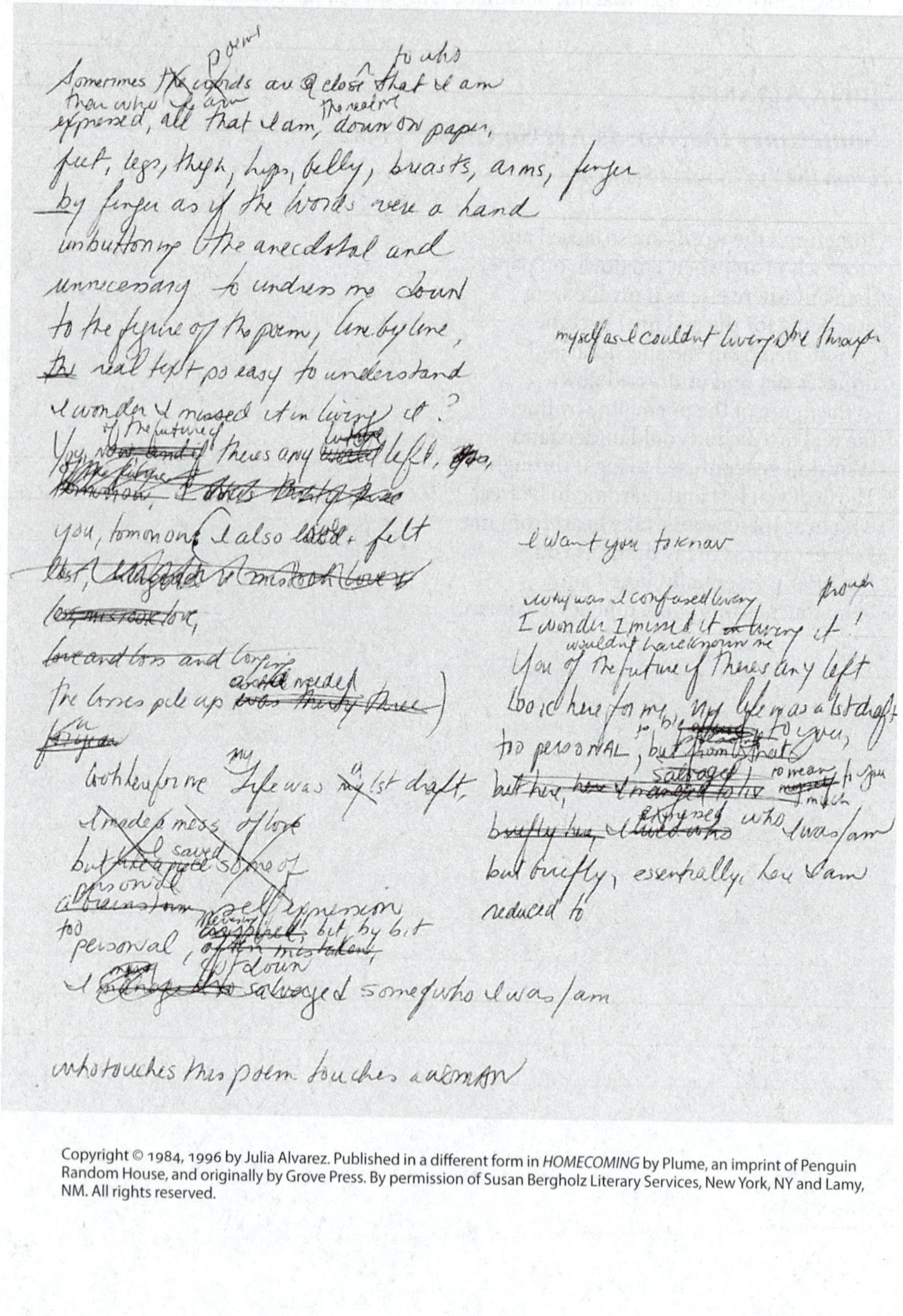

[Handwritten draft manuscript]

Sometimes the words are so close that I am
than who I am
expressed, all that I am, down on paper,
feet, legs, thigh, hips, belly, breasts, arms, finger
by finger as if the words were a hand
unbuttoning the anecdotal and
unnecessary to undress me down
to the figure of the poem, line by line,
the real text so easy to understand
I wonder I missed it in living it?
You, now of the future if there's any left,

myself as I couldn't live it the thought

I want you to know

you, tomorrow I also liked + felt

why was I confused every,
I wonder I missed it in living it!
wouldn't have known me
You of the future if there's any left
too here for me, My life was a 1st draft
too personal, but from the text
but here, salvaged to mean, you
expressed who I was/am
but briefly, essentially, here I am
reduced to

both here for me my life was my 1st draft.
I made a mess of love
but I saved some of
personal self expression
too personal, but by 6, t
I salvaged some who I was/am

who touches this poem touches a woman

Sometimes the words are so close I am
more who I am when I'm down on paper
than anywhere else as if my life were
practising for the real me I become
unbuttoned form the anecdotal and
unnecessary and undressed down
to the figure of the poem, line by line,
the real text a child can understand.
Why do I get confused living it through?
Those of you, lost and yearning to be free,
who hear these words, take heart from me.
I ~~was~~ once was in as many drafts as you.
But briefly, essentially, here I am...
Who touches this poem touches a woman.

```
Sometimes the words are so close I am
more who I am when I'm down on paper
than anywhere else as if my life were
practising for the real me I become
unbuttoned from the anecdotal and
unnecessary and undressed down
to the figure of the poem, line by line,
the real text a child could understand.
Why do I get confused living it through?
Those of you, lost and yearning to be free,
who hear these words, take heart from me.
I once was in as many drafts as you.
But briefly, essentially, here I am...
Who touches this poem touches a woman.
```

— *pretentious*

CONSIDERATIONS FOR CRITICAL THINKING AND WRITING

1. **FIRST RESPONSE.** Paraphrase lines 1–9. What produces the speaker's sense of frustration?

2. How do lines 10–14 resolve the question raised in line 9?

3. Explain how Alvarez's use of punctuation serves to reinforce the poem's meanings.

4. Discuss the elements of this poem that make it a sonnet.

5. Read carefully Alvarez's early drafts and discuss how they offer insights into your understanding and interpretation of the final version.

CONNECTION TO ANOTHER SELECTION

1. The poem's final line echoes Walt Whitman's poem "So Long," in which he addresses the reader: "Camerado, this is no book, / Who touches this touches a man." Alvarez has said that Whitman is one of her favorite poets. Read the selections by Whitman in this anthology (check the index for titles) along with "So Long" (readily available online) and explain why you think she admires his poetry.

JULIA ALVAREZ

On Writing "First Muse"   2006

I have to come clean about calling this poem, "First Muse."

I had another first muse in Spanish. Her name was Scheherazade and I read about her in a book my aunt gave me called *The Arabian Nights*. Scheherazade saves her life by telling the murderous sultan incredible tales night after night for 1001

Julia Alvarez signing a book after giving a presentation for the Portland Arts and Lectures series at the Arlene Schnitzer Concert Hall, April 3, 2014.
Noel Tendick.

nights. Listening to her stories, the sultan is transformed. He no longer wants to kill all the women in his kingdom. In fact, he falls in love with Scheherazade. This young lady saves her own life, the lives of all the women in her kingdom, and by changing him, she also saves the sultan's soul just by telling stories. Right then, I knew what I wanted to be when I grew up. You bet. A storyteller.

Of course, back then, I was growing up in the Dominican Republic, living in a cruel and dangerous dictatorship myself. My own father was a member of an underground freedom movement to depose this dictator. Like Scheherazade, my life and the life of many Dominicans was in danger. But stories like the ones in *The Arabian Nights* helped me dream that the world was a more exciting and mysterious place than I could even imagine. That I was free to travel on the magic carpet of Scheherazade's tales even if the dictatorship did not allow me to drive one town over without inspection and permission.

When I came into English and became a reader, I had new dreams. I wanted to be an American writer. But as I mentioned earlier, the United States of the early

'60s was still a long way off from the multicultural "revolution" of the late '80s and '90s. All the writers we read in my English class were Anglo Americans, and many of them were male. Still, the words they put down on paper invited everyone to partake of them. The authors were talking directly to me, asking me questions ("Who would have thought my shrivel'd heart . . . ?"), inviting me to be intimate with their words ("Who touches this [book] touches a man"). That's what I loved about reading: the great egalitarian democracy between the covers of books. The table set for all. The portable homeland. I wanted to be a part of that world. I often say that when I left the Dominican Republic in 1960, I landed, not in the United States, but in the English language, and that's where I put down deep roots by becoming a writer.

But the world beyond the covers of books did not mirror this great democracy. As you read in "Queens, 1963," the reality was disappointing. There were gated communities within this great free country. Places where immigrants and blacks need not apply. One of them was the guarded canon of literature. I still recall the famous writer who made the pronouncement that one could not write in English unless it was one's mother tongue. I was filled with self-doubt, and since I didn't have any examples in what we were reading in school that this pronouncement was wrong, I thought he was right.

Back then, Latino stories were the province of sociology, not literature. As for popular media, the only "Hispanics" on TV were Ricky Ricardo, with his laughable accent, and Chiquita Banana, selling fruit for the United Fruit Company. But as I said about writing in form, you find yourself caught in a structure or negative paradigm and you turn it on its head. You use it to get free. I listened to Chiquita singing, "I'm Chiquita Banana and I've come to say," and I began to get her message: *I'm a Latina woman, and I am claiming it openly, and what's more I've got something to say.* I felt the same rush of hope when I read Langston Hughes's "I, Too." In that poem, Mr. Hughes promised himself that "Tomorrow, / I'll be at the table" of American literature. And there he was in my English textbook. He had made good on his promise to himself, to me!

The civil rights struggle didn't just happen on buses and in places of business or on picket lines in Birmingham, Alabama, or Queens, New York. It also happened on paper. Chiquita Banana and Langston Hughes were right. There is a place for all our voices in the great inclusive world of literature. I feel honored and privileged to be part of that great liberating movement of words on paper, springing us all free with their magic and power, connecting us with ourselves and with each other.

JULIA ALVAREZ

First Muse 1999

When I heard the famous poet pronounce
"One can only write poems in the tongue
in which one first said *Mother*," I was stunned.
Lately arrived in English, I slipped down

into my seat and fought back tears, thinking   5
of all those notebooks filled with bogus poems
I'd have to burn, thinking maybe there was
a little loophole, maybe just maybe
Mami had sung me lullabies she'd learned
from wives stationed at the embassy,   10

thinking maybe she'd left the radio on
beside my crib tuned to the BBC
or Voice of America, maybe her friend
from boarding school had sent a talking doll
who spoke in English? Maybe I could be   15
the one exception to this writing rule?
For months I suffered from bad writer's-block,
which I envisioned, not as a blank page,
but as a literary border guard
turning me back to Spanish on each line.   20

I gave up writing, watched lots of TV,
and you know how it happens that advice
comes from unlikely quarters? *She* came on,
sassy, olive-skinned, hula-hooping her hips,
a basket of bananas on her head,   25
her lilting accent so full of feeling
it seemed the way the heart would speak English
if it could speak. I touched the screen and sang
my own heart out with my new muse, *I am*
Chiquita Banana and I'm here to say . . .   30

Considerations for Critical Thinking and Writing

1. **first response.** What do you think the "famous poet" had in mind by insisting that " 'One can only write poems in the tongue / in which one first said *Mother*' " (lines 2–3)? Explain why you agree or disagree with this statement.

2. How does the speaker preserve the serious nature of her bilingualism while simultaneously treating the topic humorously?

3. How and why does Chiquita Banana serve as the speaker's "new muse"?

Connections to Other Selections

1. Discuss the speakers' passion for language as it is revealed in "First Muse," "Dusting" (p. 931), and "Sometimes the Words Are So Close" (p. 935).

2. Compare the themes concerning writing and ethnicity in "First Muse" and in Julio Marzán's "Ethnic Poetry" (p. 722).

3. Consider the speakers' reactions in "First Muse" and in Judy Page Heitzman's "The Schoolroom on the Second Floor of the Knitting Mill" (p. 701) to the authoritative voice each hears. What effects do these powerful voices have on the speakers' lives?

A songbook featuring an image of the Chiquita Banana character referenced in Alvarez's "First Muse."

Chiquita Banana Songbook and Chiquita trademarks are registered trademarks and/or intellectual property of Chiquita Brands L.L.C. in the United States and other countries and are used with permission. No other use is permitted without the prior written permission of Chiquita Brands L.L.C.

CONSIDERATIONS FOR CRITICAL THINKING AND WRITING

1. How does this cover for the sheet music of Chiquita Banana's song illustrate the character's "sassy" tone (line 24) alluded to in the final stanza of "First Muse"?

2. In "First Muse," Alvarez humorously contemplates that if her mother had "left the radio on / beside my crib tuned to the BBC / or Voice of America," she might have learned English as an infant (lines 11–13). How does a careful analysis of the sheet music illustration suggest the difference between Chiquita's voice and that of the BBC or Voice of America?

3. The Chiquita Brands International corporation maintains a Web site (www .chiquita.com) that provides a history of its advertisements from the 1920s to the present, including recordings of the Chiquita song. How do you think the images of "Miss Chiquita" and her song served as a "new muse" for Alvarez when she was starting out as a writer?

Perspective

KELLI LYON JOHNSON (B. 1969)

Mapping an Identity 2005

Alvarez poses the problem of how we are to understand and represent identity within the multiple migrations that characterize an increasingly global society. By "mapping a country that's not on the map," Alvarez, a Dominican immigrant forced into exile in the United States, is undertaking a journey that places her at the forefront of contemporary American letters.

The question of identity and agency is particularly acute for women, postcolonial peoples, and others upon whom an identity has traditionally been imposed. Given Alvarez's success, both commercial and artistic, a variety of groups have claimed her as a member of their communities: as woman, ethnic, exile, diaspora, Caribbean, Dominican, Latina, and American. In the keynote address at a conference for Caribbean Studies, Doña Aída Cartagena Portalatín, "the grand woman of letters in the Dominican Republic" (*Something*[1] 171) gently chides Alvarez for writing in English. "Come back to your country, to your language," she tells Alvarez. "You are a Dominican" (171). By conflating linguistic, national, and cultural identity, Portalatín underscores the importance of these factors for constructing a literary tradition that includes displaced writers like Alvarez, who quite consciously has not adopted for writing the language of her country of origin.

In response to such comments, Alvarez has asserted her own self-definition as both (and neither) Dominican and American by writing "a new place on the map" (*Something* 173). Placing herself among a multiethnic group of postcolonial authors who write in English — "Michael Ondaatje in Toronto, Maxine Hong Kingston in San Francisco, Seamus Heaney in Boston, Bharati Mukherjee in Berkeley, Marjorie Agosín in Wellesley, Edwidge Danticat in Brooklyn" (173) — Alvarez, like these authors, has altered contemporary American literature by stretching the literary cartography of the Americas. These authors have brought, through their writings, their own countries of origin into a body of work in which the word *American* expands across continents and seas and begins to recapture its original connotation.

Alvarez has also claimed membership among a *comunidad* of U.S. Latina writers — Sandra Cisneros, Ana Castillo, Judith Ortiz Cofer, Lorna Dee Cervantes, Cherríe Moraga, Helena María Viramontes, and Denise Chávez — despite her fears that "the cage of definition" will enclose her writing "with its 'Latino subject matter,' 'Latino style,' 'Latino concerns'" (169). Like these authors, Alvarez seeks to write women into a postcolonial tradition of literature that has historically excluded women, particularly in writings of exile. To counter imposed definitions and historical silences, Alvarez has found that "the best way to define myself is through stories and poems" (169). The space that Alvarez maps is thus a narrative space: the site of her emerging cartography of identity and exile.

From Julia Alvarez: Writing a New Place on the Map

---

[1] *Something to Declare,* Alvarez's collection of essays published in 1998.

CONSIDERATIONS FOR CRITICAL THINKING AND WRITING

1. Based on your reading of the poems in this chapter, which community identity — "woman, ethnic, exile, diaspora, Caribbean, Dominican, Latina, and American" — best describes Alvarez for you?

2. In what sense does Alvarez's poetry expand "the literary cartography of the Americas"?

3. Consider "First Muse"(p. 940) as Alvarez's response to Portalatín's suggestion that she should write in Spanish rather than English and "[c]ome back to your country, to your language."

35

A CRITICAL CASE STUDY

T. S. Eliot's "The Love Song of J. Alfred Prufrock"

Genuine poetry can communicate before it is understood.

— T. S. ELIOT

This chapter provides several critical approaches to a challenging but highly rewarding poem by T. S. Eliot. After studying this poem, you're likely to find yourself quoting bits of its striking imagery. At the very least, you'll recognize the lines when you hear other people fold them into their own conversations. This poem has elicited numerous critical approaches because it raises so many issues relating to history, biography, imagery, symbolism, irony, myth, and

T. S. Eliot

Faber and Faber Ltd.

T. S. Eliot began writing poetry as a student. He is shown here in 1906 at age eighteen, during his first year at Harvard. In 1910, Eliot continued his studies abroad at the Sorbonne in Paris and at age twenty-three completed his first draft of "The Love Song of J. Alfred Prufrock" during the summer of 1911. Later in his life Eliot said, "Immature poets imitate; mature poets steal."

MS Am 2560 (177). By permission of the Houghton Library, Harvard University.

other matters. The following critical excerpts offer a small and partial sample of the possible formalist, biographical, historical, mythological, psychological, sociological, and other perspectives that have attempted to shed light on the poem (see Chapter 51, "Critical Strategies for Reading," for a discussion of a variety of critical methods). They should help you enjoy the poem more by raising questions, providing insights, and inviting you further into the text.

A BRIEF BIOGRAPHY

Born into a prominent New England family that had moved to St. Louis, Missouri, Thomas Stearns Eliot (1888–1965) was a major figure in English literature between the two world wars. He studied literature and philosophy at Harvard and on the Continent, subsequently choosing to live in England for most of his life and becoming a citizen of that country in 1927. Many writers have been powerfully influenced by his allusive and challenging poetry, particularly his treatment of postwar life in *The Waste Land* (1922) and his

This portrait of T. S. Eliot is by the Modernist painter and writer Wyndham Lewis. The Modernist movement of art and literature, dating from the late nineteenth to the mid-twentieth centuries, represented a rejection of tradition, a radical departure from Victorian sentimentality, and a move toward more experimental forms of expression. Modernist writers included T. S. Eliot, James Joyce, and Virginia Woolf. One of the themes explored by Modernist authors like Eliot is alienation. He once said, "[Poetry] may make us from time to time a little more aware of the deeper unnamed feelings which form the substratum of our being, to which we rarely penetrate; for our lives are mostly a constant evasion of ourselves."

T. S. Eliot (November 10, 1959), in a pose that suggests the Prufrock persona, holding a book containing some of his earlier work during a press conference at the University of Chicago.
© Bettmann/Corbis.

exploration of religious questions in *The Four Quartets* (1943). In addition, he wrote plays, including *Murder in the Cathedral* (1935) and *The Cocktail Party* (1950). He was awarded the Nobel Prize for Literature in 1948. In "The Love Song of J. Alfred Prufrock," Eliot presents a comic but serious figure who expresses through a series of fragmented images the futility, boredom, and meaninglessness associated with much of modern life.

T. S. ELIOT (1888–1965)

The Love Song of J. Alfred Prufrock   1917

S'io credesse che mia risposta fosse
A persona che mai tornasse al mondo,
Questa fiamma staria senza più scosse.
Ma perciocchè giammai di questo fondo

Non tornò vivo alcun, s'i'odo il vero,
Senza tema d'infamia ti rispondo.°

Let us go then, you and I,
When the evening is spread out against the sky
Like a patient etherized upon a table;
Let us go, through certain half-deserted streets,
The muttering retreats   5
Of restless nights in one-night cheap hotels
And sawdust restaurants with oyster-shells:
Streets that follow like a tedious argument
Of insidious intent
To lead you to an overwhelming question . . .   10

Oh, do not ask, "What is it?"
Let us go and make our visit.

In the room the women come and go
Talking of Michelangelo.

The yellow fog that rubs its back upon the window panes,   15
The yellow smoke that rubs its muzzle on the window panes
Licked its tongue into the corners of the evening,
Lingered upon the pools that stand in drains,
Let fall upon its back the soot that falls from chimneys,
Slipped by the terrace, made a sudden leap,   20
And seeing that it was a soft October night,
Curled once about the house, and fell asleep.

And indeed there will be time°
For the yellow smoke that slides along the street,
Rubbing its back upon the window panes;   25
There will be time, there will be time
To prepare a face to meet the faces that you meet;
There will be time to murder and create,
And time for all the works and days° of hands
That lift and drop a question on your plate: 30
Time for you and time for me,
And time yet for a hundred indecisions,
And for a hundred visions and revisions,
Before the taking of a toast and tea.

Epigraph: *S'io credesse . . . rispondo:* Dante's *Inferno,* 27:58–63. In the Eighth Chasm of the
Inferno, Dante and Virgil meet Guido da Montefeltro, one of the False Counselors, who is punished by being enveloped in an eternal flame. When Dante asks Guido to tell his life story, the
spirit replies: "If I thought that my answer were to one who might ever return to the world, this
flame would shake no more; but since from this depth none ever returned alive, if what I hear is
true, I answer you without fear of infamy." 23 *there will be time:* An allusion to Ecclesiastes
3:1–8: "To everything there is a season, and a time to every purpose under heaven. . . ." 29 *works
and days:* Hesiod's eighth-century B.C. poem *Works and Days* gives practical advice on how to
conduct one's life in accordance with the seasons.

In the room the women come and go   35
Talking of Michelangelo.

   And indeed there will be time
To wonder, "Do I dare?" and, "Do I dare?" —
Time to turn back and descend the stair,
With a bald spot in the middle of my hair —   40
(They will say: "How his hair is growing thin!")
My morning coat, my collar mounting firmly to the chin,
My necktie rich and modest, but asserted by a simple pin —
(They will say: "But how his arms and legs are thin!")
Do I dare   45
Disturb the universe?
In a minute there is time
For decisions and revisions which a minute will reverse.

   For I have known them all already, known them all:
Have known the evenings, mornings, afternoons,   50
I have measured out my life with coffee spoons;
I know the voices dying with a dying fall
Beneath the music from a farther room.
      So how should I presume?

   And I have known the eyes already, known them all —   55
The eyes that fix you in a formulated phrase.
And when I am formulated, sprawling on a pin,
When I am pinned and wriggling on the wall,
Then how should I begin
To spit out all the butt-ends of my days and ways?   60
      And how should I presume?

   And I have known the arms already, known them all —
Arms that are braceleted and white and bare
(But in the lamplight, downed with light brown hair!)
      Is it perfume from a dress   65
      That makes me so digress?
Arms that lie along a table, or wrap about a shawl.
      And should I then presume?
      And how should I begin?

      Shall I say, I have gone at dusk through narrow streets,   70
And watched the smoke that rises from the pipes
Of lonely men in shirtsleeves, leaning out of windows? . . .

I should have been a pair of ragged claws
Scuttling across the floors of silent seas.

   And the afternoon, the evening, sleeps so peacefully!   75
Smoothed by long fingers,
Asleep . . . tired . . . or it malingers,
Stretched on the floor, here beside you and me.
Should I, after tea and cakes and ices,
Have the strength to force the moment to its crisis?   80

But though I have wept and fasted, wept and prayed,
Though I have seen my head (grown slightly bald) brought in upon a platter,°
I am no prophet — and here's no great matter;
I have seen the moment of my greatness flicker,
And I have seen the eternal Footman hold my coat, and snicker,   85
    And in short, I was afraid.

    And would it have been worth it, after all,
After the cups, the marmalade, the tea,
Among the porcelain, among some talk of you and me,
Would it have been worth while   90
To have bitten off the matter with a smile,
To have squeezed the universe into a ball°
To roll it toward some overwhelming question,
To say: "I am Lazarus,° come from the dead,
Come back to tell you all, I shall tell you all" —   95
If one, settling a pillow by her head,
    Should say: "That is not what I meant at all;
        That is not it, at all."

    And would it have been worth it, after all,
Would it have been worth while,   100
After the sunsets and the dooryards and the sprinkled streets,
After the novels, after the teacups, after the skirts that trail along the floor —
And this, and so much more? —
It is impossible to say just what I mean!
But as if a magic lantern threw the nerves in patterns on a screen: 105
Would it have been worth while
If one, settling a pillow or throwing off a shawl,
And turning toward the window, should say:
    "That is not it at all,
    That is not what I meant, at all."   110

No! I am not Prince Hamlet, nor was meant to be;
Am an attendant lord,° one that will do
To swell a progress,° start a scene or two,   *state procession*
Advise the prince: withal, an easy tool,
Deferential, glad to be of use,   115
Politic, cautious, and meticulous;
Full of high sentence, but a bit obtuse;
At times, indeed, almost ridiculous —
Almost, at times, the Fool.

---

82 *head . . . upon a platter:* At Salome's request, Herod had John the Baptist decapitated and had the severed head delivered to her on a platter (see Matt. 14:1–12 and Mark 6:17–29).   92 *squeezed the universe into a ball:* See Andrew Marvell's "To His Coy Mistress" (p. 647), lines 41–42: "Let us roll all our strength and all / Our sweetness up into one ball."   94 *Lazarus:* The brother of Mary and Martha who was raised from the dead by Jesus (John 11:1–44). In Luke 16:19–31, a rich man asks that another Lazarus return from the dead to warn the living about their treatment of the poor.   112 *attendant lord:* Like Polonius in Shakespeare's *Hamlet.*

I grow old . . . I grow old . . .   120
I shall wear the bottoms of my trousers rolled.

    Shall I part my hair behind? Do I dare to eat a peach?
I shall wear white flannel trousers, and walk upon the beach.
I have heard the mermaids singing, each to each.

I do not think that they will sing to me.   125

I have seen them riding seaward on the waves,
Combing the white hair of the waves blown back
When the wind blows the water white and black.

We have lingered in the chambers of the sea
By seagirls wreathed with seaweed red and brown,   130
Till human voices wake us, and we drown.

CONSIDERATIONS FOR CRITICAL THINKING AND WRITING

1. FIRST RESPONSE. What does J. Alfred Prufrock's name connote? How would you
   characterize him?

2. What do you think is the purpose of the epigraph from Dante's *Inferno*?

3. What is it that Prufrock wants to do? How does he behave? What does he think
   of himself? Which parts of the poem answer these questions?

4. Who is the "you" of line 1 and the "we" in the final lines?

5. Discuss the poem's imagery. How does the imagery reveal Prufrock's character? Which images seem especially striking to you?

CONNECTIONS TO OTHER SELECTIONS

1. Write an essay comparing Prufrock's sense of himself as an individual with that
   of Walt Whitman's speaker in "One's-Self I Sing" (p. 1069).

2. Discuss in an essay the tone of "The Love Song of J. Alfred Prufrock" and
   Robert Frost's "Acquainted with the Night" (p. 711).

Perspectives on T. S. Eliot

ELISABETH SCHNEIDER (1897–1984)

Schneider uses a biographical approach to the poem to suggest that part of what
went into the characterization of Prufrock were some of Eliot's own sensibilities.

Hints of Eliot in Prufrock   1952

Perhaps never again did Eliot find an epigraph quite so happily suited to his use as
the passage from the *Inferno* which sets the underlying serious tone for *Prufrock* and
conveys more than one level of its meaning: "S'io credesse che mia risposta . . . ,"

lines in which Guido da Montefeltro consents to tell his story to Dante only because he believes that none ever returns to the world of the living from his depth. One in Hell can bear to expose his shame only to another of the damned; Prufrock speaks to, will be understood only by, other Prufrocks (the "you and I" of the opening, perhaps), and, I imagine the epigraph also hints, Eliot himself is speaking to those who know this kind of hell. The poem, I need hardly say, is not in a literal sense autobiographical: for one thing, though it is clear that Prufrock will never marry, the poem was published in the year of Eliot's own first marriage. Nevertheless, friends who knew the young Eliot almost all describe him, retrospectively but convincingly, in Prufrockian terms; and Eliot himself once said of dramatic monologue in general that what we normally hear in it "is the voice of the poet, who has put on the costume and make-up either of some historical character, or of one out of fiction." . . . I suppose it to be one of the many indirect clues to his own poetry planted with evident deliberation throughout his prose. "What every poet starts from," he also once said, "is his own emotions," and, writing of Dante, he asserted that the *Vita nuova* "could only have been written around a personal experience," a statement that, under the circumstances, must be equally applicable to Prufrock; Prufrock was Eliot, though Eliot was much more than Prufrock. We miss the whole tone of the poem, however, if we read it as social satire only. Eliot was not either the dedicated apostle in theory, or the great exemplar in practice, of complete "depersonalization" in poetry that one influential early essay of his for a time led readers to suppose.

From "Prufrock and After: The Theme of Change," *PMLA*, October 1952

CONSIDERATIONS FOR CRITICAL THINKING AND WRITING

1. Though Schneider concedes that the poem is not literally autobiographical, she does assert that "Prufrock was Eliot." How does she argue this point? Explain why you find her argument convincing or unconvincing.

2. Find information in the library or online about Eliot's early career when he was writing this poem. To what extent does the poem reveal his circumstances and concerns at that point in his life?

BARBARA EVERETT

Everett's discussion of tone is used to make a distinction between Eliot and his characterization of Prufrock.

The Problem of Tone in Prufrock   1974

Eliot's poetry presents a peculiar problem as far as tone is concerned. *Tone* really means the way the attitude of a speaker is manifested by the inflections of his speaking voice. Many critics have already recognized that for a mixture of reasons it is difficult, sometimes almost impossible, to ascertain Eliot's tone in this way. It is not that the poetry lacks "voice," for in fact Eliot has an extraordinarily recognizable poetic voice, often imitated and justifying his own comment in the . . . *Paris*

Review that "in a poem you're writing for your own voice, which is very important. You're thinking in terms of your own voice." It is this authoritative, idiosyncratic, and exact voice that holds our complete attention in poem after poem, however uninterested we are in what opinions it may seem or happen to be expressing. But Eliot too seems uninterested in what opinions it may happen to be expressing, for he invariably dissociates himself from his poems before they are even finished — before they are hardly begun — by balancing a derisory name or title against an "I," by reminding us that there is always going to be a moment at which detachment will take place or has taken place, a retrospective angle from which, far in the future, critical judgment alters the scene, and the speaking voice of the past has fallen silent. "I have known them all already, known them all." Thus whatever started to take place in the beginning of a poem by Eliot cannot truly be said to be Eliot's opinion because at some extremely early stage he began that process of dissociation to be loosely called "dramatization," a process reflected in the peculiar distances of the tone, as though everything spoken was in inverted commas.

From "In Search of Prufrock," *Critical Quarterly*, Summer 1974

CONSIDERATIONS FOR CRITICAL THINKING AND WRITING

1. According to Everett, why is it difficult to describe Eliot's tone in his poetry?
2. How does Eliot's tone make it difficult to make an autobiographical connection between Prufrock and Eliot?
3. How does Everett's reading of the relationship between Prufrock and Eliot differ from Schneider's in the preceding Perspective?

MICHAEL L. BAUMANN (B. 1926)

Baumann takes a close look at the poem's images in his formalist efforts to make a point about Prufrock's character.

The "Overwhelming Question" for Prufrock   1981

Most critics . . . have seen the overwhelming question related to sex. . . . They have implicitly assumed — and given their readers to understand — that Prufrock's is the male's basic question: Can I?

The poet and critic Delmore Schwartz once said that "J. Alfred Prufrock is unable to make love to women of his own class and kind because of shyness, self-consciousness, and fear of rejection."[1] This is undoubtedly true, but Prufrock's inability to *feel* love has something to do with his inability to *make* love, too. . . . A simple desire, lust, is more than honest Prufrock can cope with as he mounts the stairs.

But Prufrock is coping with another, less simple desire as well. . . . If birth, copulation, and death is all there is, then, once we are born, once we have copulated,

[1] "T. S. Eliot as the International Hero," *Partisan Review*, 12 (1945), 202; rpt. in *T. S. Eliot: A Selected Critique*, ed. Leonard Unger (New York: Rinehart & Company, Inc., 1948), 46.

only death remains (for the male of the species, at least). Prufrock, having "known them all already, known them all," having "known the evenings, mornings, afternoons," having "measured out" his life "with coffee spoons," desires death. The "overwhelming question" that assails him would no longer be the romantic rhetorical "Is life worth living?" (to which the answer is obviously No), but the more immediate shocker: "Should one commit suicide?" which is to say: "Should I?" . . .

. . . The poem makes clear that Prufrock wants more than the "entire destruction of consciousness as we understand it," a notion Prufrock expresses by wishing he were "a pair of ragged claws, / Scuttling across the floors of silent seas." Prufrock wants death itself, physical death, and the poem, I believe, is explicit about this desire.

Not only does Prufrock seem to be tired of time — "time yet for a hundred indecisions" — a tiredness that goes far beyond the acedia Prufrock is generally credited with feeling, if only because "there will be time to murder and create," time, in other words (in one sense at least) to copulate, but Prufrock is also tired of his own endless vanities, from feeling he must "prepare a face to meet the faces that you meet," to having to summon up those ironies with which to contemplate his own thin arms and legs, and, indeed, to asking if, in the rather tedious enterprise of preparing for copulation, the moment is worth "forcing to its crisis." No wonder Prufrock compares himself to John the Baptist and, in conjuring up this first concrete image of his own death, sees his head brought in upon a platter. That would be the easy way out. He had, after all, "wept and fasted, wept and prayed," but he realizes he is no prophet — and no Salome will burst into passion, will ignite for him. When the eternal Footman, Death, who holds his coat, snickers, he does so because Prufrock has let "the moment" of his "greatness" flicker, because Prufrock was unable to comply with the one imperative greatness would have thrust upon him: to kill himself. Prufrock explains: "I was afraid." Yet the achievement of his vision at the end of the poem, his being able to linger "in the chambers of the sea / By seagirls wreathed with seaweed red and brown," is an act of the imagination that only physical death can complete, unless Prufrock wants human voices to wake him, and drown him. His romantic vision demands the voluntary act: suicide. It is to be expected that he will fail in this too, as he has failed in everything else.

From "Let Us Ask 'What Is It,'" *Arizona Quarterly,* Spring 1981

Considerations for Critical Thinking and Writing

1. Describe the evidence used by Baumann to argue that Prufrock contemplates suicide.

2. Explain in an essay why you do or do not find Baumann's argument convincing.

3. Later in his essay Baumann connects Prufrock's insistence that "No, I am not Prince Hamlet" with Hamlet's "To be or not to be" speech. How do you think this reference might be used to support Baumann's argument in this excerpt?

Frederik L. Rusch (b. 1938)

Rusch makes use of the insights developed by Erich Fromm, a social psychologist who believed "psychic forces [are] a process of constant interaction between man's needs and the social and historical reality in which he participates."

Society and Character in "The Love Song of J. Alfred Prufrock" 1984

In looking at fiction, drama, and poetry from the Frommian point of view, the critic understands literature to be social portrayal as well as character portrayal or personal statement. Society and character are inextricably joined. The Frommian approach opens up the study of literary work, giving a social context to its characters, which suggests why those characters behave as they do. The Frommian approach recognizes human beings for what they are — basically gregarious individuals who are interdependent upon each other, in need of each other, and thus, to a certain degree, products of their social environments, although those environments may be inimical to their mental well-being. That is, as stated earlier, the individual's needs and drives have a social component and are not purely biological. The Frommian approach to literature assumes that a writer is — at least by implication — analyzing society and its setting as well as character. . . .

In T. S. Eliot's "The Love Song of J. Alfred Prufrock," Prufrock is talking to himself, expressing a fantasy or daydream. In his monologue, Prufrock, as noted by Grover Smith, "is addressing, as if looking into a mirror, his whole public personality."[1] Throughout the poem, Prufrock is extremely self-conscious, believing that the people in his imaginary drawing room will examine him as a specimen insect, "sprawling on a pin, / . . . pinned and wriggling on the wall. . . ." Of course, self-consciousness — being conscious of one's self — is not necessarily neurotic. Indeed, it is part of being a human being. It is only when self-consciousness, which has always led man to feel a separation from nature, becomes obsessive that we have a problem. Prufrock is certainly obsessed with his self-consciousness, convinced that everyone notices his balding head, his clothes (his prudent frocks), his thin arms and legs.

On one level, however, Prufrock is merely expressing the pain that all human beings must feel. Although his problem is extreme, he is quite representative of the human race:

> Self-awareness, reason, and imagination have disrupted the "harmony" that characterizes animal existence. Their emergence has made man into an anomaly, the freak of the universe. He is part of nature, subject to her physical laws and unable to change them, yet he transcends nature. He is set apart while being a part; he is homeless, yet chained to the home he shares with all creatures. . . . Being aware of himself, he realizes his powerlessness and the limitations of his existence. He is never free from the dichotomy of his existence: he cannot rid himself of his mind, even if he would want to; he cannot rid himself of his body as long as he is alive — and his body makes him want to be alive.[2]

This is the predicament of the human being. His self-awareness has made him feel separate from nature. This causes pain and sorrow. What, then, is the solution to the predicament? Fromm believed that mankind filled the void of alienation from nature with the creation of a culture, a society: "Man's existential, and hence unavoidable disequilibrium can be relatively stable when he has found, with the

---

[1] Grover Smith, *T. S. Eliot's Poetry and Plays: A Study in Sources and Meaning* (Chicago: U of Chicago P, 1962), 16.

[2] Erich Fromm, *The Anatomy of Human Destructiveness* (New York: Holt, Rinehart & Winston, 1973), 225.

support of his culture, a more or less adequate way of coping with his existential problems" (*Destructiveness* 225). But, unfortunately for Prufrock, his culture and society do not allow him to overcome his existential predicament. The fact is, he is bored by his modern, urban society.

In image after image, Prufrock's mind projects boredom:

> For I have known them all already, known them all:
> Have known the evenings, mornings, afternoons,
> I have measured out my life with coffee spoons. . . .
> . . . .
>
> And I have known the eyes already, known them all —
> . . . .
>
> Then how should I begin
> To spit out all the butt-ends of my days and ways?
> . . . .
>
> And I have known the arms already, known them all — . . . .

Prufrock is completely unstimulated by his social environment, to the point of near death. The evening in which he proposes to himself to make a social visit is "etherized upon a table." The fog, as a cat, falls asleep; it is "tired . . . or it malingers, / Stretched on the floor. . . ."

Prufrock, living in a city of "half-deserted streets, / . . . one-night cheap hotels / And sawdust restaurants with oyster-shells," gets no comfort, no nurturing from his environment. He is, in the words of Erich Fromm, a "modern mass man . . . isolated and lonely" (*Destructiveness* 107). He lives in a destructive environment. Instead of providing communion with fellow human beings, it alienates him through boredom. Such boredom leads to "a state of chronic depression" that can cause the pathology of "insufficient inner productivity" in the individual (*Destructiveness* 243). Such a lack of productivity is voiced by Prufrock when he confesses that he is neither Hamlet nor John the Baptist.

An interesting tension in "The Love Song of J. Alfred Prufrock" is caused by the reader's knowledge that Prufrock understands his own predicament quite well. Although he calls himself a fool, he has wisdom about himself and his predicament. This, however, only reinforces his depression and frustration. In his daydream, he is able to reveal truths about himself that, while they lead to self-understanding, apparently cannot alleviate his problems in his waking life. The poem suggests no positive movement out of the predicament. Prufrock is like a patient cited by Fromm, who under hypnosis envisioned "a black barren place with many masks," and when asked what the vision meant said "that everything was dull, dull, dull; that the masks represent the different roles he takes to fool people into thinking he is feeling well" (*Destructiveness* 246). Likewise, Prufrock understands that "There will be time, there will be time / To prepare a face to meet the faces that you meet. . . ." But despite his understanding of the nature of his existence, he cannot attain a more productive life.

It was Fromm's belief that with boredom "the decisive conditions are to be found in the overall environmental situation. . . . It is highly probable that even cases of severe depression-boredom would be less frequent and less intense . . . in a society where a mood of hope and love of life predominated. But in recent decades the opposite is increasingly the case, and thus a fertile soil for the development of individual depressive states is provided" (*Destructiveness* 251). There is no "mood of hope and love of life" in Prufrock's society. Prufrock is a lonely man, as lonely as "the lonely men in shirt-sleeves, leaning out of windows" of his fantasy. His only solution is to return to the animal state that his race was in before evolving into human beings.

Animals are one with nature, not alienated from their environments. They *are* nature, unselfconscious. Prufrock would return to a preconscious existence in the extreme: "I should have been a pair of ragged claws / Scuttling across the floors of silent seas." Claws *without a head* surely would not be alienated, bored, or depressed. They would seek and would need no psychological nurturing from their environment. And in the end Prufrock's fantasy of becoming claws is definitely more positive for him than his life as a human being. He completes his monologue with depressing irony, to say the least: It is with human voices waking us, bringing us back to human society, that we drown.

> From "Approaching Literature through the Social Psychology of
> Erich Fromm" in *Psychological Perspectives on Literature:*
> *Freudian Dissidents and Non-Freudians,* edited by Joseph Natoli

CONSIDERATIONS FOR CRITICAL THINKING AND WRITING

1. According to Rusch, why is Fromm's approach useful for understanding Prufrock's character as well as his social context?

2. In what ways is Prufrock "representative of the human race" (para. 3)? Is he like any other characters you have read about in this anthology? Explain your response.

3. In an essay consider how Rusch's analysis of Prufrock might be used to support Baumann's argument that Prufrock's "overwhelming question" is whether or not he should kill himself (p. 955).

SUGGESTED TOPICS FOR LONGER PAPERS

1. "The Love Song of J. Alfred Prufrock" has proved to be popular among generations of college students who are fond of quoting bits of the poem. What do you think accounts for that popularity among your own generation? Alternatively, why doesn't this poem speak to your concerns or those of your generation?

2. Of the four critical perspectives on the poem provided in this chapter, which did you find to be the most satisfying reading? Explain your response by describing how the one you chose opened up the poem more than the other three perspectives did.

36

A CULTURAL CASE STUDY

Harlem Renaissance Poets Claude McKay, Georgia Douglas Johnson, Langston Hughes, and Countee Cullen

I believe that poetry should be direct, comprehensible, and the epitome of simplicity.

—LANGSTON HUGHES

© Corbis.

World War I marked a steady increase of blacks migrating from the rural South to major cities in the North, such as Chicago and New York, looking for work and a more open racial environment. Returning African American soldiers helped raise black hopes and expectations because they wanted not only jobs but also respect after experiencing more liberal racial attitudes in Europe. Having fought for their country, blacks began to insist that their country stand up for them by ameliorating their civil rights through employment opportunities and an acknowledgment of black culture. In the 1920s, Harlem, a neighborhood in uptown Manhattan, became the creative center of black American literature, music, dance, painting, and sculpture. The artistic production that thrived during this period and in this section of New York City is known as the "Harlem Renaissance" and it has continued to be a vital tradition and presence in American cultural life.

In this 1932 image taken by African American photographer James VanDerZee, a Harlem couple in fur coats poses with a gleaming Cadillac on West 127th Street. VanDerZee once commented, "I tried to pose each person in such a way as to tell a story." His work offered America a dazzling view of black middle-class life in the 1920s and 1930s.
Donna Mussenden VanDerZee.

　　In 1925, Alain Locke characterized this convergence of talent as a "Mecca" of creativity; in *The New Negro*, an influential anthology showcasing writers and artists, he announced that "[t]he pulse of the Negro world has begun to beat in Harlem." Locke, a Rhodes scholar with a Ph.D. from Harvard, celebrated and encouraged the artistic and intellectual life in Harlem because he believed it was an enlargement of democratic opportunity for black Americans. He described Harlem as "the first concentration in history of so many diverse elements of Negro life. It has attracted the African, the West Indian, the Negro American; has brought together the Negro of the North and the Negro of the South; the man from the city and the man from the town and the village; the peasant, the student, the businessman, the professional man, artist, poet, musician, adventurer and worker, preacher and criminal, exploiter and social outcast." Black expression and self-determination had found a home in Harlem, a neighborhood that offered not only an enticingly exotic nightlife but also some refuge and relief from the social oppression and racism routinely encountered elsewhere. Although the Prohibition nightclubs were mostly

The famous Lafayette Theatre, located near 132nd Street on 7th Avenue, known during the Harlem Renaissance as the "Boulevard of Dreams," was one of New York's first theaters to desegregate (ca. 1912). The theater (now a church) seated two thousand people and, beginning in 1916, employed its own Lafayette Players, who performed popular and classical plays for almost exclusively black audiences. Known as the "House Beautiful" to many of its patrons, the Lafayette also showcased blues singer Bessie Smith, jazz composer Duke Ellington, and other prominent African American performers. Shown here is the vibrant opening night of Shakespeare's *Macbeth*, staged by Orson Welles, with a musical score by James P. Johnson (1936).
The Granger Collection.

for "whites only" and black workers and performers were required to enter through service doors, a good many Harlem blacks exercised their freedom in the arts and in their own assertions of self-expression, even if the many whites who frequented the clubs for blues, jazz, and raucous fun ignored the hard realities of black poverty as well as the achievements of black artists.

Ironically, the relative freedom blacks experienced in Harlem during the twenties had its origins in the racial bias and economic nervousness of the previous decades. Harlem was originally the home of well-off whites who built impressive houses lining wide boulevards and sidewalks. A *New York Times* headline from December 1911 offers a glimpse of how racism coupled with white flight made it possible for blacks to move in to Harlem: INVASION OF NEGROES CUTS HARLEM VALUES: LOSS IN ONE BLOCK BETWEEN 7TH AND 8TH AVENUES, ESTIMATED AT FROM $60,000 TO $80,000." The report goes on to explain how the "encroachment of negroes [*sic*]" into the Harlem real-estate market had brought down prices. That market decline, however, opened doors to blacks who previously had been excluded from Harlem, resulting in a vibrant opportunity for black culture to gain a foothold. In literature, the heart of that culture in the 1920s was primarily poetry—rather than fiction or drama—and Claude McKay, Langston Hughes, and Countee Cullen were three of its most significant poets. Georgia Douglas Johnson, another noteworthy poet, made important contributions to the Harlem Renaissance despite the fact that she lived in Washington, D.C., rather than New York. Her poetry, along with the meetings she orchestrated in her home for the socially and politically conscious literary elites who were at the intellectual center of the Harlem Renaissance, brought to center stage the value and importance of black cultural awareness.

Even as a child, Hughes was wrapped in that important African American legacy. He was raised by his maternal grandmother, who was the widow of Lewis Sheridan Leary, one of the band of men who participated in John Brown's raid on the federal arsenal at Harper's Ferry in 1859. The raid was a desperate attempt to ignite an insurrection that would ultimately liberate slaves in the South. It was a failure. Leary was killed, but the shawl he wore, which was returned to his wife bloodstained and riddled with bullet holes, was proudly worn by Hughes's grandmother fifty years after the raid, and she used it to cover her grandson at night when he was a young boy.

Throughout his long career as a professional writer, Hughes remained true to the African American heritage he celebrated in his writings, which were frankly "racial in theme and treatment, derived from the life I know." In an influential essay published in the *Nation*, "The Negro Artist and the Racial Mountain" (1926), he insisted on the need for black artists to draw on their heritage rather than "to run away spiritually from race":

> We younger Negro artists who create now intend to express our individual dark-skinned selves without fear or shame. If white people are pleased, we are glad. If they are not, it doesn't matter. We know we are beautiful. And ugly too. The tom-tom cries and the tom-tom laughs. If colored people are pleased we are glad. If they are not, their displeasure doesn't matter either. We build our temples for tomorrow, strong as we know how, and we stand on top of the mountain, free within ourselves.

The themes of racial pride and personal dignity work their way through some forty books that Hughes wrote, edited, or compiled during his forty-five years of writing.

Many Harlem Renaissance writers recognized the importance of reclaiming a neglected and discounted past damaged by slavery and bigotry as a means of forging a more promising future. In a famous 1925 essay, "The Negro Digs Up His Past," Arthur A. Schomburg (best known as the creator and curator of what would eventually become the Schomburg Center for Research in Black Culture of the New York Public Library) argued that "African cultural origins and sources" had to be retrieved from obscurity: "The Negro has been a man without a history because he has been considered a man without a worthy culture." This understanding and appreciation of African art helped to generate an interest in the "primitive" and more experimental styles that broke through conventional forms.

Related to this reclamation is an important anthology edited by James Weldon Johnson that includes the work of a number of new poets, such as that of Claude McKay. In *The Book of American Negro Poetry* (1922), Johnson's introductory essay called for a new, uniquely African American aesthetic that acknowledged the past but was not confined by it. He recognized and applauded the necessity for black poets to move beyond the sort of "subject-matter which went into the making of traditional dialect poetry, 'possums, watermelons, etc." and the limitations imposed by conventional "Negro dialect" expected by whites. The poet Paul Laurence Dunbar (1872–1906), for example, owed much of his literary reputation to the kind of poetry later denounced by Johnson, as illustrated by these lines from "Little Brown Baby" (1896):

> Little brown baby wif spa'klin' eyes
>   Who's pappy's darlin' an' who's pappy's chile?
> Who is it all de day nevah once tries
>   Fu' to be cross, er once loses dat smile?

Instead of writing this kind of stereotypical dialect, according to Johnson, what black poets needed to do to make a genuine contribution to American literature was

> to find a form that will express the racial spirit by symbols from within rather than by symbols from without, such as the mere mutilation of English spelling and pronunciation. He needs a form that is freer and larger than dialect, but which will still hold the racial flavor; a form expressing the imagery, the idioms, the peculiar turns of thought, and the distinctive humor and pathos, too, of the Negro, but which will also be capable of voicing the deepest and highest emotions and aspirations, and allow of the widest scope of treatment.

Two of the major ingredients of that "racial flavor" were the everyday speech of blacks and the jazz rhythms produced by musicians like Louis Armstrong and Duke Ellington. Unlike Modernists such as Ezra Pound or T. S. Eliot, whose affinity for allusion, myth, and elliptical complexity found an audience among highly sophisticated white readers, many black poets addressed themselves to the concerns of their fellow African Americans in poems that could be read with no formal training or extensive literary background, poems that were "direct, comprehensible, and the epitome of simplicity" as Hughes put it. Readers of James Weldon Johnson's *God's Trombones* (1927) did not require academic help to appreciate his free-verse arrangements adapted from the sermons of black preachers. Hughes drew on an oral tradition of working-class folk poetry that embraced vernacular street language at a time when some middle-class blacks felt that the use of the vernacular was an embarrassment and an impediment to social progress. Innovative vernacular poets, sometimes accompanied by jazz musicians or blues singers, nevertheless found appreciative audiences who reveled in the energy and freedom of the open, or free-verse, form and improvisations that incorporated suffering, yearning, and heartache, along with resilience and humor.

Much of the energy driving the Harlem Renaissance was generated by the determination of civil rights organizations located in Harlem to improve the status and dignity of African Americans by exposing whites to black artistic talent. The National Association for the Advancement of Colored People (NAACP), publisher of the *Crisis;* the National Urban League (NUL), publisher of *Opportunity;* and the Universal Negro Improvement Association (UNIA), publisher of *Negro World,* all worked to further social progress by promoting, publishing, and reviewing black writers and artists, thereby making them more creditable and worthy in the eyes of whites as well as blacks. Unfortunately, by the end of the 1920s, this energy could not sustain the level of artistic production and intensity that the decade had earlier promised. Part of the problem was that the majority of blacks, whether in Harlem or elsewhere, knew little or nothing about the awakening of the arts in Harlem; most had enough to keep them occupied just trying to earn a living. Moreover, the ebullient optimism, patronage, and publishing opportunities that created attentive audiences in the Jazz Age twenties collapsed with the stock market crash of 1929 and the economic casualties produced by the Depression. The new mood also placed a higher premium on fiction than on poetry, and though novels authored by blacks during the twenties are now less well known than their volumes of poetry, the genre culminated in Zora Neale Hurston's novel *Their Eyes Were Watching God* (1937), a prescient story about a black female protagonist who struggles to define herself in the context of a world of white assumptions. The literary legacy of the Harlem Renaissance is sustained in the continuing exploration of race, class, and gender as a central feature of American culture.

Chronology

1921   *Shuffle Along*, a popular musical revue of song, dance, and comedy created and performed by blacks, signals a growing interest in black culture.

1922   Claude McKay publishes *Harlem Shadows,* a collection of poetry that introduces early poetry of the Harlem Renaissance. Georgia Douglas Johnson publishes *Bronze,* a collection of poems centered on racial and gender experience.

1923   James Weldon Johnson publishes *Book of American Negro Poetry,* an anthology that urges blacks to establish their own distinct voices beyond stereotypical dialect.

1925   Alain Locke publishes *The New Negro,* an assessment that recognizes the emergence of the Harlem Renaissance and its relation to ethnic, cultural, and artistic identities worldwide. Countee Cullen publishes *Color,* a collection of poems that establishes him as a major writer of racial themes written in traditional forms.

1926   Langston Hughes publishes *The Weary Blues,* a poetry collection that emphasizes the centrality of jazz music in black culture. The white writer Carl Van Vechten publishes a widely read novel featuring life in Harlem, whose title, *Nigger Heaven,* creates dismay.

1927   Countee Cullen edits *Caroling Dusk,* an anthology of more than thirty contemporary black poets of the twenties.

1928   Several novels appear — such as Claude McKay's *Home to Harlem,* Rudolph Fisher's *Walls of Jericho,* and W. E. B. Du Bois's *Dark Princess* — marking a movement away from poetry and toward fiction.

1929   Nella Larsen publishes *Passing,* a novel that examines the race consciousness of women's sexuality and identity. The Wall Street stock market crash ends the Roaring Twenties and ushers in the beginning of the Great Depression, causing a profound shift in the country's economics and mood.

1930   Langston Hughes publishes his first novel, *Not without Laughter.*

Three women strolling on Seventh Avenue in Harlem, ca. 1927.
The Granger Collection.

CLAUDE McKAY (1889–1948)

© Corbis.

Claude McKay was born to peasant farmers on the island of Jamaica. His father, the son of slaves, descended from a West African tribe and familiarized him during his childhood with African folk stories. As a young man, McKay used money from the Jamaica Medal of the Institute for the Arts awarded for his two 1912 collections of dialect poetry, *Songs of Jamaica* and *Constab Ballads* (the latter about his experiences as a police constable) to immigrate to the United States. After studying at Tuskegee Institute and Kansas State College, he moved to New York City, where he placed poems in magazines such as the avant-garde *Seven Arts* and the leftist *Liberator*. In the early 1920s, he left the United States to live in Europe and North Africa for some dozen years, during which he became interested in socialism and communism and visited the Soviet Union.

Although McKay renounced Marxism and communism and converted to Catholicism in the 1940s, in the twenties he was considered radical when it came to taking on racial oppression. His reputation flourished among blacks in 1919 when he published the sonnet "If We Must Die" (p. 0000) in the *Liberator*. Written after the 1919 "Red Summer" in Chicago, during which rioters threatened the livelihoods and lives of blacks, this poem was read as a strident voice of resistance for "fighting on!"

McKay's first volume of poems published in America, *Harlem Shadows*, appeared in 1922 and established his reputation as a gifted poet writing in traditional forms, particularly sonnets, that focused on two major themes: his lyric nostalgic memories of rural life in Jamaica and his experience with racism and economic injustice in New York. A curious tension exists between his conservative fixed forms and the politicized racial consciousness that challenged the status quo in his adopted country. Nevertheless, this paradoxical blend of orthodox prosody and radical themes made him a major poet among blacks in the twenties: it satisfied traditional expectations about how poetry should be written for popular audiences while it simultaneously empowered readers who admired its defiant message to refuse racism and to reject oppression. McKay knew that his immediate audience consisted of black readers, and he was not afraid of offending genteel readers, regardless of their race.

McKay's images of the underside of life in Harlem — the poverty, desperation, prostitution, and bleakness — appeared in his prose as well as in his poetry. His first novel, *Home to Harlem*, sold extremely well but was famously criticized by the highly respected W. E. B. Du Bois, one of the founders of the NAACP, as well as a historian, sociologist, teacher, writer,

A 1925 edition of *Survey Graphic* magazine on the "Renaissance" in Harlem.
Schomburg Center, New York Public Library.

and editor. Writing in the *Crisis,* Du Bois acknowledged some success in the novel's prose style but strongly objected to the stark depiction of black life: "[F]or the most part [it] nauseates me, and after the dirtier parts of its filth, I feel distinctly like taking a bath." McKay responded by making a case for his literary art and refused to write "propaganda" or merely uplifting literature. He went on to publish two more novels that aren't set in Harlem: *Banjo* (1929) and *Banana Bottom* (1933); however, in *Gingertown,* a 1932 collection of short stories, some of the settings are located in Harlem. McKay's writing dropped off in the last decade of his life after he published his

Harlem's famous Cotton Club in 1938, where legendary jazz musicians performed throughout the Harlem Renaissance.
The Granger Collection.

autobiography, *A Long Way from Home* (1937), and his *Complete Poems* were not published until 2003.

While McKay did not publish any volumes of poetry late in life, his poems remain the bedrock on which subsequent protest poetry depicting Harlem life was built.

The Harlem Dancer   1917

Applauding youths laughed with young prostitutes
And watched her perfect, half-clothed body sway;
Her voice was like the sound of blended flutes
Blown by black players upon a picnic day.
She sang and danced on gracefully and calm,   5
The light gauze hanging loose about her form;
To me she seemed a proudly-swaying palm
Grown lovelier for passing through a storm.
Upon her swarthy neck black shiny curls
Luxuriant fell; and tossing coins in praise,   10
The wine-flushed, bold-eyed boys, and even the girls,
Devoured her shape with eager, passionate gaze;
But looking at her falsely-smiling face,
I knew her self was not in that strange place.

CONSIDERATIONS FOR CRITICAL THINKING AND WRITING

1. FIRST RESPONSE. What does the speaker think of the dancer? Is he sympathetic? Why or why not?

2. How does the speaker's language characterize the audience?

3. What do you make of the dancer's "falsely-smiling face" (line 13)? What does it say about her relationship to herself and her work?

CONNECTION TO ANOTHER SELECTION

1. Discuss the thematic significance of the respective crowds in "The Harlem Dancer" and in "The Lynching" (p. 970).

If We Must Die   1919

If we must die, let it not be like hogs
Hunted and penned in an inglorious spot,
While round us bark the mad and hungry dogs,
Making their mock at our accurséd lot.
If we must die, O let us nobly die,   5
So that our precious blood may not be shed
In vain; then even the monsters we defy
Shall be constrained to honor us though dead!
O Kinsmen! we must meet the common foe!
Though far outnumbered let us show us brave,   10
And for their thousand blows deal one deathblow!
What though before us lies the open grave?
Like men we'll face the murderous, cowardly pack,
Pressed to the wall, dying, but fighting back!

CONSIDERATIONS FOR CRITICAL THINKING AND WRITING

1. FIRST RESPONSE. How do the poem's images influence its tone?

2. Notice that this sonnet does not specifically mention race. How does that affect your reading?

3. Describe the poem's sonnet form.

CONNECTION TO ANOTHER SELECTION

1. Compare the themes in "If We Must Die" and in Langston Hughes's "Harlem" (p. 983).

The Tropics in New York   1920

Bananas ripe and green, and ginger-root,
  Cocoa in pods and alligator pears,
And tangerines and mangoes and grape fruit,
  Fit for the highest prize at parish fairs,

Set in the window, bringing memories 5
    Of fruit-trees laden by low-singing rills,
And dewy dawns, and mystical blue skies
    In benediction over nun-like hills.

My eyes grew dim, and I could no more gaze;
    A wave of longing through my body swept, 10
And, hungry for the old, familiar ways,
    I turned aside and bowed my head and wept.

CONSIDERATIONS FOR CRITICAL THINKING AND WRITING

1. FIRST RESPONSE. Explain how the title is an important element in the poem.

2. What do you think is the speaker's situation?

3. What does the fruit symbolize?

CONNECTION TO ANOTHER SELECTION

1. Compare how food is used to evoke a sense of place in this poem and in Langston Hughes's "125th Street" (p. 983).

The Lynching 1920

His spirit is smoke ascended to high heaven.
His father, by the cruelest way of pain,
Had bidden him to his bosom once again;
The awful sin remained still unforgiven.
All night a bright and solitary star 5
(Perchance the one that ever guided him,
Yet gave him up at last to Fate's wild whim)
Hung pitifully o'er the swinging char.
Day dawned, and soon the mixed crowds came to view
The ghastly body swaying in the sun. 10
The women thronged to look, but never a one
Showed sorrow in her eyes of steely blue.

And little lads, lynchers that were to be,
Danced round the dreadful thing in fiendish glee.

CONSIDERATIONS FOR CRITICAL THINKING AND WRITING

1. FIRST RESPONSE. What do you think McKay wants readers to find most disturbing about the scene depicted in the poem? What do you find most disturbing?

2. Do you think religious faith offers comfort in this poem?

3. Compare what happens at night with what the dawn reveals. Which images seem more powerful to you?

CONNECTION TO ANOTHER SELECTION

1. Compare the treatment of violence in this poem and in "If We Must Die" (p. 969).

The White City 1921

I will not toy with it nor bend an inch.
Deep in the secret chambers of my heart
I muse my life-long hate, and without flinch
I bear it nobly as I live my part.
My being would be a skeleton, a shell,   5
If this dark Passion that fills my every mood,
And makes my heaven in the white world's hell,
Did not forever feed me vital blood.
I see the mighty city through a mist —
The strident trains that speed the goaded mass,   10
The poles and spires and towers vapor-kissed,
The fortressed port through which the great ships pass,
The tides, the wharves, the dens I contemplate,
Are sweet like wanton loves because I hate.

CONSIDERATIONS FOR CRITICAL THINKING AND WRITING

1. FIRST RESPONSE. In what sense do you think the speaker's hatred provides him with "vital blood"?

2. Discuss the poem's form. Why might a closed form be useful in the context of the speaker's "dark Passion"?

CONNECTION TO ANOTHER SELECTION

1. Discuss McKay's perspective on the city in this poem and Hughes's in "125th Street" (p. 983).

America 1921

Although she feeds me bread of bitterness,
And sinks into my throat her tiger's tooth,
Stealing my breath of life, I will confess
I love this cultured hell that tests my youth.
Her vigor flows like tides into my blood,   5
Giving me strength erect against her hate,
Her bigness sweeps my being like a flood.
Yet, as a rebel fronts a king in state,

I stand within her walls with not a shred
Of terror, malice, not a word of jeer.   10
Darkly I gaze into the days ahead,
And see her might and granite wonders there,
Beneath the touch of Time's unerring hand,
Like priceless treasures sinking in the sand.

CONSIDERATIONS FOR CRITICAL THINKING AND WRITING

1. FIRST RESPONSE. According to the speaker, what is there to love about "this cultured hell" in America?

2. Is the speaker a "rebel" or simply a patriotic citizen?

3. How do the tone, diction, and imagery reveal the speaker's sense of America's future?

CONNECTION TO ANOTHER SELECTION

1. Compare the themes of this poem with those in David Hernandez's "All-American" (p. 813).

The Barrier 1922

I must not gaze at them although
Your eyes are dawning day;
I must not watch you as you go
Your sun-illumined way;

I hear but I must never heed   5
The fascinating note,
Which, fluting like a river reed,
Comes from your trembling throat;

I must not see upon your face
Love's softly glowing spark;   10
For there's the barrier of race,
You're fair and I am dark.

CONSIDERATIONS FOR CRITICAL THINKING AND WRITING

1. FIRST RESPONSE. Describe the speaker's tone in each stanza.

2. Comment on the poem's sound effects.

3. How does the light imagery in the first stanza reinforce the theme?

CONNECTION TO ANOTHER SELECTION

1. Discuss the social commentary implicit in "The Barrier" and in Countee Cullen's "For a Lady I Know" (p. 987).

GEORGIA DOUGLAS JOHNSON (1877–1966)

Born in Atlanta, Georgia, to an interracial family—an African American maternal grandfather, a Native American maternal grandmother, and an English paternal grandfather—Georgia Douglas Johnson is regarded as one of the first important African American women poets of the twentieth century. After her early education in Rome and Atlanta, Georgia, she graduated from Atlanta Normal School and then studied violin, piano, and voice at the Oberlin Conservatory and the Cleveland College of Music. She later taught in Marietta, Georgia, and became an assistant school principal in Atlanta, where in 1903 she married Henry Lincoln Johnson, an Atlanta lawyer. Seven years later they moved to Washington, D.C., where her husband served in President William Howard Taft's administration and where they raised two children.

Schomburg Center, New York Public Library.

Although she lived in Washington, D.C., Johnson was one of the major women writers to play a central role in the Harlem Renaissance. She and her husband brought together a group of African American social and political elites by hosting meetings in their home, an illustrious group that included Langston Hughes, W. E. B. Du Bois, Alain Locke, Jean Toomer, as well as faculty from Howard University. These meetings, known as the Saturday Night's Club in the S Street Salon, consisted of lively discussions, debates, and plans for literary projects affecting American blacks.

Johnson published *The Heart of Women* in 1918, the first of her four collections of poems. Written in traditional forms, these poems explored the pleasures and conflicts embedded in love relationships through a sensitive — and genteel — female voice. Her third volume of poetry, *An Autumn Love* (1928), offered similar subject matter and reflected the belief of some black writers that poetry should reflect universal concerns rather than racially based topics. In between these two volumes, however, Johnson produced a more "racially conscious" collection in 1922 titled *Bronze* that focused on a black woman's spiritual struggle in racial contexts. Some of these poems were originally published in *Crisis* and the *Liberator*. The tone of W. E. B. Du Bois's one-page foreword to this collection suggests both the esteem and the difficulties associated with gender that attended black female poets who lacked the patronage and fellow support enjoyed by their male counterparts:

> I hope Mrs. Johnson will have wide reading. Her word is simple, sometimes trite, but it is singularly sincere and true, and as a revelation of the soul struggle of the women of a race it is invaluable.

This mixed, tentative endorsement is a curious qualification that reflects the status of black women poets during the 1920s.

After her husband died in 1925, Johnson eventually went to work at the Department of Labor to support her sons while simultaneously committing herself to writing even more than she had before. From 1926 to 1932, she wrote a weekly column titled "Homely Philosophy" offering inspirational advice and wisdom that was widely distributed to African American newspapers. Although she wrote more than thirty plays, only six were published, among them *Safe* (1925) and *Sunday Morning in the South* (1925), both about the horrific lynchings during the period. Her two best-known plays, *Blue Blood* (1926) and *Plumes* (1929), dealt with, respectively, the "mixing of races" and the importance of valuing African American heritage and culture. Johnson's final collection, *Share My World* (1962), includes poems and newspaper articles confirming the hopeful sensibilities that were also present at the beginning of her writing career in her author's note to *Bronze:*

> This book is the child of a bitter earth-wound. I sit on the earth and sing — sing out, and of, my sorrow. Yet, fully conscious of the potent agencies that silently work in their healing ministries, I know that God's sun shall one day shine upon a perfected and unhampered people.

Her faith in the possibilities of an "unhampered people" makes her writing an abiding contribution to the Harlem Renaissance.

Youth   1918

The dew is on the grasses, dear,
  The blush is on the rose,
And swift across our dial-youth,°   *sundial*
  A shifting shadow goes,
The primrose moments, lush with bliss,
  Exhale and fade away,
Life may renew the Autumn time,
  But nevermore the May!

CONSIDERATIONS FOR CRITICAL THINKING AND WRITING

1. FIRST RESPONSE. Describe the traditional fixed form of this poem.

2. How do the images contribute to the poem's theme?

CONNECTION TO ANOTHER SELECTION

1. Compare the theme and tone of this poem with those of either Robert Herrick's "To the Virgins, to Make Much of Time" (p. 645) or Andrew Marvell's "To His Coy Mistress" (p. 647).

Foredoom   1918

Her life was dwarfed, and wed to blight,
Her very days were shades of night,
Her every dream was born entombed,
Her soul, a bud, — that never bloomed.

CONSIDERATIONS FOR CRITICAL THINKING AND WRITING

1. FIRST RESPONSE. How does this poem succeed in creating a kind of biography of the woman it describes?
2. What is the effect of repetition at the beginning of each line?

CONNECTION TO ANOTHER SELECTION

1. Compare the portrait of the woman in "Foredoom" with the portrait in Countee Cullen's "For a Lady I Know" (p. 987). How much do you know about each of these women?

Calling Dreams   1920

The right to make my dreams come true,
I ask, nay, I demand of life;
Nor shall fate's deadly contraband
Impede my steps, nor countermand;
Too long my heart against the ground
Has beat the dusty years around;
And now at length I rise! I wake!
And stride into the morning break!

CONSIDERATIONS FOR CRITICAL THINKING AND WRITING

1. FIRST RESPONSE. Characterize the speaker's attitude toward life.
2. Comment on the poem's rhymes and their effects.

CONNECTION TO ANOTHER SELECTION

1. Discuss the themes in "Calling Dreams" and in Langston Hughes's "Harlem" (p. 983).

Lost Illusions   1922

Oh, for the veils of my far away youth,
Shielding my heart from the blaze of the truth,
Why did I stray from their shelter and grow
Into the sadness that follows — to know!

Impotent atom with desolate gaze
Threading the tumult of hazardous ways —
Oh, for the veils, for the veils of my youth
Veils that hung low o'er the blaze of the truth!

CONSIDERATIONS FOR CRITICAL THINKING AND WRITING

1. FIRST RESPONSE. What kind of illusions do you imagine as the subject of this poem?
2. What is the speaker's attitude about knowledge? Do you think there is an acceptable alternative?

CONNECTION TO ANOTHER SELECTION

1. Discuss the perils of youth that Johnson describes in this poem and in "Youth" (p. 974).

Fusion   1922

How deftly does the gardener blend
This rose and that
To bud a new creation,
More gorgeous and more beautiful
Than any parent portion,   5
And so,
I trace within my warring blood
The tributary sources,
They potently commingle
And sweep   10
With new-born forces!

CONSIDERATIONS FOR CRITICAL THINKING AND WRITING

1. FIRST RESPONSE. Discuss the appropriateness of the poem's gardening metaphor.
2. In what sense is the speaker filled with "warring blood"?

CONNECTION TO ANOTHER SELECTION

1. Discuss the source of pride that is found in "Fusion" and in "Calling Dreams" (p. 975).

Prejudice   1922

These fell miasmic rings of mist with ghoulish menace bound,
Like noose-horizons tightening my little world around.
They still the soaring will to wing, to dance, to speed away,
And fling the soul insurgent back into its shell of clay.
Beneath incrusted silences, a seething Etna° lies,   *Sicilian volcano*
The fire of whose furnaces may sleep, but never dies!

CONSIDERATIONS FOR CRITICAL THINKING AND WRITING

1. FIRST RESPONSE. What are the emotional effects of prejudice on the speaker?
2. Discuss the tone produced by the images in each line. How does Johnson unify the images?

CONNECTION TO ANOTHER SELECTION

1. Compare the speaker's sense of place in "Prejudice" and in Claude McKay's "The Tropics in New York" (p. 969).

I Want to Die While You Love Me   1928

I want to die while you love me,
   While yet you hold me fair,
While laughter lies upon my lips
   And lights are in my hair.

I want to die while you love me   5
And bear to that still bed
Your kisses — turbulent, unspent,
   To warm me when I'm dead.

I want to die while you love me
   Oh, who would care to live   10
'Til love has nothing more to ask
   And nothing more to give.

CONSIDERATIONS FOR CRITICAL THINKING AND WRITING

1. FIRST RESPONSE. Would you consider sending this poem to a romantic partner on Valentine's Day? Why or why not?
2. Characterize the speaker. Explain why you think the speaker is male or female based on the language in the poem.

CONNECTION TO ANOTHER SELECTION

1. Write an analysis comparing this poem's style and theme with those of "To My Dear and Loving Husband" by Anne Bradstreet (p. 999).

LANGSTON HUGHES (1902–1967)

© Corbis.

Langston Hughes is the best-known writer of the Harlem Renaissance. His literary production includes volumes of poetry, novels, short stories, essays, plays, opera librettos, histories, documentaries, autobiographies, anthologies, children's books, and translations, as well as radio and television scripts. This impressive body of work makes him an important literary artist and a leading African American voice in the twentieth century. First and foremost, however, he considered himself a poet.

Born in Joplin, Missouri, Hughes grew up with his grandmother, although he did live from time to time with one or the other of his parents, who had separated early in his life. After attending Columbia University in 1921, Hughes wrote and published poetry while he worked a series of odd jobs and then traveled as a merchant seaman to Europe and Africa from 1923 to 1924. He jumped ship to work for several months as a kitchen helper in a Paris nightclub. After his return to the United States in 1925, he published poems in two black magazines, the *Crisis* and *Opportunity,* and met Carl Van Vechten, who sent his poems to the publisher Alfred A. Knopf. While working as a busboy in a Washington, D.C., hotel, he met the poet Vachel Lindsay, who was instrumental in advancing Hughes's reputation as a poet. In 1926, Hughes published his first volume of poems, *The Weary Blues,* and enrolled at Lincoln University in Pennsylvania, his education funded by a generous patron. His second volume of verse, *Fine Clothes to Jews,* appeared in 1927, and by the time he graduated from Lincoln University in 1929, he was reading his poems publicly on a book tour of the South. Hughes ended the decade as more than a promising poet; as Countee Cullen pronounced in a mixed review of *The Weary Blues* (mixed because Cullen believed that black poets should embrace universal rather than racial themes), Hughes had "arrived."

Hughes wrote more prose than poetry in the 1930s, publishing his first novel, *Not without Laughter* (1930), and a collection of stories, *The Ways of White Folks* (1934). In addition to writing a variety of magazine articles, he also worked on a number of plays and screenplays. Many of his poems from this period reflect proletarian issues. During this decade, Hughes's travels took him to all points of the compass — Cuba, Haiti, the Soviet Union, China, Japan, Mexico, France, and Spain — but his general intellectual movement was decidedly left. Hughes was attracted to the American Communist Party, owing to its insistence on equality for all working-class people regardless of race. Like many other Americans in the thirties, he turned his attention away from the exotic twenties and focused on the economic and political issues attending the Great Depression that challenged the freedom and dignity of common humanity.

(*Left*) The publication of *The Weary Blues* in 1926 established Hughes as an important figure in the Harlem Renaissance, a cultural movement characterized by an explosion of black literature, theater, music, painting, and political and racial consciousness that began after the First World War. A stamp bearing the image at left, commemorating the centennial of Hughes's birth (2002), is but one example of his lasting impact on American poetry and culture.
Henri Cartier-Bresson/Magnum Photos.

(*Below*) Langston Hughes claimed that Walt Whitman, Carl Sandburg, and Paul Laurence Dunbar were his greatest influences as a poet. However, the experience of black America from the 1920s through the 1960s, the life and language of Harlem, and a love of jazz and the blues clearly shaped the narrative and lyrical experimentation of his poetry. This image of a couple dancing in a Harlem nightclub is a snapshot of the life that influenced Hughes's work.
© Bettmann/Corbis.

To the rumble of street cars,
To the swish of rain.   10

Lenox Avenue,
Honey.
Midnight,
And the gods are laughing at us.

CONSIDERATIONS FOR CRITICAL THINKING AND WRITING

1. FIRST RESPONSE. What, in your own experience, is the equivalent of what
   Lenox Avenue is for the speaker?

2. For so brief a poem there are many sounds in these fourteen lines. What are
   they? How do they reinforce the poem's meanings?

3. What do you think is the poem's theme?

CONNECTION TO ANOTHER SELECTION

1. In an essay compare the theme of this poem with that of Emily Dickinson's
   "I know that He exists" (p. 859).

Ballad of the Landlord   1940

Landlord, landlord,
My roof has sprung a leak.
Don't you 'member I told you about it
Way last week?

Landlord, landlord,   5
These steps is broken down.
When you come up yourself
It's a wonder you don't fall down.

Ten Bucks you say I owe you?
Ten Bucks you say is due?   10
Well, that's Ten Bucks more'n I'll pay you
Till you fix this house up new.

What? You gonna get eviction orders?
You gonna cut off my heat?
You gonna take my furniture and   15
Throw it in the street?

Um-huh! You talking high and mighty.
Talk on — till you get through.
You ain't gonna be able to say a word
If I land my fist on you.   20

Police! Police!
Come and get this man!
He's trying to ruin the government
And overturn the land!

Copper's whistle!   25
Patrol bell!
Arrest.

Precinct Station.
Iron cell.
Headlines in press: 30

MAN THREATENS LANDLORD
TENANT HELD NO BAIL
JUDGE GIVES NEGRO 90 DAYS IN COUNTY JAIL

CONSIDERATIONS FOR CRITICAL THINKING AND WRITING

1. FIRST RESPONSE. The poem incorporates both humor and serious social commentary. Which do you think is dominant? Explain.
2. Why is the literary ballad an especially appropriate form for the content of this poem?
3. How does the speaker's language simultaneously characterize him and the landlord?

125th Street° 1950

Face like a chocolate bar
full of nuts and sweet.

Face like a jack-o'-lantern,
candle inside.

Face like a slice of melon,
grin that wide.

125th Street: The main street in Harlem.

CONSIDERATIONS FOR CRITICAL THINKING AND WRITING

1. FIRST RESPONSE. How do these three similes create a vivid picture of 125th Street?
2. How does this poem confirm the poet Marvin Bell's observation that "a short poem need not be small"?

CONNECTION TO ANOTHER SELECTION

1. Discuss the speaker's attitude toward the city in "125th Street" and in Claude McKay's "The Tropics in New York" (p. 969).

Harlem 1951

What happens to a dream deferred?

Does it dry up
like a raisin in the sun?

Or fester like a sore —
And then run?
Does it stink like rotten meat?   5
Or crust and sugar over —
like a syrupy sweet?

Maybe it just sags
like a heavy load.   10

Or does it explode?

CONSIDERATIONS FOR CRITICAL THINKING AND WRITING

1. FIRST RESPONSE. Could the question asked in this poem be raised by any individual or group whose dreams and aspirations are thwarted? Why or why not?

2. In some editions of Hughes's poetry, the title of this poem is "Dream Deferred." How would this change affect your reading of the poem's symbolic significance?

3. How might the final line be completed as a simile? What is the effect of the speaker's not completing the simile? Why is this an especially useful strategy?

CONNECTION TO ANOTHER SELECTION

1. Write an essay on the themes of "Harlem" and of James Merrill's "Casual Wear" (p. 724).

COUNTEE CULLEN   (1903–1946)

Getty Images.

Little is known about Countee Cullen's early life. Although he claimed to have been born in New York City, various sources who were close to him have alternately indicated that he was born in Louisville, Kentucky, or Baltimore, Maryland. In any case, Cullen, always a private person, never definitively resolved the question. Raised by his paternal grandmother as Countee Porter, Cullen was apparently adopted by the Reverend Frederick A. Cullen after she died when he was around fifteen. Reverend Cullen was an activist pastor of the Salem Methodist Episcopal Church, which was home to a large congregation in Harlem. He eventually became head of the Harlem chapter of the National Association for the Advancement of Colored People, so Cullen found himself living at one of the focal points of the black cultural and political movements near the very beginning of the Harlem Renaissance.

Cullen published his first book of poems, *Color*, in 1925, the year he graduated from New York University. This edition included a number of what were to become his major poems, some of which were simultaneously featured in Alain Locke's *The New Negro*. This remarkable success transformed an extraordinarily talented student into an important poet whose literary reputation was celebrated nationally as well as in Harlem. In 1926, he earned a master's degree in English and French from Harvard and subsequently began writing a column for *Opportunity*, the publication of the National Urban League, in which he articulated his ideas about literature and race. After publishing two more volumes of poetry in 1927, *Copper Sun* and *The Ballad of the Brown Girl*, he won a Guggenheim Fellowship to write poetry in France, one of many literary prizes he was awarded. His fourth collection of poetry, *The Black Christ and Other Poems*, appeared in 1929. Having achieved all of this, he was only twenty-six years old.

By the end of the decade, Cullen was considered a major poet of the black experience in America. Owing to his early interest in Romantic writers — John Keats was a favorite inspiration — he was also read for his treatment of traditional themes concerning love, beauty, and mutability. As he made clear in his 1927 anthology of verse showcasing black poets, he was more interested in being part of "an anthology of verse by Negro poets, rather than an anthology of Negro verse." In a poem titled "To John Keats, Poet, at Spring Time (1925)," he pledges his allegiance to a Romantic poetic tradition; consider this excerpt:

> "John Keats is dead," they say, but I
> Who hear your full insistent cry
> In bud and blossom, leaf and tree,
> Know John Keats still writes poetry.

Though Cullen habitually wrote about race consciousness and issues related to being black in an often-hostile world, he insisted on being recognized for his credentials as a poet rather than for his race, and he did so writing in traditional English forms such as the sonnet and other closed forms that he had studied in college and graduate school. He was critical of the free verse that writers like Langston Hughes coupled with the blues and jazz rhythms, as they moved away from conventional rhyme and meter (see the Perspective "On Racial Poetry" by Cullen, p. 993). Refusing to be limited by racial themes, he believed that other blacks who allowed such limitations in their work did so to their artistic disadvantage. The result was that his poetry was popular among whites as well as blacks in the 1920s.

As meteoric and brilliant as Cullen's early writing career had been, it faded almost as quickly in the 1930s. Despite publication of a satiric novel, *One Way to Heaven* (1932); *The Media and Some Poems* (1935); two books for juveniles in the early 1940s; and several dramatic and musical adaptations, his reputation steadily declined as critics began to perceive him as written out, old-fashioned, and out of touch with contemporary racial issues and the realities of black life in America. His conservative taste in conventional poetic forms was sometimes equated with staunch conservative politics. There can be no question, however, that his most successful poems are firmly based in an awareness of the social injustice produced by racism. Cullen was offered a number of opportunities teaching at the college level, but his overall influence waned as he chose in 1934 to teach French and creative writing at Frederick Douglass Junior High School in Harlem, where he worked until his poor health resulted in an early death in 1946.

Yet Do I Marvel 1925

I doubt not God is good, well-meaning, kind,
And did He stoop to quibble could tell why
The little buried mole continues blind,
Why flesh that mirrors Him must some day die,
Make plain the reason tortured Tantalus   5
Is baited by the fickle fruit, declare
If merely brute caprice dooms Sisyphus
To struggle up a never-ending stair.
Inscrutable His ways are, and immune
To catechism by a mind too strewn   10
With petty cares to slightly understand
What awful brain compels His awful hand.
Yet do I marvel at this curious thing:
To make a poet black, and bid him sing!

CONSIDERATIONS FOR CRITICAL THINKING AND WRITING

1. FIRST RESPONSE. How does the speaker envision the nature of God in lines 1–8?

2. Research the Tantalus and Sisyphus allusions. Why are these Greek myths particularly relevant in the context of the poem?

3. How do you interpret the meaning of "awful" in line 12?

CONNECTION TO ANOTHER SELECTION

1. Compare the view of God in "Yet Do I Marvel" with the perspective offered by the speaker in Emily Dickinson's "I know that He exists" (p. 859).

Incident 1925

Once riding in old Baltimore,
    Heart-filled, head-filled with glee,
I saw a Baltimorean
    Keep looking straight at me.

Now I was eight and very small.   5
    And he was no whit bigger,
And so I smiled, but he poked out
    His tongue, and called me, "Nigger."

I saw the whole of Baltimore
    From May until December;   10

Of all the things that happened there
   That's all that I remember.

CONSIDERATIONS FOR CRITICAL THINKING AND WRITING

1. FIRST RESPONSE. What does the young narrator learn from this "incident"?

2. Why do you think Cullen chose to use the word *whit* in line 6?

3. Discuss the effects of the poem's rhymes.

For a Lady I Know   1925

She even thinks that up in heaven
   Her class lies late and snores,
While poor black cherubs rise at seven
   To do celestial chores.

CONSIDERATIONS FOR CRITICAL THINKING AND WRITING

1. FIRST RESPONSE. How is social commentary made humorous in this poem?

2. Discuss the ways in which carefully chosen diction depicts the poem's characters.

CONNECTION TO ANOTHER SELECTION

1. Compare the tone in "For a Lady I Know" with that in "Incident" (p. 986).

Tableau   1925

Locked arm in arm they cross the way,
   The black boy and the white,
The golden splendor of the day,
   The sable pride of night.

From lowered blinds the dark folk stare,   5
   And here the fair folk talk,
Indignant that these two should dare
   In unison to walk.

Oblivious to look and word
   They pass, and see no wonder   10
That lightning brilliant as a sword
   Should blaze the path of thunder.

CONSIDERATIONS FOR CRITICAL THINKING AND WRITING

1. FIRST RESPONSE. Why do the "folk stare" and become "[i]ndignant"?

2. What is a tableau? Why do you think Cullen chose this as the title?

3. Is it possible to read more into this poem than issues of race? Does Cullen's use of poetic elements, such as diction, tone, or rhythm, contribute to other interpretations of this poem?

CONNECTION TO ANOTHER SELECTION

1. Consider "Tableau" alongside Claude McKay's "The Lynching" (p. 970). How might the two poems speak to each other socially and politically?

From the Dark Tower 1927

We shall not always plant while others reap
The golden increment of bursting fruit,
Not always countenance, abject and mute,
That lesser men should hold their brothers cheap;
Not everlastingly while others sleep   5
Shall we beguile their limbs with mellow flute,
Not always bend to some more subtle brute;
We were not made eternally to weep.
The night whose sable breast relieves the stark,
White stars is no less lovely being dark,   10
And there are buds that cannot bloom at all
In light, but crumple, piteous, and fall;
So in the dark we hide the heart that bleeds,
And wait, and tend our agonizing seeds.

CONSIDERATIONS FOR CRITICAL THINKING AND WRITING

1. FIRST RESPONSE. Explain how the poem's imagery enhances its themes.
2. Discuss the poem's symbols. How do they work together to enrich meaning?
3. Choose a line or phrase from the poem that you think best captures its spirit and could serve as an alternate title. Explain why.

CONNECTION TO ANOTHER SELECTION

1. Compare how issues of social justice are depicted thematically and tonally in "From the Dark Tower" and in Langston Hughes's "Ballad of the Landlord" (p. 982).

To Certain Critics 1929

Then call me traitor if you must,
Shout treason and default!
Say I betray a sacred trust
Aching beyond this vault.
I'll bear your censure as your praise,   5
For never shall the clan

Confine my singing to its ways
Beyond the ways of man.

No racial option narrows grief,
Pain is no patriot,   10
And sorrow plaits her dismal leaf
For all as lief as not.
With blind sheep groping every hill,
Searching an oriflamme,°   *a rallying banner*
How shall the shepherd heart then thrill   15
To only the darker lamb?

CONSIDERATIONS FOR CRITICAL THINKING AND WRITING

1. FIRST RESPONSE. Who is the "clan" in line 6, and why do you think Cullen uses that word to characterize them? What do they want from the speaker?

2. How does the speaker answer the critics in lines 9–16?

3. How does the very diction of this poem challenge "certain critics"?

CONNECTION TO ANOTHER SELECTION

1. Compare the speakers' attitudes toward writing in "To Certain Critics" and in "Yet Do I Marvel" (p. 986).

Perspectives

CLAUDE MCKAY (1889–1948)

On Being Neither a Classicist nor Modernist 1922

[A]lthough very conscious of the new criticisms and trends in poetry, to which I am keenly responsive and receptive, I have adhered to such of the older traditions as I find adequate for my most lawless and revolutionary passions and moods. I have not used patterns, images and words that would stamp me a classicist nor a modernist. My intellect is not scientific enough to range me on the side of either; nor is my knowledge wide enough for me to specialize in any school.

I have never studied poetics; but the forms I have used I am convinced are the ones I can work in with the highest degree of spontaneity and freedom.

I have chosen my melodies and rhythms by instinct, and I have favored words and figures which flow smoothly and harmoniously into my compositions. And in all my moods I have striven to achieve directness, truthfulness and naturalness of expression instead of an enameled originality. I have not hesitated to use words which are old, and in some circles considered poetically overworked and dead, when I thought I could make them glow alive by new manipulation. Nor have I stinted my senses of the pleasure of using the decorative metaphor where it is more truly and vividly beautiful than the exact phrase. But for me there is more quiet delight in "The golden moon of heaven" than in "The terra-cotta disc of cloud-land."

Finally, while I have welcomed criticism, friendly and unfriendly, and listened with willing attention to many varying opinions concerning other poems and my own, I have always, in the summing up, fallen back on my own ear and taste as the arbiter.

From *Harlem Shadows: The Poems of Claude McKay*

CONSIDERATIONS FOR CRITICAL THINKING AND WRITING

1. Compare McKay's description of his own poetry with Langston Hughes's aesthetics of simplicity as outlined by Karen Jackson Ford (below).

2. How accurately do you think McKay's characterization of his poetry fits the selected poems in this chapter? Choose two as the basis of your discussion.

KAREN JACKSON FORD (B. 1956)

Hughes's Aesthetics of Simplicity   1992

The repression of the great bulk of Hughes's poems is the result of chronic critical scorn for their simplicity. Throughout his long career, but especially after his first two volumes of poetry (readers were at first willing to assume that a youthful poet might grow to be more complex), his books received their harshest reviews for a variety of "flaws" that all originate in an aesthetics of simplicity. From his first book, *The Weary Blues* (1926), to his last one, *The Panther and the Lash* (1967), the reviews invoke a litany of faults: the poems are superficial, infantile, silly, small, unpoetic, common, jejune, iterative, and, of course, simple.[1] Even his admirers reluctantly conclude that Hughes's poetics failed. Saunders Redding flatly opposes simplicity and artfulness. "While Hughes's rejection of his own growth shows an admirable loyalty to his self-commitment as the poet of the 'simple, Negro commonfolk' . . . it does a disservice to his art."[2] James Baldwin, who recognizes the potential of simplicity as an artistic principle, faults the poems for "tak[ing] refuge . . . in a fake simplicity in order to avoid the very difficult simplicity of the experience."[3]

Despite a lifetime of critical disappointments, then, Hughes remained loyal to the aesthetic program he had outlined in 1926 in his decisive poetic treatise, "The Negro Artist and the Racial Mountain." There he had predicted that the common people would "give to this world its truly great Negro artist, the one who is not afraid to be himself," a poet who would explore the "great field of unused [folk] material ready for his art" and recognize that this source would provide "sufficient matter to furnish a black artist with a lifetime of creative work."[4] This is clearly a portrait of the poet Hughes would

---

[1] Reviews in which these epithets appear are collected in Edward J. Mullen, *Critical Essays on Langston Hughes* (Boston: G. K. Hall, 1986). [Ford's note.]

[2] Redding's comments appear in Mullen 74. [Ford's note.]

[3] Baldwin's comments appear in Mullen 85. [Ford's note.]

[4] *The Nation* 122 (1926): 692. [Ford's note.]

become, and he maintained his fidelity to this ideal at great cost to his literary reputation.

From "Do Right to Write Right: Langston Hughes's Aesthetics of Simplicity,"
Twentieth Century Literature 38.4 (1992)

CONSIDERATIONS FOR CRITICAL THINKING AND WRITING

1. What was Hughes's rationale for the value of simplicity in his poetry?
2. Explain whether or not you think there is any justification for regarding Hughes's poetry as "superficial" and too "simple."

DAVID CHINITZ (B. 1962)

The Romanticization of Africa in the 1920s   1997

In Europe black culture was an exotic import; in America it was domestic and increasingly mass-produced. If postwar [World War I] disillusionment judged the majority culture mannered, neurotic, and repressive, Americans had an easily accessible alternative. The need for such an Other produced a discourse in which black Americans figured as barely civilized exiles from the jungle, with — so the clichés ran — tom-toms beating in their blood and dark laughter in their souls. The African American became a model of "natural" human behavior to contrast with the falsified, constrained, and impotent modes of the "civilized."

Far from being immune to the lure of this discourse, for the better part of the 1920s Hughes asserted an open pride in the supposed primitive qualities of his race, the atavistic legacy of the African motherland. Unlike most of those who romanticized Africa, Hughes had at least some firsthand experience of the continent; yet he processed what he saw there in images conditioned by European primitivism, rendering "[the land] wild and lovely, the people dark and beautiful, the palm trees tall, the sun bright, and the rivers deep."[1] His short story "Luani of the Jungle," in attempting to glorify aboriginal African vigor as against European anemia, shows how predictable and unextraordinary even Hughes's primitivism could be. To discover in the descendants of idealized Africans the same qualities of innate health, spontaneity, and naturalness requires no great leap; one has only to identify the African American as a displaced primitive, as Hughes does repeatedly in his first book, *The Weary Blues:*

> They drove me out of the forest.
> They took me away from the jungles.
> I lost my trees.
> I lost my silver moons.
>
> Now they've caged me
> In the circus of civilization.[2]

[1] *The Big Sea.* 1940. N.Y.: Thunder's Mouth, 1986, 11. [Chinitz's note.]
[2] *The Weary Blues.* N.Y.: Knopf, 1926, 100. [Chinitz's note.]

Hughes depicts black atavism vividly and often gracefully, yet in a way that is entirely consistent with the popular iconography of the time. His African Americans retain "among the skyscrapers" the primal fears and instincts of their ancestors "among the palms in Africa."[3] The scion of Africa is still more than half primitive: "All the tom-toms of the jungles beat in my blood, / And all the wild hot moons of the jungles shine in my soul."[4]

> From "Rejuvenation through Joy: Langston Hughes, Primitivism and Jazz,"
> in *American Literary History*, Spring 1997

[3] Ibid. 101.
[4] Ibid. 102.

CONSIDERATIONS FOR CRITICAL THINKING AND WRITING

1. According to Chinitz, why did Europeans and Americans romanticize African culture?

2. Consider McKay's "The Tropics in New York" (p. 969) and Hughes's "The Negro Speaks of Rivers" (p. 980) in the context of Chinitz's discussion of "primitivism," and discuss the similarities and differences you see in their approaches.

ALAIN LOCKE (1886–1954)

Review of Georgia Douglas Johnson's Bronze: A Book of Verse   1923

One of Mrs. Johnson's literary virtues is condensation. She often distills the trite and commonplace into an elixir. Following the old-fashioned lyric strain and the sentimentalist cult of the common emotions, she succeeds because by sincerity and condensation, her poetry escapes to a large extent its own limitations. Here in the subject of these verses, there is however a double pitfall; avoiding sentimentality is to come dangerously close to propaganda. This is also deftly avoided — more by instinct than by calculation. Mrs. Johnson's silences and periods are eloquent, she stops short of the preachy and prosaic and is always lyrical and human. Almost before one has shaped his life to "Oh! the pity of it," a certain fresh breeze of faith and courage blows over the heart, and the mind revives to a healthy, humanistic optimist. Mrs. Johnson seems to me to hear a message, a message that gains through being softly but intensely insinuated between the lines of her poems — "Let the traditional instincts of women heal the world that travails under the accumulated woes of the uncompensated instincts of men," or to speak more in her way, "May the saving grace of the mother-heart save humanity."

> From *Crisis*, February 1923

CONSIDERATIONS FOR CRITICAL THINKING AND WRITING

1. What does Locke admire about Johnson's poems? How positive do you think his assessment is of her poetry?

2. What do you think Locke means when he writes, "avoiding sentimentality is to come dangerously close to propaganda"?

3. Explain whether you think Johnson avoids sentimentality in the poems reprinted in this chapter.

COUNTEE CULLEN (1903–1946)
On Racial Poetry 1926

Here is a poet with whom to reckon, to experience, and here and there, with that apologetic feeling of presumption that should companion all criticism, to quarrel.

What has always struck me most forcibly in reading Mr. Hughes' poems has been their utter spontaneity and expression of a unique personality. . . . This poet represents a transcendently emancipated spirit among a class of young writers whose particular battle-cry is freedom. With the enthusiasm of a zealot, he pursues his way, scornful, in subject matter, in photography, and rhythmical treatment, of whatever obstructions time and tradition have placed before him. To him it is essential that he be himself. Essential and commendable surely; yet the thought persists that some of these poems would have been better had Mr. Hughes held himself a bit in check. . . .

If I have the least powers of prediction, the first section of this book, *The Weary Blues,* will be most admired, even if less from intrinsic poetical worth than because of its dissociation from the traditionally poetic. Never having been one to think all subjects and forms proper for poetic consideration, I regard these jazz poems as interlopers in the company of the truly beautiful poems in other sections of the book. They move along with the frenzy and electric heat of a Methodist or Baptist revival meeting, and affect me in much the same manner. The revival meeting excites me, cooling and flushing me with alternate chills and fevers of emotion; so do these poems. But when the storm is over, I wonder if the quiet way of communing is not more spiritual for the God-seeking heart; and in the light of reflection I wonder if jazz poems really belong to that dignified company, that select and austere circle of high literary expression which we call poetry. . . .

Taken as a group the selections in this book seem one-sided to me. They tend to hurl this poet into the gaping pit that lies before all Negro writers, in the confines of which they become racial artists instead of artists pure and simple. There is too much emphasis here on strictly Negro themes; and this is probably an added reason for my coldness toward the jazz poems — they seem to set a too definite limit upon an already limited field.

From *Opportunity: A Journal of Negro Life*

CONSIDERATIONS FOR CRITICAL THINKING AND WRITING

1. In Cullen's review of *The Weary Blues,* what is his "quarrel" (para. 1) with Hughes?
2. Given the tenor of Hughes's comments on racial pride in the excerpt from "The Negro Artist and the Racial Mountain" (p. 962), what do you think his response to Cullen would be?
3. Explain why you agree or disagree with Cullen's view that Hughes's poems are "one-sided" (para. 4).
4. Do you think Cullen's argument is dated, or is it relevant to today's social climate?

ONWUCHEKWA JEMIE (B. 1940)

On Universal Poetry   1976

Hughes entertained no doubts as to the sufficiency and greatness of the molds provided by black music, nor of black life as subject matter. On the question of whether such black matter and manner could attain "universality," Hughes in his Spingarn Speech issued a definitive answer:

> There is so much richness in Negro humor, so much beauty in black dreams, so much dignity in our struggle, and so much universality in our problems, in us — in each living human being of color — that I do not understand the tendency today that some American Negro artists have of seeking to run away from themselves, of running away from us, of being afraid to sing our own songs, paint our own pictures, write about ourselves — when it is our music that has given America its greatest music, our humor that has enriched its entertainment media, our rhythm that has guided its dancing feet from plantation days to the Charleston, the Lindy Hop, and currently the Madison. . . .
>
> Could you possibly be afraid that the rest of the world will not accept it? Our spirituals are sung and loved in the great concert halls of the whole world. Our blues are played from Topeka to Tokyo. Harlem's jive talk delights Hong Kong. Those of our writers who have concerned themselves with our very special problems are translated and read around the world. The local, the regional can — and does — become universal. Sean O'Casey's Irishmen are an example. So I would say to young Negro writers, do not be afraid of yourselves. You are the world.[1]

Hughes's confidence in blackness is a major part of his legacy, for the questions he had to answer have had to be answered over again by subsequent generations of black artists. Black culture is still embattled; and Hughes provides a model for answering the questions and making the choices. Whether they say so or not, those who, like Cullen, . . . plead the need to be "universal" as an excuse for avoiding racial material, or for treating such material from perspectives rooted in alien sensibilities, invariably equate "white" or "Western" with "universal," and "black" or "non-Western" with its opposite, forgetting that the truly universal — that is, the foundation elements of human experience, the circumstances attending birth, growth, decline, and death, the emotions of joy and grief, love and hate, fear and guilt, anger and pain — are common to all humanity. The multiplicity of nations and cultures in the world makes it inevitable that the details and particulars of human experience will vary according to time, place, and circumstance, and it follows that the majority of writers will dramatize and interpret human life according to the usages of their particular nation and epoch. Indeed, the question whether a writer's work is universal or not rarely arises when that writer is European or white American. It arises so frequently in discussions of black writers for no other reason than that the long-standing myth of white superiority and black inferiority has led so many to believe that in literature, and in other areas of life as well, the black particular of universal human experience is less appropriate than the white particular.

From *Langston Hughes: An Introduction to Poetry*

[1] See Hughes, Letter to the Editor, *The Crisis*, 35:9 (September 1928), 302.

CONSIDERATIONS FOR CRITICAL THINKING AND WRITING

1. How does Jemie go beyond Hughes's own argument to make a case for the universality of poetry about black experience?

2. How might Jemie's argument be extended to other minority groups or to women?

3. Do you think that Jemie's or Cullen's argument is more persuasive? Explain your answer.

SUGGESTED TOPICS FOR LONGER PAPERS

1. Discuss the four poets' use of rhyme, meter, and sounds in eight poems of your choice. How do these elements contribute to the poems' meanings?

2. Taken together, how do the four poets' poems provide a critique of relations between blacks and whites in America?

3. Do some exploratory reading, viewing, and listening to learn more about life in Harlem in the 1920s. Based on your research, how effectively do you think Hughes's poetry evokes Harlem life?

37

A THEMATIC CASE STUDY
Love and Longing

For a man to become a poet . . .
he must be in love or miserable.
— GEORGE GORDON, LORD BYRON

© Christie's Images/Corbis.

Behind all the elements that make up a poem, and even behind its cultural contexts and critical reception, lies its theme. Its idea and the point around which the entire poem revolves, the theme is ultimately what we respond to — or fail to respond to. All the other elements, in fact, are typically there to contribute to the theme, whether or not that theme is explicitly stated. Reading thematically means extending what you have learned about the analysis of individual elements at work in the poem to make connections between the text and the world we inhabit.

This chapter, organized into a case study on love poems, focuses on a single theme as it reappears throughout various parts of poetic history. These poems have much to say about human experience — experience that is contradictory, confusing, complicated, and fascinating. You'll find diverse perspectives from different historical, cultural, generational, or political moments. You'll also discover writers who aim to entertain, to describe, to convince, and to complain. After reading these poems in the context of one another, you're likely to come away with a richer understanding of how the themes of love play out in your own life.

Poems about love have probably enchanted and intrigued their hearers since people began making poetry. Like poetry itself, love is, after all, about intensity, acute impressions, and powerful responsibilities. The emotional dimensions of love do not lend themselves to analytic expository essays. Although such writing can be satisfying intellectually, it is most inadequate for evoking and capturing the thick excitement and swooning reveries that love engenders. The poems in this section include spiritual as well as physical explorations of love that range over five centuries. As you'll see, poetic responses to love by men and women can be quite similar as well as different from one another, just as poems from different periods can reflect a variety of values and attitudes toward love. It is indeed an engaging theme — but as you read, don't forget to pay attention to the formal elements of each of these selections and how they work together to create the poem's particular points about love. Also, remember to read not only for the presence of love; many other themes can be found in these works, and many other connections can be made to the literature elsewhere in this anthology.

The oldest love poem in this case study, Christopher Marlowe's "The Passionate Shepherd to His Love," opens with the line, "Come live with me and be my love." This famous pastoral lyric set a tone for love poetry that has been replicated since its publication. Before concluding with "Then live with me and be my love," Marlowe embraces the kinds of generous pleasure that readers have traditionally and happily received for centuries. The feelings, if not the particular images, are likely to be quite familiar to you.

CHRISTOPHER MARLOWE (1564–1593)

The Passionate Shepherd to His Love   1599

Come live with me and be my love,
And we will all the pleasure prove
That valleys, groves, hills, and fields,
Woods, or steepy mountain yields.

And we will sit upon the rocks,   5
Seeing the shepherds feed their flocks,
By shallow rivers to whose falls
Melodious birds sing madrigals.

And I will make thee beds of roses
And a thousand fragrant posies,   10
A cap of flowers, and a kirtle°   *dress or skirt*
Embroidered all with leaves of myrtle;

A gown made of the finest wool
Which from our pretty lambs we pull;
Fair lined slippers for the cold,   15
With buckles of the purest gold;

A belt of straw and ivy buds,
With coral clasps and amber studs:

And if these pleasures may thee move,
Come live with me, and be my love.   20

The shepherd swains shall dance and sing
For thy delight each May morning:
If these delights thy mind may move,
Then live with me and be my love.

CONSIDERATIONS FOR CRITICAL THINKING AND WRITING

1. FIRST RESPONSE. How persuasive do you find the shepherd's arguments to his potential lover?

2. What do you think might be the equivalent of the shepherd's arguments in the twenty-first century? What kinds of appeals and images of love would be made by a contemporary lover?

3. Try writing a response to the shepherd from the female's point of view using Marlowe's rhythms, rhyme scheme, and quatrains.

While Marlowe's shepherd focuses his energies on convincing his potential love to join him (in the delights associated with love), the speaker in the following sonnet by William Shakespeare demonstrates his love for poetry as well and focuses on the beauty of the object of the poem. In doing so, he introduces a theme that has become a perennial challenge to love — the corrosive, destructive nature of what Shakespeare shockingly calls "sluttish time." His resolution of this issue is intriguing: see if you agree with it.

WILLIAM SHAKESPEARE (1564–1616)

Not marble, nor the gilded monuments   1609

Not marble, nor the gilded monuments
Of princes, shall outlive this powerful rhyme;
But you shall shine more bright in these conténts
Than unswept stone, besmeared with sluttish time.
When wasteful war shall statues overturn,   5
And broils root out the work of masonry,
Nor Mars his° swords nor war's quick fire shall burn   *possessive of Mars*
The living record of your memory.
'Gainst death and all-oblivious enmity
Shall you pace forth; your praise shall still find room   10
Even in the eyes of all posterity
That wear this world out to the ending doom.
   So, till the judgment that yourself arise,
   You live in this, and dwell in lovers' eyes.

CONSIDERATIONS FOR CRITICAL THINKING AND WRITING

1. FIRST RESPONSE. What do you think is the central point of this poem? Explain whether you agree or disagree with its theme.

2. How does "sluttish time" (line 4) represent the poem's major conflict?

3. Consider whether this poem is more about the poet's loved one or the poet's love of his own poetry.

CONNECTIONS TO OTHER SELECTIONS

1. Compare the theme of this poem with that of Andrew Marvell's "To His Coy Mistress" (p. 647), paying particular attention to the speaker's beliefs about how time affects love.

2. Discuss whether you find this love poem more or less appealing than Marlowe's "The Passionate Shepherd to His Love" (p. 997). As you make this comparison, explain what the criteria for an appealing love poem should be.

As Shakespeare's speaker presents a love that will withstand the destruction of time, Anne Bradstreet's "To My Dear and Loving Husband" evokes a marital love that confirms a connection that transcends space and matter as well as time. Although Bradstreet wrote more than three centuries ago, such devotion remains undated for many (but, of course, not all) readers of love poetry. She begins, naturally enough, with the pleasure and paradox of how two people can be one.

ANNE BRADSTREET (CA. 1612–1672)

To My Dear and Loving Husband   1678

If ever two were one, then surely we.
If ever man were loved by wife, then thee;
If ever wife was happy in a man,
Compare with me, ye women, if you can.
I prize thy love more than whole mines of gold   5
Or all the riches that the East doth hold.
My love is such that rivers cannot quench,
Nor ought but love from thee, give recompense.
Thy love is such I can no way repay,
The heavens reward thee manifold, I pray.   10
Then while we live, in love let's so persevere
That when we live no more, we may live ever.

CONSIDERATIONS FOR CRITICAL THINKING AND WRITING

1. FIRST RESPONSE. Describe the poem's tone. Is it what you'd expect from a seventeenth-century Puritan? Why or why not?

2. Explain whether Bradstreet's devotion is directed more toward her husband here on earth or toward the eternal rewards of heaven.

3. What is the paradox of the final line? How is it resolved?

CONNECTION TO ANOTHER SELECTION

1. How does the theme of this poem compare with that of Bradstreet's "Before the Birth of One of Her Children" (p. 1046)? Explain why you find the poems consistent or contradictory.

The remaining poems in this case study are modern and contemporary pieces that both maintain and revise the perspectives on love provided by Marlowe, Shakespeare, and Bradstreet. As you read them, consider what each adds to your understanding of the others and of love in general.

ELIZABETH BARRETT BROWNING (1806–1861)

How Do I Love Thee? Let Me Count the Ways   1850

How do I love thee? Let me count the ways.
I love thee to the depth and breadth and height
My soul can reach, when feeling out of sight
For the ends of being and ideal grace.
I love thee to the level of every day's   5
Most quiet need, by sun and candle-light.
I love thee freely, as men strive for right.
I love thee purely, as they turn from praise.
I love thee with the passion put to use
In my old griefs, and with my childhood's faith.   10
I love thee with a love I seemed to lose
With my lost saints. I love thee with the breath,
Smiles, tears, of all my life; and, if God choose,
I shall but love thee better after death.

CONSIDERATIONS FOR CRITICAL THINKING AND WRITING

1. FIRST RESPONSE. This poem has remained extraordinarily popular for more than 150 years. Why do you think it has been so often included in collections of love poems? What is its appeal? Does it speak to a contemporary reader? To you?

2. Comment on the effect of the diction. What kind of tone does it create?

3. Would you characterize this poem as having a religious theme — or is love a substitute for religion?

CONNECTION TO ANOTHER SELECTION

1. Compare and contrast the images, tone, and theme of this poem with those of Christina Georgina Rossetti's "Promises Like Pie-Crust" (p. 1063). Explain why you find one poem more promising than the other.

EDNA ST. VINCENT MILLAY (1892–1950)

Recuerdo°   1922

We were very tired, we were very merry —
We had gone back and forth all night on the
       ferry.

Recuerdo: I remember (Spanish).

It was bare and bright, and smelled like a
    stable —
But we looked into a fire, we leaned across a
    table,
We lay on a hill-top underneath the moon; 5
And the whistles kept blowing, and the dawn
    came soon.

We were very tired, we were very merry —
We had gone back and forth all night on the ferry;
And you ate an apple, and I ate a pear,
From a dozen of each we had bought somewhere; 10
And the sky went wan, and the wind came cold,
And the sun rose dripping, a bucketful of gold.

We were very tired, we were very merry,
We had gone back and forth all night on the ferry.
We hailed, "Good morrow, mother!" to a shawl-covered head, 15
And bought a morning paper, which neither of us read;
And she wept, "God bless you!" for the apples and pears,
And we gave her all our money but our subway fares.

CONSIDERATIONS FOR CRITICAL THINKING AND WRITING

1. FIRST RESPONSE. This poem was a very popular representation of New York City bohemian life in Greenwich Village during the 1920s. What do you think made "Recuerdo" so appealing then?
2. How does the repetition in the first two lines of each stanza connect sound to sense through the rhythm of the lines?
3. Explain how love and generosity are evoked in the poem.

CONNECTION TO ANOTHER SELECTION

1. Compare the tone in this poem with the tone in Christina Georgina Rossetti's "Promises Like Pie-Crust" (p. 1063).

EDNA ST. VINCENT MILLAY (1892–1950)

I, Being Born a Woman and Distressed 1923

I, being born a woman and distressed
By all the needs and notions of my kind,
Am urged by your propinquity to find
Your person fair, and feel a certain zest
To bear your body's weight upon my breast: 5
So subtly is the fume of life designed,
To clarify the pulse and cloud the mind,
And leave me once again undone, possessed.
Think not for this, however, the poor treason

Of my stout blood against my staggering brain,   10
I shall remember you with love, or season
My scorn with pity, — let me make it plain:
I find this frenzy insufficient reason
For conversation when we meet again.

CONSIDERATIONS FOR CRITICAL THINKING AND WRITING

1. FIRST RESPONSE. Describe the speaker's attitudes toward love and sex.

2. What kind of sonnet is this? How is the poem's theme related to this traditional form?

3. Characterize the speaker. What is your opinion of her sensibilities?

CONNECTION TO ANOTHER SELECTION

1. Discuss Millay's treatment of romantic love in this poem and in "Recuerdo" (p. 1000). Read the section on feminist criticism (pp. 1655–56) in Chapter 51, "Critical Strategies for Reading." What do you think a feminist critic would make of these two poems' coming from the same poet?

C. K. WILLIAMS (1936–2015)

Love: Beginnings   1994

They're at that stage where so much desire streams between them,
    so much frank need and want,
so much absorption in the other and the self and the self-admiring
    entity and unity, the make —
her mouth so full, breast so lifted, head thrown back *so* far in her
    laughter at his laughter,
he so solid, planted, oaky, firm, so resonantly factual in the headiness
    of being craved so,
she almost wreathed upon him as they intertwine again, touch again,
    cheek, lip, shoulder, brow,
every glance moving toward the sexual, every glance away soaring
    back in flame into the sexual —
that just to watch them is to feel again that hitching in the groin, that
    filling of the heart,
the old, sore heart, the battered, foundered, faithful heart, snorting
    again, stamping in its stall.

CONSIDERATIONS FOR CRITICAL THINKING AND WRITING

1. FIRST RESPONSE. What is the speaker's attitude toward youthful passion? How well do you think the poem captures that experience?

2. Explain how the imagery evokes the tone.

3. How do the concluding images associated with the heart affect your reading of the title?

CONNECTION TO ANOTHER SELECTION

1. Discuss love's ends and beginnings in this poem and in Luisa Lopez's "Junior Year Abroad" (p. 1006).

JOAN MURRAY (B. 1945)

Play-by-Play 1997

Yaddo°

Would it surprise the young men
playing softball on the hill to hear the women
on the terrace admiring their bodies:
the slim waist of the pitcher, the strength
of the runner's legs, the torso of the catcher   5
rising off his knees to toss the ball back to the mound?
Would it embarrass them
to hear two women, sitting together after dinner,
praising even their futile motions:
the flex of a batter's hips   10
before his missed swing, the wide-spread stride
of a man picked off his base, the intensity
on the new man's face
as he waits on deck and fans the air?

Would it annoy them, the way some women   15
take offense when men caress them with their eyes?
And why should it surprise me that these women,
well past sixty, haven't put aside desire
but sit at ease and in pleasure,
watching the young men move above the rose garden   20
where the marble Naiads
pose and yawn in their fountain?
Who better than these women, with their sweaters
draped across their shoulders, their perspectives
honed from years of lovers, to recognize   25
the beauty that would otherwise
go unnoticed on this hill?
And will it compromise their pleasure
if I sit down at their table to listen
to the play-by-play and see it through their eyes?   30

Would it distract the young men if they realized
that three women laughing softly on the terrace
above closed books and half-filled wineglasses
are moving beside them on the field?
Would they want to know how they've been   35
held to the light till some motion or expression

Yaddo: An artist's colony in Saratoga Springs, New York.

showed the unsuspected loveliness
in a common shape or face?
Wouldn't they have liked to see how they looked
down there, as they stood for a moment at the plate,   40
bathed in the light of perfect expectation,
before their shadows lengthened, before they
walked together up the darkened hill,
so beautiful they would not have
recognized themselves?   45

CONSIDERATIONS FOR CRITICAL THINKING AND WRITING

1. FIRST RESPONSE. How would you answer the series of nine questions posed by
   the speaker?
2. What do you think the young men would have to say to the older women gazing at them?
3. Explain how the "marble Naiads" (line 21) help set the tone.
4. Discuss the significance of the title.

CONNECTION TO ANOTHER SELECTION

1. Write an essay on the nature of desire in this poem and in Edna St. Vincent
   Millay's "I, Being Born a Woman and Distressed" (p. 1001).

LAURE-ANNE BOSSELAAR (B. 1943)

The Pleasures of Hating   2001

I hate Mozart. Hate him with that healthy
pleasure one feels when exasperation has

crescendoed, when lungs, heart, throat,
and voice explode at once: *I hate that!* —

there's bliss in this, rapture. My shrink   5
tried to disabuse me, convinced I use Amadeus

as a prop: *Think further, your father perhaps?*
I won't go back, think of the shrink

with a powdered wig, pinched lips, mole:
a transference, he'd say, *a relapse:* so be it.   10

I hate broccoli, chain saws, patchouli, bra-
clasps that draw dents in your back, roadblocks,

men in black kneesocks, sandals and shorts —
I *love* hating that. Loathe stickers on tomatoes,

jerky, deconstruction, nazis, doilies. I delight   15
in detesting. And love loving so much after that.

CONSIDERATIONS FOR CRITICAL THINKING AND WRITING

1. FIRST RESPONSE. In what sense can this be read as a love poem? Explain why it does or does not fit your definition of a love poem.
2. How do you interpret the poem's final two sentences?
3. Describe what you think is the relationship of love to hate in the poem.

CONNECTION TO ANOTHER SELECTION

1. How might Emily Dickinson's "Water, is taught by thirst" (p. 838) be read as a gloss on this poem?

BILLIE BOLTON (B. 1950)

Memorandum   2004

Ashley G. Stollar.

TO: My Boyfriend from Hell
FR: Me
RE: Shit I Never Want to Hear Another Word
     About as Long as I Live

1. Your Addled Thoughts. Anything about your ongoing interest in Lucy Liu's legs, Shania Twain's bellybutton, or Reese Witherspoon's whatever; your must-see TV dramas, your fantasy baseball addiction, or your addictions period. Anything about going anywhere with you at any time including, but not limited to: Sam's Club, Big Lots, Waffle House, church fish fries, local snake round-ups or Amvet turkey shoots, unless you promise to be the turkey.

2. Your Wireless Connection. Anything about your stage-four cell phone habit; the dames who have your cell phone number and why; who's on your speed-dial list or who left a voice mail message; anything about cell phone rebates, late fees, roaming charges, contracts or dropping your cell phone in the john by accident, even if you flush it and walk away.

3. Your Adolescent Only Child. Anything about his bed-wetting or fire-setting habits; his gang affiliation, court dates or swastika tattoo; anything about his tantrums, seizures or deep psychological need for video games and fruit roll-ups; anything about his pathological grudge against mankind or his particular beef against me.

4. Your Significant Others (female). Anything about the redneck redhead you banged in high school, the long-haired potheads you balled in your hippie days, the white trash airhead you married or the blue-haired battle-ax who pats you on the rump and pays for your dinner. Anything about your devotion to your long-suffering mother, your loopy sisters, or even the Blessed Virgin.

CONSIDERATIONS FOR CRITICAL THINKING AND WRITING

1. FIRST RESPONSE. What makes this a poem rather than simply a memo?
2. How do the speaker's diction and choice of details reveal her own personality?
3. CREATIVE RESPONSE. Using Bolton's style, tone, and form as inspiration, write a reply from the boyfriend's point of view.

CONNECTION TO ANOTHER SELECTION

1. Compare the use of descriptive detail to create tone in "Memorandum" and in Joan Murray's "Play-by-Play" (p. 1003).

LUISA LOPEZ (B. 1957)

Junior Year Abroad   2002

We were amateurs, that winter in Paris.

The summer before we agreed:
he would come over to keep me company at Christmas.
But the shelf life of my promise expired
before the date on his airline ticket.   5
So we ended up together under a French muslin sky.

Together alone.

Certainly I was alone, inside dark hair, inside foreign blankets,
against white sheets swirling like a cocoon,
covering my bare skin,   10
keeping me apart.
The invited man snored beside me not knowing
I didn't love him anymore.

At first I tried,
perky as a circus pony waiting at the airport gate   15
to be again as I once had been.
But even during the first night
betrayal, the snake under the evergreen,
threw me into nightmares
of floods and dying birds.   20

You see, a new boy just last month
had raised my shy hand to his warm mouth
and kissed the inside of my palm.
I thought "this is impossible,
too close to Christmas, too soon, too dangerous."   25

In Paris I concede:
deceiving my old lover, the one now stirring in his sleep
is even more dangerous.
See him opening his eyes, looking at my face,
dropping his eyes to my breasts and smiling   30
as if he were seeing two old friends? Dangerous.

When I move away and hold the sheet against
myself he,
sensing what this means,
refuses, adamant yet polite,
to traffic in the currency of my rejection.   35

He made a journey. I offered a welcome.
Why should he give me up?

CONSIDERATIONS FOR CRITICAL THINKING AND WRITING

1. **FIRST RESPONSE.** This poem is about strength and dominance as much as it is about love and attraction. Discuss the ways in which the two characters are vying for control.

2. Why is the setting important? How might the sense of the poem be different if this were happening during a typical school year as opposed to "Junior Year Abroad"?

3. Do you think the speaker has the right to reject her old boyfriend under these circumstances? Does the old boyfriend have the right to expect a "welcome" (line 37) since he was invited to visit?

4. The speaker is wrapped in sheets that are like a "cocoon" (line 9). What does this suggest about the changes she is experiencing during this encounter?

CONNECTION TO ANOTHER SELECTION

1. Compare this 2002 poem about young love with A. E. Housman's poem "When I was one-and-twenty" (p. 765), published in 1896. How much has the situation changed in a hundred years?

SUGGESTED TOPICS FOR LONGER PAPERS

1. Choose one of the love poems in this chapter and compare it with the lyrics of a contemporary love song in terms of poetic elements such as diction, tone, images, figures of speech, sounds, and rhythms.

2. Select any two poems from this chapter that were published before 1900 and compare their styles and themes with those of two poems published after 1900. Which set of poems, the early or the later, comes closest to representing your own sensibilities concerning love? Explain why.

38

A THEMATIC CASE STUDY
Humor and Satire

I think like a poet, and behave like a poet. Occasionally I need to sit in the corner for bad behavior.

— GARY SOTO

Courtesy of Gary Soto.

Poetry can be a hoot. There are plenty of poets that leave you smiling, grinning, chuckling, and laughing out loud because they use language that is witty, surprising, teasing, or satirical. Occasionally, their subject matter is unexpectedly mundane. There's a poem in this chapter, for example, titled "Suburban" (p. 1009) that reflects on a fastidious neighbor who complains about an errant dog wandering into her yard. Although this topic might seem to warrant a short leash, John Ciardi's treatment deftly shapes this unlikely material into a memorable satiric theme.

Sadly, however, poetry is too often burdened with a reputation for only being formal and serious, and readers sometimes show their deference by feeling intimidated and humbled in its earnest, weighty presence. After all, poetry frequently concerns itself with matters of great consequence: its themes contemplate subjects such as God and immortality, love and death, war and peace, injustice and outrage, racism and societal ills, deprivation and disease, alienation and angst, totalitarianism and terrorism, as well as a host of other tragic grievances and agonies that humanity might suffer. For readers of the *Onion*, a widely distributed satirical newspaper also available online, this prevailing grim reputation is humorously framed in a bogus story about National

Poetry Month, celebrated each April to increase an awareness of the value of poetry in American life. The brief article (April 27, 2005) quotes a speaker at a fund-raising meeting of the "American Poetry Prevention Society" who cautions that "we must stop this scourge before more lives are exposed to poetry." He warns that "young people, particularly morose high-school and college students, are very susceptible to this terrible affliction." The *Onion's* satire peels away the erroneous assumption that sorrow and tears are the only appropriate responses to a poetry "infection."

Poetry — at least in its clichéd popular form — is nearly always morosely dressed in black and rarely smiles. This severe image of somber profundity unfortunately tailors our expectations so that we assume that serious poetry cannot be playful and even downright funny or, putting the issue another way, that humorous poetry cannot be thoughtful and significant. The poems in this chapter demonstrate that serious poems can be funny and that comic poems can be thoughtful. Their humor, sometimes subtle, occasionally even savage, will serve to remind you that laughter engenders thought as well as pleasure.

JOHN CIARDI (1916–1986)

Suburban   1978

Yesterday Mrs. Friar phoned. "Mr. Ciardi,
  how do you do?" she said. "I am sorry to say
this isn't exactly a social call. The fact is
  your dog has just deposited — forgive me —
a large repulsive object in my petunias."   5

I thought to ask, "Have you checked the rectal grooving
  for a positive I.D.?" My dog, as it happened,
was in Vermont with my son, who had gone fishing —
  if that's what one does with a girl, two cases of beer,
and a borrowed camper. I guessed I'd get no trout.   10

But why lose out on organic gold for a wise crack?
  "Yes, Mrs. Friar," I said, "I understand."
"Most kind of you," she said. "Not at all," I said.
  I went with a spade. She pointed, looking away.
"I always have loved dogs," she said, "but really!"   15

I scooped it up and bowed. "The animal of it.
  I hope this hasn't upset you, Mrs. Friar."
"Not really," she said, "but really!" I bore the turd
  across the line to my own petunias
and buried it till the glorious resurrection   20

when even these suburbs shall give up their dead.

CONSIDERATIONS FOR CRITICAL THINKING AND WRITING

1. **FIRST RESPONSE.** How does the speaker transform Mrs. Friar into a symbolic figure of the suburbs?

2. Why do you suppose Ciardi focuses on this particular incident to make a comment on the suburbs? What is the speaker's attitude toward suburban life?

3. CREATIVE RESPONSE. Write a one-paragraph physical description of Mrs. Friar that captures her character.

CONNECTION TO ANOTHER SELECTION

1. Compare the speakers' voices in "Suburban" and in John Updike's "Dog's Death" (p. 592).

E. E. CUMMINGS (1894–1962)

when serpents bargain for the right to squirm   1950

when serpents bargain for the right to squirm
and the sun strikes to gain a living wage —
when thorns regard their roses with alarm
and rainbows are insured against old age

when every thrush may sing no new moon in   5
if all screech-owls have not okayed his voice
— and any wave signs on the dotted line
or else an ocean is compelled to close

when the oak begs permission of the birch
to make an acorn — valleys accuse their   10
mountains of having altitude — and march
denounces april as a saboteur

then we'll believe in that incredible
unanimal mankind (and not until)

CONSIDERATIONS FOR CRITICAL THINKING AND WRITING

1. FIRST RESPONSE. In what sense can this be read as a love poem? Explain why it does or does not fit your definition of a love poem.

2. How do you interpret the poem's final two sentences?

3. Describe what you think is the relationship of love to hate in the poem.

CONNECTION TO ANOTHER SELECTION

1. How might Emily Dickinson's "Water, is taught by thirst" (p. 838) be read as a gloss on this poem?

HARRYETTE MULLEN (B. 1953)

Dim Lady   2002

My honeybunch's peepers are nothing like neon. Today's special at Red Lobster is redder than her kisser. If Liquid Paper is white, her racks are institutional beige. If her mop were Slinkys, dishwater Slinkys would grow on her noggin. I have seen tablecloths in Shakey's Pizza Parlors, red and white, but no such picnic colors do I see in her mug. And in some minty-fresh mouthwashes there is more sweetness than in the garlic breeze my main squeeze wheezes. I love to hear her rap, yet I'm aware that Muzak has a hipper beat. I don't know any Marilyn Monroes. My ball and chain is plain from head to toe. And yet, by gosh, my scrumptious Twinkie has as much sex appeal for me as any lanky model or platinum movie idol who's hyped beyond belief.

© Judy Natal 2015, www.judynatal.com.

Considerations for Critical Thinking and Writing

1. FIRST RESPONSE. How does the poem's diction reveal the speaker as well as the "Lady"?

2. Why do you suppose Mullen chose to write a prose poem rather than a sonnet to praise the "Lady"?

Connection to Another Selection

1. Compare line for line "Dim Lady" with William Shakespeare's "My mistress' eyes are nothing like the sun" (p. 781). Which tribute do you prefer, the original parody of a love poem or the modern version?

Ronald Wallace (b. 1945)

In a Rut   2002

She dogs me while
I try to take a catnap.
Of course, I'm playing possum but
I can feel her watching me,
eagle-eyed, like a hawk.   5
She snakes over to my side
of the bed, and continues to
badger me. I may be a rat, but
I won't let her get my goat.
I refuse to make an   10
ass of myself, no matter
how mulish I feel.
I'm trying to make a
bee-line for sleep, but
You're a turkey! she says, and   15
I'm thinking she's no
spring chicken. She *is* a busy beaver,
though, always trying to ferret
things out. She's a bit batty,
in fact, a bit cuckoo, but   20

Unrestrained in expressing what they see,
the young are often right. She'd seen white hair.
But for me that day striding up the canyon's
steep hill, four miles into my morning walk,
old age was only a state of mind —   10
or almost so. Right before the school,
I'd detoured onto a quiet side street
and climbed among some bushes, having spent
the last mile looking for a place to pee.

CONSIDERATIONS FOR CRITICAL THINKING AND WRITING

1. FIRST RESPONSE. How does the man's choice of details to describe his encounter with the girl reveal what he thinks about getting older?

2. How would you read this poem differently if it had concluded at the end of line 10?

3. Why do you think the poet places the girl on a swing rather than on some other kind of playground equipment?

CONNECTION TO ANOTHER SELECTION

1. Compare Tilley's treatment of aging and E. E. Cummings's perspective in "old age sticks" (p. 807).

PETER SCHMITT (B. 1958)
Friends with Numbers   1995

If you make friends with numbers,
you don't need any other friends.
   — Shakuntala Devi, math genius

They are not hard to get to know:
6 and 9 keep changing their minds,
8 cuts the most graceful figure
but sleeps for an eternity,
and 7, lucky 7, takes   5
an arrow to his heart always.
5, halfway to somewhere, only
wants to patch his unicycle
tire, and 4, who'd like to stand for
something solid, has never had   10
two feet on the ground, yet flutters
gamely in the breeze like a flag.
3, for all his literary
accomplishments and pretensions
to immortality, is still   15
(I can tell you) not half the man
8 is asleep or awake. 1,

little 1. I know him better
than all the others, these numbers
who are all my friends. Only 2,   20
that strange smallest prime, can I count
as just a passing acquaintance.
Divisible by only 1
and herself, she seems on the verge,
yet, of always coming apart.   25
And though she eludes me, swanlike,
though I'd love to know her better,
still I am fine, there are others,
many, I have friends in numbers.

CONSIDERATIONS FOR CRITICAL THINKING AND WRITING

1. **FIRST RESPONSE.** How does the personification of numbers create characters in the poem?
2. Explain how the speaker's use of language helps to characterize him.
3. Discuss the various ways in which the single digits are transformed into individual visual images.

CONNECTION TO ANOTHER SELECTION

1. Discuss the originality — the fresh and unusual approach to their respective subject matter — in Schmitt's poem and in Martín Espada's poem below. What makes these poems so interesting?

MARTÍN ESPADA (B. 1957)

The Community College Revises Its Curriculum in Response to Changing Demographics   2000

SPA 100 Conversational Spanish
2 credits

The course
is especially concerned
with giving police
the ability
to express themselves
tersely
in matters of interest
to them

CONSIDERATIONS FOR CRITICAL THINKING AND WRITING

1. **FIRST RESPONSE.** What sort of political comment do you think Espada makes in this poem?

2. Would this be a poem without the title? Explain your answer.

3. CREATIVE RESPONSE. Choose a course description from your school's catalog and organize the catalog copy into poetic lines. Provide your poem with a title that offers a provocative commentary about it.

CONNECTION TO ANOTHER SELECTION

1. Compare the themes in Espada's poem and in Donald Justice's "Order in the Streets" (p. 816).

GEORGE BILGERE (B. 1951)

Stupid   2003

We were so fucked up,
She says to her friend, laughing.
We were so fucked up, it was . . .
It was like . . .
And her friend says, *yeah,*   5
We totally were.

And I wonder
What it would be like
To be permanently stupid,
To go through life   10
At that altitude, just clearing
The lowest rooftops and TV aerials,
Heading for the mountains . . .

My friends and I used to try it,
Sitting around a day-glo bong, brains   15
Turned to low, then lower,
So unmoored and adrift,
So hopelessly out of range
Of our calls to the lost
Vessels of each other,   20

We could only giggle, wondering,
Even as we did so,
Why.

Now and then
The crippled sub of an idea   25
Would try to surface out there
On the stoned moment's
Glassy horizon

Where the strawberry-scented candle
Burned like . . .   30

Like . . .

Considerations for Critical Thinking and Writing

1. FIRST RESPONSE. Describe the shift in tone from the first to the second stanza.
2. How are the metaphors in the poem related to one another?
3. What is the effect of the final line?

Connection to Another Selection

1. Discuss the themes of this poem and of Jim Tilley's "The Big Questions" (p. 612).

Gary Soto (b. 1952)

Mexicans Begin Jogging   1995

At the factory I worked
In the fleck of rubber, under the press
Of an oven yellow with flame,
Until the border patrol opened
Their vans and my boss waved for us to run.   5
"Over the fence, Soto," he shouted,
And I shouted that I was American.
"No time for lies," he said, and pressed
A dollar in my palm, hurrying me
Through the back door.   10

Since I was on his time, I ran
And became the wag to a short tail of Mexicans —
Ran past the amazed crowds that lined
The street and blurred like photographs, in rain.
I ran from that industrial road to the soft   15
Houses where people paled at the turn of an autumn sky.
What could I do but yell *vivas*
To baseball, milkshakes, and those sociologists
Who would clock me
As I jog into the next century   20
On the power of a great, silly grin.

Considerations for Critical Thinking and Writing

1. FIRST RESPONSE. What ironies are present in this poem?
2. Soto was born and raised in Fresno, California. How does this fact affect your reading of the first stanza?
3. In what different ways does the speaker become "the wag" (line 12) in this poem? (You may want to look up the word to consider all possible meanings.)
4. Explain lines 17–21. What serious point is being made in these humorous lines?

CONNECTION TO ANOTHER SELECTION

1. Compare the tone of this poem and of Martín Espada's "The Community College Revises Its Curriculum in Response to Changing Demographics" (p. 1015).

DAVID WAGONER (B. 1926)

Improving My Mind 2012

You were supposed to do it
by reading Good Books, meaning
the deep, well-meaning ones
about the Improved People
who had pure thoughts   5
    and serious, good ideas
    about what to do when
    they got up in the morning
    and went to school on time
    and studied and, after,   10
spent time sitting alone
between the covers of books
to connect each topic sentence
with the rest of its paragraph
and then were able to write   15
    an outline and précis
    to preserve it in memory —
    if you actually kept skimming
    all the way to the end
    and only skipped now and then   20
so you could feel — especially
if told to — you'd improved
your mind, which included
all those thoughts you took
to bed, to sleep, to dream with   25
    and woke up without. Of course,
    what you really liked in between
    were books about Flying Aces
    and Flatfeet and Ape Men
    and Cackling Scientists   30
who wanted to bomb the moon
and Slinky Women who wouldn't
have dreamed of wearing brassieres
and Big, Bold Men who'd been boys
only a week ago.   35

CONSIDERATIONS FOR CRITICAL THINKING AND WRITING

1. FIRST RESPONSE. What kinds of readers are described in the poem? How would you categorize your own reading?

2. How are the "Good Books" (line 2) distinguished from those in lines 28–35? Which do you prefer? Why?

3. Discuss whether or not you think there is an inevitable difference between academic reading and "what you really liked" (line 27).

CONNECTION TO ANOTHER SELECTION

1. Discuss the thematic similarities and differences in "Improving My Mind" and in Philip Larkin's "A Study of Reading Habits" (p. 601).

THOMAS R. MOORE (B. 1941)

At the Berkeley Free Speech Café   2010

The students are seated,
one to a table,
at tables for two,
ears wired,
laptops humming,   5
cell phones buzzing,
fingers texting,
iPods thumping,
toes drumming,
email flashing,   10
lattés cooling,
textbooks open,
reading for an exam
in Issues in Contemporary Culture 102.

CONSIDERATIONS FOR CRITICAL THINKING AND WRITING

1. FIRST RESPONSE. Discuss the appropriateness of the poem's title and the title of the course.

2. How do the sounds and rhythm help establish tone?

CONNECTION TO ANOTHER SELECTION

1. Write an essay comparing this poem with Tony Hoagland's "America" (p. 1032).

X. J. KENNEDY (B. 1929)

On a Young Man's Remaining an Undergraduate for Twelve Years   2006

Sweet scent of pot, the mellow smell of beer,
  Frat-house debates on sex, on God's existence
Lasting all night, vacations thrice a year,
  Pliant coeds who put up no resistance

Are all life is. Who'd give a damn for earning,   5
   Who'd struggle by degrees to lofty places
When he can loll, adrift in endless learning,
   In a warm sea of academic stasis?

He's famous now: the everlasting kid.
   After conducting an investigation,   10
Two deans resigned, to do just what he did.
   They couldn't fault his ratiocination.

CONSIDERATIONS FOR CRITICAL THINKING AND WRITING

1. FIRST RESPONSE. Comment on the description of undergraduate life in the first stanza and the effect of the enjambment in lines 4 and 5.
2. Discuss the sound effects in stanza three. How are they related to sense?
3. Why is "ratiocination" (line 12) just the right word in this context?

39

A THEMATIC CASE STUDY
The Natural World

© Bettmann/Corbis.

Writing is my salvation. If I didn't write, what would I do?
—MAXINE KUMIN

This chapter is a collection of poems thematically related to the natural environment we inhabit. Though poets may have a popular (and mistaken) reputation for being somewhat ethereal in their concerns, they still breathe the same air as the rest of us. Not surprisingly, because poets instinctively draw inspiration from nature, they are often as delighted to praise its vivid joys as they are compelled to warn us when it is abused. Having neither the technical knowledge of scientists nor the political means of legislators to defend the environment, poets nevertheless lend a voice to remind us of its pleasures, importance, and urgent fragility. The celebration of nature has always, of course, been a major poetic genre, but only fairly recently has poetry treated nature as a cause célèbre. Nature has forever aroused poets to write poems and so, given the contemporary environmental issues that have descended upon us, it is only fitting that poetry is enlisted to uphold nature.

The poems in this chapter provide some contemporary reflections on our relationship to nature. Though they are not representative of all the kinds of environmental poetry being written today, these nine poems do offer a range of voices and issues that can serve as prompts for seeing and responding to your own natural environment through poetic language. You'll find among them detailed and vivid observations of nature, as well as meditations on climate change, the sustainability of the wild, and, indeed, the future of the planet. Some of the voices are quietly thoughtful, like Wendell Berry's "The Peace of Wild Things" (p. 1023), while others are ironic or funny, and a couple will even holler at you, like Maxine Kumin's "The Whole Hog" (p. 1027).

"Optimism," by Jane Hirshfield, offers a nuanced appreciation of nature that is linked to a particular state of mind.

JANE HIRSHFIELD (B. 1953)

Optimism   2002

More and more I have come to admire resilience.
Not the simple resistance of a pillow, whose foam returns over and
over to the same shape, but the sinuous tenacity of a tree: finding the
light newly blocked on one side,
it turns in another.
A blind intelligence, true.
But out of such persistence arose turtles, rivers, mitochondria, figs —
all this resinous, unretractable earth.

CONSIDERATIONS FOR CRITICAL THINKING AND WRITING

1. FIRST RESPONSE. How do trees inform the speaker's description of optimism?
2. Discuss the way nature is envisioned in the poem.
3. How is optimism defined by the speaker? To what extent does this definition match your own perspective?

CONNECTIONS TO OTHER SELECTIONS

1. Contrast the view of nature presented in "Optimism" with that in Emily Dickinson's "Apparently with no surprise" (p. 860) and Robert Frost's "Design" (p. 885).
2. Discuss how tone affects your reading of the themes in "Optimism" and in Wendell Berry's "The Peace of Wild Things" (p. 1023). To what extent does each poem approximate your own response to nature?

The rest of the poems in this chapter explore the natural world inhabited with human beings. What is never absent, however, is the human perception that creates the poems.

WENDELL BERRY (B. 1934)

The Peace of Wild Things   1968

When despair for the world grows in me
and I wake in the night at the least sound
in fear of what my life and my children's lives may be,
I go and lie down where the wood drake
rests in his beauty on the water, and the great heron feeds.   5
I come into the peace of wild things
who do not tax their lives with forethought
of grief. I come into the presence of still water.
And I feel above me the day-blind stars
waiting with their light. For a time   10
I rest in the grace of the world, and am free.

CONSIDERATIONS FOR CRITICAL THINKING AND WRITING

1. FIRST RESPONSE. How does the diction in this poem present nature as more
   than simply an escape from despair and fear?

2. Consider this response by a student to Berry's poem: "The images are pleasant
   enough, but the overall effect seems sentimental to me." What do you think?

CONNECTION TO OTHER SELECTIONS

1. Discuss the similarities that you see in style and theme in this poem, in William Wordsworth's "A Slumber Did My Spirit Seal" (p. 1069), and in Mary
   Oliver's "Wild Geese" (p. 1028). Which poem did you prefer? Why?

GAIL WHITE (B. 1945)

Dead Armadillos   2000

> WHEN I WRITE "I'm a very
> secretive writer. Usually no
> one but me sees a poem
> before it's published. I don't
> especially recommend this. I
> probably miss a lot of helpful
> advice, but I also miss a lot of
> aggravation." — GAIL WHITE

The smart armadillo stays
on the side of the road
where it was born. The dumb ones
get a sudden urge to check the pickings
across the asphalt, and nine   5
times out of ten, collide
with a ton of moving metal.
They're on my daily route — soft shells
of land crustacea, small blind knights
in armor. No one cares.   10
There is no Save the Armadillo
Society. The Sierra Club and Greenpeace
take no interest. There are too
damned many armadillos, and beauty,

like money, is worth more when it's scarce.   15
Give us time. Let enough of them
try to cross the road.
When we're down to the last half dozen,
we'll see them with the eyes of God.

CONSIDERATIONS FOR CRITICAL THINKING AND WRITING

1. FIRST RESPONSE. Why do you think White chooses armadillos rather than, say, foxes to make her point?

2. What keeps this poem from becoming preachy?

3. How does the poem's language reveal the speaker's character?

CONNECTION TO ANOTHER SELECTION

1. Discuss the similarities in theme in "Dead Armadillos" and Walt McDonald's "Coming Across It" (p. 1025).

DAVE LUCAS (B. 1980)

November   2007

October's brief, bright gush is over.
Leaf-lisp and fetch, their cold-tea smell
raked to the curb in copper- and shale-
stained piles, or the struck-match-sweet of sulfur

becoming smoke. The overcast
sky the same slight ambergris.
Hung across it, aghast surprise
of so many clotted, orphaned nests.

WHEN I WRITE "I admire and envy writers who can keep a structured writing schedule. The lines and poems I tend to keep are those written in time stolen from other responsibilities — so that the act of writing always feels subversive, even if I'm only subverting the laundry that needs to be done." — DAVE LUCAS

CONSIDERATIONS FOR CRITICAL THINKING AND WRITING

1. FIRST RESPONSE. What overall impression does this poem convey about the month of November? How does it serve as a dramatic contrast to October?

2. Carefully examine the diction in each line to determine how the poem's images achieve their effects.

3. CREATIVE RESPONSE. Choose two consecutive months that offer striking climatic environmental changes in the region where you live and write a two-stanza poem that includes vivid diction and images.

CONNECTION TO ANOTHER SELECTION

1. Consider the thematic function of the birds in "November" and in Mary Oliver's "Wild Geese" (p. 1028).

WALT MCDONALD (B. 1934)
Coming Across It   1988

Cans rattle in the alley, a cat
prowling, or a man down on his luck
and starving. Neon on buildings

above us blinks like those eyes
in the dark, too slow for a cat,   5
lower than a man, like fangs,

yellow gold. Crowds shove us toward
something that crouches, this blind
alley like a cave. Someone shouts

Otter, and suddenly a sharp nose   10
wedges into focus, pelt shining,
webbed mammal feet begging for room.

Like a tribe, we huddle here
in the city and call *Here, otter,*
otter, asking how far to the river,   15

the police, the safest zoo. We call it
cute, call it ugly, maybe diseased
or lonely, amazed to find something wild

in the city. We wait for someone
with a gun or net to rescue it.   20
We talk to strangers like brothers,

puzzling what should be done
with dark alleys, with garbage,
with vermin that run free at night.

We keep our eyes on it, keep calling   25
softly to calm it. But if we had
clubs, we'd kill it.

CONSIDERATIONS FOR CRITICAL THINKING AND WRITING

1. **FIRST RESPONSE.** How is suspense created and sustained in the poem?
2. How do these city people respond to "something wild / in the city" (lines 18–19)?
3. How is the otter described? What is the effect of repeatedly referring to the animal as "it"?

CONNECTION TO ANOTHER SELECTION

1. Discuss how the unexpected encounter between civilization and nature produces anxiety in "Coming Across It" and in Alden Nowlan's "The Bull Moose" (p. 1026).

ALDEN NOWLAN (1933–1983)

The Bull Moose 1962

Down from the purple mist of trees on the mountain,
lurching through forests of white spruce and cedar,
stumbling through tamarack swamps,
came the bull moose
to be stopped at last by a pole-fenced pasture.   5

Too tired to turn or, perhaps, aware
there was no place left to go, he stood with the cattle.
They, scenting the musk of death, seeing his great head
like the ritual mask of a blood god, moved to the other end
of the field, and waited.   10

The neighbors heard of it, and by afternoon
cars lined the road. The children teased him
with alder switches and he gazed at them
like an old, tolerant collie. The women asked
if he could have escaped from a Fair.   15

The oldest man in the parish remembered seeing
a gelded moose yoked with an ox for plowing.
The young men snickered and tried to pour beer
down his throat, while their girl friends took their pictures.

The bull moose let them stroke his tick-ravaged flanks,   20
let them pry open his jaws with bottles, let a giggling girl
plant a little purple cap
of thistles on his head.

When the wardens came, everyone agreed it was a shame
to shoot anything so shaggy and cuddlesome.   25
He looked like the kind of pet
women put to bed with their sons.

So they held their fire. But just as the sun dropped in the river
the bull moose gathered his strength
like a scaffolded king, straightened and lifted his horns   30
so that even the wardens backed away as they raised their rifles.
When he roared, people ran to their cars. All the young men
leaned on their automobile horns as he toppled.

CONSIDERATIONS FOR CRITICAL THINKING AND WRITING

1. FIRST RESPONSE. How does the speaker present the moose and the towns-people? How are the moose and townspeople contrasted? Discuss specific lines to support your response.

2. Explain how the symbols in this poem point to a conflict between humanity and nature. What do you think the speaker's attitude toward this conflict is?

3. CRITICAL STRATEGIES. Read the section on mythological criticism (pp. 1657–59) in Chapter 51, "Critical Strategies for Reading," and write an essay on "The Bull Moose" that approaches the poem from a mythological perspective.

CONNECTION TO ANOTHER SELECTION

1. In an essay compare and contrast how the animals portrayed in "The Bull Moose" and in Kay Ryan's "Turtle" (below) are used as symbols.

KAY RYAN (B. 1945)

Turtle   2010

Who would be a turtle who could help it?
A barely mobile hard roll, a four-oared helmet,
she can ill afford the chances she must take
in rowing toward the grasses that she eats.
Her track is graceless, like dragging   5
a packing case places, and almost any slope
defeats her modest hopes. Even being practical,
she's often stuck up to the axle on her way
to something edible. With everything optimal,
she skirts the ditch which would convert   10
her shell into a serving dish. She lives
below luck-level, never imagining some lottery
will change her load of pottery to wings.
Her only levity is patience,
the sport of truly chastened things.   15

CONSIDERATIONS FOR CRITICAL THINKING AND WRITING

1. FIRST RESPONSE. Explain how the poem's imagery captures what it means to be a turtle.

2. How does Ryan transform all the perceived disadvantages of being a turtle into something positive?

3. Discuss the paradox created by the diction in the final two lines.

CONNECTION TO ANOTHER SELECTION

1. Compare Ryan's "Turtle" with Emily Dickinson's "A narrow Fellow in the Grass" (p. 2). How do the poems make you feel about the respective animal in each?

MAXINE KUMIN (1925–2014)

The Whole Hog   2010

When you go to your favorite grocery store
and this week's Special is boneless pork
tenderloin that you'll roll in a floured
paste with cracked pepper and rosemary
before you roast it in a hot oven   5
and serve it with homemade pear chutney

do you visualize up to twenty wet
pink piglets squirming out
of the sow's vagina while she is trapped
in a farrowing crate so narrow that   10
she can't turn to lick her newborns because
she might roll over and crush one as

they worm their way uphill to a teat
and do you see her being bred back to the boar
only a few days later to make more   15
piglets and the grown offspring
trucked off to slaughter in
a double-decker tractor trailer, their first

and only time in daylight, the ones
on top shitting and throwing up on the ones   20
underneath, and the whole glistening mass
of them screaming, before they're forced
down the ramp and into lines
to be killed, the way I heard

and then saw them cross the town   25
of Storm Lake, Iowa, big corn-fed hogs
bawling, knowing they were going to die,
like those guys beheaded in Iraq?
Well, this is factory farming smack
in the heart of the USA in 2008   30

so follow your star. *Bon appétit.*

CONSIDERATIONS FOR CRITICAL THINKING AND WRITING

1. FIRST RESPONSE. To whom is "The Whole Hog" addressed? How do you think the poem's images in the poem make people feel about ordering their next BLT on rye toast?

2. What is the effect of the first stanza? How does it differ in strategy from the stanzas that follow?

3. Comment on the effectiveness of the poem's final line.

CONNECTION TO ANOTHER SELECTION

1. Write an essay in which you consider the ways the conflicts between humanity and nature are presented in "The Whole Hog" and in Alden Nowlan's "The Bull Moose" (p. 1026).

MARY OLIVER (B. 1935)

Wild Geese 1986

You do not have to be good.
You do not have to walk on your knees
for a hundred miles through the desert, repenting.

You only have to let the soft animal of your body
    love what it loves.
Tell me about despair, yours, and I will tell you mine.   5
Meanwhile the world goes on.
Meanwhile the sun and the clear pebbles of the rain
are moving across the landscapes,
over the prairies and the deep trees,
the mountains and the rivers.   10
Meanwhile the wild geese, high in the clean blue air,
are heading home again.
Whoever you are, no matter how lonely,
the world offers itself to your imagination,
calls to you like the wild geese, harsh and exciting —   15
over and over announcing your place
in the family of things.

CONSIDERATIONS FOR CRITICAL THINKING AND WRITING

1. FIRST RESPONSE. Discuss the thematic significance of the wild geese. What do they offer that the poem's first three lines do not?

2. What phrases are repeated — and to what effect?

3. How would you describe the meaning of "the family of things" (last line)?

CONNECTION TO ANOTHER SELECTION

1. Discuss the treatment of imagination in "Wild Geese" and in Emily Dickinson's "To make a prairie it takes a clover and one bee" (p. 837).

SUGGESTED TOPICS FOR LONGER PAPERS

1. Write an analysis of Gail White's "Dead Armadillos" (p. 1023), Walt McDonald's "Coming Across It" (p. 1025), and Alden Nowlan's "The Bull Moose" (p. 1026) as commentaries on our civilization's problematic relationship to the wild. How does each poem add to and extend a consideration of the issue?

2. Use the Internet to find the lyrics of popular songs written within the past five years about environmental issues. Choose three and write a comparative analysis of their style and themes.

40

The World of Work

I'd like to be on record as saying that anybody can write a poem that nobody can understand. That's really easy. On the other hand, it might be really hard to write a poem that everyone in a room found meaning in.
— TED KOOSER

Chris Maddaloni/Getty Images.

This chapter offers some contemporary poems that are thematically connected to business and labor. The vicissitudes associated with making a living are not typically the subject matter chosen by poets, who have traditionally and historically preferred to write about less mundane matters, such as love, nature, spirituality, grief, death, or almost any other side of life that isn't set at a job site or in an office. However much this view of poets may be a stereotype, by the time President Calvin Coolidge confidently declared in 1925 that "the business of America is business," there was an impressive record of objections to such a narrow materialistic assertion. Consider, for example, Henry David Thoreau's assessment in this nineteenth-century journal entry: "In my experience nothing is so opposed to poetry — not crime — as business. It is a negation of life" (June 29, 1852).

Not many poems replicate the kind of exuberant optimism about the business of work to be found in this excerpt from Walt Whitman's "I Hear America Singing" (1867):

I hear America singing, the varied carols I hear,
Those of mechanics, each one singing his as it should be blithe and strong,
The carpenter singing his as he measures his plank or beam,
The mason singing his as he makes ready for work, or leaves off work,
The boatman singing what belongs to him in his boat, the deckhand singing on
    the steamboat deck,
The shoemaker singing as he sits on his bench, the hatter singing as he stands. . . .

Whitman's poem celebrates the energy he perceived in workers and business: "In modern times the new word *Business,* has been brought to the front & now dominates individuals and nations. . . . Business shall be, nay, is the word of the modern hero." In recent times in the face of economic turmoil, crushing debt, and widespread unemployment, however, Thoreau's negative critique seems to resonate more than does Whitman's cheerful expectations.

The world of work — the business of earning a living — seems to be in sharper and more problematic focus these days because it is necessarily on most people's minds, including the imaginations of many poets. The chapter's focus is not just about earning money, though the first poem, "Money," by former business executive and now poet Dana Gioia, certainly acknowledges how obsessively central money can be. The following poems about earning a living are also about personal integrity, working conditions, and the meaning of life, topics that are explored from a variety of perspectives and that evoke the misery and joy, as well as the despair and satisfaction, that going to work can pay out.

DANA GIOIA (B. 1950)

Money 1991

Money is a kind of poetry.   — *Wallace Stevens*

Money, the long green,
cash, stash, rhino, jack
or just plain dough.

Chock it up, fork it over,
shell it out. Watch it   5
burn holes through pockets.

To be made of it! To have it
to burn! Greenbacks, double eagles,
megabucks and Ginnie Maes.

It greases the palm, feathers a nest,   10
holds heads above water,
makes both ends meet.

Money breeds money.
Gathering interest, compounding daily.
Always in circulation.   15

Money. You don't know where it's been,
but you put it where your mouth is.
And it talks.

CONSIDERATIONS FOR CRITICAL THINKING AND WRITING

1. FIRST RESPONSE. Explain whether the poem supports or challenges Stevens's epigraph.
2. How does money "talk" through Gioia's choice of diction?
3. Research Wallace Stevens's biography in terms of his relationship to business. Why is he an especially appropriate source for the quotation that begins the poem?

CONNECTION TO ANOTHER SELECTION

1. Compare Gioia's poetic strategy for writing with Ronald Wallace's for "In a Rut" (p. 1011).

WHEN I READ "My advice is to read a lot of poetry; to begin with the contemporary and get an ear for contemporary poetic speech; then read your way gradually into the past. Form a strong attachment to a poet whose work you love, and immerse yourself in the work. Then find another." —TONY HOAGLAND

TONY HOAGLAND (B. 1953)

America 2003

Then one of the students with blue hair and a tongue stud
Says that America is for him a maximum-security prison

Whose walls are made of RadioShacks and Burger Kings, and MTV episodes
Where you can't tell the show from the commercials,

And as I consider how to express how full of shit I think he is,   5
He says that even when he's driving to the mall in his Isuzu

Trooper with a gang of his friends, letting rap music pour over them
Like a boiling Jacuzzi full of ballpeen hammers, even then he feels

Buried alive, captured and suffocated in the folds
Of the thick satin quilt of America   10

And I wonder if this is a legitimate category of pain,
Or whether he is just spin doctoring a better grade,

And then I remember that when I stabbed my father in the dream
        last night,
It was not blood but money

That gushed out of him, bright green hundred-dollar bills   15
Spilling from his wounds, and — this is the weird part —,

He gasped, "Thank god — those Ben Franklins were
Clogging up my heart —

And so I perish happily,
Freed from that which kept me from my liberty" —   20

Which is when I knew it was a dream, since my dad
Would never speak in rhymed couplets,

And I look at the student with his acne and cell phone and phony
    ghetto clothes
And I think, "I am asleep in America too,

And I don't know how to wake myself either,"   25
And I remember what Marx said near the end of his life:

"I was listening to the cries of the past,
When I should have been listening to the cries of the future."

But how could he have imagined 100 channels of 24-hour cable
Or what kind of nightmare it might be   30

When each day you watch rivers of bright merchandise run past you
And you are floating in your pleasure boat upon this river

Even while others are drowning underneath you
And you see their faces twisting in the surface of the waters

And yet it seems to be your own hand   35
Which turns the volume higher?

Considerations for Critical Thinking and Writing

1. **FIRST RESPONSE.** This poem consists of two sentences. How do they differ in tone
   and meaning?

2. Discuss the humor embedded in this serious poem.

3. To what extent does this poem reflect your own views about American life?

Connection to Another Selection

1. Compare the perspective offered on money in "America" with that in Dana
   Gioia's "Money" (p. 1031).

Jan Beatty (b. 1952)

My Father Teaches Me to Dream   1996

You want to know what work is?
I'll tell you what work is:
Work is work.
You get up. You get on the bus.

You don't look from side to side.   5
You keep your eyes straight ahead.
That way nobody bothers you — see?
You get off the bus. You work all day.
You get back on the bus at night. Same thing.
You go to sleep. You get up.   10
You do the same thing again.
Nothing more. Nothing less.
There's no handouts in this life.
All this other stuff you're looking for —
it ain't there.   15
Work is work.

Considerations for Critical Thinking and Writing

1. FIRST RESPONSE. How likely is it that the son or daughter of this father actually asked for a definition of work? What do you imagine prompted the start of this explanation?

2. Discuss the effect of the use of repeated words and phrases. How are they related to the father's message?

3. Consider what the title reveals about the "you" of the poem.

Connection to Another Selection

1. Compare this father's vision of work with the perspective of the young man in Baron Wormser's "Labor" (p. 1035). How might the difference between the two be explained?

MICHAEL CHITWOOD (B. 1958)

Men Throwing Bricks   2007

The one on the ground lofts two at
        a time
with just the right lift for them to
        finish
their rise as the one on the scaffold
        turns
to accept them like a gift and place
        them
on the growing stack. They chime   Derek Anderson.
        slightly
on the catch. You'd have to do this daily,
morning and afternoon, not to marvel.

Considerations for Critical Thinking and Writing

1. FIRST RESPONSE. Explain the title's ironic surprise.

2. Discuss the sounds in the poem. How does it "chime"?

3. Why is "marvel" a better choice to describe the men throwing bricks than the phrase "be impressed"?

CONNECTION TO ANOTHER SELECTION

1. Compare Chitwood's treatment of these working men with Joyce Sutphen's perspective on the men and their work in "Guys Like That" (p. 1038).

BARON WORMSER (B. 1948)

Labor   2008

I spent a couple of years during my undestined
Twenties on a north woods acreage
That grew, as the locals poetically phrased it,
"Stones and rocks." I loved it.

No real insulation in the old farmhouse,   5
Which meant ten cords of hardwood,
Which meant a muscled mantra of cutting,
Yarding, splitting, stacking and burning.

I was the maul coming down *kerchunk*
On the round of maple; I was the hellacious   10
Screeching saw; I was the fire.
I was fiber and grew imperceptibly.

I lost interest in everything except for trees.
Career, ambition and politics bored me.
I loved putting on my steel-toe, lace-up   15
Work boots in the morning. I loved the feel

Of my feet on grass slick with dew or frost
Or ice-skimmed mud or crisp snow crust.
I loved the moment after I felled a tree
When it was still again and I felt the awe   20

Of what I had done and awe for the tree that had
Stretched toward the sky for silent decades.
On Saturday night the regulars who had worked
In the woods forever mocked me as I limped into

The bar out on the state highway. "Workin' hard   25
There, sonny, or more like hardly workin'?"
I cradled my bottle between stiff raw hands,
Felt a pinching tension in the small of my back,

Inhaled ripe sweat, damp flannel,
Cheap whiskey then nodded — a happy fool.   30
They grinned back. Through their proper
Scorn I could feel it. They loved it too.

for Hayden Carruth

CONSIDERATIONS FOR CRITICAL THINKING AND WRITING

1. FIRST RESPONSE. To what extent does the poem conform to the definitions of an ode?

2. What is it about tree cutting that so enthralls the speaker?

3. Do you think this poem is sentimental? Why or why not?

4. CREATIVE RESPONSE. Write an ode concerning an activity that you know well and can express strong feelings about, using vivid images and metaphors.

CONNECTION TO ANOTHER SELECTION

1. Compare the themes in "Labor" and in Michael Chitwood's "Men Throwing Bricks" (p. 1034).

ANGELA ALAIMO O'DONNELL (B. 1960)

Touring the Mine 2009

Lackawanna Coal Company,
Scranton, Pennsylvania

Like Disney World, only true.
A tram conveys us
down the earth's dark drop.

Surprised by water and by air,
a rush of bone cold,   5
we watch the blue light telescope shut.

Hugging the curve
of the shaft's steep grade,
we roll back yards and years

to a place untouched by sun,   10
unknown to night or noon
or cloud-scudded sky,

only eons of black rock
earth's hull and hammer-
struck walls of oily coal.   15

Here among the tight-lipped men
our fathers moved in silence,
far from women and their worry,

the clamor of children
who ate their wages   20
before they'd palmed the scrip.

They split rock in the dark,
loaded it on carts,
a rough-muscled alchemy of stone.

Here heavy and inert,   25
once above the surface
it leapt to light and heat.

They made it so,
shoveled coal to feed the fire
that burnt in every man's cellar.   30

Digging down deep
they loosed the life,
bore it up and out into the blue

where we emerge squinting,
its black smoke still rising   35
against the killing cold.

CONSIDERATIONS FOR CRITICAL THINKING AND WRITING

1. FIRST RESPONSE. Why do you think O'Donnell refers to Disney World in the opening line?
2. Discuss the effect of the images used to describe the coal mine.
3. How does O'Donnell characterize the coal miners and their work?

CONNECTION TO ANOTHER SELECTION

1. Discuss the tone in "Touring the Mine" and in Michael Chitwood's "Men Throwing Bricks" (p. 1034).

DAVID IGNATOW (1914–1997)

The Jobholder   1998

I stand in the rain waiting for my bus
and in the bus I wait for my stop.
I get let off and go to work
where I wait for the day to end
and then go home, waiting for the bus,   5
of course, and my stop.

And at home I read and wait
for my hour to go to bed
and I wait for the day I can retire
and wait for my turn to die.   10

CONSIDERATIONS FOR CRITICAL THINKING AND WRITING

1. FIRST RESPONSE. How do the effects of repetition and brevity contribute to the theme of this poem?
2. Characterize the speaker's attitude toward work and life.

CONNECTION TO ANOTHER SELECTION

1. Compare Ignatow's representation of work with Baron Wormser's in "Labor" (p. 1035).

TED KOOSER (B. 1939)

Laundry 1985

A pink house trailer,
scuffed and rusted, sunken
in weeds. On the line,

five pale blue workshirts
up to their elbows   5
in raspberry canes —

a good, clean crew
of pickers, out early,
sleeves wet with dew,

and near them, a pair   10
of bright yellow panties
urging them on.

Chris Maddaloni/Getty Images.

CONSIDERATIONS FOR CRITICAL THINKING AND WRITING

1. FIRST RESPONSE. Discuss how Kooser uses color to create tonal effects.
2. Just beyond the simplicity of "Laundry," there are some ideas about work suspended from the lines. What are they?

CONNECTION TO ANOTHER SELECTION

1. Discuss the relationship between home and work in "Laundry" and in David Ignatow's "The Jobholder" (p. 1037).

JOYCE SUTPHEN (B. 1949)

Guys Like That 2007

Drive very nice cars, and from
where you sit in your dented
last-century version of the
most ordinary car in America, they

look dark-suited and neat and fast.   5
Guys like that look as if they are thinking
about wine and marble floors, but
really they are thinking about TiVo

and ESPN. Women think that guys
like that are different from the guys   10
driving the trucks that bring cattle
to slaughter, but guys like that are

planning worse things than the death
of a cow. Guys who look like that —

so clean and cool — are quietly moving 15
money across the border, cooking books,

making deals that leave some people
rich and some people poorer
than they were before guys like that
robbed them at the pump and on 20

their electricity bills, and even
now, guys like that are planning how
to divide up that little farm they just
passed, the one you used to call home.

Considerations for Critical Thinking and Writing

1. FIRST RESPONSE. How does the phrase "Guys Like That" take on different meanings as the poem progresses?

2. Discuss the poem as a critique of American business practices.

3. Why do you think Sutphen writes this poem specifically from a woman's point of view?

Connection to Another Selection

1. Consider the treatment of men's relationship to domestic life in "Guys Like That" and in Angela Alaimo O'Donnell's "Touring the Mine" (p. 1036).

MARGE PIERCY (B. 1936)

To be of use 1973

The people I love the best
jump into work head first
without dallying in the shallows
and swim off with sure strokes almost out of sight.
They seem to become natives of that element, 5
the black sleek heads of seals
bouncing like half-submerged balls.

I love people who harness themselves, an ox to a heavy cart,
who pull like water buffalo, with massive patience,
who strain in the mud and the muck to move things forward, 10
who do what has to be done, again and again.

I want to be with people who submerge
in the task, who go into the fields to harvest
and work in a row and pass the bags along,
who are not parlor generals and field deserters 15
but move in a common rhythm
when the food must come in or the fire be put out.

The work of the world is common as mud.
Botched, it smears the hands, crumbles to dust.

But the thing worth doing well done   20
has a shape that satisfies, clean and evident.
Greek amphoras for wine or oil,
Hopi vases that held corn, are put in museums
but you know they were made to be used.
The pitcher cries for water to carry   25
and a person for work that is real.

Considerations for Critical Thinking and Writing

1. **FIRST RESPONSE.** How does the poem's figurative language suggest the sort of worker the speaker admires?
2. What do you consider to be "work that is real" (line 26)?
3. What is the significance of the title?

Connection to Another Selection

1. Compare the sense of what constitutes meaningful work in this poem with that in Jan Beatty's "My Father Teaches Me to Dream" (p. 1033).

Suggested Topics for Longer Papers

1. There are many contemporary songs about work. Choose one of the poems in this chapter and in terms of poetic elements — such as diction, tone, imagery, figures of speech, sound, and rhythm — compare its themes with the lyrics of a song you admire.
2. Choose one of the writers represented in this chapter and read more poems in his or her collections. Choose five poems that you think make an interesting and coherent thematic grouping and write an analysis that reveals important elements of the poet's style and characteristic concerns.

An Anthology
of Poems

41

An Anthology
of Poems

Now the role of poetry is not simply to
hold understanding in place but to help
create and hold a realm of experience.
Poetry has become a kind of tool for
knowing the world in a particular way.
— JANE HIRSHFIELD

© Christopher Felver/Corbis.

ANONYMOUS (TRADITIONAL SCOTTISH BALLAD)

Bonny Barbara Allan   date unknown

It was in and about the Martinmas° time,
    When the green leaves were afalling,
That Sir John Graeme, in the West Country,
    Fell in love with Barbara Allan.

He sent his men down through the town,   5
    To the place where she was dwelling:
"Oh haste and come to my master dear,
    Gin° ye be Barbara Allan."   *if*

O hooly,° hooly rose she up,   *slowly*
    To the place where he was lying,   10
And when she drew the curtain by:
    "Young man, I think you're dying."

1 *Martinmas:* St. Martin's Day, November 11.

"O it's I'm sick, and very, very sick,
　　And 'tis a' for Barbara Allan." —
"O the better for me ye's never be,   15
　　Tho your heart's blood were aspilling."

"O dinna ye mind,° young man," she said,   *don't you remember*
　　"When ye was in the tavern adrinking,
That ye made the health° gae round and round,   *toasts*
　　And slighted Barbara Allan?"   20

He turned his face unto the wall,
　　And death was with him dealing:
"Adieu, adieu, my dear friends all,
　　And be kind to Barbara Allan."

And slowly, slowly raise her up,   25
　　And slowly, slowly left him,
And sighing said she could not stay,
　　Since death of life had reft him.

She had not gane a mile but twa,
　　When she heard the dead-bell ringing,   30
And every jow° that the dead-bell geid,   *stroke*
　　It cried, "Woe to Barbara Allan!"

"O mother, mother, make my bed!
　　O make it saft and narrow!
Since my love died for me today,   35
　　I'll die for him tomorrow."

W. H. AUDEN (1907–1973)

The Unknown Citizen　1940

(To JS/07/M/378
This Marble Monument
Is Erected by the State)

He was found by the Bureau of Statistics to be
One against whom there was no official complaint,
And all the reports on his conduct agree
That, in the modern sense of an old-fashioned word, he was a saint,
For in everything he did he served the Greater Community.   5
Except for the War till the day he retired
He worked in a factory and never got fired,
But satisfied his employers, Fudge Motors Inc.
Yet he wasn't a scab or odd in his views,
For his Union reports that he paid his dues,   10
(Our report on his Union shows it was sound)
And our Social Psychology workers found
That he was popular with his mates and liked a drink.
The Press are convinced that he bought a paper every day
And that his reactions to advertisements were normal in every way. 15

Policies taken out in his name prove that he was fully insured,
And his Health-card shows he was once in hospital but left it cured.
Both Producers Research and High-Grade Living declare
He was fully sensible to the advantages of the Installment Plan
And had everything necessary to the Modern Man, 20
A phonograph, radio, car and a frigidaire.
Our researchers into Public Opinion are content
That he held the proper opinions for the time of year;
When there was peace, he was for peace; when there was war, he went.
He was married and added five children to the population, 25
Which our Eugenist says was the right number for a parent of his
  generation,
And our teachers report that he never interfered with their education.
Was he free? Was he happy? The question is absurd:
Had anything been wrong, we should certainly have heard.

APHRA BEHN (1640–1689)

Song: Love Armed 1684

Love in fantastic triumph sate,
  Whilst bleeding hearts around him flowed,
For whom fresh pains he did create,
  And strange tyrannic power he showed:
From thy bright eyes he took his fire, 5
  Which round about in sport he hurled;
But 'twas from mine he took desire,
  Enough to undo the amorous world.

From me he took his sighs and tears;
  From thee, his pride and cruelty; 10
From me, his languishments and fears;
  And every killing dart from thee.
Thus thou and I the god have armed
  And set him up a deity;
But my poor heart alone is harmed,
  Whilst thine the victor is, and free. 15

WILLIAM BLAKE (1757–1827)

Infant Sorrow 1794

My mother groand! my father wept.
Into the dangerous world I leapt:
Helpless naked piping loud:
Like a fiend hid in a cloud.

Struggling in my father's hands:
Striving against my swadling bands
Bound and weary I thought best
To sulk upon my mother's breast.

ANNE BRADSTREET (CA. 1612–1672)

Before the Birth of One of Her Children 1678

All things within this fading world hath end,
Adversity doth still our joys attend;
No ties so strong, no friends so dear and sweet,
But with death's parting blow is sure to meet.
The sentence past is most irrevocable,   5
A common thing, yet oh, inevitable.
How soon, my Dear, death may my steps attend,
How soon't may be thy lot to lose thy friend,
We both are ignorant, yet love bids me
These farewell lines to recommend to thee,   10
That when that knot's untied that made us one,
I may seem thine, who in effect am none.
And if I see not half my days that's due,
What nature would, God grant to yours and you;
The many faults that well you know I have   15
Let be interred in my oblivious grave;
If any worth or virtue were in me,
Let that live freshly in thy memory
And when thou feel'st no grief, as I no harms,
Yet love thy dead, who long lay in thine arms,   20
And when thy loss shall be repaid with gains
Look to my little babes, my dear remains.
And if thou love thyself, or loved'st me,
These O protect from stepdame's° injury.   *stepmother's*
And if chance to thine eyes shall bring this verse,   25
With some sad sighs honor my absent hearse;
And kiss this paper for thy love's dear sake,
Who with salt tears this last farewell did take.

ELIZABETH BARRETT BROWNING (1806–1861)

My letters! all dead paper, mute and white 1850

My letters! all dead paper, mute and white!
And yet they seem alive and quivering
Against my tremulous hands which loose the string
And let them drop down on my knee to-night.
This said, — he wished to have me in his sight   5
Once, as a friend: this fixed a day in spring
To come and touch my hand . . . a simple thing,
Yet I wept for it! — this, . . . the paper's light . . .
Said, *Dear, I love thee*; and I sank and quailed
As if God's future thundered on my past.   10
This said, *I am thine* — and so its ink has paled
With lying at my heart that beat too fast.
and this . . . O Love, thy words have ill availed
If, what this said, I dared repeat at last!

WILLIAM CULLEN BRYANT (1794–1878)

To a Waterfowl 1818

Whither, midst falling dew,
While glow the heavens with the last steps of day,
Far, through their rosy depths, dost thou pursue
    Thy solitary way?

Vainly the fowler's eye 5
Might mark thy distant flight to do thee wrong,
As, darkly seen against the crimson sky,
    Thy figure floats along.

Seek'st thou the plashy brink
Of weedy lake, or marge of river wide, 10
Or where the rocking billows rise and sink
    On the chafed ocean side?

There is a Power whose care
Teaches thy way along that pathless coast —
The desert and illimitable air — 15
    Lone wandering, but not lost.

All day thy wings have fanned,
At that far height , the cold, thin atmosphere,
Yet stoop not , weary, to the welcome land,
    Though the dark night is near. 20

And soon that toil shall end;
Soon shalt thou find a summer home, and rest,
And scream among thy fellows; reeds shall bend,
    Soon. o'er thy sheltered nest.

Thou'rt gone, the abyss of heaven 25
Hath swallowed up thy form; yet, on my heart
Deeply has sunk the lesson thou hast given,
    And shall not soon depart.

He who, from zone to zone,
Guides through the boundless sky thy certain flight, 30
In the long way that I must tread alone,
    Will lead my steps aright.

ROBERT BURNS (1759–1796)

A Red, Red Rose 1799

O my luve's like a red, red rose
That's newly sprung in June;
O my luve's like the melodie
That's sweetly played in tune.

As fair art thou, my bonny lass,
So deep in luve am I;
And I will luve thee still my dear,
Till a' the seas gang° dry —   *go*

Till a' the seas gang dry, my dear,
And the rocks melt wi' the sun: 10
O I will luve thee still, my dear,
While the sands o' life shall run.

And fare thee weel, my only luve,
And fare thee weel awhile!
And I will come again, my luve,   15
Though it were a thousand mile.

GEORGE GORDON, LORD BYRON (1788–1824)

She Walks in Beauty   1814

From Hebrew Melodies

I

She walks in Beauty, like the night
    Of cloudless climes and starry skies;
And all that's best of dark and bright
    Meet in her aspect and her eyes:
Thus mellowed to that tender light   5
    Which Heaven to gaudy day denies.

II

One shade the more, one ray the less,
    Had half impaired the nameless grace
Which waves in every raven tress,
    Or softly lightens o'er her face;   10
Where thoughts serenely sweet express,
    How pure, how dear their dwelling-place.

III

And on that cheek, and o'er that brow,
    So soft, so calm, yet eloquent,
The smiles that win, the tints that glow,   15
    But tell of days in goodness spent,
A mind at peace with all below,
    A heart whose love is innocent!

SAMUEL TAYLOR COLERIDGE (1772–1834)

Kubla Khan: or, a Vision in a Dream°   1798

In Xanadu did Kubla Khan°
    A stately pleasure-dome decree:
Where Alph, the sacred river, ran
Through caverns measureless to man
     Down to a sunless sea.   5

So twice five miles of fertile ground
With walls and towers were girdled round:
And here were gardens bright with sinuous rills
Where blossomed many an incense-bearing tree;
And there were forests ancient as the hills,   10
Enfolding sunny spots of greenery.

But oh! that deep romantic chasm which slanted
Down the green hill athwart a cedarn cover!°
A savage place! as holy and enchanted
As e'er beneath a waning moon was haunted   15
By woman wailing for her demon-lover!
And from this chasm, with ceaseless turmoil seething,
As if this earth in fast thick pants were breathing,
A mighty fountain momently was forced,
Amid whose swift half-intermitted burst   20
Huge fragments vaulted like rebounding hail,
Of chaffy grain beneath the thresher's flail:
And 'mid these dancing rocks at once and ever
It flung up momently the sacred river.
Five miles meandering with a mazy motion   25
Through wood and dale the sacred river ran,
Then reached the caverns measureless to man,
And sank in tumult to a lifeless ocean:
And 'mid this tumult Kubla heard from far
Ancestral voices prophesying war!   30
    The shadow of the dome of pleasure
    Floated midway on the waves;
    Where was heard the mingled measure
    From the fountain and the caves.
It was a miracle of rare device,   35
A sunny pleasure-dome with caves of ice!

    A damsel with a dulcimer
    In a vision once I saw:
    It was an Abyssinian maid,
    And on her dulcimer she played,   40

Vision in a Dream: This poem came to Coleridge in an opium-induced dream, but he was interrupted by a visitor while writing it down. He was later unable to remember the rest of the poem.   1 *Kubla Khan:* The historical Kublai Khan (1216–1294, grandson of Genghis Khan) was the founder of the Mongol dynasty in China.   13 *athwart . . . cover:* Spanning a grove of cedar trees.

Singing of Mount Abora.
Could I revive within me
Her symphony and song,
To such a deep delight 'twould win me,
That with music loud and long,   45
I would build that dome in air,
That sunny dome! those caves of ice!
And all who heard should see them there,
And all should cry, Beware! Beware!
His flashing eyes, his floating hair!   50
Weave a circle round him thrice,
And close your eyes with holy dread,
For he on honey-dew hath fed,
And drunk the milk of Paradise.

JOHN DONNE (1572–1631)

Batter My Heart   1610

Batter my heart, three-personed God; for You
As yet but knock, breathe, shine, and seek to mend;
That I may rise and stand, o'erthrow me, and bend
Your force, to break, blow, burn, and make me new.
I, like an usurped town, to another due,   5
Labor to admit You, but Oh, to no end!
Reason, Your viceroy in me, me should defend,
But is captived, and proves weak or untrue.
Yet dearly I love You, and would be loved fain.
But am betrothed unto Your enemy: 10
Divorce me, untie, or break that knot again,
Take me to You, imprison me, for I,
Except You enthrall me, never shall be free,
Nor ever chaste, except You ravish me.

PAUL LAURENCE DUNBAR (1872–1906)

Sympathy   1893

I know what the caged bird feels, alas!
    When the sun is bright on the upland slopes;
When the wind stirs soft through the springing grass,
    And the river flows like a stream of glass;
        When the first bird sings and the first bud opens,   5
And the faint perfume from its chalice steals —
I know what the caged bird feels!

I know why the caged bird beats his wing
    Till its blood is red on the cruel bars;

For he must fly back to his perch and cling   10
When he fain° would be on the bough a-swing;   *rather*
   And a pain still throbs in the old, old scars
And they pulse again with a keener sting —
I know why he beats his wing!

I know why the caged bird sings, ah me,   15
   When his wing is bruised and his bosom sore, —
When he beats his bars and he would be free;
It is not a carol of joy or glee,
   But a prayer that he sends from his heart's deep core,
But a plea, that upward to Heaven he flings —   20
I know why the caged bird sings!

GEORGE ELIOT (MARY ANN EVANS / 1819–1880)

In a London Drawingroom   1865

The sky is cloudy, yellowed by the smoke.
For view there are the houses opposite,
Cutting the sky with one long line of wall
Like solid fog: far as the eye can stretch
Monotony of surface and of form   5
Without a break to hang a guess upon.
No bird can make a shadow as it flies,
For all its shadow, as in ways o'erhung
By thickest canvas, where the golden rays
Are clothed in hemp. No figure lingering   10
Pauses to feed the hunger of the eye
Or rest a little on the lap of life.
All hurry on and look upon the ground
Or glance unmarking at the passersby.
The wheels are hurrying, too, cabs, carriages   15
All closed, in multiplied identity.
The world seems one huge prison-house and court
Where men are punished at the slightest cost,
With lowest rate of color, warmth, and joy.

RALPH WALDO EMERSON (1803–1882)

Days   1867

Daughters of Time, the hypocritic° Days,
Muffled and dumb like barefoot dervishes,
And marching single in an endless file,
Bring diadems and fagots in their hands.
To each they offer gifts after his will,   5
Bread, kingdom, stars, and sky that holds them all.

---

1 *hypocritic:* The archaic meaning of *hypocrite* is "one who plays a part." The days are being compared to actors in a pomp, or procession.

I, in my pleachéd garden,° watched the pomp,
Forgot my morning wishes, hastily
Took a few herbs and apples, and the Day
Turned and departed silent. I, too late,   10
Under her solemn fillet° saw the scorn.   *headband*

7 *pleachéd garden:* A garden containing trees whose branches are artificially bent and interwoven.

CHARLOTTE PERKINS GILMAN (1860–1935)

Queer People   1899

The people people work with best
    Are often very queer
The people people own by birth
    Quite shock your first idea;
The people people choose for friends
    Your common sense appall,
But the people people marry
    Are the queerest folks of all.

THOMAS HARDY (1840–1928)

In Time of "The Breaking of Nations"°   1915

1

Only a man harrowing clods
    In a slow silent walk
With an old horse that stumbles and nods
    Half asleep as they stalk.

2

Only thin smoke without flame
    From the heaps of couch-grass;
Yet this will go onward the same   5
    Though Dynasties pass.

3

Yonder a maid and her wight°   *man*
    Come whispering by: 10
War's annals will cloud into night
    Ere their story die.

The Breaking of Nations: See Jeremiah 51:20: "Thou art my battle axe and weapons of war: for with thee will I break in pieces the nations, and with thee will I destroy kingdoms."

THOMAS HARDY (1840–1928)

I Looked Up from My Writing 1916

I looked up from my writing,
    And gave a start to see,
As if rapt in my inditing,
    The moon's full gaze on me.

Her meditative misty head   5
    Was spectral in its air,
And I involuntarily said,
    "What are you doing there?"

"Oh, I've been scanning pond and hole
    And waterway hereabout   10
For the body of one with a sunken soul
    Who has put his life-light out.

"Did you hear his frenzied tattle?
    It was sorrow for his son
Who is slain in brutish battle,   15
    Though he has injured none.

"And now I am curious to look
    Into the blinkered mind
Of one who wants to write a book
    In a world of such a kind."   20

Her temper overwrought me,
    And I edged to shun her view,
For I felt assured she thought me
    One who should drown him too.

FRANCES E. W. HARPER (1825–1911)

Learning to Read 1872

Very soon the Yankee teachers
    Came down and set up school;
But oh! how the Rebs did hate it, —
    It was agin' their rule

Our masters always tried to hide   5
    Book learning from our eyes;
Knowledge did'nt agree with slavery —
    'Twould make us all too wise.

But some of us would try to steal
    A little from the book,   10
And put the words together,
    And learn by hook or crook.

I remember Uncle Caldwell,
    Who took pot-liquor fat
And greased the pages of his book,   15
    And hid it in his hat.

And had his master ever seen
    The leaves upon his head,
He'd have thought them greasy papers,
    But nothing to be read.   20

And there was Mr. Turner's Ben
    Who heard the children spell,
And picked the words right up by heart,
    And learned to read 'em well.

Well the Northern folks kept sending   25
    The Yankee teachers down
And they stood right up and helped us,
    Though Rebs did sneer and frown,

And, I longed to read my Bible,
    For precious words it said;   30
But when I begun to learn it,
    Folks just shook their heads,

And said there is no use trying,
    Oh! Chloe, you're too late;
But as I was rising sixty,   35
    I had no time to wait.

So I got a pair of glasses,
    And straight to work I went,
And never stopped till I could read
    The hymns and Testament.   40

Then I got a little cabin —
    A place to call my own —
And I felt as independent
    As the queen upon her throne.

GERARD MANLEY HOPKINS (1844–1889)

Pied Beauty   1877

Glory be to God for dappled things —
    For skies of couple-color as a brinded cow;
        For rose-moles all in stipple upon trout that swim;
Fresh-firecoal chestnut-falls;° finches' wings;   *fallen chestnut*
    Landscape plotted and pieced — fold, fallow, and plow;   5
        And all trades, their gear and tackle and trim.

All things counter, original, spare, strange;
    Whatever is fickle, freckled (who knows how?)
      With swift, slow; sweet, sour; adazzle, dim;
He fathers-forth whose beauty is past change: 10
      Praise him.

GERARD MANLEY HOPKINS (1844–1889)

The Windhover°   1877

To Christ Our Lord

I caught this morning morning's minion,° king-   *favorite*
    dom of daylight's dauphin, dapple-dawn-drawn Falcon,
    in his riding
Of the rolling level underneath him steady air, and striding
High there, how he rung upon the rein of a wimpling wing
In his ecstasy! then off, off forth on swing,   5
    As a skate's heel sweeps smooth on a bow-bend: the hurl and gliding
Rebuffed the big wind. My heart in hiding
Stirred for a bird, — the achieve of, the mastery of the thing!

Brute beauty and valour and act, oh, air, pride, plume, here
    Buckle!° AND the fire that breaks from thee then, a billion   10
Times told lovelier, more dangerous, O my chevalier!

    No wonder of it: shéer plód makes plough down sillion°   *furrow*
Shine, and blue-bleak embers, ah my dear,
    Fall, gall themselves, and gash gold-vermilion.

The Windhover: "A name for the kestrel [a kind of small hawk], from its habit of hovering or hanging with its head to the wind" [*OED*].   10 *Buckle:* To join, to equip for battle, to crumple.

BEN JONSON (1573–1637)

To Celia   1616

Drink to me only with thine eyes,
    And I will pledge with mine;
Or leave a kiss but in the cup,
    And I'll not ask for wine.
The thirst that from the soul doth rise   5
    Doth ask a drink divine;
But might I of Jove's nectar sup,
    I would not change for thine.

I sent thee late a rosy wreath,
    Not so much honoring thee   10

As giving it a hope that there
    It could not withered be.
But thou thereon didst only breathe,
    And sent'st it back to me;
Since when it grows, and smells, I swear,   15
    Not of itself but thee.

JOHN KEATS (1795–1821)

To one who has been long in city pent   1816

To one who has been long in city pent,
    'Tis very sweet to look into the fair
    And open face of heaven, — to breathe a prayer
Full in the smile of the blue firmament.
Who is more happy, when, with heart's content,   5
    Fatigued he sinks into some pleasant lair
    Of wavy grass, and reads a debonair
And gentle tale of love and languishment?

Returning home at evening, with an ear
    Catching the notes of Philomel,° — an eye   *a nightingale* 10
Watching the sailing cloudlet's bright career,
    He mourns that day so soon has glided by:
E'en like the passage of an angel's tear
    That falls through the clear ether silently.

JOHN KEATS (1795–1821)

When I have fears that I may cease to be   1818

When I have fears that I may cease to be
    Before my pen has gleaned my teeming brain,
Before high-piled books, in charactery,°   *print*
    Hold like rich garners the full ripened grain;
When I behold, upon the night's starred face,   5
    Huge cloudy symbols of a high romance,
And think that I may never live to trace
    Their shadows, with the magic hand of chance;
And when I feel, fair creature of an hour,
    That I shall never look upon thee more,   10
Never have relish in the faery° power   *magic*
    Of unreflecting love; — then on the shore
Of the wide world I stand alone, and think
Till love and fame to nothingness do sink.

JOHN KEATS (1795–1821)

Bright star, would I were steadfast as thou art —   1819

Bright star, would I were steadfast as thou art —
    Not in lone splendor hung aloft the night
And watching, with eternal lids apart,
    Like nature's patient, sleepless Eremite,
The moving waters at their priestlike task   5
    Of pure ablution round earth's human shores,
Or gazing on the new soft fallen mask
    Of snow upon the mountains and the moors —
No — yet still steadfast, still unchangeable,
    Pillowed upon my fair love's ripening breast,   10
To feel forever its soft fall and swell,
    Awake forever in a sweet unrest,
Still, still to hear her tender-taken breath,
And so live ever — or else swoon to death.

JOHN KEATS (1795–1821)

La Belle Dame sans Merci°   1819

O what can ail thee, knight-at-arms,
    Alone and palely loitering?
The sedge has withered from the lake,
    And no birds sing.

O what can ail thee, knight-at-arms,   5
    So haggard and so woe-begone?
The squirrel's granary is full,
    And the harvest's done.

I see a lily on thy brow,
    With anguish moist and fever dew,   10
And on thy cheeks a fading rose
    Fast withereth too.

I met a lady in the meads,
    Full beautiful — a faery's child,
Her hair was long, her foot was light,   15
    And her eyes were wild.

I made a garland for her head,
    And bracelets too, and fragrant zone;°   *belt*
She looked at me as she did love,
    And made sweet moan.   20

La Belle Dame sans Merci: This title is borrowed from a medieval poem and means "The Beautiful Lady without Mercy."

I set her on my pacing steed,
 And nothing else saw all day long,
For sidelong would she bend, and sing
 A faery's song.

She found me roots of relish sweet, 25
 And honey wild, and manna dew,
And sure in language strange she said,
 "I love thee true."

She took me to her elfin grot,
 And there she wept, and sighed full sore, 30
And there I shut her wild wild eyes
 With kisses four.

And there she lullèd me asleep,
 And there I dreamed — Ah! woe betide!
The latest° dream I ever dreamed *last* 35
 On the cold hill side.

I saw pale kings and princes too,
 Pale warriors, death-pale were they all;
They cried — "La Belle Dame sans Merci
 Hath thee in thrall!" 40

I saw their starved lips in the gloam,
 With horrid warning gapèd wide,
And I awoke and found me here,
 On the cold hill's side.

And this is why I sojourn here, 45
 Alone and palely loitering,
Though the sedge has withered from the lake,
 And no birds sing.

D. H. LAWRENCE (1885–1930)

How Beastly the Bourgeois Is 1909

How beastly the bourgeois is
especially the male of the species —

Presentable, eminently presentable —
shall I make you a present of him?

Isn't he handsome? isn't he healthy? isn't he a fine specimen? 5
doesn't he look the fresh clean Englishman, outside?
Isn't it god's own image? tramping his thirty miles a day
after partridges, or a little rubber ball?
wouldn't you like to be like that, well off, and quite the thing?

Oh, but wait!   10
Let him meet a new emotion, let him be faced with another man's need,
let him come home to a bit of moral difficulty, let life face
     him with a new demand on his understanding
and then watch him go soggy, like a wet meringue.
Watch him turn into a mess; either a fool or a bully.
Just watch the display of him, confronted with a new demand
     on his intelligence,   15
a new life-demand.

How beastly the bourgeois is
especially the male of the species —

Nicely groomed , like a mushroom
standing there so sleek and erect and eyeable —   20
and like a fungus, living on the remains of bygone life
sucking his life out of the dead leaves of greater life than his own.

And even so, he's stale, he's been there too long.
Touch him, and you'll find he's all gone inside
just like an old mushroom, all wormy inside, and hollow   25
under a smooth skin and an upright appearance.

Full of seething, wormy, hollow feelings
rather nasty —
How beastly the bourgeois is!

Standing in their thousands, these appearances, in damp England   30
what a pity they can't all be kicked over
like sickening toadstools, and left to melt back, swiftly
into the soil of England.

EMMA LAZARUS (1849–1887)

The New Colossus   1883

Not like the brazen giant of Greek fame,
With conquering limbs astride from land to land;
Here at our sea-washed, sunset gates shall stand
A mighty woman with a torch, whose flame
Is the imprisoned lightning, and her name   5
Mother of Exiles. From her beacon-hand
Glows world-wide welcome; her mild eyes command
The air-bridged harbor that twin cities frame.
"Keep, ancient lands, your storied pomp!" cries she
With silent lips. "Give me your tired, your poor,   10
Your huddled masses yearning to breathe free,
The wretched refuse of your teeming shore.

Send these, the homeless, tempest-tost to me,
I lift my lamp beside the golden door!"

Amy Lowell (1874–1925)

A Decade   1919

When you came, you were like red wine and honey,
And the taste of you burnt my mouth with its sweetness.
Now you are like morning bread,
Smooth and pleasant.
I hardly taste you at all for I know your savor;
But I am completely nourished.

John Milton (1608–1674)

On the Late Massacre in Piedmont°   1655

Avenge, O Lord, thy slaughtered saints, whose bones
    Lie scattered on the Alpine mountains cold;
    Even them who kept thy truth so pure of old,
When all our fathers worshiped stocks and stones,°
Forget not: in thy book record their groans   5
    Who were thy sheep, and in their ancient fold
    Slain by the bloody Piedmontese, that rolled
Mother with infant down the rocks.° Their moans
The vales redoubled to the hills, and they
    To heaven. Their martyred blood and ashes sow   10
O'er all the Italian fields, where still doth sway
    The triple Tyrant;° that from these may grow
    A hundredfold, who, having learnt thy way,
Early may fly the Babylonian woe.°

On the Late Massacre . . . : Milton's protest against the treatment of the Waldenses, members of
a Puritan sect living in the Piedmont region of northwest Italy, was not limited to this sonnet. It
is thought that he wrote Oliver Cromwell's appeals to the duke of Savoy and to others to end the
persecution.

4 *When . . . stones:* In Milton's Protestant view, English Catholics had worshipped their stone
and wooden statues in the twelfth century, when the Waldensian sect was formed.   5–8 *in thy
book . . . rocks:* On Easter Day 1655, 1,700 members of the Waldensian sect were massacred in
Piedmont by the duke of Savoy's forces.   12 *triple Tyrant:* The Pope, with his three-crowned
tiara, has authority on earth and in heaven and hell.   14 *Babylonian woe:* The destruction of
Babylon, symbol of vice and corruption, at the end of the world (see Rev. 17–18). Protestants
interpreted the "Whore of Babylon" as the Roman Catholic Church.

JOHN MILTON (1608–1674)

When I consider how my light is spent   ca. 1655

When I consider how my light is spent,°
   Ere half my days in this dark world and wide,
   And that one talent° which is death to hide
Lodged with me useless, though my soul more bent
To serve therewith my Maker, and present   5
   My true account, lest He returning chide;
   "Doth God exact day-labor, light denied?"
I fondly° ask. But Patience, to prevent   *foolishly*
That murmur, soon replies, "God doth not need
   Either man's work or His own gifts. Who best   10
   Bear His mild yoke, they serve Him best. His state
Is kingly: thousands at His bidding speed,
   And post o'er land and ocean without rest;
   They also serve who only stand and wait."

1 *how my light is spent:* Milton had been totally blind since 1651.   3 *that one talent:* Refers to Jesus's parable of the talents (units of money), in which a servant entrusted with a talent buries it rather than invests it and is punished on his master's return (Matt. 25:14–30).

EDGAR ALLAN POE (1809–1849)

To Helen   1823

Helen, thy beauty is to me
   Like those Nicéan barks° of yore,   *Byzantine ships*
That gently, o'er a perfumed sea,
   The weary, way-worn wanderer bore
   To his own native shore.   5

On desperate seas long wont to roam,
   Thy hyacinth hair, thy classic face,
Thy Naiad° airs have brought me home   *water nymph*
   To the glory that was Greece
And the grandeur that was Rome.   10

Lo! in yon brilliant window-niche
   How statue-like I see thee stand,
   The agate lamp within thy hand!
Ah! Psyche,° from the regions which
   Are Holy Land!   15

14 *Psyche:* A princess in Greek mythology loved by Cupid.

EDWIN ARLINGTON ROBINSON (1869–1935)

Miniver Cheevy 1910

Miniver Cheevy, child of scorn,
  Grew lean while he assailed the seasons;
He wept that he was ever born,
  And he had reasons.

Miniver loved the days of old 5
  When swords were bright and steeds were prancing;
The vision of a warrior bold
  Would set him dancing.

Miniver sighed for what was not,
  And dreamed, and rested from his labors; 10
He dreamed of Thebes and Camelot,
  And Priam's neighbors.

Miniver mourned the ripe renown
  That made so many a name so fragrant;
He mourned Romance, now on the town, 15
  And Art, a vagrant.

Miniver loved the Medici,
  Albeit he had never seen one;
He would have sinned incessantly
  Could he have been one. 20

Miniver cursed the commonplace
  And eyed a khaki suit with loathing;
He missed the mediaeval grace
  Of iron clothing.

Miniver scorned the gold he sought, 25
  But sore annoyed was he without it;
Miniver thought, and thought, and thought,
  And thought about it.

Miniver Cheevy, born too late,
  Scratched his head and kept on thinking; 30
Miniver coughed, and called it fate,
  And kept on drinking.

CHRISTINA GEORGINA ROSSETTI (1830–1894)

Some Ladies Dress in Muslin Full and White ca. 1848

    Some ladies dress in muslin full and
        white,
Some gentlemen in cloth succinct and black;
Some patronise a dog-cart, some a hack,

Some think a painted clarence only
        right.
    Youth is not always such a pleasing
        sight:
Witness a man with tassels on his back;
Or woman in a great-coat like a sack,
        Towering above her sex with horrid
        height.
If all the world were water fit to drown,
        There are some whom you would not
        teach to swim,
    Rather enjoying if you saw them sink:
    Certain old ladies dressed in girlish pink,
With roses and geraniums on their gown.
        Go to the basin, poke them o'er the
        rim —

© Corbis.

CHRISTINA GEORGINA ROSSETTI (1830–1894)

Promises Like Pie-Crust°   1896

Promise me no promises,
    So will I not promise you;
Keep we both our liberties,
    Never false and never true:
Let us hold the die uncast,   5
    Free to come as free to go;
For I cannot know your past,
    And of mine what can you know?

You, so warm, may once have been
    Warmer towards another one;   10
I, so cold, may once have seen
    Sunlight, once have felt the sun:
Who shall show us if it was
    Thus indeed in time of old?
Fades the image from the glass   15
    And the fortune is not told.

If you promised, you might grieve
    For lost liberty again;
If I promised, I believe
    I should fret to break the chain: 20
Let us be the friends we were,
    Nothing more but nothing less;
Many thrive on frugal fare
    Who would perish of excess.

Pie-Crust: An old English proverb: "Promises are like pie-crust, made to be broken."

SIEGFRIED SASSOON (1886–1967)

"They" 1917

The Bishop tells us: "When the boys come back
They will not be the same; for they'll have fought
In a just cause: they lead the last attack
On Anti-Christ; their comrades' blood has bought
New right to breed an honourable race,   5
They have challenged Death and dared him face to face."

"We're none of us the same!" the boys reply.
"For George lost both his legs; and Bill's stone blind;
Poor Jim's shot through the lungs and like to die;
And Bert's gone syphilitic: you'll not find   10
A chap who's served that hasn't found *some* change."
And the Bishop said: "The ways of God are strange!"

WILLIAM SHAKESPEARE (1564–1616)

Let me not to the marriage of true minds 1609

Let me not to the marriage of true minds
Admit impediments. Love is not love
Which alters when it alteration finds,
Or bends with the remover to remove:
O, no! it is an ever-fixed mark,   5
That looks on tempests and is never shaken;
It is the star to every wandering bark,°   *ship*
Whose worth's unknown, although his height be taken.°   *measured*
Love's not Time's fool, though rosy lips and cheeks

Within his bending sickle's compass come;   10
Love alters not with his brief hours and weeks,
But bears it out even to the edge of doom.°   *Judgment Day*
    If this be error, and upon me prov'd,
    I never writ, nor no man ever lov'd.

WILLIAM SHAKESPEARE (1564–1616)

That time of year thou mayst in me behold 1609

That time of year thou mayst in me behold
When yellow leaves, or none, or few, do hang
Upon those boughs which shake against the cold,
Bare ruined choirs, where late the sweet birds sang.
In me thou see'st the twilight of such day   5
As after sunset fadeth in the west;

Which by and by black night doth take away,
Death's second self,° that seals up all in rest. *sleep*
In me thou see'st the glowing of such fire,
That on the ashes of his youth doth lie, 10
As the deathbed whereon it must expire,
Consumed with that which it was nourished by.
   This thou perceiv'st, which makes thy love more strong,
   To love that well which thou must leave ere long.

WILLIAM SHAKESPEARE (1564–1616)

When forty winters shall besiege thy brow 1609

When forty winters shall besiege thy brow
And dig deep trenches in thy beauty's field,
Thy youth's proud livery, so gazed on now,
Will be a tattered weed,° of small worth held. *garment*
Then being asked where all thy beauty lies, 5
Where all the treasure of thy lusty days,
To say within thine own deep-sunken eyes
Were an all-eating shame and thriftless praise.
How much more praise deserved thy beauty's use
If thou couldst answer, "This fair child of mine 10
Shall sum my count and make my old excuse,"
Proving his beauty by succession thine.
   This were to be new made when thou art old,
   And see thy blood warm when thou feel'st it cold.

WILLIAM SHAKESPEARE (1564–1616)

When, in disgrace with Fortune and men's eyes 1609

When, in disgrace with Fortune and men's eyes,
I all alone beweep my outcast state,
And trouble deaf heaven with my bootless cries,
And look upon myself and curse my fate,
Wishing me like to one more rich in hope, 5
Featured like him, like him with friends possessed,
Desiring this man's art, and that man's scope,
With what I most enjoy contented least,
Yet in these thoughts myself almost despising,
Haply I think on thee, and then my state, 10
Like to the lark at break of day arising
From sullen earth, sings hymns at heaven's gate;
   For thy sweet love remembered such wealth brings
   That then I scorn to change my state with kings.

Percy Bysshe Shelley (1792–1822)

Ozymandias° 1818

I met a traveler from an antique land
Who said: Two vast and trunkless legs of stone
Stand in the desert. . . . Near them, on the sand,
Half sunk, a shattered visage lies, whose frown,
And wrinkled lip, and sneer of cold command,   5
Tell that its sculptor well those passions read
Which yet survive, stamped on these lifeless things,
The hand that mocked them, and the heart that fed:
And on the pedestal these words appear:
"My name is Ozymandias, King of Kings: 10
Look on my works, ye Mighty, and despair!"
Nothing beside remains. Round the decay
Of that colossal wreck, boundless and bare
The lone and level sands stretch far away.

Ozymandias: Greek name for Ramses II, pharaoh of Egypt for sixty-seven years during the thirteenth century B.C. His colossal statue lies prostrate in the sands of Luxor. Napoleon's soldiers measured it (56 feet long, ear 3½ feet long, weight 1,000 tons). Its inscription, according to the Greek historian Diodorus Siculus, was "I am Ozymandias, King of Kings; if anyone wishes to know what I am and where I lie, let him surpass me in some of my exploits."

Lydia Huntley Sigourney (1791–1865)

Indian Names 1834

"How can the red men be forgotten, while so many of
our states and territories, bays, lakes and rivers, are
indelibly stamped by names of their giving?"

Ye say they all have passed away,
    That noble race and brave,
That their light canoes have vanished
    From off the crested wave;
That 'mid the forests where they roamed   5
    There rings no hunter shout,
But their name is on your waters,
    Ye may not wash it out.

'Tis where Ontario's billow
    Like Ocean's surge is curled,   10
Where strong Niagara's thunders wake
    The echo of the world.
Where red Missouri bringeth
    Rich tribute from the west,
And Rappahannock sweetly sleeps   15
    On green Virginia's breast.

Ye say their cone-like cabins,
    That clustered o'er the vale,

Have fled away like withered leaves
    Before the autumn gale, 20
But their memory liveth on your hills,
    Their baptism on your shore,
Your everlasting rivers speak
    Their dialect of yore.

Old Massachusetts wears it, 25
    Within her lordly crown,
And broad Ohio bears it,
    Amid his young renown;
Connecticut hath wreathed it
    Where her quiet foliage waves, 30
And bold Kentucky breathed it hoarse
    Through all her ancient caves.

Wachuset hides its lingering voice
    Within his rocky heart,
And Alleghany graves its tone 35
    Throughout his lofty chart;
Monadnock on his forehead hoar
    Doth seal the sacred trust,
Your mountains build their monument,
    Though ye destroy their dust. 40

Ye call these red-browed brethren
    The insects of an hour,
Crushed like the noteless worm amid
    The regions of their power;
Ye drive them from their father's lands, 45
    Ye break of faith the seal,
But can ye from the court of Heaven
    Exclude their last appeal?

Ye see their unresisting tribes,
    With toilsome step and slow, 50
On through the trackless desert pass,
    A caravan of woe;
Think ye the Eternal's ear is deaf?
    His sleepless vision dim?
Think ye the *soul's blood* may not cry 55
    From that far land to him?

JONATHAN SWIFT (1667–1745)

A Description of the Morning 1711

Now hardly here and there an hackney-coach,
Appearing, showed the ruddy morn's approach.
Now Betty from her master's bed had flown,
And softly stole to discompose her own.
The slipshod prentice from his master's door 5
Had pared the dirt, and sprinkled round the floor.

Now Moll had whirled her mop with dextrous airs,
Prepared to scrub the entry and the stairs.
The youth with broomy stumps began to trace
The kennel-edge, where wheels had worn the place.   10
The small-coal man was heard with cadence deep,
Till drowned in shriller notes of chimney-sweep,
Duns at his lordship's gate began to meet,
And Brickdust Moll had screamed through half the street.
The turnkey now his flock returning sees,   15
Duly let out a-nights to steal for fees;
The watchful bailiffs take their silent stands;
And schoolboys lag with satchels in their hands.

EDMUND WALLER (1606–1687)

Go, Lovely Rose   1645

Go, lovely rose,
Tell her that wastes her time and me
That now she knows,
When I resemble° her to thee,   *compare*
How sweet and fair she seems to be,   5

Tell her that's young
And shuns to have her graces spied,
That hadst thou sprung
In deserts where no men abide,
Thou must have uncommended died.   10

Small is the worth
Of beauty from the light retired:
Bid her come forth,
Suffer herself to be desired,
And not blush so to be admired.   15

Then die, that she
The common fate of all things rare
May read in thee,
How small a part of time they share
That are so wondrous sweet and fair.   20

WALT WHITMAN (1819–1892)

As Adam Early in the Morning   1861

As Adam early in the morning,
Walking forth from the bower refresh'd with sleep,
Behold me where I pass, hear my voice, approach,
Touch me, touch the palm of your hand to my body as I pass,
Be not afraid of my body.

WALT WHITMAN (1819–1892)
When I Heard the Learn'd Astronomer   1865

When I heard the learn'd astronomer,
When the proofs, the figures, were ranged in columns before me,
When I was shown the charts and diagrams, to add, divide, and measure them,
When I sitting heard the astronomer where he lectured with much applause
    in the lecture-room,
How soon unaccountable I became tired and sick,
Till rising and gliding out I wandered off by myself,
In the mystical moist night-air, and from time to time,
Looked up in perfect silence at the stars.

WALT WHITMAN (1819–1892)
One's-Self I Sing   1867

One's-Self I sing, a simple separate person,
Yet utter the word Democratic, the word En-Masse.

Of physiology from top to toe I sing,
Not physiognomy alone nor brain alone is worthy for the Muse, I say the
    Form complete is worthier far,
The Female equally with the Male I sing.

Of Life immense in passion, pulse, and power,
Cheerful, for freest action formed under the laws divine,
The Modern Man I sing.

WILLIAM WORDSWORTH (1770–1850)
A Slumber Did My Spirit Seal   1800

A slumber did my spirit seal;
  I had no human fears —
She seemed a thing that could not feel
  The touch of earthly years.

No motion has she now, no force;
  She neither hears nor sees;
Rolled round in earth's diurnal course,
  With rocks, and stones, and trees.

The Granger Collection.

WILLIAM WORDSWORTH (1770–1850)
I Wandered Lonely as a Cloud   1807

I wandered lonely as a cloud
That floats on high o'er vales and hills,
When all at once I saw a crowd,

A host, of golden daffodils,
Beside the lake, beneath the trees,   5
Fluttering and dancing in the breeze.

Continuous as the stars that shine
And twinkle on the milky way,
They stretched in never-ending line
Along the margin of a bay;   10
Ten thousand saw I at a glance,
Tossing their heads in sprightly dance.

The waves beside them danced, but they
Outdid the sparkling waves in glee;
A poet could not but be gay,   15
In such a jocund company;
I gazed — and gazed — but little thought
What wealth the show to me had brought:

For oft, when on my couch I lie
In vacant or in pensive mood,   20
They flash upon that inward eye
Which is the bliss of solitude;
And then my heart with pleasure fills,
And dances with the daffodils.

WILLIAM WORDSWORTH (1770–1850)

Composed upon Westminster Bridge 1807

Earth has not anything to show more fair:
Dull would he be of soul who could pass by
A sight so touching in its majesty:
This City now doth, like a garment, wear
The beauty of the morning; silent, bare,   5
Ships, towers, domes, theaters and temples lie
Open unto the fields, and to the sky;
All bright and glittering in the smokeless air.
Never did sun more beautifully steep
In his first splendor, valley, rock, or hill;   10
Ne'er saw I, never felt, a calm so deep!
The river glideth at his own sweet will:
Dear God! the very houses seem asleep;
And all that mighty heart is lying still!

WILLIAM WORDSWORTH (1770–1850)

Mutability 1822

From low to high doth dissolution climb,
And sink from high to low, along a scale
Of awful° notes, whose concord shall not fail;   *awe-filled*
A musical but melancholy chime,
Which they can hear who meddle not with crime,   5

Nor avarice, nor over-anxious care.
Truth fails not; but her outward forms that bear
The longest date do melt like frosty rime,
That in the morning whitened hill and plain
And is no more; drop like the tower sublime   10
Of yesterday, which royally did wear
His crown of weeds, but could not even sustain
Some casual shout that broke the silent air,
Or the unimaginable touch of Time.

STEFANIE WORTMAN (B. 1980)

Mortuary Art   2010

Again my mother makes me promise
never to have her cremated, as if I could
forget how different she and I are in our
senseless fears. I am so scared of burial,
that airless allotment of space the body   5
doesn't need. But maybe she's right
that grief should have a place to focus it.
You watch three pounds of ash dissolve
in water and suddenly, he's everywhere,
the dead father, in the rivulet rain makes   10
on your windshield. Instead, allow
the stone's symbolism, the highway
memorial cross's ruthless precision,
even if implicating the faded grass
along the margin is almost, no is,   15
too much to bear. Who knows how
the dead feel about our solicitude.
Whether we fold them, gently, lovingly,
or not, into a coffin, into a box, they are
not folded, are not there, are not.

> **WHEN I WRITE** "As I write, I move lines around, change words and phrases, and delete sections that don't seem to work. When a poem is done, I get a feeling that is similar to arriving at the last note in a musical composition. When everything falls into the right place, the poem just has a finished feeling."
> — STEFANIE WORTMAN

WILLIAM BUTLER YEATS (1865–1939)

The Lake Isle of Innisfree°   1892

I will arise and go now, and go to Innisfree,
And a small cabin build there, of clay and
    wattles made:
Nine bean-rows will I have there, a hive for the
    honey-bee,
And live alone in the bee-loud glade.

© Hulton-Deutsch Collection/Corbis.

The Lake Isle of Innisfree: An island in Lough (or Lake) Gill, in western Ireland.

And I shall have some peace there, for peace comes dropping slow,   5
Dropping from the veils of the morning to where the cricket sings;
There midnight's all a glimmer, and noon a purple glow,
And evening full of the linnet's wings.

I will arise and go now, for always night and day
I hear lake water lapping with low sounds by the shore: 10
While I stand on the roadway, or on the pavements grey,
I hear it in the deep heart's core.

WILLIAM BUTLER YEATS (1865–1939)

When You Are Old   1893

When you are old and grey and full of sleep,
And nodding by the fire, take down this book,
And slowly read, and dream of the soft look
Your eyes had once, and of their shadows deep;

How many loved your moments of glad grace,   5
And loved your beauty with love false or true,
But one man loved the pilgrim soul in you,
And loved the sorrows of your changing face;

And bending down beside the glowing bars,
Murmur, a little sadly, how Love fled   10
And paced upon the mountains overhead
And hid his face amid a crowd of stars.

WILLIAM BUTLER YEATS (1865–1939)

Leda and the Swan°   1924

A sudden blow: the great wings beating still
Above the staggering girl, her thighs caressed
By the dark webs, her nape caught in his bill,
He holds her helpless breast upon his breast.

How can those terrified vague fingers push   5
The feathered glory from her loosening thighs?
And how can body, laid in that white rush,
But feel the strange heart beating where it lies?

A shudder in the loins engenders there
The broken wall, the burning roof and tower   10
And Agamemnon dead.
                              Being so caught up,
So mastered by the brute blood of the air,
Did she put on his knowledge with his power
Before the indifferent beak could let her drop?   15

Leda and the Swan: In Greek myth, Zeus in the form of a swan seduced Leda and fathered Helen
of Troy (whose abduction started the Trojan War) and Clytemnestra, Agamemnon's wife and
murderer. Yeats thought of Zeus's appearance to Leda as a type of annunciation, like the angel
appearing to Mary.

DRAMA

The Study
of Drama

42

Reading Drama

> I regard the theater as serious business, one that makes or should make man more human, which is to say, less alone.
> — ARTHUR MILLER

© Corbis.

> There are people who ask why we need the arts. It's an intangible quality that the arts are teaching. People always want to quantify it, and you can't quantify the arts.
> — NILAJA SUN

Thos Robinson/Getty Images.

READING DRAMA RESPONSIVELY

The publication of a short story, novel, or poem represents for most writers the final step in a long creative process that might have begun with an idea, issue, emotion, or question that demanded expression. *Playwrights* — writers who make plays — may begin a work in the same way as other writers, but rarely are they satisfied with only its publication because most dramatic literature — what we call *plays* — is written to be performed by actors on a stage before an audience. Playwrights typically create a play keeping in mind not only readers but also actors, producers, directors, costumers, designers, technicians, and a theater full of other support staff who have a hand in presenting the play to a live audience.

Drama is literature equipped with arms, legs, tears, laughs, whispers, shouts, and gestures that are alive and immediate. Indeed, the word *drama* derives from the Greek word *dran*, meaning "to do" or "to perform." The text of many plays — the *script* — may come to life fully only when the written words are transformed into a performance. Although there are plays that do not invite production, they are relatively few. Such plays, written to be read rather than performed, are called *closet dramas*. In this kind of work (primarily associated with nineteenth-century English literature), literary art outweighs all other considerations. The majority of playwrights, however, view the written word as the beginning of a larger creation and hope that a producer will deem their scripts worthy of production.

Given that most playwrights intend their works to be performed, it might be argued that reading a play is a poor substitute for seeing it acted on a stage — perhaps something like reading a recipe without having access to the ingredients and a kitchen. This analogy is tempting, but it overlooks the literary dimensions of a script; the words we hear on a stage were written first. Read from a page, these words can feed an imagination in ways that a recipe cannot satisfy a hungry cook. We can fill in a play's missing faces, voices, actions, and settings in much the same way that we imagine these elements in a short story or novel. Like any play director, we are free to include as many ingredients as we have an appetite for.

This imaginative collaboration with the playwright creates a mental world that can be nearly as real and vivid as a live performance. Sometimes readers find that they prefer their own reading of a play to a director's interpretation. Shakespeare's Hamlet, for instance, has been presented as a whining son, but you may read him as a strong prince. Rich plays often accommodate a wide range of imaginative responses to their texts. Reading, then, is an excellent way to appreciate and evaluate a production of a play. Moreover, reading is valuable in its own right because it allows us to enter the playwright's created world even when a theatrical production is unavailable.

Reading a play, however, requires more creative imagining than sitting in an audience watching actors on a stage presenting lines and actions before you. As a reader you become the play's director; you construct an interpretation based on the playwright's use of language, development of character, arrangement of incidents, description of settings, and directions for staging. Keeping track of the playwright's handling of these elements will help you to organize your response to the play. You may experience suspense, fear, horror, sympathy, or humor, but whatever experience a play evokes, ask yourself why you respond to it as you do. You may discover that your assessment of Hamlet's character is different from someone else's, but whether you find him heroic, indecisive, neurotic, or a complex of competing qualities, you'll be better equipped to articulate your interpretation of him if you pay attention to your responses and ask yourself questions as you read. Consider, for example, how his reactions might be similar to or different from your own. How does his language reveal his character? Does his behavior seem justified? How would you play the role yourself? What actor do you think might best play the Hamlet that you have created in your imagination? Why would he or she (women have also played Hamlet onstage) fill the role best?

These kinds of questions (see Questions for Responsive Reading and Writing, p. 1115) can help you to think and talk about your responses to a play. Happily, such questions needn't — and often can't — be fully answered as you read the play. Frequently you must experience the entire play before you can determine how its elements work together. That's why reading a play can be such a satisfying experience. You wouldn't think of asking a live actor onstage to repeat her lines because you didn't quite comprehend their significance, but you can certainly reread a page in a book. Rereading allows you to replay language, characters, and incidents carefully and thoroughly to your own satisfaction.

Trifles

In the following play, Susan Glaspell skillfully draws on many dramatic elements and creates an intense story that is as effective on the page as it is in the theater. Glaspell wrote *Trifles* in 1916 for the Provincetown Players on Cape Cod, in Massachusetts. Their performance of the work helped her develop a reputation as a writer sensitive to feminist issues. The year after *Trifles* was produced, Glaspell transformed the play into a short story titled "A Jury of Her Peers." (A passage from the story appears on p. 1092 for comparison.)

Provided courtesy of the Lear Center for Special Collections & Archives, Connecticut College.

Glaspell's life in the Midwest provided her with the setting for *Trifles*. Born and raised in Davenport, Iowa, she graduated from Drake University in 1899 and then worked for a short time as a reporter on the *Des Moines News,* until her short stories were accepted in magazines such as *Harper's* and *Ladies' Home Journal.* Glaspell moved to the Northeast when she was in her early thirties to continue writing fiction and drama. She published novels, some twenty plays, and more than forty short stories. *Alison's House,* based on Emily Dickinson's life, earned her a Pulitzer Prize for drama in 1931. *Trifles* and "A Jury of Her Peers" remain, however, Glaspell's best-known works.

Glaspell wrote *Trifles* to complete a bill that was to feature several one-act plays by Eugene O'Neill. In *The Road to the Temple* (1926), she recalls how the play came to her as she sat in the theater looking at a bare stage. First, "the stage became a kitchen. . . . Then the door at the back opened, and people all bundled up came in — two or three men. I wasn't sure which, but sure enough about the two women, who hung back, reluctant to enter that kitchen. When I was a newspaper reporter out in Iowa, I was sent down-state to do a murder trial, and I never forgot going to the kitchen of a woman who had been locked up in town."

Trifles is about a murder committed in a midwestern farmhouse, but the play goes beyond the kinds of questions raised by most whodunit stories. The murder is the occasion instead of the focus. The play's major concerns are the moral, social, and psychological aspects of the assumptions and perceptions of the men and women who search for the murderer's motive. Glaspell is finally more interested in the meaning of Mrs. Wright's life than in the details of Mr. Wright's death.

As you read the play, keep track of your responses to the characters and note in the margin the moments when Glaspell reveals how men and women respond differently to the evidence before them. What do those moments suggest about the kinds of assumptions these men and women make about themselves and each other? How do their assumptions compare with your own?

Susan Glaspell (1882–1948)

Trifles   1916

CHARACTERS

George Henderson, county attorney
Henry Peters, sheriff
Lewis Hale, a neighboring farmer
Mrs. Peters
Mrs. Hale

SCENE: The kitchen in the now abandoned farmhouse of John Wright, a gloomy kitchen, and left without having been put in order — unwashed pans under the sink, a loaf of bread outside the breadbox, a dish towel on the table — other signs of incompleted work. At the rear the outer door opens and the Sheriff comes in followed by the County Attorney and Hale. The Sheriff and Hale are men in middle life, the County Attorney is a young man; all are much bundled up and go at once to the stove. They are followed by the two women — the Sheriff's wife first; she is a slight wiry woman, a thin nervous face. Mrs. Hale is larger and would ordinarily be called more comfortable looking, but she is disturbed now and looks fearfully about as she enters. The women have come in slowly, and stand close together near the door.

County Attorney (rubbing his hands): This feels good. Come up to the fire, ladies.
Mrs. Peters (after taking a step forward): I'm not — cold.
Sheriff (unbuttoning his overcoat and stepping away from the stove as if to mark the beginning of official business): Now, Mr. Hale, before we move things

about, you explain to Mr. Henderson just what you saw when you came here yesterday morning.

County Attorney: By the way, has anything been moved? Are things just as you left them yesterday?

Sheriff (looking about): It's just about the same. When it dropped below zero last night I thought I'd better send Frank out this morning to make a fire for us — no use getting pneumonia with a big case on, but I told him not to touch anything except the stove — and you know Frank.

County Attorney: Somebody should have been left here yesterday.

Sheriff: Oh — yesterday. When I had to send Frank to Morris Center for that man who went crazy — I want you to know I had my hands full yesterday. I knew you could get back from Omaha by today and as long as I went over everything here myself —

County Attorney: Well, Mr. Hale, tell just what happened when you came here yesterday morning.

Hale: Harry and I had started to town with a load of potatoes. We came along the road from my place and as I got here I said, "I'm going to see if I can't get John Wright to go in with me on a party telephone." I spoke to Wright about it once before and he put me off, saying folks talked too much anyway, and all he asked was peace and quiet — I guess you know about how much he talked himself; but I thought maybe if I went to the house and talked about it before his wife, though I said to Harry that I didn't know as what his wife wanted made much difference to John —

County Attorney: Let's talk about that later, Mr. Hale. I do want to talk about that, but tell now just what happened when you got to the house.

Hale: I didn't hear or see anything; I knocked at the door, and still it was all quiet inside. I knew they must be up, it was past eight o'clock. So I knocked again, and I thought I heard somebody say, "Come in." I wasn't sure, I'm not sure yet, but I opened the door — this door (*indicating the door by which the two women are still standing*) and there in that rocker — (*pointing to it*) sat Mrs. Wright. (*They all look at the rocker.*)

County Attorney: What — was she doing?

Hale: She was rockin' back and forth. She had her apron in her hand and was kind of — pleating it.

County Attorney: And how did she — look?

Hale: Well, she looked queer.

County Attorney: How do you mean — queer?

Hale: Well, as if she didn't know what she was going to do next. And kind of done up.

County Attorney: How did she seem to feel about your coming?

Hale: Why, I don't think she minded — one way or other. She didn't pay much attention. I said, "How do, Mrs. Wright, it's cold, ain't it?" And she said, "Is it?" — and went on kind of pleating at her apron. Well, I was surprised; she didn't ask me to come up to the stove, or to set down, but just sat there, not even looking at me, so I said, "I want to see John." And then she — laughed. I guess you would call it a laugh. I thought of Harry and the team outside, so I said a little sharp: "Can't I see John?" "No," she says, kind o' dull like. "Ain't he home?" says I. "Yes," says she, "he's home." "Then why can't I see him?" I asked her, out of patience. "'Cause he's dead," says she. *"Dead?"* says I. She just nodded her head, not getting a bit excited, but rockin' back and forth. "Why — where is he?" says I, not knowing what to say. She just pointed upstairs — like that *(himself pointing to the room above)*. I started for the stairs, with the idea of going up there. I walked from there to here — then I says, "Why, what did he die of?" "He died of a rope round his neck," says she, and just went on pleatin' at her apron. Well, I went out and called Harry. I thought I might — need help. We went upstairs and there he was lyin' —

County Attorney: I think I'd rather have you go into that upstairs, where you can point it all out. Just go on now with the rest of the story.

Hale: Well, my first thought was to get that rope off. It looked . . . *(stops; his face twitches)* . . . but Harry, he went up to him, and he said, "No, he's dead all right, and we'd better not touch anything." So we went back downstairs. She was still sitting that same way. "Has anybody been notified?" I asked. "No," says she, unconcerned. "Who did this, Mrs. Wright?" said Harry. He said it businesslike — and she stopped pleatin' of her apron. "I don't know," she says. "You don't *know*?" says Harry. "No," says she. "Weren't you sleepin' in the bed with him?" says Harry. "Yes," says she, "but I was on the inside." "Somebody slipped a rope round his neck and strangled him and you didn't wake up?" says Harry. "I didn't wake up," she said after him. We must 'a' looked as if we didn't see how that could be, for after a minute she said, "I sleep sound." Harry was going to ask her more questions but I said maybe we ought to let her tell her story first to the coroner, or the sheriff, so Harry went fast as he could to Rivers' place, where there's a telephone.

County Attorney: And what did Mrs. Wright do when she knew that you had gone for the coroner?

Hale: She moved from the rocker to that chair over there *(pointing to a small chair in the corner)* and just sat there with her hands held together and looking down. I got a feeling that I ought to make some conversation, so I said I had come in to see if John wanted to put in a telephone, and at that she started to laugh, and then she stopped and looked at me — scared. *(The County Attorney, who has had his notebook out, makes a note.)* I dunno, maybe it wasn't scared. I wouldn't like to say it was. Soon Harry got back, and then Dr. Lloyd came and you, Mr. Peters, and so I guess that's all I know that you don't.

County Attorney (looking around): I guess we'll go upstairs first — and then out to the barn and around there. *(To the Sheriff.)* You're convinced that there was nothing important here — nothing that would point to any motive?

Sheriff: Nothing here but kitchen things. *(The County Attorney, after again looking around the kitchen, opens the door of a cupboard closet. He gets up on a chair and looks on a shelf. Pulls his hand away, sticky.)*

County Attorney: Here's a nice mess. *(The women draw nearer.)*

Mrs. Peters (to the other woman): Oh, her fruit; it did freeze. *(To the Lawyer.)* She worried about that when it turned so cold. She said the fire'd go out and her jars would break.

Sheriff (rises): Well, can you beat the woman! Held for murder and worryin' about her preserves.

County Attorney: I guess before we're through she may have something more serious than preserves to worry about.

Hale: Well, women are used to worrying over trifles. *(The two women move a little closer together.)*

County Attorney (with the gallantry of a young politician): And yet, for all their worries, what would we do without the ladies? *(The women do not unbend. He goes to the sink, takes a dipperful of water from the pail, and pouring it into a basin, washes his hands. Starts to wipe them on the roller towel, turns it for a cleaner place.)* Dirty towels! *(Kicks his foot against the pans under the sink.)* Not much of a housekeeper, would you say, ladies?

Mrs. Hale (stiffly): There's a great deal of work to be done on a farm.

County Attorney: To be sure. And yet *(with a little bow to her)* I know there are some Dickson county farmhouses which do not have such roller towels. *(He gives it a pull to expose its full length again.)*

Mrs. Hale: Those towels get dirty awful quick. Men's hands aren't always as clean as they might be.

County Attorney: Ah, loyal to your sex, I see. But you and Mrs. Wright were neighbors. I suppose you were friends, too.

Mrs. Hale (shaking her head): I've not seen much of her of late years. I've not been in this house — it's more than a year.

County Attorney: And why was that? You didn't like her?

Mrs. Hale: I liked her all well enough. Farmers' wives have their hands full, Mr. Henderson. And then —

County Attorney: Yes — ?

Mrs. Hale (looking about): It never seemed a very cheerful place.

County Attorney: No — it's not cheerful. I shouldn't say she had the homemaking instinct.

Mrs. Hale: Well, I don't know as Wright had, either.

County Attorney: You mean that they didn't get on very well?

Mrs. Hale: No, I don't mean anything. But I don't think a place'd be any cheerfuller for John Wright's being in it.

County Attorney: I'd like to talk more of that a little later. I want to get the lay of things upstairs now. *(He goes to the left where three steps lead to a stair door.)*

Sheriff: I suppose anything Mrs. Peters does'll be all right. She was to take in some clothes for her, you know, and a few little things. We left in such a hurry yesterday.

County Attorney: Yes, but I would like to see what you take, Mrs. Peters, and keep an eye out for anything that might be of use to us.

Mrs. Peters: Yes, Mr. Henderson. *(The women listen to the men's steps on the stairs, then look about the kitchen.)*

Mrs. Hale: I'd hate to have men coming into my kitchen, snooping around and criticizing. *(She arranges the pans under sink which the lawyer had shoved out of place.)*

Mrs. Peters: Of course it's no more than their duty.

Mrs. Hale: Duty's all right, but I guess that deputy sheriff that came out to make the fire might have got a little of this on. *(Gives the roller towel a pull.)* Wish I'd thought of that sooner. Seems mean to talk about her for not having things slicked up when she had to come away in such a hurry.

Mrs. Peters (who has gone to a small table in the left rear corner of the room, and lifted one end of a towel that covers a pan): She had bread set. *(Stands still.)*

Mrs. Hale (eyes fixed on a loaf of bread beside the breadbox, which is on a low shelf at the other side of the room. Moves slowly toward it.): She was going to put this in there. *(Picks up loaf, then abruptly drops it. In a manner of returning to familiar things.)* It's a shame about her fruit. I wonder if it's all gone. *(Gets up on the chair and looks.)* I think there's some here that's all right, Mrs. Peters. Yes — here; *(holding it toward the window)* this is cherries, too. *(Looking again.)* I declare I believe that's the only one. *(Gets down, bottle in her hand. Goes to the sink and wipes it off on the outside.)* She'll feel awful bad after all her hard work in the hot weather. I remember the afternoon I put up my cherries last summer. *(She puts the bottle on the big kitchen table, center of the room. With a sigh, is about to sit down in the rocking-chair. Before she is seated realizes what chair it is; with a slow look at it, steps back. The chair which she has touched rocks back and forth.)*

Mrs. Peters: Well, I must get those things from the front room closet. *(She goes to the door at the right, but after looking into the other room, steps back.)* You coming with me, Mrs. Hale? You could help me carry them. *(They go in the other room; reappear, Mrs. Peters carrying a dress and skirt, Mrs. Hale following with a pair of shoes.)* My, it's cold in there. *(She puts the clothes on the big table, and hurries to the stove.)*

Mrs. Hale (examining the skirt): Wright was close. I think maybe that's why she kept so much to herself. She didn't even belong to the Ladies' Aid. I suppose she felt she couldn't do her part, and then you don't enjoy things when you feel shabby. I heard she used to wear pretty clothes and be lively, when she was Minnie Foster, one of the town girls singing in the choir. But that — oh, that was thirty years ago. This all you want to take in?

Mrs. Peters: She said she wanted an apron. Funny thing to want, for there isn't much to get you dirty in jail, goodness knows. But I suppose just to make her feel more natural. She said they was in the top drawer in this cupboard. Yes, here. And then her little shawl that always hung behind the door. *(Opens stair door and looks.)* Yes, here it is. *(Quickly shuts door leading upstairs.)*

Mrs. Hale (abruptly moving toward her): Mrs. Peters?

Mrs. Peters: Yes, Mrs. Hale?

Mrs. Hale: Do you think she did it?

Mrs. Peters (in a frightened voice): Oh, I don't know.

Mrs. Hale: Well, I don't think she did. Asking for an apron and her little shawl. Worrying about her fruit.

Mrs. Peters (starts to speak, glances up, where footsteps are heard in the room above. In a low voice): Mr. Peters says it looks bad for her. Mr. Henderson is awful sarcastic in a speech and he'll make fun of her sayin' she didn't wake up.

Mrs. Hale: Well, I guess John Wright didn't wake when they was slipping that rope under his neck.

Mrs. Peters: No, it's strange. It must have been done awful crafty and still. They say it was such a — funny way to kill a man, rigging it all up like that.

Mrs. Hale: That's just what Mr. Hale said. There was a gun in the house. He says that's what he can't understand.

Mrs. Peters: Mr. Henderson said coming out that what was needed for the case was a motive; something to show anger, or — sudden feeling.

Mrs. Hale (who is standing by the table): Well, I don't see any signs of anger around here. *(She puts her hand on the dish towel which lies on the table, stands looking down at table, one-half of which is clean, the other half messy.)* It's wiped to here. *(Makes a move as if to finish work, then turns and looks at loaf of bread outside the breadbox. Drops towel. In that voice of coming back to familiar things.)* Wonder how they are finding things upstairs. I hope she had it a little more red-up up there. You know, it seems kind of *sneaking.* Locking her up in town and then coming out here and trying to get her own house to turn against her!

Mrs. Peters: But, Mrs. Hale, the law is the law.

Mrs. Hale: I s'pose 'tis. *(Unbuttoning her coat.)* Better loosen up your things, Mrs. Peters. You won't feel them when you go out. *(Mrs. Peters takes off her fur tippet, goes to hang it on hook at back of room, stands looking at the under part of the small corner table.)*

Mrs. Peters: She was piecing a quilt. *(She brings the large sewing basket and they look at the bright pieces.)*

Mrs. Hale: It's a log cabin pattern. Pretty, isn't it? I wonder if she was goin' to quilt it or just knot it? *(Footsteps have been heard coming down the stairs. The Sheriff enters followed by Hale and the County Attorney.)*

Sheriff: They wonder if she was going to quilt it or just knot it! *(The men laugh, the women look abashed.)*

County Attorney (rubbing his hands over the stove): Frank's fire didn't do much up there, did it? Well, let's go out to the barn and get that cleared up. *(The men go outside.)*

Mrs. Hale (resentfully): I don't know as there's anything so strange, our takin' up our time with little things while we're waiting for them to get the evidence. *(She sits down at the big table smoothing out a block with decision.)* I don't see as it's anything to laugh about.

Mrs. Peters (apologetically): Of course they've got awful important things on their minds. *(Pulls up a chair and joins Mrs. Hale at the table.)*

Mrs. Hale (examining another block): Mrs. Peters, look at this one. Here, this is the one she was working on, and look at the sewing! All the rest of it has been so nice and even. And look at this! It's all over the place! Why, it looks as if she didn't know what she was about! *(After she has said this they look at each other, then start to glance back at the door. After an instant Mrs. Hale has pulled at a knot and ripped the sewing.)*

Mrs. Peters: Oh, what are you doing, Mrs. Hale?

Mrs. Hale (mildly): Just pulling out a stitch or two that's not sewed very good. *(Threading a needle.)* Bad sewing always made me fidgety.

Mrs. Peters (nervously): I don't think we ought to touch things.

Mrs. Hale: I'll just finish up this end. *(Suddenly stopping and leaning forward.)* Mrs. Peters?

Mrs. Peters: Yes, Mrs. Hale?

Mrs. Hale: What do you suppose she was so nervous about?

Mrs. Peters: Oh — I don't know. I don't know as she was nervous. I sometimes sew awful queer when I'm just tired. *(Mrs. Hale starts to say something, looks at Mrs. Peters, then goes on sewing.)* Well, I must get these things wrapped up. They may be through sooner than we think. *(Putting apron and other things together.)* I wonder where I can find a piece of paper, and string. *(Rises.)*

Mrs. Hale: In that cupboard, maybe.

Mrs. Peters (looking in cupboard): Why, here's a bird-cage. *(Holds it up.)* Did she have a bird, Mrs. Hale?

Mrs. Hale: Why, I don't know whether she did or not — I've not been here for so long. There was a man around last year selling canaries cheap, but I don't know as she took one; maybe she did. She used to sing real pretty herself.

Mrs. Peters (glancing around): Seems funny to think of a bird here. But she must have had one, or why would she have a cage? I wonder what happened to it?

Mrs. Hale: I s'pose maybe the cat got it.

Mrs. Peters: No, she didn't have a cat. She's got that feeling some people have about cats — being afraid of them. My cat got in her room and she was real upset and asked me to take it out.

Mrs. Hale: My sister Bessie was like that. Queer, ain't it?

Mrs. Peters (examining the cage): Why, look at this door. It's broke. One hinge is pulled apart.

Mrs. Hale (looking too): Looks as if someone must have been rough with it.

Mrs. Peters: Why, yes. *(She brings the cage forward and puts it on the table.)*

Mrs. Hale: I wish if they're going to find any evidence they'd be about it. I don't like this place.

Mrs. Peters: But I'm awful glad you came with me, Mrs. Hale. It would be lonesome for me sitting here alone.

Mrs. Hale: It would, wouldn't it? *(Dropping her sewing.)* But I tell you what I do wish, Mrs. Peters. I wish I had come over sometimes when *she* was here. I — *(looking around the room)* — wish I had.

Mrs. Peters: But of course you were awful busy, Mrs. Hale — your house and your children.

Mrs. Hale: I could've come. I stayed away because it weren't cheerful — and that's why I ought to have come. I — I've never liked this place. Maybe because it's down in a hollow and you don't see the road. I dunno what it is, but it's a lonesome place and always was. I wish I had come over to see Minnie Foster sometimes. I can see now — *(Shakes her head.)*

Mrs. Peters: Well, you mustn't reproach yourself, Mrs. Hale. Somehow we just don't see how it is with other folks until — something turns up.

Mrs. Hale: Not having children makes less work — but it makes a quiet house, and Wright out to work all day, and no company when he did come in. Did you know John Wright, Mrs. Peters?

Mrs. Peters: Not to know him; I've seen him in town. They say he was a good man.

Mrs. Hale: Yes — good; he didn't drink, and kept his word as well as most, I guess, and paid his debts. But he was a hard man, Mrs. Peters. Just to pass the time of day with him — *(Shivers.)* Like a raw wind that gets to the bone. *(Pauses, her eye falling on the cage.)* I should think she would 'a' wanted a bird. But what do you suppose went with it?

Mrs. Peters: I don't know, unless it got sick and died. *(She reaches over and swings the broken door, swings it again, both women watch it.)*

Mrs. Hale: You weren't raised round here, were you? *(Mrs. Peters shakes her head.)* You didn't know — her?

Mrs. Peters: Not till they brought her yesterday.

Mrs. Hale: She — come to think of it, she was kind of like a bird herself — real sweet and pretty, but kind of timid and — fluttery. How — she — did — change.

(Silence: then as if struck by a happy thought and relieved to get back to everyday things.) Tell you what, Mrs. Peters, why don't you take the quilt in with you? It might take up her mind.

Mrs. Peters: Why, I think that's a real nice idea, Mrs. Hale. There couldn't possibly be any objection to it could there? Now, just what would I take? I wonder if her patches are in here — and her things. *(They look in the sewing basket.)*

Mrs. Hale: Here's some red. I expect this has got sewing things in it. *(Brings out a fancy box.)* What a pretty box. Looks like something somebody would give you. Maybe her scissors are in here. *(Opens box. Suddenly puts her hand to her nose.)* Why — *(Mrs. Peters bends nearer, then turns her face away.)* There's something wrapped up in this piece of silk.

Mrs. Peters: Why, this isn't her scissors.

Mrs. Hale *(lifting the silk)*: Oh, Mrs. Peters — it's — *(Mrs. Peters bends closer.)*

Mrs. Peters: It's the bird.

Mrs. Hale *(jumping up)*: But, Mrs. Peters — look at it! Its neck! Look at its neck! It's all — other side *to.*

Mrs. Peters: Somebody — wrung — its — neck. *(Their eyes meet. A look of growing comprehension, of horror. Steps are heard outside. Mrs. Hale slips box under quilt pieces, and sinks into her chair. Enter Sheriff and County Attorney. Mrs. Peters rises.)*

County Attorney *(as one turning from serious things to little pleasantries)*: Well, ladies, have you decided whether she was going to quilt it or knot it?

Mrs. Peters: We think she was going to — knot it.

County Attorney: Well, that's interesting, I'm sure. *(Seeing the bird-cage.)* Has the bird flown?

Mrs. Hale *(putting more quilt pieces over the box)*: We think the — cat got it.

County Attorney *(preoccupied)*: Is there a cat? *(Mrs. Hale glances in a quick covert way at Mrs. Peters.)*

Mrs. Peters: Well, not *now.* They're superstitious, you know. They leave.

County Attorney *(to Sheriff Peters, continuing an interrupted conversation)*: No sign at all of anyone having come from the outside. Their own rope. Now let's go up again and go over it piece by piece. *(They start upstairs.)* It would have to have been someone who knew just the — *(Mrs. Peters sits down. The two women sit there not looking at one another, but as if peering into something and at the same time holding back. When they talk now it is in the manner of feeling their way over strange ground, as if afraid of what they are saying, but as if they cannot help saying it.)*

Mrs. Hale: She liked the bird. She was going to bury it in that pretty box.

Mrs. Peters *(in a whisper)*: When I was a girl — my kitten — there was a boy took a hatchet, and before my eyes — and before I could get there — *(Covers her face an instant.)* If they hadn't held me back I would have — *(catches herself, looks upstairs where steps are heard, falters weakly)* — hurt him.

Mrs. Hale *(with a slow look around her)*: I wonder how it would seem never to have had any children around. *(Pause.)* No, Wright wouldn't like the bird — a thing that sang. She used to sing. He killed that, too.

Mrs. Peters *(moving uneasily)*: We don't know who killed the bird.

Mrs. Hale: I knew John Wright.

Mrs. Peters: It was an awful thing was done in this house that night, Mrs. Hale. Killing a man while he slept, slipping a rope around his neck that choked the life out of him.

Mrs. Hale: His neck. Choked the life out of him. (*Her hand goes out and rests on the bird-cage.*)

Mrs. Peters (with rising voice): We don't know who killed him. We don't *know.*

Mrs. Hale (her own feeling not interrupted): If there'd been years and years of nothing, then a bird to sing to you, it would be awful — still, after the bird was still.

Mrs. Peters (something within her speaking): I know what stillness is. When we homesteaded in Dakota, and my first baby died — after he was two years old, and me with no other then —

Mrs. Hale (moving): How soon do you suppose they'll be through looking for the evidence?

Mrs. Peters: I know what stillness is. (*Pulling herself back.*) The law has got to punish crime, Mrs. Hale.

Mrs. Hale (not as if answering that): I wish you'd seen Minnie Foster when she wore a white dress with blue ribbons and stood up there in the choir and sang. (*A look around the room.*) Oh, I *wish* I'd come over here once in a while! That was a crime! That was a crime! Who's going to punish that?

Mrs. Peters (looking upstairs): We mustn't — take on.

Mrs. Hale: I might have known she needed help! I know how things can be — for women. I tell you, it's queer, Mrs. Peters. We live close together and we live far apart. We all go through the same things — it's all just a different kind of the same thing. (*Brushes her eyes, noticing the bottle of fruit, reaches out for it.*) If I was you I wouldn't tell her her fruit was gone. Tell her it *ain't.* Tell her it's all right. Take this in to prove it to her. She — she may never know whether it was broke or not.

Mrs. Peters (takes the bottle, looks about for something to wrap it in; takes petticoat from the clothes brought from the other room, very nervously begins winding this around the bottle. In a false voice): My, it's a good thing the men couldn't hear us. Wouldn't they just laugh! Getting all stirred up over a little thing like a — dead canary. As if that could have anything to do with — with — wouldn't they *laugh!* (*The men are heard coming down stairs.*)

Mrs. Hale (under her breath): Maybe they would — maybe they wouldn't.

County Attorney: No, Peters, it's all perfectly clear except a reason for doing it. But you know juries when it comes to women. If there was some definite thing. Something to show — something to make a story about — a thing that would connect up with this strange way of doing it — (*The women's eyes meet for an instant. Enter Hale from outer door.*)

Hale: Well, I've got the team around. Pretty cold out there.

County Attorney: I'm going to stay here a while by myself. (*To the Sheriff.*) You can send Frank out for me, can't you? I want to go over everything. I'm not satisfied that we can't do better.

Sheriff: Do you want to see what Mrs. Peters is going to take in? (*The Lawyer goes to the table, picks up the apron, laughs.*)

County Attorney: Oh, I guess they're not very dangerous things the ladies have picked out. (*Moves a few things about, disturbing the quilt pieces which cover the box. Steps back.*) No, Mrs. Peters doesn't need supervising. For that matter a sheriff's wife is married to the law. Ever think of it that way, Mrs. Peters?

Mrs. Peters: Not — just that way.

Sheriff (chuckling): Married to the law. *(Moves toward the other room.)* I just want you
   to come in here a minute, George. We ought to take a look at these windows.
County Attorney (scoffingly): Oh, windows!
Sheriff: We'll be right out, Mr. Hale. *(Hale goes outside. The Sheriff follows the
   County Attorney into the other room. Then Mrs. Hale rises, hands tight together,
   looking intensely at Mrs. Peters, whose eyes make a slow turn, finally meeting
   Mrs. Hale's. A moment Mrs. Hale holds her, then her own eyes point the way to
   where the box is concealed. Suddenly Mrs. Peters throws back quilt pieces and
   tries to put the box in the bag she is wearing. It is too big. She opens box, starts
   to take bird out, cannot touch it, goes to pieces, stands there helpless. Sound of
   a knob turning in the other room. Mrs. Hale snatches the box and puts it in the
   pocket of her big coat. Enter County Attorney and Sheriff.)*
County Attorney (facetiously): Well, Henry, at least we found out that she was not
   going to quilt it. She was going to — what is it you call it, ladies?
Mrs. Hale (her hand against her pocket): We call it — knot it, Mr. Henderson.

   Curtain

CONSIDERATIONS FOR CRITICAL THINKING AND WRITING

1. FIRST RESPONSE. Describe the setting of this play. What kind of atmosphere is
   established by the details in the opening scene? Does the atmosphere change
   through the course of the play?

2. Where are Mrs. Hale and Mrs. Peters while Mr. Hale explains to the county
   attorney how the murder was discovered? How does their location suggest
   the relationship between the men and the women in the play?

3. What kind of person was Minnie Foster before she married? How do you
   think her marriage affected her?

4. Characterize John Wright. Why did his wife kill him?

5. Why do the men fail to see the clues that Mrs. Hale and Mrs. Peters discover?

6. What is the significance of the birdcage and the dead bird? Why do Mrs. Hale
   and Mrs. Peters respond so strongly to them? How do you respond?

7. Why don't Mrs. Hale and Mrs. Peters reveal the evidence they have uncovered? What would you have done?

8. How do the men's conversations and actions reveal their attitudes toward
   women?

9. Why do you think Glaspell allows us only to hear about Mr. and Mrs. Wright?
   What is the effect of their never appearing onstage?

10. Does your impression of Mrs. Wright change during the course of the play? If
    so, what changes it?

11. What is the significance of the play's last line, spoken by Mrs. Hale: "We
    call it — knot it, Mr. Henderson"? Explain what you think the tone of Mrs.
    Hale's voice is when she says this line. What is she feeling? What are you
    feeling?

12. Explain the significance of the play's title. Do you think *Trifles* or "A Jury
    of Her Peers," Glaspell's title for the short story version of the play, is more
    appropriate? Can you think of other titles that capture the play's central
    concerns?

13. If possible, find a copy of "A Jury of Her Peers" online or in the library (reprinted in *The Best Short Stories of 1917*, ed. E. J. O'Brien [Boston: Small, Maynard, 1918], pp. 256–82), and write an essay that explores the differences between the play and the short story. (An alternative is to work with the excerpt on p. 1092.)

14. CRITICAL STRATEGIES. Read the section on formalist criticism (pp. 1645–47) in Chapter 51, "Critical Strategies for Reading." Several times the characters say things that they don't mean, and this creates a discrepancy between what appears to be and what is actually true. Point to instances of irony in the play and explain how they contribute to its effects and meanings. (For discussions of irony elsewhere in this book, see the Index of Terms.)

CONNECTIONS TO OTHER SELECTIONS

1. Compare and contrast how Glaspell provides background information in *Trifles* with how Sophocles does so in *Oedipus the King* (p. 1127).

2. Write an essay comparing the views of marriage in *Trifles* and in Kate Chopin's short story "The Story of an Hour" (p. 15). What similarities do you find in the themes of these two works? Are there any significant differences between the works?

3. In an essay compare Mrs. Wright's motivation for committing murder with that of Matt Fowler, the central character from Andre Dubus's short story "Killings" (p. 89). To what extent do you think they are responsible for and guilty of these crimes?

A SAMPLE CLOSE READING

An Annotated Section of Trifles

As you read a play for the first time, highlight lines, circle or underline words, and record your responses in the margins. These responses will allow you to retrieve initial reactions and questions that in subsequent readings you can pursue and resolve. Just as the play is likely to have layered meanings, so too will your own readings as you gradually piece together a variety of elements such as exposition, plot, and character that will lead you toward their thematic significance. The following annotations for an excerpt from *Trifles* offer an interpretation that was produced by several readings of the play. Of course, your annotations could be quite different, depending upon your own approach to the play.

The following excerpt appears about two pages into this nine-page play and is preceded by a significant amount of exposition that establishes the bleak midwestern farm setting and some details about Mrs. Wright, who is the prime suspect in the murder of her husband. Prior to this dialogue, only the male characters speak as they try to discover a motive for the crime.

County Attorney (looking around): I guess we'll go upstairs first — and then out to the barn and around there. *(To the Sheriff.)* You're convinced that there was nothing important here — nothing that would point to any motive?

Sheriff: Nothing here but kitchen things. *(The County Attorney, after again looking around the kitchen, opens the door of a cupboard closet. He gets up on a chair and looks on a shelf. Pulls his hand away, sticky.)*

County Attorney: Here's a nice mess. *(The women draw nearer.)*

Mrs. Peters (to the other woman): Oh, her fruit; it did freeze. *(To the Lawyer.)* She worried about that when it turned so cold. She said the fire'd go out and her jars would break.

Sheriff (rises): Well, can you beat the woman! Held for murder and worryin' about her preserves.

County Attorney: I guess before we're through she may have something more serious than preserves to worry about.

Hale: Well, women are used to worrying over trifles. *(The two women move a little closer together.)*

County Attorney (with the gallantry of a young politician): And yet, for all their worries, what would we do without the ladies? *(The women do not unbend. He goes to the sink, takes a dipperful of water from the pail, and pouring it into a basin, washes his hands. Starts to wipe them on the roller towel, turns it for a cleaner place.)* Dirty towels! *(Kicks his foot against the pans under the sink.)* Not much of a housekeeper, would you say, ladies?

Mrs. Hale (stiffly): There's a great deal of work to be done on a farm.

County Attorney: To be sure. And yet *(with a little bow to her)* I know there are some Dickson county farmhouses which do not have such roller towels. *(He gives it a pull to expose its full length again.)*

Mrs. Hale: Those towels get dirty awful quick. Men's hands aren't always as clean as they might be.

County Attorney: Ah, loyal to your sex, I see. But you and Mrs. Wright were neighbors. I suppose you were friends, too.

Mrs. Hale (shaking her head): I've not seen much of her of late years. I've not been in this house — it's more than a year.

County Attorney: And why was that? You didn't like her?

Mrs. Hale: I liked her all well enough. Farmers' wives have their hands full, Mr. Henderson. And then —

County Attorney: Yes — ?

Mrs. Hale (looking about): It never seemed a very cheerful place.

The Sheriff unknowingly announces a major conflict in the play that echoes the title: from a male point of view, there is nothing of any importance to be found in the kitchen — or in women's domestic lives. Mr. Hale confirms this by pronouncing such matters "trifles."

The County Attorney weighs in with his assessment of this "sticky" situation by calling it a "mess," from which he pulls away.

As the Attorney pulls away, the women move closer together (sides are slowly being drawn), and Mrs. Peters says more than she realizes when she observes, "Oh, her fruit; it did freeze." This anticipates our understanding of the cold, fruitless life that drove Mrs. Wright to murder.

The Sheriff's exasperation about women worrying about "preserves" will ironically help preserve the secret of Mrs. Wright — a woman who was beaten down by her husband but who cannot be beaten by these male authorities.

The Attorney has an eye for dirty towels but not for the real "dirt" embedded in the Wrights' domestic life.

The female characters are identified as "Mrs.," which emphasizes their roles as wives, while the men are autonomous and identified by their professions.

Mrs. Hale's comment begins a process of mitigating Mrs. Wright's murder of her husband. He — husbands, men — must share some of the guilt, too.

In contrast to men (a nice irony), farmers' wives' hands are full of responsibilities for which they receive little credit owing to the males' assumption that they fill their lives with trifles.

Perspective

SUSAN GLASPELL (1882–1948)

From the Short Story Version of Trifles   1917

When Martha Hale opened the storm-door and got a cut of the north wind, she ran back for her big woolen scarf. As she hurriedly wound that round her head her eye made a scandalized sweep of her kitchen. It was no ordinary thing that called her away — it was probably farther from ordinary than anything that had ever happened in Dickson County. But what her eye took in was that her kitchen was in no shape for leaving: her bread all ready for mixing, half the flour sifted and half unsifted.

She hated to see things half done; but she had been at that when the team from town stopped to get Mr. Hale, and then the sheriff came running in to say his wife wished Mrs. Hale would come too — adding, with a grin, that he guessed she was getting scarey and wanted another woman along. So she had dropped everything right where it was.

"Martha!" now came her husband's impatient voice. "Don't keep folks waiting out here in the cold."

She again opened the storm-door, and this time joined the three men and the one woman waiting for her in the big two-seated buggy.

After she had the robes tucked around her she took another look at the woman who sat beside her on the back seat. She had met Mrs. Peters the year before at the county fair, and the thing she remembered about her was that she didn't seem like a sheriff's wife. She was small and thin and didn't have a strong voice. Mrs. Gorman, sheriff's wife before Gorman went out and Peters came in, had a voice that somehow seemed to be backing up the law with every word. But if Mrs. Peters didn't look like a sheriff's wife, Peters made it up in looking like a sheriff. He was to a dot the kind of man who could get himself elected sheriff — a heavy man with a big voice, who was particularly genial with the law-abiding, as if to make it plain that he knew the difference between criminals and noncriminals. And right there it came into Mrs. Hale's mind, with a stab, that this man who was so pleasant and lively with all of them was going to the Wrights' now as a sheriff.

"The country's not very pleasant this time of year," Mrs. Peters at last ventured, as if she felt they ought to be talking as well as the men.

Mrs. Hale scarcely finished her reply, for they had gone up a little hill and could see the Wright place now, and seeing it did not make her feel like talking. It looked very lonesome this cold March morning. It had always been a lonesome-looking place. It was down in a hollow, and the poplar trees around it were lonesome-looking trees. The men were looking at it and talking about what had happened. The county attorney was bending to one side of the buggy, and kept looking steadily at the place as they drew up to it.

"I'm glad you came with me," Mrs. Peters said nervously, as the two women were about to follow the men in through the kitchen door.

Even after she had her foot on the door-step, her hand on the knob, Martha Hale had a moment of feeling she could not cross that threshold. And the reason it seemed she couldn't cross it now was simply because she hadn't crossed it before. Time and time again it had been in her mind, "I ought to go over and see Minnie

Foster" — she still thought of her as Minnie Foster, though for twenty years she had been Mrs. Wright. And then there was always something to do and Minnie Foster would go from her mind. But *now* she could come.

The men went over to the stove. The women stood close together by the door. Young Henderson, the county attorney, turned around and said, "Come up to the fire, ladies."

Mrs. Peters took a step forward, then stopped. "I'm not — cold," she said.

And so the two women stood by the door, at first not even so much as looking around the kitchen.

The men talked for a minute about what a good thing it was the sheriff had sent his deputy out that morning to make a fire for them, and then Sheriff Peters stepped back from the stove, unbuttoned his outer coat, and leaned his hands on the kitchen table in a way that seemed to mark the beginning of official business. "Now, Mr. Hale," he said in a sort of semiofficial voice, "before we move things about, you tell Mr. Henderson just what it was you saw when you came here yesterday morning."

The county attorney was looking around the kitchen.

"By the way," he said, "has anything been moved?" He turned to the sheriff. "Are things just as you left them yesterday?"

Peters looked from cupboard to sink; from that to a small worn rocker a little to one side of the kitchen table.

"It's just the same."

"Somebody should have been left here yesterday," said the county attorney.

"Oh — yesterday," returned the sheriff, with a little gesture as of yesterday having been more than he could bear to think of. "When I had to send Frank to Morris Center for that man who went crazy — let me tell you, I had my hands full *yesterday*. I knew you could get back from Omaha by to-day, George, and as long as I went over everything here myself —"

"Well, Mr. Hale," said the county attorney, in a way of letting what was past and gone go, "tell just what happened when you came here yesterday morning."

Mrs. Hale, still leaning against the door, had that sinking feeling of the mother whose child is about to speak a piece. Lewis often wandered along and got things mixed up in a story. She hoped he would tell this straight and plain, and not say unnecessary things that would just make things harder for Minnie Foster. He didn't begin at once, and she noticed that he looked queer — as if standing in that kitchen and having to tell what he had seen there yesterday morning made him almost sick.

"Yes, Mr. Hale?" the county attorney reminded.

"Harry and I had started to town with a load of potatoes," Mrs. Hale's husband began.

Harry was Mrs. Hale's oldest boy. He wasn't with them now, for the very good reason that those potatoes never got to town yesterday and he was taking them this morning, so he hadn't been home when the sheriff stopped to say he wanted Mr. Hale to come over to the Wright place and tell the county attorney his story there, where he could point it all out. With all Mrs. Hale's other emotions came the fear that maybe Harry wasn't dressed warm enough — they hadn't any of them realized how that north wind did bite.

"We come along this road," Hale was going on, with a motion of his hand to the road over which they had just come, "and as we got in sight of the house I says to Harry, 'I'm goin' to see if I can't get John Wright to take a telephone.' You see," he explained to Henderson, "unless I can get somebody to go in with me they won't come out this branch road except for a price I can't pay. I'd spoke to Wright about it once before; but he put me off, saying folks talked too much anyway, and all he asked was peace and quiet — guess you know about how much he talked himself. But I thought maybe if I went to the house and talked about it before his wife, and said all the women-folks liked the telephones, and that in this lonesome stretch of road it would be a good thing — well, I said to Harry that that was what I was going to say — though I said at the same time that I didn't know as what his wife wanted made much difference to John —"

Now, there he was! — saying things he didn't need to say. Mrs. Hale tried to catch her husband's eye, but fortunately the county attorney interrupted with:

"Let's talk about that a little later, Mr. Hale. I do want to talk about that, but I'm anxious now to get along to just what happened when you got here."

From "A Jury of Her Peers"

Considerations for Critical Thinking and Writing

1. In this opening scene from the story, how is the setting established differently from the way it is in the play (p. 1080)?

2. What kind of information is provided in the opening paragraphs of the story that is missing from the play's initial scene? What is emphasized early in the story but not in the play?

3. Which version brings us into more intimate contact with the characters? How is that achieved?

4. Does the short story's title, "A Jury of Her Peers," suggest any shift in emphasis from the play's title, *Trifles*?

5. Explain why you prefer one version over the other.

ELEMENTS OF DRAMA

Trifles is a **one-act play**; in other words, the entire play takes place in a single location and unfolds as one continuous action. As in a short story, the characters in a one-act play are presented economically, and the action is sharply focused. In contrast, full-length plays can include many characters as well as different settings in place and time. The main divisions of a full-length play are typically **acts**; their ends are indicated by lowering a curtain or turning up the houselights. Playwrights frequently employ acts to accommodate changes in time, setting, characters on stage, or mood. In many full-length plays, such as Shakespeare's *Hamlet*, acts are further divided into **scenes**; according to tradition a scene changes when the location of the action changes or when a new character enters. Acts and scenes are **conventions** that are understood and accepted by audiences because they have come, through usage and time, to be recognized as familiar techniques. The major convention of a one-act play is that it typically consists of only a single scene; nevertheless, one-act plays contain many of the elements of drama that characterize their full-length counterparts.

One-act plays create their effects through compression. They especially lend themselves to modestly budgeted productions with limited stage facilities, such as those put on by little theater groups. However, the potential of a one-act play to move audiences and readers is not related to its length. As *Trifles* shows, one-acts represent a powerful form of dramatic literature.

The single location that composes the **setting** for *Trifles* is described at the very beginning of the play; it establishes an atmosphere that will later influence our judgment of Mrs. Wright. The "gloomy" kitchen is disordered, bare, and sparsely equipped with a stove, sink, rocker, cupboard, two tables, some chairs, three doors, and a window. These details are just enough to allow us to imagine the stark, uninviting place where Mrs. Wright spent most of her time. Moreover, "signs of incompleted work," coupled with the presence of the sheriff and county attorney, create an immediate tension by suggesting that something is terribly wrong. Before a single word is spoken, **suspense** is created as the characters enter. This suspenseful situation causes an anxious uncertainty about what will happen next.

The setting is further developed through the use of **exposition**, a device that provides the necessary background information about the characters and their circumstances. For example, we immediately learn through **dialogue** — the verbal exchanges between characters — that Mr. Henderson, the county attorney, is just back from Omaha. This establishes the setting as somewhere in the Midwest, where winters can be brutally cold and barren. We also find out that John Wright has been murdered and that his wife has been arrested for the crime.

Even more important, Glaspell deftly characterizes the Wrights through exposition alone. Mr. Hale's conversation with Mr. Henderson explains how Mr. Wright's body was discovered, but it also reveals that Wright was a non-communicative man, who refused to share a "party telephone" and who did not consider "what his wife wanted." Later Mrs. Hale adds to this characterization when she tells Mrs. Peters that though Mr. Wright was an honest, good man who paid his bills and did not drink, he was a "hard man" and "Like a raw wind that gets to the bone." Mr. Hale's description of Mrs. Wright sitting in the kitchen dazed and disoriented gives us a picture of a shattered, exhausted woman. But it is Mrs. Hale who again offers further insights when she describes how Minnie Foster, a sweet, pretty, timid young woman who sang in the choir, was changed by her marriage to Mr. Wright and by her childless, isolated life on the farm.

This information about Mr. and Mrs. Wright is worked into the dialogue throughout the play in order to suggest the nature of the **conflict** or struggle between them, a motive, and, ultimately, a justification for the murder. In the hands of a skillful playwright, exposition is not merely a mechanical device; it can provide important information while simultaneously developing characterizations and moving the action forward.

The action is shaped by the *plot*, the author's arrangement of incidents in the play that gives the story a particular focus and emphasis. Plot involves more than simply what happens; it involves how and why things happen. Glaspell begins with a discussion of the murder. Why? She could have begun with the murder itself: the distraught Mrs. Wright looping the rope around her husband's neck. The moment would be dramatic and horribly vivid. We neither see the body nor hear very much about it. When Mr. Hale describes finding Mr. Wright's body, Glaspell has the county attorney cut him off by saying, "I think I'd rather have you go into that upstairs, where you can point it all out. Just go on now with the rest of the story." It is precisely the "rest of the story" that interests Glaspell. Her arrangement of incidents prevents us from sympathizing with Mr. Wright. We are, finally, invited to see Mrs. Wright instead of her husband as the victim.

Mr. Henderson's efforts to discover a motive for the murder appear initially to be the play's focus, but the real conflicts are explored in what seems to be a *subplot*, a secondary action that reinforces or contrasts with the main plot. The discussions between Mrs. Hale and Mrs. Peters and the tensions between the men and the women turn out to be the main plot because they address the issues that Glaspell chooses to explore. Those issues are not about murder but about marriage and how men and women relate to each other.

The *protagonist* of *Trifles*, the central character with whom we tend to identify, is Mrs. Hale. The *antagonist*, the character who is in some kind of opposition to the central character, is the county attorney, Mr. Henderson. These two characters embody the major conflicts presented in the play because each speaks for a different set of characters who represent disparate values. Mrs. Hale and Mr. Henderson are developed less individually than as representative types.

Mrs. Hale articulates a sensitivity to Mrs. Wright's miserable life as well as an awareness of how women are repressed in general by men; she also helps Mrs. Peters to arrive at a similar understanding. When Mrs. Hale defends Mrs. Wright's soiled towels from Mr. Henderson's criticism, Glaspell has her say more than the county attorney is capable of hearing. The *stage directions*, the playwright's instructions about how the actors are to move and behave, indicate that Mrs. Hale responds "stiffly" to Mr. Henderson's disparagements: "Men's hands aren't always as clean as they might be." Mrs. Hale eventually comes to see that the men are, in a sense, complicit because it was insensitivity like theirs that drove Mrs. Wright to murder.

Mr. Henderson, on the other hand, represents the law in a patriarchal, conventional society that blithely places a minimal value on the concerns of women. In his attempt to gather evidence against Mrs. Wright, he implicitly defends men's severe dominance over women. He also patronizes Mrs. Hale and Mrs. Peters. Like Sheriff Peters and Mr. Hale, he regards the women's world as nothing more than "kitchen things" and "trifles." Glaspell, however, patterns the plot so that the women see more about Mrs. Wright's motives than the men do and shows that the women have a deeper understanding of justice.

Many plays are plotted in what has come to be called a *pyramidal pattern*, because the plot is divided into three essential parts. Such plays begin with a *rising action*, in which complication creates conflict for the protagonist. The resulting tension builds to the second major division, known as the *climax*, when the action reaches a final *crisis*, a turning point that has a powerful effect on the protagonist. The third part consists of *falling action*; here the tensions are diminished in the *resolution* of the plot's conflicts and complications (the resolution is also referred to as the *conclusion or dénouement*, a French word meaning "unknotting"). These divisions may occur at different times. There are many variations to this pattern. The terms are helpful for identifying various moments and movements within a given plot, but they are less useful if seen as a means of reducing dramatic art to a formula.

Because *Trifles* is a one-act play, this pyramidal pattern is less elaborately worked out than it might be in a full-length play, but the basic elements of the pattern can still be discerned. The complication consists mostly of Mrs. Hale's refusal to assign moral or legal guilt to Mrs. Wright's murder of her husband. Mrs. Hale is able to discover the motive in the domestic details that are beneath the men's consideration. The men fail to see the significance of the fruit jars, messy kitchen, and badly sewn quilt.

At first Mrs. Peters seems to voice the attitudes associated with the men. Unlike Mrs. Hale, who is "more comfortable looking," Mrs. Peters is "a slight wiry woman" with "a thin nervous face" who sounds like her husband, the sheriff, when she insists, "the law is the law." She also defends the men's patronizing attitudes, because "they've got awful important things on their minds." But Mrs. Peters is a *foil* — a character whose behavior and values contrast with the protagonist's — only up to a point. When the most telling clue is discovered, Mrs. Peters suddenly understands, along with Mrs. Hale, the motive for the killing. Mrs. Wright's caged life was no longer tolerable to her after her husband had killed the bird (which was the one bright spot in her life and which represents her early life as the young Minnie Foster). This revelation brings about the climax, when the two women must decide whether to tell the men what they have discovered. Both women empathize with Mrs. Wright as they confront this crisis, and their sense of common experience leads them to withhold the evidence.

This resolution ends the play's immediate conflicts and complications. Presumably, without a motive the county attorney will have difficulty prosecuting Mrs. Wright — at least to the fullest extent of the law. However, the larger issues related to the *theme*, the central idea or meaning of the play, are left unresolved. The men have both missed the clues and failed to perceive the suffering that acquits Mrs. Wright in the minds of the two women. The play ends with Mrs. Hale's ironic answer to Mr. Henderson's question about quilting. When she says "knot it," she gives him part of the evidence he needs to connect Mrs. Wright's quilting with the knot used to strangle her husband. Mrs. Hale knows — and we know — that Mr. Henderson will miss the clue she offers because he is blinded by his own self-importance and assumptions.

Though brief, *Trifles* is a masterful representation of dramatic elements working together to keep both audiences and readers absorbed in its characters and situations.

Naked Lunch

Born in Lancaster, Pennsylvania, Michael Hollinger earned a B.A. in music at Oberlin Conservatory and a master of arts degree in theater from Villanova University, where he now teaches theater. His comedies and dramas have been widely produced in the United States and abroad. Among his plays are *An Empty Plate in the Café Du Grand Boeuf* (1994), *Red Herring* (1996), *Hot Air* (1997), *Tiny Island* (1998), *Eureka* (1999), *Opus* (2006), *Ghost-Writer* (2011), *Hope and Gravity* (2014), and *Under the Skin* (2015). He has also written three short films and coauthored *Philadelphia Diary* with Bruce Graham and Sonia Sanchez for PBS. His writing

Courtesy of Michael Hollinger.

awards include the Roger L. Stevens Award from the Kennedy Center's Fund for Outstanding New American Plays, the Barrymore Award for Outstanding New Play, and the Otto Haas Award for Emerging Theatre Artist. Hollinger's extensive music background strongly influences his work as a playwright. He has said about his own work, "Plays are music to me; characters are instruments, scenes are movements; tempo, rhythm and dynamics are critical; and melody and counterpoint are always set in relief by rests — beats, pauses, the spaces between." *Naked Lunch* (2003) is one of a group of sixteen plays written by various playwrights for *Trepidation Nation: A Phobic Anthology,* which was produced at the 2002–2003 Humana Festival by the Actor Theatre of Louisville.

> WHEN I WRITE "Conflict is the source of all drama, so I always return to the key questions when writing: Who wants what? What gets in the way? Why is it so important? Opposing forces engage our curiosity about outcome — a crucial element for an art form that requires such focused, sustained attention." — MICHAEL HOLLINGER

MICHAEL HOLLINGER (B. 1962)

Naked Lunch   2003

Lights up on Vernon and Lucy sitting at a small dining-room table, eating. There's a small vase with too many flowers in it, or a large vase with too few. A bottle of wine has been opened. Vernon regales Lucy as he vigorously devours a steak. Lucy discreetly nibbles on her corn-on-the-cob.

Vernon: Larry thinks the whole show's a fake. He says the guy's just an actor and all the crocs are trained. I said, you can't train a crocodile! It's not like some poodle you can teach to ride a bike. It's got this reptile brain, a million years old. All it knows, or wants to know, is whether or not you're juicy. Anyway, this one show the guy's sneaking up on a mother protecting her nest. And she's huge — I mean, this thing could swallow a Buick. And the guy's really playing it up: *(Australian accent.)* "Amazing — look at the size of those teeth!" But just —

(He stops, looking at Lucy. Pause. She looks up from her corn.)

Lucy: What.
Vernon: What's the matter?
Lucy: I'm listening.
Vernon: You're not eating your steak.
Lucy: Oh. No.
Vernon: How come?
Lucy: I'll just eat the corn.

    (She returns to nibbling.)

Vernon: What's wrong with the steak?
Lucy: Nothing.
Vernon: Then eat it. It's good.
Lucy: I'd . . . rather not.
Vernon: Why not?

    (Pause.)

Harlan Taylor photographer, Courtesy of Actors Theatre of Louisville.

Lucy: I'm vegetarian.

    (Beat.)

Vernon: What?
Lucy: I don't eat meat anymore.
Vernon: Since when?
Lucy: Since we, you know. Broke up.

    (Pause.)

Vernon: Just like that?
Lucy: Well —
Vernon: You break up with me and boom next day you start eating tofu?
Lucy: I'd been thinking about it for a while.
Vernon: First I ever heard of it.
Lucy: Well, I'd been thinking. *(Pause. Lucy picks up her corn again, guiding him back to the story:)* So anyway, the guy's sneaking up on the mother . . .
Vernon: Was it because of me?
Lucy: No . . .
Vernon: Something I said, or did . . .
Lucy: It's nothing like that.
Vernon: You were always fond of cataloguing the careless things I said and did . . .
Lucy: I just did some soul-searching, that's all.

    (Beat.)

Vernon: Soul-searching.
Lucy: About a lot of things.
Vernon: And your soul said to you "no more meat."

Lucy: You make it sound silly when you say it like that.

Vernon: Then what, what did your soul tell you?

(*Beat. Lucy exhales heavily and sets down her corn.*)

Lucy: I decided I didn't want to eat anything with a face.

(*Beat.*)

Vernon: A face?

(*He gets up, stands behind her and looks at her plate.*)

Lucy: Vern . . .

Vernon: I don't see any face . . .

Lucy: This doesn't have to be a big deal . . .

Vernon: I don't see a face. Do you see a face?

(*He lifts the plate toward her face.*)

Lucy: There's other reasons.

Vernon: No face.

(*He sets the plate down again.*)

Lucy: I've been reading things.

Vernon: What things?

Lucy: You know, health reports . . .

Vernon: You can't believe that stuff.

Lucy: What do you mean?

Vernon: You can't! One day they say bran's good for you — "Want to live forever? Eat more bran." — the next day they find out bran can kill you.

Lucy: Whatever.

Vernon: Too much bran boom you're dead.

Lucy: There are diseases you can get from meat.

Vernon: Like what?

Lucy: Well, listeria . . .

Vernon: That's chicken. Chicken and turkey.

Lucy: Or Mad Cow.

Vernon: Mad Cow? Did you — That's not even — that's *English,* they have that in England. This isn't English meat, this is from, I don't know, Kansas, or . . . *Wyoming.*

Lucy: Even so, —

Vernon: No. Now you're making stuff up.

Lucy: I'm not; I saw an article —

Vernon: You're just being paranoid, this whole . . . You know what this is? Do you?

Lucy: What.

Vernon: Carnophobia.

Lucy: "Carnophobia"?

Vernon: It's a word, look it up.

Lucy: It's not like I'm scared of meat . . .

Vernon: How do you think this makes me feel?

Lucy: Look, let's just drop it.

Vernon: Huh?

Lucy: We were doing so well . . .

Vernon: I invite you over, cook a nice steak, set out flowers, napkins, the whole nine yards . . .

Lucy: I appreciate the napkins.

Vernon: . . . figure I'll open a bottle of wine, apologize . . . maybe we'll get naked, be like old times.

Lucy: So let's start over.

Vernon: Then you get *carnophobic* on me.

Lucy: Can we?

Vernon: Throw it in my face.

Lucy: Please?

Vernon: Start *cataloguing* what's wrong with everything . . .

Lucy: I never meant this to be a big deal. *(Beat. She puts her hand on his. He looks at her.)* I really didn't.

(Long pause.)

Vernon: Then eat it.

(Beat.)

Lucy: Vern . . . *(He picks up her fork, jams it into her steak, and cuts off a bite with his knife.)* Why do you always have to —

(He extends the piece of meat toward Lucy's mouth.)

Vernon: Eat the meat.

Lucy: I don't want to.

Vernon: *Eat the meat.*

Lucy: Vernon . . .

Vernon: I SAID EAT THE MEAT! *(They are locked in a struggle, he menacing, she terrified. Long pause. Finally, Lucy opens her mouth and takes the bite into it. Pause.)* Chew. *(She chews for fifteen or twenty seconds.)* Swallow. *(She swallows. Cheerfully, without malice:)* Good, isn't it. *(Lucy nods obediently.)* Nice and juicy. *(He stabs his fork into his own steak, cuts off a bite and lifts it.)* See, nothing to be afraid of.

(He pops it into his mouth and begins cutting another. After a moment, Lucy goes back to her corn. They eat in absolute silence. Lights fade.)

"Naked Lunch — *a frozen moment when everyone sees what is on the end of every fork.*" — William S. Burroughs

Considerations for Critical Thinking and Writing

1. **FIRST RESPONSE.** Do you identify more with Vernon or Lucy? Which character seems more sympathetic to you? Explain why.

2. What do you think is the significance of the set directions calling for "a small vase with too many flowers in it, or a large vase with too few"?

3. Why won't Lucy eat meat?

4. Why is it so important to Vernon that Lucy eat the steak?

5. Which character would you describe as the antagonist? What do you think is the play's central conflict?

6. Discuss the tone of the final moments of the play when Vernon cuts the steak for Lucy. Is the central conflict resolved? Why or why not?

7. How would you describe the play's theme?

8. Discuss the significance of the title. How is it related to your understanding of the play's theme?

9. In the biographical headnote to the play, Hollinger describes how his plays share some of the same qualities as music. Reread his explanation of this comparison and discuss how the literary elements of *Naked Lunch* are similar to music.

CONNECTIONS TO OTHER SELECTIONS

1. Compare the theme of *Naked Lunch* with that of Susan Glaspell's *Trifles* (p. 1080).

2. Discuss the symbolic significance of the steak dinner in *Naked Lunch* and the birdcage and the dead bird in *Trifles*.

DRAMA IN POPULAR FORMS

Audiences for live performances of plays have been thinned by high ticket prices but perhaps even more significantly by the impact of motion pictures and television. Motion pictures, the original threat to live theater, have in turn been superseded by television (along with DVDs and online streaming), now the most popular form of entertainment in America. Television audiences are measured in the millions. Probably more people have seen a single weekly episode of a top-rated prime-time program such as *Modern Family* in one evening than have viewed a live performance of *Hamlet* in nearly four hundred years.

Though most of us are seated more often before a television than before live actors, our limited experience with the theater presents relatively few obstacles to appreciation because many of the basic elements of drama are similar whether the performance is on a screen or on a stage. Television has undoubtedly seduced audiences that otherwise might have been attracted to the theater, but television obviously satisfies some aspects of our desire for drama and can be seen as a potential introduction to live theater rather than as its irresistible rival.

Significant differences do, of course, exist between television and theater productions. Most obviously, television's special camera effects can capture phenomena such as earthquakes, raging fires, car chases, and space travel that cannot be realistically rendered on a live stage. The presentation of characters and the plotting of action are also handled differently owing to both the possibilities and limitations of television and the theater. Television's multiple camera angles and close-ups provide a degree of intimacy that cannot be duplicated by actors onstage, yet this intimacy does not achieve the immediacy that live actors create. On commercial television the plot must accommodate itself to breaks in the action so that advertisements can be aired at regular intervals. Beyond these and many other differences, however, there are enough important similarities that the experience of watching television shows can enhance our understanding of a theater production.

Seinfeld

Seinfeld, which aired on NBC, was first produced during the summer of 1989. Although the series ended in the spring of 1998, it remains popular in reruns. No one expected the half-hour situation comedy that evolved from the pilot to draw some twenty-seven million viewers per week who avidly watched Jerry Seinfeld playing himself as a standup comic. Nominated for numerous Emmys, the show became one of the most popular programs of the 1990s. Although *Seinfeld* portrays a relatively narrow band of contemporary urban life — four thirtysomething characters living in New York City's Upper West Side — its quirky humor and engaging characters have attracted vast numbers of devoted fans who have conferred on it a kind of cult status. If you haven't watched an episode on television, noticed the T-shirts and posters, or read *Seinlanguage* (a best-selling collection of *Seinfeld's* monologues), you can catch up with reruns, on Hulu and on TV, and on the Internet, where fans discuss the popularity and merits of the show.

The setting for *Seinfeld* is determined by its subject matter, which is everyday life in Manhattan. Most of the action alternates between two principal locations: Jerry's modest one-bedroom apartment on West 81st Street and the characters' favorite restaurant in the neighborhood. Viewers are often surprised to learn that the show was filmed on a soundstage before a live audience in Studio City, California, because the sights, sounds, and seemingly unmistakable texture of Manhattan appear in background shots so that the city functions almost as a major character in many episodes. If you ever find yourself on the corner of Broadway and 112th Street, you'll recognize the facade of Jerry's favorite restaurant; but don't bother to look for the building that matches the exterior shot of his apartment building because it is in Los Angeles, as are the scenes in which the characters actually appear on the street. The care with which the sets are created suggests how important the illusion of the New York City environment is to the show.

As the central character, Jerry begins and ends each episode with a standup comedy act delivered before a club audience. These monologues (played down in later episodes) are connected to the events in the episodes and demonstrate with humor and insight that ordinary experience — such as standing in line at a supermarket or getting something caught in your teeth — can be a source of genuine humor. For Jerry, life is filled with daily annoyances that he copes with by making sharp humorous observations. Here's a brief instance from "The Pitch" (not reprinted in the excerpt on p. 1105) in which Jerry is in the middle of a conversation with friends when he is interrupted by a phone call.

Jerry (into phone): Hello?
Man (v[oice] o[ver]): Hi, would you be interested in switching over to T.M.I. long distance service?
Jerry: Oh gee, I can't talk right now, why don't you give me your home number and I'll call you later?
Man (v[oice] o[ver]): Uh, well I'm sorry, we're not allowed to do that.

> *Jerry:* Oh, I guess you don't want people calling you at home.
> *Man (v[oice] o[ver]):* No.
> *Jerry:* Well now you know how I feel.
> *Hangs up.*

This combination of polite self-assertion and humor is Jerry's first line of defense in his ongoing skirmishes with the irritations of daily life. Unthreatening in his Nikes and neatly pressed jeans, Jerry nonetheless knows how to give it back when he is annoyed. Seinfeld has described his fictional character as a "nice, New York Jewish boy," but his character's bemused and pointed observations reveal a tough-mindedness that is often wittily on target.

Jerry's life and apartment are continually invaded by his three closest friends: George, Kramer, and Elaine. His refrigerator is the rallying point from which they feed each other lines over cardboard takeout cartons and containers of juice. Jerry's success as a standup comic is their cue to enjoy his groceries as well as his company, but they know their intrusions are welcome because the refrigerator is always restocked.

Jerry's closest friend is George Costanza (played by Jason Alexander), a frequently unemployed, balding, pudgy schlemiel. Any straightforward description of his behavior and sensibilities makes him sound starkly unappealing: he is hypochondriacal, usually upset and depressed, inept with women, embarrassingly stingy, and persistently demanding while simultaneously displaying a vain and cocky nature. As intolerable as he can be, he is nonetheless endearing. The pleasure of his character is in observing how he talks his way into trouble and then attempts to talk his way out of it to Jerry's amazement and amusement.

Across the hall from Jerry's apartment lives Kramer (played by Michael Richards), who is strategically located so as to be the mooch in Jerry's life. Known only as Kramer (until an episode later than "The Pitch" reveals his first name to be Cosmo), he amuses viewers with slapstick twitching, tripping, and falling that serve as a visual contrast to all the talking that goes on. His bizarre schemes and eccentric behavior have their physical counterpart in his vertical hair and his outrageous thrift-shop shirts from the 1960s.

Elaine Benes (played by Julia Louis-Dreyfus), on the other hand, is a sharp-tongued, smart, sexy woman who can hold her own and is very definitely a female member of this boys' club. As Jerry's ex-girlfriend, she provides some interesting romantic tension while serving as a sounding board for the relationship issues that George and Jerry obsess about. Employed at a book company at the time of the episode reprinted here, she, like George and Kramer, is also in the business of publishing her daily problems in Jerry's apartment.

The plots of most *Seinfeld* episodes are generated by the comical situations that Jerry and his friends encounter during the course of their daily lives. Minor irritations develop into huge conflicts that are offbeat, irreverent, or even absurd. The characters have plenty of time to create conflicts in their lives over such everyday situations as dealing with parents, finding an apartment, getting a date, riding the subway, ordering a meal, and losing a car in a mall parking garage. The show's screwball plots involve freewheeling misadventures that are played out in unremarkable but hilarious conversations.

The following scenes from *Seinfeld* are from a classic script titled "The Pitch" that concerns Jerry's and George's efforts to develop a television show for NBC. The script is loosely based on events that actually occurred when Jerry Seinfeld and his real-life friend Larry David (the author of "The Pitch") sat down to discuss ideas for the pilot NBC produced in 1989. As brief as these scenes are, they contain some of the dramatic elements found in a play.

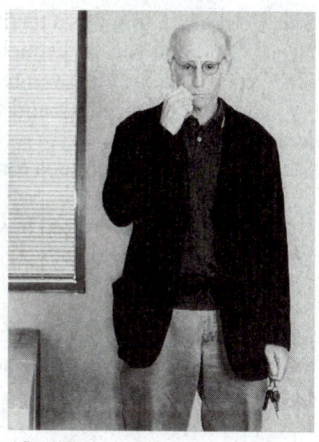

© Dan Winters.

Larry David (b. 1947)

Seinfeld   1992

"The Pitch"

[The following excerpted scenes do not appear one after the other in the original script but are interspersed through several subplots involving Kramer and Elaine.]

ACT ONE

Scene A: *Int[erior] comedy club bar — night*

> *Jerry and George are talking. Suits enter, Stu and Jay.*

Stu: Excuse me, Jerry? I'm Stu Chermak. I'm with NBC.
Jerry: Hi.
Stu: Could we speak for a few moments?
Jerry: Sure, sure.
Jay: Hi, Jay Crespi.
Jerry: Hello.
George: C-R-E-S-P-I?
Jay: That's right.
George: I'm unbelievable at spelling last names. Give me a last name.
Jay: Mm, I'm not —
Jerry: George.
George (backing off): Huh? All right, fine.

Stu: First of all, that was a terrific show.

Jerry: Oh thank you very much.

Stu: And basically, I just wanted to let you know that we've been discussing you at some of our meetings and we'd be very interested in doing something.

Jerry: Really? Wow.

Stu: So, if you have an idea for like a TV show for yourself, well, we'd just love to talk about it.

Jerry: I'd be very interested in something like that.

Stu: Well, here, why don't you give us a call and maybe we can develop a series.

> *They start to exit.*

Jerry: Okay. Great. Thanks.

Stu: It was very nice meeting you.

Jerry: Thank you.

Jay: Nice meeting you.

Jerry: Nice meeting you.

> *George returns.*

George: What was that all about?

Jerry: They said they were interested in me.

George: For what?

Jerry: You know, a TV show.

George: Your own show?

Jerry: Yeah, I guess so.

George: They want you to do a TV show?

Jerry: Well, they want me to come up with an idea. I mean, I don't have any ideas.

George: Come on, how hard is that? Look at all the junk that's on TV. You want an idea? Here's an idea. You coach a gymnastics team in high school. And you're married. And your son's not interested in gymnastics and you're pushing him into gymnastics.

Jerry: Why should I care if my son's into gymnastics?

George: Because you're a gymnastics teacher. It's only natural.

Jerry: But gymnastics is not for everybody.

George: I know, but he's your son.

Jerry: So what?

George: All right, forget that idea, it's not for you. . . . Okay, okay, I got it, I got it. You run an antique store.

Jerry: Yeah and . . . ?

George: And people come in the store and you get involved in their lives.

Jerry: What person who runs an antique store gets involved in people's lives?

George: Why not?

Jerry: So someone comes in to buy an old lamp and all of a sudden I'm getting them out of a jam? I could see if I was a pharmacist because a pharmacist knows what's wrong with everybody that comes in.

George: I know, but antiques are very popular right now.

Jerry: No they're not, they used to be.

George: Oh yeah, like you know.

Jerry: Oh like you do.

> *Cut to:*

ACT ONE

SCENE B: *Int[erior] Jerry's apartment — day*

Jerry and Kramer.

Kramer: . . . And you're the manager of the circus.

Jerry: A circus?

Kramer: Come on, this is a great idea. Look at the characters. You've got all these freaks on the show. A woman with a moustache? I mean, who wouldn't tune in to see a woman with a moustache? You've got the tallest man in the world; the guy who's just a head.

Jerry: I don't think so.

Kramer: Look Jerry, the show isn't about the circus, it's about watching freaks.

Jerry: I don't think the network will go for it.

Kramer: Why not?

Jerry: Look, I'm not pitching a show about freaks.

Kramer: Oh come on Jerry, you're wrong. People they want to watch freaks. This is a "can't miss."

ACT ONE

SCENE C: *Int[erior] coffee shop — lunchtime — day*

Jerry and George enter.

George: So, what's happening with the TV show? You come up with anything?

Jerry: No, nothing.

George: Why don't they have salsa on the table?

Jerry: What do you need salsa for?

George: Salsa is now the number one condiment in America.

Jerry: You know why? Because people like to say "salsa." "Excuse me, do you have salsa?" "We need more salsa." "Where is the salsa? No salsa?"

George: You know it must be impossible for a Spanish person to order seltzer and not get salsa. *(Angry.)* "I wanted seltzer, not salsa."

Jerry: "Don't you know the difference between seltzer and salsa? You have the seltzer after the salsa!"

George: See, this should be the show. This is the show.

Jerry: What?

George: This. Just talking.

Jerry (dismissing): Yeah, right.

George: I'm really serious. I think that's a good idea.

Jerry: Just talking? What's the show about?

George: It's about nothing.

Jerry: No story?

George: No, forget the story.

Jerry: You've got to have a story.

George: Who says you gotta have a story? Remember when we were waiting for that table in that Chinese restaurant that time? That could be a TV show.

Jerry: And who is on the show? Who are the characters?

George: I could be a character.

Jerry: You?

George: You could base a character on me.

Jerry: So on the show there's a character named George Costanza?

George: Yeah. There's something wrong with that? I'm a character. People are always saying to me, "You know you're quite a character."

Jerry: And who else is on the show?

George: Elaine could be a character. Kramer.

Jerry: Now he's a character. . . . So, everyone I know is a character on the show.

George: Right.

Jerry: And it's about nothing?

George: Absolutely nothing.

Jerry: So you're saying, I go in to NBC and tell them I got this idea for a show about nothing.

George: We go into NBC.

Jerry: We? Since when are you a writer?

George: Writer. We're talking about a sit-com.

Jerry: You want to go with me to NBC?

George: Yeah, I think we really got something here.

Jerry: What do we got?

George: An idea.

Jerry: What idea?

George: An idea for the show.

Jerry: I still don't know what the idea is.

George: It's about nothing.

Jerry: Right.

George: Everybody's doing something, we'll do nothing.

Jerry: So we go into NBC, we tell them we've got an idea for a show about nothing.

George: Exactly.

Jerry: They say, "What's your show about?" I say, "Nothing."

George: There you go.

    A beat.

Jerry: I think you may have something there.

    Cut to:

ACT ONE

SCENE D: *Int[erior] Jerry's apartment — day*

    Jerry and Kramer.

Jerry: So it would be about my real life. And one of the characters would be based on you.

Kramer (thinks): No. I don't think so.

Jerry: What do you mean you don't think so?

Kramer: I don't like it.

Jerry: I don't understand. What don't you like about it?

Kramer: I don't like the idea of a character based on me.

Jerry: Why not?

Kramer: Doesn't sit well.

Jerry: You're my neighbor. There's got to be a character based on you.

Kramer: That's your problem, buddy.

Jerry: I don't understand what the big deal is.

Kramer: Hey I'll tell you what, you can do it on one condition.

Jerry: Whatever you want.

Kramer: I get to play Kramer.

Jerry: You can't play Kramer.

Kramer: I am Kramer.

Jerry: But you can't act.

ACT ONE

SCENE G: *Int[erior] NBC reception area — day*

    Jerry and George.

Jerry (to himself): Salsa, seltzer. Hey excuse me, you got any salsa? No not seltzer, salsa. *(George doesn't react.)* What's the matter?

George (nervous): Nothing.

Jerry: You sure? You look a little pale.

George: No, I'm fine. I'm good. I'm fine. I'm very good.

Jerry: What are you, nervous?

George: No, not nervous. I'm good, very good. *(A beat, then: explodes.)* I can't do this! Can't do this!

Jerry: What?

George: I can't do this! I can't do it. I have tried. I'm here. It's impossible.

Jerry: This was your idea.

George: What idea? I just said something. I didn't know you'd listen to me.

Jerry: Don't worry about it. They're just TV executives.

George: They're men with jobs, Jerry! They wear suits and ties. They're married, they have secretaries.

Jerry: I told you not to come.

George: I need some water. I gotta get some water.

Jerry: They'll give us water inside.

George: Really? That's pretty good. . . .

    Receptionist enters.

Receptionist: They're ready for you.

George: Okay, okay, look, you do all the talking, okay?

Jerry: Relax. Who are they?

George: Yeah, they're not better than me.

Jerry: Course not.

George: Who are they?

Jerry: They're nobody.

George: What about me?

Jerry: What about you?

George: Why them? Why not me?

Jerry: Why not you?

George: I'm as good as them.

Jerry: Better.

George: You really think so?

Jerry: No.

Door opens, Jerry and George P.O.V., the four execs stand up.

Fade out.

ACT TWO

Scene G: *Int[erior] NBC president's office — day*

The mood is jovial. Stu Chermak is there — along with Susan Ross, Jay Crespi, and Russell Dalrymple, the head of the network.

Stu (to Jerry): The bit, the bit I really liked was where the parakeet flew into the mirror. Now that's funny.

George: The parakeet in the mirror. That is a good one, Stu.

Jerry: Yeah, it's one of my favorites.

Russell: What about you George, have you written anything we might know?

George: Well, possibly. I wrote an off-Broadway show, "La Cocina." . . . Actually it was off-off-Broadway. It was a comedy about a Mexican chef.

Jerry: Oh it was very funny. There was one great scene with the chef — what was his name?

George: Pepe.

Jerry: Oh Pepe, yeah Pepe. And, uh, he was making tamales.

Susan: Oh, he actually cooked on the stage?

George: No, no, he mimed it. That's what was so funny about it.

Russell: So what have you two come up with?

Jerry: Well we've thought about this in a variety of ways. But the basic idea is I will play myself.

George (interrupting, to Jerry): May I?

Jerry: Go ahead.

George: I think I can sum up the show for you with one word. NOTHING.

Russell: Nothing?

George: Nothing.

Russell: What does that mean?

George: The show is about nothing.

Jerry (to George): Well, it's not about nothing.

George (to Jerry): No, it's about nothing.

Jerry: Well, maybe in philosophy. But even nothing is something.

Jerry and George glare at each other. Receptionist sticks her head in.

Receptionist: Mr. Dalrymple, your niece is on the phone.

Russell: I'll call back.

George: D-A-L-R-I-M-P-E-L.

Russell: Not even close.

George: Is it with a "y"?

Russell: No.

Susan: What's the premise?

Jerry: . . . Well, as I was saying, I would play myself. And as a comedian, living in New York, and I have a friend and a neighbor and an ex-girlfriend, which is all true.

George: Yeah, but nothing happens on the show. You see, it's just like life. You know, you eat, you go shopping, you read. You eat, you read, you go shopping.

Russell: You read? You read on the show?

Jerry: Well I don't know about the reading. We didn't discuss the reading.

Russell: All right, tell me, tell me about the stories. What kind of stories?

George: Oh no, no stories.

Russell: No stories? So what is it?

George: What'd you do today?

Russell: I got up and came to work.

George: There's a show. That's a show.

Russell (confused): How is that a show?

Jerry: Well, uh, maybe something happens on the way to work.

George: No, no, no. Nothing happens.

Jerry: Well, something happens.

Russell: Well why am I watching it?

George: Because it's on TV.

Russell: Not yet.

George: Okay, uh, look, if you want to just keep on doing the same old thing, then maybe this idea is not for you. I for one will not compromise my artistic integrity. And I'll tell you something else. This is the show and we're not going to change it. *(To Jerry.)* Right?

Jerry: How about this? I manage a circus . . .

Considerations for Critical Thinking and Writing

1. **First response.** What does George mean when he says the proposed show should be about "nothing"? Why is George's idea both a comic and a serious proposal?

2. How does the stage direction "Suits enter" serve to characterize Stu and Jay? Write a description of how you think they would look.

3. What is revealed about George's character when he spells Crespi's and Dalrymple's names?

4. Discuss Kramer's assertion that people "want to watch freaks." Do you think this line could be used to sum up accurately audience responses to *Seinfeld*?

5. Choose a scene, and explain how humor is worked into it. What other emotions are evoked in the scene?

6. View an episode of *Seinfeld*. How does reading a script compare with watching the show? Which do you prefer? Why?

7. **Critical strategies.** Read the section on reader-response criticism (pp. 1659–61) in Chapter 51, "Critical Strategies for Reading," and discuss why you like or dislike "The Pitch" and *Seinfeld* in general. Try to account for your personal response to the script and the show.

1. In an essay explain whether you think David Ives's play *Moby-Dude, Or: The Three-Minute Whale* (p. 1483) fills George's prescription that a story should be about "nothing."

Like those of many plays, the settings for these scenes are not detailed. Jerry's apartment and the coffee shop are, to cite only two examples, not described at all. We are told only that it is lunchtime in the coffee shop. Even without a set designer's version of these scenes, we readily create a mental picture of these places that provides a background for the characters. In the coffee shop scene we can assume that Jerry and George are having lunch, but we must supply the food, the plates and cutlery, the tables and chairs, and the other customers. For the television show sets were used that replicated the details of a Manhattan coffee shop, right down to the menus and cash register. If the scene were presented on a stage, a set designer might use minimal sets and props to suggest the specific location. The director of such a production would rely on the viewers' imagination to create the details of the setting.

As brief as they are, these scenes include some exposition to provide the necessary background about the characters and their circumstances. We learn through dialogue, for example, that George is not a writer and that he doesn't think it takes very much talent to write a sitcom even though he's unemployed. These bits of information help to characterize George and allow an audience to place his attitudes and comments in a larger context that will be useful for understanding how other characters read them. Rather than dramatizing background information, the scriptwriter arranges incidents to create a particular focus and effect while working in the necessary exposition through dialogue.

The plot in these scenes shapes the conflicts to emphasize humor. As in any good play, incidents are carefully arranged to achieve a particular effect. In the first scene we learn that NBC executives are interested in having Jerry do his own television show. We also learn, through his habit of spelling people's last names when he meets them, that George is a potential embarrassment. The dialogue between Jerry and George quickly establishes the conflict. The NBC executives would like to produce a TV show with Jerry provided that he can come up with an idea for the series; Jerry, however, has no ideas (here's the complication of the pyramidal plot pattern discussed in Elements of Drama, p. 1094). This complication sets up a conflict for Jerry because George assumes that he can help Jerry develop an idea for the show, which, after all, shouldn't be any more difficult than spelling a stranger's name. As George says, "How hard is that? Look at all the junk that's on TV."

All of a sudden everyone is an expert on scriptwriting. George's off-the-wall suggestions that the premise for the show be Jerry's running an antique shop or teaching gymnastics are complemented by Kramer's idea that Jerry be "the manager of the circus" because "people they want to watch freaks." As unhelpful as Kramer's suggestion is, there is some truth here as well as humor, given his own freakish behavior. However, it is George who comes through with the most intriguing suggestion. As a result of the exuberantly funny riff he and Jerry do on "the difference between seltzer and salsa," George suddenly realizes that the show should be "about nothing" — that it should consist of nothing more than Jerry talking and hanging out with his friends George, Elaine, and Kramer. Jerry's initial skepticism gives way as he seriously considers George's proposal and is intrigued enough to bring George with him to the NBC offices to make the pitch. His decision to bring George to the meeting can only, of course, complicate matters further.

Before the meeting with the NBC executives, George is stricken with one of his crises of confidence when he compares himself to the "men with jobs" who are married and have secretaries. Characteristically, George's temporary lack of confidence shifts to an equally ill-timed arrogance once the meeting begins. He usurps Jerry's role and makes the pitch himself: "Nothing happens on the show. You see, it's just like life. You know, you eat, you go shopping, you read. You eat, you read, you go shopping." The climax occurs when George refuses even to consider any of the reservations the executives have about "nothing" happening on the show. George's insistence that he not compromise his "artistic integrity" creates a crisis for Jerry, a turning point that makes him realize that George's ridiculous arrogance might cost him his opportunity to have a TV show. Jerry's final lines to the executives — "How about this? I manage a circus . . ." — work two ways: he resignedly acknowledges that something — not "nothing" — has just happened and that George is, indeed, something of a freak.

The falling action and resolution typical of a pyramidal plot are not present in "The Pitch" because the main plot is not resolved until a later episode. "The Pitch" also contains several subplots not included in the scenes excerpted in this book. Like the main plot, these subplots involving Elaine, Kramer, and a few minor characters are not resolved until later episodes. Self-contained series episodes are increasingly rare on television, as programmers attempt to hook viewers week after week by creating suspense once associated with serialized stories that appeared weekly or monthly in magazines.

The theme of "The Pitch" is especially interesting because it self-reflexively comments on the basic premise of *Seinfeld* scripts: they are all essentially about "nothing" in that they focus on the seemingly trivial details of the four main characters' lives. The unspoken irony of this theme is that such details are in fact significant because it is just such small, everyday activities that constitute most people's lives.

43

Writing about Drama

Photo by permission of Jilly Wendell.

When you create drama, you look for the best conflict.
—JANE ANDERSON

FROM READING TO WRITING

Because dramatic literature is written to be performed, writing about reading a play may seem twice removed from what playwrights intend the experience of drama to be: a live audience responding to live actors. Although reading a play creates distance between yourself and a performance of it, reading a play can actually bring you closer to understanding that what supports a stage production of any play is the literary dimension of a script. Writing about that script — examining carefully how the language of the stage directions, setting, exposition, dialogue, plot, and other dramatic elements serve to produce effects and meanings — can enhance an imaginative re-creation of a performance. In a sense, writing about a play gauges your own interpretative response as an audience member — the difference, of course, is that instead of applauding, you are typing.

"There's the rub," as Hamlet might say, because you're working with the precision of your fingertips rather than with the hearty response of your palms. Composing an essay about drama records more than your response to a play; writing also helps you explore, clarify, and discover dimensions of the play you may not have perceived by simply watching a performance of it. Writing is work, of course, but it's the kind of work that brings you closer to your own imagination as well as to the play. That process is more accessible if you read carefully, take notes, and annotate the text to generate ideas (for a discussion of this process see Chapter 52, "Reading and the Writing Process"). This chapter offers a set of questions to help you read and write about drama and includes a sample paper that argues for a feminist reading of Susan Glaspell's *Trifles*.

Questions for Responsive Reading and Writing

The questions in this chapter can help you consider important elements that reveal a play's effects and meanings. These questions are general and will not, therefore, always be relevant to a particular play. Many of them, however, should prove to be useful for thinking, talking, and writing about drama. If you are uncertain about the meaning of a term used in a question, consult the Glossary of Literary Terms beginning on page 1716.

1. Did you enjoy the play? What, specifically, pleased or displeased you about what was expressed and how it was expressed?

2. What is the significance of the play's title? How does it suggest the author's overall emphasis?

3. What information do the stage directions provide about the characters, action, and setting? Are these directions primarily descriptive, or are they also interpretive?

4. How is the exposition presented? What does it reveal? How does the playwright's choice *not* to dramatize certain events on stage help to determine what the focus of the play is?

5. In what ways is the setting important? Would the play be altered significantly if the setting were changed?

6. Are foreshadowings used to suggest what is to come? Are flashbacks used to dramatize what has already happened?

7. What is the major conflict the protagonist faces? What complications constitute the rising action? Where is the climax? Is the conflict resolved?

8. Are one or more subplots used to qualify or complicate the main plot? Is the plot unified so that each incident somehow has a function that relates it to some other element in the play?

9. Does the author purposely avoid a pyramidal plot structure of rising action, climax, and falling action? Is the plot experimental? Is the plot logically and chronologically organized, or is it fantastical or absurd? What effects are produced by the plot? How does it reflect the author's view of life?

10. Who is the protagonist? Who (or what) is the antagonist?

(continued)

11. By what means does the playwright reveal character? What do the characters' names, physical qualities, actions, and words convey about them? What do the characters reveal about each other?

12. What is the purpose of the minor characters? Are they individualized, or do they primarily represent ideas or attitudes? Are any character foils used?

13. Do the characters all use the same kind of language, or is their speech differentiated? Is it formal or informal? How do the characters' diction and manner of speaking serve to characterize them?

14. Does your response to the characters change in the course of the play? What causes the change?

15. Are words and images repeated in the play so that they take on special meanings? Which speeches seem particularly important? Why?

16. How does the playwright's use of language contribute to the tone of the play? Is the dialogue, for example, predominantly light, humorous, relaxed, sentimental, sad, angry, intense, or violent?

17. Are any symbols used in the play? Which actions, characters, settings, objects, or words convey more than their literal meanings?

18. Are any unfamiliar theatrical conventions used that present problems in understanding the play? How does knowing more about the nature of the theater from which the play originated help to resolve these problems?

19. Is the theme stated directly, or is it developed implicitly through the plot, characters, or some other element? Does the theme confirm or challenge most people's values?

20. How does the play reflect the values of the society in which it is set and in which it was written?

21. How does the play reflect or challenge your own values?

22. Is there a sound recording, film, or online source for the play available in your library or media center? How does this version compare with your own reading?

23. How would you produce the play on a stage? Consider scenery, costumes, casting, and characterizations. What would you emphasize most in your production?

24. Is there a particular critical approach that seems especially appropriate for this play? (See Chapter 51, "Critical Strategies for Reading," which begins on p. 1641.)

25. How might biographical information about the author help the reader to grasp the central concerns of the play?

26. How might historical information about the play provide a useful context for interpretation?

27. To what extent do your own experiences, values, beliefs, and assumptions inform your interpretation?

28. What kinds of evidence from the play are you focusing on to support your interpretation? Does your interpretation leave out any important elements that might undercut or qualify your interpretation?

29. Given that there are a variety of ways to interpret the play, which one seems the most useful to you?

A SAMPLE STUDENT PAPER

The Feminist Evidence in Susan Glaspell's Trifles

The following paper was written in response to an assignment that required an analysis — about 750 words — of an assigned play. Chris Duffy's paper argues that although *Trifles* was written over ninety years ago, it should be seen as a feminist play because its treatment of the tensions between men and women deliberately reveals the oppressiveness that women have had to cope with in their everyday lives. The paper discusses a number of the play's elements, but the discussion is unified through its focus on how the women characters are bound together by a set of common concerns. Notice that page numbers are provided to document quoted passages.

Duffy 1

Chris Duffy

Professor Barrina-Barrou

English 109-2

6 March 2015

The Feminist Evidence in Susan Glaspell's *Trifles*

Despite its early publication date, Susan Glaspell's *Trifles* (1916) can be regarded as a work of feminist literature. The play depicts the life of a woman who has been suppressed, oppressed, and subjugated by a patronizing, patriarchal husband. Mrs. Wright is eventually driven to kill her "hard" (1086) husband who has stifled every last twitch of her identity. *Trifles* dramatizes the hypocrisy and ingrained discrimination of male-dominated society while simultaneously speaking to the dangers for women who succumb to such hierarchies. Because Mrs. Wright follows the role mapped by her husband and is directed by society's patriarchal expectations, her identity is lost somewhere along the way. However, Mrs. Hale and Mrs. Peters quietly insist on preserving their own identities by protecting Mrs. Wright from the men who seek to convict her of murder.

Mrs. Wright is described as someone who used to have a flair for life. Her neighbor, Mrs. Hale, comments that the last time Mrs. Wright appeared happy and vivacious was before she was married or, more important, when she was Minnie Foster and not Mrs. Wright. Mrs. Hale laments, "I heard she used to wear pretty clothes and be lively, when she was Minnie Foster,

> General thesis statement

> More specific thesis offering analysis, with supporting evidence

> Analysis of Mrs. Wright through perspectives of female characters

one of the town girls singing in the choir" (1084). But after thirty years of marriage, Mrs. Wright is now worried about her canned preserves freezing and being without an apron while she is in jail. This subservient image was so accepted in society that Mrs. Peters, the sheriff's wife, speculates that Mrs. Wright must want her apron in order to "feel more natural" (1084). Any other roles would be considered uncharacteristic.

This wifely role is predicated on the supposition that women have no ability to make complicated decisions, to think critically, or to rely on themselves. As the title suggests, the men in this story think of homemaking as much less important than a husband's breadwinning role. Mr. Hale remarks, "Well, women are used to worrying over trifles" (1083), and Sheriff Peters assumes the insignificance of "kitchen things" (1082). Hence, women are forced into a domestic, secondary role, like it or not, and are not even respected for that. Mr. Hale, Sheriff Peters, and the county attorney all dismiss the dialogue between Mrs. Peters and Mrs. Hale as feminine chitchat. Further, the county attorney allows the women to leave the Wrights' house unsupervised because he sees Mrs. Peters as merely an extension of her husband.

Analysis of role of women through perspectives of male characters

Even so, the domestic system the men have set up for their wives and their disregard for them after the rules and boundaries have been laid down prove to be the men's downfall. The evidence that Mrs. Wright killed her husband is woven into Mrs. Hale's and Mrs. Peters's conversations about Mrs. Wright's sewing and her pet bird. The knots in her quilt match those in the rope used to strangle Mr. Wright, and the bird, the last symbol of Mrs. Wright's vitality to be taken by her husband, is found dead. Unable to play the role of subservient wife anymore, Mrs. Wright is foreign to herself and therefore lives a lie. As Mrs. Hale proclaims, "Why, it looks as if she didn't know what she was about!" (1085).

Discussion of Mrs. Hale's identification with Mrs. Wright

Mrs. Hale, however, does ultimately understand what Mrs. Wright is about. She comprehends the desperation, loneliness, and pain that Mrs. Wright experienced, and she instinctively knows that the roles Mrs. Wright played—even that of murderer—are scripted by the male-dominated circumstances of her life. As Mrs. Hale shrewdly and covertly observes in the context of a discussion about housecleaning with the county attorney: "Men's

Duffy 3

hands aren't always as clean as they might be" (1083). In fact, even Mrs. Hale feels some guilt for not having made an effort to visit Mrs. Wright over the years to help relieve the monotony of Mrs. Wright's life with her husband:

> I might have known she needed help! I know how things can be—for women. I tell you, it's queer, Mrs. Peters. We live close together and we live far apart. We all go through the same things—it's all just a different kind of the same thing. (1088)

Mrs. Hale cannot help identifying with her neighbor.

In contrast, Mrs. Peters is initially reluctant to support Mrs. Wright. Not only is she married to the sheriff, but, as the county attorney puts it, "a sheriff's wife is married to the law" (1088) as well. She reminds Mrs. Hale that "the law has got to punish crime" (1088), even if it means revealing the existence of the dead bird and exposing the motive that could convict Mrs. Wright of murdering her husband. But finally Mrs. Peters also becomes complicit in keeping information from her husband and other men. She too—owing to the loss of her first child—understands what loss means and what Mrs. Hale means when she says that women "all go through the same things" (1088).

> Discussion of Mrs. Peters's identification with Mrs. Wright

The women in *Trifles* cannot, as the play reveals, be trifled with. Although Glaspell wrote the play over ninety years ago, it continues to be relevant to contemporary relationships between men and women. Its essentially feminist perspective provides a convincing case for the necessity of women to move beyond destructive stereotypes and oppressive assumptions in order to be true to their own significant—not trifling—experiences.

> Conclusion summarizing analysis

Duffy 4

Work Cited

Glaspell, Susan. "Trifles." *The Bedford Introduction to Literature*. Ed. Michael Meyer. 11th ed. Boston: Bedford/St. Martin's, 2016. 1080–89. Print.

44

A Study of Sophocles

I depict men as they ought to be . . .
— SOPHOCLES

Not all things are to be discovered;
many are better concealed.
— SOPHOCLES

© Corbis.

Sophocles lived a long, productive life (496?–406 B.C.) in Athens. During his life Athens became a dominant political and cultural power after the Persian Wars, but before he died, Sophocles witnessed the decline of Athens as a result of the Peloponnesian Wars and the city's subsequent surrender to Sparta. He saw Athenian culture reach remarkable heights as well as collapse under enormous pressures.

Sophocles embodied much of the best of Athenian culture; he enjoyed success as a statesman, general, treasurer, priest, and, of course, prize-winning dramatist. Although surviving fragments indicate that he wrote over 120 plays, only a handful remain intact. Those that survive consist of the three plays he wrote about Oedipus and his children — *Oedipus the King*, *Oedipus at Colonus*, and *Antigone* — and four additional tragedies: *Philoctetes*, *Ajax*, *Maidens of Trachis*, and *Electra*.

His plays won numerous prizes at festival competitions because of his careful, subtle plotting and the sense of inevitability with which their action is charged. Moreover, his development of character is richly complex.

Instead of relying on the extreme situations and exaggerated actions that earlier tragedians used, Sophocles created powerfully motivated characters who even today fascinate audiences with their psychological depth.

In addition to crafting sophisticated tragedies for the Greek theater, Sophocles introduced several important innovations to the stage. Most important, he broke the tradition of using only two actors; adding a third resulted in more complicated relationships and intricate dialogue among characters. As individual actors took center stage more often, Sophocles reduced the role of the chorus (discussed on p. 1122). This shift placed even more emphasis on the actors, although the chorus remained important as a means of commenting on the action and establishing its tone. Sophocles was also the first dramatist to write plays with specific actors in mind, a development that many later playwrights, including Shakespeare, exploited usefully. But without question Sophocles' greatest contribution to drama was *Oedipus the King*, which, it has been argued, is the most influential drama ever written.

Map of Ancient Greece. During Sophocles' time, the city-state of Athens (roughly in the center of this map) was the leading cultural and intellectual center of Greece — until the Peloponnesian Wars (431–404 B.C.) and Athens's defeat in 404 B.C. by the city-state of Sparta (below Athens, to the left).
Steven Wright/Shutterstock.

THEATRICAL CONVENTIONS OF GREEK DRAMA

© Corbis.

More than twenty-four hundred years have passed since 430 B.C., when Sophocles' *Oedipus the King* was probably first produced on a Greek stage. We inhabit a vastly different planet than Sophocles' audience did, yet concerns about what it means to be human in a world that frequently runs counter to our desires and aspirations have remained relatively constant. The ancient Greeks continue to speak to us. But inexperienced readers or viewers may have some initial difficulty understanding the theatrical conventions used in classical Greek tragedies such as *Oedipus the King* and *Antigone*. If Sophocles were alive today, he would very likely need some sort of assistance with the conventions of an Arthur Miller play or a television production of *Seinfeld*.

Classical Greek drama developed from religious festivals that paid homage to Dionysus, the god of wine and fertility. Most of the details of these festivals have been lost, but we do know that they included dancing and singing that celebrated legends about Dionysus. From these choral songs developed stories of both Dionysus and mortal culture-heroes. These heroes became the subject of playwrights whose works were produced in contests at the festivals. The Dionysian festivals lasted more than five hundred years, but relatively few of their plays have survived. Among the works of the three great writers of tragedy, only seven plays each by Sophocles and Aeschylus (525?–456 B.C.) and nineteen plays by Euripides (480?–406 B.C.) survive.

Plays were such important events in Greek society that they were partially funded by the state. The Greeks associated drama with religious and community values as well as entertainment. In a sense, their plays celebrate their civilization; in approving the plays, audiences applauded their own culture. The enormous popularity of the plays is indicated by the size of surviving amphitheaters. Although information about these theaters is sketchy, we do know that most of them had a common form. They were built into hillsides with rising rows of seats accommodating more than fourteen thousand people. These seats partially encircled an **orchestra** or "dancing place," where the **chorus** of a dozen or so men chanted lines and danced.

Tradition credits the Greek poet Thespis with adding an actor who was separate from the choral singing and dancing of early performances. A second actor was subsequently included by Aeschylus and a third, as noted earlier, by Sophocles. These additions made possible the conflicts and complicated relationships that evolved into the dramatic art we know today. The two or three male actors who played all the roles appeared behind the orchestra in front of the **skene**, a stage building that served as dressing rooms. As Greek theater evolved, a wall of the skene came to be painted to suggest a palace or some

Classical Greek Theater in Delphi, Greece. This photo represents the features typical of a classical theater.
© Kevin Schafer/Corbis.

other setting, and the roof was employed to indicate, for instance, a mountain location. Sometimes gods were lowered from the roof by mechanical devices to set matters right among the mortals below. This method of rescuing characters from complications beyond their abilities to resolve was known in Latin as ***deus ex machina*** ("god from the machine"), a term now used to describe any improbable means by which an author provides a too-easy resolution for a story.

Inevitably, the conventions of the Greek theaters affected how plays were presented. Few if any scene changes occurred because the amphitheater stage was set primarily for one location. If an important event happened somewhere else, it was reported by a minor character, such as a messenger. The chorus also provided necessary background information. In *Oedipus the King* and *Antigone,* the choruses, acting as townspeople, also assess the characters' strengths and weaknesses, praising them for their virtues, chiding them for their rashness, and giving them advice. The reactions of the chorus provide a connection between the actors and audience because the chorus is at once a participant in and an observer of the action. In addition, the chorus helps structure the action by indicating changes in scene or mood. Thus the chorus could be used in a variety of ways to shape the audience's response to the play's action and characters.

Actors in classical Greek amphitheaters faced considerable challenges. An intimate relationship with the audience was impossible because many spectators would have been too far away to see a facial expression or subtle gesture. Indeed, some in the audience would have had difficulty even hearing the voices of individual actors. To compensate for these disadvantages, actors wore large masks that extravagantly expressed the major characters' emotions or identified the roles of minor characters. The masks also allowed the two or three actors in a performance to play all the characters without confusing the audience. Each mask was fitted so that the mouthpiece amplified the actor's voice. The actors were further equipped with padded costumes and elevated shoes (*cothurni* or *buskins*) that made them appear larger than life.

As a result of these adaptive conventions, Greek plays tend to emphasize words — formal, impassioned speeches — more than physical action. We are invited to ponder actions and events rather than to see all of them enacted. Although the stark simplicity of Greek theater does not offer an audience realistic detail, the classical tragedies that have survived present characters in dramatic situations that transcend theatrical conventions. Tragedy, it seems, has always been compelling for human beings, regardless of the theatrical forms it has taken.

A Greek tragedy is typically divided into five parts: prologue, parodos, episodia, stasimon, and exodus. Understanding these terms provides a sense of the overall rhythm of a Greek play. The opening speech or dialogue is known as the **prologue** and usually gives the exposition necessary to follow the subsequent action. In the *parodos* the chorus makes its first entrance and gives its perspective on what the audience has learned in the prologue. Several *episodia,* or episodes, follow, in which characters engage in dialogue that frequently consists of heated debates dramatizing the play's conflicts. Following each episode is a choral ode or *stasimon,* in which the chorus responds to and interprets the preceding dialogue. The *exodus,* or last scene, follows the final episode and stasimon; in it the resolution occurs and the characters leave the stage.

The effect of alternating dialogues and choral odes has sometimes been likened to that of opera. Greek tragedies were written in verse, and the stasima were chanted or sung as the chorus moved rhythmically, so the plays have a strong musical element that is not always apparent on the printed page. If we remember their musical qualities, we are less likely to forget that no matter how terrifying or horrific the conflicts they describe, these plays are stately, measured, and dignified works that reflect a classical Greek sense of order and proportion.

TRAGEDY

Newspapers are filled with daily reports of tragedies: a child is struck and crippled by a car; an airplane plunges into a suburban neighborhood; a volcano erupts and kills thousands. These unexpected instances of suffering are commonly and accurately described as tragic, but they are not tragedies in the literary sense of the term. A literary **tragedy** presents courageous individuals who confront powerful forces within or outside themselves with a dignity that reveals the breadth and depth of the human spirit in the face of failure, defeat, and even death.

Aristotle (384–322 B.C.), in his *Poetics*, defined *tragedy* on the basis of the plays contemporary to him. His definition has generated countless variations, qualifications, and interpretations, but we still derive our literary understanding of this term from Aristotle.

The protagonist of a Greek tragedy is someone regarded as extraordinary rather than typical: a great man or woman brought from happiness to agony. The character's stature is important because it makes his or her fall all the more terrifying. The protagonist also carries mythic significance for the audience. Oedipus and Antigone, for example, are not only human beings but legendary figures from a distant, revered past. Although the gods do not appear onstage in either *Oedipus the King* or *Antigone,* their power is ever present as the characters invoke their help or attempt to defy them. In addition, Greek tragedy tends to be public rather than private. The fate of the community — the state — is often linked with that of the protagonist, as when Thebes suffers a plague as a result of Oedipus's mistaken actions.

The protagonists of classical Greek tragedies (and of those of Shakespeare) are often rulers of noble birth who represent the monarchical values of their periods, but in modern tragedies the protagonists are more likely to reflect democratic values that make it possible for anyone to be a suitable subject. What is finally important is not so much the protagonist's social stature as a greatness of character that steadfastly confronts suffering, whether it comes from supernatural, social, or psychological forces. Although Greek tragic heroes were aristocrats, the nobility of their characters was more significant than their inherited titles and privileges.

The protagonist's eminence and determination to complete some task or goal make him or her admirable in Greek tragedy, but that does not free the protagonist from what Aristotle described as "some error or frailty" that brings about his or her misfortune. The term Aristotle used for this weakness is **hamartia**. This word has frequently been interpreted to mean that the protagonist's fall is the result of an internal **tragic flaw**, such as an excess of pride, ambition, passion, or some other character trait that leads directly to disaster.

Sometimes, however, misfortunes are the result not of a character flaw but of misunderstood events that overtake and thwart the protagonist's best intentions. Thus, virtue can lead to tragedy too. *Hamartia* has also been interpreted to mean "wrong act" — a mistake based not on a personal failure but on circumstances outside the protagonist's personality and control. Many readers find that a combination of these two interpretations sheds the most light on the causes of the tragic protagonist's fall. Both internal and external forces can lead to downfall because the protagonist's personality may determine crucial judgments that result in mistaken actions.

However the idea of tragic flaw is understood, it is best not to use it as a means of reducing the qualities of a complex character to an adjective or two that labels Oedipus as guilty of "overweening pride" (the Greek term for which is **hubris** or **hybris**) or Antigone as "fated." The protagonists of tragedies require more careful characterization than a simplistic label can provide.

Whatever the causes of the tragic protagonist's downfall, he or she accepts responsibility for it. Hence, even in his or her encounter with failure (and possibly death) the tragic protagonist displays greatness of character. Perhaps it is the witnessing of this greatness, which seems both to accept and to transcend human limitations, that makes audiences feel relief rather than hopelessness at the end of a tragedy. Aristotle described this response as a **catharsis**, or purgation of the emotions of "pity and fear." We are faced with the protagonist's misfortune, which often seems out of proportion to his or her actions, and so we are likely to feel compassionate pity. Simultaneously, we may experience fear because the failure of the protagonist, who is so great in stature and power, is a frightening reminder of our own vulnerabilities. Ultimately, however, both these negative emotions are purged because the tragic protagonist's suffering is an affirmation of human values — even if they are not always triumphant — rather than a despairing denial of them.

Nevertheless, tragedies are disturbing. Instead of coming away with the reassurance of a happy ending, we must take solace in the insight produced by the hero's suffering. And just as our expectations are changed, so are the protagonist's. Aristotle described the moment in the plot when this change occurs as a **reversal** (*peripeteia*), the point when the hero's fortunes turn in an unexpected direction. He more specifically defined this term as meaning an action performed by a character that has the opposite of its intended effect. An example cited by Aristotle is the messenger's attempts to relieve Oedipus's anxieties about his relationship to his father and mother. Instead, the messenger reveals previously unknown information that eventually results in a **recognition** (*anagnorisis*); Oedipus discovers the terrible truth that he has killed his father and married his mother.

Tragedy is typically filled with ironies because there are so many moments in the plot when what seems to be turns out to be radically different from what actually is. Because of this, a particular form of irony called **dramatic irony** is also known as **tragic irony**. In dramatic irony, the meaning of a character's words or actions is understood by the audience but not by the character. Audiences of Greek tragedy shared with the playwrights a knowledge of the stories on which many tragic plots were based. Consequently, they frequently were aware of what was going to happen before the characters were. When Oedipus declares that he will seek out the person responsible for the plague that ravishes his city, the audience already knows that the person Oedipus pursues is himself.

Oedipus the King

A familiarity with the Oedipus legend allows modern readers to appreciate the series of ironies that unfolds in Sophocles' *Oedipus the King*. As an infant, Oedipus had been abandoned by his parents, Laius and Jocasta, the king and queen of Thebes, because a prophecy warned that their son would kill his father and marry his mother. They instructed a servant to leave him on a mountain to die. The infant's feet were pierced and pinned together, but he was not left on the mountain; instead the servant, out of pity, gave him to a shepherd, who in turn presented him to the king and queen of Corinth. They named him Oedipus (for "swollen foot") and raised him as their own son.

On reaching manhood, Oedipus learned from an oracle that he would kill his father and marry his mother; to avoid this horrendous fate, he left Corinth forever. In his travels, Oedipus found his way blocked by a chariot at a crossroads; in a fit of anger, he killed the servants and their passenger. That passenger, unknown to Oedipus, was his real father. In Thebes, Oedipus successfully answered the riddle of the Sphinx, a winged lion with a woman's head. The reward for defeating this dreaded monster was both the crown and the dead king's wife. Oedipus and Jocasta had four children and prospered. But when the play begins, Oedipus's rule is troubled by a plague that threatens to destroy Thebes, and he is determined to find the cause of the plague in order to save the city again.

Oedipus the King is widely recognized as the greatest of the surviving Greek tragedies. Numerous translations are available. The highly regarded translation of *Oedipus the King* by David Grene is the choice here. The play has absorbed readers for centuries because Oedipus's character — his intelligence, confidence, rashness, and suffering — represents powers and limitations that are both exhilarating and chastening. Although no reader or viewer is likely to identify with Oedipus's extreme circumstances, anyone can appreciate his heroic efforts to find the truth about himself. In that sense, he is one of us — at our best.

SOPHOCLES (496?–406 B.C.)

Oedipus the King   ca. 430 B.C.

TRANSLATED BY DAVID GRENE

CHARACTERS

Oedipus, King of Thebes
Jocasta, His Wife
Creon, His Brother-in-Law
Teiresias, an Old Blind Prophet

See Plays in Performance
insert.
© T. Charles Erickson.

A Priest
First Messenger
Second Messenger
A Herdsman
Chorus of Old Men of Thebes

SCENE: In front of the palace of Oedipus at Thebes. To the right of the stage near the altar stands the Priest with a crowd of children. Oedipus emerges from the central door.

Oedipus: Children, young sons and daughters of old Cadmus,°
    why do you sit here with your suppliant crowns?
    The town is heavy with a mingled burden
    of sounds and smells, of groans and hymns and incense;
    I did not think it fit that I should hear   5
    of this from messengers but came myself, —
    I Oedipus whom all men call the Great.   *(He turns to the Priest.)*
    You're old and they are young; come, speak for them.
    What do you fear or want, that you sit here
    suppliant? Indeed I'm willing to give all   10
    that you may need; I would be very hard
    should I not pity suppliants like these.
Priest: O ruler of my country, Oedipus,
    you see our company around the altar;
    you see our ages; some of us, like these,   15
    who cannot yet fly far, and some of us
    heavy with age; these children are the chosen
    among the young, and I the priest of Zeus.
    Within the market place sit others crowned
    with suppliant garlands, at the double shrine   20
    of Pallas° and the temple where Ismenus
    gives oracles by fire. King, you yourself
    have seen our city reeling like a wreck
    already; it can scarcely lift its prow
    out of the depths, out of the bloody surf.   25
    A blight is on the fruitful plants of the earth,
    A blight is on the cattle in the fields,
    a blight is on our women that no children
    are born to them; a God that carries fire,
    a deadly pestilence, is on our town,   30
    strikes us and spares not, and the house of Cadmus
    is emptied of its people while black Death
    grows rich in groaning and in lamentation.
    We have not come as suppliants to this altar

---

1 *Cadmus:* Founder and first king of Thebes.   21 *Pallas:* Pallas Athene, goddess of wisdom and daughter of Zeus.

because we thought of you as of a God,   35
but rather judging you the first of men
in all the chances of this life and when
we mortals have to do with more than man.
You came and by your coming saved our city,
freed us from tribute which we paid of old   40
to the Sphinx,° cruel singer. This you did
in virtue of no knowledge we could give you,
in virtue of no teaching; it was God
that aided you, men say, and you are held
with God's assistance to have saved our lives.   45
Now Oedipus, Greatest in all men's eyes,
here falling at your feet we all entreat you,
find us some strength for rescue.
Perhaps you'll hear a wise word from some God,
perhaps you will learn something from a man   50
(for I have seen that for the skilled of practice
the outcome of their counsels live the most).
Noblest of men, go, and raise up our city,
go, — and give heed. For now this land of ours
calls you its savior since you saved it once.   55
So, let us never speak about your reign
as of a time when first our feet were set
secure on high, but later fell to ruin.
Raise up our city, save it and raise it up.
Once you have brought us luck with happy omen;   60
be no less now in fortune.
If you will rule this land, as now you rule it,
better to rule it full of men than empty.
For neither tower nor ship is anything
when empty, and none live in it together.   65

Oedipus: I pity you, children. You have come full of longing,
but I have known the story before you told it
only too well. I know you are all sick,
yet there is not one of you, sick though you are,
that is as sick as I myself.   70
Your several sorrows each have single scope
and touch but one of you. My spirit groans
for city and myself and you at once.
You have not roused me like a man from sleep;
know that I have given many tears to this,   75
gone many ways wandering in thought,
but as I thought I found only one remedy
and that I took. I sent Menoeceus' son

---

41 *Sphinx:* A mythical creature with the body of a lion, wings of a bird, and the face of a woman.
The Sphinx stumped Thebans with her riddle and killed those that could not answer it. Oedipus
solved the riddle, the Sphinx killed herself, and Oedipus became king of Thebes.

Creon, Jocasta's brother, to Apollo,° 80
to his Pythian temple,
that he might learn there by what act or word
I could save this city. As I count the days,
it vexes me what ails him; he is gone
far longer than he needed for the journey.
But when he comes, then, may I prove a villain, 85
if I shall not do all the God commands.
Priest: Thanks for your gracious words. Your servants here
signal that Creon is this moment coming.
Oedipus: His face is bright. O holy Lord Apollo,
grant that his news too may be bright for us 90
and bring us safety.
Priest: It is happy news,
I think, for else his head would not be crowned
with sprigs of fruitful laurel.
Oedipus: We will know soon,
he's within hail. Lord Creon, my good brother, 95
what is the word you bring us from the God?   *(Creon enters.)*
Creon: A good word, — for things hard to bear themselves
if in the final issue all is well
I count complete good fortune.
Oedipus: What do you mean?
What you have said so far 100
leaves me uncertain whether to trust or fear.
Creon: If you will hear my news before these others
I am ready to speak, or else to go within.
Oedipus: Speak it to all;
the grief I bear, I bear it more for these 105
than for my own heart.
Creon: I will tell you, then,
what I heard from the God.
King Phoebus° in plain words commanded us
to drive out a pollution from our land,
pollution grown ingrained within the land; 110
drive it out, said the God, not cherish it,
till it's past cure.
Oedipus: What is the rite
of purification? How shall it be done?
Creon: By banishing a man, or expiation
of blood by blood, since it is murder guilt 115
which holds our city in this destroying storm.
Oedipus: Who is this man whose fate the God pronounces?
Creon: My Lord, before you piloted the state
we had a king called Laius.°

---

79 *Apollo:* Oracular god of the sun, light, and truth, and son of Zeus.   108 *King*
Phoebus: Apollo.   119 *Laius:* Former king of Thebes.

Oedipus: I know of him by hearsay. I have not seen him.   120
Creon: The God commanded clearly: let some one
   punish with force this dead man's murderers.
Oedipus: Where are they in the world? Where would a trace
   of this old crime be found? It would be hard
   to guess where.
Creon: The clue is in this land;   125
   that which is sought is found;
   the unheeded thing escapes:
   so said the God.
Oedipus: Was it at home,
   or in the country that death came upon him,
   or in another country travelling?   130
Creon: He went, he said himself, upon an embassy,
   but never returned when he set out from home.
Oedipus: Was there no messenger, no fellow traveller
   who knew what happened? Such a one might tell
   something of use.   135
Creon: They were all killed save one. He fled in terror
   and he could tell us nothing in clear terms
   of what he knew, nothing, but one thing only.
Oedipus: What was it?
   If we could even find a slim beginning   140
   in which to hope, we might discover much.
Creon: This man said that the robbers they encountered
   were many and the hands that did the murder
   were many; it was no man's single power.
Oedipus: How could a robber dare a deed like this   145
   were he not helped with money from the city,
   money and treachery?
Creon: That indeed was thought.
   But Laius was dead and in our trouble
   there was none to help.
Oedipus: What trouble was so great to hinder you   150
   inquiring out the murder of your king?
Creon: The riddling Sphinx induced us to neglect
   mysterious crimes and rather seek solution
   of troubles at our feet.
Oedipus: I will bring this to light again. King Phoebus   155
   fittingly took this care about the dead,
   and you too fittingly.
   And justly you will see in me an ally,
   a champion of my country and the God.
   For when I drive pollution from the land   160
   I will not serve a distant friend's advantage,
   but act in my own interest. Whoever
   he was that killed the king may readily
   wish to dispatch me with his murderous hand;
   so helping the dead king I help myself.   165

Come, children, take your suppliant boughs and go;
up from the altars now. Call the assembly
and let it meet upon the understanding
that I'll do everything. God will decide
whether we prosper or remain in sorrow.   170
Priest: Rise, children — it was this we came to seek,
which of himself the king now offers us.
May Phoebus who gave us the oracle
come to our rescue and stay the plague.   *(Exeunt° all but the Chorus.)*

Chorus (Strophe°): What is the sweet spoken word of God from the shrine of
Pytho° rich in gold   175
that has come to glorious Thebes?
I am stretched on the rack of doubt, and terror and trembling hold
my heart, O Delian Healer,° and I worship full of fears
for what doom you will bring to pass, new or renewed in the revolving years.
Speak to me, immortal voice,   180
child of golden Hope.

(Antistrophe°) First I call on you, Athene, deathless daughter of Zeus,
and Artemis, Earth Upholder,
who sits in the midst of the market place in the throne which men
call Fame,
and Phoebus, the Far Shooter, three averters of Fate,   185
come to us now, if ever before, when ruin rushed upon the state,
you drove destruction's flame away
out of our land.

(Strophe) Our sorrows defy number;
all the ship's timbers are rotten;   190
taking of thought is no spear for the driving away of the plague.
There are no growing children in this famous land;
there are no women bearing the pangs of childbirth.
You may see them one with another, like birds swift on the wing,
quicker than fire unmastered,   195
speeding away to the coast of the Western God.

(Antistrophe) In the unnumbered deaths
of its people the city dies;
those children that are born lie dead on the naked earth
unpitied, spreading contagion of death; and grey haired mothers
and wives   200
everywhere stand at the altar's edge, suppliant, moaning;
the hymn to the healing God rings out but with it the wailing voices
are blended.
From these our sufferings grant us, O golden Daughter of Zeus,
glad-faced deliverance.

Exeunt: Stage direction indicating that the characters have left the stage.   *Strophe:* The song sung by the Chorus, dancing from stage right to stage left.   175 *shrine of Pytho:* Delphi, site of the oracle and shrine dedicated to Apollo.   178 *Delian Healer:* Apollo.   *Antistrophe:* The song sung after the strophe by the Chorus, dancing back from stage left to stage right.

(Strophe) There is no clash of brazen shields but our fight is with
    the War God,   205
a War God ringed with the cries of men, a savage God who burns us;
grant that he turn in racing course backwards out of our country's bounds
to the great palace of Amphitrite° or where the waves of the Thracian sea
deny the stranger safe anchorage.
Whatsoever escapes the night   210
at last the light of day revisits;
so smite the War God, Father Zeus,
beneath your thunderbolt,
for you are the Lord of the lightning, the lightning that carries fire.

(Antistrophe) And your unconquered arrow shafts, winged by the golden
    corded bow,   215
Lycean King,° I beg to be at our side for help;
and the gleaming torches of Artemis with which she scours the Lycean
    hills,
and I call on the God with the turban of gold, who gave his name to this
    country of ours,
the Bacchic God° with the wind flushed face,
Evian One, who travel   220
with the Maenad company,°
combat the God that burns us
with your torch of pine;
for the God that is our enemy is a God unhonoured among the Gods.
                                 (Oedipus returns.)

Oedipus: For what you ask me — if you will hear my words,   225
and hearing welcome them and fight the plague,
you will find strength and lightening of your load.

Hark to me; what I say to you, I say
as one that is a stranger to the story
as stranger to the deed. For I would not   230
be far upon the track if I alone
were tracing it without a clue. But now,
since after all was finished, I became
a citizen among you, citizens —
now I proclaim to all the men of Thebes: 235
who so among you knows the murderer
by whose hand Laius, son of Labdacus,
died — I command him to tell everything
to me, — yes, though he fears himself to take the blame
on his own head; for bitter punishment   240
he shall have none, but leave this land unharmed.
Or if he knows the murderer, another,
a foreigner, still let him speak the truth.
For I will pay him and be grateful, too.
But if you shall keep silence, if perhaps   245

---

208 *Amphitrite:* Sea goddess and wife of Poseidon.   216 *Lycean King:* Apollo.   219 *Bacchic God:* Bacchus, also known as Dionysus, god of wine and wild celebration.   221 *Maenad company:* Female followers of Bacchus.

some one of you, to shield a guilty friend,
or for his own sake shall reject my words —
hear what I shall do then:
I forbid that man, whoever he be, my land,
my land where I hold sovereignty and throne;   250
and I forbid any to welcome him
or cry him greeting or make him a sharer
in sacrifice or offering to the Gods,
or give him water for his hands to wash.
I command all to drive him from their homes,   255
since he is our pollution, as the oracle
of Pytho's God proclaimed him now to me.
So I stand forth a champion of the God
and of the man who died.
Upon the murderer I invoke this curse —   260
whether he is one man and all unknown,
or one of many — may he wear out his life
in misery to miserable doom!
If with my knowledge he lives at my hearth
I pray that I myself may feel my curse.   265
On you I lay my charge to fulfill all this
for me, for the God, and for this land of ours
destroyed and blighted, by the God forsaken.

Even were this no matter of God's ordinance
it would not fit you so to leave it lie,   270
unpurified, since a good man is dead
and one that was a king. Search it out.
Since I am now the holder of his office,
and have his bed and wife that once was his,
and had his line not been unfortunate   275
we would have common children — (fortune leaped
upon his head) — because of all these things,
I fight in his defence as for my father,
and I shall try all means to take the murderer
of Laius the son of Labdacus   280
the son of Polydorus and before him
of Cadmus and before him of Agenor.°
Those who do not obey me, may the Gods
grant no crops springing from the ground they plough
nor children to their women! May a fate   285
like this, or one still worse than this consume them!
For you whom these words please, the other Thebans,
may Justice as your ally and all the Gods
live with you, blessing you now and for ever!
Chorus: As you have held me to my oath, I speak: 290
    I neither killed the king nor can declare

---

282 *Labdacus, Polydorus, Cadmus, and Agenor:* Referring to the father, grandfather, great-grandfather, and great-great-grandfather of Laius.

the killer; but since Phoebus set the quest
    it is his part to tell who the man is.
Oedipus: Right; but to put compulsion on the Gods
    against their will — no man can do that.   295
Chorus: May I then say what I think second best?
Oedipus: If there's a third best, too, spare not to tell it.
Chorus: I know that what the Lord Teiresias
    sees, is most often what the Lord Apollo
    sees. If you should inquire of this from him   300
    you might find out most clearly.
Oedipus: Even in this my actions have not been sluggard.
    On Creon's word I have sent two messengers
    and why the prophet is not here already
    I have been wondering.
Chorus: His skill apart   305
    there is besides only an old faint story.
Oedipus: What is it?
    I look at every story.
Chorus: It was said
    that he was killed by certain wayfarers.
Oedipus: I heard that, too, but no one saw the killer.   310
Chorus: Yet if he has a share of fear at all,
    his courage will not stand firm, hearing your curse.
Oedipus: The man who in the doing did not shrink
    will fear no word.
Chorus: Here comes his prosecutor:
    led by your men the godly prophet comes   315
    in whom alone of mankind truth is native.
                            (Enter Teiresias, led by a little boy.)
Oedipus: Teiresias, you are versed in everything,
    things teachable and things not to be spoken,
    things of the heaven and earth-creeping things.
    You have no eyes but in your mind you know   320
    with what a plague our city is afflicted.
    My lord, in you alone we find a champion,
    in you alone one that can rescue us.
    Perhaps you have not heard the messengers,
    but Phoebus sent in answer to our sending   325
    an oracle declaring that our freedom
    from this disease would only come when we
    should learn the names of those who killed King Laius,
    and kill them or expel from our country.
    Do not begrudge us oracles from birds,°   330
    or any other way of prophecy
    within your skill; save yourself and the city,
    save me; redeem the debt of our pollution

---

330 *oracles from birds:* Bird flight, a method by which prophets predicted the future using the
flight of birds.

that lies on us because of this dead man.
We are in your hands; pains are most nobly taken   335
to help another when you have means and power.
Teiresias: Alas, how terrible is wisdom when
it brings no profit to the man that's wise!
This I knew well, but had forgotten it,
else I would not have come here.
Oedipus: What is this?   340
How sad you are now you have come!
Teiresias: Let me
go home. It will be easiest for us both
to bear our several destinies to the end
if you will follow my advice.
Oedipus: You'd rob us
of this your gift of prophecy? You talk   345
as one who had no care for law nor love
for Thebes who reared you.
Teiresias: Yes, but I see that even your own words
miss the mark; therefore I must fear for mine.
Oedipus: For God's sake if you know of anything,   350
do not turn from us; all of us kneel to you,
all of us here, your suppliants.
Teiresias: All of you here know nothing. I will not
bring to the light of day my troubles, mine —
rather than call them yours.
Oedipus: What do you mean?   355
You know of something but refuse to speak.
Would you betray us and destroy the city?
Teiresias: I will not bring this pain upon us both,
neither on you nor on myself. Why is it
you question me and waste your labour? I   360
will tell you nothing.
Oedipus: You would provoke a stone! Tell us, you villain,
tell us, and do not stand there quietly
unmoved and balking at the issue.
Teiresias: You blame my temper but you do not see   365
your own that lives within you; it is me
you chide.
Oedipus: Who would not feel his temper rise
at words like these with which you shame our city?
Teiresias: Of themselves things will come, although I hide them   370
and breathe no word of them.
Oedipus: Since they will come
tell them to me.
Teiresias: I will say nothing further.
Against this answer let your temper rage
as wildly as you will.
Oedipus: Indeed I am
so angry I shall not hold back a jot   375
of what I think. For I would have you know

I think you were complotter° of the deed
and doer of the deed save in so far
as for the actual killing. Had you had eyes
I would have said alone you murdered him.   380
Teiresias: Yes? Then I warn you faithfully to keep
the letter of your proclamation and
from this day forth to speak no word of greeting
to these nor me; you are the land's pollution.
Oedipus: How shamelessly you started up this taunt!   385
How do you think you will escape?
Teiresias: I have.
I have escaped; the truth is what I cherish
and that's my strength.
Oedipus: And who has taught you truth?
Not your profession surely!
Teiresias: You have taught me,
for you have made me speak against my will.   390
Oedipus: Speak what? Tell me again that I may learn it better.
Teiresias: Did you not understand before or would you
provoke me into speaking?
Oedipus: I did not grasp it,
not so to call it known. Say it again.
Teiresias: I say you are the murderer of the king   395
whose murderer you seek.
Oedipus: Not twice you shall
say calumnies like this and stay unpunished.
Teiresias: Shall I say more to tempt your anger more?
Oedipus: As much as you desire; it will be said
in vain.
Teiresias: I say that with those you love best   400
you live in foulest shame unconsciously
and do not see where you are in calamity.
Oedipus: Do you imagine you can always talk
like this, and live to laugh at it hereafter?
Teiresias: Yes, if the truth has anything of strength.   405
Oedipus: It has, but not for you; it has no strength
for you because you are blind in mind and ears
as well as in your eyes.
Teiresias: You are a poor wretch
to taunt me with the very insults which
every one soon will heap upon yourself.   410
Oedipus: Your life is one long night so that you cannot
hurt me or any other who sees the light.
Teiresias: It is not fate that I should be your ruin,
Apollo is enough; it is his care
to work this out.
Oedipus: Was this your own design   415
or Creon's?

---

377 *complotter:* One who is part of a plot or conspiracy.

Teiresias: Creon is no hurt to you,
    but you are to yourself.
Oedipus: Wealth, sovereignty and skill outmatching skill
    for the contrivance of an envied life!
    Great store of jealousy fill your treasury chests,   420
    if my friend Creon, friend from the first and loyal,
    thus secretly attacks me, secretly
    desires to drive me out and secretly
    suborns this juggling, trick devising quack,
    this wily beggar who has only eyes   425
    for his own gains, but blindness in his skill.
    For, tell me, where have you seen clear, Teiresias,
    with your prophetic eyes? When the dark singer,
    the sphinx, was in your country, did you speak
    word of deliverance to its citizens?   430
    And yet the riddle's answer was not the province
    of a chance comer. It was a prophet's task
    and plainly you had no such gift of prophecy
    from birds nor otherwise from any God
    to glean a word of knowledge. But I came,   435
    Oedipus, who knew nothing, and I stopped her.
    I solved the riddle by my wit alone.
    Mine was no knowledge got from birds. And now
    you would expel me,
    because you think that you will find a place   440
    by Creon's throne. I think you will be sorry,
    both you and your accomplice, for your plot
    to drive me out. And did I not regard you
    as an old man, some suffering would have taught you
    that what was in your heart was treason.   445
Chorus: We look at this man's words and yours, my king,
    and we find both have spoken them in anger.
    We need no angry words but only thought
    how we may best hit the God's meaning for us.
Teiresias: If you are king, at least I have the right   450
    no less to speak in my defence against you.
    Of that much I am master. I am no slave
    of yours, but Loxias', and so I shall not
    enroll myself with Creon for my patron.
    Since you have taunted me with being blind,   455
    here is my word for you.
    You have your eyes but see not where you are
    in sin, nor where you live, nor whom you live with.
    Do you know who your parents are? Unknowing
    you are an enemy to kith and kin   460
    in death, beneath the earth, and in this life.
    A deadly footed, double striking curse,
    from father and mother both, shall drive you forth
    out of this land, with darkness on your eyes,
    that now have such straight vision. Shall there be   465

a place will not be harbour to your cries,
a corner of Cithaeron° will not ring
in echo to your cries, soon, soon, —
when you shall learn the secret of your marriage,
which steered you to a haven in this house, —　　　　　　470
haven no haven, after lucky voyage?
And of the multitude of other evils
establishing a grim equality
between you and your children, you know nothing.
So, muddy with contempt my words and Creon's!　　　　475
Misery shall grind no man as it will you.
Oedipus:　Is it endurable that I should hear
　　such words from him? Go and a curse go with you!
　　Quick, home with you! Out of my house at once!
Teiresias:　I would not have come either had you not called me.　　480
Oedipus:　I did not know then you would talk like a fool —
　　or it would have been long before I called you.
Teiresias:　I am a fool then, as it seems to you —
　　but to the parents who have bred you, wise.
Oedipus:　What parents? Stop! Who are they of all the world?　　485
Teiresias:　This day will show your birth and will destroy you.
Oedipus:　How needlessly your riddles darken everything.
Teiresias:　But it's in riddle answering you are strongest.
Oedipus:　Yes. Taunt me where you will find me great.
Teiresias:　It is this very luck that has destroyed you.　　　　490
Oedipus:　I do not care, if it has saved this city.
Teiresias:　Well, I will go. Come, boy, lead me away.
Oedipus:　Yes, lead him off. So long as you are here,
　　you'll be a stumbling block and a vexation;
　　once gone, you will not trouble me again.
Teiresias:　　　　　　　　　　　I have said　　　　　495
　　what I came here to say not fearing your
　　countenance: there is no way you can hurt me.
　　I tell you, king, this man, this murderer
　　(whom you have long declared you are in search of,
　　indicting him in threatening proclamation　　　　　500
　　as murderer of Laius) — he is here.
　　In name he is a stranger among citizens
　　but soon he will be shown to be a citizen
　　true native Theban, and he'll have no joy
　　of the discovery: blindness for sight　　　　　505
　　and beggary for riches his exchange,
　　he shall go journeying to a foreign country
　　tapping his way before him with a stick.
　　He shall be proved father and brother both
　　to his own children in his house; to her　　　　510
　　that gave him birth, a son and husband both;
　　a fellow sower in his father's bed

---

467 *Cithaeron:* Mountain in Greece and the location where Oedipus was abandoned as a baby.

with that same father that he murdered.
Go within, reckon that out, and if you find me
mistaken, say I have no skill in prophecy.   515
                    (Exeunt separately Teiresias and Oedipus.)
Chorus (Strophe): Who is the man proclaimed
        by Delphi's prophetic rock
        as the bloody handed murderer,
        the doer of deeds that none dare name?
        Now is the time for him to run   520
        with a stronger foot
        than Pegasus
        for the child of Zeus leaps in arms upon him
        with fire and the lightning bolt,
        and terribly close on his heels   525
        are the Fates that never miss.

        (Antistrophe) Lately from snowy Parnassus°
        clearly the voice flashed forth,
        bidding each Theban track him down,
        the unknown murderer.   530
        In the savage forests he lurks and in
        the caverns like
        the mountain bull.
        He is sad and lonely, and lonely his feet
        that carry him far from the navel of earth;   535
        but its prophecies, ever living,
        flutter around his head.

        (Strophe) The augur has spread confusion,
        terrible confusion;
        I do not approve what was said   540
        nor can I deny it.
        I do not know what to say;
        I am in a flutter of foreboding;
        I never heard in the present
        nor past of a quarrel between   545
        the sons of Labdacus and Polybus,
        that I might bring as proof
        in attacking the popular fame
        of Oedipus, seeking
        to take vengeance for undiscovered   550
        death in the line of Labdacus.

        (Antistrophe) Truly Zeus and Apollo are wise
        and in human things all knowing;
        but amongst men there is no
        distinct judgment, between the prophet   555
        and me — which of us is right.
        One man may pass another in wisdom

---

527 *Parnassus:* Mountain in Greece that was sacred to Apollo.

but I would never agree
with those that find fault with the king
till I should see the word   560
proved right beyond doubt. For once
in visible form the Sphinx
came on him and all of us
saw his wisdom and in that test
he saved the city. So he will not be condemned by my mind.   565

(Enter Creon.)

Creon: Citizens, I have come because I heard
deadly words spread about me, that the king
accuses me. I cannot take that from him.
If he believes that in these present troubles
he has been wronged by me in word or deed   570
I do not want to live on with the burden
of such a scandal on me. The report
injures me doubly and most vitally —
for I'll be called a traitor to my city
and traitor also to my friends and you.   575
Chorus: Perhaps it was a sudden gust of anger
that forced that insult from him, and no judgment.
Creon: But did he say that it was in compliance
with schemes of mine that the seer told him lies?
Chorus: Yes, he said that, but why, I do not know.   580
Creon: Were his eyes straight in his head? Was his mind right
when he accused me in this fashion?
Chorus: I do not know; I have no eyes to see
what princes do. Here comes the king himself.   *(Enter Oedipus.)*
Oedipus: You, sir, how is it you come here? Have you so much   585
brazen-faced daring that you venture in
my house although you are proved manifestly
the murderer of that man, and though you tried,
openly, highway robbery of my crown?
For God's sake, tell me what you saw in me,   590
what cowardice or what stupidity,
that made you lay a plot like this against me?
Did you imagine I should not observe
the crafty scheme that stole upon me or
seeing it, take no means to counter it?   595
Was it not stupid of you to make the attempt,
to try to hunt down royal power without
the people at your back or friends? For only
with the people at your back or money can
the hunt end in the capture of a crown.   600
Creon: Do you know what you're doing? Will you listen
to words to answer yours, and then pass judgment?
Oedipus: You're quick to speak, but I am slow to grasp you,
for I have found you dangerous, — and my foe.
Creon: First of all hear what I shall say to that.   605
Oedipus: At least don't tell me that you are not guilty.

Creon: If you think obstinacy without wisdom
    a valuable possession, you are wrong.
Oedipus: And you are wrong if you believe that one,
    a criminal, will not be punished only   610
    because he is my kinsman.
Creon: This is but just —
    but tell me, then, of what offense I'm guilty?
Oedipus: Did you or did you not urge me to send
    to this prophetic mumbler?
Creon: I did indeed,
    and I shall stand by what I told you.   615
Oedipus: How long ago is it since Laius. . . .
Creon: What about Laius? I don't understand.
Oedipus: Vanished — died — was murdered?
Creon: It is long,
    a long, long time to reckon.
Oedipus: Was this prophet
    in the profession then?
Creon: He was, and honoured   620
    as highly as he is today.
Oedipus: At that time did he say a word about me?
Creon: Never, at least when I was near him.
Oedipus: You never made a search for the dead man?
Creon: We searched, indeed, but never learned of anything.   625
Oedipus: Why did our wise old friend not say this then?
Creon: I don't know; and when I know nothing, I
    usually hold my tongue.
Oedipus: You know this much,
    and can declare this much if you are loyal.
Creon: What is it? If I know, I'll not deny it.   630
Oedipus: That he would not have said that I killed Laius
    had he not met you first.
Creon: You know yourself
    whether he said this, but I demand that I
    should hear as much from you as you from me.
Oedipus: Then hear, — I'll not be proved a murderer.   635
Creon: Well, then. You're married to my sister.
Oedipus: Yes,
    that I am not disposed to deny.
Creon: You rule
    this country giving her an equal share
    in the government?
Oedipus: Yes, everything she wants
    she has from me.
Creon: And I, as thirdsman to you,   640
    am rated as the equal of you two?
Oedipus: Yes, and it's there you've proved yourself false friend.
Creon: Not if you will reflect on it as I do.
    Consider, first, if you think any one
    would choose to rule and fear rather than rule   645
    and sleep untroubled by a fear if power

were equal in both cases. I, at least,
I was not born with such a frantic yearning
to be a king — but to do what kings do.
And so it is with every one who has learned   650
wisdom and self-control. As it stands now,
the prizes are all mine — and without fear.
But if I were the king myself, I must
do much that went against the grain.
How should despotic rule seem sweeter to me   655
than painless power and an assured authority?
I am not so besotted yet that I
want other honours than those that come with profit.
Now every man's my pleasure; every man greets me;
now those who are your suitors fawn on me, —   660
success for them depends upon my favour.
Why should I let all this go to win that?
My mind would not be traitor if it's wise;
I am no treason lover, of my nature,
nor would I ever dare to join a plot.   665
Prove what I say. Go to the oracle
at Pytho and inquire about the answers,
if they are as I told you. For the rest,
if you discover I laid any plot
together with the seer, kill me, I say,   670
not only by your vote but by my own.
But do not charge me on obscure opinion
without some proof to back it. It's not just
lightly to count your knaves as honest men,
nor honest men as knaves. To throw away   675
an honest friend is, as it were, to throw
your life away, which a man loves the best.
In time you will know all with certainty;
time is the only test of honest men,
one day is space enough to know a rogue.   680
Chorus: His words are wise, king, if one fears to fall.
    Those who are quick of temper are not safe.
Oedipus: When he that plots against me secretly
    moves quickly, I must quickly counterplot.
    If I wait taking no decisive measure   685
    his business will be done, and mine be spoiled.
Creon: What do you want to do then? Banish me?
Oedipus: No, certainly; kill you, not banish you.
Creon: I do not think that you've your wits about you.
Oedipus: For my own interests, yes.
Creon: But for mine, too,   690
    you should think equally.
Oedipus: You are a rogue.
Creon: Suppose you do not understand?
Oedipus: But yet
    I must be ruler.
Creon: Not if you rule badly.

Oedipus: O, city, city!

Creon: I too have some share
   in the city; it is not yours alone.   695

Chorus: Stop, my lords! Here — and in the nick of time
   I see Jocasta coming from the house;
   with her help lay the quarrel that now stirs you.   *(Enter Jocasta.)*

Jocasta: For shame! Why have you raised this foolish squabbling
   brawl? Are you not ashamed to air your private   700
   griefs when the country's sick? Go in, you, Oedipus,
   and you, too, Creon, into the house. Don't magnify
   your nothing troubles.

Creon: Sister, Oedipus,
   your husband, thinks he has the right to do
   terrible wrongs — he has but to choose between   705
   two terrors: banishing or killing me.

Oedipus: He's right, Jocasta; for I find him plotting
   with knavish tricks against my person.

Creon: That God may never bless me! May I die
   accursed, if I have been guilty of   710
   one tittle of the charge you bring against me!

Jocasta: I beg you, Oedipus, trust him in this,
   spare him for the sake of this his oath to God,
   for my sake, and the sake of those who stand here.

Chorus: Be gracious, be merciful,   715
   we beg of you.

Oedipus: In what would you have me yield?

Chorus: He has been no silly child in the past.
   He is strong in his oath now.
   Spare him.   720

Oedipus: Do you know what you ask?

Chorus: Yes.

Oedipus: Tell me then.

Chorus: He has been your friend before all men's eyes; do not cast him
   away dishonoured on an obscure conjecture.   725

Oedipus: I would have you know that this request of yours
   really requests my death or banishment.

Chorus: May the Sun God, king of Gods, forbid! May I die without God's
   blessing, without friends' help, if I had any such thought. But my
   spirit is broken by my unhappiness for my wasting country; and 730
   this would but add troubles amongst ourselves to the other troubles.

Oedipus: Well, let him go then — if I must die ten times for it,
   or be sent out dishonoured into exile.
   It is your lips that prayed for him I pitied,
   not his; wherever he is, I shall hate him.   735

Creon: I see you sulk in yielding and you're dangerous
   when you are out of temper; natures like yours
   are justly heaviest for themselves to bear.

Oedipus: Leave me alone! Take yourself off, I tell you.

Creon: I'll go, you have not known me, but they have,   740
   and they have known my innocence.   *(Exit.)*

Chorus: Won't you take him inside, lady?

Jocasta: Yes, when I've found out what was the matter.

Chorus: There was some misconceived suspicion of a story, and on the
other side the sting of injustice.   745

Jocasta: So, on both sides?

Chorus: Yes.

Jocasta: What was the story?

Chorus: I think it best, in the interests of the country, to leave it where
it ended.   750

Oedipus: You see where you have ended, straight of judgment
although you are, by softening my anger.

Chorus: Sir, I have said before and I say again — be sure that I would have
been proved a madman, bankrupt in sane council, if I should put you
away, you who steered the country I love safely when she was crazed   755
with troubles. God grant that now, too, you may prove a fortunate guide
for us.

Jocasta: Tell me, my lord, I beg of you, what was it
that roused your anger so?

Oedipus: Yes, I will tell you.
I honour you more than I honour them.   760
It was Creon and the plots he laid against me.

Jocasta: Tell me — if you can clearly tell the quarrel —

Oedipus: Creon says
that I'm the murderer of Laius.

Jocasta: Of his own knowledge or on information?

Oedipus: He sent this rascal prophet to me, since   765
he keeps his own mouth clean of any guilt.

Jocasta: Do not concern yourself about this matter;
listen to me and learn that human beings
have no part in the craft of prophecy.
Of that I'll show you a short proof.   770
There was an oracle once that came to Laius, —
I will not say that it was Phoebus' own,
but it was from his servants — and it told him
that it was fate that he should die a victim
at the hands of his own son, a son to be born   775
of Laius and me. But, see now, he,
the king, was killed by foreign highway robbers
at a place where three roads meet — so goes the story;
and for the son — before three days were out
after his birth King Laius pierced his ankles   780
and by the hands of others cast him forth
upon a pathless hillside. So Apollo
failed to fulfill his oracle to the son,
that he should kill his father, and to Laius
also proved false in that the thing he feared,   785
death at his son's hands, never came to pass.
So clear in this case were the oracles,
so clear and false. Give them no heed, I say;
what God discovers need of, easily

he shows to us himself.

Oedipus: O dear Jocasta,   790
as I hear this from you, there comes upon me
a wandering of the soul — I could run mad.

Jocasta: What trouble is it, that you turn again
and speak like this?

Oedipus: I thought I heard you say
that Laius was killed at a crossroads.   795

Jocasta: Yes, that was how the story went and still
that word goes round.

Oedipus: Where is this place, Jocasta,
where he was murdered?

Jocasta: Phocis is the country
and the road splits there, one of two roads from Delphi,
another comes from Daulia.

Oedipus: How long ago is this?   800

Jocasta: The news came to the city just before
you became king and all men's eyes looked to you.
What is it, Oedipus, that's in your mind?

Oedipus: What have you designed, O Zeus, to do with me?

Jocasta: What is the thought that troubles your heart?   805

Oedipus: Don't ask me yet — tell me of Laius —
How did he look? How old or young was he?

Jocasta: He was a tall man and his hair was grizzled
already — nearly white — and in his form
not unlike you.

Oedipus: O God, I think I have   810
called curses on myself in ignorance.

Jocasta: What do you mean? I am terrified
when I look at you.

Oedipus: I have a deadly fear
that the old seer had eyes. You'll show me more
if you can tell me one more thing.

Jocasta: I will.   815
I'm frightened, — but if I can understand,
I'll tell you all you ask.

Oedipus: How was his company?
Had he few with him when he went this journey,
or many servants, as would suit a prince?

Jocasta: In all there were but five, and among them   820
a herald; and one carriage for the king.

Oedipus: It's plain — its plain — who was it told you this?

Jocasta: The only servant that escaped safe home.

Oedipus: Is he at home now?

Jocasta: No, when he came home again
and saw you king and Laius was dead,   825
he came to me and touched my hand and begged
that I should send him to the fields to be
my shepherd and so he might see the city

as far off as he might. So I
sent him away. He was an honest man,   830
as slaves go, and was worthy of far more
than what he asked of me.
Oedipus: O, how I wish that he could come back quickly!
Jocasta: He can. Why is your heart so set on this?
Oedipus: O dear Jocasta, I am full of fears   835
that I have spoken far too much; and therefore
I wish to see this shepherd.
Jocasta: He will come;
but, Oedipus, I think I'm worthy too
to know what it is that disquiets you.
Oedipus: It shall not be kept from you, since my mind   840
has gone so far with its forebodings. Whom
should I confide in rather than you, who is there
of more importance to me who have passed
through such a fortune?
Polybus was my father, king of Corinth,   845
and Merope,° the Dorian, my mother.
I was held greatest of the citizens
in Corinth till a curious chance befell me
as I shall tell you — curious, indeed,
but hardly worth the store I set upon it.   850
There was a dinner and at it a man,
a drunken man, accused me in his drink
of being bastard. I was furious
but held my temper under for that day.
Next day I went and taxed my parents with it;   855
they took the insult very ill from him,
the drunken fellow who had uttered it.
So I was comforted for their part, but
still this thing rankled always, for the story
crept about widely. And I went at last   860
to Pytho, though my parents did not know.
But Phoebus sent me home again unhonoured
in what I came to learn, but he foretold
other and desperate horrors to befall me,
that I was fated to lie with my mother,   865
and show to daylight an accursed breed
which men would not endure, and I was doomed
to be murderer of the father that begot me.
When I heard this I fled, and in the days
that followed I would measure from the stars   870
the whereabouts of Corinth — yes, I fled
to somewhere where I should not see fulfilled
the infamies told in that dreadful oracle.

---

846 *Polybus and Merope:* King and queen that adopted and raised Oedipus.

And as I journeyed I came to the place
where, as you say, this king met with his death.   875
Jocasta, I will tell you the whole truth.
When I was near the branching of the crossroads,
going on foot, I was encountered by
a herald and a carriage with a man in it,
just as you tell me. He that led the way   880
and the old man himself wanted to thrust me
out of the road by force. I became angry
and struck the coachman who was pushing me.
When the old man saw this he watched his moment,
and as I passed he struck me from his carriage,   885
full on the head with his two pointed goad.
But he was paid in full and presently
my stick had struck him backwards from the car
and he rolled out of it. And then I killed them
all. If it happened there was any tie   890
of kinship twixt this man and Laius,
who is then now more miserable than I,
what man on earth so hated by the Gods,
since neither citizen nor foreigner
may welcome me at home or even greet me,   895
but drive me out of doors? And it is I,
I and no other have so cursed myself.
And I pollute the bed of him I killed
by the hands that killed him. Was I not born evil?
Am I not utterly unclean? I had to fly   900
and in my banishment not even see
my kindred nor set foot in my own country,
or otherwise my fate was to be yoked
in marriage with my mother and kill my father,
Polybus who begot me and had reared me.   905
Would not one rightly judge and say that on me
these things were sent by some malignant God?
O no, no, no — O holy majesty
of God on high, may I not see that day!
May I be gone out of men's sight before   910
I see the deadly taint of this disaster
come upon me.
Chorus: Sir, we too fear these things. But until you see this man face to
    face and hear his story, hope.
Oedipus: Yes, I have just this much of hope — to wait until the herdsman comes.   915
Jocasta: And when he comes, what do you want with him?
Oedipus: I'll tell you; if I find that his story is the same as yours, I at least
    will be clear of this guilt.
Jocasta: Why what so particularly did you learn from my story?
Oedipus: You said that he spoke of highway *robbers* who killed Laius. Now   920
    if he uses the same number, it was not I who killed him. One man
    cannot be the same as many. But if he speaks of a man travelling
    alone, then clearly the burden of the guilt inclines towards me.

Jocasta: Be sure, at least, that this was how he told the story. He cannot unsay
it now, for everyone in the city heard it — not I alone. But, Oedipus, even   925
if he diverges from what he said then, he shall never prove that the murder of Laius squares rightly with the prophecy — for Loxias declared that
the king should be killed by his own son. And that poor creature did not
kill him surely, — for he died himself first. So as far as prophecy goes,
henceforward I shall not look to the right hand or the left.   930
Oedipus: Right. But yet, send some one for the peasant to bring him here;
do not neglect it.
Jocasta: I will send quickly. Now let me go indoors. I will do nothing
except what pleases you.   *(Exeunt.)*
Chorus (Strophe): May destiny ever find me   935
pious in word and deed
prescribed by the laws that live on high:
laws begotten in the clear air of heaven,
whose only father is Olympus;
no mortal nature brought them to birth,   940
no forgetfulness shall lull them to sleep;
for God is great in them and grows not old.

(Antistrophe) Insolence breeds the tyrant, insolence
if it is glutted with a surfeit, unseasonable, unprofitable,
climbs to the roof-top and plunges   945
sheer down to the ruin that must be,
and there its feet are no service.
But I pray that the God may never
abolish the eager ambition that profits the state.
For I shall never cease to hold the God as our protector.   950

(Strophe) If a man walks with haughtiness
of hand or word and gives no heed
to Justice and the shrines of Gods
despises — may an evil doom
smite him for his ill-starred pride of heart!—   955
he reaps gains without justice
and will not hold from impiety
and his fingers itch for untouchable things.
When such things are done, what man shall contrive
to shield his soul from the shafts of the God?   960
When such deeds are held in honour,
why should I honour the Gods in the dance?

(Antistrophe) No longer to the holy place,
to the navel of earth I'll go
to worship, nor to Abae   965
nor to Olympia,
unless the oracles are proved to fit,
for all men's hands to point at.
O Zeus, if you are rightly called
the sovereign lord, all-mastering,   970

let this not escape you nor your ever-living power!
The oracles concerning Laius
are old and dim and men regard them not.
Apollo is nowhere clear in honour; God's service perishes.

(Enter Jocasta, carrying garlands.)

Jocasta: Princes of the land, I have had the thought to go   975
to the Gods' temples, bringing in my hand
garlands and gifts of incense, as you see.
For Oedipus excites himself too much
at every sort of trouble, not conjecturing,
like a man of sense, what will be from what was,   980
but he is always at the speaker's mercy,
when he speaks terrors. I can do no good
by my advice, and so I came as suppliant
to you, Lycaean Apollo, who are nearest.
These are the symbols of my prayer and this   985
my prayer: grant us escape free of the curse.
Now when we look to him we are all afraid;
he's pilot of our ship and he is frightened.   *(Enter Messenger.)*

Messenger: Might I learn from you, sirs, where is the house of Oedipus? Or
best of all, if you know, where is the king himself?   990

Chorus: This is his house and he is within doors. This lady is his wife and
mother of his children.

Messenger: God bless you, lady, and God bless your household! God bless
Oedipus' noble wife!

Jocasta: God bless you, sir, for your kind greeting! What do you want   995
of us that you have come here? What have you to tell us?

Messenger: Good news, lady. Good for your house and for your husband.

Jocasta: What is your news? Who sent you to us?

Messenger: I come from Corinth and the news I bring will give you pleasure.
Perhaps a little pain too.   1000

Jocasta: What is this news of double meaning?

Messenger: The people of the Isthmus will choose Oedipus to be their king.
That is the rumour there.

Jocasta: But isn't their king still old Polybus?

Messenger: No. He is in his grave. Death has got him.   1005

Jocasta: Is that the truth? Is Oedipus' father dead?

Messenger: May I die myself if it be otherwise!

Jocasta (to a servant): Be quick and run to the King with the news! O oracles
of the Gods, where are you now? It was from this man Oedipus fled, lest
he should be his murderer! And now he is dead, in the course of nature, 1010
and not killed by Oedipus.   *(Enter Oedipus.)*

Oedipus: Dearest Jocasta, why have you sent for me?

Jocasta: Listen to this man and when you hear reflect what is the outcome
of the holy oracles of the Gods.

Oedipus: Who is he? What is his message for me?   1015

Jocasta: He is from Corinth and he tells us that your father Polybus is
dead and gone.

Oedipus: What's this you say, sir? Tell me yourself.

Messenger: Since this is the first matter you want clearly told: Polybus has
    gone down to death. You may be sure of it.   1020
Oedipus: By treachery or sickness?
Messenger: A small thing will put old bodies asleep.
Oedipus: So he died of sickness, it seems, — poor old man!
Messenger: Yes, and of age — the long years he had measured.
Oedipus: Ha! Ha! O dear Jocasta, why should one   1025
    look to the Pythian hearth?° Why should one look
    to the birds screaming overhead? They prophesied
    that I should kill my father! But he's dead,
    and hidden deep in earth, and I stand here
    who never laid a hand on spear against him, —   1030
    unless perhaps he died of longing for me,
    and thus I am his murderer. But they,
    the oracles, as they stand — he's taken them
    away with him, they're dead as he himself is,
    and worthless.
Jocasta: That I told you before now.   1035
Oedipus: You did, but I was misled by my fear.
Jocasta: Then lay no more of them to heart, not one.
Oedipus: But surely I must fear my mother's bed?
Jocasta: Why should man fear since chance is all in all
    for him, and he can clearly foreknow nothing?   1040
    Best to live lightly, as one can, unthinkingly.
    As to your mother's marriage bed, — don't fear it.
    Before this, in dreams too, as well as oracles,
    many a man has lain with his own mother.
    But he to whom such things are nothing bears   1045
    his life most easily.
Oedipus: All that you say would be said perfectly
    if she were dead; but since she lives I must
    still fear, although you talk so well, Jocasta.
Jocasta: Still in your father's death there's light of comfort?   1050
Oedipus: Great light of comfort; but I fear the living.
Messenger: Who is the woman that makes you afraid?
Oedipus: Merope, old man, Polybus' wife.
Messenger: What about her frightens the queen and you?
Oedipus: A terrible oracle, stranger, from the Gods.   1055
Messenger: Can it be told? Or does the sacred law
    forbid another to have knowledge of it?
Oedipus: O no! Once on a time Loxias said
    that I should lie with my own mother and
    take on my hands the blood of my own father.   1060
    And so for these long years I've lived away
    from Corinth; it has been to my great happiness;
    but yet it's sweet to see the face of parents.

1026 *Pythian hearth:* Delphi.

Messenger: This was the fear which drove you out of Corinth?

Oedipus: Old man, I did not wish to kill my father. 1065

Messenger: Why should I not free you from this fear, sir,
    since I have come to you in all goodwill?

Oedipus: You would not find me thankless if you did.

Messenger: Why, it was just for this I brought the news, —
    to earn your thanks when you had come safe home. 1070

Oedipus: No, I will never come near my parents.

Messenger: Son,
    it's very plain you don't know what you're doing.

Oedipus: What do you mean, old man? For God's sake, tell me.

Messenger: If your homecoming is checked by fears like these.

Oedipus: Yes, I'm afraid that Phoebus may prove right. 1075

Messenger: The murder and the incest?

Oedipus: Yes, old man;
    that is my constant terror.

Messenger: Do you know
    that all your fears are empty?

Oedipus: How is that,
    if they are father and mother and I their son?

Messenger: Because Polybus was no kin to you in blood. 1080

Oedipus: What, was not Polybus my father?

Messenger: No more than I but just so much.

Oedipus: How can
    my father be my father as much as one
    that's nothing to me?

Messenger: Neither he nor I
    begat you.

Oedipus: Why then did he call me son? 1085

Messenger: A gift he took you from these hands of mine.

Oedipus: Did he love so much what he took from another's hand?

Messenger: His childlessness before persuaded him.

Oedipus: Was I a child you bought or found when I
    was given to him?

Messenger: On Cithaeron's slopes 1090
    in the twisting thickets you were found.

Oedipus: And why
    were you a traveller in those parts?

Messenger: I was
    in charge of mountain flocks.

Oedipus: You were a shepherd?
    A hireling vagrant?

Messenger: Yes, but at least at that time
    the man that saved your life, son. 1095

Oedipus: What ailed me when you took me in your arms?

Messenger: In that your ankles should be witnesses.

Oedipus: Why do you speak of that old pain?

Messenger: I loosed you;
    the tendons of your feet were pierced and fettered, —

Oedipus: My swaddling clothes brought me a rare disgrace. 1100

Messenger: So that from this you're called your present name.°
Oedipus: Was this my father's doing or my mother's?
    For God's sake, tell me.
Messenger: I don't know, but he
    who gave you to me has more knowledge than I.
Oedipus: You yourself did not find me then? You took me   1105
    from someone else?
Messenger: Yes, from another shepherd.
Oedipus: Who was he? Do you know him well enough
    to tell?
Messenger: He was called Laius' man.
Oedipus: You mean the king who reigned here in the old days?
Messenger: Yes, he was that man's shepherd.
Oedipus: Is he alive   1110
    still, so that I could see him?
Messenger: You who live here
    would know that best.
Oedipus: Do any of you here
    know of this shepherd whom he speaks about
    in town or in the fields? Tell me. It's time
    that this was found out once for all.   1115
Chorus: I think he is none other than the peasant
    whom you have sought to see already; but
    Jocasta here can tell us best of that.
Oedipus: Jocasta, do you know about this man
    whom we have sent for? Is he the man he mentions?   1120
Jocasta: Why ask of whom he spoke? Don't give it heed;
    nor try to keep in mind what has been said.
    It will be wasted labour.
Oedipus: With such clues
    I could not fail to bring my birth to light.
Jocasta: I beg you — do not hunt this out — I beg you,   1125
    if you have any care for your own life.
    What I am suffering is enough.
Oedipus: Keep up
    your heart, Jocasta. Though I'm proved a slave,
    thrice slave, and though my mother is thrice slave,
    you'll not be shown to be of lowly lineage.   1130
Jocasta: O be persuaded by me, I entreat you;
    do not do this.
Oedipus: I will not be persuaded to let be
    the chance of finding out the whole thing clearly.
Jocasta: It is because I wish you well that I   1135
    give you this counsel — and it's the best counsel.
Oedipus: Then the best counsel vexes me, and has
    for some while since.
Jocasta: O Oedipus, God help you!
    God keep you from the knowledge of who you are!

1101 *name: Oedipus* literally translates to "swollen foot."

Oedipus: Here, some one, go and fetch the shepherd for me;   1140
    and let her find her joy in her rich family!

Jocasta: O Oedipus, unhappy Oedipus!
    that is all I can call you, and the last thing
    that I shall ever call you.   *(Exit.)*

Chorus: Why has the queen gone, Oedipus, in wild   1145
    grief rushing from us? I am afraid that trouble
    will break out of this silence.

Oedipus: Break out what will! I at least shall be
    willing to see my ancestry, though humble.
    Perhaps she is ashamed of my low birth,   1150
    for she has all a woman's high-flown pride.
    But I account myself a child of Fortune,
    beneficent Fortune, and I shall not be
    dishonoured. She's the mother from whom I spring;
    the months, my brothers, marked me, now as small,   1155
    and now again as mighty. Such is my breeding,
    and I shall never prove so false to it,
    as not to find the secret of my birth.

Chorus (Strophe): If I am a prophet and wise of heart
    you shall not fail, Cithaeron,   1160
    by the limitless sky, you shall not! —
    to know at tomorrow's full moon
    that Oedipus honours you,
    as native to him and mother and nurse at once;
    and that you are honoured in dancing by us, as finding favour in sight of 1165
        our king.
    Apollo, to whom we cry, find these things pleasing!

(Antistrophe) Who was it bore you, child? One of
    the long-lived nymphs who lay with Pan —
    the father who treads the hills?   1170
    Or was she a bride of Loxias, your mother? The grassy slopes
    are all of them dear to him. Or perhaps Cyllene's king
    or the Bacchants' God that lives on the tops
    of the hills received you a gift from some
    one of the Helicon Nymphs, with whom he mostly plays?   1175
          (Enter an old man, led by Oedipus' servants.)

Oedipus: If some one like myself who never met him
    may make a guess, — I think this is the herdsman,
    whom we were seeking. His old age is consonant
    with the other. And besides, the men who bring him
    I recognize as my own servants. You   1180
    perhaps may better me in knowledge since
    you've seen the man before.

Chorus: You can be sure
    I recognize him. For if Laius
    had ever an honest shepherd, this was he.

Oedipus: You, sir, from Corinth, I must ask you first,   1185

is this the man you spoke of?
Messenger: This is he
    before your eyes.
Oedipus: Old man, look here at me
    and tell me what I ask you. Were you ever
    a servant of King Laius?
Herdsman: I was, —
    no slave he bought but reared in his own house.   1190
Oedipus: What did you do as work? How did you live?
Herdsman: Most of my life was spent among the flocks.
Oedipus: In what part of the country did you live?
Herdsman: Cithaeron and the places near to it.
Oedipus: And somewhere there perhaps you knew this man?   1195
Herdsman: What was his occupation? Who?
Oedipus: This man here,
    have you had any dealings with him?
Herdsman: No —
    not such that I can quickly call to mind.
Messenger: That is no wonder, master. But I'll make him remember what he
    does not know. For I know, that he well knows the country of 1200
    Cithaeron, how he with two flocks, I with one kept company for
    three years — each year half a year — from spring till autumn time
    and then when winter came I drove my flocks to our fold home
    again and he to Laius' steadings. Well — am I right or not in what
    I said we did?   1205
Herdsman: You're right — although it's a long time ago.
Messenger: Do you remember giving me a child
    to bring up as my foster child?
Herdsman: What's this?
    Why do you ask this question?
Messenger: Look old man,
    here he is — here's the man who was that child!
Herdsman: Death take you! Won't you hold your tongue?   1210
Oedipus: No, no,
    do not find fault with him, old man. Your words
    are more at fault than his.
Herdsman: O best of masters,
    how do I give offense?
Oedipus: When you refuse
    to speak about the child of whom he asks you.   1215
Herdsman: He speaks out of his ignorance, without meaning.
Oedipus: If you'll not talk to gratify me, you
    will talk with pain to urge you.
Herdsman: O please, sir,
    don't hurt an old man, sir.
Oedipus (to the servants):   Here, one of you,
    twist his hands behind him.
Herdsman: Why, God help me, why?   1220
    What do you want to know?

Oedipus: You gave a child
to him, — the child he asked you of?

Herdsman: I did.
I wish I'd died the day I did.

Oedipus: You will
unless you tell me truly.

Herdsman: And I'll die
far worse if I should tell you.

Oedipus: This fellow   1225
is bent on more delays, as it would seem.

Herdsman: O no, no! I have told you that I gave it.

Oedipus: Where did you get this child from? Was it your own or did you
get it from another?

Herdsman: Not
my own at all; I had it from some one.   1230

Oedipus: One of these citizens? or from what house?

Herdsman: O master, please — I beg you, master, please
don't ask me more.

Oedipus: You're a dead man if I
ask you again.

Herdsman: It was one of the children
of Laius.

Oedipus: A slave? Or born in wedlock?   1235

Herdsman: O God, I am on the brink of frightful speech.

Oedipus: And I of frightful hearing. But I must hear.

Herdsman: The child was called his child; but she within,
your wife would tell you best how all this was.

Oedipus: *She* gave it to you?

Herdsman: Yes, she did, my lord.   1240

Oedipus: To do what with it?

Herdsman: Make away with it.

Oedipus: She was so hard — its mother?

Herdsman: Aye, through fear
of evil oracles.

Oedipus: Which?

Herdsman: They said that he
should kill his parents.

Oedipus: How was it that you
gave it away to this old man?

Herdsman: O master,   1245
I pitied it, and thought that I could send it
off to another country and this man
was from another country. But he saved it
for the most terrible troubles. If you are
the man he says you are, you're bred to misery.   1250

Oedipus: O, O, O, they will all come,
all come out clearly! Light of the sun, let me
look upon you no more after today!
I who first saw the light bred of a match

accursed, and accursed in my living   1255
with them I lived with, cursed in my killing.

                                         (Exeunt all but the Chorus.)

Chorus (Strophe): O generations of men, how I
count you as equal with those who live
not at all!
What man, what man on earth wins more   1260
of happiness than a seeming
and after that turning away?
Oedipus, you are my pattern of this,
Oedipus, you and your fate!
Luckless Oedipus, whom of all men   1265
I envy not at all.

(Antistrophe) In as much as he shot his bolt
beyond the others and won the prize
of happiness complete —
O Zeus — and killed and reduced to nought   1270
the hooked taloned maid of the riddling speech,
standing a tower against death for my land:
hence he was called my king and hence
was honoured the highest of all
honours; and hence he ruled   1275
in the great city of Thebes.

(Strophe) But now whose tale is more miserable?
Who is there lives with a savager fate?
Whose troubles so reverse his life as his?

O Oedipus, the famous prince   1280
for whom a great haven
the same both as father and son
sufficed for generation,
how, O how, have the furrows ploughed
by your father endured to bear you, poor wretch,   1285
and hold their peace so long?

(Antistrophe) Time who sees all has found you out
against your will; judges your marriage accursed,
begetter and begot at one in it.

O child of Laius,   1290
would I had never seen you.
I weep for you and cry
a dirge of lamentation.

To speak directly, I drew my breath
from you at the first and so now I lull   1295
my mouth to sleep with your name.   *(Enter a second messenger.)*
Second Messenger: O Princes always honoured by our country,
what deeds you'll hear of and what horrors see,

what grief you'll feel, if you as true born Thebans
care for the house of Labdacus's sons.   1300
Phasis nor Ister cannot purge this house,
I think, with all their streams, such things
it hides, such evils shortly will bring forth
into the light, whether they will or not;
and troubles hurt the most   1305
when they prove self-inflicted.
Chorus: What we had known before did not fall short
    of bitter groaning's worth; what's more to tell?
Second Messenger: Shortest to hear and tell — our glorious queen
    Jocasta's dead.
Chorus: Unhappy woman! How?   1310
Second Messenger: By her own hand. The worst of what was done
    you cannot know. You did not see the sight.
    Yet in so far as I remember it
    you'll hear the end of our unlucky queen.
    When she came raging into the house she went   1315
    straight to her marriage bed, tearing her hair
    with both her hands, and crying upon Laius
    long dead — Do you remember, Laius,
    that night long past which bred a child for us
    to send you to your death and leave   1320
    a mother making children with her son?
    And then she groaned and cursed the bed in which
    she brought forth husband by her husband, children
    by her own child, an infamous double bond.
    How after that she died I do not know, —   1325
    for Oedipus distracted us from seeing.
    He burst upon us shouting and we looked
    to him as he paced frantically around,
    begging us always: Give me a sword, I say,
    to find this wife no wife, this mother's womb,   1330
    this field of double sowing whence I sprang
    and where I sowed my children! As he raved
    some god showed him the way — none of us there.
    Bellowing terribly and led by some
    invisible guide he rushed on the two doors, —   1335
    wrenching the hollow bolts out of their sockets,
    he charged inside. There, there, we saw his wife
    hanging, the twisted rope around her neck.
    When he saw her, he cried out fearfully
    and cut the dangling noose. Then, as she lay,   1340
    poor woman, on the ground, what happened after,
    was terrible to see. He tore the brooches —
    the gold chased brooches fastening her robe —
    away from her and lifting them up high
    dashed them on his own eyeballs, shrieking out   1345
    such things as: they will never see the crime
    I have committed or had done upon me!

Dark eyes, now in the days to come look on
forbidden faces, do not recognize
those whom you long for — with such imprecations   1350
he struck his eyes again and yet again
with the brooches. And the bleeding eyeballs gushed
and stained his beard — no sluggish oozing drops
but a black rain and bloody hail poured down.

So it has broken — and not on one head   1355
but troubles mixed for husband and for wife.
The fortune of the days gone by was true
good fortune — but today groans and destruction
and death and shame — of all ills can be named
not one is missing.   1360
Chorus: Is he now in any ease from pain?
Second Messenger: He shouts
for some one to unbar the doors and show him
to all the men of Thebes, his father's killer,
his mother's — no I cannot say the word,
it is unholy — for he'll cast himself,   1365
out of the land, he says, and not remain
to bring a curse upon his house, the curse
he called upon it in his proclamation. But
he wants for strength, aye, and some one to guide him;
his sickness is too great to bear. You, too,   1370
will be shown that. The bolts are opening.
Soon you will see a sight to waken pity
even in the horror of it.   *(Enter the blinded Oedipus.)*
Chorus: This is a terrible sight for men to see!
I never found a worse!   1375
Poor wretch, what madness came upon you!
What evil spirit leaped upon your life
to your ill-luck — a leap beyond man's strength!
Indeed I pity you, but I cannot
look at you, though there's much I want to ask   1380
and much to learn and much to see.
I shudder at the sight of you.
Oedipus: O, O,
where am I going? Where is my voice
borne on the wind to and fro?   1385
Spirit, how far have you sprung?
Chorus: To a terrible place whereof men's ears
may not hear, nor their eyes behold it.
Oedipus: Darkness!
Horror of darkness enfolding, resistless, unspeakable visitant sped by
an ill wind in haste!   1390
madness and stabbing pain and memory
of evil deeds I have done!
Chorus: In such misfortunes it's no wonder
if double weighs the burden of your grief.

Oedipus: My friend,   1395
    you are the only one steadfast, the only one that attends on me;
    you still stay nursing the blind man.
    Your care is not unnoticed. I can know
    your voice, although this darkness is my world.
Chorus: Doer of dreadful deeds, how did you dare   1400
    so far to do despite to your own eyes?
    what spirit urged you to it?
Oedipus: It was Apollo, friends, Apollo,
    that brought this bitter bitterness, my sorrows to completion.
    But the hand that struck me   1405
    was none but my own.
    Why should I see
    whose vision showed me nothing sweet to see?
Chorus: These things are as you say.
Oedipus: What can I see to love?   1410
    What greeting can touch my ears with joy?
    Take me away, and haste — to a place out of the way!
    Take me away, my friends, the greatly miserable,
    the most accursed, whom God too hates
    above all men on earth!   1415
Chorus: Unhappy in your mind and your misfortune,
    would I had never known you!
Oedipus: Curse on the man who took
    the cruel bonds from off my legs, as I lay in the field.
    He stole me from death and saved me,   1420
    no kindly service.
    Had I died then
    I would not be so burdensome to friends.
Chorus: I, too, could have wished it had been so.
Oedipus: Then I would not have come   1425
    to kill my father and marry my mother infamously.
    Now I am godless and child of impurity,
    begetter in the same seed that created my wretched self.
    If there is any ill worse than ill,
    that is the lot of Oedipus.   1430
Chorus: I cannot say your remedy was good;
    you would be better dead than blind and living.
Oedipus: What I have done here was best done — don't tell me
    otherwise, do not give me further counsel.
    I do not know with what eyes I could look   1435
    upon my father when I die and go
    under the earth, nor yet my wretched mother —
    those two to whom I have done things deserving
    worse punishment than hanging. Would the sight
    of children, bred as mine are, gladden me?   1440
    No, not these eyes, never. And my city,
    its towers and sacred places of the Gods,
    of these I robbed my miserable self
    when I commanded all to drive *him* out,

the criminal since proved by God impure   1445
and of the race of Laius.
To this guilt I bore witness against myself —
with what eyes shall I look upon my people?
No. If there were a means to choke the fountain
of hearing I would not have stayed my hand   1450
from locking up my miserable carcase,
seeing and hearing nothing; it is sweet
to keep our thoughts out of the range of hurt.

Cithaeron, why did you receive me? why
having received me did you not kill me straight?   1455
And so I had not shown to men my birth.

O Polybus and Corinth and the house,
the old house that I used to call my father's —
what fairness you were nurse to, and what foulness
festered beneath! Now I am found to be   1460
a sinner and a son of sinners. Crossroads,
and hidden glade, oak and the narrow way
at the crossroads, that drank my father's blood
offered you by my hands, do you remember
still what I did as you looked on, and what   1465
I did when I came here? O marriage, marriage!
you bred me and again when you had bred
bred children of your child and showed to men
brides, wives and mothers and the foulest deeds
that can be in this world of ours.   1470

Come — it's unfit to say what is unfit
to do. — I beg of you in God's name hide me
somewhere outside your country, yes, or kill me,
or throw me into the sea, to be forever
out of your sight. Approach and deign to touch me   1475
for all my wretchedness, and do not fear.
No man but I can bear my evil doom.
Chorus: Here Creon comes in fit time to perform
        or give advice in what you ask of us.
        Creon is left sole ruler in your stead.   1480
Oedipus: Creon! Creon! What shall I say to him?
        How can I justly hope that he will trust me?
        In what is past I have been proved towards him
        an utter liar.   (*Enter Creon.*)
Creon: Oedipus, I've come
        not so that I might laugh at you nor taunt you   1485
        with evil of the past. But if you still
        are without shame before the face of men
        reverence at least the flame that gives all life,
        our Lord the Sun, and do not show unveiled
        to him pollution such that neither land   1490
        nor holy rain nor light of day can welcome.   (*To a servant*)

Be quick and take him in. It is most decent
that only kin should see and hear the troubles
of kin.

Oedipus: I beg you, since you've torn me from   1495
my dreadful expectations and have come
in a most noble spirit to a man
that has used you vilely — do a thing for me.
I shall speak for your own good, not for my own.

Creon: What do you need that you would ask of me?   1500

Oedipus: Drive me from here with all the speed you can
to where I may not hear a human voice.

Creon: Be sure, I would have done this had not I
wished first of all to learn from the God the course
of action I should follow.

Oedipus: But his word   1505
has been quite clear to let the parricide,°
the sinner, die.

Creon: Yes, that indeed was said.
But in the present need we had best discover
what we should do.

Oedipus: And will you ask about
a man so wretched?

Creon: Now even you will trust   1510
the God.

Oedipus: So. I command you — and will beseech you —
to her that lies inside that house give burial
as you would have it; she is yours and rightly
you will perform the rites for her. For me —
never let this my father's city have me   1515
living a dweller in it. Leave me live
in the mountains where Cithaeron is, that's called
my mountain, which my mother and my father
while they were living would have made my tomb.
So I may die by their decree who sought   1520
indeed to kill me. Yet I know this much:
no sickness and no other thing will kill me.
I would not have been saved from death if not
for some strange evil fate. Well, let my fate
go where it will.

                         Creon, you need not care   1525
about my sons; they're men and so wherever
they are, they will not lack a livelihood.
But my two girls — so sad and pitiful —
whose table never stood apart from mine,
and everything I touched they always shared —   1530

1506 *parricide:* One who kills his parent or another close relative.

O Creon, have a thought for them! And most
I wish that you might suffer me to touch them
and sorrow with them.

     (Enter Antigone and Ismene, Oedipus' two daughters.)
O my lord! O true noble Creon! Can I
really be touching them, as when I saw?   1535
What shall I say?
Yes, I can hear them sobbing — my two darlings!
and Creon has had pity and has sent me
what I loved most?
Am I right?   1540

Creon: You're right: it was I gave you this
   because I knew from old days how you loved them
   as I see now.

Oedipus: God bless you for it, Creon,
   and may God guard you better on your road
   than he did me!
       O children,   1545
where are you? Come here, come to my hands,
a brother's hands which turned your father's eyes,
those bright eyes you knew once, to what you see,
a father seeing nothing, knowing nothing,
begetting you from his own source of life.   1550
I weep for you — I cannot see your faces —
I weep when I think of the bitterness
there will be in your lives, how you must live
before the world. At what assemblages
of citizens will you make one? to what   1555
gay company will you go and not come home
in tears instead of sharing in the holiday?
And when you're ripe for marriage, who will he be,
the man who'll risk to take such infamy
as shall cling to my children, to bring hurt   1560
on them and those that marry with them? What
curse is not there? "Your father killed his father
and sowed the seed where he had sprung himself
and begot you out of the womb that held him."
These insults you will hear. Then who will marry you?   1565
No one, my children; clearly you are doomed
to waste away in barrenness unmarried.
Son of Menoeceus,° since you are all the father
left these two girls, and we, their parents, both
are dead to them — do not allow them wander   1570
like beggars, poor and husbandless.
They are of your own blood.

1568 *Son of Menoeceus:* Creon.

And do not make them equal with myself
in wretchedness; for you can see them now
so young, so utterly alone, save for you only.   1575
Touch my hand, noble Creon, and say yes.
If you were older, children, and were wiser,
there's much advice I'd give you. But as it is,
let this be what you pray: give me a life
wherever there is opportunity   1580
to live, and better life than was my father's.

Creon: Your tears have had enough of scope; now go within the house.

Oedipus: I must obey, though bitter of heart.

Creon: In season, all is good.

Oedipus: Do you know on what conditions I obey?

Creon: You tell me them,   1585
and I shall know them when I hear.

Oedipus: That you shall send me out
to live away from Thebes.

Creon: That gift you must ask of the God.

Oedipus: But I'm now hated by the Gods.

Creon: So quickly you'll obtain your prayer.

Oedipus: You consent then?

Creon: What I do not mean, I do not use to say.

Oedipus: Now lead me away from here.

Creon: Let go the children, then, and come.   1590

Oedipus: Do not take them from me.

Creon: Do not seek to be master in everything,
for the things you mastered did not follow you throughout your life.

                                         (As Creon and Oedipus go out.)

Chorus: You that live in my ancestral Thebes, behold this Oedipus, —
him who knew the famous riddles and was a man most masterful;
not a citizen who did not look with envy on his lot —   1595
see him now and see the breakers of misfortune swallow him!
Look upon that last day always. Count no mortal happy till
he has passed the final limit of his life secure from pain.

CONSIDERATIONS FOR CRITICAL THINKING AND WRITING

1. FIRST RESPONSE. Is it possible for a twenty-first-century reader to identify with Oedipus's plight? What philosophic issues does he confront?

2. In the opening scene what does the priest's speech reveal about how Oedipus has been regarded as a ruler of Thebes?

3. What do Oedipus's confrontations with Teiresias and Creon indicate about his character?

4. Aristotle defined a tragic flaw as consisting of "error and frailties." What errors does Oedipus make? What are his frailties?

5. What causes Oedipus's downfall? Is he simply a pawn in a predetermined game played by the gods? Can he be regarded as responsible for the suffering and death in the play?

6. Locate instances of dramatic irony in the play. How do they serve as fore-shadowings?

7. Describe the function of the Chorus. How does the Chorus's view of life and the gods differ from Jocasta's?

8. Trace the images of vision and blindness throughout the play. How are they related to the theme? Why does Oedipus blind himself instead of joining Jocasta in suicide?

9. What is your assessment of Oedipus at the end of the play? Was he fool-ish? Heroic? Fated? To what extent can your emotions concerning him be described as "pity and fear"?

10. CRITICAL STRATEGIES. Read the section on psychological criticism (pp. 1649–51) in Chapter 51, "Critical Strategies for Reading," and Sigmund Freud's "On the Oedipus Complex" (p. 1167). Given that the *Oedipus complex* is a well-known term used in psychoanalysis, what does it mean? Does the concept offer any insights into the conflicts dramatized in the play?

CONNECTIONS TO OTHER SELECTIONS

1. Consider the endings of *Oedipus the King* and Shakespeare's *Hamlet* (p. 1237). What feelings do you have about these endings? Are they irredeem-ably unhappy? Is there anything that suggests hope for the future at the ends of these plays?

2. Sophocles does not include violence in his plays; any bloodshed occurs off-stage. Compare and contrast the effects of this strategy with the use of violence in *Hamlet*.

3. Write an essay explaining why *Oedipus the King* cannot be considered a realis-tic play in the way that Henrik Ibsen's *A Doll's House* (p. 1357) can be.

Perspectives on Sophocles

ARISTOTLE (384–322 B.C.)

On Tragic Character   ca. 340 B.C.

Now since in the finest kind of tragedy the structure should be complex and not simple, and since it should also be a representation of terrible and piteous events (that being the special mark of this type of imitation), in the first place, it is evident that good men ought not to be shown passing from happiness to misfortune, for this does not inspire either pity or fear, but only revulsion; nor evil men rising from ill fortune to prosperity, for this is the most untragic plot of all — it lacks every requirement, in that it neither elicits human sympathy nor stirs pity or fear. And again, neither should an extremely wicked man be seen falling from pros-perity into misfortune, for a plot so constructed might indeed call forth human sympathy, but would not excite pity or fear, since the first is felt for a person whose misfortune is undeserved and the second for someone like ourselves — pity for the man suffering undeservedly, fear for the man like ourselves — and hence neither pity nor fear would be aroused in this case. We are left with the man whose place is between these extremes. Such is the man who on the one hand is not preeminent in virtue and justice, and yet on the other hand does not fall into misfortune through vice or depravity, but falls because of some mistake; one among the number of the highly renowned and prosperous, such as Oedipus . . . and other famous men from families like [his].

It follows that the plot which achieves excellence will necessarily be single in outcome and not, as some say, double, and will consist in a change of fortune, not to prosperity from misfortune, but the opposite, from prosperity to misfortune, occasioned not by depravity, but by some great mistake on the part of one who is either such as I have described or better than this rather than worse. What actually has taken place has confirmed this; for though at first the poets accepted whatever myths came to hand, today the finest tragedies are founded upon the stories of only a few houses . . . and such . . . as have chanced to suffer terrible things or to do them. So then, tragedy having this construction is the finest kind of tragedy from an artistic point of view. And consequently those persons fall into the same error who bring it as a charge against Euripides° that this is what he does in his tragedies and that most of his plays have unhappy endings. For this is in fact the right procedure, as I have said; and the best proof is that on the stage and in the dramatic contests, plays of this kind seem the most tragic, provided they are successfully worked out, and Euripides, even if in everything else his management is faulty, seems at any rate to be the most tragic of the poets.

Second to this is the kind of plot that some persons place first, that which like the *Odyssey*° has a double structure and ends in opposite ways for the better characters and the worse. If it seems to be first, that is attributable to the weakness of the audience, since the poets only follow their lead and compose the kind of plays the spectators want. The pleasure it gives, however, is not that which comes from tragedy, but is rather the pleasure proper to comedy; for in comedy those who in the legend are the worst of enemies . . . end by leaving the scene as friends, and nobody is killed by anybody. . . .

With regard to the characters there are four things to aim at. First and foremost is that the characters be good. The personages will have character if, as aforesaid, they reveal in speech or in action what their moral choices are, and a good character will be one whose choices are good. It is possible to portray goodness in every class of persons; a woman may be good and a slave may be good, though perhaps as a class women are inferior and slaves utterly base. The second requisite is to make the character appropriate. Thus it is possible to portray any character as manly, but inappropriate for a female character to be manly or formidable in the way I mean. Third is to make the characters lifelike, which is something different from making them good and appropriate as described above. Fourth is to make them consistent. Even if the person being imitated is inconsistent and this is what the

---

Euripides: Fifth-century B.C. Greek playwright whose tragedies include *Electra, Medea,* and *Alcestis.* *Odyssey:* The epic by the ancient Greek poet Homer that chronicles the voyage home from the Trojan War of Odysseus (also known as Ulysses).

character is supposed to be, he should nevertheless be portrayed as consistently inconsistent. . . .

In the characters and in the plot-construction alike, one must strive for that which is either necessary or probable, so that whatever a character of any kind says or does may be the sort of thing such a character will inevitably or probably say or do and the events of the plot may follow one after another either inevitably or with probability. (Obviously, then, the *dénouement* of the plot should arise from the plot itself and not be brought about "from the machine." . . . The machine is to be used for matters lying outside the drama, either antecedents of the action which a human being cannot know, or things subsequent to the action that have to be prophesied and announced; for we accept it that the gods see everything. Within the events of the plot itself, however, there should be nothing unreasonable, or if there is, it should be kept outside the play proper as is done in the *Oedipus* of Sophocles.)

Inasmuch as tragedy is an imitation of persons who are better than the average, the example of good portrait-painters should be followed. These, while reproducing the distinctive appearance of their subjects in a recognizable likeness, make them handsomer in the picture than they are in reality. Similarly the poet when he comes to imitate men who are irascible or easygoing or have other defects of character should depict them as such and yet as good men at the same time.

From *Poetics*, translated by James Hutton

Considerations for Critical Thinking and Writing

1. Why does Aristotle insist that both virtuous and depraved characters are unsuitable as tragic figures? What kind of person constitutes a tragic character according to him?

2. Aristotle says that characters should be "lifelike" (para. 4), but he also points out that characters should be made "handsomer . . . than they are in reality" (para. 6). Is this a contradiction? Explain why or why not.

Sigmund Freud (1856–1939)

On the Oedipus Complex   1900

If *Oedipus Rex* moves a modern audience no less than it did the contemporary Greek one, the explanation can only be that its effect does not lie in the contrast between destiny and human will, but is to be looked for in the particular nature of the material on which that contrast is exemplified. There must be something which makes a voice within us ready to recognize the compelling force of destiny in the *Oedipus*. . . . His destiny moves us only because it might have been ours — because the oracle laid the same curse upon us before our birth as upon him. It is the fate of all of us, perhaps, to direct our first sexual impulse toward our mother and our first hatred and our first murderous wish against our father. Our dreams convince us that this is so. King Oedipus, who slew his father Laïus and married his mother

Jocasta, merely shows us the fulfillment of our own childhood wishes. But, more fortunate than he, we have meanwhile succeeded, in so far as we have not become psychoneurotics, in detaching our sexual impulses from our mothers and in forgetting our jealousy of our fathers. Here is one in whom these primeval wishes of our childhood have been fulfilled, and we shrink back from him with the whole force of the repression by which those wishes have since that time been held down within us. While the poet, as he unravels the past, brings to light the guilt of Oedipus, he is at the same time compelling us to recognize our own inner minds, in which those same impulses, though suppressed, are still to be found. The contrast with which the closing Chorus leaves us confronted —

> . . . Fix on Oedipus your eyes,
> Who resolved the dark enigma, noblest champion and most wise.
> Like a star his envied fortune mounted beaming far and wide:
> Now he sinks in seas of anguish, whelmed beneath a raging tide . . .[1]

— strikes as a warning at ourselves and our pride, at us who since our childhood have grown so wise and so mighty in our own eyes. Like Oedipus, we live in ignorance of these wishes, repugnant to morality, which have been forced upon us by Nature, and after their revelation we may all of us well seek to close our eyes to the scenes of our childhood.

There is an unmistakable indication in the text of Sophocles' tragedy itself that the legend of Oedipus sprang from some primeval dream material which had as its content the distressing disturbance of a child's relation to his parents owing to the first stirrings of sexuality. At a point when Oedipus, though he is not yet enlightened, has begun to feel troubled by his recollection of the oracle, Jocasta consoles him by referring to a dream which many people dream, though, as she thinks, it has no meaning:

> Many a man ere now in dreams hath lain
> With her who bare him. He hath least annoy
> Who with such omens troubleth not his mind.[2]

Today, just as then, many men dream of having sexual relations with their mothers, and speak of the fact with indignation and astonishment. It is clearly the key to the tragedy and the complement to the dream of the dreamer's father being dead. The story of Oedipus is the reaction of the imagination to these two typical dreams. And just as these dreams, when dreamt by adults, are accompanied by feelings of repulsion, so too the legend must include horror and self-punishment. Its further modification originates once again in a misconceived secondary revision of the material, which has sought to exploit it for theological purposes. . . . The attempt to harmonize divine omnipotence with human responsibility must naturally fail in connection with this subject matter just as with any other.

From *Interpretation of Dreams*, translated by James Strachey

---

[1] Lewis Campbell's translation, lines 1524ff. [in *The Bedford Introduction to Literature*, lines 1593–1596].

[2] Lewis Campbell's translation, lines 982ff. [in *The Bedford Introduction to Literature*, lines 1043–1046].

CONSIDERATIONS FOR CRITICAL THINKING AND WRITING

1. Read the section on psychological criticism in Chapter 51, "Critical Strategies for Reading" (pp. 1649–51), for additional information about Freud's theory concerning the Oedipus complex. Explain whether you agree or disagree that Freud's approach offers the "key to the tragedy" of *Oedipus the King*.

2. How does Freud's view of tragic character differ from Aristotle's?

MURIEL RUKEYSER (1913–1980)
On Oedipus the King   1973

Myth

Long afterward, Oedipus, old and blinded, walked the
roads.   He smelled a familiar smell.   It was
the Sphinx.   Oedipus said, "I want to ask one question.
Why didn't I recognize my mother?"   "You gave the
wrong answer," said the Sphinx.   "But that was what   5
made everything possible," said Oedipus.   "No," she said.
"When I asked, What walks on four legs in the morning,
two at noon, and three in the evening, you answered,
Man.   You didn't say anything about woman."
"When you say Man," said Oedipus, "you include women   10
too. Everyone knows that."   She said, "That's what
you think."

CONSIDERATIONS FOR CRITICAL THINKING AND WRITING

1. What elements of the Oedipus story does Rukeyser allude to in the poem?

2. To what does the title of Rukeyser's poem, "Myth," refer? How does the word *myth* carry more than one meaning?

3. This poem is amusing, but its ironic ending points to a serious theme. What is it? Does Sophocles' play address any of the issues raised in the poem?

DAVID WILES
On Oedipus the King *as a Political Play*   2000

Oedipus becomes a political play when we focus on the interaction of actor and chorus, and see how the chorus form a democratic mass jury. Each sequence of dialogue takes the form of a contest for the chorus' sympathy, with Oedipus sliding from the role of prosecutor to that of defendant, and each choral dance offers a provisional verdict. After Oedipus' set-to with Teiresias the soothsayer, the chorus decide to trust Oedipus on the basis of his past record; after his argument with his brother-in-law Creon, the chorus show their distress and urge compromise. Once Oedipus has confessed to a killing and Jocasta has declared that oracles have no force, the chorus are forced to think about political tyranny, torn between respect for divine law and trust in their rulers. In the next dance they assume that the contradiction is resolved and Oedipus has turned out to be the son of a god. Finally a slave's evidence reveals that the man most honoured by society is in fact the least to be envied. The political implications are clear: there is no space in democratic society for such as Oedipus. Athenians, like the chorus of the play, must reject the temptation to believe one man can calculate the future.

From *Greek Theatre Performance: An Introduction*

Considerations for Critical Thinking and Writing

1. Consider one of the scenes mentioned by Wiles and discuss in detail how "the chorus form a democratic mass jury" that judges Oedipus.
2. Discuss the "political implications" of the play that, according to Wiles, suggest "there is no space in democratic society for such as Oedipus."

45

A Study of
William Shakespeare

All the world's a stage,
And all the men and women
   merely players:
They have their exits and their
   entrances;
And one man in his time plays
   many parts . . .
— WILLIAM SHAKESPEARE

By permission of the Folger
Shakespeare Library.

Shakespeare — the nearest thing in
incarnation to the eye of God.
— SIR LAURENCE OLIVIER

© Corbis.

Although relatively little is known about William Shakespeare's life, his writings reveal him to have been an extraordinary man. His vitality, compassion, and insights are evident in his broad range of characters, who have fascinated generations of audiences, and his powerful use of the English language, which has been celebrated since his death nearly four centuries ago. Ben Jonson, his contemporary, rightly claimed that "he was not of an age, but for all time!" Shakespeare's plays have been produced so often and his writings read so widely that quotations from them have woven their way into our everyday conversations. If you have ever experienced "fear and trembling" because there was "something in the wind" or discovered that it was "a foregone conclusion" that you would "make a virtue of necessity," then it wouldn't be quite accurate for you to say that Shakespeare "was Greek to me" because these phrases come, respectively, from his plays *Much Ado about Nothing, Comedy of Errors, Othello, The Two Gentlemen of*

"First Folio" portrait (top). The image of William Shakespeare above is a portrait included on the *First Folio,* a collected edition of Shakespeare's plays published seven years after his death.

"Chandos" portrait engraving (middle). This engraving is of an image painted during Shakespeare's lifetime known as the "Chandos portrait," rumored to have been painted by Shakespeare's friend and fellow actor Richard Burbage.

Shakespeare's signature (bottom). The signature shown here is one of the bard's six authenticated signatures in existence and is from his last will and testament.

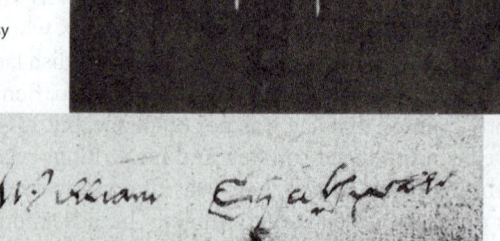

Verona, and *Julius Caesar.* Many more examples could be cited, but it is enough to say that Shakespeare's art endures. His words may give us only an oblique glimpse of his life, but they continue to give us back the experience of our own lives.

Shakespeare was born in Stratford-on-Avon on or about April 23, 1564. His father, an important citizen who held several town offices, married a woman from a prominent family; however, when their son was only a teenager, the family's financial situation became precarious. Shakespeare probably attended the Stratford grammar school, but no records of either his schooling or his early youth exist. As limited as his education was, it is clear that he was for his time a learned man. At the age of eighteen, he struck out on his own and married the twenty-six-year-old Anne Hathaway, who bore him a daughter in 1583 and twins, a boy and a girl, in 1585. Before he was twenty-one, Shakespeare had a wife and three children to support.

What his life was like for the next seven years is not known, but there is firm evidence that by 1592 he was in London enjoying some success as both an actor and a playwright. By 1594 he had also established himself as a poet with two lengthy poems, *Venus and Adonis* and *The Rape of Lucrece.* But it was in the theater that he made his living and his strongest reputation. He was well connected with a successful troupe first known as the Lord Chamberlain's Men; they built the famous Globe Theatre in 1599. Later this company, because of the patronage of King James, came to be known as the King's Men. Writing plays for this company throughout his career, Shakespeare also became one of its principal shareholders, an arrangement that allowed him to prosper in London as well as in his native Stratford, where in 1597 he bought a fine house called New Place. About 1611 he retired there with his family, although he continued writing plays. He died on April 23, 1616, and was buried at Holy Trinity Church in Stratford.

The documented details of Shakespeare's life provide barely enough information for a newspaper obituary. But if his activities remain largely unknown, his writings — among them thirty-seven plays and 154 sonnets — more than compensate for that loss. Plenty of authors have produced more work, but no writer has created so much literature that has been so universally admired. Within twenty-five years Shakespeare's dramatic works included *Hamlet, Macbeth, King Lear, Othello, Julius Caesar, Richard III, Henry IV, Romeo and Juliet, Love's Labour's Lost, A Midsummer Night's Dream, The Tempest, Twelfth Night,* and *Measure for Measure.* These plays represent a broad range of characters and actions conveyed in poetic language that reveals human nature as well as the author's genius.

SHAKESPEARE'S THEATER

Drama languished in Europe after the fall of Rome during the fifth and sixth centuries. From about A.D. 400 to 900 almost no record of dramatic productions exists except for those of minstrels and other entertainers, such as acrobats and jugglers, who traveled through the countryside. The Catholic church was instrumental in suppressing drama because the theater — represented by the excesses of Roman productions — was seen as subversive. No state-sponsored festivals brought people together in huge theaters the way they had in Greek and Roman times.

In the tenth century, however, the church helped revive theater by incorporating dialogues into the Mass as a means of dramatizing portions of the Gospels. These brief dialogues developed into more elaborate mystery plays, miracle plays, and morality plays, anonymous works that were created primarily to inculcate religious principles rather than to entertain. But these works also marked the reemergence of relatively large dramatic productions.

Mystery plays dramatize stories from the Bible, such as the Creation, the Fall of Adam and Eve, or the Crucifixion. The most highly regarded surviving example is *The Second Shepherd's Play* (ca. 1400), which dramatizes Christ's nativity. *Miracle plays* are based on the lives of saints. An extant play of the late fifteenth century, for example, is titled *Saint Mary Magdalene*. *Morality plays* present allegorical stories in which virtues and vices are personified to teach humanity how to achieve salvation. *Everyman* (ca. 1500), the most famous example, has as its central conflict every person's struggle to avoid the sins that lead to hell and practice the virtues that are rewarded in heaven.

The clergy who performed these plays gave way to trade guilds that presented them outside the church on stages featuring scenery and costumed characters. The plays' didactic content was gradually abandoned in favor of broad humor and worldly concerns. Thus by the sixteenth century religious drama had been replaced largely by secular drama.

Because theatrical productions were no longer sponsored and financed by the church or trade guilds during Shakespeare's lifetime, playwrights had to figure out ways to draw audiences willing to pay for entertainment. This necessitated some simple but important changes. Somehow, people had to be prevented from seeing a production unless they paid. Hence an enclosed space with controlled access was created. In addition, the plays had to change frequently enough to keep audiences returning, and this resulted in more experienced actors and playwrights sensitive to their audiences' tastes and interests. Plays compelling enough to attract audiences had to employ a powerful writing brought to life by convincing actors in entertaining productions. Shakespeare always wrote his dramas for the stage — for audiences who would see and hear the characters. The conventions of the theater for which he wrote are important, then, for appreciating and understanding his plays. Detailed information about Elizabethan theater (theater during the reign of Elizabeth I, from 1558 to 1603) is less than abundant, but historians have been able to piece together a good sense of what theaters were like from sources such as drawings, building contracts, and stage directions.

Early performances of various kinds took place in the courtyards of inns and taverns. These secular entertainments attracted people of all classes. To the dismay of London officials, such gatherings were also settings for the illegal activities of brawlers, thieves, and prostitutes. To avoid licensing regulations, some theaters were constructed outside the city's limits. The Globe, for instance, built by the Lord Chamberlain's Company, with which Shakespeare was closely associated, was located on the south bank of the Thames River. Regardless of the play, an Elizabethan theatergoer was likely to have an exciting time. Playwrights understood the varied nature of their audiences, so the plays appealed to a broad range of sensibilities and tastes. Philosophy and poetry rubbed shoulders with violence and sexual jokes, and somehow all were made compatible.

Physically, Elizabethan theaters resembled the courtyards where they originated, but the theaters could accommodate more people — perhaps as many as twenty-five hundred. The exterior of a theater building was many-sided or round and enclosed a yard that was only partially roofed over, to take advantage of natural light. The interior walls consisted of three galleries of seats looking onto a platform stage that extended from the rear wall. These seats were sheltered from the weather and more comfortable than the area in front of the stage, which was known as the *pit*. Here "groundlings" paid a penny to stand and watch the performance. Despite the large number of spectators, the theater created an intimate atmosphere because the audience closely surrounded the stage on three sides.

This arrangement produced two theatrical conventions: asides and soliloquies. An *aside* is a speech directed only to the audience. It makes the audience privy to a character's thoughts, allowing them to perceive ironies and intrigues that other characters know nothing about. In a large performing space, such as a Greek amphitheater, asides would be unconvincing because they would have to be declaimed loudly to be heard, but they were well suited to Elizabethan

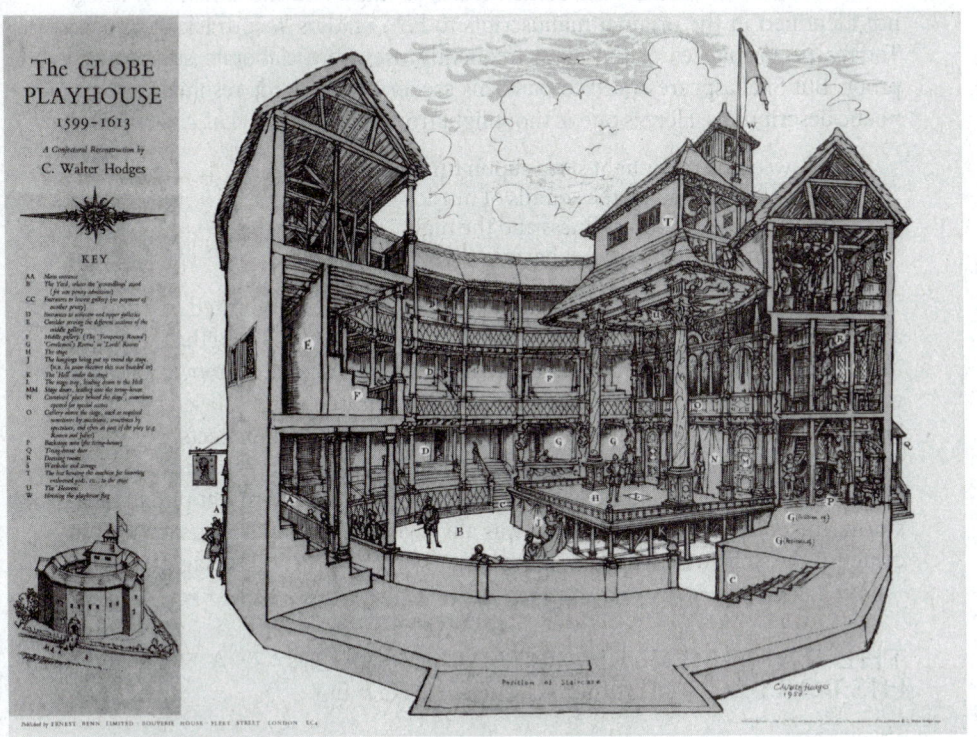

A Conjectural Reconstruction of the Globe Theatre, 1599–1613. Drawing by C. Walter Hodges from his *Globe Restored,* Oxford University Press. Folger Shakespeare Library. ART Box H688 no.12 pt.1.
By permission of the Folger Shakespeare Library.

theaters. A **soliloquy** is a speech delivered while an actor is alone on the stage; like an aside, it reveals a character's state of mind. Hamlet's "To be or not to be" speech is the most famous example of a soliloquy.

The Elizabethan platform stage was large enough — approximately twenty-five feet deep and forty feet wide — to allow a wide variety of actions, ranging from festive banquets to bloody battles. Sections of the floor could be opened or removed to create, for instance, the gravediggers' scene in *Hamlet* or to allow characters to exit through trapdoors. At the rear of the platform an inner stage was covered by curtains that could be drawn to reveal an interior setting, such as a bedroom or tomb. The curtains were also a natural location for a character to hide in order to overhear conversations. On each side of the curtains were doors through which characters entered and exited. An upper stage could be used as a watchtower, a castle wall, or a balcony. Although most of the action occurred on the main platform stage, there were opportunities for fluid movements from one acting area to another, providing a variety of settings.

These settings were not, however, elaborately indicated by scenery or props. A scene might change when one group of characters left the stage and another entered. A table and some chairs could be carried on quickly to suggest a tavern. But the action was not interrupted for set changes. Instead, the characters' speeches often identify the location of a scene. (In modern editions of Shakespeare's plays, editors indicate in brackets the scene breaks, settings, and movements of actors not identified in the original manuscripts to help readers keep track of things.) Today's performances of the plays frequently use more elaborate settings and props. But Shakespeare's need to paint his scenery with words resulted in many poetic descriptions. Here is one of moonlight from *Merchant of Venice*:

> How sweet the moonlight sleeps upon this bank!
> Here will we sit and let the sounds of music
> Creep in our ears. Soft stillness and the night
> Become the touches of sweet harmony.

Although the settings were scant and the props mostly limited to what an actor carried onto the stage (a sword, a document, a shovel), Elizabethan costuming was an elaborate visual treat that identified the characters. Moreover, because women were not permitted to act in the theater, their roles were played by young boys dressed in female costumes. In addition, elaborate sound effects were used to create atmosphere. A flourish of trumpets might accompany the entrance of a king; small cannons might be heard during a battle; thunder might punctuate a storm. In short, Elizabethan theater was alive with sights and sounds, but at the center of the stage was the playwright's language; that's where the magic began.

THE RANGE OF SHAKESPEARE'S DRAMA: HISTORY, COMEDY, AND TRAGEDY

Shakespeare's plays fall into three basic categories: histories, comedies, and tragedies. Broadly speaking, a history play is any drama based on historical materials. In this case, Shakespeare's *Antony and Cleopatra* and *Julius Caesar* would fit the definition, since they feature historical figures. More specifically, though, a *history play* is a British play based primarily on Raphael Holinshed's *Chronicles of England, Scotland, and Ireland* (1578). This account of British history was popular toward the end of the sixteenth century because of the patriotic pride that was produced by the British defeat of the Spanish Armada in 1588, and it was an important source for a series of plays Shakespeare wrote treating the reigns of British kings from Richard II to Henry VIII. The political subject matter of these plays both entertained audiences and instructed them in virtues and vices involved in England's past efforts to overcome civil war and disorder. Ambition, deception, and treason were of more than historical interest. Shakespeare's audiences saw these plays about the fifteenth century as ways of sorting through the meanings of both the calamities of the past and the uncertainties of the present.

Although Shakespeare used Holinshed's *Chronicles* as a source, he did not hesitate to make changes for dramatic purposes. In *1 Henry IV,* for example, he ages Henry IV to contrast him with the youthful Prince Hal, and he makes Hotspur younger than he actually was to have him serve as a foil to the prince. The serious theme of Hal's growth into the kind of man who would make an ideal king is counterweighted by Shakespeare's comic creation of Falstaff, that good-humored "huge hill of flesh" filled with delightful contradictions. Falstaff had historic antecedents, but the true source of his identity is the imagination of Shakespeare, a writer who was, after all, a dramatist first.

Comedy is a strong element in *1 Henry IV,* but the play's overall tone is serious. Falstaff's behavior ultimately gives way to the measured march of English history. While Shakespeare encourages us to laugh at some of the participants, we are not invited to laugh at the history of English monarchies. Comedy even appears in Shakespeare's tragedies, as in Hamlet's jests with the gravediggers or in Emilia's biting remarks in *Othello.* This use of comedy is called **comic relief**, a humorous scene or incident that alleviates tension in an otherwise serious work. In many instances these moments enhance the thematic significance of the story in addition to providing laughter. When Hamlet jokes with the gravediggers, we laugh, but something hauntingly serious about the humor also intensifies our more serious emotions.

A true comedy, however, lacks a tragedy's sense that some great disaster will finally descend on the protagonist. There are conflicts and obstacles that must be confronted, but in comedy the characters delight us by overcoming whatever initially thwarts them. We can laugh at their misfortunes because we are confident that everything will turn out fine in the end. Shakespearean comedy tends to follow this general principle; it begins with problems and ends with their resolution.

Shakespeare's comedies are called **romantic comedies** because they typically involve lovers whose hearts are set on each other but whose lives are complicated by disapproving parents, deceptions, jealousies, illusions, confused identities, disguises, or other misunderstandings. Conflicts are present, but they are more amusing than threatening. This lightness is apparent in some of the comedies' titles: the conflict in a play such as *A Midsummer Night's Dream* is, in a sense, *Much Ado about Nothing*—*As You Like It* in a comedy. Shakespeare orchestrates the problems and confusion that typify the initial plotting of a romantic comedy into harmonious wedding arrangements in the final scenes. In these comedies life is a celebration, a feast that always satisfies, because the generosity of the humor leaves us with a revived appetite for life's surprising possibilities. Discord and misunderstanding give way to concord and love. Marriage symbolizes a pledge that life itself is renewable, so we are left with a sense of new beginnings.

Although a celebration of life, comedy is also frequently used as a vehicle for criticizing human affairs. *Satire* casts a critical eye on vices and follies by holding them up to ridicule—usually to point out an absurdity so that it can be avoided or corrected. In *Twelfth Night* Malvolio is satirized for his priggishness and pomposity. He thinks himself better than almost everyone around him, but Shakespeare reveals him to be comic as well as pathetic. We come to understand what Malvolio will apparently never comprehend: that no one can take him as seriously as he takes himself. Polonius is subjected to a similar kind of scrutiny in *Hamlet*.

Malvolio's ambitious efforts to attract Olivia's affections are rendered absurd by Shakespeare's use of both high and low comedy. **High comedy** consists of verbal wit, while **low comedy** is generally associated with physical action and is less intellectual. Through puns and witty exchanges, Shakespeare's high comedy displays Malvolio's inconsistencies of character. His self-importance is deflated by low comedy. We are treated to a *farce*, a form of humor based on exaggerated, improbable incongruities, when the staid Malvolio is tricked into wearing bizarre clothing and behaving like a fool to win Olivia. Our laughter is Malvolio's pain, but though he has been "notoriously abus'd" and he vows in the final scene to be "reveng'd on the whole pack" of laughing conspirators who have tricked him, the play ends on a light note. Indeed, it concludes with a song, the last line of which reminds us of the predominant tone of the play as well as the nature of comedy: "And we'll strive to please you every day."

Tragedy, in contrast, does not promise peace and contentment. The basic characteristics of tragedy have already been outlined in the context of Greek drama (see Chapter 44). Like Greek tragic heroes, Shakespeare's protagonists are exceptional human beings whose stature makes their misfortune all the more dramatic. These characters pay a high price for their actions. Oedipus's search for the killer of Laios, Hamlet's agonized conviction that "The time is out of joint," and Othello's willingness to doubt his wife's fidelity all lead to irreversible results. Comic plots are largely free of this sense of inevitability. Instead of the festive mood that prevails once the characters in a comedy recognize their true connection to each other, tragedy gives us dark reflections that emanate from suffering. The laughter of comedy is a shared experience, a recognition of human likeness, but suffering estranges tragic heroes from the world around them.

Some of the wrenching differences between comedy and tragedy can be experienced in *Othello*. Although this play is a tragedy, Shakespeare includes in its plot many of the ingredients associated with comedy. For a time it seems possible that Othello and Desdemona will overcome the complications of a disapproving father, along with the seemingly minor deceptions, awkward misperceptions, and tender illusions that hover around them. But in *Othello* marriage is not a sign of concord displacing discord; instead, love and marriage mark the beginning of the tragic action.

Another important difference between tragedy and comedy is the way characters are presented. The tragic protagonist is portrayed as a remarkable individual whose unique qualities compel us with their power and complexity. Macbeth is not simply a murderer, nor is Othello merely a jealous husband. But despite their extreme passions, behavior, and even crimes, we identify with tragic heroes in ways that we do not with comic characters. We can laugh at pretentious fools, smug hypocrites, clumsy oafs, and thwarted lovers because we see them from a distance. They are amusing precisely because their problems are not ours; we recognize them as types instead of as ourselves (or so we think). No reader of *Twelfth Night* worries about Sir Toby Belch's excessive drinking; he is a cheerful "sot" whose passion for ale is cause for celebration rather than concern. Shakespeare's comedy is sometimes disturbing — Malvolio's character certainly is — but it is never devastating. Tragic heroes do confront devastation; they command our respect and compassion because they act in spite of terrifying risks. Their triumph is measured not by the attainment of what they seek but by the wisdom that defeat imposes on them.

A NOTE ON READING SHAKESPEARE

Readers who have had no previous experience with Shakespeare's language may find it initially daunting. They might well ask whether people ever talked the way, for example, Hamlet does in his most famous soliloquy:

> To be, or not to be: that is the question:
> Whether 'tis nobler in the mind to suffer
> The slings and arrows of outrageous fortune,
> Or to take arms against a sea of troubles,
> And by opposing end them?

People did not talk like this in Elizabethan times. Hamlet speaks poetry. Shakespeare might have had him say something like this: "The most important issue one must confront is whether the pain that life inevitably creates should be passively accepted or resisted." But Shakespeare chose poetry to reveal the depth and complexity of Hamlet's experience. This heightened language is used to clarify rather than obscure his characters' thoughts. Shakespeare has Hamlet, as well as many other characters, speak in prose too, but in general his plays are written in poetry. If you keep in mind that Shakespeare's dialogue is not typically intended to imitate everyday speech, it should be easier to understand that his language is more than simply a vehicle for expressing the action of the play.

Here are a few practical suggestions to enhance your understanding of and pleasure in reading Shakespeare's plays.

1. Keep track of the characters by referring to the *dramatis personae* (characters) listed and briefly described at the beginning of each play.

2. Remember that poetic language deserves to be read slowly and carefully. A difficult passage can sometimes be better understood if it's read aloud. Don't worry if every line isn't absolutely clear to you.

3. Pay attention to the annotations, which explain unfamiliar words, phrases, and allusions in the text. These can be distracting, but they are sometimes necessary to determine the basic meaning of a passage.

4. As you read each scene, try to imagine how it would be played on a stage.

5. If you find the reading especially difficult, try listening to a recording of the play. (Most college libraries have recordings of Shakespeare's plays.) Allowing professional actors to do the reading aloud for you can enrich your imaginative reconstruction of the action and characters. Hearing a play can help you with subsequent readings of it.

6. After reading the play, view a recording of a performance. It is important to view the performance *after* your reading, though, so that your own mental re-creation of the play is not short-circuited by a director's production.

And finally, to quote Hamlet, "Be not too tame . . . let your own discretion be your tutor." Read Shakespeare's work as best you can; it warrants such careful attention not because the language and characters are difficult to understand but because they offer so much to enjoy.

A Midsummer Night's Dream

A Midsummer Night's Dream, one of Shakespeare's most popular plays with readers and audiences, is a romantic comedy about the complex nature of love and marriage. Though some serious points about law and social order are made along the way, the action is propelled by the powers of youth, romance, love, passion, and the hilarious pursuits of characters turned about by fairies, illusions, and their own misunderstandings.

Shakespeare uses several sets of couples to dramatize love's tribulations and triumphs. The play opens with Theseus, Duke of Athens, making arrangements to wed Hippolyta, queen of the Amazons. Once enemies, they now seek love and peace in the harmony of marriage. Their union represents the happy necessity of order in the state and suggests a model of behavior that the other characters struggle to achieve.

In contrast to the serene plans for the royal wedding is the conflict produced by four Athenian youths who are thwarted in love: Helena loves Demetrius, but Demetrius loves Hermia, who wants to marry Lysander. This collision of passions is further complicated by Hermia's father, who insists in the Duke's presence that if she doesn't marry Demetrius, she must die or spend her life in a nunnery. Much of the play's conflict concerns how these two young couples align their love for one another so that each desires and is desired by the right person. When Hermia defies her father and refuses to marry Demetrius, she flees to the woods, followed by Lysander and Demetrius as well as Helena, who is in pursuit of Demetrius.

Once in the woods, the lovers find themselves in a supernatural world, the unpredictable kingdom of Oberon and Titania, the king and queen of the fairies. The fourth couple creates even more confusion through Oberon's impatience with Titania. Their quarrel results in Oberon's ordering his servant, Puck, to cast magical spells on the lovers as well as on Titania. This gives Puck the license to reveal their foolishness while eventually saving them from their own confused passions. Their reconciliations and reunions are not achieved, however, until Puck puts them through a series of comic encounters based on their illusions and vulnerabilities.

The final act includes the play within the play, "the most lamentable comedy" of two more lovers, Pyramus and Thisbe, who misunderstand one another. This travesty of a tragedy is put on by Athenian craftsmen — who are clearly better laborers than they are actors — at the Duke's request for a wedding entertainment. This play within the play reinforces the larger play's concerns about the nature of love and, indeed, of reality itself, because it raises questions about the fluid, complex relationship between art and reality. Ultimately, however, questions, issues, and conflicts give way to a generous sense of everything working out for the best as the play ends with Puck's warm assurances to the audience and his gentle urging to "Give me your hands."

WILLIAM SHAKESPEARE (1564–1616)

A Midsummer Night's Dream   ca. 1595

[DRAMATIS PERSONAE

Theseus, Duke of Athens
Hippolyta, Queen of the Amazons, betrothed to Theseus
Philostrate, Master of the Revels
Egeus, father of Hermia

Hermia, daughter of Egeus, in love with Lysander
Lysander, in love with Hermia
Demetrius, in love with Hermia and favored by Egeus
Helena, in love with Demetrius

Oberon, King of the Fairies
Titania, Queen of the Fairies
Puck, or *Robin Goodfellow*
Peaseblossom,
Cobweb,
Mote,   } fairies attending Titania
Mustardseed
Other Fairies attending

See Plays in Performance insert.
© Robbie Jack/Corbis.

Peter Quince, a carpenter, Prologue
Nick Bottom, a weaver, Pyramus
Francis Flute, a bellows mender, Thisbe
Tom Snout, a tinker, } representing Wall
Snug, a joiner, Lion
Robin Starveling, a tailor, Moonshine
Lords and Attendants on Theseus and Hippolyta

SCENE: Athens, and a wood near it.]

[ACT I

SCENE I: *Athens. Theseus' court.*]

    Enter Theseus, Hippolyta, [and Philostrate,] with others.

Theseus: Now, fair Hippolyta, our nuptial hour
    Draws on apace. Four happy days bring in
    Another moon; but, O, methinks, how slow
    This old moon wanes! She lingers° my desires,
    Like to a stepdame° or a dowager°   5
    Long withering out° a young man's revenue.
Hippolyta: Four days will quickly steep themselves° in night;
    Four nights will quickly dream away the time;
    And then the moon, like to a silver bow
    New bent in heaven, shall behold the night   10
    Of our solemnities.°
Theseus: Go Philostrate,
    Stir up the Athenian youth to merriments.
    Awake the pert and nimble spirit of mirth.
    Turn melancholy forth to funerals;
    The pale companion° is not for our pomp.°   *[Exit Philostrate.]* 15
    Hippolyta, I wooed thee with my sword°
    And won thy love doing thee injuries;
    But I will wed thee in another key,
    With pomp, with triumph,° and with reveling.

    Enter Egeus and his daughter Hermia, and Lysander, and Demetrius.

Egeus: Happy be Theseus, our renownèd duke!   20
Theseus: Thanks, good Egeus. What's the news with thee?
Egeus: Full of vexation come I, with complaint

Act I, Scene I.   4 *lingers:* Postpones, delays the fulfillment of.   5 *stepdame:* Stepmother; a *dowager:* I.e., a widow (whose right of inheritance from her dead husband is eating into her son's estate).   6 *withering out:* Causing to dwindle.   7 *steep themselves:* Saturate themselves, to be absorbed in.   11 *solemnities:* Festive ceremonies of marriage.   15 *companion:* Fellow; *pomp:* Ceremonial magnificence.   16 *with my sword:* In a military engagement against the Amazons, when Hippolyta was taken captive.   19 *triumph:* Public festivity.

Against my child, my daughter Hermia. —
Stand forth, Demetrius. — My noble lord,
This man hath my consent to marry her. —   25
Stand forth, Lysander. — And, my gracious Duke,
This man hath bewitched the bosom of my child.
Thou, thou Lysander, thou hast given her rhymes
And interchanged love tokens with my child.
Thou hast by moonlight at her window sung   30
With feigning° voice verses of feigning° love,
And stol'n the impression of her fantasy°
With bracelets of thy hair, rings, gauds,° conceits,°
Knacks,° trifles, nosegays, sweetmeats — messengers
Of strong prevailment in° unhardened youth.   35
With cunning hast thou filched my daughter's heart,
Turned her obedience, which is due to me,
To stubborn harshness. And, my gracious Duke,
Be it so° she will not here before Your Grace
Consent to marry with Demetrius,   40
I beg the ancient privilege of Athens:
As she is mine, I may dispose of her,
Which shall be either to this gentleman
Or to her death, according to our law
Immediately° provided in that case.   45
Theseus: What say you, Hermia? Be advised, fair maid.
To you your father should be as a god —
One that composed your beauties, yea, and one
To whom you are but as a form in wax
By him imprinted, and within his power   50
To leave° the figure or disfigure° it.
Demetrius is a worthy gentleman.
Hermia: So is Lysander.
Theseus: In himself he is;
But in this kind,° wanting° your father's voice,°
The other must be held the worthier.   55
Hermia: I would my father looked but with my eyes.
Theseus: Rather your eyes must with his judgment look.
Hermia: I do entreat Your Grace to pardon me.
I know not by what power I am made bold,
Nor how it may concern° my modesty   60
In such a presence here to plead my thoughts;
But I beseech Your Grace that I may know
The worst that may befall me in this case
If I refuse to wed Demetrius.

---

31 *feigning:* (1) Counterfeiting (2) faining, desirous.   32 *And . . . fantasy:* And made her
fall in love with you (imprinting your image on her imagination) by stealthy and dishonest means.
33 *gauds:* Playthings; *conceits:* Fanciful trifles.   34 *Knacks:* Knickknacks.   35 *prevail-*
ment in: Influence on.   39 *Be it so:* If.   45 *Immediately:* Directly, with nothing intervening.   51 *leave:* Leave unaltered; *disfigure:* Obliterate.   54 *kind:* Respect; *wanting:* Lacking;
voice: Approval.   60 *concern:* Befit.

Theseus: Either to die the death° or to abjure   65
    Forever the society of men.
    Therefore, fair Hermia, question your desires,
    Know of your youth, examine well your blood,°
    Whether, if you yield not to your father's choice,
    You can endure the livery° of a nun,   70
    For aye° to be in shady cloister mewed,°
    To live a barren sister all your life,
    Chanting faint hymns to the cold fruitless moon.
    Thrice blessèd they that master so their blood
    To undergo such maiden pilgrimage;   75
    But earthlier happy° is the rose distilled°
    Than that which, withering on the virgin thorn,
    Grows, lives, and dies in single blessedness.
Hermia: So will I grow, so live, so die, my lord,
    Ere I will yield my virgin patent° up   80
    Unto his lordship, whose unwishèd yoke
    My soul consents not to give sovereignty.
Theseus: Take time to pause, and by the next new moon —
    The sealing day betwixt my love and me
    For everlasting bond of fellowship —   85
    Upon that day either prepare to die
    For disobedience to your father's will,
    Or° else to wed Demetrius, as he would,
    Or on Diana's altar to protest°
    For aye austerity and single life.   90
Demetrius: Relent, sweet Hermia, and, Lysander, yield
    Thy crazèd° title to my certain right.
Lysander: You have her father's love, Demetrius;
    Let me have Hermia's. Do you marry him.
Egeus: Scornful Lysander! True, he hath my love,   95
    And what is mine my love shall render him.
    And she is mine, and all my right of her
    I do estate unto° Demetrius.
Lysander: I am, my lord, as well derived° as he,
    As well possessed;° my love is more than his;   100
    My fortunes every way as fairly° ranked,
    If not with vantage,° as Demetrius';
    And, which is more than all these boasts can be,
    I am beloved of beauteous Hermia.
    Why should not I then prosecute my right?   105
    Demetrius, I'll avouch it to his head,°

---

65 *die the death:* Be executed by legal process. 68 *blood:* Passions. 70 *livery:* Habit, costume. 71 *aye:* Ever; *mewed:* Shut in (said of a hawk, poultry, etc.). 76 *earthlier happy:* Happier as respects this world; *distilled:* Separated to make perfume. 80 *patent:* Privilege. 88 *Or:* Either. 89 *protest:* Vow. 92 *crazèd:* Cracked, unsound. 98 *estate unto:* Settle or bestow upon. 99 *as well derived:* As well born and descended. 100 *possessed:* Endowed with wealth. 101 *fairly:* Handsomely. 102 *vantage:* Superiority. 106 *head:* I.e., face.

Made love to Nedar's daughter, Helena,
And won her soul; and she, sweet lady, dotes,
Devoutly dotes, dotes in idolatry
Upon this spotted° and inconstant man. 110
Theseus: I must confess that I have heard so much,
And with Demetrius thought to have spoke thereof;
But, being overfull of self-affairs,°
My mind did lose it. But, Demetrius, come,
And come, Egeus, you shall go with me; 115
I have some private schooling° for you both.
For you, fair Hermia, look you arm° yourself
To fit your fancies° to your father's will,
Or else the law of Athens yields you up —
Which by no means we may extenuate° — 120
To death or to a vow of single life.
Come, my Hippolyta. What cheer, my love?
Demetrius and Egeus, go° along.
I must employ you in some business
Against° our nuptial, and confer with you 125
Of something nearly that° concerns yourselves.
Egeus: With duty and desire we follow you.

Exeunt [all but Lysander and Hermia].

Lysander: How now, my love, why is your cheek so pale?
How chance the roses there do fade so fast?
Hermia: Belike° for want of rain, which I could well 130
Beteem° them from the tempest of my eyes.
Lysander: Ay me! For aught that I could ever read,
Could ever hear by tale or history,
The course of true love never did run smooth;
But either it was different in blood° — 135
Hermia: O cross!° Too high to be enthralled to low.
Lysander: Or else misgrafted° in respect of years —
Hermia: O spite! Too old to be engaged to young.
Lysander: Or else it stood upon the choice of friends° —
Hermia: O hell, to choose love by another's eyes! 140
Lysander: Or if there were a sympathy° in choice,
War, death, or sickness did lay siege to it,
Making it momentany° as a sound,
Swift as a shadow, short as any dream,
Brief as the lightning in the collied° night 145
That in a spleen° unfolds° both heaven and earth,

---

110 *spotted:* I.e., morally stained. 113 *self-affairs:* My own concerns. 116 *schooling:* Admonition. 117 *look you arm:* Take care you prepare. 118 *fancies:* Likings, thoughts of love. 120 *extenuate:* Mitigate, relax. 123 *go:* I.e., come. 125 *Against:* In preparation for. 126 *nearly that:* That closely. 130 *Belike:* Very likely. 131 *Beteem:* Grant, afford. 135 *blood:* Hereditary station. 136 *cross:* Vexation. 137 *misgrafted:* Ill-grafted, badly matched. 139 *friends:* Relatives. 141 *sympathy:* Agreement. 143 *momentany:* Lasting but a moment. 145 *collied:* Blackened (as with coal dust), darkened. 146 *in a spleen:* In a swift impulse, in a violent flash; *unfolds:* Reveals.

And ere a man hath power to say "Behold!"
The jaws of darkness do devour it up.
So quick° bright things come to confusion.°
Hermia: If then true lovers have been ever crossed,°   150
It stands as an edict in destiny.
Then let us teach our trial patience,°
Because it is a customary cross,
As due to love as thoughts, and dreams, and sighs,
Wishes, and tears, poor fancy's° followers.   155
Lysander: A good persuasion.° Therefore, hear me, Hermia:
I have a widow aunt, a dowager
Of great revenue, and she hath no child.
From Athens is her house remote seven leagues;
And she respects° me as her only son.   160
There, gentle Hermia, may I marry thee,
And to that place the sharp Athenian law
Cannot pursue us. If thou lovest me, then,
Steal forth thy father's house tomorrow night;
And in the wood, a league without° the town,   165
Where I did meet thee once with Helena
To do observance to a morn of May,°
There will I stay for thee.
Hermia: My good Lysander!
I swear to thee, by Cupid's strongest bow,
By his best arrow° with the golden head,   170
By the simplicity° of Venus' doves,°
By that which knitteth souls and prospers loves,
And by that fire which burned the Carthage queen°
When the false Trojan° under sail was seen,
By all the vows that ever men have broke,   175
In number more than ever women spoke,
In that same place thou hast appointed me
Tomorrow truly will I meet with thee.
Lysander: Keep promise, love. Look, here comes Helena.

Enter Helena.

Hermia: God speed, fair° Helena! Whither away?   180
Helena: Call you me fair? That "fair" again unsay.
Demetrius loves your fair.° O happy fair!°

---

149 *quick:* Quickly; also, living, alive; *confusion:* Ruin.   150 *ever crossed:* Always thwarted.
152 *teach . . . patience:* I.e., teach ourselves patience in this trial.   155 *fancy's:* Amorous
passion's.   156 *persuasion:* Doctrine.   160 *respects:* Regards.   165 *without:* Outside.
167 *do . . . May:* Perform the ceremonies of May Day.   170 *best arrow:* Cupid's best gold-
pointed arrows were supposed to induce love; his blunt leaden arrows, aversion.   171 *simplicity:*
Innocence; *Venus' doves:* Doves that drew Venus's chariot.   173, 174 *Carthage queen, false Trojan:* (Dido, Queen of Carthage, immolated herself on a funeral pyre after having been deserted by
the Trojan hero Aeneas.)   180 *fair:* Fair-complexioned (generally regarded by the Elizabethans
as more beautiful than a dark complexion).   182 *your fair:* Your beauty (even though Hermia
is dark-complexioned); *happy fair:* Lucky fair one.

Your eyes are lodestars,° and your tongue's sweet air°
More tunable° than lark to shepherd's ear
When wheat is green, when hawthorn buds appear.   185
Sickness is catching. O, were favor° so,
Yours would I catch, fair Hermia, ere I go;
My ear should catch your voice, my eye your eye,
My tongue should catch your tongue's sweet melody.
Were the world mine, Demetrius being bated,°   190
The rest I'd give to be to you translated.°
O, teach me how you look and with what art
You sway the motion° of Demetrius' heart.

Hermia: I frown upon him, yet he loves me still.

Helena: O, that your frowns would teach my smiles such skill!   195

Hermia: I give him curses, yet he gives me love.

Helena: O, that my prayers could such affection° move!°

Hermia: The more I hate, the more he follows me.

Helena: The more I love, the more he hateth me.

Hermia: His folly, Helena, is no fault of mine.   200

Helena: None, but your beauty. Would that fault were mine!

Hermia: Take comfort. He no more shall see my face.
Lysander and myself will fly this place.
Before the time I did Lysander see
Seemed Athens as a paradise to me.°   205
O, then, what graces in my love do dwell,
That he hath turned a heaven unto a hell?

Lysander: Helen, to you our minds we will unfold.
Tomorrow night, when Phoebe° doth behold
Her silver visage in the watery glass,°   210
Decking with liquid pearl the bladed grass,
A time that lovers' flights doth still° conceal,
Through Athens' gates have we devised to steal.

Hermia: And in the wood, where often you and I
Upon faint° primrose beds were wont to lie,   215
Emptying our bosoms of their counsel° sweet,
There my Lysander and myself shall meet,
And thence from Athens turn away our eyes
To seek new friends and stranger companies.°
Farewell, sweet playfellow. Pray thou for us,   220
And good luck grant thee thy Demetrius!
Keep word, Lysander. We must starve our sight
From lovers' food till morrow deep midnight.

---

183 *lodestars:* Guiding stars; *air:* Music.   184 *tunable:* Tuneful, melodious.   186 *favor:*
Appearance, looks.   190 *bated:* Excepted.   191 *translated:* Transformed.   193 *sway the
motion:* Control the impulse.   197 *affection:* Passion; *move:* Arouse.   204–205 *Before . . .
to me:* (Hermia seemingly means that love has led to complications and jealousies, making
Athens hell for her.)   209 *Phoebe:* Diana, the moon.   210 *glass:* Mirror.   212 *still:* Always.
215 *faint:* Pale.   216 *counsel:* Secret thought.   219 *stranger companies:* The company of
strangers.

Lysander: I will, my Hermia. (*Exit Hermia.*) Helena, adieu.
 As you on him, Demetrius dote on you!   *Exit Lysander.* 225
Helena: How happy some o'er other some can be!°
 Through Athens I am thought as fair as she.
 But what of that? Demetrius thinks not so;
 He will not know what all but he do know.
 And as he errs, doting on Hermia's eyes,   230
 So I, admiring of° his qualities.
 Things base and vile, holding no quantity,°
 Love can transpose to form and dignity.
 Love looks not with the eyes, but with the mind,
 And therefore is winged Cupid painted blind.   235
 Nor hath Love's mind of any judgment taste;°
 Wings and no eyes figure° unheedy haste.
 And therefore is Love said to be a child,
 Because in choice° he is so oft beguiled.°
 As waggish° boys in game° themselves forswear,   240
 So the boy Love is perjured everywhere.
 For ere Demetrius looked on Hermia's eyne,°
 He hailed down oaths that he was only mine;
 And when this hail some heat from Hermia felt,
 So he dissolved, and showers of oaths did melt.   245
 I will go tell him of fair Hermia's flight.
 Then to the wood will he tomorrow night
 Pursue her; and for this intelligence°
 If I have thanks, it is a dear expense.°
 But herein mean I to enrich my pain,   250
 To have his sight thither and back again.   *Exit.*

[SCENE II: *Athens.*]

*Enter Quince the carpenter, and Snug the joiner, and Bottom the weaver, and
Flute the bellows mender, and Snout the tinker, and Starveling the tailor.*

Quince: Is all our company here?
Bottom: You were best to call them generally,° man by man, according to the
 scrip.°
Quince: Here is the scroll of every man's name which is thought fit,
 through all Athens, to play in our interlude° before the Duke and the 5
 Duchess on his wedding day at night.

---

226 *o'er . . . can be:* Can be in comparison to some others. 231 *admiring of:* Wondering
at. 232 *holding no quantity:* I.e., unsubstantial, unshapely. 236 *Nor . . . taste:* I.e., nor
has Love, which dwells in the fancy or imagination, any taste or least bit of judgment or reason.
237 *figure:* Are a symbol of. 239 *in choice:* In choosing; *beguiled:* Self-deluded, making
unaccountable choices. 240 *waggish:* Playful, mischievous; *game:* Sport, jest. 242 *eyne:*
Eyes (old form of plural). 248 *intelligence:* Information. 249 *a dear expense:* I.e., a
trouble worth taking on my part, or a begrudging effort on his part; *dear:* Costly.
Scene II. 2 *generally:* (Bottom's blunder for "individually.") 3 *scrip:* Scrap (Bottom's
error for "script"). 5 *interlude:* Play.

Bottom: First, good Peter Quince, say what the play treats on, then read the
names of the actors, and so grow to° a point.

Quince: Marry,° our play is "The most lamentable comedy and most cruel
death of Pyramus and Thisbe."   10

Bottom: A very good piece of work, I assure you, and a merry. Now, good
Peter Quince, call forth your actors by the scroll. Masters, spread yourselves.

Quince: Answer as I call you. Nick Bottom,° the weaver.

Bottom: Ready. Name what part I am for, and proceed.   15

Quince: You, Nick Bottom, are set down for Pyramus.

Bottom: What is Pyramus? A lover or a tyrant?

Quince: A lover, that kills himself most gallant for love.

Bottom: That will ask some tears in the true performing of it. If I do it, let the
audience look to their eyes. I will move storms; I will condole° in some   20
measure. To the rest—yet my chief humor° is for a tyrant. I could play
Ercles° rarely, or a part to tear a cat° in, to make all split.°
   "The raging rocks
   And shivering shocks
   Shall break the locks   25
      Of prison gates;
   And Phibbus' car°
   Shall shine from far
   And make and mar
      The foolish Fates."   30
This was lofty! Now name the rest of the players. This is Ercles' vein, a
tyrant's vein. A lover is more condoling.

Quince: Francis Flute, the bellows mender.

Flute: Here, Peter Quince.

Quince: Flute, you must take Thisbe on you.   35

Flute: What is Thisbe? A wandering knight?

Quince: It is the lady that Pyramus must love.

Flute: Nay, faith, let not me play a woman. I have a beard coming.

Quince: That's all one.° You shall play it in a mask, and you may speak as
small° as you will.   40

Bottom: An° I may hide my face, let me play Thisbe too. I'll speak in a monstrous little voice: "Thisne, Thisne!" "Ah, Pyramus, my lover dear! Thy
Thisbe dear, and lady dear!"

Quince: No, no, you must play Pyramus, and Flute, you Thisbe.

Bottom: Well, proceed.   45

Quince: Robin Starveling, the tailor.

Starveling: Here, Peter Quince.

Quince: Robin Starveling, you must play Thisbe's mother. Tom Snout, the
tinker.

---

8 *grow to:* Come to.   9 *Marry:* (A mild oath; originally the name of the Virgin Mary.)
14 *Bottom:* Object around which weavers wound thread.   20 *condole:* Lament, arouse pity.
21 *humor:* Inclination, whim.   22 *Ercles:* Hercules (the tradition of ranting came from Seneca's *Hercules Furens*); *tear a cat:* I.e., rant; *make all split:* I.e., cause a stir, bring the house
down.   27 *Phibbus' car:* Phoebus's, the sun god's, chariot.   39 *That's all one:* It makes no
difference.   40 *small:* High-pitched.   41 *An:* If (also at line 59).

Snout: Here, Peter Quince. 50

Quince: You, Pyramus' father; myself, Thisbe's father; Snug, the joiner, you, the lion's part; and I hope here is a play fitted.

Snug: Have you the lion's part written? Pray you, if it be, give it me, for I am slow of study.

Quince: You may do it extempore, for it is nothing but roaring. 55

Bottom: Let me play the lion too. I will roar that I will do any man's heart good to hear me. I will roar that I will make the Duke say, "Let him roar again, let him roar again."

Quince: An you should do it too terribly, you would fright the Duchess and the ladies, that they would shriek; and that were enough to hang 60 us all.

All: That would hang us, every mother's son.

Bottom: I grant you, friends, if you should fright the ladies out of their wits, they would have no more discretion but to hang us; but I will aggravate° my voice so that I will roar you° as gently as any sucking dove;° I will roar 65 you an 'twere° any nightingale.

Quince: You can play no part but Pyramus; for Pyramus is a sweet-faced man, a proper° man as one shall see in a summer's day, a most lovely gentle-manlike man. Therefore you must needs play Pyramus.

Bottom: Well, I will undertake it. What beard were I best to play it in? 70

Quince: Why, what you will.

Bottom: I will discharge° it in either your° straw-color beard, your orange-tawny beard, your purple-in-grain° beard, or your French-crown-color° beard, your perfect yellow.

Quince: Some of your French crowns° have no hair at all, and then you 75 will play barefaced. But, masters, here are your parts. *[He distributes parts.]* And I am to entreat you, request you, and desire you to con° them by tomorrow night, and meet me in the palace wood, a mile with-out the town, by moonlight. There will we rehearse; for if we meet in the city, we shall be dogged with company, and our devices° known. In the 80 meantime I will draw a bill° of properties, such as our play wants. I pray you, fail me not.

Bottom: We will meet, and there we may rehearse most obscenely° and cou-rageously. Take pains, be perfect.° Adieu.

Quince: At the Duke's oak we meet. 85

Bottom: Enough. Hold, or cut bowstrings.° *Exeunt.*

---

65 *aggravate:* (Bottom's blunder for "moderate."); *roar you:* I.e., roar for you. 66 *suck-ing dove:* (Bottom conflates *sitting dove* and *sucking lamb*, two proverbial images of inno-cence.); *an 'twere:* As if it were. 68 *proper:* Handsome. 72 *discharge:* Perform; *your:* I.e., you know the kind I mean. 73 *purple-in-grain:* Dyed a very deep red (from *grain*, the name applied to the dried insect used to make the dye). 74 *French-crown-color:* I.e., color of a French crown, a gold coin. 75 *crowns:* Heads bald from syphilis, the "French dis-ease." 77 *con:* Learn by heart. 80 *devices:* Plans. 81 *draw a bill:* Draw up a list. 83 *obscenely:* (An unintentionally funny blunder, whatever Bottom meant to say.) 84 *per-fect:* I.e., letter-perfect in memorizing your parts. 86 *Hold . . . bowstrings:* (An archer's ex-pression, not definitely explained, but probably meaning here "keep your promises, or give up the play.")

[ACT II

SCENE I: *A wood near Athens.*]

Enter a Fairy at one door, and Robin Goodfellow [Puck] at another.

Puck: How now, spirit, whither wander you?
Fairy: Over hill, over dale,
　　　Thorough° bush, thorough brier,
　　　Over park, over pale,°
　　　Thorough flood, thorough fire,   5
　　　I do wander everywhere,
　　　Swifter than the moon's sphere;°
　　　And I serve the Fairy Queen,
　　　To dew° her orbs° upon the green.
　　　The cowslips tall her pensioners° be.   10
　　　In their gold coats spots you see;
　　　Those be rubies, fairy favors;°
　　　In those freckles live their savors.°
　　　I must go seek some dewdrops here
　　　And hang a pearl in every cowslip's ear.   15
　　　Farewell, thou lob° of spirits; I'll be gone.
　　　Our Queen and all her elves come here anon.°
Puck: The King doth keep his revels here tonight.
　　　Take heed the Queen come not within his sight.
　　　For Oberon is passing fell° and wrath,°   20
　　　Because that she as her attendant hath
　　　A lovely boy, stolen from an Indian king;
　　　She ne'er had so sweet a changeling.°
　　　And jealous Oberon would have the child
　　　Knight of his train, to trace° the forests wild.   25
　　　But she perforce° withholds the lovèd boy,
　　　Crowns him with flowers, and makes him all her joy.
　　　And now they never meet in grove or green,
　　　By fountain° clear, or spangled starlight sheen,°
　　　But they do square,° that all their elves for fear   30
　　　Creep into acorn cups and hide them there.
Fairy: Either I mistake your shape and making quite,
　　　Or else you are that shrewd° and knavish sprite°
　　　Called Robin Goodfellow. Are not you he
　　　That frights the maidens of the villagery,°   35

Act II, Scene I.   3 *Thorough:* Through.   4 *pale:* Enclosure.   7 *sphere:* Orbit.   9 *dew:* Sprinkle with dew; *orbs:* Circles, i.e., fairy rings (circular bands of grass, darker than the surrounding area, caused by fungi enriching the soil).   10 *pensioners:* Retainers, members of the royal bodyguard.   12 *favors:* Love tokens.   13 *savors:* Sweet smells.   16 *lob:* Country bumpkin.   17 *anon:* At once.   20 *passing fell:* Exceedingly angry; *wrath:* Wrathful.   23 *changeling:* Child exchanged for another by the fairies.   25 *trace:* Range through.   26 *perforce:* Forcibly.   29 *fountain:* Spring; *starlight sheen:* Shining starlight.   30 *square:* Quarrel.   33 *shrewd:* Mischievous; *sprite:* Spirit.   35 *villagery:* Village population.

Skim milk,° and sometimes labor in the quern,°
And bootless° make the breathless huswife° churn,
And sometimes make the drink to bear no barm,°
Mislead night wanderers,° laughing at their harm?
Those that "Hobgoblin" call you, and "Sweet Puck,"°   40
You do their work, and they shall have good luck.
Are you not he?

Puck: Thou speakest aright;
I am that merry wanderer of the night.
I jest to Oberon and make him smile
When I a fat and bean-fed° horse beguile,   45
Neighing in likeness of a filly foal;
And sometimes lurk I in a gossip's° bowl
In very likeness of a roasted crab,°
And when she drinks, against her lips I bob
And on her withered dewlap° pour the ale.   50
The wisest aunt,° telling the saddest° tale,
Sometimes for three-foot stool mistaketh me;
Then slip I from her bum, down topples she,
And "Tailor"° cries, and falls into a cough;
And then the whole choir° hold their hips and laugh,   55
And waxen° in their mirth, and neeze,° and swear
A merrier hour was never wasted° there.
But, room,° fairy! Here comes Oberon.

Fairy: And here my mistress. Would that he were gone!

Enter [Oberon] the King of Fairies at one door, with his train, and [Titania] the
Queen at another, with hers.

Oberon: Ill met by moonlight, proud Titania.   60
Titania: What, jealous Oberon? Fairies, skip hence.
I have forsworn his bed and company.
Oberon: Tarry, rash wanton.° Am not I thy lord?
Titania: Then I must be thy lady; but I know
When thou hast stolen away from Fairyland   65
And in the shape of Corin° sat all day,
Playing on the pipes of corn° and versing love
To amorous Phillida.° Why art thou here

---

36 *Skim milk:* I.e., steal the cream; *quern:* Hand mill (where Puck presumably hampers the grinding of grain).   37 *bootless:* In vain (Puck prevents the cream from turning to butter); *huswife:* Housewife.   38 *barm:* Head on the ale (Puck prevents the barm or yeast from producing fermentation).   39 *Mislead night wanderers:* I.e., mislead with false fire those who walk abroad at night (hence earning Puck his other names of Jack o' Lantern and Will o' the Wisp).   40 *Those . . . Puck:* I.e., those who call you by the names you favor rather than those denoting the mischief you do.   45 *bean-fed:* Well fed on field beans.   47 *gossip's:* Old woman's.   48 *crab:* Crab apple.   50 *dewlap:* Loose skin on neck.   51 *aunt:* Old woman; *saddest:* Most serious.   54 *Tailor:* (Possibly because she ends up sitting cross-legged on the floor, looking like a tailor, or else referring to the *tail* or buttocks.)   55 *choir:* Company.   56 *waxen:* Increase; *neeze:* Sneeze.   57 *wasted:* Spent.   58 *room:* Stand aside, make room.   63 *wanton:* Headstrong creature.   66, 68 *Corin, Phillida:* (Conventional names of pastoral lovers.)   67 *corn:* (Here, oat stalks.)

Come from the farthest step° of India,
But that, forsooth, the bouncing Amazon,   70
Your buskined° mistress and your warrior love,
To Theseus must be wedded, and you come
To give their bed joy and prosperity.
Oberon: How canst thou thus for shame, Titania,
Glance at my credit with Hippolyta,°   75
Knowing I know thy love to Theseus?
Didst not thou lead him through the glimmering night
From Perigenia,° whom he ravishèd?
And make him with fair Aegles° break his faith,
With Ariadne° and Antiopa?°   80
Titania: These are the forgeries of jealousy;
And never, since the middle summer's spring,°
Met we on hill, in dale, forest, or mead,°
By pavèd° fountain or by rushy° brook,
Or in° the beachèd margent° of the sea,   85
To dance our ringlets to° the whistling wind,
But with thy brawls thou hast disturbed our sport.
Therefore the winds, piping to us in vain,
As in revenge, have sucked up from the sea
Contagious° fogs which, falling in the land,   90
Hath every pelting° river made so proud
That they have overborne their continents.°
The ox hath therefore stretched his yoke° in vain,
The plowman lost his sweat, and the green corn°
Hath rotted ere his youth attained a beard;   95
The fold° stands empty in the drownèd field,
And crows are fatted with the murrain° flock;
The nine-men's morris° is filled up with mud,
And the quaint mazes° in the wanton° green
For lack of tread are indistinguishable.   100

---

69 *step:* Farthest limit of travel, or, perhaps, *steep* "mountain range."   71 *buskined:* Wearing half-boots called buskins.   75 *Glance . . . Hippolyta:* Make insinuations about my favored relationship with Hippolyta.   78 *Perigenia:* I.e., Perigouna, one of Theseus's conquests. (She and the following women are named in Thomas North's translation of Plutarch's "Life of Theseus.")   79 *Aegles:* I.e., Aegle, for whom Theseus deserted Ariadne according to some accounts.   80 *Ariadne:* The daughter of Minos, King of Crete, who helped Theseus to escape the labyrinth after killing the Minotaur; later she was abandoned by Theseus; *Antiopa:* Queen of the Amazons and wife of Theseus, elsewhere identified with Hippolyta, but here thought of as a separate woman.   82 *middle summer's spring:* Beginning of midsummer.   83 *mead:* Meadow.   84 *pavèd:* With pebbled bottom; *rushy:* Bordered with rushes.   85 *in:* On; *margent:* Edge, border.   86 *ringlets to:* Dances in a ring (see *orbs* in II.i.9) to the sound of.   90 *Contagious:* Noxious.   91 *pelting:* Paltry.   92 *continents:* Banks that contain them.   93 *stretched his yoke:* I.e., pulled at his yoke in plowing.   94 *corn:* Grain of any kind.   96 *fold:* Pen for sheep or cattle.   97 *murrain:* Having died of the plague.   98 *nine-men's morris:* I.e., portion of the village green marked out in a square for a game played with nine pebbles or pegs.   99 *quaint mazes:* I.e., intricate paths marked out on the village green to be followed rapidly on foot as a kind of contest; *wanton:* Luxuriant.

The human mortals want° their winter° here;
No night is now with hymn or carol blessed.
Therefore° the moon, the governess of floods,
Pale in her anger, washes° all the air,
That rheumatic diseases° do abound.   105
And thorough this distemperature° we see
The seasons alter: hoary-headed frosts
Fall in the fresh lap of the crimson rose,
And on old Hiems'° thin and icy crown
An odorous chaplet of sweet summer buds   110
Is, as in mockery, set. The spring, the summer,
The childing° autumn, angry winter, change
Their wonted liveries,° and the mazèd° world
By their increase° now knows not which is which.
And this same progeny of evils comes   115
From our debate,° from our dissension.
We are their parents and original.°
Oberon: Do you amend it, then. It lies in you.
    Why should Titania cross her Oberon?
    I do but beg a little changeling boy   120
    To be my henchman.°
Titania: Set your heart at rest.
    The fairy land buys not the child of me.
    His mother was a vot'ress of my order,°
    And in the spicèd Indian air by night
    Full often hath she gossiped by my side   125
    And sat with me on Neptune's yellow sands,
    Marking th' embarkèd traders° on the flood,°
    When we have laughed to see the sails conceive
    And grow big-bellied with the wanton° wind;
    Which she, with pretty and with swimming° gait,   130
    Following — her womb then rich with my young squire —
    Would imitate, and sail upon the land
    To fetch me trifles, and return again
    As from a voyage, rich with merchandise.
    But she, being mortal, of that boy did die;   135
    And for her sake do I rear up her boy,
    And for her sake I will not part with him.
Oberon: How long within this wood intend you stay?

---

101 *want:* Lack; *winter:* I.e., regular winter season; or, proper observances of winter, such as the *hymn* or *carol* in the next line (?).   103 *Therefore:* I.e., as a result of our quarrel. 104 *washes:* Saturates with moisture.   105 *rheumatic diseases:* Colds, flu, and other respiratory infections.   106 *distemperature:* Disturbance in nature.   109 *Hiems':* The winter god's.   112 *childing:* Fruitful, pregnant.   113 *wonted liveries:* Usual apparel; *mazèd:* Bewildered.   114 *their increase:* Their yield, what they produce.   116 *debate:* Quarrel. 117 *original:* Origin.   121 *henchman:* Attendant, page.   123 *was . . . order:* Had taken a vow to serve me.   127 *traders:* Trading vessels; *flood:* Flood tide.   129 *wanton:* (1) Playful (2) amorous.   130 *swimming:* Smooth, gliding.

Titania: Perchance till after Theseus' wedding day.
　　　　If you will patiently dance in our round° 　　　　　　　　　　140
　　　　And see our moonlight revels, go with us;
　　　　If not, shun me, and I will spare° your haunts.
Oberon: Give me that boy, and I will go with thee.
Titania: Not for thy fairy kingdom. Fairies, away!
　　　　We shall chide downright, if I longer stay. 　　　　　　　　　145

　　　　　　　　　　　　　　Exeunt [Titania with her train].

Oberon: Well, go thy way. Thou shalt not from° this grove
　　　　Till I torment thee for this injury.
　　　　My gentle Puck, come hither. Thou rememb'rest
　　　　Since° once I sat upon a promontory,
　　　　And heard a mermaid on a dolphin's back 　　　　　　　　　150
　　　　Uttering such dulcet° and harmonious breath°
　　　　That the rude° sea grew civil at her song,
　　　　And certain stars shot madly from their spheres
　　　　To hear the sea-maid's music?
Puck: 　　　　　　　　　　I remember.
Oberon: That very time I saw, but thou couldst not, 　　　　　　155
　　　　Flying between the cold moon and the earth
　　　　Cupid, all° armed. A certain° aim he took
　　　　At a fair vestal° thronèd by° the west,
　　　　And loosed° his love shaft smartly from his bow
　　　　As° it should pierce a hundred thousand hearts; 　　　　　160
　　　　But I might° see young Cupid's fiery shaft
　　　　Quenched in the chaste beams of the watery moon,
　　　　And the imperial vot'ress passèd on,
　　　　In maiden meditation, fancy-free.°
　　　　Yet marked I where the bolt° of Cupid fell: 　　　　　　　165
　　　　It fell upon a little western flower,
　　　　Before milk-white, now purple with love's wound,
　　　　And maidens call it love-in-idleness.°
　　　　Fetch me that flower; the herb I showed thee once.
　　　　The juice of it on sleeping eyelids laid 　　　　　　　　　170
　　　　Will make or man or° woman madly dote
　　　　Upon the next live creature that it sees.
　　　　Fetch me this herb, and be thou here again
　　　　Ere the leviathan° can swim a league.
Puck: I'll put a girdle round about the earth 　　　　　　　　175
　　　　In forty° minutes. 　　　　　　　　　　　　　　*[Exit.]*
Oberon: 　　　　　　　Having once this juice,

---

140 *round:* Circular dance.　142 *spare:* Shun.　146 *from:* Go from.　149 *Since:* When.
151 *dulcet:* Sweet; *breath:* Voice, song.　152 *rude:* Rough.　157 *all:* Fully; *certain:* Sure.
158 *vestal:* Vestal virgin (contains a complimentary allusion to Queen Elizabeth as a votaress of
Diana and probably refers to an actual entertainment in her honor at Elvetham in 1591); *by:*
In the region of.　159 *loosed:* Released.　160 *As:* As if.　161 *might:* Could.　164
fancy-free: Free of love's spell.　165 *bolt:* Arrow.　168 *love-in-idleness:* Pansy, hearts-
ease.　171 *or . . . or:* Either . . . or.　174 *leviathan:* Sea monster, whale.　176 *forty:* (Used
indefinitely.)

I'll watch Titania when she is asleep
And drop the liquor of it in her eyes.
The next thing then she waking looks upon,
Be it on lion, bear, or wolf, or bull,   180
On meddling monkey, or on busy ape,
She shall pursue it with the soul of love.
And ere I take this charm from off her sight,
As I can take it with another herb,
I'll make her render up her page to me.   185
But who comes here? I am invisible,
And I will overhear their conference.

Enter Demetrius, Helena following him.

Demetrius: I love thee not; therefore pursue me not.
    Where is Lysander and fair Hermia?
    The one I'll slay; the other slayeth me.   190
    Thou toldst me they were stol'n unto this wood;
    And here am I, and wood° within this wood
    Because I cannot meet my Hermia.
    Hence, get thee gone, and follow me no more.
Helena: You draw me, you hardhearted adamant!°   195
    But yet you draw not iron, for my heart
    Is true as steel. Leave you° your power to draw,
    And I shall have no power to follow you.
Demetrius: Do I entice you? Do I speak you fair?°
    Or rather do I not in plainest truth   200
    Tell you I do not nor I cannot love you?
Helena: And even for that do I love you the more.
    I am your spaniel; and, Demetrius,
    The more you beat me I will fawn on you.
    Use me but as your spaniel, spurn me, strike me,   205
    Neglect me, lose me; only give me leave,
    Unworthy as I am, to follow you.
    What worser place can I beg in your love —
    And yet a place of high respect with me —
    Than to be usèd as you use your dog?   210
Demetrius: Tempt not too much the hatred of my spirit,
    For I am sick when I do look on thee.
Helena: And I am sick when I look not on you.
Demetrius: You do impeach° your modesty too much
    To leave° the city and commit yourself   215
    Into the hands of one that loves you not,
    To trust the opportunity of night

---

192 *and wood:* And mad, frantic (with an obvious wordplay on *wood*, meaning "woods").
195 *adamant:* Lodestone, magnet (with pun on *hardhearted,* since adamant was also thought
to be the hardest of all stones and was confused with the diamond).   197 *Leave you:* Give up.
199 *speak you fair:* Speak courteously to you.   214 *impeach:* Call into question.   215 *To
leave:* By leaving.

And the ill counsel of a desert° place
With the rich worth of your virginity.
Helena: Your virtue° is my privilege.° For that°   220
    It is not night when I do see your face,
    Therefore I think I am not in the night;
    Nor doth this wood lack worlds of company,
    For you, in my respect,° are all the world.
    Then how can it be said I am alone   225
    When all the world is here to look on me?
Demetrius: I'll run from thee and hide me in the brakes,°
    And leave thee to the mercy of wild beasts.
Helena: The wildest hath not such a heart as you.
    Run when you will. The story shall be changed: 230
    Apollo flies and Daphne holds the chase,°
    The dove pursues the griffin,° the mild hind°
    Makes speed to catch the tiger — bootless° speed,
    When cowardice pursues and valor flies!
Demetrius: I will not stay thy questions.° Let me go!   235
    Or if thou follow me, do not believe
    But I shall do thee mischief in the wood.
Helena: Ay, in the temple, in the town, the field,
    You do me mischief. Fie, Demetrius!
    Your wrongs do set a scandal on my sex.°   240
    We cannot fight for love, as men may do;
    We should be wooed and were not made to woo.   *[Exit Demetrius.]*
    I'll follow thee and make a heaven of hell,
    To die upon° the hand I love so well.   *[Exit.]*
Oberon: Fare thee well, nymph. Ere he do leave this grove   245
    Thou shalt fly him, and he shall seek thy love.

    Enter Puck.

    Has thou the flower there? Welcome, wanderer.
Puck: Aye, there it is.   *[He offers the flower.]*
Oberon: I pray thee, give it to me.
    I know a bank where the wild thyme blows,°
    Where oxlips° and the nodding violet grows,   250
    Quite overcanopied with luscious woodbine,°
    With sweet muskroses° and with eglantine.°
    There sleeps Titania sometime of° the night,

---

218 *desert:* Deserted.   220 *virtue:* Goodness or power to attract; *privilege:* Safeguard, warrant; *For that:* Because.   224 *in my respect:* As far as I am concerned, in my esteem. 227 *brakes:* Thickets.   231 *Apollo . . . chase:* (In the ancient myth, Daphne fled from Apollo and was saved from rape by being transformed into a laurel tree; here it is the female who *holds the chase,* or pursues, instead of the male.)   232 *griffin:* A fabulous monster with the head and wings of an eagle and the body of a lion; *hind:* Female deer.   233 *bootless:* Fruitless.   235 *stay thy questions:* Wait for or put up with your talk or argument. 240 *Your . . . sex:* I.e., the wrongs that you do me cause me to act in a manner that disgraces my sex.   244 *upon:* By.   249 *blows:* Blooms.   250 *oxlips:* Flowers resembling cowslip and primrose.   251 *woodbine:* Honeysuckle.   252 *muskroses:* A kind of large, sweet-scented rose; *eglantine:* Sweetbrier, another kind of rose.   253 *sometime of:* For part of.

Lulled in these flowers with dances and delight;
And there the snake throws° her enameled skin,   255
Weed° wide enough to wrap a fairy in.
And with the juice of this I'll streak° her eyes
And make her full of hateful fantasies.
Take thou some of it, and seek through this grove.

                                    [He gives some love juice.]

A sweet Athenian lady is in love   260
With a disdainful youth. Anoint his eyes,
But do it when the next thing he espies
May be the lady. Thou shalt know the man
By the Athenian garments he hath on.
Effect it with some care, that he may prove   265
More fond on° her than she upon her love;
And look thou meet me ere the first cock crow.

Puck: Fear not, my lord, your servant shall do so.   *Exeunt [separately].*

[SCENE II: *The wood.*]

Enter Titania, Queen of Fairies, with her train.

Titania: Come, now a roundel° and a fairy song;
Then, for the third part of a minute,° hence —
Some to kill cankers° in the muskrose buds,
Some war with reremice° for their leathern wings
To make my small elves coats, and some keep back   5
The clamorous owl, that nightly hoots and wonders
At our quaint° spirits. Sing me now asleep.
Then to your offices, and let me rest.

Fairies sing.

First Fairy: You spotted snakes with double° tongue,
        Thorny hedgehogs, be not seen;   10
    Newts° and blindworms,° do no wrong;
        Come not near our Fairy Queen.
Chorus [dancing]: Philomel,° with melody
        Sing in our sweet lullaby;
    Lulla, lulla, lullaby, lulla, lulla, lullaby.   15
        Never harm
        Nor spell nor charm
    Come our lovely lady nigh.
        So good night, with lullaby.

255 *throws:* Sloughs off, sheds.   256 *Weed:* Garment.   257 *streak:* Anoint, touch gently.
266 *fond on:* Doting on.   **Scene II.**   1 *roundel:* Dance in a ring.   2 *the third . . . minute:*
(Indicative of the fairies' quickness.)   3 *cankers:* Cankerworms (i.e., caterpillars or grubs).
4 *reremice:* Bats.   7 *quaint:* Dainty.   9 *double:* Forked.   11 *Newts:* Water lizards considered poisonous, as were *blindworms* — small snakes with tiny eyes — and spiders.
13 *Philomel:* The nightingale. (Philomela, daughter of King Pandion, was transformed into a
nightingale, according to Ovid's *Metamorphoses* 6, after she had been raped by her sister Procne's
husband, Tereus.)

First Fairy: Weaving spiders, come not here;   20
    Hence, you long-legged spinners, hence!
    Beetles black, approach not near;
    Worm nor snail, do no offense.°
Chorus [dancing]: Philomel, with melody
    Sing in our sweet lullaby;   25
    Lulla, lulla, lullaby, lulla, lulla, lullaby.
    Never harm
    Nor spell nor charm
    Come our lovely lady nigh.
    So good night, with lullaby.   *[Titania sleeps.]*   30
Second Fairy: Hence, away! Now all is well.
    One aloof stand sentinel.°   *[Exeunt Fairies, leaving one sentinel.]*

Enter Oberon [and squeezes the flower on Titania's eyelids].

Oberon: What thou seest when thou dost wake,
    Do it for thy true love take;
    Love and languish for his sake.
    Be it ounce,° or cat, or bear,   35
    Pard,° or boar with bristled hair,
    In thy eye that shall appear
    When thou wak'st, it is thy dear.
    Wake when some vile thing is near.   *[Exit.]*   40

Enter Lysander and Hermia.

Lysander: Fair love, you faint with wandering in the wood;
    And to speak truth, I have forgot our way.
    We'll rest us, Hermia, if you think it good,
    And tarry for the comfort of the day.
Hermia: Be it so, Lysander. Find you out a bed,   45
    For I upon this bank will rest my head.
Lysander: One turf shall serve as pillow for us both;
    One heart, one bed, two bosoms, and one troth.°
Hermia: Nay, good Lysander, for my sake, my dear,
    Lie further off yet. Do not lie so near.   50
Lysander: O, take the sense, sweet, of my innocence!°
    Love takes the meaning in love's conference.°
    I mean that my heart unto yours is knit,
    So that but one heart we can make of it;
    Two bosoms interchainèd with an oath —   55
    So then two bosoms and a single troth.
    Then by your side no bed-room me deny,
    For lying so, Hermia, I do not lie.°

---

23 *offense:* Harm.   32 *sentinel:* (Presumably Oberon is able to outwit or intimidate this guard.)   36 *ounce:* Lynx.   37 *Pard:* Leopard.   48 *troth:* Faith, trothplight.   51 *take . . . innocence:* I.e., interpret my intention as innocent.   52 *Love . . . conference:* I.e., when lovers confer, love teaches each lover to interpret the other's meaning lovingly.   58 *lie:* Tell a falsehood (with a riddling pun on *lie,* "recline").

Hermia: Lysander riddles very prettily.
    Now much beshrew° my manners and my pride 60
    If Hermia meant to say Lysander lied.
    But, gentle friend, for love and courtesy
    Lie further off, in human° modesty.
    Such separation as may well be said
    Becomes a virtuous bachelor and a maid, 65
    So far be distant; and, good night, sweet friend.
    Thy love ne'er alter till thy sweet life end!
Lysander: Amen, amen, to that fair prayer, say I,
    And then end life when I end loyalty!
    Here is my bed. Sleep give thee all his rest! 70
Hermia: With half that wish the wisher's eyes be pressed!°

              [They sleep, separated by a short distance.]

    Enter Puck.

Puck: Through the forest have I gone,
    But Athenian found I none
    On whose eyes I might approve°
    This flower's force in stirring love.
    Night and silence. — Who is here? 75
    Weeds of Athens he doth wear.
    This is he, my master said,
    Despisèd the Athenian maid;
    And here the maiden, sleeping sound,
    On the dank and dirty ground. 80
    Pretty soul, she durst not lie
    Near this lack-love, this kill-courtesy.
    Churl, upon thy eyes I throw
    All the power this charm doth owe.°   *[He applies the love juice.]* 85
    When thou wak'st, let love forbid
    Sleep his seat on thy eyelid.
    So awake when I am gone,
    For I must now to Oberon.   *Exit.*

    Enter Demetrius and Helena, running.

Helena: Stay, though thou kill me, sweet Demetrius! 90
Demetrius: I charge thee, hence, and do not haunt me thus.
Helena: O, wilt thou darkling° leave me? Do not so.
Demetrius: Stay, on thy peril!° I alone will go.   *[Exit.]*
Helena: O, I am out of breath in this fond° chase!
    The more my prayer, the lesser is my grace.° 95
    Happy is Hermia, wheresoe'er she lies,°

---

60 *beshrew:* Curse (but mildly meant).   63 *human:* Courteous (and perhaps suggesting "humane").   71 *With . . . pressed:* I.e., may we share your wish, so that your eyes too are *pressed,* closed, in sleep.   74 *approve:* Test.   85 *owe:* Own.   92 *darkling:* In the dark. 93 *on thy peril:* I.e., on pain of danger to you if you don't obey me and stay.   94 *fond:* Doting. 95 *my grace:* The favor I obtain.   96 *lies:* Dwells.

For she hath blessèd and attractive eyes.
How came her eyes so bright? Not with salt tears;
If so, my eyes are oftener washed than hers.
No, no, I am as ugly as a bear,   100
For beasts that meet me run away for fear.
Therefore no marvel though Demetrius
Do, as a monster, fly my presence thus.°
What wicked and dissembling glass of mine
Made me compare° with Hermia's sphery eyne?°   105
But who is here? Lysander, on the ground?
Dead, or asleep? I see no blood, no wound.
Lysander, if you live, good sir, awake.

Lysander [awaking]: And run through fire I will for thy sweet sake.
Transparent° Helena! Nature shows art,°   110
That through thy bosom makes me see thy heart.
Where is Demetrius? O, how fit a word
Is that vile name to perish on my sword!

Helena: Do not say so, Lysander; say not so.
What though he love your Hermia? Lord, what though?   115
Yet Hermia still loves you. Then be content.

Lysander: Content with Hermia? No! I do repent
The tedious minutes I with her have spent.
Not Hermia but Helena I love.
Who will not change a raven for a dove?   120
The will° of man is by his reason swayed,
And reason says you are the worthier maid.
Things growing are not ripe until their season;
So I, being young, till now ripe not° to reason.
And, touching° now the point° of human skill,°   125
Reason becomes the marshal to my will
And leads me to your eyes, where I o'erlook°
Love's stories written in love's richest book.

Helena: Wherefore° was I to this keen mockery born?
When at your hands did I deserve this scorn?   130
Is't not enough, is't not enough, young man,
That I did never — no, nor never can —
Deserve a sweet look from Demetrius' eye,
But you must flout my insufficiency?
Good troth,° you do me wrong, good sooth,° you do,   135
In such disdainful manner me to woo.
But fare you well. Perforce I must confess
I thought you lord of° more true gentleness.°

102–103 *no marvel . . . thus:* I.e., no wonder that Demetrius flies from me as from a monster.
105 *compare:* Vie; *sphery eyne:* Eyes as bright as stars in their spheres.   110 *Transparent:*
(1) Radiant (2) able to be seen through, lacking in deceit; *art:* Skill, magic power.   121 *will:*
Desire.   124 *ripe not:* (Am) not ripened.   125 *touching:* Reaching; *point:* Summit; *skill:*
Judgment.   127 *o'erlook:* Read.   129 *Wherefore:* Why.   135 *Good troth, good sooth:* I.e.,
indeed, truly.   138 *lord of:* I.e., possessor of; *gentleness:* Courtesy.

O, that a lady, of° one man refused,
Should of another therefore be abused!° Exit. 140
Lysander: She sees not Hermia. Hermia, sleep thou there,
And never mayst thou come Lysander near!
For as a surfeit of the sweetest things
The deepest loathing to the stomach brings,
Or as the heresies that men do leave 145
Are hated most of those they did deceive,°
So thou, my surfeit and my heresy,
Of all be hated, but the most of° me!
And, all my powers, address° your love and might
To honor Helen and to be her knight! Exit. 150
Hermia [awaking]: Help me, Lysander, help me! Do thy best
To pluck this crawling serpent from my breast!
Ay me, for pity! What a dream was here!
Lysander, look how I do quake with fear.
Methought a serpent ate my heart away, 155
And you sat smiling at his cruel prey.°
Lysander! What, removed? Lysander! Lord!
What, out of hearing? Gone? No sound, no word?
Alack, where are you? Speak, an if° you hear;
Speak, of all loves!° I swoon almost with fear. 160
No? Then I well perceive you are not nigh.
Either death, or you, I'll find immediately.
Exit. *[The sleeping Titania remains.]*

[ACT III

SCENE I: *The wood.*]

Enter the clowns° [Quince, Snug, Bottom, Flute, Snout, and Starveling].

Bottom: Are we all met?
Quince: Pat, pat,° and here's a marvelous convenient place for our rehearsal. This green plot shall be our stage, this hawthorn brake° our tiring-house,° and we will do it in action as we will do it before the Duke. 5
Bottom: Peter Quince?
Quince: What sayest thou, bully° Bottom?
Bottom: There are things in this comedy of Pyramus and Thisbe that will

---

139 *of:* By. 140 *abused:* Ill treated. 145–146 *as . . . deceive:* As renounced heresies are hated most by those persons who formerly were deceived by them. 148 *Of . . . of:* By . . . by. 149 *address:* Direct, apply. 156 *prey:* Act of preying. 159 *an if:* If. 160 *of all loves:* For love's sake. **Act III, Scene I.** *clowns:* Rustics. 2 *Pat:* On the dot, punctually. 3 *brake:* Thicket. 4 *tiring-house:* Attiring area, hence backstage. 7 *bully:* I.e., worthy, jolly, fine fellow.

never please. First, Pyramus must draw a sword to kill himself, which the
ladies cannot abide. How answer you that?   10

Snout: By 'r lakin,° a parlous° fear.

Starveling: I believe we must leave the killing out, when all is done.°

Bottom: Not a whit. I have a device to make all well. Write me° a prologue, and let the prologue seem to say, we will do no harm with our
swords, and that Pyramus is not killed indeed; and for the more better   15
assurance, tell them that I, Pyramus, am not Pyramus but Bottom the
weaver. This will put them out of fear.

Quince: Well, we will have such a prologue, and it shall be written in eight
and six.°

Bottom: No, make it two more: let it be written in eight and eight.   20

Snout: Will not the ladies be afeard of the lion?

Starveling: I fear it, I promise you.

Bottom: Masters, you ought to consider with yourself, to bring in — God
shield us! — a lion among ladies° is a most dreadful thing. For there is
not a more fearful° wildfowl than your lion living, and we ought to look   25
to 't.

Snout: Therefore another prologue must tell he is not a lion.

Bottom: Nay, you must name his name, and half his face must be seen
through the lion's neck, and he himself must speak through, saying thus or to the same defect:° "Ladies," or "Fair ladies, I would wish   30
you," or "I would request you," or "I would entreat you, not to fear, not
to tremble; my life for yours.° If you think I come hither as a lion, it were
pity of my life.° No, I am no such thing; I am a man as other men are."
And there indeed let him name his name, and tell them plainly he is Snug
the joiner.   35

Quince: Well, it shall be so. But there is two hard things: that is, to bring the
moonlight into a chamber; for, you know, Pyramus and Thisbe meet by
moonlight.

Snout: Doth the moon shine that night we play our play?

Bottom: A calendar, a calendar! Look in the almanac. Find out moon-   40
shine, find out moonshine.   *[They consult an almanac.]*

Quince: Yes, it doth shine that night.

Bottom: Why then may you leave a casement of the great chamber window
where we play open, and the moon may shine in at the casement.

Quince: Ay; or else one must come in with a bush of thorns° and a lantern   45

---

11 *By 'r lakin:* By our ladykin, i.e., the Virgin Mary; *parlous:* Perilous, alarming.   12 *when
all is done:* I.e., when all is said and done.   13 *Write me:* I.e., write at my suggestion (*me*
is used colloquially).   19 *eight and six:* Alternate lines of eight and six syllables, a common ballad measure.   24 *lion among ladies:* (A contemporary pamphlet tells how, at the
christening in 1594 of Prince Henry, eldest son of King James VI of Scotland, later James I of
England, a "blackamoor" instead of a lion drew the triumphal chariot, since the lion's presence might have "brought some fear to the nearest.")   25 *fearful:* Fear-inspiring.   30 *defect:* (Bottom's blunder for "effect.")   32 *my life for yours:* I.e., I pledge my life to make your
lives safe.   33 *it were . . . life:* I.e., I should be sorry, by my life; or, my life would be endan-
gered.   45 *bush of thorns:* Bundle of thornbush fagots (part of the accoutrements of the
man in the moon, according to the popular notions of the time, along with his lantern and
his dog).

and say he comes to disfigure,° or to present,° the person of Moonshine. Then there is another thing: we must have a wall in the great
chamber; for Pyramus and Thisbe, says the story, did talk through the
chink of a wall.

Snout: You can never bring in a wall. What say you, Bottom?   50

Bottom: Some man or other must present Wall. And let him have some plaster, or some loam, or some roughcast° about him, to signify wall; or let
him hold his fingers thus, and through that cranny shall Pyramus and
Thisbe whisper.

Quince: If that may be, then all is well. Come, sit down, every mother's son,   55
and rehearse your parts. Pyramus, you begin. When you have spoken
your speech, enter into that brake, and so everyone according to his cue.

Enter Robin [Puck].

Puck [aside]: What hempen homespuns° have we swaggering here
    So near the cradle° of the Fairy Queen?   60
    What, a play toward?° I'll be an auditor;
    An actor, too, perhaps, if I see cause.

Quince: Speak, Pyramus. Thisbe, stand forth.

Bottom [as Pyramus]: "Thisbe, the flowers of odious savors sweet —"

Quince: Odors, odors.   65

Bottom: "— Odors savors sweet;
    So hath thy breath, my dearest Thisbe dear.
    But hark, a voice! Stay thou but here awhile,
    And by and by I will to thee appear."   *Exit.*

Puck: A stranger Pyramus than e'er played here.°   *[Exit.]*   70

Flute: Must I speak now?

Quince: Ay, marry, must you; for you must understand he goes but to see a
noise that he heard, and is to come again.

Flute [as Thisbe]: "Most radiant Pyramus, most lily-white of hue,
    Of color like the red rose on triumphant° brier,   75
    Most brisky juvenal° and eke° most lovely Jew,°
    As true as truest horse that yet would never tire.
    I'll meet thee, Pyramus, at Ninny's tomb."

Quince: "Ninus'° tomb," man. Why, you must not speak that yet. That you
answer to Pyramus. You speak all your part° at once, cues and all. Pyramus,   80
enter. Your cue is past; it is "never tire."

---

46 *disfigure:* (Quince's blunder for "figure"); *present:* Represent.   52 *roughcast:* A mixture
of lime and gravel used to plaster the outside of buildings.   59 *hempen homespuns:* I.e., rustics dressed in clothes woven of coarse, homespun fabric made from hemp.   60 *cradle:* I.e.,
Titania's bower.   61 *toward:* About to take place.   70 *A stranger . . . here:* (Either Puck
refers to an earlier dramatic version played in the same theater, or he has conceived of a plan to
present a "stranger" Pyramus than ever seen before.)   75 *triumphant:* Magnificent.
76 *brisky juvenal:* Lively youth; *eke:* Also; *Jew:* (An absurd repetition of the first syllable of *juvenal* and an indication of how desperately Quince searches for his rhymes.)   79 *Ninus':* Mythical
founder of Nineveh (whose wife, Semiramis, was supposed to have built the walls of Babylon
where the story of Pyramus and Thisbe takes place).   80 *part:* (An actor's *part* was a script
consisting only of his speeches and their cues.)

Flute: O — "As true as truest horse, that yet would never tire."

[Enter Puck, and Bottom as Pyramus with the ass head.°]

Bottom: "If I were fair,° Thisbe, I were° only thine."
Quince: O, monstrous! O, strange! We are haunted. Pray, masters! Fly, mas-
ters! Help!   *[Exeunt Quince, Snug, Flute, Snout, and Starveling.]*   85
Puck: I'll follow you, I'll lead you about a round,°
   Thorough bog, thorough bush, thorough brake, thorough brier.
   Sometimes a horse I'll be, sometimes a hound,
     A hog, a headless bear, sometimes a fire;°
   And neigh, and bark, and grunt, and roar, and burn,   90
   Like horse, hound, hog, bear, fire, at every turn.   *Exit.*
Bottom: Why do they run away? This is a knavery of them to make me afeard.

   Enter Snout.

Snout: O Bottom, thou art changed! What do I see on thee?
Bottom: What do you see? You see an ass head of your own, do you?   95
                          [Exit Snout.]

   Enter Quince.

Quince: Bless thee, Bottom, bless thee! Thou art translated.°   *Exit.*
Bottom: I see their knavery. This is to make an ass of me, to fright me, if
they could. But I will not stir from this place, do what they can. I will
walk up and down here, and will sing, that they shall hear I am not
afraid.   *[He sings.]*   100
   The ouzel cock° so black of hue,
     With orange-tawny bill,
   The throstle° with his note so true,
     The wren with little quill°—
Titania [awaking]: What angel wakes me from my flowery bed?   105
Bottom [sings]:
   The finch, the sparrow, and the lark,
     The plainsong° cuckoo gray,
   Whose note full many a man doth mark,
     And dares not answer nay°—
   For indeed, who would set his wit to° so foolish a bird? Who would give a   110
   bird the lie,° though he cry "cuckoo" never so?°
Titania: I pray thee, gentle mortal, sing again.
   Mine ear is much enamored of thy note;
   So is mine eye enthrallèd to thy shape;
   And thy fair virtue's force° perforce doth move me   115
   On the first view to say, to swear, I love thee.

---

with the ass head: (This stage direction presumably refers to a standard stage property.)
83 *fair:* Handsome; *were:* Would be.   86 *about a round:* Roundabout.   89 *fire:* Will-o'-
the-wisp.   96 *translated:* Transformed.   101 *ouzel cock:* Male blackbird.   103 *throstle:*
Song thrush.   104 *quill:* (Literally, a reed pipe; hence, the bird's piping song.)   107 *plain-
song:* Singing a melody without variations.   109 *dares . . . nay:* I.e., cannot deny that he is
a cuckold.   110 *set his wit to:* Employ his intelligence to answer.   111 *give . . . lie:* Call the
bird a liar; *never so:* Ever so much.   115 *thy . . . force:* The power of your unblemished
excellence.

Bottom: Methinks, mistress, you should have little reason for that. And yet, to say the truth, reason and love keep little company together nowadays — the more the pity that some honest neighbors will not make them friends. Nay, I can gleek° upon occasion.　　　　120

Titania: Thou art as wise as thou art beautiful.

Bottom: Not so, neither. But if I had wit enough to get out of this wood, I have enough to serve mine own turn.°

Titania: Out of this wood do not desire to go.

　　Thou shalt remain here, whether thou wilt or no.　　　125
　　I am a spirit of no common rate.°
　　The summer still doth tend upon my state,°
　　And I do love thee. Therefore, go with me.
　　I'll give thee fairies to attend on thee,
　　And they shall fetch thee jewels from the deep,　　　130
　　And sing while thou on pressèd flowers dost sleep.
　　And I will purge thy mortal grossness° so
　　That thou shalt like an airy spirit go.
　　Peaseblossom, Cobweb, Mote,° and Mustardseed!

　　　Enter four Fairies [Peaseblossom, Cobweb, Mote, and Mustardseed].

Peaseblossom: Ready.　　　　135
Cobweb: And I.
Mote: 　　　　And I.
Mustardseed: 　　　　　And I.
All: 　　　　　　Where shall we go?
Titania: Be kind and courteous to this gentleman.
　　Hop in his walks and gambol in his eyes;°
　　Feed him with apricots and dewberries,°
　　With purple grapes, green figs, and mulberries;　　　140
　　The honey bags steal from the humble-bees,
　　And for night tapers crop their waxen thighs
　　And light them at the fiery glowworms' eyes,
　　To have my love to bed and to arise;
　　And pluck the wings from painted butterflies　　　145
　　To fan the moonbeams from his sleeping eyes.
　　Nod to him, elves, and do him courtesies.
Peaseblossom: Hail, mortal!
Cobweb: Hail!
Mote: Hail!　　　　150
Mustardseed: Hail!
Bottom: I cry your worships mercy,° heartily. I beseech your worship's name.
Cobweb: Cobweb.

---

120 *gleek:* Jest.　123 *serve...turn:* Answer my purpose.　126 *rate:* Rank, value.　127 *still ...state:* Always waits upon me as a part of my royal retinue.　132 *mortal grossness:* Materiality (i.e., the corporeal nature of a mortal being).　134 *Mote:* I.e., speck. (The two words *moth* and *mote* were pronounced alike, and both meanings may be present.)　138 *in his eyes:* In his sight (i.e., before him).　139 *dewberries:* Blackberries.　152 *I cry...mercy:* I beg pardon of your worships (for presuming to ask a question).

Bottom: I shall desire you of more acquaintance,° good Master Cobweb.
If I cut my finger, I shall make bold with you.° — Your name, honest 155
gentleman?

Peaseblossom: Peaseblossom.

Bottom: I pray you, commend me to Mistress Squash,° your mother,
and to Master Peascod,° your father. Good Master Peaseblossom, I
shall desire you of more acquaintance too. — Your name, I beseech 160
you, sir?

Mustardseed: Mustardseed.

Bottom: Good Master Mustardseed, I know your patience° well. That same
cowardly, giantlike ox-beef hath devoured many a gentleman of your
house. I promise you, your kindred hath made my eyes water° ere now.
I desire you of more acquaintance, good Master Mustardseed. 165

Titania: Come wait upon him; lead him to my bower.
    The moon methinks looks with a watery eye;
And when she weeps,° weeps every little flower,
    Lamenting some enforcèd° chastity. 170
Tie up my lover's tongue;° bring him silently.   *Exeunt.*

[**Scene II:** The wood.]

Enter [Oberon,] King of Fairies.

Oberon: I wonder if Titania be awaked;
    Then, what it was that next came in her eye,
Which she must dote on in extremity.

[*Enter] Robin Goodfellow [Puck].*

Here comes my messenger. How now, mad spirit?
What night-rule° now about this haunted° grove? 5

Puck: My mistress with a monster is in love.
    Near to her close° and consecrated bower,
While she was in her dull° and sleeping hour,
    A crew of patches,° rude mechanicals,°
That work for bread upon Athenian stalls,° 10
    Were met together to rehearse a play
Intended for great Theseus' nuptial day.
    The shallowest thickskin of that barren sort,°
Who Pyramus presented,° in their sport
    Forsook his scene° and entered in a brake. 15
When I did him at this advantage take,

An ass's noll° I fixèd on his head.
Anon his Thisbe must be answerèd,
And forth my mimic° comes. When they him spy,
As wild geese that the creeping fowler° eye,   20
Or russet-pated choughs,° many in sort,°
Rising and cawing at the gun's report,
Sever° themselves and madly sweep the sky,
So, at his sight, away his fellows fly;
And, at our stamp, here o'er and o'er one falls;   25
He "Murder!" cries and help from Athens calls.
Their sense thus weak, lost with their fears thus strong,
Made senseless things begin to do them wrong,
For briers and thorns at their apparel snatch;
Some, sleeves — some, hats; from yielders all things catch.°   30
I led them on in this distracted fear
And left sweet Pyramus translated there,
When in that moment, so it came to pass,
Titania waked and straightway loved an ass.

Oberon: This falls out better than I could devise.   35
But hast thou yet latched° the Athenian's eyes
With the love juice, as I did bid thee do?

Puck: I took him sleeping — that is finished too —
And the Athenian woman by his side,
That, when he waked, of force° she must be eyed.   40

Enter Demetrius and Hermia.

Oberon: Stand close. This is the same Athenian.
Puck: This is the woman, but not this the man.   *[They stand aside.]*
Demetrius: O, why rebuke you him that loves you so?
Lay breath so bitter on your bitter foe.
Hermia: Now I but chide; but I should use thee worse,   45
For thou, I fear, hast given me cause to curse.
If thou hast slain Lysander in his sleep,
Being o'er shoes° in blood, plunge in the deep,
And kill me too.
The sun was not so true unto the day   50
As he to me. Would he have stolen away
From sleeping Hermia? I'll believe as soon
This whole° earth may be bored, and that the moon
May through the center creep, and so displease
Her brother's° noontide with th' Antipodes.°   55
It cannot be but thou hast murdered him;
So should a murderer look, so dead,° so grim.

17 *noll:* Noddle, head.   19 *mimic:* Burlesque actor.   20 *fowler:* Hunter of game birds.
21 *russet-pated choughs:* Reddish brown or gray-headed jackdaws; *in sort:* In a flock.
23 *Sever:* I.e., scatter.   30 *from . . . catch:* I.e., everything preys on those who yield to fear.
36 *latched:* Fastened, snared.   40 *of force:* Perforce.   48 *Being o'er shoes:* Having waded
in so far.   53 *whole:* Solid.   55 *Her brother's:* I.e., the sun's; *th' Antipodes:* The people
on the opposite side of the earth (where the moon is imagined bringing night to noontime).
57 *dead:* Deadly, or deathly pale.

Demetrius: So should the murdered look, and so should I,
　　Pierced through the heart with your stern cruelty.
　　Yet you, the murderer, look as bright, as clear　　　　　　　　60
　　As yonder Venus in her glimmering sphere.
Hermia: What's this to° my Lysander? Where is he?
　　Ah, good Demetrius, wilt thou give him me?
Demetrius: I had rather give his carcass to my hounds.
Hermia: Out, dog! Out, cur! Thou driv'st me past the bounds　　65
　　Of maiden's patience. Hast thou slain him, then?
　　Henceforth be never numbered among men.
　　O, once° tell true, tell true, even for my sake:
　　Durst thou have looked upon him being awake?
　　And hast thou killed him sleeping? O brave touch!°　　　　　70
　　Could not a worm,° an adder, do so much?
　　An adder did it; for with doubler° tongue
　　Than thine, thou serpent, never adder stung.
Demetrius: You spend your passion° on a misprised mood.°
　　I am not guilty of Lysander's blood,　　　　　　　　　　75
　　Nor is he dead, for aught that I can tell.
Hermia: I pray thee, tell me then that he is well.
Demetrius: And if I could, what should I get therefor?°
Hermia: A privilege never to see me more.
　　And from thy hated presence part I so.　　　　　　　　80
　　See me no more, whether he be dead or no.　　　　　*Exit.*
Demetrius: There is no following her in this fierce vein.
　　Here therefore for a while I will remain.
　　So sorrow's heaviness doth heavier° grow
　　For debt that bankrupt° sleep doth sorrow owe,　　　　　85
　　Which now in some slight measure it will pay,
　　If for his tender here I make some stay.°　　*[He] lie[s] down [and sleeps].*
Oberon: What hast thou done? Thou hast mistaken quite
　　And laid the love juice on some true love's sight.
　　Of thy misprision° must perforce ensue　　　　　　　　90
　　Some true love turned, and not a false turned true.
Puck: Then fate o'errules, that, one man holding troth,°
　　A million fail, confounding oath on oath.°
Oberon: About the wood go swifter than the wind,
　　And Helena of Athens look° thou find.　　　　　　　　95
　　All fancy-sick° she is and pale of cheer°
　　With sighs of love, that cost the fresh blood° dear.

---

62 *to:* To do with.　　68 *once:* Once and for all.　　70 *brave touch!:* Fine stroke! (said ironically).　　71 *worm:* Serpent.　　72 *doubler:* (1) More forked, (2) more deceitful.　　74 *passion:* Violent feelings; *misprised mood:* Anger based on misconception.　　78 *therefor:* In return for that.　　84 *heavier:* (1) Harder to bear, (2) more drowsy.　　85 *bankrupt:* (Demetrius is saying that his sleepiness adds to the weariness caused by sorrow.)　　86–87 *Which . . . stay:* I.e., to a small extent, I will be able to "pay back" and hence find some relief from sorrow, if I pause here awhile (*make some stay*) while sleep "tenders" or offers itself by way of paying the debt owed to sorrow.　　90 *misprision:* Mistake.　　92 *that . . . troth:* In that, for each man keeping true faith in love.　　93 *confounding . . . oath:* I.e., breaking oath after oath.　　95 *look:* I.e., be sure.　　96 *fancy-sick:* Lovesick; *cheer:* Face.　　97 *sighs . . . blood:* (An allusion to the physiological theory that each sigh costs the heart a drop of blood.)

By some illusion see thou bring her here.
I'll charm his eyes against she do appear.°

Puck: I go, I go, look how I go,   100
     Swifter than arrow from the Tartar's bow.°   *[Exit.]*

Oberon [applying love juice to Demetrius' eyes]: Flower of this purple dye,
     Hit with Cupid's archery,
     Sink in apple° of his eye.
     When his love he doth espy,   105
     Let her shine as gloriously
     As the Venus of the sky.
     When thou wak'st, if she be by,
     Beg of her for remedy.

     Enter Puck.

Puck: Captain of our fairy band,   110
     Helena is here at hand,
     And the youth, mistook by me,
     Pleading for a lover's fee.°
     Shall we their fond pageant° see?
     Lord, what fools these mortals be!   115

Oberon: Stand aside. The noise they make
     Will cause Demetrius to awake.

Puck: Then will two at once woo one;
     That must needs be sport alone.°
     And those things do best please me   120
     That befall preposterously.°   *[They stand aside.]*

     Enter Lysander and Helena.

Lysander: Why should you think that I should woo in scorn?
     Scorn and derision never come in tears.
     Look when° I vow, I weep; and vows so born,
     In their nativity all truth appears.°
     How can these things in me seem scorn to you,   125
     Bearing the badge° of faith to prove them true?

Helena: You do advance° your cunning more and more.
     When truth kills truth,° O, devilish-holy fray!
     These vows are Hermia's. Will you give her o'er?
     Weigh oath with oath, and you will nothing weigh.   130
     Your vows to her and me, put in two scales,
     Will even weigh, and both as light as tales.°

Lysander: I had no judgment when to her I swore.

Helena: Nor none, in my mind, now you give her o'er.   135

Lysander: Demetrius loves her, and he loves not you.

---

99 *against . . . appear:* In anticipation of her coming.   101 *Tartar's bow:* (Tartars were famed for their skill with the bow.)   104 *apple:* Pupil.   113 *fee:* Privilege, reward.   114 *fond pageant:* Foolish spectacle.   119 *alone:* Unequaled.   121 *preposterously:* Out of the natural order.   124 *Look when:* Whenever.   124–125 *vows . . . appears:* I.e., vows made by one who is weeping give evidence thereby of their sincerity.   127 *badge:* Identifying device such as that worn on the servants' livery (here, his tears).   128 *advance:* Carry forward, display. 129 *truth kills truth:* I.e., one of Lysander's vows must invalidate the other.   133 *tales:* Lies.

Demetrius [awaking]: O Helen, goddess, nymph, perfect, divine!
    To what, my love, shall I compare thine eyne?
    Crystal is muddy. O, how ripe in show°
    Thy lips, those kissing cherries, tempting grow!
    That pure congealèd white, high Taurus'° snow,   140
    Fanned with the eastern wind, turns to a crow°
    When thou hold'st up thy hand. O, let me kiss
    This princess of pure white, this seal° of bliss!
Helena: O spite! O hell! I see you all are bent   145
    To set against° me for your merriment.
    If you were civil and knew courtesy,
    You would not do me thus much injury.
    Can you not hate me, as I know you do,
    But you must join in souls° to mock me too?   150
    If you were men, as men you are in show,
    You would not use a gentle lady so —
    To vow, and swear, and superpraise° my parts,°
    When I am sure you hate me with your hearts.
    You both are rivals, and love Hermia,   155
    And now both rivals to mock Helena.
    A trim° exploit, a manly enterprise,
    To conjure tears up in a poor maid's eyes
    With your derision! None of noble sort°
    Would so offend a virgin and extort°   160
    A poor soul's patience, all to make you sport.
Lysander: You are unkind, Demetrius. Be not so.
    For you love Hermia; this you know I know.
    And here, with all good will, with all my heart,
    In Hermia's love I yield you up my part;   165
    And yours of Helena to me bequeath,
    Whom I do love, and will do till my death.
Helena: Never did mockers waste more idle breath.
Demetrius: Lysander, keep thy Hermia; I will none.°
    If e'er I loved her, all that love is gone.   170
    My heart to her but as guestwise sojourned,°
    And now to Helen is it home returned,
    There to remain.
Lysander: Helen, it is not so.
Demetrius: Disparage not the faith thou dost not know,
    Lest, to thy peril, thou aby° it dear.   175
    Look where thy love comes; yonder is thy dear.

    Enter Hermia.

Hermia: Dark night, that from the eye his° function takes,

---

139 *show:* Appearance.   141 *Taurus:* A lofty mountain range in Asia Minor.   142 *turns to a crow:* I.e., seems black by contrast.   144 *seal:* Pledge.   146 *set against:* Attack.   150 *in souls:* I.e., heart and soul.   153 *superpraise:* Overpraise; *parts:* Qualities.   157 *trim:* Pretty, fine (said ironically).   159 *sort:* Character, quality.   160 *extort:* Twist, torture.   169 *will none:* I.e., want no part of her.   171 *to . . . sojourned:* Only visited with her.   175 *aby:* Pay for.   177 *his:* Its.

The ear more quick of apprehension makes;
Wherein it doth impair the seeing sense,
It pays the hearing double recompense. 180
Thou art not by mine eye, Lysander, found;
Mine ear, I thank it, brought me to thy sound.
But why unkindly didst thou leave me so?
Lysander: Why should he stay, whom love doth press to go?
Hermia: What love could press Lysander from my side? 185
Lysander: Lysander's love, that would not let him bide —
Fair Helena, who more engilds° the night
Than all yon fiery oes° and eyes of light.
Why seek'st thou me? Could not this make thee know
The hate I bear thee made me leave thee so? 190
Hermia: You speak not as you think. It cannot be.
Helena: Lo, she is one of this confederacy!
Now I perceive they have conjoined all three
To fashion this false sport, in spite of me.°
Injurious Hermia, most ungrateful maid! 195
Have you conspired, have you with these contrived°
To bait° me with this foul derision?
Is all the counsel° that we two have shared —
The sisters' vows, the hours that we have spent
When we have chid the hasty-footed time 200
For parting us — O, is all forgot?
All schooldays' friendship, childhood innocence?
We, Hermia, like two artificial° gods
Have with our needles created both one flower,
Both on one sampler, sitting on one cushion, 205
Both warbling of one song, both in one key,
As if our hands, our sides, voices, and minds
Had been incorporate.° So we grew together,
Like to a double cherry, seeming parted,
But yet an union in partition, 210
Two lovely° berries molded on one stem;
So, with two seeming bodies but one heart,
Two of the first, like coats in heraldry,
Due but to one and crownèd with one crest.°
And will you rend our ancient love asunder, 215
To join with men in scorning your poor friend?
It is not friendly, 'tis not maidenly.
Our sex, as well as I, may chide you for it,
Though I alone do feel the injury.
Hermia: I am amazèd at your passionate words. 220
I scorn you not. It seems that you scorn me.

---

187 *engilds:* Gilds, brightens with a golden light. 188 *oes:* Spangles (here, stars). 194 *in spite of me:* To vex me. 196 *contrived:* Plotted. 197 *bait:* Torment, as one sets on dogs to bait a bear. 198 *counsel:* Confidential talk. 203 *artificial:* Skilled in art or creation. 208 *incorporate:* Of one body. 211 *lovely:* Loving. 213–214 *Two . . . crest:* I.e., we have two separate bodies, just as a coat of arms in heraldry can be represented twice on a shield but surmounted by a single crest.

Helena: Have you not set Lysander, as in scorn,
  To follow me and praise my eyes and face?
  And made your other love, Demetrius,
  Who even but now did spurn me with his foot,   225
  To call me goddess, nymph, divine, and rare,
  Precious, celestial? Wherefore speaks he this
  To her he hates? And wherefore doth Lysander
  Deny your love, so rich within his soul,
  And tender° me, forsooth, affection,   230
  But by your setting on, by your consent?
  What though I be not so in grace° as you,
  So hung upon with love, so fortunate,
  But miserable most, to love unloved?
  This you should pity rather than despise.   235
Hermia: I understand not what you mean by this.
Helena: Ay, do! Persever, counterfeit sad° looks,
  Make mouths° upon° me when I turn my back,
  Wink each at other, hold the sweet jest up.°
  This sport, well carried,° shall be chronicled.   240
  If you have any pity, grace, or manners,
  You would not make me such an argument.°
  But fare ye well. 'Tis partly my own fault,
  Which death, or absence, soon shall remedy.
Lysander: Stay, gentle Helena; hear my excuse,   245
  My love, my life, my soul, fair Helena!
Helena: O excellent!
Hermia [to Lysander]: Sweet, do not scorn her so.
Demetrius [to Lysander]: If she cannot entreat,° I can compel.
Lysander: Thou canst compel no more than she entreat.   250
  Thy threats have no more strength than her weak prayers.
  Helen, I love thee, by my life, I do!
  I swear by that which I will lose for thee,
  To prove him false that says I love thee not.
Demetrius [to Helena]: I say I love thee more than he can do. 255
Lysander: If thou say so, withdraw, and prove it too.°
Demetrius: Quick, come!
Hermia: Lysander, whereto tends all this?
Lysander: Away, you Ethiope!°   *[He tries to break away from Hermia.]*
Demetrius: No, no; he'll
  Seem to break loose; take on as° you would follow,
  But yet come not. You are a tame man. Go!   260
Lysander [to Hermia]: Hang off,° thou cat, thou burr! Vile thing, let loose,
  Or I will shake thee from me like a serpent!

---

230 *tender:* Offer.   232 *grace:* Favor.   237 *sad:* Grave, serious.   238 *mouths:* I.e., mows, faces, grimaces; *upon:* At.   239 *hold . . . up:* Keep up the joke.   240 *carried:* Managed. 242 *argument:* Subject for a jest.   249 *entreat:* I.e., succeed by entreaty.   256 *withdraw . . . too:* I.e., withdraw with me and prove your claim in a duel (the two gentlemen are armed). 258 *Ethiope:* (Referring to Hermia's relatively dark hair and complexion; see also *tawny Tartar* six lines later.)   259 *take on as:* Act as if, make a fuss as if.   261 *Hang off:* Let go.

Hermia: Why are you grown so rude? What change is this,
    Sweet love?
Lysander: Thy love? Out, tawny Tartar, out!
    Out, lothèd med'cine!° O hated potion, hence!   265
Hermia: Do you not jest?
Helena: Yes, sooth,° and so do you.
Lysander: Demetrius, I will keep my word with thee.
Demetrius: I would I had your bond, for I perceive
    A weak bond° holds you. I'll not trust your word.
Lysander: What, should I hurt her, strike her, kill her dead?   270
    Although I hate her, I'll not harm her so.
Hermia: What, can you do me greater harm than hate?
    Hate me? Wherefore? O me, what news,° my love?
    Am not I Hermia? Are not you Lysander?
    I am as fair now as I was erewhile.°   275
    Since night you loved me; yet since night you left me.
    Why, then you left me — O, the gods forbid! —
    In earnest, shall I say?
Lysander: Ay, by my life!
    And never did desire to see thee more.
    Therefore be out of hope, of question, of doubt;   280
    Be certain, nothing truer. 'Tis no jest
    That I do hate thee and love Helena.
Hermia [to Helena]: O me! You juggler! You cankerblossom!°
    You thief of love! What, have you come by night
    And stol'n my love's heart from him?
Helena: Fine, i' faith!   285
    Have you no modesty, no maiden shame,
    No touch of bashfulness? What, will you tear
    Impatient answers from my gentle tongue?
    Fie, fie! You counterfeit, you puppet,° you!
Hermia: "Puppet"? Why, so!° Ay, that way goes the game.   290
    Now I perceive that she hath made compare
    Between our statures; she hath urged her height,
    And with her personage, her tall personage,
    Her height, forsooth, she hath prevailed with him.
    And are you grown so high in his esteem   295
    Because I am so dwarfish and so low?
    How low am I, thou painted maypole? Speak!
    How low am I? I am not yet so low
    But that my nails can reach unto thine eyes.
                        [She flails at Helena but is restrained.]
Helena: I pray you, though you mock me, gentlemen,   300
    Let her not hurt me. I was never curst;°
    I have no gift at all in shrewishness;
    I am a right° maid for my cowardice.

---

265 *med'cine:* I.e., poison.   266 *sooth:* Truly.   269 *weak bond:* I.e., Hermia's arm (with a pun on *bond,* "oath," in the previous line).   273 *what news:* What is the matter? 275 *erewhile:* Just now.   283 *cankerblossom:* Worm that destroys the flower bud, or wild rose.   289 *puppet:* (1) Counterfeit, (2) dwarfish woman (in reference to Hermia's smaller stature).   290 *Why, so:* I.e., Oh, so that's how it is.   301 *curst:* Shrewish.   303 *right:* True.

Let her not strike me. You perhaps may think,
Because she is something° lower than myself,   305
That I can match her.

Hermia: Lower? Hark, again!

Helena: Good Hermia, do not be so bitter with me.
I evermore did love you, Hermia,
Did ever keep your counsels, never wronged you,
Save that, in love unto Demetrius,   310
I told him of your stealth° unto this wood.
He followed you; for love I followed him.
But he hath chid me hence° and threatened me
To strike me, spurn me, nay, to kill me too.
And now, so° you will let me quiet go,   315
To Athens will I bear my folly back
And follow you no further. Let me go.
You see how simple and how fond° I am.

Hermia: Why, get you gone. Who is't that hinders you?

Helena: A foolish heart, that I leave here behind.   320

Hermia: What, with Lysander?

Helena: With Demetrius.

Lysander: Be not afraid; she shall not harm thee, Helena.

Demetrius: No, sir, she shall not, though you take her part.

Helena: O, when she is angry, she is keen° and shrewd.°
She was a vixen when she went to school;   325
And though she be but little, she is fierce.

Hermia: "Little" again? Nothing but "low" and "little"?
Why will you suffer her to flout me thus?
Let me come to her.

Lysander: Get you gone, you dwarf!
You minimus,° of hindering knotgrass° made!   330
You bead, you acorn!

Demetrius: You are too officious
In her behalf that scorns your services.
Let her alone. Speak not of Helena;
Take not her part. For, if thou dost intend°
Never so little show of love to her,   335
Thou shalt aby° it.

Lysander: Now she holds me not.
Now follow, if thou dar'st, to try whose right,
Of thine or mine, is most in Helena.   *[Exit.]*

Demetrius: Follow? Nay, I'll go with thee, cheek by jowl.°
                                   [Exit, following Lysander.]

Hermia: You, mistress, all this coil° is 'long of° you.   340
Nay, go not back.°

Helena: I will not trust you, I,

---

305 *something:* Somewhat.   311 *stealth:* Stealing away.   313 *chid me hence:* Driven me away with his scolding.   315 *so:* If only.   318 *fond:* Foolish.   324 *keen:* Fierce, cruel; *shrewd:* Shrewish.   330 *minimus:* Diminutive creature; *knotgrass:* A weed, an infusion of which was thought to stunt the growth.   334 *intend:* Give sign of.   336 *aby:* Pay for. 339 *cheek by jowl:* I.e., side by side.   340 *coil:* Turmoil, dissension; *'long of:* On account of. 341 *go not back:* I.e., don't retreat (Hermia is again proposing a fight).

Nor longer stay in your curst company.
Your hands than mine are quicker for a fray;
My legs are longer, though, to run away.   *[Exit.]*
Hermia: I am amazed and know not what to say.   *Exit.* 345

[Oberon and Puck come forward.]

Oberon: This is thy negligence. Still thou mistak'st,
    Or else committ'st thy knaveries willfully.
Puck: Believe me, king of shadows, I mistook.
    Did not you tell me I should know the man
    By the Athenian garments he had on?   350
    And so far blameless proves my enterprise
    That I have 'nointed an Athenian's eyes;
    And so far° am I glad it so did sort,°
    As° this their jangling I esteem a sport.
Oberon: Thou seest these lovers seek a place to fight.   355
    Hie° therefore, Robin, overcast the night;
    The starry welkin° cover thou anon
    With drooping fog as black as Acheron,°
    And lead these testy rivals so astray
    As° one come not within another's way.   360
    Like to Lysander sometimes frame thy tongue,
    Then stir Demetrius up with bitter wrong;°
    And sometimes rail thou like Demetrius.
    And from each other look thou lead them thus,
    Till o'er their brows death-counterfeiting sleep   365
    With leaden legs and batty° wings doth creep.
    Then crush this herb° into Lysander's eye,   *[giving herb]*
    Whose liquor hath this virtuous° property,
    To take from thence all error with his° might
    And make his eyeballs roll with wonted° sight.   370
    When they next wake, all this derision°
    Shall seem a dream and fruitless vision,
    And back to Athens shall the lovers wend
    With league whose date° till death shall never end.
    Whiles I in this affair do thee employ,   375
    I'll to my queen and beg her Indian boy;
    And then I will her charmèd eye release
    From monster's view, and all things shall be peace.
Puck: My fairy lord, this must be done with haste,
    For night's swift dragons° cut the clouds full fast,   380
    And yonder shines Aurora's harbinger,°
    At whose approach ghosts, wand'ring here and there,
    Troop home to churchyards. Damnèd spirits all,

---

353 *so far:* At least to this extent; *sort:* Turn out.   354 *As:* In that.   356 *Hie:* Hasten.
357 *welkin:* Sky.   358 *Acheron:* River of Hades (here representing Hades itself).   360 *As:*
That.   362 *wrong:* Insults.   366 *batty:* Batlike.   367 *this herb:* I.e., the antidote
(mentioned in II.i.184) to love-in-idleness.   368 *virtuous:* Efficacious.   369 *his:* Its.
370 *wonted:* Accustomed.   371 *derision:* Laughable business.   374 *date:* Term of existence.   380 *dragons:* (Supposed by Shakespeare to be yoked to the car of the goddess of night
or the moon.)   381 *Aurora's harbinger:* The morning star, precursor of dawn.

That in crossways and floods have burial,°
Already to their wormy beds are gone.   385
For fear lest day should look their shames upon,
They willfully themselves exile from light
And must for aye° consort with black-browed night.

Oberon: But we are spirits of another sort.
I with the Morning's love° have oft made sport,   390
And, like a forester,° the groves may tread
Even till the eastern gate, all fiery red,
Opening on Neptune with fair blessèd beams,
Turns into yellow gold his salt green streams.
But notwithstanding, haste, make no delay.   395
We may effect this business yet ere day.   *[Exit.]*

Puck: Up and down, up and down,
      I will lead them up and down.
      I am feared in field and town.
      Goblin,° lead them up and down.   400
Here comes one.

Enter Lysander.

Lysander: Where art thou, proud Demetrius? Speak thou now.
Puck [mimicking Demetrius]: Here, villain, drawn° and ready. Where art
      thou?
Lysander: I will be with thee straight.°
Puck: Follow me, then,
      To plainer° ground.   *[Lysander wanders about,° following the voice.]*

      Enter Demetrius.

Demetrius: Lysander! Speak again!   405
      Thou runaway, thou coward, art thou fled?
      Speak! In some bush? Where dost thou hide thy head?
Puck [mimicking Lysander]: Thou coward, art thou bragging to the stars,
      Telling the bushes that thou look'st for wars,
      And wilt not come? Come, recreant;° come, thou child,   410
      I'll whip thee with a rod. He is defiled
      That draws a sword on thee.
Demetrius: Yea, art thou there?
Puck: Follow my voice. We'll try° no manhood here.   *Exeunt.*

      [Lysander returns.]

Lysander: He goes before me and still dares me on.
      When I come where he calls, then he is gone.   415

---

384 *crossways . . . burial:* (Those who had committed suicide were buried at crossways, with a
stake driven through them; those who intentionally or accidentally drowned [in *floods* or deep
water] would be condemned to wander disconsolately for lack of burial rights.)   388 *for aye:*
Forever.   390 *the Morning's love:* Cephalus, a beautiful youth beloved by Aurora; or perhaps
the goddess of the dawn herself.   391 *forester:* Keeper of a royal forest.   400 *Goblin:* Hobgoblin (Puck refers to himself).   403 *drawn:* With drawn sword.   404 *straight:* Immediately.   405 *plainer:* More open.   *Lysander wanders about:* (Lysander may exit here, but
perhaps not; neither exit nor reentrance is indicated in the early texts.)   410 *recreant:* Cowardly wretch.   413 *try:* Test.

The villain is much lighter-heeled than I.
I followed fast, but faster he did fly,
That fallen am I in dark uneven way,
And here will rest me. *[He lies down.]* Come, thou gentle day!
For if but once thou show me thy gray light,   420
I'll find Demetrius and revenge this spite. *[He sleeps.]*

[Enter] Robin [Puck] and Demetrius.

Puck: Ho, ho, ho! Coward, why com'st thou not?
Demetrius: Abide° me, if thou dar'st; for well I wot°
  Thou runn'st before me, shifting every place,
  And dar'st not stand nor look me in the face.   425
  Where art thou now?
Puck: Come hither. I am here.
Demetrius: Nay, then, thou mock'st me. Thou shalt buy° this dear,°
  If ever I thy face by daylight see.
  Now go thy way. Faintness constraineth me
  To measure out my length on this cold bed.   430
  By day's approach look to be visited.   *[He lies down and sleeps.]*

Enter Helena.

Helena: O weary night, O long and tedious night,
    Abate° thy hours! Shine comforts from the east,
  That I may back to Athens by daylight
    From these that my poor company detest;   435
  And sleep, that sometimes shuts up sorrow's eye,
    Steal me awhile from mine own company.   *[She lies down and] sleep[s].*
Puck: Yet but three? Come one more;
    Two of both kinds makes up four.
    Here she comes, curst° and sad.   440
    Cupid is a knavish lad,
    Thus to make poor females mad.

  [Enter Hermia.]

Hermia: Never so weary, never so in woe,
    Bedabbled with the dew and torn with briers,
  I can no further crawl, no further go;   445
    My legs can keep no pace with my desires.
  Here will I rest me till the break of day.
  Heavens shield Lysander, if they mean a fray!   *[She lies down and sleeps.]*
Puck: On the ground
    Sleep sound.   450
    I'll apply
    To your eye,
  Gentle lover, remedy.   *[He squeezes the juice on Lysander's eyes.]*
    When thou wak'st,
    Thou tak'st   455
    True delight

---

423 *Abide:* Confront, face; *wot:* know.   427 *buy:* Aby, pay for; *dear:* Dearly.   433 *Abate:*
Lessen, shorten.   440 *curst:* Ill-tempered.

In the sight
Of thy former lady's eye;
And the country proverb known,
That every man should take his own,   460
In your waking shall be shown:
   Jack shall have Jill;°
   Naught shall go ill;
The man shall have his mare again, and all shall be well.

       [Exit. The four sleeping lovers remain.]

[ACT IV

SCENE I: *The wood. The lovers are still asleep onstage.*]

Enter [Titania,] Queen of Fairies, and [Bottom the] clown, and Fairies; and [Oberon,] the King, behind them.

Titania: Come, sit thee down upon this flowery bed,
   While I thy amiable° cheeks do coy,°
And stick muskroses in thy sleek smooth head,
   And kiss thy fair large ears, my gentle joy.   *[They recline.]*
Bottom: Where's Peaseblossom?   5
Peaseblossom: Ready.
Bottom: Scratch my head, Peaseblossom. Where's Monsieur Cobweb?
Cobweb: Ready.
Bottom: Monsieur Cobweb, good monsieur, get you your weapons in your
   hand, and kill me a red-hipped humble-bee on the top of a thistle; and,   10
   good monsieur, bring me the honey bag. Do not fret yourself too much
   in the action, monsieur; and, good monsieur, have a care the honey bag
   break not. I would be loath to have you overflown with a honey bag,
   signor. *[Exit Cobweb.]* Where's Monsieur Mustardseed?
Mustardseed: Ready.   15
Bottom: Give me your neaf,° Monsieur Mustardseed. Pray you, leave your
   courtesy,° good monsieur.
Mustardseed: What's your will?
Bottom: Nothing, good monsieur, but to help Cavalery° Cobweb° to scratch.
   I must to the barber's, monsieur, for methinks I am marvelous hairy about   20
   the face; and I am such a tender ass, if my hair do but tickle me I must
   scratch.
Titania: What, wilt thou hear some music, my sweet love?
Bottom: I have a reasonable good ear in music. Let's have the tongs and
   the bones.°   *[Music: tongs, rural music.°]*   25

---

462 *Jack shall have Jill:* (Proverbial for "boy gets girl.")   **Act IV, Scene I.**   2 *amiable:*
Lovely; *coy:* Caress.   16 *neaf:* Fist.   16–17 *leave your courtesy:* I.e., stop bowing, or put
on your hat.   19 *Cavalery:* Cavalier (form of address for a gentleman); *Cobweb:* (Seemingly
an error, since Cobweb has been sent to bring honey, while Peaseblossom has been asked to
scratch.)   24–25 *tongs . . . bones:* Instruments for rustic music (the tongs were played like a
triangle, whereas the bones were held between the fingers and used as clappers).   *Music . . .*
music: (This stage direction is added from the Folio.)

Titania: Or say, sweet love, what thou desirest to eat.

Bottom: Truly, a peck of provender.° I could munch your good dry oats. Methinks I have a great desire to a bottle° of hay. Good hay, sweet hay, hath no fellow.°

Titania: I have a venturous fairy that shall seek 30
The squirrel's hoard, and fetch thee new nuts.

Bottom: I had rather have a handful or two of dried peas. But, I pray you, let none of your people stir° me. I have an exposition of° sleep come upon me.

Titania: Sleep thou, and I will wind thee in my arms. 35
Fairies, begone, and be all ways° away. *[Exeunt Fairies.]*
So doth the woodbine° the sweet honeysuckle
Gently entwist; the female ivy so
Enrings the barky fingers of the elm.
O, how I love thee! How I dote on thee! *[They sleep.]* 40

Enter Robin Goodfellow [Puck].

Oberon [coming forward]: Welcome, good Robin. Seest thou this sweet sight?
Her dotage now I do begin to pity.
For, meeting her of late behind the wood
Seeking sweet favors° for this hateful fool,
I did upbraid her and fall out with her. 45
For she his hairy temples then had rounded
With coronet of fresh and fragrant flowers;
And that same dew, which sometime° on the buds
Was wont to swell like round and orient pearls,°
Stood now within the pretty flowerets' eyes 50
Like tears that did their own disgrace bewail.
When I had at my pleasure taunted her,
And she in mild terms begged my patience,
I then did ask of her her changeling child,
Which straight she gave me, and her fairy sent 55
To bear him to my bower in Fairyland.
And, now I have the boy, I will undo
This hateful imperfection of her eyes.
And, gentle Puck, take this transformèd scalp
From off the head of this Athenian swain, 60
That he, awaking when the other° do,
May all to Athens back again repair,°
And think no more of this night's accidents
But as the fierce vexation of a dream.
But first I will release the Fairy Queen. 65
[He squeezes an herb on her eyes.]

---

27 *peck of provender:* One-quarter bushel of grain.   28 *bottle:* Bundle.   29 *fellow:* Equal.   33 *stir:* Disturb; *exposition of:* (Bottom's phrase for "disposition to.")   36 *all ways:* In all directions.   37 *woodbine:* Bindweed, a climbing plant that twines in the opposite direction from that of honeysuckle.   44 *favors:* I.e., gifts of flowers.   48 *sometime:* Formerly.   49 *orient pearls:* I.e., the most beautiful of all pearls, those coming from the Orient.   61 *other:* Others.   62 *repair:* Return.

Be as thou wast wont to be;
See as thou wast wont to see.
Dian's bud° o'er Cupid's flower
Hath such force and blessèd power.
Now, my Titania, wake you, my sweet queen.   70
Titania [awaking]: My Oberon! What visions have I seen!
    Methought I was enamored of an ass.
Oberon: There lies your love.
Titania: How came these things to pass?
    O, how mine eyes do loathe his visage now!
Oberon: Silence awhile. Robin, take off this head.   75
    Titania, music call, and strike more dead
    Than common sleep of all these five° the sense.
Titania: Music, ho! Music, such as charmeth° sleep!   *[Music.]*
Puck [removing the ass head]: Now, when thou wak'st, with thine own fool's
    eyes peep.
Oberon: Sound, music! Come, my queen, take hands with me,   80
    And rock the ground whereon these sleepers be.   *[They dance.]*
    Now thou and I are new in amity,
    And will tomorrow midnight solemnly°
    Dance in Duke Theseus' house triumphantly,
    And bless it to all fair prosperity.   85
    There shall the pairs of faithful lovers be
    Wedded, with Theseus, all in jollity.
Puck: Fairy King, attend, and mark:
    I do hear the morning lark.
Oberon: Then, my queen, in silence sad,°   90
    Trip we after night's shade.
    We the globe can compass soon,
    Swifter than the wandering moon.
Titania: Come, my lord, and in our flight
    Tell me how it came this night   95
    That I sleeping here was found
    With these mortals on the ground.
            Exeunt [Oberon, Titania, and Puck]. Wind horn [within].

    Enter Theseus and all his train; [Hippolyta, Egeus].

Theseus: Go, one of you, find out the forester,
    For now our observation° is performed;
    And since we have the vaward° of the day,   100
    My love shall hear the music of my hounds.
    Uncouple° in the western valley; let them go.
    Dispatch, I say, and find the forester.   *[Exit an Attendant.]*
    We will, fair queen, up to the mountain's top

---

68 *Dian's bud:* (Perhaps the flower of the *agnus castus* or chaste-tree, supposed to preserve chastity; or perhaps referring simply to Oberon's herb by which he can undo the effects of "Cupid's flower," the love-in-idleness of II.i.166–168.)   77 *these five:* I.e., the four lovers and Bottom.   78 *charmeth:* Brings about, as though by a charm.   83 *solemnly:* Ceremoniously.   90 *sad:* Sober.   99 *observation:* I.e., observance to a morn of May (I.i.167). 100 *vaward:* Vanguard, i.e., earliest part.   102 *Uncouple:* Set free for the hunt.

And mark the musical confusion   105
Of hounds and echo in conjunction.
Hippolyta: I was with Hercules and Cadmus° once
When in a wood of Crete they bayed° the bear
With hounds of Sparta.° Never did I hear
Such gallant chiding;° for, besides the groves,   110
The skies, the fountains, every region near
Seemed all one mutual cry. I never heard
So musical a discord, such sweet thunder.
Theseus: My hounds are bred out of the Spartan kind,°
So flewed,° so sanded,° and their heads are hung   115
With ears that sweep away the morning dew;
Crook-kneed, and dewlapped° like Thessalian bulls;
Slow in pursuit, but matched in mouth like bells,
Each under each.° A cry° more tunable°
Was never holloed to nor cheered° with horn   120
In Crete, in Sparta, nor in Thessaly.
Judge when you hear. *[He sees the sleepers.]* But soft!° What nymphs
     are these?
Egeus: My lord, this is my daughter here asleep,
And this Lysander; this Demetrius is;
This Helena, old Nedar's Helena.   125
I wonder of° their being here together.
Theseus: No doubt they rose up early to observe
The rite of May, and hearing our intent,
Came here in grace of our solemnity.°
But speak, Egeus. Is not this the day   130
That Hermia should give answer of her choice?
Egeus: It is, my lord.
Theseus: Go bid the huntsmen wake them with their horns.

                       [Exit an Attendant.]

Shout within. Wind horns. They all start up.

Good morrow, friends. Saint Valentine° is past.
Begin these woodbirds but to couple now?   135
Lysander: Pardon, my lord.   *[They kneel.]*
Theseus: I pray you all, stand up.   *[They stand.]*
I know you two are rival enemies;
How comes this gentle concord in the world,
That hatred is so far from jealousy°
To sleep by hate and fear no enmity?   140

---

107 *Cadmus:* Mythical founder of Thebes. (This story about him is unknown.)   108 *bayed:* Brought to bay.   109 *hounds of Sparta:* (A breed famous in antiquity for their hunting skill.) 110 *chiding:* I.e., yelping.   114 *kind:* Strain, breed.   115 *So flewed:* Similarly having large hanging chaps or fleshy covering of the jaw; *sanded:* Of sandy color.   117 *dewlapped:* Having pendulous folds of skin under the neck.   118–119 *matched . . . each:* I.e., harmoniously matched in their various cries like a set of bells, from treble down to bass; *cry:* Pack of hounds; *tunable:* Well tuned, melodious.   120 *cheered:* Encouraged.   122 *soft:* I.e., gently, wait a minute.   126 *wonder of:* Wonder at.   129 *in . . . solemnity:* In honor of our wedding ceremony.   134 *Saint Valentine:* (Birds were supposed to choose their mates on Saint Valentine's Day.)   139 *jealousy:* Suspicion.

Lysander: My lord, I shall reply amazedly,
    Half sleep, half waking; but as yet, I swear,
    I cannot truly say how I came here.
    But, as I think — for truly would I speak,
    And now I do bethink me, so it is —   145
    I came with Hermia hither. Our intent
    Was to be gone from Athens, where° we might,
    Without° the peril of the Athenian law —
Egeus: Enough, enough, my lord; you have enough.
    I beg the law, the law, upon his head.   150
    They would have stol'n away; they would, Demetrius,
    Thereby to have defeated° you and me,
    You of your wife and me of my consent,
    Of my consent that she should be your wife.
Demetrius: My lord, fair Helen told me of their stealth,   155
    Of this their purpose hither° to this wood,
    And I in fury hither followed them,
    Fair Helena in fancy° following me.
    But, my good lord, I wot not by what power —
    But by some power it is — my love to Hermia,   160
    Melted as the snow, seems to me now
    As the remembrance of an idle gaud°
    Which in my childhood I did dote upon;
    And all the faith, the virtue of my heart,
    The object and the pleasure of mine eye,   165
    Is only Helena. To her, my lord,
    Was I betrothed ere I saw Hermia,
    But like a sickness did I loathe this food;
    But, as in health, come to my natural taste,
    Now I do wish it, love it, long for it,   170
    And will forevermore be true to it.
Theseus: Fair lovers, you are fortunately met.
    Of this discourse we more will hear anon.
    Egeus, I will overbear your will;
    For in the temple, by and by, with us   175
    These couples shall eternally be knit.
    And, for° the morning now is something° worn,
    Our purposed hunting shall be set aside.
    Away with us to Athens. Three and three,
    We'll hold a feast in great solemnity.°   180
    Come Hippolyta.   *[Exeunt Theseus, Hippolyta, Egeus, and train.]*
Demetrius: These things seem small and undistinguishable,
    Like far-off mountains turnèd into clouds.
Hermia: Methinks I see these things with parted° eye,
    When everything seems double.

---

147 *where:* Wherever; or, to where.   148 *Without:* Outside of, beyond.   152 *defeated:*
Defrauded.   156 *hither:* In coming hither.   158 *in fancy:* Driven by love.   162 *idle
gaud:* Worthless trinket.   177 *for:* Since; *something:* Somewhat.   180 *in great solemnity:*
With great ceremony.   184 *parted:* I.e., improperly focused.

Helena: So methinks; 185
And I have found Demetrius like a jewel,
Mine own, and not mine own.°
Demetrius: Are you sure
That we are awake? It seems to me
That yet we sleep, we dream. Do not you think
The Duke was here, and bid us follow him? 190
Hermia: Yea, and my father.
Helena: And Hippolyta.
Lysander: And he did bid us follow to the temple.
Demetrius: Why, then, we are awake. Let's follow him,
And by the way let us recount our dreams. *[Exeunt the lovers.]*
Bottom [awaking]: When my cue comes, call me, and I will answer. My 195
next is "Most fair Pyramus." Heigh-ho! Peter Quince! Flute, the bellows mender! Snout, the tinker! Starveling! God's° my life, stolen
hence and left me asleep! I have had a most rare vision. I have had a
dream, past the wit of man to say what dream it was. Man is but an ass
if he go about° to expound this dream. Methought I was — there is no 200
man can tell what. Methought I was — and methought I had — but
man is but a patched° fool if he will offer° to say what methought I
had. The eye of man hath not heard, the ear of man hath not seen,
man's hand is not able to taste, his tongue to conceive, nor his heart
to report° what my dream was. I will get Peter Quince to write a bal- 205
lad° of this dream. It shall be called "Bottom's Dream," because it hath
no bottom;° and I will sing it in the latter end of a play, before the
Duke. Peradventure, to make it the more gracious, I shall sing it at her°
death. *[Exit.]*

[SCENE II: *Athens.*]

Enter Quince, Flute, [Snout, and Starveling].

Quince: Have you sent to Bottom's house? Is he come home yet?
Starveling: He cannot be heard of. Out of doubt he is transported.°
Flute: If he come not, then the play is marred. It goes not forward. Doth it?
Quince: It is not possible. You have not a man in all Athens able to dis-
charge° Pyramus but he. 5
Flute: No, he hath simply the best wit° of any handicraft man in Athens.
Quince: Yea, and the best person° too, and he is a very paramour for a sweet
voice.
Flute: You must say "paragon." A paramour is, God bless us, a thing of
naught.° 10

186–187 *like . . . mine own:* I.e., like a jewel that one finds by chance and therefore possesses
but cannot certainly consider one's own property. 197 *God's:* May God save. 200 *go
about:* Attempt. 202 *patched:* Wearing motley, i.e., a dress of various colors; *offer:* Venture.
203–205 *The eye . . . report:* (Bottom garbles the terms of 1 Corinthians 2:9.) 206 *ballad:*
(The proper medium for relating sensational stories and preposterous events.) 207 *hath no
bottom:* Is unfathomable. 209 *her:* Thisbe's (?). **Scene II.** 2 *transported:* Carried off
by fairies; or, possibly, transformed. 5 *discharge:* Perform. 6 *wit:* Intellect. 7 *person:*
Appearance. 9–10 *a . . . naught:* A shameful thing.

Enter Snug the joiner.

Snug: Masters, the Duke is coming from the temple, and there is two or
three lords and ladies more married. If our sport had gone forward,
we had all been made men.°

Flute: O sweet bully Bottom! Thus hath he lost sixpence a day° during his
life; he could not have scaped sixpence a day. An the Duke had not given   15
him sixpence a day for playing Pyramus, I'll be hanged. He would have
deserved it. Sixpence a day in Pyramus, or nothing.

Enter Bottom.

Bottom: Where are these lads? Where are these hearts?°

Quince: Bottom! O most courageous day! O most happy hour!

Bottom: Masters, I am to discourse wonders.° But ask me not what; for if   20
I tell you, I am no true Athenian. I will tell you everything, right as it
fell out.

Quince: Let us hear, sweet Bottom.

Bottom: Not a word of° me. All that I will tell you is that the Duke hath
dined. Get your apparel together, good strings° to your beards, new   25
ribbons to your pumps;° meet presently° at the palace; every man
look o'er his part; for the short and the long is, our play is preferred.°
In any case, let Thisbe have clean linen; and let not him that plays the
lion pare his nails, for they shall hang out for the lion's claws. And,
most dear actors, eat no onions nor garlic, for we are to utter sweet   30
breath; and I do not doubt but to hear them say it is a sweet comedy.
No more words. Away! Go, away!   *[Exeunt.]*

[ACT V

Scene I: *Athens. The palace of Theseus.*]

Enter Theseus, Hippolyta, and Philostrate, [lords, and attendants].

Hippolyta: 'Tis strange, my Theseus, that° these lovers speak of.

Theseus: More strange than true. I never may° believe
These antique° fables nor these fairy toys.°
Lovers and madmen have such seething brains,
Such shaping fantasies,° that apprehend°   5
More than cool reason ever comprehends.°
The lunatic, the lover, and the poet
Are of imagination all compact.°
One sees more devils than vast hell can hold;
That is the madman. The lover, all as frantic,   10

---

13 *we ... men:* I.e., we would have had our fortunes made.   14 *sixpence a day:* I.e., as a royal
pension.   18 *hearts:* Good fellows.   20 *am ... wonders:* Have wonders to relate.   24 *of:*
Out of.   25 *strings:* (To attach the beards.)   26 *pumps:* Light shoes or slippers; *presently:*
Immediately.   27 *preferred:* Selected for consideration.   **Act V, Scene I.**   1 *that:* That
which.   2 *may:* Can.   3 *antique:* Old-fashioned (punning, too, on *antic,* "strange,"
"grotesque"); *fairy toys:* Trifling stories about fairies.   5 *fantasies:* Imaginations; *apprehend:*
Conceive, imagine.   6 *comprehends:* Understands.   8 *compact:* Formed, composed.

Sees Helen's° beauty in a brow of Egypt.°
The poet's eye, in a fine frenzy rolling,
Doth glance from heaven to earth, from earth to heaven;
And as imagination bodies forth
The forms of things unknown, the poet's pen   15
Turns them to shapes and gives to airy nothing
A local habitation and a name.
Such tricks hath strong imagination
That, if it would but apprehend some joy,
It comprehends some bringer° of that joy;   20
Or in the night, imagining some fear,°
How easy is a bush supposed a bear!

Hippolyta: But all the story of the night told over,
And all their minds transfigured so together,
More witnesseth than fancy's images°   25
And grows to something of great constancy;°
But, howsoever,° strange and admirable.°

Enter lovers: Lysander, Demetrius, Hermia, and Helena.

Theseus: Here come the lovers, full of joy and mirth.
Joy, gentle friends! Joy and fresh days of love
Accompany your hearts!

Lysander: More than to us   30
Wait in your royal walks, your board, your bed!

Theseus: Come now, what masques,° what dances shall we have,
To wear away this long age of three hours
Between our after-supper and bedtime?
Where is our usual manager of mirth?   35
What revels are in hand? Is there no play
To ease the anguish of a torturing hour?
Call Philostrate.

Philostrate: Here, mighty Theseus.

Theseus: Say, what abridgment° have you for this evening?
What masque? What music? How shall we beguile   40
The lazy time, if not with some delight?

Philostrate [giving him a paper]: There is a brief° how many sports are ripe.
Make choice of which Your Highness will see first.

Theseus [reads.]: "The battle with the Centaurs,° to be sung
By an Athenian eunuch to the harp"?   45
We'll none of that. That have I told my love,
In glory of my kinsman° Hercules.

---

11 *Helen's:* I.e., of Helen of Troy, pattern of beauty; *brow of Egypt:* I.e., face of a gypsy.
20 *bringer:* I.e., source.   21 *fear:* Object of fear.   25 *More . . . images:* Testifies to something
more substantial than mere imaginings.   26 *constancy:* Certainty.   27 *howsoever:* In any
case; *admirable:* A source of wonder.   32 *masques:* Courtly entertainments.   39 *abridgment:*
Pastime (to abridge or shorten the evening).   42 *brief:* Short written statement, summary.
44 *battle . . . Centaurs:* (Probably refers to the battle of the Centaurs and the Lapithae,
when the Centaurs attempted to carry off Hippodamia, bride of Theseus' friend Pirothous.
The story is told in Ovid's *Metamorphoses* 12.)   47 *kinsman:* (Plutarch's "Life of Theseus"
states that Hercules and Theseus were near kinsmen. Theseus is referring to a version of the
battle of the Centaurs in which Hercules was said to be present.)

[He reads.] "The riot of the tipsy Bacchanals,
Tearing the Thracian singer in their rage"?°
That is an old device;° and it was played   50
When I from Thebes came last a conqueror.
[He reads.] "The thrice three Muses mourning for the death
Of Learning, late deceased in beggary"?°
That is some satire, keen and critical,
Not sorting with° a nuptial ceremony.   55
[He reads.] "A tedious brief scene of young Pyramus
And his love Thisbe; very tragical mirth"?
Merry and tragical? Tedious and brief?
That is, hot ice and wondrous strange° snow.
How shall we find the concord of this discord?   60
Philostrate: A play there is, my lord, some ten words long,
    Which is as brief as I have known a play;
    But by ten words, my lord, it is too long,
    Which makes it tedious. For in all the play
    There is not one word apt, one player fitted.   65
    And tragical, my noble lord, it is,
    For Pyramus therein doth kill himself.
    Which, when I saw rehearsed, I must confess,
    Made mine eyes water; but more merry tears
    The passion of loud laughter never shed.   70
Theseus: What are they that do play it?
Philostrate: Hardhanded men that work in Athens here,
    Which never labored in their minds till now,
    And now have toiled° their unbreathed° memories
    With this same play, against° your nuptial.   75
Theseus: And we will hear it.
Philostrate: No, my noble lord,
    It is not for you. I have heard it over,
    And it is nothing, nothing in the world;
    Unless you can find sport in their intents,
    Extremely stretched° and conned° with cruel pain   80
    To do you service.
Theseus: I will hear that play;
    For never anything can be amiss
    When simpleness° and duty tender it.
    Go, bring them in; and take your places, ladies.
                        [Philostrate goes to summon the players.]
Hippolyta: I love not to see wretchedness o'ercharged,°   85
    And duty in his service° perishing.

48–49 *The riot . . . rage:* (This was the story of the death of Orpheus, as told in *Metamorphoses* 11.)   50 *device:* Show, performance.   52–53 *The thrice . . . beggary:* (Possibly an allusion to Spenser's *Teares of the Muses,* 1591, though "satires" deploring the neglect of learning and the creative arts were commonplace.)   55 *sorting with:* Befitting.   59 *strange:* (Sometimes emended to an adjective that would contrast with *snow,* just as *hot* contrasts with *ice.*)   74 *toiled:* Taxed; *unbreathed:* Unexercised.   75 *against:* In preparation for.   80 *stretched:* Strained; *conned:* Memorized.   83 *simpleness:* Simplicity.   85 *wretchedness o'ercharged:* Social or intellectual inferiors overburdened.   86 *his service:* Its attempt to serve.

Theseus: Why, gentle sweet, you shall see no such thing.
Hippolyta: He says they can do nothing in this kind.°
Theseus: The kinder we, to give them thanks for nothing.
    Our sport shall be to take what they mistake;   90
    And what poor duty cannot do, noble respect°
    Takes it in might, not merit.°
    Where I have come, great clerks° have purposèd
    To greet me with premeditated welcomes;
    Where I have seen them shiver and look pale,   95
    Make periods in the midst of sentences,
    Throttle their practiced accent° in their fears,
    And in conclusion dumbly have broke off,
    Not paying me a welcome. Trust me, sweet,
    Out of this silence yet I picked a welcome;   100
    And in the modesty of fearful duty
    I read as much as from the rattling tongue
    Of saucy and audacious eloquence.
    Love, therefore, and tongue-tied simplicity
    In least° speak most, to my capacity.°   105

    [Philostrate returns.]

Philostrate: So please Your Grace, the Prologue° is addressed.°
Theseus: Let him approach.   *[A flourish of trumpets.]*

    Enter the Prologue [Quince].

Prologue: If we offend, it is with our good will.
    That you should think, we come not to offend,
    But with good will. To show our simple skill,   110
    That is the true beginning of our end.
    Consider, then, we come but in despite.
    We do not come, as minding° to content you,
    Our true intent is. All for your delight
    We are not here. That you should here repent you,   115
    The actors are at hand; and, by their show,
    You shall know all that you are like to know.
Theseus: This fellow doth not stand upon points.°
Lysander: He hath rid° his prologue like a rough° colt; he knows not the
    stop.° A good moral, my lord: it is not enough to speak, but to speak 120
    true.
Hippolyta: Indeed, he hath played on his prologue like a child on a recorder:°
    a sound, but not in government.°

---

88 *kind:* Kind of thing.　　91 *respect:* Evaluation, consideration.　　92 *Takes . . . merit:* Values it for the effort made rather than for the excellence achieved.　　93 *clerks:* Learned men.
97 *practiced accent:* I.e., rehearsed speech; or, usual way of speaking.　　105 *least:* I.e., saying least; *to my capacity:* In my judgment and understanding.　　106 *Prologue:* Speaker of the prologue; *addressed:* Ready.　　113 *minding:* Intending.　　118 *stand upon points:* (1) Heed niceties or small points, (2) pay attention to punctuation in his reading. (The humor of Quince's speech is in the blunders of its punctuation.)　　119 *rid:* Ridden; *rough:* unbroken.　　120 *stop:* (1) Stopping of a colt by reining it in, (2) punctuation mark.　　123 *recorder:* Wind instrument like a flute; *government:* Control.

Theseus: His speech was like a tangled chain: nothing° impaired, but all
  disordered. Who is next?   125

  Enter Pyramus [Bottom], and Thisbe [Flute], and Wall [Snout], and
  Moonshine [Starveling], and Lion [Snug].

Prologue: Gentles, perchance you wonder at this show;
    But wonder on, till truth make all things plain.
  This man is Pyramus, if you would know;
    This beauteous lady Thisbe is, certain.
  This man with lime and roughcast doth present   130
    Wall, that vile wall which did these lovers sunder;
  And through Wall's chink, poor souls, they are content
    To whisper. At the which let no man wonder.
  This man, with lantern, dog, and bush of thorn,
    Presenteth Moonshine; for, if you will know,   135
  By moonshine did these lovers think no scorn°
    To meet at Ninus' tomb, there, there to woo.
  This grisly beast, which Lion hight° by name,
    The trusty Thisbe coming first by night
  Did scare away, or rather did affright;   140
    And as she fled, her mantle she did fall,°
  Which Lion vile with bloody mouth did stain.
    Anon comes Pyramus, sweet youth and tall,°
  And finds his trusty Thisbe's mantle slain;
  Whereat, with blade, with bloody, blameful blade,   145
    He bravely broached° his boiling bloody breast.
  And Thisbe, tarrying in mulberry shade,
    His dagger drew, and died. For all the rest,
  Let Lion, Moonshine, Wall, and lovers twain
  At large° discourse, while here they do remain.   150
                       Exeunt Lion, Thisbe, and Moonshine.

Theseus: I wonder if the lion be to speak.

Demetrius: No wonder, my lord. One lion may, when many asses do.

Wall: In this same interlude° it doth befall
  That I, one Snout by name, present a wall;
  And such a wall as I would have you think   155
  That had in it a crannied hole or chink,
  Through which the lovers, Pyramus and Thisbe,
  Did whisper often, very secretly.
  This loam, this roughcast, and this stone doth show
  That I am that same wall; the truth is so.   160
  And this the cranny is, right and sinister,°
  Through which the fearful lovers are to whisper.

Theseus: Would you desire lime and hair to speak better?

Demetrius: It is the wittiest partition° that ever I heard discourse, my lord.

  [Pyramus comes forward.]

124 *nothing:* Not at all.   136 *think no scorn:* Think it no disgraceful matter.   138 *hight:* Is
called.   141 *fall:* Let fall.   143 *tall:* Courageous.   146 *broached:* Stabbed.   150 *At large:*
In full, at length.   153 *interlude:* Play.   161 *right and sinister:* I.e., the right side of it and
the left; or, running from right to left, horizontally.   164 *partition:* (1) Wall, (2) section of a
learned treatise or oration.

Theseus: Pyramus draws near the wall. Silence!   165
Pyramus: O grim-looked° night! O night with hue so black!
     O night, which ever art when day is not!
O night, O night! Alack, alack, alack,
     I fear my Thisbe's promise is forgot.
And thou, O wall, O sweet, O lovely wall,   170
     That stand'st between her father's ground and mine,
Thou wall, O wall, O sweet and lovely wall,
     Show me thy chink, to blink through with mine eyne.
Thanks, courteous wall. Jove shield thee well for this.
     But what see I? No Thisbe do I see.   175
O wicked wall, through whom I see no bliss!
     Cursed be thy stones for thus deceiving me!
Theseus: The wall, methinks, being sensible,° should curse again.°
Pyramus: No, in truth, sir, he should not. "Deceiving me" is Thisbe's cue:
she is to enter now, and I am to spy her through the wall. You shall see,   180
it will fall pat° as I told you. Yonder she comes.

     Enter Thisbe.

Thisbe: O wall, full often hast thou heard my moans
     For parting my fair Pyramus and me.
My cherry lips have often kissed thy stones,
     Thy stones with lime and hair knit up in thee.   185
Pyramus: I see a voice. Now will I to the chink,
     To spy an° I can hear my Thisbe's face.
     Thisbe!
Thisbe: My love! Thou art my love, I think.
Pyramus: Think what thou wilt, I am thy lover's grace,°   190
     And like Limander° am I trusty still.
Thisbe: And I like Helen,° till the Fates me kill.
Pyramus: Not Shafalus to Procrus° was so true.
Thisbe: As Shafalus to Procrus, I to you.
Pyramus: O, kiss me through the hole of this vile wall!   195
Thisbe: I kiss the wall's hole, not your lips at all.
Pyramus: Wilt thou at Ninny's tomb meet me straightway?
Thisbe: 'Tide life, 'tide° death, I come without delay.
                      [Exeunt Pyramus and Thisbe.]
Wall: Thus have I, Wall, my part dischargèd so;
     And, being done, thus Wall away doth go.   *[Exit.]* 200
Theseus: Now is the mural down between the two neighbors.
Demetrius: No remedy, my lord, when walls are so willful° to hear without
     warning.°
Hippolyta: This is the silliest stuff that ever I heard.

---

166 *grim-looked:* Grim-looking.   178 *sensible:* Capable of feeling; *again:* In return.   181 *pat:*
Exactly.   187 *an:* If.   190 *lover's grace:* I.e., gracious lover.   191–192 *Limander, Helen:*
(Blunders for "Leander" and "Hero.")   193 *Shafalus, Procrus:* (Blunders for "Cephalus" and
"Procris," also famous lovers.)   198 *'tide:* Betide, come.   202 *willful:* Willing.   202–203 *without
warning:* I.e., without warning the parents. (Demetrius makes a joke on the proverb "Walls have
ears.")

Theseus: The best in this kind° are but shadows,° and the worst are no   205
    worse, if imagination amend them.
Hippolyta: It must be your imagination then, and not theirs.
Theseus: If we imagine no worse of them than they of themselves, they may
    pass for excellent men. Here come two noble beasts in, a man and a
    lion.   210

Enter Lion and Moonshine.

Lion: You, ladies, you, whose gentle hearts do fear
    The smallest monstrous mouse that creeps on floor,
May now perchance both quake and tremble here,
    When lion rough in wildest rage doth roar.
Then know that I, as Snug the joiner, am   215
A lion fell,° nor else no lion's dam;
For, if I should as lion come in strife
Into this place, 'twere pity on my life.
Theseus: A very gentle beast, and of a good conscience.
Demetrius: The very best at a beast, my lord, that e'er I saw.   220
Lysander: This lion is a very fox for his valor.°
Theseus: True; and a goose for his discretion.°
Demetrius: Not so, my lord, for his valor cannot carry his discretion, and the
    fox carries the goose.
Theseus: His discretion, I am sure, cannot carry his valor; for the goose   225
    carries not the fox. It is well. Leave it to his discretion, and let us listen
    to the moon.
Moon: This lanthorn° doth the hornèd moon present—
Demetrius: He should have worn the horns on his head.°
Theseus: He is no crescent,° and his horns are invisible within the cir-   230
    cumference.
Moon: This lanthorn doth the hornèd moon present;
    Myself the man i' the moon do seem to be.
Theseus: This is the greatest error of all the rest. The man should be put
    into the lanthorn. How is it else the man i' the moon?   235
Demetrius: He dares not come there for° the candle, for you see it is already
    in snuff.°
Hippolyta: I am weary of this moon. Would he would change!
Theseus: It appears, by his small light of discretion, that he is in the wane;
    but yet, in courtesy, in all reason, we must stay the time.   240
Lysander: Proceed, Moon.
Moon: All that I have to say is to tell you that the lanthorn is the moon, I,
    the man i' the moon, this thornbush my thornbush, and this dog my
    dog.

---

205 *in this kind:* Of this sort; *shadows:* Likenesses, representations.   216 *lion fell:* Fierce
lion (with a play on the idea of "lion skin").   221 *is . . . valor:* I.e., his valor consists of crafti-
ness and discretion.   222 *a goose . . . discretion:* I.e., as discreet as a goose, that is, more foolish than discreet.   228 *lanthorn:* (This original spelling, *lanthorn,* may suggest a play on the
horn of which lanterns were made and also on a cuckold's horns; however, the spelling *lanthorn*
is not used consistently for comic effect in this play or elsewhere. At Act V, Scene I, line 134, for
example, the word is *lantern* in the original.)   229 *on his head:* (As a sign of cuckoldry.)
230 *crescent:* A waxing moon.   236 *for:* Because of, for fear of.   237 *in snuff:* (1) Offended,
(2) in need of snuffing or trimming.

Demetrius: Why, all these should be in the lanthorn, for all these are in   245
    the moon. But silence! Here comes Thisbe.

Enter Thisbe.

Thisbe: This is old Ninny's tomb. Where is my love?
Lion [roaring]: O!
Demetrius: Well roared, Lion.   *[Thisbe runs off, dropping her mantle.]*
Theseus: Well run, Thisbe.   250
Hippolyta: Well shone, Moon. Truly, the moon shines with a good grace.
                                    [The Lion worries Thisbe's mantle.]
Theseus: Well moused,° Lion.

[Enter Pyramus; exit Lion.]

Demetrius: And then came Pyramus.
Lysander: And so the Lion vanished.
Pyramus: Sweet Moon, I thank thee for thy sunny beams;   255
    I thank thee, Moon, for shining now so bright;
    For, by thy gracious, golden, glittering gleams,
    I trust to take of truest Thisbe sight.
        But stay, O spite!
        But mark, poor knight,   260
    What dreadful dole° is here?
        Eyes, do you see?
        How can it be?
    O dainty duck! O dear!
        Thy mantle good,   265
        What, stained with blood?
    Approach, ye Furies° fell!°
        O Fates,° come, come,
        Cut thread and thrum;°
    Quail,° crush, conclude, and quell!°   270
Theseus: This passion, and the death of a dear friend, would go near to make
    a man look sad.°
Hippolyta: Beshrew my heart, but I pity the man.
Pyramus: O, wherefore, Nature, didst thou lions frame?
    Since lion vile hath here deflowered my dear,   275
    Which is — no, no, which was — the fairest dame
    That lived, that loved, that liked, that looked with cheer.°
        Come, tears, confound,
        Out, sword, and wound
    The pap° of Pyramus;   280
        Ay, that left pap,
        Where heart doth hop.   *[He stabs himself.]*
    Thus die I, thus, thus, thus.

252 *moused:* Shaken, torn, bitten.   261 *dole:* Grievous event.   267 *Furies:* Avenging
goddesses of Greek myth; *fell:* Fierce.   268 *Fates:* The three goddesses (Clotho, Lachesis,
Atropos) of Greek myth who spun, drew, and cut the thread of human life.   269 *thread and
thrum:* I.e., everything — the good and bad alike; literally, the warp in weaving and the loose
end of the warp.   270 *Quail:* Overpower; *quell:* Kill, destroy.   271–272 *This . . . sad:* I.e.,
if one had other reason to grieve, one might be sad, but not from this absurd portrayal of passion.   277 *cheer:* Countenance.   280 *pap:* Breast.

Now am I dead,
　Now am I fled;　　　　　　　　　　　　　　　　　　　285
My soul is in the sky.
　Tongue, lose thy light;
　Moon, take thy flight.　　　　　　　*[Exit Moonshine.]*
Now die, die, die, die, die.　　　　　　　　*[Pyramus dies.]*
Demetrius: No die, but an ace,° for him; for he is but one.°　　290
Lysander: Less than an ace, man; for he is dead, he is nothing.
Theseus: With the help of a surgeon he might yet recover, and yet prove
　an ass.°
Hippolyta: How chance Moonshine is gone before Thisbe comes back and
　finds her lover?　　　　　　　　　　　　　　　　　　　295
Theseus: She will find him by starlight.

[Enter Thisbe.]

Here she comes; and her passion ends the play.
Hippolyta: Methinks she should not use a long one for such a Pyramus. I
　hope she will be brief.
Demetrius: A mote° will turn the balance, which Pyramus, which° Thisbe,　300
　is the better: he for a man, God warrant us; she for a woman, God
　bless us.
Lysander: She hath spied him already with those sweet eyes.
Demetrius: And thus she means,° videlicet:°
Thisbe: Asleep, my love?　　　　　　　　　　　　　　　305
　What, dead, my dove?
O Pyramus, arise!
　Speak, speak. Quite dumb?
　Dead, dead? A tomb
Must cover thy sweet eyes.　　　　　　　　　　　　310
　These lily lips,
　This cherry nose,
　These yellow cowslip cheeks,
　Are gone, are gone!
　Lovers, make moan.　　　　　　　　　　　　　315
His eyes were green as leeks.
　O Sisters Three,°
　Come, come to me,
With hands as pale as milk;
　Lay them in gore,　　　　　　　　　　　　　320
　Since you have shore°
With shears his thread of silk.
　Tongue, not a word.
　Come, trusty sword,
Come, blade, my breast imbrue!°　　　　　*[She stabs herself.]*　325

---

290 *ace:* The side of the die featuring the single pip, or spot (the pun is on *die* as a singular of *dice;*
Bottom's performance is not worth a whole *die* but rather one single face of it, one small portion);
one: (1) An individual person, (2) unique.　293 *ass:* (With a pun on *ace.*)　300 *mote:* Small
particle; *which . . . which:* Whether . . . or.　304 *means:* Moans, laments (with a pun on
the meaning "lodge a formal complaint"); *videlicet:* To wit.　317 *Sisters Three:* The Fates.
321 *shore:* Shorn.　325 *imbrue:* Stain with blood.

And farewell, friends.
Thus Thisbe ends.
Adieu, adieu, adieu. [*She dies.*]
Theseus: Moonshine and Lion are left to bury the dead.
Demetrius: Ay, and Wall too. 330
Bottom [starting up, as Flute does also]: No, I assure you, the wall is down that
parted their fathers. Will it please you to see the epilogue, or to hear a
Bergomask dance° between two of our company?

[*The other players enter.*]

Theseus: No epilogue, I pray you; for your play needs no excuse. Never excuse;
for when the players are all dead, there need none to be blamed. Marry, if 335
he that writ it had played Pyramus and hanged himself in Thisbe's garter,
it would have been a fine tragedy; and so it is, truly, and very notably dis-
charged. But, come, your Bergomask.
Let your epilogue alone. [*A dance.*]
The iron tongue° of midnight hath told° twelve. 340
Lovers, to bed, 'tis almost fairy time.
I fear we shall outsleep the coming morn
As much as we this night have overwatched.°
This palpable-gross° play hath well beguiled
The heavy° gait of night. Sweet friends, to bed. 345
A fortnight hold we this solemnity,
In nightly revels and new jollity. *Exeunt.*

Enter Puck [carrying a broom].

Puck: Now the hungry lion roars,
And the wolf behowls the moon,
Whilst the heavy° plowman snores,
All with weary task fordone.° 350
Now the wasted brands° do glow,
Whilst the screech owl, screeching loud,
Puts the wretch that lies in woe
In remembrance of a shroud.
Now it is the time of night 355
That the graves, all gaping wide,
Every one lets forth his sprite,°
In the church-way paths to glide.
And we fairies, that do run 360
By the triple Hecate's° team
From the presence of the sun,
Following darkness like a dream,
Now are frolic.° Not a mouse

---

333 *Bergomask dance:* A rustic dance named from Bergamo, a province in the state of Venice.
340 *iron tongue:* Clapper of a bell; *told:* Counted, struck ("tolled"). 343 *overwatched:*
Stayed up too late. 344 *palpable-gross:* Palpably gross, obviously crude. 345 *heavy:* Drowsy,
dull. 350 *heavy:* Tired. 351 *fordone:* Exhausted. 352 *wasted brands:* Burned-out logs.
358 *Every . . . sprite:* Every grave lets forth its ghost. 361 *triple Hecate's:* (Hecate ruled in
three capacities: as Luna or Cynthia in heaven, as Diana on earth, and as Proserpina in hell.)
364 *frolic:* Merry.

Shall disturb this hallowed house.   365
I am sent with broom before,
To sweep the dust behind° the door.

Enter [Oberon and Titania,] King and Queen of Fairies, with all their train.

Oberon: Through the house give glimmering light,
 By the dead and drowsy fire;
 Every elf and fairy sprite   370
  Hop as light as bird from brier;
 And this ditty, after me,
 Sing, and dance it trippingly.
Titania: First, rehearse° your song by rote,
 To each word a warbling note.   375
 Hand in hand, with fairy grace,
 Will we sing, and bless this place.   *[Song and dance.]*
Oberon: Now, until the break of day,
 Through this house each fairy stray.
 To the best bride-bed will we,   380
 Which by us shall blessèd be;
 And the issue there create°
 Ever shall be fortunate.
 So shall all the couples three
 Ever true in loving be;   385
 And the blots of Nature's hand
 Shall not in their issue stand;
 Never mole, harelip, nor scar,
 Nor mark prodigious,° such as are
 Despisèd in nativity,   390
 Shall upon their children be.
 With this field dew consecrate,°
 Every fairy take his gait,°
 And each several° chamber bless,
 Through this palace, with sweet peace;   395
 And the owner of it blest
 Ever shall in safety rest.
 Trip away; make no stay;
 Meet me all by break of day.   *Exeunt [Oberon, Titania, and train].*
Puck [to the audience]: If we shadows have offended,   400
 Think but this, and all is mended,
 That you have but slumbered here°
 While these visions did appear.
 And this weak and idle theme,
 No more yielding but° a dream,   405
 Gentles, do not reprehend.

---

367 *behind:* From behind, or else like sweeping the dirt under the carpet (Robin Goodfellow
was a household spirit who helped good housemaids and punished lazy ones, but he could, of
course, be mischievous).   374 *rehearse:* Recite.   382 *create:* Created.   389 *prodigious:*
Monstrous, unnatural.   392 *consecrate:* Consecrated.   393 *take his gait:* Go his way.
394 *several:* Separate.   402 *That . . . here:* I.e., that it is a "midsummer night's dream."
405 *No . . . but:* Yielding no more than.

If you pardon, we will mend.°
And, as I am an honest Puck,
If we have unearnèd luck
Now to scape the serpent's tongue,°   410
We will make amends ere long;
Else the Puck a liar call.
So, good night unto you all.
Give me your hands,° if we be friends,
And Robin shall restore amends.°   [*Exit.*] 415

407 *mend:* Improve.   410 *serpent's tongue:* I.e., hissing.   414 *Give . . . hands:* Applaud.
415 *restore amends:* Give satisfaction in return.

Considerations for Critical Thinking and Writing

1. **FIRST RESPONSE.** Discuss the significance of the play's title. What expectations does it create for you?

2. Describe how the two settings, Athens and the nearby woods, reflect different social and physical environments as well as different types of behavior among the characters.

3. What is the symbolic function of the marriage of Theseus and Hippolyta? How is that function revealed in the scenes in which they appear?

4. Characterize the four young lovers. How individualized are their personalities? How does the extent of their characterizations suggest their function in the play?

5. What makes Bottom such a comic figure? How does his behavior shed light on the behavior of the other characters?

6. Consider how women — Hippolyta, Titania, Hermia, and Helena — are presented in the play. What characteristics do they have in common? How do they relate to the men in their lives?

7. Why does Puck describe "mortals" as "fools" (III.ii.115)? To what degree does this description fit the fairies as well?

8. How might Puck be regarded as the play's director as well as a central character?

9. How does the plot bring together the four groups of characters — Theseus and Hippolyta, the four lovers, the craftsmen, and the fairies — into a unified whole? Write a plot summary of the play that connects these four groups of characters. How does this summary resemble popular situation comedies that you've seen on television?

10. Choose a scene that you find particularly funny, and analyze how the humor is created. Describe how the scene contributes to the rest of the play.

11. What is the relationship between the play within the play, "Pyramus and Thisbe," and *A Midsummer Night's Dream*? How do the plot and theme of each serve as commentaries on each other?

12. Despite its comic scenes and happy ending, at various moments this play does raise the specter of potential tragedy. How seriously do you think we are meant to worry about the characters? What are your emotions about the young lovers as they struggle to sort things out in the woods? Discuss how this play might be transformed into a tragedy.

1. Discuss Shakespeare's use of the play within the play in both *A Midsummer Night's Dream* and *Hamlet* (below). What emotions does each produce? What conflicts and themes do they emphasize? What attitudes do they suggest about the nature of drama?

2. In an essay discuss the significance of marriage in *A Midsummer Night's Dream* and Henrik Ibsen's *A Doll's House* (p. 1357).

3. Write an essay that explores the difficulty of distinguishing between reality and illusion in *A Midsummer Night's Dream* and a very different work, Tim O'Brien's short story "How to Tell a True War Story" (p. 488). What are the similarities and differences in their perspectives on the actual and imaginary?

Hamlet, Prince of Denmark

Hamlet, the most famous play in English literature, continues to fascinate and challenge both readers and audiences. Interpretations of Hamlet's character and actions abound, because the play has produced so many intense and varied responses. No small indication of the tragedy's power is that actors long to play its title role.

A brief summary can suggest the movement of the plot but not the depth of Hamlet's character. After learning of his father's death, Prince Hamlet returns to the Danish court from his university studies to find Claudius, the dead king's brother, ruling Denmark and married to Hamlet's mother, Gertrude. Her remarriage within two months of his father's death has left Hamlet disillusioned, confused, and suspicious of Claudius. When his father's ghost appears before Hamlet to reveal that Claudius murdered the king, Hamlet is confronted with having to avenge his father's death.

Hamlet's efforts to carry out this obligation would have been a familiar kind of plot to Elizabethan audiences. **Revenge tragedy** was a well-established type of drama that traced its antecedents to Greek and Roman plays, particularly through the Roman playwright Seneca (ca. 3 B.C.–A.D. 65), whose plays were translated and produced in English in the late sixteenth century. Shakespeare's audiences knew its conventions, particularly from Thomas Kyd's popular *Spanish Tragedy* (ca. 1587). Basically, this type of play consists of a murder that has to be avenged by a relative of the victim. Typically, the victim's ghost appears to demand revenge, and invariably madness of some sort is worked into subsequent events, which ultimately result in the deaths of the murderer, the avenger, and a number of other characters. Crime, madness, ghostly anguish, poison, overheard conversations, conspiracies, and a final scene littered with corpses: *Hamlet* subscribes to the basic ingredients of the formula, but it also transcends the conventions of revenge tragedy because Hamlet contemplates not merely revenge but suicide and the meaning of life itself.

Hamlet must face not only a diseased social order but also conflicts within himself when his indecisiveness becomes as agonizing as the corruption surrounding him. However, Hamlet is also a forceful and attractive character. His intelligence is repeatedly revealed in his penetrating use of language; through images and metaphors he creates a perspective on his world that is at once satiric and profoundly painful. His astonishing and sometimes shocking wit is leveled at his mother, his beloved Ophelia, and Claudius as well as himself. Nothing escapes his critical eye and divided imagination. Hamlet, no less than the people around him, is perplexed by his alienation from life.

Hamlet's limitations as well as his virtues make him one of Shakespeare's most complex characters. His keen self-awareness is both agonizing and liberating. Although he struggles throughout the play with painful issues ranging from family loyalties to matters of state, he retains his dignity as a tragic hero, whom generations of audiences have found compelling.

WILLIAM SHAKESPEARE (1564–1616)

Hamlet, Prince of Denmark   1600

See Plays in Performance insert.

"*Hah, hha, 'To be or not to be,' and Do, Hha, 'Get a life.'*"

See Encountering Drama, pages 1347–52.

[DRAMATIS PERSONAE

Claudius, King of Denmark
Hamlet, son to the late and nephew to the
        present king
Polonius, lord chamberlain
Horatio, friend to Hamlet
Laertes, son to Polonius
Voltimand
Cornelius
Rosencrantz   } courtiers
Guildenstern
Osric
A Gentleman
A Priest
Marcellus } officers
Bernardo
Francisco, a soldier
Reynaldo, servant to Polonius
Players
Two Clowns, grave-diggers
Fortinbras, Prince of Norway
A Captain
English Ambassadors
Gertrude, Queen of Denmark, and mother to Hamlet
Ophelia, daughter to Polonius

Lords, Ladies, Officers, Soldiers, Sailors, Messengers, and other Attendants
Ghost of Hamlet's Father

SCENE: Denmark.]

[ACT I

SCENE I: *Elsinore. A platform° before the castle.*]

 Enter Bernardo and Francisco, two sentinels.

Bernardo: Who's there?
Francisco: Nay, answer me:° stand, and unfold yourself.
Bernardo: Long live the king!°
Francisco: Bernardo?
Bernardo: He.
Francisco: You come most carefully upon your hour.   5
Bernardo: 'Tis now struck twelve; get thee to bed, Francisco.
Francisco: For this relief much thanks: 'tis bitter cold,
 And I am sick at heart.
Bernardo: Have you had quiet guard?
Francisco: Not a mouse stirring.   10
Bernardo: Well, good night.
 If you do meet Horatio and Marcellus,
 The rivals° of my watch, bid them make haste.

 Enter Horatio and Marcellus.

Francisco: I think I hear them. Stand, ho! Who is there?
Horatio: Friends to this ground.
Marcellus: And liegemen to the Dane.   15
Francisco: Give you° good night.
Marcellus: O, farewell, honest soldier:
 Who hath reliev'd you?
Francisco: Bernardo hath my place.
 Give you good night.   *Exit Francisco.*
Marcellus: Holla! Bernardo!
Bernardo: Say,
 What, is Horatio there?
Horatio: A piece of him.
Bernardo: Welcome, Horatio: welcome, good Marcellus.   20
Marcellus: What, has this thing appear'd again to-night?
Bernardo: I have seen nothing.
Marcellus: Horatio says 'tis but our fantasy,

Act I, Scene I. *platform:* A level space on the battlements of the royal castle at Elsinore, a Danish seaport; now Helsingör. 2 *me:* This is emphatic, since Francisco is the sentry. 3 *Long live the king:* Either a password or greeting; Horatio and Marcellus use a different one in line 15. 13 *rivals:* Partners. 16 *Give you:* God give you.

And will not let belief take hold of him
Touching this dreaded sight, twice seen of us: 25
Therefore I have entreated him along
With us to watch the minutes of this night;
That if again this apparition come,
He may approve° our eyes and speak to it.
Horatio: Tush, tush, 'twill not appear.
Bernardo: Sit down awhile;   30
And let us once again assail your ears,
That are so fortified against our story
What we have two nights seen.
Horatio: Well, sit we down,
And let us hear Bernardo speak of this.
Bernardo: Last night of all,   35
When yond same star that's westward from the pole°
Had made his course t' illume that part of heaven
Where now it burns, Marcellus and myself,
The bell then beating one, —

Enter Ghost.

Marcellus: Peace, break thee off; look, where it comes again!   40
Bernardo: In the same figure, like the king that's dead.
Marcellus: Thou art a scholar;° speak to it, Horatio.
Bernardo: Looks 'a not like the king? mark it, Horatio.
Horatio: Most like: it harrows° me with fear and wonder.
Bernardo: It would be spoke to.°
Marcellus: Speak to it, Horatio.   45
Horatio: What art thou that usurp'st this time of night,
Together with that fair and warlike form
In which the majesty of buried Denmark°
Did sometimes march? by heaven I charge thee, speak!
Marcellus: It is offended.
Bernardo: See it stalks away!   50
Horatio: Stay! speak, speak! I charge thee, speak!   *Exit Ghost.*
Marcellus: 'Tis gone, and will not answer.
Bernardo: How now, Horatio! you tremble and look pale:
Is not this something more than fantasy?
What think you on 't?   55
Horatio: Before my God, I might not this believe
Without the sensible and true avouch
Of mine own eyes.
Marcellus: Is it not like the king?
Horatio: As thou art to thyself:
Such was the very armour he had on   60
When he the ambitious Norway combated;

29 *approve:* Corroborate.   36 *pole:* Polestar.   42 *scholar:* Exorcisms were performed in Latin, which Horatio as an educated man would be able to speak.   44 *harrows:* Lacerates the feelings.   45 *It . . . to:* A ghost could not speak until spoken to.   48 *buried Denmark:* The buried king of Denmark.

So frown'd he once, when, in an angry parle,
He smote° the sledded Polacks° on the ice.
'Tis strange.

Marcellus: Thus twice before, and jump° at this dead hour,   65
With martial stalk hath he gone by our watch.

Horatio: In what particular thought to work I know not;
But in the gross and scope° of my opinion,
This bodes some strange eruption to our state.

Marcellus: Good now,° sit down, and tell me, he that knows,   70
Why this same strict and most observant watch
So nightly toils° the subject° of the land,
And why such daily cast° of brazen cannon,
And foreign mart° for implements of war;
Why such impress° of shipwrights, whose sore task   75
Does not divide the Sunday from the week;
What might be toward, that this sweaty haste
Doth make the night joint-labourer with the day:
Who is't that can inform me?

Horatio: That can I;
At least, the whisper goes so. Our last king,   80
Whose image even but now appear'd to us,
Was, as you know, by Fortinbras of Norway,
Thereto prick'd on° by a most emulate° pride,
Dar'd to the combat; in which our valiant Hamlet —
For so this side of our known world esteem'd him —   85
Did slay this Fortinbras; who, by a seal'd compact,
Well ratified by law and heraldry,°
Did forfeit, with his life, all those his lands
Which he stood seiz'd° of, to the conqueror:
Against the which, a moiety competent°   90
Was gaged by our king; which had return'd
To the inheritance of Fortinbras,
Had he been vanquisher; as, by the same comart,°
And carriage° of the article design'd,
His fell to Hamlet. Now, sir, young Fortinbras,   95
Of unimproved° mettle hot and full,°
Hath in the skirts of Norway here and there
Shark'd up° a list of lawless resolutes,°
For food and diet,° to some enterprise
That hath a stomach in't; which is no other —   100
As it doth well appear unto our state —

---

63 *smote:* Defeated; *sledded Polacks:* Polanders using sledges.   65 *jump:* Exactly.   68 *gross and scope:* General drift.   70 *Good now:* An expression denoting entreaty or expostulation. 72 *toils:* Causes or makes to toil; *subject:* People, subjects.   73 *cast:* Casting, founding. 74 *mart:* Buying and selling, traffic.   75 *impress:* Impressment.   83 *prick'd on:* Incited; *emulate:* Rivaling.   87 *law and heraldry:* Heraldic law, governing combat.   89 *seiz'd:* Possessed.   90 *moiety competent:* Adequate or sufficient portion.   93 *comart:* Joint bargain. 94 *carriage:* Import, bearing.   96 *unimproved:* Not turned to account; *hot and full:* Full of fight.   98 *Shark'd up:* Got together in haphazard fashion; *resolutes:* Desperadoes.   99 *food and diet:* No pay but their keep.

But to recover of us, by strong hand
And terms compulsatory, those foresaid lands
So by his father lost: and this, I take it,
Is the main motive of our preparations,   105
The source of this our watch and the chief head
Of this post-haste and romage° in the land.
Bernardo: I think it be no other but e'en so:
Well may it sort° that this portentous figure
Comes armed through our watch; so like the king   110
That was and is the question of these wars.
Horatio: A mote° it is to trouble the mind's eye.
In the most high and palmy state° of Rome,
A little ere the mightiest Julius fell,
The graves stood tenantless and the sheeted dead   115
Did squeak and gibber in the Roman streets:
As stars with trains of fire° and dews of blood,
Disasters° in the sun; and the moist star°
Upon whose influence Neptune's empire° stands
Was sick almost to doomsday with eclipse: 120
And even the like precurse° of fear'd events,
As harbingers preceding still the fates
And prologue to the omen coming on,
Have heaven and earth together demonstrated
Unto our climatures and countrymen. —   125

Enter Ghost.

But soft, behold! lo, where it comes again!
I'll cross° it, though it blast me. Stay, illusion!
If thou hast any sound, or use of voice,
Speak to me!   *It° spreads his arms.*
If there be any good thing to be done,   130
That may to thee do ease and grace to me,
Speak to me!
If thou art privy to thy country's fate,
Which, happily, foreknowing may avoid,
O, speak!   135
Or if thou hast uphoarded in thy life
Extorted treasure in the womb of earth,
For which, they say, you spirits oft walk in death,   *The cock crows.*
Speak of it:° stay, and speak! Stop it, Marcellus.
Marcellus: Shall I strike at it with my partisan?°   140
Horatio: Do, if it will not stand.
Bernardo: 'Tis here!

---

107 *romage:* Bustle, commotion.   109 *sort:* Suit.   112 *mote:* Speck of dust.   113 *palmy state:* Triumphant sovereignty.   117 *stars ... fire:* I.e., comets.   118 *Disasters:* Unfavorable aspects; *moist star:* The moon, governing tides.   119 *Neptune's empire:* The sea.   121 *precurse:* Heralding.   127 *cross:* Meet, face, thus bringing down the evil influence on the person who crosses it.   129 *It:* The Ghost, or perhaps Horatio.   133–139 *If ... it:* Horatio recites the traditional reasons why ghosts might walk.   140 *partisan:* Long-handled spear with a blade having lateral projections.

Horatio: 'Tis here!
Marcellus: 'Tis gone!   *[Exit Ghost.]*
    We do it wrong, being so majestical,
    To offer it the show of violence;
    For it is, as the air, invulnerable,   145
    And our vain blows malicious mockery.
Bernardo: It was about to speak, when the cock crew.°
Horatio: And then it started like a guilty thing
    Upon a fearful summons. I have heard,
    The cock, that is the trumpet to the morn,   150
    Doth with his lofty and shrill-sounding throat
    Awake the god of day; and, at his warning,
    Whether in sea or fire, in earth or air,
    Th' extravagant and erring° spirit hies
    To his confine:° and of the truth herein   155
    This present object made probation.°
Marcellus: It faded on the crowing of the cock.
    Some say that ever 'gainst° that season comes
    Wherein our Saviour's birth is celebrated,
    The bird of dawning singeth all night long: 160
    And then, they say, no spirit dare stir abroad;
    The nights are wholesome; then no planets strike,°
    No fairy takes, nor witch hath power to charm,
    So hallow'd and so gracious° is that time.
Horatio: So have I heard and do in part believe it.   165
    But, look, the morn, in russet mantle clad,
    Walks o'er the dew of yon high eastward hill:
    Break we our watch up; and by my advice,
    Let us impart what we have seen to-night
    Unto young Hamlet; for, upon my life,   170
    This spirit, dumb to us, will speak to him.
    Do you consent we shall acquaint him with it,
    As needful in our loves, fitting our duty?
Marcellus: Let's do 't, I pray; and I this morning know
    Where we shall find him most conveniently.   *Exeunt.*   175

[SCENE II: *A room of state in the castle.*]

*Flourish. Enter Claudius, King of Denmark, Gertrude the Queen, Councilors,
Polonius and his Son Laertes, Hamlet, cum aliis° [including Voltimand and
Cornelius].*

King: Though yet of Hamlet our dear brother's death
    The memory be green, and that it us befitted
    To bear our hearts in grief and our whole kingdom

---

147 *cock crew:* According to traditional ghost lore, spirits returned to their confines at
cockcrow.   154 *extravagant and erring:* Wandering. Both words mean the same thing.
155 *confine:* Place of confinement.   156 *probation:* Proof, trial.   158 *'gainst:* Just before.
162 *planets strike:* It was thought that planets were malignant and might strike travelers by
night.   164 *gracious:* Full of goodness.   **Scene II.**   *cum aliis:* With others.

To be contracted in one brow of woe,
Yet so far hath discretion fought with nature   5
That we with wisest sorrow think on him,
Together with remembrance of ourselves.
Therefore our sometime sister, now our queen,
Th' imperial jointress° to this warlike state,
Have we, as 'twere with a defeated joy, —   10
With an auspicious and a dropping eye,
With mirth in funeral and with dirge in marriage,
In equal scale weighing delight and dole, —
Taken to wife: nor have we herein barr'd
Your better wisdoms, which have freely gone   15
With this affair along. For all, our thanks.
Now follows, that° you know, young Fortinbras,
Holding a weak supposal° of our worth,
Or thinking by our late dear brother's death
Our state to be disjoint° and out of frame,°   20
Colleagued° with this dream of his advantage,°
He hath not fail'd to pester us with message,
Importing° the surrender of those lands
Lost by his father, with all bands of law,
To our most valiant brother. So much for him.   25
Now for ourself and for this time of meeting:
Thus much the business is: we have here writ
To Norway, uncle of young Fortinbras, —
Who, impotent and bed-rid, scarcely hears
Of this his nephew's purpose, — to suppress   30
His further gait° herein; in that the levies,
The lists and full proportions, are all made
Out of his subject:° and we here dispatch
You, good Cornelius, and you, Voltimand,
For bearers of this greeting to old Norway;   35
Giving to you no further personal power
To business with the king, more than the scope
Of these delated° articles allow.
Farewell, and let your haste commend your duty.

Cornelius: }
Voltimand: }   In that and all things will we show our duty.   40

King: We doubt it nothing: heartily farewell.

                         [Exeunt Voltimand and Cornelius.]

And now, Laertes, what's the news with you?
You told us of some suit; what is't, Laertes?
You cannot speak of reason to the Dane,°
And lose your voice:° what wouldst thou beg, Laertes,   45

---

9 *jointress:* Woman possessed of a jointure, or, joint tenancy of an estate.   17 *that:* That which.   18 *weak supposal:* Low estimate.   20 *disjoint:* Distracted, out of joint; *frame:* Order.   21 *Colleagued:* Added to; *dream . . . advantage:* Visionary hope of success.   23 *Importing:* Purporting, pertaining to.   31 *gait:* Proceeding.   33 *Out of his subject:* At the expense of Norway's subjects (collectively).   38 *delated:* Expressly stated.   44 *the Dane:* Danish king.   45 *lose your voice:* Speak in vain.

That shall not be my offer, not thy asking?
The head is not more native° to the heart,
The hand more instrumental° to the mouth,
Than is the throne of Denmark to thy father.
What wouldst thou have, Laertes?

Laertes: My dread lord,   50
Your leave and favour to return to France;
From whence though willingly I came to Denmark,
To show my duty in your coronation,
Yet now, I must confess, that duty done,
My thoughts and wishes bend again toward France   55
And bow them to your gracious leave and pardon.°

King: Have you your father's leave? What says Polonius?
Polonius: He hath, my lord, wrung from me my slow leave
By laboursome petition, and at last
Upon his will I seal'd my hard consent: 60
I do beseech you, give him leave to go.
King: Take thy fair hour, Laertes; time be thine,
And thy best graces spend it at thy will!
But now, my cousin° Hamlet, and my son, —
Hamlet [aside]: A little more than kin, and less than kind!°   65
King: How is it that the clouds still hang on you?
Hamlet: Not so, my lord; I am too much in the sun.°
Queen: Good Hamlet, cast thy nighted colour off,
And let thine eye look like a friend on Denmark.
Do not for ever with thy vailed lids   70
Seek for thy noble father in the dust:
Thou know'st 'tis common; all that lives must die,
Passing through nature to eternity.
Hamlet: Ay, madam, it is common.°
Queen: If it be,
Why seems it so particular with thee?   75
Hamlet: Seems, madam! nay, it is; I know not "seems."
'Tis not alone my inky cloak, good mother,
Nor customary suits° of solemn black,
Nor windy suspiration° of forc'd breath,
No, nor the fruitful river in the eye,   80
Nor the dejected 'haviour of the visage,
Together with all forms, moods, shapes of grief,
That can denote me truly: these indeed seem,
For they are actions that a man might play:

---

47 *native:* Closely connected, related.   48 *instrumental:* Serviceable.   56 *leave and pardon:* Permission to depart.   64 *cousin:* Any kin not of the immediate family.   65 *A little . . . kind:* My relation to you has become more than kinship warrants; it has also become unnatural. 67 *I am . . . sun:* (1) I am too much out of doors, (2) I am too much in the sun of your grace (ironical), (3) I am too much of a son to you. Possibly an allusion to the proverb "Out of heaven's blessing into the warm sun"; i.e., Hamlet is out of house and home in being deprived of the kingship.   74 *Ay . . . common:* It is common, but it hurts nevertheless; possibly a reference to the commonplace quality of the queen's remark.   78 *customary suits:* Suits prescribed by custom for mourning.   79 *windy suspiration:* Heavy sighing.

But I have that within which passeth show;⠀⠀⠀⠀⠀⠀⠀⠀⠀⠀⠀⠀85
These but the trappings and the suits of woe.
King: 'Tis sweet and commendable in your nature, Hamlet,
⠀⠀To give these mourning duties to your father:
⠀⠀But, you must know, your father lost a father;
⠀⠀That father lost, lost his, and the survivor bound⠀⠀⠀⠀⠀⠀90
⠀⠀In filial obligation for some term
⠀⠀To do obsequious° sorrow: but to persever
⠀⠀In obstinate condolement° is a course
⠀⠀Of impious stubbornness; 'tis unmanly grief;
⠀⠀It shows a will most incorrect° to heaven,⠀⠀⠀⠀⠀⠀⠀⠀95
⠀⠀A heart unfortified, a mind impatient,
⠀⠀An understanding simple and unschool'd:
⠀⠀For what we know must be and is as common
⠀⠀As any the most vulgar thing° to sense,
⠀⠀Why should we in our peevish opposition⠀⠀⠀⠀⠀⠀⠀⠀100
⠀⠀Take it to heart? Fie! 'tis a fault to heaven,
⠀⠀A fault against the dead, a fault to nature,
⠀⠀To reason most absurd; whose common theme
⠀⠀Is death of fathers, and who still hath cried,
⠀⠀From the first corse till he that died to-day,⠀⠀⠀⠀⠀⠀105
⠀⠀"This must be so." We pray you, throw to earth
⠀⠀This unprevailing° woe, and think of us
⠀⠀As of a father: for let the world take note,
⠀⠀You are the most immediate° to our throne;
⠀⠀And with no less nobility° of love⠀⠀⠀⠀⠀⠀⠀⠀⠀⠀110
⠀⠀Than that which dearest father bears his son,
⠀⠀Do I impart° toward you. For your intent
⠀⠀In going back to school in Wittenberg,°
⠀⠀It is most retrograde° to our desire:
⠀⠀And we beseech you, bend you° to remain⠀⠀⠀⠀⠀⠀115
⠀⠀Here, in the cheer and comfort of our eye,
⠀⠀Our chiefest courtier, cousin, and our son.
Queen: Let not thy mother lose her prayers, Hamlet:
⠀⠀I pray thee, stay with us; go not to Wittenberg.
Hamlet: I shall in all my best obey you, madam.⠀⠀⠀⠀⠀120
King: Why, 'tis a loving and a fair reply:
⠀⠀Be as ourself in Denmark. Madam, come;
⠀⠀This gentle and unforc'd accord of Hamlet
⠀⠀Sits smiling to my heart: in grace whereof,
⠀⠀No jocund health that Denmark drinks to-day,⠀⠀⠀⠀⠀125
⠀⠀But the great cannon to the clouds shall tell,
⠀⠀And the king's rouse° the heaven shall bruit again,°
⠀⠀Re-speaking earthly thunder. Come away.

---

92 *obsequious:* Dutiful.⠀⠀93 *condolement:* Sorrowing.⠀⠀95 *incorrect:* Untrained, uncorrected.
99 *vulgar thing:* Common experience.⠀⠀107 *unprevailing:* Unavailing.⠀⠀109 *most immediate:* Next in succession.⠀⠀110 *nobility:* High degree.⠀⠀112 *impart:* The object is apparently love (l. 110).⠀⠀113 *Wittenberg:* Famous German university founded in 1502.⠀⠀114 *retrograde:* Contrary.⠀⠀115 *bend you:* Incline yourself (imperative).⠀⠀127 *rouse:* Draft of liquor; *bruit again:* Echo.

Flourish. Exeunt all but Hamlet.

Hamlet: O, that this too too sullied flesh would melt,
    Thaw and resolve itself into a dew!   130
    Or that the Everlasting had not fix'd
    His canon 'gainst self-slaughter! O God! God!
    How weary, stale, flat and unprofitable,
    Seem to me all the uses of this world!
    Fie on't! ah fie! 'tis an unweeded garden,   135
    That grows to seed; things rank and gross in nature
    Possess it merely.° That it should come to this!
    But two months dead: nay, not so much, not two:
    So excellent a king; that was, to this,
    Hyperion° to a satyr; so loving to my mother   140
    That he might not beteem° the winds of heaven
    Visit her face too roughly. Heaven and earth!
    Must I remember? why, she would hang on him,
    As if increase of appetite had grown
    By what it fed on: and yet, within a month —   145
    Let me not think on't — Frailty, thy name is woman! —
    A little month, or ere those shoes were old
    With which she followed my poor father's body,
    Like Niobe,° all tears: — why she, even she —
    O God! a beast, that wants discourse of reason,°   150
    Would have mourn'd longer — married with my uncle,
    My father's brother, but no more like my father
    Than I to Hercules: within a month:
    Ere yet the salt of most unrighteous tears
    Had left the flushing in her galled° eyes,   155
    She married. O, most wicked speed, to post
    With such dexterity° to incestuous sheets!
    It is not nor it cannot come to good:
    But break, my heart; for I must hold my tongue.

Enter Horatio, Marcellus, and Bernardo.

Horatio: Hail to your lordship!
Hamlet: I am glad to see you well: 160
    Horatio! — or I do forget myself.
Horatio: The same, my lord, and your poor servant ever.
Hamlet: Sir, my good friend; I'll change that name with you:°
    And what make you from Wittenberg, Horatio?
    Marcellus?   165
Marcellus: My good lord —
Hamlet: I am very glad to see you. Good even, sir.
    But what, in faith, make you from Wittenberg?

137 *merely:* Completely, entirely.   140 *Hyperion:* God of the sun in the older regime of ancient gods.   141 *beteem:* Allow.   149 *Niobe:* Tantalus's daughter, who boasted that she had
more sons and daughters than Leto; for this Apollo and Artemis slew her children. She was turned
into stone by Zeus on Mount Sipylus.   150 *discourse of reason:* Process or faculty of reason.
155 *galled:* Irritated.   157 *dexterity:* Facility.   163 *I'll . . . you:* I'll be your servant, you shall
be my friend; also explained as "I'll exchange the name of friend with you."

Horatio: A truant disposition, good my lord.

Hamlet: I would not hear your enemy say so,   170
   Nor shall you do my ear that violence,
   To make it truster of your own report
   Against yourself: I know you are no truant.
   But what is your affair in Elsinore?
   We'll teach you to drink deep ere you depart.   175

Horatio: My lord, I came to see your father's funeral.

Hamlet: I prithee, do not mock me, fellow-student;
   I think it was to see my mother's wedding.

Horatio: Indeed, my lord, it follow'd hard° upon.

Hamlet: Thrift, thrift, Horatio! the funeral bak'd meats°   180
   Did coldly furnish forth the marriage tables.
   Would I had met my dearest° foe in heaven
   Or ever I had seen that day, Horatio!
   My father! — methinks I see my father.

Horatio: Where, my lord!

Hamlet: In my mind's eye, Horatio.   185

Horatio: I saw him once; 'a° was a goodly king.

Hamlet: 'A was a man, take him for all in all,
   I shall not look upon his like again.

Horatio: My lord, I think I saw him yesternight.

Hamlet: Saw? who?   190

Horatio: My lord, the king your father.

Hamlet: The king my father!

Horatio: Season your admiration° for a while
   With an attent ear, till I may deliver,
   Upon the witness of these gentlemen,
   This marvel to you.

Hamlet: For God's love, let me hear.   195

Horatio: Two nights together had these gentlemen,
   Marcellus and Bernardo, on their watch,
   In the dead waste and middle of the night,
   Been thus encount'red. A figure like your father,
   Armed at point exactly, cap-a-pe,°   200
   Appears before them, and with solemn march
   Goes slow and stately by them: thrice he walk'd
   By their oppress'd° and fear-surprised eyes,
   Within his truncheon's° length; whilst they, distill'd°
   Almost to jelly with the act° of fear,   205
   Stand dumb and speak not to him. This to me
   In dreadful secrecy impart they did;
   And I with them the third night kept the watch:
   Where, as they had deliver'd, both in time,
   Form of the thing, each word made true and good,   210

---

179 *hard:* Close.   180 *bak'd meats:* Meat pies.   182 *dearest:* Direst. The adjective *dear* in Shakespeare has two different origins: O.E. *deore,* "beloved," and O.E. *deor,* "fierce." *Dearest* is the superlative of the second.   186 *'a:* He.   192 *Season your admiration:* Restrain your astonishment.   200 *cap-a-pe:* From head to foot.   203 *oppress'd:* Distressed.   204 *truncheon:* Officer's staff; *distill'd:* Softened, weakened.   205 *act:* Action.

The apparition comes: I knew your father;
These hands are not more like.
Hamlet: But where was this?
Marcellus: My lord, upon the platform where we watch'd.
Hamlet: Did you not speak to it?
Horatio: My lord, I did;
But answer made it none: yet once methought   215
It lifted up it° head and did address
Itself to motion, like as it would speak;
But even then the morning cock crew loud,
And at the sound it shrunk in haste away,
And vanish'd from our sight.
Hamlet: 'Tis very strange.   220
Horatio: As I do live, my honour'd lord, 'tis true;
And we did think it writ down in our duty
To let you know of it.
Hamlet: Indeed, indeed, sirs, but this troubles me.
Hold you the watch to-night?
Marcellus: ⎱
Bernardo: ⎰   We do, my lord.   225
Hamlet: Arm'd, say you?
Marcellus: ⎱
Bernardo: ⎰   Arm'd, my lord.
Hamlet: From top to toe?
Marcellus: ⎱
Bernardo: ⎰   My lord, from head to foot.
Hamlet: Then saw you not his face?
Horatio: O, yes, my lord; he wore his beaver° up.
Hamlet: What, look'd he frowningly?
Horatio: A countenance more   230
In sorrow than in anger.
Hamlet: Pale or red?
Horatio: Nay, very pale.
Hamlet: And fix'd his eyes upon you?
Horatio: Most constantly.
Hamlet: I would I had been there.
Horatio: It would have much amaz'd you.
Hamlet: Very like, very like. Stay'd it long?   235
Horatio: While one with moderate haste might tell a hundred.
Marcellus: ⎱
Bernardo: ⎰   Longer, longer.
Horatio: Not when I saw't.
Hamlet: His beard was grizzled,— no?
Horatio: It was, as I have seen it in his life,
A sable° silver'd.
Hamlet: I will watch to-night;   240
Perchance 'twill walk again.
Horatio: I warr'nt it will.

---

216 *it:* Its.   229 *beaver:* Visor on the helmet.   240 *sable:* Black color.

Hamlet: If it assume my noble father's person,
    I'll speak to it, though hell itself should gape
    And bid me hold my peace. I pray you all,
    If you have hitherto conceal'd this sight,   245
    Let it be tenable in your silence still;
    And whatsoever else shall hap to-night,
    Give it an understanding, but no tongue:
    I will requite your loves. So, fare you well:
    Upon the platform, 'twixt eleven and twelve,   250
    I'll visit you.
All: Our duty to your honour.
Hamlet: Your loves, as mine to you: farewell.   *Exeunt [all but Hamlet].*
    My father's spirit in arms! all is not well;
    I doubt° some foul play: would the night were come!
    Till then sit still, my soul: foul deeds will rise,   255
    Though all the earth o'erwhelm them, to men's eyes.   *Exit.*

[SCENE III: *A room in Polonius's house.*]

Enter Laertes and Ophelia, his Sister.

Laertes: My necessaries are embark'd: farewell:
    And, sister, as the winds give benefit
    And convoy is assistant,° do not sleep,
    But let me hear from you.
Ophelia: Do you doubt that?
Laertes: For Hamlet and the trifling of his favour,   5
    Hold it a fashion° and a toy in blood,°
    A violet in the youth of primy° nature,
    Forward,° not permanent, sweet, not lasting,
    The perfume and suppliance of a minute;°
    No more.
Ophelia: No more but so?
Laertes: Think it no more: 10
    For nature, crescent,° does not grow alone
    In thews° and bulk, but, as this temple° waxes,
    The inward service of the mind and soul
    Grows wide withal. Perhaps he loves you now,
    And now no soil° nor cautel° doth besmirch   15
    The virtue of his will: but you must fear,
    His greatness weigh'd,° his will is not his own;
    For he himself is subject to his birth:
    He may not, as unvalued persons do,
    Carve for himself; for on his choice depends   20

---

254 *doubt:* Fear.   **Scene III.**   3 *convoy is assistant:* Means of conveyance are available.
6 *fashion:* Custom, prevailing usage; *toy in blood:* Passing amorous fancy.   7 *primy:* In its
prime.   8 *Forward:* Precocious.   9 *suppliance of a minute:* Diversion to fill up a minute.
11 *crescent:* Growing, waxing.   12 *thews:* Bodily strength; *temple:* Body.   15 *soil:* Blemish; *cautel:* Crafty device.   17 *greatness weigh'd:* High position considered.

The safety and health of this whole state;
And therefore must his choice be circumscrib'd
Unto the voice and yielding° of that body
Whereof he is the head. Then if he says he loves you,
It fits your wisdom so far to believe it   25
As he in his particular act and place
May give his saying deed;° which is no further
Than the main voice of Denmark goes withal.
Then weigh what loss your honour may sustain,
If with too credent° ear you list his songs,   30
Or lose your heart, or your chaste treasure open
To his unmast'red° importunity.
Fear it, Ophelia, fear it, my dear sister,
And keep you in the rear of your affection,
Out of the shot and danger of desire.   35
The chariest° maid is prodigal enough,
If she unmask her beauty to the moon:
Virtue itself 'scapes not calumnious strokes:
The canker galls the infants of the spring,°
Too oft before their buttons° be disclos'd,°   40
And in the morn and liquid dew° of youth
Contagious blastments° are most imminent.
Be wary then; best safety lies in fear:
Youth to itself rebels, though none else near.

Ophelia: I shall the effect of this good lesson keep,   45
As watchman to my heart. But, good my brother,
Do not, as some ungracious° pastors do,
Show me the steep and thorny way to heaven;
Whiles, like a puff'd° and reckless libertine,
Himself the primrose path of dalliance treads,   50
And recks° not his own rede.°

    Enter Polonius.

Laertes: O, fear me not.
I stay too long: but here my father comes.
A double° blessing is a double grace;
Occasion° smiles upon a second leave.
Polonius: Yet here, Laertes? aboard, aboard, for shame!   55
The wind sits in the shoulder of your sail,
And you are stay'd for. There; my blessing with thee!
And these few precepts° in thy memory
Look thou character.° Give thy thoughts no tongue,

---

23 *voice and yielding:* Assent, approval.   27 *deed:* Effect.   30 *credent:* Credulous.   32 *unmast'red:* Unrestrained.   36 *chariest:* Most scrupulously modest.   39 *The canker . . . spring:* The cankerworm destroys the young plants of spring.   40 *buttons:* Buds; *disclos'd:* Opened.   41 *liquid dew:* I.e., time when dew is fresh.   42 *blastments:* Blights.   47 *ungracious:* Graceless.   49 *puff'd:* Bloated.   51 *recks:* Heeds; *rede:* Counsel.   53 *double:* I.e., Laertes has already bade his father good-by.   54 *Occasion:* Opportunity.   58 *precepts:* Many parallels have been found to the series of maxims which follows, one of the closer being that in Lyly's *Euphues.*   59 *character:* Inscribe.

Nor any unproportion'd° thought his act. 60
Be thou familiar, but by no means vulgar.°
Those friends thou hast, and their adoption tried,
Grapple them to thy soul with hoops of steel;
But do not dull thy palm with entertainment
Of each new-hatch'd, unfledg'd° comrade. Beware 65
Of entrance to a quarrel, but being in,
Bear't that th' opposed may beware of thee.
Give every man thy ear, but few thy voice;
Take each man's censure, but reserve thy judgement.
Costly thy habit as thy purse can buy, 70
But not express'd in fancy;° rich, not gaudy;
For the apparel oft proclaims the man,
And they in France of the best rank and station
Are of a most select and generous chief in that.°
Neither a borrower nor a lender be; 75
For loan oft loses both itself and friend,
And borrowing dulleth edge of husbandry.°
This above all: to thine own self be true,
And it must follow, as the night the day,
Thou canst not then be false to any man. 80
Farewell: my blessing season° this in thee!
Laertes: Most humbly do I take my leave, my lord.
Polonius: The time invites you; go; your servants tend.
Laertes: Farewell, Ophelia; and remember well
   What I have said to you.
Ophelia: 'Tis in my memory lock'd, 85
   And you yourself shall keep the key of it.
Laertes: Farewell.   *Exit Laertes.*
Polonius: What is 't, Ophelia, he hath said to you?
Ophelia: So please you, something touching the Lord Hamlet.
Polonius: Marry, well bethought: 90
   'Tis told me, he hath very oft of late
   Given private time to you; and you yourself
   Have of your audience been most free and bounteous:
   If it be so, as so't is put on° me,
   And that in way of caution, I must tell you, 95
   You do not understand yourself so clearly
   As it behooves my daughter and your honour.
   What is between you? give me up the truth.
Ophelia: He hath, my lord, of late made many tenders°
   Of his affection to me. 100
Polonius: Affection! pooh! you speak like a green girl,
   Unsifted° in such perilous circumstance.
   Do you believe his tenders,° as you call them?

---

60 *unproportion'd:* Inordinate.   61 *vulgar:* Common.   65 *unfledg'd:* Immature.
71 *express'd in fancy:* Fantastical in design.   74 *Are . . . that:* *Chief* is usually taken as a substantive
meaning "head," "eminence."   77 *husbandry:* Thrift.   81 *season:* Mature.   94 *put on:* Impressed on.   99, 103 *tenders:* Offers.   102 *Unsifted:* Untried.

Ophelia: I do not know, my lord, what I should think.
Polonius: Marry, I will teach you: think yourself a baby;   105
   That you have ta'en these tenders° for true pay,
   Which are not sterling.° Tender° yourself more dearly;
   Or — not to crack the wind° of the poor phrase,
   Running it thus — you'll tender me a fool.°
Ophelia: My lord, he hath importun'd me with love   110
   In honourable fashion.
Polonius: Ay, fashion° you may call it; go to, go to.
Ophelia: And hath given countenance° to his speech, my lord,
   With almost all the holy vows of heaven.
Polonius: Ay, springes° to catch woodcocks.° I do know,   115
   When the blood burns, how prodigal the soul
   Lends the tongue vows: these blazes, daughter,
   Giving more light than heat, extinct in both,
   Even in their promise, as it is a-making,
   You must not take for fire. From this time   120
   Be somewhat scanter of your maiden presence;
   Set your entreatments° at a higher rate
   Than a command to parley.° For Lord Hamlet,
   Believe so much in him,° that he is young,
   And with a larger tether may he walk   125
   Than may be given you: in few,° Ophelia,
   Do not believe his vows; for they are brokers;°
   Not of that dye° which their investments° show,
   But mere implorators of° unholy suits,
   Breathing° like sanctified and pious bawds,   130
   The better to beguile. This is for all:
   I would not, in plain terms, from this time forth,
   Have you so slander° any moment leisure,
   As to give words or talk with the Lord Hamlet.
   Look to 't, I charge you: come your ways.   135
Ophelia: I shall obey, my lord.   *Exeunt.*

[**Scene IV**: *The platform.*]

   Enter Hamlet, Horatio, and Marcellus.

Hamlet: The air bites shrewdly; it is very cold.
Horatio: It is a nipping and an eager air.
Hamlet: What hour now?
Horatio: I think it lacks of twelve.
Marcellus: No, it is struck.

---

106 *tenders:* Promises to pay.   107 *sterling:* Legal currency; *Tender:* Hold.   108 *crack the wind:* I.e., run it until it is broken-winded.   109 *tender . . . fool:* Show me a fool (for a daughter).   112 *fashion:* Mere form, pretense.   113 *countenance:* Credit, support.   115 *springes:* Snares; *woodcocks:* Birds easily caught, type of stupidity.   122 *entreatments:* Conversations, interviews.   123 *command to parley:* Mere invitation to talk.   124 *so . . . him:* This much concerning him.   126 *in few:* Briefly.   127 *brokers:* Go-betweens, procurers.   128 *dye:* Color or sort; *investments:* Clothes.   129 *implorators of:* Solicitors of.   130 *Breathing:* Speaking.   133 *slander:* Bring disgrace or reproach upon.

Horatio: Indeed? I heard it not: then it draws near the season   5
     Wherein the spirit held his wont to walk.

A flourish of trumpets, and two pieces go off.

     What does this mean, my lord?
Hamlet: The king doth wake° to-night and takes his rouse,°
     Keeps wassail,° and the swagg'ring up-spring° reels;°
     And, as he drains his draughts of Rhenish° down,   10
     The kettle-drum and trumpet thus bray out
     The triumph of his pledge.°
Horatio: Is it a custom?
Hamlet: Ay, marry, is 't:
     But to my mind, though I am native here
     And to the manner born,° it is a custom   15
     More honour'd in the breach than the observance.
     This heavy-headed revel east and west
     Makes us traduc'd and tax'd of other nations:
     They clepe° us drunkards, and with swinish phrase°
     Soil our addition;° and indeed it takes   20
     From our achievements, though perform'd at height,
     The pith and marrow of our attribute.°
     So, oft it chances in particular men,
     That for some vicious mole of nature° in them,
     As, in their birth — wherein they are not guilty,   25
     Since nature cannot choose his origin —
     By the o'ergrowth of some complexion,
     Oft breaking down the pales° and forts of reason,
     Or by some habit that too much o'er-leavens°
     The form of plausive° manners, that these men,   30
     Carrying, I say, the stamp of one defect,
     Being nature's livery,° or fortune's star,° —
     Their virtues else — be they as pure as grace,
     As infinite as man may undergo —
     Shall in the general censure take corruption   35
     From that particular fault: the dram of eale°
     Doth all the noble substance of a doubt
     To his own scandal.°

Enter Ghost.

Horatio: Look, my lord, it comes!

Scene IV.   8 *wake:* Stay awake, hold revel; *rouse:* Carouse, drinking bout.   9 *wassail:* Carousal; *up-spring:* Last and wildest dance at German merry-makings; *reels:* Reels through. 10 *Rhenish:* Rhine wine.   12 *triumph . . . pledge:* His glorious achievement as a drinker. 15 *to . . . born:* Destined by birth to be subject to the custom in question.   19 *clepe:* Call; *with swinish phrase:* By calling us swine.   20 *addition:* Reputation.   22 *attribute:* Reputation.   24 *mole of nature:* Natural blemish in one's constitution.   28 *pales:* Palings (as of a fortification).   29 *o'er-leavens:* Induces a change throughout (as yeast works in bread). 30 *plausive:* Pleasing.   32 *nature's livery; fortune's star:* The position in which one is placed by fortune, a reference to astrology. The two phrases are aspects of the same thing.   36–38 *the dram . . . scandal:* A famous crux: *dram of eale* has had various interpretations, the preferred one being probably "a dram of evil."

Hamlet: Angels and ministers of grace° defend us!
　　Be thou a spirit of health or goblin damn'd,　　　　　　　40
　　Bring with thee airs from heaven or blasts from hell,
　　Be thy intents wicked or charitable,
　　Thou com'st in such a questionable° shape
　　That I will speak to thee: I'll call thee Hamlet,
　　King, father, royal Dane: O, answer me!　　　　　　　　45
　　Let me not burst in ignorance; but tell
　　Why thy canoniz'd° bones, hearsed° in death,
　　Have burst their cerements;° why the sepulchre,
　　Wherein we saw thee quietly interr'd,
　　Hath op'd his ponderous and marble jaws,　　　　　　　50
　　To cast thee up again. What may this mean,
　　That thou, dead corse, again in complete steel
　　Revisits thus the glimpses of the moon,°
　　Making night hideous; and we fools of nature°
　　So horridly to shake our disposition　　　　　　　　　55
　　With thoughts beyond the reaches of our souls?
　　Say, why is this? wherefore? what should we do?

　　[Ghost] beckons [Hamlet].

Horatio: It beckons you to go away with it,
　　As if it some impartment° did desire
　　To you alone.
Marcellus:　　　　Look, with what courteous action　　　60
　　It waves you to a more removed° ground:
　　But do not go with it.
Horatio:　　　　　　　No, by no means.
Hamlet: It will not speak; then I will follow it.
Horatio: Do not, my lord!
Hamlet:　　　　　　Why, what should be the fear?
　　I do not set my life at a pin's fee;　　　　　　　　65
　　And for my soul, what can it do to that,
　　Being a thing immortal as itself?
　　It waves me forth again: I'll follow it.
Horatio: What if it tempt you toward the flood, my lord,
　　Or to the dreadful summit of the cliff　　　　　　　70
　　That beetles o'er° his base into the sea,
　　And there assume some other horrible form,
　　Which might deprive your sovereignty of reason°
　　And draw you into madness? think of it:
　　The very place puts toys of desperation,°　　　　　　75

---

39 *ministers of grace:* Messengers of God.　　43 *questionable:* Inviting question or conversation.　　47 *canoniz'd:* Buried according to the canons of the church; *hearsed:* Coffined. 48 *cerements:* Grave-clothes.　　53 *glimpses of the moon:* The earth by night.　　54 *fools of nature:* Mere men, limited to natural knowledge.　　59 *impartment:* Communication.　　61 *removed:* Remote.　　71 *beetles o'er:* Overhangs threateningly.　　73 *deprive . . . reason:* Take away the sovereignty of your reason. It was thought that evil spirits would sometimes assume the form of departed spirits in order to work madness in a human creature.　　75 *toys of desperation:* Freakish notions of suicide.

Without more motive, into every brain
That looks so many fathoms to the sea
And hears it roar beneath.
Hamlet: It waves me still.
    Go on; I'll follow thee.
Marcellus: You shall not go, my lord.
Hamlet: Hold off your hands! 80
Horatio: Be rul'd; you shall not go.
Hamlet: My fate cries out,
    And makes each petty artere° in this body
    As hardy as the Nemean lion's° nerve.°
    Still am I call'd. Unhand me, gentlemen.
    By heaven, I'll make a ghost of him that lets° me! 85
    I say, away! Go on; I'll follow thee. *Exeunt Ghost and Hamlet.*
Horatio: He waxes desperate with imagination.
Marcellus: Let's follow; 'tis not fit thus to obey him.
Horatio: Have after. To what issue° will this come?
Marcellus: Something is rotten in the state of Denmark. 90
Horatio: Heaven will direct it.°
Marcellus: Nay, let's follow him. *Exeunt.*

[SCENE V: *Another part of the platform.*]

    Enter Ghost and Hamlet.

Hamlet: Whither wilt thou lead me? speak; I'll go no further.
Ghost: Mark me.
Hamlet: I will.
Ghost: My hour is almost come,
    When I to sulphurous and tormenting flames
    Must render up myself.
Hamlet: Alas, poor ghost!
Ghost: Pity me not, but lend thy serious hearing 5
    To what I shall unfold.
Hamlet: Speak; I am bound to hear.
Ghost: So art thou to revenge, when thou shalt hear.
Hamlet: What?
Ghost: I am thy father's spirit,
    Doom'd for a certain term to walk the night, 10
    And for the day confin'd to fast° in fires,
    Till the foul crimes done in my days of nature
    Are burnt and purg'd away. But that I am forbid
    To tell the secrets of my prison-house,
    I could a tale unfold whose lightest word 15

---

82 *artere:* Artery. 83 *Nemean lion's:* The Nemean lion was one of the monsters slain by Hercules; *nerve:* Sinew, tendon. The point is that the arteries which were carrying the spirits out into the body were functioning and were as stiff and hard as the sinews of the lion. 85 *lets:* Hinders. 89 *issue:* Outcome. 91 *it:* I.e., the outcome. **Scene V.** 11 *fast:* Probably, do without food. It has been sometimes taken in the sense of doing general penance.

Would harrow up thy soul, freeze thy young blood,
Make thy two eyes, like stars, start from their spheres,°
Thy knotted° and combined° locks to part
And each particular hair to stand an end,
Like quills upon the fretful porpentine:°   20
But this eternal blazon° must not be
To ears of flesh and blood. List, list, O, list!
If thou didst ever thy dear father love —
Hamlet: O God!
Ghost: Revenge his foul and most unnatural° murder.   25
Hamlet: Murder!
Ghost: Murder most foul, as in the best it is;
   But this most foul, strange and unnatural.
Hamlet: Haste me to know't, that I, with wings as swift
   As meditation or the thoughts of love,   30
   May sweep to my revenge.
Ghost: I find thee apt;
   And duller shouldst thou be than the fat weed°
   That roots itself in ease on Lethe wharf,°
   Wouldst thou not stir in this. Now, Hamlet, hear:
   'Tis given out that, sleeping in my orchard,   35
   A serpent stung me; so the whole ear of Denmark
   Is by a forged process of my death
   Rankly abus'd: but know, thou noble youth,
   The serpent that did sting thy father's life
   Now wears his crown.
Hamlet: O my prophetic soul!   40
   My uncle!
Ghost: Ay, that incestuous, that adulterate° beast,
   With witchcraft of his wit, with traitorous gifts, —
   O wicked wit and gifts, that have the power
   So to seduce! — won to his shameful lust   45
   The will of my most seeming-virtuous queen:
   O Hamlet, what a falling-off was there!
   From me, whose love was of that dignity
   That it went hand in hand even with the vow
   I made to her in marriage, and to decline   50
   Upon a wretch whose natural gifts were poor
   To those of mine!
   But virtue, as it never will be moved,
   Though lewdness court it in a shape of heaven,
   So lust, though to a radiant angel link'd,   55
   Will sate itself in a celestial bed,
   And prey on garbage.

17 *spheres:* Orbits.   18 *knotted:* Perhaps intricately arranged; *combined:* Tied, bound.   20 *porpentine:* Porcupine.   21 *eternal blazon:* Promulgation or proclamation of eternity, revelation of the hereafter.   25 *unnatural:* I.e., pertaining to fratricide.   32 *fat weed:* Many suggestions have been offered as to the particular plant intended, including asphodel; probably a general figure for plants growing along rotting wharves and piles.   33 *Lethe wharf:* Bank of the river of forgetfulness in Hades.   42 *adulterate:* Adulterous.

But, soft! methinks I scent the morning air;
Brief let me be. Sleeping within my orchard,
My custom always of the afternoon,   60
Upon my secure° hour thy uncle stole,
With juice of cursed hebona° in a vial,
And in the porches of my ears did pour
The leperous° distilment; whose effect
Holds such an enmity with blood of man   65
That swift as quicksilver it courses through
The natural gates and alleys of the body,
And with a sudden vigour it doth posset°
And curd, like eager° droppings into milk,
The thin and wholesome blood: so did it mine;   70
And a most instant tetter bark'd about,
Most lazar-like,° with vile and loathsome crust,
All my smooth body.
Thus was I, sleeping, by a brother's hand
Of life, of crown, of queen, at once dispatch'd:°   75
Cut off even in the blossoms of my sin,
Unhous'led,° disappointed,° unanel'd,°
No reck'ning made, but sent to my account
With all my imperfections on my head:
O, horrible! O, horrible! most horrible!°   80
If thou hast nature in thee, bear it not;
Let not the royal bed of Denmark be
A couch for luxury° and damned incest.
But, howsomever thou pursues this act,
Taint not thy mind,° nor let thy soul contrive   85
Against thy mother aught: leave her to heaven
And to those thorns that in her bosom lodge,
To prick and sting her. Fare thee well at once!
The glow-worm shows the matin° to be near,
And 'gins to pale his uneffectual fire:°   90
Adieu, adieu, adieu! remember me.   *[Exit.]*
Hamlet: O all you host of heaven! O earth! what else?
And shall I couple° hell? O, fie! Hold, hold, my heart;
And you, my sinews, grow not instant old,
But bear me stiffly up. Remember thee!   95
Ay, thou poor ghost, whiles memory holds a seat
In this distracted globe.° Remember thee!

---

61 *secure:* Confident, unsuspicious.   62 *hebona:* Generally supposed to mean "henbane,"
conjectured *hemlock; ebenus,* meaning "yew."   64 *leperous:* Causing leprosy.   68 *posset:*
Coagulate, curdle.   69 *eager:* Sour, acid.   72 *lazar-like:* Leperlike.   75 *dispatch'd:* Suddenly bereft.   77 *Unhous'led:* Without having received the sacrament; *disappointed:* Un-
ready, without equipment for the last journey; *unanel'd:* Without having received extreme unction.   80 *O . . . horrible:* Many editors give this line to Hamlet; Garrick and Sir Henry Irving
spoke it in that part.   83 *luxury:* Lechery.   85 *Taint . . . mind:* Probably, deprave not thy
character, do nothing except in the pursuit of a natural revenge.   89 *matin:* Morning.   90
uneffectual fire: Cold light.   93 *couple:* Add.   97 *distracted globe:* Confused head.

Yea, from the table of my memory
I'll wipe away all trivial fond records,
All saws° of books, all forms, all pressures° past,   100
That youth and observation copied there;
And thy commandment all alone shall live
Within the book and volume of my brain,
Unmix'd with baser matter: yes, by heaven!
O most pernicious woman!   105
O villain, villain, smiling, damned villain!
My tables,° — meet it is I set it down,
That one may smile, and smile, and be a villain;
At least I am sure it may be so in Denmark: *[Writing.]*
So, uncle, there you are. Now to my word;°   110
It is "Adieu, adieu! remember me,"
I have sworn't.

Enter Horatio and Marcellus.

Horatio: My lord, my lord —
Marcellus: Lord Hamlet, —
Horatio: Heavens secure him!
Hamlet: So be it!
Marcellus: Hillo, ho, ho,° my lord!   115
Hamlet: Hillo, ho, ho, boy! come, bird, come.
Marcellus: How is't, my noble lord?
Horatio: What news, my lord?
Hamlet: O, wonderful!
Horatio: Good my lord, tell it.
Hamlet: No; you will reveal it.
Horatio: Not I, my lord, by heaven.
Marcellus: Nor I, my lord.   120
Hamlet: How say you, then; would heart of man once think it?
     But you'll be secret?
Horatio: ⎱
Marcellus: ⎰   Ay, by heaven, my lord.
Hamlet: There's ne'er a villain dwelling in all Denmark
     But he's an arrant° knave.
Horatio: There needs no ghost, my lord, come from the grave   125
     To tell us this.
Hamlet: Why, right; you are in the right;
     And so, without more circumstance at all,
     I hold it fit that we shake hands and part:
     You, as your business and desire shall point you;
     For every man has business and desire,   130
     Such as it is; and for my own poor part,
     Look you, I'll go pray.
Horatio: These are but wild and whirling words, my lord.
Hamlet: I am sorry they offend you, heartily;
     Yes, 'faith, heartily.

---

100 *saws:* Wise sayings; *pressures:* Impressions stamped.   107 *tables:* Probably a small portable writing-tablet carried at the belt.   110 *word:* Watchword.   115 *Hillo, ho, ho:* A fal-
coner's call to a hawk in air.   124 *arrant:* Thoroughgoing.

Horatio: There's no offence, my lord.   135

Hamlet: Yes, by Saint Patrick,° but there is, Horatio,
    And much offence too. Touching this vision here,
    It is an honest° ghost, that let me tell you:
    For your desire to know what is between us,
    O'ermaster 't as you may. And now, good friends,   140
    As you are friends, scholars and soldiers,
    Give me one poor request.

Horatio: What is 't, my lord? we will.

Hamlet: Never make known what you have seen to-night.

Horatio: }
Marcellus: } My lord, we will not.

Hamlet: Nay, but swear 't.

Horatio: In faith,   145
    My lord, not I.

Marcellus: Nor I, my lord, in faith.

Hamlet: Upon my sword.°

Marcellus: We have sworn, my lord, already.

Hamlet: Indeed, upon my sword, indeed.   *Ghost cries under the stage.*

Ghost: Swear.

Hamlet: Ah, ha, boy! say'st thou so? art thou there, truepenny?°   150
    Come on — you hear this fellow in the cellarage —
    Consent to swear.

Horatio: Propose the oath, my lord.

Hamlet: Never to speak of this that you have seen,
    Swear by my sword.

Ghost [beneath]: Swear.   155

Hamlet: Hic et ubique?° then we'll shift our ground.
    Come hither, gentlemen,
    And lay your hands again upon my sword:
    Swear by my sword,
    Never to speak of this that you have heard.   160

Ghost [beneath]: Swear by his sword.

Hamlet: Well said, old mole! canst work i' th' earth so fast?
    A worthy pioner!° Once more remove, good friends.

Horatio: O day and night, but this is wondrous strange!

Hamlet: And therefore as a stranger give it welcome.   165
    There are more things in heaven and earth, Horatio,
    Than are dreamt of in your philosophy.
    But come;
    Here, as before, never, so help you mercy,
    How strange or odd soe'er I bear myself,   170
    As I perchance hereafter shall think meet
    To put an antic° disposition on,
    That you, at such times seeing me, never shall,
    With arms encumb'red° thus, or this head-shake,

---

136 *Saint Patrick:* St. Patrick was keeper of Purgatory and patron saint of all blunders and confusion.   138 *honest:* I.e., a real ghost and not an evil spirit.   147 *sword:* I.e., the hilt in the form of a cross.   150 *truepenny:* Good old boy, or the like.   156 *Hic et ubique?:* Here and everywhere?   163 *pioner:* Digger, miner.   172 *antic:* Fantastic.   174 *encumb'red:* Folded or entwined.

Or by pronouncing of some doubtful phrase,   175
As "Well, well, we know," or "We could, an if we would,"
Or "If we list to speak," or "There be, an if they might,"
Or such ambiguous giving out,° to note°
That you know aught of me: this not to do,
So grace and mercy at your most need help you,   180
Swear.
Ghost [beneath]: Swear.
Hamlet: Rest, rest, perturbed spirit! [*They swear.*] So, gentlemen,
With all my love I do commend me to you:
And what so poor a man as Hamlet is   185
May do, t' express his love and friending° to you,
God willing, shall not lack. Let us go in together;
And still your fingers on your lips, I pray.
The time is out of joint: O cursed spite,
That ever I was born to set it right!   190
Nay, come, let's go together.   *Exeunt.*

[ACT II

SCENE I: *A room in Polonius's house.*]

Enter old Polonius with his man [Reynaldo].

Polonius: Give him this money and these notes, Reynaldo.
Reynaldo: I will, my lord.
Polonius: You shall do marvellous wisely, good Reynaldo,
Before you visit him, to make inquire
Of his behaviour.
Reynaldo: My lord, I did intend it.   5
Polonius: Marry, well said; very well said. Look you, sir,
Inquire me first what Danskers° are in Paris;
And how, and who, what means, and where they keep,°
What company, at what expense; and finding
By this encompassment° and drift° of question   10
That they do know my son, come you more nearer
Than your particular demands will touch it:°
Take° you as 'twere, some distant knowledge of him;
As thus, "I know his father and his friends,
And in part him": do you mark this, Reynaldo?   15
Reynaldo: Ay, very well, my lord.
Polonius: "And in part him; but" you may say "not well:
But, if 't be he I mean, he's very wild;
Addicted so and so": and there put on° him

---

178 *giving out:* Profession of knowledge; *to note:* To give a sign.   186 *friending:* Friend-
liness.   **Act II, Scene I.**   7 *Danskers:* Danke was a common variant for "Denmark"; hence
"Dane."   8 *keep:* Dwell.   10 *encompassment:* Roundabout talking; *drift:* Gradual approach
or course.   11–12 *come . . . it:* I.e., you will find out more this way than by asking pointed
questions.   13 *Take:* Assume, pretend.   19 *put on:* Impute to.

What forgeries° you please; marry, none so rank   20
As may dishonour him; take heed of that;
But, sir, such wanton,° wild and usual slips
As are companions noted and most known
To youth and liberty.
Reynaldo: As gaming, my lord.
Polonius: Ay, or drinking, fencing,° swearing, quarrelling,   25
  Drabbing;° you may go so far.
Reynaldo: My lord, that would dishonour him.
Polonius: 'Faith, no; as you may season it in the charge.
  You must not put another scandal on him,
  That he is open to incontinency;°   30
  That's not my meaning: but breathe his faults so quaintly°
  That they may seem the taints of liberty,°
  The flash and outbreak of a fiery mind,
  A savageness in unreclaimed° blood,
  Of general assault.°
Reynaldo: But, my good lord, —   35
Polonius: Wherefore should you do this?
Reynaldo: Ay, my lord,
  I would know that.
Polonius: Marry, sir, here's my drift;
  And, I believe, it is a fetch of wit:°
  You laying these slight sullies on my son,
  As 'twere a thing a little soil'd i' th' working,   40
  Mark you,
  Your party in converse, him you would sound,
  Having ever° seen in the prenominate° crimes
  The youth you breathe of guilty, be assur'd
  He closes with you in this consequence;°   45
  "Good sir," or so, or "friend," or "gentleman,"
  According to the phrase or the addition
  Of man and country.
Reynaldo: Very good, my lord.
Polonius: And then, sir, does 'a this — 'a does — what was I about to say? By
  the mass, I was about to say something: where did I leave?   50
Reynaldo: At "closes in the consequence," at "friend or so," and "gentle-
  man."
Polonius: At "closes in the consequence," ay, marry;
  He closes thus: "I know the gentleman;
  I saw him yesterday, or t' other day,   55
  Or then, or then; with such, or such; and, as you say,

---

20 *forgeries:* Invented tales.   22 *wanton:* Sportive, unrestrained.   25 *fencing:* Indicative of
the ill repute of professional fencers and fencing schools in Elizabethan times.   26 *Drabbing:*
Associating with immoral women.   30 *incontinency:* Habitual loose behavior.   31 *quaintly:*
Delicately, ingeniously.   32 *taints of liberty:* Blemishes due to freedom.   34 *unreclaimed:*
Untamed.   35 *general assault:* Tendency that assails all untrained youth.   38 *fetch
of wit:* Clever trick.   43 *ever:* At any time; *prenominate:* Before-mentioned.   45 *closes . . .
consequence:* Agrees with you in this conclusion.

There was 'a gaming; there o'ertook in 's rouse;°
There falling out at tennis": or perchance,
"I saw him enter such a house of sale,"
Videlicet,° a brothel, or so forth.   60
See you now;
Your bait of falsehood takes this carp of truth:
And thus do we of wisdom and of reach,°
With windlasses° and with assays of bias,°
By indirections° find directions° out: 65
So by my former lecture° and advice,
Shall you my son. You have me, have you not?
Reynaldo: My lord, I have.
Polonius: God bye ye;° fare ye well.
Reynaldo: Good my lord!
Polonius: Observe his inclination in yourself.°   70
Reynaldo: I shall, my lord.
Polonius: And let him ply his music.°
Reynaldo: Well, my lord.
Polonius: Farewell!   *Exit Reynaldo.*

     Enter Ophelia.

                     How now, Ophelia! what's the matter?
Ophelia: O, my lord, my lord, I have been so affrighted!
Polonius: With what, i' th' name of God?   75
Ophelia: My lord, as I was sewing in my closet,°
     Lord Hamlet, with his doublet° all unbrac'd;°
     No hat upon his head; his stockings foul'd,
     Ungart'red, and down-gyved° to his ankle;
     Pale as his shirt; his knees knocking each other;   80
     And with a look so piteous in purport
     As if he had been loosed out of hell
     To speak of horrors, — he comes before me.
Polonius: Mad for thy love?
Ophelia: My lord, I do not know;
     But truly, I do fear it.
Polonius: What said he?   85
Ophelia: He took me by the wrist and held me hard;
     Then goes he to the length of all his arm;
     And, with his other hand thus o'er his brow,
     He falls to such perusal of my face
     As 'a would draw it. Long stay'd he so;   90
     At last, a little shaking of mine arm

---

57 *o'ertook in 's rouse:* Overcome by drink.   60 *Videlicet:* Namely.   63 *reach:* Capacity,
ability.   64 *windlasses:* I.e., circuitous paths; *assays of bias:* Attempts that resemble the
course of the bowl, which, being weighted on one side, has a curving motion.   65 *indirec-
tions:* Devious courses; *directions:* Straight courses, i.e., the truth.   66 *lecture:* Admonition.
68 *bye ye:* Be with you.   70 *Observe . . . yourself:* In your own person, not by spies; or conform your own conduct to his inclination; or test him by studying yourself.   72 *ply his music:*
Probably to be taken literally.   76 *closet:* Private chamber.   77 *doublet:* Close-fitting
coat; *unbrac'd:* Unfastened.   79 *down-gyved:* Fallen to the ankles (like gyves or fetters).

And thrice his head thus waving up and down,
He rais'd a sigh so piteous and profound
As it did seem to shatter all his bulk°
And end his being: that done, he lets me go: 95
And, with his head over his shoulder turn'd,
He seem'd to find his way without his eyes;
For out o' doors he went without their helps,
And, to the last, bended their light on me.
Polonius: Come, go with me: I will go seek the king.   100
This is the very ecstasy of love,
Whose violent property° fordoes° itself
And leads the will to desperate undertakings
As oft as any passion under heaven
That does afflict our natures. I am sorry.   105
What, have you given him any hard words of late?
Ophelia: No, my good lord, but, as you did command,
I did repel his letters and denied
His access to me.
Polonius: That hath made him mad.
I am sorry that with better heed and judgement   110
I had not quoted° him: I fear'd he did but trifle,
And meant to wrack thee; but, beshrew my jealousy!°
By heaven, it is as proper to our age
To cast beyond° ourselves in our opinions
As it is common for the younger sort   115
To lack discretion. Come, go we to the king:
This must be known; which, being kept close, might move
More grief to hide than hate to utter love.°
Come.   *Exeunt.*

[SCENE II: *A room in the castle.*]

Flourish. Enter King and Queen, Rosencrantz, and Guildenstern [with others].

King: Welcome, dear Rosencrantz and Guildenstern!
Moreover that° we much did long to see you,
The need we have to use you did provoke
Our hasty sending. Something have you heard
Of Hamlet's transformation; so call it,   5
Sith° nor th' exterior nor the inward man
Resembles that it was. What it should be,
More than his father's death, that thus hath put him
So much from th' understanding of himself,
I cannot dream of: I entreat you both,   10
That, being of so young days° brought up with him,

94 *bulk:* Body.   102 *property:* Nature; *fordoes:* Destroys.   111 *quoted:* Observed.   112 *beshrew my jealousy:* Curse my suspicions.   114 *cast beyond:* Overshoot, miscalculate.   117–118 *might . . . love:* I.e., I might cause more grief to others by hiding the knowledge of Hamlet's love to Ophelia than hatred to me and mine by telling of it.   **Scene II.**   2 *Moreover that:* Besides the fact that.   6 *Sith:* Since.   11 *of . . . days:* From such early youth.

And sith so neighbour'd to his youth and haviour,
That you vouchsafe your rest° here in our court
Some little time: so by your companies
To draw him on to pleasures, and to gather,   15
So much as from occasion you may glean,
Whether aught, to us unknown, afflicts him thus,
That, open'd, lies within our remedy.

Queen: Good gentlemen, he hath much talk'd of you;
And sure I am two men there are not living   20
To whom he more adheres. If it will please you
To show us so much gentry° and good will
As to expend your time with us awhile,
For the supply and profit° of our hope,
Your visitation shall receive such thanks   25
As fits a king's remembrance.

Rosencrantz: Both your majesties
Might, by the sovereign power you have of us,
Put your dread pleasures more into command
Than to entreaty.

Guildenstern: But we both obey,
And here give up ourselves, in the full bent°   30
To lay our service freely at your feet,
To be commanded.

King: Thanks, Rosencrantz and gentle Guildenstern.

Queen: Thanks, Guildenstern and gentle Rosencrantz:
And I beseech you instantly to visit   35
My too much changed son. Go, some of you,
And bring these gentlemen where Hamlet is.

Guildenstern: Heavens make our presence and our practices
Pleasant and helpful to him!

Queen: Ay, amen!
    Exeunt Rosencrantz and Guildenstern [with some Attendants].

    Enter Polonius.

Polonius: Th' ambassadors from Norway, my good lord,   40
Are joyfully return'd.

King: Thou still hast been the father of good news.

Polonius: Have I, my lord? I assure my good liege,
I hold my duty, as I hold my soul,
Both to my God and to my gracious king: 45
And I do think, or else this brain of mine
Hunts not the trail of policy so sure
As it hath us'd to do, that I have found
The very cause of Hamlet's lunacy.

King: O, speak of that; that do I long to hear.   50

Polonius: Give first admittance to th' ambassadors;
My news shall be the fruit to that great feast.

King: Thyself do grace to them, and bring them in.   *[Exit Polonius.]*

---

13 *vouchsafe your rest:* Please to stay.   22 *gentry:* Courtesy.   24 *supply and profit:* Aid and successful outcome.   30 *in . . . bent:* To the utmost degree of our mental capacity.

He tells me, my dear Gertrude, he hath found
The head and source of all your son's distemper. 55
Queen: I doubt° it is no other but the main;°
His father's death, and our o'erhasty marriage.
King: Well, we shall sift him.

Enter Ambassadors [Voltimand and Cornelius, with Polonius.]

Welcome, my good friends!
Say, Voltimand, what from our brother Norway?
Voltimand: Most fair return of greetings and desires. 60
Upon our first, he sent out to suppress
His nephew's levies; which to him appear'd
To be a preparation 'gainst the Polack;
But, better look'd into, he truly found
It was against your highness: whereat griev'd, 65
That so his sickness, age and impotence
Was falsely borne in hand,° sends out arrests
On Fortinbras; which he, in brief, obeys;
Receives rebuke from Norway, and in fine°
Makes vow before his uncle never more 70
To give th' assay° of arms against your majesty.
Whereon old Norway, overcome with joy,
Gives him three score thousand crowns in annual fee,
And his commission to employ those soldiers,
So levied as before, against the Polack: 75
With an entreaty, herein further shown,   *[Giving a paper.]*
That it might please you to give quiet pass
Through your dominions for this enterprise,
On such regards of safety and allowance°
As therein are set down.
King: It likes° us well; 80
And at our more consider'd° time we'll read,
Answer, and think upon this business.
Meantime we thank you for your well-took labour:
Go to your rest; at night we'll feast together:
Most welcome home!   *Exeunt Ambassadors.*
Polonius: This business is well ended. 85
My liege, and madam, to expostulate
What majesty should be, what duty is,
Why day is day, night night, and time is time,
Were nothing but to waste night, day and time.
Therefore, since brevity is the soul of wit,° 90
And tediousness the limbs and outward flourishes,°
I will be brief: your noble son is mad:
Mad call I it; for, to define true madness

---

56 *doubt:* Fear; *main:* Chief point, principal concern.   67 *borne in hand:* Deluded.   69 *in fine:* In the end.   71 *assay:* Assault, trial (of arms).   79 *safety and allowance:* Pledges of safety to the country and terms of permission for the troops to pass.   80 *likes:* Pleases. 81 *consider'd:* Suitable for deliberation.   90 *wit:* Sound sense or judgment.   91 *flourishes:* Ostentation, embellishments.

What is 't but to be nothing else but mad?
But let that go.
Queen: More matter, with less art.   95
Polonius: Madam, I swear I use no art at all.
That he is mad, 'tis true: 'tis true 'tis pity;
And pity 'tis 'tis true: a foolish figure;°
But farewell it, for I will use no art.
Mad let us grant him, then: and now remains   100
That we find out the cause of this effect,
Or rather say, the cause of this defect,
For this effect defective comes by cause:
Thus it remains, and the remainder thus.
Perpend.°   105
I have a daughter — have while she is mine —
Who, in her duty and obedience, mark,
Hath given me this: now gather, and surmise. *[Reads the letter.]* "To the
celestial and my soul's idol,
the most beautified Ophelia," —   110
That's an ill phrase, a vile phrase; "beautified" is a vile phrase: but you
shall hear. Thus: *[Reads.]*
"In her excellent white bosom, these, & c."
Queen: Came this from Hamlet to her?
Polonius: Good madam, stay awhile; I will be faithful.   *[Reads.]* 115
            "Doubt thou the stars are fire;
                Doubt that the sun doth move;
            "Doubt truth to be a liar;
                But never doubt I love.
"O dear Ophelia, I am ill at these numbers;° I have not art to reckon°   120
my groans: but that I love thee best, O most best, believe it. Adieu.
    "Thine evermore, most dear lady, whilst this machine° is to him,
                                                                HAMLET."

This, in obedience, hath my daughter shown me,
And more above,° hath his solicitings,   125
As they fell out° by time, by means° and place,
All given to mine ear.
King: But how hath she
Receiv'd his love?
Polonius: What do you think of me?
King: As of a man faithful and honourable.
Polonius: I would fain prove so. But what might you think,   130
When I had seen this hot love on the wing —
As I perceiv'd it, I must tell you that,
Before my daughter told me — what might you,
Or my dear majesty your queen here, think,
If I had play'd the desk or table-book,°   135
Or given my heart a winking,° mute and dumb,

---

98 *figure:* Figure of speech.   105 *Perpend:* Consider.   120 *ill . . . numbers:* Unskilled at
writing verses; *reckon:* Number metrically, scan.   122 *machine:* Bodily frame.   125 *more
above:* Moreover.   126 *fell out:* Occurred; *means:* Opportunities (of access).   135 *play'd . . .
table-book:* I.e., remained shut up, concealed this information.   136 *given . . . winking:* Given
my heart a signal to keep silent.

Or look'd upon this love with idle sight;
What might you think? No, I went round to work,
And my young mistress thus I did bespeak:°
"Lord Hamlet is a prince, out of thy star;°   140
This must not be": and then I prescripts gave her,
That she should lock herself from his resort,
Admit no messengers, receive no tokens.
Which done, she took the fruits of my advice;
And he, repelled — a short tale to make —   145
Fell into a sadness, then into a fast,
Thence to a watch,° thence into a weakness,
Thence to a lightness,° and, by this declension,°
Into the madness wherein now he raves,
And all we mourn for.

King: Do you think 'tis this?   150
Queen: It may be, very like.
Polonius: Hath there been such a time — I would fain know that —
That I have positively said " 'Tis so,"
When it prov'd otherwise?
King: Not that I know.
Polonius *[pointing to his head and shoulder]:* Take this from this, if this be
          otherwise: 155
If circumstances lead me, I will find
Where truth is hid, though it were hid indeed
Within the centre.°
King: How may we try it further?
Polonius: You know, sometimes he walks four hours together
Here in the lobby.
Queen: So he does indeed.   160
Polonius: At such a time I'll loose my daughter to him:
Be you and I behind an arras° then;
Mark the encounter: if he love her not
And be not from his reason fall'n thereon,°
Let me be no assistant for a state,   165
But keep a farm and carters.
King: We will try it.

Enter Hamlet [reading on a book].

Queen: But, look, where sadly the poor wretch comes reading.
Polonius: Away, I do beseech you both, away:
                               Exeunt King and Queen [with Attendants].
I'll board° him presently. O, give me leave.
How does my good Lord Hamlet?   170
Hamlet: Well, God-a-mercy.
Polonius: Do you know me, my lord?
Hamlet: Excellent well; you are a fishmonger.°
Polonius: Not I, my lord.

---

139 *bespeak:* Address.   140 *out . . . star:* Above thee in position.   147 *watch:* State of sleep-
lessness.   148 *lightness:* Lightheadedness; *declension:* Decline, deterioration.   158 *centre:*
Middle point of the earth.   162 *arras:* Hanging, tapestry.   164 *thereon:* On that account.
169 *board:* Accost.   173 *fishmonger:* An opprobrious expression meaning "bawd," "procurer."

Hamlet: Then I would you were so honest a man.   175
Polonius: Honest, my lord!
Hamlet: Ay, sir; to be honest, as this world goes, is to be one man picked out
  of ten thousand.
Polonius: That's very true, my lord.
Hamlet: For if the sun breed maggots in a dead dog, being a good kissing   180
  carrion,° — Have you a daughter?
Polonius: I have, my lord.
Hamlet: Let her not walk i' the sun:° conception° is a blessing: but as your
  daughter may conceive — Friend, look to 't.
Polonius [aside]: How say you by° that? Still harping on my daughter: yet   185
  he knew me not at first; 'a said I was a fishmonger: 'a is far gone, far
  gone: and truly in my youth I suffered much extremity for love; very
  near this. I'll speak to him again. What do you read, my lord?
Hamlet: Words, words, words.
Polonius: What is the matter,° my lord?   190
Hamlet: Between who?°
Polonius: I mean, the matter that you read, my lord.
Hamlet: Slanders, sir: for the satirical rogue says here that old men have
  grey beards, that their faces are wrinkled, their eyes purging° thick
  amber and plum-tree gum and that they have a plentiful lack of wit,   195
  together with most weak hams: all which, sir, though I most powerfully and potently believe, yet I hold it not honesty° to have it thus set
  down, for yourself, sir, should be old as I am, if like a crab you could
  go backward.
Polonius [aside]: Though this be madness, yet there is method in 't. — Will   200
  you walk out of the air, my lord?
Hamlet: Into my grave.
Polonius: Indeed, that's out of the air. *(Aside.)* How pregnant sometimes
  his replies are! a happiness° that often madness hits on, which reason and sanity could not so prosperously° be delivered of. I will leave   205
  him, and suddenly contrive the means of meeting between him and
  my daughter. — My honourable lord, I will most humbly take my
  leave of you.
Hamlet: You cannot, sir, take from me any thing that I will more willingly
  part withal: except my life, except my life, except my life.   210

  Enter Guildenstern and Rosencrantz.

Polonius: Fare you well, my lord.
Hamlet: These tedious old fools!
Polonius: You go to seek the Lord Hamlet; there he is.
Rosencrantz [to Polonius]: God save you, sir!   *[Exit Polonius.]*
Guildenstern: My honoured lord!   215
Rosencrantz: My most dear lord!
Hamlet: My excellent good friends! How dost thou, Guildenstern? Ah, Ros-
  encrantz! Good lads, how do ye both?

180–181 *good kissing carrion:* I.e., a good piece of flesh for kissing (?).   183 *i' the sun:* In the
sunshine of princely favors; *conception:* Quibble on "understanding" and "pregnancy."
185 *by:* Concerning.   190 *matter:* Substance.   191 *Between who:* Hamlet deliberately
takes *matter* as meaning "basis of dispute."   194 *purging:* discharging.   197 *honesty:*
Decency.   204 *happiness:* Felicity of expression.   205 *prosperously:* Successfully.

Rosencrantz: As the indifferent° children of the earth.

Guildenstern: Happy, in that we are not over-happy; 220
On Fortune's cap we are not the very button.

Hamlet: Nor the soles of her shoe?

Rosencrantz: Neither, my lord.

Hamlet: Then you live about her waist, or in the middle of her favours?

Guildenstern: 'Faith, her privates° we. 225

Hamlet: In the secret parts of Fortune? O, most true; she is a strumpet. What's the news?

Rosencrantz: None, my lord, but that the world's grown honest.

Hamlet: Then is doomsday near: but your news is not true. Let me question more in particular: what have you, my good friends, deserved at 230 the hands of Fortune, that she sends you to prison hither?

Guildenstern: Prison, my lord!

Hamlet: Denmark's a prison.

Rosencrantz: Then is the world one.

Hamlet: A goodly one; in which there are many confines,° wards and dun- 235 geons, Denmark being one o' the worst.

Rosencrantz: We think not so, my lord.

Hamlet: Why, then, 'tis none to you; for there is nothing either good or bad, but thinking makes it so: to me it is a prison.

Rosencrantz: Why then, your ambition makes it one; 'tis too narrow for 240 your mind.

Hamlet: O God, I could be bounded in a nutshell and count myself a king of infinite space, were it not that I have bad dreams.

Guildenstern: Which dreams indeed are ambition, for the very substance of the ambitious° is merely the shadow of a dream. 245

Hamlet: A dream itself is but a shadow.

Rosencrantz: Truly, and I hold ambition of so airy and light a quality that it is but a shadow's shadow.

Hamlet: Then are our beggars bodies, and our monarchs and out-stretched heroes the beggars' shadows. Shall we to the court? for, by 250 my fay,° I cannot reason.°

Rosencrantz: ⎫
⎬ We'll wait upon you.°
Guildenstern: ⎭

Hamlet: No such matter: I will not sort° you with the rest of my servants, for, to speak to you like an honest man, I am most dreadfully attended.° But, in the beaten way of friendship,° what make you at 255 Elsinore?

Rosencrantz: To visit you, my lord: no other occasion.

Hamlet: Beggar that I am, I am ever poor in thanks; but I thank you: and sure, dear friends, my thanks are too dear a° halfpenny. Were you not sent for? Is it your own inclining? Is it a free visitation? Come, come, 260 deal justly with me: come, come; nay, speak.

Guildenstern: What should we say, my lord?

---

219 *indifferent:* Ordinary.   225 *privates:* I.e., ordinary men (sexual pun on *private parts*). 235 *confines:* Places of confinement.   244–245 *very ... ambitious:* That seemingly most substantial thing which the ambitious pursue.   251 *fay:* Faith; *reason:* Argue.   252 *wait upon:* Accompany.   253 *sort:* Class.   254–255 *dreadfully attended:* Poorly provided with servants.   255 *in the ... friendship:* As a matter of course among friends.   259 *a:* I.e., at a.

Hamlet: Why, any thing, but to the purpose. You were sent for; and there is a kind of confession in your looks which your modesties have not craft enough to colour: I know the good king and queen have sent for 265 you.

Rosencrantz: To what end, my lord?

Hamlet: That you must teach me. But let me conjure° you, by the rights of our fellowship, by the consonancy of our youth,° by the obligation of our ever-preserved love, and by what more dear a better proposer° 270 could charge you withal, be even and direct with me, whether you were sent for, or no?

Rosencrantz [aside to Guildenstern]: What say you?

Hamlet [aside]: Nay, then, I have an eye of you. — If you love me, hold not off.   275

Guildenstern: My lord, we were sent for.

Hamlet: I will tell you why; so shall my anticipation prevent your discovery,° and your secrecy to the king and queen moult no feather. I have of late — but wherefore I know not — lost all my mirth, forgone all custom of exercises; and indeed it goes so heavily with my disposition 280 that this goodly frame, the earth, seems to me a sterile promontory, this most excellent canopy, the air, look you, this brave o'erhanging firmament, this majestical roof fretted° with golden fire, why, it appeareth nothing to me but a foul and pestilent congregation of vapours. What a piece of work is a man! how noble in reason! how 285 infinite in faculties!° in form and moving how express° and admirable! in action how like an angel! in apprehension° how like a god! the beauty of the world! the paragon of animals! And yet, to me, what is this quintessence° of dust? man delights not me: no, nor woman neither, though by your smiling you seem to say so.   290

Rosencrantz: My lord, there was no such stuff in my thoughts.

Hamlet: Why did you laugh then, when I said "man delights not me"?

Rosencrantz: To think, my lord, if you delight not in man, what lenten° entertainment the players shall receive from you: we coted° them on the way; and hither are they coming, to offer you service.   295

Hamlet: He that plays the king shall be welcome; his majesty shall have tribute of me; the adventurous knight shall use his foil and target;° the lover shall not sigh gratis; the humorous man° shall end his part in peace; the clown shall make those laugh whose lungs are tickle o' the sere;° and the lady shall say her mind freely, or the blank verse 300 shall halt for 't.° What players are they?

Rosencrantz: Even those you were wont to take delight in, the tragedians of the city.

---

268 *conjure:* Adjure, entreat.   269 *consonancy of our youth:* The fact that we are of the same age.   270 *better proposer:* One more skillful in finding proposals.   277–278 *prevent your discovery:* Forestall your disclosure.   283 *fretted:* Adorned.   286 *faculties:* Capacity; *express:* Well-framed (?), exact (?).   287 *apprehension:* Understanding.   289 *quintessence:* The fifth essence of ancient philosophy, supposed to be the substance of the heavenly bodies and to be latent in all things.   293 *lenten:* Meager.   294 *coted:* Overtook and passed beyond.   297 *foil and target:* Sword and shield.   298 *humorous man:* Actor who takes the part of the humor characters.   299–300 *tickle o' the sere:* Easy on the trigger. 300–301 *the lady . . . for 't:* The lady (fond of talking) shall have opportunity to talk, blank verse or no blank verse.

Hamlet: How chances it they travel? their residence,° both in reputation
and profit, was better both ways.   305

Rosencrantz: I think their inhibition° comes by the means of the late
innovation.°

Hamlet: Do they hold the same estimation they did when I was in the city?
are they so followed?

Rosencrantz: No, indeed, are they not.   310

Hamlet: How° comes it? do they grow rusty?

Rosencrantz: Nay, their endeavour keeps in the wonted pace: but there is,
sir, an aery° of children, little eyases,° that cry out on the top of question,° and are most tyrannically° clapped for 't: these are now the fashion, and so berattle° the common stages° — so they call them — that   315
many wearing rapiers° are afraid of goose-quills° and dare scarce come
thither.

Hamlet: What, are they children? who maintains 'em? how are they escoted?° Will they pursue the quality° no longer than they can sing?°
will they not say afterwards, if they should grow themselves to com-   320
mon° players — as it is most like, if their means are no better — their
writers do them wrong, to make them exclaim against their own
succession?°

Rosencrantz: 'Faith, there has been much to do on both sides; and the nation holds it no sin to tarre° them to controversy: there was, for a   325
while, no money bid for argument,° unless the poet and the player
went to cuffs° in the question.°

Hamlet: Is't possible?

Guildenstern: O, there has been much throwing about of brains.

Hamlet: Do the boys carry it away?°   330

Rosencrantz: Ay, that they do, my lord; Hercules and his load° too.

Hamlet: It is not very strange; for my uncle is king of Denmark, and those
that would make mows° at him while my father lived, give twenty,
forty, fifty, a hundred ducats° a-piece for his picture in little.° 'Sblood,
there is something in this more than natural, if philosophy could find   335
it out.   *A flourish [of trumpets within].*

Guildenstern: There are the players.

---

304 *residence:* Remaining in one place.   306 *inhibition:* Formal prohibition (from acting plays in the city or, possibly, at court).   307 *innovation:* The new fashion in satirical
plays performed by boy actors in the "private" theaters.   311–331 *How . . . load:* The passage is the famous one dealing with the War of the Theatres (1599–1602); namely, the rivalry
between the children's companies and the adult actors.   313 *aery:* Nest; *eyases:* Young
hawks.   313–314 *cry . . . question:* Speak in a high key dominating conversation; clamor forth
the height of controversy; probably "excel"; perhaps intended to decry leaders of the dramatic
profession.   314 *tyrannically:* Outrageously.   315 *berattle:* Berate; *common stages:* Public
theaters.   316 *many wearing rapiers:* Many men of fashion, who were afraid to patronize the
common players for fear of being satirized by the poets who wrote for the children; *goose-quills:* I.e.,
pens of satirists.   318–319 *escoted:* Maintained.   319 *quality:* Acting profession; *no
longer . . . sing:* I.e., until their voices change.   320–321 *common:* Regular, adult.   323 *succession:* Future careers.   325 *tarre:* Set on (as dogs).   326 *argument:* Probably, plot for a play.
327 *went to cuffs:* Came to blows; *question:* Controversy.   330 *carry it away:* Win the day.
331 *Hercules . . . load:* Regarded as an allusion to the sign of the Globe Theatre, which was Hercules bearing the world on his shoulder.   333 *mows:* Grimaces.   334 *ducats:* Gold coins
worth 9s. 4d; *in little:* In miniature.

Hamlet: Gentlemen, you are welcome to Elsinore. Your hands, come then: the appurtenance of welcome is fashion and ceremony: let me comply° with you in this garb,° lest my extent° to the players, which, I tell 340 you, must show fairly outwards, should more appear like entertainment than yours. You are welcome: but my uncle-father and auntmother are deceived.

Guildenstern: In what, my dear lord?

Hamlet: I am but mad north-north-west:° when the wind is southerly I 345 know a hawk from a handsaw.°

Enter Polonius.

Polonius: Well be with you, gentlemen!

Hamlet: Hark you, Guildenstern; and you too: at each ear a hearer: that great baby you see there is not yet out of his swaddling-clouts.°

Rosencrantz: Happily he is the second time come to them; for they say an 350 old man is twice a child.

Hamlet: I will prophesy he comes to tell me of the players; mark it. — You say right, sir: o' Monday morning;° 'twas then indeed.

Polonius: My lord, I have news to tell you.

Hamlet: My lord, I have news to tell you. When Roscius° was an actor in 355 Rome, —

Polonius: The actors are come hither, my lord.

Hamlet: Buz, buz!°

Polonius: Upon my honour, —

Hamlet: Then came each actor on his ass, — 360

Polonius: The best actors in the world, either for tragedy, comedy, history, pastoral, pastoral-comical, historical-pastoral, tragical-historical, tragical-comical-historical-pastoral, scene individable,° or poem unlimited:° Seneca° cannot be too heavy, nor Plautus° too light. For the law of writ and the liberty,° these are the only men. 365

Hamlet: O Jephthah, judge of Israel,° what a treasure hadst thou!

Polonius: What a treasure had he, my lord?

Hamlet: Why,

"One fair daughter, and no more,
The which he loved passing well." 370

Polonius [aside]: Still on my daughter.

Hamlet: Am I not i' the right, old Jephthah?

339–340 *comply:* Observe the formalities of courtesy.   340 *garb:* Manner; *extent:* Showing of kindness.   345 *I am . . . north-north-west:* I am only partly mad, i.e., in only one point of the compass.   346 *handsaw:* A proposed reading of *hernshaw* would mean "heron"; *handsaw* may be an early corruption of *hernshaw.* Another view regards *hawk* as the variant of *hack,* a tool of the pickax type, and *handsaw* as a saw operated by hand.   349 *swaddling-clouts:* Cloths in which to wrap a newborn baby.   353 *o' Monday morning:* Said to mislead Polonius. 355 *Roscius:* A famous Roman actor.   358 *Buz, buz:* An interjection used at Oxford to denote stale news.   363 *scene individable:* A play observing the unity of place.   364 *poem unlimited:* A play disregarding the unities of time and place; *Seneca:* Writer of Latin tragedies, model of early Elizabethan writers of tragedy; *Plautus:* Writer of Latin comedy.   365 *law . . . liberty:* Pieces written according to rules and without rules, i.e., "classical" and "romantic" dramas.   366 *Jephthah . . . Israel:* Jephthah had to sacrifice his daughter; see Judges 11.

Polonius: If you call me Jephthah, my lord, I have a daughter that I love pass-
ing° well.

Hamlet: Nay, that follows not. 375

Polonius: What follows, then, my lord?

Hamlet: Why,

"As by lot, God wot,"

and then, you know,

"It came to pass, as most like° it was," — 380

the first row° of the pious chanson° will show you more; for look,
where my abridgement comes.°

Enter the Players.

You are welcome, masters; welcome, all. I am glad to see thee well. Welcome, good friends. O, old friend! why, thy face is valanced° since I saw
thee last: comest thou to beard me in Denmark? What, my young lady 385
and mistress! By'r lady, your ladyship is nearer to heaven than when I saw
you last, by the altitude of a chopine.° Pray God, your voice, like a piece
of uncurrent° gold, be not cracked within the ring.° Masters, you are all
welcome. We'll e'en to 't like French falconers, fly at any thing we see: we'll
have a speech straight: come, give us a taste of your quality; come, a pas- 390
sionate speech.

First Player: What speech, my good lord?

Hamlet: I heard thee speak me a speech once, but it was never acted; or, if
it was, not above once; for the play, I remember, pleased not the million; 'twas caviary to the general:° but it was — as I received it, and 395
others, whose judgements in such matters cried in the top of°
mine — an excellent play, well digested in the scenes, set down with
as much modesty as cunning.° I remember, one said there were no
sallets° in the lines to make the matter savoury, nor no matter in the
phrase that might indict° the author of affectation; but called it an 400
honest method, as wholesome as sweet, and by very much more handsome than fine.° One speech in 't I chiefly loved: 'twas Æneas' tale to
Dido;° and thereabout of it especially, where he speaks of Priam's
slaughter: if it live in your memory, begin at this line: let me see, let
me see — 405

"The rugged Pyrrhus,° like th' Hyrcanian beast,"° —

'tis not so: — it begins with Pyrrhus: —

---

374 *passing:* Surpassingly.　　380 *like:* Probable.　　381 *row:* Stanza; *chanson:* Ballad.
382 *abridgement comes:* Opportunity comes for cutting short the conversation. 384 *valanced:*
Fringed (with a beard).　　387 *chopine:* Kind of shoe raised by the thickness of the heel;
worn in Italy, particularly at Venice.　　388 *uncurrent:* Not passable as lawful coinage.
388–389 *cracked within the ring:* In the center of coins were rings enclosing the sovereign's
head; if the coin was cracked within this ring, it was unfit for currency.　　395 *caviary to the
general:* Not relished by the multitude.　　396 *cried in the top of:* Spoke with greater authority
than.　　398 *cunning:* Skill.　　398–399 *sallets:* Salads: here, spicy improprieties. 400 *indict:*
Convict.　　401–402 *as wholesome ... fine:* Its beauty was not that of elaborate ornament, but
that of order and proportion.　　402–403 *Æneas' tale to Dido:* The lines recited by the player
are imitated from Marlowe and Nashe's *Dido Queen of Carthage* (II.i.214 ff.). They are written
in such a way that the conventionality of the play within a play is raised above that of ordinary
drama.　　406 *Pyrrhus:* A Greek hero in the Trojan War; *Hyrcanian beast:* The tiger; see Virgil,
Aeneid, IV.266.

"The rugged Pyrrhus, he whose sable arms,
Black as his purpose, did the night resemble
When he lay couched in the ominous horse,°   410
Hath now this dread and black complexion smear'd
With heraldry more dismal; head to foot
Now is he total gules;° horridly trick'd°
With blood of fathers, mothers, daughters, sons,
Bak'd and impasted° with the parching streets,   415
That lend a tyrannous and a damned light
To their lord's murder: roasted in wrath and fire,
And thus o'er-sized° with coagulate gore,
With eyes like carbuncles, the hellish Pyrrhus
Old grandsire Priam seeks."   420
So, proceed you.

Polonius: 'Fore God, my lord, well spoken, with good accent and good
discretion.

First Player: "Anon he finds him
Striking too short at Greeks; his antique sword,   425
Rebellious to his arm, lies where it falls,
Repugnant° to command: unequal match'd,
Pyrrhus at Priam drives; in rage strikes wide;
But with the whiff and wind of his fell sword
Th' unnerved father falls. Then senseless Ilium,°   430
Seeming to feel this blow, with flaming top
Stoops to his base, and with a hideous crash
Takes prisoner Pyrrhus' ear: for, lo! his sword
Which was declining on the milky head
Of reverend Priam, seem'd i' th' air to stick: 435
So, as a painted tyrant,° Pyrrhus stood,
And like a neutral to his will and matter,°
Did nothing.
But, as we often see, against° some storm,
A silence in the heavens, the rack° stand still,   440
The bold winds speechless and the orb below
As hush as death, anon the dreadful thunder
Doth rend the region,° so, after Pyrrhus' pause,
Aroused vengeance sets him new a-work;
And never did the Cyclops' hammers fall   445
On Mars's armour forg'd for proof eterne°
With less remorse than Pyrrhus' bleeding sword
Now falls on Priam.
Out, out, thou strumpet, Fortune! All you gods,
In general synod,° take away her power;   450
Break all the spokes and fellies° from her wheel,

---

410 *ominous horse:* Trojan horse.   413 *gules:* Red, a heraldic term; *trick'd:* Spotted, smeared.
415 *impasted:* Made into a paste.   418 *o'er-sized:* Covered as with size or glue.   427 *Repugnant:* Disobedient.   430 *Then senseless Ilium:* Insensate Troy.   436 *painted tyrant:* Tyrant in a picture.   437 *matter:* Task.   439 *against:* Before.   440 *rack:* Mass of clouds.
443 *region:* Assembly.   446 *proof eterne:* External resistance to assault.   450 *synod:* Assembly.   451 *fellies:* Pieces of wood forming the rim of a wheel.

And bowl the round nave° down the hill of heaven,
> As low as to the fiends!"

Polonius: This is too long.

Hamlet: It shall to the barber's, with your beard. Prithee, say on: he's for a   455
jig° or a tale of bawdry,° or he sleeps: say on: come to Hecuba.°

First Player: "But who, ah woe! had seen the mobled° queen —"

Hamlet: "The mobled queen?"

Polonius: That's good; "mobled queen" is good.

First Player: "Run barefoot up and down, threat'ning the flames   460
> With bisson rheum;° a clout° upon that head
> Where late the diadem stood, and for a robe,
> About her lank and all o'er-teemed° loins,
> A blanket, in the alarm of fear caught up;
> Who this had seen, with tongue in venom steep'd,   465
> 'Gainst Fortune's state would treason have pronounc'd:°
> But if the gods themselves did see her then
> When she saw Pyrrhus make malicious sport
> In mincing with his sword her husband's limbs,
> The instant burst of clamour that she made,   470
> Unless things mortal move them not at all,
> Would have made milch° the burning eyes of heaven,
> And passion in the gods."

Polonius: Look, whe'r he has not turned° his colour and has tears in 's eyes.
Prithee, no more.   475

Hamlet: 'Tis well; I'll have thee speak out the rest soon. Good my lord,
will you see the players well bestowed? Do you hear, let them be well
used; for they are the abstract° and brief chronicles of the time: after
your death you were better have a bad epitaph than their ill report
while you live.   480

Polonius: My lord, I will use them according to their desert.

Hamlet: God's bodykins,° man, much better: use every man after his desert,
and who shall 'scape whipping? Use them after your own honour and
dignity: the less they deserve, the more merit is in your bounty. Take
them in.   485

Polonius: Come, sirs.

Hamlet: Follow him, friends: we'll hear a play tomorrow. *[Aside to First
Player.]* Dost thou hear me, old friend; can you play the Murder of
Gonzago?

First Player: Ay, my lord.   490

Hamlet: We'll ha 't to-morrow night. You could, for a need, study a speech
of some dozen or sixteen lines,° which I would set down and insert in 't,
could you not?

First Player: Ay, my lord.

---

452 *nave:* Hub.   456 *jig:* Comic performance given at the end or in an interval of a play; *bawdry:* Indecency; *Hecuba:* Wife of Priam, king of Troy.   457 *mobled:* Muffled.   461 *bisson rheum:* Blinding tears; *clout:* Piece of cloth.   463 *o'er-teemed:* Worn out with bearing children.   466 *pronounc'd:* Proclaimed.   472 *milch:* Moist with tears.   474 *turned:* Changed.   478 *abstract:* Summary account.   482 *bodykins:* Diminutive form of the oath "by God's body."   492 *dozen or sixteen lines:* Critics have amused themselves by trying to locate Hamlet's lines. Lucianus's speech III.ii.229–234 is the best guess.

Hamlet: Very well. Follow that lord; and look you mock him not. — My good   495
  friends, I'll leave you till night: you are welcome to Elsinore.

                                      Exeunt Polonius and Players.

Rosencrantz: Good my lord!   *Exeunt [Rosencrantz and Guildenstern.]*
Hamlet: Ay, so, God bye to you. — Now I am alone.
  O, what a rogue and peasant° slave am I!
  Is it not monstrous that this player here,   500
  But in a fiction, in a dream of passion,
  Could force his soul so to his own conceit
  That from her working all his visage wann'd,°
  Tears in his eyes, distraction in 's aspect,
  A broken voice, and his whole function suiting   505
  With forms to his conceit?° and all for nothing!
  For Hecuba!
  What's Hecuba to him, or he to Hecuba,
  That he should weep for her? What would he do,
  Had he the motive and the cue for passion   510
  That I have? He would drown the stage with tears
  And cleave the general ear with horrid speech,
  Make mad the guilty and appall the free,
  Confound the ignorant, and amaze indeed
  The very faculties of eyes and ears.   515
  Yet I,
  A dull and muddy-mettled° rascal, peak,°
  Like John-a-dreams,° unpregnant of° my cause,
  And can say nothing; no, not for a king.
  Upon whose property° and most dear life   520
  A damn'd defeat was made. Am I a coward?
  Who calls me villain? breaks my pate across?
  Plucks off my beard, and blows it in my face?
  Tweaks me by the nose? gives me the lie i' th' throat,
  As deep as to the lungs? who does me this?   525
  Ha!
  'Swounds, I should take it: for it cannot be
  But I am pigeon-liver'd° and lack gall
  To make oppression bitter, or ere this
  I should have fatted all the region kites°   530
  With this slave's offal: bloody, bawdy villain!
  Remorseless, treacherous, lecherous, kindless° villain!
  O, vengeance!
  Why, what an ass am I! This is most brave,
  That I, the son of a dear father murder'd,   535

---

499 *peasant:* Base.   503 *wann'd:* Grew pale.   505–506 *his whole . . . conceit:* His whole
being responded with forms to suit his thought.   517 *muddy-mettled:* Dull-spirited; *peak:*
Mope, pine.   518 *John-a-dreams:* An expression occurring elsewhere in Elizabethan literature to indicate a dreamer; *unpregnant of:* Not quickened by.   520 *property:* Proprietor-
ship (of crown and life).   528 *pigeon-liver'd:* The pigeon was supposed to secrete no gall; if
Hamlet, so he says, had had gall, he would have felt the bitterness of oppression, and avenged it.
530 *region kites:* Kites of the air.   532 *kindless:* Unnatural.

Prompted to my revenge by heaven and hell,
Must, like a whore, unpack my heart with words,
And fall a-cursing, like a very drab,°
A stallion!°
Fie upon 't! foh! About,° my brains! Hum, I have heard   540
That guilty creatures sitting at a play
Have by the very cunning of the scene
Been struck so to the soul that presently
They have proclaim'd their malefactions;
For murder, though it have no tongue, will speak   545
With most miraculous organ. I'll have these players
Play something like the murder of my father
Before mine uncle: I'll observe his looks:
I'll tent° him to the quick: if 'a do blench,°
I know my course. The spirit that I have seen   550
May be the devil:° and the devil hath power
T' assume a pleasing shape; yea, and perhaps
Out of my weakness and my melancholy,
As he is very potent with such spirits,°
Abuses me to damn me: I'll have grounds   555
More relative° than this:° the play's the thing
Wherein I'll catch the conscience of the king.   *Exit.*

[ACT III

SCENE I: *A room in the castle.*]

Enter King, Queen, Polonius, Ophelia, Rosencrantz, Guildenstern, Lords.

King: And can you, by no drift of conference,°
    Get from him why he puts on this confusion,
    Grating so harshly all his days of quiet
    With turbulent and dangerous lunacy?
Rosencrantz: He does confess he feels himself distracted;   5
    But from what cause 'a will by no means speak.
Guildenstern: Nor do we find him forward° to be sounded,
    But, with a crafty madness, keeps aloof,
    When we would bring him on to some confession
    Of his true state.
Queen: Did he receive you well?   10
Rosencrantz: Most like a gentleman.
Guildenstern: But with much forcing of his disposition.°

---

538 *drab:* Prostitute.   539 *stallion:* Prostitute (male or female).   540 *About:* About it,
or turn thou right about.   549 *tent:* Probe; *blench:* Quail, flinch.   551 *May be the*
devil: Hamlet's suspicion is properly grounded in the belief of the time.   554 *spirits:*
Humors.   556 *relative:* Closely related, definite; *this:* I.e., the ghost's story.   **Act III,**
Scene I.   1 *drift of conference:* Device of conversation.   7 *forward:* Willing.   12 *forc-*
ing of his disposition: I.e., against his will.

Rosencrantz: Niggard of question;° but, of our demands,
    Most free in his reply.
Queen: Did you assay° him
    To any pastime?   15
Rosencrantz: Madam, it so fell out, that certain players
    We o'er-raught° on the way: of these we told him;
    And there did seem in him a kind of joy
    To hear of it: they are here about the court,
    And, as I think, they have already order   20
    This night to play before him.
Polonius: 'Tis most true:
    And he beseech'd me to entreat your majesties
    To hear and see the matter.
King: With all my heart; and it doth much content me
    To hear him so inclin'd.   25
    Good gentlemen, give him a further edge,°
    And drive his purpose into these delights.
Rosencrantz: We shall, my lord.   *Exeunt Rosencrantz and Guildenstern.*
King: Sweet Gertrude, leave us too;
    For we have closely° sent for Hamlet hither,
    That he, as 'twere by accident, may here   30
    Affront° Ophelia:
    Her father and myself, lawful espials,°
    Will so bestow ourselves that, seeing, unseen,
    We may of their encounter frankly judge,
    And gather by him, as he is behav'd,   35
    If 't be th' affliction of his love or no
    That thus he suffers for.
Queen: I shall obey you.
    And for your part, Ophelia, I do wish
    That your good beauties be the happy cause
    Of Hamlet's wildness:° so shall I hope your virtues   40
    Will bring him to his wonted way again,
    To both your honours.
Ophelia: Madam, I wish it may.   *[Exit Queen.]*
Polonius: Ophelia, walk you here. Gracious,° so please you,
    We will bestow ourselves. *[To Ophelia.]* Read on this book;
    That show of such an exercise° may colour°   45
    Your loneliness. We are oft to blame in this, —
    'Tis too much prov'd — that with devotion's visage
    And pious action we do sugar o'er
    The devil himself.
King: *[aside]* O, 'tis too true!
    How smart a lash that speech doth give my conscience!   50

---

13 *Niggard of question:* Sparing of conversation.   14 *assay:* Try to win.   17 *o'er-raught:* Overtook.   26 *edge:* Incitement.   29 *closely:* Secretly.   31 *Affront:* Confront.   32 *lawful espials:* Legitimate spies.   40 *wildness:* Madness.   43 *Gracious:* Your grace (addressed to the king).   45 *exercise:* Act of devotion (the book she reads is one of devotion); *colour:* Give a plausible appearance to.

The harlot's cheek, beautied with plast'ring art,
Is not more ugly to° the thing° that helps it
Than is my deed to my most painted word:
O heavy burthen!
Polonius: I hear him coming: let's withdraw, my lord.   55

                                 [Exeunt King and Polonius.]

    Enter Hamlet.

Hamlet: To be, or not to be: that is the question:
Whether 'tis nobler in the mind to suffer
The slings and arrows of outrageous fortune,
Or to take arms against a sea° of troubles,
And by opposing end them? To die: to sleep;   60
No more; and by a sleep to say we end
The heart-ache and the thousand natural shocks
That flesh is heir to, 'tis a consummation
Devoutly to be wish'd. To die, to sleep;
To sleep: perchance to dream: ay, there's the rub;   65
For in that sleep of death what dreams may come
When we have shuffled° off this mortal coil,°
Must give us pause: there's the respect°
That makes calamity of so long life;°
For who would bear the whips and scorns of time,°   70
Th' oppressor's wrong, the proud man's contumely,
The pangs of despis'd° love, the law's delay,
The insolence of office° and the spurns°
That patient merit of th' unworthy takes,
When he himself might his quietus° make   75
With a bare bodkin?° who would fardels° bear,
To grunt and sweat under a weary life,
But that the dread of something after death,
The undiscover'd country from whose bourn°
No traveller returns, puzzles the will   80
And makes us rather bear those ills we have
Than fly to others that we know not of?
Thus conscience° does make cowards of us all;
And thus the native hue° of resolution
Is sicklied o'er° with the pale cast° of thought,   85
And enterprises of great pitch° and moment°

---

52 *to:* Compared to; *thing:* I.e., the cosmetic.   59 *sea:* The mixed metaphor of this speech has often been commented on; a later emendation *siege* has sometimes been spoken on the stage.   67 *shuffled:* Sloughed, cast; *coil:* Usually means "turmoil"; here, possibly "body" (conceived of as wound about the soul like rope); *clay, soil, veil,* have been suggested as emendations.   68 *respect:* Consideration.   69 *of . . . life:* So long-lived.   70 *time:* The world.   72 *despis'd:* Rejected.   73 *office:* Office-holders; *spurns:* Insults.   75 *quietus:* Acquittance; here, death.   76 *bare bodkin:* Mere dagger; *bare* is sometimes understood as "unsheathed"; *fardels:* Burdens.   79 *bourn:* Boundary.   83 *conscience:* Probably, inhibition by the faculty of reason restraining the will from doing wrong.   84 *native hue:* Natural color; metaphor derived from the color of the face.   85 *sicklied o'er:* Given a sickly tinge; *cast:* Shade of color.   86 *pitch:* Height (as of a falcon's flight); *moment:* Importance.

With this regard° their currents° turn awry,
And lose the name of action — Soft you now!
The fair Ophelia! Nymph, in thy orisons°
Be all my sins rememb'red.

Ophelia: Good my lord,   90
How does your honour for this many a day?

Hamlet: I humbly thank you; well, well, well.

Ophelia: My lord, I have remembrances of yours,
That I have longed long to re-deliver;
I pray you, now receive them.

Hamlet: No, not I;   95
I never gave you aught.

Ophelia: My honour'd lord, you know right well you did;
And, with them, words of so sweet breath compos'd
As made the things more rich: their perfume lost,
Take these again; for to the noble mind   100
Rich gifts wax poor when givers prove unkind.
There, my lord.

Hamlet: Ha, ha! are you honest?°

Ophelia: My lord?

Hamlet: Are you fair?   105

Ophelia: What means your lordship?

Hamlet: That if you be honest and fair, your honesty° should admit no
discourse to° your beauty.

Ophelia: Could beauty, my lord, have better commerce° than with honesty?

Hamlet: Ay, truly; for the power of beauty will sooner transform honesty   110
from what it is to a bawd than the force of honesty can translate beauty
into his likeness: this was sometime a paradox, but now the time° gives it
proof. I did love you once.

Ophelia: Indeed, my lord, you made me believe so.

Hamlet: You should not have believed me; for virtue cannot so inoculate° our   115
old stock but we shall relish of it:° I loved you not.

Ophelia: I was the more deceived.

Hamlet: Get thee to a nunnery: why wouldst thou be a breeder of sinners? I am myself indifferent honest;° but yet I could accuse me of
such things that it were better my mother had not borne me: I am very   120
proud, revengeful, ambitious, with more offences at my beck° than I
have thoughts to put them in, imagination to give them shape, or time
to act them in. What should such fellows as I do crawling between earth and heaven? We are arrant knaves, all; believe none of us.
Go thy ways to a nunnery. Where's your father?   125

---

87 *regard:* Respect, consideration; *currents:* Courses.   89 *orisons:* Prayers.   103–108 *are you honest ... beauty: Honest* meaning "truthful" and "chaste" and *fair* meaning "just, honorable" (line 105) and "beautiful" (line 107) are not mere quibbles; the speech has the irony of a *double entendre.*   107 *your honesty:* Your chastity.   108 *discourse to:* Familiar intercourse with.   109 *commerce:* Intercourse.   113 *the time:* The present age.   115 *inoculate:* Graft (meta-phorical).   116 *but ... it:* I.e., that we do not still have about us a taste of the old stock; i.e., retain our sinfulness.   119 *indifferent honest:* Moderately virtuous.   121 *beck:* Command.

Ophelia: At home, my lord.

Hamlet: Let the doors be shut upon him, that he may play the fool no where but in 's own house. Farewell.

Ophelia: O, help him, you sweet heavens!

Hamlet: If thou dost marry, I'll give thee this plague for thy dowry: be   130
thou as chaste as ice, as pure as snow, thou shalt not escape calumny.
Get thee to a nunnery, go: farewell. Or, if thou wilt needs marry, marry
a fool; for wise men know well enough what monsters° you make of
them. To a nunnery, go, and quickly too. Farewell.

Ophelia: O heavenly powers, restore him!   135

Hamlet: I have heard of your° paintings too, well enough; God hath given
you one face, and you make yourselves another: you jig,° you amble,
and you lisp; you nick-name God's creatures, and make your wantonness your ignorance.° Go to, I'll no more on 't; it hath made me mad. I
say, we will have no more marriage: those that are married already, all   140
but one,° shall live; the rest shall keep as they are. To a nunnery, go.

Exit.

Ophelia: O, what a noble mind is here o'er-thrown!
The courtier's, soldier's, scholar's, eye, tongue, sword;
Th' expectancy and rose° of the fair state,
The glass of fashion and the mould of form,°   145
Th' observ'd of all observers,° quite, quite down!
And I, of ladies most deject and wretched,
That suck'd the honey of his music vows,
Now see that noble and most sovereign reason,
Like sweet bells jangled, out of time and harsh;   150
That unmatch'd form and feature of blown° youth
Blasted with ecstasy:° O, woe is me,
T' have seen what I have seen, see what I see!

Enter King and Polonius.

King: Love! his affections do not that way tend;
Nor what he spake, though it lack'd form a little,   155
Was not like madness. There's something in his soul,
O'er which his melancholy sits on brood;
And I do doubt° the hatch and the disclose°
Will be some danger: which for to prevent,
I have in quick determination   160
Thus set it down: he shall with speed to England,
For the demand of our neglected tribute:
Haply the seas and countries different
With variable° objects shall expel

---

133 *monsters:* An allusion to the horns of a cuckold.   136 *your:* Indefinite use.   137 *jig:*
Move with jerky motion; probably allusion to the *jig*, or song and dance, of the current stage.
138–139 *make . . . ignorance:* I.e., excuse your wantonness on the ground of your ignorance.
141 *one:* I.e., the king.   144 *expectancy and rose:* Source of hope.   145 *The glass . . .*
form: The mirror of fashion and the pattern of courtly behavior.   146 *observ'd . . . observers:*
I.e., the center of attention in the court.   151 *blown:* Blooming.   152 *ecstasy:* Madness.
158 *doubt:* Fear; *disclose:* Disclosure or revelation (by chipping of the shell).   164 *variable:*
Various.

This something-settled° matter in his heart,   165
Whereon his brains still beating puts him thus
From fashion of himself.° What think you on 't?
Polonius: It shall do well: but yet do I believe
The origin and commencement of his grief
Sprung from neglected love. How now, Ophelia!   170
You need not tell us what Lord Hamlet said;
We heard it all. My lord, do as you please;
But, if you hold it fit, after the play
Let his queen mother all alone entreat him
To show his grief: let her be round° with him;   175
And I'll be plac'd, so please you, in the ear
Of all their conference. If she find him not,
To England send him, or confine him where
Your wisdom best shall think.
King: It shall be so: 180
Madness in great ones must not unwatch'd go.   *Exeunt.*

[SCENE II: *A hall in the castle.*]

Enter Hamlet and three of the Players.

Hamlet: Speak the speech, I pray you, as I pronounced it to you, trippingly on the tongue: but if you mouth it, as many of your° players
do, I had as lief the town-crier spoke my lines. Nor do not saw the
air too much with your hand, thus, but use all gently; for in the very
torrent, tempest, and, as I may say, whirlwind of your passion, you   5
must acquire and beget a temperance that may give it smoothness.
O, it offends me to the soul to hear a robustious° periwig-pated°
fellow tear a passion to tatters, to very rags, to split the ears of the
groundlings,° who for the most part are capable of° nothing but
inexplicable° dumb-shows and noise: I would have such a fellow   10
whipped for o'er-doing Termagant;° it out-herods Herod:° pray you,
avoid it.
First Player: I warrant your honour.
Hamlet: Be not too tame neither, but let your own discretion be your
tutor: suit the action to the word, the word to the action; with this spe- 15
cial observance, that you o'er-step not the modesty of nature: for any
thing so overdone is from the purpose of playing, whose end, both
at the first and now, was and is, to hold, as 't were, the mirror up to
nature; to show virtue her own feature, scorn her own image, and
the very age and body of the time his form and pressure.° Now this   20

---

165 *something-settled:* Somewhat settled.   167 *From . . . himself:* Out of his natural manner.   175 *round:* Blunt. **Scene II.**   2 *your:* Indefinite use.   7 *robustious:* Violent,
boisterous; *periwig-pated:* Wearing a wig.   9 *groundlings:* Those who stood in the yard of
the theater; *capable of:* Susceptible of being influenced by.   10 *inexplicable:* Of no significance worth explaining.   11 *Termagant:* A god of the Saracens; a character in the St. Nicholas
play, where one of his worshipers, leaving him in charge of goods, returns to find them
stolen; whereupon he beats the god (or idol), which howls vociferously; *Herod:* Herod of Jewry;
a character in *The Slaughter of the Innocents* and other cycle plays. The part was played with great
noise and fury.   20 *pressure:* Stamp, impressed character.

overdone, or come tardy off,° though it make the unskilful laugh,
cannot but make the judicious grieve; the censure of the which one°
must in your allowance o'erweigh a whole theatre of others. O, there
be players that I have seen play, and heard others praise, and that
highly, not to speak it profanely, that, neither having the accent of   25
Christians nor the gait of Christian, pagan, nor man, have so strut-
ted and bellowed that I have thought some of nature's journeymen°
had made men and not made them well, they imitated humanity so
abominably.

First Player: I hope we have reformed that indifferently° with us, sir.   30

Hamlet: O, reform it altogether. And let those that play your clowns speak
no more than is set down for them; for there be of° them that will themselves laugh, to set on some quantity of barren° spectators to laugh too;
though, in the mean time, some necessary question of the play be then to
be considered: that's villanous, and shows a most pitiful ambition in the   35
fool that uses it. Go, make you ready.

[Exeunt Players.]

Enter Polonius, Guildenstern, and Rosencrantz.

How now, my lord! will the king hear this piece of work?

Polonius: And the queen too, and that presently.

Hamlet: Bid the players make haste.   [*Exit Polonius.*]
    Will you two help to hasten them?   40

Rosencrantz: ⎫
Guildenstern: ⎬   We will, my lord.   *Exeunt they two.*

Hamlet: What ho! Horatio!

Enter Horatio.

Horatio: Here, sweet lord, at your service.

Hamlet: Horatio, thou art e'en as just° a man
    As e'er my conversation cop'd withal.

Horatio: O, my dear lord, —

Hamlet: Nay, do not think I flatter;   45
    For what advancement may I hope from thee
    That no revenue hast but thy good spirits,
    To feed and clothe thee? Why should the poor be flatter'd?
    No, let the candied tongue lick absurd pomp,
    And crook the pregnant° hinges of the knee   50
    Where thrift° may follow fawning. Dost thou hear?
    Since my dear soul was mistress of her choice
    And could of men distinguish her election,
    S' hath seal'd thee for herself; for thou hast been
    As one, in suff'ring all, that suffers nothing,   55
    A man that fortune's buffets and rewards
    Hast ta'en with equal thanks: and blest are those
    Whose blood and judgement are so well commeddled,

---

21 *come tardy off*: Inadequately done.   22 *the censure . . . one*: The judgment of even one of
whom.   27 *journeymen*: Laborers not yet masters in their trade.   30 *indifferently*: Fairly,
tolerably.   32 *of*: I.e., some among them.   33 *barren*: I.e., of wit.   43 *just*: Honest, honorable.   50 *pregnant*: Pliant.   51 *thrift*: Profit.

That they are not a pipe for fortune's finger
To sound what stop° she please. Give me that man　　　60
That is not passion's slave, and I will wear him
In my heart's core, ay, in my heart of heart,
As I do thee. — Something too much of this. —
There is a play to-night before the king;
One scene of it comes near the circumstance　　　65
Which I have told thee of my father's death:
I prithee, when thou seest that act afoot,
Even with the very comment of thy soul°
Observe my uncle: if his occulted° guilt
Do not itself unkennel in one speech,　　　70
It is a damned° ghost that we have seen,
And my imaginations are as foul
As Vulcan's stithy.° Give him heedful note;
For I mine eyes will rivet to his face,
And after we will both our judgements join　　　75
In censure of his seeming.°
Horatio:　　　　　　　　　Well, my lord:
　If 'a steal aught the whilst this play is playing,
　And 'scape detecting, I will pay the theft.

Enter trumpets and kettledrums, King, Queen, Polonius, Ophelia,
[Rosencrantz, Guildenstern, and others].

Hamlet: They are coming to the play; I must be idle:° Get you a place.
King: How fares our cousin Hamlet?　　　80
Hamlet: Excellent, i' faith; of the chameleon's dish:° I eat the air, promise-
　crammed: you cannot feed capons so.
King: I have nothing with° this answer, Hamlet; these words are not
　mine.°
Hamlet: No, nor mine now. *[To Polonius.]* My lord, you played once i' the　　85
　university, you say?
Polonius: That did I, my lord; and was accounted a good actor.
Hamlet: What did you enact?
Polonius: I did enact Julius Cæsar: I was killed i' the Capitol; Brutus killed
　me.　　　90
Hamlet: It was a brute part of him to kill so capital a calf there. Be the players
　ready?
Rosencrantz: Ay, my lord; they stay upon your patience.
Queen: Come hither, my dear Hamlet, sit by me.
Hamlet: No, good mother, here's metal more attractive.　　　95
Polonius [to the king]: O, ho! do you mark that?
Hamlet: Lady, shall I lie in your lap?　　　　　　　*[Lying down at Ophelia's feet.]*

---

60 *stop:* Hole in a wind instrument for controlling the sound.　68 *very . . . soul:* Inward and
sagacious criticism.　69 *occulted:* Hidden.　71 *damned:* In league with Satan.　73 *stithy:*
Smithy, place of *stiths* (anvils).　76 *censure . . . seeming:* Judgment of his appearance or behavior.　79 *idle:* Crazy, or not attending to anything serious.　81 *chameleon's dish:* Cha-
meleons were supposed to feed on air. (Hamlet deliberately misinterprets the king's "fares" as
"feeds.")　83 *have . . . with:* Make nothing of.　83–84 *are not mine:* Do not respond to
what I ask.

Ophelia: No, my lord.

Hamlet: I mean, my head upon your lap?

Ophelia: Ay, my lord.   100

Hamlet: Do you think I meant country° matters?

Ophelia: I think nothing, my lord.

Hamlet: That's a fair thought to lie between maids' legs.

Ophelia: What is, my lord?

Hamlet: Nothing.   105

Ophelia: You are merry, my lord.

Hamlet: Who, I?

Ophelia: Ay, my lord.

Hamlet: O God, your only° jig-maker.° What should a man do but be
merry? for, look you, how cheerfully my mother looks, and my father 110
died within's two hours.

Ophelia: Nay, 'tis twice two months, my lord.

Hamlet: So long? Nay then, let the devil wear black, for I'll have a suit of
sables.° O heavens! die two months ago, and not forgotten yet? Then
there's hope a great man's memory may outlive his life half a year: but, 115
by 'r lady, 'a must build churches, then; or else shall 'a suffer not thinking
on,° with the hobbyhorse, whose epitaph is "For, O, for, O, the hobbyhorse is forgot."°

The trumpets sound. Dumb show follows.

> *Enter a King and a Queen [very lovingly]; the Queen embracing him,
> and he her. [She kneels, and makes show of protestation unto him.] He takes
> her up, and declines his head upon her neck: he lies him down upon a bank
> of flowers: she, seeing him asleep, leaves him. Anon comes in another man,
> takes off his crown, kisses it, pours poison in the sleeper's ears, and leaves
> him. The Queen returns; finds the King dead, makes passionate action. The
> Poisoner, with some three or four come in again, seem to condole with her.
> The dead body is carried away. The Poisoner woos the Queen with gifts: she
> seems harsh awhile, but in the end accepts love. [Exeunt.]*

Ophelia: What means this, my lord?

Hamlet: Marry, this is miching mallecho;° it means mischief.   120

Ophelia: Belike this show imports the argument of the play.

> *Enter Prologue.*

Hamlet: We shall know by this fellow: the players cannot keep counsel; they'll
tell all.

Ophelia: Will 'a tell us what this show meant?

Hamlet: Ay, or any show that you'll show him: be not you ashamed to 125
show, he'll not shame to tell you what it means.

Ophelia: You are naught, you are naught:° I'll mark the play.

Prologue: For us, and for our tragedy,

---

101 *country:* With a bawdy pun.   109 *your only:* Only your; *jig-maker:* Composer of
jigs (song and dance).   113–114 *suit of sables:* Garments trimmed with the fur of the sable,
with a quibble on *sable* meaning "black."   116–117 *suffer . . . on:* Undergo oblivion.   117–118 *"For . . . forgot":* Verse of a song occurring also in *Love's Labour's Lost,*
III.i.30. The hobbyhorse was a character in the Morris Dance.   120 *miching mallecho:*
Sneaking mischief.   127 *naught:* Indecent.

Here stooping° to your clemency,
We beg your hearing patiently.   *[Exit.]* 130
Hamlet: Is this a prologue, or the posy° of a ring?
Ophelia: 'Tis brief, my lord.
Hamlet: As woman's love.

Enter [two Players as] King and Queen.

Player King: Full thirty times hath Phoebus' cart gone round
Neptune's salt wash° and Tellus'° orbed ground,   135
And thirty dozen moons with borrowed° sheen
About the world have times twelve thirties been,
Since love our hearts and Hymen° did our hands
Unite commutual° in most sacred bands.
Player Queen: So many journeys may the sun and moon   140
Make us again count o'er ere love be done!
But, woe is me, you are so sick of late,
So far from cheer and from your former state,
That I distrust° you. Yet, though I distrust,
Discomfort you, my lord, it nothing must: 145
For women's fear and love holds quantity;°
In neither aught, or in extremity.
Now, what my love is, proof hath made you know;
And as my love is siz'd, my fear is so:
Where love is great, the littlest doubts are fear;   150
Where little fears grow great, great love grows there.
Player King: 'Faith, I must leave thee, love, and shortly too;
My operant° powers their functions leave° to do:
And thou shalt live in this fair world behind,
Honour'd, belov'd; and haply one as kind   155
For husband shalt thou —
Player Queen: O, confound the rest!
Such love must needs be treason in my breast:
In second husband let me be accurst!
None wed the second but who kill'd the first.
Hamlet (aside): Wormwood, wormwood.   160
Player Queen: The instances that second marriage move
Are base respects of thrift, but none of love:
A second time I kill my husband dead,
When second husband kisses me in bed.
Player King: I do believe you think what now you speak;   165
But what we do determine oft we break.
Purpose is but the slave to memory,
Of violent birth, but poor validity:
Which now, like fruit unripe, sticks on the tree;
But fall, unshaken, when they mellow be.   170
Most necessary 'tis that we forget
To pay ourselves what to ourselves is debt:

---

129 *stooping:* Bowing.   131 *posy:* Motto.   135 *salt wash:* The sea; *Tellus:* Goddess of the
earth (*orbed ground*).   136 *borrowed:* I.e., reflected.   138 *Hymen:* God of matrimony.
139 *commutual:* Mutually.   144 *distrust:* Am anxious about.   146 *holds quantity:* Keeps
proportion between.   153 *operant:* Active; *leave:* Cease.

What to ourselves in passion we propose,
The passion ending, doth the purpose lose.
The violence of either grief or joy 175
Their own enactures° with themselves destroy:
Where joy most revels, grief doth most lament;
Grief joys, joy grieves, on slender accident.
This world is not for aye,° nor 'tis not strange
That even our loves should with our fortunes change; 180
For 'tis a question left us yet to prove,
Whether love lead fortune, or else fortune love.
The great man down, you mark his favourite flies;
The poor advanc'd makes friends of enemies.
And hitherto doth love on fortune tend; 185
For who° not needs shall never lack a friend,
And who in want a hollow friend doth try,
Directly seasons° him his enemy.
But, orderly to end where I begun,
Our wills and fates do so contrary run 190
That our devices still are overthrown;
Our thoughts are ours, their ends° none of our own:
So think thou wilt no second husband wed;
But die thy thoughts when thy first lord is dead.
Player Queen: Nor earth to me give food, nor heaven light! 195
Sport and repose lock from me day and night!
To desperation turn my trust and hope!
An anchor's° cheer° in prison be my scope!
Each opposite° that blanks° the face of joy
Meet what I would have well and it destroy! 200
Both here and hence pursue me lasting strife,
If, once a widow, ever I be wife!
Hamlet: If she should break it now!
Player King: 'Tis deeply sworn. Sweet, leave me here awhile;
My spirits grow dull, and fain I would beguile 205
The tedious day with sleep. *[Sleeps.]*
Player Queen: Sleep rock thy brain;
And never come mischance between us twain! *Exit.*
Hamlet: Madam, how like you this play?
Queen: The lady doth protest too much, methinks.
Hamlet: O, but she'll keep her word. 210
King: Have you heard the argument? Is there no offence in 't?
Hamlet: No, no, they do but jest, poison in jest; no offence i' the world.
King: What do you call the play?
Hamlet: The Mouse-trap. Marry, how? Tropically.° This play is the image of a
murder done in Vienna: Gonzago° is the duke's name; his wife, Baptista: 215
you shall see anon; 't is a knavish piece of work: but what o' that? your

---

176 *enactures:* Fulfillments.   179 *aye:* Ever.   186 *who:* Whoever.   188 *seasons:* Matures,
ripens.   192 *ends:* Results.   198 *An anchor's:* An anchorite's; *cheer:* Fare; sometimes printed as
chair.   199 *opposite:* Adverse thing; *blanks:* Causes to *blanch* or grow pale.   214 *Tropically:*
Figuratively, *tropically* suggests a pun on *trap* in *Mouse-trap* (l. 214).   215 *Gonzago:* In 1538
Luigi Gonzago murdered the Duke of Urbano by pouring poisoned lotion in his ears.

majesty and we that have free souls, it touches us not: let the galled jade°
winch,° our withers° are unwrung.°

Enter Lucianus.

This is one Lucianus, nephew to the king.
Ophelia: You are as good as a chorus,° my lord.   220
Hamlet: I could interpret between you and your love, if I could see the pup-
pets dallying.°
Ophelia: You are keen, my lord, you are keen.
Hamlet: It would cost you a groaning to take off my edge.
Ophelia: Still better, and worse.°   225
Hamlet: So you mistake° your husbands. Begin, murderer; pox,° leave thy
damnable faces, and begin. Come: the croaking raven doth bellow for
revenge.
Lucianus: Thoughts black, hands apt, drugs fit, and time agreeing;
Confederate° season, else no creature seeing;   230
Thou mixture rank, of midnight weeds collected,
With Hecate's° ban° thrice blasted, thrice infected,
Thy natural magic and dire property,
On wholesome life usurp immediately.
                                 [Pours the poison into the sleeper's ears.]
Hamlet: 'A poisons him i' the garden for his estate. His name's Gonzago: 235
the story is extant, and written in very choice Italian: you shall see
anon how the murderer gets the love of Gonzago's wife.
Ophelia: The king rises.
Hamlet: What, frighted with false fire!°
Queen: How fares my lord?   240
Polonius: Give o'er the play.
King: Give me some light: away!
Polonius: Lights, lights, lights!   *Exeunt all but Hamlet and Horatio.*
Hamlet: Why, let the strucken deer go weep,
The hart ungalled play;   245
For some must watch, while some must sleep:
Thus runs the world away.°
Would not this,° sir, and a forest of feathers° — if the rest of my for-
tunes turn Turk with° me — with two Provincial roses° on my razed°
shoes, get me a fellowship in a cry° of players,° sir?   250

---

218 *galled jade:* Horse whose hide is rubbed by saddle or harness; *winch:* Wince; *withers:* The
part between the horse's shoulder blades; *unwrung:* Not wrung or twisted.   220 *chorus:* In
many Elizabethan plays the action was explained by an actor known as the "chorus"; at a puppet show the actor who explained the action was known as an "interpreter," as indicated by the
lines following.   222 *dallying:* With sexual suggestion, continued in *keen* (sexually aroused),
groaning (i.e., in pregnancy), and *edge* (i.e., sexual desire or impetuosity).   225 *Still . . . worse:*
More keen, less decorous.   226 *mistake:* Err in taking; *pox:* An imprecation.   230 *Confederate:* Conspiring (to assist the murderer).   232 *Hecate:* The goddess of witchcraft; *ban:* Curse.
239 *false fire:* Fireworks, or a blank discharge.   244–247 *Why . . . away:* Probably from an
old ballad, with allusion to the popular belief that a wounded deer retires to weep and die. Cf. *As
You Like It,* II.i.66.   248 *this:* I.e., the play; *feathers:* Allusion to the plumes which Elizabethan
actors were fond of wearing.   249 *turn Turk with:* Go back on; *two Provincial roses:* Rosettes
of ribbon like the roses of Provins near Paris, or else the roses of Provence; *razed:* Cut, slashed
(by way of ornament).   250 *cry:* Pack (as of hounds); *fellowship . . . players:* Partnership in a
theatrical company.

Horatio: Half a share.°
Hamlet: A whole one, I.
> For thou dost know, O Damon dear,
>> This realm dismantled° was
> Of Jove himself; and now reigns here   255
>> A very, very° — pajock.°

Horatio: You might have rhymed.
Hamlet: O good Horatio, I'll take the ghost's word for a thousand pound.
> Didst perceive?

Horatio: Very well, my lord.   260
Hamlet: Upon the talk of the poisoning?
Horatio: I did very well note him.
Hamlet: Ah, ha! Come, some music! come, the recorders!°
> For if the king like not the comedy,
> Why then, belike, he likes it not, perdy.°   265
> Come, some music!

Enter Rosencrantz and Guildenstern.

Guildenstern: Good my lord, vouchsafe me a word with you.
Hamlet: Sir, a whole history.
Guildenstern: The king, sir, —
Hamlet: Ay, sir, what of him?   270
Guildenstern: Is in his retirement marvellous distempered.
Hamlet: With drink, sir?
Guildenstern: No, my lord, rather with choler.°
Hamlet: Your wisdom should show itself more richer to signify this to
> his doctor; for, for me to put him to his purgation would perhaps   275
> plunge him into far more choler.

Guildenstern: Good my lord, put your discourse into some frame° and start
> not so wildly from my affair.

Hamlet: I am tame, sir: pronounce.
Guildenstern: The queen, your mother, in most great affliction of spirit, 280
> hath sent me to you.

Hamlet: You are welcome.
Guildenstern: Nay, good my lord, this courtesy is not of the right breed.
> If it shall please you to make me a wholesome° answer, I will do your
> mother's commandment; if not, your pardon and my return shall be   285
> the end of my business.

Hamlet: Sir, I cannot.
Guildenstern: What, my lord?
Hamlet: Make you a wholesome answer; my wit's diseased: but, sir, such
> answer as I can make, you shall command; or, rather, as you say, my   290
> mother: therefore no more, but to the matter:° my mother, you say, —

---

251 *Half a share:* Allusion to the custom in dramatic companies of dividing the ownership into a number of shares among the householders.   254 *dismantled:* Stripped, divested. 253–256 *For . . . very:* Probably from an old ballad having to do with Damon and Pythias. 256 *pajock:* Peacock (a bird with a bad reputation). Possibly the word was *patchock*, diminutive of *patch*, clown.   263 *recorders:* Wind instruments of the flute kind.   265 *perdy:* Corruption of *par dieu.*   273 *choler:* Bilious disorder, with quibble on the sense "anger." 277 *frame:* Order.   284 *wholesome:* Sensible.   291 *matter:* Matter in hand.

Rosencrantz: Then thus she says; your behaviour hath struck her into amazement and admiration.

Hamlet: O wonderful son, that can so 'stonish a mother! But is there no sequel at the heels of this mother's admiration? Impart.   295

Rosencrantz: She desires to speak with you in her closet, ere you go to bed.

Hamlet: We shall obey, were she ten times our mother. Have you any further trade with us?

Rosencrantz: My lord, you once did love me.

Hamlet: And do still, by these pickers and stealers.°   300

Rosencrantz: Good my lord, what is your cause of distemper? you do, surely, bar the door upon your own liberty, if you deny your griefs to your friend.

Hamlet: Sir, I lack advancement.

Rosencrantz: How can that be, when you have the voice° of the king him-   305
self for your succession in Denmark?

Hamlet: Ay, sir, but "While the grass grows,"° — the proverb is something musty.

Enter the Players with recorders.

O, the recorders! let me see one. To withdraw° with you: — why do you go about to recover the wind° of me, as if you would drive me into   310
a toil?°

Guildenstern: O, my lord, if my duty be too bold, my love is too unmannerly.°

Hamlet: I do not well understand that. Will you play upon this pipe?

Guildenstern: My lord, I cannot.   315

Hamlet: I pray you.

Guildenstern: Believe me, I cannot.

Hamlet: I beseech you.

Guildenstern: I know no touch of it, my lord.

Hamlet: 'Tis as easy as lying: govern these ventages° with your fingers   320
and thumb, give it breath with your mouth, and it will discourse most eloquent music. Look you, these are the stops.

Guildenstern: But these cannot I command to any utterance of harmony; I have not the skill.

Hamlet: Why, look you now, how unworthy a thing you make of me! You   325
would play upon me; you would seem to know my stops; you would pluck out the heart of my mystery; you would sound me from my lowest note to the top of my compass:° and there is much music, excellent voice, in this little organ;° yet cannot you make it speak. 'Sblood, do you think I am easier to be played on than a pipe? Call   330
me what instrument you will, though you can fret° me, you cannot play upon me.

---

300 *pickers and stealers:* Hands, so called from the catechism "to keep my hands from picking and stealing."   305 *voice:* Support.   307 *"While . . . grows":* The rest of the proverb is "the silly horse starves." Hamlet may be destroyed while he is waiting for the succession to the kingdom.   309 *withdraw:* Speak in private.   310 *recover the wind:* Get to the windward side. 311 *toil:* Snare.   312–313 *if . . . unmannerly:* If I am using an unmannerly boldness, it is my love which occasions it.   320 *ventages:* Stops of the recorders.   328 *compass:* Range of voice. 329 *organ:* Musical instrument, i.e., the pipe.   331 *fret:* Quibble on meaning "irritate" and the piece of wood, gut, or metal which regulates the fingering.

Enter Polonius.

God bless you, sir!

Polonius: My lord, the queen would speak with you, and presently.

Hamlet: Do you see yonder cloud that's almost in shape of a camel? 335

Polonius: By the mass, and 'tis like a camel, indeed.

Hamlet: Methinks it is like a weasel.

Polonius: It is backed like a weasel.

Hamlet: Or like a whale?

Polonius: Very like a whale. 340

Hamlet: Then I will come to my mother by and by. *[Aside.]* They fool me to
the top of my bent.° — I will come by and by.°

Polonius: I will say so. *[Exit.]*

Hamlet: By and by is easily said.

Leave me, friends. *[Exeunt all but Hamlet.]* 345

'Tis now the very witching time° of night,

When churchyards yawn and hell itself breathes out

Contagion to this world: now could I drink hot blood,

And do such bitter business as the day

Would quake to look on. Soft! now to my mother. 350

O heart, lose not thy nature; let not ever

The soul of Nero° enter this firm bosom:

Let me be cruel, not unnatural:

I will speak daggers to her, but use none;

My tongue and soul in this be hypocrites; 355

How in my words somever she be shent,°

To give them seals° never, my soul, consent! *Exit.*

[SCENE III: *A room in the castle.*]

Enter King, Rosencrantz, and Guildenstern.

King: I like him not, nor stands it safe with us

To let his madness range. Therefore prepare you;

I your commission will forthwith dispatch,°

And he to England shall along with you:

The terms° of our estate° may not endure 5

Hazard so near us as doth hourly grow

Out of his brows.°

Guildenstern: We will ourselves provide:

Most holy and religious fear it is

To keep those many many bodies safe

That live and feed upon your majesty. 10

Rosencrantz: The single and peculiar° life is bound,

With all the strength and armour of the mind,

---

342 *top of my bent:* Limit of endurance, i.e., extent to which a bow may be bent; *by and by:*
Immediately. 346 *witching time:* I.e., time when spells are cast. 352 *Nero:* Murderer of
his mother, Agrippina. 356 *shent:* Rebuked. 357 *give them seals:* Confirm with deeds.
Scene III. 3 *dispatch:* Prepare. 5 *terms:* Condition, circumstances; *estate:* State.
7 *brows:* Effronteries. 11 *single and peculiar:* Individual and private.

To keep itself from noyance;° but much more
That spirit upon whose weal depend and rest
The lives of many. The cess° of majesty   15
Dies not alone; but, like a gulf,° doth draw
What's near it with it: it is a massy wheel,
Fix'd on the summit of the highest mount,
To whose huge spokes ten thousand lesser things
Are mortis'd and adjoin'd; which, when it falls,   20
Each small annexment, petty consequence,
Attends° the boist'rous ruin. Never alone
Did the king sigh, but with a general groan.
King: Arm° you, I pray you, to this speedy voyage;
For we will fetters put about this fear,   25
Which now goes too free-footed.
Rosencrantz: We will haste us.
                    Exeunt Gentlemen [Rosencrantz and Guildenstern].

        Enter Polonius.

Polonius: My lord, he's going to his mother's closet:
Behind the arras° I'll convey° myself,
To hear the process;° I'll warrant she'll tax him home:°
And, as you said, and wisely was it said,   30
'Tis meet that some more audience than a mother,
Since nature makes them partial, should o'erhear
The speech, of vantage.° Fare you well, my liege:
I'll call upon you ere you go to bed,
And tell you what I know.
King: Thanks, dear my lord.   *Exit [Polonius].*   35
O, my offence is rank, it smells to heaven;
It hath the primal eldest curse° upon't,
A brother's murder. Pray can I not,
Though inclination be as sharp as will:°
My stronger guilt defeats my strong intent;   40
And, like a man to double business bound,
I stand in pause where I shall first begin,
And both neglect. What if this cursed hand
Were thicker than itself with brother's blood,
Is there not rain enough in the sweet heavens   45
To wash it white as snow? Whereto serves mercy
But to confront° the visage of offence?
And what's in prayer but this two-fold force,
To be forestalled° ere we come to fall,
Or pardon'd being down? Then I'll look up;   50

---

13 *noyance:* Harm.   15 *cess:* Decease.   16 *gulf:* Whirlpool.   22 *Attends:* Participates
in.   24 *Arm:* Prepare.   28 *arras:* Screen of tapestry placed around the walls of household
apartments; *convey:* Implication of secrecy, *convey* was often used to mean "steal."   29 *process:*
Proceedings; *tax him home:* Reprove him severely.   33 *of vantage:* From an advantageous place.
37 *primal eldest curse:* The curse of Cain, the first to kill his brother.   39 *sharp as will:* I.e.,
his desire is as strong as his determination.   47 *confront:* Oppose directly.   49 *forestalled:*
Prevented.

My fault is past. But, O, what form of prayer
Can serve my turn? "Forgive me my foul murder"?
That cannot be: since I am still possess'd
Of those effects for which I did the murder,
My crown, mine own ambition° and my queen.   55
May one be pardon'd and retain th' offence?°
In the corrupted currents° of this world
Offence's gilded hand° may shove by justice,
And oft 'tis seen the wicked prize° itself
Buys out the law: but 'tis not so above;   60
There is no shuffling,° there the action lies°
In his true nature; and we ourselves compell'd,
Even to the teeth and forehead° of our faults,
To give in evidence. What then? what rests?°
Try what repentance can: what can it not?   65
Yet what can it when one can not repent?
O wretched state! O bosom black as death!
O limed° soul, that, struggling to be free,
Art more engag'd!° Help, angels! Make assay!°
Bow, stubborn knees; and, heart with strings of steel, 70
Be soft as sinews of the new-born babe!
All may be well.   *[He kneels.]*

Enter Hamlet.

Hamlet: Now might I do it pat,° now he is praying;
And now I'll do't. And so 'a goes to heaven;
And so am I reveng'd. That would be scann'd:°   75
A villain kills my father; and for that,
I, his sole son, do this same villain send
To heaven.
Why, this is hire and salary, not revenge.
'A took my father grossly, full of bread;°   80
With all his crimes broad blown,° as flush° as May;
And how his audit stands who knows save heaven?
But in our circumstance and course° of thought,
'Tis heavy with him: and am I then reveng'd,
To take him in the purging of his soul,   85
When he is fit and season'd for his passage?°
No!
Up, sword; and know thou a more horrid hent:°
When he is drunk asleep,° or in his rage,
Or in th' incestuous pleasure of his bed;   90

55 *ambition:* I.e., realization of ambition.   56 *offence:* Benefit accruing from offense.   57 *currents:* Courses.   58 *gilded hand:* Hand offering gold as a bribe.   59 *wicked prize:* Prize won by wickedness.   61 *shuffling:* Escape by trickery; *lies:* Is sustainable.   63 *teeth and forehead:* Very face.   64 *rests:* Remains.   68 *limed:* Caught as with birdlime.   69 *engag'd:* Embedded; *assay:* Trial.   73 *pat:* Opportunely.   75 *would be scann'd:* Needs to be looked into.   80 *full of bread:* Enjoying his worldly pleasures (see Ezekiel 16:49).   81 *broad blown:* In full bloom; *flush:* Lusty.   83 *in . . . course:* As we see it in our mortal situation.   86 *fit . . . passage:* I.e., reconciled to heaven by forgiveness of his sins.   88 *hent:* Seizing; or more probably, occasion of seizure.   89 *drunk asleep:* In a drunken sleep.

> At game, a-swearing, or about some act
> That has no relish of salvation in't;
> Then trip him, that his heels may kick at heaven,
> And that his soul may be as damn'd and black
> As hell, whereto it goes. My mother stays: 95
> This physic° but prolongs thy sickly days.   *Exit.*

King: [Rising] My words fly up, my thoughts remain below:
> Words without thoughts never to heaven go.   *Exit.*

[SCENE IV: *The Queen's closet.*]

Enter [Queen] Gertrude and Polonius.

Polonius: 'A will come straight. Look you lay° home to him:
> Tell him his pranks have been too broad° to bear with,
> And that your grace hath screen'd and stood between
> Much heat° and him. I'll sconce° me even here.
> Pray you, be round° with him.   5

Hamlet (within): Mother, mother, mother!

Queen: I'll warrant you,
> Fear me not: withdraw, I hear him coming.
>   [*Polonius hides behind the arras.*]

Enter Hamlet.

Hamlet: Now, mother, what's the matter?

Queen: Hamlet, thou hast thy father much offended.

Hamlet: Mother, you have my father° much offended.   10

Queen: Come, come, you answer with an idle tongue.

Hamlet: Go, go, you question with a wicked tongue.

Queen: Why, how now, Hamlet!

Hamlet: What's the matter now?

Queen: Have you forgot me?

Hamlet: No, by the rood,° not so:
> You are the queen, your husband's brother's wife;   15
> And — would it were not so! — you are my mother.

Queen: Nay, then, I'll set those to you that can speak.

Hamlet: Come, come, and sit you down; you shall not budge;
> You go not till I set you up a glass
> Where you may see the inmost part of you.   20

Queen: What wilt thou do? thou wilt not murder me?
> Help, help, ho!

Polonius [behind]: What, ho! help, help; help!

Hamlet [drawing]: How now! a rat? Dead, for a ducat, dead!
>   [*Makes a pass through the arras.*]

Polonius [behind]: O, I am slain!   [*Falls and dies.*]   25

Queen: O me, what hast thou done?

96 *physic:* Purging (by prayer).   **Scene IV.**   1 *lay:* Thrust.   2 *broad:* Unrestrained.
4 *Much heat:* I.e., the king's anger; *sconce:* Hide.   5 *round:* Blunt.   9–10 *thy father, my father:* I.e., Claudius, the elder Hamlet.   14 *rood:* Cross.

Hamlet: Nay, I know not:
    Is it the king?
Queen: O, what a rash and bloody deed is this!
Hamlet: A bloody deed! almost as bad, good mother,
As kill a king, and marry with his brother.   30
Queen: As kill a king!
Hamlet: Ay, lady, it was my word.
              [Lifts up the arras and discovers Polonius.]
    Thou wretched, rash, intruding fool, farewell!
    I took thee for thy better: take thy fortune;
    Thou find'st to be too busy is some danger.
    Leave wringing of your hands: peace! sit you down,   35
    And let me wring your heart; for so I shall,
    If it be made of penetrable stuff,
    If damned custom have not braz'd° it so
    That it be proof and bulwark against sense.
Queen: What have I done, that thou dar'st wag thy tongue   40
    In noise so rude against me?
Hamlet: Such an act
    That blurs the grace and blush of modesty,
    Calls virtue hypocrite, takes off the rose
    From the fair forehead of an innocent love
    And sets a blister° there, makes marriage-vows   45
    As false as dicers' oaths: O, such a deed
    As from the body of contraction° plucks
    The very soul, and sweet religion° makes
    A rhapsody° of words: heaven's face does glow
    O'er this solidity and compound mass   50
    With heated visage, as against the doom
    Is thought-sick at the act.°
Queen: Ay me, what act,
    That roars so loud, and thunders in the index?°
Hamlet: Look here, upon this picture, and on this.
    The counterfeit presentment° of two brothers.   55
    See, what a grace was seated on this brow;
    Hyperion's° curls; the front° of Jove himself;
    An eye like Mars, to threaten and command;
    A station° like the herald Mercury
    New-lighted on a heaven-kissing hill;   60
    A combination and a form indeed,
    Where every god did seem to set his seal,
    To give the world assurance° of a man:
    This was your husband. Look you now, what follows:

---

38 *braz'd:* Brazened, hardened.   45 *sets a blister:* Brands as a harlot.   47 *contraction:* The marriage contract.   48 *religion:* Religious vows.   49 *rhapsody:* Senseless string. 49–52 *heaven's . . . act:* Heaven's face blushes to look down on this world, and Gertrude's marriage makes heaven feel as sick as though the day of doom were near.   53 *index:* Prelude or preface.   55 *counterfeit presentment:* Portrayed representation.   57 *Hyperion's:* The sun god's; *front:* Brow.   59 *station:* Manner of standing.   63 *assurance:* Pledge, guarantee.

Here is your husband; like a mildew'd ear,°   65
Blasting his wholesome brother. Have you eyes?
Could you on this fair mountain leave to feed,
And batten° on this moor?° Ha! have you eyes?
You cannot call it love; for at your age
The hey-day° in the blood is tame, it's humble,   70
And waits upon the judgement: and what judgement
Would step from this to this? Sense, sure, you have,
Else could you not have motion;° but sure, that sense
Is apoplex'd;° for madness would not err,
Nor sense to ecstasy was ne'er so thrall'd°   75
But it reserv'd some quantity of choice,°
To serve in such a difference. What devil was't
That thus hath cozen'd° you at hoodman-blind?°
Eyes without feeling, feeling without sight,
Ears without hands or eyes, smelling sans° all,   80
Or but a sickly part of one true sense
Could not so mope.°
O shame! where is thy blush? Rebellious hell,
If thou canst mutine° in a matron's bones,
To flaming youth let virtue be as wax,   85
And melt in her own fire: proclaim no shame
When the compulsive ardour gives the charge,°
Since frost itself as actively doth burn
And reason panders will.°
Queen: O Hamlet, speak no more:
Thou turn'st mine eyes into my very soul;   90
And there I see such black and grained° spots
As will not leave their tinct.
Hamlet: Nay, but to live
In the rank sweat of an enseamed° bed,
Stew'd in corruption, honeying and making love
Over the nasty sty, —
Queen: O, speak to me no more;   95
These words, like daggers, enter in mine ears;
No more, sweet Hamlet!
Hamlet: A murderer and a villain;
A slave that is not twentieth part the tithe
Of your precedent lord;° a vice of kings;°

65 *mildew'd ear:* See Genesis 41:5–7.   68 *batten:* Grow fat; *moor:* Barren upland.   70 *hey-day:* State of excitement.   72–73 *Sense . . . motion:* Sense and motion are functions of the middle or sensible soul, the possession of sense being the basis of motion.   74 *apoplex'd:* Paralyzed. Mental derangement was thus of three sorts: apoplexy, ecstasy, and diabolic possession.   75 *thrall'd:* Enslaved.   76 *quantity of choice:* Fragment of the power to choose.   78 *cozen'd:* Tricked, cheated; *hoodman-blind:* Blindman's buff.   80 *sans:* Without.   82 *mope:* Be in a depressed, spiritless state, act aimlessly.   84 *mutine:* Mutiny, rebel.   87 *gives the charge:* Delivers the attack.   89 *reason panders will:* The normal and proper situation was one in which reason guided the will in the direction of good; here, reason is perverted and leads in the direction of evil.   91 *grained:* Dyed in grain.   93 *enseamed:* Loaded with grease, greased.   99 *precedent lord:* I.e., the elder Hamlet; *vice of kings:* Buffoon of kings; a reference to the Vice, or clown, of the morality plays and interludes.

A cutpurse of the empire and the rule, 100
That from a shelf the precious diadem stole,
And put it in his pocket!
Queen: No more!

Enter Ghost.

Hamlet: A king of shreds and patches,° —
Save me, and hover o'er me with your wings,
You heavenly guards! What would your gracious figure? 105
Queen: Alas, he's mad!
Hamlet: Do you not come your tardy son to chide,
That, laps'd in time and passion,° lets go by
Th' important° acting of your dread command?
O, say! 110
Ghost: Do not forget: this visitation
Is but to whet thy almost blunted purpose.
But, look, amazement° on thy mother sits:
O, step between her and her fighting soul:
Conceit in weakest bodies strongest works: 115
Speak to her, Hamlet.
Hamlet: How is it with you, lady?
Queen: Alas, how is 't with you,
That you do bend your eye on vacancy
And with th' incorporal° air do hold discourse?
Forth at your eyes your spirits wildly peep; 120
And, as the sleeping soldiers in th' alarm,
Your bedded° hair, like life in excrements,°
Start up, and stand an° end. O gentle son,
Upon the heat and flame of thy distemper
Sprinkle cool patience. Whereon do you look? 125
Hamlet: On him, on him! Look you, how pale he glares!
His form and cause conjoin'd,° preaching to stones,
Would make them capable. — Do not look upon me;
Lest with this piteous action you convert
My stern effects:° then what I have to do 130
Will want true colour;° tears perchance for blood.
Queen: To whom do you speak this?
Hamlet: Do you see nothing there?
Queen: Nothing at all; yet all that is I see.
Hamlet: Nor did you nothing hear?
Queen: No, nothing but ourselves.
Hamlet: Why, look you there! look, how it steals away! 135

103 *shreds and patches:* I.e., motley, the traditional costume of the Vice. 108 *laps'd . . . passion:* Having suffered time to slip and passion to cool; also explained as "engrossed in casual events and lapsed into mere fruitless passion, so that he no longer entertains a rational purpose." 109 *important:* Urgent. 113 *amazement:* Frenzy, distraction. 119 *incorporal:* Immaterial. 122 *bedded:* Laid in smooth layers; *excrements:* The hair was considered an excrement or voided part of the body. 123 *an:* On. 127 *conjoin'd:* United. 129–130 *convert . . . effects:* Divert me from my stern duty. For *effects*, possibly *affects* (affections of the mind). 131 *want true colour:* Lack good reason so that (with a play on the normal sense of *colour*) I shall shed tears instead of blood.

My father, in his habit as he liv'd!
Look, where he goes, even now, out at the portal!   *Exit Ghost.*
Queen: This is the very coinage of your brain:
    This bodiless creation ecstasy
    Is very cunning in.
Hamlet: Ecstasy!   140
    My pulse, as yours, doth temperately keep time,
    And makes as healthful music: it is not madness
    That I have utt'red: bring me to the test,
    And I the matter will re-word,° which madness
    Would gambol° from. Mother, for love of grace,   145
    Lay not that flattering unction° to your soul,
    That not your trespass, but my madness speaks:
    It will but skin and film the ulcerous place,
    Whiles rank corruption, mining° all within,
    Infects unseen. Confess yourself to heaven;   150
    Repent what's past; avoid what is to come;°
    And do not spread the compost° on the weeds,
    To make them ranker. Forgive me this my virtue;°
    For in the fatness° of these pursy° times
    Virtue itself of vice must pardon beg,   155
    Yea, curb° and woo for leave to do him good.
Queen: O Hamlet, thou hast cleft my heart in twain.
Hamlet: O, throw away the worser part of it,
    And live the purer with the other half.
    Good night: but go not to my uncle's bed;   160
    Assume a virtue, if you have it not.
    That monster, custom, who all sense doth eat,
    Of habits devil, is angel yet in this,
    That to the use of actions fair and good
    He likewise gives a frock or livery,   165
    That aptly is put on. Refrain to-night,
    And that shall lend a kind of easiness
    To the next abstinence: the next more easy;
    For use almost can change the stamp of nature,
    And either . . . the devil, or throw him out°   170
    With wondrous potency. Once more, good night:
    And when you are desirous to be bless'd,°
    I'll blessing beg of you. For this same lord,   *[Pointing to Polonius.]*
    I do repent: but heaven hath pleas'd it so,
    To punish me with this and this with me,   175
    That I must be their scourge and minister.
    I will bestow him, and will answer well

---

144 *re-word:* Repeat in words.   145 *gambol:* Skip away.   146 *unction:* Ointment used medicinally or as a rite; suggestion that forgiveness for sin may not be so easily achieved. 149 *mining:* Working under the surface.   151 *what is to come:* I.e., the sins of the future. 152 *compost:* Manure.   153 *this my virtue:* My virtuous talk in reproving you. 154 *fatness:* Grossness; *pursy:* Short-winded, corpulent.   156 *curb:* Bow, bend the knee. 170 Defective line usually emended by inserting *master* after *either.*   172 *be bless'd:* Become blessed, i.e., repentant.

The death I gave him. So, again, good night.
I must be cruel, only to be kind:
Thus bad begins and worse remains behind.   180
One word more, good lady.
Queen: What shall I do?
Hamlet: Not this, by no means, that I bid you do:
Let the bloat° king tempt you again to bed;
Pinch wanton on your cheek; call you his mouse;
And let him, for a pair of reechy° kisses,   185
Or paddling in your neck with his damn'd fingers,
Make you to ravel all this matter out,
That I essentially° am not in madness,
But mad in craft. 'Twere good you let him know;
For who, that's but a queen, fair, sober, wise,   190
Would from a paddock,° from a bat, a gib,°
Such dear concernings° hide? who would do so?
No, in despite of sense and secrecy,
Unpeg the basket on the house's top,
Let the birds fly, and, like the famous ape,°   195
To try conclusions,° in the basket creep,
And break your own neck down.
Queen: Be thou assur'd, if words be made of breath,
And breath of life, I have no life to breathe
What thou hast said to me.   200
Hamlet: I must to England; you know that?
Queen: Alack,
I had forgot: 'tis so concluded on.
Hamlet: There's letters seal'd: and my two schoolfellows,
Whom I will trust as I will adders fang'd,
They bear the mandate; they must sweep my way,°   205
And marshal me to knavery. Let it work;
For 'tis the sport to have the enginer°
Hoist° with his own petar:° and 't shall go hard
But I will delve one yard below their mines,
And blow them at the moon: O, 'tis most sweet,   210
When in one line two crafts° directly meet.
This man shall set me packing:°
I'll lug the guts into the neighbour room.
Mother, good night. Indeed this counsellor
Is now most still, most secret and most grave,   215

---

183 *bloat:* Bloated.   185 *reechy:* Dirty, filthy.   188 *essentially:* In my essential nature.
191 *paddock:* Toad; *gib:* Tomcat.   192 *dear concernings:* Important affairs.   195 *the famous
ape:* A letter from Sir John Suckling seems to supply other details of the story, otherwise not identified: "It is the story of the jackanapes and the partridges; thou starest after a beauty till it be lost
to thee, then let'st out another, and starest after that till it is gone too."   196 *conclusions:* Experiments.   205 *sweep my way:* Clear my path.   207 *enginer:* Constructor of military works, or
possibly, artilleryman.   208 *Hoist:* Blown up; *petar:* Defined as a small engine of war used to
blow in a door or make a breach, and as a case filled with explosive materials.   211 *two crafts:*
Two acts of guile, with quibble on the sense of "two ships."   212 *set me packing:* Set me to making schemes, and set me to lugging (him), and, also, send me off in a hurry.

Who was in life a foolish prating knave.
Come, sir, to draw° toward an end with you.
Good night, mother.   *Exeunt [severally; Hamlet dragging in Polonius.]*

[ACT IV

SCENE I: *A room in the castle.*]

Enter King and Queen, with Rosencrantz and Guildenstern.

King: There's matter in these sighs, these profound heaves:
     You must translate: 'tis fit we understand them.
     Where is your son?
Queen: Bestow this place on us a little while.
                         [Exeunt Rosencrantz and Guildenstern.]
     Ah, mine own lord, what have I seen to-night!   5
King: What, Gertrude? How does Hamlet?
Queen: Mad as the sea and wind, when both contend
     Which is the mightier: in his lawless fit,
     Behind the arras hearing something stir,
     Whips out his rapier, cries, "A rat, a rat!"   10
     And, in this brainish° apprehension,° kills
     The unseen good old man.
King: O heavy deed!
     It had been so with us, had we been there:
     His liberty is full of threats to all;
     To you yourself, to us, to every one.   15
     Alas, how shall this bloody deed be answer'd?
     It will be laid to us, whose providence°
     Should have kept short,° restrain'd and out of haunt,°
     This mad young man: but so much was our love,
     We would not understand what was most fit;   20
     But, like the owner of a foul disease,
     To keep it from divulging,° let it feed
     Even on the pith of life. Where is he gone?
Queen: To draw apart the body he hath kill'd:
     O'er whom his very madness, like some ore   25
     Among a mineral° of metals base,
     Shows itself pure; 'a weeps for what is done.
King: O Gertrude, come away!
     The sun no sooner shall the mountains touch,
     But we will ship him hence: and this vile deed   30
     We must, with all our majesty and skill,
     Both countenance and excuse. Ho, Guildenstern!

---

217 *draw:* Come, with quibble on literal sense.   **Act IV, Scene I.**   11 *brainish:* Headstrong,
passionate; *apprehension:* Conception, imagination.   17 *providence:* Foresight.   18 *short:*
I.e., on a short tether; *out of haunt:* Secluded.   22 *divulging:* Becoming evident.   26 *min-eral:* Mine.

Enter Rosencrantz and Guildenstern.

Friends both, go join you with some further aid:
Hamlet in madness hath Polonius slain,
And from his mother's closet hath he dragg'd him: 35
Go seek him out; speak fair, and bring the body
Into the chapel. I pray you, haste in this.
                        [Exeunt Rosencrantz and Guildenstern.]
Come, Gertrude, we'll call up our wisest friends;
And let them know, both what we mean to do,
And what's untimely done . . .° 40
Whose whisper o'er the world's diameter,°
As level° as the cannon to his blank,°
Transports his pois'ned shot, may miss our name,
And hit the woundless° air. O, come away!
My soul is full of discord and dismay. *Exeunt.* 45

[SCENE II: *Another room in the castle.*]

Enter Hamlet.

Hamlet: Safely stowed.
Rosencrantz: ⎱
Guildenstern: ⎰ *(within)* Hamlet! Lord Hamlet!
Hamlet: But soft, what noise? who calls on Hamlet? O, here they come.

Enter Rosencrantz and Guildenstern.

Rosencrantz: What have you done, my lord, with the dead body?
Hamlet: Compounded it with dust, whereto 'tis kin.
Rosencrantz: Tell us where 'tis, that we may take it thence 5
And bear it to the chapel.
Hamlet: Do not believe it.
Rosencrantz: Believe what?
Hamlet: That I can keep your counsel° and not mine own. Besides, to be
demanded of a sponge! what replication° should be made by the son 10
of a king?
Rosencrantz: Take you me for a sponge, my lord?
Hamlet: Ay, sir, that soaks up the king's countenance, his rewards, his
authorities.° But such officers do the king best service in the end:
he keeps them, like an ape an apple, in the corner of his jaw; first 15
mouthed, to be last swallowed: when he needs what you have gleaned,
it is but squeezing you, and, sponge, you shall be dry again.
Rosencrantz: I understand you not, my lord.
Hamlet: I am glad of it: a knavish speech sleeps in a foolish ear.
Rosencrantz: My lord, you must tell us where the body is, and go with us 20
to the king.

40 Defective line; some editors add: *so, haply, slander;* others add: *for, haply, slander;* other
conjectures.   41 *diameter:* Extent from side to side.   42 *level:* Straight; *blank:* White
spot in the center of a target.   44 *woundless:* Invulnerable.   **Scene II.**   9 *keep your counsel:* Hamlet is aware of their treachery but says nothing about it.   10 *replication:* Reply.
14 *authorities:* Authoritative backing.

Hamlet: The body is with the king, but the king is not with the body.° The
　　king is a thing—
Guildenstern: A thing, my lord!
Hamlet: Of nothing: bring me to him. Hide fox, and all after.°　　　　*Exeunt.*　25

[**SCENE III:** *Another room in the castle.*]

　　Enter King, and two or three.

King: I have sent to seek him, and to find the body.
　　How dangerous is it that this man goes loose!
　　Yet must not we put the strong law on him:
　　He's lov'd of the distracted° multitude,
　　Who like not in their judgement, but their eyes;　　　　　　　　　　5
　　And where 'tis so, th' offender's scourge° is weigh'd,°
　　But never the offence. To bear all smooth and even,
　　This sudden sending him away must seem
　　Deliberate pause:° diseases desperate grown
　　By desperate appliance are reliev'd,　　　　　　　　　　　　　　　10
　　Or not at all.

　　Enter Rosencrantz, [Guildenstern,] and all the rest.

　　　　　　　How now! what hath befall'n?
Rosencrantz: Where the dead body is bestow'd, my lord,
　　We cannot get from him.
King:　　　　　　　　　But where is he?
Rosencrantz: Without, my lord; guarded, to know your pleasure.
King: Bring him before us.　　　　　　　　　　　　　　　　　　15
Rosencrantz: Ho! bring in the lord.

　　They enter [with Hamlet].

King: Now, Hamlet, where's Polonius?
Hamlet: At supper.
King: At supper! where?
Hamlet: Not where he eats, but where 'a is eaten: a certain convocation of　20
　　politic° worms° are e'en at him. Your worm is your only emperor for diet:
　　we fat all creatures else to fat us, and we fat ourselves for maggots: your fat
　　king and your lean beggar is but variable service,° two dishes, but to one
　　table: that's the end.
King: Alas, alas!　　　　　　　　　　　　　　　　　　　　　　25

---

22 *The body . . . body:* There are many interpretations; possibly, "The body lies in death with
the king, my father; but my father walks disembodied"; or "Claudius has the bodily possession
of kingship, but kingliness, or justice of inheritance, is not with him."　　25 *Hide . . . after:* An
old signal cry in the game of hide-and-seek.　**Scene III.**　　4 *distracted:* I.e., without power
of forming logical judgments.　　6 *scourge:* Punishment; *weigh'd:* Taken into consideration.
9 *Deliberate pause:* Considered action.　20–21 *convocation . . . worms:* Allusion to the Diet of
Worms (1521).　　21 *politic:* Crafty.　　23 *variable service:* A variety of dishes.

Hamlet: A man may fish with the worm that hath eat of a king, and eat of the
fish that hath fed of that worm.

King: What dost thou mean by this?

Hamlet: Nothing but to show you how a king may go a progress° through
the guts of a beggar. 30

King: Where is Polonius?

Hamlet: In heaven; send thither to see: if your messenger find him not
there, seek him i' the other place yourself. But if indeed you find him
not within this month, you shall nose him as you go up the stairs
into the lobby. 35

King [to some Attendants]: Go seek him there.

Hamlet: 'A will stay till you come. *[Exeunt Attendants.]*

King: Hamlet, this deed, for thine especial safety, —
 Which we do tender,° as we dearly grieve
 For that which thou hast done, — must send thee hence 40
 With fiery quickness: therefore prepare thyself;
 The bark is ready, and the wind at help,
 Th' associates tend, and everything is bent
 For England.

Hamlet: For England!

King: Ay, Hamlet.

Hamlet: Good.

King: So is it, if thou knew'st our purposes. 45

Hamlet: I see a cherub° that sees them. But, come; for England! Farewell, dear
 mother.

King: Thy loving father, Hamlet.

Hamlet: My mother: father and mother is man and wife; man and wife is
 one flesh; and so, my mother. Come, for England! *Exit.* 50

King: Follow him at foot;° tempt him with speed aboard;
 Delay it not; I'll have him hence to-night:
 Away! for every thing is seal'd and done
 That else leans on th' affair: pray you, make haste.
                    [Exeunt all but the King.]
 And, England, if my love thou hold'st at aught — 55
 As my great power thereof may give thee sense,
 Since yet thy cicatrice° looks raw and red
 After the Danish sword, and thy free awe°
 Pays homage to us — thou mayst not coldly set
 Our sovereign process; which imports at full, 60
 By letters congruing to that effect,
 The present death of Hamlet. Do it, England;
 For like the hectic° in my blood he rages,
 And thou must cure me: till I know 'tis done,
 Howe'er my haps,° my joys were ne'er begun. *Exit.* 65

29 *progress:* Royal journey of state.   39 *tender:* Regard, hold dear.   46 *cherub:* Cherubim
are angels of knowledge.   51 *at foot:* Close behind, at heel.   57 *cicatrice:* Scar.   58 *free
awe:* Voluntary show of respect.   63 *hectic:* Fever.   65 *haps:* Fortunes.

[SCENE IV: *A plain in Denmark.*]

Enter Fortinbras with his Army over the stage.

Fortinbras: Go, captain, from me greet the Danish king;
    Tell him that, by his license,° Fortinbras
    Craves the conveyance° of a promis'd march
    Over his kingdom. You know the rendezvous.
    If that his majesty would aught with us,   5
    We shall express our duty in his eye;°
    And let him know so.
Captain: I will do't, my lord.
Fortinbras: Go softly° on.   *[Exeunt all but Captain.]*

Enter Hamlet, Rosencrantz, [Guildenstern,] &c.

Hamlet: Good sir, whose powers are these?
Captain: They are of Norway, sir.   10
Hamlet: How purpos'd, sir, I pray you?
Captain: Against some part of Poland.
Hamlet: Who commands them, sir?
Captain: The nephew to old Norway, Fortinbras.
Hamlet: Goes it against the main° of Poland, sir,   15
    Or for some frontier?
Captain: Truly to speak, and with no addition,
    We go to gain a little patch of ground
    That hath in it no profit but the name.
    To pay five ducats, five, I would not farm it;°   20
    Nor will it yield to Norway or the Pole
    A ranker rate, should it be sold in fee.°
Hamlet: Why, then the Polack never will defend it.
Captain: Yes, it is already garrison'd.
Hamlet: Two thousand souls and twenty thousand ducats   25
    Will not debate the question of this straw:°
    This is th' imposthume° of much wealth and peace,
    That inward breaks, and shows no cause without
    Why the man dies. I humbly thank you, sir.
Captain: God be wi' you, sir.   *[Exit.]*
Rosencrantz: Will 't please you go, my lord?   30
Hamlet: I'll be with you straight. Go a little before.

                             [Exeunt all except Hamlet.]
    How all occasions° do inform against° me,
    And spur my dull revenge! What is a man,
    If his chief good and market of his time°

Scene IV.   2 *license:* Leave.   3 *conveyance:* Escort, convoy.   6 *in his eye:* In his presence.   8 *softly:* Slowly.   15 *main:* Country itself.   20 *farm it:* Take a lease of it.   22 *fee:* Fee simple.   26 *debate . . . straw:* Settle this trifling matter.   27 *imposthume:* Purulent abscess or swelling.   32 *occasions:* Incidents, events; *inform against:* Generally defined as "show," "betray" (i.e., his tardiness); more probably *inform* means "take shape," as in *Macbeth,* II.i.48.   34 *market of his time:* The best use he makes of his time, or, that for which he sells his time.

Be but to sleep and feed? a beast, no more. 35
Sure, he that made us with such large discourse,
Looking before and after, gave us not
That capability and god-like reason
To fust° in us unus'd. Now, whether it be
Bestial oblivion, or some craven scruple 40
Of thinking too precisely on th' event,
A thought which, quarter'd, hath but one part wisdom
And ever three parts coward, I do not know
Why yet I live to say "This thing 's to do";
Sith I have cause and will and strength and means 45
To do 't. Examples gross as earth exhort me:
Witness this army of such mass and charge
Led by a delicate and tender prince,
Whose spirit with divine ambition puff'd
Makes mouths at the invisible event, 50
Exposing what is mortal and unsure
To all that fortune, death and danger dare,
Even for an egg-shell. Rightly to be great
Is not to stir without great argument,
But greatly to find quarrel in a straw 55
When honour's at the stake. How stand I then,
That have a father kill'd, a mother stain'd,
Excitements of° my reason and my blood,
And let all sleep? while, to my shame, I see
The imminent death of twenty thousand men, 60
That, for a fantasy and trick° of fame,
Go to their graves like beds, fight for a plot°
Whereon the numbers cannot try the cause,
Which is not tomb enough and continent
To hide the slain? O, from this time forth, 65
My thoughts be bloody, or be nothing worth!   *Exit.*

[SCENE V: *Elsinore. A room in the castle.*]

Enter Horatio, [Queen] Gertrude, and a Gentleman.

Queen: I will not speak with her.
Gentleman: She is importunate, indeed distract:
  Her mood will needs be pitied.
Queen: What would she have?
Gentleman: She speaks much of her father; says she hears
  There's tricks° i' th' world; and hems, and beats her heart;° 5
  Spurns enviously at straws;° speaks things in doubt,
  That carry but half sense: her speech is nothing,
  Yet the unshaped° use of it doth move

---

39 *fust:* Grow moldy.   58 *Excitements of:* Incentives to.   61 *trick:* Toy, trifle.   62 *plot:*
Piece of ground.   **Scene V.**   5 *tricks:* Deceptions; *heart:* I.e., breast.   6 *Spurns . . . straws:*
Kicks spitefully at small objects in her path.   8 *unshaped:* Unformed, artless.

The hearers to collection;° they yawn° at it,
And botch° the words up fit to their own thoughts;   10
Which, as her winks, and nods, and gestures yield° them,
Indeed would make one think there might be thought,
Though nothing sure, yet much unhappily.°
Horatio: 'Twere good she were spoken with: for she may strew
Dangerous conjectures in ill-breeding minds.°   15
Queen: Let her come in.   *[Exit Gentleman.]*
    [Aside.] To my sick soul, as sin's true nature is,
Each toy seems prologue to some great amiss:°
So full of artless jealousy is guilt,
It spills itself in fearing to be spilt.°   20

Enter Ophelia [distracted].

Ophelia: Where is the beauteous majesty of Denmark?
Queen: How now, Ophelia!
Ophelia (she sings): How should I your true love know
        From another one?
    By his cockle hat° and staff,   25
        And his sandal shoon.°
Queen: Alas, sweet lady, what imports this song?
Ophelia: Say you? nay, pray you mark.
    (Song) He is dead and gone, lady,
        He is dead and gone;   30
    At his head a grass-green turf,
        At his heels a stone.
    O, ho!
Queen: Nay, but, Ophelia —
Ophelia: Pray you, mark   35
    [Sings.] White his shroud as the mountain snow, —

    Enter King.

Queen: Alas, look here, my lord.
Ophelia (Song): Larded° all with flowers;
    Which bewept to the grave did not go
        With true-love showers.   40
King: How do you, pretty lady?
Ophelia: Well, God 'ild° you! They say the owl° was a baker's daughter.
    Lord, we know what we are, but know not what we may be. God be at
    your table!
King: Conceit upon her father.   45

9 *collection:* Inference, a guess at some sort of meaning; *yawn:* Wonder.   10 *botch:* Patch.
11 *yield:* Deliver, bring forth (her words).   13 *much unhappily:* Expressive of much unhappiness.   15 *ill-breeding minds:* Minds bent on mischief.   18 *great amiss:* Calamity, disaster.
19–20 *So . . . spilt:* Guilt is so full of suspicion that it unskillfully betrays itself in fearing to be
betrayed.   25 *cockle hat:* Hat with cockleshell stuck in it as a sign that the wearer has been a
pilgrim to the shrine of St. James of Compostella. The pilgrim's garb was a conventional disguise
for lovers.   26 *shoon:* Shoes.   38 *Larded:* Decorated.   42 *God 'ild:* God yield or reward;
owl: Reference to a monkish legend that a baker's daughter was turned into an owl for refusing
bread to the Savior.

Ophelia: Pray let's have no words of this; but when they ask you what it
    means, say you this:
    (Song) To-morrow is Saint Valentine's day,
      All in the morning betime,
    And I a maid at your window,   50
      To be your Valentine.°
    Then up he rose, and donn'd his clothes,
      And dupp'd° the chamber-door;
    Let in the maid, that out a maid
      Never departed more.   55
King: Pretty Ophelia!
Ophelia: Indeed, la, without an oath, I'll make an end on 't:
    [Sings.] By Gis° and by Saint Charity,
      Alack, and fie for shame!
    Young men will do 't, if they come to 't;   60
      By cock,° they are to blame.
    Quoth she, before you tumbled me,
      You promis'd me to wed.
    So would I ha' done, by yonder sun,
      An thou hadst not come to my bed.   65
King: How long hath she been thus?
Ophelia: I hope all will be well. We must be patient: but I cannot choose
    but weep, to think they would lay him i' the cold ground. My brother
    shall know of it: and so I thank you for your good counsel. Come, my
    coach! Good night, ladies; good night, sweet ladies; good night, good   70
    night.   *[Exit.]*
King: Follow her close; give her good watch, I pray you.   *[Exit Horatio.]*
    O, this is the poison of deep grief; it springs
    All from her father's death. O Gertrude, Gertrude,
    When sorrows come, they come not single spies,   75
    But in battalions. First, her father slain;
    Next your son gone; and he most violent author
    Of his own just remove: the people muddied,
    Thick and unwholesome in their thoughts and whispers,
    For good Polonius' death; and we have done but greenly,°   80
    In hugger-mugger° to inter him: poor Ophelia
    Divided from herself and her fair judgement,
    Without the which we are pictures, or mere beasts:
    Last, and as much containing as all these,
    Her brother is in secret come from France;   85
    Feeds on his wonder, keeps himself in clouds,°
    And wants not buzzers° to infect his ear
    With pestilent speeches of his father's death;
    Wherein necessity, of matter beggar'd,°
    Will nothing stick° our person to arraign   90

51 *Valentine:* This song alludes to the belief that the first girl seen by a man on the morning of
this day was his valentine or true love.   53 *dupp'd:* Opened.   58 *Gis:* Jesus.   61 *cock:*
Perversion of "God" in oaths.   80 *greenly:* Foolishly.   81 *hugger-mugger:* Secret haste.
86 *in clouds:* Invisible.   87 *buzzers:* Gossipers.   89 *of matter beggar'd:* Unprovided with
facts.   90 *nothing stick:* Not hesitate.

In ear and ear.° O my dear Gertrude, this,
Like to a murd'ring-piece,° in many places
Gives me superfluous death.   *A noise within.*
Queen: Alack, what noise is this?
King: Where are my Switzers?° Let them guard the door.

Enter a Messenger.

What is the matter?
Messenger: Save yourself, my lord: 95
The ocean, overpeering° of his list,°
Eats not the flats with more impiteous haste
Than young Laertes, in a riotous head,
O'erbears your officers. The rabble call him lord;
And, as the world were now but to begin,   100
Antiquity forgot, custom not known,
The ratifiers and props of every word,°
They cry "Choose we: Laertes shall be king":
Caps, hands, and tongues, applaud it to the clouds:
"Laertes shall be king, Laertes king!"   *A noise within.* 105
Queen: How cheerfully on the false trail they cry!
O, this is counter,° you false Danish dogs!
King: The doors are broke.

Enter Laertes with others.

Laertes: Where is this king? Sirs, stand you all without.
Danes: No, let's come in.
Laertes: I pray you, give me leave.   110
Danes: We will, we will.   *[They retire without the door.]*
Laertes: I thank you: keep the door. O thou vile king,
    Give me my father!
Queen: Calmly, good Laertes.
Laertes: That drop of blood that's calm proclaims me bastard,
Cries cuckold to my father, brands the harlot   115
Even here, between the chaste unsmirched brow
Of my true mother.
King: What is the cause, Laertes,
That thy rebellion looks so giant-like?
Let him go, Gertrude; do not fear our person:
There's such divinity doth hedge a king,   120
That treason can but peep to° what it would,°
Acts little of his will. Tell me, Laertes,
Why thou art thus incens'd. Let him go, Gertrude.
Speak, man.
Laertes: Where is my father?
King: Dead.
Queen: But not by him.   125

---

91 *In ear and ear:* In everybody's ears.   92 *murd'ring-piece:* Small cannon or mortar; suggestion of numerous missiles fired.   94 *Switzers:* Swiss guards, mercenaries.   96 *overpeering:* Overflowing; *list:* Shore.   102 *word:* Promise.   107 *counter:* A hunting term meaning to follow the trail in a direction opposite to that which the game has taken.   121 *peep to:* I.e., look at from afar off; *would:* Wishes to do.

King: Let him demand his fill.

Laertes: How came he dead? I'll not be juggled with:
    To hell, allegiance! vows, to the blackest devil!
    Conscience and grace, to the profoundest pit!
    I dare damnation. To this point I stand,   130
    That both the worlds I give to negligence,°
    Let come what comes; only I'll be reveng'd
    Most throughly° for my father.

King: Who shall stay you?

Laertes: My will,° not all the world's:
    And for my means, I'll husband them so well,   135
    They shall go far with little.

King: Good Laertes,
    If you desire to know the certainty
    Of your dear father, is 't writ in your revenge,
    That, swoopstake,° you will draw both friend and foe,
    Winner and loser?   140

Laertes: None but his enemies.

King: Will you know them then?

Laertes: To his good friends thus wide I'll ope my arms;
    And like the kind life-rend'ring pelican,°
    Repast° them with my blood.

King: Why, now you speak
    Like a good child and a true gentleman.   145
    That I am guiltless of your father's death,
    And am most sensibly in grief for it,
    It shall as level to your judgement 'pear
    As day does to your eye.   *A noise within:* "Let her come in."

Laertes: How now! what noise is that?   150

    Enter Ophelia.

    O heat,° dry up my brains! tears seven times salt,
    Burn out the sense and virtue of mine eye!
    By heaven, thy madness shall be paid with weight,
    Till our scale turn the beam. O rose of May!
    Dear maid, kind sister, sweet Ophelia!   155
    O heavens! is 't possible, a young maid's wits
    Should be as mortal as an old man's life?
    Nature is fine in love, and where 'tis fine,
    It sends some precious instance of itself
    After the thing it loves.   160

Ophelia (Song): They bore him barefac'd on the bier;
    Hey non nonny, nonny, hey nonny;
    And in his grave rain'd many a tear: —
    Fare you well, my dove!

---

131 *give to negligence:* He despises both the here and the hereafter.   133 *throughly:* thoroughly.   134 *My will:* He will not be stopped except by his own will.   139 *swoopstake:* Literally, drawing the whole stake at once, i.e., indiscriminately.   143 *pelican:* Reference to the belief that the pelican feeds its young with its own blood.   144 *Repast:* Feed.   151 *heat:* Probably the heat generated by the passion of grief.

Laertes: Hadst thou thy wits, and didst persuade revenge,   165
      It could not move thus.
Ophelia [sings]: You must sing a-down a-down,
          An you call him a-down-a.
      O, how the wheel° becomes it! It is the false steward,° that stole his
      master's daughter.   170
Laertes: This nothing's more than matter.
Ophelia: There's rosemary,° that's for remembrance; pray you, love,
      remember: and there is pansies,° that's for thoughts.
Laertes: A document° in madness, thoughts and remembrance fitted.
Ophelia: There's fennel° for you, and columbines:° there's rue° for you; and   175
      here's some for me: we may call it herb of grace° o' Sundays: O, you must
      wear your rue with a difference. There's a daisy:° I would give you some
      violets,° but they withered all when my father died: they say 'a made a
      good end, —
      [*Sings.*] For bonny sweet Robin is all my joy.°   180
Laertes: Thought° and affliction, passion, hell itself,
      She turns to favour and to prettiness.
Ophelia (Song): And will 'a not come again?°
      And will 'a not come again?
          No, no, he is dead: 185
          Go to thy death-bed:
      He never will come again.

      His beard was as white as snow,
      All flaxen was his poll:°
          He is gone, he is gone,   190
          And we cast away° moan:
      God ha' mercy on his soul!
      And of all Christian souls, I pray God. God be wi' you.   [*Exit.*]
Laertes: Do you see this, O God?
King: Laertes, I must commune with your grief,   195
      Or you deny me right.° Go but apart,
      Make choice of whom your wisest friends you will,
      And they shall hear and judge 'twixt you and me:
      If by direct or by collateral° hand
      They find us touch'd,° we will our kingdom give,   200
      Our crown, our life, and all that we call ours,
      To you in satisfaction; but if not,

---

169 *wheel:* Spinning wheel as accompaniment to the song refrain; *false steward:* The story is unknown.   172 *rosemary:* Used as a symbol of remembrance both at weddings and at funerals.   173 *pansies:* Emblems of love and courtship (from the French *pensée*).   174 *document:* Piece of instruction or lesson.   175, 176 *fennel:* Emblem of flattery; *columbines:* Emblem of unchastity (?) or ingratitude (?); *rue:* Emblem of repentance. It was usually mingled with holy water and then known as *herb of grace*. Ophelia is probably playing on the two meanings of *rue*, "repentant" and "even for ruth (pity)"; the former signification is for the queen, the latter for herself.   177 *daisy:* Emblem of dissembling, faithlessness.   178 *violets:* Emblems of faithfulness.   180 *For . . . joy:* Probably a line from a Robin Hood ballad.   181 *Thought:* Melancholy thought.   183 *And . . . again:* This song appeared in the songbooks as "The Merry Milkmaids' Dumps."   189 *poll:* Head.   191 *cast away:* Shipwrecked.   196 *right:* My rights.   199 *collateral:* Indirect.   200 *touch'd:* Implicated.

Be you content to lend your patience to us,
And we shall jointly labour with your soul
To give it due content.
Laertes: Let this be so;   205
His means of death, his obscure funeral —
No trophy, sword, nor hatchment° o'er his bones,
No noble rite nor formal ostentation —
Cry to be heard, as 'twere from heaven to earth,
That I must call 't in question.
King: So you shall;   210
And where th' offence is let the great axe fall.
I pray you, go with me.   *Exeunt.*

[SCENE VI: *Another room in the castle.*]

Enter Horatio and others.

Horatio: What are they that would speak with me?
Gentleman: Sea-faring men, sir: they say they have letters for you.
Horatio: Let them come in.   *[Exit Gentleman.]*
I do not know from what part of the world
I should be greeted, if not from lord Hamlet.   5

Enter Sailors.

First Sailor: God bless you, sir.
Horatio: Let him bless thee too.
First Sailor: 'A shall sir, an 't please him. There's a letter for you, sir; it
comes from the ambassador that was bound for England; if your
name be Horatio, as I am let to know it is.   10
Horatio [reads]: "Horatio, when thou shalt have overlooked this, give
these fellows some means° to the king: they have letters for him. Ere
we were two days old at sea, a pirate of very warlike appointment gave
us chase. Finding ourselves too slow of sail, we put on a compelled
valour, and in the grapple I boarded them: on the instant they got   15
clear of our ship; so I alone became their prisoner. They have dealt
with me like thieves of mercy:° but they knew what they did; I am to
do a good turn for them. Let the king have the letters I have sent; and
repair thou to me with as much speed as thou wouldest fly death. I
have words to speak in thine ear will make thee dumb; yet are they   20
much too light for the bore° of the matter. These good fellows will
bring thee where I am. Rosencrantz and Guildenstern hold their
course for England: of them I have much to tell thee. Farewell.
                "He that thou knowest thine, HAMLET."
Come, I will give you way for these your letters;   25
And do 't the speedier, that you may direct me
To him from whom you brought them.   *Exeunt.*

---

207 *hatchment:* Tablet displaying the armorial bearings of a deceased person.   **Scene VI.**
12 *means:* Means of access.   17 *thieves of mercy:* Merciful thieves.   21 *bore:* Caliber, importance.

[SCENE VII: *Another room in the castle.*]

    Enter King and Laertes.

King: Now must your conscience° my acquittance seal,
    And you must put me in your heart for friend,
    Sith you have heard, and with a knowing ear,
    That he which hath your noble father slain
    Pursued my life.
Laertes: It well appears: but tell me   5
    Why you proceeded not against these feats,
    So criminal and so capital° in nature,
    As by your safety, wisdom, all things else,
    You mainly° were stirr'd up.
King: O, for two special reasons;
    Which may to you, perhaps, seem much unsinew'd,°   10
    But yet to me th' are strong. The queen his mother
    Lives almost by his looks; and for myself —
    My virtue or my plague, be it either which —
    She's so conjunctive° to my life and soul,
    That, as the star moves not but in his sphere,°   15
    I could not but by her. The other motive,
    Why to a public count° I might not go,
    Is the great love the general gender° bear him;
    Who, dipping all his faults in their affection,
    Would, like the spring° that turneth wood to stone,   20
    Convert his gyves° to graces; so that my arrows,
    Too slightly timber'd° for so loud° a wind,
    Would have reverted to my bow again,
    And not where I had aim'd them.
Laertes: And so have I a noble father lost;   25
    A sister driven into desp'rate terms,°
    Whose worth, if praises may go back° again,
    Stood challenger on mount° of all the age°
    For her perfections: but my revenge will come.
King: Break not your sleeps for that: you must not think   30
    That we are made of stuff so flat and dull
    That we can let our beard be shook with danger
    And think it pastime. You shortly shall hear more:
    I lov'd your father, and we love ourself;
    And that, I hope, will teach you to imagine —   35

Scene VII.   1 *conscience:* Knowledge that this is true.   7 *capital:* Punishable by death. 9 *mainly:* Greatly.   10 *unsinew'd:* Weak.   14 *conjunctive:* Conformable (the next line suggesting planetary conjunction).   15 *sphere:* The hollow sphere in which, according to Ptolemaic astronomy, the planets were supposed to move.   17 *count:* Account, reckoning. 18 *general gender:* Common people.   20 *spring:* I.e., one heavily charged with lime. 21 *gyves:* Fetters; here, faults, or possibly, punishments inflicted (on him).   22 *slightly timber'd:* Light; *loud:* Strong.   26 *terms:* State, condition.   27 *go back:* Return to Ophelia's former virtues.   28 *on mount:* Set up on high, *mounted* (on horseback); *of all the age:* Qualifies *challenger* and not *mount.*

Enter a Messenger with letters.

How now! what news?

Messenger: Letters, my lord, from Hamlet:
These to your majesty; this to the queen.°

King: From Hamlet! who brought them?

Messenger: Sailors, my lord, they say; I saw them not:
They were given me by Claudio;° he receiv'd them   40
Of him that brought them.

King: Laertes, you shall hear them.
Leave us.   *[Exit Messenger.]*
[Reads.] "High and mighty, You shall know I am set naked° on your
kingdom. To-morrow shall I beg leave to see your kingly eyes: when I
shall, first asking your pardon thereunto, recount the occasion of my   45
sudden and more strange return."   "HAMLET."
What should this mean? Are all the rest come back?
Or is it some abuse, and no such thing?

Laertes: Know you the hand?

King: 'Tis Hamlet's character. "Naked!"
And in a postscript here, he says "alone."   50
Can you devise° me?

Laertes: I'm lost in it, my lord. But let him come;
It warms the very sickness in my heart,
That I shall live and tell him to his teeth,
"Thus didst thou."

King: If it be so, Laertes —   55
As how should it be so? how otherwise?° —
Will you be rul'd by me?

Laertes: Ay, my lord;
So you will not o'errule me to a peace.

King: To thine own peace. If he be now return'd,
As checking at° his voyage, and that he means   60
No more to undertake it, I will work him
To an exploit, now ripe in my device,
Under the which he shall not choose but fall:
And for his death no wind of blame shall breathe,
But even his mother shall uncharge the practice°   65
And call it accident.

Laertes: My lord, I will be rul'd;
The rather, if you could devise it so
That I might be the organ.°

King: It falls right.
You have been talk'd of since your travel much,

---

37 *to the queen:* One hears no more of the letter to the queen.   40 *Claudio:* This character
does not appear in the play.   43 *naked:* Unprovided (with retinue).   51 *devise:* Explain to.
56 *As . . . otherwise?* How can this (Hamlet's return) be true? (yet) how otherwise than true
(since we have the evidence of his letter)? Some editors read *How should it not be so,* etc., making
the words refer to Laertes's desire to meet with Hamlet.   60 *checking at:* Used in falconry of a
hawk's leaving the quarry to fly at a chance bird; turn aside.   65 *uncharge the practice:* Acquit
the stratagem of being a plot.   68 *organ:* Agent, instrument.

And that in Hamlet's hearing, for a quality   70
Wherein, they say, you shine: your sum of parts
Did not together pluck such envy from him
As did that one, and that, in my regard,
Of the unworthiest siege.°
Laertes: What part is that, my lord?
King: A very riband in the cap of youth,   75
Yet needful too; for youth no less becomes
The light and careless livery that it wears
Than settled age his sables° and his weeds,
Importing health and graveness. Two months since,
Here was a gentleman of Normandy: —   80
I have seen myself, and serv'd against, the French,
And they can well° on horseback: but this gallant
Had witchcraft in 't; he grew unto his seat;
And to such wondrous doing brought his horse,
As had he been incorps'd and demi-natur'd°   85
With the brave beast: so far he topp'd° my thought,
That I, in forgery° of shapes and tricks,
Come short of what he did.
Laertes: A Norman was 't?
King: A Norman.
Laertes: Upon my life, Lamord.°
King: The very same.   90
Laertes: I know him well: he is the brooch indeed
And gem of all the nation.
King: He made confession° of you,
And gave you such a masterly report
For art and exercise° in your defence°   95
And for your rapier most especial,
That he cried out, 'twould be a sight indeed,
If one could match you: the scrimers° of their nation,
He swore, had neither motion, guard, nor eye,
If you oppos'd them. Sir, this report of his   100
Did Hamlet so envenom with his envy
That he could nothing do but wish and beg
Your sudden coming o'er, to play° with you.
Now, out of this, —
Laertes: What out of this, my lord?
King: Laertes, was your father dear to you?   105
Or are you like the painting of a sorrow,
A face without a heart?

---

74 *siege:* Rank.   78 *sables:* Rich garments.   82 *can well:* Are skilled.   85 *incorps'd and demi-natur'd:* Of one body and nearly of one nature (like the centaur).   86 *topp'd:* Surpassed. 87 *forgery:* Invention.   90 *Lamord:* This refers possibly to Pietro Monte, instructor to Louis XII's master of the horse.   93 *confession:* Grudging admission of superiority.   95 *art and exercise:* Skillful exercise; *defence:* Science of defense in sword practice.   98 *scrimers:* Fencers. 103 *play:* Fence.

Laertes: Why ask you this?
King: Not that I think you did not love your father;
    But that I know love is begun by time;
    And that I see, in passages of proof,°   110
    Time qualifies the spark and fire of it.
    There lives within the very flame of love
    A kind of wick or snuff that will abate it;
    And nothing is at a like goodness still;
    For goodness, growing to a plurisy,°   115
    Dies in his own too much:° that we would do,
    We should do when we would; for this "would" changes
    And hath abatements° and delays as many
    As there are tongues, are hands, are accidents;°
    And then this "should" is like a spendthrift° sigh,   120
    That hurts by easing. But, to the quick o' th' ulcer:° —
    Hamlet comes back: what would you undertake,
    To show yourself your father's son in deed
    More than in words?
Laertes: To cut his throat i' th' church.
King: No place, indeed, should murder sanctuarize;°   125
    Revenge should have no bounds. But, good Laertes,
    Will you do this, keep close within your chamber.
    Hamlet return'd shall know you are come home:
    We'll put on those shall praise your excellence
    And set a double varnish on the fame   130
    The Frenchman gave you, bring you in fine together
    And wager on your heads: he, being remiss,
    Most generous and free from all contriving,
    Will not peruse the foils; so that, with ease,
    Or with a little shuffling, you may choose   135
    A sword unbated,° and in a pass of practice°
    Requite him for your father.
Laertes: I will do 't:
    And, for that purpose, I'll anoint my sword.
    I bought an unction of a mountebank,°
    So mortal that, but dip a knife in it,
    Where it draws blood no cataplasm° so rare,   140
    Collected from all simples° that have virtue
    Under the moon,° can save the thing from death
    That is but scratch'd withal: I'll touch my point

---

110 *passages of proof:* Proved instances.   115 *plurisy:* Excess, plethora.   116 *in his own too much:* Of its own excess.   118 *abatements:* Diminutions.   119 *accidents:* Occurrences, incidents.   120 *spendthrift:* An allusion to the belief that each sigh cost the heart a drop of blood.   121 *quick o' th' ulcer:* Heart of the difficulty.   125 *sanctuarize:* Protect from punishment; allusion to the right of sanctuary with which certain religious places were invested. 136 *unbated:* Not blunted, having no button; *pass of practice:* Treacherous thrust. 139 *mountebank:* Quack doctor.   141 *cataplasm:* Plaster or poultice.   142 *simples:* Herbs. 143 *Under the moon:* I.e., when collected by moonlight to add to their medicinal value.

With this contagion, that, if I gall° him slightly,   145
It may be death.
King: Let's further think of this;
   Weigh what convenience both of time and means
   May fit us to our shape:° if this should fail,
   And that our drift look through our bad performance,°
   'Twere better not assay'd: therefore this project   150
   Should have a back or second, that might hold,
   If this should blast in proof.° Soft! let me see:
   We'll make a solemn wager on your cunnings:°
   I ha 't:
   When in your motion you are hot and dry —   155
   As make your bouts more violent to that end —
   And that he calls for drink, I'll have prepar'd him
   A chalice° for the nonce, whereon but sipping,
   If he by chance escape your venom'd stuck,°
   Our purpose may hold there. But stay, what noise?   160

Enter Queen.

Queen: One woe doth tread upon another's heel,
   So fast they follow: your sister's drown'd, Laertes.
Laertes: Drown'd! O, where?
Queen: There is a willow° grows askant° the brook,
   That shows his hoar° leaves in the glassy stream;   165
   There with fantastic garlands did she make
   Of crow-flowers,° nettles, daisies, and long purples°
   That liberal° shepherds give a grosser name,
   But our cold maids do dead men's fingers call them:
   There, on the pendent boughs her crownet° weeds   170
   Clamb'ring to hang, an envious sliver° broke;
   When down her weedy° trophies and herself
   Fell in the weeping brook. Her clothes spread wide;
   And, mermaid-like, awhile they bore her up:
   Which time she chanted snatches of old lauds;°   175
   As one incapable° of her own distress,
   Or like a creature native and indued°
   Upon that element: but long it could not be
   Till that her garments, heavy with their drink,
   Pull'd the poor wretch from her melodious lay   180
   To muddy death.
Laertes: Alas, then, she is drown'd?
Queen: Drown'd, drown'd.

---

145 *gall:* Graze, wound.   148 *shape:* Part we propose to act.   149 *drift ... performance:* Intention be disclosed by our bungling.   152 *blast in proof:* Burst in the test (like a cannon).   153 *cunnings:* Skills.   158 *chalice:* Cup.   159 *stuck:* Thrust (from *stoccado*). 164 *willow:* For its significance of forsaken love; *askant:* Aslant.   165 *hoar:* White (i.e., on the underside).   167 *crow-flowers:* Buttercups; *long purples:* Early purple orchids. 168 *liberal:* Probably, free-spoken.   170 *crownet:* Coronet; made into a chaplet.   171 *sliver:* Branch.   172 *weedy:* I.e., of plants.   175 *lauds:* Hymns.   176 *incapable:* Lacking capacity to apprehend.   177 *indued:* Endowed with qualities fitting her for living in water.

Laertes: Too much of water hast thou, poor Ophelia,
  And therefore I forbid my tears: but yet
  It is our trick;° nature her custom holds,   185
  Let shame say what it will: when these are gone,
  The woman will be out.° Adieu, my lord:
  I have a speech of fire, that fain would blaze,
  But that this folly drowns it.   *Exit.*
King: Let's follow, Gertrude:
  How much I had to do to calm his rage!   190
  Now fear I this will give it start again;
  Therefore let 's follow.   *Exeunt.*

[ACT V

Scene I: *A churchyard.*]

  Enter two Clowns° [with spades, &c.].

First Clown: Is she to be buried in Christian burial when she wilfully seeks
  her own salvation?

Second Clown: I tell thee she is; therefore make her grave straight:° the
  crowner° hath sat on her, and finds it Christian burial.

First Clown: How can that be, unless she drowned herself in her own   5
  defence?

Second Clown: Why, 'tis found so.

First Clown: It must be "se offendendo";° it cannot be else. For here lies
  the point: if I drown myself wittingly,° it argues an act: and an act
  hath three branches;° it is, to act, to do, and to perform: argal,° she   10
  drowned herself wittingly.

Second Clown: Nay, but hear you, goodman delver,°—

First Clown: Give me leave. Here lies the water; good: here stands the
  man; good: if the man go to this water, and drown himself, it is, will
  he, nill he, he goes,—mark you that; but if the water come to him and   15
  drown him, he drowns not himself: argal, he that is not guilty of his
  own death shortens not his own life.

Second Clown: But is this law?

First Clown: Ay, marry, is 't; crowner's quest° law.

Second Clown: Will you ha' the truth on 't? If this had not been a gentle- 20
  woman, she should have been buried out o' Christian burial.

First Clown: Why, there thou say'st:° and the more pity that great folk
  should have countenance° in this world to drown or hang themselves,

---

185 *trick:* Way.   186–187 *when . . . out:* When my tears are all shed, the woman in me will
be satisfied.   **Act V, Scene I.**   *Clowns:* The word *clown* was used to denote peasants as
well as humorous characters; here applied to the rustic type of clown.   3 *straight:* Straightway, immediately; some interpret "from east to west in a direct line, parallel with the church."
4 *crowner:* Coroner.   8 *"se offendendo":* For *se defendendo,* term used in verdicts of justifiable homicide.   9 *wittingly:* Intentionally.   10 *three branches:* Parody of legal phraseology;
argal: Corruption of *ergo,* therefore.   12 *delver:* Digger.   19 *quest:* Inquest.   22 *there
thou say'st:* That's right.   23 *countenance:* Privilege.

more than their even° Christian. Come, my spade. There is no ancient
gentlemen but gardeners, ditchers, and grave-makers: they hold up°   25
Adam's profession.

Second Clown: Was he a gentleman?

First Clown: 'A was the first that ever bore arms.

Second Clown: Why, he had none.

First Clown: What, art a heathen? How dost thou understand the Scripture?   30
The Scripture says "Adam digged": could he dig without arms? I'll put another question to thee: if thou answerest me not to the purpose, confess
thyself°—

Second Clown: Go to.°

First Clown: What is he that builds stronger than either the mason, the ship-   35
wright, or the carpenter?

Second Clown: The gallows-maker; for that frame outlives a thousand
tenants.

First Clown: I like thy wit well, in good faith: the gallows does well; but
how does it well? it does well to those that do ill: now thou dost ill to   40
say the gallows is built stronger than the church: argal, the gallows
may do well to thee. To 't again, come.

Second Clown: "Who builds stronger than a mason, a shipwright, or a
carpenter?"

First Clown: Ay, tell me that, and unyoke.°   45

Second Clown: Marry, now I can tell.

First Clown: To 't.

Second Clown: Mass,° I cannot tell.

Enter Hamlet and Horatio [at a distance].

First Clown: Cudgel thy brains no more about it, for your dull ass will not
mend his pace with beating; and, when you are asked this question   50
next, say "a grave-maker": the houses he makes lasts till doomsday.
Go, get thee in, and fetch me a stoup° of liquor.

[Exit Second Clown.] Song. [He digs.]

In youth, when I did love, did love,
   Methought it was very sweet,
To contract — O — the time, for — a — my behove,°   55
   O, methought, there — a — was nothing — a — meet.

Hamlet: Has this fellow no feeling of his business, that 'a sings at grave-
making?

Horatio: Custom hath made it in him a property of easiness.°

Hamlet: 'Tis e'en so: the hand of little employment hath the daintier   60
sense.

First Clown: (*Song.*) But age, with his stealing steps,
   Hath claw'd me in his clutch,
And hath shipped me into the land
   As if I had never been such.   *[Throws up a skull.]*   65

---

24 *even:* Fellow.   25 *hold up:* Maintain, continue.   33 *confess thyself:* "And be hanged"
completes the proverb.   34 *Go to:* Perhaps, "begin," or some other form of concession.
45 *unyoke:* After this great effort you may unharness the team of your wits.   48 *Mass:* By the
Mass.   52 *stoup:* Two-quart measure.   55 *behove:* Benefit.   59 *property of easiness:* A
peculiarity that now is easy.

Hamlet: That skull had a tongue in it, and could sing once: how the knave jowls° it to the ground, as if 'twere Cain's jaw-bone,° that did the first murder! This might be the pate of a politician,° which this ass now o'er-reaches;° one that would circumvent God, might it not?

Horatio: It might, my lord.   70

Hamlet: Or of a courtier; which could say "Good morrow, sweet lord! How dost thou, sweet lord?" This might be my lord such-a-one, that praised my lord such-a-one's horse, when he meant to beg it; might it not?

Horatio: Ay, my lord.   75

Hamlet: Why, e'en so: and now my Lady Worm's; chapless,° and knocked about the mazzard° with a sexton's spade: here's fine revolution, an we had the trick to see 't. Did these bones cost no more the breeding, but to play at loggats° with 'em? mine ache to think on 't.

First Clown: (*Song.*) A pick-axe, and a spade, a spade,   80
    For and° a shrouding sheet:
  O, a pit of clay for to be made
    For such a guest is meet.   *[Throws up another skull.]*

Hamlet: There's another: why may not that be the skull of a lawyer? Where be his quiddities° now, his quillities,° his cases, his tenures,°   85
and his tricks? why does he suffer this mad knave now to knock him about the sconce° with a dirty shovel, and will not tell him of his action of battery? Hum! This fellow might be in 's time a great buyer of land, with his statutes, his recognizances,° his fines, his double vouchers,° his recoveries:° is this the fine° of his fines, and the re-   90
covery of his recoveries, to have his fine pate full of fine dirt? will his vouchers vouch him no more of his purchases, and double ones too, than the length and breadth of a pair of indentures?° The very conveyances of his lands will scarcely lie in this box; and must the inheritor° himself have no more, ha?   95

Horatio: Not a jot more, my lord.

Hamlet: Is not parchment made of sheep-skins?

Horatio: Ay, my lord, and of calf-skins° too.

Hamlet: They are sheep and calves which seek out assurance in that.°
  I will speak to this fellow. Whose grave's this, sirrah?   100

First Clown: Mine, sir.
  [Sings.] O, a pit of clay for to be made
    For such a guest is meet.

Hamlet: I think it be thine, indeed; for thou liest in 't.

---

67 *jowls:* Dashes; *Cain's jaw-bone:* Allusion to the old tradition that Cain slew Abel with the jawbone of an ass.   68 *politician:* Schemer, plotter.   69 *o'er-reaches:* Quibble on the literal sense and the sense "circumvent."   76 *chapless:* Having no lower jaw.   77 *mazzard:* Head.   79 *loggats:* A game in which six sticks are thrown to lie as near as possible to a stake fixed in the ground, or block of wood on a floor.   81 *For and:* And moreover.   85 *quiddities:* Subtleties, quibbles; *quillities:* Verbal niceties, subtle distinctions; *tenures:* The holding of a piece of property or office or the conditions or period of such holding.   87 *sconce:* Head. 89 *statutes, recognizances:* Legal terms connected with the transfer of land.   90 *vouchers:* Persons called on to warrant a tenant's title; *recoveries:* Process for transfer of entailed estate; *fine:* The four uses of this word are as follows: (1) end, (2) legal process, (3) elegant, (4) small. 93 *indentures:* Conveyances or contracts.   95 *inheritor:* Possessor, owner.   98 *calf-skins:* Parchments.   99 *assurance in that:* Safety in legal parchments.

First Clown: You lie out on 't, sir, and therefore 't is not yours: for my part,   105
    I do not lie in 't, yet it is mine.

Hamlet: Thou dost lie in 't, to be in 't and say it is thine: 'tis for the dead, not
    for the quick; therefore thou liest.

First Clown: 'Tis a quick lie, sir; 'twill away again, from me to you.

Hamlet: What man dost thou dig it for?   110

First Clown: For no man, sir.

Hamlet: What woman, then?

First Clown: For none, neither.

Hamlet: Who is to be buried in 't?

First Clown: One that was a woman, sir; but, rest her soul, she's dead.   115

Hamlet: How absolute° the knave is! we must speak by the card,° or equivoca-
    tion° will undo us. By the Lord, Horatio, these three years I have taken
    note of it; the age is grown so picked° that the toe of the peasant comes so
    near the heel of the courtier, he galls° his kibe.° How long hast thou been
    a grave-maker?   120

First Clown: Of all the day i' the year, I came to 't that day that our last king
    Hamlet overcame Fortinbras.

Hamlet: How long is that since?

First Clown: Cannot you tell that? every fool can tell that: it was the
    very day that young Hamlet was born; he that is mad, and sent into   125
    England.

Hamlet: Ay, marry, why was he sent into England?

First Clown: Why, because 'a was mad: 'a shall recover his wits there; or, if 'a
    do not, 'tis no great matter there.

Hamlet: Why?   130

First Clown: 'Twill not be seen in him there; there the men are as mad as he.

Hamlet: How came he mad?

First Clown: Very strangely, they say.

Hamlet: How strangely?   135

First Clown: Faith, e'en with losing his wits.

Hamlet: Upon what ground?

First Clown: Why, here in Denmark: I have been sexton here, man and boy,
    thirty years.°

Hamlet: How long will a man lie i' the earth ere he rot?   140

First Clown: Faith, if 'a be not rotten before 'a die — as we have many pocky°
    corses now-a-days, that will scarce hold the laying in — 'a will last you
    some eight year or nine year: a tanner will last you nine year.

Hamlet: Why he more than another?

First Clown: Why, sir, his hide is so tanned with his trade, that 'a will keep   145
    out water a great while; and your water is a sore decayer of your whore-
    son dead body. Here's a skull now hath lain you i' th' earth three and
    twenty years.

Hamlet: Whose was it?

---

116 *absolute:* Positive, decided; *by the card:* With precision, i.e., by the mariner's card on which
the points of the compass were marked.   117 *equivocation:* Ambiguity in the use of terms.
118 *picked:* Refined, fastidious.   119 *galls:* Chafes; *kibe:* Chilblain.   139 *thirty years:* This
statement with that in line 125 shows Hamlet's age to be thirty years.   141 *pocky:* Rotten,
diseased.

First Clown: A whoreson mad fellow's it was: whose do you think it was? 150
Hamlet: Nay, I know not.
First Clown: A pestilence on him for a mad rogue! 'a poured a flagon of
Rhenish on my head once. This same skull, sir, was Yorick's skull, the
king's jester.
Hamlet: This? 155
First Clown: E'en that.
Hamlet: Let me see. *[Takes the skull.]* Alas, poor Yorick! I knew him, Horatio: a fellow of infinite jest, of most excellent fancy: he hath borne me
on his back a thousand times; and now, how abhorred in my imagi- 160
nation it is! my gorge rises at it. Here hung those lips that I have
kissed I know not how oft. Where be your gibes now? your gam-
bols? your songs? your flashes of merriment, that were wont to set
the table on a roar? Not one now, to mock your own grinning? quite
chap-fallen? Now get you to my lady's chamber, and tell her, let her
paint an inch thick, to this favour she must come; make her laugh at 165
that. Prithee, Horatio, tell me one thing.
Horatio: What's that, my lord?
Hamlet: Dost thou think Alexander looked o' this fashion i' the earth?
Horatio: E'en so.
Hamlet: And smelt so? pah! *[Puts down the skull.]* 170
Horatio: E'en so, my lord.
Hamlet: To what base uses we may return, Horatio! Why may not imagination trace the noble dust of Alexander, till 'a find it stopping a bung-
hole?
Horatio: 'Twere to consider too curiously,° to consider so. 175
Hamlet: No, faith, not a jot; but to follow him thither with modesty
enough, and likelihood to lead it: as thus: Alexander died, Alexander
was buried, Alexander returneth into dust; the dust is earth; of earth
we make loam;° and why of that loam, whereto he was converted,
might they not stop a beer-barrel? 180
    Imperious° Cæsar, dead and turn'd to clay,
    Might stop a hole to keep the wind away:
    O, that that earth, which kept the world in awe,
    Should patch a wall t'expel the winter's flaw!°
But soft! but soft awhile! here comes the king, 185

*Enter King, Queen, Laertes, and the Corse of [Ophelia, in procession, with
Priest, Lords, etc.].*

The queen, the courtiers: who is this they follow?
And with such maimed rites? This doth betoken
The corse they follow did with desp'rate hand
Fordo° it° own life: 'twas of some estate.
Couch° we awhile, and mark. *[Retiring with Horatio.]* 190
Laertes: What ceremony else?
Hamlet: That is Laertes,
    A very noble youth: mark.

---

175 *curiously:* Minutely.   179 *loam:* Clay paste for brickmaking.   181 *Imperious:* Imperial.   184 *flaw:* Gust of wind.   189 *Fordo:* Destroy; *it:* Its.   190 *Couch:* Hide, lurk.

Laertes: What ceremony else?
First Priest: Her obsequies have been as far enlarg'd°
    As we have warranty: her death was doubtful;   195
    And, but that great command o'ersways the order,
    She should in ground unsanctified have lodg'd
    Till the last trumpet; for charitable prayers,
    Shards,° flints and pebbles should be thrown on her:
    Yet here she is allow'd her virgin crants,°   200
    Her maiden strewments° and the bringing home
    Of bell and burial.°
Laertes: Must there no more be done?
First Priest: No more be done:
    We should profane the service of the dead
    To sing a requiem and such rest to her   205
    As to peace-parted° souls.
Laertes: Lay her i' th' earth:
    And from her fair and unpolluted flesh
    May violets spring! I tell thee, churlish priest,
    A minist'ring angel shall my sister be,
    When thou liest howling.°
Hamlet: What, the fair Ophelia!   210
Queen: Sweets to the sweet: farewell!   *[Scattering flowers.]*
    I hop'd thou shouldst have been my Hamlet's wife;
    I thought thy bride-bed to have deck'd, sweet maid,
    And not have strew'd thy grave.
Laertes: O, treble woe
    Fall ten times treble on that cursed head,   215
    Whose wicked deed thy most ingenious sense°
    Depriv'd thee of! Hold off the earth awhile,
    Till I have caught her once more in mine arms: *[Leaps into the grave.]*
    Now pile your dust upon the quick and dead,
    Till of this flat a mountain you have made,   220
    T' o'ertop old Pelion,° or the skyish head
    Of blue Olympus.
Hamlet: *[Advancing]* What is he whose grief
    Bears such an emphasis? whose phrase of sorrow
    Conjures the wand'ring stars,° and makes them stand
    Like wonder-wounded hearers? This is I,   225
    Hamlet the Dane.   *[Leaps into the grave.]*
Laertes: The devil take thy soul!   *[Grappling with him.]*
Hamlet: Thou pray'st not well.
    I prithee, take thy fingers from my throat;

---

194 *enlarg'd:* Extended, referring to the fact that suicides are not given full burial rites. 199 *Shards:* Broken bits of pottery.   200 *crants:* Garlands customarily hung upon the biers of unmarried women.   201 *strewments:* Traditional strewing of flowers.   201–202 *bringing . . . burial:* The laying to rest of the body, to the sound of the bell.   206 *peace-parted:* Allusion to the text "Lord, now lettest thou thy servant depart in peace."   210 *howling:* I.e., in hell.   216 *ingenious sense:* Mind endowed with finest qualities.   221 *Pelion:* Olympus, Pelion, and Ossa are mountains in the north of Thessaly.   224 *wand'ring stars:* Planets.

For, though I am not splenitive° and rash,
Yet have I in me something dangerous,   230
Which let thy wisdom fear: hold off thy hand.
King: Pluck them asunder.
Queen: Hamlet, Hamlet!
All: Gentlemen, —
Horatio: Good my lord, be quiet.

[The Attendants part them, and they come out of the grave.]

Hamlet: Why, I will fight with him upon this theme
Until my eyelids will no longer wag.°   235
Queen: O my son, what theme?
Hamlet: I lov'd Ophelia: forty thousand brothers
Could not, with all their quantity° of love,
Make up my sum. What wilt thou do for her?
King: O, he is mad, Laertes.   240
Queen: For love of God, forbear° him.
Hamlet: 'Swounds,° show me what thou 'lt do:
Woo 't° weep? woo 't fight? woo 't fast? woo 't tear thyself?
Woo 't drink up eisel?° eat a crocodile?
I'll do 't. Dost thou come here to whine?   245
To outface me with leaping in her grave?
Be buried quick with her, and so will I:
And, if thou prate of mountains, let them throw
Millions of acres on us, till our ground,
Singeing his pate against the burning zone,°   250
Make Ossa like a wart! Nay, an thou 'lt mouth,
I'll rant as well as thou.
Queen: This is mere madness:
And thus awhile the fit will work on him;
Anon, as patient as the female dove.
When that her golden couplets° are disclos'd,   255
His silence will sit drooping.
Hamlet: Hear you, sir;
What is the reason that you use me thus?
I lov'd you ever: but it is no matter;
Let Hercules himself do what he may,
The cat will mew and dog will have his day.   260
King: I pray thee, good Horatio, wait upon him.   *Exit Hamlet and Horatio.*
[To Laertes.] Strengthen your patience in° our last night's speech;
We'll put the matter to the present push.°
Good Gertrude, set some watch over your son.

---

229 *splenitive:* Quick-tempered.   235 *wag:* Move (not used ludicrously).   238 *quantity:*
Some suggest that the word is used in a deprecatory sense (little bits, fragments).   241 *for-*
bear: Leave alone.   242 *'Swounds:* Oath, "God's wounds."   243 *Woo 't:* Wilt thou.
244 *eisel:* Vinegar. Some editors have taken this to be the name of a river, such as the Yssel, the
Weissel, and the Nile.   250 *burning zone:* Sun's orbit.   255 *golden couplets:* The pigeon
lays two eggs; the young when hatched are covered with golden down.   262 *in:* By recalling.
263 *present push:* Immediate test.

This grave shall have a living° monument: 265
An hour of quiet shortly shall we see;
Till then, in patience our proceeding be.   *Exeunt.*

[SCENE II: *A hall in the castle.*]

Enter Hamlet and Horatio.

Hamlet: So much for this, sir: now shall you see the other;
    You do remember all the circumstance?
Horatio: Remember it, my lord!
Hamlet: Sir, in my heart there was a kind of fighting,
    That would not let me sleep: methought I lay   5
    Worse than the mutines in the bilboes.° Rashly,°
    And prais'd be rashness for it, let us know,
    Our indiscretion sometime serves us well,
    When our deep plots do pall:° and that should learn us
    There's a divinity that shapes our ends,   10
    Rough-hew° them how we will, —
Horatio: That is most certain.
Hamlet: Up from my cabin,
    My sea-gown° scarf'd about me, in the dark
    Grop'd I to find out them; had my desire,
    Finger'd° their packet, and in fine° withdrew   15
    To mine own room again; making so bold,
    My fears forgetting manners, to unseal
    Their grand commission; where I found, Horatio, —
    O royal knavery! — an exact command,
    Larded° with many several sorts of reasons   20
    Importing Denmark's health and England's too,
    With, ho! such bugs° and goblins in my life,°
    That, on the supervise,° no leisure bated,°
    No, not to stay the grinding of the axe,
    My head should be struck off.
Horatio: Is 't possible?   25
Hamlet: Here's the commission: read it at more leisure.
    But wilt thou hear me how I did proceed?
Horatio: I beseech you.
Hamlet: Being thus be-netted round with villanies, —
    Ere I could make a prologue to my brains,   30
    They had begun the play° — I sat me down,

---

265 *living:* Lasting; also refers (for Laertes's benefit) to the plot against Hamlet. **Scene II.**
6 *mutines in the bilboes:* Mutineers in shackles; *Rashly:* Goes with line 12.   9 *pall:* Fail.
11 *Rough-hew:* Shape roughly; it may mean "bungle."   13 *sea-gown:* "A sea-gown, or a
coarse, high-collered, and short-sleeved gowne, reaching down to the mid-leg, and used most
by seamen and saylors" (Cotgrave, quoted by Singer).   15 *Finger'd:* Pilfered, filched; *in fine:*
Finally.   20 *Larded:* Enriched.   22 *bugs:* Bugbears; *such . . . life:* Such imaginary dangers if I
were allowed to live.   23 *supervise:* Perusal; *leisure bated:* Delay allowed.   30–31 *prologue . . .
play:* I.e., before I could begin to think, my mind had made its decision.

Devis'd a new commission, wrote it fair:
I once did hold it, as our statists° do,
A baseness to write fair° and labour'd much
How to forget that learning, but, sir, now   35
It did me yeoman's° service: wilt thou know
Th' effect of what I wrote?
Horatio: Ay, good my lord.
Hamlet: An earnest conjuration from the king,
    As England was his faithful tributary,
    As love between them like the palm might flourish,   40
    As peace should still her wheaten garland° wear
    And stand a comma° 'tween their amities,
    And many such-like 'As'es° of great charge,°
    That, on the view and knowing of these contents,
    Without debatement further, more or less,   45
    He should the bearers put to sudden death,
    Not shriving-time° allow'd.
Horatio: How was this seal'd?
Hamlet: Why, even in that was heaven ordinant.°
    I had my father's signet in my purse,
    Which was the model of that Danish seal;   50
    Folded the writ up in the form of th' other,
    Subscrib'd it, gave 't th' impression, plac'd it safely,
    The changeling never known. Now, the next day
    Was our sea-fight; and what to this was sequent°
    Thou know'st already.   55
Horatio: So Guildenstern and Rosencrantz go to 't.
Hamlet: Why, man, they did make love to this employment;
    They are not near my conscience; their defeat
    Does by their own insinuation° grow:
    'Tis dangerous when the baser nature comes   60
    Between the pass° and fell incensed° points
    Of mighty opposites.
Horatio: Why, what a king is this!
Hamlet: Does it not, think thee, stand° me now upon —
    He that hath kill'd my king and whor'd my mother,
    Popp'd in between th' election° and my hopes,   65
    Thrown out his angle° for my proper life,
    And with such coz'nage° — is 't not perfect conscience,
    To quit° him with this arm? and is 't not to be damn'd,

---

33 *statists:* Statesmen.   34 *fair:* In a clear hand.   36 *yeoman's:* I.e., faithful.   41 *wheaten garland:* Symbol of peace.   42 *comma:* Smallest break or separation. Here *amity* begins and *amity* ends the period, and *peace* stands between like a dependent clause. The comma indicates continuity, link.   43 *'As'es:* The "whereases" of a formal document, with play on the word *ass; charge:* Import, and burden.   47 *shriving-time:* Time for absolution.   48 *ordinant:* Directing.   54 *sequent:* Subsequent.   59 *insinuation:* Interference.   61 *pass:* Thrust; *fell incensed:* Fiercely angered.   63 *stand:* Become incumbent.   65 *election:* The Danish throne was filled by election.   66 *angle:* Fishing line.   67 *coz'nage:* Trickery.   68 *quit:* Repay.

To let this canker° of our nature come
  In further evil?   70
Horatio: It must be shortly known to him from England
  What is the issue of the business there.
Hamlet: It will be short: the interim is mine;
  And a man's life's no more than to say "One."
  But I am very sorry, good Horatio,   75
  That to Laertes I forgot myself;
  For, by the image of my cause, I see
  The portraiture of his: I'll court his favours:
  But, sure, the bravery° of his grief did put me
  Into a tow'ring passion.
Horatio: Peace! who comes here?   80

   Enter a Courtier [Osric].

Osric: Your lordship is right welcome back to Denmark.
Hamlet: I humbly thank you, sir. *[To Horatio.]* Dost know this water-fly?°
Horatio: No, my good lord.
Hamlet: Thy state is the more gracious; for 'tis a vice to know him. He
  hath much land, and fertile: let a beast be lord of beasts,° and his crib   85
  shall stand at the king's mess:° 'tis a chough;° but, as I say, spacious
  in the possession of dirt.
Osric: Sweet lord, if your lordship were at leisure, I should impart a thing to
  you from his majesty.
Hamlet: I will receive it, sir, with all diligence of spirit. Put your bonnet to   90
  his right use; 'tis for the head.
Osric: I thank your lordship, it is very hot.
Hamlet: No, believe me, 'tis very cold; the wind is northerly.
Osric: It is indifferent° cold, my lord, indeed.
Hamlet: But yet methinks it is very sultry and hot for my complexion.   95
Osric: Exceedingly, my lord; it is very sultry, — as 'twere, — I cannot tell
  how. But, my lord, his majesty bade me signify to you that 'a has laid a
  great wager on your head: sir, this is the matter, —
Hamlet: I beseech you, remember° —
                  [Hamlet moves him to put on his hat.]
Osric: Nay, good my lord; for mine ease,° in good faith. Sir, here is newly   100
  come to court Laertes; believe me, an absolute gentleman, full of
  most excellent differences, of very soft° society and great showing:°
  indeed, to speak feelingly° of him, he is the card° or calendar of gentry,° for you shall find in him the continent of what part a gentleman
  would see.   105

---

69 *canker:* Ulcer, or possibly the worm which destroys buds and leaves.   79 *bravery:*
Bravado.   82 *water-fly:* Vain or busily idle person.   85 *lord of beasts:* See Genesis 1:26, 28.
85–86 *his crib . . . mess:* He shall eat at the king's table and be one of the group of persons
(usually four) constituting a *mess* at a banquet.   86 *chough:* Probably, chattering jackdaw;
also explained as *chuff,* provincial boor or churl.   94 *indifferent:* Somewhat.   99 *remember:*
I.e., remember thy courtesy; conventional phrase for "Be covered."   100 *mine ease:* Conventional reply declining the invitation of "Remember thy courtesy."   102 *soft:* Gentle; *showing:*
Distinguished appearance.   103 *feelingly:* With just perception; *card:* Chart, map.   103–104 *gentry:*
Good breeding.

Hamlet: Sir, his definement° suffers no perdition° in you; though, I know,
to divide him inventorially° would dozy° the arithmetic of memory,
and yet but yaw° neither, in respect of his quick sail. But, in the ver-
ity of extolment, I take him to be a soul of great article;° and his infu-
sion° of such dearth and rareness,° as, to make true diction of him,   110
his semblable° is his mirror; and who else would trace° him, his umbrage,° nothing more.

Osric: Your lordship speaks most infallibly of him.

Hamlet: The concernancy,° sir? why do we wrap the gentleman in our
more rawer breath?°   115

Osric: Sir?

Horatio [aside to Hamlet]: Is 't not possible to understand in another tongue?°
You will do 't, sir, really.

Hamlet: What imports the nomination° of this gentleman?

Osric: Of Laertes?   120

Horatio [aside to Hamlet]: His purse is empty already; all 's golden words are
spent.

Hamlet: Of him, sir.

Osric: I know you are not ignorant —

Hamlet: I would you did, sir; yet, in faith, if you did, it would not much 125
approve° me. Well, sir?

Osric: You are not ignorant of what excellence Laertes is —

Hamlet: I dare not confess that, lest I should compare with him in excellence;
but, to know a man well, were to know himself.°

Osric: I mean, sir, for his weapon; but in the imputation° laid on him by 130
them, in his meed° he's unfellowed.

Hamlet: What's his weapon?

Osric: Rapier and dagger.

Hamlet: That's two of his weapons: but, well.

Osric: The king, sir, hath wagered with him six Barbary horses: against 135
the which he has impawned,° as I take it, six French rapiers and poniards,
with their assigns, as girdle, hangers,° and so: three of the carriages, in
faith, are very dear to fancy,° very responsive° to the hilts, most delicate°
carriages, and of very liberal conceit.°

Hamlet: What call you the carriages?   140

Horatio [aside to Hamlet]: I knew you must be edified by the margent° ere
you had done.

Osric: The carriages, sir, are the hangers.

---

106 *definement:* Definition; *perdition:* Loss, diminution.   107 *divide him inventorially:* I.e.,
enumerate his graces; *dozy:* Dizzy.   108 *yaw:* To move unsteadily (of a ship).   109 *article:*
Moment or importance.   109–110 *infusion:* Infused temperament, character imparted by
nature.   110 *dearth and rareness:* Rarity.   111 *semblable:* True likeness; *trace:* Follow.
111–112 *umbrage:* Shadow.   114 *concernancy:* Import.   115 *breath:* Speech. 117–118 *Is
't . . . tongue?:* I.e., can one converse with Osric only in this outlandish jargon?   119 *nomi-
nation:* Naming.   126 *approve:* Command.   129 *but . . . himself:* But to know a man as
excellent were to know Laertes.   130 *imputation:* Reputation.   131 *meed:* Merit.   136 *he
has impawned:* He has wagered.   137 *hangers:* Straps on the sword belt from which the
sword hung.   138 *dear to fancy:* Fancifully made; *responsive:* Probably, well balanced, corresponding closely.   139 *delicate:* Fine in workmanship; *liberal conceit:* Elaborate design.
141 *margent:* Margin of a book, place for explanatory notes.

Hamlet: The phrase would be more german° to the matter, if we could
carry cannon by our sides: I would it might be hangers till then. But, 145
on: six Barbary horses against six French swords, their assigns, and
three liberal-conceited carriages; that's the French bet against the Danish. Why is this "impawned," as you call it?

Osric: The king, sir, hath laid, that in a dozen passes between yourself
and him, he shall not exceed you three hits: he hath laid on twelve for 150
nine; and it would come to immediate trial, if your lordship would
vouchsafe the answer.

Hamlet: How if I answer "no"?

Osric: I mean, my lord, the opposition of your person in trial.

Hamlet: Sir, I will walk here in the hall: if it please his majesty, it is the 155
breathing time° of day with me; let the foils be brought, the gentleman willing, and the king hold his purpose, I will win for him as I
can; if not, I will gain nothing but my shame and the odd hits.

Osric: Shall I re-deliver you e'en so?

Hamlet: To this effect, sir; after what flourish your nature will. 160

Osric: I commend my duty to your lordship.

Hamlet: Yours, yours. *[Exit Osric.]* He does well to commend it himself; there
are no tongues else for 's turn.

Horatio: This lapwing° runs away with the shell on his head.

Hamlet: 'A did comply, sir, with his dug,° before 'a sucked it. Thus has 165
he — and many more of the same breed that I know the drossy° age
dotes on — only got the tune° of the time and out of an habit of encounter;° a kind of yesty° collection, which carries them through
and through the most fann'd and winnowed° opinions; and do but
blow them to their trial, the bubbles are out.° 170

Enter a Lord.

Lord: My lord, his majesty commended him to you by young Osric, who
brings back to him, that you attend him in the hall: he sends to know
if your pleasure hold to play with Laertes, or that you will take longer
time.

Hamlet: I am constant to my purposes; they follow the king's pleasure: if 175
his fitness speaks, mine is ready; now or whensoever, provided I be so
able as now.

Lord: The king and queen and all are coming down.

Hamlet: In happy time.°

Lord: The queen desires you to use some gentle entertainment to Laertes 180
before you fall to play.

Hamlet: She well instructs me.   *[Exit Lord.]*

Horatio: You will lose this wager, my lord.

---

144 *german:* Germane, appropriate.   156 *breathing time:* Exercise period.   164 *lapwing:*
Peewit; noted for its wiliness in drawing a visitor away from its nest and its supposed habit of
running about when newly hatched with its head in the shell; possibly an allusion to Osric's hat.
165 *did comply . . . dug:* Paid compliments to his mother's breast.   166 *drossy:* Frivolous.
167 *tune:* Temper, mood.   167–168 *habit of encounter:* Demeanor of social intercourse.
168 *yesty:* Frothy.   169 *fann'd and winnowed:* Select and refined.   170 *blow . . . out:* I.e.,
put them to the test, and their ignorance is exposed.   179 *In happy time:* A phrase of courtesy.

Hamlet: I do not think so; since he went into France, I have been in continual practice; I shall win at the odds. But thou wouldst not think 185 how ill all 's here about my heart: but it is no matter.

Horatio: Nay, good my lord, —

Hamlet: It is but foolery; but it is such a kind of gain-giving,° as would perhaps trouble a woman.

Horatio: If your mind dislike any thing, obey it: I will forestall their repair 190 hither, and say you are not fit.

Hamlet: Not a whit, we defy augury: there's a special providence in the fall of a sparrow. If it be now, 'tis not to come; if it be not to come, it will be now; if it be not now, yet it will come: the readiness is all:° since no man of aught he leaves knows, what is 't to leave betimes? 195 Let be.

A table prepared. [Enter] Trumpets, Drums, and Officers with cushions; King, Queen, [Osric,] and all the State; foils, daggers, [and wine borne in;] and Laertes.

King: Come, Hamlet, come, and take this hand from me.

[The King puts Laertes's hand into Hamlet's.]

Hamlet: Give me your pardon, sir: I have done you wrong;
But pardon 't as you are a gentleman.
This presence° knows, 200
And you must needs have heard, how I am punish'd
With a sore distraction. What I have done,
That might your nature, honour and exception°
Roughly awake, I here proclaim was madness.
Was 't Hamlet wrong'd Laertes? Never Hamlet: 205
If Hamlet from himself be ta'en away,
And when he's not himself does wrong Laertes,
Then Hamlet does it not, Hamlet denies it.
Who does it, then? His madness: if 't be so,
Hamlet is of the faction that is wrong'd; 210
His madness is poor Hamlet's enemy.
Sir, in this audience,
Let my disclaiming from a purpos'd evil
Free me so far in your most generous thoughts,
That I have shot mine arrow o'er the house, 215
And hurt my brother.

Laertes: I am satisfied in nature,°
Whose motive, in this case, should stir me most
To my revenge: but in my terms of honour
I stand aloof; and will no reconcilement,
Till by some elder masters, of known honour, 220
I have a voice° and precedent of peace,
To keep my name ungor'd. But till that time,
I do receive your offer'd love like love,
And will not wrong it.

---

188 *gain-giving:* Misgiving.   194 *all:* All that matters.   200 *presence:* Royal assembly.
203 *exception:* Disapproval.   216 *nature:* I.e., he is personally satisfied, but his honor must be
satisfied by the rules of the code of honor.   221 *voice:* Authoritative pronouncement.

Hamlet: I embrace it freely;
  And will this brother's wager frankly play.   225
  Give us the foils. Come on.
Laertes: Come, one for me.
Hamlet: I'll be your foil,° Laertes: in mine ignorance
  Your skill shall, like a star i' th' darkest night,
  Stick fiery off° indeed.
Laertes: You mock me, sir.
Hamlet: No, by this hand.   230
King: Give them the foils, young Osric. Cousin Hamlet,
  You know the wager?
Hamlet: Very well, my lord;
  Your grace has laid the odds o' th' weaker side.
King: I do not fear it; I have seen you both:
  But since he is better'd, we have therefore odds.   235
Laertes: This is too heavy, let me see another.
Hamlet: This likes me well. These foils have all a length?

  [They prepare to play.]

Osric: Ay, my good lord.
King: Set me the stoups of wine upon that table.
  If Hamlet give the first or second hit,   240
  Or quit in answer of the third exchange,
  Let all the battlements their ordnance fire;
  The king shall drink to Hamlet's better breath;
  And in the cup an union° shall he throw,
  Richer than that which four successive kings   245
  In Denmark's crown have worn. Give me the cups;
  And let the kettle° to the trumpet speak,
  The trumpet to the cannoneer without,
  The cannons to the heavens, the heavens to earth,
  "Now the king drinks to Hamlet." Come begin: *Trumpets the while.* 250
  And you, the judges, bear a wary eye.
Hamlet: Come on, sir.
Laertes: Come, my lord.   *[They play.]*
Hamlet: One.
Laertes: No.
Hamlet: Judgement.
Osric: A hit, a very palpable hit.

  Drum, trumpets, and shot. Flourish. A piece goes off.

Laertes: Well; again.
King: Stay; give me drink. Hamlet, this pearl° is thine;
  Here's to thy health. Give him the cup.   255
Hamlet: I'll play this bout first; set it by awhile.
  Come. *[They play.]* Another hit; what say you?
Laertes: A touch, a touch, I do confess 't.

---

227 *foil:* Quibble on the two senses: "background which sets something off," and "blunted rapier for fencing."   229 *Stick fiery off:* Stand out brilliantly.   244 *union:* Pearl.   247 *kettle:* Kettledrum.   254 *pearl:* I.e., the poison.

King: Our son shall win.
Queen: He's fat,° and scant of breath.
   Here, Hamlet, take my napkin, rub thy brows: 260
   The queen carouses° to thy fortune, Hamlet.
Hamlet: Good madam!
King: Gertrude, do not drink.
Queen: I will, my lord; I pray you, pardon me.   *[Drinks.]*
King [aside]: It is the poison'd cup: it is too late.
Hamlet: I dare not drink yet, madam; by and by.   265
Queen: Come, let me wipe thy face.
Laertes: My lord, I'll hit him now.
King: I do not think 't.
Laertes [aside]: And yet 'tis almost 'gainst my conscience.
Hamlet: Come, for the third, Laertes: you but dally;
   I pray you, pass with your best violence;   270
   I am afeard you make a wanton° of me.
Laertes: Say you so? come on.   *[They play.]*
Osric: Nothing, neither way.
Laertes: Have at you now!

   [Laertes wounds Hamlet; then, in scuffling, they change rapiers,° and Hamlet
   wounds Laertes.]

King: Part them; they are incens'd.
Hamlet: Nay, come again.   *[The Queen falls.]*
Osric: Look to the queen there, ho!   275
Horatio: They bleed on both sides. How is it, my lord?
Osric: How is 't, Laertes?
Laertes: Why, as a woodcock° to mine own springe,° Osric;
   I am justly kill'd with mine own treachery.
Hamlet: How does the queen?
King: She swounds° to see them bleed.   280
Queen: No, no, the drink, the drink, — O my dear Hamlet, —
   The drink, the drink! I am poison'd.   *[Dies.]*
Hamlet: O villany! Ho! let the door be lock'd:
   Treachery! Seek it out.   *[Laertes falls.]*
Laertes: It is here, Hamlet: Hamlet, thou art slain;   285
   No med'cine in the world can do thee good;
   In thee there is not half an hour of life;
   The treacherous instrument is in thy hand,
   Unbated° and envenom'd: the foul practice
   Hath turn'd itself on me; lo, here I lie,   290
   Never to rise again: thy mother's poison'd:
   I can no more: the king, the king's to blame.

---

259 *fat:* Not physically fit, out of training. Some earlier editors speculated that the term applied to the corpulence of Richard Burbage, who originally played the part, but the allusion now appears unlikely. *Fat* may also suggest "sweaty."   261 *carouses:* Drinks a toast.   271 *wanton:* Spoiled child.   *in scuffling, they change rapiers:* According to a widespread stage tradition, Hamlet receives a scratch, realizes that Laertes's sword is unbated, and accordingly forces an exchange.   278 *woodcock:* As type of stupidity or as decoy; *springe:* Trap, snare.   280 *swounds:* Swoons.   289 *Unbated:* Not blunted with a button.

Hamlet: The point envenom'd too!
    Then, venom, to thy work.   *[Stabs the King.]*
All: Treason! treason!   295
King: O, yet defend me, friends; I am but hurt.
Hamlet: Here, thou incestuous, murd'rous, damned Dane,
    Drink off this potion. Is thy union here?
    Follow my mother.   *[King dies.]*
Laertes: He is justly serv'd;
    It is a poison temper'd° by himself.
    Exchange forgiveness with me, noble Hamlet: 300
    Mine and my father's death come not upon thee,
    Nor thine on me!   *[Dies.]*
Hamlet: Heaven make thee free of it! I follow thee.
    I am dead, Horatio. Wretched queen, adieu!   305
    You that look pale and tremble at this chance,
    That are but mutes° or audience to this act,
    Had I but time — as this fell sergeant,° Death,
    Is strict in his arrest — O, I could tell you —
    But let it be. Horatio, I am dead;   310
    Thou livest; report me and my cause aright
    To the unsatisfied.
Horatio: Never believe it:
    I am more an antique Roman° than a Dane:
    Here 's yet some liquor left.
Hamlet: As th' art a man,
    Give me the cup: let go, by heaven, I'll ha 't.
    O God! Horatio, what a wounded name,   315
    Things standing thus unknown, shall live behind me!
    If thou didst ever hold me in thy heart,
    Absent thee from felicity awhile,
    And in this harsh world draw thy breath in pain,   320
    To tell my story.   *A march afar off.*
          What warlike noise is this?
Osric: Young Fortinbras, with conquest come from Poland,
    To the ambassadors of England gives
    This warlike volley.
Hamlet: O, I die, Horatio;
    The potent poison quite o'er-crows° my spirit: 325
    I cannot live to hear the news from England;
    But I do prophesy th' election lights
    On Fortinbras: he has my dying voice;
    So tell him, with th' occurrents,° more and less,
    Which have solicited.° The rest is silence.   *[Dies.]* 330
Horatio: Now cracks a noble heart. Good night, sweet prince;
    And flights of angels sing thee to thy rest!
    Why does the drum come hither?   *[March within.]*

---

300 *temper'd:* Mixed.   307 *mutes:* Performers in a play who speak no words.   308 *sergeant:* Sheriff's officer.   313 *Roman:* It was the Roman custom to follow masters in death.   325 *o'er-crows:* Triumphs over.   329 *occurrents:* Events, incidents.   330 *solicited:* Moved, urged.

Enter Fortinbras, with the [English] Ambassadors [and others].

Fortinbras: Where is this sight?

Horatio: What is it you would see?
If aught of woe or wonder, cease your search. 335

Fortinbras: This quarry° cries on havoc.° O proud Death,
What feast is toward in thine eternal cell,
That thou so many princes at a shot
So bloodily hast struck?

First Ambassador: The sight is dismal;
And our affairs from England come too late: 340
The ears are senseless that should give us hearing,
To tell him his commandment is fulfill'd,
That Rosencrantz and Guildenstern are dead:
Where should we have our thanks?

Horatio: Not from his mouth,°
Had it th' ability of life to thank you: 345
He never gave commandment for their death.
But since, so jump° upon this bloody question,°
You from the Polack wars, and you from England,
Are here arriv'd, give order that these bodies
High on a stage° be placed to the view; 350
And let me speak to th' yet unknowing world
How these things came about: so shall you hear
Of carnal, bloody, and unnatural acts,
Of accidental judgements, casual slaughters,
Of deaths put on by cunning and forc'd cause, 355
And, in this upshot, purposes mistook
Fall'n on th' inventors' heads: all this can I
Truly deliver.

Fortinbras: Let us haste to hear it,
And call the noblest to the audience.
For me, with sorrow I embrace my fortune: 360
I have some rights of memory° in this kingdom,
Which now to claim my vantage doth invite me.

Horatio: Of that I shall have also cause to speak,
And from his mouth whose voice will draw on more:°
But let this same be presently perform'd, 365
Even while men's minds are wild; lest more mischance,
On° plots and errors, happen.

Fortinbras: Let four captains
Bear Hamlet, like a soldier, to the stage;
For he was likely, had he been put on,
To have prov'd most royal: and, for his passage,° 370
The soldiers' music and the rites of war
Speak loudly for him.

---

336 *quarry:* Heap of dead; *cries on havoc:* Proclaims a general slaughter. 344 *his mouth:* I.e., the king's. 347 *jump:* Precisely; *question:* Dispute. 350 *stage:* Platform. 361 *of memory:* Traditional, remembered. 364 *voice . . . more:* Vote will influence still others. 367 *On:* On account of, or possibly, on top of, in addition to. 370 *passage:* Death.

Take up the bodies: such a sight as this
Becomes the field,° but here shows much amiss.
Go, bid the soldiers shoot.   375

*Exeunt [marching, bearing off the dead bodies; after which a peal of ordnance
is shot off].*

---

374 *field:* I.e., of battle.

CONSIDERATIONS FOR CRITICAL THINKING AND WRITING

1. **FIRST RESPONSE.** Why does Hamlet find avenging his father's death so difficult? Why doesn't he take decisive action as soon as he seems convinced of Claudius's guilt?

2. Claudius urges Hamlet to leave behind his "obstinate condolement" and give up grieving for his dead father because it represents "impious stubbornness" (I.ii.93–94). Consider Claudius's advice in this speech (lines 87–117). Is it sensible? Why won't Hamlet heed this advice?

3. Are Polonius's admonitions to Laertes and Ophelia good advice (I.iii.55–81, 115–135)? What does his advice suggest about life at court, given that he is the chief counselor to the king?

4. When the ghost tells Hamlet that Claudius murdered him, Hamlet cries out, "O my prophetic soul!" (I.v.40). Why? What does the ghost demand of Hamlet?

5. What is known about the kind of person Hamlet was before his father's death? Does he have the stature of a tragic hero such as Oedipus? How does news of the murder and his mother's remarriage affect his behavior and view of life? Is he mad, as Polonius assumes, or is he pretending to be mad? Is there a "method in 't" (II.ii.200)? What do we learn from Hamlet's soliloquies?

6. What is the purpose of the play within the play? How does it provide a commentary on the action of the larger play?

7. Is Ophelia connected in any way with the crime Hamlet seeks to avenge? Why is he so brutal to Ophelia in Act III, Scene i? Why does she go mad?

8. Does Hamlet think Gertrude is as guilty as Claudius? Why is Hamlet so thoroughly disgusted by her in Act III, Scene iv?

9. Why doesn't Hamlet kill Claudius as he prays (III.iii)? Do you feel any sympathy for Claudius in this scene, or is he presented as a callous murderer?

10. If Hamlet had killed Claudius in Act III and the play had ended there, what would be missing in Hamlet's perceptions of himself and the world? How does his character develop in Acts IV and V? What softens our realization that Hamlet is in various degrees responsible for the deaths of Polonius, Ophelia, Laertes, Rosencrantz, Guildenstern, Claudius, and Gertrude?

11. What purpose does Fortinbras serve in the action? Would anything be lost if he were edited out of the play?

12. Despite its tragic dimensions, *Hamlet* includes humorous scenes and many witty lines delivered by the title character himself. Locate those scenes and lines, and then determine the tone and purpose of the play's humor.

13. **CRITICAL STRATEGIES.** Read the section on formalist criticism (pp. 1645–47) in Chapter 51, "Critical Strategies for Reading." Choose a soliloquy by Hamlet and write an analysis of its images so that you reveal some significant portion of his character.

CONNECTIONS TO OTHER SELECTIONS

1. Compare in an essay Hamlet's attitudes about revenge with Matt Fowler's in Andre Dubus's short story "Killings" (p. 89).

2. Here's a long reach but a potentially interesting one: write an essay that considers Gertrude as a wife and mother alongside Nora in Henrik Ibsen's *A Doll's House* (p. 1357). How responsible are they to themselves and to others? Can they be discussed in the same breath, or are they from such different worlds that nothing useful can be said about comparing them? Either way, explain your response.

Perspectives on Shakespeare

THE MAYOR OF LONDON (1597)

Objections to the Elizabethan Theater 1597

The inconueniences that grow by Stage playes abowt the Citie of London.

1. They are a speaciall cause of corrupting their Youth, conteninge nothinge but vnchast matters, lascivious devices, shiftes of Coozenage,° & other lewd & vngodly practizes, being so as that they impresse the very qualitie & corruption of manners which they represent, Contrary to the rules & art prescribed for the makinge of Comedies eauen amonge the Heathen, who vsd them seldom & at certen sett tymes, and not all the year longe as our manner is. Whearby such as frequent them, beinge of the base & refuze sort of people or such young gentlemen as have small regard of credit or conscience, drawe the same into imitacion and not to the avoidinge the like vices which they represent.

2. They are the ordinary places for vagrant persons, Maisterles men, thieves, horse stealers, whoremongers, Coozeners, Conycatchers,° contrivers of treason, and other idele and daungerous persons to meet together & to make theire matches to the great displeasure of Almightie God & the hurt & annoyance of her Maiesties people, which cannot be prevented nor discovered by the Gouernours of the Citie for that they are owt of the Citiees iurisdiction.

3. They maintaine idlenes in such persons as haue no vocation & draw apprentices and other seruantes from theire ordinary workes and all sortes of people from the resort vnto sermons and other Christian exercises, to the great hinderance of traides & prophanation of religion established by her highnes within this Realm.

4. In the time of sickness it is fownd by experience, that many hauing sores and yet not hart sicke take occasion hearby to walk abroad & to recreat themselves by heareinge a play Whearby others are infected, and them selves also many things miscarry.

From Edmund K. Chambers, *The Elizabethan Stage*

---

shiftes of Coozenage: Perverse behavior.   *Conycatchers:* Tricksters.

1. Summarize the mayor's objections to the theater. Do any of his reasons for protesting theatrical productions seem reasonable to you? Why or why not?

2. Are any of these concerns reflected in attitudes about the theater today? Why or why not?

3. How would you defend *Hamlet* or *A Midsummer Night's Dream* against charges that they draw some people into "imitacion and not to the avoidinge the like vices which they represent"?

LISA JARDINE (B. 1944)
On Boy Actors in Female Roles 1989

Every schoolchild knows that there were no women actors on the Elizabethan stage; the female parts were taken by young male actors. But every schoolchild also learns that this fact is of little consequence for the twentieth-century reader of Shakespeare's plays. Because the taking of female parts by boys was universal and commonplace, we are told, it was accepted as "verisimilitude" by the Elizabethan audience, who simply disregarded it, as we would disregard the creaking of stage scenery and accept the backcloth forest as "real" for the duration of the play.

Conventional or not, the taking of female parts by boy players actually occasioned a good deal of contemporary comment and created considerable moral uneasiness, even amongst those who patronized and supported the theaters. Amongst those who opposed them, transvestism on stage was a main plank in the anti-stage polemic. "The appareil of wemen is a great provocation of men to lust and leacherie," wrote Dr. John Rainoldes, a leading Oxford divine (quoting the Bishop of Paris), in *Th' Overthrow of Stage-Playes* (Middleburgh, 1599). And he continues with an unhealthy interest which infuses the entire pamphlet: "A womans garment beeing put on a man doeth vehemently touch and moue him with the remembrance and imagination of a woman; and the imagination of a thing desirable doth stirr up the desire."

According to Rainoldes, and the authorities with whose independent testimony he lards his polemic, the wearing of female dress by boy players "is an occasion of wantonnes and lust." Sexuality, misdirected toward the boy masquerading in female dress, is "stirred" by attire and gesture; male prostitution and perverted sexual activity is the inevitable accompaniment of female impersonation.

From *Still Harping on Daughters*, Second Edition

1. How does Jardine complicate the Elizabethan convention of boy actors assuming female roles? To what extent does it add to the representation of Elizabethan theater put forward by the mayor of London?

2. What do you think would be your own response to a boy actor playing a female role? Consider, for example, Hippolyta in *A Midsummer Night's Dream* or Ophelia in *Hamlet*.

SAMUEL JOHNSON (1709–1784)
On Shakespeare's Characters 1765

Shakespeare is above all writers, at least above all modern writers, the poet of nature: the poet that holds up to his readers a faithful mirror of manners and life. His characters are not modified by the customs of particular places, unpracticed by the rest of the world; by the peculiarities of studies or professions, which can operate but upon small numbers; or by the accidents of transient fashions or temporary opinions: they are the genuine progeny of common humanity, such as the world will always supply, and observation will always find. His persons act and speak by the influence of those general passions and principles by which all minds are agitated, and the whole system of life is continued in motion. In the writings of other poets a character is too often an individual; in those of Shakespeare it is commonly a species.

From the preface to Johnson's edition of Shakespeare's works

CONSIDERATIONS FOR CRITICAL THINKING AND WRITING

1. Johnson made this famous assessment of Shakespeare's ability to portray "common humanity" in the eighteenth century. As a twenty-first-century reader, explain why you agree or disagree with Johnson's view that Shakespeare's characters have universal appeal.

2. Write an essay discussing whether you think it is desirable or necessary for characters to be "a faithful mirror of manners and life." Along the way consider whether you encountered any characters in *Hamlet* or *A Midsummer Night's Dream* who do not provide what you consider to be an accurate mirror of human life.

SIGMUND FREUD (1856–1939)
On Repression in Hamlet 1900

Another of the great creations of tragic poetry, Shakespeare's *Hamlet,* has its roots in the same soil as *Oedipus Rex*. But the changed treatment of the same material reveals the whole difference in the mental life of these two widely separated epochs of civilization: the secular advance of repression in the emotional life of mankind. In the *Oedipus* the child's wishful fantasy that underlies it is brought into the open and realized as it would be in a dream. In *Hamlet* it remains repressed; and — just as in the case of a neurosis — we only learn of its existence from its inhibiting consequences. Strangely enough, the overwhelming effect produced by the more modern tragedy has turned out to be compatible with the fact that people have remained completely in the dark as to the hero's character. The play is built up on Hamlet's hesitations over fulfilling the task of revenge that is assigned to him; but its text offers no reasons or motives for these hesitations and an immense variety of attempts at interpreting them have failed to produce a result. According to the view which was originated by Goethe and is still the prevailing one today, Hamlet represents the type of man whose power of direct action is paralyzed by an excessive development of his intellect. (He is "sicklied o'er with the pale cast of thought.") According to another view, the dramatist has tried to portray a pathologically irresolute character which might be classed as neurasthenic. The plot of the drama shows us, however, that Hamlet is far from being represented as a person incapable of taking any action. We see him doing so on two occasions: first in a sudden outburst of temper, when he runs his sword through the eavesdropper behind the arras, and secondly, in a premeditated and even crafty fashion, when, with all the callousness of a Renaissance prince, he sends the two courtiers to the death that had been planned for himself. What is it, then, that inhibits him in fulfilling the task set him by his father's ghost? The answer, once again, is that it is the peculiar nature of the task. Hamlet is able to do anything — except take vengeance on the man who did away with his father and took that father's place with his mother, the man who shows him the repressed wishes of his own childhood realized. Thus the loathing which should drive him on to revenge is replaced in him by self-reproaches, by scruples of conscience, which remind him that he himself is literally no better than the sinner whom he is to punish. Here I have translated into conscious terms what was bound to remain unconscious in Hamlet's mind; and if anyone is inclined to call him a hysteric, I can only accept the fact as one that is implied by my interpretation. The distaste for sexuality expressed by Hamlet in his conversation with Ophelia fits in very well with this: the same distaste which was destined to take possession of the poet's mind more and more during the years that followed, and which reached its extreme expression in *Timon of Athens*. For it can of course only be the poet's own mind which confronts us in Hamlet. I observe in a book on Shakespeare by Georg Brandes (1896) a statement that *Hamlet* was written immediately after the death of Shakespeare's father (in 1601), that is, under the immediate impact of his bereavement and, as we may well assume, while his childhood feelings about his father had been freshly revived. It is known, too, that Shakespeare's own son who died at an early age bore the name "Hamnet," which is identical with "Hamlet." Just as *Hamlet* deals with the relation of a son to his parents, so *Macbeth* (written at approximately the same period) is concerned with the subject of childlessness. But just as all neurotic symptoms, and, for that matter, dreams, are capable of being "overinterpreted" and indeed need to be, if they are to be fully understood, so all genuinely creative writings are the product of more than a single motive and more than a single impulse in the poet's mind, and are open to more than a single interpretation. In what I have written I have only attempted to interpret the deepest layer of impulses in the mind of the creative writer.

From *The Interpretation of Dreams*, translated by James Strachey

CONSIDERATIONS FOR CRITICAL THINKING AND WRITING

1. What reason does Freud offer for Hamlet's inability to avenge his father's death? Explain whether you find Freud's reasoning convincing.

2. Read the section on psychological criticism (pp. 1649–51) in Chapter 51, "Critical Strategies for Reading," and then discuss Freud's assertion that "it can of course only be the poet's own mind which confronts us in Hamlet." Explain why you agree or disagree.

3. Write an essay discussing whether you think Freud's approach to Hamlet opens up perspectives on the play or narrowly limits them.

JAN KOTT (1914–2001)

On Producing Hamlet   1964

No Dane of flesh and blood has been written about so extensively as Hamlet. Shakespeare's prince is certainly the best known representative of his nation. Innumerable glossaries and commentaries have grown round Hamlet, and he is one of the few literary heroes who live apart from the text, apart from the theater. His name means something even to those who have never seen or read Shakespeare's play. In this respect he is rather like Leonardo's Mona Lisa. We know she is smiling even before we have seen the picture, as it were. It contains not only what Leonardo expressed in it but also everything that has been written about it. Too many people — girls, women, poets, painters — have tried to solve the mystery of that smile. It is not just Mona Lisa that is smiling at us now, but all those who have tried to analyze, or imitate, that smile.

This is also the case with *Hamlet,* or rather — with *Hamlet* in the theater. For we have been separated from the text not only by Hamlet's "independent life" in our culture, but simply by the size of the play. *Hamlet* cannot be performed in its entirety, because the performance would last nearly six hours. One has to select, curtail, and cut. One can perform only one of several *Hamlets* potentially existing in this arch-play. It will always be a poorer *Hamlet* than Shakespeare's *Hamlet* is; but it may also be a *Hamlet* enriched by being of our time. It may, but I would rather say — it must be so.

For *Hamlet* cannot be played simply. This may be the reason why it is so tempting to producers and actors. Many generations have seen their own reflections in this play. The genius of *Hamlet* consists, perhaps, in the fact that the play can serve as a mirror. An ideal *Hamlet* would be one most true to Shakespeare and most modern at the same time. Is this possible? I do not know. But we can only appraise any Shakespearean production by asking how much there is of Shakespeare in it, and how much of us.

What I have in mind is not a forced topicality, a *Hamlet* that would be set in a cellar of young existentialists. *Hamlet* has been performed for that matter in evening dress and in circus tights; in medieval armor and in Renaissance costume. Costumes do not matter. What matters is that through Shakespeare's text we ought to get at our modern experience, anxiety, and sensibility.

There are many subjects in *Hamlet.* There is politics, force opposed to morality; there is discussion of the divergence between the theory and practice, of the ultimate purpose of life; there is tragedy of love, as well as family drama, political, eschatological, and metaphysical problems are considered. There is everything you want, including deep psychological analysis, a bloody story, a duel, and general slaughter. One can select at will. But one must know what one selects, and why.

From "*Hamlet* of the Mid-Century" in *Shakespeare Our Contemporary,*
translated by Boleslaw Taborski

CONSIDERATIONS FOR CRITICAL THINKING AND WRITING

1. "Many generations have seen their own reflections in this play." Use this statement as a basis for researching productions of *Hamlet*. How have events contemporary to the play's performances influenced the ways it has been presented?

2. Explain why you think it is good or bad for a producer to interpret a play in light of events contemporary to it.

3. If you were to produce *Hamlet* today, what would you emphasize? Consider how you would handle the setting, costuming, casting, and theme.

4. What do you think a reader-response critic would have to say about Kott's comments on producing *Hamlet*? Base your answer on the discussion of reader-response criticism (pp. 1659–61) in Chapter 51, "Critical Strategies for Reading."

RUSSELL JACKSON (B. 1949)

A Film Diary of the Shooting of Kenneth Branagh's Hamlet   1996

Wednesday 3 January
Rehearsals Begin

First morning in Shepperton. This may be one of the major British studios but it's not, on first sight, impressive. Located in a semi-suburban hinterland southwest of London, it seems at first like an industrial estate, a jumble of sheds, hangars, workshops, and what look like builders' yards, with a mansion trapped in the middle of it all like a genteel hostage from Edwardian England. . . .

We're in the elegant boardroom of the old house, round a long green-baize covered table. First session is with Derek Jacobi (Claudius) and Julie Christie (Gertrude), plus Ken [Branagh], Orlando Seale (his "acting double"), Annie Wotton (Script Supervisor), Simon Mosley (First A.D.), and Hugh Cruttwell.

Ken distributes phials [vials] of a herbal "Rescue Remedy" (only half a joke, admitting nervous apprehension). Everyone has read the screenplay, and the actors have already had some discussion of their roles with Ken, but these days of rehearsal before we begin shooting will give everyone time for reappraisal, adjustments, and (most important) finding out how the story will be told by *this* company of actors, in *these* circumstances. We won't start with a read-through: better to edge toward the play. We discuss royal families (including the current one), privacy, politics, and draw toward a reading of the scenes when Claudius and Gertrude are together. There's talk about the issue of complicity between them (not at all, so far as murder is concerned) and the "essential" Claudius, which she took (and part of him still takes) as loving, kind, a "good" man. Derek goes along with this, though he and Hugh Cruttwell remind us of Hamlet's very different point of view. Gertrude and Claudius feel responsible for Hamlet but Claudius has another agenda she knows nothing about — concerning the potential threat posed by her son.

After lunch the Polonius family join us, with Horatio. By now we feel able to discuss frankly and simply (and off the record) our own experiences of family, bereavement, grief. (This is not just to canvass ideas about the emotions of the play to draw on them in performance: it also establishes common ground among us.) Then we try to imagine an "ideal" family, successful and well-balanced according to current middle-class notions, professional but not competitive, materially well-off but not showy — which (we agree) turns out quite repulsive. Then on to the Polonius family.

Polonius (Richard Briers) was promoted by new king. Laertes (Michael Maloney) is in Paris getting the gentlemanly accomplishments (N.B. not at Wittenberg).

Ophelia (Kate Winslet) and Hamlet have been having an affair (yes, they have been to bed together, because we want this relationship to be as serious as possible) since the death of Hamlet senior. (Effect of a surge of feeling in time of bereavement and crisis?)

Thursday 4–Monday 8 January

We work through scenes, trying various approaches, finding snags, problems, opportunities. Ophelia's motivations in returning Hamlet's love tokens are considered: she is going further than Polonius suggested in any instructions we have heard, and whatever her father and the king expect from this confrontation, she has her own agenda (perhaps to find out why Hamlet is behaving this way to her, to put him on the spot?). The kinder and more circumspect Polonius seems, the harder it will be for her to betray him — hence her lying to Hamlet ("Where's your father? — At home, my lord"). In "To be or not to be" Ken wants to show Hamlet alone with his mirror image(s) in the vast space of the mirrored hall. He has to be careful not to give the soliloquy an energy or momentum that it does not need — those qualities are coming soon enough in what follows when he encounters Ophelia. Ken steers Derek toward seeming even more vulnerable as Claudius, "quietly anxious" about Hamlet after "nunnery" scene, rarely openly angry, even when Rosencrantz and Guildenstern have screwed up. So, when he does flare up, becomes desperate, it will be more shocking.

On 8 January we go over each actor's list of their character's priorities. Claudius has specific aims: inspiring confidence and trust in himself; loving Gertrude; making Hamlet look indulgent and neurotic (and thus defusing him); creating a new, strong, triumphalist Denmark (a military regime). Gertrude's aims are more general: decorum, sense of behaving properly in public; *noblesse oblige*, etiquette; sense of culture, confidence; loving Hamlet. Old Hamlet (Brian Blessed) points out that when he was alive he never let Claudius see how little he mattered — there has to be an underlying bitterness in what Claudius has done to get the crown as well as intense love for Gertrude. We consider different ways of showing these relationships in a short flashback — perhaps Old Hamlet and his son playing chess while Gertrude and Claudius watch, or some other activity (perhaps outdoors) that will focus their various feelings for each other.

> From *Hamlet*. Screenplay and Introduction by
> Kenneth Branagh. Film diary by Russell Jackson.

CONSIDERATIONS FOR CRITICAL THINKING AND WRITING

1. In what sense can the actors' discussions of character motivation and background be considered an interpretation of *Hamlet*? Why do you suppose the actors find these kinds of discussions useful?

2. Create a list of "priorities" for characters *not* already discussed by the actors on Branagh's set. Consider, for example, Horatio, Laertes, Rosencrantz, Guildenstern, Marcellus, or Bernardo.

3. How does Jackson's comment that it was essential for the actors to determine "how the story will be told by *this* company of actors, in *these* circumstances" compare with Jan Kott's observations on producing *Hamlet* (p. 1340)?

4. Watch Branagh's *Hamlet* (available via many streaming services) and write an essay that focuses on a single character or scene that you find especially effective (or not).

LINDA BAMBER (B. 1945)

Feminine Rebellion and Masculine Authority *in* A Midsummer Night's Dream 1981

In the comedies, the feminine challenges the status quo either overtly or through its command of socially subversive forces like sexuality, romantic passion, household revels, and so forth.

The best example of the relationship between male dominance and the status quo comes in *A Midsummer Night's Dream*, which begins with a rebellion of the feminine against the power of masculine authority. Hermia refuses the man both Aegeus and Theseus order her to marry; her refusal sends us off into the forest, beyond the power of the father and the masculine state. Once in the forest, of course, we find the social situation metaphorically repeated in this world of imagination and nature. The fairy king, Oberon, rules the forest. His rule, too, is troubled by the rebellion of the feminine. Titania has refused to give him her page, the child of a human friend who died in childbirth. But by the end of the story Titania is conquered, the child relinquished, and order restored. Even here the comic upheavals, whether we see them as May games or bad dreams, are associated with an uprising of women. David P. Young has pointed out how firmly this play connects order with masculine dominance and the disruption of order with the rebellion of the feminine:

> It is appropriate that Theseus, as representative of daylight and right reason, should have subdued his bride-to-be to the rule of his masculine will. That is the natural order of things. It is equally appropriate that Oberon, as king of darkness and fantasy, should have lost control of his wife, and that the corresponding natural disorder described by Titania should ensue.[1]

The natural order, the status quo, is for men to rule women. When they fail to do so, we have the exceptional situation, the festive, disruptive, disorderly moment of comedy.

A Midsummer Night's Dream is actually an anomaly among the festive comedies. It is unusual for the forces of the green world to be directed, as they are here, by a masculine figure. Because the green world here is a partial reproduction of the social world, the feminine is reduced to a kind of first cause of the action while a masculine power directs it. In the other festive comedies the feminine Other presides. She does not *command* the forces of the alternative world, as Oberon does, but since she acts in harmony with these forces her will and desire often prevail.

Where are we to bestow our sympathies? On the forces that make for the disruption of the status quo and therefore for the plot? Or on the force that asserts itself against the disruption and reestablishes a workable social order? Of course we cannot choose. We can only say that in comedy we owe our holiday to such forces as the tendency of the feminine to rebel, whereas to the successful reassertion of masculine power we owe our everyday order. Shakespearean comedy endorses both sides. Holiday is, of course, the subject and the analogue of each play; but the plays always end in a return to everyday life. The optimistic reading of Shakespearean comedy says that everyday life is clarified and enriched by our holiday from it; according to the pessimistic reading the temporary subversion of the social order has revealed how much that order excludes, how high a price we

---

[1] David P. Young, *Something of Great Constancy* (New Haven, CT: Yale UP, 1966), 183.

pay for it. But whether our return to everyday life is a comfortable one or not, the return itself is the inevitable conclusion to the journey out.

From *Comic Women, Tragic Men:*
A Study of Gender and Genre in Shakespeare

CONSIDERATIONS FOR CRITICAL THINKING AND WRITING

1. What distinctions does Bamber make between the "optimistic" and "pessimistic" readings of Shakespearean comedy? In an essay explain how you would categorize your own reading of *A Midsummer Night's Dream.*

2. Compare Bamber's view of the "disruptive, disorderly moment of comedy" with James Kincaid's view of comedy (p. 1345). How do Bamber and Kincaid define the comic?

LOUIS ADRIAN MONTROSE (B. 1946)

On Amazonian Mythology in A Midsummer Night's Dream 1983

The beginning of *A Midsummer Night's Dream* coincides with the end of a struggle in which Theseus has been victorious over the Amazon warrior:

> Hippolyta, I woo'd thee with my sword,
> And won thy love doing thee injuries;
> But I will wed thee in another key,
> With pomp, with triumph, and with revelling.
>
> (I.i.16–19)

Descriptions of the Amazons are ubiquitous in Elizabethan texts. . . .

Sixteenth-century travel narratives often recreate the ancient Amazons of Scythia in South America or in Africa. Invariably, the Amazons are relocated just beyond the receding boundary of *terra incognita.*° Thus, in Sierra Leone in 1582, the chaplain of an English expedition to the Spice Islands recorded the report of a Portuguese trader that "near the mountains of the moon there is a queen, empress of all these Amazons, a witch and a cannibal who daily feeds on the flesh of boys. She ever remains unmarried, but she has intercourse with a great number of men by whom she begets offspring. The kingdom, however, remains hereditary to the daughters, not to the sons."[1] This cultural fantasy assimilates Amazonian myth, witchcraft, and cannibalism into an anticulture which precisely inverts European norms of political authority, sexual license, marriage practices, and inheritance rules.[2] The attitude toward the Amazons expressed in such Renaissance texts is

---

terra incognita: Unknown land.

[1] *An Elizabethan in 1582: The Diary of Richard Madox, Fellow of All Souls,* ed. Elizabeth Story Donno, Hakluyt Society, second ser., no. 47 (London, 1977), p. 183. I owe this reference to Stephen Greenblatt, *Renaissance Self-Fashioning: From More to Shakespeare* (Chicago, 1980), p. 181.
[2] The linkage of Amazon, witch, and cannibal exemplifies a logic of inversion ingrained in European categories of thought. It has been suggested recently that sixteenth- and seventeenth-century witchcraft beliefs were a coherent, meaningful, and indeed necessary component of a larger intellectual system based upon principles of hierarchy, opposition, and inversion. This system linked together demonism, political sedition and rebellion, and female misrule as inversions of the divinely sanctioned order in the cosmos, state, and family. See Stuart Clark, "Inversion, Misrule and the Meaning of Witchcraft," *Past & Present* no. 87 (May 1980), 98–127. . . .

a mixture of fascination and horror. Amazonian mythology seems symbolically to embody and to control a collective anxiety about the power of the female not only to dominate or reject the male but to create and destroy him. It is an ironic acknowledgment by an androcentric° culture of the degree to which men are in fact dependent upon women: upon mothers and nurses, for their birth and nurture; upon mistresses and wives, for the validation of their manhood.

Shakespeare engages his wedding play in a dialectic with this mythological formation. The Amazons have been defeated before the play begins; and nuptial rites are to be celebrated when it ends. *A Midsummer Night's Dream* focuses upon different crucial transitions in the male and female life cycles: the fairy plot, upon taking "a little changeling boy" from childhood into youth, from the world of the mother into the world of the father; the Athenian plot, upon taking a maiden from youth into maturity, from the world of the father into the world of the husband. The pairing of the four Athenian lovers is made possible by the magical powers of Oberon and made lawful by the political authority of Theseus. Each of these rulers is preoccupied with the fulfillment of his own desires in the possession or repossession of a wife. Only after Hippolyta has been mastered by Theseus may marriage seal them "in everlasting bond of fellowship" (I.i.85). And only after "proud Titania" has been degraded by "jealous Oberon" (II.i.60, 61), has "in mild terms begg'd" (IV.i.53) his patience, and has readily yielded the changeling boy to him, may they be "new in amity" (IV.i.82).

The . . . structure of *A Midsummer Night's Dream* eventually restores the inverted Amazonian system of gender and nurture to a patriarchal norm.

> From "'Shaping Fantasies': Figurations of Gender and Power
> in Elizabethan Culture," *Representations,* Spring 1983

androcentric: Male-centered.

Considerations for Critical Thinking and Writing

1. How does Montrose use "Amazonian mythology" to account for the plot elements in the play?

2. In an essay use the insights provided in Montrose's perspective to explore how order is associated with masculinity and rebellion is associated with femininity in *A Midsummer Night's Dream.*

James Kincaid (b. 1937)

On the Value of Comedy in the Face of Tragedy   1991

[O]ur current hierarchical arrangement (tragedy high — comedy low) betrays an acquiescence in the most smothering of political conservatisms. Put another way, by coupling tragedy with the sublime, the ineffable, the metaphysical and by aligning comedy with the mundane, the quotidian, and the material we manage to muffle, even to erase, the most powerful narratives of illumination and liberation we have. . . .

The point is comic relief, the *concept* of comic relief and who it relieves. Now we usually refer to comic relief in the same tone we use for academic deans, other people's children, Melanie Griffith, the new criticism, jogging, Big Macs, the *New York Times Book Review,* leisure suits, people who go on cruises, realtors, and the MLA: bemused contempt. (Which is what we think about comic relief.) Comedy is that which attends on, offers relaxation from, prepares us for more of — something else, something serious and demanding. Comedy is not demanding — it does not demand or take, it gives. And we know that any agency which gives cannot be worth much. Tragedy's seriousness is guaranteed by its bullying greed, its insistence on having things its own way and pulling from us not only our tears, which we value little, but our attention, which we hate to give. Comedy, on the other hand, doesn't care if we attend closely. Tragedy is sleek and single-minded, comedy rumpled and hospitable to any idea or agency. Tragedy stares us out of countenance; comedy winks and leers and drools. Tragedy is all dressed up; comedy is always taking things off, mooning us. We find it inevitable that we associate tragedy with the high, comedy with the low. What is at issue here is the nature of that inevitability, our willingness to conspire in a discourse which pays homage to tragic grandeur and reduces comedy to release, authorized license, periodic relief — like a sneeze or yawn or belch. By allowing such discourse to flow through us, we add our bit of cement to the cultural edifice that sits on top of comedy, mashes it down into a mere adjunct to tragedy, its reverse and inferior half, its silly little carnival. By cooperating in this move, we relieve orthodox and conservative power structures of any pressure that might be exercised against them. Comic relief relieves the status quo, in other words, contains the power of comedy. . . .

Let's put it this way, comedy is not a mode that stands in opposition to tragedy. Comedy is the *whole* story, the narrative which refuses to leave things out. Tragedy insists on a formal structure that is unified and coherent, formally balanced and elegantly tight. Only that which is coordinate is allowed to adorn the tragic body. With comedy, nothing is sacrificed, nothing lost; the discoordinate and the discontinuous are especially welcome. Tragedy protects itself by its linearity, its tight conclusiveness; comedy's generosity and ability never to end make it gloriously vulnerable. Pitting tragedy against comedy is running up algebra against recess. . . .

> From a paper read at the 1991 meeting of the Modern Language Association,
> "Who Is Relieved by the Idea of Comic Relief?"

CONSIDERATIONS FOR CRITICAL THINKING AND WRITING

1. What distinctions does Kincaid make between comedy and tragedy? How does his description of tragedy compare with Aristotle's (see p. 1165)?

2. How does Kincaid's description of comedy fit *A Midsummer Night's Dream*?

3. According to Kincaid, why is the denigration of comedy a conservative impulse? In an essay explain why you agree or disagree with the argument.

ENCOUNTERING DRAMA: A VISUAL PORTFOLIO
HAMLET IN POPULAR CULTURE AND PERFORMANCE

Although William Shakespeare wrote *Hamlet* more than four hundred years ago, its impact on contemporary life — on literature, visual art, theater and film, and even everyday language — is wide-reaching and profound. *Hamlet* is the most famous play written in the English language, and its timeless themes and memorable characters continue to make it the subject of fine art, popular art, and numerous adaptations onstage and on film. This portfolio, which features multiple portrayals of the characters of Hamlet and Ophelia, offers a sense of *Hamlet*'s cultural presence and significance. In the following images, the character Hamlet is represented in fine art and in multiple performances — from Sarah Bernhardt to Ethan Hawke — and the character Ophelia is represented in nineteenth-century paintings, a contemporary performance, and a cartoon from the *New Yorker*. How do these portrayals compare with your reading of the play and its characters?

Hamlet and Horatio in the Cemetery (1839). Inspired by an 1827 English production of *Hamlet* in Paris, the French Romantic painter Eugène Delacroix (1798–1863) rendered a series of images from the play, including this painting of the graveyard scene (Act V, Scene i). Here, under a brooding sky, a gravedigger hands Hamlet the skull of Yorick. "Alas, poor Yorick!" says Hamlet, "I knew him, Horatio: a fellow of infinite jest. . . ." (See also Delacroix's *The Death of Ophelia*, page 1352.)

Alfredo Dagli Orti / The Art Archive at Art Resource, New York.

CONSIDERATIONS AND CONNECTIONS

1. Given your own reading of the character Hamlet, how does the portrayal of Hamlet by Delacroix compare with how you imagine him?

2. Discuss the representations of death in this painting and in Delacroix's treatment of Ophelia (p. 1352). How does Delacroix's depiction of death compare with Shakespeare's?

Ethan Hawke as Hamlet (1999). Directed by Michael Almeryeda, this contemporary vision ▶ of *Hamlet* sets the tragedy in New York City, in the context of corporate America. Ethan Hawke (left) portrays Hamlet as a young filmmaker struggling to gain control over his deceased father's business. Hawke comments: "I always thought that in a modern sense Hamlet was mostly a kind of Holden Caulfield or Kurt Cobain, and I wanted to evoke that spirit. . . . Many of his dilemmas are a young man's dilemmas. He's concerned about his relationship with his father and his mother. He doesn't really know who he is or what he's about. He's got this girlfriend situation. These are all a young man's issues . . . seeking meaning and being confused and overwhelmed by events you don't feel you control."
The Kobal Collection at Art Resource, New York.

CONSIDERATIONS AND CONNECTIONS

1. How accurately do you think Hawke's comments about Hamlet's dilemmas sum up his character? Explain why you think a contemporary treatment of the play enhances or damages it.

2. Except to identify Hawke as Hamlet, the caption does not indicate who the other three figures are. Who do you think those actors portray? Explain why.

Sarah Bernhardt as Hamlet (1900). In his book *Shakespeare in the Movies*, the film critic Douglas Brode writes, "[Shakespeare's plays] aren't plays at all; rather, they are screenplays, written, ironically, three centuries before the birth of cinema." The first film version of the play was a bold interpretation titled *Le Duel d'Hamlet*, produced for the Paris Exhibition of 1900. Playing the lead was Sarah Bernhardt (known as "The Divine Sarah"), the most famous, or at least most scandalous, actress of the nineteenth century. One of the earliest films with sound, the dialogue of *Le Duel* was dubbed (in French), and sound effects for swordfighting were made by clacking knives behind the screen.
© Corbis.

CONSIDERATIONS AND CONNECTIONS

1. What advantages and/ or disadvantages do you think there are when the role of Hamlet is played by a woman?

2. Comment on Bernhardt's costuming and that of Ethan Hawke (p. 1349). What are the effects of each costume upon your perception of Hamlet's character? Which do you prefer? Explain why.

Laurence Olivier as Hamlet
(1948). Since the first staging of
Hamlet by Shakespeare's acting
troupe (probably between 1600
and 1601, before the Quarto was
first published in 1603), the role
of the Prince of Denmark has
been interpreted by countless
performers. Sir Laurence Olivier,
who directed, produced, and
played the lead in this famous
film version, called *Hamlet* "the
tragedy of a man who couldn't
make up his mind."
© Corbis.

CONSIDERATIONS AND CONNECTIONS

1. How does this scene of Hamlet (Laurence Olivier) with Yorick's skull compare with Delacroix's (p. 1347)? Which scene emphasizes more dramatically the grim reality of death to you? Explain why.

2. How old is Hamlet in the play? Compare this image of Olivier with that of Ethan Hawke (above). Explain why you would choose one or the other actor as closer to your own sense of Hamlet's age.

Ophelia: Here Is Rosemary ▶ (mid- to late nineteenth century). Undone by the death of her father and abandonment by Hamlet, Ophelia behaves in an increasingly erratic manner. In Act IV, Scene v, she offers the grieving Laertes a sprig of rosemary: "There's rosemary, that's for remembrance; pray you, love, remember: and there is pansies, that's for thoughts." Laertes calls her speech "a document in madness," and the King, earlier in the scene, asks the Queen to "follow her close; give her good watch," as Ophelia is "divided from herself and her fair judgement." Ophelia's madness and sexuality were popular subjects among artists of the nineteenth century, and this painting by William Gorman Wills (Irish, 1828–91) offers an especially provocative reading of Ophelia and her relationship to Laertes.
© Christie's Images/Corbis.

Considerations and Connections

1. Discuss the manner in which Ophelia and Laertes are posed together in this painting. What do you think Wills is suggesting about the nature of the connection between them? Does the play's text support that depiction of them?

2. Of the three images of Ophelia — Wills's, Delacroix's (p. 1352), and Winslet's (p. 1351) — which do you find to be the most in line with your reading of the character? Explain why.

"He's, like, 'To be or not to be,' and I'm, like, 'Get a life.'"

Ophelia Cartoon from the *New Yorker* (Lee Lorenz, 1995). In "Reading Ophelia's Madness,"
Gabrielle Dane writes: "Ophelia has been shaped to conform to external demands, to reflect
others' desires . . . she appears condemned to martyrdom on the altar of male fantasies and
priorities." In the play, the character Ophelia is manipulated by those closest to her — by her
father Polonius, her brother Laertes, and her beloved Hamlet. Not so the Ophelia of this *New
Yorker* cartoon — here we see a rebellious and sassy version of the character, one who is fed
up with Hamlet's turmoil and dramatic speeches, and far from mad.

CONSIDERATIONS AND CONNECTIONS

1. Are there any passages in the play that
   warrant Lorenz's cartoon representation of
   Ophelia? Why or why not?

2. Try creating your own cartoon of another
   character in Hamlet that captures some
   of the contemporary humorous tone that
   Lorenz evokes.

Kate Winslet as Ophelia (1996). Set in the late
nineteenth century, with Victorian-inspired
costumes and sets, Kenneth Branagh's epic
film version of *Hamlet* intensifies the relationship between Hamlet and Ophelia by including
an explicit sex scene. Ophelia (played by Kate
Winslet) flashes back to this encounter when her
father asks her about Hamlet: "Do you believe
his tenders, as you call them?" She answers:
"I do not know, my lord, what I should think"
(Act I, Scene iii). Another twist is Ophelia's mad
scene — Winslet performs it bound in a strait-
jacket (Act IV, Scene v). "Winslet plays Ophelia
like Laura from *The Glass Menagerie*," wrote the
film critic Chris Hewitt; "she's a delicate piece of
glass, slowly breaking into a million pieces." (See
also "A Film Diary of the Shooting of Kenneth
Branagh's *Hamlet*," page 1341.)

The Kobal Collection at Art Resource, New York.

CONSIDERATIONS AND CONNECTIONS

1. Name at least two other contemporary actors who you think could effectively play the role of Ophelia, and explain your choices.

2. View Kenneth Branagh's version of *Hamlet* and write a review that assesses Winslet's role as Ophelia.

The Death of Ophelia (1853, by Eugène Delacroix). There is much scholarly debate about the nature of Ophelia's death — was it an accident? a suicide? perhaps a murder by the Queen? In Delacroix's vision of Ophelia's final moments, a passive figure, bathed in light and loosely clad, is both etherealized and eroticized. The image is, arguably, a departure from the "muddy death" described by Queen Gertrude (Act IV, Scene vii). (See also *Hamlet and Horatio in the Cemetery,* page 1347.)

Alfredo Dagli Orti / The Art Archive at Art Resource, New York.

CONSIDERATIONS AND CONNECTIONS

1. Explain why you think Delacroix's image of Ophelia's death points to suicide, an accident, or ambiguity.

2. Compare the Queen's description of Ophelia's drowning (Act IV, Scene vii, lines 164–81) with the visual details of this painting. What important similarities and differences do you find in each rendering?

46

Modern Drama

A play should give you something to think about. When I see a play and understand it the first time, then I know it can't be much good.

—T. S. ELIOT

MS Am 2560 (177). By permission of the Houghton Library, Harvard University.

REALISM

Realism is a literary technique that attempts to create the appearance of life as it is actually experienced. Characters in modern realistic plays (written during and after the last quarter of the nineteenth century) speak dialogue that we might hear in our daily lives. These characters are not larger than life but representative of it; they seem to speak the way we do rather than in highly poetic language, formal declarations, asides, or soliloquies. It is impossible to imagine a heroic figure such as Oedipus inhabiting a comfortably furnished living room and chatting about his wife's household budget the way Torvald Helmer does in Henrik Ibsen's *A Doll's House*. Realism brings into focus commonplace, everyday life rather than the extraordinary kinds of events that make up Sophocles' *Oedipus the King* or Shakespeare's *Hamlet*.

Realistic characters can certainly be heroic, but like Nora Helmer, they find that their strength and courage are tested in the context of events ordinary people might experience. Work, love, marriage, children, and death are often the focus of realistic dramas. These subjects can also constitute much of the material in nonrealistic plays, but modern realistic dramas present such material in the realm of the probable. Conflicts in realistic plays are likely to reflect problems in our own lives. Hence, making ends meet takes precedence over saving a kingdom; middle- and lower-class individuals take center stage as primary characters in main plots rather than being secondary characters in subplots. Thus we can see why the nineteenth-century movement toward realism paralleled the rise of a middle class eagerly seeking representations of its concerns in the theater.

Before the end of the nineteenth century, however, few attempts were made in the theater to present life as it is actually lived. The chorus's role in Sophocles' *Oedipus the King*, the allegorical figures in morality plays, the remarkable mistaken identities in Shakespeare's comedies, or the rhymed couplets spoken in seventeenth-century plays such as Molière's *Tartuffe* represent theatrical conventions rather than life. Theatergoers have understood and appreciated these conventions for centuries — and still do — but in the nineteenth century social, political, and industrial revolutions helped create an atmosphere in which some playwrights found it necessary to create works that more directly reflected their audiences' lives.

Playwrights such as Henrik Ibsen and Anton Chekhov refused to join the ranks of their romantic contemporaries, who they felt falsely idealized life. The most popular plays immediately preceding the works of these realistic writers consisted primarily of love stories and action-packed plots. Such **melodramas** offer audiences thrills and chills as well as happy endings. They typically include a virtuous individual struggling under the tyranny of a wicked oppressor, who is defeated only at the last moment. Suspense is reinforced by a series of pursuits, captures, and escapes that move the plot quickly and de-emphasize character or theme. These representations of extreme conflicts enjoyed wide popularity in the nineteenth century — indeed, they still do — because their formula was varied enough to be entertaining yet their outcomes were always comforting to the audience's sense of justice. From the realists' perspective, melodramas were merely escape fantasies that distorted life by refusing to examine the real world closely and objectively. But an indication of the popularity of such happy endings can be seen in Chekhov's farcical comedies, such as *The Proposal*, a one-act play filled with exaggerated characters and action. Despite his realist's values, Chekhov was also sometimes eager to please audiences.

Realists attempted to open their audiences' eyes; to their minds, the only genuine comfort was in knowing the truth. Many of their plays concern controversial issues of the day and focus on people who fall prey to indifferent societal institutions. English dramatist John Galsworthy (1867–1933) examined social values in *Strife* (1909) and *Justice* (1910), two plays whose titles broadly suggest the nature of his concerns. British playwright George Bernard Shaw (1856–1950) often used comedy and irony as a means of awakening his audiences to contemporary problems: *Arms and the Man* (1894) satirizes romantic attitudes toward war, and *Mrs. Warren's Profession* (1898) indicts a social and economic system that drives a woman to prostitution. Chekhov's major plays are populated by characters frustrated by their social situations and their own sensibilities; they are ordinary people who long for happiness but become entangled in everyday circumstances that limit their lives. Ibsen also took a close look at his characters' daily lives. His plays attack social conventions and challenge popular attitudes toward marriage; he stunned audiences by dramatizing the suffering of a man dying of syphilis.

With these kinds of materials, Ibsen and his contemporaries popularized the **problem play**, a drama that represents a social issue in order to awaken the audience to it. These plays usually reject romantic plots in favor of holding up a mirror that reflects not simply what audiences want to see but what the playwright sees in them. Nineteenth-century realistic theater was no refuge from the social, economic, and psychological problems that melodrama ignored or sentimentalized.

NATURALISM

Related to realism is another movement, called *naturalism*. Essentially more of a philosophical attitude than a literary technique, naturalism derives its name from the idea that human beings are part of nature and subject to its laws. According to naturalists, heredity and environment shape and control people's lives; their behavior is determined more by instinct than by reason. This deterministic view argues that human beings have no transcendent identity because there is no soul or spiritual world that ultimately distinguishes humanity from any other form of life. Characters in naturalistic plays are generally portrayed as victims overwhelmed by internal and external forces. Thus literary naturalism tends to include not only the commonplace but the sordid, destructive, and chaotic aspects of life. Naturalism, then, is an extreme form of realism.

The earliest and most articulate voice of naturalism was that of French author Émile Zola (1840–1902), who urged artists to draw their characters from life and present their histories as faithfully as scientists report laboratory findings. Zola's best-known naturalistic play, *Thérèse Raquin* (1873), is a dramatization of an earlier novel involving a woman whose passion causes her to take a lover and plot with him to kill her husband. In his preface to the novel, Zola explains that his purpose is to take "a strong man and unsatisfied woman," "throw them into a violent drama and note scrupulously the sensations and acts of these creatures." The diction of Zola's statement reveals his nearly clinical approach, which becomes even more explicit when Zola likens his method of revealing character to that of an autopsy: "I have simply done on two living bodies the work which surgeons do on corpses."

Although some naturalistic plays have been successfully produced and admired (notably Maxim Gorky's *The Lower Depths* [1902], set in a grim boardinghouse occupied by characters who suffer poverty, crime, betrayal, disease, and suicide), few important dramatists fully subscribed to naturalism's extreme methods and values. Nevertheless, the movement significantly influenced playwrights. Because of its insistence on the necessity of closely observing characters' environment, playwrights placed a new emphasis on detailed settings and natural acting. This verisimilitude became a significant feature of realistic drama.

THEATRICAL CONVENTIONS OF MODERN DRAMA

The picture-frame stage that is often used for realistic plays typically reproduces the setting of a room in some detail. Within the stage, framed by a proscenium arch (from which the curtain hangs), scenery and props are used to create an illusion of reality. Whether the "small book-case with well-bound books" described in the opening setting of Ibsen's *A Doll's House* is only painted scenery or an actual case with books, it will probably look real to the audience. Removing the fourth wall of a room so that an audience can look in fosters the illusion that the actions onstage are real events happening before unseen spectators. The texture of Nora's life is communicated by the set as well as by what she says and does. That doesn't happen in a play like Sophocles' *Oedipus the King*. Technical effects can make us believe there is wood burning in a fireplace or snow falling outside a window. Outdoor settings are made similarly realistic by props and painted sets. In one of Chekhov's full-length plays, for example, the second act opens in a meadow with the faint outline of a city on the horizon.

In addition to lifelike sets, a particular method of acting is used to create a realistic atmosphere. Actors address each other instead of directing formal speeches toward the audience; they act within the setting, not merely before it. At the beginning of the twentieth century Konstantin Stanislavsky (1863–1938), a Russian director, teacher, and actor, developed a system of acting that was an important influence in realistic theater. He trained actors to identify with the inner emotions of the characters they played. They were encouraged to recall from their own lives emotional responses similar to those they were portraying. The goal was to present a role truthfully by first feeling and then projecting the character's situation. Among Stanislavsky's early successes in this method were the plays of Chekhov.

There are, however, degrees of realism on the stage. Tennessee Williams's *The Glass Menagerie* (1945), for example, is a partially realistic portrayal of characters whose fragile lives are founded on illusions. Williams's dialogue rings true, and individual scenes resemble the kind of real-life action we would imagine such vulnerable characters engaging in, but other elements of the play are nonrealistic. For instance, Williams uses Tom as a major character in the play as well as narrator and stage manager. Here is part of Williams's stage directions: "The narrator is an undisguised convention of the play. He takes whatever license with dramatic convention as is convenient to his purposes." Although this play can be accurately described as including realistic elements,

Williams, like many other contemporary playwrights, does not attempt an absolute fidelity to reality. He uses flashbacks — as does Arthur Miller in *Death of a Salesman* (p. 1496) — to present incidents that occurred before the opening scene because the past impinges so heavily on the present. Most playwrights don't attempt to duplicate reality, since that can now be done so well by motion pictures.

Realism needn't lock a playwright into a futile attempt to make everything appear as it is in life. There is no way to avoid theatrical conventions: actors impersonate characters in a setting that is, after all, a stage. Indeed, even the dialogue in a realistic play is quite different from the pauses, sentence fragments, repetitions, silences, and incoherencies that characterize the way people usually speak. Realistic dialogue may seem like ordinary speech, but it, like Shakespeare's poetic language, is constructed. If we remember that realistic drama represents only the appearance of reality and that what we read on a page or see and hear onstage is the result of careful selecting, editing, and even distortion, then we are more likely to appreciate the playwright's art.

A Doll's House

Henrik Ibsen was born in Skien, Norway, to wealthy parents, who lost their money while he was a young boy. His early experiences with small-town life and genteel poverty sensitized him to the problems that he subsequently dramatized in a number of his plays. At age sixteen he was apprenticed to a druggist; he later thought about studying medicine, but by his early twenties he was earning a living writing and directing plays in various Norwegian cities. By the time of his death he enjoyed an international reputation for his treatment of social issues related to middle-class life.

Time Life Pictures/Mansell/Getty Images.

Ibsen's earliest dramatic works were historical and romantic plays, some in verse. His first truly realistic work was *The Pillars of Society* (1877), whose title ironically hints at the corruption and hypocrisy exposed in it. The realistic social-problem plays for which he is best known followed. These dramas at once fascinated and shocked international audiences. Among his most produced and admired works are *A Doll's House* (1879), *Ghosts* (1881), *An Enemy of the People* (1882), *The Wild Duck* (1884), and *Hedda Gabler* (1890). The common denominator in many of Ibsen's dramas is his interest in individuals struggling for an authentic identity in the face of tyrannical social conventions. This conflict often results in his characters' being divided between a sense of duty to themselves and their responsibility to others.

Ibsen used such external and internal conflicts to propel his plays' action. Like many of his contemporaries who wrote realistic plays, he adopted the form of the ***well-made play***. A dramatic structure popularized in France by Eugène Scribe (1791–1861) and Victorien Sardou (1831–1908), the well-made play employs conventions including plenty of suspense created by meticulous plotting. Extensive exposition explains past events that ultimately lead to an inevitable climax. Tension is released when a secret that reverses the protagonist's fortunes is revealed. Ibsen, having directed a number of Scribe's plays in Norway, knew their cause-to-effect plot arrangements and used them for his own purposes in his problem plays.

A Doll's House dramatizes the tensions of a nineteenth-century middle-class marriage in which a wife struggles to step beyond the limited identity imposed on her by her husband and society. Although the Helmers' pleasant apartment seems an unlikely setting for the fierce conflicts that develop, the issues raised in the play are unmistakably real. *A Doll's House* affirms the necessity to reject hypocrisy, complacency, cowardice, and stifling conventions if life is to have dignity and meaning. Several critical approaches to the play can be found in Chapter 47, "A Critical Case Study: Henrik Ibsen's *A Doll's House.*"

Henrik Ibsen (1828–1906)

A Doll's House   1879

TRANSLATED BY R. FARQUHARSON SHARP

DRAMATIS PERSONAE

Torvald Helmer
Nora, his wife
Doctor Rank
Mrs. Linde
Nils Krogstad
Helmer's three small children
Anne, their nurse
A Housemaid
A Porter

See Plays in Performance insert.
Joan Marcus.

SCENE: The action takes place in Helmer's house.

ACT I

SCENE: *A room furnished comfortably and tastefully, but not extravagantly. At the back, a door to the right leads to the entrance-hall, another to the left leads to Helmer's study. Between the doors stands a piano. In the middle of the left-hand wall is a door, and beyond it a window. Near the window are a round table, arm-chairs, and a small sofa. In the right-hand wall, at the farther end, another door; and* on the same side, nearer the footlights, a stove, two easy chairs, and a rocking-chair; between the stove and the door, a small table. Engravings on the walls; a cabinet with china and other small objects; a small book-case with well-bound books. The floors are carpeted, and a fire burns in the stove. It is winter.

    A bell rings in the hall; shortly afterwards the door is heard to open. Enter Nora, humming a tune and in high spirits. She is in outdoor dress and carries a number of parcels; these she lays on the table to the right. She leaves the outer door open after her, and through it is seen a Porter who is carrying a Christmas Tree and a basket, which he gives to the Maid who has opened the door.

Nora: Hide the Christmas Tree carefully, Helen. Be sure the children do not see it until this evening, when it is dressed. *(To the Porter, taking out her purse.)* How much?

Porter: Sixpence.

Nora: There is a shilling. No, keep the change. *(The Porter thanks her, and goes out. Nora shuts the door. She is laughing to herself, as she takes off her hat and coat. She takes a packet of macaroons from her pocket and eats one or two; then goes cautiously to her husband's door and listens.)* Yes, he is in. *(Still humming, she goes to the table on the right.)*

Helmer (calls out from his room): Is that my little lark twittering out there?

Nora (busy opening some of the parcels): Yes, it is!

Helmer: Is it my little squirrel bustling about?

Nora: Yes!

Helmer: When did my squirrel come home?

Nora: Just now. *(Puts the bag of macaroons into her pocket and wipes her mouth.)* Come in here, Torvald, and see what I have bought.

Helmer: Don't disturb me. *(A little later, he opens the door and looks into the room, pen in hand.)* Bought, did you say? All these things? Has my little spendthrift been wasting money again?

Nora: Yes but, Torvald, this year we really can let ourselves go a little. This is the first Christmas that we have not needed to economise.

Helmer: Still, you know, we can't spend money recklessly.

Nora: Yes, Torvald, we may be a wee bit more reckless now, mayn't we? Just a tiny wee bit! You are going to have a big salary and earn lots and lots of money.

Helmer: Yes, after the New Year; but then it will be a whole quarter before the salary is due.

Nora: Pooh! we can borrow until then.

Helmer: Nora! *(Goes up to her and takes her playfully by the ear.)* The same little featherhead! Suppose, now, that I borrowed fifty pounds to-day, and you spent it all in the Christmas week, and then on New Year's Eve a slate fell on my head and killed me, and —

Nora (putting her hands over his mouth): Oh! don't say such horrid things.

Helmer: Still, suppose that happened, — what then?

Nora: If that were to happen, I don't suppose I should care whether I owed money or not.

Helmer: Yes, but what about the people who had lent it?

Nora: They? Who would bother about them? I should not know who they were.

Helmer: That is like a woman! But seriously, Nora, you know what I think about that. No debt, no borrowing. There can be no freedom or beauty about a home life that depends on borrowing and debt. We two have kept bravely on the straight road so far, and we will go on the same way for the short time longer that there need be any struggle.

Nora (moving towards the stove): As you please, Torvald.

Helmer (following her): Come, come, my little skylark must not droop her wings. What is this! Is my little squirrel out of temper? *(Taking out his purse.)* Nora, what do you think I have got here?

Nora (turning round quickly): Money!

Helmer: There you are. *(Gives her some money.)* Do you think I don't know what a lot is wanted for housekeeping at Christmas-time?

Nora (counting): Ten shillings — a pound — two pounds! Thank you, thank you, Torvald; that will keep me going for a long time.

Helmer: Indeed it must.

Nora: Yes, yes, it will. But come here and let me show you what I have bought. And all so cheap! Look, here is a new suit for Ivar, and a sword; and a horse and a trumpet for Bob; and a doll and dolly's bedstead for Emmy, — they are very plain, but anyway she will soon break them in pieces. And here are dress-lengths and handkerchiefs for the maids; old Anne ought really to have something better.

Helmer: And what is in this parcel?

Nora (crying out): No, no! you mustn't see that until this evening.

Helmer: Very well. But now tell me, you extravagant little person, what would you like for yourself?

Nora: For myself? Oh, I am sure I don't want anything.

Helmer: Yes, but you must. Tell me something reasonable that you would particularly like to have.

Nora: No, I really can't think of anything — unless, Torvald —

Helmer: Well?

Nora (playing with his coat buttons, and without raising her eyes to his): If you really want to give me something, you might — you might —

Helmer: Well, out with it!

Nora (speaking quickly): You might give me money, Torvald. Only just as much as you can afford; and then one of these days I will buy something with it.

Helmer: But, Nora —

Nora: Oh, do! dear Torvald; please, please do! Then I will wrap it up in beautiful gilt paper and hang it on the Christmas Tree. Wouldn't that be fun?

Helmer: What are little people called that are always wasting money?

Nora: Spendthrifts — I know. Let us do as you suggest, Torvald, and then I shall have time to think what I am most in want of. That is a very sensible plan, isn't it?

Helmer (smiling): Indeed it is — that is to say, if you were really to save out of the money I give you, and then really buy something for yourself. But if you spend it all on the housekeeping and any number of unnecessary things, then I merely have to pay up again.

Nora: Oh but, Torvald —

Helmer: You can't deny it, my dear little Nora. *(Puts his arm round her waist.)* It's a sweet little spendthrift, but she uses up a deal of money. One would hardly believe how expensive such little persons are!

Nora: It's a shame to say that. I do really save all I can.

Helmer (laughing): That's very true, — all you can. But you can't save anything!

Nora (smiling quietly and happily): You haven't any idea how many expenses we skylarks and squirrels have, Torvald.

Helmer: You are an odd little soul. Very like your father. You always find some new way of wheedling money out of me, and, as soon as you have got it, it seems to melt in your hands. You never know where it has gone. Still, one must take you as you are. It is in the blood; for indeed it is true that you can inherit these things, Nora.

Nora: Ah, I wish I had inherited many of papa's qualities.

Helmer: And I would not wish you to be anything but just what you are, my sweet little skylark. But, do you know, it strikes me that you are looking rather — what shall I say — rather uneasy today?

Nora: Do I?

Helmer: You do, really. Look straight at me.

Nora (looks at him): Well?

Helmer (wagging his finger at her): Hasn't Miss Sweet Tooth been breaking rules in town today?

Nora: No; what makes you think that?

Helmer: Hasn't she paid a visit to the confectioner's?

Nora: No, I assure you, Torvald —

Helmer: Not been nibbling sweets?

Nora: No, certainly not.

Helmer: Not even taken a bite at a macaroon or two?

Nora: No, Torvald, I assure you really —

Helmer: There, there, of course I was only joking.

Nora (going to the table on the right): I should not think of going against your wishes.

Helmer: No, I am sure of that; besides, you gave me your word — (*Going up to her.*) Keep your little Christmas secrets to yourself, my darling. They will all be revealed to-night when the Christmas Tree is lit, no doubt.

Nora: Did you remember to invite Doctor Rank?

Helmer: No. But there is no need; as a matter of course he will come to dinner with us. However, I will ask him when he comes in this morning. I have ordered some good wine. Nora, you can't think how I am looking forward to this evening.

Nora: So am I! And how the children will enjoy themselves, Torvald!

Helmer: It is splendid to feel that one has a perfectly safe appointment, and a big enough income. It's delightful to think of, isn't it?

Nora: It's wonderful!

Helmer: Do you remember last Christmas? For a full three weeks beforehand you shut yourself up every evening until long after midnight, making ornaments for the Christmas Tree, and all the other fine things that were to be a surprise to us. It was the dullest three weeks I ever spent!

Nora: I didn't find it dull.

Helmer (smiling): But there was precious little result, Nora.

Nora: Oh, you shouldn't tease me about that again. How could I help the cat's going in and tearing everything to pieces?

Helmer: Of course you couldn't, poor little girl. You had the best of intentions to please us all, and that's the main thing. But it is a good thing that our hard times are over.

Nora: Yes, it is really wonderful.

Helmer: This time I needn't sit here and be dull all alone, and you needn't ruin your dear eyes and your pretty little hands —

Nora (clapping her hands): No, Torvald, I needn't any longer, need I! It's wonderfully lovely to hear you say so! *(Taking his arm.)* Now I will tell you how I have been thinking we ought to arrange things, Torvald. As soon as Christmas is over — *(A bell rings in the hall.)* There's the bell. *(She tidies the room a little.)* There's some one at the door. What a nuisance!

Helmer: If it is a caller, remember I am not at home.

Maid (in the doorway): A lady to see you, ma'am, — a stranger.

Nora: Ask her to come in.

Maid (to Helmer): The doctor came at the same time, sir.

Helmer: Did he go straight into my room?

Maid: Yes, sir.

> *Helmer goes into his room. The Maid ushers in Mrs. Linde, who is in travelling dress, and shuts the door.*

Mrs. Linde (in a dejected and timid voice): How do you do, Nora?

Nora (doubtfully): How do you do —

Mrs. Linde: You don't recognise me, I suppose.

Nora: No, I don't know — yes, to be sure, I seem to — *(Suddenly.)* Yes! Christine! Is it really you?

Mrs. Linde: Yes, it is I.

Nora: Christine! To think of my not recognising you! And yet how could I — *(In a gentle voice.)* How you have altered, Christine!

Mrs. Linde: Yes, I have indeed. In nine, ten long years —

Nora: Is it so long since we met? I suppose it is. The last eight years have been a happy time for me, I can tell you. And so now you have come into the town, and have taken this long journey in winter — that was plucky of you.

Mrs. Linde: I arrived by steamer this morning.

Nora: To have some fun at Christmas-time, of course. How delightful! We will have such fun together! But take off your things. You are not cold, I hope. *(Helps her.)* Now we will sit down by the stove, and be cosy. No, take this arm-chair; I will sit here in the rocking-chair. *(Takes her hands.)* Now you look like your old self again; it was only the first moment — You are a little paler, Christine, and perhaps a little thinner.

Mrs. Linde: And much, much older, Nora.

Nora: Perhaps a little older; very, very little; certainly not much. *(Stops suddenly and speaks seriously.)* What a thoughtless creature I am, chattering away like this. My poor, dear Christine, do forgive me.

Mrs. Linde: What do you mean, Nora?

Nora (gently): Poor Christine, you are a widow.

Mrs. Linde: Yes; it is three years ago now.

Nora: Yes, I knew; I saw it in the papers. I assure you, Christine, I meant ever so often to write to you at the time, but I always put it off and something always prevented me.

Mrs. Linde: I quite understand, dear.

Nora: It was very bad of me, Christine. Poor thing, how you must have suffered. And he left you nothing?

Mrs. Linde: No.

Nora: And no children?

Mrs. Linde: No.

Nora: Nothing at all, then.

Mrs. Linde: Not even any sorrow or grief to live upon.

Nora (looking incredulously at her): But, Christine, is that possible?

Mrs. Linde (smiles sadly and strokes her hair): It sometimes happens, Nora.

Nora: So you are quite alone. How dreadfully sad that must be. I have three lovely children. You can't see them just now, for they are out with their nurse. But now you must tell me all about it.

Mrs. Linde: No, no; I want to hear about you.

Nora: No, you must begin. I mustn't be selfish today; today I must only think of your affairs. But there is one thing I must tell you. Do you know we have just had a great piece of good luck?

Mrs. Linde: No, what is it?

Nora: Just fancy, my husband has been made manager of the Bank!

Mrs. Linde: Your husband? What good luck!

Nora: Yes, tremendous! A barrister's profession is such an uncertain thing, especially if he won't undertake unsavoury cases; and naturally Torvald has never been willing to do that, and I quite agree with him. You may imagine how pleased we are! He is to take up his work in the Bank at the New Year, and then he will have a big salary and lots of commissions. For the future we can live quite differently — we can do just as we like. I feel so relieved and so happy, Christine! It will be splendid to have heaps of money and not need to have any anxiety, won't it?

Mrs. Linde: Yes, anyhow I think it would be delightful to have what one needs.

Nora: No, not only what one needs, but heaps and heaps of money.

Mrs. Linde (smiling): Nora, Nora, haven't you learned sense yet? In our schooldays you were a great spendthrift.

Nora (laughing): Yes, that is what Torvald says now. *(Wags her finger at her.)* But "Nora, Nora" is not so silly as you think. We have not been in a position for me to waste money. We have both had to work.

Mrs. Linde: You too?

Nora: Yes; odds and ends, needlework, crotchet-work, embroidery, and that kind of thing. *(Dropping her voice.)* And other things as well. You know Torvald left his office when we were married? There was no prospect of promotion there, and he had to try and earn more than before. But during the first year he over-worked himself dreadfully. You see, he had to make money every way he could, and he worked early and late; but he couldn't stand it, and fell dreadfully ill, and the doctors said it was necessary for him to go south.

Mrs. Linde: You spent a whole year in Italy, didn't you?

Nora: Yes. It was no easy matter to get away, I can tell you. It was just after Ivar was born; but naturally we had to go. It was a wonderfully beautiful journey, and it saved Torvald's life. But it cost a tremendous lot of money, Christine.

Mrs. Linde: So I should think.

Nora: It cost about two hundred and fifty pounds. That's a lot, isn't it?

Mrs. Linde: Yes, and in emergencies like that it is lucky to have the money.

Nora: I ought to tell you that we had it from papa.

Mrs. Linde: Oh, I see. It was just about that time that he died, wasn't it?

Nora: Yes; and, just think of it, I couldn't go and nurse him. I was expecting little Ivar's birth every day and I had my poor sick Torvald to look after. My dear, kind father — I never saw him again, Christine. That was the saddest time I have known since our marriage.

Mrs. Linde: I know how fond you were of him. And then you went off to Italy?

Nora: Yes; you see we had money then, and the doctors insisted on our going, so we started a month later.

Mrs. Linde: And your husband came back quite well?

Nora: As sound as a bell!

Mrs. Linde: But — the doctor?

Nora: What doctor?

Mrs. Linde: I thought your maid said the gentleman who arrived here just as I did, was the doctor?

Nora: Yes, that was Doctor Rank, but he doesn't come here professionally. He is our greatest friend, and comes in at least once everyday. No, Torvald has not had an hour's illness since then, and our children are strong and healthy and so am I. *(Jumps up and claps her hands.)* Christine! Christine! it's good to be alive and happy! — But how horrid of me; I am talking of nothing but my own affairs. *(Sits on a stool near her, and rests her arms on her knees.)* You mustn't be angry with me. Tell me, is it really true that you did not love your husband? Why did you marry him?

Mrs. Linde: My mother was alive then, and was bedridden and helpless, and I had to provide for my two younger brothers; so I did not think I was justified in refusing his offer.

Nora: No, perhaps you were quite right. He was rich at that time, then?

Mrs. Linde: I believe he was quite well off. But his business was a precarious one; and, when he died, it all went to pieces and there was nothing left.

Nora: And then? —

Mrs. Linde: Well, I had to turn my hand to anything I could find — first a small shop, then a small school, and so on. The last three years have seemed like one long working-day, with no rest. Now it is at an end, Nora. My poor mother needs me no more, for she is gone; and the boys do not need me either; they have got situations and can shift for themselves.

Nora: What a relief you must feel it —

Mrs. Linde: No, indeed; I only feel my life unspeakably empty. No one to live for anymore. *(Gets up restlessly.)* That was why I could not stand the life in my little backwater any longer. I hope it may be easier here to find something which will busy me and occupy my thoughts. If only I could have the good luck to get some regular work — office work of some kind —

Nora: But, Christine, that is so frightfully tiring, and you look tired out now. You had far better go away to some watering-place.

Mrs. Linde (walking to the window): I have no father to give me money for a journey, Nora.

Nora (rising): Oh, don't be angry with me!

Mrs. Linde (going up to her): It is you that must not be angry with me, dear. The worst of a position like mine is that it makes one so bitter. No one to work for, and yet obliged to be always on the lookout for chances. One must live, and so one becomes selfish. When you told me of the happy turn your fortunes have taken — you will hardly believe it — I was delighted not so much on your account as on my own.

Nora: How do you mean? — Oh, I understand. You mean that perhaps Torvald could get you something to do.

Mrs. Linde: Yes, that was what I was thinking of.

Nora: He must, Christine. Just leave it to me; I will broach the subject very cleverly — I will think of something that will please him very much. It will make me so happy to be of some use to you.

Mrs. Linde: How kind you are, Nora, to be so anxious to help me! It is doubly kind in you, for you know so little of the burdens and troubles of life.

Nora: I — ? I know so little of them?

Mrs. Linde (smiling): My dear! Small household cares and that sort of thing! — You are a child, Nora.

Nora (tosses her head and crosses the stage): You ought not to be so superior.

Mrs. Linde: No?

Nora: You are just like the others. They all think that I am incapable of anything really serious —

Mrs. Linde: Come, come —

Nora: — that I have gone through nothing in this world of cares.

Mrs. Linde: But, my dear Nora, you have just told me all your troubles.

Nora: Pooh! — those were trifles. *(Lowering her voice.)* I have not told you the important thing.

Mrs. Linde: The important thing? What do you mean?

Nora: You look down upon me altogether, Christine — but you ought not to. You are proud, aren't you, of having worked so hard and so long for your mother?

Mrs. Linde: Indeed, I don't look down on anyone. But it is true that I am both proud and glad to think that I was privileged to make the end of my mother's life almost free from care.

Nora: And you are proud to think of what you have done for your brothers?

Mrs. Linde: I think I have the right to be.

Nora: I think so, too. But now, listen to this; I too have something to be proud and glad of.

Mrs. Linde: I have no doubt you have. But what do you refer to?

Nora: Speak low. Suppose Torvald were to hear! He mustn't on any account — no one in the world must know, Christine, except you.

Mrs. Linde: But what is it?

Nora: Come here. *(Pulls her down on the sofa beside her.)* Now I will show you that I too have something to be proud and glad of. It was I who saved Torvald's life.

Mrs. Linde: "Saved"? How?

Nora: I told you about our trip to Italy. Torvald would never have recovered if he had not gone there —

Mrs. Linde: Yes, but your father gave you the necessary funds.

Nora (smiling): Yes, that is what Torvald and all the others think, but —

Mrs. Linde: But —

Nora: Papa didn't give us a shilling. It was I who procured the money.

Mrs. Linde: You? All that large sum?

Nora: Two hundred and fifty pounds. What do you think of that?

Mrs. Linde: But, Nora, how could you possibly do it? Did you win a prize in the Lottery?

Nora (contemptuously): In the Lottery? There would have been no credit in that.

Mrs. Linde: But where did you get it from, then?

Nora (humming and smiling with an air of mystery): Hm, hm! Aha!

Mrs. Linde: Because you couldn't have borrowed it.

Nora: Couldn't I? Why not?

Mrs. Linde: No, a wife cannot borrow without her husband's consent.

Nora (tossing her head): Oh, if it is a wife who has any head for business — a wife who has the wit to be a little bit clever —

Mrs. Linde: I don't understand it at all, Nora.

Nora: There is no need you should. I never said I had borrowed the money. I may have got it some other way. *(Lies back on the sofa.)* Perhaps I got it from some other admirer. When anyone is as attractive as I am —

Mrs. Linde: You are a mad creature.

Nora: Now, you know you're full of curiosity, Christine.

Mrs. Linde: Listen to me, Nora dear. Haven't you been a little bit imprudent?

Nora (sits up straight): Is it imprudent to save your husband's life?

Mrs. Linde: It seems to me imprudent, without his knowledge, to —

Nora: But it was absolutely necessary that he should not know! My goodness, can't you understand that? It was necessary he should have no idea what a dangerous condition he was in. It was to me that the doctors came and said that his life was in danger, and that the only thing to save him was to live in the south. Do you suppose I didn't try, first of all, to get what I wanted as if it were for myself? I told him how much I should love to travel abroad like other young wives; I tried tears and entreaties with him; I told him that he ought to remember the condition I was in, and that he ought to be kind and indulgent to me; I even hinted that he might raise a loan. That nearly made him angry, Christine. He said I was thoughtless, and that it was his duty as my husband not to indulge me in my whims and caprices — as I believe he called them. Very well, I thought, you must be saved — and that was how I came to devise a way out of the difficulty —

Mrs. Linde: And did your husband never get to know from your father that the money had not come from him?

Nora: No, never. Papa died just at that time. I had meant to let him into the secret and beg him never to reveal it. But he was so ill then — alas, there never was any need to tell him.

Mrs. Linde: And since then have you never told your secret to your husband?

Nora: Good Heavens, no! How could you think so? A man who has such strong opinions about these things! And besides, how painful and humiliating it would be for Torvald, with his manly independence, to know that he owed me anything! It would upset our mutual relations altogether; our beautiful happy home would no longer be what it is now.

Mrs. Linde: Do you mean never to tell him about it?

Nora (meditatively, and with a half smile): Yes — someday, perhaps, after many years, when I am no longer as nice-looking as I am now. Don't laugh at me! I mean, of course, when Torvald is no longer as devoted to me as he is now; when my dancing and dressing-up and reciting have palled on him; then it may be a good thing to have something in reserve — *(Breaking off.)* What nonsense! That time will never come. Now, what do you think of my great secret, Christine? Do you still think I am of no use? I can tell you, too, that this affair has caused me a lot of worry. It has been by no means easy for me to meet my engagements punctually. I may tell you that there is something that is called, in business, quarterly interest, and another thing called payment in installments, and it is always so dreadfully difficult to manage them. I have had to save a little here and there, where I could, you understand. I have not been able to put aside much from my housekeeping money, for Torvald must have a good table. I couldn't let my children be shabbily dressed; I have felt obliged to use up all he gave me for them, the sweet little darlings!

Mrs. Linde: So it has all had to come out of your own necessaries of life, poor Nora?

Nora: Of course. Besides, I was the one responsible for it. Whenever Torvald has given me money for new dresses and such things, I have never spent more than half of it; I have always bought the simplest and cheapest things. Thank Heaven, any clothes look well on me, and so Torvald has never noticed it. But it was often very hard on me, Christine — because it is delightful to be really well dressed, isn't it?

Mrs. Linde: Quite so.

Nora: Well, then I have found other ways of earning money. Last winter I was lucky enough to get a lot of copying to do; so I locked myself up and sat writing every evening until quite late at night. Many a time I was desperately tired; but all the same it was a tremendous pleasure to sit there working and earning money. It was like being a man.

Mrs. Linde: How much have you been able to pay off in that way?

Nora: I can't tell you exactly. You see, it is very difficult to keep an account of a business matter of that kind. I only know that I have paid every penny that I could scrape together. Many a time I was at my wits' end. *(Smiles.)* Then I used to sit here and imagine that a rich old gentleman had fallen in love with me —

Mrs. Linde: What! Who was it?

Nora: Be quiet! — that he had died; and that when his will was opened it contained, written in big letters, the instruction: "The lovely Mrs. Nora Helmer is to have all I possess paid over to her at once in cash."

Mrs. Linde: But, my dear Nora — who could the man be?

Nora: Good gracious, can't you understand? There was no old gentleman at all; it was only something that I used to sit here and imagine, when I couldn't think of any way of procuring money. But it's all the same now; the tiresome old person can stay where he is, as far as I am concerned; I don't care about him or his will either, for I am free from care now. *(Jumps up.)* My goodness, it's delightful to think of, Christine! Free from care! To be able to be free from care, quite free from care; to be able to play and romp with the children; to be able to keep the house beautifully and have everything just as Torvald likes it! And, think of it, soon the spring will come and the big blue sky! Perhaps we shall be able to take a little trip — perhaps I shall see the sea again! Oh, it's a wonderful thing to be alive and be happy. *(A bell is heard in the hall.)*

Mrs. Linde (rising): There is the bell; perhaps I had better go.

Nora: No, don't go; no one will come in here; it is sure to be for Torvald.

Servant (at the hall door): Excuse me, ma'am — there is a gentleman to see the master, and as the doctor is with him —

Nora: Who is it?

Krogstad (at the door): It is I, Mrs. Helmer *(Mrs. Linde starts, trembles, and turns to the window.)*

Nora (takes a step towards him, and speaks in a strained, low voice): You? What is it? What do you want to see my husband about?

Krogstad: Bank business — in a way. I have a small post in the Bank, and I hear your husband is to be our chief now —

Nora: Then it is —

Krogstad: Nothing but dry business matters, Mrs. Helmer; absolutely nothing else.

Nora: Be so good as to go into the study, then. *(She bows indifferently to him and shuts the door into the hall; then comes back and makes up the fire in the stove.)*

Mrs. Linde: Nora — who was that man?

Nora: A lawyer, of the name of Krogstad.

Mrs. Linde: Then it really was he.

Nora: Do you know the man?

Mrs. Linde: I used to — many years ago. At one time he was a solicitor's clerk in our town.

Nora: Yes, he was.

Mrs. Linde: He is greatly altered.

Nora: He made a very unhappy marriage.

Mrs. Linde: He is a widower now, isn't he?

Nora: With several children. There now, it is burning up. (*Shuts the door of the stove and moves the rocking-chair aside.*)

Mrs. Linde: They say he carries on various kinds of business.

Nora: Really! Perhaps he does; I don't know anything about it. But don't let us think of business; it is so tiresome.

Doctor Rank (comes out of Helmer's study. Before he shuts the door he calls to him): No, my dear fellow, I won't disturb you; I would rather go in to your wife for a little while. (*Shuts the door and sees Mrs. Linde.*) I beg your pardon; I am afraid I am disturbing you too.

Nora: No, not at all. (*Introducing him.*) Doctor Rank, Mrs. Linde.

Rank: I have often heard Mrs. Linde's name mentioned here. I think I passed you on the stairs when I arrived, Mrs. Linde?

Mrs. Linde: Yes, I go up very slowly; I can't manage stairs well.

Rank: Ah! some slight internal weakness?

Mrs. Linde: No, the fact is I have been overworking myself.

Rank: Nothing more than that? Then I suppose you have come to town to amuse yourself with our entertainments?

Mrs. Linde: I have come to look for work.

Rank: Is that a good cure for overwork?

Mrs. Linde: One must live, Doctor Rank.

Rank: Yes, the general opinion seems to be that it is necessary.

Nora: Look here, Doctor Rank — you know you want to live.

Rank: Certainly. However wretched I may feel, I want to prolong the agony as long as possible. All my patients are like that. And so are those who are morally diseased; one of them, and a bad case too, is at this very moment with Helmer —

Mrs. Linde (sadly): Ah!

Nora: Whom do you mean?

Rank: A lawyer of the name of Krogstad, a fellow you don't know at all. He suffers from a diseased moral character, Mrs. Helmer; but even he began talking of its being highly important that he should live.

Nora: Did he? What did he want to speak to Torvald about?

Rank: I have no idea; I only heard that it was something about the Bank.

Nora: I didn't know this — what's his name — Krogstad had anything to do with the Bank.

Rank: Yes, he has some sort of appointment there. (*To Mrs. Linde.*) I don't know whether you find also in your part of the world that there are certain people who go zealously snuffing about to smell out moral corruption, and, as soon as they have found some, put the person concerned into some lucrative position where they can keep their eye on him. Healthy natures are left out in the cold.

Mrs. Linde: Still I think the sick are those who most need taking care of.

Rank (shrugging his shoulders): Yes, there you are. That is the sentiment that is turning Society into a sick-house.

Nora, who has been absorbed in her thoughts, breaks out into smothered laughter and claps her hands.

Rank: Why do you laugh at that? Have you any notion what Society really is?

Nora: What do I care about tiresome Society? I am laughing at something quite different, something extremely amusing. Tell me, Doctor Rank, are all the people who are employed in the Bank dependent on Torvald now?

Rank: Is that what you find so extremely amusing?

Nora (smiling and humming): That's my affair! *(Walking about the room.)* It's perfectly glorious to think that we have — that Torvald has so much power over so many people. *(Takes the packet from her pocket.)* Doctor Rank, what do you say to a macaroon?

Rank: What, macaroons? I thought they were forbidden here.

Nora: Yes, but these are some Christine gave me.

Mrs. Linde: What! I? —

Nora: Oh, well, don't be alarmed! You couldn't know that Torvald had forbidden them. I must tell you that he is afraid they will spoil my teeth. But, bah! — once in a way — That's so, isn't it, Doctor Rank? By your leave! *(Puts a macaroon into his mouth.)* You must have one too, Christine. And I shall have one, just a little one — or at most two. *(Walking about.)* I am tremendously happy. There is just one thing in the world now that I should dearly love to do.

Rank: Well, what is that?

Nora: It's something I should dearly love to say, if Torvald could hear me.

Rank: Well, why can't you say it?

Nora: No, I daren't; it's so shocking.

Mrs. Linde: Shocking?

Rank: Well, I should not advise you to say it. Still, with us you might. What is it you would so much like to say if Torvald could hear you?

Nora: I should just love to say — Well, I'm damned!

Rank: Are you mad?

Mrs. Linde: Nora, dear — !

Rank: Say it, here he is!

Nora (hiding the packet): Hush! Hush! Hush! *(Helmer comes out of his room, with his coat over his arm and his hat in his hand.)*

Nora: Well, Torvald dear, have you got rid of him?

Helmer: Yes, he has just gone.

Nora: Let me introduce you — this is Christine, who has come to town.

Helmer: Christine — ? Excuse me, but I don't know —

Nora: Mrs. Linde, dear; Christine Linde.

Helmer: Of course. A school friend of my wife's, I presume?

Mrs. Linde: Yes, we have known each other since then.

Nora: And just think, she has taken a long journey in order to see you.

Helmer: What do you mean?

Mrs. Linde: No, really, I —

Nora: Christine is tremendously clever at book-keeping, and she is frightfully anxious to work under some clever man, so as to perfect herself —

Helmer: Very sensible, Mrs. Linde.

Nora: And when she heard you had been appointed manager of the Bank — the news was telegraphed, you know — she travelled here as quick as she could.

Torvald, I am sure you will be able to do something for Christine, for my sake, won't you?

Helmer: Well, it is not altogether impossible. I presume you are a widow, Mrs. Linde?

Mrs. Linde: Yes.

Helmer: And have had some experience of book-keeping?

Mrs. Linde: Yes, a fair amount.

Helmer: Ah! well, it's very likely I may be able to find something for you —

Nora (clapping her hands): What did I tell you? What did I tell you?

Helmer: You have just come at a fortunate moment, Mrs. Linde.

Mrs. Linde: How am I to thank you?

Helmer: There is no need. *(Puts on his coat.)* But to-day you must excuse me —

Rank: Wait a minute; I will come with you. *(Brings his fur coat from the hall and warms it at the fire.)*

Nora: Don't be long away, Torvald dear.

Helmer: About an hour, not more.

Nora: Are you going too, Christine?

Mrs. Linde (putting on her cloak): Yes, I must go and look for a room.

Helmer: Oh, well then, we can walk down the street together.

Nora (helping her): What a pity it is we are so short of space here; I am afraid it is impossible for us —

Mrs. Linde: Please don't think of it! Good-bye, Nora dear, and many thanks.

Nora: Good-bye for the present. Of course you will come back this evening. And you too, Dr. Rank. What do you say? If you are well enough? Oh, you must be! Wrap yourself up well. *(They go to the door all talking together. Children's voices are heard on the staircase.)*

Nora: There they are! There they are! *(She runs to open the door. The Nurse comes in with the children.)* Come in! Come in! *(Stoops and kisses them.)* Oh, you sweet blessings! Look at them, Christine! Aren't they darlings?

Rank: Don't let us stand here in the draught.

Helmer: Come along, Mrs. Linde; the place will only be bearable for a mother now!

Rank, Helmer, and Mrs. Linde go downstairs. The Nurse comes forward with the children; Nora shuts the hall door.

Nora: How fresh and well you look! Such red cheeks like apples and roses. *(The children all talk at once while she speaks to them.)* Have you had great fun? That's splendid! What, you pulled both Emmy and Bob along on the sledge? — both at once? — that was good. You are a clever boy, Ivar. Let me take her for a little, Anne. My sweet little baby doll! *(Takes the baby from the Maid and dances it up and down.)* Yes, yes, mother will dance with Bob too. What! Have you been snowballing? I wish I had been there too! No, no, I will take their things off, Anne; please let me do it, it is such fun. Go in now, you look half frozen. There is some hot coffee for you on the stove.

The Nurse goes into the room on the left. Nora takes off the children's things and throws them about, while they all talk to her at once.

Nora: Really! Did a big dog run after you? But it didn't bite you? No, dogs don't bite nice little dolly children. You mustn't look at the parcels, Ivar. What are they? Ah, I daresay you would like to know. No, no — it's something nasty!

Come, let us have a game! What shall we play at? Hide and Seek? Yes, we'll play Hide and Seek. Bob shall hide first. Must I hide? Very well, I'll hide first. *(She and the children laugh and shout, and romp in and out of the room; at last Nora hides under the table, the children rush in and out for her, but do not see her; they hear her smothered laughter, run to the table, lift up the cloth and find her. Shouts of laughter. She crawls forward and pretends to frighten them. Fresh laughter. Meanwhile there has been a knock at the hall door, but none of them has noticed it. The door is half opened, and Krogstad appears. He waits a little; the game goes on.)*

Krogstad: Excuse me, Mrs. Helmer.

Nora (with a stifled cry, turns round and gets up on to her knees): Ah! what do you want?

Krogstad: Excuse me, the outer door was ajar; I suppose someone forgot to shut it.

Nora (rising): My husband is out, Mr. Krogstad.

Krogstad: I know that.

Nora: What do you want here, then?

Krogstad: A word with you.

Nora: With me? — *(To the children, gently.)* Go in to nurse. What? No, the strange man won't do mother any harm. When he has gone we will have another game. *(She takes the children into the room on the left, and shuts the door after them.)* You want to speak to me?

Krogstad: Yes, I do.

Nora: To-day? It is not the first of the month yet.

Krogstad: No, it is Christmas Eve, and it will depend on yourself what sort of a Christmas you will spend.

Nora: What do you mean? To-day it is absolutely impossible for me —

Krogstad: We won't talk about that until later on. This is something different. I presume you can give me a moment?

Nora: Yes — yes, I can — although —

Krogstad: Good. I was in Olsen's Restaurant and saw your husband going down the street —

Nora: Yes?

Krogstad: With a lady.

Nora: What then?

Krogstad: May I make so bold as to ask if it was a Mrs. Linde?

Nora: It was.

Krogstad: Just arrived in town?

Nora: Yes, to-day.

Krogstad: She is a great friend of yours, isn't she?

Nora: She is. But I don't see —

Krogstad: I knew her too, once upon a time.

Nora: I am aware of that.

Krogstad: Are you? So you know all about it; I thought as much. Then I can ask you, without beating about the bush — is Mrs. Linde to have an appointment in the Bank?

Nora: What right have you to question me, Mr. Krogstad? — You, one of my husband's subordinates! But since you ask, you shall know. Yes, Mrs. Linde *is* to have an appointment. And it was I who pleaded her cause, Mr. Krogstad, let me tell you that.

Krogstad: I was right in what I thought, then.

Nora (walking up and down the stage): Sometimes one has a tiny little bit of influence, I should hope. Because one is a woman, it does not necessarily follow
that — . When anyone is in a subordinate position, Mr. Krogstad, they should
really be careful to avoid offending anyone who — who —

Krogstad: Who has influence?

Nora: Exactly.

Krogstad (changing his tone): Mrs. Helmer, you will be so good as to use your
influence on my behalf.

Nora: What? What do you mean?

Krogstad: You will be so kind as to see that I am allowed to keep my subordinate
position in the Bank.

Nora: What do you mean by that? Who proposes to take your post away from you?

Krogstad: Oh, there is no necessity to keep up the pretence of ignorance. I can
quite understand that your friend is not very anxious to expose herself to the
chance of rubbing shoulders with me; and I quite understand, too, whom I
have to thank for being turned off.

Nora: But I assure you —

Krogstad: Very likely; but, to come to the point, the time has come when I should
advise you to use your influence to prevent that.

Nora: But, Mr. Krogstad, I *have* no influence.

Krogstad: Haven't you? I thought you said yourself just now —

Nora: Naturally I did not mean you to put that construction on it. What should
make you think I have any influence of that kind with my husband?

Krogstad: Oh, I have known your husband from our student days. I don't suppose
he is any more unassailable than other husbands.

Nora: If you speak slightingly of my husband, I shall turn you out of the house.

Krogstad: You are bold, Mrs. Helmer.

Nora: I am not afraid of you any longer. As soon as the New Year comes, I shall in
a very short time be free of the whole thing.

Krogstad (controlling himself): Listen to me, Mrs. Helmer. If necessary, I am prepared to fight for my small post in the Bank as if I were fighting for my life.

Nora: So it seems.

Krogstad: It is not only for the sake of the money; indeed, that weighs least with
me in the matter. There is another reason — well, I may as well tell you. My
position is this. I daresay you know, like everybody else, that once, many years
ago, I was guilty of an indiscretion.

Nora: I think I have heard something of the kind.

Krogstad: The matter never came into court; but every way seemed to be closed
to me after that. So I took to the business that you know of. I had to do something; and, honestly, I don't think I've been one of the worst. But now I must
cut myself free from all that. My sons are growing up; for their sake I must try
and win back as much respect as I can in the town. This post in the Bank was
like the first step up for me — and now your husband is going to kick me downstairs again into the mud.

Nora: But you must believe me, Mr. Krogstad; it is not in my power to help you
at all.

Krogstad: Then it is because you haven't the will; but I have means to compel you.

Nora: You don't mean that you will tell my husband that I owe you money?

Krogstad: Hm! — suppose I were to tell him?

Nora: It would be perfectly infamous of you. *(Sobbing.)* To think of his learning my
secret, which has been my joy and pride, in such an ugly, clumsy way — that

he should learn it from you! And it would put me in a horribly disagreeable
 position —

Krogstad: Only disagreeable?

Nora (impetuously): Well, do it, then! — and it will be the worse for you. My husband will see for himself what a blackguard you are, and you certainly won't
 keep your post then.

Krogstad: I asked you if it was only a disagreeable scene at home that you were
 afraid of?

Nora: If my husband does get to know of it, of course he will at once pay you what
 is still owing, and we shall have nothing more to do with you.

Krogstad (coming a step nearer): Listen to me, Mrs. Helmer. Either you have a very
 bad memory or you know very little of business. I shall be obliged to remind
 you of a few details.

Nora: What do you mean?

Krogstad: When your husband was ill, you came to me to borrow two hundred
 and fifty pounds.

Nora: I didn't know anyone else to go to.

Krogstad: I promised to get you that amount —

Nora: Yes, and you did so.

Krogstad: I promised to get you that amount, on certain conditions. Your mind
 was so taken up with your husband's illness, and you were so anxious to get
 the money for your journey, that you seem to have paid no attention to the
 conditions of our bargain. Therefore it will not be amiss if I remind you of
 them. Now, I promised to get the money on the security of a bond which I
 drew up.

Nora: Yes, and which I signed.

Krogstad: Good. But below your signature there were a few lines constituting your
 father a surety for the money; those lines your father should have signed.

Nora: Should? He did sign them.

Krogstad: I had left the date blank; that is to say, your father should himself have
 inserted the date on which he signed the paper. Do you remember that?

Nora: Yes, I think I remember —

Krogstad: Then I gave you the bond to send by post to your father. Is that not so?

Nora: Yes.

Krogstad: And you naturally did so at once, because five or six days afterwards
 you brought me the bond with your father's signature. And then I gave you
 the money.

Nora: Well, haven't I been paying it off regularly?

Krogstad: Fairly so, yes. But — to come back to the matter in hand — that must
 have been a very trying time for you, Mrs. Helmer.

Nora: It was, indeed.

Krogstad: Your father was very ill, wasn't he?

Nora: He was very near his end.

Krogstad: And he died soon afterwards?

Nora: Yes.

Krogstad: Tell me, Mrs. Helmer, can you by any chance remember what day your
 father died? — on what day of the month, I mean.

Nora: Papa died on the 29th of September.

Krogstad: That is correct; I have ascertained it for myself. And, as that is so, there
 is a discrepancy *(taking a paper from his pocket)* which I cannot account for.

Nora: What discrepancy? I don't know —

Krogstad: The discrepancy consists, Mrs. Helmer, in the fact that your father signed this bond three days after his death.

Nora: What do you mean? I don't understand —

Krogstad: Your father died on the 29th of September. But, look here; your father has dated his signature the 2nd of October. It is a discrepancy, isn't it? (*Nora is silent.*) Can you explain it to me? (*Nora is still silent.*) It is a remarkable thing, too, that the words "2nd of October," as well as the year, are not written in your father's handwriting but in one that I think I know. Well, of course it can be explained; your father may have forgotten to date his signature, and someone else may have dated it haphazard before they knew of his death. There is no harm in that. It all depends on the signature of the name; and *that* is genuine, I suppose, Mrs. Helmer? It was your father himself who signed his name here?

Nora (after a short pause, throws her head up and looks defiantly at him): No, it was not. It was I that wrote papa's name.

Krogstad: Are you aware that is a dangerous confession?

Nora: In what way? You shall have your money soon.

Krogstad: Let me ask you a question; why did you not send the paper to your father?

Nora: It was impossible; papa was so ill. If I had asked him for his signature, I should have had to tell him what the money was to be used for; and when he was so ill himself I couldn't tell him that my husband's life was in danger — it was impossible.

Krogstad: It would have been better for you if you had given up your trip abroad.

Nora: No, that was impossible. That trip was to save my husband's life; I couldn't give that up.

Krogstad: But did it never occur to you that you were committing a fraud on me?

Nora: I couldn't take that into account; I didn't trouble myself about you at all. I couldn't bear you, because you put so many heartless difficulties in my way, although you knew what a dangerous condition my husband was in.

Krogstad: Mrs. Helmer, you evidently do not realise clearly what it is that you have been guilty of. But I can assure you that my one false step, which lost me all my reputation, was nothing more or nothing worse than what you have done.

Nora: You? Do you ask me to believe that you were brave enough to run a risk to save your wife's life?

Krogstad: The law cares nothing about motives.

Nora: Then it must be a very foolish law.

Krogstad: Foolish or not, it is the law by which you will be judged, if I produce this paper in court.

Nora: I don't believe it. Is a daughter not to be allowed to spare her dying father anxiety and care? Is a wife not to be allowed to save her husband's life? I don't know much about law; but I am certain that there must be laws permitting such things as that. Have you no knowledge of such laws — you who are a lawyer? You must be a very poor lawyer, Mr. Krogstad.

Krogstad: Maybe. But matters of business — such business as you and I have had together — do you think I don't understand that? Very well. Do as you please. But let me tell you this — if I lose my position a second time, you shall lose yours with me. (*He bows, and goes out through the hall.*)

Nora (appears buried in thought for a short time, then tosses her head): Nonsense! Trying to frighten me like that! — I am not so silly as he thinks. (*Begins to busy herself putting the children's things in order.*) And yet — ? No, it's impossible! I did it for love's sake.

Children (in the doorway on the left): Mother, the stranger man has gone out through the gate.

Nora: Yes, dears, I know. But, don't tell anyone about the stranger man. Do you hear? Not even papa.

Children: No, mother; but will you come and play again?

Nora: No, no, — not now.

Children: But, mother, you promised us.

Nora: Yes, but I can't now. Run away in; I have such a lot to do. Run away in, my sweet little darlings. *(She gets them into the room by degrees and shuts the door on them; then sits down on the sofa, takes up a piece of needlework and sews a few stitches, but soon stops.)* No! *(Throws down the work, gets up, goes to the hall door and calls out.)* Helen! bring the Tree in. *(Goes to the table on the left, opens a drawer, and stops again.)* No, no! it is quite impossible!

Maid (coming in with the Tree): Where shall I put it, ma'am?

Nora: Here, in the middle of the floor.

Maid: Shall I get you anything else?

Nora: No, thank you. I have all I want. *(Exit Maid.)*

Nora (begins dressing the tree): A candle here — and flowers here — . The horrible man! It's all nonsense — there's nothing wrong. The Tree shall be splendid! I will do everything I can think of to please you, Torvald! — I will sing for you, dance for you — *(Helmer comes in with some papers under his arm.)* Oh! are you back already?

Helmer: Yes. Has anyone been here?

Nora: Here? No.

Helmer: That is strange. I saw Krogstad going out of the gate.

Nora: Did you? Oh yes, I forgot, Krogstad was here for a moment.

Helmer: Nora, I can see from your manner that he has been here begging you to say a good word for him.

Nora: Yes.

Helmer: And you were to appear to do it of your own accord; you were to conceal from me the fact of his having been here; didn't he beg that of you too?

Nora: Yes, Torvald, but —

Helmer: Nora, Nora, and you would be a party to that sort of thing? To have any talk with a man like that, and give him any sort of promise? And to tell me a lie into the bargain?

Nora: A lie — ?

Helmer: Didn't you tell me no one had been here? *(Shakes his finger at her.)* My little song-bird must never do that again. A song-bird must have a clean beak to chirp with — no false notes! *(Puts his arm around her waist.)* That is so, isn't it? Yes, I am sure it is. *(Lets her go.)* We will say no more about it. *(Sits down by the stove.)* How warm and snug it is here! *(Turns over his papers.)*

Nora (after a short pause, during which she busies herself with the Christmas Tree): Torvald!

Helmer: Yes.

Nora: I am looking forward tremendously to the fancy-dress ball at the Stenborgs' the day after to-morrow.

Helmer: And I am tremendously curious to see what you are going to surprise me with.

Nora: It was very silly of me to want to do that.

Helmer: What do you mean?

Nora: I can't hit upon anything that will do; everything I think of seems so silly and insignificant.

Helmer: Does my little Nora acknowledge that at last?

Nora (standing behind his chair with her arms on the back of it): Are you very busy, Torvald?

Helmer: Well —

Nora: What are all those papers?

Helmer: Bank business.

Nora: Already?

Helmer: I have got authority from the retiring manager to undertake the necessary changes in the staff and in the rearrangement of the work; and I must make use of the Christmas week for that, so as to have everything in order for the new year.

Nora: Then that was why this poor Krogstad —

Helmer: Hm!

Nora (leans against the back of his chair and strokes his hair): If you hadn't been so busy I should have asked you a tremendously big favour, Torvald.

Helmer: What is that? Tell me.

Nora: There is no one has such good taste as you. And I do so want to look nice at the fancy-dress ball. Torvald, couldn't you take me in hand and decide what I shall go as, and what sort of a dress I shall wear?

Helmer: Aha! so my obstinate little woman is obliged to get someone to come to her rescue?

Nora: Yes, Torvald, I can't get along a bit without your help.

Helmer: Very well, I will think it over, we shall manage to hit upon something.

Nora: That is nice of you. *(Goes to the Christmas Tree. A short pause.)* How pretty the red flowers look — . But, tell me, was it really something very bad that this Krogstad was guilty of?

Helmer: He forged someone's name. Have you any idea what that means?

Nora: Isn't it possible that he was driven to do it by necessity?

Helmer: Yes; or, as in so many cases, by imprudence. I am not so heartless as to condemn a man altogether because of a single false step of that kind.

Nora: No, you wouldn't, would you, Torvald?

Helmer: Many a man has been able to retrieve his character, if he has openly confessed his fault and taken his punishment.

Nora: Punishment —?

Helmer: But Krogstad did nothing of that sort; he got himself out of it by a cunning trick, and that is why he has gone under altogether.

Nora: But do you think it would —?

Helmer: Just think how a guilty man like that has to lie and play the hypocrite with every one, how he has to wear a mask in the presence of those near and dear to him, even before his own wife and children. And about the children — that is the most terrible part of it all, Nora.

Nora: How?

Helmer: Because such an atmosphere of lies infects and poisons the whole life of a home. Each breath the children take in such a house is full of the germs of evil.

Nora (coming nearer him): Are you sure of that?

Helmer: My dear, I have often seen it in the course of my life as a lawyer. Almost everyone who has gone to the bad early in life has had a deceitful mother.

Nora: Why do you only say — mother?

Helmer: It seems most commonly to be the mother's influence, though naturally a
  bad father's would have the same result. Every lawyer is familiar with the fact.
  This Krogstad, now, has been persistently poisoning his own children with
  lies and dissimulation; that is why I say he has lost all moral character. *(Holds
  out his hands to her.)* That is why my sweet little Nora must promise me not to
  plead his cause. Give me your hand on it. Come, come, what is this? Give me
  your hand. There now, that's settled. I assure you it would be quite impossible
  for me to work with him; I literally feel physically ill when I am in the company of such people.

*Nora (takes her hand out of his and goes to the opposite side of the Christmas
  Tree):* How hot it is in here; and I have such a lot to do.

Helmer (getting up and putting his papers in order): Yes, and I must try and read
  through some of these before dinner; and I must think about your costume,
  too. And it is just possible I may have something ready in gold paper to hang
  up on the Tree. *(Puts his hand on her head.)* My precious little singing-bird!
  (He goes into his room and shuts the door after him.)

Nora (after a pause, whispers): No, no — it isn't true. It's impossible; it must be
  impossible.

  The Nurse opens the door on the left.

Nurse: The little ones are begging so hard to be allowed to come in to mamma.

Nora: No, no, no! Don't let them come in to me! You stay with them, Anne.

Nurse: Very well, ma'am. *(Shuts the door.)*

Nora (pale with terror): Deprave my little children? Poison my home? *(A short
  pause. Then she tosses her head.)* It's not true. It can't possibly be true.

ACT II

THE SAME SCENE: *The Christmas Tree is in the corner by the piano, stripped of its
ornaments and with burnt-down candle-ends on its dishevelled branches. Nora's
cloak and hat are lying on the sofa. She is alone in the room, walking about uneasily.
She stops by the sofa and takes up her cloak.*

Nora (drops her cloak): Someone is coming now! *(Goes to the door and listens.)*
  No — it is no one. Of course, no one will come to-day, Christmas Day — nor
  to-morrow either. But, perhaps — *(opens the door and looks out).* No, nothing
  in the letter-box; it is quite empty. *(Comes forward.)* What rubbish! of course
  he can't be in earnest about it. Such a thing couldn't happen; it is impossible —
  I have three little children.

  Enter the Nurse from the room on the left, carrying a big cardboard box.

Nurse: At last I have found the box with the fancy dress.

Nora: Thanks; put it on the table.

Nurse (doing so): But it is very much in want of mending.

Nora: I should like to tear it into a hundred thousand pieces.

Nurse: What an idea! It can easily be put in order — just a little patience.

Nora: Yes, I will go and get Mrs. Linde to come and help me with it.

Nurse: What, out again? In this horrible weather? You will catch cold, ma'am, and
  make yourself ill.

Nora: Well, worse than that might happen. How are the children?

Nurse: The poor little souls are playing with their Christmas presents, but—

Nora: Do they ask much for me?

Nurse: You see, they are so accustomed to have their mamma with them.

Nora: Yes, but, nurse, I shall not be able to be so much with them now as I was before.

Nurse: Oh well, young children easily get accustomed to anything.

Nora: Do you think so? Do you think they would forget their mother if she went away altogether?

Nurse: Good heavens!—went away altogether?

Nora: Nurse, I want you to tell me something I have often wondered about—how could you have the heart to put your own child out among strangers?

Nurse: I was obliged to, if I wanted to be little Nora's nurse.

Nora: Yes, but how could you be willing to do it?

Nurse: What, when I was going to get such a good place by it? A poor girl who has got into trouble should be glad to. Besides, that wicked man didn't do a single thing for me.

Nora: But I suppose your daughter has quite forgotten you.

Nurse: No, indeed she hasn't. She wrote to me when she was confirmed, and when she was married.

Nora (putting her arms round her neck): Dear old Anne, you were a good mother to me when I was little.

Nurse: Little Nora, poor dear, had no other mother but me.

Nora: And if my little ones had no other mother, I am sure you would—What nonsense I am talking! *(Opens the box.)* Go in to them. Now I must—. You will see to-morrow how charming I shall look.

Nurse: I am sure there will be no one at the ball so charming as you, ma'am. *(Goes into the room on the left.)*

Nora (begins to unpack the box, but soon pushes it away from her): If only I dared go out. If only no one would come. If only I could be sure nothing would happen here in the meantime. Stuff and nonsense! No one will come. Only I mustn't think about it. I will brush my muff. What lovely, lovely gloves! Out of my thoughts, out of my thoughts! One, two, three, four, five, six—*(Screams.)* Ah! there is someone coming—. *(Makes a movement towards the door, but stands irresolute.)*

Enter Mrs. Linde from the hall, where she has taken off her cloak and hat.

Nora: Oh, it's you, Christine. There is no one else out there, is there? How good of you to come!

Mrs. Linde: I heard you were up asking for me.

Nora: Yes, I was passing by. As a matter of fact, it is something you could help me with. Let us sit down here on the sofa. Look here. To-morrow evening there is to be a fancy-dress ball at the Stenborgs', who live above us; and Torvald wants me to go as a Neapolitan fisher-girl, and dance the Tarantella that I learned at Capri.

Mrs. Linde: I see; you are going to keep up the character.

Nora: Yes, Torvald wants me to. Look, here is the dress; Torvald had it made for me there, but now it is all so torn, and I haven't any idea—

Mrs. Linde: We will easily put that right. It is only some of the trimming come unsewn here and there. Needle and thread? Now then, that's all we want.

Nora: It *is* nice of you.

Mrs. Linde (sewing): So you are going to be dressed up to-morrow, Nora. I will tell you what — I shall come in for a moment and see you in your fine feathers. But I have completely forgotten to thank you for a delightful evening yesterday.

Nora (gets up, and crosses the stage): Well, I don't think yesterday was as pleasant as usual. You ought to have come to town a little earlier, Christine. Certainly Torvald does understand how to make a house dainty and attractive.

Mrs. Linde: And so do you, it seems to me; you are not your father's daughter for nothing. But tell me, is Doctor Rank always as depressed as he was yesterday?

Nora: No; yesterday it was very noticeable. I must tell you that he suffers from a very dangerous disease. He has consumption of the spine, poor creature. His father was a horrible man who committed all sorts of excesses; and that is why his son was sickly from childhood, do you understand?

Mrs. Linde (dropping her sewing): But, my dearest Nora, how do you know anything about such things?

Nora (walking about): Pooh! When you have three children, you get visits now and then from — from married women, who know something of medical matters, and they talk about one thing and another.

Mrs. Linde (goes on sewing. A short silence): Does Doctor Rank come here everyday?

Nora: Everyday regularly. He is Torvald's most intimate friend, and a great friend of mine too. He is just like one of the family.

Mrs. Linde: But tell me this — is he perfectly sincere? I mean, isn't he the kind of man that is very anxious to make himself agreeable?

Nora: Not in the least. What makes you think that?

Mrs. Linde: When you introduced him to me yesterday, he declared he had often heard my name mentioned in this house; but afterwards I noticed that your husband hadn't the slightest idea who I was. So how could Doctor Rank — ?

Nora: That is quite right, Christine. Torvald is so absurdly fond of me that he wants me absolutely to himself, as he says. At first he used to seem almost jealous if I mentioned any of the dear folk at home, so naturally I gave up doing so. But I often talk about such things with Doctor Rank, because he likes hearing about them.

Mrs. Linde: Listen to me, Nora. You are still very like a child in many things, and I am older than you in many ways and have a little more experience. Let me tell you this — you ought to make an end of it with Doctor Rank.

Nora: What ought I to make an end of?

Mrs. Linde: Of two things, I think. Yesterday you talked some nonsense about a rich admirer who was to leave you money —

Nora: An admirer who doesn't exist, unfortunately! But what then?

Mrs. Linde: Is Doctor Rank a man of means?

Nora: Yes, he is.

Mrs. Linde: And has no one to provide for?

Nora: No, no one; but —

Mrs. Linde: And comes here everyday?

Nora: Yes, I told you so.

Mrs. Linde: But how can this well-bred man be so tactless?

Nora: I don't understand you at all.

Mrs. Linde: Don't prevaricate, Nora. Do you suppose I don't guess who lent you the two hundred and fifty pounds?

Nora: Are you out of your senses? How can you think of such a thing! A friend of ours, who comes here everyday! Do you realise what a horribly painful position that would be?

Mrs. Linde: Then it really isn't he?

Nora: No, certainly not. It would never have entered into my head for a moment. Besides, he had no money to lend then; he came into his money afterwards.

Mrs. Linde: Well, I think that was lucky for you, my dear Nora.

Nora: No, it would never have come into my head to ask Doctor Rank. Although I am quite sure that if I had asked him —

Mrs. Linde: But of course you won't.

Nora: Of course not. I have no reason to think it could possibly be necessary. But I am quite sure that if I told Doctor Rank —

Mrs. Linde: Behind your husband's back?

Nora: I must make an end of it with the other one, and that will be behind his back too. I *must* make an end of it with him.

Mrs. Linde: Yes, that is what I told you yesterday, but —

Nora (walking up and down): A man can put a thing like that straight much easier than a woman —

Mrs. Linde: One's husband, yes.

Nora: Nonsense! *(Standing still.)* When you pay off a debt you get your bond back, don't you?

Mrs. Linde: Yes, as a matter of course.

Nora: And can tear it into a hundred thousand pieces, and burn it up — the nasty dirty paper!

Mrs. Linde (looks hard at her, lays down her sewing and gets up slowly): Nora, you are concealing something from me.

Nora: Do I look as if I were?

Mrs. Linde: Something has happened to you since yesterday morning. Nora, what is it?

Nora (going nearer to her): Christine! *(Listens.)* Hush! there's Torvald come home. Do you mind going in to the children for the present? Torvald can't bear to see dressmaking going on. Let Anne help you.

Mrs. Linde (gathering some of the things together): Certainly — but I am not going away from here until we have had it out with one another. *(She goes into the room on the left, as Helmer comes in from the hall.)*

Nora (going up to Helmer): I have wanted you so much, Torvald dear.

Helmer: Was that the dressmaker?

Nora: No, it was Christine; she is helping me to put my dress in order. You will see I shall look quite smart.

Helmer: Wasn't that a happy thought of mine, now?

Nora: Splendid! But don't you think it is nice of me, too, to do as you wish?

Helmer: Nice? — because you do as your husband wishes? Well, well, you little rogue, I am sure you did not mean it in that way. But I am not going to disturb you; you will want to be trying on your dress, I expect.

Nora: I suppose you are going to work.

Helmer: Yes. *(Shows her a bundle of papers.)* Look at that. I have just been into the bank. *(Turns to go into his room.)*

Nora: Torvald.

Helmer: Yes.

Nora: If your little squirrel were to ask you for something very, very prettily —?

Helmer: What then?

Nora: Would you do it?

Helmer: I should like to hear what it is, first.

Nora: Your squirrel would run about and do all her tricks if you would be nice, and do what she wants.

Helmer: Speak plainly.

Nora: Your skylark would chirp about in every room, with her song rising and falling—

Helmer: Well, my skylark does that anyhow.

Nora: I would play the fairy and dance for you in the moonlight, Torvald.

Helmer: Nora—you surely don't mean that request you made to me this morning?

Nora (going near him): Yes, Torvald, I beg you so earnestly—

Helmer: Have you really the courage to open up that question again?

Nora: Yes, dear, you *must* do as I ask; you *must* let Krogstad keep his post in the bank.

Helmer: My dear Nora, it is his post that I have arranged Mrs. Linde shall have.

Nora: Yes, you have been awfully kind about that; but you could just as well dismiss some other clerk instead of Krogstad.

Helmer: This is simply incredible obstinacy! Because you chose to give him a thoughtless promise that you would speak for him, I am expected to—

Nora: That isn't the reason, Torvald. It is for your own sake. This fellow writes in the most scurrilous newspapers; you have told me so yourself. He can do you an unspeakable amount of harm. I am frightened to death of him—

Helmer: Ah, I understand; it is recollections of the past that scare you.

Nora: What do you mean?

Helmer: Naturally you are thinking of your father.

Nora: Yes—yes, of course. Just recall to your mind what these malicious creatures wrote in the papers about papa, and how horribly they slandered him. I believe they would have procured his dismissal if the Department had not sent you over to inquire into it, and if you had not been so kindly disposed and helpful to him.

Helmer: My little Nora, there is an important difference between your father and me. Your father's reputation as a public official was not above suspicion. Mine is, and I hope it will continue to be so, as long as I hold my office.

Nora: You never can tell what mischief these men may contrive. We ought to be so well off, so snug and happy here in our peaceful home, and have no cares— you and I and the children, Torvald! That is why I beg you so earnestly—

Helmer: And it is just by interceding for him that you make it impossible for me to keep him. It is already known at the Bank that I mean to dismiss Krogstad. Is it to get about now that the new manager has changed his mind at his wife's bidding—

Nora: And what if it did?

Helmer: Of course!—if only this obstinate little person can get her way! Do you suppose I am going to make myself ridiculous before my whole staff, to let people think that I am a man to be swayed by all sorts of outside influence? I should very soon feel the consequences of it, I can tell you! And besides, there is one thing that makes it quite impossible for me to have Krogstad in the Bank as long as I am manager.

Nora: Whatever is that?

Helmer: His moral failings I might perhaps have overlooked, if necessary—

Nora: Yes, you could — couldn't you?

Helmer: And I hear he is a good worker, too. But I knew him when we were boys. It was one of those rash friendships that so often prove an incubus in afterlife. I may as well tell you plainly, we were once on very intimate terms with one another. But this tactless fellow lays no restraint on himself when other people are present. On the contrary, he thinks it gives him the right to adopt a familiar tone with me, and every minute it is "I say, Helmer, old fellow!" and that sort of thing. I assure you it is extremely painful for me. He would make my position in the Bank intolerable.

Nora: Torvald, I don't believe you mean that.

Helmer: Don't you? Why not?

Nora: Because it is such a narrow-minded way of looking at things.

Helmer: What are you saying? Narrow-minded? Do you think I am narrow-minded?

Nora: No, just the opposite, dear — and it is exactly for that reason.

Helmer: It's the same thing. You say my point of view is narrow-minded, so I must be so too. Narrow-minded! Very well — I must put an end to this. *(Goes to the hall door and calls.)* Helen!

Nora: What are you going to do?

Helmer (looking among his papers): Settle it. *(Enter Maid.)* Look here; take this letter and go downstairs with it at once. Find a messenger and tell him to deliver it, and be quick. The address is on it, and here is the money.

Maid: Very well, sir. *(Exit with the letter.)*

Helmer (putting his papers together): Now then, little Miss Obstinate.

Nora (breathlessly): Torvald — what was that letter?

Helmer: Krogstad's dismissal.

Nora: Call her back, Torvald! There is still time. Oh Torvald, call her back! Do it for my sake — for your own sake — for the children's sake! Do you hear me, Torvald? Call her back! You don't know what that letter can bring upon us.

Helmer: It's too late.

Nora: Yes, it's too late.

Helmer: My dear Nora, I can forgive the anxiety you are in, although really it is an insult to me. It is, indeed. Isn't it an insult to think that I should be afraid of a starving quill-driver's vengeance? But I forgive you nevertheless, because it is such eloquent witness to your great love for me. *(Takes her in his arms.)* And that is as it should be, my own darling Nora. Come what will, you may be sure I shall have both courage and strength if they be needed. You will see I am man enough to take everything upon myself.

Nora (in a horror-stricken voice): What do you mean by that?

Helmer: Everything, I say —

Nora (recovering herself): You will never have to do that.

Helmer: That's right. Well, we will share it, Nora, as man and wife should. That is how it shall be. *(Caressing her.)* Are you content now? There! there! — not these frightened dove's eyes! The whole thing is only the wildest fancy! — Now, you must go and play through the Tarantella and practise with your tambourine. I shall go into the inner office and shut the door, and I shall hear nothing; you can make as much noise as you please. *(Turns back at the door.)* And when Rank comes, tell him where he will find me. *(Nods to her, takes his papers and goes into his room, and shuts the door after him.)*

Nora (bewildered with anxiety, stands as if rooted to the spot, and whispers): He was capable of doing it. He will do it. He will do it in spite of everything. — No, not that! Never, never! Anything rather than that! Oh, for some help, some way out of it! *(The door-bell rings.)* Doctor Rank! Anything rather than that — anything, whatever it is! *(She puts her hands over her face, pulls herself together, goes to the door and opens it. Rank is standing without, hanging up his coat. During the following dialogue it begins to grow dark.)*

Nora: Good-day, Doctor Rank. I knew your ring. But you mustn't go in to Torvald now; I think he is busy with something.

Rank: And you?

Nora (brings him in and shuts the door after him): Oh, you know very well I always have time for you.

Rank: Thank you. I shall make use of as much of it as I can.

Nora: What do you mean by that? As much of it as you can?

Rank: Well, does that alarm you?

Nora: It was such a strange way of putting it. Is anything likely to happen?

Rank: Nothing but what I have long been prepared for. But I certainly didn't expect it to happen so soon.

Nora (gripping him by the arm): What have you found out? Doctor Rank, you must tell me.

Rank (sitting down by the stove): It is all up with me. And it can't be helped.

Nora (with a sigh of relief): Is it about yourself?

Rank: Who else? It is no use lying to one's self. I am the most wretched of all my patients, Mrs. Helmer. Lately I have been taking stock of my internal economy. Bankrupt! Probably within a month I shall lie rotting in the churchyard.

Nora: What an ugly thing to say!

Rank: The thing itself is cursedly ugly, and the worst of it is that I shall have to face so much more that is ugly before that. I shall only make one more examination of myself; when I have done that, I shall know pretty certainly when it will be that the horrors of dissolution will begin. There is something I want to tell you. Helmer's refined nature gives him an unconquerable disgust at everything that is ugly; I won't have him in my sick-room.

Nora: Oh, but, Doctor Rank —

Rank: I won't have him there. Not on any account. I bar my door to him. As soon as I am quite certain that the worst has come, I shall send you my card with a black cross on it, and then you will know that the loathsome end has begun.

Nora: You are quite absurd to-day. And I wanted you so much to be in a really good humour.

Rank: With death stalking beside me? — To have to pay this penalty for another man's sin? Is there any justice in that? And in every single family, in one way or another, some such inexorable retribution is being exacted —

Nora (putting her hands over her ears): Rubbish! Do talk of something cheerful.

Rank: Oh, it's a mere laughing matter, the whole thing. My poor innocent spine has to suffer for my father's youthful amusements.

Nora (sitting at the table on the left): I suppose you mean that he was too partial to asparagus and pâté de foie gras, don't you?

Rank: Yes, and to truffles.

Nora: Truffles, yes. And oysters too, I suppose?

Rank: Oysters, of course, that goes without saying.

Nora: And heaps of port and champagne. It is sad that all these nice things should take their revenge on our bones.

Rank: Especially that they should revenge themselves on the unlucky bones of those who have not had the satisfaction of enjoying them.

Nora: Yes, that's the saddest part of it all.

Rank (with a searching look at her): Hm! —

Nora (after a short pause): Why did you smile?

Rank: No, it was you that laughed.

Nora: No, it was you that smiled, Doctor Rank!

Rank (rising): You are a greater rascal than I thought.

Nora: I am in a silly mood to-day.

Rank: So it seems.

Nora (putting her hands on his shoulders): Dear, dear Doctor Rank, death mustn't take you away from Torvald and me.

Rank: It is a loss you would easily recover from. Those who are gone are soon forgotten.

Nora (looking at him anxiously): Do you believe that?

Rank: People form new ties, and then —

Nora: Who will form new ties?

Rank: Both you and Helmer, when I am gone. You yourself are already on the high road to it, I think. What did that Mrs. Linde want here last night?

Nora: Oho! — you don't mean to say you are jealous of poor Christine?

Rank: Yes, I am. She will be my successor in this house. When I am done for, this woman will —

Nora: Hush! don't speak so loud. She is in that room.

Rank: To-day again. There, you see.

Nora: She has only come to sew my dress for me. Bless my soul, how unreasonable you are! *(Sits down on the sofa.)* Be nice now, Doctor Rank, and to-morrow you will see how beautifully I shall dance, and you can imagine I am doing it all for you — and for Torvald too, of course. *(Takes various things out of the box.)* Doctor Rank, come and sit down here, and I will show you something.

Rank (sitting down): What is it?

Nora: Just look at those!

Rank: Silk stockings.

Nora: Flesh-coloured. Aren't they lovely? It is so dark here now, but to-morrow —. No, no, no! you must only look at the feet. Oh well, you may have leave to look at the legs too.

Rank: Hm! —

Nora: Why are you looking so critical? Don't you think they will fit me?

Rank: I have no means of forming an opinion about that.

Nora (looks at him for a moment): For shame! *(Hits him lightly on the ear with the stockings.)* That's to punish you. *(Folds them up again.)*

Rank: And what other nice things am I to be allowed to see?

Nora: Not a single thing more, for being so naughty. *(She looks among the things, humming to herself.)*

Rank (after a short silence): When I am sitting here, talking to you as intimately as this, I cannot imagine for a moment what would have become of me if I had never come into this house.

Nora (smiling): I believe you do feel thoroughly at home with us.

Rank (in a lower voice, looking straight in front of him): And to be obliged to leave it all —

Nora: Nonsense, you are not going to leave it.

Rank (as before): And not be able to leave behind one the slightest token of one's gratitude, scarcely even a fleeting regret — nothing but an empty place which the first comer can fill as well as any other.

Nora: And if I asked you now for a —? No!

Rank: For what?

Nora: For a big proof of your friendship —

Rank: Yes, yes!

Nora: I mean a tremendously big favour.

Rank: Would you really make me so happy for once?

Nora: Ah, but you don't know what it is yet.

Rank: No — but tell me.

Nora: I really can't, Doctor Rank. It is something out of all reason; it means advice, and help, and a favour —

Rank: The bigger a thing it is the better. I can't conceive what it is you mean. Do tell me. Haven't I your confidence?

Nora: More than anyone else. I know you are my truest and best friend, and so I will tell you what it is. Well, Doctor Rank, it is something you must help me to prevent. You know how devotedly, how inexpressibly deeply Torvald loves me; he would never for a moment hesitate to give his life for me.

Rank (leaning towards her): Nora — do you think he is the only one —?

Nora (with a slight start): The only one —?

Rank: The only one who would gladly give his life for your sake.

Nora (sadly): Is that it?

Rank: I was determined you should know it before I went away, and there will never be a better opportunity than this. Now you know it, Nora. And now you know, too, that you can trust me as you would trust no one else.

Nora (rises, deliberately and quietly): Let me pass.

Rank (makes room for her to pass him, but sits still): Nora!

Nora (at the hall door): Helen, bring in the lamp. *(Goes over to the stove.)* Dear Doctor Rank, that was really horrid of you.

Rank: To have loved you as much as anyone else does? Was that horrid?

Nora: No, but to go and tell me so. There was really no need —

Rank: What do you mean? Did you know —? *(Maid enters with lamp, puts it down on the table, and goes out.)* Nora — Mrs. Helmer — tell me, had you any idea of this?

Nora: Oh, how do I know whether I had or whether I hadn't? I really can't tell you — To think you could be so clumsy, Doctor Rank! We were getting on so nicely.

Rank: Well, at all events you know now that you can command me, body and soul. So won't you speak out?

Nora (looking at him): After what happened?

Rank: I beg you to let me know what it is.

Nora: I can't tell you anything now.

Rank: Yes, yes. You mustn't punish me in that way. Let me have permission to do for you whatever a man may do.

Nora: You can do nothing for me now. Besides, I really don't need any help at all. You will find that the whole thing is merely fancy on my part. It really is so — of course it is! *(Sits down in the rocking-chair, and looks at him with a smile.)* You are a nice sort of man, Doctor Rank! — don't you feel ashamed of yourself, now the lamp has come?

Rank: Not a bit. But perhaps I had better go — for ever?

Nora: No, indeed, you shall not. Of course you must come here just as before. You know very well Torvald can't do without you.

Rank: Yes, but you?

Nora: Oh, I am always tremendously pleased when you come.

Rank: It is just that, that put me on the wrong track. You are a riddle to me. I have often thought that you would almost as soon be in my company as in Helmer's.

Nora: Yes — you see there are some people one loves best, and others whom one would almost always rather have as companions.

Rank: Yes, there is something in that.

Nora: When I was at home, of course I loved papa best. But I always thought it tremendous fun if I could steal down into the maids' room, because they never moralised at all, and talked to each other about such entertaining things.

Rank: I see — it is *their* place I have taken.

Nora (jumping up and going to him): Oh, dear, nice Doctor Rank, I never meant that at all. But surely you can understand that being with Torvald is a little like being with papa —

Enter Maid from the hall.

Maid: If you please, ma'am. *(Whispers and hands her a card.)*

Nora (glancing at the card): Oh! *(Puts it in her pocket.)*

Rank: Is there anything wrong?

Nora: No, no, not in the least. It is only something — it is my new dress —

Rank: What? Your dress is lying there.

Nora: Oh, yes, that one; but this is another. I ordered it. Torvald mustn't know about it —

Rank: Oho! Then that was the great secret.

Nora: Of course. Just go in to him; he is sitting in the inner room. Keep him as long as —

Rank: Make your mind easy; I won't let him escape. *(Goes into Helmer's room.)*

Nora (to the Maid): And he is standing waiting in the kitchen?

Maid: Yes; he came up the back stairs.

Nora: But didn't you tell him no one was in?

Maid: Yes, but it was no good.

Nora: He won't go away?

Maid: No; he says he won't until he has seen you, ma'am.

Nora: Well, let him come in — but quietly. Helen, you mustn't say anything about it to anyone. It is a surprise for my husband.

Maid: Yes, ma'am, I quite understand. *(Exit.)*

Nora: This dreadful thing is going to happen! It will happen in spite of me! No, no, no, it can't happen — it shan't happen! *(She bolts the door of Helmer's room. The Maid opens the hall door for Krogstad and shuts it after him. He is wearing a fur coat, high boots and a fur cap.)*

Nora (advancing towards him): Speak low — my husband is at home.

Krogstad: No matter about that.

Nora: What do you want of me?

Krogstad: An explanation of something.

Nora: Make haste then. What is it?

Krogstad: You know, I suppose, that I have got my dismissal.

Nora: I couldn't prevent it, Mr. Krogstad. I fought as hard as I could on your side, but it was no good.

Krogstad: Does your husband love you so little, then? He knows what I can expose you to, and yet he ventures —

Nora: How can you suppose that he has any knowledge of the sort?

Krogstad: I didn't suppose so at all. It would not be the least like our dear Torvald Helmer to show so much courage —

Nora: Mr. Krogstad, a little respect for my husband, please.

Krogstad: Certainly — all the respect he deserves. But since you have kept the matter so carefully to yourself, I make bold to suppose that you have a little clearer idea, than you had yesterday, of what it actually is that you have done?

Nora: More than you could ever teach me.

Krogstad: Yes, such a bad lawyer as I am.

Nora: What is it you want of me?

Krogstad: Only to see how you were, Mrs. Helmer. I have been thinking about you all day long. A mere cashier, a quill-driver, a — well, a man like me — even he has a little of what is called feeling, you know.

Nora: Show it, then; think of my little children.

Krogstad: Have you and your husband thought of mine? But never mind about that. I only wanted to tell you that you need not take this matter too seriously. In the first place there will be no accusation made on my part.

Nora: No, of course not; I was sure of that.

Krogstad: The whole thing can be arranged amicably; there is no reason why anyone should know anything about it. It will remain a secret between us three.

Nora: My husband must never get to know anything about it.

Krogstad: How will you be able to prevent it? Am I to understand that you can pay the balance that is owing?

Nora: No, not just at present.

Krogstad: Or perhaps that you have some expedient for raising the money soon?

Nora: No expedient that I mean to make use of.

Krogstad: Well, in any case, it would have been of no use to you now. If you stood there with ever so much money in your hand, I would never part with your bond.

Nora: Tell me what purpose you mean to put it to.

Krogstad: I shall only preserve it — keep it in my possession. No one who is not concerned in the matter shall have the slightest hint of it. So that if the thought of it has driven you to any desperate resolution —

Nora: It has.

Krogstad: If you had it in your mind to run away from your home —

Nora: I had.

Krogstad: Or even something worse —

Nora: How could you know that?

Krogstad: Give up the idea.

Nora: How did you know I had thought of *that*?

Krogstad: Most of us think of that at first. I did, too — but I hadn't the courage.

Nora (faintly): No more had I.

Krogstad (in a tone of relief): No, that's it, isn't it — you hadn't the courage either?

Nora: No, I haven't — I haven't.

Krogstad: Besides, it would have been a great piece of folly. Once the first storm at home is over — . I have a letter for your husband in my pocket.

Nora: Telling him everything?

Krogstad: In as lenient a manner as I possibly could.

Nora (quickly): He mustn't get the letter. Tear it up. I will find some means of getting money.

Krogstad: Excuse me, Mrs. Helmer, but I think I told you just now —

Nora: I am not speaking of what I owe you. Tell me what sum you are asking my husband for, and I will get the money.

Krogstad: I am not asking your husband for a penny.

Nora: What do you want, then?

Krogstad: I will tell you. I want to rehabilitate myself, Mrs. Helmer; I want to get on; and in that your husband must help me. For the last year and a half I have not had a hand in anything dishonourable, and all that time I have been struggling in most restricted circumstances. I was content to work my way up step by step. Now I am turned out, and I am not going to be satisfied with merely being taken into favour again. I want to get on, I tell you. I want to get into the Bank again, in a higher position. Your husband must make a place for me —

Nora: That he will never do!

Krogstad: He will; I know him; he dare not protest. And as soon as I am in there again with him, then you will see! Within a year I shall be the manager's right hand. It will be Nils Krogstad and not Torvald Helmer who manages the Bank.

Nora: That's a thing you will never see!

Krogstad: Do you mean that you will — ?

Nora: I have courage enough for it now.

Krogstad: Oh, you can't frighten me. A fine, spoilt lady like you —

Nora: You will see, you will see.

Krogstad: Under the ice, perhaps? Down into the cold, coal-black water? And then, in the spring, to float up to the surface, all horrible and unrecognisable, with your hair fallen out —

Nora: You can't frighten me.

Krogstad: Nor you me. People don't do such things, Mrs. Helmer. Besides, what use would it be? I should have him completely in my power all the same.

Nora: Afterwards? When I am no longer —

Krogstad: Have you forgotten that it is I who have the keeping of your reputation? *(Nora stands speechlessly looking at him.)* Well, now, I have warned you. Do not do anything foolish. When Helmer has had my letter, I shall expect a message from him. And be sure you remember that it is your husband himself who has forced me into such ways as this again. I will never forgive him for that. Good-bye, Mrs. Helmer. *(Exit through the hall.)*

Nora (goes to the hall door, opens it slightly and listens): He is going. He is not putting the letter in the box. Oh no, no! that's impossible! *(Opens the door by degrees.)* What is that? He is standing outside. He is not going downstairs. Is he hesitating? Can he — ? *(A letter drops into the box; then Krogstad's footsteps are heard, till they die away as he goes downstairs. Nora utters a stifled cry, and runs across the room to the table by the sofa. A short pause.)*

Nora: In the letter-box. *(Steals across to the hall door.)* There it lies — Torvald, Torvald, there is no hope for us now!

Mrs. Linde comes in from the room on the left, carrying the dress.

Mrs. Linde: There, I can't see anything more to mend now. Would you like to try it on — ?

Nora (in a hoarse whisper): Christine, come here.

Mrs. Linde (throwing the dress down on the sofa): What is the matter with you? You look so agitated!

Nora: Come here. Do you see that letter? There, look — you can see it through the glass in the letter-box.

Mrs. Linde: Yes, I see it.

Nora: That letter is from Krogstad.

Mrs. Linde: Nora — it was Krogstad who lent you the money!

Nora: Yes, and now Torvald will know all about it.

Mrs. Linde: Believe me, Nora, that's the best thing for both of you.

Nora: You don't know all. I forged a name.

Mrs. Linde: Good heavens — !

Nora: I only want to say this to you, Christine — you must be my witness.

Mrs. Linde: Your witness? What do you mean? What am I to — ?

Nora: If I should go out of my mind — and it might easily happen —

Mrs. Linde: Nora!

Nora: Or if anything else should happen to me — anything, for instance, that might prevent my being here —

Mrs. Linde: Nora! Nora! you are quite out of your mind.

Nora: And if it should happen that there were some one who wanted to take all the responsibility, all the blame, you understand —

Mrs. Linde: Yes, yes — but how can you suppose — ?

Nora: Then you must be my witness, that it is not true, Christine. I am not out of my mind at all! I am in my right senses now, and I tell you no one else has known anything about it; I, and I alone, did the whole thing. Remember that.

Mrs. Linde: I will, indeed. But I don't understand all this.

Nora: How should you understand it? A wonderful thing is going to happen!

Mrs. Linde: A wonderful thing?

Nora: Yes, a wonderful thing! — But it is so terrible, Christine; it *mustn't* happen, not for all the world.

Mrs. Linde: I will go at once and see Krogstad.

Nora: Don't go to him; he will do you some harm.

Mrs. Linde: There was a time when he would gladly do anything for my sake.

Nora: He?

Mrs. Linde: Where does he live?

Nora: How should I know — ? Yes *(feeling in her pocket),* here is his card. But the letter, the letter — !

Helmer (calls from his room, knocking at the door): Nora!

Nora (cries out anxiously): Oh, what's that? What do you want?

Helmer: Don't be so frightened. We are not coming in; you have locked the door. Are you trying on your dress?

Nora: Yes, that's it. I look so nice, Torvald.

Mrs. Linde (who has read the card): I see he lives at the corner here.

Nora: Yes, but it's no use. It is hopeless. The letter is lying there in the box.

Mrs. Linde: And your husband keeps the key?

Nora: Yes, always.

Mrs. Linde: Krogstad must ask for his letter back unread, he must find some pretence —

Nora: But it is just at this time that Torvald generally —

Mrs. Linde: You must delay him. Go in to him in the meantime. I will come back as soon as I can. *(She goes out hurriedly through the hall door.)*

Nora (goes to Helmer's door, opens it and peeps in): Torvald!

Helmer (from the inner room): Well? May I venture at last to come into my own room again? Come along, Rank, now you will see — *(Halting in the doorway.)* But what is this?

Nora: What is what, dear?

Helmer: Rank led me to expect a splendid transformation.

Rank (in the doorway): I understood so, but evidently I was mistaken.

Nora: Yes, nobody is to have the chance of admiring me in my dress until to-morrow.

Helmer: But, my dear Nora, you look so worn out. Have you been practising too much?

Nora: No, I have not practised at all.

Helmer: But you will need to —

Nora: Yes, indeed I shall, Torvald. But I can't get on a bit without you to help me; I have absolutely forgotten the whole thing.

Helmer: Oh, we will soon work it up again.

Nora: Yes, help me, Torvald. Promise that you will! I am so nervous about it — all the people —. You must give yourself up to me entirely this evening. Not the tiniest bit of business — you mustn't even take a pen in your hand. Will you promise, Torvald dear?

Helmer: I promise. This evening I will be wholly and absolutely at your service, you helpless little mortal. Ah, by the way, first of all I will just — *(Goes towards the hall door.)*

Nora: What are you going to do there?

Helmer: Only see if any letters have come.

Nora: No, no! don't do that, Torvald!

Helmer: Why not?

Nora: Torvald, please don't. There is nothing there.

Helmer: Well, let me look. *(Turns to go to the letter-box. Nora, at the piano, plays the first bars of the Tarantella. Helmer stops in the doorway.)* Aha!

Nora: I can't dance tomorrow if I don't practise with you.

Helmer (going up to her): Are you really so afraid of it, dear?

Nora: Yes, so dreadfully afraid of it. Let me practise at once; there is time now, before we go to dinner. Sit down and play for me, Torvald dear; criticise me, and correct me as you play.

Helmer: With great pleasure, if you wish me to. *(Sits down at the piano.)*

Nora (takes out of the box a tambourine and a long variegated shawl. She hastily drapes the shawl round her. Then she springs to the front of the stage and calls out): Now play for me! I am going to dance!

Helmer plays and Nora dances. Rank stands by the piano behind Helmer, and looks on.

Helmer (as he plays): Slower, slower!

Nora: I can't do it any other way.

Helmer: Not so violently, Nora!

Nora: This is the way.

Helmer (stops playing): No, no — that is not a bit right.

Nora (laughing and swinging the tambourine): Didn't I tell you so?

Rank: Let me play for her.

Helmer (getting up): Yes, do. I can correct her better then.

Rank sits down at the piano and plays. Nora dances more and more wildly. Helmer has taken up a position beside the stove, and during her dance gives her frequent instructions. She does not seem to hear him; her hair comes down and falls over her shoulders; she pays no attention to it, but goes on dancing. Enter Mrs. Linde.

Mrs. Linde (standing as if spell-bound in the doorway): Oh! —

Nora (as she dances): Such fun, Christine!

Helmer: My dear darling Nora, you are dancing as if your life depended on it.

Nora: So it does.

Helmer: Stop, Rank; this is sheer madness. Stop, I tell you! *(Rank stops playing, and Nora suddenly stands still. Helmer goes up to her.)* I could never have believed it. You have forgotten everything I taught you.

Nora (throwing away the tambourine): There, you see.

Helmer: You will want a lot of coaching.

Nora: Yes, you see how much I need it. You must coach me up to the last minute. Promise me that, Torvald!

Helmer: You can depend on me.

Nora: You must not think of anything but me, either to-day or to-morrow; you mustn't open a single letter — not even open the letter-box —

Helmer: Ah, you are still afraid of that fellow —

Nora: Yes, indeed I am.

Helmer: Nora, I can tell from your looks that there is a letter from him lying there.

Nora: I don't know; I think there is; but you must not read anything of that kind now. Nothing horrid must come between us until this is all over.

Rank (whispers to Helmer): You mustn't contradict her.

Helmer (taking her in his arms): The child shall have her way. But to-morrow night, after you have danced —

Nora: Then you will be free. *(The Maid appears in the doorway to the right.)*

Maid: Dinner is served, ma'am.

Nora: We will have champagne, Helen.

Maid: Very good, ma'am.   [*Exit.*]

Helmer: Hullo! — are we going to have a banquet?

Nora: Yes, a champagne banquet until the small hours. *(Calls out.)* And a few macaroons, Helen — lots, just for once!

Helmer: Come, come, don't be so wild and nervous. Be my own little skylark, as you used.

Nora: Yes, dear, I will. But go in now and you too, Doctor Rank. Christine, you must help me to do up my hair.

Rank (whispers to Helmer as they go out): I suppose there is nothing — she is not expecting anything?

Helmer: Far from it, my dear fellow; it is simply nothing more than this childish nervousness I was telling you of. *(They go into the right-hand room.)*

Nora: Well!

Mrs. Linde: Gone out of town.

Nora: I could tell from your face.

Mrs. Linde: He is coming home to-morrow evening. I wrote a note for him.

Nora: You should have let it alone; you must prevent nothing. After all, it is splendid to be waiting for a wonderful thing to happen.

Mrs. Linde: What is it that you are waiting for?

Nora: Oh, you wouldn't understand. Go in to them, I will come in a moment. *(Mrs. Linde goes into the dining-room. Nora stands still for a little while, as if to compose herself. Then she looks at her watch.)* Five o'clock. Seven hours until midnight; and then four-and-twenty hours until the next midnight. Then the Tarantella will be over. Twenty-four and seven? Thirty-one hours to live.

Helmer (from the doorway on the right): Where's my little skylark?

Nora (going to him with her arms outstretched): Here she is!

ACT III

THE SAME SCENE: *The table has been placed in the middle of the stage, with chairs round it. A lamp is burning on the table. The door into the hall stands open. Dance music is heard in the room above. Mrs. Linde is sitting at the table idly turning over the leaves of a book; she tries to read, but does not seem able to collect her thoughts. Every now and then she listens intently for a sound at the outer door.*

Mrs. Linde (looking at her watch): Not yet — and the time is nearly up. If only he does not —. (*Listens again.*) Ah, there he is. (*Goes into the hall and opens the outer door carefully. Light footsteps are heard on the stairs. She whispers.*) Come in. There is no one here.

Krogstad (in the doorway): I found a note from you at home. What does this mean?

Mrs. Linde: It is absolutely necessary that I should have a talk with you.

Krogstad: Really? And is it absolutely necessary that it should be here?

Mrs. Linde: It is impossible where I live; there is no private entrance to my rooms. Come in; we are quite alone. The maid is asleep, and the Helmers are at the dance upstairs.

Krogstad (coming into the room): Are the Helmers really at a dance to-night?

Mrs. Linde: Yes, why not?

Krogstad: Certainly — why not?

Mrs. Linde: Now, Nils, let us have a talk.

Krogstad: Can we two have anything to talk about?

Mrs. Linde: We have a great deal to talk about.

Krogstad: I shouldn't have thought so.

Mrs. Linde: No, you have never properly understood me.

Krogstad: Was there anything else to understand except what was obvious to all the world — a heartless woman jilts a man when a more lucrative chance turns up?

Mrs. Linde: Do you believe I am as absolutely heartless as all that? And do you believe that I did it with a light heart?

Krogstad: Didn't you?

Mrs. Linde: Nils, did you really think that?

Krogstad: If it were as you say, why did you write to me as you did at the time?

Mrs. Linde: I could do nothing else. As I had to break with you, it was my duty also to put an end to all that you felt for me.

Krogstad (wringing his hands): So that was it. And all this — only for the sake of money!

Mrs. Linde: You must not forget that I had a helpless mother and two little brothers. We couldn't wait for you, Nils; your prospects seemed hopeless then.

Krogstad: That may be so, but you had no right to throw me over for anyone else's sake.

Mrs. Linde: Indeed I don't know. Many a time did I ask myself if I had the right to do it.

Krogstad (more gently): When I lost you, it was as if all the solid ground went from under my feet. Look at me now — I am a shipwrecked man clinging to a bit of wreckage.

Mrs. Linde: But help may be near.

Krogstad: It *was* near; but then you came and stood in my way.

Mrs. Linde: Unintentionally, Nils. It was only to-day that I learned it was your place I was going to take in the Bank.

Krogstad: I believe you, if you say so. But now that you know it, are you not going to give it up to me?

Mrs. Linde: No, because that would not benefit you in the least.

Krogstad: Oh, benefit, benefit — I would have done it whether or no.

Mrs. Linde: I have learned to act prudently. Life, and hard, bitter necessity have taught me that.

Krogstad: And life has taught me not to believe in fine speeches.

Mrs. Linde: Then life has taught you something very reasonable. But deeds you must believe in?

Krogstad: What do you mean by that?

Mrs. Linde: You said you were like a shipwrecked man clinging to some wreckage.

Krogstad: I had good reason to say so.

Mrs. Linde: Well, I am like a shipwrecked woman clinging to some wreckage — no one to mourn for, no one to care for.

Krogstad: It was your own choice.

Mrs. Linde: There was no other choice — then.

Krogstad: Well, what now?

Mrs. Linde: Nils, how would it be if we two shipwrecked people could join forces?

Krogstad: What are you saying?

Mrs. Linde: Two on the same piece of wreckage would stand a better chance than each on their own.

Krogstad: Christine!

Mrs. Linde: What do you suppose brought me to town?

Krogstad: Do you mean that you gave me a thought?

Mrs. Linde: I could not endure life without work. All my life, as long as I can re- member, I have worked, and it has been my greatest and only pleasure. But now I am quite alone in the world — my life is so dreadfully empty and I feel so forsaken. There is not the least pleasure in working for one's self. Nils, give me someone and something to work for.

Krogstad: I don't trust that. It is nothing but a woman's overstrained sense of gen- erosity that prompts you to make such an offer of yourself.

Mrs. Linde: Have you ever noticed anything of the sort in me?

Krogstad: Could you really do it? Tell me — do you know all about my past life?

Mrs. Linde: Yes.

Krogstad: And do you know what they think of me here?

Mrs. Linde: You seemed to me to imply that with me you might have been quite another man.

Krogstad: I am certain of it.

Mrs. Linde: Is it too late now?

Krogstad: Christine, are you saying this deliberately? Yes, I am sure you are. I see it in your face. Have you really the courage, then — ?

Mrs. Linde: I want to be a mother to someone, and your children need a mother. We two need each other. Nils, I have faith in your real character — I can dare anything together with you.

Krogstad (grasps her hands): Thanks, thanks, Christine! Now I shall find a way to clear myself in the eyes of the world. Ah, but I forgot —

Mrs. Linde (listening): Hush! The Tarantella! Go, go!

Krogstad: Why? What is it?

Mrs. Linde: Do you hear them up there? When that is over, we may expect them back.

Krogstad: Yes, yes — I will go. But it is all no use. Of course you are not aware what steps I have taken in the matter of the Helmers.

Mrs. Linde: Yes, I know all about that.

Krogstad: And in spite of that have you the courage to —?

Mrs. Linde: I understand very well to what lengths a man like you might be driven by despair.

Krogstad: If I could only undo what I have done!

Mrs. Linde: You cannot. Your letter is lying in the letter-box now.

Krogstad: Are you sure of that?

Mrs. Linde: Quite sure, but —

Krogstad (with a searching look at her): Is that what it all means? — that you want to save your friend at any cost? Tell me frankly. Is that it?

Mrs. Linde: Nils, a woman who has once sold herself for another's sake, doesn't do it a second time.

Krogstad: I will ask for my letter back.

Mrs. Linde: No, no.

Krogstad: Yes, of course I will. I will wait here until Helmer comes; I will tell him he must give me my letter back — that it only concerns my dismissal — that he is not to read it —

Mrs. Linde: No, Nils, you must not recall your letter.

Krogstad: But, tell me, wasn't it for that very purpose that you asked me to meet you here?

Mrs. Linde: In my first moment of fright, it was. But twenty-four hours have elapsed since then, and in that time I have witnessed incredible things in this house. Helmer must know all about it. This unhappy secret must be disclosed; they must have a complete understanding between them, which is impossible with all this concealment and falsehood going on.

Krogstad: Very well, if you will take the responsibility. But there is one thing I can do in any case, and I shall do it at once.

Mrs. Linde (listening): You must be quick and go! The dance is over; we are not safe a moment longer.

Krogstad: I will wait for you below.

Mrs. Linde: Yes, do. You must see me back to my door.

Krogstad: I have never had such an amazing piece of good fortune in my life! (*Goes out through the outer door. The door between the room and the hall remains open.*)

Mrs. Linde (tidying up the room and laying her hat and cloak ready): What a difference! what a difference! Some-one to work for and live for — a home to bring comfort into. That I will do, indeed. I wish they would be quick and come — (*Listens.*) Ah, there they are now. I must put on my things. (*Takes up her hat and cloak. Helmer's and Nora's voices are heard outside; a key is turned, and*

Helmer brings Nora almost by force into the hall. She is in an Italian costume
with a large black shawl around her; he is in evening dress, and a black domino°
which is flying open.)

Nora (hanging back in the doorway, and struggling with him): No, no, no! — don't
take me in. I want to go upstairs again; I don't want to leave so early.

Helmer: But, my dearest Nora —

Nora: Please, Torvald dear — please, *please* — only an hour more.

Helmer: Not a single minute, my sweet Nora. You know that was our agreement.
Come along into the room; you are catching cold standing there. (He brings
her gently into the room, in spite of her resistance.)

Mrs. Linde: Good-evening.

Nora: Christine!

Helmer: You here, so late, Mrs. Linde?

Mrs. Linde: Yes, you must excuse me; I was so anxious to see Nora in her dress.

Nora: Have you been sitting here waiting for me?

Mrs. Linde: Yes, unfortunately I came too late, you had already gone upstairs; and
I thought I couldn't go away again without having seen you.

Helmer (taking off Nora's shawl): Yes, take a good look at her. I think she is worth
looking at. Isn't she charming, Mrs. Linde?

Mrs. Linde: Yes, indeed she is.

Helmer: Doesn't she look remarkably pretty? Everyone thought so at the dance.
But she is terribly self-willed, this sweet little person. What are we to do with
her? You will hardly believe that I had almost to bring her away by force.

Nora: Torvald, you will repent not having let me stay, even if it were only for half
an hour.

Helmer: Listen to her, Mrs. Linde! She had danced her Tarantella, and it had been a
tremendous success, as it deserved — although possibly the performance was
a trifle too realistic — a little more so, I mean, than was strictly compatible
with the limitations of art. But never mind about that! The chief thing is, she
had made a success — she had made a tremendous success. Do you think I
was going to let her remain there after that, and spoil the effect? No, indeed!
I took my charming little Capri maiden — my capricious little Capri maiden,
I should say — on my arm; took one quick turn round the room; a curtsey on
either side, and, as they say in novels, the beautiful apparition disappeared.
An exit ought always to be effective, Mrs. Linde; but that is what I cannot
make Nora understand. Pooh! this room is hot. (Throws his domino on a chair,
and opens the door of his room.) Hullo! it's all dark in here. Oh, of course —
excuse me —. (He goes in, and lights some candles.)

Nora (in a hurried and breathless whisper): Well?

Mrs. Linde (in a low voice): I have had a talk with him.

Nora: Yes, and —

Mrs. Linde: Nora, you must tell your husband all about it.

Nora (in an expressionless voice): I knew it.

Mrs. Linde: You have nothing to be afraid of as far as Krogstad is concerned; but
you must tell him.

Nora: I won't tell him.

Mrs. Linde: Then the letter will.

Nora: Thank you, Christine. Now I know what I must do. Hush —!

---

domino: A loose cloak, worn with a mask for the upper part of the face at masquerades.

Helmer (coming in again): Well, Mrs. Linde, have you admired her?

Mrs. Linde: Yes, and now I will say good-night.

Helmer: What, already? Is this yours, this knitting?

Mrs. Linde (taking it): Yes, thank you, I had very nearly forgotten it.

Helmer: So you knit?

Mrs. Linde: Of course.

Helmer: Do you know, you ought to embroider.

Mrs. Linde: Really? Why?

Helmer: Yes, it's far more becoming. Let me show you. You hold the embroidery thus in your left hand, and use the needle with the right — like this — with a long, easy sweep. Do you see?

Mrs. Linde: Yes, perhaps —

Helmer: But in the case of knitting — that can never be anything but ungraceful; look here — the arms close together, the knitting-needles going up and down — it has a sort of Chinese effect — . That was really excellent champagne they gave us.

Mrs. Linde: Well, — good-night, Nora, and don't be self-willed any more.

Helmer: That's right, Mrs. Linde.

Mrs. Linde: Good-night, Mr. Helmer.

Helmer (accompanying her to the door): Good-night, good-night. I hope you will get home all right. I should be very happy to — but you haven't any great distance to go. Good-night, good-night. *(She goes out; he shuts the door after her, and comes in again.)* Ah! — at last we have got rid of her. She is a frightful bore, that woman.

Nora: Aren't you very tired, Torvald?

Helmer: No, not in the least.

Nora: Nor sleepy?

Helmer: Not a bit. On the contrary, I feel extraordinarily lively. And you? — you really look both tired and sleepy.

Nora: Yes, I am very tired. I want to go to sleep at once.

Helmer: There, you see it was quite right of me not to let you stay there any longer.

Nora: Everything you do is quite right, Torvald.

Helmer (kissing her on the forehead): Now my little skylark is speaking reasonably. Did you notice what good spirits Rank was in this evening?

Nora: Really? Was he? I didn't speak to him at all.

Helmer: And I very little, but I have not for a long time seen him in such good form. *(Looks for a while at her and then goes nearer to her.)* It is delightful to be at home by ourselves again, to be all alone with you — you fascinating, charming little darling!

Nora: Don't look at me like that, Torvald.

Helmer: Why shouldn't I look at my dearest treasure? — at all the beauty that is mine, all my very own?

Nora (going to the other side of the table): You mustn't say things like that to me to-night.

Helmer (following her): You have still got the Tarantella in your blood, I see. And it makes you more captivating than ever. Listen — the guests are beginning to go now. *(In a lower voice.)* Nora — soon the whole house will be quiet.

Nora: Yes, I hope so.

Helmer: Yes, my own darling Nora. Do you know, when I am out at a party with you like this, why I speak so little to you, keep away from you, and only send a stolen glance in your direction now and then? — do you know why I do that?

It is because I make believe to myself that we are secretly in love, and you are my secretly promised bride, and that no one suspects there is anything between us.

Nora: Yes, yes — I know very well your thoughts are with me all the time.

Helmer: And when we are leaving, and I am putting the shawl over your beautiful young shoulders — on your lovely neck — then I imagine that you are my young bride and that we have just come from the wedding, and I am bringing you for the first time into our home — to be alone with you for the first time — quite alone with my shy little darling! All this evening I have longed for nothing but you. When I watched the seductive figures of the Tarantella, my blood was on fire; I could endure it no longer, and that was why I brought you down so early —

Nora: Go away, Torvald! You must let me go. I won't —

Helmer: What's that? You're joking, my little Nora! You won't — you won't? Am I not your husband — ? *(A knock is heard at the outer door.)*

Nora (starting): Did you hear — ?

Helmer (going into the hall): Who is it?

Rank (outside): It is I. May I come in for a moment?

Helmer (in a fretful whisper): Oh, what does he want now? *(Aloud.)* Wait a minute! *(Unlocks the door.)* Come, that's kind of you not to pass by our door.

Rank: I thought I heard your voice, and felt as if I should like to look in. *(With a swift glance round.)* Ah, yes! — these dear familiar rooms. You are very happy and cosy in here, you two.

Helmer: It seems to me that you looked after yourself pretty well upstairs too.

Rank: Excellently. Why shouldn't I? Why shouldn't one enjoy everything in this world? — at any rate as much as one can, and as long as one can. The wine was capital —

Helmer: Especially the champagne.

Rank: So you noticed that too? It is almost incredible how much I managed to put away!

Nora: Torvald drank a great deal of champagne to-night too.

Rank: Did he?

Nora: Yes, and he is always in such good spirits afterwards.

Rank: Well, why should one not enjoy a merry evening after a well-spent day?

Helmer: Well spent? I am afraid I can't take credit for that.

Rank (clapping him on the back): But I can, you know!

Nora: Doctor Rank, you must have been occupied with some scientific investigation to-day.

Rank: Exactly.

Helmer: Just listen! — little Nora talking about scientific investigations!

Nora: And may I congratulate you on the result?

Rank: Indeed you may.

Nora: Was it favourable, then?

Rank: The best possible, for both doctor and patient — certainty.

Nora (quickly and searchingly): Certainty?

Rank: Absolute certainty. So wasn't I entitled to make a merry evening of it after that?

Nora: Yes, you certainly were, Doctor Rank.

Helmer: I think so too, so long as you don't have to pay for it in the morning.

Rank: Oh well, one can't have anything in this life without paying for it.

Nora: Doctor Rank — are you fond of fancy-dress balls?

Rank: Yes, if there is a fine lot of pretty costumes.

Nora: Tell me — what shall we two wear at the next?

Helmer: Little featherbrain! — are you thinking of the next already?

Rank: We two? Yes, I can tell you. You shall go as a good fairy —

Helmer: Yes, but what do you suggest as an appropriate costume for that?

Rank: Let your wife go dressed just as she is in everyday life.

Helmer: That was really very prettily turned. But can't you tell us what you will be?

Rank: Yes, my dear friend, I have quite made up my mind about that.

Helmer: Well?

Rank: At the next fancy-dress ball I shall be invisible.

Helmer: That's a good joke!

Rank: There is a big black hat — have you never heard of hats that make you invisible? If you put one on, no one can see you.

Helmer (suppressing a smile): Yes, you are quite right.

Rank: But I am clean forgetting what I came for. Helmer, give me a cigar — one of the dark Havanas.

Helmer: With the greatest pleasure. (*Offers him his case.*)

Rank (takes a cigar and cuts off the end): Thanks.

Nora (striking a match): Let me give you a light.

Rank: Thank you. (*She holds the match for him to light his cigar.*) And now good-bye!

Helmer: Good-bye, good-bye, dear old man!

Nora: Sleep well, Doctor Rank.

Rank: Thank you for that wish.

Nora: Wish me the same.

Rank: You? Well, if you want me to sleep well! And thanks for the light. (*He nods to them both and goes out.*)

Helmer (in a subdued voice): He has drunk more than he ought.

Nora (absently): Maybe. (*Helmer takes a bunch of keys out of his pocket and goes into the hall.*) Torvald! what are you going to do there?

Helmer: Empty the letter-box; it is quite full; there will be no room to put the newspaper in to-morrow morning.

Nora: Are you going to work to-night?

Helmer: You know quite well I'm not. What is this? Someone has been at the lock.

Nora: At the lock —?

Helmer: Yes, someone has. What can it mean? I should never have thought the maid —. Here is a broken hairpin. Nora, it is one of yours.

Nora (quickly): Then it must have been the children —

Helmer: Then you must get them out of those ways. There, at last I have got it open. (*Takes out the contents of the letter-box, and calls to the kitchen.*) Helen! — Helen, put out the light over the front door. (*Goes back into the room and shuts the door into the hall. He holds out his hand full of letters.*) Look at that — look what a heap of them there are. (*Turning them over.*) What on earth is that?

Nora (at the window): The letter — No! Torvald, no!

Helmer: Two cards — of Rank's.

Nora: Of Doctor Rank's?

Helmer (looking at them): Doctor Rank. They were on the top. He must have put them in when he went out.

Nora: Is there anything written on them?

Helmer: There is a black cross over the name. Look there — what an uncomfortable idea! It looks as if he were announcing his own death.

Nora: It is just what he is doing.

Helmer: What? Do you know anything about it? Has he said anything to you?

Nora: Yes. He told me that when the cards came it would be his leave-taking from us. He means to shut himself up and die.

Helmer: My poor old friend! Certainly I knew we should not have him very long with us. But so soon! And so he hides himself away like a wounded animal.

Nora: If it has to happen, it is best it should be without a word — don't you think so, Torvald?

Helmer (walking up and down): He had so grown into our lives. I can't think of him as having gone out of them. He, with his sufferings and his loneliness, was like a cloudy background to our sunlit happiness. Well, perhaps it is best so. For him, anyway. *(Standing still.)* And perhaps for us too, Nora. We two are thrown quite upon each other now. *(Puts his arms round her.)* My darling wife, I don't feel as if I could hold you tight enough. Do you know, Nora, I have often wished that you might be threatened by some great danger, so that I might risk my life's blood, and everything, for your sake.

Nora (disengages herself, and says firmly and decidedly): Now you must read your letters, Torvald.

Helmer: No, no; not to-night. I want to be with you, my darling wife.

Nora: With the thought of your friend's death —

Helmer: You are right, it has affected us both. Something ugly has come between us — the thought of the horrors of death. We must try and rid our minds of that. Until then — we will each go to our own room.

Nora (hanging on his neck): Good-night, Torvald — Good-night!

Helmer (kissing her on the forehead): Good-night, my little singing-bird. Sleep sound, Nora. Now I will read my letters through. *(He takes his letters and goes into his room, shutting the door after him.)*

Nora (gropes distractedly about, seizes Helmer's domino, throws it round her, while she says in quick, hoarse, spasmodic whispers): Never to see him again. Never! Never! *(Puts her shawl over her head.)* Never to see my children again either — never again. Never! Never! — Ah! the icy, black water — the unfathomable depths — If only it were over! He has got it now — now he is reading it. Good-bye, Torvald and my children! *(She is about to rush out through the hall, when Helmer opens his door hurriedly and stands with an open letter in his hand.)*

Helmer: Nora!

Nora: Ah! —

Helmer: What is this? Do you know what is in this letter?

Nora: Yes, I know. Let me go! Let me get out!

Helmer (holding her back): Where are you going?

Nora (trying to get free): You shan't save me, Torvald!

Helmer (reeling): True? Is this true, that I read here? Horrible! No, no — it is impossible that it can be true.

Nora: It is true. I have loved you above everything else in the world.

Helmer: Oh, don't let us have any silly excuses.

Nora (taking a step towards him): Torvald — !

Helmer: Miserable creature — what have you done?

Nora: Let me go. You shall not suffer for my sake. You shall not take it upon yourself.

Helmer: No tragedy airs, please. *(Locks the hall door.)* Here you shall stay and give me an explanation. Do you understand what you have done? Answer me! Do you understand what you have done?

Nora (looks steadily at him and says with a growing look of coldness in her face): Yes, now I am beginning to understand thoroughly.

Helmer (walking about the room): What a horrible awakening! All these eight years — she who was my joy and pride — a hypocrite, a liar — worse, worse — a criminal! The unutterable ugliness of it all! — For shame! For shame! *(Nora is silent and looks steadily at him. He stops in front of her.)* I ought to have suspected that something of the sort would happen. I ought to have foreseen it. All your father's want of principle — be silent! — all your father's want of principle has come out in you. No religion, no morality, no sense of duty —. How I am punished for having winked at what he did! I did it for your sake, and this is how you repay me.

Nora: Yes, that's just it.

Helmer: Now you have destroyed all my happiness. You have ruined all my future. It is horrible to think of! I am in the power of an unscrupulous man; he can do what he likes with me, ask anything he likes of me, give me any orders he pleases — I dare not refuse. And I must sink to such miserable depths because of a thoughtless woman!

Nora: When I am out of the way, you will be free.

Helmer: No fine speeches, please. Your father had always plenty of those ready, too. What good would it be to me if you were out of the way, as you say? Not the slightest. He can make the affair known everywhere; and if he does, I may be falsely suspected of having been a party to your criminal action. Very likely people will think I was behind it all — that it was I who prompted you! And I have to thank you for all this — you whom I have cherished during the whole of our married life. Do you understand now what it is you have done for me?

Nora (coldly and quietly): Yes.

Helmer: It is so incredible that I can't take it in. But we must come to some understanding. Take off that shawl. Take it off, I tell you. I must try and appease him some way or another. The matter must be hushed up at any cost. And as for you and me, it must appear as if everything between us were just as before — but naturally only in the eyes of the world. You will still remain in my house, that is a matter of course. But I shall not allow you to bring up the children; I dare not trust them to you. To think that I should be obliged to say so to one whom I have loved so dearly, and whom I still —. No, that is all over. From this moment happiness is not the question; all that concerns us is to save the remains, the fragments, the appearance —

A ring is heard at the front-door bell.

Helmer (with a start): What is that? So late! Can the worst —? Can he —? Hide yourself, Nora. Say you are ill.

Nora stands motionless. Helmer goes and unlocks the hall door.

Maid (half-dressed, comes to the door): A letter for the mistress.

Helmer: Give it to me. *(Takes the letter, and shuts the door.)* Yes, it is from him. You shall not have it; I will read it myself.

Nora: Yes, read it.

Helmer (standing by the lamp): I scarcely have the courage to do it. It may mean ruin for both of us. No, I must know. *(Tears open the letter, runs his eye over a few lines, looks at a paper enclosed, and gives a shout of joy.)* Nora! *(She looks at him questioningly.)* Nora! — No, I must read it once again —. Yes, it is true! I am saved! Nora, I am saved!

Nora: And I?

Helmer: You too, of course; we are both saved, both you and I. Look, he sends you your bond back. He says he regrets and repents — that a happy change in his life — never mind what he says! We are saved, Nora! No one can do anything to you. Oh, Nora, Nora! — no, first I must destroy these hateful things. Let me see —. *(Takes a look at the bond.)* No, no, I won't look at it. The whole thing shall be nothing but a bad dream to me. *(Tears up the bond and both letters, throws them all into the stove, and watches them burn.)* There — now it doesn't exist any longer. He says that since Christmas Eve you —. These must have been three dreadful days for you, Nora.

Nora: I have fought a hard fight these three days.

Helmer: And suffered agonies, and seen no way out but —. No, we won't call any of the horrors to mind. We will only shout with joy, and keep saying, "It's all over! It's all over!" Listen to me, Nora. You don't seem to realise that it is all over. What is this? — such a cold, set face! My poor little Nora, I quite understand; you don't feel as if you could believe that I have forgiven you. But it is true, Nora, I swear it; I have forgiven you everything. I know that what you did, you did out of love for me.

Nora: That is true.

Helmer: You have loved me as a wife ought to love her husband. Only you had not sufficient knowledge to judge of the means you used. But do you suppose you are any the less dear to me, because you don't understand how to act on your own responsibility? No, no; only lean on me; I will advise you and direct you. I should not be a man if this womanly helplessness did not just give you a double attractiveness in my eyes. You must not think anymore about the hard things I said in my first moment of consternation, when I thought everything was going to overwhelm me. I have forgiven you, Nora; I swear to you I have forgiven you.

Nora: Thank you for your forgiveness. *(She goes out through the door to the right.)*

Helmer: No, don't go —. *(Looks in.)* What are you doing in there?

Nora (from within): Taking off my fancy dress.

Helmer (standing at the open door): Yes, do. Try and calm yourself, and make your mind easy again, my frightened little singing-bird. Be at rest, and feel secure; I have broad wings to shelter you under. *(Walks up and down by the door.)* How warm and cosy our home is, Nora. Here is shelter for you; here I will protect you like a hunted dove that I have saved from a hawk's claws; I will bring peace to your poor beating heart. It will come, little by little, Nora, believe me. Tomorrow morning you will look upon it all quite differently; soon everything will be just as it was before. Very soon you won't need me to assure you that I have forgiven you; you will yourself feel the certainty that I have done so. Can you suppose I should ever think of such a thing as repudiating you, or even reproaching you? You have no idea what a true man's heart is like, Nora. There is something so indescribably sweet and satisfying, to a man, in the knowledge that he has forgiven his wife — forgiven her freely, and with all his heart. It seems as if that had made her, as it were, doubly his own; he has given her a new life, so to speak; and she has in a way become both wife and child to him. So you shall be for me after this, my little scared, helpless darling. Have no anxiety about anything, Nora; only be frank and open with me, and I will serve as will and conscience both to you —. What is this? Not gone to bed? Have you changed your things?

Nora (in everyday dress): Yes, Torvald, I have changed my things now.

Helmer: But what for? — so late as this.

Nora: I shall not sleep to-night.

Helmer: But, my dear Nora —

Nora (looking at her watch): It is not so very late. Sit down here, Torvald. You and I have much to say to one another. *(She sits down at one side of the table.)*

Helmer: Nora — what is this? — this cold, set face?

Nora: Sit down. It will take some time; I have a lot to talk over with you.

Helmer (sits down at the opposite side of the table): You alarm me, Nora! — and I don't understand you.

Nora: No, that is just it. You don't understand me, and I have never understood you either — before to-night. No, you mustn't interrupt me. You must simply listen to what I say. Torvald, this is a settling of accounts.

Helmer: What do you mean by that?

Nora (after a short silence): Isn't there one thing that strikes you as strange in our sitting here like this?

Helmer: What is that?

Nora: We have been married now eight years. Does it not occur to you that this is the first time we two, you and I, husband and wife, have had a serious conversation?

Helmer: What do you mean by serious?

Nora: In all these eight years — longer than that — from the very beginning of our acquaintance, we have never exchanged a word on any serious subject.

Helmer: Was it likely that I would be continually and forever telling you about worries that you could not help me to bear?

Nora: I am not speaking about business matters. I say that we have never sat down in earnest together to try and get at the bottom of anything.

Helmer: But, dearest Nora, would it have been any good to you?

Nora: That is just it; you have never understood me. I have been greatly wronged, Torvald — first by papa and then by you.

Helmer: What! By us two — by us two, who have loved you better than anyone else in the world?

Nora (shaking her head): You have never loved me. You have only thought it pleasant to be in love with me.

Helmer: Nora, what do I hear you saying?

Nora: It is perfectly true, Torvald. When I was at home with papa, he told me his opinion about everything, and so I had the same opinions; and if I differed from him I concealed the fact, because he would not have liked it. He called me his doll-child, and he played with me just as I used to play with my dolls. And when I came to live with you —

Helmer: What sort of an expression is that to use about our marriage?

Nora (undisturbed): I mean that I was simply transferred from papa's hands into yours. You arranged everything according to your own taste, and so I got the same tastes as you — or else I pretended to, I am really not quite sure which — I think sometimes the one and sometimes the other. When I look back on it, it seems to me as if I had been living here like a poor woman — just from hand to mouth. I have existed merely to perform tricks for you, Torvald. But you would have it so. You and papa have committed a great sin against me. It is your fault that I have made nothing of my life.

Helmer: How unreasonable and how ungrateful you are, Nora! Have you not been happy here?

Nora: No, I have never been happy. I thought I was, but it has never really been so.

Helmer: Not — not happy!

Nora: No, only merry. And you have always been so kind to me. But our home has been nothing but a playroom. I have been your doll-wife, just as at home I was papa's doll-child; and here the children have been my dolls. I thought it great fun when you played with me, just as they thought it great fun when I played with them. That is what our marriage has been, Torvald.

Helmer: There is some truth in what you say — exaggerated and strained as your view of it is. But for the future it shall be different. Playtime shall be over, and lesson-time shall begin.

Nora: Whose lessons? Mine, or the children's?

Helmer: Both yours and the children's, my darling Nora.

Nora: Alas, Torvald, you are not the man to educate me into being a proper wife for you.

Helmer: And you can say that!

Nora: And I — how am I fitted to bring up the children?

Helmer: Nora!

Nora: Didn't you say so yourself a little while ago — that you dare not trust me to bring them up?

Helmer: In a moment of anger! Why do you pay any heed to that?

Nora: Indeed, you were perfectly right. I am not fit for the task. There is another task I must undertake first. I must try and educate myself — you are not the man to help me in that. I must do that for myself. And that is why I am going to leave you now.

Helmer (springing up): What do you say?

Nora: I must stand quite alone, if I am to understand myself and everything about me. It is for that reason that I cannot remain with you any longer.

Helmer: Nora, Nora!

Nora: I am going away from here now, at once. I am sure Christine will take me in for the night —

Helmer: You are out of your mind! I won't allow it! I forbid you!

Nora: It is no use forbidding me anything any longer. I will take with me what belongs to myself. I will take nothing from you, either now or later.

Helmer: What sort of madness is this!

Nora: To-morrow I shall go home — I mean, to my old home. It will be easiest for me to find something to do there.

Helmer: You blind, foolish woman!

Nora: I must try and get some sense, Torvald.

Helmer: To desert your home, your husband and your children! And you don't consider what people will say!

Nora: I cannot consider that at all. I only know that it is necessary for me.

Helmer: It's shocking. This is how you would neglect your most sacred duties.

Nora: What do you consider my most sacred duties?

Helmer: Do I need to tell you that? Are they not your duties to your husband and your children?

Nora: I have other duties just as sacred.

Helmer: That you have not. What duties could those be?

Nora: Duties to myself.

Helmer: Before all else, you are a wife and a mother.

Nora: I don't believe that any longer. I believe that before all else I am a reasonable human being, just as you are — or, at all events, that I must try and become one. I know quite well, Torvald, that most people would think you right, and that views of that kind are to be found in books; but I can no longer content myself with what most people say, or with what is found in books. I must think over things for myself and get to understand them.

Helmer: Can you not understand your place in your own home? Have you not a reliable guide in such matters as that? — have you no religion?

Nora: I am afraid, Torvald, I do not exactly know what religion is.

Helmer: What are you saying?

Nora: I know nothing but what the clergyman said, when I went to be confirmed. He told us that religion was this, and that, and the other. When I am away from all this, and am alone, I will look into that matter too. I will see if what the clergyman said is true, or at all events if it is true for me.

Helmer: This is unheard of in a girl of your age! But if religion cannot lead you aright, let me try and awaken your conscience. I suppose you have some moral sense? Or — answer me — am I to think you have none?

Nora: I assure you, Torvald, that is not an easy question to answer. I really don't know. The thing perplexes me altogether. I only know that you and I look at it in quite a different light. I am learning, too, that the law is quite another thing from what I supposed; but I find it impossible to convince myself that the law is right. According to it a woman has no right to spare her old dying father, or to save her husband's life. I can't believe that.

Helmer: You talk like a child. You don't understand the conditions of the world in which you live.

Nora: No, I don't. But now I am going to try. I am going to see if I can make out who is right, the world or I.

Helmer: You are ill, Nora; you are delirious; I almost think you are out of your mind.

Nora: I have never felt my mind so clear and certain as to-night.

Helmer: And is it with a clear and certain mind that you forsake your husband and your children?

Nora: Yes, it is.

Helmer: Then there is only one possible explanation.

Nora: What is that?

Helmer: You do not love me anymore.

Nora: No, that is just it.

Helmer: Nora! — and you can say that?

Nora: It gives me great pain, Torvald, for you have always been so kind to me, but I cannot help it. I do not love you any more.

Helmer (regaining his composure): Is that a clear and certain conviction too?

Nora: Yes, absolutely clear and certain. That is the reason why I will not stay here any longer.

Helmer: And can you tell me what I have done to forfeit your love?

Nora: Yes, indeed I can. It was to-night, when the wonderful thing did not happen; then I saw you were not the man I had thought you.

Helmer: Explain yourself better. I don't understand you.

Nora: I have waited so patiently for eight years; for, goodness knows, I knew very well that wonderful things don't happen every day. Then this horrible misfortune came upon me; and then I felt quite certain that the wonderful thing was going to happen at last. When Krogstad's letter was lying out there, never for a moment did I imagine that you would consent to accept this man's conditions.

I was so absolutely certain that you would say to him: Publish the thing to the whole world. And when that was done —

Helmer: Yes, what then? — when I had exposed my wife to shame and disgrace?

Nora: When that was done, I was so absolutely certain, you would come forward and take everything upon yourself, and say: I am the guilty one.

Helmer: Nora—!

Nora: You mean that I would never have accepted such a sacrifice on your part? No, of course not. But what would my assurances have been worth against yours? That was the wonderful thing which I hoped for and feared; and it was to prevent that, that I wanted to kill myself.

Helmer: I would gladly work night and day for you, Nora — bear sorrow and want for your sake. But no man would sacrifice his honour for the one he loves.

Nora: It is a thing hundreds of thousands of women have done.

Helmer: Oh, you think and talk like a heedless child.

Nora: Maybe. But you neither think nor talk like the man I could bind myself to. As soon as your fear was over — and it was not fear for what threatened me, but for what might happen to you — when the whole thing was past, as far as you were concerned it was exactly as if nothing at all had happened. Exactly as before, I was your little skylark, your doll, which you would in future treat with doubly gentle care, because it was so brittle and fragile. *(Getting up.)* Torvald — it was then it dawned upon me that for eight years I had been living here with a strange man, and had borne him three children—. Oh, I can't bear to think of it! I could tear myself into little bits!

Helmer (sadly): I see, I see. An abyss has opened between us — there is no denying it. But, Nora, would it not be possible to fill it up?

Nora: As I am now, I am no wife for you.

Helmer: I have it in me to become a different man.

Nora: Perhaps — if your doll is taken away from you.

Helmer: But to part! — to part from you! No, no, Nora, I can't understand that idea.

Nora (going out to the right): That makes it all the more certain that it must be done. *(She comes back with her cloak and hat and a small bag which she puts on a chair by the table.)*

Helmer: Nora, Nora, not now! Wait until to-morrow.

Nora (putting on her cloak): I cannot spend the night in a strange man's room.

Helmer: But can't we live here like brother and sister — ?

Nora (putting on her hat): You know very well that would not last long. *(Puts the shawl round her.)* Good-bye, Torvald. I won't see the little ones. I know they are in better hands than mine. As I am now, I can be of no use to them.

Helmer: But some day, Nora — some day?

Nora: How can I tell? I have no idea what is going to become of me.

Helmer: But you are my wife, whatever becomes of you.

Nora: Listen, Torvald. I have heard that when a wife deserts her husband's house, as I am doing now, he is legally freed from all obligations towards her. In any case, I set you free from all your obligations. You are not to feel yourself bound in the slightest way, any more than I shall. There must be perfect freedom on both sides. See, here is your ring back. Give me mine.

Helmer: That too?

Nora: That too.

Helmer: Here it is.

Nora: That's right. Now it is all over. I have put the keys here. The maids know all about everything in the house — better than I do. To-morrow, after I have left her, Christine will come here and pack up my own things that I brought with me from home. I will have them sent after me.

Helmer: All over! All over! — Nora, shall you never think of me again?

Nora: I know I shall often think of you, the children, and this house.

Helmer: May I write to you, Nora?

Nora: No — never. You must not do that.

Helmer: But at least let me send you —

Nora: Nothing — nothing —

Helmer: Let me help you if you are in want.

Nora: No. I can receive nothing from a stranger.

Helmer: Nora — can I never be anything more than a stranger to you?

Nora (taking her bag): Ah, Torvald, the most wonderful thing of all would have to happen.

Helmer: Tell me what that would be!

Nora: Both you and I would have to be so changed that —. Oh, Torvald, I don't believe any longer in wonderful things happening.

Helmer: But I will believe in it. Tell me! So changed that — ?

Nora: That our life together would be a real wedlock. Good-bye. *(She goes out through the hall.)*

Helmer (sinks down on a chair at the door and buries his face in his hands): Nora! Nora! *(Looks round, and rises.)* Empty. She is gone. *(A hope flashes across his mind.)* The most wonderful thing of all — ?

The sound of a door shutting is heard from below.

CONSIDERATIONS FOR CRITICAL THINKING AND WRITING

1. FIRST RESPONSE. What is the significance of the play's title?

2. Nora lies several times during the play. What kinds of lies are they? Do her lies indicate that she is not to be trusted, or are they a sign of something else about her personality?

3. What kind of wife does Helmer want Nora to be? He affectionately calls her names such as "skylark" and "squirrel." What does this reveal about his attitude toward her?

4. Why is Nora "pale with terror" at the end of Act I? What is the significance of the description of the Christmas tree now "stripped of its ornaments and with burnt-down candle-ends on its dishevelled branches" that opens Act II? What other symbols are used in the play?

5. What is Doctor Rank's purpose in the play?

6. How does the relationship between Krogstad and Mrs. Linde serve to emphasize certain qualities in the Helmers' marriage?

7. Is Krogstad's decision not to expose Nora's secret convincing? Does his shift from villainy to generosity seem adequately motivated?

8. Why does Nora reject Helmer's efforts to smooth things over between them and start again? Do you have any sympathy for Helmer?

9. Would you describe the ending as essentially happy or unhappy? Is the play more like a comedy or a tragedy?

10. Ibsen believed that a "dramatist's business is not to answer questions, but only to ask them." What questions are raised in the play? Does Ibsen propose any specific answers?

11. What makes this play a work of realism? Are there any elements that seem not to be realistic?

12. CRITICAL STRATEGIES. Read the section on new historicist criticism (pp. 1653–54) in Chapter 51, "Critical Strategies for Reading," and consider the following: Ibsen once wrote a different ending for the play to head off producers who might have been tempted to change the final scene to placate the public's sense of morality. In the second conclusion, Helmer forces Nora to look in on their sleeping children. This causes her to realize that she cannot leave her family even though it means sacrificing herself. Ibsen called this version of the ending a "barbaric outrage" and didn't use it. How do you think the play reflects or refutes social values contemporary to it?

CONNECTIONS TO OTHER SELECTIONS

1. What does Nora have in common with the protagonist in Gail Godwin's "A Sorrowful Woman" (p. 39)? What significant differences are there between them?

2. Explain how Torvald's attitude toward Nora is similar to the men's attitudes toward women in Susan Glaspell's *Trifles* (p. 1079). Write an essay exploring how the assumptions the men make about women in both plays contribute to the plays' conflicts.

Perspective

HENRIK IBSEN (1828–1906)

Notes for A Doll House   1878

There are two kinds of spiritual law, two kinds of conscience, one in man and another, altogether different, in woman. They do not understand each other; but in practical life the woman is judged by man's law, as though she were not a woman but a man.

The wife in the play ends by having no idea of what is right or wrong; natural feeling on the one hand and belief in authority on the other have altogether bewildered her.

A woman cannot be herself in the society of the present day, which is an exclusively masculine society, with laws framed by men and with a judicial system that judges feminine conduct from a masculine point of view.

She has committed forgery, and she is proud of it; for she did it out of love for her husband, to save his life. But this husband with his commonplace principles of honor is on the side of the law and looks at the question from the masculine point of view.

Spiritual conflicts. Oppressed and bewildered by the belief in authority, she loses faith in her moral right and ability to bring up her children. Bitterness. A mother in modern society, like certain insects who go away and die when she has done her duty in the propagation of the race. Love of life, of home, of husband and children and family. Now and then a womanly shaking off of her thoughts. Sudden return of anxiety and terror. She must bear it all alone. The catastrophe approaches, inexorably, inevitably. Despair, conflict, and destruction.

From From Ibsen's Workshop, translated by A. G. Chater

CONSIDERATIONS FOR CRITICAL THINKING AND WRITING

1. Given the ending of *A Doll's House*, what do you think of Ibsen's early view in his notes that "the wife in the play ends by having no idea of what is right or wrong" (para. 2)? Would you describe Nora as "altogether bewildered" (para. 2)? Why or why not?

2. "A woman cannot be herself in the society of the present day, which is an exclusively masculine society" (para. 3). Why is this statement true of Nora? Explain why you agree or disagree that this observation is accurate today.

3. How does oppressive "authority" (para. 5) loom large for Nora? What kind of authority creates "spiritual conflicts" for her?

More Perspectives appear in the next chapter, "A Critical Case Study: Henrik Ibsen's *A Doll's House*," page 1413.

BEYOND REALISM

Realistic drama remained popular throughout the twentieth century, but from its beginnings it has been continually challenged by nonrealistic modes of theater. By the end of the nineteenth century, playwrights reacting against realism began to develop a variety of new approaches to setting, action, and character. Instead of creating a slice of life onstage, modern experimental playwrights drew on purely theatrical devices, ranging from stark sets and ritualistic actions to symbolic characterizations and audience participation. In general, such devices were designed to jar audiences' expectations and to heighten their awareness that what appeared before them was indeed a theatrical production. A glimpse of some of the nonrealistic movements in drama suggests how the possibilities for affecting audiences have been broadened by experimental theater.

Symbolist drama rejected the realists' assumption that life can be understood objectively and scientifically. The symbolists emphasized a subjective, emotional response to life because they believed that ultimate realities can be recognized only intuitively. Since absolute truth cannot be directly perceived, symbolists such as the Belgian playwright Maurice Maeterlinck (1862–1949) sought to express spiritual truth through settings, characters, and actions that suggest a transcendent reality. Maeterlinck's most famous symbolist play, *Pelléas and Mélisande* (1892), is a story of love and vengeance that includes mysterious forebodings, symbolic objects, and unexplained powerful forces. The elements of the play make no attempt to create the texture of ordinary life.

Other playwrights — such as William Butler Yeats (1865–1939) in Ireland, Paul Claudel (1868–1955) in France, Leonid Andreyev (1871–1919) in Russia, and Federico García Lorca (1898–1936) in Spain — also used some of the techniques associated with symbolist plays, but the movement never enjoyed wide popularity because audiences often found the plays' action too vague and their language too cryptic. Nevertheless, symbolist drama had an important influence on the work of subsequent playwrights, such as Tennessee Williams's *The Glass Menagerie* and Arthur Miller's *Death of a Salesman* (p. 1496); these dramatists effectively used symbols in plays that contain both realistic and nonrealistic qualities.

Another nonrealistic movement, known as *expressionism*, was popular from the end of World War I until the mid-1920s. Expressionist playwrights emphasized the internal lives of their characters and deliberately distorted reality by creating an outward manifestation of an inner state of being. The late plays of Swedish dramatist August Strindberg (1849–1912) anticipate expressionistic techniques. Strindberg's preface to *A Dream Play* (1902) reflects the impact that Freudian psychology would eventually have on the theater:

> The author has tried to imitate the disconnected but seemingly logical form of the dream. Anything may happen; everything is possible and probable. Time and space do not exist. On an insignificant background of reality, imagination designs and embroiders novel patterns: a medley of memories, experiences, free fancies, absurdities, and improvisations.

In such nonrealistic drama the action does not have to proceed chronologically because the playwright dramatizes the emotional life of the characters, which blends the past with the present rather than moving in a fixed, linear way. This fluidity of development can be seen in the *flashbacks* of Williams's *The Glass Menagerie* and Miller's *Death of a Salesman*.

The *epic theater* of Bertolt Brecht (1898–1956) is, like symbolism and expressionism, a long way from the realistic elements in Ibsen's *A Doll's House*. Brecht kept a distance between his characters and the audience. This strategy of alienation was designed to alert audiences to important social problems that might be overlooked if an individual's struggles became too emotionally absorbing. Brecht's drama, by casting new light on chronic human problems such as poverty, injustice, and war, was a means to convey hope and evidence that society could be changed for the better. Brecht called his drama "epic" to distinguish it from Aristotle's notion of drama. The episodic structure was designed to prevent the audience from being swept up in the action or losing themselves in an inevitable tragedy. Instead, Brecht wanted the audience to analyze the action and realize that certain consequences weren't inevitable but could be avoided. This distancing, the dramatization of societal issues, and the use of loosely connected scenes sometimes narrated by a kind of stage manager are the hallmarks of epic drama.

Epic theater revels in stylized theatricality. The major action in *The Caucasian Chalk Circle*, for example, consists of a play within a play. Brecht's dramas use suggestive rather than detailed settings, and their scenery and props are frequently changed as the audience watches. His actors make clear that they are pretending to be characters. They may speak or sing in verse, address the audience, or comment on issues with other characters who are not participants in the immediate action. In brief, Brecht's theater is keenly conscious of itself as theater.

In contrast to this didactic theater, the *theater of the absurd* was a response to the twentieth century's loss of faith in reason, religion, and life itself. These doubts produced an approach to drama that emphasizes chaotic, irrational forces and portrays human beings as more the victims than the makers of their world.

Absurdists such as Samuel Beckett (1906–1989), French dramatist Eugène Ionesco (1912–1994), English playwright Harold Pinter (1930–2008), and American writer Edward Albee (b. 1928) employ a variety of approaches to drama, but they share some assumptions about what subjects are important. Absurdism challenges the belief that life is ordered and meaningful. Instead of positing traditional values that give human beings a sense of purpose in life, absurdists dramatize our inability to comprehend fully our identities and destinies. Unlike heroic characters such as Oedipus or Hamlet, who retain their dignity despite their defeats, the characters in absurdist dramas frequently seem pathetically comic as they drift from one destructive moment to the next. These **antiheroes** are often bewildered, ineffectual, deluded, and lost. If they learn anything, it is that the world isolates them in an existence devoid of God and absolute values.

The basic premise of absurdism — that life is meaningless — is often presented in a nonrealistic manner to disrupt our expectations. In a realistic play such as Ibsen's *A Doll's House*, characters act pretty much the way we believe people behave. The motivation of these characters and the plausibility of their actions are comprehensible, but in an absurdist drama we are confronted with characters who appear in a series of disconnected incidents that lead to deeper confusion. What would we make of Nora if Ibsen had her appear in the final act costumed as a doll? This would be not only bizarre but unacceptable in a realistic play. However, it could make dramatic sense in an absurdist adaptation that sought to dramatize Nora's loss of identity and dehumanization as a result of her marriage.

Nora's appearance as a doll would, of course, be laughably inconsistent with what we judge to be real or reasonable. And yet we might find ourselves sympathizing with her situation. Suppose that instead of slamming the door and leaving her husband in the final scene, Nora moved stiffly about the room costumed as a doll while Helmer complacently sipped sherry and read the evening paper. Such an ending would suggest that she had been defeated by the circumstances in her life. Her condition — being nothing more than someone's toy — would be both absurd and pathetic. If we laughed at this scene, we would do so because Nora's situation is grotesquely humorous, a parody of her assumptions, hopes, and expectations. This is the world of **tragicomedy**, where laughter and pain coexist and where there is neither the happy resolution that typifies comic plots nor the transformational suffering that brings clarification to the tragic hero. It is the world dramatized, for example, in the opening scene of Harold Pinter's *The Dumb Waiter* when Ben tells Gus about an item he's read in the paper.

> *Ben:* A man of eighty-seven wanted to cross the road. But there was a lot of traffic, see? He couldn't see how he was going to squeeze through. So he crawled under a lorry [truck].
> *Gus:* He what?
> *Ben:* He crawled under a lorry. A stationary lorry.
> *Gus:* No?
> *Ben:* The lorry started and ran over him.
> *Gus:* Go on!
> *Ben:* That's what it says here.
> *Gus:* Get away.
> *Ben:* It's enough to make you want to puke, isn't it?
> *Gus:* Who advised him to do a thing like that?
> *Ben:* A man of eighty-seven crawling under a lorry!
> *Gus:* It's unbelievable.
> *Ben:* It's down here in black and white.
> *Gus:* Incredible.

As much as Gus finds the story difficult to believe and Ben is sickened by it, it is a fact that the old man was crushed under ridiculous circumstances. His death is unexpected, accidental, incomprehensible, and meaningless — except that what happened to the old man is, from an absurdist's perspective, really no different from what life has in store for all of us one way or the other.

An absurdist playwright may, as Pinter does, employ realistic settings and speech, but he or she goes beyond realistic conventions to challenge the rational assumptions we make about our lives. Pinter insists that "a play is not an essay." Background information, character motivation, action — nothing presented on an absurdist's stage is governed by the conventions of realism. The absurdists typically refuse to create the illusion of reality because there is, finally, no reality to imitate. If conversations in their plays are sometimes fragmented and seemingly inconsequential, the reason is that absurdists dramatize people's combined inability and unwillingness to communicate with one another. Indeed, Samuel Beckett's *Act without Words* contains no dialogue, and in his *Krapp's Last Tape* a single character addresses only his own tape-recorded voice. To some extent we must suspend common sense and logic if we are to appreciate the visions and voices in an absurdist play.

Although many other nonrealistic movements developed in the twentieth century, these four — symbolism, expressionism, epic theater, and the theater of the absurd — embrace the major differences between nonrealistic and realistic drama. The theater continually tests its own possibilities. In the 1960s and 1970s, for example, some acting companies in New York completely collapsed the usual distinctions between audience and actors. The Living Theater went even further by moving into the streets, where the actors and audiences engaged in dramatic political statements aimed at raising the social consciousness of people wherever they were. Some critics argued that this was not really theater but merely an exuberant kind of political rally. However, proponents of these productions — known as *guerrilla theater* — argued that protest drama is both politically and artistically valid. In any case, although today's playwrights seem considerably less inclined to take to the streets, there is a tolerance for a wide range of possible relationships between actors and audiences. Audiences (and readers) can expect symbolic characters, expressionistic settings, poetic language, monologues, and extreme actions in productions that also contain realistic elements. In *Route 1 & 9* (1981), a piece created by an experimental theater company called the Wooster Group, for example, audiences found themselves confronted with passages from Thornton Wilder's idealized version of America in *Our Town* that were coupled with a pornographic film and a black vaudeville act. This unlikely combination was used to comment on Wilder's conception of America in which issues of sex and race are largely ignored. Increasingly, experimental theater has cultivated an eclectic approach to drama, using a variety of media, cultures, playwrights, and even languages to enrich an audience's experience. Parts of Robert Wilson's *CIVIL warS* (1984) — a work never staged in its entirety in any one place — were performed in several countries, including France, Italy, and the United States, and drew on different languages as well as cultures to evoke a wide range of experiences from history, literature, myths, and even dreams. Chapter 49, "A Thematic Case Study: An Album of Contemporary Humor and Satire," attests to the traditions and innovations that contemporary dramatists have incorporated into their dramatic art.

47

A CRITICAL CASE STUDY

Henrik Ibsen's
A Doll's House

Time Life Pictures/Mansell/Getty Images.

Spiritual conflicts. Oppressed and bewildered by the belief in authority, she loses faith in her moral right and ability to bring up her children. Bitterness . . . Now and then a womanly shaking off of her thoughts. Sudden return of anxiety and terror. She must bear it all alone. The catastrophe approaches, inexorably, inevitably. Despair, conflict, and destruction.

— HENRIK IBSEN, from his notes for
A Doll's House

This chapter provides several critical approaches to Henrik Ibsen's *A Doll's House,* which appears in Chapter 46, page 1357. There have been numerous critical approaches to this play because it raises so many issues relating to matters such as relationships between men and women, history, and biography, as well as imagery, symbolism, and irony. The following critical excerpts offer a small and partial sample of the possible biographical, historical, mythological, psychological, sociological, and other perspectives that have attempted to shed light on the play (see Chapter 51, "Critical Strategies for Reading," for a discussion of a variety of critical methods). They should help you to enjoy the play more by raising questions, providing insights, and inviting you to delve further into the text.

The following letter offers a revealing vignette of the historical contexts for *A Doll's House.* Professor Richard Panofsky of the University of Massachusetts Dartmouth has provided the letter and this background information: "The translated letter was written in 1844 by Marcus (1807–1865) to his wife Ulrike (1816–1888), after six children had been born. This upper-middle-class Jewish family lived in Hamburg, Germany, where Marcus was a doctor. As the letter implies, Ulrike had left home and children: the letter establishes conditions for her to return. A woman in upper-class society of the time had few choices in an unhappy marriage. Divorce or separation meant ostracism; as Marcus writes, 'your husband, children, and the entire city threaten indifference or even contempt.' And she could not take a job, as she would have no profession to step into. In any case, Ulrike did return home. Between 1846 and 1857 the marriage produced eight more children. Beyond what the letter shows, we do not know the reasons for the separation or what the later marriage relationship was like."

Perspectives

A Nineteenth-Century Husband's Letter to His Wife   1844

Dear Wife,   June 23, 1844
    You have sinned greatly — and maybe I too; but this much is certain: Adam sinned after Eve had already sinned. So it is with us; you, alone, carry the guilt of all the misfortune which, however, I helped to enlarge later by my behavior. Listen now, since I still believe certain things to be necessary in order that we may have a peaceful life. If we want not only to be content for a day but forever, you will have to follow my wishes. So examine yourself and determine if you are strong enough to conquer your false ambitions and your stubbornness to submit to all the conditions, the fulfillment of which I cannot ignore. Every sensible person will tell you that all I ask of you is what is easily understood. If you insist on remaining stubborn, then do not return to my house, for you will never be happy with me; your husband, children, and the entire city threaten indifference or even contempt.
    But if you decide to act *sensibly* and *correctly,* that is *justly* and *kindly,* then be certain that many in the world will envy you.
    I am including here the paper which I read to you in front of the rabbi; ask anyone in your residence if the wishes expressed by me are not quite reasonable, and are of a kind to which every wife can agree for the welfare of domestic happiness. In any case, act in a way you think best.
    When you decide to return, write to tell me on which day and hour you depart from Berlin and give me your itinerary whether by way of Kuestrin and Pinne or by way of Wollstein. I will then meet you at Wollstein or Pinne. I expect you will bring Solomon with you.
    Don't travel unprepared. If you need money, ask your father.
    May God enlighten your heart and mind
                                                    I remain your so far unhappy,   [Marcus]
    Greetings to my parents, brothers, and sisters; also your brother. Show them what you wish, this letter, the enclosure, whatever you want. The children are fortunately healthy.

If you want to return with joy and peace, write me by return mail. In that case, I would rather send you a carriage. Maybe Madam Fraenkel will come along. . . .

[Enclosure]

My wife promises — for which every wife is obligated to her husband — to follow my wishes in everything and to strictly obey my orders. It is already self-evident that our marital relations have often been disturbed by the fact that my wife does not follow my wishes but believes herself to be entitled to act on her own, even if this is totally against my orders. In order not to have to remind my wife every second what my wishes are regarding homemaking and public conduct — wishes which I have often expressed — I want to make here a few rules which shall serve as a code of conduct. A home is best run if the work for each hour is planned ahead of time, if possible.

Servants get up no later than 5:00 A.M. in summer and 6:00 A.M. in winter, the children an hour later. The cook prepares breakfast. The nursemaid puts out clothes for every child, prepares water and sponge, cleans the combs, etc. The cook should stay in the kitchen unless there is time to clean the rooms. At least once a week the rooms should be cleaned whenever possible, but not all on the same day.

Every Wednesday, the people in the house should do a laundry. Every last Wednesday in the month, there shall be a large laundry with an outside washerwoman. At least every Monday, the seamstress shall come into the house to fix what is necessary.

Every Thursday or Friday, bread is baked for the week; I think it is best to buy grain and have it ground, but to knead it at home.

Every Friday special bread (Barches) should be bought for the evening meal.

The kitchen list will be prepared and discussed every Thursday evening, jointly, by me and my wife; but my wish is to be decisive.

After this, provisions are to be bought every Friday at the market. For this purpose, my wife, herself, will go to the market on Fridays, accompanied by a servant; she can substitute a special woman who does errands (*Faktorfrau*) if she wishes, but not a servant.

All expenditures have to be written down daily and punctually.

The children receive a bath every Thursday evening. The children's clothes must be kept in a specially appointed chest, with a separate compartment for each child with the child's name upon it. The boys' suits and girls' dresses are to be kept separately. To keep used laundry, there must be a hamper easily accessible. Equally important is the food storage box in which provisions are kept in order, locked and safe from vermin.

The kitchen should be kept in order. Once a week all woodwork and copper must be scoured. The lights and lamps have to be cleaned daily. Toward servants, one has to be strict and just. Therefore, one should not call them names which aren't suitable for a decent wife. One should give them enough nourishing food. Disobedience and obstinacy are to be referred to me.

My wife will never make visits in my absence. However, she should visit the synagogue every Saturday — at least once a month; also she should go for a walk with the children at least once a week.

CONSIDERATIONS FOR CRITICAL THINKING AND WRITING

1. Describe the tone of Marcus's letter to his wife. To what extent does he accept responsibility for their separation? What significant similarities and differences do you find between Marcus and Torvald Helmer?

2. Read the discussion on historical criticism in Chapter 51, "Critical Strategies for Reading" (pp. 1651–55). How do you think a new historicist would use this letter to shed light on *A Doll's House*?

3. Write a response to the letter from what you imagine the wife's point of view to be.

4. No information is available about this couple's marriage after Ulrike returned home. In an essay, speculate on what you think their relationship was like later in their marriage.

BARRY WITHAM (B. 1939) AND
JOHN LUTTERBIE (B. 1948)

Witham and Lutterbie describe how they use a Marxist approach to teach *A Doll's House* in their drama class, in which they teach plays from a variety of critical perspectives.

A Marxist Approach to A Doll House   1985

A principal tenet of Marxist criticism is that human consciousness is a product of social conditions and that human relationships are often subverted by and through economic considerations. Mrs. Linde has sacrificed a genuine love to provide for her brothers, and Krogstad has committed a crime to support his children. Anne-Marie, the maid, has also been the victim of her economic background. Because she's "a girl who's poor and gotten in trouble," her relationship with her child has been interrupted and virtually destroyed. In each instance the need for money is linked with the ability to exist. But while the characters accept the social realities of their misfortunes, they do not appear to question how their human attitudes have been thoroughly shaped by socioeconomic considerations.

Once students begin to perceive how consciousness is affected by economics, a Marxist reading of Ibsen's play can illuminate a number of areas. Krogstad, for example, becomes less of a traditional villain when we realize that he is fighting for his job at the bank "as if it were life itself." And his realization of the senselessness of their lives is poignantly revealed when he reflects on Mrs. Linde's past, "all this simply for money." Even Dr. Rank speaks about his failing health and imminent death in entirely financial terms. "These past few days I've been auditing my internal accounts. Bankrupt! Within a month I'll probably be laid out and rotting in the churchyard."

All these characters, however, serve as foils for the central struggle between Nora and Torvald and highlight the pilgrimage that Nora makes in the play. At the outset two things are clear: (1) Nora is enslaved by Torvald in economic terms, and

(2) she equates personal freedom with the acquisition of wealth. The play begins joyfully not only because it is the holiday season but also because Torvald's promotion to bank manager will ensure "a safe, secure job with a comfortable salary." Nora is happy because she sees the future in wholly economic terms. "Won't it be lovely to have stacks of money and not a care in the world?"

What she learns, however, is that financial enslavement is symptomatic of other forms of enslavement — master-slave, male-female, sexual objectification, all of which characterize her relationship with Torvald — and that money is no guarantee of happiness. At the end of the play she renounces not only her marital vows but also her financial dependence because she has discovered that personal and human freedom are not measured in economic terms.

This discovery also prompts her to reexamine the society of which she is a part and leads us into a consideration of the ideology in the play. In what sense has Nora committed a criminal offense in forging her father's name? Is it indeed just that she should be punished for an altruistic act, one that cost her dearly both in terms of self-denial and the destruction of her family? Ibsen's defense of Nora is clear, of course, and his implicit indictment of a society that encourages this kind of injustice stimulates a discussion of the assumptions that created the law.

One of the striking things about *A Doll House* is how Anne-Marie accepts her alienation from her child as if it were natural, given the circumstances of class and money. It does not occur to her that laws were framed by other people and thus are capable of imperfection and susceptible to change. Nora broke a law that not only tries to stop thievery (the appropriation of capital) by outlawing forgery but also discriminates against anyone deemed a bad risk. Question leads to question as the class investigates why women were bad risks and why they had difficulty finding employment. It becomes obvious that the function of women in this society was not "natural" but artificial, a role created by their relationship to the family and by their subservience to men. In the marketplace they were a labor force expecting subsistence wages and providing an income to supplement that earned by their husbands or fathers.

An even clearer picture of Nora's society emerges when the Marxist critic examines those features or elements that are not in the play. These "absences" become valuable clues in understanding the ideology in the text. In the words of Fredric Jameson, absences are

> terms or nodal points implicit in the ideological system which have, however, remained unrealized in the surface of the text, which have failed to become manifest in the logic of the narrative, and which we can therefore read as what the text represses.[1]

The notion of absences is particularly intriguing for students, who learn quickly to apply it to such popular media as films and television (what can we learn about the experience of urban black Americans from sitcoms like *Julia* and *The Jeffersons*?). Absent from *A Doll House* is Nora's mother, an omission that ties her more firmly to a male-dominated world and the bank owners who promoted Torvald. These

---

[1] Fredric Jameson, *The Political Unconscious: Narrative as a Socially Symbolic Act* (Ithaca: Cornell UP, 1981), p. 48.

absences shape our view because they form a layer of reality that is repressed in the play. And an examination of this "repressed" material leads us to our final topic of discussion: What is the relation between this play and the society in which it was created and produced?

Most Marxist critics believe that there are only three possible answers: the play supports the status quo, argues for reforms in an essentially sound system, or advocates a radical restructuring. Though these options are seemingly reductive, discussion reveals the complexities of reaching any unanimous agreement, and students frequently disagree about Ibsen's intentions regarding reform or revolution. Nora's leaving is obviously a call for change, but many students are not sure whether this leave-taking is a way forward or a cul-de-sac for a system that is thoroughly controlled by the prevailing power structure. . . .

Viewing the play through the lens of Marxist atheists does make one thing clear. Nora's departure had ramifications for her society that went beyond the marriage bed. By studying the play within the context of its socioeconomic structure, we can see how the ideology in the text affects the characters and how they perpetuate the ideology. The conclusion of *A Doll House* was a challenge to the economic superstructures that had controlled and excluded the Noras of the world by manipulating their economic status and, by extension, their conscious estimation of themselves and their place in society.

From "A Marxist Approach to *A Doll House*"
in *Approaches to Teaching Ibsen's* A Doll House

CONSIDERATIONS FOR CRITICAL THINKING AND WRITING

1. To what extent do you agree or disagree with the Marxist "tenet" (para. 1) that "consciousness is affected by economics" (para. 2)?

2. Do you think that Nora's "leave-taking is a way forward or a cul-de-sac for a system that is thoroughly controlled by the prevailing power structure" (para. 8)? Explain your response.

3. Consider whether "A Nineteenth-Century Husband's Letter to His Wife" (p. 1414) supports or challenges Witham and Lutterbie's Marxist reading of *A Doll's House*.

CAROL STRONGIN TUFTS (B. 1947)

A Psychoanalytic Reading of Nora   1986

I am not a member of the Women's Rights League. Whatever I have written has been without any conscious thought of making propaganda. I have been more the poet and less the social philosopher than people generally seem inclined to believe. . . . To me it has seemed a problem of mankind in general. And if you read my books carefully you will understand this. . . . My task has been the *description of humanity.* To be sure, whenever such a description is felt to be reasonably true, the reader will read his own feelings and sentiments into the work of the poet.

These are then attributed to the poet; but incorrectly so. Every reader remolds the work beautifully and neatly, each according to his own personality. Not only those who write but also those who read are poets. They are collaborators.[1]

To look again at Ibsen's famous and often-quoted words — his assertion that *A Doll House* was not intended as propaganda to promote the cause of women's rights — is to realize the sarcasm aimed by the playwright at those nineteenth-century "collaborators" who insisted on viewing his play as a treatise and Nora, his heroine, as the romantic standard-bearer for the feminist cause. Yet there is also a certain irony implicit in such a realization, for directors, actors, audiences, and critics turning to this play a little over one hundred years after its first performance bring with them the historical, cultural, and psychological experience which itself places them in the role of Ibsen's collaborators. Because it is a theatrical inevitability that each dramatic work which survives its time and place of first performance does so to be recast in productions mounted in succeeding times and different places, *A Doll House* can never so much be simply reproduced as it must always be re-envisioned. And if the spectacle of a woman walking out on her husband and children in order to fulfill her "duties to (her)self" is no longer the shock for us today that it was for audiences at the end of the nineteenth century, a production of *A Doll House* which resonates with as much immediacy and power for us as it did for its first audiences may do so through the discovery within Ibsen's text of something of our own time and place. For in *A Doll House*, as Rolf Fjelde has written, "(i)t is the entire house . . . which is on trial, the total complex of relationships, including husband, wife, children, servants, upstairs and downstairs, that is tested by the visitors that come and go, embodying aspects of the inescapable reality outside."[2] And a production which approaches that reality through the experience of Western culture in the last quarter of the twentieth century may not only discover how uneasy was Ibsen's relationship to certain aspects of the forces of Romanticism at work in his own society, but, in so doing, may also come to fashion *A Doll House* which shifts emphasis away from the celebration of the Romantic belief in the sovereignty of the individual to the revelation of an isolating narcissism — a narcissism that has become all too familiar to us today.[3]

The characters of *A Doll House* are, to be sure, not alone in dramatic literature in being self-preoccupied, for self-preoccupation is a quality shared by characters from Oedipus to Hamlet and on into modern drama. Yet if a contemporary production is to suggest the narcissistic self-absorption of Ibsen's characters, it must do so in

---

[1] Speech delivered at the Banquet of the Norwegian League for Women's Rights, Christiana, 26 May 1898, in *Ibsen: Letters and Speeches,* ed. Evert Sprinchorn (New York: Hill and Wang, 1964), p. 337.
[2] Rolf Fjelde, Introduction to *A Doll House,* in Henrik Ibsen, *The Complete Major Prose Plays* (New York: Farrar, Straus, Giroux, 1978), p. 121.
[3] For studies of the prevalence of the narcissistic personality disorder in contemporary psychoanalytic literature, see Otto F. Kernberg, *Borderline Conditions and Pathological Narcissism* (New York: J. Aronson, 1975); Heinz Kohut, *The Analysis of the Self* (New York: International Universities Press, 1971); and Peter L. Giovachinni, *Psychoanalysis of Character Disorders* (New York: J. Aronson, 1975). See also Christopher Lasch, *The Culture of Narcissism* (New York: Norton, 1979), for a discussion of narcissism as the defining characteristic of contemporary American society.

such a way as to imply motivations for their actions and delineate their relationships with one another. Thus it is important to establish a conceptual framework which will provide a degree of precision for the use of the term "narcissism" in this discussion so as to distinguish it from the kind of self-absorption which is an inherent quality necessarily shared by all dramatic characters. For that purpose, it is useful to turn to the criteria established by the Task Force on Nomenclature and Statistics of the American Psychiatric Association for diagnosing the narcissistic personality:

A. Grandiose sense of self-importance and uniqueness, e.g., exaggerates achievements and talents, focuses on how special one's problems are.
B. Preoccupation with fantasies of unlimited success, power, brilliance, beauty, or ideal love.
C. Exhibitionistic: requires constant attention and admiration.
D. Responds to criticism, indifference of others, or defeat with either cool indifference, or with marked feelings of rage, inferiority, shame, humiliation, or emptiness.
E. At least two of the following are characteristics of disturbances in interpersonal relationships:

1. Lack of empathy: inability to recognize how others feel, e.g., unable to appreciate the distress of someone who is seriously ill.
2. Entitlement: expectation of special favors without assuming reciprocal responsibilities, e.g., surprise and anger that people won't do what he wants.
3. Interpersonal exploitiveness: takes advantage of others to indulge own desires for self-aggrandizement, with disregard for the personal integrity and rights of others.
4. Relationships characteristically vacillate between the extremes of over-idealization and devaluation.[4]

These criteria, as they provide a background against which to consider Nora's relationship with both Kristine Linde and Dr. Rank, will serve to illuminate not only those relationships themselves, but also the relationship of Nora and her husband which is at the center of the play. Moreover, if these criteria are viewed as outlines for characterization—but not as reductive psychoanalytic constructs leading to "case studies"—it becomes possible to discover a Nora of greater complexity than the totally sympathetic victim turned romantic heroine who has inhabited most productions of the play. And, most important of all, as Nora and her relationships within the walls of her "doll house" come to imply a paradigm of the dilemma of all human relationships in the greater society outside, the famous sound of the slamming door may come to resonate even more loudly for us than it did for the audiences of the nineteenth century with a profound and immediate sense of irony and ambiguity, an irony and ambiguity which could not have escaped Ibsen himself.

> From "Recasting *A Doll House:* Narcissism as Character Motivation
> in Ibsen's Play," *Comparative Drama,* Summer 1986

CONSIDERATIONS FOR CRITICAL THINKING AND WRITING

1. What is Tufts's purpose in arguing that Nora be seen as narcissistic?

---

[4] Task Force on Nomenclature and Statistics, American Psychiatric Association, *DSM-III: Diagnostic Criteria Draft* (New York, 1978), pp. 103–04.

2. Using the criteria of the American Psychiatric Association, consider Nora's personality. Write an essay either refuting the assertion that she has a narcissistic personality or supporting it.

3. How does Tufts's reading compare with Joan Templeton's feminist reading of Nora in the Perspective that follows? Which do you find more convincing? Why?

JOAN TEMPLETON (B. 1942)

This feminist perspective summarizes the arguments against reading the play as a dramatization of a feminist heroine.

Is A Doll House *a Feminist Text?*   1989

A Doll House *is no more about women's rights than Shakespeare's* Richard II *is about the divine right of kings, or* Ghosts *about syphilis. . . . Its theme is the need of every individual to find out the kind of person he or she is and to strive to become that person.*[1]

Ibsen has been resoundingly saved from feminism, or, as it was called in his day, "the woman question." His rescuers customarily cite a statement the dramatist made on 26 May 1898 at a seventieth-birthday banquet given in his honor by the Norwegian Women's Rights League:

> I thank you for the toast, but must disclaim the honor of having consciously worked for the women's rights movement. . . . True enough, it is desirable to solve the woman problem, along with all the others; but that has not been the whole purpose. My task has been the description of humanity.[2]

Ibsen's champions like to take this disavowal as a precise reference to his purpose in writing *A Doll House* twenty years earlier, his "original intention," according to Maurice Valency.[3] Ibsen's biographer Michael Meyer urges all reviewers of *A Doll House* revivals to learn Ibsen's speech by heart,[4] and James McFarlane, editor of *The Oxford Ibsen,* includes it in his explanatory material on *A Doll House,* under "Some Pronouncements of the Author," as though Ibsen had been speaking of the play.[5] Whatever propaganda feminists may have made of *A Doll House,* Ibsen, it is argued, never meant to write a play about the highly topical subject of women's rights; Nora's conflict represents something other than, or something more than, woman's. In an article commemorating the half century of Ibsen's death,

[1] Michael Meyer, *Ibsen* (Garden City: Doubleday, 1971), 457. [This is not the Michael Meyer who is editor of *The Bedford Introduction to Literature.*]

[2] Henrik Ibsen, *Letters and Speeches,* ed. and trans. Evert Sprinchorn (New York: Hill, 1964), 337.

[3] Maurice Valency, *The Flower and the Castle: An Introduction to Modern Drama* (New York: Schocken, 1982), 151.

[4] Meyer, 774.

[5] James McFarlane, "*A Doll's House:* Commentary" in *The Oxford Ibsen,* ed. McFarlane (Oxford UP, 1961), V, 456.

R. M. Adams explains, "*A Doll House* represents a woman imbued with the idea of becoming a person, but it proposes nothing categorical about women becoming people; in fact, its real theme has nothing to do with the sexes."[6] Over twenty years later, after feminism had resurfaced as an international movement, Einar Haugen, the doyen of American Scandinavian studies, insisted that "Ibsen's Nora is not just a woman arguing for female liberation; she is much more. She embodies the comedy as well as the tragedy of modern life."[7] In the Modern Language Association's *Approaches to Teaching* A Doll House, the editor speaks disparagingly of "reductionist views of *(A Doll House)* as a feminist drama." Summarizing a "major theme" in the volume as "the need for a broad view of the play and a condemnation of a static approach," she warns that discussions of the play's "connection with feminism" have value only if they are monitored, "properly channeled and kept firmly linked to Ibsen's text."[8]

Removing the woman question from *A Doll House* is presented as part of a corrective effort to free Ibsen from his erroneous reputation as a writer of thesis plays, a wrongheaded notion usually blamed on Shaw, who, it is claimed, mistakenly saw Ibsen as the nineteenth century's greatest iconoclast and offered that misreading to the public as *The Quintessence of Ibsenism*. Ibsen, it is now de rigueur to explain, did not stoop to "issues." He was a poet of the truth of the human soul. That Nora's exit from her dollhouse has long been the principal international symbol for women's issues, including many that far exceed the confines of her small world, is irrelevant to the essential meaning of *A Doll House*, a play, in Richard Gilman's phrase, "pitched beyond sexual difference."[9] Ibsen, explains Robert Brustein, "was completely indifferent to (the woman question) except as a metaphor for individual freedom."[10] Discussing the relation of *A Doll House* to feminism, Halvdan Koht, author of the definitive Norwegian Ibsen life, says in summary, "Little by little the topical controversy died away; what remained was the work of art, with its demand for truth in every human relation."[11]

Thus, it turns out, the *Uncle Tom's Cabin* of the women's rights movement is not really about women at all. "Fiddle-faddle," pronounced R. M. Adams, dismissing feminist claims for the play.[12] Like angels, Nora has no sex. Ibsen meant her to be Everyman.

> From "The *Doll House* Backlash: Criticism, Feminism, and Ibsen,"
>
> *PMLA,* January 1989

---

[6] R. M. Adams, "The Fifty-First Anniversary," *Hudson Review* 10 (1957): 416.
[7] Einar Haugen, *Ibsen's Drama: Author to Audience* (Minneapolis: U of Minnesota P, 1979), vii.
[8] Yvonne Shafer, ed., *Approaches to Teaching Ibsen's* A Doll House (New York: MLA, 1985), 32.
[9] Richard Gilman, *The Making of Modern Drama* (New York: Farrar, 1972), 65.
[10] Robert Brustein, *The Theatre of Revolt* (New York: Little, 1962), 105.
[11] Halvdan Koht, *Life of Ibsen* (New York: Blom, 1971), 323.
[12] Adams, 416.

CONSIDERATIONS FOR CRITICAL THINKING AND WRITING

1. According to Templeton, what kinds of arguments are used to reject *A Doll's House* as a feminist text?

2. From the tone of the summaries provided, what would you say is Templeton's attitude toward these arguments?

3. Read the section on feminist criticism in Chapter 51, "Critical Strategies for Reading" (pp. 1655–56), and write an essay addressing the summarized arguments as you think a feminist critic might respond.

APPLYING A CRITICAL STRATEGY

This section offers advice about developing an argument that draws on the different strategies, or schools of literary theory, covered in Chapter 51. The following list of questions and suggestions will help you to apply one or more of these critical strategies to a work in order to shed light on it. Following the questions is a sample paper based on *A Doll's House* (p. 1425).

There are many possible lenses through which to read a literary work. The Perspectives and Critical Case Studies in this anthology suggest a variety of approaches — including formalist, biographical, psychological, Marxist, new historicist, feminist, mythological, reader-response, and deconstructionist strategies — that can be used to explore the effects, meanings, and significances of a poem, short story, or play (see Chapter 51 for a discussion of these strategies).

Once you have generated a central idea about a work, you will need to choose the critical approach(es) that will allow you to develop your argument. In the following sample paper, the writer chose a new historicist approach because she was interested in speculating about what Nora faced after she left her husband on the other side of the slammed door in *A Doll's House*. By using evidence external to the play, from a letter written by a nineteenth-century husband to his wife, the writer was able to re-create some of the historical context for *A Doll's House* in order to argue that Nora's leaving home is a more risky, problematic action than her simple declaration of freedom from her husband. This historical approach allowed the writer to offer a substantive argument about what Nora might have faced beyond the slammed door.

Regardless of the approach — or combination of approaches — you find helpful, it is essential that you be thoroughly familiar with the text of the literary work before examining it through the lens of a particular critical strategy. Without a strong familiarity with the literary work, you will not be able to judge the accuracy and validity of a critic's arguments, and you might find your own insights immediately superseded by those of the first critic you read. For additional advice on how to incorporate material from critical essays into your writing without losing track of your own argument about a work, see Questions for Writing: Incorporating the Critics (p. 425).

1. Which of the critical strategies discussed in Chapter 51 seems the most appropriate to the literary work under consideration? Why do you prefer one particular approach over another? Do any critical strategies seem especially inappropriate? Why?

2. Does the historical context of a literary work suggest that certain critical strategies, such as Marxism or feminism, might be particularly productive?

3. Does the literary work reflect or challenge the cultural assumptions contemporary to it in such a way as to suggest a critical approach for your paper?

4. Does the author comment on his or her own literary work in letters, interviews, or lectures? If so, how might these comments help you to develop an approach for your paper?

5. Are you able to formulate an interpretation of the work you want to discuss before reading the critics extensively? If so, how might the critics' discussions help you to develop, enhance, or qualify your argument about how to interpret the work?

6. If you haven't developed an argument before reading the critics, how might some exploratory reading lead you into significant questions and controversial issues that would offer topics that could be developed into a thesis?

7. If you are drawing on the work of a number of critics, how are their critical strategies — whether formalist, biographical, psychological, historical, or other — relevant to your own? How can you use their insights to support your own argument?

8. Is it possible and desirable to combine approaches — such as psychological and historical or biographical and feminist — so that multiple perspectives can be used to support your argument?

9. If the strategies or approaches the critics use to interpret the literary work tend to be similar, are there questions and issues that have been neglected or ignored that can become the focus of your argument about the literary work?

10. If the critics' approaches are very different from one another, is there a way to use those differences to argue your own critical approach that allows you to support one critic rather than another or to resolve a controversy among the critics?

11. Is your argument adequately supported with specific evidence from the literary text? Have you been careful not to avoid discussing parts of the text that do not seem to support your argument?

12. Is your own discussion of the literary text free of simple plot summary? Does each paragraph include a thesis statement that advances your argument rather than merely consisting of facts and plot summary?

13. Have you accurately and fairly represented the critics' arguments?

14. Have you made your own contributions, qualifications, or disagreements with the critics clear to your reader?

A SAMPLE STUDENT PAPER

On the Other Side of the Slammed Door in Henrik Ibsen's A Doll's House

The following sample paper focuses on the magnitude of Nora Helmer's decision to leave her husband in *A Doll's House*. Kathy Atner uses a new historicist perspective to show just how difficult Nora's decision would have been in the context of nineteenth-century attitudes toward marriage and women. The paper develops an argument primarily from evidence supplied by "A Nineteenth-Century Husband's Letter to His Wife" (p. 1414). By drawing on a source that ordinarily might have been ignored by literary critics, Atner is able to suggest how difficult Nora's life would have been after abandoning her husband and family. This historical strategy is combined with a feminist perspective that gives the modern reader a greater understanding of the issues Nora must inevitably confront once she slams the door shut on her conventional and accepted life as devoted wife and mother. By using both new historicist and feminist perspectives, Atner suggests that contemporary readers should be sensitive to the tragic as well as the heroic dimension of Nora's life.

Atner 1

Kathy Atner

Professor Porter

English 216

6 April 2015

On the Other Side of the Slammed Door

in Henrik Ibsen's *A Doll's House*

Nora Helmer's decision to leave her family in Henrik Ibsen's 1879 play *A Doll's House* reflects the dilemma faced by many nineteenth-century women who were forced either to conform to highly restrictive gender roles or to abandon these roles in order to realize their value as individuals. Although Ibsen brings his audience to the moment that Nora chooses to disregard her social role and opt for her "freedom," his play does not clearly reveal the true fate of women who followed Nora's path in the nineteenth century. Historically, most women who chose not to acquiesce to the socially prescribed roles of marriage were treated as unnatural creatures and shunned by the respectable public. An actual letter, written in 1844 by a man named Marcus to his estranged wife, Ulrike,

> Thesis placing play in historical context

reveals the effects of this severe social condemnation (1414). His

letter implies the desperate fate that inevitably befalls women who reject their prescribed duties as wives and mothers. Through Marcus's letter to his wife, the painful ramifications of Nora's decision to accommodate her own personal desires instead of those of her family become even more poignant, courageous, and tragic.

In the nineteenth century, women had few alternatives to marriage, and women who "failed" at marriage were thought to have failed in their most important duty. In his letter, Marcus articulates society's deep disgust for women who reject what it believes is the sacred female role of home-maker. His letter, while on one level an angry condemnation of his wife's

"stubbornness" (1414) and a cruelly condescending list of conditions to be met on her return, is on another level a plea for her to accept again the role that society has assigned her. He is clearly shaken by his wife's abandonment and interprets it as a betrayal of a social "law" or tradition, which, to Marcus's mind, ought to be carved in stone. He responds to this betrayal by demanding complete obedience from his wife in the form of a promise "to follow my wishes in everything and to strictly obey my orders" (1415). Only when she acquiesces to his conditions and returns to her role as docile and obedient wife will Marcus in turn be able to resume the comfortably familiar, socially sanctioned role of dominant, morally superior husband.

Like Ulrike, Nora decides to leave the security and comfort of her restrictive domestic life to try to become a human being. Ibsen neglects, however, to show his audience the actual result of that decision. At the conclusion of *A Doll's House,* Nora slams the door on her past life, hoping to begin a new life that will somehow be more satisfying. Yet the modern

audience has no genuine sense of what she may have found beyond that door, and perhaps neither did Nora. Through Ulrike's story, however, the reader understands the historical truth that the world awaiting Nora was hostile and unsympathetic. Marcus warns his wife that "your husband, children, and the entire city threaten indifference or even contempt" (1414) if she refuses to return immediately to her socially acceptable domestic role. This pressure to conform, combined with the bleak prospects of a single woman, results in

Atner 3

Ulrike's ultimate choice to keep up "appearances" rather than further subject herself to a contemptuous world that neither wants nor understands her. Although we cannot know Nora's fate after she leaves Torvald, we may assume that her future would be as bleak as Ulrike's and that the pressure to return to her domestic life would be equally strong.

When *A Doll's House* was first produced in 1879, audiences had no more sympathy for Nora's predicament than they did for the real-life stories of women such as Ulrike. As Errol Durbach points out, in the nineteenth century, Ibsen's play "did not precipitate heated debate about feminism, women's rights, or male domination. The sound and the fury were addressed to the very question . . . What credible wife and mother would ever walk out this way on her family?" (14). A great many readers and audience members tended to side with Torvald, who seemed, to them, the innocent victim of Nora's consuming selfishness. The audience's repulsion toward Nora's apparently "unnatural" action of abandoning her family mirrors the responses of Marcus and Torvald Helmer, the bereft, perplexed, and angry husbands. Nora and Ulrike radically disrupt their husbands' perceptions of family relationships by walking out of their lives, preferring to recognize their own needs before any others. These women suggest that Torvald's claim that "Before all else, you are a wife and a mother" (1403) may not necessarily be true for all women, but their brave rejections of domestic life cannot force society to condone their behavior.

> Analysis of status of women and audience of the nineteenth century

Ibsen maintains that *A Doll's House* is not about women's rights specifically but encompasses a more universal "description of humanity" (*Letters* 337). In showing a human being trying to create a new identity for herself, however, Ibsen reveals the extent to which people are trapped in societal norms and expectations. Nora's acknowledgment that she "can no longer content myself with what most people say, or with what is found in books" (1404) suggests a profound social upheaval that has the potential to subvert long-established gender roles. If Nora and Ulrike relinquish the role of the subservient and helpless wife, then Torvald and Marcus can no longer play the role of the dominating, protective husband. Without this role, the men are as helpless as they want their wives to be, and the traditional gender

> Analysis of play in context of nineteenth-century reality

expectations are no longer beyond question. Yet the historical reality is that in spite of Nora's daring escape from her oppressive family, the world was not ready to accommodate women who rejected their feminine duties. Ulrike was thwarted in her attempt to free herself from her family; history suggests that Nora may have met a similar fate.

Modern audiences tend to see Nora as a strong, admirable woman who is courageous enough to sacrifice everything in order to fulfill her own needs as an individual and as a woman. She shatters gender stereotypes through her defiant disregard for all that society demands of her. Yet, taken in the context of nineteenth-century life, perhaps Nora's story is more tragic than we might initially like to believe. Ulrike's story, told through her husband's letter, suggests that in a time of turbulent social upheaval, what was interpreted as a collapse of what we now call "family values" was shocking, scandalous, and deeply frightening to many. In the nineteenth century, Nora was not the sympathetic character that she is today; instead, she symbolized many negative attributes—what Marcus calls "false ambitions" and "stubbornness" (1414)—that were often ascribed to women. Ulrike's forced return to her role as dutiful wife and mother suggests that society was quick to punish disobedient women and that the slamming door at the end of *A Doll's House* was not necessarily the sound of freedom for Nora.

Concluding historical analysis of play as tragedy

Works Cited

Durbach, Errol. *A Doll's House: Ibsen's Myth of Transformation*. Boston: Twayne, 1991. Print.

Ibsen, Henrik. *A Doll's House*. Trans. R. Farquharson Sharp. Meyer 1358–1406. Print.

———. *Letters and Speeches*. Ed. and trans. Evert Sprinchorn. New York: Hill, 1964. Print.

Meyer, Michael, ed. *The Bedford Introduction to Literature*. 11th ed. Boston: Bedford/St. Martin's, 2016. Print.

"A Nineteenth-Century Husband's Letter to His Wife." Meyer 1414–15. Print.

48

A CRITICAL CASE STUDY

John Patrick Shanley's
Doubt: A Parable

Doubt is nothing less than an
opportunity to reenter the Present.

— JOHN PATRICK SHANLEY

© Fairchild Photo Service/Condé Nast/
CORBIS.

This chapter offers several perspectives on John Patrick Shanley's provocative play *Doubt: A Parable*. A tightly written and traditional well-made play, the tensions produced in *Doubt* have fascinated theater and film audiences as well as readers owing to the trembling balance that Shanley creates between the two main characters, Sister Aloysius and Father Flynn. Though set in a Catholic grammar school in 1964, the play transcends any potentially parochial limitations by presenting deeply personal conflicts embedded in basic human concerns that explore moral certainty and doubt. The Perspectives following the play offer some biographical, cultural, and performance contexts that should enhance your reading of the text.

A BRIEF BIOGRAPHY

A playwright, screenwriter, and director, John Patrick Shanley was born the son of an Irish immigrant meatpacker and raised in the east Bronx, where he attended St. Anthony's Grammar School, was expelled from Cardinal Spellman High School, and subsequently graduated from Thomas More Preparatory School in New Hampshire. Shanley's life and writing has been steeped in the tumultuous blue-collar world of his Bronx youth. A former marine, he has worked, among other jobs, as a bartender, locksmith, house painter, and elevator operator; in 1977 he gradu-

© Fairchild Photo Service/Condé Nast/ CORBIS.

ated from New York University as valedictorian. He has written more than two dozen plays, including *Women of Manhattan* (1986), *Dirty Story* (2003), and *Outside Mullinger* (2014), as well as a number of successful film and television screenplays. His breakthrough screenplay, *Moonstruck* (1987), won the Academy Award for Best Original Screenplay and the Writers Guild of America Award for Best Screenplay Written Directly for the Screen.

In *Doubt: A Parable*, all of Shanley's talents are apparent in an absorbing drama that he wrote for the stage, adapted as a screenplay, and then directed as a film starring Meryl Streep and Philip Seymour Hoffman. The play and film have been showered with recognition, including the Obie Award for Playwriting (2005), the Drama Critics' Circle Award (2005), the Tony Award for Best Play (2005), the Pulitzer Prize for Drama (2005), and the Academy Award for Best Adapted Screenplay (2008). Set in a 1964 Bronx Catholic school, the play is about a stern nun's suspicions concerning a popular liberal priest's relationship with a new young black student. Shanley substitutes our preconceptions about what we think we know about these characters with ambiguities and uncertainties so that what seems predictable becomes equivocal. Shanley has explained in a number of interviews that he likes to attack the notion that plays and films must affirm certainties or validate what audiences already believe. That's not what his work sets out to do: "The theme should arise like smoke off a play. It shouldn't be stated, or if it is, it should go by just like another line."

JOHN PATRICK SHANLEY (B. 1950)

Doubt: A Parable 2005

CHARACTERS

Father Brendan Flynn, late thirties
Sister Aloysius Beauvier, fifties/sixties
Sister James, twenties
Mrs. Muller, around thirty-eight

SETTING: St. Nicholas, a Catholic church and school in the Bronx, New York, 1964

The bad sleep well.
— *Title of Kurosawa film*

In much wisdom is much grief:
and he that increaseth knowledge increaseth
sorrow.
　　　　　　　　　　　　　　— *Ecclesiastes*

See Plays in Performance insert.
Sara Krulwich/*The New York Times*/Redux.

Everything that is hard to attain
is easily assailed by the mob.
　　　　　　　　　　　　— *Ptolemy*

I

A Priest, Father Flynn, in his late thirties, in green and gold vestments, gives a sermon. He is working class, from the Northeast.

Flynn: What do you do when you're not sure? That's the topic of my sermon today. You look for God's direction and can't find it. Last year when President Kennedy was assassinated, who among us did not experience the most profound disorientation. Despair. "What now? Which way? What do I say to my kids? What do I tell myself?" It was a time of people sitting together, bound together by a common feeling of hopelessness. But think of that! Your *bond* with your fellow beings was your *despair.* It was a public experience, shared by everyone in our society. It was awful, but we were in it together! How much worse is it then for the lone man, the lone woman, stricken by a private calamity? "No one knows I'm sick. No one knows I've lost my last real friend. No one knows I've done something wrong." Imagine the isolation. You see the world as through a window. On the one side of the glass: happy, untroubled people. On the other side: you. Something has happened, you have to carry it, and it's incommunicable. For those so afflicted, only God knows their pain. Their secret. The secret of their alienating sorrow. And when such a person, as they must, howls to the sky, to God: "Help me!" What if no answer comes? Silence. I want to tell you a story. A cargo ship sank and all her crew was drowned. Only this one sailor survived. He made a raft of some spars and, being of a nautical discipline, turned his eyes to the Heavens and read the stars. He set a course for his home, and, exhausted, fell asleep. Clouds rolled in and blanketed the sky. For the next twenty nights, as he floated on the vast ocean, he could no longer see the stars. He thought he was on course but there was no way to be certain. As the days rolled on, and he wasted away with fevers, thirst and starvation, he began to have doubts. Had he set his course right? Was he still going on towards his home? Or was he horribly lost and doomed to a terrible death? No way to know. The message of the constellations — had he imagined it because of his desperate circumstance? Or had he seen Truth once, and now had to hold on to it without further reassurance? That was his dilemma on a voyage without apparent end. There are those of you in church today who know exactly the crisis of faith I describe. I want to say to you: Doubt can be a bond as powerful and sustaining as certainty. When you are lost, you are not alone. In the name of the Father, the Son, and the Holy Ghost. Amen.

(He exits.)

II

The lights crossfade to a corner office in a Catholic school in the Bronx. The principal, Sister Aloysius Beauvier, sits at her desk, writing in a ledger with a fountain pen. She is in her fifties or sixties. She is watchful, reserved, unsentimental. She is of the order of the Sisters of Charity. She wears a black bonnet and floor-length black habit, rimless glasses. A knock at the door.

Sister Aloysius: Come in.

(Sister James, also of the Sisters of Charity, pokes her head in. She is in her twenties. There's a bit of sunshine in her heart, though she's reserved as well.)

Sister James: Have you a moment, Sister Aloysius?
Sister Aloysius: Come in, Sister James.

(She enters.)

Who's watching your class?
Sister James: They're having Art.
Sister Aloysius: Art. Waste of time.
Sister James: It's only an hour a week.
Sister Aloysius: Much can be accomplished in sixty minutes.
Sister James: Yes, Sister Aloysius. I wondered if I might know what you did about William London?
Sister Aloysius: I sent him home.
Sister James: Oh dear. So he's still bleeding?
Sister Aloysius: Oh yes.
Sister James: His nose just let loose and started gushing during The Pledge of Allegiance.
Sister Aloysius: Was it spontaneous?
Sister James: What else would it be?
Sister Aloysius: Self-induced.
Sister James: You mean, you think he might've intentionally given himself a nosebleed?
Sister Aloysius: Exactly.
Sister James: No!
Sister Aloysius: You are a very innocent person, Sister James. William London is a fidgety boy and if you do not keep right on him, he will do anything to escape his chair. He would set his foot on fire for half a day out of school.
Sister James: But why?
Sister Aloysius: He has a restless mind.
Sister James: But that's good.
Sister Aloysius: No, it's not. His father's a policeman and the last thing he wants is a rowdy boy. William London is headed for trouble. Puberty has got hold of him. He will be imagining all the wrong things, and I strongly suspect he will not graduate high school. But that's beyond our jurisdiction. We simply have

to get him through, out the door, and then he's somebody else's project. Ordinarily, I assign my most experienced sisters to eighth grade but I'm working within constraints. Are you in control of your class?

Sister James: I think so.

Sister Aloysius: Usually more children are sent down to me.

Sister James: I try to take care of things myself.

Sister Aloysius: That can be an error. You are answerable to me, I to the monsignor, he to the bishop, and so on up to the Holy Father. There's a chain of discipline. Make use of it.

Sister James: Yes, Sister.

Sister Aloysius: How's Donald Muller doing?

Sister James: Steady.

Sister Aloysius: Good. Has anyone hit him?

Sister James: No.

Sister Aloysius: Good. That girl Linda Conte, have you seated her away from the boys?

Sister James: As far as space permits. It doesn't do much good.

Sister Aloysius: Just get her through. Intact.

(*Pause. Sister Aloysius is staring absently at Sister James. A silence falls.*)

Sister James: So. Should I go? (*No answer*) Is something the matter?

Sister Aloysius: No. Why? Is something the matter?

Sister James: I don't think so.

Sister Aloysius: Then nothing's the matter then.

Sister James: Well. Thank you, Sister. I just wanted to check on William's nose.

(*She starts to go.*)

Sister Aloysius: He had a ballpoint pen.

Sister James: Excuse me, Sister?

Sister Aloysius: William London had a ballpoint pen. He was fiddling with it while he waited for his mother. He's not using it for assignments, I hope.

Sister James: No, of course not.

Sister Aloysius: I'm sorry I allowed even cartridge pens into the school. The students really should only be learning script with true fountain pens. Always the easy way out these days. What does that teach? Every easy choice today will have its consequence tomorrow. Mark my words.

Sister James: Yes, Sister.

Sister Aloysius: Ballpoints make them press down, and when they press down, they write like monkeys.

Sister James: I don't allow them ballpoint pens.

Sister Aloysius: Good. Penmanship is dying all across the country. You have some time. Sit down.

(*Sister James hesitates and sits down.*)

We might as well have a talk. I've been meaning to talk to you. I observed your lesson on the New Deal at the beginning of the term. Not bad. But I caution you. Do not idealize Franklin Delano Roosevelt. He was a good president, but he did attempt to pack the Supreme Court. I do not approve of making heroes of lay historical figures. If you want to talk about saints, do it in Religion.

Sister James: Yes, Sister.

Sister Aloysius: Also. I question your enthusiasm for History.

Sister James: But I love History!

Sister Aloysius: That is exactly my meaning. You favor History and risk swaying the children to value it over their other subjects. I think this is a mistake.

Sister James: I never thought of that. I'll try to treat my other lessons with more enthusiasm.

Sister Aloysius: No. Give them their History without putting sugar all over it. That's the point. Now. Tell me about your class. How would you characterize the condition of 8-B?

Sister James: I don't know where to begin. What do you want to know?

Sister Aloysius: Let's begin with Stephen Inzio.

Sister James: Stephen Inzio has the highest marks in the class.

Sister Aloysius: Noreen Horan?

Sister James: Second highest marks.

Sister Aloysius: Brenda McNulty?

Sister James: Third highest.

Sister Aloysius: You see I am making a point, Sister James. I know that Stephen Inzio, Noreen Horan and Brenda McNulty are one, two and three in your class. School-wide, there are forty-eight such students each grade period. I make it my business to know all forty-eight of their names. I do not say this to aggrandize myself, but to illustrate the importance of paying attention. You must pay attention as well.

Sister James: Yes, Sister Aloysius.

Sister Aloysius: I cannot be everywhere.

Sister James: Am I falling short, Sister?

Sister Aloysius: These three students with the highest marks. Are they the most intelligent children in your class?

Sister James: No, I wouldn't say they are. But they work the hardest.

Sister Aloysius: Very good! That's right! That's the ethic. What good's a gift if it's left in the box? What good is a high IQ if you're staring out the window with your mouth agape? Be hard on the bright ones, Sister James. Don't be charmed by cleverness. Not theirs. And not yours. I think you are a competent teacher, Sister James, but maybe not our best teacher. The best teachers do not perform, they cause the students to perform.

Sister James: Do I perform?

Sister Aloysius: As if on a Broadway stage.

Sister James: Oh dear. I had no conception!

Sister Aloysius: You're showing off. You like to see yourself ten feet tall in their eyes. Another thing occurs to me. Where were you before?

Sister James: Mount St. Margaret's.

Sister Aloysius: All girls.

Sister James: Yes.

Sister Aloysius: I feel I must remind you. Boys are made of gravel, soot and tar paper. Boys are a different breed.

Sister James: I feel I know how to handle them.

Sister Aloysius: But perhaps you are wrong. And perhaps you are not working hard enough.

Sister James: Oh.

(Sister James cries a little.)

Sister Aloysius: No tears.

Sister James: I thought you were satisfied with me.

Sister Aloysius: Satisfaction is a vice. Do you have a handkerchief?

Sister James: Yes.

Sister Aloysius: Use it. Do you think that Socrates was satisfied? Good teachers are never content. We have some three hundred and seventy-two students in this school. It is a society which requires constant educational, spiritual and human vigilance. I cannot afford an excessively innocent instructor in my eighth grade class. It's self-indulgent. Innocence is a form of laziness. Innocent teachers are easily duped. You must be canny, Sister James.

Sister James: Yes, Sister.

Sister Aloysius: When William London gets a nosebleed, be skeptical. Don't let a little blood fuddle your judgment. God gave you a brain and a heart. The heart is warm, but your wits must be cold. Liars should be frightened to lie to you. They should be uncomfortable in your presence. I doubt they are.

Sister James: I don't know. I've never thought about it.

Sister Aloysius: The children should think you see right through them.

Sister James: Wouldn't that be a little frightening?

Sister Aloysius: Only to the ones that are up to no good.

Sister James: But I want my students to feel they can talk to me.

Sister Aloysius: They're children. They can talk to each other. It's more important they have a fierce moral guardian. You stand at the door, Sister. You are the gatekeeper. If you are vigilant, they will not need to be.

Sister James: I'm not sure what you want me to do.

Sister Aloysius: And if things occur in your classroom which you sense require understanding, but you don't understand, come to me.

Sister James: Yes, Sister.

Sister Aloysius: That's why I'm here. That's why I'm the principal of this school. Do you stay when the specialty instructors come in?

Sister James: Yes.

Sister Aloysius: But you're here now while the Art class is going on.

Sister James: I was a little concerned about William's nose.

Sister Aloysius: Right. So you have Art in class.

Sister James: She comes in. Mrs. Bell. Yes.

Sister Aloysius: And you take them down to the basement for Dance with Mrs. Shields.

Sister James: On Thursdays.

Sister Aloysius: Another waste of time.

Sister James: Oh, but everyone loves the Christmas pageant.

Sister Aloysius: I don't love it. Frankly it offends me. Last year the girl playing Our Lady was wearing lipstick. I was waiting in the wings for that little jade.

Sister James: Then there's Music.

Sister Aloysius: That strange woman with the portable piano. What's wrong with her neck?

Sister James: Some kind of goiter. Poor woman.

Sister Aloysius: Yes. Mrs. Carolyn.

Sister James: That's right.

Sister Aloysius: We used to have a Sister teaching that. Not enough Sisters. What else?

Sister James: Physical Education and Religion.

Sister Aloysius: And for that we have Father Flynn. Two hours a week. And you stay for those?

Sister James: Mostly. Unless I have reports to fill out or . . .

Sister Aloysius: What do you think of Father Flynn?

Sister James: Oh, he's a brilliant man. What a speaker!

Sister Aloysius: Yes. His sermon this past Sunday was poetic.

Sister James: He's actually very good, too, at teaching basketball. I was surprised. I wouldn't think a man of the cloth the personality type for basketball, but he has a way he has, very natural with dribbling and shooting.

Sister Aloysius: What do you think that sermon was about?

Sister James: What?

Sister Aloysius: This past Sunday. What was he talking about?

Sister James: Well, Doubt. He was talking about Doubt.

Sister Aloysius: Why?

Sister James: Excuse me, Sister?

Sister Aloysius: Well, sermons come from somewhere, don't they? Is Father Flynn in Doubt, is he concerned that someone else is in Doubt?

Sister James: I suppose you'd have to ask him.

Sister Aloysius: No. That would not be appropriate. He is my superior. And if he were troubled, he should confess it to a fellow priest, or the monsignor. We do not share intimate information with priests.

(*A pause.*)

Sister James: I'm a little concerned.

(*Sister Aloysius leans forward.*)

Sister Aloysius: About what?

Sister James: The time. Art class will be over in a few minutes. I should go up.

Sister Aloysius: Have you noticed anything, Sister James?

Sister James: About what?

Sister Aloysius: I want you to be alert.

Sister James: I don't believe I'm following you, Sister.

Sister Aloysius: I'm sorry I'm not more forthright, but I must be careful not to create something by saying it. I can only say I am concerned, perhaps needlessly, about matters in St. Nicholas School.

Sister James: Academically?

Sister Aloysius: I wasn't inviting a guessing game. I want you to pay attention to your class.

Sister James: Well, of course I'll pay attention to my class, Sister. And I'll try not to perform. And I'll try to be less innocent. I'm sorry you're disappointed in me. Please know that I will try my best. Honestly.

Sister Aloysius: Look at you. You'd trade anything for a warm look. I'm telling you here and now, I want to see the starch in your character cultivated. If you are looking for reassurance, you can be fooled. If you forget yourself and study others, you will not be fooled. It's important. One final matter and then you really must get back. Sister Veronica is going blind.

Sister James: Oh how horrible!

Sister Aloysius: This is not generally known and I don't want it known. If they find out in the rectory, she'll be gone. I cannot afford to lose her. But now if you see her making her way down those stone stairs into the courtyard, for the love of Heaven, lightly take her hand as if in fellowship and see that she doesn't destroy herself. All right, go.

III

The lights crossfade to Father Flynn, whistle around his neck, in a sweatshirt and pants, holding a basketball.

Flynn: All right, settle down, boys. Now the thing about shooting from the foul line: It's psychological. The rest of the game you're cooperating with your teammates, you're competing against the other team. But at the foul line, it's you against yourself. And the danger is: You start to think. When you think, you stop breathing. Your body locks up. So you have to remember to relax. Take a breath, unlock your knees — this is something for you to watch, Jimmy. You stand like a parking meter. Come up with a routine of what you do. Shift your weight, move your hips . . . You think that's funny, Ralph? What's funny is you never getting a foul shot. Don't worry if you look silly. They won't think you're silly if you get the basket. Come up with a routine, concentrate on the routine, and you'll forget to get tensed up. Now on another matter, I've noticed several of you guys have dirty nails. I don't want to see that. I'm not talking about the length of your nails, I'm talking about cleanliness. See? Look at my nails. They're long, I like them a little long, but look at how clean they are. That makes it okay. There was a kid I grew up with, Timmy Mathisson, never had clean nails, and he'd stick his fingers up his nose, in his mouth. — This is a true story, learn to listen! He got spinal meningitis and died a horrible death. Sometimes it's the little things that get you. You try to talk to a girl with those filthy paws, Mr. Conroy, she's gonna take off like she's being chased by the Red Chinese! *(Reacting genially to laughter)* All right, all right. You guys, what am I gonna do with you? Get dressed, come on over to the rectory, have some Kool-Aid and cookies, we'll have a bull session. *(Blows his whistle)* Go!

IV

Crossfade to a bit of garden, a bench, brick walls. Sister Aloysius, in full habit and a black shawl, is wrapping a pruned rosebush in burlap. Sister James enters.

Sister James: Good afternoon, Sister.
Sister Aloysius: Good afternoon, Sister James. Mr. McGinn pruned this bush, which was the right thing to do, but he neglected to protect it from the frost.
Sister James: Have we had a frost?
Sister Aloysius: When it comes, it's too late.
Sister James: You know about gardening?
Sister Aloysius: A little. Where is your class?
Sister James: The girls are having Music.
Sister Aloysius: And the boys?
Sister James: They're in the rectory.

(*Sister James indicates the rectory, which is out of view, just on the other side of the garden.*)

Sister Aloysius: With Father Flynn.

Sister James: Yes. He's giving them a talk.

Sister Aloysius: On what subject?

Sister James: How to be a man.

Sister Aloysius: Well, if Sisters were permitted in the rectory, I would be interested to hear that talk. I don't know how to be a man. I would like to know what's involved. Have you ever given the girls a talk on how to be a woman?

Sister James: No. I wouldn't be competent.

Sister Aloysius: Why not?

Sister James: I just don't think I would. I took my vows at the beginning . . . Before . . . At the beginning.

Sister Aloysius: The founder of our order, The Blessed Mother Seton, was married and had five children before embarking on her vows.

Sister James: I've often wondered how she managed so much in one life.

Sister Aloysius: Life perhaps is longer than you think and the dictates of the soul more numerous. I was married.

Sister James: You were!

(Sister Aloysius smiles for the first time.)

Sister Aloysius: You could at least hide your astonishment.

Sister James: I . . . didn't know.

Sister Aloysius: When one takes on the habit, one must close the door on secular things. My husband died in the war against Adolph Hitler.

Sister James: Really! Excuse me, Sister.

Sister Aloysius: But I'm like you. I'm not sure I would feel competent to lecture tittering girls on the subject of womanhood. I don't come into this garden often. What is it, forty feet across? The convent here, the rectory there. We might as well be separated by the Atlantic Ocean. I used to potter around out here, but Monsignor Benedict does his reverie at quixotic times and we are rightly discouraged from crossing paths with priests unattended. He is seventy-nine, but nevertheless.

Sister James: The monsignor is very good, isn't he?

Sister Aloysius: Yes. But he is oblivious.

Sister James: To what?

Sister Aloysius: I don't believe he knows who's President of the United States. I mean him no disrespect of course. It's just that he's otherworldly in the extreme.

Sister James: Is it that he's innocent, Sister Aloysius?

Sister Aloysius: You have a slyness at work, Sister James. Be careful of it. How is your class? How is Donald Muller?

Sister James: He is thirteenth in class.

Sister Aloysius: I know. That's sufficient. Is he being accepted?

Sister James: He has no friends.

Sister Aloysius: That would be a lot to expect after only two months. Has anyone hit him?

Sister James: No.

Sister Aloysius: Someone will. And when it happens, send them right down to me.

Sister James: I'm not so sure anyone will.

Sister Aloysius: There is a statue of St. Patrick on one side of the church altar and a statue of St. Anthony on the other. This parish serves Irish and Italian families. Someone will hit Donald Muller.

Sister James: He has a protector.
Sister Aloysius: Who?
Sister James: Father Flynn.

(*Sister Aloysius, who has been fussing with mulch, is suddenly rigid. She rises.*)

Sister Aloysius: What?
Sister James: He's taken an interest. Since Donald went on the altar boys. (*Pause*) I thought I should tell you.
Sister Aloysius: I told you to come to me, but I hoped you never would.
Sister James: Maybe I shouldn't have.
Sister Aloysius: I knew once you did, something would be set in motion. So it's happened.
Sister James: What?! I'm not telling you that! I'm not even certain what you mean.
Sister Aloysius: Yes, you are.
Sister James: I've been trying to become more cold in my thinking as you suggested . . . I feel as if I've lost my way a little, Sister Aloysius. I had the most terrible dream last night. I want to be guided by you and responsible to the children, but I want my peace of mind. I must tell you I have been longing for the return of my peace of mind.
Sister Aloysius: You may not have it. It is not your place to be complacent. That's for the children. That's what we give them.
Sister James: I think I'm starting to understand you a little. But it's so unsettling to look at things and people with suspicion. It feels as if I'm less close to God.
Sister Aloysius: When you take a step to address wrongdoing, you are taking a step away from God, but in His service. Dealing with such matters is hard and thankless work.
Sister James: I've become more reserved in class. I feel separated from the children.
Sister Aloysius: That's as it should be.
Sister James: But I feel. Wrong. And about this other matter, I don't have any evidence. I'm not at all certain that anything's happened.
Sister Aloysius: We can't wait for that.
Sister James: But what if it's nothing?
Sister Aloysius: Then it's nothing. I wouldn't mind being wrong. But I doubt I am.
Sister James: Then what's to be done?
Sister Aloysius: I don't know.
Sister James: You'll know what to do.
Sister Aloysius: I don't know what to do. There are parameters which protect him and hinder me.
Sister James: But he can't be safe if it's established. I doubt he could recover from the shame.
Sister Aloysius: What have you seen?
Sister James: I don't know.
Sister Aloysius: What have you seen?
Sister James: He took Donald to the rectory.
Sister Aloysius: What for?
Sister James: A talk.
Sister Aloysius: Alone?
Sister James: Yes.
Sister Aloysius: When?
Sister James: A week ago.
Sister Aloysius: Why didn't you tell me?

Sister James: I didn't think there was anything wrong with it. It never came into my mind that he . . . that there could be anything wrong.

Sister Aloysius: Of all the children. Donald Muller. I suppose it makes sense.

Sister James: How does it make sense?

Sister Aloysius: He's isolated. The little sheep lagging behind is the one the wolf goes for.

Sister James: I don't know that anything's wrong!

Sister Aloysius: Our first Negro student. I thought there'd be fighting, a parent or two to deal with . . . I should've foreseen this possibility.

Sister James: How could you imagine it?

Sister Aloysius: It is my job to outshine the fox in cleverness! That's my job!

Sister James: But maybe it's nothing!

Sister Aloysius: Then why do you look like you've seen the Devil?

Sister James: It's just the way the boy acted when he came back to class.

Sister Aloysius: He said something?

Sister James: No. It was his expression. He looked frightened and . . . he put his head on the desk in the most peculiar way. (*Struggles*) And one other thing. I think there was alcohol on his breath. There was alcohol on his breath.

(Sister Aloysius looks toward the rectory.)

Sister Aloysius: Eight years ago at St. Boniface we had a priest who had to be stopped. But I had Monsignor Scully then . . . who I could rely on. Here, there's no man I can go to, and men run everything. We are going to have to stop him ourselves.

Sister James: Can't you just . . . report your suspicions?

Sister Aloysius: To Monsignor Benedict? The man's guileless! He would just ask Father Flynn!

Sister James: Well, would that be such a bad idea?

Sister Aloysius: And he would believe whatever Father Flynn told him. He would think the matter settled.

Sister James: But maybe that is all that needs to be done. If it's true. If I had done something awful, and I was confronted with it, I'd be so repentant.

Sister Aloysius: Sister James, my dear, you must try to imagine a very different kind of person than yourself. A man who would do this has already denied a great deal. If I tell the monsignor and he is satisfied with Father Flynn's rebuttal, the matter is suppressed.

Sister James: Well then tell the bishop.

Sister Aloysius: The hierarchy of the Church does not permit my going to the bishop. No. Once I tell the monsignor, it's out of my hands, I'm helpless. I'm going to have to come up with a pretext, get Father Flynn into my office. Try to force it. You'll have to be there.

Sister James: Me? No! Why? Oh no, Sister! I couldn't!

Sister Aloysius: I can't be closeted alone with a priest. Another Sister must be in attendance and it has to be you. The circle of confidence mustn't be made any wider. Think of the boy if this gets out.

Sister James: I can't do it!

Sister Aloysius: Why not? You're squeamish?

Sister James: I'm not equipped! It's . . . I would be embarrassed. I couldn't possibly be present if the topic were spoken of!

Sister Aloysius: Please, Sister, do not indulge yourself in witless adolescent scruples. I assure you I would prefer a more seasoned confederate. But you are the one who came to me.

Sister James: You told me to!

Sister Aloysius: Would you rather leave the boy to be exploited? And don't think this will be the only story. If you close your eyes, you will be a party to all that comes after.

Sister James: You're supposed to tell the monsignor!

Sister Aloysius: That you saw a look in a boy's eye? That *perhaps* you smelled something on his breath? Monsignor Benedict thinks the sun rises and sets on Father Flynn. You'd be branded an hysteric and transferred.

Sister James: We can ask him.

Sister Aloysius: Who?

Sister James: The boy. Donald Muller.

Sister Aloysius: He'll deny it.

Sister James: Why?

Sister Aloysius: Shame.

Sister James: You can't know that.

Sister Aloysius: And if he does point the finger, how do you think that will be received in this community? A black child. *(No answer)* I am going to think this through. Then I'm going to invite Father Flynn to my office on an unrelated matter. You will be there.

Sister James: But what good can I do?

Sister Aloysius: Aside from the unacceptability of a priest and nun being alone, I need a witness.

Sister James: To what?

Sister Aloysius: He may tell the truth and lie afterwards.

(*Sister James looks toward the rectory.*)

Sister James: The boys are coming out of the rectory. They look happy enough.

Sister Aloysius: They look smug. Like they have a secret.

Sister James: There he is.

Sister Aloysius: If I could, Sister James, I would certainly choose to live in innocence. But innocence can only be wisdom in a world without evil. Situations arise and we are confronted with wrongdoing and the need to act.

Sister James: I have to take the boys up to class.

Sister Aloysius: Go on, then. Take them. I will be talking to you.

(*The sound of wind. Sister Aloysius pulls her shawl tightly about her and goes. After a moment, Sister James goes as well.*)

V

The principal's office. A phone rings. Sister Aloysius enters with a pot of tea, walking quickly to answer the phone.

Sister Aloysius: Hello, St. Nicholas School? Oh yes, Mr. McGinn. Thank you for calling back. That was quite a windstorm we had last night. No, I didn't know there was a Great Wind in Ireland and you were there for it. That's fascinating. Yes. I was wondering if you would be so kind as to remove a tree limb that's fallen in the courtyard of the church. Sister Veronica tripped on it this morning and fell on her face. I think she's all right. She doesn't look any worse, Mr. McGinn. Thank you, Mr. McGinn.

(*She hangs up the phone and looks at her watch, a bit anxious. A knock at the door.*)

Come in.

(The door opens. Father Flynn is standing there in his black cassock. He doesn't come in.)

Flynn: Good morning, Sister Aloysius! How are you today?

Sister Aloysius: Good morning, Father Flynn. Very well. Good of you to come by.

(Father Flynn takes a step into the office.)

Flynn: Are we ready for the meeting?

Sister Aloysius: We're just short Sister James. *(Father Flynn steps back into the doorway)* Did you hear that wind last night?

Flynn: I certainly did. Imagine what it must've been like in the frontier days when a man alone in the woods sat by a fire in his buckskins and listened to a sound like that. Imagine the loneliness! The immense darkness pressing in! How frightening it must've been!

Sister Aloysius: If one lacked faith in God's protection, I suppose it would be frightening.

Flynn: Did I hear Sister Veronica had an accident?

Sister Aloysius: Yes. Sister Veronica fell on a piece of wood this morning and practically killed herself.

Flynn: Is she all right?

Sister Aloysius: Oh, she's fine.

Flynn: Her sight isn't good, is it?

Sister Aloysius: Her sight is fine. Nuns fall, you know.

Flynn: No, I didn't know that.

Sister Aloysius: It's the habit. It catches us up more often than not. What with our being in black and white, and so prone to falling, we're more like dominos than anything else.

(Sister James appears at the door, breathless.)

Sister James: Am I past the time?

(Father Flynn takes a step into the office.)

Flynn: Not at all. Sister Aloysius and I were just having a nice chat.

Sister James: Good morning, Father Flynn. Good morning, Sister. I'm sorry I was delayed. Mr. McGinn has closed the courtyard to fix something so I had to go back through the convent and out the side door and then I ran into Sister Veronica.

Flynn: How is she?

Sister James: She has a bit of a bloody nose.

Sister Aloysius: I'm beginning to think you're punching people.

Sister James: Sister?

Sister Aloysius: Well, after the incident with . . . Never mind. Well, come in, please. Sit down.

(They come in and sit down. Father Flynn takes Sister Aloysius's chair. He's sitting at her desk. She reacts, but says nothing.)

I actually have a hot pot of tea. *(Closes the door but for an inch)* And close this but not quite for form's sake. Would you have a cup of tea, Father?

Flynn: I would love a cup of tea.

Sister Aloysius: Perhaps you could serve him, Sister?

Sister James: Of course.

Sister Aloysius: And yourself of course.

Sister James: Would you like tea, Sister Aloysius?

Sister Aloysius: I've already had my cup.

Flynn: Is there sugar?

Sister Aloysius: Sugar? Yes! *(Rummages in her desk)* It's here somewhere. I put it in the drawer for Lent last year and never remembered to take it out.

Flynn: It mustn't have been much to give up then.

Sister Aloysius: No, I'm sure you're right. Here it is. I'll serve you, though for want of practice, I'm . . . *(Clumsy)*

> *(She's got the sugar bowl and is poised to serve him a lump of sugar with a small pair of tongs when she sees his nails.)*

Your fingernails.

Flynn: I wear them a little long. The sugar?

Sister Aloysius: Oh yes. One?

Flynn: Three.

Sister Aloysius: Three.

> *(She's appalled but tries to hide it.)*

Flynn: Sweet tooth.

Sister Aloysius: One, two, three. Sister, do you take sugar?

> *(Sister Aloysius looks at Sister James.)*

Sister James (To Sister Aloysius): Never! *(To Father Flynn)* Not that there's anything wrong with sugar. *(To Sister Aloysius again)* Thank you.

> *(Sister Aloysius puts the sugar away in her desk.)*

Sister Aloysius: Well, thank you, Father, for making the time for us. We're at our wit's end.

Flynn: I think it's an excellent idea to rethink the Christmas pageant. Last year's effort was a little woebegone.

Sister James: No! I loved it! *(Becomes self-conscious)* But I love all Christmas pageants. I just love the Nativity. The birth of the Savior. And the hymns of course. "O Little Town of Bethlehem," "O Come, O Come Emmanuel" . . .

Sister Aloysius: Thank you, Sister James. Sister James will be co-directing the pageant with Mrs. Shields this year. So what do you think, Father Flynn? Is there something new we could do?

Flynn: Well, we all love the Christmas hymns, but it might be jolly to include a secular song.

Sister Aloysius: Secular.

Flynn: Yes. "It's Beginning to Look a Lot Like Christmas." Something like that.

Sister Aloysius: What would be the point of performing a secular song?

Flynn: Fun.

Sister James: Or "Frosty the Snowman."

Flynn: That's a good one. We could have one of the boys dress as a snowman and dance around.

Sister Aloysius: Which boy?

Flynn: We'd do tryouts.

Sister Aloysius: "Frosty the Snowman" espouses a pagan belief in magic. The snowman comes to life when an enchanted hat is put on his head. If the music were more somber, people would realize the images are disturbing and the song heretical.

(Sister James and Father Flynn exchange a look.)

Sister James: I've never thought about "Frosty the Snowman" like that.

Sister Aloysius: It should be banned from the airwaves.

Flynn: So. Not "Frosty the Snowman."

(Father Flynn writes something in a small notebook.)

Sister Aloysius: I don't think so. "It's Beginning to Look a Lot Like Christmas" would be fine I suppose. The parents would like it. May I ask what you wrote down? With that ballpoint pen.

Flynn: Oh. Nothing. An idea for a sermon.

Sister Aloysius: You had one just now?

Flynn: I get them all the time.

Sister Aloysius: How fortunate.

Flynn: I forget them so I write them down.

Sister Aloysius: What is the idea?

Flynn: Intolerance.

(Sister James tries to break a bit of tension.)

Sister James: Would you like a little more tea, Father?

Flynn: Not yet. I think a message of the Second Ecumenical Council was that the Church needs to take on a more familiar face. Reflect the local community. We should sing a song from the radio now and then. Take the kids out for ice cream.

Sister Aloysius: Ice cream.

Flynn: Maybe take the boys on a camping trip. We should be friendlier. The children and the parents should see us as members of their family rather than emissaries from Rome. I think the pageant should be charming, like a community theatre doing a show.

Sister Aloysius: But we are not members of their family. We're different.

Flynn: Why? Because of our vows?

Sister Aloysius: Precisely.

Flynn: I don't think we're so different. *(To Sister James)* You know, I would take some more tea, Sister. Thank you.

Sister Aloysius: And they think we're different. The working-class people of this parish trust us to be different.

Flynn: I think we're getting off the subject.

Sister Aloysius: Yes, you're right, back to it. The Christmas pageant. We must be careful how Donald Muller is used in the pageant.

(Sister James shakes as she pours the tea.)

Flynn: Easy there, Sister, you don't spill.

Sister James: Oh, uh, yes, Father.

Flynn: What about Donald Muller?

Sister Aloysius: We must be careful, in the pageant, that we neither hide Donald Muller nor put him forward.

Flynn: Because of the color of his skin.

Sister Aloysius: That's right.

Flynn: Why?

Sister Aloysius: Come, Father. You're being disingenuous.

Flynn: I think he should be treated like every other boy.

Sister Aloysius: You yourself singled the boy out for special attention. You held a private meeting with him at the rectory. *(Turning to Sister James)* A week ago?

Sister James: Yes.

(He realizes something's up.)

Flynn: What are we talking about?

Sister James: Donald Muller?

Sister Aloysius: The boy acted strangely when he returned to class.

(Father Flynn turns to Sister James.)

Flynn: He did?

Sister James: When he returned from the rectory. A little odd, yes.

Sister Aloysius: Can you tell us why?

Flynn: How did he act strangely?

Sister James: I'm not sure how to explain it. He laid his head on the desk . . .

Flynn: You mean you had some impression?

Sister James: Yes.

Flynn: And he'd come from the rectory so you're asking me if I know anything about it?

Sister James: That's it.

Flynn: Hmmm. Did you want to discuss the pageant, is that why I'm here, or is this what you wanted to discuss?

Sister Aloysius: This.

Flynn: Well. I feel a little uncomfortable.

Sister Aloysius: Why?

Flynn: Why do you think? Something about your tone.

Sister Aloysius: I would prefer a discussion of fact rather than tone.

Flynn: Well. If I had judged my conversation with Donald Muller to be of concern to you, Sister, I would have sat you down and talked to you about it. But I did not judge it to be of concern to you.

Sister Aloysius: Perhaps you are mistaken in your understanding of what concerns me. The boy is in my school and his well-being is my responsibility.

Flynn: His well-being is not at issue.

Sister Aloysius: I am not satisfied that that is true. He was upset when he returned to class.

Flynn: Did he say something?

Sister James: No.

Sister Aloysius: What happened in the rectory?

Flynn: Happened? Nothing happened. I had a talk with a boy.

Sister Aloysius: What about?

Flynn: It was a private matter.

Sister Aloysius: He's twelve years old. What could be private?

Flynn: I'll say it again, Sister. I object to your tone.

Sister Aloysius: This is not about my tone or your tone, Father Flynn. It's about arriving at the truth.

Flynn: Of what?

Sister Aloysius: You know what I'm talking about. Don't you? You're controlling the expression on your face right now. Aren't you?

Flynn: My face? You said you wanted to talk about the pageant, Sister. That's why I'm here. Am I to understand that you brought me into your office to confront me in some way? It's outrageous. I'm not answerable to you. What exactly are you accusing me of?

Sister Aloysius: I am not accusing you of anything, Father Flynn. I am asking you to tell me what happened in the rectory.

(Father Flynn stands.)

Flynn: I don't wish to continue this conversation at all further. And if you are dissatisfied with that, I suggest you speak to Monsignor Benedict. I can only imagine that your unfortunate behavior this morning is the result of over-work. Perhaps you need a leave of absence. I may suggest it. Have a good morning. *(To Sister James)* Sister?

Sister James: Good morning, Father.

(Sister Aloysius's next words stop him.)

Sister Aloysius: There was alcohol on his breath. *(He turns)* When he returned from his meeting with you.

(He comes back and sits down. He rubs his eyes.)

Flynn: Alcohol.

Sister James: I did smell it on his breath.

Sister Aloysius: Well?

Flynn: Can't you let this alone?

Sister Aloysius: No.

Flynn: I see there's no way out of this.

Sister James: Take your time, Father. Would you like some more tea?

Flynn: You should've let it alone.

Sister Aloysius: Not possible.

Flynn: Donald Muller served as altar boy last Tuesday morning. After Mass, Mr. McGinn caught him in the sacristy drinking altar wine. When I found out, I sent for him. There were tears. He begged not to be removed from the altar boys. And I took pity on him. I told him if no one else found out, I would let him stay on.

(Sister James is overjoyed. Sister Aloysius is unmoved.)

Sister James: Oh, what a relief! That explains everything! Thanks be to God! Oh, Sister, look, it's all a mistake!

Sister Aloysius: And if I talk to Mr. McGinn?

Flynn: Talk to Mr. McGinn by all means. But now that the boy's secret's out, I'm going to have to remove him from the altar boys. Which I think is too bad. That's what I was trying to avoid.

Sister James: You were trying to protect the boy!

Flynn: That's right.

Sister James: I might've done the same thing! *(To Sister Aloysius)* Is there a way Donald could stay on the altar boys?

Sister Aloysius: No. If the boy drank altar wine, he cannot continue as an altar boy.

Flynn: Of course you're right. I'm just not the disciplinarian you are, Sister. And he is the only Negro in the school. That did affect my thinking on the matter. It will be commented on that he's no longer serving at Mass. It's a public thing. A certain ignorant element in the parish will be confirmed in their beliefs.

Sister Aloysius: He must be held to the same standard as the others.

Flynn: Of course. Do we need to discuss the pageant or was that just . . .

Sister Aloysius: No, this was the issue.

Flynn: Are you satisfied?

Sister Aloysius: Yes.
Flynn: Then I'll be going. I have some writing to do.
Sister Aloysius: Intolerance.
Flynn: That's right.

(*He goes, then stops at the door.*)

I'm not pleased with how you handled this, Sister. Next time you are troubled by dark ideas, I suggest you speak to the monsignor.

(*He goes. After a moment, Sister James weakly launches into optimism.*)

Sister James: Well. What a relief! He cleared it all up.
Sister Aloysius: You believe him?
Sister James: Of course.
Sister Aloysius: Isn't it more that it's easier to believe him?
Sister James: But we can corroborate his story with Mr. McGinn!
Sister Aloysius: Yes. These types of people are clever. They're not so easily undone.
Sister James: Well, I'm convinced!
Sister Aloysius: You're not. You just want things to be resolved so you can have simplicity back.
Sister James: I want no further part of this.
Sister Aloysius: I'll bring him down. With or without your help.
Sister James: How can you be so sure he's lying?
Sister Aloysius: Experience.
Sister James: You just don't like him! You don't like it that he uses a ballpoint pen. You don't like it that he takes three lumps of sugar in his tea. You don't like it that he likes "Frosty the Snowman." And you're letting that convince you of something terrible, just terrible! Well, I like "Frosty the Snowman"! And it would be nice if this school weren't run like a prison! And I think it's a good thing that I love to teach History and that I might inspire my students to love it, too! And if you judge that to mean I'm not fit to be a teacher, then so be it!
Sister Aloysius: Sit down. (*Sister James does*) In ancient Sparta, important matters were decided by who shouted loudest. Fortunately, we are not in ancient Sparta. Now. Do you honestly find the students in this school to be treated like inmates in a prison?
Sister James (Relenting): No, I don't. Actually, by and large, they seem to be fairly happy. But they're all uniformly terrified of you!
Sister Aloysius: Yes. That's how it works. Sit there.

(*Sister Aloysius looks in a notebook, picks up the phone, dials.*)

Hello, this is Sister Aloysius Beauvier, the principal of St. Nicholas. Is this Mrs. Muller? I'm calling about your son, Donald. I would like you and your husband to come down here for a talk. When would be convenient?

(*Lights fade.*)

VI

Father Flynn, in blue and white vestments, is at the pulpit.

Flynn: A woman was gossiping with a friend about a man she hardly knew — I know none of you have ever done this — and that night she had a dream. A great hand appeared over her and pointed down at her. She was immediately seized with an overwhelming sense of guilt. The next day she went to confession. She got the old parish priest, Father O'Rouke, and she told him the whole thing. "Is gossiping a sin?" she asked the old man. "Was that the Hand of God Almighty pointing a finger at me? Should I be asking your absolution? Father, tell me, have I done something wrong?" *(Irish brogue)* "Yes!" Father O'Rouke answered her. "Yes, you ignorant, badly brought-up female! You have borne false witness against your neighbor, you have played fast and loose with his reputation, and you should be heartily ashamed!" So the woman said she was sorry and asked forgiveness. "Not so fast!" says O'Rouke. "I want you to go home, take a pillow up on your roof, cut it open with a knife, and return here to me!" So she went home, took the pillow off her bed, a knife from the drawer, went up the fire escape to the roof, and stabbed the pillow. Then she went back to the old priest as instructed. "Did you gut the pillow with the knife?" he says. "Yes, Father." "And what was the result?" "Feathers," she said. "Feathers"? he repeated. "Feathers everywhere, Father!" "Now I want you to go back and gather up every last feather that flew out on the wind!" "Well," she says, "it can't be done. I don't know where they went. The wind took them all over." "And that," said Father O'Rouke, "is *gossip!*" In the name of the Father, Son, and the Holy Ghost, Amen.

VII

The lights crossfade to the garden. A crow caws. Sister James sits on the bench, deep in thought. Father Flynn enters.

Flynn: Good afternoon, Sister James.

Sister James: Good afternoon, Father.

Flynn: What is that bird complaining about? What kind of bird is that? A starling? A grackle?

Sister James: A crow?

Flynn: Of course it is. Are you praying? I didn't mean to interrupt.

Sister James: I'm not praying, no.

Flynn: You seem subdued.

Sister James: Oh. I can't sleep.

Flynn: Why not?

Sister James: Bad dreams. Actually one bad dream, and then I haven't slept right since.

Flynn: What about?

Sister James: I looked in a mirror and there was a darkness where my face should be. It frightened me.

Flynn: I can't sleep on occasion.

Sister James: No? Do you see that big hand pointing a finger at you?

Flynn: Yes. Sometimes.

Sister James: Was your sermon directed at anyone in particular?

Flynn: What do you think?

Sister James: Did you make up that story about the pillow?

Flynn: Yes. You make up little stories to illustrate. In the tradition of the parable.

Sister James: Aren't the things that actually happen in life more worthy of interpretation than a made-up story?

Flynn: No. What actually happens in life is beyond interpretation. The truth makes for a bad sermon. It tends to be confusing and have no clear conclusion.

Sister James: I received a letter from my brother in Maryland yesterday. He's very sick.

Flynn: Maybe you should go and see him.

Sister James: I can't leave my class.

Flynn: How's Donald Muller doing?

Sister James: I don't know.

Flynn: You don't see him?

Sister James: I see him every day, but I don't know how he's doing. I don't know how to judge these things. Now.

Flynn: I stopped speaking to him for fear of it being misunderstood. Isn't that a shame? I actually avoided him the other day when I might've passed him in the hall. He doesn't understand why. I noticed you didn't come to me for confession.

Sister James: No. I went to Monsignor Benedict. He's very kind.

Flynn: I wasn't?

Sister James: It wasn't that. As you know. You know why.

Flynn: You're against me?

Sister James: No.

Flynn: You're not convinced?

Sister James: It's not for me to be convinced, one way or the other. It's Sister Aloysius.

Flynn: Are you just an extension of her?

Sister James: She's my superior.

Flynn: But what about you?

Sister James: I wish I knew nothing whatever about it. I wish the idea had never entered my mind.

Flynn: How did it enter your mind?

Sister James: Sister Aloysius.

Flynn: I feel as if my reputation has been damaged through no fault of my own. But I'm reluctant to take the steps necessary to repair it for fear of doing further harm. It's frustrating, I can tell you that.

Sister James: Is it true?

Flynn: What?

Sister James: You know what I'm asking.

Flynn: No, it's not true.

Sister James: Oh, I don't know what to believe.

Flynn: How can you take sides against me?

Sister James: It doesn't matter.

Flynn: It does matter! I've done nothing. There's no substance to any of this. The most innocent actions can appear sinister to the poisoned mind. I had to throw that poor boy off the altar. He's devastated. The only reason I haven't gone to the monsignor is I don't want to tear apart the school. Sister Aloysius would most certainly lose her position as principal if I made her accusations known. Since they're baseless. You might lose your place as well.

Sister James: Are you threatening me?

Flynn: What do you take me for? No.

Sister James: I want to believe you.

Flynn: Then do. It's as simple as that.

Sister James: It's not me that has to be convinced.

Flynn: I don't have to prove anything to her.

Sister James: She's determined.

Flynn: To what?

Sister James: Protect the boy.

Flynn: It's me that cares about that boy, not her. Has she ever reached out a hand to that child or any child in this school? She's like a block of ice! Children need warmth, kindness, understanding! What does she give them? Rules. That black boy needs a helping hand or he's not going to make it here! But if she has her way, he'll be left to his own undoing. Why do you think he was in the sacristy drinking wine that day? He's in trouble! She sees me talk in a human way to these children and she immediately assumes there must be something wrong with it. Something dirty. Well, I'm not going to let her keep this parish in the Dark Ages! And I'm not going to let her destroy my spirit of compassion!

Sister James: I'm sure that's not her intent.

Flynn: I care about this congregation!

Sister James: I know you do.

Flynn: Like you care about your class! You love them, don't you?

Sister James: Yes.

Flynn: That's natural. How else would you relate to children? I can look at your face and know your philosophy: kindness.

Sister James: I don't know. I mean, of course.

Flynn: What is Sister Aloysius's philosophy do you suppose?

   (A pause.)

Sister James: I don't have to suppose. She's told me. She discourages . . . warmth. She's suggested I be more . . . formal.

Flynn: There are people who go after your humanity, Sister James, who tell you the light in your heart is a weakness. That your soft feelings betray you. I don't believe that. It's an old tactic of cruel people to kill kindness in the name of virtue. Don't believe it. There's nothing wrong with love.

Sister James: Of course not, but . . .

Flynn: Have you forgotten that was the message of the Savior to us all. Love. Not suspicion, disapproval and judgment. Love of people. Have you found Sister Aloysius a positive inspiration?

Sister James: I don't want to misspeak, but no. She's taken away my joy of teaching. And I loved teaching more than anything. *(She cries a little. He pats her uneasily, looking around)*

Flynn: It's all right. You're going to be all right.

Sister James: I feel as if everything is upside down.

Flynn: It isn't though. There are just times in life when we feel lost. You're not alone with it. It happens to many of us.

Sister James: A bond. *(Becomes self-conscious)* I'd better go in.

Flynn: I'm sorry your brother is ill.

Sister James: Thank you, Father. *(Starts to go, stops)* I don't believe it!

Flynn: You don't?

Sister James: No.

Flynn: Thank you, Sister. That's a great relief to me. Thank you very much.

(She goes. He takes out his little black book and writes in it. The crow caws. He yells at it:)

Oh, be quiet.

(Then he opens a prayer book and walks away.)

VIII

Crossfade to the principal's office. Sister Aloysius is sitting looking out the window, very still. A knock at the door. She doesn't react. A second knock, louder. She pulls a small earplug out of her ear and scurries to the door. She opens it. There stands Mrs. Muller, a black woman of about thirty-eight, in her Sunday best, dressed for church. She's on red alert.

Sister Aloysius: Mrs. Muller?
Mrs. Muller: Yes.
Sister Aloysius: Come in.

(Sister Aloysius closes the door.)

Please have a seat.
Mrs. Muller: I thought I might a had the wrong day when you didn't answer the door.
Sister Aloysius: Oh. Yes. Well, just between us, I was listening to a transistor radio with an earpiece.

(She shows Mrs. Muller a very small transistor radio.)

Look at how tiny they're making them now. I confiscated it from one of the students and now I can't stop using it.
Mrs. Muller: You like music?
Sister Aloysius: Not really. News reports. Years ago I used to listen to all the news reports because my husband was in Italy in the war. When I came into possession of this little radio, I found myself doing it again. Though there is no war and the voices have changed.
Mrs. Muller: You were a married woman?
Sister Aloysius: Yes. But then he was killed. Is your husband coming?
Mrs. Muller: Couldn't get off work.
Sister Aloysius: I see. Of course. It was a lot to ask.
Mrs. Muller: How's Donald doing?
Sister Aloysius: He's passing his subjects. He has average grades.
Mrs. Muller: Oh. Good. He was upset about getting taken off the altar boys.
Sister Aloysius: Did he explain why?
Mrs. Muller: He said he was caught drinking wine.
Sister Aloysius: That is the reason.
Mrs. Muller: Well, that seems fair. But he's a good boy, Sister. He fell down there, but he's a good boy pretty much down the line. And he knows what an opportunity he has here. I think the whole thing was just a bit much for him.
Sister Aloysius: What do you mean, the whole thing?
Mrs. Muller: He's the only colored here. He's the first in this school. That'd be a lot for a boy.
Sister Aloysius: I suppose it is. But he has to do the work of course.

Mrs. Muller: He is doing it though, right?

Sister Aloysius: Yes. He's getting by. He's getting through. How is he at home?

Mrs. Muller: His father beat the hell out of him over that wine.

Sister Aloysius: He shouldn't do that.

Mrs. Muller: You don't tell my husband what to do. You just stand back. He didn't want Donald to come here.

Sister Aloysius: Why not?

Mrs. Muller: Thought he'd have a lot of trouble with the other boys. But that hasn't really happened as far as I can make out.

Sister Aloysius: Good.

Mrs. Muller: That priest, Father Flynn, been watching out for him.

Sister Aloysius: Yes. Have you met Father Flynn?

Mrs. Muller: Not exactly, no. I seen him on the altar, but I haven't met him face to face. No. Just, you know, heard from Donald.

Sister Aloysius: What does he say?

Mrs. Muller: You know, Father Flynn, Father Flynn. He looks up to him. The man gives him his time, which is what the boy needs. He needs that.

Sister Aloysius: Mrs. Muller, we may have a problem.

Mrs. Muller: Well, I thought you must a had a reason for asking me to come in. Principal's a big job. If you stop your day to talk to me, must be something. I just want to say though, it's just till June.

Sister Aloysius: Excuse me?

Mrs. Muller: Whatever the problem is, Donald just has to make it here till June. Then he's off into high school.

Sister Aloysius: Right.

Mrs. Muller: If Donald can graduate from here, he has a better chance of getting into a good high school. And that would mean an opportunity at college. I believe he has the intelligence. And he wants it, too.

Sister Aloysius: I don't see anything at this time standing in the way of his graduating with his class.

Mrs. Muller: Well, that's all I care about. Anything else is all right with me.

Sister Aloysius: I doubt that.

Mrs. Muller: Try me.

Sister Aloysius: I'm concerned about the relationship between Father Flynn and your son.

Mrs. Muller: You don't say. Concerned. What do you mean, concerned?

Sister Aloysius: That it may not be right.

Mrs. Muller: Uh-huh. Well, there's something wrong with everybody, isn't that so? Got to be forgiving.

Sister Aloysius: I'm concerned, to be frank, that Father Flynn may have made advances on your son.

Mrs. Muller: *May* have made.

Sister Aloysius: I can't be certain.

Mrs. Muller: No evidence?

Sister Aloysius: No.

Mrs. Muller: Then maybe there's nothing to it?

Sister Aloysius: I think there is something to it.

Mrs. Muller: Well, I would prefer not to see it that way if you don't mind.

Sister Aloysius: I can understand that this is hard to hear. I think Father Flynn gave Donald that altar wine.

Mrs. Muller: Why would he do that?

Sister Aloysius: Has Donald been acting strangely?

Mrs. Muller: No.

Sister Aloysius: Nothing out of the ordinary?

Mrs. Muller: He's been himself.

Sister Aloysius: All right.

Mrs. Muller: Look, Sister, I don't want any trouble, and I feel like you're on the march somehow.

Sister Aloysius: I'm not sure you completely understand.

Mrs. Muller: I think I understand the kind of thing you're talking about. But I don't want to get into it.

Sister Aloysius: What's that?

Mrs. Muller: Not to be disagreeing with you, but if we're talking about something floating around between this priest and my son, that ain't my son's fault.

Sister Aloysius: I'm not suggesting it is.

Mrs. Muller: He's just a boy.

Sister Aloysius: I know.

Mrs. Muller: Twelve years old. If somebody should be taking blame for anything, it should be the man, not the boy.

Sister Aloysius: I agree with you completely.

Mrs. Muller: You're agreeing with me but I'm sitting in the principal's office talking about my son. Why isn't the priest in the principal's office, if you know what I'm saying and you'll excuse my bringing it up.

Sister Aloysius: You're here because I'm concerned about Donald's welfare.

Mrs. Muller: You think I'm not?

Sister Aloysius: Of course you are.

Mrs. Muller: Let me ask you something. You honestly think that priest gave Donald that wine to drink?

Sister Aloysius: Yes, I do.

Mrs. Muller: Then how come my son got kicked off the altar boys if it was the man that gave it to him?

Sister Aloysius: The boy got caught, the man didn't.

Mrs. Muller: How come the priest didn't get kicked off the priesthood?

Sister Aloysius: He's a grown man, educated. And he knows what's at stake. It's not so easy to pin someone like that down.

Mrs. Muller: So you give my son the whole blame. No problem my son getting blamed and punished. That's easy. You know why that is?

Sister Aloysius: Perhaps you should let me talk. I think you're getting upset.

Mrs. Muller: That's because that's the way it is. You're just finding out about it, but that's the way it is and the way it's been, Sister. You're not going against no *man* in a *robe* and win, Sister. He's got the position.

Sister Aloysius: And he's got your son.

Mrs. Muller: Let him have 'im then.

Sister Aloysius: What?

Mrs. Muller: It's just till June.

Sister Aloysius: Do you know what you're saying?

Mrs. Muller: Know more about it than you.

Sister Aloysius: I believe this man is creating or has already brought about an improper relationship with your son.

Mrs. Muller: I don't know.

Sister Aloysius: I know I'm right.

Mrs. Muller: Why you need to know something like that for sure when you don't? Please, Sister. You got some kind a righteous cause going with this priest and now you want to drag my boy into it. My son doesn't need additional difficulties. Let him take the good and leave the rest when he leaves this place in June. He knows how to do that. I taught him how to do that.

Sister Aloysius: What kind of mother are you?

Mrs. Muller: Excuse me, but you don't know enough about life to say a thing like that, Sister.

Sister Aloysius: I know enough.

Mrs. Muller: You know the rules maybe, but that don't cover it.

Sister Aloysius: I know what I won't accept!

Mrs. Muller: You accept what you gotta accept and you work with it. That's the truth I know. Sorry to be so sharp, but you're in here in this room . . .

Sister Aloysius: This man is in my school.

Mrs. Muller: Well, he's gotta be somewhere and maybe he's doing some good too. You ever think of that?

Sister Aloysius: He's after the boys.

Mrs. Muller: Well, maybe some of them boys want to get caught. Maybe what you don't know maybe is my son is . . . that way. That's why his father beat him up. Not the wine. He beat Donald for being what he is.

Sister Aloysius: What are you telling me?

Mrs. Muller: I'm his mother. I'm talking about his nature now, not anything he's done. But you can't hold a child responsible for what God gave him to be.

Sister Aloysius: Listen to me with care, Mrs. Muller. I'm only interested in actions. It's hopeless to discuss a child's possible inclination. I'm finding it difficult enough to address a man's deeds. This isn't about what the boy may be, but what the man is. It's about the man.

Mrs. Muller: But there's the boy's nature.

Sister Aloysius: Let's leave that out of it.

Mrs. Muller: Forget it then. You're the one forcing people to say these things out loud. Things are in the air and you leave them alone if you can. That's what I know. My boy came to this school 'cause they were gonna kill him at the public school. So we were lucky enough to get him in here for his last year. Good. His father don't like him. He comes here, the kids don't like him. One man is good to him. This priest. Puts out a hand to the boy. Does the man have his reasons? Yes. Everybody has their reasons. *You* have your reasons. But do I ask the man why he's good to my son? No. I don't care why. My son needs some man to care about him and see him through to where he wants to go. And thank God, this educated man with some kindness in him wants to do just that.

Sister Aloysius: This will not do.

Mrs. Muller: It's just till June. Sometimes things aren't black and white.

Sister Aloysius: And sometimes they are. I'll throw your son out of this school. Make no mistake.

Mrs. Muller: But why would you do that? If nothing started with him?

Sister Aloysius: Because I will stop this whatever way I must.

Mrs. Muller: You'd hurt my son to get your way?

Sister Aloysius: It won't end with your son. There will be others, if there aren't already.

Mrs. Muller: Throw the priest out then.

Sister Aloysius: I'm trying to do just that.
Mrs. Muller: Well, what do you want from me?

(*A pause.*)

Sister Aloysius: Nothing. As it turns out. I was hoping you might know something that would help me, but it seems you don't.
Mrs. Muller: Please leave my son out of this. My husband would kill that child over a thing like this.
Sister Aloysius: I'll try.

(*Mrs. Muller stands up.*)

Mrs. Muller: I don't know, Sister. You may think you're doing good, but the world's a hard place. I don't know that you and me are on the same side. I'll be standing with my son and those who are good with my son. It'd be nice to see you there. Nice talking with you, Sister. Good morning.

(*She goes, leaving the door open behind her. Sister Aloysius is shaken. After a moment, Father Flynn appears at the door. He's in a controlled fury.*)

Flynn: May I come in?
Sister Aloysius: We would require a third party.
Flynn: What was Donald's mother doing here?
Sister Aloysius: We were having a chat.
Flynn: About what?
Sister Aloysius: A third party is truly required, Father.
Flynn: No, Sister. No third party. You and me are due for a talk.

(*He comes in and slams the door behind him. They face each other.*)

You have to stop this campaign against me!
Sister Aloysius: You can stop it at any time.
Flynn: How?
Sister Aloysius: Confess and resign.
Flynn: You are attempting to destroy my reputation! But the result of all this is going to be your removal, not mine!
Sister Aloysius: What are you doing in this school?
Flynn: I am trying to do good!
Sister Aloysius: Or even more to the point, what are you doing in the priesthood?
Flynn: You are single-handedly holding this school and this parish back!
Sister Aloysius: From what?
Flynn: Progressive education and a welcoming church.
Sister Aloysius: You can't distract me, Father Flynn. This isn't about my behavior, it's about yours.
Flynn: It's about your unfounded suspicions.
Sister Aloysius: That's right. I have suspicions.
Flynn: You know what I haven't understood through all this? *Why* do you suspect me? What have I done?
Sister Aloysius: You gave that boy wine to drink. And you let him take the blame.
Flynn: That's completely untrue! Did you talk to Mr. McGinn?
Sister Aloysius: All McGinn knows is the boy drank wine. He doesn't how he came to drink it.
Flynn: Did his mother have something to add to that?
Sister Aloysius: No.

Flynn: So that's it. There's nothing there.

Sister Aloysius: I'm not satisfied.

Flynn: Well, if you're not satisfied, ask the boy then!

Sister Aloysius: No, he'd protect you. That's what he's been doing.

Flynn: Oh, and why would he do that?

Sister Aloysius: Because you have seduced him.

Flynn: You're insane! You've got it in your head that I've corrupted this child after giving him wine, and nothing I say will change that.

Sister Aloysius: That's right.

Flynn: But correct me if I'm wrong. This has nothing to do with the wine, not really. You had a fundamental mistrust of me before this incident! It was you that warned Sister James to be on the lookout, wasn't it?

Sister Aloysius: That's true.

Flynn: So you admit it!

Sister Aloysius: Certainly.

Flynn: Why?

Sister Aloysius: I know people.

Flynn: That's not good enough!

Sister Aloysius: It won't have to be.

Flynn: How's that?

Sister Aloysius: You will tell me what you've done.

Flynn: Oh I will?

Sister Aloysius: Yes.

Flynn: I'm not one of your truant boys, you know. Sister James is convinced I'm innocent.

Sister Aloysius: So you talked to Sister James? Well, of course you talked to Sister James.

Flynn: Did you know that Donald's father beats him?

Sister Aloysius: Yes.

Flynn: And might that not account for the odd behavior Sister James noticed in the boy?

Sister Aloysius: It might.

Flynn: Then what is it? What? What did you hear, what did you see that convinced you so thoroughly?

Sister Aloysius: What does it matter?

Flynn: I want to know.

Sister Aloysius: On the first day of the school year, I saw you touch William London's wrist. And I saw him pull away.

Flynn: That's all?

Sister Aloysius: That was all.

Flynn: But that's nothing.

(*He writes in his book.*)

Sister Aloysius: What are you writing now?

Flynn: You leave me no choice. I'm writing down what you say. I tend to get too flustered to remember the details of an upsetting conversation, and this may be important. When I talk to the monsignor and explain why you have to be removed as the principal of this school.

Sister Aloysius: This morning, before I spoke with Mrs. Muller, I took the precaution of calling the last parish to which you were assigned.

Flynn: What did he say?

Sister Aloysius: Who?

Flynn: The pastor?

Sister Aloysius: I did not speak to the pastor. I spoke to one of the nuns.

Flynn: You should've spoken to the pastor.

Sister Aloysius: I spoke to a nun.

Flynn: That's not the proper route for you to have taken, Sister! The Church is very clear. You're supposed to go through the pastor.

Sister Aloysius: Why? Do you have an understanding, you and he? Father Flynn, you have a history.

Flynn: You have no right to go rummaging through my past!

Sister Aloysius: This is your third parish in five years.

Flynn: Call the pastor and ask him why I left! It was perfectly innocent.

Sister Aloysius: I'm not calling the pastor.

Flynn: I am a good priest! And there is nothing in my record to suggest otherwise.

Sister Aloysius: You will go after another child and another, until you are stopped.

Flynn: What nun did you speak to?

Sister Aloysius: I won't say.

Flynn: I've not touched a child.

Sister Aloysius: You have.

Flynn: You have not the slightest proof of anything.

Sister Aloysius: But I have my certainty, and armed with that, I will go to your last parish, and the one before that if necessary. I will find a parent, Father Flynn! Trust me I will. A parent who probably doesn't know that you are *still working with children*! And once I do that, you will be exposed. You may even be attacked, metaphorically or otherwise.

Flynn: You have no right to act on your own! You are a member of a religious order. You have taken vows, obedience being one! You answer to us! You have no right to step outside the Church!

Sister Aloysius: I will step outside the Church if that's what needs to be done, though the door should shut behind me! I will do what needs to be done, Father, if it means I'm damned to Hell! You should understand that, or you will mistake me. Now, did you give Donald Muller wine to drink?

Flynn: Have you never done anything wrong?

Sister Aloysius: I have.

Flynn: Mortal sin?

Sister Aloysius: Yes.

Flynn: And?

Sister Aloysius: I confessed it! Did you give Donald Muller wine to drink?

Flynn: Whatever I have done, I have left in the healing hands of my confessor. As have you! We are the same!

Sister Aloysius: We are not the same! A dog that bites is a dog that bites! I do not justify what I do wrong and go on. I admit it, desist, and take my medicine. Did you give Donald Muller wine to drink?

Flynn: No.

Sister Aloysius: Mental reservation?

Flynn: No.

Sister Aloysius: You lie. Very well then. If you won't leave my office, I will. And once I go, I will not stop.

(She goes to the door. Suddenly, a new tone comes into his voice.)

Flynn: Wait!

Sister Aloysius: You will request a transfer from this parish. You will take a leave of absence until it is granted.

Flynn: And do what for the love of God? My life is here.

Sister Aloysius: Don't.

Flynn: Please! Are we people? Am I a person flesh and blood like you? Or are we just ideas and convictions. I can't say everything. Do you understand? There are things I can't say. Even if you can't imagine the explanation, Sister, remember that there are circumstances beyond your knowledge. Even if you feel certainty, it is an emotion and not a fact. In the spirit of charity, I appeal to you. On behalf of my life's work. You have to behave responsibly. I put myself in your hands.

Sister Aloysius: I don't want you.

Flynn: My reputation is at stake.

Sister Aloysius: You can preserve your reputation.

Flynn: If you say these things, I won't be able to do my work in the community.

Sister Aloysius: Your work in the community should be discontinued.

Flynn: You'd leave me with nothing.

Sister Aloysius: That's not true. It's Donald Muller who has nothing, and you took full advantage of that.

Flynn: I have not done anything wrong. I care about that boy very much.

Sister Aloysius: Because you smile at him and sympathize with him, and talk to him as if you were the same?

Flynn: That child needed a friend!

Sister Aloysius: You are a cheat. The warm feeling you experienced when that boy looked at you with trust was not the sensation of virtue. It can be got by a drunkard from his tot of rum. You're a disgrace to the collar. The only reason you haven't been thrown out of the Church is the decline in vocations.

Flynn: I can fight you.

Sister Aloysius: You will lose.

Flynn: You can't know that.

Sister Aloysius: I know.

Flynn: Where's your compassion?

Sister Aloysius: Nowhere you can get at it. Stay here. Compose yourself. Use the phone if you like. Good day, Father. I have no sympathy for you. I know you're invulnerable to true regret. *(Starts to go. Pause)* And cut your nails.

(She goes, closing the door behind her. After a moment, he goes to the phone and dials.)

Flynn: Yes. This is Father Brendan Flynn of St. Nicholas parish. I need to make an appointment to see the bishop.

(Lights fade.)

IX

The lights crossfade to Sister Aloysius walking into the garden. It's a sunny day. She sits on the bench. Sister James enters.

Sister Aloysius: How's your brother?

Sister James: Better. Much better.

Sister Aloysius: I'm very glad. I prayed for him.

Sister James: It was good to get away. I needed to see my family. It had been too long.

Sister Aloysius: Then I'm glad you did it.

Sister James: And Father Flynn is gone.

Sister Aloysius: Yes.

Sister James: Where?

Sister Aloysius: St. Jerome's.

Sister James: So you did it. You got him out.

Sister Aloysius: Yes.

Sister James: Donald Muller is heartbroken that he's gone.

Sister Aloysius: Can't be helped. It's just till June.

Sister James: I don't think Father Flynn did anything wrong.

Sister Aloysius: No? He convinced you?

Sister James: Yes, he did.

Sister Aloysius: Hmmm.

Sister James: Did you ever prove it?

Sister Aloysius: What?

Sister James: That he interfered with Donald Muller?

Sister Aloysius: Did I ever prove it to whom?

Sister James: Anyone but yourself?

Sister Aloysius: No.

Sister James: But you were sure.

Sister Aloysius: Yes.

Sister James: I wish I could be like you.

Sister Aloysius: Why?

Sister James: Because I can't sleep at night anymore. Everything seems uncertain to me.

Sister Aloysius: Maybe we're not supposed to sleep so well. They've made Father Flynn the pastor of St. Jerome.

Sister James: Who?

Sister Aloysius: The bishop appointed Father Flynn the pastor of St. Jerome Church and School. It's a promotion.

Sister James: You didn't tell them?

Sister Aloysius: I told our good Monsignor Benedict. I crossed the garden and told him. He did not believe it to be true.

Sister James: Then why did Father Flynn leave? What did you say to him to make him go?

Sister Aloysius: That I had called a nun in his previous parish. That I had found out his prior history of infringements.

Sister James: So you did prove it!

Sister Aloysius: I was lying. I made no such call.

Sister James: You lied?

Sister Aloysius: Yes. But if he had no such history, the lie wouldn't have worked. His resignation was his confession. He was what I thought he was. And he's gone.

Sister James: I can't believe you lied.

Sister Aloysius: In the pursuit of wrongdoing, one steps away from God. Of course there's a price.

Sister James: I see. So now he's in another school.

Sister Aloysius: Yes. Oh, Sister James!

Sister James: What is it, Sister?

Sister Aloysius: I have doubts! I have such doubts!

(Sister Aloysius is bent with emotion. Sister James comforts her. Lights fade.)

End of play

Considerations for Critical Thinking and Writing

1. FIRST RESPONSE. Which character do you find to be the more sympathetic, Father Flynn or Sister Aloysius? Explain why your opinion remains constant or shifts over the course of the play.

2. Discuss the significance of Father Flynn's sermon at the beginning of Scene I. How does it anticipate the thematic conflicts that follow?

3. Why do you think Shanley sets the play in a Catholic school in 1964 rather than in the twenty-first century? How relevant is the period in which the drama takes place?

4. How do Father Flynn's long monologues in Scenes I, III, and VI help establish his character?

5. What significant details about Sister Aloysius reveal her character and values? What motivates her behavior?

6. How does Sister James serve as a foil to Sister Aloysius? What, if anything, do they share in common?

7. How would you describe Father Flynn's relationship with Donald Muller?

8. Explain whether or not you find Mrs. Muller's defense of Father Flynn's connection to her son, Donald, convincing in the face of Sister Aloysius's charges (Scene VIII).

9. How do you interpret Sister Aloysius's final line in the play?

10. In Scene VII, Father Flynn explains why he creates "little stories to illustrate" his sermons "[i]n the tradition of a parable." What is his rationale for using this technique and how does it relate to the play's themes?

Connections to Other Selections

1. Discuss the ways in which ambiguity is used to complicate the plot and the theme of *Doubt: A Parable* and Nathaniel Hawthorne's "Young Goodman Brown" (p. 321).

2. Compare the school settings created in Shanley's play and in Nilaja Sun's *No Child . . .* (p. 1565). How are the assumptions, values, and characteristic experiences associated with these settings crucial to the tone of each play?

Perspectives

John Patrick Shanley (b. 1950)

On the Value of Doubt   2005

I have been led by the bitter necessities of an interesting life to value that age-old practice of the wise: Doubt.

There is an uneasy time when belief has begun to slip, but hypocrisy has yet to take hold, when the consciousness is disturbed but not yet altered. It is the most dangerous, important, and ongoing experience of life. The beginning of change is the moment of Doubt. It is that crucial moment when I renew my humanity or become a lie.

Doubt requires more courage than conviction does, and more energy; because conviction is a resting place and doubt is infinite — it is a passionate exercise. You may come out of my play uncertain. You may want to be sure. Look down on that feeling. We've got to learn to live with a full measure of uncertainty. There is no last word. That's the silence under the chatter of our time.

From Preface to *Doubt: A Parable* (New York: Theatre Communications Group, 2005)

CONSIDERATIONS FOR CRITICAL THINKING AND WRITING

1. How does Shanley make a case for doubt's being a form of wisdom?
2. Explain why you agree or disagree with the assertion that "Doubt requires more courage than conviction does." How does your response affect your interpretation of the final lines of *Doubt*?

ALEX WITCHEL (B. 1958)

On Shanley's Experiences in Catholic School   2004

From the beginning, Shanley went to Catholic schools. The Sisters of Charity, who ran St. Anthony's Grammar School, which he attended in the Bronx and has written about in *Doubt*, were the sympathetic antithesis to the Irish Christian Brothers who ran Cardinal Spellman High School. "They beat children with their fists," Shanley said. "I saw a 220-pound brother put a boy, a little gangly boy, against a wall and hit him in the stomach as hard as he could."

Shanley's response to that environment was to become a professional problem child. In religion class, he insisted he did not believe in God. In the cafeteria, he flung mashed potatoes over his shoulder often enough to get banned from the hot-lunch program. He read science fiction books during all his classes and spent five days a week, every week for most of the two years he was there in detention before the brothers finally kicked him out.

He went instead to the Thomas Moore Preparatory School, a private school with a Catholic orientation, in Harrisville, N.H., which afforded him a few humane teachers. It was their kindness, actually, that was among the reasons he wrote *Doubt*, in which a nun suspects a priest of being a bit too interested in a young boy. The strength of the play is how skillfully Shanley exposes the two sides to every suspicion. "It was homosexual teachers for the most part who saved me," Shanley said. "The head of discipline at Thomas Moore was gay, and he was my friend and protector. Did he have his reasons for being interested in me? Everybody has their reasons. Passion fuels many things, and it's used in many ways. Many of these people never cross the line."

Shanley's relative, unfortunately, was not as lucky. "A child in my family was molested by a priest," he said. "The parents went first to the local level, then up the chain of command to a highly placed church official, who took them by the hands and said: 'I'm so sorry this happened to you. I will take care of it.' And then he promoted him. They were so shocked that they left the church for 10 years. But they missed it, so they returned to a parish where the monsignor gave a sermon saying that with these church scandals it was the parents, not the clergy, who were responsible. They had to leave the church again."

From "The Confessions of John Patrick Shanley,"
New York Times, November 7, 2004

1. To what extent does this description of the playwright as a student influence your understanding of Shanley's characterization of Sister Aloysius?

2. How does this biographical information suggest why "Shanley exposes the two sides to every suspicion" in *Doubt*?

ELIZABETH CULLINGFORD (B. 1948)

On the Whiplash Climax of Doubt 2010

In a climax that threatens the audience with whiplash, Sister Aloysius accuses Father Flynn of seducing Donald, he threatens to get her dismissed, and she claims to have spoken to a nun from his last parish who revealed his "prior history of infringements." Her subversive woman-to-woman strategy infuriates him: "That's not the proper route for you to have taken, Sister! . . . You're supposed to go through the pastor." Armed with the knowledge that "this is your third parish in five years," a damning fact that he does not dispute, she snarls: "I will find a parent, Father Flynn! Trust me I will. A parent who probably doesn't know that you are *still working with children*! And once I do that, you will be exposed." Father Flynn explodes, towering over his accuser: "You have taken vows, obedience being one! You answer to us!" — "us" being the chain of male hierarchy that Sister Aloysius has circumvented by her call to another nun. When she stands her ground, he switches from bullying to abjection, begging for charity without admitting guilt: "Even if you can't imagine the explanation, Sister, remember that there are circumstances beyond your knowledge. Even if you feel certainty, it is an emotion and not a fact." Her compassion is inaccessible, however. As he calls the bishop to request a transfer, it appears that Sister Aloysius is right — that Father Flynn is an abuser.

But the brief final scene throws everything into doubt once more. Father Flynn has left St. Nicholas, only to be promoted to pastor of St. Jerome Church and School. The homosocial hierarchy has discounted a woman and closed ranks around one of its own, who is still working in close contact with children. Yet Donald Muller is "heartbroken," not relieved, by the departure of his supposed molester. And shockingly, Sister Aloysius reveals to Sister James that she never called the other nun. She insists that her untruth paid off: "[I]f he had no such history, the lie wouldn't have worked. His resignation was his confession. He was what I thought he was." But Father Flynn could have been the closeted priest she thought he was without being a child abuser. His relationship with Donald might have provided a vulnerable gay child with invaluable positive mentoring from a sympathetic gay adult: permission (as the film suggests) to play with toy ballerinas and dream of dressing up in priestly skirts. The priest's flight might not have been an admission of guilt, but a recognition that his steely antagonist would never relent.

Sister Aloysius's own certainty crumbles in the last lines of the play: "Oh, Sister James! . . . I have doubts! I have such doubts!" but Shanley maintains ambiguity to the last: she does not reveal what they are. Was she wrong to equate homosexuality with pedophilia, and to conflate orientation (tragic though not sinful) with action (always sinful)? Was Father Flynn innocent after all? Or was she wrong to drive him away from St. Nicholas into a school perhaps less well equipped with suspicious sisters? Has she unintentionally engineered the transfer of a problem priest into a new arena of sexual opportunity? Even more shockingly, was she wrong to equate pedophilia with abuse? Neither Sister Aloysius nor the audience will ever know for sure.

From *"Evil, Sin, or Doubt?* The Dramas of Clerical Child Abuse," *Theatre Journal,*
May 2010

CONSIDERATIONS FOR CRITICAL THINKING AND WRITING

1. Explore Cullingford's dual observation that "Father Flynn could have been the closeted priest she thought he was without being a child abuser." Explain whether or not you think the play supports this assessment.

2. A number of questions are raised in Cullingford's third paragraph. Which question do you think is the most important and crucial to your interpretation of the play, and how do you answer it?

KENNETH TURAN (B. 1946)
On the Film Version of Doubt   2008

Doubt is a film with many fine elements, but its director, John Patrick Shanley, doesn't seem to trust them. Which is rather odd, because it was Shanley who wrote both the script and the play on which it's based. . . .

Shanley the writer has carefully constructed this drama like the delicately balanced house of cards it is. On the stage as well as on the screen, *Doubt* is a highly polished piece of business, with every speech and every action calculated for maximum effect, a well-made play if ever there was one.

Although a did-he-or-didn't-he mystery is *Doubt*'s central plot mechanism, the play and the film are about a whole lot more. Philosophical questions about conservative versus progressive religious values, about rigidity versus openness and suspicion versus proof, about how far it's appropriate to go when you are sure you are right, are what got Shanley to write the piece in the first place.

But in the process of opening this story up, of changing it from a four-actor stage play to a film with multiple characters and numerous extras, Shanley seems to have lost a certain amount of faith in what he'd written. As a director he's ended up pushing the drama harder than he needs to. He hasn't done anything fatal, but he has tampered with and hampered it.

For one thing, Shanley has chosen to bring too much of the outside world into St. Nicholas' cloistered halls. Having a cat physically catch a mouse at a key juncture is too literal a metaphor by half, and *Doubt* threatens to become meteorologically overwrought by putting all kinds of wind, rain and even thunder into the story whenever it feels the proceedings won't work on their own. . . .

The only place where this kind of literalism works is *Doubt*'s setting. Cinematographer Roger Deakins, production designer David Gropman and costume designer Ann Roth have combined to carefully re-create the look of the Bronx and the bonnet-wearing Sisters of Charity who call the borough home. An image of the nightgowned nuns coming out of their rooms en masse in the early morning is especially fine.

Inhabiting this world are two particularly well-matched antagonists. Streep's Sister Aloysius is the showier role, a literal holy terror who hasn't smiled since Pius XII was pope and inflicts old school discipline as disapproval and suspicion oozes from every pore. It's a part that verges on caricature, but Streep is adept at walking up to that line without crossing over.

In the other corner is Father Flynn. As played by Hoffman, who looks just fleshy enough to be Pat O'Brien's younger brother, Father Flynn is a priest who likes his pleasures, whether it be rare beef and red wine at dinner or three lumps of sugar in his tea.

These two are not just poles apart personally, they differ on the future of the church. Sister Aloysius is old-fashioned enough to consider "Frosty the Snowman" a pagan anthem (really), while Father Flynn thinks "It's a new time, Sister, the church needs to change."

This philosophical difference is heightened by a conflict over the situation of one particular boy, 12-year-old Donald Miller (Joseph Foster II), the school's first black student.

Father Flynn takes an interest, saying he just wants to protect the friendless boy, but Sister Aloysius suspects that something akin to molestation might be going on. Father Flynn has a plausible answer for everything, but just because we feel closer to his worldview doesn't mean he is without blame. As Sister Aloysius goes into overdrive, Hoffman's nuanced performance gives nothing away.

From "*Doubt* Has a Crisis of Faith," *Los Angeles Times,* December 12, 2008

CONSIDERATIONS FOR CRITICAL THINKING AND WRITING

1. In what sense does Turan think that Shanley's film version of *Doubt* "lost a certain amount of faith"? Even without having seen the film, discuss whether or not you think he makes a valid point.

2. View the film version of *Doubt* and write a review that compares your reading of the play with your experience of it on the screen. Are they both satisfying? Why or why not?

PLAYS IN PERFORMANCE

Oedipus the King: At center stage is Iokaste (Ching Valdes-Aran) in a scene from the 1993 production of *Oedipus the King* (p. 1127) at Philadelphia's Wilma Theater, directed by Blanka Zizka and Jiri Zizka. © T. Charles Erickson.

A Midsummer Night's Dream (right): Titania, Queen of the Fairies (Fiona Victory), and Bottom (Graham Sinclair), in a 1988 performance of *A Midsummer Night's Dream* (p. 1180) at the Edinburgh International Arts Festival.
© Robbie Jack/Corbis.

Hamlet (below): The "play within the play" scene from *Hamlet* (p. 1237).
Nat Farbman/The LIFE Picture Collection/Getty Images.

A Doll's House: Owen Teale and Janet McTeer in a scene from the 1997 Bill Kenwright London production of *A Doll's House* (p. 1357) performed at New York's Belasco Theatre — winner of the 1997 Tony Award for Best Revival of a Play. Joan Marcus.

Doubt (above): Cherry Jones as Sister Aloysius and Brian F. O'Byrne as Father Flynn in the 2004 world premiere of *Doubt* (p. 1430) at the Manhattan Theatre Club.

Sara Krulwich/*The New York Times*/Redux.

Rodeo (right): Margo Martindale in *Rodeo* (p. 1474), during the Sixth Annual Humana Festival of New American Plays, at the Actors Theatre of Louisville, Kentucky, in 1982.

Richard C. Trigg, photographer. Courtesy of The Actors Theatre of Louisville.

Fences (left): Mary Alice and James Earl Jones in the Yale Repertory Theatre's 1985 production of *Fences* (p. 1589).
Ron Schert/The Image Works.

Trying to Find Chinatown (below): Richard Thompson as Benjamin and Zar Acayan as Ronnie in *Trying to Find Chinatown* (p. 1491), during the 20th Annual Humana Festival of New American Plays, at the Actor's Theatre of Louisville, Kentucky, in 1996.
Courtesy of The Actors Theatre of Louisville.

Death of a Salesman (above):
Willy (Lee J. Cobb) with sons
Hap (Cameron Mitchell) and
Biff (Arthur Kennedy) in
Death of a Salesman (p. 1495).
Photo by W. Eugene Smith, The LIFE
Picture Collection/Getty Images.

No Child . . . (right):
Playwright and actor Nilaja
Sun performs a scene from
her solo show, *No Child* . . .
(p. 1563), in a 2008 Berkeley
Repertory Theatre production.
Carol Rosegg.

Playwriting 101: A scene from the 2003 Kaleidoscope Theatre Company production (New York) of Rich Orloff's *Playwriting 101* (p. 1477).
Photo by Rick Tormone.

Naked Lunch: A scene from the 2004 Humana Festival production of *Naked Lunch* (p. 1098).
Harlan Taylor photographer, Courtesy of The Actors Theatre of Louisville.

A THEMATIC CASE STUDY

An Album of Contemporary
Humor and Satire

I write plays because they're fun.
— RICH ORLOFF

Photo by Rich Tormone.

In contrast to the darkness and suffering that surrounds, for example, Hamlet's tragedy, comedy typically works out in the end: the hero triumphs; a sense of renewal flourishes; life is better, yielding to human hopes and aspirations; the implausible is happily possible and characters find freedom, acceptance, and love. Life in a comedy is, as Shakespeare would have it, a midsummer night's dream. Comedy does not mean, however, that there isn't trouble along the way. Humor in comedy can embody anger, criticism, and indignation in its response to life's absurdities and pretentiousness. Toothy wide grins can also produce biting satire.

Humor, satire, and social commentary ride together in Jane Martin's *Rodeo* (p. 1474), a rich monologue that reveals a powerful woman's character as well as the corrosive commercialization of a genuinely American sport. In Jane Anderson's *The Reprimand* (p. 1467), a short play in which humor serves as a corrective, two women engage in a strained phone conversation over an offhanded remark about one's body weight. Their subsequent dialogue is spiced with acid reflux and carefully measured pretenses that leave a bad aftertaste. These satiric plays make moral, social, and political points through humor, but they do not harangue or lecture audiences. There are no seats available for the presumptuous and the pretentious in comedy's theater.

Comedy is sometimes associated with another kind of bad taste. The essential differences between comedy and tragedy can be clearly discerned in the plot, characters, and themes of two plays like *A Midsummer Night's Dream* and *Hamlet*, but there are also important differences in style. James Kincaid neatly summarizes a crucial difference in his discussion of "Who Is Relieved by the Idea of Comic Relief?" (an excerpt from this essay appears on p. 1345). He shrewdly distinguishes between them: "Tragedy is sleek and single-minded, comedy rumpled and hospitable to any idea or agency. Tragedy stares us out of countenance; comedy winks and leers and drools. Tragedy is all dressed up; comedy is always taking things off, mooning us." Kincaid deftly puts his finger on the unruly nature of comedy without pointing his finger at it. Comedy celebrates the messy, untidy, confused disarrangements that life presents to us as it does in Sharon E. Cooper's *Mistaken Identity* (p. 1469). Rich Orloff even makes fun of playwriting in his *Playwriting 101: The Rooftop Lesson* (p. 1477). This is not to say that satirizing one's own satire renders everything meaningless but rather to acknowledge that everything is fair game for comedy. As you'll see, even tragedy is figuratively mooned by comedy in David Ives's *Moby-Dude, Or: The Three-Minute Whale* (p. 1484). Bon voyage.

The Reprimand

Writer and director Jane Anderson started her career as an actor. She left college at the age of nineteen to pursue acting and was cast in the David Mamet hit play *Sexual Perversity in Chicago*. The experience familiarized Anderson with scriptwriting, and eventually she founded a writing group called New York Writers' Block. She later wrote and performed in a number of one-woman comedic plays, whose success afforded her the opportunity to write for the television sitcoms *The Facts of Life* and *The Wonder Years*.

Photo by permission of Jilly Wendell.

In 1986, Anderson wrote the play *Defying Gravity*, a composite of monologues about the space shuttle *Challenger* explosion. Her first screenplay, *The Positively True Adventures of the Alleged Texas Cheerleader-Murdering Mom*, was a satirical look at the true story of a Texas mother who tried to hire a contract killer to murder her daughter's rival (and her mother) for the junior high school cheerleading squad. The HBO movie starred Holly Hunter and gave Anderson instant notoriety as a screenwriter. She has written the screenplays for a number of movies since, including *The Baby Dance,* starring Jody Foster, and *When Billie Beat Bobby,* the story of tennis champion Billie Jean King beating an aging Bobby Riggs. In 2009 she was nominated for the Writer's Guild of America Award for Best Dramatic Series for her writing on the second season of the television series *Mad Men.*

The Reprimand was one of five "phone plays" that premiered in February 2000 at the annual Humana Festival of New American Plays held at Actors Theatre in Louisville, Kentucky. The phone call is a traditional stage convention that consists of an actor providing one side of a conversation, but for the Humana Festival performances, the actors conversed offstage and the audience heard both sides of the three-minute conversation. In *The Reprimand,* the overheard conversation reveals a complicated power struggle between two women.

JANE ANDERSON (B. 1954)

The Reprimand   2000

CHARACTERS

Rhona
Mim

Rhona: . . . we need to talk about what you did in the meeting this morning.
Mim: My God, what?
Rhona: That reference you made about my weight.
Mim: What reference?
Rhona: When we came into the room and Jim was making the introductions, you said, "Oh Rhona, why don't you take the bigger chair."
Mim: But that was — I thought since this was your project that you should sit in the better chair.
Rhona: But you didn't say better, you said bigger.
Mim: I did? Honest to God, that isn't what I meant. I'm so sorry if it hurt your feelings.
Rhona: You didn't hurt my feelings. This has nothing to do with my feelings. What concerns me — and concerns Jim by the way — is how this could have undermined the project.
Mim: Jim said something about it?
Rhona: Yes.
Mim: What did he say?
Rhona: He thought your comment was inappropriate.
Mim: Really? How? I was talking about a chair.
Rhona: Mim, do you honestly think anyone in that room was really listening to what I had to say after you made that comment?
Mim: I thought they were very interested in what you had to say.
Rhona: Honey, there was a reason why Dick and Danny asked you all the follow-up questions.

Mim: But that's because I hadn't said anything up to that point. Look, I'm a little confused about Jim's reaction, because after the meeting he said he liked what I did with the follow-up.

Rhona: He should acknowledge what you do. And I know the reason why he's finally said something is because I've been telling him that you deserve more credit.

Mim: Oh, thank you. But I think Jim already respects what I do.

Rhona: He should respect you. But from what I've observed, I think — because you're an attractive woman — that he still uses you for window dressing. Especially when you're working with me. You know what I'm saying?

Mim: Well, if that's the case, Jim is a jerk.

Rhona: I know that. And I know you know that. But I think you still have a lot of anger about the situation and sometimes it really shows.

Mim: I don't mean it to show.

Rhona: I know that. Look, I consider you — regardless of what Jim thinks — I think you're really talented and I really love working with you.

Mim: And I enjoy working with you.

Rhona: Thank you. And that's why I want to keep things clear between us. Especially when we're working for men like Jim.

Mim: No, I agree, absolutely.

Rhona: *(To someone off-phone.)* Tell him I'll be right there. *(Back to Mim.)* Mim, sorry — I have Danny on the phone.

Mim: Oh — do you want to conference me in?

Rhona: I can handle it, but thank you. Mim, I'm so glad we had this talk.

Mim: Well, thank you for being so honest with me.

Rhona: And thank you for hearing me. I really appreciate it. Let's talk later?

Mim: Sure. *(Rhona hangs up. A beat.) (Mumbling.)* Fat pig. *(Hangs up.)*

CONSIDERATIONS FOR CRITICAL THINKING AND WRITING

1. FIRST RESPONSE. Do you identify with one character more than the other? Consider whether Rhona or Mim is more sympathetic.

2. What is humorous about the nature of the conflict? Is there a resolution to the conflict?

3. How is the exposition presented? What does it reveal? How does Anderson's choice not to dramatize events onstage help to determine the focus of the play?

4. What can be said about the setting? Explain whether you think setting has any role in this play.

5. Discuss the significance of the title. To whom does it apply?

6. CREATIVE RESPONSE. Write a three-minute phone or e-mail conversation between a student and professor that captures some dramatic tension in their relationship.

CONNECTIONS TO OTHER SELECTIONS

1. Compare the power relationship that exists between Rhona and Mim and that of Mrs. Peters and Mrs. Hale in Susan Glaspell's *Trifles* (p. 1080).

2. Discuss the ways in which hostility is manifested in characters' dialogue in *The Reprimand* and in Michael Hollinger's *Naked Lunch* (p. 1098).

Mistaken Identity

Sharon E. Cooper is an award-winning play-wright and teacher whose work has been produced in India, Germany, England, Hungary, and across the United States. Her work has appeared in *Laugh Lines: Short Comic Plays* and in the 2010 and 2014 editions of *The Best Ten-Minute Plays*. Cooper is an English tutor, writing coach, fitness instructor, screenwriter, Resident Playwright at The CRY HAVOC Company in New York City, and a member of the Dramatist Guild. Her full-length screenplay, *The Golden Age of Kali*, was inspired by *Mistaken Identity*. *Mistaken Identity* starts the way a good many shaky blind dates begin but then takes an interesting turn.

Virginia Zapar.

> **WHEN I WRITE** "Don't be scared to write the truth as you know it and as you see it. Find like-minded, thoughtful people — people you can trust, who will listen and help you write the story you want to write. But if someone tries to rewrite or 'fix' your story, stop listening." — SHARON E. COOPER

SHARON E. COOPER (B. 1975)
Mistaken Identity   2004
(2008 Revised)

CHARACTERS

Kali Patel, 29. Single lesbian Hindu of Indian heritage; social worker who works as much as possible; lives in Leicester, England.

Steve Dodd, 32. Single straight guy, desperate to marry, raised Baptist but attends church only on Christmas and Easter; studying abroad for his final year as an undergraduate.

SETTING: The Castle, a pub in Kirby Muxlowe in Leicester, England.

TIME: The present.

> *(Lights up on Steve and Kali in a busy pub on their first date. They are in the middle of dinner.)*

Steve: You must get tired of fish and chips all the time. Why do y'all call them "chips"? When they're french fries, I mean. And you ever notice when people swear, they say, "Excuse my French." Not me. Nope. I have nothing against the French.

Kali: Right, well, I'm not French, Steve, now am I?

Steve: I just didn't want you to think I was prejudiced against the French or *anyone else*. . . . They're like your neighbors, the French. And your neighbors are like my neighbors. And like a good neighbor, State Farm is there. Have you heard that commercial?

Kali: What? No. Steve —

Steve: It's for insurance. Y'all must not play it here. *(Pause.)* So I know that you all do the "arranged marriage thing." Rashid and I had a long talk about it. Of course, Rashid and I wanted you to approve, too, Kali.

Kali: How twenty-first century of you and my brother. Steve . . .

Kali: I'm gay. / *Steve:* Will you marry me?

Kali: Come again? / *Steve:* What?

Kali: How could you ask me to . . . / *Steve:* Well, I can't believe this.

Kali: Bloody hell, stop talking while I'm talking . . . / *Steve:* This is very strange.

Kali: So — what?

Steve: This new information is, well, new, and changes things, I guess.

Kali: You guess? What the hell is wrong with you? I'm sorry, Steve, you just happened to show up at the end of a very long line of a lot of very bad dates. You know, movies where the bloke negotiates holding your hand while you're just trying to eat popcorn; running across De Montfort University in the pouring rain; dropping a bowling ball on the bloke's pizza.

Steve: You had me until the bowling ball. Kali, this doesn't make sense. I invite you out on a lovely date. We eat fish and chips — when I would rather be eating a burger or lasagna —

Kali: Steve, I'm sorry.

Steve: I figured we would have a nice long traditional wedding with the colorful tents. All of my family would be there. We're more of the Christmas/ Easter Christians, so we'd do your religion and I would wear —

Kali: *(Overlapping.)* You don't know anything about my people. What are you —

Steve: *(Overlapping.)* Ooohhh, yes, I do. I saw *Monsoon Wedding*. And the director's cut! And I saw *Slumdog Millionaire* like three times. Three times. Unbelievable!

Kali: Yes, this makes loads of sense at the end of the day. I am a lesbian who has to date every Hindu bloke in England until her brother gets so desperate that he sets her up with a cowboy —

Steve: I take offense to that.

Kali: *(Overlapping.)* But I should feel sorry for *you* because *you* watched *two*, count them, *two* movies about Indian people in your entire life and ordered fish when there are hamburgers on the menu! Forgive *me* for being so insensitive.

Steve: I ordered fish because I wanted you to like me. And I'm sure I've seen other Asian movies. Like all those fighting movies. You know, the ones where women are jumping through the air —

Kali: Aaahhh! Do you see how all of this is a moot point now?

Steve: I'm confused. Let's review.

Kali: Please, no, bloody hell, let's not review. Let's get the waiter. Haven't you had enough?

(She gets up. He follows.)

Steve: *(Overlapping.)* Why is your brother setting up his *lesbian* sister —

Kali: *(Overlapping.)* Will you please keep your voice down?

Steve: *(Overlapping.)* — up on dates for marriage and tricking well-meaning men — specifically me — into proposing to her? I'm here to finish my business degree, but I wasn't born yesterday. So I took a few years off and changed careers a few times, was a fireman —

Kali: *(Overlapping.)* What does that have to do with anything?

Steve: And I'm thirty-two years old, but that doesn't mean —

Kali: Mate, are you going to keep on and on?

Steve: Why did your brother put me through this? This isn't one of those new reality shows: "Little Brothers Set Up Their Lesbian Sisters." Is there a camera under the table? *(He looks.)* Let's talk about this. *(He sits back down.)* I'm a good listener. Go ahead. *(Pause.)* I'm listening. *(Pause.)* You have to say something if you want this to continue with what we call in America, a conversation.

Kali: Are you done?

Steve: Go ahead.

(She sits.)

Kali: I guess I was hoping you wouldn't tell Rashid.

Steve: He doesn't know?

Kali: You are finishing your bachelor's degree, is that right?

Steve: If you're so "bloody" smart, I'm wondering why you would tell me, a man that is friends with your brother and sits next to him twice a week in eight A.M. classes — why would you tell *me* you're a lesbian and *not* your brother?

Kali: Maybe for the same reason you would ask a woman you've never met before to marry you.

Steve: Your brother made it sound like it would be easy. I've been looking for that.

Kali: *(Overlapping.)* Look, you seem very nice, you do.

Steve: I am very nice.

Kali: And at the end of the day, I hope you find someone you like.

Steve: I like how you say "at the end of the day" and I like how you say "bloke" and "mate." It's so endearing. And you're beautiful and small and your hair falls on your back so.

Kali: Steve, being a lesbian is not negotiable. And don't start with how sexy it would be to be with me or to watch me and another woman —

Steve: *(Overlapping.)* Kali, I didn't say any of that.

Kali: You didn't have to. Up until a few minutes ago, you thought I was a quiet, subservient Asian toy for sale from her brother. Steve, go get a doll. She can travel with you to America whenever you want. In the meantime, I'll continue to be a loud, abrasive *(Whispering.)* lesbian while my brother sets me up with every bloke on the street — and they don't even have to be Hindu anymore! Do you have any idea what that's like? *(Pause.)* How would you know?

Steve: You're right. I wouldn't.

Kali: Steve, why did you want to be with me? I mean, before.

Steve: I figured that we would have visited my family in the winter when it's so cold here. I would have been willing to stay here when I'm done with school and we would get a nice little place by the —

Kali: Steve, we hadn't even shared dessert yet.

Steve: Don't blame me for all of this. Five minutes ago, we were on a date.

Kali: We're just two people in a pub.

Steve: Kali, do you remember the last time someone — man, woman, I don't care — had their hand down the small of your back or leaned into you like it didn't matter where you ended and they began?

Kali: Yes, I do remember that. And that was strangely poetic.

Steve: You don't have to sound so surprised. Anyway, I remember that feeling. Three years ago, at a Fourth of July celebration — you know, that's the holiday —

Kali: Yes, Steve, I know the holiday.

Steve: She was the only woman I ever really loved. I knew it was ending. Could taste it. I just held her as the fireworks went off and the dust got in our skin. Figured I would hold on, hoping that would keep me for a while. You know how they say babies will die if they're left alone too long. Always wondered if it's true for bigger people, too. Like how long would we last? . . . She left with her Pilates mat and Snoopy slippers a few days later. I bet it hasn't been three years for you.

Kali: No, it hasn't. But you wouldn't want to hear about that.

Steve: Why not?

Kali: Come on, Steve, I'm not here for your fantasies —

Steve: This thing where you assume you know what I'm thinking — it's gettin' old.

Kali: I'm . . . sorry. I do have a woman in my life, Michele — She's a teacher for people that are deaf. We've been together for eleven months. The longest we were away from each other was this one time for three weeks. She was at a retreat where they weren't allowed to talk — you know, total immersion. So she would call and I would say, "Is it beautiful there, love?" and she would hit a couple of buttons. Sometimes she would leave me messages: "beep, beep, beep beep beep beep." It didn't matter that she didn't say anything . . . But I can't take her home for Diwali.

Steve: What's that?

Kali: It's a festival of lights where —

Steve: You mean like Hanukkah.

Kali: No, like Diwali. It's a New Year's celebration where we remember ancestors, family, and friends. And reflect back and look to the future.

Steve: It sounds nice. You know, my mother has been asking me for grandchildren since I turned twenty-seven. Every year at Christmas, it's the same: "I can't wait to hang another stocking for my grandchildren, if I ever get to have them."

Kali: Now, imagine that same conversation, well, not about Christmas, and what if you could never give that to them — could never bring someone home for any holiday for the rest of your life?

Steve: Then why don't you just tell them the truth?

Kali: I can't say, Mum, Daddy, Rashid, I've chosen women over men — it's not a hamburger over fish. You just don't know how they'll react. I'd run the risk of not being allowed to see my nieces. I'm so exhausted from hiding, I can barely breathe.

Steve: So stop hiding.

Kali: Have you been listening to what I've been saying?

Steve: Have you?

Kali: Are you going to tell my brother?

Steve: Do you want me to?

Kali: I don't know.

Steve: I've never thought about that thing that you said.

Kali: Which thing would that be?

Steve: The one where maybe you can't see your nieces 'cause you're gay. That must suck.

Kali: Yes, well, thanks for trying to make me feel better.

Steve: Listen, you get to decide what you tell your family and when. As far as I'm concerned, I'll tell Rashid tomorrow that we're getting married. Or I can tell him you're a lesbian, and if he doesn't let you be with his kids anymore, I'll punch him in the face. That was me kidding.

Kali: You're funny. *(Pause.)* Maybe I told you because somewhere deep down, I do want him to know. But I don't know if I can take the risk.

Steve: You don't have to rush.

Kali: I just wish it could be more simple. Like, why can't what I want be part of the whole picket-fence thing? That's pretty ridiculous, huh?

Steve: We're all looking for that. My grandparents met before World War II, dated for seven days in a row, and my grandfather asked my grandmother to go with him to Louisiana, where he'd be stationed. She said, "Is that a proposal?" And he said, "Of course it is." And they've been together ever since. And I just want that, too. Huh — asking you to marry me on a first date! You must think I'm pretty desperate, huh?

Kali: Not any more than the rest of us . . . Oh, hell, do you want to have some dessert?

Steve: Oh, hell, sure. You know, we're going to share dessert.

Kali: Hey, mate, no one said anything about sharing.

Steve: I would go home with you for Diwali. I mean, as friends. If you ever wanted one around. You're a nice girl, Kali. I mean woman, mate, bloke. I mean —

Kali: Sssshhhh. Let's just get some dessert.

(Lights fade as they motion for the waiter. Blackout.)

Considerations for Critical Thinking and Writing

1. **FIRST RESPONSE.** Did you find this play humorous and enjoyable? Why or why not?

2. How does Cooper establish Steve's character in his first few speeches? At what point is his character made more complex?

3. How important is the brother's role in the plot?

4. What serious issues — and conflicts — emerge from the humor of this play?

5. Is there a climax? Are the conflicts resolved?

6. Discuss the potential meanings of the title.

Connections to Other Selections

1. Compare Steve's character with that of Vernon's in Michael Hollinger's *Naked Lunch* (p. 1098). What is the essential difference between them? Are there any significant similarities?

2. **CREATIVE RESPONSE.** Write the dessert scene that ends *Mistaken Identity* so that it matches the tone of *Naked Lunch*.

Rodeo

Jane Martin is a pseudonym. The author's identity is known only to a handful of administrators at the Actors Theatre of Louisville who handle permissions for productions and reprints of the play. *Rodeo* is one of eleven monologues in *Talking With. . . .* Martin has also published other plays conveniently grouped in two volumes: *Jane Martin: Collected Plays 1980–1995* (1996) and *Jane Martin: Collected Plays 1996–2001* (2001).

Although only one character appears in *Rodeo,* the monologue is surprisingly moving as she describes what the rodeo once was, how it has changed, and what it means to her. At first glance the subject matter may not seem very promising for drama, but the character's energy, forthrightness, and colorful language transform seemingly trivial details into significant meanings.

Jane Martin

Rodeo 1981

A young woman in her late twenties sits working on a piece of tack. Beside her is a Lone Star beer in the can. As the lights come up we hear the last verse of a Tanya Tucker song or some other female country-western vocalist. She is wearing old worn jeans and boots plus a long-sleeved workshirt with the sleeves rolled up. She works until the song is over and then speaks.

See Plays in Performance insert.

Richard C. Trigg, photographer. Courtesy of The Actors Theatre of Louisville.

Big Eight: Shoot — Rodeo's just goin' to hell in a handbasket. Rodeo used to be somethin'. I loved it. I did. Once Daddy an' a bunch of 'em was foolin' around with some old bronc over to our place and this ol' red nose named Cinch got bucked off and my Daddy hooted and said he had him a nine-year-old girl, namely me, wouldn't have no damn trouble cowboyin' that horse. Well, he put me on up there, stuck that ridin' rein in my hand, gimme a kiss, and said, "Now there's only one thing t' remember Honey Love, if ya fall off you jest don't come home." Well I stayed up. You gotta stay on a bronc eight seconds. Otherwise the ride don't count. So from that day on my daddy called me Big Eight. Heck! That's all the name I got anymore . . . Big Eight.

Used to be fer cowboys, the rodeo did. Do it in some open field, folks would pull their cars and pick-ups round it, sit on the hoods, some ranch hand'd bulldog him some rank steer and everybody'd wave their hats and call him by name. Ride us some buckin' stock, rope a few calves, git throwed off a bull, and then we'd jest git us to a bar and tell each other lies about how good we were.

Used to be a family thing. Wooly Billy Tilson and Tammy Lee had them five kids on the circuit. Three boys, two girls and Wooly and Tammy. Wasn't no two-beer rodeo in Oklahoma didn't have a Tilson entered. Used to call the oldest girl Tits. Tits Tilson. Never seen a girl that top-heavy could ride so well. Said she only fell off when the gravity got her. Cowboys used to say if she

landed face down you could plant two young trees in the holes she'd leave. Ha!
Tits Tilson.

Used to be people came to a rodeo had a horse of their own back home.
Farm people, ranch people — lord, they *knew* what they were lookin' at.
Knew a good ride from a bad ride, knew hard from easy. You broke some
bones er spent the day eatin' dirt, at least ya got appreciated.

Now they bought the rodeo. Them. Coca-Cola, Pepsi Cola, Marlboro
damn cigarettes. You know the ones I mean. Them. Hire some New York faggot t' sit on some ol' stuffed horse in front of a sagebrush photo n' smoke that
junk. Hell, tobacco wasn't made to smoke, honey, it was made to chew. Lord
wanted ya filled up with smoke he would've set ya on fire. Damn it gets me!

There's some guy in a banker's suit runs the rodeo now. Got him a pinky
ring and a digital watch, honey. Told us we oughta have a watchamacallit, cho-
riographus or somethin', some ol' ballbuster used to be with the Ice damn Capades. Wants us to ride around dressed up like Mickey Mouse, Pluto, crap like
that. Told me I had to haul my butt through the barrel race done up like Minnie
damn Mouse in a tu-tu. Huh uh, honey! Them people is so screwed-up they
probably eat what they run over in the road.

Listen, they got the clowns wearin' Astronaut suits! I ain't lyin'. You
know what a rodeo clown does! You go down, fall off whatever — the clown
runs in front of the bull so's ya don't git stomped. Pin-stripes, he got 'em in
space suits tellin' jokes on a microphone. First horse see 'em, done up like
the Star Wars went crazy. Best buckin' horse on the circuit, name of Piss 'N'
Vinegar, took one look at them clowns, had him a heart attack and died.
Cowboy was ridin' him got hisself squashed. Twelve hundred pounds of cor-
onary arrest jes fell right through 'em. Blam! Vio con dios. Crowd thought
that was funnier than the astronauts. I swear it won't be long before they're
strappin' ice-skates on the ponies. Big crowds now. Ain't hardly no ranch
people, no farm people, nobody I know. Buncha disco babies and dee-vorce
lawyers — designer jeans and day-glo Stetsons. Hell, the whole bunch of 'em
wears French perfume. Oh it smells like money now! Got it on the cable T
and V — hey, you know what, when ya rodeo yer just bound to kick yerself
up some dust — well now, seems like that fogs up the ol' TV camera, so they
told us a while back that from now on we was gonna ride on some new stuff
called Astro-dirt. Dust free. Artificial damn dirt, honey. Lord have mercy.

Banker Suit called me in the other day said "Lurlene . . ." "Hold it," I said,
"Who's this Lurlene? Round here they call me Big Eight." "Well, Big Eight,"
he said, "My name's Wallace." "Well that's a real surprise t' me," I said, "Cause
aroun' here everybody jes calls you Dumb-ass." My, he laughed real big, slapped
his big ol' desk, an' then he said I wasn't suitable for the rodeo no more. Said
they was lookin' fer another type, somethin' a little more in the showgirl line,
like the Dallas Cowgirls maybe. Said the ridin' and ropin' wasn't the thing no
more. Talked on about floats, costumes, dancin' choreog-aphy. If I was a man
I woulda pissed on his shoe. Said he'd give me a lifetime pass though. Said I
could come to his rodeo any time I wanted.

Rodeo used to be people ridin' horses for the pleasure of people who rode
horses — made you feel good about what you could do. Rodeo wasn't worth
no money to nobody. Money didn't have nothing to do with it! Used to be
seven Tilsons riding in the rodeo. Wouldn't none of 'em dress up like Donald
damn Duck so they quit. That there's the law of gravity!

There's a bunch of assholes in this country sneak around until they see ya havin' fun and then they buy the fun and start in sellin' it. See, they figure if ya love it, they can sell it. Well you look out, honey! They want to make them a dollar out of what you love. Dress *you* up like Minnie Mouse. Sell your rodeo. Turn *yer* pleasure into Ice damn Capades. You hear what I'm sayin'? You're jus' merchandise to them, sweetie. You're jus' merchandise to them.

Blackout.

CONSIDERATIONS FOR CRITICAL THINKING AND WRITING

1. FIRST RESPONSE. Big Eight is presented as an old-fashioned rodeo type. What associations or stereotypes do you have about such people? What assumptions do you make about them? How does the author use those expectations to heighten your understanding of Big Eight's character?

2. How has the rodeo changed from how it "used to be"? How do you account for those changes?

3. Comment on Big Eight's use of language. Why is it appropriate for her character?

4. How would you describe Big Eight's brand of humor? How does it affect your understanding of her?

5. How do your feelings about Big Eight develop during the course of the monologue?

6. What does the rodeo mean to Big Eight?

CONNECTIONS TO OTHER SELECTIONS

1. Compare and contrast a Shakespeare monologue from either *Hamlet* (p. 1238) or *A Midsummer Night's Dream* (p. 1181) with the style and content of *Rodeo*.

2. In an essay discuss the nostalgic tone in *Rodeo* and Stephen Crane's short story "The Bride Comes to Yellow Sky" (p. 251). In your response consider each work's treatment of the West.

3. Compare the attitudes expressed about merchandising in *Rodeo* with those expressed in Arthur Miller's *Death of a Salesman* (p. 1497).

Photo by Rick Tormone.

Playwriting 101: The Rooftop Lesson

Born in Chicago, Rich Orloff graduated from Oberlin College in 1973 and has built a successful career as a comedic playwright. He has written thirteen full-length plays, seven collections of one-act plays, and more than seventy short plays, four of which have appeared in *Best American Short Plays*. His works are produced throughout the United States and have won a number of awards, including the 2002–03

Dramatists Guild Playwriting Fellowship. On his Web site <www.richorloff.com> Orloff explains what prompted him to write *Playwriting 101: The Rooftop Lesson:* "The play was originally produced as part of a series of short plays produced on an actual rooftop in Manhattan. When I was invited to submit to the festival, every idea I came up with seemed completely clichéd. So I gathered the clichés into one story and satirized them. Voila, an original play!"

WHEN I WRITE "One of the joys of writing plays is knowing that it's always a draft. I keep revising until I sense the play is connecting well with an audience, that they're laughing at the funny parts and are engaged in the story." — RICHARD ORLOFF

RICH ORLOFF (B. 1951)

Playwriting 101: The Rooftop Lesson 2000

NOTE: The characters [the Teacher, the Jumper, and the Good Samaritan] can be of either sex, but the Jumper and Good Samaritan should be of the same sex. References are written as if the characters are male, but that can be changed.

TIME: The present.

PLACE: The rooftop of a large urban building.

See Plays in Performance insert.

Photo by Rick Tormone.

(As the play begins, The Jumper is on the ledge of the roof and is about to jump.)

The Jumper: I'm going to jump, and nobody can stop me!

(The Good Samaritan enters quickly.)

The Good Samaritan: Don't!!!!!

(The Teacher enters and stands to the side. The Teacher points a clicker at the others and clicks, freezing the action.)

The Teacher (addressing the audience): A typical dramatic scenario: Two people in conflict — at least one in deep inner conflict — with high stakes, suspense, and affordable cast size. How will this situation play out? That depends, of course, on the level of craft and creativity in that remarkable art form known as playwriting. Let's rewind from the start — *(The Teacher clicks, and The Jumper and Good Samaritan return to their places at the top of the play, quickly reversing their initial movements.)* And see what happens.

(The Teacher clicks again to resume the action. The Jumper is on the ledge of the roof and is about to jump.)

The Jumper: I'm going to jump, and nobody can stop me!

(The Good Samaritan enters quickly.)

The Good Samaritan: Don't!!!!!
The Jumper: Okay.

(The Teacher clicks to freeze the action.)

The Teacher: Not very satisfying, is it? Where's the suspense? Where's the tension? And what audience member will want to pay today's ticket prices for a play whose conflict resolves in forty-five seconds? But most importantly, where can you go from here?

(The Teacher clicks to unfreeze the action.)

The Good Samaritan: Gee, you could've hurt yourself.
The Jumper: Gosh, you're right.
The Good Samaritan: Want to grab a brew?
The Jumper: Sure.

(The Teacher clicks to freeze the action.)

The Teacher: Without intense oppositional desires, more commonly known as "conflict," there is no play. When Nora leaves in *A Doll's House*, nobody wants her husband to reply — *(upbeat)* "Call when you get work!" So let's start this scene over — *(The Teacher clicks. The Jumper and Good Samaritan rewind to their initial places.)* maintaining conflict.

(The Teacher clicks again.)

The Jumper: I'm going to jump, and nobody can stop me!

(The Good Samaritan enters quickly.)

The Good Samaritan: Don't!!!!!
The Jumper: Fuck you!
The Good Samaritan *(giving an obscene gesture)*: No, you asshole, fuck you!

(The Teacher clicks and freezes the action.)

The Teacher: Let's rise above profanity, shall we? It alienates conservatives and makes liberals think you're second-rate David Mamet. *(Clicks.)* Rewind . . . And again: *(Clicks.)*
The Jumper: I'm going to jump, and nobody can stop me!

(The Good Samaritan enters quickly.)

The Good Samaritan: Don't!!!!!
The Jumper: Why not?!!!

(The Teacher clicks.)

The Teacher: Oooo, you can just feel the suspense rising now, can't you?

(The Teacher clicks again.)

The Good Samaritan: Because suicide is a sin!

(The Teacher clicks.)

The Teacher: Big deal. Theatre is written by sinners about sinners for sinners. Nobody goes to *Othello* to hear, "Iago, you're so naughty!" Always let the audience form their own judgments. Rewind a bit. *(Clicks.)* Now let's try a different tack. *(Clicks.)*
The Jumper: Why not?!
The Good Samaritan: Because I love you.
The Jumper: I didn't know!

(The Teacher clicks.)

The Teacher: I don't care! Let's see if we can find something less clichéd.

(*The Teacher clicks again.*)

The Jumper: Why not?!

The Good Samaritan: Because if you jump there, you'll land on my little girl's lemonade stand. And my little girl!

(*The Jumper looks over the ledge and moves over two feet.*)

The Jumper: Is this better?

(*The Teacher clicks.*)

The Teacher: Now what have we gained? Be wary of minor obstacles. Unless, of course, you need to fill time. Again.

(*The Teacher clicks again.*)

The Jumper: Why not?!

The Good Samaritan: Because life is worth living.

The Jumper: Mine isn't!

(*The Teacher clicks.*)

The Teacher: Excellent. We don't just have a plot anymore, we have a theme. Theme, the difference between entertainment and art. No theme, add a car chase and sell it to the movies. But with theme, you have the potential to create something meaningful, something memorable, something college students can write term papers about. So let's rewind a bit and see where this thematically rich drama goes now.

(*The Teacher clicks to rewind and clicks again to resume.*)

The Good Samaritan: Because life is worth living!

The Jumper: Mine isn't!

The Good Samaritan: Gosh. Tell me all about it.

(*The Teacher clicks.*)

The Teacher: Some expositional subtlety, please.

(*The Teacher clicks again.*)

The Good Samaritan: Because life is worth living!

The Jumper: Mine isn't!

The Good Samaritan: Are you sure?

(*The Teacher clicks.*)

The Teacher: Better.

(*The Teacher clicks again.*)

The Jumper: Yes, I'm sure. I'm broke, I have no friends, and I see no reason to continue.

The Good Samaritan: Look, so you're broke and friendless. All experiences are transient. Detach, as the Buddha once did.

(*The Teacher clicks.*)

The Teacher: Of all the world's great religions, Buddhism is the least entertaining. Let's try again.

(*The Teacher clicks again.*)

The Good Samaritan: So you're broke and you're friendless. Why not try Prozac?

(The Teacher clicks.)

The Teacher: The popularity and effectiveness of modern antidepressants is one of the great challenges of contemporary dramaturgy. We no more want Willy Loman to solve his problems with Prozac than we want Stanley and Stella Kowalski to get air-conditioning. How can today's playwright deal with today's medicinal deus ex machinas? Let's see.

(The Teacher clicks again.)

The Jumper: I tried Prozac once, and it made my mouth really dry.

(The Teacher clicks.)

The Teacher: Not great, but we'll let it slide.

(The Teacher clicks again.)

The Good Samaritan: Let me help you.
The Jumper: It's too late.
The Good Samaritan: No, it's not.
The Jumper: You don't understand. I haven't told you the worst.

(The Teacher clicks.)

The Teacher: Fictional characters are rarely straightforward.

(The Teacher clicks again.)

The Jumper: You see, until a few weeks ago, I was in love. Deep love. True love. I was involved with two of the most wonderful gals in the world. One was sexy, rich, generous and caring. The other was streetwise, daring and even sexier. Between the two of them, I had everything. Then they found out about each other, and they both dumped me. Not just one, but both.

(The Teacher clicks.)

The Teacher: Excellent playwriting. Here's a heartbreaking situation with which we can all identify. Maybe not in the specifics, but in the universal experience of rejection.

(The Teacher clicks again.)

The Good Samaritan: At least you've had two exciting affairs. I haven't gotten laid in a year.

(The Teacher clicks.)

The Teacher: A superb response. Another situation with which, um, well, we've all had friends who've had that problem.

(The Teacher clicks again.)

The Jumper: So what are you telling me? That life can get *worse*? That's supposed to get me off this ledge?
The Good Samaritan: Hey, I'm just trying to help!
The Jumper: Well, you're doing a lousy job.
The Good Samaritan: At least I've got some money in the bank!
The Jumper: You've also got rocks in your head!

(The Teacher clicks.)

The Teacher: A common beginner's mistake. Two characters in hostile disagreement isn't conflict, it's just bickering. We don't go to the theatre to hear petty, puerile antagonism; that's why we have families. Let's hope this goes somewhere interesting, or I'll have to rewind.

(The Teacher clicks again.)

The Jumper: You've only got money in the bank because you're cheap.
The Good Samaritan: I am not.
The Jumper: Well, you certainly dress like you are.
The Teacher: Now this is really degenerating.

(The Teacher clicks, but the action continues.)

The Good Samaritan: Listen, you stupid twerp —
The Jumper: At least I'm a twerp with a decent sex life.
The Good Samaritan: And if it was decent for *them,* maybe you'd still have a sex life.

(The Teacher continues to click, but the action continues.)

The Teacher (as the action continues): Now stop it . . . Stop it! . . . Stop it!! *(Etc.)*

(Shouting above The Teacher's "Stop it"s, which they ignore:)

The Jumper: Loser!
The Good Samaritan: Pervert!
The Jumper: Cheapskate!
The Good Samaritan: Cretin!
The Jumper: Asshole!
The Good Samaritan: Imbecile!
The Jumper: Shithead!
The Teacher (clicking in vain): Stop it!!!!

(The Good Samaritan takes out a clicker and freezes The Teacher.)

The Good Samaritan: Notice how organically the teacher's frustration has increased. What began as a minor irritation became unbearable when the human desire to control was thwarted.

(The Good Samaritan clicks again.)

The Teacher: What are you doing?! I hold the clicker around here. How dare —

(The Good Samaritan clicks. The Teacher freezes.)

The Good Samaritan: See how frustration becomes "anger"? Although the real life stakes are minor, the character's emotional investment is intense. That's good playwriting.

(The Good Samaritan clicks again.)

The Teacher: Stop that. What do you think this is, a Pirandello° play?
The Good Samaritan: Well, how do you think *we* feel? We can't say more than two lines without being interrupted by your self-important pronouncements. How'd you like it if I did that to you?
The Teacher: You have no dra — *(The Good Samaritan clicks and stops/starts The Teacher during the following:)* matically vi — able rea — son to inter — rupt me. Damn it, will you get back in the play?

Luigi Pirandello (1867–1936): Italian playwright famous for exploring illusion and reality in his plays.

The Good Samaritan: No, and you can't make me!

(The Good Samaritan clicks at The Teacher, who dodges the clicker.)

The Teacher: Aha, missed. You superficial stereotype!

(The Teacher clicks at The Good Samaritan and vice versa during the following, both successfully dodging the other.)

The Good Samaritan: Control freak!

The Teacher: Cliché!

The Good Samaritan: Semi-intellectual!

The Teacher: Contrivance!

The Good Samaritan: Academic tapeworm!

The Teacher: First draft mistake!

(The Jumper, who has been watching this, takes out a gun and shoots it into the air.)

The Jumper: Hey!!! I'm the one with the problem. This play's supposed to be about me.

The Good Samaritan: Tough. The well-made play died with Ibsen.

The Teacher (to The Good Samaritan): Damn it, get back into the play!

The Good Samaritan: Don't tell me what to do. Ever since I was a kid, everyone's told me how I'm supposed to behave. When I was five, my mom sent me to my room *(The Teacher starts clicking manically at The Good Samaritan.)* four thousand times because I wouldn't be the kid she wanted me —

The Teacher: This monologue is not justified!

The Good Samaritan: Tough shit, it's my life!

The Teacher: It's bad drama!

The Good Samaritan: I'll show you bad drama!

(The Good Samaritan and The Teacher begin to fight.)

The Jumper: Stop it! Come on, stop it, you're pulling focus.

The Teacher: Butt out!

(The Jumper tries to break up the fight.)

The Jumper: Come on, guys, cool it!

The Good Samaritan: Get away from us!

The Jumper: Just stop it!

The Good Samaritan: Leave us alone!

(The three of them are in a tight cluster. We hear a gunshot. The Teacher pulls away. There's blood on The Teacher's chest.)

The Teacher: I just got tenure.

(The Teacher collapses.)

The Good Samaritan: Oh my God.

The Jumper: He's dead.

(The Good Samaritan looks at The Jumper.)

The Good Samaritan: How horrible. Is that good playwriting or bad playwriting?

The Jumper: I, I don't know. It just happened.

(The Good Samaritan and The Jumper look at The Teacher.)

The Jumper and The Good Samaritan (simultaneously): Hmmmmmmm.

(The Good Samaritan and The Jumper begin to exit.)

The Good Samaritan: Gee, you could've hurt yourself.
The Jumper: Gosh, you're right.
The Good Samaritan: Want to grab a brew?
The Jumper: Sure.

(The Teacher comes to life for a moment, clicks into the air and: Blackout.)

CONSIDERATIONS FOR CRITICAL THINKING AND WRITING

1. FIRST RESPONSE. Comment on Orloff's statement that his purpose in *Playwriting 101* was to satirize dramatic clichés to make an "original play." Explain why you think he was or was not successful.

2. Why do you think the stage directions call for the Jumper and Good Samaritan to be of the same sex?

3. What do you learn from the Teacher about developing conflict and suspense?

4. What is the conflict in the play? Is there a resolution?

5. Describe the theme. Is it implicit or explicitly stated?

6. The Good Samaritan asks at the end, "Is that good playwriting or bad playwriting?" (above). What do you think?

CONNECTIONS TO OTHER SELECTIONS

1. The Teacher claims that "When [Ibsen's] Nora leaves in *A Doll's House* [p. 1358], nobody wants her husband to reply — *(upbeat)* 'Call when you get work!'" Why not?

2. The Teacher also claims, "Two characters in hostile disagreement isn't conflict, it's just bickering. We don't go to the theatre to hear petty, puerile antagonism; that's why we have families." Consider the value of this assertion in relation to Jane Anderson's *The Reprimand* (p. 1467).

Moby-Dude, Or: The Three-Minute Whale

Born in Chicago and educated at Northwestern University and the Yale School of Drama, David Ives writes for television, film, and opera. A recipient of a Guggenheim Fellowship in playwriting, he has created a number of one-act plays for the annual comedy festival called Manhattan Punch Line. Many of his one-

Peter Sumner Walton Bellamy.

act plays are available in *All in the Timing* (1994), *Lives of the Saints* (2000), and *Time Flies and Other Plays* (2001); his full-length plays are collected in *Polish Joke and Other Plays* (2004). *Venus in Fur*, another full-length play, is an erotic comic drama that opened in 2010. *Moby-Dude, Or: The Three-Minute*

Whale is a very brief play about a student trying to convince his teacher that he actually completed reading a very long novel. In the introduction to *Talk to Me: Monologue Plays,* from which *Moby-Dude* is reprinted, the editors, Nina Shengold and Eric Lane, offer a valuable perspective on the nature of monologue plays by describing them as a "modern form of that most ancient of human entertainments, storytelling. Our paleolithic ancestors listened to hunters enacting their sagas in front of a campfire, and members of every human community since have stood up in front of their peers and performed their trades." Here's Ives's updated version of classic storytelling.

WHEN I WRITE "I have worked on writing schedules covering every hour of the day. All schedules are good. All rituals are good. All writing superstitions are good. The point is not to have a writing schedule; the point is to write." — DAVID IVES

DAVID IVES (B. 1950)

Moby-Dude, Or: The Three-Minute Whale   2004

SFX: sound of waves and gulls. Distant ship's bell.
Our Narrator is a stoned-out surfer of seventeen.

Our Narrator: Call me Ishmael, dude. Yes, Mrs. Podgorski, I *did* read *Moby-Dick* over the summer like I was supposed to. It was bohdacious. Actually, y'know, it's "*Moby-hyphen-Dick.*" The title's got a little hyphen before the "Dick." And what is the meaning of this dash before the "Dick"? *WHOAAA!* Another mystery in this awesome American masterpiece, a peerless allegorical saga of mortal courage, metaphysical ambiguity and maniacal obsession! *What,* Mrs. Podgorski? You don't believe I really *read* Herman Melville's *Moby-Dick Or The Whale?* Five hundred sixty-two pages, fourteen ounces, published 1851, totally tanked its first weekend, rereleased in the 1920s as one of the world's gnarliest works of Art? You think I copped all this like off the back of the tome or by watching the crappy 1956 film starring Gregory Peck? Mrs. P., you been chasing my tail since middle school, do *I* get all testy? Do *I* say, what is the plot in under two minutes — besides a whale and a hyphen? *Moby-Dick* in two minutes, huh? Okay, kyool. Let's rip.

(*SFX: ship's bell, close up and sharp, to signal the start and a ticking watch, underneath. Very fast.*)

Fade in the boonies of Massachusetts, eighteen-something. Young dude possibly named Ishmael, like the Bible, meets-cute with, TAA-DAA!, *Queequeg,* a South Sea cannibal with a heart of gold.

(*SFX: cutesy voice going, "Awwww."*)

Maybe they're gay.

(*SFX: tongue slurp.*)

Or maybe they represent some east-west, pagan-Christian duality action. Anyway, the two newfound bros go to Mass and hear a sermon about Jonah . . .

(*SFX: one second of church organ.*)

Biblical tie-in, then ship out on Christmas Day *(could be symbolical!)* aboard the USS *Pequod* with its mysterious wacko Captain Ahab . . .

(SFX: madman laughter.)

. . . who — *backstory* — is goofyfoot because the equally mysterious mom-boosaloid white whale Moby-like-the-singer Dick bit his leg off.

(SFX: chomp.)

Freudian castration action. I mean he's big and he's got sperm and his last name is "Dick," right? Moby is also a metaphor for God, Nature, Truth, obses-sisical love, the world, the past, and white people. Check out Pip the Negro cabin boy who by a *fluke* . . .

(SFX: rimshot.)

. . . goes wacko too. Ahab says,

(SFX: echo effect.)

"Bring me the head of the Great White Whale and you win this prize!"

(SFX: echo effect out, cash register sound.)

The crew is stoked, by *NOT* first-mate like-the-coffee-Starbuck. Ahab wants the big one, Starbuck wants the whale juice. Idealism versus capitalism.

(SFX: an impressed "Whoo.")

Radical. Queequeg tells the carpenter to build him a coffin shaped like a canoe.

(SFX: theremin.)

Foreshadowing! Then lots of chapters everybody skips about the scientology of whales.

(SFX: yawn.)

Cut to . . .

(SFX: trumpet fanfare.)

Page 523, the Pacific Ocean. *"Surf's up!"* Ahab sights the Dick. He's totally amped. The boards hit the waves, the crew snakes the Dick for three whole days, bottom of the third Ahab is ten-toes-on-the-nose, he's aggro, Moby goes aerial, Ahab's in the zone, he fires his choicest harpoon, the rope does a 360 round his neck, Ahab crushes out, Moby totals the *Pequod*, everybody eats it 'cept our faithful narrator Ishmael who boogies to safety on Queequeg's coffin . . .

(SFX: resounding echo effect, deeper voice.)

"AND I ONLY AM ESCAPED ALONE TO TELL THEE!"

(Resume normal voice.)

Roll final credits. The End.

(SFX: ship's bell to signal end of fight. End ticking watch.)

So what do you say, Mrs. Podgorski? You want to like hang and catch a cup of Starbucks sometime . . . ? — *Tubular!*

End of play

CONSIDERATIONS FOR CRITICAL THINKING AND WRITING

1. FIRST RESPONSE. Discuss whether you think it is necessary to have read Melville's *Moby-Dick* in order to appreciate the narrator's monologue.

2. How do the narrator's diction and style contribute to the play's humor?

3. In what sense is Mrs. Podgorski the antagonist?

4. Comment on the appropriateness of the sound effects.

5. CREATIVE RESPONSE. Write a monologue in which Mrs. Podgorski responds to the student.

CONNECTION TO ANOTHER SELECTION

1. How are the narrators' sensibilities revealed by their respective monologues in *Moby-Dude* and Jane Martin's *Rodeo* (p. 1474)?

2. Compare the tone of the narrator's monologue with that of Martin's *Rodeo* (p. 1474).

A Collection
of Plays

50

Plays for Further Reading

My plays are about love, honor, duty, betrayal — things humans have written about since the beginning of time.
— AUGUST WILSON

Joan Marcus.

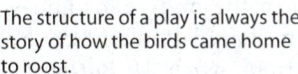

The structure of a play is always the story of how the birds came home to roost.
— ARTHUR MILLER

© Corbis.

Trying to Find Chinatown

Born in Los Angeles, David Henry Hwang is the son of immigrant Chinese American parents; his father worked as a banker, and his mother was a professor of piano. Educated at Stanford University, from which he earned his B.A. in English in 1979, he became interested in theater after attending plays at the American Conservatory in San Francisco. His marginal interest in a law career quickly gave way to his involvement in the engaging world of live theater. By his senior year, he had written and produced his first play, *FOB* (an acronym for "fresh off the boat"), which marked the beginning of a meteoric rise as a playwright. After a brief stint as a writing teacher at a Menlo Park high school, Hwang attended the Yale University School of Drama from 1980 to 1981. Although he didn't stay to complete a degree, he studied theater history before leaving for New York City, where he thought the professional theater would provide a richer education than the student workshops at Yale.

© Michal Daniel.

In New York Hwang's work received a warm reception. In 1980 an off-Broadway production of *FOB* won an Obie Award for the best new play of the season. The play incorporates many of Hwang's characteristic concerns as a playwright. Growing up in California as a Chinese American made him politically conscious during his college years in the late 1970s; this interest in his Chinese roots is evident in the central conflicts of *FOB,* which focuses on a Chinese immigrant's relationship with two Chinese American students he meets in Los Angeles. Hwang's early plays are populated with Chinese Americans attempting to find the center of their own lives as they seesaw between the conventions, traditions, and values of East and West.

Hwang's next two dramas, produced in 1983, consist of two one-act plays set in Japan. Together they are titled *Sound and Beauty,* but each has its own title — *The House of Sleeping Beauties* and *The Sound of a Voice.* In these plays Hwang moves away from tales of Chinese American immigrants and themes of race and assimilation to stories about tragic love based on Japanese materials. Although Hwang was successful in having additional plays produced in the mid-1980s and won prestigious fellowships from the Guggenheim Foundation and the National Endowment for the Arts, it was not until 1988, when *M. Butterfly* — a complex treatment of social, political, racial, cultural, and sexual issues — was produced on Broadway, that he achieved astonishing commercial success as well as widespread acclaim. His awards for this play include the Outer Critics Circle Award for best Broadway play, the Drama Desk Award for best new play, the John Gassner Award for best American play, and the Tony Award for best play of the year. By the end of 1988, Hwang was regarded by many critics as the most talented young playwright in the United States. One of his recent plays, *Chinglish* (2011), is a humorous treatment of an American businessman in China. *Trying to Find Chinatown* is a brief but complicated confrontation between two young men who argue about racial identity in unexpected ways. Hwang's strategy is to challenge the polemical stereotyping that often passes for discussions of ethnic and cultural heritage in the United States.

DAVID HENRY HWANG (B. 1957)

Trying to Find Chinatown 1996

See Plays in Performance insert.
Courtesy of The Actors Theatre of Louisville.

CHARACTERS

Benjamin, Caucasian male, early twenties.
Ronnie, Asian-American male,
  mid-twenties.

TIME AND PLACE A street corner on the Lower East Side, New York City. The present.

NOTE ON MUSIC Obviously, it would be foolish to require that the actor portraying Ronnie perform the specified violin music live. The score of this play can be played on tape over the house speakers, and the actor can feign playing the violin using a bow treated with soap. However, in order to effect a convincing illusion, it is desirable that the actor possess some familiarity with the violin or another stringed instrument.

> *Darkness. Over the house speakers, sound fades in: Hendrix-like virtuoso rock 'n' roll riffs — heavy feedback, distortion, phase shifting, wah-wah — amplified over a tiny Fender pug-nose.*

> *Lights fade up to reveal that the music's being played over a solid-body electric violin by Ronnie, a Chinese-American male in his mid-twenties; he is dressed in retro-'60s clothing and has a few requisite '90s body mutilations. He's playing on a sidewalk for money, his violin case open before him; change and a few stray bills have been left by previous passersby.*
> *Benjamin enters; he's in his early twenties, blond, blue-eyed, a Midwestern tourist in the big city. He holds a scrap of paper in his hands, scanning street signs for an address. He pauses before Ronnie, listens for a while. With a truly bravura run, Ronnie concludes the number and falls to his knees, gasping. Benjamin applauds.*

Benjamin: Good. That was really great. *(Pause)* I didn't . . . I mean, a fiddle . . . I mean, I'd heard them at square dances, on country stations and all, but I never . . . wow, this must really be New York City!

> *(Benjamin applauds, starts to walk on. Still on his knees, Ronnie clears his throat loudly.)*

Oh, I . . . you're not just doing this for your health, right?

> *(Benjamin reaches in his pocket, pulls out a couple of coins. Ronnie clears his throat again.)*

Look, I'm not a millionaire, I'm just . . .

> *(Benjamin pulls out his wallet, removes a dollar bill. Ronnie nods his head and gestures toward the violin case as he takes out a pack of cigarettes, lights one.)*

Ronnie: And don't call it a "fiddle," OK?

Benjamin: Oh. Well, I didn't mean to —

Ronnie: You sound like a wuss. A hick. A dipshit.

Benjamin: It just slipped out. I didn't really —

Ronnie: If this was a fiddle, I'd be sitting here with a cob pipe, stomping my cowboy boots and kicking up hay. Then I'd go home and fuck my cousin.

Benjamin: Oh! Well, I don't really think —

Ronnie: Do you see a cob pipe? Am I fucking my cousin?

Benjamin: Well, no, not at the moment, but —

Ronnie: All right. Then this is a violin, now you give me your money, and I ignore the insult. Herein endeth the lesson.

(Pause.)

Benjamin: Look, a dollar's more than I've ever given to a . . . to someone asking for money.

Ronnie: Yeah, well, this is New York. Welcome to the cost of living.

Benjamin: What I mean is, maybe in exchange, you could help me — ?

Ronnie: Jesus Christ! Do you see a sign around my neck reading "Big Apple Fucking Tourist Bureau"?

Benjamin: I'm just looking for an address, I don't think it's far from here, maybe you could . . . ?

(Benjamin holds out his scrap of paper, Ronnie snatches it away.)

Ronnie: You're lucky I'm such a goddamn softy. *(He looks at the paper)* Oh, fuck you. Just suck my dick, you and the cousin you rode in on.

Benjamin: I don't get it! What are you — ?

Ronnie: Eat me. You know exactly what I —

Benjamin: I'm just asking for a little —

Ronnie: "13 Doyers Street"? Like you don't know where that is?

Benjamin: Of course I don't know! That's why I'm asking —

Ronnie: C'mon, you trailer-park refugee. You don't know that's Chinatown?

Benjamin: Sure I know that's Chinatown.

Ronnie: I know you know that's Chinatown.

Benjamin: So? That doesn't mean I know where Chinatown —

Ronnie: So why is it that you picked *me*, of all the street musicians in the city — to point you in the direction of Chinatown? Lemme guess — is it the earring? No, I don't think so. The Hendrix riffs? Guess again, you fucking moron.

Benjamin: Now, wait a minute. I see what you're —

Ronnie: What are you gonna ask me next? Where you can find the best dim sum in the city? Whether I can direct you to a genuine opium den? Or do I happen to know how you can meet Miss Saigon for a night of nookie-nookie followed by a good old-fashioned ritual suicide? Now, get your white ass off my sidewalk. One dollar doesn't even begin to make up for all this aggravation. Why don't you go back home and race bullfrogs, or whatever it is you do for — ?

Benjamin: Brother, I can absolutely relate to your anger. Righteous rage, I suppose, would be a more appropriate term. To be marginalized, as we are, by a white racist patriarchy, to the point where the accomplishments of our people are obliterated from the history books, this is cultural genocide of the first order, leading to the fact that you must do battle with all of Euro-America's emasculating and brutal stereotypes of Asians — the opium den, the sexual objectification of the Asian female, the exoticized image of a tourist's

Chinatown which ignores the exploitation of workers, the failure to unionize, the high rate of mental illness and tuberculosis — against these, each day, you rage, no, not as a victim, but as a survivor, yes, brother, a glorious warrior survivor!

(Silence.)

Ronnie: Say what?
Benjamin: So, I hope you can see that my request is not —
Ronnie: Wait, wait.
Benjamin: — motivated by the sorts of racist assumptions —
Ronnie: But, but where . . . how did you learn all that?
Benjamin: All what?
Ronnie: All that — you know — oppression stuff — tuberculosis . . .
Benjamin: It's statistically irrefutable. TB occurs in the community at a rate —
Ronnie: Where did *you* learn it?
Benjamin: I took Asian-American studies. In college.
Ronnie: Where did you go to college?
Benjamin: University of Wisconsin. Madison.
Ronnie: Madison, Wisconsin?
Benjamin: That's not where the bridges are, by the way.
Ronnie: Huh? Oh, right . . .
Benjamin: You wouldn't believe the number of people who —
Ronnie: They have Asian-American studies in Madison, Wisconsin? Since when?
Benjamin: Since the last Third World Unity hunger strike. *(Pause)* Why do you look so surprised? We're down.
Ronnie: I dunno. It just never occurred to me, the idea of Asian students in the Midwest going on a hunger strike.
Benjamin: Well, a lot of them had midterms that week, so they fasted in shifts. *(Pause)* The administration never figured it out. The Asian students put that "They all look alike" stereotype to good use.
Ronnie: OK, so they got Asian-American studies. That still doesn't explain —
Benjamin: What?
Ronnie: Well . . . what *you* were doing taking it?
Benjamin: Just like everyone else. I wanted to explore my roots. And, you know, the history of oppression which is my legacy. After a lifetime of assimilation, I wanted to find out who I really am.

(Pause.)

Ronnie: And did you?
Benjamin: Sure. I learned to take pride in my ancestors who built the railroads, my Popo who would make me a hot bowl of jok with thousand-day-old eggs when the white kids chased me home yelling, "Gook! Chink! Slant-eyes!"
Ronnie: OK, OK, that's enough!
Benjamin: Painful to listen to, isn't it?
Ronnie: I don't know what kind of bullshit ethnic studies program they're running over in Wuss-consin, but did they bother to teach you that in order to find your Asian "roots," it's a good idea to first be Asian?

(Pause.)

Benjamin: Are you speaking metaphorically?
Ronnie: No! Literally! Look at your skin!

Benjamin: You know, it's very stereotypical to think that all Asian skin tones conform to a single hue.

Ronnie: You're white! Is this some kind of redneck joke or something? Am I the first person in the world to tell you this?

Benjamin: Oh! Oh! Oh!

Ronnie: I know real Asians are scarce in the Midwest, but . . . Jesus!

Benjamin: No, of course, I . . . I see where your misunderstanding arises.

Ronnie: Yeah. It's called, "You white."

Benjamin: It's just that — in my hometown of Tribune, Kansas, and then at school — see, everyone knows me — so this sort of thing never comes up. *(He offers his hand)* Benjamin Wong. I forget that a society wedded to racial constructs constantly forces me to explain my very existence.

Ronnie: Ronnie Chang. Otherwise known as "The Bow Man."

Benjamin: You see, I was adopted by Chinese-American parents at birth. So, clearly, I'm an Asian-American —

Ronnie: Even though you're blond and blue-eyed.

Benjamin: Well, you can't judge my race by my genetic heritage alone.

Ronnie: If genes don't determine race, what does?

Benjamin: Perhaps you'd prefer that I continue in denial, masquerading as a white man?

Ronnie: You can't just wake up and say, "Gee, I *feel* black today."

Benjamin: Brother, I'm just trying to find what you've already got.

Ronnie: What do I got?

Benjamin: A home. With your people. Picketing with the laundry workers. Taking refuge from the daily slights against your masculinity in the noble image of Gwan Gung.

Ronnie: Gwan who?

Benjamin: C'mon — the Chinese god of warriors and — what do you take me for? There're altars to him up all over the community.

Ronnie: I dunno what community you're talking about, but it's sure as hell not mine.

(Pause.)

Benjamin: What do you mean?

Ronnie: I mean, if you wanna call Chinatown *your* community, OK, knock yourself out, learn to use chopsticks, big deal. Go ahead, try and find your "roots" in some dim sum parlor with headless ducks hanging in the window. Those places don't tell you a thing about who *I* am.

Benjamin: Oh, I get it.

Ronnie: You get what?

Benjamin: You're one of those self-hating, *assimilated* Chinese-Americans, aren't you?

Ronnie: Oh, Jesus.

Benjamin: You probably call yourself "Oriental," huh? Look, maybe I can help you. I have some books I can —

Ronnie: Hey, I read all those Asian identity books when you were still slathering on industrial-strength sunblock. *(Pause)* Sure, I'm Chinese. But folks like you act like that means something. Like, all of a sudden, you know who I am. You think identity's that simple? That you can wrap it all up in a neat package and say, "I have ethnicity, therefore I am"? All you fucking ethnic fundamentalists.

Always settling for easy answers. You say you're looking for identity, but you can't begin to face the real mysteries of the search. So instead, you go skin-deep, and call it a day. *(Pause. He turns away from Benjamin and starts to play his violin — slow and bluesy.)*

Benjamin: So what are you? "Just a human being"? That's like saying you *have* no identity. If you asked me to describe my dog, I'd say more than, "He's just a dog."

Ronnie: What — you think if I deny the importance of my race, I'm nobody? There're worlds out there, worlds you haven't even begun to understand. Open your eyes. Hear with your ears.

(Ronnie holds his violin at chest level, but does not attempt to play during the following monologue. As he speaks, rock and jazz violin tracks fade in and out over the house speakers, bringing to life the styles of music he describes.)

I concede — it was called a fiddle long ago — but that was even before the birth of jazz. When the hollering in the fields, the rank injustice of human bondage, the struggle of God's children against the plagues of the devil's white man, when all these boiled up into that bittersweet brew, called by later generations, the blues. That's when fiddlers like Son Sims held their chin rests at their chests, and sawed away like the hillbillies still do today. And with the coming of ragtime appeared the pioneer Stuff Smith, who sang as he stroked the catgut, with his raspy, Louis Armstrong–voice — gruff and sweet like the timber of horsehair riding south below the fingerboard — and who finally sailed for Europe to find ears that would hear. Europe — where Stephane Grappelli initiated a magical French violin, to be passed from generation to generation — first he, to Jean-Luc Ponty, then Ponty to Didier Lockwood. Listening to Grappelli play "A Nightingale Sang in Berkeley Square" is to understand not only the song of birds, but also how they learn to fly, fall in love on the wing, and finally falter one day, to wait for darkness beneath a London street lamp. And Ponty — he showed how the modern violin man can accompany the shadow of his own lead lines, which cascade, one over another, into some nether world beyond the range of human hearing. Joe Venuti. Noel Pointer. Sven Asmussen. Even the Kronos Quartet, with their arrangement of "Purple Haze." Now, tell me, could any legacy be more rich, more crowded with mythology and heroes to inspire pride? What can I say if the banging of a gong or the clinking of a pickax on the Transcontinental Railroad fails to move me even as much as one note, played through a violin MIDI controller by Michael Urbaniak? *(He puts his violin to his chin, begins to play a jazz composition of his own invention)* Does it have to sound like Chinese opera before people like you decide I know who I am?

(Benjamin stands for a long moment, listening to Ronnie play. Then, he drops his dollar into the case, turns and exits right. Ronnie continues to play a long moment. Then Benjamin enters downstage left, illuminated in his own spotlight. He sits on the floor of the stage, his feet dangling off the lip. As he speaks, Ronnie continues playing his tune, which becomes underscoring for Benjamin's monologue. As the music continues, does it slowly begin to reflect the influence of Chinese music?)

Benjamin: When I finally found Doyers Street, I scanned the buildings for Number 13. Walking down an alley where the scent of freshly steamed char siu bao lingered in the air, I felt immediately that I had entered a world where all things were finally familiar. *(Pause)* An old woman bumped me with her shopping bag — screaming to her friend in Cantonese, though they walked no more than a few inches apart. Another man — shouting to a vendor in Sze-Yup. A youth, in white undershirt, perhaps a recent newcomer, bargaining with a grocer in Hokkien. I walked through this ocean of dialects, breathing in the richness with deep gulps, exhilarated by the energy this symphony brought to my step. And when I finally saw the number 13, I nearly wept at my good fortune. An old tenement, paint peeling, inside walls no doubt thick with a century of grease and broken dreams — and yet, to me, a temple — the house where my father was born. I suddenly saw it all: Gung Gung, coming home from his sixteen-hour days pressing shirts he could never afford to own, bringing with him candies for my father, each sweet wrapped in the hope of a better life. When my father left the ghetto, he swore he would never return. But he had, this day, in the thoughts and memories of his son, just six months after his death. And as I sat on the stoop, I pulled a hua-moi° from my pocket, sucked on it, and felt his spirit returning. To this place where his ghost, and the dutiful hearts of all his descendants, would always call home. *(He listens for a long moment)* And I felt an ache in my heart for all those lost souls, denied this most important of revelations: to know who they truly are.

(Benjamin sucks his salted plum and listens to the sounds around him. Ronnie continues to play. The two remain oblivious of one another. Lights fade slowly to black.)

End of play

Hua-moi: A dry, sour plum that is a Cantonese specialty food.

CONNECTIONS TO OTHER SELECTIONS

1. How do you think Ronnie in *Trying to Find Chinatown* would assess August Wilson's treatment of race in *Fences* (p. 1589)?

2. Discuss the perspective offered on white attitudes toward race in Hwang's play and in Nilaja Sun's *No Child . . .* (p. 1565).

Death of a Salesman

Arthur Miller was born in New York City to middle-class Jewish parents. His mother was a teacher and his father a clothing manufacturer. In 1938 he graduated from the University of Michigan, where he had begun writing plays. Six years later his first Broadway play, *The Man Who Had All the Luck,* closed after only a few performances, but *All My Sons* (1947) earned the admiration of both critics and audiences. This drama of family life launched his career, and his next play was even more successful. *Death of a Salesman* (1949) won a Pulitzer Prize and established

© Corbis.

his international reputation so that Miller, along with Tennessee Williams, became one of the most successful American playwrights of the 1940s and 1950s. During this period, his plays included an adaptation of Henrik Ibsen's *Enemy of the People* (1951), *The Crucible* (1953), and *A View from the Bridge* (1955). Among his later works are *The Misfits* (1961, a screenplay), *After the Fall* (1964), *Incident at Vichy* (1964), *The Price* (1968), *The Creation of the World and Other Business* (1972), *The Archbishop's Ceiling* (1976), *The American Clock* (1980), *Time Bends* (1987, essays), *The Ride Down Mt. Morgan* (1991), and *Broken Glass* (1994).

In *Death of a Salesman* Miller's concerns and techniques are similar to those of social realism. His characters' dialogue sounds much like ordinary speech and deals with recognizable family problems ranging from feelings about one another to personal aspirations. Like Ibsen and Chekhov, Miller places his characters in a social context so that their behavior within the family suggests larger implications: the death of this salesman raises issues concerning the significance and value of the American dream of success.

Although such qualities resemble some of the techniques and concerns of realistic drama, Miller also uses other techniques to express Willy Loman's thoughts. In a sense, the play allows the audience to observe what goes on inside the protagonist's head. (At one point Miller was going to title the play *The Inside of His Head.*) When Willy thinks of the past, we see those events reenacted onstage in the midst of present events. This reenactment is achieved through the use of symbolic nonrealistic sets that appear or disappear as the stage lighting changes to reveal Willy's state of mind.

Willy Loman is in many ways an ordinary human being—indeed, painfully so. He is neither brilliant nor heroic, and his life is made up of unfulfilled dreams and self-deceptions. Yet Miller conceived of him as a tragic figure because, as he wrote in "Tragedy and the Common Man" (see p. 1561), "the common man is as apt a subject for tragedy . . . as kings." Willy's circumstances are radically different from those of Oedipus or Hamlet, but Miller manages to create a character whose human dignity evokes tragic feelings for many readers and viewers.

Arthur Miller (1915–2005)

Death of a Salesman   1949

Certain Private Conversations in Two Acts and a Requiem

CAST

Willy Loman	Uncle Ben
Linda	Howard Wagner
Biff	Jenny
Happy	Stanley
Bernard	Miss Forsythe
The Woman	Letta
Charley	

See Plays in Performance insert.

Photo by W. Eugene Smith, The LIFE Picture Collection/Getty Images.

SCENE: The action takes place in Willy Loman's house and yard and in various places he visits in the New York and Boston of today.

Throughout the play, in the stage directions, left and right mean stage left and stage right.

ACT I

A melody is heard, played upon a flute. It is small and fine, telling of grass and trees and the horizon. The curtain rises.

Before us is the Salesman's house. We are aware of towering, angular shapes behind it, surrounding it on all sides. Only the blue light of the sky falls upon the house and forestage; the surrounding area shows an angry glow of orange. As more light appears, we see a solid vault of apartment houses around the small, fragile-seeming home. An air of the dream clings to the place, a dream rising out of reality. The kitchen at center seems actual enough, for there is a kitchen table with three chairs, and a refrigerator. But no other fixtures are seen. At the back of the kitchen there is a draped entrance, which leads to the living-room. To the right of the kitchen, on a level raised two feet, is a bedroom furnished only with a brass bed-stead and a straight chair. On a shelf over the bed a silver athletic trophy stands. A window opens onto the apartment house at the side.

Behind the kitchen, on a level raised six and a half feet, is the boys' bed-room, at present barely visible. Two beds are dimly seen, and at the back of the room a dormer window. (This bedroom is above the unseen living-room.) At the left a stairway curves up to it from the kitchen.

The entire setting is wholly or, in some places, partially transparent. The roof-line of the house is one-dimensional; under and over it we see the apartment buildings. Before the house lies an apron, curving beyond the forestage into the orchestra. This forward area serves as the back yard as well as the locale of all Willy's imaginings and of his city scenes. Whenever the action is in the present the actors observe the imaginary wall-lines, entering the house only through its door at the left. But in the scenes of the past these boundaries are broken, and charac-ters enter or leave a room by stepping "through" a wall onto the forestage.

From the right, Willy Loman, the Salesman, enters, carrying two large sample cases. The flute plays on. He hears but is not aware of it. He is past sixty years of age, dressed quietly. Even as he crosses the stage to the doorway of the house, his exhaustion is apparent. He unlocks the door, comes into the kitchen, and thankfully lets his burden down, feeling the soreness of his palms. A word-sigh escapes his lips—it might be "Oh, boy, oh, boy." He closes the door, then carries his cases out into the living-room, through the draped kitchen doorway.

Linda, his wife, has stirred in her bed at the right. She gets out and puts on a robe, listening. Most often jovial, she has developed an iron repression of her exceptions to Willy's behavior—she more than loves him, she admires him, as though his mercurial nature, his temper, his massive dreams and little cruelties, served her only as sharp reminders of the turbulent longings within him, long-ings which she shares but lacks the temperament to utter and follow to their end.

Linda (*hearing Willy outside the bedroom, calls with some trepidation*): Willy!
Willy: It's all right. I came back.

Linda: Why? What happened? *(Slight pause.)* Did something happen, Willy?

Willy: No, nothing happened.

Linda: You didn't smash the car, did you?

Willy (with casual irritation): I said nothing happened. Didn't you hear me?

Linda: Don't you feel well?

Willy: I'm tired to the death. *(The flute has faded away. He sits on the bed beside her, a little numb.)* I couldn't make it. I just couldn't make it, Linda.

Linda (very carefully, delicately): Where were you all day? You look terrible.

Willy: I got as far as a little above Yonkers. I stopped for a cup of coffee. Maybe it was the coffee.

Linda: What?

Willy (after a pause): I suddenly couldn't drive any more. The car kept going off onto the shoulder, y'know?

Linda (helpfully): Oh. Maybe it was the steering again. I don't think Angelo knows the Studebaker.

Willy: No, it's me, it's me. Suddenly I realize I'm goin' sixty miles an hour and I don't remember the last five minutes. I'm — I can't seem to — keep my mind to it.

Linda: Maybe it's your glasses. You never went for your new glasses.

Willy: No, I see everything. I came back ten miles an hour. It took me nearly four hours from Yonkers.

Linda (resigned): Well, you'll just have to take a rest, Willy, you can't continue this way.

Willy: I just got back from Florida.

Linda: But you didn't rest your mind. Your mind is overactive, and the mind is what counts, dear.

Willy: I'll start out in the morning. Maybe I'll feel better in the morning. *(She is taking off his shoes.)* These goddam arch supports are killing me.

Linda: Take an aspirin. Should I get you an aspirin? It'll soothe you.

Willy (with wonder): I was driving along, you understand? And I was fine. I was even observing the scenery. You can imagine, me looking at scenery, on the road every week of my life. But it's so beautiful up there, Linda, the trees are so thick, and the sun is warm. I opened the windshield and just let the warm air bathe over me. And then all of a sudden I'm goin' off the road! I'm tellin' ya, I absolutely forgot I was driving. If I'd've gone the other way over the white line I might've killed somebody. So I went on again — and five minutes later I'm dreamin' again, and I nearly — *(He presses two fingers against his eyes.)* I have such thoughts, I have such strange thoughts.

Linda: Willy, dear. Talk to them again. There's no reason why you can't work in New York.

Willy: They don't need me in New York. I'm the New England man. I'm vital in New England.

Linda: But you're sixty years old. They can't expect you to keep traveling every week.

Willy: I'll have to send a wire to Portland. I'm supposed to see Brown and Morrison tomorrow morning at ten o'clock to show the line. Goddammit, I could sell them! *(He starts putting on his jacket.)*

Linda (taking the jacket from him): Why don't you go down to the place tomorrow and tell Howard you've simply got to work in New York? You're too accommodating, dear.

Willy: If old man Wagner was alive I'd a been in charge of New York now! That man was a prince, he was a masterful man. But that boy of his, that Howard, he don't appreciate. When I went north the first time, the Wagner Company didn't know where New England was!

Linda: Why don't you tell those things to Howard, dear?

Willy (encouraged): I will, I definitely will. Is there any cheese?

Linda: I'll make you a sandwich.

Willy: No, go to sleep. I'll take some milk. I'll be up right away. The boys in?

Linda: They're sleeping. Happy took Biff on a date tonight.

Willy (interested): That so?

Linda: It was so nice to see them shaving together, one behind the other, in the bathroom. And going out together. You notice? The whole house smells of shaving lotion.

Willy: Figure it out. Work a lifetime to pay off a house. You finally own it, and there's nobody to live in it.

Linda: Well, dear, life is a casting off. It's always that way.

Willy: No, no, some people — some people accomplish something. Did Biff say anything after I went this morning?

Linda: You shouldn't have criticized him, Willy, especially after he just got off the train. You mustn't lose your temper with him.

Willy: When the hell did I lose my temper? I simply asked him if he was making any money. Is that a criticism?

Linda: But, dear, how could he make any money?

Willy (worried and angered): There's such an undercurrent in him. He became a moody man. Did he apologize when I left this morning?

Linda: He was crestfallen, Willy. You know how he admires you. I think if he finds himself, then you'll both be happier and not fight any more.

Willy: How can he find himself on a farm? Is that a life? A farmhand? In the beginning, when he was young, I thought, well, a young man, it's good for him to tramp around, take a lot of different jobs. But it's more than ten years now and he has yet to make thirty-five dollars a week!

Linda: He's finding himself, Willy.

Willy: Not finding yourself at the age of thirty-four is a disgrace!

Linda: Shh!

Willy: The trouble is he's lazy, goddammit!

Linda: Willy, please!

Willy: Biff is a lazy bum!

Linda: They're sleeping. Get something to eat. Go on down.

Willy: Why did he come home? I would like to know what brought him home.

Linda: I don't know. I think he's still lost, Willy. I think he's very lost.

Willy: Biff Loman is lost. In the greatest country in the world a young man with such — personal attractiveness, gets lost. And such a hard worker. There's one thing about Biff — he's not lazy.

Linda: Never.

Willy (with pity and resolve): I'll see him in the morning; I'll have a nice talk with him. I'll get him a job selling. He could be big in no time. My God! Remember how they used to follow him around in high school? When he smiled at one of them their faces lit up. When he walked down the street . . . *(He loses himself in reminiscences.)*

Linda (trying to bring him out of it): Willy, dear, I got a new kind of American-type cheese today. It's whipped.

Willy: Why do you get American when I like Swiss?

Linda: I just thought you'd like a change —

Willy: I don't want a change! I want Swiss cheese. Why am I always being contradicted?

Linda (with a covering laugh): I thought it would be a surprise.

Willy: Why don't you open a window in here, for God's sake?

Linda (with infinite patience): They're all open, dear.

Willy: The way they boxed us in here. Bricks and windows, windows and bricks.

Linda: We should've bought the land next door.

Willy: The street is lined with cars. There's not a breath of fresh air in the neighborhood. The grass don't grow any more, you can't raise a carrot in the back yard. They should've had a law against apartment houses. Remember those two beautiful elm trees out there? When I and Biff hung the swing between them?

Linda: Yeah, like being a million miles from the city.

Willy: They should've arrested the builder for cutting those down. They massacred the neighborhood. *(Lost.)* More and more I think of those days, Linda. This time of year it was lilac and wisteria. And then the peonies would come out, and the daffodils. What fragrance in this room!

Linda: Well, after all, people had to move somewhere.

Willy: No, there's more people now.

Linda: I don't think there's more people. I think —

Willy: There's more people! That's what's ruining this country! Population is getting out of control. The competition is maddening! Smell the stink from that apartment house! And another one on the other side . . . How can they whip cheese?

> *On Willy's last line, Biff and Happy raise themselves up in their beds, listening.*

Linda: Go down, try it. And be quiet.

Willy (turning to Linda, guiltily): You're not worried about me, are you, sweetheart?

Biff: What's the matter?

Happy: Listen!

Linda: You've got too much on the ball to worry about.

Willy: You're my foundation and my support, Linda.

Linda: Just try to relax, dear. You make mountains out of molehills.

Willy: I won't fight with him any more. If he wants to go back to Texas, let him go.

Linda: He'll find his way.

Willy: Sure. Certain men just don't get started till later in life. Like Thomas Edison, I think. Or B. F. Goodrich. One of them was deaf. *(He starts for the bedroom doorway.)* I'll put my money on Biff.

Linda: And Willy — if it's warm Sunday we'll drive in the country. And we'll open the windshield, and take lunch.

Willy: No, the windshields don't open on the new cars.

Linda: But you opened it today.

Willy: Me? I didn't. *(He stops.)* Now isn't that peculiar! Isn't that a remarkable — *(He breaks off in amazement and fright as the flute is heard distantly.)*

Linda: What, darling?

Willy: That is the most remarkable thing.

Linda: What, dear?

Willy: I was thinking of the Chevy. *(Slight pause.)* Nineteen twenty-eight . . . when I had that red Chevy — *(Breaks off.)* That funny? I coulda sworn I was driving that Chevy today.

Linda: Well, that's nothing. Something must've reminded you.

Willy: Remarkable. Ts. Remember those days? The way Biff used to simonize that car? The dealer refused to believe there was eighty thousand miles on it. *(He shakes his head.)* Heh! *(To Linda.)* Close your eyes, I'll be right up. *(He walks out of the bedroom.)*

Happy (to Biff): Jesus, maybe he smashed up the car again!

Linda (calling after Willy): Be careful on the stairs, dear! The cheese is on the middle shelf! *(She turns, goes over to the bed, takes his jacket, and goes out of the bedroom.)*

Light has risen on the boys' room. Unseen, Willy is heard talking to himself, "Eighty thousand miles," and a little laugh. Biff gets out of bed, comes downstage a bit, and stands attentively. Biff is two years older than his brother Happy, well built, but in these days bears a worn air and seems less self-assured. He has succeeded less, and his dreams are stronger and less acceptable than Happy's. Happy is tall, powerfully made. Sexuality is like a visible color on him, or a scent that many women have discovered. He, like his brother, is lost, but in a different way, for he has never allowed himself to turn his face toward defeat and is thus more confused and hard-skinned, although seemingly more content.

Happy (getting out of bed): He's going to get his license taken away if he keeps that up. I'm getting nervous about him, y'know, Biff?

Biff: His eyes are going.

Happy: No, I've driven with him. He sees all right. He just doesn't keep his mind on it. I drove into the city with him last week. He stops at a green light and then it turns red and he goes. *(He laughs.)*

Biff: Maybe he's color-blind.

Happy: Pop? Why he's got the finest eye for color in the business. You know that.

Biff (sitting down on his bed): I'm going to sleep.

Happy: You're not still sour on Dad, are you, Biff?

Biff: He's all right, I guess.

Willy (underneath them, in the living-room): Yes, sir, eighty thousand miles — eighty-two thousand!

Biff: You smoking?

Happy (holding out a pack of cigarettes): Want one?

Biff (taking a cigarette): I can never sleep when I smell it.

Willy: What a simonizing job, heh!

Happy (with deep sentiment): Funny, Biff, y'know? Us sleeping in here again? The old beds. *(He pats his bed affectionately.)* All the talk that went across those two beds, huh? Our whole lives.

Biff: Yeah. Lotta dreams and plans.

Happy (with a deep and masculine laugh): About five hundred women would like to know what was said in this room.

They share a soft laugh.

Biff: Remember that big Betsy something — what the hell was her name — over on Bushwick Avenue?

Happy (combing his hair): With the collie dog!

Biff: That's the one. I got you in there, remember?

Happy: Yeah, that was my first time — I think. Boy, there was a pig! *(They laugh, almost crudely.)* You taught me everything I know about women. Don't forget that.

Biff: I bet you forgot how bashful you used to be. Especially with girls.

Happy: Oh, I still am, Biff.

Biff: Oh, go on.

Happy: I just control it, that's all. I think I got less bashful and you got more so. What happened, Biff? Where's the old humor, the old confidence? *(He shakes Biff's knee. Biff gets up and moves restlessly about the room.)* What's the matter?

Biff: Why does Dad mock me all the time?

Happy: He's not mocking you, he —

Biff: Everything I say there's a twist of mockery on his face. I can't get near him.

Happy: He just wants you to make good, that's all. I wanted to talk to you about Dad for a long time, Biff. Something's — happening to him. He — talks to himself.

Biff: I noticed that this morning. But he always mumbled.

Happy: But not so noticeable. It got so embarrassing I sent him to Florida. And you know something? Most of the time he's talking to you.

Biff: What's he say about me?

Happy: I can't make it out.

Biff: What's he say about me?

Happy: I think the fact that you're not settled, that you're still kind of up in the air . . .

Biff: There's one or two other things depressing him, Happy.

Happy: What do you mean?

Biff: Never mind. Just don't lay it all to me.

Happy: But I think if you just got started — I mean — is there any future for you out there?

Biff: I tell ya, Hap, I don't know what the future is. I don't know — what I'm supposed to want.

Happy: What do you mean?

Biff: Well, I spent six or seven years after high school trying to work myself up. Shipping clerk, salesman, business of one kind or another. And it's a measly manner of existence. To get on that subway on the hot mornings in summer. To devote your whole life to keeping stock, or making phone calls, or selling or buying. To suffer fifty weeks of the year for the sake of a two-week vacation, when all you really desire is to be outdoors, with your shirt off. And always to have to get ahead of the next fella. And still — that's how you build a future.

Happy: Well, you really enjoy it on a farm? Are you content out there?

Biff (with rising agitation): Hap, I've had twenty or thirty different kinds of jobs since I left home before the war, and it always turns out the same. I just realized it lately. In Nebraska when I herded cattle, and the Dakotas, and Arizona, and now in Texas. It's why I came home now, I guess, because I realized it. This farm I work on, it's spring there now, see? And they've got about fifteen new colts. There's nothing more inspiring or — beautiful than the sight of a mare and a new colt. And it's cool there now, see? Texas is cool now, and it's spring. And whenever spring comes to where I am, I suddenly get the feeling, my God, I'm not gettin' anywhere! What the hell am I doing, playing around with horses, twenty-eight dollars a week! I'm thirty-four years old, I oughta be makin' my future. That's when I come running home. And now, I get here, and I don't know what to do with myself. *(After a pause.)* I've always made a point of not wasting my life, and everytime I come back here I know that all I've done is to waste my life.

Happy: You're a poet, you know that, Biff? You're a — you're an idealist!

Biff: No, I'm mixed up very bad. Maybe I oughta get married. Maybe I oughta get stuck into something. Maybe that's my trouble. I'm like a boy. I'm not married. I'm not in business, I just — I'm like a boy. Are you content, Hap? You're a success, aren't you? Are you content?

Happy: Hell, no!

Biff: Why? You're making money, aren't you?

Happy (moving about with energy, expressiveness): All I can do now is wait for the merchandise manager to die. And suppose I get to be merchandise manager? He's a good friend of mine, and he just built a terrific estate on Long Island. And he lived there about two months and sold it, and now he's building another one. He can't enjoy it once it's finished. And I know that's just what I would do. I don't know what the hell I'm workin' for. Sometimes I sit in my apartment — all alone. And I think of the rent I'm paying. And it's crazy. But then, it's what I always wanted. My own apartment, a car, and plenty of women. And still, goddammit, I'm lonely.

Biff (with enthusiasm): Listen, why don't you come out West with me?

Happy: You and I, heh?

Biff: Sure, maybe we could buy a ranch. Raise cattle, use our muscles. Men built like we are should be working out in the open.

Happy (avidly): The Loman Brothers, heh?

Biff (with vast affection): Sure, we'd be known all over the counties!

Happy (enthralled): That's what I dream about, Biff. Sometimes I want to just rip my clothes off in the middle of the store and outbox that goddam merchandise manager. I mean I can outbox, outrun, and outlift anybody in that store, and I have to take orders from those common, petty sons-of-bitches till I can't stand it any more.

Biff: I'm tellin' you, kid, if you were with me I'd be happy out there.

Happy (enthused): See, Biff, everybody around me is so false that I'm constantly lowering my ideals . . .

Biff: Baby, together we'd stand up for one another, we'd have someone to trust.

Happy: If I were around you —

Biff: Hap, the trouble is we weren't brought up to grub for money. I don't know how to do it.

Happy: Neither can I!

Biff: Then let's go!

Happy: The only thing is — what can you make out there?

Biff: But look at your friend. Builds an estate and then hasn't the peace of mind to live in it.

Happy: Yeah, but when he walks into the store the waves part in front of him. That's fifty-two thousand dollars a year coming through the revolving door, and I got more in my pinky finger than he's got in his head.

Biff: Yeah, but you just said —

Happy: I gotta show some of those pompous, self-important executives over there that Hap Loman can make the grade. I want to walk into the store the way he walks in. Then I'll go with you, Biff. We'll be together yet, I swear. But take those two we had tonight. Now weren't they gorgeous creatures?

Biff: Yeah, yeah, most gorgeous I've had in years.

Happy: I get that any time I want, Biff. Whenever I feel disgusted. The trouble is, it gets like bowling or something. I just keep knockin' them over and it doesn't mean anything. You still run around a lot?

Biff: Naa. I'd like to find a girl — steady, somebody with substance.

Happy: That's what I long for.

Biff: Go on! You'd never come home.

Happy: I would! Somebody with character, with resistance! Like Mom, y'know? You're gonna call me a bastard when I tell you this. That girl Charlotte I was with tonight is engaged to be married in five weeks. *(He tries on his new hat.)*

Biff: No kiddin'!

Happy: Sure, the guy's in line for the vice-presidency of the store. I don't know what gets into me, maybe I just have an overdeveloped sense of competition or something, but I went and ruined her, and furthermore I can't get rid of her. And he's the third executive I've done that to. Isn't that a crummy characteristic? And to top it all, I go to their weddings! *(Indignantly, but laughing.)* Like I'm not supposed to take bribes. Manufacturers offer me a hundred-dollar bill now and then to throw an order their way. You know how honest I am, but it's like this girl, see. I hate myself for it. Because I don't want the girl, and, still, I take it and — I love it!

Biff: Let's go to sleep.

Happy: I guess we didn't settle anything, heh?

Biff: I just got one idea that I think I'm going to try.

Happy: What's that?

Biff: Remember Bill Oliver?

Happy: Sure, Oliver is very big now. You want to work for him again?

Biff: No, but when I quit he said something to me. He put his arm on my shoulder, and he said, "Biff, if you ever need anything, come to me."

Happy: I remember that. That sounds good.

Biff: I think I'll go to see him. If I could get ten thousand or even seven or eight thousand dollars I could buy a beautiful ranch.

Happy: I bet he'd back you. 'Cause he thought highly of you, Biff. I mean, they all do. You're well liked, Biff. That's why I say to come back here, and we both have the apartment. And I'm tellin' you, Biff, any babe you want . . .

Biff: No, with a ranch I could do the work I like and still be something. I just wonder though. I wonder if Oliver still thinks I stole that carton of basketballs.

Happy: Oh, he probably forgot that long ago. It's almost ten years. You're too sensitive. Anyway, he didn't really fire you.

Biff: Well, I think he was going to. I think that's why I quit. I was never sure whether he knew or not. I know he thought the world of me, though. I was the only one he'd let lock up the place.

Willy (below): You gonna wash the engine, Biff?

Happy: Shh!

Biff looks at Happy, who is gazing down, listening. Willy is mumbling in the parlor.

Happy: You hear that?

They listen. Willy laughs warmly.

Biff (growing angry): Doesn't he know Mom can hear that?

Willy: Don't get your sweater dirty, Biff!

A look of pain crosses Biff's face.

Happy: Isn't that terrible? Don't leave again, will you? You'll find a job here. You gotta stick around. I don't know what to do about him, it's getting embarrassing.

Willy: What a simonizing job!

Biff: Mom's hearing that!

Willy: No kiddin', Biff, you got a date? Wonderful!

Happy: Go on to sleep. But talk to him in the morning, will you?

Biff (reluctantly getting into bed): With her in the house. Brother!

Happy (getting into bed): I wish you'd have a good talk with him.

The light on their room begins to fade.

Biff (to himself in bed): That selfish, stupid . . .

Happy: Sh . . . Sleep, Biff.

Their light is out. Well before they have finished speaking, Willy's form is dimly seen below in the darkened kitchen. He opens the refrigerator, searches in there, and takes out a bottle of milk. The apartment houses are fading out, and the entire house and surroundings become covered with leaves. Music insinuates itself as the leaves appear.

Willy: Just wanna be careful with those girls, Biff, that's all. Don't make any promises. No promises of any kind. Because a girl, y'know, they always believe what you tell 'em, and you're very young, Biff, you're too young to be talking seriously to girls.

Light rises on the kitchen. Willy, talking, shuts the refrigerator door and comes downstage to the kitchen table. He pours milk into a glass. He is totally immersed in himself, smiling faintly.

Willy: Too young entirely, Biff. You want to watch your schooling first. Then when you're all set, there'll be plenty of girls for a boy like you. *(He smiles broadly at a kitchen chair.)* That so? The girls pay for you? *(He laughs.)* Boy, you must really be makin' a hit.

Willy is gradually addressing—physically—a point offstage, speaking through the wall of the kitchen, and his voice has been rising in volume to that of a normal conversation.

Willy: I been wondering why you polish the car so careful. Ha! Don't leave the hubcaps, boys. Get the chamois to the hubcaps. Happy, use newspaper on the windows, it's the easiest thing. Show him how to do it, Biff! You see, Happy? Pad it up, use it like a pad. That's it, that's it, good work. You're doin' all right, Hap. *(He pauses, then nods in approbation for a few seconds, then looks upward.)* Biff, first thing we gotta do when we get time is clip that big branch over the house. Afraid it's gonna fall in a storm and hit the roof. Tell you what. We get a rope and sling her around, and then we climb up there with a couple of saws and take her down. Soon as you finish the car, boys, I wanna see ya. I got a surprise for you, boys.

Biff (offstage): Whatta ya got, Dad?

Willy: No, you finish first. Never leave a job till you're finished — remember that. (*Looking toward the "big trees."*) Biff, up in Albany I saw a beautiful hammock. I think I'll buy it next trip, and we'll hang it right between those two elms. Wouldn't that be something? Just swingin' there under those branches. Boy, that would be . . .

Young Biff and Young Happy appear from the direction Willy was addressing. Happy carries rags and a pail of water. Biff, wearing a sweater with a block "S," carries a football.

Biff (pointing in the direction of the car offstage): How's that, Pop, professional?
Willy: Terrific. Terrific job, boys. Good work, Biff.
Happy: Where's the surprise, Pop?
Willy: In the back seat of the car.
Happy: Boy! (*He runs off.*)
Biff: What is it, Dad? Tell me, what'd you buy?
Willy (laughing, cuffs him): Never mind, something I want you to have.
Biff (turns and starts off): What is it, Hap?
Happy (offstage): It's a punching bag!
Biff: Oh, Pop!
Willy: It's got Gene Tunney's signature on it!

Happy runs onstage with a punching bag.

Biff: Gee, how'd you know we wanted a punching bag?
Willy: Well, it's the finest thing for the timing.
Happy (lies down on his back and pedals with his feet): I'm losing weight, you notice, Pop?
Willy (to Happy): Jumping rope is good too.
Biff: Did you see the new football I got?
Willy (examining the ball): Where'd you get a new ball?
Biff: The coach told me to practice my passing.
Willy: That so? And he gave you the ball, heh?
Biff: Well, I borrowed it from the locker room. (*He laughs confidentially.*)
Willy (laughing with him at the theft): I want you to return that.
Happy: I told you he wouldn't like it!
Biff (angrily): Well, I'm bringing it back!
Willy (stopping the incipient argument, to Happy): Sure, he's gotta practice with a regulation ball, doesn't he? (*To Biff.*) Coach'll probably congratulate you on your initiative!
Biff: Oh, he keeps congratulating my initiative all the time, Pop.
Willy: That's because he likes you. If somebody else took that ball there'd be an uproar. So what's the report, boys, what's the report?
Biff: Where'd you go this time, Dad? Gee we were lonesome for you.
Willy (pleased, puts an arm around each boy and they come down to the apron): Lonesome, heh?
Biff: Missed you every minute.
Willy: Don't say? Tell you a secret, boys. Don't breathe it to a soul. Someday I'll have my own business, and I'll never have to leave home any more.
Happy: Like Uncle Charley, heh?
Willy: Bigger than Uncle Charley! Because Charley is not — liked. He's liked, but he's not — well liked.

Biff: Where'd you go this time, Dad?

Willy: Well, I got on the road, and I went north to Providence. Met the Mayor.

Biff: The Mayor of Providence!

Willy: He was sitting in the hotel lobby.

Biff: What'd he say?

Willy: He said, "Morning!" And I said, "You got a fine city here, Mayor." And then he had coffee with me. And then I went to Waterbury. Waterbury is a fine city. Big clock city, the famous Waterbury clock. Sold a nice bill there. And then Boston — Boston is the cradle of the Revolution. A fine city. And a couple of other towns in Mass., and on to Portland and Bangor and straight home!

Biff: Gee, I'd love to go with you sometime, Dad.

Willy: Soon as summer comes.

Happy: Promise?

Willy: You and Hap and I, and I'll show you all the towns. America is full of beautiful towns and fine, upstanding people. And they know me, boys, they know me up and down New England. The finest people. And when I bring you fellas up, there'll be open sesame for all of us, 'cause one thing, boys: I have friends. I can park my car in any street in New England, and the cops protect it like their own. This summer, heh?

Biff and Happy (together): Yeah! You bet!

Willy: We'll take our bathing suits.

Happy: We'll carry your bags, Pop!

Willy: Oh, won't that be something! Me comin' into the Boston stores with you boys carryin' my bags. What a sensation!

Biff is prancing around, practicing passing the ball.

Willy: You nervous, Biff, about the game?

Biff: Not if you're gonna be there.

Willy: What do they say about you in school, now that they made you captain?

Happy: There's a crowd of girls behind him everytime the classes change.

Biff (taking Willy's hand): This Saturday, Pop, this Saturday — just for you, I'm going to break through for a touchdown.

Happy: You're supposed to pass.

Biff: I'm takin' one play for Pop. You watch me, Pop, and when I take off my helmet, that means I'm breakin' out. Then you watch me crash through that line!

Willy (kisses Biff): Oh, wait'll I tell this in Boston!

Bernard enters in knickers. He is younger than Biff, earnest and loyal, a worried boy.

Bernard: Biff, where are you? You're supposed to study with me today.

Willy: Hey, looka Bernard. What're you lookin' so anemic about, Bernard?

Bernard: He's gotta study, Uncle Willy. He's got Regents next week.

Happy (tauntingly, spinning Bernard around): Let's box, Bernard!

Bernard: Biff! (He gets away from Happy.) Listen, Biff, I heard Mr. Birnbaum say that if you don't start studyin' math, he's gonna flunk you, and you won't graduate. I heard him!

Willy: You better study with him, Biff. Go ahead now.

Bernard: I heard him!

Biff: Oh, Pop, you didn't see my sneakers! (He holds up a foot for Willy to look at.)

Willy: Hey, that's a beautiful job of printing!

Bernard (wiping his glasses): Just because he printed University of Virginia on his
    sneakers doesn't mean they've got to graduate him, Uncle Willy!

Willy (angrily): What're you talking about? With scholarships to three universities
    they're gonna flunk him?

Bernard: But I heard Mr. Birnbaum say —

Willy: Don't be a pest, Bernard! *(To his boys.)* What an anemic!

Bernard: Okay, I'm waiting for you in my house, Biff.

    Bernard goes off. The Lomans laugh.

Willy: Bernard is not well liked, is he?

Biff: He's liked, but he's not well liked.

Happy: That's right, Pop.

Willy: That's just what I mean. Bernard can get the best marks in school,
    y'understand, but when he gets out in the business world, y'understand, you
    are going to be five times ahead of him. That's why I thank Almighty God
    you're both built like Adonises.° Because the man who makes an appearance
    in the business world, the man who creates personal interest, is the man who
    gets ahead. Be liked and you will never want. You take me, for instance. I
    never have to wait in line to see a buyer. "Willy Loman is here!" That's all they
    have to know, and I go right through.

Biff: Did you knock them dead, Pop?

Willy: Knocked 'em cold in Providence, slaughtered 'em in Boston.

Happy (on his back, pedaling again): I'm losing weight, you notice, Pop?

    Linda enters, as of old, a ribbon in her hair, carrying a basket of washing.

Linda (with youthful energy): Hello, dear!

Willy: Sweetheart!

Linda: How'd the Chevy run?

Willy: Chevrolet, Linda, is the greatest car ever built. *(To the boys.)* Since when do
    you let your mother carry wash up the stairs?

Biff: Grab hold there, boy!

Happy: Where to, Mom?

Linda: Hang them up on the line. And you better go down to your friends, Biff.
    The cellar is full of boys. They don't know what to do with themselves.

Biff: Ah, when Pop comes home they can wait!

Willy (laughs appreciatively): You better go down and tell them what to do, Biff.

Biff: I think I'll have them sweep out the furnace room.

Willy: Good work, Biff.

Biff (goes through wall-line of kitchen to doorway at back and calls down): Fellas!
    Everybody sweep out the furnace room! I'll be right down!

Voices: All right! Okay, Biff.

Biff: George and Sam and Frank, come out back! We're hangin' up the wash! Come
    on, Hap, on the double! *(He and Happy carry out the basket.)*

Linda: The way they obey him!

Willy: Well, that's training, the training. I'm tellin' you, I was sellin' thousands and
    thousands, but I had to come home.

Linda: Oh, the whole block'll be at that game. Did you sell anything?

Willy: I did five hundred gross in Providence and seven hundred gross in Boston.

Adonis: In Greek mythology, a young man known for his good looks and favored by Aphrodite,
goddess of love and beauty.

Linda: No! Wait a minute, I've got a pencil. *(She pulls pencil and paper out of her apron pocket.)* That makes your commission . . . Two hundred — my God! Two hundred and twelve dollars!

Willy: Well, I didn't figure it yet, but . . .

Linda: How much did you do?

Willy: Well, I — I did — about a hundred and eighty gross in Providence. Well, no — it came to — roughly two hundred gross on the whole trip.

Linda (without hesitation): Two hundred gross. That's . . . *(She figures.)*

Willy: The trouble was that three of the stores were half closed for inventory in Boston. Otherwise I woulda broke records.

Linda: Well, it makes seventy dollars and some pennies. That's very good.

Willy: What do we owe?

Linda: Well, on the first there's sixteen dollars on the refrigerator —

Willy: Why sixteen?

Linda: Well, the fan belt broke, so it was a dollar eighty.

Willy: But it's brand new.

Linda: Well, the man said that's the way it is. Till they work themselves in, y'know.

They move through the wall-line into the kitchen.

Willy: I hope we didn't get stuck on that machine.

Linda: They got the biggest ads of any of them!

Willy: I know, it's a fine machine. What else?

Linda: Well, there's nine-sixty for the washing machine. And for the vacuum cleaner there's three and a half due on the fifteenth. Then the roof, you got twenty-one dollars remaining.

Willy: It don't leak, does it?

Linda: No, they did a wonderful job. Then you owe Frank for the carburetor.

Willy: I'm not going to pay that man! That goddam Chevrolet, they ought to prohibit the manufacture of that car!

Linda: Well, you owe him three and a half. And odds and ends, comes to around a hundred and twenty dollars by the fifteenth.

Willy: A hundred and twenty dollars! My God, if business don't pick up I don't know what I'm gonna do!

Linda: Well, next week you'll do better.

Willy: Oh, I'll knock 'em dead next week. I'll go to Hartford. I'm very well liked in Hartford. You know, the trouble is, Linda, people don't seem to take to me.

They move onto the forestage.

Linda: Oh, don't be foolish.

Willy: I know it when I walk in. They seem to laugh at me.

Linda: Why? Why would they laugh at you? Don't talk that way, Willy.

Willy moves to the edge of the stage. Linda goes into the kitchen and starts to darn stockings.

Willy: I don't know the reason for it, but they just pass me by. I'm not noticed.

Linda: But you're doing wonderful, dear. You're making seventy to a hundred dollars a week.

Willy: But I gotta be at it ten, twelve hours a day. Other men — I don't know — they do it easier. I don't know why — I can't stop myself — I talk too much. A man oughta come in with a few words. One thing about Charley. He's a man of few words, and they respect him.

Linda: You don't talk too much, you're just lively.

Willy (smiling): Well, I figure, what the hell, life is short, a couple of jokes. *(To himself.)* I joke too much! *(The smile goes.)*

Linda: Why? You're —

Willy: I'm fat. I'm very — foolish to look at, Linda. I didn't tell you, but Christmas time I happened to be calling on F. H. Stewarts, and a salesman I know, as I was going in to see the buyer I heard him say something about — walrus. And I — I cracked him right across the face. I won't take that. I simply will not take that. But they do laugh at me. I know that.

Linda: Darling . . .

Willy: I gotta overcome it. I know I gotta overcome it. I'm not dressing to advantage, maybe.

Linda: Willy, darling, you're the handsomest man in the world —

Willy: Oh, no, Linda.

Linda: To me you are. *(Slight pause.)* The handsomest.

From the darkness is heard the laughter of a woman. Willy doesn't turn to it, but it continues through Linda's lines.

Linda: And the boys, Willy. Few men are idolized by their children the way you are.

Music is heard as behind a scrim, to the left of the house, The Woman, dimly seen, is dressing.

Willy (with great feeling): You're the best there is, Linda, you're a pal, you know that? On the road — on the road I want to grab you sometimes and just kiss the life outa you.

The laughter is loud now, and he moves into a brightening area at the left, where The Woman has come from behind the scrim and is standing, putting on her hat, looking into a "mirror" and laughing.

Willy: 'Cause I get so lonely — especially when business is bad and there's nobody to talk to. I get the feeling that I'll never sell anything again, that I won't make a living for you, or a business, a business for the boys. *(He talks through The Woman's subsiding laughter; The Woman primps at the "mirror.")* There's so much I want to make for —

The Woman: Me? You didn't make me, Willy. I picked you.

Willy (pleased): You picked me?

The Woman (who is quite proper-looking, Willy's age): I did. I've been sitting at that desk watching all the salesmen go by, day in, day out. But you've got such a sense of humor, and we do have such a good time together, don't we?

Willy: Sure, sure. *(He takes her in his arms.)* Why do you have to go now?

The Woman: It's two o'clock . . .

Willy: No, come on in! *(He pulls her.)*

The Woman: . . . my sisters'll be scandalized. When'll you be back?

Willy: Oh, two weeks about. Will you come up again?

The Woman: Sure thing. You do make me laugh. It's good for me. *(She squeezes his arm, kisses him.)* And I think you're a wonderful man.

Willy: You picked me, heh?

The Woman: Sure. Because you're so sweet. And such a kidder.

Willy: Well, I'll see you next time I'm in Boston.

The Woman: I'll put you right through to the buyers.

Willy (slapping her bottom): Right. Well, bottoms up!

The Woman (slaps him gently and laughs): You just kill me, Willy. *(He suddenly grabs her and kisses her roughly.)* You kill me. And thanks for the stockings. I love a lot of stockings. Well, good night.

Willy: Good night. And keep your pores open!

The Woman: Oh, Willy!

The Woman bursts out laughing, and Linda's laughter blends in. The Woman disappears into the dark. Now the area at the kitchen table brightens. Linda is sitting where she was at the kitchen table, but now is mending a pair of her silk stockings.

Linda: You are, Willy. The handsomest man. You've got no reason to feel that —

Willy (coming out of The Woman's dimming area and going over to Linda): I'll make it all up to you, Linda, I'll —

Linda: There's nothing to make up, dear. You're doing fine, better than —

Willy (noticing her mending): What's that?

Linda: Just mending my stockings. They're so expensive —

Willy (angrily, taking them from her): I won't have you mending stockings in this house! Now throw them out!

Linda puts the stockings in her pocket.

Bernard (entering on the run): Where is he? If he doesn't study!

Willy (moving to the forestage, with great agitation): You'll give him the answers!

Bernard: I do, but I can't on a Regents! That's a state exam! They're liable to arrest me!

Willy: Where is he? I'll whip him, I'll whip him!

Linda: And he'd better give back that football, Willy, it's not nice.

Willy: Biff! Where is he? Why is he taking everything?

Linda: He's too rough with the girls, Willy. All the mothers are afraid of him!

Willy: I'll whip him!

Bernard: He's driving the car without a license!

The Woman's laugh is heard.

Willy: Shut up!

Linda: All the mothers —

Willy: Shut up!

Bernard (backing quietly away and out): Mr. Birnbaum says he's stuck up.

Willy: Get outa here!

Bernard: If he doesn't buckle down he'll flunk math! *(He goes off.)*

Linda: He's right, Willy, you've gotta —

Willy (exploding at her): There's nothing the matter with him! You want him to be a worm like Bernard? He's got spirit, personality . . .

As he speaks, Linda, almost in tears, exits into the living-room. Willy is alone in the kitchen, wilting and staring. The leaves are gone. It is night again, and the apartment houses look down from behind.

Willy: Loaded with it. Loaded! What is he stealing? He's giving it back, isn't he? Why is he stealing? What did I tell him? I never in my life told him anything but decent things.

Happy in pajamas has come down the stairs; Willy suddenly becomes aware of Happy's presence.

Happy: Let's go now, come on.

Willy (sitting down at the kitchen table): Huh! Why did she have to wax the floors herself? Everytime she waxes the floors she keels over. She knows that!

Happy: Shh! Take it easy. What brought you back tonight?

Willy: I got an awful scare. Nearly hit a kid in Yonkers. God! Why didn't I go to Alaska with my brother Ben that time! Ben! That man was a genius, that man was success incarnate! What a mistake! He begged me to go.

Happy: Well, there's no use in —

Willy: You guys! There was a man started with the clothes on his back and ended up with diamond mines!

Happy: Boy, someday I'd like to know how he did it.

Willy: What's the mystery? The man knew what he wanted and went out and got it! Walked into a jungle, and comes out, the age of twenty-one, and he's rich! The world is an oyster, but you don't crack it open on a mattress!

Happy: Pop, I told you I'm gonna retire you for life.

Willy: You'll retire me for life on seventy goddam dollars a week? And your women and your car and your apartment, and you'll retire me for life! Christ's sake, I couldn't get past Yonkers today! Where are you guys, where are you? The woods are burning! I can't drive a car!

Charley has appeared in the doorway. He is a large man, slow of speech, laconic, immovable. In all he says, despite what he says, there is pity, and, now, trepidation. He has a robe over pajamas, slippers on his feet. He enters the kitchen.

Charley: Everything all right?

Happy: Yeah, Charley, everything's . . .

Willy: What's the matter?

Charley: I heard some noise. I thought something happened. Can't we do something about the walls? You sneeze in here, and in my house hats blow off.

Happy: Let's go to bed, Dad. Come on.

Charley signals to Happy to go.

Willy: You go ahead, I'm not tired at the moment.

Happy (to Willy): Take it easy, huh? *(He exits.)*

Willy: What're you doin' up?

Charley (sitting down at the kitchen table opposite Willy): Couldn't sleep good. I had a heartburn.

Willy: Well, you don't know how to eat.

Charley: I eat with my mouth.

Willy: No, you're ignorant. You gotta know about vitamins and things like that.

Charley: Come on, let's shoot. Tire you out a little.

Willy (hesitantly): All right. You got cards?

Charley (taking a deck from his pocket): Yeah, I got them. Someplace. What is it with those vitamins?

Willy (dealing): They build up your bones. Chemistry.

Charley: Yeah, but there's no bones in a heartburn.

Willy: What are you talkin' about? Do you know the first thing about it?

Charley: Don't get insulted.

Willy: Don't talk about something you don't know anything about.

They are playing. Pause.

Charley: What're you doin' home?

Willy: A little trouble with the car.

Charley: Oh. *(Pause.)* I'd like to take a trip to California.

Willy: Don't say.

Charley: You want a job?

Willy: I got a job, I told you that. *(After a slight pause.)* What the hell are you offering me a job for?

Charley: Don't get insulted.

Willy: Don't insult me.

Charley: I don't see no sense in it. You don't have to go on this way.

Willy: I got a good job. *(Slight pause.)* What do you keep comin' in here for?

Charley: You want me to go?

Willy (after a pause, withering): I can't understand it. He's going back to Texas again. What the hell is that?

Charley: Let him go.

Willy: I got nothin' to give him, Charley, I'm clean, I'm clean.

Charley: He won't starve. None a them starve. Forget about him.

Willy: Then what have I got to remember?

Charley: You take it too hard. To hell with it. When a deposit bottle is broken you don't get your nickel back.

Willy: That's easy enough for you to say.

Charley: That ain't easy for me to say.

Willy: Did you see the ceiling I put up in the living-room?

Charley: Yeah, that's a piece of work. To put up a ceiling is a mystery to me. How do you do it?

Willy: What's the difference?

Charley: Well, talk about it.

Willy: You gonna put up a ceiling?

Charley: How could I put up a ceiling?

Willy: Then what the hell are you bothering me for?

Charley: You're insulted again.

Willy: A man who can't handle tools is not a man. You're disgusting.

Charley: Don't call me disgusting, Willy.

> *Uncle Ben, carrying a valise and an umbrella, enters the forestage from around the right corner of the house. He is a stolid man, in his sixties, with a mustache and an authoritative air. He is utterly certain of his destiny, and there is an aura of far places about him. He enters exactly as Willy speaks.*

Willy: I'm getting awfully tired, Ben.

> *Ben's music is heard. Ben looks around at everything.*

Charley: Good, keep playing; you'll sleep better. Did you call me Ben?

> *Ben looks at his watch.*

Willy: That's funny. For a second there you reminded me of my brother Ben.

Ben: I only have a few minutes. *(He strolls, inspecting the place. Willy and Charley continue playing.)*

Charley: You never heard from him again, heh? Since that time?

Willy: Didn't Linda tell you? Couple of weeks ago we got a letter from his wife in Africa. He died.

Charley: That so.

Ben (chuckling): So this is Brooklyn, eh?

Charley: Maybe you're in for some of his money.

Willy: Naa, he had seven sons. There's just one opportunity I had with that man . . .

Ben: I must make a train, William. There are several properties I'm looking at in Alaska.

Willy: Sure, sure! If I'd gone with him to Alaska that time, everything would've been totally different.

Charley: Go on, you'd froze to death up there.

Willy: What're you talking about?

Ben: Opportunity is tremendous in Alaska, William. Surprised you're not up there.

Willy: Sure, tremendous.

Charley: Heh?

Willy: There was the only man I ever met who knew the answers.

Charley: Who?

Ben: How are you all?

Willy (taking a pot, smiling): Fine, fine.

Charley: Pretty sharp tonight.

Ben: Is Mother living with you?

Willy: No, she died a long time ago.

Charley: Who?

Ben: That's too bad. Fine specimen of a lady, Mother.

Willy (to Charley): Heh?

Ben: I'd hoped to see the old girl.

Charley: Who died?

Ben: Heard anything from Father, have you?

Willy (unnerved): What do you mean, who died?

Charley (taking a pot): What're you talkin' about?

Ben (looking at his watch): William, it's half-past eight!

Willy (as though to dispel his confusion he angrily stops Charley's hand): That's my build!

Charley: I put the ace —

Willy: If you don't know how to play the game I'm not gonna throw my money away on you!

Charley (rising): It was my ace, for God's sake!

Willy: I'm through, I'm through!

Ben: When did Mother die?

Willy: Long ago. Since the beginning you never knew how to play cards.

Charley (picks up the cards and goes to the door): All right! Next time I'll bring a deck with five aces.

Willy: I don't play that kind of game!

Charley (turning to him): You ought to be ashamed of yourself!

Willy: Yeah?

Charley: Yeah! *(He goes out.)*

Willy (slamming the door after him): Ignoramus!

Ben (as Willy comes toward him through the wall-line of the kitchen): So you're William.

Willy (shaking Ben's hand): Ben! I've been waiting for you so long! What's the answer? How did you do it?

Ben: Oh, there's a story in that.

Linda enters the forestage, as of old, carrying the wash basket.

Linda: Is this Ben?

Ben (gallantly): How do you do, my dear.

Linda: Where've you been all these years? Willy's always wondered why you —

Willy (pulling Ben away from her impatiently): Where is Dad? Didn't you follow him? How did you get started?

Ben: Well, I don't know how much you remember.

Willy: Well, I was just a baby, of course, only three or four years old —

Ben: Three years and eleven months.

Willy: What a memory, Ben!

Ben: I have many enterprises, William, and I have never kept books.

Willy: I remember I was sitting under the wagon in — was it Nebraska?

Ben: It was South Dakota, and I gave you a bunch of wild flowers.

Willy: I remember you walking away down some open road.

Ben (laughing): I was going to find Father in Alaska.

Willy: Where is he?

Ben: At that age I had a very faulty view of geography, William. I discovered after a few days that I was heading due south, so instead of Alaska, I ended up in Africa.

Linda: Africa!

Willy: The Gold Coast!

Ben: Principally diamond mines.

Linda: Diamond mines!

Ben: Yes, my dear. But I've only a few minutes —

Willy: No! Boys! Boys! *(Young Biff and Happy appear.)* Listen to this. This is your Uncle Ben, a great man! Tell my boys, Ben!

Ben: Why, boys, when I was seventeen I walked into the jungle, and when I was twenty-one I walked out. *(He laughs.)* And by God I was rich.

Willy (to the boys): You see what I been talking about? The greatest things can happen!

Ben (glancing at his watch): I have an appointment in Ketchikan Tuesday next week.

Willy: No, Ben! Please tell about Dad. I want my boys to hear. I want them to know the kind of stock they spring from. All I remember is a man with a big beard, and I was in Mamma's lap, sitting around a fire, and some kind of high music.

Ben: His flute. He played the flute.

Willy: Sure, the flute, that's right!

New music is heard, a high, rollicking tune.

Ben: Father was a very great and a very wild-hearted man. We would start in Boston, and he'd toss the whole family into the wagon, and then he'd drive the team right across the country; through Ohio, and Indiana, Michigan, Illinois, and all the Western states. And we'd stop in the towns and sell the flutes that he'd made on the way. Great inventor, Father. With one gadget he made more in a week than a man like you could make in a lifetime.

Willy: That's just the way I'm bringing them up, Ben — rugged, well liked, all-around.

Ben: Yeah? *(To Biff.)* Hit that, boy — hard as you can. *(He pounds his stomach.)*

Biff: Oh, no, sir!

Ben (taking boxing stance): Come on, get to me. *(He laughs.)*

Willy: Go to it, Biff! Go ahead, show him!

Biff: Okay! *(He cocks his fists and starts in.)*

Linda (to Willy): Why must he fight, dear?

Ben (sparring with Biff): Good boy! Good boy!

Willy: How's that, Ben, heh?

Happy: Give him the left, Biff!

Linda: Why are you fighting?

Ben: Good boy! *(Suddenly comes in, trips Biff, and stands over him, the point of his umbrella poised over Biff's eye.)*

Linda: Look out, Biff!

Biff: Gee!

Ben (patting Biff's knee): Never fight fair with a stranger, boy. You'll never get out of the jungle that way. *(Taking Linda's hand and bowing):* It was an honor and a pleasure to meet you, Linda.

Linda (withdrawing her hand coldly, frightened): Have a nice — trip.

Ben (to Willy): And good luck with your — what do you do?

Willy: Selling.

Ben: Yes. Well . . . *(He raises his hand in farewell to all.)*

Willy: No, Ben, I don't want you to think . . . *(He takes Ben's arm to show him.)* It's Brooklyn, I know, but we hunt too.

Ben: Really, now.

Willy: Oh, sure, there's snakes and rabbits and — that's why I moved out here. Why, Biff can fell any one of these trees in no time! Boys! Go right over to where they're building the apartment house and get some sand. We're gonna rebuild the entire front stoop now! Watch this, Ben!

Biff: Yes, sir! On the double, Hap!

Happy (as he and Biff run off): I lost weight, Pop, you notice?

> *Charley enters in knickers, even before the boys are gone.*

Charley: Listen, if they steal any more from that building the watchman'll put the cops on them!

Linda (to Willy): Don't let Biff . . .

> *Ben laughs lustily.*

Willy: You shoulda seen the lumber they brought home last week. At least a dozen six-by-tens worth all kinds a money.

Charley: Listen, if that watchman —

Willy: I gave them hell, understand. But I got a couple of fearless characters there.

Charley: Willy, the jails are full of fearless characters.

Ben (clapping Willy on the back, with a laugh at Charley): And the stock exchange, friend!

Willy (joining in Ben's laughter): Where are the rest of your pants?

Charley: My wife bought them.

Willy: Now all you need is a golf club and you can go upstairs and go to sleep. *(To Ben).* Great athlete! Between him and his son Bernard they can't hammer a nail!

Bernard (rushing in): The watchman's chasing Biff!

Willy (angrily): Shut up! He's not stealing anything!

Linda (alarmed, hurrying off left): Where is he? Biff, dear! *(She exits.)*

Willy (moving toward the left, away from Ben): There's nothing wrong. What's the matter with you?

Ben: Nervy boy. Good!

Willy (laughing): Oh, nerves of iron, that Biff!

Charley: Don't know what it is. My New England man comes back and he's bleedin', they murdered him up there.

Willy: It's contacts, Charley, I got important contacts!

Charley (sarcastically): Glad to hear it, Willy. Come in later, we'll shoot a little casino. I'll take some of your Portland money. *(He laughs at Willy and exits.)*

Willy (turning to Ben): Business is bad, it's murderous. But not for me, of course.

Ben: I'll stop by on my way back to Africa.

Willy (longingly): Can't you stay a few days? You're just what I need, Ben, because I—I have a fine position here, but I—well, Dad left when I was such a baby and I never had a chance to talk to him and I still feel—kind of temporary about myself.

Ben: I'll be late for my train.

> *They are at opposite ends of the stage.*

Willy: Ben, my boys—can't we talk? They'd go into the jaws of hell for me, see, but I—

Ben: William, you're being first-rate with your boys. Outstanding, manly chaps!

Willy (hanging on to his words): Oh, Ben, that's good to hear! Because sometimes I'm afraid that I'm not teaching them the right kind of—Ben, how should I teach them?

Ben (giving great weight to each word, and with a certain vicious audacity): William, when I walked into the jungle, I was seventeen. When I walked out I was twenty-one. And, by God, I was rich! *(He goes off into darkness around the right corner of the house.)*

Willy: . . . was rich! That's just the spirit I want to imbue them with! To walk into a jungle! I was right! I was right! I was right!

> *Ben is gone, but Willy is still speaking to him as Linda, in nightgown and robe, enters the kitchen, glances around for Willy, then goes to the door of the house, looks out, and sees him. Comes down to his left. He looks at her.*

Linda: Willy, dear? Willy?

Willy: I was right!

Linda: Did you have some cheese? *(He can't answer.)* It's very late, darling. Come to bed, heh?

Willy (looking straight up): Gotta break your neck to see a star in this yard.

Linda: You coming in?

Willy: Whatever happened to that diamond watch fob? Remember? When Ben came from Africa that time? Didn't he give me a watch fob with a diamond in it?

Linda: You pawned it, dear. Twelve, thirteen years ago. For Biff's radio correspondence course.

Willy: Gee, that was a beautiful thing. I'll take a walk.

Linda: But you're in your slippers.

Willy (starting to go around the house at the left): I was right! I was! *(Half to Linda, as he goes, shaking his head.)* What a man! There was a man worth talking to. I was right!

Linda (calling after Willy): But in your slippers, Willy!

    Willy is almost gone when Biff, in his pajamas, comes down the stairs and enters the kitchen.

Biff: What is he doing out there?

Linda: Sh!

Biff: God Almighty, Mom, how long has he been doing this?

Linda: Don't, he'll hear you.

Biff: What the hell is the matter with him?

Linda: It'll pass by morning.

Biff: Shouldn't we do anything?

Linda: Oh, my dear, you should do a lot of things, but there's nothing to do, so go to sleep.

    Happy comes down the stairs and sits on the steps.

Happy: I never heard him so loud, Mom.

Linda: Well, come around more often; you'll hear him. *(She sits down at the table and mends the lining of Willy's jacket.)*

Biff: Why didn't you ever write me about this, Mom?

Linda: How would I write to you? For over three months you had no address.

Biff: I was on the move. But you know I thought of you all the time. You know that, don't you, pal?

Linda: I know, dear, I know. But he likes to have a letter. Just to know that there's still a possibility for better things.

Biff: He's not like this all the time, is he?

Linda: It's when you come home he's always the worst.

Biff: When I come home?

Linda: When you write you're coming, he's all smiles, and talks about the future, and — he's just wonderful. And then the closer you seem to come, the more shaky he gets, and then, by the time you get here, he's arguing, and he seems angry at you. I think it's just that maybe he can't bring himself to — to open up to you. Why are you so hateful to each other? Why is that?

Biff (evasively): I'm not hateful, Mom.

Linda: But you no sooner come in the door than you're fighting!

Biff: I don't know why. I mean to change. I'm tryin', Mom, you understand?

Linda: Are you home to stay now?

Biff: I don't know. I want to look around, see what's doin'.

Linda: Biff, you can't look around all your life, can you?

Biff: I just can't take hold, Mom. I can't take hold of some kind of a life.

Linda: Biff, a man is not a bird, to come and go with the springtime.

Biff: Your hair . . . *(He touches her hair.)* Your hair got so gray.

Linda: Oh, it's been gray since you were in high school. I just stopped dyeing it, that's all.

Biff: Dye it again, will ya? I don't want my pal looking old. *(He smiles.)*

Linda: You're such a boy! You think you can go away for a year and . . . You've got to get it into your head now that one day you'll knock on this door and there'll be strange people here —

Biff: What are you talking about? You're not even sixty, Mom.

Linda: But what about your father?

Biff (lamely): Well, I meant him too.

Happy: He admires Pop.

Linda: Biff, dear, if you don't have any feeling for him, then you can't have any feeling for me.

Biff: Sure I can, Mom.

Linda: No. You can't just come to see me, because I love him. (*With a threat, but only a threat, of tears.*) He's the dearest man in the world to me, and I won't have anyone making him feel unwanted and low and blue. You've got to make up your mind now, darling, there's no leeway any more. Either he's your father and you pay him that respect, or else you're not to come here. I know he's not easy to get along with — nobody knows that better than me — but . . .

Willy (from the left, with a laugh): Hey, hey, Biffo!

Biff (starting to go out after Willy): What the hell is the matter with him? (*Happy stops him.*)

Linda: Don't — don't go near him!

Biff: Stop making excuses for him! He always, always wiped the floor with you. Never had an ounce of respect for you.

Happy: He's always had respect for —

Biff: What the hell do you know about it?

Happy (surlily): Just don't call him crazy!

Biff: He's got no character — Charley wouldn't do this. Not in his own house — spewing out that vomit from his mind.

Happy: Charley never had to cope with what he's got to.

Biff: People are worse off than Willy Loman. Believe me, I've seen them!

Linda: Then make Charley your father, Biff. You can't do that, can you? I don't say he's a great man. Willy Loman never made a lot of money. His name was never in the paper. He's not the finest character that ever lived. But he's a human being, and a terrible thing is happening to him. So attention must be paid. He's not to be allowed to fall into his grave like an old dog. Attention, attention must be finally paid to such a person. You called him crazy —

Biff: I didn't mean —

Linda: No, a lot of people think he's lost his — balance. But you don't have to be very smart to know what his trouble is. The man is exhausted.

Happy: Sure!

Linda: A small man can be just as exhausted as a great man. He works for a company thirty-six years this March, opens up unheard-of territories to their trademark, and now in his old age they take his salary away.

Happy (indignantly): I didn't know that, Mom.

Linda: You never asked, my dear! Now that you get your spending money someplace else you don't trouble your mind with him.

Happy: But I gave you money last —

Linda: Christmas time, fifty dollars! To fix the hot water it cost ninety-seven fifty! For five weeks he's been on straight commission, like a beginner, an unknown!

Biff: Those ungrateful bastards!

Linda: Are they any worse than his sons? When he brought them business, when he was young, they were glad to see him. But now his old friends, the old buyers that loved him so and always found some order to hand him in a pinch — they're all dead, retired. He used to be able to make six, seven calls a day in Boston. Now he takes his valises out of the car and puts them back and takes them out again and he's exhausted. Instead of walking he talks now. He drives seven hundred miles, and when he gets there no one knows him any more, no one welcomes him. And what goes through a man's mind, driving seven hundred miles home without having earned a cent? Why shouldn't he talk to himself? Why? When he has to go to Charley and borrow fifty dollars a week and pretend to me that it's his pay? How long can that go on? How long? You see what I'm sitting here and waiting for? And you tell me he has no character? The man who never worked a day but for your benefit? When does he get the medal for that? Is this his reward — to turn around at the age of sixty-three and find his sons, who he loved better than his life, one a philandering bum —

Happy: Mom!

Linda: That's all you are, my baby! *(To Biff.)* And you! What happened to the love you had for him? You were such pals! How you used to talk to him on the phone every night! How lonely he was till he could come home to you!

Biff: All right, Mom. I'll live here in my room, and I'll get a job. I'll keep away from him, that's all.

Linda: No, Biff. You can't stay here and fight all the time.

Biff: He threw me out of this house, remember that.

Linda: Why did he do that? I never knew why.

Biff: Because I know he's a fake and he doesn't like anybody around who knows!

Linda: Why a fake? In what way? What do you mean?

Biff: Just don't lay it all at my feet. It's between me and him — that's all I have to say. I'll chip in from now on. He'll settle for half my pay check. He'll be all right. I'm going to bed. *(He starts for the stairs.)*

Linda: He won't be all right.

Biff (turning on the stairs, furiously): I hate this city and I'll stay here. Now what do you want?

Linda: He's dying, Biff.

Happy turns quickly to her, shocked.

Biff (after a pause): Why is he dying?

Linda: He's been trying to kill himself.

Biff (with great horror): How?

Linda: I live from day to day.

Biff: What're you talking about?

Linda: Remember I wrote you that he smashed up the car again? In February?

Biff: Well?

Linda: The insurance inspector came. He said that they have evidence. That all these accidents in the last year — weren't — weren't — accidents.

Happy: How can they tell that? That's a lie.

Linda: It seems there's a woman . . . *(She takes a breath as):*

    Biff (sharply but contained): What woman?

    Linda (simultaneously): . . . and this woman . . .

Linda: What?

Biff: Nothing. Go ahead.

Linda: What did you say?

Biff: Nothing. I just said what woman?

Happy: What about her?

Linda: Well, it seems she was walking down the road and saw his car. She says that he wasn't driving fast at all, and that he didn't skid. She says he came to that little bridge, and then deliberately smashed into the railing, and it was only the shallowness of the water that saved him.

Biff: Oh, no, he probably just fell asleep again.

Linda: I don't think he fell asleep.

Biff: Why not?

Linda: Last month . . . *(With great difficulty.)* Oh, boys, it's so hard to say a thing like this! He's just a big stupid man to you, but I tell you there's more good in him than in many other people. *(She chokes, wipes her eyes.)* I was looking for a fuse. The lights blew out, and I went down the cellar. And behind the fuse box — it happened to fall out — was a length of rubber pipe — just short.

Happy: No kidding?

Linda: There's a little attachment on the end of it. I knew right away. And sure enough, on the bottom of the water heater there's a new little nipple on the gas pipe.

Happy (angrily): That — jerk.

Biff: Did you have it taken off?

Linda: I'm — I'm ashamed to. How can I mention it to him? Every day I go down and take away that little rubber pipe. But, when he comes home, I put it back where it was. How can I insult him that way? I don't know what to do. I live from day to day, boys. I tell you, I know every thought in his mind. It sounds so old-fashioned and silly, but I tell you he put his whole life into you and you've turned your backs on him. *(She is bent over in chair, weeping, her face in her hands.)* Biff, I swear to God! Biff, his life is in your hands!

Happy (to Biff): How do you like that damned fool!

Biff (kissing her): All right, pal, all right. It's all settled now. I've been remiss. I know that, Mom. But now I'll stay, and I swear to you, I'll apply myself. *(Kneeling in front of her, in a fever of self-reproach.)* It's just — you see, Mom, I don't fit in business. Not that I won't try. I'll try, and I'll make good.

Happy: Sure you will. The trouble with you in business was you never tried to please people.

Biff: I know, I —

Happy: Like when you worked for Harrison's. Bob Harrison said you were tops, and then you go and do some damn fool thing like whistling whole songs in the elevator like a comedian.

Biff (against Happy): So what? I like to whistle sometimes.

Happy: You don't raise a guy to a responsible job who whistles in the elevator!

Linda: Well, don't argue about it now.

Happy: Like when you'd go off and swim in the middle of the day instead of taking the line around.

Biff (his resentment rising): Well, don't you run off? You take off sometimes, don't you? On a nice summer day?

Happy: Yeah, but I cover myself!

Linda: Boys!

Happy: If I'm going to take a fade the boss can call any number where I'm supposed to be and they'll swear to him that I just left. I'll tell you something that I hate to say, Biff, but in the business world some of them think you're crazy.

Biff (angered): Screw the business world!

Happy: All right, screw it! Great, but cover yourself!

Linda: Hap, Hap!

Biff: I don't care what they think! They've laughed at Dad for years, and you know why? Because we don't belong in this nuthouse of a city! We should be mixing cement on some open plain, or — or carpenters. A carpenter is allowed to whistle!

Willy walks in from the entrance of the house, at left.

Willy: Even your grandfather was better than a carpenter. *(Pause. They watch him.)* You never grew up. Bernard does not whistle in the elevator, I assure you.

Biff *(as though to laugh Willy out of it)*: Yeah, but you do, Pop.

Willy: I never in my life whistled in an elevator! And who in the business world thinks I'm crazy?

Biff: I didn't mean it like that, Pop. Now don't make a whole thing out of it, will ya?

Willy: Go back to the West! Be a carpenter, a cowboy, enjoy yourself!

Linda: Willy, he was just saying —

Willy: I heard what he said!

Happy *(trying to quiet Willy)*: Hey, Pop, come on now . . .

Willy *(continuing over Happy's line)*: They laugh at me, heh? Go to Filene's, go to the Hub, go to Slattery's, Boston. Call out the name Willy Loman and see what happens! Big shot!

Biff: All right, Pop.

Willy: Big!

Biff: All right!

Willy: Why do you always insult me?

Biff: I didn't say a word. *(To Linda.)* Did I say a word?

Linda: He didn't say anything, Willy.

Willy *(going to the doorway of the living-room)*: All right, good night, good night.

Linda: Willy, dear, he just decided . . .

Willy *(to Biff)*: If you get tired hanging around tomorrow, paint the ceiling I put up in the living-room.

Biff: I'm leaving early tomorrow.

Happy: He's going to see Bill Oliver, Pop.

Willy *(interestedly)*: Oliver? For what?

Biff *(with reserve, but trying, trying)*: He always said he'd stake me. I'd like to go into business, so maybe I can take him up on it.

Linda: Isn't that wonderful?

Willy: Don't interrupt. What's wonderful about it? There's fifty men in the City of New York who'd stake him. *(To Biff.)* Sporting goods?

Biff: I guess so. I know something about it and —

Willy: He knows something about it! You know sporting goods better than Spalding, for God's sake! How much is he giving you?

Biff: I don't know, I didn't even see him yet, but —

Willy: Then what're you talkin' about?

Biff *(getting angry)*: Well, all I said was I'm gonna see him, that's all!

Willy *(turning away)*: Ah, you're counting your chickens again.

Biff *(starting left for the stairs)*: Oh, Jesus, I'm going to sleep!

Willy *(calling after him)*: Don't curse in this house!

Biff *(turning)*: Since when did you get so clean?

Happy *(trying to stop them)*: Wait a . . .

Willy: Don't use that language to me! I won't have it!

Happy *(grabbing Biff, shouts)*: Wait a minute! I got an idea. I got a feasible idea. Come here, Biff, let's talk this over now, let's talk some sense here. When I was down in Florida last time, I thought of a great idea to sell sporting goods. It just came back to me. You and I, Biff — we have a line, the Loman Line. We train a couple of weeks, and put on a couple of exhibitions, see?

Willy: That's an idea!

Happy: Wait! We form two basketball teams, see? Two water-polo teams. We play each other. It's a million dollars' worth of publicity. Two brothers, see? The Loman Brothers. Displays in the Royal Palms — all the hotels. And banners over the ring and the basketball court: "Loman Brothers." Baby, we could sell sporting goods!

Willy: That is a one-million-dollar idea!

Linda: Marvelous!

Biff: I'm in great shape as far as that's concerned.

Happy: And the beauty of it is, Biff, it wouldn't be like a business. We'd be out playin' ball again . . .

Biff (enthused): Yeah, that's . . .

Willy: Million-dollar . . .

Happy: And you wouldn't get fed up with it, Biff. It'd be the family again. There'd be the old honor, and comradeship, and if you wanted to go off for a swim or some-thin' — well, you'd do it! Without some smart cooky gettin' up ahead of you!

Willy: Lick the world! You guys together could absolutely lick the civilized world.

Biff: I'll see Oliver tomorrow. Hap, if we could work that out . . .

Linda: Maybe things are beginning to —

Willy (wildly enthused, to Linda): Stop interrupting! *(To Biff.)* But don't wear sport jacket and slacks when you see Oliver.

Biff: No, I'll —

Willy: A business suit, and talk as little as possible, and don't crack any jokes.

Biff: He did like me. Always liked me.

Linda: He loved you!

Willy (to Linda): Will you stop! *(To Biff.)* Walk in very serious. You are not apply-ing for a boy's job. Money is to pass. Be quiet, fine, and serious. Everybody likes a kidder, but nobody lends him money.

Happy: I'll try to get some myself, Biff. I'm sure I can.

Willy: I see great things for you kids, I think your troubles are over. But remember, start big and you'll end big. Ask for fifteen. How much you gonna ask for?

Biff: Gee, I don't know —

Willy: And don't say "Gee." "Gee" is a boy's word. A man walking in for fifteen thousand dollars does not say "Gee!"

Biff: Ten, I think, would be top though.

Willy: Don't be so modest. You always started too low. Walk in with a big laugh. Don't look worried. Start off with a couple of your good stories to lighten things up. It's not what you say, it's how you say it — because personality al-ways wins the day.

Linda: Oliver always thought the highest of him —

Willy: Will you let me talk?

Biff: Don't yell at her, Pop, will ya?

Willy (angrily): I was talking, wasn't I?

Biff: I don't like you yelling at her all the time, and I'm tellin' you, that's all.

Willy: What're you, takin' over this house?

Linda: Willy —

Willy (turning on her): Don't take his side all the time, goddammit!

Biff (furiously): Stop yelling at her!

Willy (suddenly pulling on his cheek, beaten down, guilt ridden): Give my best to Bill Oliver — he may remember me. *(He exits through the living-room doorway.)*

Linda *(her voice subdued):* What'd you have to start that for? *(Biff turns away.)*
You see how sweet he was as soon as you talked hopefully? *(She goes over to
Biff.)* Come up and say good night to him. Don't let him go to bed that way.
Happy: Come on, Biff, let's buck him up.
Linda: Please, dear. Just say good night. It takes so little to make him happy.
Come. *(She goes through the living-room doorway, calling upstairs from within
the living-room.)* Your pajamas are hanging in the bathroom, Willy!
Happy *(looking toward where Linda went out):* What a woman! They broke the
mold when they made her. You know that, Biff?
Biff: He's off salary. My God, working on commission!
Happy: Well, let's face it: he's no hot-shot selling man. Except that sometimes, you
have to admit, he's a sweet personality.
Biff *(deciding):* Lend me ten bucks, will ya? I want to buy some new ties.
Happy: I'll take you to a place I know. Beautiful stuff. Wear one of my striped
shirts tomorrow.
Biff: She got gray. Mom got awful old. Gee, I'm gonna go in to Oliver tomorrow
and knock him for a —
Happy: Come on up. Tell that to Dad. Let's give him a whirl. Come on.
Biff *(steamed up):* You know, with ten thousand bucks, boy!
Happy *(as they go into the living-room):* That's the talk, Biff, that's the first time I've
heard the old confidence out of you! *(From within the living-room, fading off.)*
You're gonna live with me, kid, and any babe you want just say the word . . .
*(The last lines are hardly heard. They are mounting the stairs to their parents'
bedroom.)*
Linda *(entering her bedroom and addressing Willy, who is in the bathroom. She is
straightening the bed for him):* Can you do anything about the shower? It drips.
Willy *(from the bathroom):* All of a sudden everything falls to pieces! Goddam
plumbing, oughta be sued, those people. I hardly finished putting it in and the
thing . . . *(His words rumble off.)*
Linda: I'm just wondering if Oliver will remember him. You think he might?
Willy *(coming out of the bathroom in his pajamas):* Remember him? What's the
matter with you, you crazy? If he'd've stayed with Oliver he'd be on top by now!
Wait'll Oliver gets a look at him. You don't know the average caliber any more.
The average young man today — *(he is getting into bed)* — is got a caliber of
zero. Greatest thing in the world for him was to bum around.

Biff and Happy enter the bedroom. Slight pause.

Willy *(stops short, looking at Biff):* Glad to hear it, boy.
Happy: He wanted to say good night to you, sport.
Willy *(to Biff):* Yeah. Knock him dead, boy. What'd you want to tell me?
Biff: Just take it easy, Pop. Good night. *(He turns to go.)*
Willy *(unable to resist):* And if anything falls off the desk while you're talking to
him — like a package or something — don't you pick it up. They have office
boys for that.
Linda: I'll make a big breakfast —
Willy: Will you let me finish? *(To Biff.)* Tell him you were in the business in the
West. Not farm work.
Biff: All right, Dad.
Linda: I think everything —
Willy *(going right through her speech):* And don't undersell yourself. No less than
fifteen thousand dollars.

Biff (unable to bear him): Okay. Good night, Mom. *(He starts moving.)*

Willy: Because you got a greatness in you, Biff, remember that. You got all kinds a greatness . . . *(He lies back, exhausted. Biff walks out.)*

Linda (calling after Biff): Sleep well, darling!

Happy: I'm gonna get married, Mom. I wanted to tell you.

Linda: Go to sleep, dear.

Happy (going): I just wanted to tell you.

Willy: Keep up the good work. *(Happy exits.)* God . . . remember that Ebbets Field game? The championship of the city?

Linda: Just rest. Should I sing to you?

Willy: Yeah. Sing to me. *(Linda hums a soft lullaby.)* When that team came out — he was the tallest, remember?

Linda: Oh, yes. And in gold.

> *Biff enters the darkened kitchen, takes a cigarette, and leaves the house. He comes downstage into a golden pool of light. He smokes, staring at the night.*

Willy: Like a young god. Hercules — something like that. And the sun, the sun all around him. Remember how he waved to me? Right up from the field, with the representatives of three colleges standing by? And the buyers I brought, and the cheers when he came out — Loman, Loman, Loman! God Almighty, he'll be great yet. A star like that, magnificent, can never really fade away!

> *The light on Willy is fading. The gas heater begins to glow through the kitchen wall, near the stairs, a blue flame beneath red coils.*

Linda (timidly): Willy dear, what has he got against you?

Willy: I'm so tired. Don't talk any more.

> *Biff slowly returns to the kitchen. He stops, stares toward the heater.*

Linda: Will you ask Howard to let you work in New York?

Willy: First thing in the morning. Everything'll be all right.

> *Biff reaches behind the heater and draws out a length of rubber tubing. He is horrified and turns his head toward Willy's room, still dimly lit, from which the strains of Linda's desperate but monotonous humming rise.*

Willy (staring through the window into the moonlight): Gee, look at the moon moving between the buildings!

> *Biff wraps the tubing around his hand and quickly goes up the stairs.*

> *Curtain.*

ACT II

> *Music is heard, gay and bright. The curtain rises as the music fades away. Willy, in shirt sleeves, is sitting at the kitchen table, sipping coffee, his hat in his lap. Linda is filling his cup when she can.*

Willy: Wonderful coffee. Meal in itself.

Linda: Can I make you some eggs?

Willy: No. Take a breath.

Linda: You look so rested, dear.

Willy: I slept like a dead one. First time in months. Imagine, sleeping till ten on a Tuesday morning. Boys left nice and early, heh?

Linda: They were out of here by eight o'clock.

Willy: Good work!

Linda: It was so thrilling to see them leaving together. I can't get over the shaving lotion in this house!

Willy (smiling): Mmm —

Linda: Biff was very changed this morning. His whole attitude seemed to be hopeful. He couldn't wait to get downtown to see Oliver.

Willy: He's heading for a change. There's no question, there simply are certain men that take longer to get — solidified. How did he dress?

Linda: His blue suit. He's so handsome in that suit. He could be a — anything in that suit!

Willy gets up from the table. Linda holds his jacket for him.

Willy: There's no question, no question at all. Gee, on the way home tonight I'd like to buy some seeds.

Linda (laughing): That'd be wonderful. But not enough sun gets back there. Nothing'll grow any more.

Willy: You wait, kid, before it's all over we're gonna get a little place out in the country, and I'll raise some vegetables, a couple of chickens . . .

Linda: You'll do it yet, dear.

Willy walks out of his jacket. Linda follows him.

Willy: And they'll get married, and come for a weekend. I'd build a little guest house. 'Cause I got so many fine tools, all I'd need would be a little lumber and some peace of mind.

Linda (joyfully): I sewed the lining . . .

Willy: I could build two guest houses, so they'd both come. Did he decide how much he's going to ask Oliver for?

Linda (getting him into the jacket): He didn't mention it, but I imagine ten or fifteen thousand. You going to talk to Howard today?

Willy: Yeah. I'll put it to him straight and simple. He'll just have to take me off the road.

Linda: And Willy, don't forget to ask for a little advance, because we've got the insurance premium. It's the grace period now.

Willy: That's a hundred . . . ?

Linda: A hundred and eight, sixty-eight. Because we're a little short again.

Willy: Why are we short?

Linda: Well, you had the motor job on the car . . .

Willy: That goddam Studebaker!

Linda: And you got one more payment on the refrigerator . . .

Willy: But it just broke again!

Linda: Well, it's old, dear.

Willy: I told you we should've bought a well-advertised machine. Charley bought a General Electric and it's twenty years old and it's still good, that son-of-a-bitch.

Linda: But, Willy —

Willy: Whoever heard of a Hastings refrigerator? Once in my life I would like to own something outright before it's broken! I'm always in a race with the junkyard! I just finished paying for the car and it's on its last legs. The refrigerator consumes belts like a goddam maniac. They time those things. They time them so when you finally paid for them, they're used up.

Linda (buttoning up his jacket as he unbuttons it): All told, about two hundred dollars would carry us, dear. But that includes the last payment on the mortgage. After this payment, Willy, the house belongs to us.

Willy: It's twenty-five years!

Linda: Biff was nine years old when we bought it.

Willy: Well, that's a great thing. To weather a twenty-five-year mortgage is —

Linda: It's an accomplishment.

Willy: All the cement, the lumber, the reconstruction I put in this house! There ain't a crack to be found in it any more.

Linda: Well, it served its purpose.

Willy: What purpose? Some stranger'll come along, move in, and that's that. If only Biff would take this house, and raise a family . . . *(He starts to go.)* Goodby, I'm late.

Linda (suddenly remembering): Oh, I forgot! You're supposed to meet them for dinner.

Willy: Me?

Linda: At Frank's Chop House on Forty-eighth near Sixth Avenue.

Willy: Is that so! How about you?

Linda: No, just the three of you. They're gonna blow you to a big meal!

Willy: Don't say! Who thought of that?

Linda: Biff came to me this morning, Willy, and he said, "Tell Dad, we want to blow him to a big meal." Be there six o'clock. You and your two boys are going to have dinner.

Willy: Gee whiz! That's really somethin'. I'm gonna knock Howard for a loop, kid. I'll get an advance, and I'll come home with a New York job. Goddammit, now I'm gonna do it!

Linda: Oh, that's the spirit, Willy!

Willy: I will never get behind a wheel the rest of my life!

Linda: It's changing, Willy, I can feel it changing!

Willy: Beyond a question. G'by, I'm late. *(He starts to go again.)*

Linda (calling after him as she runs to the kitchen table for a handkerchief): You got your glasses?

Willy (feels for them, then comes back in): Yeah, yeah, got my glasses.

Linda (giving him the handkerchief): And a handkerchief.

Willy: Yeah, handkerchief.

Linda: And your saccharine?

Willy: Yeah, my saccharine.

Linda: Be careful on the subway stairs.

> She kisses him, and a silk stocking is seen hanging from her hand. Willy notices it.

Willy: Will you stop mending stockings? At least while I'm in the house. It gets me nervous. I can't tell you. Please.

> Linda hides the stocking in her hand as she follows Willy across the forestage in front of the house.

Linda: Remember, Frank's Chop House.

Willy (passing the apron): Maybe beets would grow out there.

Linda (laughing): But you tried so many times.

Willy: Yeah. Well, don't work hard today. *(He disappears around the right corner of the house.)*

Linda: Be careful!

As Willy vanishes, Linda waves to him. Suddenly the phone rings. She runs across the stage and into the kitchen and lifts it.

Linda: Hello? Oh, Biff! I'm so glad you called, I just . . . Yes, sure, I just told him. Yes, he'll be there for dinner at six o'clock, I didn't forget. Listen, I was just dying to tell you. You know that little rubber pipe I told you about? That he connected to the gas heater? I finally decided to go down the cellar this morning and take it away and destroy it. But it's gone! Imagine? He took it away himself, it isn't there! *(She listens.)* When? Oh, then you took it. Oh — nothing, it's just that I'd hoped he'd taken it away himself. Oh, I'm not worried, darling, because this morning he left in such high spirits, it was like the old days! I'm not afraid any more. Did Mr. Oliver see you? . . . Well, you wait there then. And make a nice impression on him, darling. Just don't perspire too much before you see him. And have a nice time with Dad. He may have big news too! . . . That's right, a New York job. And be sweet to him tonight, dear. Be loving to him. Because he's only a little boat looking for a harbor. *(She is trembling with sorrow and joy.)* Oh, that's wonderful, Biff, you'll save his life. Thanks, darling. Just put your arm around him when he comes into the restaurant. Give him a smile. That's the boy . . . Good-by, dear. . . . You got your comb? . . . That's fine. Good-by, Biff dear.

In the middle of her speech, Howard Wagner, thirty-six, wheels in a small type-writer table on which is a wire-recording machine and proceeds to plug it in. This is on the left forestage. Light slowly fades on Linda as it rises on Howard. Howard is intent on threading the machine and only glances over his shoulder as Willy appears.

Willy: Pst! Pst!

Howard: Hello, Willy, come in.

Willy: Like to have a little talk with you, Howard.

Howard: Sorry to keep you waiting. I'll be with you in a minute.

Willy: What's that, Howard?

Howard: Didn't you ever see one of these? Wire recorder.

Willy: Oh. Can we talk a minute?

Howard: Records things. Just got delivery yesterday. Been driving me crazy, the most terrific machine I ever saw in my life. I was up all night with it.

Willy: What do you do with it?

Howard: I bought it for dictation, but you can do anything with it. Listen to this. I had it home last night. Listen to what I picked up. The first one is my daughter. Get this. *(He flicks the switch and "Roll Out the Barrel" is heard being whistled.)* Listen to that kid whistle.

Willy: That is lifelike, isn't it?

Howard: Seven years old. Get that tone.

Willy: Ts, ts. Like to ask a little favor if you . . .

The whistling breaks off, and the voice of Howard's daughter is heard.

His Daughter: "Now you, Daddy."

Howard: She's crazy for me! *(Again the same song is whistled.)* That's me! Ha! *(He winks.)*

Willy: You're very good!

The whistling breaks off again. The machine runs silent for a moment.

Howard: Sh! Get this now, this is my son.

His Son: "The capital of Alabama is Montgomery; the capital of Arizona is Phoenix; the capital of Arkansas is Little Rock; the capital of California is Sacramento . . ." *(and on, and on).*

Howard (holding up five fingers): Five years old, Willy!

Willy: He'll make an announcer some day!

His Son (continuing): "The capital . . ."

Howard: Get that — alphabetical order! *(The machine breaks off suddenly.)* Wait a minute. The maid kicked the plug out.

Willy: It certainly is a —

Howard: Sh, for God's sake!

His Son: "It's nine o'clock, Bulova watch time. So I have to go to sleep."

Willy: That really is —

Howard: Wait a minute! The next is my wife.

They wait.

Howard's Voice: "Go on, say something." *(Pause.)* "Well, you gonna talk?"

His Wife: "I can't think of anything."

Howard's Voice: "Well, talk — it's turning."

His Wife (shyly, beaten): "Hello." *(Silence.)* "Oh, Howard, I can't talk into this . . ."

Howard (snapping the machine off): That was my wife.

Willy: That is a wonderful machine. Can we —

Howard: I tell you, Willy, I'm gonna take my camera, and my bandsaw, and all my hobbies, and out they go. This is the most fascinating relaxation I ever found.

Willy: I think I'll get one myself.

Howard: Sure, they're only a hundred and a half. You can't do without it. Supposing you wanna hear Jack Benny, see? But you can't be at home at that hour. So you tell the maid to turn the radio on when Jack Benny comes on, and this automatically goes on with the radio . . .

Willy: And when you come home you . . .

Howard: You can come home twelve o'clock, one o'clock, any time you like, and you get yourself a Coke and sit yourself down, throw the switch, and there's Jack Benny's program in the middle of the night!

Willy: I'm definitely going to get one. Because lots of time I'm on the road, and I think to myself, what I must be missing on the radio!

Howard: Don't you have a radio in the car?

Willy: Well, yeah, but who ever thinks of turning it on?

Howard: Say, aren't you supposed to be in Boston?

Willy: That's what I want to talk to you about, Howard. You got a minute? *(He draws a chair in from the wing.)*

Howard: What happened? What're you doing here?

Willy: Well . . .

Howard: You didn't crack up again, did you?

Willy: Oh, no. No . . .

Howard: Geez, you had me worried there for a minute. What's the trouble?

Willy: Well, tell you the truth, Howard. I've come to the decision that I'd rather not travel any more.

Howard: Not travel! Well, what'll you do?

Willy: Remember, Christmas time, when you had the party here? You said you'd try to think of some spot for me here in town.

Howard: With us?

Willy: Well, sure.

Howard: Oh, yeah, yeah. I remember. Well, I couldn't think of anything for you, Willy.

Willy: I tell ya, Howard. The kids are all grown up, y'know. I don't need much any more. If I could take home — well, sixty-five dollars a week, I could swing it.

Howard: Yeah, but Willy, see I —

Willy: I tell ya why, Howard. Speaking frankly and between the two of us, y'know — I'm just a little tired.

Howard: Oh, I could understand that, Willy. But you're a road man, Willy, and we do a road business. We've only got a half-dozen salesmen on the floor here.

Willy: God knows, Howard, I never asked a favor of any man. But I was with the firm when your father used to carry you in here in his arms.

Howard: I know that, Willy, but —

Willy: Your father came to me the day you were born and asked me what I thought of the name of Howard, may he rest in peace.

Howard: I appreciate that, Willy, but there just is no spot here for you. If I had a spot I'd slam you right in, but I just don't have a single solitary spot.

He looks for his lighter. Willy has picked it up and gives it to him. Pause.

Willy (with increasing anger): Howard, all I need to set my table is fifty dollars a week.

Howard: But where am I going to put you, kid?

Willy: Look, it isn't a question of whether I can sell merchandise, is it?

Howard: No, but it's a business, kid, and everybody's gotta pull his own weight.

Willy (desperately): Just let me tell you a story, Howard —

Howard: 'Cause you gotta admit, business is business.

Willy (angrily): Business is definitely business, but just listen for a minute. You don't understand this. When I was a boy — eighteen, nineteen — I was already on the road. And there was a question in my mind as to whether selling had a future for me. Because in those days I had a yearning to go to Alaska. See, there were three gold strikes in one month in Alaska, and I felt like going out. Just for the ride, you might say.

Howard (barely interested): Don't say.

Willy: Oh, yeah, my father lived many years in Alaska. He was an adventurous man. We've got quite a little streak of self-reliance in our family. I thought I'd go out with my older brother and try to locate him, and maybe settle in the North with the old man. And I was almost decided to go, when I met a salesman in the Parker House. His name was Dave Singleman. And he was eighty-four years old, and he'd drummed merchandise in thirty-one states. And old Dave, he'd go up to his room, y'understand, put on his green velvet slippers — I'll never forget — and pick up his phone and call the buyers, and without ever leaving his room, at the age of eighty-four, he made his living. And when I saw that, I realized that selling was the greatest career a man could want. 'Cause what could be more satisfying than to be able to go, at the age of eighty-four, into twenty or thirty different cities, and pick up a phone, and be remembered and loved and helped by so many different people? Do you know? when he died — and by the way he died the death of a salesman, in his green velvet slippers in the smoker of the New York, New Haven, and

Hartford, going into Boston — when he died, hundreds of salesmen and buyers were at his funeral. Things were sad on a lotta trains for months after that. *(He stands up. Howard has not looked at him.)* In those days there was personality in it, Howard. There was respect, and comradeship, and gratitude in it. Today, it's all cut and dried, and there's no chance for bringing friendship to bear — or personality. You see what I mean? They don't know me any more.

Howard (moving away, to the right): That's just the thing, Willy.

Willy: If I had forty dollars a week — that's all I'd need. Forty dollars, Howard.

Howard: Kid, I can't take blood from a stone, I —

Willy (desperation is on him now): Howard, the year Al Smith° was nominated, your father came to me and —

Howard (starting to go off): I've got to see some people, kid.

Willy (stopping him): I'm talking about your father! There were promises made across this desk! You mustn't tell me you've got people to see — I put thirty-four years into this firm, Howard, and now I can't pay my insurance! You can't eat the orange and throw the peel away — a man is not a piece of fruit! *(After a pause.)* Now pay attention. Your father — in 1928 I had a big year. I averaged a hundred and seventy dollars a week in commissions.

Howard (impatiently): Now, Willy, you never averaged —

Willy (banging his hand on the desk): I averaged a hundred and seventy dollars a week in the year of 1928! And your father came to me — or rather, I was in the office here — it was right over this desk — and he put his hand on my shoulder —

Howard (getting up): You'll have to excuse me, Willy, I gotta see some people. Pull yourself together. *(Going out.)* I'll be back in a little while.

On Howard's exit, the light on his chair grows very bright and strange.

Willy: Pull myself together! What the hell did I say to him? My God, I was yelling at him! How could I! *(Willy breaks off, staring at the light, which occupies the chair, animating it. He approaches this chair, standing across the desk from it.)* Frank, Frank, don't you remember what you told me that time? How you put your hand on my shoulder, and Frank . . . *(He leans on the desk and as he speaks the dead man's name he accidentally switches on the recorder, and instantly:)*

Howard's Son: ". . . of New York is Albany. The capital of Ohio is Cincinnati, the capital of Rhode Island is . . ." *(The recitation continues.)*

Willy (leaping away with fright, shouting): Ha! Howard! Howard! Howard!

Howard (rushing in): What happened?

Willy (pointing at the machine, which continues nasally, childishly, with the capital cities): Shut it off! Shut it off!

Howard (pulling the plug out): Look, Willy . . .

Willy (pressing his hands to his eyes): I gotta get myself some coffee. I'll get some coffee . . .

Willy starts to walk out. Howard stops him.

Howard (rolling up the cord): Willy, look . . .

Willy: I'll go to Boston.

Howard: Willy, you can't go to Boston for us.

Al Smith: Democratic candidate for president of the United States in 1928 who lost the election to Herbert Hoover.

Willy: Why can't I go?

Howard: I don't want you to represent us. I've been meaning to tell you for a long time now.

Willy: Howard, are you firing me?

Howard: I think you need a good long rest, Willy.

Willy: Howard —

Howard: And when you feel better, come back, and we'll see if we can work something out.

Willy: But I gotta earn money, Howard. I'm in no position to —

Howard: Where are your sons? Why don't your sons give you a hand?

Willy: They're working on a very big deal.

Howard: This is no time for false pride, Willy. You go to your sons and you tell them that you're tired. You've got two great boys, haven't you?

Willy: Oh, no question, no question, but in the meantime . . .

Howard: Then that's that, heh?

Willy: All right, I'll go to Boston tomorrow.

Howard: No, no.

Willy: I can't throw myself on my sons. I'm not a cripple!

Howard: Look, kid, I'm busy this morning.

Willy (grasping Howard's arm): Howard, you've got to let me go to Boston!

Howard (hard, keeping himself under control): I've got a line of people to see this morning. Sit down, take five minutes, and pull yourself together, and then go home, will ya? I need the office, Willy. *(He starts to go, turns, remembering the recorder, starts to push off the table holding the recorder.)* Oh, yeah. Whenever you can this week, stop by and drop off the samples. You'll feel better, Willy, and then come back and we'll talk. Pull yourself together, kid, there's people outside.

Howard exits, pushing the table off left. Willy stares into space, exhausted. Now the music is heard — Ben's music — first distantly, then closer, closer. As Willy speaks, Ben enters from the right. He carries valise and umbrella.

Willy: Oh, Ben, how did you do it? What is the answer? Did you wind up the Alaska deal already?

Ben: Doesn't take much time if you know what you're doing. Just a short business trip. Boarding ship in an hour. Wanted to say good-by.

Willy: Ben, I've got to talk to you.

Ben (glancing at his watch): Haven't the time, William.

Willy (crossing the apron to Ben): Ben, nothing's working out. I don't know what to do.

Ben: Now, look here, William. I've bought timberland in Alaska and I need a man to look after things for me.

Willy: God, timberland! Me and my boys in those grand outdoors!

Ben: You've a new continent at your doorstep, William. Get out of these cities, they're full of talk and time payments and courts of law. Screw on your fists and you can fight for a fortune up there.

Willy: Yes, yes! Linda, Linda!

Linda enters as of old, with the wash.

Linda: Oh, you're back?

Ben: I haven't much time.

Willy: No, wait! Linda, he's got a proposition for me in Alaska.

Linda: But you've got — *(To Ben.)* He's got a beautiful job here.

Willy: But in Alaska, kid, I could —

Linda: You're doing well enough, Willy!

Ben (to Linda): Enough for what, my dear?

Linda (frightened of Ben and angry at him): Don't say those things to him! Enough to be happy right here, right now. *(To Willy, while Ben laughs.)* Why must everybody conquer the world? You're well liked, and the boys love you, and someday — *(to Ben)* — why, old man Wagner told him just the other day that if he keeps it up he'll be a member of the firm, didn't he, Willy?

Willy: Sure, sure. I am building something with this firm, Ben, and if a man is building something he must be on the right track, mustn't he?

Ben: What are you building? Lay your hand on it. Where is it?

Willy (hesitantly): That's true, Linda, there's nothing.

Linda: Why? *(To Ben.)* There's a man eighty-four years old —

Willy: That's right, Ben, that's right. When I look at that man I say, what is there to worry about?

Ben: Bah!

Willy: It's true, Ben. All he has to do is go into any city, pick up the phone, and he's making his living and you know why?

Ben (picking up his valise): I've got to go.

Willy (holding Ben back): Look at this boy!

Biff, in his high school sweater, enters carrying suitcase. Happy carries Biff's shoulder guards, gold helmet, and football pants.

Willy: Without a penny to his name, three great universities are begging for him, and from there the sky's the limit, because it's not what you do, Ben. It's who you know and the smile on your face! It's contacts, Ben, contacts! The whole wealth of Alaska passes over the lunch table at the Commodore Hotel, and that's the wonder, the wonder of this country, that a man can end with diamonds here on the basis of being liked! *(He turns to Biff.)* And that's why when you get out on that field today it's important. Because thousands of people will be rooting for you and loving you. *(To Ben, who has again begun to leave.)* And Ben! when he walks into a business office his name will sound out like a bell and all the doors will open to him! I've seen it, Ben, I've seen it a thousand times! You can't feel it with your hand like timber, but it's there!

Ben: Good-by, William.

Willy: Ben, am I right? Don't you think I'm right? I value your advice.

Ben: There's a new continent at your doorstep, William. You could walk out rich. Rich! *(He is gone.)*

Willy: We'll do it here, Ben! You hear me? We're gonna do it here!

Young Bernard rushes in. The gay music of the Boys is heard.

Bernard: Oh, gee, I was afraid you left already!

Willy: Why? What time is it?

Bernard: It's half-past one!

Willy: Well, come on, everybody! Ebbets Field next stop! Where's the pennants? *(He rushes through the wall-line of the kitchen and out into the living-room.)*

Linda (to Biff): Did you pack fresh underwear?

Biff (who has been limbering up): I want to go!

Bernard: Biff, I'm carrying your helmet, ain't I?

Happy: I'm carrying the helmet.

Bernard: How am I going to get in the locker room?

Linda: Let him carry the shoulder guards. *(She puts her coat and hat on in the kitchen.)*

Bernard: Can I, Biff? 'Cause I told everybody I'm going to be in the locker room.

Happy: In Ebbets Field it's the clubhouse.

Bernard: I meant the clubhouse. Biff!

Happy: Biff!

Biff (grandly, after a slight pause): Let him carry the shoulder guards.

Happy (as he gives Bernard the shoulder guards): Stay close to us now.

> *Willy rushes in with the pennants.*

Willy (handing them out): Everybody wave when Biff comes out on the field. *(Happy and Bernard run off.)* You set now, boy?

> *The music has died away.*

Biff: Ready to go, Pop. Every muscle is ready.

Willy (at the edge of the apron): You realize what this means?

Biff: That's right, Pop.

Willy (feeling Biff's muscles): You're comin' home this afternoon captain of the All Scholastic Championship Team of the City of New York.

Biff: I got it, Pop. And remember, pal, when I take off my helmet, that touchdown is for you.

Willy: Let's go! *(He is starting out, with his arm around Biff, when Charley enters, as of old, in knickers.)* I got no room for you, Charley.

Charley: Room? For what?

Willy: In the car.

Charley: You goin' for a ride? I wanted to shoot some casino.

Willy (furiously): Casino! *(Incredulously.)* Don't you realize what today is?

Linda: Oh, he knows, Willy. He's just kidding you.

Willy: That's nothing to kid about!

Charley: No, Linda, what's goin' on?

Linda: He's playing in Ebbets Field.

Charley: Baseball in this weather?

Willy: Don't talk to him. Come on, come on! *(He is pushing them out.)*

Charley: Wait a minute, didn't you hear the news?

Willy: What?

Charley: Don't you listen to the radio? Ebbets Field just blew up.

Willy: You go to hell! *(Charley laughs. Pushing them out.)* Come on, come on! We're late.

Charley (as they go): Knock a homer, Biff, knock a homer!

Willy (the last to leave, turning to Charley): I don't think that was funny, Charley. This is the greatest day of his life.

Charley: Willy, when are you going to grow up?

Willy: Yeah, heh? When this game is over, Charley, you'll be laughing out of the other side of your face. They'll be calling him another Red Grange. Twenty-five thousand a year.

Charley (kidding): Is that so?

Willy: Yeah, that's so.

Charley: Well, then, I'm sorry, Willy. But tell me something.

Willy: What?

Charley: Who is Red Grange?

Willy: Put up your hands. Goddam you, put up your hands!

> *Charley, chuckling, shakes his head and walks away, around the left corner of the stage. Willy follows him. The music rises to a mocking frenzy.*

Willy: Who the hell do you think you are, better than everybody else? You don't know everything, you big, ignorant, stupid . . . Put up your hands!

> *Light rises, on the right side of the forestage, on a small table in the reception room of Charley's office. Traffic sounds are heard. Bernard, now mature, sits whistling to himself. A pair of tennis rackets and an overnight bag are on the floor beside him.*

Willy (offstage): What are you walking away for? Don't walk away! If you're going to say something say it to my face! I know you laugh at me behind my back. You'll laugh out of the other side of your goddam face after this game. Touch-down! Touchdown! Eighty thousand people! Touchdown! Right between the goal posts.

> *Bernard is a quiet, earnest, but self-assured young man. Willy's voice is coming from right upstage now. Bernard lowers his feet off the table and listens. Jenny, his father's secretary, enters.*

Jenny (distressed): Say, Bernard, will you go out in the hall?

Bernard: What is that noise? Who is it?

Jenny: Mr. Loman. He just got off the elevator.

Bernard (getting up): Who's he arguing with?

Jenny: Nobody. There's nobody with him. I can't deal with him any more, and your father gets all upset everytime he comes. I've got a lot of typing to do, and your father's waiting to sign it. Will you see him?

Willy (entering): Touchdown! Touch — *(He sees Jenny.)* Jenny, Jenny, good to see you. How're ya? Workin'? Or still honest?

Jenny: Fine. How've you been feeling?

Willy: Not much any more, Jenny. Ha, ha! *(He is surprised to see the rackets.)*

Bernard: Hello, Uncle Willy.

Willy (almost shocked): Bernard! Well, look who's here! *(He comes quickly, guiltily, to Bernard and warmly shakes his hand.)*

Bernard: How are you? Good to see you.

Willy: What are you doing here?

Bernard: Oh, just stopped by to see Pop. Get off my feet till my train leaves. I'm going to Washington in a few minutes.

Willy: Is he in?

Bernard: Yes, he's in his office with the accountant. Sit down.

Willy (sitting down): What're you going to do in Washington?

Bernard: Oh, just a case I've got there, Willy.

Willy: That so? *(Indicating the rackets.)* You going to play tennis there?

Bernard: I'm staying with a friend who's got a court.

Willy: Don't say. His own tennis court. Must be fine people, I bet.

Bernard: They are, very nice. Dad tells me Biff's in town.

Willy (with a big smile): Yeah, Biff's in. Working on a very big deal, Bernard.

Bernard: What's Biff doing?

Willy: Well, he's been doing very big things in the West. But he decided to establish himself here. Very big. We're having dinner. Did I hear your wife had a
boy?

Bernard: That's right. Our second.

Willy: Two boys! What do you know!

Bernard: What kind of a deal has Biff got?

Willy: Well, Bill Oliver — very big sporting-goods man — he wants Biff very badly.
Called him in from the West. Long distance, carte blanche, special deliveries.
Your friends have their own private tennis court?

Bernard: You still with the old firm, Willy?

Willy (after a pause): I'm — I'm overjoyed to see how you made the grade, Bernard, overjoyed. It's an encouraging thing to see a young man really —
really — Looks very good for Biff — very — *(He breaks off, then.)* Bernard —
(He is so full of emotion, he breaks off again.)

Bernard: What is it, Willy?

Willy (small and alone): What — what's the secret?

Bernard: What secret?

Willy: How — how did you? Why didn't he ever catch on?

Bernard: I wouldn't know that, Willy.

Willy (confidentially, desperately): You were his friend, his boyhood friend. There's
something I don't understand about it. His life ended after that Ebbets Field
game. From the age of seventeen nothing good ever happened to him.

Bernard: He never trained himself for anything.

Willy: But he did, he did. After high school he took so many correspondence
courses. Radio mechanics; television; God knows what, and never made the
slightest mark.

Bernard (taking off his glasses): Willy, do you want to talk candidly?

Willy (rising, faces Bernard): I regard you as a very brilliant man, Bernard. I value
your advice.

Bernard: Oh, the hell with the advice, Willy. I couldn't advise you. There's just one
thing I've always wanted to ask you. When he was supposed to graduate, and
the math teacher flunked him —

Willy: Oh, that son-of-a-bitch ruined his life.

Bernard: Yeah, but, Willy, all he had to do was go to summer school and make up
that subject.

Willy: That's right, that's right.

Bernard: Did you tell him not to go to summer school?

Willy: Me? I begged him to go. I ordered him to go!

Bernard: Then why wouldn't he go?

Willy: Why? Why! Bernard, that question has been trailing me like a ghost for the
last fifteen years. He flunked the subject, and laid down and died like a hammer hit him!

Bernard: Take it easy, kid.

Willy: Let me talk to you — I got nobody to talk to. Bernard, Bernard, was it my
fault? Y'see? It keeps going around in my mind, maybe I did something to
him. I got nothing to give him.

Bernard: Don't take it so hard.

Willy: Why did he lay down? What is the story there? You were his friend!

Bernard: Willy, I remember, it was June, and our grades came out. And he'd
flunked math.

Willy: That son-of-a-bitch!

Bernard: No, it wasn't right then. Biff just got very angry, I remember, and he was ready to enroll in summer school.

Willy (surprised): He was?

Bernard: He wasn't beaten by it at all. But then, Willy, he disappeared from the block for almost a month. And I got the idea that he'd gone up to New England to see you. Did he have a talk with you then?

Willy stares in silence.

Bernard: Willy?

Willy (with a strong edge of resentment in his voice): Yeah, he came to Boston. What about it?

Bernard: Well, just that when he came back—I'll never forget this, it always mystifies me. Because I'd thought so well of Biff, even though he'd always taken advantage of me. I loved him, Willy, y'know? And he came back after that month and took his sneakers—remember those sneakers with "University of Virginia" printed on them? He was so proud of those, wore them every day. And he took them down in the cellar, and burned them up in the furnace. We had a fist fight. It lasted at least half an hour. Just the two of us, punching each other down the cellar, and crying right through it. I've often thought of how strange it was that I knew he'd given up his life. What happened in Boston, Willy?

Willy looks at him as at an intruder.

Bernard: I just bring it up because you asked me.

Willy (angrily): Nothing. What do you mean, "What happened?" What's that got to do with anything?

Bernard: Well, don't get sore.

Willy: What are you trying to do, blame it on me? If a boy lays down is that my fault?

Bernard: Now, Willy, don't get—

Willy: Well, don't—don't talk to me that way! What does that mean, "What happened?"

Charley enters. He is in his vest, and he carries a bottle of bourbon.

Charley: Hey, you're going to miss that train. *(He waves the bottle.)*

Bernard: Yeah, I'm going. *(He takes the bottle.)* Thanks, Pop. *(He picks up his rackets and bag.)* Good-by, Willy, and don't worry about it. You know. "If at first you don't succeed . . ."

Willy: Yes, I believe in that.

Bernard: But sometimes, Willy, it's better for a man just to walk away.

Willy: Walk away?

Bernard: That's right.

Willy: But if you can't walk away?

Bernard (after a slight pause): I guess that's when it's tough. *(Extending his hand.)* Good-by, Willy.

Willy (shaking Bernard's hand): Good-by, boy.

Charley (an arm on Bernard's shoulder): How do you like this kid? Gonna argue a case in front of the Supreme Court.

Bernard (protesting): Pop!

Willy (genuinely shocked, pained, and happy): No! The Supreme Court!

Bernard: I gotta run. 'By, Dad!

Charley: Knock 'em dead, Bernard!

> *Bernard goes off.*

Willy (as Charley takes out his wallet): The Supreme Court! And he didn't even mention it!

Charley (counting out money on the desk): He don't have to — he's gonna do it.

Willy: And you never told him what to do, did you? You never took any interest in him.

Charley: My salvation is that I never took any interest in any thing. There's some money — fifty dollars. I got an accountant inside.

Willy: Charley, look . . . *(With difficulty.)* I got my insurance to pay. If you can manage it — I need a hundred and ten dollars.

> *Charley doesn't reply for a moment; merely stops moving.*

Willy: I'd draw it from my bank but Linda would know, and I . . .

Charley: Sit down, Willy.

Willy (moving toward the chair): I'm keeping an account of everything, remember. I'll pay every penny back. *(He sits.)*

Charley: Now listen to me, Willy.

Willy: I want you to know I appreciate . . .

Charley (sitting down on the table): Willy, what're you doin'? What the hell is goin' on in your head?

Willy: Why? I'm simply . . .

Charley: I offered you a job. You can make fifty dollars a week. And I won't send you on the road.

Willy: I've got a job.

Charley: Without pay? What kind of a job is a job without pay? *(He rises.)* Now, look, kid, enough is enough. I'm no genius but I know when I'm being insulted.

Willy: Insulted!

Charley: Why don't you want to work for me?

Willy: What's the matter with you? I've got a job.

Charley: Then what're you walkin' in here every week for?

Willy (getting up): Well, if you don't want me to walk in here —

Charley: I am offering you a job.

Willy: I don't want your goddam job!

Charley: When the hell are you going to grow up?

Willy (furiously): You big ignoramus, if you say that to me again I'll rap you one! I don't care how big you are! *(He's ready to fight.)*

> *Pause.*

Charley (kindly, going to him): How much do you need, Willy?

Willy: Charley, I'm strapped. I'm strapped. I don't know what to do. I was just fired.

Charley: Howard fired you?

Willy: That snotnose. Imagine that? I named him. I named him Howard.

Charley: Willy, when're you gonna realize that them things don't mean anything? You named him Howard, but you can't sell that. The only thing you got in this world is what you can sell. And the funny thing is that you're a salesman, and you don't know that.

Willy: I've always tried to think otherwise, I guess. I always felt that if a man was impressive, and well liked, that nothing —

Charley: Why must everybody like you? Who liked J. P. Morgan? Was he impressive? In a Turkish bath he'd look like a butcher. But with his pockets on he was very well liked. Now listen, Willy, I know you don't like me, and nobody can say I'm in love with you, but I'll give you a job because — just for the hell of it, put it that way. Now what do you say?

Willy: I — I just can't work for you, Charley.

Charley: What're you, jealous of me?

Willy: I can't work for you, that's all, don't ask me why.

Charley (angered, takes out more bills): You been jealous of me all your life, you damned fool! Here, pay your insurance. *(He puts the money in Willy's hand.)*

Willy: I'm keeping strict accounts.

Charley: I've got some work to do. Take care of yourself. And pay your insurance.

Willy (moving to the right): Funny, y'know? After all the highways, and the trains, and the appointments, and the years, you end up worth more dead than alive.

Charley: Willy, nobody's worth nothin' dead. *(After a slight pause.)* Did you hear what I said?

Willy stands still, dreaming.

Charley: Willy!

Willy: Apologize to Bernard for me when you see him. I didn't mean to argue with him. He's a fine boy. They're all fine boys, and they'll end up big — all of them. Someday they'll all play tennis together. Wish me luck, Charley. He saw Bill Oliver today.

Charley: Good luck.

Willy (on the verge of tears): Charley, you're the only friend I got. Isn't that a remarkable thing? *(He goes out.)*

Charley: Jesus!

Charley stares after him a moment and follows. All light blacks out. Suddenly raucous music is heard, and a red glow rises behind the screen at right. Stanley, a young waiter, appears, carrying a table, followed by Happy, who is carrying two chairs.

Stanley (putting the table down): That's all right, Mr. Loman, I can handle it myself. *(He turns and takes the chairs from Happy and places them at the table.)*

Happy (glancing around): Oh, this is better.

Stanley: Sure, in the front there you're in the middle of all kinds a noise. Whenever you got a party, Mr. Loman, you just tell me and I'll put you back here. Y'know, there's a lotta people they don't like it private, because when they go out they like to see a lotta action around them because they're sick and tired to stay in the house by theirself. But I know you, you ain't from Hackensack. You know what I mean?

Happy (sitting down): So how's it coming, Stanley?

Stanley: Ah, it's a dog's life. I only wish during the war they'd a took me in the Army. I coulda been dead by now.

Happy: My brother's back, Stanley.

Stanley: Oh, he come back, heh? From the Far West.

Happy: Yeah, big cattle man, my brother, so treat him right. And my father's coming too.

Stanley: Oh, your father too!

Happy: You got a couple of nice lobsters?

Stanley: Hundred per cent, big.

Happy: I want them with the claws.

Stanley: Don't worry, I don't give you no mice. *(Happy laughs.)* How about some wine? It'll put a head on the meal.

Happy: No. You remember, Stanley, that recipe I brought you from overseas? With the champagne in it?

Stanley: Oh, yeah, sure. I still got it tacked up yet in the kitchen. But that'll have to cost a buck apiece anyways.

Happy: That's all right.

Stanley: What'd you, hit a number or somethin'?

Happy: No, it's a little celebration. My brother is — I think he pulled off a big deal today. I think we're going into business together.

Stanley: Great! That's the best for you. Because a family business, you know what I mean? — that's the best.

Happy: That's what I think.

Stanley: 'Cause what's the difference? Somebody steals? It's in the family. Know what I mean? *(Sotto voce.°)* Like this bartender here. The boss is goin' crazy what kinda leak he's got in the cash register. You put it in but it don't come out.

Happy (raising his head): Sh!

Stanley: What?

Happy: You notice I wasn't lookin' right or left, was I?

Stanley: No.

Happy: And my eyes are closed.

Stanley: So what's the — ?

Happy: Strudel's comin'.

Stanley (catching on, looks around): Ah, no, there's no —

> He breaks off as a furred, lavishly dressed girl enters and sits at the next table. Both follow her with their eyes.

Stanley: Geez, how'd ya know?

Happy: I got radar or something. *(Staring directly at her profile.)* Oooooooo . . . Stanley.

Stanley: I think that's for you, Mr. Loman.

Happy: Look at that mouth. Oh, God. And the binoculars.

Stanley: Geez, you got a life, Mr. Loman.

Happy: Wait on her.

Stanley (going to the girl's table): Would you like a menu, ma'am?

Girl: I'm expecting someone, but I'd like a —

Happy: Why don't you bring her — excuse me, miss, do you mind? I sell champagne, and I'd like you to try my brand. Bring her a champagne, Stanley.

Girl: That's awfully nice of you.

Happy: Don't mention it. It's all company money. *(He laughs.)*

Girl: That's a charming product to be selling, isn't it?

Happy: Oh, gets to be like everything else. Selling is selling, y'know.

Girl: I suppose.

Happy: You don't happen to sell, do you?

Girl: No, I don't sell.

Sotto voce: Softly, "under the breath" (Italian).

Happy: Would you object to a compliment from a stranger? You ought to be on a magazine cover.

Girl (looking at him a little archly): I have been.

    Stanley comes in with a glass of champagne.

Happy: What'd I say before, Stanley? You see? She's a cover girl.

Stanley: Oh, I could see, I could see.

Happy (to the Girl): What magazine?

Girl: Oh, a lot of them. *(She takes the drink.)* Thank you.

Happy: You know what they say in France, don't you? "Champagne is the drink of the complexion" — Hya, Biff!

    Biff has entered and sits with Happy.

Biff: Hello, kid. Sorry I'm late.

Happy: I just got here. Uh, Miss — ?

Girl: Forsythe.

Happy: Miss Forsythe, this is my brother.

Biff: Is Dad here?

Happy: His name is Biff. You might've heard of him. Great football player.

Girl: Really? What team?

Happy: Are you familiar with football?

Girl: No, I'm afraid I'm not.

Happy: Biff is quarterback with the New York Giants.

Girl: Well, that is nice, isn't it? *(She drinks.)*

Happy: Good health.

Girl: I'm happy to meet you.

Happy: That's my name. Hap. It's really Harold, but at West Point they called me Happy.

Girl (now really impressed): Oh, I see. How do you do? *(She turns her profile.)*

Biff: Isn't Dad coming?

Happy: You want her?

Biff: Oh, I could never make that.

Happy: I remember the time that idea would never come into your head. Where's the old confidence, Biff?

Biff: I just saw Oliver —

Happy: Wait a minute. I've got to see that old confidence again. Do you want her? She's on call.

Biff: Oh, no. *(He turns to look at the Girl.)*

Happy: I'm telling you. Watch this. *(Turning to the Girl.)* Honey? *(She turns to him.)* Are you busy?

Girl: Well, I am . . . but I could make a phone call.

Happy: Do that, will you, honey? And see if you can get a friend. We'll be here for a while. Biff is one of the greatest football players in the country.

Girl (standing up): Well, I'm certainly happy to meet you.

Happy: Come back soon.

Girl: I'll try.

Happy: Don't try, honey, try hard.

    The Girl exits. Stanley follows, shaking his head in bewildered admiration.

Happy: Isn't that a shame now? A beautiful girl like that? That's why I can't get married. There's not a good woman in a thousand. New York is loaded with them, kid!

Biff: Hap, look—

Happy: I told you she was on call!

Biff (strangely unnerved): Cut it out, will ya? I want to say something to you.

Happy: Did you see Oliver?

Biff: I saw him all right. Now look, I want to tell Dad a couple of things and I want you to help me.

Happy: What? Is he going to back you?

Biff: Are you crazy? You're out of your goddam head, you know that?

Happy: Why? What happened?

Biff (breathlessly): I did a terrible thing today, Hap. It's been the strangest day I ever went through. I'm all numb, I swear.

Happy: You mean he wouldn't see you?

Biff: Well, I waited six hours for him, see? All day. Kept sending my name in. Even tried to date his secretary so she'd get me to him, but no soap.

Happy: Because you're not showin' the old confidence, Biff. He remembered you, didn't he?

Biff (stopping Happy with a gesture): Finally, about five o'clock, he comes out. Didn't remember who I was or anything. I felt like such an idiot, Hap.

Happy: Did you tell him my Florida idea?

Biff: He walked away. I saw him for one minute. I got so mad I could've torn the walls down! How the hell did I ever get the idea I was a salesman there? I even believed myself that I'd been a salesman for him! And then he gave me one look and — I realized what a ridiculous lie my whole life has been! We've been talking in a dream for fifteen years. I was a shipping clerk.

Happy: What'd you do?

Biff (with great tension and wonder): Well, he left, see. And the secretary went out. I was all alone in the waiting-room. I don't know what came over me, Hap. The next thing I know I'm in his office — paneled walls, everything. I can't explain it. I — Hap, I took his fountain pen.

Happy: Geez, did he catch you?

Biff: I ran out. I ran down all eleven flights. I ran and ran and ran.

Happy: That was an awful dumb — what'd you do that for?

Biff (agonized): I don't know, I just — wanted to take something, I don't know. You gotta help me, Hap, I'm gonna tell Pop.

Happy: You crazy? What for?

Biff: Hap, he's got to understand that I'm not the man somebody lends that kind of money to. He thinks I've been spiting him all these years and it's eating him up.

Happy: That's just it. You tell him something nice.

Biff: I can't.

Happy: Say you got a lunch date with Oliver tomorrow.

Biff: So what do I do tomorrow?

Happy: You leave the house tomorrow and come back at night and say Oliver is thinking it over. And he thinks it over for a couple of weeks, and gradually it fades away and nobody's the worse.

Biff: But it'll go on forever!

Happy: Dad is never so happy as when he's looking forward to something!

    Willy enters.

Happy: Hello, scout!

Willy: Gee, I haven't been here in years!

Stanley has followed Willy in and sets a chair for him. Stanley starts off but Happy stops him.

Happy: Stanley!

Stanley stands by, waiting for an order.

Biff *(going to Willy with guilt, as to an invalid):* Sit down, Pop. You want a drink?

Willy: Sure, I don't mind.

Biff: Let's get a load on.

Willy: You look worried.

Biff: N-no. *(To Stanley.)* Scotch all around. Make it doubles.

Stanley: Doubles, right. *(He goes.)*

Willy: You had a couple already, didn't you?

Biff: Just a couple, yeah.

Willy: Well, what happened, boy? *(Nodding affirmatively, with a smile.)* Everything go all right?

Biff *(takes a breath, then reaches out and grasps Willy's hand):* Pal . . . *(He is smiling bravely, and Willy is smiling too.)* I had an experience today.

Happy: Terrific, Pop.

Willy: That so? What happened?

Biff *(high, slightly alcoholic, above the earth):* I'm going to tell you everything from first to last. It's been a strange day. *(Silence. He looks around, composes himself as best he can, but his breath keeps breaking the rhythm of his voice.)* I had to wait quite a while for him, and —

Willy: Oliver.

Biff: Yeah, Oliver. All day, as a matter of cold fact. And a lot of — instances —facts, Pop, facts about my life came back to me. Who was it, Pop? Who ever said I was a salesman with Oliver?

Willy: Well, you were.

Biff: No, Dad, I was a shipping clerk.

Willy: But you were practically —

Biff *(with determination):* Dad, I don't know who said it first, but I was never a salesman for Bill Oliver.

Willy: What're you talking about?

Biff: Let's hold on to the facts tonight, Pop. We're not going to get anywhere bullin' around. I was a shipping clerk.

Willy *(angrily):* All right, now listen to me —

Biff: Why don't you let me finish?

Willy: I'm not interested in stories about the past or any crap of that kind because the woods are burning, boys, you understand? There's a big blaze going on all around. I was fired today.

Biff *(shocked):* How could you be?

Willy: I was fired, and I'm looking for a little good news to tell your mother, because the woman has waited and the woman has suffered. The gist of it is that I haven't got a story left in my head, Biff. So don't give me a lecture about facts and aspects. I am not interested. Now what've you got to say to me?

Stanley enters with three drinks. They wait until he leaves.

Willy: Did you see Oliver?

Biff: Jesus, Dad!

Willy: You mean you didn't go up there?

Happy: Sure he went up there.

Biff: I did. I — saw him. How could they fire you?

Willy (on the edge of his chair): What kind of a welcome did he give you?

Biff: He won't even let you work on commission?

Willy: I'm out! *(Driving.)* So tell me, he gave you a warm welcome?

Happy: Sure, Pop, sure!

Biff (driven): Well, it was kind of —

Willy: I was wondering if he'd remember you. *(To Happy.)* Imagine, man doesn't see him for ten, twelve years and gives him that kind of a welcome!

Happy: Damn right!

Biff (trying to return to the offensive): Pop, look —

Willy: You know why he remembered you, don't you? Because you impressed him in those days.

Biff: Let's talk quietly and get this down to the facts, huh?

Willy (as though Biff had been interrupting): Well, what happened? It's great news, Biff. Did he take you into his office or'd you talk in the waiting-room?

Biff: Well, he came in, see, and —

Willy (with a big smile): What'd he say? Betcha he threw his arm around you.

Biff: Well, he kinda —

Willy: He's a fine man. *(To Happy.)* Very hard man to see, y'know.

Happy (agreeing): Oh, I know.

Willy (to Biff): Is that where you had the drinks?

Biff: Yeah, he gave me a couple of — no, no!

Happy (cutting in): He told him my Florida idea.

Willy: Don't interrupt. *(To Biff.)* How'd he react to the Florida idea?

Biff: Dad, will you give me a minute to explain?

Willy: I've been waiting for you to explain since I sat down here! What happened? He took you into his office and what?

Biff: Well — I talked. And — and he listened, see.

Willy: Famous for the way he listens, y'know. What was his answer?

Biff: His answer was — *(He breaks off, suddenly angry.)* Dad, you're not letting me tell you what I want to tell you!

Willy (accusing, angered): You didn't see him, did you?

Biff: I did see him!

Willy: What'd you insult him or something? You insulted him, didn't you?

Biff: Listen, will you let me out of it, will you just let me out of it!

Happy: What the hell!

Willy: Tell me what happened!

Biff (to Happy): I can't talk to him!

> *A single trumpet note jars the ear. The light of green leaves stains the house, which holds the air of night and a dream. Young Bernard enters and knocks on the door of the house.*

Young Bernard (frantically): Mrs. Loman, Mrs. Loman!

Happy: Tell him what happened!

Biff (to Happy): Shut up and leave me alone!

Willy: No, no! You had to go and flunk math!

Biff: What math? What're you talking about?

Young Bernard: Mrs. Loman, Mrs. Loman!

> *Linda appears in the house, as of old.*

Willy (wildly): Math, math, math!

Biff: Take it easy, Pop!

Young Bernard: Mrs. Loman!

Willy (furiously): If you hadn't flunked you'd've been set by now!

Biff: Now, look, I'm gonna tell you what happened, and you're going to listen to me.

Young Bernard: Mrs. Loman!

Biff: I waited six hours —

Happy: What the hell are you saying?

Biff: I kept sending in my name but he wouldn't see me. So finally he . . . *(He continues unheard as light fades low on the restaurant.)*

Young Bernard: Biff flunked math!

Linda: No!

Young Bernard: Birnbaum flunked him! They won't graduate him!

Linda: But they have to. He's gotta go to the university. Where is he? Biff! Biff!

Young Bernard: No, he left. He went to Grand Central.

Linda: Grand — You mean he went to Boston!

Young Bernard: Is Uncle Willy in Boston?

Linda: Oh, maybe Willy can talk to the teacher. Oh, the poor, poor boy!

> *Light on house area snaps out.*

Biff (at the table, now audible, holding up a gold fountain pen): . . . so I'm washed up with Oliver, you understand? Are you listening to me?

Willy (at a loss): Yeah, sure. If you hadn't flunked —

Biff: Flunked what? What're you talking about?

Willy: Don't blame everything on me! I didn't flunk math — you did! What pen?

Happy: That was awful dumb, Biff, a pen like that is worth —

Willy (seeing the pen for the first time): You took Oliver's pen?

Biff (weakening): Dad, I just explained it to you.

Willy: You stole Bill Oliver's fountain pen!

Biff: I didn't exactly steal it! That's just what I've been explaining to you!

Happy: He had it in his hand and just then Oliver walked in, so he got nervous and stuck it in his pocket!

Willy: My God, Biff!

Biff: I never intended to do it, Dad!

Operator's Voice: Standish Arms, good evening!

Willy (shouting): I'm not in my room!

Biff (frightened): Dad, what's the matter? *(He and Happy stand up.)*

Operator: Ringing Mr. Loman for you!

Willy: I'm not there, stop it!

Biff (horrified, gets down on one knee before Willy): Dad, I'll make good, I'll make good. *(Willy tries to get to his feet. Biff holds him down.)* Sit down now.

Willy: No, you're no good, you're no good for anything.

Biff: I am, Dad, I'll find something else, you understand? Now don't worry about anything. *(He holds up Willy's face.)* Talk to me, Dad.

Operator: Mr. Loman does not answer. Shall I page him?

Willy (attempting to stand, as though to rush and silence the Operator): No, no, no!

Happy: He'll strike something, Pop.

Willy: No, no . . .

Biff (desperately, standing over Willy): Pop, listen! Listen to me! I'm telling you something good. Oliver talked to his partner about the Florida idea. You listening? He—he talked to his partner, and he came to me . . . I'm going to be all right, you hear? Dad, listen to me, he said it was just a question of the amount!

Willy: Then you . . . got it?

Happy: He's gonna be terrific, Pop!

Willy (trying to stand): Then you got it, haven't you? You got it! You got it!

Biff (agonized, holds Willy down): No, no. Look, Pop. I'm supposed to have lunch with them tomorrow. I'm just telling you this so you'll know that I can still make an impression, Pop. And I'll make good somewhere, but I can't go tomorrow, see?

Willy: Why not? You simply—

Biff: But the pen, Pop!

Willy: You give it to him and tell him it was an oversight!

Happy: Sure, have lunch tomorrow!

Biff: I can't say that—

Willy: You were doing a crossword puzzle and accidentally used his pen!

Biff: Listen, kid, I took those balls years ago, now I walk in with his fountain pen? That clinches it, don't you see? I can't face him like that! I'll try elsewhere.

Page's Voice: Paging Mr. Loman!

Willy: Don't you want to be anything?

Biff: Pop, how can I go back?

Willy: You don't want to be anything, is that what's behind it?

Biff (now angry at Willy for not crediting his sympathy): Don't take it that way! You think it was easy walking into that office after what I'd done to him? A team of horses couldn't have dragged me back to Bill Oliver!

Willy: Then why'd you go?

Biff: Why did I go? Why did I go! Look at you! Look at what's become of you!

Off left, The Woman laughs.

Willy: Biff, you're going to lunch tomorrow, or—

Biff: I can't go. I've got no appointment!

Happy: Biff, for . . . !

Willy: Are you spiting me?

Biff: Don't take it that way! Goddammit!

Willy (strikes Biff and falters away from the table): You rotten little louse! Are you spiting me?

The Woman: Someone's at the door, Willy!

Biff: I'm no good, can't you see what I am?

Happy (separating them): Hey, you're in a restaurant! Now cut it out, both of you! *(The girls enter.)* Hello, girls, sit down.

The Woman laughs, off left.

Miss Forsythe: I guess we might as well. This is Letta.

The Woman: Willy, are you going to wake up?

Biff (ignoring Willy): How're ya, miss, sit down. What do you drink?

Miss Forsythe: Letta might not be able to stay long.

Letta: I gotta get up very early tomorrow. I got jury duty. I'm so excited! Were you fellows ever on a jury?

Biff: No, but I been in front of them! *(The girls laugh.)* This is my father.

Letta: Isn't he cute? Sit down with us, Pop.

Happy: Sit him down, Biff!

Biff (going to him): Come on, slugger, drink us under the table. To hell with it! Come on, sit down, pal.

On Biff's last insistence, Willy is about to sit.

The Woman (now urgently): Willy, are you going to answer the door!

The Woman's call pulls Willy back. He starts right, befuddled.

Biff: Hey, where are you going?
Willy: Open the door.
Biff: The door?
Willy: The washroom . . . the door . . . where's the door?
Biff (leading Willy to the left): Just go straight down.

Willy moves left.

The Woman: Willy, Willy, are you going to get up, get up, get up, get up?

Willy exits left.

Letta: I think it's sweet you bring your daddy along.
Miss Forsythe: Oh, he isn't really your father!
Biff (at left, turning to her resentfully): Miss Forsythe, you've just seen a prince walk by. A fine, troubled prince. A hard-working, unappreciated prince. A pal, you understand? A good companion. Always for his boys.
Letta: That's so sweet.
Happy: Well, girls, what's the program? We're wasting time. Come on, Biff. Gather round. Where would you like to go?
Biff: Why don't you do something for him?
Happy: Me!
Biff: Don't you give a damn for him, Hap?
Happy: What're you talking about? I'm the one who —
Biff: I sense it, you don't give a good goddamn about him. *(He takes the rolled-up hose from his pocket and puts it on the table in front of Happy.)* Look what I found in the cellar, for Christ's sake. How can you bear to let it go on?
Happy: Me? Who goes away? Who runs off and —
Biff: Yeah, but he doesn't mean anything to you. You could help him — I can't! Don't you understand what I'm talking about? He's going to kill himself, don't you know that?
Happy: Don't I know it! Me!
Biff: Hap, help him! Jesus . . . help him . . . Help me, help me, I can't bear to look at his face! *(Ready to weep, he hurries out, up right.)*
Happy (starting after him): Where are you going?
Miss Forsythe: What's he so mad about?
Happy: Come on, girls, we'll catch up with him.
Miss Forsythe (as Happy pushes her out): Say, I don't like that temper of his!
Happy: He's just a little overstrung, he'll be all right!
Willy (off left, as The Woman laughs): Don't answer! Don't answer!
Letta: Don't you want to tell your father —
Happy: No, that's not my father. He's just a guy. Come on, we'll catch Biff, and, honey, we're going to paint this town! Stanley, where's the check! Hey, Stanley!

They exit. Stanley looks toward left.

Stanley (calling to Happy indignantly): Mr. Loman! Mr. Loman!

Stanley picks up a chair and follows them off. Knocking is heard off left. The Woman enters, laughing. Willy follows her. She is in a black slip; he is buttoning his shirt. Raw, sensuous music accompanies their speech.

Willy: Will you stop laughing? Will you stop?

The Woman: Aren't you going to answer the door? He'll wake the whole hotel.

Willy: I'm not expecting anybody.

The Woman: Whyn't you have another drink, honey, and stop being so damn self-centered?

Willy: I'm so lonely.

The Woman: You know you ruined me, Willy? From now on, whenever you come to the office, I'll see that you go right through to the buyers. No waiting at my desk any more, Willy. You ruined me.

Willy: That's nice of you to say that.

The Woman: Gee, you are self-centered! Why so sad? You are the saddest, self-centeredest soul I ever did see-saw. *(She laughs. He kisses her.)* Come on inside, drummer boy. It's silly to be dressing in the middle of the night. *(As knocking is heard.)* Aren't you going to answer the door?

Willy: They're knocking on the wrong door.

The Woman: But I felt the knocking. And he heard us talking in here. Maybe the hotel's on fire!

Willy (his terror rising): It's a mistake.

The Woman: Then tell him to go away!

Willy: There's nobody there.

The Woman: It's getting on my nerves, Willy. There's somebody standing out there and it's getting on my nerves!

Willy (pushing her away from him): All right, stay in the bathroom here, and don't come out. I think there's a law in Massachusetts about it, so don't come out. It may be that new room clerk. He looked very mean. So don't come out. It's a mistake, there's no fire.

The knocking is heard again. He takes a few steps away from her, and she vanishes into the wing. The light follows him, and now he is facing Young Biff, who carries a suitcase. Biff steps toward him. The music is gone.

Biff: Why didn't you answer?

Willy: Biff! What are you doing in Boston?

Biff: Why didn't you answer? I've been knocking for five minutes, I called you on the phone —

Willy: I just heard you. I was in the bathroom and had the door shut. Did anything happen home?

Biff: Dad — I let you down.

Willy: What do you mean?

Biff: Dad . . .

Willy: Biffo, what's this about? *(Putting his arm around Biff.)* Come on, let's go downstairs and get you a malted.

Biff: Dad, I flunked math.

Willy: Not for the term?

Biff: The term. I haven't got enough credits to graduate.

Willy: You mean to say Bernard wouldn't give you the answers?

Biff: He did, he tried, but I only got a sixty-one.

Willy: And they wouldn't give you four points?

Biff: Birnbaum refused absolutely. I begged him, Pop, but he won't give me those points. You gotta talk to him before they close the school. Because if he saw the kind of man you are, and you just talked to him in your way, I'm sure he'd come through for me. The class came right before practice, see, and I didn't go enough. Would you talk to him? He'd like you, Pop. You know the way you could talk.

Willy: You're on. We'll drive right back.

Biff: Oh, Dad, good work! I'm sure he'll change it for you!

Willy: Go downstairs and tell the clerk I'm checkin' out. Go right down.

Biff: Yes, sir! See, the reason he hates me, Pop — one day he was late for class so I got up at the blackboard and imitated him. I crossed my eyes and talked with a lithp.

Willy (laughing): You did? The kids like it?

Biff: They nearly died laughing!

Willy: Yeah? What'd you do?

Biff: The thquare root of thixthy twee is . . . *(Willy bursts out laughing; Biff joins him.)* And in the middle of it he walked in!

Willy laughs and The Woman joins in offstage.

Willy (without hesitation): Hurry downstairs and —

Biff: Somebody in there?

Willy: No, that was next door.

The Woman laughs offstage.

Biff: Somebody got in your bathroom!

Willy: No, it's the next room, there's a party —

The Woman (enters, laughing. She lisps this): Can I come in? There's something in the bathtub, Willy, and it's moving!

Willy looks at Biff, who is staring open-mouthed and horrified at The Woman.

Willy: Ah — you better go back to your room. They must be finished painting by now. They're painting her room so I let her take a shower here. Go back, go back . . . *(He pushes her.)*

The Woman (resisting): But I've got to get dressed, Willy, I can't —

Willy: Get out of here! Go back, go back . . . *(Suddenly striving for the ordinary):* This is Miss Francis, Biff, she's a buyer. They're painting her room. Go back, Miss Francis, go back . . .

The Woman: But my clothes, I can't go out naked in the hall!

Willy (pushing her offstage): Get outa here! Go back, go back!

Biff slowly sits down on his suitcase as the argument continues offstage.

The Woman: Where's my stockings? You promised me stockings, Willy!

Willy: I have no stockings here!

The Woman: You had two boxes of size nine sheers for me, and I want them!

Willy: Here, for God's sake, will you get outa here!

The Woman (enters holding a box of stockings): I just hope there's nobody in the hall. That's all I hope. *(To Biff.)* Are you football or baseball?

Biff: Football.

The Woman (angry, humiliated): That's me too. G'night. *(She snatches her clothes from Willy, and walks out.)*

Willy (after a pause): Well, better get going. I want to get to the school first thing in the morning. Get my suits out of the closet. I'll get my valise. *(Biff doesn't* move.) What's the matter? (*Biff remains motionless, tears falling.*) She's a buyer. Buys for J. H. Simmons. She lives down the hall — they're painting. You don't imagine — (*He breaks off. After a pause.*) Now listen, pal, she's just a buyer. She sees merchandise in her room and they have to keep it looking just so . . . (*Pause. Assuming command.*) All right, get my suits. (*Biff doesn't move.*) Now stop crying and do as I say. I gave you an order. Biff, I gave you an order! Is that what you do when I give you an order? How dare you cry! (*Putting his arm around Biff.*) Now look, Biff, when you grow up you'll understand about these things. You mustn't — you mustn't overemphasize a thing like this. I'll see Birnbaum first thing in the morning.

Biff: Never mind.

Willy (getting down beside Biff): Never mind! He's going to give you those points. I'll see to it.

Biff: He wouldn't listen to you.

Willy: He certainly will listen to me. You need those points for the U. of Virginia.

Biff: I'm not going there.

Willy: Heh? If I can't get him to change that mark you'll make it up in summer school. You've got all summer to —

Biff (his weeping breaking from him): Dad . . .

Willy (infected by it): Oh, my boy . . .

Biff: Dad . . .

Willy: She's nothing to me, Biff. I was lonely, I was terribly lonely.

Biff: You — you gave her Mama's stockings! (*His tears break through and he rises to go.*)

Willy (grabbing for Biff): I gave you an order!

Biff: Don't touch me, you — liar!

Willy: Apologize for that!

Biff: You fake! You phony little fake! You fake! (*Overcome, he turns quickly and weeping fully goes out with his suitcase. Willy is left on the floor on his knees.*)

Willy: I gave you an order! Biff, come back here or I'll beat you! Come back here! I'll whip you!

Stanley comes quickly in from the right and stands in front of Willy.

Willy (shouts at Stanley): I gave you an order . . .

Stanley: Hey, let's pick it up, pick it up, Mr. Loman. (*He helps Willy to his feet.*) Your boys left with the chippies. They said they'll see you home.

A second waiter watches some distance away.

Willy: But we were supposed to have dinner together.

Music is heard, Willy's theme.

Stanley: Can you make it?

Willy: I'll — sure, I can make it. (*Suddenly concerned about his clothes.*) Do I — I look all right?

Stanley: Sure, you look all right. (*He flicks a speck off Willy's lapel.*)

Willy: Here — here's a dollar.

Stanley: Oh, your son paid me. It's all right.

Willy (putting it in Stanley's hand): No, take it. You're a good boy.

Stanley: Oh, no, you don't have to . . .

Willy: Here — here's some more, I don't need it any more. (*After a slight pause.*) Tell me — is there a seed store in the neighborhood?

Stanley: Seeds? You mean like to plant?

As Willy turns, Stanley slips the money back into his jacket pocket.

Willy: Yes. Carrots, peas . . .

Stanley: Well, there's hardware stores on Sixth Avenue, but it may be too late now.

Willy (anxiously): Oh, I'd better hurry. I've got to get some seeds. *(He starts off to the right.)* I've got to get some seeds, right away. Nothing's planted. I don't have a thing in the ground.

Willy hurries out as the light goes down. Stanley moves over to the right after him, watches him off. The other waiter has been staring at Willy.

Stanley (to the waiter): Well, whatta you looking at?

The waiter picks up the chairs and moves off right. Stanley takes the table and follows him. The light fades on this area. There is a long pause, the sound of the flute coming over. The light gradually rises on the kitchen, which is empty. Happy appears at the door of the house, followed by Biff. Happy is carrying a large bunch of long-stemmed roses. He enters the kitchen, looks around for Linda. Not seeing her, he turns to Biff, who is just outside the house door, and makes a gesture with his hands, indicating "Not here, I guess." He looks into the living-room and freezes. Inside, Linda, unseen, is seated, Willy's coat on her lap. She rises ominously and quietly and moves toward Happy, who backs up into the kitchen, afraid.

Happy: Hey, what're you doing up? *(Linda says nothing but moves toward him implacably.)* Where's Pop? *(He keeps backing to the right, and now Linda is in full view in the doorway to the living-room.)* Is he sleeping?

Linda: Where were you?

Happy (trying to laugh it off): We met two girls, Mom, very fine types. Here, we brought you some flowers. *(Offering them to her.)* Put them in your room, Ma.

She knocks them to the floor at Biff's feet. He has now come inside and closed the door behind him. She stares at Biff, silent.

Happy: Now what'd you do that for? Mom, I want you to have some flowers —

Linda (cutting Happy off, violently to Biff): Don't you care whether he lives or dies?

Happy (going to the stairs): Come upstairs, Biff.

Biff (with a flare of disgust, to Happy): Go away from me! *(To Linda.)* What do you mean, lives or dies? Nobody's dying around here, pal.

Linda: Get out of my sight! Get out of here!

Biff: I wanna see the boss.

Linda: You're not going near him!

Biff: Where is he? *(He moves into the living-room and Linda follows.)*

Linda (shouting after Biff): You invite him for dinner. He looks forward to it all day — *(Biff appears in his parents' bedroom, looks around, and exits.)* — and then you desert him there. There's no stranger you'd do that to!

Happy: Why? He had a swell time with us. Listen, when I — *(Linda comes back into the kitchen)* — desert him I hope I don't outlive the day!

Linda: Get out of here!

Happy: Now look, Mom . . .

Linda: Did you have to go to women tonight? You and your lousy rotten whores!

Biff re-enters the kitchen.

Happy: Mom, all we did was follow Biff around trying to cheer him up! *(To Biff.)* Boy, what a night you gave me!

Linda: Get out of here, both of you, and don't come back! I don't want you tormenting him any more. Go on now, get your things together! *(To Biff.)* You can sleep in his apartment. *(She starts to pick up the flowers and stops herself.)* Pick up this stuff, I'm not your maid any more. Pick it up, you bum, you!

Happy turns his back to her in refusal. Biff slowly moves over and gets down on his knees, picking up the flowers.

Linda: You're a pair of animals! Not one, not another living soul would have had the cruelty to walk out on that man in a restaurant!

Biff (not looking at her): Is that what he said?

Linda: He didn't have to say anything. He was so humiliated he nearly limped when he came in.

Happy: But, Mom, he had a great time with us —

Biff (cutting him off violently): Shut up!

Without another word, Happy goes upstairs.

Linda: You! You didn't even go in to see if he was all right!

Biff (still on the floor in front of Linda, the flowers in his hand; with self-loathing): No. Didn't. Didn't do a damned thing. How do you like that, heh? Left him babbling in a toilet.

Linda: You louse. You . . .

Biff: Now you hit it on the nose! *(He gets up, throws the flowers in the wastebasket.)* The scum of the earth, and you're looking at him!

Linda: Get out of here!

Biff: I gotta talk to the boss, Mom. Where is he?

Linda: You're not going near him. Get out of this house!

Biff (with absolute assurance, determination): No. We're gonna have an abrupt conversation, him and me.

Linda: You're not talking to him!

Hammering is heard from outside the house, off right. Biff turns toward the noise.

Linda (suddenly pleading): Will you please leave him alone?

Biff: What's he doing out there?

Linda: He's planting the garden!

Biff (quietly): Now? Oh, my God!

Biff moves outside, Linda following. The light dies down on them and comes up on the center of the apron as Willy walks into it. He is carrying a flashlight, a hoe, and handful of seed packets. He raps the top of the hoe sharply to fix it firmly, and then moves to the left, measuring off the distance with his foot. He holds the flashlight to look at the seed packets, reading off the instructions. He is in the blue of night.

Willy: Carrots . . . quarter-inch apart. Rows . . . one-foot rows. *(He measures it off.)* One foot. *(He puts down a package and measures off.)* Beets. *(He puts down another package and measures again.)* Lettuce. *(He reads the package, puts it down.)* One foot — *(He breaks off as Ben appears at the right and moves slowly down to him.)* What a proposition, ts, ts. Terrific, terrific. 'Cause she's suffered, Ben, the woman has suffered. You understand me? A man can't go out the way he came in, Ben, a man has got to add up to something. You can't, you can't — (*Ben moves toward him as though to interrupt.*) You gotta consider, now. Don't answer so quick. Remember, it's a guaranteed twenty-thousand-dollar proposition. Now look, Ben, I want you to go through the ins and outs of this thing with me. I've got nobody to talk to, Ben, and the woman has suffered, you hear me?

Ben (standing still, considering): What's the proposition?

Willy: It's twenty thousand dollars on the barrelhead. Guaranteed, gilt-edged, you understand?

Ben: You don't want to make a fool of yourself. They might not honor the policy.

Willy: How can they dare refuse? Didn't I work like a coolie to meet every premium on the nose? And now they don't pay off? Impossible!

Ben: It's called a cowardly thing, William.

Willy: Why? Does it take more guts to stand here the rest of my life ringing up a zero?

Ben (yielding): That's a point, William. (*He moves, thinking, turns.*) And twenty thousand — that *is* something one can feel with the hand, it is there.

Willy (now assured, with rising power): Oh, Ben, that's the whole beauty of it! I see it like a diamond, shining in the dark, hard and rough, that I can pick up and touch in my hand. Not like — like an appointment! This would not be another damned-fool appointment, Ben, and it changes all the aspects. Because he thinks I'm nothing, see, and so he spites me. But the funeral —(*Straightening up.*) Ben, that funeral will be massive! They'll come from Maine, Massachusetts, Vermont, New Hampshire! All the old-timers with the strange license plates — that boy will be thunder-struck, Ben, because he never realized — I am known! Rhode Island, New York, New Jersey — I am known, Ben, and he'll see it with his eyes once and for all. He'll see what I am, Ben! He's in for a shock, that boy!

Ben (coming to the edge of the garden): He'll call you a coward.

Willy (suddenly fearful): No, that would be terrible.

Ben: Yes. And a damned fool.

Willy: No, no, he mustn't, I won't have that! (*He is broken and desperate.*)

Ben: He'll hate you William.

The gay music of the Boys is heard.

Willy: Oh, Ben, how do we get back to all the great times? Used to be so full of light, and comradeship, the sleigh-riding in winter, and the ruddiness on his cheeks. And always some kind of good news coming up, always something nice coming up ahead. And never even let me carry the valises in the house, and simonizing, simonizing that little red car! Why, why can't I give him something and not have him hate me?

Ben: Let me think about it. (*He glances at his watch.*) I still have a little time. Remarkable proposition, but you've got to be sure you're not making a fool of yourself.

Ben drifts off upstage and goes out of sight. Biff comes down from the left.

Willy (suddenly conscious of Biff, turns and looks up at him, then begins picking up the packages of seeds in confusion): Where the hell is that seed? (*Indignantly.*) You can't see nothing out here! They boxed in the whole goddamn neighborhood!

Biff: There are people all around here. Don't you realize that?

Willy: I'm busy. Don't bother me.

Biff (taking the hoe from Willy): I'm saying good-by to you, Pop. *(Willy looks at him, silent, unable to move.)* I'm not coming back any more.

Willy: You're not going to see Oliver tomorrow?

Biff: I've got no appointment, Dad.

Willy: He put his arm around you, and you've got no appointment?

Biff: Pop, get this now, will you? Everytime I've left it's been a fight that sent me out of here. Today I realized something about myself and I tried to explain it to you and I — I think I'm just not smart enough to make any sense out of it for you. To hell with whose fault it is or anything like that. *(He takes Willy's arm.)* Let's just wrap it up, heh? Come on in, we'll tell Mom. *(He gently tries to pull Willy to left.)*

Willy (frozen, immobile, with guilt in his voice): No, I don't want to see her.

Biff: Come on! *(He pulls again, and Willy tries to pull away.)*

Willy (highly nervous): No, no, I don't want to see her.

Biff (tries to look into Willy's face, as if to find the answer there): Why don't you want to see her?

Willy (more harshly now): Don't bother me, will you?

Biff: What do you mean, you don't want to see her? You don't want them calling you yellow, do you? This isn't your fault; it's me, I'm a bum. Now come inside! *(Willy strains to get away.)* Did you hear what I said to you?

Willy pulls away and quickly goes by himself into the house. Biff follows.

Linda (to Willy): Did you plant, dear?

Biff (at the door, to Linda): All right, we had it out. I'm going and I'm not writing any more.

Linda (going to Willy in the kitchen): I think that's the best way, dear. 'Cause there's no use drawing it out, you'll just never get along.

Willy doesn't respond.

Biff: People ask where I am and what I'm doing, you don't know, and you don't care. That way it'll be off your mind and you can start brightening up again. All right? That clears it, doesn't it? *(Willy is silent, and Biff goes to him.)* You gonna wish me luck, scout? *(He extends his hand.)* What do you say?

Linda: Shake his hand, Willy.

Willy (turning to her, seething with hurt): There's no necessity to mention the pen at all, y'know.

Biff (gently): I've got no appointment, Dad.

Willy (erupting fiercely): He put his arm around . . . ?

Biff: Dad, you're never going to see what I am, so what's the use of arguing? If I strike oil I'll send you a check. Meantime forget I'm alive.

Willy (to Linda): Spite, see?

Biff: Shake hands, Dad.

Willy: Not my hand.

Biff: I was hoping not to go this way.

Willy: Well, this is the way you're going. Good-by.

Biff looks at him a moment, then turns sharply and goes to the stairs.

Willy (stops him with): May you rot in hell if you leave this house!

Biff (turning): Exactly what is it that you want from me?

Willy: I want you to know, on the train, in the mountains, in the valleys, wherever you go, that you cut down your life for spite!

Biff: No, no.

Willy: Spite, spite, is the word of your undoing! And when you're down and out, remember what did it. When you're rotting somewhere beside the railroad tracks, remember, and don't you dare blame it on me!

Biff: I'm not blaming it on you!

Willy: I won't take the rap for this, you hear?

Happy comes down the stairs and stands on the bottom step, watching.

Biff: That's just what I'm telling you!

Willy (sinking into a chair at the table, with full accusation): You're trying to put a knife in me — don't think I don't know what you're doing!

Biff: All right, phony! Then let's lay it on the line. (*He whips the rubber tube out of his pocket and puts it on the table.*)

Happy: You crazy —

Linda: Biff! (*She moves to grab the hose, but Biff holds it down with his hand.*)

Biff: Leave it there! Don't move it!

Willy (not looking at it): What is that?

Biff: You know goddam well what that is.

Willy (caged, wanting to escape): I never saw that.

Biff: You saw it. The mice didn't bring it into the cellar! What is this supposed to do, make a hero out of you? This supposed to make me sorry for you?

Willy: Never heard of it.

Biff: There'll be no pity for you, you hear it? No pity!

Willy (to Linda): You hear the spite!

Biff: No, you're going to hear the truth — what you are and what I am!

Linda: Stop it!

Willy: Spite!

Happy (coming down toward Biff): You cut it now!

Biff (to Happy): The man don't know who we are! The man is gonna know! (*To Willy.*) We never told the truth for ten minutes in this house!

Happy: We always told the truth!

Biff (turning on him): You big blow, are you the assistant buyer? You're one of the two assistants to the assistant, aren't you?

Happy: Well, I'm practically —

Biff: You're practically full of it! We all are! And I'm through with it. (*To Willy.*) Now hear this, Willy, this is me.

Willy: I know you!

Biff: You know why I had no address for three months? I stole a suit in Kansas City and I was in jail. (*To Linda, who is sobbing.*) Stop crying. I'm through with it.

Linda turns away from them, her hands covering her face.

Willy: I suppose that's my fault!

Biff: I stole myself out of every good job since high school!

Willy: And whose fault is that?

Biff: And I never got anywhere because you blew me so full of hot air I could never stand taking orders from anybody! That's whose fault it is!

Willy: I hear that!

Linda: Don't, Biff!

Biff: It's goddam time you heard that! I had to be boss big shot in two weeks, and I'm through with it!

Willy: Then hang yourself! For spite, hang yourself!

Biff: No! Nobody's hanging himself, Willy! I ran down eleven flights with a pen in my hand today. And suddenly I stopped, you hear me? And in the middle of that office building, do you hear this? I stopped in the middle of that building and I saw — the sky. I saw the things that I love in this world. The work and the food and time to sit and smoke. And I looked at the pen and said to myself, what the hell am I grabbing this for? Why am I trying to become what I don't want to be? What am I doing in an office, making a contemptuous, begging fool of myself, when all I want is out there, waiting for me the minute I say I know who I am! Why can't I say that, Willy? *(He tries to make Willy face him, but Willy pulls away and moves to the left.)*

Willy (with hatred, threateningly): The door of your life is wide open!

Biff: Pop! I'm a dime a dozen, and so are you!

Willy (turning on him now in an uncontrolled outburst): I am not a dime a dozen! I am Willy Loman, and you are Biff Loman!

Biff starts for Willy, but is blocked by Happy. In his fury, Biff seems on the verge of attacking his father.

Biff: I am not a leader of men, Willy, and neither are you. You were never anything but a hard-working drummer who landed in the ash can like all the rest of them! I'm one dollar an hour, Willy! I tried seven states and couldn't raise it. A buck an hour! Do you gather my meaning? I'm not bringing home any prizes any more, and you're going to stop waiting for me to bring them home!

Willy (directly to Biff): You vengeful, spiteful mutt!

Biff breaks from Happy. Willy, in fright, starts up the stairs. Biff grabs him.

Biff (at the peak of his fury): Pop, I'm nothing! I'm nothing, Pop. Can't you understand that? There's no spite in it any more. I'm just what I am, that's all.

Biff's fury has spent itself, and he breaks down, sobbing, holding on to Willy, who dumbly fumbles for Biff's face.

Willy (astonished): What're you doing? What're you doing? *(To Linda.)* Why is he crying?

Biff (crying, broken): Will you let me go, for Christ's sake? Will you take that phony dream and burn it before something happens? *(Struggling to contain himself, he pulls away and moves to the stairs.)* I'll go in the morning. Put him — put him to bed. *(Exhausted, Biff moves up the stairs to his room.)*

Willy (after a long pause, astonished, elevated): Isn't that — isn't that remarkable? Biff — he likes me!

Linda: He loves you, Willy!

Happy (deeply moved): Always did, Pop.

Willy: Oh, Biff! *(Staring wildly.)* He cried! Cried to me. *(He is choking with his love, and now cries out his promise.)* That boy — that boy is going to be magnificent!

Ben appears in the light just outside the kitchen.

Ben: Yes, outstanding, with twenty thousand behind him.

Linda (sensing the racing of his mind, fearfully, carefully): Now come to bed, Willy. It's all settled now.

Willy (finding it difficult not to rush out of the house): Yes, we'll sleep. Come on. Go to sleep, Hap.

Ben: And it does take a great kind of a man to crack the jungle.

In accents of dread, Ben's idyllic music starts up.

Happy (his arm around Linda): I'm getting married, Pop, don't forget it. I'm changing everything. I'm gonna run that department before the year is up. You'll see, Mom. *(He kisses her.)*

Ben: The jungle is dark but full of diamonds, Willy.

Willy turns, moves, listening to Ben.

Linda: Be good. You're both good boys, just act that way, that's all.

Happy: 'Night, Pop. *(He goes upstairs.)*

Linda (to Willy): Come, dear.

Ben (with greater force): One must go in to fetch a diamond out.

Willy (to Linda, as he moves slowly along the edge of the kitchen, toward the door): I just want to get settled down, Linda. Let me sit alone for a little.

Linda (almost uttering her fear): I want you upstairs.

Willy (taking her in his arms): In a few minutes, Linda. I couldn't sleep right now. Go on, you look awful tired. *(He kisses her.)*

Ben: Not like an appointment at all. A diamond is rough and hard to the touch.

Willy: Go on now. I'll be right up.

Linda: I think this is the only way, Willy.

Willy: Sure, it's the best thing.

Ben: Best thing!

Willy: The only way. Everything is gonna be — go on, kid, get to bed. You look so tired.

Linda: Come right up.

Willy: Two minutes.

Linda goes into the living-room, then reappears in her bedroom. Willy moves just outside the kitchen door.

Willy: Loves me. *(Wonderingly.)* Always loved me. Isn't that a remarkable thing? Ben, he'll worship me for it!

Ben (with promise): It's dark there, but full of diamonds.

Willy: Can you imagine that magnificence with twenty thousand dollars in his pocket?

Linda (calling from her room): Willy! Come up!

Willy (calling into the kitchen): Yes! Yes. Coming! It's very smart, you realize that, don't you, sweetheart? Even Ben sees it. I gotta go, baby. 'By! 'By! *(Going over to Ben, almost dancing.)* Imagine? When the mail comes he'll be ahead of Bernard again!

Ben: A perfect proposition all around.

Willy: Did you see how he cried to me? Oh, if I could kiss him, Ben!

Ben: Time, William, time!

Willy: Oh, Ben, I always knew one way or another we were gonna make it, Biff and I!

Ben (looking at his watch): The boat. We'll be late. *(He moves slowly off into the darkness.)*

Willy (elegiacally, turning to the house): Now when you kick off, boy, I want a seventy-yard boot, and get right down the field under the ball, and when you hit, hit low and hit hard, because it's important, boy. *(He swings around and faces the audience.)* There's all kinds of important people in the stands, and the first thing you know . . . *(Suddenly realizing he is alone.)* Ben! Ben, where do I . . . ? *(He makes a sudden movement of search.)* Ben, how do I . . . ?

Linda (calling): Willy, you coming up?

Willy (uttering a gasp of fear, whirling about as if to quiet her): Sh! *(He turns around as if to find his way; sounds, faces, voices, seem to be swarming in upon him and he flicks at them, crying.)* Sh! Sh! *(Suddenly music, faint and high, stops him. It rises in intensity, almost to an unbearable scream. He goes up and down on his toes, and rushes off around the house.)* Shhh!

Linda: Willy?

> *There is no answer. Linda waits. Biff gets up off his bed. He is still in his clothes. Happy sits up. Biff stands listening.*

Linda (with real fear): Willy, answer me! Willy!

> *There is the sound of a car starting and moving away at full speed.*

Linda: No!

Biff (rushing down the stairs): Pop!

> *As the car speeds off, the music crashes down in a frenzy of sound, which becomes the soft pulsation of a single cello string. Biff slowly returns to his bedroom. He and Happy gravely don their jackets. Linda slowly walks out of her room. The music has developed into a dead march. The leaves of day are appearing over everything. Charley and Bernard, somberly dressed, appear and knock on the kitchen door. Biff and Happy slowly descend the stairs to the kitchen as Charley and Bernard enter. All stop a moment when Linda, in clothes of mourning, bearing a little bunch of roses, comes through the draped doorway into the kitchen. She goes to Charley and takes his arm. Now all move toward the audience, through the wall-line of the kitchen. At the limit of the apron, Linda lays down the flowers, kneels, and sits back on her heels. All stare down at the grave.*

REQUIEM

Charley: It's getting dark, Linda.

> *Linda doesn't react. She stares at the grave.*

Biff: How about it, Mom? Better get some rest, heh? They'll be closing the gate soon.

> *Linda makes no move. Pause.*

Happy (deeply angered): He had no right to do that. There was no necessity for it. We would've helped him.

Charley (grunting): Hmmm.

Biff: Come along, Mom.

Linda: Why didn't anybody come?

Charley: It was a very nice funeral.

Linda: But where are all the people he knew? Maybe they blame him.

Charley: Naa. It's a rough world, Linda. They wouldn't blame him.

Linda: I can't understand it. At this time especially. First time in thirty-five years we were just about free and clear. He only needed a little salary. He was even finished with the dentist.

Charley: No man only needs a little salary.

Linda: I can't understand it.

Biff: There were a lot of nice days. When he'd come home from a trip; or on Sundays, making the stoop; finishing the cellar; putting on the new porch; when he built the extra bathroom; and put up the garage. You know something, Charley, there's more of him in that front stoop than in all the sales he ever made.

Charley: Yeah. He was a happy man with a batch of cement.

Linda: He was so wonderful with his hands.

Biff: He had the wrong dreams. All, all, wrong.

Happy (almost ready to fight Biff): Don't say that!

Biff: He never knew who he was.

Charley (stopping Happy's movement and reply. To Biff): Nobody dast blame this man. You don't understand: Willy was a salesman. And for a salesman, there is no rock bottom to the life. He don't put a bolt to a nut, he don't tell you the law or give you medicine. He's a man way out there in the blue, riding on a smile and a shoeshine. And when they start not smiling back — that's an earthquake. And then you get yourself a couple of spots on your hat, and you're finished. Nobody dast blame this man. A salesman is got to dream, boy. It comes with the territory.

Biff: Charley, the man didn't know who he was.

Happy (infuriated): Don't say that!

Biff: Why don't you come with me, Happy?

Happy: I'm not licked that easily. I'm staying right in this city, and I'm gonna beat this racket! *(He looks at Biff, his chin set.)* The Loman Brothers!

Biff: I know who I am, kid.

Happy: All right, boy. I'm gonna show you and everybody else that Willy Loman did not die in vain. He had a good dream. It's the only dream you can have — to come out number-one man. He fought it out here, and this is where I'm gonna win it for him.

Biff (with a hopeless glance at Happy, bends toward his mother): Let's go, Mom.

Linda: I'll be with you in a minute. Go on, Charley. *(He hesitates.)* I want to, just for a minute. I never had a chance to say good-by.

Charley moves away, followed by Happy. Biff remains a slight distance up and left of Linda. She sits there, summoning herself. The flute begins, not far away, playing behind her speech.

Linda: Forgive me, dear. I can't cry. I don't know what it is, but I can't cry. I don't understand it. Why did you ever do that? Help me, Willy, I can't cry. It seems to me that you're just on another trip. I keep expecting you. Willy, dear, I can't cry. Why did you do it? I search and search and I search, and I can't understand it, Willy. I made the last payment on the house today. Today, dear. And there'll be nobody home. *(A sob rises in her throat.)* We're free and clear. *(Sobbing more fully, released.)* We're free. *(Biff comes slowly toward her.)* We're free . . . We're free . . .

Biff lifts her to her feet and moves out up right with her in his arms. Linda sobs quietly. Bernard and Charley come together and follow them, followed by Happy. Only the music of the flute is left on the darkening stage as over the house the hard towers of the apartment buildings rise into sharp focus, and

The Curtain Falls.

CONNECTIONS TO OTHER SELECTIONS

1. Compare and contrast Willy Loman with Polonius in Shakespeare's *Hamlet* (p. 1238). To what extent is each character wise, foolish, deluded, and hypocritical? Explain why Loman can be seen as a tragic character while Polonius cannot be.

2. Read David Hernandez's poem "All-American" (p. 813), and compare its treatment of the American dream with the one in *Death of a Salesman*. How do the tones of the two works differ?

3. What similarities do you find between the endings of *Death of a Salesman* and August Wilson's *Fences* (p. 1589)? Are the endings happy, unhappy, or something else?

Perspectives

ARTHUR MILLER (1915–2005)
Tragedy and the Common Man 1949

In this age few tragedies are written. It has often been held that the lack is due to a paucity of heroes among us, or else that modern man has had the blood drawn out of his organs of belief by the skepticism of science, and the heroic attack on life cannot feed on an attitude of reserve and circumspection. For one reason or another, we are often held to be below tragedy — or tragedy above us. The inevitable conclusion is, of course, that the tragic mode is archaic, fit only for the very highly placed, the kings or the kingly, and where this admission is not made in so many words it is most often implied.

I believe that the common man is as apt a subject for tragedy in its highest sense as kings were. On the face of it this ought to be obvious in the light of modern psychiatry, which bases its analysis upon classic formulations, such as the Oedipus and Orestes complexes, for instance, which were enacted by royal beings, but which apply to everyone in similar emotional situations.

More simply, when the question of tragedy in art is not at issue, we never hesitate to attribute to the well-placed and the exalted the very same mental processes as the lowly. And finally, if the exaltation of tragic action were truly a property of the high-bred character alone, it is inconceivable that the mass of mankind should cherish tragedy above all other forms, let alone be capable of understanding it.

As a general rule, to which there may be exceptions unknown to me, I think the tragic feeling is evoked in us when we are in the presence of a character who is ready to lay down his life, if need be, to secure one thing — his sense of personal dignity. From Orestes to Hamlet, Medea to Macbeth, the underlying struggle is that of the individual attempting to gain his "rightful" position in his society.

Sometimes he is one who has been displaced from it, sometimes one who seeks to attain it for the first time, but the fateful wound from which the inevitable events spiral is the wound of indignity, and its dominant force is indignation. Tragedy, then, is the consequence of a man's total compulsion to evaluate himself justly.

In the sense of having been initiated by the hero himself, the tale always reveals what has been called his "tragic flaw," a failing that is not peculiar to grand or elevated characters. Nor is it necessarily a weakness. The flaw, or crack in the character, is really nothing — and need be nothing — but his inherent unwillingness to remain passive in the face of what he conceives to be a challenge to his dignity, his image of his rightful status. Only the passive, only those who accept their lot without active retaliation, are "flawless." Most of us are in that category.

But there are among us today, as there always have been, those who act against the scheme of things that degrades them, and in the process of action, everything we have accepted out of fear or insensitivity or ignorance is shaken before us and examined, and from this total onslaught by an individual against the seemingly stable cosmos surrounding us — from this total examination of the "unchangeable" environment — comes the terror and the fear that is classically associated with tragedy.

More important, from this total questioning of what has been previously unquestioned, we learn. And such a process is not beyond the common man. In revolutions around the world, these past thirty years, he has demonstrated again and again this inner dynamic of all tragedy.

Insistence upon the rank of the tragic hero, or the so-called nobility of his character, is really but a clinging to the outward forms of tragedy. If rank or nobility of character was indispensable, then it would follow that the problems of those with rank were the particular problems of tragedy. But surely the right of one monarch to capture the domain from another no longer raises our passions, nor are our concepts of justice what they were to the mind of an Elizabethan king.

The quality in such plays that does shake us, however, derives from the underlying fear of being displaced, the disaster inherent in being torn away from our chosen image of what and who we are in this world. Among us today this fear is as strong, and perhaps stronger, than it ever was. In fact, it is the common man who knows this fear best.

Now, if it is true that tragedy is the consequence of a man's total compulsion to evaluate himself justly, his destruction in the attempt posits a wrong or an evil in his environment. And this is precisely the morality of tragedy and its lesson. The discovery of the moral law, which is what the enlightenment of tragedy consists of, is not the discovery of some abstract or metaphysical quantity.

The tragic right is a condition of life, a condition in which the human personality is able to flower and realize itself. The wrong is the condition which suppresses man, perverts the flowing out of his love and creative instinct. Tragedy enlightens — and it must, in that it points the heroic finger at the enemy of man's freedom. The thrust for freedom is the quality in tragedy which exalts. The revolutionary questioning of the stable environment is what terrifies. In no way is the common man debarred from such thoughts or such actions.

Seen in this light, our lack of tragedy may be partially accounted for by the turn which modern literature has taken toward the purely psychiatric view of life, or the purely sociological. If all our miseries, our indignities, are born and bred within our minds, then all action, let alone the heroic action, is obviously impossible.

And if society alone is responsible for the cramping of our lives, then the protagonist must needs be so pure and faultless as to force us to deny his validity as a character. From neither of these views can tragedy derive, simply because neither represents a balanced concept of life. Above all else, tragedy requires the finest appreciation by the writer of cause and effect.

No tragedy can therefore come about when its author fears to question absolutely everything, when he regards any institution, habit, or custom as being either everlasting, immutable, or inevitable. In the tragic view the need of man to wholly realize himself is the only fixed star, and whatever it is that hedges his nature and lowers it is ripe for attack and examination. Which is not to say that tragedy must preach revolution.

The Greeks could probe the very heavenly origin of their ways and return to confirm the rightness of laws. And Job could face God in anger, demanding his right, and end in submission. But for a moment everything is in suspension, nothing is accepted, and in this stretching and tearing apart of the cosmos, in the very action of so doing, the character gains "size," the tragic stature which is spuriously attached to the royal or the high born in our minds. The commonest of men may take on that stature to the extent of his willingness to throw all he has into the contest, the battle to secure his rightful place in his world.

There is a misconception of tragedy with which I have been struck in review after review, and in many conversations with writers and readers alike. It is the idea that tragedy is of necessity allied to pessimism. Even the dictionary says nothing more about the word than that it means a story with a sad or unhappy ending. This impression is so firmly fixed that I almost hesitate to claim that in truth tragedy implies more optimism in its author than does comedy, and that its final result ought to be the reinforcement of the onlooker's brightest opinions of the human animal.

For, if it is true to say that in essence the tragic hero is intent upon claiming his whole due as a personality, and if this struggle must be total and without reservation, then it automatically demonstrates the indestructible will of man to achieve his humanity.

The possibility of victory must be there in tragedy. Where pathos rules, where pathos is finally derived, a character has fought a battle he could not possibly have won. The pathetic is achieved when the protagonist is, by virtue of his witlessness, his insensitivity, or the very air he gives off, incapable of grappling with a much superior force.

Pathos truly is the mode for the pessimist. But tragedy requires a nicer balance between what is possible and what is impossible. And it is curious, although edifying, that the plays we revere, century after century, are the tragedies. In them, and in them alone, lies the belief — optimistic, if you will — in the perfectibility of man.

It is time, I think, that we who are without kings, took up this bright thread of our history and followed it to the only place it can possibly lead in our time — the heart and spirit of the average man.

From *Theater Essays of Arthur Miller*

CONSIDERATIONS FOR CRITICAL THINKING AND WRITING

1. According to Miller, why is there a "lack" (para. 1) of tragedy in modern literature? Why do psychological and sociological accounts of human behavior limit the possibilities for tragedy?

2. Why is the "common man" (para. 2) a suitable subject for tragedy? How does Miller's view of tragedy compare with Aristotle's (p. 1165)?

3. What distinction does Miller make between tragedy and pathos? Which term best characterizes Willy Loman in *Death of a Salesman*? Explain why.

ARTHUR MILLER (1915–2005)

On Biff and Willy Loman 1950

A serious theme is entertaining to the extent that it is not trifled with, not cleverly angled, but met in head-on collision. [The audience] will not consent to suffer while the creators stand by with tongue in cheek. They have a way of knowing. Nobody can blame them.

And there have been certain disappointments, one above all. I am sorry the self-realization of the older son, Biff, is not a weightier counterbalance to Willy's disaster in the audience's mind.

And certain things are more clearly known, or so it seems now. We want to give of ourselves, and yet all we train for is to take, as though nothing less will keep the world at a safe distance. Every day we contradict our will to create, which is to give. The end of man is not security, but without security we are without the elementary condition of humaneness.

To me the tragedy of Willy Loman is that he gave his life, or sold it, in order to justify the waste of it. It is the tragedy of a man who did believe that he alone was not meeting the qualifications laid down for mankind by those clean-shaven frontiersmen who inhabit the peaks of broadcasting and advertising offices. From those forests of canned goods high up near the sky, he heard the thundering command to succeed as it ricocheted down the newspaper-lined canyons of his city, heard not a human voice, but a wind of a voice to which no human can reply in kind, except to stare into the mirror at a failure.

From the *New York Times*, February 5, 1950

CONSIDERATIONS FOR CRITICAL THINKING AND WRITING

1. Discuss what you think Miller has in mind when he refers to Biff's "self-realization" (para. 2).
2. According to Miller, what influences Willy to make him feel like a failure?
3. How is Miller's description of "the tragedy of Willy Loman" (para. 4) dramatized in the play?

No Child . . .

Raised in the multicultural Lower East Side of Manhattan, Nilaja Sun has always been at home with the energy, variety, and ethnic richness that New York City has to offer. A graduate of Franklin and Marshall College, she has appeared in a number of New York plays and in television shows such as *30 Rock* and *Law and Order: SVU*. She has worked as a teaching artist in New York City's Epic Theatre Company's "Journeys" program, which introduces theater to city students through the study and

Thos Robinson/Getty Images.

production of a single play in their school. Written and first produced when she was only twenty-six years old, *No Child . . .* reflects some of Sun's experience as a teaching artist and has won a number of prizes, including an Outer Critics Circle Award, an Obie Award, a John Gassner Award, and a San Francisco Bay Area Theatre Critics Circle Award.

The raucous class depicted in this play is both a challenge and an eye-opener into the comic and chaotic lives of students that Sun takes seriously. She manages to teach — and learn — from an unlikely, unpromising group of kids who take for granted that they will be left behind.

Nilaja Sun (b. 1974)

No Child . . .   2007

NOTES: *This play may be performed with one actor or with as many as sixteen actors. The play takes place in several locations but is best staged in a fluid style with lights and sounds suggesting scene changes.*

CHARACTERS

(In order of appearance:)
Janitor Baron, eighties, Narrator
Ms. Sun, thirties, teaching artist
Ms. Tam, twenties, teacher
Coca, sixteen, student
Jerome, eighteen, student
Brian, sixteen, student
Shondrika, sixteen, student
Xiomara, sixteen, student
Jose, seventeen, student
Chris, fifteen, student
Mrs. Kennedy, school principal
Security Guard, any age
Phillip, sixteen, student
Mrs. Projensky, substitute teacher
Mr. Johnson, Teacher
Doña Guzman, seventies, grandmother to Jose Guzman

See Plays in Performance insert.
Carol Rosegg.

TIME: Now

PLACE: New York

SCENE 1

School. Morning. Janitor enters, mopping floor as he sings.

Janitor: Trouble in mind.
    I'm Blue.
    But I won't be blue always.

Cuz the sun's gonna shine
In my back door someday.
(To audience.)

Hear that? Silence. Beautiful silence, pure silence. The kind of silence that only comes from spending years in the back woods. We ain't in the back woods (though I'm thinking 'bout retirin' there). It's 8:04 AM — five minutes before the start of the day. And, we on the second floor of Malcolm X High School in the Bronx, U.S.A. Right over there is my Janitor's closet, just right of the girls' bathroom where the smell of makeup, hair pomade, and gossip fills the air in the morning light. There's Mrs. Kennedy's room — she the principal. For seventeen years, been leading this group of delinquents — Oh I'm sorry, academically and emotionally challenged youth. She got a lot to work with! Seventeen feet below my very own, lay one hundred-thousand-dollar worth of a security system. This include two metal-detecting machines, seven metal-detecting wands, five school guards, and three N.Y.C. police officers. All armed. Guess all we missing is a bomb-sniffing dog. Right over there's Ms. Tam's class, she one of them new teachers. Worked as an associate in the biggest investment firm in New York then coming home from a long dreary day at work, read an ad on the subway — ya'll know the ones that offer you a lifetime of glorious purpose and meaning if you just become a New York City teacher. Uh-huh — the devil's lair on the IRT. I adore Ms. Tam, she kind, docile, but I don't think she know what she got herself into. See, I been working here since 1958 and I done seen some teachers come and go, I said I seen teachers come and go. Ah! One more time for good luck, I seen teachers come and go and I do believe it is one of the hardest jobs in the whole wide world. Shoot, I don't gotta tell you that, y'all look like smart folk! The most underpaid, underappreciated, *underpaid* job in this crazy universe. But for some miracle, every year God creates people that grow up knowing that's what they gonna do for the rest of they life. God, ain't He sometin'! Now, you might say to me, "Jackson Baron Copeford the Third. Boy, what you doin' up dere on dat stage? You ain't no actor." That I know and neither are these kids you about to meet. *(He clears his throat.)* What you about to see is a story about a play within a play within a play. And a teacher (or as she likes to call herself — a teaching artist — just so as people know she do somethin' else on her free time). The kids call her Ms. Sun and in two minutes from now she gonna walk up them stairs towards the janitor's room and stop right at Ms. Tam's class. She gonna be something they done never seen before. Now I know what you're thinking: "Oh, Baron. I know about the public schools. I watch Eyewitness News." What I got to say to that? HUSH! You don't know unless you been in the schools on a day-to-day basis. HUSH! You don't know unless you been a teacher, administrator, student, or custodial staff. HUSH! Cuz you could learn a little sometin'. Here's lesson number one: Taking the 6 train, in eighteen minutes, you can go from Fifty-ninth Street, one of the richest congressional districts in the nation, all the way up to Brook Ave. in the Bronx, where Malcolm X High is, the poorest congressional district in the nation. In only eighteen minutes. HUSH!

SCENE 2

Before class.

Ms. Sun (On the phone in the hallway.): Mr. Pulaski! Hi, it's Nilaja Sun from Bergen Street. 280 Bergen. Apartment four? Hey! Mr. Pulaski, thanks for being so patient, I know how late my rent is . . . By the way, how's your wife Margaret? Cool. And your son Josh? Long Island University. That's serious. Oh he's gonna love it and he'll be close to home. But yes, I apologize for not getting you last month's rent on time, but see the IRS put a levy on my bank account and I just can't retrieve any money from it right now. Well, it should be cleared by Tuesday but the real reason why I called was to say I'm startin' a new teaching program up here in the Bronx and it's a six-week-long workshop and they're paying me exactly what I owe you so . . . what's that? Theater. I'm teaching theater. A play actually. It's called *Our Country's Good* . . . Have you heard of it? Well it's about a group of convicts that put on a play . . . So the kids are actually gonna be doing a play within a play within . . . What's that? Ah, yes, kids today need more discipline and less self-expression. Less "lulalula" and more daily structure like Catholic school during Pope Pius the Twelfth. On the flip side of the matter, having gone to Catholic school for thirteen years, I didn't even know I was black until college. *(She roars her laughter.)* Sir? Sir, are you still there? *(Bell rings.)* I gotta go teach, sir. Are we cool with getting you that money by the twenty-fifth? How about the thirtieth? Thirty-first? I know, don't push it. You rock. Yes, I'm still an actor. No, not in anything right now. But soon. Yes, sir, happy Lent to you too, sir.

SCENE 3

Classroom.

Ms. Tam: Ms. Sun? Come on in. I'm Cindy Tam and I'm so excited to have your program here in our English class. Sorry we weren't able to meet the last four times you set up a planning meeting but so much has been going on in my life. Is it true you've been a teaching artist for seven years? In New York City? Wow. That's amazing. I'm a new teacher. They don't know that. It's a *challenge.* The kids are really *spirited.* Kaswan, where are you going? Well, we're going to be starting in a few minutes and I would strongly suggest you not leave. *(Listens.)* OK, but be back in five minutes, um, Veronica, stop hitting Chris and calling him a motherfucker. I'm sorry, please stop hitting Chris and calling him a motherfucker. Thanks, Veronica. Sorry, like I said, very excited you're here. Where is everyone? The kids usually come in twenty to thirty minutes late because it's so early. I know it's only a forty-one-minute class but I've been installing harsher penalties for anyone who comes in after fifteen. After five? OK, we'll try that. Well, what we *can* do today is start the program in ten minutes and wait for the bulk of them to come in, eat their breakfast, and . . . You wanna start now? But there are only seven kids here. The rest of them will ask what's going on and what am I gonna say to each late student? *(Scared out of her wits.)* OK. Then, we'll start. Now. Class! Please welcome Ms. Sun. She's going to be teaching you a play, and teaching you about acting, and how to act and we're gonna do a play and it's gonna be fun.

Coca: Fun? This is stupid already. I don't wanna act. I wanna do vocabulary.

Jerome: Vocab? Hello, Ms. Sun. Thank you for starting the class on time. Since we usually be the only ones on time.

Brian: Niggah, you ain't never on time.

Jerome: Shut up, bitch motherfucker.

Ms. Tam: Jerome, Brian? What did I tell you about the offensive language?

Jerome: Yo, yo. We know. Pork-fried rice wonton coming up.

Ms. Tam: I heard that, Jerome.

Jerome: Sorry, Ms. Tam.

Brian: (Accent.) Solly, Ms. Tam.

Ms. Tam: Go on, Ms. Sun! *(Beat.)*

Ms. Sun: Ah, well, I'm Ms. Sun and I will be with you all for the next six weeks and by the end of those glorious weeks, you would have read a play, analyzed the play, been cast in it, rehearsed it and lastly performed it. It's gonna be a whirl-wind spectacle that I want you to start inviting your parents and friends and loved ones to come see . . . What's that? No, it's not *Raisin in the Sun* . . . No, not *West Side Story.* It's a play called *Our Country's Good.*

Coca: Ew. This is some patrionism?

Ms. Sun: Patriotism? No. It's a play based in Australia in 1788 and it's written by a woman named Timberlake Wertenbaker.

Brian: Yo, Justin Timberlake done wrote himself a play. "Gonna rock yo' body. Today. Dance with me."

Ms. Tam: Brian, focus?

Brian: "People say she a gold digga, but she don't mess with no broke niggas."

Ms. Tam: Brian!!! Put down the Red Bull.

Brian: Beef-fried rice.

Ms. Tam: Brian.

Brian: Vegetable-fried rice.

Jerome: Ay yo! This some white shit. Ain't this illegal to teach this white shit no mo'?

Ms. Sun: Are you done?

Jerome: Huh?

Ms. Sun: Are you done?

Jerome: What?

Ms. Sun: With your spiel? With your little spiel?

Jerome: Yeah.

Ms. Sun: Because I'm trying to tell you what the play is about and I can't when you keep on interrupting.

Jerome: Oh my bad. Damn. She got attitude. I like that.

Shondrika: I don't. What's this play about anyway?

Ms. Sun: Well, what's your name?

Shondrika: Shondrika.

Ms. Sun: Well, Shondrika . . .

Shondrika: Shondrika!

Ms. Sun: Shondrika?

Shondrika: Shondrika!!!

Ms. Sun: Shondrika!!!

Shondrika: Close enough.

Ms. Sun: Ah-hah . . . *Our Country's Good* is about a group of convicts.

Xiomara: What are convicts?

Jerome: Jailbirds, you dumb in a can. Get it? *(Laugh/clap.)* Dominican! Dominican!

Ms. Sun: . . . And they put on a play called *The Recruiting Officer.* You'll be reading . . .

Coca: We gotta read?

Jerome: Aw hell no.

Ms. Tam: Yes, you'll be reading, but you're also gonna be creating a community.

Jerome: Ay yo! Last time I created a community the cops came. *(Latecomers enter.)*

Ms. Tam: Kaswan, Jose, Jennifer, Malika, Talifa, Poughkeepsie, come on in, you're late. What's your excuse this time, Jose?

Jose: Sorry, Miss. But that faggot Mr. Smith was yelling at us to stop running to class. Fucking faggot.

Ms. Sun: ENOUGH!

Jose: Who? Who this?

Ms. Sun: Hi. I'm Ms. Sun. Take your seats *now.* And as of today and for the next six weeks, when I'm in this classroom, you will not be using the word *faggot* or *bitch* or *nigga* or *motherfucker* or *motherfuckerniggabitchfaggot.* Anymore. Dominicans shall not be called and will not call each other dumb in a cans or platanos.

Coca: *Ah, y pero quien e heta? Esa prieta?*

Ms. Sun: *La prieta soy yo, senorita. (Coca is speechless.)*

Brian: Shwimp fwy why! Shwimp fwy why!

Ms. Sun: We will respect our teacher's ethnicity.

Brian: Shwimp fwy why??? *(No one else laughs.)*

Ms. Sun: Ladies will not call each other heifers or hos.

Shondrika: Shoot! That's what I'm talkin' about.

Ms. Sun: We will start class on time. We will eat our breakfast beforehand. And from now on we are nothing but thespians.

Xiomara: Lesbians? I ain't no Rosie O'Donnell.

Ms. Sun: No, no! Thespian! It means actor, citizen, lover of all things great.

Xiomara: I love that hard cash that bling-bling.

Ms. Sun: Say it with me, class, thespian.

Xiomara: *(Bored.)* Thespian.

Ms. Sun: Thespian!

Jerome: *(Bored.)* Thespian.

Ms. Sun: Thespian!

Coca: Thespian, already, damn!

Ms. Sun: Now, let's get up and form a circle.

Shondrika: Get up? Aw hell no!

Jose: Miss, we not supposed to do exercises this early.

Ms. Tam: Come on guys, stand up. Stand up.

Coca: Miss, this is mad boring.

Ms. Sun: Boredom, my love, usually comes from boring people.

Brian: OOOOOOOOOOOOH!

Coca: *(Dissed.)* What's that supposed to mean?

Brian: That's O.D., yo! Oh she played you, yo!

Jerome: Ay yo, shut yo trap! Miss, I could be the lovable and charming leading man that gets all the honies' numbers?

Ms. Sun: We'll see.

Jerome: Miss, can I get your number? *(Beat.)* Nah, I'm just playing. Let's do this, yo. Get up. *(They get up.)*

Ms. Sun: OK, thank you . . .

Jerome: Jerome!

Ms. Sun: Jerome. Great circle! Let's take a deep breath in and out. In . . .

Brian: Ohm! Nah! I'm just playing. Keep going. Keep going. Keep going. Keep going.

Ms. Sun: . . . and out . . . In . . .

Coca: I'm hungry. What time it is?

Ms. Sun: . . . and out . . . stretch with me, will you? Now, who here has ever seen a play? *(No one raises their hand . . . but Chris.)* Really? Which show?

Chris: Star Wars. It was a live reenactment.

Ms. Sun: Was it in a theater?

Chris: Yeah. We all wore outfits and costumes and acted alongside the movie.

Jerome: Damn, Chris, you like SupaDupaJamaicanNerdNegro.

Chris: And for that, I zap you. *(To Ms. Sun.)* You really gonna make us act onstage?

Ms. Sun: Yup.

Chris: I'm scared.

Ms. Sun: Yeah, well guess what? Before I walked in here, even with all my acting and teaching experience, I was scared and nervous too, but you get over it once you get a feel for the audience and you see all of your parents and your friends and your teachers smiling at you. Did you guys know that public speaking is the number one fear for all humans — even greater than death?

Jerome: What? They ain't never lived in the hood.

Jose: But, Miss, you should be scared of this class, cuz we supposed to be the worst class in the school.

Ms. Tam: It's true. They are.

Ms. Sun: Really, well, in the past thirty-five minutes, I've met some pretty amazing young adults, thinkers, debaters, thespians . . .

Brian: Lesbians.

Ms. Sun: Keep breathing! *(Bell rings.)* Oh no, listen, read scenes one through five for the next time. Thanks guys, you are great.

Ms. Tam: Wow. That was amazing. You're really great with the kids. *(Beat.)* Just to let you know. They're probably not going to read the play and they are probably going to lose the handout and probably start to cut your class and their parents probably won't come to the show. Probably. OK, bye.

Ms. Sun: Bye. *(She watches her leave.)* For all our sake, Ms. Tam, I hope you're probably wrong.

Scene 4

School hallway.

Mrs. Kennedy: Ms. Sun, hi, Mrs. Kennedy — the principal, so glad to meet you. Sorry about the attendance, Ms. Tam is a new teacher and we need all these kids to pass five Regents exams in the next two months. The pressure's on. Let me know when you'll be needing the auditorium. There are four schools in this building and it's like fighting diseased lions to book a night in it. But, you're priority. We've given you one of the most challenging classes. But I believe in them. I believe in you. Tyesha, can I have a word? *(She walks off. Security guard stops Sun.)*

Security Guard: Y'ave pass ta leave. I said do you have a pass to leave? Oh, you a teaching artist? Oh. Cuz you look like one a them. Well, excuse me for livin'! *(To other guards.)* Just trying to do mi job. I don't know the difference 'tween the teachers, teaching artists, parents, Board of Ed people, and these animals comin' in here. I don' know da difference. Just tryin' to do mi job. *(To student.)* Girl, girl! Whatcha t'ink dis is? You can't go in wifoot goin' tru da detector. I don care if you just walked out and now you come back in. Rules are rules. Put ya bag in and yo wallet and your selfish phone.

(Beep.) Go back. Ya belt.

(Beep.) Go back. Ya earrings.

(Beep.) Go back. Ya shoes. Don't sass me!

(Beep.) Go back. Ya hair . . . t'ings.

(Beep.) Go back. Ya jewelry. Oh, oh I don' have time for your attitude. Open your arms, spread your legs. Oh, oh I don' care about your science class. Should know betta' than to just waltz in 'ere ten minutes 'fore class. Got ta give it one whole hour. Lemme see yo I.D. Don' have? Can't come in. Excuse?!!! What ya name is? Shondrika Jones! I don' care about ya Regents. Go, Go, Go back home. Next time don' bring all dat bling and don' bring all dat belt and don' bring all dat sass. Who ya t'ink ya is? The mayor of New York City? Slut! *(To another student.)* Boy, boy, don't you pass me! *(Light shift.)*

Janitor: *(To audience.)* Your tax dollars at work! As Ms. Sun makes her way back home on the train, she thinks to herself.

SCENE 5

Subway car.

Ms. Sun: What will these six weeks bring? How will I persuade them to act onstage? *(Beat.)* Why did I choose a play about convicts? These kids aren't convicts. The kids in Rikers are convicts. These kids are just in tenth grade. They've got the world telling them they are going to end up in jail. Why would I choose a play about convicts? Why couldn't I choose a play about kings and queens in Africa or the triumphs of the Taino Indian? This totally wouldn't jive if I were white and trying to do this. How dare I! Why would I choose to do a play about convicts?

SCENE 6

Classroom.

Jerome: Because we treated like convicts every day.

Ms. Tam: Jerome, raise your hand.

Jerome: *(Raises hand.)* We treated like convicts every day.

Ms. Sun: How do you mean?

Shondrika: First, we wake up to bars on our windows.

Coca: Then, our moms and dads.

Shondrika: You got a dad?

Coca: Yeah . . . so? Then our mom tells us where to go, what to do, and blah, blah, blah.

Jerome: Then, we walk in a uniformed line towards the subways, cramming into a ten-by-forty-foot cell *(Laughs.)* checking out the fly honies.

Brian: But there ain't no honies in jail, know what I'm saying?

Jerome: Unless, you there long enough, what, what!

Ms. Sun: Then, class, you'll walk into another line at the bodega at the corner store, to get what?

Xiomara: Breakfast.

Ms. Sun: And what's for breakfast?

Xiomara: Welch's Orange and a Debbie snack cake.

Ms. Sun: Exactly, then what?

Shondrika: Then, we go to school.

Chris: . . . Where a cool electronic object points out our every metal flaw.

Jerome: Damn, Chris, you read way too much sci-fi!

Shondrika: Then we go to a class they tell us we gotta go to, with a teacher we gotta learn from and a play we gotta do.

Ms. Sun: And now that you feel like prisoners . . . open to page twenty-seven. Phillip says, "Watkin: Man is born free, and everywhere he is in chains." What *don't* people expect from prisoners?

Jose: For them to succeed in life . . .

Ms. Sun: But, in the play . . .

Coca: They succeed by doing the exact opposite of what people expect.

Ms. Sun: And so . . . how does that relate to your lives?

Shondrika: Shoot, don't nobody expect us to do nothing but drop out, get pregnant, go to jail . . .

Brian: . . . or work for the MTA.

Xiomara: My mom works for the MTA, nigga. Sorry, Miss . . . NEGRO.

Shondrika: So, dese characters is kinda going through what we kinda going through right now.

Ms. Sun: Kinda, yeah. And so . . . Brian . . .

Brian: By us doing the show, see what I'm saying, we could prove something to ourselves and our moms and her dad and Mrs. Kennedy and Ms. Tam that we is the shi . . . shining stars of the school, see what I'm saying?

Ms. Sun: Great, turn to Act One, Scene Six. Can I have a volunteer to read? (*Sun looks around.*)

Shondrika: Shoot, I'll read, give me this: "We are talking about criminals, often hardened criminals. They have a habit of vice and crime. Habits . . ."

Jose: Damn, Ma, put some feeling into that!

Shondrika: I don't see you up here reading, Jose.

Jose: Cuz you the actress of the class.

Shondrika: (*Realizing she is the "actress" of the class.*) "Habits are difficult to BREAK! And it can be more than habit, an I-nate —"

Ms. Tam: (*Correcting.*) Innate . . .

Shondrika: See, Ms. Tam why you had to mess up my flow? Now I gotta start from the beginning since you done messed up my flow. (*Class sighs.*)

Brian: Aw. Come on!!!

Ms. Tam: Sorry, Shondrika.

Shondrika: Right. "Habits are difficult to break. And it can be more than habit, an innate tendency. Many criminals seem to have been born that way. It is in their nature." Thank you. (*Applause.*)

Ms. Sun: Beautiful, Shondrika. And is it in your nature to live like you're a convict?

Shondrika: No!

Ms. Sun: Well, what is in your nature? Coca?

Coca: Love.

Ms. Sun: What else? Chris?

Chris: Success. And real estate.

Ms. Sun: Jose, how about you?

Jose: Family. Yo. My brother and my *buela.*°

Ms. Sun: Brian?

Brian: And above all, money, see what I'm sayin', know what I mean, see what I'm saying?

Ms. Sun: Yes, Brian, we see what you're saying . . . and now that you know that you actually *can* succeed, let's get up and stretch!

Coca: Get up? Aw — hell no!

Jose: This is mad boring.

Xiomara: I just ate. I hate this part.

Jerome: Can I go to the bathroom? *(Bell rings. Lights shift.)*

Janitor: Not so bad for a second class. Although, due to discipline issues, attention problems, lateness and resistance to the project on the whole, Ms. Sun is already behind in her teaching lesson. And, the show is only four weeks away. Let's watch as Ms. Sun enters her third week of classes. The show must go on! (I'm good at this. I am!)

SCENE 7

Classroom.

Coca: Miss. Did you hear? Most of our class is gone for the day . . . They went on an important school trip. To the UniverSoul Circus. There's only five of us here.

Ms. Sun: That's OK, Coca. We'll make do with the five of us, including Ms. Tam.

Ms. Tam: *(Tired.)* Ewww . . .

Ms. Sun: So, we will start the rehearsal section for *Our Country's Good.* We have the lovely Xiomara as Mary Brenham.

Xiomara: *(Deep voice.)* I don't want to be Mary Brenham, I want to be Liz . . . the pretty one.

Ms. Sun: I think I can make that happen. Chris as the Aborigine.

Chris: It's good.

Ms. Sun: And Phillip as . . . Phillip as . . . Ralph! Phillip, do me a favor, go to page thirty-one and read your big monologue about the presence of women on the stage.

Phillip: *(Inaudibly.)* "In my own small way in just a few hours I have seen something change. I asked some of the convict women to read me some lines, these women who behave often no better than animals." *(Pause.)*

Ms. Sun: Good, Phillip, good. Do me a favor and read the first line again but pretend that you are speaking to a group of a hundred people.

Phillip: *(Inaudibly.)* "In my own small way in just a few hours I have seen something change."

Ms. Sun: Thank you, Phillip. You can sit down now. *(She goes to work on another student.)* No, Phillip, get back up. Someone is stealing your brand new . . . what kind of car do you like, Phillip?

Phillip: *(Inaudibly.)* Mercedes LX 100, Limited edition.

---

buela: Short for the Spanish word *abuela* (grandmother).

Ms. Sun: That! And, you have to, with that line there, stop him from taking your prized possession. Read it again.

Phillip: *(Inaudibly.)* "In my own small way I have seen something change."

Ms. Sun: Now open your mouth . . .

Phillip: *(Inaudibly but with mouth wide.)* "In my own small way . . ."

Ms. Sun: Your tongue, your tongue is a living breathing animal thrashing about in your mouth — it's not just lying there on the bottom near your jaw — it's got a life of its own, man. Give it life.

Phillip: *(Full on.)* "In my own small way I have seen something change!" *(The bell rings.)*

Ms. Sun: That's it. That's it. Right there . . . *(She is alone now.)* God, I need a Vicodin.

SCENE 8

School. Night.

Janitor: It may not look it, but this school has gone through many transformations. When I first arrived at its pristine steps, I marveled at the architecture . . . like a castle. Believe it or not, there were nothin' but Italian kids here and it was called Robert Moses High back then. Humph! See, I was the first Negro janitor here and ooh that made them other custodians upset. But I did my job, kept my courtesies intact. Them janitors all gone now . . . and I'm still here. Then came the 60s, civil rights, the assassination of President Kennedy right there on the TV, Vietnam. Those were some hot times. Italians started moving out and Blacks and Puerto Ricans moved right on in. Back then, landlords was burning up they own buildings just so as to collect they insurance. And, the Black Panthers had a breakfast program — would say "Brotha Baron! How you gonna fight the MAN today?" I say "With my broom and my grade D ammonia, ya dig?" They'd laugh. They all gone, I'm still here. Then came the 70s when they renamed the school Malcolm X after our great revolutionary. I say, "Alright, here we go. True change has got to begin now." Lesson number two: Revolution has its upside and its downside. Try not to stick around for the downside. Eighties brought Reagan, that goddamn crack ('scuse my cussin') and hip-hop. Ain't nothing like my Joe King Oliver's Creole Jazz Band but what you gonna do. And here we come to today. Building fallin' apart, paint chipping, water damage, kids running around here talking loud like crazy folk, half of them is raising themselves. Let me tell ya, I don't know nothing about no No Child, Yes Child, Who Child What Child. I do know there's a hole in the fourth-floor ceiling ain't been fixed since '87, all the bathrooms on the third floor, they all broke. Now, who's accountable for dat? Heck, they even asked me to give up my closet, make it into some science lab class cuz ain't got no room. I say, "This my sanctuary. You can't take away my zen. Shoot, I read *O* magazine." They complied for now. Phew! Everything's falling apart . . . But these floors, these windows, these chalkboards — they clean . . . why? Cuz I'm still here!

SCENE 9

Classroom.

Coca: Miss, did you hear? Someone stole Ms. Tam's bag and she quit for good. We got some Russian teacher now.

Mrs. Projensky: Quiet Quiet Quiet Quiet Quiet Quiet Quiet. Quiet!

Ms. Sun: Miss, Miss, Miss. I'm the teaching artist for . . .

Mrs. Projensky: Sit down, you.

Shondrika: Aw, snap, she told her.

Mrs. Projensky: Sit down, quiet. Quiet, sit down.

Ms. Sun: No, I'm the teaching artist for this period. Maybe Miss Tam or Mrs. Kennedy told you something about me?

Jerome: *(Shadowboxes.)* Ah, hah, you being replaced, Russian lady.

Ms. Sun: Jerome, you're not helping right now.

Jerome: What?! You don't gotta tell me jack. We ain't got a teacher no more or haven't you heard? *(He flings a chair.)* We are the worst class in school.

Mrs. Projensky: Sit down! Sit down!

Ms. Sun: Guys, quiet down and focus. We have a show to do in a few weeks.

Coca: Ooee, I don't wanna do this no more. It's stupid.

Chris: I still want to do it.

Jerome: Shut the fuck up, Chris.

Jose: Yo man, she's right. This shit is mad fucking boring yo.

Coca: Yeah!

Xiomara: Yeah!

Brian: Yeah!

Shondrika: Yeah!

Coca: Mad boring.

Jerome: Fuckin' stupid.

Mrs. Projensky: Quiet! Quiet! Quiet!

Ms. Sun: What has gotten into all you? The first two classes were amazing, you guys were analyzing the play, making parallels to your lives. So, we missed a week when you went to go see, uh . . .

Shondrika: UniverSoul Circus.

Ms. Sun: Right! But, just because we missed a week doesn't mean we have to start from square one. Does it? Jerome, Jerome! where are you going?

Mrs. Projensky: Sit down, sit down, you! Sit down!

Jerome: I don't gotta listen to none of y'all. *(He flings another chair.)* I'm eighteen years old.

Brian: Yeah, and still in the tenth grade, nigga. *(Brian flings a chair.)*

Ms. Sun: Brian!

Jerome: I most definitely ain't gonna do no stupid-ass motha fuckin' Australian play from the goddamn seventeen-hundreds!

Ms. Sun: Fine, Jerome. You don't wanna be a part of something really special? There are others here who do.

Jerome: Who? Who in here want to do this show, memorize your lines, look like stupid fucking dicks on the stage for the whole school to laugh at us like they always do anyhow when can't none of us speak no goddamn English.

Ms. Sun: Jerome, that's not fair, no one is saying you don't speak English. You all invited your parents . . .

Coca: Ooee, my moms can't come to this. She gotta work. Plus the Metrocard ends at seven.

Xiomara: My mom ain't never even been to this school.

Jerome: That's what I'm sayin'! Who the fuck wanna do this? Who the fuck wanna do this?

Ms. Sun: I'll take the vote, Jerome, if you sit down. Everyone sit down.

Mrs. Projensky: Sit down!

Ms. Sun: Thank you, ma'am. OK, so, who, after all the hard work we've done so far building a team, analyzing the play in your own words (that is not easy, I know), developing self-esteem *y coraje* as great thespians . . .

Brian: Lesbians.

Ms. Sun: Who wants to quit . . . after all this? *(She looks around as they all raise their hands . . . except for Chris.)* I see.

Chris: Miss. No. I still wanna do the show.

Jerome: That's cuz you gay, Chris. Yo, I'm out! One. Niggas. *(Pause. Ms. Sun is hurt.)*

Ms. Sun: OK . . . Well . . . Ms.?

Mrs. Projensky: Projensky.

Ms. Sun: Ms. Projensky.

Mrs. Projensky: Projensky!

Ms. Sun: Projensky.

Mrs. Projensky: Projensky!!!

Ms. Sun: Projensky!!!

Mrs. Projensky: Is close.

Ms. Sun: Do they have any sample Regents to take?

Mrs. Projensky: Yes, they do.

Ms. Sun: Great. I'll alert Mrs. Kennedy of your vote.

Phillip: *(Audibly.)* Ms. Sun?

Ms. Sun: Yes, Phillip, what is it?

Phillip: Can I still do the show? *(Beat.)*

SCENE 10

Principal's office.

Mrs. Kennedy: So they voted you out? Well, Malcolm X Vocational High School did not get an eight-thousand-dollar grant from the Department of Education of the City of New York for these students to choose democracy now. They will do the show. Because I will tell them so tomorrow. If they do not do the show, each student in 10F will be suspended and *not* be able to join their friends in their beloved Great Adventures trip in May. The horror. Look, I understand that they consider themselves the worst class in school. News flash — They're not even close. I know that they've had five different teachers in the course of seven months. I also can wrap my brain around the fact that seventy-nine percent of those kids in there have been physically, emotionally, and sexually abused in their tender little sixteen-year-old lives. But that does not give them the right to disrespect someone who is stretching them to give them something beautiful. Something challenging. Something Jay-Z and P Diddly only *wish* they could offer them. Now, I will call all their parents this weekend and notify them of their intolerable behavior as well as invite them to *Our Country's Good.* Done. See you next Wednesday, Ms. Sun?

Ms. Sun: Yes, yes. Thanks! Yes! . . . Uh, no, Mrs. Kennedy. You won't be seeing me next Wednesday. I quit. I came to teaching to touch lives and educate and be this enchanting artist in the classroom and I have done nothing but lose ten pounds in a month and develop a disgusting smoking habit. Those kids in there? They need something much greater than anything I can give them — *they need a miracle* . . . and they need a miracle like every day. Sometimes, I dream of going to Connecticut and teaching the rich white kids there. All I'd have to battle against is soccer moms, bulimia, and everyone asking me how I wash my hair. But, I chose to teach in my city, this city that raised me . . . and I'm tired, and I'm not even considered a "real" teacher. I don't know how I would survive as a real teacher. But they do . . . on what, God knows. And, the worst thing, the worst thing is that all those kids in there are *me*. Brown skin, brown eyes, stuck. I can't even help my own people. Really revolutionary, huh?

It seems to me that this whole school system, not just here but the whole system is falling apart from under us and then there are these testing and accountability laws that have nothing to do with any real solutions and if we expect to stay some sort of grand nation for the next fifty years, we got another thing coming. *Because we're not teaching these kids how to be leaders.* We're getting them ready for jail! Take off your belt, take off your shoes, go back, go back, go back. We're totally abandoning these kids and we have been for thirty years and then we get annoyed when they're running around in the subway calling themselves bitches and niggas, we get annoyed when their math scores don't pair up to a five-year-old's in China, we get annoyed when they don't graduate in time. It's because we've abandoned them. And, I'm no different, I'm abandoning them too. (*Beat.*) I just need a break to be an actor, get health insurance, go on auditions, pay the fucking IRS. Sorry. Look, I'm sorry about the big grant from the Department of Ed. but perhaps we could make it up somehow next year. I can't continue this program any longer, even if it is for our country's good. Bye! (*Light shift.*)

Janitor: (*Sings.*)
    I'm gonna lay. Lay my head
    On some lonesome railroad line.
    Let that 2:19 train—

SCENE 11

Outside of school.

Ms. Sun: (*Sings.*)
    Ease my troubled mind—
Jerome: Ms. Sun?
Ms. Sun: Hi. Jerome.
Jerome: You singing? (*Beat.*) We were talking about you in the cafeteria. Had a power lunch. (*He laughs.*) Most of us were being assholes . . . sorry . . . bad thespians when we did that to you.
Ms. Sun: You were the leader, do you know that, Jerome? Do you know that we teachers, we have feelings. And we try our best not to break in front of you all?
Jerome: Yeah, I know, my mom tells me that all the time.
Ms. Sun: Listen to her, sweetheart, she's right. (*Beat.*) Look, the show is off. I'll be here next year, and we'll start again on another more tangible play, maybe even *Raisin in the Sun*. Now, if you'll excuse me, I have an audition to prepare for. (*She turns to leave.*)
Jerome: Ms. Sun, "The theater is an expression of civilization . . ."
Ms. Sun: What?

Jerome: I said, "The theater is an expression of civilization. We belong to a great country which has spawned great playwrights: Shakespeare, Marlowe, Jonson, and even in our own time, Sheridan. The convicts will be speaking a refined, literate language and expressing sentiments of a delicacy they are not used to. It will remind them that there is more to life than crime, punishment. And we, this colony of a few hundred, will be watching this together. For a few hours we will no longer be despised prisoners and hated gaolers. We will laugh, we may be moved. We may even think a little. Can you suggest something else that would provide such an evening, Watkin?" *(Beat.)* Thank you.

Ms. Sun: Jerome, I didn't know . . .

Jerome: . . . that I had the part of Second Lieutenant Ralph Clark memorized. I do my thang. Guess I won't be doing it this year though. Shoot, every teacher we have runs away. *(Beat.)*

Ms. Sun: Listen, Jerome, you tell all your cafeteria buddies in there, OK, to have all their lines memorized from Acts One and Two and be completely focused when I walk into that room next week — that means no talking, no hidden conversations and blurting out random nonsense, no gum, and for crying out loud, no one should be drinking Red Bull.

Jerome: Aight. So you back?

Ms. Sun: . . . Yeah, and I'm bad. *(She does some Michael Jackson moves.)*

Jerome: Miss, you really do need an acting job soon. *(Light shift.)*

Janitor: Things are looking up for our little teaching artist. She got a new lease on life. Got on a payment plan with the IRS. Stopped smoking, ate a good breakfast, even took the early train to school this mornin'.

SCENE 12

Classroom.

Coca: Miss, did you hear? We got a new teacher permanently. He's kinda . . . good!

Mr. Johnson: What do we say when Ms. Sun walks in?

Shondrika: Good morning, Ms. Sun.

Mr. Johnson: Hat off, Jerome.

Jerome: Damn, he got attitude! *(Beat.)* I like that!

Ms. Sun: Wow, wow. You guys are lookin' really, really good.

Mr. Johnson: Alright, let's get in the formation that we created. First, the tableau.

Ms. Sun: *(Intimate.)* Tableau, you got them to do a tableau.

Mr. Johnson: *(Intimate.)* I figured you'd want to see them in a frozen non-speaking state for a while. Oh, Kaswan, Xiomara, and Brian are in the auditorium building the set.

Ms. Sun: *(Intimate.)* Wow. This is amazing. Thank you.

Mr. Johnson: Don't thank me. Thank Mrs. Kennedy, thank yourself, thank these kids. *(To class.)* And we're starting from the top, top, top. Only one more week left. Shondrika, let's see those fliers you're working on.

Shondrika: I been done. "Come see *Our Country's Good* cuz it's for your *own* good."

Ms. Sun: Beautiful, Shondrika. Let's start from the top. *(Sound of noise.)* What's all that noise out in the hallway?

Brian: Ay, yo. Janitor Baron had a heart attack in his closet last night. He died there.

Coca: What? He was our favorite . . .

Jerome: How old was he, like a hundred or something?

Shondrika: I just saw him yesterday. He told me he would come to the show. He died all alone, ya'll. *(Long pause.)*

Ms. Sun: Thespians, I can give you some time . . .

Jerome: Nah, nah we done wasted enough time. Let's rehearse. Do the show. Dedicate it to Janitor Baron, our pops, may you rest in peace.

Ms. Sun: Alright, then, we're taking it from the top. Chris, that's you, sweetheart.

Chris: "A giant canoe drifts onto the sea, clouds billowing from upright oars. This is a dream that has lost its way. Best to leave it alone." *(Light shift.)*

Janitor: My, My, My . . . them kids banded together over me. Memorized, rehearsed, added costumes, a small set, even added a rap or two at the end — don't tell the playwright! And, I didn't even think they knew my name. Ain't that something? I think I know what you saying to yourselves: I see dead people. Shoot, this is a good story, I wanna finish telling it! Plus, my new friend up here, Arthur Miller, tells me ain't no rules say a dead man can't make a fine narrator. Say he wish he thought of it himself. Meanwhile, like most teachers, even after-hours, Ms. Sun's life just ain't her own.

SCENE 13

Sun's apartment. Night.

Ms. Sun: *(On phone.)* Hi. This is Ms. Sun from Malcolm X High. I'm looking for Jose Guzman. He's a lead actor in *Our Country's Good* but I haven't seen him in class or after-school rehearsals since last week. My number is . . . *(Light shift. On phone:)* Hi. This is Ms. Sun again from Malcolm X High. I know it's probably dinner time but I'm still trying to reach Jose or his grandmother, Doña Guzman . . . *(Light shift. On phone:)* Hi. Ms. Sun here. Sorry, I know it's early and Mrs. Kennedy called last night, but the show is in less than two days . . . *(Light shift. On phone:)* Hi. It's midnight. You can probably imagine who this is. Does anyone answer this phone? Why have a machine, I mean really . . . Hello, hello, yes. This is Ms. Sun from Malcolm X High, oh . . . Puedo hablar con Doña Guzman. Ah Hah! Finally. Doña Guzman, ah ha, bueno, Ingles, OK. I've been working with your grandson now for six weeks on a play that you might have heard of. *(Beat.)* Un espectaculo . . . ah ha, pero Ingles, OK. I haven't seen him in a week and the show is in twenty-four hours. Mañana actually . . . Como? His brother was killed. Ave Maria, Lo siento, señora . . . How? Gangs . . . no, no, olvidate, forget about it. I'll send out prayers to you y tu familia. Buenas. *(She hangs up. Light shift.)*

Janitor: Chin up now!

SCENE 14

School auditorium.

Janitor: Cuz, it's opening night in the auditorium . . . I'm not even gonna talk about the logistics behind booking a high school auditorium for a night. Poor Mrs. Kennedy became a dictator.

Mrs. Kennedy: I booked this auditorium for the night and no one shall take it from me!!!

Janitor: The stage is ablaze with fear, apprehension, doubt, nervousness, and, well, drama.

Mr. Johnson: Anyone seen Jerome?

Ms. Sun: Anyone seen Jerome?

Coca: His mom called him at four. Told him he had to babysit for the night.

Ms. Sun: But, he's got a show tonight. Couldn't they find someone else? Couldn't he just bring the brats? Sorry.

Mr. Johnson: What are we going to do now? His part is enormous.

Phillip: Ms. Sun?

Ms. Sun: What, Phillip?

Phillip: . . . I could do his part.

Ms. Sun: *(With apprehension.)* OK, Phillip. You're on. Just remember . . .

Phillip: I know . . . someone is stealing my Mercedes LX one hundred Limited Edition.

Ms. Sun: And . . . ?

Phillip: . . . Let my tongue be alive!

Doña Guzman: Doña Guzman, buenas. Buenas. Doña Guzman. The abuela de Jose.

Ms. Sun: Jose, you made it. I'm so sorry about your brother.

Jose: Yeah, I know. Where's my costume at? Buela, no ta allí.

Doña Guzman: Mira pa ya, muchacho. We had very long week pero he love this class. He beg me "mami, mami, mami, Our Country Goo, Our Country Goo, Our Country Goo." What can I do? I say yes. What I can do, you know.

Ms. Sun: Oh señora. It's parents like you . . . thank you. Muchissima gracias por todo. Sit, sit in the audience por favor.

Mrs. Kennedy: Ms. Sun, everyone is in place, there are about seventy-five people in that audience, including some parents I desperately need to speak to. We're glad you're back. Good luck!

Shondrika: Miss, you want me to get the kids together before we start?

Ms. Sun: Yeah, Shondrika, would you?

Shondrika: Uh huh.

Janitor: Now, here's a teacher's moment of truth. The last speech before the kids go on!

Ms. Sun: Alright. This is it. We're here. We have done the work. We have lived this play inside and out. I officially have a hernia.

Coca: *(Laughing.)* She so stupid. I like her.

Ms. Sun: We are a success . . . no matter what happens on this stage tonight. No matter which actors are missing or if your parents couldn't make it. I see before me twenty-seven amazingly talented young men and women. And I never thought I'd say this but I'm gonna miss you all.

Shondrika: Ooh, she gonna make me cry!

Ms. Sun: Tonight is your night.

Coca: Ooee, I'm nervous.

Phillip: Me too.

Ms. Sun: I am too. That just means you care. Now let's take a deep breath in and out. In . . .

Brian: OHM! Nah, I'm just kiddin'. Keep going. Focus Focus.

Ms. Sun: . . . and out. In and out.

Shondrika: Miss, let's do this for Jose's brother and Janitor Baron.

Ms. Sun: Oh, Shondrika, that's beautiful. OK, gentlemen, be with us tonight! PLACES. *(Light shift.)*

Chris: A giant canoe drifts out onto the sea, best to leave it alone.

Coca: This hateful hary-scary, topsy-turvy outpost. This is not a civilization.

Xiomara: It's two hours, possibly of amusement, possibly of boredom. It's a waste, an unnecessary waste.

Phillip: The convicts will feel nothing has changed and will go back to their old ways.

Jose: You have to be careful OH DAMN. *(Nervously, he regains his thought.)* You have to be careful with words that begin with IN. It can turn everything upside down. INjustice, most of that word is taken up with justice, but the IN turns it inside out making it the ugliest word in the English language.

Shondrika: Citizens must be taught to obey the law of their own will. I want to rule over responsible human beings.

Phillip: Unexpected situations are often matched by unexpected virtues in people. Are they not?

Brian: A play should make you understand something new.

Shondrika: Human beings —

Xiomara: —have an intelligence —

Brian: —that has nothing to do —

Jose: —with the circumstances —

Coca: —into which they were born.

Chris: THE END. *(Raucous applause. Light shift.)*

Janitor: And the show did go on. A show that sparked a mini-revolution in the hearts of everyone in that auditorium. Sure, some crucial lines were fumbled, and some entrances missed and three cell phones went off in the audience. But, my God, if those kids weren't a success.

SCENE 15

Backstage.

Coca: Miss, I did good, right? I did good? I did good. I did my lines right. I did my motivations right. I did good, right. I did good? I did good? I did good? *(Assured.)* I did good. I did good. I did good. Oh, Miss. I been wantin' to tell you. You know I'm pregnant right? . . . Oh don't cry . . . Damn. Why do everyone cry when I say that? No, I wanted to tell you because my baby will not live like a prisoner, like a convict. I mean we still gotta put the baby-proof bars on the windows but that's state law. But that's it. We gonna travel, explore, see somethin' new for a change. I mean I love the Bronx but there's more to life right? You taught me that. "Man is born free" right . . . I mean, even though it's gonna be a girl. *(Beat.)* I know we was mad hard so thank you.

Jose: Ms.? I don't know but, that class was still mad boring to me.

Phillip: *(Audibly.)* Ms. Sun?! I wanna be an actor now!

Security Guard: O, O! We gotta clear out the auditorium. You can't be lollygagging in here. Clear it out. Clear it out. Clear it out! By the way, I never done seen dem kids shine like they did tonight. They did good. You did good. Now, you got ta clear it out!

Ms. Sun: (*To herself.*) Jerome . . . Jerome. (*Beat.*) "And we, this colony of a few hundred, will be watching this together, and we will no longer be despised prisoners and hated gaolers. We will laugh, we may be moved. We may . . ."

Jerome: (*Gasping.*) ". . . even think a little!"

Ms. Sun: Jerome? What are you doing here?

Jerome: (*Panting.*) Mom came home early. Told me to run over here fast as I could
. . . (*He realizes.*) I missed it. I missed it all. And I worked *hard* to learn my
lines.

Ms. Sun: Yes, you did Jerome. You worked very hard. (*Long beat.*)

Jerome: You gonna be teaching here again next year?

Ms. Sun: That's the plan. But, only tenth-graders again. Sorry.

Jerome: Oh no worries. I'm definitely gonna get left back for you. Psyche . . .
Lemme go shout out to all them other thespians. You gonna be around?

Ms. Sun: No, actually I have a commercial shoot early tomorrow morning.

Jerome: Really, for what?

Ms. Sun: (*Slurring.*) It's nothing . . .

Jerome: Aw, come on you could tell me.

Ms. Sun: Really, it's nothing.

Jerome: Lemme know. Lemme know. Come on lemme know.

Ms. Sun: It's for Red Bull, damn it. Red Bull.

Jerome: Aight! Ms. Sun's finally getting paid. (*Light shift.*)

SCENE 16

Janitor: And on to our third and final lesson of the evening: Something interesting
happens when you die. You still care about the ones you left behind and wanna
see how life ended up for them. Ms. Tam went back to the firm and wound up
investing 2.3 million dollars towards arts in education with a strong emphasis
on cultural diversity. Phillip proudly works as a conductor for the MTA. Shondrika Jones graduated *summa cum laude* from Harvard University and became
the first black woman mayor of New York City. Alright now. Jose Guzman lost
his life a week after the show when he decided to take vengeance on the Blood
that killed his brother. Jerome. I might be omnipresent but I sure as heck ain't
omniscient. Some of the brightest just slip through the cracks sometime. Do
me a favor — you ever see him around town, tell him we thinkin' about him.
And Ms. Sun. Well, she went on to win an NAACP Award, a Hispanic Heritage
Award, a Tony Award, and an Academy Award. She was also in charge of restructuring of the nation's No Child Left Behind law *and* lives happily with her
husband, Denzel Washington. His first wife never had a chance, poor thang.
She still comes back every year to teach at Malcolm X High; oh, oh, oh, recently
renamed Saint Tupac Shakur Preparatory. Times — they are a-changin'! (*He
grabs his broom and sings. Lights shift as he walks toward a bright light offstage.*)
Trouble in mind
It's true
I had almost lost my way
(*Offstage light brightens as if the heavens await. He knows to walk "into" it.*)
But, the sun's gonna shine
In my back door someday
That's alright, Lord. That's alright!

End of play

CONNECTIONS TO ANOTHER SELECTION

1. Discuss the purpose of the play within the play in *No Child . . .* and in Shakespeare's *Hamlet* (p. 1238). Why do you think this device has been a favorite strategy of playwrights over the years?

Tender Offer

Born in Brooklyn, New York, in 1950, Wendy Wasserstein studied at Mount Holyoke College, City College of New York, and the Yale School of Drama. She was a resident playwright off-Broadway, at New York's Playwrights Horizon Theatre, where many of her plays were per-

Jack Mitchell/Getty Images.

formed before audiences receptive to Wasserstein's humorous treatment of feminist issues. Among her plays are *Uncommon Women* (1977), *Isn't It Romantic* (1980), *The Sisters Rosenzweig* (1993), and the enormously successful *The Heidi Chronicles* (1988), which won numerous honors including a Tony Award, a Pulitzer Prize, and the New York Drama Critics' Circle Award. In 1990 her book of essays, *Bachelor Girl,* was published. Her last play, *Third* (2005), explores the politics of academic life. She received National Endowment for the Arts and Guggenheim grants in support of her work.

Tender Offer, which appeared in a special issue of one-act plays in the Spring 1991 *Antaeus,* is a brief but absorbing treatment of the tentative relationship between a father and daughter. Characteristic of Wasserstein's work, this play uses humor deftly to present a serious moment that requires a "good deal" to resolve it.

WENDY WASSERSTEIN (1950–2006)

Tender Offer 1991

A girl of around nine is alone in a dance studio. She is dressed in traditional leotards and tights. She begins singing to herself, "Nothing Could Be Finer Than to Be in Carolina." She maps out a dance routine, including parts for the chorus. She builds to a finale. A man, Paul, around thirty-five, walks in. He has a sweet, though distant, demeanor. As he walks in, Lisa notices him and stops.

Paul: You don't have to stop, sweetheart.
Lisa: That's okay.
Paul: Looked very good.
Lisa: Thanks.

Paul: Don't I get a kiss hello?

Lisa: Sure.

Paul (embraces her): Hi, Tiger.

Lisa: Hi, Dad.

Paul: I'm sorry I'm late.

Lisa: That's okay.

Paul: How'd it go?

Lisa: Good.

Paul: Just good?

Lisa: Pretty good.

Paul: "Pretty good." You mean you got a lot of applause or "pretty good" you could have done better?

Lisa: Well, Courtney Palumbo's mother thought I was pretty good. But you know the part in the middle when everybody's supposed to freeze and the big girl comes out. Well, I think I moved a little bit.

Paul: I thought what you were doing looked very good.

Lisa: Daddy, that's not what I was doing. That was tap-dancing. I made that up.

Paul: Oh. Well it looked good. Kind of sexy.

Lisa: Yuch!

Paul: What do you mean "yuch"?

Lisa: Just yuch!

Paul: You don't want to be sexy?

Lisa: I don't care.

Paul: Let's go, Tiger. I promised your mother I'd get you home in time for dinner.

Lisa: I can't find my leg warmers.

Paul: You can't find your what?

Lisa: Leg warmers. I can't go home till I find my leg warmers.

Paul: I don't see you looking for them.

Lisa: I was waiting for you.

Paul: Oh.

Lisa: Daddy.

Paul: What?

Lisa: Nothing.

Paul: Where do you think you left them?

Lisa: Somewhere around here. I can't remember.

Paul: Well, try to remember, Lisa. We don't have all night.

Lisa: I told you. I think somewhere around here.

Paul: I don't see them. Let's go home now. You'll call the dancing school tomorrow.

Lisa: Daddy, I can't go home till I find them. Miss Judy says it's not professional to leave things.

Paul: Who's Miss Judy?

Lisa: She's my ballet teacher. She once danced the lead in *Swan Lake,* and she was a June Taylor dancer.

Paul: Well, then, I'm sure she'll understand about the leg warmers.

Lisa: Daddy, Miss Judy wanted to know why you were late today.

Paul: Hmmmmmmmmm?

Lisa: Why were you late?

Paul: I was in a meeting. Business. I'm sorry.

Lisa: Why did you tell Mommy you'd come instead of her if you knew you had business?

Paul: Honey, something just came up. I thought I'd be able to be here. I was looking forward to it.

Lisa: I wish you wouldn't make appointments to see me.

Paul: Hmmmmmmm.

Lisa: You shouldn't make appointments to see me unless you know you're going
to come.

Paul: Of course I'm going to come.

Lisa: No, you're not. Talia Robbins told me she's much happier living without her
father in the house. Her father used to come home late and go to sleep early.

Paul: Lisa, stop it. Let's go.

Lisa: I can't find my leg warmers.

Paul: Forget your leg warmers.

Lisa: Daddy.

Paul: What is it?

Lisa: I saw this show on television, I think it was WPIX Channel 11. Well, the
father was crying about his daughter.

Paul: Why was he crying? Was she sick?

Lisa: No. She was at school. And he was at business. And he just missed her, so he
started to cry.

Paul: What was the name of this show?

Lisa: I don't know. I came in in the middle.

Paul: Well, Lisa, I certainly would cry if you were sick or far away, but I know that
you're well and you're home. So no reason to get maudlin.

Lisa: What's maudlin?

Paul: Sentimental, soppy. Frequently used by children who make things up to get
attention.

Lisa: I am sick! I am sick! I have Hodgkin's disease and a bad itch on my leg.

Paul: What do you mean you have Hodgkin's disease? Don't say things like that.

Lisa: Swoosie Kurtz, she had Hodgkin's disease on a TV movie last year, but she
got better and now she's on *Love Sidney*.

Paul: Who is Swoosie Kurtz?

Lisa: She's an actress named after an airplane. I saw her on *Live at Five*.

Paul: You watch too much television; you should do your homework. Now, put
your coat on.

Lisa: Daddy, I really do have a bad itch on my leg. Would you scratch it?

Paul: Lisa, you're procrastinating.

Lisa: Why do you use words I don't understand? I hate it. You're like Daria Feldman's
mother. She always talks in Yiddish to her husband so Daria won't understand.

Paul: *Procrastinating* is not Yiddish.

Lisa: Well, I don't know what it is.

Paul: Procrastinating means you don't want to go about your business.

Lisa: I don't go to business. I go to school.

Paul: What I mean is you want to hang around here until you and I are late for
dinner and your mother's angry and it's too late for you to do your homework.

Lisa: I do not.

Paul: Well, it sure looks that way. Now put your coat on and let's go.

Lisa: Daddy.

Paul: Honey, I'm tired. Really, later.

Lisa: Why don't you want to talk to me?

Paul: I do want to talk to you. I promise when we get home we'll have a nice talk.

Lisa: No, we won't. You'll read the paper and fall asleep in front of the news.

Paul: Honey, we'll talk on the weekend, I promise. Aren't I taking you to the theater this weekend? Let me look. (*He takes out appointment book.*) Yes; Sunday. *Joseph and the Amazing Technicolor Raincoat* with Lisa. Okay, Tiger?

Lisa: Sure. It's *Dreamcoat*.

Paul: What?

Lisa: Nothing. I think I see my leg warmers. (*She goes to pick them up, and an odd-looking trophy.*)

Paul: What's that?

Lisa: It's stupid. I was second best at the dance recital, so they gave me this thing. It's stupid.

Paul: Lisa.

Lisa: What?

Paul: What did you want to talk about?

Lisa: Nothing.

Paul: Was it about my missing your recital? I'm really sorry, Tiger. I would have liked to have been here.

Lisa: That's okay.

Paul: Honest?

Lisa: Daddy, you're prostrastinating.

Paul: I'm procrastinating. Sit down. Let's talk. So. How's school?

Lisa: Fine.

Paul: You like it?

Lisa: Yup.

Paul: You looking forward to camp this summer?

Lisa: Yup.

Paul: Is Daria Feldman going back?

Lisa: Nope.

Paul: Why not?

Lisa: I don't know. We can go home now. Honest, my foot doesn't itch anymore.

Paul: Lisa, you know what you do in business when it seems like there's nothing left to say? That's when you really start talking. Put a bid on the table.

Lisa: What's a bid?

Paul: You tell me what you want and I'll tell you what I've got to offer. Like Monopoly. You want Boardwalk, but I'm only willing to give you the Railroads. Now, because you are my daughter I'd throw in Water Works and Electricity. Understand, Tiger?

Lisa: No. I don't like board games. You know, Daddy, we could get Space Invaders for our home for thirty-five dollars. In fact, we could get Osborne System for two thousand. Daria Feldman's parents . . .

Paul: Daria Feldman's parents refuse to talk to Daria, so they bought a computer to keep Daria busy so they won't have to speak in Yiddish. Daria will probably grow up to be a homicidal maniac lesbian prostitute.

Lisa: I know what that word *prostitute* means.

Paul: Good. (*Pause.*) You still haven't told me about school. Do you still like your teacher?

Lisa: She's okay.

Paul: Lisa, if we're talking try to answer me.

Lisa: I am answering you. Can we go home now, please?

Paul: Damn it, Lisa, if you want to talk to me . . . Talk to me!

Lisa: I can't wait till I'm old enough so I can make my own money and never have to see you again. Maybe I'll become a prostitute.

Paul: Young lady, that's enough.

Lisa: I hate you, Daddy! I hate you! (*She throws her trophy into the trash bin.*)

Paul: What'd you do that for?

Lisa: It's stupid.

Paul: Maybe I wanted it.

Lisa: What for?

Paul: Maybe I wanted to put it where I keep your dinosaur and the picture you made of Mrs. Kimbel with the chicken pox.

Lisa: You got mad at me when I made that picture. You told me I had to respect Mrs. Kimbel because she was my teacher.

Paul: That's true. But she wasn't my teacher. I liked her better with the chicken pox. (*Pause.*) Lisa, I'm sorry. I was very wrong to miss your recital, and you don't have to become a prostitute. That's not the type of profession Miss Judy has in mind for you.

Lisa (mumbles): No.

Paul: No. (*Pause.*) So Talia Robbins is really happy her father moved out?

Lisa: Talia Robbins picks open the eighth-grade lockers during gym period. But she did that before her father moved out.

Paul: You can't always judge someone by what they do or what they don't do. Sometimes you come home from dancing school and run upstairs and shut the door, and when I finally get to talk to you, everything is "okay" or "fine." Yup or nope?

Lisa: Yup.

Paul: Sometimes, a lot of times, I come home and fall asleep in front of the television. So you and I spend a lot of time being a little scared of each other. Maybe?

Lisa: Maybe.

Paul: Tell you what. I'll make you a tender offer.

Lisa: What?

Paul: I'll make you a tender offer. That's when one company publishes in the newspaper that they want to buy another company. And the company that publishes is called the Black Knight because they want to gobble up the poor little company. So the poor little company needs to be rescued. And then a White Knight comes along and makes a bigger and better offer so the shareholders won't have to tender shares to the Big Black Knight. You with me?

Lisa: Sort of.

Paul: I'll make you a tender offer like the White Knight. But I don't want to own you. I just want to make a much better offer. Okay?

Lisa (sort of understanding): Okay. (*Pause. They sit for a moment.*) Sort of, Daddy, what do you think about? I mean, like when you're quiet what do you think about?

Paul: Oh, business usually. If I think I made a mistake or if I think I'm doing okay. Sometimes I think about what I'll be doing five years from now and if it's what I hoped it would be five years ago. Sometimes I think about what your life will be like, if Mount Saint Helens will erupt again. What you'll become if you'll study penmanship or word processing. If you speak kindly of me to your psychiatrist when you are in graduate school. And how the hell I'll pay for your graduate school. And sometimes I try and think what it was I thought about when I was your age.

Lisa: Do you ever look out your window at the clouds and try to see which kinds of shapes they are? Like one time, honest, I saw the head of Walter Cronkite in a flower vase. Really! Like look don't those kinda look like if you turn it upside down, two big elbows or two elephant trunks dancing?

Paul: Actually still looks like Walter Cronkite in a flower vase to me. But look up a little. See the one that's still moving? That sorta looks like a whale on a thimble.

Lisa: Where?

Paul: Look up. To your right.

Lisa: I don't see it. Where?

Paul: The other way.

Lisa: Oh, yeah! There's the head and there's the stomach. Yeah! (*Lisa picks up her trophy.*) Hey, Daddy.

Paul: Hey, Lisa.

Lisa: You can have this thing if you want it. But you have to put it like this, because if you put it like that it is gross.

Paul: You know what I'd like? So I can tell people who come into my office why I have this gross stupid thing on my shelf, I'd like it if you could show me your dance recital.

Lisa: Now?

Paul: We've got time. Mother said she won't be home till late.

Lisa: Well, Daddy, during a lot of it I freeze and the big girl in front dances.

Paul: Well, how 'bout the number you were doing when I walked in?

Lisa: Well, see, I have parts for a lot of people in that one, too.

Paul: I'll dance the other parts.

Lisa: You can't dance.

Paul: Young lady, I played Yvette Mimieux in a *Hasty Pudding Show.*

Lisa: Who's Yvette Mimieux?

Paul: Watch more television. You'll find out. (*Paul stands up.*) So I'm ready. (*He begins singing.*) "Nothing could be finer than to be in Carolina."

Lisa: Now I go. In the morning. And now you go. Dum-da.

Paul (*obviously not a tap dancer*): Da-da-dum.

Lisa (*whines*): Daddy!

Paul (*mimics her*): Lisa! Nothing could be finer . . .

Lisa: That looks dumb.

Paul: Oh, yeah? You think they do this better in *The Amazing Minkcoat?* No way! Now you go — da da da dum.

Lisa: Da da da dum.

Paul: If I had Aladdin's lamp for only a day, I'd make a wish . . .

Lisa: Daddy, that's maudlin!

Paul: I know it's maudlin. And here's what I'd say:

Lisa and Paul: I'd say that "nothing could be finer than to be in Carolina in the mooooooooooornin'."

CONNECTIONS TO OTHER SELECTIONS

1. Compare the fathers in *Tender Offer* and Arthur Miller's *Death of a Salesman* (p. 1497). What conflicts are associated with the father in each work? To what extent are the conflicts resolved or not resolved?

2. *Tender Offer* and Jane Martin's *Rodeo* (p. 1474) are extremely brief dramatic works that present conflicts in which business serves as an antagonist. Write an essay on the nature of the conflicts in each play and how business is the source of those conflicts.

Fences

August Wilson, who, as a young poet, "wanted to be Dylan Thomas," went on to become a major force in the American theater. Between the 1980s and 2005, Wilson wrote a sequence of ten plays that chronicled the black experience in the United States in each decade of the twentieth century. *Ma Rainey's Black Bottom,* the first of these to be completed, premiered at the Yale Repertory Theatre in 1984, went to Broadway shortly thereafter, and eventually won the New York Drama Critics' Circle Award. Other plays in the sequence include *Joe Turner's Come and Gone* (1986), *The Piano Lesson* (1987), *Two Trains Running* (1989), and Wilson's last play, *Radio Golf* (2005).

Joan Marcus.

Born in Pittsburgh, Pennsylvania, Wilson grew up in the Hill, a black neighborhood to which his mother had come from North Carolina. His white father never lived with the family. Wilson quit school at sixteen and worked in a variety of menial jobs, meanwhile submitting poetry to a number of local publications. He didn't begin to find his writing voice, however, until he moved to Minneapolis–St. Paul, where he founded the Black Horizons Theatre Company in 1968 and later started the Playwrights Center. He supported himself during part of this time by writing skits for the Science Museum of Minnesota.

Fences offers a complex look at the internal and external pressures on a black tenement family living in Pittsburgh during the 1950s.

AUGUST WILSON (1945–2005)

Fences 1985

CHARACTERS

Troy Maxson
Jim Bono, Troy's friend
Rose, Troy's wife
Lyons, Troy's oldest son by previous marriage
Gabriel, Troy's brother
Cory, Troy and Rose's son
Raynell, Troy's daughter

SETTING: The setting is the yard which fronts the only entrance to the Maxson household, an ancient two-story brick house set back off a small alley in a big-city neighborhood. The entrance to the house is gained by two or three steps leading to a wooden porch badly in need of paint.

See Plays in Performance insert.
Ron Scherl/The Image Works.

A relatively recent addition to the house and running its full width, the porch lacks congruence. It is a sturdy porch with a flat roof. One or two chairs of dubious value sit at one end where the kitchen window opens onto the porch. An old-fashioned icebox stands silent guard at the opposite end.

The yard is a small dirt yard, partially fenced, except for the last scene, with a wooden sawhorse, a pile of lumber, and other fence-building equipment set off to the side. Opposite is a tree from which hangs a ball made of rags. A baseball bat leans against the tree. Two oil drums serve as garbage receptacles and sit near the house at right to complete the setting.

THE PLAY: Near the turn of the century, the destitute of Europe sprang on the city with tenacious claws and an honest and solid dream. The city devoured them. They swelled its belly until it burst into a thousand furnaces and sewing machines, a thousand butcher shops and bakers' ovens, a thousand churches and hospitals and funeral parlors and money-lenders. The city grew. It nourished itself and offered each man a partnership limited only by his talent, his guile, and his willingness and capacity for hard work. For the immigrants of Europe, a dream dared and won true.

The descendants of African slaves were offered no such welcome or participation. They came from places called the Carolinas and the Virginias, Georgia, Alabama, Mississippi, and Tennessee. They came strong, eager, searching. The city rejected them and they fled and settled along the riverbanks and under bridges in shallow, ramshackle houses made of sticks and tarpaper. They collected rags and wood. They sold the use of their muscles and their bodies. They cleaned houses and washed clothes, they shined shoes, and in quiet desperation and vengeful pride, they stole, and lived in pursuit of their own dream. That they could breathe free, finally, and stand to meet life with the force of dignity and whatever eloquence the heart could call upon.

By 1957, the hard-won victories of the European immigrants had solidified the industrial might of America. War had been confronted and won with new energies that used loyalty and patriotism as its fuel. Life was rich, full, and flourishing. The Milwaukee Braves won the World Series, and the hot winds of change that would make the sixties a turbulent, racing, dangerous, and provocative decade had not yet begun to blow full.

ACT I

SCENE I

It is 1957. Troy and Bono enter the yard, engaged in conversation. Troy is fifty-three years old, a large man with thick, heavy hands; it is this largeness that he strives to fill out and make an accommodation with. Together with his black-ness, his largeness informs his sensibilities and the choices he has made in his life.

Of the two men, Bono is obviously the follower. His commitment to their friendship of thirty-odd years is rooted in his admiration of Troy's honesty, ca-pacity for hard work, and his strength, which Bono seeks to emulate.

It is Friday night, payday, and the one night of the week the two men engage in a ritual of talk and drink. Troy is usually the most talkative and at times he can be crude and almost vulgar, though he is capable of rising to profound heights of expression. The men carry lunch buckets and wear or carry burlap aprons and are dressed in clothes suitable to their jobs as garbage collectors.

Bono: Troy, you ought to stop that lying!

Troy: I ain't lying! The nigger had a watermelon this big. *(He indicates with his hands.)* Talking about . . . "What watermelon, Mr. Rand?" I liked to fell out! "What watermelon, Mr. Rand?" . . . And it sitting there big as life.

Bono: What did Mr. Rand say?

Troy: Ain't said nothing. Figure if the nigger too dumb to know he carrying a watermelon, he wasn't gonna get much sense out of him. Trying to hide that great big old watermelon under his coat. Afraid to let the white man see him carry it home.

Bono: I'm like you . . . I ain't got no time for them kind of people.

Troy: Now what he look like getting mad cause he see the man from the union talking to Mr. Rand?

Bono: He come to me talking about . . . "Maxson gonna get us fired." I told him to get away from me with that. He walked away from me calling you a trouble-maker. What Mr. Rand say?

Troy: Ain't said nothing. He told me to go down the Commissioner's office next Friday. They called me down there to see them.

Bono: Well, as long as you got your complaint filed, they can't fire you. That's what one of them white fellows tell me.

Troy: I ain't worried about them firing me. They gonna fire me cause I asked a question? That's all I did. I went to Mr. Rand and asked him, "Why? Why you got the white mens driving and the colored lifting?" Told him, "what's the matter, don't I count? You think only white fellows got sense enough to drive a truck. That ain't no paper job! Hell, anybody can drive a truck. How come you got all whites driving and the colored lifting?" He told me "take it to the union." Well, hell, that's what I done! Now they wanna come up with this pack of lies.

Bono: I told Brownie if the man come and ask him any questions . . . just tell the truth! It ain't nothing but something they done trumped up on you cause you filed a complaint on them.

Troy: Brownie don't understand nothing. All I want them to do is change the job description. Give everybody a chance to drive the truck. Brownie can't see that. He ain't got that much sense.

Bono: How you figure he be making out with that gal be up at Taylors' all the time . . . that Alberta gal?

Troy: Same as you and me. Getting just as much as we is. Which is to say nothing.

Bono: It is, huh? I figure you doing a little better than me . . . and I ain't saying what I'm doing.

Troy: Aw, nigger, look here . . . I know you. If you had got anywhere near that gal, twenty minutes later you be looking to tell somebody. And the first one you gonna tell . . . that you gonna want to brag to . . . is me.

Bono: I ain't saying that. I see where you be eyeing her.

Troy: I eye all the women. I don't miss nothing. Don't never let nobody tell you Troy Maxson don't eye the women.

Bono: You been doing more than eyeing her. You done bought her a drink or two.

Troy: Hell yeah, I bought her a drink! What that mean? I bought you one, too. What that mean cause I buy her a drink? I'm just being polite.

Bono: It's all right to buy her one drink. That's what you call being polite. But when you wanna be buying two or three . . . that's what you call eyeing her.

Troy: Look here, as long as you known me . . . you ever known me to chase after women?

Bono: Hell yeah! Long as I done known you. You forgetting I knew you when.

Troy: Naw, I'm talking about since I been married to Rose?

Bono: Oh, not since you been married to Rose. Now, that's the truth, there. I can say that.

Troy: All right then! Case closed.

Bono: I see you be walking up around Alberta's house. You supposed to be at Taylors' and you be walking up around there.

Troy: What you watching where I'm walking for? I ain't watching after you.

Bono: I seen you walking around there more than once.

Troy: Hell, you liable to see me walking anywhere! That don't mean nothing cause you see me walking around there.

Bono: Where she come from anyway? She just kinda showed up one day.

Troy: Tallahassee. You can look at her and tell she one of them Florida gals. They got some big healthy women down there. Grow them right up out the ground. Got a little bit of Indian in her. Most of them niggers down in Florida got some Indian in them.

Bono: I don't know about that Indian part. But she damn sure big and healthy. Woman wear some big stockings. Got them great big old legs and hips as wide as the Mississippi River.

Troy: Legs don't mean nothing. You don't do nothing but push them out of the way. But them hips cushion the ride!

Bono: Troy, you ain't got no sense.

Troy: It's the truth! Like you riding on Goodyears!

> *Rose enters from the house. She is ten years younger than Troy, her devotion to him stems from her recognition of the possibilities of her life without him: a succession of abusive men and their babies, a life of partying and running the streets, the Church, or aloneness with its attendant pain and frustration. She recognizes Troy's spirit as a fine and illuminating one and she either ignores or forgives his faults, only some of which she recognizes. Though she doesn't drink, her presence is an integral part of the Friday night rituals. She alternates between the porch and the kitchen, where supper preparations are under way.*

Rose: What you all out here getting into?

Troy: What you worried about what we getting into for? This is men talk, woman.

Rose: What I care what you all talking about? Bono, you gonna stay for supper?

Bono: No, I thank you, Rose. But Lucille say she cooking up a pot of pigfeet.

Troy: Pigfeet! Hell, I'm going home with you! Might even stay the night if you got some pigfeet. You got something in there to top them pigfeet, Rose?

Rose: I'm cooking up some chicken. I got some chicken and collard greens.

Troy: Well, go on back in the house and let me and Bono finish what we was talking about. This is men talk. I got some talk for you later. You know what kind of talk I mean. You go on and powder it up.

Rose: Troy Maxson, don't you start that now!

Troy (puts his arm around her): Aw, woman . . . come here. Look here, Bono . . . when I met this woman . . . I got out that place, say, "Hitch up my pony, saddle up my mare . . . there's a woman out there for me somewhere. I looked here.

Looked there. Saw Rose and latched on to her." I latched on to her and told her — I'm gonna tell you the truth — I told her, "Baby, I don't wanna marry, I just wanna be your man." Rose told me . . . tell him what you told me, Rose.

Rose: I told him if he wasn't the marrying kind, then move out the way so the marrying kind could find me.

Troy: That's what she told me. "Nigger, you in my way. You blocking the view! Move out the way so I can find me a husband." I thought it over two or three days. Come back —

Rose: Ain't no two or three days nothing. You was back the same night.

Troy: Come back, told her . . . "Okay, baby . . . but I'm gonna buy me a banty rooster and put him out there in the backyard . . . and when he see a stranger come, he'll flap his wings and crow . . ." Look here, Bono, I could watch the front door by myself . . . it was that back door I was worried about.

Rose: Troy, you ought not talk like that. Troy ain't doing nothing but telling a lie.

Troy: Only thing is . . . when we first got married . . . forget the rooster . . . we ain't had no yard!

Bono: I hear you tell it. Me and Lucille was staying down there on Logan Street. Had two rooms with the outhouse in the back. I ain't mind the outhouse none. But when that goddamn wind blow through there in the winter . . . that's what I'm talking about! To this day I wonder why in the hell I ever stayed down there for six long years. But see, I didn't know I could do no better. I thought only white folks had inside toilets and things.

Rose: There's a lot of people don't know they can do no better than they doing now. That's just something you got to learn. A lot of folks still shop at Bella's.

Troy: Ain't nothing wrong with shopping at Bella's. She got fresh food.

Rose: I ain't said nothing about if she got fresh food. I'm talking about what she charge. She charge ten cents more than the A&P.

Troy: The A&P ain't never done nothing for me. I spends my money where I'm treated right. I go down to Bella, say, "I need a loaf of bread, I'll pay you Friday." She give it to me. What sense that make when I got money to go and spend it somewhere else and ignore the person who done right by me? That ain't in the Bible.

Rose: We ain't talking about what's in the Bible. What sense it make to shop there when she overcharge?

Troy: You shop where you want to. I'll do my shopping where the people been good to me.

Rose: Well, I don't think it's right for her to overcharge. That's all I was saying.

Bono: Look here . . . I got to get on. Lucille going be raising all kind of hell.

Troy: Where you going, nigger? We ain't finished this pint. Come here, finish this pint.

Bono: Well, hell, I am . . . if you ever turn the bottle loose.

Troy (hands him the bottle): The only thing I say about the A&P is I'm glad Cory got that job down there. Help him take care of his school clothes and things. Gabe done moved out and things getting tight around here. He got that job. . . . He can start to look out for himself.

Rose: Cory done went and got recruited by a college football team.

Troy: I told that boy about that football stuff. The white man ain't gonna let him get nowhere with that football. I told him when he first come to me with it. Now you come telling me he done went and got more tied up in it. He ought to go and get recruited in how to fix cars or something where he can make a living.

Rose: He ain't talking about making no living playing football. It's just something the boys in school do. They gonna send a recruiter by to talk to you. He'll tell you he ain't talking about making no living playing football. It's a honor to be recruited.

Troy: It ain't gonna get him nowhere. Bono'll tell you that.

Bono: If he be like you in the sports . . . he's gonna be all right. Ain't but two men ever played baseball as good as you. That's Babe Ruth° and Josh Gibson.° Them's the only two men ever hit more home runs than you.

Troy: What it ever get me? Ain't got a pot to piss in or a window to throw it out of.

Rose: Times have changed since you was playing baseball, Troy. That was before the war. Times have changed a lot since then.

Troy: How in hell they done changed?

Rose: They got lots of colored boys playing ball now. Baseball and football.

Bono: You right about that, Rose. Times have changed, Troy. You just come along too early.

Troy: There ought not never have been no time called too early! Now you take that fellow . . . what's that fellow they had playing right field for the Yankees back then? You know who I'm talking about, Bono. Used to play right field for the Yankees.

Rose: Selkirk?

Troy: Selkirk! That's it! Man batting .269, understand? .269. What kind of sense that make? I was hitting .432 with thirty-seven home runs! Man batting .269 and playing right field for the Yankees! I saw Josh Gibson's daughter yesterday. She walking around with raggedy shoes on her feet. Now I bet you Selkirk's daughter ain't walking around with raggedy shoes on her feet! I bet you that!

Rose: They got a lot of colored baseball players now. Jackie Robinson° was the first. Folks had to wait for Jackie Robinson.

Troy: I done seen a hundred niggers play baseball better than Jackie Robinson. Hell, I know some teams Jackie Robinson couldn't even make! What you talking about Jackie Robinson. Jackie Robinson wasn't nobody. I'm talking about if you could play ball then they ought to have let you play. Don't care what color you were. Come telling me I come along too early. If you could play . . . then they ought to have let you play.

Troy takes a long drink from the bottle.

Rose: You gonna drink yourself to death. You don't need to be drinking like that.

Troy: Death ain't nothing. I done seen him. Done wrassled with him. You can't tell me nothing about death. Death ain't nothing but a fastball on the outside corner. And you know what I'll do to that! Lookee here, Bono . . . am I lying? You get one of them fastballs, about waist high, over the outside corner of the plate where you can get the meat of the bat on it . . . and good god! You can kiss it goodbye. Now, am I lying?

Bono: Naw, you telling the truth there. I seen you do it.

Troy: If I'm lying . . . that 450 feet worth of lying! *(Pause.)* That's all death is to me. A fastball on the outside corner.

Rose: I don't know why you want to get on talking about death.

Troy: Ain't nothing wrong with talking about death. That's part of life. Everybody gonna die. You gonna die, I'm gonna die. Bono's gonna die. Hell, we all gonna die.

Babe Ruth (1895–1948): One of the greatest American baseball players. *Josh Gibson* (1911–1947): Powerful baseball player known in the 1930s as the Babe Ruth of the Negro leagues. *Jackie Robinson* (1919–1972): The first black baseball player in the major leagues (1947).

Rose: But you ain't got to talk about it. I don't like to talk about it.

Troy: You the one brought it up. Me and Bono was talking about baseball . . . you tell me I'm gonna drink myself to death. Ain't that right, Bono? You know I don't drink this but one night out of the week. That's Friday night. I'm gonna drink just enough to where I can handle it. Then I cuts it loose. I leave it alone. So don't you worry about me drinking myself to death. 'Cause I ain't worried about Death. I done seen him. I done wrestled with him.

Look here, Bono . . . I looked up one day and Death was marching straight at me. Like Soldiers on Parade! The Army of Death was marching straight at me. The middle of July, 1941. It got real cold just like it be winter. It seem like Death himself reached out and touched me on the shoulder. He touch me just like I touch you. I got cold as ice and Death standing there grinning at me.

Rose: Troy, why don't you hush that talk.

Troy: I say . . . what you want, Mr. Death? You be wanting me? You done brought your army to be getting me? I looked him dead in the eye. I wasn't fearing nothing. I was ready to tangle. Just like I'm ready to tangle now. The Bible say be ever vigilant. That's why I don't get but so drunk. I got to keep watch.

Rose: Troy was right down there in Mercy Hospital. You remember he had pneumonia? Laying there with a fever talking plumb out of his head.

Troy: Death standing there staring at me . . . carrying that sickle in his hand. Finally he say, "You want bound over for another year?" See, just like that . . . "You want bound over for another year?" I told him, "Bound over hell! Let's settle this now!"

It seem like he kinda fell back when I said that, and all the cold went out of me. I reached down and grabbed that sickle and threw it just as far as I could throw it . . . and me and him commenced to wrestling.

We wrestled for three days and three nights. I can't say where I found the strength from. Every time it seemed like he was gonna get the best of me, I'd reach way down deep inside myself and find the strength to do him one better.

Rose: Every time Troy tell that story he find different ways to tell it. Different things to make up about it.

Troy: I ain't making up nothing. I'm telling you the facts of what happened. I wrestled with Death for three days and three nights and I'm standing here to tell you about it. *(Pause.)* All right. At the end of the third night we done weakened each other to where we can't hardly move. Death stood up, throwed on his robe . . . had him a white robe with a hood on it. He throwed on that robe and went off to look for his sickle. Say, "I'll be back." Just like that. "I'll be back." I told him, say, "Yeah, but . . . you gonna have to find me!" I wasn't no fool. I wan't going looking for him. Death ain't nothing to play with. And I know he's gonna get me. I know I got to join his army . . . his camp followers. But as long as I keep my strength and see him coming . . . as long as I keep up my vigilance . . . he's gonna have to fight to get me. I ain't going easy.

Bono: Well, look here, since you got to keep up your vigilance . . . let me have the bottle.

Troy: Aw hell, I shouldn't have told you that part. I should have left out that part.

Rose: Troy be talking that stuff and half the time don't even know what he be talking about.

Troy: Bono know me better than that.

Bono: That's right. I know you. I know you got some Uncle Remus° in your blood.
You got more stories than the devil got sinners.

Troy: Aw hell, I done seen him too! Done talked with the devil.

Rose: Troy, don't nobody wanna be hearing all that stuff.

> *Lyons enters the yard from the street. Thirty-four years old, Troy's son by a
> previous marriage, he sports a neatly trimmed goatee, sport coat, white shirt,
> tieless and buttoned at the collar. Though he fancies himself a musician, he is
> more caught up in the rituals and "idea" of being a musician than in the actual
> practice of the music. He has come to borrow money from Troy, and while he
> knows he will be successful, he is uncertain as to what extent his lifestyle will be
> held up to scrutiny and ridicule.*

Lyons: Hey, Pop.

Troy: What you come "Hey, Popping" me for?

Lyons: How you doing, Rose? *(He kisses her.)* Mr. Bono. How you doing?

Bono: Hey, Lyons . . . how you been?

Troy: He must have been doing all right. I ain't seen him around here last week.

Rose: Troy, leave your boy alone. He come by to see you and you wanna start all
that nonsense.

Troy: I ain't bothering Lyons. *(Offers him the bottle.)* Here . . . get you a drink. We
got an understanding. I know why he come by to see me and he know I know.

Lyons: Come on, Pop . . . I just stopped by to say hi . . . see how you was doing.

Troy: You ain't stopped by yesterday.

Rose: You gonna stay for supper, Lyons? I got some chicken cooking in the oven.

Lyons: No, Rose . . . thanks. I was just in the neighborhood and thought I'd stop
by for a minute.

Troy: You was in the neighborhood all right, nigger. You telling the truth there.
You was in the neighborhood cause it's my payday.

Lyons: Well, hell, since you mentioned it . . . let me have ten dollars.

Troy: I'll be damned! I'll die and go to hell and play blackjack with the devil before
I give you ten dollars.

Bono: That's what I wanna know about . . . that devil you done seen.

Lyons: What . . . Pop done seen the devil? You too much, Pops.

Troy: Yeah, I done seen him. Talked to him too!

Rose: You ain't seen no devil. I done told you that man ain't had nothing to do with
the devil. Anything you can't understand, you want to call it the devil.

Troy: Look here, Bono . . . I went down to see Hertzberger about some furniture.
Got three rooms for two-ninety-eight. That what it say on the radio. "Three
rooms . . . two-ninety-eight." Even made up a little song about it. Go down
there . . . man tell me I can't get no credit. I'm working every day and can't get
no credit. What to do? I got an empty house with some raggedy furniture in
it. Cory ain't got no bed. He's sleeping on a pile of rags on the floor. Working
every day and can't get no credit. Come back here — Rose'll tell you — mad-
der than hell. Sit down . . . try to figure what I'm gonna do. Come a knock
on the door. Ain't been living here but three days. Who know I'm here? Open
the door . . . devil standing there bigger than life. White fellow . . . white fellow . . . got on good clothes and everything. Standing there with a clipboard

---

Uncle Remus: Black storyteller who recounts traditional black tales in the book by Joel Chandler
Harris.

in his hand. I ain't had to say nothing. First words come out of his mouth was . . . "I understand you need some furniture and can't get no credit." I liked to fell over. He say, "I'll give you all the credit you want, but you got to pay the interest on it." I told him, "Give me three rooms worth and charge whatever you want." Next day a truck pulled up here and two men unloaded them three rooms. Man what drove the truck give me a book. Say send ten dollars, first of every month to the address in the book and everything will be all right. Say if I miss a payment the devil was coming back and it'll be hell to pay. That was fifteen years ago. To this day . . . the first of the month I send my ten dollars, Rose'll tell you.

Rose: Troy lying.

Troy: I ain't never seen that man since. Now you tell me who else that could have been but the devil? I ain't sold my soul or nothing like that, you understand. Naw, I wouldn't have truck with the devil about nothing like that. I got my furniture and pays my ten dollars the first of the month just like clockwork.

Bono: How long you say you been paying this ten dollars a month?

Troy: Fifteen years!

Bono: Hell, ain't you finished paying for it yet? How much the man done charged you?

Troy: Ah hell, I done paid for it. I done paid for it ten times over! The fact is I'm scared to stop paying it.

Rose: Troy lying. We got that furniture from Mr. Glickman. He ain't paying no ten dollars a month to nobody.

Troy: Aw hell, woman. Bono know I ain't that big a fool.

Lyons: I was just getting ready to say . . . I know where there's a bridge for sale.

Troy: Look here, I'll tell you this . . . it don't matter to me if he was the devil. It don't matter if the devil give credit. Somebody has got to give it.

Rose: It ought to matter. You going around talking about having truck with the devil . . . God's the one you gonna have to answer to. He's the one gonna be at the Judgment.

Lyons: Yeah, well, look here, Pop . . . let me have that ten dollars. I'll give it back to you. Bonnie got a job working at the hospital.

Troy: What I tell you, Bono? The only time I see this nigger is when he wants something. That's the only time I see him.

Lyons: Come on, Pop, Mr. Bono don't want to hear all that. Let me have the ten dollars. I told you Bonnie working.

Troy: What that mean to me? "Bonnie working." I don't care if she working. Go ask her for the ten dollars if she working. Talking about "Bonnie working." Why ain't you working?

Lyons: Aw, Pop, you know I can't find no decent job. Where am I gonna get a job at? You know I can't get no job.

Troy: I told you I know some people down there. I can get you on the rubbish if you want to work. I told you that the last time you came by here asking me for something.

Lyons: Naw, Pop . . . thanks. That ain't for me. I don't wanna be carrying nobody's rubbish. I don't wanna be punching nobody's time clock.

Troy: What's the matter, you too good to carry people's rubbish? Where you think that ten dollars you talking about come from? I'm just supposed to haul people's rubbish and give my money to you cause you too lazy to work. You too lazy to work and wanna know why you ain't got what I got.

Rose: What hospital Bonnie working at? Mercy?

Lyons: She's down at Passavant working in the laundry.

Troy: I ain't got nothing as it is. I give you that ten dollars and I got to eat beans the rest of the week. Naw . . . you ain't getting no ten dollars here.

Lyons: You ain't got to be eating no beans. I don't know why you wanna say that.

Troy: I ain't got no extra money. Gabe done moved over to Miss Pearl's paying her the rent and things done got tight around here. I can't afford to be giving you every payday.

Lyons: I ain't asked you to give me nothing. I asked you to loan me ten dollars. I know you got ten dollars.

Troy: Yeah, I got it. You know why I got it? Cause I don't throw my money away out there in the streets. You living the fast life . . . wanna be a musician . . . running around in them clubs and things . . . then, you learn to take care of yourself. You ain't gonna find me going and asking nobody for nothing. I done spent too many years without.

Lyons: You and me is two different people, Pop.

Troy: I done learned my mistake and learned to do what's right by it. You still trying to get something for nothing. Life don't owe you nothing. You owe it to yourself. Ask Bono. He'll tell you I'm right.

Lyons: You got your way of dealing with the world . . . I got mine. The only thing that matters to me is the music.

Troy: Yeah, I can see that! It don't matter how you gonna eat . . . where your next dollar is coming from. You telling the truth there.

Lyons: I know I got to eat. But I got to live too. I need something that gonna help me to get out of the bed in the morning. Make me feel like I belong in the world. I don't bother nobody. I just stay with the music cause that's the only way I can find to live in the world. Otherwise there ain't no telling what I might do. Now I don't come criticizing you and how you live. I just come by to ask you for ten dollars. I don't wanna hear all that about how I live.

Troy: Boy, your mamma did a hell of a job raising you.

Lyons: You can't change me, Pop. I'm thirty-four years old. If you wanted to change me, you should have been there when I was growing up. I come by to see you . . . ask for ten dollars and you want to talk about how I was raised. You don't know nothing about how I was raised.

Rose: Let the boy have ten dollars, Troy.

Troy (to Lyons): What the hell you looking at me for? I ain't got no ten dollars. You know what I do with my money. *(To Rose.)* Give him ten dollars if you want him to have it.

Rose: I will. Just as soon as you turn it loose.

Troy (handing Rose the money): There it is. Seventy-six dollars and forty-two cents. You see this, Bono? Now, I ain't gonna get but six of that back.

Rose: You ought to stop telling that lie. Here, Lyons. *(She hands him the money.)*

Lyons: Thanks, Rose. Look . . . I got to run . . . I'll see you later.

Troy: Wait a minute. You gonna say, "thanks, Rose" and ain't gonna look to see where she got that ten dollars from? See how they do me, Bono?

Lyons: I know she got it from you, Pop. Thanks. I'll give it back to you.

Troy: There he go telling another lie. Time I see that ten dollars . . . he'll be owing me thirty more.

Lyons: See you, Mr. Bono.

Bono: Take care, Lyons!

Lyons: Thanks, Pop. I'll see you again.

> *Lyons exits the yard.*

Troy: I don't know why he don't go and get him a decent job and take care of that woman he got.

Bono: He'll be all right, Troy. The boy is still young.

Troy: The *boy* is thirty-four years old.

Rose: Let's not get off into all that.

Bono: Look here . . . I got to be going. I got to be getting on. Lucille gonna be waiting.

Troy (puts his arm around Rose): See this woman, Bono? I love this woman. I love this woman so much it hurts. I love her so much . . . I done run out of ways of loving her. So I got to go back to basics. Don't you come by my house Monday morning talking about time to go to work . . . 'cause I'm still gonna be stroking!

Rose: Troy! Stop it now!

Bono: I ain't paying him no mind, Rose. That ain't nothing but gin-talk. Go on, Troy. I'll see you Monday.

Troy: Don't you come by my house, nigger! I done told you what I'm gonna be doing.

> *The lights go down to black.*

SCENE II

> *The lights come up on Rose hanging up clothes. She hums and sings softly to herself. It is the following morning.*

Rose (sings): Jesus, be a fence all around me every day
Jesus, I want you to protect me as I travel on my way.
Jesus, be a fence all around me every day.

> *Troy enters from the house.*

Jesus, I want you to protect me
As I travel on my way.
(To Troy.) 'Morning. You ready for breakfast? I can fix it soon as I finish hanging up these clothes?

Troy: I got the coffee on. That'll be all right. I'll just drink some of that this morning.

Rose: That 651 hit yesterday. That's the second time this month. Miss Pearl hit for a dollar . . . seem like those that need the least always get lucky. Poor folks can't get nothing.

Troy: Them numbers don't know nobody. I don't know why you fool with them. You and Lyons both.

Rose: It's something to do.

Troy: You ain't doing nothing but throwing your money away.

Rose: Troy, you know I don't play foolishly. I just play a nickel here and a nickel there.

Troy: That's two nickels you done thrown away.

Rose: Now I hit sometimes . . . that makes up for it. It always comes in handy when I do hit. I don't hear you complaining then.

Troy: I ain't complaining now. I just say it's foolish. Trying to guess out of six hundred ways which way the number gonna come. If I had all the money niggers, these Negroes, throw away on numbers for one week — just one week — I'd be a rich man.

Rose: Well, you wishing and calling it foolish ain't gonna stop folks from playing numbers. That's one thing for sure. Besides . . . some good things come from playing numbers. Look where Pope done bought him that restaurant off of numbers.

Troy: I can't stand niggers like that. Man ain't had two dimes to rub together. He walking around with his shoes all run over bumming money for cigarettes. All right. Got lucky there and hit the numbers . . .

Rose: Troy, I know all about it.

Troy: Had good sense, I'll say that for him. He ain't throwed his money away. I seen niggers hit the numbers and go through two thousand dollars in four days. Man bought him that restaurant down there . . . fixed it up real nice . . . and then didn't want nobody to come in it! A Negro go in there and can't get no kind of service. I seen a white fellow come in there and order a bowl of stew. Pope picked all the meat out the pot for him. Man ain't had nothing but a bowl of meat! Negro come behind him and ain't got nothing but the potatoes and carrots. Talking about what numbers do for people, you picked a wrong example. Ain't done nothing but make a worser fool out of him than he was before.

Rose: Troy, you ought to stop worrying about what happened at work yesterday.

Troy: I ain't worried. Just told me to be down there at the Commissioner's office on Friday. Everybody think they gonna fire me. I ain't worried about them firing me. You ain't got to worry about that. *(Pause.)* Where's Cory? Cory in the house? *(Calls.)* Cory?

Rose: He gone out.

Troy: Out, huh? He gone out 'cause he know I want him to help me with this fence. I know how he is. That boy scared of work.

Gabriel enters. He comes halfway down the alley and, hearing Troy's voice, stops.

Troy (continues): He ain't done a lick of work in his life.

Rose: He had to go to football practice. Coach wanted them to get in a little extra practice before the season start.

Troy: I got his practice . . . running out of here before he get his chores done.

Rose: Troy, what is wrong with you this morning? Don't nothing set right with you. Go on back in there and go to bed . . . get up on the other side.

Troy: Why something got to be wrong with me? I ain't said nothing wrong with me.

Rose: You got something to say about everything. First it's the numbers . . . then it's the way the man runs his restaurant . . . then you done got on Cory. What's it gonna be next? Take a look up there and see if the weather suits you . . . or is it gonna be how you gonna put up the fence with the clothes hanging in the yard.

Troy: You hit the nail on the head then.

Rose: I know you like I know the back of my hand. Go on in there and get you some coffee . . . see if that straighten you up. 'Cause you ain't right this morning.

Troy starts into the house and sees Gabriel. Gabriel starts singing. Troy's brother, he is seven years younger than Troy. Injured in World War II, he has a metal plate in his head. He carries an old trumpet tied around his waist and believes with every fiber of his being that he is the Archangel Gabriel.° He carries a chipped basket with an assortment of discarded fruits and vegetables he has picked up in the strip district and which he attempts to sell.

Gabriel (singing): Yes, ma am, I got plums
    You ask me how I sell them
    Oh ten cents apiece
    Three for a quarter
    Come and buy now
    'Cause I'm here today
    And tomorrow I'll be gone

Gabriel enters.

Hey, Rose!
Rose: How you doing, Gabe?
Gabriel: There's Troy . . . Hey, Troy!
Troy: Hey, Gabe.

Exit into kitchen.

Rose (to Gabriel): What you got there?
Gabriel: You know what I got, Rose. I got fruits and vegetables.
Rose (looking in basket): Where's all these plums you talking about?
Gabriel: I ain't got no plums today, Rose. I was just singing that. Have some tomorrow. Put me in a big order for plums. Have enough plums tomorrow for St. Peter and everybody.

Troy reenters from kitchen, crosses to steps.

(To Rose.) Troy's mad at me.
Troy: I ain't mad at you. What I got to be mad at you about? You ain't done nothing to me.
Gabriel: I just moved over to Miss Pearl's to keep out from in your way. I ain't mean no harm by it.
Troy: Who said anything about that? I ain't said anything about that.
Gabriel: You ain't mad at me, is you?
Troy: Naw . . . I ain't mad at you, Gabe. If I was mad at you I'd tell you about it.
Gabriel: Got me two rooms. In the basement. Got my own door too. Wanna see my key? *(He holds up a key.)* That's my own key! Ain't nobody else got a key like that. That's my key! My two rooms!
Troy: Well, that's good, Gabe. You got your own key . . . that's good.
Rose: You hungry, Gabe? I was just fixing to cook Troy his breakfast.
Gabriel: I'll take some biscuits. You got some biscuits? Did you know when I was in heaven . . . every morning me and St. Peter° would sit down by the gate and eat some big fat biscuits? Oh, yeah! We had us a good time. We'd sit there and eat us them biscuits and then St. Peter would go off to sleep and tell me to wake him up when it's time to open the gates for the judgment.
Rose: Well, come on . . . I'll make up a batch of biscuits.

Rose exits into the house.

Archangel Gabriel: Considered one of God's primary messengers in the Old and New Testaments.   *St. Peter:* One of Jesus's disciples, believed to be the keeper of the gates of Heaven.

Gabriel: Troy . . . St. Peter got your name in the book. I seen it. It say . . . Troy Maxson. I say . . . I know him! He got the same name like what I got. That's my brother!

Troy: How many times you gonna tell me that, Gabe?

Gabriel: Ain't got my name in the book. Don't have to have my name. I done died and went to heaven. He got your name though. One morning St. Peter was looking at his book . . . marking it up for the judgment . . . and he let me see your name. Got it in there under M. Got Rose's name . . . I ain't seen it like I seen yours . . . but I know it's in there. He got a great big book. Got everybody's name what was ever been born. That's what he told me. But I seen your name. Seen it with my own eyes.

Troy: Go on in the house there. Rose going to fix you something to eat.

Gabriel: Oh, I ain't hungry. I done had breakfast with Aunt Jemimah. She come by and cooked me up a whole mess of flapjacks. Remember how we used to eat them flapjacks?

Troy: Go on in the house and get you something to eat now.

Gabriel: I got to sell my plums. I done sold some tomatoes. Got me two quarters. Wanna see? *(He shows Troy his quarters.)* I'm gonna save them and buy me a new horn so St. Peter can hear me when it's time to open the gates. *(Gabriel stops suddenly. Listens.)* Hear that? That's the hellhounds. I got to chase them out of here. Go on get out of here! Get out!

Gabriel exits singing.

Better get ready for the judgment
Better get ready for the judgment
My Lord is coming down

Rose enters from the house.

Troy: He's gone off somewhere.

Gabriel (offstage): Better get ready for the judgment
Better get ready for the judgment morning
Better get ready for the judgment
My God is coming down

Rose: He ain't eating right. Miss Pearl say she can't get him to eat nothing.

Troy: What you want me to do about it, Rose? I done did everything I can for the man. I can't make him get well. Man got half his head blown away . . . what you expect?

Rose: Seem like something ought to be done to help him.

Troy: Man don't bother nobody. He just mixed up from that metal plate he got in his head. Ain't no sense for him to go back into the hospital.

Rose: Least he be eating right. They can help him take care of himself.

Troy: Don't nobody wanna be locked up, Rose. What you wanna lock him up for? Man go over there and fight the war . . . messin' around with them Japs, get half his head blown off . . . and they give him a lousy three thousand dollars. And I had to swoop down on that.

Rose: Is you fixing to go into that again?

Troy: That's the only way I got a roof over my head . . . cause of that metal plate.

Rose: Ain't no sense you blaming yourself for nothing. Gabe wasn't in no condition to manage that money. You done what was right by him. Can't nobody say you ain't done what was right by him. Look how long you took care of him . . . till he wanted to have his own place and moved over there with Miss Pearl.

Troy: That ain't what I'm saying, woman! I'm just stating the facts. If my brother didn't have that metal plate in his head . . . I wouldn't have a pot to piss in or a window to throw it out of. And I'm fifty-three years old. Now see if you can understand that!

Troy gets up from the porch and starts to exit the yard.

Rose: Where you going off to? You been running out of here every Saturday for weeks. I thought you was gonna work on this fence?

Troy: I'm gonna walk down to Taylors'. Listen to the ball game. I'll be back in a bit. I'll work on it when I get back.

He exits the yard. The lights go to black.

SCENE III

The lights come up on the yard. It is four hours later. Rose is taking down the clothes from the line. Cory enters carrying his football equipment.

Rose: Your daddy like to had a fit with you running out of here this morning without doing your chores.

Cory: I told you I had to go to practice.

Rose: He say you were supposed to help him with this fence.

Cory: He been saying that the last four or five Saturdays, and then he don't never do nothing, but go down to Taylors. Did you tell him about the recruiter?

Rose: Yeah, I told him.

Cory: What he say?

Rose: He ain't said nothing too much. You get in there and get started on your chores before he gets back. Go on and scrub down them steps before he gets back here hollering and carrying on.

Cory: I'm hungry. What you got to eat, Mama?

Rose: Go on and get started on your chores. I got some meat loaf in there. Go on and make you a sandwich . . . and don't leave no mess in there.

Cory exits into the house. Rose continues to take down the clothes. Troy enters the yard and sneaks up and grabs her from behind.

Troy! Go on, now. You liked to scared me to death. What was the score of the game? Lucille had me on the phone and I couldn't keep up with it.

Troy: What I care about the game? Come here, woman. (*He tries to kiss her.*)

Rose: I thought you went down Taylors' to listen to the game. Go on, Troy! You supposed to be putting up this fence.

Troy (attempting to kiss her again): I'll put it up when I finish with what is at hand.

Rose: Go on, Troy. I ain't studying you.

Troy (chasing after her): I'm studying you . . . fixing to do my homework!

Rose: Troy, you better leave me alone.

Troy: Where's Cory? That boy brought his butt home yet?

Rose: He's in the house doing his chores.

Troy (calling): Cory! Get your butt out here, boy!

Rose exits into the house with the laundry. Troy goes over to the pile of wood, picks up a board, and starts sawing. Cory enters from the house.

Troy: You just now coming in here from leaving this morning?

Cory: Yeah, I had to go to football practice.

Troy: Yeah, what?

Cory: Yessir.

Troy: I ain't but two seconds off you noway. The garbage sitting in there over-flowing . . . you ain't done none of your chores . . . and you come in here talking about "Yeah."

Cory: I was just getting ready to do my chores now, Pop . . .

Troy: Your first chore is to help me with this fence on Saturday. Everything else come after that. Now get that saw and cut them boards.

Cory takes the saw and begins cutting the boards. Troy continues working. There is a long pause.

Cory: Hey, Pop . . . why don't you buy a TV?

Troy: What I want with a TV? What I want one of them for?

Cory: Everybody got one. Earl, Ba Bra . . . Jesse!

Troy: I ain't asked you who had one. I say what I want with one?

Cory: So you can watch it. They got lots of things on TV. Baseball games and everything. We could watch the World Series.

Troy: Yeah . . . and how much this TV cost?

Cory: I don't know. They got them on sale for around two hundred dollars.

Troy: Two hundred dollars, huh?

Cory: That ain't that much, Pop.

Troy: Naw, it's just two hundred dollars. See that roof you got over your head at night? Let me tell you something about that roof. It's been over ten years since that roof was last tarred. See now . . . the snow come this winter and sit up there on that roof like it is . . . and it's gonna seep inside. It's just gonna be a little bit . . . ain't gonna hardly notice it. Then the next thing you know, it's gonna be leaking all over the house. Then the wood rot from all that water and you gonna need a whole new roof. Now, how much you think it cost to get that roof tarred?

Cory: I don't know.

Troy: Two hundred and sixty-four dollars . . . cash money. While you thinking about a TV, I got to be thinking about the roof . . . and whatever else go wrong here. Now if you had two hundred dollars, what would you do . . . fix the roof or buy a TV?

Cory: I'd buy a TV. Then when the roof started to leak . . . when it needed fixing . . . I'd fix it.

Troy: Where you gonna get the money from? You done spent it for a TV. You gonna sit up and watch the water run all over your brand new TV.

Cory: Aw, Pop. You got money. I know you do.

Troy: Where I got it at, huh?

Cory: You got it in the bank.

Troy: You wanna see my bankbook? You wanna see that seventy-three dollars and twenty-two cents I got sitting up in there.

Cory: You ain't got to pay for it all at one time. You can put a down payment on it and carry it on home with you.

Troy: Not me. I ain't gonna owe nobody nothing if I can help it. Miss a payment and they come and snatch it right out your house. Then what you got? Now, soon as I get two hundred dollars clear, then I'll buy a TV. Right now, as soon as I get two hundred and sixty-four dollars, I'm gonna have this roof tarred.

Cory: Aw . . . Pop!

Troy: You go on and get you two hundred dollars and buy one if ya want it. I got better things to do with my money.

Cory: I can't get no two hundred dollars. I ain't never seen two hundred dollars.

Troy: I'll tell you what . . . you get you a hundred dollars and I'll put the other hundred with it.

Cory: All right, I'm gonna show you.

Troy: You gonna show me how you can cut them boards right now.

Cory begins to cut the boards. There is a long pause.

Cory: The Pirates won today. That makes five in a row.

Troy: I ain't thinking about the Pirates. Got an all-white team. Got that boy . . . that Puerto Rican boy . . . Clemente. Don't even half-play him. That boy could be something if they give him a chance. Play him one day and sit him on the bench the next.

Cory: He gets a lot of chances to play.

Troy: I'm talking about playing regular. Playing every day so you can get your timing. That's what I'm talking about.

Cory: They got some white guys on the team that don't play every day. You can't play everybody at the same time.

Troy: If they got a white fellow sitting on the bench . . . you can bet your last dollar he can't play! The colored guy got to be twice as good before he get on the team. That's why I don't want you to get all tied up in them sports. Man on the team and what it get him? They got colored on the team and don't use them. Same as not having them. All them teams the same.

Cory: The Braves got Hank Aaron and Wes Covington. Hank Aaron hit two home runs today. That makes forty-three.

Troy: Hank Aaron ain't nobody. That what you supposed to do. That's how you supposed to play the game. Ain't nothing to it. It's just a matter of timing . . . getting the right follow-through. Hell, I can hit forty-three home runs right now!

Cory: Not off no major-league pitching, you couldn't.

Troy: We had better pitching in the Negro leagues. I hit seven home runs off of Satchel Paige.° You can't get no better than that!

Cory: Sandy Koufax. He's leading the league in strikeouts.

Troy: I ain't thinking of no Sandy Koufax.

Cory: You got Warren Spahn and Lew Burdette. I bet you couldn't hit no home runs off of Warren Spahn.

Troy: I'm through with it now. You go on and cut them boards. *(Pause.)* Your mama tell me you done got recruited by a college football team? Is that right?

Cory: Yeah. Coach Zellman say the recruiter gonna be coming by to talk to you. Get you to sign the permission papers.

Troy: I thought you supposed to be working down there at the A&P. Ain't you suppose to be working down there after school?

Cory: Mr. Stawicki say he gonna hold my job for me until after the football season. Say starting next week I can work weekends.

Troy: I thought we had an understanding about this football stuff? You suppose to keep up with your chores and hold that job down at the A&P. Ain't been

Satchel Paige (1906?–1982): Legendary black pitcher in the Negro leagues.

around here all day on a Saturday. Ain't none of your chores done . . . and now you telling me you done quit your job.

Cory: I'm going to be working weekends.

Troy: You damn right you are! And ain't no need for nobody coming around here to talk to me about signing nothing.

Cory: Hey, Pop . . . you can't do that. He's coming all the way from North Carolina.

Troy: I don't care where he coming from. The white man ain't gonna let you get nowhere with that football noway. You go on and get your book-learning so you can work yourself up in that A&P or learn how to fix cars or build houses or something, get you a trade. That way you have something can't nobody take away from you. You go on and learn how to put your hands to some good use. Besides hauling people's garbage.

Cory: I get good grades, Pop. That's why the recruiter wants to talk with you. You got to keep up your grades to get recruited. This way I'll be going to college. I'll get a chance . . .

Troy: First you gonna get your butt down there to the A&P and get your job back.

Cory: Mr. Stawicki done already hired somebody else 'cause I told him I was play-ing football.

Troy: You a bigger fool than I thought . . . to let somebody take away your job so you can play some football. Where you gonna get your money to take out your girlfriend and whatnot? What kind of foolishness is that to let somebody take away your job?

Cory: I'm still gonna be working weekends.

Troy: Naw . . . naw. You getting your butt out of here and finding you another job.

Cory: Come on, Pop! I got to practice. I can't work after school and play football too. The team needs me. That's what Coach Zellman say . . .

Troy: I don't care what nobody else say. I'm the boss . . . you understand? I'm the boss around here. I do the only saying what counts.

Cory: Come on, Pop!

Troy: I asked you . . . did you understand?

Cory: Yeah . . .

Troy: What?!

Cory: Yessir.

Troy: You go on down there to that A&P and see if you can get your job back. If you can't do both . . . then you quit the football team. You've got to take the crookeds with the straights.

Cory: Yessir. *(Pause.)* Can I ask you a question?

Troy: What the hell you wanna ask me? Mr. Stawicki the one you got the questions for.

Cory: How come you ain't never liked me?

Troy: Liked you? Who the hell say I got to like you? What law is there say I got to like you? Wanna stand up in my face and ask a damn fool-ass question like that. Talking about liking somebody. Come here, boy, when I talk to you.

Cory comes over to where Troy is working. He stands slouched over and Troy shoves him on his shoulder.

Straighten up, goddammit! I asked you a question . . . what law is there say I got to like you?

Cory: None.

Troy: Well, all right then! Don't you eat every day? *(Pause.)* Answer me when I talk to you! Don't you eat every day?

Cory: Yeah.

Troy: Nigger, as long as you in my house, you put that sir on the end of it when you talk to me!

Cory: Yes . . . sir.

Troy: You eat every day.

Cory: Yessir!

Troy: Got a roof over your head.

Cory: Yessir!

Troy: Got clothes on your back.

Cory: Yessir.

Troy: Why you think that is?

Cory: Cause of you.

Troy: Ah, hell I know it's cause of me . . . but why do you think that is?

Cory (hesitant): Cause you like me.

Troy: Like you? I go out of here every morning . . . bust my butt . . . putting up with them crackers° every day . . . cause I like you? You are the biggest fool I ever saw. *(Pause.)* It's my job. It's my responsibility! You understand that? A man got to take care of his family. You live in my house . . . sleep you behind on my bedclothes . . . fill you belly up with my food . . . cause you my son. You my flesh and blood. Not cause I like you! Cause it's my duty to take care of you. I owe a responsibility to you! Let's get this straight right here . . . before it go along any further . . . I ain't got to like you. Mr. Rand don't give me my money come payday cause he likes me. He give me cause he owe me. I done give you everything I had to give you. I gave you your life! Me and your mama worked that out between us. And liking your black ass wasn't part of the bargain. Don't you try and go through life worrying about if somebody like you or not. You best be making sure they doing right by you. You understand what I'm saying, boy?

Cory: Yessir.

Troy: Then get the hell out of my face, and get on down to that A&P.

Rose has been standing behind the screen door for much of the scene. She enters as Cory exits.

Rose: Why don't you let the boy go ahead and play football, Troy? Ain't no harm in that. He's just trying to be like you with the sports.

Troy: I don't want him to be like me! I want him to move as far away from my life as he can get. You the only decent thing that ever happened to me. I wish him that. But I don't wish him a thing else from my life. I decided seventeen years ago that boy wasn't getting involved in no sports. Not after what they did to me in the sports.

Rose: Troy, why don't you admit you was too old to play in the major leagues? For once . . . why don't you admit that?

Troy: What do you mean too old? Don't come telling me I was too old. I just wasn't the right color. Hell, I'm fifty-three years old and can do better than Selkirk's .269 right now!

---

crackers: White people, often used to refer disparagingly to poor whites.

Rose: How's was you gonna play ball when you were over forty? Sometimes I can't get no sense out of you.

Troy: I got good sense, woman. I got sense enough not to let my boy get hurt over playing no sports. You been mothering that boy too much. Worried about if people like him.

Rose: Everything that boy do . . . he do for you. He wants you to say "Good job, son." That's all.

Troy: Rose, I ain't got time for that. He's alive. He's healthy. He's got to make his own way. I made mine. Ain't nobody gonna hold his hand when he get out there in that world.

Rose: Times have changed from when you was young, Troy. People change. The world's changing around you and you can't even see it.

Troy (slow, methodical): Woman . . . I do the best I can do. I come in here every Friday. I carry a sack of potatoes and a bucket of lard. You all line up at the door with your hands out. I give you the lint from my pockets. I give you my sweat and my blood. I ain't got no tears. I done spent them. We go upstairs in that room at night . . . and I fall down on you and try to blast a hole into forever. I get up Monday morning . . . find my lunch on the table. I go out. Make my way. Find my strength to carry me through to the next Friday. *(Pause.)* That's all I got, Rose. That's all I got to give. I can't give nothing else.

Troy exits into the house. The lights go down to black.

Scene IV

It is Friday. Two weeks later. Cory starts out of the house with his football equipment. The phone rings.

Cory (calling): I got it! *(He answers the phone and stands in the screen door talking.)* Hello? Hey, Jesse. Naw . . . I was just getting ready to leave now.

Rose (calling): Cory!

Cory: I told you, man, them spikes is all tore up. You can use them if you want, but they ain't no good. Earl got some spikes.

Rose (calling): Cory!

Cory (calling to Rose): Mam? I'm talking to Jesse. *(Into phone.)* When she say that? *(Pause.)* Aw, you lying, man. I'm gonna tell her you said that.

Rose (calling): Cory, don't you go nowhere!

Cory: I got to go to the game, Ma! *(Into the phone.)* Yeah, hey, look, I'll talk to you later. Yeah, I'll meet you over Earl's house. Later. Bye, Ma.

Cory exits the house and starts out the yard.

Rose: Cory, where you going off to? You got that stuff all pulled out and thrown all over your room.

Cory (in the yard): I was looking for my spikes. Jesse wanted to borrow my spikes.

Rose: Get up there and get that cleaned up before your daddy get back in here.

Cory: I got to go to the game! I'll clean it up *when I get back.*

Cory exits.

Rose: That's all he need to do is see that room all messed up.

Rose exits into the house. Troy and Bono enter the yard. Troy is dressed in clothes other than his work clothes.

Bono: He told him the same thing he told you. Take it to the union.

Troy: Brownie ain't got that much sense. Man wasn't thinking about nothing. He wait until I confront them on it . . . then he wanna come crying seniority. *(Calls.)* Hey, Rose!

Bono: I wish I could have seen Mr. Rand's face when he told you.

Troy: He couldn't get it out of his mouth! Liked to bit his tongue! When they called me down there to the Commissioner's office . . . he thought they was gonna fire me. Like everybody else.

Bono: I didn't think they was gonna fire you. I thought they was gonna put you on the warning paper.

Troy: Hey, Rose! *(To Bono.)* Yeah, Mr. Rand like to bit his tongue.

Troy breaks the seal on the bottle, takes a drink, and hands it to Bono.

Bono: I see you run right down to Taylors' and told that Alberta gal.

Troy (calling): Hey Rose! *(To Bono.)* I told everybody. Hey, Rose! I went down there to cash my check.

Rose (entering from the house): Hush all that hollering, man! I know you out here. What they say down there at the Commissioner's office?

Troy: You supposed to come when I call you, woman. Bono'll tell you that. *(To Bono.)* Don't Lucille come when you call her?

Rose: Man, hush your mouth. I ain't no dog . . . talk about "come when you call me."

Troy (puts his arm around Rose): You hear this, Bono? I had me an old dog used to get uppity like that. You say, "C'mere, Blue!" . . . and he just lay there and look at you. End up getting a stick and chasing him away trying to make him come.

Rose: I ain't studying you and your dog. I remember you used to sing that old song.

Troy (he sings): Hear it ring! Hear it ring! I had a dog his name was Blue.

Rose: Don't nobody wanna hear you sing that old song.

Troy (sings): You know Blue was mighty true.

Rose: Used to have Cory running around here singing that song.

Bono: Hell, I remember that song myself.

Troy (sings): You know Blue was a good old dog.
     Blue treed a possum in a hollow log.
     That was my daddy's song. My daddy made up that song.

Rose: I don't care who made it up. Don't nobody wanna hear you sing it.

Troy (makes a song like calling a dog): Come here, woman.

Rose: You come in here carrying on, I reckon they ain't fired you. What they say down there at the Commissioner's office?

Troy: Look here, Rose . . . Mr. Rand called me into his office today when I got back from talking to them people down there . . . it come from up top . . . he called me in and told me they was making me a driver.

Rose: Troy, you kidding!

Troy: No I ain't. Ask Bono.

Rose: Well, that's great, Troy. Now you don't have to hassle them people no more.

Lyons enters from the street.

Troy: Aw hell, I wasn't looking to see you today. I thought you was in jail. Got it all over the front page of the *Courier* about them raiding Sefus's place . . . where you be hanging out with all them thugs.

Lyons: Hey, Pop . . . that ain't got nothing to do with me. I don't go down there gambling. I go down there to sit in with the band. I ain't got nothing to do with the gambling part. They got some good music down there.

Troy: They got some rogues . . . is what they got.

Lyons: How you been, Mr. Bono? Hi, Rose.

Bono: I see where you playing down at the Crawford Grill tonight.

Rose: How come you ain't brought Bonnie like I told you? You should have brought Bonnie with you, she ain't been over in a month of Sundays.

Lyons: I was just in the neighborhood . . . thought I'd stop by.

Troy: Here he come . . .

Bono: Your daddy got a promotion on the rubbish. He's gonna be the first colored driver. Ain't got to do nothing but sit up there and read the paper like them white fellows.

Lyons: Hey, Pop . . . if you knew how to read you'd be all right.

Bono: Naw . . . naw . . . you mean if the nigger knew how to *drive* he'd be all right. Been fighting with them people about driving and ain't even got a license. Mr. Rand know you ain't got no driver's license?

Troy: Driving ain't nothing. All you do is point the truck where you want it to go. Driving ain't nothing.

Bono: Do Mr. Rand know you ain't got no driver's license? That's what I'm talking about. I ain't asked if driving was easy. I asked if Mr. Rand know you ain't got no driver's license.

Troy: He ain't got to know. The man ain't got to know my business. Time he find out, I have two or three driver's licenses.

Lyons (going into his pocket): Say, look here, Pop . . .

Troy: I knew it was coming. Didn't I tell you, Bono? I know what kind of "Look here, Pop" that was. The nigger fixing to ask me for some money. It's Friday night. It's my payday. All them rogues down there on the avenue . . . the ones that ain't in jail . . . and Lyons is hopping in his shoes to get down there with them.

Lyons: See, Pop . . . if you give somebody else a chance to talk sometimes, you'd see that I was fixing to pay you back your ten dollars like I told you. Here . . . I told you I'd pay you when Bonnie got paid.

Troy: Naw . . . you go ahead and keep that ten dollars. Put it in the bank. The next time you feel like you wanna come by here and ask me for something . . . you go on down there and get that.

Lyons: Here's your ten dollars, Pop. I told you I don't want you to give me nothing. I just wanted to borrow ten dollars.

Troy: Naw . . . you go on and keep that for the next time you want to ask me.

Lyons: Come on, Pop . . . here go your ten dollars.

Rose: Why don't you go on and let the boy pay you back, Troy?

Lyons: Here you go, Rose. If you don't take it I'm gonna have to hear about it for the next six months. *(He hands her the money.)*

Rose: You can hand yours over here too, Troy.

Troy: You see this, Bono. You see how they do me.

Bono: Yeah, Lucille do me the same way.

Gabriel is heard singing offstage. He enters.

Gabriel: Better get ready for the Judgment! Better get ready for . . . Hey! . . . Hey! . . . There's Troy's boy!

Lyons: How are you doing, Uncle Gabe?

Gabriel: Lyons . . . The King of the Jungle! Rose . . . hey, Rose. Got a flower for you. *(He takes a rose from his pocket.)* Picked it myself. That's the same rose like you is!

Rose: That's right nice of you, Gabe.

Lyons: What you been doing, Uncle Gabe?

Gabriel: Oh, I been chasing hellhounds and waiting on the time to tell St. Peter to open the gates.

Lyons: You been chasing hellhounds, huh? Well . . . you doing the right thing, Uncle Gabe. Somebody got to chase them.

Gabriel: Oh, yeah . . . I know it. The devil's strong. The devil ain't no pushover. Hellhounds snipping at everybody's heels. But I got my trumpet waiting on the judgment time.

Lyons: Waiting on the Battle of Armageddon, huh?

Gabriel: Ain't gonna be too much of a battle when God get to waving that Judgment sword. But the people's gonna have a hell of a time trying to get into heaven if them gates ain't open.

Lyons (putting his arm around Gabriel): You hear this, Pop. Uncle Gabe, you all right!

Gabriel (laughing with Lyons): Lyons! King of the Jungle.

Rose: You gonna stay for supper, Gabe? Want me to fix you a plate?

Gabriel: I'll take a sandwich, Rose. Don't want no plate. Just wanna eat with my hands. I'll take a sandwich.

Rose: How about you, Lyons? You staying? Got some short ribs cooking.

Lyons: Naw, I won't eat nothing till after we finished playing. *(Pause.)* You ought to come down and listen to me play Pop.

Troy: I don't like that Chinese music. All that noise.

Rose: Go on in the house and wash up, Gabe . . . I'll fix you a sandwich.

Gabriel (to Lyons, as he exits): Troy's mad at me.

Lyons: What you mad at Uncle Gabe for, Pop?

Rose: He thinks Troy's mad at him cause he moved over to Miss Pearl's.

Troy: I ain't mad at the man. He can live where he want to live at.

Lyons: What he move over there for? Miss Pearl don't like nobody.

Rose: She don't mind him none. She treats him real nice. She just don't allow all that singing.

Troy: She don't mind that rent he be paying . . . that's what she don't mind.

Rose: Troy, I ain't going through that with you no more. He's over there cause he want to have his own place. He can come and go as he please.

Troy: Hell, he could come and go as he please here. I wasn't stopping him. I ain't put no rules on him.

Rose: It ain't the same thing, Troy. And you know it.

Gabriel comes to the door.

Now, that's the last I wanna hear about that. I don't wanna hear nothing else about Gabe and Miss Pearl. And next week . . .

Gabriel: I'm ready for my sandwich, Rose.

Rose: And next week . . . when that recruiter come from that school . . . I want you to sign that paper and go on and let Cory play football. Then that'll be the last I have to hear about that.

Troy (to Rose as she exits into the house): I ain't thinking about Cory nothing.

Lyons: What . . . Cory got recruited? What school he going to?

Troy: That boy walking around here smelling his piss . . . thinking he's grown. Thinking he's gonna do what he want, irrespective of what I say. Look here, Bono . . . I left the Commissioner's office and went down to the A&P . . . that boy ain't working down there. He lying to me. Telling me he got his job back . . . telling me he working weekends . . . telling me he working after school . . . Mr. Stawicki tell me he ain't working down there at all!

Lyons: Cory just growing up. He's just busting at the seams trying to fill out your shoes.

Troy: I don't care what he's doing. When he get to the point where he wanna disobey me . . . then it's time for him to move on. Bono'll tell you that. I bet he ain't never disobeyed his daddy without paying the consequences.

Bono: I ain't never had a chance. My daddy came on through . . . but I ain't never knew him to see him . . . or what he had on his mind or where he went. Just moving on through. Searching out the New Land. That's what the old folks used to call it. See a fellow moving around from place to place . . . woman to woman . . . called it searching out the New Land. I can't say if he ever found it. I come along, didn't want no kids. Didn't know if I was gonna be in one place long enough to fix on them right as their daddy. I figured I was going searching too. As it turned out I been hooked up with Lucille near about as long as your daddy been with Rose. Going on sixteen years.

Troy: Sometimes I wish I hadn't known my daddy. He ain't cared nothing about no kids. A kid to him wasn't nothing. All he wanted was for you to learn how to walk so he could start you to working. When it come time for eating . . . he ate first. If there was anything left over, that's what you got. Man would sit down and eat two chickens and give you the wing.

Lyons: You ought to stop that, Pop. Everybody feed their kids. No matter how hard times is . . . everybody care about their kids. Make sure they have something to eat.

Troy: The only thing my daddy cared about was getting them bales of cotton in to Mr. Lubin. That's the only thing that mattered to him. Sometimes I used to wonder why he was living. Wonder why the devil hadn't come and got him. "Get them bales of cotton in to Mr. Lubin" and find out he owe him money . . .

Lyons: He should have just went on and left when he saw he couldn't get nowhere. That's what I would have done.

Troy: How he gonna leave with eleven kids? And where he gonna go? He ain't knew how to do nothing but farm. No, he was trapped and I think he knew it. But I'll say this for him . . . he felt a responsibility toward us. Maybe he ain't treated us the way I felt he should have . . . but without that responsibility he could have walked off and left us . . . made his own way.

Bono: A lot of them did. Back in those days what you talking about . . . they walk out their front door and just take on down one road or another and keep on walking.

Lyons: There you go! That's what I'm talking about.

Bono: Just keep on walking till you come to something else. Ain't you never heard of nobody having the walking blues? Well, that's what you call it when you just take off like that.

Troy: My daddy ain't had them walking blues! What you talking about? He stayed right there with his family. But he was just as evil as he could be. My mama couldn't stand him. Couldn't stand that evilness. She run off when I was about eight. She sneaked off one night after he had gone to sleep. Told me she was coming back for me. I ain't never seen her no more. All his women run off and left him. He wasn't good for nobody.

When my turn come to head out, I was fourteen and got to sniffing around Joe Canewell's daughter. Had us an old mule we called Greyboy. My daddy sent me out to do some plowing and I tied up Greyboy and went to fooling around with Joe Canewell's daughter. We done found us a nice little spot, got real cozy with each other. She about thirteen and we done figured we was grown anyway . . . so we down there enjoying ourselves . . . ain't thinking about nothing. We didn't know Greyboy had got loose and wandered back to the house and my daddy was looking for me. We down there by the creek enjoying ourselves when my daddy come up on us. Surprised us. He had them leather straps off the mule and commenced to whupping me like there was no tomorrow. I jumped up, mad and embarrassed. I was scared of my daddy. When he commenced to whupping on me . . . quite naturally I run to get out of the way. *(Pause.)* Now I thought he was mad cause I ain't done my work. But I see where he was chasing me off so he could have the gal for himself. When I see what the matter of it was, I lost all fear of my daddy. Right there is where I become a man . . . at fourteen years of age. *(Pause.)* Now it was my turn to run him off. I picked up them same reins that he had used on me. I picked up them reins and commenced to whupping on him. The gal jumped up and run off . . . and when my daddy turned to face me, I could see why the devil had never come to get him . . . cause he was the devil himself. I don't know what happened. When I woke up, I was laying right there by the creek, and Blue . . . this old dog we had . . . was licking my face. I thought I was blind. I couldn't see nothing. Both my eyes were swollen shut. I laid there and cried. I didn't know what I was gonna do. The only thing I knew was the time had come for me to leave my daddy's house. And right there the world suddenly got big. And it was a long time before I could cut it down to where I could handle it.

Part of that cutting down was when I got to the place where I could feel him kicking in my blood and knew that the only thing that separated us was the matter of a few years.

Gabriel enters from the house with a sandwich.

Lyons: What you got there, Uncle Gabe?

Gabriel: Got me a ham sandwich. Rose gave me a ham sandwich.

Troy: I don't know what happened to him. I done lost touch with everybody except Gabriel. But I hope he's dead. I hope he found some peace.

Lyons: That's a heavy story, Pop. I didn't know you left home when you was fourteen.

Troy: And didn't know nothing. The only part of the world I knew was the forty-two acres of Mr. Lubin's land. That's all I knew about life.

Lyons: Fourteen's kinda young to be out on your own. *(Phone rings.)* I don't even think I was ready to be out on my own at fourteen. I don't know what I would have done.

Troy: I got up from the creek and walked on down to Mobile. I was through with farming. Figured I could do better in the city. So I walked the two hundred miles to Mobile.

Lyons: Wait a minute . . . you ain't walked no two hundred miles, Pop. Ain't nobody gonna walk no two hundred miles. You talking about some walking there.

Bono: That's the only way you got anywhere back in them days.

Lyons: Shhh. Damn if I wouldn't have hitched a ride with somebody!

Troy: Who you gonna hitch it with? They ain't had no cars and things like they got now. We talking about 1918.

Rose (entering): What you all out here getting into?

Troy (to Rose): I'm telling Lyons how good he got it. He don't know nothing about this I'm talking.

Rose: Lyons, that was Bonnie on the phone. She say you supposed to pick her up.

Lyons: Yeah, okay, Rose.

Troy: I walked on down to Mobile and hitched up with some of them fellows that was heading this way. Got up here and found out . . . not only couldn't you get a job . . . you couldn't find no place to live. I thought I was in freedom. Shhh. Colored folks living down there on the riverbanks in whatever kind of shelter they could find for themselves. Right down there under the Brady Street Bridge. Living in shacks made of sticks and tarpaper. Messed around there and went from bad to worse. Started stealing. First it was food. Then I figured, hell, if I steal money I can buy me some food. Buy me some shoes too! One thing led to another. Met your mama. I was young and anxious to be a man. Met your mama and had you. What I do that for? Now I got to worry about feeding you and her. Got to steal three times as much. Went out one day looking for somebody to rob . . . that's what I was, a robber. I'll tell you the truth. I'm ashamed of it today. But it's the truth. Went to rob this fellow . . . pulled out my knife . . . and he pulled out a gun. Shot me in the chest. I felt just like somebody had taken a hot branding iron and laid it on me. When he shot me I jumped at him with my knife. They told me I killed him and they put me in the penitentiary and locked me up for fifteen years. That's where I met Bono. That's where I learned how to play baseball. Got out that place and your mama had taken you and went on to make life without me. Fifteen years was a long time for her to wait. But that fifteen years cured me of that robbing stuff. Rose'll tell you. She asked me when I met her if I had gotten all that foolishness out of my system. And I told her, "Baby, it's you and baseball all what count with me." You hear me, Bono? I meant it too. She say, "Which one comes first?" I told her, "Baby, ain't no doubt it's baseball . . . but you stick and get old with me and we'll both outlive this baseball." Am I right, Rose? And it's true.

Rose: Man, hush your mouth. You ain't said no such thing. Talking about, "Baby, you know you'll always be number one with me." That's what you was talking.

Troy: You hear that, Bono. That's why I love her.

Bono: Rose'll keep you straight. You get off the track, she'll straighten you up.

Rose: Lyons, you better get on up and get Bonnie. She waiting on you.

Lyons (gets up to go): Hey, Pop, why don't you come on down to the Grill and hear me play?

Troy: I ain't going down there. I'm too old to be sitting around in them clubs.

Bono: You got to be good to play down at the Grill.

Lyons: Come on, Pop . . .

Troy: I got to get up in the morning.

Lyons: You ain't got to stay long.

Troy: Naw, I'm gonna get my supper and go on to bed.

Lyons: Well, I got to go. I'll see you again.

Troy: Don't you come around my house on my payday.

Rose: Pick up the phone and let somebody know you coming. And bring Bonnie with you. You know I'm always glad to see her.

Lyons: Yeah, I'll do that, Rose. You take care now. See you, Pop. See you, Mr. Bono. See you, Uncle Gabe.

Gabriel: Lyons! King of the Jungle!

Lyons exits.

Troy: Is supper ready, woman? Me and you got some business to take care of. I'm gonna tear it up too.

Rose: Troy, I done told you now!

Troy (puts his arm around Bono): Aw hell, woman . . . this is Bono. Bono like family. I done known this nigger since . . . how long I done know you?

Bono: It's been a long time.

Troy: I done know this nigger since Skippy was a pup. Me and him done been through some times.

Bono: You sure right about that.

Troy: Hell, I done know him longer than I known you. And we still standing shoulder to shoulder. Hey, look here, Bono . . . a man can't ask for no more than that. *(Drinks to him.)* I love you, nigger.

Bono: Hell, I love you too . . . I got to get home see my woman. You got yours in hand. I got to go get mine.

Bono starts to exit as Cory enters the yard, dressed in his football uniform. He gives Troy a hard, uncompromising look.

Cory: What you do that for, Pop?

He throws his helmet down in the direction of Troy.

Rose: What's the matter? Cory . . . what's the matter?

Cory: Papa done went up to the school and told Coach Zellman I can't play football no more. Wouldn't even let me play the game. Told him to tell the recruiter not to come.

Rose: Troy . . .

Troy: What you Troying me for. Yeah, I did it. And the boy know why I did it.

Cory: Why you wanna do that to me? That was the one chance I had.

Rose: Ain't nothing wrong with Cory playing football, Troy.

Troy: The boy lied to me. I told the nigger if he wanna play football . . . to keep up his chores and hold down that job at the A&P. That was the conditions. Stopped down there to see Mr. Stawicki . . .

Cory: I can't work after school during the football season, Pop! I tried to tell you that Mr. Stawicki's holding my job for me. You don't never want to listen to nobody. And then you wanna go and do this to me!

Troy: I ain't done nothing to you. You done it to yourself.

Cory: Just cause you didn't have a chance! You just scared I'm gonna be better than you, that's all.

Troy: Come here.

Rose: Troy . . .

Cory reluctantly crosses over to Troy.

Troy: All right! See. You done made a mistake.

Cory: I didn't even do nothing!

Troy: I'm gonna tell you what your mistake was. See . . . you swung at the ball and didn't hit it. That's strike one. See, you in the batter's box now. You swung and you missed. That's strike one. Don't you strike out!

Lights fade to black.

ACT II

SCENE I

The following morning. Cory is at the tree hitting the ball with the bat. He tries to mimic Troy, but his swing is awkward, less sure. Rose enters from the house.

Rose: Cory, I want you to help me with this cupboard.

Cory: I ain't quitting the team. I don't care what Poppa say.

Rose: I'll talk to him when he gets back. He had to go see about your Uncle Gabe. The police done arrested him. Say he was disturbing the peace. He'll be back directly. Come on in here and help me clean out the top of this cupboard.

Cory exits into the house. Rose sees Troy and Bono coming down the alley.

Troy . . . what they say down there?

Troy: Ain't said nothing. I give them fifty dollars and they let him go. I'll talk to you about it. Where's Cory?

Rose: He's in there helping me clean out these cupboards.

Troy: Tell him to get his butt out here.

Troy and Bono go over to the pile of wood. Bono picks up the saw and begins sawing.

Troy (to Bono): All they want is the money. That makes six or seven times I done went down there and got him. See me coming they stick out their hands.

Bono: Yeah. I know what you mean. That's all they care about . . . that money. They don't care about what's right. *(Pause.)* Nigger, why you got to go and get some hard wood? You ain't doing nothing but building a little old fence. Get you some soft pine wood. That's all you need.

Troy: I know what I'm doing. This is outside wood. You put pine wood inside the house. Pine wood is inside wood. This here is outside wood. Now you tell me where the fence is gonna be?

Bono: You don't need this wood. You can put it up with pine wood and it'll stand as long as you gonna be here looking at it.

Troy: How you know how long I'm gonna be here, nigger? Hell, I might just live forever. Live longer than old man Horsely.

Bono: That's what Magee used to say.

Troy: Magee's a damn fool. Now you tell me who you ever heard of gonna pull their own teeth with a pair of rusty pliers.

Bono: The old folks . . . my granddaddy used to pull his teeth with pliers. They ain't had no dentists for the colored folks back then.

Troy: Get clean pliers! You understand? Clean pliers! Sterilize them! Besides we ain't living back then. All Magee had to do was walk over to Doc Goldblum's.

Bono: I see where you and that Tallahassee gal . . . that Alberta . . . I see where you all done got tight.

Troy: What you mean "got tight"?

Bono: I see where you be laughing and joking with her all the time.

Troy: I laughs and jokes with all of them, Bono. You know me.

Bono: That ain't the kind of laughing and joking I'm talking about.

> *Cory enters from the house.*

Cory: How you doing, Mr. Bono?

Troy: Cory? Get that saw from Bono and cut some wood. He talking about the wood's too hard to cut. Stand back there, Jim, and let that young boy show you how it's done.

Bono: He's sure welcome to it.

> *Cory takes the saw and begins to cut the wood.*

Whew-e-e! Look at that. Big old strong boy. Look like Joe Louis.° Hell, must be getting old the way I'm watching that boy whip through that wood.

Cory: I don't see why Mama want a fence around the yard noways.

Troy: Damn if I know either. What the hell she keeping out with it? She ain't got nothing nobody want.

Bono: Some people build fences to keep people out . . . and other people build fences to keep people in. Rose wants to hold on to you all. She loves you.

Troy: Hell, nigger, I don't need nobody to tell me my wife loves me. Cory . . . go on in the house and see if you can find that other saw.

Cory: Where's it at?

Troy: I said find it! Look for it till you find it!

> *Cory exits into the house.*

What's that supposed to mean? Wanna keep us in?

Bono: Troy . . . I done known you seem like damn near my whole life. You and Rose both. I done know both of you all for a long time. I remember when you met Rose. When you was hitting them baseball out the park. A lot of them old gals was after you then. You had the pick of the litter. When you picked Rose, I was happy for you. That was the first time I knew you had any sense. I said . . . My man Troy knows what he's doing . . . I'm gonna follow this nigger . . . he might take me somewhere. I been following you too. I done learned a whole heap of things about life watching you. I done learned how to tell where the shit lies. How to tell it from the alfalfa. You done learned me a lot of things. You showed me how to not make the same mistakes . . . to take life as it comes along and keep putting one foot in front of the other. *(Pause.)* Rose a good woman, Troy.

Troy: Hell, nigger, I know she a good woman. I been married to her for eighteen years. What you got on your mind, Bono?

Bono: I just say she a good woman. Just like I say anything. I ain't got to have nothing on my mind.

Troy: You just gonna say she a good woman and leave it hanging out there like that? Why you telling me she a good woman?

Bono: She loves you, Troy. Rose loves you.

Joe Louis (1914–1981): Black American boxer who held the world heavyweight championship title.

Troy: You saying I don't measure up. That's what you trying to say. I don't measure up cause I'm seeing this other gal. I know what you trying to say.

Bono: I know what Rose means to you, Troy. I'm just trying to say I don't want to see you mess up.

Troy: Yeah, I appreciate that, Bono. If you was messing around on Lucille I'd be telling you the same thing.

Bono: Well, that's all I got to say. I just say that because I love you both.

Troy: Hell, you know me . . . I wasn't out there looking for nothing. You can't find a better woman than Rose. I know that. But seems like this woman just stuck onto me where I can't shake her loose. I done wrestled with it, tried to throw her off me . . . but she just stuck on tighter. Now she's stuck on for good.

Bono: You's in control . . . that's what you tell me all the time. You responsible for what you do.

Troy: I ain't ducking the responsibility of it. As long as it sets right in my heart . . . then I'm okay. Cause that's all I listen to. It'll tell me right from wrong every time. And I ain't talking about doing Rose no bad turn. I love Rose. She done carried me a long ways and I love and respect her for that.

Bono: I know you do. That's why I don't want to see you hurt her. But what you gonna do when she find out? What you got then? If you try and juggle both of them . . . sooner or later you gonna drop one of them. That's common sense.

Troy: Yeah, I hear what you saying, Bono. I been trying to figure a way to work it out.

Bono: Work it out right, Troy. I don't want to be getting all up between you and Rose's business . . . but work it so it come out right.

Troy: Ah hell, I get all up between you and Lucille's business. When you gonna get that woman that refrigerator she been wanting? Don't tell me you ain't got no money now. I know who your banker is. Mellon don't need that money bad as Lucille want that refrigerator. I'll tell you that.

Bono: Tell you what I'll do . . . when you finish building this fence for Rose . . . I'll buy Lucille that refrigerator.

Troy: You done stuck your foot in your mouth now!

Troy grabs up a board and begins to saw. Bono starts to walk out the yard.

Hey, nigger . . . where you going?

Bono: I'm going home. I know you don't expect me to help you now. I'm protecting my money. I wanna see you put that fence up by yourself. That's what I want to see. You'll be here another six months without me.

Troy: Nigger, you ain't right.

Bono: When it comes to my money . . . I'm right as fireworks on the Fourth of July.

Troy: All right, we gonna see now. You better get out your bankbook.

Bono exits, and Troy continues to work. Rose enters from the house.

Rose: What they say down there? What's happening with Gabe?

Troy: I went down there and got him out. Cost me fifty dollars. Say he was disturbing the peace. Judge set up a hearing for him in three weeks. Say to show cause why he shouldn't be recommitted.

Rose: What was he doing that cause them to arrest him?

Troy: Some kids was teasing him and he run them off home. Say he was howling and carrying on. Some folks seen him and called the police. That's all it was.

Rose: Well, what's you say? What'd you tell the judge?

Troy: Told him I'd look after him. It didn't make no sense to recommit the man. He stuck out his big greasy palm and told me to give him fifty dollars and take him on home.

Rose: Where's he at now? Where'd he go off to?

Troy: He's gone about his business. He don't need nobody to hold his hand.

Rose: Well, I don't know. Seem like that would be the best place for him if they did put him into the hospital. I know what you're gonna say. But that's what I think would be best.

Troy: The man done had his life ruined fighting for what? And they wanna take and lock him up. Let him be free. He don't bother nobody.

Rose: Well, everybody got their own way of looking at it I guess. Come on and get your lunch. I got a bowl of lima beans and some cornbread in the oven. Come and get something to eat. Ain't no sense you fretting over Gabe.

Rose turns to go into the house.

Troy: Rose . . . got something to tell you.

Rose: Well, come on . . . wait till I get this food on the table.

Troy: Rose!

She stops and turns around.

I don't know how to say this. *(Pause.)* I can't explain it none. It just sort of grows on you till it gets out of hand. It starts out like a little bush . . . and the next thing you know it's a whole forest.

Rose: Troy . . . what is you talking about?

Troy: I'm talking, woman, let me talk. I'm trying to find a way to tell you . . . I'm gonna be a daddy. I'm gonna be somebody's daddy.

Rose: Troy . . . you're not telling me this? You're gonna be . . . what?

Troy: Rose . . . now . . . see . . .

Rose: You telling me you gonna be somebody's daddy? You telling your *wife* this?

Gabriel enters from the street. He carries a rose in his hand.

Gabriel: Hey, Troy! Hey, Rose!

Rose: I have to wait eighteen years to hear something like this.

Gabriel: Hey, Rose . . . I got a flower for you. *(He hands it to her.)* That's a rose. Same rose like you is.

Rose: Thanks, Gabe.

Gabriel: Troy, you ain't mad at me is you? Them bad mens come and put me away. You ain't mad at me is you?

Troy: Naw, Gabe, I ain't mad at you.

Rose: Eighteen years and you wanna come with this.

Gabriel (takes a quarter out of his pocket): See what I got? Got a brand new quarter.

Troy: Rose . . . it's just . . .

Rose: Ain't nothing you can say, Troy. Ain't no way of explaining that.

Gabriel: Fellow that give me this quarter had a whole mess of them. I'm gonna keep this quarter till it stop shining.

Rose: Gabe, go on in the house there. I got some watermelon in the Frigidaire. Go on and get you a piece.

Gabriel: Say, Rose . . . you know I was chasing hellhounds and them bad mens come and get me and take me away. Troy helped me. He come down there and told them they better let me go before he beat them up. Yeah, he did!

Rose: You go on and get you a piece of watermelon, Gabe. Them bad mens is gone now.

Gabriel: Okay, Rose . . . gonna get me some watermelon. The kind with the stripes on it.

Gabriel exits into the house.

Rose: Why, Troy? Why? After all these years to come dragging this in to me now. It don't make no sense at your age. I could have expected this ten or fifteen years ago, but not now.

Troy: Age ain't got nothing to do with it, Rose.

Rose: I done tried to be everything a wife should be. Everything a wife could be. Been married eighteen years and I got to live to see the day you tell me you been seeing another woman and done fathered a child by her. And you know I ain't never wanted no half nothing in my family. My whole family is half. Everybody got different fathers and mothers . . . my two sisters and my brother. Can't hardly tell who's who. Can't never sit down and talk about Papa and Mama. It's your papa and your mama and my papa and my mama . . .

Troy: Rose . . . stop it now.

Rose: I ain't never wanted that for none of my children. And now you wanna drag your behind in here and tell me something like this.

Troy: You ought to know. It's time for you to know.

Rose: Well, I don't want to know, goddamn it!

Troy: I can't just make it go away. It's done now. I can't wish the circumstance of the thing away.

Rose: And you don't want to either. Maybe you want to wish me and my boy away. Maybe that's what you want? Well, you can't wish us away. I've got eighteen years of my life invested in you. You ought to have stayed upstairs in my bed where you belong.

Troy: Rose . . . now listen to me . . . we can get a handle on this thing. We can talk this out . . . come to an understanding.

Rose: All of a sudden it's "we." Where was "we" at when you was down there rolling around with some godforsaken woman? "We" should have come to an understanding before you started making a damn fool of yourself. You're a day late and a dollar short when it comes to an understanding with me.

Troy: It's just . . . She gives me a different idea . . . a different understanding about myself. I can step out of this house and get away from the pressures and problems . . . be a different man. I ain't got to wonder how I'm gonna pay the bills or get the roof fixed. I can just be a part of myself that I ain't never been.

Rose: What I want to know . . . is do you plan to continue seeing her. That's all you can say to me.

Troy: I can sit up in her house and laugh. Do you understand what I'm saying. I can laugh out loud . . . and it feels good. It reaches all the way down to the bottom of my shoes. *(Pause.)* Rose, I can't give that up.

Rose: Maybe you ought to go on and stay down there with her . . . if she's a better woman than me.

Troy: It ain't about nobody being a better woman or nothing. Rose, you ain't the blame. A man couldn't ask for no woman to be a better wife than you've been. I'm responsible for it. I done locked myself into a pattern trying to take care of you all that I forgot about myself.

Rose: What the hell was I there for? That was my job, not somebody else's.

Troy: Rose, I done tried all my life to live decent . . . to live a clean . . . hard . . . useful life. I tried to be a good husband to you. In every way I knew how. Maybe I come into the world backwards, I don't know. But . . . you born with two strikes on you before you come to the plate. You got to guard it closely . . . always looking for the curve ball on the inside corner. You can't afford to let none get past you. You can't afford a call strike. If you going down . . . you going down swinging. Everything lined up against you. What you gonna do. I fooled them, Rose. I bunted. When I found you and Cory and a halfway decent job . . . I was safe. Couldn't nothing touch me. I wasn't gonna strike out no more. I wasn't going back to the penitentiary. I wasn't gonna lay in the streets with a bottle of wine. I was safe. I had me a family. A job. I wasn't gonna get that last strike. I was on first looking for one of them boys to knock me in. To get me home.

Rose: You should have stayed in my bed, Troy.

Troy: Then when I saw that gal . . . she firmed up my backbone. And I got to thinking that if I tried . . . I just might be able to steal second. Do you understand after eighteen years I wanted to steal second.

Rose: You should have held me tight. You should have grabbed me and held on.

Troy: I stood on first base for eighteen years and I thought . . . well, goddamn it . . . go on for it!

Rose: We're not talking about baseball! We're talking about you going off to lay in bed with another woman . . . and then bring it home to me. That's what we're talking about. We ain't talking about no baseball.

Troy: Rose, you're not listening to me. I'm trying the best I can to explain it to you. It's not easy for me to admit that I been standing in the same place for eighteen years.

Rose: I been standing with you! I been right here with you, Troy. I got a life too. I gave eighteen years of my life to stand in the same spot with you. Don't you think I ever wanted other things? Don't you think I had dreams and hopes? What about my life? What about me. Don't you think it ever crossed my mind to want to know other men? That I wanted to lay up somewhere and forget about my responsibilities? That I wanted someone to make me laugh so I could feel good? You not the only one who's got wants and needs. But I held on to you, Troy. I took all my feelings, my wants and needs, my dreams . . . and I buried them inside you. I planted a seed and watched and prayed over it. I planted myself inside you and waited to bloom. And it didn't take me no eighteen years to find out the soil was hard and rocky and it wasn't never gonna bloom.

But I held on to you, Troy. I held you tighter. You was my husband. I owed you everything I had. Every part of me I could find to give you. And upstairs in that room . . . with the darkness falling in on me . . . I gave everything I had to try and erase the doubt that you wasn't the finest man in the world. And wherever you was going . . . I wanted to be there with you. Cause you was my husband. Cause that's the only way I was gonna survive as your wife. You always talking about what you give . . . and what you don't have to give. But you take too. You take . . . and don't even know nobody's giving!

Rose turns to exit into the house; Troy grabs her arm.

Troy: You say I take and don't give!

Rose: Troy! You're hurting me!

Troy: You say I take and don't give!

Rose: Troy . . . you're hurting my arm! Let go!

Troy: I done give you everything I got. Don't you tell that lie on me.

Rose: Troy!

Troy: Don't you tell that lie on me!

> *Cory enters from the house.*

Cory: Mama!

Rose: Troy. You're hurting me.

Troy: Don't you tell me about no taking and giving.

> *Cory comes up behind Troy and grabs him. Troy, surprised, is thrown off balance just as Cory throws a glancing blow that catches him on the chest and knocks him down. Troy is stunned, as is Cory.*

Rose: Troy. Troy. No!

> *Troy gets to his feet and starts at Cory.*

Troy . . . no. Please! Troy!

> *Rose pulls on Troy to hold him back. Troy stops himself.*

Troy (to Cory): All right. That's strike two. You stay away from around me, boy. Don't you strike out. You living with a full count. Don't you strike out.

> *Troy exits out the yard as the lights go down.*

Scene II

> *It is six months later, early afternoon. Troy enters from the house and starts to exit the yard. Rose enters from the house.*

Rose: Troy, I want to talk to you.

Troy: All of a sudden, after all this time, you want to talk to me, huh? You ain't wanted to talk to me for months. You ain't wanted to talk to me last night. You ain't wanted no part of me then. What you wanna talk to me about now?

Rose: Tomorrow's Friday.

Troy: I know what day tomorrow is. You think I don't know tomorrow's Friday? My whole life I ain't done nothing but look to see Friday coming and you got to tell me it's Friday.

Rose: I want to know if you're coming home.

Troy: I always come home, Rose. You know that. There ain't never been a night I ain't come home.

Rose: That ain't what I mean . . . and you know it. I want to know if you're coming straight home after work.

Troy: I figure I'd cash my check . . . hang out at Taylors' with the boys . . . maybe play a game of checkers . . .

Rose: Troy, I can't live like this. I won't live like this. You livin' on borrowed time with me. It's been going on six months now you ain't been coming home.

Troy: I be here every night. Every night of the year. That's 365 days.

Rose: I want you to come home tomorrow after work.

Troy: Rose . . . I don't mess up my pay. You know that now. I take my pay and I give it to you. I don't have no money but what you give me back. I just want to have a little time to myself . . . a little time to enjoy life.

Rose: What about me? When's my time to enjoy life?

Troy: I don't know what to tell you, Rose. I'm doing the best I can.

Rose: You ain't been home from work but time enough to change your clothes and run out . . . and you wanna call that the best you can do?

Troy: I'm going over to the hospital to see Alberta. She went into the hospital this afternoon. Look like she might have the baby early. I won't be gone long.

Rose: Well, you ought to know. They went over to Miss Pearl's and got Gabe today. She said you told them to go ahead and lock him up.

Troy: I ain't said no such thing. Whoever told you that is telling a lie. Pearl ain't doing nothing but telling a big fat lie.

Rose: She ain't had to tell me. I read it on the papers.

Troy: I ain't told them nothing of the kind.

Rose: I saw it right there on the papers.

Troy: What it say, huh?

Rose: It said you told them to take him.

Troy: Then they screwed that up, just the way they screw up everything. I ain't worried about what they got on the paper.

Rose: Say the government send part of his check to the hospital and the other part to you.

Troy: I ain't got nothing to do with that if that's the way it works. I ain't made up the rules about how it work.

Rose: You did Gabe just like you did Cory. You wouldn't sign the paper for Cory . . . but you signed for Gabe. You signed that paper.

The telephone is heard ringing inside the house.

Troy: I told you I ain't signed nothing, woman! The only thing I signed was the release form. Hell, I can't read, I don't know what they had on that paper! I ain't signed nothing about sending Gabe away.

Rose: I said send him to the hospital . . . you said let him be free . . . now you done went down there and signed him to the hospital for half his money. You went back on yourself, Troy. You gonna have to answer for that.

Troy: See now . . . you been over there talking to Miss Pearl. She done got mad cause she ain't getting Gabe's rent money. That's all it is. She's liable to say anything.

Rose: Troy, I seen where you signed the paper.

Troy: You ain't seen nothing I signed. What she doing got papers on my brother anyway? Miss Pearl telling a big fat lie. And I'm gonna tell her about it too! You ain't seen nothing I signed. Say . . . you ain't seen nothing I signed.

Rose exits into the house to answer the telephone. Presently she returns.

Rose: Troy . . . that was the hospital. Alberta had the baby.

Troy: What she have? What is it?

Rose: It's a girl.

Troy: I better get on down to the hospital to see her.

Rose: Troy . . .

Troy: Rose . . . I got to go see her now. That's only right . . . what's the matter . . . the baby's all right, ain't it?

Rose: Alberta died having the baby.

Troy: Died . . . you say she's dead? Alberta's dead?

Rose: They said they done all they could. They couldn't do nothing for her.

Troy: The baby? How's the baby?

Rose: They say it's healthy. I wonder who's gonna bury her.

Troy: She had family, Rose. She wasn't living in the world by herself.

Rose: I know she wasn't living in the world by herself.

Troy: Next thing you gonna want to know if she had any insurance.

Rose: Troy, you ain't got to talk like that.

Troy: That's the first thing that jumped out your mouth. "Who's gonna bury her?" Like I'm fixing to take on that task for myself.

Rose: I am your wife. Don't push me away.

Troy: I ain't pushing nobody away. Just give me some space. That's all. Just give me some room to breathe.

Rose exits into the house. Troy walks about the yard.

Troy (with a quiet rage that threatens to consume him): All right . . . Mr. Death. See now . . . I'm gonna tell you what I'm gonna do. I'm gonna take and build me a fence around this yard. See? I'm gonna build me a fence around what belongs to me. And then I want you to stay on the other side. See? You stay over there until you're ready for me. Then you come on. Bring your army. Bring your sickle. Bring your wrestling clothes. I ain't gonna fall down on my vigilance this time. You ain't gonna sneak up on me no more. When you ready for me . . . when the top of your list say Troy Maxson . . . that's when you come around here. You come up and knock on the front door. Ain't nobody else got nothing to do with this. This is between you and me. Man to man. You stay on the other side of that fence until you ready for me. Then you come up and knock on the front door. Anytime you want. I'll be ready for you.

The lights go down to black.

SCENE III

The lights come up on the porch. It is late evening three days later. Rose sits listening to the ball game waiting for Troy. The final out of the game is made and Rose switches off the radio. Troy enters the yard carrying an infant wrapped in blankets. He stands back from the house and calls.

Rose enters and stands on the porch. There is a long, awkward silence, the weight of which grows heavier with each passing second.

Troy: Rose . . . I'm standing here with my daughter in my arms. She ain't but a wee bittie little old thing. She don't know nothing about grownups' business. She innocent . . . and she ain't got no mama.

Rose: What you telling me for, Troy?

She turns and exits into the house.

Troy: Well . . . I guess we'll just sit out here on the porch.

He sits down on the porch. There is an awkward indelicateness about the way he handles the baby. His largeness engulfs and seems to swallow it. He speaks loud enough for Rose to hear.

A man's got to do what's right for him. I ain't sorry for nothing I done. It felt right in my heart. *(To the baby.)* What you smiling at? Your daddy's a big man. Got these great big old hands. But sometimes he's scared. And right now your daddy's scared cause we sitting out here and ain't got no home. Oh, I been homeless before. I ain't had no little baby with me. But I been homeless. You just be out on the road by your lonesome and you see one of them trains coming and you just kinda go like this . . .

He sings as a lullaby.

Please, Mr. Engineer let a man ride the line
Please, Mr. Engineer let a man ride the line
I ain't got no ticket please let me ride the blinds

Rose enters from the house. Troy, hearing her steps behind him, stands and faces her.

She's my daughter, Rose. My own flesh and blood. I can't deny her no more than I can deny them boys. *(Pause.)* You and them boys is my family. You and them and this child is all I got in the world. So I guess what I'm saying is . . . I'd appreciate it if you'd help me take care of her.

Rose: Okay, Troy . . . you're right. I'll take care of your baby for you . . . cause . . . like you say . . . she's innocent . . . and you can't visit the sins of the father upon the child. A motherless child has got a hard time. *(She takes the baby from him.)* From right now . . . this child got a mother. But you a womanless man.

Rose turns and exits into the house with the baby. Lights go down to black.

SCENE IV

It is two months later. Lyons enters from the street. He knocks on the door and calls.

Lyons: Hey, Rose! *(Pause.)* Rose!

Rose (from inside the house): Stop that yelling. You gonna wake up Raynell. I just got her to sleep.

Lyons: I just stopped by to pay Papa this twenty dollars I owe him. Where's Papa at?

Rose: He should be here in a minute. I'm getting ready to go down to the church. Sit down and wait on him.

Lyons: I got to go pick up Bonnie over her mother's house.

Rose: Well, sit it down there on the table. He'll get it.

Lyons (enters the house and sets the money on the table): Tell Papa I said thanks. I'll see you again.

Rose: All right, Lyons. We'll see you.

Lyons starts to exit as Cory enters.

Cory: Hey, Lyons.

Lyons: What's happening, Cory? Say man, I'm sorry I missed your graduation. You know I had a gig and couldn't get away. Otherwise, I would have been there, man. So what you doing?

Cory: I'm trying to find a job.

Lyons: Yeah I know how that go, man. It's rough out here. Jobs are scarce.

Cory: Yeah, I know.

Lyons: Look here, I got to run. Talk to Papa . . . he know some people. He'll be able to help get you a job. Talk to him . . . see what he say.

Cory: Yeah . . . all right, Lyons.

Lyons: You take care. I'll talk to you soon. We'll find some time to talk.

> *Lyons exits the yard. Cory wanders over to the tree, picks up the bat, and assumes a batting stance. He studies an imaginary pitcher and swings. Dissatisfied with the result, he tries again. Troy enters. They eye each other for a beat. Cory puts the bat down and exits the yard. Troy starts into the house as Rose exits with Raynell. She is carrying a cake.*

Troy: I'm coming in and everybody's going out.

Rose: I'm taking this cake down to the church for the bake sale. Lyons was by to see you. He stopped by to pay you your twenty dollars. It's laying in there on the table.

Troy (going into his pocket): Well . . . here go this money.

Rose: Put it in there on the table, Troy. I'll get it.

Troy: What time you coming back?

Rose: Ain't no use in you studying me. It don't matter what time I come back.

Troy: I just asked you a question, woman. What's the matter . . . can't I ask you a question?

Rose: Troy, I don't want to go into it. Your dinner's in there on the stove. All you got to do is heat it up. And don't you be eating the rest of them cakes in there. I'm coming back for them. We having a bake sale at the church tomorrow.

> *Rose exits the yard. Troy sits down on the steps, takes a pint bottle from his pocket, opens it, and drinks. He begins to sing.*

Troy: Hear it ring! Hear it ring!
Had an old dog his name was Blue
You know Blue was mighty true
You know Blue was a good old dog
Blue trees a possum in a hollow log
You know from that he was a good old dog

> *Bono enters the yard.*

Bono: Hey, Troy.

Troy: Hey, what's happening, Bono?

Bono: I just thought I'd stop by to see you.

Troy: What you stop by and see me for? You ain't stopped by in a month of Sundays. Hell, I must owe you money or something.

Bono: Since you got your promotion I can't keep up with you. Used to see you every day. Now I don't even know what route you working.

Troy: They keep switching me around. Got me out in Greentree now . . . hauling white folks' garbage.

Bono: Greentree, huh? You lucky, at least you ain't got to be lifting them barrels. Damn if they ain't getting heavier. I'm gonna put in my two years and call it quits.

Troy: I'm thinking about retiring myself.

Bono: You got it easy. You can *drive* for another five years.

Troy: It ain't the same, Bono. It ain't like working the back of the truck. Ain't got nobody to talk to . . . feel like you working by yourself. Naw, I'm thinking about retiring. How's Lucille?

Bono: She all right. Her arthritis get to acting up on her sometime. Saw Rose on my way in. She going down to the church, huh?

Troy: Yeah, she took up going down there. All them preachers looking for some-body to fatten their pockets. *(Pause.)* Got some gin here.

Bono: Naw, thanks. I just stopped by to say hello.

Troy: Hell, nigger . . . you can take a drink. I ain't never known you to say no to a drink. You ain't got to work tomorrow.

Bono: I just stopped by. I'm fixing to go over to Skinner's. We got us a domino game going over his house every Friday.

Troy: Nigger, you can't play no dominoes. I used to whup you four games out of five.

Bono: Well, that learned me. I'm getting better.

Troy: Yeah? Well, that's all right.

Bono: Look here . . . I got to be getting on. Stop by sometime, huh?

Troy: Yeah, I'll do that, Bono. Lucille told Rose you bought her a new refrigerator.

Bono: Yeah, Rose told Lucille you had finally built your fence . . . so I figured we'd call it even.

Troy: I knew you would.

Bono: Yeah . . . okay. I'll be talking to you.

Troy: Yeah, take care, Bono. Good to see you. I'm gonna stop over.

Bono: Yeah. Okay, Troy.

Bono exits. Troy drinks from the bottle.

Troy: Old Blue died and I dig his grave
Let him down with a golden chain
Every night when I hear old Blue bark
I know Blue treed a possum in Noah's Ark.
Hear it ring! Hear it ring!

Cory enters the yard. They eye each other for a beat. Troy is sitting in the middle of the steps. Cory walks over.

Cory: I got to get by.

Troy: Say what? What's you say?

Cory: You in my way. I got to get by.

Troy: You got to get by where? This is my house. Bought and paid for. In full. Took me fifteen years. And if you wanna go in my house and I'm sitting on the steps . . . you say excuse me. Like your mama taught you.

Cory: Come on, Pop . . . I got to get by.

Cory starts to maneuver his way past Troy. Troy grabs his leg and shoves him back.

Troy: You just gonna walk over top of me?

Cory: I live here too!

Troy (advancing toward him): You just gonna walk over top of me in my own house?

Cory: I ain't scared of you.

Troy: I ain't asked if you was scared of me. I asked you if you was fixing to walk over top of me in my own house? That's the question. You ain't gonna say excuse me? You just gonna walk over top of me?

Cory: If you wanna put it like that.

Troy: How else am I gonna put it?

Cory: I was walking by you to go into the house cause you sitting on the steps drunk, singing to yourself. You can put it like that.

Troy: Without saying excuse me???

> *Cory doesn't respond.*

I asked you a question. Without saying excuse me???

Cory: I ain't got to say excuse me to you. You don't count around here no more.

Troy: Oh, I see . . . I don't count around here no more. You ain't got to say excuse me to your daddy. All of a sudden you done got so grown that your daddy don't count around here no more . . . Around here in his own house and yard that he done paid for with the sweat of his brow. You done got so grown to where you gonna take over. You gonna take over my house. Is that right? You gonna wear my pants. You gonna go in there and stretch out on my bed. You ain't got to say excuse me cause I don't count around here no more. Is that right?

Cory: That's right. You always talking this dumb stuff. Now, why don't you just get out my way?

Troy: I guess you got someplace to sleep and something to put in your belly. You got that, huh? You got that? That's what you need. You got that, huh?

Cory: You don't know what I got. You ain't got to worry about what I got.

Troy: You right! You one hundred percent right! I done spent the last seventeen years worrying about what you got. Now it's your turn, see? I'll tell you what to do. You grown . . . we done established that. You a man. Now, let's see you act like one. Turn your behind around and walk out this yard. And when you get out there in the alley . . . you can forget about this house. See? Cause this is my house. You go on and be a man and get your own house. You can forget about this. Cause this is mine. You go on and get yours cause I'm through with doing for you.

Cory: You talking about what you did for me . . . what'd you ever give me?

Troy: Them feet and bones! That pumping heart, nigger! I give you more than anybody else is ever gonna give you.

Cory: You ain't never gave me nothing! You ain't never done nothing but hold me back. Afraid I was gonna be better than you. All you ever did was try and make me scared of you. I used to tremble every time you called my name. Every time I heard your footsteps in the house. Wondering all the time . . . what's Papa gonna say if I do this? . . . What's he gonna say if I do that? . . . What's Papa gonna say if I turn on the radio? And Mama, too . . . she tries . . . but she's scared of you.

Troy: You leave your mama out of this. She ain't got nothing to do with this.

Cory: I don't know how she stand you . . . after what you did to her.

Troy: I told you to leave your mama out of this!

> *He advances toward Cory.*

Cory: What you gonna do . . . give me a whupping? You can't whup me no more. You're too old. You just an old man.

Troy (shoves him on his shoulder): Nigger! That's what you are. You just another nigger on the street to me!

Cory: You crazy! You know that?

Troy: Go on now! You got the devil in you. Get on away from me!

Cory: You just a crazy old man . . . talking about I got the devil in me.

Troy: Yeah, I'm crazy! If you don't get on the other side of that yard . . . I'm gonna show you how crazy I am! Go on . . . get the hell out of my yard.

Cory: It ain't your yard. You took Uncle Gabe's money he got from the army to buy this house and then you put him out.

Troy (advances on Cory): Get your black ass out of my yard!

> *Troy's advance backs Cory up against the tree. Cory grabs up the bat.*

Cory: I ain't going nowhere! Come on . . . put me out! I ain't scared of you.

Troy: That's my bat!

Cory: Come on!

Troy: Put my bat down!

Cory: Come on, put me out.

> *Cory swings at Troy, who backs across the yard.*

What's the matter? You so bad . . . put me out!

> *Troy advances toward Cory.*

Cory (backing up): Come on! Come on!

Troy: You're gonna have to use it! You wanna draw that bat back on me . . . you're gonna have to use it.

Cory: Come on! . . . Come on!

> *Cory swings the bat at Troy a second time. He misses. Troy continues to advance toward him.*

Troy: You're gonna have to kill me! You wanna draw that bat back on me. You're gonna have to kill me.

> *Cory, backed up against the tree, can go no farther. Troy taunts him. He sticks out his head and offers him a target.*

Come on! Come on!

> *Cory is unable to swing the bat. Troy grabs it.*

Troy: Then I'll show you.

> *Cory and Troy struggle over the bat. The struggle is fierce and fully engaged. Troy ultimately is the stronger and takes the bat from Cory and stands over him ready to swing. He stops himself.*

Go on and get away from around my house.

> *Cory, stung by his defeat, picks himself up, walks slowly out of the yard and up the alley.*

Cory: Tell Mama I'll be back for my things.

Troy: They'll be on the other side of that fence.

> *Cory exits.*

Troy: I can't taste nothing. Helluljah! I can't taste nothing no more. *(Troy assumes a batting posture and begins to taunt Death, the fastball on the outside corner.)* Come on! It's between you and me now! Come on! Anytime you want! Come on! I be ready for you . . . but I ain't gonna be easy.

> *The lights go down on the scene.*

SCENE V

> *The time is 1965. The lights come up in the yard. It is the morning of Troy's funeral. A funeral plaque with a light hangs beside the door. There is a small garden plot off to the side. There is noise and activity in the house as Rose, Gabriel,*

and Bono have gathered. The door opens and Raynell, seven years old, enters dressed in a flannel nightgown. She crosses to the garden and pokes around with a stick. Rose calls from the house.

Rose: Raynell!
Raynell: Mam?
Rose: What you doing out there?
Raynell: Nothing.

> *Rose comes to the door.*

Rose: Girl, get in here and get dressed. What you doing?
Raynell: Seeing if my garden growed.
Rose: I told you it ain't gonna grow overnight. You got to wait.
Raynell: It don't look like it never gonna grow. Dag!
Rose: I told you a watched pot never boils. Get in here and get dressed.
Raynell: This ain't even no pot, Mama.
Rose: You just have to give it a chance. It'll grow. Now you come on and do what I told you. We got to be getting ready. This ain't no morning to be playing around. You hear me?
Raynell: Yes, mam.

> *Rose exits into the house. Raynell continues to poke at her garden with a stick. Cory enters. He is dressed in a Marine corporal's uniform, and carries a duffel bag. His posture is that of a military man, and his speech has a clipped sternness.*

Cory (to Raynell): Hi. (Pause.) I bet your name is Raynell.
Raynell: Uh huh.
Cory: Is your mama home?

> *Raynell runs up on the porch and calls through the screen door.*

Raynell: Mama . . . there's some man out here. Mama?

> *Rose comes to the door.*

Rose: Cory? Lord have mercy! Look here, you all!

> *Rose and Cory embrace in a tearful reunion as Bono and Lyons enter from the house dressed in funeral clothes.*

Bono: Aw, looka here . . .
Rose: Done got all grown up!
Cory: Don't cry, Mama. What you crying about?
Rose: I'm just so glad you made it.
Cory: Hey Lyons. How you doing, Mr. Bono.

> *Lyons goes to embrace Cory.*

Lyons: Look at you, man. Look at you. Don't he look good, Rose. Got them Corporal stripes.
Rose: What took you so long?
Cory: You know how the Marines are, Mama. They got to get all their paperwork straight before they let you do anything.
Rose: Well, I'm sure glad you made it. They let Lyons come. Your Uncle Gabe's still in the hospital. They don't know if they gonna let him out or not. I just talked to them a little while ago.

Lyons: A Corporal in the United States Marines.

Bono: Your daddy knew you had it in you. He used to tell me all the time.

Lyons: Don't he look good, Mr. Bono?

Bono: Yeah, he remind me of Troy when I first met him. *(Pause.)* Say, Rose, Lucille's down at the church with the choir. I'm gonna go down and get the pallbearers lined up. I'll be back to get you all.

Rose: Thanks, Jim.

Cory: See you, Mr. Bono.

Lyons (with his arm around Raynell): Cory . . . look at Raynell. Ain't she precious? She gonna break a whole lot of hearts.

Rose: Raynell, come and say hello to your brother. This is your brother, Cory. You remember Cory.

Raynell: No, Mam.

Cory: She don't remember me, Mama.

Rose: Well, we talk about you. She heard us talk about you. *(To Raynell.)* This is your brother, Cory. Come on and say hello.

Raynell: Hi.

Cory: Hi. So you're Raynell. Mama told me a lot about you.

Rose: You all come on into the house and let me fix you some breakfast. Keep up your strength.

Cory: I ain't hungry, Mama.

Lyons: You can fix me something, Rose. I'll be in there in a minute.

Rose: Cory, you sure you don't want nothing? I know they ain't feeding you right.

Cory: No, Mama . . . thanks. I don't feel like eating. I'll get something later.

Rose: Raynell . . . get on upstairs and get that dress on like I told you.

Rose and Raynell exit into the house.

Lyons: So . . . I hear you thinking about getting married.

Cory: Yeah, I done found the right one, Lyons. It's about time.

Lyons: Me and Bonnie been split up about four years now. About the time Papa retired. I guess she just got tired of all them changes I was putting her through. *(Pause.)* I always knew you was gonna make something out yourself. Your head was always in the right direction. So . . . you gonna stay in . . . make it a career . . . put in your twenty years?

Cory: I don't know. I got six already, I think that's enough.

Lyons: Stick with Uncle Sam and retire early. Ain't nothing out here. I guess Rose told you what happened with me. They got me down the workhouse. I thought I was being slick cashing other people's checks.

Cory: How much time you doing?

Lyons: They give me three years. I got that beat now. I ain't got but nine more months. It ain't so bad. You learn to deal with it like anything else. You got to take the crookeds with the straights. That's what Papa used to say. He used to say that when he struck out. I seen him strike out three times in a row . . . and the next time up he hit the ball over the grandstand. Right out there in Homestead Field. He wasn't satisfied hitting in the seats . . . he want to hit it over everything! After the game he had two hundred people standing around waiting to shake his hand. You got to take the crookeds with the straights. Yeah, Papa was something else.

Cory: You still playing?

Lyons: Cory . . . you know I'm gonna do that. There's some fellows down there we got us a band . . . we gonna try and stay together when we get out . . . but yeah, I'm still playing. It still helps me to get out of bed in the morning. As long as it do that I'm gonna be right there playing and trying to make some sense out of it.

Rose (calling): Lyons, I got these eggs in the pan.

Lyons: Let me go on and get these eggs, man. Get ready to go bury Papa. *(Pause.)* How you doing? You doing all right?

Cory nods. Lyons touches him on the shoulder and they share a moment of silent grief. Lyons exits into the house. Cory wanders about the yard. Raynell enters.

Raynell: Hi.

Cory: Hi.

Raynell: Did you used to sleep in my room?

Cory: Yeah . . . that used to be my room.

Raynell: That's what Papa call it. "Cory's room." It got your football in the closet.

Rose comes to the door.

Rose: Raynell, get in there and get them good shoes on.

Raynell: Mama, can't I wear these? Them other one hurt my feet.

Rose: Well, they just gonna have to hurt your feet for a while. You ain't said they hurt your feet when you went down to the store and got them.

Raynell: They didn't hurt then. My feet done got bigger.

Rose: Don't you give me no backtalk now. You get in there and get them shoes on.

Raynell exits into the house.

Ain't too much changed. He still got that piece of rag tied to that tree. He was out here swinging that bat. I was just ready to go back in the house. He swung that bat and then he just fell over. Seem like he swung it and stood there with this grin on his face . . . and then he just fell over. They carried him on down to the hospital, but I knew there wasn't no need . . . why don't you come on in the house?

Cory: Mama . . . I got something to tell you. I don't know how to tell you this . . . but I've got to tell you . . . I'm not going to Papa's funeral.

Rose: Boy, hush your mouth. That's your daddy you talking about. I don't want hear that kind of talk this morning. I done raised you to come to this? You standing there all healthy and grown talking about you ain't going to your daddy's funeral?

Cory: Mama . . . listen . . .

Rose: I don't want to hear it, Cory. You just get that thought out of your head.

Cory: I can't drag Papa with me everywhere I go. I've got to say no to him. One time in my life I've got to say no.

Rose: Don't nobody have to listen to nothing like that. I know you and your daddy ain't seen eye to eye, but I ain't got to listen to that kind of talk this morning. Whatever was between you and your daddy . . . the time has come to put it aside. Just take it and set it over there on the shelf and forget about it. Disrespecting your daddy ain't gonna make you a man, Cory. You got to find a way to come to that on your own. Not going to your daddy's funeral ain't gonna make you a man.

Cory: The whole time I was growing up . . . living in his house . . . Papa was like a shadow that followed you everywhere. It weighed on you and sunk into your flesh. It would wrap around you and lay there until you couldn't tell which one was you anymore. That shadow digging in your flesh. Trying to crawl in. Trying to live through you. Everywhere I looked, Troy Maxson was staring back at me . . . hiding under the bed . . . in the closet. I'm just saying I've got to find a way to get rid of that shadow, Mama.

Rose: You just like him. You got him in you good.

Cory: Don't tell me that, Mama.

Rose: You Troy Maxson all over again.

Cory: I don't want to be Troy Maxson. I want to be me.

Rose: You can't be nobody but who you are, Cory. That shadow wasn't nothing but you growing into yourself. You either got to grow into it or cut it down to fit you. But that's all you got to make life with. That's all you got to measure yourself against that world out there. Your daddy wanted you to be everything he wasn't . . . and at the same time he tried to make you into everything he was. I don't know if he was right or wrong . . . but I do know he meant to do more good than he meant to do harm. He wasn't always right. Sometimes when he touched he bruised. And sometimes when he took me in his arms he cut.

When I first met your daddy I thought . . . Here is a man I can lay down with and make a baby. That's the first thing I thought when I seen him. I was thirty years old and had done seen my share of men. But when he walked up to me and said, "I can dance a waltz that'll make you dizzy," I thought, Rose Lee, here is a man that you can open yourself up to and be filled to bursting. Here is a man that can fill all them empty spaces you been tipping around the edges of. One of them empty spaces was being somebody's mother.

I married your daddy and settled down to cooking his supper and keeping clean sheets on the bed. When your daddy walked through the house he was so big he filled it up. That was my first mistake. Not to make him leave some room for me. For my part in the matter. But at that time I wanted that. I wanted a house that I could sing in. And that's what your daddy gave me. I didn't know to keep up his strength I had to give up little pieces of mine. I did that. I took on his life as mine and mixed up the pieces so that you couldn't hardly tell which was which anymore. It was my choice. It was my life and I didn't have to live it like that. But that's what life offered me in the way of being a woman and I took it. I grabbed hold of it with both hands.

By the time Raynell came into the house, me and your daddy had done lost touch with one another. I didn't want to make my blessing off of nobody's misfortune . . . but I took on to Raynell like she was all them babies I had wanted and never had.

The phone rings.

Like I'd been blessed to relive a part of my life. And if the Lord see fit to keep up my strength . . . I'm gonna do her just like your daddy did you . . . I'm gonna give her the best of what's in me.

Raynell (entering, still with her old shoes): Mama . . . Reverend Tollivier on the phone.

Rose exits into the house.

Raynell: Hi.

Cory: Hi.

Raynell: You in the Army or the Marines?

Cory: Marines.

Raynell: Papa said it was the Army. Did you know Blue?

Cory: Blue? Who's Blue?

Raynell: Papa's dog what he sing about all the time.

Cory (singing): Hear it ring! Hear it ring!
> I had a dog his name was Blue
> You know Blue was mighty true
> You know Blue was a good old dog
> Blue treed a possum in a hollow log
> You know from that he was a good old dog.
> Hear it ring! Hear it ring!

> *Raynell joins in singing.*

Cory and Raynell: Blue treed a possum out on a limb
> Blue looked at me and I looked at him
> Grabbed that possum and put him in a sack
> Blue stayed there till I came back
> Old Blue's feets was big and round
> Never allowed a possum to touch the ground.

> Old Blue died and I dug his grave
> I dug his grave with a silver spade
> Let him down with a golden chain
> And every night I call his name
> Go on Blue, you good dog you
> Go on Blue, you good dog you

Raynell: Blue laid down and died like a man
> Blue laid down and died . . .

Both: Blue laid down and died like a man
> Now he's treeing possums in the Promised Land
> I'm gonna tell you this to let you know
> Blue's gone where the good dogs go
> When I hear old Blue bark
> When I hear old Blue bark
> Blue treed a possum in Noah's Ark
> Blue treed a possum in Noah's Ark.

> *Rose comes to the screen door.*

Rose: Cory, we gonna be ready to go in a minute.

Cory (to Raynell): You go on in the house and change them shoes like Mama told you so we can go to Papa's funeral.

Raynell: Okay, I'll be back.

> *Raynell exits into the house. Cory gets up and crosses over to the tree. Rose stands in the screen door watching him. Gabriel enters from the alley.*

Gabriel (calling): Hey, Rose!

Rose: Gabe?

Gabriel: I'm here, Rose. Hey Rose, I'm here!

> *Rose enters from the house.*

Rose: Lord . . . Look here, Lyons!

Lyons: See, I told you, Rose . . . I told you they'd let him come.

Cory: How you doing, Uncle Gabe?

Lyons: How you doing, Uncle Gabe?

Gabriel: Hey, Rose. It's time. It's time to tell St. Peter to open the gates. Troy, you ready? You ready, Troy. I'm gonna tell St. Peter to open the gates. You get ready now.

> *Gabriel, with great fanfare, braces himself to blow. The trumpet is without a mouthpiece. He puts the end of it into his mouth and blows with great force, like a man who has been waiting some twenty-odd years for this single moment. No sound comes out of the trumpet. He braces himself and blows again with the same result. A third time he blows. There is a weight of impossible description that falls away and leaves him bare and exposed to a frightful realization. It is a trauma that a sane and normal mind would be unable to withstand. He begins to dance. A slow, strange dance, eerie and life-giving. A dance of atavistic signature and ritual. Lyons attempts to embrace him. Gabriel pushes Lyons away. He begins to howl in what is an attempt at song, or perhaps a song turning back into itself in an attempt at speech. He finishes his dance and the gates of heaven stand open as wide as God's closet.*

That's the way that go!

CONNECTIONS TO OTHER SELECTIONS

1. Compare and contrast Troy Maxson with Willy Loman in Miller's *Death of a Salesman* (p. 1497). How do these protagonists relate to their sons?
2. How might the narrator's experiences in Ralph Ellison's short story "Battle Royal" (p. 227) be used to shed light on Troy's conflicts in *Fences*?

Perspective

DAVID SAVRAN (B. 1950)

An Interview with August Wilson   1987

Savran: In reading *Fences,* I came to view Troy more and more critically as the play progressed, sharing Rose's point of view. We see that Troy has been crippled by his father. That's being replayed in Troy's relationship with Cory. Do you think there's a way out of that cycle?

Wilson: Surely. First of all, we're all like our parents. The things we are taught early in life, how to respond to the world, our sense of morality—everything, we get from them. Now you can take that legacy and do with it anything you want to do. It's in your hands. Cory is Troy's son. How can he be Troy's son without sharing Troy's values? I was trying to get at why Troy made the choices he made, how they have influenced his values, and how he attempts to pass those along to his son. Each generation gives the succeeding generation what they think they need. One question in the play is "Are the tools we are given sufficient to compete in a world that is different from the one our parents knew?" I think they are — it's just that we have to do different things with the tools. That's all Troy has to give. Troy's flaw is that he does not recognize that the world was changing. That's because he spent fifteen years in a penitentiary.

As African-Americans, we should demand to participate in society as Africans. That's the way out of the vicious cycle of poverty and neglect that exists in 1987 in America, where you have a huge percentage of blacks living in the equivalent of South African townships, in housing projects. No one is inviting these people to participate in society. Look at the poverty levels — $8,500 for a family of four, if you have $8,501 you're not counted. Those statistics would go up enormously if we had an honest assessment of the cost of living in America. I don't know how anybody can support a family of four on $8,500. What I'm saying is that 85 or 90 percent of blacks in America are living in abject poverty and, for the most part, are crowded into what amount to concentration camps. The situation for blacks in America is worse than it was forty years ago. Some sociologists will tell you about the tremendous progress we've made. They didn't put me out when I walked in the door. And you can always point to someone who works on Wall Street, or is a doctor. But they don't count in the larger scheme of things.

Savran: Do you have any idea how these political changes could take place?

Wilson: I'm not sure. I know that blacks must be allowed their cultural differences. I think the process of assimilation to white American society was a big mistake. We don't want to be like you. Blacks living in housing projects are isolated from the society, for the most part — living as they choose, as Africans. Only they don't realize the value in what they're doing because they have accepted their victimization. They've marked themselves as victims. Once they recognize that, they can begin to move through society in a different manner, from a stronger position, and claim what is theirs.

Savran: A project of yours is to point up what happens when oppression is internalized.

Wilson: Yes, transfer of aggression to the wrong target. I think it's interesting that the two roads open to blacks for "full participation" are entertainment and sports. *Ma Rainey* and *Fences*, and I didn't plan it that way. I don't think that they're the correct roads. I think Troy's right. Now with the benefit of historical perspective, I can say that the athletic scholarship was actually a way of exploiting. Now you've got two million kids who think they're going to play in the NBA. In the sixties the universities made a lot of money off of athletics. You had kids playing for free who, by and large, were not getting educated, were taking courses in basketweaving. Some of them could barely read.

Savran: Troy may be right about that issue, but it seems that he has passed on certain destructive traits in spite of himself. Take the hostility between father and son.

Wilson: I think every generation says to the previous generation: you're in my way, I've got to get by. The father-son conflict is actually a normal generational conflict that happens all the time.

Savran: So it's a healthy and a good thing?

Wilson: Oh, sure. Troy is seeing this boy walk around, smelling his piss. Two men cannot live in the same household. Troy would have been tremendously disappointed if Cory had not challenged him. Troy knows that this boy has to go out and do battle with that world: "So I had best prepare him because I know that's a harsh, cruel place out there. But that's going to be easy compared to what he's getting here. Ain't nobody gonna whip your ass like I'm gonna whip it." He has a tremendous love for the kid. But he's not going to say, "I love you," he's going to demonstrate it. He's carrying garbage for seventeen years just for the kid. The only world Troy knows is the one that he made. Cory's going to go on to find another one, he's going to arrive at the same place as Troy. I think one of the most important lines in the play is when Troy is talking about his father: "I got to the place where I could feel him kicking in my blood and knew that the only thing that separated us was the matter of a few years."

Hopefully, Cory will do things a bit differently with his son. For Troy, sports was not the way to go, the white man wouldn't let him get away with that. "Get you a job, with your hands, something that nobody can take away from you." The idea of school — he doesn't know what that is. That's for white folks. Very few blacks had paperwork jobs. But if you knew how to fix cars, you could always make some money. That's what Troy wants for Cory. There aren't many people who ever jumped up in Troy's face. So he's proud of the kid at the same time that he expresses a hurt that all men feel. You got to cut your kid loose at some point. There's that sense of loss and separation. You find out how Troy left his father's house and you see how Cory leaves his house. I suspect with Cory it will repeat with some differences and maybe, after five or six generations, they'll find a different way to do it.

Savran: Where Cory ends up is very ambiguous, as a marine in 1965.

Wilson: Yes. For the average black kid on the street, that was an alternative. You went into the army because you could learn how to do something. I can remember my parents talking about the son of some friends: "He's in the navy. He *did* something" — as opposed to standing on the street corner, shooting drugs, drinking wine, and robbing stores. Lyons says to Cory, "I always knew you were going to make something out of yourself." It really wounds me. He's a corporal in the marines. For blacks, that is a sense of accomplishment. Therein lies one of the tragedies of blacks in America. Cory says, "I don't know. I put in six years. That's enough." Anyone who goes into the army and makes a career out of it is a loser. They sit there and are nurtured by the army and they don't have to confront life. Then they get out of the army and find there's nothing to do. They didn't learn any skills. And if they did, they can't find a job. Four months later, they're shooting dope. In the sixties a whole bunch of blacks went over, fought, and died in the Vietnam War. The survivors came back to the same street corners and found out nothing had changed. They still couldn't get a job.

At the end of *Fences* every person, with the exception of Raynell, is institutionalized. Rose is in a church. Lyons is in a penitentiary. Gabriel's in a mental hospital, and Cory's in the marines. The only free person is the girl, Troy's daughter, the hope for the future. That was conscious on my part because in '57 that's what I saw. Blacks have relied on institutions which are really foreign — except for the black church, which has been our saving grace. I have some problems with it but I recognize it as a central social organization and sometimes an economic organization for the black community. I would like to see blacks develop their own institutions that respond to their needs.

From *In Their Own Voices*

Considerations for Critical Thinking and Writing

1. Wilson describes Troy's "flaw" as an inability to "recognize that the world was changing" (para. 2). Discuss how completely this assessment describes Troy.

2. Write an essay discussing how Wilson uses the hostility between father and son in *Fences* as a means of treating larger social issues for blacks in America.

3. Read the section on historical criticism (pp. 1651–55) in Chapter 51, "Critical Strategies for Reading." Discuss how useful and accurate you think *Fences* is in depicting black life in America for the past several decades.

CRITICAL THINKING AND WRITING

Credits, clockwise from top left: © Bettmann/Corbis; © Bettmann/CORBIS; © Beth Gwinn; Everett Collection/Newscom; © Michael Nicholson/CORBIS; Boston Globe/Getty Images.

51

Critical Strategies
for Reading

Great literature is simply language
charged with meaning to the utmost
possible degree.
—EZRA POUND

Courtesy of George
Eastman House,
International Museum
of Photography and
Film.

The answers you get from literature
depend upon the questions you pose.
—MARGARET ATWOOD

© Kathy deWitt/Alamy.

CRITICAL THINKING

Maybe this has happened to you: the assignment is to write an analysis of
some aspect of a work — let's say, Nathaniel Hawthorne's *The Scarlet Letter* —
that interests you and takes into account critical sources that comment on and
interpret the work. You cheerfully begin research in the library but quickly
find yourself bewildered by several seemingly unrelated articles. The first
traces the thematic significance of images of light and darkness in the novel;
the second makes a case for Hester Prynne as a liberated woman; the third
argues that Arthur Dimmesdale's guilt is a projection of Hawthorne's own
emotions; and the fourth analyzes the introduction, "The Custom-House," as
an attack on bourgeois values. These disparate treatments may seem random

and capricious — a confirmation of your worst suspicions that interpretations of literature are hit-or-miss excursions into areas that you know little about or didn't know even existed. But if you understand that the four articles are written from four different perspectives — formalist, feminist, psychological, and Marxist — and that the purpose of each is to enhance your understanding of the novel by discussing a particular element of it, then you can see that the articles' varying strategies represent potentially interesting ways of opening up the text that might otherwise never have occurred to you. There are many ways to approach a text, and a useful first step is to develop a sense of direction, an understanding of how a perspective — your own or a critic's — shapes a discussion of a text.

This chapter offers an introduction to critical approaches to literature by outlining a variety of strategies for reading fiction, poetry, or drama. These strategies include approaches that have long been practiced by readers who have used, for example, the insights gleaned from biography and history to illuminate literary works as well as more recent approaches, such as those used by gender, reader-response, and deconstructionist critics. Each of these perspectives is sensitive to point of view, symbol, tone, irony, and other literary elements that you have been studying, but each also casts those elements in a special light. The formalist approach emphasizes how the elements within a work achieve their effects, whereas biographical and psychological approaches lead outward from the work to consider the author's life and other writings. Even broader approaches, such as historical and cultural perspectives, connect the work to historic, social, and economic forces. Mythological readings represent the broadest approach because they discuss the cultural and universal responses readers have to a work.

Any given strategy raises its own types of questions and issues while seeking particular kinds of evidence to support itself. An awareness of the assumptions and methods that inform an approach can help you to understand better the validity and value of a given critic's strategy for making sense of a work. More important, such an understanding can widen and deepen the responses of your own reading.

The critical thinking that goes into understanding a professional critic's approach to a work is not foreign to you because you have already used essentially the same kind of thinking to understand the work itself. You have developed skills to produce a literary *analysis* that, for example, describes how a character, symbol, or rhyme scheme supports a theme. These same skills are also useful for reading literary criticism because they allow you to keep track of how the parts of a critical approach create a particular reading of a literary work. When you analyze a story, poem, or play by closely examining how its various elements relate to the whole, your *interpretation* — your articulation of what the work means to you as supported by an analysis of its elements — necessarily involves choosing what you focus on in the work. The same is true of professional critics.

Critical readings presuppose choices in the kinds of materials that are discussed. An analysis of the setting of John Updike's "A & P" (p. 200) would probably focus on the oppressive environment the protagonist associates with the store rather than, say, the economic history of that supermarket chain. (For a student's analysis of the setting in "A & P," see p. 1684.) The economic history of a supermarket chain might be useful to a Marxist critic concerned with how class relations are revealed in "A & P," but for a formalist critic interested in identifying the unifying structures of the story, such information would be irrelevant.

The Perspectives and Critical Case Studies in this anthology offer opportunities to read critics using a wide variety of approaches to analyze and interpret texts. In the Critical Case Study on Ibsen's *A Doll's House* (Chapter 47), for instance, Carol Strongin Tufts (p. 1418) offers a psychoanalytic reading of Nora that characterizes her as a narcissistic personality rather than as a feminist heroine. The criteria she uses to evaluate Nora's behavior are drawn from the language used by the American Psychiatric Association. In contrast, Joan Templeton (p. 1421) places Nora in the context of women's rights issues to argue that Nora must be read from a feminist perspective if the essential meaning of the play is to be understood. Each of these critics raises different questions, examines different evidence, and employs different assumptions to interpret Nora's character. Being aware of those differences — teasing them out so that you can see how they lead to competing conclusions — is a useful way to analyze the analysis itself. What is left out of an interpretation is sometimes as significant as what is included. As you read the critics, it's worth reminding yourself that your own critical thinking skills can help you to determine the usefulness of a particular approach.

The following overview of critical strategies for reading is neither exhaustive in the types of critical approaches covered nor complete in its presentation of the complexities inherent in them, but it should help you to develop an appreciation of the intriguing possibilities that attend literary interpretation. The emphasis in this chapter is on ways of thinking about literature rather than on daunting lists of terms, names, and movements. Although a working knowledge of critical schools may be valuable and necessary for a fully informed use of a given critical approach, the aim here is more modest and practical. This chapter is no substitute for the shelves of literary criticism that can be found in your library, but it does suggest how readers using different perspectives organize their responses to texts.

The summaries of critical approaches that follow are descriptive, not evaluative. Each approach has its advantages and limitations. In practice, many critical approaches overlap and complement each other, but those matters are best left to further study. Like literary artists, critics have their personal values, tastes, and styles. The appropriateness of a specific critical approach will depend, at least in part, on the nature of the literary work under discussion as well as on your own sensibilities and experience. However, any approach, if it is to enhance understanding, requires sensitivity, tact, and an awareness of the various literary elements of the text, including, of course, its use of language.

Successful critical approaches avoid eccentric decodings that reveal so-called hidden meanings that are not only hidden but totally absent from the text. For a parody of this sort of critical excess, see "A Parodic Interpretation of 'Stopping by Woods on a Snowy Evening'" (p. 889), in which Herbert R. Coursen Jr. has some fun with a Robert Frost poem and Santa Claus while making a serious point about the dangers of overly ingenious readings. Literary criticism attempts, like any valid hypothesis, to account for phenomena — the text — without distorting or misrepresenting what it describes.

THE LITERARY CANON: DIVERSITY AND CONTROVERSY

Before looking at the various critical approaches discussed in this chapter, it makes sense to consider first which literature has been traditionally considered worthy of such analysis. The discussion in the introduction called The Changing Literary Canon (p. 6) may have already alerted you to the fact that in recent years many more works by women, minorities, and writers from around the world have been considered by scholars, critics, and teachers to merit serious study and inclusion in what is known as the literary canon. This increasing diversity has been celebrated by those who believe that multiculturalism taps new sources for the discovery of great literature while raising significant questions about language, culture, and society. At the same time, others have perceived this diversity as a threat to the established, traditional canon of Western culture.

The debates concerning who should be read, taught, and written about have sometimes been acrimonious as well as lively and challenging. Bitter arguments have been waged on campuses and in the press over what has come to be called *political correctness*. Two main camps have formed around these debates — liberals and conservatives (the appropriateness of these terms is debatable, but the oppositional positioning is unmistakable). The liberals are said to insist on encouraging tolerant attitudes about race, class, gender, and sexual orientation, and opening up the curriculum to multicultural texts from Asia, Africa, Latin America, and elsewhere. These revisionists, seeking a change in traditional attitudes, are sometimes accused of trying to substitute ideological dogma for reason and truth and to intimidate opposing colleagues and students into silence and acceptance of their politically correct views. The conservatives are also portrayed as ideologues; in their efforts to preserve what they regard as the best from the past, they fail to acknowledge that Western classics, mostly written by white male Europeans, represent only a portion of human experience. These traditionalists are seen as advocating values that are neither universal nor eternal but merely privileged and entrenched. Conservatives are charged with ignoring the political agenda that their values represent and that is implicit in their preference for the works of canonical authors such as Homer, Virgil, Shakespeare, Milton, Tolstoy, and Faulkner. The reductive and contradictory nature of this national debate between liberals and conservatives has been neatly summed up by Katha Pollitt: "Read the conservatives' list and produce a nation of sexists and racists — or a nation of philosopher kings. Read the liberals' list and produce a nation of spiritual relativists — or a nation of open-minded world citizens" ("Canon to the Right of Me . . . ," *Nation*, Sept. 23, 1991, p. 330).

These troubling and extreme alternatives can be avoided, of course, if the issues are not approached from such absolutist positions. Solutions to these issues cannot be suggested in this limited space, and, no doubt, solutions will evolve over time, but we can at least provide a perspective. Books — regardless of what list they are on — are not likely to unite a fragmented nation or to disunite a unified one. It is perhaps more useful and accurate to see issues of canonicity as reflecting political changes rather than being the primary causes of them. This is not to say that books don't have an impact on readers — that *Uncle Tom's Cabin,* for instance, did not galvanize antislavery sentiments in nineteenth-century America — but that book lists do not by themselves preserve or destroy the status quo.

It's worth noting that the curricula of American universities have always undergone significant and, some would say, wrenching changes. Only a little more than one hundred years ago there was strong opposition to teaching English, as well as other modern languages, alongside programs dominated by Greek and Latin. Only since the 1920s has American literature been made a part of the curriculum, and just five decades ago including twentieth-century writers such as James Joyce, Virginia Woolf, Franz Kafka, and Ernest Hemingway in the curriculum was regarded with raised eyebrows. New voices do not drown out the past; they build on it and eventually become part of the past as newer writers take their place beside them. Neither resistance to change nor a denial of the past will have its way with the canon. Though both impulses are widespread, neither is likely to dominate the other because there are too many reasonable, practical readers and teachers who instead of replacing Shakespeare, Melville, and other canonical writers have supplemented them with neglected writers from Western and other cultures. These readers experience the current debates about the canon not as a binary opposition but as an opportunity to explore important questions about continuity and change in our literature, culture, and society.

FORMALIST STRATEGIES

Formalist critics focus on the formal elements of a work — its language, structure, and tone. A formalist reads literature as an independent work of art rather than as a reflection of the author's state of mind or as a representation of a moment in history. Historic influences on a work, an author's intentions, or anything else outside the work are generally not treated by formalists (this is particularly true of the most famous modern formalists, known as the **New Critics**, who dominated American criticism from the 1940s through the 1960s). Instead, formalists offer intense examinations of the relationship between form and meaning within a work, emphasizing the subtle complexity of how a work is arranged. This kind of close reading pays special attention to what are often described as *intrinsic* matters in a literary work, such as diction, irony, paradox, metaphor, and symbol, as well as larger elements, such as plot, characterization, and narrative technique. Formalists examine how these elements work together to give a coherent shape to a work while contributing to its meaning. The answers to the questions formalists raise about how the shape and effect of a work are related come from the work itself. Other kinds of information that go beyond the text — biography, history, politics, economics, and so on — are typically regarded by formalists as *extrinsic* matters, which are considerably less important than what goes on within the autonomous text.

Poetry especially lends itself to close readings because a poem's relative brevity allows for detailed analyses of nearly all its words and how they achieve their effects. For a student's formalist reading of how a pervasive sense of death is worked into a poem, see "A Reading of Emily Dickinson's 'There's a certain Slant of light'" (p. 1681).

Formalist strategies are also useful for analyzing drama and fiction. In his well-known essay "The World of *Hamlet*," Maynard Mack explores Hamlet's character and predicament by paying close attention to the words and images that Shakespeare uses to build a world in which appearances mask reality and mystery is embedded in scene after scene. Mack points to recurring terms, such as *apparition, seems, assume,* and *put on,* as well as repeated images of acting, clothing, disease, and painting, to indicate the treacherous surface world Hamlet must penetrate to get to the truth. This pattern of deception provides an organizing principle around which Mack offers a reading of the entire play:

> Hamlet's problem, in its crudest form, is simply the problem of the avenger: he must carry out the injunction of the ghost and kill the king. But this problem . . . is presented in terms of a certain kind of world. The ghost's injunction to act becomes so inextricably bound up for Hamlet with the character of the world in which the action must be taken — its mysteriousness, its baffling appearances, its deep consciousness of infection, frailty, and loss — that he cannot come to terms with either without coming to terms with both.

Although Mack places *Hamlet* in the tradition of revenge tragedy, his reading of the play emphasizes Shakespeare's arrangement of language rather than literary history as a means of providing an interpretation that accounts for various elements of the play. Mack's formalist strategy explores how diction reveals meaning and how repeated words and images evoke and reinforce important thematic significances.

For an example of a work in which the shape of the plot serves as the major organizing principle, let's examine Kate Chopin's "The Story of an Hour" (p. 15), a two-page short story that takes only a few minutes to read. With the story fresh in your mind, consider how you might approach it from a formalist perspective. A first reading probably results in surprise at the story's ending: a grieving wife "afflicted with a heart trouble" suddenly dies of a heart attack, not because she's learned that her kind and loving husband has been killed in a terrible train accident but because she discovers that he is very much alive.

Clearly, we are faced with an ironic situation since there is such a powerful incongruity between what is expected to happen and what actually happens. A likely formalist strategy for analyzing this story would be to raise questions about the ironic ending. Is this merely a trick ending, or is it a carefully wrought culmination of other elements in the story so that in addition to creating surprise the ending snaps the story shut on an interesting and challenging theme? Formalists value such complexities over simple surprise effects.

A second, closer reading indicates that Chopin's third-person narrator presents the story in a manner similar to Josephine's gentle attempts to break the news about Brently Mallard's death. The story is told in "veiled hints that [reveal] in half concealing." But unlike Josephine, who tries to protect her sister's fragile heart from stress, the narrator seeks to reveal Mrs. Mallard's complex heart. A formalist would look back over the story for signs of the ending in the imagery. Although Mrs. Mallard grieves immediately and unreservedly when she hears about the train disaster, she soon begins to feel a different emotion as she looks out the window at "the tops of trees . . . all aquiver with the new spring life." This symbolic evocation of renewal and rebirth — along with "the delicious breath of rain," the sounds of life in the street, and the birds singing — causes her to feel, in spite of her own efforts to repress her thoughts and emotions, "free, free, free!" She feels alive with a sense of possibility, with a "clear and exalted perception" that she "would live for herself" instead of for and through her husband.

It is ironic that this ecstatic "self-assertion" is interpreted by Josephine as grief, but the crowning irony for this "goddess of Victory" is the doctors' assumption that she dies of joy rather than of the shock of having to abandon her newly discovered self once she realizes her husband is still alive. In the course of an hour, Mrs. Mallard's life is irretrievably changed: her husband's assumed accidental death frees her, but the fact that he lives and all the expectations imposed on her by his continued life kill her. She does, indeed, die of a broken heart, but only Chopin's readers know the real ironic meaning of that explanation.

Although this brief discussion of some of the formal elements of Chopin's story does not describe all there is to say about how they produce an effect and create meaning, it does suggest the kinds of questions, issues, and evidence that a formalist strategy might raise in providing a close reading of the text itself.

BIOGRAPHICAL STRATEGIES

A knowledge of an author's life can help readers understand his or her work more fully. Events in a work might follow actual events in a writer's life just as characters might be based on people known by the author. Ernest Hemingway's "Soldier's Home" (p. 162) is a story about the difficulties of a World War I veteran named Krebs returning to his small hometown in Oklahoma, where he cannot adjust to the pious assumptions of his family and neighbors.

He refuses to accept their innocent blindness to the horrors he has witnessed during the war. They have no sense of the brutality of modern life; instead they insist he resume his life as if nothing has happened. There is plenty of biographical evidence to indicate that Krebs's unwillingness to lie about his war experiences reflects Hemingway's own responses on his return to Oak Park, Illinois, in 1919. Krebs, like Hemingway, finds he has to leave the sentimentality, repressiveness, and smug complacency that threaten to render his experiences unreal: "the world they were in was not the world he was in."

An awareness of Hemingway's own war experiences and subsequent disillusionment with his hometown can be readily developed through available biographies, letters, and other works he wrote. Consider, for example, this passage from *By Force of Will: The Life and Art of Ernest Hemingway,* in which Scott Donaldson describes Hemingway's response to World War I:

> In poems, as in [*A Farewell to Arms*], Hemingway expressed his distaste for the first war. The men who had to fight the war did not die well:
>
> > Soldiers pitch and cough and twitch —
> > All the world roars red and black;
> > Soldiers smother in a ditch,
> > Choking through the whole attack.
>
> And what did they die for? They were "sucked in" by empty words and phrases —
>
> > King and country,
> > Christ Almighty,
> > And the rest,
> > Patriotism,
> > Democracy,
> > Honor —
>
> which spelled death. The bitterness of these outbursts derived from the distinction Hemingway drew between the men on the line and those who started the wars that others had to fight.

This kind of information can help to deepen our understanding of just how empathetically Krebs is presented in the story. Relevant facts about Hemingway's life will not make "Soldier's Home" a better-written story than it is, but such information can make clearer the source of Hemingway's convictions and how his own experiences inform his major concerns as a storyteller.

Some formalist critics — some New Critics, for example — argue that interpretation should be based exclusively on internal evidence rather than on any biographical information outside the work. They argue that it is not possible to determine an author's intention and that the work must stand by itself. Although this is a useful caveat for keeping the work in focus, a reader who finds biography relevant would argue that biography can at the very least serve as a control on interpretation. A reader who, for example, finds Krebs at fault for not subscribing to the values of his hometown would be misreading the story, given both its tone and the biographical information available about the author. Although the narrator never *tells* the reader that Krebs is right or wrong for leaving town, the story's tone sides with his view of things.

If, however, someone were to argue otherwise, insisting that the tone is not decisive and that Krebs's position is problematic, a reader familiar with Hemingway's own reactions could refute that argument with a powerful confirmation of Krebs's instincts to withdraw. Hence, many readers find biography useful for interpretation.

However, it is also worth noting that biographical information can complicate a work. Chopin's "The Story of an Hour" presents a repressed wife's momentary discovery of what freedom from her husband might mean to her. She awakens to a new sense of herself when she learns of her husband's death, only to collapse of a heart attack when she sees that he is alive. Readers might be tempted to interpret this story as Chopin's fictionalized commentary about her own marriage because her husband died twelve years before she wrote the story and seven years before she began writing fiction seriously. Biographers seem to agree, however, that Chopin's marriage was evidently satisfying to her and that she was not oppressed by her husband and did not feel oppressed.

Moreover, consider this diary entry from only one month after Chopin wrote the story (quoted by Per Seyersted in *Kate Chopin: A Critical Biography*):

> If it were possible for my husband and my mother to come back to earth, I feel that I would unhesitatingly give up everything that has come into my life since they left it and join my existence again with theirs. To do that, I would have to forget the past ten years of my growth — my real growth. But I would take back a little wisdom with me; it would be the spirit of perfect acquiescence.

This passage raises provocative questions instead of resolving them. How does that "spirit of perfect acquiescence" relate to Mrs. Mallard's insistence that she "would live for herself"? Why would Chopin be willing to "forget the past ten years of . . . growth" given her protagonist's desire for "self-assertion"? Although these and other questions raised by the diary entry cannot be answered here, this kind of biographical perspective certainly adds to the possibilities of interpretation.

Sometimes biographical information does not change our understanding so much as it enriches our appreciation of a work. It matters, for instance, that much of John Milton's poetry, so rich in visual imagery, was written after he became blind; and it is just as significant — to shift to a musical example — that a number of Ludwig van Beethoven's greatest works, including the Ninth Symphony, were composed after he succumbed to total deafness.

PSYCHOLOGICAL STRATEGIES

Given the enormous influence that Sigmund Freud's psychoanalytic theories have had on twentieth-century interpretations of human behavior, it is nearly inevitable that most people have some familiarity with his ideas concerning dreams, unconscious desires, and sexual repression, as well as his terms for different aspects of the psyche — the id, ego, and superego. Psychological approaches to literature draw on Freud's theories and other psychoanalytic theories to understand more fully the text, the writer, and the reader.

Critics use such approaches to explore the motivations of characters and the symbolic meanings of events, while biographers speculate about a writer's own motivations — conscious or unconscious — in a literary work. Psychological approaches are also used to describe and analyze the reader's personal responses to a text.

Although it is not feasible to explain psychoanalytic terms and concepts in so brief a space as this, it is possible to suggest the nature of a psychological approach. It is a strategy based heavily on the idea of the existence of a human unconscious — those impulses, desires, and feelings that a person is unaware of but that influence emotions and behavior.

Central to a number of psychoanalytic critical readings is Freud's concept of what he called the *Oedipus complex*, a term derived from Sophocles' tragedy *Oedipus the King* (p. 1127). This complex is predicated on a boy's unconscious rivalry with his father for his mother's love and his desire to eliminate his father in order to take his father's place with his mother. The female version of the psychological conflict is known as the *Electra complex*, a term used to describe a daughter's unconscious rivalry for her father. The name comes from a Greek legend about Electra, who avenged the death of her father, Agamemnon, by plotting the death of her mother. In *The Interpretation of Dreams*, Freud explains why *Oedipus the King* "moves a modern audience no less than it did the contemporary Greek one." What unites their powerful attraction to the play is an unconscious response:

> There must be something which makes a voice within us ready to recognize the compelling force of destiny in the *Oedipus*. . . . His destiny moves us only because it might have been ours — because the oracle laid the same curse upon us before our birth as upon him. It is the fate of all of us, perhaps, to direct our first sexual impulse towards our mother and our first hatred and our first murderous wish against our father. Our dreams convince us that this is so. King Oedipus, who slew his father Laios and married his mother Iokaste, merely shows us the fulfillment of our own childhood wishes . . . and we shrink back from him with the whole force of the repression by which those wishes have since that time been held down within us.

In this passage Freud interprets the unconscious motives of Sophocles in writing the play, Oedipus in acting within it, and the audience in responding to it.

A further application of the Oedipus complex can be observed in a classic interpretation of *Hamlet* by Ernest Jones, who used this concept to explain why Hamlet delays in avenging his father's death. This reading has been tightly summarized by Norman Holland, a psychoanalytic critic, in *The Shakespearean Imagination*. Holland shapes the issues into four major components:

> One, people over the centuries have been unable to say why Hamlet delays in killing the man who murdered his father and married his mother. Two, psychoanalytic experience shows that every child wants to do just exactly that. Three, Hamlet delays because he cannot punish Claudius for doing what he himself wished to do as a child and, unconsciously, still wishes to do: he would be punishing himself. Four, the fact that this wish is unconscious explains why people could not explain Hamlet's delay.

Although the Oedipus complex is, of course, not relevant to all psychological interpretations of literature, interpretations involving this complex do offer a useful example of how psychoanalytic critics tend to approach a text. (For Freud's discussion of *Hamlet,* see p. 1338.)

The situation in which Mrs. Mallard finds herself in Chopin's "The Story of an Hour" is not related to an Oedipus complex, but it is clear that news of her husband's death has released powerful unconscious desires for freedom that she had previously suppressed. As she grieved, "something" was "coming to her and she was waiting for it, fearfully." What comes to her is what she senses about the life outside her window; that's the stimulus, but the true source of what was to "possess her," which she strove to "beat . . . back with her [conscious] will," is her desperate desire for the autonomy and fulfillment she had been unable to admit did not exist in her marriage. A psychological approach to her story amounts to a case study in the destructive nature of self-repression. Moreover, the story might reflect Chopin's own views of her marriage — despite her conscious statements about her loving husband. And what about the reader's response? How might a psychological approach account for different responses in female and male readers to Mrs. Mallard's death? One needn't be versed in psychoanalytic terms to entertain this question.

HISTORICAL STRATEGIES

Historians sometimes use literature as a window onto the past because literature frequently provides the nuances of a historic period that cannot be readily perceived through other sources. The characters in Harriet Beecher Stowe's *Uncle Tom's Cabin* (1852) display, for example, a complex set of white attitudes toward blacks in mid-nineteenth-century America that is absent from more traditional historic documents, such as census statistics or state laws. Another way of approaching the relationship between literature and history, however, is to use history as a means of understanding a literary work more clearly. The plot pattern of pursuit, escape, and capture in nineteenth-century slave narratives had a significant influence on Stowe's plotting of action in *Uncle Tom's Cabin.* This relationship demonstrates that the writing contemporary to an author is an important element of the history that helps to shape a work. There are many ways to talk about the historical and cultural dimensions of a work. Such readings treat a literary text as a document reflecting, producing, or being produced by the social conditions of its time, giving equal focus to the social milieu and the work itself. Four historical strategies that have been especially influential are literary history criticism, Marxist criticism, new historicist criticism, and cultural criticism.

Literary History Criticism

Literary historians shift the emphasis from the period to the work. Hence a literary historian might also examine mid-nineteenth-century abolitionist attitudes toward blacks to determine whether Stowe's novel is representative of those views or significantly to the right or left of them. Such a study might even indicate how closely the book reflects racial attitudes of twentieth-century readers. A work of literature may transcend time to the extent that it addresses the concerns of readers over a span of decades or centuries, but it remains for the literary historian a part of the past in which it was composed, a past that can reveal more fully a work's language, ideas, and purposes.

Literary historians move beyond both the facts of an author's personal life and the text itself to the social and intellectual currents in which the author composed the work. They place the work in the context of its time (as do many critical biographers, who write "life and times" studies), and sometimes they make connections with other literary works that may have influenced the author. The basic strategy of literary historians is to illuminate the historic background in order to shed light on some aspect of the work itself.

In Hemingway's "Soldier's Home" we learn that Krebs had been at Belleau Wood, Soissons, the Champagne, St. Mihiel, and the Argonne. Although nothing is said of these battles in the story, they were among the bloodiest of the war; the wholesale butchery and staggering casualties incurred by both sides make credible the way Krebs's unstated but lingering memories have turned him into a psychological prisoner of war. Knowing something about the ferocity of those battles helps us account for Krebs's response in the story. Moreover, we can more fully appreciate Hemingway's refusal to have Krebs lie about the realities of war for the folks back home if we are aware of the numerous poems, stories, and plays published during World War I that presented war as a glorious, manly, transcendent sacrifice for God and country. Juxtaposing those works with "Soldier's Home" brings the differences into sharp focus.

Similarly, a reading of William Blake's poem "London" (p. 679) is less complete if we do not know of the horrific social conditions — the poverty, disease, exploitation, and hypocrisy — that characterized the city Blake laments in the late eighteenth century.

One last example: the repression expressed in the lines on Mrs. Mallard's face is more distinctly seen if Chopin's "The Story of an Hour" is placed in the context of "the women's question" as it continued to develop in the 1890s. Mrs. Mallard's impulse toward "self-assertion" runs parallel with a growing women's movement away from the role of long-suffering housewife. This desire was widely regarded by traditionalists as a form of dangerous selfishness that was considered as unnatural as it was immoral. It is no wonder that Chopin raises the question of whether Mrs. Mallard's sense of freedom owing to her husband's death isn't a selfish, "monstrous joy." Mrs. Mallard, however, dismisses this question as "trivial" in the face of her new perception of life, a dismissal that Chopin endorses by way of the story's ironic ending. The larger social context of this story would have been more apparent to Chopin's readers in 1894 than it is to readers in the 2000s. That is why a historical reconstruction of the limitations placed on married women helps to explain the pressures, tensions, and momentary — only momentary — release that Mrs. Mallard experiences.

Marxist Criticism

Marxist readings developed from the heightened interest in radical reform during the 1930s, when many critics looked to literature as a means of furthering proletarian social and economic goals, based largely on the writings of Karl Marx. *Marxist critics* focus on the ideological content of a work — its explicit and implicit assumptions and values about matters such as culture, race, class, and power. Marxist studies typically aim at revealing and clarifying ideological issues and also correcting social injustices. Some Marxist critics have used literature to describe the competing socioeconomic interests that too often advance capitalist money and power rather than socialist morality and justice. They argue that criticism, like literature, is essentially political because it either challenges or supports economic oppression. Even if criticism attempts to ignore class conflicts, it is politicized, according to Marxists, because it supports the status quo.

It is not surprising that Marxist critics pay more attention to the content and themes of literature than to its form. A Marxist critic would more likely be concerned with the exploitive economic forces that cause Willy Loman to feel trapped in Miller's *Death of a Salesman* (p. 1497) than with the playwright's use of nonrealistic dramatic techniques to reveal Loman's inner thoughts. Similarly, a Marxist reading of Chopin's "The Story of an Hour" might draw on the evidence made available in a book published only a few years after the story by Charlotte Perkins Gilman titled *Women and Economics: A Study of the Economic Relation between Men and Women as a Factor in Social Evolution* (1898). An examination of this study could help explain how some of the "repression" Mrs. Mallard experiences was generated by the socioeconomic structure contemporary to her and how Chopin challenges the validity of that structure by having Mrs. Mallard resist it with her very life. A Marxist reading would see the protagonist's conflict as not only an individual issue but part of a larger class struggle.

New Historicist Criticism

Since the 1960s a development in historical approaches to literature known as *new historicism* has emphasized the interaction between the historic context of a work and a modern reader's understanding and interpretation of the work. In contrast to many traditional literary historians, however, new historicists attempt to describe the culture of a period by reading many different kinds of texts that traditional literary historians might have previously left for economists, sociologists, and anthropologists. New historicists attempt to read a period in all its dimensions, including political, economic, social, and aesthetic concerns. These considerations could be used to explain the pressures that destroy Mrs. Mallard. A new historicist might examine the story and the public attitudes toward women contemporary to "The Story of an Hour" as well as documents such as suffragist tracts and medical diagnoses to explore how the same forces — expectations about how women are supposed to feel, think, and behave — shape different kinds of texts and how these texts influence each other. A new historicist might, for example, examine medical records for evidence of "nervousness" and "hysteria" as common diagnoses for women who led lives regarded as too independent by their contemporaries.

Without an awareness of just how selfish and self-destructive Mrs. Mallard's impulses would have been in the eyes of her contemporaries, readers in the twenty-first century might miss the pervasive pressures embedded not only in her marriage but in the social fabric surrounding her. Her death is made more understandable by such an awareness. The doctors who diagnose her as suffering from "the joy that kills" are not merely insensitive or stupid; they represent a contrasting set of assumptions and values that are as historic and real as Mrs. Mallard's yearnings.

New historicist criticism acknowledges more fully than traditional historical approaches the competing nature of readings of the past and thereby tends to offer new emphases and perspectives. New historicism reminds us that there is not only one historic context for "The Story of an Hour." Those doctors reveal additional dimensions of late-nineteenth-century social attitudes that warrant our attention, whether we agree with them or not. By emphasizing that historical perceptions are governed, at least in part, by our own concerns and preoccupations, new historicists sensitize us to the fact that the history on which we choose to focus is colored by being reconstructed from our own present moment. This reconstructed history affects our reading of texts.

Cultural Criticism

Cultural critics, like new historicists, focus on the historical contexts of a literary work, but they pay particular attention to popular manifestations of social, political, and economic contexts. Popular culture — mass-produced and consumed cultural artifacts, today ranging from advertising to popular fiction to television to rock music — and "high" culture are given equal emphasis. A cultural critic might be interested in looking at how Baz Luhrmann's movie version of *Romeo + Juliet* (1996) was influenced by the fragmentary nature of MTV videos. Adding the "low" art of everyday life to "high" art opens up previously unexpected and unexplored areas of criticism. Cultural critics use widely eclectic strategies drawn from new historicism, psychology, gender studies, and deconstructionism (to name only a handful of approaches) to analyze not only literary texts but radio talk shows, comic strips, calendar art, commercials, travel guides, and baseball cards. Because all human activity falls within the ken of cultural criticism, nothing is too minor or major, obscure or pervasive, to escape the range of its analytic vision.

Cultural criticism also includes *postcolonial criticism*, the study of cultural behavior and expression in relationship to the formerly colonized world. Postcolonial criticism refers to the analysis of literary works written by writers from countries and cultures that at one time were controlled by colonizing powers — such as Indian writers during or after British colonial rule. The term also refers to the analysis of literary works written about colonial cultures by writers from the colonizing country. Many of these kinds of analyses point out how writers from colonial powers sometimes misrepresent colonized cultures by reflecting more their own values: Joseph Conrad's *Heart of Darkness* (published in 1899) represents African culture differently than Chinua Achebe's *Things Fall Apart* does, for example. Cultural criticism and postcolonial criticism represent a broad range of approaches to examining race, gender, and class in historical contexts in a variety of cultures.

A cultural critic's approach to Chopin's "The Story of an Hour" might emphasize how the story reflects the potential dangers and horrors of train travel in the 1890s or it might examine how heart disease was often misdiagnosed by physicians or used as a metaphor in Mrs. Mallard's culture for a variety of emotional conditions. Each of these perspectives can serve to create a wider and more informed understanding of the story. For a sense of the range of documents used by cultural critics to shed light on literary works and the historical contexts in which they are written and read, see the Cultural Case Study on James Joyce's short story "Eveline" (p. 436).

GENDER STRATEGIES

Gender critics explore how ideas about men and women — what is masculine and feminine — can be regarded as socially constructed by particular cultures. According to some critics, sex is determined by simple biological and anatomical categories of male or female, and gender is determined by a culture's values. Thus, ideas about gender and what constitutes masculine and feminine behavior are created by cultural institutions and conditioning. A gender critic might, for example, focus on Chopin's characterization of an emotionally sensitive Mrs. Mallard and a rational, composed husband in "The Story of an Hour" as a manifestation of socially constructed gender identity in the 1890s. *Gender criticism* expands categories and definitions of what is masculine or feminine and tends to regard sexuality as more complex than merely masculine or feminine, heterosexual or homosexual. Gender criticism, therefore, has come to include gay and lesbian criticism as well as feminist criticism. Although there are complex and sometimes problematic relationships among these approaches because some critics argue that heterosexuals and homosexuals are profoundly biologically different, gay and lesbian criticism, like feminist criticism, can be usefully regarded as a subset of gender criticism.

Feminist Criticism

Like Marxist critics, *feminist critics* reading "The Story of an Hour" would also be interested in Charlotte Perkins Gilman's *Women and Economics: A Study of the Economic Relation between Men and Women as a Factor in Social Evolution* (1898) because they seek to correct or supplement what they regard as a predominantly male-dominated critical perspective with a feminist consciousness. Like other forms of sociological criticism, feminist criticism places literature in a social context, and, like those of Marxist criticism, its analyses often have sociopolitical purposes — explaining, for example, how images of women in literature reflect the patriarchal social forces that have impeded women's efforts to achieve full equality with men.

Feminists have analyzed literature by both men and women in an effort to understand literary representations of women as well as the writers and cultures that create them. Related to concerns about how gender affects the way men and women write about each other is an interest in whether women use language differently from the way men do. Consequently, feminist critics' approach to literature is characterized by the use of a broad range of disciplines, including history, sociology, psychology, and linguistics, to provide a perspective sensitive to feminist issues.

A feminist approach to Chopin's "The Story of an Hour" might explore the psychological stress created by the expectations that marriage imposes on Mrs. Mallard, expectations that literally and figuratively break her heart. Given that her husband is kind and loving, the issue is not her being married to Brently but her being married at all. Chopin presents marriage as an institution that creates in both men and women the assumed "right to impose a private will upon a fellow-creature." That "right," however, is seen, especially from a feminist perspective, as primarily imposed on women by men. A feminist critic might note, for instance, that the protagonist is introduced as "Mrs. Mallard" (we learn that her first name is Louise only later); she is defined by her marital status and her husband's name, a name whose origin from the Old French is related to the word *masle*, which means "male." The appropriateness of her name points up the fact that her emotions and the cause of her death are interpreted in male terms by the doctors. The value of a feminist perspective on this work can be readily discerned if a reader imagines Mrs. Mallard's story being told from the point of view of one of the doctors who diagnoses the cause of her death as a weak heart rather than as a fierce struggle.

Gay and Lesbian Criticism

Gay and lesbian critics focus on a variety of issues, including how gays and lesbians are represented in literature, how they read literature, and whether sexuality and gender are culturally constructed or innate. Gay critics have produced new readings of works by and discovered homosexual concerns in writers such as Herman Melville and Henry James, while lesbian critics have done the same for the works of writers such as Emily Dickinson and Toni Morrison. A lesbian reading of "The Story of an Hour," for example, might consider whether Mrs. Mallard's ecstatic feeling of relief — produced by the belief that her marriage is over owing to the presumed death of her husband — isn't also a rejection of her heterosexual identity. Perhaps her glimpse of future freedom, evoked by feminine images of a newly discovered nature "all aquiver with the new spring of life," embraces a repressed new sexual identity that "was too subtle and elusive to name" but that was "approaching to possess her" no matter how much she "was striving to beat it back with her will." Although gay and lesbian readings often raise significant interpretive controversies among critics, they have opened up provocative discussions of seemingly familiar texts.

MYTHOLOGICAL STRATEGIES

Mythological approaches to literature attempt to identify what in a work creates deep universal responses in readers. Whereas psychological critics interpret the symbolic meanings of characters and actions in order to understand more fully the unconscious dimensions of an author's mind, a character's motivation, or a reader's response, *mythological critics* (also frequently referred to as *archetypal critics*) interpret the hopes, fears, and expectations of entire cultures.

In this context myth is not to be understood simply as referring to stories about imaginary gods who perform astonishing feats in the causes of love, jealousy, or hatred. Nor are myths to be judged as merely erroneous, primitive accounts of how nature runs its course and humanity its affairs. Instead, literary critics use myths as a strategy for understanding how human beings try to account for their lives symbolically. Myths can be a window into a culture's deepest perceptions about itself because myths attempt to explain what otherwise seems unexplainable: a people's origin, purpose, and destiny.

All human beings have a need to make sense of their lives, whether they are concerned about their natural surroundings, the seasons, sexuality, birth, death, or the very meaning of existence. Myths help people organize their experiences; these systems of belief (less formally held than religious or political tenets but no less important) embody a culture's assumptions and values. What is important to the mythological critic is not the validity or truth of those assumptions and values; what matters is that they reveal common human concerns.

It is not surprising that although the details of mythic stories vary enormously, the essential patterns are often similar because these myths attempt to explain universal experiences. There are, for example, numerous myths that redeem humanity from permanent death through a hero's resurrection and rebirth. The resurrection of Jesus symbolizes for Christians the ultimate defeat of death and coincides with the rebirth of nature's fertility in spring. Features of this rebirth parallel the Greek myths of Adonis and Hyacinth, who die but are subsequently transformed into living flowers; there are also similarities that connect these stories to the reincarnation of the Indian Buddha or the rebirth of the Egyptian Osiris. Important differences exist among these stories, but each reflects a basic human need to limit the power of death and to hope for eternal life.

Mythological critics look for underlying, recurrent patterns in literature that reveal universal meanings and basic human experiences for readers regardless of when or where they live. The characters, images, and themes that symbolically embody these meanings and experiences are called *archetypes*. This term designates universal symbols that evoke deep and perhaps unconscious responses in a reader because archetypes bring with them our hopes and fears since the beginning of human time. Surely one of the most powerfully compelling archetypes is the death and rebirth theme that relates the human life cycle to the cycle of the seasons. Many others could be cited and would be exhausted only after all human concerns were cataloged, but a few examples can suggest some of the range of plots, images, and characters addressed.

Among the most common literary archetypes are stories of quests, initiations, scapegoats, meditative withdrawals, descents to the underworld, and heavenly ascents. These stories are often filled with archetypal images — bodies of water that may symbolize the unconscious or eternity or baptismal rebirth; rising suns, suggesting reawakening and enlightenment; setting suns, pointing toward death; colors such as green, evocative of growth and fertility, or black, indicating chaos, evil, and death. Along the way are earth mothers, fatal women, wise old men, desert places, and paradisal gardens. No doubt your own reading has introduced you to any number of archetypal plots, images, and characters.

Mythological critics attempt to explain how archetypes are embodied in literary works. Employing various disciplines, these critics articulate the power a literary work has over us. Some critics are deeply grounded in classical literature, whereas others are more conversant with philology, anthropology, psychology, or cultural history. Whatever their emphases, however, mythological critics examine the elements of a work in order to make larger connections that explain the work's lasting appeal.

A mythological reading of Sophocles' *Oedipus the King*, for example, might focus on the relationship between Oedipus's role as a scapegoat and the plague and drought that threaten to destroy Thebes. The city is saved and the fertility of its fields restored only after the corruption is located in Oedipus. His subsequent atonement symbolically provides a kind of rebirth for the city. Thus, the plot recapitulates ancient rites in which the well-being of a king was directly linked to the welfare of his people. If a leader was sick or corrupt, he had to be replaced in order to guarantee the health of the community.

A similar pattern can be seen in the rottenness that Shakespeare exposes in Hamlet's Denmark. *Hamlet* reveals an archetypal pattern similar to that of *Oedipus the King*: not until the hero sorts out the corruption in his world and in himself can vitality and health be restored in his world. Hamlet avenges his father's death and becomes a scapegoat in the process. When he fully accepts his responsibility to set things right, he is swept away along with the tide of intrigue and corruption that has polluted life in Denmark. The new order — established by Fortinbras at the play's end — is achieved precisely because Hamlet is willing and finally able to sacrifice himself in a necessary purgation of the diseased state.

These kinds of archetypal patterns exist potentially in any literary period. Consider how in Chopin's "The Story of an Hour" Mrs. Mallard's life parallels the end of winter and the earth's renewal in spring. When she feels a surge of new life after grieving over her husband's death, her own sensibilities are closely aligned with the "new spring life" that is "all aquiver" outside her window. Although she initially tries to resist that renewal by "beat[ing] it back with her will," she cannot control the life force that surges within her and all around her. When she finally gives herself to the energy and life she experiences, she feels triumphant — like a "goddess of Victory." But this victory is short lived when she learns that her husband is still alive and with him all the obligations that made her marriage feel like a wasteland. Her death is an ironic version of a rebirth ritual. The coming of spring is an ironic contrast to her own discovery that she can no longer live a repressed, circumscribed life with her husband. Death turns out to be preferable to the living death that her marriage means to her. Although spring will go on, this "goddess of Victory" is defeated by a devastating social contract. The old, corrupt order continues, and that for Chopin is a cruel irony that mythological critics would see as an unnatural disruption of the nature of things.

READER-RESPONSE STRATEGIES

Reader-response criticism, as its name implies, focuses its attention on the reader rather than the work itself. This approach to literature describes what goes on in the reader's mind during the process of reading a text. In a sense, all critical approaches (especially psychological and mythological criticism) concern themselves with a reader's response to literature, but there is a stronger emphasis in reader-response criticism on the reader's active construction of the text. Although many critical theories inform reader-response criticism, all *reader-response critics* aim to describe the reader's experience of a work: in effect we get a reading of the reader, who comes to the work with certain expectations and assumptions, which are either met or not met. Hence the consciousness of the reader — produced by reading the work — is the subject matter of reader-response critics. Just as writing is a creative act, reading is, since it also produces a text.

Reader-response critics do not assume that a literary work is a finished product with fixed formal properties, as, for example, formalist critics do. Instead, the literary work is seen as an evolving creation of the reader as he or she processes characters, plots, images, and other elements while reading. Some reader-response critics argue that this act of creative reading is, to a degree, controlled by the text, but it can produce many interpretations of the same text by different readers. There is no single definitive reading of a work, because the crucial assumption is that readers create rather than discover meanings in texts. Readers who have gone back to works they had read earlier in their lives often find that a later reading draws very different responses from them. What earlier seemed unimportant is now crucial; what at first seemed central is now barely worth noting. The reason, put simply, is that two different people have read the same text. Reader-response critics are not after the "correct" reading of the text or what the author presumably intended; instead they are interested in the reader's experience with the text.

These experiences change with readers; although the text remains the same, the readers do not. Social and cultural values influence readings, so that, for example, an avowed Marxist would be likely to come away from Miller's

Death of a Salesman with a very different view of American capitalism than that of, say, a successful sales representative, who might attribute Willy Loman's fall more to his character than to the American economic system. Moreover, readers from different time periods respond differently to texts. An Elizabethan — concerned perhaps with the stability of monarchical rule — might respond differently to Hamlet's problems than would a twenty-first-century reader well versed in psychology and concepts of what Freud called the Oedipus complex. This is not to say that anything goes, that Miller's play can be read as an amoral defense of cheating and rapacious business practices or that *Hamlet* is about the dangers of living away from home. The text does, after all, establish some limits that allow us to reject certain readings as erroneous. But reader-response critics do reject formalist approaches that describe a literary work as a self-contained object, the meaning of which can be determined without reference to any extrinsic matters, such as the social and cultural values assumed by either the author or the reader.

Reader-response criticism calls attention to how we read and what influences our readings. It does not attempt to define what a literary work means on the page but rather what it does to an informed reader, a reader who understands the language and conventions used in a given work. Reader-response criticism is not a rationale for mistaken or bizarre readings of works but an exploration of the possibilities for a plurality of readings shaped by readers' experiences with the text. This kind of strategy can help us understand how our responses are shaped by both the text and ourselves.

Chopin's "The Story of an Hour" illustrates how reader-response critical strategies read the reader. Chopin doesn't say that Mrs. Mallard's marriage is repressive; instead, that troubling fact dawns on the reader at the same time that the recognition forces its way into Mrs. Mallard's consciousness. Her surprise is also the reader's because although she remains in the midst of intense grief, she is on the threshold of a startling discovery about the new possibilities life offers. How the reader responds to that discovery, however, is not entirely controlled by Chopin. One reader, perhaps someone who has recently lost a spouse, might find Mrs. Mallard's "joy" indeed "monstrous" and selfish. Certainly that's how Mrs. Mallard's doctors — the seemingly authoritative diagnosticians in the story — would very likely read her. But for other readers — especially twenty-first-century readers steeped in feminist values — Mrs. Mallard's feelings require no justification. Such readers might find Chopin's ending to the story more ironic than she seems to have intended because Mrs. Mallard's death could be read as Chopin's inability to envision a protagonist who has the strength of her convictions. In contrast, a reader in 1894 might have seen the ending as Mrs. Mallard's only escape from the repressive marriage her husband's assumed death suddenly allowed her to see. A reader in our times probably would argue that it was the marriage that should have died rather than Mrs. Mallard, that she had other alternatives, not just obligations (as the doctors would have insisted), to consider.

By imagining different readers, we can imagine a variety of responses to the story that are influenced by the readers' own impressions, memories, or experiences with marriage. Such imagining suggests the ways in which reader-response criticism opens up texts to a number of interpretations. As one final example, consider how readers' responses to "The Story of an Hour" would be affected if it were printed in two different magazines, read in the context of either *Ms.* or *Good Housekeeping.* What assumptions and beliefs would each magazine's readership be likely to bring to the story? How do you think the respective experiences and values of each magazine's readers would influence their readings? For a sample reader-response student paper on "The Story of an Hour," see page 20.

DECONSTRUCTIONIST STRATEGIES

Deconstructionist critics insist that literary works do not yield fixed, single meanings. They argue that there can be no absolute knowledge about anything because language can never say what we intend it to mean. Anything we write conveys meanings we did not intend, so the deconstructionist argument goes. Language is not a precise instrument but a power whose meanings are caught in an endless web of possibilities that cannot be untangled. Accordingly, any idea or statement that insists on being understood separately can ultimately be "deconstructed" to reveal its relations and connections to contradictory and opposite meanings.

Unlike other forms of criticism, ***deconstructionism*** seeks to destabilize meanings instead of establishing them. In contrast to formalists such as the New Critics, who closely examine a work in order to call attention to how its various components interact to establish a unified whole, deconstructionists try to show how a close examination of the language in a text inevitably reveals conflicting, contradictory impulses that "deconstruct" or break down its apparent unity.

Although deconstructionists and New Critics both examine the language of a text closely, deconstructionists focus on the gaps and ambiguities that reveal a text's instability and indeterminacy, whereas New Critics look for patterns that explain how the text's fixed meaning is structured. Deconstructionists painstakingly examine the competing meanings within the text rather than attempting to resolve them into a unified whole.

The questions deconstructionists ask are aimed at discovering and describing how a variety of possible readings are generated by the elements of a text. In contrast to a New Critic's concerns about the ultimate meaning of a work, a deconstructionist is primarily interested in how the use of language — diction, tone, metaphor, symbol, and so on — yields only provisional, not definitive, meanings. Consider, for example, the following excerpt from an American Puritan poet, Anne Bradstreet. The excerpt is from "The Flesh and the Spirit" (1678), which consists of an allegorical debate between two sisters, the body and the soul. During the course of the debate, Flesh, a consummate materialist, insists that Spirit values ideas that do not exist and that her faith in idealism is both unwarranted and insubstantial in the face of the material values that earth has to offer — riches, fame, and physical pleasure. Spirit, however, rejects the materialistic worldly argument that the only ultimate reality is physical reality and pledges her faith in God:

> Mine eye doth pierce the heavens and see
> What is invisible to thee.
> My garments are not silk nor gold,
> Nor such like trash which earth doth hold,
> But royal robes I shall have on,
> More glorious than the glist'ning sun;
> My crown not diamonds, pearls, and gold,
> But such as angels' heads enfold
> The city where I hope to dwell,
> There's none on earth can parallel;
> The stately walls both high and strong,
> Are made of precious jasper stone;
> The gates of pearl, both rich and clear,
> And angels are for porters there;
> The streets thereof transparent gold,
> Such as no eye did e'er behold;
> A crystal river there doth run,
> Which doth proceed from the Lamb's throne.

A deconstructionist would point out that Spirit's language — her use of material images such as jasper stone, pearl, gold, and crystal — cancels the explicit meaning of the passage by offering a supermaterialistic reward to the spiritually faithful. Her language, in short, deconstructs her intended meaning by employing the same images that Flesh would use to describe the rewards of the physical world. A deconstructionist reading, then, reveals the impossibility of talking about the invisible and spiritual worlds without using materialistic (that is, metaphoric) language. Thus Spirit's very language demonstrates a contradiction and conflict in her conviction that the world of here and now must be rejected for the hereafter. Her language deconstructs her meaning.

Deconstructionists look for ways to question and extend the meanings of a text. A deconstructionist might find, for example, the ironic ending of Chopin's "The Story of an Hour" less tidy and conclusive than would a New Critic, who might attribute Mrs. Mallard's death to her sense of lost personal freedom. A deconstructionist might use the story's ending to suggest that the narrative shares the doctors' inability to imagine a life for Mrs. Mallard apart from her husband. As difficult as it is controversial, deconstructionism is not easily summarized or paraphrased.

52

Reading and the Writing Process

I can't write five words but that I change
seven.
— DOROTHY PARKER

© Bettmann/Corbis.

THE PURPOSE AND VALUE
OF WRITING ABOUT LITERATURE

Introductory literature courses typically include three components — reading, discussion, and writing. Students usually find the readings a pleasure, the class discussions a revelation, and the writing assignments — at least initially — a little intimidating. Writing an analysis of Herman Melville's use of walls in "Bartleby, the Scrivener" (p. 130), for example, may seem considerably more daunting than making a case for animal rights or analyzing a campus newspaper editorial that calls for grade reforms. Like Bartleby, you might want to respond with "I would prefer not to." Literary topics are not, however, all that different from the kinds of papers assigned in English composition courses; many of the same skills are required for both. Regardless of the type of paper, you must develop a thesis and support it with evidence in language that is clear and persuasive.

Whether the subject matter is a marketing survey, a political issue, or a literary work, writing is a method of communicating information and perceptions. Writing teaches. But before writing becomes an instrument for informing the reader, it serves as a means of learning for the writer. An essay is a process of discovery as well as a record of what has been discovered. One of the chief benefits of writing is that we frequently realize what we want to say only after trying out ideas on a page and seeing our thoughts take shape in language.

More specifically, writing about a literary work encourages us to be better readers because it requires a close examination of the elements of a short story, poem, or play. To determine how plot, character, setting, point of view, style, tone, irony, or any number of other literary elements function in a work, we must study them in relation to one another as well as separately. Speed-reading won't do. To read a text accurately and validly — neither ignoring nor distorting significant details — we must return to the work repeatedly to test our responses and interpretations. By paying attention to details and being sensitive to the author's use of language, we develop a clearer understanding of how the work conveys its effects and meanings.

Nevertheless, students sometimes ask why it is necessary or desirable to write about a literary work. Why not allow stories, poems, and plays to speak for themselves? Isn't it presumptuous to interpret Hemingway, Dickinson, or Shakespeare? These writers do, of course, speak for themselves, but they do so indirectly. Literary criticism seeks not to replace the text by explaining it but to enhance our readings of works by calling attention to elements that we might have overlooked or only vaguely sensed.

Another misunderstanding about the purpose of literary criticism is that it crankily restricts itself to finding faults in a work. Critical essays are sometimes mistakenly equated with newspaper and magazine reviews of recently published works. Reviews typically include summaries and evaluations to inform readers about a work's nature and quality, but critical essays assume that readers are already familiar with a work. Although a critical essay may point out limitations and flaws, most criticism — and certainly the kind of essay usually written in an introductory literature course — is designed to explain, analyze, and reveal the complexities of a work. Such sensitive consideration increases our appreciation of the writer's achievement and significantly adds to our enjoyment of a short story, poem, or play. In short, the purpose and value of writing about literature are that doing so leads to greater understanding and pleasure.

READING THE WORK CLOSELY

Know the piece of literature you are writing about before you begin your essay. Think about how the work makes you feel and how it is put together. The more familiar you are with how the various elements of the text convey effects and meanings, the more confident you will be explaining whatever perspective on it you ultimately choose. Do not insist that everything make sense on a first reading. Relax and enjoy yourself; you can be attentive and still allow the author's words to work their magic on you. With subsequent readings, however, go more slowly and analytically as you try to establish relations between characters, actions, images, or whatever else seems important. Ask yourself why you respond as you do. Think as you read, and notice how the parts of a work contribute to its overall nature. Whether the work is a short story, poem, or play, you will read relevant portions of it over and over, and you will very likely find more to discuss in each review if the work is rich.

It's best to avoid reading other critical discussions of a work before you are thoroughly familiar with it. There are several good reasons for following this advice. By reading interpretations before you know a work, you deny yourself the pleasure of discovery. That is a bit like starting with the last chapter in a mystery novel. But perhaps even more important than protecting the surprise and delight that a work might offer is that a premature reading of a critical discussion will probably short-circuit your own responses. You will see the work through the critic's eyes and have to struggle with someone else's perceptions and ideas before you can develop your own.

Reading criticism can be useful, but not until you have thought through your own impressions of the text. A guide should not be permitted to become a tyrant. This does not mean, however, that you should avoid background information about a work — for example, that Blanche Farley's "The Lover Not Taken" (p. 797) is a parody of Robert Frost's "The Road Not Taken" (p. 871). Knowing something about the author as well as historic and literary contexts can help to create expectations that enhance your reading.

ANNOTATING THE TEXT AND JOURNAL NOTE TAKING

As you read, get in the habit of annotating your texts. Whether you write marginal notes, highlight, underline, or draw boxes and circles around important words and phrases, you'll eventually develop a system that allows you to retrieve significant ideas and elements from the text. Another way to record your impressions of a work — as with any other experience — is to keep a journal. By writing down your reactions to characters, images, language, actions, and other matters in a reading journal, you can often determine why you like or dislike a work or feel sympathetic or antagonistic to an author or discover paths into a work that might have eluded you if you hadn't preserved your impressions. Your journal notes and annotations may take whatever form you find useful; full sentences and grammatical correctness are not essential (unless they are to be handed in and your instructor requires that), though they might allow you to make better sense of your own reflections days later. The point is simply to put in writing thoughts that you can retrieve when you need them for class discussion or a writing assignment. Consider the following student annotation of the first twenty-four lines of Andrew Marvell's "To His Coy Mistress" (p. 647) and the journal entry that follows it:

Annotated Text

If we had time . . .

(Had we but world enough, and time,   *Waste life and you*
  This coyness, lady, were no (crime.)   *steal from yourself.*
  We would sit down, and think which way
  To walk, and pass our long love's day.
  Thou by the Indian (Ganges') side   5
  Shouldst rubies find; I by the tide
  Of (Humber) would complain.° I would   *Measurements*   *write love songs*
  Love you ten years before the Flood,   *of time*
  And you should, if you please, refuse
  Till the conversion of the Jews.   10
  My vegetable love should grow,°   *slow, unconscious growth*
  Vaster than empires, and more slow;
  An hundred years should go to praise
  Thine eyes and on thy forehead gaze,
  Two hundred to adore each breast,   15
  But thirty thousand to the rest:
  An age at least to every part,
  And the last age should show your heart.
  For, lady, you deserve this state,

contrast   Nor would I love at lower rate.   20
river   (But) at my back I always hear
and   Time's wingèd chariot hurrying near;   *Lines move faster here —*
desert   And yonder all before us lie   *tone changes.*
images   (Deserts) of vast (eternity.)   —— *This eternity rushes in.*

Journal Note

He'd be patient and wait for his "mistress" if they had the time—sing songs, praise her, adore her, etc. But they don't have that much time according to him. He *seems* to be patient but he actually begins by calling patience—her coyness—a "crime." Looks to me like he's got his mind made up from the beginning of the poem. Where's her response? I'm not sure about him.

     This journal note responds to some of the effects noted in the annotations of the poem; it's an excellent beginning for making sense of the speaker's argument in the poem.

     Taking notes will preserve your initial reactions to the work. Many times first impressions are the best. Your response to a peculiar character in a story, a striking phrase in a poem, or a subtle bit of stage business in a play might lead to larger perceptions. The student paper on John Updike's "A & P" (p. 1686), for example, began with the student writing "how come?" next to the story's title in her textbook. She thought it strange that the title didn't refer to a character or the story's conflict. That annotated response eventually led her to examine the significance of the setting, which became the central idea of her paper.

You should take detailed notes only after you've read through the work. If you write too many notes during the first reading, you're likely to disrupt your response. Moreover, until you have a sense of the entire work, it will be difficult to determine how connections can be made among its various elements. In addition to recording your first impressions and noting significant passages, characters, actions, and so on, you should consult the Questions for Responsive Reading and Writing about fiction (p. 47), poetry (p. 628), and drama (p. 1115). These questions can assist you in getting inside a work as well as organizing your notes.

Inevitably, you will take more notes than you finally use in the paper. Note taking is a form of thinking aloud, but because your ideas are on paper you don't have to worry about forgetting them. As you develop a better sense of a potential topic, your notes will become more focused and detailed.

CHOOSING A TOPIC

If your instructor assigns a topic or offers a choice from among an approved list of topics, some of your work is already completed. Instead of being asked to come up with a topic about *Oedipus the King* (p. 1127), you may be asked to write a three-page essay that specifically discusses whether Oedipus's downfall is a result of fate or foolish pride. You also have the assurance that a specified topic will be manageable within the suggested number of pages. Unless you ask your instructor for permission to write on a different or related topic, be certain to address yourself to the assignment. An essay that does not discuss Oedipus's downfall but instead describes his relationship with his wife Iokaste would be missing the point. Notice too that there is room even in an assigned topic to develop your own approach. One question that immediately comes to mind is whether Oedipus's plight is relevant to a twenty-first-century reader. Assigned topics do not relieve you of thinking about an aspect of a work, but they do focus your thinking.

At some point during the course, you may have to begin an essay from scratch. You might, for example, be asked to write about a short story that somehow impressed you or that seemed particularly well written or filled with insights. Before you start considering a topic, you should have a sense of how long the paper will be because the assigned length can help to determine the extent to which you should develop your topic. Ideally, the paper's length should be based on how much space you deem necessary to present your discussion clearly and convincingly, but if you have any doubts and no specific guidelines have been indicated, ask. The question is important; a topic that might be appropriate for a three-page paper could be too narrow for ten pages. Three pages would probably be adequate for a discussion of why Emily murders Homer in Faulkner's "A Rose for Emily" (p. 78). Conversely, it would be futile to try to summarize Faulkner's use of the South in his fiction in even ten pages; this would have to be narrowed to something like "Images of the South in 'A Rose for Emily.'" Be sure that the topic you choose can be adequately covered in the assigned number of pages.

Once you have a firm sense of how much you are expected to write, you can begin to decide on your topic. If you are to choose what work to write about, select one that genuinely interests you. Too often students pick a story, poem, or play because it is mercifully short or seems simple. Such works can certainly be the subjects of fine essays, but simplicity should not be the major reason for selecting them. Choose a work that has moved you so that you have something to say about it. The student who wrote about "A & P" was initially attracted to the story's title because she had once worked in a similar store. After reading the story, she became fascinated with its setting because Updike's descriptions seemed so accurate. Her paper then grew out of her curiosity about the setting's purpose. When a writer is engaged in a topic, the paper has a better chance of being interesting to a reader.

After you have settled on a particular work, your notes and annotations of the text should prove useful for generating a topic. The paper on "John Updike's A & P as a State of Mind" developed naturally from the notes (p. 1684) that the student jotted down about the setting and antagonist. If you think with a pen in your hand, you are likely to find when you review your notes that your thoughts have clustered into one or more topics. Perhaps there are patterns of imagery that seem to make a point about life. There may be scenes that are ironically paired or secondary characters who reveal certain qualities about the protagonist. Your notes and annotations on such aspects can lead you to a particular effect or impression. Having chuckled your way through "A & P," you may discover that your notations about the story's humor point to a serious satire of society's values.

DEVELOPING A THESIS

When you are satisfied that you have something interesting to say about a work and that your notes have led you to a focused topic, you can formulate a *thesis*, the central idea of the paper. Whereas the topic indicates what the paper focuses on (the setting in "A & P"), the thesis explains what you have to say about the topic (because the intolerant setting of "A & P" is the antagonist in the story, it is crucial to our understanding of Sammy's decision to quit his job). The thesis should be a complete sentence (though sometimes it may require more than one sentence) that establishes your topic in clear, unambiguous language. The thesis may be revised as you get further into the topic and discover what you want to say about it, but once the thesis is firmly established, it will serve as a guide for you and your reader because all the information and observations in your essay should be related to the thesis.

One student on an initial reading of Andrew Marvell's "To His Coy Mistress" (p. 647) saw that the male speaker of the poem urges a woman to love now before time runs out for them. This reading gave him the impression that the poem is a simple celebration of the pleasures of the flesh, but on subsequent readings he underlined or noted these images: "Time's wingèd chariot hurrying near"; "Deserts of vast eternity"; "marble vault"; "worms"; "dust"; "ashes"; and these two lines: "The grave's a fine and private place, / But none, I think, do there embrace."

By listing these images associated with time and death, he established an inventory that could be separated from the rest of his notes on point of view, character, sounds, and other subjects. Inventorying notes allows patterns to emerge that you might have only vaguely perceived otherwise. Once these images are grouped, they call attention to something darker and more complex in Marvell's poem than a first impression might suggest.

These images may create a different feeling about the poem, but they still don't explain very much. One simple way to generate a thesis about a literary work is to ask the question "why?" Why do these images appear in the poem? Why does Hamlet hesitate to avenge his father's death? Why does Hemingway choose the Midwest as the setting of "Soldier's Home"? Your responses to these kinds of questions can lead to a thesis.

Writers sometimes use freewriting to help themselves explore possible answers to such questions. It can be an effective way of generating ideas. Freewriting is exactly that: the technique calls for nonstop writing without concern for mechanics or editing of any kind. Freewriting for ten minutes or so on a question will result in fragments and repetitions, but it can also produce some ideas. Here's an example of a student's response to the question about the images in "To His Coy Mistress":

He wants her to make love. Love poem. There's little time. Her crime. He exaggerates. Sincere? Sly? What's he want? She says nothing—he says it all. What about deserts, ashes, graves, and worms? Some love poem. Sounds like an old Vincent Price movie. Full of sweetness but death creeps in. Death—hurry hurry! Tear pleasures. What passion! Where's death in this? How can a love poem be so ghoulish? She does nothing. Maybe frightened? Convinced? Why death? Love and death—time—death.

This freewriting contains several ideas; it begins by alluding to the poem's plot and speaker, but the central idea seems to be death. This emphasis led the student to five potential thesis statements for his essay about the poem:

1. "To His Coy Mistress" is a difficult poem.
2. Death in "To His Coy Mistress."
3. There are many images of death in "To His Coy Mistress."
4. "To His Coy Mistress" celebrates the pleasures of the flesh, but it also recognizes the power of death to end that pleasure.
5. On the surface, "To His Coy Mistress" is a celebration of the pleasures of the flesh, but this witty seduction is tempered by a chilling recognition of the reality of death.

The first statement is too vague to be useful. In what sense is the poem difficult? A more precise phrasing, indicating the nature of the difficulty, is needed. The second statement is a topic rather than a thesis. Because it is not a sentence, it does not express a complete idea about how the poem treats death. Although this could be an appropriate title, it is inadequate as a thesis statement. The third statement, like the first one, identifies the topic, but even though it is a sentence, it is not a complete idea that tells us anything significant beyond the fact it states. After these preliminary attempts to develop a thesis, the student remembered his first impression of the poem and incorporated it into his thesis statement. The fourth thesis is a useful approach to the poem because it limits the topic and indicates how it will be treated in the paper: the writer will begin with an initial impression of the poem and then go on to qualify it. However, the fifth thesis is better than the fourth because it indicates a shift in tone produced by the ironic relationship between death and flesh. An effective thesis, like this one, makes a clear statement about a manageable topic and provides a firm sense of direction for the paper.

Most writing assignments in a literature course require you to persuade readers that your thesis is reasonable and supported with evidence. Papers that report information without comment or evaluation are simply summaries. A plot summary of Shakespeare's *The Tempest,* for example, would have no thesis, but a paper that discussed how Prospero's oppression of Caliban represents European imperialism and colonialism would argue a thesis. Similarly, a paper that merely pointed out the death images in "To His Coy Mistress" would not contain a thesis, but a paper that attempted to make a case for the death imagery as a grim reminder of how vulnerable flesh is would involve persuasion. In developing a thesis, remember that you are expected not merely to present information but to argue a point.

ARGUING ABOUT LITERATURE

An argumentative essay is designed to make persuasive your interpretation of a work. Arguing about literature doesn't mean that you're engaged in an angry, antagonistic dispute (though controversial topics do sometimes engender heated debates; see, for example, Joan Templeton's comments in the Critical Case Study on Ibsen's *A Doll's House* [p. 1421]). Instead, argumentation requires that you present your interpretation of a work (or a portion of it) by supporting your discussion with clearly defined terms, ample evidence, and a detailed analysis of relevant portions of the text.

If you have a choice, it's generally best to write about a topic that you feel strongly about. If you're not fascinated by Bartleby the Scrivener's haunting presence in Melville's short story, then perhaps you'll find chilling Emily Grierson's behavior in Faulkner's "A Rose for Emily," or maybe you can explain why Bartleby's character is so excruciatingly boring to you. If your essay is to be interesting and convincing, what is important is that it be written from a strong point of view that persuasively argues your evaluation, analysis, and interpretation of a work. It is not enough to say that you like or dislike a work; instead you must give your reader some ideas and evidence that can be accepted or rejected based on the quality of the answers to the questions you raise.

One way to come up with persuasive answers is to generate good questions that will lead you further into the text and to critical issues related to it. Notice how the Perspectives, Critical Case Studies, and Cultural Case Studies in this anthology raise significant questions and issues about texts from a variety of points of view. Moreover, the Critical Strategies for Reading summarized in Chapter 51 can be a resource for raising questions that can be shaped into an argument, and the Questions for Writing: Incorporating the Critics (p. 425) can help you to incorporate a critic's perspective into your own argument. The following lists of questions for the critical approaches covered in Chapter 51 should be useful for discovering arguments you might make about a short story, poem, or play. The page number that follows each heading refers to the discussion in the anthology for that particular approach.

Questions for Arguing about Literature

FORMALIST QUESTIONS (P. 1645)

1. How do various elements of the work — plot, character, point of view, setting, tone, diction, images, symbol, and so on — reinforce its meanings?

2. How are the elements related to the whole?

3. What is the work's major organizing principle? How is its structure unified?

4. What issues does the work raise? How does the work's structure resolve those issues?

BIOGRAPHICAL QUESTIONS (P. 1647)

1. Are facts about the writer's life relevant to your understanding of the work?

2. Are characters and incidents in the work versions of the writer's own experiences? Are they treated factually or imaginatively?

3. How do you think the writer's values are reflected in the work?

PSYCHOLOGICAL QUESTIONS (P. 1649)

1. How does the work reflect the author's personal psychology?

2. What do the characters' emotions and behavior reveal about their psychological states? What types of personalities are they?

3. Are psychological matters such as repression, dreams, and desire presented consciously or unconsciously by the author?

HISTORICAL QUESTIONS (P. 1651)

1. How does the work reflect the period in which it is written?

(continued)

2. What literary or historical influences helped to shape the form and content of the work?

3. How important is the historical context to interpreting the work?

Marxist Questions (p. 1653)

1. How are class differences presented in the work? Are characters aware or unaware of the economic and social forces that affect their lives?

2. How do economic conditions determine the characters' lives?

3. What ideological values are explicit or implicit?

4. Does the work challenge or affirm the social order it describes?

New Historicist Questions (p. 1653)

1. What kinds of documents outside the work seem especially relevant for shedding light on the work?

2. How are social values contemporary to the work reflected or refuted in the work?

3. How does your own historical moment affect your reading of the work and its historical reconstruction?

Cultural Studies Questions (p. 1654)

1. What does the work reveal about the cultural behavior contemporary to it?

2. How does popular culture contemporary to the work reflect or challenge the values implicit or explicit in the work?

3. What kinds of cultural documents contemporary to the work add to your reading of it?

4. How do your own cultural assumptions affect your reading of the work and the culture contemporary to it?

Gender Studies Questions (p. 1655)

1. How are the lives of men and women portrayed in the work? Do the men and women in the work accept or reject these roles?

2. Are the form and content of the work influenced by the author's gender?

3. What attitudes are explicit or implicit concerning heterosexual, homosexual, or lesbian relationships? Are these relationships sources of conflict? Do they provide resolutions to conflicts?

4. Does the work challenge or affirm traditional ideas about men and women and same-sex relationships?

Mythological Questions (p. 1657)

1. How does the story resemble other stories in plot, character, setting, or use of symbols?

2. Are archetypes presented, such as quests, initiations, scapegoats, or withdrawals and returns?

3. Does the protagonist undergo any kind of transformation such as a movement from innocence to experience that seems archetypal?

4. Do any specific allusions to myths shed light on the text?

READER-RESPONSE QUESTIONS (P. 1659)

1. How do you respond to the work?
2. How do your own experiences and expectations affect your reading and interpretation?
3. What is the work's original or intended audience? To what extent are you similar to or different from that audience?
4. Do you respond in the same way to the work after more than one reading?

DECONSTRUCTIONIST QUESTIONS (P. 1661)

1. How are contradictory and opposing meanings expressed in the work?
2. How does meaning break down or deconstruct itself in the language of the text?
3. Would you say that ultimate definitive meanings are impossible to determine and establish in the text? Why? How does that affect your interpretation?
4. How are implicit ideological values revealed in the work?

These questions will not apply to all texts; and they are not mutually exclusive. They can be combined to explore a text from several critical perspectives simultaneously. A feminist approach to Kate Chopin's "The Story of an Hour" could also use Marxist concerns about class to make observations about the oppression of women's lives in the historical context of the nineteenth century. Your use of these questions should allow you to discover significant issues from which you can develop an argumentative essay that is organized around clearly defined terms, relevant evidence, and a persuasive analysis.

ORGANIZING A PAPER

After you have chosen a manageable topic and developed a thesis, a central idea about it, you can begin to organize your paper. Your thesis, even if it is still somewhat tentative, should help you decide what information will need to be included and provide you with a sense of direction.

Consider again the sample thesis in the section on developing a thesis:

On the surface, "To His Coy Mistress" is a celebration of the pleasures of the flesh, but this witty seduction is tempered by a chilling recognition of the reality of death.

This thesis indicates that the paper can be divided into two parts — the pleasures of the flesh and the reality of death. It also indicates an order: because the central point is to show that the poem is more than a simple celebration, the pleasures of the flesh should be discussed first so that another, more complex, reading of the poem can follow. If the paper began with the reality of death, its point would be anticlimactic.

Having established such a broad and informal outline, you can draw on your underlinings, margin notations, and note cards for the subheadings and evidence required to explain the major sections of your paper. This next level of detail would look like the following:

1. Pleasures of the flesh
   Part of the traditional tone of love poetry
2. Recognition of death
   Ironic treatment of love
      Diction
      Images
      Figures of speech
      Symbols
      Tone

This list was initially a jumble of terms, but the student arranged the items so that each of the two major sections leads to a discussion of tone. (The student also found it necessary to drop some biographical information from his notes because it was irrelevant to the thesis.) The list indicates that the first part of the paper will establish the traditional tone of love poetry that celebrates the pleasures of the flesh, while the second part will present a more detailed discussion about the ironic recognition of death. The emphasis is on the latter because that is the point to be argued in the paper. Hence, the thesis has helped to organize the parts of the paper, establish an order, and indicate the paper's proper proportions.

The next step is to fill in the subheadings with information from your notes. Many experienced writers find that making lists of information to be included under each subheading is an efficient way to develop paragraphs. For a longer paper (perhaps a research paper), you should be able to develop a paragraph or more on each subheading. On the other hand, a shorter paper may require that you combine several subheadings in a paragraph. You may also discover that while an informal list is adequate for a brief paper, a ten-page assignment could require a more detailed outline. Use the method that is most productive for you. Whatever the length of the essay, your presentation must be in a coherent and logical order that allows your reader to follow the argument and evaluate the evidence. The quality of your reading can be demonstrated only by the quality of your writing.

WRITING A DRAFT

Be flexible. Your outline should smoothly conduct you from one point to the next, but do not permit it to railroad you. If a relevant and important idea occurs to you now, work it into the draft. By using the first draft as a means of thinking about what you want to say, you will very likely discover more than your notes originally suggested. Plenty of good writers don't use outlines at all but discover ordering principles as they write. Do not attempt to compose a perfectly correct draft the first time around. Grammar, punctuation, and spelling can wait until you revise. Concentrate on what you are saying. Good writing most often occurs when you are in hot pursuit of an idea rather than in a nervous search for errors.

Once you have a first draft on paper, you can delete material that is unrelated to your thesis and add material necessary to illustrate your points and make your paper convincing. The student who wrote "John Updike's A & P as a State of Mind" (p. 1684) wisely dropped a paragraph that questioned whether Sammy displays chauvinistic attitudes toward women. Although this is an interesting issue, it has nothing to do with the thesis, which explains how the setting influences Sammy's decision to quit his job. Instead of including that paragraph, she added one that described Lengel's crabbed response to the girls so that she could lead up to the A & P "policy" he enforces.

Remember that your initial draft is only that. You should go through the paper many times — and then again — working to substantiate and clarify your ideas. You may even end up with several entire versions of the paper. Rewrite. The sentences within each paragraph should be related to a single topic. Transitions should connect one paragraph to the next so that there are no abrupt or confusing shifts. Awkward or wordy phrasing or unclear sentences and paragraphs should be mercilessly poked and prodded into shape.

Writing the Introduction and Conclusion

After you have clearly and adequately developed the body of your paper, pay particular attention to the introductory and concluding paragraphs. It's probably best to write the introduction — at least the final version of it — last, after you know precisely what you are introducing. Because this paragraph is crucial for generating interest in the topic, it should engage the reader and provide a sense of what the paper is about. There is no formula for writing effective introductory paragraphs because each writing situation is different — depending on the audience, topic, and approach — but if you pay attention to the introductions of the essays you read, you will notice a variety of possibilities. The introductory paragraph to "John Updike's A & P as a State of Mind," for example, is a straightforward explanation of why the story's setting is important for understanding Updike's treatment of the antagonist. The rest of the paper then offers evidence to support this point.

Concluding paragraphs demand equal attention because they leave the reader with a final impression. The conclusion should provide a sense of closure instead of starting a new topic or ending abruptly. In the final paragraph about the significance of the setting in "A & P," the student brings together the reasons Sammy quit his job by referring to his refusal to accept Lengel's store policies. At the same time she makes this point, she also explains the significance of Sammy ringing up the "No Sale" mentioned in her introductory paragraph. Thus, we are brought back to where we began, but we now have a greater understanding of why Sammy quits his job. Of course, the body of your paper is the most important part of your presentation, but do remember that first and last impressions have a powerful impact on readers.

Using Quotations

Quotations can be a valuable means of marshaling evidence to illustrate and support your ideas. A judicious use of quoted material will make your points clearer and more convincing. Here are some guidelines that should help you use quotations effectively.

1. Brief quotations (four lines or fewer of prose or three lines or fewer of poetry) should be carefully introduced and integrated into the text of your paper with quotation marks around them:

According to the narrator, Bertha "had a reputation for strictness." He tells us that she always "wore dark clothes, dressed her hair simply, and expected contrition and obedience from her pupils."

For brief poetry quotations, use a slash to indicate a division between lines:

The concluding lines of Blake's "The Tyger" pose a disturbing question: "What immortal hand or eye / Dare frame thy fearful symmetry?"

Lengthy quotations should be separated from the text of your paper. More than three lines of poetry should be double spaced and centered on the page. More than four lines of prose should be double spaced and indented one inch from the left margin, with the right margin the same as for the text. Do *not* use quotation marks for the passage; the indentation indicates that the passage is a quotation. Lengthy quotations should not be used in place of your own writing. Use them only if they are absolutely necessary.

2. If any words are added to a quotation, use brackets to distinguish your addition from the original source:

"He [Young Goodman Brown] is portrayed as self-righteous and disillusioned."

Any words inside quotation marks and not in brackets must be precisely those of the author. Brackets can also be used to change the grammatical structure of a quotation so that it fits into your sentence:

Smith argues that Chekhov "present[s] the narrator in an ambivalent light."

If you drop any words from the source, use ellipses to indicate the omission:

"Early to bed . . . makes a man healthy, wealthy, and wise."

Use ellipses following a period to indicate an omission at the end of a sentence:

"Early to bed and early to rise makes a man healthy. . . ."

Use a single line of spaced periods to indicate the omission of a line or more of poetry or more than one paragraph of prose:

Nothing would sleep in that cellar, dank as a ditch,

Bulbs broke out of boxes hunting for chinks in the dark,

. . . .

Nothing would give up life:

Even the dirt kept breathing a small breath.

3. You will be able to punctuate quoted material accurately and confidently if you observe these conventions.

Place commas and periods inside quotation marks:

"Even the dirt," Roethke insists, "kept breathing a small breath."

Even though a comma does not appear after "dirt" in the original quotation, it is placed inside the quotation mark. The exception to this rule occurs when a parenthetical reference to a source follows the quotation:

"Even the dirt," Roethke insists, "kept breathing a small breath" (11).

Punctuation marks other than commas or periods go outside the quotation marks unless they are part of the material quoted:

What does Roethke mean when he writes that "the dirt kept breathing a small breath"?

Yeats asked, "How can we know the dancer from the dance?"

REVISING AND EDITING

Put some distance — a day or so if you can — between yourself and each draft of your paper. The phrase that seemed just right on Wednesday may be revealed as all wrong on Friday. You'll have a better chance of detecting lumbering sentences and thin paragraphs if you plan ahead and give yourself the time to read your paper from a fresh perspective. Through the process of revision, you can transform a competent paper into an excellent one.

Begin by asking yourself if your approach to the topic requires any rethinking. Is the argument carefully thought out and logically presented? Are there any gaps in the presentation? How well is the paper organized? Do the paragraphs lead into one another? Does the body of the paper deliver what the thesis promises? Is the interpretation sound? Are any relevant and important elements of the work ignored or distorted to advance the thesis? Are the points supported with evidence? These large questions should be addressed before you focus on more detailed matters. If you uncover serious problems as a result of considering these questions, you'll probably have quite a lot of rewriting to do, but at least you will have the opportunity to correct the problems — even if doing so takes several drafts.

The following checklist offers questions to ask about your paper as you revise and edit it. Most of these questions will be familiar to you; however, if you need help with any of them, ask your instructor or review the appropriate section in a composition handbook.

Questions for Writing: A Revision Checklist

1. Is the topic manageable? Is it too narrow or too broad?
2. Is the thesis clear? Is it based on a careful reading of the work?
3. Is the paper logically organized? Does it have a firm sense of direction?
4. Is your argument persuasive?
5. Should any material be deleted? Do any important points require further illustration or evidence?
6. Does the opening paragraph introduce the topic in an interesting manner?
7. Are the paragraphs developed, unified, and coherent? Are any too short or long?
8. Are there transitions linking the paragraphs?
9. Does the concluding paragraph provide a sense of closure?
10. Is the tone appropriate? Is it, for example, flippant or pretentious?
11. Is the title engaging and suggestive?
12. Are the sentences clear, concise, and complete?
13. Are simple, complex, and compound sentences used for variety?
14. Have technical terms been used correctly? Are you certain of the meanings of all the words in the paper? Are they spelled correctly?
15. Have you documented any information borrowed from books, articles, or other sources? Have you quoted too much instead of summarizing or paraphrasing secondary material?
16. Have you used a standard format for citing sources (see p. 1701)?
17. Have you followed your instructor's guidelines for the manuscript format of the final draft?
18. Have you carefully proofread the final draft?

When you proofread your final draft, you may find a few typographical errors that must be corrected but do not warrant reprinting an entire paper. Provided there are not more than a handful of such errors throughout the paper, they can be corrected as shown in the following passage. This example condenses a short paper's worth of errors; no single passage should be this shabby in your essay:

To add a letter or word, use a caret on the line where the addition is needed. To delete a word draw a single line through ~~through~~ it. Run-on words are separated by a vertical line, and inadvertent spaces are closed like t his. Transposed letters are indicated this wa. New paragraphs are noted with the sign ¶ in front of where the next paragraph is to begin. ¶Unless you . . .

These sorts of errors can be minimized by proofreading on the screen and simply entering corrections as you go along.

TYPES OF WRITING ASSIGNMENTS

The types of papers most frequently assigned in literature classes are explication, analysis, and comparison and contrast. Most writing about literature involves some combination of these skills. This section includes a sample explication, an analysis, and a comparison and contrast paper. For a sample research paper that demonstrates a variety of strategies for documenting outside sources, see page 1707. For genre-based assignments, see the sample papers for writing about fiction (p. 20), poetry (p. 632), and drama (p. 1117).

Explication

The purpose of this approach to a literary work is to make the implicit explicit. *Explication* is a detailed explanation of a passage of poetry or prose. Because explication is an intensive examination of a text line by line, it is mostly used to interpret a short poem in its entirety or a brief passage from a long poem, short story, or play. Explication can be used in any kind of paper when you want to be specific about how a writer achieves a certain effect. An explication pays careful attention to language — the connotations of words, allusions, figurative language, irony, symbol, rhythm, sound, and so on. These elements are examined in relation to one another and to the overall effect and meaning of the work.

The simplest way to organize an explication is to move through the passage line by line, explaining whatever seems significant. It is wise to avoid, however, an assembly-line approach that begins each sentence with "In line one (two, three) . . ." Instead, organize your paper in whatever way best serves your thesis. You might find that the right place to start is with the final lines, working your way back to the beginning of the poem or passage. The following sample explication on Dickinson's "There's a certain Slant of light" does just that. The student's opening paragraph refers to the final line of the poem in order to present her thesis. She explains that though the poem begins with an image of light, it is not a bright or cheery poem but one concerned with "the look of Death." Since the last line prompted her thesis, that is where she begins the explication.

You might also find it useful to structure a paper by discussing various elements of literature, so that you have a paragraph on connotative words followed by one on figurative language and so on. However your paper is organized, keep in mind that the aim of an explication is not simply to summarize the passage but to comment on the effects and meanings produced by the author's use of language in it. An effective explication (the Latin word *explicare* means "to unfold") displays a text to reveal how it works and what it signifies. Although writing an explication requires some patience and sensitivity, it is an excellent method for coming to understand and appreciate the elements and qualities that constitute literary art.

A SAMPLE STUDENT EXPLICATION

A Reading of Emily Dickinson's "There's a certain Slant of light"

The sample paper by Bonnie Katz is the result of an assignment calling for an explication of about 750 words on any poem by Emily Dickinson. Katz selected "There's a certain Slant of light."

EMILY DICKINSON (1830–1886)

There's a certain Slant of light   ca. 1861

There's a certain Slant of light,
Winter Afternoons —
That oppresses, like the Heft
Of Cathedral Tunes —

Heavenly Hurt, it gives us —   5
We can find no scar,
But internal difference,
Where the Meanings, are —

None may teach it — Any —
'Tis the Seal Despair —   10
An imperial affliction
Sent us of the Air —

When it comes, the Landscape listens —
Shadows — hold their breath —
When it goes, 'tis like the Distance   15
On the look of Death —

This essay comments on every line of the poem and provides a coherent reading that relates each line to the speaker's intense awareness of death. Although the essay discusses each stanza in the order that it appears, the introductory paragraph provides a brief overview explaining how the poem's images contribute to its total meaning. In addition, the student does not hesitate to discuss a line out of sequence when it can be usefully connected to another phrase. This is especially apparent in the third paragraph, in her discussion of stanzas 2 and 3. The final paragraph describes some of the formal elements of the poem. It might be argued that this discussion could have been integrated into the previous paragraphs rather than placed at the end, but the student does make a connection in her concluding sentence between the pattern of language and its meaning.

Several other matters are worth noticing. The student works quotations into her own sentences to support her points. She quotes exactly as the words appear in the poem, even Dickinson's irregular use of capital letters. When something is added to a quotation to clarify it, it is enclosed in brackets so that the essayist's words will not be mistaken for the poet's: "Seal [of] Despair." A slash is used to indicate line divisions as in "imperial affliction / Sent us of the Air."

Bonnie Katz

Professor Quiello

English 109-2

26 January 2015

A Reading of Emily Dickinson's

"There's a certain Slant of light"

Because Emily Dickinson did not provide titles for her poetry, editors follow the customary practice of using the first line of a poem as its title. However, a more appropriate title for "There's a certain Slant of light," one that suggests what the speaker in the poem is most concerned about, can be drawn from the poem's last line, which ends with "the look of Death" (line 16). Although the first line begins with an image of light, nothing bright, carefree, or cheerful appears in the poem. Instead, the predominant mood and images are darkened by a sense of despair resulting from the speaker's awareness of death.

In the first stanza, the "certain Slant of light" is associated with "Winter Afternoons" (2), a phrase that connotes the end of a day, a season,

[Margin note: Thesis providing overview of explication]

and even life itself. Such light is hardly warm or comforting. Not a ray or beam, this slanting light suggests something unusual or distorted and creates in the speaker a certain slant on life that is consistent with the cold, dark mood that winter afternoons can produce. Like the speaker, most of us have seen and felt this sort of light: it "oppresses" (3) and pervades our sense of things when we encounter it. Dickinson uses the senses of hearing and touch as well as sight to describe the overwhelming oppressiveness that the speaker experiences. The light is transformed into sound by a simile that tells us it is "like the Heft / Of Cathedral Tunes" (3–4). Moreover, the "Heft" of that sound—the slow, solemn measures of tolling church bells and organ music— weighs heavily on our spirits. Through the use of shifting imagery, Dickinson evokes a kind of spiritual numbness that we keenly feel and perceive through our senses.

> Line-by-line explication of first stanza, focusing on connotations of words and imagery, in relation to mood and meaning of poem as a whole; supported with references to the text.

By associating the winter light with "Cathedral Tunes," Dickinson lets us know that the speaker is concerned about more than the weather. Whatever it is that "oppresses" is related by connotation to faith, mortality, and God. The second and third stanzas offer several suggestions about this connection. The pain caused by the light is a "Heavenly Hurt" (5). This "imperial affliction / Sent us of the Air" (11–12) apparently comes from God above, and yet it seems to be part of the very nature of life. The oppressiveness we feel is in the air, and it can neither be specifically identified at this point in the poem nor be eliminated, for "None may teach it—Any" (9). All we know is that existence itself seems depressing under the weight of this "Seal [of] Despair" (10). The impression left by this "Seal" is stamped within the mind or soul rather than externally. "We can find no scar" (6), but once experienced this oppressiveness challenges our faith in life and its "Meanings" (8).

> Explication of second, third, and fourth stanzas, focusing on connotations of words and imagery in relation to mood and meaning of poem as a whole. Supported with references to the text.

The final stanza does not explain what those "Meanings" are, but it does make clear that the speaker is acutely aware of death. As the winter daylight fades, Dickinson projects the speaker's anxiety onto the surrounding landscape and shadows, which will soon be engulfed by the darkness that follows this light: "the Landscape listens— / Shadows—hold their breath—" (13–14). This image firmly aligns the winter light in the first stanza with darkness. Paradoxically, the light in this poem illuminates the nature of darkness. Tension is released when the light is completely gone, but what remains is the despair that the "imperial affliction" has imprinted on the speaker's sensibilities, for it is "like the Distance / On the look of Death—" (15–16). There can be no relief from what that "certain Slant of light" has revealed because what has been experienced is permanent—like the fixed stare in the eyes of someone who is dead.

The speaker's awareness of death is conveyed in a thoughtful, hushed tone. The lines are filled with fluid *l* and smooth *s* sounds that are appropriate for the quiet, meditative voice in the poem. The voice sounds tentative and uncertain—perhaps a little frightened. This seems to be reflected in the slightly irregular meter of the lines. The stanzas are trochaic with the second and fourth lines of each stanza having five syllables, but no stanza is identical because each works a slight variation on the first stanza's seven syllables in the first and third lines. The rhymes also combine exact patterns with variations. The first and third lines of each stanza are not exact rhymes, but the second and fourth lines are exact so that the paired words are more closely related: *Afternoons, Tunes; scar, are; Despair, Air; and breath, Death.* There is a pattern to the poem, but it is unobtrusively woven into the speaker's voice in much the same way that "the look of Death" (16) is subtly present in the images and language of the poem.

> Explication of the elements of rhythm and sound throughout poem

> Conclusion tying explication of rhythm and sound with explication of words and imagery in previous paragraphs

Work Cited

Dickinson, Emily. "There's a certain Slant of light." *The Bedford Introduction to Literature.* Ed. Michael Meyer. 11th ed. Boston: Bedford/St. Martin's, 2016. 1680. Print.

Analysis

The preceding sample essay shows how an explication examines in detail the important elements in a work and relates them to the whole. An analysis, however, usually examines only a single element — such as plot, character, point of view, symbol, tone, or irony—and relates it to the entire work. An analytic topic separates the work into parts and focuses on a specific one; you might consider "Point of View in 'A Rose for Emily,'" "Patterns of Rhythm in Browning's 'My Last Duchess,'" or "The Significance of Fortinbras in *Hamlet*." The specific element must be related to the work as a whole or it will appear irrelevant. It is not enough to point out that there are many death images in Marvell's "To His Coy Mistress"; the images must somehow be connected to the poem's overall effect.

Whether an analytic paper is just a few pages or many, it cannot attempt to discuss everything about the work it is considering. Only those elements that are relevant to the topic can be treated. This kind of focusing makes the topic manageable; this is why most papers that you write will probably be some form of analysis. Explications are useful for a short passage, but a line-by-line commentary on a story, play, or long poem simply isn't practical. Because analysis allows you to consider the central effect or meaning of an entire work by studying a single important element, it is a useful and common approach to longer works.

A SAMPLE STUDENT ANALYSIS

John Updike's A & P as a State of Mind

Nancy Lager's paper analyzes the setting in John Updike's "A & P" (the entire story appears on p. 200). The assignment simply asked for an essay of approximately 750 words on a short story written in the twentieth century. The approach was left to the student.

The idea for this essay began with Lager asking herself why Updike used "A & P" as the title. The initial answer to the question was that "the setting is important in this story." This answer was the rough beginning of a tentative thesis. What still had to be explained, though, was how the setting is important. To determine the significance of the setting, Lager jotted down some notes based on her underlinings and marginal notations:

A & P

"usual traffic"

lights and tile

"electric eye"

shoppers like "sheep," "houseslaves," "pigs"

"Alexandrov and Petrooshki" — Russia

New England Town	*Lengel*
typical: bank, church, etc.	"manager"
traditional	"doesn't miss that much"

conservative	(like lady shopper)
proper	Sunday school
near Salem — witch trials	"It's our policy"
puritanical	spokesman for A & P values
intolerant	

From these notes Lager saw that Lengel serves as the voice of the A & P. He is, in a sense, a personification of the intolerant atmosphere of the setting. This insight led to another version of her thesis statement: "The setting of 'A & P' is the antagonist of the story." That explained at least some of the setting's importance. By seeing Lengel as a spokesman for A & P policies, Lager could view him as a voice that articulates the morally smug atmosphere created by the setting. Finally, she considered why it is significant that the setting is the antagonist, and this generated her last thesis: "Because the intolerant setting of 'A & P' is the antagonist in the story, it is crucial to our understanding of Sammy's decision to quit his job." This thesis sentence does not appear precisely in these words in the essay, but it is the backbone of the introductory paragraph.

The remaining paragraphs consist of details that describe the A & P in the second paragraph, the New England town in the third, Lengel in the fourth, and Sammy's reasons for quitting in the concluding paragraph. Paragraphs 2, 3, and 4 are largely based on Lager's notes, which she used as an outline once her thesis was established. The essay is sharply focused, well organized, and generally well written. In addition, it suggests a number of useful guidelines for analytic papers:

1. Only the points related to the thesis are included. In another type of paper the role of the girls in the bathing suits, for example, might have been considerably more prominent.
2. The analysis keeps the setting in focus while at the same time indicating how it is significant in the major incident in the story — Sammy's quitting.
3. The title is a useful lead into the paper; it provides a sense of what the topic is. In addition, the title is drawn from a sentence (the final one of the first paragraph) that clearly explains its meaning.
4. The introductory paragraph is direct and clearly indicates the paper will argue that the setting serves as the antagonist of the story.
5. Brief quotations are deftly incorporated into the text of the paper to illustrate points. We are told what we need to know about the story as evidence is provided to support ideas. There is no unnecessary plot summary. Even though "A & P" is only a few pages in length and is an assigned topic, page numbers are included after quoted phrases. If the story were longer, page numbers would be especially helpful for the reader.
6. The paragraphs are well developed, unified, and coherent. They flow naturally from one to another. Notice, for example, the smooth transition worked into the final sentence of the third paragraph and the first sentence of the fourth paragraph.

7. Lager makes excellent use of her careful reading and notes by finding revealing connections among the details she has observed. The store's "electric eye," for instance, is related to the woman's and Lengel's watchfulness.
8. As events are described, the present tense is used. This avoids awkward tense shifts and lends an immediacy to the discussion.
9. The concluding paragraph establishes the significance of why the setting should be seen as the antagonist and provides a sense of closure by referring again to Sammy's "No Sale," which has been mentioned at the end of the first paragraph.
10. In short, Lager has demonstrated that she has read the work closely, has understood the relation of the setting to the major action, and has argued her thesis convincingly by using evidence from the story.

Lager 1

Nancy Lager

Professor Taylor

English 102-12

2 February 2015

John Updike's A & P as a State of Mind

The setting of John Updike's "A & P" is crucial to our understanding of Sammy's decision to quit his job. Although Sammy is the central character in the story and we learn that he is a principled, good-natured nineteen-year-old with a sense of humor, Updike seems to invest as much effort in describing the setting as he does in Sammy. The setting is the antagonist and plays a role that is as important as Sammy's. The title, after all, is not "Youthful Rebellion" or "Sammy Quits" but "A & P." Even though Sammy knows that his quitting will make life more difficult for him, he instinctively insists on rejecting what the A & P comes to represent in the story. When he rings up a "No Sale" and "saunter[s]" (204) out of the store, he leaves behind not only a job but the rigid state of mind associated with the A & P.

Sammy's descriptions of the A & P present a setting that is ugly, monotonous, and rigidly regulated. The fluorescent light is as blandly cool as the "checkerboard green-and-cream rubber-tile floor" (202). We can see the uniformity Sammy describes because we have all been in chain stores. The "usual traffic" moves in one direction (except for the swimsuited girls, who move against it), and everything is neatly ordered and categorized in tidy aisles. The dehumanizing routine of this environment is suggested by Sammy's offhand references to the typical shoppers as "sheep" (201), "houseslaves" (202), and "pigs" (204). They seem to pace through the store in a stupor; as Sammy tells us, not even dynamite could move them.

The A & P is appropriately located "right in the middle" (202) of a proper, conservative, traditional New England town north of Boston. This location, coupled with the fact that the town is only five miles from Salem, the site of the famous seventeenth-century witch trials, suggests a narrow, intolerant social atmosphere in which there is no room for stepping beyond the boundaries of what is regarded as normal and proper. The importance of this setting can be appreciated even more if we imagine the action taking place in, say, a mellow suburb of southern California. In this prim New England setting, the girls in their bathing suits are bound to offend somebody's sense of propriety.

As soon as Lengel sees the girls, the inevitable conflict begins. He embodies the dull conformity represented by the A & P. As "manager" (203), he is both the guardian and enforcer of "policy" (203). When he gives the girls "that sad Sunday-school-superintendent stare" (203), we know we are in the presence of the A & P version of a dreary bureaucrat who "doesn't miss that much" (203). He is as unsympathetic and unpleasant as the woman "with rouge on her cheeks and no eyebrows" (201) who pounces on Sammy for ringing up her "HiHo crackers" twice. Like the "electric eye" (204) in the doorway, her vigilant eyes allow nothing to escape their notice. For Sammy the logical extension of Lengel's "policy" is the half-serious notion that one day the A & P might be known as the "Great Alexandrov and Petrooshki Tea Company" (202). Sammy's connection between what he regards as mindless "policy" (203) and Soviet oppression is obviously an exaggeration, but the reader is invited to entertain the similarities anyway.

The reason Sammy quits his job has less to do with defending the girls than with his own sense of what it means to be a decent human being. His decision is not an easy one. He doesn't want to make trouble or disappoint his parents, and he knows his independence and self-reliance (the other side of New England tradition) will make life more complex for him. In spite of his own hesitations, he finds himself blurting out "Fiddle-de-doo" (204) to Lengel's policies and in doing so knows that his grandmother "would have been pleased" (204). Sammy's "No Sale" rejects the crabbed perspective on life that Lengel represents as manager of the A & P. This gesture is more than just a negative, however, for as he punches in that last entry on the cash register, "the machine whirs 'pee-pul'" (204). His decision to quit his job at the A & P is an expression of his refusal to regard policies as more important than people.

Work Cited

Updike, John. "A & P." *The Bedford Introduction to Literature*. Ed. Michael Meyer. 11th ed. Boston: Bedford/St. Martin's, 2016. 200–04. Print.

Comparison and Contrast

Another essay assignment in literature courses often combined with analytic topics is the type that requires you to write about similarities and differences between or within works. You might be asked to discuss "How Sounds Express Meanings in John Updike's 'Player Piano' and Lewis Carroll's 'Jabberwocky,'" or "Sammy's and Stokesie's Attitudes about Conformity in Updike's 'A & P.'" A *comparison* of either topic would emphasize their similarities, while a *contrast* would stress their differences. It is possible, of course, to include both perspectives in a paper if you find significant likenesses and differences. A comparison of Andrew Marvell's "To His Coy Mistress" and Ann Lauinger's "Marvell Noir" would, for example, yield similarities because each poem describes a man urging his lover to make the most of their precious time together; however, important differences also exist in the tone and theme of each poem that would constitute a contrast. (You should, incidentally, be aware that the term *comparison* is sometimes used inclusively to refer to both similarities and differences. If you are assigned a comparison of two works, be sure that you understand what your instructor's expectations are; you may be required to include both approaches in the essay.)

When you choose your own topic, the paper will be more successful — more manageable — if you write on works that can be meaningfully related to each other. Although Robert Herrick's "To the Virgins, to Make Much of Time" and Shakespeare's *Hamlet* both have something to do with hesitation, the likelihood of anyone making a connection between the two that reveals something interesting and important is remote — though perhaps not impossible if the topic were conceived imaginatively and tactfully. That is not to say that comparisons of works from different genres should be avoided, but the relation between them should be strong, as would a treatment of African American identity in Ralph Ellison's "Battle Royal" and August Wilson's *Fences*. Choose a topic that encourages you to ask significant questions about each work; the purpose of a comparison or contrast is to understand the works more clearly for having examined them together. Despite the obvious differences between Henrik Ibsen's *A Doll's House* and Gail Godwin's "A Sorrowful Woman," the two are closely related if we ask why the wife in each work withdraws from her family.

Choose works to compare or contrast that intersect with each other in some significant way. They may, for example, be written by the same author, in the same genre, or about the same subject. Perhaps you can compare their use of some technique, such as irony or point of view. Regardless of the specific topic, be sure to have a thesis that allows you to organize your paper around a central idea that argues a point about the two works. If you merely draw up a list of similarities or differences without a thesis in mind, your paper will be little more than a series of observations with no apparent purpose. Keep in the foreground of your thinking what the comparison or contrast reveals about the works.

There is no single way to organize comparative papers since each topic is likely to have its own particular issues to resolve, but it is useful to be aware of two basic patterns that can be helpful with a comparison, a contrast, or a combination of both. One method that can be effective for relatively short papers consists of dividing the paper in half, first discussing one work and then the other. Here, for example, is a partial informal outline for a discussion of Sophocles' *Oedipus the King* and Shakespeare's *Hamlet;* the topic is a comparison and contrast: "Oedipus and Hamlet as Tragic Figures."

1. Oedipus

    a. The nature of the conflict

    b. Strengths and stature

    c. Weaknesses and mistakes

    d. What is learned

2. Hamlet

    a. The nature of the conflict

    b. Strengths and stature

    c. Weaknesses and mistakes

    d. What is learned

This organizational strategy can be effective provided that the second part of the paper combines the discussion of Hamlet with references to Oedipus so that the thesis is made clear and the paper unified without being repetitive. If the two characters were treated entirely separately, then the discussion would be merely parallel rather than integrated. In a lengthy paper, this organization probably would not work well because a reader would have difficulty remembering the points made in the first half as he or she reads on.

Thus, for a longer paper it is usually better to create a more integrated structure that discusses both works as you take up each item in your outline. Here is the second basic pattern using the elements in the partial outline just cited:

1. The nature of the conflict
   a. Oedipus
   b. Hamlet
2. Strengths and stature
   a. Oedipus
   b. Hamlet
3. Weaknesses and mistakes
   a. Oedipus
   b. Hamlet
4. What is learned
   a. Oedipus
   b. Hamlet

This pattern allows you to discuss any number of topics without requiring that your reader recall what you first said about the conflict Oedipus confronts before you discuss Hamlet's conflicts fifteen pages later. However you structure your comparison or contrast paper, make certain that a reader can follow its elements and keep track of its thesis.

A SAMPLE STUDENT COMPARISON

The Struggle for Women's Self-Definition in Henrik Ibsen's A Doll's House *and James Joyce's* "Eveline"

The following paper was written in response to an assignment that required a comparison and contrast — about 750 words — of two works of literature. The student chose to write an analysis of how the women in each work respond to being defined by men.

Monica Casis

Professor Matthews

English 105-4

4 February 2015

The Struggle for Women's Self-Definition

in Henrik Ibsen's *A Doll's House* and James Joyce's "Eveline"

Although Henrik Ibsen's *A Doll's House* (1879) and James Joyce's "Eveline" (1914) were written more than thirty years apart and portray radically different characters and circumstances, both works raise similar questions about the role of women and how they are defined in their respective worlds. Each work presents a woman who conforms to society's ideas of gender in an effort to be accepted and loved. While both Ibsen's Nora Helmer and Joyce's Eveline are intelligent and resourceful, Nora is able to break free of society's hold; Eveline cannot. Nevertheless, these narratives show the emergence of each woman's identity—Nora's refusal to be a submissive and belittled housewife and Eveline's awareness of the constraints placed upon her by her father and community. From the beginning, these women are more intelligent and self-aware than the people who oppress them; unfortunately, that does not necessarily lead to complete autonomy.

In *A Doll House*, Nora is treated as her father's, then her husband's, doll. She is called "squirrel," "spendthrift," and "skylark" and is admonished for such things as eating sweets or asking her husband to take her ideas into consideration (1360). Torvald's concept of the ideal woman is a showpiece who can dress up, recite, and dance. As a mother, Nora only plays with her children; it is Anne Marie who takes care of them. As a housewife, she has no control over the household finances; her husband gives her an allowance.

Although Nora continually conforms to her husband's expectations, she has the strength and courage to borrow money for a trip to Italy to save his life and does odd jobs to pay the debt that she has committed forgery to secure. She is proud of her sacrifice for her family. At the same time, she plays the role of a frivolous, helpless, dependent woman in order to coax her husband into giving her money and to keep him away from Krogstad's incriminating letter; she lies in order to keep him happy. Though Nora appears to be a woman trapped within her husband's expectations of her, she does have a will of her own. Once she sees and understands Torvald's superficiality and selfishness—that he is concerned only with what threatens him—Nora realizes she must abandon him and the role he has defined for her. Eveline, who submits to her overbearing father for most of Joyce's story, ultimately sees the need for change—the need to break out of her current life. However, unlike Nora, Eveline does not imagine an independent life; she sees marriage to Frank as her only way out. It is marriage that she believes will bring respect, happiness, and a kind of freedom: "People would treat her with respect then. She would not be treated as her mother had been" (437).

The turning points in *A Doll's House* and in "Eveline" occur when the women protagonists are faced with the choice of whether to leave the men in their lives. Nora is convinced that she will corrupt her children and home with the guilt she bears—for being with a man whom she no longer respects. When Torvald learns the truth from Krogstad, he regards her as a liar, hypocrite, and criminal and therefore repudiates her. Once Nora realizes the selfishness of her husband, she knows she cannot stay with him. She must leave him and her children in order to search for her own identity.

Eveline's turning point, on the other hand, results in inaction. She cannot bring herself to leave her home or her father, however unpleasant her daily life. The reasons are not entirely clear, but we can assume that her reluctance stems from the fear of such overwhelming change. Leaving her home and the people she has known her entire life is understandably daunt- ing, especially for such a young person. However, there is also the possibility that Eveline recognizes the problem with her plan. Relocating and marrying Frank will only substitute one dependence with another. Leaving would force her to, once again, rely on the male presence in her life. As a married woman she would never truly gain her own identity.

When Nora and Eveline come to terms with themselves, their situations are no less problematic than when they falsely fulfilled the expectations imposed on them by the men in their lives. Nora leaves to pursue what may seem to be selfish desires, yet this bold move is necessary to gain independence and self-reliance. Eveline, however, cannot free herself from

Casis 3

her father's control or leave Dublin with Frank, because her fear and guilt entrap her "like a helpless animal" (439). She lacks Nora's strength and determination to embark on a new life of risky possibilities; instead, Eveline remains passive and unable to choose a different life for herself.

At the end of each work, both women face the struggles that will inform the rest of their lives, but whereas Nora's circumstances might be understood as potentially hopeful, Eveline's condition almost certainly must be considered as hopeless.

Casis 4

Works Cited

Ibsen, Henrik. *A Doll's House*. Meyer 1358–1406.

Joyce, James. "Eveline." Meyer 436–39.

Meyer, Michael, ed. *The Bedford Introduction to Literature*. 11th ed. Boston: Bedford/St. Martin's, 2016. Print.

53

The Literary Research Paper

Nancy Crampton.

Does anyone know a good poet who's a vegetarian?

—DONALD HALL

A close reading of a primary source such as a short story, poem, or play can give insights into a work's themes and effects, but sometimes you will want to know more. A published commentary by a critic who knows the work well and is familiar with the author's life and times can provide insights that otherwise may not be available. Such comments and interpretations — known as *secondary sources* — are, of course, not a substitute for the work itself, but they often can take you into a work further than if you made the journey by yourself.

After imagination, good sense, and energy, perhaps the next most important quality for writing a research paper is the ability to organize material. A research paper on a literary topic requires a writer to take account of quite a lot at once: the text, ideas, sources, and documentation techniques all make demands on one's efforts to present a topic clearly and convincingly.

The following list should give you a sense of what goes into creating a research paper. Although some steps on the list can be folded into one another, they offer an overview of the work that will involve you:

1. Choosing a topic
2. Finding sources
3. Evaluating sources
4. Taking notes
5. Developing a thesis
6. Organizing an outline
7. Writing drafts
8. Revising
9. Documenting sources
10. Preparing the final draft and proofreading

Even if you have never written a research paper, you most likely have already had experience choosing a topic, developing a thesis, organizing an outline, and writing a draft that you then revised, proofread, and handed in. Those skills represent six of the ten items on the list. This chapter briefly reviews some of these steps and focuses on the remaining tasks, unique to research paper assignments.

CHOOSING A TOPIC

Chapter 52 discussed the importance of reading a work closely and taking careful notes as a means of generating topics for writing about literature. If you know a work well and record your understanding of it in notes, you'll have impressions and ideas to choose from for potential topics. You may find it useful to review the information on pages 1641–62 before reading the advice about putting together a research paper in this chapter.

The student author of the sample research paper "How William Faulkner's Narrator Cultivates a Rose for Emily" (p. 1707) was asked to write a five-page paper that demonstrated some familiarity with published critical perspectives on a Faulkner story of his choice. Before looking into critical discussions of the story, he read "A Rose for Emily" several times, taking notes and making comments in the margin of his textbook on each reading.

What prompted his choice of "A Rose for Emily" was a class discussion in which many of his classmates found the story's title inappropriate or misleading because they could not understand how and why the story constituted a tribute to Emily given that she murdered a man and slept with his dead body over many years. The gruesome surprise ending revealing Emily as a murderer and necrophiliac hardly seemed to warrant a rose and a tribute for the central character. Why did Faulkner use such a title? Only after having thoroughly examined the story did the student go to the library to see what professional critics had to say about this question.

FINDING SOURCES

Whether your college library is large or small, its reference librarians can usually help you locate secondary sources about a particular work or author. Unless you choose a very recently published story, poem, play, or essay about which little or nothing has been written, you should be able to find out more about a literary work efficiently and quickly. Even if a work has been published recently, you can probably find relevant information on the Internet (see Electronic Sources, below).

Electronic Sources

Researchers can locate materials in a variety of sources, including card catalogs, specialized encyclopedias, bibliographies, and indexes to periodicals. Libraries also provide online databases that you can access from home. This can be an efficient way to establish a bibliography on a specific topic. Consult a reference librarian about how to use your library's online resources and to determine how they will help you research your topic.

In addition to the many electronic databases available from your library's computerized holdings, such as *MLA International Bibliography* (a major source for articles and books on literary topics), the Internet also connects millions of sites with primary sources (the full texts of stories, poems, plays, and essays) and secondary sources (biography or criticism). If you have not had practice with research on the Web, it is a good idea to get guidance from your instructor or a librarian, and by using your library's home page as a starting point. Browsing on the Internet can be absorbing as well as informative, but unless you have plenty of time to spare, don't wait until the last minute to locate your electronic sources. You might find yourself trying to find reliable, professional sources among thousands of sites if you enter an unqualified entry such as "Charles Dickens." Here are several especially useful electronic databases that will provide you with bibliographic information in literature studies. Your school's English Department home page may offer online support as well.

> *Internet Public Library Online Criticism.* <ipl.org/div/litcrit>. Maintained by the University of Michigan, this site provides links to literary criticism by author, work, country, or period.
>
> *JSTOR.* An index that also offers abstracts of journal articles on language and literature.
>
> *MLA International Bibliography.* This is a standard resource for articles and books on literary subjects that allows topical and keyword searches.
>
> *Voice of the Shuttle.* <vos.ucsb.edu>. Maintained by the University of California, this site is a wide-ranging resource for British and American literary studies.

Do remember that your own college library offers a broad range of electronic sources. If you're feeling uncertain or intimidated, your reference librarians are there to help you to get started.

EVALUATING SOURCES AND TAKING NOTES

Evaluate your sources for their reliability and the quality of their evidence. Check to see whether an article or book has been superseded by later studies; try to use up-to-date sources. A popular magazine article will probably not be as authoritative as an article in a scholarly journal. Sources that are well documented with primary and secondary materials usually indicate that the author has done his or her homework. Books printed by university presses and established trade presses are preferable to books privately printed. But there are always exceptions. If you are uncertain about how to assess a book, try to find out something about the author. Are there any other books listed in your library's electronic catalog that indicate the author's expertise? What do book reviews say about the work? Three valuable indexes to book reviews of literary studies are *Book Review Digest, Book Review Index,* and *Index to Book Reviews in the Humanities.* Your reference librarian can show you how to use these important tools for evaluating books. Reviews can be a quick means to gain a broad perspective on writers and their works because reviewers often survey previous approaches to the topic under discussion.

A cautionary note: assessing online sources can be more problematic than evaluating print sources because anyone with a computer and online access can publish on the Internet. Be sure to determine the nature of your sources and their authority. Is the site the work of a professional or an amateur? Is the information likely to be reliable? Is it documented? Before placing your trust in an Internet source, make sure that it warrants your confidence.

As you prepare a list of reliable sources relevant to your topic, record the necessary bibliographic information so that it will be available when you make up the list of works cited for your paper. For a book, include the author, complete title, place of publication, publisher, and date. For an article, include the author, complete title, name of periodical, volume number, date of issue, and page numbers. For an Internet source, include the author, complete title, database title, periodical or site name, date of posting of the site (or last update), name of the institution or organization, and date when you accessed the source.

Once you have assembled a tentative bibliography, you will need to take notes on your readings. Be sure to keep track of where the information comes from by writing the author's name and page number. If you use more than one work by the same author, include a brief title as well as the author's name.

DEVELOPING A THESIS AND ORGANIZING THE PAPER

As the notes on "A Rose for Emily" accumulated, the student sorted them into topics:

1. Publication history of the story
2. Faulkner on the title of "A Rose for Emily"
3. Is Emily simply insane?
4. The purpose of Emily's servant
5. The narrator
6. The townspeople's view of Emily
7. The surprise ending
8. Emily's admirable qualities
9. Homer's character

The student quickly saw that items 1, 4, and 9 were not directly related to his topic concerning the significance of the story's title. The remaining numbers (2, 3, 5, 6, 7, 8) are the topics taken up in the paper. The student had begun his reading of secondary sources with a tentative thesis that stemmed from his question about the appropriateness of the title. That "why" shaped itself into the expectation that he would have a thesis something like this: "The title justifies Emily's murder of Homer because . . ."

The assumption was that he would find information that indicated some specific reason. But the more he read, the more he discovered that it was possible to speak only about how the narrator prevents the reader from making a premature judgment about Emily rather than justifying her actions. Hence, he wisely changed his tentative thesis to this final thesis: "The narrator describes incidents and withholds information in such a way as to cause the reader to sympathize with Emily before her crime is revealed." This thesis helped the student explain why the title is accurate and useful rather than misleading.

Because the assignment was relatively brief, the student did not write up a formal outline but instead organized his notes and proceeded to write the first draft from them.

REVISING

After writing your first draft, you should review the advice and revision checklist on pages 1677–78 so that you can read your paper with an objective eye. Two days after writing his next-to-last draft, the writer of "How William Faulkner's Narrator Cultivates a Rose for Emily" realized that he had allotted too much space for critical discussions of the narrator that were not directly related to his approach. He wanted to demonstrate a familiarity with these studies, but it was not essential that he summarize or discuss them. He corrected this by consolidating parenthetical references: "Though a number of studies discuss the story's narrator (see, for example, Curry; Kempton; Sullivan; and Watkins). . . ." His earlier draft had included summaries of these studies that were tangential to his argument. The point is that he saw this himself after he took some time to approach the paper from a fresh perspective.

DOCUMENTING SOURCES AND AVOIDING PLAGIARISM

You must acknowledge the use of a source when you (1) quote someone's exact words, (2) summarize or borrow someone's opinions or ideas, or (3) use information and facts that are not considered to be common knowledge. The purpose of this documentation is to acknowledge your sources, to demonstrate that you are familiar with what others have thought about the topic, and to provide your reader access to the same sources. If your paper is not adequately documented, it will be vulnerable to a charge of *plagiarism* — the presentation of someone else's work as your own. Conscious plagiarism is easy to avoid; honesty takes care of that for most people. However, there is a more problematic form of plagiarism that is often inadvertent. Whether inadequate documentation is conscious or not, plagiarism is a serious matter and must be avoided. Papers can be evaluated only by what is on the page, not by their writers' intentions.

Let's look more closely at what constitutes plagiarism. Consider the following passage quoted from John Gassner's introduction to *Four Great Plays by Henrik Ibsen* (New York: Bantam, 1959), p. viii:

Today it seems incredible that *A Doll's House* should have created the furor it did. In exploding Victorian ideals of feminine dependency the play seemed revolutionary in 1879. When its heroine Nora left her home in search of self-development it seemed as if the sanctity of marriage had been flouted by a playwright treading the stage with cloven-feet.

Now read this plagiarized version:

A Doll's House created a furor in 1879 by blowing up Victorian ideals about a woman's place in the world. Nora's search for self-fulfillment outside her home appeared to be an attack on the sanctity of marriage by a cloven-footed playwright.

Though the writer has shortened the passage and made some changes in the wording, this paragraph is basically the same as Gassner's. Indeed, several of his phrases are lifted almost intact. Even if a parenthetical reference had been included at the end of the passage and the source included in the Works Cited, the language of this passage would still be plagiarism because it is presented as the writer's own. Both language and ideas must be acknowledged.

Here is an adequately documented version of the passage:

John Gassner has observed how difficult it is for today's readers to comprehend the intense reaction against *A Doll's House* in 1879. When Victorian audiences watched Nora walk out of her stifling marriage, they assumed that Ibsen was expressing a devilish contempt for the "sanctity of marriage" (viii).

This passage makes absolutely clear that the observation is Gassner's, and it is written in the student's own language with the exception of one quoted phrase. Had Gassner not been named in the passage, the parenthetical reference would have included his name: (Gassner viii).

Some mention should be made of the notion of common knowledge before we turn to the standard format for documenting sources. Observations and facts that are widely known and routinely included in many of your sources do not require documentation. It is not necessary to cite a source for the fact that Alfred, Lord Tennyson, was born in 1809 or that Ernest Hemingway loved to fish and hunt. Sometimes it will be difficult for you to determine what common knowledge is for a topic that you know little about. If you are in doubt, the best strategy is to supply a reference.

There are two basic ways to document sources. Traditionally, sources have been cited in footnotes at the bottom of each page or in endnotes grouped together at the end of the paper. Here is how a portion of the sample paper would look if footnotes were used instead of parenthetical documentation:

As Heller points out, before we learn of Emily's bizarre behavior we see her as a sympathetic—if antiquated—figure in a town whose life and concerns have passed her by; hence, "we are disposed to see Emily as victimized."[1]

[1] Terry Heller, "The Telltale Hair: A Critical Study of William Faulkner's 'A Rose for Emily,'" *Arizona Quarterly* 28.4 (1972): 306. Print.

Unlike endnotes, which are double spaced throughout under the title of "Notes" on separate pages at the end of the paper, footnotes appear four spaces below the text. They are single spaced with double spaces between notes.

No doubt you will have encountered these documentation methods in your reading. A different style is recommended, however, in the Modern Language Association's *MLA Handbook for Writers of Research Papers,* 7th ed. (2009). This style employs parenthetical references within the text of the paper; these are keyed to an alphabetical list of Works Cited at the end of the paper. This method is designed to be less distracting for the reader. Unless you are instructed to follow the footnote or endnote style for documentation, use the parenthetical method explained in the next section.

The List of Works Cited

Items in the list of works cited are arranged alphabetically according to the author's last name and indented a half inch after the first line. This allows the reader to locate quickly the complete bibliographic information for the author's name cited within the parenthetical reference in the text. The following are common entries for literature papers and should be used as models. If some of your sources are of a different nature, consult the *MLA Handbook for Writers of Research Papers,* 7th ed. (New York: MLA, 2009); or, for the latest updates, check MLA's Web site at <mlahandbook.org>.

The following entries include examples to follow when citing electronic sources. For electronic sources, include as many of the following elements as apply and as are available:

- Author's name
- Title of work (if it's a book, italicized; if it's a short work, such as an article or poem, use quotation marks)
- Title of the site (or of the publication, if you're citing an online periodical, for example), italicized
- Sponsor or publisher of the site (if not named as the author)
- Date of publication or last update
- Medium of publication
- Date you accessed the source

A BOOK BY ONE AUTHOR

Hendrickson, Robert. *The Literary Life and Other Curiosities.* New York: Viking, 1981. Print.

AN ONLINE BOOK

Frost, Robert. *A Boy's Will.* New York: Holt, 1915. *Bartleby.com: Great Books Online.* Web.
11 May 2015.

PART OF AN ONLINE BOOK

Frost, Robert. "Into My Own." *A Boy's Will.* New York: Holt, 1915. N. pag. *Bartleby.com: Great Books Online.* Web. 11 May 2015.

Notice that the author's name is in reverse order. This information, along with the full title, place of publication, publisher, and date, should be taken from the title and copyright pages of the book. The title is italicized and is also followed by a period. It is unnecessary to include the state, country, or province after the city name. Use the publication date on the title page; if none appears there, use the copyright date (after ©) on the back of the title page. Include the medium of publication.

A BOOK BY TWO AUTHORS

Horton, Rod W., and Herbert W. Edwards. *Backgrounds of American Literary Thought*. 3rd

    ed. Englewood Cliffs: Prentice, 1974. Print.

Only the first author's name is given in reverse order. The edition number
appears after the title.

A BOOK WITH MORE THAN THREE AUTHORS

Gates, Henry Louis, Jr., et al., eds. *The Norton Anthology of African American Literature*.

    3rd ed. New York: Norton, 2014. Print.

(Note: The abbreviation *et al.* means "and others.")

A WORK IN A COLLECTION BY THE SAME AUTHOR

O'Connor, Flannery. "Greenleaf." *The Complete Stories*. By O'Connor. New York: Farrar,

    1971. 311–34. Print.

Page numbers are given because the reference is to only a single story in the
collection.

A WORK IN A COLLECTION BY DIFFERENT WRITERS

Frost, Robert. "Design." *The Bedford Introduction to Literature*. Ed. Michael Meyer. 11th

    ed. Boston: Bedford/St. Martin's, 2016. 885. Print.

Sun, Nilaja. *No Child. . . . The Bedford Introduction to Literature*. Ed. Michael Meyer. 11th

    ed. Boston: Bedford/St. Martin's, 2016. 1565–82. Print.

The titles of poems and short stories are enclosed in quotation marks; plays
and novels are italicized.

CROSS-REFERENCE TO A COLLECTION

Frost, Robert. "Design." Meyer 885.

Meyer, Michael, ed. *The Bedford Introduction to Literature*. 11th ed. Boston: Bedford/

    St. Martin's, 2016. Print.

O'Connor, Flannery. "Revelation." Meyer 385–99.

Sun, Nilaja. *No Child. . . .* Meyer 1565–82.

When citing more than one work from the same collection, use a cross-
reference to avoid repeating the same bibliographic information that appears
in the main entry for the collection.

A TRANSLATED BOOK

Grass, Günter. *The Tin Drum*. Trans. Ralph Manheim. New York: Vintage-Random, 1962. Print.

AN INTRODUCTION, PREFACE, FOREWORD, OR AFTERWORD

Johnson, Thomas H. Introduction. *Final Harvest: Emily Dickinson's Poems*. By Emily Dickinson. Boston: Little, Brown, 1961. vii–xiv. Print.

This cites the introduction by Johnson. Notice that a colon is used between the book's main title and subtitle. To cite a poem in this book, use this method:

Dickinson, Emily. "A Tooth upon Our Peace." *Final Harvest: Emily Dickinson's Poems*. Ed. Thomas H. Johnson. Boston: Little, Brown, 1961. 110. Print.

AN ENTRY IN AN ENCYCLOPEDIA

"Wordsworth, William." *The New Encyclopedia Britannica*. 1984 ed. Print.

Because this encyclopedia is organized alphabetically, no page number or other information is given, only the edition number (if available) and date.

AN ARTICLE IN A MAGAZINE

Morrow, Lance. "Scribble, Scribble, Eh, Mr. Toad." *Time* 24 Feb. 1986: 84. Print.

AN ARTICLE FROM AN ONLINE MAGAZINE

Wasserman, Elizabeth. "The Byron Complex." *Atlantic Online*. The Atlantic Monthly Group, 22 Sept. 2002. Web. 4 Feb. 2015.

The citation for an unsigned article would begin with the title and be alphabetized by the first word of the title other than "a," "an," or "the."

AN ARTICLE IN A SCHOLARLY JOURNAL WITH CONTINUOUS PAGINATION BEYOND A SINGLE ISSUE

Mahar, William J. "Black English in Early Blackface Minstrelsy: A New Interpretation of the Sources of Minstrel Show Dialect." *American Quarterly* 37.2 (1985): 260–85. Print.

Regardless of whether the journal uses continuous pagination or separate pagination for each issue, it is necessary to include the volume number and the issue number for every entry (for example, "11.5" indicates volume 11, issue 5). If a journal does not offer an issue number, use only the volume number, as in the next entry. If a journal uses *only* issue numbers, use that in place of the volume number.

AN ARTICLE IN A SCHOLARLY JOURNAL WITH SEPARATE
PAGINATION FOR EACH ISSUE

Updike, John. "The Cultural Situation of the American Writer." *American Studies*
    International 15 (1977): 19–28. Print.

In the following citation, noting the winter issue helps a reader find the correct
article among all of the articles published by the online journal in 2004.

AN ARTICLE FROM AN ONLINE SCHOLARLY JOURNAL

Mamet, David. "Secret Names." *Threepenny Review* 96 (Winter 2004): n. pag. Web.
    4 Feb. 2015.

The following citation indicates that the article appears on page 1 of section 7
and continues onto another page.

AN ARTICLE IN A NEWSPAPER

Ziegler, Philip. "The Lure of Gossip, the Rules of History." *New York Times* 23 Feb. 1986:
    sec. 7: 1+. Print.

AN ARTICLE FROM AN ONLINE NEWSPAPER

Brantley, Ben. "Souls Lost and Doomed Enliven London Stages." *New York Times.* New
    York Times, 4 Feb. 2004. Web. 5 Feb. 2015.

A LECTURE

Tilton, Robert. "The Beginnings of American Studies." English 270 class lecture.
    University of Connecticut, Storrs. 12 Mar. 2012. Lecture.

LETTER, E-MAIL, OR INTERVIEW

Vellenga, Carolyn. Letter to the author. 9 Oct. 2013.

Harter, Stephen P. E-mail to the author. 28 Dec. 2014.

McConagha, Bill. Personal interview. 9 May 2013.

Following are additional examples for citing electronic sources.

WORK FROM A SUBSCRIPTION SERVICE

Libraries pay for access to databases such as *LexisNexis, ProQuest,* and
Expanded Academic ASAP. When you retrieve an article or other work from a
subscription database, cite your source based on this model:

Vendler, Helen Hennessey. "The Passion of Emily Dickinson." *New Republic* 3 Aug. 1992:

34–38. *Expanded Academic ASAP*. Web. 4 Feb. 2015.

A DOCUMENT FROM A WEB SITE

When citing sources from the Internet, include as much publication information as possible (see guidelines on p. 1701). In some cases, as in the following example, a date of publication for the document "Dickens in America" is not available. The entry provides the author, title of document, title of site, sponsor of the site, medium, and access date:

Perdue, David. "Dickens in America." *David Perdue's Charles Dickens Page*. David A.

Perdue, 1 Apr. 2009. Web. 13 Apr. 2015.

AN ENTIRE WEB SITE

Perdue, David. *David Perdue's Charles Dickens Page*. David A. Perdue, 1 Apr. 2009. Web. 13 Apr.

2015.

Treat a CD-ROM as you would any other source, but name the medium at the end of the entry.

A WORK FROM A CD-ROM

Aaron, Belèn V. "The Death of Theory." *Scholarly Book Reviews* 4.3 (1997): 146–47.

CD-ROM. *ERIC*. SilverPlatter. Dec. 1997.

AN ONLINE POSTING

Shuck, John. "Hamlet." *PBS Discussions*. PBS, 16 May 2005. Web. 13 Apr. 2015.

Parenthetical References

A list of works cited is not an adequate indication of how you have used sources in your paper. You must also provide the precise location of quotations and other information by using parenthetical references within the text of the paper. You do this by citing the author's name (or the source's title if the work is anonymous) and the page number:

Collins points out that "Nabokov was misunderstood by early reviewers of his work" (28).

or

Nabokov's first critics misinterpreted his stories (Collins 28).

Either way a reader will find the complete bibliographic entry in the list of works cited under Collins's name and know that the information cited in the paper appears on page 28. Notice that the end punctuation comes after the parentheses.

If you have listed more than one work by the same author, you would add a brief title to the parenthetical reference to distinguish between them. You could also include the full title in your text:

Nabokov's first critics misinterpreted his stories (Collins, "Early Reviews" 28).

or

Collins points out in "Early Reviews of Nabokov's Fiction" that Nabokov's early work was misinterpreted by reviewers (28).

For electronic sources, provide the author's name. Unless your online source is a stable, paginated document (such as a pdf file), do not include page numbers in your parenthetical references. The following example shows an in-text citation to William Faulkner's acceptance speech for the Nobel Prize for Literature, found at the Nobel Web site.

William Faulkner believed that it was his duty as a writer to "help man endure by lifting his heart" (Faulkner).

This reference would appear in the works cited list as follows:

Faulkner, William. "Banquet Speech: The Nobel Prize in Literature." *The Nobel E-Museum.* The Nobel Foundation, 10 Dec. 1950. Web. 4 Feb. 2012.

There can be many variations on what is included in a parenthetical reference, depending on the nature of the entry in the list of works cited. But the general principle is simple enough: provide enough parenthetical information for a reader to find the work in "Works Cited." Examine the sample research paper for more examples of works cited and strategies for including parenthetical references. If you are puzzled by a given situation, refer to the *MLA Handbook.*

A SAMPLE STUDENT RESEARCH PAPER

How William Faulkner's Narrator Cultivates a Rose for Emily

The following research paper by Tony Groulx follows the format described in the *MLA Handbook for Writers of Research Papers,* 7th ed. (2009). This format is discussed in the preceding section on documentation. Though the sample paper is short, it illustrates many of the techniques and strategies useful for writing an essay that includes secondary sources. (Faulkner's "A Rose for Emily" is reprinted on p. 78.)

Tony Groulx

Professor Hugo

English 109-3

4 February 2015

How William Faulkner's Narrator Cultivates a Rose for Emily

William Faulkner's "A Rose for Emily" is an absorbing mystery story whose chilling ending contains a gruesome surprise. When we discover, along with the narrator and townspeople, what was left of Homer Barron's body, we may be surprised or not, depending on how carefully we have been reading the story and keeping track of details such as Emily Grierson's purchase of rat poison and Homer's disappearance. Probably most readers anticipate finding Homer's body at the end of the story because Faulkner carefully prepares the groundwork for the discovery as the townspeople force their way into that mysterious upstairs room where a "thin, acrid pall as of the tomb seemed to lie everywhere" (83). But very few readers, if any, are prepared for the story's final paragraph, when we realize that the strand of "iron-gray hair" (the last three words of the story) on the second pillow indicates that Emily has slept with Homer since she murdered him. This last paragraph produces the real horror in the story and an extraordinary revelation about Emily's character.

> Reference to text of the story

The final paragraph seems like the right place to begin a discussion of this story because the surprise ending not only creates a powerful emotional effect in us but also raises an important question about what we are to think of Emily. Is this isolated, eccentric woman simply mad? All the circumstantial evidence indicates that she is a murderer and necrophiliac, and yet Faulkner titles the story "A Rose for Emily," as if she is due some kind of tribute. The title somehow qualifies the gasp of horror that the story leads up to in the final paragraph. Why would anyone offer this woman a "rose"? What's behind the title?

Faulkner was once directly asked the meaning of the title and replied:

> Oh it's simply the poor woman had had no life at all. Her father had kept her more or less locked up and then she had a lover who was about to quit her, she had to murder him. It was just "A Rose for Emily"—that's all. (qtd. in Gwynn and Blotner 87-88)

> Reference to secondary source (Gwynn and Blotner)

This reply explains some of Emily's motivation for murdering Homer, but it doesn't actually address the purpose and meaning of the title. If Emily killed

Homer out of a kind of emotional necessity—out of a fear of abandonment—how does that explain the fact that the title seems to suggest that the story is a way of paying respect to Emily? The question remains.

Whatever respect the story creates for Emily cannot be the result of her actions. Surely there can be no convincing excuse made for murder and necrophilia; there is nothing to praise about what she does. Instead, the tribute comes in the form of how her story is told rather than what we are told about her. To do this Faulkner uses a narrator who tells Emily's story in such a way as to maximize our sympathy for her. The grim information about Emily's "iron-gray hair" on the pillow is withheld until the very end and not only to produce a surprise but to permit the reader to develop a sympathetic understanding of her before we are shocked and disgusted by her necrophilia.

Significantly, the narrator begins the story with Emily's death rather than Homer's. Though a number of studies discuss the story's narrator (see, for example, Curry; Kempton; Sullivan; and Watkins), Terry Heller's is one of the most comprehensive in its focus on the narrator's effects on the readers' response to Emily. As Heller points out, before we learn of Emily's bizarre behavior we see her as a sympathetic—if antiquated—figure in a town whose life and concerns have passed her by; hence, "we are disposed to see Emily as victimized" (306). Her refusal to pay her taxes is an index to her isolation and eccentricity, but this incident also suggests a degree of dignity and power lacking in the town officials who fail to collect her taxes. Her encounters with the officials of Jefferson—whether in the form of the sneaking aldermen who try to cover up the smell around her house or the druggist who unsuccessfully tries to get her to conform to the law when she buys arsenic—place her in an admirable light because her willfulness is based on her personal strength. Moreover, it is relatively easy to side with Emily when the townspeople are described as taking pleasure in her being reduced to poverty as a result of her father's death because "now she too would know the old thrill and the old despair of a penny more or less" (Faulkner 80). The narrator's account of their pettiness, jealousy, and inability to make sense of Emily causes the reader to sympathize with Emily's eccentricities before we must judge her murderous behavior. We admire her for taking life on her own terms, and the narrator makes sure this response is in place prior to our realization that she also takes life.

Reference to secondary sources (Curry; Kempton; Sullivan; Watkins) with signal phrase for Heller

Reference to secondary source (Heller) with signal phrase ("As Heller points out...")

Reference to text of the story

Groulx 3

We don't really know much about Emily because the narrator arranges the details of her life so that it's difficult to know what she's been up to. We learn, for example, about the smell around the house before she buys the poison and Homer disappears, so that the cause-and-effect relationship among these events is a bit slippery (for a detailed reconstruction of the chronology, see McGlynn; Nebecker), but the effect is to suspend judgment of Emily. By the time we realize what she has done, we are already inclined to see her as outside community values almost out of necessity. That's not to say that the murdering of Homer is justified by the narrator, but it is to say that her life maintains its private—though no longer secret—dignity. Despite the final revelation, Emily remains "dear, inescapable, impervious, tranquil, and perverse" (Faulkner 82).

> Reference to secondary sources (McGlynn and Nebecker)

> References to text of the story

The narrator's "rose" to Emily is his recognition that Emily is all these things—including "perverse." She evokes "a sort of respectful affection for a fallen monument" (Faulkner 78). She is, to be sure, "fallen," but she is also somehow central—a "monument"—to the life of the community. Faulkner does not offer a definitive reading of Emily, but he does have the narrator pay tribute to her by attempting to provide a complex set of contexts for her actions—contexts that include a repressive father, resistance to a changing South and impinging North, the passage of time and its influence on the present, and relations between men and women as well as relations between generations. Robert Crosman discusses the narrator's efforts to understand Emily:

> The narrator is himself a "reader" of Emily's story, trying to put together from fragments a complete picture, trying to find the meaning of her life in its impact upon an audience, the citizens of Jefferson, of which he is a member. (212)

> Reference to secondary source (Crosman)

The narrator refuses to dismiss Emily as simply mad or to treat her life as merely a grotesque, sensational horror story. Instead, his narrative method brings us into her life before we too hastily reject her, and in doing so it offers us a complex imaginative treatment of fierce determination and strength coupled with illusions and shocking eccentricities. The narrator's rose for Emily is paying her the tribute of placing that "long strand of iron-gray hair" in the context of her entire life.

Works Cited

Crosman, Robert. "How Readers Make Meaning." *College Literature* 9.3
    (1982): 207–15. Print.

Curry, Renee R. "Gender and Authorial Limitation in Faulkner's 'A Rose for
    Emily.'" *Mississippi Quarterly* 47.3 (1994): 391–402. *Expanded Academic
    ASAP*. Web. 4 Jan. 2015.

Faulkner, William. "A Rose for Emily." *The Bedford Introduction to Literature*.
    Ed. Michael Meyer. 11th ed. Boston: Bedford/St. Martin's, 2016.
    78–83. Print.

Gwynn, Frederick, and Joseph Blotner, eds. *Faulkner in the University: Class
    Conferences at the University of Virginia, 1957–58*. Charlottesville:
    U of Virginia P, 1959. Print.

Heller, Terry. "The Telltale Hair: A Critical Study of William Faulkner's 'A Rose
    for Emily.'" *Arizona Quarterly* 28.4 (1972): 301–18. Print.

Kempton, K. P. *The Short Story*. Cambridge: Harvard UP, 1954. 104–06. Print.

McGlynn, Paul D. "The Chronology of 'A Rose for Emily.'" *Studies in Short
    Fiction* 6.4 (1969): 461–62. Print.

Nebecker, Helen E. "Chronology Revised." *Studies in Short Fiction* 8.4 (1971):
    471–73. Print.

Sullivan, Ruth. "The Narrator in 'A Rose for Emily.'" *Journal of Narrative
    Technique* 1.3 (1971): 159–78. Print.

Watkins, F. C. "The Structure of 'A Rose for Emily.'" *Modern Language Notes*
    69.6 (1954): 508–10. Print.

54

Taking Essay
Examinations

You must write. It's not enough to start
by thinking. You become a writer by
writing.
—R. K. NARAYAN

© Dinodia Photos/Alamy.

PREPARING FOR AN ESSAY EXAM

Keep Up with the Reading

The best way to prepare for an examination is to keep up with the reading. If
you begin the course with a commitment to completing the reading assignments on time, you will not have to read in a frenzy and cram just days before
the test. The readings will be a pleasure, not a frantic ordeal. Moreover, you
will find that your instructor's comments and class discussion will make more
sense to you and that you'll be able to participate in class discussion. As you
prepare for the exam, you should be rereading texts rather than reading for the
first time. It may not be possible to reread everything, but you'll at least be able
to scan a familiar text and reread passages that are particularly important.

Take Notes and Annotate the Text

Don't rely exclusively on your memory. The typical literature class includes a hefty amount of reading, so unless you take notes, annotate the text with your own comments, and underline important passages, you're likely to forget material that could be useful for responding to an examination question (see pp. 1665–67 for a discussion of these matters). The more you can retrieve from your reading, the more prepared you'll be for reviewing significant material for the exam. These notes can be used to illustrate points that were made in class. By briefly quoting an important phrase or line from the text, you can provide supporting evidence that will make your argument convincing. Consider, for example, the difference between writing that "Marvell's speaker in 'To His Coy Mistress' says that they won't be able to love after they die" and writing that "the speaker intones that 'The grave's a fine and private place / But none, I think, do there embrace.'" No one expects you to memorize the entire poem, but recalling a few lines here and there can transform a sleepy generality into an illustrative, persuasive argument.

Anticipate Questions

As you review the readings, keep in mind the class discussions and the focus provided by your instructor. Class discussions and the instructor's emphasis often become the basis for essay questions. You may not see the exact same topics on the exam, but you might find that the matters you've discussed in class will serve as a means of responding to an essay question. If, for example, class discussion of John Updike's "A & P" (see p. 200) centered on the story's small-town New England setting, you could use that conservative, traditional, puritanical setting to answer a question such as "Discuss how the conflicts that Sammy encounters in 'A & P' are related to the story's theme." A discussion of the intolerant rigidity of this New England town could be connected to A & P "policy" and the crabbed values associated with Lengel that lead to Sammy's quitting his job in protest of such policies. The point is that you'll be well prepared for an essay exam when you can shape the material you've studied so that it is responsive to whatever kinds of reasonable questions you encounter on the exam. Reasonable questions? Yes, your instructor is more likely to offer you an opportunity to demonstrate your familiarity with and understanding of the text than to set a trap that, for instance, demands you discuss how Updike's work experience as an adolescent informs the story when no mention was ever made of that in class or in your reading.

You can also anticipate questions by considering the generic Questions for Responsive Reading and Writing about fiction (p. 47), poetry (p. 628), and drama (p. 1115) and the Questions for Arguing about Literature (p. 1671), along with the Questions for Writing about an Author in Depth (p. 858). Not all of these questions will necessarily be relevant to every work that you read, but they cover a wide range of concerns that should allow you to organize your reading, note taking, and reviewing so that you're not taken by surprise during the exam.

Studying with a classmate or a small group from class can be a stimulating and fruitful means of discovering and organizing the major topics and themes of the course. This method of brainstorming can be useful not only for studying for exams but for understanding and reviewing course readings throughout the semester. And, finally, you needn't be shy about asking your instructor what types of questions might appear on the exam and how best to study for them. You may not get a very specific reply, but almost any information is more useful than none.

TYPES OF EXAMS

Closed-Book versus Open-Book Exams

Closed-book exams require more memorization and recall than open-book exams, which permit you to use your text and perhaps even your notes to answer questions. Dates, names, definitions, and other details play less of a role in an open-book exam. An open-book exam requires no less preparation, however, because you'll need to be intimately familiar with the texts and the major ideas, themes, and issues that you've studied in order to quickly and efficiently support your points with relevant, specific evidence. Since every student has the same advantage of having access to the text, preparation remains the key to answering the questions. Some students find open-book exams more difficult than closed-book tests because they risk spending too much time reading, scanning, and searching for material and not enough time writing a response that draws on the knowledge and understanding that their reading and studying has provided them. It's best to limit the time you allow yourself to review the text and notes so that you devote an adequate amount of time to getting your ideas on paper.

Essay Questions

Essay questions generally fall within one of the following categories. If you can recognize quickly what is being asked of you, you will be able to respond to them more efficiently.

1. **Explication** Explication calls for a line-by-line explanation of a passage of poetry or prose that considers, for example, diction, figures of speech, symbolism, sound, form, and theme in an effort to describe how language creates meaning. (For a more detailed discussion of explication, see p. 1679.)

2. **Definition** Defining a term and then applying it to a writer or work is a frequent exam exercise. Consider: "Define *romanticism*. To what extent can Hawthorne's *The Scarlet Letter* be regarded as a romantic story?" This sort of question requires that you first describe what constitutes a romantic literary work and then explain how *The Scarlet Letter* does (and doesn't) fit the bill.

3. **Analysis** An analytical question focuses on a particular part of a literary work. You might be asked, for example, to analyze the significance of

images in John Keats's poem "Ode on a Grecian Urn" (p. 660). This sort of question requires you to discuss a specific element of the poem and also to explain how that element contributes to the poem's overall effect. (For a more detailed discussion of analysis, see p. 1683.)

4. **Comparison and Contrast** Comparison and contrast calls for a discussion of the similarities and/or differences between writers, works, or elements of works — for example, "Compare and contrast Lengel's sensibilities in John Updike's 'A & P' (p. 200) with John Wright's in Susan Glaspell's *Trifles* (p. 1080)." Despite the obvious differences in age and circumstances between these characters, a discussion of their responses to people — particularly to women — reveals some intriguing similarities. (For a more detailed discussion of comparison and contrast, see pp. 1688–90.)

5. **Discussion of a Critical Perspective** A brief quotation by a critic about a work is usually designed to stimulate a response that requires you to agree with, disagree with, or qualify a critic's perspective. Usually it is not important whether you agree or disagree with the critic; what matters is the quality of your argument. Think about how you might wrestle with this assessment of Robert Frost written by Lionel Trilling: "The manifest America of Mr. Frost's poems may be pastoral; the actual America is tragic." With some qualifications (surely not all of Frost's poems are "tragic") this could provide a useful way of talking about a poem such as "Mending Wall" (p. 874).

6. **Imaginative Questions** To a degree every question requires imagination regardless of whether it's being asked or answered. However, some questions require more imaginative leaps to arrive at the center of an issue than others do. Consider, for example, the intellectual agility needed to respond to this question: "How do you think Dickens's Mr. Gradgrind from *Hard Times* and the narrator of Frost's 'Mending Wall' would respond to Sammy's character in Updike's 'A & P'?" As tricky as this triangulation of topics may seem, there is plenty to discuss concerning Gradgrind's literal-mindedness, the narrator's imagination, and Sammy's rejection of "policy." Or try a simpler but no less interesting version: "How do you think Frost would review Marvell's 'To His Coy Mistress' and Keats's 'Ode on a Grecian Urn'?" Such questions certainly require detailed, reasoned responses, but they also leave room for creativity and even wit.

STRATEGIES FOR WRITING ESSAY EXAMS

Your hands may be sweaty and your heart pounding as you begin the exam, but as long as you're prepared and you keep in mind some basic strategies for writing essay exams, you should be able to respond to questions with confidence and a genuine sense of accomplishment.

1. Before you begin writing, read through the entire exam. If there are choices to be made, make certain you know how many questions must be answered (only one out of four, not two). Note how many points each question

is worth; spend more time on the two worth forty points each, and perhaps leave the twenty-point question for last.

2. Budget your time. If there are short-answer questions, do not allow them to absorb you so that you cannot do justice to the longer essay questions. Follow the suggested time limit for each question; if none is offered, then create your own schedule in proportion to the points allotted for each question.

3. Depending on your own sensibilities, you may want to begin with the easiest or hardest questions. It doesn't really matter which you begin with as long as you pace yourself to avoid running out of time.

4. Be sure that you understand the question. Does it ask you to compare and/or contrast, define, analyze, explicate, or use some other approach? Determine how many elements there are to the question so that you don't inadvertently miss part of the question. Do not spend time copying the question.

5. Make some brief notes about how you plan to answer the question; even a simple list of what you'll need to cover can serve as a useful outline.

6. Address the question; avoid unnecessary summaries or irrelevant asides. Focus on the particular elements enumerated or implied by the question.

7. After beginning the essay, write a clear thesis that describes the major topics you will discuss: "*The Scarlet Letter* is typical of Hawthorne's concerns as a writer owing to its treatment of sin, guilt, isolation, and secrecy."

8. Support and illustrate your answer with specific, relevant references to the text. The more specificity — the more you demonstrate a familiarity with the text (rather than simply provide a plot summary) — the better the answer.

9. Don't overlap and repeat responses to questions; your instructor will recognize such padding. If two different questions are about the same work or writer, demonstrate the breadth and depth of your knowledge of the subject.

10. Allow time to proofread and to qualify and to add more supporting material if necessary. At this final stage, too, it's worth remembering that Mark Twain liked to remind his readers that the difference between the right word and the almost right word is the difference between lightning and a lightning bug.

Glossary of Literary Terms

Accent The emphasis, or stress, given a syllable in pronunciation. We say "*syllable*" not "sy*llable*," "*emphasis*" not "em*phasis*." Accents can also be used to emphasize a particular word in a sentence: *Is* she con*tent* with the con*tents* of the *yellow pack*age? See also METER.

Act A major division in the action of a play. The ends of acts are typically indicated by lowering the curtain or turning up the houselights. Playwrights frequently employ acts to accommodate changes in time, setting, characters onstage, or mood. In many full-length plays, acts are further divided into scenes, which often mark a point in the action when the location changes or when a new character enters. See also SCENE.

Allegory A narration or description usually restricted to a single meaning because its events, actions, characters, settings, and objects represent specific abstractions or ideas. Although the elements in an allegory may be interesting in themselves, the emphasis tends to be on what they ultimately mean. Characters may be given names such as Hope, Pride, Youth, and Charity; they have few if any personal qualities beyond their abstract meanings. These personifications are not symbols because, for instance, the meaning of a character named Charity is precisely that virtue. See also SYMBOL.

Alliteration The repetition of the same consonant sounds in a sequence of words, usually at the beginning of a word or stressed syllable: "*descending dew drops*"; "*luscious lemons*." Alliteration is based on the sounds of letters, rather than the spelling of words; for example, "*keen*" and "*car*" alliterate, but "*car*" and "*cite*" do not. Used sparingly, alliteration can intensify ideas by emphasizing key words, but when used too self-consciously, it can be distracting, even ridiculous, rather than effective. See also ASSONANCE, CONSONANCE.

Allusion A brief reference to a person, place, thing, event, or idea in history or literature. Allusions conjure up biblical authority, scenes from Shakespeare's plays, historic figures, wars, great love stories, and anything else that might enrich an author's work. Allusions imply reading and cultural experiences shared by the writer and reader, functioning as a kind of shorthand whereby the recalling of something outside the work supplies an emotional or intellectual context, such as a poem about current racial struggles calling up the memory of Abraham Lincoln.

Ambiguity Allows for two or more simultaneous interpretations of a word, phrase, action, or situation, all of which can be supported by the context of a work. Deliberate ambiguity can contribute to the effectiveness and richness of a work, for example, in the open-ended conclusion to Hawthorne's "Young Goodman Brown." However, unintentional ambiguity obscures meaning and can confuse readers.

Anagram A word or phrase made from the letters of another word or phrase, as "heart" is an anagram of "earth." Anagrams have often been considered merely an exercise of one's ingenuity, but sometimes writers use anagrams to conceal proper names or veiled messages, or to suggest important connections between words, as in "hated" and "death."

Anapestic meter See FOOT.

Antagonist The character, force, or collection of forces in fiction or drama that opposes the PROTAGONIST and gives rise to the conflict of the story; an opponent of the protagonist, such as Claudius in Shakespeare's play *Hamlet*. See also CHARACTER, CONFLICT.

Antihero A protagonist who has the opposite of most of the traditional attributes of a hero. He or she may be bewildered, ineffectual, deluded, or merely pathetic. Often what antiheroes learn, if they learn anything at all, is that the world isolates them in an existence devoid of God and absolute values. Yossarian from Joseph Heller's *Catch-22* is an example of an antihero. See also CHARACTER.

Apostrophe An address, either to someone who is absent and therefore cannot hear the speaker or to something nonhuman that cannot comprehend. Apostrophe often provides a speaker the opportunity to think aloud.

Approximate rhyme See RHYME.

Archetype A term used to describe universal symbols that evoke deep and sometimes unconscious responses in a reader. In literature, characters, images, and themes that symbolically embody universal meanings and basic human experiences, regardless of when or where they live, are considered archetypes. Common literary archetypes include stories of quests, initiations, scapegoats, descents to the underworld, and ascents to heaven. See also MYTHOLOGICAL CRITICISM.

Aside In drama, a speech directed to the audience that supposedly is not audible to the other characters onstage at the time. When Hamlet first appears onstage, for example, his aside "A little more than kin, and less than kind!" gives the audience a strong sense of his alienation from King Claudius. See also SOLILOQUY.

Assonance The repetition of internal vowel sounds in nearby words that do not end the same, for example, "asl*ee*p under a tr*ee*," or "*each* evening." Similar endings result in rhyme, as in "asl*eep* in the d*eep*." Assonance is a strong means of emphasizing important words in a line. See also ALLITERATION, CONSONANCE.

Ballad Traditionally, a ballad is a song, transmitted orally from generation to generation, that tells a story and that eventually is written down. As such, ballads usually cannot be traced to a particular author or group of authors. Typically, ballads are dramatic, condensed, and impersonal narratives, such as "Bonny Barbara Allan." A **literary ballad** is a narrative poem that is written in deliberate imitation of the language, form, and spirit of the traditional ballad, such as Keats's "La Belle Dame sans Merci." See also BALLAD STANZA, QUATRAIN.

Ballad stanza A four-line stanza, known as a QUATRAIN, consisting of alternating eight- and six-syllable lines. Usually only the second and fourth lines rhyme (an *abcb* pattern). Coleridge adopted the ballad stanza in "The Rime of the Ancient Mariner."

All in a hot and copper sky
The bloody Sun, at noon,
Right up above the mast did stand,
No bigger than the Moon.

See also BALLAD, QUATRAIN.

Biographical criticism An approach to literature that suggests that knowledge of the author's life experiences can aid in the understanding of his or her work. While biographical information can sometimes complicate one's interpretation of a work, and some formalist critics (such as the New Critics) disparage the use of the author's biography as a tool for textual interpretation, learning about the life of the author can often enrich a reader's appreciation for that author's work. See also CULTURAL CRITICISM, FORMALIST CRITICISM, NEW CRITICISM.

Blank verse Unrhymed iambic pentameter. Blank verse is the English verse form closest to the natural rhythms of English speech and therefore is the most common pattern found in traditional English narrative and dramatic poetry from Shakespeare to the early twentieth century. Shakespeare's plays use blank verse extensively. See also IAMBIC PENTAMETER.

Cacophony Language that is discordant and difficult to pronounce, such as this line from John Updike's "Player Piano": "never my numb plunker fumbles." Cacophony ("bad sound") may be unintentional in the writer's sense of music, or it may be used consciously for deliberate dramatic effect. See also EUPHONY.

Caesura A pause within a line of poetry that contributes to the rhythm of the line. A caesura can occur anywhere within a line and need not be indicated by punctuation. In scanning a line, caesuras are indicated by a double vertical line (||). See also METER, RHYTHM, SCANSION.

Canon Those works generally considered by scholars, critics, and teachers to be the most important to read and study, which collectively constitute the "masterpieces" of literature. Since the 1960s, the traditional English and American literary canon, consisting mostly of works by white male writers, has been rapidly expanding to include many female writers and writers of varying ethnic backgrounds.

Carpe diem The Latin phrase meaning "seize the day." This is a very common literary theme, especially in lyric poetry, which emphasizes that life is short, time is fleeting, and that one should make the most of present pleasures. Robert Herrick's poem "To the Virgins, to Make Much of Time" employs the *carpe diem* theme.

Catharsis Meaning "purgation," *catharsis* describes the release of the emotions of pity and fear by the audience at the end of a tragedy. In his *Poetics,* Aristotle discusses the importance of catharsis. The audience faces the misfortunes of the protagonist, which elicit pity and compassion. Simultaneously, the audience also confronts the failure of the protagonist, thus receiving a frightening reminder of human limitations and frailties. Ultimately, however, both these negative emotions are purged, because the tragic protagonist's suffering is an affirmation of human values rather than a despairing denial of them. See also TRAGEDY.

Character, characterization A character is a person presented in a dramatic or narrative work, and characterization is the process by which a writer makes that character seem real to the reader. A **hero** or **heroine**, often called the PROTAGONIST, is the central character who engages the reader's interest and empathy. The ANTAGONIST is the character, force, or collection of forces that stands directly opposed to the protagonist and gives rise to the conflict of the story. A **static character** does not change throughout the work, and the reader's knowledge of that character does not grow, whereas a **dynamic character** undergoes some kind of change because of the action in the plot. **Flat characters** embody one or two qualities, ideas, or traits that can be readily described in a brief summary. They are not psychologically complex characters and therefore are readily accessible to readers. Some flat characters are recognized as **stock characters**; they embody stereotypes such as the "dumb blonde" or the "mean stepfather." They become types rather than individuals. **Round characters** are more complex than flat or stock characters, and often display the inconsistencies and internal conflicts found in most real people. They are more fully developed, and therefore are harder to summarize. Authors have two major methods of presenting characters: **showing** and **telling**. **Showing** allows the author to present a character talking and acting, and lets the reader infer what kind of person the character is. In **telling**, the author intervenes to describe and sometimes evaluate the character for the reader. Characters can be convincing whether they are presented by showing or by telling, as long as their actions are motivated. **Motivated action** by the characters occurs when the reader or audience is offered reasons for how the characters behave, what they say, and the decisions they make. **Plausible action** is action by a character in a story that seems reasonable, given the motivations presented. See also PLOT.

Chorus In Greek tragedies (especially those of Aeschylus and Sophocles), a group of people who serve mainly as commentators on the characters and events. They add to the audience's understanding of the play by expressing traditional moral, religious, and social attitudes. The role of the chorus in dramatic works evolved through the sixteenth century, and the chorus occasionally is still used by modern playwrights such as T. S. Eliot in *Murder in the Cathedral*. See also DRAMA.

Cliché An idea or expression that has become tired and trite from overuse, its freshness and clarity having worn off. Clichés often anesthetize readers and are usually a sign of weak writing. See also SENTIMENTALITY, STOCK RESPONSES.

Climax See PLOT.

Closet drama A play that is written to be read rather than performed onstage. In this kind of drama, literary art outweighs all other considerations. See also DRAMA.

Colloquial Refers to a type of informal diction that reflects casual, conversational language and often includes slang expressions. See also DICTION.

Comedy A work intended to interest, involve, and amuse the reader or audience, in which no terrible disaster occurs and that ends happily for the main characters. **High comedy** refers to verbal wit, such as puns, whereas **low comedy** is generally associated with physical action and is less intellectual. **Romantic comedy** involves a love affair that meets with various obstacles (like disapproving parents, mistaken identities, deceptions, or other sorts of misunderstandings) but overcomes them to end in a blissful union. Shakespeare's comedies, such as *A Midsummer Night's Dream,* are considered romantic comedies.

Comic relief A humorous scene or incident that alleviates tension in an otherwise serious work. In many instances these moments enhance the thematic significance of the story in addition to providing laughter. When Hamlet jokes with the gravediggers, we laugh, but something hauntingly serious about the humor also intensifies our more serious emotions.

Conflict The struggle within the plot between opposing forces. The PROTAGONIST engages in the conflict with the ANTAGONIST, which may take the form of a character, society, nature, or an aspect of the protagonist's personality. See also CHARACTER, PLOT.

Connotation Associations and implications that go beyond the literal meaning of a word, which derive from how the word has been commonly used and the associations people make with it. For example, the word *eagle* connotes ideas of liberty and freedom that have little to do with the word's literal meaning. See also DENOTATION.

Consonance A common type of near rhyme that consists of identical consonant sounds preceded by different vowel sounds: *home, same; worth, breath.* See also RHYME.

Contextual symbol See SYMBOL.

Controlling metaphor See METAPHOR.

Convention A characteristic of a literary genre (often unrealistic) that is understood and accepted by audiences because it has come, through usage and time, to be recognized as a familiar technique. For example, the division of a play into acts and scenes is a dramatic convention, as are soliloquies and asides. FLASH-BACKS and FORESHADOWING are examples of literary conventions.

Conventional symbol See SYMBOL.

Cosmic irony See IRONY.

Couplet Two consecutive lines of poetry that usually rhyme and have the same meter. A **heroic couplet** is a couplet written in rhymed iambic pentameter.

Crisis A turning point in the action of a story that has a powerful effect on the protagonist. Opposing forces come together decisively to lead to the climax of the plot. See also PLOT.

Cultural criticism An approach to literature that focuses on the historical as well as social, political, and economic contexts of a work. Popular culture — mass-produced and mass-consumed cultural artifacts ranging from advertising to popular fiction to television to rock music — is given equal emphasis with "high culture." **Cultural critics** use widely eclectic strategies such as new historicism, psychology, gender studies, and deconstructionism to analyze not only literary texts but everything from radio talk shows, comic strips, calendar art, and commercials, to travel guides and baseball cards. See also HISTORICAL CRITICISM, MARXIST CRITICISM, POSTCOLONIAL CRITICISM.

Dactylic meter See FOOT.

Deconstructionism An approach to literature that suggests that literary works do not yield fixed, single meanings, because language can never say exactly what we intend it to mean. Deconstructionism seeks to destabilize meaning by examining the gaps and ambiguities of the language of a text. Deconstructionists pay close attention to language in order to discover and describe how a variety of possible readings are generated by the elements of a text. See also NEW CRITICISM.

Denotation The dictionary meaning of a word. See also CONNOTATION.

Dénouement A French term meaning "unraveling" or "unknotting," used to describe the resolution of the plot following the climax. See also PLOT, RESOLUTION.

Dialect A type of informational diction. Dialects are spoken by definable groups of people from a particular geographic region, economic group, or social class. Writers use dialect to contrast and express differences in educational, class, social, and regional backgrounds of their characters. See also DICTION.

Dialogue The verbal exchanges between characters. Dialogue makes the characters seem real to the reader or audience by revealing firsthand their thoughts, responses, and emotional states. See also DICTION.

Diction A writer's choice of words, phrases, sentence structures, and figurative language, which combine to help create meaning. **Formal diction** consists of a dignified, impersonal, and elevated use of language; it follows the rules of syntax exactly and is often characterized by complex words and lofty tone. **Middle diction** maintains correct language usage, but is less elevated than formal diction; it reflects the way most educated people speak. **Informal diction** represents the plain language of everyday use, and often includes idiomatic expressions, slang, contractions, and many simple, common words. **Poetic diction** refers to the way poets sometimes employ an elevated diction that deviates significantly from the common speech and writing of their time, choosing words for their supposedly inherent poetic qualities. Since the eighteenth century, however, poets have been incorporating all kinds of diction in their work and so there is no longer an automatic distinction between the language of a poet and the language of everyday speech. See also DIALECT.

Didactic poetry Poetry designed to teach an ethical, moral, or religious lesson. Michael Wigglesworth's Puritan poem *Day of Doom* is an example of didactic poetry.

Doggerel A derogatory term used to describe poetry whose subject is trite and whose rhythm and sounds are monotonously heavy-handed.

Drama Derived from the Greek word *dram*, meaning "to do" or "to perform," the term *drama* may refer to a single play, a group of plays ("Jacobean drama"), or to all plays ("world drama"). Drama is designed for performance in a theater; actors take on the roles of characters, perform indicated actions, and speak the dialogue written in the script. **Play** is a general term for a work of dramatic literature, and a **playwright** is a writer who makes plays.

Dramatic irony See IRONY.

Dramatic monologue A type of lyric poem in which a character (the speaker) addresses a distinct but silent audience imagined to be present in the poem in such a way as to reveal a dramatic situation and, often unintentionally, some aspect of his or her temperament or personality. See also LYRIC.

Dynamic character See CHARACTER.

Editorial omniscience See NARRATOR.

Electra complex The female version of the Oedipus complex. *Electra complex* is a term used to describe the psychological conflict of a daughter's unconscious rivalry with her mother for her father's attention. The name comes from the Greek legend of Electra, who avenged the death of her father, Agamemnon, by plotting the death of her mother. See also OEDIPUS COMPLEX, PSYCHOLOGICAL CRITICISM.

Elegy A mournful, contemplative lyric poem written to commemorate someone who is dead, often ending in a consolation. Tennyson's *In Memoriam,* written on the death of Arthur Hallam, is an elegy. *Elegy* may also refer to a serious meditative poem produced to express the speaker's melancholy thoughts. See also LYRIC.

End rhyme See RHYME.

End-stopped line A poetic line that has a pause at the end. End-stopped lines reflect normal speech patterns and are often marked by punctuation. The first line of Keats's "Endymion" is an example of an end-stopped line; the natural pause coincides with the end of the line, and is marked by a period:

A thing of beauty is a joy forever.

English sonnet See SONNET.

Enjambment In poetry, when one line ends without a pause and continues into the next line for its meaning. This is also called a **run-on line**. The transition between the first two lines of Wordsworth's poem "My Heart Leaps Up" demonstrates enjambment:

My heart leaps up when I behold
   A rainbow in the sky:

Envoy See SESTINA.

Epic A long narrative poem, told in a formal, elevated style, that focuses on a serious subject and chronicles heroic deeds and events important to a culture or nation. Milton's *Paradise Lost,* which attempts to "justify the ways of God to man," is an epic. See also NARRATIVE POEM.

Epigram A brief, pointed, and witty poem that usually makes a satiric or humorous point. Epigrams are most often written in couplets, but take no prescribed form.

Epiphany In fiction, when a character suddenly experiences a deep realization about himself or herself; a truth that is grasped in an ordinary rather than a melodramatic moment.

Escape literature See FORMULA FICTION.

Euphony *Euphony* ("good sound") refers to language that is smooth and musically pleasant to the ear. See also CACOPHONY.

Exact rhyme See RHYME.

Exposition A narrative device, often used at the beginning of a work, that provides necessary background information about the characters and their circumstances. Exposition explains what has gone on before, the relationships between characters, the development of a theme, and the introduction of a conflict. See also FLASHBACK.

Extended metaphor See METAPHOR.

Eye rhyme See RHYME.

Falling action See PLOT.

Falling meter See METER.

Farce A form of humor based on exaggerated, improbable incongruities. Farce involves rapid shifts in action and emotion, as well as slapstick comedy and extravagant dialogue. Malvolio, in Shakespeare's *Twelfth Night*, is a farcical character.

Feminine rhyme See RHYME.

Feminist criticism An approach to literature that seeks to correct or supplement what may be regarded as a predominantly male critical perspective with a feminist consciousness. Feminist criticism places literature in a social context and uses a broad range of disciplines, including history, sociology, psychology, and linguistics, to provide a perspective sensitive to feminist issues. Feminist theories also attempt to understand representation from a woman's point of view and to explain women's writing strategies as specific to their social conditions. See also GAY AND LESBIAN CRITICISM, GENDER CRITICISM, SOCIOLOGICAL CRITICISM.

Figures of speech Ways of using language that deviate from the literal, denotative meanings of words in order to suggest additional meanings or effects. Figures of speech say one thing in terms of something else, such as when an eager funeral director is described as a vulture. See also METAPHOR, SIMILE.

First-person narrator See NARRATOR.

Fixed form A poem that may be categorized by the pattern of its lines, meter, rhythm, or stanzas. A sonnet is a fixed form of poetry because by definition it must have fourteen lines. Other fixed forms include LIMERICK, SESTINA, and VILLANELLE. However, poems written in a fixed form may not always fit into categories precisely, because writers sometimes vary traditional forms to create innovative effects. See also OPEN FORM.

Flashback A narrated scene that marks a break in the narrative in order to inform the reader or audience member about events that took place before the opening scene of a work. See also EXPOSITION.

Flat character See CHARACTER.

Foil A character in a work whose behavior and values contrast with those of another character in order to highlight the distinctive temperament of that character (usually the protagonist). In Shakespeare's *Hamlet*, Laertes acts as a foil to Hamlet, because his willingness to act underscores Hamlet's inability to do so.

Foot The metrical unit by which a line of poetry is measured. A foot usually consists of one stressed and one or two unstressed syllables. An *iambic foot,* which consists of one unstressed syllable followed by one stressed syllable ("away"), is the most common metrical foot in English poetry. A *trochaic foot* consists of one stressed syllable followed by an unstressed syllable ("lovely"). An *anapestic foot* is two unstressed syllables followed by one stressed one ("understand"). A *dactylic foot* is one stressed syllable followed by two unstressed ones ("desperate"). A *spondee* is a foot consisting of two stressed syllables ("dead set"), but is not a sustained metrical foot and is used mainly for variety or emphasis. See also IAMBIC PENTAMETER, LINE, METER.

Foreshadowing The introduction early in a story of verbal and dramatic hints that suggest what is to come later.

Form The overall structure or shape of a work, which frequently follows an established design. Forms may refer to a literary type (narrative form, short story form) or to patterns of meter, lines, and rhymes (stanza form, verse form). See also FIXED FORM, OPEN FORM.

Formal diction See DICTION.

Formalist criticism An approach to literature that focuses on the formal elements of a work, such as its language, structure, and tone. Formalist critics offer intense examinations of the relationship between form and meaning in a work, emphasizing the subtle complexity in how a work is arranged. Formalists pay special attention to diction, irony, paradox, metaphor, and symbol, as well as larger elements such as plot, characterization, and narrative technique. Formalist critics read literature as an independent work of art rather than as a reflection of the author's state of mind or as a representation of a moment in history. Therefore, anything outside of the work, including historical influences and authorial intent, is generally not examined by formalist critics. See also NEW CRITICISM.

Formula fiction Often characterized as "escape literature," formula fiction follows a pattern of conventional reader expectations. Romance novels, westerns, science fiction, and detective stories are all examples of formula fiction; while the details of individual stories vary, the basic ingredients of each kind of story are the same. Formula fiction offers happy endings (the hero "gets the girl," the detective cracks the case), entertains wide audiences, and sells tremendously well.

Found poem An unintentional poem discovered in a nonpoetic context, such as a conversation, news story, or advertisement. Found poems serve as reminders that everyday language often contains what can be considered poetry, or that poetry is definable as any text read as a poem.

Free verse Also called OPEN FORM poetry, *free verse* refers to poems characterized by their nonconformity to established patterns of meter, rhyme, and stanza. Free verse uses elements such as speech patterns, grammar, emphasis, and breath pauses to decide line breaks, and usually does not rhyme. See OPEN FORM.

Gay and lesbian criticism An approach to literature that focuses on how gays and lesbians are represented in literature, how they read literature, and whether sexuality, as well as gender, is culturally constructed or innate. See also FEMINIST CRITICISM, GENDER CRITICISM.

Gender criticism An approach to literature that explores how ideas about men and women — what is masculine and feminine — can be regarded as socially constructed by particular cultures. Gender criticism expands categories and definitions of what is masculine or feminine and tends to regard sexuality as more complex than merely masculine or feminine, heterosexual or homosexual. See also FEMINIST CRITICISM, GAY AND LESBIAN CRITICISM.

Genre A French word meaning kind or type. The major genres in literature are poetry, fiction, drama, and essays. Genre can also refer to more specific types of literature such as comedy, tragedy, epic poetry, or science fiction.

Haiku A style of lyric poetry borrowed from the Japanese that typically presents an intense emotion or vivid image of nature, which, traditionally, is designed to lead to a spiritual insight. Haiku is a fixed poetic form, consisting of seventeen syllables organized into three unrhymed lines of five, seven, and five syllables. Today, however, many poets vary the syllabic count in their haiku. See also FIXED FORM.

Hamartia A term coined by Aristotle to describe "some error or frailty" that brings about misfortune for a tragic hero. The concept of *hamartia* is closely related to that of the tragic flaw: both lead to the downfall of the protagonist in a tragedy. *Hamartia* may be interpreted as an internal weakness in a character (like greed or passion or HUBRIS); however, it may also refer to a mistake that a character makes that is based not on a personal failure, but on circumstances outside the protagonist's personality and control. See also TRAGEDY.

Hero, heroine See CHARACTER.

Heroic couplet See COUPLET.

High comedy See COMEDY.

Historical criticism An approach to literature that uses history as a means of understanding a literary work more clearly. Such criticism moves beyond both the facts of an author's personal life and the text itself in order to examine the social and intellectual currents in which the author composed the work. See also CULTURAL CRITICISM, MARXIST CRITICISM, NEW HISTORICISM, POSTCOLONIAL CRITICISM.

Hubris or Hybris Excessive pride or self-confidence that leads a protagonist to disregard a divine warning or to violate an important moral law. In tragedies, hubris is a very common form of *hamartia*. See also HAMARTIA, TRAGEDY.

Hyperbole A boldly exaggerated statement that adds emphasis without intending to be literally true, as in the statement "He ate everything in the house." Hyperbole (also called **overstatement**) may be used for serious, comic, or ironic effect. See also FIGURES OF SPEECH.

Iambic meter See FOOT.

Iambic pentameter A metrical pattern in poetry that consists of five iambic feet per line. (An iamb, or iambic foot, consists of one unstressed syllable followed by a stressed syllable.) See also FOOT, METER.

Image A word, phrase, or figure of speech (especially a SIMILE or a METAPHOR) that addresses the senses, suggesting mental pictures of sights, sounds, smells, tastes, feelings, or actions. Images offer sensory impressions to the reader and also convey emotions and moods through their verbal pictures. See also FIGURES OF SPEECH.

Implied metaphor See METAPHOR.

In medias res See PLOT.

Informal diction See DICTION.

Internal rhyme See RHYME.

Irony A literary device that uses contradictory statements or situations to reveal a reality different from what appears to be true. It is ironic for a firehouse to burn down or for a police station to be burglarized. **Verbal irony** is a figure of speech that occurs when a person says one thing but means the opposite. **Sarcasm** is a strong form of verbal irony that is calculated to hurt someone through, for example, false praise. **Dramatic irony** creates a discrepancy between what a character believes or says and what the reader or audience member knows to be true. **Tragic irony** is a form of dramatic irony found in tragedies such as *Oedipus the King*, in which Oedipus searches for the person responsible for the plague that ravishes his city and ironically ends up hunting himself. **Situational irony** exists when there is an incongruity between what is expected to happen and what actually happens due to forces beyond human comprehension or control. The suicide of the seemingly successful main character in Edwin Arlington Robinson's poem "Richard Cory" is an example of situational irony. **Cosmic irony** occurs when a writer uses God, destiny, or fate to dash the hopes and expectations of a character or of humankind in general. In cosmic irony, a discrepancy exists between what a character aspires to and what universal forces provide. Stephen Crane's poem "A Man Said to the Universe" is a good example of cosmic irony, because the universe acknowledges no obligation to the man's assertion of his own existence.

Italian sonnet See SONNET.

Limerick A light, humorous style of fixed form poetry. Its usual form consists of five lines with the rhyme scheme *aabba;* lines 1, 2, and 5 contain three feet, while lines 3 and 4 usually contain two feet. Limericks range in subject matter from the silly to the obscene, and since Edward Lear popularized them in the nineteenth century, children and adults have enjoyed these comic poems. See also FIXED FORM.

Limited omniscient narrator See NARRATOR.

Line A sequence of words printed as a separate entity on the page. In poetry, lines are usually measured by the number of feet they contain. The names for various line lengths are as follows:

monometer: one foot	pentameter: five feet
dimeter: two feet	hexameter: six feet
trimeter: three feet	heptameter: seven feet
tetrameter: four feet	octameter: eight feet

The number of feet in a line, coupled with the name of the foot, describes the metrical qualities of that line. See also END-STOPPED LINE, ENJAMBMENT, FOOT, METER.

Literary ballad See BALLAD.

Literary symbol See SYMBOL.

Low comedy See COMEDY.

Lyric A type of brief poem that expresses the personal emotions and thoughts of a single speaker. It is important to realize, however, that although the lyric is uttered in the first person, the speaker is not necessarily the poet. There are many varieties of lyric poetry, including the DRAMATIC MONOLOGUE, ELEGY, HAIKU, ODE, and SONNET forms.

Marxist criticism An approach to literature that focuses on the ideological content of a work — its explicit and implicit assumptions and values about matters such as culture, race, class, and power. Marxist criticism, based largely on the writings of Karl Marx, typically aims at not only revealing and clarifying ideological issues but also correcting social injustices. Some Marxist critics use literature to describe the competing socioeconomic interests that too often advance capitalist interests such as money and power rather than socialist interests such as morality and justice. They argue that literature and literary criticism are essentially political because they either challenge or support economic oppression. Because of this strong emphasis on the political aspects of texts, Marxist criticism focuses more on the content and themes of literature than on its form. See also CULTURAL CRITICISM, HISTORICAL CRITICISM, SOCIOLOGICAL CRITICISM.

Masculine rhyme See RHYME.

Melodrama A term applied to any literary work that relies on implausible events and sensational action for its effect. The conflicts in melodramas typically arise out of plot rather than characterization; often a virtuous individual must somehow confront and overcome a wicked oppressor. Usually, a melodramatic story ends happily, with the protagonist defeating the antagonist at the last possible moment. Thus, melodramas entertain the reader or audience with exciting action while still conforming to a traditional sense of justice. See also SENTIMENTALITY.

Metafiction The literary term used to describe a work that explores the nature, structure, logic, status, and function of storytelling.

Metaphor A metaphor is a figure of speech that makes a comparison between two unlike things, without using the word *like* or *as*. Metaphors assert the identity of dissimilar things, as when Macbeth asserts that life *is* a "brief candle." Metaphors can be subtle and powerful, and can transform people, places, objects, and ideas into whatever the writer imagines them to be. An **implied metaphor** is a more subtle comparison; the terms being compared are not so specifically explained. For example, to describe a stubborn man unwilling to leave, one could say that he was "a mule standing his ground." This is a fairly explicit metaphor; the man is being compared to a mule. But to say that the man "brayed his refusal to leave" is to create an implied metaphor, because the subject (the man) is never overtly identified as a mule. Braying is associated with the mule, a notoriously stubborn creature, and so the comparison between the stubborn man and the mule is sustained. Implied metaphors can slip by inattentive readers who are not sensitive to such carefully chosen, highly concentrated language. An **extended metaphor** is a sustained comparison in which part or all of a poem consists of a series of related metaphors. Robert Francis's poem "Catch" relies on an extended metaphor that compares poetry to playing catch. A **controlling metaphor** runs through an entire work and determines the form or nature of that work. The controlling metaphor in Anne Bradstreet's poem "The Author to Her Book" likens her book to a child. **Synecdoche** is a kind of metaphor in which a part of something is used to signify the whole, as when a gossip is called a "wagging tongue," or when ten ships are called "ten sails." Sometimes, synecdoche refers to the whole being used to signify the part, as in the phrase "Boston won the baseball game." Clearly, the entire city of Boston did not participate in the game; the whole of Boston is being used to signify the individuals who played and won the game. **Metonymy** is a type of metaphor in which something closely associated with a subject is substituted for it. In this way, we speak of the "silver screen" to mean motion pictures, "the crown" to stand for the king, "the White House" to stand for the activities of the president. See also FIGURES OF SPEECH, PERSONIFICATION, SIMILE.

Meter When a rhythmic pattern of stresses recurs in a poem, it is called *meter*. Metrical patterns are determined by the type and number of feet in a line of verse; combining the name of a line length with the name of a foot concisely describes the meter of the line. **Rising meter** refers to metrical feet that move from unstressed to stressed sounds, such as the iambic foot and the anapestic foot. **Falling meter** refers to metrical feet that move from stressed to unstressed sounds, such as the trochaic foot and the dactylic foot. See also ACCENT, FOOT, IAMBIC PENTAMETER, LINE.

Metonymy See METAPHOR.

Middle diction See DICTION.

Motivated action See CHARACTER.

Mythological criticism An approach to literature that seeks to identify what in a work creates deep universal responses in readers, by paying close attention to the hopes, fears, and expectations of entire cultures. Mythological critics (sometimes called *archetypal critics*) look for underlying, recurrent patterns in literature that reveal universal meanings and basic human experiences for readers regardless of when and where they live. These critics attempt to explain how archetypes (the characters, images, and themes that symbolically embody universal meanings and experiences) are embodied in literary works in order to make larger connections that explain a particular work's lasting appeal. Mythological critics may specialize in areas such as classical literature, philology, anthropology, psychology, and cultural history, but they all emphasize the assumptions and values of various cultures. See also ARCHETYPE.

Naive narrator See NARRATOR.

Narrative poem A poem that tells a story. A narrative poem may be short or long, and the story it relates may be simple or complex. See also BALLAD, EPIC.

Narrator The voice of the person telling the story, not to be confused with the author's voice. With a **first-person narrator**, the *I* in the story presents the point of view of only one character. The reader is restricted to the perceptions, thoughts, and feelings of that single character. For example, in Melville's "Bartleby, the Scrivener," the lawyer is the first-person narrator of the story. First-person narrators can play either a major or a minor role in the story they are telling. An **unreliable narrator** reveals an interpretation of events that is somehow different from the author's own interpretation of those events. Often, the unreliable narrator's perception of plot, characters, and setting becomes the actual subject of the story, as in Melville's "Bartleby, the Scrivener." Narrators can be unreliable for a number of reasons: they might lack self-knowledge (like Melville's lawyer), they might be inexperienced, they might even be insane. **Naive narrators** are usually characterized by youthful innocence, such as Mark Twain's Huck Finn or J. D. Salinger's Holden Caulfield. An **omniscient narrator** is an all-knowing narrator who is not a character in the story and who can move from place to place and pass back and forth through time, slipping into and out of characters as no human being possibly could in real life. Omniscient narrators can report the thoughts and feelings of the characters, as well as their words and actions. The narrator of *The Scarlet Letter* is an omniscient narrator. **Editorial omniscience** refers to an intrusion by the narrator in order to evaluate a character for a reader, as when the narrator of *The Scarlet Letter* describes Hester's relationship to the Puritan community. Narration that allows the characters' actions and thoughts to speak for themselves is called **neutral omniscience**. Most modern writers use neutral omniscience so that readers can reach their own conclusions. **Limited omniscience** occurs when an author restricts a narrator to the single perspective of either a major or minor character. The way people, places, and events appear to that character is the way they appear to the reader. Sometimes a limited omniscient narrator can see into more than one character, particularly in a work that focuses on two characters alternately from one chapter to the next. Short stories, however, are frequently limited to a single character's point of view. See also PERSONA, POINT OF VIEW, STREAM-OF-CONSCIOUSNESS TECHNIQUE.

Near rhyme See RHYME.

Neutral omniscience See NARRATOR.

New Criticism An approach to literature made popular between the 1940s and the 1960s that evolved out of formalist criticism. New Critics suggest that detailed analysis of the language of a literary text can uncover important layers of meaning in that work. New Criticism consciously downplays the historical influences, authorial intentions, and social contexts that surround texts in order to focus on explication — extremely close textual analysis. Critics such as John Crowe Ransom, I. A. Richards, and Robert Penn Warren are commonly associated with New Criticism. See also FORMALIST CRITICISM.

New historicism An approach to literature that emphasizes the interaction between the historic context of the work and a modern reader's understanding and interpretation of the work. New historicists attempt to describe the culture of a period by reading many different kinds of texts and paying close attention to many different dimensions of a culture, including political, economic, social, and aesthetic concerns. They regard texts not simply as a reflection of the culture that produced them but also as contributing to that culture by playing an active role in the social and political conflicts of an age. New historicism acknowledges and then explores various versions of "history," sensitizing us to the fact that the history on which we choose to focus is colored by being reconstructed from our present circumstances. See also HISTORICAL CRITICISM.

Objective point of view See POINT OF VIEW.

Octave A poetic stanza of eight lines, usually forming one part of a sonnet. See also SONNET, STANZA.

Ode A relatively lengthy lyric poem that often expresses lofty emotions in a dignified style. Odes are characterized by a serious topic, such as truth, art, freedom, justice, or the meaning of life; their tone tends to be formal. There is no prescribed pattern that defines an ode; some odes repeat the same pattern in each stanza, while others introduce a new pattern in each stanza. See also LYRIC.

Oedipus complex A Freudian term derived from Sophocles' tragedy *Oedipus the King*. It describes a psychological complex that is predicated on a boy's unconscious rivalry with his father for his mother's love and his desire to eliminate his father in order to take his father's place with his mother. The female equivalent of this complex is called the **Electra complex**. See also ELECTRA COMPLEX, PSYCHOLOGICAL CRITICISM.

Off rhyme See RHYME.

Omniscient narrator See NARRATOR.

One-act play A play that takes place in a single location and unfolds as one continuous action. The characters in a one-act play are presented economically and the action is sharply focused. See also DRAMA.

Onomatopoeia A term referring to the use of a word that resembles the sound it denotes. *Buzz, rattle, bang,* and *sizzle* all reflect onomatopoeia. Onomatopoeia can also consist of more than one word; writers sometimes create lines or whole passages in which the sound of the words helps to convey their meanings.

Open form Sometimes called **free verse**, open form poetry does not conform to established patterns of METER, RHYME, and STANZA. Such poetry derives its rhythmic qualities from the repetition of words, phrases, or grammatical structures, the arrangement of words on the printed page, or by some other means. The poet E. E. Cummings wrote open form poetry; his poems do not have measurable meters, but they do have rhythm. See also FIXED FORM.

Organic form Refers to works whose formal characteristics are not rigidly predetermined but follow the movement of thought or emotion being expressed. Such works are said to grow like living organisms, following their own individual patterns rather than external fixed rules that govern, for example, the form of a SONNET.

Overstatement See HYPERBOLE.

Oxymoron A condensed form of paradox in which two contradictory words are used together, as in "sweet sorrow" or "original copy." See also PARADOX.

Paradox A statement that initially appears to be contradictory but then, on closer inspection, turns out to make sense. For example, John Donne ends his sonnet "Death, Be Not Proud" with the paradoxical statement "Death, thou shalt die." To solve the paradox, it is necessary to discover the sense that underlies the statement. Paradox is useful in poetry because it arrests a reader's attention by its seemingly stubborn refusal to make sense.

Paraphrase A prose restatement of the central ideas of a poem, in your own language.

Parody A humorous imitation of another, usually serious, work. It can take any fixed or open form, because parodists imitate the tone, language, and shape of the original in order to deflate the subject matter, making the original work seem absurd. Anthony Hecht's poem "Dover Bitch" is a famous parody of Matthew Arnold's well-known "Dover Beach." Parody may also be used as a form of literary criticism to expose the defects in a work. But sometimes parody becomes an affectionate acknowledgment that a well-known work has become both institutionalized in our culture and fair game for some fun. For example, Peter De Vries's "To His Importunate Mistress" gently mocks Andrew Marvell's "To His Coy Mistress."

Persona Literally, a *persona* is a mask. In literature, a *persona* is a speaker created by a writer to tell a story or to speak in a poem. A persona is not a character in a story or narrative, nor does a persona necessarily directly reflect the author's personal voice. A persona is a separate self, created by and distinct from the author, through which he or she speaks. See also NARRATOR.

Personification A form of metaphor in which human characteristics are attributed to nonhuman things. Personification offers the writer a way to give the world life and motion by assigning familiar human behaviors and emotions to animals, inanimate objects, and abstract ideas. For example, in Keats's "Ode on a Grecian Urn," the speaker refers to the urn as an "unravished bride of quietness." See also METAPHOR.

Petrarchan sonnet See SONNET.

Picture poem A type of open form poetry in which the poet arranges the lines of the poem so as to create a particular shape on the page. The shape of the poem embodies its subject; the poem becomes a picture of what the poem is describing. Michael McFee's "In Medias Res" is an example of a picture poem. See also OPEN FORM.

Plausible action See CHARACTER.

Play See DRAMA.

Playwright See DRAMA.

Plot An author's selection and arrangement of incidents in a story to shape the action and give the story a particular focus. Discussions of plot include not just what happens, but also how and why things happen the way they do. Stories that are written in a **pyramidal pattern** divide the plot into three essential parts. The first part is the **rising action**, in which complication creates some sort of conflict for the protagonist. The second part is the **climax**, the moment of greatest emotional tension in a narrative, usually marking a turning point in the plot at which the **rising action** reverses to become the falling action. The third part, the **falling action** (or RESOLUTION), is characterized by diminishing tensions and the resolution of the plot's conflicts and complications. *In medias res* is a term used to describe the common strategy of beginning a story in the middle of the action. In this type of plot, we enter the story on the verge of some important moment. See also CHARACTER, CRISIS, RESOLUTION, SUBPLOT.

Poetic diction See DICTION.

Point of view Refers to who tells us a story and how it is told. What we know and how we feel about the events in a work are shaped by the author's choice of point of view. The teller of the story, the narrator, inevitably affects our understanding of the characters' actions by filtering what is told through his or her own perspective. The various points of view that writers draw upon can be grouped into two broad categories: (1) the third-person narrator uses *he, she,* or *they* to tell the story and does not participate in the action; and (2) the first-person narrator uses *I* and is a major or minor participant in the action. In addition, a second-person narrator, *you,* is also possible, but is rarely used because of the awkwardness of thrusting the reader into the story, as in "You are minding your own business on a park bench when a drunk steps out and demands your lunch bag." An **objective point of view** employs a third-person narrator who does not see into the mind of any character. From this detached and impersonal perspective, the narrator reports action and dialogue without telling us directly what the characters think and feel. Since no analysis or interpretation is provided by the narrator, this point of view places a premium on dialogue, actions, and details to reveal character to the reader. See also NARRATOR, STREAM-OF-CONSCIOUSNESS TECHNIQUE.

Postcolonial criticism An approach to literature that focuses on the study of cultural behavior and expression in relationship to the colonized world. Postcolonial criticism refers to the analysis of literary works written by writers from countries and cultures that at one time have been controlled by colonizing powers — such as Indian writers during or after British colonial rule. Postcolonial criticism also refers to the analysis of literary works written about colonial cultures by writers from the colonizing country. Many of these kinds of analyses point out how writers from colonial powers sometimes misrepresent colonized cultures by reflecting their own values. See also CULTURAL CRITICISM, HISTORICAL CRITICISM, MARXIST CRITICISM.

Problem play Popularized by Henrik Ibsen, a problem play is a type of drama that presents a social issue in order to awaken the audience to it. These plays usually reject romantic plots in favor of holding up a mirror that reflects not simply what the audience wants to see but what the playwright sees in them. Often, a problem play will propose a solution to the problem that does not coincide with prevailing opinion. The term is also used to refer to certain Shakespeare plays that do not fit the categories of tragedy, comedy, or romance. See also DRAMA.

Prologue The opening speech or dialogue of a play, especially a classic Greek play, that usually gives the exposition necessary to follow the subsequent action. Today the term also refers to the introduction to any literary work. See also DRAMA, EXPOSITION.

Prose poem A kind of open form poetry that is printed as prose and represents the most clear opposite of fixed form poetry. Prose poems are densely compact and often make use of striking imagery and figures of speech. See also FIXED FORM, OPEN FORM.

Prosody The overall metrical structure of a poem. See also METER.

Protagonist The main character of a narrative; its central character who engages the reader's interest and empathy. See also CHARACTER.

Psychological criticism An approach to literature that draws upon psychoanalytic theories, especially those of Sigmund Freud or Jacques Lacan, to understand more fully the text, the writer, and the reader. The basis of this approach is the idea of the existence of a human unconscious — those impulses, desires, and feelings about which a person is unaware but which influence emotions and behavior. Critics use psychological approaches to explore the motivations of characters and the symbolic meanings of events, while biographers speculate about a writer's own motivations — conscious or unconscious — in a literary work. Psychological approaches are also used to describe and analyze the reader's personal responses to a text.

Pun A play on words that relies on a word's having more than one meaning or sounding like another word. Shakespeare and other writers use puns extensively, for serious and comic purposes; in *Romeo and Juliet* (III.i.101), the dying Mercutio puns, "Ask for me tomorrow and you shall find me a grave man." Puns have serious literary uses, but since the eighteenth century, puns have been used almost purely for humorous effect. See also COMEDY.

Pyramidal pattern See PLOT.

Quatrain A four-line stanza. Quatrains are the most common stanzaic form in the English language; they can have various meters and rhyme schemes. See also METER, RHYME, STANZA.

Reader-response criticism An approach to literature that focuses on the reader rather than the work itself, by attempting to describe what goes on in the reader's mind during the reading of a text. Hence, the consciousness of the reader — produced by reading the work — is the actual subject of reader-response criticism. These critics are not after a "correct" reading of the text or what the author presumably intended; instead, they are interested in the reader's individual experience with the text. Thus, there is no single definitive reading of a work, because readers create rather than discover absolute meanings in texts. However, this approach is not a rationale for mistaken or bizarre readings, but an exploration of the possibilities for a plurality of readings. This kind of strategy calls attention to how we read and what influences our readings, and what that reveals about ourselves.

Recognition The moment in a story when previously unknown or withheld information is revealed to the protagonist, resulting in the discovery of the truth of his or her situation and, usually, a decisive change in course for that character. In *Oedipus the King*, the moment of recognition comes when Oedipus finally realizes that he has killed his father and married his mother.

Resolution The conclusion of a plot's conflicts and complications. The resolution, also known as the **falling action**, follows the climax in the plot. See also DÉNOUEMENT, PLOT.

Revenge tragedy See TRAGEDY.

Reversal The point in a story when the protagonist's fortunes turn in an unexpected direction. See also PLOT.

Rhyme The repetition of identical or similar concluding syllables in different words, most often at the ends of lines. Rhyme is predominantly a function of sound rather than spelling; thus, words that end with the same vowel sounds rhyme, for instance, *day, prey, bouquet, weigh,* and words with the same consonant ending rhyme, for instance *vain, feign, rein, lane.* Words do not have to be spelled the same way or look alike to rhyme. In fact, words may look alike but not rhyme at all. This is called **eye rhyme**, as with *bough* and *cough,* or *brow* and *blow*. **End rhyme** is the most common form of rhyme in poetry; the rhyme comes at the end of the lines:

> It runs through the reeds
>   And away it proceeds,
> Through meadow and glade,
>   In sun and in shade.

The **rhyme scheme** of a poem describes the pattern of end rhymes. Rhyme schemes are mapped out by noting patterns of rhyme with small letters: the first rhyme sound is designated *a*, the second becomes *b*, the third *c*, and so on. Thus, the rhyme scheme of the stanza above is *aabb*. **Internal rhyme** places at least one of the rhymed words within the line, as in "Dividing and gliding and sliding" or "In mist or cloud, on mast or shroud." **Masculine rhyme** describes the rhyming of single-syllable words, such as *grade* or *shade*. Masculine rhyme also occurs when rhyming words of more than one syllable, when the same sound occurs in a final stressed syllable, as in *defend* and *contend, betray* and *away*. **Feminine rhyme** consists of a rhymed stressed syllable followed by one or more identical unstressed syllables, as in *butter, clutter; gratitude, attitude; quivering, shivering*. All the examples so far have illustrated **exact rhymes**, because they share the same stressed vowel sounds as well as sharing sounds that follow the vowel. In **near rhyme** (also called **off rhyme, slant rhyme**, and **approximate rhyme**), the sounds are almost but not exactly alike. A common form of near rhyme is CONSONANCE, which consists of identical consonant sounds preceded by different vowel sounds: *home, same; worth, breath.*

Rhyme scheme See RHYME.

Rhythm A term used to refer to the recurrence of stressed and unstressed sounds in poetry. Depending on how sounds are arranged, the rhythm of a poem may be fast or slow, choppy or smooth. Poets use rhythm to create pleasurable sound patterns and to reinforce meanings. Rhythm in prose arises from pattern repetitions of sounds and pauses that create looser rhythmic effects. See also METER.

Rising action See PLOT.

Rising meter See METER.

Romantic comedy See COMEDY.

Round character See CHARACTER.

Run-on line See ENJAMBMENT.

Sarcasm See IRONY.

Satire The literary art of ridiculing a folly or vice in order to expose or correct it. The object of satire is usually some human frailty; people, institutions, ideas, and things are all fair game for satirists. Satire evokes attitudes of amusement, contempt, scorn, or indignation toward its faulty subject in the hope of somehow improving it. See also IRONY, PARODY.

Scansion The process of measuring the stresses in a line of verse in order to determine the metrical pattern of the line. See also LINE, METER.

Scene In drama, a scene is a subdivision of an ACT. In modern plays, scenes usually consist of units of action in which there are no changes in the setting or breaks in the continuity of time. According to traditional conventions, a scene changes when the location of the action shifts or when a new character enters. See also ACT, CONVENTION, DRAMA.

Script The written text of a play, which includes the dialogue between characters, stage directions, and often other expository information. See also DRAMA, EXPOSITION, PROLOGUE, STAGE DIRECTIONS.

Sentimentality A pejorative term used to describe the effort by an author to induce emotional responses in the reader that exceed what the situation warrants. Sentimentality especially pertains to such emotions as pathos and sympathy; it cons readers into falling for the mass murderer who is devoted to stray cats, and it requires that readers do not examine such illogical responses. Clichés and stock responses are the key ingredients of sentimentality in literature. See also CLICHÉ, STOCK RESPONSES.

Sestet A stanza consisting of exactly six lines. See also STANZA.

Sestina A type of fixed form poetry consisting of thirty-six lines of any length divided into six sestets and a three-line concluding stanza called an ENVOY. The six words at the end of the first sestet's lines must also appear at the ends of the other five sestets, in varying order. These six words must also appear in the envoy, where they often resonate important themes. An example of this highly demanding form of poetry is Algernon Charles Swinburne's "Sestina." See also SESTET.

Setting The physical and social context in which the action of a story occurs. The major elements of setting are the time, the place, and the social environment that frames the characters. Setting can be used to evoke a mood or atmosphere that will prepare the reader for what is to come, as in Nathaniel Hawthorne's short story "Young Goodman Brown." Sometimes, writers choose a particular setting because of traditional associations with that setting that are closely related to the action of a story. For example, stories filled with adventure or romance often take place in exotic locales.

Shakespearean sonnet See SONNET.

Showing See CHARACTER.

Simile A common figure of speech that makes an explicit comparison between two things by using words such as *like, as, than, appears,* and *seems:* "A sip of Mrs. Cook's coffee is like a punch in the stomach." The effectiveness of this simile is created by the differences between the two things compared. There would be no simile if the comparison were stated this way: "Mrs. Cook's coffee is as strong as the cafeteria's coffee." This is a literal translation because Mrs. Cook's coffee is compared with something like it — another kind of coffee. See also FIGURES OF SPEECH, METAPHOR.

Situational irony See IRONY.

Slant rhyme See RHYME.

Sociological criticism An approach to literature that examines social groups, relationships, and values as they are manifested in literature. Sociological approaches emphasize the nature and effect of the social forces that shape power relationships between groups or classes of people. Such readings treat literature as either a document reflecting social conditions or a product of those conditions. The former view brings into focus the social milieu; the latter emphasizes the work. Two important forms of sociological criticism are Marxist and feminist approaches. See also FEMINIST CRITICISM, MARXIST CRITICISM.

Soliloquy A dramatic convention by means of which a character, alone onstage, utters his or her thoughts aloud. Playwrights use soliloquies as a convenient way to inform the audience about a character's motivations and state of mind. Shakespeare's Hamlet delivers perhaps the best known of all soliloquies, which begins: "To be or not to be." See also ASIDE, CONVENTION.

Sonnet A fixed form of lyric poetry that consists of fourteen lines, usually written in iambic pentameter. There are two basic types of sonnets, the Italian and the English. The **Italian sonnet**, also known as the **Petrarchan sonnet**, is divided into an octave, which typically rhymes *abbaabba*, and a sestet, which may have varying rhyme schemes. Common rhyme patterns in the sestet are *cdecde, cdcdcd,* and *cdccdc.* Very often the octave presents a situation, attitude, or problem that the sestet comments upon or resolves, as in John Keats's "On First Looking into Chapman's Homer." The **English sonnet**, also known as the **Shakespearean sonnet**, is organized into three quatrains and a couplet, which typically rhyme *abab cdcd efef gg.* This rhyme scheme is more suited to English poetry because English has fewer rhyming words than Italian. English sonnets, because of their four-part organization, also have more flexibility with respect to where thematic breaks can occur. Frequently, however, the most pronounced break or turn comes with the concluding couplet, as in Shakespeare's "Shall I compare thee to a summer's day?" See also COUPLET, IAMBIC PENTAMETER, LINE, OCTAVE, QUATRAIN, SESTET.

Speaker The voice used by an author to tell a story or speak a poem. The speaker is often a created identity, and should not automatically be equated with the author's self. See also NARRATOR, PERSONA, POINT OF VIEW.

Spondee See FOOT.

Stage directions A playwright's written instructions about how the actors are to move and behave in a play. They explain in which direction characters should move, what facial expressions they should assume, and so on. See also DRAMA, SCRIPT.

Stanza In poetry, *stanza* refers to a grouping of lines, set off by a space, that usually has a set pattern of meter and rhyme. See also LINE, METER, RHYME.

Static character See CHARACTER.

Stock character See CHARACTER.

Stock responses Predictable, conventional reactions to language, characters, symbols, or situations. The flag, motherhood, puppies, God, and peace are common objects used to elicit stock responses from unsophisticated audiences. See also CLICHÉ, SENTIMENTALITY.

Stream-of-consciousness technique The most intense use of a central consciousness in narration. The stream-of-consciousness technique takes a reader inside a character's mind to reveal perceptions, thoughts, and feelings on a conscious or unconscious level. This technique suggests the flow of thought as well as its content; hence, complete sentences may give way to fragments as the character's mind makes rapid associations free of conventional logic or transitions.

James Joyce's novel *Ulysses* makes extensive use of this narrative technique. See also NARRATOR, POINT OF VIEW.

Stress The emphasis, or accent, given a syllable in pronunciation. See also ACCENT.

Style The distinctive and unique manner in which a writer arranges words to achieve particular effects. Style essentially combines the idea to be expressed with the individuality of the author. These arrangements include individual word choices as well as matters such as the length of sentences, their structure, tone, and use of irony. See also DICTION, IRONY, TONE.

Subplot The secondary action of a story, complete and interesting in its own right, that reinforces or contrasts with the main plot. There may be more than one subplot, and sometimes as many as three, four, or even more, running through a piece of fiction. Subplots are generally either analogous to the main plot, thereby enhancing our understanding of it, or extraneous to the main plot, to provide relief from it. See also PLOT.

Suspense The anxious anticipation of a reader or an audience as to the outcome of a story, especially concerning the character or characters with whom sympathetic attachments are formed. Suspense helps to secure and sustain the interest of the reader or audience throughout a work.

Symbol A person, object, image, word, or event that evokes a range of additional meaning beyond and usually more abstract than its literal significance. Symbols are educational devices for evoking complex ideas without having to resort to painstaking explanations that would make a story more like an essay than an experience. **Conventional symbols** have meanings that are widely recognized by a society or culture. Some conventional symbols are the Christian cross, the Star of David, a swastika, or a nation's flag. Writers use conventional symbols to reinforce meanings. Kate Chopin, for example, emphasizes the spring setting in "The Story of an Hour" as a way of suggesting the renewed sense of life that Mrs. Mallard feels when she thinks herself free from her husband. A **literary** or **contextual symbol** can be a setting, character, action, object, name, or anything else in a work that maintains its literal significance while suggesting other meanings. Such symbols go beyond conventional symbols; they gain their symbolic meaning within the context of a specific story. For example, the white whale in Melville's *Moby-Dick* takes on multiple symbolic meanings in the work, but these meanings do not automatically carry over into other stories about whales. The meanings suggested by Melville's whale are specific to that text; therefore, it becomes a contextual symbol. See also ALLEGORY.

Synecdoche See METAPHOR.

Syntax The ordering of words into meaningful verbal patterns such as phrases, clauses, and sentences. Poets often manipulate syntax, changing conventional word order, to place certain emphasis on particular words. Emily Dickinson, for instance, writes about being surprised by a snake in her poem "A narrow Fellow in the Grass," and includes this line: "His notice sudden is." In addition to creating the alliterative hissing *s*-sounds here, Dickinson also effectively manipulates the line's syntax so that the verb *is* appears unexpectedly at the end, making the snake's hissing presence all the more "sudden."

Telling See CHARACTER.

Tercet A three-line stanza. See also STANZA, TRIPLET.

Terza rima An interlocking three-line rhyme scheme: *aba, bcb, cdc, ded,* and so on. Dante's *The Divine Comedy* and Frost's "Acquainted with the Night" are written in *terza rima.* See also RHYME, TERCET.

Theme The central meaning or dominant idea in a literary work. A theme provides a unifying point around which the plot, characters, setting, point of view, symbols, and other elements of a work are organized. It is important not to mistake the theme for the actual subject of the work; the theme refers to the abstract concept that is made concrete through the images, characterization, and action of the text. In nonfiction, however, the theme generally refers to the main topic of the discourse.

Thesis The central idea of an essay. The thesis is a complete sentence (although sometimes it may require more than one sentence) that establishes the topic of the essay in clear, unambiguous language.

Tone The author's implicit attitude toward the reader or the people, places, and events in a work as revealed by the elements of the author's style. Tone may be characterized as serious or ironic, sad or happy, private or public, angry or affectionate, bitter or nostalgic, or any other attitudes and feelings that human beings experience. See also STYLE.

Tragedy A story that presents courageous individuals who confront powerful forces within or outside themselves with a dignity that reveals the breadth and depth of the human spirit in the face of failure, defeat, and even death. Tragedies recount an individual's downfall; they usually begin high and end low. Shakespeare is known for his tragedies, including *Macbeth, King Lear, Othello,* and *Hamlet.* The **revenge tragedy** is a well-established type of drama that can be traced back to Greek and Roman plays, particularly through the Roman playwright Seneca (ca. 3 B.C.–A.D. 63). Revenge tragedies basically consist of a murder that has to be avenged by a relative of the victim. Typically, the victim's ghost appears to demand revenge, and invariably madness of some sort is worked into subsequent events, which ultimately end in the deaths of the murderer, the avenger, and a number of other characters. Shakespeare's *Hamlet* subscribes to the basic ingredients of revenge tragedy, but it also transcends these conventions because Hamlet contemplates not merely revenge but suicide and the meaning of life itself. A **tragic flaw** is an error or defect in the tragic hero that leads to his downfall, such as greed, pride, or ambition. This flaw may be a result of bad character, bad judgment, an inherited weakness, or any other defect of character. **Tragic irony** is a form of dramatic irony found in tragedies such as *Oedipus the King,* in which Oedipus ironically ends up hunting himself. See also COMEDY, DRAMA.

Tragic flaw See TRAGEDY.

Tragic irony See IRONY, TRAGEDY.

Tragicomedy A type of drama that combines certain elements of both tragedy and comedy. The play's plot tends to be serious, leading to a terrible catastrophe, until an unexpected turn in events leads to a reversal of circumstance, and the story ends happily. Tragicomedy often employs a romantic, fast-moving plot dealing with love, jealousy, disguises, treachery, intrigue, and surprises, all moving toward a melodramatic resolution. Shakespeare's *Merchant of Venice* is a tragicomedy. See also COMEDY, DRAMA, MELODRAMA, TRAGEDY.

Triplet A tercet in which all three lines rhyme. See also TERCET.

Trochaic meter See FOOT.

Understatement The opposite of hyperbole, understatement (or litotes) refers to a figure of speech that says less than is intended. Understatement usually has an ironic effect, and sometimes may be used for comic purposes, as in Mark Twain's statement, "The reports of my death are greatly exaggerated." See also HYPERBOLE, IRONY.

Unreliable narrator See NARRATOR.

Verbal irony See IRONY.

Verse A generic term used to describe poetic lines composed in a measured rhythmical pattern that are often, but not necessarily, rhymed. See also LINE, METER, RHYME, RHYTHM.

Villanelle A type of fixed form poetry consisting of nineteen lines of any length divided into six stanzas: five tercets and a concluding quatrain. The first and third lines of the initial tercet rhyme; these rhymes are repeated in each subsequent tercet (*aba*) and in the final two lines of the quatrain (*abaa*). Line 1 appears in its entirety as lines 6, 12, and 18, while line 3 reappears as lines 9, 15, and 19. Dylan Thomas's "Do Not Go Gentle into That Good Night" is a villanelle. See also FIXED FORM, QUATRAIN, RHYME, TERCET.

Well-made play A realistic style of play that employs conventions including plenty of suspense created by meticulous plotting. Well-made plays are tightly and logically constructed, and lead to a logical resolution that is favorable to the protagonist. This dramatic structure was popularized in France by Eugène Scribe (1791–1861) and Victorien Sardou (1831–1908) and was adopted by Henrik Ibsen. See also CHARACTER, PLOT.

Acknowledgments (continued from p. iv)

Gaylord Brewer. "The Joys of Secret Sin" from *The Martini Diet* (Dream Horse Press, 2008). Copyright © 2008 by Gaylord Brewer. Reprinted with the permission of the author.

Mark Budman. "The Diary of a Salaryman" from *You Have Time for This: Contemporary American Short-Short Stories*, edited by Mark Budman and Tom Hazuka. Copyright © 2007 by Mark Budman. Reprinted by permission of the author.

Ron Carlson. "Max" from *A Kind of Flying: Selected Stories* by Ron Carlson. Copyright © 2003, 1997, 1992, 1987 by Ron Carlson. Used by permission of the author and W. W. Norton & Company, Inc.

Raymond Carver. "Popular Mechanics" from *What We Talk about When We Talk about Love* by Raymond Carver. Copyright © 1974, 1976, 1978, 1980, 1981 by Raymond Carver. Used by permission of Alfred A. Knopf, an imprint of the Knopf Doubleday Publishing Group, a division of Penguin Random House LLC. All rights reserved. Any third party use of this material, outside of this publication, is prohibited. Interested parties must apply directly to Penguin Random House LLC for permission.

May-lee Chai. "Saving Sourdi," *ZYZZYVA*, no. 3 (Winter 2001), pp. 139–58. Copyright © 2001 by May-lee Chai. Used by permission of the author.

Lydia Davis. "Negative Emotions" from *Can't and Won't: Stories* by Lydia Davis. Copyright © 2014 by Lydia Davis. Reprinted by permission of Farrar, Straus & Giroux, LLC.

Benjamin DeMott. "Abner Snopes as a Victim of Class" from *Close Imaginings: An Introduction to Literature* by Benjamin DeMott, copyright © 1988. Reprinted by permission of Margaret DeMott.

Andre Dubus. "Killings" from *Finding a Girl in America* by Andre Dubus. Copyright © 1980 by Andre Dubus. Reprinted by permission of David R. Godine, Publisher, Inc.

Ralph Ellison. "Battle Royal" from *Invisible Man* by Ralph Ellison. Copyright © 1948 and renewed 1976 by Ralph Ellison. Used by permission of Random House, an imprint and division of Penguin Random House LLC. All rights reserved. Any third party use of this material, outside of this publication, is prohibited. Interested parties must apply directly to Penguin Random House LLC for permission.

William Faulkner. "Barn Burning" from *Collected Stories of William Faulkner* by William Faulkner. Copyright 1950 by Random House, Inc. Copyright renewed 1977 by Jill Faulkner Summers. "A Rose for Emily" from *Collected Stories of William Faulkner* by William Faulkner. Copyright © 1930 and renewed 1958 by William Faulkner. Used by permission of Random House, an imprint and division of Penguin Random House LLC. All rights reserved. Any third party use of this material, outside of this publication, is prohibited. Interested parties must apply directly to Penguin Random House LLC for permission. "On 'A Rose for Emily'" from *Faulkner in the University*, edited by Frederick L. Gwynn and Joseph L. Blotner. Copyright © 1995 by the Rector and Visitors of the University of Virginia. Reprinted by permission of the University of Virginia Press.

Dagoberto Gilb. "Love in L.A." from *The Magic of Blood* by Dagoberto Gilb. Copyright © 1993. Story originally published in *Buffalo*. "On Distortions of Mexican American Culture," from "La Próxima Parada Is Next," *American Book Review* vol. 32, no. 3 (March/April 2011). Copyright © 2011 by Dagoberto Gilb. "On Physical Labor," from "Work Union" in *Gritos* by Dagoberto Gilb. Copyright © 2003 by Dagoberto Gilb. Originally appeared in *The Carpenter* (magazine of the United Brotherhood of Carpenters). "Romero's Shirt" from *The Magic of Blood* by Dagoberto Gilb. Copyright © 1993. Story originally published in *New Chicana/Chicano Writing*. "Shout" from *Woodcuts of Women* by Dagoberto Gilb. Copyright © 2001 by Dagoberto Gilb. "Uncle Rock" from *Before the End, After the Beginning* by Dagoberto Gilb. Copyright © 2011 by Dagoberto Gilb. All selections reprinted by permission of the author.

Gail Godwin. "A Sorrowful Woman," published in 1971 in *Esquire* magazine. Copyright © 1971 by Gail Godwin. Reprinted by permission of John Hawkins & Associates, Inc.

Mark Halliday. "Young Man on Sixth Avenue," from *The Pushcart Prize XXI: 1997 Best of the Small Presses* (Pushcart Press, 1996), pp. 358–60. Originally appeared in *Chicago Review* 1995. Copyright © 1995 by Mark Halliday. Reprinted by permission of the author.

Ron Hansen. "My Kid's Dog" from *She Loves Me Not: New and Selected Stories*. Copyright © 2012 by Ron Hansen. Originally appeared in *Harper's*, March 2003. Reprinted by permission of SLL/Sterling Lord Literistic, Inc.

Ernest Hemingway. "Soldier's Home" from *In Our Time* by Ernest Hemingway. Copyright © 1925, 1930 by Charles Scribner's Sons; copyright renewed © 1953, 1958 by Ernest Hemingway. Reprinted with the permission of Scribner, a division of Simon & Schuster, Inc. All rights reserved.

Jane Hiles. "Blood Ties in 'Barn Burning'" from "Kinship and Heredity in Faulkner's 'Barn Burning,'" *Mississippi Quarterly* 38, no. 3 (Summer 1985), pp. 329–37. Copyright © 1985 Mississippi State University, Mississippi State, Mississippi. Reprinted by permission of *Mississippi Quarterly: The Journal of Southern Culture.*

Claire Katz. "The Function of Violence in O'Connor's Fiction" from "Flannery O'Connor's Rage of Vision," *American Literature* 46.1 (March 1974), pp. 545–67. Copyright 1974, Duke University Press. All rights reserved. Republished by permission of the copyright holder, Duke University Press, www.dukeupress.edu.

Jamaica Kincaid. "Girl" from *At the Bottom of the River* by Jamaica Kincaid. Copyright © 1983 by Jamaica Kincaid. Reprinted by permission of Farrar, Straus & Giroux, LLC.

Phil Klay. "Redeployment" from *Redeployment* by Phil Klay. Copyright © 2014 by Phil Klay. Used by permission of Penguin Press, an imprint of Penguin Publishing Group, a division of Penguin Random House LLC.

Gavin Ford Kovite. "When Engaging Targets, Remember." First published in *Fire and Forget: Short Stories from the Long War*, ed. Roy Scranton and Matt Gallagher (Da Capo, 2013). Copyright © 2013 by Gavin Ford Kovite. Reprinted by permission of the author.

"A Letter Home from an Irish Emigrant in Australia" [Bridget Burke], from *Oceans of Consolation: Personal Accounts of Irish Migration to Australia* by David Fitzpatrick (Cornell UP, 1994). Reprinted by permission of David Fitzpatrick.

Li Ho. Excerpt from "A Beautiful Girl Combs Her Hair," translated by David Young, from *Five T'ang Poets.* Copyright © 1990 by Oberlin College. Reprinted with the permission of The Permissions Company, Inc., on behalf of Oberlin College Press, www.oberlin.edu/ocpress/.

Mordecai Marcus. "What Is an Initiation Story?" from *The Journal of Aesthetics and Art Criticism* 19.2 (Winter 1960), pp. 222–23. Copyright © 1960. Reprinted with the permission of John Wiley & Sons Ltd.

Dan McCall. "On the Lawyer's Character in 'Bartleby the Scrivener'" from *The Silence of Bartleby* by Dan McCall. Copyright © 1989 Cornell University. Used by permission of the publisher, Cornell University Press.

Peter Meinke. "The Cranes." Copyright © 1986 by Peter Meinke. Reprinted by permission of Ann Rittenberg Literary Agency, Inc.

Susan Minot. "Lust" from *Lust and Other Stories* by Susan Minot. Copyright © 1989 by Susan Minot. Reprinted by permission of Houghton Mifflin Harcourt Publishing Company. All rights reserved.

Maggie Mitchell. "It Would Be Different If." Originally appeared in *New South* vol. 4, no. 2 (2011). Copyright © 2011 by Margaret E. Mitchell. Reprinted by permission of the author.

Rick Moody. "Boys" from *Demonology: Stories* by Rick Moody. Copyright © 2001 by Rick Moody. Used by permission of Little, Brown & Company.

Alice Munro. "Wild Swans" from *Selected Stories* by Alice Munro. Copyright © 1996 by Alice Munro. Used by permission of Alfred A. Knopf, an imprint of the Knopf Doubleday Publishing Group, a division of Penguin Random House LLC. All rights reserved. Any third party use of this material, outside of this publication, is prohibited. Interested parties must apply directly to Penguin Random House LLC for permission. Also reprinted by permission of William Morris Endeavor Entertainment, LLC.

Kay Mussell. "Are Feminism and Romance Novels Mutually Exclusive?" from "All about Romance: The Back Fence for Lovers of Romance Novels" at <http://www.likesbooks.com/mussell.html>. Reprinted by permission of the author.

Joyce Carol Oates. "Hi Howya Doin" from *Ploughshares* 32.1 (Spring 2007). Copyright © 2007 by Ontario Review, Inc. Reprinted by permission of John Hawkins & Associates, Inc.

Tim O'Brien. "How to Tell a True War Story" from *The Things They Carried* by Tim O'Brien. Copyright © 1990 by Tim O'Brien. Reprinted by permission of Houghton Mifflin Harcourt Publishing Company. All rights reserved.

Flannery O'Connor. "Good Country People" from *A Good Man Is Hard to Find and Other Stories.* Copyright © 1953 by Flannery O'Connor. Copyright © renewed 1981 by Regina O'Connor. Reprinted by permission of Houghton Mifflin Harcourt Publishing Company. All rights reserved. "A Good Man Is Hard to Find" from *A Good Man Is Hard to Find and Other Stories.* Copyright © 1953 by Flannery O'Connor. Copyright © renewed 1981 by Regina O'Connor. Reprinted by permission of Houghton Mifflin Harcourt Publishing Company. All rights reserved. "Revelation" from *The Complete Stories* by Flannery O'Connor. Copyright © 1971 by the Estate of Mary Flannery O'Connor. Reprinted by permission of Farrar, Straus & Giroux, LLC.

Michael Oppenheimer. "The Paring Knife." First published in *Sundog* vol. 4, no. 1 (1982). Copyright © Michael Oppenheimer. Reprinted by permission of the author.

Annie Proulx. "55 Miles to the Gas Pump." Reprinted with the permission of Scribner, a division of Simon & Schuster, Inc., from *Close Range: Wyoming Stories* by Annie Proulx. Copyright © 1999 by Dead Line Ltd. All rights reserved.

Muriel Spark. "The First Year of My Life" from *Open to the Public.* Copyright © 1953, 1957, 1958, 1961, 1964, 1967, 1985, 1987, 1989, 1994, 1995, 1996, 1997 by Muriel Spark. Copyright © 1985 by Copyright Administration Limited. First appeared in the *New Yorker.* Reprinted by permission of New Directions Publishing Corp.

Terry Tilton. "That Settles That" from *The World's Shortest Stories*, ed. Steve Moss. Copyright © 1998. Reproduced with permission of RUNNING PRESS BOOK PUBLISHERS via Copyright Clearance Center.

David Updike. "Summer" from *Out on the Marsh* by David Updike. Copyright © 1988 by David Updike. Used by permission of the Wylie Agency LLC.

John Updike. "A & P" from *Pigeon Feathers and Other Stories* by John Updike. Copyright © 1962 and renewed 1990 by John Updike. Used by permission of Alfred A. Knopf, an imprint of the Knopf Doubleday Publishing Group, a division of Penguin Random House LLC. All rights reserved. Any third party use of this material, outside of this publication, is prohibited. Interested parties must apply directly to Penguin Random House LLC for permission.

Karen van der Zee. *A Secret Sorrow.* Text copyright © 1981 by Karen van der Zee. Permission to reproduce text granted by Harlequin Books S.A.

Alice Walker. "The Flowers," from *In Love & Trouble: Stories of Black Women* by Alice Walker. Copyright © 1973 by Alice Walker. Reprinted by permission of Houghton Mifflin Harcourt Publishing Company. All rights reserved.

David Foster Wallace. "Incarnations of Burned Children" from *Oblivion* by David Foster Wallace. Copyright © 2004 by David Foster Wallace. Used by permission of Little, Brown & Company.

Fay Weldon. "IND AFF, or Out of Love in Sarajevo." Copyright © 1988 by Fay Weldon. First published in *The Observer* magazine (August 7, 1988). Reprinted by permission of the author.

Gayle Edward Wilson. "Conflict in 'Barn Burning'" from "'Being Pulled Two Ways': The Nature of Sarty's Choice in 'Barn Burning.'" *Mississippi Quarterly* 24, no. 3 (Summer 1971), pp. 279–88. Copyright © 1971 Mississippi State University, Mississippi State, Mississippi. Reprinted by permission of *Mississippi Quarterly: The Journal of Southern Culture.*

Tobias Wolff. "That Room" from *Our Story Begins: New and Selected Stories* by Tobias Wolff. Copyright © 2008 by Tobias Wolff. Used by permission of Alfred A. Knopf, an imprint of the Knopf Doubleday Publishing Group, a division of Penguin Random House LLC. All rights reserved. Any third party use of this material, outside of this publication, is prohibited. Interested parties must apply directly to Penguin Random House LLC for permission.

Geoff Wyss. "How to Be a Winner" from *How* by Geoff Wyss. Copyright © 2012 by Geoff Wyss. Copyright © 2012 by The Ohio State University. Reprinted by permission of the Ohio State University Press. All rights reserved.

Xu Xi. "Famine." Copyright © 2004, 2005 by Xu Xi. Reprinted by permission of the Harold Matson Co., Inc. All rights reserved.

Inc., on behalf of the University of Arkansas Press, www.uapress.com. "Litany" from *Nine Horses: Poems* by Billy Collins. Copyright © 2008 by Billy Collins. Used by permission of Random House, an imprint and division of Penguin Random House LLC. Any third party use of this material, outside of this publication, is prohibited. Interested parties must apply directly to Penguin Random House, Inc., for permission. "Nostalgia" from *Questions About Angels* by Billy Collins. Copyright © 1991. Reprinted by permission of the University of Pittsburgh Press. "On 'Building with Its Face Blown Off,'" "On Writing 'Litany,'" "On Writing 'Nostalgia,'" "On Writing 'Osso Buco,'" "On Writing 'Questions About Angels,'" copyright © Billy Collins. Reprinted by permission of the Chris Calhoun Agency. "Osso Buco" from *The Art of Drowning* by Billy Collins. Copyright © 1995. Reprinted by permission of the University of Pittsburgh Press. "Questions About Angels" from *Questions About Angels* by Billy Collins. Copyright © 1991. Reprinted by permission of the University of Pittsburgh Press.

Edmund Conti. "Pragmatist" from *Light Year '86*. Reprinted by permission of the author.

Sally Croft. "Home-Baked Bread" from *Light Year '86*. Reprinted by permission of Bruce Croft.

Countee Cullen. "For a Lady I Know" from *Color* by Countee Cullen. Copyright © 1925 by Harper & Brothers; copyright renewed 1952 by Ida M. Cullen. "From the Dark Tower" from *Copper Sun* by Countee Cullen. Copyright © 1927 by Harper & Brothers; copyright renewed 1954 by Ida M. Cullen. "Incident" from *Color* by Countee Cullen. Copyright © 1925 by Harper & Brothers; copyright renewed 1952 by Ida M. Cullen. "On Racial Poetry" from *Opportunity: A Journal of Negro Life*, February 1926 issue. Copyright © 1926 by *Opportunity* magazine; copyright renewed 1954 by Ida M. Cullen. Reprinted by permission of the National Urban League. "Tableau" from *Color* by Countee Cullen. Copyright © 1925 by Harper & Brothers; copyright renewed 1952 by Ida M. Cullen. "To Certain Critics" from *My Soul's High Song: The Collected Writings of Countee Cullen* (Anchor Books, 1991). Originally published in *The Black Christ and Other Poems*. Copyright © 1929 by Harper & Brothers, copyright renewed 1956 by Ida M. Cullen. "Yet Do I Marvel" from *Color* by Countee Cullen. Copyright © 1925 by Harper & Brothers; copyright renewed 1952 by Ida M. Cullen. Copyrights held by the Amistad Research Center, Tulane University, administered by Thompson and Thompson, Brooklyn, NY.

E. E. Cummings. "l(a," copyright © 1958, 1986, 1991 by the Trustees for the E. E. Cummings Trust. "next to of course god america i," copyright © 1926, 1954, © 1991 by the Trustees for the E. E. Cummings Trust. Copyright © 1985 by George James Firmage. "old age sticks" and "when serpents bargain for the right to squirm," copyright © 1948, © 1976, 1991 by the Trustees for the E. E. Cummings Trust. Copyright © 1979 by George J. Firmage. All selections from *Complete Poems: 1904–1962* by E. E. Cummings, edited by George J. Firmage. Copyright 1923, 1925, 1926, 1931, 1935, 1938, 1939, 1940, 1944, 1945, 1946, 1947, 1948, 1949, 1950, 1951, 1952, 1953, 1954, © 1955, 1956, 1957, 1958, 1959, 1960, 1961, 1962, 1963, 1966, 1967, 1968, 1972, 1973, 1974, 1975, 1976, 1977, 1978, 1979, 1980, 1981, 1982, 1983, 1984, 1985, 1986, 1987, 1988, 1989, 1990, 1991 by the Trustees for the E. E. Cummings Trust. Copyright © 1973, 1976, 1978, 1979, 1981, 1983, 1985, 1991 by George James Firmage. Used by permission of Liveright Publishing Corporation.

Joanne Diaz. "On My Father's Loss of Hearing" from *The Lessons* by Joanne Diaz. Originally published in the *Southern Review* 42, no. 3 (Summer 2006). Copyright © 2011 by Silverfish Review Press. Reprinted by permission of the publisher.

Emily Dickinson. "After great pain, a formal feeling comes —," "Because I could not stop for Death —," "A Bird came down the Walk —," "From all the Jails the Boys and Girls," "Heaven' — is what I cannot reach!," "I dwell in Possibility —," "I felt a Cleaving in my Mind —," "If I shouldn't be alive," "I heard a Fly buzz — when I died —," "I never saw a Moor —," "I taste a liquor never brewed —," "Much Madness is divinest Sense —," "A narrow Fellow in the Grass," "Papa Above!," "The Soul selects her own Society —," "Success is counted sweetest," "Tell all the Truth but tell it slant —," and "There's a certain Slant of light." Reprinted by permission of the publishers and the Trustees of Amherst College from *The Poems of Emily Dickinson*, edited by Thomas H. Johnson, Cambridge, Mass.: The Belknap Press of Harvard University Press. Copyright © 1951, 1955 by the President and Fellows of Harvard College. Copyright © renewed 1979, 1983 by the President and Fellows of Harvard College. Copyright © 1914, 1918, 1919, 1924, 1929, 1930, 1932, 1935, 1937, 1942 by Martha Dickinson Bianchi. Copyright © 1952, 1957, 1958, 1963, 1965 by Mary L. Hampson.

Cornelius Eady. "The Supremes" from *The Gathering of My Name*. Copyright © 1991 by Cornelius Eady. Reprinted with the permission of The Permissions Company, Inc., on behalf of Carnegie Mellon University Press.

Martín Espada. "The Community College Revises Its Curriculum in Response to Changing Demographics" from *A Mayan Astronomer in Hell's Kitchen* by Martín Espada. Copyright © 2000 by Martín Espada. Used by permission of the author and W. W. Norton & Company, Inc. "Latin Night at the Pawn Shop" from *Rebellion Is the Circle of a Lover's Hands / Rebelión es el giro de manos del amante* by Martín Espada. Copyright © 1990 by Martín Espada. Translation copyright © by Camilo Pérez-Bustillo and Martín Espada. First printed in 1990 by Curbstone Press. Reprinted with the permission of the author and Northwestern University Press. "The Mexican Cabdriver's Poem for His Wife, Who Has Left Him" from *A Mayan Astronomer in Hell's Kitchen* by Martín Espada. Copyright © 2000 by Martín Espada. Used by permission of the author and W. W. Norton & Company, Inc.

Barbara Everett. "The Problem of Tone in Prufrock" excerpted from "In Search of Prufrock," *Critical Quarterly* 16.2 (June 1974). Reprinted with the permission of John Wiley & Sons Ltd.

Ruth Fainlight. "Crocuses" from *New & Collected Poems* by Ruth Fainlight (Bloodaxe Books, 2010). Copyright © 2010 by Ruth Fainlight. Reprinted with permission of Bloodaxe Books on behalf of the author. www.bloodaxebooks.com.

Blanche Farley. "The Lover Not Taken" from *Light Year '86*. Reprinted by permission of the author.

Kenneth Fearing. "AD" from *Kenneth Fearing Complete Poems*, ed. by Robert Ryely (Orono, ME: National Poetry Foundation, 1997). Copyright © 1938 by Kenneth Fearing, renewed in 1966 by the Estate of Kenneth Fearing. Reprinted by the permission of Russell & Volkening as agents for the author.

Karen Jackson Ford. "Hughes's Aesthetics of Simplicity" from "Do Right to Write Right: Langston Hughes's Aesthetics of Simplicity," *Twentieth Century Literature* 38, no. 4 (Winter 1992), pp. 436–456. Copyright 1992, Hofstra

University. All rights reserved. Republished by permission of the copyright holder, and the present publisher, Duke University Press, www.dukeupress.edu.

Ruth Forman. "Poetry Should Ride the Bus." From *We Are the Young Magicians* (Boston: Beacon Press, 1993). Copyright © 1993 by Ruth Forman. Reprinted with the permission of the author.

Robert Francis. "Catch" and "The Pitcher" from *The Orb Weaver*. Copyright © 1960 by Robert Francis. Reprinted with permission of Wesleyan University Press.

Robert Frost. "Acquainted with the Night," "Design," "Dust of Snow," "Fire and Ice," "The Gift Outright," "The Need of Being Versed in Country Things," "Neither Out Far nor In Deep," "Nothing Gold Can Stay," "Once by the Pacific," and "Stopping by Woods on a Snowy Evening," from *The Poetry of Robert Frost*, edited by Edward Connery Lathem. Copyright © 1923, 1928, 1942, 1956, 1969 by Henry Holt and Company, copyright © 1936, 1951, 1956 by Robert Frost, copyright © 1964, 1970 by Lesley Frost Ballantine. Reprinted by permission of Henry Holt and Company, LLC. All rights reserved.

Christina Gerogiannis. "Headland." Copyright © 2007 by Christina Gerogiannis. Reprinted by permission of the author.

Sandra M. Gilbert and Susan Gubar. "On Dickinson's White Dress" from *The Madwoman in the Attic*. Copyright © 1979 by Yale University Press. Reprinted by permission of Yale University Press.

Dana Gioia. "Money" from *The Gods of Winter*. Copyright © 1991 by Dana Gioia. Reprinted with the permission of The Permissions Company, Inc., on behalf of Graywolf Press, Minneapolis, Minnesota, www.graywolfpress.org.

R. S. Gwynn. "Shakespearean Sonnet." Originally appeared in *Formalist* 12.2 (2001). Copyright © 2001 by R. S. Gwynn. Reprinted by permission of the author.

Rachel Hadas. "The Red Hat" from *Halfway Down the Hall*. Copyright © 1998 by Rachel Hadas. Reprinted with permission of Wesleyan University Press.

Richard Hague. "Directions for Resisting the SAT" from *Ohio Teachers Write* (Ohio Council of Teachers of English, 1996). Copyright © 1996 by Richard Hague. Reprinted by permission of the author.

Mark Halliday. "Graded Paper," *Michigan Quarterly Review*. Reprinted by permission of the author.

William Hathaway. "Oh, Oh" from *Light Year '86*. This poem was originally published in the *Cincinnati Poetry Review*. Reprinted by permission of the author.

Robert Hayden. "Those Winter Sundays," copyright © 1966 by Robert Hayden, from *Collected Poems of Robert Hayden* by Robert Hayden, edited by Frederick Glaysher. Used by permission of Liveright Publishing Corporation.

Seamus Heaney. "The Pitchfork" from *Opened Ground: Selected Poems 1966–1996* by Seamus Heaney. Copyright © 1998 by Seamus Heaney. Reprinted by permission of Farrar, Straus and Giroux, LLC, and Faber and Faber, Ltd.

Judy Page Heitzman. "The Schoolroom on the Second Floor of the Knitting Mill." Copyright © 1991 by Judy Page Heitzman. Originally appeared in the *New Yorker*, December 2, 1992, p. 102. Reprinted by permission of the author.

David Hernandez. "All-American," *Southern Review* 48.4 (Autumn 2012). Copyright © 2012 by David Hernandez. Used by permission of the author.

William Heyen. "The Trains" from *The Host: Selected Poems 1965–1990* by William Heyen. Copyright © 1994 by Time Being Press. Reprinted by permission of the author.

Bob Hicok. "Making it in poetry," copyright © 2004 by Bob Hicok. "Making it in poetry" first appeared in the *Georgia Review* 58.2 (Summer 2004), and is reprinted here with the acknowledgment of the editors and the permission of the author.

Jane Hirshfield. "Optimism" from *Given Sugar, Given Salt* by Jane Hirshfield. Copyright © 2001 by Jane Hirshfield. Reprinted by permission of HarperCollins Publishers.

Edward Hirsch. "Edward Hopper and the House by the Railroad (1925)" from *Wild Gratitude* by Edward Hirsch. Copyright © 1985 by Edward Hirsch. Used by permission of Alfred A. Knopf, an imprint of the Knopf Doubleday Publishing Group, a division of Penguin Random House LLC. All rights reserved. Any third party use of this material, outside of this publication, is prohibited. Interested parties must apply directly to Penguin Random House LLC for permission.

Tony Hoagland. "America" from *What Narcissism Means to Me*. Copyright © 2003 by Tony Hoagland. Reprinted with the permission of The Permissions Company, Inc., on behalf of Graywolf Press, Minneapolis, Minnesota, www.graywolfpress.org.

Andrew Hudgins. "Elegy for My Father, Who Is Not Dead" from *The Never-Ending: New Poems* by Andrew Hudgins. Copyright © 1991 by Andrew Hudgins. Reprinted by permission of Houghton Mifflin Harcourt Publishing Company. All rights reserved. "The Ice-Cream Truck" from *Shut Up, You're Fine! Poems for Very, Very Bad Children* by Andrew Hudgins. Copyright © 2009 by Andrew Hudgins. Reprinted by permission of the author.

Langston Hughes. "Ballad of the Landlord," "Harlem," "Jazzonia," "Lenox Avenue: Midnight," "The Negro Speaks of Rivers," and "125th Street," from *The Collected Poems of Langston Hughes* by Langston Hughes, edited by Arnold Rampersad with David Roessel, Associate Editor. Copyright © 1994 by the Estate of Langston Hughes. Used by permission of Alfred A. Knopf, an imprint of the Knopf Doubleday Publishing Group, a division of Penguin Random House LLC. All rights reserved. Any third party use of this material, outside of this publication, is prohibited. Interested parties must apply directly to Penguin Random House LLC for permission.

Paul Humphrey. "Blow" from *Light Year '86*. Reprinted with the permission of Eleanor Humphrey.

David Ignatow. "The Jobholder" from *At My Ease: Uncollected Poems of the Fifties and Sixties*. Copyright © 1998 by the Estate of David Ignatow. Reprinted with the permission of The Permissions Company, Inc., on behalf of BOA Editions Ltd., www.boaeditions.org.

Randall Jarrell. "The Death of the Ball Turret Gunner" from *The Complete Poems* by Randall Jarrell. Copyright © 1969, renewed 1997 by Mary von S. Jarrell. Reprinted by permission of Farrar, Straus and Giroux, LLC.

Kelli Lyon Johnson. "Mapping an Identity" excerpted from *Julia Alvarez: Writing a New Place on the Map* by Kelli Lyon Johnson. Copyright © 2005 University of New Mexico Press. Reprinted by permission of the author and University of New Mexico Press.

Alice Jones. "The Foot" and "The Lungs," from *Anatomy* by Alice Jones (San Francisco: Bullnettle Press, 1997). Copyright © 1997 by Alice Jones. Reprinted by permission of the author.

Donald Justice. "Order in the Streets" from *Losers Weepers: Poems Found Practically Everywhere*, edited by George Hitchcock. Reprinted by permission of Jean Ross Justice.

Garrison Keillor. "The Anthem." Originally published in the January/February 2006 issue of the *Atlantic*. Copyright © 2006 by Garrison Keillor. Reprinted by permission of Garrison Keillor.

Jane Kenyon. "Not Writing" from *Collected Poems*. Copyright © 2005 by the Estate of Jane Kenyon. Reprinted with the permission of The Permissions Company, Inc., on behalf of Graywolf Press, Minneapolis, Minnesota, www.graywolfpress.org.

Carolyn Kizer. "After Bashō" from *Cool, Calm & Collected: Poems 1960–2000*. Copyright © 2001 by Carolyn Kizer. Reprinted with the permission of The Permissions Company, Inc., on behalf of Copper Canyon Press, www.coppercanyonpress.org.

Yusef Komunyakaa. "Facing It" from *Dien Cai Dau*. Copyright © 1988 by Yusef Komunyakaa. Reprinted with permission of Wesleyan University Press.

Ted Kooser. "Laundry" from *One World at a Time* by Ted Kooser. Copyright © 1985. Reprinted by permission of the University of Pittsburgh Press. "Selecting a Reader" from *Sure Signs: New and Selected Poems* by Ted Kooser. Copyright © 1980. Reprinted by permission of the University of Pittsburgh Press.

Maxine Kumin. "The Whole Hog" from *Where I Live: New and Selected Poems, 1990–2010* by Maxine Kumin. Copyright © 2010 by Maxine Kumin. Used by permission of the author and W. W. Norton & Company, Inc.

Danusha Laméris. "Names" from *The Moons of August* by Danusha Laméris. Copyright © 2014 by Danusha Laméris. Reprinted with the permission of The Permissions Company, Inc., on behalf of Autumn House Press, www.autumnhouse.org.

Philip Larkin. "A Study of Reading Habits" from *The Complete Poems of Philip Larkin* by Philip Larkin, edited by Archie Burnett. Copyright © 2012 by the Estate of Philip Larkin. Reprinted by permission of Farrar, Straus and Giroux, LLC, and Faber and Faber, Ltd.

Ann Lauinger. "Marvell Noir." First appeared in *Parnassus: Poetry in Review* 28, no. 1 & 2 (2005). Copyright © 2005 by Ann Lauinger. Reprinted by permission of the author.

David Lenson. "On the Contemporary Use of Rhyme" from "The Battle Is Joined: Formalists Take On Defenders of Free Verse," *The Chronicle of Higher Education* (February 24, 1988). Reprinted by permission of the author.

Li Ho. Excerpt from "A Beautiful Girl Combs Her Hair," translated by David Young, from *Five T'ang Poets*. Copyright © 1990 by Oberlin College. Reprinted with the permission of The Permissions Company, Inc., on behalf of Oberlin College Press, www.oberlin.edu/ocpress/.

Alain LeRoy Locke. "Review of Georgia Douglas Johnson's *Bronze: A Book of Verse*," excerpted from "Notes on the New Books" by Alain LeRoy Locke and Jessie Fauset, *The Crisis* 25, no. 4 (February 1923): 161. Bedford/St. Martin's/Macmillan Higher Education wishes to thank the Crisis Publishing Co., Inc., the publisher of the magazine of the National Association for the Advancement of Colored People, for the use of this material.

Diane Lockward. "Linguini" from *What Feeds Us* by Diane Lockward (Wind Publications, 2006). Copyright © 2006 by Diane Lockward. First appeared in *Poet Lore*. Reprinted by permission of the author.

Dave Lucas. "November," originally appeared in *Shenandoah* 57.1 (Spring 2007). Copyright © 2007 by Dave Lucas. Reprinted by permission of the author.

Katharyn Howd Machan. "Hazel Tells LaVerne" from *Light Year '85*. Copyright © 1977 by Katharyn Howd Machan. Reprinted by permission of the author.

Elaine Magarrell. "The Joy of Cooking" from *Sometime the Cow Kick Your Head, Light Year 88/89*. Reprinted by permission.

John Maloney. "Good!" from *Proposal* by John Maloney. Zoland Books, 1999. Copyright © 1999 by John Maloney. Reprinted by permission of the author.

Julio Marzán. "Ethnic Poetry." Originally appeared in *Parnassus: Poetry in Review*. "The Translator at the Reception for Latin American Writers." Reprinted by permission of the author.

Florence Cassen Mayers. "All-American Sestina," © 1996 Florence Cassen Mayers, as first published in the *Atlantic Monthly*. Reprinted with permission of the author.

David McCord. "Epitaph on a Waiter" from *Odds Without Ends*, copyright © 1954 by David T. W. McCord. Reprinted by permission of the estate of David T. W. McCord.

Walt McDonald. "Coming Across It" from *Embers* Vol. 13, no. 1 (1988), p. 17. Copyright © 1988 by Walt McDonald. Reprinted with the permission of the author.

Michael McFee. "In Medias Res" from *Colander* by Michael McFee. Copyright © 1996 by Michael McFee. Reprinted by permission of Michael McFee. "Spitwads" from *Shinemaster*. Copyright © 2006 by Michael McFee. Reprinted with the permission of The Permissions Company, Inc., on behalf of Carnegie Mellon University Press, www.cmu.edu/universitypress.

James Merrill. Excerpt: "1/Casual Wear" from "Topics," from *Collected Poems* by James Merrill. Copyright © 2001 by the Literary Estate of James Merrill at Washington University. Used by permission of Alfred A. Knopf, an imprint of the Knopf Doubleday Publishing Group, a division of Penguin Random House LLC. All rights reserved. Any third party use of this material, outside of this publication, is prohibited. Interested parties must apply directly to Penguin Random House LLC for permission.

Edna St. Vincent Millay. "I, being born a woman and distressed" and "I will put Chaos into fourteen lines," from *Collected Poems*. Copyright 1954, © 1982 by Edna St. Vincent Millay and Norma Millay Ellis. Reprinted with the permission of The Permissions Company, Inc., on behalf of Holly Peppe, Literary Executor, The Millay Society, www.millay.org.

Elaine Mitchell. "Form" from *Light 9* (Spring 1994). Reprinted by permission of the Literary Estate of Elaine Mitchell.

Janice Townley Moore. "To a Wasp" first appeared in *Light Year,* Bits Press. Reprinted by permission of the author.

Robert Morgan. "Mountain Graveyard" from *Sigodlin.* Copyright © 1990 by Robert Morgan. Reprinted by permission of the author.

Paul Muldoon. "Symposium" from *Poems: 1968–1998* by Paul Muldoon. Copyright © 2001 by Paul Muldoon. Reprinted by permission of Farrar, Straus and Giroux, LLC.

Harryette Mullen. "Dim Lady" from *Sleeping with the Dictionary* by Harryette Romell Mullen. Copyright © 2002 by Harryette Mullen. Reproduced with permission of University of California Press via Copyright Clearance Center.

Joan Murray. "Play-By-Play." Reprinted by permission from *The Hudson Review* Vol. XLIX, No. 4 (Winter 1997). Copyright © 1997 by Joan Murray. "We Old Dudes," copyright © 2006 by Joan Murray. First appeared in the July/ August 2006 issue of *Poetry* magazine. Reprinted by permission of the author.

Marilyn Nelson. "How I Discovered Poetry" from *The Fields of Praise: New and Selected Poems* by Marilyn Nelson. Copyright © 1997 by Marilyn Nelson. Reprinted by permission of the author and Louisiana State University Press.

Howard Nemerov. "Because You Asked about the Line between Prose and Poetry" from *Sentences* by Howard Nemerov. Copyright © 1980. "Walking the Dog" from *Trying Conclusions: New and Selected Poems 1961–1991.* Copyright © 1991. Reprinted by permission of the Estate of Howard Nemerov.

John Frederick Nims. "Love Poem" from *Selected Poems.* Copyright © 1982 by the University of Chicago. Reprinted by permission of the University of Chicago Press.

Alden Nowlan. "The Bull Moose" from *Alden Nowlan: Selected Poems* by Alden Nowlan. Copyight © 1967. Reprinted by permission of the Estate of Alden Nowlan.

Angela Alaimo O'Donnell. "Messenger" from *Waking My Mother* by Angela Alaimo O'Donnell, published in 2013 by Word Poetry, Cincinnati, Ohio. Copyright © 2013 by Angela Alaimo O'Donnell. "Touring the Mine" from *Moving House* by Angela Alaimo O'Donnell (Cincinnati, OH: Word Press, 2009). Copyright © 2009 by Angela Alaimo O'Donnell. Reprinted by permission of WordTech Communications LLC.

Sharon Olds. "Last Night" from *The Wellspring: Poems* by Sharon Olds. Copyright © 1996 by Sharon Olds. Used by permission of Alfred A. Knopf, an imprint of the Knopf Doubleday Publishing Group, a division of Penguin Random House LLC. All rights reserved. Any third party use of this material, outside of this publication, is prohibited. Interested parties must apply directly to Penguin Random House LLC for permission.

Mary Oliver. "Oxygen" and "The Poet with His Face in His Hands," from *New and Selected Poems, Volume Two* by Mary Oliver. Published by Beacon Press, Boston. Copyright © 2005 by Mary Oliver. Reprinted by permission of the Charlotte Sheedy Literary Agency, Inc. "Wild Geese" from *Dream Work* by Mary Oliver. Copyright © 1986 by Mary Oliver. Used by permission of Grove/Atlantic, Inc. Any third party use of this material, outside of this publication, is prohibited.

Lisa Parker. "Snapping Beans" from the collection *This Gone Place* by Lisa Parker. Originally appeared in *Parnassus* 23, no. 2 (1998). Reprinted by permission of the author.

Linda Pastan. "Marks" from *PM/AM: New and Selected Poems* by Linda Pastan. Copyright © 1978 by Linda Pastan. Used by permission of W. W. Norton & Company, Inc.

Laurence Perrine. "The limerick's never averse." Copyright © Laurence Perrine. Reprinted by permission of Douglas Perrine.

Kevin Pierce. "Proof of Origin" from *Light 50* (Autumn 2005). Copyright © 2005 by Kevin Pierce. Reprinted with the permission of the author.

Marge Piercy. "To be of use" from *Circles on the Water* by Marge Piercy. Copyright © 1982 by Middlemarsh, Inc. Used by permission of Alfred A. Knopf, an imprint of the Knopf Doubleday Publishing Group, a division of Penguin Random House LLC. Any third party use of this material, outside of this publication, is prohibited. Interested parties must apply directly to Penguin Random House LLC, for permission.

Peter D. Poland. "On 'Neither Out Far nor In Deep,'" from *The Explicator* 52, no. 2 (Winter 1994). Copyright © 1994. Reproduced by permission of Taylor & Francis Group, LLC (http://www.taylorandfrancis.com).

Henry Reed. "Naming of Parts" from *Henry Reed: Collected Poems,* ed. Jon Stallworthy. Copyright © 1946, 1947, 1970, 1991, 2007 by the Executor of Henry Reed's Estate. Reprinted by permission of Carcanet Press Ltd.

Marny Requa. "From an Interview with Julia Alvarez" excerpted from "The Politics of Fiction," *Frontera* 5 (1997). 29 January 1997, http://www.fronteramag.com/issue5/Alvarez/index.htm. Reprinted with permission of Marny Requa.

Alberto Ríos. "Seniors" from *Five Indiscretions.* Copyright © 1985 by Alberto Ríos. Reprinted by permission of the author.

Theodore Roethke. "My Papa's Waltz," copyright 1942 by Hearst Magazines, Inc. "Root Cellar," copyright 1943 by Modern Poetry Association, Inc. From *Collected Poems* by Theodore Roethke. Used by permission of Doubleday, an imprint of the Knopf Doubleday Publishing Group, a division of Penguin Random House LLC. All rights reserved. Any third party use of this material, outside of this publication, is prohibited. Interested parties must apply directly to Penguin Random House LLC for permission.

Frederik L. Rusch. "Society and Character in 'The Love Song of J. Alfred Prufrock'" from "Approaching Literature through the Social Psychology of Erich Fromm" in *Psychological Perspectives on Literature: Freudian Dissidents and Non-Freudians,* edited by Joseph Natoli. Copyright © 1984. Reprinted by permission of the author.

Kay Ryan. "Dew" and "Learning," from *Elephant Rocks* by Kay Ryan. Copyright © 1996 by Kay Ryan. Used by permission of Grove/Atlantic, Inc. Any third party use of this material, outside of this publication, is prohibited. "Turtle" from *Flamingo Watching* by Kay Ryan. Copyright © 1994 by Kay Ryan. Used by permission of Copper Beech Press.

Michael Ryan. "I" from *Poetry* 202.4 (July/August 2013). Copyright © 2013 by Michael Ryan. Reprinted with the permission of the author.

Sappho. "Prayer to my lady of Paphos" (Fragment #38) from *Sappho: A New Translation* by Mary Barnard. Copyright © 1958 by the Regents of the University of California, renewed © 1986 by Mary Barnard. Reproduced with permission of University of California Press via Copyright Clearance Center.

Peter Schmitt. "Friends with Numbers" from *Hazard Duty*. Copyright © 1995 by Peter Schmitt. Used by permission of Copper Beech Press.

Elisabeth Schneider. "Hints of Eliot in Prufrock." Reprinted by permission of the Modern Language Association of America from "Prufrock and After: The Theme of Change," *PMLA* 87 (1982): 1103–1117.

David Shumate. "Shooting the Horse" from *High Water Mark: Prose Poems* by David Shumate. Copyright © 2004. Reprinted by permission of the University of Pittsburgh Press.

Charles Simic. "Fork" from *Selected Early Poems* by Charles Simic. Copyright © 1999 by Charles Simic. Reprinted with the permission of George Braziller, Inc., www.georgebraziller.com.

Louis Simpson. "In the Suburbs" from *The Owner of the House: New Collected Poems, 1940–2001*. Copyright © 1963, 2001 by Louis Simpson. Reprinted with the permission of The Permissions Company, Inc., on behalf of BOA Editions Ltd., www.boaeditions.org.

David R. Slavitt. "Titanic" from *Change of Address: Poems New and Selected* by David R. Slavitt. Copyright © 2005 by David R. Slavitt. Reprinted by permission of Louisiana State University Press.

Ernest Slyman. "Lightning Bugs" from *Sometime the Cow Kick Your Head, Light Year 88/89*. Reprinted by permission of the author.

Patricia Smith. "What It's Like to Be a Black Girl (For Those of You Who Aren't)" from *Life According to Motown* by Patricia Smith. Copyright © 1991 by Patricia Smith. Reprinted by permission of the author.

Gary Snyder. "A Dent in the Bucket" from *Danger on Peaks* by Gary Snyder. Copyright © 2004 by Gary Snyder. Reprinted by permission of Counterpoint. "How Poetry Comes to Me" from *No Nature* by Gary Snyder. Copyright © 1992 by Gary Snyder. Used by permission of Pantheon Books, an imprint of the Knopf Doubleday Publishing Group, a division of Penguin Random House LLC. All rights reserved. Any third party use of this material, outside of this publication, is prohibited. Interested parties must apply directly to Penguin Random House LLC for permission.

David Solway. "Windsurfing." Reprinted by permission of the author.

Cathy Song. "Girl Powdering Her Neck" and "The Youngest Daughter," from *Picture Bride*. Copyright © 1983 by Yale University Press. Reprinted by permission of Yale University Press.

Timothy Steele. "Waiting for the Storm" from *Sapphics and Uncertainties: Poems, 1970–1986*. Copyright © 1986, 1995 by Timothy Steele. Reprinted with the permission of The Permissions Company, Inc., on behalf of the University of Arkansas Press, www.uapress.com.

Jim Stevens. "Schizophrenia." Originally appeared in *Light: The Quarterly of Light Verse* (Spring 1992). Copyright © 1992 by Jim Stevens. Reprinted by permission.

Wallace Stevens. "Anecdote of the Jar" from *The Collected Poems of Wallace Stevens* by Wallace Stevens. Copyright © 1954 by Wallace Stevens and copyright renewed 1982 by Holly Stevens. Used by permission of Alfred A. Knopf, an imprint of the Knopf Doubleday Publishing Group, a division of Penguin Random House LLC. All rights reserved. Any third party use of this material, outside of this publication, is prohibited. Interested parties must apply directly to Penguin Random House LLC for permission.

John Stone. "American Gothic" from *Where Water Begins: New Poems and Prose* by John Stone. Copyright © 1986, 1987, 1990, 1992, 1995, 1996, 1997, 1998 by John Stone. Reprinted by permission of Louisiana State University Press. First published in the *Georgia Journal*.

Joyce Sutphen. "Guys Like That" from *The Writer's Almanac* online, January 7, 2007. Copyright © 2007 by Joyce Sutphen. Reprinted by permission of the author.

Wisława Szymborska. "Brueghel's Two Monkeys" from *View with a Grain of Sand: Selected Poems* by Wisława Szymborska, translated from the Polish by Stanisław Barańczak & Clare Cavanagh. Copyright © 1995 by Houghton Mifflin Harcourt Publishing Company. Copyright © 1976 Czytelnik, Warszawa. "Vermeer," from *Here: New Poems* by Wisława Szymborska. Translated by Clare Cavanagh and Stanisław Baranczak. Copyright © 2010 by Wisława Szymborska. English translation © 2010 by Houghton Mifflin Harcourt Publishing Company. Both selections reprinted by permission of Houghton Mifflin Harcourt Publishing Company. All rights reserved.

Dylan Thomas. "Do not go gentle into that good night" from *The Poems of Dylan Thomas*. Copyright © 1952 by Dylan Thomas. "The Hand That Signed the Paper" from *The Poems of Dylan Thomas*. Copyright © 1939 by New Directions Publishing Corp. Both selections reprinted by permission of New Directions Publishing Corp.

Jim Tilley. "The Big Questions" from *In Confidence* by Jim Tilley (Pasadena, CA: Red Hen Press, 2011). Copyright © 2011 by Jim Tilley. "Hello, Old Man" from *Cruising at Sixty to Seventy* by Jim Tilley (Pasadena, CA: Red Hen Press, 2014). Copyright © 2014 by Jim Tilley. Both selections reprinted by permission of Red Hen Press.

Jean Toomer. "Unsuspecting." Reprinted from the Jean Toomer Papers, James Weldon Johnson Memorial Collection, Beinecke Rare Book and Manuscript Library, with the permission of the Yale Committee on Literary Property as owner of the literary property rights.

Natasha Trethewey. "On Captivity" from *Thrall: Poems* by Natasha Trethewey. Copyright © 2012 by Natasha Trethewey. Reprinted by permission of Houghton Mifflin Harcourt Publishing Company. All rights reserved.

William Trowbridge. "Drumming Behind You in the High School Band" from *Enter Dark Stranger*. Copyright © 1989 by William Trowbridge. Reprinted with the permission of The Permissions Company, Inc., on behalf of the University of Arkansas Press, www.uapress.com.

John Updike. "Dog's Death" and "Player Piano," from *Collected Poems, 1953–1993* by John Updike. Copyright © 1993 by John Updike. Used by permission of Alfred A. Knopf, an imprint of the Knopf Doubleday Publishing Group, a division of Penguin Random House LLC. All rights reserved. Any third party use of this material, outside of this publication, is prohibited. Interested parties must apply directly to Penguin Random House LLC for permission.

David Wagoner. "Improving My Mind," *Georgia Review* 66.2 (Summer 2012). Copyright © 2012 by David Wagoner. Reprinted by permission.

Richard Wakefield. "The Bell Rope" from *East of Early Winters: Poems* by Richard Wakefield (University of Evansville Press, 2006). Copyright © 2006 by Richard Wakefield. Reprinted with permission from the author.

Ronald Wallace. "Building an Outhouse" from *The Makings of Happiness* by Ronald Wallace. Copyright © 1991. Reprinted by permission of the University of Pittsburgh Press. "Dogs (1)" from *The Uses of Adversity* by Ronald Wallace. Copyright © 1998. Reprinted by permission of the University of Pittsburgh Press. "In a Rut" from *The Best American Poetry 2003*, ed. Yusef Komunyakaa. Originally published in *Poetry Northwest*. Copyright © 2003. Reprinted by permission of the author.

Charles Harper Webb. "Descent" from *Liver* by Charles Harper Webb. Copyright © 1999 The Board of Regents of the University of Wisconsin System. Reprinted by permission of the University of Wisconsin Press.

Gail White. "Dead Armadillos." Copyright © 2000 by Gail White. Reprinted by permission of the author.

Richard Wilbur. "The Writer" from *The Mind-Reader* by Richard Wilbur. Copyright © 1971 and renewed 1999 by Richard Wilbur. Reprinted by permission of Houghton Mifflin Harcourt Publishing Company. All rights reserved.

C. K. Williams. "Love: Beginnings" from *Collected Poems* by C. K. Williams. Copyright © 2006 by C. K. Williams. Reprinted by permission of Farrar, Straus and Giroux, LLC.

William Carlos Williams. "Poem" and "The Red Wheelbarrow," from *The Collected Poems: Volume 1, 1909–1939*. Copyright © 1938 by New Directions Publishing Corp. Reprinted by permission of New Directions Publishing Corp.

Cynthia Griffin Wolff. "On the Many Voices in Dickinson's Poetry," excerpted from *Emily Dickinson* by Cynthia Griffin Wolff. Copyright © 1986 by Cynthia Griffin Wolff. Used by permission of Alfred A. Knopf, an imprint of the Knopf Doubleday Publishing Group, a division of Penguin Random House LLC. All rights reserved. Any third party use of this material, outside of this publication, is prohibited. Interested parties must apply directly to Penguin Random House LLC for permission.

Baron Wormser. "Labor" from *Scattered Chapters: New and Selected Poems*. Copyright © 2008 by Baron Wormser. Reprinted with the permission of The Permissions Company, Inc., on behalf of Sarabande Books, www.sarabandebooks.org.

Stefanie Wortman. "Mortuary Art," first published in *Smartish Pace* and collected in the book *In the Permanent Collection* (University of North Texas Press, 2014). Copyright © 2010 by Stefanie Wortman. Reprinted by permission of the publisher.

William Butler Yeats. "Leda and the Swan" from *The Collected Works of W. B. Yeats, Volume I: The Poems, Revised*, by W. B. Yeats, edited by Richard J. Finneran. Copyright © 1928 by the Macmillan Company, renewed © 1956 by Georgie Yeats. All rights reserved. Reprinted with the permission of Scribner, a division of Simon & Schuster, Inc.

Kevin Young. "Eddie Priest's Barbershop & Notary" from *Most Way Home* by Kevin Young. Copyright © 1995 by Kevin Young. Reprinted with permission from Steerforth Press.

DRAMA

Jane Anderson. *The Reprimand*. Copyright © 2000 by Jane Anderson. Reprinted by permission of William Morris Endeavor Entertainment, LLC, on behalf of the author.

Aristotle. "On Tragic Character" from *Aristotle's Poetics*, trans. James Hutton. Copyright © 1982 by W. W. Norton & Company, Inc. Used by permission of W. W. Norton & Company, Inc.

Linda Bamber. "Feminine Rebellion and Masculine Authority in *A Midsummer Night's Dream*," excerpted from *Comic Women, Tragic Men: A Study of Gender and Genre in Shakespeare* by Linda Bamber. Copyright © 1982 by the Board of Trustees of Leland Stanford Jr. University. Used with the permission of Stanford University Press, www.sup.org.

David Bevington. Notes to accompany *Hamlet, Prince of Denmark* and *A Midsummer Night's Dream*, from David Bevington, *The Complete Works of Shakespeare*, 4th edition. Copyright © 1992. Reprinted by permission of Pearson Education, Inc., New York, New York.

Sharon E. Cooper. *Mistaken Identity*. Copyright © 2003, 2009 by Sharon E. Cooper. Originally published by Vintage Press in the anthology *Laugh Lines: Short Comic Plays*, ed. by Eric Lane and Nina Shengold. Reprinted by permission of the author. For inquiries regarding producing, please contact the author at secooper1@yahoo.com, or visit her Web site, www.sharonecooper.com.

Elizabeth Cullingford. "On the Whiplash Climax of *Doubt*," excerpted from *"Evil, Sin, or Doubt? The Dramas of Clerical Child Abuse," Theatre Journal* 62.2 (2010), p. 262. Copyright © 2010 The Johns Hopkins University Press. Reprinted with permission of Johns Hopkins University Press.

Larry David. Episode entitled "The Pitch" from the television series *Seinfeld* © 1992 Castle Rock Entertainment, written by Larry David. All Rights Reserved. Reprinted by permission of Castle Rock Entertainment.

Michael Hollinger. *Naked Lunch* from *Humana Festival 2003*, ed. Tanya Palmer and Amy Wegener. Copyright © 2003 by Michael Hollinger. Reprinted by permission.

David Henry Hwang. *Trying to Find Chinatown*. Published in *Trying to Find Chinatown: The Selected Plays of David Henry Hwang*. Copyright © 2000 by David Henry Hwang. Published by Theatre Communications Group. Used by permission of Theatre Communications Group.

David Ives. *Moby-Dude, or: The Three-Minute Whale* from *Talk to Me: Monologue Plays*, ed. Nina Shengold and Eric Lane. Copyright © 2004 by David Ives. Reprinted by permission of Abrams Artists Agency.

Russell Jackson. "A Film Diary of the Shooting of Kenneth Branagh's *Hamlet*" from *Hamlet: Screenplay and Introduction* by William Shakespeare, Kenneth Branagh, and Russell Jackson. Copyright © 1996 by Russell Jackson. Used by permission of the author.

Lisa Jardine. "On Boy Actors in Female Roles" from *Still Harping on Daughters: Women and Drama in the Age of Shakespeare* by Lisa Jardine. Copyright © 1983. Reprinted by permission.

James R. Kincaid. "On the Value of Comedy in the Face of Tragedy," excerpted from "Who Is Relieved by Comic Relief?" in *Annoying the Victorians* (New York: Routledge, 1995). Reprinted by permission of the author.

Jan Kott. "On Producing *Hamlet*" from *Shakespeare: Our Contemporary* by Jan Kott, trans. Boleslaw Taborski. Copyright © 1964 by Panstwowe Wydawnictwo Naukowe and Doubleday, an imprint of Penguin Random House

Index of First Lines

Index of Authors and Titles

Index of Terms

Boldface numbers refer to the Glossary of Literary Terms.